Official
BASEBALL
REGISTER

1991 EDITION

Editor/Baseball Register
BARRY SIEGEL

Contributing Editors/Baseball Register
CRAIG CARTER
JOHN DUXBURY
STEVE ZESCH

Publisher
THOMAS G. OSENTON

Director, Specialized Publications
GARY LEVY

Published by

The Sporting News

1212 North Lindbergh Boulevard
P.O. Box 56 — St. Louis, MO 63166

Copyright © 1991
The Sporting News Publishing Company

A Times Mirror
Company

ISBN 0-89204-383-0   ISSN 0067-4281

Table
of
CONTENTS

Players included are those who played in at least one game in the major leagues in 1990, plus selected invitees to spring training.

ON THE COVER: Pittsburgh outfielder Barry Bonds, who connected for 33 homers, drove in 114 runs and swiped 52 bases in 1990, led the Pirates to a division title and was named National League Most Valuable Player and The Sporting News Major League Player of the Year.

— Photo by Rich Pilling/The Sporting News

EXPLANATION OF ABBREVIATIONS

G—Games played. Pos.—Position. AB—At Bats. R—Runs. H—Hits. 2B—Two-Base Hits. 3B—Three-Base Hits. HR—Home Runs. RBI—Runs Batted In. B.A.—Batting Average. PO—Putouts. A—Assists. E—Errors. F.A.—Fielding Average. IP—Innings Pitched. W—Won. L—Lost. Pct.—Winning percentage. ER—Earned Runs. SO—Strikeouts. BB—Bases on Balls. ERA—Earned-Run Average.

Players

Please note for statistical comparisons: In 1972, 10 days were missed, as well as 50 days in 1981, due to the cancellation of games because of players' strike.

*Denotes led league. ●Tied for lead. Mark before position (where more than one position is given) denotes where played as leader in department shown.

DONALD WILLIAM AASE

Name pronounced AH-see.

(Don)

Born September 8, 1954, at Orange, Calif.
Height, 6.03. Weight, 222.
Throws and bats righthanded.
Attended California State University, Fullerton, Calif.

Major League saves: 1979 (2), 1980 (2), 1981 (11), 1982 (4), 1984 (8), 1985 (14), 1986 (34), 1987 (2), 1989 (2), 1990 (3). Total—82.

Led International League pitchers in games started with 29 in 1975.

Led Carolina League pitchers in games started with 30, complete games with 18 and tied for lead in shutouts with 4 in 1974.

Named Carolina League Pitcher of the Year, 1974.

Year Club	League	G.	IP.	W.	L.	Pct.	H.	R.	ER.	SO.	BB.	ERA.
1972—Williamsport	NYP	12	62	0	*10	.000	60	48	40	40	34	5.81
1973—Winter Haven	Florida St.	29	170	12	●15	.444	153	82	68	127	73	3.60
1974—Winston-Salem	Carolina	32	*230	*17	8	.680	185	72	62	*176	84	*2.43
1975—Pawtucket	Int'national	29	186	8	13	.381	173	85	75	125	88	3.63
1976—Rhode Island†	Int'national	10	54	5	2	.714	42	23	20	40	34	3.33
1977—Pawtucket	Int'national	18	109	6	6	.500	118	67	61	64	60	5.04
1977—Boston‡	American	13	92	6	2	.750	85	36	32	49	19	3.13
1978—California	American	29	179	11	8	.579	185	88	80	93	80	4.02
1979—California	American	37	185	9	10	.474	200	104	99	96	77	4.82
1980—California	American	40	175	8	13	.381	193	83	79	74	66	4.06
1981—California	American	39	65	4	4	.500	56	17	17	38	24	2.35
1982—California§	American	24	52	3	3	.500	45	20	20	40	23	3.46
1983—California x	American					(Did not play)						
1984—Redwood y	California	4	12⅓	0	1	.000	9	9	7	10	7	5.11
1984—California z	American	23	39	4	1	.800	30	7	7	28	19	1.62
1985—Baltimore	American	54	88	10	6	.625	83	44	37	67	35	3.78
1986—Baltimore	American	66	81⅔	6	7	.462	71	29	27	67	28	2.98
1987—Baltimore a	American	7	8	1	0	1.000	8	2	2	3	4	2.25
1988—Rochester b	Int'national	7	7⅓	0	0	.000	5	1	1	6	3	1.23
1988—Baltimore c	American	35	46⅔	0	0	.000	40	22	21	28	37	4.05
1989—New York d	National	49	59⅓	1	5	.167	56	27	26	34	26	3.94
1990—Los Angeles e	National	32	38	3	1	.750	33	24	21	24	19	4.97
1990—Bakersfield f	California	6	9	0	0	.000	6	1	1	4	2	1.00
American League Totals—11 Years		367	1011⅓	62	54	.534	996	452	421	583	412	3.75
National League Totals—2 Years		81	97⅓	4	6	.400	89	51	47	58	45	4.35
Major League Totals—13 Years		448	1108⅔	66	60	.524	1085	503	468	641	457	3.80

Selected by Boston Red Sox' organization in 6th round of free-agent draft, June 6, 1972.

†On disabled list, June 23, 1976 through remainder of season.

‡Traded with cash to California Angels for Second Baseman Jerry Remy, December 8, 1977.

§On disabled list, June 3 to June 27 and July 20 to September 7, 1982.

xOn disabled list, March 30, 1983 through remainder of season.

yOn California disabled list, March 27 to June 13, 1984; included rehabilitation disability assignment to Redwood, May 10 to May 30, 1984.

zGranted free agency, November 8, 1984; signed by Baltimore Orioles, December 13, 1984.

aOn disabled list, April 15 to May 13 and May 27, 1987 through remainder of season.

bOn Baltimore disabled list, March 30 to May 10, 1988; included rehabilitation disability assignment to Rochester, April 21 to May 10, 1988.

cReleased, October 3, 1988; signed by Tidewater (New York Mets' organization), February 20, 1989.

dGranted free agency, November 13, 1989; signed by Albuquerque (Los Angeles Dodgers' organization), February 20, 1990.

eOn disabled list, July 2 to August 18, 1990; included rehabilitation disability assignment to Bakersfield, August 3 to August 18, 1990.

fGranted free agency, October 8, 1990.

CHAMPIONSHIP SERIES RECORD

Year Club	League	G.	IP.	W.	L.	Pct.	H.	R.	ER.	SO.	BB.	ERA.
1979—California	American	2	5	1	0	1.000	4	1	1	6	2	1.80

ALL-STAR GAME RECORD

Year League	IP.	W.	L.	Pct.	H.	R.	ER.	SO.	BB.	ERA.
1986—American	⅔	0	0	.000	0	0	0	0	0	0.00

JAMES ANTHONY ABBOTT
(Jim)

Born September 19, 1967, at Flint, Mich.
Height, 6.03. Weight, 210.
Throws and bats lefthanded.
Attended University of Michigan, Ann Arbor, Mich.

Member of 1988 U.S. Olympic baseball team.
Named lefthanded pitcher on THE SPORTING NEWS College Baseball All-America Team, 1988.

Year Club	League	G.	IP.	W.	L.	Pct.	H.	R.	ER.	SO.	BB.	ERA.
1989—California	American	29	181⅓	12	12	.500	190	95	79	115	74	3.92
1990—California	American	33	211⅔	10	14	.417	⋆246	116	106	105	72	4.51
Major League Totals—2 Years		62	393	22	26	.458	436	211	185	220	146	4.24

Selected by Toronto Blue Jays' organization in 36th round of free-agent draft, June 3, 1985.
Selected by California Angels' organization in 1st round (eighth player selected) of free-agent draft, June 1, 1988.

PAUL DAVID ABBOTT

Born September 15, 1967, at Van Nuys, Calif.
Height, 6.03. Weight, 185.
Throws and bats righthanded.

Pitched 3-0 no-hit victory against Palm Springs, June 26, 1988 (seven innings).
Tied for California League lead in games started by pitchers with 28 in 1988.

Year Club	League	G.	IP.	W.	L.	Pct.	H.	R.	ER.	SO.	BB.	ERA.
1985—Elizabethton	Ap'lachian	10	35	1	5	.167	33	32	27	34	32	6.94
1986—Kenosha	Midwest	25	98	6	10	.375	102	62	49	73	73	4.50
1987—Kenosha	Midwest	26	145⅓	13	6	.684	102	76	59	138	103	3.65
1988—Visalia	California	28	172⅓	11	9	.550	141	95	80	⋆205	⋆143	4.18
1989—Orlando	Southern	17	90⅔	9	3	.750	71	48	44	102	48	4.37
1990—Portland	P. Coast	23	128½	5	14	.263	110	75	65	129	82	4.56
1990—Minnesota	American	7	34⅔	0	5	.000	37	24	23	25	28	5.97
Major League Totals—1 Year		7	34⅔	0	5	.000	37	24	23	25	28	5.97

Selected by Minnesota Twins' organization in 3rd round of free-agent draft, June 3, 1985.

SHAWN WESLEY ABNER

Born June 17, 1966, at Hamilton, O.
Height, 6.01. Weight, 190.
Throws and bats righthanded.
Brother of Ben Abner, outfielder in Montreal Expos' and Pittsburgh Pirates' organizations,
1984 through 1987.

Major League stolen bases: 1987 (1), 1989 (1), 1990 (2). Total—4.
Tied for Texas League lead in being hit by pitch with 7 in 1986.
Led Texas League outfielders in total chances with 352 in 1986.
Led Carolina League outfielders in total chances with 352 in 1985.
Named Carolina League Player of the Year, 1985.

Year Club	League	Pos.	G.	AB.	R.	H.	2B.	3B.	HR.	RBI.	B.A.	PO.	A.	E.	F.A.
1984—Kingsport	Appal.	OF	46	183	32	50	8	0	10	35	.273	87	1	1	.989
1984—Little Falls	NYP	OF	18	68	7	18	2	0	1	5	.265	40	2	1	.977
1985—Lynchburg	Carol.	OF	139	⋆542	71	⋆163	⋆30	⋆11	16	⋆89	.301	⋆332	8	12	.966
1986—Jackson†	Texas	OF	⋆134	511	80	136	29	●8	14	76	.266	⋆338	10	4	.989
1987—Las Vegas	P. C.	OF	105	406	60	122	14	11	11	85	.300	238	9	4	.984
1987—San Diego	Nat.	OF	16	47	5	13	3	1	2	7	.277	23	2	2	.926
1988—San Diego	Nat.	OF	37	83	6	15	3	0	2	5	.181	55	1	1	.982
1988—Las Vegas	P. C.	OF	63	252	35	64	16	2	4	34	.254	147	1	6	.961
1989—Las Vegas	P. C.	OF	56	223	31	60	11	2	8	31	.269	129	6	1	.993
1989—San Diego	Nat.	OF	57	102	13	18	4	0	2	14	.176	67	0	0	1.000
1990—San Diego	Nat.	OF	91	184	17	45	9	0	1	15	.245	108	1	1	.991
Major League Totals—4 Years			201	416	41	91	19	1	7	41	.219	175	1	1	.994

Selected by New York Mets' organization in 1st round (first player selected) of free-agent draft, June 4, 1984.
†Traded with Outfielders Stanley Jefferson and Kevin Mitchell and Pitchers Kevin Armstrong and Kevin Brown to San Diego Padres for Outfielder Kevin McReynolds, Pitcher Gene Walter and Infielder Adam Ging, December 11, 1986.

JAMES JUSTIN ACKER
(Jim)

Born September 24, 1958, at Freer, Tex.
Height, 6.02. Weight, 212.
Throws and bats righthanded.
Attended University of Texas, Austin, Tex.
Brother of Bill Acker, nose tackle with St. Louis Cardinals, Kansas City Chiefs, Cincinnati Bengals and
Buffalo Bills, 1980 through 1984.

Major League saves: 1983 (1), 1984 (1), 1985 (10), 1987 (14), 1989 (2), 1990 (1). Total—29.

Year Club	League	G.	IP.	W.	L.	Pct.	H.	R.	ER.	SO.	BB.	ERA.
1980—Bradenton Braves	Gulf Coast	1	5	1	0	1.000	1	0	0	5	0	0.00
1980—Savannah	Southern	13	95	5	5	.500	84	33	28	47	29	2.65
1981—Savannah	Southern	10	77	5	5	.500	57	34	23	37	34	2.69

Year	Club	League	G.	IP.	W.	L.	Pct.	H.	R.	ER.	SO.	BB.	ERA.
1981—Richmond	Int'national	21	118	8	7	.533	112	63	55	72	74	4.19
1982—Savannah†‡	Southern	26	142	9	14	.391	120	96	70	96	86	4.44
1983—Toronto	American	38	97⅔	5	1	.833	103	52	47	44	38	4.33
1984—Toronto§	American	32	72	3	5	.375	79	39	35	33	25	4.38
1985—Toronto	American	61	86⅓	7	2	.778	86	35	31	42	43	3.23
1986—Toronto x	American	23	60	2	4	.333	63	34	29	32	22	4.35
1986—Atlanta	National	21	95	3	8	.273	100	47	40	37	26	3.79
1987—Atlanta	National	68	114⅔	4	9	.308	109	57	53	68	51	4.16
1988—Atlanta y	National	21	42	0	4	.000	45	26	22	25	14	4.71
1988—Greenville z	Southern	8	15⅔	0	0	.000	7	3	3	5	3	1.72
1989—Atlanta a	National	59	97⅔	0	6	.000	84	29	29	68	20	2.67
1989—Toronto	American	14	28⅓	2	1	.667	24	7	5	24	12	1.59
1990—Toronto	American	59	91⅔	4	4	.500	103	49	39	54	30	3.83
American League Totals—6 Years		227	436	23	17	.575	458	216	186	229	170	3.84
National League Totals—4 Years		169	349⅓	7	27	.206	338	159	144	198	111	3.71
Major League Totals—8 Years		396	785⅓	30	44	.405	796	375	330	427	281	3.78

Selected by Atlanta Braves' organization in 1st round (21st player selected) of free-agent draft, June 3, 1980.

†On disabled list, April 9 to April 20, 1982.

‡Drafted by Toronto Blue Jays, December 6, 1982.

§On disabled list, August 16 to September 1, 1984.

xTraded to Atlanta Braves for Pitcher Joe Johnson, July 6, 1986.

yOn disabled list, May 9 to August 19, 1988; included rehabilitation disability assignment to Greenville, July 30 to August 18, 1988.

zGranted free agency, November 4, 1988; re-signed by Richmond (Atlanta Braves' organization), January 6, 1989.

aTraded to Toronto Blue Jays for Pitcher Tony Castillo and a player to be named later, August 24, 1989; Atlanta Braves' organization acquired Catcher Francisco Cabrera to complete deal, August 24, 1989.

CHAMPIONSHIP SERIES RECORD

Shares Championship Series record for most games pitched, series (5), 1989.

Year	Club	League	G.	IP.	W.	L.	Pct.	H.	R.	ER.	SO.	BB.	ERA.
1985—Toronto	American	2	6	0	0	.000	2	0	0	5	0	0.00
1989—Toronto	American	5	6⅓	0	0	.000	4	2	1	4	1	1.42
Championship Series Totals—2 Years		7	12⅓	0	0	.000	6	2	1	9	1	0.73

STEVEN THOMAS ADKINS
(Steve)

Born October 26, 1964, at Chicago, Ill.
Height, 6.06. Weight, 210.
Throws and bats lefthanded.
Received bachelor of science degree in mechanical
engineering from University of Pennsylvania in 1986.

Tied for Eastern League lead in shutouts with 5 in 1989.

Year	Club	League	G.	IP.	W.	L.	Pct.	H.	R.	ER.	SO.	BB.	ERA.
1986—Oneonta	NYP	14	80⅓	8	2	.800	59	23	15	74	36	1.68
1987—Fort Lauderdale	Florida St.	5	21⅓	1	1	.500	26	11	11	7	8	4.64
1987—Prince William	Carolina	21	115⅔	9	8	.529	120	72	62	84	70	4.82
1988—Prince William	Carolina	31	94⅓	6	4	.600	88	44	35	92	40	3.34
1989—Fort Lauderdale	Florida St.	11	45⅔	3	3	.500	40	15	12	48	14	2.36
1989—Albany	Eastern	16	117⅔	12	1	★.923	67	31	27	132	58	★2.07
1990—Columbus	Int'national	27	177	15	7	.682	153	72	57	138	★98	2.90
1990—New York	American	5	24	1	2	.333	19	18	17	14	29	6.38
Major League Totals—1 Year		5	24	1	2	.333	19	18	17	14	29	6.38

Selected by New York Yankees' organization in 15th round of free-agent draft, June 2, 1986.

MICHAEL TROY AFENIR

(Known by middle name.)
Name pronounced AFF-nur.
Born September 21, 1963, at Escondido, Calif.
Height, 6.04. Weight, 200.
Throws and bats righthanded.
Attended Palomar College, San Marcos, Calif.

Led South Atlantic League in passed balls with 32 in 1984.

Year	Club	League	Pos.	G.	AB.	R.	H.	2B.	3B.	HR.	RBI.	B.A.	PO.	A.	E.	F.A.
1983—Sarasota Astros	Gulf C.	C	27	89	16	26	5	1	5	24	.292	101	19	3	.976
1983—Auburn	NYP	C	7	26	2	3	0	0	0	0	.115	48	2	0	1.000
1984—Asheville	S. Atl.	C-1B	115	358	44	69	16	0	16	69	.193	656	61	12	.984
1985—Osceola	Fla. St.	★C-SS	99	323	38	80	19	1	6	41	.248	557	72	★16	.975
1986—Columbus†	South.	C-1B	91	313	50	68	15	3	14	45	.217	492	38	14	.974
1987—Osceola	Fla. St.	C-1B	79	294	60	81	20	1	14	68	.276	353	30	5	.987
1987—Columbus	South.	C-1B	31	99	15	20	8	0	2	11	.202	142	16	3	.981
1987—Houston	Nat.	C	10	20	1	6	1	0	0	1	.300	35	2	1	.974
1988—Columbus‡	South.	OF-C-1B	137	494	61	122	21	5	16	66	.247	313	29	9	.974
1989—Huntsville§	South.	OF-C-1B	65	225→	31	57	15	1	13	45	.253	142	11	3	.981
1990—Tacoma	P. C.	C	88	289	44	72	14	2	15	47	.249	457	60	7	.987

Year	Club	League	Pos.	G.	AB.	R.	H.	2B.	3B.	HR.	RBI.	B.A.	PO.	A.	E.	F.A.
1990—Oakland.................	Amer.	C	14	14	0	2	0	0	0	2	.143	13	0	0	1.000
National League Totals—1 Year			10	20	1	6	1	0	0	1	.300	35	2	1	.974
American League Totals—1 Year			14	14	0	2	0	0	0	2	.143	13	0	0	1.000
Major League Totals—2 Years................			24	34	1	8	1	0	0	3	.235	48	2	1	.980

Selected by Chicago Cubs' organization in 1st round (second player selected) of free-agent draft, January 12, 1982.
Selected by Baltimore Orioles' organization in secondary phase of free-agent draft, June 7, 1982.
Selected by Houston Astros' organization in secondary phase of free-agent draft, January 11, 1983.
†On disabled list, June 21 to July 7, 1986.
‡Traded to Huntsville (Oakland Athletics' organization) for Catcher Matt Sinatro, April 6, 1989.
§On disabled list, April 22 to May 1 and May 9 to June 14, 1989.

JUAN ROBERTO AGOSTO

Born February 23, 1958, at Rio Piedras, P.R.
Height, 6.02. Weight, 190.
Throws and bats lefthanded.

Major League saves: 1983 (7), 1984 (7), 1985 (1), 1986 (1), 1987 (2), 1988 (4), 1989 (1), 1990 (4). Total—27.
Led Carolina League in balks with 4 in 1977 and 5 in 1978.

Year	Club	League	G.	IP.	W.	L.	Pct.	H.	R.	ER.	SO.	BB.	ERA.
1975—Winter Haven................	Florida St.		6	28	0	4	.000	35	23	18	19	24	5.79
1975—Elmira	NYP		9	23	1	4	.200	27	37	22	22	34	8.61
1976—Winter Haven................	Florida St.		28	107	5	11	.313	97	70	55	80	69	4.63
1977—Winston-Salem	Carolina		30	119	4	9	.308	128	106	79	98	*111	5.97
1978—Winter Haven................	Florida St.		1	1	0	0	.000	5	2	2	0	0	27.00
1978—Winston-Salem†	Carolina		23	120	5	11	.313	114	76	51	74	89	3.83
1979—Puerto Rico‡................	Int.-Amer.		10	31	3	2	.600	31	13	9	9	17	2.61
1980—Glens Falls	Eastern		8	22	1	0	1.000	26	18	17	8	18	6.95
1980—Appleton	Midwest		23	144	11	6	.647	118	60	43	93	52	2.69
1981—Edmonton................	P. Coast		48	120	7	10	.412	128	61	52	57	49	3.90
1981—Chicago.................	American		2	6	0	0	.000	5	3	3	3	0	4.50
1982—Edmonton................	P. Coast		50	95⅓	3	4	.429	101	63	53	39	49	5.00
1982—Chicago.................	American		1	2	0	0	.000	7	4	4	1	0	18.00
1983—Denver	Am. Assoc.		19	26	4	1	.800	19	8	6	19	10	2.08
1983—Chicago.................	American		39	41⅔	2	2	.500	41	20	19	29	11	4.10
1984—Chicago.................	American		49	55⅓	2	1	.667	54	20	19	26	34	3.09
1985—Chicago.................	American		54	60⅓	4	3	.571	45	27	24	39	23	3.58
1985—Buffalo	Am. Assoc.		6	12⅔	0	0	.000	13	3	3	11	2	2.13
1986—Chicago§-Minnesota	American		26	25	1	4	.200	49	30	24	12	18	8.64
1986—Toledo x................	Int'national		21	35	4	3	.571	33	11	9	29	14	2.31
1987—Tucson.................	P. Coast		44	50	4	2	.667	48	16	11	31	19	1.98
1987—Houston................	National		27	27⅓	1	1	.500	26	12	8	6	10	2.63
1988—Houston................	National		75	91⅔	10	2	.833	74	27	23	33	30	2.26
1989—Houston................	National		71	83	4	5	.444	81	32	27	46	32	2.93
1990—Houston y................	National		*82	92⅓	9	8	.529	91	46	44	50	39	4.29
American League Totals—6 Years			171	190⅓	9	10	.474	201	104	93	110	86	4.40
National League Totals—4 Years......................			255	294⅓	24	16	.600	272	117	102	135	111	3.12
Major League Totals—10 Years................			426	484⅔	33	26	.559	473	221	195	245	197	3.62

Signed as free agent by Boston Red Sox' organization, August 29, 1974.
†Released, September 21, 1978; signed by Puerto Rico of Inter-American League, March 10, 1979.
‡Declared free agent when Inter-American League folded, June 15, 1979; signed by Chicago White Sox' organization, January 18, 1980.
§Sold to Minnesota Twins in exchange for loaning Pitcher Pete Filson to Buffalo (Chicago White Sox' organization), April 30, 1986; Filson was returned to Minnesota and traded to Chicago White Sox for Pitcher Kurt Walker, September 3, 1986.
xReleased, December 20, 1986; signed by Tucson (Houston Astros' organization), February 13, 1987.
yGranted free agency, November 5, 1990; signed by St. Louis Cardinals, December 14, 1990.

CHAMPIONSHIP SERIES RECORD

Year	Club	League	G.	IP.	W.	L.	Pct.	H.	R.	ER.	SO.	BB.	ERA.
1983—Chicago...............................	American		1	⅓	0	0	.000	0	0	0	0	0	0.00

RICHARD WARREN AGUILERA

Name pronounced Ag-ah-lair-uh.

(Rick)

Born December 31, 1961, at San Gabriel, Calif.
Height, 6.05. Weight, 205.
Throws and bats righthanded.
Attended Brigham Young University, Provo, Utah.

Major League saves: 1989 (7), 1990 (32). Total—39.
Tied for Carolina League lead in shutouts with 3 in 1984.
Tied for New York-Pennsylvania League lead in shutouts with 2 in 1983.

Year	Club	League	G.	IP.	W.	L.	Pct.	H.	R.	ER.	SO.	BB.	ERA.
1983—Little Falls......................	NYP		16	104	5	6	.455	*109	55	43	84	26	3.72
1984—Lynchburg......................	Carolina		13	88⅓	8	3	.727	72	29	23	101	28	2.34
1984—Jackson†........................	Texas		11	67	4	4	.500	68	37	34	71	19	4.57
1985—Tidewater......................	Int'national		11	79	6	4	.600	64	24	22	55	17	2.51

Year Club	League	G.	IP.	W.	L.	Pct.	H.	R.	ER.	SO.	BB.	ERA.
1985—New York	National	21	122⅓	10	7	.588	118	49	44	74	37	3.24
1986—New York	National	28	141⅔	10	7	.588	145	70	61	104	36	3.88
1987—New York‡	National	18	115	11	3	.786	124	53	46	77	33	3.60
1987—Tidewater	Int'national	3	13	1	1	.500	8	2	1	10	1	0.69
1988—New York§	National	11	24⅔	0	4	.000	29	20	19	16	10	6.93
1988—St. Lucie	Florida St.	2	7	0	0	.000	8	1	1	5	1	1.29
1988—Tidewater	Int'national	1	6	0	0	.000	6	1	1	4	1	1.50
1989—New York x	National	36	69⅓	6	6	.500	59	19	18	80	21	2.34
1989—Minnesota	American	11	75⅔	3	5	.375	71	32	27	57	17	3.21
1990—Minnesota	American	56	65⅓	5	3	.625	55	27	20	61	19	2.76
National League Totals—5 Years		114	473	37	27	.578	475	211	188	351	137	3.58
American League Totals—2 Years		67	141	8	8	.500	126	59	47	118	36	3.00
Major League Totals—6 Years		181	614	45	35	.563	601	270	235	469	173	3.44

Selected by St. Louis Cardinals' organization in 37th round of free-agent draft, June 3, 1980.

Selected by New York Mets' organization in 3rd round of free-agent draft, June 6, 1983.

†On disabled list, September 3 to September 15, 1985.

‡On disabled list, May 23 to August 24, 1987; included rehabilitation disability assignment to Tidewater, August 10 to August 24, 1987.

§On disabled list, April 19 to June 19 and July 12 to September 7, 1988; included rehabilitation disability assignment to St. Lucie, June 7 to June 14, 1988; and Tidewater, June 15 to June 19, 1988.

xTraded with Pitcher David West and three players to be named later to Minnesota Twins for Pitcher Frank Viola, July 31, 1989; Portland (Minnesota Twins' organization) acquired Pitchers Kevin Tapani and Tim Drummond on August 1, 1989, and Minnesota acquired Pitcher Jack Savage to complete deal, October 16, 1989.

CHAMPIONSHIP SERIES RECORD

Year Club	League	G.	IP.	W.	L.	Pct.	H.	R.	ER.	SO.	BB.	ERA.
1986—New York	National	2	5	0	0	.000	2	1	0	2	2	0.00
1988—New York	National	3	7	0	0	.000	3	1	1	4	2	1.29
Championship Series Totals—2 Years		5	12	0	0	.000	5	2	1	6	4	0.75

WORLD SERIES RECORD

Year Club	League	G.	IP.	W.	L.	Pct.	H.	R.	ER.	SO.	BB.	ERA.
1986—New York	National	2	3	1	0	1.000	8	4	4	4	1	12.00

DARREL WAYNE AKERFELDS

Born June 12, 1962, at Denver, Colo.
Height, 6.02. Weight, 210.
Throws and bats righthanded.
Attended Mesa College, Grand Junction, Colo., and
University of Arkansas, Fayetteville, Ark.

Major League saves: 1990 (3).

Tied for Midwest League lead in wild pitches with 19 in 1984.

Year Club	League	G.	IP.	W.	L.	Pct.	H.	R.	ER.	SO.	BB.	ERA.
1983—Bellingham†	Northwest	12	68⅓	5	3	.625	62	36	34	85	36	4.48
1984—Madison	Midwest	24	151	11	6	.647	156	86	74	137	74	4.41
1985—Huntsville‡	Southern	17	96⅓	9	6	.600	75	42	37	56	64	3.46
1986—Tacoma	P. Coast	25	150	8	12	.400	158	91	79	91	62	4.74
1986—Oakland	American	2	5⅓	0	0	.000	7	5	4	5	3	6.75
1987—Tacoma§	P. Coast	19	129⅔	10	3	.769	117	52	51	84	57	3.54
1987—Cleveland	American	16	74⅔	2	6	.250	84	60	56	42	38	6.75
1988—Colorado Springs x	P. Coast	49	58	3	7	.300	70	43	28	50	26	4.34
1989—Oklahoma City	Am. Assoc.	33	108	5	5	.500	89	45	40	75	59	3.33
1989—Texas y	American	6	11	0	1	.000	11	6	4	9	5	3.27
1990—Philadelphia	National	71	93	5	2	.714	65	45	39	42	54	3.77
American League Totals—3 Years		24	91	2	7	.222	102	71	64	56	46	6.33
National League Totals—1 Year		71	93	5	2	.714	65	45	39	42	54	3.77
Major League Totals—4 Years		95	184	7	9	.438	167	116	103	98	100	5.04

Selected by Atlanta Braves' organization in 9th round of free-agent draft, June 3, 1980.

Selected by Seattle Mariners' organization in 1st round (seventh player selected) of free-agent draft, June 6, 1983.

†Traded to Oakland A's, December 7, 1983, completing deal in which Seattle Mariners traded Pitcher Bill Caudill and a player to be named later to Oakland for Pitcher Dave Beard and Catcher Bob Kearney, November 21, 1983.

‡On disabled list, May 22 to June 13 and July 5 to August 20, 1985.

§Traded with Catcher Brian Dorsett to Cleveland Indians for Second Baseman Tony Bernazard, July 15, 1987.

xDrafted by Texas Rangers, December 5, 1988; deal settled with future considerations.

ySold to Philadelphia Phillies, March 31, 1990.

SCOTT PHILLIP ALDRED

Born June 12, 1968, at Flint, Mich.
Height, 6.04. Weight, 195.
Throws and bats lefthanded.

Led International League pitchers in games started with 29 in 1990.

Year Club	League	G.	IP.	W.	L.	Pct.	H.	R.	ER.	SO.	BB.	ERA.
1987—Fayetteville	S. Atlantic	21	110	4	9	.308	101	56	44	91	69	3.57
1988—Lakeland	Florida St.	25	131⅓	8	7	.533	122	61	52	102	72	3.56

Year	Club	League	G.	IP.	W.	L.	Pct.	H.	R.	ER.	SO.	BB.	ERA.
1989—London		Eastern	20	122	10	6	.625	98	55	52	97	59	3.84
1990—Toledo		Int'national	29	158	6	15	.286	145	93	86	133	81	4.90
1990—Detroit		American	4	14⅓	1	2	.333	13	6	6	7	10	3.77
Major League Totals—1 Year			4	14⅓	1	2	.333	13	6	6	7	10	3.77

Selected by Detroit Tigers' organization in 16th round of free-agent draft, June 2, 1986.

MICHAEL PETER ALDRETE
Name pronounced Owl-DRET-ee.

(Mike)

Born January 29, 1961, at Carmel, Calif.
Height, 5.11. Weight, 185.
Throws and bats lefthanded.
Received bachelor of arts degree in communication from
Stanford University, Stanford, Calif.
Brother of Rich Aldrete, first baseman in San Francisco Giants' organization.

Major League stolen bases: 1986 (1), 1987 (6), 1988 (6), 1989 (1), 1990 (1). Total—15.
Led California League in total bases with 225 in 1984.

Year	Club	League	Pos.	G.	AB.	R.	H.	2B.	3B.	HR.	RBI.	B.A.	PO.	A.	E.	F.A.
1983—Great Falls		Pion.	1B-OF	38	132	30	55	11	2	4	31	.417	257	17	4	.986
1983—Fresno		Calif.	1B	20	68	5	14	4	0	1	12	.206	189	9	2	.990
1984—Fresno		Calif.	1B	136	457	89	155	28	3	12	72	.339	1180	74	8	*.994
1985—Shreveport		Texas	1B-OF	127	441	80	147	32	1	15	77	.333	854	41	9	.990
1985—Phoenix		P. C.	OF	3	8	0	1	1	0	0	1	.125	3	0	0	1.000
1986—Phoenix		P. C.	OF-1B	47	159	36	59	14	0	6	35	.371	131	8	1	.993
1986—San Francisco		Nat.	1B-OF	84	216	27	54	18	3	2	25	.250	317	36	1	.997
1987—San Francisco		Nat.	OF-1B	126	357	50	116	18	2	9	51	.325	328	18	3	.991
1988—San Francisco†		Nat.	OF-1B	139	389	44	104	15	0	3	50	.267	272	8	4	.986
1989—Montreal‡		Nat.	OF-1B	76	136	12	30	8	1	1	12	.221	109	9	1	.992
1989—Indianapolis		A. A.	1B-OF	10	31	4	4	1	0	0	2	.129	41	3	0	1.000
1990—Montreal		Nat.	OF-1B	96	161	22	39	7	1	1	18	.242	160	12	1	.994
Major League Totals—5 Years				521	1259	155	343	66	7	16	156	.272	1186	83	10	.992

Selected by San Francisco Giants' organization in 7th round of free-agent draft, June 6, 1983.
†Traded to Montreal Expos for Outfielder Tracy Jones, December 8, 1988.
‡On disabled list, August 16 to September 1, 1989; included rehabilitation disability assignment to Indianapolis, August 21 to September 1, 1989.

CHAMPIONSHIP SERIES RECORD

Year	Club	League	Pos.	G.	AB.	R.	H.	2B.	3B.	HR.	RBI.	B.A.	PO.	A.	E.	F.A.
1987—San Francisco		Nat.	PH-OF	5	10	0	1	0	0	0	1	.100	5	0	0	1.000

JAY ROBERT ALDRICH

Born April 14, 1961, at Alexandria, La.
Height, 6.03. Weight, 210.
Throws and bats righthanded.
Attended Monclair State College, Upper Montclair, N.J.

Major League saves: 1989 (1), 1990 (1). Total—2.
Tied for California League lead in intentional bases on balls issued with 10 in 1984.

Year	Club	League	G.	IP.	W.	L.	Pct.	H.	R.	ER.	SO.	BB.	ERA.
1982—Pikeville		Ap'lachian	11	53⅔	1	2	.333	44	33	25	37	28	4.19
1983—Beloit		Midwest	28	103⅔	7	4	.636	114	59	48	96	35	4.17
1984—Stockton		California	54	105⅔	11	●14	.440	107	46	34	78	44	2.90
1985—El Paso		Texas	42	63⅓	4	1	.800	61	28	25	35	13	3.55
1986—El Paso		Texas	40	54⅓	3	3	.500	60	24	21	34	18	3.48
1987—Denver		Am. Assoc.	20	29	1	0	1.000	26	13	11	16	6	3.41
1987—Milwaukee		American	31	58⅓	3	1	.750	71	33	32	22	13	4.94
1988—Denver		Am. Assoc.	50	72	3	7	.300	83	40	37	53	20	4.63
1989—Denver		Am. Assoc.	31	42⅔	2	4	.333	44	15	13	24	13	2.74
1989—Milwaukee†		American	16	26	1	0	1.000	24	11	11	12	13	3.81
1989—Atlanta‡		National	8	12⅓	1	2	.333	7	5	3	7	6	2.19
1990—Baltimore		American	7	12	1	2	.333	17	13	11	5	7	8.25
1990—Rochester§		Int'national	30	53⅔	4	1	.800	72	38	32	34	7	5.37
1990—Phoenix x		P. Coast	8	16⅔	0	0	.000	19	8	8	9	2	4.32
American League Totals—3 Years			54	96⅓	5	3	.625	112	57	54	39	33	5.04
National League Totals—1 Year			8	12⅓	1	2	.333	7	5	3	7	6	2.19
Major League Totals—3 Years			62	108⅔	6	5	.545	119	62	57	46	39	4.72

Selected by Milwaukee Brewers' organization in 10th round of free-agent draft, June 7, 1982.
†Traded to Atlanta Braves, September 1, 1989, completing deal in which Atlanta traded Infielder Ed Romero to Milwaukee Brewers for a player to be named later, August 23, 1989.
‡Released, November 15, 1989; signed by Rochester (Baltimore Orioles' organization), December 5, 1989.
§Sold to Phoenix (San Francisco Giants' organization), August 8, 1990.
xGranted free agency, October 15, 1990.

GERALD PAUL ALEXANDER

Born March 26, 1968, at Baton Rouge, La.
Height, 5.11. Weight, 190.
Throws and bats righthanded.
Attended Tulane University, New Orleans, La.

Year	Club	League	G.	IP.	W.	L.	Pct.	H.	R.	ER.	SO.	BB.	ERA.
1989—Sarasota Rangers	Gulf Coast	6	6⅓	0	0	.000	3	0	0	9	0	0.00
1989—Port Charlotte	Florida St.	14	53	2	3	.400	36	12	10	41	16	1.70
1990—Charlotte	Florida St.	7	42⅔	6	1	.857	24	7	3	39	14	0.63
1990—Oklahoma City	Am. Assoc.	20	118⅔	13	2	.867	126	58	54	94	45	4.10
1990—Texas	American	3	7	0	0	.000	14	6	6	8	5	7.71
Major League Totals—1 Year		3	7	0	0	.000	14	6	6	8	5	7.71

Selected by Texas Rangers' organization in 21st round of free-agent draft, June 5, 1989.

LUIS RENE ALICEA

Born July 29, 1965, at Santurce, Puerto Rico.
Height, 5.09. Weight, 165.
Throws right and bats left and righthanded.
Attended Florida State University, Tallahassee, Fla.

Major League stolen bases: 1988 (1).
Named second baseman on THE SPORTING NEWS College Baseball All-America Team, 1986.

Year	Club	League	Pos.	G.	AB.	R.	H.	2B.	3B.	HR.	RBI.	B.A.	PO.	A.	E.	F.A.
1986—Erie	NYP	2B	47	163	40	46	6	1	3	18	.282	94	163	12	.955
1986—Arkansas	Texas	2B-SS	25	68	8	16	3	0	0	3	.235	39	63	4	.962
1987—Arkansas	Texas	2B	101	337	57	91	14	3	4	47	.270	184	251	11	★.975
1987—Louisville	A. A.	2B	29	105	18	32	10	2	2	20	.305	69	81	4	.974
1988—Louisville	A. A.	2B-SS-OF	49	191	21	53	11	6	1	21	.277	116	165	0	1.000
1988—St. Louis	Nat.	2B	93	297	20	63	10	4	1	24	.212	206	240	14	.970
1989—Louisville	A. A.	2B	124	412	53	102	20	3	8	48	.248	240	310	16	.972
1990—Arkansas	Texas	2B	14	49	11	14	3	1	0	4	.286	24	34	4	.935
1990—St. Petersburg	Fla. St.	2B	29	95	14	22	1	4	0	12	.232	20	23	0	1.000
1990—Louisville†	A. A.	3B	25	92	10	32	6	3	0	10	.348	14	39	6	.898
Major League Totals—1 Year			93	297	20	63	10	4	1	24	.212	206	240	14	.970

Selected by St. Louis Cardinals' organization in 1st round (23rd player selected) of free-agent draft, June 2, 1986.
†On disabled list, April 6 to June 4, 1990.

DALE LeBEAU ALLRED
(Beau)

Born June 4, 1965, at Mesa, Ariz.
Height, 6.00. Weight, 195.
Throws and bats lefthanded.
Attended Cochise County Community College, Douglas,
Ariz., and Lamar University, Beaumont, Tex.

Year	Club	League	Pos.	G.	AB.	R.	H.	2B.	3B.	HR.	RBI.	B.A.	PO.	A.	E.	F.A.
1987—Burlington	W. Car.	OF	54	167	39	57	14	1	10	38	★.341	61	2	4	.940
1988—Kinston	Carol.	OF	126	397	66	100	23	3	15	74	.252	187	10	10	.952
1989—Canton-Akron	East.	OF	118	412	67	125	23	5	14	75	.303	204	7	8	.963
1989—Colorado Springs	P. C.	OF	11	47	8	13	3	0	1	4	.277	27	1	0	1.000
1989—Cleveland	Amer.	OF	13	24	0	6	3	0	0	1	.250	11	1	0	1.000
1990—Colorado Springs	P. C.	OF	115	378	79	105	23	6	13	74	.278	203	12	●11	.951
1990—Cleveland	Amer.	OF	4	16	2	3	1	0	1	2	.188	5	0	1	.833
Major League Totals—2 Years			17	40	2	9	4	0	1	3	.225	16	1	1	.944

Selected by Cleveland Indians' organization in 25th round of free-agent draft, June 2, 1987.

ROBERTO ALOMAR (VELAZQUEZ)

Born February 5, 1968, at Salinas, Puerto Rico.
Height, 6.00. Weight, 185.
Throws right and bats left and righthanded.
Son of Sandy Alomar Sr., infielder with Milwaukee-Atlanta Braves, New York Mets, Chicago White Sox,
California Angels, New York Yankees and Texas Rangers, 1964 through 1978; minor league instructor,
San Diego Padres' organization, 1985; and coach with San Diego Padres, 1986 through 1990;
and brother of Sandy Alomar, Jr., catcher with Cleveland Indians.

Major League stolen bases: 1988 (24), 1989 (42), 1990 (24). Total—90.
Led National League in sacrifice hits with 17 in 1989.
Led National League second basemen in errors with 17 in 1990.
Led Texas League shortstops in putouts with 167 and errors with 34 in 1987.
Led South Atlantic League second basemen in errors with 35 in 1985.

Year	Club	League	Pos.	G.	AB.	R.	H.	2B.	3B.	HR.	RBI.	B.A.	PO.	A.	E.	F.A.
1985—Charleston	S. Atl.	2B-SS	★137	★546	89	160	14	3	0	54	.293	298	339	36	.947
1986—Reno	Calif.	2B	90	356	53	123	16	4	4	49	★.346	198	265	18	.963
1987—Wichita	Texas	SS-2B	130	536	88	171	41	4	12	68	.319	188	309	36	.932
1988—Las Vegas	P. C.	2B	9	37	5	10	1	0	2	14	.270	22	29	1	.981
1988—San Diego	Nat.	2B	143	545	84	145	24	6	9	41	.266	319	459	16	.980
1989—San Diego	Nat.	2B	158	623	82	184	27	1	7	56	.295	341	472	★28	.967
1990—San Diego†	Nat.	2B-SS	147	586	80	168	27	5	6	60	.287	316	404	19	.974
Major League Totals—3 Years			448	1754	246	497	78	12	22	157	.283	976	1335	63	.973

Signed as free agent by San Diego Padres' organization, February 16, 1985.

†Traded with Outfielder Joe Carter to Toronto Blue Jays for First Baseman Fred McGriff and Shortstop Tony Fernandez, December 5, 1990.

ALL-STAR GAME RECORD

Year League	Pos.	AB.	R.	H.	2B.	3B.	HR.	RBI.	B.A.	PO.	A.	E.	F.A.
1990—National	2B	1	0	0	0	0	0	0	.000	1	2	0	1.000

SANTOS ALOMAR JR. (VELAZQUEZ)
(Sandy)

Born June 18, 1966, at Salinas, Puerto Rico.
Height, 6.05. Weight, 200.
Throws and bats righthanded.
Son of Sandy Alomar, Sr., infielder with Milwaukee-Atlanta Braves, New York Mets,
Chicago White Sox, California Angels, New York Yankees and Texas Rangers, 1964 through 1978;
minor league instructor, San Diego Padres' organization, 1985; and coach with San Diego Padres, 1986 through 1990;
and brother of Roberto Alomar, second baseman with Toronto Blue Jays.

Major League stolen bases: 1990 (4).
Led Pacific Coast League catchers in putouts with 573 in 1988 and 702 in 1989.
Led Pacific Coast League catchers in total chances with 633 in 1988 and 761 in 1989.
Led Northwest League catchers in putouts with 421 in 1984.
Named American League Rookie of the Year by THE SPORTING NEWS, 1990.
Named American League Rookie of the Year by Baseball Writers' Association of America, 1990.
Named catcher on THE SPORTING NEWS American League All-Star fielding team, 1990.
Named Minor League Player of the Year by THE SPORTING NEWS, 1989.
Named Minor League Co-Player of the Year by THE SPORTING NEWS, 1988.
Named Pacific Coast League Player of the Year, 1988 and 1989.

Year Club	League	Pos.	G.	AB.	R.	H.	2B.	3B.	HR.	RBI.	B.A.	PO.	A.	E.	F.A.
1984—Spokane†	N'west	*C-1B	59	219	13	47	5	0	0	21	.215	465	51	8	*.985
1985—Charleston†	S. Atl.	C-OF	100	352	38	73	7	0	3	43	.207	779	75	18	.979
1986—Beaumont†	Texas	C	100	346	36	83	15	1	4	27	.240	505	60	*18	.969
1987—Wichita	Texas	C	103	375	50	115	19	1	8	65	.307	*606	50	*15	.978
1988—Las Vegas	P. C.	C-OF	93	337	59	100	9	5	16	71	.297	574	46	*14	.978
1988—San Diego	Nat.	PH	1	1	0	0	0	0	0	0	.000	0	0	0	.000
1989—Las Vegas	P. C.	C-OF	131	*523	88	160	33	8	13	101	.306	706	47	12	.984
1989—San Diego‡	Nat.	C	7	19	1	4	1	0	1	6	.211	33	1	0	1.000
1990—Cleveland	Amer.	C	132	445	60	129	26	2	9	66	.290	686	46	*14	.981
National League Totals—2 Years			8	20	1	4	1	0	1	6	.200	33	1	0	1.000
American League Totals—1 Year			132	445	60	129	26	2	9	66	.290	686	46	14	.981
Major League Totals—3 Years			140	465	61	133	27	2	10	72	.286	719	47	14	.982

Signed as free agent by San Diego Padres' organization, October 21, 1983.
†Batted left and righthanded.
‡Traded with Outfielder Chris James and Third Baseman Carlos Baerga to Cleveland Indians for Outfielder Joe Carter, December 6, 1989.

ALL-STAR GAME RECORD

Year League	Pos.	AB.	R.	H.	2B.	3B.	HR.	RBI.	B.A.	PO.	A.	E.	F.A.
1990—American	C	3	1	2	0	0	0	0	.667	3	0	0	1.000

MOISES ROJAS ALOU

First name pronounced MOY-ses.

Born July 3, 1966, at Atlanta, Ga.
Height, 6.03. Weight, 175.
Throws and bats righthanded.
Attended Canada College, Redwood City, Calif.
Son of Felipe Alou, outfielder with San Francisco, Milwaukee-Atlanta Braves, Oakland, New York Yankees, Montreal and Milwaukee Brewers, 1958 through 1974; coach with Montreal Expos, 1979, 1980 and 1984; and minor league manager in Montreal Expos' organization, 1977, 1978, 1981 through 1983 and since 1985; Nephew of Jesus Alou, outfielder with San Francisco, Houston, Oakland and New York Yankees, 1963 through 1975, 1978 and 1979, and scout with Montreal Expos since 1983; Nephew of Matty Alou, outfielder with San Francisco, Pittsburgh, St. Louis, Oakland, New York Yankees and San Diego, 1960 through 1974; and brother of Jose Alou, outfielder in Montreal Expos' organization, 1987 through 1989.

Led American Association outfielders in double plays with 7 in 1990.

Year Club	League	Pos.	G.	AB.	R.	H.	2B.	3B.	HR.	RBI.	B.A.	PO.	A.	E.	F.A.
1986—Watertown	NYP	OF	69	254	30	60	9	*8	6	35	.236	134	6	7	.952
1987—Macon	S. Atl.	OF	4	8	1	1	0	0	0	0	.125	6	0	0	1.000
1987—Wichita	NYP	OF	39	117	20	25	6	2	4	8	.214	43	1	2	.957
1988—Augusta	S. Atl.	OF	105	358	58	112	23	5	7	62	.313	220	10	9	.962
1989—Salem	Carol.	OF	86	321	50	97	29	2	14	53	.302	166	12	10	.947
1989—Harrisburg	East.	OF	54	205	36	60	5	2	3	19	.293	89	1	2	.978
1990—Harrisburg	East.	OF	36	132	19	39	12	2	3	22	.295	93	2	1	.990
1990—Buff.†-Ind.	A. A.	OF	90	326	44	86	5	6	5	37	.264	196	12	8	.963
1990—Pitt.-Mont.	Nat.	OF	16	20	4	4	0	1	0	0	.200	9	1	0	1.000
Major League Totals—1 Year			16	20	4	4	0	1	0	0	.200	9	1	0	1.000

Selected by Pittsburgh Pirates' organization in 1st round (second player selected) of free agent draft, January 14, 1986.

†Traded to Montreal Expos, August 16, 1990, completing deal in which Montreal traded Pitcher Zane Smith to Pittsburgh Pirates for Pitcher Scott Ruskin, Shortstop Willie Greene and a player to be named later, August 8, 1990.

WILSON EDUARDO ALVAREZ

Born March 24, 1970, at Maracaibo, Venezuela.
Height, 6.01. Weight, 175.
Throws and bats lefthanded.

Tied for Gulf Coast League lead in home runs allowed with 6 in 1987.

Year Club	League	G.	IP.	W.	L.	Pct.	H.	R.	ER.	SO.	BB.	ERA.
1987—Gastonia	S. Atlantic	8	32	1	5	.167	39	24	23	19	23	6.47
1987—Sarasota Rangers	Gulf Coast	10	44⅔	2	5	.286	41	29	26	46	21	5.24
1988—Gastonia	S. Atlantic	23	127	4	11	.267	113	63	42	134	49	2.98
1988—Oklahoma City	Am. Assoc.	5	16⅔	1	1	.500	17	8	7	9	6	3.78
1989—Tulsa	Texas	7	48	2	2	.500	40	14	11	29	16	2.06
1989—Texas†	American	1	0	0	1	.000	3	3	3	0	2	....
1989—Birmingham	Southern	6	35⅔	2	1	.667	32	12	12	18	16	3.03
1990—Birmingham	Southern	7	46⅓	5	1	.833	44	24	22	36	25	4.27
1990—Vancouver	P. Coast	17	75	7	7	.500	91	54	50	35	51	6.00
Major League Totals—1 Year		1	0	0	1	.000	3	3	3	0	2	....

Signed as free agent by Texas Rangers' organization, September 23, 1986.

†Traded with Infielder Scott Fletcher and Outfielder Sammy Sosa to Chicago White Sox for Outfielder Harold Baines and Infielder Fred Manrique, July 29, 1989.

LARRY EUGENE ANDERSEN

Born May 6, 1953, at Portland, Ore.
Height, 6.03. Weight, 205.
Throws and bats righthanded.
Attended Bellevue Community College, Bellevue, Wash.

Pitched 6-0 no-hit victory against Victoria, June 1, 1974.
Major League saves: 1981 (5), 1982 (1), 1984 (4), 1985 (3), 1986 (1), 1987 (5), 1988 (5), 1989 (3), 1990 (7). Total—34.
Led Pacific Coast League in saves with 25 in 1978 and 22 in 1983.
Led American Association in balks with 4 in 1975.

Year Club	League	G.	IP.	W.	L.	Pct.	H.	R.	ER.	SO.	BB.	ERA.
1971—Reno	California	7	24	1	0	1.000	37	20	18	10	9	6.75
1971—Sarasota Indians	Gulf Coast	4	15	0	3	.000	15	7	5	10	7	3.00
1972—Reno	California	27	124	4	14	.222	166	102	90	79	57	6.53
1973—Reno	California	29	164	10	8	.556	173	91	72	115	67	3.95
1974—San Antonio	Texas	25	169	10	6	.625	176	84	72	64	51	3.83
1975—Oklahoma City	Am. Assoc.	25	156	10	11	.476	179	87	73	64	52	4.21
1975—Cleveland	American	3	6	0	0	.000	4	3	3	4	2	4.50
1976—Toledo	Int'national	6	23	0	2	.000	47	33	33	8	6	12.91
1976—Williamsport	Eastern	21	133	9	6	.600	117	47	40	74	34	2.71
1977—Toledo†	Int'national	45	65	5	6	.455	52	20	14	40	37	1.94
1977—Cleveland	American	11	14	0	1	.000	10	7	5	8	9	3.21
1978—Portland	P. Coast	57	99	10	7	.588	92	42	38	65	45	3.45
1979—Tacoma	P. Coast	27	112	10	6	.625	124	59	50	52	32	4.02
1979—Cleveland‡	American	8	17	0	0	.000	25	14	14	7	4	7.41
1980—Portland§	P. Coast	52	93	5	7	.417	78	24	18	65	16	1.74
1981—Seattle	American	41	68	3	3	.500	57	27	20	40	18	2.65
1982—Seattle x	American	40	79⅔	0	0	.000	100	56	53	32	23	5.99
1982—Salt Lake City y	P. Coast	5	6⅔	1	0	1.000	2	0	0	8	3	0.00
1983—Portland	P. Coast	52	70⅓	7	8	.467	63	35	16	64	30	2.05
1983—Philadelphia	National	17	26⅓	1	0	1.000	19	7	7	14	9	2.39
1984—Philadelphia	National	64	90⅔	3	7	.300	85	32	24	54	25	2.38
1985—Philadelphia	National	57	73	3	3	.500	78	41	35	50	26	4.32
1986—Philadelphia z-Houston a	National	48	77½	2	1	.667	83	30	26	42	26	3.03
1987—Houston b	National	67	101⅔	9	5	.643	95	46	39	94	41	3.45
1988—Houston c	National	53	82⅔	2	4	.333	82	29	27	66	20	2.94
1989—Houston d	National	60	87⅔	4	4	.500	63	19	15	85	24	1.54
1990—Houston e	National	50	73⅔	5	2	.714	61	19	16	68	24	1.95
1990—Boston f	American	15	22	0	0	.000	18	3	3	25	3	1.23
American League Totals—6 Years		118	206⅔	3	4	.429	214	110	98	116	59	4.27
National League Totals—8 Years		416	613	29	26	.527	566	223	189	473	195	2.77
Major League Totals—13 Years		534	819⅔	32	30	.516	780	333	287	589	254	3.15

Selected by Cleveland Indians' organization in 7th round of free-agent draft, June 8, 1971.

†Appeared as first baseman with no chances.

‡Traded to Pittsburgh Pirates for Outfielder Larry Littleton and Pitcher John Burden, December 21, 1979.

§Traded to Seattle Mariners, October 29, 1980, completing deal in which Seattle traded Pitcher Odell Jones to Pittsburgh Pirates for a player to be named later, April 1, 1980.

xOn disabled list, August 11 to September 1, 1982; included rehabilitation disability assignment to Salt Lake City August 11 to August 31, 1982.

yLoaned to Portland (Philadelphia Phillies' organization), April 1, 1983; sold to Philadelphia Phillies, July 29, 1983.

zReleased, May 13, 1986; signed by Houston Astros, May 16, 1986.

aGranted free agency, November 12, 1986; re-signed by Astros, December 21, 1986.

bGranted free agency, November 9, 1987; re-signed by Astros, January 8, 1988.

cOn disabled list, April 26 to May 11, 1988.

dOn disabled list, April 25 to May 10 and August 20 to September 4, 1989.

eTraded to Boston Red Sox for Third Baseman Jeff Bagwell, August 30, 1990.

fGranted free agency, December 7, 1990; signed by San Diego Padres, December 21, 1990.

CHAMPIONSHIP SERIES RECORD

Year Club	League	G.	IP.	W.	L.	Pct.	H.	R.	ER.	SO.	BB.	ERA.
1986—Houston	National	2	5	0	0	.000	1	0	0	3	2	0.00
1990—Boston	American	3	3	0	1	.000	3	2	2	3	3	6.00
Championship Series Totals—2 Years		5	8	0	1	.000	4	2	2	6	5	2.25

WORLD SERIES RECORD

Year Club	League	G.	IP.	W.	L.	Pct.	H.	R.	ER.	SO.	BB.	ERA.
1983—Philadelphia	National	2	4	0	0	.000	4	1	1	1	0	2.25

ALLAN LEE ANDERSON

Born January 7, 1964, at Lancaster, O.
Height, 6.00. Weight, 194.
Throws and bats lefthanded.

Led California League in shutouts with 5 in 1984.

Year Club	League	G.	IP.	W.	L.	Pct.	H.	R.	ER.	SO.	BB.	ERA.
1983—Wisconsin Rapids	Midwest	7	30⅓	0	4	.000	36	28	23	46	17	6.82
1983—Elizabethton	Ap'lachian	6	12⅔	1	3	.250	17	12	12	12	7	8.53
1984—Visalia	California	26	188⅔	12	7	.632	152	80	60	151	105	2.86
1985—Toledo	Int'national	27	176	7	11	.389	176	81	67	94	79	3.43
1986—Toledo	Int'national	11	67	2	5	.286	78	39	34	37	31	4.57
1986—Minnesota†	American	21	84⅓	3	6	.333	106	54	52	51	30	5.55
1987—Portland	P. Coast	19	98	4	8	.333	127	77	61	45	49	5.60
1987—Minnesota	American	4	12⅓	1	0	1.000	20	15	15	3	10	10.95
1988—Portland	P. Coast	3	14⅓	1	1	.500	11	4	2	9	5	1.26
1988—Minnesota	American	30	202⅓	16	9	.640	199	70	55	83	37	*2.45
1989—Minnesota‡	American	33	196⅔	17	10	.630	214	97	83	69	53	3.80
1990—Minnesota	American	31	188⅔	7	18	.280	214	106	95	82	39	4.53
Major League Totals—5 Years		119	684⅓	44	43	.506	753	342	300	288	169	3.95

Selected by Minnesota Twins' organization in 2nd round of free-agent draft, June 7, 1982.
†Appeared in one game as a pinch-runner.
‡Struck out in only appearance as a pinch-hitter.

BRADY KEVIN ANDERSON

Born January 18, 1964, at Silver Spring, Md.
Height, 6.01. Weight, 186.
Throws and bats lefthanded.
Attended University of California, Irvine, Calif.

Major League stolen bases: 1988 (10), 1989 (16), 1990 (15). Total—41.
Led New York-Pennsylvania League in bases on balls received with 67 in 1985.
Led Florida State League in bases on balls received with 107 in 1986.

Year Club	League	Pos.	G.	AB.	R.	H.	2B.	3B.	HR.	RBI.	B.A.	PO.	A.	E.	F.A.
1985—Elmira	NYP	OF	71	215	36	55	7	●6	5	21	.256	119	5	3	.976
1986—Winter Haven	Fla. St.	OF	126	417	86	133	19	11	12	87	.319	280	5	1	*.997
1987—New Britain	East.	OF	52	170	30	50	4	3	6	35	.294	127	2	2	.985
1987—Pawtucket	Int.	OF	23	79	18	30	4	0	2	8	.380	48	1	0	1.000
1988—Bos.†-Balt.	Amer.	OF	94	325	31	69	13	4	1	21	.212	243	4	4	.984
1988—Pawtucket	Int.	OF	49	167	27	48	6	1	4	19	.287	115	4	2	.983
1989—Baltimore	Amer.	OF	94	266	44	55	12	2	4	16	.207	191	3	3	.985
1989—Rochester	Int.	OF	21	70	14	14	1	2	1	8	.200	1	0	0	1.000
1990—Baltimore‡	Amer.	OF	89	234	24	54	5	2	3	24	.231	149	3	2	.987
1990—Hagerstown	East.	OF	9	34	8	13	0	2	1	5	.382	8	1	0	1.000
1990—Frederick	Carol.	OF	2	7	2	3	1	0	0	3	.429	1	0	0	1.000
Major League Totals—3 Years			277	825	99	178	30	8	8	61	.216	583	10	9	.985

Selected by Boston Red Sox' organization in 10th round of free-agent draft, June 3, 1985.
†Traded with Pitcher Curt Schilling to Baltimore Orioles for Pitcher Mike Boddicker, July 29, 1988.
‡On disabled list, June 8 to July 20, 1990; included rehabilitation disability assignment to Hagerstown, July 5 to July 12, 1990; and Frederick, July 13 to July 17, 1990.

DAVID CARTER ANDERSON
(Dave)

Born August 1, 1960, at Louisville, Ky.
Height, 6.02. Weight, 184.
Throws and bats righthanded.
Attended Memphis State University, Memphis, Tenn.

Major League stolen bases: 1983 (6), 1984 (15), 1985 (5), 1986 (5), 1987 (9), 1988 (4), 1989 (2), 1990 (1). Total—47.
Led Pacific Coast League shortstops in double plays with 81 in 1982.

Year Club	League	Pos.	G.	AB.	R.	H.	2B.	3B.	HR.	RBI.	B.A.	PO.	A.	E.	F.A.
1981—Vero Beach	Fla. St.	SS	65	200	44	54	8	1	0	18	.270	109	218	23	.934
1982—Albuquerque	P. C.	SS	132	507	100	174	19	7	5	76	.343	223	397	*34	.948
1983—Albuquerque	P. C.	SS	9	27	10	11	1	1	0	3	.407	17	26	1	.977
1983—Los Angeles	Nat.	SS-3B	61	115	12	19	4	2	1	2	.165	56	100	5	.969
1984—Los Angeles	Nat.	SS-3B	121	374	51	94	16	2	3	34	.251	176	359	19	.966
1985—Los Angeles†	Nat.	3B-SS-2B	77	221	24	44	6	0	4	18	.199	61	187	9	.965
1985—Albuquerque	P. C.	SS-3B-2B	28	97	23	28	7	0	3	16	.289	29	62	11	.892

Year Club	League	Pos.	G.	AB.	R.	H.	2B.	3B.	HR.	RBI.	B.A.	PO.	A.	E.	F.A.
1986—Los Angeles‡ .... Nat.		3B-SS-2B	92	216	31	53	9	0	1	15	.245	77	159	11	.955
1987—Los Angeles§ .... Nat.		SS-3B-2B	108	265	32	62	12	3	1	13	.234	103	207	7	.978
1988—Los Angeles .... Nat.		SS-3B-2B	116	285	31	71	10	2	2	20	.249	139	244	5	.987
1989—Los Angeles x .... Nat.		SS-3B-2B	87	140	15	32	2	0	1	14	.229	61	73	1	.993
1990—San Francisco ...... Nat.		S-2-1-3	60	100	14	35	5	1	1	6	.350	33	59	1	.989
Major League Totals—8 Years			722	1716	210	410	64	10	14	122	.239	706	1388	58	.973

Selected by Los Angeles Dodgers' organization in 1st round (22nd player selected) of free-agent draft, June 8, 1981.

†On disabled list, April 29 to June 2 and July 31 to September 1, 1985; included rehabilitation disability assignment to Albuquerque, May 17 to June 1 and August 17 to August 31, 1985.

‡On disabled list, June 22 to August 19, 1986.

§On disabled list, August 11 to September 2, 1987.

xGranted free agency, November 13, 1989; signed by San Francisco Giants, November 29, 1989.

CHAMPIONSHIP SERIES RECORD

Year Club	League	Pos.	G.	AB.	R.	H.	2B.	3B.	HR.	RBI.	B.A.	PO.	A.	E.	F.A.
1985—Los Angeles .... Nat.		PR-SS-3B	4	5	1	0	0	0	0	0	.000	3	4	0	1.000

WORLD SERIES RECORD

Year Club	League	Pos.	G.	AB.	R.	H.	2B.	3B.	HR.	RBI.	B.A.	PO.	A.	E.	F.A.
1988—Los Angeles .... Nat.		PH-DH	1	1	0	0	0	0	0	0	.000	0	0	0	.000

KENT McKAY ANDERSON

Born August 12, 1963, at Florence, S.C.
Height, 6.01. Weight, 187.
Throws and bats righthanded.
Attended University of South Carolina, Columbia, S.C.

Major League stolen bases: 1989 (1).

Year Club	League	Pos.	G.	AB.	R.	H.	2B.	3B.	HR.	RBI.	B.A.	PO.	A.	E.	F.A.
1984—Peoria.................... Midw.		SS	67	223	24	50	9	1	1	16	.224	124	189	18	.946
1985—Redwood............ Calif.		SS	117	420	53	105	17	1	1	47	.250	182	316	29	★.945
1986—Palm Springs† ..... Calif.		SS-OF-3B	69	240	37	67	14	0	2	35	.279	131	166	19	.940
1987—Edmonton............. P. C.		SS	57	181	27	42	4	5	3	20	.232	112	154	9	.967
1988—Edmonton............. P. C.		SS	113	374	50	94	22	3	2	39	.251	175	283	30	.939
1989—Edmonton............. P. C.		SS	4	12	3	4	0	0	0	1	.333	7	17	1	.960
1989—California.............. Amer.		S-2-3-O	86	223	27	51	6	1	0	17	.229	102	233	10	.971
1990—California‡............ Amer.		SS-3B-2B	49	143	16	44	6	1	1	5	.308	75	129	9	.958
1990—Edmonton............. P. C.		2B-3B-SS	18	59	10	16	6	1	0	7	.271	31	55	3	.966
Major League Totals—2 Years			135	366	43	95	12	2	1	22	.260	177	362	19	.966

Selected by California Angels' organization in 4th round of free-agent draft, June 4, 1984.

†On disabled list, May 12 to June 23, 1986.

‡On disabled list, May 20 to June 11 and August 16 to September 1, 1990.

SCOTT RICHARD ANDERSON

Born August 1, 1962, at Corvallis, Ore.
Height, 6.06. Weight, 190.
Throws and bats righthanded.
Attended Oregon State University, Corvallis, Ore.

Led American Association in complete games with 6 in 1990.
Tied for Texas League lead in games started by pitchers with 27 in 1985.

Year Club	League	G.	IP.	W.	L.	Pct.	H.	R.	ER.	SO.	BB.	ERA.
1984—Burlington .... Midwest		14	86⅓	3	6	.333	79	33	24	81	28	2.50
1985—Tulsa.............................. Texas		28	174⅓	9	6	.600	177	87	71	123	51	3.67
1986—Tulsa.............................. Texas		10	18⅔	0	0	.000	11	4	3	13	8	1.45
1986—Oklahoma City .... Am. Assoc.		48	82	5	7	.417	82	36	27	51	28	2.96
1987—Texas............................. American		8	11⅓	0	1	.000	17	12	12	6	8	9.53
1987—Oklahoma City .... Am. Assoc.		49	64	5	3	.625	79	44	40	39	35	5.63
1988—Oklahoma City† .... Am. Assoc.		38	97	4	6	.400	101	51	49	44	49	4.55
1989—Indianapolis .... Am. Assoc.		29	127⅔	7	8	.467	139	62	45	88	44	3.17
1990—Indianapolis .... Am. Assoc.		27	182	12	10	.545	166	74	67	116	61	3.31
1990—Montreal‡ .... National		4	18	0	1	.000	12	6	6	16	5	3.00
American League Totals—1 Year		8	11⅓	0	1	.000	17	12	12	6	8	9.53
National League Totals—1 Year		4	18	0	1	.000	12	6	6	16	5	3.00
Major League Totals—2 Years		12	29⅓	0	2	.000	29	18	18	22	13	5.52

Selected by Oakland A's organization in 16th round of free-agent draft, June 3, 1980.

Selected by Texas Rangers' organization in 7th round of free-agent draft, June 4, 1984.

†Traded to Indianapolis (Montreal Expos' organization) for Outfielder-First Baseman Mike Berger, December 19, 1988.

‡Released, November 1, 1990.

—DID YOU KNOW—

That Oakland's Mark McGwire is the only major leaguer to hit 30 or more home runs in each of his first four seasons?

ERIC TODD ANTHONY

Born November 8, 1967, at San Diego, Calif.
Height, 6.02. Weight, 195.
Throws and bats lefthanded.

Major League stolen bases: 1990 (5).
Led Southern League in slugging percentage with .558 in 1989.
Led South Atlantic League in slugging percentage with .558 in 1988.
Led Gulf Coast League in total bases with 110 in 1987.
Named Southern League Most Valuable Player, 1989.

Year Club	League	Pos.	G.	AB.	R.	H.	2B.	3B.	HR.	RBI.	B.A.	PO.	A.	E.	F.A.
1986—Sarasota Astros....	Gulf C.	OF	13	12	2	3	0	0	0	0	.250	2	1	0	1.000
1987—Sarasota Astros....	Gulf C.	OF	60	216	38	57	11	6	★10	★46	.264	100	●11	5	.957
1988—Asheville...............	S. Atl.	OF	115	439	73	120	★36	1	★29	89	.273	152	8	14	.920
1989—Columbus..............	South.	OF	107	403	67	121	16	2	★28	79	.300	178	17	8	.961
1989—Houston.................	Nat.	OF	25	61	7	11	2	0	4	7	.180	34	1	0	1.000
1989—Tucson...................	P. C.	OF	12	46	10	10	3	0	3	11	.217	21	0	0	1.000
1990—Houston†...............	Nat.	OF	84	239	26	46	8	0	10	29	.192	124	5	4	.970
1990—Columbus..............	South.	OF	4	12	2	2	0	0	1	3	.167	3	0	0	1.000
1990—Tucson...................	P. C.	OF	40	161	28	46	10	2	6	26	.286	84	7	4	.958
Major League Totals—2 Years.................			109	300	33	57	10	0	14	36	.190	158	6	4	.976

Selected by Houston Astros' organization in 34th round of free-agent draft, June 2, 1986.
†On disabled list, April 10 to April 30, 1990; included rehabilitation disability assignment to Columbus, April 25 to April 30, 1990.

ROBERT KEVIN APPIER

(Known by middle name.)

Born December 6, 1967, at Lancaster, Calif.
Height, 6.01. Weight, 190.
Throws and bats righthanded.
Attended Fresno State University, Fresno, Calif.,
and Antelope Valley College, Lancaster, Calif.

Tied for Northwest League lead in games started by pitchers with 15 in 1987.
Named American League Rookie Pitcher of the Year by THE SPORTING NEWS, 1990.

Year Club	League	G.	IP.	W.	L.	Pct.	H.	R.	ER.	SO.	BB.	ERA.
1987—Eugene..............................	Northwest	15	77	5	2	.714	81	43	26	72	29	3.04
1988—Baseball City	Florida St.	24	147⅓	10	9	.526	134	58	45	112	39	2.75
1988—Memphis.........................	Southern	3	19⅔	2	0	1.000	11	5	4	18	7	1.83
1989—Omaha.............................	Am. Assoc.	22	139	8	8	.500	141	70	61	109	42	3.95
1989—Kansas City.....................	American	6	21⅔	1	4	.200	34	22	22	10	12	9.14
1990—Omaha.............................	Am. Assoc.	3	18	2	0	1.000	15	3	3	17	3	1.50
1990—Kansas City.....................	American	32	185⅔	12	8	.600	179	67	57	127	54	2.76
Major League Totals—2 Years............................		38	207⅓	13	12	.520	213	89	79	137	66	3.43

Selected by Kansas City Royals' organization in 1st round (ninth player selected) of free-agent draft, June 2, 1987.

LUIS ANTONIO AQUINO (COLON)

Name pronounced A-Keno.

Born May 19, 1965, at Rio Piedras, Puerto Rico.
Height, 6.01. Weight, 190.
Throws and bats righthanded.

Pitched 2-0 no-hit victory against Columbus, June 20, 1988.
Led Southern League in saves with 20 and tied for lead in games finished in relief with 42 in 1985.
Led Carolina League in games finished in relief with 42 in 1984.

Year Club	League	G.	IP.	W.	L.	Pct.	H.	R.	ER.	SO.	BB.	ERA.
1982—Bradenton Blue Jays...................	Gulf Coast	13	73⅓	4	7	.364	60	33	27	52	17	3.31
1983—Florence............................	S. Atlantic	29	133⅔	7	9	.438	128	91	78	104	61	5.25
1984—Kinston............................	Carolina	★53	70	5	6	.455	50	21	21	78	37	2.70
1984—Knoxville	Southern	3	4	0	0	.000	3	4	4	7	3	9.00
1985—Knoxville	Southern	50	83	5	7	.417	58	29	24	82	32	2.60
1986—Syracuse	Int'national	43	84⅓	3	7	.300	70	30	27	60	34	2.88
1986—Toronto	American	7	11⅓	1	1	.500	14	8	8	5	3	6.35
1987—Syracuse†	Int'national	26	84⅔	6	7	.462	75	46	45	68	51	4.78
1987—Omaha.............................	Am. Assoc.	14	50⅔	3	2	.600	42	15	13	29	16	2.31
1988—Omaha.............................	Am. Assoc.	25	129⅓	8	3	.727	106	43	41	93	50	2.85
1988—Kansas City.....................	American	7	29	1	0	1.000	33	15	9	11	17	2.79
1989—Kansas City‡...................	American	34	141⅓	6	8	.429	148	62	55	68	35	3.50
1990—Kansas City§...................	American	20	68⅓	4	1	.800	59	25	24	28	27	3.16
Major League Totals—4 Years............................		68	250	12	10	.545	254	110	96	112	82	3.46

Signed as free agent by Toronto Blue Jays' organization, June 15, 1981.
†Traded to Kansas City Royals' organization for Outfielder Juan Beniquez, July 14, 1987.
‡On disabled list, May 31 to June 15, 1989.
§On disabled list, July 21 to September 24, 1990.

BRONI JOHN ARD
(Johnny)

Born June 1, 1967, at Las Vegas, Nev.
Height, 6.05. Weight, 220.
Throws and bats righthanded.
Attended Francis Marion College, Florence, S.C., and Manatee Junior College, Bradenton, Fla.

Pitched 2-0 no-hit victory against Chattanooga, August 30, 1990 (first game).
Tied for California League lead in games started by pitchers with 28 in 1989.
Received reported $92,000 bonus to sign with Minnesota Twins, 1988.

Year	Club	League	G.	IP.	W.	L.	Pct.	H.	R.	ER.	SO.	BB.	ERA.
1988—Elizabethton	Ap'lachian	9	59⅓	4	1	.800	40	17	13	71	26	1.97
1988—Kenosha	Midwest	4	25⅔	3	0	1.000	14	3	3	16	4	1.05
1989—Visalia	California	28	186	●13	7	.650	155	87	68	153	84	3.29
1990—Orlando†	Southern	29	180⅓	12	9	.571	167	90	76	101	85	3.79

Selected by Minnesota Twins' organization in 1st round (20th player selected) of free-agent draft, June 1, 1988.
†Traded with a player to be named later to San Francisco Giants for Pitcher Steve Bedrosian, December 5, 1990; San Francisco acquired Pitcher Jimmy Williams to complete deal, December 18, 1990.

JACK WILLIAM ARMSTRONG

Born March 7, 1965, at Englewood, N.J.
Height, 6.05. Weight, 220.
Throws and bats righthanded.
Attended Rider College, Lawrenceville, N.J., and received degree in economics
from University of Oklahoma, Norman, Okla., in 1987.

Pitched 4-0 no-hit victory against Indianapolis, August 7, 1988.
Tied for National League lead in balks with 5 in 1990.
Led American Association in shutouts with 6 and complete games with 12 in 1989.

Year	Club	League	G.	IP.	W.	L.	Pct.	H.	R.	ER.	SO.	BB.	ERA.
1987—Billings	Pioneer	5	20⅓	2	1	.667	16	7	6	29	12	2.66
1987—Vermont	Eastern	5	35⅔	1	2	.333	24	12	12	39	23	3.03
1988—Nashville	Am. Assoc.	17	120	5	5	.500	84	44	40	116	38	3.00
1988—Cincinnati	National	14	65⅓	4	7	.364	63	44	42	45	38	5.79
1989—Nashville	Am. Assoc.	25	182⅔	●13	9	.591	144	63	59	152	58	2.91
1989—Cincinnati	National	9	42⅔	2	3	.400	40	24	22	23	21	4.64
1990—Cincinnati†	National	29	166	12	9	.571	151	72	63	110	59	3.42
Major League Totals—3 Years		52	274	18	19	.486	254	140	127	178	118	4.17

Selected by San Francisco Giants' organization in 3rd round of free-agent draft, June 2, 1986.
Selected by Cincinnati Reds' organization in 1st round (18th player selected) of free-agent draft, June 2, 1987.
†On disabled list, August 25 to September 9, 1990.

WORLD SERIES RECORD

Year	Club	League	G.	IP.	W.	L.	Pct.	H.	R.	ER.	SO.	BB.	ERA.
1990—Cincinnati	National	1	3	0	0	.000	1	0	0	3	0	0.00

ALL-STAR GAME RECORD

Year	League	IP.	W.	L.	Pct.	H.	R.	ER.	SO.	BB.	ERA.
1990—National		2	0	0	.000	1	0	0	2	0	0.00

BRADLEY JAMES ARNSBERG
(Brad)

Born August 20, 1963, at Seattle, Wash.
Height, 6.04. Weight, 210.
Throws and bats righthanded.
Attended Merced College, Merced, Calif.
Brother of Tim Arnsberg, pitcher in Houston Astros' organization, 1985 through 1987.

Major League saves: 1989 (1), 1990 (5). Total—6.
Pitched 5-0 no-hit victory against Savannah, May 24, 1984.
Led International League in complete games with 9 and tied for lead in shutouts with 2 in 1987.
Led International League pitchers in games started with 28 and balks with 5 in 1986.
Tied for South Atlantic League lead in complete games with 10 and shutouts with 4 in 1984.
Named International League Pitcher of the Year, 1987.
Named Eastern League Pitcher of the Year, 1985.

Year	Club	League	G.	IP.	W.	L.	Pct.	H.	R.	ER.	SO.	BB.	ERA.
1984—Greensboro	S. Atlantic	23	158⅔	12	5	.706	121	61	52	112	59	2.95
1985—Albany†	Eastern	20	141¼	●14	2	*.875	105	34	25	82	35	*1.59
1986—Columbus	Int'national	28	*177⅓	8	●12	.400	168	*106	●83	96	53	4.21
1986—New York	American	2	8	0	0	.000	13	3	3	3	1	3.38
1987—Columbus	Int'national	19	144	12	5	.706	140	55	46	83	37	2.88
1987—New York‡§	American	6	19⅓	1	3	.250	22	12	12	14	13	5.59
1988—Texas x	American					(Did not play)						
1989—Texas	American	16	48	2	1	.667	45	27	22	26	22	4.13
1989—Oklahoma City	Am. Assoc.	18	115⅓	6	8	.429	117	58	52	61	34	4.06
1990—Oklahoma City	Am. Assoc.	14	29⅔	0	4	.000	35	19	17	17	10	5.16
1990—Texas	American	53	62⅔	6	1	.857	56	20	15	44	33	2.15
Major League Totals—4 Years		77	138	9	5	.643	136	62	52	87	69	3.39

Selected by Cleveland Indians' organization in 19th round of free-agent draft, June 8, 1981.
Selected by St. Louis Cardinals' organization in secondary phase of free-agent draft, January 12, 1982.
Selected by Baltimore Orioles' organization in secondary phase of free-agent draft, June 7, 1982.
Selected by California Angels' organization in secondary phase of free-agent draft, January 11, 1983.
Selected by New York Yankees' organization in secondary phase of free-agent draft, June 6, 1983.
†On disabled list, May 12 to May 24 and June 23 to July 22, 1985.
‡On disabled list, August 23 to September 14, 1987.
§Traded to Texas Rangers, November 10, 1987, completing deal in which Texas traded Catcher Don Slaught to New York Yankees for a player to be named later, November 2, 1987.
xOn disabled list, March 29 to September 1, 1988.

ANDREW JASON ASHBY
(Andy)

Born July 11, 1967, at Kansas City, Mo.
Height, 6.05. Weight, 180.
Throws and bats righthanded.
Attended Crowder College, Neosho, Mo.

Year Club	League	G.	IP.	W.	L.	Pct.	H.	R.	ER.	SO.	BB.	ERA.
1986—Bend	Northwest	16	60	1	2	.333	56	40	33	45	34	4.95
1987—Spartanburg	S. Atlantic	13	64⅓	4	6	.400	73	45	40	52	38	5.60
1987—Utica	NYP	13	60	3	7	.300	56	38	27	51	36	4.05
1988—Spartanburg†	S. Atlantic	3	16⅔	1	1	.500	13	7	5	16	7	2.70
1988—Batavia	NYP	6	44⅔	3	1	.750	25	11	8	32	16	1.61
1989—Spartanburg	S. Atlantic	17	106⅔	5	9	.357	95	48	34	100	49	2.87
1989—Clearwater‡	Florida St.	6	43⅔	1	4	.200	28	9	6	44	21	1.24
1990—Reading	Eastern	23	139⅔	10	7	.588	134	65	53	94	48	3.42

Signed as free agent by Philadelphia Phillies' organization, May 4, 1986.
†On disabled list, April 7 to July 10, 1988.
‡On disabled list, April 6 to April 26, 1989.

PAUL ANDRE ASSENMACHER

Born December 10, 1960, at Detroit, Mich.
Height, 6.03. Weight, 200.
Throws and bats lefthanded.
Received degree in business administration from Aquinas College, Grand Rapids, Mich.

Shares major league record for most strikeouts, inning (4), August 22, 1989, fifth inning.
Major League saves: 1986 (7), 1987 (2), 1988 (5), 1990 (10). Total—24.

Year Club	League	G.	IP.	W.	L.	Pct.	H.	R.	ER.	SO.	BB.	ERA.
1983—Bradenton Braves	Gulf Coast	10	36⅔	1	0	1.000	35	14	9	44	4	2.21
1984—Durham	Carolina	26	147⅓	6	11	.353	153	78	70	147	52	4.28
1985—Durham	Carolina	14	38⅓	3	2	.600	38	16	14	36	13	3.29
1985—Greenville	Southern	29	52⅔	6	0	1.000	47	16	15	59	11	2.56
1986—Atlanta	National	61	68⅓	7	3	.700	61	23	19	56	26	2.50
1987—Atlanta†	National	52	54⅔	1	1	.500	58	41	31	39	24	5.10
1987—Richmond	Int'national	4	24⅔	1	2	.333	30	11	10	21	8	3.65
1988—Atlanta‡	National	64	79⅓	8	7	.533	72	28	27	71	32	3.06
1989—Atlanta§-Chicago	National	63	76⅔	3	4	.429	74	37	34	79	28	3.99
1990—Chicago	National	74	103	7	2	.778	90	33	32	95	36	2.80
Major League Totals—5 Years		314	382	26	17	.605	355	162	143	340	146	3.37

Signed as free agent by Atlanta Braves' organization, July 10, 1983.
†On disabled list, April 29 to May 9, 1987.
‡On disabled list, August 10 to August 25, 1988.
§Traded to Chicago Cubs for two players to be named later, August 24, 1989; Atlanta Braves acquired Catcher Kelly Mann and Pitcher Pat Gomez to complete deal, September 1, 1989.

CHAMPIONSHIP SERIES RECORD

Year Club	League	G.	IP.	W.	L.	Pct.	H.	R.	ER.	SO.	BB.	ERA.
1989—Chicago	National	2	⅔	0	0	.000	3	1	1	0	0	13.50

DONALD GLENN AUGUST
(Don)

Born July 3, 1963, at Inglewood, Calif.
Height, 6.03. Weight, 190.
Throws and bats righthanded.
Attended Chapman College, Orange, Calif.

Tied for Pacific Coast League lead in games started by pitchers with 27 in 1986.
Member of 1984 U.S. Olympic baseball team.

Year Club	League	G.	IP.	W.	L.	Pct.	H.	R.	ER.	SO.	BB.	ERA.
1985—Columbus	Southern	27	176⅓	14	8	.636	183	77	58	78	49	2.96
1986—Tucson†-Vancouver	P. Coast	27	179	10	10	.500	192	88	67	70	51	3.37
1987—Denver	Am. Assoc.	28	179½	10	9	.526	★220	★124	★111	91	55	5.57
1988—Denver	Am. Assoc.	10	71⅔	4	1	.800	79	37	28	58	14	3.52
1988—Milwaukee	American	24	148⅓	13	7	.650	137	55	51	66	48	3.09
1989—Milwaukee	American	31	142⅓	12	12	.500	175	93	84	51	58	5.31
1989—Denver	Am. Assoc.	4	23⅔	1	1	.500	35	18	13	12	5	4.94

Year	Club	League	G.	IP.	W.	L.	Pct.	H.	R.	ER.	SO.	BB.	ERA.
1990—Milwaukee	American	5	11	0	3	.000	13	10	8	2	5	6.55
1990—Denver	Am. Assoc.	22	124	7	7	.500	164	98	*93	67	27	6.75
Major League Totals—3 Years		60	301⅔	25	22	.532	325	158	143	119	111	4.27

Selected by Houston Astros' organization in 1st round (17th player selected) of free-agent draft, June 4, 1984.

†Traded with a player to be named later to Milwaukee Brewers for Pitcher Danny Darwin, August 15, 1986; Milwaukee organization acquired Pitcher Mark Knudson to complete deal, August 21, 1986.

JOSEPH JOHN AUSANIO JR.
(Joe)

Born December 9, 1965, at Kingston, N.Y.
Height, 6.01. Weight, 200.
Throws and bats righthanded.
Attended Jacksonville University, Jacksonville, Fla.

Led Carolina League in saves with 20 and games finished in relief with 51 in 1989.
Led New York-Pennsylvania League in saves with 13 in 1988.

Year	Club	League	G.	IP.	W.	L.	Pct.	H.	R.	ER.	SO.	BB.	ERA.
1988—Watertown	NYP	28	47⅔	2	4	.333	29	10	7	56	27	1.32
1989—Salem	Carolina	54	89	5	4	.556	51	29	21	97	44	2.12
1990—Harrisburg	Eastern	43	54	3	2	.600	36	15	11	50	16	1.83

Selected by Atlanta Braves' organization in 30th round of free-agent draft, June 4, 1984.
Selected by Pittsburgh Pirates' organization in 11th round of free-agent draft, June 1, 1988.

JAMES PARKER AUSTIN

Born December 7, 1963, at Farmville, Va.
Height, 6.02. Weight, 200.
Throws and bats righthanded.
Attended Virginia Commonwealth University, Richmond, Va.

Year	Club	League	G.	IP.	W.	L.	Pct.	H.	R.	ER.	SO.	BB.	ERA.
1986—Spokane	N'west	28	59⅔	5	4	.556	53	24	15	74	22	2.26
1987—Charleston, S.C.	S. Atlantic	31	152	7	10	.412	138	89	71	123	56	4.20
1988—Riverside	California	12	80	6	2	.750	65	31	24	73	35	2.70
1988—Wichita†	Texas	12	73	5	6	.455	76	46	39	52	23	4.81
1989—Stockton	California	7	48⅓	3	3	.500	51	19	14	44	14	2.61
1989—El Paso	Texas	22	85	3	10	.231	121	60	55	69	34	5.82
1990—El Paso	Texas	38	92⅓	11	3	.786	91	36	25	77	26	2.44

Selected by San Diego Padres' organization in 6th round of free-agent draft, June 2, 1986.
†Traded with Pitcher Todd Simmons to Milwaukee Brewers' organization for Pitcher Dan Murphy, February 15, 1989.

STEVEN THOMAS AVERY
(Steve)

Born April 14, 1970, at Trenton, Mich.
Height, 6.04. Weight, 180.
Throws and bats lefthanded.

Tied for Appalachian League lead in shutouts with 2 in 1988.

Year	Club	League	G.	IP.	W.	L.	Pct.	H.	R.	ER.	SO.	BB.	ERA.
1988—Pulaski	Ap'lachian	10	66	7	1	.875	38	16	11	80	19	1.50
1989—Durham	Carolina	13	86⅔	6	4	.600	59	22	14	90	20	1.45
1989—Greenville	Southern	13	84⅓	6	3	.667	68	32	26	75	34	2.77
1990—Richmond	Int'national	13	82⅓	5	5	.500	85	35	31	69	21	3.39
1990—Atlanta	National	21	99	3	11	.214	121	79	62	75	45	5.64
Major League Totals—1 Year		21	99	3	11	.214	121	79	62	75	45	5.64

Selected by Atlanta Braves' organization in 1st round (third player selected) of free-agent draft, June 1, 1988.

OSCAR AZOCAR (AZOCAR)

Born February 21, 1965, at Caracas, Venezuela.
Height, 6.01. Weight, 195.
Throws and bats lefthanded.

Major League stolen bases: 1990 (7).

Year	Club	League	Pos.	G.	AB.	R.	H.	2B.	3B.	HR.	RBI.	B.A.	PO.	A.	E.	F.A.
1987—Fort Lauderdale	Fla. St.	OF-1B	53	192	25	69	11	3	6	39	.359	112	4	3	.975
1988—Albany	East.	*OF-P	*138	*543	60	148	22	*9	6	66	.273	264	13	*15	.949
1989—Albany	East.	OF	92	362	50	101	15	2	4	47	.279	158	2	4	.976
1989—Columbus	Int.	OF	37	130	14	38	9	3	1	12	.292	41	2	1	.977
1990—Columbus	Int.	OF-1B	94	374	49	109	20	5	5	52	.291	228	10	4	.983
1990—New York†	Amer.	OF	65	214	18	53	8	0	5	19	.248	105	4	1	.991
Major League Totals—1 Year			65	214	18	53	8	0	5	19	.248	105	4	1	.991

Signed as free agent by New York Yankees' organization, November 22, 1983.
†Traded to San Diego Padres for a player to be named later, December 3, 1990.

Year Club	League	G.	IP.	W.	L.	Pct.	H.	R.	ER.	SO.	BB.	ERA.
1984—Sarasota Yankees	Gulf Coast	11	56⅓	4	1	.800	37	12	8	60	17	1.28
1985—Sarasota Yankees	Gulf Coast	5	37⅓	4	0	1.000	30	8	6	36	14	1.45
1985—Oneonta	NYP	14	16⅔	0	2	.000	21	16	9	13	9	4.86
1986—Sarasota Yankees	Gulf Coast	6	36	4	2	.667	29	17	13	22	12	3.25
1986—Oneonta	NYP	10	22	2	0	1.000	27	9	7	19	9	2.86
1988—Albany	Eastern	3	3	0	0	.000	4	1	1	1	1	3.00

WALTER WAYNE BACKMAN
(Wally)

Born September 22, 1959, at Hillsboro, Ore.
Height, 5.09. Weight, 168.
Throws right and bats right and lefthanded.

Major League stolen bases: 1980 (2), 1981 (1), 1982 (8), 1984 (32), 1985 (30), 1986 (13), 1987 (11), 1988 (9), 1989 (1), 1990 (6). Total—113.
Collected six hits in one game, April 27, 1990.
Tied for National League lead in sacrifice hits with 14 in 1985.
Led International League in bases on balls received with 87 in 1980.
Led Carolina League in caught stealing with 17 in 1978.

Year Club	League	Pos.	G.	AB.	R.	H.	2B.	3B.	HR.	RBI.	B.A.	PO.	A.	E.	F.A.
1977—Little Falls	NYP	SS-3B	69	255	44	83	10	2	6	30	.325	96	185	19	.937
1978—Lynchburg	Carol.	SS	132	494	86	149	19	●9	3	38	.302	★202	★329	30	★.947
1979—Jackson	Texas	SS-2B	110	404	63	114	11	5	2	19	.282	184	259	31	.935
1980—Tidewater	Int.	2B-SS	125	400	53	117	15	5	1	51	.293	237	320	22	.962
1980—New York	Nat.	2B-SS	27	93	12	30	1	1	0	9	.323	62	55	1	.992
1981—New York	Nat.	2B-3B	26	36	5	10	2	0	0	0	.278	14	21	2	.946
1981—Tidewater†‡	Int.	SS-3B-2B	21	59	6	9	3	1	0	6	.153	12	38	1	.980
1982—New York§	Nat.	2B-3B-SS	96	261	37	71	13	2	3	22	.272	173	209	16	.960
1983—New York	Nat.	2B-3B	26	42	6	7	0	1	0	3	.167	16	15	2	.939
1983—Tidewater	Int.	2B-SS-3B	101	361	69	114	11	3	1	28	.316	175	278	13	.972
1984—New York	Nat.	2B-SS	128	436	68	122	19	2	1	26	.280	223	306	10	.981
1985—New York	Nat.	★2B-SS	145	520	77	142	24	5	1	38	.275	273	370	7	★.989
1986—New York	Nat.	2B	124	387	67	124	18	2	1	27	.320	186	290	17	.966
1987—New Yorkx	Nat.	2B	94	300	43	75	6	1	1	23	.250	131	210	6	.983
1988—New York yz	Nat.	2B	99	294	44	89	12	0	0	17	.303	128	219	4	.989
1989—Minnesota ab	Amer.	2B	87	299	33	69	9	2	1	26	.231	146	187	6	.982
1990—Pittsburgh c	Nat.	3B-2B	104	315	62	92	21	3	2	28	.292	56	136	12	.941
National League Totals—10 Years			869	2684	421	762	116	17	9	193	.284	1242	1831	77	.976
American League Totals—1 Year			87	299	33	69	9	2	1	26	.231	146	187	6	.982
Major League Totals—11 Years			956	2983	454	831	125	19	10	219	.279	1408	2018	83	.976

Selected by New York Mets' organization in 1st round (16th player selected) of free-agent draft, June 7, 1977.
†On suspended list, June 18 to June 20, 1981.
‡On disabled list, July 9 to September 1, 1981.
§On disabled list, August 15 to September 8, 1982.
xOn disabled list, June 9 to June 29, 1987.
yOn disabled list, August 27 to September 11, 1988.
zTraded with Pitcher Mike Santiago to Minnesota Twins for Pitchers Jeff Bumgarner, Steve Gasser and Toby Nivens, December 7, 1988.
aOn disabled list, May 8 to May 25 and July 9 to August 14, 1989.
bGranted free agency, November 13, 1989; signed by Pittsburgh Pirates, January 31, 1990.
cGranted free agency, November 5, 1990.

CHAMPIONSHIP SERIES RECORD

Year Club	League	Pos.	G.	AB.	R.	H.	2B.	3B.	HR.	RBI.	B.A.	PO.	A.	E.	F.A.
1986—New York	Nat.	2B-PH	6	21	5	5	0	0	0	2	.238	9	17	0	1.000
1988—New York	Nat.	2B	7	22	2	6	1	0	0	2	.273	7	19	2	.929
1990—Pittsburgh	Nat.	3B-PH	3	7	1	1	1	0	0	0	.143	1	3	0	1.000
Championship Series Totals—3 Years			16	50	8	12	2	0	0	4	.240	17	39	2	.966

WORLD SERIES RECORD

Year Club	League	Pos.	G.	AB.	R.	H.	2B.	3B.	HR.	RBI.	B.A.	PO.	A.	E.	F.A.
1986—New York	Nat.	PR-2B	6	18	4	6	0	0	0	1	.333	9	13	0	1.000

CARLOS O. BAERGA (ORTIZ)

Born November 4, 1968, at San Juan, Puerto Rico.
Height, 5.11. Weight, 165.
Throws right and bats left and righthanded.

Led Pacific Coast League third basemen in total chances with 380 in 1989.
Led Texas League shortstops in double plays with 61 in 1988.
Led South Atlantic League second basemen in errors with 29 in 1987.

Year Club	League	Pos.	G.	AB.	R.	H.	2B.	3B.	HR.	RBI.	B.A.	PO.	A.	E.	F.A.
1986—Charleston	S. Atl.	2B-SS	111	378	57	102	14	4	7	41	.270	202	245	27	.943
1987—Charleston, S. C.	S. Atl.	2B-SS	134	515	83	157	23	●9	7	50	.305	253	341	36	.943
1988—Wichita	Texas	SS-2B	122	444	67	121	28	1	12	65	.273	221	325	33	.943
1989—Las Vegas†	P. C.	3B	132	520	63	143	28	2	10	74	.275	★92	256	★32	.916
1990—Cleveland	Amer.	3B-SS-2B	108	312	46	81	17	2	7	47	.260	79	164	17	.935
1990—Colorado Springs	P. C.	3B	12	50	11	19	2	1	1	11	.380	18	31	4	.925
Major League Totals—1 Year			108	312	46	81	17	2	7	47	.260	79	164	17	.935

Signed as free agent by San Diego Padres' organization, November 4, 1985.

†Traded with Catcher Sandy Alomar and Outfielder Chris James to Cleveland Indians for Outfielder Joe Carter, December 6, 1989.

KEVIN RICHARD BAEZ

Born January 10, 1967, at Brooklyn, N.Y.
Height, 6.00. Weight, 160.
Throws and bats righthanded.
Received degree from Dominican College, Orangeburg, N.Y.

Led Texas League shortstops in total chances with 509 in 1990.
Led New York-Pennsylvania League shortstops in total chances with 317 in 1988.

Year	Club	League	Pos.	G.	AB.	R.	H.	2B.	3B.	HR.	RBI.	B.A.	PO.	A.	E.	F.A.
1988—Little Falls	NYP	SS	70	218	23	58	7	1	1	19	.266	93	198	26	.918
1989—Columbia	S. Atl.	SS	123	426	59	108	20	1	5	44	.254	181	327	36	★.934
1990—Jackson†	Texas	SS	106	326	29	76	11	0	2	29	.233	★184	301	24	.953
1990—New York	Nat.	SS	5	12	0	2	1	0	0	0	.167	5	7	0	1.000
Major League Totals—1 Year			5	12	0	2	1	0	0	0	.167	5	7	0	1.000

Selected by New York Mets' organization in 7th round of free-agent draft, June 1, 1988.
†On disabled list, July 26 to August 12, 1990.

SCOTT ALAN BAILES

Born December 18, 1962, at Chillicothe, O.
Height, 6.02. Weight, 171.
Throws and bats lefthanded.
Attended St. Louis Community College at Meramec, St. Louis, Mo.

Major League saves: 1986 (7), 1987 (6). Total—13.

Year	Club	League	G.	IP.	W.	L.	Pct.	H.	R.	ER.	SO.	BB.	ERA.
1982—Greenwood†	S. Atlantic	3	13⅔	0	1	.000	17	12	11	8	6	7.24
1983—Alexandria	Carolina	52	75	5	2	.714	67	38	28	101	45	3.36
1984—Nashua	Eastern	54	87	6	8	.429	80	43	33	61	46	3.41
1985—Nashua‡-Waterbury	Eastern	42	126⅓	9	6	.600	123	58	38	93	43	2.71
1986—Cleveland	American	62	112⅔	10	10	.500	123	70	62	60	43	4.95
1987—Cleveland	American	39	120⅓	7	8	.467	145	75	62	65	47	4.64
1988—Cleveland	American	37	145	9	14	.391	149	89	79	53	46	4.90
1989—Cleveland§x	American	34	113⅔	5	9	.357	116	57	54	47	29	4.28
1990—California	American	27	35⅓	2	0	1.000	46	30	25	16	20	6.37
1990—Edmonton	P. Coast	9	18	0	1	.000	21	13	12	12	8	6.00
Major League Totals—5 Years		199	527	33	41	.446	579	321	282	241	185	4.82

Selected by Texas Rangers' organization in 7th round of free-agent draft, January 12, 1982.
Selected by Pittsburgh Pirates' organization in secondary phase of free-agent draft, June 7, 1982.
†On disabled list, August 12, 1982 through remainder of season.
‡Traded to Cleveland Indians' organization, July 3, 1985, completing deal in which Cleveland traded Shortstop Johnnie LeMaster to Pittsburgh Pirates for a player to be named later, May 30, 1985.
§On disabled list, August 13 to September 6, 1989.
xTraded to California Angels for Infielder Jeff Manto and Pitcher Colin Charland, January 9, 1990.

JOHN MARK BAILEY

(Known by middle name.)

Born November 4, 1961, at Springfield, Mo.
Height, 6.05. Weight, 200.
Throws right and bats right and lefthanded.
Attended Southwest Missouri State University, Springfield, Mo.

Major League stolen bases: 1986 (1), 1987 (1). Total—2.
Switch-hit home runs in one game, September 16, 1984.
Led National League in passed balls with 17 in 1984 and 19 in 1985.
Led South Atlantic League catchers in fielding percentage with .989 in 1983.

Year	Club	League	Pos.	G.	AB.	R.	H.	2B.	3B.	HR.	RBI.	B.A.	PO.	A.	E.	F.A.
1982—Auburn	NYP	1B-3B-OF	65	230	46	69	10	1	11	40	.300	195	29	5	.978
1983—Asheville	S. Atl.	C-1B	122	410	68	108	23	1	19	62	.263	767	77	7	.992
1984—Columbus	South.	C-1B-OF	17	53	5	15	3	2	0	9	.283	83	11	0	1.000
1984—Houston	Nat.	C	108	344	38	73	16	1	9	34	.212	629	56	12	.983
1985—Houston	Nat.	●C-1B	114	332	47	88	14	0	10	45	.265	566	52	●13	.979
1986—Houston	Nat.	C-1B	57	153	9	27	5	0	4	15	.176	322	33	4	.989
1986—Tucson†	P. C.	C-1B	35	123	22	42	8	1	1	19	.341	120	10	3	.977
1987—Houston	Nat.	C	35	64	5	13	1	0	0	3	.203	126	7	2	.985
1987—Tucson	P. C.	C-1B	11	29	1	4	0	0	0	2	.138	32	6	1	.974
1988—Houston‡	Nat.	C	8	23	1	3	0	0	0	0	.130	48	3	1	.981
1988—Tucson§	P. C.	C-1B-OF	37	111	6	19	7	1	0	9	.171	113	9	1	.992
1988—Indianapolis x	A. A.	C	20	51	10	12	2	0	2	6	.235	99	7	3	.972
1989—Tidewater y	Int.	C-1B	72	190	17	46	7	1	2	25	.242	291	17	3	.990
1990—Phoenix	P. C.	C-1B	57	175	19	39	4	0	7	28	.223	226	23	2	.992
1990—San Francisco	Nat.	C	5	7	1	1	0	0	1	3	.143	3	0	0	1.000
Major League Totals—6 Years			327	923	101	205	36	1	24	100	.222	1694	151	32	.983

Selected by Houston Astros' organization in 6th round of free-agent draft, June 7, 1982.

‡ On disabled list, May 9 to June 2, 1988.
§ Traded to Montreal Expos for Infielder Casey Candaele, July 23, 1988.
x Traded with Third Baseman Tom O'Malley to New York Mets for Pitcher Steve Frey, March 28, 1989.
y Granted free agency, October 15, 1989; signed by Phoenix (San Francisco Giants' organization), December 12, 1989.

HAROLD DOUGLAS BAINES

Born March 15, 1959, at Easton, Md.
Height, 6.02. Weight, 195.
Throws and bats lefthanded.

Shares major league record for most plate appearances, game (12), May 8, finished May 9, 1984 (25 innings).
Shares American League records for longest errorless game and most innings by outfielder, game (25), May 8, finished May 9, 1984.
Major League stolen bases: 1980 (2), 1981 (6), 1982 (10), 1983 (7), 1984 (1), 1985 (1), 1986 (2). Total—29.
Hit three home runs in a game, July 7, 1982 and September 17, 1984.
Led American League in slugging percentage with .541 in 1984.
Led American League in game-winning RBIs with 22 in 1983.
Tied for American Association lead in double plays by outfielders with 4 in 1979.
Named designated hitter on THE SPORTING NEWS American League All-Star Team, 1988 and 1989.
Named outfielder on THE SPORTING NEWS American League All-Star Team, 1985.
Named designated hitter on THE SPORTING NEWS American League Silver Slugger team, 1989.

Year	Club	League	Pos.	G.	AB.	R.	H.	2B.	3B.	HR.	RBI.	B.A.	PO.	A.	E.	F.A.
1977—Appleton	Midw.		OF	69	222	37	58	11	2	5	29	.261	94	10	7	.937
1978—Knoxville	South.		OF-1B	137	502	70	138	16	6	13	72	.275	291	22	13	.960
1979—Iowa	A. A.		OF	125	466	87	139	25	8	22	87	.298	222	●16	11	.956
1980—Chicago	Amer.		OF	141	491	55	125	23	6	13	49	.255	229	6	9	.963
1981—Chicago	Amer.		OF	82	280	42	80	11	7	10	41	.286	120	10	2	.985
1982—Chicago	Amer.		OF	161	608	89	165	29	8	25	105	.271	326	10	7	.980
1983—Chicago	Amer.		OF	156	596	76	167	33	2	20	99	.280	312	10	9	.973
1984—Chicago	Amer.		OF	147	569	72	173	28	10	29	94	.304	307	8	6	.981
1985—Chicago	Amer.		OF	160	640	86	198	29	3	22	113	.309	318	8	2	.994
1986—Chicago	Amer.		OF	145	570	72	169	29	2	21	88	.296	295	15	5	.984
1987—Chicago†	Amer.		OF	132	505	59	148	26	4	20	93	.293	13	0	0	1.000
1988—Chicago	Amer.		OF	158	599	55	166	39	1	13	81	.277	14	1	2	.882
1989—Chicago‡-Texas	Amer.		OF	146	505	73	156	29	1	16	72	.309	54	0	2	.964
1990—Texas§-Oakland	Amer.		OF	135	415	52	118	15	1	16	65	.284	5	0	1	.833
Major League Totals—11 Years				1563	5778	731	1665	291	45	205	900	.288	1993	68	45	.979

Selected by Chicago White Sox' organization in 1st round (first player selected) of free-agent draft, June 7, 1977.
† On disabled list, April 7 to May 8, 1987.
‡ Traded with Infielder Fred Manrique to Texas Rangers for Shortstop Scott Fletcher, Outfielder Sammy Sosa and Pitcher Wilson Alvarez, July 29, 1989.
§ Traded to Oakland Athletics for two players to be named later, August 29, 1990; Texas Rangers acquired Pitchers Joe Bitker and Scott Chiamparino to complete deal, September 4, 1990.

CHAMPIONSHIP SERIES RECORD

Year	Club	League	Pos.	G.	AB.	R.	H.	2B.	3B.	HR.	RBI.	B.A.	PO.	A.	E.	F.A.
1983—Chicago	Amer.		OF	4	16	0	2	0	0	0	0	.125	5	1	0	1.000
1990—Oakland	Amer.		DH	4	14	2	5	1	0	0	3	.357	0	0	0	.000
Championship Series Totals—2 Years				8	30	2	7	1	0	0	3	.233	5	1	0	1.000

WORLD SERIES RECORD

Year	Club	League	Pos.	G.	AB.	R.	H.	2B.	3B.	HR.	RBI.	B.A.	PO.	A.	E.	F.A.
1990—Oakland	Amer.		PH-DH	3	7	1	1	0	0	1	2	.143	0	0	0	.000

ALL-STAR GAME RECORD

Year	League	Pos.	AB.	R.	H.	2B.	3B.	HR.	RBI.	B.A.	PO.	A.	E.	F.A.
1985—American		PH	1	0	1	0	0	0	0	1.000	0	0	0	.000
1986—American		PH	1	0	0	0	0	0	0	.000	0	0	0	.000
1987—American		PH	1	0	0	0	0	0	0	.000	0	0	0	.000
1989—American		DH	3	1	1	0	0	0	1	.333	0	0	0	.000
All-Star Game Totals—4 Years			6	1	2	0	0	0	1	.333	0	0	0	.000

CHARLES DOUGLAS BAIR
(Doug)

Born August 22, 1949, at Defiance, O.
Height, 6.00. Weight, 185.
Throws and bats righthanded.
Received bachelor of science degree in industrial education from
Bowling Green State University, Bowling Green, O.

Major League saves: 1977 (8), 1978 (28), 1979 (16), 1980 (6), 1981 (1), 1982 (8), 1983 (5), 1984 (4), 1986 (4), 1989 (1).
Total—81.
Led Carolina League in complete games with 15 in 1972.
Named Carolina League Pitcher of the Year, 1972.

Year	Club	League	G.	IP.	W.	L.	Pct.	H.	R.	ER.	SO.	BB.	ERA.
1971—Salem†	Carolina		6	29	2	3	.400	35	22	19	18	26	5.90
1971—Waterbury	Eastern		1	7	1	0	1.000	5	0	0	2	0	0.00

Year Club	League	G.	IP.	W.	L.	Pct.	H.	R.	ER.	SO.	BB.	ERA.
1972—Salem	Carolina	24	180	15	7	.682	170	•86	57	186	★95	2.85
1972—Charleston	Int'national	1	4	0	1	.000	5	3	3	5	0	6.75
1973—Charleston	Int'national	26	158	7	11	.389	173	103	77	94	87	4.39
1974—Charleston‡	Int'national	26	170	7	★16	.304	166	87	77	117	91	4.08
1975—Charleston	Int'national	26	167	9	12	.429	157	72	56	113	58	3.02
1976—Charleston	Int'national	45	122	7	10	.412	102	48	43	108	57	3.17
1976—Pittsburgh§	National	4	6	0	0	.000	4	4	4	4	5	6.00
1977—San Jose	P. Coast	20	33	5	2	.714	24	8	8	49	17	2.18
1977—Oakland x	American	45	83	4	6	.400	78	39	32	68	57	3.47
1978—Cincinnati	National	70	100	7	6	.538	87	23	22	91	38	1.98
1979—Cincinnati	National	65	94	11	7	.611	93	47	45	86	51	4.31
1980—Cincinnati	National	61	85	3	6	.333	91	42	40	62	39	4.24
1981—Cincinnati y-St. Louis	National	35	55	4	2	.667	55	34	31	30	19	5.07
1982—St. Louis	National	63	91⅔	5	3	.625	69	27	26	68	36	2.55
1983—St. Louis z	National	26	29⅔	1	1	.500	24	11	10	21	13	3.03
1983—Detroit a	American	27	55⅔	7	3	.700	51	27	24	39	19	3.88
1984—Detroit	American	47	93⅔	5	3	.625	82	42	39	57	36	3.75
1985—Detroit b	American	21	49	2	0	1.000	54	38	34	30	25	6.24
1985—St. Louis c	National	2	2	0	0	.000	1	0	0	0	2	0.00
1986—Tacoma	P. Coast	8	12	3	1	.750	8	3	0	13	6	0.00
1986—Oakland d	American	31	45	2	3	.400	37	15	15	40	18	3.00
1987—Maine	Int'national	45	72⅓	6	3	.667	56	27	24	63	32	2.99
1987—Philadelphia e	National	11	13⅔	2	0	1.000	17	9	9	10	5	5.93
1988—Syracuse	Int'national	39	65⅓	3	4	.429	41	19	17	60	20	2.34
1988—Toronto f	American	10	13⅓	0	0	.000	14	6	6	8	3	4.05
1989—Syracuse g	Int'national	19	25	2	0	1.000	11	3	2	16	8	0.72
1989—Pittsburgh h	National	44	67⅓	2	3	.400	52	19	17	56	28	2.27
1990—Buffalo	Am. Assoc.	29	52⅓	4	2	.667	53	19	16	29	18	2.75
1990—Pittsburgh i	National	22	24⅓	0	0	.000	30	15	13	19	11	4.81
National League Totals—11 Years		403	568⅔	35	28	.556	523	231	217	447	247	3.43
American League Totals—6 Years		181	339⅔	20	15	.571	316	167	150	242	158	3.97
Major League Totals—15 Years		584	908⅓	55	43	.561	839	398	367	689	405	3.64

Selected by Pittsburgh Pirates' organization in 2nd round of free-agent draft, June 8, 1971.

†On temporary inactive list, June 23 to July 22, 1971.

‡Conditionally released to Detroit Tigers' organization, December 17, 1974; returned, March 28, 1975.

§Traded with Pitchers Doc Medich, Dave Giusti and Rick Langford, Outfielders Mitchell Page and Tony Armas to Oakland A's for Infielders Phil Garner and Tommy Helms, and Pitcher Chris Batton, March 15, 1977.

xTraded to Cincinnati Reds for First Baseman Dave Revering and cash, February 25, 1978.

yTraded to St. Louis Cardinals for Pitcher Joe Edelen and Second Baseman Neil Fiala, September 10, 1981.

zTraded to Detroit Tigers for a player to be named later, June 21, 1983; St. Louis Cardinals acquired Pitcher Dave Rucker to complete deal, July 5, 1983.

aGranted free agency, November 7, 1983; re-signed by Tigers, December 23, 1983.

bReleased, August 22, 1985; signed by St. Louis Cardinals, September 2, 1985.

cGranted free agency, November 12, 1985; signed by Oakland A's organization, May 19, 1986.

dGranted free agency, November 10, 1986; signed by Maine (Philadelphia Phillies' organization), July 23, 1987.

eReleased, March 26, 1988; signed by Syracuse (Toronto Blue Jays' organization), April 7, 1988.

fReleased, October 31, 1988; re-signed by Blue Jays' organization, February 17, 1989.

gSold to Pittsburgh Pirates, June 16, 1989.

hGranted free agency, November 13, 1989; re-signed by Pirates, November 14, 1989.

iGranted free agency, November 5, 1990.

CHAMPIONSHIP SERIES RECORD

Year Club	League	G.	IP.	W.	L.	Pct.	H.	R.	ER.	SO.	BB.	ERA.
1979—Cincinnati	National	1	1	0	1	.000	2	1	1	0	1	9.00
1982—St. Louis	National	1	1	0	0	.000	2	0	0	0	3	0.00
Championship Series Totals—2 Years		2	2	0	1	.000	4	1	1	0	4	4.50

WORLD SERIES RECORD

Year Club	League	G.	IP.	W.	L.	Pct.	H.	R.	ER.	SO.	BB.	ERA.
1982—St. Louis	National	3	2	0	1	.000	2	2	2	3	2	9.00
1984—Detroit	American	1	⅔	0	0	.000	0	0	0	1	0	0.00
World Series Totals—2 Years		4	2⅔	0	1	.000	2	2	2	4	2	6.75

DOUGLAS LEE BAKER
(Doug)

Born April 3, 1961, at Fullerton, Calif.
Height, 5.09. Weight, 165.
Throws right and bats left and righthanded.
Attended Arizona State University, Tempe, Ariz.
Brother of Dave Baker, third baseman with Toronto Blue Jays, 1982.

Major League stolen bases: 1984 (3).
Led Southern League in sacrifice hits with 18 and being hit by pitch with 13 in 1983.
Led Pacific Coast League shortstops in double plays with 80 in 1988.
Led Southern League shortstops in total chances with 747 in 1983.

Year Club	League	Pos.	G.	AB.	R.	H.	2B.	3B.	HR.	RBI.	B.A.	PO.	A.	E.	F.A.
1982—Birmingham	South.	SS	70	213	28	48	3	4	1	21	.225	115	190	14	.956
1983—Birmingham	South.	SS	★146	452	72	109	18	3	5	51	.241	238	★482	27	.964
1984—Evansville†	A. A.	SS	77	243	34	63	21	1	8	30	.259	152	270	16	.963

Year Club	League	Pos.	G.	AB.	R.	H.	2B.	3B.	HR.	RBI.	B.A.	PO.	A.	E.	F.A.
1984—Detroit..................	Amer.	SS-2B	43	108	15	20	4	1	0	12	.185	56	86	5	.966
1985—Detroit..................	Amer.	SS-2B	15	27	4	5	1	0	0	1	.185	12	12	1	.960
1985—Nashville..............	A. A.	SS	107	325	42	71	9	4	2	30	.218	179	318	22	.958
1986—Detroit..................	Amer.	SS-2B	13	24	1	3	1	0	0	0	.125	17	21	1	.974
1986—Nashville..............	A. A.	SS	112	369	46	101	14	6	2	40	.274	*208	291	15	*.971
1987—Toledo	Int.	SS	117	376	40	93	14	2	2	27	.247	190	342	*24	.957
1987—Detroit‡................	Amer.	SS-2B-3B	8	1	0	0	0	0	0	0	.000	2	8	0	1.000
1988—Portland...............	P. C.	*SS-3B	121	417	52	102	17	4	2	45	.245	194	340	21	*.962
1988—Minnesota............	Amer.	SS-3B-2B	11	7	1	0	0	0	0	0	.000	5	7	0	1.000
1989—Portland...............	P. C.	SS-OF-1B	84	312	38	74	10	4	2	27	.237	143	295	13	.971
1989—Minnesota............	Amer.	2B-SS	43	78	17	23	5	1	0	9	.295	42	63	2	.981
1990—Minnesota............	Amer.	2B	3	1	0	0	0	0	0	0	.000	1	2	0	1.000
1990—Portland§..............	P. C.	1-O-P	91	301	46	65	15	2	3	18	.216	141	184	5	.985
Major League Totals—7 Years.................			136	246	38	51	11	2	0	22	.207	135	199	9	.974

Selected by Oakland A's organization in 9th round of free-agent draft, January 13, 1981.
Selected by Detroit Tigers' organization in 9th round of free-agent draft, June 7, 1982.
†On disabled list, June 10 to June 21, 1984.
‡Traded to Minnesota Twins for Shortstop Julius McDougal, February 24, 1988.
§Granted free agency, October 15, 1990.

CHAMPIONSHIP SERIES RECORD

Year Club	League	Pos.	G.	AB.	R.	H.	2B.	3B.	HR.	RBI.	B.A.	PO.	A.	E.	F.A.
1984—Detroit..................	Amer.	SS	1	0	0	0	0	0	0	0	.000	0	0	0	.000

WORLD SERIES RECORD

Eligible for 1984 World Series with Detroit Tigers; did not play.

PITCHING RECORD

Year Club	League	G.	IP.	W.	L.	Pct.	H.	R.	ER.	SO.	BB.	ERA.
1990—Portland..	P. Coast	1	1	0	0	.000	1	0	0	0	0	0.00

STEPHEN CHARLES BALBONI
(Steve)

Born January 16, 1957, at Brockton, Mass.
Height, 6.03. Weight, 250.
Throws and bats righthanded.
Attended Eckerd College, St. Petersburg, Fla.

Major League stolen bases: 1985 (1).
Led American League batters in strikeouts with 166 in 1985.
Led American League first basemen in total chances with 1,686 in 1985.
Led International League batters in strikeouts with 146 in 1981.
Led Southern League in total bases with 288 and intentional bases on balls received with 17 in 1980.
Led Florida State League batters in strikeouts with 154 in 1979.
Led Florida State League first basemen in double plays with 106 in 1979 and Southern League first basemen with 125 in 1980.
Named Southern League Most Valuable Player, 1980.
Named Florida State League Most Valuable Player, 1979.
Named designated hitter on THE SPORTING NEWS College Baseball All-America Team, 1978.

Year Club	League	Pos.	G.	AB.	R.	H.	2B.	3B.	HR.	RBI.	B.A.	PO.	A.	E.	F.A.
1978—West Haven	East.	DH	2	2	0	0	0	0	0	0	.000	0	0	0	.000
1978—Fort Lauderdale ..	Fla. St.	1B	60	176	19	36	5	0	1	19	.205	475	19	4	.992
1979—Fort Lauderdale ..	Fla. St.	1B	*140	*504	69	127	19	2	*26	*91	.252	*1297	*97	11	*.992
1980—Nashville..............	South.	1B	141	521	*101	157	25	2	*34	*122	.301	*1218	76	13	*.990
1981—Columbus..............	Int.	1B	125	434	68	107	21	2	*33	*98	.247	631	55	*14	.980
1981—New York..............	Amer.	1B	4	7	2	2	1	1	0	2	.286	14	1	0	1.000
1982—Columbus..............	Int.	1B	83	313	57	89	17	1	*32	86	.284	426	38	8	.983
1982—New York..............	Amer.	1B	33	107	8	20	2	1	2	4	.187	194	13	2	.990
1983—Columbus..............	Int.	1B	84	317	72	87	14	0	27	81	.274	479	47	11	.980
1983—New York†............	Amer.	1B	32	86	8	20	2	0	5	17	.233	178	9	3	.984
1984—Kansas City..........	Amer.	1B	126	438	58	107	23	2	28	77	.244	1102	79	●15	.987
1985—Kansas City..........	Amer.	1B	160	600	74	146	28	2	36	88	.243	*1573	101	12	.993
1986—Kansas City‡.........	Amer.	1B	138	512	54	117	25	1	29	88	.229	1236	98	*18	.987
1987—Kansas City§.........	Amer.	1B	121	386	44	80	11	1	24	60	.207	521	41	6	.989
1988—K.C.x-Sea.y	Amer.	1B	118	413	46	97	17	1	23	66	.235	428	30	4	.991
1989—New York..............	Amer.	1B	110	300	33	71	12	2	17	59	.237	150	7	1	.994
1990—New York..............	Amer.	1B	116	266	24	51	6	0	17	34	.192	183	7	3	.984
Major League Totals—10 Years..............			958	3115	351	711	127	11	181	495	.228	5579	386	64	.989

Selected by New York Yankees' organization in 4th round of free-agent draft, June 6, 1978.
†Traded with Pitcher Roger Erickson to Kansas City Royals for Pitcher Mike Armstrong and Catcher Duane Dewey, December 8, 1983.
‡Released, December 18, 1986; re-signed by Royals, February 25, 1987.
§Released, December 21, 1987; re-signed by Royals, February 18, 1988.
xReleased, May 27, 1988; signed by Seattle Mariners, June 1, 1988.
yTraded to New York Yankees for Pitcher Dana Ridenour, March 27, 1989.

Shares American League Championship Series record for most strikeouts, series (8), 1985.

Year Club	League	Pos.	G.	AB.	R.	H.	2B.	3B.	HR.	RBI.	B.A.	PO.	A.	E.	F.A.
1984—Kansas City.......... Amer.		1B	3	11	0	1	0	0	0	0	.091	20	3	1	.958
1985—Kansas City.......... Amer.		1B	7	25	1	3	0	0	0	1	.120	72	7	2	.975
Championship Series Totals—2 Years.....			10	36	1	4	0	0	0	1	.111	92	10	3	.971

WORLD SERIES RECORD

Shares World Series record for most at-bats, inning (2), October 27, 1985, fifth inning.

Year Club	League	Pos.	G.	AB.	R.	H.	2B.	3B.	HR.	RBI.	B.A.	PO.	A.	E.	F.A.
1985—Kansas City.......... Amer.		1B	7	25	2	8	0	0	0	3	.320	70	3	0	1.000

JEFFREY ALLEN BALDWIN
(Jeff)

Born September 5, 1965, at Milford, Del.
Height, 6.01. Weight, 190.
Throws and bats lefthanded.
Attended Camden County College, Blackwood, N.J.

Year Club	League	Pos.	G.	AB.	R.	H.	2B.	3B.	HR.	RBI.	B.A.	PO.	A.	E.	F.A.
1985—Sarasota Astros.... Gulf C.		1B-OF	47	138	17	36	2	2	0	12	.261	222	15	8	.967
1986—Asheville............... S. Atl.		OF	118	346	66	94	14	3	13	69	.272	119	9	2	.985
1987—Osceola................. Fla. St.		OF	127	437	70	133	20	5	1	56	.304	201	6	5	.976
1988—Osceola................. Fla. St.		OF	55	168	23	45	8	1	1	25	.268	40	0	0	1.000
1988—Columbus............... South.		OF	39	91	7	20	1	0	0	6	.220	29	1	1	.968
1989—Columbus............... South.		OF	96	256	31	70	13	0	1	23	.273	82	6	5	.946
1990—Columbus............... South.		OF-1B	77	250	43	79	11	1	7	37	.316	135	5	3	.979
1990—Houston................. Nat.		OF	7	8	1	0	0	0	0	0	.000	1	0	0	1.000
1990—Tucson................... P. C.		OF	19	37	4	5	1	0	0	5	.135	18	2	2	.909
Major League Totals—1 Year.................			7	8	1	0	0	0	0	0	.000	1	0	0	1.000

Selected by Houston Astros' organization in 14th round of free-agent draft, January 9, 1985.

JEFFREY SCOTT BALLARD
(Jeff)

Born August 13, 1963, at Billings, Mont.
Height, 6.02. Weight, 203.
Throws and bats lefthanded.
Received degree in geophysics from Stanford University, Stanford, Calif.

Tied for New York-Pennsylvania League lead in shutouts with 3 in 1985.

Year Club	League	G.	IP.	W.	L.	Pct.	H.	R.	ER.	SO.	BB.	ERA.
1985—Newark	NYP	13	96	●10	2	.833	78	20	15	91	20	1.41
1986—Hagerstown	Carolina	17	112	9	5	.643	106	39	23	115	32	★1.85
1986—Charlotte......................	Southern	10	59⅔	5	2	.714	70	29	22	35	20	3.32
1986—Rochester.....................	Int'national	2	6⅓	0	2	.000	11	6	5	7	3	7.11
1987—Rochester.....................	Int'national	23	160⅓	13	4	.765	151	60	55	114	35	3.09
1987—Baltimore.....................	American	14	69⅔	2	8	.200	100	60	51	27	35	6.59
1988—Rochester.....................	Int'national	9	60⅔	4	3	.571	56	26	20	32	11	2.97
1988—Baltimore.....................	American	25	153⅓	8	12	.400	167	83	75	41	42	4.40
1989—Baltimore.....................	American	35	215⅓	18	8	.692	240	95	82	62	57	3.43
1990—Baltimore.....................	American	44	133⅓	2	11	.154	152	79	73	50	42	4.93
Major League Totals—4 Years............................		118	571⅔	30	39	.435	659	317	281	180	176	4.42

Selected by Milwaukee Brewers' organization in 16th round of free-agent draft, June 8, 1981.
Selected by Baltimore Orioles' organization in 27th round of free-agent draft, June 4, 1984.
Selected by Baltimore Orioles' organizaton in 7th round of free-agent draft, June 3, 1985.

JAY SCOT BALLER

Born October 6, 1960, at Stayton, Ore.
Height, 6.07. Weight, 225.
Throws and bats righthanded

Major League saves: 1985 (1), 1986 (5). Total—6.
Led American Association in games finished in relief with 40 in 1987 and 59 in 1989.
Led International League in hit batsmen with 12 in 1983.
Led Eastern League in hit batsmen with 12 in 1982.
Led South Atlantic League in hit batsmen with 10 in 1980.
Led Pioneer League in home runs allowed with 9 in 1979.

Year Club	League	G.	IP.	W.	L.	Pct.	H.	R.	ER.	SO.	BB.	ERA.
1979—Helena.............................	Pioneer	13	67	5	6	.455	89	59	43	68	34	5.78
1980—Spartanburg...................	S. Atlantic	26	139	10	5	.667	132	69	55	95	72	3.56
1981—Peninsula......................	Carolina	27	147	9	14	.391	119	85	64	166	78	3.92
1982—Reading.........................	Eastern	50	151⅓	9	8	.529	110	64	45	155	85	★2.68
1982—Philadelphia†	National	4	8	0	0	.000	7	4	3	7	2	3.38
1983—Charleston......................	Int'national	20	78⅔	4	12	.250	91	79	77	62	66	8.81
1983—Buffalo...........................	Eastern	16	34⅔	1	2	.333	32	34	29	35	35	7.53
1984—Buffalo...........................	Eastern	14	79⅓	4	5	.444	73	50	40	74	48	4.54
1984—Maine‡............................	Int'national	15	83⅔	9	4	.692	82	57	50	52	48	5.38
1085—Iowa...............................	Am. Assoc.	24	149	8	9	.471	140	77	70	119	63	4.23

Year Club	League	G.	IP.	W.	L.	Pct.	H.	R.	ER.	SO.	BB.	ERA.
1985—Chicago	National	20	52	2	3	.400	52	21	20	31	17	3.46
1986—Chicago	National	36	53⅔	2	4	.333	58	37	32	42	28	5.37
1986—Iowa	Am. Assoc.	27	59⅓	3	7	.300	63	32	29	51	32	4.40
1987—Iowa	Am. Assoc.	44	59⅓	4	3	.571	50	24	24	62	24	3.64
1987—Chicago§x	National	23	29⅓	0	1	.000	38	22	22	27	20	6.75
1988—Calgary y	P. Coast	★66	98⅓	10	7	.588	91	48	41	82	33	3.75
1989—Indianapolis z	Am. Assoc.	62	62⅓	1	5	.167	49	19	14	53	20	2.02
1990—Omaha	Am. Assoc.	52	75	3	6	.333	69	35	27	68	33	3.24
1990—Kansas City	American	3	2⅓	0	1	.000	4	4	4	1	2	15.43
National League Totals—4 Years		83	143	4	8	.333	155	84	77	107	67	4.85
American League Totals—1 Year		3	2⅓	0	1	.000	4	4	4	1	2	15.43
Major League Totals—5 Years		86	145⅓	4	9	.308	159	88	81	108	69	5.02

Selected by Philadelphia Phillies' organization in 3rd round of free-agent draft, June 5, 1979.

†Traded with Second Baseman Manny Trillo, Outfielder George Vukovich, Infielder Julio Franco and Catcher Jerry Willard to Cleveland Indians for Outfielder Von Hayes, December 9, 1982.

‡Traded to Chicago Cubs' organization for Infielder Dan Rohn, April 1, 1985.

§Released, December 21, 1987; re-signed by Cubs, February 17, 1988.

xReleased, March, 1988; signed by Calgary (Seattle Mariners' organization), March, 1988.

yGranted free agency, October 15, 1988; signed by Indianapolis (Montreal Expos' organization), December 7, 1988.

zGranted free agency, October 15, 1989; signed by Omaha (Kansas City Royals' organization), January, 1990.

MICHAEL SCOTT BANKHEAD

(Known by middle name.)

Born July 31, 1963, at Raleigh, N.C.
Height, 5.10. Weight, 185.
Throws and bats righthanded.
Attended University of North Carolina, Chapel Hill, N.C.

Member of 1984 U.S. Olympic baseball team.

Year Club	League	G.	IP.	W.	L.	Pct.	H.	R.	ER.	SO.	BB.	ERA
1985—Memphis	Southern	24	140⅓	8	6	.571	117	63	56	●128	56	3.59
1986—Omaha	Am. Assoc.	7	48⅓	2	2	.500	31	11	8	34	14	1.49
1986—Kansas City†	American	24	121	8	9	.471	121	66	62	94	37	4.61
1987—Seattle‡	American	27	149⅓	9	8	.529	168	96	90	95	37	5.42
1988—San Bernardino§	California	2	11	0	0	.000	6	3	2	6	4	1.64
1988—Calgary	P. Coast	2	11	1	1	.500	15	9	9	5	5	7.36
1988—Seattle	American	21	135	7	9	.438	115	53	46	102	38	3.07
1989—Seattle	American	33	210⅓	14	6	.700	187	84	78	140	63	3.34
1990—Seattle x	American	4	13	0	2	.000	18	16	16	10	7	11.08
1990—Calgary	P. Coast	2	7	0	1	.000	9	6	5	7	3	6.43
Major League Totals—5 Years		109	628⅔	38	34	.528	609	315	292	441	182	4.18

Selected by Pittsburgh Pirates' organization in 17th round of free-agent draft, June 8, 1981.

Selected by Kansas City Royals' organization in 1st round (16th player selected) of free-agent draft, June 4, 1984.

†Traded with Pitcher Steve Shields and Outfielder Mike Kingery to Seattle Mariners for Outfielder Danny Tartabull and Pitcher Rick Luecken, December 10, 1986.

‡On disabled list, June 24 to July 13, 1987.

§On Seattle disabled list, March 20 to May 14, 1988; included rehabilitation disability assignment to San Bernardino, April 23 to May 2, 1988, and Calgary, May 3 to May 10, 1988.

xOn disabled list, April 16 to May 18 and June 3, 1990 through remainder of season; included rehabilitation disability assignment to Calgary, May 1 to May 7, 1990.

WILLIE ANTHONY BANKS

Born February 27, 1969, at Jersey City, N.J.
Height, 6.01. Weight, 190.
Throws and bats righthanded.

Pitched 1-0 no-hit victory against Palm Springs, May 24, 1989.
Led California League in wild pitches with 22 and tied for lead in shutouts with 4 in 1989.
Led Appalachian League in wild pitches with 28 and tied for lead in balks with 3 in 1987.
Received reported $160,000 bonus to sign with Minnesota Twins, 1987.

Year Club	League	G.	IP.	W.	L.	Pct.	H.	R.	ER.	SO.	BB.	ERA.
1987—Elizabethton	Ap'lachian	13	65⅔	1	8	.111	73	★71	★51	71	★62	6.99
1988—Kenosha	Midwest	24	125⅔	10	10	.500	109	73	52	113	★107	3.72
1989—Visalia	California	27	174	12	9	.571	122	70	50	★173	85	2.59
1989—Orlando	Southern	1	7	1	0	1.000	10	4	4	9	0	5.14
1990—Orlando	Southern	28	162⅔	7	9	.438	161	93	71	114	98	3.93

Selected by Minnesota Twins' organization in 1st round (third player selected) of free-agent draft, June 2, 1987.

FLOYD FRANKLIN BANNISTER

Born June 10, 1955, at Pierre, S. Dakota.
Height, 6.01. Weight, 190.
Throws and bats lefthanded.
Attended Arizona State University, Tempe, Ariz.
Brother-in-law of Greg Cochran, pitcher in Oakland A's and New York Yankees' organizations, 1975 through 1982.

Named College Player of the Year by THE SPORTING NEWS, 1976.
Named lefthanded pitcher on THE SPORTING NEWS College Baseball All-America Team, 1975 and 1976.

Year	Club	League	G.	IP.	W.	L.	Pct.	H.	R.	ER.	SO.	BB.	ERA.
1976—Covington	Ap'lachian	3	13	0	0	.000	3	0	0	27	2	0.00
1976—Columbus	Southern	3	24	1	0	1.000	16	4	4	20	14	1.50
1976—Memphis	Int'national	1	6	1	0	1.000	7	1	1	6	3	1.50
1977—Houston†	National	24	143	8	9	.471	138	70	64	112	68	4.03
1978—Houston‡	National	28	110	3	9	.250	120	59	59	94	63	4.83
1979—Seattle	American	30	182	10	15	.400	185	92	82	115	68	4.05
1980—Seattle	American	32	218	9	13	.409	200	96	84	155	66	3.47
1981—Seattle§	American	21	121	9	9	.500	128	62	60	85	39	4.46
1982—Seattle x	American	35	247	12	13	.480	225	112	94	★209	77	3.43
1983—Chicago	American	34	217⅓	16	10	.615	191	88	81	193	71	3.35
1984—Chicago y	American	34	218	14	11	.560	211	127	117	152	80	4.83
1985—Chicago	American	34	210⅔	10	14	.417	211	121	114	198	100	4.87
1986—Chicago z	American	28	165⅓	10	14	.417	162	81	65	92	48	3.54
1987—Chicago a	American	34	228⅔	16	11	.593	216	100	91	124	49	3.58
1988—Kansas City	American	31	189⅓	12	13	.480	182	102	91	113	68	4.33
1989—Kansas City bc	American	14	75⅓	4	1	.800	87	40	39	35	18	4.66
1990—Yakult d	Central	9	49	3	2	.600	52	25	22	31	22	4.04
National League Totals—2 Years		52	253	11	18	.379	258	129	123	206	131	4.38
American League Totals—11 Years		327	2072⅔	122	124	.496	1998	1021	918	1471	684	3.99
Major League Totals—13 Years		379	2325⅔	133	142	.484	2256	1150	1041	1677	815	4.03

Selected by Oakland A's organization in 3rd round of free-agent draft, June 5, 1973.
Selected by Houston Astros' organization in 1st round (first player selected) of free-agent draft, June 8, 1976.
†On disabled list, July 26 to August 22, 1977.
‡Traded to Seattle Mariners for Shortstop Craig Reynolds, December 8, 1978.
§On disabled list, August 8 to August 29, 1981.
xGranted free agency, November 10, 1982; signed by Chicago White Sox, December 13, 1982.
yHad one at-bat with no hits.
zOn disabled list, May 19 to June 17, 1986.
aTraded with Infielder Dave Cochrane to Kansas City Royals for Pitchers John Davis, Melido Perez, Chuck Mount and Greg Hibbard, December 10, 1987.
bOn disabled list, June 12, 1989 through remainder of season.
cGranted free agency, November 13, 1989; signed by Yakult Swallows of Japanese Baseball League, December 4, 1989.
dSigned by California Angels, December 12, 1990.

CHAMPIONSHIP SERIES RECORD

Year	Club	League	G.	IP.	W.	L.	Pct.	H.	R.	ER.	SO.	BB.	ERA.
1983—Chicago	American	1	6	0	1	.000	5	4	3	5	1	4.50

ALL-STAR GAME RECORD

Year	League	IP.	W.	L.	Pct.	H.	R.	ER.	SO.	BB.	ERA.
1982—American		1	0	0	.000	1	0	0	0	0	0.00

JESSE LEE BARFIELD

Born October 29, 1959, at Joliet, Ill.
Height, 6.01. Weight, 206.
Throws and bats righthanded.

Major League stolen bases: 1981 (4), 1982 (1), 1983 (2), 1984 (8), 1985 (22), 1986 (8), 1987 (3), 1988 (7), 1989 (5), 1990 (4). Total—64.
Led American League outfielders in double plays with 8 in 1985 and 1986.
Led Florida State League batters in strikeouts with 125 in 1978.
Named outfielder on THE SPORTING NEWS American League All-Star fielding team, 1986 and 1987.
Named outfielder on THE SPORTING NEWS American League Silver Slugger team, 1986.

Year	Club	League	Pos.	G.	AB.	R.	H.	2B.	3B.	HR.	RBI.	B.A.	PO.	A.	E.	F.A.
1977—Utica	NYP	OF	70	234	37	53	9	3	5	35	.226	122	6	●13	.908
1978—Dunedin	Fla. St.	OF	133	441	40	91	12	3	2	34	.206	229	★22	★15	.944
1979—Kinston	Carol.	OF	136	477	66	126	24	5	8	71	.264	284	19	17	.947
1980—Knoxville†	South.	OF	124	433	63	104	12	8	14	65	.240	309	14	12	.964
1981—Knoxville	South.	OF	141	524	83	137	24	13	16	70	.261	270	★23	6	.980
1981—Toronto	Amer.	OF	25	95	7	22	3	2	2	9	.232	71	2	0	1.000
1982—Toronto	Amer.	OF	139	394	54	97	13	2	18	58	.246	217	15	9	.963
1983—Toronto	Amer.	OF	128	388	58	98	13	3	27	68	.253	213	16	8	.966
1984—Toronto‡	Amer.	OF	110	320	51	91	14	1	14	49	.284	190	9	10	.952
1985—Toronto	Amer.	OF	155	539	94	156	34	9	27	84	.289	349	★22	4	.989
1986—Toronto	Amer.	OF	158	589	107	170	35	2	★40	108	.289	368	★20	3	.992
1987—Toronto	Amer.	OF	159	590	89	155	25	3	28	84	.263	341	●17	3	.992
1988—Toronto‡	Amer.	OF	137	468	62	114	21	5	18	56	.244	325	12	4	.988
1989—Tor.§-N.Y.	Amer.	OF	150	521	79	122	23	1	23	67	.234	340	★20	●10	.973
1990—New York	Amer.	OF	153	476	69	117	21	2	25	78	.246	305	★16	9	.973
Major League Totals—10 Years			1314	4380	670	1142	202	30	222	661	.261	2719	149	60	.980

Selected by Toronto Blue Jays' organization in 9th round of free-agent draft, June 7, 1977.
†On disabled list, August 15 to August 29, 1980.
‡On disabled list, May 16 to May 31, 1988.
§Traded to New York Yankees for Pitcher Al Leiter, April 30, 1989.

CHAMPIONSHIP SERIES RECORD

Year	Club	League	Pos.	G.	AB.	R.	H.	2B.	3B.	HR.	RBI.	B.A.	PO.	A.	E.	F.A.
1985—Toronto	Amer.	OF	7	25	3	7	1	0	1	4	.280	21	0	1	.955

Year League	Pos.	AB.	R.	H.	2B.	3B.	HR.	RBI.	B.A.	PO.	A.	E.	F.A.
1986—American	PH-OF	3	0	0	0	0	0	0	.000	2	0	0	1.000

JOHN DAVID BARFIELD

Born October 15, 1964, at Little Rock, Ark.
Height, 6.01. Weight, 195.
Throws and bats lefthanded.
Attended Crowder College, Neosho, Mo.; and Oklahoma City University, Oklahoma City, Okla.

Major League saves: 1990 (1).

Year Club	League	G.	IP.	W.	L.	Pct.	H.	R.	ER.	SO.	BB.	ERA.
1986—Daytona Beach	Florida St.	3	17⅓	1	1	.500	14	9	8	13	1	4.15
1986—Salem	Carolina	13	56	2	5	.286	71	43	31	39	22	4.98
1987—Charlotte	Florida St.	25	153⅔	10	7	.588	145	75	63	79	55	3.69
1988—Tulsa	Texas	24	169	9	9	.500	159	69	54	125	66	2.88
1989—Oklahoma City	Am. Assoc.	28	175⅓	10	8	.556	178	93	79	58	68	4.06
1989—Texas	American	4	11⅔	0	1	.000	15	10	8	9	4	6.17
1990—Oklahoma City	Am. Assoc.	19	43⅓	1	6	.143	44	21	17	25	21	3.53
1990—Texas	American	33	44⅓	4	3	.571	42	25	23	17	13	4.67
Major League Totals—2 Years		37	56	4	4	.500	57	35	31	26	17	4.98

Selected by Philadelphia Phillies' organization in 17th round of free-agent draft, January 9, 1985.
Selected by Texas Rangers' organization in 11th round of free-agent draft, June 2, 1986.

BRIAN KEITH BARNES

Born March 25, 1967, at Roanoke Rapids, N.C.
Height, 5.09. Weight, 170.
Throws and bats lefthanded.
Attended Clemson University, Clemson, S.C.

Named Southern League Pitcher of the Year, 1990.

Year Club	League	G.	IP.	W.	L.	Pct.	H.	R.	ER.	SO.	BB.	ERA.
1989—Jamestown	NYP	2	9	1	0	1.000	4	1	1	15	3	1.00
1989—West Palm Beach	Florida St.	7	50	4	3	.571	25	9	4	67	16	0.72
1989—Indianapolis	Am. Assoc.	1	6	1	0	1.000	5	1	1	5	2	1.50
1990—Jacksonville	Southern	29	★201⅓	13	7	.650	144	78	62	★213	87	2.77
1990—Montreal	National	4	28	1	1	.500	25	10	9	23	7	2.89
Major League Totals—1 Year		4	28	1	1	.500	25	10	9	23	7	2.89

Selected by Baltimore Orioles' organization in 25th round of free-agent draft, June 1, 1988.
Selected by Montreal Expos' organization in 4th round of free-agent draft, June 5, 1989.

MARTIN GLENN BARRETT
(Marty)

Born June 23, 1958, at Arcadia, Calif.
Height, 5.10. Weight, 175.
Throws and bats righthanded.
Attended Mesa Community College, Mesa, Ariz. and Arizona State University, Tempe, Ariz.
Brother of Charlie Barrett, pitcher in Los Angeles Dodgers' organization, 1973 through 1978;
and Tom Barrett, second baseman with Philadelphia Phillies, 1988 and 1989.

Major League stolen bases: 1984 (5), 1985 (7), 1986 (15), 1987 (15), 1988 (7), 1989 (4), 1990 (4). Total—57.
Led American League in sacrifice hits with 18 in 1986, 22 in 1987 and 20 in 1988.
Led American League second basemen in double plays with 110 in 1985.
Led Eastern League in sacrifice hits with 15 in 1980.
Led Florida State League in sacrifice flies with 9 in 1979.
Led International League second basemen in double plays with 99 in 1982.

Year Club	League	Pos.	G.	AB.	R.	H.	2B.	3B.	HR.	RBI.	B.A.	PO.	A.	E.	F.A.
1979—Winter Haven	Fla. St.	2B	57	178	25	53	7	0	1	28	.298	124	144	6	.978
1980—Bristol	East.	★2B-SS	128	475	72	130	17	2	1	41	.274	279	372	10	★.985
1981—Pawtucket†	Int.	2B	88	343	36	91	12	2	1	28	.265	186	254	10	.978
1982—Pawtucket	Int.	2B	131	477	72	143	27	1	5	57	.300	303	★415	11	★.985
1982—Boston	Amer.	2B	8	18	0	1	0	0	0	0	.056	11	21	0	1.000
1983—Boston	Amer.	2B	33	44	7	10	1	1	0	2	.227	32	28	1	.984
1983—Pawtucket	Int.	2B	36	119	24	41	4	2	1	18	.345	70	115	1	.995
1984—Boston	Amer.	2B	139	475	56	144	23	3	3	45	.303	245	417	9	★.987
1985—Boston	Amer.	2B	156	534	59	142	26	0	5	56	.266	★355	479	11	.987
1986—Boston	Amer.	2B	158	625	94	179	39	4	4	60	.286	303	★450	14	.982
1987—Boston‡	Amer.	2B	137	559	72	164	23	0	3	43	.293	320	438	9	★.988
1988—Boston	Amer.	2B	150	612	83	173	28	1	1	65	.283	317	402	7	.990
1989—Boston§	Amer.	2B	86	336	31	86	18	0	1	27	.256	152	245	10	.975
1989—Pawtucket	Int.	2B	11	35	4	10	1	1	0	4	.286	22	25	2	.959
1990—Boston x	Amer.	2B-3B	62	159	15	36	4	0	0	13	.226	90	148	2	.992
Major League Totals—9 Years			929	3362	417	935	162	9	17	311	.278	1820	2628	63	.986

Selected by California Angels' organization in 11th round of free-agent draft, January 11, 1977.
Selected by New York Mets' organization in 3rd round of free-agent draft, January 10, 1978.
Selected by Boston Red Sox' organization in secondary phase of free-agent draft, June 5, 1979.
†On disabled list, June 25 to July 15 and July 17 to August 4, 1981.
‡On disabled list, April 11 to April 27, 1987.

§On disabled list, June 5 to August 5, 1989; included rehabilitation disability assignment to Pawtucket, July 24 to August 5, 1989.
xReleased, December 14, 1990.

CHAMPIONSHIP SERIES RECORD

Shares American League Championship Series record for most singles, series (9), 1986.

Year	Club	League	Pos.	G.	AB.	R.	H.	2B.	3B.	HR.	RBI.	B.A.	PO.	A.	E.	F.A.
1986—Boston	Amer.	2B	7	30	4	11	2	0	0	5	.367	19	21	0	1.000
1988—Boston	Amer.	2B	4	15	2	1	0	0	0	0	.067	6	8	0	1.000
1990—Boston	Amer	2B	3	0	0	0	0	0	0	0	.000	2	0	0	1.000
Championship Series Totals—3 Years			14	45	6	12	2	0	0	5	.267	27	29	0	1.000

WORLD SERIES RECORD

Shares World Series record for most hits, series (13), 1986.

Year	Club	League	Pos.	G.	AB.	R.	H.	2B.	3B.	HR.	RBI.	B.A.	PO.	A.	E.	F.A.
1986—Boston	Amer.	2B	7	30	1	13	2	0	0	4	.433	13	25	0	1.000

KEVIN CHARLES BASS

Born May 12, 1959, at Redwood City, Calif.
Height, 6.00. Weight, 190.
Throws right and bats right and lefthanded.
Brother of Richard Bass, minor league outfielder, 1976 and 1977;
cousin of James Lofton, wide receiver with Buffalo Bills.
Shares major league record for most games, switch-hit home runs, season (2), 1987.
Shares National League record for most games, switch-hit home runs, lifetime (3).
Major League stolen bases: 1983 (2), 1984 (5), 1985 (19), 1986 (22), 1987 (21), 1988 (31), 1989 (11), 1990 (2). Total—113.
Switch-hit home runs in one game, August 3, 1987, September 2, 1987 and August 20, 1989.
Led Midwest League in being hit by pitch with 10 in 1978.
Led Eastern League outfielders in double plays with 7 in 1980.

Year	Club	League	Pos.	G.	AB.	R.	H.	2B.	3B.	HR.	RBI.	B.A.	PO.	A.	E.	F.A.
1977—Newark	NYP	OF	48	189	30	56	11	●7	1	33	.296	56	2	3	.951
1978—Burlington	Midw.	OF	129	499	81	132	27	5	18	69	.265	★281	14	11	.964
1979—Holyoke	East.	OF	135	490	69	129	15	4	8	54	.263	280	●16	★17	.946
1980—Holyoke	East.	OF	136	490	79	147	★31	7	4	51	.300	305	14	★18	.947
1981—Vancouver†	P. C.	OF	97	339	40	87	10	5	2	30	.257	175	14	7	.964
1982—Milwaukee	Amer.	OF	18	9	4	0	0	0	0	0	.000	7	0	0	1.000
1982—Vancouver‡	P. C.	OF	102	413	70	130	23	7	17	65	.315	199	15	10	.955
1982—Houston	Nat.	OF	12	24	2	1	0	0	0	1	.042	11	0	1	.917
1983—Houston	Nat.	OF	88	195	25	46	7	3	2	18	.236	68	1	4	.945
1984—Houston§	Nat.	OF	121	331	33	86	17	5	2	29	.260	149	4	4	.975
1985—Houston	Nat.	OF	150	539	72	145	27	5	16	68	.269	328	10	1	★.997
1986—Houston	Nat.	OF	157	591	83	184	33	5	20	79	.311	303	12	5	.984
1987—Houston	Nat.	OF	157	592	83	168	31	5	19	85	.284	287	11	4	.987
1988—Houston	Nat.	OF	157	541	57	138	27	2	14	72	.255	267	7	6	.979
1989—Houston x	Nat.	OF	87	313	42	94	19	4	5	44	.300	186	6	3	.985
1989—Tucson y	P. C.	OF	6	17	1	5	1	0	0	2	.294	8	0	0	1.000
1990—San Francisco z	Nat.	OF	61	214	25	54	9	1	7	32	.252	88	2	3	.968
1990—San Jose	Calif.	OF	6	22	2	8	1	0	4	.364	3	0	0	1.000
1990—Phoenix	P. C.	OF	8	33	2	8	2	0	0	4	.242	5	2	0	1.000
American League Totals—1 Year			18	9	4	0	0	0	0	0	.000	7	0	0	1.000
National League Totals—9 Years			990	3340	422	916	170	30	85	428	.274	1687	53	31	.982
Major League Totals—9 Years			1008	3349	426	916	170	30	85	428	.274	1694	53	31	.983

Selected by Milwaukee Brewers' organization in 2nd round of free-agent draft, June 7, 1977.
†On disabled list, July 29 to September 1, 1981.
‡Traded with Pitchers Mike Madden and Frank DiPino to Houston Astros, September 3, 1982, completing deal in which Houston traded Pitcher Don Sutton to Milwaukee Brewers for three players to be named later, August 30, 1982.
§On disabled list, March 29 to April 13, 1984.
xOn disabled list, May 28 to August 11, 1989; included rehabilitation disability assignment to Tucson, August 4 to August 11, 1989.
yGranted free agency, November 13, 1989; signed by San Francisco Giants, November 16, 1989.
zOn disabled list, May 27 to September 3, 1990; included rehabilitation disability assignment to San Jose, August 20 to August 26, 1990; and Phoenix, August 27 to September 3, 1990.

CHAMPIONSHIP SERIES RECORD

Shares Championship Series records for most times caught stealing, series (3), 1986 and game (2), October 15, 1986 (16 innings).

Year	Club	League	Pos.	G.	AB.	R.	H.	2B.	3B.	HR.	RBI.	B.A.	PO.	A.	E.	F.A.
1986—Houston	Nat.	OF	6	24	0	7	2	0	0	0	.292	16	0	1	.941

ALL-STAR GAME RECORD

Year	League	Pos.	AB.	R.	H.	2B.	3B.	HR.	RBI.	B.A.	PO.	A.	E.	F.A.
1986—National		PH	1	0	0	0	0	0	0	.000	0	0	0	.000

—DID YOU KNOW—

That none of the 1991 Hall of Fame inductees—Rod Carew, Gaylord Perry or Ferguson Jenkins—ever played in a World Series?

WILLIAM DERRICK BATES
(Billy)

Born December 7, 1963, at Houston, Tex.
Height, 5.07. Weight, 165.
Throws right and bats lefthanded.
Attended University of Texas, Austin, Tex.

Major League stolen bases: 1989 (2), 1990 (6). Total—8.
Led American Association second basemen in total chances with 636 in 1988.
Led Texas League second basemen in double plays with 96 in 1986.
Named second baseman on THE SPORTING NEWS College Baseball All-America Team, 1984.

Year Club	League	Pos.	G.	AB.	R.	H.	2B.	3B.	HR.	RBI.	B.A.	PO.	A.	E.	F.A.
1985—Stockton	Calif.	2B-OF	59	218	36	65	8	1	3	31	.298	117	175	8	.973
1986—El Paso†	Texas	2B	122	511	104	151	26	4	8	75	.295	★286	362	21	.969
1987—Denver†	A. A.	●2B-SS	130	506	★117	160	25	5	3	62	.316	254	●393	17	.974
1988—Denver†	A. A.	★2B-OF	119	472	74	122	16	★12	2	44	.258	★252	369	15	.976
1989—Denver	A. A.	2B-OF	95	363	50	99	11	2	1	38	.273	192	285	13	.973
1989—Milwaukee‡	Amer.	2B	7	14	3	3	0	0	0	0	.214	14	16	2	.938
1990—Milwaukee	Amer.	2B	14	29	6	3	1	0	0	2	.103	18	33	2	.962
1990—Denver§-Nash.	A. A.	2B-OF	98	362	51	106	15	3	0	34	.293	170	240	7	.983
1990—Cincinnati	Nat.	2B	8	5	2	0	0	0	0	0	.000	0	1	0	1.000
American League Totals—2 Years			21	43	9	6	1	0	0	2	.140	32	49	4	.953
National League Totals—1 Year			8	5	2	0	0	0	0	0	.000	0	1	0	1.000
Major League Totals—2 Years			29	48	11	6	1	0	0	2	.125	32	50	4	.953

Selected by Philadelphia Phillies' organization in 8th round of free-agent draft, June 7, 1982.
Selected by Milwaukee Brewers' organization in 4th round of free-agent draft, June 3, 1985.
†Switch-hitter.
‡On disabled list, August 23 to September 12, 1989.
§Traded with Outfielder Glenn Braggs to Cincinnati Reds for Pitchers Ron Robinson and Bob Sebra, June 9, 1990.

CHAMPIONSHIP SERIES RECORD

Year Club	League	Pos.	G.	AB.	R.	H.	2B.	3B.	HR.	RBI.	B.A.	PO.	A.	E.	F.A.
1990—Cincinnati	Nat.	PR	2	0	1	0	0	0	0	0	.000	0	0	0	.000

WORLD SERIES RECORD

Year Club	League	Pos.	G.	AB.	R.	H.	2B.	3B.	HR.	RBI.	B.A.	PO.	A.	E.	F.A.
1990—Cincinnati	Nat.	PH	1	1	1	1	0	0	0	0	1.000	0	0	0	.000

WILLIAM DAVID BATHE
Name pronounced Bayth.
(Bill)

Born October 14, 1960, at Downey, Calif.
Height, 6.02. Weight, 200.
Throws and bats righthanded.
Attended Rio Hondo College, Whittier, Calif.; California State University,
Fullerton, Calif.; and Pepperdine University, Malibu, Calif.
Twin brother of Bob Bathe, third baseman in Oakland A's and Chicago Cubs'
organizations, 1982 through 1986.

Led Pacific Coast League catchers in total chances with 702 in 1983 and 684 in 1985.
Led Pacific Coast League catchers in putouts with 632 and tied for lead in double plays with 9 in 1983.

Year Club	League	Pos.	G.	AB.	R.	H.	2B.	3B.	HR.	RBI.	B.A.	PO.	A.	E.	F.A.
1981—San Jose†	Calif.	C-OF	51	177	20	45	9	1	4	22	.254	234	42	8	.972
1982—West Haven	East.	C	128	370	57	104	22	0	17	57	.281	★763	55	9	★.989
1983—Tacoma	P. C.	C-1B	116	399	56	101	18	1	16	62	.253	633	55	15	.979
1984—Tacoma	P. C.	C-3B-1B	84	245	27	63	12	1	3	42	.257	381	29	7	.983
1985—Tacoma	P. C.	C	108	359	43	100	26	0	6	45	.279	★613	64	7	.990
1986—Oakland	Amer.	C	39	103	9	19	3	0	5	11	.184	211	11	2	.991
1986—Tacoma‡	P. C.	C	40	135	13	26	7	1	1	13	.193	120	21	2	.986
1987—Iowa	A. A.	C-1B	46	130	17	43	7	1	3	22	.331	176	10	4	.979
1988—Iowa§	A. A.	C-1B	106	385	48	120	27	2	8	49	.312	434	33	8	.983
1989—Phoenix	P. C.	C-OF-1B	76	270	30	94	21	5	6	40	.348	145	11	1	.994
1989—San Francisco	Nat.	C	30	32	3	9	1	0	0	6	.281	13	0	0	1.000
1990—San Francisco x	Nat.	C	52	48	3	11	0	1	3	12	.229	10	1	0	1.000
1990—Phoenix y	P. C.	DH-PH	18	56	9	16	5	0	1	9	.286	0	0	0	.000
American League Totals—1 Year			39	103	9	19	3	0	5	11	.184	211	11	2	.991
National League Totals—2 Years			82	80	6	20	1	1	3	18	.250	23	1	0	1.000
Major League Totals—3 Years			121	183	15	39	4	1	8	29	.213	234	12	2	.992

Selected by Pittsburgh Pirates' organization in 10th round of free-agent draft, January 8, 1980.
Selected by Oakland A's organization in 8th round of free-agent draft, June 8, 1981.
†Loaned to San Jose (Co-op), June 23, 1981; returned, October 22, 1981.
‡Traded to Chicago Cubs for First Baseman Joe Hicks, December 17, 1986.
§Granted free agency, October 15, 1988; signed by Phoenix (San Francisco Giants' organization), November 8, 1988.
xOn disabled list, May 3 to July 1, 1990; included rehabilitation disability assignment to Phoenix, May 20 to June 8, 1990.
yReleased, October 4, 1990.

Year	Club	League	Pos.	G.	AB.	R.	H.	2B.	3B.	HR.	RBI.	B.A.	PO.	A.	E.	F.A.
1989—San Francisco		Nat.	PH	2	1	0	0	0	0	0	0	.000	0	0	0	.000

WORLD SERIES RECORD
Shares record for hitting home run in first series at-bat, October 27, 1989.

Year	Club	League	Pos.	G.	AB.	R.	H.	2B.	3B.	HR.	RBI.	B.A.	PO.	A.	E.	F.A.
1989—San Francisco		Nat.	PH	2	2	1	1	0	0	1	3	.500	0	0	0	.000

JOSE JOAQUIN BAUTISTA

Name pronounced Bough-TEES-tuh.
Born July 25, 1964, at Bani, Dominican Republic.
Height, 6.02. Weight, 207.
Throws and bats righthanded.

Pitched 6-0 no-hit victory against Prince William, May 26, 1985 (first game).

Year	Club	League	G.	IP.	W.	L.	Pct.	H.	R.	ER.	SO.	BB.	ERA.
1981—Kingsport	Ap'lachian	13	66	3	6	.333	84	54	34	34	17	4.64
1982—Kingsport	Ap'lachian	14	38⅓	0	4	.000	61	44	38	13	19	8.92
1983—Sarasota Mets	Gulf Coast	13	81⅔	4	3	.571	66	31	21	44	32	2.31
1984—Columbia	S. Atlantic	19	135	13	4	.765	121	52	47	96	35	3.13
1985—Lynchburg	Carolina	27	169	15	8	.652	145	49	44	109	33	2.34
1986—Jackson	Texas	7	21⅔	0	1	.000	36	22	20	13	8	8.31
1986—Lynchburg	Carolina	18	118⅔	8	8	.500	120	58	52	62	24	3.94
1987—Jackson†	Texas	28	169⅓	10	5	.667	174	76	61	95	43	3.24
1988—Baltimore	American	33	171⅔	6	15	.286	171	86	82	76	45	4.30
1989—Baltimore‡	American	15	78	3	4	.429	84	46	46	30	15	5.31
1989—Rochester	Int'national	15	98⅔	4	4	.500	84	41	31	47	26	2.83
1990—Baltimore	American	22	26⅔	1	0	1.000	28	15	12	15	7	4.05
1990—Rochester	Int'national	27	108⅔	7	8	.467	115	51	49	50	15	4.06
Major League Totals—3 Years		70	276½	10	19	.345	283	147	140	121	67	4.56

Signed as free agent by New York Mets' organization, April 25, 1981.
†Drafted by Baltimore Orioles, December 7, 1987.
‡On disabled list, May 20 to June 11, 1989; included rehabilitation disability assignment to Rochester, May 29 to June 11, 1989.

KEVIN GERARD BEARSE

Born November 7, 1965, at Jersey City, N.J.
Height, 6.02. Weight, 195.
Throws and bats lefthanded.
Attended Old Dominion University, Norfolk, Va.

Led Carolina League in games finished in relief with 56 and saves with 22 in 1988.
Tied for Pacific Coast League lead in shutouts with 2 and complete games with 6 in 1990.
Tied for Appalachian League lead in saves with 8 in 1987.
Named Carolina League co-Pitcher of the Year, 1988.

Year	Club	League	G.	IP.	W.	L.	Pct.	H.	R.	ER.	SO.	BB.	ERA.
1987—Burlington	Ap'lachian	22	63	7	1	.875	45	13	12	81	15	1.71
1988—Kinston	Carolina	*62	103	10	8	.556	76	19	15	127	28	1.31
1989—Canton-Akron	Eastern	14	101	9	3	.750	90	29	23	67	16	2.05
1989—Colorado Springs	P. Coast	13	89	5	2	.714	87	44	39	51	32	3.94
1990—Cleveland	American	3	7⅔	0	2	.000	16	11	11	2	5	12.91
1990—Colorado Springs†	P. Coast	25	145⅔	11	9	.550	170	92	81	79	49	5.00
Major League Totals—1 Year		3	7⅔	0	2	.000	16	11	11	2	5	12.91

Selected by Cleveland Indians' organization in 27th round of free-agent draft, June 2, 1986.
Selected by Cleveland Indians' organization in 22nd round of free-agent draft, June 2, 1987.
†Claimed on waivers by Montreal Expos, September 4, 1990.

GORDON BLAINE BEATTY

(Known by middle name.)
Born April 25, 1964, at Victoria, Tex.
Height, 6.02. Weight, 190.
Throws and bats lefthanded.
Attended San Jacinto College, Pasadena, Tex.,
and Baylor University, Waco, Tex.

Led Texas League pitchers in shutouts with 5, complete games with 12 and tied for lead in games started with 28 in 1988.
Led New York-Pennsylvania League pitchers in complete games with 8 in 1986.
Tied for International League lead in games started by pitchers with 27 and shutouts with 3 in 1989.
Named Texas League Pitcher of the Year, 1988.
Named Carolina League Pitcher of the Year, 1987.

Year	Club	League	G.	IP.	W.	L.	Pct.	H.	R.	ER.	SO.	BB.	ERA.
1986—Newark	NYP	15	*119⅓	*11	3	.786	98	37	28	93	30	2.11
1987—Hagerstown	Carolina	13	100	11	1	*.917	81	32	28	65	11	2.52
1987—Charlotte†	Southern	15	105⅔	6	5	.545	110	38	36	57	20	3.07
1988—Jackson	Texas	30	*208⅔	*16	8	.667	191	64	57	103	34	2.40

Year	Club	League	G.	IP.	W.	L.	Pct.	H.	R.	ER.	SO.	BB.	ERA.
1989—Tidewater	Int'national	27	185	12	10	.545	173	86	68	90	43	3.31
1989—New York	National	2	6	0	0	.000	5	1	1	3	2	1.50
1990—New York‡	National					(Did not play)						
Major League Totals—1 Year		2	6	0	0	.000	5	1	1	3	2	1.50

Selected by Baltimore Orioles' organization in 5th round of free-agent draft, January 17, 1984.
Selected by Baltimore Orioles' organization in secondary phase of free-agent draft, June 4, 1984.
Selected by St. Louis Cardinals' organization in secondary phase of free-agent draft, June 3, 1985.
Selected by Baltimore Orioles' organization in 9th round of free-agent draft, June 2, 1986.
†Traded with a player to be named later to New York Mets for Pitcher Doug Sisk, December 8, 1987; New York acquired Pitcher Greg Talamantez to complete deal, December 11, 1987.
‡On disabled list, April 6, 1990 through entire season.

STEPHEN WAYNE BEDROSIAN
Name pronounced Bed-ROHZ-ee-un.

(Steve)

Born December 6, 1957, at Methuen, Mass.
Height, 6.03. Weight, 210.
Throws and bats righthanded.
Attended North Essex Community College, Haverhill, Mass., and
University of New Haven, New Haven, Conn.

Holds major league record for most games taken out as starting pitcher, season (37), 1985.
Major League saves: 1982 (11), 1983 (19), 1984 (11), 1986 (29), 1987 (40), 1988 (28), 1989 (23), 1990 (17). Total—178.
Led National League in saves with 40 in 1987.
Tied for Southern League lead in games started by pitchers with 29 in 1980.
Won National League Cy Young Memorial Award, 1987.
Named National League Fireman of the Year by THE SPORTING NEWS, 1987.
Named National League Rookie Pitcher of the Year by THE SPORTING NEWS, 1982.

Year	Club	League	G.	IP.	W.	L.	Pct.	H.	R.	ER.	SO.	BB.	ERA.
1978—Kingsport	Ap'lachian	6	38	2	2	.500	38	18	13	29	25	3.08
1978—Greenwood	W. Carol.	8	55	5	1	.833	45	17	13	58	34	2.13
1979—Savannah†	Southern	13	89	5	5	.500	71	36	30	73	58	3.03
1980—Savannah	Southern	29	*203	14	10	.583	167	91	72	*161	96	3.19
1981—Richmond	Int'national	26	184	10	10	.500	143	76	55	144	99	2.69
1981—Atlanta	National	15	24	1	2	.333	15	14	12	9	15	4.50
1982—Atlanta	National	64	137⅔	8	6	.571	102	39	37	123	57	2.42
1983—Atlanta	National	70	120	9	10	.474	100	50	48	114	51	3.60
1984—Atlanta‡	National	40	83⅔	9	6	.600	65	23	22	81	33	2.37
1985—Atlanta§	National	37	206⅔	7	15	.318	198	101	88	134	111	3.83
1986—Philadelphia	National	68	90⅓	8	6	.571	79	39	34	82	34	3.39
1987—Philadelphia	National	65	89	5	3	.625	79	31	28	74	28	2.83
1988—Maine x	Int'national	5	6⅔	0	0	.000	6	0	0	5	2	0.00
1988—Philadelphia	National	57	74⅓	6	6	.500	75	34	31	61	27	3.75
1989—Philadelphia y-San Francisco	National	68	84⅔	3	7	.300	56	31	27	58	39	2.87
1990—San Francisco z	National	68	79⅓	9	9	.500	72	40	37	43	44	4.20
Major League Totals—10 Years		552	989⅔	65	70	.481	841	402	364	779	439	3.31

Selected by Atlanta Braves' organization in 3rd round of free-agent draft, June 6, 1978.
†On disabled list, June 24 to September 18, 1979.
‡On disabled list, August 20 to September 4, 1984.
§Traded with Outfielder Milt Thompson to Philadelphia Phillies for Catcher Ozzie Virgil and Pitcher Pete Smith, December 10, 1985.
xOn Philadelphia disabled list, March 21 to May 20, 1988; included rehabilitation disability assignment to Maine, May 9 to May 19, 1988.
yTraded with a player to be named later to San Francisco Giants for Pitchers Dennis Cook and Terry Mulholland and Third Baseman Charlie Hayes, June 18, 1989; San Francisco organization acquired Infielder Rick Parker to complete deal, August 7, 1989.
zTraded to Minnesota Twins for Pitcher Johnny Ard and a player to be named later, December 5, 1990; San Francisco Giants acquired Pitcher Jimmy Williams to complete deal, December 18, 1990.

CHAMPIONSHIP SERIES RECORD
Shares National League Championship Series record for most saves, series (3), 1989.

Year	Club	League	G.	IP.	W.	L.	Pct.	H.	R.	ER.	SO.	BB.	ERA.
1982—Atlanta	National	2	1	0	0	.000	3	2	2	2	1	18.00
1989—San Francisco	National	4	3⅓	0	0	.000	4	1	1	2	2	2.70
Championship Series Totals—2 Years		6	4⅓	0	0	.000	7	3	3	4	3	6.23

WORLD SERIES RECORD

Year	Club	League	G.	IP.	W.	L.	Pct.	H.	R.	ER.	SO.	BB.	ERA.
1989—San Francisco	National	2	2⅔	0	0	.000	0	0	0	2	2	0.00

ALL-STAR GAME RECORD

Year	League	IP.	W.	L.	Pct.	H.	R.	ER.	SO.	BB.	ERA.
1987—National		1	0	0	.000	0	0	0	0	2	0.00

—DID YOU KNOW—
That the N.L. East champion Pirates had 19 different pitchers win at least one game in 1990?

KEVIN D. BELCHER

Born August 8, 1967, at Waco, Tex.
Height, 6.00. Weight, 175.
Throws and bats righthanded.
Attended Navarro College, Corsicana, Tex.

Year Club League	Pos.	G.	AB.	R.	H.	2B.	3B.	HR.	RBI.	B.A.	PO.	A.	E.	F.A.
1987—Sarasota Rangers Gulf C.	OF	58	215	32	45	8	2	2	10	.209	89	6	●7	.931
1988—Gastonia................ S. Atl.	OF	105	392	56	96	13	1	8	44	.245	190	8	7	.966
1989—Gastonia†............. S. Atl.	OF	93	338	61	100	21	1	14	59	.296	172	5	4	.978
1990—Tulsa..................... Texas	OF	110	423	66	124	18	7	11	43	.293	107	9	5	.959
1990—Texas.................... Amer.	OF	16	15	4	2	1	0	0	0	.133	12	0	0	1.000
Major League Totals—1 Year..................		16	15	4	2	1	0	0	0	.133	12	0	0	1.000

Selected by Texas Rangers' organization in 6th round of free-agent draft, June 2, 1987.
†On disabled list, July 15, 1989 through remainder of season.

TIMOTHY WAYNE BELCHER
(Tim)

Born October 19, 1961, at Mount Gilead, O.
Height, 6.03. Weight, 223.
Throws and bats righthanded.
Attended Mt. Vernon Nazarene College, Mt. Vernon, O.

Shares major league record for fewest complete games for leader, season (10), 1989.
Major League saves: 1988 (4), 1989 (1). Total—5.
Led National League in shutouts with 8 and tied for complete games with 10 in 1989.
Named National League Rookie Pitcher of the Year by THE SPORTING NEWS, 1988.
Named righhanded pitcher on THE SPORTING NEWS College Baseball All-America Team, 1983.

Year Club	League	G.	IP.	W.	L.	Pct.	H.	R.	ER.	SO.	BB.	ERA.
1984—Madison	Midwest	16	98⅓	9	4	.692	80	45	39	111	48	3.57
1984—Albany............................	Eastern	10	54	3	4	.429	37	30	20	40	41	3.33
1985—Huntsville	Southern	29	149⅔	11	10	.524	145	99	78	90	99	4.69
1986—Huntsville†	Southern	9	37	2	5	.286	50	28	27	25	22	6.57
1987—Tacoma‡........................	P. Coast	29	163	9	11	.450	143	89	80	136	★133	4.42
1987—Los Angeles	National	6	34	4	2	.667	30	11	9	23	7	2.38
1988—Los Angeles	National	36	179⅔	12	6	.667	143	65	58	152	51	2.91
1989—Los Angeles§................	National	39	230	15	12	.556	182	81	72	200	80	2.82
1990—Los Angeles§................	National	24	153	9	9	.500	136	76	68	102	48	4.00
Major League Totals—4 Years...........................		105	596⅔	40	29	.580	491	233	207	477	186	3.12

Selected by Minnesota Twins' organization in 1st round (first player selected) of free-agent draft, June 6, 1983.
Selected by New York Yankees' organization in secondary phase of free-agent draft, January 17, 1984.
Selected by Oakland A's organization in player compensation pool draft, February 8, 1984. (Oakland received compensation for Baltimore Orioles' signing of free-agent Pitcher Tom Underwood, a Type A player, February 7, 1984.)
†On disabled list, April 10 to May 4 and May 5 to July 23, 1986.
‡Traded to Los Angeles Dodgers, September 3, 1987, completing deal in which Los Angeles traded Pitcher Rick Honeycutt to Oakland Athletics for a player to be named later, August 29, 1987.
§On disabled list, August 17, 1990 through remainder of season.

CHAMPIONSHIP SERIES RECORD

Year Club	League	G.	IP.	W.	L.	Pct.	H.	R.	ER.	SO.	BB.	ERA.
1988—Los Angeles	National	2	15⅓	2	0	1.000	12	7	7	16	4	4.11

WORLD SERIES RECORD

Year Club	League	G.	IP.	W.	L.	Pct.	H.	R.	ER.	SO.	BB.	ERA.
1988—Los Angeles	National	2	8⅔	1	0	1.000	10	7	6	10	6	6.23

STANLEY PETER BELINDA
(Stan)

Born August 6, 1966, at State College, Pa.
Height, 6.03. Weight, 200.
Throws and bats righthanded.
Attended Allegany Community College, Cumberland, Md.

Major League saves: 1990 (8).

Year Club	League	G.	IP.	W.	L.	Pct.	H.	R.	ER.	SO.	BB.	ERA.
1986—Watertown	NYP	5	8	0	0	.000	5	3	3	5	2	3.38
1986—Bradenton Pirates†	Gulf Coast	17	20⅓	3	2	.600	23	12	6	17	2	2.66
1987—Macon..	S. Atlantic	50	82	6	4	.600	59	26	19	75	27	2.09
1988—Salem..	Carolina	53	71⅔	6	4	.600	54	33	22	63	32	2.76
1989—Harrisburg	Eastern	32	38⅔	1	4	.200	32	13	10	33	25	2.33
1989—Buffalo..	Am. Assoc.	19	28⅓	2	2	.500	13	5	3	28	13	0.95
1989—Pittsburgh..................................	National	8	10⅓	0	1	.000	13	8	7	10	2	6.10
1990—Buffalo..	Am. Assoc.	15	23⅔	3	1	.750	20	8	5	25	8	1.90
1990—Pittsburgh..................................	National	55	58⅓	3	4	.429	48	23	23	55	29	3.55
Major League Totals—2 Years........................		63	68⅔	3	5	.375	61	31	30	65	31	3.93

Selected by Pittsburgh Pirates' organization in 10th round of free-agent draft, June 2, 1986.
†On disabled list, June 21 to June 30, 1986.

Year Club	League	G.	IP.	W.	L.	Pct.	H.	R.	ER.	SO.	BB.	ERA.
1990—Pittsburgh	National	3	3⅔	0	0	.000	3	1	1	4	0	2.45

GEORGE ANTONIO BELL (MATHEY)

Born October 21, 1959, at San Pedro de Macoris, D. R.
Height, 6.01. Weight, 202.
Throws and bats righthanded.
Brother of Juan Bell, shortstop in Baltimore Orioles' organization;
and Rolando Bell, infielder in Los Angeles Dodgers' organization, 1985 through 1987.

Shares major league record for most sacrifice flies, game (3), August 14, 1990.
Major League stolen bases: 1981 (3), 1983 (1), 1984 (11), 1985 (21), 1986 (7), 1987 (5), 1988 (4), 1989 (4), 1990 (3). Total—59.
Hit three home runs in a game, April 4, 1988.
Led American League in sacrifice flies with 14 in 1989.
Led American League in total bases with 369 in 1987.
Tied for American League lead in game-winning RBIs with 15 in 1986.
Tied for International League lead in double plays by outfielders with 4 in 1983.
Led Western Carolinas League in total bases with 270 in 1979.
Named Major League Player of the Year by THE SPORTING NEWS, 1987.
Named American League Player of the Year by THE SPORTING NEWS, 1987.
Named American League Most Valuable Player by Baseball Writers' Association of America, 1987.
Named outfielder on THE SPORTING NEWS American League All-Star Team, 1986 and 1987.
Named outfielder on THE SPORTING NEWS American League Silver Slugger team, 1985 through 1987.

Year Club	League	Pos.	G.	AB.	R.	H.	2B.	3B.	HR.	RBI.	B.A.	PO.	A.	E.	F.A.
1978—Helena	Pion.	OF	33	106	20	33	6	1	0	14	.311	39	4	4	.915
1979—Spartanburg	W. Car.	OF	130	491	78	150	24	★15	22	★102	.305	206	14	8	.965
1980—Reading†‡	East.	OF	22	55	11	17	5	2	0	11	.309	24	0	1	.960
1981—Toronto	Amer.	OF	60	163	19	38	2	1	5	12	.233	92	3	3	.969
1982—Syracuse§	Int.	OF	37	125	11	25	5	4	3	19	.200	72	3	1	.987
1983—Syracuse	Int.	OF	85	317	37	86	11	4	15	59	.271	135	12	6	.961
1983—Toronto	Amer.	OF	39	112	5	30	5	4	2	17	.268	61	1	3	.954
1984—Toronto	Amer.	OF-3B	159	606	85	177	39	4	26	87	.292	289	13	9	.971
1985—Toronto	Amer.	●OF-1B	157	607	87	167	28	6	28	95	.275	320	14	●11	.968
1986—Toronto	Amer.	OF-3B	159	641	101	198	38	6	31	108	.309	270	17	10	.966
1987—Toronto	Amer.	OF-2B-3B	156	610	111	188	32	4	47	★134	.308	249	14	11	.960
1988—Toronto	Amer.	OF	156	614	78	165	27	5	24	97	.269	253	8	15	.946
1989—Toronto x	Amer.	OF	153	613	88	182	41	2	18	104	.297	258	4	●10	.963
1990—Toronto y	Amer.	OF	142	562	67	149	25	0	21	86	.265	226	4	5	.979
Major League Totals—9 Years			1181	4528	641	1294	237	32	202	740	.286	2018	78	77	.965

Signed as free agent by Philadelphia Phillies' organization, June 23, 1978.
†On disabled list, June 22, 1980 through remainder of season.
‡Drafted by Toronto Blue Jays, December 8, 1980.
§On disabled list, April 20 to May 1, June 14 to June 30 and July 8, 1982 through remainder of season.
xOn suspended list, July 31 to August 2, 1989.
yGranted free agency, November 5, 1990; signed by Chicago Cubs, December 6, 1990.

CHAMPIONSHIP SERIES RECORD

Year Club	League	Pos.	G.	AB.	R.	H.	2B.	3B.	HR.	RBI.	B.A.	PO.	A.	E.	F.A.
1985—Toronto	Amer.	OF	7	28	4	9	3	0	0	1	.321	13	0	0	1.000
1989—Toronto	Amer.	OF-DH	5	20	2	4	0	0	1	2	.200	3	1	0	1.000
Championship Series Totals—2 Years			12	48	6	13	3	0	1	3	.271	16	1	0	1.000

ALL-STAR GAME RECORD

Year League	Pos.	AB.	R.	H.	2B.	3B.	HR.	RBI.	B.A.	PO.	A.	E.	F.A.
1987—American	OF	3	0	0	0	0	0	0	.000	1	0	0	1.000
1990—American	PH-OF	2	0	0	0	0	0	0	.000	2	0	0	1.000
All-Star Games Totals—2 Years		5	0	0	0	0	0	0	.000	3	0	0	1.000

JAY STUART BELL

Born December 11, 1965, at Pensacola, Fla.
Height, 6.01. Weight, 180.
Throws and bats righthanded.

Shares major league record by hitting home run in first major league at-bat, September 29, 1986.
Major League stolen bases: 1987 (2), 1988 (4), 1989 (5), 1990 (10). Total—21.
Led National League in sacrifice hits with 39 in 1990.
Led National League shortstops in total chances with 741 in 1990.
Led American Association shortstops in putouts with 198, assists with 322 and total chances with 550 in 1987.
Led National League in sacrifice hits with 39 in 1990.
Led National League shortstops in total chances with 741 in 1990.
Led Eastern League shortstops in total chances with 613 in 1986.
Led California League shortstops in double plays with 84 in 1985.
Led Appalachian League shortstops in double plays with 43 and total chances with 352 in 1984.

Year Club League	Pos.	G.	AB.	R.	H.	2B.	3B.	HR.	RBI.	B.A.	PO.	A.	E.	F.A.
1984—Elizabethton .... Appal.	SS	66	245	43	54	12	1	6	30	.220	★109	★218	25	.929
1985—Visalia† .... Calif.	SS	106	376	56	106	16	6	9	59	.282	176	330	53	.905
1985—Waterbury............. East.	SS	29	114	13	34	11	2	1	14	.298	41	79	6	.952
1986—Waterbury............. East.	SS	138	494	86	137	28	4	7	74	.277	197	★371	★45	.927
1986—Cleveland.............. Amer.	2B	5	14	3	5	2	0	1	4	.357	1	6	2	.778
1987—Buffalo................... A. A.	★SS-2B	110	362	71	94	15	4	17	60	.260	201	325	★30	.946
1987—Cleveland.............. Amer.	SS	38	125	14	27	9	1	2	13	.216	67	93	9	.947
1988—Cleveland.............. Amer.	SS	73	211	23	46	5	1	2	21	.218	103	170	10	.965
1988—Colorado Springs‡ P. C.	SS	49	181	35	50	12	2	7	24	.276	87	171	18	.935
1989—Pittsburgh.............. Nat.	SS	78	271	33	70	13	3	2	27	.258	109	197	10	.968
1989—Buffalo................... A. A.	SS-3B	86	298	49	85	15	3	10	54	.285	110	223	16	.954
1990—Pittsburgh.............. Nat.	SS	159	583	93	148	28	7	7	52	.254	★260	459	22	.970
American League Totals—3 Years		116	350	40	78	16	2	5	38	.223	171	269	21	.954
National League Totals—2 Years		237	854	126	218	41	10	9	79	.255	369	656	32	.970
Major League Totals—5 Years		353	1204	166	296	57	12	14	117	.246	540	925	53	.965

Selected by Minnesota Twins' organization in 1st round (eighth player selected) of free-agent draft, June 4, 1984.

†Traded with Pitcher Curt Wardle, Outfielder Jim Weaver and a player to be named later to Cleveland Indians for Pitcher Bert Blyleven, August 1, 1985; Cleveland organization acquired Pitcher Rich Yett to complete deal, September 17, 1985.

‡Traded to Pittsburgh Pirates for Shortstop Felix Fermin, March 25, 1989.

CHAMPIONSHIP SERIES RECORD

Year Club League	Pos.	G.	AB.	R.	H.	2B.	3B.	HR.	RBI.	B.A.	PO.	A.	E.	F.A.
1990—Pittsburgh.............. Nat.	SS	6	20	3	5	1	0	1	1	.250	4	22	1	.963

JUAN BELL (MATHEY)

Born March 29, 1968 at San Pedro de Macoris, D. R.
Height, 5.11. Weight, 172.
Throws right and bats left and righthanded.
Brother of George Bell, outfielder with Chicago Cubs; and Rolando Bell,
infielder in Los Angeles Dodgers' organization, 1985 through 1987.

Major League stolen bases: 1989 (1).
Led Gulf Coast League shortstops in total chances with 293 in 1986.
Led California League shortstops in total chances with 719 in 1987.

Year Club League	Pos.	G.	AB.	R.	H.	2B.	3B.	HR.	RBI.	B.A.	PO.	A.	E.	F.A.
1985—Bradenton Dodg.. Gulf C.	SS-2B	42	106	11	17	0	0	0	8	.160	56	73	20	.866
1986—Sarasota Dodg.†... Gulf C.	SS	59	217	38	52	6	2	0	26	.240	78	★193	22	.925
1987—Bakersfield........... Calif.	SS	134	473	54	116	15	3	4	58	.245	235	★431	★53	.926
1988—San Antonio†........ Texas	SS	61	215	37	60	4	2	5	21	.279	106	182	20	.935
1988—Albuquerque‡ .... P. C.	SS	73	257	42	77	9	3	8	45	.300	114	249	23	.940
1989—Rochester.............. Int.	SS	116	408	50	107	15	6	2	32	.262	190	297	36	.931
1989—Baltimore .... Amer.	2B-SS	8	4	2	0	0	0	0	0	.000	2	6	0	1.000
1990—Rochester§........... Int.	SS	82	326	59	93	12	5	6	35	.285	131	240	22	.944
1990—Baltimore .... Amer.	SS	5	2	1	0	0	0	0	0	.000	1	1	0	1.000
Major League Totals—2 Years		13	6	3	0	0	0	0	0	.000	3	7	0	1.000

Signed as free agent by Los Angeles Dodgers' organization, September 1, 1984.

†Batted righthanded only.

‡Traded with Pitchers Brian Holton and Ken Howell to Baltimore Orioles for First Baseman Eddie Murray, December 4, 1988.

§On disabled list, July 6 to August 27, 1990.

MICHAEL ALLEN BELL

(Mike)

Born April 22, 1968, at Lewiston, N.J.
Height, 6.01. Weight, 175.
Throws and bats lefthanded.

Led Southern League first basemen in total chances with 1,316 in 1989.
Led Carolina League first basemen in total chances with 1,014 in 1988.

Year Club League	Pos.	G.	AB.	R.	H.	2B.	3B.	HR.	RBI.	B.A.	PO.	A.	E.	F.A.
1987—Sumter................... S. Atl.	1B	133	443	54	108	17	3	5	51	.244	1007	70	16	.985
1988—Durham................. Carol.	1B	126	440	72	113	18	3	17	84	.257	★924	76	14	★.986
1988—Greenville .... South.	1B	4	12	1	3	1	0	0	4	.250	44	1	0	1.000
1989—Greenville .... South.	1B	132	472	63	115	26	3	6	57	.244	★1209	★94	13	.990
1990—Greenville .... South.	1B	106	405	50	118	24	2	6	42	.291	981	85	8	★.993
1990—Atlanta .... Nat.	1B	36	45	8	11	5	1	1	5	.244	97	9	2	.981
Major League Totals—1 Year.................		36	45	8	11	5	1	1	5	.244	97	9	2	.981

Selected by Atlanta Braves' organization in 4th round of free-agent draft, June 2, 1986.

ALBERT JOJUAN BELLE

(Joey)

Born August 25, 1966, at Shreveport, La.
Height, 6.02. Weight, 200.
Throws and bats righthanded.
Attended Louisiana State University, Baton Rouge, La.

Major League stolen bases: 1989 (2).

Year Club League	Pos.	G.	AB.	R.	H.	2B.	3B.	HR.	RBI.	B.A.	PO.	A.	E.	F.A.
1987—Kinston..................Carol.	OF	10	37	5	12	2	0	3	9	.324	5	0	0	1.000
1988—Kinston..................Carol.	OF	41	153	21	46	16	0	8	39	.301	43	5	5	.906
1988—Waterloo...............Midw.	OF	9	28	2	7	1	0	1	2	.250	11	1	0	1.000
1989—Canton-Akron...... East.	OF	89	312	48	88	20	0	20	69	.282	136	4	3	.979
1989—Cleveland.............. Amer.	OF	62	218	22	49	8	4	7	37	.225	92	3	2	.979
1990—Cleveland.............. Amer.	OF	9	23	1	4	0	0	1	3	.174	0	0	0	.000
1990—Colorado Springs. P. C.	OF	24	96	16	33	3	1	5	19	.344	31	0	2	.939
1990—Canton-Akron ...... East.	DH	9	32	4	8	1	0	0	3	.250	0	0	0	.000
Major League Totals—2 Years................		71	241	23	53	8	4	8	40	.220	92	3	2	.979

Selected by Cleveland Indians' organization in 2nd round of free-agent draft, June 2, 1987.

RAFAEL LEONIDAS BELLIARD (MATIAS)

Name pronounced BELL-ee-ard.

Born October 24, 1961, at Pueblo Nuevo, Mao, D. R.
Height, 5.06. Weight, 150.
Throws and bats righthanded.

Major League stolen bases: 1982 (1), 1984 (4), 1986 (12), 1987 (5), 1988 (7), 1989 (5), 1990 (1). Total—35.
Led National League shortstops in fielding percentage with .977 in 1988.
Led Carolina League in sacrifice hits with 12 and tied for lead in caught stealing with 15 in 1981.
Tied for Eastern League lead in double plays by shortstops with 69 in 1983.

Year Club League	Pos.	G.	AB.	R.	H.	2B.	3B.	HR.	RBI.	B.A.	PO.	A.	E.	F.A.
1980—Bradenton Pir. ..... Gulf C.	SS-2B-3B	12	42	6	9	1	0	0	2	.214	24	39	1	.984
1980—Shelby.................... S. Atl.	SS	8	24	1	3	0	0	0	2	.125	10	27	5	.881
1981—Alexandria .... Carol.	SS	127	472	58	102	6	5	0	33	.216	●205	330	29	.949
1982—Buffalo†................. East.	SS	40	124	14	34	1	1	0	19	.274	56	87	5	.966
1982—Pittsburgh.............. Nat.	SS	9	2	3	1	0	0	0	0	.500	2	2	0	1.000
1983—Lynn...................... East.	SS-2B	127	431	63	113	13	2	2	37	.262	203	307	26	.951
1983—Pittsburgh.............. Nat.	SS	4	1	1	0	0	0	0	0	.000	1	3	0	1.000
1984—Pittsburgh‡........... Nat.	SS-2B	20	22	3	5	0	0	0	0	.227	12	13	3	.893
1985—Pittsburgh.............. Nat.	SS	17	20	1	4	0	0	0	1	.200	13	23	2	.947
1985—Hawaii.................. P. C.	SS-2B	100	341	35	84	12	4	1	18	.246	172	289	5	.989
1986—Pittsburgh§........... Nat.	SS-2B	117	309	33	72	5	2	0	31	.233	147	317	12	.975
1987—Pittsburgh x .... Nat.	SS-2B	81	203	26	42	4	3	1	15	.207	113	191	6	.981
1987—Harrisburg............. East.	SS	37	145	24	49	5	2	0	9	.338	59	115	7	.961
1988—Pittsburgh y .... Nat.	SS-2B	122	286	28	61	0	4	0	11	.213	134	261	9	.978
1989—Pittsburgh.............. Nat.	SS-2B-3B	67	154	10	33	4	0	0	8	.214	71	138	3	.986
1990—Pittsburgh z .... Nat.	2B-SS-3B	47	54	10	11	3	0	0	6	.204	37	36	2	.973
Major League Totals—9 Years................		484	1051	115	229	16	9	1	72	.218	530	984	37	.976

Signed as free agent by Pittsburgh Pirates' organization, July 10, 1980.
†On disabled list, April 19 to July 24, 1982.
‡On disabled list, June 28 to August 28, 1984.
§On disabled list, July 28 to August 12, 1986.
xOn disabled list, August 27, 1987 through remainder of season.
yOn disabled list, May 19 to June 3, 1988.
zGranted free agency, November 5, 1990; signed by Atlanta Braves, December 18, 1990.

ANDREW CHARLES BENES
(Andy)

Born August 20, 1967, at Evansville, Ind.
Height, 6.06. Weight, 235.
Throws and bats righthanded.
Attended University of Evansville, Evansville, Ind.

Tied for National League lead in balks with 5 in 1990.
Led Texas League in shutouts with 3 in 1989.
Named National League Rookie Pitcher of the Year by THE SPORTING NEWS, 1989.
Named Texas League Pitcher of the Year, 1989.
Member of 1988 U.S. Olympic baseball team.
Received reported $230,000 bonus to sign with San Diego Padres, 1988.

Year Club League	G.	IP.	W.	L.	Pct.	H.	R.	ER.	SO.	BB.	ERA.
1989—Wichita......................Texas	16	108⅓	8	4	.667	79	32	26	115	39	2.16
1989—Las Vegas.....................P. Coast	5	26⅔	2	1	.667	41	29	24	29	12	8.10
1989—San Diego ....National	10	66⅔	6	3	.667	51	28	26	66	31	3.51
1990—San Diego ....National	32	192⅓	10	11	.476	177	87	77	140	69	3.60
Major League Totals—2 Years........	42	259	16	14	.533	228	115	103	206	100	3.58

Selected by San Diego Padres' organization in 1st round (first player selected) of free-agent draft, June 1, 1988.

MICHAEL PAUL BENJAMIN
(Mike)

Born November 22, 1965, at Euclid, O.
Height, 6.03. Weight, 195.
Throws and bats righthanded.
Attended Cerritos College, Norwalk, Calif., and Arizona State University, Tempe, Ariz.

Major League stolen bases: 1990 (1).
Led Pacific Coast League shortstops in total chances with 626 in 1990.

Year Club	League	Pos.	G.	AB.	R.	H.	2B.	3B.	HR.	RBI.	B.A.	PO.	A.	E.	F.A.
1987—Fresno	Calif.	SS	64	212	25	51	6	4	6	24	.241	89	188	21	.930
1988—Shreveport	Texas	SS	89	309	48	73	19	5	6	37	.236	134	248	11	.972
1988—Phoenix	P. C.	SS	37	106	13	18	4	1	0	6	.170	41	74	4	.966
1989—Phoenix	P. C.	SS-2B	113	363	44	94	17	6	3	36	.259	149	332	15	.970
1989—San Francisco	Nat.	SS	14	6	6	1	0	0	0	0	.167	4	4	0	1.000
1990—Phoenix	P. C.	SS	118	419	61	105	21	7	5	39	.251	★216	★386	24	.962
1990—San Francisco	Nat.	SS	22	56	7	12	3	1	2	3	.214	29	53	1	.988
Major League Totals—2 Years			36	62	13	13	3	1	2	3	.210	33	57	1	.989

Selected by Minnesota Twins' organization in 7th round of free-agent draft, January 9, 1985.
Selected by San Francisco Giants' organization in 3rd round of free-agent draft, June 2, 1987.

TODD ERIC BENZINGER

Born February 11, 1963, at Dayton, Ky.
Height, 6.01. Weight, 190.
Throws right and bats left and righthanded.
Nephew of Don Gross, pitcher with Cincinnati Reds and Pittsburgh Pirates, 1955 through 1960.
Major League stolen bases: 1987 (5), 1988 (2), 1989 (3), 1990 (3). Total—13.

Year Club	League	Pos.	G.	AB.	R.	H.	2B.	3B.	HR.	RBI.	B.A.	PO.	A.	E.	F.A.
1981—Elmira	NYP	OF-1B	41	141	21	34	10	1	2	8	.241	131	9	2	.986
1982—Winston-Salem	Carol.	OF-1B	121	443	54	97	19	1	5	46	.219	438	28	8	.983
1983—Winter Haven	Fla. St.	OF-1B-3B	125	480	56	134	34	5	7	68	.279	206	10	8	.964
1984—New Britain†	East.	OF-1B	110	391	49	101	25	5	10	60	.258	465	29	14	.972
1985—Pawtucket‡	Int.	OF	70	256	31	64	13	1	11	47	.250	106	3	3	.973
1986—Pawtucket§	Int.	OF-1B	90	314	41	79	13	2	11	32	.252	156	4	2	.988
1987—Pawtucket	Int.	OF-1B	65	257	47	83	17	3	13	49	.323	256	16	2	.993
1987—Boston	Amer.	OF-1B	73	223	36	62	11	1	8	43	.278	155	7	2	.988
1988—Boston xy	Amer.	1B-OF	120	405	47	103	28	1	13	70	.254	602	38	6	.991
1989—Cincinnati	Nat.	1B	161	★628	79	154	28	3	17	76	.245	1417	73	7	.995
1990—Cincinnati	Nat.	1B-OF	118	376	35	95	14	2	5	46	.253	733	52	6	.992
American League Totals—2 Years			193	628	83	165	39	2	21	113	.263	757	45	8	.990
National League Totals—2 Years			279	1004	114	249	42	5	22	122	.248	2150	125	13	.994
Major League Totals—4 Years			472	1632	197	414	81	7	43	235	.254	2907	170	21	.993

Selected by Boston Red Sox' organization in 4th round of free-agent draft, June 8, 1981.
†On disabled list, August 10, 1984 through remainder of season.
‡On disabled list, April 10 to June 11, 1985.
§On disabled list, April 11 to April 21 and June 26 to July 17, 1986.
xOn disabled list, June 3 to June 22, 1988.
yTraded with Pitcher Jeff Sellers and a player to be named later to Cincinnati Reds for First Baseman Nick Esasky and Pitcher Rob Murphy, December 13, 1988; Cincinnati acquired Pitcher Luis Vasquez to complete deal, January 12, 1989.

CHAMPIONSHIP SERIES RECORD

Year Club	League	Pos.	G.	AB.	R.	H.	2B.	3B.	HR.	RBI.	B.A.	PO.	A.	E.	F.A.
1988—Boston	Amer.	1B-PH	4	11	0	1	0	0	0	0	.091	21	1	0	1.000
1990—Cincinnati	Nat.	PH-1B	5	9	0	3	0	0	0	0	.333	17	0	0	1.000
Championship Series Total—2 Years			9	20	0	4	0	0	0	0	.200	38	1	0	1.000

WORLD SERIES RECORD

Year Club	League	Pos.	G.	AB.	R.	H.	2B.	3B.	HR.	RBI.	B.A.	PO.	A.	E.	F.A.
1990—Cincinnati	Nat.	PH-1B	4	11	1	2	0	0	0	0	.182	24	0	0	1.000

JUAN BAUTISTA BERENGUER JR.

Name pronounced Bare-en-GARE.

Born November 30, 1954, at Aguadulce, Panama.
Height, 5.11. Weight, 223.
Throws and bats righthanded.
Major League saves: 1983 (1), 1986 (4), 1987 (4), 1988 (2), 1989 (3). Total—14.
Led Carolina League pitchers in games started with 28 and hit batsmen with 13 in 1976.
Tied for American Association lead in complete games with 9 in 1982.
Tied for Texas League pitchers lead in games started with 26 in 1977.
Tied for Midwest League lead in hit batsmen with 8 in 1975.
Named International League Pitcher of the Year, 1978.

Year Club	League	G.	IP.	W.	L.	Pct.	H.	R.	ER.	SO.	BB.	ERA.
1975—Wausau	Midwest	18	95	5	4	.556	83	41	31	58	50	2.94
1976—Lynchburg	Carolina	28	187	10	13	.435	★175	89	★75	114	★118	3.61
1977—Jackson	Texas	26	181	9	8	.529	143	89	69	★160	★126	3.43
1978—Tidewater	Int'national	24	147	10	7	.588	117	60	60	130	91	3.67
1978—New York†	National	5	13	0	2	.000	17	12	12	8	11	8.31
1979—Tacoma	P. Coast	26	166	8	8	.500	128	101	90	★220	129	4.88
1979—New York	National	5	31	1	1	.500	28	13	10	25	12	2.90
1980—Tidewater	Int'national	27	157	9	●15	.375	122	78	67	★178	76	3.84
1980—New York‡	National	6	9	0	1	.000	9	9	6	7	10	6.00
1981—Kansas City§-Toronto x	American	20	91	2	★13	.133	84	62	53	49	51	5.24
1982—Evansville	Am. Assoc.	25	156⅓	11	10	.524	152	85	80	127	80	4.61

Year Club	League	G.	IP.	W.	L.	Pct.	H.	R.	ER.	SO.	BB.	ERA.
1982—Detroit	American	2	6⅔	0	0	.000	5	5	5	8	9	6.75
1983—Detroit	American	37	157⅔	9	5	.643	110	58	55	129	71	3.14
1984—Detroit	American	31	168⅓	11	10	.524	146	75	65	118	79	3.48
1985—Detroit y	American	31	95	5	6	.455	96	67	59	82	48	5.59
1986—San Francisco za	National	46	73⅓	2	3	.400	64	23	22	72	44	2.70
1987—Minnesota bc	American	47	112	8	1	.889	100	51	49	110	47	3.94
1988—Minnesota	American	57	100	8	4	.667	74	44	44	99	61	3.96
1989—Minnesota	American	56	106	9	3	.750	96	44	41	93	47	3.48
1990—Minnesota d	American	51	100⅓	8	5	.615	85	43	38	77	58	3.41
National League Totals—4 Years		62	126⅓	3	7	.300	118	57	50	112	77	3.56
American League Totals—9 Years		332	937	60	47	.561	796	449	409	765	471	3.93
Major League Totals—13 Years		394	1063⅓	63	54	.538	914	506	459	877	548	3.88

Signed as free agent by New York Mets' organization, February 22, 1975.
†Loaned to Tacoma (Cleveland Indians' organization), March 24, 1979; returned August 29, 1979.
‡Traded to Kansas City for Outfielder Marvell Wynne and Pitcher John Skinner, March 31, 1981.
§Sold on waivers to Toronto Blue Jays, August 8, 1981.
xReleased, March 28, 1982; signed by Evansville (Detroit Tigers' organization), April 4, 1982.
yTraded with Catcher Bob Melvin and a player to be named later to San Francisco Giants for Pitchers Dave LaPoint and Eric King and Catcher Matt Nokes, October 7, 1985; San Francisco acquired Pitcher Scott Medvin to complete deal, December 11, 1985.
zOn disabled list, April 7 to April 28, 1986.
aReleased, December 9, 1986; signed by Minnesota Twins, January 9, 1987.
bOn disabled list, August 3 to August 22, 1987.
cGranted free agency, November 9, 1987; re-signed by Twins, December 22, 1987.
dGranted free agency, December 7, 1990.

CHAMPIONSHIP SERIES RECORD

Shares American League Championship Series record for most games pitched, series (4), 1987.

Year Club	League	G.	IP.	W.	L.	Pct.	H.	R.	ER.	SO.	BB.	ERA.
1987—Minnesota	American	4	6	0	0	.000	1	1	1	6	3	1.50

WORLD SERIES RECORD

Year Club	League	G.	IP.	W.	L.	Pct.	H.	R.	ER.	SO.	BB.	ERA.
1987—Minnesota	American	3	4⅓	0	1	.000	10	5	5	1	0	10.38

Eligible for 1984 World Series with Detroit Tigers; did not play.

DAVID BRUCE BERGMAN
(Dave)

Born June 6, 1953, at Evanston, Ill.
Height, 6.02. Weight, 190.
Throws and bats lefthanded.
Received bachelor of arts degree in business administration
from Illinois State University, Normal, Ill., in 1974.

Major League stolen bases: 1978 (2), 1980 (1), 1981 (2), 1982 (3), 1983 (2), 1984 (3), 1989 (1), 1990 (3). Total—17.
Led International League in bases on balls received with 95 in 1979.
Led International League first basemen in putouts with 1,199 in 1976.
Led Eastern League first basemen in assists with 58 in 1975.
Named Eastern League Most Valuable Player, 1975.
Named outfielder on THE SPORTING NEWS College Baseball All-America Team, 1974.

Year Club	League	Pos.	G.	AB.	R.	H.	2B.	3B.	HR.	RBI.	B.A.	PO.	A.	E.	F.A.
1974—Oneonta	NYP	1B	56	201	60	70	6	•7	10	48	★.348	494	★29	8	★.985
1975—West Haven	East.	1B-OF	124	399	76	124	15	6	11	60	★.311	610	61	5	.993
1975—New York	Amer.	OF	7	17	0	0	0	0	0	0	.000	10	1	1	.917
1976—Syracuse	Int.	★1B-OF	134	455	68	134	23	2	7	65	.295	1201	82	10	★.992
1977—Syracuse	Int.	OF-1B	132	468	88	146	29	4	16	59	.312	534	39	8	.986
1977—New York†	Amer.	OF-1B	5	4	1	1	0	0	0	1	.250	8	0	0	1.000
1978—Houston	Nat.	1B-OF	104	186	15	43	5	1	0	12	.231	328	16	4	.989
1979—Charleston	Int.	1B-OF	138	461	78	129	23	3	6	58	.280	910	61	11	.989
1979—Houston	Nat.	1B	13	15	4	6	0	0	1	2	.400	8	0	0	1.000
1980—Houston	Nat.	1B-OF	90	78	12	20	6	1	0	3	.256	187	16	1	.995
1981—Hou.‡-S.F.	Nat.	1B-OF	69	151	17	38	9	0	4	14	.252	255	25	3	.989
1982—San Francisco	Nat.	1B-OF	100	121	22	33	3	1	4	14	.273	321	20	4	.988
1983—San Francisco§	Nat.	1B-OF	90	140	16	40	4	1	6	24	.286	299	27	2	.994
1984—Detroit	Amer.	1B-OF	120	271	42	74	8	5	7	44	.273	658	75	8	.989
1985—Detroit x	Amer.	1B-OF	69	140	8	25	2	0	3	7	.179	306	25	3	.991
1985—Nashville	A. A.	1B	11	39	6	9	1	0	1	6	.231	87	8	1	.990
1986—Detroit	Amer.	1B-OF	65	130	14	30	6	1	1	9	.231	255	29	4	.986
1987—Detroit y	Amer.	1B-OF	91	172	25	47	7	3	6	22	.273	357	29	3	.992
1988—Detroit z	Amer.	1B-OF	116	289	37	85	14	0	5	35	.294	386	37	4	.991
1989—Detroit	Amer.	1B-OF	137	385	38	103	13	1	7	37	.268	912	85	7	.993
1990—Detroit	Amer.	1B-OF	100	205	21	57	10	1	2	26	.278	203	13	1	.995
National League Totals—6 Years			466	691	86	180	27	4	15	69	.260	1398	104	14	.991
American League Totals—9 Years			710	1613	186	422	60	11	31	181	.262	3095	294	31	.991
Major League Totals—15 Years			1176	2304	272	602	87	15	46	250	.261	4493	398	45	.991

Selected by Chicago Cubs' organization in 12th round of free-agent draft, June 8, 1971.
Selected by New York Yankees' organization in 2nd round of free-agent draft, June 5, 1974.

†Traded to Houston Astros, November 23, 1977, completing deal in which Houston traded First Baseman-Catcher Cliff Johnson to New York Yankees for Infielder Mike Fischlin, Pitcher Randy Niemann and a player to be named later, June 15, 1977.

‡Traded with Outfielder Jeff Leonard to San Francisco Giants for First Baseman Mike Ivie, April 20, 1981.

§Traded to Philadelphia Phillies for Outfielder Alejandro Sanchez, March 24, 1984; Traded by Philadelphia with Pitcher Willie Hernandez to Detroit Tigers for Outfielder Glenn Wilson and Catcher-First Baseman John Wockenfuss, March 24, 1984.

xOn disabled list, April 22 to May 29, 1985; included rehabilitation disability assignment to Nashville, May 15 to May 29, 1985.

yOn disabled list, June 7 to June 22, 1987.

zGranted free agency, November 4, 1988; re-signed by Tigers, December 7, 1988.

CHAMPIONSHIP SERIES RECORD

Year	Club	League	Pos.	G.	AB.	R.	H.	2B.	3B.	HR.	RBI.	B.A.	PO.	A.	E.	F.A.
1980—Houston	Nat.	PR-1B	4	3	0	1	0	1	0	2	.333	8	2	1	.909
1984—Detroit	Amer.	PR-1B	2	1	1	1	0	0	0	0	1.000	5	0	0	1.000
1987—Detroit	Amer.	PH-DH-1	4	4	0	1	0	0	0	2	.250	6	0	0	1.000
Championship Series Totals—3 Years			10	8	1	3	0	1	0	4	.375	19	2	1	.955

WORLD SERIES RECORD

Year	Club	League	Pos.	G.	AB.	R.	H.	2B.	3B.	HR.	RBI.	B.A.	PO.	A.	E.	F.A.
1984—Detroit	Amer.	PR-1B	5	5	0	0	0	0	0	0	.000	22	4	0	1.000

ANTONIO BERNAZARD (GARCIA)
(Tony)

Born August 24, 1956, at Caguas, Puerto Rico.
Height, 5.09. Weight, 160.
Throws right and bats right and lefthanded.
Attended University of Florida, Gainesville, Fla., and Humacao College, Humacao, P.R.
Brother of Oscar Bernazard, outfielder in Pittsburgh Pirates'
and Montreal Expos' organizations, 1975 through 1978.

Major League stolen bases: 1979 (1), 1980 (9), 1981 (4), 1982 (11), 1983 (23), 1984 (20), 1985 (17), 1986 (17), 1987 (11). Total—113.

Switch-hit home runs in one game, July 1, 1986.

Led American League second basemen in total chances with 810 in 1986.

Led Eastern League in caught stealing with 20 in 1977.

Led American Association second basemen in putouts with 297, assists with 386 and double plays with 101 in 1978.

Led Eastern League second basemen in double plays with 70 in 1976.

Led Florida State League second basemen in assists with 386 in 1975.

Named second baseman on THE SPORTING NEWS American League All-Star Team, 1986.

Year	Club	League	Pos.	G.	AB.	R.	H.	2B.	3B.	HR.	RBI.	B.A.	PO.	A.	E.	F.A.
1974—Kinston†	Carol.	2B	56	225	22	45	3	1	0	16	.200	129	142	19	.934
1974—Sarasota Expos‡	Gulf C.	2B	34	109	11	18	2	1	1	6	.165	95	71	7	.960
1975—W. Palm Beach	Fla. St.	2B-SS	★134	★509	65	121	16	2	6	50	.238	282	389	28	.960
1976—Quebec City	East.	2B	106	334	35	72	8	3	1	26	.216	227	257	18	.964
1977—Quebec City	East.	2B	125	425	68	119	11	6	1	34	.280	273	379	25	.963
1978—Denver	A. A.	★2-3-O	128	479	★107	137	30	9	9	65	.286	302	390	★32	.956
1979—Denver	A. A.	2B	82	273	58	82	15	2	3	29	.300	178	275	●19	.960
1979—Montreal	Nat.	2B	22	40	11	12	2	0	1	8	.300	22	34	1	.982
1980—Montreal§	Nat.	2B-SS	82	183	26	41	7	1	5	18	.224	82	151	9	.963
1981—Chicago	Amer.	2B-SS	106	384	53	106	14	4	6	34	.276	228	320	7	.987
1982—Chicago x	Amer.	2B	137	540	90	138	25	9	11	56	.256	353	443	12	.985
1983—Chi. y-Sea. z	Amer.	2B	139	533	65	141	34	3	8	56	.265	262	422	19	.973
1984—Cleveland	Amer.	2B	140	439	44	97	15	4	2	38	.221	264	397	★20	.971
1985—Cleveland a	Amer.	2B-SS	153	500	73	137	26	3	11	59	.274	313	399	16	.978
1986—Cleveland	Amer.	2B	146	562	88	169	28	4	17	73	.301	★351	442	17	.979
1987—Cle.b-Oak.c	Amer.	2B	140	507	73	127	26	2	14	49	.250	243	335	17	.971
1988—Daiei	Pacific	....	....	....	....	....	....	....	....	....	....	....	....	....	....
1989—Daiei	Pacific	....	....	....	....	....	....	....	....	....	....	....	....	....	....
1990—Daiei d	Pacific	....	75	276	...	76	....	...	13	40	.275	....	....	....	....
National League Totals—2 Years			104	223	37	53	9	1	6	26	.238	104	185	10	.967
American League Totals—7 Years			961	3465	486	915	168	29	69	365	.264	2014	2758	108	.978
Major League Totals—9 Years			1065	3688	523	968	177	30	75	391	.262	2118	2943	118	.977

Signed as free agent by Montreal Expos' organization, November 13, 1973.

†On disabled list, June 10 to June 17, 1974.

‡On temporary inactive list, August 15 to September 25, 1974.

§Traded to Chicago White Sox for Pitcher Richard Wortham, December 12, 1980.

xOn disabled list, September 13, 1982 through remainder of season.

yTraded to Seattle Mariners for Second Baseman Julio Cruz, June 15, 1983.

zTraded to Cleveland Indians for Outfielder Gorman Thomas and Second Baseman Jack Perconte, December 7, 1983.

aGranted free agency, November 12, 1985; re-signed by Indians, January 8, 1986.

bTraded to Oakland Athletics for Pitcher Darrel Akerfelds and Catcher Brian Dorsett, July 15, 1987.

cReleased, December 21, 1987; signed by Fukuoka Daiei Hawks of Japanese Baseball League, February, 1988.

dSigned by Detroit Tigers, December 5, 1990.

CESAR ENRIQUILLO BERNHARDT

Born January 18, 1969, at San Pedro de Macoris, Dominican Republic.
Height, 5.09. Weight, 150.
Throws and bats righthanded.

Led Midwest League in total bases with 206 in 1989.
Led Southern League second basemen in total chances with 674 and double plays with 93 in 1990.
Led Midwest League second basemen in double plays with 70 in 1989.

Year Club	League	Pos.	G.	AB.	R.	H.	2B.	3B.	HR.	RBI.	B.A.	PO.	A.	E.	F.A.
1986—Appleton	Midw.	2B	19	76	9	21	2	2	1	12	.276	29	37	8	.892
1986—Sarasota W. S.†.....	Gulf C.	2B	42	103	6	19	3	0	0	10	.184	46	42	8	.917
1987—Charleston, W.Va.	S. Atl.	2B	122	444	56	112	28	5	5	53	.252	225	255	21	.958
1988—South Bend	Midw.	OF-2B	124	482	47	136	17	2	1	51	.282	158	100	9	.966
1989—South Bend	Midw.	2B	127	493	73	★148	26	7	6	●81	.300	193	324	20	.963
1990—Birmingham	South.	2B ●142		★574	96	160	26	9	6	82	.279	★277	★371	★26	.961

Signed as free agent by Chicago White Sox' organization, December 18, 1985.
†Switch-hitter.

GERONIMO EMILIANO BERROA

Born March 18, 1965, at Santo Domingo, D. R.
Height, 6.00. Weight, 195.
Throws and bats righthanded.

Led International League in being hit by pitch with 10 and tied for lead in sacrifice flies with 8 in 1988.
Led International League in grounding into double plays with 17 in 1990.
Led Southern League in total bases with 297 in 1987.

Year Club	League	Pos.	G.	AB.	R.	H.	2B.	3B.	HR.	RBI.	B.A.	PO.	A.	E.	F.A.
1984—Bradenton Jays....	Gulf C.	OF	62	235	31	59	16	1	3	34	.251	75	2	5	.939
1985—Kinston.................	Carol.	OF	19	43	4	8	0	0	1	4	.186	13	1	1	.933
1985—Medicine Hat.......	Pion.	OF	54	201	39	69	★22	2	6	45	.343	58	3	3	.953
1985—Florence	S. Atl.	OF	19	66	7	21	2	0	3	20	.318	24	0	2	.923
1986—Ventura...............	Calif.	OF	128	459	76	137	22	5	21	73	.298	194	9	14	.935
1986—Knoxville	South.	OF	1	4	0	0	0	0	0	0	.000	2	0	0	1.000
1987—Knoxville	South.	OF	134	523	87	150	33	3	36	108	.287	236	6	●15	.942
1988—Syracuse†	Int.	OF	131	470	55	122	●29	1	8	64	.260	243	12	5	.981
1989—Atlanta	Nat.	OF	81	136	7	36	4	0	2	9	.265	67	1	2	.971
1990—Richmond.............	Int.	OF	135	499	56	134	17	2	12	80	.269	200	10	7	.968
1990—Atlanta	Nat.	OF	7	4	0	0	0	0	0	0	.000	1	0	0	1.000
Major League Totals—2 Years................			88	140	7	36	4	0	2	9	.257	68	1	2	.972

Signed as free agent by Toronto Blue Jays' organization, September 4, 1983.
†Drafted by Atlanta Braves, December 5, 1988.

SEAN ROBERT BERRY

Born March 22, 1966, at Santa Monica, Calif.
Height, 5.11. Weight, 200.
Throws and bats righthanded.
Attended UCLA, Los Angeles, Calif.

Led Northwest League third basemen in double plays with 11 in 1986.

Year Club	League	Pos.	G.	AB.	R.	H.	2B.	3B.	HR.	RBI.	B.A.	PO.	A.	E.	F.A.
1986—Eugene...................	N'west	3B	65	238	53	76	20	2	5	44	.319	★63	96	21	.883
1987—Fort Myers†..........	Fla. St.	3B	66	205	26	52	7	2	2	30	.259	39	101	23	.859
1988—Baseball City	Fla. St.	3B-SS-OF	94	304	34	71	6	4	4	30	.234	84	161	28	.897
1989—Baseball City	Fla. St.	3-O-2-S	116	394	67	106	19	7	4	44	.266	100	199	24	.926
1990—Memphis...............	South.	3B	135	487	73	142	25	4	14	77	.292	79	238	27	.922
1990—Kansas City..........	Amer.	3B	8	23	2	5	1	1	0	4	.217	7	10	1	.944
Major League Totals—1 Year...................			8	23	2	5	1	1	0	4	.217	7	10	1	.944

Selected by Boston Red Sox' organization in 4th round of free-agent draft, June 4, 1984.
Selected by Kansas City Royals' organization in secondary phase of free-agent draft, January 14, 1986.
†On disabled list, April 16 to May 3, 1987.

DAMON SCOTT BERRYHILL

Born December 3, 1963, at South Laguna, Calif.
Height, 6.00. Weight, 205.
Throws right and bats right and lefthanded.
Attended Orange Coast College, Costa Mesa, Calif.

Major League stolen bases: 1988 (1), 1989 (1). Total—2.
Led American Association catchers in putouts with 603, assists with 66, double plays with 11, passed balls with 15 and total chances with 676 in 1987.
Led Carolina League in passed balls with 18 in 1985.

Year Club	League	Pos.	G.	AB.	R.	H.	2B.	3B.	HR.	RBI.	B.A.	PO.	A.	E.	F.A.
1984—Quad Cities†.........	Midw.	C-1B	62	217	30	60	14	0	0	31	.276	314	31	8	.977
1985—Winston-Salem	Carol.	C-1B	117	386	31	90	25	1	9	50	.233	625	71	11	.984
1986—Pittsfield	East.	C-OF	112	345	33	71	13	1	6	35	.206	449	61	12	.977
1987—Iowa	A. A.	★C-1B	121	429	54	123	22	1	18	67	.287	607	67	7	★.990
1987—Chicago	Nat.	C	12	28	2	5	1	0	0	1	.179	37	3	4	.909
1988—Iowa	A. A.	C	21	73	11	16	5	1	2	11	.219	117	15	0	1.000
1988—Chicago‡	Nat.	C	95	309	19	80	19	1	7	38	.259	448	54	9	.982

Year Club	League	Pos.	G.	AB.	R.	H.	2B.	3B.	HR.	RBI.	B.A.	PO.	A.	E.	F.A.
1989—Iowa§	A. A.	C	7	30	4	6	1	0	2	4	.200	40	5	2	.957
1989—Chicago	Nat.	C	91	334	37	86	13	0	5	41	.257	473	41	4	.992
1990—Peoria x	Midw.	C	7	26	10	10	2	0	3	8	.385	75	4	1	.988
1990—Iowa	A. A.	C	22	79	8	17	1	0	3	6	.215	115	13	2	.985
1990—Chicago	Nat.	C	17	53	6	10	4	0	1	9	.189	87	3	2	.978
Major League Totals—4 Years			215	724	64	181	37	1	13	89	.250	1045	101	19	.984

Selected by Chicago White Sox' organization in 13th round of free-agent draft, January 11, 1983.
Selected by Chicago Cubs' organization in 1st round (fourth player selected) of free-agent draft, January 17, 1984.
†Batted righthanded only.
‡On disabled list, June 30 to July 15, 1988.
§On Chicago disabled list, March 9 to May 1 and August 19 to September 29, 1989; included rehabilitation disability assignment to Iowa, April 24 to May 1, 1989.
xOn Chicago disabled list, April 8 to August 15, 1990; included rehabilitation disability assignment to Peoria, July 16 to July 23, 1990; and Iowa, July 24 to August 4, 1990.

ALPHONSE DANTE BICHETTE

(Known by middle name.)
Name pronounced Bi-SHETT.
Born November 18, 1963, at West Palm Beach, Fla.
Height, 6.03. Weight, 225.
Throws and bats righthanded.
Attended Palm Beach Junior College, Lake Worth, Fla.

Major League stolen bases: 1989 (3), 1990 (5). Total—8.
Led Midwest League in game-winning RBIs with 13 in 1985.

Year Club	League	Pos.	G.	AB.	R.	H.	2B.	3B.	HR.	RBI.	B.A.	PO.	A.	E.	F.A.
1984—Salem	N'west	OF-1B-3B	64	250	27	58	9	2	4	30	.232	224	24	11	.958
1985—Quad Cities	Midw.	1B-OF-C	137	547	58	145	28	4	11	78	.265	300	21	15	.955
1986—Palm Springs	Calif.	OF-3B	68	290	39	79	15	0	10	73	.272	78	68	11	.930
1986—Midland	Texas	OF-3B	62	243	43	69	16	2	12	36	.284	131	30	11	.936
1987—Edmonton	P. C.	OF-3B	92	360	54	108	20	3	13	50	.300	169	21	9	.955
1988—Edmonton	P. C.	OF	132	509	64	136	29	●10	14	81	.267	218	★22	★15	.941
1988—California	Amer.	OF	21	46	1	12	2	0	0	8	.261	44	2	1	.979
1989—California	Amer.	OF	48	138	13	29	7	0	3	15	.210	95	6	1	.990
1989—Edmonton	P. C.	OF	61	226	39	55	11	2	11	40	.243	92	9	1	.990
1990—California	Amer.	OF	109	349	40	89	15	1	15	53	.255	183	12	7	.965
Major League Totals—3 Years			178	533	54	130	24	1	18	76	.244	322	20	9	.974

Selected by California Angels' organization in 16th round of free-agent draft, June 4, 1984.

MICHAEL JOSEPH BIELECKI

Name pronounced Bill-LECK-ee.

(Mike)

Born July 31, 1959, at Baltimore, Md.
Height, 6.03. Weight, 195.
Throws and bats righthanded.
Attended Loyola College, Baltimore, Md. and Valencia Community College, Orlando, Fla.

Major League saves: 1990 (1).
Tied for Eastern League lead in home runs allowed with 24 in 1982.
Tied for South Atlantic League lead in games started with 28 in 1981.

Year Club	League	G.	IP.	W.	L.	Pct.	H.	R.	ER.	SO.	BB.	ERA.
1979—Bradenton Pirates	Gulf Coast	9	51	1	4	.200	48	21	13	35	21	2.29
1980—Shelby	S. Atlantic	29	99	3	5	.375	106	60	50	78	58	4.55
1981—Greenwood	S. Atlantic	28	192	12	11	.522	172	95	73	163	82	3.42
1982—Buffalo	Eastern	25	157⅓	7	12	.368	165	96	●85	135	75	4.86
1983—Lynn	Eastern	25	163⅔	●15	7	.682	126	73	58	★143	69	3.19
1984—Hawaii	P. Coast	28	187⅓	★19	3	★.864	162	70	62	★162	88	2.97
1984—Pittsburgh	National	4	4⅓	0	0	.000	4	0	0	1	0	0.00
1985—Pittsburgh	National	12	45⅔	2	3	.400	45	26	23	22	31	4.53
1985—Hawaii	P. Coast	20	129⅓	8	6	.571	117	58	55	111	56	3.83
1986—Pittsburgh	National	31	148⅔	6	11	.353	149	87	77	83	83	4.66
1987—Vancouver	P. Coast	26	181	12	10	.545	194	89	76	140	78	3.78
1987—Pittsburgh†	National	8	45⅔	2	3	.400	43	25	24	25	12	4.73
1988—Chicago	National	19	48⅓	2	2	.500	55	22	18	33	16	3.35
1988—Iowa	Am. Assoc.	23	54⅔	3	2	.600	34	19	16	50	20	2.63
1989—Chicago	National	33	212⅓	18	7	.720	187	82	74	147	81	3.14
1990—Chicago	National	36	168	8	11	.421	188	101	92	103	70	4.93
Major League Totals—7 Years		143	673	38	37	.507	671	343	308	414	293	4.12

Selected by Kansas City Royals' organization in 6th round of free-agent draft, January 9, 1979.
Selected by Pittsburgh Pirates' organization in secondary phase of free-agent draft, June 5, 1979.
†Traded to Chicago Cubs for Pitcher Mike Curtis, March 31, 1988.

CHAMPIONSHIP SERIES RECORD

Year Club	League	G.	IP.	W.	L.	Pct.	H.	R.	ER.	SO.	BB.	ERA.
1989—Chicago	National	2	12⅓	0	1	.000	7	5	5	11	6	3.65

CRAIG ALAN BIGGIO
Name pronounced BIJ-ee-oh.

Born December 14, 1965, at Smithtown, N. Y.
Height, 5.11. Weight, 180.
Throws and bats righthanded.
Attended Seton Hall University, South Orange, N. J.

Major League stolen bases: 1988 (6), 1989 (21), 1990 (25). Total—52.
Named catcher on THE SPORTING NEWS National League Silver Slugger team, 1989.
Named catcher on THE SPORTING NEWS College Baseball All-America Team, 1987.

Year	Club	League	Pos.	G.	AB.	R.	H.	2B.	3B.	HR.	RBI.	B.A.	PO.	A.	E.	F.A.
1987—Asheville	S. Atl.	C-OF	64	216	59	81	17	2	9	49	.375	378	46	2	.995
1988—Tucson	P. C.	C-OF	77	281	60	90	21	4	3	41	.320	318	33	6	.983
1988—Houston	Nat.	C	50	123	14	26	6	1	3	5	.211	292	28	3	.991
1989—Houston	Nat.	C-OF	134	443	64	114	21	2	13	60	.257	742	56	9	.989
1990—Houston	Nat.	C-OF	150	555	53	153	24	2	4	42	.276	657	60	13	.982
Major League Totals—3 Years			334	1121	131	293	51	5	20	107	.261	1691	144	25	.987

Selected by Houston Astros' organization in 1st round (22nd player selected) of free-agent draft, June 2, 1987.

DANN JAMES BILARDELLO
Named pronounced Bill-ar-DELL-oh.

Born May 26, 1959, at Santa Cruz, Calif.
Height, 6.00. Weight, 190.
Throws and bats righthanded.
Attended Cabrillo College, Aptos, Calif.

Major League stolen bases: 1983 (2), 1986 (1), 1989 (1). Total—4.
Led Texas League catchers in double plays with 15 in 1982.
Led Pioneer League catchers in double plays with 5 in 1978.

Year	Club	League	Pos.	G.	AB.	R.	H.	2B.	3B.	HR.	RBI.	B.A.	PO.	A.	E.	F.A.
1978—Lethbridge	Pion.	C	42	133	21	33	8	1	2	20	.248	210	36	7	.972
1979—Clinton†	Midw.	C	52	142	18	34	4	0	2	15	.239	283	31	3	.991
1980—Lodi‡	Calif.	C	41	117	22	36	4	0	6	15	.308	169	30	8	.961
1981—Lodi	Calif.	C	105	352	72	108	19	2	21	80	.307	203	39	9	.964
1981—San Antonio	Texas	C	6	19	0	1	0	0	0	1	.053	34	2	1	.973
1982—San Antonio§	Texas	C	103	347	49	99	14	2	17	48	.285	546	★80	15	.977
1983—Cincinnati	Nat.	C	109	298	27	71	18	0	9	38	.238	494	72	5	.991
1984—Cincinnati	Nat.	C	68	182	16	38	7	0	2	10	.209	323	34	3	.992
1984—Wichita	A. A.	C	49	167	21	40	9	0	5	17	.240	290	31	3	.991
1985—Cincinnati	Nat.	C	42	102	6	17	0	0	1	9	.167	198	20	3	.986
1985—Denver x	A. A.	C-1B-3B	67	236	41	57	5	3	10	37	.242	365	50	6	.986
1986—Montreal	Nat.	C	79	191	12	37	5	0	4	17	.194	391	38	8	.982
1986—Indianapolis yz	A. A.	C	2	5	1	3	0	1	0	0	.600	6	0	0	1.000
1987—Vancouver a	P. C.	C	37	97	7	21	3	0	1	11	.216	186	30	4	.982
1987—Omaha	A. A.	C-3B	22	71	6	13	5	1	2	7	.183	96	13	1	.991
1988—Omaha b	A. A.	C	71	235	27	57	14	0	8	45	.243	395	31	5	.988
1989—Buffalo	A. A.	C-1B	66	180	11	37	8	0	3	17	.206	364	33	7	.983
1989—Pittsburgh c	Nat.	C	33	80	11	18	6	0	2	8	.225	150	14	5	.970
1990—Buffalo	A. A.	C-1B	52	154	19	44	8	1	5	26	.286	295	26	5	.985
1990—Pittsburgh d	Nat.	C	19	37	1	2	0	0	0	3	.054	69	9	0	1.000
Major League Totals—6 Years			350	890	73	183	36	0	18	85	.206	1625	187	24	.987

Selected by Seattle Mariners' organization in 3rd round of free-agent draft, January 10, 1978.
Selected by Los Angeles Dodgers' organization in secondary phase of free-agent draft, June 6, 1978.
†On disabled list, May 9 to June 14, 1979.
‡On disabled list, June 12 to August 13, 1980.
§Drafted by Cincinnati Reds, December 6, 1982.
xTraded with Pitchers Jay Tibbs, Andy McGaffigan and John Stuper to Montreal Expos for Pitcher Bill Gullickson and Catcher Sal Butera, December 19, 1985.
yReleased, December 20, 1986; re-signed by Expos' organization, March 22, 1987.
zSold to Pittsburgh Pirates, March 22, 1987.
aSold to Omaha (Kansas City Royals' organization), July 23, 1987.
bGranted free agency, October 15, 1988; signed by Buffalo (Pittsburgh Pirates' organization), January 25, 1989.
cReleased, November 21, 1989; re-signed by Pirates' organization, January 30, 1990.
dGranted free agency, December 20, 1990.

TIMOTHY DEAN BIRTSAS
(Tim)

Born September 5, 1960, at Clarkston, Mich.
Height, 6.07. Weight, 245.
Throws and bats lefthanded.
Received bachelor of science degree in recreation from Michigan State University, East Lansing, Mich.

Major League saves: 1989 (1).

Year	Club	League	G.	IP.	W.	L.	Pct.	H.	R.	ER.	SO.	BB.	ERA.
1982—Oneonta	NYP	6	16⅓	1	1	.500	19	13	7	24	17	3.86
1983—Fort Lauderdale	Florida St.	23	167⅔	12	8	.600	120	57	44	★160	88	2.36
1984—Fort Lauderdale†	Florida St.	11	57⅔	5	1	.833	51	23	23	62	37	3.59
1985—Tacoma	P. Coast	4	26⅔	2	2	.500	21	10	9	25	14	3.04
1985—Oakland	American	29	141⅓	10	6	.625	124	72	63	94	91	4.01

Year Club	League	G.	IP.	W.	L.	Pct.	H.	R.	ER.	SO.	BB.	ERA.
1986—Oakland	American	2	2	0	0	.000	2	5	5	1	4	22.50
1986—Tacoma‡	P. Coast	19	91⅓	3	7	.300	94	59	52	75	71	5.07
1987—Huntsville	Southern	17	114⅔	5	10	.333	109	54	46	75	53	3.61
1987—Tacoma§	P. Coast	10	66⅓	7	2	.778	46	26	23	50	54	3.12
1988—Nashville	Am. Assoc.	8	49⅔	1	3	.250	33	20	17	48	21	3.08
1988—Cincinnati	National	36	64⅓	1	3	.250	61	34	30	38	24	4.20
1989—Cincinnati	National	42	69⅔	2	2	.500	68	33	29	57	27	3.75
1990—Cincinnati	National	29	51⅓	1	3	.250	69	24	22	41	24	3.86
1990—Nashville x	Am. Assoc.	8	35	2	4	.333	33	21	17	34	16	4.37
American League Totals—2 Years		31	143⅓	10	6	.625	126	77	68	95	95	4.27
National League Totals—3 Years		107	185⅓	4	8	.333	198	91	81	136	75	3.93
Major League Totals—5 Years		138	328⅔	14	14	.500	324	168	149	231	170	4.08

Selected by New York Yankees' organization in 2nd round of free-agent draft, June 7, 1982.

†Traded with Outfielder Stan Javier and Pitchers Jay Howell, Eric Plunk and Jose Rijo to Oakland A's for Outfielder Rickey Henderson, Pitcher Bert Bradley and cash, December 5, 1984.

‡On disabled list, July 18 to August 26, 1986.

§Traded with Pitcher Jose Rijo to Cincinnati Reds for Outfielder Dave Parker, December 8, 1987.

xReleased, December 11, 1990.

JOSEPH ANTHONY BITKER
(Joe)

Born February 12, 1964, at Glendale, Calif.
Height, 6.01. Weight, 175.
Throws and bats righthanded.
Attended Sacramento City College, Sacramento, Calif.

Led Pacific Coast League in saves with 26 in 1990.
Tied for South Atlantic League lead in shutouts with 4 in 1985.

Year Club	League	G.	IP.	W.	L.	Pct.	H.	R.	ER.	SO.	BB.	ERA.
1984—Spokane	Northwest	14	87	4	4	.500	85	48	33	60	33	3.41
1985—Charleston	S. Atlantic	13	90⅓	9	3	.750	74	35	26	85	31	2.59
1985—Beaumont	Texas	15	98	8	1	.889	91	43	34	64	41	3.12
1986—Beaumont	Texas	18	114⅔	7	7	.500	114	55	45	91	52	3.53
1986—Las Vegas	P. Coast	5	27⅓	2	0	1.000	24	10	10	19	9	3.29
1987—Las Vegas	P. Coast	36	160⅓	11	9	.550	184	97	86	80	79	4.83
1988—Las Vegas	P. Coast	28	178⅓	8	10	.444	195	98	71	106	41	3.58
1989—Las Vegas†-Tacoma	P. Coast	42	73⅔	3	4	.429	67	38	30	48	20	3.67
1990—Tacoma	P. Coast	48	56⅓	2	3	.400	51	22	20	52	20	3.20
1990—Oakland‡-Texas	American	6	12	0	0	.000	8	3	3	8	4	2.25
Major League Totals—1 Year		6	12	0	0	.000	8	3	3	8	4	2.25

Selected by Detroit Tigers' organization in 3rd round of free-agent draft, January 11, 1983.

Selected by Minnesota Twins' organization in 6th round of free-agent draft, January 17, 1984.

Selected by San Diego Padres' organization in secondary phase of free-agent draft, June 4, 1984.

†Released, June 1, 1989; signed by Tacoma (Oakland Athletics' organization), June 22, 1989.

‡Traded with Pitcher Scott Chiamparino to Texas Rangers, September 4, 1990, completing deal in which Texas traded Outfielder/Designated Hitter Harold Baines to Oakland Athletics for two players to be named later, August 29, 1990.

HARRY RALSTON BLACK
(Bud)

Born June 30, 1957, at San Mateo, Calif.
Height, 6.02. Weight, 185.
Throws and bats lefthanded.
Attended Lower Columbia College, Longview, Wash. and received bachelor of arts degree
in finance from San Diego State University, San Diego, Calif. in 1979.
Son of Harry Black, Sr., former minor league hockey player.

Major League saves: 1986 (9), 1987 (1), 1988 (1). Total—11.
Led American League in balks with 7 in 1982.

Year Club	League	G.	IP.	W.	L.	Pct.	H.	R.	ER.	SO.	BB.	ERA.
1979—Bellingham	Northwest	2	5	0	0	.000	3	0	0	8	5	0.00
1979—San Jose	California	17	27	0	1	.000	17	11	9	24	16	3.00
1980—San Jose	California	32	86	5	3	.625	67	34	33	73	49	3.45
1981—Lynn	Eastern	22	87	2	6	.250	78	38	29	86	23	3.00
1981—Spokane	P. Coast	4	8	1	0	1.000	12	4	4	4	2	4.50
1981—Seattle†	American	2	1	0	0	.000	2	0	0	0	3	0.00
1982—Kansas City	American	22	88⅓	4	6	.400	92	48	45	40	34	4.58
1982—Omaha	Am. Assoc.	4	29	3	1	.750	23	9	8	20	10	2.48
1983—Omaha	Am. Assoc.	5	35	3	1	.750	31	13	13	32	13	3.34
1983—Kansas City	American	24	161⅓	10	7	.588	159	75	68	58	43	3.79
1984—Kansas City	American	35	257	17	12	.586	226	99	89	140	64	3.12
1985—Kansas City	American	33	205⅔	10	15	.400	216	111	99	122	59	4.33
1986—Kansas City	American	56	121	5	10	.333	100	49	43	68	43	3.20
1987—Kansas City‡	American	29	122⅓	8	6	.571	126	63	49	61	35	3.60
1988—Kansas City§-Cleveland x	American	33	81	4	4	.500	82	47	45	63	34	5.00
1988—Williamsport y	Eastern	1	5	1	0	1.000	0	0	0	5	0	0.00
1989—Cleveland	American	33	222⅓	12	11	.522	213	95	83	88	52	3.36
1990—Cleveland z-Toronto a	American	32	206⅔	13	11	.542	181	86	82	106	61	3.57
Major League Totals—10 Years		299	1466⅔	83	82	.503	1397	673	603	746	428	3.70

Selected by San Francisco Giants' organization in 3rd round of free-agent draft, January 11, 1977.
Selected by New York Mets' organization in secondary phase of free-agent draft, June 7, 1977.
Selected by Seattle Mariners' organization in 17th round of free-agent draft, June 5, 1979.
†Traded to Kansas City Royals, March 2, 1982, completing deal in which Kansas City traded Infielder Manny Castillo to Seattle Mariners for a player to be named later, October 23, 1981.
‡On disabled list, June 8 to July 4, 1987.
§Traded to Cleveland Indians for First Baseman Pat Tabler, June 3, 1988.
xOn disabled list, July 19 to August 21, 1988; included rehabilitation disability assignment to Williamsport, August 16 to August 21, 1988.
yGranted free agency, November 4, 1988; re-signed by Indians, December 5, 1988.
zTraded to Toronto Blue Jays for Pitcher Mauro Gozzo and two players to be named later, September 16, 1990; Cleveland Indians acquired Pitcher Steve Cummings on September 21, 1990 and Pitcher Alex Sanchez on September 24, 1990 to complete deal.
aGranted free agency, November 5, 1990; signed by San Francisco Giants, November 9, 1990.

CHAMPIONSHIP SERIES RECORD

Year Club	League	G.	IP.	W.	L.	Pct.	H.	R.	ER.	SO.	BB.	ERA.
1984—Kansas City	American	1	5	0	1	.000	7	4	4	3	1	7.20
1985—Kansas City	American	3	10⅔	0	0	.000	11	3	2	8	4	1.69
Championship Series Totals—2 Years		4	15⅔	0	1	.000	18	7	6	11	5	3.45

WORLD SERIES RECORD

Year Club	League	G.	IP.	W.	L.	Pct.	H.	R.	ER.	SO.	BB.	ERA.
1985—Kansas City	American	2	5⅓	0	1	.000	4	3	3	4	5	5.06

WILLIAM ALLEN BLAIR
(Willie)

Born December 18, 1965, at Paintsville, Ky.
Height, 6.01. Weight, 185.
Throws and bats righthanded.
Attended Morehead State University, Morehead, Ky.

Led New York-Pennsylvania League in saves with 12 in 1986.

Year Club	League	G.	IP.	W.	L.	Pct.	H.	R.	ER.	SO.	BB.	ERA.
1986—St. Catharines	NYP	21	53⅔	5	0	1.000	32	10	10	55	20	1.68
1987—Dunedin	Florida St.	50	85⅓	2	9	.182	99	51	42	72	29	4.43
1988—Dunedin	Florida St.	4	6⅔	2	0	1.000	5	2	2	5	4	2.70
1988—Knoxville	Southern	34	102	5	5	.500	94	49	41	76	35	3.62
1989—Syracuse	Int'national	19	106⅔	5	6	.455	94	55	47	76	38	3.97
1990—Toronto	American	27	68⅔	3	5	.375	66	33	31	43	28	4.06
1990—Syracuse†	Int'national	3	19	0	2	.000	20	13	10	6	8	4.74
Major League Totals—1 Year		27	68⅔	3	5	.375	66	33	31	43	28	4.06

Selected by Toronto Blue Jays' organization in 11th round of free-agent draft, June 2, 1986.
†Traded to Cleveland Indians for Pitcher Alex Sanchez, November 6, 1990.

KEVIN DeWAYNE BLANKENSHIP

Born January 26, 1963, at Anaheim, Calif.
Height, 6.00. Weight, 185.
Throws and bats righthanded.
Attended University of Arizona, Tucson, Ariz.

Year Club	League	G.	IP.	W.	L.	Pct.	H.	R.	ER.	SO.	BB.	ERA.
1984—Bradenton Braves	Gulf Coast	19	53⅔	3	1	.750	48	20	8	27	16	1.34
1985—Durham	Carolina	29	116⅔	8	8	.500	124	63	49	89	53	3.78
1986—Greenville	Southern	38	123	6	7	.462	132	78	67	83	84	4.90
1987—Greenville	Southern	40	102⅓	4	7	.364	96	51	47	78	53	4.13
1988—Greenville	Southern	28	177	13	9	.591	132	58	46	127	83	2.34
1988—Atlanta†-Chicago	National	3	15⅔	1	1	.500	14	8	8	9	8	4.60
1989—Iowa	Am. Assoc.	35	162	●13	7	.650	155	79	67	110	79	3.72
1989—Chicago	National	2	5⅓	0	0	.000	4	1	1	2	2	1.69
1990—Iowa	Am. Assoc.	27	163	10	9	.526	175	79	62	101	●78	3.42
1990—Chicago‡	National	3	12⅓	0	2	.000	13	10	8	5	6	5.84
Major League Totals—3 Years		8	33⅓	1	3	.250	31	19	17	16	16	4.59

Signed as free agent by Atlanta Braves' organization, June 19, 1984.
†Traded with Pitcher Kevin Coffman to Chicago Cubs for Catcher Jody Davis, September 29, 1988.
‡Granted free agency, October 15, 1990; signed by Buffalo (Pittsburgh Pirates' organization), November 20, 1990.

LANCE ROBERT BLANKENSHIP

Born December 6, 1963, at Portland, Ore.
Height, 6.00. Weight, 185.
Throws and bats righthanded.
Attended University of California, Berkeley, Calif.

Major League stolen bases: 1989 (5), 1990 (3). Total—8.
Led Pacific Coast League in bases on balls received with 96 in 1988.
Led Pacific Coast League second basemen in total chances with 682 in 1988.
Named third baseman on THE SPORTING NEWS College Baseball All-America Team, 1985.

Year	Club	League	Pos.	G.	AB.	R.	H.	2B.	3B.	HR.	RBI.	B.A.	PO.	A.	E.	F.A.
1986—Medford	N'west	OF	14	52	22	21	3	0	2	17	.404	22	1	1	.958
1986—Modesto	Calif.	OF-3B	55	171	47	50	5	3	6	25	.292	88	27	7	.943
1987—Modesto	Calif.	3-O-S-2	22	84	14	23	9	2	0	17	.274	26	30	8	.875
1987—Huntsville	South.	OF-2B-3B	107	390	64	99	21	3	4	39	.254	185	99	8	.973
1988—Tacoma	P. C.	2B-OF	131	437	84	116	21	8	9	52	.265	272	★390	21	.969
1988—Oakland	Amer.	2B	10	3	1	0	0	0	0	0	.000	1	1	0	1.000
1989—Tacoma	P. C.	2B	25	98	25	29	8	2	2	9	.296	39	81	2	.984
1989—Oakland	Amer.	OF-2B	58	125	22	29	5	1	1	4	.232	69	49	1	.992
1990—Oakland	Amer.	3-O-2-1	86	136	18	26	3	0	0	10	.191	66	69	5	.964
1990—Tacoma	P. C.	2B-OF-3B	24	93	18	24	7	1	1	9	.258	39	57	2	.980
Major League Totals—3 Years			154	264	41	55	8	1	1	14	.208	136	119	6	.977

Selected by Oakland Athletics' organization in 10th round of free-agent draft, June 2, 1986.

CHAMPIONSHIP SERIES RECORD

Year	Club	League	Pos.	G.	AB.	R.	H.	2B.	3B.	HR.	RBI.	B.A.	PO.	A.	E.	F.A.
1989—Oakland	Amer.	2B	1	0	0	0	0	0	0	0	.000	0	1	0	1.000
1990—Oakland	Amer.	PR	3	0	1	0	0	0	0	0	.000	0	0	0	.000
Championship Series Totals—2 Years			4	0	1	0	0	0	0	0	.000	0	1	0	1.000

WORLD SERIES RECORD

Year	Club	League	Pos.	G.	AB.	R.	H.	2B.	3B.	HR.	RBI.	B.A.	PO.	A.	E.	F.A.
1989—Oakland	Amer.	PH-2B	1	2	1	1	0	0	0	0	.500	1	0	0	1.000
1990—Oakland	Amer.	PH	1	1	0	0	0	0	0	0	.000	0	0	0	.000
World Series Totals—2 Years			2	3	1	1	0	0	0	0	.333	1	0	0	1.000

JEFFREY MICHAEL BLAUSER
(Jeff)

Born November 8, 1965, at Los Gatos, Calif.
Height, 6.00. Weight, 170.
Throws and bats righthanded.
Attended Sacramento City College, Sacramento, Calif.

Major League stolen bases: 1987 (7), 1989 (5), 1990 (3). Total—15.
Led Carolina League shortstops in total chances with 506 in 1986.

Year	Club	League	Pos.	G.	AB.	R.	H.	2B.	3B.	HR.	RBI.	B.A.	PO.	A.	E.	F.A.
1984—Pulaski	Appal.	SS	62	217	41	54	6	1	3	24	.249	61	162	24	.903
1985—Sumter	S. Atl.	SS	125	422	74	99	19	0	5	49	.235	150	306	35	.929
1986—Durham	Carol.	SS	123	447	94	128	27	3	13	52	.286	167	★314	25	★.951
1987—Richmond	Int.	SS-2B	33	113	11	20	1	0	1	12	.177	56	106	9	.947
1987—Atlanta	Nat.	SS	51	165	11	40	6	3	2	15	.242	65	166	9	.962
1987—Greenville	South.	SS	72	265	35	66	13	3	4	32	.249	101	225	8	.976
1988—Richmond	Int.	SS	69	271	40	77	19	1	5	23	.284	93	156	15	.943
1988—Atlanta	Nat.	2B-SS	18	67	7	16	3	1	2	7	.239	35	59	4	.959
1989—Atlanta	Nat.	3-2-S-O	142	456	63	123	24	2	12	46	.270	137	254	21	.949
1990—Atlanta†	Nat.	S-2-3-O	115	386	46	104	24	3	8	39	.269	169	288	16	.966
Major League Totals—4 Years			326	1074	127	283	57	9	24	107	.264	406	767	50	.959

Selected by St. Louis Cardinals' organization in 1st round (eighth player selected) of free-agent draft, January 17, 1984.
Selected by Atlanta Braves' organization in secondary phase of free-agent draft, June 4, 1984.
†On disabled list, May 14 to May 30, 1990.

MICHAEL ROY BLOWERS
(Mike)

Born April 24, 1965, at Wurzburg, West Germany.
Height, 6.02. Weight, 210.
Throws and bats righthanded.
Attended Tacoma Community College, Tacoma, Wash.,
and University of Washington, Seattle, Wash.

Shares American League record for most errors, game (4), May 3, 1990.
Major League stolen bases: 1990 (1).
Led Southern League third basemen in double plays with 27 in 1988.
Led Florida State League third basemen in double plays with 27 and fielding percentage with .944 in 1987.

Year	Club	League	Pos.	G.	AB.	R.	H.	2B.	3B.	HR.	RBI.	B.A.	PO.	A.	E.	F.A.
1986—Jamestown	NYP	SS-3B	32	95	13	24	9	2	1	6	.253	48	73	16	.883
1986—Bradenton Expos	Gulf C.	SS	31	115	14	25	3	1	2	17	.217	50	84	15	.899
1987—W. Palm Beach	Fla. St.	3B-SS-1B	136	491	68	124	30	3	16	71	.253	75	239	18	.946
1988—Jacksonville	South.	★3B-SS-2B	137	460	58	115	20	6	15	60	.250	★125	241	34	.915
1989—Indianapolis†	A. A.	★3B-SS	131	461	49	123	29	6	14	56	.267	91	214	23	★.930
1989—New York	Amer.	3B	13	38	2	10	0	0	0	3	.263	9	14	4	.852
1990—New York	Amer.	3B	48	144	16	27	4	0	5	21	.188	26	63	10	.899
1990—Columbus	Int.	3B-1B-2B	62	230	30	78	20	6	6	50	.339	64	89	8	.950
Major League Totals—2 Years			61	182	18	37	4	0	5	24	.203	35	77	14	.889

Selected by Seattle Mariners' organization in 8th round of free-agent draft, January 17, 1984.
Selected by San Francisco Giants' organization in secondary phase of free-agent draft, June 4, 1984.
Selected by Baltimore Orioles' organization in secondary phase of free-agent draft, January 9, 1985.

Selected by Montreal Expos' organization in 10th round of free-agent draft, June 2, 1986.
†Traded to New York Yankees, August 31, 1989, completing deal in which New York traded Pitcher John Candelaria to Montreal Expos for a player to be named later, August 29, 1989.

RIK AALBERT BLYLEVEN
(Bert)

Born April 6, 1951, at Zeist, The Netherlands.
Height, 6.03. Weight, 220.
Throws and bats righthanded.

Holds major league record for most home runs allowed, season (50), 1986.
Shares major league record for most putouts by pitcher, nine-inning game (6), June 24, 1984.
Shares American League record for longest one-hit complete game (10 innings), June 21, 1976.
Pitched 6-0 no-hit victory against California Angels, September 22, 1977.
Led American League in home runs allowed with 50 in 1986 and 46 in 1987.
Led American League pitchers in complete games with 24 and tied for lead in games started with 37 in 1985.
Led American League in hit batsmen with 12 in 1976 and 16 in 1988.
Led American League in shutouts with 9 in 1973 and 5 in both 1985 and 1989.
Tied for American League lead in balks with 3 in 1970.
Named American League Comeback Player of the Year by THE SPORTING NEWS, 1989.
Named American League Rookie Pitcher of the Year by THE SPORTING NEWS, 1970.

Year	Club	League	G.	IP.	W.	L.	Pct.	H.	R.	ER.	SO.	BB.	ERA.
1969—Sarasota Twins	Gulf Coast	7	32	2	2	.500	31	13	10	39	11	2.81
1969—Orlando	Florida St.	6	37	5	0	1.000	36	6	6	41	14	1.46
1970—Evansville	Am. Assoc.	8	54	4	2	.667	48	18	15	63	12	2.50
1970—Minnesota	American	27	164	10	9	.526	143	66	58	135	47	3.18
1971—Minnesota	American	38	278	16	15	.516	267	95	87	224	59	2.82
1972—Minnesota	American	39	287	17	17	.500	247	93	87	228	69	2.73
1973—Minnesota	American	40	325	20	17	.541	296	109	91	258	67	2.52
1974—Minnesota	American	37	281	17	17	.500	244	99	83	249	77	2.66
1975—Minnesota	American	35	276	15	10	.600	219	104	92	233	84	3.00
1976—Minnesota†-Texas	American	36	298	13	16	.448	283	106	95	219	81	2.87
1977—Texas‡	American	30	235	14	12	.538	181	81	71	182	69	2.72
1978—Pittsburgh	National	34	244	14	10	.583	217	94	82	182	66	3.02
1979—Pittsburgh	National	37	237	12	5	.706	238	102	95	172	92	3.61
1980—Pittsburgh§	National	34	217	8	13	.381	219	102	92	168	59	3.82
1981—Cleveland	American	20	159	11	7	.611	145	52	51	107	40	2.89
1982—Cleveland x	American	4	20⅓	2	2	.500	16	14	11	19	11	4.87
1983—Cleveland y	American	24	156⅓	7	10	.412	160	74	68	123	44	3.91
1984—Cleveland y	American	33	245	19	7	.731	204	86	78	170	74	2.87
1985—Cleveland z-Minnesota	American	37	★293⅔	17	16	.515	264	121	103	★206	75	3.16
1986—Minnesota	American	36	★271⅔	17	14	.548	262	134	121	215	58	4.01
1987—Minnesota	American	37	267	15	12	.556	249	132	119	196	101	4.01
1988—Minnesota ab	American	33	207⅓	10	★17	.370	240	128	★125	145	51	5.43
1989—California	American	33	241	17	5	.773	225	76	73	131	44	2.73
1990—California c	American	23	134	8	7	.533	163	85	78	69	25	5.24
National League Totals—3 Years		105	698	34	28	.548	674	298	269	522	217	3.47
American League Totals—18 Years		562	4139⅓	245	210	.538	3808	1655	1491	3109	1076	3.24
Major League Totals—21 Years		667	4837⅓	279	238	.540	4482	1953	1760	3631	1293	3.27

Selected by Minnesota Twins' organization in 3rd round of free-agent draft, June 5, 1969.
†Traded with Shortstop Danny Thompson to Texas Rangers for Pitcher Bill Singer, Infielders Roy Smalley and Mike Cubbage, Pitcher Jim Gideon and a reported $250,000 cash, June 1, 1976.
‡Traded with First Baseman-Outfielder John Milner to Pittsburgh Pirates for Outfielder-First Baseman Al Oliver and Infielder Nelson Norman, December 8, 1977.
§Traded with Catcher Manny Sanguillen to Cleveland Indians for Pitchers Bob Owchinko, Rafael Vasquez and Victor Cruz and Catcher Gary Alexander, December 9, 1980.
xOn disabled list, May 2, 1982 through remainder of season.
yOn disabled list, May 23 to June 10, 1984.
zTraded to Minnesota Twins for Pitcher Curt Wardle, Outfielder Jim Weaver, Infielder Jay Bell and a player to be named later, August 1, 1985; Cleveland Indians' organization acquired Pitcher Rich Yett to complete deal, September 17, 1985.
aOn disabled list, July 30 to August 15, 1988.
bTraded with Pitcher Kevin Trudeau to California Angels for Pitchers Mike Cook and Rob Wassenaar and First Baseman Paul Sorrento, November 3, 1988.
cOn disabled list, August 11, 1990 through remainder of season.

CHAMPIONSHIP SERIES RECORD

Year	Club	League	G.	IP.	W.	L.	Pct.	H.	R.	ER.	SO.	BB.	ERA.
1970—Minnesota	American	1	2	0	0	.000	2	1	0	2	0	0.00
1979—Pittsburgh	National	1	9	1	0	1.000	8	1	1	9	0	1.00
1987—Minnesota	American	2	13⅓	2	0	1.000	12	6	6	9	3	4.05
Championship Series Totals—3 Years		4	24⅓	3	0	1.000	22	8	7	20	3	2.59

WORLD SERIES RECORD

Year	Club	League	G.	IP.	W.	L.	Pct.	H.	R.	ER.	SO.	BB.	ERA.
1979—Pittsburgh	National	2	10	1	0	1.000	8	2	2	4	3	1.80
1987—Minnesota	American	2	13	1	1	.500	13	5	4	12	2	2.77
World Series Totals—2 Years		4	23	2	1	.667	21	7	6	16	5	2.35

Year	League	IP.	W.	L.	Pct.	H.	R.	ER.	SO.	BB.	ERA.
1973—American		1	0	1	.000	2	2	2	0	2	18.00
1985—American		2	0	0	.000	3	2	2	1	1	9.00
All-Star Game Totals—2 Years		3	0	1	.000	5	4	4	1	3	12.00

MICHAEL JAMES BODDICKER

Name pronounced BOD-dick-er

(Mike)

Born August 23, 1957, at Cedar Rapids, Iowa.
Height, 5.11. Weight, 186.
Throws and bats righthanded.
Attended University of Iowa, Iowa City, Iowa.

Shares modern major league record for most putouts by pitcher, season (49), 1984.
Led American League in shutouts with 5 in 1983.
Named American League Rookie Pitcher of the Year by THE SPORTING NEWS, 1983.
Named righthanded pitcher on THE SPORTING NEWS American League All-Star Team, 1984.
Named pitcher on THE SPORTING NEWS American League All-Star fielding team, 1990.

Year	Club	League	G.	IP.	W.	L.	Pct.	H.	R.	ER.	SO.	BB.	ERA.
1978—Bluefield	Ap'lachian	8	19	2	1	.667	9	2	1	28	10	0.47
1978—Charlotte	Southern	10	65	4	3	.571	42	15	14	48	17	1.94
1978—Rochester	Int'national	1	5	1	0	1.000	4	1	1	3	2	1.80
1979—Charlotte	Southern	14	102	9	3	.750	82	40	34	89	36	3.00
1979—Rochester	Int'national	15	72	4	6	.400	88	48	48	48	27	6.00
1980—Rochester	Int'national	25	190	12	9	.571	149	57	46	109	35	2.18
1980—Baltimore	American	1	7	0	1	.000	6	6	5	4	5	6.43
1981—Rochester	Int'national	30	182	10	10	.500	182	91	85	109	66	4.20
1981—Baltimore	American	2	6	0	0	.000	6	4	3	2	2	4.50
1982—Rochester	Int'national	20	133⅓	10	5	.667	121	59	53	82	36	3.58
1982—Baltimore	American	7	25⅔	1	0	1.000	25	10	10	20	12	3.51
1983—Rochester	Int'national	4	23⅔	3	1	.750	17	6	5	18	13	1.90
1983—Baltimore†	American	27	179	16	8	.667	141	65	55	120	52	2.77
1984—Baltimore†	American	34	261⅓	★20	11	.645	218	95	81	128	81	★2.79
1985—Baltimore‡	American	32	203⅓	12	17	.414	227	104	92	135	89	4.07
1986—Baltimore§	American	33	218⅓	14	12	.538	214	125	114	175	74	4.70
1987—Baltimore	American	33	226	10	12	.455	212	114	105	152	78	4.18
1988—Baltimore x-Boston	American	36	236	13	15	.464	234	102	89	156	77	3.39
1989—Boston	American	34	211⅔	15	11	.577	217	101	94	145	71	4.00
1990—Boston y	American	34	228	17	8	.680	225	92	85	143	69	3.36
Major League Totals—11 Years		273	1802⅓	118	95	.554	1725	818	733	1180	610	3.66

Selected by Montreal Expos' organization in 8th round of free-agent draft, June 4, 1975.
Selected by Baltimore Orioles' organization in 6th round of free-agent draft, June 6, 1978.
†Appeared in one game as a pinch-runner.
‡Appeared in two games as a pinch-runner.
§On disabled list, April 20 to May 10, 1986.
xTraded to Boston Red Sox for Outfielder Brady Anderson and Pitcher Curt Schilling, July 29, 1988.
yGranted free agency, November 5, 1990; signed by Kansas City Royals, November 21, 1990.

CHAMPIONSHIP SERIES RECORD

Shares Championship Series record for most strikeouts, game (14), October 6, 1983.

Year	Club	League	G.	IP.	W.	L.	Pct.	H.	R.	ER.	SO.	BB.	ERA.
1983—Baltimore	American	1	9	1	0	1.000	5	0	0	14	3	0.00
1988—Boston	American	1	2⅔	0	1	.000	8	6	6	2	1	20.25
1990—Boston	American	1	8	0	1	.000	6	4	2	7	3	2.25
Championship Series Totals—3 Years		3	19⅔	1	2	.333	19	10	8	23	7	3.66

WORLD SERIES RECORD

Year	Club	League	G.	IP.	W.	L.	Pct.	H.	R.	ER.	SO.	BB.	ERA.
1983—Baltimore	American	1	9	1	0	1.000	3	1	0	6	0	0.00

ALL-STAR GAME RECORD

Member of American League All-Star Team in 1984; did not play.

JOSEPH MARTIN BOEVER

Name pronounced BAY-vur.

(Joe)

Born October 4, 1960, at St. Louis, Mo.
Height, 6.01. Weight, 200.
Throws and bats righthanded.
Attended Crowder College, Neosho, Mo., St. Louis Community College at
Meramec, St. Louis, Mo., and University of Nevada, Las Vegas, Nev.

Major League saves: 1988 (1), 1989 (21), 1990 (14). Total—36.
Led International League in saves with 22 in 1988.
Led American Association in saves with 21 in 1987.

Led Florida State League in games finished in relief with 38 and tied for lead in saves with 14 in 1984.
Led Florida State League in games finished in relief with 46, saves with 26 and intentional bases on balls issued with 12 in 1983.
Tied for New York-Pennsylvania League lead in intentional bases on balls issued with 5 in 1982.

Year Club	League	G.	IP.	W.	L.	Pct.	H.	R.	ER.	SO.	BB.	ERA.
1982—Erie	NYP	19	32⅔	2	3	.400	20	8	7	63	12	1.93
1982—Springfield	Midwest	3	4	0	0	.000	3	1	1	7	2	2.25
1983—St. Petersburg	Florida St.	53	80⅓	5	6	.455	61	29	27	57	37	3.02
1984—Arkansas	Texas	8	11	0	1	.000	10	11	10	12	12	8.18
1984—St. Petersburg	Florida St.	48	77⅔	6	4	.600	52	31	26	81	45	3.01
1985—Arkansas	Texas	27	37⅔	3	1	.750	21	5	5	45	23	1.19
1985—Louisville	Am. Assoc.	21	35⅓	3	2	.600	28	11	8	37	22	2.04
1985—St. Louis	National	13	16½	0	0	.000	17	8	8	20	4	4.41
1986—St. Louis	National	11	21⅔	0	1	.000	19	5	4	8	11	1.66
1986—Louisville	Am. Assoc.	51	88	4	5	.444	71	25	22	75	48	2.25
1987—Louisville†	Am. Assoc.	43	59	3	2	.600	52	22	22	79	27	3.36
1987—Atlanta	National	14	18⅓	1	0	1.000	29	15	15	18	12	7.36
1987—Richmond	Int'national	6	9	1	0	1.000	8	1	1	8	4	1.00
1988—Richmond	Int'national	48	71⅓	6	3	.667	47	17	17	71	22	2.14
1988—Atlanta	National	16	20⅓	0	2	.000	12	4	4	7	1	1.77
1989—Atlanta	National	66	82⅓	4	11	.267	78	37	36	68	34	3.94
1990—Atlanta‡-Philadelphia	National	67	88⅓	3	6	.333	77	35	33	75	51	3.36
Major League Totals—6 Years		187	247⅓	8	20	.286	232	104	100	196	113	3.64

Signed as free agent by St. Louis Cardinals' organization, June 25, 1982.
†Traded to Atlanta Braves for Pitcher Randy O'Neal, July 25, 1987.
‡Traded to Philadelphia Phillies for Pitcher Marvin Freeman, July 23, 1990.

WADE ANTHONY BOGGS

Born June 15, 1958, at Omaha, Neb.
Height, 6.02. Weight, 197.
Throws right and bats lefthanded.
Attended Hillsborough Community College, Tampa, Fla.

Shares major league records for most games, one or more hits, season (135), 1985; most years leading league in intentional bases on balls (4).
Holds American League records for highest batting average, rookie season, 100 or more games (.349), 1982; most consecutive years with 200 or more hits (7); most singles, season (187), 1985.
Shares American League records for most seasons and most consecutive seasons leading league, intentional bases on balls (3); fewest double plays, third baseman, season, 150 or more games (17), 1988.
Major League stolen bases: 1982 (1), 1983 (3), 1984 (3), 1985 (2), 1987 (1), 1988 (2), 1989 (2). Total—14.
Led American League in intentional bases on balls received with 19 in 1987, 1989 and 1990 and tied for lead with 18 in 1988.
Led American League in bases on balls received with 105 in 1986 and 125 in 1988.
Led American League in grounding into double plays with 23 in 1988.
Led American league third basemen in total chances with 486 in 1985.
Led American League third basemen in double plays with 30 in 1984, 37 in 1987 and 29 in 1989.
Named third baseman on THE SPORTING NEWS American League All-Star Team, 1983 and 1985 through 1988.
Named third baseman on THE SPORTING NEWS American League Silver Slugger team, 1983 and 1986 through 1989.

Year Club	League	Pos.	G.	AB.	R.	H.	2B.	3B.	HR.	RBI.	B.A.	PO.	A.	E.	F.A.
1976—Elmira	NYP	3B	57	179	29	47	6	0	0		.263	36	75	16	.874
1977—Winston-Salem	Carol.	3B-2B-SS	117	422	67	140	13	1	2	55	.332	145	223	27	.932
1978—Bristol	East.	3-S-2-O	109	354	63	110	14	2	1	32	.311	62	107	7	.960
1979—Bristol†	East.	*3-S-2	113	406	56	132	17	2	0	41	.325	94	213	15	*.953
1980—Pawtucket	Int.	3B-1B	129	418	51	128	21	0	1	45	.306	108	156	12	.957
1981—Pawtucket	Int.	3B-1B	137	498	67	*167	*41	3	5	60	*.335	359	238	26	.958
1982—Boston	Amer.	1B-3B-OF	104	338	51	118	14	1	5	44	.349	489	168	8	.988
1983—Boston	Amer.	3B	153	582	100	210	44	7	5	74	*.361	118	368	*27	.947
1984—Boston	Amer.	3B	158	625	109	203	31	4	6	55	.325	141	330	•20	.959
1985—Boston	Amer.	3B	161	653	107	*240	42	3	8	78	*.368	134	335	17	.965
1986—Boston	Amer.	3B	149	580	107	207	47	2	8	71	*.357	*121	267	19	.953
1987—Boston	Amer.	3B-1B	147	551	108	200	40	6	24	89	*.363	112	277	14	.965
1988—Boston	Amer.	3B	155	584	*128	214	*45	6	5	58	*.366	*122	250	11	.971
1989—Boston	Amer.	3B	156	621	•113	205	*51	7	3	54	.330	*123	264	17	.958
1990—Boston	Amer.	3B	155	619	89	187	44	5	6	63	.302	108	241	20	.946
Major League Totals—9 Years			1338	5153	912	1784	358	41	70	586	.346	1468	2500	153	.963

Selected by Boston Red Sox' organization in 7th round of free-agent draft, June 8, 1976.
†On disabled list, April 20 to May 2, 1979.

CHAMPIONSHIP SERIES RECORD

Shares Championship Series record for most sacrifice flies, series (2), 1988.

Year Club	League	Pos.	G.	AB.	R.	H.	2B.	3B.	HR.	RBI.	B.A.	PO.	A.	E.	F.A.
1986—Boston	Amer.	3B	7	30	3	7	1	1	0	2	.233	7	13	2	.909
1988—Boston	Amer.	3B	4	13	2	5	0	0	0	3	.385	6	6	0	1.000
1990—Boston	Amer.	3B	4	16	1	7	1	0	1	1	.438	6	10	0	1.000
Championship Series Totals—3 Years			15	59	6	19	2	1	1	6	.322	19	29	2	.960

WORLD SERIES RECORD

Year Club	League	Pos.	G.	AB.	R.	H.	2B.	3B.	HR.	RBI.	B.A.	PO.	A.	E.	F.A.
1986—Boston	Amer.	3B	7	31	3	9	3	0	0	3	.290	4	15	0	1.000

Year	League	Pos.	AB.	R.	H.	2B.	3B.	HR.	RBI.	B.A.	PO.	A.	E.	F.A.
1985—American		3B	0	0	0	0	0	0	0	.000	0	0	0	.000
1986—American		3B	3	0	1	0	0	0	0	.333	0	1	0	1.000
1987—American		3B	3	0	0	0	0	0	0	.000	0	3	0	1.000
1988—American		3B	3	0	1	0	0	0	0	.333	0	1	0	1.000
1989—American		3B	3	1	1	0	0	1	1	.333	1	1	0	1.000
1990—American		3B	2	0	2	0	0	0	0	1.000	0	4	0	1.000
All-Star Game Totals—6 Years			14	1	5	0	0	1	1	.357	1	10	0	1.000

BRIAN EDWARD BOHANON

Born August 1, 1968, at Denton, Tex.
Height, 6.02. Weight, 215.
Throws and bats lefthanded.

Year	Club	League	G.	IP.	W.	L.	Pct.	H.	R.	ER.	SO.	BB.	ERA.
1987—Sarasota Rangers	Gulf Coast	5	21	0	2	.000	15	13	11	21	5	4.71
1988—Port Charlotte†	Florida St.	2	6⅔	0	1	.000	6	4	4	9	5	5.40
1989—Charlotte‡	Florida St.	11	54⅔	0	3	.000	40	16	11	33	20	1.81
1989—Tulsa	Texas	11	73⅔	5	0	1.000	59	20	18	44	27	2.20
1990—Texas	American	11	34	0	3	.000	40	30	25	15	18	6.62
1990—Oklahoma City	Am. Assoc.	14	32	1	2	.333	35	16	13	22	8	3.66
Major League Totals—1 Year		11	34	0	3	.000	40	30	25	15	18	6.62

Selected by Texas Rangers' organization in 1st round (19th player selected) of free-agent draft, June 2, 1987.
†On disabled list, April 17, 1988 through remainder of season.
‡On disabled list, April 7 to May 2, 1989.

THOMAS EDWARD BOLTON
(Tom)

Born May 6, 1962, at Nashville, Tenn.
Height, 6.03. Weight, 175.
Throws and bats lefthanded.

Major League saves: 1988 (1).

Year	Club	League	G.	IP.	W.	L.	Pct.	H.	R.	ER.	SO.	BB.	ERA.
1980—Elmira	NYP	23	56	6	2	.750	43	26	15	43	22	2.41
1981—Winter Haven	Florida St.	24	92	2	9	.182	125	62	46	41	41	4.50
1982—Winter Haven	Florida St.	28	162⅔	9	8	.529	161	67	54	77	63	2.99
1983—New Britain†	Eastern	16	99⅔	7	3	.700	93	36	32	62	41	2.89
1983—Pawtucket	Int'national	6	29	0	5	.000	33	26	21	20	25	6.52
1984—New Britain	Eastern	33	87	4	5	.444	87	54	40	66	34	4.14
1985—New Britain	Eastern	34	101	5	6	.455	106	53	48	74	40	4.28
1986—Pawtucket‡	Int'national	29	86	3	4	.429	80	30	26	58	25	2.72
1987—Pawtucket	Int'national	5	21⅔	2	1	.667	25	14	13	8	12	5.40
1987—Boston	American	29	61⅔	1	0	1.000	83	33	30	49	27	4.38
1988—Pawtucket	Int'national	18	19⅓	3	0	1.000	17	7	6	15	10	2.79
1988—Boston	American	28	30⅓	1	3	.250	35	17	16	21	14	4.75
1989—Pawtucket	Int'national	25	143⅓	12	5	.706	140	57	46	99	47	2.89
1989—Boston	American	4	17⅓	0	4	.000	21	18	16	9	10	8.31
1990—Pawtucket	Int'national	4	11⅔	1	0	1.000	9	6	5	8	7	3.86
1990—Boston	American	21	119⅔	10	5	.667	111	46	45	65	47	3.38
Major League Totals—4 Years		82	229	12	12	.500	250	114	107	144	98	4.21

Selected by Boston Red Sox organization in 20th round of free-agent draft, June 3, 1980.
†On disabled list, June 27 to July 9, 1983.
‡On disabled list, April 11 to May 26, 1986.

CHAMPIONSHIP SERIES RECORD

Year	Club	League	G.	IP.	W.	L.	Pct.	H.	R.	ER.	SO.	BB.	ERA.
1990—Boston	American	2	3	0	0	.000	2	0	0	3	2	0.00

BARRY LAMAR BONDS

Born July 24, 1964, at Riverside, Calif.
Height, 6.01. Weight, 185.
Throws and bats lefthanded.
Attended Arizona State University, Tempe, Ariz.
Son of Bobby Bonds, outfielder with San Francisco, New York Yankees, California,
Chicago White Sox, Texas, Cleveland, St. Louis and Chicago Cubs,
1968 through 1981; and coach with Cleveland Indians, 1984 through 1987.

Shares major league record for fewest assists by outfielder for leader, season (14), 1990.
Major League stolen bases: 1986 (36), 1987 (32), 1988 (17), 1989 (32), 1990 (52). Total—169.
Led National League in slugging percentage with .565 in 1990.
Named Major League Player of the Year by THE SPORTING NEWS, 1990.
Named National League Player of the Year by THE SPORTING NEWS, 1990.
Named National League Most Valuable Player by Baseball Writers' Association of America, 1990.
Named outfielder on THE SPORTING NEWS National League All-Star Team, 1990.
Named outfielder on THE SPORTING NEWS National League All-Star fielding team, 1990.
Named outfielder on THE SPORTING NEWS National League Silver Slugger team, 1990.
Named outfielder on THE SPORTING NEWS College Baseball All-America Team, 1985.

Year Club	League	Pos.	G.	AB.	R.	H.	2B.	3B.	HR.	RBI.	B.A.	PO.	A.	E.	F.A.
1985—Prince William	Carol.	OF	71	254	49	76	16	4	13	37	.299	202	4	5	.976
1986—Hawaii..................	P. C.	OF	44	148	30	46	7	2	7	37	.311	109	4	2	.983
1986—Pittsburgh.............	Nat.	OF	113	413	72	92	26	3	16	48	.223	280	9	5	.983
1987—Pittsburgh.............	Nat.	OF	150	551	99	144	34	9	25	59	.261	330	15	5	.986
1988—Pittsburgh.............	Nat.	OF	144	538	97	152	30	5	24	58	.283	292	5	6	.980
1989—Pittsburgh.............	Nat.	OF	159	580	96	144	34	6	19	58	.248	365	14	6	.984
1990—Pittsburgh.............	Nat.	OF	151	519	104	156	32	3	33	114	.301	338	●14	6	.983
Major League Totals—5 Years................			717	2601	468	688	156	26	117	337	.265	1605	57	28	.983

Selected by San Francisco Giants' organization in 2nd round of free-agent draft, June 7, 1982.
Selected by Pittsburgh Pirates' organization in 1st round (sixth player selected) of free-agent draft, June 3, 1985.

CHAMPIONSHIP SERIES RECORD

Year Club	League	Pos.	G.	AB.	R.	H.	2B.	3B.	HR.	RBI.	B.A.	PO.	A.	E.	F.A.
1990—Pittsburgh.............	Nat.	OF	6	18	4	3	0	0	0	1	.167	13	0	0	1.000

ALL-STAR GAME RECORD

Year League	Pos.	AB.	R.	H.	2B.	3B.	HR.	RBI.	B.A.	PO.	A.	E.	F.A.
1990—National.........................	OF	1	0	0	0	0	0	0	.000	2	0	0	1.000

RICARDO BONES

Name pronounced Bo-NAY.

(Ricky)

Born April 7, 1969, at Salinas, Puerto Rico.
Height, 5.10. Weight, 175.
Throws and bats righthanded.

Led Texas League in home runs allowed with 22 in 1989.

Year Club	League	G.	IP.	W.	L.	Pct.	H.	R.	ER.	SO.	BB.	ERA.
1986—Spokane	Northwest	18	58	1	3	.250	63	44	36	46	29	5.59
1987—Charleston, S.C.	S. Atlantic	26	170⅓	12	5	.706	★183	81	69	130	45	3.65
1988—Riverside	California	25	175⅓	15	6	.714	162	80	71	129	64	3.64
1989—Wichita	Texas	24	136⅓	10	9	.526	162	103	87	88	47	5.74
1990—Wichita	Texas	21	137	6	4	.600	138	66	53	96	45	3.48
1990—Las Vegas.......................	P. Coast	5	36⅓	2	1	.667	45	17	14	25	10	3.47

Signed as free agent by San Diego Padres' organization, May 13, 1986.

ROBERTO MARTIN ANTONIO BONILLA

Name pronounced Boh-NEE-yah.

(Bobby)

Born February 23, 1963, at New York, N.Y.
Height, 6.03. Weight, 230.
Throws right and bats left and righthanded.
Attended New York Technical College, Westbury, N.Y.

Major League stolen bases: 1986 (8), 1987 (3), 1988 (3), 1989 (8), 1990 (4). Total—26.
Switch-hit home runs in one game, July 3, 1987 and April 6, 1988.
Led National League in sacrifice flies with 15 in 1990.
Led National League third basemen in double plays with 31 in 1989.
Led National League third basemen in total chances with 489 in 1989.
Named outfielder on THE SPORTING NEWS National League All-Star Team, 1990.
Named third baseman on THE SPORTING NEWS National League All-Star Team, 1988.
Named outfielder on THE SPORTING NEWS National League Silver Slugger team, 1990.
Named third baseman on THE SPORTING NEWS National League Silver Slugger team, 1988.

Year Club	League	Pos.	G.	AB.	R.	H.	2B.	3B.	HR.	RBI.	B.A.	PO.	A.	E.	F.A.
1981—Bradenton Pir.	Gulf C.	1B-C-3B	22	69	6	15	5	0	0	7	.217	124	23	5	.967
1982—Bradenton Pir.	Gulf C.	1B	47	167	20	38	3	0	5	26	.228	318	36	★14	.962
1983—Alexandria	Carol.	OF-1B	●136	504	88	129	19	7	11	59	.256	259	12	15	.948
1984—Nashua	East.	★OF-1B	136	484	74	128	19	5	11	71	.264	312	8	★15	.955
1985—Prince William†‡	Carol.	1B-3B	39	130	15	34	4	1	3	11	.262	180	9	2	.990
1986—Chicago§	Amer.	OF-1B	75	234	27	63	10	2	2	26	.269	361	22	2	.995
1986—Pittsburgh	Nat.	OF-1B-3B	63	192	28	46	6	2	1	17	.240	90	16	3	.972
1987—Pittsburgh.............	Nat.	3B-OF-1B	141	466	58	140	33	3	15	77	.300	142	139	16	.946
1988—Pittsburgh.............	Nat.	3B	159	584	87	160	32	7	24	100	.274	121	★336	★32	.935
1989—Pittsburgh.............	Nat.	★3-1-0	●163	616	96	173	37	10	24	86	.281	190	334	★35	.937
1990—Pittsburgh.............	Nat.	OF-3B-1B	160	625	112	175	39	7	32	120	.280	315	35	15	.959
American League Totals—1 Year			75	234	27	63	10	2	2	26	.269	361	22	2	.995
National League Totals—5 Years...........			686	2483	381	694	147	29	96	400	.280	858	860	101	.944
Major League Totals—5 Years................			761	2717	408	757	157	31	98	426	.279	1219	882	103	.953

Signed as free agent by Pittsburgh Pirates' organization, July 11, 1981.
†On Pittsburgh disabled list, March 25 to July 19, 1985.
‡Drafted by Chicago White Sox, December 10, 1985.
§Traded to Pittsburgh Pirates for Pitcher Jose DeLeon, July 23, 1986.

CHAMPIONSHIP SERIES RECORD

Year Club	League	Pos.	G.	AB.	R.	H.	2B.	3B.	HR.	RBI.	B.A.	PO.	A.	E.	F.A.
1990—Pittsburgh.............	Nat.	OF-3B	6	21	0	4	1	0	0	1	.190	4	5	1	.900

Year League	Pos.	AB.	R.	H.	2B.	3B.	HR.	RBI.	B.A.	PO.	A.	E.	F.A.
1988—National	3B	4	0	0	0	0	0	0	.000	0	2	0	1.000
1989—National	DH	2	0	2	0	0	0	0	1.000	0	0	0	.000
1990—National	1B	1	0	0	0	0	0	0	.000	1	0	0	1.000
All-Star Game Totals—3 Years		7	0	2	0	0	0	0	.286	1	2	0	1.000

GREGORY SCOTT BOOKER
(Greg)

Born June 22, 1960, at Lynchburg, Va.
Height, 6.06. Weight, 245.
Throws and bats righthanded.
Attended Elon College, Elon College, N.C.
Son-in-law of Jack McKeon, minor league catcher, 1949 through 1959; scout with Minnesota Twins, 1965 through 1967;
manager with Kansas City Royals, Oakland A's and San Diego Padres, 1973 through 1975, 1977, 1978
and 1988 through 1990; coach with Oakland A's, 1978; scout and Assistant to General
Manager with San Diego Padres, 1980; and Vice-President of Baseball Operations
with San Diego Padres, 1981 through 1988; and related to Richard (Buddy)
Booker, catcher with Cleveland Indians and Chicago
White Sox, 1966 and 1968.

Major League saves: 1987 (1).
Led California League in wild pitches with 20 in 1982.

Year Club	League	G.	IP.	W.	L.	Pct.	H.	R.	ER.	SO.	BB.	ERA.
1981—Walla Walla	Northwest	11	53	2	3	.400	55	41	31	25	35	5.26
1982—Reno	California	27	161⅔	8	*13	.381	160	*133	*114	81	*157	6.35
1983—Las Vegas	P. Coast	46	102⅓	5	6	.455	120	77	63	58	68	5.54
1983—San Diego	National	6	11⅔	0	1	.000	18	10	10	5	9	7.71
1984—Las Vegas	P. Coast	9	55⅔	4	3	.571	66	39	34	23	24	5.50
1984—San Diego	National	32	57⅓	1	1	.500	67	27	21	28	27	3.30
1985—San Diego	National	17	22⅓	0	1	.000	20	17	17	7	17	6.85
1985—Las Vegas†	P. Coast	10	45	1	1	.500	46	34	27	16	34	5.40
1986—Las Vegas	P. Coast	36	128⅔	8	9	.471	148	89	75	71	65	5.25
1986—San Diego	National	9	11	1	0	1.000	10	5	2	7	4	1.64
1987—San Diego‡	National	44	68⅓	1	1	.500	62	29	24	17	30	3.16
1988—San Diego	National	34	63⅔	2	2	.500	68	31	24	43	19	3.39
1989—San Diego§	National	11	19	0	1	.000	15	10	9	8	10	4.26
1989—Portland	P. Coast	14	46	0	3	.000	57	35	31	23	22	6.07
1989—Minnesota xy	American	6	8⅔	0	0	.000	11	4	4	3	2	4.15
1990—Phoenix	P. Coast	49	72⅔	2	4	.333	83	46	37	29	36	4.58
1990—San Francisco	National	2	2	0	0	.000	7	3	3	1	0	13.50
National League Totals—8 Years		155	255⅓	5	7	.417	267	132	110	116	116	3.88
American League Totals—1 Year		6	8⅔	0	0	.000	11	4	4	3	2	4.15
Major League Totals—8 Years		161	264	5	7	.417	278	136	114	119	118	3.89

Selected by Oakland A's organization in 32nd round of free-agent draft, June 6, 1978.
Selected by San Diego Padres' organization in 10th round of free-agent draft, June 8, 1981.
†On disabled list, July 18 to August 21, 1985.
‡On disabled list, March 29 to April 15, 1987.
§Traded to Portland (Minnesota Twins' organization) for Pitcher Fred Toliver, June 29, 1989.
xGranted free agency, October 15, 1989; signed by Iowa (Chicago Cubs' organization), December 19, 1989.
yReleased, April 3, 1990; signed by Phoenix (San Francisco Giants' organization), April 5, 1990.

CHAMPIONSHIP SERIES RECORD

Year Club	League	G.	IP.	W.	L.	Pct.	H.	R.	ER.	SO.	BB.	ERA.
1984—San Diego	National	1	2	0	0	.000	2	0	0	2	1	0.00

WORLD SERIES RECORD

Year Club	League	G.	IP.	W.	L.	Pct.	H.	R.	ER.	SO.	BB.	ERA.
1984—San Diego	National	1	1	0	0	.000	0	1	1	0	4	9.00

RECORD AS INFIELDER

Year Club League	Pos.	G.	AB.	R.	H.	2B.	3B.	HR.	RBI.	B.A.	PO.	A.	E.	F.A.
1981—Walla Walla .... N'west	*P-1B	31	64	8	12	0	0	4	15	.188	26	14	0	*1.000

RODERICK STEWART BOOKER
(Rod)

Born September 4, 1958, at Los Angeles, Calif.
Height, 6.00. Weight, 175.
Throws right and bats lefthanded.
Attended Pasadena City College, Pasadena, Calif., and
University of California, Berkeley, Calif.

Major League stolen bases: 1987 (2), 1988 (2), 1990 (3). Total—7.

Year Club League	Pos.	G.	AB.	R.	H.	2B.	3B.	HR.	RBI.	B.A.	PO.	A.	E.	F.A.
1980—Visalia .... Calif.	SS	69	242	45	68	5	4	0	26	.281	91	198	18	.941
1981—Orlando .... South.	SS-3B	111	331	56	85	8	3	0	33	.257	145	304	30	.937
1982—Toledo† .... Int.	SS-2B-3B	104	292	38	73	8	1	0	19	.250	177	272	36	.926
1983—Arkansas............... Texas	SS-3B-2B	127	469	75	128	15	3	3	60	.273	153	343	19	.963

Year Club	League	Pos.	G.	AB.	R.	H.	2B.	3B.	HR.	RBI.	B.A.	PO.	A.	E.	F.A.
1984—Louisville	A. A.	2B-SS-3B	63	185	19	47	3	1	0	14	.254	100	167	8	.971
1984—Arkansas...............	Texas	SS	52	209	10	43	4	3	0	22	.206	87	160	15	.943
1985—Arkansas...............	Texas	SS	129	466	59	123	18	3	1	47	.264	198	362	26	*.956
1986—Arkansas...............	Texas	SS	36	151	20	48	7	2	0	20	.318	66	121	10	.949
1986—Louisville	A. A.	2B-SS-3B	78	289	51	81	11	5	1	30	.280	151	205	10	.973
1987—Louisville	A. A.	2B-SS-3B	34	135	25	47	3	1	1	21	.348	50	95	5	.967
1987—St. Louis.................	Nat.	2B-3B-SS	44	47	9	13	1	1	0	8	.277	25	28	2	.964
1988—St. Louis.................	Nat.	3B-2B	18	35	6	12	3	0	0	3	.343	3	15	2	.900
1988—Louisville	A. A.	2B-SS-OF	111	370	50	96	12	1	4	31	.259	197	330	20	.963
1989—St. Louis.................	Nat.	2B-3B	10	8	1	2	0	0	0	0	.250	4	9	2	.867
1989—Louisville‡	A. A.	SS-3B-2B	94	276	37	64	9	2	2	30	.232	123	232	14	.962
1990—Philadelphia	Nat.	SS-2B-3B	73	131	19	29	5	2	0	10	.221	57	74	4	.970
Major League Totals—4 Years.................			145	221	35	56	9	3	0	21	.253	89	126	10	.956

Selected by Detroit Tigers' organization in 14th round of free-agent draft, June 8, 1976.
Selected by Baltimore Orioles' organization in 10th round of free-agent draft, June 5, 1979.
Selected by Minnesota Twins' organization in 4th round of free-agent draft, June 3, 1980.
†Sold to St. Louis Cardinals' organization, April 5, 1983.
‡Released, October 5, 1989; signed by Scranton/Wilkes-Barre (Philadelphia Phillies' organization), December 14, 1989.

DANIEL HUGH BOONE
(Dan)

Born January 14, 1954, at Long Beach, Calif.
Height, 5.08. Weight, 140.
Throws and bats lefthanded.
Attended Cerritos College, Norwalk, Calif., and California State University, Fullerton, Calif.
Descendant of American Pioneer Daniel Boone.

Pitched 2-0 no-hit victory against Syracuse, July 23, 1990 (second game).
Tied for National League lead in balks with 5 in 1981.
Led Texas League in saves with 26 in 1980.

Year Club	League	G.	IP.	W.	L.	Pct.	H.	R.	ER.	SO.	BB.	ERA.
1977—Salinas..........................	California	17	21	0	0	.000	20	8	7	19	3	3.00
1977—El Paso..........................	Texas	23	35	2	1	.667	45	12	11	32	13	2.83
1977—Salt Lake City................	P. Coast	8	16	0	0	.000	25	16	15	8	5	8.44
1978—El Paso..........................	Texas	36	54	3	2	.600	49	19	16	51	10	2.67
1978—Salt Lake City................	P. Coast	26	43	4	1	.800	52	24	21	21	10	4.40
1979—Salt Lake City†‡............	P. Coast	50	83	9	2	.818	90	35	28	48	23	3.04
1980—Amarillo.........................	Texas	46	73	5	4	.556	68	27	24	62	16	2.96
1980—Hawaii...........................	P. Coast	8	14	2	0	1.000	10	2	2	7	3	1.29
1981—San Diego......................	National	37	63	1	0	1.000	63	23	20	43	21	2.86
1982—San Diego§-Houston.....................National		20	28⅔	1	1	.500	28	16	15	12	7	4.71
1982—Tucson...........................	P. Coast	25	49	5	4	.556	51	19	18	43	13	3.31
1983—Tucson x-Vancouver ....P. Coast		43	75⅓	7	6	.538	96	49	42	58	10	5.02
1984—Vancouver y...................	P. Coast	27	57	4	4	.500	63	35	30	22	25	4.74
1985-89—					(Out of Organized Baseball)							
1990—Rochester	Int'national	47	121	11	5	.688	96	44	35	65	30	2.60
1990—Baltimore	American	4	9⅔	0	0	.000	12	3	3	2	3	2.79
National League Totals—2 Years......................		57	91⅔	2	1	.667	91	39	35	55	28	3.44
American League Totals—1 Year		4	9⅔	0	0	.000	12	3	3	2	3	2.79
Major League Totals—3 Years.....................		61	101⅓	2	1	.667	103	42	38	57	31	3.38

Selected by California Angels' organization in 15th round of free-agent draft, June 5, 1973.
Selected by California Angels' organization in secondary phase of free-agent draft, January 9, 1974.
Selected by New York Yankees' organization in 14th round of free-agent draft, June 4, 1975.
Selected by San Diego Padres' organization in secondary phase of free-agent draft, January 7, 1976.
Selected by California Angels' organization in secondary phase of free-agent draft, June 8, 1976.
†On disabled list, June 7 to July 2, 1979.
‡Released, March 30, 1980; signed by Amarillo (San Diego Padres' organization), April 2, 1980.
§Traded to Houston Astros for Infielder Joe Pittman, June 8, 1982.
xReleased, June 17, 1983; signed by Vancouver (Milwaukee Brewers' organization), July 15, 1983.
yReleased, July 3, 1984; signed by Rochester (Baltimore Orioles' organization), February 22, 1990.

ROBERT RAYMOND BOONE
(Bob)

Born November 19, 1947, at San Diego, Calif.
Height, 6.02. Weight, 207.
Throws and bats righthanded.
Received bachelor of arts degree in psychology from Stanford University, Palo Alto, Calif. in 1969.
Son of Ray Boone, infielder with Cleveland, Detroit, Chicago A.L., Kansas City,
Milwaukee and Boston, 1948 through 1960; and scout with Boston Red Sox since 1961;
brother of Rodney Alan Boone, catcher-outfielder in Kansas City Royals' and
Houston Astros' organization, 1972 through 1975; and father of Bret Boone,
second baseman in Seattle Mariners' organization.

Holds major league records for most games (2,225), putouts (11,260) and chances accepted (12,434) by catcher, lifetime; most years, 100 or more games, catcher (15).
Major League stolen bases: 1972 (1), 1973 (3), 1974 (3), 1975 (1), 1976 (2), 1977 (5), 1978 (2), 1979 (1), 1980 (3), 1981 (2), 1983 (4), 1984 (3), 1985 (1), 1986 (1), 1988 (2), 1989 (3), 1990 (1). Total—38.

Led American League catchers in double plays with 12 in 1983, 15 in 1985 and 16 in 1986.
Led American League catchers in total chances with 745 in 1982 and 823 in 1989.
Led National League catchers in fielding percentage with .991 in 1978.
Led National League catchers in total chances with 924 in 1974.
Led Pacific Coast League catchers in passed balls with 18 and double plays with 13 in 1972.
Tied for Carolina League lead in double plays by third basemen with 18 in 1969.
Named catcher on THE SPORTING NEWS National League All-Star Team, 1976.
Named catcher on THE SPORTING NEWS American League All-Star fielding team, 1982 and 1986 through 1989.
Named catcher on THE SPORTING NEWS National League All-Star fielding team, 1978 and 1979.

Year	Club	League	Pos.	G.	AB.	R.	H.	2B.	3B.	HR.	RBI.	B.A.	PO.	A.	E.	F.A.
1969—Raleigh-Durham	Carol.		3B	80	300	45	90	13	1	5	46	.300	71	160	20	.920
1970—Reading†	East.		3B	20	80	12	23	2	0	2	10	.288	28	38	7	.904
1971—Reading‡	East.		3B-C-SS	92	328	41	87	14	3	4	37	.265	206	138	17	.953
1972—Eugene	P. C.		C	138	513	77	158	32	4	17	67	.308	★699	★77	★24	.970
1972—Philadelphia	Nat.		C	16	51	4	14	1	0	1	4	.275	66	7	5	.936
1973—Philadelphia	Nat.		C	145	521	42	136	20	2	10	61	.261	868	★89	10	.990
1974—Philadelphia	Nat.		C	146	488	41	118	24	3	3	52	.242	★825	77	★22	.976
1975—Philadelphia	Nat.		C-3B	97	289	28	71	14	2	2	20	.246	459	48	5	.990
1976—Philadelphia	Nat.		C-1B	121	361	40	98	18	2	4	54	.271	587	39	6	.990
1977—Philadelphia	Nat.		C-3B	132	440	55	125	26	4	11	66	.284	654	83	8	.989
1978—Philadelphia	Nat.		C-1B-OF	132	435	48	123	18	4	12	62	.283	650	55	8	.989
1979—Philadelphia	Nat.		C-3B	119	398	38	114	21	3	9	58	.286	527	66	8	.987
1980—Philadelphia	Nat.		C	141	480	34	110	23	1	9	55	.229	741	88	★18	.979
1981—Philadelphia§	Nat.		C	76	227	19	48	7	0	4	24	.211	365	32	6	.985
1982—California	Amer.		C	143	472	42	121	17	0	7	58	.256	★650	★87	8	.989
1983—California	Amer.		C	142	468	46	120	18	0	9	52	.256	606	★83	★14	.980
1984—California	Amer.		C	139	450	33	91	16	1	3	32	.202	660	★71	12	.984
1985—California	Amer.		C	150	460	37	114	17	0	5	55	.248	670	71	10	.987
1986—California x	Amer.		C	144	442	48	98	12	2	7	49	.222	812	★84	11	.988
1987—Palm Springs	Calif.		C	3	9	0	1	1	0	0	0	.111	17	4	1	.955
1987—California	Amer.		C	128	389	42	94	18	0	3	33	.242	684	56	★13	.983
1988—California y	Amer.		C	122	352	38	104	17	0	5	39	.295	506	★66	8	.986
1989—Kansas City	Amer.		C	131	405	33	111	13	2	1	43	.274	★752	64	7	.991
1990—Kansas City za	Amer.		C	40	117	11	28	3	0	0	9	.239	243	19	4	.985
National League Totals—10 Years				1125	3690	349	957	172	21	65	456	.259	5742	584	96	.958
American League Totals—9 Years				1139	3555	330	881	131	5	40	370	.248	5583	601	87	.986
Major League Totals—19 Years				2264	7245	679	1838	303	26	105	826	.254	11325	1185	183	.986

Selected by Philadelphia Phillies' organization in 20th round of free-agent draft, June 5, 1969.
†On military list, May 26, 1970 through remainder of season.
‡On disabled list, April 10 to June 4, 1971.
§Sold to California Angels, December 6, 1981.
xGranted free agency, November 12, 1986; re-signed by Angels, May 1, 1987.
yGranted free agency, October 24, 1988; signed by Kansas City Royals, November 30, 1988.
zOn disabled list, May 17 to July 20, 1990.
aGranted free agency, November 5, 1990.

DIVISION SERIES RECORD

Year	Club	League	Pos.	G.	AB.	R.	H.	2B.	3B.	HR.	RBI.	B.A.	PO.	A.	E.	F.A.
1981—Philadelphia	Nat.		C	3	5	0	0	0	0	0	0	.000	10	2	0	1.000

CHAMPIONSHIP SERIES RECORD

Holds Championship Series record for most sacrifice hits, total series (5).
Shares Championship Series records for most consecutive hits, series (5) and most singles, series (9), 1986; most sacrifice hits, series (2), 1982.
Shares American League Championship Series record for most consecutive hits, total series (5).

Year	Club	League	Pos.	G.	AB.	R.	H.	2B.	3B.	HR.	RBI.	B.A.	PO.	A.	E.	F.A.
1976—Philadelphia	Nat.		C	3	7	0	2	0	0	0	1	.286	8	2	0	1.000
1977—Philadelphia	Nat.		C	4	10	1	4	0	0	0	0	.400	18	2	0	1.000
1978—Philadelphia	Nat.		C	3	11	0	2	0	0	0	0	.182	16	2	1	.947
1980—Philadelphia	Nat.		C	5	18	1	4	0	0	0	2	.222	22	3	0	1.000
1982—California	Amer.		C	5	16	3	4	0	0	1	4	.250	30	3	0	1.000
1986—California	Amer.		C	7	22	4	10	0	0	1	2	.455	33	3	0	1.000
Championship Series Totals—6 Years				27	84	9	26	0	0	2	9	.310	127	15	1	.993

WORLD SERIES RECORD

Year	Club	League	Pos.	G.	AB.	R.	H.	2B.	3B.	HR.	RBI.	B.A.	PO.	A.	E.	F.A.
1980—Philadelphia	Nat.		C	6	17	3	7	2	0	0	4	.412	49	3	0	1.000

ALL-STAR GAME RECORD

Year	League	Pos.	AB.	R.	H.	2B.	3B.	HR.	RBI.	B.A.	PO.	A.	E.	F.A.
1976—National		C	2	0	0	0	0	0	0	.000	5	0	0	1.000
1978—National‡		C	1	1	1	0	0	0	2	1.000	3	1	0	1.000
1979—National‡		C	2	1	1	0	0	0	0	.500	0	0	0	.000
1983—American		C	0	0	0	0	0	0	0	.000	1	0	0	1.000
All-Star Game Totals—4 Years			5	2	2	0	0	0	2	.400	9	1	0	1.000

—DID YOU KNOW—

That Los Angeles owned the majors' best record in extra-inning games in 1990, finishing 10-3 for a .769 winning percentage?

PATRICK LANCE BORDERS
(Pat)

Born May 14, 1963, at Columbus, O.
Height, 6.02. Weight, 200.
Throws and bats righthanded.
Brother of Todd Borders, catcher in Chicago Cubs' organization, 1988 and 1989.

Major League stolen bases: 1989 (2).
Tied for Southern League in passed balls with 16 in 1987.

Year—Club	League	Pos.	G.	AB.	R.	H.	2B.	3B.	HR.	RBI.	B.A.	PO.	A.	E.	F.A.
1982—Medicine Hat	Pion.	3B	61	217	30	66	12	2	5	33	.304	23	96	*25	.826
1983—Florence	S. Atl.	3B	131	457	62	125	31	4	5	54	.274	70	233	*41	.881
1984—Florence	S. Atl.	1B-3B-OF	131	467	69	129	32	5	12	85	.276	650	77	25	.967
1985—Kinston	Carol.	1B	127	460	43	120	16	1	10	60	.261	854	42	*20	.978
1986—Florence	S. Atl.	C-OF	16	40	8	15	7	0	3	9	.375	22	1	0	1.000
1986—Knoxville	South.	C-1B	12	34	3	12	1	0	2	5	.353	45	5	3	.943
1986—Kinston	Carol.	C-1B-OF	49	174	24	57	10	0	6	26	.328	211	26	7	.971
1987—Dunedin	Fla. St.	1B	3	11	0	4	0	0	0	1	.364	21	1	0	1.000
1987—Knoxville	South.	C-3B	94	349	44	102	14	1	11	51	.292	432	49	12	.976
1988—Toronto†	Amer.	C-2B-3B	56	154	15	42	6	3	5	21	.273	205	19	7	.970
1988—Syracuse	Int.	C	35	120	11	29	8	0	3	14	.242	202	17	2	.991
1989—Toronto	Amer.	C	94	241	22	62	11	1	3	29	.257	261	27	6	.980
1990—Toronto	Amer.	C	125	346	36	99	24	2	15	49	.286	515	46	4	.993
Major League Totals—3 Years			275	741	73	203	41	6	23	99	.274	981	92	17	.984

Selected by Toronto Blue Jays' organization in sixth round of free-agent draft, June 7, 1982.

†On disabled list, July 5 to August 19, 1988; included rehabilitation disability assignment to Syracuse, July 30 to August 19, 1988.

CHAMPIONSHIP SERIES RECORD

Year—Club	League	Pos.	G.	AB.	R.	H.	2B.	3B.	HR.	RBI.	B.A.	PO.	A.	E.	F.A.
1989—Toronto	Amer.	PH-C	1	1	0	1	0	0	0	1	1.000	1	0	0	1.000

MICHAEL TODD BORDICK
(Mike)

Born July 21, 1965, at Marquette, Mich.
Height, 5.11. Weight, 170.
Throws and bats righthanded.
Attended University of Maine, Orono, Me.

Led Pacific Coast League shortstops in fielding percentage with .972 and double plays with 82 in 1990.

Year—Club	League	Pos.	G.	AB.	R.	H.	2B.	3B.	HR.	RBI.	B.A.	PO.	A.	E.	F.A.
1986—Medford	N'west	SS	46	187	30	48	3	1	0	19	.257	68	143	18	.921
1987—Modesto	Calif.	SS	133	497	73	133	17	0	3	75	.268	216	305	17	*.968
1988—Huntsville	South.	2B-SS-3B	132	481	48	130	13	2	0	28	.270	260	406	24	.965
1989—Tacoma	P. C.	2B-SS-3B	136	487	55	117	17	1	1	43	.240	261	431	33	.954
1990—Oakland	Amer.	3B-SS-2B	25	14	0	1	0	0	0	0	.071	9	8	0	1.000
1990—Tacoma	P. C.	SS-2B	111	348	49	79	16	1	2	30	.227	210	366	16	.973
Major League Totals—1 Year			25	14	0	1	0	0	0	0	.071	9	8	0	1.000

Signed as free agent by Oakland Athletics' organization, July 10, 1986.

WORLD SERIES RECORD

Year—Club	League	Pos.	G.	AB.	R.	H.	2B.	3B.	HR.	RBI.	B.A.	PO.	A.	E.	F.A.
1990—Oakland	Amer.	PR-SS	3	0	0	0	0	0	0	0	.000	0	2	0	1.000

CHRISTOPHER LOUIS BOSIO

Name pronounced Boz-e-o.

(Chris)

Born April 3, 1963, at Carmichael, Calif.
Height, 6.03. Weight, 225.
Throws and bats righthanded.
Attended Sacramento City College, Sacramento, Calif.

Major League saves: 1987 (2), 1988 (6). Total—8.
Tied for Pacific Coast League lead in saves with 16 in 1986.

Year—Club	League	G.	IP.	W.	L.	Pct.	H.	R.	ER.	SO.	BB.	ERA.
1982—Pikeville	Ap'lachian	13	51⅓	3	2	.600	60	31	28	53	17	4.91
1983—Beloit	Midwest	17	107⅔	3	10	.231	125	82	67	71	41	5.60
1983—Paintsville	Ap'lachian	7	44⅓	2	2	.500	30	18	14	43	18	2.84
1984—Beloit	Midwest	26	181	*17	6	.739	159	83	55	156	56	2.73
1985—El Paso	Texas	28	181⅓	11	6	.647	186	108	77	*155	49	3.82
1986—Vancouver	P. Coast	44	67	7	3	.700	47	18	17	60	13	2.28
1986—Milwaukee	American	10	34⅔	0	4	.000	41	27	27	29	13	7.01
1987—Milwaukee	American	46	170	11	8	.579	187	102	99	150	50	5.24
1988—Milwaukee	American	38	182	7	15	.318	190	80	68	84	38	3.36
1988—Denver	Am. Assoc.	2	14	1	0	1.000	13	6	6	12	4	3.86
1989—Milwaukee	American	33	234⅔	15	10	.600	225	90	77	173	48	2.95
1990—Milwaukee†	American	20	132⅔	4	9	.308	131	67	59	76	38	4.00
1990—Beloit	Midwest	1	3	0	0	.000	4	2	1	2	1	3.00
Major League Totals—5 Years		147	754	37	46	.446	774	366	330	512	187	3.94

Selected by Pittsburgh Pirates' organization in 29th round of free-agent draft, June 8, 1981.
Selected by Milwaukee Brewers' organization in secondary phase of free-agent draft, January 12, 1982.
†On disabled list, June 29 to July 15 and August 2, 1990 through remainder of season; included rehabilitation disability assignment to Beloit, July 9 to July 15, 1990.

SHAWN KEALOHA BOSKIE

Born March 28, 1967, at Hawthorne, Nev.
Height, 6.03. Weight, 205.
Throws and bats righthanded.
Attended Modesto Junior College, Modesto, Calif.

Led Southern League in hit batsmen with 19 in 1989.
Led Carolina League in hit batsmen with 17 in 1988.
Led Appalachian League in wild pitches with 15 in 1986.

Year Club	League	G.	IP.	W.	L.	Pct.	H.	R.	ER.	SO.	BB.	ERA.
1986—Wytheville	Ap'lachian	14	54	4	4	.500	42	41	32	40	57	5.33
1987—Peoria	Midwest	26	149	9	11	.450	149	91	72	100	56	4.35
1988—Winston-Salem	Carolina	27	186	12	7	.632	176	83	70	164	89	3.39
1989—Charlotte	Southern	28	181	11	8	.579	*196	105	88	*164	84	4.38
1990—Iowa	Am. Assoc.	8	51	4	2	.667	46	22	18	51	21	3.18
1990—Chicago†	National	15	97⅔	5	6	.455	99	42	40	49	31	3.69
Major League Totals—1 Year		15	97⅔	5	6	.455	99	42	40	49	31	3.69

Selected by Chicago Cubs' organization in 1st round (10th player selected) of free-agent draft, January 14, 1986.
†On disabled list, August 5 to September 26, 1990.

THADDIS BOSLEY JR.

Name pronounced BAHZ-lee.

(Thad)

Born September 17, 1956, at Oceanside, Calif.
Height, 6.03. Weight, 175.
Throws and bats lefthanded.
Attended Mira Costa Community College, Oceanside, Calif.

Major League stolen bases: 1977 (5), 1978 (12), 1979 (4), 1980 (3), 1981 (2), 1982 (3), 1983 (1), 1984 (5), 1985 (5), 1986 (3), 1988 (1), 1989 (2), 1990 (1). Total—47.
Led California League in stolen bases with 90 and caught stealing with 17 in 1976.
Led Pioneer League in bases on balls received with 71 in 1974.
Named California League Most Valuable Player, 1976.

Year Club	League	Pos.	G.	AB.	R.	H.	2B.	3B.	HR.	RBI.	B.A.	PO.	A.	E.	F.A.
1974—Idaho Falls	Pion.	OF	68	223	55	54	3	4	0	14	.242	101	4	*11	.905
1975—Quad Cities†	Midw.	OF	108	379	67	113	12	3	1	50	.298	206	2	4	*.981
1976—Salinas	Calif.	OF	134	527	105	171	26	4	2	72	*.324	285	13	7	*.977
1977—Salt Lake City	P. C.	OF	69	298	55	97	22	2	2	38	.326	169	6	5	.972
1977—California‡§	Amer.	OF	58	212	19	63	10	2	0	19	.297	130	1	5	.963
1978—Iowa x	A. A.	OF	47	179	27	52	3	0	3	15	.291	77	5	2	.976
1978—Chicago x	Amer.	OF	66	219	25	59	5	1	2	13	.269	155	3	4	.975
1979—Iowa y	A. A.	OF	95	382	62	101	14	5	1	24	.264	140	6	5	.967
1979—Chicago	Amer.	OF	36	77	13	24	1	1	1	8	.312	57	2	2	.967
1980—Chicago za	Amer.	OF	70	147	12	33	2	0	2	14	.224	91	1	4	.958
1981—Vancouver	P. C.	OF	34	122	15	39	5	2	0	14	.320	75	0	5	.938
1981—Milwaukee b	Amer.	OF	42	105	11	24	2	0	0	3	.229	55	1	2	.966
1982—Seattle	Amer.	OF	22	46	3	8	1	0	0	2	.174	12	1	0	1.000
1982—Salt Lake C. cdef	P. C.	OF	22	84	15	25	2	2	3	9	.298	24	2	0	1.000
1983—Mexico City	Mex.	OF	31	107	24	35	7	3	4	18	.327	24	1	0	1.000
1983—Iowa	A. A.	OF	39	124	22	36	11	0	7	24	.290	3	0	1	.750
1983—Chicago	Nat.	OF	43	72	12	21	4	1	2	12	.292	27	1	0	1.000
1984—Iowa	A. A.	OF	51	162	23	58	16	1	6	43	.358	31	4	2	.946
1984—Chicago	Nat.	OF	55	98	17	29	2	2	2	14	.296	39	2	1	.976
1985—Chicago	Nat.	OF	108	180	25	59	6	3	7	27	.328	84	0	1	.988
1986—Chicago g	Nat.	OF	87	120	15	33	4	1	1	9	.275	31	0	1	.969
1987—Kansas City h	Amer.	OF	80	140	13	39	6	1	1	16	.279	28	0	1	.966
1988—K.C. ij-Calif.	Amer.	OF	50	96	10	25	5	0	0	9	.260	59	0	2	.967
1988—Edmonton k	P. C.	OF	18	52	13	16	5	1	0	9	.308	20	1	0	1.000
1989—Oklahoma City	A. A.	OF	30	101	17	31	7	0	2	12	.307	35	2	1	.974
1989—Texas l	Amer.	OF	37	40	5	9	2	0	1	9	.225	12	1	0	1.000
1990—Texas m	Amer.	OF	30	29	3	4	0	0	1	3	.138	4	0	0	1.000
American League Totals—10 Years			491	1111	114	288	34	5	8	96	.259	603	10	20	.968
National League Totals—4 Years			293	470	69	142	16	7	12	62	.302	181	3	3	.984
Major League Totals—14 Years			784	1581	183	430	50	12	20	158	.272	784	13	23	.972

Selected by California Angels' organization in 4th round of free-agent draft, June 5, 1974.
†On disabled list, April 19 to May 6, 1975.
‡On disabled list, June 29 to July 10, 1977.
§Traded with Outfielder Bobby Bonds and Pitcher Richard Dotson to Chicago White Sox for Pitchers Chris Knapp and Dave Frost and Catcher Brian Downing, December 5, 1977.
xOn disabled list, June 29 to July 17, 1978.
yOn disabled list, July 15 to July 25, 1979.
zOn disabled list, August 12, 1980 through remainder of season.
aTraded to Milwaukee Brewers' organization for First Baseman-Outfielder John Poff, April 1, 1981.

bTraded to Seattle Mariners for Pitcher Mike Parrott, March 5, 1982.
cOn disabled list, June 6 to July 1 and August 3 to September 2, 1982.
dGranted free agency, September 5, 1982; signed by Tacoma (Oakland A's organization), February 14, 1983.
eSold to Iowa (Chicago Cubs' organization), March 30, 1983.
fLoaned to Mexico City Tigers, April 3, 1983; returned, May 28, 1983.
gTraded with Pitcher Dave Gumpert to Kansas City Royals for Catcher Jim Sundberg, March 30, 1987.
hGranted free agency, November 9, 1987; re-signed by Royals, January 5, 1988.
iOn disabled list, May 11 to May 27, 1988.
jReleased, May 27, 1988; signed by Edmonton (California Angels' organization), June 7, 1988.
kGranted free agency, November 4, 1988; signed by Oklahoma City (Texas Rangers' organization), June 8, 1989.
lReleased, October 2, 1989; re-signed by Rangers, December 19, 1989.
mReleased, June 2, 1990.

DIVISION SERIES RECORD

Year	Club	League	Pos.	G.	AB.	R.	H.	2B.	3B.	HR.	RBI.	B.A.	PO.	A.	E.	F.A.
1981—Milwaukee		Amer.	PR-DH	1	0	0	0	0	0	0	0	.000	0	0	0	.000

CHAMPIONSHIP SERIES RECORD

Year	Club	League	Pos.	G.	AB.	R.	H.	2B.	3B.	HR.	RBI.	B.A.	PO.	A.	E.	F.A.
1984—Chicago		Nat.	PH	2	2	0	0	0	0	0	0	.000	0	0	0	.000

DARYL LAMONT BOSTON

Born January 4, 1963, at Cincinnati, O.
Height, 6.03. Weight, 195.
Throws and bats lefthanded.

Major League stolen bases: 1984 (6), 1985 (8), 1986 (9), 1987 (12), 1988 (9), 1989 (7), 1990 (19). Total—70.
Led Eastern League batters in strikeouts with 133 in 1983.
Led Midwest League outfielders in total chances with 312 in 1982.
Tied for American Association lead in sacrifice flies with 11 in 1984.
Tied for American Association lead in double plays by outfielders with 4 in 1984.

Year	Club	League	Pos.	G.	AB.	R.	H.	2B.	3B.	HR.	RBI.	B.A.	PO.	A.	E.	F.A.
1981—Sarasota W. S.		Gulf C.	OF	56	189	30	55	6	3	1	30	.291	84	9	3	.969
1982—Appleton		Midw.	OF	★139	512	86	143	19	9	15	77	.279	★293	9	10	.968
1983—Glens Falls		East.	OF	113	435	65	104	15	1	18	50	.239	271	8	13	.955
1983—Denver		A. A.	OF	14	51	11	13	4	1	2	7	.255	26	1	5	.844
1984—Denver		A. A.	OF	127	471	94	147	21	★19	15	82	.312	311	11	●10	.970
1984—Chicago		Amer.	OF	35	83	8	14	3	1	0	3	.169	59	2	6	.910
1985—Chicago		Amer.	OF	95	232	20	53	13	1	3	15	.228	179	7	2	.989
1985—Buffalo		A. A.	OF	63	241	45	66	12	1	10	36	.274	151	3	3	.981
1986—Buffalo		A. A.	OF	96	360	57	109	16	3	5	41	.303	210	1	5	.977
1986—Chicago		Amer.	OF	56	199	29	53	11	3	5	22	.266	152	3	5	.969
1987—Chicago		Amer.	OF	103	337	51	87	21	2	10	29	.258	207	3	2	.991
1987—Hawaii		P. C.	OF	21	77	14	23	3	0	5	13	.299	43	3	0	1.000
1988—Chicago		Amer.	OF	105	281	37	61	12	2	15	31	.217	190	4	10	.951
1989—Chicago		Amer.	OF	101	218	34	55	3	4	5	23	.252	134	2	4	.971
1990—Chicago†		Amer.	OF	5	1	0	0	0	0	0	0	.000	0	0	0	.000
1990—New York		Nat.	OF	115	366	65	100	21	2	12	45	.273	203	3	3	.986
American League Totals—7 Years				500	1351	179	323	63	13	38	123	.239	921	21	29	.970
National League Totals—1 Year				115	366	65	100	21	2	12	45	.273	203	3	3	.986
Major League Totals—7 Years				615	1717	244	423	84	15	50	168	.246	1124	24	32	.973

Selected by Chicago White Sox' organization in 1st round (seventh player selected) of free-agent draft, June 8, 1981.
†Claimed on waivers by New York Mets, April 30, 1990.

DENIS BOUCHER

Born March 7, 1968, at Montreal, Quebec, Canada.
Height, 6.01. Weight, 195.
Throws left and bats righthanded.

Led South Atlantic League in balks with 21 and tied for lead in games started by pitchers with 32 in 1988.

Year	Club	League	G.	IP.	W.	L.	Pct.	H.	R.	ER.	SO.	BB.	ERA.
1988—Myrtle Beach		S. Atlantic	33	196⅔	13	12	.520	161	81	62	169	63	2.84
1989—Dunedin		Florida St.	33	164⅔	10	10	.500	142	80	56	117	58	3.06
1990—Dunedin		Florida St.	9	60	7	0	1.000	45	8	5	62	8	0.75
1990—Syracuse		Int'national	17	107⅔	8	5	.615	100	52	46	80	37	3.85

Signed as free agent by Toronto Blue Jays' organization, August 18, 1987.

DENNIS RAY BOYD
(Oil Can)

(Given nickname from beer drinking friends in Meridian, Miss.
where beer is referred to as oil.)
Born October 6, 1959, at Meridian, Miss.
Height, 6.01. Weight, 160.
Throws and bats righthanded.
Attended Jackson State University, Jackson, Miss.
Brother of Don Boyd, outfielder in St. Louis Cardinals' organization, 1973.

Led Florida State League pitchers in games started with 28 and home runs allowed with 11 in 1981.
Tied for Eastern League lead in games started by pitchers with 27 and complete games with 13 in 1982.

Year Club	League	G.	IP.	W.	L.	Pct.	H.	R.	ER.	SO.	BB.	ERA.
1980—Elmira	NYP	12	69	7	1	.875	54	20	19	79	30	2.48
1981—Winter Haven	Florida St.	28	186	14	8	.636	★195	90	75	154	54	3.63
1982—Bristol	Eastern	27	★205	14	8	.636	190	71	64	★191	49	2.81
1982—Boston	American	3	8⅓	0	1	.000	11	5	5	2	2	5.40
1983—Pawtucket	Int'national	20	122⅔	5	8	.385	119	69	55	129	41	4.04
1983—Boston	American	15	98⅔	4	8	.333	103	46	36	43	23	3.28
1984—Boston	American	29	197⅔	12	12	.500	207	109	96	134	53	4.37
1984—Pawtucket	Int'national	5	37⅓	3	1	.750	30	12	12	45	12	2.89
1985—Boston	American	35	272⅓	15	13	.536	★273	117	112	154	67	3.70
1986—Boston	American	30	214⅓	16	10	.615	222	99	90	129	45	3.78
1987—Pawtucket†	Int'national	3	12	1	1	.500	12	6	6	8	4	4.50
1987—Boston	American	7	36⅔	1	3	.250	47	31	24	12	9	5.89
1988—Boston‡	American	23	129⅔	9	7	.563	147	82	77	71	41	5.34
1989—Boston§	American	10	59	3	2	.600	57	31	29	26	19	4.42
1989—Pawtucket	Int'national	2	7	0	0	.000	4	0	0	11	0	0.00
1989—New Britain x	Eastern	1	5	0	1	.000	3	1	1	8	1	1.80
1990—Montreal	National	31	190⅔	10	6	.625	164	64	62	113	52	2.93
American League Totals—8 Years		152	1016⅔	60	56	.517	1067	520	469	571	259	4.15
National League Totals—1 Year		31	190⅔	10	6	.625	164	64	62	113	52	2.93
Major League Totals—9 Years		183	1207⅓	70	62	.530	1231	584	531	684	311	3.96

Selected by Boston Red Sox' organization in 16th round of free-agent draft, June 3, 1980.

†On Boston disabled list, March 29 to June 22 and July 31, 1987 through remainder of season; included rehabilitation disability assignment to Pawtucket, June 8 to June 22, 1987.

‡On disabled list, July 27 to August 20 and August 31, 1988 through remainder of season.

§On disabled list, May 2 to September 1, 1989; included rehabilitation disability assignment to Pawtucket, August 18 to August 27, 1989; and to New Britain, August 28 to September 1, 1989.

xGranted free agency, November 13, 1989; signed by Montreal Expos, December 7, 1989.

CHAMPIONSHIP SERIES RECORD

Year Club	League	G.	IP.	W.	L.	Pct.	H.	R.	ER.	SO.	BB.	ERA.
1986—Boston	American	2	13⅔	1	1	.500	17	7	7	8	3	4.61

WORLD SERIES RECORD

Year Club	League	G.	IP.	W.	L.	Pct.	H.	R.	ER.	SO.	BB.	ERA.
1986—Boston	American	1	7	0	1	.000	9	6	6	3	1	7.71

PHILIP POOLE BRADLEY
(Phil)

Born March 11, 1959, at Bloomington, Ind.
Height, 6.00. Weight, 185.
Throws and bats righthanded.
Received bachelor of science degree in personnel management from
University of Missouri, Columbia, Mo., in 1982.

Shares major league records for most doubles, inning (2), August 30, 1989, first inning; most strikeouts, nine-inning game (5), September 7, 1989, first game.

Major League stolen bases: 1983 (3), 1984 (21), 1985 (22), 1986 (21), 1987 (40), 1988 (11), 1989 (20), 1990 (17). Total—155.

Led American League in being hit by pitch with 11 in 1990.
Led National League in being hit by pitch with 16 in 1988.
Named outfielder on THE SPORTING NEWS American League All-Star Team, 1985.

Year Club	League	Pos.	G.	AB.	R.	H.	2B.	3B.	HR.	RBI.	B.A.	PO.	A.	E.	F.A.
1981—Bellingham	N'west	OF	53	193	38	58	12	5	1	20	.301	94	3	1	★.990
1982—Bakersfield	Calif.	OF	109	405	98	134	17	10	0	37	.331	226	13	6	.976
1983—Salt Lake City	P. Coast	OF	130	458	100	148	14	4	2	41	.323	284	13	1	★.997
1983—Seattle	Amer.	OF	23	67	8	18	2	0	0	5	.269	36	1	1	.974
1984—Seattle	Amer.	OF	124	322	49	97	12	4	0	24	.301	235	3	2	.992
1985—Seattle	Amer.	OF	159	641	100	192	33	8	26	88	.300	336	10	5	.986
1986—Seattle†	Amer.	OF	143	526	88	163	27	4	12	50	.310	250	11	1	.996
1987—Seattle‡	Amer.	OF	158	603	101	179	38	10	14	67	.297	273	13	5	.983
1988—Philadelphia§	Nat.	OF	154	569	77	150	30	5	11	56	.264	298	14	3	.990
1989—Baltimore	Amer.	OF	144	545	83	151	23	10	11	55	.277	284	4	3	.990
1990—Balt.xy-Chi.z	Amer.	OF	117	422	59	108	14	2	4	31	.256	219	4	4	.982
American League Totals—7 Years			868	3126	488	908	149	38	67	320	.290	1633	46	21	.988
National League Totals—1 Year			154	569	77	150	30	5	11	56	.264	298	14	3	.990
Major League Totals—8 Years			1022	3695	565	1058	179	43	78	376	.286	1931	60	24	.988

Selected by Seattle Mariners' organization in 3rd round of free-agent draft, June 8, 1981.

†On disabled list, May 26 to June 12, 1986.

‡Traded with Pitcher Tim Fortugno to Philadelphia Phillies for Outfielders Glenn Wilson and Dave Brundage and Pitcher Mike Jackson, December 9, 1987.

§Traded to Baltimore Orioles for Pitchers Ken Howell and Gordon Dillard, December 8, 1988.

xOn disabled list, June 17 to July 13, 1990.

yTraded to Chicago White Sox for Designated Hitter/First Baseman Ron Kittle, July 30, 1990.

zGranted free agency, November 5, 1990.

ALL-STAR GAME RECORD

Year League	Pos.	AB.	R.	H.	2B.	3B.	HR.	RBI.	B.A.	PO.	A.	E.	F.A.
1985—American	OF	1	0	0	0	0	0	0	.000	1	0	0	1.000

SCOTT WILLIAM BRADLEY

Born March 22, 1960, at Montclair, N.J.
Height, 5.11. Weight, 185.
Throws right and bats lefthanded.
Received bachelor of science degree in business administration
from University of North Carolina, Chapel Hill, N.C.

Major League stolen bases: 1986 (1), 1988 (1), 1989 (1). Total—3.
Tied for International League lead in game-winning RBIs with 14 in 1984.
Tied for Florida State League lead in game-winning RBIs with 13 in 1982.
Named International League Player of the Year, 1984.

Year Club	League	Pos.	G.	AB.	R.	H.	2B.	3B.	HR.	RBI.	B.A.	PO.	A.	E.	F.A.
1981—Oneonta	NYP	C-OF	71	276	48	85	17	4	4	54	.308	323	40	9	.976
1982—Nashville	South.	C	5	19	2	2	1	0	0	0	.105	44	2	2	.958
1982—Fort Lauderdale	Fla. St.	C-1B-3B	121	439	52	130	28	4	3	66	.296	407	57	10	.979
1983—Nashville	South.	C-3B	137	525	83	142	33	4	8	76	.270	475	88	13	.977
1984—Columbus	Int.	C-OF-3B	★138	★538	84	★180	31	2	6	●84	★.335	432	50	9	.982
1984—New York	Amer.	OF-C	9	21	3	6	1	0	0	2	.286	10	0	0	1.000
1985—New York†	Amer.	C	19	49	4	8	2	1	0	1	.163	12	0	1	.923
1985—Albany	East.	3B	6	24	2	3	1	0	0	2	.125	8	14	4	.846
1985—Columbus‡	Int.	C-3B	43	163	17	49	10	0	4	27	.301	118	53	4	.977
1986—Buffalo	A. A.	C-OF	33	126	14	42	3	3	5	20	.333	165	9	0	1.000
1986—Chicago§-Seattle	Amer.	C-OF	77	220	20	66	8	3	5	28	.300	281	21	3	.990
1987—Seattle	Amer.	C-3B-OF	102	342	34	95	15	1	5	43	.278	438	39	8	.984
1988—Seattle	Amer.	C-O-3-1	103	335	45	86	17	1	4	33	.257	543	42	6	.990
1989—Seattle	Amer.	C-1B-OF	103	270	21	74	16	0	3	37	.274	400	26	4	.988
1990—Seattle	Amer.	C-3B-1B	101	233	11	52	9	0	1	28	.223	354	30	2	.995
Major League Totals—7 Years			514	1470	138	387	68	6	18	172	.263	2038	158	24	.989

Selected by Minnesota Twins' organization in 12th round of free-agent draft, June 6, 1978.
Selected by New York Yankees' organization in 3rd round of free-agent draft, June 8, 1981.
†On disabled list, April 24 to June 17, 1985; included rehabilitation disability assignment to Sarasota, June 5 and June 6, 1985, and Albany, June 7 to June 17, 1985.
‡Traded with Pitcher Neil Allen, Outfielder Glen Braxton and cash to Chicago White Sox for Catchers Ron Hassey and Chris Alvarez, Pitcher Eric Schmidt and Outfielder Matt Winters, February 13, 1986.
§Traded to Seattle Mariners for a player to be named later, June 26, 1986; Chicago White Sox' organization acquired Outfielder Ivan Calderon to complete deal, July 1, 1986.

GLENN ERICK BRAGGS

Born October 17, 1962, at San Bernardino, Calif.
Height, 6.03. Weight, 220.
Throws and bats righthanded.
Attended University of Hawaii, Honolulu, Haw.

Major League stolen bases: 1986 (1), 1987 (12), 1988 (6), 1989 (17), 1990 (8). Total—44.
Led Texas League in being hit by pitch with 10 in 1985.
Led Appalachian League in total bases with 164, bases on balls received with 54 and intentional bases on balls received with 6 in 1983.
Named California League Most Valuable Player, 1984.
Named Appalachian League Player of the Year, 1983.
Received reported $50,000 bonus to sign with Milwaukee Brewers, 1983.

Year Club	League	Pos.	G.	AB.	R.	H.	2B.	3B.	HR.	RBI.	B.A.	PO.	A.	E.	F.A.
1983—Paintsville	Appal.	OF	●73	241	★65	★94	★20	1	●16	★74	★.390	115	8	6	.953
1984—Stockton	Calif.	OF	108	399	76	118	29	2	15	86	.296	158	4	6	.964
1985—El Paso	Texas	OF	117	448	105	139	26	4	20	103	.310	239	10	11	.958
1986—Vancouver	P. C.	OF	90	325	80	117	26	6	15	75	.360	218	8	2	.991
1986—Milwaukee	Amer.	OF	58	215	19	51	8	2	4	18	.237	116	5	12	.910
1987—Milwaukee	Amer.	OF	132	505	67	136	28	7	13	77	.269	301	6	9	.972
1988—Milwaukee†	Amer.	OF	72	272	30	71	14	0	10	42	.261	134	1	3	.978
1989—Milwaukee	Amer.	OF	144	514	77	127	12	3	15	66	.247	267	6	8	.972
1990—Milwaukee‡	Amer.	OF	37	113	17	28	5	0	3	13	.248	81	1	3	.965
1990—Cincinnnati	Nat.	OF	72	201	22	60	9	1	6	28	.299	110	10	4	.968
American League Totals—5 Years			443	1619	210	413	67	12	45	216	.255	899	19	35	.963
National League Totals—1 Year			72	201	22	60	9	1	6	28	.299	110	10	4	.968
Major League Totals—5 Years			515	1820	232	473	76	13	51	244	.260	1009	29	39	.964

Selected by New York Yankees' organization in 6th round of free-agent draft, June 3, 1980.
Selected by Milwaukee Brewers' organization in 2nd round of free-agent draft, June 6, 1983.
†On disabled list, July 2, 1988 through remainder of season.
‡Traded with Infielder Billy Bates to Cincinnati Reds for Pitchers Ron Robinson and Bob Sebra, June 9, 1990.

CHAMPIONSHIP SERIES RECORD

Year Club	League	Pos.	G.	AB.	R.	H.	2B.	3B.	HR.	RBI.	B.A.	PO.	A.	E.	F.A.
1990—Cincinnati	Nat.	OF	2	5	0	1	0	0	0	0	.200	2	0	0	1.000

WORLD SERIES RECORD

Year Club	League	Pos.	G.	AB.	R.	H.	2B.	3B.	HR.	RBI.	B.A.	PO.	A.	E.	F.A.
1990—Cincinnati	Nat.	PH-OF	2	4	0	0	0	0	0	2	.000	0	0	0	.000

JEFFREY HOKE BRANTLEY
(Jeff)

Born September 5, 1963, at Florence, Ala.
Height, 5.11. Weight, 190.
Throws and bats righthanded.
Attended Mississippi State University, Mississippi State, Miss.

Major League saves: 1988 (1), 1990 (19). Total—20.
Tied for Pacific Coast League lead in hit batsmen with 11 in 1987.
Tied for Texas League lead in complete games with 8 in 1986.

Year Club	League	G.	IP.	W.	L.	Pct.	H.	R.	ER.	SO.	BB.	ERA.
1985—Fresno	California	14	94⅔	8	2	.800	83	39	35	85	37	3.33
1986—Shreveport	Texas	26	165⅔	8	10	.444	139	78	64	125	68	3.48
1987—Shreveport	Texas	2	11⅔	0	1	.000	12	7	4	7	4	3.09
1987—Phoenix	P. Coast	29	170⅓	6	11	.353	187	110	88	111	82	4.65
1988—Phoenix	P. Coast	27	122⅔	9	5	.643	130	65	59	83	39	4.33
1988—San Francisco	National	9	20⅔	0	1	.000	22	13	13	11	6	5.66
1989—San Francisco	National	59	97⅓	7	1	.875	101	50	44	69	37	4.07
1989—Phoenix	P. Coast	7	14⅓	1	1	.500	6	2	2	20	6	1.26
1990—San Francisco	National	55	86⅔	5	3	.625	77	18	15	61	33	1.56
Major League Totals—3 Years		123	204⅔	12	5	.706	200	81	72	141	76	3.17

Selected by Montreal Expos' organization in 13th round of free-agent draft, June 4, 1984.
Selected by San Francisco Giants' organization in 6th round of free-agent draft, June 3, 1985.

CHAMPIONSHIP SERIES RECORD

Year Club	League	G.	IP.	W.	L.	Pct.	H.	R.	ER.	SO.	BB.	ERA.
1989—San Francisco	National	3	5	0	0	.000	1	0	0	3	2	0.00

WORLD SERIES RECORD

Year Club	League	G.	IP.	W.	L.	Pct.	H.	R.	ER.	SO.	BB.	ERA.
1989—San Francisco	National	3	4⅓	0	0	.000	5	2	2	1	3	4.15

ALL-STAR GAME RECORD

Year League	IP.	W.	L.	Pct.	H.	R.	ER.	SO.	BB.	ERA.
1990—National	⅓	0	1	.000	2	2	2	0	0	54.00

MICHAEL CHARLES BRANTLEY
(Mickey)

Born June 17, 1961, at Catskill, N.Y.
Height, 5.10. Weight, 187.
Throws and bats righthanded.
Attended Columbia-Greene Community College, Hudson, N.Y., and
Coastal Carolina Community College, Jacksonville, N.C.

Major League stolen bases: 1986 (1), 1987 (13), 1988 (18), 1989 (2). Total—34.
Hit three home runs in a game, September 14, 1987.
Tied for Southern League lead in sacrifice flies with 10 in 1984.

Year Club	League	Pos.	G.	AB.	R.	H.	2B.	3B.	HR.	RBI.	B.A.	PO.	A.	E.	F.A.
1983—Bakersfield	Calif.	OF	53	185	33	55	9	3	6	29	.297	59	3	1	.984
1984—Chattanooga	South.	OF-3B	131	472	73	149	21	9	11	76	.316	211	14	8	.966
1984—Salt Lake City	P. C.	OF	4	17	2	4	0	0	0	1	.235	8	0	0	1.000
1985—Calgary†	P. C.	OF	74	279	52	68	13	6	11	45	.244	165	1	3	.982
1986—Calgary	P. C.	OF	106	396	*104	126	18	4	30	92	.318	201	9	4	.981
1986—Seattle	Amer.	OF	27	102	12	20	3	2	3	7	.196	54	3	1	.983
1987—Seattle‡	Amer.	OF	92	351	52	106	23	2	14	54	.302	163	3	3	.982
1987—Calgary	P. C.	OF	13	50	13	12	0	1	2	6	.240	6	1	1	.875
1988—Seattle	Amer.	OF	149	577	76	152	25	4	15	56	.263	327	5	6	.982
1989—Seattle	Amer.	OF	34	108	14	17	5	0	0	8	.157	50	1	0	1.000
1989—Calgary	P. C.	OF	49	178	33	44	12	3	4	21	.247	97	5	1	.990
1990—Calgary§x	P. C.	OF	29	103	17	24	3	0	1	8	.233	52	0	2	.963
1990—Denver	A. A.	OF	20	72	14	19	3	2	2	10	.264	37	1	0	1.000
Major League Totals—4 Years			302	1138	154	295	56	8	32	125	.259	594	12	10	.984

Selected by Cincinnati Reds' organization in 8th round of free-agent draft, June 7, 1982.
Selected by Seattle Mariners' organization in 2nd round of free-agent draft, June 6, 1983.
†On disabled list, August 20 to September 9, 1985.
‡On disabled list, April 19 to June 4, 1987; included rehabilitation disability assignment to Calgary, May 9 to May 29, 1987.
§On Seattle disabled list, April 6 to April 15, 1990.
xTraded to Denver (Milwaukee Brewers' organization) for Third Baseman Frank Bolick, June 6, 1990.

SIDNEY EUGENE BREAM
(Sid)

Born August 3, 1960, at Carlisle, Pa.
Height, 6.04. Weight, 220.
Throws and bats lefthanded.
Attended Liberty Baptist College, Lynchburg, Va.

Holds National League record for most assists by first baseman, season (166), 1986.

Major League stolen bases: 1984 (1), 1986 (13), 1987 (9), 1988 (9), 1990 (8). Total—40.
Led National League first basemen in total chances with 1,503 in 1986.
Led Pacific Coast League first basemen in total chances with 1,411 in 1983 and 1,200 in 1984.
Led Pacific Coast League first basemen in double plays with 106 in 1984.

Year	Club	League	Pos.	G.	AB.	R.	H.	2B.	3B.	HR.	RBI.	B.A.	PO.	A.	E.	F.A.
1981—Vero Beach	Fla. St.	1B	70	260	35	85	12	5	1	47	.327	613	45	10	.985
1982—Vero Beach	Fla. St.	1B	63	226	41	70	13	5	4	43	.310	523	40	5	.991
1982—San Antonio	Texas	1B	70	259	43	83	18	0	8	50	.320	621	40	12	.982
1982—Albuquerque	P. C.	1B	3	8	3	3	1	0	1	2	.375	11	0	0	1.000
1983—Albuquerque	P. C.	1B	138	485	115	149	23	4	●32	★118	.307	1264	★123	24	.983
1983—Los Angeles	Nat.	1B	15	11	0	2	0	0	0	2	.182	8	0	0	1.000
1984—Albuquerque	P. C.	1B	114	429	82	147	25	4	20	90	.343	1071	★112	17	.986
1984—Los Angeles	Nat.	1B	27	49	2	9	3	0	0	6	.184	95	11	0	1.000
1985—L.A.†-Pitt.	Nat.	1B	50	148	18	34	7	0	6	21	.230	367	35	3	.993
1985—Albuquerque	P. C.	1B-OF	85	297	51	110	25	3	17	57	.370	381	51	2	.995
1986—Pittsburgh	Nat.	★1B-OF	154	522	73	140	37	5	16	77	.268	1320	★166	★17	.989
1987—Pittsburgh	Nat.	1B	149	516	64	142	25	3	13	65	.275	1236	127	★17	.988
1988—Pittsburgh	Nat.	1B	148	462	50	122	37	0	10	65	.264	1118	★140	6	.995
1989—Pittsburgh‡	Nat.	1B	19	36	3	8	3	0	0	4	.222	111	7	1	.992
1990—Pittsburgh§	Nat.	1B	147	389	39	105	23	2	15	67	.270	971	104	8	.993
Major League Totals—8 Years			709	2133	249	562	135	10	60	307	.263	5226	590	52	.991

Selected by Los Angeles Dodgers' organization in 2nd round of free-agent draft, June 8, 1981.

†Traded with Outfielder Cecil Espy, September 9, 1985, completing deal in which Los Angeles Dodgers acquired Third Baseman Bill Madlock for three players to be named later, August 31, 1985. Pittsburgh Pirates acquired Outfielder R. J. Reynolds as partial completion of deal, September 3, 1985.

‡On disabled list, April 16 to May 9 and May 29, 1989 through remainder of season

§Granted free agency, November 5, 1990; signed by Atlanta Braves, December 5, 1990.

CHAMPIONSHIP SERIES RECORD

Year	Club	League	Pos.	G.	AB.	R.	H.	2B.	3B.	HR.	RBI.	B.A.	PO.	A.	E.	F.A.
1990—Pittsburgh	Nat.	1B-PH	4	8	1	4	1	0	1	3	.500	26	3	0	1.000

GEORGE HOWARD BRETT

Born May 15, 1953, at Glen Dale, W. Va.
Height, 6.00. Weight, 200.
Throws right and bats lefthanded.
Attended Longview Community College, Lee's Summit, Mo. and
El Camino College, Torrance, Calif.
Brother of Ken Brett, pitcher with Boston, Milwaukee, Philadelphia, Pittsburgh, New York AL,
Chicago AL, California, Minnesota, Los Angeles and Kansas City, 1967 and 1969 through 1981;
and manager of Utica (Co-op) in New York-Pennsylvania League, 1985;
John Brett, third baseman in Boston Red Sox' organization, 1968;
and Bob Brett, outfielder in Kansas City Royals' organization, 1972.

Holds major league record for most consecutive games, three or more hits, season (6), May 8 through 13, 1976.
Shares major league records for most consecutive seasons leading major league in triples (2), 1975 and 1976; most home runs, month of October (4), 1985.
Holds American League record for fewest putouts by third baseman for leader in most putouts, season (140), 1976.
Became sixth major-league player to collect 20 or more doubles, triples and home runs in one season, 1979.
Hit three home runs in a game, July 22, 1979 and April 20, 1983.
Hit for the cycle, May 28, 1979 and July 25, 1990.
Major League stolen bases: 1974 (8), 1975 (13), 1976 (21), 1977 (14), 1978 (23), 1979 (17), 1980 (15), 1981 (14), 1982 (6), 1985 (9), 1986 (1), 1987 (6), 1988 (14), 1989 (14), 1990 (9). Total—184.
Led American League in intentional bases on balls received with 31 in 1985 and 18 in 1986.
Led American League in slugging percentage with .664 in 1980, .563 in 1983 and .585 in 1985.
Led American League in total bases with 298 in 1976.
Led American League third basemen in double plays with 33 in 1985.
Led American League third basemen in assists with 373, errors with 30 and total chances with 532 in 1979.
Led American League third baseman in putouts with 140 in 1976.
Led California League in sacrifice hits with 8 in 1972.
Led California League third basemen in assists with 172 in 1972.
Named Man of the Year by THE SPORTING NEWS, 1980.
Named Major League Player of the Year by THE SPORTING NEWS, 1980.
Named American League Player of the Year by THE SPORTING NEWS, 1980.
Named American League Most Valuable Player by Baseball Writers' Association of America, 1980.
Named first baseman on THE SPORTING NEWS American League All-Star Team, 1988.
Named third baseman on THE SPORTING NEWS American League All-Star Team, 1976, 1979 and 1980.
Named third baseman on THE SPORTING NEWS American League All-Star fielding team, 1985.
Named first baseman on THE SPORTING NEWS American League Silver Slugger Team, 1988.
Named third baseman on THE SPORTING NEWS Silver Slugger team, 1980 and 1985.

Year	Club	League	Pos.	G.	AB.	R.	H.	2B.	3B.	HR.	RBI.	B.A.	PO.	A.	E.	F.A.
1971—Billings	Pion.	SS-3B	68	258	44	75	8	5	5	44	.291	87	140	28	.890
1972—San Jose†	Calif.	★3-S-2	117	431	66	118	13	5	10	68	.274	101	213	★30	.913
1973—Omaha	A. A.	3B-OF	117	405	66	115	16	4	8	64	.284	92	219	26	.923
1973—Kansas City	Amer.	3B	13	40	2	5	2	0	0	0	.125	9	28	1	.974
1974—Omaha	A. A.	3B	16	64	9	17	2	0	2	14	.266	8	31	4	.907
1974—Kansas City	Amer.	3B-SS	133	457	49	129	21	5	2	47	.282	102	279	21	.948
1975—Kansas City	Amer.	●3B-SS	159	★634	84	★195	35	●13	11	89	.308	132	356	●26	.949
1976—Kansas City	Amer.	3B-SS	159	★645	94	★215	34	★14	7	67	★.333	146	350	26	.950
1977—Kansas City	Amer.	3B-SS	139	564	105	176	32	13	22	88	.312	115	325	21	.954
1978—Kansas City‡	Amer.	3B-SS	128	510	79	150	★45	8	9	62	.294	104	289	16	.961

Year	Club	League	Pos.	G.	AB.	R.	H.	2B.	3B.	HR.	RBI.	B.A.	PO.	A.	E.	F.A.
1979—Kansas City		Amer.	3B-1B	154	645	119	★212	42	★20	23	107	.329	176	378	31	.947
1980—Kansas City§		Amer.	3B-1B	117	449	87	175	33	9	24	118	★.390	107	256	17	.955
1981—Kansas City		Amer.	3B	89	347	42	109	27	7	6	43	.314	74	170	14	.946
1982—Kansas City		Amer.	3B-OF	144	552	101	166	32	9	21	82	.301	130	295	17	.962
1983—Kansas City x		Amer.	3B-1B-OF	123	464	90	144	38	2	25	93	.310	210	192	25	.941
1984—Kansas City y		Amer.	3B	104	377	42	107	21	3	13	69	.284	59	201	14	.949
1985—Kansas City		Amer.	3B	155	550	108	184	38	5	30	112	.335	107	★339	15	.967
1986—Kansas City		Amer.	3B-SS	124	441	70	128	28	4	16	73	.290	97	218	16	.952
1987—Kansas City z		Amer.	1B-3B	115	427	71	124	18	2	22	78	.290	805	69	9	.990
1988—Kansas City		Amer.	1B-SS	157	589	90	180	42	3	24	103	.306	1126	70	10	.992
1989—Kansas City a		Amer.	1B-OF	124	457	67	129	26	3	12	80	.282	898	80	2	.998
1990—Kansas City		Amer.	1B-OF-3B	142	544	82	179	●45	7	14	87	★.329	880	67	7	.993
Major League Totals—18 Years				2279	8692	1382	2707	559	127	281	1398	.311	5277	3962	288	.970

Selected by Kansas City Royals' organization in 2nd round of free-agent draft, June 8, 1971.
†On disabled list, April 29 to May 11, 1972.
‡On disabled list, May 4 to May 19 and July 27 to August 14, 1978.
§On disabled list, June 11 to July 10, 1980.
xOn disabled list, June 8 to June 29, 1983.
yOn disabled list, April 1 to May 18, 1984.
zOn disabled list, April 20 to May 13 and May 16 to June 12, 1987.
aOn disabled list, April 30 to June 10, 1989.

DIVISION SERIES RECORD

Year	Club	League	Pos.	G.	AB.	R.	H.	2B.	3B.	HR.	RBI.	B.A.	PO.	A.	E.	F.A.
1981—Kansas City		Amer.	3B	3	12	0	2	0	0	0	0	.167	1	6	1	.876

CHAMPIONSHIP SERIES RECORD

Holds Championship Series records for highest slugging average, 50 or more at-bats (.728), most runs (22), triples (4), home runs (9), total bases (75), long hits (18), total series; most total bases, game (12), October 6, 1978.

Shares Championship Series records for most runs, game (4), October 11, 1985; most home runs, game (3), October 6, 1978; most triples (2), 1977, game-winning RBIs (2) and bases on balls (7), 1985, series; most game-winning RBIs, total series (3).

Holds American League Championship Series record for highest slugging average, series (1.056), 1978.

Shares American League Championship Series records for most home runs, series (3), 1978 and 1985; most long hits, game (3), October 6, 1978 and October 11, 1985.

Year	Club	League	Pos.	G.	AB.	R.	H.	2B.	3B.	HR.	RBI.	B.A.	PO.	A.	E.	F.A.
1976—Kansas City		Amer.	3B	5	18	4	8	1	1	1	5	.444	3	7	3	.769
1977—Kansas City		Amer.	3B	5	20	2	6	0	2	0	2	.300	5	12	2	.895
1978—Kansas City		Amer.	3B	4	18	7	7	1	1	3	3	.389	3	8	1	.917
1980—Kansas City		Amer.	3B	3	11	3	3	1	0	2	4	.273	2	7	0	1.000
1984—Kansas City		Amer.	3B	3	13	0	3	0	0	0	0	.231	2	7	0	1.000
1985—Kansas City		Amer.	3B	7	23	6	8	2	0	3	5	.348	7	8	2	.882
Championship Series Totals—6 Years				27	103	22	35	5	4	9	19	.340	22	49	8	.899

WORLD SERIES RECORD

Year	Club	League	Pos.	G.	AB.	R.	H.	2B.	3B.	HR.	RBI.	B.A.	PO.	A.	E.	F.A.
1980—Kansas City		Amer.	3B	6	24	3	9	2	1	3	3	.375	4	17	1	.955
1985—Kansas City		Amer.	3B	7	27	5	10	1	0	1	1	.370	10	19	1	.967
World Series Totals—2 Years				13	51	8	19	3	1	1	4	.373	14	36	2	.962

ALL-STAR GAME RECORD

Holds All-Star Game record for most sacrifice flies, lifetime (3).

Year	League	Pos.	AB.	R.	H.	2B.	3B.	HR.	RBI.	B.A.	PO.	A.	E.	F.A.
1976—American		3B	2	0	0	0	0	0	0	.000	0	1	0	1.000
1977—American		3B	2	0	0	0	0	0	0	.000	2	1	0	1.000
1978—American		3B	3	1	2	1	0	0	2	.667	0	2	0	1.000
1979—American		3B	3	1	0	0	0	0	0	.000	1	2	0	1.000
1981—American		3B	3	0	0	0	0	0	0	.000	0	1	0	1.000
1982—American		3B	2	0	2	0	0	0	0	1.000	0	0	0	.000
1983—American		3B	4	2	2	1	1	0	1	.500	1	5	0	1.000
1984—American		3B	3	1	1	0	0	1	1	.333	3	0	0	1.000
1985—American		3B	1	0	0	0	0	0	1	.000	2	1	0	1.000
1988—American		PH	1	0	0	0	0	0	0	.000	0	0	0	.000
All-Star Game Totals—10 Years			24	5	7	2	1	1	5	.292	9	13	0	1.000

Named to American League All-Star Team in 1980 game; replaced due to injury.
Named to American League All-Star Team for 1986 game; replaced due to injury by Brook Jacoby.
Named to American League All-Star Team for 1987 game; replaced due to injury by Kevin Seitzer.

RODNEY LEE BREWER
(Rod)

Born February 24, 1966, at Zellwood, Fla.
Height, 6.03. Weight, 210.
Throws and bats lefthanded.
Attended University of Florida, Gainesville, Fla.

Led American Association first basemen in total chances with 1,292 and double plays with 118 in 1990.
Led Appalachian League in intentional bases on balls received with 5 in 1987.

Led Midwest League first basemen in double plays with 106 in 1988.
Led Appalachian League first basemen in putouts with 554 and total chances with 605 in 1987.
Named first baseman on THE SPORTING NEWS College Baseball All-America Team, 1987.

Year Club	League	Pos.	G.	AB.	R.	H.	2B.	3B.	HR.	RBI.	B.A.	PO.	A.	E.	F.A.
1987—Johnson City	Appal.	*1B-OF	67	238	33	60	11	2	10	42	.252	557	*45	6	*.990
1988—Springfield	Midw.	1B	133	457	57	136	25	2	8	64	.298	*1249	78	10	*.993
1989—Arkansas................	Texas	1B	128	470	71	130	25	2	10	93	.277	1084	97	●12	.990
1990—Louisville	A. A.	*1B-P	●144	514	60	129	15	5	12	83	.251	*1153	*126	13	.990
1990—St. Louis................	Nat.	1B	14	25	4	6	1	0	0	2	.240	46	6	1	.981
Major League Totals—1 Year................			14	25	4	6	1	0	0	2	.240	46	6	1	.981

Selected by Toronto Blue Jays' organization in 25th round of free-agent draft, June 4, 1984.
Selected by St. Louis Cardinals' organization in 5th round of free-agent draft, June 2, 1987.

PITCHING RECORD

Year Club	League	G.	IP.	W.	L.	Pct.	H.	R.	ER.	SO.	BB.	ERA.
1990—Louisville	Am. Assoc.	1	1	0	0	.000	0	0	0	0	0	0.00

GREGORY BRILEY
(Greg)

Born May 24, 1965, at Bethel, N. C.
Height, 5.08. Weight, 165.
Throws right and bats righthanded.
Attended Louisburg College, Louisburg, N. C., and
North Carolina State University, Raleigh, N. C.

Major League stolen bases: 1989 (11), 1990 (16). Total—27.

Year Club	League	Pos.	G.	AB.	R.	H.	2B.	3B.	HR.	RBI.	B.A.	PO.	A.	E.	F.A.
1986—Bellingham	N'west	2B	63	218	52	65	12	●4	7	46	.298	132	146	24	.921
1987—Chattanooga	South.	2B	137	539	81	148	21	5	7	61	.275	221	346	*29	.951
1988—Calgary	P. C.	OF-2B	112	445	74	139	29	9	11	66	.312	237	132	15	.961
1988—Seattle..................	Amer.	OF	13	36	6	9	2	0	1	4	.250	13	0	1	.929
1989—Seattle..................	Amer.	OF-2B	115	394	52	105	22	4	13	52	.266	197	38	9	.963
1989—Calgary	P. C.	3B-2B-OF	25	94	27	32	8	1	4	20	.340	22	44	5	.930
1990—Seattle..................	Amer.	OF	125	337	40	83	18	2	5	29	.246	177	4	2	.989
Major League Totals—3 Years................			253	767	98	197	42	6	19	85	.257	387	42	12	.973

Selected by Los Angeles Dodgers' organization in 3rd round of free-agent draft, January 9, 1985.
Selected by Cleveland Indians' organization in secondary phase of free-agent draft, June 3, 1985.
Selected by Seattle Mariners' organization in secondary phase of free-agent draft, June 2, 1986.

MARIO DIONISIO BRITO

Born April 9, 1966, at Bonao, Dominican Republic.
Height, 6.03. Weight, 185.
Throws and bats righthanded.

Year Club	League	G.	IP.	W.	L.	Pct.	H.	R.	ER.	SO.	BB.	ERA.
1986—Bradenton Expos	Gulf Coast	11	59⅓	5	3	.625	58	29	27	40	24	4.10
1987—Jamestown.......................	NYP	15	95⅓	6	5	.545	83	50	32	89	40	3.02
1988—Rockford............................	Midwest	27	186	13	8	.619	161	83	62	144	52	3.00
1989—West Palm Beach	Florida St.	23	149⅓	11	8	.579	134	64	48	90	49	2.89
1990—Jacksonville....................................	Southern	18	115⅔	9	7	.563	100	57	41	49	34	3.19

Signed as free agent by Montreal Expos' organization, March 2, 1985.

GREGORY ALLEN BROCK
(Greg)

Born June 14, 1957, at McMinnville, Ore.
Height, 6.03. Weight, 205.
Throws right and bats lefthanded.
Attended University of Wyoming, Laramie, Wyo.
Brother of Eric Brock, shortstop in Los Angeles Dodgers' organization, 1983 and 1984.

Major League stolen bases: 1983 (5), 1984 (8), 1985 (4), 1986 (2), 1987 (5), 1988 (6), 1989 (6), 1990 (4). Total—40.
Led Pacific Coast League in bases on balls received with 105 and intentional bases on balls received with 15 in 1982.
Led Pioneer League in bases on balls received with 54 in 1979.
Led Pacific Coast League first basemen in double plays with 106 in 1982.

Year Club	League	Pos.	G.	AB.	R.	H.	2B.	3B.	HR.	RBI.	B.A.	PO.	A.	E.	F.A.
1979—Lethbridge	Pion.	1B	66	247	61	88	18	2	16	77	.356	543	*36	8	*.986
1980—Lodi	Calif.	1B	121	418	72	125	19	3	*29	95	.299	906	*79	5	*.995
1981—San Antonio..........	Texas	1B	128	499	86	147	25	3	*32	106	.295	1071	*90	9	.992
1982—Albuquerque	P. C.	1B	135	480	118	149	21	8	44	138	.310	*1076	*106	*20	.983
1982—Los Angeles	Nat.	1B	18	17	1	2	1	0	0	1	.118	9	0	0	1.000
1983—Los Angeles	Nat.	1B	146	455	64	102	14	2	20	66	.224	1162	106	12	.991
1984—Los Angeles†	Nat.	1B	88	271	33	61	6	0	14	34	.225	703	65	4	.995
1984—Albuquerque	P. C.	1B-3B	24	93	19	29	7	0	6	15	.312	134	38	11	.940
1985—Los Angeles	Nat.	1B	129	438	64	110	19	0	21	66	.251	1113	84	7	.994
1986—Los Angeles‡§.......	Nat.	1B	115	325	33	76	13	0	16	52	.234	726	87	3	.996
1987—Milwaukee x	Amer.	1B	141	532	81	159	29	3	13	85	.299	1065	109	8	.993
1988—Milwaukee y	Amer.	1B	115	364	53	77	16	1	6	50	.212	915	102	7	.993

Year	Club	League	Pos.	G.	AB.	R.	H.	2B.	3B.	HR.	RBI.	B.A.	PO.	A.	E.	F.A.
1989—Beloit z	Midw.	1B	16	52	10	18	2	0	2	10	.346	80	8	2	.978
1989—Milwaukee	Amer.	1B	107	373	40	99	16	0	12	52	.265	850	58	5	.995
1990—Milwaukee	Amer.	1B	123	367	42	91	23	0	7	50	.248	885	63	5	.995
National League Totals—5 Years			496	1506	195	351	53	2	71	219	.233	3713	342	26	.994
American League Totals—4 Years			486	1636	216	426	84	4	38	237	.260	3715	332	25	.994
Major League Totals—9 Years			982	3142	411	777	137	6	109	456	.247	7428	674	51	.994

Selected by Los Angeles Dodgers' organization in 13th round of free-agent draft, June 5, 1979.
†On disabled list, May 12 to June 7, 1984.
‡On disabled list, June 19 to July 10, 1986.
§Traded to Milwaukee Brewers for Pitchers Tim Leary and Tim Crews, December 10, 1986.
xOn disabled list, June 12 to June 27, 1987.
yOn disabled list, June 7 to July 23, 1988.
zOn Milwaukee disabled list, April 2 to May 31, 1989; included rehabilitation disability assignment to Beloit, May 10 to May 28, 1989.

CHAMPIONSHIP SERIES RECORD

Year	Club	League	Pos.	G.	AB.	R.	H.	2B.	3B.	HR.	RBI.	B.A.	PO.	A.	E.	F.A.
1983—Los Angeles	Nat.	1B	3	9	1	0	0	0	0	0	.000	13	0	0	1.000
1985—Los Angeles	Nat.	1B-PH	5	12	2	1	0	0	1	2	.083	35	4	0	1.000
Championship Series Totals—2 Years			8	21	3	1	0	0	1	2	.048	48	4	0	1.000

THOMAS DALE BROOKENS
(Tom)

Born August 10, 1953, at Chambersburg, Pa.
Height, 5.10. Weight, 170.
Throws and bats righthanded.
Attended Mansfield State College, Mansfield, Pa.
Twin brother of Tim Brookens, infielder-outfielder in Detroit Tigers' organization, 1975 through 1978; cousin of Ike Brookens, pitcher with Detroit Tigers, 1975.

Shares American League record for most errors by third baseman, game (4), September 6, 1980.
Major League stolen bases: 1979 (10), 1980 (13), 1981 (5), 1982 (5), 1983 (10), 1984 (6), 1985 (14), 1986 (11), 1987 (7), 1988 (4), 1989 (1). Total—86.
Tied for American League lead in errors by third basemen with 23 in 1985.

Year	Club	League	Pos.	G.	AB.	R.	H.	2B.	3B.	HR.	RBI.	B.A.	PO.	A.	E.	F.A.
1975—Montgomery	South.	SS	100	329	37	73	11	2	7	36	.222	139	298	31	.934
1976—Montgomery	South.	2B	137	492	76	127	22	5	11	56	.258	310	★389	★25	.965
1977—Evansville	A. A.	3B-2B	118	440	70	127	22	5	8	52	.289	132	250	25	.939
1978—Evansville†	A. A.	3B-2B-1B	65	206	27	58	11	1	6	25	.282	76	100	20	.898
1979—Evansville	A. A.	3B-2B	77	265	51	81	23	2	14	46	.306	71	166	16	.937
1979—Detroit	Amer.	3B-2B	60	190	23	50	5	2	4	21	.263	76	141	11	.952
1980—Detroit	Amer.	★3-2-S	151	509	64	140	25	9	10	66	.275	127	307	★29	.937
1981—Detroit‡	Amer.	3B	71	239	19	58	10	1	4	25	.243	58	139	10	.952
1982—Detroit	Amer.	3-2-S-O	140	398	40	92	15	3	9	58	.231	119	276	20	.952
1983—Detroit	Amer.	3B-SS-2B	138	332	50	71	13	3	6	32	.214	97	254	22	.941
1984—Detroit§	Amer.	3B-SS-2B	113	224	32	55	11	4	5	26	.246	98	187	12	.960
1985—Detroit x	Amer.	3-S-2-C	156	485	54	115	34	6	7	47	.237	135	277	24	.944
1986—Detroit	Amer.	3-2-S-O	98	281	42	76	11	2	3	25	.270	106	144	7	.973
1987—Detroit y	Amer.	3B-SS-2B	143	444	59	107	15	3	13	59	.241	119	256	19	.952
1988—Detroit	Amer.	3B-SS-2B	136	441	62	107	23	5	5	38	.243	101	235	17	.952
1989—New York zab	Amer.	3-S-2-O	66	168	14	38	6	0	4	14	.226	27	85	7	.941
1990—Cleveland cd	Amer.	3-2-S-1	64	154	18	41	7	2	1	20	.266	57	104	6	.964
Major League Totals—12 Years			1336	3865	477	950	175	40	71	431	.246	1120	2405	184	.950

Selected by Detroit Tigers' organization in 1st round (fourth player selected) of free-agent draft, January 9, 1975.
†On disabled list, April 14 to May 9 and June 4 to June 21, 1978.
‡On disabled list, March 30 to May 4, 1981.
§On disabled list, August 19 to September 4, 1984.
xGranted free agency, November 12, 1985; re-signed by Tigers, January 8, 1986.
yGranted free agency, January 22, 1988; re-signed by Tigers, February 9, 1988.
zTraded to New York Yankees for Pitcher Charles Hudson, March 23, 1989.
aOn disabled list, July 29 to September 6, 1989.
bReleased, November 20, 1989; signed by Cleveland Indians, December 8, 1989.
cOn disabled list, May 14 to May 29, 1990.
dGranted free agency, November 5, 1990.

CHAMPIONSHIP SERIES RECORD

Year	Club	League	Pos.	G.	AB.	R.	H.	2B.	3B.	HR.	RBI.	B.A.	PO.	A.	E.	F.A.
1984—Detroit	Amer.	2B-3B	2	2	0	0	0	0	0	0	.000	0	2	1	.667
1987—Detroit	Amer.	3B	5	13	0	0	0	0	0	0	.000	3	15	0	1.000
Championship Series Totals—2 Years			7	15	0	0	0	0	0	0	.000	3	17	1	.952

WORLD SERIES RECORD

Year	Club	League	Pos.	G.	AB.	R.	H.	2B.	3B.	HR.	RBI.	B.A.	PO.	A.	E.	F.A.
1984—Detroit	Amer.	PH-3B	3	3	0	0	0	0	0	0	.000	0	3	0	1.000

—DID YOU KNOW—
That Cincinnati's Herm Winningham and the Cubs' Shawon Dunston tied a major league record with three-triple games in 1990?

HUBERT BROOKS JR.
(Hubie)

Born September 24, 1956, at Los Angeles, Calif.
Height, 6.00. Weight, 205.
Throws and bats righthanded.
Attended Mesa Community College, Mesa, Ariz., and received bachelor of science
degree in health science from Arizona State University, Tempe, Ariz.
Grandson of Leandrus Brooks, player with Philadelphia of Negro National League; and
cousin of Donnie Moore, pitcher with Chicago Cubs, St. Louis Cardinals,
Milwaukee Brewers, Atlanta Braves and California Angels, 1975 and 1977 through 1988.

Major League stolen bases: 1980 (1), 1981 (9), 1982 (6), 1983 (6), 1984 (6), 1985 (6), 1986 (4), 1987 (4), 1988 (7), 1989 (6),
1990 (2). Total—57.
Led International League in game-winning RBIs with 12 in 1980.
Named shortstop on THE SPORTING NEWS National League Silver Slugger team, 1985 and 1986.
Named shortstop on THE SPORTING NEWS College Baseball All-America Team, 1978.
Named outfielder on THE SPORTING NEWS College Baseball All-America Team, 1977.

Year Club	League	Pos.	G.	AB.	R.	H.	2B.	3B.	HR.	RBI.	B.A.	PO.	A.	E.	F.A.
1978—Jackson	Texas	SS-OF-3B	45	153	19	33	8	1	3	16	.216	49	84	14	.905
1979—Jackson	Texas	3B-SS	112	406	68	124	21	2	3	28	.305	92	218	29	.942
1979—Tidewater	Int.	SS-3B-OF	5	15	1	6	1	0	1	3	.400	4	8	1	.923
1980—Tidewater	Int.	OF-3B-SS	113	417	50	124	18	5	3	50	.297	152	90	18	.931
1980—New York	Nat.	3B	24	81	8	25	2	1	1	10	.309	16	40	2	.966
1981—New York	Nat.	*3-O-S	98	358	34	110	21	2	4	38	.307	67	193	*21	.925
1982—New York†	Nat.	3B	126	457	40	114	21	2	2	40	.249	89	237	24	.931
1983—New York	Nat.	3B-2B	150	586	53	147	18	4	5	58	.251	116	303	21	.952
1984—New York‡	Nat.	3B-SS	153	561	61	159	23	2	16	73	.283	112	284	29	.932
1985—Montreal	Nat.	SS	156	605	67	163	34	7	13	100	.269	203	441	28	.958
1986—Montreal §	Nat.	SS	80	306	50	104	18	5	14	58	.340	116	222	15	.958
1987—Montreal x	Nat.	SS	112	430	57	113	22	3	14	72	.263	131	271	20	.953
1988—Montreal	Nat.	OF	151	588	61	164	35	2	20	90	.279	261	8	9	.968
1989—Montreal y	Nat.	OF	148	542	56	145	30	1	14	70	.268	234	6	9	.964
1990—Los Angeles z	Nat.	OF	153	568	74	151	28	1	20	91	.266	255	9	10	.964
Major League Totals—11 Years			1351	5082	561	1395	252	30	123	700	.274	1600	2014	188	.951

Selected by Montreal Expos' organization in 19th round of free-agent draft, June 5, 1974.
Selected by Kansas City Royals' organization in secondary phase of free-agent draft, January 7, 1976.
Selected by Chicago White Sox' organization in secondary phase of free-agent draft, June 8, 1976.
Selected by Oakland A's organization in secondary phase of free-agent draft, January 11, 1977.
Selected by Chicago White Sox' organization in secondary phase of free-agent draft, June 7, 1977.
Selected by New York Mets' organization in 1st round (third player selected) of free-agent draft, June 6, 1978.
†On disabled list, June 28 to July 22, 1982.
‡Traded with Catcher Mike Fitzgerald, Outfielder Herm Winningham and Pitcher Floyd Youmans to Montreal
Expos for Catcher Gary Carter, December 10, 1984.
§On disabled list, August 2, 1986 through remainder of season.
xOn disabled list, April 11 to May 25, 1987.
yGranted free agency, November 13, 1989; signed by Los Angeles Dodgers, December 21, 1989.
zTraded to New York Mets for Pitchers Bob Ojeda and Greg Hansell, December 15, 1990.

ALL-STAR GAME RECORD

Year League	Pos.	AB.	R.	H.	2B.	3B.	HR.	RBI.	B.A.	PO.	A.	E.	F.A.
1986—National	PH-SS	2	1	0	0	0	0	0	.000	1	0	0	1.000
1987—National	SS	3	1	1	0	0	0	0	.333	1	2	0	1.000
All-Star Game Totals—2 Years		5	2	1	0	0	0	0	.200	2	2	0	1.000

SCOTT DAVID BROSIUS

Born August 15, 1966, at Hillsboro, Ore.
Height, 6.01. Weight, 185.
Throws and bats righthanded.
Attended Linfield College, McMinnville, Ore.

Led Southern League in total bases with 274 in 1990.
Led Northwest League in sacrifice flies with 7 in 1987.

Year Club	League	Pos.	G.	AB.	R.	H.	2B.	3B.	HR.	RBI.	B.A.	PO.	A.	E.	F.A.
1987—Medford	N'west	3-S-2-1	65	255	34	73	18	1	3	49	.286	123	148	38	.877
1988—Madison	Midw.	S-3-O-1	132	504	82	153	28	2	9	58	.304	151	305	61	.882
1989—Huntsville	South.	2-3-S-1	128	461	68	125	22	2	7	60	.271	225	316	34	.941
1990—Huntsville	South.	SS-2B-3B	●142	547	94	*162	*39	2	23	88	.296	253	419	41	.942
1990—Tacoma	P. C.	2B	3	7	2	1	0	1	0	0	.143	3	5	0	1.000

Selected by Oakland Athletics' organization in 20th round of free-agent draft, June 2, 1987.

TERRENCE PAUL BROSS
(Terry)

Born March 30, 1966, at El Paso, Tex.
Height, 6.09. Weight, 234.
Throws and bats righthanded.
Attended St. John's University, Jamaica, N.Y.

Led Texas League in saves with 28 and games finished in relief with 48 in 1990.

Year Club	League	G.	IP.	W.	L.	Pct.	H.	R.	ER.	SO.	BB.	ERA.
1987—Little Falls................	NYP	10	28	2	0	1.000	22	23	12	21	20	3.86
1988—Little Falls................	NYP	20	55⅓	2	1	.667	43	25	19	59	38	3.09
1989—St. Lucie†	Florida St.	35	58	8	2	●.800	39	21	18	47	26	2.79
1990—Jackson	Texas	58	71⅔	3	4	.429	46	21	21	51	40	2.64

Selected by New York Mets' organization in 13th round of free-agent draft, June 2, 1987.
†On disabled list, May 31 to June 29, 1989.

JAMES KEVIN BROWN

(Known by middle name.)
Born March 14, 1965, at McIntyre, Ga.
Height, 6.04. Weight, 195.
Throws and bats righthanded.
Attended Georgia Tech, Atlanta, Ga.

Named as righthanded pitcher on THE SPORTING NEWS College Baseball All-America Team, 1986.

Year Club	League	G.	IP.	W.	L.	Pct.	H.	R.	ER.	SO.	BB.	ERA.
1986—Sarasota Rangers..............	Gulf Coast	3	6	0	0	.000	7	4	4	1	2	6.00
1986—Tulsa....................................	Texas	3	10	0	0	.000	9	7	5	10	5	4.50
1986—Texas..................................	American	1	5	1	0	1.000	6	2	2	4	0	3.60
1987—Tulsa....................................	Texas	8	42	1	4	.200	53	36	34	26	18	7.29
1987—Oklahoma City	Am. Assoc.	5	24⅓	0	5	.000	32	32	29	9	17	10.73
1987—Port Charlotte..................	Florida St.	6	36⅓	0	2	.000	33	14	11	21	17	2.72
1988—Tulsa....................................	Texas	26	174⅓	12	10	.545	174	94	68	118	61	3.51
1988—Texas..................................	American	4	23⅓	1	1	.500	33	15	11	12	8	4.24
1989—Texas..................................	American	28	191	12	9	.571	167	81	71	104	70	3.35
1990—Texas††............................	American	26	180	12	10	.545	175	84	72	88	60	3.60
Major League Totals—4 Years............................		59	399⅓	26	20	.565	381	182	156	208	138	3.52

Selected by Texas Rangers' organization in 1st round (fourth player selected) of free-agent draft, June 2, 1986.
†On disabled list, August 14 to August 29, 1990.
‡Made an out in only appearance as pinch-hitter.

KEITH EDWARD BROWN

Born February 14, 1964, at Flagstaff, Ariz.
Height, 6.04. Weight, 210.
Throws right and bats left and righthanded.
Attended College of the Siskiyous, Weed, Calif.,
and California State University, Sacramento, Calif.

Year Club	League	G.	IP.	W.	L.	Pct.	H.	R.	ER.	SO.	BB.	ERA.
1986—Sarasota Reds	Gulf Coast	7	47⅓	4	1	.800	29	15	5	26	5	0.95
1986—Billings	Pioneer	4	21⅓	2	0	1.000	18	6	5	14	7	2.11
1986—Vermont..........................	Eastern	4	14	1	1	.500	12	10	8	11	8	5.14
1987—Cedar Rapids................	Midwest	17	124⅓	13	4	.765	91	28	22	86	27	*1.59
1988—Chattanooga	Southern	10	69⅔	9	1	*.900	47	11	11	34	20	1.42
1988—Nashville.........................	Am. Assoc.	12	85⅓	6	3	.667	72	33	18	43	28	1.90
1988—Cincinnati.......................	National	4	16⅓	2	1	.667	14	5	5	6	4	2.76
1989—Nashville.........................	Am. Assoc.	29	161⅓	8	13	.381	171	99	86	85	51	4.80
1990—Nashville.........................	Am. Assoc.	39	94⅓	7	8	.467	83	37	25	50	24	2.39
1990—Cincinnati.......................	National	8	11⅓	0	0	.000	12	6	6	8	3	4.76
Major League Totals—2 Years............................		12	27⅔	2	1	.667	26	11	11	14	7	3.58

Selected by Cincinnati Reds' organization in 21st round of free-agent draft, June 2, 1986.

KEVIN DEWAYNE BROWN

Born March 5, 1966, at Oroville, Calif.
Height, 6.01. Weight, 185.
Throws and bats lefthanded.
Attended Sacramento City College, Sacramento, Calif.

Year Club	League	G.	IP.	W.	L.	Pct.	H.	R.	ER.	SO.	BB.	ERA.
1986—Idaho Falls......................	Pioneer	12	68	3	6	.333	65	48	38	44	41	5.03
1987—Sumter............................	S. Atlantic	9	56	7	1	.875	53	14	12	45	19	1.93
1987—Durham†.........................	Carolina	13	72⅔	4	4	.500	78	46	42	48	42	5.20
1988—St. Lucie	Florida St.	20	134	5	7	.417	96	42	27	113	37	*1.81
1988—Jackson	Texas	5	32⅔	1	2	.333	24	9	8	24	11	2.20
1989—Jackson	Texas	8	51⅔	5	2	.714	51	15	13	40	11	2.26
1989—Tidewater........................	Int'national	13	75	6	6	.500	81	41	37	46	31	4.44
1990—Tidewater........................	Int'national	26	134⅓	10	6	.625	138	71	53	109	60	3.55
1990—New York‡......................	National	2	2	0	0	.000	2	0	0	0	1	0.00
1990—Milwaukee......................	American	5	21	1	1	.500	14	7	6	12	7	2.57
National League Totals—1 Year.........................		2	2	0	0	.000	2	0	0	0	1	0.00
American League Totals—1 Year......................		5	21	1	1	.500	14	7	6	12	7	2.57
Major League Totals—1 Year.........................		7	23	1	1	.500	16	7	6	12	8	2.35

Selected by Kansas City Royals' organization in 4th round of free-agent draft, January 9, 1985.
Selected by Philadelphia Phillies' organization in secondary phase of free-agent draft, June 3, 1985.
Selected by Atlanta Braves' organization in secondary phase of free-agent draft, January 14, 1986.
†Traded to New York Mets, December 8, 1987, to complete deal in which Atlanta Braves acquired Outfielder Terry Blocker for a player to be named later, November 11, 1987.

‡Traded with Pitcher Julio Machado to Milwaukee Brewers, September 7, 1990, as partial completion of deal in which Milwaukee traded Catcher Charlie O'Brien and a player to be named later to New York Mets for two players to be named later, August 30, 1990; New York acquired Pitcher Kevin Carmody to complete deal, September 11, 1990.

MARTY LEO BROWN

Born January 23, 1963, at Lawton, Okla.
Height, 6.01. Weight, 195.
Throws and bats righthanded.
Attended Crowder College, Neosho, Mo., and
University of Georgia, Athens, Ga.

Tied for Midwest League lead in caught stealing with 20 in 1986.
Led Eastern League third basemen in assists with 234 and fielding percentage with .957 in 1987.
Led Pioneer League first basemen in assists with 49 in 1985.

Year Club	League	Pos.	G.	AB.	R.	H.	2B.	3B.	HR.	RBI.	B.A.	PO.	A.	E.	F.A.
1985—Billings	Pion.	1B-OF	68	248	50	84	21	3	10	45	.339	592	50	10	.985
1986—Cedar Rapids	Midw.	3B-1B	●139	508	85	152	19	8	18	83	.299	86	249	40	.893
1987—Vermont	East.	3B-1B	134	470	69	124	17	5	15	74	.264	132	237	14	.963
1988—Nashville	A. A.	3B-OF-SS	135	484	50	128	15	4	7	55	.264	93	227	22	.936
1988—Cincinnati	Nat.	3B	10	16	0	3	1	0	0	2	.188	1	9	0	1.000
1989—Nashville	A. A.	3-O-1-S	120	422	61	103	21	2	12	46	.244	202	162	28	.929
1989—Cincinnati†	Nat.	3B	16	30	2	5	1	0	0	4	.167	2	19	2	.913
1990—Baltimore	Amer.	2B-3B	9	15	1	3	0	0	0	0	.200	1	3	0	1.000
1990—Rochester	Int.	I-O-C-P	67	211	32	51	8	4	5	25	.242	144	83	11	.954
National League Totals—2 Years			26	46	2	8	2	0	0	6	.174	3	28	2	.939
American League Totals—1 Year			9	15	1	3	0	0	0	0	.200	1	3	0	1.000
Major League Totals—3 Years			35	61	3	11	2	0	0	6	.180	4	31	2	.946

Selected by Cincinnati Reds' organization in 12th round of free-agent draft, June 3, 1985.
†Drafted by Baltimore Orioles, December 4, 1989.

PITCHING RECORD

Year Club	League	G.	IP.	W.	L.	Pct.	H.	R.	ER.	SO.	BB.	ERA.
1990—Rochester	Int'national	1	1	0	0	.000	0	0	0	2	1	0.00

JEROME A. BROWNE
(Jerry)

Born February 13, 1966, at St. Croix, Virgin Islands.
Height, 5.10. Weight, 170.
Throws right and bats left and righthanded.

Holds American League record for fewest double plays, second baseman, season, 150 or more games (67), 1989.
Major League stolen bases: 1987 (27), 1988 (7), 1989 (14), 1990 (12). Total—60.
Led Texas League second basemen in fielding percentage with .984 in 1986.
Led Carolina League second basemen in total chances with 675 in 1985.

Year Club	League	Pos.	G.	AB.	R.	H.	2B.	3B.	HR.	RBI.	B.A.	PO.	A.	E.	F.A.
1983—Sarasota Rangers	Gulf C.	2B	48	181	34	51	2	2	0	20	.282	92	123	14	.939
1984—Burlington	Midw.	SS-2B	127	420	70	99	10	1	0	18	.236	231	311	43	.926
1985—Salem	Carol.	2B	122	460	69	123	18	4	3	58	.267	★265	★390	20	.970
1986—Tulsa	Texas	2B-SS	128	491	82	149	15	7	2	57	.303	282	307	19	.969
1986—Texas	Amer.	2B	12	24	6	10	2	0	0	3	.417	9	15	2	.923
1987—Texas†	Amer.	2B	132	454	63	123	16	6	1	38	.271	258	338	12	.980
1988—Texas	Amer.	2B	73	214	26	49	9	2	1	17	.229	112	139	11	.958
1988—Oklahoma City‡	A. A.	2B	76	286	45	72	15	2	5	34	.252	190	231	10	.977
1989—Cleveland	Amer.	2B	153	598	83	179	31	4	5	45	.299	305	380	15	.979
1990—Cleveland	Amer.	2B	140	513	92	137	26	5	6	50	.267	286	382	10	.985
Major League Totals—5 Years			510	1803	270	498	84	17	13	153	.276	970	1254	50	.978

Signed as free agent by Texas Rangers' organization, March 3, 1983.
†On disabled list, August 24 to September 8, 1987.
‡Traded with First Baseman Pete O'Brien and Outfielder Oddibe McDowell to Cleveland Indians for Second Baseman Julio Franco, December 6, 1988.

THOMAS LEO BROWNING
(Tom)

Born April 28, 1960, at Casper, Wyo.
Height, 6.01. Weight, 190.
Throws and bats lefthanded.
Attended Tennessee Wesleyan College, Athens, Tenn., and
Le Moyne College, Syracuse, N.Y.

Pitched 1-0 perfect game against Los Angeles Dodgers, September 16, 1988.
Pitched seven-inning, 2-0 no-hit victory against Iowa, July 31, 1984.
Led National League in home runs allowed with 36 in 1988 and 31 in 1989.
Led National League pitchers in games started with 37 in 1989 and tied for lead with 39 in 1986, 36 in 1988 and 35 in 1990.
Tied for American Association lead in home runs allowed with 24 in 1984.
Named National League Rookie Pitcher of the Year by THE SPORTING NEWS, 1985.

Year Club	League	G.	IP.	W.	L.	Pct.	H.	R.	ER.	SO.	BB.	ERA.
1982—Billings	Pioneer	14	88	4	●8	.333	96	53	38	⋆87	41	3.89
1983—Tampa	Florida St.	11	78⅔	8	1	.889	53	19	13	101	36	1.49
1983—Waterbury	Eastern	18	117⅓	4	10	.286	100	62	46	101	63	3.53
1984—Wichita	Am. Assoc.	30	189⅓	12	10	.545	169	88	83	⋆160	73	3.95
1984—Cincinnati	National	3	23⅓	1	0	1.000	27	4	4	14	5	1.54
1985—Cincinnati	National	38	261⅓	20	9	.690	242	111	103	155	73	3.55
1986—Cincinnati	National	39	243⅓	14	13	.519	225	123	103	147	70	3.81
1987—Cincinnati	National	32	183	10	13	.435	201	107	102	117	61	5.02
1987—Nashville	Am. Assoc.	5	29⅔	2	3	.400	37	22	20	28	12	6.07
1988—Cincinnati	National	36	250⅔	18	5	.783	205	98	95	124	64	3.41
1989—Cincinnati	National	37	249⅔	15	12	.556	241	109	94	118	64	3.39
1990—Cincinnati†	National	35	227⅔	15	9	.625	235	98	96	99	52	3.80
Major League Totals—7 Years		220	1439	93	61	.604	1376	650	597	774	389	3.73

Selected by Cincinnati Reds' organization in 9th round of free-agent draft, June 7, 1982.
†Granted free agency, November 5, 1990; re-signed by Reds, November 21, 1990.

CHAMPIONSHIP SERIES RECORD

Year Club	League	G.	IP.	W.	L.	Pct.	H.	R.	ER.	SO.	BB.	ERA.
1990—Cincinnati	National	2	11	1	1	.500	9	4	4	5	6	3.27

WORLD SERIES RECORD

Year Club	League	G.	IP.	W.	L.	Pct.	H.	R.	ER.	SO.	BB.	ERA.
1990—Cincinnati	National	1	6	1	0	1.000	6	3	3	2	2	4.50

ANTHONY MICHAEL BRUMLEY
(Mike)

Born April 9, 1963, at Oklahoma City, Okla.
Height, 5.10. Weight, 165.
Throws right and bats left and righthanded.
Attended University of Texas, Austin, Tex.
Son of Mike Brumley, catcher with Washington Senators, 1964 through 1966.

Major League stolen bases: 1987 (7) 1989 (8), 1990 (2). Total—17.
Led American Association shortstops in total chances with 597 in 1986.

Year Club	League	Pos.	G.	AB.	R.	H.	2B.	3B.	HR.	RBI.	B.A.	PO.	A.	E.	F.A.
1983—Winter Haven	Fla. St.	SS-OF	44	153	25	48	6	4	1	18	.314	51	92	20	.877
1984—New Britain†	East.	OF-SS	34	121	14	28	6	2	0	9	.231	71	6	6	.928
1984—Midland	Texas	OF	73	255	37	55	11	3	6	21	.216	128	4	5	.964
1985—Pittsfield	East.	SS-OF	131	460	66	127	23	⋆14	3	58	.276	182	333	33	.940
1986—Iowa	A. A.	SS	139	458	74	103	21	5	10	44	.225	177	⋆400	20	.966
1987—Iowa	A. A.	SS-2B-OF	92	319	44	81	20	5	6	42	.254	147	240	24	.942
1987—Chicago‡	Nat.	SS-2B	39	104	8	21	2	2	1	9	.202	43	93	5	.965
1988—Las Vegas§	P. C.	S-O-3-2	113	425	77	134	16	7	3	41	.315	139	322	28	.943
1989—Detroit	Amer.	S-2-3-O	92	212	33	42	5	2	1	11	.198	80	160	12	.952
1989—Toledo xy	Int.	SS	8	26	4	6	2	2	0	1	.231	9	14	2	.920
1990—Seattle z	Amer.	S-2-3-O	62	147	19	33	5	4	0	7	.224	63	123	5	.974
1990—Calgary a	P. C.	SS	8	28	4	9	1	0	0	1	.321	13	23	2	.947
National League Totals—1 Year			39	104	8	21	2	2	1	9	.202	43	93	5	.965
American League Totals—2 Years			154	359	52	75	10	6	1	18	.209	143	283	17	.962
Major League Totals—3 Years			193	463	60	96	12	8	2	27	.207	186	376	22	.962

Selected by Philadelphia Phillies' organization in 16th round of free-agent draft, June 3, 1980.
Selected by Boston Red Sox' organization in 2nd round of free-agent draft, June 6, 1983.
†Traded with Pitcher Dennis Eckersley to Chicago Cubs for First Baseman-Outfielder Bill Buckner, May 25, 1984.
‡Traded with Infielder Keith Moreland to San Diego Padres for Pitchers Rich Gossage and Ray Hayward, February 12, 1988.
§Traded to Detroit Tigers for Infielder Luis Salazar, March 23, 1989.
xTraded to Baltimore Orioles for Designated Hitter Larry Sheets, January 10, 1990.
yReleased, April 3, 1990; signed by Seattle Mariners, April 6, 1990.
zOn disabled list, June 6 to July 11, 1990; included rehabilitation disability assignment to Calgary, July 4 to July 11, 1990.
aReleased, September 27, 1990.

THOMAS ANDREW BRUNANSKY
(Tom)

Born August 20, 1960, at Covina, Calif.
Height, 6.04. Weight, 216.
Throws and bats righthanded.
Attended California State Poly University, Pomona, Calif.
Brother-in-law of Dave Engle, catcher with Minnesota Twins,
Detroit Tigers, Montreal Expos and Milwaukee Brewers, 1981 through 1989.

Major League stolen bases: 1981 (1), 1982 (1), 1983 (2), 1984 (4), 1985 (5), 1986 (12), 1987 (11), 1988 (17), 1989 (5), 1990 (5). Total—63.
Hit three home runs in a game, September 29, 1990.
Led American League outfielders in double plays with 8 in 1983 and 6 in 1984.
Tied for Texas League lead in double plays by outfielders with 4 in 1980.
Received reported $100,000 bonus to sign with California Angels, 1978.

Year	Club	League	Pos.	G.	AB.	R.	H.	2B.	3B.	HR.	RBI.	B.A.	PO.	A.	E.	F.A.
1978—Idaho Falls	Pioneer	OF	48	190	55	63	14	4	6	45	.332	85	1	8	.915
1979—Salinas	Calif.	OF	*140	485	85	131	23	1	23	76	.270	279	11	6	.980
1980—El Paso	Texas	OF	128	495	103	160	24	8	24	97	.323	306	17	*14	.958
1980—Salt Lake City	P. C.	OF	9	32	7	11	2	2	1	8	.344	28	1	0	1.000
1981—Salt Lake City†	P. C.	OF	96	343	61	114	17	10	22	81	.332	250	14	5	.981
1981—California	Amer.	OF	11	33	7	5	0	0	3	6	.152	27	3	2	.938
1982—Spokane‡	P. C.	OF	25	88	12	18	6	1	1	6	.205	44	7	1	.981
1982—Minnesota	Amer.	OF	127	463	77	126	30	1	20	46	.272	343	8	5	.986
1983—Minnesota	Amer.	OF	151	542	70	123	24	5	28	82	.227	375	16	6	.985
1984—Minnesota	Amer.	OF	155	567	75	144	21	0	32	85	.254	304	13	5	.984
1985—Minnesota	Amer.	OF	157	567	71	137	28	4	27	90	.242	300	14	5	.984
1986—Minnesota	Amer.	OF	157	593	69	152	28	1	23	75	.256	315	10	6	.982
1987—Minnesota	Amer.	OF	155	532	83	138	22	2	32	85	.259	273	10	3	.990
1988—Minnesota§	Amer.	OF	14	49	5	9	1	0	1	6	.184	19	0	3	.864
1988—St. Louis	Nat.	OF	143	523	69	128	22	4	22	79	.245	267	10	1	*.996
1989—St. Louis	Nat.	OF-1B	158	556	67	133	29	3	20	85	.239	291	9	7	.977
1990—St. Louis x	Nat.	OF	19	57	5	9	3	0	1	2	.158	37	1	2	.950
1990—Boston y	Amer.	OF	129	461	61	123	24	5	15	71	.267	267	7	5	.982
American League Totals—9 Years			1056	3807	518	957	178	18	181	546	.251	2223	81	40	.983
National League Totals—3 Years			320	1136	141	270	54	7	43	166	.238	595	20	10	.984
Major League Totals—10 Years			1376	4943	659	1227	232	25	224	712	.248	2818	101	50	.983

Selected by California Angels' organization in 1st round (14th player selected) of free-agent draft, June 6, 1978.

†On disabled list, August 8 to August 31, 1981.

‡Traded with Pitcher Mike Walters and cash to Minnesota Twins for Pitcher Doug Corbett and Second Baseman Rob Wilfong, May 12, 1982.

§Traded to St. Louis Cardinals for Second Baseman Tom Herr, April 22, 1988.

xTraded to Boston Red Sox for Pitcher Lee Smith, May 4, 1990.

yGranted free agency, November 5, 1990; re-signed by Red Sox, December 19, 1990.

CHAMPIONSHIP SERIES RECORD

Shares Championship Series records for most doubles (4) and long hits (6), series, 1987.

Year	Club	League	Pos.	G.	AB.	R.	H.	2B.	3B.	HR.	RBI.	B.A.	PO.	A.	E.	F.A.
1987—Minnesota	Amer.	OF	5	17	5	7	4	0	2	9	.412	10	0	0	1.000
1990—Boston	Amer.	OF	4	12	0	1	0	0	0	1	.083	13	0	0	1.000
Major League Totals—2 Years			9	29	5	8	4	0	2	10	.276	23	0	0	1.000

WORLD SERIES RECORD

Year	Club	League	Pos.	G.	AB.	R.	H.	2B.	3B.	HR.	RBI.	B.A.	PO.	A.	E.	F.A.
1987—Minnesota	Amer.	OF	7	25	5	5	0	0	0	2	.200	14	0	0	1.000

ALL-STAR GAME RECORD

Year	League	Pos.	AB.	R.	H.	2B.	3B.	HR.	RBI.	B.A.	PO.	A.	E.	F.A.
1985—American		OF	1	0	0	0	0	0	0	.000	0	0	0	.000

WILLIAM JOSEPH BUCKNER
(Bill)

Born December 14, 1949, at Vallejo, Calif.
Height, 6.01. Weight, 195.
Throws and bats lefthanded.
Attended University of Southern California, Los Angeles, Calif., and
Arizona State University, Tempe, Ariz.
Brother of Jim Buckner, minor league outfielder, 1972 through 1981;
and Bob Buckner, minor league infielder, 1966 through 1970;
and part-time scout with Chicago Cubs, 1977 through 1979.

Holds major league record for most assists, first baseman, season (184), 1985.

Shares major league record for most games, first baseman, season (162), 1985.

Shares National League records for fewest double plays, first baseman, season, 150 or more games (89), 1982; fewest errors by first baseman for leader in errors, season (13), 1983.

Major League stolen bases: 1971 (4), 1972 (10), 1973 (12), 1974 (31), 1975 (8), 1976 (28), 1977 (7), 1978 (7), 1979 (9), 1980 (1), 1981 (5), 1982 (15), 1983 (12), 1984 (2), 1985 (18), 1986 (6), 1987 (2), 1988 (5), 1989 (1). Total—183.

Led Pioneer League first basemen in double plays with 37 in 1968.

Year	Club	League	Pos.	G.	AB.	R.	H.	2B.	3B.	HR.	RBI.	B.A.	PO.	A.	E.	F.A.
1968—Ogden	Pion.	1B	*64	*256	54	*88	10	*8	4	41	*.344	468	28	4	*.992
1969—Albuquerque	Texas	OF-1B	70	257	44	79	7	3	7	50	.307	220	15	3	.987
1969—Spokane	P. C.	OF-1B	36	143	21	45	1	1	2	27	.315	128	12	5	.966
1969—Los Angeles	Nat.	PH	1	1	0	0	0	0	0	0	.000	0	0	0	.000
1970—Spokane	P. C.	1B-OF	111	465	78	156	33	2	3	74	.335	582	22	7	.989
1970—Los Angeles	Nat.	OF-1B	28	68	6	13	3	1	0	4	.191	37	1	0	1.000
1971—Los Angeles	Nat.	OF-1B	108	358	37	99	15	1	5	41	.277	235	11	1	.996
1972—Los Angeles	Nat.	OF-1B	105	383	47	122	14	3	5	37	.319	434	22	4	.991
1973—Los Angeles	Nat.	1B-OF	140	575	68	158	20	0	8	46	.275	981	50	3	.997
1974—Los Angeles	Nat.	OF-1B	145	580	83	182	30	3	7	58	.314	284	5	7	.976
1975—Los Angeles†	Nat.	OF	92	288	30	70	11	2	6	31	.243	138	4	2	.986
1976—Los Angeles‡	Nat.	OF-1B	154	642	76	193	28	4	7	60	.301	315	7	5	.985
1977—Chicago§	Nat.	1B	122	426	40	121	27	0	11	60	.284	966	58	10	.990
1978—Chicago x	Nat.	1B	117	446	47	144	26	1	5	74	.323	1075	83	6	.995
1979—Chicago	Nat.	1B	149	591	72	168	34	7	14	66	.284	1258	124	7	.995

Year Club	League	Pos.	G.	AB.	R.	H.	2B.	3B.	HR.	RBI.	B.A.	PO.	A.	E.	F.A.
1980—Chicago	Nat.	1B-OF	145	578	69	187	41	3	10	68	★.324	916	78	8	.992
1981—Chicago	Nat.	1B	106	421	45	131	★35	3	10	75	.311	996	81	★17	.984
1982—Chicago	Nat.	1B	161	★657	93	201	34	5	15	105	.306	1547	★159	12	.993
1983—Chicago	Nat.	★●1B-OF	153	626	79	175	●38	6	16	66	.280	1391	★161	●13	.992
1984—Chicago y	Nat.	1B-OF	21	43	3	9	0	0	0	2	.209	71	6	0	1.000
1984—Boston	Amer.	1B	114	439	51	122	21	2	11	67	.278	974	96	●15	.986
1985—Boston	Amer.	1B	162	673	89	201	46	3	16	110	.299	1384	★184	12	.992
1986—Boston	Amer.	1B	153	629	73	168	39	2	18	102	.267	1067	★157	14	.989
1987—Bos. za-Cal.	Amer.	1B	132	469	39	134	18	2	5	74	.286	640	60	6	.992
1988—Cal.b-K.C.c	Amer.	1B	108	285	19	71	14	0	3	43	.249	161	13	1	.994
1989—Kansas City d	Amer.	1B	79	176	7	38	4	1	1	16	.216	181	13	3	.985
1990—Boston e	Amer.	1B	22	43	4	8	0	0	1	3	.186	75	6	0	1.000
National League Totals—16 Years			1747	6683	795	1973	356	39	119	793	.295	10644	850	95	.992
American League Totals—7 Years			770	2714	282	742	142	10	55	415	.273	4482	529	51	.990
Major League Totals—22 Years			2517	9397	1077	2715	498	49	174	1208	.289	15126	1379	146	.991

Selected by Los Angeles Dodgers' organization in 2nd round of free-agent draft, June 7, 1968.
†On disabled list, April 21 to May 12, 1975.
‡Traded with Infielder Ivan DeJesus and Pitcher Jeff Albert to Chicago Cubs for Outfielder Rick Monday and Pitcher Mike Garman, January 11, 1977.
§On disabled list, March 28 to April 19, 1977.
xOn disabled list, June 22 to July 7, 1978.
yTraded to Boston Red Sox for Pitcher Dennis Eckersley and Outfielder Mike Brumley, May 25, 1984.
zOn disabled list, June 10 to June 26, 1987.
aReleased, July 23, 1987; signed by California Angels, July 28, 1987.
bReleased, May 9, 1988; signed by Kansas City Royals, May 13, 1988.
cGranted free agency, November 4, 1988; re-signed by Royals, December 6, 1988.
dGranted free agency, November 13, 1989; signed by Pawtucket (Boston Red Sox' organization), February 15, 1990.
eReleased, June 5, 1990.

CHAMPIONSHIP SERIES RECORD

Year Club	League	Pos.	G.	AB.	R.	H.	2B.	3B.	HR.	RBI.	B.A.	PO.	A.	E.	F.A.
1974—Los Angeles	Nat.	OF	4	18	0	3	1	0	0	0	.167	6	0	0	1.000
1986—Boston	Amer.	1B	7	28	3	6	1	0	0	3	.214	49	5	0	1.000
Championship Series Totals—2 Years			11	46	3	9	2	0	0	3	.196	55	5	0	1.000

WORLD SERIES RECORD

Year Club	League	Pos.	G.	AB.	R.	H.	2B.	3B.	HR.	RBI.	B.A.	PO.	A.	E.	F.A.
1974—Los Angeles	Nat.	OF	5	20	1	5	1	0	1	1	.250	11	0	0	1.000
1986—Boston	Amer.	1B	7	32	2	6	0	0	0	1	.188	53	7	1	.984
World Series Totals—2 Years			12	52	3	11	1	0	1	2	.212	64	7	1	.986

ALL-STAR GAME RECORD

Year League	Pos.	AB.	R.	H.	2B.	3B.	HR.	RBI.	B.A.	PO.	A.	E.	F.A.
1981—National	PH	1	0	0	0	0	0	0	.000	0	0	0	.000

STEVEN BERNARD BUECHELE

Name pronounced BOO-shell.

(Steve)

Born September 26, 1961, at Lancaster, Calif.
Height, 6.02. Weight, 200.
Throws and bats righthanded.
Attended Stanford University, Stanford, Calif.

Major League stolen bases: 1985 (3), 1986 (5), 1987 (2), 1988 (2), 1989 (1), 1990 (1). Total—14.
Named American Association Most Valuable Player, 1985.

Year Club	League	Pos.	G.	AB.	R.	H.	2B.	3B.	HR.	RBI.	B.A.	PO.	A.	E.	F.A.
1982—Tulsa	Texas	2B-3B	62	213	21	63	12	2	5	33	.296	111	174	8	.973
1983—Tulsa	Texas	2B-3B	117	437	62	121	12	4	14	62	.277	182	259	18	.961
1983—Oklahoma City	A. A.	2B-3B	9	34	6	9	5	0	1	4	.265	17	22	1	.975
1984—Oklahoma City	A. A.	2B-3B	131	447	48	118	25	3	7	59	.264	236	329	17	.971
1985—Oklahoma City	A. A.	3B-2B	89	350	56	104	20	7	9	64	.297	84	170	7	.973
1985—Texas	Amer.	3B-2B	69	219	22	48	6	3	6	21	.219	52	138	6	.969
1986—Texas	Amer.	3B-2B-OF	153	461	54	112	19	2	18	54	.243	174	292	12	.975
1987—Texas	Amer.	3B-2B-OF	136	363	45	86	20	0	13	50	.237	89	211	9	.971
1988—Texas	Amer.	3B-2B	155	503	68	126	21	4	16	58	.250	114	300	16	.963
1989—Texas	Amer.	3B-2B-SS	155	486	60	114	22	2	16	59	.235	128	288	12	.972
1990—Texas†‡	Amer.	3B-2B	91	251	30	54	10	0	7	30	.215	72	160	8	.967
1990—Oklahoma City	A. A.	3B	6	21	1	3	0	0	1	1	.143	4	15	0	1.000
Major League Totals—6 Years			759	2283	279	540	98	11	76	272	.237	629	1389	63	.970

Selected by Chicago White Sox' organization in 1st round (ninth player selected) of free-agent draft, June 5, 1979.
Selected by Texas Rangers' organization in 5th round of free-agent draft, June 7, 1982.
†On disabled list, April 22 to May 25 and June 18 to July 20, 1990; included rehabilitation disability assignment to Oklahoma City, July 16 to July 20, 1990.
‡On suspended list, August 24 to August 27, 1990.

JAY CAMPBELL BUHNER

Born August 13, 1964, at Louisville, Ky.
Height, 6.03. Weight, 205.
Throws and bats righthanded.
Attended McLennan Community College, Waco, Tex.

Shares major league records for most strikeouts, two consecutive nine-inning games (8), August 23, 24, 1990; most strikeouts, three consecutive games (10), August 23, 24, 25, 1990.
Major League stolen bases: 1988 (1), 1989 (1), 1990 (2). Total—4.
Led Florida State League in game-winning RBIs with 15 in 1985.
Tied for International League lead in double plays by outfielders with 6 in 1987.

Year Club	League	Pos.	G.	AB.	R.	H.	2B.	3B.	HR.	RBI.	B.A.	PO.	A.	E.	F.A.
1984—Watertown†	NYP	OF	65	229	43	74	16	3	9	●58	.323	106	8	1	.991
1985—Fort Lauderdale ..	Fla. St.	OF	117	409	65	121	18	10	11	76	.296	235	12	7	.972
1986—Fort Lauderdale‡	Fla. St.	OF	36	139	24	42	9	1	7	31	.302	84	7	3	.968
1987—Columbus.............	Int.	OF	134	502	83	140	23	1	★31	85	.279	275	★20	6	.980
1987—New York.............	Amer.	OF	7	22	0	5	2	0	0	1	.227	11	1	0	1.000
1988—Columbus.............	Int.	OF	38	129	26	33	5	0	8	18	.256	83	3	1	.989
1988—N.Y.§-Sea.	Amer.	OF	85	261	36	56	13	1	13	38	.215	186	9	3	.985
1989—Calgary	P. C.	OF	56	196	43	61	12	1	11	45	.311	97	8	2	.981
1989—Seattle x................	Amer.	OF	58	204	27	56	15	1	9	33	.275	106	6	4	.966
1990—Calgary y..............	P. C.	OF	13	34	6	7	1	0	2	5	.206	14	1	0	1.000
1990—Seattle...................	Amer.	OF	51	163	16	45	12	0	7	33	.276	55	1	2	.966
Major League Totals—4 Years...............			201	650	79	162	42	2	29	105	.249	358	17	9	.977

Selected by Atlanta Braves' organization in 9th round of free-agent draft, June 6, 1983.
Selected by Pittsburgh Pirates' organization in secondary phase of free-agent draft, January 17, 1984.
†Traded with Infielder Dale Berra and Pitcher Alfonso Pulido to New York Yankees for Outfielder Steve Kemp, Infielder Tim Foli and $800,000, December 20, 1984.
‡On disabled list, April 11 to July 28, 1986.
§Traded with Pitcher Rich Balabon and a player to be named later to Seattle Mariners for Designated Hitter Ken Phelps, July 21, 1988; Seattle acquired Pitcher Troy Evers to complete deal, October 12, 1988.
xOn disabled list, June 29 to August 19, 1989; included rehabilitation disability assignment to Calgary, August 16 to August 19, 1989.
yOn Seattle disabled list, March 31 to June 1 and June 17 to August 23, 1990, included rehabilitation disability assignment to Calgary, May 18 to June 1, 1990.

ERIC JERALD BULLOCK

Born February 16, 1960, at Los Angeles, Calif.
Height, 5.11. Weight, 185.
Throws and bats lefthanded.
Attended Los Angeles Harbor Junior College, Woodland Hills, Calif.
and California State University, Fullerton, Calif.
Son of Eddie Bullock, minor league outfielder, 1955.

Major League stolen bases: 1986 (2), 1988 (1). Total—3.
Led Pacific Coast League in stolen bases with 51 and caught stealing with 18 in 1988.
Tied for Pacific Coast League lead in being hit by pitch with 7 in 1985.

Year Club	League	Pos.	G.	AB.	R.	H.	2B.	3B.	HR.	RBI.	B.A.	PO.	A.	E.	F.A.
1981—Sarasota Orange..	Gulf C.	OF	56	184	38	54	8	3	1	15	.293	67	6	3	.961
1981—Daytona Beach....	Fla. St.	DH	1	2	1	1	0	0	0	1	.500	0	0	0	.000
1982—Daytona Beach....	Fla. St.	OF	117	442	90	150	24	11	5	●85	.339	180	11	5	.974
1982—Columbus.............	South.	OF	18	66	6	20	1	0	2	13	.303	21	1	0	1.000
1983—Columbus.............	South.	OF	130	475	65	131	15	6	9	59	.276	196	9	3	.986
1984—Columbus.............	South.	OF	71	265	47	77	15	2	3	41	.291	133	3	4	.971
1984—Tucson..................	P. C.	OF	60	185	22	51	6	2	1	16	.276	96	2	5	.951
1985—Tucson..................	P. C.	OF	124	467	81	149	26	8	4	57	.319	199	5	7	.967
1985—Houston	Nat.	OF	18	25	3	7	2	0	0	2	.280	6	0	2	.750
1986—Houston	Nat.	OF	6	21	0	1	0	0	0	1	.048	7	0	1	.875
1986—Tucson†................	P. C.	OF	42	151	28	58	8	2	3	21	.384	73	2	1	.987
1987—Tuc.‡-Port.§..........	P. C.	OF	106	330	42	88	13	6	2	34	.267	145	5	2	.987
1988—Portland..............	P. C.	OF	117	434	69	134	20	8	2	46	.309	211	11	3	★.987
1988—Minnesota x..........	Amer.	OF	16	17	3	5	0	0	0	3	.294	7	0	1	.875
1989—Scr./Wil-Barre y..	Int.	OF	80	281	37	77	10	8	3	40	.274	119	4	1	.992
1989—Philadelphia z......	Nat.	OF	6	4	1	0	0	0	0	0	.000	2	0	0	1.000
1990—Indianapolis..........	A. A.	OF	107	434	62	122	19	7	3	32	.281	185	5	5	.974
1990—Montreal..............	Nat.	PH-PR	4	2	0	1	0	0	0	0	.500	0	0	0	.000
National League Totals—4 Years...........			34	52	4	9	2	0	0	3	.173	15	0	3	.833
American League Totals—1 Year...........			16	17	3	5	0	0	0	3	.294	7	0	1	.875
Major League Totals—5 Years............			50	69	7	14	2	0	0	6	.203	22	0	4	.846

Selected by Los Angeles Dodgers' organization in 18th round of free-agent draft, June 6, 1978.
Selected by San Diego Padres' organization in 1st round (fifth player selected) of free-agent draft, January 13, 1981.
Selected by Houston Astros' organization in secondary phase of free-agent draft, June 8, 1981.
†On disabled list, May 6 to July 7, 1986.
‡Traded to Minnesota Twins' organization for Pitcher Clay Christiansen, June 2, 1987.
§Granted free agency, October 15, 1987; re-signed by Twins' organization, November 7, 1987.
xTraded with Second Baseman Tom Herr and Catcher Tom Nieto to Philadelphia Phillies for Pitcher Shane Rawley and cash, October 24, 1988.
yOn disabled list, April 6 to May 27, 1989.
zGranted free agency, October 15, 1989; signed by Indianapolis (Montreal Expos' organization), March 17, 1990.

DAVID ALLEN BURBA

Born July 7, 1966, at Dayton, O.
Height, 6.04. Weight, 220.
Throws and bats righthanded.
Attended Ohio State University, Columbus, O.
Nephew of Ray Hathaway, pitcher with Brooklyn Dodgers, 1945.

Year Club	League	G.	IP.	W.	L.	Pct.	H.	R.	ER.	SO.	BB.	ERA.
1987—Bellingham	Northwest	5	23⅓	3	1	.750	20	10	5	24	3	1.93
1987—Salinas	California	9	54⅔	1	6	.143	53	31	28	46	29	4.61
1988—San Bernardino	California	20	114	5	7	.417	106	41	34	102	54	2.68
1989—San Bernardino	California	25	156⅔	11	7	.611	138	69	55	89	55	3.16
1990—Calgary	P. Coast	31	113⅔	10	6	.625	124	64	59	47	45	4.67
1990—Seattle	American	6	8	0	0	.000	8	6	4	4	2	4.50
Major League Totals—1 Year		6	8	0	0	.000	8	6	4	4	2	4.50

Selected by Seattle Mariners' organization in 2nd round of free-agent draft, June 2, 1987.

TIMOTHY PHILIP BURKE
(Tim)

Born February 19, 1959, at Omaha, Neb.
Height, 6.03. Weight, 205.
Throws and bats righthanded.
Attended University of Nebraska, Lincoln, Neb.

Holds National League record for most games pitched by rookie, season (78), 1985.
Major League saves: 1985 (8), 1986 (4), 1987 (18), 1988 (18), 1989 (28), 1990 (20). Total—96.

Year Club	League	G.	IP.	W.	L.	Pct.	H.	R.	ER.	SO.	BB.	ERA.
1980—Salem†	Carolina					(Did not play)						
1981—Alexandria	Carolina	23	149	8	10	.444	139	67	57	111	48	3.44
1982—Buffalo‡	Eastern	25	144	7	10	.412	162	93	83	93	57	5.19
1983—Columbus	Eastern	4	12	1	0	1.000	15	9	9	6	8	6.75
1983—Nashville§x	Southern	20	129	12	4	.750	124	63	46	64	37	3.21
1984—Indianapolis	Am. Assoc.	35	180⅔	11	8	.579	192	81	70	108	61	3.49
1985—Montreal	National	★78	120⅓	9	4	.692	86	32	32	87	44	2.39
1986—Montreal	National	68	101⅓	9	7	.563	103	37	33	82	46	2.93
1987—Montreal y	National	55	91	7	0	1.000	64	18	12	58	17	1.19
1988—Montreal	National	61	82	3	5	.375	84	36	31	42	25	3.40
1989—Montreal	National	68	84⅔	9	3	.750	68	24	24	54	22	2.55
1990—Montreal z	National	58	75	3	3	.500	71	29	21	47	21	2.52
Major League Totals—6 Years		388	554⅓	40	22	.645	476	176	153	370	175	2.48

Selected by Pittsburgh Pirates' organization in 2nd round of free-agent draft, June 3, 1980.
†On disabled list, July 12, 1980 through remainder of season.
‡Traded with Catcher John Holland, Infielder Jose Rivera and Outfielder Don Aubin to New York Yankees' organization for Outfielder Lee Mazzilli, December 22, 1982.
§On disabled list, May 4 to May 23, 1983.
xTraded to Montreal Expos' organization for Outfielder Pat Rooney, December 19, 1983.
yOn disabled list, March 28 to April 22, 1987.
zOn disabled list, May 31 to July 12, 1990.

ALL-STAR GAME RECORD

Year League	IP.	W.	L.	Pct.	H.	R.	ER.	SO.	BB.	ERA.
1989—National	2	0	0	.000	2	0	0	1	0	0.00

JOHN DAVID BURKETT

Born November 28, 1964, at New Brighton, Pa.
Height, 6.02. Weight, 210.
Throws and bats righthanded.

Major League saves: 1990 (1).
Tied for Pacific Coast League lead in games started by pitchers with 28 in 1989.

Year Club	League	G.	IP.	W.	L.	Pct.	H.	R.	ER.	SO.	BB.	ERA.
1983—Great Falls	Pioneer	13	50⅓	2	6	.250	73	44	35	38	30	6.26
1984—Clinton	Midwest	20	126⅔	7	6	.538	128	81	61	83	38	4.33
1985—Fresno	California	20	109⅔	7	4	.636	98	43	35	72	46	2.87
1986—Fresno	California	4	24⅔	0	3	.000	34	19	15	14	8	5.47
1986—Shreveport	Texas	22	128⅔	10	6	.625	99	46	38	73	42	2.66
1987—Shreveport	Texas	27	★177⅔	●14	8	.636	181	75	66	126	53	3.34
1987—San Francisco	National	3	6	0	0	.000	7	4	3	5	3	4.50
1988—Phoenix	P. Coast	21	114	5	11	.313	141	79	66	74	49	5.21
1988—Shreveport	Texas	7	50⅔	5	1	.833	33	15	12	34	18	2.13
1989—Phoenix	P. Coast	28	167⅔	10	11	.476	197	111	94	105	59	5.05
1990—Phoenix	P. Coast	3	23	2	1	.667	18	8	7	9	3	2.74
1990—San Francisco	National	33	204	14	7	.667	201	92	86	118	61	3.79
Major League Totals—2 Years		36	210	14	7	.667	208	96	89	123	64	3.81

Selected by San Francisco Giants' organization in 6th round of free-agent draft, June 6, 1983.

ELLIS RENA BURKS

Born September 11, 1964, at Vicksburg, Miss.
Height, 6.02. Weight, 202.
Throws and bats righthanded.
Attended Ranger Junior College, Ranger, Tex.

Shares major league record for most home runs, inning (2), August 27, 1990, fourth inning.
Major League stolen bases: 1987 (27), 1988 (25), 1989 (21), 1990 (9). Total—82.
Tied for Florida State League lead in double plays by outfielders with 6 in 1984.
Named outfielder on THE SPORTING NEWS American League All-Star Team, 1990.
Named outfielder on THE SPORTING NEWS American League All-Star fielding team, 1990.
Named outfielder on THE SPORTING NEWS American League Silver Slugger team, 1990.

Year Club	League	Pos.	G.	AB.	R.	H.	2B.	3B.	HR.	RBI.	B.A.	PO.	A.	E.	F.A.
1983—Elmira	NYP	OF	53	174	30	42	9	0	2	23	.241	89	5	2	.979
1984—Winter Haven	Fla. St.	OF	112	375	52	96	15	4	6	43	.256	196	12	5	.977
1985—New Britain	East.	OF	133	476	66	121	25	7	10	61	.254	306	9	8	.975
1986—New Britain	East.	OF	124	462	70	126	20	3	14	55	.273	318	5	5	.985
1987—Pawtucket	Int.	OF	11	40	11	9	3	1	3	6	.225	25	0	0	1.000
1987—Boston	Amer.	OF	133	558	94	152	30	2	20	59	.272	320	15	4	.988
1988—Boston†	Amer.	OF	144	540	93	159	37	5	18	92	.294	370	9	9	.977
1989—Boston‡	Amer.	OF	97	399	73	121	19	6	12	61	.303	245	7	6	.977
1989—Pawtucket	Int.	OF	5	21	4	3	1	0	0	0	.143	16	0	0	1.000
1990—Boston	Amer.	OF	152	588	89	174	33	8	21	89	.296	324	7	2	.994
Major League Totals—4 Years			526	2085	349	606	119	21	71	301	.291	1259	38	21	.984

Selected by Boston Red Sox' organization in 1st round (20th player selected) of free agent draft, January 11, 1983.
†On disabled list, March 26 to April 12, 1988.
‡On disabled list, June 15 to August 1, 1989; included rehabilitation disability assignment to Pawtucket, July 26 to August 1, 1989.

CHAMPIONSHIP SERIES RECORD

Year Club	League	Pos.	G.	AB.	R.	H.	2B.	3B.	HR.	RBI.	B.A.	PO.	A.	E.	F.A.
1988—Boston	Amer.	OF	4	17	2	4	1	0	0	1	.235	10	0	0	1.000
1990—Boston	Amer.	OF	4	15	1	4	2	0	0	0	.267	9	1	0	1.000
Championship Series Totals—2 Years			8	32	3	8	3	0	0	1	.250	19	1	0	1.000

ALL-STAR GAME RECORD

Named to American League All-Star Team for 1990 game; replaced due to injury by Brook Jacoby.

TODD EDWARD BURNS

Born July 6, 1963, at Maywood, Calif.
Height, 6.02. Weight, 190.
Throws and bats righthanded.
Attended Oral Roberts University, Tulsa, Okla.

Major League saves: 1988 (1), 1989 (8), 1990 (3). Total—12.
Tied for Southern League lead in shutouts with 3 in 1986.

Year Club	League	G.	IP.	W.	L.	Pct.	H.	R.	ER.	SO.	BB.	ERA.
1984—Medford	Northwest	22	36⅓	3	0	1.000	21	4	2	63	12	0.50
1984—Madison	Midwest	10	14	3	2	.600	11	4	4	20	3	2.57
1985—Madison	Midwest	20	123	8	8	.500	109	55	50	94	40	3.66
1985—Huntsville	Southern	4	22⅔	3	1	.750	16	6	3	8	13	1.19
1986—Huntsville	Southern	20	124⅔	7	7	.500	122	59	52	77	39	3.75
1986—Tacoma	P.Coast	11	16⅔	0	1	.000	11	4	4	14	12	2.16
1987—Huntsville	Southern	34	63⅔	3	4	.429	49	24	21	54	17	2.97
1987—Tacoma	P. Coast	21	27⅔	2	2	.500	27	16	15	30	16	4.88
1988—Tacoma	P. Coast	21	73⅓	4	3	.571	74	39	30	59	26	3.68
1988—Oakland	American	17	102⅔	8	2	.800	93	38	36	57	34	3.16
1989—Oakland	American	50	96⅓	6	5	.545	66	27	24	49	28	2.24
1990—Oakland	American	43	78⅔	3	3	.500	78	28	26	43	32	2.97
Major League Totals—3 Years		110	277⅔	17	10	.630	237	93	86	149	94	2.79

Selected by Oakland A's organization in 7th round of free-agent draft, June 4, 1984.

WORLD SERIES RECORD

Year Club	League	G.	IP.	W.	L.	Pct.	H.	R.	ER.	SO.	BB.	ERA.
1988—Oakland	American	1	⅓	0	0	.000	0	0	0	0	0	0.00
1989—Oakland	American	2	1⅔	0	0	.000	1	0	0	0	1	0.00
1990—Oakland	American	2	1⅔	0	0	.000	5	3	3	0	2	16.20
World Series Totals—3 Years		5	3⅔	0	0	.000	6	3	3	0	3	7.36

ROBERT RANDALL BUSH
(Randy)

Born October 5, 1958, at Dover, Del.
Height, 6.01. Weight, 184.
Throws and bats lefthanded.
Attended Miami-Dade Community College (North), Miami, Fla.,
and University of New Orleans, New Orleans, La.

Shares American League record for most home runs by pinch-hitter, consecutive at-bats (2), June 20 and 23, 1986.

Major League stolen bases: 1984 (1), 1985 (3), 1986 (5), 1987 (10), 1988 (8), 1989 (5). Total—32.
Led Southern League in being hit by pitch with 8 in 1979 and 12 in 1981.

Year Club	League	Pos.	G.	AB.	R.	H.	2B.	3B.	HR.	RBI.	B.A.	PO.	A.	E.	F.A.
1979—Orlando	South.	1B	76	243	33	62	12	2	6	34	.255	653	38	13	.982
1980—Toledo†	Int.	OF-1B	40	108	11	21	1	0	1	7	.194	112	6	1	.992
1980—Orlando	South.	1B	51	175	32	41	2	1	7	26	.234	458	28	4	.992
1981—Orlando	South.	OF-1B	136	482	98	140	26	3	22	94	.290	174	7	5	.973
1982—Toledo	Int.	OF	49	160	21	52	14	0	8	27	.325	68	0	1	.986
1982—Minnesota	Amer.	OF	55	119	13	29	6	1	4	13	.244	7	0	0	1.000
1983—Minnesota	Amer.	1B	124	373	43	93	24	3	11	56	.249	21	3	0	1.000
1984—Minnesota	Amer.	1B	113	311	46	69	17	1	11	43	.222	5	0	0	1.000
1985—Minnesota	Amer.	OF-1B	97	234	26	56	13	3	10	35	.239	79	0	2	.975
1986—Minnesota	Amer.	OF-1B	130	357	50	96	19	7	7	45	.269	182	2	4	.979
1987—Minnesota	Amer.	OF-1B	122	293	46	74	10	2	11	46	.253	164	5	4	.977
1988—Minnesota‡	Amer.	OF-1B	136	394	51	103	20	3	14	51	.261	206	5	4	.981
1989—Minnesota	Amer.	OF-1B	141	391	60	103	17	4	14	54	.263	339	14	3	.992
1990—Minnesota§	Amer.	OF-1B	73	181	17	44	8	0	6	18	.243	64	3	0	1.000
1990—Portland x	P. C.	OF	3	9	2	2	2	0	0	1	.222	0	0	0	.000
Major League Totals—9 Years			991	2653	352	667	134	24	88	361	.251	1067	32	17	.985

Selected by Minnesota Twins' organization in 2nd round of free-agent draft, June 5, 1979.
†On disabled list, May 25 to June 27, 1980.
‡Granted free agency, November 4, 1988; re-signed by Twins, December 12, 1988.
§On disabled list, May 19 to July 19 and August 23 to September 7, 1990; included rehabilitation disability assignment to Portland, June 27 to June 30, 1990.
xGranted free agency, November 5, 1990; re-signed by Twins, December 18, 1990.

CHAMPIONSHIP SERIES RECORD

Shares Championship Series record for most stolen bases, inning (2), October 8, 1987, fourth inning.

Year Club	League	Pos.	G.	AB.	R.	H.	2B.	3B.	HR.	RBI.	B.A.	PO.	A.	E.	F.A.
1987—Minnesota	Amer.	DH	4	12	4	3	0	1	0	2	.250	0	0	0	.000

WORLD SERIES RECORD

Year Club	League	Pos.	G.	AB.	R.	H.	2B.	3B.	HR.	RBI.	B.A.	PO.	A.	E.	F.A.
1987—Minnesota	Amer.	DH-PH	4	6	1	1	1	0	0	2	.167	0	0	0	.000

BRETT MORGAN BUTLER

Born June 15, 1957, at Los Angeles, Calif.
Height, 5.10. Weight, 160.
Throws and bats lefthanded.
Attended Arizona State University, Tempe, Ariz., and received bachelor of science degree in
education from Southeastern Oklahoma State University, Durant, Okla., in 1979.

Shares major league records for fewest double plays by outfielder, season, for leader in most double plays (4), 1983; fewest double plays by outfielder, season, 150 or more games (0), 1990.
Shares National League record for fewest assists, outfielder, season, 150 or more games (3), 1988.
Shares modern National League record for most bases on balls, game (5), April 12, 1990.
Major League stolen bases: 1981 (9), 1982 (21), 1983 (39), 1984 (52), 1985 (47), 1986 (32), 1987 (33), 1988 (43), 1989 (31), 1990 (51). Total—358.
Led American League in caught stealing with 22 in 1984 and 20 in 1985.
Tied for National League lead in double plays by outfielders with 4 in 1983.
Led International League in bases on balls received with 103 in 1981.
Named International League Most Valuable Player, 1981.

Year Club	League	Pos.	G.	AB.	R.	H.	2B.	3B.	HR.	RBI.	B.A.	PO.	A.	E.	F.A.
1979—Greenwood	W. Car.	OF	35	117	26	37	2	4	1	11	.316	45	2	0	1.000
1979—Bradenton	Gulf C.	OF	30	111	36	41	7	5	3	20	.369	66	5	0	1.000
1980—Anderson	S. Atl.	OF	70	255	73	76	12	6	1	26	.298	190	5	1	.995
1980—Durham	Carol.	OF	66	224	47	82	15	6	2	39	.366	156	4	3	.982
1981—Richmond	Int.	OF	125	466	★93	156	19	4	3	36	.335	286	15	3	.990
1981—Atlanta	Nat.	OF	40	126	17	32	2	3	0	4	.254	76	2	1	.987
1982—Atlanta	Nat.	OF	89	240	35	52	2	0	0	7	.217	129	2	0	1.000
1982—Richmond	Int.	OF	41	157	22	57	8	3	1	22	.363	101	2	1	.990
1983—Atlanta†	Nat.	OF	151	549	84	154	21	★13	5	37	.281	284	13	4	.987
1984—Cleveland	Amer.	OF	159	602	108	162	25	9	3	49	.269	448	13	4	.991
1985—Cleveland	Amer.	OF	152	591	106	184	28	14	5	50	.311	437	19	1	★.998
1986—Cleveland	Amer.	OF	161	587	92	163	17	★14	4	51	.278	434	9	3	.993
1987—Cleveland‡§	Amer.	OF	137	522	91	154	25	8	9	41	.295	393	4	4	.990
1988—San Francisco	Nat.	OF	157	568	★109	163	27	9	6	43	.287	395	3	5	.988
1989—San Francisco	Nat.	OF	154	594	100	168	22	4	4	36	.283	407	11	6	.986
1990—San Francisco x	Nat.	OF	160	622	108	●192	20	9	3	44	.309	420	4	6	.986
National League Totals—6 Years			751	2699	453	761	94	38	18	171	.282	1711	35	22	.988
American League Totals—4 Years			609	2302	397	663	95	45	21	191	.288	1712	45	12	.993
Major League Totals—10 Years			1360	5001	850	1424	189	83	39	362	.285	3423	80	34	.990

Selected by Atlanta Braves' organization in 23rd round of free-agent draft, June 5, 1979.
†Traded with Infielder Brook Jacoby to Cleveland Indians, October 21, 1983, completing deal in which Atlanta Braves acquired Pitcher Len Barker for three players to be named later, August 28, 1983. Cleveland acquired Pitcher Rick Behenna as partial completion of deal, September 2, 1983.
‡On disabled list, April 11 to April 30, 1987.
§Granted free agency, November 9, 1987; signed by San Francisco Giants, December 1, 1987.
xGranted free agency, December 7, 1990; signed by Los Angeles Dodgers, December 14, 1990.

Year Club	League	Pos.	G.	AB.	R.	H.	2B.	3B.	HR.	RBI.	B.A.	PO.	A.	E.	F.A.
1982—Atlanta	Nat.	OF-PH	2	1	0	0	0	0	0	0	.000	0	0	0	.000
1989—San Francisco	Nat.	OF	5	19	6	4	0	0	0	0	.211	9	0	0	1.000
Championship Series Totals—2 Years.....			7	20	6	4	0	0	0	0	.200	9	0	0	1.000

WORLD SERIES RECORD

Year Club	League	Pos.	G.	AB.	R.	H.	2B.	3B.	HR.	RBI.	B.A.	PO.	A.	E.	F.A.
1989—San Francisco	Nat.	OF	4	14	1	4	1	0	0	1	.286	9	0	0	1.000

FRANCISCO CABRERA (PAULINO)

Born October 10, 1966, at Santo Domingo, D.R.
Height, 6.04. Weight, 195.
Throws and bats righthanded.

Major League stolen bases: 1990 (1).
Led International League in sacrifice flies with 8 in 1989.
Tied for New York-Pennsylvania League lead in game-winning RBIs with 10 in 1986.
Led International League in passed balls with 13 in 1989.
Led Southern League catchers in total chances with 874 and tied for lead in double plays with 6 in 1988.
Led South Atlantic League catchers in total chances with 959 in 1987.

Year Club	League	Pos.	G.	AB.	R.	H.	2B.	3B.	HR.	RBI.	B.A.	PO.	A.	E.	F.A.
1986—Ventura County ...	Calif.	C	6	12	2	2	1	0	0	3	.167	26	3	1	.967
1986—St. Catherines	NYP	C	68	246	31	73	13	2	6	35	.297	449	50	6	.988
1987—Myrtle Beach	S. Atl.	C	129	449	61	124	27	1	14	72	.276	★849	89	●21	.978
1988—Dunedin	Fla. St.	C	9	35	2	14	4	0	1	9	.400	74	9	3	.965
1988—Knoxville	South.	C	119	429	59	122	19	1	20	54	.284	★783	★68	★230	.974
1989—Syr.-Rich.	Int.	★C-1B	116	434	59	130	31	5	9	72	.300	554	35	★12	.980
1989—Toronto†	Amer.	DH	3	12	1	2	1	0	0	0	.167	0	0	0	.000
1989—Atlanta	Nat.	C-1B	4	14	0	3	2	0	0	0	.214	27	1	1	.966
1990—Richmond.............	Int.	1B-C-OF	35	132	12	30	3	1	7	20	.227	269	25	4	.987
1990—Atlanta	Nat.	1B-C	63	137	14	38	5	1	7	25	.277	269	19	3	.990
American League Totals—1 Year			3	12	1	2	1	0	0	0	.167	0	0	0	.000
National League Totals—2 Years............			67	151	14	41	7	1	7	25	.272	296	20	4	.988
Major League Totals—2 Years.................			70	163	15	43	8	1	7	25	.264	296	20	4	.988

Signed as free agent by Toronto Blue Jays' organization, February 28, 1986.

†Traded to Atlanta Braves' organization, August 24, 1989, completing deal in which Atlanta traded Pitcher Jim Acker to Toronto Blue Jays for Pitcher Tony Castillo and a player to be named later, August 24, 1989.

GREGORY JAMES CADARET

Name pronounced CAD-uh-ray.

(Greg)

Born February 27, 1962, at Detroit, Mich.
Height, 6.03. Weight, 214.
Throws and bats lefthanded.
Attended Grand Valley State College, Allendale, Mich.

Major League saves: 1988 (3), 1990 (3). Total—6.

Year Club	League	G.	IP.	W.	L.	Pct.	H.	R.	ER.	SO.	BB.	ERA.
1983—Medford..	Northwest	12	64	7	3	.700	73	36	31	51	36	4.36
1984—Modesto..	California	26	171⅓	13	8	.619	162	79	58	138	82	3.05
1985—Huntsville..	Southern	17	82⅓	3	7	.300	96	61	56	60	57	6.12
1985—Modesto..	California	12	61⅓	3	9	.250	59	50	40	43	54	5.87
1986—Huntsville..	Southern	28	141⅓	12	5	.706	166	106	85	110	98	5.41
1987—Huntsville..	Southern	24	40⅓	5	2	.714	31	16	13	48	20	2.90
1987—Tacoma..	P. Coast	7	13	1	2	.333	5	6	5	12	13	3.46
1987—Oakland...	American	29	39⅔	6	2	.750	37	22	20	30	24	4.54
1988—Oakland...	American	58	71⅔	5	2	.714	60	26	23	64	36	2.89
1989—Oakland†-New York.....................	American	46	120	5	5	.500	130	62	54	80	57	4.05
1990—New York..	American	54	121⅓	5	4	.556	120	62	56	80	64	4.15
Major League Totals—4 Years..................		187	352⅔	21	13	.618	347	172	153	254	181	3.90

Selected by Oakland A's organization in 11th round of free-agent draft, June 6, 1983.

†Traded with Pitcher Eric Plunk and Outfielder Luis Polonia to New York Yankees for Outfielder Rickey Henderson, June 21, 1989.

CHAMPIONSHIP SERIES RECORD

Year Club	League	G.	IP.	W.	L.	Pct.	H.	R.	ER.	SO.	BB.	ERA.
1988—Oakland..	American	1	⅓	0	0	.000	1	1	1	0	0	27.00

WORLD SERIES RECORD

Year Club	League	G.	IP.	W.	L.	Pct.	H.	R.	ER.	SO.	BB.	ERA.
1988—Oakland..	American	3	2	0	0	.000	2	0	0	3	0	0.00

IVAN CALDERON (PEREZ)

Name pronounced Call-durh-OWN.

Born March 19, 1962, at Fajardo, Puerto Rico.
Height, 6.01. Weight, 221.
Throws and bats righthanded.

Major League stolen bases: 1984 (1), 1985 (4), 1986 (3), 1987 (10), 1988 (4), 1989 (7), 1990 (32). Total—61.
Led American League in grounding into double plays with 26 in 1990.
Tied for Southern League lead in total bases with 267 in 1983.

Year	Club	League	Pos.	G.	AB.	R.	H.	2B.	3B.	HR.	RBI.	B.A.	PO.	A.	E.	F.A.
1980—Bellingham	N'west	OF	57	195	44	62	7	⋆9	4	32	.318	56	4	7	.896
1981—Wausau	Midw.	OF-SS	117	402	79	123	19	1	20	62	.306	130	17	6	.961
1982—Wausau	Midw.	S-O-3-1	126	461	91	132	22	5	24	89	.286	215	202	45	.903
1983—Chattanooga	South.	OF	139	546	92	●170	34	⋆15	11	80	⋆.311	251	10	13	.953
1984—Salt Lake City†	P. C.	OF	66	255	61	93	7	9	4	45	.365	132	9	8	.946
1984—Seattle‡	Amer.	OF	11	24	2	5	1	0	1	1	.208	22	0	0	1.000
1985—Seattle	Amer.	OF-1B	67	210	37	60	16	4	8	28	.286	108	5	2	.983
1986—Seattle§-Chicago	Amer.	OF	50	164	16	41	7	1	2	15	.250	64	4	5	.932
1986—Calgary	P. C.	OF	24	81	17	27	3	0	3	18	.333	34	2	1	.973
1986—Buffalo	A. A.	OF	27	105	11	23	9	0	5	22	.219	30	1	5	.861
1987—Chicago x	Amer.	OF	144	542	93	159	38	2	28	83	.293	295	8	5	.984
1988—Chicago y	Amer.	OF	73	264	40	56	14	0	14	35	.212	141	5	7	.954
1989—Chicago	Amer.	OF-1B	157	622	83	178	34	9	14	87	.286	384	17	9	.978
1990—Chicago z	Amer.	OF	158	607	85	166	44	2	14	74	.273	269	7	7	.975
Major League Totals—7 Years			660	2433	356	665	154	18	81	323	.273	1283	46	35	.974

Signed as free agent by Seattle Mariners' organization, July 30, 1979.
†On disabled list, May 25 to July 2, 1984.
‡On disabled list, August 26 to September 12, 1984.
§Traded to Chicago White Sox' organization, July 1, 1986, completing deal in which Chicago traded Catcher Scott Bradley to Seattle Mariners for a player to be named later, June 26, 1986.
xOn disabled list, May 16 to May 31, 1987.
yOn disabled list, June 27 to July 12 and July 31, 1988 through remainder of season.
zTraded with Pitcher Barry Jones to Montreal Expos for Outfielder Tim Raines, Pitcher Jeff Carter and a player to be named later, December 23, 1990.

ERNIE CARLOS CAMACHO

Born February 1, 1956, at Salinas, Calif.
Height, 6.01. Weight, 180.
Throws and bats righthanded.
Attended Hartnell Junior College, Salinas, Calif.

Major League saves: 1984 (23), 1986 (20), 1987 (1), 1988 (1). Total—45.

Year	Club	League	G.	IP.	W.	L.	Pct.	H.	R.	ER.	SO.	BB.	ERA.
1976—Modesto	California	10	56	3	4	.429	69	47	35	29	39	5.63
1977—Modesto†	California	5	32	2	1	.667	30	19	14	21	23	3.94
1977—Chattanooga	Southern	11	60	3	8	.273	74	50	43	20	28	6.45
1978—Modesto‡	California	1	2	0	0	.000	0	0	0	2	2	0.00
1979—Ogden	P. Coast	21	97	7	9	.438	102	86	71	60	70	6.59
1980—Ogden	P. Coast	33	64	5	3	.625	60	29	28	58	26	3.94
1980—Oakland§	American	5	12	0	0	.000	20	9	9	9	5	6.75
1981—Portland x	P. Coast	18	38	2	3	.400	45	24	20	31	22	4.74
1981—Pittsburgh y	National	7	22	0	1	.000	23	13	12	11	15	4.91
1982—Edmonton zab	P. Coast	7	19⅔	0	0	.000	10	8	7	18	16	3.20
1982—Mexico City Reds	Mexican	15	20⅓	3	1	.750	21	12	12	15	6	5.31
1982—Rochester c	Int'national	8	17⅔	0	1	.000	16	7	4	11	10	2.04
1983—Vancouver d	P. Coast	11	23⅔	0	2	.000	31	21	18	16	12	6.85
1983—Charleston	Int'national	24	33⅓	4	0	1.000	19	5	5	27	17	1.35
1983—Cleveland	American	4	5⅓	0	1	.000	9	5	3	3	2	5.06
1984—Cleveland	American	69	100	5	9	.357	83	31	27	48	37	2.43
1985—Cleveland e	American	2	3⅓	0	1	.000	4	3	3	2	1	8.10
1986—Cleveland f	American	51	57⅓	2	4	.333	60	26	26	36	31	4.08
1987—Cleveland	American	15	13⅔	0	1	.000	21	14	14	9	5	9.22
1987—Buffalo g	Am. Assoc.	23	29⅓	1	3	.250	33	14	6	18	16	1.84
1988—Tucson	P. Coast	36	42⅓	1	5	.167	47	24	20	26	27	4.25
1988—Houston h	National	13	17⅔	0	3	.000	25	15	15	13	12	7.64
1989—Phoenix	P. Coast	40	55	3	0	1.000	33	10	9	59	16	1.47
1989—San Francisco	National	13	16⅓	3	0	1.000	10	5	5	14	11	2.76
1990—Phoenix	P. Coast	13	15	1	0	1.000	12	4	3	17	11	1.80
1990—San Francisco i-St. Louis	National	14	15⅔	0	0	.000	17	10	9	15	9	5.17
1990—Louisville j	Am. Assoc.	15	16⅓	1	1	.500	16	10	8	15	7	4.41
American League Totals—6 Years		146	191⅔	7	16	.304	193	86	82	106	81	3.85
National League Totals—4 Years		47	71⅔	3	4	.429	75	43	41	53	47	5.15
Major League Totals—10 Years		193	263⅓	10	20	.333	268	129	123	159	128	4.20

Selected by Pittsburgh Pirates' organization in 12th round of free-agent draft, June 4, 1975.
Selected by California Angels' organization in secondary phase of free-agent draft, January 7, 1976.
Selected by Oakland A's organization in secondary phase of free-agent draft, June 8, 1976.
†On disabled list, April 23 to June 14, 1977.
‡On Jersey City temporary inactive list, April 14 to July 18, 1978; on Modesto temporary inactive list, July 18 to August 30, 1978.
§Traded to Pittsburgh Pirates, April 10, 1981, completing deal in which Pittsburgh traded Pitcher Bob Owchinko to Oakland A's for cash and player to be named later, April 6, 1981.
xOn disabled list, June 23 to July 15, 1981.
yTraded with Infielder Vance Law to Chicago White Sox for Pitchers Ross Baumgarten and Butch Edge, March 21, 1982.
zOn suspended list, April 5 to April 25, 1982.
aLoaned to Mexico City Reds, May 16, 1982; returned, August 2, 1982.

bLoaned to Rochester (Baltimore Orioles' organization), August 5, 1982; returned, September 17, 1982.

cGranted free agency, October 22, 1982; signed by Vancouver (Milwaukee Brewers' organization), December 19, 1982.

dTraded with Outfielder Gorman Thomas and Pitcher Jamie Easterly to Cleveland Indians for Outfielder Rick Manning and Pitcher Rick Waits, June 6, 1983.

eOn disabled list, April 13, 1985 through remainder of season.

fOn disabled list, May 14 to May 29, 1986.

gGranted free agency, October 15, 1987; signed by Houston Astros, March 10, 1988.

hGranted free agency, October 15, 1988; signed by Phoenix (San Francisco Giants' organization), February 27, 1989.

iReleased, June 23, 1990; signed by Louisville (St. Louis Cardinals' organization), July 2, 1990.

jReleased, October 11, 1990.

KENNETH GENE CAMINITI
(Ken)

Born April 21, 1963, at Hanford, Calif.
Height, 6.00. Weight, 200.
Throws right and bats left and righthanded.
Attended San Jose State University, San Jose, Calif.

Major League stolen bases: 1989 (4), 1990 (9). Total—13.
Led Pacific Coast League third basemen in double plays with 25 and total chances with 382 in 1988.
Led Southern League third basemen in double plays with 34 in 1986.
Named third baseman on THE SPORTING NEWS College Baseball All-America Team, 1984.

Year	Club	League	Pos.	G.	AB.	R.	H.	2B.	3B.	HR.	RBI.	B.A.	PO.	A.	E.	F.A.
1985—Osceola	Fla. St.	3B	126	468	83	133	26	9	4	73	.284	53	193	20	.925
1986—Columbus	South.	3B	137	513	82	154	29	3	12	81	.300	105	*299	33	.924
1987—Columbus	South.	3B	95	375	66	122	25	2	15	69	.325	55	205	21	.925
1987—Houston	Nat.	3B	63	203	10	50	7	1	3	23	.246	50	98	8	.949
1988—Tucson	P. C.	3B	109	416	54	113	24	7	5	66	.272	*105	*250	27	.929
1988—Houston	Nat.	3B	30	83	5	15	2	0	1	7	.181	12	43	3	.948
1989—Houston	Nat.	3B	161	585	71	149	31	3	10	72	.255	126	335	22	.954
1990—Houston	Nat.	3B	153	541	52	131	20	2	4	51	.242	118	243	21	.945
Major League Totals—4 Years			407	1412	138	345	60	6	18	153	.244	306	719	54	.950

Selected by Houston Astros' organization in 3rd round of free-agent draft, June 4, 1984.

JAMES MARCUS CAMPBELL
(Jim)

Born May 19, 1966, at Santa Maria, Calif.
Height, 5.11. Weight, 175.
Throws and bats lefthanded.
Attended Butte College, Oroville, Calif., and
San Diego State University, San Diego, Calif.

Year	Club	League	G.	IP.	W.	L.	Pct.	H.	R.	ER.	SO.	BB.	ERA.
1987—Eugene	Northwest	32	62	6	0	1.000	32	5	5	75	12	*0.73
1988—Memphis	Southern	53	85	4	3	.571	80	39	34	81	25	3.60
1989—Memphis	Southern	49	104	7	10	.412	96	58	52	78	38	4.50
1990—Memphis	Southern	40	99⅔	5	5	.500	78	38	27	79	32	2.44
1990—Omaha	Am. Assoc.	4	27⅓	2	2	.500	25	4	4	19	10	1.32
1990—Kansas City†	American	2	9⅔	1	0	1.000	15	9	9	2	1	8.38
Major League Totals—1 Year		2	9⅔	1	0	1.000	15	9	9	2	1	8.38

Selected by Kansas City Royals' organization in 32nd round of free-agent draft, June 2, 1987.
†On disabled list, September 16, 1990 through remainder of season.

SILVESTRE CAMPUSANO
(Sil)

Born December 31, 1966, at Mano Guayabo, D. R.
Height, 6.00. Weight, 190.
Throws and bats righthanded.

Major League stolen bases: 1990 (1).
Tied for Gulf Coast League lead in stolen bases with 21 in 1984.
Tied for International League lead in caught stealing with 15 in 1987.
Led Southern League outfielders in total chances with 437 and tied for lead in double plays with 6 in 1986.
Led South Atlantic League outfielders in double plays with 5 in 1985.
Named South Atlantic League Most Valuable Player, 1985.

Year	Club	League	Pos.	G.	AB.	R.	H.	2B.	3B.	HR.	RBI.	B.A.	PO.	A.	E.	F.A.
1984—Bradenton Jays	Appal.	OF	●63	236	42	63	17	2	0	22	.267	128	7	*8	.944
1985—Florence	S. Atl.	OF	88	348	80	109	31	1	15	56	.313	188	12	4	.980
1985—Knoxville	South.	OF	45	178	30	54	9	0	6	29	.303	135	3	4	.972
1986—Knoxville	South.	OF	132	493	89	126	32	6	14	59	.256	*401	21	15	.966
1987—Syracuse	Int.	OF	129	481	70	127	28	●10	14	63	.264	324	8	*11	.968
1988—Toronto†	Amer.	OF	73	142	14	31	10	2	2	12	.218	111	2	8	.934
1988—Syracuse	Int.	OF	17	62	8	13	3	0	0	3	.210	44	0	1	.978
1989—Syracuse‡	Int.	OF	112	356	46	86	19	4	6	30	.242	256	9	5	.981
1990—Philadelphia	Nat.	OF	66	85	10	18	1	1	2	9	.212	40	1	1	.976
American League Totals—1 Year			73	142	14	31	10	2	2	12	.218	111	2	8	.934
National League Totals—1 Year			66	85	10	18	1	1	2	9	.212	40	1	1	.976
Major League Totals—2 Years			139	227	24	49	11	3	4	21	.216	151	3	9	.945

Signed as free agent by Toronto Blue Jays' organization, November 14, 1983.

†On disabled list, August 4 to September 2, 1988; included rehabilitation disability assignment to Syracuse, August 19 to September 2, 1988.

‡Drafted by Philadelphia Phillies, December 4, 1989.

GEORGE ANTHONY CANALE IV

Name pronounced Ca-NAL-lee.

Born August 11, 1965, at Memphis, Tenn.
Height, 6.01. Weight, 190.
Throws right and bats lefthanded.
Attended Virginia Tech, Blacksburg, Va.

Led American Association batters in strikeouts with 134 and total bases with 245 in 1989.
Led Texas League batters in strikeouts with 152 in 1988.
Led Pioneer League in bases on balls received with 54 in 1986.
Led American Association first basemen in total chances with 1,391 and double plays with 122 in 1989.
Led Texas League first basemen in double plays with 106 in 1988.
Led Pioneer League first basemen in double plays with 47 in 1986.
Named first baseman on THE SPORTING NEWS College Baseball All-America Team, 1986.

Year Club	League	Pos.	G.	AB.	R.	H.	2B.	3B.	HR.	RBI.	B.A.	PO.	A.	E.	F.A.
1986—Helena	Pion.	1B	65	221	48	72	19	0	9	49	.326	*554	29	6	*.990
1987—El Paso	Texas	1B	65	253	38	65	10	2	7	36	.257	639	35	3	.996
1987—Stockton	Calif.	1B	66	246	42	69	18	1	7	48	.280	615	33	4	.994
1988—El Paso	Texas	1B-3B-OF	132	496	77	120	23	2	23	93	.242	1231	71	12	.991
1989—Denver	A. A.	*1B-3B	●144	503	80	140	33	●9	18	71	.278	*1287	*94	10	*.993
1989—Milwaukee	Amer.	1B	13	26	5	5	1	0	1	3	.192	86	4	1	.989
1990—Denver	A. A.	1B	134	468	76	119	17	6	12	60	.254	1073	63	10	*.991
1990—Milwaukee	Amer.	1B	10	13	4	1	1	0	0	0	.077	32	4	0	1.000
Major League Totals—2 Years			23	39	9	6	2	0	1	3	.154	118	8	1	.992

Selected by Milwaukee Brewers' organization in 6th round of free-agent draft, June 2, 1986.

CASEY TODD CANDAELE

Named pronounced Kan-DELL.

Born January 12, 1961, at Lompoc, Calif.
Height, 5.09. Weight, 165.
Throws right and bats right and lefthanded.
Attended University of Arizona, Tucson, Ariz.
Son of Helen St. Aubin, former professional women's baseball player.

Major League stolen bases: 1986 (3), 1987 (7), 1988 (1), 1990 (7). Total—18.
Led American Association in sacrifice hits with 11 in 1986.
Led Florida State League second basemen in assists with 391, double plays with 87 and errors with 30 in 1983.
Tied for American Association lead in double plays by second basemen with 68 in 1986.

Year Club	League	Pos.	G.	AB.	R.	H.	2B.	3B.	HR.	RBI.	B.A.	PO.	A.	E.	F.A.
1983—W. Palm Beach	Fla. St.	2-O-3-S	127	*511	77	156	26	9	0	45	.305	271	403	32	.955
1983—Memphis	South.	3B	5	19	4	4	1	0	0	1	.211	2	11	0	1.000
1984—Jacksonville	South.	S-O-2-3	132	532	68	145	23	2	2	53	.273	224	352	18	.970
1985—Indianapolis	A. A.	O-2-S-3	127	390	55	101	13	5	0	35	.259	266	160	6	.986
1986—Indianapolis	A. A.	2B-OF	119	480	77	145	32	6	2	42	.302	240	319	13	.977
1986—Montreal	Nat.	2B-3B	30	104	9	24	4	1	0	6	.231	45	74	2	.983
1987—Montreal	Nat.	2-O-S-1	138	449	62	122	23	4	1	23	.272	237	176	8	.981
1988—Mon.†-Hou.	Nat.	2B-OF-3B	57	147	11	25	8	1	0	5	.170	79	126	2	.990
1988—Indianapolis	A. A.	SS-2B-OF	60	239	23	63	11	6	2	36	.264	105	161	3	.989
1988—Tucson	P. C.	O-2-S-3	17	66	8	17	3	0	0	5	.258	35	29	3	.955
1989—Tucson‡	P. C.	O-3-2-S-1	68	206	22	45	6	1	0	17	.218	94	59	5	.968
1990—Tucson	P. C.	2B	7	28	2	6	1	0	0	2	.214	14	24	1	.974
1990—Houston	Nat.	O-2-S-3	130	262	30	75	8	6	3	22	.286	147	120	3	.989
Major League Totals—4 Years			355	962	112	246	43	12	4	56	.256	508	496	15	.985

Signed as free agent by Montreal Expos' organization, August 15, 1982.

†Traded to Houston Astros for Catcher Mak Bailey, July 23, 1988.

‡On disabled list, June 9 to July 22, 1989.

JOHN ROBERT CANDELARIA

Born November 6, 1953, at Brooklyn, N.Y.
Height, 6.06. Weight, 225.
Throws left and bats righthanded.

Pitched 2-0 no-hit victory against Los Angeles Dodgers, August 9, 1976.
Major League saves: 1976 (1), 1978 (1), 1980 (1), 1982 (1), 1984 (2), 1985 (9), 1988 (1), 1990 (5). Total—21.
Tied for National League lead in home runs allowed with 29 in 1977.
Led Carolina League in home runs allowed with 17 in 1974.
Named American League Comeback Player of the Year by THE SPORTING NEWS, 1986.
Received reported $40,000 bonus to sign with Pittsburgh Pirates, 1973.

Year Club	League	G.	IP.	W.	L.	Pct.	H.	R.	ER.	SO.	BB.	ERA.
1973—Charleston	W. Carol.	18	95	10	2	*.833	84	45	40	60	38	3.79
1974—Salem	Carolina	25	154	11	8	.579	146	80	63	147	63	3.68
1974—Charleston	Int'national	1	11	0	0	.000	7	2	2	10	1	1.64
1975—Charleston	Int'national	10	61	7	1	.875	53	15	12	48	17	1.77
1975—Pittsburgh	National	18	121	8	6	.571	95	47	37	95	36	2.75

Year Club	League	G.	IP.	W.	L.	Pct.	H.	R.	ER.	SO.	BB.	ERA.
1976—Pittsburgh	National	32	220	16	7	.696	173	87	77	138	60	3.15
1977—Pittsburgh	National	33	231	20	5	*.800	197	64	60	133	52	*2.34
1978—Pittsburgh	National	30	189	12	11	.522	191	73	68	94	49	3.24
1979—Pittsburgh	National	33	207	14	9	.609	201	83	74	101	41	3.22
1980—Pittsburgh	National	35	233	11	14	.440	246	114	104	97	50	4.02
1981—Pittsburgh†	National	6	41	2	2	.500	42	17	16	14	11	3.51
1982—Pittsburgh	National	31	174⅔	12	7	.632	166	62	57	133	37	2.94
1983—Pittsburgh	National	33	197⅔	15	8	.652	191	73	71	157	45	3.23
1984—Pittsburgh	National	33	185⅓	12	11	.522	179	69	56	133	34	2.72
1985—Pittsburgh‡	National	37	54⅓	2	4	.333	57	23	22	47	14	3.64
1985—California	American	13	71	7	3	.700	70	33	30	53	24	3.80
1986—California§	American	16	91⅔	10	2	.833	68	30	26	81	26	2.55
1986—Palm Springs	California	2	7	0	0	.000	4	2	2	8	2	2.57
1987—California xy	American	20	116⅔	8	6	.571	127	70	61	74	20	4.71
1987—New York z	National	3	12⅓	2	0	1.000	17	8	8	10	3	5.84
1988—New York	American	25	157	13	7	.650	150	69	59	121	23	3.38
1989—New York a	American	10	49	3	3	.500	49	28	28	37	12	5.14
1989—Sarasota Yankees b	Gulf Coast	2	8	1	0	1.000	6	0	0	12	1	0.00
1989—Montreal c	National	12	16⅓	0	2	.000	17	8	6	14	4	3.31
1990—Minnesota d-Toronto e	American	47	79⅔	7	6	.538	87	36	35	63	20	3.95
National League Totals—13 Years		336	1882⅔	126	86	.594	1772	728	656	1166	434	3.14
American League Totals—6 Years		131	565	48	27	.640	551	266	239	429	125	3.81
Major League Totals—16 Years		467	2447⅔	174	113	.606	2323	994	895	1595	559	3.29

Selected by Pittsburgh Pirates' organization in 2nd round of free-agent draft, June 6, 1972.

†On disabled list, May 11, 1981 through remainder of season.

‡Traded with Pitcher AI Holland and Outfielder George Hendrick to California Angels for Pitcher Pat Clements, Outfielder Mike Brown and a player to be named later, August 2, 1985; Pittsburgh Pirates' organization acquired Pitcher Bob Kipper to complete deal, August 16, 1985.

§On disabled list, April 15 to July 8, 1986; included rehabilitation disability assignment to Palm Springs, June 26 to July 2, 1986.

xOn disabled list, May 14 to May 29 and June 19 to August 5, 1987.

yTraded to New York Mets for Pitchers Shane Young and Jeff Richardson, September 15, 1987.

zGranted free agency, November 9, 1987; signed by New York Yankees, January 15, 1988.

aOn disabled list, May 6 to August 19, 1989; included rehabilitation disability assignment to Sarasota Yankees, August 11 to August 19, 1989.

bTraded to Montreal Expos for a player to be named later, August 29, 1989; New York Yankees acquired Third Baseman Mike Blowers to complete deal, August 31, 1989.

cReleased, January 24, 1990; signed by Minnesota Twins, February 28, 1990.

dTraded to Toronto Blue Jays for Second Baseman Nelson Liriano and Outfielder Pedro Munoz, July 27, 1990.

eGranted free agency, November 5, 1990.

CHAMPIONSHIP SERIES RECORD

Shares Championship Series records for most strikeouts (14) and most consecutive strikeouts (4), game, October 7, 1975.

Year Club	League	G.	IP.	W.	L.	Pct.	H.	R.	ER.	SO.	BB.	ERA.
1975—Pittsburgh	National	1	7⅔	0	0	.000	3	3	3	14	2	3.52
1979—Pittsburgh	National	1	7	0	0	.000	5	2	2	4	1	2.57
1986—California	American	2	10⅔	1	1	.500	11	8	1	7	6	0.84
Championship Series Totals—3 Years		4	25⅓	1	1	.500	19	13	6	25	9	2.13

WORLD SERIES RECORD

Year Club	League	G.	IP.	W.	L.	Pct.	H.	R.	ER.	SO.	BB.	ERA.
1979—Pittsburgh	National	2	9	1	1	.500	14	6	5	4	2	5.00

ALL-STAR GAME RECORD

Member of National League All-Star Team in 1977; did not play.

THOMAS CAESAR CANDIOTTI

(Tom)

Born August 31, 1957, at Walnut Creek, Calif.
Height, 6.02. Weight, 200.
Throws and bats righthanded.
Received bachelor of science degree in business administration
from St. Mary's College, Moraga, Calif., in 1979.
Brother-in-law of Brad Wellman, infielder with San Francisco Giants,
Los Angeles Dodgers and Kansas City Royals, 1982 through 1989.

Led American League in complete games with 17 in 1986.

Year Club	League	G.	IP.	W.	L.	Pct.	H.	R.	ER.	SO.	BB.	ERA.
1979—Victoria†	Northwest	12	70	5	1	.833	63	23	19	66	16	2.44
1980—Fort Myers	Florida St.	7	44	3	2	.600	32	16	11	31	9	2.25
1980—Jacksonville‡§	Southern	17	117	7	8	.467	98	45	36	93	40	2.77
1981—El Paso x	Texas	21	119	7	6	.538	137	51	37	68	27	2.80
1982—Vancouver y	P. Coast						(Did not play)					
1983—El Paso	Texas	7	24⅔	1	0	1.000	23	10	8	18	7	2.92
1983—Vancouver	P. Coast	15	99½	6	4	.600	87	35	31	61	16	2.81
1983—Milwaukee	American	10	55⅔	4	4	.500	62	21	20	21	16	3.23
1984—Vancouver z	P. Coast	15	96⅔	8	4	.667	96	36	31	53	22	2.89

Year Club	League	G.	IP.	W.	L.	Pct.	H.	R.	ER.	SO.	BB.	ERA.
1984—Milwaukee a	American	8	32⅓	2	2	.500	38	21	19	23	10	5.29
1984—Beloit	Midwest	2	10	0	1	.000	12	5	3	12	5	2.70
1985—El Paso	Texas	4	29⅓	1	0	1.000	29	11	9	16	7	2.76
1985—Vancouver b	P. Coast	24	150⅔	9	13	.409	178	83	66	97	36	3.94
1986—Cleveland	American	36	252⅓	16	12	.571	234	112	100	167	106	3.57
1987—Cleveland	American	32	201⅔	7	18	.280	193	132	107	111	93	4.78
1988—Cleveland c	American	31	216⅔	14	8	.636	225	86	79	137	53	3.28
1989—Cleveland d	American	31	206	13	10	.565	188	80	71	124	55	3.10
1990—Cleveland e	American	31	202	15	11	.577	207	92	82	128	55	3.65
Major League Totals—7 Years		179	1166⅔	71	65	.522	1147	544	478	711	388	3.69

Signed as free-agent by Victoria (Independent), July 17, 1979.
†Released, January 4, 1980; signed by Ft. Myers (Kansas City Royals' organization), January 5, 1980.
‡On disabled list, June 7 to June 26, 1980.
§Drafted by Vancouver (Milwaukee Brewers' organization), December 9, 1980.
xOn disabled list, April 10 to May 12, 1981.
yOn disabled list, April 13, 1982 through remainder of season.
zOn disabled list, May 30 to June 15, 1984.
aOn disabled list, August 2 to September 1, 1984; included rehabilitation disability assignment to Beloit, August 24 to August 31, 1984.
bGranted free agency, October 15, 1985; signed by Cleveland Indians, December 12, 1985.
cOn disabled list, August 4 to August 19, 1988.
dOn disabled list, July 2 to July 17, 1989.
eOn disabled list, May 7 to May 22, 1990.

JOHN ANTHONY CANGELOSI

Born March 10, 1963, at Brooklyn, N.Y.
Height, 5.08. Weight, 160.
Throws left and bats righthanded.
Attended Miami-Dade Community College (North), Miami, Fla.

Holds American League record for most stolen bases by rookie (50), 1986.
Major League stolen bases: 1986 (50), 1987 (21), 1988 (9), 1989 (11), 1990 (7), Total—98.
Led Eastern League in bases on balls received with 101 in 1984.
Led Midwest League in stolen bases with 87 and caught stealing with 35 in 1983.
Tied for New York-Pennsylvania League lead in bases on balls received with 56 in 1982.

Year Club	League	Pos.	G.	AB.	R.	H.	2B.	3B.	HR.	RBI.	B.A.	PO.	A.	E.	F.A.
1982—Niagara Falls	NYP	OF	●76	277	60	80	15	4	5	38	.289	118	5	4	.969
1983—Appleton	Midw.	OF	128	439	87	124	12	4	1	48	.282	262	10	6	.978
1984—Glens Falls†	East.	OF	138	464	91	133	17	1	1	38	.287	310	11	11	.967
1985—Mex. City Reds	Mex.	OF	61	201	46	71	9	4	1	30	.353	127	7	6	.957
1985—Chicago	Amer.	OF	5	2	2	0	0	0	0	0	.000	1	0	0	1.000
1985—Buffalo	A. A.	OF	78	244	34	58	8	5	1	21	.238	148	9	2	.987
1986—Chicago‡	Amer.	OF	137	438	65	103	16	3	2	32	.235	276	7	9	.969
1987—Pittsburgh	Nat.	OF	104	182	44	50	8	3	4	18	.275	74	3	3	.962
1988—Pittsburgh§	Nat.	OF-P	75	118	18	30	4	1	0	8	.254	52	0	2	.963
1988—Buffalo	A. A.	OF	37	145	23	48	6	0	0	10	.331	89	3	0	1.000
1989—Pittsburgh	Nat.	OF	112	160	18	35	4	2	0	9	.219	71	1	2	.973
1990—Pittsburgh	Nat.	OF	58	76	13	15	2	0	0	1	.197	24	0	0	1.000
1990—Buffalo x	A. A.	OF	24	89	17	31	2	2	0	7	.348	49	0	1	.980
American League Totals—2 Years			142	440	67	103	16	3	2	32	.234	277	7	9	.969
National League Totals—4 Years			349	536	93	130	18	6	4	36	.243	221	4	7	.970
Major League Totals—6 Years			491	976	160	233	34	9	6	68	.239	498	11	16	.970

Selected by Chicago White Sox' organization in 4th round of free-agent draft, January 12, 1982.
†Loaned with Infielder Manny Salinas to Mexico City Reds, March 4, 1985, as part of deal in which Infielder Nelson Barrera was purchased by Chicago White Sox; returned, June 1, 1985.
‡Traded to Pittsburgh Pirates, March 30, 1987, completing deal in which Pittsburgh traded Pitcher Jim Winn to Chicago White Sox for a player to be named later, March 27, 1987.
§On disabled list, June 6 to June 27, 1988; included rehabilitation disability assignment to Buffalo, June 20 to June 27, 1988.
xGranted free agency, December 20, 1990.

PITCHING RECORD

Year Club	League	G.	IP.	W.	L.	Pct.	H.	R.	ER.	SO.	BB.	ERA.
1988—Pittsburgh	National	1	2	0	0	.000	1	0	0	0	0	0.00

JOSE CANSECO JR.

Name pronounced Can-SAY-co.

Born July 2, 1964, at Havana, Cuba.
Height, 6.03. Weight, 240.
Throws and bats righthanded.
Identical twin of Ozzie Canseco, outfielder in Oakland Athletics' organization.

Major League stolen bases: 1985 (1), 1986 (15), 1987 (15), 1988 (40), 1989 (6), 1990 (19). Total—96.
Hit three home runs in a game, July 3, 1988.
Led American League in slugging percentage with .569 in 1988.
Led Northwest League batters in strikeouts with 78 in 1983.
Led California League outfielders in double plays with 8 in 1984.
Named American League Player of the Year by THE SPORTING NEWS, 1988.

— 77 —

Named American League Most Valuable Player by Baseball Writers' Association of America, 1988.
Named outfielder on THE SPORTING NEWS American League All-Star Team, 1988 and 1990.
Named outfielder on THE SPORTING NEWS American League Silver Slugger team, 1988 and 1990.
Named American League Rookie Player of the Year by THE SPORTING NEWS, 1986.
Named American League Rookie of the Year by Baseball Writers' Association of America, 1986.
Named Minor League Player of the Year by THE SPORTING NEWS, 1985.
Named Southern League Most Valuable Player, 1985.

Year Club	League	Pos.	G.	AB.	R.	H.	2B.	3B.	HR.	RBI.	B.A.	PO.	A.	E.	F.A.
1982—Miami	Fla. St.	3B	6	9	0	1	0	0	0	0	.111	3	1	1	.800
1982—Idaho Falls	Pion.	3B-OF	28	57	13	15	3	0	2	7	.263	6	17	3	.885
1983—Madison	Midw.	OF	34	88	8	14	4	0	3	10	.159	23	2	1	.962
1983—Medford	N'west	OF	59	197	34	53	15	2	11	40	.269	46	5	5	.911
1984—Modesto	Calif.	OF	116	410	61	113	21	2	15	73	.276	216	17	9	.963
1985—Huntsville†	South.	OF	58	211	47	67	10	2	25	80	.318	117	9	7	.947
1985—Tacoma	P.C.	OF	60	233	41	81	16	1	11	47	.348	81	7	2	.978
1985—Oakland	Amer.	OF	29	96	16	29	3	0	5	13	.302	56	2	3	.951
1986—Oakland	Amer.	OF	157	600	85	144	29	1	33	117	.240	319	4	●14	.958
1987—Oakland	Amer.	OF	159	630	81	162	35	3	31	113	.257	263	12	7	.975
1988—Oakland	Amer.	OF	158	610	120	187	34	0	∗42	∗124	.307	304	11	7	.978
1989—Huntsville‡	South.	OF	9	29	2	6	0	0	3	3	.207	9	0	0	1.000
1989—Oakland	Amer.	OF	65	227	40	61	9	1	17	57	.269	119	5	3	.976
1990—Oakland§	Amer.	OF	131	481	83	132	14	2	37	101	.274	182	7	1	.995
Major League Totals—6 Years			699	2644	425	715	124	7	165	525	.270	1243	41	35	.973

Selected by Oakland A's organization in 15th round of free-agent draft, June 7, 1982.
†On disabled list, May 14 to June 3, 1985.
‡On Oakland disabled list, March 23 to July 13, 1989; included rehabilitation disability assignment to Huntsville, May 6, 1989 and June 28 to July 13, 1989.
§On disabled list, June 8 to June 23, 1990.

CHAMPIONSHIP SERIES RECORD

Shares American League Championship Series record for most home runs, series (3), 1988.

Year Club	League	Pos.	G.	AB.	R.	H.	2B.	3B.	HR.	RBI.	B.A.	PO.	A.	E.	F.A.
1988—Oakland	Amer.	OF	4	16	4	5	1	0	3	4	.313	6	0	0	1.000
1989—Oakland	Amer.	OF-PH	5	17	1	5	0	0	1	3	.294	6	1	1	.875
1990—Oakland	Amer.	OF	4	11	3	2	0	0	0	1	.182	14	0	0	1.000
Championship Series Totals—3 Years			13	44	8	12	1	0	4	8	.273	26	1	1	.964

WORLD SERIES RECORD

Shares World Series records for hitting home run in first series at-bat, October 15, 1988; most grand slams, game (1), October 15, 1988; most runs batted in, inning (4), October 15, 1988, second inning.

Year Club	League	Pos.	G.	AB.	R.	H.	2B.	3B.	HR.	RBI.	B.A.	PO.	A.	E.	F.A.
1988—Oakland	Amer.	OF	5	19	1	1	0	0	1	5	.053	8	0	0	1.000
1989—Oakland	Amer.	OF	4	14	5	5	0	0	1	3	.357	6	0	0	1.000
1990—Oakland	Amer.	O-PH-DH	4	12	1	1	0	0	1	2	.083	4	0	0	1.000
World Series Totals—3 Years			13	45	7	7	0	0	3	10	.156	18	0	0	1.000

ALL-STAR GAME RECORD

Year League		Pos.	AB.	R.	H.	2B.	3B.	HR.	RBI.	B.A.	PO.	A.	E.	F.A.
1988—American		OF	4	0	0	0	0	0	0	.000	3	0	0	1.000
1990—American		OF	4	0	0	0	0	0	0	.000	1	0	0	1.000
All-Star Game Totals—2 Years			8	0	0	0	0	0	0	.000	4	0	0	1.000

Member of American League All-Star Team in 1986; did not play.
Named to American League All-Star Team for 1989 game; did not play due to injury.

OSVALDO CAPAS CANSECO

Name pronounced Can-SAY-co.

(Ozzie)

Born July 2, 1964, at Havana, Cuba.
Height, 6.03. Weight, 220.
Throws and bats righthanded.
Attended Miami-Dade Community College (South), Miami, Fla.
Identical twin of Jose Canseco, outfielder with Oakland Athletics.

Year Club	League	Pos.	G.	AB.	R.	H.	2B.	3B.	HR.	RBI.	B.A.	PO.	A.	E.	F.A.
1983—Greensboro	S. Atl.	P	27	0	0	0	0	0	0	0	.000	2	15	4	.810
1984—Greensboro†	S. Atl.	P-OF	8	1	1	0	0	0	0	0	.000	3	1	2	.667
1984—Oneonta	NYP	P	14	0	0	0	0	0	0	0	.000	4	6	3	.769
1985—Fort Lauderdale	Fla. St.	P	11	0	0	0	0	0	0	0	.000	0	6	3	.667
1985—Sarasota Yankees	Gulf C.	P-OF	20	39	2	7	0	1	1	5	.179	4	15	4	.826
1986—Sarasota Yanks‡	Gulf C.	OF	7	15	3	2	1	0	1	3	.133	4	0	1	.800
1986—Madison	Midw.	OF-P-1B	42	128	17	20	1	1	3	17	.156	72	1	2	.973
1987—Madison	Midw.	OF	92	309	64	82	12	4	11	54	.265	131	6	13	.913
1988—Madison	Midw.	OF	99	359	63	98	17	7	12	68	.273	187	9	5	.975
1988—Huntsville	South.	OF	27	99	6	22	7	0	3	12	.222	29	0	1	.967
1989—Huntsville§	South.	OF-P	91	317	52	74	17	2	12	52	.233	148	8	4	.975
1990—Huntsville	South.	OF	97	325	50	73	21	0	20	67	.225	157	5	8	.953
1990—Oakland	Amer.	OF	9	19	1	2	1	0	0	1	.105	3	0	0	1.000
Major League Totals—1 Year			9	19	1	2	1	0	0	1	.105	3	0	0	1.000

Selected by New York Yankees' organization in 2nd round of free-agent draft, January 11, 1983.
†On temporary inactive list, April 18 to May 14 and June 2 to June 6, 1984.
‡Released, July 4, 1986; signed by Oakland Athletics' organization, July 10, 1986.
§On Oakland disabled list, March 19 to April 27, 1989.

RECORD AS PITCHER

Year Club	League	G.	IP.	W.	L.	Pct.	H.	R.	ER.	SO.	BB.	ERA.
1983—Greensboro	S. Atlantic	27	87⅓	3	6	.333	98	62	49	59	49	5.05
1984—Greensboro	S. Atlantic	6	16⅔	1	1	.500	19	13	9	9	22	4.86
1984—Oneonta	NYP	14	43⅓	1	6	.143	44	29	17	40	21	3.53
1985—Fort Lauderdale	Florida St.	11	57⅓	5	4	.556	42	33	23	37	42	3.61
1985—Sarasota Yankees	Gulf Coast	13	84⅔	5	4	.556	93	37	29	48	11	3.08
1986—Madison	Midwest	2	4	1	0	1.000	2	0	0	3	2	0.00
1989—Huntsville	Southern	3	5	0	0	.000	5	4	4	1	1	7.20

MICHAEL LEE CAPEL
(Mike)

Born October 13, 1961, at Marshall, Tex.
Height, 6.01. Weight, 175.
Throws and bats righthanded.
Attended University of Texas, Austin, Tex.

Led American Association in intentional bases on balls issued with 11 in 1987.

Year Club	League	G.	IP.	W.	L.	Pct.	H.	R.	ER.	SO.	BB.	ERA.
1983—Midland	Texas	3	14⅓	1	1	.500	22	12	11	8	8	6.91
1983—Quad Cities	Midwest	8	44⅔	3	2	.600	32	15	12	35	14	2.42
1984—Midland	Texas	16	61⅓	1	10	.091	69	53	43	20	37	6.31
1984—Lodi	California	20	69	0	7	.000	54	38	28	46	35	3.65
1985—Pittsfield	Eastern	33	73⅓	3	6	.333	74	44	40	53	47	4.91
1986—Pittsfield†	Eastern	38	62⅔	4	4	.500	51	20	13	50	22	1.87
1987—Iowa	Am. Assoc.	53	108⅓	7	10	.412	117	72	69	75	43	5.73
1988—Iowa	Am. Assoc	32	57⅔	3	2	.600	60	24	22	49	23	3.43
1988—Chicago	National	22	29⅓	2	1	.667	34	19	16	19	13	4.91
1989—Iowa‡	Am. Assoc.	64	97	4	7	.364	87	43	35	62	41	3.25
1990—Denver	Am. Assoc.	41	101⅓	4	3	.571	98	55	48	60	39	4.26
1990—Milwaukee	American	2	⅓	0	0	.000	6	6	5	1	1	135.00
National League Totals—1 Year		22	29⅓	2	1	.667	34	19	16	19	13	4.91
American League Totals—1 Year		2	⅓	0	0	.000	6	6	5	1	1	135.00
Major League Totals—2 Years		24	29⅔	2	1	.667	40	25	21	20	14	6.37

Selected by Philadelphia Phillies' organization in 24th round of free-agent draft, June 3, 1980.
Selected by Chicago Cubs' organization in 13th round of free-agent draft, June 6, 1983.
†On disabled list, May 26 to June 16, 1986.
‡Granted free agency, October 15, 1989; signed by Denver (Milwaukee Brewers' organization), December 13, 1989.

DONALD WAYNE CARMAN
(Don)

Born August 14, 1959, at Oklahoma City, Okla.
Height, 6.03. Weight, 201.
Throws and bats lefthanded.
Attended Seminole Junior College, Seminole, Okla.,
and University of Oklahoma, Norman, Okla.

Shares National League records for fewest games lost for leader, season (15), 1989; most consecutive home runs allowed, inning (3), April 17, 1989, third inning.
Major League saves: 1983 (1), 1985 (7), 1986 (1), 1990 (1). Total—10.

Year Club	League	G.	IP.	W.	L.	Pct.	H.	R.	ER.	SO.	BB.	ERA.
1979—Spartanburg	W. Carol.	37	78	6	3	.667	72	36	34	70	28	3.92
1980—Peninsula	Carolina	27	150	14	5	.737	149	73	57	*141	53	3.42
1981—Reading	Eastern	28	176	12	13	.480	167	93	79	105	75	4.04
1982—Oklahoma City	Am. Assoc.	10	33	0	1	.000	37	29	25	29	23	6.82
1982—Reading	Eastern	20	97⅓	6	7	.462	99	58	45	81	62	4.16
1983—Reading	Eastern	*56	124⅓	8	5	.615	85	51	41	93	71	2.97
1983—Philadelphia	National	1	1	0	0	.000	0	0	0	0	0	0.00
1984—Portland	P. Coast	39	55⅔	3	3	.500	66	36	33	53	22	5.34
1984—Philadelphia	National	11	13⅓	0	1	.000	14	9	8	16	6	5.40
1985—Philadelphia	National	71	86⅓	9	4	.692	52	25	20	87	38	2.08
1986—Philadelphia	National	50	134⅓	10	5	.667	113	50	48	98	52	3.22
1987—Philadelphia	National	35	211	13	11	.542	194	110	99	125	69	4.22
1988—Philadelphia	National	36	201⅓	10	14	.417	211	101	96	116	70	4.29
1989—Philadelphia	National	49	149⅓	5	●15	.250	152	98	87	81	86	5.24
1990—Philadelphia†	National	59	86⅔	6	2	.750	69	43	40	58	38	4.15
Major League Totals—8 Years		312	883⅓	53	52	.505	805	436	398	581	359	4.06

Signed as free agent by Philadelphia Phillies' organization, August 25, 1978.
†Granted free agency, November 5, 1990.

—DID YOU KNOW—
That Atlanta's 162 home runs in 1990 were the club's most since 1973?

CRIS HOWELL CARPENTER

Born April 5, 1965, at St. Augustine, Fla.
Height, 6.01. Weight, 185.
Throws and bats righthanded.
Attended University of Georgia, Athens, Ga.

Received reported $160,000 bonus to sign with St. Louis Cardinals, 1987.

Year Club	League	G.	IP.	W.	L.	Pct.	H.	R.	ER.	SO.	BB.	ERA.
1988—Louisville	Am. Assoc.	13	87⅔	6	2	.750	81	28	28	45	26	2.87
1988—St. Louis	National	8	47⅔	2	3	.600	56	27	25	24	9	4.72
1989—St. Louis	National	36	68	4	4	.500	70	30	24	35	26	3.18
1989—Louisville	Am. Assoc.	27	36⅔	5	3	.625	39	17	13	29	9	3.19
1990—St. Louis	National	4	8	0	0	.000	5	4	4	6	2	4.50
1990—Louisville	Am. Assoc.	22	143⅓	10	8	.556	146	61	59	100	21	3.70
Major League Totals—3 Years		48	123⅔	6	7	.462	131	61	53	65	37	3.86

Selected by Toronto Blue Jays' organization in 7th round of free-agent draft, June 2, 1986.
Selected by St. Louis Cardinals' organization in 1st round (14th player selected) of free-agent draft, June 2, 1987.

CHARLES LEE GLENN CARR JR.
(Chuck)

Born August 10, 1968, at San Bernardino, Calif.
Height, 5.10. Weight, 155.
Throws right and bats left and righthanded.

Major League stolen bases: 1990 (1).

Year Club	League	Pos.	G.	AB.	R.	H.	2B.	3B.	HR.	RBI.	B.A.	PO.	A.	E.	F.A.
1986—Sarasota Reds†	Gulf C.	2B	44	123	13	21	5	0	0	10	.171	75	100	11	.941
1987—Bellingham	N'west	S-O-2-3	44	165	31	40	1	1	1	11	.242	50	58	14	.885
1988—Wausau	Midw.	OF-SS	82	304	58	91	14	2	6	30	.299	170	17	12	.940
1988—Vermont‡	East.	OF	41	159	26	39	4	2	1	13	.245	105	6	6	.949
1989—Jackson	Texas	OF	116	444	45	107	13	1	0	22	.241	280	11	8	.973
1990—Jackson	Texas	OF	93	361	60	93	19	9	3	24	.258	226	12	8	.967
1990—Tidewater	Int.	OF	20	81	13	21	5	1	0	8	.259	40	3	0	1.000
1990—New York	Nat.	OF	4	2	0	0	0	0	0	0	.000	0	0	0	.000
Major League Totals—1 Year			4	2	0	0	0	0	0	0	.000	0	0	0	.000

Selected by Cincinnati Reds' organization in 9th round of free-agent draft, June 2, 1986.
†Released, March, 1987; signed by Bellingham (Seattle Mariners' organization) June 15, 1987.
‡Traded to New York Mets' organization for Pitcher Reggie Dobie, November 18, 1988.

MARK STEVEN CARREON

Name pronounced CAIR-ee-on.

Born July 9, 1963, at Chicago, Ill.
Height, 6.00. Weight, 194.
Throws left and bats righthanded.
Son of Camilo Carreon, catcher with Chicago White Sox,
Cleveland Indians and Baltimore Orioles, 1959 through 1966.

Major League stolen bases: 1989 (2), 1990 (1). Totals—3.
Led International League in game-winning RBIs with 19 in 1987 and tied for lead with 11 in 1988.
Led Carolina League in sacrifice flies with 11 in 1983.
Tied for South Atlantic League lead in game-winning RBIs with 12 in 1982.

Year Club	League	Pos.	G.	AB.	R.	H.	2B.	3B.	HR.	RBI.	B.A.	PO.	A.	E.	F.A.
1981—Kingsport	Appal.	OF-C	64	232	30	67	8	0	1	36	.289	101	7	4	.964
1982—Shelby	S. Atl.	OF	133	486	★120	160	29	6	2	79	.329	183	8	5	.974
1983—Lynchburg	Carol.	OF	128	491	94	164	13	8	1	67	.334	173	8	14	.928
1984—Jackson	Texas	OF	119	435	64	122	14	3	1	43	.280	146	1	4	.974
1985—Tidewater	Int.	OF	7	15	1	2	1	0	1	2	.133	2	0	0	1.000
1985—Jackson	Texas	OF	123	447	96	140	23	5	6	51	.313	201	8	1	.995
1986—Tidewater	Int.	OF	115	426	62	123	23	2	10	64	.289	192	6	6	.971
1987—Tidewater	Int.	OF	133	525	83	164	★41	5	10	89	.312	237	8	5	.980
1987—New York	Nat.	OF	9	12	0	3	0	0	0	1	.250	4	0	1	.800
1988—Tidewater	Int.	OF	102	365	48	96	13	3	14	55	.263	111	6	2	.983
1988—New York	Nat.	OF	7	9	5	5	2	0	1	1	.556	1	0	0	1.000
1989—Tidewater†	Int.	OF-1B	32	122	22	34	4	0	1	21	.279	26	0	0	1.000
1989—New York	Nat.	OF	68	133	20	41	6	0	6	16	.308	57	0	1	.983
1990—New York‡	Nat.	OF	82	188	30	47	12	0	10	26	.250	87	1	0	1.000
Major League Totals—4 Years			166	342	55	96	20	0	17	44	.281	149	1	2	.987

Selected by New York Mets' organization in 8th round of free-agent draft, June 8, 1981.
†On New York disabled list, March 28 to April 24, 1989; included rehabilitation disability assignment to Tidewater, April 5 to April 24, 1989.
‡On disabled list, August 21, 1990 through remainder of season.

GARY EDMUND CARTER

Born April 8, 1954, at Culver City, Calif.
Height, 6.02. Weight, 210.
Throws and bats righthanded.
Brother of Gordon Carter, outfielder in San Francisco Giants'
organization, 1972 and 1973.

Holds major league records for fewest passed balls, season, 150 or more games (1), 1978.

Shares major league records for most home runs, two consecutive games (5), September 3 and 4, 1985; most years leading league in chances accepted, catcher (8).

Holds National League records for most seasons leading league in games by catcher (6); most years leading league in putouts by catcher (8); most years leading league in chances accepted by catcher (7); most games (1,903), putouts (10,949) and chances accepted (12,055), catcher, lifetime.

Major League stolen bases: 1974 (2), 1975 (5), 1977 (5), 1978 (10), 1979 (3), 1980 (3), 1981 (1), 1982 (2), 1983 (1), 1984 (2), 1985 (1), 1986 (1), 1990 (1). Total—37.

Hit three home runs in a game, April 20, 1977 and September 3, 1985.

Led National League in sacrifice flies with 15 and tied for lead in game-winning RBIs with 16 and grounding into double plays with 21 in 1986.

Led National League catchers in assists with 107 in 1983.

Led National League catchers in total chances with 921 in 1977, 874 in 1978, 848 in 1979, 937 in 1980, 571 in 1981, 1,068 in 1982 and 860 in 1988.

Led National League in passed balls with 12 in 1979.

Led National League catchers in putouts with 811 in 1977, 781 in 1978, 509 in 1981, 956 in 1985 and 797 in 1988.

Led National League catchers in double plays with 14 in 1977, 9 in 1978, 12 in 1979, 14 in 1983 and 13 in 1987.

Led International League catchers in putouts with 794, assists with 65, double plays with 15 and fielding percentage with .990 in 1974.

Named National League Rookie Player of the Year by THE SPORTING NEWS, 1975.

Named catcher on THE SPORTING NEWS National League All-Star Team, 1980 through 1982 and 1984 through 1986.

Named catcher on THE SPORTING NEWS National League All-Star fielding team, 1980 through 1982.

Named catcher on THE SPORTING NEWS National League Silver Slugger team, 1981, 1982 and 1984 through 1986.

Year	Club	League	Pos.	G.	AB.	R.	H.	2B.	3B.	HR.	RBI.	B.A.	PO.	A.	E.	F.A.
1972—Cocoa Expos	Fla.E.C.	C-1B-3B	18	71	6	17	3	0	2	9	.239	111	12	10	.925
1972—W. Palm Beach	Fla. St.	C	20	50	9	16	2	2	0	5	.320	84	12	2	.980
1973—Quebec City	East.	C-1B-OF	130	439	65	111	16	1	15	68	.253	823	75	20	.978
1973—Peninsula	Int.	C	8	25	2	7	2	0	0	1	.280	5	1	0	1.000
1974—Memphis	Int.	C-1B-3B	135	441	62	118	14	7	23	83	.268	908	76	12	.988
1974—Montreal	Nat.	C-OF	9	27	5	11	0	1	1	6	.407	28	4	0	1.000
1975—Montreal	Nat.	OF-C-3B	144	503	58	136	20	1	17	68	.270	430	38	9	.981
1976—Montreal†	Nat.	C-OF	91	311	31	68	8	1	6	38	.219	364	42	2	.995
1977—Montreal	Nat.	⋆C-OF	154	522	86	148	29	2	31	84	.284	813	⋆101	9	.990
1978—Montreal	Nat.	C-1B	157	533	76	136	27	1	20	72	.255	787	83	10	.989
1979—Montreal	Nat.	C	141	505	74	143	26	5	22	75	.283	⋆751	⋆88	9	.989
1980—Montreal	Nat.	C	154	549	76	145	25	5	29	101	.264	⋆822	⋆108	7	⋆.993
1981—Montreal	Nat.	C-1B	100	374	48	94	20	2	16	68	.251	515	58	4	.993
1982—Montreal	Nat.	C	154	557	91	163	32	1	29	97	.293	⋆954	⋆104	10	.991
1983—Montreal	Nat.	⋆C-1B	145	541	63	146	37	3	17	79	.270	855	108	5	⋆.995
1984—Montreal‡	Nat.	C-1B	159	596	75	175	32	1	27	●106	.294	990	78	7	.993
1985—New York	Nat.	C-1B-OF	149	555	83	156	17	1	32	100	.281	987	70	8	.992
1986—New York§	Nat.	C-1-O-3	132	490	81	125	14	2	24	105	.255	943	70	9	.991
1987—New York	Nat.	C-1B-OF	139	523	55	123	18	2	20	83	.235	886	70	9	.991
1988—New York	Nat.	C-1B-3B	130	455	39	110	16	2	11	46	.242	842	58	10	.989
1989—New York x	Nat.	C-1B	50	153	14	28	8	0	2	15	.183	266	31	6	.980
1989—Tidewater y	Int.	C-1B	5	16	2	3	0	0	1	3	.188	26	1	1	.964
1990—San Francisco za	Nat.	C-1B	92	244	24	62	10	0	9	27	.254	348	31	3	.992
Major League Totals—17 Years			2100	7438	979	1969	339	30	313	1170	.265	11581	1142	117	.991

Selected by Montreal Expos' organization in 3rd round of free-agent draft, June 6, 1972.

†On disabled list, June 6 to July 22, 1976.

‡Traded to New York Mets for Infielder Hubie Brooks, Catcher Mike Fitzgerald, Outfielder Herm Winningham and Pitcher Floyd Youmans, December 10, 1984.

§On disabled list, August 17 to September 1, 1986.

xOn disabled list, May 10 to July 25, 1989; included rehabilitation disability assignment to Tidewater, July 19 to July 25, 1989.

yReleased, November 14, 1989; signed by San Francisco Giants, January 19, 1990.

zOn disabled list, July 9 to July 25, 1990.

aGranted free agency, November 5, 1990.

DIVISION SERIES RECORD

Year	Club	League	Pos.	G.	AB.	R.	H.	2B.	3B.	HR.	RBI.	B.A.	PO.	A.	E.	F.A.
1981—Montreal	Nat.	C	5	19	3	8	3	0	2	6	.421	21	5	0	1.000

CHAMPIONSHIP SERIES RECORD

Shares Championship Series records for most game-winning RBIs, total series (3) and series (2), 1986.

Year	Club	League	Pos.	G.	AB.	R.	H.	2B.	3B.	HR.	RBI.	B.A.	PO.	A.	E.	F.A.
1981—Montreal	Nat.	C	5	16	3	7	1	0	0	0	.438	27	3	0	1.000
1986—New York	Nat.	C	6	27	1	4	1	0	0	2	.148	42	5	0	1.000
1988—New York	Nat.	C	7	27	0	6	1	1	0	4	.222	58	1	0	1.000
Championship Series Totals—3 Years			18	70	4	17	3	1	0	6	.243	127	9	0	1.000

WORLD SERIES RECORD

Year	Club	League	Pos.	G.	AB.	R.	H.	2B.	3B.	HR.	RBI.	B.A.	PO.	A.	E.	F.A.
1986—New York	Nat.	C	7	29	4	8	2	0	2	9	.276	57	1	0	1.000

ALL-STAR GAME RECORD

Shares All-Star Game record for most home runs, game (2), August 9, 1981.

Year	League	Pos.	AB.	R.	H.	2B.	3B.	HR.	RBI.	B.A.	PO.	A.	E.	F.A.
1975—National		OF	0	0	0	0	0	0	0	.000	1	0	0	1.000
1979—National		C	2	0	1	0	0	0	1	.500	6	1	0	1.000

Year	League	Pos.	AB.	R.	H.	2B.	3B.	HR.	RBI.	B.A.	PO.	A.	E.	F.A.
1980—National		C	1	0	0	0	0	0	0	.000	1	0	0	1.000
1981—National		C	3	2	2	0	0	2	2	.667	5	1	0	1.000
1982—National		C	3	0	1	0	0	0	1	.333	7	0	0	1.000
1983—National		C	2	0	0	0	0	0	0	.000	3	0	0	1.000
1984—National		C	2	1	1	0	0	1	1	.500	9	0	0	1.000
1986—National		C	3	0	0	0	0	0	0	.000	9	0	0	1.000
1987—National		C	1	0	0	0	0	0	0	.000	1	0	0	1.000
1988—National		C	3	0	1	0	0	0	0	.333	3	0	0	1.000
All-Star Game Totals—10 Years			20	3	6	0	0	3	5	.300	45	2	0	1.000

Named to National League All-Star Team for 1985 game; replaced due to injury by Terry Kennedy.

JEFFREY ALLEN CARTER
(Jeff)

Born December 3, 1964, at Tampa, Fla.
Height, 6.03. Weight, 195.
Throws and bats righthanded.
Attended South Florida Community College, Avon Park, Fla., and received
degree from University of Tampa, Tampa, Fla.

Year	Club	League	G.	IP.	W.	L.	Pct.	H.	R.	ER.	SO.	BB.	ERA.
1987—Jamestown	NYP	31	42⅓	2	3	.400	39	15	11	42	17	2.34
1988—Rockford	Midwest	39	107⅓	11	5	.688	100	38	33	91	35	2.77
1989—West Palm Beach	Florida St.	7	35	4	1	.800	36	14	10	29	8	2.57
1989—Jacksonville	Southern	6	36	1	4	.200	23	11	10	21	14	2.50
1990—Jacksonville	Southern	52	117⅓	8	3	.727	90	36	24	76	33	*1.84

Selected by Montreal Expos' organization in 19th round of free-agent draft, June 2, 1987.

JOSEPH CARTER
(Joe)

Born March 7, 1960, at Oklahoma City, Okla.
Height, 6.03. Weight, 225.
Throws and bats righthanded.
Brother of Fred Carter, outfielder in New York Yankees' and
Cleveland Indians' organizations, 1985 through 1988.

Shares major league records for most home runs, two consecutive games (5), July 18 (2), 19 (3), 1989; most games with three or more home runs, season (2), 1989.
Shares American League record for most games with three or more home runs, lifetime (4).
Major League stolen bases: 1983 (1), 1984 (2), 1985 (24), 1986 (29), 1987 (31), 1988 (27), 1989 (13), 1990 (22). Total—149.
Hit three home runs in a game, August 29, 1986, May 28, 1987, June 24, 1989 and July 19, 1989.
Led American League first basemen in errors with 12 in 1987.
Led American Association in total bases with 265 and tied for lead in strikeouts by batters with 103 in 1983.
Named College Player of the Year by THE SPORTING NEWS, 1981.
Named outfielder on THE SPORTING NEWS College Baseball All-America Team, 1980 and 1981.
Received reported $150,000 bonus to sign with Chicago Cubs, 1981.

Year	Club	League	Pos.	G.	AB.	R.	H.	2B.	3B.	HR.	RBI.	B.A.	PO.	A.	E.	F.A.
1981—Midland	Texas	OF	67	249	42	67	15	3	5	35	.269	100	10	4	.965
1982—Midland†	Texas	OF	110	427	84	136	22	8	25	98	.319	182	6	5	.974
1983—Iowa	A. A.	OF	124	*522	82	160	27	6	22	83	.307	204	9	12	.947
1983—Chicago	Nat.	OF	23	51	6	9	1	1	0	1	.176	26	0	0	1.000
1984—Iowa‡	A. A.	OF	61	248	45	77	12	7	14	67	.310	142	6	2	.987
1984—Cleveland§	Amer.	OF-1B	66	244	32	67	6	1	13	41	.275	169	11	6	.968
1985—Cleveland	Amer.	O-1-2-3	143	489	64	128	27	0	15	59	.262	311	17	6	.982
1986—Cleveland	Amer.	OF-1B	162	663	108	200	36	9	29	*121	.302	800	55	10	.988
1987—Cleveland	Amer.	1B-OF	149	588	83	155	27	2	32	106	.264	782	46	17	.980
1988—Cleveland	Amer.	OF	157	621	85	168	36	6	27	98	.271	444	8	7	.985
1989—Cleveland x	Amer.	OF-1B	●162	●651	84	158	32	4	35	105	.243	443	20	9	.981
1990—San Diego y	Nat.	OF-1B	*162	*634	79	147	27	1	24	115	.232	492	16	11	.979
National League Totals—2 Years			185	685	85	156	28	2	24	116	.228	518	16	11	.980
American League Totals—6 Years			839	3256	456	876	164	22	151	530	.269	2949	157	55	.983
Major League Totals—8 Years			1024	3941	541	1032	192	24	175	646	.262	3467	173	66	.982

Selected by Chicago Cubs' organization in 1st round (second player selected) of free-agent draft, June 8, 1981.
†On disabled list, April 9 to April 19, 1982.
‡Traded with Outfielder Mel Hall and Pitchers Don Schulze and Darryl Banks to Cleveland Indians for Catcher Ron Hassey and Pitchers Rick Sutcliffe and George Frazier, June 13, 1984.
§On disabled list, July 2 to July 17, 1984.
xTraded to San Diego Padres for Catcher Sandy Alomar, Outfielder Chris James and Third Baseman Carlos Baerga, December 6, 1989.
yTraded with Second Baseman Roberto Alomar to Toronto Blue Jays for First Baseman Fred McGriff and Shortstop Tony Fernandez, December 5, 1990.

—DID YOU KNOW—
That San Francisco's Kevin Mitchell homered against every N.L. opponent in 1990 for the second consecutive season?

STEVEN JEROME CARTER
(Steve)

Born December 3, 1964, at Charlottesville, Va.
Height, 6.04. Weight, 200.
Throws right and bats lefthanded.
Attended Hagerstown Junior College, Hagerstown, Md.,
and University of Georgia, Athens, Ga.

Year Club	League	Pos.	G.	AB.	R.	H.	2B.	3B.	HR.	RBI.	B.A.	PO.	A.	E.	F.A.
1987—Watertown	NYP	OF	66	242	50	75	18	1	0	30	.310	132	4	8	.944
1988—Harrisburg	East.	OF	9	35	7	10	2	0	0	2	.286	18	1	1	.950
1988—Augusta	S. Atl.	OF	74	278	47	83	18	6	3	43	.299	89	3	4	.958
1988—Salem	Carol.	OF	6	21	4	6	0	0	0	1	.286	15	2	0	1.000
1989—Buffalo	A. A.	OF	100	356	53	105	24	6	1	43	.295	188	3	6	.970
1989—Pittsburgh	Nat.	OF	9	16	2	2	1	0	1	3	.125	4	0	0	1.000
1990—Buffalo	A. A.	OF	120	426	62	129	19	*12	8	45	.303	222	9	4	.983
1990—Pittsburgh	Nat.	OF	5	5	0	1	0	0	0	0	.200	4	0	0	1.000
Major League Totals—2 Years			14	21	2	3	1	0	1	3	.143	8	0	0	1.000

Selected by Pittsburgh Pirates' organization in 21st round of free-agent draft, June 6, 1983.
Selected by Kansas City Royals' organization in secondary phase of free-agent draft, January 17, 1984.
Selected by Milwaukee Brewers' organization in 3rd round of free-agent draft, January 9, 1985.
Selected by Milwaukee Brewers' organization in secondary phase of free-agent draft, June 3, 1985.
Selected by Pittsburgh Pirates' organization in 17th round of free-agent draft, June 2, 1987.

CHARLES DOUGLAS CARY
(Chuck)

Born March 3, 1960, at Whittier, Calif.
Height, 6.04. Weight, 216.
Throws and bats lefthanded.
Attended University of California, Berkeley, Calif.

Major League saves: 1985 (2), 1987 (1). Total—3.
Tied for Southern League lead in balks with 3 in 1982.

Year Club	League	G.	IP.	W.	L.	Pct.	H.	R.	ER.	SO.	BB.	ERA.
1981—Macon	S. Atlantic	13	87	5	5	.500	77	32	25	55	19	2.59
1982—Birmingham	Southern	28	166	8	14	.364	162	93	77	125	64	4.17
1983—Birmingham†	Southern	17	104⅔	6	8	.429	103	50	42	69	42	3.61
1983—Evansville	Am. Assoc.	15	16⅓	1	1	.500	21	10	8	8	8	4.41
1984—Birmingham‡	Southern	22	108⅓	6	4	.600	118	61	58	62	46	4.82
1985—Nashville	Am. Assoc.	48	66	2	1	.667	55	27	22	54	27	3.00
1985—Detroit	American	16	23⅔	0	1	.000	16	9	9	22	8	3.42
1986—Detroit	American	22	31⅔	1	2	.333	33	18	12	21	15	3.41
1986—Nashville§	Am. Assoc.	22	26⅓	1	4	.200	29	21	16	19	15	5.47
1987—Richmond	Int'national	40	105⅔	4	6	.400	104	64	55	128	43	4.68
1987—Atlanta	National	13	16⅓	1	1	.500	17	7	7	15	4	3.78
1988—Atlanta x	National	7	8⅓	0	0	.000	8	6	6	7	4	6.48
1988—Bradenton Braves	Gulf Coast	4	12	0	2	.000	11	10	5	18	2	3.75
1988—Richmond y	Int'national	5	6⅓	0	0	.000	4	1	1	3	2	1.42
1989—Columbus	Int'national	11	23⅓	1	1	.500	17	9	8	27	13	3.09
1989—New York z	American	22	99⅓	4	4	.500	78	42	36	79	29	3.26
1990—New York a	American	28	156⅔	6	12	.333	155	77	73	134	55	4.19
American League Totals—4 Years		88	311⅓	11	19	.367	282	146	130	256	107	3.76
National League Totals—2 Years		20	25	1	1	.500	25	13	13	22	8	4.68
Major League Totals—6 Years		108	336⅓	12	20	.375	307	159	143	278	115	3.83

Selected by Detroit Tigers' organization in 7th round of free-agent draft, June 8, 1981.
†On disabled list, April 18 to May 12, 1983.
‡On disabled list, June 24 to July 11 and August 4 to August 17, 1984.
§Traded with Pitcher Randy O'Neal to Atlanta Braves for Outfielders Terry Harper and Freddy Tiburcio, January 27, 1987.
xOn disabled list, April 10 to August 17, 1988; included rehabilitation disability assignment to Bradenton, July 29 to August 10, 1988, and to Richmond, August 11 to August 17, 1988.
yReleased, December 4, 1988; signed by Columbus (New York Yankees' organization), January, 1989.
zOn disabled list, June 15 to July 11, 1989; included rehabilitation disability assignment to Columbus, July 4 to July 11, 1989.
aOn New York disabled list, April 9 to May 15, 1990; included rehabilitation disability assignment to Tampa (did not play), May 1 to May 14, 1990.

LAWRENCE PAUL CASIAN
Name pronounced CASS-ee-un.
(Larry)

Born October 28, 1965, at Lynwood, Calif.
Height, 6.00. Weight, 170.
Throws left and bats righthanded.
Attended California State University, Fullerton, Calif.

Year Club	League	G.	IP.	W.	L.	Pct.	H.	R.	ER.	SO.	BB.	ERA.
1987—Visalia	California	18	97	10	3	.769	89	35	27	96	49	2.51
1988—Orlando	Southern	27	174	9	9	.500	165	72	57	104	62	2.95
1988—Portland	P. Coast	1	2⅔	0	1	.000	5	3	0	2	0	0.00
1989—Portland	P. Coast	28	169⅓	7	12	.368	201	97	85	65	63	4.52
1990—Portland	P. Coast	37	156⅔	9	9	.500	171	90	78	89	59	4.48
1990—Minnesota	American	5	22⅓	2	1	.667	26	9	8	11	4	3.22
Major League Totals—1 Year		5	22⅓	2	1	.667	26	9	8	11	4	3.22

Selected by Minnesota Twins' organization in 6th round of free-agent draft, June 2, 1987.

ANTONIO CASTILLO

Name pronounced Cas-TEE-yoh.

(Tony)

Born March 1, 1963, at Lara, Venezuela.
Height, 5.10. Weight, 188.
Throws and bats lefthanded.

Major League saves: 1989 (1), 1990 (1). Total—2.

Year Club	League	G.	IP.	W.	L.	Pct.	H.	R.	ER.	SO.	BB.	ERA.
1983—Bradenton Jays	Gulf Coast	1	3	0	0	.000	3	1	1	4	0	3.00
1984—Florence	S. Atlantic	25	137⅓	11	8	.579	123	71	52	96	50	3.41
1985—Kinston	Carolina	36	127⅔	11	7	.611	111	44	27	136	48	1.90
1986—Knoxville†	Southern					(Did not play)						
1987—Dunedin	Florida St.	39	69⅔	6	2	.750	62	30	26	62	19	3.36
1988—Dunedin	Florida St.	30	42⅔	4	3	.571	31	9	7	46	10	1.48
1988—Knoxville	Southern	5	8	1	0	1.000	2	0	0	11	1	0.00
1988—Toronto	American	14	15	1	0	1.000	10	5	5	14	2	3.00
1989—Toronto	American	17	17⅔	1	1	.500	23	14	12	10	10	6.11
1989—Syracuse‡	Int'national	27	41⅔	1	3	.250	33	15	13	37	15	2.81
1989—Atlanta	National	12	9⅓	0	1	.000	8	5	5	5	4	4.82
1990—Atlanta	National	52	76⅔	5	1	.833	93	41	36	64	20	4.23
1990—Richmond	Int'national	5	25	3	1	.750	14	7	7	27	6	2.52
American League Totals—2 Years		31	32⅔	2	1	.667	33	19	17	24	12	4.68
National League Totals—2 Years		64	86	5	2	.714	101	46	41	69	24	4.29
Major League Totals—3 Years		95	118⅔	7	3	.700	134	65	58	93	36	4.40

Signed as free agent by Toronto Blue Jays' organization, February 16, 1983.
†On disabled list, April 10, 1986 through entire season.
‡Traded with a player to be named later to Atlanta Braves for Pitcher Jim Acker, August 24, 1989; Atlanta organization acquired Catcher Francisco Cabrera to complete deal, August 24, 1989.

FRANK ANTHONY CASTILLO

Name pronounced Cas-TEE-yoh.

Born April 1, 1969, at El Paso, Tex.
Height, 6.01. Weight, 180.
Throws and bats righthanded.

Pitched 4-0 no-hit victory against Huntsville, July 13, 1990 (first game).
Tied for Appalachian League lead in complete games with 5 in 1987.
Named Appalachian League Player of the Year, 1987.

Year Club	League	G.	IP.	W.	L.	Pct.	H.	R.	ER.	SO.	BB.	ERA.
1987—Wytheville	Ap'lachian	12	90⅓	*10	1	*.909	86	31	23	83	21	2.29
1987—Geneva	NYP	1	6	1	0	1.000	3	1	0	6	1	0.00
1988—Peoria†	Midwest	9	51	6	1	.857	25	5	4	58	10	0.71
1989—Winston-Salem	Carolina	18	129⅓	9	6	.600	118	42	36	114	24	2.51
1989—Charlotte	Southern	10	68	3	4	.429	73	35	29	43	12	3.84
1990—Charlotte	Southern	18	111⅓	6	6	.500	113	54	48	112	27	3.88

Selected by Chicago Cubs' organization in 6th round of free-agent draft, June 2, 1987.
†On disabled list, April 1 to July 23, 1988.

MONTE CARMELO CASTILLO

Name pronounced Cas-TEE-yoh.

(Carmen)

Born June 8, 1958, at San Francisco de Macoris, D. R.
Height, 6.01. Weight, 201.
Throws and bats righthanded.

Major League stolen bases: 1983 (1), 1984 (1), 1985 (3), 1987 (1), 1988 (6), 1989 (1). Total—15.

Year Club	League	Pos.	G.	AB.	R.	H.	2B.	3B.	HR.	RBI.	B.A.	PO.	A.	E.	F.A.
1978—Auburn†	NYP	OF	53	174	37	41	10	2	4	21	.236	109	6	11	.913
1978—Helena	Pion.	OF	5	15	1	6	2	0	0	2	.400	2	0	1	.667
1979—Waterloo	Midw.	OF	49	138	25	28	5	1	3	12	.203	54	1	7	.887
1979—Batavia	NYP	OF	36	128	29	43	8	1	8	28	.336	56	4	5	.923
1980—Waterloo	Midw.	OF	117	390	69	103	14	1	11	64	.264	173	10	14	.929
1981—Chattanooga	South.	OF	119	441	63	124	17	6	11	58	.281	236	13	15	.943
1982—Charleston	Int.	OF	71	281	46	78	12	1	9	39	.278	159	10	11	.939
1982—Cleveland	Amer.	OF	47	120	11	25	4	0	2	11	.208	91	0	2	.978
1983—Charleston‡	Int.	OF	36	148	29	40	5	2	4	22	.270	85	6	6	.938

Year Club	League	Pos.	G.	AB.	R.	H.	2B.	3B.	HR.	RBI.	B.A.	PO.	A.	E.	F.A.
1983—Cleveland............	Amer.	OF	23	36	9	10	2	1	1	3	.278	23	3	2	.929
1984—Cleveland............	Amer.	OF	87	211	36	55	9	2	10	36	.261	123	2	9	.933
1985—Cleveland............	Amer.	OF	67	184	27	45	5	1	11	25	.245	101	0	5	.953
1985—Maine....................	Int.	OF	26	96	12	23	2	2	2	18	.240	9	0	0	1.000
1986—Cleveland............	Amer.	OF	85	205	34	57	9	0	8	32	.278	58	4	4	.939
1987—Cleveland............	Amer.	OF	89	220	27	55	17	0	11	31	.250	29	3	0	1.000
1988—Cleveland§..........	Amer.	OF	66	176	12	48	8	0	4	14	.273	69	1	5	.933
1989—Minnesota x	Amer.	OF	94	218	23	56	13	3	8	33	.257	119	3	3	.976
1990—Minnesota............	Amer.	OF	64	137	11	30	4	0	0	12	.219	24	0	2	.923
Major League Totals—9 Years................			622	1507	190	381	71	7	55	197	.253	637	16	32	.953

Signed as free agent by Philadelphia Phillies' organization, June 30, 1978.

†Drafted by Chattanooga (Cleveland Indians' organization), December 5, 1978.

‡On disabled list, May 5 to July 4, 1983.

§Traded to Minnesota Twins for Pitcher Keith Atherton, March 26, 1989.

xGranted free agency, November 13, 1989; re-signed by Twins, January 8, 1990.

ANDUJAR CEDENO

Name pronounced Seh-DAIN-yo.

Born August 21, 1969, at La Romana, Dominican Republic.

Height, 6.01. Weight, 170.

Throws and bats righthanded.

Led Southern League shortstops in total chances with 572 in 1990.

Year Club	League	Pos.	G.	AB.	R.	H.	2B.	3B.	HR.	RBI.	B.A.	PO.	A.	E.	F.A.
1988—Sarasota Rangers	Gulf C.	SS	46	165	25	47	5	2	1	20	.285	58	145	25	.890
1989—Asheville...............	S. Atl.	SS-3B	126	487	76	*146	23	6	14	93	.300	182	346	62	.895
1990—Columbus..............	South.	SS	132	495	57	119	21	*11	19	64	.240	167	354	*51	.911
1990—Houston.................	Nat.	SS	7	8	0	0	0	0	0	0	.000	3	2	1	.833
Major League Totals—1 Year................			7	8	0	0	0	0	0	0	.000	3	2	1	.833

Signed as free agent by Houston Astros' organization, October 1, 1986.

RICHARD ALDO CERONE

Name pronounced Ce-RONE.

(Rick)

Born May 19, 1954, at Newark, N. J.

Height, 5.11. Weight, 195.

Throws and bats righthanded.

Received bachelor of science degree in physical education from
Seton Hall University, South Orange, N. J. in 1975.

Holds major league record for most consecutive errorless games, catcher, lifetime (159), July 5, 1987 through May 8, 1989.

Major league stolen bases: 1979 (1), 1980 (1), 1984 (1), 1985 (1). Total—4.

Named catcher on THE SPORTING NEWS American League All-Star Team, 1980.

Received reported $60,000 bonus to sign with Cleveland Indians, 1975.

Year Club	League	Pos.	G.	AB.	R.	H.	2B.	3B.	HR.	RBI.	B.A.	PO.	A.	E.	F.A.
1975—Oklahoma City	A. A.	C-OF	46	140	22	35	6	1	2	13	.250	178	30	3	.986
1975—Cleveland..............	Amer.	C	7	12	1	3	1	0	0	0	.250	18	1	0	1.000
1976—Toledo†.................	Int.	C	96	339	38	86	19	0	11	49	.254	351	50	*18	.957
1976—Cleveland‡...........	Amer.	C	7	16	1	2	0	0	0	1	.125	25	1	1	.963
1977—Charleston............	Int.	C-OF	70	231	30	54	10	1	6	40	.234	254	32	5	.983
1977—Toronto	Amer.	C	31	100	7	20	4	0	1	10	.200	146	15	1	.944
1978—Toronto	Amer.	C	88	282	25	63	8	2	3	20	.223	426	44	4	.992
1979—Toronto§	Amer.	C	136	469	47	112	27	4	7	61	.239	560	68	13	.980
1980—New York..............	Amer.	C	147	519	70	144	30	4	14	85	.277	800	73	9	.990
1981—New York x	Amer.	C	71	234	23	57	13	2	2	21	.244	353	26	3	.992
1982—New York y	Amer.	C	89	300	29	68	10	0	5	28	.227	509	25	6	.989
1983—New York..............	Amer.	C-3B	80	246	18	54	7	0	2	22	.220	412	18	4	.991
1984—New York z	Amer.	C	38	120	8	25	3	0	2	13	.208	230	9	1	.996
1984—Columbus a	Int.	C	8	25	2	5	2	0	0	1	.200	42	5	1	.979
1985—Atlanta bc.............	Nat.	C	96	282	15	61	9	0	3	25	.216	384	48	6	.986
1986—Milwaukee d	Amer.	C	68	216	22	56	14	0	4	18	.259	391	44	4	.991
1987—New York e	Amer.	*C-1B-P	113	284	28	69	12	1	4	23	.243	542	38	1	*.998
1988—Boston...................	Amer.	C	84	264	31	71	13	1	3	27	.269	471	28	0	*1.000
1989—Boston f................	Amer.	C-OF	102	296	28	72	16	1	4	48	.243	579	41	10	.984
1990—New York g	Amer.	C-2B	49	139	12	42	6	0	2	11	.302	179	14	1	.995
1990—Sarasota Yanks....	Gulf C.	C	3	7	0	1	0	0	0	0	.143	11	1	0	1.000
1990—Columbus..............	Int.	C	4	11	0	1	0	0	0	1	.091	13	0	1	.929
American League Totals—15 Years			1110	3497	350	858	164	15	53	388	.245	5641	445	58	.991
National League Totals—1 Year.............			96	282	15	61	9	0	3	25	.216	384	48	6	.986
Major League Totals—16 Years..............			1206	3779	365	919	173	15	56	413	.243	6025	493	64	.990

Selected by Cleveland Indians' organization in 1st round (seventh player selected) of free-agent draft, June 4, 1975.

†On disabled list, May 13 to May 24, 1976.

‡Traded with Infielder-Outfielder John Lowenstein to Toronto Blue Jays for Outfielder Rico Carty, December 6, 1976.

§Traded with Pitcher Tom Underwood and Outfielder Ted Wilborn to New York Yankees for First Baseman Chris Chambliss, Infielder Damaso Garcia and Pitcher Paul Mirabella, November 1, 1979.

xOn disabled list, April 19 to May 24, 1981.
yOn disabled list, May 12 to July 15, 1982.
zOn disabled list, May 7 to July 5, 1984; included rehabilitation disability assignment to Columbus, June 25 to July 5, 1984.
aTraded to Atlanta Braves for Pitcher Brian Fisher, December 5, 1984.
bOn disabled list, June 17 to July 2, 1985.
cTraded with Pitcher David Clay and Shortstop Flavio Alfaro to Milwaukee Brewers for Catcher Ted Simmons, March 5, 1986.
dGranted free agency, November 12, 1986; signed by New York Yankees, February 13, 1987.
eReleased, April 4, 1988; signed by Boston Red Sox, April 15, 1988.
fReleased, December 19, 1989; signed by New York Yankees, December 20, 1989.
gOn disabled list, June 8 to August 11, 1990; included rehabilitation disability assignment to Sarasota Yankees, July 9 to July 11, 1990; and Columbus, July 12 to July 24, 1990.

DIVISION SERIES RECORD

Year Club	League	Pos.	G.	AB.	R.	H.	2B.	3B.	HR.	RBI.	B.A.	PO.	A.	E.	F.A.
1981—New York	Amer.	C	5	18	1	6	2	0	1	5	.333	42	1	1	.977

CHAMPIONSHIP SERIES RECORD

Shares Championship Series record for hitting home run in first series at-bat, October 8, 1980.

Year Club	League	Pos.	G.	AB.	R.	H.	2B.	3B.	HR.	RBI.	B.A.	PO.	A.	E.	F.A.
1980—New York	Amer.	C	3	12	1	4	0	0	1	2	.333	14	4	0	1.000
1981—New York	Amer.	C	3	10	1	1	0	0	0	0	.100	23	2	0	1.000
Championship Series Totals—2 Years			6	22	2	5	0	0	1	2	.227	37	6	0	1.000

WORLD SERIES RECORD

Year Club	League	Pos.	G.	AB.	R.	H.	2B.	3B.	HR.	RBI.	B.A.	PO.	A.	E.	F.A.
1981—New York	Amer.	C	6	21	2	4	1	0	1	3	.190	42	4	0	1.000

PITCHING RECORD

Year Club	League	G.	IP.	W.	L.	Pct.	H.	R.	ER.	SO.	BB.	ERA.
1987—New York	American	2	2	0	0	.000	0	0	0	1	1	0.00

JOHN JOSEPH CERUTTI

Born April 28, 1960, at Albany, N. Y.
Height, 6.02. Weight, 195.
Throws and bats lefthanded.
Received bachelor of arts degree in economics from Amherst College, Amherst, Mass.

Major League saves: 1986 (1), 1988 (1). Total—2.
Tied for Southern League lead in shutouts with 3 in 1983.
Tied for Pioneer League lead in home runs allowed with 8 and games started by pitchers with 14 in 1981.

Year Club	League	G.	IP.	W.	L.	Pct.	H.	R.	ER.	SO.	BB.	ERA.
1981—Medicine Hat	Pioneer	14	*107	8	4	.667	87	45	36	120	43	3.03
1982—Kinston	Carolina	16	113	10	5	.667	88	47	40	136	49	3.19
1982—Knoxville	Southern	4	32⅓	4	0	1.000	18	4	4	17	10	1.11
1982—Syracuse	Int'national	6	30	0	3	.000	42	25	22	20	16	6.60
1983—Knoxville	Southern	29	188⅔	9	13	.409	182	89	72	131	65	3.43
1984—Syracuse	Int'national	29	148	7	●13	.350	152	89	73	114	52	4.44
1985—Syracuse	Int'national	28	182	11	9	.550	165	84	60	110	60	2.97
1985—Toronto	American	4	6⅔	0	2	.000	10	7	4	5	4	5.40
1986—Syracuse	Int'national	7	43⅔	1	3	.250	44	27	20	22	16	4.12
1986—Toronto	American	34	145⅓	9	4	.692	150	73	67	89	47	4.15
1987—Toronto	American	44	151⅓	11	4	*.733	144	75	74	92	59	4.40
1988—Toronto	American	46	123⅔	6	7	.462	120	56	43	65	42	3.13
1989—Toronto	American	33	205⅓	11	11	.500	214	90	70	69	53	3.07
1990—Toronto†	American	30	140	9	9	.500	162	77	74	49	49	4.76
Major League Totals—6 Years		191	772⅓	46	37	.554	800	378	332	369	254	3.87

Selected by Toronto Blue Jays' organization in 1st round (21st player selected) of free-agent draft, June 8, 1981.
†Granted free agency, December 20, 1990.

CHAMPIONSHIP SERIES RECORD

Year Club	League	G.	IP.	W.	L.	Pct.	H.	R.	ER.	SO.	BB.	ERA.
1989—Toronto	American	2	2⅔	0	0	.000	0	0	0	1	3	0.00

WESLEY POLK CHAMBERLAIN
(Wes)

Born April 13, 1966, at Chicago, Ill.
Height, 6.02. Weight, 210.
Throws and bats righthanded.
Attended Jackson State University, Jackson, Miss.

Major League stolen bases: 1990 (4).
Led Eastern League in total bases with 239 in 1989.
Tied for New York-Pennsylvania League lead in double plays by outfielders with 3 in 1987.
Named Eastern League Most Valuable Player, 1989.

Year Club	League	Pos.	G.	AB.	R.	H.	2B.	3B.	HR.	RBI.	B.A.	PO.	A.	E.	F.A.
1987—Watertown .... NYP		OF	66	258	50	67	13	4	5	35	.260	121	9	7	.949
1988—Augusta .... S. Atl.		OF	27	107	22	36	7	2	1	17	.336	49	4	1	.981
1988—Salem .... Carol.		OF	92	365	66	100	15	1	11	50	.274	161	11	9	.950
1989—Harrisburg .... East.		OF	129	471	65	*144	26	3	21	*87	.306	205	*14	*15	.936
1990—Buffalo† .... A. A.		OF	123	416	43	104	24	2	6	52	.250	203	16	9	.961
1990—Philadelphia .... Nat.		OF	18	46	9	13	3	0	2	4	.283	23	0	1	.958
Major League Totals—1 Year			18	46	9	13	3	0	2	4	.283	23	0	1	.958

Selected by Pittsburgh Pirates' organization in 5th round of free-agent draft, June 4, 1984.

Selected by Pittsburgh Pirates' organization in 4th round of free-agent draft, June 2, 1987.

†Traded with Outfielder Julio Peguero and a player to be named later to Philadelphia Phillies for Outfielder/First Baseman Carmelo Martinez, August 30, 1990; Philadelphia acquired Outfielder Tony Longmire to complete deal, September 28, 1990.

DARRIN JOHN CHAPIN

Born February 1, 1966, at Warren, O.
Height, 6.00. Weight, 170.
Throws and bats righthanded.
Attended Cuyahoga Community College, Cleveland, O.,
and Cleveland State University, Cleveland, O.

Led Eastern League in saves with 21 and games finished in relief with 40 in 1990.

Tied for New York-Pennsylvania League lead in intentional bases on balls issued with 5 in 1987.

Year Club	League	G.	IP.	W.	L.	Pct.	H.	R.	ER.	SO.	BB.	ERA.
1986—Sarasota Yankees .... Gulf Coast		13	83⅓	4	3	.571	71	●42	30	67	27	3.24
1987—Oneonta .... NYP		25	40	1	1	.500	31	8	3	26	17	0.68
1988—Fort Lauderdale .... Florida St.		38	63	6	4	.600	39	8	6	57	19	0.86
1988—Albany .... Eastern		3	4	0	0	.000	11	7	5	4	2	11.25
1989—Albany .... Eastern		7	8⅔	1	0	1.000	5	0	0	16	1	0.00
1989—Columbus .... Int'national		27	40	2	4	.333	33	15	13	38	15	2.93
1990—Albany .... Eastern		43	52⅔	3	2	.600	43	20	16	61	21	2.73
1990—Columbus .... Int'national		6	8⅔	0	1	.000	10	8	7	8	6	7.27

Selected by New York Yankees' organization in 6th round of free-agent draft, January 14, 1986.

NORMAN WOOD CHARLTON III
(Norm)

Born January 6, 1963, at Fort Polk, La.
Height, 6.03. Weight, 205.
Throws left and bats left and righthanded.
Received degree in political science, religion, and physical education
from Rice University, Houston, Tex.

Major League saves: 1990 (2).

Led American Association in wild pitches with 13 in 1988.

Year Club	League	G.	IP.	W.	L.	Pct.	H.	R.	ER.	SO.	BB.	ERA.
1984—West Palm Beach .... Florida St.		8	39⅓	1	4	.200	51	27	20	27	22	4.58
1985—West Palm Beach† .... Florida St.		24	128	7	10	.412	135	79	65	71	79	4.57
1986—Vermont .... Eastern		22	136⅔	10	6	.625	109	55	43	96	74	2.83
1987—Nashville‡ .... Am. Assoc.		18	98⅓	2	8	.200	97	57	47	74	44	4.30
1988—Nashville .... Am. Assoc.		27	182	11	10	.524	149	69	61	*161	56	3.02
1988—Cincinnati .... National		10	61⅓	4	5	.444	60	27	27	39	20	3.96
1989—Cincinnati .... National		69	95⅓	8	3	.727	67	38	31	98	40	2.93
1990—Cincinnati .... National		56	154⅓	12	9	.571	131	53	47	117	70	2.74
Major League Totals—3 Years		135	311	24	17	.585	258	118	105	254	130	3.04

Selected by Montreal Expos' organization in 1st round (27th player selected) of free-agent draft, June 4, 1984.

†Traded with a player to be named later to Cincinnati Reds for Infielder Wayne Krenchicki, March 31, 1986; Cincinnati acquired Second Baseman Tim Barker to complete deal, April 2, 1986.

‡On Cincinnati disabled list, April 6 to June 26, 1987; included rehabilitation disability assignment to Nashville, June 9 to June 26, 1987.

CHAMPIONSHIP SERIES RECORD

Year Club	League	G.	IP.	W.	L.	Pct.	H.	R.	ER.	SO.	BB.	ERA.
1990—Cincinnati .... National		4	5	1	1	.500	4	2	1	3	3	1.80

WORLD SERIES RECORD

Year Club	League	G.	IP.	W.	L.	Pct.	H.	R.	ER.	SO.	BB.	ERA.
1990—Cincinnati .... National		1	1	0	0	.000	1	0	0	0	0	0.00

SCOTT MICHAEL CHIAMPARINO

Name pronounced CHAMP-uh-ree-no.
Born August 22, 1966, at San Mateo, Calif.
Height, 6.02. Weight, 200.
Throws right and bats lefthanded.
Attended Santa Clara University, Santa Clara, Calif.

Tied for Pacific Coast League lead in shutouts with 2 in 1990.

Year Club	League	G.	IP.	W.	L.	Pct.	H.	R.	ER.	SO.	BB.	ERA.
1987—Medford	Northwest	13	67⅔	5	4	.556	64	29	19	65	20	2.53
1988—Modesto	California	16	106⅔	5	7	.417	89	40	32	117	56	2.70
1988—Huntsville	Southern	13	84	4	5	.444	88	36	30	49	26	3.21
1989—Huntsville	Southern	17	101⅔	8	6	.571	109	60	52	87	29	4.60
1990—Tacoma†	P. Coast	26	173	13	9	.591	174	79	63	110	72	3.28
1990—Texas	American	6	37⅔	1	2	.333	36	14	11	19	12	2.63
Major League Totals—1 Year		6	37⅔	1	2	.333	36	14	11	19	12	2.63

Selected by Oakland Athletics' organization in 4th round of free-agent draft, June 2, 1987.

†Traded with Pitcher Joe Bitker to Texas Rangers, September 4, 1990, completing deal in which Texas traded Outfielder/Designated Hitter Harold Baines to Oakland Athletics for two players to be named later, August 29, 1990.

STEPHEN VINCENT CHITREN
(Steve)

Born June 8, 1967, at Tokyo, Japan.
Height, 6.00. Weight, 180.
Throws and bats righthanded.
Attended Stanford University, Stanford, Calif.

Led Southern League in saves with 27 in 1990.

Year Club	League	G.	IP.	W.	L.	Pct.	H.	R.	ER.	SO.	BB.	ERA.
1989—Madison	Midwest	20	22⅔	2	1	.667	13	3	3	17	4	1.19
1989—Southern Oregon	Northwest	2	5	0	0	.000	3	2	1	3	2	1.80
1990—Huntsville	Southern	48	53⅔	2	4	.333	32	18	10	61	22	1.68
1990—Tacoma	P. Coast	1	⅔	0	0	.000	1	0	0	2	0	0.00
1990—Oakland	American	8	17⅔	1	0	1.000	7	2	2	19	4	1.02
Major League Totals—1 Year		8	17⅔	1	0	1.000	7	2	2	19	4	1.02

Selected by Seattle Mariners' organization in 9th round of free-agent draft, June 1, 1988.
Selected by Oakland Athletics' organization in 6th round of free-agent draft, June 5, 1989.

JAMES CLANCY
(Jim)

Born December 18, 1955, at Chicago, Ill.
Height, 6.04. Weight, 220.
Throws and bats righthanded.

Major League saves: 1988 (1), 1990 (1). Total—2.
Led American League pitchers in games started with 40 in 1982 and tied for lead with 36 in 1984.
Tied for National League lead in intentional bases on balls issued with 15 in 1989.
Tied for Gulf Coast League lead in shutouts with 2 in 1974.

Year Club	League	G.	IP.	W.	L.	Pct.	H.	R.	ER.	SO.	BB.	ERA.
1974—Sarasota Rangers	Gulf Coast	9	53	3	3	.500	40	21	16	58	28	2.72
1975—Anderson	W. Carol.	23	148	6	13	.316	139	85	63	109	91	3.83
1976—San Antonio†‡	Texas	23	125	6	8	.429	133	94	★89	77	98	6.41
1977—Jersey City	Eastern	20	118	5	13	.278	116	87	64	99	75	4.88
1977—Toronto	American	13	77	4	9	.308	80	47	43	44	47	5.03
1978—Toronto	American	31	194	10	12	.455	199	96	88	106	91	4.08
1979—Toronto§	American	12	64	2	7	.222	65	44	39	33	31	5.48
1980—Toronto	American	34	251	13	16	.448	217	108	92	152	★128	3.30
1981—Toronto	American	22	125	6	12	.333	126	77	68	56	64	4.90
1982—Toronto	American	40	266⅔	16	14	.533	251	122	110	139	77	3.71
1983—Toronto	American	34	223	15	11	.577	238	115	97	99	61	3.91
1984—Toronto	American	36	219⅔	13	15	.464	249	★132	★125	118	88	5.12
1985—Toronto x	American	23	128⅔	9	6	.600	117	54	54	66	37	3.78
1985—Knoxville	Southern	2	8	1	0	1.000	7	3	3	2	2	3.38
1986—Toronto y	American	34	219⅓	14	14	.500	202	100	96	126	63	3.94
1987—Toronto	American	37	241⅓	15	11	.577	234	103	95	180	80	3.54
1988—Toronto z	American	36	196⅓	11	13	.458	207	106	98	118	47	4.49
1989—Houston	National	33	147	7	14	.333	155	100	83	91	66	5.08
1990—Houston	National	33	76	2	8	.200	100	58	55	44	33	6.51
1990—Tucson	P. Coast	10	42⅓	3	2	.600	48	17	14	34	9	2.98
American League Totals—12 Years		352	2206	128	140	.478	2185	1104	1005	1237	814	4.10
National League Totals—2 Years		66	223	9	22	.290	255	158	138	135	99	5.57
Major League Totals—14 Years		418	2429	137	162	.458	2440	1262	1143	1372	913	4.24

Selected by Texas Rangers' organization in 4th round of free-agent draft, June 5, 1974.

†On disabled list, June 15 to June 26, 1976.

‡Selected by Toronto Blue Jays from Texas Rangers in American League expansion draft, November 5, 1976.

§On disabled list, May 12 to July 4 and August 5, 1979 through remainder of season.

xOn disabled list, March 25 to April 30 and July 27 to September 2, 1985; included rehabilitation disability assignment to Knoxville, April 21 to April 30, 1985.

yGranted free agency, November 12, 1986; re-signed by Blue Jays, January 6, 1987.

zGranted free agency, October 24, 1988; signed by Houston Astros, December 16, 1988.

CHAMPIONSHIP SERIES RECORD

Year Club	League	G.	IP.	W.	L.	Pct.	H.	R.	ER.	SO.	BB.	ERA.
1985—Toronto	American	1	1	0	1	.000	2	1	1	0	1	9.00

Year League	IP.	W.	L.	Pct.	H.	R.	ER.	SO.	BB.	ERA.
1982—American	1	0	0	.000	0	0	0	0	0	0.00

BRYAN DONALD CLARK

Born July 12, 1956, at Madera, Calif.
Height, 6.02. Weight, 200.
Throws and bats lefthanded.
Attended Fresno City College, Fresno, Calif.

Major League saves: 1981 (2), 1985 (2). Total—4.
Led Carolina League in wild pitches with 24 in 1977 and 27 in 1979.
Led Western Carolinas League in wild pitches with 31 in 1976.
Led New York-Pennsylvania League in wild pitches with 24 in 1975.
Tied for Pacific Coast League lead in games started by pitchers with 28 in 1989.
Tied for American Association lead in shutouts with 2 in 1986.
Tied for Carolina League lead in shutouts with 3 in 1979.
Tied for Gulf Coast League lead in shutouts with 2 in 1974.

Year Club	League	G.	IP.	W.	L.	Pct.	H.	R.	ER.	SO.	BB.	ERA.
1974—Bradenton Pirates	Gulf Coast	11	62	4	6	.400	49	35	23	47	*40	3.34
1975—Charleston	W. Carol.	12	57	4	7	.364	56	48	34	38	67	5.37
1975—Niagara Falls	NYP	13	74	3	*10	.231	47	49	37	59	*71	4.50
1976—Charleston	W. Carol.	22	103	1	13	.071	97	87	70	79	104	6.12
1977—Salem	Carolina	26	125	5	*13	.278	135	105	66	108	105	4.75
1978—Charleston†	W. Carol.	12	56	1	6	.143	55	53	38	44	55	6.11
1978—Bellingham	Northwest	2	4	0	0	.000	4	1	1	6	3	2.25
1978—Stockton	California	11	27	0	4	.000	30	32	22	18	39	7.33
1979—Alexandria	Carolina	23	167	●14	5	.737	124	57	49	116	*112	2.64
1980—Spokane	P. Coast	8	41	2	5	.286	43	35	24	19	37	5.27
1980—Lynn..	Eastern	16	116	9	5	.643	102	49	40	93	50	3.10
1981—Seattle.....................................	American	29	93	2	5	.286	92	54	45	52	55	4.35
1982—Salt Lake City	P. Coast	4	5⅓	1	1	.500	5	6	6	2	5	10.13
1982—Seattle.....................................	American	37	114⅔	5	2	.714	104	44	35	70	58	2.75
1983—Seattle‡	American	41	162⅓	7	10	.412	160	82	71	76	72	3.94
1984—Syracuse	Int'national	6	34	3	1	.750	32	16	13	26	26	3.44
1984—Toronto§	American	20	45⅔	1	2	.333	66	33	30	21	22	5.91
1985—Maine	Int'national	4	18⅔	1	0	1.000	15	2	2	9	8	0.96
1985—Cleveland x	American	31	62⅔	3	4	.429	78	47	44	24	34	6.32
1986—Buffalo.....................................	Am. Assoc.	34	122	7	6	.538	124	54	44	85	54	3.25
1986—Chicago....................................	American	5	8	0	0	.000	8	4	4	5	2	4.50
1987—Hawaii......................................	P. Coast	19	122⅓	4	10	.286	113	58	48	64	56	3.53
1987—Chicago yz................................	American	11	18⅔	0	0	.000	19	5	5	8	8	2.41
1988—Tacoma	P. Coast	19	92⅔	5	6	.455	104	50	34	46	44	3.30
1989—Tacoma a	P. Coast	28	174⅔	*15	7	.682	154	77	61	112	85	3.14
1990—Calgary	P. Coast	18	57	4	3	.571	55	40	25	27	29	3.95
1990—Seattle.....................................	American	12	11	2	0	1.000	9	4	4	3	10	3.27
Major League Totals—8 Years............................		186	516	20	23	.465	536	273	238	259	261	4.15

Selected by Pittsburgh Pirates' organization in 10th round of free-agent draft, June 5, 1974.
†Sold to Seattle Mariners' organization, June 12, 1978.
‡Traded to Toronto Blue Jays for Outfielder Barry Bonnell, December 9, 1983.
§Released, April 1, 1985; signed by Cleveland Indians' organization, April 15, 1985.
xReleased, November 12, 1985; signed by Buffalo (Chicago White Sox' organization), February 25, 1986.
yGranted free agency, October 15, 1987; signed by Minnesota Twins, December 7, 1987.
zReleased, March, 1988; signed by Tacoma (Oakland Athletics' organization), May 22, 1988.
aGranted free agency, October 15, 1989; signed by Calgary (Seattle Mariners' organization), December 27, 1989.

DAVID EARL CLARK
(Dave)

Born September 3, 1962, at Tupelo, Miss.
Height, 6.02. Weight, 210.
Throws right and bats lefthanded.
Attended Jackson State University, Jackson, Miss.
Brother of Lewis Clark, wide receiver with Seattle Seahawks.

Major League stolen bases: 1986 (1), 1987 (1), 1990 (7). Total—9.
Named outfielder on THE SPORTING NEWS College Baseball All-America Team, 1983.

Year Club	League	Pos.	G.	AB.	R.	H.	2B.	3B.	HR.	RBI.	B.A.	PO.	A.	E.	F.A.
1983—Waterloo...............	Midw.	OF	58	159	20	44	8	1	4	20	.277	37	4	1	.976
1984—Waterloo...............	Midw.	OF	110	363	74	112	16	3	15	63	.309	128	10	4	.972
1984—Buffalo..................	East.	OF	17	56	12	10	1	0	3	10	.179	23	2	1	.962
1985—Waterbury............	East.	OF	132	463	75	140	24	7	12	64	.302	204	11	11	.951
1986—Maine...................	Int.	OF	106	355	56	99	17	2	19	58	.279	150	4	6	.963
1986—Cleveland..............	Amer.	OF	18	58	10	16	1	0	3	9	.276	26	0	0	1.000
1987—Buffalo..................	A. A.	OF	108	420	83	143	22	3	30	80	.340	181	*22	6	.971
1987—Cleveland..............	Amer.	OF	29	87	11	18	5	0	3	12	.207	24	1	0	1.000
1988—Cleveland..............	Amer.	OF	63	156	11	41	4	1	3	18	.263	36	0	2	.947
1988—Colorado Springs.	P. C.	OF	47	165	27	49	10	2	4	31	.297	85	6	3	.968
1989—Cleveland†............	Amer.	OF	102	253	21	60	12	0	8	29	.237	27	0	1	.964

Year	Club	League	Pos.	G.	AB.	R.	H.	2B.	3B.	HR.	RBI.	B.A.	PO.	A.	E.	F.A.
1990—Chicago		Nat.	OF	84	171	22	47	4	2	5	20	.275	60	2	0	1.000
	American League Totals—4 Years			212	554	53	135	22	1	17	68	.244	113	1	3	.974
	National League Totals—1 Year			84	171	22	47	4	2	5	20	.275	60	2	0	1.000
	Major League Totals—5 Years			296	725	75	182	26	3	22	88	.251	173	3	3	.983

Selected by Cleveland Indians' organization in 1st round (11th player selected) of free-agent draft, June 6, 1983.
†Traded to Chicago Cubs for Outfielder Mitch Webster, November 20, 1989.

JACK ANTHONY CLARK

Born November 10, 1955, at New Brighton, Pa.
Height, 6.03. Weight, 226.
Throws and bats righthanded.

Shares major league records for most strikeouts, two consecutive games (9), June 11 (5) (12 innings), 13 (4), 1989; most errors by first baseman, inning (3), May 25, 1987, second inning.

Holds National League record for most consecutive games, one or more bases on balls (16), July 18 through August 10, 1987.

Shares National League record for most bases on balls, doubleheader (6), July 8, 1987 (19 innings).

Major League stolen bases: 1975 (1), 1976 (6), 1977 (12), 1978 (15), 1979 (11), 1980 (2), 1981 (1), 1982 (6), 1983 (5), 1984 (1), 1985 (1), 1986 (1), 1987 (1), 1988 (3), 1989 (6), 1990 (4). Total—76.

Led National League in bases on balls received with 136 in 1987, 132 in 1989 and 104 in 1990.

Led National League in slugging percentage with .597 in 1987.

Led National League in game-winning RBIs with 18 in 1980 and tied for lead with 21 in 1982.

Tied for National League lead in double plays by outfielders with 5 in 1978, 7 in 1979 and 4 in 1981.

Led Texas League in total bases with 239 in 1975.

Led California League in total bases with 254 in 1974.

Led Texas League third basemen in putouts with 102, assists with 278, double plays with 29 and fielding percentage with .872 in 1975.

Named first baseman on THE SPORTING NEWS National League All-Star Team, 1987.

Named outfielder on THE SPORTING NEWS National League All-Star Team, 1978.

Named first baseman on THE SPORTING NEWS National League Silver Slugger team, 1985 and 1987.

Year	Club	League	Pos.	G.	AB.	R.	H.	2B.	3B.	HR.	RBI.	B.A.	PO.	A.	E.	F.A.
1973—Great Falls		Pion.	OF-P-3B	65	234	46	75	20	1	9	54	.321	73	9	1	.988
1974—Fresno		Calif.	3B	131	495	88	156	23	9	19	★117	.315	100	204	★53	.852
1975—Lafayette		Texas	★3B-OF	126	466	94	141	25	2	●23	77	.303	107	279	★56	.873
1975—San Francisco		Nat.	OF-3B	8	17	3	4	0	0	0	2	.235	8	1	0	1.000
1976—Phoenix		P. C.	OF-3B	131	470	111	152	29	★16	17	86	.323	188	23	9	.959
1976—San Francisco		Nat.	OF	26	102	14	23	6	2	2	10	.225	71	3	1	.987
1977—San Francisco		Nat.	OF	136	413	64	104	17	4	13	51	.252	226	11	6	.975
1978—San Francisco		Nat.	OF	156	592	90	181	46	8	25	98	.306	320	16	6	.982
1979—San Francisco		Nat.	OF-3B	143	527	84	144	25	2	26	86	.273	262	13	5	.971
1980—San Francisco†		Nat.	OF	127	437	77	124	20	8	22	82	.284	229	7	8	.967
1981—San Francisco		Nat.	OF	99	385	60	103	19	2	17	53	.268	193	●14	4	.981
1982—San Francisco		Nat.	OF	157	563	90	154	30	3	27	103	.274	281	10	6	.980
1983—San Francisco		Nat.	OF-1B	135	492	82	132	25	0	20	66	.268	262	20	9	.969
1984—San Francisco‡§		Nat.	OF-1B	57	203	33	65	9	1	11	44	.320	120	9	2	.985
1985—St. Louis x		Nat.	★1B-OF	126	442	71	124	26	3	22	87	.281	1128	66	★14	.988
1986—St. Louis y		Nat.	1B	65	232	34	55	12	2	9	23	.237	623	35	3	.995
1987—St. Louis z		Nat.	1B-OF	131	419	93	120	23	1	35	106	.286	1152	77	14	.989
1988—New York ab		Amer.	OF-1B	150	496	81	120	14	0	27	93	.242	129	8	5	.965
1989—San Diego		Nat.	●1B-OF	142	455	76	110	19	1	26	94	.242	1157	89	●15	.988
1990—San Diego cde		Nat.	1B	115	334	59	89	12	1	25	62	.266	855	69	6	.994
	National League Totals—15 Years			1623	5613	930	1532	289	38	280	967	.273	6887	440	99	.987
	American League Totals—1 Year			150	496	81	120	14	0	27	93	.242	129	8	5	.965
	Major League Totals—16 Years			1773	6109	1011	1652	303	38	307	1060	.270	7016	448	104	.986

Selected by San Francisco Giants' organization in 13th round of free-agent draft, June 5, 1973.
†On disabled list, August 23 to September 8, 1980.
‡On disabled list, June 25 to September 5, 1984.
§Traded to St. Louis Cardinals for First Basemen David Green and Gary Rajsich, Pitcher Dave LaPoint and Shortstop Jose Gonzalez (Jose Uribe), February 1, 1985.
xOn disabled list, August 24 to September 8, 1985.
yOn disabled list, June 25, 1986 through remainder of season.
zGranted free agency, November 9, 1987; signed by New York Yankees, January 6, 1988.
aOn disabled list, March 21 to April 15, 1988.
bTraded with Pitcher Pat Clements to San Diego Padres for Pitchers Jimmy Jones and Lance McCullers and Outfielder Stan Jefferson, October 24, 1988.
cOn disabled list, May 6 to June 4, 1990.
dOn suspended list, October 2 and October 3, 1990.
eGranted free agency, December 7, 1990; signed by Boston Red Sox, December 15, 1990.

CHAMPIONSHIP SERIES RECORD

Shares Championship Series records for most at-bats (2), hits (2) and singles (2), inning, October 13, 1985, second inning.

Year	Club	League	Pos.	G.	AB.	R.	H.	2B.	3B.	HR.	RBI.	B.A.	PO.	A.	E.	F.A.
1985—St. Louis		Nat.	1B	6	21	4	8	0	0	1	4	.381	55	0	0	1.000
1987—St. Louis		Nat.	PH	1	1	0	0	0	0	0	0	.000	0	0	0	.000
	Championship Series Totals—2 Years			7	22	4	8	0	0	1	4	.364	55	0	0	1.000

WORLD SERIES RECORD

Year	Club	League	Pos.	G.	AB.	R.	H.	2B.	3B.	HR.	RBI.	B.A.	PO.	A.	E.	F.A.
1985—St. Louis	Nat.		1B	7	25	1	6	2	0	0	4	.240	49	4	0	1.000

ALL-STAR GAME RECORD

Year	League	Pos.	AB.	R.	H.	2B.	3B.	HR.	RBI.	B.A.	PO.	A.	E.	F.A.
1978—National		OF	1	0	0	0	0	0	0	.000	0	0	0	.000
1979—National		PH	1	0	0	0	0	0	0	.000	0	0	0	.000
1985—National		1B	1	0	0	0	0	0	0	.000	4	0	0	1.000
1987—National		1B	3	0	0	0	0	0	0	.000	7	1	0	1.000
All-Star Game Totals—4 Years			6	0	0	0	0	0	0	.000	11	1	0	1.000

PITCHING RECORD

Year	Club	League	G.	IP.	W.	L.	Pct.	H.	R.	ER.	SO.	BB.	ERA.
1973—Great Falls	Pioneer		5	15	0	2	.000	24	24	10	17	19	6.00

JERALD DWAYNE CLARK

Born August 10, 1963, at Crockett, Tex.
Height, 6.04. Weight, 202.
Throws and bats righthanded.
Attended Lamar University, Beaumont, Tex.
Brother of Phil Clark, catcher-outfielder in Detroit Tigers' organization;
and Isaiah Clark, shortstop in Seattle Mariners' organization.

Named Northwest League Most Valuable Player, 1985.

Year	Club	League	Pos.	G.	AB.	R.	H.	2B.	3B.	HR.	RBI.	B.A.	PO.	A.	E.	F.A.
1985—Spokane	N'west		OF	73	283	45	92	●24	3	2	50	.325	145	7	6	.962
1986—Reno	Calif.		OF	95	389	76	118	34	3	7	58	.303	135	6	5	.966
1986—Beaumont	Texas		OF	16	56	9	18	4	1	0	6	.321	39	1	2	.952
1987—Wichita	Texas		OF	132	531	86	165	36	8	18	95	.311	262	10	3	.989
1988—Las Vegas	P. C.		OF-3B-1B	107	408	65	123	27	7	9	67	.301	194	11	7	.967
1988—San Diego	Nat.		OF	6	15	0	3	1	0	0	3	.200	10	1	0	1.000
1989—Las Vegas	P. C.		OF-1B	107	419	84	131	27	4	22	83	.313	213	8	8	.965
1989—San Diego	Nat.		OF	17	41	5	8	2	0	1	7	.195	16	2	1	.947
1990—San Diego	Nat.		1B-OF	53	101	12	27	4	1	5	11	.267	102	6	1	.991
1990—Las Vegas	P. C.		1B-OF	40	161	30	49	7	4	12	32	.304	236	10	2	.992
Major League Totals—3 Years				76	157	17	38	7	1	6	21	.242	128	9	2	.986

Selected by Los Angeles Dodgers' organization in 23rd round of free-agent draft, June 4, 1984.
Selected by San Diego Padres' organization in 12th round of free-agent draft, June 3, 1985.

MARK WILLIAM CLARK

Born May 12, 1968, at Bath, Ill.
Height, 6.05. Weight, 225.
Throws and bats righthanded.
Attended Lincoln Land Community College, Springfield, Ill.

Led Texas League in complete games with 5 in 1990.

Year	Club	League	G.	IP.	W.	L.	Pct.	H.	R.	ER.	SO.	BB.	ERA.
1988—Hamilton	NYP		15	94⅓	6	7	.462	88	39	32	60	32	3.05
1989—Savannah	S. Atlantic		27	173⅔	●14	9	.609	143	61	47	132	52	2.44
1990—St. Petersburg	Florida St.		10	62	3	2	.600	63	33	21	58	14	3.05
1990—Arkansas	Texas		19	115⅓	5	11	.313	111	56	49	87	37	3.82

Selected by St. Louis Cardinals' organization in 9th round of free-agent draft, June 1, 1988.

TERRY LEE CLARK

Born October 10, 1960, at Los Angeles, Calif.
Height, 6.02. Weight, 196.
Throws and bats righthanded.
Attended Mount San Antonio College, Walnut, Calif.

Led Florida State League in games finished in relief with 51 in 1982.
Led South Atlantic League in games finished in relief with 51 in 1981.
Led Appalachian League in saves with 8 in 1979.

Year	Club	League	G.	IP.	W.	L.	Pct.	H.	R.	ER.	SO.	BB.	ERA.
1979—Johnson City	Ap'lachian		●23	32	4	2	.667	31	10	7	22	11	1.97
1980—Gastonia	S. Atlantic		49	88	4	7	.364	82	34	31	50	22	3.17
1981—Gastonia	S. Atlantic		★53	75	4	5	.444	56	23	18	66	25	2.16
1982—St. Petersburg	Florida St.		★58	88⅓	10	7	.588	81	32	25	61	34	2.55
1983—Arkansas	Texas		52	81⅓	6	6	.500	68	31	29	63	19	3.21
1984—Louisville†	Am. Assoc.		18	34⅓	1	3	.250	41	19	18	24	12	4.72
1985—Arkansas‡	Texas		42	96⅔	6	5	.545	102	64	53	67	38	4.93
1986—Midland	Texas		57	90⅓	9	4	.692	98	49	33	66	28	3.29
1987—Edmonton	P. Coast		33	154⅔	8	9	.471	140	79	66	88	56	3.84
1988—Edmonton	P. Coast		16	113⅔	7	6	.538	128	62	57	59	33	4.51
1988—California	American		15	94	6	6	.500	120	54	53	39	31	5.07
1989—Edmonton§	P. Coast		21	138⅓	11	5	.688	130	62	55	90	33	3.58
1989—California x	American		4	11	0	2	.000	13	8	6	7	3	4.91
1990—Tucson	P. Coast		29	155	11	4	.733	172	73	61	80	41	3.54

Year Club	League	G.	IP.	W.	L.	Pct.	H.	R.	ER.	SO.	BB.	ERA.
1990—Houston	National	1	4	0	0	.000	9	7	6	2	3	13.50
American League Totals—2 Years		19	105	6	8	.429	133	62	59	46	34	5.06
National League Totals—1 Year		1	4	0	0	.000	9	7	6	2	3	13.50
Major League Totals—3 Years		20	109	6	8	.429	142	69	65	48	37	5.37

Selected by St. Louis Cardinals' organization in 22nd round of free-agent draft, June 5, 1979.

†On disabled list, May 27 to August 22, 1984.

‡Granted free agency, October 15, 1985; signed by Midland (California Angels' organization), February 25, 1986.

§On California disabled list, March 19 to May 3, 1989; included rehabilitation disability assignment to Palm Springs, April 12 to April 20, 1989; and Edmonton, April 21 to May 1, 1989.

xReleased, October 6, 1989; signed by Tucson (Houston Astros' organization), January 26, 1990.

WILLIAM NUSCHLER CLARK JR.
(Will)

Born March 13, 1964, at New Orleans, La.
Height, 6.01. Weight, 190.
Throws and bats lefthanded.
Attended Mississippi State University, Starkville, Miss.

Shares major league record by hitting home run in first major league at-bat, April 8, 1986.
Major League stolen bases: 1986 (4), 1987 (5), 1988 (9), 1989 (8), 1990 (8). Total—34.
Led National League in bases on balls received with 100 and intentional bases on balls received with 27 in 1988.
Led National League first basemen in total chances with 1,608 in 1988, 1,566 in 1989 and 1,587 in 1990.
Led National League first baseman in double plays with 130 in 1987, 126 in 1988 and 118 in 1990.
Named first baseman on THE SPORTING NEWS National League All-Star Team, 1988 and 1989.
Named first baseman on THE SPORTING NEWS National League Silver Slugger team, 1989.
Named first baseman on THE SPORTING NEWS College Baseball All-America Team, 1985.
Member of 1984 U.S. Olympic baseball team.
Named designated hitter on THE SPORTING NEWS College Baseball All-America Team, 1984.

Year Club	League	Pos.	G.	AB.	R.	H.	2B.	3B.	HR.	RBI.	B.A.	PO.	A.	E.	F.A.
1985—Fresno	Calif.	1B-OF	65	217	41	67	14	0	10	48	.309	523	51	6	.990
1986—San Francisco†	Nat.	1B	111	408	66	117	27	2	11	41	.287	942	72	11	.989
1986—Phoenix.................	P. C.	DH	6	20	3	5	0	0	0	1	.250	0	0	0	.000
1987—San Francisco	Nat.	1B	150	529	89	163	29	5	35	91	.308	1253	103	13	.991
1988—San Francisco	Nat.	1B	★162	575	102	162	31	6	29	★109	.282	★1492	104	12	.993
1989—San Francisco	Nat.	1B	159	588	●104	196	38	9	23	111	.333	★1445	111	10	.994
1990—San Francisco	Nat.	1B	154	600	91	177	25	5	19	95	.295	★1456	119	12	.992
Major League Totals—5 Years			736	2700	452	815	150	27	117	447	.302	6588	509	58	.992

Selected by Kansas City Royals' organization in 4th round of free-agent draft, June 7, 1982.

Selected by San Francisco Giants' organization in 1st round (second player selected) of free-agent draft, June 3, 1985.

†On disabled list, June 4 to July 24, 1986; included rehabilitation disability assignment to Phoenix, July 7 to July 24, 1986.

CHAMPIONSHIP SERIES RECORD

Holds Championship Series records for most hits (13) and total bases (24), series, 1989; most runs batted in, game (6), October 4, 1989.

Shares Championship Series records for most runs (8), consecutive hits (5) and long hits (6), series, 1989; most runs (4) and grand slams (1), game, October 4, 1989; most runs batted in, inning (4), October 4, 1989, fourth inning.

Shares National League Championship Series record for most hits, game (4), October 4, 1989.

Year Club	League	Pos.	G.	AB.	R.	H.	2B.	3B.	HR.	RBI.	B.A.	PO.	A.	E.	F.A.
1987—San Francisco	Nat.	1B	7	25	3	9	2	0	1	3	.360	63	7	1	.986
1989—San Francisco	Nat.	1B	5	20	8	13	3	1	2	8	.650	43	6	0	1.000
Championship Series Totals—2 Years.....			12	45	11	22	5	1	3	11	.489	106	13	1	.992

WORLD SERIES RECORD

Year Club	League	Pos.	G.	AB.	R.	H.	2B.	3B.	HR.	RBI.	B.A.	PO.	A.	E.	F.A.
1989—San Francisco	Nat.	1B	4	16	2	4	1	0	0	0	.250	40	2	0	1.000

ALL-STAR GAME RECORD

Year League	Pos.	AB.	R.	H.	2B.	3B.	HR.	RBI.	B.A.	PO.	A.	E.	F.A.
1988—National	1B	2	0	0	0	0	0	0	.000	4	1	0	1.000
1989—National	1B	2	0	0	0	0	0	0	.000	5	0	0	1.000
1990—National	1B	3	0	1	0	0	0	0	.333	6	0	0	1.000
All-Star Game Totals—3 Years....................		7	0	1	0	0	0	0	.143	15	1	0	1.000

STANLEY MARTEN CLARKE
(Stan)

Born August 9, 1960, at Toledo, O.
Height, 6.00. Weight, 190.
Throws and bats lefthanded.
Attended University of Toledo, Toledo, O.

Led International League in home runs allowed with 19 and balks with 16 in 1988.
Led Pioneer League in balks with 6 and tied for lead in complete games with 6 in 1981.
Tied for American Association lead in home runs allowed with 20 in 1990.

Year Club	League	G.	IP.	W.	L.	Pct.	H.	R.	ER.	SO.	BB.	ERA.
1981—Medicine Hat	Pioneer	17	94	8	4	.667	96	54	42	112	35	4.02
1982—Florence	S. Atlantic	50	95	6	4	.600	60	26	20	136	52	1.89
1982—Knoxville	Southern	11	16	0	1	.000	11	3	3	12	3	1.69
1983—Knoxville	Southern	26	43⅓	2	4	.333	30	18	12	51	20	2.49
1983—Toronto	American	10	11	1	1	.500	10	4	4	7	5	3.27
1983—Syracuse	Int'national	33	53	0	3	.000	39	26	17	58	34	2.89
1984—Syracuse†	Int'national	29	56⅔	2	3	.400	40	32	26	55	46	4.13
1985—Syracuse	Int'national	43	117⅔	●14	4	★.778	106	52	44	98	66	3.37
1985—Toronto	American	4	4	0	0	.000	3	2	2	2	2	4.50
1986—Syracuse	Int'national	31	138⅔	8	9	.471	138	68	60	64	57	3.89
1986—Toronto‡	American	10	12⅔	0	1	.000	18	13	13	9	10	9.24
1987—Calgary	P. Coast	31	64⅔	4	4	.500	46	23	21	42	34	2.92
1987—Seattle§	American	22	23	2	2	.500	31	14	14	13	10	5.48
1988—Toledo x	Int'national	31	189	12	13	.480	★184	80	73	133	61	3.48
1989—Omaha	Am. Assoc.	26	171⅔	12	6	.667	157	72	67	145	31	3.51
1989—Kansas City y	American	2	7	0	2	.000	14	12	12	2	4	15.43
1990—Louisville	Am. Assoc.	32	150	10	9	.526	159	82	76	93	51	4.56
1990—St. Louis z	National	2	3⅓	0	0	.000	2	1	1	3	0	2.70
American League Totals—5 Years		48	57⅔	3	6	.333	76	45	45	33	31	7.02
National League Totals—1 Year		2	3⅓	0	0	.000	2	1	1	3	0	2.70
Major League Totals—6 Years		50	61	3	6	.333	78	46	46	36	31	6.79

Selected by Toronto Blue Jays' organization in 6th round of free-agent draft, June 8, 1981.
†On disabled list, June 6 to July 3 and August 23, 1984 through remainder of season.
‡Drafted by Seattle Mariners, December 8, 1986.
§Traded to Detroit Tigers for Outfielder Bruce Fields, October 5, 1987.
xGranted free agency, October 15, 1989; signed by Omaha (Kansas City Royals' organization), November 20, 1988.
yGranted free agency, October 15, 1989; signed by Louisville (St. Louis Cardinals' organization), November 16, 1989.
zReleased, October 11, 1990.

MARTIN KEITH CLARY
(Marty)

Born April 3, 1962, at Detroit, Mich.
Height, 6.04. Weight, 195.
Throws and bats righthanded.
Attended Northwestern University, Evanston, Ill.
Led Southern League pitchers in games started with 30 in 1984.

Year Club	League	G.	IP.	W.	L.	Pct.	H.	R.	ER.	SO.	BB.	ERA.
1983—Durham	Carolina	15	89⅔	3	8	.273	101	65	50	58	39	5.02
1984—Greenville	Southern	30	186⅓	14	9	.609	172	77	66	125	82	3.19
1985—Richmond	Int'national	26	156⅔	8	12	.400	155	81	73	76	77	4.19
1986—Richmond	Int'national	24	132⅓	7	6	.538	118	72	64	56	82	4.35
1987—Richmond	Int'national	26	178	11	10	.524	180	86	74	91	75	3.74
1987—Atlanta	National	7	14⅔	0	1	.000	20	13	10	7	4	6.14
1988—Richmond	Int'national	27	143⅔	6	11	.353	142	65	54	73	37	3.38
1989—Richmond	Int'national	15	101⅓	7	5	.583	87	33	23	70	28	2.04
1989—Atlanta	National	18	108⅔	4	3	.571	103	47	38	30	31	3.15
1990—Atlanta†	National	33	101⅔	1	10	.091	128	72	64	44	39	5.67
Major League Totals—3 Years		58	225	5	14	.263	251	132	112	81	74	4.48

Selected by Atlanta Braves' organization in 3rd round of free-agent draft, June 6, 1983.
†Released, November 13, 1990.

MARK ALAN CLEAR

Born May 27, 1956, at Los Angeles, Calif.
Height, 6.04. Weight, 215.
Throws and bats righthanded.
Attended Mount Antonio College, Walnut, Calif.
Nephew of Bob Clear, minor league pitcher, 1945 through 1955; minor league player-manager,
1956 through 1961; minor league manager, 1962 through 1973; scout with California Angels,
1974 and 1975; and coach with California Angels, 1976 through 1987.
Major League saves: 1979 (14), 1980 (9), 1981 (9), 1982 (14), 1983 (4), 1984 (8), 1985 (3), 1986 (16), 1987 (6). Total—83.
Led Appalachian League in hit batsmen with 11 in 1974.
Named American League Rookie of the Year by THE SPORTING NEWS, 1979.

Year Club	League	G.	IP.	W.	L.	Pct.	H.	R.	ER.	SO.	BB.	ERA.
1974—Pulaski†	Ap'lachian	14	51	0	7	.000	73	★69	49	38	43	8.65
1975—Idaho Falls	Pioneer	13	28	1	2	.333	24	14	6	29	30	1.93
1976—Quad Cities	Midwest	30	144	8	10	.444	135	84	63	109	111	3.94
1977—Quad Cities	Midwest	13	74	6	3	.667	64	47	40	48	50	4.86
1977—Salinas	California	13	44	1	4	.200	49	36	32	26	45	6.55
1978—Salinas	California	10	53	3	5	.375	51	38	32	55	40	5.43
1978—El Paso	Texas	31	52	4	2	.667	28	14	14	80	32	2.42
1979—California	American	52	109	11	5	.688	87	48	44	98	68	3.63
1980—California‡	American	58	106	11	11	.500	82	51	39	105	65	3.31
1981—Boston	American	34	77	8	3	.727	69	36	35	82	51	4.09
1982—Boston	American	55	105	14	9	.609	92	39	35	109	61	3.00
1983—Boston	American	48	96	4	5	.444	101	71	67	81	68	6.28
1984—Boston	American	47	67	8	3	.727	47	38	30	76	70	4.03

Year Club	League	G.	IP.	W.	L.	Pct.	H.	R.	ER.	SO.	BB.	ERA.
1985—Boston§	American	41	55⅔	1	3	.250	45	26	23	55	50	3.72
1986—Milwaukee	American	59	73⅔	5	5	.500	53	23	18	85	36	2.20
1987—Milwaukee x	American	58	78⅓	8	5	.615	70	46	39	81	55	4.48
1988—Milwaukee yz	American	25	29	1	0	1.000	23	12	9	26	21	2.79
1989—California ab	American					(Did not play)						
1990—Edmonton	P. Coast	12	14⅔	1	0	1.000	14	5	5	21	8	3.07
1990—California c	American	4	7⅔	0	0	.000	5	7	5	6	9	5.87
1990—Iowa de	Am. Assoc.	2	1	0	0	.000	1	1	1	0	1	9.00
Major League Totals—11 Years		481	804⅓	71	49	.592	674	397	344	804	554	3.85

Selected by Philadelphia Phillies' organization in 8th round of free-agent draft, June 5, 1974.

†Released, April 2, 1975; signed by California Angels' organization, June 16, 1975.

‡Traded with Third Baseman Carney Lansford and Outfielder Rick Miller to Boston Red Sox for Shortstop Rick Burleson and Third Baseman Butch Hobson, December 10, 1980.

§Traded to Milwaukee Brewers for Infielder Ed Romero, December 11, 1985.

xGranted free agency, November 9, 1987; re-signed by Brewers, December 14, 1987.

yOn disabled list, July 21 to August 11 and August 22, 1988 through remainder of season.

zReleased, October 13, 1988; signed by California Angels, January 28, 1989.

aOn disabled list, April 1, 1989 through entire season.

bReleased, December 20, 1989; re-signed by Angels, February 2, 1990.

cReleased, June 6, 1990; signed by Iowa (Chicago Cubs' organization), June 22, 1990.

dOn suspended list, July 1, 1990 through remainder of season.

eReleased, September 21, 1990.

CHAMPIONSHIP SERIES RECORD

Year Club	League	G.	IP.	W.	L.	Pct.	H.	R.	ER.	SO.	BB.	ERA.
1979—California	American	1	5⅔	0	0	.000	4	3	3	3	2	4.76

ALL-STAR GAME RECORD

Year League	IP.	W.	L.	Pct.	H.	R.	ER.	SO.	BB.	ERA.
1979—American	2	0	0	.000	2	1	1	0	1	4.50

Member of American League All-Star Team in 1982; did not play.

WILLIAM ROGER CLEMENS

(Known by middle name.)
Born August 4, 1962, at Dayton, O.
Height, 6.04. Weight, 220.
Throws and bats righthanded.
Attended San Jacinto College (North), Houston, Tex.,
and University of Texas, Austin, Tex.

Holds major league record for most strikeouts, nine-inning game (20), April 29, 1986.
Shares American League record for most consecutive strikeouts, game (8), April 29, 1986.
Led American League in shutouts with 7 in 1987, 8 in 1988 and tied for lead with 4 in 1990.
Led American League in complete games with 18 in 1987 and tied for lead with 14 in 1988.
Named Major League Player of the Year by THE SPORTING NEWS, 1986.
Named American League Pitcher of the Year by THE SPORTING NEWS, 1986.
Won American League Cy Young Memorial Award, 1986 and 1987.
Named American League Most Valuable Player by Baseball Writers' Association of America, 1986.
Named righthanded pitcher on THE SPORTING NEWS American League All-Star Team, 1986 and 1987.

Year Club	League	G.	IP.	W.	L.	Pct.	H.	R.	ER.	SO.	BB.	ERA.
1983—Winter Haven	Florida St.	4	29	3	1	.750	22	4	4	36	0	1.24
1983—New Britain	Eastern	7	52	4	1	.800	31	8	8	59	12	1.38
1984—Pawtucket	Int'national	7	46⅔	2	3	.400	39	12	10	50	14	1.93
1984—Boston	American	21	133⅓	9	4	.692	146	67	64	126	29	4.32
1985—Boston†	American	15	98⅓	7	5	.583	83	38	36	74	37	3.29
1986—Boston	American	33	254	★24	4	★.857	179	77	70	238	67	★2.48
1987—Boston	American	36	281⅔	●20	9	.690	248	100	93	256	83	2.97
1988—Boston	American	35	264	18	12	.600	217	93	86	★291	62	2.93
1989—Boston	American	35	253⅓	17	11	.607	215	101	88	230	93	3.13
1990—Boston§	American	31	228⅓	21	6	.778	193	59	49	209	54	★1.93
Major League Totals—7 Years		206	1513	116	51	.695	1281	535	486	1424	425	2.89

Selected by New York Mets' organization in 12th round of free-agent draft, June 8, 1981.
Selected by Boston Red Sox' organization in 1st round (19th player selected) of free-agent draft, June 6, 1983.
†On disabled list, July 8 to August 3 and August 21, 1985 through remainder of season.

CHAMPIONSHIP SERIES RECORD

Holds Championship Series record for most hits allowed (22), series, 1986.
Shares Championship Series records for most earned runs allowed, series (11), most earned runs allowed, game (7), October 7, 1986; most consecutive strikeouts, game (4), October 6, 1988.
Holds American League Championship Series record for most innings pitched (22⅔), 1986.
Shares American League Championship Series record for most runs allowed, game (8), October 7, 1986.

Year Club	League	G.	IP.	W.	L.	Pct.	H.	R.	ER.	SO.	BB.	ERA.
1986—Boston	American	3	22⅔	1	1	.500	22	12	11	17	7	4.37
1988—Boston	American	1	7	0	0	.000	6	3	3	8	0	3.86
1990—Boston	American	2	7⅔	0	1	.000	7	3	3	4	5	3.52
Championship Series Totals—3 Years		6	37⅓	1	2	.333	35	18	17	29	12	4.10

WORLD SERIES RECORD

Year Club	League	G.	IP.	W.	L.	Pct.	H.	R.	ER.	SO.	BB.	ERA.
1986—Boston	American	2	11⅓	0	0	.000	9	5	4	11	6	3.18

Year League	IP.	W.	L.	Pct.	H.	R.	ER.	SO.	BB.	ERA.
1986—American	3	1	0	1.000	0	0	0	2	0	0.00
1988—American	1	0	0	.000	0	0	0	1	0	0.00
All-Star Game Totals—2 Years	4	1	0	1.000	0	0	0	3	0	0.00

Member of American League All-Star Team in 1990; did not play.

PATRICK BRIAN CLEMENTS
(Pat)

Born February 2, 1962, at McCloud, Calif.
Height, 6.00. Weight, 187.
Throws left and bats righthanded.
Attended UCLA.

Major League saves: 1985 (3), 1986 (2), 1987 (7). Total—12.

Year Club	League	G.	IP.	W.	L.	Pct.	H.	R.	ER.	SO.	BB.	ERA.
1983—Peoria	Midwest	15	92⅓	4	7	.364	113	56	46	67	24	4.48
1984—Waterbury	Eastern	43	67	4	2	.667	59	28	20	44	29	2.69
1985—California†	American	41	62	5	0	1.000	47	23	23	19	25	3.34
1985—Pittsburgh	National	27	34⅓	0	2	.000	39	14	14	17	15	3.67
1986—Pittsburgh‡	National	65	61	0	4	.000	53	20	19	31	32	2.80
1987—New York	American	55	80	3	3	.500	91	45	44	36	30	4.95
1987—Columbus	Int'national	4	19	1	0	1.000	19	8	8	7	2	3.79
1988—Columbus	Int'national	32	144	6	7	.462	136	55	44	69	34	2.75
1988—New York§	American	6	8⅓	0	0	.000	12	8	6	3	4	6.48
1989—Las Vegas	P. Coast	18	55	3	1	.750	57	31	25	34	24	4.09
1989—San Diego	National	23	39	4	1	.800	39	17	17	18	15	3.92
1990—San Diego	National	9	13	0	0	.000	20	9	6	6	7	4.15
1990—Las Vegas x	P. Coast	26	86⅓	4	3	.571	106	68	58	57	34	6.05
American League Totals—2 Years		102	150⅓	8	3	.727	150	76	73	58	59	4.37
National League Totals—4 Years		124	147⅓	4	7	.364	151	60	56	72	69	3.42
Major League Totals—6 Years		226	297⅔	12	10	.545	301	136	129	130	128	3.90

Selected by New York Yankees' organization in 32nd round of free-agent draft, June 3, 1980.
Selected by California Angels' organization in 4th round of free-agent draft, June 6, 1983.
†Traded with Outfielder Mike Brown and a player to be named later to Pittsburgh Pirates for Pitchers John Candelaria and Al Holland and Outfielder George Hendrick, August 2, 1985; Pittsburgh organization acquired Pitcher Bob Kipper to complete deal, August 16, 1985.
‡Traded with Pitchers Rick Rhoden and Cecilio Guante to New York Yankees for Pitchers Doug Drabek, Brian Fisher and Logan Easley, November 26, 1986.
§Traded with First Baseman-Outfielder Jack Clark to San Diego Padres for Pitchers Jimmy Jones and Lance McCullers and Outfielder Stan Jefferson, October 24, 1988.
xGranted free agency, December 20, 1990.

BOBBY DEAN COACHMAN
(Pete)

Born November 11, 1961, at Cottonwood, Ala.
Height, 5.09. Weight, 175.
Throws and bats righthanded.
Attended University of South Alabama, Mobile, Ala.

Led Midwest League in stolen bases with 69 in 1985.
Led Midwest League second basemen in double plays with 87 and total chances with 742 in 1985.
Led Northwest League second basemen in double plays with 35 in 1984.

Year Club	League	Pos.	G.	AB.	R.	H.	2B.	3B.	HR.	RBI.	B.A.	PO.	A.	E.	F.A.
1984—Salem	N'west	2B-3B	65	231	44	60	10	2	0	21	.260	129	162	10	.967
1985—Quad Cities	Midw.	2B	135	530	93	140	21	4	1	38	.264	*353	*370	19	.974
1986—Palm Springs	Calif.	2B	68	274	74	85	12	4	3	41	.310	146	206	14	.962
1986—Midland	Texas	2B	61	249	53	87	17	3	5	35	.349	125	171	11	.964
1987—Edmonton	P. C.	2B	115	440	82	136	26	3	4	43	.309	228	342	11	.981
1988—Edmonton	P. C.	2B-3B	129	486	80	128	21	2	6	61	.263	226	303	10	.981
1989—Edmonton	P. C.	3B-2B	127	477	69	136	17	10	2	43	.285	71	118	10	.950
1990—Edmonton	P. C.	3B-2B-OF	111	419	78	122	15	2	5	51	.291	72	122	11	.946
1990—California	Amer.	3B-2B	16	45	3	14	3	0	0	5	.311	6	23	2	.935
Major League Totals—1 Year			16	45	3	14	3	0	0	5	.311	6	23	2	.935

Selected by California Angels' organization in 11th round of free-agent draft, June 4, 1984.

DAVID CARTER COCHRANE
(Dave)

Born January 31, 1963, at Riverside, Calif.
Height, 6.02. Weight, 180.
Throws right and bats left and righthanded.
Attended California State University, Fullerton, Calif.

Led Texas League batters in strikeouts with 133 in 1984.
Led Carolina League in game-winning RBIs with 18 in 1983.
Led New York-Pennsylvania League batters in strikeouts with 117 and intentional bases on balls received with 7 in 1982.

Year Club	League	Pos.	G.	AB.	R.	H.	2B.	3B.	HR.	RBI.	B.A.	PO.	A.	E.	F.A.
1982—Little Falls............	NYP	3B	70	269	51	81	16	2	22	62	.301	49	110	*29	.846
1983—Lynchburg............	Carol.	3B	120	445	73	117	16	1	25	*102	.263	66	167	26	.900
1984—Jackson................	Texas	3B-SS	129	454	66	121	29	3	22	77	.267	79	167	32	.885
1985—Jackson†‡§...........	Texas	SS	33	103	14	23	1	0	4	20	.223	39	87	14	.900
1986—Birmingham	South.	3B-SS	93	349	66	95	23	5	17	74	.272	82	201	36	.887
1986—Buffalo..................	A. A.	3B-SS-OF	38	124	15	28	7	0	6	16	.226	25	58	4	.954
1986—Chicago................	Amer.	3B-SS	19	62	4	12	2	0	1	2	.194	10	31	6	.872
1987—Hawaii xy	P. C.	3-O-P-1	129	451	60	122	23	3	15	66	.271	106	83	15	.926
1988—Calgary	P. C.	1-O-3-C-S	120	406	55	116	27	3	15	61	.286	387	106	29	.944
1989—Calgary	P. C.	3-1-S-C-O	32	125	22	34	10	0	6	35	.272	86	43	6	.956
1989—Seattle..................	Amer.	I-O-C	54	102	13	24	4	1	3	7	.235	78	41	5	.960
1990—Calgary	P. C.	3-O-S-2-C	69	262	43	72	14	4	8	36	.275	104	101	14	.936
1990—Seattle..................	Amer.	S-3-1-C	15	20	0	3	0	0	0	0	.150	8	10	0	1.000
Major League Totals—3 Years			88	184	17	39	6	1	4	9	.212	96	82	11	.942

Selected by New York Mets' organization in 4th round of free-agent draft, June 8, 1981.

†On disabled list, May 25 to July 16, 1985.

‡Traded to Chicago White Sox' organization for Outfielder Tom Paciorek, July 16, 1985.

§On Glens Falls disabled list, July 16, 1985 through remainder of season.

xTraded with Pitcher Floyd Bannister to Kansas City Royals for Pitchers John Davis, Melido Perez, Chuck Mount and Greg Hibbard, December 10, 1987.

yTraded to Calgary (Seattle Mariners' organization) for Pitcher Ken Spratke, February 3, 1988.

PITCHING RECORD

Year Club	League	G.	IP.	W.	L.	Pct.	H.	R.	ER.	SO.	BB.	ERA.
1987—Hawaii..............................	P. Coast	8	11⅓	1	1	.500	15	9	9	6	11	7.15

CHRISTOPHER ALLEN CODIROLI

Name pronounced Coda-RO-lee.

(Chris)

Born March 26, 1958, at Oxnard, Calif.
Height, 6.01. Weight, 160.
Throws and bats righthanded.
Attended San Jose City College, San Jose, Calif., and San Jose State University, San Jose, Calif.

Major League saves: 1983 (1), 1984 (1), 1988 (1). Total—3.

Tied for American League lead in games started by pitchers with 37 in 1985.

Year Club	League	G.	IP.	W.	L.	Pct.	H.	R.	ER.	SO.	BB.	ERA.
1978—Lakeland........................	Florida St.	16	102	4	6	.400	93	44	37	72	40	3.26
1978—Montgomery...................	Southern	10	78	5	2	.714	60	20	17	57	24	1.96
1979—Montgomery†.................	Southern	8	49	2	3	.400	41	24	18	34	27	3.31
1980—Lakeland‡......................	Florida St.	9	50	1	1	.500	33	13	10	26	19	1.80
1980—Montgomery§.................	Southern	2	4	0	1	.000	6	7	6	1	4	13.50
1981—San Jose.......................	California	14	35	3	2	.600	23	8	6	26	24	1.54
1981—West Haven	Eastern	21	50	3	2	.600	35	25	15	47	25	2.70
1982—West Haven x................	Eastern	12	45	6	1	.857	37	14	12	45	19	2.40
1982—Tacoma.........................	P. Coast	16	123⅓	10	3	*.769	100	36	26	85	21	*1.90
1982—Oakland........................	American	3	16⅔	1	2	.333	16	8	8	5	4	4.32
1983—Oakland........................	American	37	205⅔	12	12	.500	208	115	102	85	72	4.46
1984—Oakland........................	American	28	89⅓	6	4	.600	111	67	58	44	34	5.84
1984—Tacoma.........................	P. Coast	9	57	2	1	.667	49	35	24	52	30	3.79
1985—Oakland........................	American	37	226	14	14	.500	228	125	112	111	78	4.46
1986—Oakland y......................	American	16	91⅔	5	8	.385	91	54	41	43	38	4.03
1987—Oakland z......................	American	3	11⅓	0	2	.000	12	11	11	4	8	8.74
1987—Tacoma z.......................	P. Coast	19	67⅔	2	7	.222	77	56	46	34	52	6.12
1988—Cleveland......................	American	14	19⅓	0	4	.000	32	22	20	12	10	9.31
1988—Colorado Springs a........	P. Coast	17	96⅓	5	4	.556	104	64	52	51	42	4.86
1989—		(Out of Organized Baseball)										
1990—Memphis.......................	Southern	4	13⅓	1	1	.500	16	12	12	13	10	8.10
1990—Omaha..........................	Am. Assoc.	4	16	1	1	.500	19	10	10	9	9	5.63
1990—Kansas City b................	American	6	10⅓	0	1	.000	13	11	11	8	17	9.58
Major League Totals—8 Years		144	670⅓	38	47	.447	711	413	363	312	261	4.87

Selected by Detroit Tigers' organization in 1st round (11th player selected) of free-agent draft, January 10, 1978.

†On disabled list, May 25, 1979 through remainder of season.

‡On disabled list, April 11 to June 10, 1980.

§Released, April 3, 1981; signed by Oakland A's organization, April 14, 1981.

xOn disabled list, April 19 to April 29, 1982.

yOn disabled list, June 28, 1966 through remainder of season.

zGranted free agency, October 15, 1987; signed by Colorado Springs (Cleveland Indians' organization), February 22, 1988.

aReleased, September 6, 1988; signed by Omaha (Kansas City Royals' organization), June, 1990.

bReleased, October 4, 1990.

KEVIN REESE COFFMAN

Born January 19, 1965, at Austin, Tex.
Height, 6.03. Weight, 206.
Throws and bats righthanded.

Led Southern League in wild pitches with 21 in 1987.

Year Club	League	G.	IP.	W.	L.	Pct.	H.	R.	ER.	SO.	BB.	ERA.
1983—Bradenton Braves	Gulf Coast	6	28⅔	2	4	.333	27	29	21	25	39	6.59
1984—Anderson	S. Atlantic	7	32⅔	1	4	.200	37	23	17	23	26	4.68
1984—Pulaski	Ap'lachian	11	48	1	4	.200	41	26	22	41	33	4.13
1985—Durham†	Carolina	3	4⅓	0	1	.000	4	5	5	1	11	10.38
1985—Sumter‡	S. Atlantic	24	62⅔	1	3	.250	42	25	22	43	26	3.16
1986—Durham	Carolina	3	13⅓	1	2	.333	11	12	11	7	17	7.43
1986—Sumter	S. Atlantic	18	114⅓	10	3	.769	99	56	39	120	64	3.07
1986—Greenville	Southern	8	48⅔	3	4	.429	43	24	24	43	30	4.44
1987—Greenville	Southern	30	181⅔	11	11	.500	162	102	89	153	★130	4.41
1987—Atlanta	National	5	25⅓	2	3	.400	31	14	13	14	22	4.62
1988—Atlanta	National	18	67	2	6	.250	62	52	43	24	54	5.78
1988—Durham	Carolina	8	10	1	1	.500	12	6	5	10	3	4.50
1988—Richmond§	Int'national	9	19⅓	1	1	.500	15	10	9	18	20	4.19
1989—Charlotte	Southern	7	21⅔	0	3	.000	15	15	9	12	26	3.74
1989—Iowa	Am. Assoc.	14	17⅔	0	2	.000	17	19	16	11	26	8.15
1989—Winston-Salem	Carolina	7	36	2	3	.400	23	24	18	47	34	4.50
1990—Charlotte	Southern	14	93	7	3	.700	77	28	21	84	54	2.03
1990—Iowa	Am. Assoc.	9	60⅓	2	5	.286	43	26	23	49	40	3.43
1990—Chicago x	National	8	18⅓	0	2	.000	26	24	23	9	19	11.29
Major League Totals—3 Years		31	110⅔	4	11	.267	119	90	79	47	95	6.42

Selected by Atlanta Braves' organization in 11th round of free-agent draft, June 6, 1983.
†On disabled list, April 24 to May 4, 1985.
‡On disabled list, May 4 to May 28, 1985.
§Traded with Pitcher Kevin Blankenship to Chicago Cubs for Catcher Jody Davis, September 29, 1988.
xReleased, December 3, 1990.

ALEXANDER COLE JR.

(Alex)

Born August 17, 1965, at Fayetteville, N. C.
Height, 6.02. Weight, 170.
Throws and bats lefthanded.
Attended Manatee Junior College, Bradenton, Fla.

Major League stolen bases: 1990 (40).
Led American Association in stolen bases with 47 in 1989.
Led Texas League in stolen bases with 68 and caught stealing with 29 in 1987.
Led Florida State League in caught stealing with 22 in 1986.
Led Appalachian League in stolen bases with 46 and caught stealing with 8 in 1985.
Tied for Pacific Coast League lead in caught stealing with 18 in 1990.
Led American Association outfielders in total chances with 342 in 1989.
Led Appalachian League outfielders in total chances with 142 in 1985.
Tied for Texas League lead in double plays by outfielders with 5 in 1987.

Year Club	League	Pos.	G.	AB.	R.	H.	2B.	3B.	HR.	RBI.	B.A.	PO.	A.	E.	F.A.
1985—Johnson City	Appal.	OF	66	232	★60	61	5	1	1	13	.263	★127	★12	3	.979
1986—St. Petersburg	Fla. St.	OF	74	286	76	98	9	1	0	26	.343	201	4	8	.962
1986—Louisville	A. A.	OF	63	200	25	50	2	4	1	16	.250	135	6	9	.940
1987—Arkansas	Texas	OF	125	477	68	122	12	4	2	27	.256	289	14	10	.968
1988—Louisville	A. A.	OF	120	392	44	91	7	8	0	24	.232	276	13	1	.997
1989—St. Petersburg	Fla. St.	OF	8	32	2	6	0	0	0	1	.188	13	0	0	1.000
1989—Louisville†	A. A.	OF	127	455	75	128	5	5	2	29	.281	★320	14	8	.977
1990—L.V.‡-Colo. Spr.	P. C.	OF	104	390	71	120	9	4	0	31	.308	181	6	9	.954
1990—Cleveland	Amer.	OF	63	227	43	68	5	4	0	13	.300	145	3	6	.961
Major League Totals—1 Year			63	227	43	68	5	4	0	13	.300	145	3	6	.961

Selected by Pittsburgh Pirates' organization in 11th round of free-agent draft, January 17, 1984.
Selected by St. Louis Cardinals' organization in 2nd round of free-agent draft, January 9, 1985.
†Traded with Pitcher Steve Peters to San Diego Padres for Pitcher Omar Olivares, February 27, 1990.
‡Traded to Cleveland Indians for Catcher Tom Lampkin, July 11, 1990.

VICTOR ALEXANDER COLE

Born January 23, 1968, at Leningrad, Russia.
Height, 5.10. Weight, 160.
Throws right and bats left and righthanded.
Attended Santa Clara University, Santa Clara, Calif.

Year Club	League	G.	IP.	W.	L.	Pct.	H.	R.	ER.	SO.	BB.	ERA.
1988—Eugene	Northwest	15	23⅔	1	0	1.000	16	6	4	39	8	1.52
1988—Baseball City	Florida St.	10	35	5	0	1.000	27	9	8	29	21	2.06
1989—Baseball City	Florida St.	9	42	3	1	.750	43	23	18	30	22	3.86
1989—Memphis	Southern	13	63⅔	1	9	.100	67	53	45	52	51	6.36
1990—Memphis	Southern	46	107⅔	3	8	.273	91	61	52	102	70	4.35

Selected by Kansas City Royals' organization in 14th round of free-agent draft, June 1, 1988.

—DID YOU KNOW—

That Kansas City rookie Kevin Appier fired a one-hitter against Detroit last July 7, one night after the Tigers' Jack Morris one-hit the Royals?

VINCENT MAURICE COLEMAN
(Vince)

Born September 22, 1961, at Jacksonville, Fla.
Height, 6.00. Weight, 170.
Throws right and bats left and righthanded.
Received degree in physical education from Florida A&M University, Tallahassee, Fla.
Cousin of Greg Coleman, punter with Cleveland Browns, Minnesota Vikings
and Washington Redskins, 1977 through 1988.

Holds major league records for most stolen bases (110) and most caught stealing (25), rookie season, 1985; most consecutive stolen bases without caught stealing, lifetime (50), September 18, 1988 through July 26, 1989.

Shares major league records for most sacrifice flies, game (3), May 1, 1986; fewest errors by outfielder, season, for leader in errors (9), 1986.

Shares National League record for most consecutive years leading league in stolen bases (6), 1985 through 1990.

Major League stolen bases: 1985 (110), 1986 (107), 1987 (109), 1988 (81), 1989 (65), 1990 (77). Total—549.

Led National League in stolen bases with 110 in 1985, 107 in 1986, 109 in 1987, 81 in 1988, 65 in 1989 and 77 in 1990.

Led National League in caught stealing with 25 in 1985, 22 in 1987 and tied for lead with 27 in 1988.

Led American Association in stolen bases with 101 and caught stealing with 36 in 1984.

Led South Atlantic League in stolen bases with 145 and caught stealing with 31 in 1983.

Tied for Appalachian League lead in stolen bases with 43 in 1982.

Led American Association outfielders in total chances with 381 in 1984.

Named National League Rookie Player of the Year by THE SPORTING NEWS, 1985.

Named National League Rookie of the Year by Baseball Writers' Association of America, 1985.

Named South Atlantic League Most Valuable Player, 1983.

Year Club	League	Pos.	G.	AB.	R.	H.	2B.	3B.	HR.	RBI.	B.A.	PO.	A.	E.	F.A.
1982—Johnson City	Appal.	OF	58	212	40	53	2	1	0	16	.250	123	7	8	.942
1983—Macon	S. Atl.	OF	113	446	99	156	8	7	0	53	★.350	225	18	8	.968
1984—Louisville	A. A.	OF	152	★608	★97	156	21	7	4	48	.257	357	14	●10	.974
1985—Louisville	A. A.	OF	5	21	1	3	0	0	0	0	.143	8	0	0	1.000
1985—St. Louis	Nat.	OF	151	636	107	170	20	10	1	40	.267	305	16	7	.979
1986—St. Louis	Nat.	OF	154	600	94	139	13	8	0	29	.232	300	12	●9	.972
1987—St. Louis	Nat.	OF	151	623	121	180	14	10	3	43	.289	274	16	9	.970
1988—St. Louis	Nat.	OF	153	616	77	160	20	10	3	38	.260	290	14	9	.971
1989—St. Louis	Nat.	OF	145	563	94	143	21	9	2	28	.254	247	5	●10	.962
1990—St. Louis†	Nat.	OF	124	497	73	145	18	9	6	39	.292	244	12	5	.981
Major League Totals—6 Years			878	3535	566	937	106	56	15	217	.265	1660	75	49	.973

Selected by Philadelphia Phillies' organization in 20th round of free-agent draft, June 8, 1981.

Selected by St. Louis Cardinals' organization in 10th round of free-agent draft, June 7, 1982.

†Granted free agency, November 5, 1990; signed by New York Mets, December 5, 1990.

CHAMPIONSHIP SERIES RECORD

Shares National League Championship Series record for most times caught stealing, total series (4).

Year Club	League	Pos.	G.	AB.	R.	H.	2B.	3B.	HR.	RBI.	B.A.	PO.	A.	E.	F.A.
1985—St. Louis	Nat.	OF	3	14	2	4	0	0	0	1	.286	8	0	0	1.000
1987—St. Louis	Nat.	OF	7	26	3	7	1	0	0	4	.269	9	1	0	1.000
Championship Series Totals—2 Years			10	40	5	11	1	0	0	5	.275	17	1	0	1.000

WORLD SERIES RECORD

Year Club	League	Pos.	G.	AB.	R.	H.	2B.	3B.	HR.	RBI.	B.A.	PO.	A.	E.	F.A.
1987—St. Louis	Nat.	OF	7	28	5	4	2	0	0	2	.143	10	2	0	1.000

Eligible for 1985 World Series with St. Louis Cardinals; did not play.

ALL-STAR GAME RECORD

Year League	Pos.	AB.	R.	H.	2B.	3B.	HR.	RBI.	B.A.	PO.	A.	E.	F.A.
1988—National	OF	2	1	1	0	0	0	0	.500	3	0	0	1.000
1989—National	PR-OF	0	0	0	0	0	0	0	.000	0	0	0	.000
All-Star Game Totals—2 Years		2	1	1	0	0	0	0	.500	3	0	0	1.000

DARNELL COLES

First name pronounced Darr-NELL.

Born June 2, 1962, at San Bernardino, Calif.
Height, 6.01. Weight, 185.
Throws and bats righthanded.
Attended Orange Coast College, Costa Mesa, Calif.

Major League stolen bases: 1984 (2), 1986 (6), 1987 (1), 1988 (4), 1989 (5). Total—18.

Hit three home runs in a game, September 20, 1987.

Led Midwest League shortstops in double plays with 66 in 1981.

Year Club	League	Pos.	G.	AB.	R.	H.	2B.	3B.	HR.	RBI.	B.A.	PO.	A.	E.	F.A.
1980—Bellingham	N'west	SS	35	117	23	25	3	1	2	12	.214	37	80	★28	.807
1981—Wausau	Midw.	SS	111	354	53	97	20	3	9	48	.274	154	335	52	.904
1982—Bakersfield	Calif.	SS	136	482	91	146	24	4	11	55	.303	200	419	★73	.895
1983—Chattanooga	South.	SS	72	261	49	75	10	4	5	24	.287	131	232	30	.924
1983—Salt Lake City	P. C.	SS	61	234	43	74	12	5	10	41	.316	100	178	25	.917
1983—Seattle	Amer.	3B	27	92	9	26	7	0	1	6	.283	17	47	4	.941
1984—Salt Lake City†	P. C.	3B	69	242	57	77	22	3	14	68	.318	45	164	16	.929
1984—Seattle	Amer.	3B-OF	48	143	15	23	3	1	0	6	.161	31	63	8	.922
1985—Calgary‡	P. C.	3B-SS-OF	31	97	16	31	8	0	4	24	.320	16	49	5	.929

Year	Club	League	Pos.	G.	AB.	R.	H.	2B.	3B.	HR.	RBI.	B.A.	PO.	A.	E.	F.A.
1985—Seattle§	Amer.	SS-3B-OF	27	59	8	14	4	0	1	5	.237	25	44	6	.920	
1986—Detroit x	Amer.	3B-OF-SS	142	521	67	142	30	2	20	86	.273	111	242	23	.939	
1987—Detroit y	Amer.	3-1-O-S	53	149	14	27	5	1	4	15	.181	84	67	17	.899	
1987—Toledo z	Int.	3B-OF-SS	10	37	7	12	5	0	1	8	.324	7	8	1	.938	
1987—Pittsburgh	Nat.	OF-3B-1B	40	119	20	27	8	0	6	24	.227	39	20	3	.952	
1988—Pittsburgh a	Nat.	OF-1B-3B	68	211	20	49	13	1	5	36	.232	100	0	2	.980	
1988—Seattle	Amer.	OF-1B	55	195	32	57	10	1	10	34	.292	66	3	1	.986	
1989—Seattle	Amer.	OF-3B-1B	146	535	54	135	21	3	10	59	.252	317	76	12	.970	
1990—Sea.b-Det.c	Amer.	OF-3B-1B	89	215	22	45	7	1	3	20	.209	69	42	9	.925	
American League Totals—8 Years			587	1909	221	469	87	9	49	231	.246	720	584	80	.942	
National League Totals—2 Years			108	330	40	76	21	1	11	60	.230	139	20	5	.970	
Major League Totals—8 Years			695	2239	261	545	108	10	60	291	.243	859	604	85	.945	

Selected by Seattle Mariners' organization in 1st round (sixth player selected) of free-agent draft, June 3, 1980.

†On Seattle disabled list, March 29 to April 24, 1984; included rehabilitation disability assignment to Salt Lake City, April 12 to April 24, 1984.

‡On disabled list, August 8 to September 9, 1985.

§Traded to Detroit Tigers for Pitcher Rich Monteleone, December 12, 1985.

xOn disabled list, June 16 to July 1, 1986.

yOn disabled list, May 25 to June 27, 1987; included rehabilitation disability assignment to Toledo, June 16 to June 27, 1987.

zTraded with a player to be named later to Pittsburgh Pirates for Third Baseman Jim Morrison, August 7, 1987; Pittsburgh organization acquired Pitcher Morris Madden to complete deal, August 12, 1987.

aTraded to Seattle Mariners for Outfielder Glenn Wilson, July 22, 1988.

bTraded to Detroit Tigers for Outfielder Tracy Jones, June 18, 1990.

cGranted free agency, November 5, 1990.

DAVID S. COLLINS
(Dave)

Born October 20, 1952, at Rapid City, S. D.
Height, 5.10. Weight, 175.
Throws left and bats left and righthanded.
Attended Mesa Community College, Mesa, Ariz.

Major League stolen bases: 1975 (24), 1976 (32), 1977 (25), 1978 (7), 1979 (16), 1980 (79), 1981 (26), 1982 (13), 1983 (31), 1984 (60), 1985 (29), 1986 (27), 1987 (9), 1988 (7), 1989 (3), 1990 (7). Total—395.

Led Pioneer League outfielders in double plays with 3 in 1972.

Named Pioneer League Most Valuable Player, 1972.

Year	Club	League	Pos.	G.	AB.	R.	H.	2B.	3B.	HR.	RBI.	B.A.	PO.	A.	E.	F.A.
1972—Idaho Falls	Pion.	★OF-1B	68	252	40	69	8	★8	1	27	.274	101	★11	3	.974	
1973—Quad Cities†	Midw.	OF	110	387	61	100	15	7	4	49	.258	229	10	11	.956	
1974—Salinas	Calif.	OF-1B	39	143	30	49	3	5	1	21	.343	109	0	5	.956	
1974—El Paso	Texas	1B-OF	82	324	64	114	15	4	4	49	★.352	381	14	12	.971	
1975—Salt Lake City	P. C.	OF	51	193	41	60	7	6	0	24	.311	58	2	1	.984	
1975—California	Amer.	OF	93	319	41	85	13	4	3	29	.266	159	3	2	.988	
1976—Salt Lake City	P. C.	OF	35	136	28	49	13	4	0	12	.360	50	3	2	.964	
1976—California‡	Amer.	OF	99	365	45	96	12	1	4	28	.263	160	3	1	.994	
1977—Seattle§	Amer.	OF	120	402	46	96	9	3	5	28	.239	124	6	2	.985	
1978—Cincinnati	Nat.	OF	102	102	13	22	1	0	0	7	.216	30	1	1	.969	
1979—Cincinnati	Nat.	OF-1B	122	396	59	126	16	4	3	35	.318	223	3	4	.983	
1980—Cincinnati	Nat.	OF	144	551	94	167	20	4	3	35	.303	337	5	5	.986	
1981—Cincinnati x	Nat.	OF	95	360	63	98	18	6	3	23	.272	167	4	4	.977	
1982—New York y	Amer.	OF-1B	111	348	41	88	12	3	3	25	.253	498	28	7	.987	
1983—Toronto z	Amer.	OF-1B	118	402	55	109	12	4	1	34	.271	270	9	3	.989	
1984—Toronto a	Amer.	OF-1B	128	441	59	136	24	●15	2	44	.308	237	11	2	.992	
1985—Oakland b	Amer.	OF	112	379	52	95	16	4	4	29	.251	221	1	5	.978	
1986—Detroit cd	Amer.	OF	124	419	44	113	18	2	1	27	.270	211	2	1	.995	
1987—Nashville e	A. A.	DH-PH	13	40	8	8	6	0	0	9	.200	0	0	0	.000	
1987—Cincinnati e	Nat.	OF	57	85	19	25	5	0	0	5	.294	36	0	0	1.000	
1988—Cincinnati f	Nat.	OF-1B	99	174	12	41	6	2	0	14	.236	66	2	4	.944	
1989—Cincinnati gh	Nat.	OF	78	106	12	25	4	0	0	7	.236	41	0	0	1.000	
1990—St. Louis ij	Nat.	1B-OF	99	58	12	13	1	0	0	3	.224	89	0	1	.989	
National League Totals—8 Years			796	1832	284	517	71	16	9	129	.282	989	15	19	.981	
American League Totals—8 Years			905	3075	383	818	116	36	23	244	.266	1880	63	23	.988	
Major League Totals—16 Years			1701	4907	667	1335	187	52	32	373	.272	2869	78	42	.986	

Selected by Cincinnati Reds' organization in 23rd round of free-agent draft, June 8, 1971.

Selected by Kansas City Royals' organization in secondary phase of free-agent draft, January 12, 1972.

Selected by California Angels' organization in secondary phase of free-agent draft, June 6, 1972.

†On disabled list, May 21 to May 31, 1973.

‡Selected by Seattle Mariners in special American League expansion draft, November 5, 1976.

§Traded to Cincinnati Reds for Pitcher Shane Rawley, December 9, 1977.

xGranted free agency, November 13, 1981; signed by New York Yankees, December 23, 1981.

yTraded with Pitcher Mike Morgan, First Baseman Fred McGriff and a reported $400,000 to Toronto Blue Jays for Pitcher Dale Murray and Outfielder-Catcher Tom Dodd, December 9, 1982.

zOn disabled list, June 4 to June 22, 1983.

aTraded with Shortstop Alfredo Griffin and cash to Oakland A's for Pitcher Bill Caudill, December 8, 1984.

bTraded to Detroit Tigers for Infielder Barbaro Garbey, November 13, 1985.

cReleased, October 16, 1986; signed by Montreal Expos, November 13, 1986.

dReleased, March 31, 1987; signed by Nashville (Cincinnati Reds' organization), June 19, 1987.

eGranted free agency, November 9, 1987; re-signed by Reds, December 8, 1987.
fGranted free agency, November 4, 1988; re-signed by Reds, December 7, 1988.
gReleased, June 23, 1989; re-signed by Reds, July 30, 1989.
hGranted free agency, November 13, 1989; signed by Louisville (St. Louis Cardinals' organization), February 16, 1990.
iOn voluntarily retired list, October 10, 1990.
jNamed coach with St. Louis Cardinals for 1991 season.

CHAMPIONSHIP SERIES RECORD

Year	Club	League	Pos.	G.	AB.	R.	H.	2B.	3B.	HR.	RBI.	B.A.	PO.	A.	E.	F.A.
1979—Cincinnati		Nat.	OF	3	14	0	5	1	0	0	1	.357	5	0	0	1.000

PATRICK DENNIS COMBS
(Pat)

Born September 29, 1966, at Newport, R.I.
Height, 6.04. Weight, 200.
Throws and bats lefthanded.
Attended Rice University, Houston, Tex., and
Baylor University, Waco, Tex.

Led Eastern League in home runs allowed with 16 in 1989.

Year	Club	League	G.	IP.	W.	L.	Pct.	H.	R.	ER.	SO.	BB.	ERA.
1989—Reading		Eastern	19	125	8	7	.533	104	57	47	77	40	3.38
1989—Scranton/Wilkes-Barre		Int'national	3	24⅓	3	0	1.000	15	4	1	20	7	0.37
1989—Philadelphia		National	6	38⅔	4	0	1.000	36	10	9	30	6	2.09
1990—Philadelphia		National	32	183⅓	10	10	.500	179	90	83	108	86	4.07
Major League Totals—2 Years			38	222	14	10	.583	215	100	92	138	92	3.73

Selected by Philadelphia Phillies' organization in 1st round (11th player selected) of free-agent draft, June 1, 1988.

KEITH MARTIN COMSTOCK

Born December 23, 1955, at San Francisco, Calif.
Height, 6.00. Weight, 174.
Throws and bats lefthanded.
Attended Canada College, Redwood City, Calif.
Brother of Brad Comstock, pitcher in San Francisco Giants' organization, 1987 and 1988.

Major League saves: 1987 (1), 1990 (2). Total—3.
Tied for Southern League lead in shutouts with 3 in 1983.

Year	Club	League	G.	IP.	W.	L.	Pct.	H.	R.	ER.	SO.	BB.	ERA.
1976—Idaho Falls†		Pioneer	15	37	1	4	.200	33	18	16	45	32	3.89
1977—Quad Cities		Midwest	18	32	1	0	1.000	22	18	18	39	18	5.06
1977—Salinas		California	23	33	1	1	.500	35	26	17	41	18	4.64
1978—Salinas		California	27	82	6	4	.600	70	31	26	71	46	2.85
1979—El Paso‡		Texas	16	63	2	5	.286	95	64	50	18	35	7.14
1980—West Haven		Eastern	29	73	2	4	.333	64	40	34	52	37	4.19
1981—West Haven		Eastern	35	145	8	7	.533	123	76	66	133	80	4.10
1982—West Haven		Eastern	24	125	9	5	.643	99	48	42	132	69	3.02
1982—Tacoma§		P. Coast	5	27⅔	1	2	.333	34	24	22	22	12	7.16
1983—Birmingham x		Southern	37	145⅔	12	3	●.800	130	58	52	136	63	3.21
1984—Minnesota		American	4	6⅓	0	0	.000	6	6	6	2	4	8.53
1984—Toledo y		Int'national	23	164⅓	12	6	.667	132	58	51	154	56	2.79
1985—Yomiuri z		Central	21	124	8	8	.500	....	....	58	87	76	4.19
1986—Yomiuri z		Central	3	10	0	2	.000	....	....	9	7	7	7.83
1987—Phoenix		P. Coast	17	39	4	2	.667	24	12	12	35	23	2.77
1987—San Francisco ab-San Diego		National	41	56⅔	2	1	.667	52	30	29	59	31	4.61
1988—Las Vegas		P. Coast	50	71⅓	5	4	.556	67	32	25	78	31	3.14
1988—San Diego		National	7	8	0	0	.000	8	6	6	9	3	6.75
1989—Las Vegas c-Calgary		P. Coast	33	55⅓	9	2	.818	45	19	18	64	21	2.93
1989—Seattle		American	31	25⅔	1	2	.333	26	8	8	22	10	2.81
1990—Seattle		American	60	56	7	4	.636	40	22	18	50	26	2.89
American League Totals—3 Years			95	88	8	6	.571	72	36	32	74	40	3.27
National League Totals—2 Years			48	64⅔	2	1	.667	60	36	35	68	34	4.87
Major League Totals—5 Years			143	152⅔	10	7	.588	132	72	67	142	74	3.95

Selected by California Angels' organization in 5th round of free-agent draft, January 7, 1976.
†On disabled list, July 29, 1976 through remainder of season.
‡Released, July 6, 1979; signed by West Haven (Oakland A's organization), February 29, 1980.
§Sold to Detroit Tigers' organization, March 28, 1983.
xGranted free agency, October 23, 1983; signed by Minnesota Twins' organization, October 23, 1983.
yReleased, November 6, 1984; signed by Yomiuri Giants of Japanese Baseball League.
zReleased by Yomiuri Giants; signed by San Francisco Giants, November 24, 1986.
aAppeared in one game as an outfielder with no chances.
bTraded with Third Baseman Chris Brown and Pitchers Mark Davis and Mark Grant to San Diego Padres for Pitchers Dave Dravecky and Craig Lefferts and Infielder Kevin Mitchell, July 4, 1987.
cReleased, June 18, 1989; signed by Seattle Mariners, June 20, 1989.

—DID YOU KNOW—

That the 1990 San Francisco Giants used 26 pitchers, one shy of the major league record shared by three teams?

DAVID BRIAN CONE

Born January 2, 1963, at Kansas City, Mo.
Height, 6.01. Weight, 190.
Throws right and bats lefthanded.

Major League saves: 1987 (1).
Tied for National League lead in balks with 10 in 1988.
Led Southern League in wild pitches with 27 in 1984.

Year Club	League	G.	IP.	W.	L.	Pct.	H.	R.	ER.	SO.	BB.	ERA.
1981—Sarasota Royals-Blue	Gulf Coast	14	67	6	4	.600	52	24	19	45	33	2.55
1982—Charleston	S. Atlantic	16	104⅔	9	2	.818	84	38	24	87	47	2.06
1982—Fort Myers	Florida St.	10	72⅓	7	1	.875	56	21	17	57	25	2.12
1983—Jacksonville†	Southern						(Did not play)					
1984—Memphis	Southern	29	178⅔	8	12	.400	162	103	85	110	114	4.28
1985—Omaha	Am. Assoc.	28	158⅔	9	15	.375	157	90	82	115	★93	4.65
1986—Omaha	Am. Assoc.	39	71	8	4	.667	60	23	22	63	25	2.79
1986—Kansas City‡	American	11	22⅔	0	0	.000	29	14	14	21	13	5.56
1987—New York§	National	21	99⅓	5	6	.455	87	46	41	68	44	3.71
1987—Tidewater	Int'national	3	11	0	1	.000	10	8	7	7	6	5.73
1988—New York	National	35	231⅓	20	3	★.870	178	67	57	213	80	2.22
1989—New York	National	34	219⅔	14	8	.636	183	92	86	190	74	3.52
1990—New York	National	31	211⅔	14	10	.583	177	84	76	★233	65	3.23
American League Totals—1 Year		11	22⅔	0	0	.000	29	14	14	21	13	5.56
National League Totals—4 Years		121	762	53	27	.663	625	289	260	704	263	3.07
Major League Totals—5 Years		132	784⅔	53	27	.663	654	303	274	725	276	3.14

Selected by Kansas City Royals' organization in 3rd round of free-agent draft, June 8, 1981.
†On disabled list, April 8, 1983 through entire season.
‡Traded with Catcher Chris Jelic to New York Mets for Catcher Ed Hearn and Pitchers Rick Anderson and Mauro Gozzo, March 27, 1987.
§On disabled list, May 28 to August 14, 1987; included rehabilitation disability assignment to Tidewater, July 30 to August 14, 1987.

CHAMPIONSHIP SERIES RECORD

Year Club	League	G.	IP.	W.	L.	Pct.	H.	R.	ER.	SO.	BB.	ERA.
1988—New York	National	3	12	1	1	.500	10	6	6	9	5	4.50

ALL-STAR GAME RECORD

Year League	IP.	W.	L.	Pct.	H.	R.	ER.	SO.	BB.	ERA.
1988—National	1	0	0	.000	0	0	0	1	0	0.00

JEFFREY GUY CONINE
(Jeff)

Born June 27, 1966, at Tacoma, Wash.
Height, 6.01. Weight, 205.
Throws and bats righthanded.
Attended UCLA, Los Angeles, Calif.

Led Southern League first baseman in total chances with 1,281 and double plays with 108 in 1990.
Named Southern League Most Valuable Player, 1990.

Year Club	League	Pos.	G.	AB.	R.	H.	2B.	3B.	HR.	RBI.	B.A.	PO.	A.	E.	F.A.
1988—Baseball City	Fla. St.	1B-3B	118	415	63	113	23	9	10	59	.272	661	51	22	.970
1989—Baseball City	Fla. St.	1B	113	425	68	116	12	7	14	60	.273	830	65	18	.980
1990—Memphis	South.	★1B-3B	137	487	89	156	37	8	15	95	.320	★1164	★95	★22	.983
1990—Kansas City	Amer.	1B	9	20	3	5	2	0	0	2	.250	39	4	1	.977
Major League Totals—1 Year			9	20	3	5	2	0	0	2	.250	39	4	1	.977

Selected by Kansas City Royals' organization in 58th round of free-agent draft, June 2, 1987.

DENNIS BRYAN COOK

Born October 4, 1962, at Lamarque, Texas.
Height, 6.03. Weight, 185.
Throws and bats lefthanded.
Attended Angelina College, Lufkin, Tex., and University of Texas, Austin, Tex.

Major League saves: 1990 (1).
Named Texas League Pitcher of the Year, 1987.

Year Club	League	G.	IP.	W.	L.	Pct.	H.	R.	ER.	SO.	BB.	ERA.
1985—Clinton	Midwest	13	83	5	4	.556	73	35	31	40	27	3.36
1986—Fresno	California	27	170	12	7	.632	141	92	75	★173	100	3.97
1987—Shreveport	Texas	16	105⅔	9	2	.818	94	32	25	98	20	2.13
1987—Phoenix	P. Coast	12	62	2	5	.286	72	45	36	24	26	5.23
1988—Phoenix	P. Coast	26	141⅓	11	9	.550	138	73	61	110	51	3.88
1988—San Francisco	National	4	22	2	1	.667	9	8	7	13	11	2.86
1989—Phoenix	P. Coast	12	78	7	4	.636	73	29	27	85	19	3.12
1989—San Francisco†-Philadelphia	National	23	121	7	8	.467	110	59	50	67	38	3.72
1990—Philadelphia‡-Los Angeles	National	47	156	9	4	.692	155	74	68	64	56	3.92
Major League Totals—3 Years		74	299	18	13	.581	274	141	125	144	105	3.76

Selected by San Diego Padres' organization in 6th round of free-agent draft, January 11, 1983.
Selected by San Francisco Giants' organization in 18th round of free-agent draft, June 3, 1985.

†Traded with Pitcher Terry Mulholland and Third Baseman Charlie Hayes to Philadelphia Phillies for Pitcher Steve Bedrosian and a player to be named later, June 18, 1989; San Francisco Giants' organization acquired Infielder Rick Parker to complete deal, August 7, 1989.

‡Traded to Los Angeles Dodgers for Catcher Darrin Fletcher, September 13, 1990.

SCOTT ROBERT COOLBAUGH

Born June 13, 1966, at Binghamton, N.Y.
Height, 5.11. Weight, 195.
Throws and bats righthanded.
Attended University of Texas, Austin, Tex.

Major League stolen bases: 1990 (1).

Tied for Texas League lead in sacrifice flies with 8 in 1988.

Led American Association third basemen in putouts with 105, assists with 278, total chances with 413 and double plays with 32 in 1989.

Led Texas League third basemen in double plays with 28 and total chances with 421 in 1988.

Year Club	League	Pos.	G.	AB.	R.	H.	2B.	3B.	HR.	RBI.	B.A.	PO.	A.	E.	F.A.
1987—Charlotte	Fla. St.	3B-2B	66	233	27	64	21	0	2	20	.275	42	151	16	.923
1988—Tulsa	Texas	3B	136	470	52	127	15	4	13	75	.270	72	★324	25	.941
1989—Oklahoma City	A. A.	3B-2B	●144	★527	66	137	28	0	18	74	.260	108	279	30	.928
1989—Texas	Amer.	3B	25	51	7	14	1	0	2	7	.275	7	39	2	.958
1990—Oklahoma City	A. A.	3-1-2-O	76	293	39	66	17	2	6	30	.225	91	144	15	.940
1990—Texas†	Amer.	3B	67	180	21	36	6	0	2	13	.200	42	118	10	.941
Major League Totals—2 Years			92	231	28	50	7	0	4	20	.216	49	157	12	.945

Selected by Texas Rangers' organization in 3rd round of free-agent draft, June 2, 1987.

†Traded to San Diego Padres for Catcher Mark Parent, December 12, 1990.

SCOTT KENDRICK COOPER

Born October 13, 1967, at St. Louis, Mo.
Height, 6.03. Weight, 200.
Throws right and bats lefthanded.

Led Carolina League in total bases with 234 in 1988.

Led International League third basemen in putouts with 94 and tied for lead in assists with 240 in 1990.

Year Club	League	Pos.	G.	AB.	R.	H.	2B.	3B.	HR.	RBI.	B.A.	PO.	A.	E.	F.A.
1986—Elmira	NYP	3B	51	191	23	55	9	0	9	43	.288	22	62	9	.903
1987—Greensboro	S. Atl.	3B-1B	119	370	52	93	21	2	15	63	.251	150	153	21	.935
1988—Lynchburg	Carol.	3B-1B-OF	130	497	90	●148	★45	7	9	73	.298	116	198	27	.921
1989—New Britain	East.	3B	124	421	50	104	24	2	7	39	.247	91	212	22	.932
1990—Pawtucket	Int.	3B-SS	124	433	56	115	17	1	12	44	.266	96	244	22	.939
1990—Boston	Amer.	PH-PR	2	1	0	0	0	0	0	0	.000	0	0	0	.000
Major League Totals—1 Year			2	1	0	0	0	0	0	0	.000	0	0	0	.000

Selected by Boston Red Sox' organization in 3rd round of free-agent draft, June 2, 1986.

JOSE MANUEL CORA
(Joey)

Born May 14, 1965, at Cuguas, Puerto Rico.
Height, 5.08. Weight, 150.
Throws right and bats left and righthanded.
Attended Vanderbilt University, Nashville, Tenn.

Major League stolen bases: 1987 (15), 1989 (1), 1990 (8). Total—24.

Led Pacific Coast League second basemen in errors with 24 in both 1988 and 1989.

Year Club	League	Pos.	G.	AB.	R.	H.	2B.	3B.	HR.	RBI.	B.A.	PO.	A.	E.	F.A.
1985—Spokane	N'west	2B	43	170	48	55	11	2	3	26	.324	92	123	9	.960
1986—Beaumont†	Texas	2B-SS	81	315	54	96	5	5	3	41	.305	217	267	19	.962
1987—San Diego	Nat.	2B-SS	77	241	23	57	7	2	0	13	.237	123	200	10	.970
1987—Las Vegas	P. C.	2B-SS	81	293	50	81	9	1	1	24	.276	186	249	9	.980
1988—Las Vegas	P. C.	2B-3B-OF	127	460	73	136	15	3	3	55	.296	285	346	26	.960
1989—Las Vegas	P. C.	2B-SS	119	507	79	157	25	4	0	37	.310	245	349	27	.957
1989—San Diego	Nat.	SS-3B-2B	12	19	5	6	1	0	0	1	.316	11	15	2	.929
1990—San Diego	Nat.	SS-2B-C	51	100	12	27	3	0	0	2	.270	59	49	11	.908
1990—Las Vegas	P. C.	SS-2B	51	211	41	74	13	9	0	24	.351	125	148	14	.951
Major League Totals—3 Years			140	360	40	90	11	2	0	16	.250	193	264	23	.952

Selected by San Diego Padres' organization in 1st round (23rd player selected) of free-agent draft, June 3, 1985.

†On disabled list, June 22 to August 15, 1986.

SHERMAN STANLEY CORBETT

Born November 3, 1962, at New Braunfels, Tex.
Height, 6.04. Weight, 203.
Throws and bats lefthanded.
Attended Texas A&M University, College Station, Tex.

Major League saves: 1988 (1).

Tied for Pacific Coast League lead in intentional bases on balls issued with 8 in 1989.

Tied for California League lead in shutouts with 3 and games started by pitchers with 28 in 1985.

Tied for Northwest League lead in shutouts with 2 in 1984.

Year Club	League	G.	IP.	W.	L.	Pct.	H.	R.	ER.	SO.	BB.	ERA.
1984—Salem	Northwest	15	100⅓	7	6	.538	75	42	35	97	43	3.14
1985—Redwood	California	28	174	11	12	.478	165	108	78	122	101	4.03
1986—Midland	Texas	26	147⅔	7	10	.412	168	94	80	82	56	4.88
1987—Edmonton	P. Coast	41	55⅔	6	6	.500	61	37	34	29	49	5.50
1988—Midland	Texas	18	47⅔	3	2	.600	48	21	18	40	11	3.40
1988—California	American	34	45⅔	2	1	.667	47	23	21	28	23	4.14
1989—Edmonton	P. Coast	52	63⅓	6	7	.462	58	33	31	43	45	4.41
1989—California	American	4	5⅓	0	0	.000	3	2	2	3	1	3.38
1990—Edmonton	P. Coast	47	69⅓	3	1	.750	64	31	27	44	25	3.50
1990—California†	American	4	5	0	0	.000	8	5	5	2	3	9.00
Major League Totals—3 Years		42	56	2	1	.667	58	30	28	33	27	4.50

Selected by California Angels' organization in 3rd round of free-agent draft, June 4, 1984.

†Granted free agency, October 15, 1990.

JAMES BERNARD CORSI
(Jim)

Born September 9, 1961, at Newton, Mass.
Height, 6.01. Weight, 210.
Throws and bats righthanded.
Received bachelor of arts degree in management from St. Leo College, St. Leo, Fla.

Led Pacific Coast League in games finished in relief with 45 in 1988.

Year Club	League	G.	IP.	W.	L.	Pct.	H.	R.	ER.	SO.	BB.	ERA.
1982—Oneonta	NYP	1	3⅓	0	0	.000	5	4	4	6	2	10.80
1982—Paintsville	Ap'lachian	8	31	0	2	.000	32	11	10	20	13	2.90
1983—Greensboro†	S. Atlantic	12	50⅔	2	2	.500	59	37	23	37	33	4.09
1983—Oneonta‡	NYP	11	59⅓	3	6	.333	76	38	28	47	21	4.25
1984—						(Out of Organized Baseball)						
1985—Greensboro§	S. Atlantic	41	78⅔	5	8	.385	94	49	37	84	23	4.23
1986—New Britain x	Eastern	29	51⅓	2	3	.400	52	13	13	38	20	2.28
1987—Modesto	California	19	30	3	1	.750	23	16	12	45	10	3.60
1987—Huntsville	Southern	28	48	8	1	.889	30	17	15	33	15	2.81
1988—Tacoma	P. Coast	50	59	2	5	.286	60	25	18	48	23	2.75
1988—Oakland	American	11	21⅓	0	1	.000	20	10	9	10	6	3.80
1989—Tacoma	P. Coast	23	28⅓	2	3	.400	40	17	13	23	9	4.13
1989—Oakland	American	22	38½	1	2	.333	26	8	8	21	10	1.88
1990—Tacoma yz	P. Coast	5	6	0	0	.000	9	2	1	3	1	1.50
Major League Totals—2 Years		33	59⅔	1	3	.250	46	18	17	31	16	2.56

Selected by New York Yankees' organization in 25th round of free-agent draft, June 7, 1982.

†On Fort Lauderdale disabled list, April 8 to May 11, 1983.

‡Released, April 3, 1984; signed by Greensboro (Boston Red Sox' organization), April 1, 1985.

§Released, January 31, 1986; re-signed by Red Sox' organization, April 5, 1986.

xReleased, April 2, 1987; signed by Modesto (Oakland Athletics' organization), April 12, 1987.

yOn Oakland disabled list, March 29, 1990 through entire season; included rehabilitation disability assignment to Tacoma, June 29 to July 25, 1990.

zGranted free agency, December 20, 1990.

JOHN REILLY COSTELLO

Born December 24, 1960, at New York, N. Y.
Height, 6.01. Weight, 180.
Throws and bats righthanded.
Received degree in police science from Mercyhurst College, Erie, Pa.

Major League saves: 1988 (1), 1989 (3). Total—4.

Year Club	League	G.	IP.	W.	L.	Pct.	H.	R.	ER.	SO.	BB.	ERA.
1983—Erie	NYP	15	63⅔	2	5	.286	79	51	47	41	21	6.64
1984—Savannah	S. Atlantic	26	166	13	9	.591	142	80	62	114	86	3.36
1985—Springfield	Midwest	28	188	8	13	.381	188	105	∗87	127	60	4.16
1986—St. Petersburg	Florida St.	15	71⅔	8	2	.800	65	21	19	32	24	2.39
1986—Arkansas	Texas	10	15	0	0	.000	17	11	9	10	6	5.40
1987—Arkansas	Texas	44	74	5	2	.714	64	27	19	67	22	2.31
1987—Louisville	Am. Assoc.	6	10⅓	2	0	1.000	14	6	5	8	7	4.35
1988—Louisville	Am. Assoc.	20	29⅓	1	1	.500	17	7	6	34	7	1.84
1988—St. Louis	National	36	49⅔	5	2	.714	44	15	10	38	25	1.81
1989—St. Louis†	National	48	62⅓	5	4	.556	48	24	23	40	20	3.32
1989—Louisville	Am. Assoc.	4	5	0	0	.000	5	1	1	4	1	1.80
1990—St. Louis‡§-Montreal x	National	8	10⅔	0	0	.000	12	8	7	2	2	5.91
1990—Indianapolis y	Am. Assoc.	22	30⅔	0	3	.000	36	26	24	32	20	7.04
Major League Totals—3 Years		92	122⅔	10	6	.625	104	47	40	80	47	2.93

Selected by St. Louis Cardinals' organization in 24th round of free-agent draft, June 6, 1983.

†On disabled list, April 30 to May 21, 1989; included rehabilitation disability assignment to Louisville, May 13 to May 21, 1989.

‡On disabled list, March 31 to April 15, 1990.

§Traded to Montreal Expos for Infielder Rex Hudler, April 23, 1990.

xOn disabled list, April 25 to May 26 and May 27 to June 10, 1990; included rehabilitation disability assignment to Indianapolis, May 17 to May 24 and June 8 to June 9, 1990.

yTraded to San Diego Padres for Pitcher Brian Harrison, November 9, 1990.

HENRY COTTO (SUAREZ)

Name pronounced KOTT-oh.

Born January 5, 1961, at New York, N. Y.
Height, 6.02. Weight, 180.
Throws and bats righthanded.

Major League stolen bases: 1984 (9), 1985 (1), 1986 (3), 1987 (4), 1988 (27), 1989 (10), 1990 (21). Total—75.
Led Texas League in stolen bases with 52 in 1982.
Tied for American Association lead in caught stealing with 17 in 1983.
Led Texas League outfielders in total chances with 333 in 1982.
Tied for International League lead in double plays by outfielders with 3 in 1986.

Year Club	League	Pos.	G.	AB.	R.	H.	2B.	3B.	HR.	RBI.	B.A.	PO.	A.	E.	F.A.
1980—Sarasota Cubs	Gulf C.	OF	43	166	24	47	7	5	0	30	.283	93	6	3	.971
1980—Quad Cities	Midw.	OF	19	78	9	22	1	1	0	5	.282	27	2	4	.879
1981—Quad Cities	Midw.	OF	128	493	80	144	15	6	1	46	.292	249	★23	13	.954
1982—Midland	Texas	OF	130	524	103	161	12	5	1	36	.307	★310	16	7	.979
1983—Iowa†	A. A.	OF	104	426	52	111	7	10	0	35	.261	253	8	7	.974
1984—Chicago	Nat.	OF	105	146	24	40	5	0	0	8	.274	117	3	2	.984
1984—Iowa‡	A. A.	OF	8	30	3	6	2	0	0	0	.200	12	3	0	1.000
1985—New York§	Amer.	OF	34	56	4	17	1	0	1	6	.304	41	2	1	.977
1985—Columbus	Int.	OF	75	272	38	70	16	2	7	36	.257	158	5	2	.988
1986—New York	Amer.	OF	35	80	11	17	3	0	1	6	.213	59	1	0	1.000
1986—Columbus	Int.	OF	97	359	45	89	17	6	7	48	.248	215	5	8	.965
1987—Columbus	Int.	OF	34	129	26	39	13	2	3	20	.302	73	3	2	.974
1987—New York x	Amer.	OF	68	149	21	35	10	0	5	20	.235	89	2	1	.989
1988—Seattle	Amer.	OF	133	386	50	100	18	1	8	33	.259	253	6	2	.992
1989—Seattle	Amer.	OF	100	295	44	78	11	2	9	33	.264	153	9	2	.988
1990—Seattle	Amer.	OF	127	355	40	92	14	3	4	33	.259	194	4	2	.990
National League Totals—1 Year			105	146	24	40	5	0	0	8	.274	117	3	2	.984
American League Totals—6 Years			497	1321	170	339	57	6	28	131	.257	789	24	8	.990
Major League Totals—7 Years			602	1467	194	379	62	6	28	139	.258	906	27	10	.989

Signed as free agent by Chicago Cubs' organization, June 7, 1980.

†On disabled list, May 10 to May 30, 1983.

‡Traded with Catcher Ron Hassey and Pitchers Rich Bordi and Porfi Altamirano to New York Yankees for Pitcher Ray Fontenot and Outfielder Brian Dayett, December 4, 1984.

§On disabled list, May 25 to July 5, 1985; included rehabilitation disability assignment to Columbus, June 19 to July 5, 1985.

xTraded with Pitcher Steve Trout to Seattle Mariners for Pitchers Lee Guetterman, Clay Parker and Wade Taylor, December 22, 1987.

CHAMPIONSHIP SERIES RECORD

Year Club	League	Pos.	G.	AB.	R.	H.	2B.	3B.	HR.	RBI.	B.A.	PO.	A.	E.	F.A.
1984—Chicago	Nat.	OF-PR	3	1	1	1	0	0	0	0	1.000	2	0	0	1.000

DANNY BRADFORD COX

Born September 21, 1959, at Northhampton, England.
Height, 6.04. Weight, 225.
Throws and bats righthanded.
Attended Chattahoochee Valley Community College, Phenix City, Ala.,
and Troy State University, Troy, Ala.

Pitched 11-0 no-hit victory against Bristol, August 9, 1981.
Tied for National League lead in hit batsmen with 7 in 1984.
Led Appalachian League in complete games with 10 and shutouts with 4 in 1981.
Named Appalachian League Player of the Year, 1981.

Year Club	League	G.	IP.	W.	L.	Pct.	H.	R.	ER.	SO.	BB.	ERA.
1981—Johnson City	Ap'lachian	13	★109	9	4	.692	80	27	25	★87	36	★2.06
1982—Springfield	Midwest	15	84⅓	5	3	.625	82	46	24	68	29	2.56
1983—St. Petersburg†	Florida St.	5	32	2	2	.500	26	10	9	22	14	2.53
1983—Arkansas	Texas	11	86⅓	8	3	.727	60	31	22	73	24	2.29
1983—Louisville	Am. Assoc.	2	11	0	0	.000	10	3	3	8	0	2.45
1983—St. Louis	National	12	83	3	6	.333	92	38	30	36	23	3.25
1984—St. Louis	National	29	156⅓	9	11	.450	171	81	70	70	54	4.03
1984—Louisville	Am. Assoc.	6	42⅓	4	1	.800	34	16	10	34	7	2.13
1985—St. Louis	National	35	241	18	9	.667	226	91	77	131	64	2.88
1986—St. Louis‡	National	32	220	12	13	.480	189	85	71	108	60	2.90
1987—St. Louis§	National	31	199⅓	11	9	.550	224	99	86	101	71	3.88
1988—St. Louis x	National	13	86	3	8	.273	89	40	38	47	25	3.98
1988—Louisville	Am. Assoc.	3	11⅔	0	0	.000	11	7	4	7	6	3.09
1989—St. Louis yz	National					(Did not play)						
1990—Louisville a	Am. Assoc.	4	11	0	3	.000	22	20	19	6	10	15.55
1990—Springfield	Midwest	1	5	0	0	.000	1	0	0	3	0	0.00
1990—Arkansas b	Texas	1	7	1	0	1.000	3	1	1	3	1	1.29
Major League Totals—6 Years		152	985⅔	56	56	.500	991	434	372	493	297	3.40

Selected by St. Louis Cardinals' organization in 13th round of free-agent draft, June 8, 1981.

†On Arkansas disabled list, April 8 to April 21, 1983.

‡On disabled list, March 30 to April 24, 1986; included rehabilitation disability assignment to Louisville, April 17 to April 24, 1986.

§On disabled list, July 10 to August 8, 1987.

xOn disabled list, April 30 to June 27 and August 7, 1988 through remainder of season; included rehabilitation disability assignment to Louisville, June 16 to June 27, 1988.

yOn disabled list, March 27, 1989 through entire season.

zGranted free agency, November 13, 1989; re-signed by Cardinals, November 30, 1989.

aOn St. Louis disabled list, March 31, 1990 through entire season; included rehabilitation disability assignment to Louisville, May 17 to May 31 and June 13 to June 18, 1990; to Springfield, June 6 and June 7, 1990; and Arkansas, June 8 to June 12, 1990.

bGranted free agency, October 19, 1990; signed by Scranton/Wilkes-Barre (Philadelphia Phillies' organization), December 17, 1990.

CHAMPIONSHIP SERIES RECORD

Shares Championship Series record for most complete games pitched, series (2), 1987.
Shares National League Championship Series record for most complete games pitched, total series (2).

Year	Club	League	G.	IP.	W.	L.	Pct.	H.	R.	ER.	SO.	BB.	ERA.
1985—St. Louis	National	1	6	1	0	1.000	4	1	1	4	5	1.50
1987—St. Louis	National	2	17	1	1	.500	17	4	4	11	3	2.12
Championship Series Totals—2 Years			3	23	2	1	.667	21	5	5	15	8	1.96

WORLD SERIES RECORD

Shares World Series records for most earned runs allowed, game (7), October 18, 1987; most earned runs allowed, inning (6), October 18, 1987, fourth inning.

Year	Club	League	G.	IP.	W.	L.	Pct.	H.	R.	ER.	SO.	BB.	ERA.
1985—St. Louis	National	2	14	0	0	.000	14	2	2	13	4	1.29
1987—St. Louis	National	3	11⅔	1	2	.333	13	10	10	9	8	7.71
World Series Totals—2 Years			5	25⅔	1	2	.333	27	12	12	22	12	4.21

STEVEN RAY CRAWFORD
(Steve)

Born April 29, 1958, at Pryor, Okla.
Height, 6.05. Weight, 225.
Throws and bats righthanded.
Attended Claremore Junior College, Claremore, Okla., and
Northeastern Oklahoma State University, Tahlequah, Okla.

Major League saves: 1984 (1), 1985 (12), 1986 (4), 1990 (1). Total—18.
Led Carolina League pitchers in games started with 28 and complete games with 15 in 1979.
Tied for Carolina League lead in shutouts with 3 in 1979.

Year	Club	League	G.	IP.	W.	L.	Pct.	H.	R.	ER.	SO.	BB.	ERA.
1978—Winston-Salem	Carolina	19	110	9	5	.643	109	53	42	60	48	3.44
1979—Winston-Salem	Carolina	29	*211	11	11	.500	*208	88	●69	127	67	2.94
1980—Bristol†	Eastern	24	177	9	7	.563	170	68	52	97	64	2.64
1980—Boston	American	6	32	2	0	1.000	41	14	13	10	8	3.66
1981—Boston	American	14	58	0	5	.000	69	38	32	29	18	4.97
1982—Boston‡	American	5	9	1	0	1.000	14	3	2	2	0	2.00
1982—Pawtucket	Int'national	10	46	1	4	.200	55	25	21	20	15	4.11
1983—Pawtucket§	Int'national	27	154⅔	8	11	.421	181	98	89	104	80	5.18
1984—Pawtucket	Int'national	7	18⅓	2	1	.667	11	10	4	8	9	1.96
1984—Boston	American	35	62	5	0	1.000	69	31	23	21	21	3.34
1985—Boston x	American	44	91	6	5	.545	103	47	38	58	28	3.76
1986—Boston y	American	40	57⅓	0	2	.000	69	29	25	32	19	3.92
1986—Pawtucket	Int'national	5	6	1	1	.500	10	4	4	2	1	6.00
1987—Boston za	American	29	72⅔	5	4	.556	91	48	43	43	32	5.33
1988—San Antonio b	Texas	3	6	1	0	1.000	2	0	0	4	0	0.00
1988—Albuquerque c	P. Coast	32	54⅓	3	6	.333	59	31	23	36	25	3.81
1989—Omaha	Am. Assoc.	22	43	3	1	.750	41	18	14	32	9	2.93
1989—Kansas City d	American	25	54	3	1	.750	48	19	17	33	19	2.83
1990—Kansas City e	American	46	80	5	4	.556	79	38	37	54	23	4.16
1990—Omaha f	Am. Assoc.	4	6	0	0	.000	2	0	0	11	2	0.00
Major League Totals—9 Years			244	516	27	21	.563	583	267	230	282	168	4.01

Signed as free agent by Boston Red Sox' organization, May 6, 1978.

†On disabled list, April 14 to May 2, 1980.

‡On disabled list, April 1 to August 12, 1982; included rehabilitation disability assignment to Pawtucket, July 21 to August 9, 1982.

§On disabled list, July 26 to August 5, 1983.

xOn disabled list, May 7 to May 22 and June 23 to July 8, 1985.

yOn disabled list, July 18 to September 1, 1986; included rehabilitation disability assignment to Pawtucket, August 15 to September 1, 1986.

zOn disabled list, July 16 to July 31, 1987.

aGranted free agency, November 9, 1987; signed by San Antonio (Los Angeles Dodgers' organization), May 12, 1988.

bOn disabled list, May 12 to May 25, 1988.

cGranted free agency, October 15, 1988; signed by Omaha (Kansas City Royals' organization), March 7, 1989.

dGranted free agency, November 13, 1989; re-signed by Royals, December 5, 1989.

eOn disabled list, April 25 to May 24, 1990; included rehabilitation disability assignment to Omaha, May 12 to May 23, 1990.

fGranted free agency, November 5, 1990; re-signed by Royals, December 6, 1990.

CHAMPIONSHIP SERIES RECORD

Year	Club	League	G.	IP.	W.	L.	Pct.	H.	R.	ER.	SO.	BB.	ERA.
1986—Boston	American	1	1⅔	1	0	1.000	1	0	0	1	2	0.00

Year	Club	League	G.	IP.	W.	L.	Pct.	H.	R.	ER.	SO.	BB.	ERA.
1986—Boston		American	3	4⅓	1	0	1.000	5	3	3	4	0	6.23

STANLEY TIMOTHY CREWS
(Tim)

Born April 3, 1961, at Tampa, Fla.
Height, 6.00. Weight, 195.
Throws and bats righthanded.
Attended Valencia Community College, Orlando, Fla.

Major League saves: 1987 (3), 1989 (1), 1990 (5). Total—9.
Led Texas League in home runs allowed with 25 and tied for lead in balks with 4 in 1983.
Tied for Midwest League lead in home runs allowed with 16 in 1981.

Year	Club	League	G.	IP.	W.	L.	Pct.	H.	R.	ER.	SO.	BB.	ERA.
1981—Burlington		Midwest	21	144	10	4	.714	148	82	67	98	27	4.19
1982—Stockton		California	19	139	10	4	.714	151	66	52	83	28	3.37
1983—El Paso		Texas	27	163⅓	9	8	.529	*207	*129	*119	99	53	6.56
1984—El Paso†		Texas	8	36	2	3	.400	56	32	27	22	10	6.75
1985—Stockton‡		California	16	90	8	1	.889	101	46	33	56	17	3.30
1986—El Paso		Texas	15	90⅔	5	5	.500	114	53	48	50	18	4.76
1986—Vancouver§		P. Coast	10	33⅓	2	1	.667	39	15	15	28	14	4.05
1987—Albuquerque		P. Coast	42	72	7	2	.778	73	34	29	60	25	3.63
1987—Los Angeles		National	20	29	1	1	.500	30	9	8	20	8	2.48
1988—Albuquerque		P. Coast	10	13⅓	1	1	.500	13	5	4	7	2	2.70
1988—Los Angeles		National	42	71⅔	4	0	1.000	77	29	25	45	16	3.14
1989—Los Angeles		National	44	61⅔	0	1	.000	69	27	22	56	23	3.21
1989—Albuquerque		P. Coast	2	2⅓	0	1	.000	3	2	2	2	0	7.71
1990—Los Angeles		National	66	107⅓	4	5	.444	98	40	33	76	24	2.77
Major League Totals—4 Years			172	269⅔	9	7	.563	274	105	88	197	71	2.94

Selected by Kansas City Royals' organization in 2nd round of free-agent draft, January 8, 1980.
Selected by Milwaukee Brewers' organization in 2nd round of free-agent draft, January 13, 1981.
†On disabled list, June 9, 1984 through remainder of season.
‡On disabled list, May 17 to July 12, 1985.
§Traded with Pitcher Tim Leary to Los Angeles Dodgers for First Baseman Greg Brock, December 10, 1986.

CHARLES ROBERT CRIM
(Chuck)

Born July 23, 1961, at Van Nuys, Calif.
Height, 6.00. Weight, 185.
Throws and bats righthanded.
Attended University of Hawaii, Honolulu, Haw.

Major League saves: 1987 (12), 1988 (9), 1989 (7), 1990 (11). Total—39.
Led Appalachian League in complete games with 8 in 1982.
Tied for Midwest League lead in complete games with 11 in 1983.

Year	Club	League	G.	IP.	W.	L.	Pct.	H.	R.	ER.	SO.	BB.	ERA.
1982—Pikeville		Ap'lachian	11	77⅓	4	6	.400	62	32	22	76	18	2.56
1983—Beloit		Midwest	25	163⅓	11	10	.524	150	83	63	154	50	3.47
1984—El Paso		Texas	55	90	7	4	.636	77	20	15	69	25	1.50
1985—Vancouver		P. Coast	48	106⅔	3	6	.333	110	58	54	68	38	4.56
1986—Vancouver		P. Coast	26	45⅓	0	3	.000	64	32	25	26	15	4.96
1986—El Paso		Texas	16	39	2	4	.333	35	16	12	32	2	2.77
1987—Milwaukee		American	53	130	6	8	.429	133	60	53	56	39	3.67
1988—Milwaukee		American	*70	105	7	6	.538	95	38	34	58	28	2.91
1989—Milwaukee†		American	*76	117⅔	9	7	.563	114	42	37	59	36	2.83
1990—Milwaukee‡		American	67	85⅔	3	5	.375	88	39	33	39	23	3.47
1990—Beloit		Midwest	1	2	0	0	.000	3	2	1	0	0	4.50
Major League Totals—4 Years			266	438⅓	25	26	.490	430	179	157	212	126	3.22

Selected by Chicago Cubs' organization in 3rd round of free-agent draft, June 5, 1979.
Selected by Milwaukee Brewers' organization in 17th round of free-agent draft, June 7, 1982.
†Appeared as first baseman in one game with no chances.
‡On disabled list, July 22 to August 10, 1990; included rehabilitation disability assignment to Beloit, August 7, 1990.

CHRISTOPHER JOHN CRON
(Chris)

Born March 31, 1964, at Albuquerque, N.M.
Height, 6.02. Weight, 200.
Throws and bats righthanded.
Attended Santa Ana Junior College, Santa Ana, Calif.

Led California League in being hit by pitch with 27 in 1988.
Led Midwest League in being hit by pitch with 17 in 1987.
Tied for South Atlantic League lead in being hit by pitch with 18 in 1985.
Led California League third basemen in double plays with 27 in 1988.
Tied for Texas League lead in errors by third basemen with 12 in 1989.

Year	Club	League	Pos.	G.	AB.	R.	H.	2B.	3B.	HR.	RBI.	B.A.	PO.	A.	E.	F.A.
1984—Pulaski	Appal.	1B	32	114	22	42	8	0	7	37	.368	241	18	5	.981
1985—Sumter	S. Atl.	1B	119	425	53	102	20	0	7	59	.240	930	68	*25	.976
1986—Durham†	Carol.	1B	90	265	26	55	10	0	7	34	.208	527	41	9	.984
1987—Palm Springs	Calif.	3B	26	92	6	25	3	0	2	9	.272	21	60	8	.910
1987—Quad City	Midw.	3B-SS	111	398	53	110	20	1	11	62	.276	88	225	36	.897
1988—Palm Springs	Calif.	*3B-1B	127	467	71	117	28	3	14	84	.251	99	225	*31	.913
1989—Midland	Texas	1B-3B	128	491	80	148	*33	3	22	*103	.301	932	116	17	.984
1990—Edmonton	P. C.	1B-3B	104	401	54	115	31	0	17	75	.287	847	84	7	.993

Selected by Atlanta Braves' organization in 7th round of free-agent draft, January 11, 1983.
Selected by Detroit Tigers' organization in secondary phase of free-agent draft, June 6, 1983.
Selected by Atlanta Braves' organization in secondary phase of free-agent draft, January 17, 1984.
†Released, October 16, 1986; signed by California Angels' organization, January 19, 1987.

STEVEN BRENT CUMMINGS
(Steve)

Born July 15, 1964, at Houston, Tex.
Height, 6.02. Weight, 205.
Throws right and bats left and righthanded.
Attended Blinn College, Brenham, Tex.,
and University of Houston, Houston, Tex.

Led Southern League in games started by pitchers with 33 in 1988.
Led Florida State League pitchers in games started with 29 in 1987.
Tied for New York-Pennsylvania League lead in games started by pitchers with 18 in 1986.

Year	Club	League	G.	IP.	W.	L.	Pct.	H.	R.	ER.	SO.	BB.	ERA.
1986—St. Catharines	NYP	18	110⅓	9	5	.643	80	36	25	86	34	2.04
1987—Dunedin	Florida St.	32	186⅔	*18	8	.692	189	80	61	111	60	2.94
1988—Knoxville	Southern	35	*212⅔	14	11	.560	*206	88	65	131	64	2.75
1989—Syracuse	Int'national	19	106	7	5	.583	97	46	37	60	41	3.14
1989—Toronto	American	5	21	2	0	1.000	18	9	7	8	11	3.00
1990—Syracuse	Int'national	16	81	5	3	.625	76	31	28	34	37	3.11
1990—Toronto†	American	6	12⅓	0	0	.000	22	7	7	4	5	5.11
Major League Totals—2 Years		11	33⅓	2	0	1.000	40	16	14	12	16	3.78

Selected by Texas Rangers' organization in 5th round of free-agent draft, January 17, 1984.
Selected by Atlanta Braves' organization in secondary phase of free-agent draft, June 4, 1984.
Selected by Toronto Blue Jays' organization in 2nd round of free-agent draft, June 2, 1986.
†Traded to Cleveland Indians, September 21, 1990, as partial completion of deal in which Cleveland traded Pitcher Bud Black to Toronto Blue Jays for Pitcher Mauro Gozzo and two players to be named later, September 16, 1990; Cleveland acquired Pitcher Alex Sanchez to complete deal, September 24, 1990.

MILTON CUYLER JR.
(Milt)

Born October 7, 1968, at Macon, Ga.
Height, 5.10. Weight, 175.
Throws right and bats left and righthanded.

Major League stolen bases: 1990 (1).
Led International League in stolen bases with 52 and caught stealing with 14 in 1990.
Led Florida State League in caught stealing with 25 in 1988.
Led South Atlantic League in sacrifice hits with 17 in 1987.
Led Eastern League outfielders in total chances with 293 in 1989.

Year	Club	League	Pos.	G.	AB.	R.	H.	2B.	3B.	HR.	RBI.	B.A.	PO.	A.	E.	F.A.
1986—Bristol	Appal.	OF	45	174	24	40	3	5	1	11	.230	97	0	4	.960
1987—Fayetteville	S. Atl.	OF	94	366	65	107	8	4	2	34	.292	237	13	7	.973
1988—Lakeland	Fla. St.	OF	132	483	*100	143	11	3	2	32	.296	257	8	4	.985
1989—Toledo	Int.	OF	24	83	4	14	3	2	0	6	.169	48	3	2	.962
1989—London	East.	OF	98	366	69	96	8	7	7	34	.262	*272	13	8	.973
1990—Toledo	Int.	OF	124	461	77	119	11	8	2	42	.258	290	4	7	.977
1990—Detroit	Amer.	OF	19	51	8	13	3	1	0	8	.255	38	2	1	.976
Major League Totals—1 Year		19	51	8	13	3	1	0	8	.255	38	2	1	.976

Selected by Detroit Tigers' organization in 2nd round of free-agent draft, June 2, 1986.

KALVOSKI DANIELS
(Kal)

Born August 20, 1963, at Vienna, Ga.
Height, 5.11. Weight, 205.
Throws right and bats lefthanded.
Attended Middle Georgia College, Cochran, Ga.

Major League stolen bases: 1986 (15), 1987 (26), 1988 (27), 1989 (9), 1990 (4). Total—81.
Led Eastern League in slugging percentage with .525 in 1984.
Tied for Pioneer League lead in game-winning RBIs with 9 and stolen bases with 27 in 1982.

Year	Club	League	Pos.	G.	AB.	R.	H.	2B.	3B.	HR.	RBI.	B.A.	PO.	A.	E.	F.A.
1982—Billings	Pion.	OF	67	240	43	88	14	4	3	38	.367	104	4	5	.956
1983—Cedar Rapids	Midw.	OF	101	342	51	86	14	5	5	28	.251	130	5	2	.985
1984—Vermont	East.	OF	122	415	81	130	29	4	17	62	.313	143	2	5	.967

Year Club	League	Pos.	G.	AB.	R.	H.	2B.	3B.	HR.	RBI.	B.A.	PO.	A.	E.	F.A.
1985—Denver†	A. A.	OF	76	285	59	86	12	9	15	43	.302	83	5	4	.957
1986—Cincinnati	Nat.	OF	74	181	34	58	10	4	6	23	.320	88	0	3	.967
1986—Denver	A. A.	OF	42	132	33	49	12	2	8	32	.371	78	4	3	.965
1987—Cincinnati‡	Nat.	OF	108	368	73	123	24	1	26	64	.334	178	5	6	.968
1988—Cincinnati	Nat.	OF	140	495	95	144	29	1	18	64	.291	256	10	5	.982
1989—Cinc.§x-L.A.y	Nat.	OF	55	171	33	42	13	0	4	17	.246	88	4	0	1.000
1990—Los Angeles	Nat.	OF	130	450	81	133	23	1	27	94	.296	207	13	3	.987
Major League Totals—5 Years.................			507	1665	316	500	99	7	81	262	.300	817	32	17	.980

Selected by New York Mets' organization in 3rd round of free-agent draft, January 12, 1982.
Selected by Cincinnati Reds' organization in secondary phase of free-agent draft, June 7, 1982.
†On disabled list, July 7, 1985 through remainder of season.
‡On disabled list, July 6 to August 6, 1987.
§On disabled list, May 15 to June 21, 1989.
xTraded with Infielder Lenny Harris to Los Angeles Dodgers for Pitcher Tim Leary and Shortstop Mariano Duncan, July 18, 1989.
yOn disabled list, August 7, 1989 through remainder of season.

RONALD MAURICE DARLING JR.
(Ron)

Born August 19, 1960, at Honolulu, Haw.
Height, 6.03. Weight, 195.
Throws and bats righthanded.
Attended Yale University, New Haven, Conn.
Brother of Eddie Darling, first baseman in New York Yankees' organization, 1981 and 1982.

Shares National League record for fewest assists by pitcher, season, for leader in assists (47), 1985 and 1986.
Named pitcher on THE SPORTING NEWS National League All-Star fielding team, 1989.

Year Club	League	G.	IP.	W.	L.	Pct.	H.	R.	ER.	SO.	BB.	ERA.
1981—Tulsa†	Texas	13	71	4	2	.667	72	43	35	53	33	4.44
1982—Tidewater.....................	Int'national	26	152	7	9	.438	143	76	63	114	95	3.73
1983—Tidewater.....................	Int'national	27	159	10	9	.526	137	83	71	107	102	4.02
1983—New York......................	National	5	35⅓	1	3	.250	31	11	11	23	17	2.80
1984—New York......................	National	33	205⅔	12	9	.571	179	97	87	136	104	3.81
1985—New York......................	National	36	248	16	6	.727	214	93	80	167	★114	2.90
1986—New York......................	National	34	237	15	6	.714	203	84	74	184	81	2.81
1987—New York‡...................	National	32	207⅔	12	8	.600	183	101	99	167	96	4.29
1988—New York......................	National	34	240⅔	17	9	.654	218	97	87	161	60	3.25
1989—New York......................	National	33	217⅓	14	14	.500	214	100	85	153	70	3.52
1990—New York......................	National	33	126	7	9	.438	135	73	63	99	44	4.50
Major League Totals—8 Years.....................		240	1517⅔	94	64	.595	1377	666	586	1090	586	3.48

Selected by Texas Rangers' organization in 1st round (ninth player selected) of free-agent draft, June 8, 1981.
†Traded with Pitcher Walt Terrell to New York Mets' organization for Outfielder Lee Mazzilli, April 1, 1982.
‡On disabled list, September 12, 1987 through remainder of season.

CHAMPIONSHIP SERIES RECORD

Year Club	League	G.	IP.	W.	L.	Pct.	H.	R.	ER.	SO.	BB.	ERA.
1986—New York..................................	National	1	5	0	0	.000	6	4	4	5	2	7.20
1988—New York..................................	National	2	7	0	1	.000	11	9	6	7	4	7.71
Championship Series Totals—2 Years.................		3	12	0	1	.000	17	13	10	12	6	7.50

Appeared as pinch-runner for New York Mets in one game of 1988 Championship Series.

WORLD SERIES RECORD

Shares World Series record for most wild pitches, game (2), October 18, 1986.

Year Club	League	G.	IP.	W.	L.	Pct.	H.	R.	ER.	SO.	BB.	ERA.
1986—New York......................................	National	3	17⅔	1	1	.500	13	4	3	12	10	1.53

ALL-STAR GAME RECORD

Member of National League All-Star Team in 1985; did not play.

DANIEL WAYNE DARWIN
(Danny)

Born October 25, 1955, at Bonham, Tex.
Height, 6.03. Weight, 190.
Throws and bats righthanded.
Attended Grayson County College, Denison, Tex.
Brother of Jeff Darwin, pitcher in Seattle Mariners' organization.

Major League saves: 1980 (8), 1982 (7), 1985 (2), 1988 (3), 1989 (7), 1990 (2). Total—29.
Tied for American League lead in home runs allowed with 34 in 1985.
Tied for Texas League lead in shutouts with 4 and hit batsmen with 8 in 1977.
Tied for Western Carolinas League lead in balks with 5 in 1976.

Year Club	League	G.	IP.	W.	L.	Pct.	H.	R.	ER.	SO.	BB.	ERA.
1976—Asheville	W. Carol.	16	102	6	3	.667	96	54	41	76	48	3.62
1977—Tulsa†	Texas	23	154	13	4	.765	130	53	43	129	72	2.51
1978—Tucson	P. Coast	23	125	8	9	.471	147	100	87	126	83	6.26
1978—Texas	American	3	9	1	0	1.000	11	4	4	8	1	4.00
1979—Tucson	P. Coast	13	95	6	6	.500	89	43	38	65	42	3.60

Year Club	League	G.	IP.	W.	L.	Pct.	H.	R.	ER.	SO.	BB.	ERA.
1979—Texas	American	20	78	4	4	.500	50	36	35	58	30	4.04
1980—Texas‡	American	53	110	13	4	.765	98	37	32	104	50	2.62
1981—Texas	American	22	146	9	9	.500	115	67	59	98	57	3.64
1982—Texas	American	56	89	10	8	.556	95	38	34	61	37	3.44
1983—Texas§	American	28	183	8	13	.381	175	86	71	92	62	3.49
1984—Texas x	American	35	233⅓	8	12	.400	249	110	98	123	54	3.94
1985—Milwaukee y	American	39	217⅔	8	18	.308	212	112	92	125	65	3.80
1986—Milwaukee z	American	27	130⅓	6	8	.429	120	62	51	80	35	3.52
1986—Houston	National	12	54⅓	5	2	.714	50	19	14	40	9	2.32
1987—Houston a	National	33	195⅔	9	10	.474	184	87	78	134	69	3.59
1988—Houston	National	44	192	8	13	.381	189	86	82	129	48	3.84
1989—Houston	National	68	122	11	4	.733	92	34	32	104	33	2.36
1990—Houston b	National	48	162⅔	11	4	.733	136	42	40	109	31	*2.21
American League Totals—9 Years		283	1186⅔	67	76	.469	1125	552	476	749	391	3.61
National League Totals—5 Years		205	726⅔	44	33	.571	651	268	246	516	190	3.05
Major League Totals—13 Years		488	1913⅓	111	109	.505	1776	820	722	1265	581	3.40

Signed as free agent by Texas Rangers' organization, May 10, 1976.
†On disabled list, April 25 to May 4 and May 22 to June 11, 1977.
‡On disabled list, June 5 to June 26, 1980.
§On disabled list, March 25 to April 10 and August 9 to September 1, 1983.
xTraded with a player to be named later to Milwaukee Brewers as part of a six-player, four-team deal in which Kansas City Royals acquired Catcher Jim Sundberg from Milwaukee, Texas Rangers acquired Catcher Don Slaught from Kansas City, New York Mets' organization acquired Pitcher Frank Wills from Kansas City and Milwaukee organization acquired Pitcher Tim Leary from New York, January 18, 1985; Milwaukee organization acquired Catcher Bill Hance from Texas to complete deal, January 30, 1985.
yGranted free agency, November 12, 1985; re-signed by Brewers, December 22, 1985.
zTraded to Houston Astros for Pitcher Don August and a player to be named later, August 15, 1986; Milwaukee Brewers' organization acquired Pitcher Mark Knudson to complete deal, August 21, 1986.
aGranted free agency, November 9, 1987; re-signed by Astros, January 8, 1988.
bGranted free agency, December 7, 1990; signed by Boston Red Sox, December 19, 1990.

DOUGLAS CRAIG DASCENZO

Name pronounced Duh-SEN-zoh.

(Doug)

Born June 30, 1964, at Cleveland, O.
Height, 5.08. Weight, 160.
Throws left and bats left and righthanded.
Attended Florida College, Temple Terrace, Fla., and
Oklahoma State University, Stillwater, Okla.

Major League stolen bases: 1988 (6), 1989 (6), 1990 (15). Total—27.
Led American Association in caught stealing with 21 in 1989.
Led Carolina League in sacrifice hits with 12 in 1986.
Led Eastern League outfielders in total chances with 308 in 1987.

Year Club	League	Pos.	G.	AB.	R.	H.	2B.	3B.	HR.	RBI.	B.A.	PO.	A.	E.	F.A.
1985—Geneva	NYP	OF-1B	70	252	*59	84	15	1	3	23	.333	133	7	4	.972
1986—Winston-Salem	Carol.	OF	138	545	107	*178	29	11	6	83	.327	299	15	8	.975
1987—Pittsfield	East.	OF	134	496	84	152	32	6	3	56	.306	*299	5	4	*.987
1988—Iowa	A. A.	OF	132	505	73	149	22	5	6	49	.295	261	6	4	.985
1988—Chicago	Nat.	OF	26	75	9	16	3	0	0	4	.213	55	1	0	1.000
1989—Iowa	A. A.	OF	111	431	59	121	18	4	4	33	.281	273	15	6	.980
1989—Chicago	Nat.	OF	47	139	20	23	1	0	1	12	.165	96	0	0	1.000
1990—Chicago	Nat.	OF-P	113	241	27	61	9	5	1	26	.253	174	2	0	1.000
Major League Totals—3 Years			186	455	56	100	13	5	2	42	.220	325	3	0	1.000

Selected by Chicago Cubs' organization in 12th round of free-agent draft, June 3, 1985.

PITCHING RECORD

Year Club	League	G.	IP.	W.	L.	Pct.	H.	R.	ER.	SO.	BB.	ERA.
1990—Chicago	National	1	1	0	0	.000	1	0	0	0	0	0.00

JOHN MICHAEL DAUGHERTY

Name pronounced DAW-er-tee.

(Jack)

Born July 3, 1960, at Hialeah, Fla.
Height, 6.00. Weight, 190.
Throws left and bats right and lefthanded.
Attended San Diego Mesa College, San Diego, Calif.,
and University of Arizona, Tucson, Ariz.

Major League stolen bases: 1989 (2).
Led Florida State League in total bases with 213 in 1985.
Led Pioneer League in total bases with 179 and intentional bases on balls received with 10 in 1984.
Tied for Pioneer League lead in bases on balls received with 52 in 1984.
Led Pioneer League first basemen in total chances with 624 in 1984.
Named Florida State League Most Valuable Player, 1985.

Year Club	League	Pos.	G.	AB.	R.	H.	2B.	3B.	HR.	RBI.	B.A.	PO.	A.	E.	F.A.
1983—San José†	Calif.	1B	116	364	46	95	17	2	2	45	.261	670	25	7	.990
1984—Helena§	Pion.	1B	66	259	*77	*104	*26	2	15	*82	*.402	*583	33	8	.987
1985—W. Palm Beach....	Fla. St.	1B	133	481	76	152	25	3	10	*87	.316	1041	50	14	.987
1986—Jacksonville.........	South.	1B	138	502	87	159	37	4	4	63	.317	1007	64	*19	.983
1987—Indianapolis	A. A.	1B-OF	117	420	65	131	35	3	7	50	.312	754	76	7	.992
1987—Montreal	Nat.	1B	11	10	1	1	1	0	0	1	.100	1	1	0	1.000
1988—Indianapolis§	A. A.	1B-OF	137	481	82	137	33	2	6	67	.285	896	62	8	.992
1989—Oklahoma City	A. A.	1B-OF	82	311	28	78	15	3	3	32	.251	728	54	6	.992
1989—Texas	Amer.	1B-OF	52	106	15	32	4	2	1	10	.302	132	14	0	1.000
1990—Texas	Amer.	OF-1B	125	310	36	93	20	2	6	47	.300	225	22	3	.988
National League Totals—1 Year.............			11	10	1	1	1	0	0	1	.100	1	1	0	1.000
American League Totals—2 Years			177	416	51	125	24	4	7	57	.300	357	36	3	.992
Major League Totals—3 Years.............			188	426	52	126	25	4	7	58	.296	358	37	3	.992

Signed as free agent by Oakland A's organization, October 9, 1982.

†Released, January 16, 1984; signed by Helena (Independent), June 13, 1984.

§Sold to West Palm Beach (Montreal Expos' organization), December 4, 1984.

§Traded to Texas Rangers' organization, September 13, 1988, completing deal in which Texas traded Infielder Tom O'Malley to Montreal Expos for a player to be named later, September 1, 1988.

DARREN ARTHUR DAULTON

Born January 3, 1962, at Arkansas City, Kan.
Height, 6.02. Weight, 190.
Throws right and bats lefthanded.
Attended Cowley County Community College, Arkansas City, Kan.

Major League stolen bases: 1985 (3), 1986 (2), 1988 (2), 1989 (2), 1990 (7). Total—16.
Tied for National League lead in double plays by catchers with 10 in 1990.
Tied for Eastern League lead in sacrifice flies with 10 in 1983.

Year Club	League	Pos.	G.	AB.	R.	H.	2B.	3B.	HR.	RBI.	B.A.	PO.	A.	E.	F.A.
1980—Helena	Pion.	C	37	100	13	20	2	1	1	10	.200	224	17	4	.984
1981—Spartanburg.........	S. Atl.	C-OF-3B	98	270	44	62	11	1	3	29	.230	378	34	4	.990
1982—Peninsula..............	Carol.	C-1B	110	324	65	78	21	2	11	44	.241	654	63	9	.990
1983—Reading.................	East.	C-1B-OF	113	362	77	95	16	4	19	83	.262	557	57	14	.978
1983—Philadelphia	Nat.	C	2	3	1	1	0	0	0	0	.333	8	0	0	1.000
1984—Portland†	P. C.	C	80	252	45	75	19	4	7	38	.298	322	26	6	.983
1985—Portland...............	P. C.	C	23	64	13	19	5	3	2	10	.297	110	9	0	1.000
1985—Philadelphia‡	Nat.	C	36	103	14	21	3	1	4	11	.204	160	15	1	.994
1986—Philadelphia§	Nat.	C	49	138	18	31	4	0	8	21	.225	244	21	4	.985
1987—Clearwater x.........	Fla. St.	C-1B	9	22	1	5	3	0	1	5	.227	27	5	3	.914
1987—Maine....................	Int.	C-1B	20	70	9	15	1	1	3	10	.214	138	12	0	1.000
1987—Philadelphia y......	Nat.	C-1B	53	129	10	25	6	0	3	13	.194	210	13	2	.991
1988—Philadelphia y......	Nat.	C-1B	58	144	13	30	6	0	1	12	.208	205	15	6	.973
1989—Philadelphia	Nat.	C	131	368	29	74	12	2	8	44	.201	627	56	11	.984
1990—Philadelphia	Nat.	C	143	459	62	123	30	1	12	57	.268	683	*70	8	.989
Major League Totals—7 Years.................			472	1344	147	305	61	4	36	158	.227	2137	190	32	.986

Selected by Philadelphia Phillies' organization in 25th round of free-agent draft, June 3, 1980.

†On disabled list, July 20 to August 28, 1984.

‡On disabled list, May 17 to August 9, 1985; included rehabilitation disability assignment to Portland, July 20 to August 7, 1985.

§On Philadelphia disabled list, June 22, 1986 through remainder of season.

xOn Philadelphia disabled list, April 1 to April 16, 1987.

yOn disabled list, August 28, 1988 through remainder of season.

JOHN MARK DAVIDSON

(Known by middle name.)

Born February 15, 1961, at Knoxville, Tenn.
Height, 6.02. Weight, 190.
Throws and bats righthanded.
Attended University of North Carolina, Charlotte, N.C.,
and Clemson University, Clemson, S.C.
Son of Max Davidson, minor league outfielder, 1947 through 1954.

Major League stolen bases: 1986 (2), 1987 (9), 1988 (3), 1989 (1). Total—15.
Led Southern League in game-winning RBIs with 16 in 1985.

Year Club	League	Pos.	G.	AB.	R.	H.	2B.	3B.	HR.	RBI.	B.A.	PO.	A.	E.	F.A.
1982—Wisconsin Rapids	Midw.	OF	79	247	54	74	11	0	10	41	.300	166	13	5	.973
1983—Wis. Rapids†	Midw.	OF	111	363	63	80	15	1	13	48	.220	181	6	6	.969
1984—Orlando‡	South.	OF-1B-3B	114	348	55	99	11	6	4	37	.284	243	13	3	.988
1985—Orlando	South.	OF-3B	134	453	93	137	17	2	25	106	.302	305	14	6	.982
1986—Toledo	Int.	OF	108	383	55	95	16	1	10	38	.248	290	8	8	.974
1986—Minnesota.............	Amer.	OF	36	68	5	8	3	0	0	2	.118	48	0	1	.980
1987—Minnesota.............	Amer.	OF	102	150	32	40	4	1	1	14	.267	102	3	0	1.000
1988—Minnesota.............	Amer.	OF-3B	100	106	22	23	7	0	1	10	.217	103	3	5	.955
1988—Portland	P. C.	OF-P	15	56	6	18	4	2	0	5	.321	35	2	0	1.000
1989—Portland§-Tucson	P. C.	OF	69	237	26	58	9	2	5	24	.245	145	9	0	1.000
1989—Houston	Nat.	OF	33	65	7	13	2	1	1	5	.200	36	0	0	1.000

Year Club	League	Pos.	G.	AB.	R.	H.	2B.	3B.	HR.	RBI.	B.A.	PO.	A.	E.	F.A.
1990—Tucson....................	P. C.	OF	56	182	35	61	13	1	6	46	.335	98	4	1	.990
1990—Houston x	Nat.	OF	57	130	12	38	5	1	1	11	.292	103	1	2	.981
American League Totals—3 Years			238	324	59	71	14	1	2	26	.219	253	6	6	.977
National League Totals—2 Years............			90	195	19	51	7	2	2	16	.262	139	1	2	.986
Major League Totals—5 Years.................			328	519	78	122	21	3	4	42	.235	392	7	8	.980

Selected by Minnesota Twins' organization in 11th round of free-agent draft, June 7, 1982.
†On disabled list, April 15 to May 4, 1983.
‡On disabled list, July 16 to July 26, 1984.
§Traded to Tucson (Houston Astros' organization) for a player to be named later, May 16, 1989; Minnesota Twins acquired Pitcher Greg Johnson to complete deal, September 6, 1989.
xOn disabled list, April 30 to May 28, 1990; included rehabilitation disability assignment to Tucson, May 10 to May 28, 1990.

CHAMPIONSHIP SERIES RECORD

Year Club	League	Pos.	G.	AB.	R.	H.	2B.	3B.	HR.	RBI.	B.A.	PO.	A.	E.	F.A.
1987—Minnesota..............	Amer.	PR	1	0	0	0	0	0	0	0	.000	0	0	0	.000

WORLD SERIES RECORD

Year Club	League	Pos.	G.	AB.	R.	H.	2B.	3B.	HR.	RBI.	B.A.	PO.	A.	E.	F.A.
1987—Minnesota..............	Amer.	OF-PH	2	1	0	0	0	0	0	0	.000	0	0	0	.000

PITCHING RECORD

Year Club	League	G.	IP.	W.	L.	Pct.	H.	R.	ER.	SO.	BB.	ERA.
1988—Portland...	P. Coast	1	1⅓	0	1	.000	2	1	1	0	2	6.75

ALVIN GLENN DAVIS

Born September 9, 1960, at Riverside, Calif.
Height, 6.01. Weight, 190.
Throws right and bats lefthanded.
Received bachelor of science degree in finance from Arizona State University, Tempe, Ariz.

Shares major league record for most putouts, first baseman, nine-inning game (22), May 28, 1988.
Shares American League record for most home runs, first two major league games (2), April 11 and 13, 1984.
Major League stolen bases: 1984 (5), 1985 (1), 1988 (1). Total—7.
Led Southern League in bases on balls received with 120 and sacrifice flies with 12 in 1983.
Led Southern League first basemen in total chances with 1,348 and double plays with 118 in 1983.
Named American League Rookie Player of the Year by THE SPORTING NEWS, 1984.
Named American League Rookie of the Year by Baseball Writers' Association of America, 1984.

Year Club	League	Pos.	G.	AB.	R.	H.	2B.	3B.	HR.	RBI.	B.A.	PO.	A.	E.	F.A.
1982—Lynn......................	East	1B	74	225	37	64	10	1	12	56	.284	579	51	6	.991
1983—Chattanooga†	South.	★●1B-OF	131	422	87	125	24	3	18	83	.296	★1233	★99	●16	.988
1984—Salt Lake City.......	P. C.	1B	1	3	2	2	0	0	0	1	.667	2	0	0	1.000
1984—Seattle..................	Amer.	1B	152	567	80	161	34	3	27	116	.284	1271	94	11	.992
1985—Seattle..................	Amer.	1B	155	578	78	166	33	1	18	78	.287	1438	103	13	.992
1986—Seattle‡................	Amer.	1B	135	479	66	130	18	1	18	72	.271	880	82	14	.986
1987—Seattle..................	Amer.	1B	157	580	86	171	37	2	29	100	.295	1386	96	9	.994
1988—Seattle§................	Amer.	1B	140	478	67	141	24	1	18	69	.295	980	65	6	.994
1989—Seattle x	Amer.	1B	142	498	84	152	30	1	21	95	.305	1106	81	10	.992
1990—Seattle y	Amer.	1B	140	494	63	140	21	0	17	68	.283	435	31	3	.994
Major League Totals—7 Years.................			1021	3674	524	1061	197	9	148	598	.289	7496	552	66	.992

Selected by San Francisco Giants' organization in 8th round of free-agent draft, June 6, 1978.
Selected by Oakland A's organization in 6th round of free-agent draft, June 8, 1981.
Selected by Seattle Mariners' organization in 6th round of free-agent draft, June 7, 1982.
†On disabled list, July 21 to July 31, 1983.
‡On disabled list, June 25 to July 17, 1986.
§On disabled list, June 26 to July 15, 1988.
xOn disabled list, May 21 to June 6, 1989.
yOn disabled list, June 26 to July 11, 1990.

ALL-STAR GAME RECORD

Year League	Pos.	AB.	R.	H.	2B.	3B.	HR.	RBI.	B.A.	PO.	A.	E.	F.A.
1984—American	PH	1	0	0	0	0	0	0	.000	0	0	0	.000

CHARLES THEODORE DAVIS
(Chili)

(Original nickname was Chili Bowl, which was prompted by a friend who saw Davis after he received a haircut back in the sixth grade. The nickname was later shortened to Chili.)

Born January 17, 1960, at Kingston, Jamaica.
Height, 6.03. Weight, 215.
Throws right and bats left and righthanded.

Shares major league record for fewest errors by outfielder, season, for leader in errors (9), 1986.
Holds National League record for most games, switch-hit home runs, lifetime (3).
Shares National League record for most games, switch-hit home runs, season (2), 1987.
Major League stolen bases: 1981 (2), 1982 (24), 1983 (10), 1984 (12), 1985 (15), 1986 (16), 1987 (16), 1988 (9), 1989 (3), 1990 (1). Total—108.
Switch-hit home runs in one game, June 5, 1983, June 27, 1987, September 15, 1987, July 30, 1988 and July 1, 1989.
Tied for American League lead in sacrifice flies with 10 in 1988.

Year	Club	League	Pos.	G.	AB.	R.	H.	2B.	3B.	HR.	RBI.	B.A.	PO.	A.	E.	F.A.
1978—Cedar Rapids	Midw.	C-OF	124	424	63	119	18	5	16	73	.281	365	45	25	.943
1979—Fresno	Calif.	OF-C	134	490	91	132	24	5	21	95	.269	339	43	20	.950
1980—Shreveport	Texas	OF-C	129	442	50	130	30	4	12	67	.294	184	20	12	.944
1981—San Francisco	Nat.	OF	8	15	1	2	0	0	0	0	.133	7	0	0	1.000
1981—Phoenix†	P. C.	OF	88	334	76	117	16	6	19	75	.350	175	7	6	.968
1982—San Francisco	Nat.	OF	154	641	86	167	27	6	19	76	.261	404	●16	12	.972
1983—San Francisco	Nat.	OF	137	486	54	113	21	2	11	59	.233	357	7	9	.976
1983—Phoenix	P. C.	OF	10	44	12	13	2	0	2	9	.295	15	0	2	.882
1984—San Francisco	Nat.	OF	137	499	87	157	21	6	21	81	.315	292	9	9	.971
1985—San Francisco	Nat.	OF	136	481	53	130	25	2	13	56	.270	279	10	6	.980
1986—San Francisco	Nat.	OF	153	526	71	146	28	3	13	70	.278	303	9	●9	.972
1987—San Francisco‡	Nat.	OF	149	500	80	125	22	1	24	76	.250	265	6	7	.975
1988—California	Amer.	OF	158	600	81	161	29	3	21	93	.268	299	10	★19	.942
1989—California	Amer.	OF	154	560	81	152	24	1	22	90	.271	270	5	6	.979
1990—California§x	Amer.	OF	113	412	58	109	17	1	12	58	.265	77	5	3	.965
National League Totals—7 Years			874	3148	432	840	144	20	101	418	.267	1907	57	52	.974
American League Totals—3 Years			425	1572	220	422	70	5	55	241	.268	646	20	28	.960
Major League Totals—10 Years			1299	4720	652	1262	214	25	156	659	.267	2553	77	80	.970

Selected by San Francisco Giants' organization in 11th round of free-agent draft, June 7, 1977.
†On disabled list, August 19 to August 28, 1982.
‡Granted free agency, November 9, 1987; signed by California Angels, December 1, 1987.
§On disabled list, July 17 to August 9, 1990.
xGranted free agency, December 7, 1990.

CHAMPIONSHIP SERIES RECORD

Year	Club	League	Pos.	G.	AB.	R.	H.	2B.	3B.	HR.	RBI.	B.A.	PO.	A.	E.	F.A.
1987—San Francisco	Nat.	OF	6	20	2	3	1	0	0	0	.150	11	1	1	.923

ALL-STAR GAME RECORD

Year	League	Pos.	AB.	R.	H.	2B.	3B.	HR.	RBI.	B.A.	PO.	A.	E.	F.A.
1984—National	PH	1	0	0	0	0	0	0	.000	0	0	0	.000
1986—National	OF	1	0	0	0	0	0	0	.000	0	0	0	.000
All-Star Game Totals—2 Years		2	0	0	0	0	0	0	.000	0	0	0	.000

ERIC KEITH DAVIS

Born May 29, 1962, at Los Angeles, Calif.
Height, 6.03. Weight, 185.
Throws and bats righthanded.

Holds major league record for most strikeouts, two consecutive games (9), April 24 and 25, 1987 (21 innings).
Shares major league record for most grand slams, one month (3), May, 1987.
Major League stolen bases: 1984 (10), 1985 (16), 1986 (80), 1987 (50), 1988 (35), 1989 (21), 1990 (21). Total—233.
Hit three home runs in a game, September 10, 1986 and May 3, 1987.
Hit for the cycle, June 2, 1989.
Led National League in game-winning RBIs with 21 in 1988.
Led National League outfielders in total chances with 394 in 1987.
Led Northwest League in stolen bases with 40 in 1981.
Named outfielder on THE SPORTING NEWS National League All-Star Team, 1987 and 1989.
Named outfielder on THE SPORTING NEWS National League All-Star fielding team, 1987 through 1989.
Named outfielder on THE SPORTING NEWS National League Silver Slugger team, 1987 and 1989.

Year	Club	League	Pos.	G.	AB.	R.	H.	2B.	3B.	HR.	RBI.	B.A.	PO.	A.	E.	F.A.
1980—Eugene	N'west	SS-2B	33	73	12	16	1	0	1	11	.219	24	35	11	.843
1981—Eugene	N'west	OF	62	214	★67	69	10	4	11	39	.322	94	11	4	.963
1982—Cedar Rapids	Midw.	OF	111	434	80	120	20	5	15	56	.276	239	9	9	.965
1983—Waterbury	East.	OF	89	293	56	85	13	1	15	43	.290	214	8	2	.991
1983—Indianapolis	A. A.	OF	19	77	18	23	4	0	7	19	.299	61	1	1	.984
1984—Wichita	A. A.	OF	52	194	42	61	9	5	14	34	.314	110	5	5	.958
1984—Cincinnati†	Nat.	OF	57	174	33	39	10	1	10	30	.224	125	4	1	.992
1985—Cincinnati	Nat.	OF	56	122	26	30	3	3	8	18	.246	75	3	1	.987
1985—Denver	A. A.	OF	64	206	48	57	10	2	15	38	.277	94	5	3	.971
1986—Cincinnati	Nat.	OF	132	415	97	115	15	3	27	71	.277	274	2	7	.975
1987—Cincinnati	Nat.	OF	129	474	120	139	23	4	37	100	.293	★380	10	4	.990
1988—Cincinnati	Nat.	OF	135	472	81	129	18	3	26	93	.273	300	2	6	.981
1989—Cincinnati‡	Nat.	OF	131	462	74	130	14	2	34	101	.281	298	2	5	.984
1990—Cincinnati§	Nat.	OF	127	453	84	118	26	2	24	86	.260	257	11	2	.993
Major League Totals—7 Years			767	2572	515	700	109	18	166	499	.272	1709	34	26	.985

Selected by Cincinnati Reds' organization in 8th round of free-agent draft, June 3, 1980.
†On disabled list, August 16 to September 1, 1984.
‡On disabled list, May 3 to May 18, 1989.
§On disabled list, April 25 to May 19, 1990.

CHAMPIONSHIP SERIES RECORD

Year	Club	League	Pos.	G.	AB.	R.	H.	2B.	3B.	HR.	RBI.	B.A.	PO.	A.	E.	F.A.
1990—Cincinnati	Nat.	OF	6	23	2	4	1	0	0	2	.174	12	1	0	1.000

WORLD SERIES RECORD

Shares record by hitting home run in first series at-bat, October 16, 1990.

Year	Club	League	Pos.	G.	AB.	R.	H.	2B.	3B.	HR.	RBI.	B.A.	PO.	A.	E.	F.A.
1990—Cincinnati	Nat.	OF	4	14	3	4	0	0	1	5	.286	4	0	0	1.000

ALL-STAR GAME RECORD

Year	League	Pos.	AB.	R.	H.	2B.	3B.	HR.	RBI.	B.A.	PO.	A.	E.	F.A.
1987—National		OF	3	0	0	0	0	0	0	.000	1	0	0	1.000
1989—National		OF	2	0	0	0	0	0	0	.000	1	0	0	1.000
All-Star Game Totals—2 Years			5	0	0	0	0	0	0	.000	2	0	0	1.000

GEORGE EARL DAVIS JR.
(Storm)

(Nicknamed by mother after "Dr. Storm", a character in "Dates on Trial",
a book she was reading while pregnant with Storm.)
Born December 26, 1961, at Dallas, Tex.
Height, 6.04. Weight, 200.
Throws and bats righthanded.

Major League saves: 1984 (1).
Tied for American League lead in wild pitches with 16 in 1988.
Named American League Comeback Player of the Year by THE SPORTING NEWS, 1988.

Year	Club	League	G.	IP.	W.	L.	Pct.	H.	R.	ER.	SO.	BB.	ERA.
1979—Bluefield	Ap'lachian.	10	58	4	4	.500	44	34	25	54	30	3.88
1980—Miami	Florida St.	25	151	9	12	.429	157	85	59	90	55	3.52
1981—Charlotte	Southern	28	187	14	10	.583	★215	86	72	119	65	3.47
1982—Rochester	Int'national	4	26⅔	2	1	.667	25	13	11	27	7	3.71
1982—Baltimore	American	29	100⅔	8	4	.667	96	40	39	67	28	3.49
1983—Baltimore	American	34	200⅓	13	7	.650	180	90	80	125	64	3.59
1984—Baltimore	American	35	225	14	9	.609	205	86	78	105	71	3.12
1985—Baltimore	American	31	175	10	8	.556	172	92	88	93	70	4.53
1986—Baltimore†	American	25	154	9	12	.429	166	70	62	96	49	3.62
1986—Hagerstown‡	Carolina	1	4	0	0	.000	3	0	0	6	3	0.00
1987—San Diego§	National	21	62⅔	2	7	.222	70	48	43	37	36	6.18
1987—Wichita	Texas	1	4	0	1	.000	4	3	0	2	0	0.00
1987—Reno x	California	1	5	0	0	.000	2	2	2	5	6	3.60
1987—Oakland	American	5	30⅓	1	1	.500	28	13	11	28	11	3.26
1988—Oakland	American	33	201⅔	16	7	.696	211	86	83	127	91	3.70
1989—Oakland yz	American	31	169⅓	19	7	.731	187	91	82	91	68	4.36
1990—Kansas City a	American	21	112	7	10	.412	129	66	59	62	35	4.74
American League Totals—9 Years		244	1368⅓	97	65	.599	1374	634	582	794	487	3.83
National League Totals—1 Year		21	62⅔	2	7	.222	70	48	43	37	36	6.18
Major League Totals—9 Years		265	1431	99	72	.579	1444	682	625	831	523	3.93

Selected by Baltimore Orioles' organization in 7th round of free-agent draft, June 5, 1979.
†On disabled list, July 4 to July 22, 1986; included rehabilitation disability assignment to Hagerstown, July 18 to July 22, 1986.
‡Traded to San Diego Padres for Catcher Terry Kennedy and Pitcher Mark Williamson, October 30, 1986.
§On disabled list, June 30 to August 17, 1987; included rehabilitation disability assignment to Wichita, August 7 to August 11, and Reno, August 12 to August 17, 1987.
xTraded to Oakland Athletics for two players to be named later, August 30, 1987; San Diego Padres acquired Pitcher Dave Leiper, August 31, 1987, and First Baseman Rob Nelson, September 8, 1987, to complete deal.
yOn disabled list, May 18 to June 10, 1989.
zGranted free agency, November 13, 1989; signed by Kansas City Royals, December 7, 1989.
aOn disabled list, May 31 to June 21 and July 1 to July 17, 1990.

CHAMPIONSHIP SERIES RECORD

Year	Club	League	G.	IP.	W.	L.	Pct.	H.	R.	ER.	SO.	BB.	ERA.
1983—Baltimore	American	1	6	0	0	.000	5	0	0	2	2	0.00
1988—Oakland	American	1	6⅓	0	0	.000	2	2	0	4	5	0.00
1989—Oakland	American	1	6⅓	0	1	.000	5	6	5	3	2	7.11
Championship Series Totals—3 Years		3	18⅔	0	1	.000	12	8	5	9	9	2.41

WORLD SERIES RECORD

Year	Club	League	G.	IP.	W.	L.	Pct.	H.	R.	ER.	SO.	BB.	ERA.
1983—Baltimore	American	1	5	1	0	1.000	6	3	3	3	1	5.40
1988—Oakland	American	2	8	0	2	.000	14	10	10	7	1	11.25
World Series Totals—2 Years		3	13	1	2	.333	20	13	13	10	2	9.00

Eligible for 1989 World Series with Oakland Athletics; did not play.

GLENN EARL DAVIS

Born March 28, 1961, at Jacksonville, Fla.
Height, 6.03. Weight, 210.
Throws and bats righthanded.
Attended Manatee Junior College, Bradenton, Fla.,
and University of Georgia, Athens, Ga.

Shares major league record for most times hit by pitch, game (3), April 9, 1990.
Shares National League record for fewest double plays by first baseman, season, 150 or more games (89), 1987.
Major League stolen bases: 1986 (3), 1987 (4), 1988 (4), 1989 (4), 1990 (8). Total—23.
Hit three home runs in a game, September 10, 1987 and June 1, 1990.
Led National League in being hit by pitch with 8 in 1990.
Tied for National League lead in game-winning RBIs with 16 in 1986.
Led Gulf Coast League first basemen in total chances with 520 and tied for lead in double plays with 35 in 1981.
Named first baseman on THE SPORTING NEWS National League Silver Slugger team, 1986.

Year Club	League	Pos.	G.	AB.	R.	H.	2B.	3B.	HR.	RBI.	B.A.	PO.	A.	E.	F.A.
1981—Sara. Astros-Or.....	Gulf C.	*1B-OF	54	188	27	49	7	1	6	35	.261	*469	*37	*14	.973
1982—Daytona Beach	Fla. St.	1B-3B	103	378	70	119	28	3	●19	79	.315	759	70	16	.981
1982—Columbus..............	South.	1B	26	97	14	24	6	1	4	8	.247	257	11	2	.993
1983—Columbus..............	South.	OF	118	445	68	133	19	3	●25	85	.299	186	17	9	.958
1983—Tucson..................	P. C.	OF-1B-3B	15	57	5	12	3	0	1	8	.211	52	4	2	.966
1984—Tucson..................	P. C.	1B-OF	131	471	66	140	28	7	16	94	.297	922	94	22	.979
1984—Houston..............	Nat.	1B	18	61	6	13	5	0	2	8	.213	151	15	2	.988
1985—Tucson..................	P. C.	1B-OF	60	220	22	67	24	2	5	35	.305	420	29	5	.989
1985—Houston................	Nat.	1B-OF	100	350	51	95	11	0	20	64	.271	766	57	12	.986
1986—Houston................	Nat.	1B	158	574	91	152	32	3	31	101	.265	1253	111	11	.992
1987—Houston................	Nat.	1B	151	578	70	145	35	2	27	93	.251	1283	112	12	.991
1988—Houston................	Nat.	1B	152	561	78	152	26	0	30	99	.271	1355	103	6	*.996
1989—Houston................	Nat.	1B	158	581	87	156	26	1	34	89	.269	1347	113	12	.992
1990—Houston†..............	Nat.	1B	93	327	44	82	15	4	22	64	.251	796	55	4	.995
1990—Columbus..............	South.	1B	12	37	3	11	0	0	1	8	.297	79	7	3	.966
Major League Totals—7 Years................			830	3032	427	795	150	10	166	518	.262	6951	566	59	.992

Selected by Baltimore Orioles' organization in 32nd round of free-agent draft, June 5, 1979.
Selected by Houston Astros' organization in secondary phase of free-agent draft, January 13, 1981.
†On disabled list, June 25 to August 29, 1990; included rehabilitation disability assignment to Columbus, July 28 to August 3 and August 18 to August 28, 1990.

CHAMPIONSHIP SERIES RECORD

Shares Championship Series records for most at-bats, game (7), October 15, 1986 (16 innings); hitting home run in first series at-bat, October 8, 1986.

Year Club	League	Pos.	G.	AB.	R.	H.	2B.	3B.	HR.	RBI.	B.A.	PO.	A.	E.	F.A.
1986—Houston..................	Nat.	1B	6	26	3	7	1	0	1	3	.269	62	3	1	.985

ALL-STAR GAME RECORD

Year League	Pos.	AB.	R.	H.	2B.	3B.	HR.	RBI.	B.A.	PO.	A.	E.	F.A.
1986—National..	PH	1	0	0	0	0	0	0	.000	0	0	0	.000
1989—National..	1B	1	1	1	0	0	0	0	1.000	7	0	0	1.000
All-Star Game Totals—2 Years...................		2	1	1	0	0	0	0	.500	7	0	0	1.000

JODY RICHARD DAVIS

Born November 12, 1956, at Gainesville, Ga.
Height, 6.03. Weight, 210.
Throws and bats righthanded.
Attended Middle Georgia College, Cochran, Ga.

Major League stolen bases: 1984 (5), 1985 (1), 1987 (1). Total—7.
Led National League catchers in total chances with 998 and double plays with 14 in 1986.
Led National League in passed balls with 21 in 1983.
Tied for National League lead in double plays by catchers with 11 in 1982.
Led Carolina League in sacrifice flies with 13 in 1978.
Led Carolina League catchers in double plays with 8 in 1978.
Named catcher on THE SPORTING NEWS National League All-Star fielding team, 1986.

Year Club	League	Pos.	G.	AB.	R.	H.	2B.	3B.	HR.	RBI.	B.A.	PO.	A.	E.	F.A.
1976—Marion..................	Appal.	C	50	164	20	38	5	1	5	19	.232	290	30	*13	.961
1977—Little Falls.............	NYP	C-1B	64	214	37	62	11	2	11	46	.290	369	50	12	.972
1978—Lynchburg.............	Carol.	C-1B-3B	120	408	57	107	24	2	16	94	.262	595	79	15	.978
1979—Jackson†..............	Texas	C-1B	132	433	57	128	23	4	21	91	.296	661	81	15	.980
1980—St. Petersburg.......	Fla. St.	C-1B	45	155	27	43	4	0	6	27	.277	171	20	5	.974
1980—Springfield‡§........	A. A.	C-1B	13	36	3	6	1	0	0	2	.167	59	7	1	.985
1981—Chicago	Nat.	C	56	180	14	46	5	1	4	21	.256	274	44	9	.972
1982—Chicago	Nat.	C	130	418	41	109	20	2	12	52	.261	598	89	11	.984
1983—Chicago	Nat.	C	151	510	56	138	31	2	24	84	.271	730	75	13	.984
1984—Chicago	Nat.	C	150	523	55	134	25	2	19	94	.256	811	89	*15	.984
1985—Chicago	Nat.	C	142	482	47	112	30	0	17	58	.232	694	84	8	.990
1986—Chicago	Nat.	*C-1B	148	528	61	132	27	2	21	74	.250	*885	*105	8	.992
1987—Chicago	Nat.	C	125	428	57	106	12	2	19	51	.248	749	79	9	.989
1988—Chi. xy-Atl.............	Nat.	C	90	257	21	59	9	0	7	36	.230	396	34	2	.995
1989—Atlanta	Nat.	C-1B	78	231	12	39	5	0	4	19	.169	376	40	6	.986
1990—Atlanta z................	Nat.	1B-C	12	28	0	2	0	0	0	1	.071	64	6	0	1.000
1990—Toledo ab..............	A. A.	C	3	8	1	1	0	0	0	0	.125	20	0	0	1.000
Major League Totals—10 Years..............			1082	3585	364	877	164	11	127	490	.245	5577	645	81	.987

Selected by New York Mets' organization in 3rd round of free-agent draft, January 7, 1976.
†Traded to St. Louis Cardinals' organization for Pitcher Ray Searage, December 10, 1979.
‡On disabled list, April 14 to June 20, 1980.
§Drafted by Chicago Cubs, December 8, 1980.
xOn disabled list, May 3 to May 19, 1988.
yTraded to Atlanta Braves for Pitchers Kevin Coffman and Kevin Blankenship, September 29, 1988.
zReleased, May 16, 1990; signed by Toledo (Detroit Tigers' organization), May 28, 1990.
aOn temporary inactive list, May 28 to June 5 and June 9, 1990 through remainder of season.
bReleased, September 30, 1990.

CHAMPIONSHIP SERIES RECORD

Year Club	League	Pos.	G.	AB.	R.	H.	2B.	3B.	HR.	RBI.	B.A.	PO.	A.	E.	F.A.
1984—Chicago	Nat.	C	5	18	3	7	2	0	2	6	.389	23	2	0	1.000

Year	League	Pos.	AB.	R.	H.	2B.	3B.	HR.	RBI.	B.A.	PO.	A.	E.	F.A.
1984—National		C	1	0	0	0	0	0	0	.000	1	0	0	1.000
1986—National		C	1	0	1	0	0	0	0	1.000	3	0	0	1.000
All-Star Game Totals—2 Years			2	0	1	0	0	0	0	.500	4	0	0	1.000

JOHN KIRK DAVIS

Born January 5, 1963, at Chicago, Ill.
Height, 6.07. Weight 215.
Throws and bats righthanded.

Major League saves: 1987 (2), 1988 (1), 1989 (1). Total—4.
Tied for American League lead in intentional bases on balls issued with 10 in 1988.
Led Pioneer League in wild pitches with 12 in 1982.

Year	Club	League	G.	IP.	W.	L.	Pct.	H.	R.	ER.	SO.	BB.	ERA.
1981—Sarasota Royals-Blue		Gulf Coast	10	30	2	2	.500	28	21	17	13	23	5.10
1982—Butte		Pioneer	14	80⅔	7	1	.875	100	62	★55	.38	37	6.14
1983—Charleston		S. Atlantic	20	78	5	6	.455	104	64	57	48	40	6.58
1984—Fort Myers		Florida St.	25	153	7	11	.389	170	91	77	84	70	4.53
1985—Memphis		Southern	27	160⅓	6	15	.286	186	113	96	103	75	5.39
1986—Memphis		Southern	41	111⅓	6	6	.500	99	63	58	70	69	4.69
1986—Omaha		Am. Assoc.	2	2	0	0	.000	2	1	1	1	1	4.50
1987—Omaha		Am. Assoc.	43	50⅔	4	3	.571	34	16	15	44	27	2.66
1987—Kansas City†		American	27	43⅔	5	2	.714	29	13	11	24	26	2.27
1988—Chicago		American	34	63⅔	2	5	.286	77	58	47	37	50	6.64
1988—Vancouver		P. Coast	15	17⅓	1	0	1.000	15	7	6	9	7	3.06
1989—Vancouver		P. Coast	35	49⅓	4	3	.571	33	24	13	57	33	2.37
1989—Chicago‡		American	4	6	0	1	.000	5	4	3	5	2	4.50
1990—Denver§		Am. Assoc.	6	4½	1	3	.250	4	7	6	3	8	12.46
1990—Las Vegas		P. Coast	18	74⅔	2	4	.333	68	40	36	68	43	4.34
1990—San Diego x		National	6	9⅓	0	1	.000	9	7	6	7	4	5.79
American League Totals—3 Years			65	113⅓	7	8	.467	111	75	61	66	78	4.84
National League Totals—1 Year			6	9⅓	0	1	.000	9	7	6	7	4	5.79
Major League Totals—3 Years			71	122⅔	7	9	.438	120	82	67	73	82	4.92

Selected by Kansas City Royals' organization in 7th round of free-agent draft, June 8, 1981.
†Traded with Pitchers Melido Perez, Chuck Mount and Greg Hibbard to Chicago White Sox for Pitcher Floyd Bannister and Infielder Dave Cochrane, December 10, 1987.
‡Released, April 2, 1990; signed by Denver (Milwaukee Brewers' organization), April 7, 1990.
§Released, April 26, 1990; signed by Las Vegas (San Diego Padres' organization), May 1, 1990.
xGranted free agency, October 15, 1990.

MARK ANTHONY DAVIS

Born November 25, 1964, at Lemon Grove, Calif.
Height, 6.00. Weight, 170.
Throws and bats righthanded.
Attended Stanford University, Stanford, Calif.
Brother of Mike Davis, outfielder with Oakland A's and Los Angeles Dodgers, 1980 through 1989;
cousin of Dave Grayson, Sr., defensive back with Dallas Texans,
Kansas City Chiefs and Oakland Raiders, 1961 through 1970; and
related to Dave Grayson, Jr., linebacker with Cleveland Browns.

Year	Club	League	Pos.	G.	AB.	R.	H.	2B.	3B.	HR.	RBI.	B.A.	PO.	A.	E.	F.A.
1986—Appleton		Midw.	OF	77	272	37	62	10	4	3	22	.228	105	5	3	.973
1987—Peninsula		Carol.	OF	134	507	91	149	24	6	16	72	.294	214	9	7	.970
1988—Birmingham		South.	OF	66	248	52	72	18	3	6	27	.290	142	5	6	.961
1988—Vancouver		P. C.	OF	68	241	24	51	9	2	4	29	.212	114	6	5	.960
1989—Vancouver		P. C.	OF	39	123	13	16	4	1	0	8	.130	64	2	0	1.000
1989—Birmingham†		South.	OF	56	192	35	49	10	3	5	26	.255	102	1	3	.972
1989—Midland		Texas	OF	19	58	9	14	1	0	1	7	.241	37	1	0	1.000
1990—Midland		Texas	OF	92	353	66	94	16	1	12	41	.266	194	8	2	.990
1990—Edmonton		P. C.	OF	35	133	30	49	10	5	9	34	.368	56	2	3	.951

Selected by St. Louis Cardinals' organization in 5th round of free-agent draft, June 7, 1982.
Selected by San Diego Padres' organization in 9th round of free-agent draft, June 3, 1985.
Selected by Chicago White Sox' organization in 12th round of free-agent draft, June 2, 1986.
†Traded to Midland (California Angels' organization) for Outfielder Mark Doran, August 4, 1989.

MARK WILLIAM DAVIS

Born October 19, 1960, at Livermore, Calif.
Height, 6.04. Weight, 205.
Throws and bats lefthanded.
Attended Chabot College, Hayward, Calif.

Major League saves: 1985 (7), 1986 (4), 1987 (2), 1988 (28), 1989 (44), 1990 (6). Total—91.
Led National League in games finished in relief with 65 and saves with 44 in 1989.
Led Western Carolinas League in shutouts with 5, home runs allowed with 18 and tied for lead in balks with 5 in 1979.
Tied for Eastern League lead in shutouts with 4 and in games started by pitchers with 28 in 1980.
Named National League Pitcher of the Year by THE SPORTING NEWS, 1989.
Won National League Cy Young Memorial Award, 1989.

Named National League Fireman of the Year by THE SPORTING NEWS, 1989.
Named lefthanded pitcher on THE SPORTING NEWS National League All-Star Team, 1989.
Named Eastern League Most Valuable Player, 1980.

Year	Club	League	G.	IP.	W.	L.	Pct.	H.	R.	ER.	SO.	BB.	ERA.
1979—Spartanburg	W. Carol.	26	166	11	9	.550	147	76	59	135	49	3.20
1980—Reading	Eastern	28	★193	★19	6	★.760	140	63	53	★185	75	★2.47
1980—Philadelphia	National	2	7	0	0	.000	4	2	2	5	5	2.57
1981—Oklahoma City†	Am. Assoc.	13	65	5	2	.714	66	34	28	56	47	3.88
1981—Philadelphia	National	9	43	1	4	.200	49	37	37	29	24	7.74
1982—Oklahoma City‡§	Am. Assoc.	21	96⅔	5	12	.294	111	75	67	95	50	6.24
1983—Phoenix	P. Coast	13	72⅔	6	3	.667	89	57	51	64	33	6.32
1983—San Francisco	National	20	111	6	4	.600	93	51	43	83	50	3.49
1984—San Francisco	National	46	174⅔	5	17	.227	201	113	★104	124	54	5.36
1985—San Francisco	National	77	114⅓	5	12	.294	89	49	45	131	41	3.54
1986—San Francisco	National	67	84⅓	5	7	.417	63	33	28	90	34	2.99
1987—San Francisco x - San Diego	National	63	133	9	8	.529	123	64	59	98	59	3.99
1988—San Diego	National	62	98⅓	5	10	.333	70	24	22	102	42	2.01
1989—San Diego y	National	70	92⅔	4	3	.571	66	21	19	92	31	1.85
1990—Kansas City z	American	53	68⅔	2	7	.222	71	43	39	73	52	5.11
National League Totals—9 Years		416	858⅓	40	65	.381	758	394	359	754	340	3.76
American League Totals—1 Year		53	68⅔	2	7	.222	71	43	39	73	52	5.11
Major League Totals—10 Years		469	927	42	72	.368	829	437	398	827	392	3.86

Selected by New York Mets' organization in 21st round of free-agent draft, June 6, 1978.
Selected by Philadelphia Phillies' organization in secondary phase of free-agent draft, January 9, 1979.
†On disabled list, April 14 to June 11, 1981.
‡On disabled list, August 3 to August 30, 1982.
§Traded with Pitcher Mike Krukow and Outfielder Charles Penigar to San Francisco Giants for Second Baseman Joe Morgan and Pitcher Al Holland, December 14, 1982.
xTraded with third Baseman Chris Brown and Pitchers Keith Comstock and Mark Grant to San Diego Padres for Pitchers Dave Dravecky and Craig Lefferts and Infielder Kevin Mitchell, July 4, 1987.
yGranted free agency, November 13, 1989; signed by Kansas City Royals, December 11, 1989.
zOn disabled list, August 10 to September 5, 1990.

ALL-STAR GAME RECORD

Year League	IP.	W.	L.	Pct.	H.	R.	ER.	SO.	BB.	ERA.
1988—National	⅔	0	0	.000	1	0	0	0	0	0.00
1989—National	1	0	0	.000	0	0	0	2	0	0.00
All-Star Game Totals—2 Years	1⅔	0	0	.000	1	0	0	2	0	0.00

ANDRE NOLAN DAWSON

Born July 10, 1954, at Miami, Fla.
Height, 6.03. Weight, 195.
Throws and bats righthanded.
Attended Florida A&M University, Tallahassee, Fla.
Nephew of Theodore Taylor, third baseman-outfielder in Pittsburgh Pirates'
organization, 1967 through 1969.

Holds major league record for most intentional bases on balls, game (5), May 22, 1990 (16 innings).
Shares major league records for most total bases, inning (8); most home runs, inning (2), July 30, 1978, third inning, and September 24, 1985, fifth inning; most runs batted in, inning (6), September 24, 1985, fifth inning; fewest double plays by outfielder, season, 150 or more games (0), 1987.
Major League stolen bases: 1976 (1), 1977 (21), 1978 (28), 1979 (35), 1980 (34), 1981 (26), 1982 (39), 1983 (25), 1984 (13), 1985 (13), 1986 (18), 1987 (11), 1988 (12), 1989 (8), 1990 (16). Total—300.
Hit for the cycle, April 29, 1987.
Hit three home runs in a game, September 24, 1985 and August 1, 1987.
Led National League in total bases with 341 in 1983 and 353 in 1987.
Led National League in sacrifice flies with 18 in 1983.
Led National League in being hit by pitch with 12 in 1978, 7 in 1981 and tied for lead with 6 in 1980 and 9 in 1983.
Tied for National League lead in intentional bases on balls received with 21 in 1990.
Tied for National League lead in game-winning RBIs with 16 in 1987.
Led National League outfielders in total chances with 344 in 1981, 435 in 1982 and 450 in 1983.
Led Pioneer League in total bases with 166, in being hit by pitch with 6 and tied for lead in sacrifice flies with 5 in 1975.
Named National League Player of the Year by THE SPORTING NEWS, 1981 and 1987.
Named National League Most Valuable Player by Baseball Writers' Association of America, 1987.
Named National League Rookie Player of the Year by THE SPORTING NEWS, 1977.
Named National League Rookie of the Year by Baseball Writers' Association of America, 1977.
Named outfielder on THE SPORTING NEWS National League All-Star Team, 1981, 1983 and 1987.
Named outfielder on THE SPORTING NEWS National League All-Star fielding team, 1980 through 1985, 1987 and 1988.
Named outfielder on THE SPORTING NEWS National League Silver Slugger team, 1980, 1981, 1983 and 1987.

Year	Club	League	Pos.	G.	AB.	R.	H.	2B.	3B.	HR.	RBI.	B.A.	PO.	A.	E.	F.A.
1975—Lethbridge	Pion.	OF	●72	★300	52	★99	14	7	★13	50	.330	★142	7	★10	.937
1976—Quebec City	East.	OF	40	143	27	51	6	0	8	27	.357	89	3	6	.939
1976—Denver	A. A.	OF	74	240	51	84	19	4	20	46	.350	97	2	2	.980
1976—Montreal	Nat.	OF	24	85	9	20	4	1	0	7	.235	61	1	2	.969
1977—Montreal	Nat.	OF	139	525	64	148	26	9	19	65	.282	352	9	4	.989
1978—Montreal	Nat.	OF	157	609	84	154	24	8	25	72	.253	411	17	5	.988
1979—Montreal	Nat.	OF	155	639	90	176	24	12	25	92	.275	394	7	5	.988
1980—Montreal	Nat.	OF	151	577	96	178	41	7	17	87	.308	410	14	6	.986
1981—Montreal	Nat.	OF	103	394	71	119	21	3	24	64	.302	★327	10	7	.980

Year Club League	Pos.	G.	AB.	R.	H.	2B.	3B.	HR.	RBI.	B.A.	PO.	A.	E.	F.A.
1982—Montreal .... Nat.	OF	148	608	107	183	37	7	23	83	.301	★419	8	8	.982
1983—Montreal .... Nat.	OF	159	633	104	●189	36	10	32	113	.299	★435	6	9	.980
1984—Montreal .... Nat.	OF	138	533	73	132	23	6	17	86	.248	297	11	8	.975
1985—Montreal .... Nat.	OF	139	529	65	135	27	2	23	91	.255	248	9	7	.973
1986—Montreal†‡ .... Nat.	OF	130	496	65	141	32	2	20	78	.284	200	11	3	.986
1987—Chicago .... Nat.	OF	153	621	90	178	24	2	★49	★137	.287	271	12	4	.986
1988—Chicago .... Nat.	OF	157	591	78	179	31	8	24	79	.303	267	7	3	.989
1989—Chicago§ .... Nat.	OF	118	416	62	105	18	6	21	77	.252	227	4	3	.987
1990—Chicago .... Nat.	OF	147	529	72	164	28	5	27	100	.310	250	10	5	.981
Major League Totals—15 Years		2018	7785	1130	2201	396	88	346	1231	.283	4569	136	79	.983

Selected by Montreal Expos' organization in 11th round of free-agent draft, June 4, 1975.

†On disabled list, June 5 to June 30, 1986.

‡Granted free agency, November 12, 1986; signed by Chicago Cubs, March 9, 1987.

§On disabled list, May 7 to June 12, 1989.

DIVISION SERIES RECORD

Year Club League	Pos.	G.	AB.	R.	H.	2B.	3B.	HR.	RBI.	B.A.	PO.	A.	E.	F.A.
1981—Montreal .... Nat.	OF	5	20	1	6	0	1	0	0	.300	12	1	1	.929

CHAMPIONSHIP SERIES RECORD

Year Club League	Pos.	G.	AB.	R.	H.	2B.	3B.	HR.	RBI.	B.A.	PO.	A.	E.	F.A.
1981—Montreal .... Nat.	OF	5	20	2	3	0	0	0	0	.150	12	0	0	1.000
1989—Chicago .... Nat.	OF	5	19	0	2	1	0	0	3	.105	4	0	0	1.000
Championship Series Totals—2 Years		10	39	2	5	1	0	0	3	.128	16	0	0	1.000

ALL-STAR GAME RECORD

Year League	Pos.	AB.	R.	H.	2B.	3B.	HR.	RBI.	B.A.	PO.	A.	E.	F.A.
1981—National	OF	4	0	1	0	0	0	0	.250	4	0	0	1.000
1982—National	OF	4	0	1	0	0	0	0	.250	4	0	0	1.000
1983—National	OF	3	0	0	0	0	0	0	.000	3	0	0	1.000
1987—National	OF	3	0	1	1	0	0	0	.333	3	0	0	1.000
1988—National	OF	2	0	1	0	0	0	0	.500	0	0	0	.000
1989—National	OF	1	0	0	0	0	0	0	.000	1	0	0	1.000
1990—National	OF	2	0	0	0	0	0	0	.000	1	0	0	1.000
All-Star Game Totals—7 Years		19	0	4	1	0	0	0	.211	16	0	0	1.000

KENNETH GRANT DAYLEY II
(Ken)

Born February 25, 1959, at Jerome, Ida.
Height, 6.00. Weight, 180.
Throws and bats lefthanded.
Attended University of Portland, Portland, Ore.

Major League saves: 1985 (11), 1986 (5), 1987 (4), 1988 (5), 1989 (12), 1990 (2). Total—39.

Led International League pitchers in games started with 31 in 1981.

Received reported $100,000 bonus to sign with Atlanta Braves, 1980.

Named lefthanded pitcher on THE SPORTING NEWS College Baseball All-America Team, 1980.

Year Club	League	G.	IP.	W.	L.	Pct.	H.	R.	ER.	SO.	BB.	ERA.
1980—Savannah	Southern	16	105	8	3	.727	86	38	30	104	54	2.57
1981—Richmond	Int'national	31	★200	●13	8	.619	180	82	74	★162	★117	3.33
1982—Richmond	Int'national	13	98⅓	8	3	.727	89	43	34	79	47	3.11
1982—Atlanta	National	20	71⅓	5	6	.455	79	39	36	34	25	4.54
1983—Richmond	Int'national	14	90⅔	9	3	.750	79	39	33	74	49	3.28
1983—Atlanta	National	24	104⅔	5	8	.385	100	59	50	70	39	4.30
1984—Atlanta†-St. Louis	National	7	23⅔	0	5	.000	44	28	21	10	11	7.99
1984—Atlanta	Int'national	9	62⅓	5	1	.833	66	31	28	45	24	4.04
1984—Louisville	Am. Assoc.	13	96⅓	4	6	.400	86	42	35	79	22	3.27
1985—St. Louis	National	57	65⅓	4	4	.500	65	24	20	62	18	2.76
1986—St. Louis‡§	National	31	38⅔	0	3	.000	42	19	14	33	11	3.26
1987—Louisville	Am. Assoc.	1	2	0	0	.000	1	1	1	1	1	4.50
1987—Springfield	Midwest	2	3⅔	0	0	.000	1	0	0	3	1	0.00
1987—St. Louis x	National	53	61	9	5	.643	52	21	18	63	33	2.66
1988—St. Louis y	National	54	55⅓	2	7	.222	48	20	17	38	19	2.77
1989—St. Louis	National	71	75⅓	4	3	.571	63	26	24	40	30	2.87
1990—St. Louis z	National	58	73⅓	4	4	.500	63	32	29	51	30	3.56
Major League Totals—9 Years		375	568⅔	33	45	.423	556	268	229	401	216	3.62

Selected by Atlanta Braves' organization in 1st round (third player selected) of free-agent draft, June 3, 1980.

†Traded with First Baseman Mike Jorgensen to St. Louis Cardinals for Third Baseman Ken Oberkfell, June 15, 1984.

‡On disabled list, July 13, 1986 through remainder of season.

§Released, December 20, 1986; re-signed by Cardinals, January 19, 1987.

xOn St. Louis disabled list, April 5 to May 21, 1987; included rehabilitation disability assignment to Louisville, May 12 to May 21, 1987.

yOn disabled list, April 5 to May 9, 1988.

zGranted free agency, November 5, 1990; signed by Toronto Blue Jays, November 26, 1990.

CHAMPIONSHIP SERIES RECORD

Shares Championship Series record for most games pitched, series (5), 1985.

Year Club	League	G.	IP.	W.	L.	Pct.	H.	R.	ER.	SO.	BB.	ERA.
1985—St. Louis..........................	National	5	6	0	0	.000	2	0	0	3	1	0.00
1987—St. Louis..........................	National	3	4	0	0	.000	1	0	0	4	2	0.00
Championship Series Totals—2 Years.................		8	10	0	0	.000	3	0	0	7	3	0.00

WORLD SERIES RECORD

Year Club	League	G.	IP.	W.	L.	Pct.	H.	R.	ER.	SO.	BB.	ERA.
1985—St. Louis..........................	National	4	6	1	0	1.000	1	0	0	5	3	0.00
1987—St. Louis..........................	National	4	4⅔	0	0	.000	2	1	1	3	0	1.93
World Series Totals—2 Years		8	10⅔	1	0	1.000	3	1	1	8	3	0.84

STEVEN M. DECKER
(Steve)

Born October 25, 1965, at Rock Island, Ill.
Height, 6.03. Weight, 205.
Throws and bats righthanded.
Attended Lewis-Clark State College, Lewiston, Ida.

Year Club	League	Pos.	G.	AB.	R.	H.	2B.	3B.	HR.	RBI.	B.A.	PO.	A.	E.	F.A.
1988—Everett..................	N'west	C	13	42	11	22	2	0	2	13	.524	37	3	2	.952
1988—San Jose	Calif.	C	47	175	31	56	9	0	4	34	.320	199	26	5	.978
1989—San Jose	Calif.	C-1B	64	225	27	65	12	0	3	46	.289	417	51	7	.985
1989—Shreveport	Texas	C-1B	44	142	19	46	8	0	1	18	.324	229	22	5	.981
1990—Shreveport	Texas	C	116	403	52	118	22	1	15	80	.293	650	71	10	.986
1990—San Francisco	Nat.	C	15	54	5	16	2	0	3	8	.296	75	11	1	.989
Major League Totals—1 Year.................			15	54	5	16	2	0	3	8	.296	75	11	1	.989

Selected by San Francisco Giants' organization in 21st round of free-agent draft, June 1, 1988.

ROBERT GEORGE DEER
(Rob)

Born September 29, 1960, at Orange, Calif.
Height, 6.03. Weight, 225.
Throws and bats righthanded.
Attended Fresno City College, Fresno, Calif.

Shares major league records for most grand slams, two consecutive games (2), August 19 and 20, 1987; most strikeouts, nine-inning game (5), August 8, first game, 1987.
Holds American League record for most strikeouts, season (186), 1987.
Major League stolen bases: 1984 (1), 1986 (5), 1987 (12), 1988 (9), 1989 (4), 1990 (2). Total—33.
Led American League batters in strikeouts with 186 in 1987 and tied for lead with 153 in 1988.
Led American League outfielders in double plays with 7 in 1990.
Led Pacific Coast League batters in strikeouts with 175 in 1984.
Led Texas League batters in strikeouts with 177 in 1982 and 185 in 1983.
Tied for Texas League lead in game-winning RBIs with 13 in 1983.
Led California League batters in strikeouts with 146 in 1981.

Year Club	League	Pos.	G.	AB.	R.	H.	2B.	3B.	HR.	RBI.	B.A.	PO.	A.	E.	F.A.
1978—Great Falls...........	Pion.	OF	48	137	20	34	6	5	0	18	.248	83	3	4	.956
1979—Cedar Rapids.......	Midw.	OF	29	86	7	18	0	1	1	16	.209	35	1	4	.900
1979—Great Falls...........	Pion.	OF	63	218	49	69	18	7	7	44	.317	95	10	5	.955
1980—Clinton..................	Midw.	OF	127	434	60	114	31	5	13	58	.263	184	●17	11	.948
1981—Fresno	Calif.	OF	135	479	86	137	24	4	*33	107	.286	211	14	6	.974
1982—Shreveport	Texas	OF-1B	128	410	58	85	26	0	27	73	.207	184	10	11	.946
1983—Shreveport	Texas	OF	132	448	89	97	15	1	*35	99	.217	252	13	7	.974
1984—Phoenix..................	P. C.	OF	133	449	88	102	21	1	*31	69	.227	251	*19	9	.968
1984—San Francisco	Nat.	OF	13	24	5	4	0	0	3	3	.167	19	0	2	.905
1985—San Francisco†	Nat.	OF-1B	78	162	22	30	5	1	8	20	.185	127	2	2	.985
1986—Milwaukee............	Amer.	OF-1B	134	466	75	108	17	3	33	86	.232	312	8	8	.976
1987—Milwaukee............	Amer.	OF-1B	134	474	71	113	15	2	28	80	.238	304	16	8	.976
1988—Milwaukee‡...........	Amer.	OF	135	492	71	124	24	0	23	85	.252	284	10	3	.990
1989—Milwaukee§..........	Amer.	OF	130	466	72	98	18	2	26	65	.210	267	10	8	.972
1990—Milwaukee x	Amer.	OF-1B	134	440	57	92	15	1	27	69	.209	373	25	10	.975
National League Totals—2 Years........			91	186	27	34	5	1	11	23	.183	146	2	4	.974
American League Totals—5 Years			667	2338	346	535	89	8	137	385	.229	1540	69	37	.978
Major League Totals—7 Years.................			758	2524	373	569	94	9	148	408	.225	1686	71	41	.977

Selected by San Francisco Giants' organization in 4th round of free-agent draft, June 6, 1978.
†Traded to Milwaukee Brewers for Pitchers Dean Freeland and Eric Pilkington, December 18, 1985.
‡On disabled list, July 4 to July 27, 1988.
§On disabled list, August 9 to August 25, 1989.
xGranted free agency, November 5, 1990; signed by Detroit Tigers, November 23, 1990.

—DID YOU KNOW—

That the six no-hitters pitched in the majors before the 1990 All-Star break matched the total thrown in the previous six seasons combined?

JOSE LUIS DeJESUS (VELAZQUEZ)

Born January 6, 1965, at Brooklyn, N.Y.
Height, 6.05. Weight, 195.
Throws and bats righthanded.

Year Club	League	G.	IP.	W.	L.	Pct.	H.	R.	ER.	SO.	BB.	ERA.
1983—Sarasota Royals	Gulf Coast	10	24	1	2	.333	17	18	11	10	17	4.13
1984—Charleston	S. Atlantic	27	163	11	12	.478	152	98	80	85	69	4.42
1985—Fort Myers†	Florida St.	27	129⅔	8	10	.444	119	70	62	94	59	4.30
1986—Fort Myers	Florida St.	22	110	4	9	.308	87	64	42	97	82	3.44
1987—Memphis	Southern	25	130⅓	4	11	.267	106	78	65	79	99	4.49
1988—Memphis	Southern	20	116	9	9	.500	88	56	50	149	70	3.88
1988—Omaha	Am. Assoc.	7	49⅔	2	3	.400	44	22	19	57	14	3.44
1988—Kansas City	American	2	2⅔	0	1	.000	6	10	8	2	5	27.00
1989—Omaha	Am. Assoc.	31	145⅓	8	11	.421	112	78	61	158	*98	3.78
1989—Kansas City‡	American	3	8	0	0	.000	7	4	4	2	8	4.50
1990—Scranton/Wilkes-Barre	Int'national	10	56	1	4	.200	41	30	21	45	39	3.38
1990—Philadelphia	National	22	130	7	8	.467	97	63	54	87	73	3.74
American League Totals—2 Years		5	10⅔	0	1	.000	13	14	12	4	13	10.13
National League Totals—1 Year		22	130	7	8	.467	97	63	54	87	73	3.74
Major League Totals—3 Years		27	140⅔	7	9	.438	110	77	66	91	86	4.22

Signed as free agent by Kansas City Royals' organization, May 9, 1983.
†Drafted by Toronto Blue Jays, December 10, 1985; returned, April 3, 1986.
‡Traded to Philadelphia Phillies for Shortstop Steve Jeltz, March 31, 1990.

FRANCISCO DeLaROSA

Born March 3, 1966, at La Romana, Dominican Republic.
Height, 5.11. Weight, 185.
Throws right and bats left and righthanded.

Year Club	League	G.	IP.	W.	L.	Pct.	H.	R.	ER.	SO.	BB.	ERA.
1985—Bradenton Blue Jays†	Gulf Coast	16	31	0	1	.000	43	24	19	19	5	5.52
1986-87—						(Out of Organized Baseball)						
1988—Hagerstown	Carolina	29	41	3	4	.429	34	21	21	47	29	4.61
1989—Frederick	Carolina	23	22⅔	3	4	.429	17	9	6	31	11	2.38
1989—Hagerstown	Eastern	18	29⅔	1	1	.500	27	15	15	34	20	4.55
1990—Hagerstown	Eastern	23	131	9	5	.643	97	42	30	105	51	2.06
1990—Rochester	Int'national	2	⅔	0	0	.000	0	0	0	1	1	0.00

Signed as free agent by Toronto Blue Jays' organization, March 4, 1985.
†Released, September 28, 1985; signed by Baltimore Orioles' organization, October 24, 1987.

JOSE DeLEON (CHESTARO)

Born December 20, 1960, at Rancho Viejo, LaVega, D.R.
Height, 6.03. Weight, 215.
Throws and bats righthanded.

Major League saves: 1985 (3), 1986 (1). Total—4.
Led Gulf Coast League in home runs allowed with 7 in 1979.
Tied for South Atlantic League lead in home runs allowed with 19 in 1980.
Tied for Gulf Coast League lead in wild pitches with 9 in 1979.

Year Club	League	G.	IP.	W.	L.	Pct.	H.	R.	ER.	SO.	BB.	ERA.
1979—Bradenton Pirates	Gulf Coast	11	59	2	4	.333	76	47	42	33	38	6.41
1980—Shelby	S. Atlantic	26	168	10	15	.400	160	108	*90	118	69	4.82
1981—Buffalo	Eastern	25	159	12	6	.667	136	72	55	158	94	3.11
1982—Portland†	P. Coast	24	119	10	7	.588	138	81	79	94	65	5.97
1983—Hawaii	P. Coast	20	127⅓	11	6	.647	90	50	43	128	68	*3.04
1983—Pittsburgh	National	15	108	7	3	.700	75	36	34	118	47	2.83
1984—Pittsburgh	National	30	192⅓	7	13	.350	147	86	80	153	92	3.74
1985—Pittsburgh	National	31	162⅔	2	*19	.095	138	93	85	149	89	4.70
1985—Hawaii	P. Coast	5	41	4	0	1.000	15	4	4	45	10	0.88
1986—Hawaii	P. Coast	15	106	5	8	.385	87	32	29	83	44	2.46
1986—Pittsburgh‡	National	9	16⅓	1	3	.250	17	16	15	11	17	8.27
1986—Chicago	American	13	79	4	5	.444	49	30	26	68	42	2.96
1987—Chicago§	American	33	206	11	12	.478	177	106	92	153	97	4.02
1988—St. Louis x	National	34	225⅓	13	10	.565	198	95	92	208	86	3.67
1989—St. Louis	National	36	244⅔	16	12	.571	173	96	83	*201	80	3.05
1990—St. Louis	National	32	182⅔	7	*19	.269	168	96	90	164	86	4.43
National League Totals—7 Years		187	1132	53	79	.402	916	518	479	1004	497	3.81
American League Totals—2 Years		46	285	15	17	.469	226	136	118	221	139	3.73
Major League Totals—8 Years		233	1417	68	96	.415	1142	654	597	1225	636	3.79

Selected by Pittsburgh Pirates' organization in 3rd round of free-agent draft June 5, 1979.
†On disabled list, July 5 to July 29, 1982.
‡Traded to Chicago White Sox for Outfielder Bobby Bonilla, July 23, 1986.
§Traded to St. Louis Cardinals for Pitcher Rick Horton, Outfielder Lance Johnson and cash, February 9, 1988.
xAppeared in one game as an outfielder with one putout.

LUIS MANUEL de los SANTOS

Born December 29, 1966, at San Cristobal, D.R.
Height, 6.05. Weight, 200.
Throws and bats righthanded.

Led American Association in sacrifice flies with 12 in 1990.
Led American Association in grounding into double plays with 20 in 1987, 17 in 1988 and 19 in 1989.
Led American Association first basemen in total chances with 1,050 in 1988.
Named American Association Most Valuable Player, 1988.

Year	Club	League	Pos.	G.	AB.	R.	H.	2B.	3B.	HR.	RBI.	B.A.	PO.	A.	E.	F.A.
1984—Eugene	N'west	3B	67	257	27	69	10	2	2	30	.268	67	93	22	.879
1985—Fort Myers	Fla. St.	3B	123	454	44	120	18	2	0	48	.264	87	141	32	.877
1986—Memphis	South.	3B	135	525	72	159	21	5	3	84	.303	*136	244	*50	.884
1987—Omaha	A. A.	3B-1B	135	518	53	152	29	6	2	67	.293	401	116	27	.950
1988—Omaha	A. A.	1B	136	*535	62	*164	25	4	6	●87	.307	*971	68	*11	.990
1988—Kansas City	Amer.	1B	11	22	1	2	1	1	0	1	.091	31	1	0	1.000
1989—Omaha	A. A.	1B-3B	99	387	45	115	31	3	3	62	.297	842	57	9	.990
1989—Kansas City	Amer.	1B	28	87	6	22	3	1	0	6	.253	203	16	3	.986
1990—Omaha	A. A.	3B-1B	135	521	55	146	23	1	5	74	.280	242	171	16	.963
Major League Totals—2 Years				39	109	7	24	4	2	0	7	.220	234	17	3	.988

Selected by Kansas City Royals' organization in 2nd round of free-agent draft, June 4, 1984.

RICHARD ANTHONY DeLUCIA
(Rich)

Born October 7, 1964, at Wyomissing, Pa.
Height, 6.00. Weight, 180.
Throws and bats righthanded.
Attended University of Tennessee, Knoxville, Tenn.

Pitched seven-inning, 1-0 no-hit victory against Everett, July 17, 1986.
Tied for Northwest League lead in shutouts with 1 in 1986.

Year	Club	League	G.	IP.	W.	L.	Pct.	H.	R.	ER.	SO.	BB.	ERA.
1986—Bellingham	Northwest	13	74	8	2	.800	44	20	14	69	24	*1.70
1987—Salinas†	California	1	1	0	0	.000	2	1	1	1	0	9.00
1988—San Bernardino	California	22	127⅔	7	8	.467	110	57	44	118	59	3.10
1989—Williamsport‡	Eastern	10	54⅔	3	4	.429	59	28	23	41	13	3.79
1990—San Bernardino	California	5	30⅔	4	1	.800	19	9	7	35	3	2.05
1990—Williamsport	Eastern	18	115	6	6	.500	92	30	27	76	30	2.11
1990—Calgary	P. Coast	5	32⅓	2	2	.500	30	17	13	23	12	3.62
1990—Seattle	American	5	36	1	2	.333	30	9	8	20	9	2.00
Major League Totals—1 Year		5	36	1	2	.333	30	9	8	20	9	2.00

Selected by Toronto Blue Jays' organization in 15th round of free-agent draft, June 3, 1985.
Selected by Seattle Mariners' organization in 6th round of free-agent draft, June 2, 1986.
†On disabled list, April 10, 1987 through remainder of season.
‡On disabled list, May 31 to July 2 and July 7, 1989 through remainder of season.

JOHN RIKARD DEMPSEY
(Rick)

Born September 13, 1949, at Fayetteville, Tenn.
Height, 6.00. Weight, 199.
Throws and bats righthanded.
Attended Pierce Junior College, Woodland Hills, Calif.
Brother of Pat Dempsey, catcher in Oakland A's, Baltimore Orioles', New York Yankees', Cleveland Indians'
and Minnesota Twins' organizations, 1977 through 1987.

Shares major league record for most double plays by catcher, game (3), June 1, 1977.
Major League stolen bases: 1974 (1), 1976 (1), 1977 (2), 1978 (7), 1980 (3), 1983 (1), 1984 (1), 1986 (1), 1988 (1), 1989 (1), 1990 (1). Total—20.
Tied for American League lead in double plays by catchers with 14 in 1978.
Led International League in passed balls with 14 in 1973.
Led New York-Pennsylvania League catchers in putouts with 468, assists with 35, fielding percentage with .990 and tied for lead in double plays with 4 in 1968.

Year	Club	League	Pos.	G.	AB.	R.	H.	2B.	3B.	HR.	RBI.	B.A.	PO.	A.	E.	F.A.
1967—Sarasota Twins	Gulf C.	C-OF-1B	40	102	9	21	4	3	0	9	.206	133	16	2	.987
1968—Wisconsin Rapids	Midw.	C	11	35	12	8	2	0	1	6	.229	68	2	1	.986
1968—Auburn	NYP	C-1B-OF	73	270	48	79	10	7	7	61	.293	505	38	7	.987
1969—Wisconsin Rapids	Midw.	C	50	151	35	55	11	2	6	31	.364	341	30	●13	.966
1969—Minnesota	Amer.	C	5	6	1	3	1	0	0	0	.500	5	0	1	.833
1970—Charlotte	South	C-OF-2B	105	351	28	86	20	6	4	42	.245	506	76	18	.970
1970—Minnesota	Amer.	C	5	7	1	0	0	0	0	0	.000	12	0	1	.923
1971—Charlotte	South	C-OF	105	338	39	82	16	2	8	47	.243	599	65	8	.988
1971—Minnesota	Amer.	C	6	13	2	4	1	0	0	0	.308	30	4	2	.944
1972—Minnesota†	Amer.	C	25	40	0	8	1	0	0	0	.200	67	5	1	.986
1972—Tacoma	P. C.	C-OF	48	161	13	38	6	2	3	18	.236	284	33	5	.984
1973—Syracuse	Int.	C-OF-3B	122	387	53	96	14	4	6	47	.248	585	69	9	.986
1973—New York	Amer.	C	6	11	0	2	0	0	0	0	.182	9	0	2	.818
1974—New York	Amer.	C-OF	43	109	12	26	3	0	2	12	.239	152	22	4	.978
1975—New York	Amer.	C-OF-3B	71	145	18	38	8	0	1	11	.262	92	9	3	.971
1976—N.Y.‡-Balt.	Amer.	C-OF	80	216	12	42	2	0	0	12	.194	302	39	4	.988

Year	Club	League	Pos.	G.	AB.	R.	H.	2B.	3B.	HR.	RBI.	B.A.	PO.	A.	E.	F.A.
1977—Baltimore§	Amer.	C	91	270	27	61	7	4	3	34	.226	416	52	11	.977
1978—Baltimore	Amer.	C	136	441	41	114	25	0	6	32	.259	636	79	11	.985
1979—Baltimore	Amer.	C	124	368	48	88	23	0	6	41	.239	615	*81	7	.990
1980—Baltimore	Amer.	C-OF-1B	119	362	51	95	26	3	9	40	.262	544	55	8	.987
1981—Baltimore	Amer.	C	92	251	24	54	10	1	6	15	.215	384	35	1	*.998
1982—Baltimore	Amer.	C	125	344	35	88	15	1	5	36	.256	491	46	5	.991
1983—Baltimore	Amer.	C	128	347	33	80	16	2	4	32	.231	591	65	2	*.997
1984—Baltimore	Amer.	C	109	330	37	76	11	0	11	34	.230	453	43	4	.992
1985—Baltimore	Amer.	C	132	362	54	92	19	0	12	52	.254	575	49	8	.987
1986—Baltimore x	Amer.	C	122	327	42	68	15	1	13	29	.208	659	53	7	.990
1987—Cleveland yz	Amer.	C	60	141	16	25	10	0	1	9	.177	293	18	5	.984
1988—Los Angeles	Nat.	C	77	167	25	42	13	0	7	30	.251	333	29	4	.989
1989—Los Angeles	Nat.	C	79	151	16	27	7	0	4	16	.179	265	35	5	.984
1990—Los Angeles ab	Nat.	C	62	128	13	25	5	0	2	15	.195	213	27	2	.992
American League Totals—19 Years			1479	4090	454	964	193	12	79	389	.236	6326	655	87	.988
National League Totals—3 Years			218	446	54	94	25	0	13	61	.211	811	91	11	.988
Major League Totals—22 Years			1697	4536	508	1058	218	12	92	450	.233	7137	746	98	.988

Selected by Minnesota Twins' organization in 12th round of free-agent draft, June 6, 1967.
†Traded to New York Yankees' organization for Outfielder Danny Walton, October 27, 1972.
‡Traded with Pitchers Rudy May, Tippy Martinez, Dave Pagan and Scott McGregor to Baltimore Orioles for Pitchers Ken Holtzman, Doyle Alexander and Grant Jackson, Catcher Ellie Hendricks and Pitcher Jimmy Freeman, June 15, 1976.
§On disabled list, July 9 to August 21, 1977.
xGranted free agency, November 12, 1986; signed by Cleveland Indians, February 6, 1987.
yOn disabled list, July 22 to September 11, 1987.
zReleased, October 29, 1987; signed by Los Angeles Dodgers, March 30, 1988.
aOn disabled list, April 16 to May 3, 1990.
bGranted free agency, November 5, 1990.

CHAMPIONSHIP SERIES RECORD

Year	Club	League	Pos.	G.	AB.	R.	H.	2B.	3B.	HR.	RBI.	B.A.	PO.	A.	E.	F.A.
1979—Baltimore	Amer.	C	3	10	3	4	2	0	0	2	.400	10	1	0	1.000
1983—Baltimore	Amer.	C	4	12	1	2	0	0	0	0	.167	29	5	1	.971
1988—Los Angeles	Nat.	PH-C	4	5	1	2	2	0	0	2	.400	7	0	0	1.000
Championship Series Totals—3 Years			11	27	5	8	4	0	0	4	.296	46	6	1	.981

WORLD SERIES RECORD

Year	Club	League	Pos.	G.	AB.	R.	H.	2B.	3B.	HR.	RBI.	B.A.	PO.	A.	E.	F.A.
1979—Baltimore	Amer.	C-PR	7	21	3	6	3	0	0	0	.286	38	2	0	1.000
1983—Baltimore	Amer.	C	5	13	3	5	4	0	1	2	.385	27	4	0	1.000
1988—Los Angeles	Nat.	C	2	5	0	1	1	0	0	1	.200	13	1	0	1.000
World Series Totals—3 Years			14	39	6	12	7	0	1	3	.308	78	7	0	1.000

JAMES JOSEPH DESHAIES

Name pronounced Duh-SHAYS.

(Jim)

Born June 23, 1960, at Massena, N.Y.
Height, 6.04. Weight, 222.
Throws and bats lefthanded.
Received bachelor of arts degree from Le Moyne College, Syracuse, N.Y., in 1982.

Holds modern major league record for most consecutive strikeouts at start of game (8), September 23, 1986.
Pitched seven-inning, 5-1 no-hit victory for Nashville against Columbus, May 4, 1984.
Led National League in balks with 7 in 1986.
Led International League in balks with 4 in 1985.
Tied for International League lead in shutouts with 4 in 1984.

Year	Club	League	G.	IP.	W.	L.	Pct.	H.	R.	ER.	SO.	BB.	ERA.
1982—Oneonta	NYP	15	108⅓	6	5	.545	93	50	40	*137	40	3.32
1983—Fort Lauderdale	Florida St.	20	117⅔	11	3	.786	105	44	33	128	58	2.52
1984—Nashville	Southern	7	45	3	2	.600	33	20	14	42	29	2.80
1984—Columbus	Int'national	18	135⅔	10	5	.667	99	45	36	117	62	*2.39
1984—New York	American	2	7	0	1	.000	14	9	9	5	7	11.57
1985—Columbus†‡	Int'national	21	131⅔	8	6	.571	124	67	63	106	59	4.31
1985—Houston	National	2	3	0	0	.000	1	0	0	2	0	0.00
1986—Houston§	National	26	144	12	5	.706	124	58	52	128	59	3.25
1987—Houston x	National	26	152	11	6	.647	149	81	78	104	57	4.62
1988—Houston	National	31	207	11	14	.440	164	77	69	127	72	3.00
1989—Houston	National	34	225⅔	15	10	.600	180	80	73	153	79	2.91
1990—Houston	National	34	209⅓	7	12	.368	186	93	88	119	84	3.78
American League Totals—1 Year		2	7	0	1	.000	14	9	9	5	7	11.57
National League Totals—6 Years		153	941	56	47	.544	804	389	360	633	351	3.44
Major League Totals—7 Years		155	948	56	48	.538	818	398	369	638	358	3.50

Selected by Montreal Expos' organization in 13th round of free-agent draft, June 6, 1978.
Selected by New York Yankees' organization in 21st round of free-agent draft, June 7, 1982.
†On disabled list, April 10 to April 26 and August 4 to August 14, 1985.

‡Traded with a player to be named later to Houston Astros for Pitcher Joe Niekro, September 15, 1985; Houston organization acquired Infielder Neder Horta, September 24, 1985, and Pitcher Dody Rather, January 11, 1986, to complete deal.
§On disabled list, April 21 to May 7, 1986.
xOn disabled list, July 26 to August 16, 1987.

DELINO LAMONT DeSHIELDS
First name pronounced Duh-LYNE-oh.

Born January 15, 1969, at Seaford, Del.
Height, 6.01. Weight, 170.
Throws right and bats lefthanded.
Attended Villanova University, Villanova, Pa.

Shares modern National League record for most hits, first major league game (4), April 9, 1990.
Major League stolen bases: 1990 (42).

Year	Club	League	Pos.	G.	AB.	R.	H.	2B.	3B.	HR.	RBI.	B.A.	PO.	A.	E.	F.A.
1987—Bradenton Expos	Gulf C.	★SS-3B	31	111	17	24	5	2	1	4	.216	47	90	★22	.862
1987—Jamestown	NYP	SS	34	96	16	21	1	2	1	5	.219	25	57	21	.796
1988—Rockford	Midw.	SS	129	460	97	116	26	6	12	46	.252	173	344	42	.925
1989—Jacksonville	South.	SS	93	307	55	83	10	6	3	35	.270	127	218	34	.910
1989—Indianapolis	A. A.	SS	47	181	29	47	8	4	2	14	.260	73	101	13	.930
1990—Montreal†	Nat.	2B	129	499	69	144	28	6	4	45	.289	236	371	12	.981
Major League Totals—1 Year			129	499	69	144	28	6	4	45	.289	236	371	12	.981

Selected by Montreal Expos' organization in 1st round (12th player selected) of free-agent draft, June 2, 1987.
†On disabled list, June 16 to July 12, 1990.

MICHAEL DEVEREAUX
Name pronounced DEH-ver-oh.
(Mike)
Born April 10, 1963, at Casper, Wyo.
Height, 6.00. Weight, 195.
Throws and bats righthanded.
Attended Mesa Community College, Mesa, Ariz., and received bachelor of arts degree in finance from Arizona State University, Tempe, Ariz.

Major League stolen bases: 1987 (3), 1989 (22), 1990 (13). Total—38.
Led Texas League in sacrifice flies with 11 in 1987.
Led Pioneer League in total bases with 152 and stolen bases with 40 in 1985.
Led Texas League outfielders in total chances with 349 in 1987.

Year	Club	League	Pos.	G.	AB.	R.	H.	2B.	3B.	HR.	RBI.	B.A.	PO.	A.	E.	F.A.
1985—Great Falls	Pion.	OF	●70	★289	★73	★103	17	10	4	★67	.356	100	4	5	.954
1986—San Antonio	Texas	OF	115	431	69	130	22	2	10	53	.302	292	13	4	.987
1987—San Antonio	Texas	OF	★135	★562	90	169	28	9	26	91	.301	★339	7	3	★.991
1987—Albuquerque	P. C.	OF	3	11	2	3	1	0	1	1	.273	4	1	0	1.000
1987—Los Angeles	Nat.	OF	19	54	7	12	3	0	0	4	.222	21	1	0	1.000
1988—Albuquerque	P. C.	OF	109	423	88	144	26	4	13	76	.340	211	5	7	.969
1988—Los Angeles†	Nat.	OF	30	43	4	5	1	0	0	2	.116	29	0	0	1.000
1989—Baltimore	Amer.	OF	122	391	55	104	14	3	8	46	.266	288	1	5	.983
1990—Baltimore‡	Amer.	OF	108	367	48	88	18	1	12	49	.240	281	4	5	.983
1990—Frederick	Carol.	OF	2	8	3	4	0	0	1	3	.500	4	2	0	1.000
1990—Hagerstown	East.	OF	4	20	4	5	3	0	0	3	.250	13	0	1	.929
National League Totals—2 Years			49	97	11	17	4	0	0	6	.175	50	1	0	1.000
American League Totals—2 Years			230	758	103	192	32	4	20	95	.253	569	5	10	.983
Major League Totals—4 Years			279	855	114	209	36	4	20	101	.244	619	6	10	.984

Selected by Cleveland Indians' organization in 26th round of free-agent draft, June 4, 1984.
Selected by Los Angeles Dodgers' organization in 5th round of free-agent draft, June 3, 1985.
†Traded to Baltimore Orioles for Pitcher Mike Morgan, March 12, 1989.
‡On disabled list, May 17 to June 15, 1990; included rehabilitation disability assignment to Frederick, June 9 and June 10, 1990; and Hagerstown, June 11 to June 15, 1990.

MARK ALAN DEWEY
Born January 3, 1965, at Grand Rapids, Mich.
Height, 6.00. Weight, 185.
Throws and bats righthanded.
Attended Grand Valley State University, Allendale, Mich.

Led California League in saves with 30 and games finished in relief with 57 in 1989.

Year	Club	League	G.	IP.	W.	L.	Pct.	H.	R.	ER.	SO.	BB.	ERA.
1987—Everett	Northwest	19	84⅔	7	3	.700	88	39	31	67	26	3.30
1988—Clinton	Midwest	37	119⅓	10	4	.714	95	36	19	76	14	★1.43
1989—San Jose	California	59	68⅔	1	6	.143	62	35	24	60	23	3.15
1990—Shreveport	Texas	33	38⅓	1	5	.167	37	11	8	23	10	1.88
1990—Phoenix	P. Coast	19	30⅓	2	3	.400	26	14	9	27	10	2.67
1990—San Francisco	National	14	22⅔	1	1	.500	22	7	7	11	5	2.78
Major League Totals—1 Year		14	22⅔	1	1	.500	22	7	7	11	5	2.78

Selected by San Francisco Giants' organization in 23rd round of free-agent draft, June 2, 1987.

CARLOS FRANCISCO DIAZ

Name pronounced DEE-az.

Born December 24, 1964, at Elizabeth, N.J.
Height, 6.03. Weight, 190.
Throws and bats righthanded.
Attended Oklahoma State University, Stillwater, Okla.

Tied for Southern League lead in double plays by catchers with 8 in 1989.

Year	Club	League	Pos.	G.	AB.	R.	H.	2B.	3B.	HR.	RBI.	B.A.	PO.	A.	E.	F.A.
1986—Ventura County	...	Calif.	C	2	5	1	2	1	0	0	0	.400	17	3	1	.952
1986—Medicine Hat		Pion	C-1B	20	83	11	26	5	2	0	16	.313	87	10	4	.960
1986—St. Catharines		NYP	C-1B	24	74	9	13	3	1	1	5	.176	145	14	3	.981
1987—Dunedin		Fla. St.	C-1B	73	230	24	53	6	0	0	27	.230	432	43	7	.985
1988—Knoxville		South.	C	7	23	2	5	1	0	0	0	.217	51	6	1	.983
1988—Dunedin		Fla. St.	C-1B	68	235	20	46	11	0	6	23	.196	472	52	7	.987
1988—Syracuse		Int.	C	27	83	4	14	5	0	1	8	.169	174	13	0	1.000
1989—Knoxville		South.	C	100	320	28	80	12	1	6	36	.250	608	75	11	.984
1990—Syracuse		Int.	C	77	251	18	51	10	0	1	19	.203	421	37	8	.983
1990—Toronto		Amer.	C	9	3	1	1	0	0	0	0	.333	13	3	0	1.000
Major League Totals—1 Year				9	3	1	1	0	0	0	0	.333	13	3	0	1.000

Selected by Cleveland Indians' organization in 7th round of free-agent draft, June 7, 1982.
Selected by Toronto Blue Jays' organization in 14th round of free-agent draft, June 2, 1986.

EDGAR SERRANO DIAZ

Name pronounced DEE-az.

Born February 8, 1964, at Santurce, Puerto Rico.
Height, 6.00. Weight, 160.
Throws and bats righthanded.

Major League stolen bases: 1990 (3).
Led Texas League shortstops in total chances with 743 and double plays with 101 in 1985.

Year	Club	League	Pos.	G.	AB.	R.	H.	2B.	3B.	HR.	RBI.	B.A.	PO.	A.	E.	F.A.
1982—Pikeville		Appal.	SS	24	4	2	0	0	0	0	0	.083	12	30	3	.933
1983—Beloit		Midw.	SS	107	307	29	64	2	0	0	15	.208	173	258	42	.911
1984—Stockton		Calif.	SS	123	419	58	108	1	7	0	35	.258	189	381	40	.934
1985—El Paso		Texas	SS	132	501	90	134	14	4	0	55	.267	★217	★489	37	.950
1986—Vancouver†		P. C.	★SS-2B	108	346	44	109	2	4	0	43	.315	173	311	★31	.940
1986—Milwaukee		Amer.	SS	5	13	0	3	0	0	0	0	.231	6	8	2	.875
1987—Denver‡		A. A.	SS	48	162	24	44	10	2	0	15	.272	95	144	10	.960
1988—Denver§		A. A.	SS	79	278	44	65	7	0	0	21	.234	161	221	18	.955
1989—Denver		A. A.	SS	105	316	29	68	8	1	1	22	.215	198	307	24	.955
1989—El Paso		Texas	SS	23	78	16	24	0	0	0	6	.308	49	78	8	.941
1990—Milwaukee		Amer.	SS-2B-3B	86	218	27	59	2	2	0	14	.271	125	197	17	.950
Major League Totals—2 Years				91	231	27	62	2	2	0	14	.268	131	205	19	.946

Signed as free agent by Milwaukee Brewers' organization, March 3, 1982.
†On disabled list, July 3 to July 17, 1986.
‡On Milwaukee disabled list, March 29 to June 3, 1987; included rehabilitation disability assignment to Denver, May 15 to June 3, 1987.
§On restricted list, July 28, 1988 through remainder of season.

MARIO RAFAEL DIAZ (TORRES)

Name pronounced DEE-az.

Born January 10, 1962, at Humacao, P. R.
Height, 5.10. Weight, 160.
Throws and bats righthanded.

Led Southern League in sacrifice hits with 14 in 1985.

Year	Club	League	Pos.	G.	AB.	R.	H.	2B.	3B.	HR.	RBI.	B.A.	PO.	A.	E.	F.A.
1979—Bellingham		N'west	SS-3B-2B	32	96	12	19	2	0	1	5	.198	28	69	8	.924
1980—Wausau		Midw.	SS-2B	110	349	28	63	5	0	3	21	.181	172	328	41	.924
1981—Lynn		East.	SS	106	314	16	63	8	1	1	22	.201	163	318	18	★.964
1982—Lynn		East.	SS-1B	53	162	19	35	7	1	1	13	.216	384	172	18	.969
1982—Salt Lake City		P. C.	SS	5	19	2	7	1	0	0	2	.368	4	15	1	.950
1982—Wausau		Midw.	SS	56	187	15	49	8	1	1	23	.262	78	148	16	.934
1983—Bakersfield		Calif.	SS-2B	51	171	23	41	5	1	0	10	.240	92	146	22	.915
1983—Chattanooga		South.	SS	33	111	18	30	6	5	2	13	.270	48	80	10	.928
1984—Chattanooga		South.	SS-2B	108	322	23	67	7	1	1	19	.208	179	313	26	.950
1985—Chattanooga		South.	SS	115	400	38	101	6	7	0	38	.253	186	314	31	.942
1986—Calgary		P. C.	SS	109	379	40	107	17	6	1	41	.282	194	302	16	.969
1987—Calgary		P. C.	SS	108	376	52	106	17	3	4	52	.282	195	280	21	.958
1987—Seattle		Amer.	SS	11	23	4	7	0	1	0	3	.304	10	25	1	.972
1988—Calgary		P. C.	SS	46	164	16	54	18	0	1	30	.329	65	138	12	.944
1988—Seattle†		Amer.	S-2-1-3	28	72	6	22	5	0	0	9	.306	31	47	1	.987
1989—Seattle		Amer.	SS-2B-3B	52	74	9	10	0	0	1	7	.135	35	54	5	.947
1989—Calgary		P. C.	2B-SS-1B	37	127	22	43	8	1	2	9	.339	64	73	9	.938
1990—Calgary‡§		P. C.	3B-SS-2B	32	105	10	35	5	1	1	19	.333	35	61	2	.980
1990—Tidewater		Int.	SS-3B	29	104	15	33	8	0	1	9	.317	38	92	6	.956

Year	Club	League	Pos.	G.	AB.	R.	H.	2B.	3B.	HR.	RBI.	B.A.	PO.	A.	E.	F.A.
1990—New York x		Nat.	SS-2B	16	22	0	3	1	0	0	1	.136	5	18	1	.958
	American League Totals—3 Years			91	169	19	39	5	1	1	19	.231	76	126	7	.967
	National League Totals—1 Year			16	22	0	3	1	0	0	1	.136	5	18	1	.958
	Major League Totals—4 Years			107	191	19	42	6	1	1	20	.220	81	144	8	.966

Signed as free agent by Seattle Mariners' organization, December 21, 1978.

†On disabled list, May 6 to May 23, 1988; included rehabilitation disability assignment to Calgary, May 16 to May 23, 1988.

‡On Seattle disabled list, March 31 to May 4, 1990.

§Traded to Tidewater (New York Mets' organization) for Pitcher Brian Givens, June 19, 1990.

xGranted free agency, October 15, 1990.

ROBERT KEITH DIBBLE
(Rob)

Born January 24, 1964, at Bridgeport, Conn.
Height, 6.04. Weight, 235.
Throws right and bats lefthanded.
Attended Florida Southern College, Lakeland, Fla.

Major League saves: 1989 (2), 1990 (11). Total—13.

Year	Club	League	G.	IP.	W.	L.	Pct.	H.	R.	ER.	SO.	BB.	ERA.
1983—Billings		Pioneer	5	12⅔	0	1	.000	18	13	11	7	11	7.82
1983—Eugene		Northwest	7	37⅔	3	2	.600	38	28	24	17	18	5.73
1984—Tampa		Florida St.	15	64⅔	5	2	.714	59	31	21	39	29	2.92
1985—Cedar Rapids		Midwest	45	65⅔	5	5	.500	67	37	28	73	28	3.84
1986—Vermont		Eastern	31	55⅓	3	2	.600	53	29	19	37	28	3.09
1986—Denver		Am. Assoc.	5	6⅔	1	0	1.000	9	4	4	3	2	5.40
1987—Nashville		Am. Assoc.	44	61	2	4	.333	72	34	32	51	27	4.72
1988—Nashville		Am. Assoc.	31	35	2	1	.667	21	9	9	41	14	2.31
1988—Cincinnati		National	37	59⅓	1	1	.500	43	12	12	59	21	1.82
1989—Cincinnati†‡		National	74	99	10	5	.667	62	23	23	141	39	2.09
1990—Cincinnati		National	68	98	8	3	.727	62	22	19	136	34	1.74
	Major League Totals—3 Years		179	256⅓	19	9	.679	167	57	54	336	94	1.90

Selected by St. Louis Cardinals' organization in 11th round of free-agent draft, June 7, 1982.

Selected by Cincinnati Reds' organization in secondary phase of free-agent draft, June 6, 1983.

†On suspended list, May 31 to June 2 and July 25 to July 28, 1989.

‡On disabled list, July 10 to July 25, 1989.

CHAMPIONSHIP SERIES RECORD

Year	Club	League	G.	IP.	W.	L.	Pct.	H.	R.	ER.	SO.	BB.	ERA.
1990—Cincinnati		National	4	5	0	0	.000	0	0	0	10	1	0.00

WORLD SERIES RECORD

Year	Club	League	G.	IP.	W.	L.	Pct.	H.	R.	ER.	SO.	BB.	ERA.
1990—Cincinnati		National	3	4⅔	1	0	1.000	3	0	0	4	1	0.00

ALL-STAR GAME RECORD

Year	League	IP.	W.	L.	Pct.	H.	R.	ER.	SO.	BB.	ERA.
1990—National		1	0	0	.000	1	0	0	0	1	0.00

LANCE MICHAEL DICKSON

Born October 19, 1969, at Fullerton, Calif.
Height, 6.01. Weight, 185.
Throws left and bats righthanded.
Attended University of Arizona, Tucson, Ariz.

Received reported bonus of $202,000 to sign with Chicago Cubs, 1990.

Year	Club	League	G.	IP.	W.	L.	Pct.	H.	R.	ER.	SO.	BB.	ERA.
1990—Geneva		NYP	3	17	2	1	.667	5	1	1	29	4	0.53
1990—Peoria		Midwest	5	35⅔	3	1	.750	22	9	6	54	11	1.51
1990—Charlotte		Southern	3	23⅔	2	1	.667	13	1	1	28	3	0.38
1990—Chicago†		National	3	13⅔	0	3	.000	20	12	11	4	4	7.24
	Major League Total—1 Year		3	13⅔	0	3	.000	20	12	11	4	4	7.24

Selected by Houston Astros' organization in 37th round of free-agent draft, June 2, 1987.

Selected by Chicago Cubs' organization in 1st round (23rd player selected) of free-agent draft, June 4, 1990.

†On disabled list, August 19 to September 11, 1990.

FRANK MICHAEL DiPINO

Born October 22, 1956, at Syracuse, N.Y.
Height, 6.00. Weight, 180.
Throws and bats lefthanded.
Attended St. Leo College, St. Leo, Fla.

Pitched seven-inning, 6-0 no-hit victory against Reading, June 8, 1980 (second game).

Major League saves: 1983 (20), 1984 (14), 1985 (6), 1986 (3), 1987 (4), 1988 (6), 1990 (3). Total—56.

Year	Club	League	G.	IP.	W.	L.	Pct.	H.	R.	ER.	SO.	BB.	ERA.
1977—Newark	NYP	14	29	1	3	.250	14	12	8	41	22	2.48
1978—Burlington	Midwest	15	88	5	4	.556	98	58	46	68	36	4.70
1979—Stockton†	California	16	99	5	3	.625	92	45	38	67	46	3.45
1980—Holyoke	Eastern	16	76	7	0	1.000	46	13	11	58	27	1.30
1980—Vancouver	P. Coast	24	28	3	1	.750	24	10	7	32	14	2.25
1981—Vancouver‡	P. Coast	27	81	3	5	.375	83	45	39	81	39	4.33
1981—Milwaukee	American	2	2	0	0	.000	0	0	0	3	3	0.00
1982—Vancouver§	P. Coast	26	189⅔	13	9	.591	187	102	85	115	86	4.03
1982—Houston	National	6	28⅓	2	2	.500	32	20	19	25	11	6.04
1983—Houston	National	53	71⅓	3	4	.429	52	21	21	67	20	2.65
1984—Houston	National	57	75⅓	4	9	.308	74	32	28	65	36	3.35
1985—Houston	National	54	76	3	7	.300	69	44	34	49	43	4.03
1986—Houston x-Chicago	National	61	80⅓	3	7	.300	74	45	39	70	30	4.37
1987—Chicago	National	69	80	3	3	.500	75	31	28	61	34	3.15
1988—Chicago y	National	63	90⅓	2	3	.400	102	54	50	69	32	4.98
1989—St. Louis z	National	67	88⅓	9	0	1.000	73	26	24	44	20	2.45
1990—St. Louis	National	62	81	5	2	.714	92	45	41	49	31	4.56
American League Totals—1 Year		2	2	0	0	.000	0	0	0	3	3	0.00
National League Totals—9 Years		492	671	34	37	.479	643	318	284	499	257	3.81
Major League Totals—10 Years		494	673	34	37	.479	643	318	284	502	260	3.80

Signed as free agent by Milwaukee Brewers' organization, July 11, 1977.

†On disabled list, May 19 to June 11, 1979.

‡On disabled list, May 9 to June 10, 1981.

§Traded with Outfielder Kevin Bass and Pitcher Mike Madden to Houston Astros, September 3, 1982, completing deal in which Houston traded Pitcher Don Sutton to Milwaukee Brewers for three players to be named later, August 30, 1982.

xTraded to Chicago Cubs for Outfielder Davey Lopes, July 21, 1986.

yGranted free agency, November 4, 1988; signed by St. Louis Cardinals, December 21, 1988.

zGranted free agency, November 13, 1989; re-signed by Cardinals, December 13, 1989.

GARY THOMAS DISARCINA

Name pronounced Dee-sar-SEE-na.

Born November 19, 1967, at Malden, Mass.
Height, 6.01. Weight, 178.
Throws and bats righthanded.
Attended University of Massachusetts, Amherst, Mass.

Major League stolen bases: 1990 (1).

Year	Club	League	Pos.	G.	AB.	R.	H.	2B.	3B.	HR.	RBI.	B.A.	PO.	A.	E.	F.A.
1988—Bend	N'west	SS	71	295	40	90	11	●5	2	39	.305	104	★237	27	.927
1989—Midland	Texas	SS	126	441	65	126	18	7	4	54	.286	206	★411	30	★.954
1989—California	Amer.	SS	2	0	0	0	0	0	0	0	.000	0	0	0	.000
1990—Edmonton	P. C.	SS	97	330	46	70	12	2	4	37	.212	165	289	24	.950
1990—California	Amer.	SS-2B	18	57	8	8	1	1	0	0	.140	17	57	4	.949
Major League Totals—2 Years			20	57	8	8	1	1	0	0	.140	17	57	4	.949

Selected by California Angels' organization in 6th round of free-agent draft, June 1, 1988.

CHRIS BARTON DONNELS

Name pronounced DONN-uls.

Born April 21, 1966, at Los Angeles, Calif.
Height, 6.00. Weight, 185.
Throws right and bats lefthanded.
Attended Loyola Marymount University, Los Angeles, Calif.

Led Texas League in bases on balls received with 111 in 1990.

Led Florida State League in slugging percentage with .510 and intentional bases on balls received with 15 in 1989.

Led Texas League third basemen in putouts with 79, assists with 242, errors with 31, total chances with 352 and double plays with 24 in 1990.

Led Florida State League third basemen in putouts with 93, assists with 202 and total chances with 320 in 1989.

Named Florida State League Most Valuable Player, 1989.

Year	Club	League	Pos.	G.	AB.	R.	H.	2B.	3B.	HR.	RBI.	B.A.	PO.	A.	E.	F.A.
1987—Kingsport	Appal.	3B	26	86	18	26	4	0	3	16	.302	16	44	6	.909
1987—Columbia	S. Atl.	3B	41	136	20	35	7	0	2	17	.257	32	86	10	.922
1988—St. Lucie	Fla. St.	3B	65	198	25	43	14	2	3	22	.217	40	116	15	.912
1988—Columbia	S. Atl.	3B	42	133	19	32	6	0	2	13	.241	29	84	7	.942
1989—St. Lucie	Fla. St.	3B-1B	117	386	70	121	23	1	17	★78	.313	242	209	28	.942
1990—Jackson	Texas	3B-1B-2B	130	419	66	114	24	0	12	63	.272	95	244	32	.914

Selected by New York Mets' organization in 1st round (24th player selected) of free agent draft, June 2, 1987.

JOHN ROBERT DOPSON JR.

Born July 14, 1963, at Baltimore, Md.
Height, 6.04. Weight, 225.
Throws right and bats lefthanded.

Led American League in balks with 15 in 1989.

Year	Club	League	G.	IP.	W.	L.	Pct.	H.	R.	ER.	SO.	BB.	ERA.
1982—Jamestown	NYP		15	106⅔	6	●8	.429	117	58	47	62	34	3.97
1983—West Palm Beach	Florida St.		23	146⅔	13	6	.684	141	82	56	69	38	3.44
1984—Jacksonville†	Southern		26	170⅔	10	8	.556	198	83	70	76	41	3.69
1985—Jacksonville	Southern		5	32⅓	3	0	1.000	27	5	4	20	10	1.11
1985—Indianapolis‡	Am. Assoc.		18	95⅓	4	7	.364	88	44	40	48	44	3.78
1985—Montreal	National		4	13	0	2	.000	25	17	16	4	4	11.08
1986—West Palm Beach§	Florida St.		2	10⅔	2	0	1.000	8	0	0	8	4	0.00
1986—Indianapolis	Am. Assoc.		4	16	0	3	.000	18	12	8	6	11	4.50
1987—Jacksonville	Southern		21	118⅓	7	5	.583	123	58	50	75	30	3.80
1988—Indianapolis	Am. Assoc.		3	18	0	0	.000	19	7	7	15	5	3.50
1988—Montreal x	National		26	168⅔	3	11	.214	150	69	57	101	58	3.04
1989—Boston y	American		29	169⅓	12	8	.600	166	84	75	95	69	3.99
1989—Pawtucket	Int'national		2	8⅔	0	2	.000	13	9	7	9	1	7.27
1990—Boston z	American		4	17⅔	0	0	.000	13	7	4	9	9	2.04
1990—Pawtucket	Int'national		5	22	2	1	.667	28	12	12	13	8	4.91
National League Totals—2 Years			30	181⅔	3	13	.188	175	86	73	105	62	3.62
American League Totals—2 Years			33	187	12	8	.600	179	91	79	104	78	3.80
Major League Totals—4 Years			63	368⅔	15	21	.417	354	177	152	209	140	3.71

Selected by Montreal Expos' organization in 2nd round of free-agent draft, June 7, 1982.

†On suspended list, May 24 to May 31, 1984.

‡On disabled list, June 24 to July 15, 1985.

§On Indianapolis disabled list, April 10 to May 12, May 29 to June 23 and July 7, 1986 through remainder of season.

xTraded with Shortstop Luis Rivera to Boston Red Sox for Shortstop Spike Owen and Pitcher Dan Gakeler, December 8, 1988.

yOn disabled list, August 2 to August 28, 1989; included rehabilitation disability assignment to Pawtucket, August 18 to August 28, 1989.

zOn disabled list, April 28, 1990 through remainder of season; included rehabilitation disability assignment to Pawtucket, May 15 to June 4 and August 10 to August 22, 1990.

WILLIAM DONALD DORAN

Name pronounced DOOR-un.

(Bill)

Born May 28, 1958, at Cincinnati, O.
Height, 6.00. Weight, 175.
Throws right and bats right and lefthanded.
Attended Miami University, Oxford, O.

Major League stolen bases: 1982 (5), 1983 (12), 1984 (21), 1985 (23), 1986 (42), 1987 (31), 1988 (17), 1989 (22), 1990 (23). Total—196.

Led National League in caught stealing with 19 in 1986.

Led National League second basemen in fielding percentage with .992 in 1987.

Led Pacific Coast League second basemen in double plays with 123 in 1982.

Led Gulf Coast League second basemen in double plays with 33 in 1979.

Year	Club	League	Pos.	G.	AB.	R.	H.	2B.	3B.	HR.	RBI.	B.A.	PO.	A.	E.	F.A.
1979—Sarasota Astros	Gulf C.		2B	44	164	21	42	6	0	1	16	.256	107	★144	11	.958
1980—Daytona Beach	Fla. St.		2B-SS	102	369	62	90	11	3	2	45	.244	232	259	21	.959
1981—Columbus	South.		2B-SS	124	427	83	120	17	7	5	56	.281	263	355	17	.973
1982—Tucson	P. C.		2B	★142	559	100	169	32	7	1	65	.302	★361	★424	★23	.972
1982—Houston	Nat.		2B	26	97	11	27	3	0	0	6	.278	41	78	3	.975
1983—Houston	Nat.		2B	154	535	70	145	12	7	8	39	.271	★347	461	17	.979
1984—Houston	Nat.		2B-SS	147	548	92	143	18	11	4	41	.261	274	440	12	.983
1985—Houston	Nat.		2B	148	578	84	166	31	6	14	59	.287	345	440	16	.980
1986—Houston	Nat.		2B	145	550	92	152	29	3	6	37	.276	262	329	16	.974
1987—Houston	Nat.		2B-SS	★162	625	82	177	23	3	16	79	.283	300	432	7	.991
1988—Houston	Nat.		2B	132	480	66	119	18	1	7	53	.248	260	371	4	★.987
1989—Houston	Nat.		2B	142	507	65	111	25	2	8	58	.219	254	345	12	.980
1990—Hou.†‡-Cinc.§	Nat.		2B-3B	126	403	59	121	29	2	7	37	.300	198	306	8	.984
Major League Totals—9 Years				1182	4323	621	1161	188	35	70	409	.269	2281	3202	99	.982

Selected by Houston Astros' organization in 6th round of free-agent draft, June 5, 1979.

†On disabled list, July 4 to July 19, 1990.

‡Traded to Cincinnati Reds for three players to be named later, August 30, 1990; Houston Astros acquired Catcher Terry McGriff and Pitchers Keith Kaiser and Butch Henry to complete deal, September 7, 1990.

§Granted free agency, November 5, 1990; re-signed by Reds, December 5, 1990.

CHAMPIONSHIP SERIES RECORD

Shares Championship Series record for most at-bats, game (7), October 15, 1986 (16 innings).

Year	Club	League	Pos.	G.	AB.	R.	H.	2B.	3B.	HR.	RBI.	B.A.	PO.	A.	E.	F.A.
1986—Houston	Nat.		2B	6	27	3	6	0	0	1	3	.222	9	17	0	1.000

BRIAN RICHARD DORSETT

Born April 9, 1961, at Terre Haute, Ind.
Height, 6.03. Weight, 215.
Throws and bats righthanded.
Attended Indiana State University, Terre Haute, Ind.

Led International League in passed balls with 13 in 1990.

Year	Club	League	Pos.	G.	AB.	R.	H.	2B.	3B.	HR.	RBI.	B.A.	PO.	A.	E.	F.A.
1983—Medford		N'west	C	14	48	11	13	2	1	1	10	.271	85	8	2	.979
1983—Madison		Midw.	C	58	204	16	52	7	0	3	27	.255	337	51	6	.985
1984—Modesto†		Calif.	C-1B	99	375	39	99	19	0	8	52	.264	511	76	13	.978
1985—Madison		Midw.	C	40	161	15	43	11	0	2	30	.267	194	40	5	.979
1985—Huntsville		South.	C	88	313	38	84	18	3	11	43	.268	437	51	10	.980
1986—Tacoma		P. C.	C	117	426	49	111	33	1	10	51	.261	420	54	18	.963
1987—Tacoma‡		P. C.	C	78	282	31	66	14	1	6	39	.234	341	51	4	.990
1987—Buffalo		A. A.	C	26	86	9	22	5	1	4	14	.256	119	9	1	.992
1987—Cleveland		Amer.	C	5	11	2	3	0	0	1	3	.273	12	0	0	1.000
1988—C. S. §x -Edm.		P. C.	C-1B	53	163	21	43	7	0	11	32	.264	283	37	5	.985
1988—California y		Amer.	C	7	11	0	1	0	0	0	2	.091	19	3	0	1.000
1989—Columbus		Int.	C	110	388	45	97	21	1	17	62	.250	482	47	7	.987
1989—New York		Amer.	C	8	22	3	8	1	0	0	4	.364	29	3	0	1.000
1990—Columbus		Int.	C	114	415	44	113	28	1	14	67	.272	548	37	11	.982
1990—New York z		Amer.	C	14	35	2	5	2	0	0	0	.143	31	0	0	1.000
Major League Totals—4 Years				34	79	7	17	3	0	1	9	.215	91	6	0	1.000

Selected by Oakland A's organization in 10th round of free-agent draft, June 6, 1983.

†On disabled list, June 18 to July 24, 1984.

‡Traded with Pitcher Darrel Akerfelds to Cleveland Indians for Second Baseman Tony Bernazard, July 15, 1987.

§On Cleveland disabled list, March 26 to June 7, 1988.

xTraded to California Angels for a player to be named later, June 7, 1988.

yTraded to New York Yankees for Pitcher Eric Schmidt, November 17, 1988.

zReleased, November 19, 1990.

RICHARD ELLIOTT DOTSON

Born January 10, 1959, at Cincinnati, O.
Height, 6.00. Weight, 203.
Throws and bats righthanded.

Tied for American League lead in shutouts with 4 in 1981.

Year	Club	League	G.	IP.	W.	L.	Pct.	H.	R.	ER.	SO.	BB.	ERA.
1977—Idaho Falls†		Pioneer	13	66	4	5	.444	65	61	42	83	63	5.73
1978—Knoxville		Southern	26	145	11	10	.524	128	85	69	152	∗105	4.28
1979—Knoxville		Southern	25	163	9	9	.500	133	81	67	133	88	3.70
1979—Chicago		American	5	24	2	0	1.000	28	13	10	13	6	3.75
1980—Chicago		American	33	198	12	10	.545	185	105	94	109	87	4.27
1981—Chicago		American	24	141	9	8	.529	145	67	59	73	49	3.77
1982—Chicago		American	34	196⅔	11	15	.423	219	97	84	109	73	3.84
1983—Chicago		American	35	240	22	7	∗.759	209	92	86	137	∗106	3.23
1984—Chicago‡		American	32	245⅔	14	15	.483	216	110	98	120	103	3.59
1985—Chicago§		American	9	52⅓	3	4	.429	53	30	26	33	17	4.47
1986—Chicago		American	34	197	10	●17	.370	226	125	120	110	69	5.48
1987—Chicago x		American	31	211⅓	11	12	.478	201	109	98	114	86	4.17
1988—New York y		American	32	171	12	9	.571	178	103	95	77	72	5.00
1989—New York z-Chicago a		American	28	151⅓	5	12	.294	181	84	75	69	58	4.46
1990—Kansas City b		American	8	28⅔	0	4	.000	43	29	27	9	14	8.48
Major League Totals—12 Years			305	1857	111	113	.496	1884	964	872	973	740	4.23

Selected by California Angels' organization in 1st round (seventh player selected) of free-agent draft, June 7, 1977.

†Traded with Outfielders Bobby Bonds and Thad Bosley to Chicago White Sox for Catcher Brian Downing and Pitchers Chris Knapp and Dave Frost, December 5, 1977.

‡Appeared in one game as a pinch-runner.

§On disabled list, April 7 to April 22 and June 11, 1985 through remainder of season.

xTraded with Pitcher Scott Nielsen to New York Yankees for Outfielder Dan Pasqua, Catcher Mark Salas and Pitcher Steve Rosenberg, November 12, 1987.

yOn disabled list, July 1 to July 18, 1988.

zReleased, June 22, 1989; signed by Chicago White Sox, July 1, 1989.

aGranted free agency, November 13, 1989; signed by Kansas City Royals, December 5, 1989.

bReleased, June 21, 1990.

CHAMPIONSHIP SERIES RECORD

Year	Club	League	G.	IP.	W.	L.	Pct.	H.	R.	ER.	SO.	BB.	ERA.
1983—Chicago		American	1	5	0	1	.000	6	6	6	3	3	10.80

ALL-STAR GAME RECORD

Year	League	IP.	W.	L.	Pct.	H.	R.	ER.	SO.	BB.	ERA.
1984—American		2	0	0	.000	2	0	0	2	1	0.00

BRIAN JAY DOWNING

Born October 9, 1950, at Los Angeles, Calif.
Height, 5.10. Weight, 194.
Throws and bats righthanded.
Attended Cypress Junior College, Cypress, Calif.

Shares major league records for highest fielding percentage by outfielder, season, 150 or more games (1.000), 1982; fewest errors by outfielder, season, 150 or more games (0), 1982; fewest double plays by outfielder, season, 150 or more games (0), 1982.

Holds American League record for most consecutive errorless games by an outfielder (244), May 25, 1981 through July 21, second game, 1983.

Major League stolen bases: 1975 (13), 1976 (7), 1977 (1), 1978 (3), 1979 (3), 1981 (1), 1982 (2), 1983 (1), 1985 (5), 1986 (4), 1987 (5), 1988 (3). Total—48.

Tied for American League lead in bases on balls received with 106 in 1987.

Year Club	League	Pos.	G.	AB.	R.	H.	2B.	3B.	HR.	RBI.	B.A.	PO.	A.	E.	F.A.
1970—Sarasota W. S........	Gulf C.	C-OF	34	96	16	21	1	1	0	14	.219	167	11	1	.994
1971—Appleton...............	Midw.	3B-C-OF	99	333	51	82	6	3	3	22	.246	353	98	13	.972
1972—Knoxville...............	South.	OF-3B-C	135	442	75	123	24	7	15	67	.278	250	123	21	.947
1973—Iowa......................	A. A.	3B-OF-C	68	228	34	56	6	1	7	27	.246	84	90	8	.956
1973—Chicago†...............	Amer.	OF-C-3B	34	73	5	13	1	0	2	4	.178	72	17	5	.947
1974—Chicago.................	Amer.	C-OF	108	293	41	66	12	1	10	39	.225	337	30	2	.995
1975—Chicago.................	Amer.	C	138	420	58	101	12	1	7	41	.240	730	84	8	.990
1976—Chicago‡...............	Amer.	C	104	317	38	81	14	0	3	30	.256	450	38	6	.988
1977—Chicago§..............	Amer.	C-OF	69	169	28	48	4	2	4	25	.284	325	28	6	.983
1978—California...............	Amer.	C	133	412	42	105	15	0	7	46	.255	681	82	5	.993
1979—California...............	Amer.	C	148	509	87	166	27	3	12	75	.326	669	35	11	.985
1980—California x	Amer.	C	30	93	5	27	6	0	2	25	.290	69	6	0	1.000
1981—California...............	Amer.	OF-C	93	317	47	79	14	0	9	41	.249	237	18	2	.992
1982—California...............	Amer.	OF	158	623	109	175	37	2	28	84	.281	321	9	0	●1.000
1983—California y	Amer.	OF	113	403	68	99	15	1	19	53	.246	160	9	1	.994
1984—California...............	Amer.	OF	156	539	65	148	28	2	23	91	.275	272	5	0	★1.000
1985—California...............	Amer.	OF	150	520	80	137	23	1	20	85	.263	244	5	2	.992
1986—California z...........	Amer.	OF	152	513	90	137	27	4	20	95	.267	267	5	3	.989
1987—California...............	Amer.	OF	155	567	110	154	29	3	29	77	.272	47	2	0	1.000
1988—California a	Amer.	DH	135	484	80	117	18	2	25	64	.242	0	0	0	.000
1989—California...............	Amer.	DH	142	544	59	154	25	2	14	59	.283	0	0	0	.000
1990—California b	Amer.	DH	96	330	47	90	18	2	14	51	.273	0	0	0	.000
Major League Totals—18 Years...............			2114	7126	1059	1897	325	26	248	985	.266	4881	391	51	.990

Signed as free agent by Chicago White Sox' organization, August 19, 1969.

†On disabled list, June 1 to July 9, 1973.

‡On disabled list, July 30 to August 15, 1976.

§Traded with Pitchers Chris Knapp and Dave Frost to California Angels for Outfielders Bobby Bonds and Thad Bosley and Pitcher Richard Dotson, December 5, 1977.

xOn disabled list, April 20 to September 1, 1980.

yOn disabled list, May 10 to June 20, 1983.

zGranted free agency, November 12, 1986; re-signed by Angels, January 8, 1987.

aOn disabled list, April 20 to May 6, 1988.

bGranted free agency, November 5, 1990.

CHAMPIONSHIP SERIES RECORD

Year Club	League	Pos.	G.	AB.	R.	H.	2B.	3B.	HR.	RBI.	B.A.	PO.	A.	E.	F.A.
1979—California...............	Amer.	C	4	15	1	3	0	0	1	1	.200	27	0	0	1.000
1982—California...............	Amer.	OF	5	19	3	3	1	0	0	0	.158	5	0	0	1.000
1986—California...............	Amer.	OF	7	27	2	6	0	0	1	7	.222	18	0	0	1.000
Championship Series Totals—3 Years.....			16	61	6	12	1	0	1	8	.197	50	0	0	1.000

ALL-STAR GAME RECORD

Year League	Pos.	AB.	R.	H.	2B.	3B.	HR.	RBI.	B.A.	PO.	A.	E.	F.A.
1979—American	C	1	0	1	0	0	0	0	1.000	3	0	0	1.000

KELLY ROBERT DOWNS

Born October 25, 1960, at Ogden, Utah.
Height, 6.04. Weight, 205.
Throws and bats righthanded.
Brother of Dave Downs, pitcher with Philadelphia Phillies, 1972.

Major League saves: 1987 (1).

Tied for Pacific Coast League lead in games started by pitchers with 29 in 1983.

Year Club	League	G.	IP.	W.	L.	Pct.	H.	R.	ER.	SO.	BB.	ERA.
1980—Spartanburg..................	W. Carol.	14	90	5	7	.417	85	41	26	40	17	2.60
1981—Peninsula.....................	Carolina	25	175	13	7	.650	176	79	58	124	35	2.98
1982—Oklahoma City	Am. Assoc.	32	156⅔	2	★15	.118	182	★116	93	70	72	5.34
1983—Portland†......................	P. Coast	29	159⅓	9	●13	.409	186	98	79	71	61	4.46
1984—Portland†......................	P. Coast	30	163	7	12	.368	166	106	96	104	65	5.30
1985—Phoenix........................	P. Coast	37	137	9	10	.474	138	69	61	109	56	4.01
1986—Phoenix........................	P. Coast	18	108	8	5	.615	116	54	41	68	28	3.42
1986—San Francisco	National	14	88⅓	4	4	.500	78	29	27	64	30	2.75
1987—San Francisco	National	41	186	12	9	.571	185	83	75	137	67	3.63
1988—San Francisco‡	National	27	168	13	9	.591	140	67	62	118	47	3.32
1989—San Francisco§	National	18	82⅔	8	8	.333	82	47	44	49	26	4.79
1989—Phoenix........................	P. Coast	3	9⅓	1	1	.500	11	9	9	9	5	8.68
1989—San Jose.......................	California	1	5	0	0	.000	1	0	0	7	4	0.00
1990—San Jose x.....................	California	1	5	0	1	.000	5	2	1	3	0	1.80
1990—Phoenix........................	P. Coast	1	5	0	0	.000	5	3	1	4	0	1.80
1990—San Francisco	National	13	63	3	2	.600	56	26	24	31	20	3.43
Major League Totals—5 Years.......		113	588	36	32	.529	541	252	232	399	190	3.55

Selected by Philadelphia Phillies' organization in 26th round of free-agent draft, June 5, 1979.

†Traded with Pitcher George Riley to San Francisco Giants for First Baseman Al Oliver and a player to be named later, August 20, 1984; Philadelphia Phillies acquired Pitcher Renie Martin to complete deal, August 30, 1984.

‡On disabled list, August 31, 1988 through remainder of season.

§On disabled list, May 2 to August 13, 1989; included rehabilitation disability assignment to Phoenix, May 17 to May 23 and August 3 to August 7, 1989; and San Jose, August 8 to August 12, 1989.

xOn San Francisco disabled list, April 3 to August 10, 1990; included rehabilitation disability assignment to San Jose, July 31 to August 6, 1990; and Phoenix, August 7 to August 9, 1990.

CHAMPIONSHIP SERIES RECORD

Year Club	League	G.	IP.	W.	L.	Pct.	H.	R.	ER.	SO.	BB.	ERA.
1987—San Francisco	National	1	1⅓	0	0	.000	1	0	0	0	0	0.00
1989—San Francisco	National	2	8⅔	1	0	1.000	8	3	3	6	6	3.12
Championship Series Totals—2 Years		3	10	1	0	1.000	9	3	3	6	6	2.70

WORLD SERIES RECORD

Year Club	League	G.	IP.	W.	L.	Pct.	H.	R.	ER.	SO.	BB.	ERA.
1989—San Francisco	National	3	4⅔	0	0	.000	3	4	4	4	2	7.71

DOUGLAS DEAN DRABEK
(Doug)

Born July 25, 1962, at Victoria, Tex.
Height, 6.01. Weight, 185.
Throws and bats righthanded.
Attended University of Houston, Houston, Tex.

Named National League Pitcher of the Year by THE SPORTING NEWS, 1990.
Won National League Cy Young Memorial Award, 1990.
Named righthanded pitcher on THE SPORTING NEWS National League All-Star Team, 1990.

Year Club	League	G.	IP.	W.	L.	Pct.	H.	R.	ER.	SO.	BB.	ERA.
1983—Niagara Falls	NYP	16	103⅔	6	7	.462	99	52	42	103	48	3.65
1984—Appleton	Midwest	1	5	1	0	1.000	3	1	1	6	3	1.80
1984—Glens Falls†	Eastern	19	124⅔	12	5	.706	90	34	31	75	44	2.24
1984—Nashville	Southern	4	31	1	2	.333	30	11	8	22	10	2.32
1985—Albany	Eastern	26	*192⅔	13	7	.650	153	71	64	*153	55	2.99
1986—Columbus	Int'national	8	42	1	4	.200	50	36	34	23	25	7.29
1986—New York‡	American	27	131⅔	7	8	.467	126	64	60	76	50	4.10
1987—Pittsburgh§	National	29	176⅓	11	12	.478	165	86	76	120	46	3.88
1988—Pittsburgh	National	33	219⅓	15	7	.682	194	83	75	127	50	3.08
1989—Pittsburgh	National	35	244⅓	14	12	.538	215	83	76	123	69	2.80
1990—Pittsburgh	National	33	231⅓	*22	6	*.786	190	78	71	131	56	2.76
American League Totals—1 Year		27	131⅔	7	8	.467	126	64	60	76	50	4.10
National League Totals—4 Years		130	871⅓	62	37	.626	764	330	298	501	221	3.08
Major League Totals—5 Years		157	1003	69	45	.605	890	394	358	577	271	3.21

Selected by Cleveland Indians' organization in 4th round of free-agent draft, June 3, 1980.
Selected by Chicago White Sox' organization in 11th round of free-agent draft, June 6, 1983.
†Traded with Pitcher Kevin Hickey to New York Yankees' organization, August 13, 1984, completing deal in which New York traded Infielder Roy Smalley to Chicago White Sox for two players to be named later, July 18, 1984.
‡Traded with Pitchers Brian Fisher and Logan Easley to Pittsburgh Pirates for Pitchers Rick Rhoden, Cecilio Guante and Pat Clements, November 26, 1986.
§On disabled list, April 26 to May 18, 1987.

CHAMPIONSHIP SERIES RECORD

Year Club	League	G.	IP.	W.	L.	Pct.	H.	R.	ER.	SO.	BB.	ERA.
1990—Pittsburgh	National	2	16⅓	1	1	.500	12	4	3	13	3	1.65

TIMOTHY DARNELL DRUMMOND
(Tim)

Born December 24, 1964, at La Plata, Md.
Height, 6.03. Weight, 195.
Throws and bats righthanded.
Attended Charles County Community College, La Plata, Md.

Major League saves: 1989 (1), 1990 (1). Total—2.

Year Club	League	G.	IP.	W.	L.	Pct.	H.	R.	ER.	SO.	BB.	ERA.
1983—Bradenton Pirates	Gulf Coast	14	88	7	2	.778	73	20	14	40	21	1.43
1984—Macon	S. Atlantic	27	154⅔	7	*15	.318	139	93	67	76	81	3.90
1985—Macon	S. Atlantic	27	168⅓	8	11	.421	171	100	77	91	73	4.12
1986—Prince William	Carolina	47	73⅔	6	4	.600	71	39	31	55	34	3.79
1987—Vancouver	P. Coast	46	63⅔	2	6	.250	62	35	21	49	43	2.97
1987—Pittsburgh†	National	6	6	0	0	.000	5	3	3	5	3	4.50
1988—Tidewater	Int'national	38	82⅓	6	3	.667	71	33	30	62	28	3.28
1989—Tidewater‡	Int'national	35	63⅓	5	1	.833	63	29	23	42	26	3.27
1989—Portland	P. Coast	10	22	1	1	.500	19	9	8	21	8	3.27
1989—Minnesota	American	8	16⅓	0	0	.000	16	7	7	9	8	3.86
1990—Minnesota	American	35	91	3	5	.375	104	46	44	49	36	4.35
National League Totals—1 Year		6	6	0	0	.000	5	3	3	5	3	4.50
American League Totals—2 Years		43	107⅓	3	5	.375	120	53	51	58	44	4.28
Major League Totals—3 Years		49	113⅓	3	5	.375	125	56	54	63	47	4.29

Selected by Pittsburgh Pirates' organization in 12th round of free-agent draft, January 11, 1983.
†Traded with Catcher Mackey Sasser to New York Mets for First Baseman Randy Milligan and Pitcher Scott Henion, March 26, 1988.

BRIAN ANDREW DuBOIS

Name pronounced Doo-BOYS.

Born April 18, 1967, at Joliet, Ill.
Height, 5.10. Weight, 194.
Throws and bats lefthanded.

Major League saves: 1989 (1).
Tied for Carolina League lead in games started by pitchers with 28 and complete games with 7 in 1988.

Year—Club	League	G.	IP.	W.	L.	Pct.	H.	R.	ER.	SO.	BB.	ERA.
1985—Bluefield	Ap'lachian	10	57⅔	5	4	.556	42	23	16	67	20	2.50
1986—Hagerstown†	Carolina	5	20⅓	1	2	.333	29	19	16	17	11	7.08
1986—Bluefield	Ap'lachian	3	9⅓	1	1	.500	8	2	1	8	2	0.96
1987—Hagerstown‡	Carolina	27	155	8	9	.471	162	81	67	96	73	3.89
1988—Virginia-Hagerstown	Carolina	28	183⅔	●14	9	.609	★195	★113	★85	147	50	4.17
1989—Hagerstown	Eastern	15	112	6	4	.600	93	36	31	82	18	2.49
1989—Detroit	American	6	36	0	4	.000	29	14	7	13	17	1.75
1989—Rochester§-Toledo	Int'national	7	54	4	2	.667	41	14	12	29	18	2.00
1990—Toledo	Int'national	13	69⅔	5	4	.556	67	27	21	47	26	2.71
1990—Detroit xy	American	12	58⅓	3	5	.375	70	37	33	34	22	5.09
Major League Totals—2 Years		18	94⅓	3	9	.250	99	51	40	47	39	3.82

Selected by Baltimore Orioles' organization in 4th round of free-agent draft, June 3, 1985.
†On disabled list, May 9 to June 30, 1986.
‡Loaned to Virginia (Independent), April, 1988; returned, June, 1988.
§Traded to Detroit Tigers for First Baseman Keith Moreland, July 29, 1989.
xClaimed on waivers by Baltimore Orioles, August 29, 1990.
yOn disabled list, September 5, 1990 through remainder of season.

ROBERT THOMAS DUCEY
(Rob)

Born May 24, 1965, at Toronto, Canada.
Height, 6.02. Weight, 180.
Throws right and bats lefthanded.
Attended Seminole Community College, Sanford, Fla.

Major League stolen bases: 1987 (2), 1988 (1), 1989 (2), 1990 (1). Total—6.
Tied for International League lead in double plays by outfielders with 4 in 1990.
Tied for Southern League lead in double plays by outfielders with 6 in 1986.

Year—Club	League	Pos.	G.	AB.	R.	H.	2B.	3B.	HR.	RBI.	B.A.	PO.	A.	E.	F.A.
1984—Medicine Hat	Pion.	OF-1B	63	235	49	71	10	3	12	49	.302	185	11	6	.970
1985—Florence	S. Atl.	OF-1B	134	529	78	133	22	2	13	86	.251	228	8	9	.963
1986—Ventura	Calif.	OF-1B	47	178	36	60	11	3	12	38	.337	97	3	2	.980
1986—Knoxville	South.	OF	88	344	49	106	22	3	11	58	.308	186	10	6	.970
1987—Syracuse	Int.	OF	100	359	62	102	14	●10	10	60	.284	171	13	6	.968
1987—Toronto	Amer.	OF	34	48	12	9	1	0	1	6	.188	31	0	0	1.000
1988—Syracuse	Int.	OF	90	317	40	81	14	4	7	42	.256	233	6	4	.984
1988—Toronto	Amer.	OF	27	54	15	17	4	1	0	6	.315	35	1	0	1.000
1989—Toronto†	Amer.	OF	41	76	5	16	4	0	0	7	.211	56	3	0	1.000
1989—Syracuse	Int.	OF	10	29	0	3	0	1	0	3	.103	14	0	1	.933
1990—Syracuse	Int.	OF	127	438	53	117	32	7	7	47	.267	262	13	13	.955
1990—Toronto	Amer.	OF	19	53	7	16	5	0	0	7	.302	37	0	0	1.000
Major League Totals—4 Years			121	231	39	58	14	1	1	26	.251	159	4	0	1.000

Signed as free agent by Toronto Blue Jays' organization, May 16, 1984.

†On disabled list, June 9 to September 2, 1989; included rehabilitation disability assignment to Syracuse, July 5 to July 14 and August 24 to September 2, 1989.

MARIANO DUNCAN

Born March 13, 1963, at San Pedro de Macoris, D. R.
Height, 6.00. Weight, 185.
Throws and bats righthanded.

Major League stolen bases: 1985 (38), 1986 (48), 1987 (11), 1989 (9), 1990 (13). Total—119.
Led Florida State League in stolen bases with 56 in 1983.
Led Texas League second basemen in double plays with 84 in 1984.

Year—Club	League	Pos.	G.	AB.	R.	H.	2B.	3B.	HR.	RBI.	B.A.	PO.	A.	E.	F.A.
1982—Lethbridge†	Pion.	SS-2B	30	55	9	13	3	1	1	8	.236	23	35	15	.795
1983—Vero Beach†	Fla. St.	OF-SS-2B	109	384	73	102	10	★15	0	42	.266	169	157	37	.898
1984—San Antonio†	Texas	2B-OF-SS	125	502	80	127	14	●11	2	44	.253	283	335	22	.966
1985—Los Angeles†	Nat.	SS-2B	142	562	74	137	24	6	6	39	.244	224	430	30	.956
1986—Los Angeles†‡	Nat.	SS	109	407	47	93	7	0	8	30	.229	172	317	25	.951
1987—Los Angeles†§	Nat.	★S-2-O	76	261	31	56	8	1	6	18	.215	101	213	★21	.937
1987—Albuquerque†	P. C.	SS	6	22	6	6	0	0	0	0	.273	8	15	2	.920
1988—Albuquerque†	P. C.	SS-2B	56	227	48	65	4	8	0	25	.286	104	153	18	.935

Year	Club	League	Pos.	G.	AB.	R.	H.	2B.	3B.	HR.	RBI.	B.A.	PO.	A.	E.	F.A.
1989—L.A.xy-Cin.	Nat.	SS-2B-OF	94	258	32	64	15	2	3	21	.248	101	155	14	.948	
1990—Cincinnati z	Nat.	2B-SS-OF	125	435	67	133	22	*11	10	55	.306	265	303	18	.969	
Major League Totals—5 Years			546	1923	251	483	76	20	33	163	.251	863	1418	108	.955	

Signed as free agent by Los Angeles Dodgers' organization, January 17, 1982.

†Switch-hitter.

‡On disabled list, August 19 to September 17, 1986.

§On disabled list, June 19 to July 4 and August 16, 1987 through remainder of season.

xOn disabled list, May 28 to June 12 and July 1 to July 16, 1989.

yTraded with Pitcher Tim Leary to Cincinnati Reds for Outfielder Kal Daniels and Infielder Lenny Harris, July 18, 1989.

zOn disabled list, May 14 to May 30, 1990.

CHAMPIONSHIP SERIES RECORD

Year	Club	League	Pos.	G.	AB.	R.	H.	2B.	3B.	HR.	RBI.	B.A.	PO.	A.	E.	F.A.
1985—Los Angeles	Nat.	SS	5	18	2	4	2	1	0	1	.222	7	16	1	.958	
1990—Cincinnati	Nat.	2B	6	20	1	6	0	0	1	4	.300	6	11	1	.944	
Championship Series Totals—2 Years			11	38	3	10	2	1	1	5	.263	13	27	2	.952	

WORLD SERIES RECORD

Year	Club	League	Pos.	G.	AB.	R.	H.	2B.	3B.	HR.	RBI.	B.A.	PO.	A.	E.	F.A.
1990—Cincinnati	Nat.	2B	4	14	1	2	0	0	0	1	.143	9	9	0	1.000	

MICHAEL DENNIS DUNNE
(Mike)

Born October 27, 1962, at South Bend, Ind.
Height, 6.04. Weight, 221.
Throws right and bats lefthanded.
Attended Bradley University, Peoria, Ill.

Led American Association pitchers in balks with 9 and tied for lead in games started with 28 in 1986.

Named National League Rookie Pitcher of the Year by THE SPORTING NEWS, 1987.

Member of 1984 U.S. Olympic baseball team.

Named righthanded pitcher on THE SPORTING NEWS College Baseball All-America Team, 1984.

Year	Club	League	G.	IP.	W.	L.	Pct.	H.	R.	ER.	SO.	BB.	ERA.
1985—Arkansas†	Texas	23	146	4	9	.308	133	72	50	91	57	3.08	
1986—Louisville‡	Am. Assoc.	28	*185⅔	9	●12	.429	182	102	*94	94	82	4.56	
1987—Vancouver	P. Coast	9	61⅓	3	5	.375	61	21	12	41	23	1.76	
1987—Pittsburgh	National	23	163⅓	13	6	.684	143	66	55	72	68	3.03	
1988—Pittsburgh§	National	30	170	7	11	.389	163	88	74	70	88	3.92	
1989—Pittsburgh x	National	3	14⅓	1	1	.500	21	12	12	4	9	7.53	
1989—Seattle	American	15	85⅓	2	9	.182	104	61	50	38	37	5.27	
1989—Calgary y	P. Coast	9	51⅔	4	0	1.000	54	26	19	19	25	3.31	
1990—Las Vegas z	P. Coast	4	28	1	2	.333	20	12	10	12	10	3.21	
1990—San Diego	National	10	28⅔	0	3	.000	28	21	18	15	17	5.65	
National League Totals—4 Years		66	376⅓	21	21	.500	355	187	159	161	182	3.80	
American League Totals—1 Year		15	85⅓	2	9	.182	104	61	50	38	37	5.27	
Major League Totals—4 Years		81	461⅔	23	30	.434	459	248	209	199	219	4.07	

Selected by St. Louis Cardinals' organization in 1st round (seventh player selected) of free-agent draft, June 4, 1984.

†On disabled list, May 31 to June 10, 1985.

‡Traded with Outfielder Andy Van Slyke and Catcher Mike LaValliere to Pittsburgh Pirates for Catcher Tony Pena, April 1, 1987.

§On disabled list, April 6 to April 28, 1988.

xTraded with Pitcher Mike Walker and Outfielder Mark Merchant to Seattle Mariners for Shortstop Rey Quinones and Pitcher Bill Wilkinson, April 21, 1989.

yDrafted by San Diego Padres, December 4, 1989.

zOn San Diego disabled list, April 1 to May 14 and July 19 to September 13, 1990; included rehabilitation disability assignment to Las Vegas, April 25 to May 14, 1990.

SHAWON DONNELL DUNSTON

Born March 21, 1963, at Brooklyn, N.Y.
Height, 6.01. Weight, 175.
Throws and bats righthanded.

Shares modern major league record for most triples, game (3), July 28, 1990.

Major League stolen bases: 1985 (11), 1986 (13), 1987 (12), 1988 (30), 1989 (19), 1990 (25). Total—110.

Led National League shortstops in total chances with 817 and tied for lead in double plays with 96 in 1986.

Named shortstop on THE SPORTING NEWS National League All-Star Team, 1989.

Received reported $150,000 bonus to sign with Chicago Cubs, 1982.

Year	Club	League	Pos.	G.	AB.	R.	H.	2B.	3B.	HR.	RBI.	B.A.	PO.	A.	E.	F.A.
1982—Sarasota Cubs	Gulf C.	SS-3B	53	190	27	61	11	0	2	28	.321	61	129	24	.888	
1983—Quad Cities†	Midw.	SS	117	455	65	141	17	8	4	62	.310	172	326	47	.914	
1984—Midland	Texas	SS	73	298	44	98	13	3	3	34	.329	164	203	32	.920	
1984—Iowa	A. A.	SS	61	210	25	49	11	1	7	27	.233	90	165	26	.907	
1985—Chicago	Nat.	SS	74	250	40	65	12	4	4	18	.260	144	248	17	.958	
1985—Iowa	A. A.	SS	73	272	24	73	9	6	2	28	.268	138	176	12	.963	
1986—Chicago	Nat.	SS	150	581	66	145	36	3	17	68	.250	*320	*465	*32	.961	
1987—Chicago‡	Nat.	SS	95	346	40	85	18	3	5	22	.246	160	271	14	.969	
1987—Iowa	A. A.	SS	5	19	1	8	1	0	0	2	.421	6	12	1	.947	

Year Club League	Pos.	G.	AB.	R.	H.	2B.	3B.	HR.	RBI.	B.A.	PO.	A.	E.	F.A.
1988—Chicago .... Nat.	SS	155	575	69	143	23	6	9	56	.249	★257	455	20	.973
1989—Chicago .... Nat.	SS	138	471	52	131	20	6	9	60	.278	213	379	17	.972
1990—Chicago .... Nat.	SS	146	545	73	143	22	8	17	66	.262	255	392	20	.970
Major League Totals—6 Years		758	2768	340	712	131	30	61	290	.257	1349	2210	120	.967

Selected by Chicago Cubs' organization in 1st round (first player selected) of free-agent draft, June 7, 1982.

†On disabled list, May 31 to June 10, 1983.

‡On disabled list, June 16 to August 21, 1987; included rehabilitation disability assignment to Iowa, August 14 to August 21, 1987.

CHAMPIONSHIP SERIES RECORD

Year Club League	Pos.	G.	AB.	R.	H.	2B.	3B.	HR.	RBI.	B.A.	PO.	A.	E.	F.A.
1989—Chicago .... Nat.	SS	5	19	2	6	0	0	0	0	.316	10	14	1	.960

ALL-STAR GAME RECORD

Year League	Pos.	AB.	R.	H.	2B.	3B.	HR.	RBI.	B.A.	PO.	A.	E.	F.A.
1990—National	SS	2	0	0	0	0	0	0	.000	0	0	0	.000

Member of National League All-Star Team in 1988; did not play.

JAMES EDWARD DWYER
(Jim)

Born January 3, 1950, at Evergreen Park, Ill.
Height, 5.10. Weight, 196.
Throws and bats lefthanded.
Received bachelor of arts degree in accounting from Southern Illinois University, Carbondale, Ill., in 1973.
Nephew of Don Dwyer, second baseman in New York Giants' organization, 1947.

Major League stolen bases: 1975 (4), 1978 (7), 1979 (3), 1980 (3), 1982 (2), 1983 (1), 1987 (4), 1989 (2). Total—26.
Tied for American Association lead in caught stealing with 13 in 1977.

Year Club League	Pos.	G.	AB.	R.	H.	2B.	3B.	HR.	RBI.	B.A.	PO.	A.	E.	F.A.
1971—Cedar Rapids........ Midw.	OF	58	201	30	63	6	6	2	15	.313	73	3	3	.962
1972—Modesto .... Calif.	OF	92	354	87	115	15	★13	9	45	.325	149	8	4	.975
1972—Arkansas................ Texas	OF	44	162	16	41	1	0	2	14	.253	101	6	2	.982
1973—Tulsa .... A. A.	OF	87	349	63	135	22	8	1	40	★.387	127	8	5	.964
1973—St. Louis................. Nat.	OF	28	57	7	11	1	1	0	0	.193	32	0	0	1.000
1974—Tulsa .... A. A.	OF-1B	36	119	20	40	7	2	1	15	.336	120	13	3	.978
1974—St. Louis................. Nat.	OF-1B	74	86	13	24	1	0	2	11	.279	31	3	0	1.000
1975—Tulsa .... A. A.	OF	33	109	17	44	8	2	1	17	.404	49	2	2	.962
1975—St.L.†-Mont. .... Nat.	OF	81	206	26	56	8	1	3	21	.272	104	8	4	.966
1976—Mont.‡-N.Y.§ .... Nat.	OF	61	105	9	19	3	1	0	5	.181	35	0	1	.972
1976—Tidewater............ Int.	OF	8	26	0	5	1	0	0	1	.192	14	0	1	.933
1977—Wichita x.............. A. A.	OF	130	464	★113	★154	★38	12	18	70	★.332	245	6	8	.969
1977—St. Louis................. Nat.	OF	13	31	3	7	1	0	0	2	.226	16	0	0	1.000
1978—St.L. y-S.F. z .... Nat.	OF-1B	107	238	30	53	12	2	6	26	.223	216	15	3	.987
1979—Boston .... Amer.	1B-OF	76	113	19	30	7	0	2	14	.265	167	16	4	.979
1980—Boston a .... Amer.	OF-1B	93	260	41	74	11	1	9	38	.285	143	15	4	.975
1981—Baltimore .... Amer.	OF-1B	68	134	16	30	0	1	3	10	.224	97	2	2	.980
1982—Baltimore .... Amer.	OF-1B	71	148	28	45	4	3	6	15	.304	87	0	2	.978
1983—Baltimore .... Amer.	OF-1B	100	196	37	56	17	1	8	38	.286	123	2	4	.969
1984—Baltimore b .... Amer.	OF	76	161	22	41	9	1	2	21	.255	83	3	3	.966
1985—Baltimore c .... Amer.	OF	101	233	35	58	8	3	7	36	.249	131	4	1	.993
1986—Baltimore d.......... Amer.	OF-1B	94	160	18	39	13	1	8	31	.244	33	4	0	1.000
1987—Baltimore .... Amer.	OF	92	241	54	66	7	1	15	33	.274	57	1	0	1.000
1988—Balt.ef-Minn. .... Amer.	OF	55	94	9	24	1	0	2	18	.255	3	0	0	1.000
1988—Rochester g.......... Int.	DH	8	27	7	8	3	1	0	4	.296	0	0	0	.000
1989—Minnesota h .... Amer.	OF	88	225	34	71	11	0	3	23	.316	0	0	0	.000
1989—Montreal i............ Nat.	PH	13	10	1	3	1	0	0	2	.300	0	0	0	.000
1990—Minnesota j .... Amer.	OF	37	63	7	12	0	0	1	5	.190	2	0	0	1.000
National League Totals—7 Years		377	733	89	173	27	5	11	67	.236	434	26	8	.983
American League Totals—12 Years		951	2028	320	546	88	12	66	282	.269	926	47	20	.980
Major League Totals—18 Years		1328	2761	409	719	115	17	77	349	.260	1360	73	28	.981

Selected by St. Louis Cardinals' organization in 11th round of free-agent draft, June 8, 1971.

†Traded to Montreal Expos for Infielder Larry Lintz, July 25, 1975.

‡Traded with Outfielder Jose (Pepe) Mangual to New York Mets for Outfielder Del Unser and Infielder Wayne Garrett, July 21, 1976.

§In three-club deal, Chicago Cubs traded Outfielder-First Baseman Pete LaCock to Kansas City Royals, the New York Mets traded Outfielder Jim Dwyer to Chicago Cubs' organization, and New York received a player to be named later, December 8, 1976; New York acquired Outfielder Sheldon Mallory from Kansas City to complete deal, December 13, 1976.

xReleased, September 7, 1977, signed by St. Louis Cardinals, September 13, 1977.

yTraded to San Francisco Giants, June 15, 1978, completing deal in which San Francisco traded Pitcher Frank Riccelli to St. Louis Cardinals for a player to be named later, October 25, 1977.

zSold to Boston Red Sox, March 15, 1979.

aGranted free agency, October 22, 1980; signed by Baltimore Orioles, December 23, 1980.

bOn disabled list, July 19 to August 29, 1984.

cGranted free agency, November 12, 1985; re-signed by Orioles, February 5, 1986.

dGranted free agency, November 12, 1986; re-signed by Orioles, November 20, 1986.

eOn disabled list, April 15 to May 14 and July 11 to August 1, 1988; included rehabilitation disability assignment to Rochester, May 6 to May 14, 1988.

fTraded to Minnesota Twins for a player to be named later, August 29, 1988; Baltimore Orioles acquired Pitcher Doug Kline to complete deal, August 31, 1988.

gGranted free agency, November 4, 1988; re-signed by Twins, December 6, 1988.

hTraded to Montreal Expos for a player to be named later, August 28, 1989; Minnesota Twins acquired Outfielder Alonzo Powell to complete deal, September 16, 1989.

iTraded to Minnesota Twins for Pitcher Jim Davins, January 12, 1990.

jReleased, June 22, 1990.

CHAMPIONSHIP SERIES RECORD

Year	Club	League	Pos.	G.	AB.	R.	H.	2B.	3B.	HR.	RBI.	B.A.	PO.	A.	E.	F.A.
1983—Baltimore		Amer.	PH-OF	2	4	1	1	1	0	0	0	.250	4	0	0	1.000

WORLD SERIES RECORD

Shares World Series record for hitting home run in first series at-bat, October 11, 1983.

Year	Club	League	Pos.	G.	AB.	R.	H.	2B.	3B.	HR.	RBI.	B.A.	PO.	A.	E.	F.A.
1983—Baltimore		Amer.	OF	2	8	3	3	1	0	1	1	.375	2	0	0	1.000

MICHAEL LAWRENCE DYER
(Mike)

Born September 8, 1966, at Upland, Calif.
Height, 6.03. Weight, 195.
Throws and bats righthanded.
Attended Citrus College, Glendora, Calif.

Tied for Appalachian League lead in games started by pitchers with 14 in 1986.

Year	Club	League	G.	IP.	W.	L.	Pct.	H.	R.	ER.	SO.	BB.	ERA.
1986—Elizabethton		Ap'lachian	14	72⅓	5	7	.417	70	50	28	62	42	3.48
1987—Kenosha		Midwest	27	167	16	5	.762	124	72	57	163	84	3.07
1988—Orlando		Southern	27	162⅓	11	13	.458	155	84	72	125	86	3.99
1989—Portland		P. Coast	15	89⅓	3	6	.333	80	56	44	63	51	4.43
1989—Minnesota		American	16	71	4	7	.364	74	43	38	37	37	4.82
1990—Portland†		P. Coast	2	2⅓	0	1	.000	6	10	9	0	9	34.71
Major League Totals—1 Year			16	71	4	7	.364	74	43	38	37	37	4.82

Selected by Minnesota Twins' organization in 4th round of free-agent draft, January 14, 1986.

†On disabled list, April 15, 1990 through remainder of season.

LEONARD KYLE DYKSTRA

Name pronounced DYK-struh.

(Lenny)

Born February 10, 1963, at Santa Ana, Calif.
Height, 5.10. Weight, 170.
Throws and bats lefthanded.
Grandson of Pete Leswick, forward with New York Americans and Boston Bruins of NHL,
1936-37 and 1944-45; nephew of Tony Leswick, forward with New York Rangers,
Detroit Red Wings and Chicago Black Hawks of NHL, 1945-46
through 1955-56 and 1957-58; and brother of Kevin Dykstra, umpire in Northwest League, 1988.

Major League stolen bases: 1985 (15), 1986 (31), 1987 (27), 1988 (30), 1989 (30), 1990 (33). Total—166.
Led National League outfielders in total chances with 452 in 1990.
Led Carolina League in bases on balls received with 107, stolen bases with 105 and caught stealing with 23 in 1983.
Named Carolina League Player of the Year, 1983.

Year	Club	League	Pos.	G.	AB.	R.	H.	2B.	3B.	HR.	RBI.	B.A.	PO.	A.	E.	F.A.
1981—Shelby		S. Atl.	OF-SS	48	157	34	41	7	2	0	18	.261	86	3	4	.957
1982—Shelby		S. Atl.	OF	120	413	95	120	13	7	3	38	.291	239	11	14	.947
1983—Lynchburg		Carol.	OF	●136	*525	*132	*188	24	*14	8	81	*.358	268	9	7	.975
1984—Jackson		Texas	OF	131	501	*100	138	25	7	6	52	.275	256	5	2	*.992
1985—Tidewater		Int.	OF	58	229	44	71	8	6	1	25	.310	184	4	5	.974
1985—New York		Nat.	OF	83	236	40	60	9	3	1	19	.254	165	6	1	.994
1986—New York		Nat.	OF	147	431	77	127	27	7	8	45	.295	283	8	3	.990
1987—New York		Nat.	OF	132	431	86	123	37	3	10	43	.285	239	4	3	.988
1988—New York		Nat.	OF	126	429	57	116	19	3	8	33	.270	270	3	1	.996
1989—N.Y.†-Phi.		Nat.	OF	146	511	66	121	32	4	7	32	.237	332	10	4	.988
1990—Philadelphia		Nat.	OF	149	590	106	●192	35	3	9	60	.325	*439	7	6	.987
Major League Totals—6 Years			783	2628	432	739	159	23	43	232	.281	1728	38	18	.990

Selected by New York Mets' organization in 12th round of free-agent draft, June 8, 1981.

†Traded with Pitcher Roger McDowell and a player to be named later to Philadelphia Phillies for Outfielder Juan Samuel, June 18, 1989; Philadelphia organization acquired Pitcher Tom Edens to complete deal, July 27, 1989.

CHAMPIONSHIP SERIES RECORD

Shares Championship Series record for most times hit by pitch, series (2), 1988.

Year	Club	League	Pos.	G.	AB.	R.	H.	2B.	3B.	HR.	RBI.	B.A.	PO.	A.	E.	F.A.
1986—New York		Nat.	OF-PH	6	23	3	7	1	1	1	3	.304	10	0	0	1.000
1988—New York		Nat.	PH-OF	7	14	6	6	3	0	1	3	.429	9	0	0	1.000
Championship Series Totals—2 Years			13	37	9	13	4	1	2	6	.351	19	0	0	1.000

WORLD SERIES RECORD

Year	Club	League	Pos.	G.	AB.	R.	H.	2B.	3B.	HR.	RBI.	B.A.	PO.	A.	E.	F.A.
1986—New York		Nat.	OF-PH	7	27	4	8	0	0	2	3	.296	14	0	0	1.000

Year League	Pos.	AB.	R.	H.	2B.	3B.	HR.	RBI.	B.A.	PO.	A.	E.	F.A.
1990—National	OF	4	0	1	0	0	0	0	.250	3	0	0	1.000

GARY LOUIS EAVE

Born July 22, 1963, at Monroe, La.
Height, 6.04. Weight, 190.
Throws and bats righthanded.
Attended Grambling State University, Grambling, La.

Year Club	League	G.	IP.	W.	L.	Pct.	H.	R.	ER.	SO.	BB.	ERA.
1985—Bradenton Braves	Gulf Coast	6	30⅔	2	1	.667	28	7	6	21	8	1.76
1986—Sumter	S. Atlantic	25	47	4	1	.800	34	18	15	61	21	2.87
1987—Durham	Carolina	16	87⅓	5	4	.556	90	51	47	82	35	4.84
1987—Greenville	Southern	25	54⅓	2	5	.286	39	19	17	52	23	2.82
1988—Richmond	Int'national	34	101	5	9	.357	100	49	40	81	31	3.56
1988—Atlanta	National	5	5	0	0	.000	7	5	5	0	3	9.00
1989—Richmond	Int'national	23	141⅓	●13	3	⋆.813	111	48	44	93	57	2.80
1989—Atlanta†	National	3	20⅔	2	0	1.000	15	3	3	9	12	1.31
1990—Seattle	American	8	30	0	3	.000	27	16	14	16	20	4.20
1990—Calgary‡-Phoenix§	P. Coast	11	50⅔	3	3	.500	63	47	44	27	40	7.82
National League Totals—2 Years		8	25⅔	2	0	1.000	22	8	8	9	15	2.81
American League Totals—1 Year		8	30	0	3	.000	27	16	14	16	20	4.20
Major League Totals—3 Years		16	55⅔	2	3	.400	49	24	22	25	35	3.56

Selected by Atlanta Braves' organization in 12th round of free-agent draft, June 3, 1985.

†Traded with Third Baseman Ken Pennington to Calgary (Seattle Mariners' organization) for Third Baseman Jim Presley, January 24, 1990.

‡Traded to San Francisco Giants for Pitcher Russ Swan, May 24, 1990.

§Granted free agency, December 20, 1990.

DENNIS LEE ECKERSLEY

Born October 3, 1954, at Oakland, Calif.
Height, 6.02. Weight, 195.
Throws and bats righthanded.
Son-in-law of Al Jacinto, second baseman in Chicago White Sox' organization, 1947 through 1954.
Pitched 1-0 no-hit victory against California Angels, May 30, 1977.
Major League saves: 1975 (2), 1976 (1), 1987 (16), 1988 (45), 1989 (33), 1990 (48). Total—145.
Led American League in saves with 45 in 1988.
Led American League in home runs allowed with 30 in 1978.
Tied for American League lead in intentional bases on balls issued with 11 in 1977.
Led Texas League in hit batsmen with 10 in 1974.
Led California League pitchers in games started with 31 and tied for lead in shutouts with 5 in 1973.
Named American League Fireman of the Year by THE SPORTING NEWS, 1988.
Named American League Rookie Pitcher of the Year by THE SPORTING NEWS, 1975.
Received reported $32,000 bonus to sign with Cleveland Indians, 1972.

Year Club	League	G.	IP.	W.	L.	Pct.	H.	R.	ER.	SO.	BB.	ERA.
1972—Reno	California	12	75	5	5	.500	87	46	40	56	33	4.80
1973—Reno	California	31	202	12	8	.600	182	97	82	218	91	3.65
1974—San Antonio	Texas	23	167	●14	3	⋆.824	141	66	63	⋆163	60	3.40
1975—Cleveland	American	34	187	13	7	.650	147	61	54	152	90	2.60
1976—Cleveland	American	36	199	13	12	.520	155	82	76	200	78	3.44
1977—Cleveland†	American	33	247	14	13	.519	214	100	97	191	54	3.53
1978—Boston	American	35	268	20	8	.714	258	99	89	162	71	2.99
1979—Boston	American	33	247	17	10	.630	234	89	82	150	59	2.99
1980—Boston	American	30	198	12	14	.462	188	101	94	121	44	4.27
1981—Boston	American	23	154	9	8	.529	160	82	73	79	35	4.27
1982—Boston	American	33	224⅓	13	13	.500	228	101	93	127	43	3.73
1983—Boston	American	28	176⅓	9	13	.409	223	119	110	77	39	5.61
1984—Boston‡	American	9	64⅔	4	4	.500	71	38	36	33	13	5.01
1984—Chicago§	National	24	160⅓	10	8	.556	152	59	54	81	36	3.03
1985—Chicago x	National	25	169⅓	11	7	.611	145	61	58	117	19	3.08
1986—Chicago y	National	33	201	6	11	.353	226	109	102	137	43	4.57
1987—Oakland	American	54	115⅔	6	8	.429	99	41	39	113	17	3.03
1988—Oakland	American	60	72⅔	4	2	.667	52	20	19	70	11	2.35
1989—Oakland z	American	51	57⅔	4	0	1.000	32	10	10	55	3	1.56
1990—Oakland	American	63	73⅓	4	2	.667	41	9	5	73	4	0.61
American League Totals—14 Years		522	2284⅔	142	114	.555	2102	952	877	1603	561	3.45
National League Totals—3 Years		82	530⅔	27	26	.509	523	229	214	335	98	3.63
Major League Totals—16 Years		604	2815⅓	169	140	.547	2625	1181	1091	1938	659	3.49

Selected by Cleveland Indians' organization in 3rd round of free-agent draft, June 6, 1972.

†Traded with Catcher Fred Kendall to Boston Red Sox for Pitchers Rick Wise and Mike Paxton, Third Baseman Ted Cox and Catcher Bo Diaz, March 30, 1978.

‡Traded with Outfielder Mike Brumley to Chicago Cubs for First Baseman-Outfielder Bill Buckner, May 25, 1984.

§Granted free agency, November 6, 1984; re-signed by Cubs, November 28, 1984.

xOn disabled list, August 11 to September 7, 1985.

yTraded with Infielder Dan Rohn to Oakland Athletics for Outfielder Dave Wilder, Infielder Brian Guinn and Pitcher Mark Leonette, April 3, 1987.

zOn disabled list, May 29 to July 13, 1989.

Holds record for most saves, lifetime (9) and series (4), 1988.
Holds American League record for most saves, total series (4).
Shares American League record for most games pitched, lifetime (11) and series (4), 1988.

Year	Club	League	G.	IP.	W.	L.	Pct.	H.	R.	ER.	SO.	BB.	ERA.
1984—Chicago	National	1	5⅓	0	1	.000	9	5	5	0	0	8.44
1988—Oakland	American	4	6	0	0	.000	1	0	0	5	2	0.00
1989—Oakland	American	4	5⅔	0	0	.000	4	1	1	2	0	1.59
1990—Oakland	American	3	3⅓	0	0	.000	2	0	0	3	0	0.00
Championship Series Totals—4 Years			12	20⅓	0	1	.000	16	6	6	10	2	2.66

WORLD SERIES RECORD

Year	Club	League	G.	IP.	W.	L.	Pct.	H.	R.	ER.	SO.	BB.	ERA.
1988—Oakland	American	2	1⅔	0	1	.000	2	2	2	2	1	10.80
1989—Oakland	American	2	1⅔	0	0	.000	0	0	0	0	0	0.00
1990—Oakland	American	2	1⅓	0	1	.000	3	1	1	1	0	6.75
World Series Totals—3 Years			6	4⅔	0	2	.000	5	3	3	3	1	5.79

ALL-STAR GAME RECORD

Year	League	IP.	W.	L.	Pct.	H.	R.	ER.	SO.	BB.	ERA.
1977—American	2	0	0	.000	0	0	0	1	0	0.00
1982—American	3	0	1	.000	2	3	3	1	2	9.00
1988—American	1	0	0	.000	0	0	0	1	0	0.00
1990—American	1	0	0	.000	1	0	0	1	0	0.00
All-Star Game Totals—4 Years	7	0	1	.000	3	3	3	4	2	3.86

THOMAS PATRICK EDENS
(Tom)

Born June 9, 1961, at Ontario, Ore.
Height, 6.02. Weight, 185.
Throws and bats righthanded.
Received degree in business from Lewis-Clark State College, Lewiston, Ida.

Pitched seven-inning, 6-1 no-hit victory against Helena, August 22, 1983 (second game).
Major League saves: 1990 (2).

Year	Club	League	G.	IP.	W.	L.	Pct.	H.	R.	ER.	SO.	BB.	ERA.
1983—Butte†	Pioneer	13	58⅓	2	3	.400	65	47	28	44	33	4.32
1984—Columbia‡	S. Atlantic	16	95⅓	7	4	.636	65	44	33	60	58	3.12
1984—Lynchburg	Carolina	3	14⅓	1	1	.500	11	6	4	15	8	2.51
1985—Lynchburg§	Carolina	16	82	6	4	.600	86	40	35	48	34	3.84
1986—Jackson	Texas	16	106	9	4	.692	76	36	30	72	41	2.55
1986—Tidewater	Int'national	11	61⅓	5	3	.625	71	33	31	31	28	4.55
1987—Tidewater	Int'national	25	138	9	7	.563	140	69	55	61	55	3.59
1987—New York	National	2	8	0	0	.000	15	6	6	4	4	6.75
1988—Tidewater	Int'national	24	135⅓	7	6	.538	128	67	52	89	53	3.46
1989—Tidewater x-Scranton/W.-B.y	Int'national	25	107⅓	2	6	.250	121	59	53	47	39	4.44
1990—Denver	Am. Assoc.	19	36⅔	1	1	.500	32	23	22	26	22	5.40
1990—Milwaukee z	American	35	89	4	5	.444	89	52	44	40	33	4.45
National League Totals—1 Year		2	8	0	0	.000	15	6	6	4	4	6.75
American League Totals—1 Year		35	89	4	5	.444	89	52	44	40	33	4.45
Major League Totals—2 Years		37	97	4	5	.444	104	58	50	44	37	4.64

Selected by Cincinnati Reds' organization in 12th round of free-agent draft, June 5, 1979.
Selected by Kansas City Royals' organization in 14th round of free-agent draft, June 6, 1983.
†Traded to New York Mets' organization for Infielder Tucker Ashford, April 1, 1984.
‡On disabled list, April 9 to April 19 and May 21 to June 18, 1984.
§On disabled list, June 25 to August 12, 1985.
xTraded to Philadelphia Phillies' organization, July 27, 1989, completing deal in which Philadelphia traded Second Baseman Juan Samuel to New York Mets for Outfielder Lenny Dykstra, Pitcher Roger McDowell and a player to be named later, June 18, 1989.
yGranted free agency, October 15, 1989; signed by Denver (Milwaukee Brewers' organization), December 6, 1989.
zGranted free agency, December 20, 1990.

WAYNE MAURICE EDWARDS

Born March 7, 1964, at Burbank, Calif.
Height, 6.05. Weight, 185.
Throws and bats lefthanded.
Attended Azusa Pacific University, Azusa, Calif.

Major League saves: 1990 (2).
Led Southern League in wild pitches with 16 in 1988.
Led Florida State League in complete games with 15 and tied for lead in wild pitches with 17 in 1987.

Year	Club	League	G.	IP.	W.	L.	Pct.	H.	R.	ER.	SO.	BB.	ERA.
1985—Sarasota White Sox	Gulf Coast	11	68⅔	•7	3	.700	52	26	19	61	18	2.49
1986—Peninsula	Carolina	24	128⅓	8	8	.500	149	80	60	86	68	4.21
1987—Daytona Beach	Florida St.	29	⋆199⅔	16	8	.667	⋆211	91	80	121	68	3.61
1988—Birmingham	Southern	27	167	9	12	.429	176	108	91	136	92	4.90
1988—Vancouver	P. Coast	2	3	0	0	.000	0	0	0	2	0	0.00
1989—Birmingham	Southern	24	158	10	4	.714	131	69	56	122	65	3.19

Year Club	League	G.	IP.	W.	L.	Pct.	H.	R.	ER.	SO.	BB.	ERA.
1989—Chicago	American	7	7⅓	0	0	.000	7	3	3	9	3	3.68
1990—Chicago	American	42	95	5	3	.625	81	39	34	63	41	3.22
Major League Totals—2 Years		49	102⅓	5	3	.625	88	42	37	72	44	3.25

Selected by Chicago White Sox' organization in 10th round of free agent draft, June 3, 1985.

BRUCE EDWARD EGLOFF

Born April 10, 1965, at Denver, Colo.
Height, 6.02. Weight, 215.
Throws and bats righthanded.
Attended Merced College, Merced, Calif., and
University of California, Santa Barbara, Calif.

Year Club	League	G.	IP.	W.	L.	Pct.	H.	R.	ER.	SO.	BB.	ERA.
1986—Batavia	NYP	12	70	1	2	.333	79	42	31	62	17	3.99
1987—Waterloo†	Midwest	7	22⅔	1	2	.333	30	14	13	14	10	5.16
1988—Burlington‡	Midwest					(Did not play)						
1989—Waterloo§	NYP	22	48⅔	1	1	.500	33	19	14	63	24	2.59
1990—Canton-Akron x	Eastern	34	54⅔	3	2	.600	44	16	12	53	15	1.98

Selected by Cleveland Indians' organization in 5th round of free-agent draft, June 2, 1986.
†On disabled list, June 11 to August 8, 1987.
‡On disabled list, June 19, 1988 through remainder of season.
§On Canton disabled list, April 7 to June 16, 1989.
xOn disabled list, July 12 to August 2 and August 10, 1990 through remainder of season.

MARK ANTHONY EICHHORN

Name pronounced IKE-horn
Born November 21, 1960, at San Jose, Calif.
Height, 6.03. Weight, 210.
Throws and bats righthanded.
Attended Cabrillo Junior College, Aptos, Calif.

Shares American League record for most games, relief pitcher, season (89), 1987.
Major League saves: 1986 (10), 1987 (4), 1988 (1), 1990 (13). Total—28.
Led American League in intentional bases on balls issued with 14 in 1986.
Tied for International League lead in saves with 19 in 1989.
Tied for Southern League lead in games started by pitchers with 29 in 1981.
Named American League Rookie Pitcher of the Year by THE SPORTING NEWS, 1986.

Year Club	League	G.	IP.	W.	L.	Pct.	H.	R.	ER.	SO.	BB.	ERA.
1979—Medicine Hat	Pioneer	16	93	7	6	.538	101	62	35	66	26	3.39
1980—Kinston	Carolina	26	183	14	10	.583	158	72	59	119	56	2.90
1981—Knoxville	Southern	30	192	10	14	.417	202	112	85	99	57	3.98
1982—Syracuse	Int'national	27	156⅔	10	11	.476	158	92	79	71	83	4.54
1982—Toronto	American	7	38	0	3	.000	40	28	23	16	14	5.45
1983—Syracuse	Int'national	7	30⅔	0	5	.000	36	32	27	12	21	7.92
1983—Knoxville	Southern	21	120⅔	6	12	.333	124	65	58	54	47	4.33
1984—Syracuse	Int'national	36	117⅔	5	9	.357	147	92	78	54	51	5.97
1985—Knoxville	Southern	26	116⅓	5	1	.833	101	49	39	76	34	3.02
1985—Syracuse	Int'national	8	37⅓	2	5	.286	38	24	20	27	7	4.82
1986—Toronto†	American	69	157	14	6	.700	105	32	30	166	45	1.72
1987—Toronto	American	★89	127⅔	10	6	.625	110	47	45	96	52	3.17
1988—Toronto	American	37	66⅔	0	3	.000	79	32	31	28	27	4.19
1988—Syracuse‡	Int'national	18	38⅓	4	4	.500	35	9	5	34	15	1.17
1989—Atlanta	National	45	68⅓	5	5	.500	70	36	33	49	19	4.35
1989—Richmond§	Int'national	25	41	1	0	1.000	29	6	6	33	6	1.32
1990—California	American	60	84⅔	2	5	.286	98	36	29	69	23	3.08
American League Totals—5 Years		262	474	26	23	.531	432	175	158	375	161	3.00
National League Totals—1 Year		45	68⅓	5	5	.500	70	36	33	49	19	4.35
Major League Totals—6 Years		307	542⅓	31	28	.525	502	211	191	424	180	3.17

Selected by Toronto Blue Jays' organization in 2nd round of free-agent draft, January 9, 1979.
†On disabled list, June 16 to July 1, 1986.
‡Sold to Atlanta Braves, March 29, 1989.
§Released, November 20, 1989; signed by Edmonton (California Angels' organization), December 19, 1989.

DAVID WILLIAM EILAND

Name pronounced EYE-land.

(Dave)

Born July 5, 1966, at Dade City, Fla.
Height, 6.03. Weight, 205.
Throws and bats righthanded.
Attended University of Florida, Gainesville, Fla., and
University of South Florida, Tampa, Fla.

Led International League in complete games with 11 and tied for lead in shutouts with 3 in 1990.
Tied for Eastern League lead in complete games with 7 in 1988.
Named International League Pitcher of the Year, 1990.

Year Club	League	G.	IP.	W.	L.	Pct.	H.	R.	ER.	SO.	BB.	ERA.
1987—Oneonta	NYP	5	29⅓	4	0	1.000	20	6	6	16	3	1.84
1987—Fort Lauderdale	Florida St.	8	62½	5	3	.625	57	17	13	28	8	1.88
1988—Albany	Eastern	18	119⅓	9	5	.643	95	39	34	66	22	2.56
1988—Columbus	Int'national	4	24⅓	1	1	.500	25	8	7	13	6	2.59
1988—New York	American	3	12⅔	0	0	.000	15	9	9	7	4	6.39
1989—Columbus	Int'national	18	103	9	4	.692	107	47	43	45	21	3.76
1989—New York	American	6	34⅓	1	3	.250	44	25	22	11	13	5.77
1990—Columbus	Int'national	27	175⅓	*16	5	.762	155	63	56	96	32	2.87
1990—New York	American	5	30⅓	2	1	.667	31	14	12	16	5	3.56
Major League Totals—3 Years		14	77⅓	3	4	.429	90	48	43	34	22	5.00

Selected by New York Yankees' organization in 7th round of free-agent draft, June 2, 1987.

JAMES MICHAEL EISENREICH

Name pronounced EYES-en-rike.

(Jim)

Born April 18, 1959, at St. Cloud, Minn.
Height, 5.11. Weight, 195.
Throws and bats lefthanded.
Attended St. Cloud State University, St. Cloud, Minn.

Major League stolen bases: 1984 (2), 1987 (1), 1988 (9), 1989 (27), 1990 (12). Total—51.
Named Appalachian League Co-Player of the Year, 1980.

Year Club	League	Pos.	G.	AB.	R.	H.	2B.	3B.	HR.	RBI.	B.A.	PO.	A.	E.	F.A.
1980—Elizabethton	Appal.	OF	67	258	47	77	12	●4	3	41	.298	151	7	3	.981
1980—Wis. Rapids	Midw.	DH	5	16	4	7	0	0	0	5	.438	0	0	0	.000
1981—Wis. Rapids	Midw.	OF	*134	489	101	●152	*27	0	23	99	.311	*295	17	9	.972
1982—Minnesota†	Amer.	OF	34	99	10	30	6	0	2	9	.303	72	0	2	.973
1983—Minnesota‡	Amer.	OF	2	7	1	2	1	0	0	0	.286	6	1	0	1.000
1984—Minnesota§x	Amer.	OF	12	32	1	7	1	0	0	3	.219	5	0	0	1.000
1985-86—y							(Out of Organized Baseball)								
1987—Memphis	South.	DH	70	275	60	105	36	●10	11	57	.382	0	0	0	.000
1987—Kansas City z	Amer.	DH	44	105	10	25	8	2	4	21	.238	0	0	0	.000
1988—Kansas City	Amer.	OF	82	202	26	44	8	1	1	19	.218	109	0	4	.965
1988—Omaha	A. A.	OF	36	142	28	41	8	3	4	14	.289	73	1	1	.987
1989—Kansas City a	Amer.	OF	134	475	64	139	33	7	9	59	.293	273	4	3	.989
1990—Kansas City	Amer.	OF	142	496	61	139	29	7	5	51	.280	261	6	1	*.996
Major League Totals—7 Years			450	1416	173	386	86	17	21	162	.273	726	11	10	.987

Selected by Minnesota Twins' organization in 16th round of free-agent draft, June 3, 1980.
†On disabled list, May 6 to May 28 and June 18 to September 1, 1982.
‡On disabled list, April 7, 1983; then transferred to voluntarily retired list, May 27, 1983 through remainder of season.
§On disabled list, April 26 to May 18, 1984.
xOn voluntarily retired list, June 4, 1984 through September 29, 1986.
yClaimed on waivers by Kansas City Royals, October 2, 1986.
zOn disabled list, August 25 to September 9, 1987.
aOn disabled list, July 22 to August 6, 1989.

KEVIN DANIEL ELSTER

Born August 3, 1964, at San Pedro, Calif.
Height, 6.02. Weight, 200.
Throws and bats righthanded.
Attended Golden West College, Huntington Beach, Calif.

Holds major league records for most consecutive errorless games, shortstop, lifetime (88), July 20, 1988 through May 8, 1989; fewest putouts for leader, shortstop, season (235), 1989.
Major League stolen bases: 1988 (2), 1989 (4), 1990 (2). Total—8.
Led Texas League shortstops in total chances with 589 and double plays with 83 in 1986.
Led New York-Pennsylvania League shortstops in double plays with 45 and total chances with 358 in 1984.

Year Club	League	Pos.	G.	AB.	R.	H.	2B.	3B.	HR.	RBI.	B.A.	PO.	A.	E.	F.A.
1984—Little Falls	NYP	SS	71	257	35	66	7	3	3	35	.257	*128	214	16	*.955
1985—Lynchburg	Carol.	SS	59	224	41	66	9	0	7	26	.295	82	195	16	.945
1985—Jackson†	Texas	SS	59	214	30	55	13	0	2	22	.257	107	220	10	.970
1986—Jackson	Texas	SS	127	435	69	117	19	3	2	52	.269	*196	*365	28	*.952
1986—New York	Nat.	SS	19	30	3	5	1	0	0	0	.167	16	35	2	.962
1987—Tidewater	Int.	SS	134	*549	83	*170	33	7	8	74	.310	219	419	21	.968
1987—New York	Nat.	SS	5	10	1	4	2	0	0	1	.400	4	6	1	.909
1988—New York	Nat.	SS	149	406	41	87	11	1	9	37	.214	196	345	13	.977
1989—New York	Nat.	SS	151	458	52	106	25	2	10	55	.231	*235	374	15	.976
1990—New York‡	Nat.	SS	92	314	36	65	20	1	9	45	.207	159	251	17	.960
Major League Totals—5 Years			416	1218	133	267	59	4	28	138	.219	610	1011	48	.971

Selected by New York Mets' organization in 2nd round of free-agent draft, January 17, 1984.
†On disabled list, August 11, 1985 through remainder of season.
‡On disabled list, August 4, 1990 through remainder of season.

Year Club	League	Pos.	G.	AB.	R.	H.	2B.	3B.	HR.	RBI.	B.A.	PO.	A.	E.	F.A.
1986—New York.............	Nat.	PR-SS	4	3	0	0	0	0	0	0	.000	2	3	0	1.000
1988—New York.............	Nat.	SS-PR	5	8	1	2	1	0	0	1	.250	7	7	2	.875
Championship Series Totals—2 Years.....			9	11	1	2	1	0	0	1	.182	9	10	2	.905

WORLD SERIES RECORD

Year Club	League	Pos.	G.	AB.	R.	H.	2B.	3B.	HR.	RBI.	B.A.	PO.	A.	E.	F.A.
1986—New York.............	Nat.	SS	1	1	0	0	0	0	0	0	.000	3	3	1	.857

NARCISO ELVIRA

Born October 29, 1967, at Vera Cruz, Mexico.
Height, 5.10. Weight, 160.
Throws and bats lefthanded.

Year Club	League	G.	IP.	W.	L.	Pct.	H.	R.	ER.	SO.	BB.	ERA.
1986—Leon†................................	Mexican	31	127⅓	8	5	.615	128	81	68	84	84	4.81
1987—Beloit‡................................	Midwest	4	27	3	0	1.000	15	5	4	29	12	1.33
1987—Leon................................	Mexican	33	109⅓	6	8	.429	104	75	64	80	62	5.27
1988—Stockton............................	California	25	135⅓	7	6	.538	87	49	44	161	79	2.93
1989—El Paso................................	Texas	7	33	2	2	.500	48	34	28	18	23	7.64
1989—Stockton............................	California	17	115⅓	8	5	.615	92	45	39	135	43	3.04
1990—El Paso§............................	Texas	4	18	0	2	.000	17	11	9	12	6	4.50
1990—Beloit................................	Midwest	8	38⅓	3	2	.600	37	16	10	45	9	2.35
1990—Milwaukee............................	American	4	5	0	0	.000	6	3	3	6	5	5.40
Major League Totals—1 Year............................		4	5	0	0	.000	6	3	3	6	5	5.40

†Sold to Milwaukee Brewers' organization, December, 1986.
‡Loaned to Leon of Mexican League.
§On disabled list, May 17 to July 20, 1990.

LUIS MARTIN ENCARNACION

Born October 20, 1963, at Santo Domingo, Dominican Republic.
Height, 5.11. Weight, 180.
Throws and bats righthanded.

Led Midwest League in saves with 24 and tied for lead in games finished in relief with 49 in 1985.

Year Club	League	G.	IP.	W.	L.	Pct.	H.	R.	ER.	SO.	BB.	ERA.
1984—Batavia................................	NYP	21	60⅔	5	2	.714	48	25	21	65	33	3.12
1985—Waterloo............................	Midwest	53	92	8	5	.615	63	31	27	108	36	2.64
1986—Waterbury............................	Eastern	46	67⅔	8	9	.471	58	38	30	75	42	3.99
1987—Williamsport†................................	Eastern	43	55⅓	4	5	.444	61	24	24	34	22	3.90
1988—Memphis............................	Southern	49	78	4	3	.571	60	27	24	64	28	2.77
1989—Memphis............................	Southern	20	47⅓	4	4	.500	32	21	11	44	20	2.09
1989—Omaha............................	Am. Assoc.	31	50⅔	3	5	.375	39	10	10	41	18	1.78
1990—Omaha................................	Am. Assoc.	44	76	6	5	.545	70	30	25	62	30	2.96
1990—Kansas City............................	American	4	10⅓	0	0	.000	14	10	9	8	4	7.84
Major League Totals—1 Year............................		4	10⅓	0	0	.000	14	10	9	8	4	7.84

Signed as free agent by Cleveland Indians' organization, June 2, 1984.
†Drafted by Kansas City Royals' organization, December 8, 1987.

JAMES GERHARD EPPARD
(Jim)

Born April 27, 1960, at South Bend, Ind.
Height, 6.02. Weight, 180.
Throws and bats lefthanded.
Attended Citrus College, Azusa, Calif., and University of California, Berkeley, Calif.

Tied for California League lead in grounding into double plays with 19 in 1985.
Led International League first basemen in total chances with 1,113 and double plays with 100 in 1990.
Led California League first basemen in total chances with 1,341 in 1985.

Year Club	League	Pos.	G.	AB.	R.	H.	2B.	3B.	HR.	RBI.	B.A.	PO.	A.	E.	F.A.
1982—Medford.............	N'west	*1B-OF	64	242	58	*91	13	2	1	41	*.376	459	*38	10	.980
1983—Modesto.................	Calif.	1B	134	488	68	138	18	4	4	45	.283	1086	74	10	*.991
1984—Albany....................	East.	OF-1B	118	417	58	130	14	6	0	51	.312	551	41	4	.993
1985—Modesto.................	Calif.	1B	141	531	97	*183	23	4	3	88	*.345	1204	*125	12	.991
1986—Tacoma††.............	P. C.	OF-1B	95	321	39	88	15	1	0	34	.274	204	11	2	.991
1987—Edmonton.............	P. C.	1B-OF	132	446	68	152	*33	3	3	94	*.341	947	85	11	.989
1987—California.............	Amer.	OF	8	9	2	3	0	0	0	0	.333	1	0	0	1.000
1988—Edmonton.............	P. C.	1B	41	141	18	37	6	1	0	16	.262	322	31	4	.989
1988—California.............	Amer.	OF-1B	56	113	7	32	3	1	0	14	.283	63	4	2	.971
1989—Edmonton.............	P. C.	1B-OF	90	292	40	80	16	1	2	34	.274	599	52	6	.991
1989—California§.............	Amer.	1B	12	12	0	3	0	0	0	2	.250	12	0	0	1.000
1990—Syracuse	Int.	1B	133	461	72	*143	18	3	4	48	*.310	*1010	*93	10	*.991
1990—Toronto x.............	Amer.	PH	6	5	0	1	0	0	0	0	.200	0	0	0	.000
Major League Totals—4 Years.................			82	139	9	39	3	1	0	16	.281	76	4	2	.976

Selected by Chicago Cubs' organization in 11th round of free-agent draft, January 8, 1980.
Selected by Oakland A's organization in 13th round of free-agent draft, June 7, 1982.
†On disabled list, April 11 to April 21, 1986.

‡Sold to California Angels' organization, January 12, 1987.
§Released, October 6, 1989; signed by Syracuse (Toronto Blue Jays' organization), January 29, 1990.
xReleased, October 24, 1990.

JOHN EDWARD ERICKS III

Born September 16, 1967, at Oak Lawn, Ill.
Height, 6.07. Weight, 220.
Throws and bats righthanded.
Attended University of Illinois, Champaign, Ill.

Received reported $100,000 bonus to sign with St. Louis Cardinals, 1988.

Year Club	League	G.	IP.	W.	L.	Pct.	H.	R.	ER.	SO.	BB.	ERA.
1988—Johnson City	Ap'lachian	9	41	3	2	.600	27	20	17	41	27	3.73
1989—Savannah	S. Atlantic	28	167⅓	11	10	.524	90	59	38	*211	101	2.04
1990—St. Petersburg	Florida St.	4	23	2	1	.667	16	5	4	25	6	1.57
1990—Arkansas†	Texas	4	15⅓	1	2	.333	17	19	16	19	19	9.39

Selected by St. Louis Cardinals' organization in 1st round (22nd player selected) of free-agent draft, June 1, 1988.
†On disabled list, May 19, 1990 through remainder of season.

SCOTT GAVIN ERICKSON

Born February 2, 1968, at Long Beach, Calif.
Height, 6.04. Weight, 220.
Throws and bats righthanded.
Attended San Jose City College, San Jose, Calif., and
University of Arizona, Tucson, Ariz.

Year Club	League	G.	IP.	W.	L.	Pct.	H.	R.	ER.	SO.	BB.	ERA.
1989—Visalia	California	12	78⅔	3	4	.429	79	29	26	59	22	2.97
1990—Orlando	Southern	15	101	8	3	.727	75	38	34	69	24	3.03
1990—Minnesota	American	19	113	8	4	.667	108	49	36	53	51	2.87
Major League Totals—1 Year		19	113	8	4	.667	108	49	36	53	51	2.87

Selected by New York Mets' organization in 36th round of free-agent draft, June 2, 1986.
Selected by Houston Astros' organization in 34th round of free-agent draft, June 2, 1987.
Selected by Toronto Blue Jays' organization in 44th round of free-agent draft, June 1, 1988.
Selected by Minnesota Twins' organization in 4th round of free-agent draft, June 5, 1989.

NICHOLAS ANDREW ESASKY

Name pronounced Ee-SASS-kee.

(Nick)

Born February 24, 1960, at Hialeah, Fla.
Height, 6.03. Weight, 215.
Throws and bats righthanded.

Major League stolen bases: 1983 (6), 1984 (1), 1985 (3), 1988 (7), 1989 (1). Total—18.
Led Eastern League batters in strikeouts with 131 and game-winning RBIs with 14 in 1980.

Year Club	League	Pos.	G.	AB.	R.	H.	2B.	3B.	HR.	RBI.	B.A.	PO.	A.	E.	F.A.
1978—Billings	Pion.	3B	64	213	38	65	10	5	4	48	.305	*62	88	22	.872
1979—Tampa	Fla. St.	3B	124	439	52	118	16	3	10	66	.269	91	234	27	.923
1980—Waterbury	East.	3B	135	425	79	115	18	4	*30	79	.271	98	241	23	.936
1981—Indianapolis	A. A.	3B	121	423	55	112	22	4	17	62	.265	99	220	*37	.896
1982—Indianapolis	A. A.	3B	105	341	59	90	15	3	27	62	.264	77	150	21	*.915
1983—Indianapolis	A. A.	3B	49	158	33	44	5	0	14	37	.278	27	71	14	.875
1983—Cincinnati	Nat.	3B	85	302	41	80	10	5	12	46	.265	53	133	13	.935
1984—Cincinnati	Nat.	3B-1B	113	322	30	62	10	5	10	45	.193	220	137	18	.952
1985—Cincinnati	Nat.	3B-OF-1B	125	413	61	108	21	0	21	66	.262	169	106	8	.972
1986—Cincinnati†	Nat.	1B-OF-3B	102	330	35	76	17	2	12	41	.230	585	33	5	.992
1987—Nashville‡	A. A.	1B	13	52	13	23	6	0	5	18	.442	102	7	0	1.000
1987—Cincinnati	Nat.	1B-3B-OF	100	346	48	94	19	2	22	59	.272	773	41	6	.993
1988—Cincinnati§x	Nat.	1B	122	391	40	95	17	2	15	62	.243	982	52	6	.994
1989—Boston y	Amer.	1B-OF	154	564	79	156	26	5	30	108	.277	1319	107	6	.996
1990—Atlanta z	Nat.	1B	9	35	2	6	0	0	0	0	.171	79	5	5	.944
National League Totals—7 Years			656	2139	257	521	94	16	92	319	.244	2861	507	61	.982
American League Totals—1 Year			154	564	79	156	26	5	30	108	.277	1319	107	6	.996
Major League Totals—8 Years			810	2703	336	677	120	21	122	427	.250	4180	614	67	.986

Selected by Cincinnati Reds' organization in 1st round (17th player selected) of free-agent draft, June 6, 1978.
†On disabled list, June 15 to July 17, 1986.
‡On Cincinnati disabled list, March 23 to May 19, 1987; included rehabilitation disability assignment to Nashville, May 5 to May 19, 1987.
§On disabled list, May 11 to June 3, 1988.
xTraded with Pitcher Rob Murphy to Boston Red Sox for First Baseman Todd Benzinger, Pitcher Jeff Sellers and a player to be named later, December 13, 1988; Cincinnati Reds acquired Pitcher Luis Vasquez to complete deal, January 12, 1989.
yGranted free agency, November 13, 1989; signed by Atlanta Braves, November 17, 1989.
zOn disabled list, April 22, 1990 through remainder of season.

DANIEL PERRY ESKEW
(Dan)

Born February 2, 1966, at Nashville, Tenn.
Height, 6.01. Weight, 200.
Throws and bats righthanded.
Attended Indian River Community College, Fort Pierce, Fla.,
and University of Tennessee, Knoxville, Tenn.

Year Club	League	G.	IP.	W.	L.	Pct.	H.	R.	ER.	SO.	BB.	ERA.
1988—Southern Oregon	Northwest	9	48⅔	4	2	.667	29	20	13	61	21	2.40
1988—Modesto	California	6	26½	1	2	.333	30	24	18	30	21	6.15
1989—Modesto	California	15	75⅓	3	5	.375	70	39	34	58	31	4.06
1990—Huntsville	Southern	25	148⅓	14	3	*.824	133	62	55	128	60	3.34

Selected by New York Mets' organization in 16th round of free-agent draft, June 4, 1984.
Selected by Milwaukee Brewers' organization in secondary phase of free-agent draft, January 14, 1986.
Selected by Cleveland Indians' organization in secondary phase of free-agent draft, June 2, 1986.
Selected by Cleveland Indians' organization in 18th round of free-agent draft, June 2, 1987.
Selected by Oakland Athletics' organization in 6th round of free-agent draft, June 1, 1988.

ALVARO ALBERTO ESPINOZA (RAMIREZ)
Name pronounced Ess-pin-OH-zuh.

Born February 19, 1962, at Valencia, Carabobo, Venezuela.
Height, 6.00. Weight, 189.
Throws and bats righthanded.

Shares major league record for fewest runs batted in, season, 150 or more games (20), 1990.
Major League stolen bases: 1989 (3), 1990 (1). Total—4.
Tied for International League lead in sacrifice hits with 16 in 1984.
Led International League shortstops in putouts with 159 in 1986.
Led California League shortstops in total chances with 660 in 1983.
Led Gulf Coast League shortstops in assists with 217, double plays with 33 and total chances with 356 in 1980.

Year Club	League	Pos.	G.	AB.	R.	H.	2B.	3B.	HR.	RBI.	B.A.	PO.	A.	E.	F.A.
1979—Sarasota Astros	Gulf C.	SS-2B-3B	11	32	3	7	0	0	0	5	.219	18	27	1	.978
1980—Sara. Astros-O.†	Gulf C.	*SS-3B	59	200	24	43	5	0	0	14	.215	*114	219	*25	.930
1981—							(Out of Organized Baseball)								
1982—Wisconsin Rapids	Midw.	SS-3B-1B	112	379	41	101	9	0	5	29	.266	237	241	33	.935
1983—Visalia	Calif.	SS	130	486	57	155	20	1	4	57	.319	*256	364	40	.939
1984—Toledo‡	Int.	SS	104	344	22	80	12	5	0	30	.233	157	293	19	.959
1984—Minnesota	Amer.	SS	1	0	0	0	0	0	0	0	.000	0	0	0	.000
1985—Toledo§	Int.	SS	82	266	24	61	11	0	1	33	.229	132	245	16	.959
1985—Minnesota	Amer.	SS	32	57	5	15	2	0	0	9	.263	25	69	5	.949
1986—Toledo	Int.	SS-2B	73	253	18	71	8	1	2	27	.281	170	205	12	.969
1986—Minnesota	Amer.	2B-SS	37	42	4	9	1	0	0	1	.214	23	52	4	.949
1987—Portland x	P. C.	SS-3B-1B	91	291	28	80	3	2	4	28	.275	158	236	20	.952
1988—Columbus	Int.	SS-2B-3B	119	435	42	107	10	5	2	30	.246	221	404	19	.970
1988—New York	Amer.	2B-SS	3	3	0	0	0	0	0	0	.000	5	2	0	1.000
1989—New York	Amer.	SS	146	503	51	142	23	1	0	41	.282	237	471	22	.970
1990—New York	Amer.	SS	150	438	31	98	12	2	2	20	.224	268	447	17	.977
Major League Totals—6 Years			368	1043	91	264	38	3	2	71	.253	558	1041	48	.971

Signed as free agent by Houston Astros' organization, October 30, 1978.
†Released, September 30, 1980; signed by Wisconsin Rapids (Minnesota Twins' organization), March 18, 1982.
‡On disabled list, June 7 to June 25, 1984.
§On disabled list, June 6 to July 2, 1985.
xGranted free agency, October 15, 1987; signed by Columbus (New York Yankees' organization), November 17, 1987.

CECIL EDWARD ESPY

Born January 20, 1963, at San Diego, Calif.
Height, 6.03. Weight, 195.
Throws right and bats left and righthanded.
Son of Cecil Espy, scout with St. Louis Cardinals since 1979.

Major League stolen bases: 1987 (2), 1988 (33), 1989 (45), 1990 (11). Total—91.
Led American League in caught stealing with 20 in 1989.
Led Florida State League in stolen bases with 74 in 1982.
Tied for Texas League lead in caught stealing with 17 in 1985.
Led Texas League shortstops in errors with 50 in 1985.
Led Texas League outfielders in total chances with 365 in 1984.

Year Club	League	Pos.	G.	AB.	R.	H.	2B.	3B.	HR.	RBI.	B.A.	PO.	A.	E.	F.A.
1980—Sarasota W. Sox	Gulf C.	OF	58	212	33	58	7	3	0	26	.274	138	4	7	.953
1981—Appleton	Midw.	OF	72	273	37	55	2	2	1	19	.201	143	5	5	.967
1981—Sarasota W. Sox†	Gulf C.	OF	43	142	24	40	3	1	0	16	.282	54	1	4	.932
1982—Vero Beach	Fla. St.	OF	131	*523	*100	*166	14	7	1	34	.317	275	9	10	.966
1983—San Antonio	Texas	OF	133	*564	88	151	16	11	4	38	.268	258	12	10	.964
1983—Los Angeles	Nat.	OF	20	11	4	3	1	0	0	1	.273	11	0	0	1.000
1984—San Antonio	Texas	*O-2-S	*133	*535	99	146	19	8	8	60	.273	*348	16	5	.986
1985—San Antonio‡	Texas	SS-OF	124	461	64	129	24	3	5	49	.280	183	346	51	.912
1986—Hawaii§	P. C.	OF-2B-SS	106	384	49	101	19	3	4	38	.263	172	8	5	.973
1987—Oklahoma City	A. A.	OF-SS	118	443	76	134	18	6	1	37	.302	195	161	16	.957
1987—Texas	Amer.	OF	14	8	1	0	0	0	0	0	.000	8	1	0	1.000

Year Club	League	Pos.	G.	AB.	R.	H.	2B.	3B.	HR.	RBI.	B.A.	PO.	A.	E.	F.A.
1988—Texas x	Amer.	O-S-C-1-2	123	347	46	86	17	6	2	39	.248	200	11	7	.968
1989—Texas.....................	Amer.	OF	142	475	65	122	12	7	3	31	.257	281	5	3	.990
1990—Texas.....................	Amer.	OF-2B	52	71	10	9	0	0	0	1	.127	56	1	0	1.000
1990—Oklahoma City ..... A. A.		OF-SS	34	126	15	34	4	1	2	20	.270	69	8	5	.939
National League Totals—1 Year............			20	11	4	3	1	0	0	1	.273	11	0	0	1.000
American League Totals—4 Years			331	901	122	217	29	13	5	71	.241	545	18	10	.983
Major League Totals—5 Years.................			351	912	126	220	30	13	5	72	.241	556	18	10	.983

Selected by Chicago White Sox' organization in 1st round (eighth player selected) of free-agent draft, June 3, 1980.
†Traded with Pitcher Burt Geiger to Los Angeles Dodgers' organization for Outfielder Rudy Law, March 30, 1982.
‡Traded with First Baseman Sid Bream to Pittsburgh Pirates, September 9, 1985, completing deal in which Los Angeles Dodgers acquired Third Baseman Bill Madlock for three players to be named later, R. J. Reynolds as partial completion of deal, September 3, 1985.
§Drafted by Texas Rangers, December 8, 1986.
xOn disabled list, May 3 to May 18, 1988.

RAUL ANTONIO EUSEBIO

Born April 27, 1967, at Boca Chica, Dominican Republic.
Height, 6.02. Weight, 180.
Throws and bats righthanded.
Tied for Southern League lead in double plays by catchers with 8 in 1989.

Year Club	League	Pos.	G.	AB.	R.	H.	2B.	3B.	HR.	RBI.	B.A.	PO.	A.	E.	F.A.
1985—Sarasota Astros....	Gulf C.	C	1	1	0	0	0	0	0	0	.000	4	0	0	1.000
1986—..................................				(Played in Dominican Summer League)											
1987—Sarasota Astros....	Gulf C.	C-1B	42	125	26	26	1	2	1	15	.208	204	24	4	.983
1988—Osceola.................	Fla. St.	C-OF	118	392	45	96	6	3	0	40	.245	611	66	8	.988
1989—Columbus..............	South.	C	65	203	20	38	6	1	0	18	.187	355	46	7	.983
1989—Osceola.................	Fla. St.	C	52	175	22	50	6	3	0	30	.286	290	40	5	.985
1990—Columbus†............	South.	C	92	318	36	90	18	0	4	37	.283	558	69	4	*.994

Signed as free agent by Houston Astros' organization, May 30, 1985.
†On disabled list, August 5, 1990 through remainder of season.

DWIGHT MICHAEL EVANS

Born November 3, 1951, at Santa Monica, Calif.
Height, 6.03. Weight, 208.
Throws and bats righthanded.
Major League stolen bases: 1973 (5), 1974 (4), 1975 (3), 1976 (6), 1977 (4), 1978 (8), 1979 (6), 1980 (3), 1981 (3), 1982 (3), 1983 (3), 1984 (3), 1985 (7), 1986 (3), 1987 (4), 1988 (5), 1989 (3), 1990 (3). Total—76.
Hit for the cycle, June 28, 1984.
Led American League in bases on balls received with 85 in 1981, 114 in 1985 and tied for lead with 106 in 1987.
Led American League in total bases with 215 in 1981.
Led American League outfielders in double plays with 8 in 1975 and 7 in 1980.
Tied for American League lead in errors by first basemen with 12 in 1987.
Led Western Carolinas League in sacrifice flies with 8 in 1970.
Tied for Carolina League lead in double plays by outfielders with 3 in 1971.
Named outfielder on THE SPORTING NEWS American League All-Star Team, 1982, 1984 and 1987.
Named outfielder on THE SPORTING NEWS American League All-Star fielding team, 1976, 1978, 1979 and 1981 through 1985.
Named outfielder on THE SPORTING NEWS American League Silver Slugger team, 1981 and 1987.
Named International League Most Valuable Player, 1972.

Year Club	League	Pos.	G.	AB.	R.	H.	2B.	3B.	HR.	RBI.	B.A.	PO.	A.	E.	F.A.
1969—Jamestown............	NYP	OF-3B	34	100	13	28	3	2	1	12	.280	44	10	3	.947
1970—Greenville	W. Car.	OF-3B	108	355	69	98	14	*11	7	68	.276	130	11	7	.953
1971—Winston-Salem	Carol.	OF-1B	118	402	63	115	20	4	12	63	.286	219	17	10	.959
1972—Louisville	Int.	OF	●144	496	90	149	23	8	17	*95	.300	270	12	6	.979
1972—Boston	Amer.	OF	18	57	2	15	3	1	1	6	.263	25	3	0	1.000
1973—Boston	Amer.	OF	119	282	46	63	13	1	10	32	.223	178	4	1	.995
1974—Boston	Amer.	OF	133	463	60	130	19	8	10	70	.281	294	8	3	.990
1975—Boston	Amer.	OF	128	412	61	113	24	6	13	56	.274	281	15	4	.987
1976—Boston	Amer.	OF	146	501	61	121	34	5	17	62	.242	324	15	2	*.994
1977—Boston†	Amer.	OF	73	230	39	66	9	2	14	36	.287	126	2	1	.992
1978—Boston	Amer.	OF	147	497	75	123	24	2	24	63	.247	305	14	6	.982
1979—Boston	Amer.	OF	152	489	69	134	24	1	21	58	.274	307	15	4	.988
1980—Boston	Amer.	OF	148	463	72	123	37	5	18	60	.266	268	11	5	.982
1981—Boston	Amer.	OF	108	412	84	122	19	4	●22	71	.296	259	9	2	.993
1982—Boston	Amer.	OF	●162	609	122	178	37	7	32	98	.292	346	9	10	.973
1983—Boston‡	Amer.	OF	126	470	74	112	19	4	22	58	.238	222	6	3	.987
1984—Boston	Amer.	OF	●162	630	*121	186	37	8	32	104	.295	311	7	2	.994
1985—Boston	Amer.	OF	159	617	110	162	29	1	29	78	.263	291	9	3	.990
1986—Boston	Amer.	OF	152	529	86	137	33	2	26	97	.259	280	10	5	.983
1987—Boston	Amer.	1B-OF	154	541	109	165	37	2	34	123	.305	753	46	13	.984
1988—Boston	Amer.	OF-1B	149	559	96	164	31	7	21	111	.293	611	34	9	.986
1989—Boston	Amer.	OF	146	520	82	148	27	3	20	100	.285	153	5	3	.981
1990—Boston§x	Amer.	DH	123	445	66	111	18	3	13	63	.249	0	0	0	.000
Major League Totals—19 Years.............			2505	8726	1435	2373	474	72	379	1346	.272	5334	222	76	.987

Selected by Boston Red Sox' organization in 5th round of free-agent draft, June 5, 1969.
†On disabled list, June 21 to July 8 and August 25 to September 21, 1977.

‡On disabled list, August 13 to September 1, 1983.
§On disabled list, July 14 to July 30, 1990.
xReleased, October 26, 1990; signed by Baltimore Orioles, December 6, 1990.

CHAMPIONSHIP SERIES RECORD

Year Club	League	Pos.	G.	AB.	R.	H.	2B.	3B.	HR.	RBI.	B.A.	PO.	A.	E.	F.A.
1975—Boston	Amer.	OF	3	10	1	1	1	0	0	0	.100	7	0	0	1.000
1986—Boston	Amer.	OF	7	28	2	6	1	0	1	4	.214	11	0	0	1.000
1988—Boston	Amer.	OF	4	12	1	2	1	0	0	1	.167	11	0	0	1.000
1990—Boston	Amer.	DH	4	13	0	3	1	0	0	0	.231	0	0	0	.000
Championship Series Totals—4 Years			18	63	4	12	4	0	1	5	.190	29	0	0	1.000

WORLD SERIES RECORD

Year Club	League	Pos.	G.	AB.	R.	H.	2B.	3B.	HR.	RBI.	B.A.	PO.	A.	E.	F.A.
1975—Boston	Amer.	OF	7	24	3	7	1	1	1	5	.292	23	1	0	1.000
1986—Boston	Amer.	OF	7	26	4	8	2	0	2	9	.308	16	1	1	.944
World Series Totals—2 Years			14	50	7	15	3	1	3	14	.300	39	2	1	.976

ALL-STAR GAME RECORD

Year League	Pos.	AB.	R.	H.	2B.	3B.	HR.	RBI.	B.A.	PO.	A.	E.	F.A.
1978—American	OF	1	0	0	0	0	0	0	.000	3	0	0	1.000
1981—American	PH-OF	2	1	1	0	0	0	0	.500	2	0	0	1.000
1987—American	OF	2	0	2	0	0	0	0	1.000	2	0	0	1.000
All-Star Game Totals—3 Years		5	1	3	0	0	0	0	.600	7	0	0	1.000

PAUL TYRRELL FARIES

Born February 20, 1965, at Berkeley, Calif.
Height, 5.10. Weight, 165.
Throws and bats righthanded.
Attended Pepperdine University, Malibu, Calif.

Led Northwest League in stolen bases with 30 in 1987.
Led Pacific Coast League second basemen in assists with 363 in 1990.
Led Texas League second basemen in fielding percentage with .979 and putouts with 258 in 1989.
Led California League second basemen in assists with 469, double plays with 81 and total chances with 764 in 1988.
Led Northwest League second basemen in total chances with 377 in 1987.
Named California League Most Valuable Player, 1988.

Year Club	League	Pos.	G.	AB.	R.	H.	2B.	3B.	HR.	RBI.	B.A.	PO.	A.	E.	F.A.
1987—Spokane	N'west	2B	74	280	★67	86	9	3	0	27	.307	★169	★197	11	★.971
1988—Riverside	Calif.	★2B-SS	141	★579	108	183	39	4	2	77	.316	288	486	20	★.975
1989—Wichita	Texas	2B-SS	130	★513	79	136	25	8	6	52	.265	284	391	18	.974
1990—Las Vegas	P. C.	2B-SS-3B	137	★552	★109	★172	29	3	5	64	.312	277	418	25	.965
1990—San Diego	Nat.	2B-SS-3B	14	37	4	7	1	0	0	2	.189	21	34	2	.965
Major League Totals—1 Year			14	37	4	7	1	0	0	2	.189	21	34	2	.965

Selected by San Diego Padres' organization in 22nd round of free-agent draft, June 2, 1987.

MONTY TED FARISS

Born October 13, 1967, at Cordell, Okla.
Height, 6.04. Weight, 180.
Throws and bats righthanded.
Attended Oklahoma State University, Stillwater, Okla.

Led Texas League shortstops in double plays with 94 and total chances with 712 in 1988.
Received reported $170,000 bonus to sign with Texas Rangers, 1988.
Named shortstop on THE SPORTING NEWS College Baseball All-America Team, 1988.

Year Club	League	Pos.	G.	AB.	R.	H.	2B.	3B.	HR.	RBI.	B.A.	PO.	A.	E.	F.A.
1988—Butte	Pion.	SS	17	53	16	21	1	0	4	22	.396	36	52	4	.957
1988—Tulsa	Texas	SS	49	165	21	37	6	6	3	31	.224	77	147	18	.926
1989—Tulsa	Texas	SS	132	497	72	135	27	2	5	52	.272	★260	401	★51	.928
1990—Tulsa	Texas	SS	71	244	45	73	15	6	7	34	.299	141	190	24	.932
1990—Oklahoma City	A. A.	S-2-1-3	62	225	30	68	12	3	4	31	.302	138	151	22	.929

Selected by New York Mets' organization in 7th round of free-agent draft, June 3, 1985.
Selected by Texas Rangers' organization in 1st round (sixth player selected) of free-agent draft, June 1, 1988.

HOWARD EARL FARMER

Born January 18, 1966, at Gary, Ind.
Height, 6.03. Weight, 190.
Throws and bats righthanded.
Attended Utica Junior College, Utica, Miss., and
Jackson State University, Jackson, Miss.

Tied for Southern League lead in shutouts with 2 in 1989.

Year Club	League	G.	IP.	W.	L.	Pct.	H.	R.	ER.	SO.	BB.	ERA.
1987—Jamestown	NYP	15	96⅓	9	6	.600	93	42	35	63	30	3.27
1988—Rockford	Midwest	27	193⅔	15	7	.682	153	70	54	145	58	2.51
1989—Jacksonville	Southern	26	184	12	9	.571	122	59	45	151	50	2.20
1989—Indianapolis	Am. Assoc.	1	7	1	0	1.000	3	1	0	3	3	0.00

Year Club	League	G.	IP.	W.	L.	Pct.	H.	R.	ER.	SO.	BB.	ERA.
1990—Indianapolis	Am. Assoc.	26	148	7	9	.438	150	84	64	99	48	3.89
1990—Montreal	National	6	23	0	3	.000	26	18	18	14	10	7.04
Major League Totals—1 Year		6	23	0	3	.000	26	18	18	14	10	7.04

Selected by Toronto Blue Jays' organization in 1st round (25th player selection) of free-agent draft, January 9, 1985.
Selected by Montreal Expos' organization in 7th round of free-agent draft, June 2, 1987.

STEVEN MICHAEL FARR
(Steve)

Born December 12, 1956, at Cheverly, Md.
Height, 5.11. Weight, 200.
Throws and bats righthanded.
Attended American University, Washington, D. C.,
and Charles County Community College, La Plata, Md.

Major League saves: 1984 (1), 1985 (1), 1986 (8), 1987 (1), 1988 (20), 1989 (18), 1990 (1). Total—50.

Year Club	League	G.	IP.	W.	L.	Pct.	H.	R.	ER.	SO.	BB.	ERA.
1977—Niagara Falls	NYP	10	52	1	5	.167	53	30	23	43	30	3.98
1978—Charleston	W. Carol.	21	77	5	3	.625	72	45	36	54	63	4.21
1978—Salem	Ap'lachian	2	16	2	0	1.000	13	2	1	12	1	0.56
1979—Salem†	Carolina	26	119	3	10	.231	138	81	66	105	47	4.99
1980—Buffalo	Eastern	23	161	11	6	.647	158	84	71	71	64	3.97
1980—Portland	P. Coast	2	7	0	1	.000	11	9	8	0	2	10.29
1981—Buffalo	Eastern	29	106	8	3	.727	102	50	44	82	48	3.74
1981—Portland	P. Coast	4	23	0	3	.000	39	28	20	19	12	7.83
1982—Buffalo‡§	Eastern	25	76⅓	5	8	.385	72	40	34	84	38	4.01
1983—Buffalo	Eastern	18	112	13	1	★.929	88	28	20	108	50	★1.61
1984—Maine	Int'national	6	45	4	0	1.000	37	14	13	40	8	2.60
1984—Cleveland xy	American	31	116	3	11	.214	106	61	59	83	46	4.58
1985—Omaha	Am. Assoc.	17	133⅔	10	4	.714	105	36	30	98	41	★2.02
1985—Kansas City	American	16	37⅔	2	1	.667	34	15	13	36	20	3.11
1986—Kansas City	American	56	109⅓	8	4	.667	90	39	38	83	39	3.13
1987—Kansas City	American	47	91	4	3	.571	97	47	42	88	44	4.15
1987—Omaha	Am. Assoc.	8	12⅔	0	0	.000	6	3	2	15	6	1.42
1988—Kansas City	American	62	82⅔	5	4	.556	74	25	23	72	30	2.50
1989—Kansas City z	American	51	63⅓	2	5	.286	75	35	29	56	22	4.12
1990—Kansas City a	American	57	127	13	7	.650	99	32	28	94	48	1.98
Major League Totals—7 Years		320	627	37	35	.514	575	254	232	512	249	3.33

Signed as a free agent by Pittsburgh Pirates' organization, December 13, 1976.
†On disabled list, June 6 to June 22, 1979.
‡On Lynn suspended list, April 16, 1983; then transferred to restricted list, April 27 to June 8, 1983.
§Traded to Buffalo (Cleveland Indians' organization) for Catcher John Malkin, June 8, 1983.
xOn disabled list, June 20 to July 5, 1984.
yReleased, March 31, 1985; signed by Kansas City Royals' organization, May 9, 1985.
zOn disabled list, August 21 to September 13, 1989.
aGranted free agency, November 5, 1990; signed by New York Yankees, November 26, 1990.

CHAMPIONSHIP SERIES RECORD

Year Club	League	G.	IP.	W.	L.	Pct.	H.	R.	ER.	SO.	BB.	ERA.
1985—Kansas City	American	2	6⅓	1	0	1.000	4	1	1	3	1	1.42

WORLD SERIES RECORD

Eligible for 1985 World Series with Kansas City Royals; did not play.

JOHN EDWARD FARRELL

Born August 4, 1962, at Monmouth Park, N. J.
Height, 6.04. Weight, 210.
Throws and bats righthanded.
Attended Oklahoma State University, Stillwater, Okla.

Led American Association in home runs allowed with 26 in 1987.
Tied for Eastern League lead in shutouts with 3 and hit batsmen with 10 in 1986.

Year Club	League	G.	IP.	W.	L.	Pct.	H.	R.	ER.	SO.	BB.	ERA.
1984—Waterloo	Midwest	9	43⅓	0	5	.000	59	34	31	29	33	6.44
1984—Maine	Int'national	5	26⅓	2	1	.667	20	11	11	12	20	3.76
1985—Waterbury	Eastern	25	149	7	13	.350	161	★106	86	75	76	5.19
1986—Waterbury	Eastern	26	173⅓	9	10	.474	158	82	59	104	54	3.06
1987—Buffalo	Am. Assoc.	25	156	6	12	.333	155	109	101	91	64	5.83
1987—Cleveland	American	10	69	5	1	.833	68	29	26	28	22	3.39
1988—Cleveland†	American	31	210⅓	14	10	.583	216	106	99	92	67	4.24
1989—Cleveland‡	American	31	208	9	14	.391	196	97	84	132	71	3.63
1990—Cleveland§	American	17	96⅔	4	5	.444	108	49	46	44	33	4.28
1990—Canton-Akron	Eastern	2	10	1	1	.500	13	8	8	5	2	7.20
Major League Totals—4 Years		89	584	32	30	.516	588	281	255	296	193	3.93

Selected by Oakland A's organization in 9th round of free-agent draft, June 3, 1980.
Selected by Cleveland Indians' organization in 16th round of free-agent draft, June 6, 1983.
Selected by Cleveland Indians' organization in 2nd round of free-agent draft, June 4, 1984.

†On disabled list, August 28 to September 20, 1988.
‡On disabled list, March 19 to April 16, 1989.
§On disabled list, June 25 to September 21, 1990; included rehabilitation disability assignment to Canton-Akron, July 16 to July 30, 1990.

MICHAEL OTIS FELDER
(Mike)

Born November 18, 1962, at Richmond, Calif.
Height, 5.08. Weight, 160.
Throws right and bats left and righthanded.
Attended Contra Costa College, San Pablo, Calif.

Major League stolen bases: 1985 (4), 1986 (16), 1987 (34), 1988 (8), 1989 (26), 1990 (20). Total—108.
Led Pacific Coast League in stolen bases with 61 in 1985.
Led Texas League in sacrifice flies with 9 in 1984.
Led Texas League in stolen bases with 71 in 1983 and 58 in 1984.
Led California League in stolen bases with 92 in 1982.
Led Texas League outfielders in putouts with 332, total chances with 363 and tied for lead in assists with 18 in 1983.

Year Club	League	Pos.	G.	AB.	R.	H.	2B.	3B.	HR.	RBI.	B.A.	PO.	A.	E.	F.A.
1981—Stockton	Calif.	2B-OF	91	338	66	91	8	1	3	30	.269	172	162	13	.963
1982—Stockton	Calif.	OF	137	524	102	138	18	11	7	47	.263	314	9	10	.970
1983—El Paso	Texas	●OF-2B	133	554	108	156	23	10	9	78	.282	334	24	●13	.965
1984—El Paso†	Texas	OF	122	496	98	144	19	2	9	72	.290	321	13	6	.982
1985—Vancouver	P. C.	OF-2B	137	563	91	177	16	11	2	43	.314	294	15	4	.987
1985—Milwaukee	Amer.	OF	15	56	8	11	1	0	0	0	.196	32	1	0	1.000
1986—Milwaukee‡	Amer.	OF	44	155	24	37	2	4	1	13	.239	98	0	0	1.000
1986—El Paso	Texas	OF	8	31	10	14	3	0	0	2	.452	14	0	0	1.000
1986—Vancouver	P. C.	OF	39	153	21	40	3	4	1	15	.261	83	4	4	.956
1987—Milwaukee	Amer.	OF-2B	108	289	48	77	5	7	2	31	.266	190	10	5	.976
1987—Denver	A. A.	OF-2B	27	113	26	41	6	2	2	20	.363	75	3	1	.987
1988—Milwaukee§	Amer.	OF-2B	50	81	14	14	1	0	0	5	.173	40	1	1	.976
1988—Denver	A. A.	OF	20	78	10	21	4	1	0	5	.269	55	1	1	.982
1989—Milwaukee	Amer.	OF-2B	117	315	50	76	11	3	3	23	.241	203	24	4	.983
1990—Milwaukee x	Amer.	OF-2B-3B	121	237	38	65	7	2	3	27	.274	167	9	5	.972
Major League Totals—6 Years			455	1133	182	280	27	16	9	99	.247	730	45	15	.981

Selected by Milwaukee Brewers' organization in 3rd round of free-agent draft, January 13, 1981.
†On disabled list, April 15 to April 26, 1984.
‡On disabled list, May 3 to June 5, 1986; included rehabilitation disability assignment to El Paso, May 23 to June 5, 1986.
§On disabled list, May 31 to August 2, 1988; included rehabilitation disability assignment to Denver, June 24 to July 1 and July 15 to July 28, 1988.
xOn suspended list, August 27 to August 30, 1990.

JUNIOR FRANCISCO FELIX (SANCHEZ)

Born October 3, 1967, at Laguna Sabada, Dominican Republic.
Height, 5.11. Weight, 180.
Throws right and bats left and righthanded.

Shares major league record by hitting home run in first major league at-bat, May 4, 1989.
Major League stolen bases: 1989 (18), 1990 (13). Totals—31.
Led South Atlantic League in caught stealing with 28 in 1987.
Led Pioneer League batters in strikeouts with 84, stolen bases with 37, caught stealing with 9 and tied for lead in being hit by pitch with 6 in 1986.
Led Pioneer League outfielders in total chances with 165 in 1986.

Year Club	League	Pos.	G.	AB.	R.	H.	2B.	3B.	HR.	RBI.	B.A.	PO.	A.	E.	F.A.
1986—Medicine Hat	Pion.	OF	67	263	57	75	9	3	4	28	.285	★152	8	5	.970
1987—Myrtle Beach	S. Atl.	OF	124	466	70	135	15	●9	12	51	.290	188	8	9	.956
1988—Knoxville†	South.	OF	93	360	52	91	16	5	3	25	.253	190	13	11	.949
1989—Syracuse	Int.	OF	21	87	17	24	4	2	1	10	.276	42	0	1	.977
1989—Toronto	Amer.	OF	110	415	62	107	14	8	9	46	.258	243	9	9	.966
1990—Toronto‡§	Amer.	OF	127	463	73	122	23	7	15	65	.263	244	11	9	.966
Major League Totals—2 Years			237	878	135	229	37	15	24	111	.261	487	20	18	.966

Signed as free agent by Toronto Blue Jays' organization, September 15, 1985.
†On suspended list, July 15, 1988 through remainder of season.
‡On disabled list, July 13 to August 9, 1990.
§Traded with Infielder Luis Sojo and a player to be named later to California Angels for Outfielder Devon White, Pitcher Willie Fraser and a player to be named later, December 2, 1990; Toronto Blue Jays acquired Pitcher Marcus Moore and California acquired Catcher Ken Rivers to complete deal, December 4, 1990.

CHAMPIONSHIP SERIES RECORD

Year Club	League	Pos.	G.	AB.	R.	H.	2B.	3B.	HR.	RBI.	B.A.	PO.	A.	E.	F.A.
1989—Toronto	Amer.	OF	3	11	0	3	1	0	0	3	.273	8	0	0	1.000

FELIX JOSE FERMIN

Born October 9, 1963, at Mao, Valverde, D. R.
Height, 5.11 Weight, 170.
Throws and bats righthanded.

Shares major league record for most sacrifice hits, game (4), August 22, 1989 (10 innings).

Holds American League record for fewest long hits, season, 150 or more games (10), 1989.
Major League stolen bases: 1988 (3), 1989 (6), 1990 (3). Total—12.
Led American League in sacrifice hits with 32 in 1989.
Led Eastern League shortstops in fielding percentage with .968 in 1987.
Led Eastern League shortstops in total chances with 661 in 1985.
Tied for New York-Pennsylvania League lead in double plays by shortstops with 38 in 1983.

Year	Club	League	Pos.	G.	AB.	R.	H.	2B.	3B.	HR.	RBI.	B.A.	PO.	A.	E.	F.A.
1983—Watertown	NYP	SS	67	234	27	46	6	1	0	14	.197	94	223	30	.914
1983—Bradenton Pir.	Gulf C.	SS	1	4	1	1	0	0	0	1	.250	1	4	0	1.000
1984—Prince William	Carol.	SS	119	382	34	94	13	1	0	41	.246	181	376	23	★.960
1985—Nashua	East.	★SS-2B	137	443	32	100	10	2	0	27	.226	★251	387	24	★.964
1986—Hawaii	P.C.	SS-2B	39	125	13	32	5	0	0	9	.256	60	99	7	.958
1986—Prince William	Carol.	SS	84	322	58	90	10	1	0	26	.280	158	205	19	.950
1987—Harrisburg	East.	SS-2B	100	399	62	107	9	5	0	35	.268	177	288	15	.969
1987—Pittsburgh†	Nat.	SS	23	68	6	17	0	0	0	4	.250	36	62	2	.980
1988—Buffalo	A. A.	SS	87	352	38	92	11	1	0	31	.261	131	268	10	.976
1988—Pittsburgh‡	Nat.	SS	43	87	9	24	0	2	0	2	.276	51	76	6	.955
1989—Cleveland	Amer.	SS-2B	156	484	50	115	9	1	0	21	.238	253	517	★26	.967
1990—Cleveland	Amer.	SS-2B	148	414	47	106	13	2	1	40	.256	214	423	16	.975
National League Totals—2 Years			66	155	15	41	0	2	0	6	.265	87	138	8	.966
American League Totals—2 Years			304	898	97	221	22	3	1	61	.246	467	940	42	.971
Major League Totals—4 Years			370	1053	112	262	22	5	1	67	.249	554	1078	50	.970

Signed as free agent by Pittsburgh Pirates' organization, June 11, 1983.
†On disabled list, July 19 to August 24, 1987; included rehabilitation disability assignment to Harrisburg, August 12 to August 24, 1987.
‡Traded to Cleveland Indians for Shortstop Jay Bell, March 25, 1989.

ALEXANDER FERNANDEZ
(Alex)

Born August 13, 1969, at Miami Beach, Fla.
Height, 6.01. Weight, 205.
Throws and bats righthanded.
Attended University of Miami, Coral Gables, Fla., and
Miami-Dade Community College (South), Miami, Fla.

Received reported $350,000 bonus to sign with Chicago White Sox, 1990.

Year	Club	League	G.	IP.	W.	L.	Pct.	H.	R.	ER.	SO.	BB.	ERA.
1990—Sarasota White Sox	Gulf Coast	2	10	1	0	1.000	11	4	4	16	1	3.60
1990—Sarasota	Florida St.	2	14⅔	1	1	.500	8	4	3	23	3	1.84
1990—Birmingham	Southern	4	25	3	0	1.000	20	7	3	27	6	1.08
1990—Chicago	American	13	87⅔	5	5	.500	89	40	37	61	34	3.80
Major League Totals—1 Year		13	87⅔	5	5	.500	89	40	37	61	34	3.80

Selected by Milwaukee Brewers' organization in 1st round (24th player selected) of free-agent draft, June 1, 1988.
Selected by Chicago White Sox' organization in 1st round (fourth player selected) of free-agent draft, June 4, 1990.

CHARLES SIDNEY FERNANDEZ
(Sid)

Born October 12, 1962, at Honolulu, Haw.
Height, 6.01. Weight, 230.
Throws and bats lefthanded.

Pitched 1-0 no-hit victory against Fort Lauderdale, June 8, 1982.
Pitched 5-0 no-hit victory against Winter Haven, April 24, 1982.
Major League saves: 1986 (1).
Named Texas League Pitcher of the Year, 1983.

Year	Club	League	G.	IP.	W.	L.	Pct.	H.	R.	ER.	SO.	BB.	ERA.
1981—Lethbridge	Pioneer	11	76	5	1	.833	43	21	13	★128	31	★1.54
1982—Vero Beach	Florida St.	12	84⅔	8	1	.889	38	19	18	★137	38	1.91
1982—Albuquerque	P. Coast	13	88	6	5	.545	76	54	53	86	52	5.42
1983—San Antonio	Texas	24	153	●13	4	.765	111	61	48	★209	96	★2.82
1983—Los Angeles†	National	2	6	0	1	.000	7	4	4	9	7	6.00
1984—Tidewater	Int'national	17	105⅔	6	5	.545	69	39	30	123	63	2.56
1984—New York	National	15	90	6	6	.500	74	40	35	62	34	3.50
1985—Tidewater	Int'national	5	35⅓	4	1	.800	17	8	8	42	21	2.04
1985—New York	National	26	170⅓	9	9	.500	108	56	53	180	80	2.80
1986—New York	National	32	204⅓	16	6	.727	161	82	80	200	91	3.52
1987—New York‡	National	28	156	12	8	.600	130	75	66	134	67	3.81
1988—New York	National	31	187	12	10	.545	127	69	63	189	70	3.03
1989—New York	National	35	219⅓	14	5	★.737	157	73	69	198	75	2.83
1990—New York	National	30	179⅓	9	14	.391	130	79	69	181	67	3.46
Major League Totals—8 Years		199	1212⅓	78	59	.569	894	478	439	1153	491	3.26

Selected by Los Angeles Dodgers' organization in 3rd round of free-agent draft, June 8, 1981.
†Traded with Infielder Ross Jones to New York Mets for Pitcher Carlos Diaz and a player to be named later, December 8, 1983; Los Angeles Dodgers acquired Infielder Bob Bailor to complete deal, December 12, 1983.
†On disabled list, August 4 to August 22, 1987.

Year	Club	League	G.	IP.	W.	L.	Pct.	H.	R.	ER.	SO.	BB.	ERA.
1986—New York		National	1	6	0	1	.000	3	3	3	5	1	4.50
1988—New York		National	1	4	0	1	.000	7	6	6	5	1	13.50
Championship Series Totals—2 Years			2	10	0	2	.000	10	9	9	10	2	8.10

WORLD SERIES RECORD

Year	Club	League	G.	IP.	W.	L.	Pct.	H.	R.	ER.	SO.	BB.	ERA.
1986—New York		National	3	6⅔	0	0	.000	6	1	1	10	1	1.35

ALL-STAR GAME RECORD

Year	League	IP.	W.	L.	Pct.	H.	R.	ER.	SO.	BB.	ERA.
1986—National		1	0	0	.000	0	0	0	3	2	0.00
1987—National		1	0	0	.000	0	0	0	1	1	0.00
All-Star Game Totals—2 Years		2	0	0	.000	0	0	0	4	3	0.00

OCTAVIO ANTONIO FERNANDEZ (CASTRO)
(Tony)

Born June 30, 1962, at San Pedro de Macoris, D. R.
Height, 6.02. Weight, 175.
Throws right and bats right and lefthanded.

Holds major league record for highest fielding average, shortstop, season, 100 or more games (.992), 1989.
Holds American League record for most games by shortstop, season (163), 1986.
Shares American League record for most games by switch-hitter, season (163), 1986.
Major League stolen bases: 1984 (5), 1985 (13), 1986 (25), 1987 (32), 1988 (15), 1989 (22), 1990 (26). Total—138.
Led American League shortstops in total chances with 791 in 1985 and 786 in 1990.
Led International League shortstops in double plays with 87 in 1983.
Named shortstop on THE SPORTING NEWS American League All-Star Team, 1986.
Named shortstop on THE SPORTING NEWS American League All-Star fielding team, 1986 through 1989.

Year	Club	League	Pos.	G.	AB.	R.	H.	2B.	3B.	HR.	RBI.	B.A.	PO.	A.	E.	F.A.
1980—Kinston		Carol.	SS	62	187	28	52	6	2	0	12	.278	93	205	28	.914
1981—Kinston		Carol.	SS	75	280	57	89	10	6	1	13	.318	121	227	19	.948
1981—Syracuse†		Int.	SS	31	115	13	32	6	2	1	9	.278	69	80	3	.980
1982—Syracuse		Int.	SS	134	523	78	158	21	6	4	56	.302	★246	364	23	★.964
1983—Syracuse		Int.	SS	117	437	65	131	18	6	5	38	.300	★211	361	26	.957
1983—Toronto		Amer.	SS	15	34	5	9	1	1	0	2	.265	16	17	0	1.000
1984—Syracuse		Int.	SS	26	94	12	24	1	0	0	6	.255	46	72	5	.959
1984—Toronto		Amer.	SS-3B	88	233	29	63	5	3	3	19	.269	119	195	9	.972
1985—Toronto		Amer.	SS	161	564	71	163	31	10	2	51	.289	283	★478	30	.962
1986—Toronto		Amer.	SS	★163	★687	91	213	33	9	10	65	.310	★294	445	13	★.983
1987—Toronto		Amer.	SS	146	578	90	186	29	8	5	67	.322	★270	396	14	.979
1988—Toronto		Amer.	SS	154	648	76	186	41	4	5	70	.287	247	470	14	.981
1989—Toronto‡		Amer.	SS	140	573	64	147	25	9	11	64	.257	260	475	6	★.992
1990—Toronto§		Amer.	SS	161	635	84	175	27	★17	4	66	.276	★297	★480	9	.989
Major League Totals—8 Years				1028	3952	510	1142	192	61	40	404	.289	1786	2956	95	.980

Signed as free agent by Toronto Blue Jays' organization, April 24, 1979.
†On disabled list, August 10 to August 27, 1981.
‡On disabled list, April 8 to May 2, 1989.
§Traded with First Baseman Fred McGriff to San Diego Padres for Outfielder Joe Carter and Second Baseman Roberto Alomar, December 5, 1990.

CHAMPIONSHIP SERIES RECORD

Year	Club	League	Pos.	G.	AB.	R.	H.	2B.	3B.	HR.	RBI.	B.A.	PO.	A.	E.	F.A.
1985—Toronto		Amer.	SS	7	24	2	8	2	0	0	2	.333	11	15	2	.929
1989—Toronto		Amer.	SS	5	20	6	7	3	0	0	1	.350	9	15	0	1.000
Championship Series Totals—2 Years				12	44	8	15	5	0	0	3	.341	20	30	2	.962

ALL-STAR GAME RECORD

Year	League	Pos.	AB.	R.	H.	2B.	3B.	HR.	RBI.	B.A.	PO.	A.	E.	F.A.
1986—American		SS	0	0	0	0	0	0	0	.000	0	0	0	.000
1987—American		SS	2	0	0	0	0	0	0	.000	1	3	0	1.000
1989—American		PR-SS	1	0	0	0	0	0	0	.000	2	2	0	1.000
All-Star Game Totals—3 Years			3	0	0	0	0	0	0	.000	3	5	0	1.000

MICHAEL LEE FETTERS
(Mike)

Born December 19, 1964, at Van Nuys, Calif.
Height, 6.04. Weight, 212.
Throws and bats righthanded.
Attended Pepperdine University, Malibu, Calif.

Major League saves: 1990 (1).
Tied for Pacific Coast League lead in complete games with 6 in 1989.

Year	Club	League	G.	IP.	W.	L.	Pct.	H.	R.	ER.	SO.	BB.	ERA.
1986—Salem		Northwest	12	72	4	2	.667	60	39	27	72	51	3.38
1987—Palm Springs		California	19	116	9	7	.563	106	62	46	105	73	3.57

Year Club	League	G.	IP.	W.	L.	Pct.	H.	R.	ER.	SO.	BB.	ERA.
1988—Midland	Texas	20	114	8	8	.500	116	78	75	101	67	5.92
1988—Edmonton	P. Coast	2	14	2	0	1.000	8	3	3	11	10	1.93
1989—Edmonton	P. Coast	26	168	12	8	.600	160	80	71	★144	72	3.80
1989—California	American	1	3⅓	0	0	.000	5	4	3	4	1	8.10
1990—Edmonton	P. Coast	5	27⅓	1	1	.500	22	9	3	26	13	0.99
1990—California	American	26	67⅔	1	1	.500	77	33	31	35	20	4.12
Major League Totals—2 Years		27	71	1	1	.500	82	37	34	39	21	4.31

Selected by Los Angeles Dodgers' organization in 22nd round of free-agent draft, June 6, 1983.
Selected by California Angels' organization in 1st round (compensation selection) of free-agent draft, June 2, 1986.

CECIL GRANT FIELDER

Born September 21, 1963, at Los Angeles, Calif.
Height 6.03. Weight, 240.
Throws and bats righthanded.
Attended University of Nevada, Las Vegas, Nev.

Shares major league record for most games with three home runs, season (2), 1990.
Hit three home runs in a game, May 6, 1990 and June 6, 1990.
Led American League hitters in total bases with 339, slugging percentage with .592 and strikeouts with 182 in 1990.
Led American League first basemen in double plays with 137 in 1990.
Led Pioneer League in total bases with 176 and being hit by pitch with 8 in 1982.
Named American League Player of the Year by THE SPORTING NEWS, 1990.
Named first baseman on THE SPORTING NEWS American League All-Star Team, 1990.
Named first baseman on THE SPORTING NEWS American League Silver Slugger team, 1990.

Year Club	League	Pos.	G.	AB.	R.	H.	2B.	3B.	HR.	RBI.	B.A.	PO.	A.	E.	F.A.
1982—Butte†	Pion.	1B	69	273	73	88	★28	0	★20	68	.322	247	18	4	.985
1983—Florence	S. Atl.	1B	140	500	81	156	28	2	16	94	.312	957	64	16	.985
1984—Kinston	Carol.	1B	61	222	42	63	12	1	19	49	.284	533	24	9	.984
1984—Knoxville	South.	1B	64	236	33	60	12	2	9	44	.254	173	10	4	.979
1985—Knoxville	South.	1B	96	361	52	106	26	2	18	81	.294	444	26	6	.987
1985—Toronto	Amer.	1B	30	74	6	23	4	0	4	16	.311	171	17	4	.979
1986—Toronto	Amer.	1B-3B-OF	34	83	7	13	2	0	4	13	.157	37	4	1	.976
1986—Syracuse	Int.	OF-1B	88	325	47	91	13	3	18	68	.280	117	5	1	.992
1987—Toronto	Amer.	1B-3B	82	175	30	47	7	1	14	32	.269	98	6	0	1.000
1988—Toronto‡	Amer.	1B-3B-2B	74	174	24	40	6	1	9	23	.230	101	12	1	.991
1989—Hanshin§	Central	.....	106	384	60	116	11	0	38	81	.302	Figures Unavailable			
1990—Detroit	Amer.	1B	159	573	104	159	25	1	★51	★132	.277	1190	111	14	.989
Major League Totals—5 Years			379	1079	171	282	44	3	82	216	.261	1597	150	20	.989

Selected by Baltimore Orioles' organization in 31st round of free-agent draft, June 8, 1981.
Selected by Kansas City Royals' organization in secondary phase of free-agent draft, June 7, 1982.
†Traded to Toronto Blue Jays' organization for Outfielder Leon Roberts, February 4, 1983.
‡Sold to Hanshin Tigers of Japanese Baseball League, December 22, 1988.
§Signed by Detroit Tigers, January 15, 1990.

CHAMPIONSHIP SERIES RECORD

Year Club	League	Pos.	G.	AB.	R.	H.	2B.	3B.	HR.	RBI.	B.A.	PO.	A.	E.	F.A.
1985—Toronto	Amer.	PH	3	3	0	1	1	0	0	0	.333	0	0	0	.000

ALL-STAR GAME RECORD

Year League	Pos.	AB.	R.	H.	2B.	3B.	HR.	RBI.	B.A.	PO.	A.	E.	F.A.
1990—American	PH-1B	1	0	0	0	0	0	0	.000	3	1	0	1.000

THOMAS CARSON FILER III
(Tom)

Born December 1, 1956, at Philadelphia, Pa.
Height, 6.01. Weight, 198.
Throws and bats righthanded.
Received bachelor of science degree in marketing from
La Salle College, Philadelphia, Pa., in 1978.

Tied for American Association lead in wild pitches with 11 in 1981.

Year Club	League	G.	IP.	W.	L.	Pct.	H.	R.	ER.	SO.	BB.	ERA.
1978—Oneonta	NYP	9	43	2	3	.400	30	14	8	34	14	1.67
1979—West Haven	Eastern	24	154	12	8	.600	132	73	62	80	53	3.62
1980—Nashville†	Southern	27	187	13	9	.591	168	94	61	112	86	2.94
1981—Columbus‡	Int'national	1	3	0	1	.000	6	5	5	3	4	15.00
1981—Iowa	Am. Assoc.	21	109	4	9	.308	123	64	58	61	57	4.79
1982—Iowa	Am. Assoc.	17	92⅓	6	7	.462	109	74	69	51	31	6.73
1982—Chicago	National	8	40⅔	1	2	.333	50	25	25	15	18	5.53
1983—Iowa	Am. Assoc.	27	108	5	6	.455	128	56	50	56	44	4.17
1984—Iowa §x	Am. Assoc.	26	123⅓	9	7	.563	149	86	67	80	48	4.89
1985—Syracuse y	Int'national	12	78⅓	7	2	.778	67	24	22	31	22	2.53
1985—Toronto z	American	11	48⅔	7	0	1.000	38	21	21	24	18	3.88
1986—Toronto a	American					(Did not play)						
1987—Syracuse	Int'national	8	24⅔	1	0	1.000	23	6	4	9	6	1.46
1987—Knoxville	Southern	6	20⅔	2	0	1.000	13	2	2	14	4	0.87
1987—Dunedin b	Florida St.	6	23	0	0	.000	20	5	2	13	0	0.78
1988—Denver	Am. Assoc.	8	55⅔	4	2	.667	40	14	13	34	9	2.10

Year Club	League	G.	IP.	W.	L.	Pct.	H.	R.	ER.	SO.	BB.	ERA.
1988—Milwaukee..................	American	19	101⅔	5	8	.385	108	54	50	39	33	4.43
1989—Denver c................	Am. Assoc.	12	83⅔	5	1	.833	77	28	26	34	14	2.80
1989—Milwaukee d..............	American	13	72⅓	7	3	.700	74	30	29	20	23	3.61
1990—Milwaukee e..............	American	7	22	2	3	.400	26	17	15	8	9	6.14
1990—Denver f................	Am. Assoc.	9	51⅓	3	5	.375	70	39	37	22	9	6.49
National League Totals—1 Year............		8	40⅔	1	2	.333	50	25	25	15	18	5.53
American League Totals—4 Years..........		50	244⅔	21	14	.600	246	122	115	91	83	4.23
Major League Totals—5 Years............		58	285⅓	22	16	.579	296	147	140	106	101	4.42

Signed as free agent by New York Yankees' organization, June 28, 1978.
†Drafted by Oakland A's, December 8, 1980; returned, April 9, 1981.
‡Traded with cash to Chicago Cubs' organization for Catcher Barry Foote, April 27, 1981.
§On disabled list, April 20 to May 12 and August 11 to August 22, 1984.
xGranted free agency, October 15, 1984; signed by Syracuse (Toronto Blue Jays' organization), November 21, 1984.
yOn disabled list, April 24 to May 4 and May 16 to May 26, 1985.
zOn disabled list, August 28 to September 12, 1985.
aOn disabled list, March 27, 1986 through entire season.
bSold to Denver (Milwaukee Brewers' organization), October 6, 1987.
cOn Milwaukee disabled list, April 2 to May 8, 1989.
dAppeared in one game as a pinch-runner.
eOn disabled list, April 30 to May 15 and June 3 to August 20, 1990; included rehabilitation disability assignment to Denver, July 20 to August 18, 1990.
fReleased, October 16, 1990.

WILLIAM PETER FILSON
(Pete)

Born September 28, 1958, at Darby, Pa.
Height, 6.02. Weight, 185.
Throws left and bats left and righthanded.
Attended Temple University, Philadelphia, Pa.

Pitched seven-inning, 4-0 no-hit victory against Gastonia, April 25, 1980 (first game).
Pitched seven-inning, 10-0 no-hit victory against Kingsport, August 7, 1979 (second game).
Major League saves: 1983 (1), 1984 (1), 1985 (2). Total—4.
Led International League in complete games with 11 and balks with 8 in 1982.
Led Appalachian League in complete games with 9, shutouts with 3 and balks with 4 in 1979.
Named American Association Pitcher of the Year, 1986.

Year Club	League	G.	IP.	W.	L.	Pct.	H.	R.	ER.	SO.	BB.	ERA.
1979—Paintsville................	Ap'lachian	13	*91	*9	0	*1.000	51	19	17	*118	39	*1.68
1979—Oneonta................	NYP	1	1	0	0	.000	0	0	0	1	0	0.00
1980—Greensboro................	S. Atlantic	4	27	3	0	1.000	13	5	5	34	14	1.67
1980—Fort Lauderdale...........	Florida St.	23	144	10	9	.526	105	56	48	86	69	3.00
1981—Fort Lauderdale...........	Florida St.	11	68	7	1	.875	56	20	15	68	20	1.99
1981—Nashville................	Southern	14	99	10	2	●.833	73	30	20	77	28	1.82
1982—Columbus†-Toledo.........	Int'national	23	150⅔	8	10	.444	168	87	77	84	53	4.60
1982—Minnesota................	American	5	12⅓	0	2	.000	17	12	12	10	8	8.76
1983—Minnesota‡................	American	26	90	4	1	.800	87	34	34	49	29	3.40
1983—Toledo................	Int'national	2	7	0	1	.000	8	6	6	6	3	7.71
1984—Minnesota................	American	55	118⅔	6	5	.545	106	56	54	59	54	4.10
1985—Minnesota................	American	40	95⅔	4	5	.444	93	42	39	42	30	3.67
1986—Minnesota§-Chicago.......	American	7	18	0	1	.000	27	13	12	8	7	6.00
1986—Buffalo x................	Am. Assoc.	36	139	*14	3	.824	116	46	35	81	32	*2.27
1987—Columbus................	Int'national	22	135	12	4	.750	153	62	56	73	43	3.73
1987—New York y................	American	7	22	1	0	1.000	26	10	8	10	9	3.27
1988—Sarasota Yankees za......	Gulf Coast	1	1	0	0	.000	0	0	0	1	0	0.00
1989—Baseball City............	Florida St.	8	46	4	0	1.000	47	20	17	20	12	3.33
1989—Memphis................	Southern	10	58⅔	6	2	.750	67	34	27	31	18	4.14
1990—Omaha................	Am. Assoc.	17	107	12	2	.857	107	41	33	66	31	2.78
1990—Kansas City bc............	American	8	35	0	4	.000	42	31	23	9	13	5.91
Major League Totals—7 Years............		148	391⅔	15	18	.455	398	198	182	187	150	4.18

Selected by New York Yankees' organization in 8th round of free-agent draft, June 5, 1979.
†Traded with infielder Larry Milbourne and Pitcher John Pacella to Minnesota Twins for Catcher Butch Wynegar and Pitcher Roger Erickson, May 12, 1982.
‡On disabled list, July 13 to August 3, 1983.
§Loaned to Buffalo (Chicago White Sox' organization) in exchange for sale of Pitcher Juan Agosto to Minnesota Twins and traded to Chicago White Sox for Pitcher Kurt Walker, September 3, 1986.
xTraded with infielder Randy Velarde to New York Yankees for Pitcher Scott Nielson and Infielder Mike Soper, January 5, 1987.
yReleased, March 29, 1988; signed by Columbus (New York Yankees' organization), April 4, 1988.
zOn Columbus disabled list, April 7, 1988 through remainder of season.
aGranted free agency, October 15, 1988; signed by Memphis (Kansas City Royals' organization), May 31, 1989.
bOn disabled list, August 12, 1990 through remainder of season.
cReleased, October 4, 1990.

—DID YOU KNOW—

That last year, the Cubs had their first trio of .300 hitters (Andre Dawson, Mark Grace, Ryne Sandberg) since 1945 (Phil Cavarretta, Stan Hack, Don Johnson)?

CHARLES EDWARD FINLEY
(Chuck)

Born November 26, 1962 at Monroe, La.
Height, 6.06. Weight, 215.
Throws and bats lefthanded.
Attended Northeast Louisiana State University, Monroe, La.

Named lefthanded pitcher on THE SPORTING NEWS American League All-Star Team, 1989 and 1990.

Year Club	League	G.	IP.	W.	L.	Pct.	H.	R.	ER.	SO.	BB.	ERA.
1985—Salem	Northwest	18	29	3	1	.750	34	21	15	32	10	4.66
1986—Quad Cities	Midwest	10	12	1	0	1.000	4	0	0	16	3	0.00
1986—California	American	25	46⅓	3	1	.750	40	17	17	37	23	3.30
1987—California	American	35	90⅔	2	7	.222	102	54	47	63	43	4.67
1988—California	American	31	194⅓	9	15	.375	191	95	90	111	82	4.17
1989—California†	American	29	199⅔	16	9	.640	171	64	57	156	82	2.57
1990—California	American	32	236	18	9	.667	210	77	63	177	81	2.40
Major League Totals—5 Years		152	767	48	41	.539	714	307	274	544	311	3.22

Selected by California Angels' organization in 15th round of free-agent draft, June 4, 1984.
Selected by California Angels' organization in secondary phase of free-agent draft, January 9, 1985.
†On disabled list, August 22 to September 15, 1989.

CHAMPIONSHIP SERIES RECORD

Year Club	League	G.	IP.	W.	L.	Pct.	H.	R.	ER.	SO.	BB.	ERA.
1986—California	American	3	2	0	0	.000	1	0	0	1	0	0.00

ALL-STAR GAME RECORD

Year League	IP.	W.	L.	Pct.	H.	R.	ER.	SO.	BB.	ERA.
1990—American	1	0	0	.000	0	0	0	1	1	0.00

Member of American League All-Star Team in 1989; did not play.

STEVEN ALLEN FINLEY
(Steve)

Born March 12, 1965, at Union City, Tenn.
Height, 6.02. Weight, 175.
Throws and bats lefthanded.
Attended Southern Illinois University, Carbondale, Ill.

Major League stolen bases: 1989 (17), 1990 (22). Total—39.
Led International League outfielders in total chances with 315 in 1988.

Year Club	League	Pos.	G.	AB.	R.	H.	2B.	3B.	HR.	RBI.	B.A.	PO.	A.	E.	F.A.
1987—Newark	NYP	OF	54	222	40	65	13	2	3	33	.293	122	7	4	.970
1987—Hagerstown	Carol.	OF	15	65	9	22	3	2	1	5	.338	32	3	0	1.000
1988—Hagerstown	Carol.	OF	8	28	2	6	2	0	0	3	.214	17	0	0	1.000
1988—Charlotte	South.	OF	10	40	7	12	4	2	1	6	.300	14	0	0	1.000
1988—Rochester	Int.	OF	120	456	61	★143	19	7	5	54	★.314	★289	14	★12	.962
1989—Baltimore†	Amer.	OF	81	217	35	54	5	2	2	25	.249	144	1	2	.986
1989—Rochester	Int.	OF	7	25	2	4	0	0	0	2	.160	17	2	0	1.000
1989—Hagerstown	East.	OF	11	48	11	20	3	1	0	7	.417	35	2	3	.925
1990—Baltimore	Amer.	OF	142	464	46	119	16	4	3	37	.256	298	4	7	.977
Major League Totals—2 Years			223	681	81	173	21	6	5	62	.254	442	5	9	.980

Selected by Atlanta Braves' organization in 11th round of free-agent draft, June 2, 1986.
Selected by Baltimore Orioles' organization in 13th round of free-agent draft, June 2, 1987.
†On disabled list, April 4 to April 22 and July 29 to September 1, 1989; included rehabilitation disability assignment to Hagerstown, August 21 to August 23, 1989.

BRIAN KEVIN FISHER

Born March 18, 1962, at Honolulu, Haw.
Height, 6.04. Weight, 210.
Throws and bats righthanded.
Attended Columbia College, Aurora, Colo.

Major League saves: 1985 (14), 1986 (6), 1988 (1), 1989 (1). Total—22.
Led International League pitchers in games started with 29 in 1984.
Tied for South Atlantic League lead in balks with 4 in 1981.

Year Club	League	G.	IP.	W.	L.	Pct.	H.	R.	ER.	SO.	BB.	ERA.
1980—Bradenton Braves	Gulf Coast	12	61	5	3	.625	55	34	26	48	★53	3.84
1981—Anderson	S. Atlantic	25	152	6	8	.429	139	96	72	152	94	4.26
1982—Durham†	Carolina	18	104	6	6	.500	72	43	32	129	43	2.77
1983—Savannah	Southern	27	150	8	11	.421	172	101	87	103	56	5.22
1984—Richmond‡	Int'national	29	183	9	11	.450	188	●101	★87	122	●100	4.28
1985—Columbus	Int'national	7	11⅓	0	0	.000	8	4	3	12	7	2.38
1985—New York	American	55	98⅓	4	4	.500	77	32	26	85	29	2.38
1986—New York	American	62	96⅔	9	5	.643	105	61	53	67	37	4.93
1986—Columbus§	Int'national	6	8⅔	0	0	.000	8	4	4	4	3	4.15
1987—Pittsburgh	National	37	185⅓	11	9	.550	185	99	93	117	72	4.52
1988—Pittsburgh x	National	33	146⅓	8	10	.444	157	78	75	66	57	4.61
1989—Buffalo y	Am. Assoc.	5	28	3	0	1.000	30	17	16	15	7	5.14
1989—Pittsburgh z	National	9	17	0	3	.000	25	17	15	8	10	7.94

Year	Club	League	G.	IP.	W.	L.	Pct.	H.	R.	ER.	SO.	BB.	ERA.
1990—Tucson		P. Coast	30	87⅓	8	8	.500	113	72	66	47	36	6.80
1990—Houston a		National	4	5	0	0	.000	9	5	4	1	0	7.20
American League Totals—2 Years			117	195	13	9	.591	182	93	79	152	66	3.65
National League Totals—4 Years			83	353⅔	19	22	.463	376	199	187	192	139	4.76
Major League Totals—6 Years			200	548⅔	32	31	.508	558	292	266	344	205	4.36

Selected by Atlanta Braves' organization in 2nd round of free-agent draft, June 3, 1980.
†On disabled list, May 18 to July 1, 1982.
‡Traded to New York Yankees for Catcher Rick Cerone, December 5, 1984.
§Traded with Pitchers Doug Drabek and Logan Easley to Pittsburgh Pirates for Pitchers Rick Rhoden, Cecilio Guante and Pat Clements, November 26, 1986.
xOn disabled list, April 30 to May 15, 1988.
yOn Pittsburgh disabled list, March 30 to April 16, June 12 to July 13 and July 25 to September 20, 1989; included rehabilitation disability assignment to Buffalo, June 16 to July 4, 1989.
zReleased, November 29, 1989; signed by Houston Astros, February 1, 1990.
aReleased, August 28, 1990.

THOMAS JOHN FISCHER
(Tom)

Born March 23, 1967, at West Bend, Wis.
Height, 5.11. Weight, 195.
Throws and bats lefthanded.
Attended University of Wisconsin, Madison, Wis.
Nephew of Bill Fischer, pitcher with Chicago White Sox, Detroit Tigers, Washington Senators, Kansas City Athletics and Minnesota Twins, 1956 through 1964; scout, Kansas City Royals, 1969 through 1974; minor league pitching instructor, Kansas City Royals, 1975 through 1978 and 1984; coach, Cincinnati Reds, 1979 through 1983; and coach with Boston Red Sox since 1985.

Tied for Carolina League lead in games started by pitchers with 27 in 1989.
Received reported $110,000 bonus to sign with Boston Red Sox, 1988.

Year	Club	League	G.	IP.	W.	L.	Pct.	H.	R.	ER.	SO.	BB.	ERA.
1988—Lynchburg		Carolina	14	76⅔	7	4	.636	72	37	30	63	25	3.52
1989—Lynchburg		Carolina	28	171⅓	12	13	.480	178	94	★91	138	79	4.78
1990—New Britain		Eastern	27	163⅓	13	10	.565	166	★89	★76	116	64	4.19

Selected by Boston Red Sox' organization in 1st round (10th player selected) of free-agent draft, June 1, 1988.

CARLTON ERNEST FISK

Born December 26, 1947, at Bellows Falls, Vt.
Height, 6.02. Weight, 225.
Throws and bats righthanded.
Attended University of New Hampshire, Durham, N. H.
Brother of Calvin Fisk, former catcher in Baltimore Orioles' organization;
brother-in-law of Rick Miller, outfielder with Boston Red Sox and California Angels, 1971 through 1985;
and cousin of Dave Jennings, punter with New York Giants and New York Jets, 1974 through 1987.

Holds major league records for most home runs by catcher, lifetime (332), longest game with no passed balls (25 innings), and most innings played by catcher, game (25), May 8, finished May 9, 1984.
Shares major league records for most at-bats (11) and plate appearances (12), game, May 8, finished May 9, 1984 (25 innings); most home runs, opening game of season (2), April 6, 1973.
Shares modern major league record for most long hits, inning (2), May 15, 1975, eighth inning; and June 30, 1977, eighth inning.
Holds American League records for most years (21), games (2,041), putouts (10,505), chances accepted (11,469), catcher, lifetime; home runs, catcher, season (33), 1985.
Shares American League records for most seasons, catcher (20); fewest passed balls, season, 150 or more games (4), 1977.
Major League stolen bases: 1972 (5), 1973 (7), 1974 (5), 1975 (4), 1976 (12), 1977 (7), 1978 (7), 1979 (3), 1980 (11), 1981 (3), 1982 (17), 1983 (9), 1984 (6), 1985 (17), 1986 (2), 1987 (1), 1989 (1), 1990 (7). Total—124.
Hit for the cycle, May 16, 1984.
Led American League in being hit by pitch with 13 in 1980.
Led American League in passed balls with 11 in 1983.
Led American League catchers in double plays with 10 in 1981 and 15 in 1987.
Led American League catches in putouts with 470 in 1981.
Led American League catchers in errors with 10 in 1980.
Led American League catchers in total chances with 933 in 1972, 803 in 1973, 519 in 1981 and 871 in 1985.
Led International League catchers in double plays with 12 in 1971.
Named THE SPORTING NEWS American League Rookie Player of the Year, 1972.
Named American League Rookie of the Year by Baseball Writers' Association of America, 1972.
Named catcher on THE SPORTING NEWS American League All-Star Team, 1972, 1977, 1983, 1985 and 1990.
Named catcher on THE SPORTING NEWS American League All-Star fielding team, 1972.
Named catcher on THE SPORTING NEWS American League Silver Slugger team, 1981, 1985 and 1988.

Year	Club	League	Pos.	G.	AB.	R.	H.	2B.	3B.	HR.	RBI.	B.A.	PO.	A.	E.	F.A.
1967—Greenville†		W. Car.					(In Military Service)								
1968—Waterloo‡		Midw.	C	62	195	31	66	11	2	12	34	.338	385	42	8	.982
1969—Pittsfield		East.	C	97	309	38	75	18	3	10	41	.243	551	65	★22	.966
1969—Boston		Amer.	C	2	5	0	0	0	0	0	0	.000	2	0	0	1.000
1970—Pawtucket		East.	C-OF-1B	93	284	43	65	18	1	12	44	.229	482	50	7	.987
1971—Louisville		Int.	C-OF-3B	94	308	45	81	10	4	10	43	.263	588	51	13	.980
1971—Boston		Amer.	C	14	48	7	15	2	1	2	6	.313	72	6	2	.975
1972—Boston		Amer.	C	131	457	74	134	28	●9	22	61	.293	★846	★72	●15	.984
1973—Boston		Amer.	C	135	508	65	125	21	0	26	71	.246	★739	50	★14	.983

Year	Club	League	Pos.	G.	AB.	R.	H.	2B.	3B.	HR.	RBI.	B.A.	PO.	A.	E.	F.A.
1974—Boston§	Amer.	C	52	187	36	56	12	1	11	26	.299	267	26	6	.980
1975—Boston x	Amer.	C	79	263	47	87	14	4	10	52	.331	347	30	8	.979
1976—Boston	Amer.	C	134	487	76	124	17	5	17	58	.255	649	73	12	.984
1977—Boston	Amer.	C	152	536	106	169	26	3	26	102	.315	779	69	11	.987
1978—Boston	Amer.	★C-OF	157	571	94	162	39	5	20	88	.284	734	90	★17	.980
1979—Boston y	Amer.	C-OF	91	320	49	87	23	2	10	42	.272	155	8	3	.982
1980—Boston z	Amer.	C-1-O-3	131	478	73	138	25	3	18	62	.289	543	56	11	.982
1981—Chicago	Amer.	C-1-3-O	96	338	44	89	12	0	7	45	.263	479	46	6	.989
1982—Chicago	Amer.	C-1B	135	476	66	127	17	3	14	65	.267	648	63	5	.993
1983—Chicago	Amer.	C	138	488	85	141	26	4	26	86	.289	★709	46	7	.991
1984—Chicago a	Amer.	C	102	359	54	83	20	1	21	43	.231	421	38	6	.987
1985—Chicago b	Amer.	C	153	543	85	129	23	1	37	107	.238	★801	60	10	.989
1986—Chicago	Amer.	C-OF	125	457	42	101	11	0	14	63	.221	455	44	8	.984
1987—Chicago c	Amer.	C-1B-OF	135	454	68	116	22	1	23	71	.256	597	66	7	.990
1988—Chicago d	Amer.	C	76	253	37	70	8	1	19	50	.277	338	36	2	.995
1989—Chicago e	Amer.	C	103	375	47	110	25	2	13	68	.293	419	37	3	★.993
1990—Chicago	Amer.	C	137	452	65	129	21	0	18	65	.285	660	63	4	.994
Major League Totals—21 Years				2278	8055	1220	2192	392	46	354	1231	.272	10660	979	157	.987

Selected by Baltimore Orioles' organization in 36th round of free-agent draft, June, 1965.
Selected by Boston Red Sox' organization in 1st round (fourth player selected) of free-agent draft, January, 1967.
†On temporary inactive list, April 17, 1967; transferred to military list, May 18, 1967 through April 9, 1968.
‡On temporary inactive list, August 5 to August 20, 1968.
§On disabled list, March 21 to April 26 and June 28, 1974 through remainder of season.
xOn disabled list, March 24 to June 23, 1975.
yOn disabled list, April 14 to May 21, 1979.
zGranted free agency by arbitrator's ruling, February 12, 1981; signed by Chicago White Sox, March 18, 1981.
aOn disabled list, June 13 to July 5, 1984.
bGranted free agency, November 12, 1985; re-signed by White Sox, January 8, 1986.
cGranted free agency, January 22, 1988; re-signed by White Sox, February 9, 1988.
dOn disabled list, May 11 to July 28, 1988.
eOn disabled list, April 11 to June 1, 1989.

CHAMPIONSHIP SERIES RECORD

Year	Club	League	Pos.	G.	AB.	R.	H.	2B.	3B.	HR.	RBI.	B.A.	PO.	A.	E.	F.A.
1975—Boston	Amer.	C	3	12	4	5	1	0	0	2	.417	15	0	0	1.000
1983—Chicago	Amer.	C	4	17	0	3	1	0	0	0	.176	27	3	0	1.000
Championship Series Totals—2 Years			7	29	4	8	2	0	0	2	.276	42	3	0	1.000

WORLD SERIES RECORD

Shares World Series record for most at-bats, inning (2), October 15, 1975, fourth inning.

Year	Club	League	Pos.	G.	AB.	R.	H.	2B.	3B.	HR.	RBI.	B.A.	PO.	A.	E.	F.A.
1975—Boston	Amer.	C	7	25	5	6	0	0	2	4	.240	37	3	2	.952

ALL-STAR GAME RECORD

Year	League	Pos.	AB.	R.	H.	2B.	3B.	HR.	RBI.	B.A.	PO.	A.	E.	F.A.
1972—American		C	2	1	1	0	0	0	0	.500	2	0	0	1.000
1973—American		C	2	0	0	0	0	0	0	.000	3	0	0	1.000
1976—American		C	1	0	0	0	0	0	0	.000	1	0	0	1.000
1977—American		C	2	0	0	0	0	0	0	.000	6	1	0	1.000
1978—American		C	2	0	0	0	0	0	1	.000	4	0	0	1.000
1980—American		C	2	0	0	0	0	0	0	.000	5	0	0	1.000
1981—American		C	3	1	1	0	0	0	0	.333	4	0	0	1.000
1982—American		C	2	0	0	0	0	0	0	.000	2	0	0	1.000
1985—American		C	2	0	0	0	0	0	0	.000	2	0	0	1.000
All-Star Game Totals—9 Years			18	2	2	0	0	0	1	.111	29	1	0	1.000

Named to American League All-Star Team for 1974 game; replaced due to injury.

MICHAEL ROY FITZGERALD
(Mike)

Born July 13, 1960, at Long Beach, Calif.
Height, 5.11. Weight, 190.
Throws and bats righthanded.
Nephew of Dan Gausepohl, outfielder in San Diego
Padres' organization, 1979 through 1982.

Shares major league record by hitting home run in first major league at-bat, September 13, 1983.
Major League stolen bases: 1984 (1), 1985 (5), 1986 (3), 1987 (3), 1988 (2), 1989 (3), 1990 (8). Total—25.
Tied for National League lead in double plays by catchers with 10 in 1990.
Led Carolina League in sacrifice flies with 11 in 1979.

Year	Club	League	Pos.	G.	AB.	R.	H.	2B.	3B.	HR.	RBI.	B.A.	PO.	A.	E.	F.A.
1978—Little Falls	NYP	C	48	140	25	36	10	0	5	21	.257	230	37	1	.996
1979—Lynchburg	Carol.	C	117	368	55	93	16	4	13	★75	.253	424	60	10	.980
1980—Alex.†-Lynch.	Carol.	C-1B-OF	105	338	36	71	10	2	10	44	.210	438	45	7	.986
1981—Jackson	Texas	C-1-O-3	66	218	28	68	14	2	4	29	.312	344	52	3	.992
1981—Tidewater	Int.	C-OF	24	58	9	9	2	0	1	3	.155	124	9	2	.985
1982—Tidewater	Int.	C-1-O-3	94	302	33	74	9	2	4	36	.245	451	34	7	.986
1983—Tidewater	Int.	C-1-3-O	111	370	64	105	17	1	14	65	.284	588	62	8	.988

Year Club	League	Pos.	G.	AB.	R.	H.	2B.	3B.	HR.	RBI.	B.A.	PO.	A.	E.	F.A.
1983—New York	Nat.	C	8	20	1	2	0	0	1	2	.100	37	8	2	.957
1984—New York‡	Nat.	C	112	360	20	87	15	1	2	33	.242	715	47	4	★.995
1985—Montreal	Nat.	C	108	295	25	61	7	1	5	34	.207	542	46	8	.987
1986—Indianapolis	A. A.	C	10	32	4	11	3	0	0	4	.344	58	5	1	.984
1986—Montreal§	Nat.	C	73	209	20	59	13	1	6	37	.282	415	35	3	.993
1987—Montreal x	Nat.	C-1B-2B	107	287	32	69	11	0	3	36	.240	603	27	12	.981
1988—Montreal	Nat.	C-OF	63	155	17	42	6	1	5	23	.271	262	21	6	.979
1988—Indianapolis	A. A.	C	32	96	12	24	6	1	1	13	.250	234	11	2	.992
1989—Montreal	Nat.	C-3B-OF	100	290	33	69	18	2	7	42	.238	465	44	8	.985
1990—Montreal	Nat.	C-OF	111	313	36	76	18	1	9	41	.243	565	42	6	.990
Major League Totals—8 Years			682	1929	184	465	88	7	38	248	.241	3604	270	49	.988

Selected by New York Mets' organization in 6th round of free-agent draft, June 6, 1978.

†Loaned to Alexandria (Co-op), April 8, 1980; returned, May 31, 1980.

‡Traded with Infielder Hubie Brooks, Outfielder Herm Winningham and Pitcher Floyd Youmans to Montreal Expos for Catcher Gary Carter, December 10, 1984.

§On disabled list, August 2, 1986 through remainder of season.

xOn disabled list, March 28 to April 20, 1987.

MICHAEL KENDALL FLANAGAN
(Mike)

Born December 16, 1951, at Manchester, N. H.
Height, 6.00. Weight, 195.
Throws and bats lefthanded.
Attended University of Massachusetts, Amherst, Mass.
Son of Ed Flanagan, Jr., minor league pitcher, 1947 through 1952.

Major League saves: 1977 (1).
Tied for American League lead in shutouts with 5 in 1979.
Tied for American League lead in games started by pitchers with 40 in 1978.
Tied for International League lead in shutouts with 4 in 1975.
Tied for Southern League lead in shutouts with 3 in 1974.
Named American League Pitcher of the Year by THE SPORTING NEWS, 1979.
Won American League Cy Young Memorial Award, 1979.
Named lefthanded pitcher on THE SPORTING NEWS American League All-Star Team, 1979.

Year Club	League	G.	IP.	W.	L.	Pct.	H.	R.	ER.	SO.	BB.	ERA.
1973—Miami	Florida St.	11	61	4	1	.800	39	21	15	61	25	2.21
1974—Miami	Florida St.	14	103	6	6	.500	67	32	24	119	48	2.10
1974—Asheville	Southern	11	84	6	4	.600	61	19	17	62	18	1.82
1975—Rochester	Int'national	27	173	13	4	★.765	155	58	48	135	64	2.50
1975—Baltimore	American	2	10	0	1	.000	9	4	3	7	6	2.70
1976—Baltimore	American	20	85	3	5	.375	83	41	39	56	33	4.13
1976—Rochester	Int'national	7	51	6	1	.857	40	16	12	24	14	2.12
1977—Baltimore	American	36	235	15	10	.600	235	100	95	149	70	3.64
1978—Baltimore	American	40	281	19	15	.559	271	128	★126	167	87	4.04
1979—Baltimore	American	39	266	★23	9	.719	245	107	91	190	70	3.08
1980—Baltimore	American	37	251	16	13	.552	★278	121	115	128	71	4.12
1981—Baltimore	American	20	116	9	6	.600	108	55	54	72	37	4.19
1982—Baltimore	American	36	236	15	11	.577	233	110	104	103	76	3.97
1983—Baltimore†	American	20	125⅓	12	4	.750	135	53	46	50	31	3.30
1984—Baltimore	American	34	226⅔	13	13	.500	213	103	89	115	81	3.53
1985—Hagerstown‡	Carolina	1	6	0	0	.000	1	0	0	5	4	0.00
1985—Baltimore	American	15	86	4	5	.444	101	49	49	42	28	5.13
1986—Baltimore§	American	29	172	7	11	.389	179	95	81	96	66	4.24
1987—Baltimore xy-Toronto	American	23	144	6	8	.429	148	72	65	93	51	4.06
1987—Rochester	Int'national	3	12	0	0	.000	12	5	4	10	3	3.00
1988—Toronto z	American	34	211	13	13	.500	220	106	98	99	80	4.18
1989—Toronto	American	30	171⅔	8	10	.444	186	82	75	47	47	3.93
1990—Toronto a	American	5	20⅓	2	2	.500	28	14	12	5	8	5.31
Major League Totals—16 Years		420	2637	165	136	.548	2672	1240	1142	1419	842	3.90

Selected by Houston Astros' organization in 15th round of free-agent draft, June 8, 1971.

Selected by Baltimore Orioles' organization in 7th round of free-agent draft, June 5, 1973.

†On disabled list, May 18 to August 7, 1983.

‡On Baltimore disabled list, March 26 to July 20, 1985; included rehabilitation disability assignment to Hagerstown, July 10 to July 20, 1985.

§On disabled list, May 31 to June 19, 1986.

xOn disabled list, May 18 to July 17, 1987; included rehabilitation disability assignment to Rochester, July 3 to July 17, 1987.

yTraded to Toronto Blue Jays for Pitcher Oswald Peraza and a player to be named later, August 31, 1987; Baltimore Orioles acquired Pitcher Jose Mesa to complete deal, September 4, 1987.

zGranted free agency, November 4, 1988; re-signed by Blue Jays, December 24, 1988.

aReleased, May 8, 1990.

CHAMPIONSHIP SERIES RECORD

Year Club	League	G.	IP.	W.	L.	Pct.	H.	R.	ER.	SO.	BB.	ERA.
1979—Baltimore	American	1	7	1	0	1.000	6	6	4	2	1	5.14
1983—Baltimore	American	1	5	1	0	1.000	5	1	1	1	0	1.80
1989—Toronto	American	1	4⅓	0	1	.000	7	5	5	3	1	10.38
Championship Series Totals—3 Years		3	16⅓	2	1	.667	18	12	10	6	2	5.51

WORLD SERIES RECORD

Year Club	League	G.	IP.	W.	L.	Pct.	H.	R.	ER.	SO.	BB.	ERA.
1979—Baltimore	American	3	15	1	1	.500	18	7	5	13	2	3.00
1983—Baltimore	American	1	4	0	0	.000	6	2	2	1	1	4.50
World Series Totals—2 Years		4	19	1	1	.500	24	9	7	14	3	3.32

ALL-STAR GAME RECORD

Named to American League All-Star Team for 1978 game; did not play.

DARRIN GLEN FLETCHER

Born October 3, 1966, at Elmhurst, Ill.
Height, 6.01. Weight, 199.
Throws right and bats lefthanded.
Attended University of Illinois, Champaign, Ill.
Son of Tom Fletcher, pitcher with Detroit Tigers, 1962.

Led Pacific Coast League catchers in total chances with 787 in 1990.
Tied for Texas League lead in double plays by catchers with 9 in 1988.

Year Club	League	Pos.	G.	AB.	R.	H.	2B.	3B.	HR.	RBI.	B.A.	PO.	A.	E.	F.A.
1987—Vero Beach	Fla. St.	C	43	124	13	33	7	0	0	15	.266	212	35	3	.988
1988—San Antonio	Texas	C	89	279	19	58	8	0	1	20	.208	529	64	5	*.992
1989—Albuquerque	P. C.	C	100	315	34	86	16	1	5	44	.273	632	63	9	.987
1989—Los Angeles	Nat.	C	5	8	1	4	0	0	1	2	.500	16	1	0	1.000
1990—Albuquerque	P. C.	C	105	350	58	102	23	1	13	65	.291	*715	64	8	.990
1990—L.A.†-Phi.	Nat.	C	11	23	3	3	1	0	0	1	.130	30	3	0	1.000
Major League Totals—2 Years		16	31	4	7	1	0	1	3	.226	46	4	0	1.000

Selected by Los Angeles Dodgers' organization in 6th round of free-agent draft, June 2, 1987.
†Traded to Philadelphia Phillies for Pitcher Dennis Cook, September 13, 1990.

SCOTT BRIAN FLETCHER

Born July 30, 1958, at Fort Walton Beach, Fla.
Height, 5.11. Weight, 173.
Throws and bats righthanded.
Attended University of Toledo, Toledo, O.; Valencia Community College,
Orlando, Fla., and Georgia Southern College, Statesboro, Ga.
Son of Richard W. Fletcher, minor league pitcher, 1952 through 1959.

Major League stolen bases: 1982 (1), 1983 (5), 1984 (10), 1985 (5), 1986 (12), 1987 (13), 1988 (8), 1989 (2), 1990 (1). Total—57.
Led American League second basemen in double plays with 115 in 1990.
Led American Association in being hit by pitch with 9 and grounding into double plays with 20 in 1981.
Led American Association shortstops in total chances with 607 in 1982.
Led Texas League second basemen in double plays with 112 in 1980.

Year Club	League	Pos.	G.	AB.	R.	H.	2B.	3B.	HR.	RBI.	B.A.	PO.	A.	E.	F.A.
1979—Geneva	NYP	SS	67	261	59	81	12	3	4	43	.310	99	195	18	*.942
1980—Midland	Texas	*2B-SS	130	501	*111	164	16	*11	6	65	.327	*354	*390	*29	.962
1981—Iowa	A. A.	SS	119	458	66	117	26	4	4	33	.255	*222	337	28	.952
1981—Chicago	Nat.	2B-SS-3B	19	46	6	10	4	0	0	1	.217	34	44	3	.963
1982—Iowa	A. A.	SS	129	502	90	157	26	3	4	60	.313	224	•357	26	.957
1982—Chicago†	Nat.	SS	11	24	4	4	0	0	0	1	.167	11	23	0	1.000
1983—Chicago	Amer.	SS-2B-3B	114	262	42	62	16	5	3	31	.237	126	308	16	.964
1984—Chicago	Amer.	SS-2B-3B	149	456	46	114	13	3	3	35	.250	234	439	19	.973
1985—Chicago‡	Amer.	3B-SS-2B	119	301	38	77	8	1	2	31	.256	123	208	8	.976
1986—Texas	Amer.	SS-3B-2B	147	530	82	159	34	5	3	50	.300	216	388	16	.974
1987—Texas	Amer.	SS	156	588	82	169	28	4	5	63	.287	249	413	23	.966
1988—Texas§	Amer.	SS	140	515	59	142	19	4	0	47	.276	215	414	11	.983
1989—Texas xy-Chicago	Amer.	SS-2B	142	546	77	138	25	2	1	43	.253	241	362	15	.976
1990—Chicago	Amer.	2B	151	509	54	123	18	3	4	56	.242	305	436	9	.988
National League Totals—2 Years		30	70	10	14	4	0	0	2	.200	45	67	3	.974
American League Totals—8 Years		1118	3707	480	984	161	27	21	356	.265	1709	2968	117	.976
Major League Totals—10 Years		1148	3777	490	998	165	27	21	358	.264	1754	3035	120	.976

Selected by Los Angeles Dodgers' organization in 33rd round of free-agent draft, June 8, 1976.
Selected by Oakland A's organization in secondary phase of free-agent draft, January 10, 1978.
Selected by Houston Astros' organization in secondary phase of free-agent draft, June 6, 1978.
Selected by Chicago Cubs' organization in secondary phase of free-agent draft, June 5, 1979.
†Traded with Pitchers Dick Tidrow and Randy Martz and Infielder Pat Tabler to Chicago White Sox for Pitchers Steve Trout and Warren Brusstar, January 25, 1983.
‡Traded with Pitcher Ed Correa and a player to be named later to Texas Rangers for Infielder Wayne Tolleson and Pitcher Dave Schmidt, November 25, 1985; Texas acquired Infielder Jose Mota to complete deal, December 12, 1985.
§Granted free agency, November 4, 1988; re-signed by Rangers, November 30, 1988.
xOn disabled list, July 5 to July 20, 1989.
yTraded with Outfielder Sammy Sosa and Pitcher Wilson Alvarez to Chicago White Sox for Outfielder Harold Baines and Infielder Fred Manrique, July 29, 1989.

CHAMPIONSHIP SERIES RECORD

Year Club	League	Pos.	G.	AB.	R.	H.	2B.	3B.	HR.	RBI.	B.A.	PO.	A.	E.	F.A.
1983—Chicago	Amer.	SS	3	7	0	0	0	0	0	0	.000	3	8	0	1.000

THOMAS MICHAEL FOLEY
(Tom)

Born September 9, 1959, at Columbus, Ga.
Height, 6.01. Weight, 180.
Throws right and bats lefthanded.
Attended Miami-Dade Community College (South), Miami, Fla.

Major League stolen bases: 1983 (1), 1984 (3), 1985 (2), 1986 (10), 1987 (6), 1988 (2), 1989 (2). Total—26.
Led Pioneer League in caught stealing with 10 in 1977.
Led Florida State League shortstops in double plays with 71 in 1979.
Led Western Carolinas League shortstops in double plays with 98 in 1978.

Year Club	League	Pos.	G.	AB.	R.	H.	2B.	3B.	HR.	RBI.	B.A.	PO.	A.	E.	F.A.
1977—Billings	Pion.	3B-SS	59	209	37	53	7	1	2	21	.254	53	109	24	.871
1978—Shelby	W. Car.	SS	124	424	55	98	19	1	2	41	.231	*217	●352	30	*.950
1979—Tampa	Fla. St.	SS	125	414	38	95	12	6	0	37	.229	223	*394	35	.946
1980—Waterbury	East.	2B	131	477	49	119	16	4	4	41	.249	*222	329	31	.947
1981—Indianapolis	A. A.	SS	103	347	47	81	12	2	6	27	.233	175	267	27	.942
1982—Indianapolis	A. A.	SS	129	427	65	115	20	9	8	63	.269	*227	343	27	.955
1983—Cincinnati	Nat.	SS-2B	68	98	7	20	4	1	0	9	.204	54	76	2	.985
1984—Cincinnati	Nat.	SS-2B-3B	106	277	26	70	8	3	5	27	.253	119	228	11	.969
1985—Cinc.†-Phil.	Nat.	SS-2B-3B	89	250	24	60	13	1	3	23	.240	127	202	7	.979
1986—Reading‡	East.	SS-2B	3	11	2	2	2	0	0	0	.182	2	11	0	1.000
1986—Phil.§ - Mon.	Nat.	SS-2B-3B	103	263	26	70	15	3	1	23	.266	117	190	6	.981
1987—Montreal x	Nat.	SS-2B-3B	106	280	35	82	18	3	5	28	.293	134	190	9	.973
1988—Montreal	Nat.	2B-SS-3B	127	377	33	100	21	3	5	43	.265	204	324	15	.972
1989—Montreal y	Nat.	2-3-S-P	122	375	34	86	19	2	7	39	.229	203	317	8	.985
1990—Montreal	Nat.	S-2-3-1	73	164	11	35	2	1	0	12	.213	80	123	5	.976
Major League Totals—8 Years			794	2084	196	523	100	17	26	204	.251	1038	1650	63	.977

Selected by Cincinnati Reds' organization in 7th round of free-agent draft, June 7, 1977.
†Traded with Catcher Alan Knicely, a player to be named later and cash to Philadelphia Phillies for Catcher Bo Diaz and Pitcher Greg Simpson, August 8, 1985; Philadelphia acquired Pitcher Freddie Toliver to complete deal, August 27, 1985.
‡On Philadelphia disabled list, March 23 to April 29, 1986; included rehabilitation disability assignment to Reading, April 25 to April 29, 1986.
§Traded with Pitcher Lary Sorensen to Montreal Expos for Pitcher Dan Schatzeder and Infielder Skeeter Barnes, July 24, 1986.
xOn disabled list, May 17 to June 2, 1987.
yOn disabled list, July 26 to August 12, 1989.

PITCHING RECORD

Year Club	League	G.	IP.	W.	L.	Pct.	H.	R.	ER.	SO.	BB.	ERA.
1989—Montreal	National	1	⅓	0	0	.000	1	1	1	0	0	27.00

CURTIS GLENN FORD
(Curt)

Born October 11, 1960, at Jackson, Miss.
Height, 5.10. Weight, 158.
Throws right and bats lefthanded.
Attended Jackson State University, Jackson, Miss.

Major League stolen bases: 1985 (1), 1986 (13), 1987 (11), 1988 (6), 1989 (5). Total—36.
Led American Association in stolen bases with 45 and tied for lead in caught stealing with 17 in 1985.
Led Midwest League in total bases with 236 in 1983.
Named Midwest League Most Valuable Player, 1983.

Year Club	League	Pos.	G.	AB.	R.	H.	2B.	3B.	HR.	RBI.	B.A.	PO.	A.	E.	F.A.
1981—Johnson City	Appal.	*2B-1B	63	218	36	65	11	2	5	38	.298	115	149	*18	.936
1982—St. Petersburg	Fla. St.	2B-OF	133	447	59	123	18	8	1	49	.275	292	294	22	.964
1983—Springfield	Midw.	OF-2B	126	465	80	135	27	7	20	*91	.290	181	7	8	.960
1984—Arkansas	Texas	OF-2B-3B	118	442	62	143	23	1	10	78	.324	224	102	8	.976
1984—Louisville	A. A.	OF-2B	13	38	5	10	2	0	0	1	.263	13	2	0	1.000
1985—Louisville	A. A.	OF-3B	127	475	73	121	20	6	7	45	.255	243	25	8	.971
1985—St. Louis	Nat.	OF	11	12	2	6	2	0	0	3	.500	3	0	1	.750
1986—Louisville	A. A.	OF	53	200	47	59	9	2	4	31	.295	120	2	1	.992
1986—St. Louis	Nat.	OF	85	214	30	53	15	2	2	29	.248	109	7	3	.975
1987—St. Louis†	Nat.	OF	89	228	32	65	9	5	3	26	.285	157	2	3	.981
1988—St. Louis‡	Nat.	OF-1B	91	128	11	25	6	0	1	18	.195	95	6	2	.981
1989—Philadelphia	Nat.	OF-1B-2B	108	142	13	31	5	1	1	13	.218	46	5	0	1.000
1990—Philadelphia	Nat.	OF	22	18	0	2	0	0	0	0	.111	2	0	0	1.000
1990—Scranton/W.-B.§	Int.	OF	56	194	28	43	5	3	5	12	.222	107	2	1	.991
Major League Totals—6 Years			406	742	88	182	37	8	7	89	.245	412	20	9	.980

Selected by St. Louis Cardinals' organization in 4th round of free-agent draft, June 8, 1981.
†On disabled list, August 10 to September 18, 1987.
‡Traded with Catcher Steve Lake to Philadelphia for Outfielder Milt Thompson, December 16, 1988.
§Granted free agency, October 15, 1990.

CHAMPIONSHIP SERIES RECORD

Year Club	League	Pos.	G.	AB.	R.	H.	2B.	3B.	HR.	RBI.	B.A.	PO.	A.	E.	F.A.
1987—St. Louis	Nat.	OF-PH	4	9	2	3	0	0	0	0	.333	6	0	0	1.000

Year	Club	League	Pos.	G.	AB.	R.	H.	2B.	3B.	HR.	RBI.	B.A.	PO.	A.	E.	F.A.
1987—St. Louis	Nat.	OF-PH	5	13	1	4	0	0	0	2	.308	5	0	0	1.000

EMILO ANTHONY FOSSAS
(Tony)

Born September 23, 1957, at Havana, Cuba.
Height, 6.00. Weight, 187.
Throws and bats lefthanded.
Attended University of South Florida, Tampa, Fla.

Major League saves: 1989 (1).
Tied for South Atlantic League in games started by pitchers with 27 in 1980.

Year	Club	League	G.	IP.	W.	L.	Pct.	H.	R.	ER.	SO.	BB.	ERA.
1979—Sarasota Rangers	Gulf Coast	10	60	6	3	.667	54	28	20	49	26	3.00
1979—Tulsa	Texas	2	11	1	1	.500	14	10	8	3	4	6.55
1980—Asheville	S. Atlantic	30	*197	8	2	.600	*187	84	69	140	69	3.15
1981—Tulsa†‡§	Texas	38	106	5	6	.455	113	65	49	57	44	4.16
1982—Burlington	Midwest	25	146⅓	8	9	.471	121	63	50	115	33	3.08
1983—Tulsa	Texas	24	133	8	7	.533	123	77	62	103	46	4.20
1983—Oklahoma City	Am. Assoc.	10	35⅓	1	2	.333	55	33	31	23	12	7.90
1984—Tulsa	Texas	4	10	0	1	.000	12	5	5	7	3	4.50
1984—Oklahoma City	Am. Assoc.	29	121	5	9	.357	143	65	58	74	34	4.31
1985—Oklahoma City x	Am. Assoc.	30	110	7	6	.538	121	65	58	49	36	4.75
1986—Edmonton y	P. Coast	7	43⅓	3	3	.500	53	23	22	15	12	4.57
1987—Edmonton z	P. Coast	40	117⅓	6	8	.429	152	76	65	54	29	4.99
1988—Oklahoma City	Am. Assoc.	52	66⅔	3	0	1.000	64	21	21	42	16	2.84
1988—Texas a	American	5	5⅔	0	0	.000	11	3	3	0	2	4.76
1989—Denver	Am. Assoc.	24	35⅓	5	1	.833	27	9	8	35	11	2.04
1989—Milwaukee	American	51	61	2	2	.500	57	27	24	42	22	3.54
1990—Milwaukee	American	32	29⅓	2	3	.400	44	23	21	24	10	6.44
1990—Denver b	Am. Assoc.	25	35⅔	5	2	.714	29	8	6	45	10	1.51
Major League Totals—3 Years		88	96	4	5	.444	112	53	48	66	34	4.50

Selected by Minnesota Twins' organization in 9th round of free-agent draft, June 6, 1978.
Selected by Texas Rangers' organization in 12th round of free-agent draft, June 5, 1979.
†Released, February 18, 1982; signed by Midland (Chicago Cubs' organization), March 11, 1982.
‡Loaned to Tabasco of Mexican League, March 15, 1982; returned, April 7, 1982.
§Released, April 7, 1982; signed by Burlington (Texas Rangers' organization), May 3, 1982.
xGranted free agency, October 15, 1985; signed by Edmonton (California Angels' organization), December 13, 1985.
yOn disabled list, June 2, 1986 through remainder of season.
zGranted free agency, October 15, 1987; signed by Oklahoma City (Texas Rangers' organization), December 1, 1987.
aGranted free agency, October 15, 1988; signed by Denver (Milwaukee Brewers' organization), January 21, 1989.
bReleased, December 6, 1990.

JOHN ANTHONY FRANCO

Born September 17, 1960, at Brooklyn, N.Y.
Height, 5.10. Weight, 185.
Throws and bats lefthanded.
Attended St. John's University, Jamaica, N.Y.

Major League saves: 1984 (4), 1985 (12), 1986 (29), 1987 (32), 1988 (39), 1989 (32), 1990 (33). Total—181.
Led National League in saves with 39 in 1988 and 33 in 1990.
Led National League in games finished in relief with 60 in 1987 and 61 in 1988.
Named National League Fireman of the Year by THE SPORTING NEWS, 1988 and 1990.

Year	Club	League	G.	IP.	W.	L.	Pct.	H.	R.	ER.	SO.	BB.	ERA.
1981—Vero Beach	Florida St.	13	79	7	4	.636	78	41	31	60	41	3.53
1982—Albuquerque	P. Coast	5	27⅓	1	2	.333	41	22	22	24	15	7.24
1982—San Antonio	Texas	17	105⅓	10	5	.667	137	70	58	76	46	4.96
1983—Albuquerque†	P. Coast	11	15	0	0	.000	10	11	9	8	11	5.40
1983—Indianapolis	Am. Assoc.	23	115	6	10	.375	148	69	62	54	42	4.85
1984—Wichita	Am. Assoc.	6	9⅓	1	0	1.000	8	6	6	11	4	5.79
1984—Cincinnati	National	54	79⅓	6	2	.750	74	28	23	55	36	2.61
1985—Cincinnati	National	67	99	12	3	.800	83	27	24	61	40	2.18
1986—Cincinnati	National	74	101	6	6	.500	90	40	33	84	44	2.94
1987—Cincinnati	National	68	82	8	5	.615	76	26	23	61	27	2.52
1988—Cincinnati	National	70	86	6	6	.500	60	18	15	46	27	1.57
1989—Cincinnati‡	National	60	80⅔	4	8	.333	77	35	28	60	36	3.12
1990—New York	National	55	67⅔	5	3	.625	66	22	19	56	21	2.53
Major League Totals—7 Years		448	595⅓	47	33	.588	526	196	165	423	231	2.49

Selected by Los Angeles Dodgers' organization in 5th round of free-agent draft, June 8, 1981.
†Traded with Pitcher Brett Wise to Cincinnati Reds' organization for Infielder Rafael Landestoy, May 9, 1983.
‡Traded with Outfielder Don Brown to New York Mets for Pitchers Randy Myers and Kip Gross, December 6, 1989.

ALL-STAR GAME RECORD

Year	League	IP.	W.	L.	Pct.	H.	R.	ER.	SO.	BB.	ERA.
1987—National	⅔	0	0	.000	0	0	0	0	0	0.00
1990—National	1	0	0	.000	0	0	0	0	0	0.00
All-Star Game Totals—2 Years	1⅔	0	0	.000	0	0	0	0	0	0.00

Member of National League All-Star Team in 1986; did not play.
Member of National League All-Star Team in 1989; did not play.

JULIO CESAR FRANCO

Name pronounced FRANHK-oh.
Born August 23, 1961, at San Pedro de Macoris, D. R.
Height, 6.01. Weight, 188.
Throws and bats righthanded.

Major League stolen bases: 1983 (32), 1984 (19), 1985 (13), 1986 (10), 1987 (32), 1988 (25), 1989 (21), 1990 (31). Total—183.
Led American League in grounding into double plays with 28 in 1986 and 27 in 1989.
Led American League shortstops in errors with 35 in 1985.
Led Northwest League in total bases with 153 in 1979.
Led Carolina League shortstops in double plays with 73 in 1980.
Led Northwest League shortstops in double plays with 45 in 1979.
Named second baseman on THE SPORTING NEWS American League All-Star Team, 1989 and 1990.
Named second baseman on THE SPORTING NEWS American League Silver Slugger team, 1988 through 1990.
Named Carolina League Most Valuable Player, 1980.

Year Club	League	Pos.	G.	AB.	R.	H.	2B.	3B.	HR.	RBI.	B.A.	PO.	A.	E.	F.A.
1978—Butte	Pion.	SS	47	141	34	43	5	2	3	28	.305	37	52	25	.781
1979—Central Oregon	N'west	SS	●71	299	57	⋆98	15	5	●10	45	.328	103	⋆256	31	.921
1980—Peninsula	Carol.	SS	●140	⋆555	105	178	25	6	11	⋆99	.321	179	⋆412	42	.934
1981—Reading	East.	SS	⋆139	⋆532	70	160	17	3	8	74	.301	246	437	30	.958
1982—Oklahoma City	A. A.	⋆SS-3B	120	463	80	139	19	5	21	66	.300	211	350	⋆42	.930
1982—Philadelphia†	Nat.	SS-3B	16	29	3	8	1	0	0	3	.276	8	25	0	1.000
1983—Cleveland	Amer.	SS	149	560	68	153	24	8	8	80	.273	247	438	28	.961
1984—Cleveland	Amer.	SS	160	⋆658	82	188	22	5	3	79	.286	280	481	⋆36	.955
1985—Cleveland	Amer.	SS-2B	160	636	97	183	33	4	6	90	.288	252	437	36	.950
1986—Cleveland	Amer	SS-2B	149	599	80	183	30	5	10	74	.306	248	413	19	.972
1987—Cleveland‡	Amer.	SS-2B	128	495	86	158	24	3	8	52	.319	175	313	18	.964
1988—Cleveland§	Amer.	2B	152	613	88	186	23	6	10	54	.303	310	434	14	.982
1989—Texas	Amer.	2B	150	548	80	173	31	5	13	92	.316	256	386	13	.980
1990—Texas	Amer.	2B	157	582	96	172	27	1	11	69	.296	310	444	●19	.975
National League Totals—1 Year			16	29	3	8	1	0	0	3	.276	8	25	0	1.000
American League Totals—8 Years			1205	4691	677	1396	214	37	69	590	.298	2078	3346	183	.967
Major League Totals—9 Years			1221	4720	680	1404	215	37	69	593	.297	2086	3371	183	.968

Signed as free agent by Philadelphia Phillies' organization, June 23, 1978.
†Traded with Second Baseman Manny Trillo, Outfielder George Vukovich, Pitcher Jay Baller and Catcher Jerry Willard to Cleveland Indians for Outfielder Von Hayes, December 9, 1982.
‡On disabled list, July 13 to August 8, 1987.
§Traded to Texas Rangers for First Baseman Pete O'Brien, Outfielder Oddibe McDowell and Second Baseman Jerry Browne, December 6, 1988.

ALL-STAR GAME RECORD

Year League	Pos.	AB.	R.	H.	2B.	3B.	HR.	RBI.	B.A.	PO.	A.	E.	F.A.
1989—American	2B	3	0	1	0	0	0	0	.333	1	1	0	1.000
1990—American	PH-2B	3	0	1	1	0	0	2	.333	1	0	0	1.000
All-Star Game Totals—2 Years		6	0	2	1	0	0	2	.333	2	1	0	1.000

TERRY JON FRANCONA

Born April 22, 1959, at New Brighton, Pa.
Height, 6.01. Weight, 175.
Throws and bats lefthanded.
Attended University of Arizona, Tucson, Ariz.
Son of John (Tito) Francona, outfielder-first baseman with Baltimore, Chicago A.L., Detroit, Cleveland, St. Louis, Philadelphia, Atlanta, Oakland and Milwaukee, 1956 through 1970.

Major League stolen bases: 1981 (1), 1982 (2), 1985 (5), 1987 (2), 1989 (2). Total—12.
Named College Player of the Year by THE SPORTING NEWS, 1980.
Named outfielder on THE SPORTING NEWS College Baseball All-America Team, 1980.

Year Club	League	Pos.	G.	AB.	R.	H.	2B.	3B.	HR.	RBI.	B.A.	PO.	A.	E.	F.A.
1980—Memphis	South.	OF	60	210	20	63	13	2	1	23	.300	59	4	4	.940
1981—Memphis	South.	OF-1B	41	161	20	56	8	1	0	18	.348	102	7	5	.956
1981—Denver	A. A.	OF	93	355	53	125	17	⋆9	1	58	.352	158	7	3	.982
1981—Montreal	Nat.	OF-1B	34	95	11	26	0	1	1	8	.274	41	5	0	1.000
1982—Montreal†	Nat.	OF-1B	46	131	14	42	3	0	0	9	.321	65	0	3	.956
1983—Montreal	Nat.	OF-1B	120	230	21	59	11	1	3	22	.257	172	10	3	.984
1984—Montreal‡	Nat.	1B-OF	58	214	18	74	19	2	1	18	.346	431	50	3	.994
1985—Montreal§	Nat.	1B-OF-3B	107	281	19	75	15	1	2	31	.267	431	40	6	.987
1986—Chicago	Nat.	OF-1B	86	124	13	31	3	0	2	8	.250	123	7	0	1.000
1986—Iowa x	A. A.	1B-OF	17	60	7	15	3	2	0	8	.250	82	3	1	.988
1987—Cincinnati y	Nat.	1B-OF	102	207	16	47	5	0	3	12	.227	377	45	2	.995
1988—Colorado Springs . P. C.		OF-1B	68	235	29	76	15	5	0	32	.329	115	11	3	.977
1988—Cleveland z	Amer.	1B-OF	62	212	24	66	8	0	1	12	.311	47	5	1	.981
1989—Milwaukee a	Amer.	1B-OF-P	90	233	26	54	10	1	3	23	.232	339	26	4	.989
1990—Milwaukee b	Amer.	1B	3	4	1	0	0	0	0	0	.000	6	0	0	1.000
1990—Louisville	A. A.	OF-1B-P	86	285	29	75	9	3	6	30	.263	126	7	2	.985
National League Totals—7 Years			553	1282	112	354	56	5	12	108	.276	1640	157	17	.991
American League Totals—3 Years			155	449	51	120	18	1	4	35	.267	392	31	5	.988
Major League Totals—10 Years			708	1731	163	474	74	6	16	143	.274	2032	188	22	.990

Selected by Chicago Cubs' organization in 2nd round of free-agent draft, June 7, 1977.
Selected by Montreal Expos' organization in 1st round (22nd player selected) of free-agent draft, June 3, 1980.
†On disabled list, June 17 to September 27, 1982.
‡On disabled list, June 15 to September 5, 1984.
§Released, April 1, 1986; signed by Chicago Cubs' organization, May 2, 1986.
xGranted free agency, October 18, 1986; signed by Cincinnati Reds, March 23, 1987.
yGranted free agency, November 12, 1987; signed by Colorado Springs (Cleveland Indians' organization), February 28, 1988.
zGranted free agency, November 4, 1988; signed by Milwaukee Brewers, March 30, 1989.
aGranted free agency, November 13, 1989; re-signed by Brewers, December 12, 1989.
b Released, April 27, 1990; signed by Louisville (St. Louis Cardinals' organization), May 5, 1990.

DIVISION SERIES RECORD

Year	Club	League	Pos.	G.	AB.	R.	H.	2B.	3B.	HR.	RBI.	B.A.	PO.	A.	E.	F.A.
1981—Montreal		Nat.	OF	5	12	0	4	0	0	0	0	.333	8	0	0	1.000

CHAMPIONSHIP SERIES RECORD

Year	Club	League	Pos.	G.	AB.	R.	H.	2B.	3B.	HR.	RBI.	B.A.	PO.	A.	E.	F.A.
1981—Montreal		Nat.	PH-OF	2	1	0	0	0	0	0	0	.000	0	0	0	.000

PITCHING RECORD

Year	Club	League	G.	IP.	W.	L.	Pct.	H.	R.	ER.	SO.	BB.	ERA.
1989—Milwaukee	American		1	1	0	0	.000	0	0	0	1	0	0.00
1990—Louisville	Am. Assoc.		5	7⅔	0	0	.000	4	1	1	6	2	1.17
Major League Totals—1 Year			1	1	0	0	.000	0	0	0	1	0	0.00

WILLIAM PATRICK FRASER
(Willie)

Born May 26, 1964, at New York, N.Y.
Height, 6.01. Weight, 208.
Throws and bats righthanded.
Attended Concordia College, Bronxville, N.Y.
Major League saves: 1987 (1), 1989 (2), 1990 (2). Total—5.
Led American League in home runs allowed with 33 in 1988.

Year	Club	League	G.	IP.	W.	L.	Pct.	H.	R.	ER.	SO.	BB.	ERA.
1985—Quad Cities	Midwest		13	81⅔	2	6	.250	95	53	49	72	32	5.40
1986—Palm Springs	California		19	124⅓	9	2	.818	115	60	49	99	29	3.55
1986—Edmonton	P. Coast		6	40	4	1	.800	25	15	14	24	8	3.15
1986—California	American		1	4⅓	0	0	.000	6	4	4	2	1	8.31
1987—California	American		36	176⅔	10	10	.500	160	85	77	106	63	3.92
1988—California	American		34	194⅔	12	13	.480	203	129	117	86	80	5.41
1989—California	American		44	91⅔	4	7	.364	80	33	33	46	23	3.24
1990—California	American		45	76	5	4	.556	69	29	26	32	24	3.08
1990—Edmonton†	P. Coast		3	14⅓	1	0	1.000	11	8	5	12	6	3.14
Major League Totals—5 Years			160	543⅓	31	34	.477	518	280	257	272	191	4.26

Selected by California Angels' organization in 1st round (15th player selected) of free-agent draft, June 3, 1985.
†Traded with Outfielder Devon White and a player to be named later to Toronto Blue Jays for Outfielder Junior Felix, Infielder Luis Sojo and a player to be named later, December 2, 1990; Toronto acquired Pitcher Marcus Moore and California Angels acquired Catcher Ken Rivers to complete deal, December 4, 1990.

MARVIN FREEMAN

Born April 10, 1963, at Chicago, Ill.
Height, 6.07. Weight, 222.
Throws and bats righthanded.
Attended Jackson State University, Jackson, Miss.
Pitched 6-0 no-hit victory against Richmond, July 28, 1988 (second game).
Major League saves: 1990 (1).
Tied for Eastern League lead in games started by pitchers with 27 in 1986.
Tied for Northwest League lead in games started by pitchers with 15 in 1984.

Year	Club	League	G.	IP.	W.	L.	Pct.	H.	R.	ER.	SO.	BB.	ERA.
1984—Bend	Northwest		15	89⅔	8	5	.615	64	41	26	79	52	2.61
1985—Clearwater	Florida St.		14	88⅓	6	5	.545	72	32	30	55	36	3.06
1985—Reading	Eastern		11	65⅓	1	7	.125	51	41	39	35	52	5.37
1986—Reading	Eastern		27	163	13	6	.684	130	89	73	*111	113	4.03
1986—Philadelphia	National		3	16	2	0	1.000	6	4	4	8	10	2.25
1987—Maine	Int'national		10	46	0	7	.000	56	38	32	29	30	6.26
1987—Reading	Eastern		9	49⅔	3	3	.500	45	30	28	40	32	5.07
1988—Maine	Int'national		18	74	5	5	.500	62	43	38	37	46	4.62
1988—Philadelphia	National		11	51⅔	2	3	.400	55	36	35	37	43	6.10
1989—Scranton/Wilkes-Barre	Int'national		5	14	1	1	.500	11	8	7	8	5	4.50
1989—Philadelphia†	National		1	3	0	0	.000	2	2	2	0	5	6.00
1990—Scranton/W.-B.‡—Richmond	Int'national		14	74⅓	4	7	.364	72	43	40	56	41	4.84
1990—Philadelphia-Atlanta	National		25	48	1	2	.333	41	24	23	38	17	4.31
Major League Totals—4 Years			40	118⅔	5	5	.500	104	66	64	83	75	4.85

Selected by Montreal Expos' organization in 9th round of free-agent draft, June 8, 1981.
Selected by Philadelphia Phillies' organization in 2nd round of free-agent draft, June 4, 1984.

‡Traded to Richmond (Atlanta Braves' organization) for Pitcher Joe Boever, July 23, 1990.

STEVEN FRANCIS FREY
(Steve)

Born July 29, 1963, at Meadowbrook, Pa.
Height, 5.09. Weight, 170.
Throws left and bats righthanded.
Attended Bucks County Community College, Newton, Pa.

Major League saves: 1990 (9).

Year	Club	League	G.	IP.	W.	L.	Pct.	H.	R.	ER.	SO.	BB.	ERA.
1983—Oneonta	NYP	28	72⅓	4	6	.400	47	27	22	86	35	2.74
1984—Fort Lauderdale	Florida St.	47	64⅔	4	2	.667	46	26	15	66	34	2.09
1985—Fort Lauderdale	Florida St.	19	22⅓	1	1	.500	11	4	3	15	12	1.21
1985—Albany	Eastern	40	61⅓	4	7	.364	53	30	26	54	25	3.82
1986—Albany	Eastern	40	73	3	4	.429	50	25	17	62	18	2.10
1986—Columbus	Int'national	11	19	0	2	.000	29	17	17	11	10	8.05
1987—Albany	Eastern	14	28	0	2	.000	20	6	6	19	7	1.93
1987—Columbus†	Int'national	23	47⅓	2	1	.667	45	19	16	35	10	3.04
1988—Tidewater‡	Int'national	58	54⅔	6	3	.667	38	23	19	58	25	3.13
1989—Indianapolis	Am. Assoc.	21	25⅓	2	1	.667	18	7	5	23	6	1.78
1989—Montreal	National	20	21⅓	3	2	.600	29	15	13	15	11	5.48
1990—Montreal§	National	51	55⅔	8	2	.800	44	15	13	29	29	2.10
1990—Indianapolis	Am. Assoc.	2	3	0	0	.000	0	0	0	3	1	0.00
Major League Totals—2 Years		71	77	11	4	.733	73	30	26	44	40	3.04

Selected by New York Yankees' organization in 15th round of free-agent draft, June 6, 1983.
†Traded with Outfielder Darren Reed and Catcher Phil Lombardi to New York Mets for Shortstop Rafael Santana and Pitcher Victor Garica, December 11, 1987.
‡Traded to Indianapolis (Montreal Expos' organization) for Catcher Mark Bailey and Third Baseman Tom O'Malley, March 28, 1989.
§On disabled list, May 25 to June 15, 1990; included rehabilitation disability assignment to Indianapolis, June 11 to June 15, 1990.

TODD GERALD FROHWIRTH

Born September 28, 1962, at Milwaukee, Wis.
Height, 6.04. Weight, 204.
Throws and bats righthanded.
Attended Northwest Missouri State University, Maryville, Mo.

Led International League in saves with 21 and games finished in relief with 52 in 1990.
Led Eastern League in saves with 19 in 1987.
Led Carolina League in games finished in relief with 48 and saves with 18 in 1985.
Led Northwest League in games finished in relief with 25 and tied for lead in saves with 11 in 1984.
Tied for International League lead in intentional bases on balls issued with 7 in 1987.

Year	Club	League	G.	IP.	W.	L.	Pct.	H.	R.	ER.	SO.	BB.	ERA.
1984—Bend	Northwest	29	49⅔	4	4	.500	26	17	9	60	31	1.63
1985—Peninsula	Carolina	*54	82	7	5	.583	70	33	20	74	48	2.20
1986—Clearwater	FloridaSt.	32	52	3	3	.500	54	29	23	39	18	3.98
1986—Reading	Eastern	29	42	0	4	.000	39	20	15	23	10	3.21
1987—Reading	Eastern	36	58	2	4	.333	36	14	12	44	13	1.86
1987—Maine	Int'national	27	32⅓	1	4	.200	30	12	9	21	15	2.51
1987—Philadelphia	National	10	11	1	0	1.000	12	0	0	9	2	0.00
1988—Philadelphia	National	12	12	1	2	.333	16	11	11	11	11	8.25
1988—Maine	Int'national	49	62⅔	7	3	.700	52	21	17	39	19	2.44
1989—Scranton/Wilkes-Barre	Int'national	21	32⅓	3	2	.600	29	11	8	29	11	2.23
1989—Philadelphia	National	45	62⅔	1	0	1.000	56	26	25	39	18	3.59
1990—Philadelphia	National	5	1	0	1	.000	3	2	2	1	6	18.00
1990—Scranton/Wilkes-Barre†	Int'national	*67	83	9	7	.563	76	34	28	56	32	3.04
Major League Totals—4 Years		72	86⅔	3	3	.500	87	39	38	60	37	3.95

Selected by Philadelphia Phillies' organization in 13th round of free-agent draft, June 4, 1984.
†Granted free agency, October 15, 1990.

DAVID TRAVIS FRYMAN
(Known by middle name.)

Born April 25, 1969, at Lexington, Ky.
Height, 6.01. Weight, 180.
Throws and bats righthanded.

Major League stolen bases: 1990 (3).
Led Appalachian League shortstops in total chances with 313 in 1987.

Year	Club	League	Pos.	G.	AB.	R.	H.	2B.	3B.	HR.	RBI.	B.A.	PO.	A.	E.	F.A.
1987—Bristol	Appal.	SS	67	248	25	58	9	0	2	20	.234	*103	187	●23	.927
1988—Fayetteville	S. Atl.	SS-2B	123	411	44	96	17	4	0	47	.234	174	390	32	.946
1989—London	East.	SS	118	426	52	113	*30	1	9	56	.265	192	346	*27	.952
1990—Toledo	Int.	SS	87	327	38	84	22	2	10	53	.257	128	277	26	.940
1990—Detroit	Amer.	3B-SS	66	232	32	69	11	1	9	27	.297	47	145	14	.932
Major League Totals—1 Year			66	232	32	69	11	1	9	27	.297	47	145	14	.932

Selected by Detroit Tigers' organization in 1st round (30th player selected) of free-agent draft, June 2, 1987.

GARY JOSEPH GAETTI

Name pronounced Guy-ETT-ee.

Born August 19, 1958, at Centralia, Ill.
Height, 6.00. Weight, 200.
Throws and bats righthanded.
Attended Lake Land College, Mattoon, Ill., and Northwest
Missouri State University, Maryville, Mo.

Shares major league records by hitting home run in first major league at-bat, September 20, 1981; most home runs, opening day of season (2), April 6, 1982; most sacrifice flies, rookie season (13), 1982.
Major League stolen bases: 1983 (7), 1984 (11), 1985 (13), 1986 (14), 1987 (10), 1988 (7), 1989 (6), 1990 (6). Total—74.
Led American League in grounding into double plays with 25 in 1987.
Led American League in sacrifice flies with 13 in 1982.
Led American League third basemen in putouts with 142 in 1984 and 146 in 1985.
Led American League third basemen in total chances with 496 in 1984, 473 in 1986 and 438 in 1990.
Led American League third basemen in assists with 334 in both 1984 and 1986 and 318 in 1990.
Led American League third basemen in double plays with 46 in 1983 and 36 in both 1986 and 1990.
Tied for American League lead in errors by third basemen with 20 in 1984.
Led Southern League third basemen in putouts with 122 and assists with 281 in 1981.
Led Midwest League third basemen in double plays with 35 in 1980.
Tied for Appalachian League lead in errors by third basemen with 18 in 1979.
Named third baseman on THE SPORTING NEWS American League All-Star fielding team, 1986 through 1989.

Year—Club	League	Pos.	G.	AB.	R.	H.	2B.	3B.	HR.	RBI.	B.A.	PO.	A.	E.	F.A.
1979—Elizabethton	Appal.	3B-SS	66	230	50	59	15	2	14	42	.257	70	134	21	.907
1980—Wisconsin Rapids	Midw.	3B	138	503	77	134	27	3	*22	82	.266	*94	*363	●35	.929
1981—Orlando	South.	*3B-1B	137	495	92	137	19	2	30	93	.277	143	283	*32	.930
1981—Minnesota	Amer.	3B	9	26	4	5	0	0	2	3	.192	5	17	0	1.000
1982—Minnesota	Amer.	3B-SS	145	508	59	117	25	4	25	84	.230	106	291	17	.959
1983—Minnesota	Amer.	3B-SS	157	584	81	143	30	3	21	78	.245	*131	361	17	.967
1984—Minnesota	Amer.	3B-OF-SS	●162	588	55	154	29	4	5	65	.262	163	335	21	.960
1985—Minnesota	Amer.	3B-OF-1B	160	560	71	138	31	0	20	63	.246	162	316	18	.964
1986—Minnesota	Amer.	3-S-O-2	157	596	91	171	34	1	34	108	.287	120	335	21	.956
1987—Minnesota†	Amer.	3B	154	584	95	150	36	2	31	109	.257	●134	261	11	.973
1988—Minnesota‡	Amer.	3B-SS	133	468	66	141	29	2	28	88	.301	105	191	7	.977
1989—Minnesota§	Amer.	3B-1B	130	498	63	125	11	4	19	75	.251	115	253	10	.974
1990—Minnesota x	Amer.	3B-SS	154	577	61	132	27	5	16	85	.229	125	319	18	.961
Major League Totals—10 Years			1361	4989	646	1276	252	25	201	758	.256	1166	2679	140	.965

Selected by St. Louis Cardinals' organization in 4th round of free-agent draft, January 10, 1978.
Selected by Chicago White Sox' organization in secondary phase of free-agent draft, June 6, 1978.
Selected by Minnesota Twins' organization in secondary phase of free-agent draft, June 5, 1979.
†Granted free agency, November 9, 1987; re-signed by Twins, January 7, 1988.
‡On disabled list, August 21 to September 5, 1988.
§On disabled list, August 26 to September 13, 1989.
xGranted free agency, December 7, 1990.

CHAMPIONSHIP SERIES RECORD

Shares Championship Series record for hitting home run in first at-bat, October 7, 1987.

Year—Club	League	Pos.	G.	AB.	R.	H.	2B.	3B.	HR.	RBI.	B.A.	PO.	A.	E.	F.A.
1987—Minnesota	Amer.	3B	5	20	5	6	1	0	2	5	.300	8	7	0	1.000

WORLD SERIES RECORD

Shares World Series records for most at-bats (2) and most hits (2), inning, October 17, 1987, fourth inning.

Year—Club	League	Pos.	G.	AB.	R.	H.	2B.	3B.	HR.	RBI.	B.A.	PO.	A.	E.	F.A.
1987—Minnesota	Amer.	3B	7	27	4	7	2	1	1	4	.259	6	15	0	1.000

ALL-STAR GAME RECORD

Year—League	Pos.	AB.	R.	H.	2B.	3B.	HR.	RBI.	B.A.	PO.	A.	E.	F.A.
1988—American	PH	1	0	0	0	0	0	0	.000	0	0	0	.000
1989—American	3B	1	0	0	0	0	0	0	.000	1	0	0	1.000
All-Star Game Totals—2 Years		2	0	0	0	0	0	0	.000	1	0	0	1.000

GREGORY CARPENTER GAGNE

Name pronounced GAG-nee.

(Greg)

Born November 12, 1961, at Fall River, Mass.
Height, 5.11. Weight, 172.
Throws and bats righthanded.

Shares Major League record for most inside-the-park home runs, game (2), October 4, 1986.
Major League stolen bases: 1985 (10), 1986 (12), 1987 (6), 1988 (15), 1989 (11), 1990 (8). Total—62.
Led International League shortstops in total chances with 599 in 1983.

Year—Club	League	Pos.	G.	AB.	R.	H.	2B.	3B.	HR.	RBI.	B.A.	PO.	A.	E.	F.A.
1979—Paintsville	Appal.	SS	41	106	10	19	2	3	0	7	.179	28	62	14	.865
1980—Greensboro†	S. Atl.	SS-3B-2B	98	337	39	91	20	5	3	32	.270	133	233	35	.913
1981—Greensboro	S. Atl.	2B-SS-3B	104	364	71	108	21	3	9	48	.297	172	280	25	.948
1982—Fort Lauderdale‡	Fla. St.	SS	1	3	0	1	0	0	0	0	.333	3	5	0	1.000
1982—Orlando	South.	SS-2B	136	504	73	117	23	5	11	57	.232	185	403	39	.938
1983—Toledo	Int.	SS	119	392	61	100	22	4	17	66	.255	201	*364	*34	.943

Year	Club	League	Pos.	G.	AB.	R.	H.	2B.	3B.	HR.	RBI.	B.A.	PO.	A.	E.	F.A.
1983—Minnesota	Amer.		SS	10	27	2	3	1	0	0	3	.111	10	14	2	.923
1984—Toledo§	Int.		3B-SS-2B	70	236	31	66	7	2	9	27	.280	58	168	20	.926
1984—Minnesota	Amer.		PR-PH	2	1	0	0	0	0	0	0	.000	0	0	0	.000
1985—Minnesota x	Amer.		SS	114	293	37	66	15	3	2	23	.225	149	269	14	.968
1986—Minnesota	Amer.		*SS-2B	156	472	63	118	22	6	12	54	.250	228	381	*26	.959
1987—Minnesota	Amer.		SS-OF-2B	137	437	68	116	28	7	10	40	.265	196	391	18	.970
1988—Minnesota	Amer.		S-O-2-3	149	461	70	109	20	6	14	48	.236	202	373	18	.970
1989—Minnesota	Amer.		SS-OF	149	460	69	125	29	7	9	48	.272	218	389	18	.971
1990—Minnesota	Amer.		SS-OF	138	388	38	91	22	3	7	38	.235	184	377	14	.976
Major League Totals—8 Years				855	2539	347	628	137	32	54	254	.247	1187	2194	110	.968

Selected by New York Yankees' organization in 5th round of free-agent draft, June 5, 1979.

†On disabled list, September 4 to September 22, 1980.

‡Traded with Pitchers Ron Davis and Paul Boris and a reported $400,000 to Minnesota Twins for Shortstop Roy Smalley, April 10, 1982.

§On disabled list, June 13 to July 18, 1984.

xOn disabled list, August 10 to September 1, 1985.

CHAMPIONSHIP SERIES RECORD

Year	Club	League	Pos.	G.	AB.	R.	H.	2B.	3B.	HR.	RBI.	B.A.	PO.	A.	E.	F.A.
1987—Minnesota	Amer.		SS	5	18	5	5	3	0	2	3	.278	9	13	2	.917

WORLD SERIES RECORD

Shares World Series record for most at-bats, inning (2), October 18, 1987, fourth inning.

Year	Club	League	Pos.	G.	AB.	R.	H.	2B.	3B.	HR.	RBI.	B.A.	PO.	A.	E.	F.A.
1987—Minnesota	Amer.		SS	7	30	5	6	1	0	1	3	.200	6	20	2	.929

ANDRES JOSE GALARRAGA

Name pronounced Gahl-ah-RAH-guh.

Born June 18, 1961, at Caracas, Venezuela.
Height, 6.03. Weight, 235.
Throws and bats righthanded.

Major League stolen bases: 1985 (1), 1986 (6), 1987 (7), 1988 (13), 1989 (12), 1990 (10). Total—49.

Led National League batters in strikeouts with 153 in 1988, 158 in 1989 and 169 in 1990.

Led National League in total bases with 329 in 1988.

Led National League in being hit by pitch with 10 in 1987 and tied for lead with 13 in 1989.

Led Southern League in total bases with 271, slugging percentage with .508, intentional bases on balls received with 10 and tied for lead in being hit by pitch with 9 in 1984.

Tied for American Association lead in game-winning RBIs with 13 in 1985.

Led Southern League first basemen in total chances with 1,428 and double plays with 130 in 1984.

Named first baseman on THE SPORTING NEWS National League All-Star fielding team, 1989 and 1990.

Named first baseman on THE SPORTING NEWS National League Silver Slugger team, 1988.

Named Southern League Most Valuable Player, 1984.

Year	Club	League	Pos.	G.	AB.	R.	H.	2B.	3B.	HR.	RBI.	B.A.	PO.	A.	E.	F.A.
1979—W. Palm Beach	Fla. St.		1B	7	23	3	3	0	0	0	1	.130	2	1	0	1.000
1979—Calgary	Pion.		1B-3B-C	42	112	14	24	3	1	4	16	.214	187	21	5	.976
1980—Calgary	Pion.		1-3-C-O	59	190	27	50	11	4	4	22	.263	287	52	21	.942
1981—Jamestown	NYP		C-1-O-3	47	154	24	40	5	4	6	26	.260	154	15	0	1.000
1982—W. Palm Beach	Fla. St.		1B-OF	105	338	39	95	20	2	14	51	.281	462	36	9	.982
1983—W. Palm Beach	Fla. St.		1B-OF-3B	104	401	55	116	18	3	10	66	.289	861	77	13	.986
1984—Jacksonville	South.		1B	143	533	81	154	28	4	27	87	.289	*1302	*110	16	.989
1985—Indianapolis	A. A.		1B-OF	121	439	*75	118	15	8	25	87	.269	930	63	14	.986
1985—Montreal	Nat.		1B	24	75	9	14	1	0	2	4	.187	173	22	1	.995
1986—Montreal†	Nat.		1B	105	321	39	87	13	0	10	42	.271	805	40	4	.995
1987—Montreal	Nat.		1B	147	551	72	168	40	3	13	90	.305	*1300	103	10	.993
1988—Montreal	Nat.		1B	157	609	99	*184	*42	8	29	92	.302	1464	103	15	.991
1989—Montreal	Nat.		1B	152	572	76	147	30	1	23	85	.257	1335	91	11	.992
1990—Montreal	Nat.		1B	155	579	65	148	29	0	20	87	.256	1300	94	10	.993
Major League Totals—6 Years				740	2707	360	748	155	12	97	400	.276	6377	453	51	.993

Signed as free agent by Montreal Expos' organization, January 19, 1979.

†On disabled list, July 10 to August 19 and August 20 to September 4, 1986.

ALL-STAR GAME RECORD

Year	League	Pos.	AB.	R.	H.	2B.	3B.	HR.	RBI.	B.A.	PO.	A.	E.	F.A.
1988—National		1B	2	0	0	0	0	0	0	.000	6	0	0	1.000

DAVID THOMAS GALLAGHER
(Dave)

Born September 20, 1960, at Trenton, N.J.
Height, 6.00. Weight, 185.
Throws and bats righthanded.
Attended Mercer County Community College, Trenton, N.J.

Major League stolen bases: 1987 (2), 1988 (5), 1989 (5), 1990 (1). Total—13.

Led International League in sacrifice hits with 12 in 1986.

Led Midwest League in sacrifice hits with 21 in 1982.

Led International League outfielders in total chances with 369 in 1985.

Tied for Eastern League lead in double plays by outfielders with 4 in 1983.

Year Club	League	Pos.	G.	AB.	R.	H.	2B.	3B.	HR.	RBI.	B.A.	PO.	A.	E.	F.A.
1980—Batavia..................	NYP	OF	69	241	33	66	6	3	5	36	.274	114	4	2	.983
1981—Waterloo...............	Midw.	OF-3B	127	435	55	102	22	1	3	34	.234	224	22	7	.972
1982—Chattanooga	South.	OF	15	54	10	12	2	1	0	4	.222	32	1	0	1.000
1982—Waterloo...............	Midw.	OF	110	409	61	118	25	7	6	47	.289	232	15	4	★.984
1983—Buffalo†...............	East.	OF-3B	107	376	64	127	21	3	2	47	★.338	223	13	5	.979
1984—Maine....................	Int.	OF	116	380	49	94	19	5	6	49	.247	208	7	3	.986
1985—Maine....................	Int.	OF	132	488	71	118	22	3	9	55	.242	★357	9	3	★.992
1986—Maine....................	Int.	OF	132	497	59	145	23	5	8	44	.292	341	★14	1	★.997
1987—Cleveland..............	Amer.	OF	15	36	2	4	1	1	0	1	.111	34	1	1	.972
1987—Buffalo‡...............	A. A.	OF	12	46	10	12	4	0	0	6	.261	34	1	0	1.000
1987—Calgary§................	P. C.	OF	75	268	45	82	27	2	3	46	.306	143	5	4	.974
1988—Vancouver............	P. C.	OF	34	131	23	44	8	1	4	27	.336	79	2	0	1.000
1988—Chicago	Amer.	OF	101	347	59	105	15	3	5	31	.303	228	5	0	1.000
1989—Chicago	Amer.	OF	161	601	74	160	22	2	1	46	.266	390	8	3	.993
1990—Chi.xy-Balt.z.........	Amer.	OF	68	126	12	32	4	1	0	7	.254	96	3	2	.980
Major League Totals—4 Years.................			345	1110	147	301	42	7	6	85	.271	748	17	6	.992

Selected by Oakland A's organization in 1st round (third player selected) of free-agent draft, January 8, 1980.
Selected by Cleveland Indians' organization in secondary phase of free-agent draft, June 3, 1980.
†On disabled list, May 2 to June 6, 1983.
‡Traded to Seattle Mariners' organization for Pitcher Mark Huismann, May 12, 1987.
§Released, September 30, 1987; signed by Vancouver (Chicago White Sox' organization), December 7, 1987.
xOn disabled list, April 29 to May 28, 1990.
yClaimed on waivers by Baltimore Orioles, August 1, 1990.
zTraded to California Angels for Pitchers David Martinez and Mike Hook, December 4, 1990.

MICHAEL ANTHONY GALLEGO
Name pronounced Guy-YEGG-oh.

(Mike)

Born October 31, 1960, at Whittier, Calif.
Height, 5.08. Weight, 160.
Throws and bats righthanded.
Attended University of California, Los Angeles, Calif.

Major League stolen bases: 1985 (1), 1988 (2), 1989 (7), 1990 (5). Total—15.
Tied for American League lead in sacrifice hits with 17 in 1990.
Led Pacific Coast League in being hit by pitch with 8 in 1986.

Year Club	League	Pos.	G.	AB.	R.	H.	2B.	3B.	HR.	RBI.	B.A.	PO.	A.	E.	F.A.
1981—Modesto................	Calif.	2B	60	202	38	55	9	3	0	23	.272	127	161	13	.957
1982—West Haven	East.	2B-SS	54	139	17	25	1	0	0	5	.180	85	111	4	.980
1982—Tacoma.................	P. C.	2B-3B-SS	44	136	12	30	3	1	0	11	.221	73	111	8	.958
1983—Tacoma†...............	P. C.	2B	2	2	0	0	0	0	0	0	.000	0	1	0	1.000
1983—Albany..................	East.	2B-SS-3B	90	274	31	61	6	0	0	18	.223	184	260	4	.991
1984—Tacoma.................	P. C.	2B-SS-3B	101	288	29	70	8	1	0	18	.243	167	231	13	.968
1985—Oakland................	Amer.	2B-SS-3B	76	77	13	16	5	1	1	9	.208	57	94	1	.993
1985—Modesto................	Calif.	2B-SS-3B	6	25	1	5	1	0	0	2	.200	12	11	1	.958
1986—Tacoma.................	P. C.	SS-3B-2B	132	443	58	122	16	5	4	46	.275	197	417	23	.964
1986—Oakland................	Amer.	2B-3B-SS	20	37	2	10	2	0	0	4	.270	24	51	1	.987
1987—Tacoma.................	P. C.	2B	10	41	6	11	0	2	0	6	.268	15	25	1	.976
1987—Oakland‡..............	Amer.	2B-3B-SS	72	124	18	31	6	0	2	14	.250	75	122	8	.961
1988—Oakland................	Amer.	2B-SS-3B	129	277	38	58	8	0	2	20	.209	155	254	8	.981
1989—Oakland................	Amer.	SS-2B-3B	133	357	45	90	14	2	3	30	.252	211	363	19	.968
1990—Oakland................	Amer.	2-S-3-O	140	389	36	80	13	2	3	34	.206	207	379	13	.978
Major League Totals—6 Years.................			570	1261	152	285	48	5	11	111	.226	729	1263	50	.976

Selected by Oakland A's organization in 2nd round of free-agent draft., June 8, 1981.
†On temporary inactive list, April 10 to May 20, 1983.
‡On disabled list, June 13 to July 29, 1987.

CHAMPIONSHIP SERIES RECORD
Shares American League Championship Series record for most sacrifice hits, series (2), 1989.

Year Club	League	Pos.	G.	AB.	R.	H.	2B.	3B.	HR.	RBI.	B.A.	PO.	A.	E.	F.A.
1988—Oakland................	Amer.	2B	4	12	1	1	0	0	0	0	.083	7	6	0	1.000
1989—Oakland................	Amer.	SS-2B	4	11	3	3	1	0	0	1	.273	6	14	0	1.000
1990—Oakland................	Amer.	2B-SS	4	10	1	4	1	0	0	2	.400	8	9	0	1.000
Championship Series Totals—3 Years.....			12	33	5	8	2	0	0	3	.242	21	29	0	1.000

WORLD SERIES RECORD

Year Club	League	Pos.	G.	AB.	R.	H.	2B.	3B.	HR.	RBI.	B.A.	PO.	A.	E.	F.A.
1988—Oakland................	Amer.	PR-2B	1	0	0	0	0	0	0	0	.000	0	0	0	.000
1989—Oakland................	Amer.	2B-3B	2	1	0	0	0	0	0	0	.000	0	0	0	.000
1990—Oakland................	Amer.	SS	4	11	0	1	0	0	0	1	.091	7	10	1	.944
World Series Totals—3 Years			7	12	0	1	0	0	0	1	.083	7	10	1	.944

—DID YOU KNOW—
That Bobby Thigpen of the White Sox saved more games (57) than the entire bull-pens of every other A.L. team but Oakland, which notched 64 saves?

RONALD EDWIN GANT
(Ronnie)

Born March 2, 1965, at Victoria, Tex.
Height, 6.00. Weight, 172.
Throws and bats righthanded.

Major League stolen bases: 1987 (4), 1988 (19), 1989 (9), 1990 (33). Total—65.
Led National League second baseman in errors with 26 in 1988.
Led Carolina League in total bases with 271 in 1986.
Led Southern League second basemen in double plays with 108 and total chances with 783 in 1987.
Led South Atlantic League second basemen in double plays with 75 in 1984.

Year	Club	League	Pos.	G.	AB.	R.	H.	2B.	3B.	HR.	RBI.	B.A.	PO.	A.	E.	F.A.
1983—Bradenton Brav...	Gulf C.	SS	56	193	32	45	2	2	1	14	.233	68	134	22	.902
1984—Anderson	S. Atl.	2B	105	359	44	85	14	6	3	38	.237	248	263	31	.943
1985—Sumter	S. Atl.	2B-SS	102	305	46	78	14	4	7	37	.256	160	200	10	.973
1986—Durham	Carol.	2B	137	512	108	142	31	10	*26	102	.277	240	384	26	.960
1987—Greenville	South.	2B	140	527	78	130	27	3	14	82	.247	*328	*434	21	*.973
1987—Atlanta	Nat.	2B	21	83	9	22	4	0	2	9	.265	45	59	3	.972
1988—Richmond	Int.	2B	12	45	3	14	2	2	0	4	.311	22	23	5	.900
1988—Atlanta	Nat.	2B-3B	146	563	85	146	28	8	19	60	.259	316	417	31	.959
1989—Atlanta	Nat.	3B-OF	75	260	26	46	8	3	9	25	.177	70	103	17	.911
1989—Sumter	S. Atl.	OF	12	39	13	15	4	1	1	5	.385	19	1	2	.909
1989—Richmond	Int.	OF-3B	63	225	42	59	13	2	11	27	.262	111	14	5	.962
1990—Atlanta	Nat.	OF	152	575	107	174	34	3	32	84	.303	357	7	8	.978
Major League Totals—4 Years			394	1481	227	388	74	14	62	178	.262	788	586	59	.959

Selected by Atlanta Braves' organization in 4th round of free-agent draft, June 6, 1983.

JAMES ELMER GANTNER
(Jim)

Born January 5, 1954, at Eden, Wis.
Height, 5.11. Weight, 175.
Throws right and bats lefthanded.
Attended University of Wisconsin, Oshkosh, Wis.

Shares major league record for longest errorless game by second baseman (25 innings), May 8, finished May 9, 1984; fielded 24⅓ innings.
Holds American League record for highest fielding average, second baseman, lifetime (.985).
Shares American League record for most innings played by second baseman, game (25), May 8, finished May 9, 1984; fielded 24⅓ innings.
Major League stolen bases: 1976 (1), 1977 (2), 1978 (2), 1979 (3), 1980 (11), 1981 (3), 1982 (6), 1983 (5), 1984 (6), 1985 (11), 1986 (13), 1987 (6), 1988 (20), 1989 (20), 1990 (18). Total—127.
Led American League in being hit by pitch with 10 in 1989.
Led American League second basemen in total chances with 613 in 1981, 900 in 1983 and 844 in 1984.
Led American League second basemen in double plays with 95 in 1981 and 128 in 1983.
Led Pacific Coast League third basemen in putouts with 136 and in fielding percentage with .936 in 1977.
Led Eastern League third basemen in fielding percentage with .953 in 1976.
Led Eastern League third basemen in putouts with 310 and assists with 310 in 1975.

Year	Club	League	Pos.	G.	AB.	R.	H.	2B.	3B.	HR.	RBI.	B.A.	PO.	A.	E.	F.A.
1974—Newark	NYP	SS-3B	62	177	35	54	6	2	5	21	.305	64	134	14	.934
1975—Thetford Mines	East.	3B-SS ●138		456	61	117	17	0	12	48	.257	129	317	33	.931
1976—Berkshire	East.	3B-SS	126	403	56	118	21	1	6	53	.293	120	294	20	.954
1976—Milwaukee	Amer.	3B	26	69	6	17	1	0	0	7	.246	17	37	1	.982
1977—Spokane	P. C.	*3B-OF ●143		541	98	152	35	5	15	80	.281	137	*321	31	.937
1977—Milwaukee	Amer.	3B	14	47	4	14	1	0	1	2	.298	8	29	4	.902
1978—Milwaukee	Amer.	2-3-S-1	43	97	14	21	1	0	1	8	.216	46	82	5	.962
1979—Milwaukee	Amer.	3-2-S-P	70	208	29	59	10	3	2	22	.284	80	161	7	.972
1980—Milwaukee	Amer.	3B-2B-SS	132	415	47	117	21	3	4	40	.282	159	335	15	.971
1981—Milwaukee	Amer.	2B	107	352	35	94	14	1	2	33	.267	251	352	10	.984
1982—Milwaukee	Amer.	2B	132	447	48	132	17	2	4	43	.295	307	398	13	.982
1983—Milwaukee	Amer.	2B	161	603	85	170	23	8	.11	74	.282	374	*512	14	.984
1984—Milwaukee	Amer.	2B	153	613	61	173	27	1	3	56	.282	*362	469	13	.985
1985—Milwaukee	Amer.	2B-3B-SS	143	523	63	133	15	4	5	44	.254	278	436	11	.985
1986—Milwaukee	Amer.	2B-3B-SS	139	497	58	136	25	1	7	38	.274	309	353	10	.985
1987—Milwaukee†	Amer.	2B-3B	81	265	37	72	14	0	4	30	.272	119	193	6	.981
1988—Milwaukee‡	Amer.	*2B-3B	155	539	67	149	28	2	0	47	.276	*325	430	11	.986
1989—Milwaukee§	Amer.	2B	116	409	51	112	18	3	0	34	.274	241	362	8	.987
1990—Beloit x	Midw.	2B	9	29	10	11	1	0	2	6	.379	2	1	1	.750
1990—Denver	A. A.	2B-3B	6	22	1	8	1	0	0	1	.364	7	14	0	1.000
1990—Milwaukee	Amer.	2B-3B	88	323	36	85	8	5	0	25	.263	167	240	9	.978
Major League Totals—15 Years			1560	5407	641	1484	223	33	44	503	.274	3043	4389	137	.982

Selected by Milwaukee Brewers' organization in 12th round of free-agent draft, June 5, 1974.
†On disabled list, July 31 to September 3, 1987.
‡Granted free agency, November 4, 1988; re-signed by Brewers, December 20, 1988.
§On disabled list, August 16, 1989 through remainder of season.
xOn Milwaukee disabled list, March 31 to June 14, 1990; included rehabilitation disability assignment to Beloit, May 24 to June 5, 1990; and Denver, June 6 to June 12, 1990.

DIVISION SERIES RECORD

Year	Club	League	Pos.	G.	AB.	R.	H.	2B.	3B.	HR.	RBI.	B.A.	PO.	A.	E.	F.A.
1981—Milwaukee	Amer.	2B	4	14	1	2	1	0	0	0	.143	3	15	2	.900

Year Club	League	Pos.	G.	AB.	R.	H.	2B.	3B.	HR.	RBI.	B.A.	PO.	A.	E.	F.A.
1982—Milwaukee............	Amer.	2B	5	16	1	3	0	0	0	2	.188	12	8	0	1.000

WORLD SERIES RECORD

Year Club	League	Pos.	G.	AB.	R.	H.	2B.	3B.	HR.	RBI.	B.A.	PO.	A.	E.	F.A.
1982—Milwaukee............	Amer.	2B	7	24	5	8	4	1	0	4	.333	9	33	5	.894

PITCHING RECORD

Year Club	League	G.	IP.	W.	L.	Pct.	H.	R.	ER.	SO.	BB.	ERA.
1979—Milwaukee......................................	American	1	1	0	0	.000	2	0	0	0	0	0.00

RICHARD ARON GARCES
(Rich)

Born May 18, 1971, at Maracay, Venezuela.
Height, 6.00. Weight, 187.
Throws and bats righthanded.

Major League saves: 1990 (2).
Led California League in saves with 28 in 1990.

Year Club	League	G.	IP.	W.	L.	Pct.	H.	R.	ER.	SO.	BB.	ERA.
1988—Elizabethton	Ap'lachian	17	59	5	4	.556	51	22	15	69	27	2.29
1989—Kenosha..	Midwest	24	142⅔	9	10	.474	117	70	54	84	62	3.41
1990—Visalia	California	47	54⅔	2	2	.500	33	14	11	75	16	1.81
1990—Orlando	Southern	15	17⅓	2	1	.667	17	4	4	22	14	2.08
1990—Minnesota....................................	American	5	5⅔	0	0	.000	4	2	1	1	4	1.59
Major League Totals—1 Year..............................		5	5⅔	0	0	.000	4	2	1	1	4	1.59

Signed as free agent by Minnesota Twins' organization, December 29, 1987.

CARLOS JESUS GARCIA

Born October 15, 1967, at Tachira, Venezuela.
Height, 6.01. Weight, 185.
Throws and bats righthanded.

Year Club	League	Pos.	G.	AB.	R.	H.	2B.	3B.	HR.	RBI.	B.A.	PO.	A.	E.	F.A.
1987—Macon....................	S. Atl.	SS	110	373	44	95	14	3	3	38	.255	161	262	42	.910
1988—Augusta	S. Atl.	SS	73	269	32	78	13	2	1	45	.290	138	207	29	.922
1988—Salem.....................	Carol.	SS	62	236	21	65	9	3	1	28	.275	131	151	24	.922
1989—Salem.....................	Carol.	SS	81	304	45	86	12	4	7	49	.283	137	262	32	.926
1989—Harrisburg	East.	SS	54	188	28	53	5	5	3	25	.282	84	131	7	.968
1990—Harrisburg	East.	SS	65	242	36	67	11	2	5	25	.277	101	209	14	.957
1990—Buffalo...................	A. A.	SS	63	197	23	52	10	0	5	18	.264	106	170	19	.936
1990—Pittsburgh.............	Nat.	SS	4	4	1	2	0	0	0	0	.500	0	4	0	1.000
Major League Totals—1 Year..................		4	4	1	2	0	0	0	0	.500	0	4	0	1.000

Signed as free agent by Pittsburgh Pirates' organization, January 9, 1987.

RAMON ANTONIO GARCIA

Born December 9, 1969, at Guanare, Venezuela.
Height, 6.02. Weight, 200.
Throws and bats righthanded.

Pitched 2-0 no-hit victory against Sarasota Mets, August 3, 1989.
Led Florida State League in home runs allowed with 10 in 1990.
Tied for Gulf Coast League lead in shutouts with 1 in 1989.

Year Club	League	G.	IP.	W.	L.	Pct.	H.	R.	ER.	SO.	BB.	ERA.
1987—Sarasota White Sox.....................Gulf Coast		6	12	1	0	1.000	8	3	2	6	5	1.50
1988—Sarasota White Sox.....................Gulf Coast		13	22	2	1	.667	15	9	6	17	4	2.45
1989—Sarasota White Sox.....................Gulf Coast		14	53	6	4	.600	34	21	18	52	17	3.06
1990—Sarasota .... Florida St.		26	157⅓	9	*14	.391	155	84	69	130	45	3.95
1990—Vancouver................................... P. Coast		1	1	0	0	.000	2	0	0	1	0	0.00

Signed as free agent by Chicago White Sox' organization, June 30, 1987.

MICHAEL JAMES GARDINER
(Mike)

Born October 19, 1965, at Sarnia, Ontario, Canada.
Height, 6.00. Weight, 185.
Throws right and bats left and righthanded.
Received bachelor's degree in business from Indiana State University,
Terre Haute, Ind., in 1987.

Named Eastern League Pitcher of the Year, 1990.
Member of Canadian Olympic baseball team, 1984.

Year Club	League	G.	IP.	W.	L.	Pct.	H.	R.	ER.	SO.	BB.	ERA.
1987—Bellingham .... Northwest		2	10	2	0	1.000	6	0	0	11	1	0.00
1987—Wausau.. Midwest		13	81	3	5	.375	91	54	47	80	33	5.22
1988—Wausau†....................................... Midwest		11	31⅓	2	1	.667	31	16	11	24	13	3.16
1989—Wausau.. Midwest		15	30⅓	4	0	1.000	21	5	2	48	11	0.59

Year Club	League	G.	IP.	W.	L.	Pct.	H.	R.	ER.	SO.	BB.	ERA.
1989—Williamsport	Eastern	30	63⅓	4	6	.400	54	25	20	60	32	2.84
1990—Williamsport	Eastern	26	*179⅔	12	8	.600	136	47	38	*149	29	*1.90
1990—Seattle	American	5	12⅔	0	2	.000	22	17	15	6	5	10.66
Major League Totals—1 Year		5	12⅔	0	2	.000	22	17	15	6	5	10.66

Selected by Seattle Mariners' organization in 18th round of free-agent draft, June 2, 1987.
†On disabled list, May 9 to June 10, 1988.

MARK ALLAN GARDNER

Born March 1, 1962, at Clovis, Calif.
Height, 6.01. Weight, 200.
Throws and bats righthanded.
Attended Fresno City College, Fresno, Calif., and Fresno State University, Fresno, Calif.

Led National League in hit batsmen with 9 in 1990.
Named American Association Pitcher of the Year, 1989.

Year Club	League	G.	IP.	W.	L.	Pct.	H.	R.	ER.	SO.	BB.	ERA.
1985—Jamestown	NYP	3	13	0	0	.000	9	4	4	16	4	2.77
1985—West Palm Beach	Florida St.	10	60⅔	5	4	.556	54	24	16	44	18	2.37
1986—Jacksonville	Southern	29	168⅔	10	11	.476	144	88	72	140	90	3.84
1987—Indianapolis	Am. Assoc.	9	46	3	3	.500	48	32	29	41	28	5.67
1987—Jacksonville	Southern	17	101	4	6	.400	101	50	47	78	42	4.19
1988—Jacksonville	Southern	15	112⅓	6	3	.667	72	24	20	130	36	1.60
1988—Indianapolis	Am. Assoc.	13	84⅓	4	2	.667	65	30	26	71	32	2.77
1989—Indianapolis	Am. Assoc.	24	163⅓	12	4	*.750	122	51	43	*175	59	2.37
1989—Montreal	National	7	26⅓	0	3	.000	26	16	15	21	11	5.13
1990—Montreal†	National	27	152⅔	7	9	.438	129	62	58	135	61	3.42
Major League Totals—2 Years		34	179	7	12	.368	155	78	73	156	72	3.67

Selected by California Angels' organization in 6th round of free-agent draft, January 11, 1983.
Selected by Cleveland Indians' organization in 17th round of free-agent draft, June 4, 1984.
Selected by Montreal Expos' organization in 8th round of free-agent draft, June 3, 1985.
†On disabled list, September 20, 1990 through remainder of season.

WESLEY BRIAN GARDNER
(Wes)

Born April 29, 1961, at Benton, Ark.
Height, 6.04. Weight, 203.
Throws and bats righthanded.
Attended University of Central Arkansas, Conway, Ark.

Major League saves: 1984 (1), 1987 (10), 1988 (2). Total—13.
Led International League in saves with 20 in 1984 and tied for lead with 18 in 1985.
Led International League in games finished in relief with 37 in 1984.

Year Club	League	G.	IP.	W.	L.	Pct.	H.	R.	ER.	SO.	BB.	ERA.
1982—Little Falls	NYP	23	77⅔	3	6	.333	73	48	32	77	29	3.71
1983—Lynchburg	Carolina	49	62⅔	6	3	.667	55	16	13	67	32	1.87
1984—Tidewater	Int'national	40	56	1	2	.333	40	11	10	36	19	1.61
1984—New York	National	21	25⅓	1	1	.500	34	19	18	19	8	6.39
1985—Tidewater	Int'national	53	76⅔	7	6	.538	57	31	24	75	34	2.82
1985—New York†	National	9	12	0	2	.000	18	14	7	11	8	5.25
1986—Boston‡	American	1	1	0	0	.000	1	1	1	1	0	9.00
1987—Boston	American	49	89⅔	3	6	.333	98	55	54	70	42	5.42
1987—Pawtucket	Int'national	5	8⅔	1	0	1.000	8	3	3	9	3	3.12
1988—Boston§	American	36	149	8	6	.571	119	61	58	106	64	3.50
1989—Boston x	American	22	86	3	7	.300	97	64	57	81	47	5.97
1990—Boston yz	American	34	77⅓	3	7	.300	77	43	42	58	35	4.89
National League Totals—2 Years		30	37⅓	1	3	.250	52	33	25	30	16	6.03
American League Totals—5 Years		142	403	17	26	.395	392	224	212	316	188	4.73
Major League Totals—7 Years		172	440⅓	18	29	.383	444	257	237	346	204	4.84

Selected by New York Mets' organization in 22nd round of free-agent draft, June 7, 1982.
†Traded with Pitcher Calvin Schiraldi and Outfielders John Christensen and LaSchelle Tarver to Boston Red Sox for Pitchers Bob Ojeda, Tom McCarthy, John Mitchell and Chris Bayer, November 13, 1985.
‡On disabled list, April 14, 1986 through remainder of season; included rehabilitation disability assignment to Pawtucket, June 24 to July 1, 1986.
§On disabled list, May 29 to June 13, 1988.
xOn disabled list, May 21 to June 12 and August 28, 1989 through remainder of season.
yOn disabled list, April 13 to April 28 and July 28 to August 12, 1990.
zTraded to San Diego Padres for First Baseman-Outfielder Steve Hendricks and Pitcher Brad Hoyer, December 15, 1990.

CHAMPIONSHIP SERIES RECORD

Year Club	League	G.	IP.	W.	L.	Pct.	H.	R.	ER.	SO.	BB.	ERA.
1988—Boston	American	1	4⅔	0	0	.000	6	3	3	8	2	5.79

—DID YOU KNOW—

That Minnesota's Gene Larkin led all designated hitters last season with a .336 batting average?

SCOTT WILLIAM GARRELTS
Name pronounced Guh-RELTZ.

Born October 30, 1961, at Urbana, Ill.
Height, 6.04. Weight, 210.
Throws and bats righthanded.

Pitched seven-inning, 1-0 no-hit victory against Tacoma, August 20, 1983.
Major League saves: 1985 (13), 1986 (10), 1987 (12), 1988 (13). Total—48.
Tied for Midwest League lead in games started by pitchers with 27 in 1980.

Year Club	League	G.	IP.	W.	L.	Pct.	H.	R.	ER.	SO.	BB.	ERA.
1979—Great Falls	Pioneer	8	43	1	4	.200	45	37	28	26	40	5.86
1980—Clinton	Midwest	27	176	11	11	.500	155	98	76	*159	*149	3.89
1981—Shreveport†	Texas	14	71	3	8	.273	56	43	35	73	43	4.44
1982—Shreveport	Texas	27	151⅓	9	10	.474	131	76	64	159	90	3.81
1982—San Francisco	National	1	2	0	0	.000	3	3	3	4	2	13.50
1983—Phoenix‡	P. Coast	21	97⅔	5	5	.500	86	64	50	89	81	4.61
1983—San Francisco	National	5	35⅔	2	2	.500	33	11	10	16	19	2.52
1984—Phoenix	P. Coast	21	97⅔	5	7	.417	97	75	64	69	82	5.90
1984—San Francisco	National	21	43	2	3	.400	45	33	27	32	34	5.65
1985—San Francisco	National	74	105⅔	9	6	.600	76	37	27	106	58	2.30
1986—San Francisco	National	53	173⅔	13	9	.591	144	65	60	125	74	3.11
1987—San Francisco	National	64	106⅓	11	7	.611	70	41	38	127	55	3.22
1988—San Francisco	National	65	98	5	9	.357	80	42	39	86	46	3.58
1989—San Francisco§	National	30	193⅓	14	5	*.737	149	58	49	119	46	*2.28
1990—San Francisco	National	31	182	12	11	.522	190	91	84	80	70	4.15
Major League Totals—9 Years		344	939⅔	68	52	.567	790	381	337	695	404	3.23

Selected by San Francisco Giants' organization in 1st round (15th player selected) of free-agent draft, June 5, 1979.
†On disabled list, July 15 to August 16, 1981.
‡On disabled list, May 12 to June 6 and July 8 to July 24, 1983.
§On disabled list, June 30 to July 16, 1989.

CHAMPIONSHIP SERIES RECORD

Year Club	League	G.	IP.	W.	L.	Pct.	H.	R.	ER.	SO.	BB.	ERA.
1987—San Francisco	National	2	2⅔	0	0	.000	2	2	2	4	4	6.75
1989—San Francisco	National	2	11⅔	1	0	1.000	16	7	7	8	2	5.40
Championship Series Totals—2 Years		4	14⅓	1	0	1.000	18	9	9	12	6	5.65

WORLD SERIES RECORD

Year Club	League	G.	IP.	W.	L.	Pct.	H.	R.	ER.	SO.	BB.	ERA.
1989—San Francisco	National	2	7⅓	0	2	.000	13	9	8	8	1	9.82

ALL-STAR GAME RECORD

Member of National League All-Star Team in 1985; did not play.

RICHARD LEO GEDMAN JR.
(Rich)

Born September 26, 1959, at Worcester, Mass.
Height, 6.00. Weight, 222.
Throws right and bats lefthanded.

Holds major league records for most putouts (36) and chances accepted (37) by catcher, two consecutive nine-inning games, April 29, 30, 1986.
Shares major league record for most putouts by catcher, nine-inning game (20), April 29, 1986.
Shares American League record for most chances accepted by catcher, nine-inning game (20), April 29, 1986.
Major League stolen bases: 1985 (2), 1986 (1). Total—3.
Hit for the cycle, September 18, 1985.
Led American League catchers in total chances with 937 and passed balls with 14 in 1986.
Led International League catchers in double plays with 13 in 1980.
Named catcher on THE SPORTING NEWS American League All-Star Team, 1986.
Named American League Rookie Player of the Year by THE SPORTING NEWS, 1981.

Year Club	League	Pos.	G.	AB.	R.	H.	2B.	3B.	HR.	RBI.	B.A.	PO.	A.	E.	F.A.
1978—Winter Haven	Fla. St.	C	98	297	35	89	17	3	3	32	.300	377	39	2	*.995
1979—Bristol	East.	C	130	470	48	129	25	1	12	63	.274	497	58	11	*.981
1980—Pawtucket	Int.	C	111	347	43	82	18	2	11	29	.236	367	*65	7	.984
1980—Boston	Amer.	C	9	24	2	5	0	0	0	1	.208	13	0	2	.867
1981—Pawtucket	Int.	C	25	81	8	24	3	0	2	11	.296	176	20	6	.969
1981—Boston	Amer.	C	62	205	22	59	15	0	5	26	.288	275	30	3	.990
1982—Boston	Amer.	C	92	289	30	72	17	2	4	26	.249	397	29	10	.977
1983—Boston	Amer.	C	81	204	21	60	16	1	2	18	.294	274	26	6	.980
1984—Boston	Amer.	C	133	449	54	121	26	4	24	72	.269	693	58	*18	.977
1985—Boston	Amer.	C	144	498	66	147	30	5	18	80	.295	768	*78	*15	.983
1986—Boston†	Amer.	C	135	462	49	119	29	0	16	65	.258	*866	65	6	.994
1987—Boston†	Amer.	C	52	151	11	31	8	0	1	13	.205	306	14	8	.976
1988—Boston§	Amer.	C	95	299	33	69	14	0	9	39	.231	570	40	5	.992
1988—Pawtucket	Int.	C	4	15	2	7	1	0	1	1	.467	13	1	1	.933
1989—Boston	Amer.	C	93	260	24	55	9	0	4	16	.212	486	36	10	.981
1990—Boston x	Amer.	C	10	15	3	3	0	0	0	0	.200	27	5	1	.970

Year Club League	Pos.	G.	AB.	R.	H.	2B.	3B.	HR.	RBI.	B.A.	PO.	A.	E.	F.A.
1990—Houston y .... Nat.	C	40	104	4	21	7	0	1	10	.202	180	25	0	1.000
American League Totals—11 Years		906	2856	315	741	164	12	83	356	.259	4675	381	84	.984
National League Totals—1 Year.............		40	104	4	21	7	0	1	10	.202	180	25	0	1.000
Major League Totals—11 Years...............		946	2960	319	762	171	12	84	366	.257	4855	406	84	.984

Signed as free agent by Boston Red Sox' organization, August 5, 1977.

†Granted free agency, November 12, 1986; re-signed by Red Sox, May 2, 1987.

‡On disabled list, July 7 to July 22 and July 30, 1987 through remainder of season.

§On disabled list, April 26 to May 20, 1988; included rehabilitation disability assignment to Pawtucket, May 14 to May 20, 1988.

xTraded to Houston Astros for a player to be named later, June 8, 1990; deal settled with cash.

yGranted free agency, November 5, 1990.

CHAMPIONSHIP SERIES RECORD

Year Club League	Pos.	G.	AB.	R.	H.	2B.	3B.	HR.	RBI.	B.A.	PO.	A.	E.	F.A.
1986—Boston................... Amer.	C	7	28	4	10	1	0	1	6	.357	45	4	0	1.000
1988—Boston................... Amer.	C	4	14	1	5	0	0	1	1	.357	34	5	0	1.000
Championship Series Totals—2 Years.....		11	42	5	15	1	0	2	7	.357	79	9	0	1.000

WORLD SERIES RECORD

Year Club League	Pos.	G.	AB.	R.	H.	2B.	3B.	HR.	RBI.	B.A.	PO.	A.	E.	F.A.
1986—Boston................... Amer.	C	7	30	1	6	1	0	1	1	.200	46	3	2	.961

ALL-STAR GAME RECORD

Year League	Pos.	AB.	R.	H.	2B.	3B.	HR.	RBI.	B.A.	PO.	A.	E.	F.A.
1985—American	C	1	0	0	0	0	0	0	.000	4	0	0	1.000
1986—American	C	0	0	0	0	0	0	0	.000	1	1	0	1.000
All-Star Game Totals—2 Years....................		1	0	0	0	0	0	0	.000	5	1	0	1.000

CHRISTOPHER SEAN GEORGE
(Chris)

Born September 24, 1966, at Pittsburgh, Pa.
Height, 6.02. Weight, 200.
Throws and bats righthanded.
Attended Kent State University, Kent, O.

Led Texas League in intentional bases on balls issued with 7 in 1990.

Year Club	League	G.	IP.	W.	L.	Pct.	H.	R.	ER.	SO.	BB.	ERA.
1988—Beloit...	Midwest	22	58	7	4	.636	52	27	19	58	14	2.95
1989—Stockton...	California	55	79⅔	7	7	.500	61	30	19	85	37	2.15
1990—El Paso..	Texas	39	55⅔	8	3	.727	41	16	11	38	20	1.78
1990—Denver...	Am. Assoc.	7	5⅓	1	1	.500	17	11	11	4	4	18.56

Selected by Milwaukee Brewers' organization in 7th round of free-agent draft, June 1, 1988.

ROBERT PETER GEREN III
(Bob)

Born September 22, 1961, at San Diego, Calif.
Height, 6.03. Weight, 228.
Throws and bats righthanded.

Led Eastern League catchers in fielding percentage with .994 in 1987.
Led Texas League catchers in fielding percentage with .996 in 1985.
Led Midwest League catchers in putouts with 826, assists with 102 and total chances with 939 in 1983.

Year Club	League	Pos.	G.	AB.	R.	H.	2B.	3B.	HR.	RBI.	B.A.	PO.	A.	E.	F.A.
1979—Walla Walla .... N'west	C	54	151	19	26	5	0	0	16	.172	183	23	9	.958
1980—Reno .... Calif.	C	48	157	24	45	7	1	4	23	.287	89	17	4	.964
1980—Walla Walla† .... N'west	C	51	177	19	45	8	1	2	28	.254	306	40	10	.972
1981—St. Petersburg....... Fla. St.	C	64	167	15	37	9	1	0	13	.222	204	24	3	.987
1982—St. Petersburg....... Fla. St.	★C-OF-1B	110	352	38	86	24	1	1	45	.244	500	★72	10	.983
1983—Springfield............ Midw.	C-1B	124	434	67	115	21	3	24	73	.265	829	104	11	.988
1984—Arkansas................ Texas	C-1B-3B	86	292	39	72	12	0	15	40	.247	545	56	8	.987
1984—Louisville .... A. A.	C	15	40	3	7	1	0	0	3	.175	80	6	1	.989
1985—Arkansas................ Texas	C-1B-OF	103	315	38	71	18	1	5	40	.225	562	60	4	.994
1985—Louisville‡ .... A. A.	C	5	14	2	5	2	0	1	3	.357	27	1	0	1.000
1986—Albany.................... East.	C-1B	11	27	3	4	1	0	0	0	.148	51	7	0	1.000
1986—Columbus.............. Int.	C-1B	68	205	24	52	15	3	7	25	.254	270	36	5	.984
1987—Albany.................... East.	C-1B-3B	78	213	33	47	7	2	11	31	.221	319	45	3	.992
1987—Columbus.............. Int.	C	5	20	1	3	0	0	1	3	.150	20	3	1	.958
1988—Columbus.............. Int.	C	95	321	37	87	13	2	8	35	.271	478	72	8	.986
1988—New York.............. Amer.	C	10	10	0	1	0	0	0	0	.100	18	3	0	1.000
1989—Columbus.............. Int.	C	27	95	11	24	4	1	2	13	.253	137	18	2	.987
1989—New York.............. Amer.	C	65	205	26	59	5	1	9	27	.288	308	24	3	.991
1990—New York.............. Amer.	C	110	277	21	59	7	0	8	31	.213	487	55	4	.993
Major League Totals—3 Years.................		185	492	47	119	12	1	17	58	.242	813	82	7	.992

Selected by San Diego Padres' organization in 1st round (24th player selected) of free-agent draft, June 5, 1979.

†Traded to St. Louis Cardinals' organization, December 10, 1980, completing deal in which San Diego Padres traded Pitchers Rollie Fingers and Bob Shirley, Catcher-First Baseman Gene Tenace and a player to be named later to

St. Louis Cardinals for Catchers Terry Kennedy and Steve Swisher, Pitchers John Littlefield, Al Olmsted, Kim Seaman and John Urrea and Infielder Mike Phillips, December 8, 1980.

‡Granted free agency, October 15, 1985; signed by Columbus (New York Yankees' organization), November 7, 1985.

KIRK HAROLD GIBSON

Born May 28, 1957, at Pontiac, Mich.
Height, 6.03. Weight, 215.
Throws and bats lefthanded.
Attended Michigan State University, East Lansing, Mich.

Shares major league record for most home runs, opening day of season (2), April 7, 1986.
Major League stolen bases: 1979 (3), 1980 (4), 1981 (17), 1982 (9), 1983 (14), 1984 (29), 1985 (30), 1986 (34), 1987 (26), 1988 (31), 1989 (12), 1990 (26). Total—235.
Named National League Most Valuable Player by Baseball Writers' Association of America, 1988.
Named outfielder on THE SPORTING NEWS National League Silver Slugger team, 1988.
Received reported $200,000 bonus to sign with Detroit Tigers, 1978.
Named outfielder on THE SPORTING NEWS College Baseball All-America Team, 1978.
Selected by St. Louis Cardinals in 7th round (173rd player selected) of 1979 NFL draft.
Named as wide receiver on THE SPORTING NEWS College Football All-America Team, 1978.

Year Club	League	Pos.	G.	AB.	R.	H.	2B.	3B.	HR.	RBI.	B.A.	PO.	A.	E.	F.A.
1978—Lakeland†	Fla. St.	OF	54	175	27	42	5	4	8	40	.240	115	2	6	.951
1979—Evansville‡	A. A.	OF	89	327	50	80	13	5	9	42	.245	100	5	9	.921
1979—Detroit	Amer.	OF	12	38	3	9	3	0	1	4	.237	15	0	0	1.000
1980—Detroit§	Amer.	OF	51	175	23	46	2	1	9	16	.263	122	1	1	.992
1981—Detroit	Amer.	OF	83	290	41	95	11	3	9	40	.328	142	1	4	.973
1982—Detroit x	Amer.	OF	69	266	34	74	16	2	8	35	.278	167	4	1	.994
1983—Detroit	Amer.	OF	128	401	60	91	12	9	15	51	.227	116	2	3	.975
1984—Detroit	Amer.	OF	149	531	92	150	23	10	27	91	.282	245	4	●12	.954
1985—Detroit y	Amer.	OF	154	581	96	167	37	5	29	97	.287	286	1	●11	.963
1986—Detroit z	Amer.	OF	119	441	84	118	11	2	28	86	.268	190	2	2	.990
1987—Toledo	Int.	DH	6	17	2	4	0	0	0	3	.235	0	0	0	.000
1987—Detroit ab	Amer.	OF	128	487	95	135	25	3	24	79	.277	253	6	7	.974
1988—Los Angeles	Nat.	OF	150	542	106	157	28	1	25	76	.290	311	6	★12	.964
1989—Los Angeles c	Nat.	OF	71	253	35	54	8	2	9	28	.213	146	3	3	.980
1990—Albuquerque d	P. C.	OF	5	14	6	6	2	0	1	4	.429	2	0	1	.667
1990—Los Angeles e	Nat.	OF	89	315	59	82	20	0	8	38	.260	191	4	1	.995
American League Totals—9 Years			893	3210	528	885	140	35	150	499	.276	1536	21	41	.974
National League Totals—3 Years			310	1110	200	293	56	3	42	142	.264	648	13	16	.976
Major League Totals—12 Years			1203	4320	728	1178	196	38	192	641	.273	2184	34	57	.975

Selected by Detroit Tigers' organization in 1st round (12th player selected) of free-agent draft, June 6, 1978.
†On restricted list, August 15, 1978, to March 1, 1979.
‡On disabled list, April 13 to May 21, 1979.
§On disabled list, June 18 to October 6, 1980.
xOn disabled list, July 11, 1982 through remainder of season.
yGranted free agency, November 12, 1985; re-signed by Tigers, January 8, 1986.
zOn disabled list, April 23 to June 2, 1986.
aOn Detroit disabled list, March 30 to May 5, 1987; included rehabilitation disability assignment to Toledo, April 28 to May 5, 1987.
bGranted free agency, January 22, 1988; signed by Los Angeles Dodgers, January 29, 1988.
cOn disabled list, April 26 to May 23 and July 23, 1989 through remainder of season.
dOn Los Angeles disabled list, March 31 to June 2, 1990; included rehabilitation disability assignment to Albuquerque, May 24 to June 2, 1990.
eGranted free agency, November 5, 1990; signed by Kansas City Royals, December 1, 1990.

CHAMPIONSHIP SERIES RECORD

Shares Championship Series record for most game-winning RBIs, series (2), 1988.
Shares American League Championship Series record for most strikeouts, series (8), 1987.

Year Club	League	Pos.	G.	AB.	R.	H.	2B.	3B.	HR.	RBI.	B.A.	PO.	A.	E.	F.A.
1984—Detroit	Amer.	OF	3	12	2	5	1	0	1	2	.417	7	0	0	1.000
1987—Detroit	Amer.	OF	5	21	4	6	1	0	1	4	.286	10	1	0	1.000
1988—Los Angeles	Nat.	OF	7	26	2	4	0	0	2	6	.154	17	1	1	.947
Championship Series Totals—3 Years			15	59	8	15	2	0	4	12	.254	34	2	1	.973

WORLD SERIES RECORD

Year Club	League	Pos.	G.	AB.	R.	H.	2B.	3B.	HR.	RBI.	B.A.	PO.	A.	E.	F.A.
1984—Detroit	Amer.	OF	5	18	4	6	0	0	2	7	.333	5	1	2	.750
1988—Los Angeles	Nat.	PH	1	1	1	1	0	0	1	2	1.000	0	0	0	.000
World Series Totals—2 Years			6	19	5	7	0	0	3	9	.368	5	1	2	.750

PAUL MARSHALL GIBSON

Born January 4, 1960, at Southampton, N.Y.
Height, 6.00. Weight, 185.
Throws left and bats righthanded.
Attended Suffolk County Community College, Selden, N.Y.

Major League saves: 1990 (3).
Tied for International League lead in shutouts with 2 in 1987.

Year Club	League	G.	IP.	W.	L.	Pct.	H.	R.	ER.	SO.	BB.	ERA.
1978—Shelby	W. Carol.	24	140	9	6	.600	106	57	47	71	71	3.02
1979—Tampa	Florida St.	24	129	3	8	.273	121	56	44	58	46	3.07
1980—Cedar Rapids†	Midwest	28	146	6	•15	.286	171	97	80	74	53	4.93
1981—Lakeland	Florida St.	20	64	4	3	.571	64	25	21	38	21	2.95
1982—Birmingham‡	Southern	44	77⅓	3	3	.500	60	25	23	71	39	2.68
1983—Orlando§	Southern	40	76⅔	1	7	.125	91	59	52	45	56	6.10
1984—Orlando x	Southern	27	121	7	7	.500	125	71	52	64	54	3.87
1985—Birmingham	Southern	36	144⅓	8	8	.500	135	73	66	79	63	4.12
1986—Glens Falls	Eastern	9	19⅔	3	1	.750	16	3	3	21	7	1.37
1986—Nashville	Am. Assoc.	30	113⅓	5	6	.455	121	58	50	91	40	3.97
1987—Toledo	Int'national	27	179	⋆14	7	.667	173	83	69	118	57	3.47
1988—Detroit	American	40	92	4	2	.667	83	33	30	50	34	2.93
1989—Detroit	American	45	132	4	8	.333	129	71	68	77	57	4.64
1990—Detroit	American	61	97⅓	5	4	.556	99	36	33	56	44	3.05
Major League Totals—3 Years		146	321⅓	13	14	.481	311	140	131	183	135	3.67

Selected by Cincinnati Reds' organization in 3rd round of free-agent draft, January 10, 1978.
†Released, April 8, 1981; signed by Lakeland (Detroit Tigers' organization), May 23, 1981.
‡Drafted by Minnesota Twins, December 6, 1982.
§On disabled list, August 4 to August 14, 1983.
xGranted free agency, October 15, 1984; signed by Birmingham (Detroit Tigers' organization), November 9, 1984.

BYRON BRETT GIDEON

(Known by middle name.)
Born August 8, 1963, at Ozona, Tex.
Height, 6.02. Weight, 195.
Throws and bats righthanded.
Attended Bee County College, Beeville, Tex., and University of Mary Hardin-Baylor, Belton, Tex.

Major League saves: 1987 (3).

Year Club	League	G.	IP.	W.	L.	Pct.	H.	R.	ER.	SO.	BB.	ERA.
1985—Macon	S. Atlantic	15	82⅓	4	7	.364	71	38	30	62	46	3.28
1986—Prince William	Carolina	26	55⅔	1	6	.143	60	43	34	41	37	5.50
1986—Macon	S. Atlantic	6	48	5	1	.833	33	16	14	38	35	2.63
1986—Nashua	Eastern	4	11⅔	0	1	.000	13	6	4	6	5	3.09
1987—Harrisburg	Eastern	26	36⅓	4	3	.571	27	10	8	39	10	1.98
1987—Pittsburgh	National	29	36⅔	1	5	.167	34	22	19	31	10	4.66
1988—Harrisburg	Eastern	25	39⅔	3	2	.600	27	8	6	30	21	1.36
1988—Buffalo†	Am. Assoc.	24	42	1	6	.143	33	17	17	41	19	3.64
1989—Indianapolis	Am. Assoc.	47	71⅔	7	2	.778	41	24	18	71	23	2.26
1989—Montreal	National	4	4⅔	0	0	.000	5	1	1	2	5	1.93
1990—Montreal‡	National	1	1	0	0	.000	2	1	1	0	4	9.00
Major League Totals—3 Years		34	42⅓	1	5	.167	41	24	21	33	19	4.46

Selected by Houston Astros' organization in 8th round of free-agent draft, January 11, 1983.
Selected by Pittsburgh Pirates' organization in 6th round of free-agent draft, June 3, 1985.
†Traded to Montreal Expos, March 30, 1989, completing deal in which Montreal traded Pitcher Neal Heaton to Pittsburgh Pirates for a player to be named later, March 28, 1989.
‡On disabled list, April 11, 1990 through remainder of season.

BRIAN JEFFREY GILES

Born April 27, 1960, at Manhattan, Kan.
Height, 6.01. Weight, 175.
Throws and bats righthanded.
Grandson of George F. Giles, first baseman in Negro National and American Leagues, 1927 through 1938; son of George F. Giles, Jr., minor league infielder, 1953 through 1955.

Major League stolen bases: 1982 (6), 1983 (17), 1985 (2), 1990 (2). Total—27.

Year Club	League	Pos.	G.	AB.	R.	H.	2B.	3B.	HR.	RBI.	B.A.	PO.	A.	E.	F.A.
1978—Little Falls	NYP	2B	61	195	36	44	5	5	4	21	.226	⋆135	144	16	.946
1979—Lynchburg†	Carol.	2B	86	278	40	83	16	2	2	33	.299	180	271	13	.972
1980—Jackson	Texas	2B	132	448	76	128	30	8	10	57	.286	291	325	26	.960
1981—Tidewater	Int.	2B-SS	121	400	60	107	17	3	7	40	.268	267	384	24	.964
1981—New York	Nat.	SS-2B	9	7	0	0	0	0	0	0	.000	5	8	0	1.000
1982—Tidewater	Int.	2B-SS	108	352	48	98	32	4	11	54	.278	240	354	17	.972
1982—New York	Nat.	2B-SS	45	138	14	29	5	0	3	10	.210	122	133	2	.992
1983—New York	Nat.	2B-SS	145	400	39	98	15	0	2	27	.245	309	390	14	.980
1984—Tidewater‡	Int.	2B-SS-3B	118	384	59	93	24	1	6	37	.242	248	344	16	.974
1985—Milwaukee	Amer.	SS-2B	34	58	6	10	1	0	1	1	.172	48	58	2	.981
1985—Vancouver§	P. C.	SS	40	128	21	30	7	1	2	15	.234	47	125	9	.950
1986—Buffalo x	A. A.	SS	30	98	10	28	5	1	3	9	.286	44	82	7	.947
1986—Chicago y	Amer.	2B-SS	9	11	0	3	0	0	0	1	.273	15	11	0	1.000
1987—Hawaii z	P. C.	SS-2B-3B	132	449	60	99	21	3	6	47	.220	244	392	38	.944
1988—Calgary a	P. C.	S-2-3-1-O	120	383	76	105	20	2	13	56	.274	198	272	19	.961
1989—Colo. Springs b	P. C.	S-3-2-O	105	318	58	94	23	5	10	40	.296	155	237	12	.970
1990—Seattle	Amer.	SS-2B-3B	45	95	15	22	6	0	4	11	.232	57	88	3	.980
1990—Calgary c	P. C.	SS-2B	38	122	28	32	8	0	5	19	.262	53	106	7	.958
National League Totals—3 Years			199	545	53	127	20	0	5	37	.233	436	531	16	.984
American League Totals—3 Years			88	164	21	35	7	0	5	13	.213	120	157	5	.982
Major League Totals—6 Years			287	709	74	162	27	0	10	50	.228	556	688	21	.983

Selected by New York Mets' organization in 2nd round of free-agent draft, June 6, 1978.
†On disabled list, July 10 to August 11, 1979.
‡Drafted by Milwaukee Brewers, December 3, 1984.
§Granted free agency, October 15, 1985; signed by Buffalo (Chicago White Sox' organization), December 12, 1985.
xOn disabled list, May 6 to July 17, 1986.
yOn disabled list, August 25, 1986 through remainder of season.
zGranted free agency, October 15, 1987; signed by Calgary (Seattle Mariners' organization), January 11, 1988.
aGranted free agency, October 15, 1988; signed by Colorado Springs (Cleveland Indians' organization), February 21, 1989.
bGranted free agency, October 15, 1989; signed by Calgary (Seattle Mariners' organization), November 2, 1989.
cGranted free agency, October 15, 1990.

OTIS BERNARD GILKEY
(Known by middle name.)

Born September 24, 1966, at St. Louis, Mo.
Height, 6.00. Weight, 170.
Throws and bats righthanded.

Major League stolen bases: 1990 (6).
Led American Association batters in bases on balls received with 75 and caught stealing with 33 in 1990.
Led Texas League in stolen bases with 53 and caught stealing with 22 in 1989.
Led New York-Pennsylvania League outfielders in total chances with 185 in 1985.

Year Club	League	Pos.	G.	AB.	R.	H.	2B.	3B.	HR.	RBI.	B.A.	PO.	A.	E.	F.A.
1985—Erie	NYP	OF	•77	★294	57	60	9	1	7	27	.204	★164	★13	★8	.957
1986—Savannah†	S. Atl.	OF	105	374	64	88	15	4	6	36	.235	220	7	5	.978
1987—Springfield‡	Midw.	OF	46	162	30	37	5	0	0	9	.228	79	5	4	.955
1988—Springfield	Midw.	OF	125	491	84	120	18	7	6	36	.244	165	10	6	.967
1989—Arkansas	Texas	OF	131	500	★104	139	25	3	6	57	.278	236	★22	9	.966
1990—Louisville	A. A.	OF	132	499	83	147	26	8	3	46	.295	236	18	•11	.958
1990—St. Louis	Nat.	OF	18	64	11	19	5	2	1	3	.297	47	2	2	.961
Major League Totals—1 Year			18	64	11	19	5	2	1	3	.297	47	2	2	.961

Signed as free agent by St. Louis Cardinals' organization, August 22, 1984.
†On disabled list, April 10 to April 25, 1986.
‡On disabled list, May 29, 1987 through remainder of season.

THOMAS BRADFORD GILLES
(Tom)

Born July 2, 1962, at Peoria, Ill.
Height, 6.01. Weight, 185.
Throws and bats righthanded.
Attended Indiana State University, Terre Haute, Ind.

Year Club	League	G.	IP.	W.	L.	Pct.	H.	R.	ER.	SO.	BB.	ERA.
1987—Appleton‡	Midwest	1	3	0	0	.000	2	0	0	1	2	0.00
1988—Kenosha	Midwest	21	89⅔	6	3	.667	77	40	33	41	15	3.31
1988—Orlando§	Southern	7	25⅔	3	0	1.000	27	13	11	7	5	3.86
1989—Knoxville	Southern	12	52	5	1	.833	42	21	17	27	14	2.94
1989—Syracuse	Int'national	29	83⅔	4	4	.500	85	38	33	41	28	3.55
1990—Syracuse	Int'national	43	71⅓	3	3	.500	58	21	16	44	21	2.02
1990—Toronto x	American	2	1⅓	1	0	1.000	2	1	1	1	0	6.75
Major League Totals—1 Year		2	1⅓	1	0	1.000	2	1	1	1	0	6.75

Selected by New York Yankees' organization in 47th round of free-agent draft, June 4, 1984.
†Released, March 25, 1986; signed by Appleton (Kansas City Royals' organization), January 1, 1987.
‡Released, March 30, 1988; signed by Kenosha (Minnesota Twins' organization), April 6, 1988.
§Drafted by Toronto Blue Jays' organization, December 6, 1988.
xGranted free agency, October 15, 1990.

RECORD AS INFIELDER

Year Club	League	Pos.	G.	AB.	R.	H.	2B.	3B.	HR.	RBI.	B.A.	PO.	A.	E.	F.A.
1984—Sarasota Yankees	Gulf C.	1B-3B	42	145	14	35	4	2	2	13	.241	342	42	2	.995
1985—Fort Lauderdale	Fla. St.	3B-1B	2	5	1	1	0	0	0	2	.200	4	1	1	.833
1985—Oneonta†	NYP	1B-3B-OF	40	118	16	26	6	2	1	19	.220	160	28	3	.984

JOSEPH ELLIOTT GIRARDI
(Joe)

Born October 14, 1964, at Peoria, Ill.
Height, 5.11. Weight, 195.
Throws and bats righthanded.
Received degree in industrial engineering from Northwestern University, Evanston, Ill., in 1986.

Major League stolen bases: 1989 (2), 1990 (8). Total—10.
Tied for National League lead in passed balls with 16 in 1990.
Led Eastern League catchers in putouts with 448, fielding percentage with .992, total chances with 528 and tied for lead in double plays with 5 in 1988.
Led Carolina League catchers in total chances with 661 and tied for lead in passed balls with 17 in 1987.

Year Club	League	Pos.	G.	AB.	R.	H.	2B.	3B.	HR.	RBI.	B.A.	PO.	A.	E.	F.A.
1986—Peoria†	Midw.	C	68	230	36	71	13	1	3	28	.309	405	34	5	.989
1987—Winston-Salem	Carol.	C	99	364	51	102	9	8	8	46	.280	★569	★74	18	.973

Year Club	League	Pos.	G.	AB.	R.	H.	2B.	3B.	HR.	RBI.	B.A.	PO.	A.	E.	F.A.
1988—Pittsfield‡	East.	*C-OF	104	357	44	97	14	1	7	41	.272	460	*76	6	.989
1989—Chicago	Nat.	C	59	157	15	39	10	0	1	14	.248	332	28	7	.981
1989—Iowa	A. A.	C	32	110	12	27	4	2	2	11	.245	172	21	1	.995
1990—Chicago	Nat.	C	133	419	36	113	24	2	1	38	.270	653	61	11	.985
Major League Totals—2 Years			192	576	51	152	34	2	2	52	.264	985	89	18	.984

Selected by Chicago Cubs' organization in 5th round of free-agent draft, June 2, 1986.
†On disabled list, August 27, 1986 through remainder of season.
‡On disabled list, August 7, 1988 through remainder of season.

CHAMPIONSHIP SERIES RECORD

Year Club	League	Pos.	G.	AB.	R.	H.	2B.	3B.	HR.	RBI.	B.A.	PO.	A.	E.	F.A.
1989—Chicago	Nat.	C	4	10	1	1	0	0	0	0	.100	20	0	0	1.000

CLINTON DANIEL GLADDEN III
(Dan)

Born July 7, 1957, at San Jose, Calif.
Height, 5.11. Weight, 181.
Throws and bats righthanded.
Attended DeAnza College, Cupertino, Calif., and
Fresno State University, Fresno, Calif.
Brother of Jeff Gladden, pitcher in Kansas City Royals' and
San Francisco Giants' organization, 1980 through 1984.

Major League stolen bases: 1983 (4), 1984 (31), 1985 (32), 1986 (27), 1987 (25), 1988 (28), 1989 (23), 1990 (25). Total—195.
Tied for American League lead in double plays by outfielders with 5 in 1988.
Led Texas League in stolen bases with 52 and caught stealing with 26 in 1981.

Year Club	League	Pos.	G.	AB.	R.	H.	2B.	3B.	HR.	RBI.	B.A.	PO.	A.	E.	F.A.
1979—Fresno	Calif.	OF-2B-SS	60	228	41	70	9	1	3	31	.307	56	16	3	.960
1980—Fresno	Calif.	OF	62	237	46	72	10	2	9	41	.304	68	3	1	.986
1980—Shreveport	Texas	OF-SS	74	292	51	86	11	2	9	35	.295	169	14	5	.973
1981—Shreveport	Texas	OF-SS-2B	124	472	81	148	23	9	8	44	.314	211	12	3	.987
1982—Phoenix	P. C.	OF	130	503	93	155	40	5	10	74	.308	264	16	7	.976
1983—Phoenix	P. C.	OF	127	505	113	153	30	9	12	80	.303	319	6	7	.979
1983—San Francisco	Nat.	OF	18	63	6	14	2	0	1	9	.222	53	0	0	1.000
1984—Phoenix†	P. C.	OF	59	234	70	93	11	7	3	27	.397	130	4	2	.985
1984—San Francisco	Nat.	OF	86	342	71	120	17	2	4	31	.351	232	8	3	.988
1985—San Francisco	Nat.	OF	142	502	64	122	15	8	7	41	.243	273	3	7	.975
1986—San Francisco‡	Nat.	OF	102	351	55	97	16	1	4	29	.276	226	7	3	.987
1986—Phoenix§ x............	P. C.	OF	7	27	5	9	4	0	0	0	.333	11	0	0	1.000
1987—Minnesota	Amer.	OF	121	438	69	109	21	2	8	38	.249	223	9	3	.987
1988—Minnesota	Amer.	O-2-3-P	141	576	91	155	32	6	11	62	.269	319	12	3	.991
1989—Minnesota y	Amer.	OF-P	121	461	69	136	23	3	8	46	.295	245	8	9	.966
1990—Minnesota	Amer.	OF	136	534	64	147	27	6	5	40	.275	286	12	6	.980
National League Totals—4 Years			348	1258	196	353	50	11	16	110	.281	784	18	13	.984
American League Totals—4 Years			519	2009	293	547	103	17	32	186	.272	1073	41	21	.981
Major League Totals—8 Years			867	3267	489	900	153	28	48	296	.275	1857	59	34	.983

Signed as free agent by San Francisco Giants' organization, June 17, 1979.
†On disabled list, April 19 to May 1, 1984.
‡On disabled list, June 4 to July 23, 1986; included rehabilitation disability assignment to Phoenix, July 14 to July 23, 1986.
§Batted left and righthanded.
xTraded with Pitcher David Blakley to Minnesota Twins for Pitchers Jose Dominguez and Ray Velasquez and a player to be named later, March 31 1987; San Francisco Giants' organization acquired Pitcher Bryan Hickerson to complete deal, June 15, 1987.
yOn disabled list, June 25 to July 10 and July 17 to August 7, 1989.

CHAMPIONSHIP SERIES RECORD

Shares Championship Series records for most times hit by pitch, series (2), 1987 and game (2), October 11, 1987.

Year Club	League	Pos.	G.	AB.	R.	H.	2B.	3B.	HR.	RBI.	B.A.	PO.	A.	E.	F.A.
1987—Minnesota	Amer.	OF	5	20	5	7	2	0	0	5	.350	12	0	0	1.000

WORLD SERIES RECORD

Shares World Series records for most grand slams, game (1), October 17, 1987; most runs batted in, inning (4), October 17, 1987, fourth inning.

Year Club	League	Pos.	G.	AB.	R.	H.	2B.	3B.	HR.	RBI.	B.A.	PO.	A.	E.	F.A.
1987—Minnesota	Amer.	OF	7	31	3	9	2	1	1	7	.290	12	0	0	1.000

PITCHING RECORD

Year Club	League	G.	IP.	W.	L.	Pct.	H.	R.	ER.	SO.	BB.	ERA.
1988—Minnesota	American	1	1	0	0	.000	0	0	0	0	0	0.00
1989—Minnesota	American	1	1	0	0	.000	2	1	1	0	1	9.00
Major League Totals—2 Years		2	2	0	0	.000	2	1	1	0	1	4.50

—DID YOU KNOW—
That every one of the 10 runs the Yankees scored against Minnesota last July 22 was unearned? The Yanks were helped by five Minnesota errors?

THOMAS MICHAEL GLAVINE

Name pronounced GLA-vin.

(Tom)

Born March 25, 1966, at Concord, Mass.
Height, 6.01. Weight, 190.
Throws and bats lefthanded.

Led Gulf Coast League in wild pitches with 12 in 1984.
Drafted by Los Angeles Kings in 1984 NHL entry draft. Fourth Kings pick, 69th player overall, fourth round.

Year Club	League	G.	IP.	W.	L.	Pct.	H.	R.	ER.	SO.	BB.	ERA.
1984—Bradenton Braves	Gulf Coast	8	32⅓	2	3	.400	29	17	12	34	13	3.34
1985—Sumter	S. Atlantic	26	168⅔	9	6	.600	114	58	44	174	73	*2.35
1986—Greenville	Southern	22	145⅓	11	6	.647	129	62	55	114	70	3.41
1986—Richmond	Int'national	7	40	1	5	.167	40	29	25	12	27	5.63
1987—Richmond	Int'national	22	150⅓	6	12	.333	142	70	56	91	56	3.35
1987—Atlanta	National	9	50⅓	2	4	.333	55	34	31	20	33	5.54
1988—Atlanta	National	34	195⅓	7	*17	.292	201	111	99	84	63	4.56
1989—Atlanta	National	29	186	14	8	.636	172	88	76	90	40	3.68
1990—Atlanta	National	33	214⅓	10	12	.455	232	111	102	129	78	4.28
Major League Totals—4 Years		105	646	33	41	.446	660	344	308	323	214	4.29

Selected by Atlanta Braves' organization in 2nd round of free-agent draft, June 4, 1984.

JERRY DON GLEATON

(Jerry Don)

Born September 14, 1957, at Brownwood, Tex.
Height, 6.03. Weight, 210.
Throws and bats lefthanded.
Attended University of Texas, Austin, Tex.

Major League saves: 1984 (2), 1985 (1), 1987 (5), 1988 (3), 1990 (13). Total—24.
Tied for Eastern League lead in complete games with 13 in 1982.
Tied for Texas League lead in home runs allowed with 17 in 1980.

Year Club	League	G.	IP.	W.	L.	Pct.	H.	R.	ER.	SO.	BB.	ERA.
1979—Tulsa	Texas	5	35	3	2	.600	37	19	19	21	15	4.89
1979—Texas	American	5	10	0	1	.000	15	7	7	2	2	6.30
1980—Tulsa	Texas	25	178	13	7	.650	179	83	72	138	68	3.64
1980—Texas†	American	5	7	0	0	.000	5	2	2	2	4	2.57
1981—Seattle	American	20	85	4	7	.364	88	50	45	31	38	4.76
1981—Spokane	P. Coast	13	91	5	7	.417	104	53	42	57	39	4.15
1982—Lynn	Eastern	24	182	15	7	.682	175	71	55	132	54	2.72
1982—Seattle	American	3	4⅔	0	0	.000	7	7	7	1	2	13.50
1983—Salt Lake City	P. Coast	24	137⅓	9	9	.500	189	112	102	73	81	6.68
1984—Salt Lake City‡	P. Coast	29	49⅔	4	1	.800	62	39	32	39	17	5.80
1984—Denver	Am. Assoc.	12	20	1	1	.500	20	5	4	10	4	1.80
1984—Chicago	American	11	18⅓	1	2	.333	20	12	7	4	6	3.44
1985—Buffalo	Am. Assoc.	38	55⅓	8	2	*.800	62	17	15	37	21	2.44
1985—Chicago	American	31	29⅔	1	0	1.000	37	19	19	22	13	5.76
1986—Buffalo§	Am. Assoc.	46	78⅓	4	3	.571	79	34	28	77	35	3.22
1987—Omaha	Am. Assoc.	6	15	2	0	1.000	14	6	5	9	6	3.00
1987—Kansas City	American	48	50⅔	4	4	.500	38	28	24	44	28	4.26
1988—Omaha	Am. Assoc.	15	37⅓	4	2	.667	30	7	6	40	14	1.45
1988—Kansas City	American	42	38	0	4	.000	33	17	15	29	17	3.55
1989—Kansas City	American	15	14⅓	0	0	.000	20	10	9	9	6	5.65
1989—Omaha x	Am. Assoc.	24	56⅔	3	3	.500	40	12	7	57	22	1.11
1990—Detroit	American	57	82⅔	1	3	.250	62	27	27	56	25	2.94
Major League Totals—10 Years		237	340⅓	11	21	.344	325	179	162	200	141	4.28

Selected by Baltimore Orioles' organization in 2nd round of free-agent draft, June 8, 1976.
Selected by Texas Rangers' organization in 1st round (17th player selected) of free-agent draft, June 5, 1979.
†Traded with Pitchers Brian Allard, Ken Clay and Steve Finch, Shortstop Rick Auerbach and Outfielder Richie Zisk to Seattle Mariners for Catcher Larry Cox, Pitcher Rick Honeycutt, Outfielders Willie Horton and Leon Roberts and Shortstop Mario Mendoza, December 12, 1980.
‡Traded with Pitcher Gene Nelson to Chicago White Sox for Pitcher Salome Barojas, June 27, 1984.
§Granted free agency, October 15, 1986; signed by Kansas City Royals, November 15, 1986.
xTraded to Detroit Tigers for Pitcher Greg Everson, April 2, 1990.

JERRY LEROY GOFF

Born April 12, 1964, at San Rafael, Calif.
Height. 6.03. Weight, 205.
Throws right and bats lefthanded.
Attended Marin Community College, Kentfield, Calif.,
and University of California, Berkeley, Calif.

Led Pacific Coast League in passed balls with 14 in 1989.
Led Northwest League catchers in double plays with 7 in 1986.
Led Midwest League in passed balls with 32 in 1987.

Year Club	League	Pos.	G.	AB.	R.	H.	2B.	3B.	HR.	RBI.	B.A.	PO.	A.	E.	F.A.
1986—Bellingham	N'west	C	54	168	26	32	7	2	7	25	.190	286	35	12	.964
1987—Waunau	Midw.	C-1B	109	336	51	78	17	2	13	47	.232	583	73	15	.978

Year	Club	League	Pos.	G.	AB.	R.	H.	2B.	3B.	HR.	RBI.	B.A.	PO.	A.	E.	F.A.
1988—San Bernardino....	Calif.		C	65	215	38	62	11	0	13	43	.288	383	64	6	.987
1988—Vermont	East.		★C-OF	63	195	27	41	7	1	7	23	.210	283	40	★17	..950
1989—Williamsport.........	East.		C-OF	33	119	9	22	5	0	3	8	.185	180	21	6	.971
1989—Calgary†	P. C.		C-1-3-O	76	253	40	59	16	0	11	50	.233	346	63	12	.971
1990—Indianapolis	A. A.		C-3-1-2	39	143	23	41	10	2	5	26	.287	162	24	6	.969
1990—Montreal	Nat.		C-1B-3B	52	119	14	27	1	0	3	7	.227	216	17	9	.963
Major League Totals—1 Year..................				52	119	14	27	1	0	3	7	.227	216	17	9	.963

Selected by Oakland A's organization in 7th round of free-agent draft, January 11, 1983.
Selected by New York Yankees' organization in 12th round of free-agent draft, January 17, 1984.
Selected by Seattle Mariners' organization in 3rd round of free-agent draft, June 2, 1986.
†Traded to Montreal Expos for Pitcher Pat Pacillo, February 27, 1990.

LEONARDO GOMEZ
(Leo)

Born March 2, 1967, in Puerto Rico.
Height, 6.00. Weight, 202.
Throws and bats righthanded.

Led Eastern League in bases on balls received with 89 in 1989.
Led International League third basemen in double plays with 26 in 1990.
Led Eastern League third basemen in assists with 256 in 1989.

Year	Club	League	Pos.	G.	AB.	R.	H.	2B.	3B.	HR.	RBI.	B.A.	PO.	A.	E.	F.A.
1986—Bluefield†	Appal.		3B-2B-SS	27	88	23	31	7	1	7	28	.352	15	38	7	.883
1987—Hagerstown	Carol.		3B-SS	131	466	94	152	★38	2	19	110	★.326	75	233	33	.903
1988—Charlotte‡	South.		3B-1B	24	89	6	26	5	0	1	10	.292	19	50	8	.896
1989—Hagerstown	East.		3B-SS	134	448	71	126	23	3	18	78	.281	79	257	25	.931
1990—Rochester	Int.		3B-1B	131	430	★97	119	26	4	26	★97	.277	92	204	20	.937
1990—Baltimore	Amer.		3B	12	39	3	9	0	0	0	1	.231	11	20	4	.886
Major League Totals—1 Year..................				12	39	3	9	0	0	0	1	.231	11	20	4	.886

Signed as free agent by Baltimore Orioles' organization, December 13, 1985.
†On disabled list, July 3 to July 31, 1986.
‡On disabled list, May 3, 1988 through remainder of season.

RENE ADRIAN GONZALES

Born September 3, 1961, at Austin, Tex.
Height, 6.03. Weight, 201.
Throws and bats righthanded.
Attended Glendale College, Glendale, Calif.; and California State University, Los Angeles, Calif.

Major League stolen bases: 1987 (1), 1988 (2), 1989 (5), 1990 (1). Total—9.
Led American Association shortstops in double plays with 79 in 1985.
Led Southern League shortstops in double plays with 102 in 1983.

Year	Club	League	Pos.	G.	AB.	R.	H.	2B.	3B.	HR.	RBI.	B.A.	PO.	A.	E.	F.A.
1982—Memphis	South.		SS	56	183	10	39	3	1	1	11	.213	77	183	14	.949
1983—Memphis	South.		SS	144	476	67	128	12	2	2	44	.269	★258	449	20	★.972
1984—Indianapolis	A. A.		SS-3B-2B	114	359	41	84	12	2	2	32	.234	161	349	13	.975
1984—Montreal	Nat.		SS	29	30	5	7	1	0	0	2	.233	17	28	2	.957
1985—Indianapolis	A. A.		SS	130	340	21	77	11	1	0	25	.226	203	★345	23	.960
1986—Indianapolis	A. A.		3B-SS-2B	116	395	57	108	14	2	3	43	.273	208	297	23	.956
1986—Montreal†	Nat.		SS-3B	11	26	1	3	0	0	0	0	.115	7	19	0	1.000
1987—Baltimore	Amer.		3B-2B-SS	37	60	14	16	2	1	1	7	.267	22	43	2	.970
1987—Rochester	Int.		3-S-2-1-O	42	170	20	51	9	3	0	24	.300	72	108	3	.984
1988—Baltimore	Amer.		3-2-S-1-O	92	237	13	51	6	0	2	15	.215	66	185	8	.969
1989—Baltimore	Amer.		2B-3B-SS	71	166	16	36	4	0	1	11	.217	103	146	7	.973
1990—Baltimore	Amer.		2-3-S-O	67	103	13	22	3	1	1	12	.214	68	114	2	.989
National League Totals—2 Years				40	56	6	10	1	0	0	2	.179	24	47	2	.973
American League Totals—4 Years				267	566	56	125	15	2	5	45	.221	259	488	19	.975
Major League Totals—6 Years				307	622	62	135	16	2	5	47	.217	283	535	21	.975

Selected by Montreal Expos' organization in 5th round of free-agent draft, June 7, 1982.
†Traded to Baltimore Orioles, December 16, 1986, completing deals in which Baltimore traded Pitcher Dennis Martinez to Montreal Expos on June 16, 1986 and Catcher John Stefero to Montreal on December 8, 1986, both for a player to be named later.

JOSE RAFAEL GONZALEZ

Born November 23, 1964, at Puerto Plata, Dominican Republic.
Height, 6.02. Weight, 201.
Throws and bats righthanded.

Major League stolen bases: 1985 (1), 1986 (4), 1987 (5), 1988 (3), 1989 (9), 1990 (3). Total—25.
Tied for Texas League lead in caught stealing with 17 in 1985.
Led Texas League outfielders in total chances with 320 in 1985.

Year	Club	League	Pos.	G.	AB.	R.	H.	2B.	3B.	HR.	RBI.	B.A.	PO.	A.	E.	F.A.
1981—Lethbridge	Pion.		OF	34	103	11	14	1	1	0	7	.136	65	6	5	.934
1982—Lethbridge	Pion.		OF	55	209	35	63	14	1	4	47	.301	112	7	1	.992
1983—Lodi†	Calif.		OF	76	310	48	91	17	4	6	36	.294	182	7	4	.979
1984—Bakersfield...........	Calif.		OF	129	484	86	107	26	1	11	59	.221	264	13	9	.969

Year	Club	League	Pos.	G.	AB.	R.	H.	2B.	3B.	HR.	RBI.	B.A.	PO.	A.	E.	F.A.
1985—San Antonio	Texas	OF	128	448	82	137	22	6	13	62	.306	★294	15	11	.966
1985—Los Angeles	Nat.	OF	23	11	6	3	2	0	0	0	.273	10	0	0	1.000
1986—Albuquerque	P. C.	OF	89	303	39	84	20	3	6	37	.277	171	10	6	.968
1986—Los Angeles	Nat.	OF	57	93	15	20	5	1	2	6	.215	73	0	6	.924
1987—Albuquerque	P. C.	OF	116	339	67	95	22	3	13	61	.280	225	10	9	.963
1987—Los Angeles	Nat.	OF	18	16	2	3	2	0	0	1	.188	19	1	0	1.000
1988—Albuquerque	P. C.	OF	84	288	57	88	15	2	5	22	.306	177	7	6	.968
1988—Los Angeles	Nat.	OF	37	24	7	2	1	0	0	0	.083	15	0	1	.938
1989—Albuquerque	P. C.	OF	50	180	32	48	12	4	4	31	.267	98	3	2	.981
1989—Los Angeles	Nat.	OF	95	261	31	70	11	2	3	18	.268	171	8	6	.968
1990—Los Angeles	Nat.	OF	106	99	15	23	5	3	2	8	.232	62	1	0	1.000
Major League Totals—6 Years			336	504	76	121	26	6	7	33	.240	350	10	13	.965

Signed as free agent by Los Angeles Dodgers' organization, August 12, 1980.
†On disabled list, July 7, 1983 through remainder of season.

CHAMPIONSHIP SERIES RECORD

Year	Club	League	Pos.	G.	AB.	R.	H.	2B.	3B.	HR.	RBI.	B.A.	PO.	A.	E.	F.A.
1988—Los Angeles	Nat.	OF-PR	5	0	2	0	0	0	0	0	.000	3	0	0	1.000

WORLD SERIES RECORD

Year	Club	League	Pos.	G.	AB.	R.	H.	2B.	3B.	HR.	RBI.	B.A.	PO.	A.	E.	F.A.
1988—Los Angeles	Nat.	PH-OF	4	2	0	0	0	0	0	0	.000	2	0	0	1.000

JUAN A. GONZALEZ (VAZQUEZ)

Born October 16, 1969, at Vega Baja, Puerto Rico.
Height, 6.03. Weight, 200.
Throws and bats righthanded.

Led Texas League in total bases with 254 in 1989.
Led American Association in total bases with 252 in 1990.
Named American Association Most Valuable Player, 1990.

Year	Club	League	Pos.	G.	AB.	R.	H.	2B.	3B.	HR.	RBI.	B.A.	PO.	A.	E.	F.A.
1986—Sarasota Rangers	Gulf C.	OF	60	★233	24	56	4	1	0	36	.240	89	6	●6	.941
1987—Gastonia	S. Atl.	OF	127	509	69	135	21	2	14	74	.265	234	10	12	.953
1988—Port Charlotte†	Fla. St.	OF	77	277	25	71	14	3	8	43	.256	139	5	4	.973
1989—Tulsa	Texas	OF	133	502	73	147	30	7	21	85	.293	292	15	9	.972
1989—Texas	Amer.	OF	24	60	6	9	3	0	1	7	.150	53	0	2	.964
1990—Oklahoma City	A. A.	OF	128	496	78	128	29	4	★29	★101	.258	220	7	8	.966
1990—Texas	Amer.	OF	25	90	11	26	7	1	4	12	.289	33	0	0	1.000
Major League Totals—2 Years			49	150	17	35	10	1	5	19	.233	86	0	2	.977

Signed as free agent by Texas Rangers' organization, May 30, 1986.
†On disabled list, April 27 to June 17, 1988.

LUIS EMILIO GONZALEZ

Born September 3, 1967, at Tampa, Fla.
Height, 6.02. Weight, 180.
Throws right and bats lefthanded.
Attended University of South Alabama, Mobile, Ala.

Tied for Southern League lead in sacrifice flies with 12 and intentional bases on balls received with 9 in 1990.

Year	Club	League	Pos.	G.	AB.	R.	H.	2B.	3B.	HR.	RBI.	B.A.	PO.	A.	E.	F.A.
1988—Asheville	S. Atl.	3B	31	115	13	29	7	1	2	14	.252	19	62	6	.931
1988—Auburn	NYP	3B-SS-1B	39	157	32	49	10	3	5	27	.312	37	83	13	.902
1989—Osceola	Fla. St.	DH	86	287	46	82	16	7	6	38	.286	0	0	0	.000
1990—Columbus	South.	1B-3B	138	495	86	131	30	6	●24	89	.265	1039	88	23	.980
1990—Houston	Nat.	3B-1B	12	21	1	4	2	0	0	1	.190	22	10	0	1.000
Major League Totals—1 Year			12	21	1	4	2	0	0	1	.190	22	10	0	1.000

Selected by Houston Astros' organization in 4th round of free-agent draft, June 1, 1988.

DWIGHT EUGENE GOODEN

Born November 16, 1964, at Tampa, Fla.
Height, 6.03. Weight, 210.
Throws and bats righthanded.
Uncle of Gary Sheffield, third baseman with Milwaukee Brewers.

Holds major league record for most strikeouts by rookie, season (276), 1984.
Shares modern major league record for most strikeouts, two consecutive games (32), September 12, 17, 1984.
Holds National League record for most strikeouts, three consecutive games (43), September 7, 12, 17, 1984.
Major League saves: 1989 (1).
Led National League in complete games with 16 in 1985.
Tied for National League lead in balks with 7 in 1984.
Led Carolina League in shutouts with 6 in 1983.
Named National League Pitcher of the Year by THE SPORTING NEWS, 1985.
Won National League Cy Young Memorial Award, 1985.
Named righthanded pitcher on THE SPORTING NEWS National League All-Star Team, 1985.
Named National League Rookie Pitcher of the Year by THE SPORTING NEWS, 1984.
Named National League Rookie Pitcher of the Year by Baseball Writers' Association of America, 1984.
Named Carolina League Pitcher of the Year, 1983.
Received reported $125,000 bonus to sign with New York Mets, 1982.

Year Club	League	G.	IP.	W.	L.	Pct.	H.	R.	ER.	SO.	BB.	ERA.
1982—Kingsport	Ap'lachian	9	65⅔	5	4	.556	53	34	18	66	25	2.47
1982—Little Falls	NYP	2	13	0	1	.000	11	6	6	18	3	4.15
1983—Lynchburg	Carolina	27	191	*19	4	.826	121	58	53	*300	*112	*2.50
1984—New York	National	31	218	17	9	.654	161	72	63	*276	73	2.60
1985—New York	National	35	*276⅔	*24	4	.857	198	51	47	*268	69	*1.53
1986—New York	National	33	250	17	6	.739	197	92	79	200	80	2.84
1987—Tidewater†	Int'national	4	22	3	0	1.000	20	7	5	24	9	2.05
1987—Lynchburg	Carolina	1	4	0	0	.000	2	0	0	3	2	0.00
1987—New York	National	25	179⅔	15	7	.682	162	68	64	148	53	3.21
1988—New York	National	34	248⅓	18	9	.667	242	98	88	175	57	3.19
1989—New York‡	National	19	118⅓	9	4	.692	93	42	38	101	47	2.89
1990—New York	National	34	232⅔	19	7	.731	229	106	99	223	70	3.83
Major League Totals—7 Years		211	1523⅔	119	46	.721	1282	529	478	1391	449	2.82

Selected by New York Mets' organization in 1st round (fifth player selected) of free-agent draft, June 7, 1982.

†On New York disabled list, April 1 to June 5, 1987; included rehabilitation disability assignment to Tidewater, May 12 to May 17 and May 21 to June 1, 1987.

‡On disabled list, July 2 to September 2, 1989.

CHAMPIONSHIP SERIES RECORD

Holds Championship Series record for most strikeouts, series (20), 1988.
Shares National League Championship Series record for most innings pitched, game (10), October 14, 1986.

Year Club	League	G.	IP.	W.	L.	Pct.	H.	R.	ER.	SO.	BB.	ERA.
1986—New York	National	2	17	0	1	.000	16	2	2	9	5	1.06
1988—New York	National	3	18⅓	0	0	.000	10	6	6	20	8	2.95
Championship Series Totals—2 Years		5	35⅓	0	1	.000	26	8	8	29	13	2.04

WORLD SERIES RECORD

Year Club	League	G.	IP.	W.	L.	Pct.	H.	R.	ER.	SO.	BB.	ERA.
1986—New York	National	2	9	0	2	.000	17	10	8	9	4	8.00

ALL-STAR GAME RECORD

Holds All-Star Game record for most balks, lifetime (2).
Shares All-Star Game record for most games lost, lifetime (2).

Year League	IP.	W.	L.	Pct.	H.	R.	ER.	SO.	BB.	ERA.
1984—National	2	0	0	.000	1	0	0	3	0	0.00
1986—National	3	0	1	.000	3	2	2	2	0	6.00
1988—National	3	0	1	.000	3	1	1	1	1	3.00
All-Star Game Totals—3 Years	8	0	2	.000	7	3	3	6	1	3.38

Member of National League All-Star Team in 1985; did not play.

THOMAS GORDON
(Tom)

Born November 18, 1967, at Sebring, Fla.
Height, 5.09. Weight, 160.
Throws and bats righthanded.

Major League saves: 1989 (1).
Tied for Northwest League lead in balks with 4 in 1987.
Named American League Rookie Pitcher of the Year by THE SPORTING NEWS, 1989.

Year Club	League	G.	IP.	W.	L.	Pct.	H.	R.	ER.	SO.	BB.	ERA.
1986—Sarasota Royals	Gulf Coast	9	44	3	1	.750	31	12	5	47	23	1.02
1986—Omaha	Am. Assoc.	1	1⅓	0	0	.000	6	7	7	3	2	47.25
1987—Eugene	Northwest	15	72⅓	●9	0	●1.000	48	33	23	91	47	2.86
1987—Fort Myers	Florida St.	3	13⅔	1	0	1.000	5	4	4	11	17	2.63
1988—Appleton	Midwest	17	118	7	5	.583	69	30	27	*172	43	2.06
1988—Memphis	Southern	6	47⅓	6	0	1.000	16	3	2	62	17	0.38
1988—Omaha	Am. Assoc.	3	20⅓	3	0	1.000	11	3	3	29	15	1.33
1988—Kansas City	American	5	15⅔	0	2	.000	16	9	9	18	7	5.17
1989—Kansas City	American	49	163	17	9	.654	122	67	66	153	86	3.64
1990—Kansas City	American	32	195⅓	12	11	.522	192	99	81	175	99	3.73
Major League Totals—3 Years		86	374	29	22	.569	330	175	156	346	192	3.75

Selected by Kansas City Royals' organization in 6th round of free-agent draft, June 2, 1986.

JAMES WILLIAM GOTT
(Jim)

Born August 3, 1959, at Hollywood, Calif.
Height, 6.04. Weight, 220.
Throws and bats righthanded.
Attended Brigham Young University, Provo, Utah.

Major League saves: 1984 (2), 1986 (1), 1987 (13), 1988 (34), 1990 (3). Total—53.
Led Western Carolinas League in wild pitches with 21 in 1979.
Tied for Pioneer League lead in games started by pitchers with 14 in 1977.

Year Club	League	G.	IP.	W.	L.	Pct.	H.	R.	ER.	SO.	BB.	ERA.
1977—Calgary	Pioneer	14	65	3	4	.429	71	*82	*69	60	*83	9.55
1978—Gastonia	W. Carol.	22	145	9	6	.600	100	67	64	130	●113	3.97

Year Club	League	G.	IP.	W.	L.	Pct.	H.	R.	ER.	SO.	BB.	ERA.
1978—St. Petersburg	Florida St.	5	28	1	3	.250	23	9	4	15	12	1.29
1979—St. Petersburg	Florida St.	4	18	0	3	.000	18	13	13	9	13	6.50
1979—Gastonia	W. Carol.	19	77	5	5	.500	63	57	48	102	88	5.61
1979—Arkansas†	Texas	2	5	0	1	.000	3	6	3	7	13	5.40
1980—St. Petersburg	Florida St.	25	137	5	11	.313	138	96	70	103	113	4.60
1981—Arkansas‡	Texas	28	131	5	9	.357	133	68	50	93	65	3.44
1982—Toronto	American	30	136	5	10	.333	134	76	67	82	66	4.43
1983—Toronto	American	34	176⅔	9	14	.391	195	103	93	121	68	4.74
1984—Toronto§	American	35	109⅔	7	6	.538	93	54	49	73	49	4.02
1985—San Francisco	National	26	148⅓	7	10	.412	144	73	64	78	51	3.88
1986—San Francisco x	National	9	13	0	0	.000	16	12	11	9	13	7.62
1986—Phoenix y	P. Coast	2	2⅔	0	0	.000	2	2	2	2	3	6.75
1987—San Francisco z-Pittsburgh	National	55	87	1	2	.333	81	43	33	90	40	3.41
1988—Pittsburgh	National	67	77⅓	6	6	.500	68	30	30	76	22	3.49
1989—Pittsburgh ab	National	1	⅔	0	0	.000	1	0	0	1	1	0.00
1990—Bakersfield c	California	7	13	0	0	.000	13	5	4	16	4	2.77
1990—Los Angeles	National	50	62	3	5	.375	59	27	20	44	34	2.90
American League Totals—3 Years		99	422⅓	21	30	.412	422	233	209	276	183	4.45
National League Totals—6 Years		208	388⅓	17	23	.425	369	185	158	298	161	3.66
Major League Totals—9 Years		307	810⅔	38	53	.418	791	418	367	574	344	4.07

Selected by St. Louis Cardinals' organization in 4th round of free-agent draft, June 7, 1977.

†On disabled list, August 16 to September 1, 1979.

‡Drafted by Toronto Blue Jays, December 7, 1981.

§Traded with Pitcher Jack McKnight and Infielder Augie Schmidt to San Francisco Giants for Pitcher Gary Lavelle, January 26, 1985.

xOn disabled list, May 9, 1986 through remainder of season; included rehabilitation disability assignment to Phoenix, June 9 to June 24, 1986.

yReleased, December 19, 1986; re-signed by Giants, April 7, 1987.

zClaimed on waivers by Pittsburgh Pirates, August 3, 1987.

aOn disabled list, April 7, 1989 through remainder of season.

bGranted free agency, November 13, 1989; signed by Los Angeles Dodgers, December 7, 1989.

cOn Los Angeles disabled list, April 7 to May 25, 1990; included rehabilitation disability assignment to Bakersfield, May 4 to May 25, 1990.

MAURO PAUL GOZZO

Born March 7, 1966, at New Britain, Conn.
Height, 6.03. Weight, 210.
Throws and bats righthanded.

Tied for South Atlantic League lead in intentional bases on balls issued with 7 in 1985.

Year Club	League	G.	IP.	W.	L.	Pct.	H.	R.	ER.	SO.	BB.	ERA.
1984—Little Falls	NYP	24	38⅓	4	3	.571	40	27	24	30	28	5.63
1985—Columbia	S. Atlantic	49	78	11	4	.733	62	22	22	66	39	2.54
1986—Lynchburg†	Carolina	60	78⅓	9	4	.692	80	30	27	50	35	3.10
1987—Memphis	Southern	19	91⅓	6	5	.545	95	58	46	56	36	4.53
1988—Memphis‡	Southern	33	92⅔	4	9	.308	127	64	59	48	36	5.73
1989—Knoxville	Southern	18	60⅓	7	0	1.000	59	27	20	37	12	2.98
1989—Syracuse	Int'national	12	62	5	1	.833	56	22	19	34	19	2.76
1989—Toronto	American	9	31⅔	4	1	.800	35	19	17	10	9	4.83
1990—Syracuse	Int'national	34	98	3	8	.273	87	46	39	62	44	3.58
1990—Toronto§-Cleveland	American	2	3	0	0	.000	2	0	0	2	2	0.00
Major League Totals—2 Years		11	34⅔	4	1	.800	37	19	17	12	11	4.41

Selected by New York Mets' organization in 13th round of free-agent draft, June 4, 1984.

†Traded with Catcher Ed Hearn and Pitcher Rich Anderson to Kansas City Royals for Catcher Chris Jelic and Pitcher David Cone, March 27, 1987.

‡Drafted by Toronto Blue Jays' organization, December 6, 1988.

§Traded with two players to be named later to Cleveland Indians for Pitcher Bud Black, September 16, 1990; Cleveland acquired Pitcher Steve Cummings on September 21, 1990 and Pitcher Alex Sanchez on September 24, 1990 to complete deal.

MARK EUGENE GRACE

Born June 28, 1964, at Winston-Salem, N. C.
Height, 6.02. Weight, 190.
Throws and bats lefthanded.
Attended Saddleback College, Mission Viejo, Calif., and
San Diego State University, San Diego, Calif.

Holds National League record for most assists by first baseman, season (180), 1990.
Major League stolen bases: 1988 (3), 1989 (14), 1990 (15). Total—32.
Led Eastern League in slugging percentage with .545 in 1987.
Led Midwest League first basemen in double plays with 103 in 1986.
Named National League Rookie Player of the Year by THE SPORTING NEWS, 1988.
Named Eastern League Most Valuable Player, 1987.

Year Club	League	Pos.	G.	AB.	R.	H.	2B.	3B.	HR.	RBI.	B.A.	PO.	A.	E.	F.A.
1986—Peoria	Midw.	1B-OF	126	465	81	159	30	4	15	95	*.342	1050	69	13	.989
1987—Pittsfield	East.	1B	123	453	81	151	29	8	17	*101	.333	1054	*96	6	*.995
1988—Iowa	A.A.	1B	21	67	11	17	4	0	0	14	.254	189	20	1	.995
1988—Chicago	Nat.	1B	134	486	65	144	23	4	7	57	.296	1182	87	●17	.987

Year Club	League	Pos.	G.	AB.	R.	H.	2B.	3B.	HR.	RBI.	B.A.	PO.	A.	E.	F.A.
1989—Chicago†	Nat.	1B	142	510	74	160	28	3	13	79	.314	1230	126	6	.996
1990—Chicago	Nat.	1B	157	589	72	182	32	1	9	82	.309	1324	*180	12	.992
Major League Totals—3 Years			433	1585	211	486	83	8	29	218	.307	3736	393	35	.992

Selected by Minnesota Twins' organization in 15th round of free-agent draft, January 17, 1984.
Selected by Chicago Cubs' organization in 24th round of free-agent draft, June 3, 1985.
†On disabled list, June 5 to June 23, 1989.

CHAMPIONSHIP SERIES RECORD

Shares Championship Series record for hitting home run in first series at-bat, October 4, 1989.

Year Club	League	Pos.	G.	AB.	R.	H.	2B.	3B.	HR.	RBI.	B.A.	PO.	A.	E.	F.A.
1989—Chicago	Nat.	1B	5	17	3	11	3	1	1	8	.647	44	3	0	1.000

JOSEPH MILTON GRAHE
(Joe)

Born June 14, 1967, at West Palm Beach, Fla.
Height, 6.00. Weight, 200.
Throws and bats righthanded.
Attended Palm Beach Junior College, Lake Worth, Fla.,
and University of Miami, Coral Gables, Fla.

Year Club	League	G.	IP.	W.	L.	Pct.	H.	R.	ER.	SO.	BB.	ERA.
1990—Midland	Texas	18	119	7	5	.583	145	75	70	58	34	5.29
1990—Edmonton	P. Coast	5	40	3	0	1.000	35	10	6	21	11	1.35
1990—California	American	8	43⅓	3	4	.429	51	30	24	25	23	4.98
Major League Totals—1 Year		8	43⅓	3	4	.429	51	30	24	25	23	4.98

Selected by Milwaukee Brewers' organization in 28th round of free-agent draft, June 2, 1986.
Selected by Oakland Athletics' organization in 5th round of free-agent draft, June 1, 1988.
Selected by California Angels' organization in 2nd round of free-agent draft, June 5, 1989.

MARK ANDREW GRANT

Born October 24, 1963, at Aurora, Ill.
Height, 6.02. Weight, 215.
Throws and bats righthanded.
Cousin of Rick Ramos, pitcher in Montreal Expos' organization, 1978 through 1983; and nephew
of Richard Ramos, pitcher in Chicago White Sox' organization, 1953 through 1958.
Pitched 9-0 no-hit victory against Danville, August 12, 1982.
Major League saves: 1984 (1), 1987 (1), 1989 (2), 1990 (3). Total—7.
Led Pacific Coast League pitchers in complete games with 10 and tied for lead in games started with 27 in 1986.
Led Pacific Coast League pitchers in wild pitches with 18 and tied for league lead in games started with 29 in 1985.
Tied for Pacific Coast League lead in shutouts with 3 in 1985 and 1986.
Tied for Midwest League lead in shutouts with 4 in 1982.

Year Club	League	G.	IP.	W.	L.	Pct.	H.	R.	ER.	SO.	BB.	ERA.
1981—Great Falls	Pioneer	10	64	2	6	.250	63	36	31	50	35	4.36
1982—Clinton	Midwest	27	*198⅔	*16	5	*.762	139	63	52	*243	60	2.36
1983—Shreveport	Texas	26	*186⅔	10	8	.556	182	83	76	159	71	3.66
1984—Phoenix	P. Coast	17	111⅓	5	7	.417	102	64	49	78	61	3.96
1984—San Francisco†	National	11	53⅔	1	4	.200	56	40	38	32	19	6.37
1985—Phoenix	P. Coast	29	183	8	●15	.348	182	101	92	133	90	4.52
1986—Phoenix	P. Coast	28	181⅔	*14	7	.667	204	105	99	93	46	4.90
1986—San Francisco	National	4	10	0	1	.000	6	4	4	5	5	3.60
1987—San Francisco‡-San Diego	National	33	163⅓	7	9	.438	170	88	77	90	73	4.24
1987—Phoenix	P. Coast	3	23	2	1	.667	20	8	8	12	5	3.13
1988—San Diego	National	33	97⅔	2	8	.200	97	41	40	61	36	3.69
1989—San Diego	National	50	116⅓	8	2	.800	105	45	43	69	32	3.33
1990—San Diego§-Atlanta	National	59	91⅓	2	3	.400	108	53	48	69	37	4.73
Major League Totals—6 Years		190	532⅓	20	27	.426	542	271	250	326	202	4.23

Selected by San Francisco Giants' organization in 1st round (10th player selected) of free-agent draft, June 8, 1981.
†On disabled list, May 4 to May 23, 1984.
‡Traded with Third Baseman Chris Brown and Pitchers Keith Comstock and Mark Davis to San Diego Padres for Pitchers Dave Dravecky and Craig Lefferts and Infielder Kevin Mitchell, July 4, 1987.
§Traded to Atlanta Braves for Pitcher Derek Lilliquist, July 12, 1990.

JEFFREY EDWARD GRAY
(Jeff)

Born April 10, 1963, at Richmond, Va.
Height, 6.01. Weight, 190.
Throws and bats righthanded.
Attended Florida State University, Tallahassee, Fla.
Major League saves: 1990 (9).
Led Florida State League in games finished in relief with 47 in 1985.
Tied for Gulf Coast League lead in intentional bases on balls issued with 5 in 1984.

Year Club	League	G.	IP.	W.	L.	Pct.	H.	R.	ER.	SO.	BB.	ERA.
1984—Sarasota Phillies	Gulf Coast	26	41⅓	6	4	.600	35	9	6	26	10	1.31
1985—Clearwater†	Florida St.	55	87⅔	5	9	.357	80	38	31	80	33	3.18
1986—Vermont	Eastern	*55	84⅓	*14	2	*.875	71	24	22	65	26	2.35

Year Club	League	G.	IP.	W.	L.	Pct.	H.	R.	ER.	SO.	BB.	ERA.
1987—Nashville	Am. Assoc.	53	83⅓	4	10	.286	97	52	45	70	26	4.86
1988—Nashville	Am. Assoc.	42	73	8	5	.615	59	17	16	73	18	1.97
1988—Cincinnati	National	5	9⅓	0	0	.000	12	4	4	5	4	3.86
1989—Nashville‡§	Am. Assoc.	44	66⅓	4	4	.500	76	33	27	58	12	3.66
1990—Pawtucket	Int'national	21	31⅔	0	0	.000	20	14	12	35	7	3.41
1990—Boston	American	41	50⅔	2	4	.333	53	27	25	50	15	4.44
National League Totals—1 Year		5	9⅓	0	0	.000	12	4	4	5	4	3.86
American League Totals—1 Year		41	50⅔	2	4	.333	53	27	25	50	15	4.44
Major League Totals—2 Years		46	60	2	4	.333	65	31	29	55	19	4.35

Signed as free agent by Philadelphia Phillies' organization, June 14, 1984.

†Traded with Pitcher John Denny to Cincinnati Reds for Outfielder Gary Redus and Pitcher Tom Hume, December 11, 1985.

‡Traded to Philadelphia Phillies' organization, September 6, 1989, completing deal in which Philadelphia traded Pitcher Bob Sebra to Cincinnati Reds for a player to be named later, July 13, 1989.

§Released, March 30, 1990; signed by Pawtucket (Boston Red Sox' organization), April 7, 1990.

CHAMPIONSHIP SERIES RECORD

Year Club	League	G.	IP.	W.	L.	Pct.	H.	R.	ER.	SO.	BB.	ERA.
1990—Boston	American	2	3⅓	0	0	.000	4	2	1	2	1	2.70

CRAIG ALLEN GREBECK

Born December 29, 1964, at Cerritos, Calif.
Height, 5.08. Weight, 160.
Throws and bats righthanded.
Attended California State University at Dominguez Hills, Carson, Calif.

Led Southern League in grounding into double plays with 15 in 1989.

Year Club	League	Pos.	G.	AB.	R.	H.	2B.	3B.	HR.	RBI.	B.A.	PO.	A.	E.	F.A.
1987—Peninsula	Carol.	SS	104	378	63	106	22	3	15	67	.280	137	278	16	.963
1988—Birmingham	South.	2B	133	450	57	126	21	1	9	53	.280	238	368	19	.970
1989—Birmingham	South.	SS-3B-2B	●143	●533	85	★153	25	4	5	80	.287	234	364	28	.955
1990—Chicago	Amer.	3B-SS-2B	59	119	7	20	3	1	1	9	.168	36	98	3	.978
1990—Vancouver	P. C.	SS-3B-2B	12	41	8	8	0	0	1	3	.195	28	26	1	.982
Major League Totals—1 Year			59	119	7	20	3	1	1	9	.168	36	98	3	.978

Signed as free agent by Chicago White Sox' organization, August 13, 1986.

GARY ALLAN GREEN

Born January 14, 1962, at Pittsburgh, Pa.
Height, 6.03. Weight, 175.
Throws and bats righthanded.
Attended Oklahoma State University, Stillwater, Okla.
Son of Freddie Green, pitcher with Pittsburgh Pirates and
Washington Senators, 1959 through 1962 and 1964.

Major League stolen bases: 1990 (1).
Led Pacific Coast League in sacrifice hits with 14 in 1987.
Led Texas League in sacrifice hits with 15 in 1985.
Led Pacific Coast League shortstops in double plays with 75 in 1987.
Member of 1984 U.S. Olympic baseball team.

Year Club	League	Pos.	G.	AB.	R.	H.	2B.	3B.	HR.	RBI.	B.A.	PO.	A.	E.	F.A.
1985—Beaumont†	Texas	SS	119	409	44	105	17	1	1	51	.257	157	405	30	.949
1986—Las Vegas	P. C.	SS	129	416	42	104	11	3	0	41	.250	158	390	24	.958
1986—San Diego	Nat.	SS	13	33	2	7	1	0	0	2	.212	16	35	0	1.000
1987—Las Vegas	P. C.	SS	111	337	32	80	8	2	1	32	.237	164	306	13	★.973
1988—Las Vegas	P. C.	SS-3B	88	302	39	82	16	2	0	37	.272	79	194	18	.938
1989—San Diego	Nat.	SS-3B	15	27	4	7	3	0	0	0	.259	6	29	3	.921
1989—Las Vegas‡	P. C.	SS-1B	62	191	18	40	6	0	0	18	.209	71	177	19	.929
1990—Oklahoma City	A. A.	SS	55	167	19	39	11	0	4	25	.234	101	145	10	.961
1990—Texas	Amer.	SS	62	88	10	19	3	0	0	8	.216	61	112	5	.972
National League Totals—2 Years			28	60	6	14	4	0	0	2	.233	22	64	3	.966
American League Totals—1 Year			62	88	10	19	3	0	0	8	.216	61	112	5	.972
Major League Totals—3 Years			90	148	16	33	7	0	0	10	.223	83	176	8	.970

Selected by San Francisco Giants' organization in 29th round of free-agent draft, June 3, 1980.
Selected by St. Louis Cardinals' organization in 2nd round of free-agent draft, June 6, 1983.
Selected by San Diego Padres' organization in 1st round (26th player selected) of free-agent draft, June 4, 1984.
†On disabled list, July 19 to July 28, 1985.
‡Drafted by Oklahoma City (Texas Rangers' organization), December 5, 1989.

IRA THOMAS GREENE
(Tommy)

Born April 6, 1967, at Lumberton, N. C.
Height, 6.05. Weight, 225.
Throws and bats righthanded.

Led South Atlantic League pitchers in games started with 28 and tied for lead in shutouts with 3 in 1986.
Tied for International League lead in shutouts with 3 in 1988.

Year Club	League	G.	IP.	W.	L.	Pct.	H.	R.	ER.	SO.	BB.	ERA.
1985—Pulaski	Ap'lachian	12	50⅔	2	5	.286	49	45	43	32	27	7.64
1986—Sumter	S. Atlantic	28	174⅔	11	7	.611	162	95	91	169	82	4.69
1987—Greenville	Southern	23	142⅓	11	8	.579	103	60	52	101	66	3.29
1988—Richmond	Int'national	29	177⅓	7	17	.292	169	98	94	130	70	4.77
1989—Richmond	Int'national	26	152	9	12	.429	136	74	61	125	50	3.61
1989—Atlanta	National	4	26⅓	1	2	.333	22	12	12	17	6	4.10
1990—Atlanta†-Philadelphia	National	15	51⅓	3	3	.500	50	31	29	21	26	5.08
1990—Richmond-Scranton/W.-B.	Int'national	20	116	5	8	.385	93	49	45	69	67	3.49
Major League Totals—2 Years		19	77⅔	4	5	.444	72	43	41	38	32	4.75

Selected by Atlanta Braves' organization in 1st round (14th player selected) of free-agent draft, June 3, 1985.

†Traded to Scranton/Wilkes-Barre (Philadelphia Phillies' organization), August 9, 1990, as partial completion of deal in which Atlanta Braves traded Outfielder Dale Murphy and a player to be named later to Philadelphia for Pitcher Jeff Parrett and two players to be named later, August 3, 1990. Atlanta acquired Outfielder Jim Vatcher on August 9, 1990 and Shortstop Victor Rosario on September 4, 1990 to complete deal.

MICHAEL LEWIS GREENWELL
(Mike)

Born July 18, 1963, at Louisville, Ky.
Height, 6.00. Weight, 200.
Throws right and bats lefthanded.

Holds American League record for most game-winning runs batted in, season (23), 1988.
Hit for the cycle, September 14, 1988.
Major League stolen bases: 1985 (1), 1987 (5), 1988 (16), 1989 (13), 1990 (8). Total—43.
Led American League in game-winning RBIs with 23 and tied for lead in intentional bases on balls received with 18 in 1988.
Led Carolina League in being hit by pitch with 15 in 1984.
Named outfielder on THE SPORTING NEWS American League All-Star Team, 1988.
Named outfielder on THE SPORTING NEWS American League Silver Slugger team, 1988.

Year Club	League	Pos.	G.	AB.	R.	H.	2B.	3B.	HR.	RBI.	B.A.	PO.	A.	E.	F.A.
1982—Elmira	NYP	3B-2B	72	268	57	72	10	1	6	36	.269	96	151	31	.888
1983—Winston-Salem†	Carol.	OF	48	158	23	44	8	0	3	21	.278	28	1	1	.967
1984—Winston-Salem	Carol.	3B-OF	130	454	70	139	23	6	16	84	.306	126	132	30	.896
1985—Pawtucket	Int.	OF	117	418	47	107	21	1	13	52	.256	178	8	7	.964
1985—Boston	Amer.	OF	17	31	7	10	1	0	4	8	.323	14	0	0	1.000
1986—Pawtucket	Int.	OF-3B	89	320	62	96	21	1	18	59	.300	130	20	8	.949
1986—Boston	Amer.	OF	31	35	4	11	2	0	4	4	.314	18	1	0	1.000
1987—Boston	Amer.	OF-C	125	412	71	135	31	6	19	89	.328	165	8	6	.966
1988—Boston	Amer.	OF	158	590	86	192	39	8	22	119	.325	302	6	6	.981
1989—Boston‡	Amer.	OF	145	578	87	178	36	0	14	95	.308	220	11	8	.967
1990—Boston	Amer.	OF	159	610	71	181	30	6	14	73	.297	287	13	7	.977
Major League Totals—6 Years			635	2256	326	707	139	20	73	388	.313	1006	39	27	.975

Selected by Boston Red Sox' organization in 3rd round of free-agent draft, June 7, 1982.
†On disabled list, April 21 to May 2 and May 13 to July 25, 1983.
‡On disabled list, July 30 to August 14, 1989.

CHAMPIONSHIP SERIES RECORD

Year Club	League	Pos.	G.	AB.	R.	H.	2B.	3B.	HR.	RBI.	B.A.	PO.	A.	E.	F.A.
1986—Boston	Amer.	PH	2	2	0	1	0	0	0	0	.500	0	0	0	.000
1988—Boston	Amer.	OF	4	14	2	3	1	0	1	3	.214	4	0	0	1.000
1990—Boston	Amer.	OF	4	14	1	0	0	0	0	0	.000	3	0	1	.750
Championship Series Totals—3 Years			10	30	3	4	1	0	1	3	.133	7	0	1	.875

WORLD SERIES RECORD

Year Club	League	Pos.	G.	AB.	R.	H.	2B.	3B.	HR.	RBI.	B.A.	PO.	A.	E.	F.A.
1986—Boston	Amer.	PH	4	3	0	0	0	0	0	0	.000	0	0	0	.000

ALL-STAR GAME RECORD

Year League	Pos.	AB.	R.	H.	2B.	3B.	HR.	RBI.	B.A.	PO.	A.	E.	F.A.
1988—American	OF	1	0	0	0	0	0	0	.000	1	0	0	1.000
1989—American	OF	0	0	0	0	0	0	0	.000	1	0	0	1.000
All-Star Game Totals—2 Years		1	0	0	0	0	0	0	.000	2	0	0	1.000

WILLIAM THOMAS GREGG JR.
(Tommy)

Born July 29, 1963, at Boone, N. C.
Height, 6.01. Weight, 190.
Throws and bats lefthanded.
Attended Wake Forest University, Winston-Salem, N. C.

Major League stolen bases: 1989 (3), 1990 (4). Total—7.
Led Eastern League in intentional bases on balls received with 14 in 1987.

Year Club	League	Pos.	G.	AB.	R.	H.	2B.	3B.	HR.	RBI.	B.A.	PO.	A.	E.	F.A.
1985—Macon	S. Atl.	OF	72	259	43	81	14	2	1	18	.313	117	4	1	.992
1986—Nashua	East.	OF-1B	126	421	55	113	13	4	1	29	.268	216	7	4	.982
1987—Harrisburg	East.	OF	133	461	99	171	22	9	10	82	*.371	242	12	7	.973
1987—Pittsburgh	Nat.	OF	10	8	3	2	1	0	0	0	.250	1	0	0	1.000

Year	Club	League	Pos.	G.	AB.	R.	H.	2B.	3B.	HR.	RBI.	B.A.	PO.	A.	E.	F.A.
1988—Buffalo	A. A.		OF	72	252	34	74	12	0	6	27	.294	134	3	2	.986
1988—Pitt.†-Atl.	Nat.		OF	25	44	5	13	4	0	1	7	.295	26	1	0	1.000
1989—Atlanta‡	Nat.		OF-1B	102	276	24	67	8	0	6	23	.243	321	17	2	.994
1990—Atlanta	Nat.		1B-OF	124	239	18	63	13	1	5	32	.264	356	34	6	.985
Major League Totals—4 Years				261	567	50	145	26	1	12	62	.256	704	52	8	.990

Selected by Cleveland Indians' organization in 9th round of free-agent draft, June 8, 1981.
Selected by Cleveland Indians' organization in 32nd round of free-agent draft, June 4, 1984.
Selected by Pittsburgh Pirates' organization in 7th round of free-agent draft, June 3, 1985.
†Traded to Atlanta Braves, September 1, 1988, completing deal in which Atlanta traded Infielder Ken Oberkfell and cash to Pittsburgh Pirates for a player to be named later, August 28, 1988.
‡On disabled list, April 20 to June 2, 1989.

GEORGE KENNETH GRIFFEY SR.
(Ken)

Born April 10, 1950, at Donora, Pa.
Height, 6.00. Weight, 210.
Throws and bats lefthanded.
Father of Ken Griffey Jr., outfielder with Seattle Mariners; and
Craig Griffey, defensive back at Ohio State University.

Shares modern major league record for most at-bats, nine inning game (7), June 13, 1975.
Major League stolen bases: 1973 (4), 1974 (9), 1975 (16), 1976 (34), 1977 (17), 1978 (23), 1979 (12), 1980 (23), 1981 (12), 1982 (10), 1983 (5), 1984 (2), 1985 (7), 1986 (14), 1987 (4), 1988 (1), 1989 (4), 1990 (2). Total—199.
Hit three home runs in a game, July 22, 1986.
Led American Association in stolen bases with 43 in 1973.
Tied for Eastern League lead in double plays by outfielders with 6 in 1972.
Named as outfielder on THE SPORTING NEWS National League All-Star Team, 1976.

Year	Club	League	Pos.	G.	AB.	R.	H.	2B.	3B.	HR.	RBI.	B.A.	PO.	A.	E.	F.A.
1969—Bradenton Reds	Gulf C.		★OF-1B	49	153	22	43	★11	1	1	12	.281	57	4	★10	.859
1970—Sioux Falls	North.		OF	51	164	20	40	2	1	2	24	.244	76	2	7	.918
1971—Tampa	Fla. St.		OF	88	281	60	96	7	11	3	33	.342	137	13	8	.949
1971—Three Rivers	East.		OF	9	32	1	13	1	2	0	4	.406	17	0	1	.944
1972—Three Rivers	East.		●OF-SS	128	472	★96	150	21	3	14	52	.318	212	10	●15	.937
1973—Indianapolis	A. A.		OF	107	397	88	130	18	5	10	58	.327	171	11	6	.968
1973—Cincinnati	Nat.		OF	25	86	19	33	5	1	3	14	.384	25	1	0	1.000
1974—Indianapolis	A. A.		OF	43	162	34	54	6	4	5	18	.333	70	4	1	.987
1974—Cincinnati	Nat.		OF	88	227	24	57	9	5	2	19	.251	115	5	0	1.000
1975—Cincinnati	Nat.		OF	132	463	95	141	15	9	4	46	.305	202	6	7	.967
1976—Cincinnati	Nat.		OF	148	562	111	189	28	9	6	74	.336	270	10	6	.976
1977—Cincinnati	Nat.		OF	154	585	117	186	35	8	12	57	.318	298	10	3	.990
1978—Cincinnati	Nat.		OF	158	614	90	177	33	8	10	63	.288	296	13	10	.969
1979—Cincinnati†	Nat.		OF	95	380	62	120	27	4	8	32	.316	175	8	3	.984
1980—Cincinnati	Nat.		OF	146	544	89	160	28	10	13	85	.294	266	5	6	.978
1981—Cincinnati‡	Nat.		OF	101	396	65	123	21	6	2	34	.311	268	8	3	.989
1982—New York	Amer.		OF	127	484	70	134	23	2	12	54	.277	282	8	5	.983
1983—New York§	Amer.		1B-OF	118	458	60	140	21	3	11	46	.306	870	57	8	.991
1984—New York	Amer.		OF-1B	120	399	44	109	20	1	7	56	.273	422	22	16	.965
1985—New York x	Amer.		OF-1B	127	438	68	120	28	4	10	69	.274	227	8	7	.971
1986—New York y	Amer.		OF	59	198	33	60	7	0	9	26	.303	96	5	3	.971
1986—Atlanta	Nat.		OF-1B	80	292	36	90	15	3	12	32	.308	136	2	2	.986
1987—Atlanta	Nat.		OF-1B	122	399	65	114	24	1	14	64	.286	205	8	2	.991
1988—Atl. b - Cinc. c	Nat.		OF-1B	94	243	26	62	6	0	4	23	.255	193	16	4	.981
1989—Cincinnati	Nat.		OF-1B	106	236	26	62	8	3	8	30	.263	122	2	2	.984
1990—Cincinnati de	Nat.		1B-OF	46	63	6	13	2	0	1	8	.206	54	4	1	.983
1990—Seattle f	Amer.		OF	21	77	13	29	2	0	3	18	.377	25	1	1	.963
National League Totals—14 Years				1495	5090	831	1527	256	67	99	581	.300	2625	98	49	.982
American League Totals—6 Years				572	2054	288	592	101	10	52	269	.288	1922	101	40	.981
Major League Totals—18 Years				2067	7144	1119	2119	357	77	151	850	.297	4547	199	89	.982

Selected by Cincinnati Reds' organization in 29th round of free-agent draft, June 5, 1969.
†On disabled list, August 14 to September 7, 1979.
‡Traded to New York Yankees for Pitcher Brian Ryder and a player to be named later, November 4, 1981; Cincinnati Reds' organization acquired Pitcher Freddie Toliver to complete deal, December 10, 1981.
§On disabled list, July 2 to August 2, 1983.
xOn disabled list, May 28 to June 12, 1985.
yTraded to Atlanta Braves for Outfielder Claudell Washington and Shortstop Paul Zuvella, June 30, 1986.
zOn disabled list, May 5 to May 20, 1987.
aGranted free agency, November 9, 1987; re-signed by Braves, November 13, 1987.
bReleased, July 28, 1988; signed by Cincinnati Reds, August 2, 1988.
cReleased, December 21, 1988; re-signed by Reds, March 30, 1989.
dOn voluntarily retired list, August 18, 1990.
eReleased, August 24, 1990; signed by Seattle Mariners, August 29, 1990.
fGranted free agency, November 5, 1990; re-signed by Mariners, December 17, 1990.

CHAMPIONSHIP SERIES RECORD

Shares Championship Series records for most stolen bases, inning (2), October 5, 1975, sixth inning.
Shares National League Championship Series record for most stolen bases, game (3), October 5, 1975.

Year	Club	League	Pos.	G.	AB.	R.	H.	2B.	3B.	HR.	RBI.	B.A.	PO.	A.	E.	F.A.
1973—Cincinnati	Nat.		OF-PH	3	7	0	1	1	0	0	0	.143	3	0	0	1.000

Year Club League	Pos.	G.	AB.	R.	H.	2B.	3B.	HR.	RBI.	B.A.	PO.	A.	E.	F.A.
1975—Cincinnati............. Nat.	OF	3	12	3	4	1	0	0	4	.333	4	1	0	1.000
1976—Cincinnati............. Nat.	OF	3	13	2	5	0	1	0	2	.385	11	0	0	1.000
Championship Series Totals—3 Years....		9	32	5	10	2	1	0	6	.313	17	1	0	1.000

WORLD SERIES RECORD

Year Club League	Pos.	G.	AB.	R.	H.	2B.	3B.	HR.	RBI.	B.A.	PO.	A.	E.	F.A.
1975—Cincinnati............. Nat.	OF	7	26	4	7	3	1	0	4	.269	10	1	0	1.000
1976—Cincinnati............. Nat.	OF	4	17	2	1	0	0	0	1	.059	5	0	0	1.000
World Series Totals—2 Years..................		11	43	6	8	3	1	0	5	.186	15	1	0	1.000

ALL-STAR GAME RECORD

Year League	Pos.	AB.	R.	H.	2B.	3B.	HR.	RBI.	B.A.	PO.	A.	E.	F.A.
1976—National.......................................	OF	1	1	1	0	0	0	1	1.000	1	0	0	1.000
1980—National.......................................	OF	3	1	2	0	0	1	1	.667	0	0	0	.000
All-Star Game Totals—2 Years....................		4	2	3	0	0	1	2	.750	1	0	0	1.000

Member of National League All-Star Team in 1977; did not play.

GEORGE KENNETH GRIFFEY JR.
(Ken)

Born November 21, 1969, at Donora, Pa.
Height, 6.03. Weight, 200.
Throws and bats lefthanded.
Son of Ken Griffey, Sr., outfielder with Seattle Mariners; and
brother of Craig Griffey, defensive back at Ohio State University.

Major League stolen bases: 1989 (16), 1990 (16). Total—32.
Led American League outfielders in double plays with 6 in 1989.
Named outfielder on THE SPORTING NEWS American League All-Star fielding team, 1990.

Year Club League	Pos.	G.	AB.	R.	H.	2B.	3B.	HR.	RBI.	B.A.	PO.	A.	E.	F.A.
1987—Bellingham .... N'west	OF	54	182	43	57	9	1	14	40	.313	117	4	1	★.992
1988—San Bernardino†.. Calif.	OF	58	219	50	74	13	3	11	42	.338	145	3	2	.987
1988—Vermont .... East.	OF	17	61	10	17	5	1	2	10	.279	40	2	1	.977
1989—Seattle‡................... Amer.	OF	127	455	61	120	23	0	16	61	.264	302	12	●10	.969
1990—Seattle.................... Amer.	OF	155	597	91	179	28	7	22	80	.300	330	8	7	.980
Major League Totals—2 Years................		282	1052	152	299	51	7	38	141	.284	632	20	17	.975

Selected by Seattle Mariners' organization in 1st round (first player selected) of free-agent draft, June 2, 1987.
†On disabled list, June 9 to August 15, 1988.
†On disabled list, July 24 to August 20, 1989.

ALL-STAR GAME RECORD

Year League	Pos.	AB.	R.	H.	2B.	3B.	HR.	RBI.	B.A.	PO.	A.	E.	F.A.
1990—American	OF	2	0	0	0	0	0	0	.000	2	0	0	1.000

ALFREDO CLAUDINO GRIFFIN

Born March 6, 1957, at Santo Domingo, D. R.
Height, 5.11. Weight, 165.
Throws right and bats left and righthanded.

Major League stolen bases: 1977 (2), 1979 (21), 1980 (18), 1981 (8), 1982 (10), 1983 (8), 1984 (11), 1985 (24), 1986 (33), 1987 (26), 1988 (7), 1989 (10), 1990 (6). Total—184.
Led American League shortstops in putouts with 280 in 1983.
Led American League shortstops in total chances with 824 in 1982.
Named shortstop on THE SPORTING NEWS American League All-Star fielding team, 1985.
Named American League Co-Rookie of the Year by the Baseball Writers' Association of America, 1979.

Year Club League	Pos.	G.	AB.	R.	H.	2B.	3B.	HR.	RBI.	B.A.	PO.	A.	E.	F.A.
1974—Reno .... Calif.	SS	11	35	4	9	0	0	1	.257	10	22	9	.780
1974—Sarasota Indians...Gulf C.	SS	49	158	17	41	1	0	0	11	.259	67	133	★25	.889
1975—San Jose .... Calif.	SS	124	358	42	82	4	3	0	25	.229	189	281	47	.909
1976—San Jose .... Calif.	SS	64	224	40	58	3	1	0	17	.259	91	145	24	.908
1976—Williamsport........ East.	SS	58	200	22	55	3	0	0	17	.275	86	172	17	.938
1976—Toledo .... Int.	SS	22	88	5	19	7	1	0	6	.216	44	71	7	.943
1976—Cleveland.............. Amer.	SS	12	4	0	1	0	0	0	0	.250	1	2	1	.750
1977—Toledo .... Int.	SS	125	457	60	114	14	5	1	32	.249	★223	398	★49	.927
1977—Cleveland.............. Amer.	SS	14	41	5	6	1	0	0	3	.146	17	30	3	.940
1978—Portland .... P. C.	★SS-OF	133	474	82	138	22	10	5	48	.291	201	395	★40	.937
1978—Cleveland†............ Amer.	SS	5	4	1	2	1	0	0	0	.500	4	7	1	.917
1979—Toronto .... Amer.	SS	153	624	81	179	22	10	2	31	.287	272	501	★36	.956
1980—Toronto .... Amer.	SS	155	653	63	166	26	●15	2	41	.254	295	489	★37	.955
1981—Toronto .... Amer.	★SS-3B-2B	101	388	30	81	19	6	0	21	.209	191	279	★31	.938
1982—Toronto .... Amer.	SS	●162	539	57	130	20	8	1	48	.241	★319	479	●26	.968
1983—Toronto .... Amer.	SS-2B	●162	528	62	132	22	9	4	47	.250	287	422	25	.966
1984—Toronto‡ .... Amer.	SS-2B	140	419	53	101	8	2	4	30	.241	230	320	21	.963
1985—Oakland................ Amer.	SS	162	614	75	166	18	7	2	64	.270	278	440	30	.960
1986—Oakland................ Amer.	SS	162	594	74	169	23	6	4	51	.285	282	421	25	.966
1987—Oakland§............... Amer.	SS-2B	144	494	69	130	23	5	3	60	.263	250	389	24	.964
1988—Los Angeles xy..... Nat.	SS	95	316	39	63	8	3	1	27	.199	145	264	15	.965
1989—Los Angeles z .... Nat.	SS	136	506	49	125	27	2	0	29	.247	208	333	14	.975

Year	Club	League	Pos.	G.	AB.	R.	H.	2B.	3B.	HR.	RBI.	B.A.	PO.	A.	E.	F.A.
1990—Los Angeles		Nat.	SS	141	461	38	97	11	3	1	35	.210	221	382	●26	.959
American League Totals—12 Years			1372	4902	570	1263	183	68	22	396	.258	2426	3779	260	.960
National League Totals—3 Years			372	1283	126	285	46	8	2	91	.222	574	979	55	.966
Major League Totals—15 Years			1744	6185	696	1548	229	76	24	487	.250	3000	4758	315	.961

Signed as free agent by Cleveland Indians' organization, August 22, 1973.
†Traded with Third Baseman Phil Lansford to Toronto Blue Jays for Pitcher Victor Cruz, December 6, 1978.
‡Traded with Outfielder Dave Collins and cash to Oakland A's for Pitcher Bill Caudill, December 8, 1984.
§As part of an eight-player, three-team deal, New York Mets traded Pitcher Jesse Orosco to Oakland Athletics, December 11, 1987. Oakland then traded Orosco along with Shortstop Alfredo Griffin and Pitcher Jay Howell to Los Angeles Dodgers for Pitchers Bob Welch, Matt Young and Jack Savage. Oakland then traded Savage along with Pitchers Wally Whitehurst and Kevin Tapani to New York.
xOn disabled list, May 22 to July 25, 1988.
yGranted free agency, November 4, 1988; re-signed by Dodgers, November 7, 1988.
zOn disabled list, May 8 to May 28, 1989.

CHAMPIONSHIP SERIES RECORD

Year	Club	League	Pos.	G.	AB.	R.	H.	2B.	3B.	HR.	RBI.	B.A.	PO.	A.	E.	F.A.
1988—Los Angeles		Nat.	SS	7	25	1	4	1	0	0	3	.160	17	13	0	1.000

WORLD SERIES RECORD

Year	Club	League	Pos.	G.	AB.	R.	H.	2B.	3B.	HR.	RBI.	B.A.	PO.	A.	E.	F.A.
1988—Los Angeles		Nat.	SS	5	16	2	3	0	0	0	0	.188	7	13	1	.952

ALL-STAR GAME RECORD

Year	League	Pos.	AB.	R.	H.	2B.	3B.	HR.	RBI.	B.A.	PO.	A.	E.	F.A.
1984—American		SS	0	0	0	0	0	0	0	.000	0	1	0	1.000

JASON ALAN GRIMSLEY

Born August 7, 1967, at Cleveland, Tex.
Height, 6.03. Weight, 180.
Throws and bats righthanded.

Pitched 3-0 no-hit victory against Harrisburg, May 3, 1989 (first game).
Led International League in wild pitches with 18 in 1990.
Led New York-Pennsylvania League in hit batsmen with 11 and wild pitches with 18 in 1986.
Tied for Eastern League lead in games started by pitchers with 26 in 1989.

Year	Club	League	G.	IP.	W.	L.	Pct.	H.	R.	ER.	SO.	BB.	ERA.
1985—Bend	Northwest	6	11⅓	0	1	.000	12	21	17	10	25	13.50
1986—Utica	NYP	14	64⅔	1	●10	.091	63	61	46	46	★77	6.40
1987—Spartanburg	S. Atlantic	23	88⅓	7	4	.636	59	48	31	98	54	3.16
1988—Clearwater	Florida St.	16	101⅓	4	7	.364	80	48	42	90	37	3.73
1988—Reading	Eastern	5	21⅓	1	3	.250	20	19	17	14	13	7.17
1989—Reading	Eastern	26	172	11	8	.579	121	65	57	134	★109	2.98
1989—Philadelphia	National	4	18⅓	1	3	.250	19	13	12	7	19	5.89
1990—Scranton/Wilkes-Barre	Int'national	22	128⅓	8	5	.615	111	68	56	99	78	3.93
1990—Philadelphia	National	11	57⅓	3	2	.600	47	21	21	41	43	3.30
Major League Totals—2 Years		15	75⅔	4	5	.444	66	34	33	48	62	3.93

Selected by Philadelphia Phillies' organization in 10th round of free-agent draft, June 3, 1985.

MARQUIS DEAN GRISSOM

First name pronounced Mar-KEESE.
Born April 17, 1967, at Atlanta, Ga.
Height, 5.11. Weight, 190.
Throws and bats righthanded.
Attended Florida A&M University, Tallahassee, Fla.

Major League stolen bases: 1989 (1), 1990 (22). Total—23.
Led New York-Pennsylvania League in total bases with 146 in 1988.

Year	Club	League	Pos.	G.	AB.	R.	H.	2B.	3B.	HR.	RBI.	B.A.	PO.	A.	E.	F.A.
1988—Jamestown		NYP	OF	74	★291	★69	94	14	7	8	39	.323	123	●11	3	.978
1989—Jacksonville		South.	OF	78	278	43	83	15	4	3	31	.299	141	7	3	.980
1989—Indianapolis		A. A.	OF	49	187	28	52	10	4	2	21	.278	106	5	0	1.000
1989—Montreal		Nat.	OF	26	74	16	19	2	0	1	2	.257	32	1	2	.943
1990—Montreal†		Nat.	OF	98	288	42	74	14	2	3	29	.257	165	5	2	.988
1990—Indianapolis		A. A.	OF	5	22	3	4	0	0	2	3	.182	16	0	0	1.000
Major League Totals—2 Years			124	362	58	93	16	2	4	31	.257	197	6	4	.981

Selected by Montreal Expos' organization in 3rd round of free-agent draft, June 1, 1988.

†On disabled list, May 29 to June 30, 1990; included rehabilitation disability assignment to Indianapolis, June 25 to June 30, 1990.

KEVIN FRANK GROSS

Born June 8, 1961, at Downey, Calif.
Height, 6.05. Weight, 215.
Throws and bats righthanded.
Attended Oxnard College, Oxnard, Calif., and
California Lutheran College, Thousand Oaks, Calif.

Major League saves: 1984 (1).
Led National League in home runs allowed with 28 in 1986.
Led National League in hit batsmen with 11 in 1988 and tied for lead with 8 in 1986 and 10 in 1987.
Tied for South Atlantic League lead in games started by pitchers with 28 in 1981.

Year Club	League	G.	IP.	W.	L.	Pct.	H.	R.	ER.	SO.	BB.	ERA.
1981—Spartanburg	S. Atlantic	28	192	13	12	.520	173	94	76	123	62	3.56
1982—Reading	Eastern	26	151	10	15	.400	138	81	71	136	89	4.23
1983—Portland	P. Coast	15	80	3	5	.375	82	60	60	61	45	6.75
1983—Philadelphia	National	17	96	4	6	.400	100	46	38	66	35	3.56
1984—Philadelphia	National	44	129	8	5	.615	140	66	59	84	44	4.12
1985—Philadelphia	National	38	205⅔	15	13	.536	194	86	78	151	81	3.41
1986—Philadelphia	National	37	241⅔	12	12	.500	240	115	108	154	94	4.02
1987—Philadelphia	National	34	200⅔	9	16	.360	205	107	97	110	87	4.35
1988—Philadelphia†	National	33	231⅔	12	14	.462	209	101	95	162	*89	3.69
1989—Montreal	National	31	201⅓	11	12	.478	188	105	*98	158	88	4.38
1990—Montreal‡§	National	31	163⅓	9	12	.429	171	86	83	111	65	4.57
Major League Totals—8 Years		265	1469⅓	80	90	.471	1447	712	656	996	583	4.02

Selected by Baltimore Orioles' organization in 32nd round of free-agent draft, June 5, 1979.
Selected by Philadelphia Phillies' organization in secondary phase of free-agent draft, January 13, 1981.
†Traded to Montreal Expos for Pitchers Floyd Youmans and Jeff Parrett, December 6, 1988.
‡On disabled list, June 28 to July 20, 1990.
§Granted free agency, November 5, 1990; signed by Los Angeles Dodgers, December 3, 1990.

WORLD SERIES RECORD
Eligible for 1983 World Series with Philadelphia Phillies; did not play.

ALL-STAR GAME RECORD

Year League	IP.	W.	L.	Pct.	H.	R.	ER.	SO.	BB.	ERA.
1988—National	1	0	0	.000	0	0	0	1	0	0.00

KIP LEE GROSS

Born August 24, 1964, at Scottsbluff, Neb.
Height, 6.02. Weight, 190.
Throws and bats righthanded.
Attended Murray State College, Tishomingo, Okla., and
University of Nebraska, Lincoln, Neb.

Year Club	League	G.	IP.	W.	L.	Pct.	H.	R.	ER.	SO.	BB.	ERA.
1987—Lynchburg	Carolina	16	89⅓	7	4	.636	92	37	27	39	22	2.72
1988—St. Lucie	Florida St.	28	178⅓	13	9	.591	153	72	52	124	53	2.62
1989—Jackson	Texas	16	112	6	5	.545	96	47	31	60	13	2.49
1989—Tidewater†	Int'national	12	70⅓	4	4	.500	72	33	31	39	17	3.97
1990—Nashville	Am. Assoc.	40	127	12	7	.632	113	54	47	62	47	3.33
1990—Cincinnati	National	5	6⅓	0	0	.000	6	3	3	3	2	4.26
Major League Totals—1 Year		5	6⅓	0	0	.000	6	3	3	3	2	4.26

Selected by St. Louis Cardinals' organization in 3rd round of free-agent draft, January 9, 1985.
Selected by New York Mets' organization in 4th round of free-agent draft, June 2, 1986.
†Traded with Pitcher Randy Myers to Cincinnati Reds for Pitcher John Franco and Outfielder Don Brown, December 6, 1989.

KELLY WAYNE GRUBER

Born February 26, 1962, at Bellaire, Tex.
Height, 6.00. Weight, 185.
Throws and bats righthanded.
Attended University of Texas, Austin, Tex.

Major League stolen bases: 1986 (2), 1987 (12), 1988 (23), 1989 (10), 1990 (14). Total—61.
Hit for the cycle, April 16, 1989.
Led American League third basemen in putouts with 123 in 1990.
Led American League third basemen in assists with 349 and total chances with 477 in 1988.
Led International League in slugging percentage with .500 in 1984.
Led International League third basemen in total chances with 309 in 1985.
Led Southern League shortstops in errors with 43 in 1982.
Named third baseman on THE SPORTING NEWS American League All-Star Team, 1990.
Named third baseman on THE SPORTING NEWS American League All-Star fielding team, 1990.
Named third baseman on THE SPORTING NEWS American League Silver Slugger team, 1990.

Year Club	League	Pos.	G.	AB.	R.	H.	2B.	3B.	HR.	RBI.	B.A.	PO.	A.	E.	F.A.
1980—Batavia	NYP	SS	61	212	27	46	3	2	2	19	.217	87	155	21	.920
1981—Waterloo	Midw.	SS	127	458	64	133	25	4	14	59	.290	*180	*389	*56	.910
1982—Chattanooga	South.	SS-3B	128	441	53	107	18	4	13	54	.243	161	333	44	.918
1983—Buffalo†	East.	3B-SS-OF	111	403	60	106	20	4	15	54	.263	98	170	27	.908
1984—Toronto	Amer.	3B-OF-SS	15	16	1	1	0	0	1	2	.063	6	12	2	.900
1984—Syracuse	Int.	3B-OF	97	342	53	92	12	2	21	55	.269	76	156	18	.928
1985—Syracuse	Int.	3B	121	473	71	118	16	5	21	69	.249	78	*217	14	.955
1985—Toronto	Amer.	3B-2B	5	13	0	3	0	0	0	1	.231	2	6	0	1.000
1986—Toronto	Amer.	3-2-O-S	87	143	20	28	4	1	5	15	.196	43	77	7	.945
1987—Toronto	Amer.	3-S-2-O	138	341	50	80	14	3	12	36	.235	76	200	13	.955
1988—Toronto	Amer.	3-2-O-S	158	569	75	158	33	5	16	81	.278	121	365	16	.968
1989—Toronto‡	Amer.	*3-O-S	135	545	83	158	24	4	18	73	.290	121	295	*22	.950

Year	Club	League	Pos.	G.	AB.	R.	H.	2B.	3B.	HR.	RBI.	B.A.	PO.	A.	E.	F.A.
1990—Toronto		Amer.	3B-OF	150	592	92	162	36	6	31	118	.274	129	280	19	.956
Major League Totals—7 Years				688	2219	321	590	111	19	83	326	.266	498	1235	79	.956

Selected by Cleveland Indians' organization in 1st round (10th player selected) of free-agent draft, June 3, 1980.
†Drafted by Toronto Blue Jays, December 5, 1983.
‡On disabled list, August 10 to August 25, 1989.

CHAMPIONSHIP SERIES RECORD

Shares Championship Series record for most singles, game (4), October 7, 1989.

Year	Club	League	Pos.	G.	AB.	R.	H.	2B.	3B.	HR.	RBI.	B.A.	PO.	A.	E.	F.A.
1989—Toronto		Amer.	3B	5	17	2	5	1	0	0	1	.294	4	8	0	1.000

ALL-STAR GAME RECORD

Shares record for most stolen bases, game (2), July 10, 1990.

Year	League	Pos.	AB.	R.	H.	2B.	3B.	HR.	RBI.	B.A.	PO.	A.	E.	F.A.
1990—American		PR-3B	1	0	0	0	0	0	0	.000	0	1	0	1.000

Member of American League All-Star Team in 1989; did not play.

CECILIO GUANTE (MAGALLANES)

Name pronounced Goo-AHN-tay.

Born February 2, 1960, at Jacagua, D. R.
Height, 6.03. Weight, 205.
Throws and bats righthanded.

Major League saves: 1983 (9), 1984 (2), 1985 (5), 1986 (4), 1987 (1), 1988 (12), 1989 (2). Total—35.
Led South Atlantic League in saves with 19 in 1980.

Year	Club	League	G.	IP.	W.	L.	Pct.	H.	R.	ER.	SO.	BB.	ERA.
1980—Shelby		S. Atlantic	39	90	6	6	.500	58	32	29	114	25	2.90
1980—Salem		Carolina	6	14	0	0	.000	7	2	2	18	8	1.29
1981—Buffalo		Eastern	10	14	1	1	.500	8	3	1	17	9	0.64
1981—Portland†		P. Coast	19	104	6	6	.500	110	64	62	70	58	5.37
1982—Portland		P. Coast	21	35	3	2	.600	34	17	15	29	26	3.86
1982—Pittsburgh		National	10	27	0	0	.000	28	16	10	26	5	3.33
1983—Hawaii		P. Coast	15	25⅔	2	1	.667	22	12	10	24	12	3.51
1983—Pittsburgh		National	49	100⅓	2	6	.250	90	45	37	82	46	3.32
1984—Pittsburgh‡		National	27	41⅓	2	3	.400	32	12	12	30	16	2.61
1984—Nashua		Eastern	1	3	0	0	.000	5	1	1	2	0	3.00
1985—Pittsburgh		National	63	109	4	6	.400	84	34	33	92	40	2.72
1986—Pittsburgh§x		National	52	78	5	2	.714	65	32	29	63	29	3.35
1987—New York y		American	23	44	3	2	.600	42	30	28	46	20	5.73
1988—New York z-Texas a		American	63	79⅔	5	6	.455	67	26	25	65	26	2.82
1989—Texas bc		American	50	69	6	6	.500	66	35	30	69	36	3.91
1990—Cleveland d		American	26	46⅔	2	3	.400	38	26	26	30	18	5.01
1990—Pawtucket		Int'national	2	5	0	0	.000	1	0	0	4	2	0.00
National League Totals—5 Years			201	355⅔	13	17	.433	299	139	121	293	136	3.06
American League Totals—4 Years			162	239⅓	16	17	.485	213	117	109	210	100	4.10
Major League Totals—9 Years			363	595	29	34	.460	512	256	230	503	236	3.48

Signed as free agent by Pittsburgh Pirates' organization, November 24, 1979.
†On disabled list, July 25 to August 5, 1981.
‡On disabled list, July 13 to July 30, 1984.
§On disabled list, August 25 to September 24, 1986.
xTraded with Pitchers Rick Rhoden and Pat Clements to New York Yankees for Pitchers Doug Drabek, Brian Fisher and Logan Easley, November 26, 1986.
yOn disabled list, May 25 to June 9 and July 7 to September 14, 1987.
zTraded to Texas Rangers for Pitcher Dale Mohorcic, August 30, 1988.
aGranted free agency, November 4, 1988; re-signed by Rangers, January 6, 1989.
bOn disabled list, August 19 to September 3, 1989.
cReleased, October 2, 1989; signed by Cleveland Indians, November 21, 1989.
dReleased, August 12, 1990; signed by Pawtucket (Boston Red Sox' organization), August 23, 1990.

MARK STEVEN GUBICZA

Name pronounced GOO-ba-zah.

Born August 14, 1962, at Philadelphia, Pa.
Height, 6.05. Weight, 220.
Throws and bats righthanded.
Son of Anthony F. Gubicza, minor league pitcher, 1950 and 1951.

Tied for American League lead in games started by pitchers with 36 in 1989.

Year	Club	League	G.	IP.	W.	L.	Pct.	H.	R.	ER.	SO.	BB.	ERA.
1981—Sarasota Royals-Gold		Gulf Coast	11	56	●8	1	★.889	39	18	14	40	23	2.25
1982—Fort Myers†		Florida St.	11	48	2	5	.286	49	33	22	36	25	4.13
1983—Jacksonville		Southern	28	196	14	12	.538	146	81	67	★146	93	3.08
1984—Kansas City		American	29	189	10	14	.417	172	90	85	111	75	4.05
1985—Kansas City		American	29	177⅓	14	10	.583	160	88	80	99	77	4.06
1986—Kansas City‡		American	35	180⅔	12	6	.667	155	77	73	118	84	3.64
1987—Kansas City		American	35	241⅔	13	18	.419	231	114	107	166	120	3.98
1988—Kansas City		American	35	269⅔	20	8	.714	237	94	81	183	83	2.70

Year Club	League	G.	IP.	W.	L.	Pct.	H.	R.	ER.	SO.	BB.	ERA.
1989—Kansas City	American	36	255	15	11	.577	252	100	86	173	63	3.04
1990—Kansas City§	American	16	94	4	7	.364	101	48	47	71	38	4.50
Major League Totals—7 Years		215	1407⅓	88	74	.543	1308	611	559	921	540	3.57

Selected by Kansas City Royals' organization in 2nd round of free-agent draft, June 8, 1981.
†On disabled list, June 29, 1982 through remainder of season.
‡On disabled list, June 6 to June 21, 1986.
§On disabled list, July 1, 1990 through remainder of season.

CHAMPIONSHIP SERIES RECORD

Year Club	League	G.	IP.	W.	L.	Pct.	H.	R.	ER.	SO.	BB.	ERA.
1985—Kansas City	American	2	8⅓	1	0	1.000	4	3	3	4	4	3.24

WORLD SERIES RECORD

Eligible for 1985 World Series with Kansas City Royals; did not play.

ALL-STAR GAME RECORD

Year League	IP.	W.	L.	Pct.	H.	R.	ER.	SO.	BB.	ERA.
1988—American	2	0	0	.000	3	1	1	2	0	4.50
1989—American	1	0	0	.000	0	0	0	1	0	0.00
All-Star Game Totals—2 Years	3	0	0	.000	3	1	1	3	0	3.00

PEDRO GUERRERO
Name pronounced Guh-RAIR-oh.

Born June 29, 1956, at San Pedro de Macoris, D. R.
Height, 6.00. Weight, 195.
Throws and bats righthanded.
Half-brother of Domingo Michel, outfielder in Detroit Tigers' organization.

Holds National League records for most home runs, month of June (15), 1985; most consecutive times reached base safely, season (14), July 23 through 26, 1985.
Shares National League record for fewest errors by first baseman for leader in errors, season (13), 1990.
Major League stolen bases: 1979 (2), 1980 (2), 1981 (5), 1982 (22), 1983 (23), 1984 (9), 1985 (12), 1987 (9), 1988 (4), 1989 (2), 1990 (1). Total—91.
Led National League in sacrifice flies with 12 in 1989.
Led National League in slugging percentage with .577 in 1985.
Led National League third basemen in errors with 30 and tied for lead in total chances with 458 in 1983.
Led Pacific Coast League in sacrifice flies with 15 in 1978.
Tied for Northwest League lead in double plays by third basemen with 13 in 1974.
Named outfielder on THE SPORTING NEWS National League All-Star Team, 1981 and 1982.
Named outfielder on THE SPORTING NEWS National League Silver Slugger team, 1982.

Year Club	League	Pos.	G.	AB.	R.	H.	2B.	3B.	HR.	RBI.	B.A.	PO.	A.	E.	F.A.
1973—Sarasota Ind.†	Gulf C.	3B-SS	44	153	13	39	2	3	2	22	.255	32	82	11	.912
1974—Orangeburg	W. Car.	3B	19	55	3	8	1	0	0	1	.145	11	22	5	.868
1974—Bellingham	N'west	3B	82	297	49	94	●23	2	3	55	.316	★69	124	23	.894
1975—Danville	Midw.	3B-OF	104	351	81	121	25	5	10	76	★.345	111	168	31	.900
1976—Waterbury	East.	1B	132	495	73	151	★30	10	5	66	.305	1129	★96	★19	.985
1977—Albuquerque‡	P. C.	1B	32	129	30	52	11	4	4	39	.403	329	17	10	.972
1978—Albuquerque	P. C.	1B-3B	134	492	92	166	28	4	14	★116	.337	982	80	10	.991
1978—Los Angeles	Nat.	1B	5	8	3	5	0	1	0	1	.625	25	1	0	1.000
1979—Albuquerque	P. C.	OF-3B-1B	113	453	94	151	33	9	22	★103	.333	188	9	5	.975
1979—Los Angeles	Nat.	OF-1B-3B	25	62	7	15	2	0	2	9	.242	53	4	1	.983
1980—Los Angeles§	Nat.	O-2-3-1	75	183	27	59	9	1	7	31	.322	103	110	3	.986
1981—Los Angeles	Nat.	OF-3B-1B	98	347	46	104	17	2	12	48	.300	165	55	11	.952
1982—Los Angeles	Nat.	OF-3B	150	575	87	175	27	5	32	100	.304	282	53	12	.965
1983—Los Angeles	Nat.	3B-1B	160	584	87	174	28	6	32	103	.298	130	308	31	.934
1984—Los Angeles x	Nat.	3B-OF-1B	144	535	85	162	29	4	16	72	.303	271	151	22	.950
1985—Los Angeles	Nat.	OF-3B-1B	137	487	99	156	22	2	33	87	.320	251	123	13	.966
1986—Los Angeles y	Nat.	OF-1B	31	61	7	15	3	0	5	10	.246	39	1	0	1.000
1987—Los Angeles	Nat.	OF-1B	152	545	89	184	25	2	27	89	.338	482	44	12	.978
1988—L.A.zab-St.L.	Nat.	1B-3B-OF	103	364	40	104	14	2	10	65	.286	466	99	12	.979
1988—Albuquerque	P. C.	1B	5	12	3	5	0	0	1	4	.417	30	2	0	1.000
1989—St. Louis	Nat.	1B	162	570	60	177	●42	1	17	117	.311	★1445	72	●15	.990
1990—St. Louis c	Nat.	1B	136	498	42	140	31	1	13	80	.281	1083	73	★13	.989
Major League Totals—13 Years			1378	4819	679	1470	249	27	206	812	.305	4795	1094	145	.976

Signed as free agent by Cleveland Indians' organization, January 15, 1973.
†Traded to Los Angeles Dodgers for Pitcher Bruce Ellingsen, April 4, 1974.
‡On disabled list, May 19 to August 30, 1977.
§On disabled list, August 23 to September 15, 1980.
xOn disabled list, July 22 to August 6, 1984.
yOn disabled list, April 4 to July 30 and August 11 to September 3, 1986.
zOn suspended list, May 24 to May 28, 1988.
aOn disabled list, June 5 to July 29, 1988; included rehabilitation disability assignment to Albuquerque, July 23 to July 29, 1988.
bTraded to St. Louis Cardinals for Pitcher John Tudor, August 16, 1988.
cOn disabled list, August 19 to September 3, 1990.

DIVISION SERIES RECORD

Year Club	League	Pos.	G.	AB.	R.	H.	2B.	3B.	HR.	RBI.	B.A.	PO.	A.	E.	F.A.
1981—Los Angeles	Nat.	3B	5	17	1	3	1	0	1	1	.176	3	15	0	1.000

Holds Championship Series records for most times grounded into double play, total series (5) and series (4), 1981. Shares National League Championship Series record for most times grounded into double play (2), October 16, 1981.

Year Club League	Pos.	G.	AB.	R.	H.	2B.	3B.	HR.	RBI.	B.A.	PO.	A.	E.	F.A.
1981—Los Angeles .... Nat.	OF	5	19	1	2	0	0	1	2	.105	9	2	0	1.000
1983—Los Angeles .... Nat.	3B	4	12	1	3	1	1	0	2	.250	0	9	0	1.000
1985—Los Angeles .... Nat.	OF	6	20	2	5	1	0	0	4	.250	11	0	0	1.000
Championship Series Totals—3 Years.....		15	51	4	10	2	1	1	8	.196	20	11	0	1.000

WORLD SERIES RECORD

Year Club League	Pos.	G.	AB.	R.	H.	2B.	3B.	HR.	RBI.	B.A.	PO.	A.	E.	F.A.
1981—Los Angeles .... Nat.	OF	6	21	2	7	1	1	2	7	.333	17	1	0	1.000

ALL-STAR GAME RECORD

Year League	Pos.	AB.	R.	H.	2B.	3B.	HR.	RBI.	B.A.	PO.	A.	E.	F.A.
1981—National	PH	1	0	0	0	0	0	0	.000	0	0	0	.000
1983—National	3B-OF	1	0	0	0	0	0	0	.000	0	0	1	.000
1987—National	PH	1	0	0	0	0	0	0	.000	0	0	0	.000
1989—National	DH	2	0	0	0	0	0	0	.000	0	0	0	.000
All-Star Game Totals—4 Years..................		5	0	0	0	0	0	0	.000	0	0	1	.000

Named to National League All-Star Team for 1985 game; replaced due to injury by Glenn Wilson.

ARTHUR LEE GUETTERMAN
(Known by middle name.)

Born November 22, 1958, at Chattanooga, Tenn.
Height, 6.08. Weight, 235.
Throws and bats lefthanded.
Received bachelor of science degree in physical education from
Liberty Baptist College, Lynchburg, Va. in 1981.

Major League saves: 1989 (13), 1990 (2). Total—15.

Year Club League	G.	IP.	W.	L.	Pct.	H.	R.	ER.	SO.	BB.	ERA.
1981—Bellingham .... Northwest	13	84	6	4	.600	85	36	25	55	42	2.68
1982—Bakersfield .... California	26	154	7	11	.389	172	100	76	82	69	4.44
1983—Bakersfield...................... California	25	156⅓	12	6	.667	164	72	56	93	45	3.22
1984—Chattanooga† .... Southern	24	157	11	7	.611	174	68	59	47	38	3.38
1984—Seattle............................ American	3	4⅓	0	0	.000	9	2	2	2	2	4.15
1985—Calgary‡ .... P. Coast	20	110⅓	5	8	.385	138	86	71	48	44	5.79
1986—Seattle............................ American	41	76	0	4	.000	108	67	62	38	30	7.34
1986—Calgary .... P. Coast	4	19⅓	1	0	1.000	24	12	12	8	7	5.59
1987—Calgary .... P. Coast	16	44	5	1	.833	41	14	14	29	17	2.86
1987—Seattle§.......................... American	25	113⅓	11	4	*.733	117	60	48	42	35	3.81
1988—New York .... American	20	40⅔	1	2	.333	49	21	21	15	14	4.65
1988—Columbus........................ Int'national	18	120⅔	9	6	.600	109	46	37	49	26	2.76
1989—New York .... American	70	103	5	5	.500	98	31	28	51	26	2.45
1990—New York x .... American	64	93	11	7	.611	80	37	35	48	26	3.39
Major League Totals—6 Years..........................	223	430⅓	28	22	.560	461	218	196	196	133	4.10

Selected by Seattle Mariners' organization in 4th round of free-agent draft, June 8, 1981.
†On disabled list, August 1 to August 15, 1984.
‡On disabled list, April 11 to May 31, 1985.
§Traded with Pitchers Clay Parker and Wade Taylor to New York Yankees for Pitcher Steve Trout and Outfielder Henry Cotto, December 22, 1987.
xOn disabled list, July 19 to August 3, 1990.

OSWALDO JOSE GUILLEN (BARRIOS)
Name pronounced GEY-un.

(Ozzie)

Born January 20, 1964, at Ocumare del Tuy, Miranda, Venezuela.
Height, 5.11. Weight, 153.
Throws right and bats lefthanded.

Shares major league record for fewest bases on balls received, 150 or more games, season (12), 1985, 1986.
Holds American League record for fewest putouts, shortstop, season, 150 or more games (220), 1985.
Major League stolen bases: 1985 (7), 1986 (8), 1987 (25), 1988 (25), 1989 (36), 1990 (13). Total—114.
Led American League shortstops in total chances with 760 in 1987 and 863 in 1988.
Led American League shortstops in double plays with 105 in 1987.
Led Pacific Coast League shortstops in assists with 362 and total chances with 549 in 1984.
Tied for California League lead in sacrifice hits with 14 in 1982.
Named American League Rookie Player of the Year by THE SPORTING NEWS, 1985.
Named American League Rookie of the Year by Baseball Writers' Association of America, 1985.
Named shortstop on THE SPORTING NEWS American League All-Star fielding team, 1990.

Year Club League	Pos.	G.	AB.	R.	H.	2B.	3B.	HR.	RBI.	B.A.	PO.	A.	E.	F.A.
1981—Bradenton Padr.† Gulf C.	SS-2B	55	189	26	49	4	1	0	16	.259	105	135	15	.941
1982—Reno† .... Calif.	SS	130	528	*103	*183	33	1	2	54	.347	*240	399	41	.940
1983—Beaumont† .... Texas	SS	114	427	62	126	20	4	2	48	.295	185	327	*38	.931
1984—Las Vegas†‡......... P. C.	SS-2B	122	463	81	137	26	6	5	53	.296	172	364	17	.969
1985—Chicago .... Amer.	SS	150	491	71	134	21	9	1	33	.273	220	382	12	*.980

Year Club	League	Pos.	G.	AB.	R.	H.	2B.	3B.	HR.	RBI.	B.A.	PO.	A.	E.	F.A.
1986—Chicago	Amer.	SS	159	547	58	137	19	4	2	47	.250	261	459	22	.970
1987—Chicago	Amer.	SS	149	560	64	156	22	7	2	51	.279	266	475	19	.975
1988—Chicago	Amer.	SS	156	566	58	148	16	7	0	39	.261	273	*570	20	.977
1989—Chicago	Amer.	SS	155	597	63	151	20	8	1	54	.253	272	512	22	.973
1990—Chicago	Amer.	SS	160	516	61	144	21	4	1	58	.279	252	474	17	.977
Major League Totals—6 Years			929	3277	375	870	119	39	7	282	.265	1544	2872	112	.975

Signed as free agent by San Diego Padres' organization, December 17, 1980.

†Switch-hitter.

‡Traded with Pitchers Tim Lollar and Bill Long and Third Baseman Luis Salazar to Chicago White Sox for Pitchers LaMarr Hoyt, Kevin Kristan and Todd Simmons, December 6, 1984.

ALL-STAR GAME RECORD

Year League	Pos.	AB.	R.	H.	2B.	3B.	HR.	RBI.	B.A.	PO.	A.	E.	F.A.
1990—American	SS	2	0	0	0	0	0	0	.000	0	2	0	1.000

Named to American League All-Star Team for 1988 game; replaced due to injury by Kurt Stillwell.

WILLIAM LEE GULLICKSON
(Bill)

Born February 20, 1959, at Marshall, Minn.
Height, 6.03. Weight, 205.
Throws and bats righthanded.

Shares modern major league record for most wild pitches, game (6), April 10, 1982.
Led National League in intentional bases on balls issued with 14 in 1990.
Led National League in home runs allowed with 27 in 1984.
Named National League Rookie Pitcher of the Year by THE SPORTING NEWS, 1980.

Year Club	League	G.	IP.	W.	L.	Pct.	H.	R.	ER.	SO.	BB.	ERA.
1977—West Palm Beach	Florida St.	10	56	3	3	.500	67	30	25	35	17	4.02
1978—West Palm Beach	Florida St.	20	148	9	9	.500	121	45	30	127	52	1.82
1978—Memphis	Southern	8	50	1	4	.200	44	19	17	43	19	3.06
1979—Denver	Am. Assoc.	11	54	3	3	.500	65	44	40	31	26	6.67
1979—Memphis	Southern	16	116	10	3	.769	110	52	47	115	42	3.65
1979—Montreal	National	1	1	0	0	.000	2	0	0	0	0	0.00
1980—Denver	Am. Assoc.	9	66	6	2	.750	47	14	14	64	29	1.91
1980—Montreal	National	24	141	10	5	.667	127	53	47	120	50	3.00
1981—Montreal	National	22	157	7	9	.438	142	54	49	115	34	2.81
1982—Montreal	National	34	236⅔	12	14	.462	231	101	94	155	61	3.57
1983—Montreal	National	34	242⅓	17	12	.586	230	108	101	120	59	3.75
1984—Montreal†	National	32	226⅔	12	9	.571	230	100	91	100	37	3.61
1985—Montreal‡§	National	29	181⅓	14	12	.538	187	78	71	68	47	3.52
1986—Cincinnati	National	37	244⅔	15	12	.556	245	103	92	121	60	3.38
1987—Cincinnati x	National	27	165	10	11	.476	172	99	89	89	39	4.85
1987—New York y	American	8	48	4	2	.667	46	29	26	28	11	4.88
1988—Yomiuri Giants	Central	26	203⅓	14	9	.609	173	77	70	134	51	3.10
1989—Yomiuri Giants z	Central	15	111	7	5	.583	97	47	45	97	34	3.65
1990—Houston a	National	32	193⅓	10	14	.417	221	100	82	73	61	3.82
National League Totals—10 Years		272	1789	107	98	.522	1787	796	716	961	448	3.60
American League Totals—1 Year		8	48	4	2	.667	46	29	26	28	11	4.88
Major League Totals—10 Years		280	1837	111	100	.526	1833	825	742	989	459	3.64

Selected by Montreal Expos' organization in 1st round (second player selected) of free-agent draft, June 7, 1977.

†On disabled list, April 20 to May 8, 1984.

‡On disabled list, June 17 to July 8, 1985.

§Traded with Catcher Sal Butera to Cincinnati Reds for Pitchers Jay Tibbs, Andy McGaffigan and John Stuper and Catcher Dann Bilardello, December 19, 1985.

xTraded to New York Yankees for Pitcher Dennis Rasmussen, August 26, 1987.

yGranted free agency, November 9, 1987; signed by Yomiuri Giants of Japanese Baseball League, January 13, 1988.

zSigned by Houston Astros, December 6, 1989.

aReleased, October 4, 1990; signed by Detroit Tigers, December 3, 1990.

DIVISION SERIES RECORD

Year Club	League	G.	IP.	W.	L.	Pct.	H.	R.	ER.	SO.	BB.	ERA.
1981—Montreal	National	1	7⅔	1	0	1.000	6	1	1	3	1	1.17

CHAMPIONSHIP SERIES RECORD

Shares Championship Series record for most games lost, series (2), 1981.

Year Club	League	G.	IP.	W.	L.	Pct.	H.	R.	ER.	SO.	BB.	ERA.
1981—Montreal	National	2	14⅓	0	2	.000	12	5	4	12	6	2.51

ERIC ANDREW GUNDERSON

Born March 29, 1966, at Portland, Ore.
Height, 6.00. Weight, 175.
Throws left and bats righthanded.
Attended Portland State University, Portland, Ore.

Led Northwest League pitchers in complete games with 5 and tied for lead in games started with 15 and shutouts with 3 in 1987.

Led California League in hit batsmen with 17 in 1988.

Year Club	League	G.	IP.	W.	L.	Pct.	H.	R.	ER.	SO.	BB.	ERA.
1987—Everett	Northwest	15	98⅔	8	4	.667	80	34	27	*99	34	2.46
1988—San Jose	California	20	149⅓	12	5	.706	131	56	44	151	52	2.65
1988—Shreveport	Texas	7	36⅔	1	2	.333	45	25	21	28	13	5.15
1989—Shreveport	Texas	11	72⅔	8	2	*.800	68	24	22	61	23	2.72
1989—Phoenix	P. Coast	14	85⅔	2	4	.333	93	51	48	56	36	5.04
1990—San Francisco	National	7	19⅔	1	2	.333	24	14	12	14	11	5.49
1990—Phoenix	P. Coast	16	82	5	7	.417	137	87	75	41	46	8.23
1990—Shreveport	Texas	8	52⅔	2	2	.500	51	24	19	44	17	3.25
Major League Totals—1 Year		7	19⅔	1	2	.333	24	14	12	14	11	5.49

Selected by San Francisco Giants' organization in 2nd round of free-agent draft, June 2, 1987.

MARK ANDREW GUTHRIE

Born September 22, 1965, at Buffalo, N.Y.
Height, 6.04. Weight, 205.
Throws left and bats left and righthanded.
Attended Louisiana State University, Baton Rouge, La.

Year Club	League	G.	IP.	W.	L.	Pct.	H.	R.	ER.	SO.	BB.	ERA.
1987—Visalia	California	4	12	2	1	.667	10	7	6	9	5	4.50
1988—Visalia	California	25	171⅓	12	9	.571	169	81	63	182	86	3.31
1989—Orlando	Southern	14	96	8	3	.727	75	32	21	103	38	1.97
1989—Portland	P. Coast	7	44⅓	3	4	.429	45	21	18	35	16	3.65
1989—Minnesota	American	13	57⅓	2	4	.333	66	32	29	38	21	4.55
1990—Minnesota	American	24	144⅔	7	9	.438	154	65	61	101	39	3.79
1990—Portland	P. Coast	9	42⅓	1	3	.250	47	19	14	39	12	2.98
Major League Totals—2 Years		37	202	9	13	.409	220	97	90	139	60	4.01

Selected by St. Louis Cardinals' organization in 4th round of free-agent draft, June 2, 1986.
Selected by Minnesota Twins' organization in 7th round of free-agent draft, June 2, 1987.

JOSE ALBERTO GUZMAN (MIRABEL)

Born April 9, 1963, at Santa Isabel, Puerto Rico.
Height, 6.03. Weight, 198.
Throws and bats righthanded.

Year Club	League	G.	IP.	W.	L.	Pct.	H.	R.	ER.	SO.	BB.	ERA.
1981—Sarasota Rangers	Gulf Coast	14	39	3	3	.500	44	30	23	13	14	5.31
1982—Sarasota Rangers	Gulf Coast	12	66	5	4	.556	51	21	16	42	13	2.18
1983—Burlington	Midwest	25	154⅔	12	8	.600	135	68	51	146	52	2.97
1984—Tulsa	Texas	25	140⅓	7	9	.438	137	75	65	82	55	4.17
1985—Oklahoma City	Am. Assoc.	25	149⅔	10	5	.667	131	60	52	76	40	3.13
1985—Texas	American	5	32⅔	3	2	.600	27	13	10	24	14	2.76
1986—Texas	American	29	172⅓	9	15	.375	199	101	87	87	60	4.54
1987—Texas	American	37	208⅓	14	14	.500	196	115	108	143	82	4.67
1988—Texas	American	30	206⅔	11	13	.458	180	99	85	157	82	3.70
1989—Texas†	American					(Did not play)						
1990—Charlotte‡	Florida St.	2	8⅓	0	1	.000	10	3	2	7	4	2.16
1990—Oklahoma City	Am. Assoc.	7	28⅔	0	3	.000	35	20	18	26	9	5.65
1990—Tulsa	Texas	1	3	0	0	.000	3	2	2	2	0	6.00
Major League Totals—4 Years		101	620	37	44	.457	602	328	290	411	238	4.21

Signed as free agent by Texas Rangers' organization, February 10, 1981.
†On disabled list, March 26 to September 1, 1989.
‡On Texas disabled list, March 31 to August 9, 1990; included rehabilitation disability assignment to Charlotte, June 6 to June 19, 1990; to Oklahoma City, July 17 to July 19 and July 29 to July 30, 1990; and Tulsa, July 20 to July 25, 1990.

ANTHONY KEITH GWYNN

Name pronounced Gwin.

(Tony)

Born May 9, 1960, at Los Angeles, Calif.
Height, 5.11. Weight, 216.
Throws and bats lefthanded.
Attended San Diego State University, San Diego, Calif.
Brother of Chris Gwynn, outfielder with Los Angeles Dodgers.

Holds National League record for lowest average by batting leader, season (.313), 1988.
Shares National League record for most years leading league, singles (4).
Shares modern National League record for most stolen bases, game (5), September 20, 1986.
Major League stolen bases: 1982 (8), 1983 (7), 1984 (33), 1985 (14), 1986 (37), 1987 (56), 1988 (26), 1989 (40), 1990 (17). Total—238.
Led National League outfielders in total chances with 360 in 1986.
Named outfielder on THE SPORTING NEWS National League All-Star Team, 1984, 1986, 1987 and 1989.
Named outfielder on THE SPORTING NEWS National League All-Star fielding team, 1986, 1987, 1989 and 1990.
Named outfielder on THE SPORTING NEWS National League Silver Slugger team, 1984, 1986, 1987 and 1989.
Named Northwest League Most Valuable Player, 1981.
Drafted by San Diego Clippers in 10th round (210th player selected) of NBA draft, June 9, 1981.

Year Club League	Pos.	G.	AB.	R.	H.	2B.	3B.	HR.	RBI.	B.A.	PO.	A.	E.	F.A.
1981—Walla Walla .... N'west	OF	42	178	46	59	12	1	12	37	*.331	76	2	3	.963
1981—Amarillo .... Texas	OF	23	91	22	42	8	2	4	19	.462	41	1	0	1.000
1982—Hawaii .... P. C.	OF	93	366	65	120	23	2	5	46	.328	208	11	4	.982
1982—San Diego† .... Nat.	OF	54	190	33	55	12	2	1	17	.289	110	1	1	.991
1983—Las Vegas‡ .... P. C.	OF	17	73	15	25	6	0	0	7	.342	23	2	3	.893
1983—San Diego .... Nat.	OF	86	304	34	94	12	2	1	37	.309	163	9	1	.994
1984—San Diego .... Nat.	OF	158	606	88	*213	21	10	5	71	*.351	345	11	4	.989
1985—San Diego .... Nat.	OF	154	622	90	197	29	5	6	46	.317	337	14	4	.989
1986—San Diego .... Nat.	OF	160	*642	•107	*211	33	7	14	59	.329	*337	19	4	.989
1987—San Diego .... Nat.	OF	157	589	119	*218	36	13	7	54	*.370	298	13	6	.981
1988—San Diego§ .... Nat.	OF	133	521	64	163	22	5	7	70	*.313	264	8	5	.982
1989—San Diego .... Nat.	OF	158	604	82	*203	27	7	4	62	*.336	353	13	6	.984
1990—San Diego .... Nat.	OF	141	573	79	177	29	10	4	72	.309	327	11	5	.985
Major League Totals—9 Years		1201	4651	696	1531	221	61	49	488	.329	2534	99	36	.987

Selected by San Diego Padres' organization in 3rd round of free-agent draft, June 8, 1981.
†On disabled list, August 26 to September 10, 1982.
‡On San Diego disabled list, March 26 to June 21, 1983; included rehabilitation assignment to Las Vegas, May 31 to June 20, 1983.
§On disabled list, May 8 to May 29, 1988.

CHAMPIONSHIP SERIES RECORD

Year Club League	Pos.	G.	AB.	R.	H.	2B.	3B.	HR.	RBI.	B.A.	PO.	A.	E.	F.A.
1984—San Diego .... Nat.	OF	5	19	6	7	3	0	0	3	.368	9	0	0	1.000

WORLD SERIES RECORD

Year Club League	Pos.	G.	AB.	R.	H.	2B.	3B.	HR.	RBI.	B.A.	PO.	A.	E.	F.A.
1984—San Diego .... Nat.	OF	5	19	1	5	0	0	0	0	.263	12	1	1	.929

ALL-STAR GAME RECORD

Year League	Pos.	AB.	R.	H.	2B.	3B.	HR.	RBI.	B.A.	PO.	A.	E.	F.A.
1984—National	OF	3	0	1	0	0	0	0	.333	0	0	0	.000
1985—National	OF	1	0	0	0	0	0	0	.000	1	0	0	1.000
1986—National	OF	3	0	0	0	0	0	0	.000	1	0	0	1.000
1987—National	PH	1	0	0	0	0	0	0	.000	0	0	0	.000
1989—National	OF	2	1	1	0	0	0	0	.500	2	0	0	1.000
1990—National	PH	0	0	0	0	0	0	0	.000	0	0	0	.000
All-Star Game Totals—6 Years		10	1	2	0	0	0	0	.200	4	0	0	1.000

CHRISTOPHER KARLTON GWYNN
Name pronounced Gwin.

(Chris)

Born October 13, 1964, at Los Angeles, Calif.
Height, 6.00. Weight, 210.
Throws and bats lefthanded.
Attended San Diego State University, San Diego, Calif.
Brother of Tony Gwynn, outfielder with San Diego Padres.

Major League stolen bases: 1989 (1).
Named outfielder on THE SPORTING NEWS College Baseball All-America Team, 1985.
Member of 1984 U.S. Olympic baseball team.

Year Club League	Pos.	G.	AB.	R.	H.	2B.	3B.	HR.	RBI.	B.A.	PO.	A.	E.	F.A.
1985—Vero Beach .... Fla. St.	OF	52	179	19	46	8	6	0	17	.257	43	2	0	1.000
1986—San Antonio .... Texas	OF	111	401	46	115	22	1	6	67	.287	186	11	2	.990
1987—Albuquerque .... P. C.	OF	110	362	54	101	12	3	5	41	.279	141	5	1	.993
1987—Los Angeles .... Nat.	OF	17	32	2	7	1	0	0	2	.219	12	0	0	1.000
1988—Albuquerque .... P. C.	OF	112	411	57	123	22	•10	5	61	.299	134	3	4	.972
1988—Los Angeles .... Nat.	OF	12	11	1	2	0	0	0	0	.182	0	0	0	.000
1989—Albuquerque .... P. C.	OF	26	89	14	29	9	1	0	12	.326	27	0	0	1.000
1989—Los Angeles† .... Nat.	OF	32	68	8	16	4	1	0	7	.235	26	1	0	1.000
1990—Los Angeles .... Nat.	OF	101	141	19	40	2	1	5	22	.284	39	1	0	1.000
Major League Totals—4 Years		162	252	30	65	7	2	5	31	.258	65	2	0	1.000

Selected by California Angels' organization in 5th round of free-agent draft, June 7, 1982.
Selected by Los Angeles Dodgers' organization in 1st round (10th player selected) of free-agent draft, June 3, 1985.
†On disabled list, June 12 to July 6 and July 16, 1989 through remainder of season; included rehabilitation disability assignment to Albuquerque, August 3 to August 11, 1989.

ROBERT DAVID HAAS
(Dave)

Born October 19, 1965, at Independence, Mo.
Height, 6.01. Weight, 200.
Throws and bats righthanded.
Attended Wichita State University, Wichita, Kan.

Pitched 5-0 no-hit victory against Clearwater, April 14, 1989.
Led Eastern League pitchers in games started with 27 in 1990.

Year Club	League	G.	IP.	W.	L.	Pct.	H.	R.	ER.	SO.	BB.	ERA.
1988—Fayetteville	S. Atlantic	11	54⅔	4	3	.571	59	20	11	46	19	1.81
1989—Lakeland	Florida St.	10	62	4	1	.800	50	16	14	46	16	2.03
1989—London	Eastern	18	103⅔	3	11	.214	107	69	65	75	51	5.64
1990—London	Eastern	27	177⅔	13	8	.619	151	64	59	116	74	2.99

Selected by Baltimore Orioles' organization in 28th round of free-agent draft, June 4, 1984.
Selected by Toronto Blue Jays' organization in 18th round of free-agent draft, June 2, 1987.
Selected by Detroit Tigers' organization in 15th round of free-agent draft, June 1, 1988.

JOHN GABRIEL HABYAN
Name pronounced HAY-bee-un.

Born January 29, 1964, at Bayshore, N. Y.
Height, 6.02. Weight, 195.
Throws and bats righthanded.

Pitched 6-0 no-hit victory against Columbus, May 13, 1985.
Major League saves: 1987 (1).

Year Club	League	G.	IP.	W.	L.	Pct.	H.	R.	ER.	SO.	BB.	ERA.
1982—Bluefield	Ap'lachian	12	81⅓	●9	2	.818	68	35	32	55	24	3.54
1982—Hagerstown	Carolina	1	⅔	0	0	.000	5	5	5	1	2	67.50
1983—Hagerstown	Carolina	11	48	2	3	.400	54	41	31	42	29	5.81
1983—Newark	NYP	11	71⅔	5	3	.625	68	34	27	64	29	3.39
1984—Hagerstown	Carolina	13	81⅓	9	4	.692	64	41	32	81	33	3.54
1984—Charlotte	Southern	13	77	4	7	.364	84	46	38	55	34	4.44
1985—Charlotte	Southern	28	189⅔	13	5	.722	157	73	69	123	90	3.27
1985—Baltimore	American	2	2⅔	1	0	1.000	3	1	0	2	0	0.00
1986—Rochester	Int'national	26	157⅓	12	7	.632	168	82	75	93	69	4.29
1986—Baltimore	American	6	26⅓	1	3	.250	24	17	13	14	18	4.44
1987—Rochester	Int'national	7	49	3	2	.600	47	23	21	39	20	3.86
1987—Baltimore	American	27	116⅓	6	7	.462	110	67	62	64	40	4.80
1988—Rochester	Int'national	23	147⅓	9	9	.500	161	78	73	91	46	4.46
1988—Baltimore	American	7	14⅔	1	0	1.000	22	10	7	4	4	4.30
1989—Rochester†‡-Columbus	Int'national	15	83⅔	3	5	.375	103	44	37	52	14	3.98
1990—Columbus	Int'national	36	112	7	7	.500	99	52	40	77	30	3.21
1990—New York	American	6	8⅔	0	0	.000	10	2	2	4	2	2.08
Major League Totals—5 Years		48	168⅔	9	10	.474	169	97	84	88	64	4.48

Selected by Baltimore Orioles' organization in 3rd round of free-agent draft, June 7, 1982.
†On Baltimore disabled list, March 30 to June 9, 1989.
‡Traded to New York Yankees' organization for Outfielder Stanley Jefferson, July 20, 1989.

WALTER WILLIAM HALE
(Chip)

Born December 2, 1964, at Santa Clara, Calif.
Height, 5.11. Weight, 180.
Throws right and bats lefthanded.
Received degree from University of Arizona, Tucson, Ariz.

Led Pacific Coast League second basemen in putouts with 311, total chances with 679, fielding percentage with .982 and double plays with 101 in 1990.
Led Pacific Coast League second basemen in assists with 332 in 1989.

Year Club	League	Pos.	G.	AB.	R.	H.	2B.	3B.	HR.	RBI.	B.A.	PO.	A.	E.	F.A.
1987—Kenosha	Midw.	2B	87	339	65	117	12	7	7	65	★.345	164	233	10	.975
1988—Orlando	South.	2B	133	482	62	126	20	1	11	65	.261	254	322	★23	.962
1989—Portland	P. C.	2B-3B	108	411	49	112	16	9	2	34	.273	217	333	10	.982
1989—Minnesota	Amer.	2B-3B	28	67	6	14	3	0	0	4	.209	15	40	1	.982
1990—Portland	P. C.	2B-SS-3B	130	479	71	134	24	2	3	40	.280	312	362	13	.981
1990—Minnesota	Amer.	2B	1	2	0	0	0	0	0	2	.000	2	6	0	1.000
Major League Totals—2 Years			29	69	6	14	3	0	0	6	.203	17	46	1	.984

Selected by Minnesota Twins' organization in 17th round of free-agent draft, June 2, 1987.

ANDREW CLARK HALL
(Drew)

Born March 27, 1963, at Louisville, Ky.
Height, 6.05. Weight, 220.
Throws and bats lefthanded.
Attended Morehead State University, Morehead, Ky.

Major League saves: 1986 (1), 1988 (1), 1990 (3). Total—5.
Tied for Eastern League lead in shutouts with 3 in 1986.
Named lefthanded pitcher on THE SPORTING NEWS College Baseball All-America Team, 1984.

Year Club	League	G.	IP.	W.	L.	Pct.	H.	R.	ER.	SO.	BB.	ERA.
1984—Lodi	California	8	48	3	3	.500	43	31	26	43	44	4.88
1985—Winston-Salem	Carolina	24	140⅔	10	7	.588	131	92	73	135	83	4.67
1986—Pittsfield	Eastern	24	158⅓	8	11	.421	130	77	63	115	84	3.58
1986—Chicago	National	5	23⅔	1	2	.333	24	12	12	21	10	4.56
1987—Iowa	Am. Assoc.	35	66⅓	6	3	.667	74	42	33	66	45	4.48
1987—Chicago	National	21	32⅔	1	1	.500	40	31	25	20	14	6.89
1988—Chicago	National	19	22⅓	1	1	.500	26	20	19	22	9	7.66

Year Club	League	G.	IP.	W.	L.	Pct.	H.	R.	ER.	SO.	BB.	ERA.
1988—Iowa†	Am. Assoc.	49	65⅓	4	3	.571	41	20	17	75	26	2.34
1989—Oklahoma City	Am. Assoc.	11	17⅔	1	0	1.000	7	3	3	18	6	1.53
1989—Texas‡	American	38	58⅓	2	1	.667	42	24	24	45	33	3.70
1990—Montreal§	National	42	58⅓	4	7	.364	52	35	33	40	29	5.09
National League Totals—4 Years		87	137	7	11	.389	142	98	89	103	62	5.85
American League Totals—1 Year		38	58⅓	2	1	.667	42	24	24	45	33	3.70
Major League Totals—5 Years		125	195⅓	9	12	.429	184	122	113	148	95	5.21

Selected by Chicago Cubs' organization in 1st round (third player selected) of free-agent draft, June 4, 1984.

†Traded with Outfielder Rafael Palmeiro and Pitcher Jamie Moyer to Texas Rangers for Pitchers Mitch Williams, Paul Kilgus and Steve Wilson, Infielder Curtis Wilkerson and Luis Benitez and Outfielder Pablo Delgado, December 5, 1988.

‡Traded to Montreal Expos for Infielder Jeff Huson, April 2, 1990.

§On disabled list, July 21 to September 4, 1990.

GARDNER CARLILE HALL
(Grady)

Born May 29, 1964, at Findlay, O.
Height, 6.04. Weight, 200.
Throws left and bats righthanded.
Attended Northwestern University, Evanston, Ill.

Led Southern League in complete games with 9 in 1989.
Led Southern League in balks with 11 in 1988.
Tied for Pacific Coast League lead in games started by pitchers with 28 in 1990.

Year Club	League	G.	IP.	W.	L.	Pct.	H.	R.	ER.	SO.	BB.	ERA.
1986—Buffalo	Am. Assoc.	12	71⅓	4	5	.444	84	52	48	37	27	6.06
1987—Birmingham†	Southern	10	58	3	5	.375	54	28	24	30	20	3.72
1987—Sarasota White Sox	Gulf Coast	3	11	1	1	.500	12	7	5	11	2	4.09
1988—Birmingham	Southern	20	137	9	8	.529	132	59	45	69	42	2.96
1988—Vancouver	P. Coast	8	46	2	2	.500	43	24	21	13	21	4.11
1989—Birmingham	Southern	27	190⅔	12	8	.600	173	97	73	147	68	3.45
1990—Vancouver	P. Coast	28	∗184⅔	13	8	.619	185	100	87	106	89	4.24

Selected by Boston Red Sox' organization in 27th round of free-agent draft, June 3, 1985.
Selected by Chicago White Sox' organization in 1st round (20th player selected) of free-agent draft, June 2, 1986.
†On disabled list, April 16 to July 24, 1987.

MELVIN HALL JR.
(Mel)

Born September 16, 1960, at Lyons, N. Y.
Height, 6.01. Weight, 218.
Throws and bats lefthanded.
Son of Melvin Hall Sr., minor league player in Cincinnati Reds' organization, 1949.

Major League stolen bases: 1983 (6), 1984 (3), 1986 (6), 1987 (5), 1988 (7). Total—27.
Led American Association in game-winning RBIs with 17 in 1982.
Led Texas League in total bases with 286 in 1981.
Led American Association outfielders in total chances with 339 in 1982.
Led Texas League outfielders in total chances with 324 and double plays with 5 in 1981.

Year Club	League	Pos.	G.	AB.	R.	H.	2B.	3B.	HR.	RBI.	B.A.	PO.	A.	E.	F.A.
1978—Bradenton Cubs	Gulf C.	OF	43	145	30	42	7	3	2	17	.290	∗97	5	4	.962
1979—Geneva	NYP	OF	66	251	49	79	18	5	3	53	.315	113	5	7	.944
1980—Midland	Texas	OF	37	128	17	34	7	3	1	14	.266	58	3	3	.953
1980—Quad Cities	Midw.	OF	97	347	54	102	14	4	6	42	.294	171	9	5	.973
1981—Midland	Texas	OF	131	533	●98	∗170	34	5	24	95	.319	∗302	14	8	.975
1981—Chicago	Nat.	OF	10	11	1	1	0	0	1	2	.091	0	0	0	.000
1982—Iowa	A. A.	OF	133	502	∗116	165	∗34	6	32	125	.329	∗317	13	●9	.973
1982—Chicago	Nat.	OF	24	80	6	21	3	2	0	4	.263	42	4	3	.939
1983—Chicago†	Nat.	OF	112	410	60	116	23	5	17	56	.283	239	8	3	.988
1983—Midland	Texas	OF	6	19	9	9	2	1	3	7	.474	8	0	0	1.000
1984—Chicago‡	Nat.	OF	48	150	25	42	11	3	4	22	.280	69	5	3	.961
1984—Cleveland	Amer.	OF	83	257	43	66	13	1	7	30	.257	143	3	1	.993
1985—Cleveland§	Amer.	OF	23	66	7	21	6	0	0	12	.318	18	0	0	1.000
1986—Cleveland	Amer.	OF	140	442	68	131	29	2	18	77	.296	233	7	7	.972
1987—Cleveland	Amer.	OF	142	485	57	136	21	1	18	76	.280	264	3	3	.989
1988—Cleveland x	Amer.	OF	150	515	69	144	32	4	6	71	.280	288	3	10	.967
1989—New York yz	Amer.	OF	113	361	54	94	9	0	17	58	.260	141	3	1	.993
1990—New York a	Amer.	OF	113	360	41	93	23	2	12	46	.258	70	2	2	.973
National League Totals—4 Years			194	651	92	180	37	10	22	84	.276	350	17	9	.976
American League Totals—7 Years			764	2486	339	685	133	10	78	370	.276	1157	21	24	.980
Major League Totals—10 Years			958	3137	431	865	170	20	100	454	.276	1507	38	33	.979

Selected by Chicago Cubs' organization in 2nd round of free-agent draft, June 6, 1978.

†On disabled list, April 15 to May 31, 1983; included rehabilitation disability assignment to Midland, May 25 to May 31, 1983.

‡Traded with Outfielder Joe Carter and Pitchers Don Schulze and Darryl Banks to Cleveland Indians for Catcher Ron Hassey and Pitchers Rick Sutcliffe and George Frazier, June 13, 1984.

§On disabled list, May 10, 1985 through remainder of season.

xTraded to New York Yankees for Catcher Joel Skinner and Outfielder Turner Ward, March 19, 1989.

yOn disabled list, April 26 to May 26, 1989.
zGranted free agency, November 13, 1989; re-signed by Yankees, November 30, 1989.
aOn disabled list, July 16 to August 1, 1990.

ROBERT JAMES HAMELIN III
(Bob)

Born November 29, 1967, at Elizabeth, N.J.
Height, 6.00. Weight, 240.
Throws and bats lefthanded.
Attended UCLA, Los Angeles, Calif., and Rancho
Santiago College, Santa Ana, Calif.
Led Northwest League first basemen in total chances with 682 in 1988.

Year Club	League	Pos.	G.	AB.	R.	H.	2B.	3B.	HR.	RBI.	B.A.	PO.	A.	E.	F.A.
1988—Eugene	N'west	1B	70	235	42	70	19	1	*17	61	.298	*642	25	*15	.978
1989—Memphis†	South.	1B	68	211	45	62	12	5	16	47	.308	487	27	8	.985
1990—Omaha‡	A. A.	1B	90	271	31	63	11	2	8	30	.232	396	32	4	.991

Selected by Kansas City Royals' organization in 2nd round of free-agent draft, June 1, 1988.
†On disabled list, June 25 to July 2 and August 3, 1989 through remainder of season.
‡On disabled list, August 8, 1990 through remainder of season.

DARRYL QUINN HAMILTON

Born December 3, 1964, at Baton Rouge, La.
Height, 6.01. Weight, 180.
Throws right and bats lefthanded.
Attended Nicholls State University, Thibodaux, La.
Major League stolen bases: 1988 (7), 1990 (10). Total—17.
Led California League in intentional bases on balls received with 9 in 1987.

Year Club	League	Pos.	G.	AB.	R.	H.	2B.	3B.	HR.	RBI.	B.A.	PO.	A.	E.	F.A.
1986—Helena	Pion.	OF	65	248	*72	●97	12	●6	0	35	*.391	132	9	0	*1.000
1987—Stockton	Calif.	OF	125	494	102	162	17	6	8	61	.328	221	8	1	*.996
1988—Denver	A. A.	OF	72	277	55	90	11	4	0	32	.325	160	2	2	.988
1988—Milwaukee	Amer.	OF	44	103	14	19	4	0	1	11	.184	75	1	0	1.000
1989—Denver	A. A.	OF	129	497	72	142	24	4	2	40	.286	263	11	0	*1.000
1990—Milwaukee	Amer.	OF	89	156	27	46	5	0	1	18	.295	120	1	1	.992
Major League Totals—2 Years			133	259	41	65	9	0	2	29	.251	195	2	1	.995

Selected by Milwaukee Brewers' organization in 11th round of free-agent draft, June 2, 1986.

JEFFREY ROBERT HAMILTON
(Jeff)

Born March 19, 1964, at Flint, Mich.
Height, 6.03. Weight, 207.
Throws and bats righthanded.
Led Florida State League third basemen in total chances with 395 and double plays with 25 in 1984.
Led Pioneer League third basemen in double plays with 16 in 1983.

Year Club	League	Pos.	G.	AB.	R.	H.	2B.	3B.	HR.	RBI.	B.A.	PO.	A.	E.	F.A.
1983—Lodi	Calif.	3B-OF	44	141	15	28	4	0	0	10	.199	26	62	17	.838
1983—Lethbridge	Pion.	3B	68	*281	48	●94	*23	2	3	61	.335	38	118	17	.902
1984—Vero Beach	Fla. St.	3B	127	466	51	121	31	4	4	59	.260	*109	*259	*27	*.932
1985—San Antonio	Texas	3B-OF	101	377	48	125	14	3	13	59	.332	69	186	16	.941
1986—Albuquerque	P. C.	3B	71	288	40	90	21	3	10	42	.313	39	151	19	.909
1986—Los Angeles	Nat.	3B-SS	71	147	22	33	5	0	5	19	.224	40	87	4	.969
1987—Albuquerque	P. C.	3B	65	236	52	85	17	1	12	48	.360	43	102	11	.929
1987—Los Angeles†	Nat.	3B-SS	39	83	5	18	3	0	0	1	.217	27	60	6	.935
1988—Los Angeles‡	Nat.	3B-SS-1B	111	309	34	73	14	2	6	33	.236	67	160	14	.942
1989—Los Angeles	Nat.	*3-P-2-S	151	548	45	134	35	1	12	56	.245	*139	234	19	.952
1990—Los Angeles§	Nat.	3B	7	24	1	3	0	0	0	1	.125	3	12	0	1.000
Major League Totals—5 Years			375	1111	107	261	57	3	23	110	.235	276	553	43	.951

Selected by Los Angeles Dodgers' organization in 29th round of free-agent draft, June 7, 1982.
†On disabled list, August 14, 1987 through remainder of season.
‡On disabled list, July 27 to September 1, 1988.
§On disabled list, April 21, 1990 through remainder of season.

CHAMPIONSHIP SERIES RECORD

Shares Championship Series record for most at-bats, inning (2), October 12, 1988, second inning.

Year Club	League	Pos.	G.	AB.	R.	H.	2B.	3B.	HR.	RBI.	B.A.	PO.	A.	E.	F.A.
1988—Los Angeles	Nat.	3B	7	23	2	5	0	0	1	.217	9	10	2	.905

WORLD SERIES RECORD

Year Club	League	Pos.	G.	AB.	R.	H.	2B.	3B.	HR.	RBI.	B.A.	PO.	A.	E.	F.A.
1988—Los Angeles	Nat.	3B	5	19	1	2	0	0	0	0	.105	2	5	1	.875

PITCHING RECORD

Year Club	League	G.	IP.	W.	L.	Pct.	H.	R.	ER.	SO.	BB.	ERA.
1989—Los Angeles	National	1	1⅔	0	1	.000	2	1	1	2	1	5.40

CHARLTON ATLEE HAMMAKER
(Known by middle name.)

Born January 24, 1958, at Carmel, Calif.
Height, 6.02. Weight, 200.
Throws left and bats right and lefthanded.
Attended East Tennessee State University, Johnson City, Tenn.

Major League saves: 1988 (5).

Year Club	League	G.	IP.	W.	L.	Pct.	H.	R.	ER.	SO.	BB.	ERA.
1979—Sarasota Royals-Gold	Gulf Coast	1	5	1	0	1.000	3	1	1	6	1	1.80
1979—Fort Myers†	Florida St.	1	5	0	1	.000	9	5	1	5	0	1.80
1980—Jacksonville‡	Southern	20	137	8	9	.471	131	64	51	88	37	3.35
1981—Omaha	Am. Assoc.	21	146	11	5	.688	147	70	59	63	40	3.64
1981—Kansas City§	American	10	39	1	3	.250	44	24	24	11	12	5.54
1982—Phoenix	P. Coast	1	5⅔	0	1	.000	13	5	4	6	2	6.35
1982—San Francisco	National	29	175	12	8	.600	189	86	80	102	28	4.11
1983—San Francisco x	National	23	171⅓	10	9	.526	147	57	43	127	32	⋆2.25
1984—Phoenix y	P. Coast	2	8	0	1	.000	14	7	4	5	2	4.50
1984—San Francisco	National	6	33	2	0	1.000	32	10	8	24	9	2.18
1985—San Francisco	National	29	170⅔	5	12	.294	161	81	71	100	47	3.74
1986—San Francisco za	National					(Did not play)						
1987—Phoenix b	P. Coast	3	17⅓	1	2	.333	19	9	8	8	6	4.15
1987—Shreveport	Texas	1	7	0	1	.000	6	2	1	3	0	1.29
1987—San Francisco c	National	31	168⅓	10	10	.500	159	73	67	107	57	3.58
1988—San Francisco	National	43	144⅔	9	9	.500	136	68	60	65	41	3.73
1989—San Francisco d	National	28	76⅔	6	6	.500	78	34	32	30	23	3.76
1990—San Francisco ef-San Diego	National	34	86⅔	4	9	.308	85	44	42	44	27	4.36
American League Totals—1 Year		10	39	1	3	.250	44	24	24	11	12	5.54
National League Totals—8 Years		223	1027⅓	58	63	.479	987	453	403	599	264	3.53
Major League Totals—9 Years		233	1066⅓	59	66	.472	1031	477	427	610	276	3.60

Selected by Kansas City Royals' organization in 1st round (21st player selected) of free-agent draft, June 5, 1979.
†On disabled list, July 6 to October 26, 1979.
‡On disabled list, August 3 to August 22, 1980.
§Traded with Pitchers Craig Chamberlain and Renie Martin and a player to be named later to San Francisco Giants for Pitchers Vida Blue and Bob Tufts, March 30, 1982; San Francisco organization acquired Second Baseman Brad Wellman to complete deal, April 19, 1982.
xOn disabled list, July 26 to August 21, 1983.
yOn San Francisco disabled list, April 2 to June 26 and August 4 to September 1, 1984; included rehabilitation disability assignment to Phoenix, June 16 to June 25, 1984.
zOn disabled list, April 7, 1986 through entire season.
aReleased, December 9, 1986; re-signed by Giants, February 4, 1987.
bOn San Francisco disabled list, April 2 to April 30, 1987; included rehabilitation disability assignment to Phoenix, April 10 to April 30, 1987.
cGranted free agency, November 9, 1987; re-signed by Giants, January 8, 1988.
dOn disabled list, June 19 to July 17 and August 3 to September 21, 1989.
eOn disabled list, June 18 to July 11, 1990.
fReleased, August 12, 1990; signed by San Diego Padres, August 24, 1990.

CHAMPIONSHIP SERIES RECORD

Year Club	League	G.	IP.	W.	L.	Pct.	H.	R.	ER.	SO.	BB.	ERA.
1987—San Francisco	National	2	8	0	1	.000	12	7	7	7	0	7.88
1989—San Francisco	National	1	1	0	0	.000	1	0	0	0	0	0.00
Championship Series Totals—2 Years		3	9	0	1	.000	13	7	7	7	0	7.00

WORLD SERIES RECORD

Year Club	League	G.	IP.	W.	L.	Pct.	H.	R.	ER.	SO.	BB.	ERA.
1989—San Francisco	National	2	2⅓	0	0	.000	8	4	4	2	0	15.43

ALL-STAR GAME RECORD

Holds All-Star Game records for most runs and earned runs allowed, game and inning (7), July 6, 1983, third inning; most hits allowed, inning (6), July 6, 1983, third inning.
Shares All-Star Game record for most home runs allowed, inning (2), July 6, 1983, third inning.

Year League	IP.	W.	L.	Pct.	H.	R.	ER.	SO.	BB.	ERA.
1983—National	⅔	0	0	.000	6	7	7	0	1	94.50

CHRISTOPHER ANDREW HAMMOND
(Chris)

Born January 21, 1966, at Atlanta, Ga.
Height, 6.00. Weight, 190.
Throws and bats lefthanded.
Attended Gulf Coast Community College, Panama City, Fla.,
and University of Alabama, Birmingham, Ala.
Brother of Steve Hammond, outfielder with Kansas City Royals, 1982.

Led American Association in shutouts with 3 in 1990.
Named American Association Pitcher of the Year, 1990.

Year Club	League	G.	IP.	W.	L.	Pct.	H.	R.	ER.	SO.	BB.	ERA.
1986—Sarasota Reds	Gulf Coast	7	41⅔	3	2	.600	27	21	13	53	17	2.81
1986—Tampa	Florida St.	5	21⅔	0	2	.000	25	8	8	5	13	3.32

Year Club	League	G.	IP.	W.	L.	Pct.	H.	R.	ER.	SO.	BB.	ERA.
1987—Tampa	Florida St.	25	170	11	11	.500	174	81	67	126	60	3.55
1988—Chattanooga	Southern	26	182⅔	*16	5	.762	127	48	35	127	77	*1.72
1989—Nashville	Am. Assoc.	24	157⅓	11	7	.611	144	69	59	142	96	3.38
1990—Nashville	Am. Assoc.	24	149	*15	1	*.938	118	43	36	*149	63	*2.17
1990—Cincinnati	National	3	11⅓	0	2	.000	13	9	8	4	12	6.35
Major League Totals—1 Year		3	11⅓	0	2	.000	13	9	8	4	12	6.35

Selected by Cincinnati Reds' organization in 6th round of free-agent draft, January 14, 1986.

DAVID ANDREW HANSEN
(Dave)

Born November 24, 1968, at Long Beach, Calif.
Height, 6.00. Weight, 180.
Throws right and bats lefthanded.
Led Pacific Coast League batters in bases on balls received with 90 in 1990.
Led Florida State League in total bases with 210, game-winning RBIs with 19 and tied for lead in sacrifice flies with 9 in 1988.
Led Pacific Coast League third basemen in assists with 254, total chances with 349 and double plays with 25 in 1990.
Led Florida State League third basemen in total chances with 383 and double plays with 24 in 1988.

Year Club	League	Pos.	G.	AB.	R.	H.	2B.	3B.	HR.	RBI.	B.A.	PO.	A.	E.	F.A.
1986—Great Falls	Pion.	OF-3B-C	61	204	39	61	7	3	1	36	.299	54	10	7	.901
1987—Bakersfield	Calif.	*3B-OF	132	432	68	113	22	1	3	38	.262	79	198	*45	.860
1988—Vero Beach	Fla. St.	3B	135	512	68	*149	●28	6	7	*81	.291	*102	*263	18	*.953
1989—San Antonio	Texas	3B	121	464	72	138	21	4	6	52	.297	*92	208	16	*.949
1989—Albuquerque	P. C.	3B	6	30	6	8	1	0	2	10	.267	3	8	3	.786
1990—Albuquerque	P. C.	*3-O-S	135	487	90	154	20	3	11	92	.316	71	255	26	*.926
1990—Los Angeles	Nat.	3B	5	7	0	1	0	0	0	1	.143	0	1	1	.500
Major League Totals—1 Year			5	7	0	1	0	0	0	1	.143	0	1	1	.500

Selected by Los Angeles Dodgers' organization in 2nd round of free-agent draft, June 2, 1986.

TERREL ERNEST HANSEN

Born September 25, 1966, at Bremerton, Wash.
Height, 6.03. Weight, 210.
Throws and bats righthanded.
Attended Washington State University, Pullman, Wash.
Led Midwest League in being hit by pitch with 23 in 1989.

Year Club	League	Pos.	G.	AB.	R.	H.	2B.	3B.	HR.	RBI.	B.A.	PO.	A.	E.	F.A.
1987—Jamestown	NYP	OF-1B	29	67	8	16	3	0	1	14	.239	21	2	3	.885
1988—W. Palm Beach	Fla. St.	OF-1B	58	190	17	49	9	0	4	28	.258	80	4	2	.977
1989—Rockford	Midw.	OF-1B	125	468	60	126	24	3	16	●81	.269	205	14	4	.982
1990—Jacksonville	South.	OF-1B	123	420	72	109	26	2	●24	83	.260	289	12	9	.971

Selected by New York Mets' organization in 14th round of free-agent draft, June 4, 1984.
Selected by Montreal Expos' organization in 14th round of free-agent draft, June 2, 1987.

ERIK B. HANSON

Born May 18, 1965, at Kinnelon, N. J.
Height, 6.06. Weight, 210.
Throws and bats righthanded.
Attended Wake Forest University, Winston-Salem, N. C.
Pitched 5-0 no-hit victory against Las Vegas, August 21, 1988 (second game).

Year Club	League	G.	IP.	W.	L.	Pct.	H.	R.	ER.	SO.	BB.	ERA.
1986—Chattanooga†	Southern	3	9⅓	0	0	.000	10	4	4	11	4	3.86
1987—Chattanooga	Southern	21	131⅓	8	10	.444	102	56	38	131	43	2.60
1987—Calgary	P. Coast	8	47⅓	1	3	.250	38	23	19	43	21	3.61
1988—Calgary	P. Coast	27	161⅔	12	7	.632	167	92	76	*154	57	4.23
1988—Seattle	American	6	41⅔	2	3	.400	35	17	15	36	12	3.24
1989—Seattle‡	American	17	113⅓	9	5	.643	103	44	40	75	32	3.18
1989—Calgary	P. Coast	8	38	4	2	.667	51	30	29	37	11	6.87
1990—Seattle	American	33	236	18	9	.667	205	88	85	211	68	3.24
Major League Totals—3 Years		56	391	29	17	.630	343	149	140	322	112	3.22

Selected by Montreal Expos' organization in 7th round of free-agent draft, June 6, 1983.
Selected by Seattle Mariners' organization in 2nd round of free-agent draft, June 2, 1986.
†On inactive list, June 12 to August 18, 1986.
‡On disabled list, May 25 to August 4, 1989; included rehabilitation disability assignment to Calgary, June 14 to June 22 and July 24 to August 4, 1989.

MICHAEL ANTHONY HARKEY
(Mike)

Born October 25, 1966, at San Diego, Calif.
Height, 6.05. Weight, 220.
Throws and bats righthanded.
Attended California State University, Fullerton, Calif.
Named National League Rookie Pitcher of the Year by THE SPORTING NEWS, 1990.

Year Club	League	G.	IP.	W.	L.	Pct.	H.	R.	ER.	SO.	BB.	ERA.
1987—Peoria	Midwest	12	76	2	3	.400	81	45	30	48	28	3.55
1987—Pittsfield	Eastern	1	2	0	0	.000	1	0	0	2	0	0.00
1988—Pittsfield	Eastern	13	85⅔	9	2	*.818	66	29	13	73	35	1.37
1988—Iowa	Am. Assoc.	12	78⅔	7	2	.778	55	36	31	62	33	3.55
1988—Chicago	National	5	34⅔	0	3	.000	33	14	10	18	15	2.60
1989—Iowa†	Am. Assoc.	12	63	2	7	.222	67	37	31	37	35	4.43
1990—Chicago‡	National	27	173⅔	12	6	.667	153	71	63	94	59	3.26
Major League Totals—2 Years		32	208⅓	12	9	.571	186	85	73	112	74	3.15

Selected by San Diego Padres' organization in 18th round of free-agent draft, June 4, 1984.
Selected by Chicago Cubs' organization in 1st round (fourth player selected) of free-agent draft, June 2, 1987.
†On disabled list, April 5 to April 28 and July 4, 1989 through remainder of season.
‡On disabled list, May 29 to June 13, 1990.

PETER THOMAS HARNISCH
(Pete)

Born September 23, 1966, at Commack, N. Y.
Height, 6.00. Weight, 219.
Throws and bats righthanded.
Attended Fordham University, Bronx, N. Y.

Year Club	League	G.	IP.	W.	L.	Pct.	H.	R.	ER.	SO.	BB.	ERA.
1987—Bluefield	Ap'lachian	9	52⅔	3	1	.750	38	19	15	64	26	2.56
1987—Hagerstown	Carolina	4	20	1	2	.333	17	7	5	18	14	2.25
1988—Charlotte	Southern	20	132⅓	7	6	.538	113	55	38	141	52	2.58
1988—Rochester	Int'national	7	58⅓	4	1	.800	44	16	14	43	14	2.16
1988—Baltimore	American	2	13	0	2	.000	13	8	8	10	9	5.54
1989—Baltimore	American	18	103⅓	5	9	.357	97	55	53	70	64	4.62
1989—Rochester	Int'national	12	87⅓	5	5	.500	60	27	25	59	35	2.58
1990—Baltimore	American	31	188⅔	11	11	.500	189	96	91	122	86	4.34
Major League Totals—3 Years		51	305	16	22	.421	299	159	152	202	159	4.49

Selected by Baltimore Orioles' organization in 1st round (27th player selected) of free-agent draft, June 2, 1987.

BRIAN DAVID HARPER

Born October 16, 1959, at Los Angeles, Calif.
Height, 6.02. Weight, 208.
Throws and bats righthanded.
Major League stolen bases: 1981 (1), 1989 (2), 1990 (3). Total—6.
Led Pacific Coast League in total bases with 339 in 1981.
Led Pacific Coast League in sacrifice flies with 12 in 1987.
Led Pacific Coast League catchers in errors with 19 in 1981.
Led Texas League in passed balls with 19 in 1979.
Tied for American Association lead in errors by catchers with 13 in 1986.

Year Club	League	Pos.	G.	AB.	R.	H.	2B.	3B.	HR.	RBI.	B.A.	PO.	A.	E.	F.A.
1977—Idaho Falls	Pion.	C	52	186	28	60	9	3	1	33	.323	352	36	13	.968
1978—Quad Cities	Midw.	C	129	508	80	149	31	2	24	*101	.293	430	46	16	.967
1979—El Paso	Texas	C	132	531	85	167	*37	3	14	90	.315	443	66	*29	.946
1979—California	Amer.	DH	1	2	0	0	0	0	0	0	.000	0	0	0	.000
1980—El Paso†	Texas	C	105	400	61	114	23	3	12	66	.285	214	30	7	.972
1981—Salt Lake City	P. C.	C-OF-1B	134	549	99	*192	45	9	28	122	.350	421	30	24	.949
1981—California‡	Amer.	OF	4	11	1	3	0	0	0	1	.273	5	0	1	.833
1982—Pittsburgh	Nat.	OF	20	29	4	8	1	0	2	4	.276	10	0	0	1.000
1982—Portland	P. C.	OF-3B-C	101	395	71	112	29	8	17	73	.284	164	36	8	.962
1983—Pittsburgh	Nat.	OF-1B	61	131	16	29	4	1	7	20	.221	40	0	0	1.000
1984—Pittsburgh§ x	Nat.	OF-C	46	112	4	29	4	0	2	11	.259	57	3	1	.984
1985—St. Louis y	Nat.	O-3-C-1	43	52	5	13	4	0	0	8	.250	15	5	0	1.000
1986—Nashville	A. A.	C-OF-1B	95	317	41	83	11	1	11	45	.262	377	55	15	.966
1986—Detroit z	Amer.	OF-1B-C	19	36	2	5	1	0	0	3	.139	25	2	1	.964
1987—San Jose a	Calif.	3B-OF-C	8	29	5	9	0	0	3	8	.310	21	12	5	.868
1987—Tacoma	P. C.	OF-C-P	94	323	41	100	17	0	9	62	.310	163	10	5	.972
1987—Oakland b	Amer.	OF	11	17	1	4	1	0	0	3	.235	0	0	0	.000
1988—Portland	P. C.	C-3-O-P	46	170	34	60	10	1	13	42	.353	181	25	5	.976
1988—Minnesota	Amer.	C-3B	60	166	15	49	11	1	3	20	.295	208	15	2	.991
1989—Minnesota	Amer.	*C-O-1-3	126	385	43	125	24	0	8	57	.325	462	36	*11	.978
1990—Minnesota	Amer.	C-3B-1B	134	479	61	141	42	3	6	54	.294	686	58	11	.985
American League Totals—7 Years			355	1096	123	327	79	4	17	138	.298	1386	111	26	.983
National League Totals—4 Years			170	324	29	79	13	1	11	43	.244	122	8	1	.992
Major League Totals—11 Years			525	1420	152	406	92	5	28	181	.286	1508	119	27	.984

Selected by California Angels' organization in 4th round of free-agent draft, June 7, 1977.
†On disabled list, July 1 to July 17, 1980.
‡Traded to Pittsburgh Pirates for Shortstop Tim Foli, December 11, 1981.
§On disabled list, April 12 to May 10 and May 16 to June 4, 1984.
xTraded with Pitcher John Tudor to St. Louis Cardinals for Outfielder-First Baseman George Hendrick and Catcher Steve Barnard, December 12, 1984.
yReleased, April 1, 1986; signed by Detroit Tigers, April 25, 1986.
zReleased, March 23, 1987; signed by San Jose (Independent), May 3, 1987.
aSold to Oakland Athletics' organization, May 12, 1987.
bReleased, October 12, 1987; signed by Portland (Minnesota Twins' organization), January 4, 1988.

Year	Club	League	Pos.	G.	AB.	R.	H.	2B.	3B.	HR.	RBI.	B.A.	PO.	A.	E.	F.A.
1985—St. Louis		Nat.	PH	1	1	0	0	0	0	0	0	.000	0	0	0	.000

WORLD SERIES RECORD

Year	Club	League	Pos.	G.	AB.	R.	H.	2B.	3B.	HR.	RBI.	B.A.	PO.	A.	E.	F.A.
1985—St. Louis		Nat.	PH	4	4	0	1	0	0	0	1	.250	0	0	0	.000

PITCHING RECORD

Year	Club	League	G.	IP.	W.	L.	Pct.	H.	R.	ER.	SO.	BB.	ERA.
1987—Tacoma		P. Coast	1	3	0	0	.000	3	1	1	1	0	3.00
1988—Portland		P. Coast	1	1	0	0	.000	2	1	1	0	2	9.00

GREG ALLEN HARRIS

Born November 2, 1955, at Lynwood, Calif.
Height, 6.00. Weight, 175.
Throws and bats righthanded.
Attended Long Beach City College, Long Beach, Calif.

Major League saves: 1981 (1), 1982 (1), 1984 (3), 1985 (11), 1986 (20), 1988 (1), 1989 (1). Total—38.

Year	Club	League	G.	IP.	W.	L.	Pct.	H.	R.	ER.	SO.	BB.	ERA.
1977—Jackson		Texas	30	83	3	6	.333	96	63	50	56	36	5.42
1978—Lynchburg		Carolina	21	154	8	9	.471	114	52	37	102	74	2.16
1978—Jackson		Texas	6	33	2	3	.400	24	13	11	18	10	3.00
1979—Jackson		Texas	25	163	9	11	.450	125	58	41	89	81	*2.26
1980—Tidewater		Int'national	39	110	2	9	.182	99	45	33	92	40	2.70
1981—Tidewater		Int'national	7	48	4	0	1.000	37	14	11	26	16	2.06
1981—New York†		National	16	69	3	5	.375	65	36	34	54	28	4.43
1982—Indianapolis		Am. Assoc.	8	48	4	1	.800	27	18	16	44	24	3.00
1982—Cincinnati		National	34	91⅓	2	6	.250	96	56	49	67	37	4.83
1983—Indianapolis		Am. Assoc.	28	152⅓	9	12	.429	155	83	70	*146	66	4.14
1983—Cincinnati‡		National	1	1	0	0	.000	2	3	3	1	3	27.00
1984—Montreal§-San Diego		National	34	54⅓	2	2	.500	38	18	15	45	25	2.48
1984—Indianapolis x		Am. Assoc.	14	44⅔	4	4	.500	44	27	22	45	29	4.43
1985—Texas		American	58	113	5	4	.556	74	35	31	111	43	2.47
1986—Texas		American	73	111⅓	10	8	.556	103	40	35	95	42	2.83
1987—Texas yz		American	42	140⅔	5	10	.333	157	92	76	106	56	4.86
1988—Maine		Int'national	3	4⅔	0	1	.000	5	3	1	5	1	1.93
1988—Philadelphia a		National	66	107	4	6	.400	80	34	28	71	52	2.36
1989—Philadelphia b		National	44	75⅓	2	2	.500	64	34	30	51	43	3.58
1989—Boston c		American	15	28	2	2	.500	21	12	8	25	15	2.57
1990—Boston		American	34	184⅓	13	9	.591	186	90	82	117	77	4.00
National League Totals—6 Years			195	398	13	21	.382	345	181	159	289	188	3.60
American League Totals—5 Years			222	577⅓	35	33	.515	541	269	232	454	233	3.62
Major League Totals—10 Years			417	975⅓	48	54	.471	886	450	391	743	421	3.61

Selected by California Angels' organization in 10th round of free-agent draft, June 5, 1974.
Selected by New York Mets' organization in secondary phase of free-agent draft, January 9, 1975.
Selected by New York Mets' organization in 7th round of free-agent draft, January 7, 1976.
Signed as free agent by New York Mets' organization, September 17, 1976.
†Traded with Catcher Alex Trevino and Pitcher Jim Kern to Cincinnati Reds for Outfielder George Foster, February 10, 1982.
‡Claimed on waivers by Montreal Expos, September 27, 1983.
§Traded to San Diego Padres for Infielder Al Newman, July 20, 1984.
xSold to Texas Rangers, February 13, 1985.
yReleased, December 21, 1987; signed by Cleveland Indians, January 19, 1988.
zReleased, March 24, 1988; signed by Maine (Philadelphia Phillies' organization), April 1, 1988.
aGranted free agency, November 4, 1988; re-signed by Phillies, December 7, 1988.
bClaimed on waivers by Boston Red Sox, August 7, 1989.
cGranted free agency, November 13, 1989; re-signed by Red Sox, February 15, 1990.

CHAMPIONSHIP SERIES RECORD

Shares Championship Series records for most earned runs allowed, game (7), October 2, 1984; most earned runs (6) and hits (6) allowed, inning, October 2, 1984, fifth inning.

Year	Club	League	G.	IP.	W.	L.	Pct.	H.	R.	ER.	SO.	BB.	ERA.
1984—San Diego		National	1	2	0	0	.000	9	8	7	2	3	31.50
1990—Boston		American	1	⅓	0	1	.000	3	1	1	0	0	27.00
Championship Series Totals—2 Years			2	2⅓	0	1	.000	12	9	8	2	3	30.86

WORLD SERIES RECORD

Year	Club	League	G.	IP.	W.	L.	Pct.	H.	R.	ER.	SO.	BB.	ERA.
1984—San Diego		National	1	5⅓	0	0	.000	3	0	0	5	3	0.00

—DID YOU KNOW—

That the Mets' Dave Magadan led all major league hitters in 1990 with a .372 average on the road and a .409 mark in pinch-hitting spots?

GREGORY WADE HARRIS
(Greg)

Born December 1, 1963, at Greensboro, N. C.
Height, 6.02. Weight, 190.
Throws and bats righthanded.
Attended Elon College, Elon College, N. C.

Pitched 7-0 no-hit victory against Midland, August 26, 1987.
Major League saves: 1989 (6), 1990 (9). Total—15.
Led Texas League in complete games with 7, home runs allowed with 32, balks with 6 and tied for lead in shutouts with 2 in 1987.

Year	Club	League	G.	IP.	W.	L.	Pct.	H.	R.	ER.	SO.	BB.	ERA.
1985—Spokane		Northwest	13	87⅓	5	4	.556	80	36	33	90	36	3.40
1986—Charleston		S. Atlantic	27	*191⅓	13	7	.650	176	69	56	176	54	2.63
1987—Wichita		Texas	27	174⅓	12	11	.522	205	103	83	170	49	4.28
1988—Las Vegas		P. Coast	26	159⅔	9	5	.643	160	84	73	147	65	4.11
1988—San Diego		National	3	18	2	0	1.000	13	3	3	15	3	1.50
1989—San Diego		National	56	135	8	9	.471	106	43	39	106	52	2.60
1990—San Diego		National	73	117⅓	8	8	.500	92	35	30	97	49	2.30
Major League Totals—3 Years			132	270⅓	18	17	.514	211	81	72	218	104	2.40

Selected by San Diego Padres' organization in 10th round of free-agent draft, June 3, 1985.

LEONARD ANTHONY HARRIS
(Lenny)

Born October 28, 1964, at Miami, Fla.
Height, 5.10. Weight, 204.
Throws right and bats lefthanded.
Attended Miami-Dade Community College (North), Miami, Fla.

Major League stolen bases: 1988 (4), 1989 (14), 1990 (15). Total—33.
Led American Association in stolen bases with 45 and caught stealing with 22 in 1988.
Led Eastern League in game-winning RBIs with 13 in 1986.
Led American Association second basemen in errors with 23 in 1988.
Led Eastern League third basemen in putouts with 116 and total chances with 360 in 1986.
Led Florida State League third basemen in double plays with 34 in 1985.

Year	Club	League	Pos.	G.	AB.	R.	H.	2B.	3B.	HR.	RBI.	B.A.	PO.	A.	E.	F.A.
1983—Billings		Pion.	3B	56	224	37	63	8	1	1	26	.281	34	95	22	.854
1984—Cedar Rapids		Midw.	3B	132	468	52	115	15	3	6	53	.246	111	204	*34	.903
1985—Tampa		Fla. St.	3B	132	499	66	129	11	8	3	51	.259	89	*277	*35	.913
1986—Vermont		East.	*3B-SS	119	450	68	114	17	2	10	52	.253	119	220	*28	.924
1987—Nashville		A. A.	SS-3B	120	403	45	100	12	3	2	31	.248	124	210	34	.908
1988—Nashville†		A. A.	2B-SS-3B	107	422	46	117	20	2	0	35	.277	203	247	25	.947
1988—Glens Falls		East.	2B	17	65	9	22	5	1	1	7	.338	40	49	5	.947
1988—Cincinnati		Nat.	3B-2B	16	43	7	16	1	0	0	8	.372	14	33	1	.979
1989—Cinc.‡-L.A.		Nat.	2-3-O-S	115	335	36	79	10	1	3	26	.236	147	168	15	.955
1989—Nashville		A. A.	2B	8	34	6	9	2	0	3	6	.265	23	20	0	1.000
1990—Los Angeles		Nat.	3-2-O-S	137	431	61	131	16	4	2	29	.304	140	205	11	.969
Major League Totals—3 Years				268	809	104	226	27	5	5	63	.279	301	406	27	.963

Selected by Cincinnati Reds' organization in 5th round of free-agent draft, June 6, 1983.
†Loaned to Glens Falls (Detroit Tigers' organization), May 6, 1988; returned, June 26, 1988.
‡Traded with Outfielder Kal Daniels to Los Angeles Dodgers for Pitcher Tim Leary and Shortstop Mariano Duncan, July 18, 1989.

REGINALD ALLEN HARRIS
(Reggie)

Born August 12, 1968, at Waynesboro, Va.
Height, 6.01. Weight, 180.
Throws and bats righthanded.

Year	Club	League	G.	IP.	W.	L.	Pct.	H.	R.	ER.	SO.	BB.	ERA.
1987—Elmira		NYP	9	46⅔	2	3	.400	50	29	26	25	22	5.01
1988—Lynchburg		Carolina	17	64	1	8	.111	86	60	53	48	34	7.45
1988—Elmira		NYP	10	54⅓	3	6	.333	56	37	32	46	28	5.30
1989—Winter Haven†		Florida St.	29	153⅓	10	13	.435	144	81	68	85	77	3.99
1990—Huntsville‡		Southern	5	29⅔	0	2	.000	26	12	10	34	16	3.03
1990—Oakland		American	16	41⅓	1	0	1.000	25	16	16	31	21	3.48
Major League Totals—1 Year			16	41⅓	1	0	1.000	25	16	16	31	21	3.48

Selected by Boston Red Sox' organization in 1st round (26th player selected) of free-agent draft, June 2, 1987.
†Drafted by Oakland Athletics, December 4, 1989.
‡On Oakland disabled list, March 29 through July 3, 1990; included rehabilitation disability assignment to Huntsville, May 26 to June 24, 1990.

TYRONE EUGENE HARRIS
(Gene)

Born December 5, 1964, at Sebring, Fla.
Height, 5.11. Weight, 190.
Throws and bats righthanded.
Attended Tulane University, New Orleans, La.

Major League saves: 1989 (1).
Led Southern League in complete games with 7 in 1988.

Year	Club	League	G.	IP.	W.	L.	Pct.	H.	R.	ER.	SO.	BB.	ERA.
1986—Jamestown	NYP	4	20⅓	0	2	.000	15	8	5	16	11	2.21
1986—Burlington	Midwest	7	53⅓	4	2	.667	37	12	8	32	15	1.35
1986—West Palm Beach	Florida St.	2	11	0	0	.000	14	7	5	5	7	4.09
1987—West Palm Beach	Florida St.	26	179	9	7	.563	178	101	87	121	77	4.37
1988—Jacksonville	Southern	18	126⅔	9	5	.643	95	43	37	103	45	2.63
1989—Montreal	National	11	20	1	1	.500	16	11	11	11	10	4.95
1989—Indianapolis†	Am. Assoc.	6	11	2	0	1.000	4	0	0	9	10	0.00
1989—Calgary	P. Coast	5	6	0	0	.000	4	0	0	4	1	0.00
1989—Seattle‡§	American	10	33⅓	1	4	.200	47	27	24	14	15	6.48
1990—Calgary	P. Coast	6	7⅔	3	0	1.000	7	2	2	9	4	2.35
1990—Seattle	American	25	38	1	2	.333	31	25	20	43	30	4.74
National League Totals—1 Year		11	20	1	1	.500	16	11	11	11	10	4.95
American League Totals—2 Years		35	71⅓	2	6	.250	78	52	44	57	45	5.55
Major League Totals—2 Years		46	91⅓	3	7	.300	94	63	55	68	55	5.42

Selected by Montreal Expos' organization in 5th round of free-agent draft, June 2, 1986.
†Traded with Pitchers Randy Johnson and Brian Holman to Seattle Mariners for Pitcher Mark Langston and a player to be named later, May 25, 1989; Indianapolis (Montreal Expos' organization) acquired Pitcher Mike Campbell to complete deal, July 31, 1989.
‡On disabled list, July 29, 1989 through remainder of season.
§Appeared in one game as a pinch-runner.

BRIAN LEE HARRISON

Born November 26, 1966, at Bluefield, W.Va.
Height, 6.01. Weight, 180.
Throws and bats lefthanded.
Attended Ventura Junior College, Ventura, Calif.

Tied for Northwest League lead in balks with 3 in 1986.

Year	Club	League	G.	IP.	W.	L.	Pct.	H.	R.	ER.	SO.	BB.	ERA.
1986—Spokane†-Tri-Cities	Northwest	22	61	3	5	.375	66	56	42	64	60	6.20
1987—Charleston, S.C.	S. Atlantic	37	72⅔	4	0	1.000	64	31	22	87	30	2.72
1987—Reno	California	1	3⅔	0	0	.000	6	5	3	2	5	7.36
1988—Riverside	California	21	101⅔	5	8	.385	92	61	47	95	60	4.17
1989—Riverside	California	42	71	2	7	.222	69	42	33	81	43	4.18
1990—Riverside‡§	California	37	45⅓	5	2	.714	32	9	6	55	20	1.19

Selected by San Francisco Giants' organization in 26th round of free-agent draft, June 3, 1985.
Selected by San Diego Padres' organization in secondary phase of free-agent draft, January 14, 1986.
†Loaned to Tri-Cities (Co-op), July 16, 1986; returned, September 1, 1986.
‡Traded to Montreal Expos' organization for Pitcher John Costello, November 9, 1990.
§Drafted by Chicago White Sox, December 3, 1990.

MICHAEL EDWARD HARTLEY
(Mike)

Born August 31, 1961, at Hawthorne, Calif.
Height, 6.01. Weight, 197.
Throws and bats righthanded.
Attended Grossmont College, El Cajon, Calif.

Major League saves: 1990 (1).
Led Pacific Coast League in games finished in relief with 50 in 1989.

Year	Club	League	G.	IP.	W.	L.	Pct.	H.	R.	ER.	SO.	BB.	ERA.
1982—Johnson City	Ap'lachian	8	29	3	1	.750	32	12	9	13	8	2.79
1983—St. Petersburg	Florida St.	9	29⅔	1	3	.250	25	14	11	18	24	3.34
1983—Macon	S. Atlantic	7	29	2	3	.400	36	36	33	12	30	10.24
1983—Erie	NYP	7	32	1	3	.250	36	27	24	25	31	6.75
1984—St. Petersburg	Florida St.	31	139⅓	8	14	.364	142	81	65	88	84	4.20
1985—Springfield	Midwest	33	114⅓	2	7	.222	119	77	65	100	62	5.12
1986—Springfield	Midwest	8	15	0	0	.000	22	17	16	10	14	9.60
1986—Savannah†	S. Atlantic	39	56	5	7	.417	38	31	18	55	37	2.89
1987—Bakersfield	California	33	56	5	4	.556	44	19	16	72	24	2.57
1987—San Antonio	Texas	25	41	3	4	.429	21	8	6	37	18	1.32
1987—Albuquerque	P. Coast	2	2⅔	0	1	.000	5	3	2	3	3	6.75
1988—San Antonio	Texas	30	45	5	1	.833	25	5	4	57	18	0.80
1988—Albuquerque	P. Coast	18	20⅔	2	2	.500	22	11	10	16	12	4.35
1989—Albuquerque	P. Coast	58	77⅓	7	4	.636	53	31	24	76	34	2.79
1989—Los Angeles	National	5	6	0	1	.000	2	1	1	4	0	1.50
1990—Los Angeles	National	32	79⅓	6	3	.667	58	32	26	76	30	2.95
1990—Albuquerque	P. Coast	3	3	0	0	.000	3	0	0	3	2	0.00
Major League Totals—2 Years		37	85⅓	6	4	.600	60	33	27	80	30	2.85

Signed as free agent by St. Louis Cardinals' organization, November 27, 1981.
†Drafted by San Antonio (Los Angeles Dodgers' organization), December 9, 1986.

BRYAN STANLEY HARVEY

Born June 2, 1963, at Chattanooga, Tenn.
Height, 6.02. Weight, 219.
Throws and bats righthanded.
Attended University of North Carolina, Charlotte, N. C.

Major League saves: 1988 (17), 1989 (25), 1990 (25). Total—67.
Named American League Rookie Pitcher of the Year by THE SPORTING NEWS, 1988.

Year Club	League	G.	IP.	W.	L.	Pct.	H.	R.	ER.	SO.	BB.	ERA
1985—Quad City†	Midwest	30	81⅔	5	6	.455	66	37	32	111	37	3.53
1986—Palm Springs	California	43	57	3	4	.429	38	24	17	68	38	2.68
1987—Midland	Texas	43	53	2	2	.500	40	14	12	78	28	2.04
1987—California	American	3	5	0	0	.000	6	0	0	3	2	0.00
1988—Edmonton	P. Coast	5	5⅔	0	0	.000	7	2	2	10	4	3.18
1988—California	American	50	76	7	5	.583	59	22	18	67	20	2.13
1989—California	American	51	55	3	3	.500	36	21	21	78	41	3.44
1990—California	American	54	64⅓	4	4	.500	45	24	23	82	35	3.22
Major League Totals—4 Years		158	200⅓	14	12	.538	146	67	62	230	98	2.79

Signed as free agent by California Angels' organization, August 20, 1984.
†On disabled list, April 12 to April 22, 1985.

WILLIAM JOSEPH HASELMAN
(Bill)

Born May 25, 1966, at Long Branch, N.J.
Height, 6.03. Weight, 205.
Throws and bats righthanded.
Attended UCLA, Los Angeles, Calif.

Led Texas League catchers in putouts with 676, assists with 90, total chances with 786 and passed balls with 20 in 1990.
Led Texas League in passed balls with 12 in 1989.

Year Club	League	Pos.	G.	AB.	R.	H.	2B.	3B.	HR.	RBI.	B.A.	PO.	A.	E.	F.A.
1987—Gastonia	S. Atl.	C	61	235	35	72	13	1	8	33	.306	26	2	2	.933
1988—Port Charlotte	Fla. St.	C	122	453	56	111	17	2	10	54	.245	249	30	6	.979
1989—Tulsa	Texas	C	107	352	38	95	17	2	7	36	.270	508	63	9	.984
1990—Tulsa	Texas	★C-1-O-3	120	430	68	137	39	2	18	80	.319	722	93	★20	.976
1990—Texas	Amer.	C	7	13	0	2	0	0	0	3	.154	8	0	0	1.000
Major League Totals—1 Year		7	13	0	2	0	0	0	3	.154	8	0	0	1.000

Selected by Texas Rangers' organization in 1st round (23rd player selected) of free-agent draft, June 2, 1987.

RONALD WILLIAM HASSEY
(Ron)

Born February 27, 1953, at Tucson, Ariz.
Height, 6.02. Weight, 195.
Throws right and bats lefthanded.
Received degree in public administration from University of Arizona, Tucson, Ariz.
Son of Bill Hassey, minor league outfielder, 1949 through 1952.

Major League stolen bases: 1978 (2), 1979 (1), 1982 (3), 1983 (2), 1984 (1), 1986 (1), 1988 (2), 1989 (1). Total—13.
Led American League in passed balls with 15 in 1985.

Year Club	League	Pos.	G.	AB.	R.	H.	2B.	3B.	HR.	RBI.	B.A.	PO.	A.	E.	F.A.
1976—San Jose	Calif.	C-3B	22	62	7	19	4	0	1	7	.306	55	2	2	.966
1976—Williamsport	East.	C	21	68	6	19	3	0	0	8	.279	63	10	4	.948
1977—Toledo	Int.	C-3-1-O	129	446	50	132	21	1	10	57	.296	484	82	21	.964
1978—Portland	P. C.	C-3B	72	235	42	76	12	1	12	52	.323	312	32	7	.980
1978—Cleveland	Amer.	C	25	74	5	15	0	0	2	9	.203	130	15	1	.993
1979—Tacoma	P. C.	C-3B	44	157	25	53	10	0	3	27	.338	282	44	2	.994
1979—Cleveland	Amer.	C-1B	75	223	20	64	14	0	4	32	.287	368	29	3	.993
1980—Cleveland	Amer.	C-1B	130	390	43	124	18	4	8	65	.318	564	52	4	.994
1981—Cleveland	Amer.	C-1B	61	190	8	44	4	0	1	25	.232	327	44	3	.992
1982—Cleveland	Amer.	C-1B	113	323	33	81	18	0	5	34	.251	566	38	4	.993
1983—Cleveland	Amer.	C	117	341	48	92	21	0	6	42	.270	514	43	3	.995
1984—Cleveland†	Amer.	C-1B	48	149	11	38	5	1	0	19	.255	210	16	1	.996
1984—Chicago‡§	Nat.	C-1B	19	33	5	11	0	0	2	5	.333	53	2	1	.982
1985—New York xy	Amer.	C-1B	92	267	31	79	16	1	13	42	.296	420	20	7	.984
1986—N.Y.z-Chi.	Amer.	C	113	341	45	110	25	1	9	49	.323	318	14	4	.988
1987—Chicago a	Amer.	C	49	145	15	31	9	0	3	12	.214	114	12	0	1.000
1987—Hawaii b	P. C.	DH	6	21	3	3	2	0	0	4	.143	0	0	0	.000
1988—Oakland	Amer.	C	107	323	32	83	15	0	7	45	.257	465	31	3	.994
1989—Oakland	Amer.	C-1B	97	268	29	61	12	0	5	23	.228	425	25	4	.991
1990—Oakland c	Amer.	C-1B	94	254	18	54	7	0	5	22	.213	312	18	1	.997
American League Totals—13 Years		1121	3288	338	876	164	7	68	419	.266	4733	357	38	.993
National League Totals—1 Year		19	33	5	11	0	0	2	5	.333	53	2	1	.982
Major League Totals—13 Years		1140	3321	343	887	164	7	70	424	.267	4786	359	39	.992

Selected by Cincinnati Reds' organization in 23rd round of free-agent draft, June 6, 1972.
Selected by Kansas City Royals' organization in 22nd round of free-agent draft, June 4, 1975.
Selected by Cleveland Indians' organization in 18th round of free-agent draft, June 8, 1976.
†Traded with Pitchers Rick Sutcliffe and George Frazier to Chicago Cubs for Outfielders Mel Hall and Joe Carter and Pitchers Don Schulze and Darryl Banks, June 13, 1984.

‡On disabled list, July 5 to September 1, 1984.
§Traded with Outfielder Henry Cotto and Pitchers Rich Bordi and Porfi Altamirano to New York Yankees for Pitcher Ray Fontenot and Outfielder Brian Dayett, December 4, 1984.
xTraded with Pitcher Joe Cowley to Chicago White Sox for Pitcher Britt Burns, Shortstop Mike Soper and Outfielder Glen Braxton, December 12, 1985.
yTraded with Catcher Chris Alvarez, Pitcher Eric Schmidt and Outfielder Matt Winters to New York Yankees for Pitcher Neil Allen, Catcher Scott Bradley, Outfielder Glen Braxton and cash, February 13, 1986.
zTraded with Shortstop Carlos Martinez and a player to be named later to Chicago White Sox for Outfielder Ron Kittle, Infielder Wayne Tolleson and Catcher Joel Skinner, July 30, 1986; New York Yankees traded Catcher Bill Lindsey to Chicago organization to complete deal, December 24, 1986.
aOn disabled list, June 1 to August 7, 1987; included rehabilitation disability assignment to Hawaii, June 28 to August 2, 1987.
bGranted free agency, November 30, 1987; signed by Oakland Athletics, December 9, 1987.
cGranted free agency, November 5, 1990.

CHAMPIONSHIP SERIES RECORD

Year Club	League	Pos.	G.	AB.	R.	H.	2B.	3B.	HR.	RBI.	B.A.	PO.	A.	E.	F.A.
1988—Oakland	Amer.	C	4	8	2	4	1	0	1	3	.500	13	0	0	1.000
1989—Oakland	Amer.	C	2	6	0	1	0	0	0	1	.167	10	0	0	1.000
1990—Oakland	Amer.	C-PH	2	3	0	1	0	0	0	0	.333	6	0	0	1.000
Championship Series Totals—3 Years			8	17	2	6	1	0	1	4	.353	29	0	0	1.000

WORLD SERIES RECORD

Year Club	League	Pos.	G.	AB.	R.	H.	2B.	3B.	HR.	RBI.	B.A.	PO.	A.	E.	F.A.
1988—Oakland	Amer.	C-PH	5	8	0	2	0	0	0	1	.250	28	1	0	1.000
1990—Oakland	Amer.	PH-C	3	6	0	2	0	0	0	1	.333	2	0	1	.667
World Series Totals—2 Years			8	14	0	4	0	0	0	2	.286	30	1	1	.969

Eligible for 1989 World Series with Oakland Athletics; did not play.

MICHAEL VAUGHN HATCHER JR.
(Mickey)

Born March 15, 1955, at Cleveland, O.
Height, 6.02. Weight, 202.
Throws and bats righthanded.
Attended Mesa Community College, Mesa, Ariz., and
University of Oklahoma, Norman, Okla.
Brother of Hal Hatcher, catcher in Kansas City Royals' organization, 1980 through 1985.

Major League stolen bases: 1979 (1), 1981 (3), 1983 (2), 1986 (2), 1987 (2), 1989 (1). Total—11.

Year Club	League	Pos.	G.	AB.	R.	H.	2B.	3B.	HR.	RBI.	B.A.	PO.	A.	E.	F.A.
1977—Clinton	Midw.	OF	78	288	47	89	12	4	11	53	.309	126	9	4	.971
1978—San Antonio†	Texas	3B	83	334	60	111	12	6	8	62	.332	55	124	22	.891
1978—Albuquerque	P. C.	3B-OF	41	155	25	51	11	5	7	39	.329	24	63	8	.916
1979—Albuquerque	P. C.	3B-OF	103	420	88	156	29	12	10	93	★.371	127	156	12	.959
1979—Los Angeles	Nat.	OF-3B	33	93	9	25	4	1	1	5	.269	47	24	5	.934
1980—Albuquerque	P. C.	OF-3B	43	181	28	65	7	2	7	40	.359	52	32	9	.903
1980—Los Angeles‡	Nat.	3B-OF	57	84	4	19	2	0	1	5	.226	31	23	3	.947
1981—Minnesota	Amer.	OF-1B-3B	99	377	36	96	23	2	3	37	.255	296	11	3	.990
1982—Minnesota	Amer.	OF-3B	84	277	23	69	13	2	3	26	.249	81	17	1	.990
1983—Minnesota§	Amer.	OF-1B-3B	106	375	50	119	15	3	9	47	.317	199	11	3	.986
1984—Minnesota	Amer.	OF-1B-3B	152	576	61	174	35	5	5	69	.302	364	20	9	.977
1985—Minnesota x	Amer.	OF-1B	116	444	46	125	28	0	3	49	.282	246	7	3	.988
1986—Minnesota y	Amer.	OF-1B-3B	115	317	40	88	13	3	3	32	.278	220	16	4	.983
1987—Los Angeles	Nat.	3B-1B-OF	101	287	27	81	19	1	7	42	.282	277	105	11	.972
1988—Los Angeles z	Nat.	OF-1B-3B	88	191	22	56	8	0	1	25	.293	189	19	3	.986
1989—Los Angeles a	Nat.	O-3-1-P	94	224	18	66	9	2	2	25	.295	89	21	4	.965
1990—Los Angeles b	Nat.	1B-3B-OF	85	132	12	28	3	1	0	13	.212	86	17	3	.972
National League Totals—6 Years			458	1011	92	275	45	5	12	115	.272	719	209	29	.970
American League Totals—6 Years			672	2366	256	671	127	15	26	260	.284	1406	82	23	.985
Major League Totals—12 Years			1130	3377	348	946	172	20	38	375	.280	2125	291	52	.979

Selected by Houston Astros' organization in 14th round of free-agent draft, June 5, 1974.
Selected by New York Mets' organization in 2nd round of free-agent draft, January 7, 1976.
Selected by Los Angeles Dodgers' organization in 5th round of free-agent draft, June 7, 1977.
†On disabled list, July 13 to July 23, 1978.
‡Traded with First Baseman Kelly Snider and Pitcher Matt Reeves to Minnesota Twins for Outfielder Ken Landreaux, March 30, 1981.
§On disabled list, June 21 to July 8 and August 1 to August 23, 1983.
xOn disabled list, July 10 to July 25, 1985.
yReleased, March 31, 1987; signed by Los Angeles Dodgers, April 10, 1987.
zOn disabled list, July 7 to July 22, 1988.
aOn disabled list, June 4 to June 19 and August 7 to August 22, 1989.
bGranted free agency, November 5, 1990; re-signed by Dodgers, December 19, 1990.

CHAMPIONSHIP SERIES RECORD

Year Club	League	Pos.	G.	AB.	R.	H.	2B.	3B.	HR.	RBI.	B.A.	PO.	A.	E.	F.A.
1988—Los Angeles	Nat.	1B-OF	6	21	4	5	2	0	0	3	.238	34	1	2	.946

Shares World Series record for hitting home run in first series at-bat, October 15, 1988.

Year Club	League	Pos.	G.	AB.	R.	H.	2B.	3B.	HR.	RBI.	B.A.	PO.	A.	E.	F.A.
1988—Los Angeles	Nat.	OF	5	19	5	7	1	0	2	5	.368	8	0	0	1.000

PITCHING RECORD

Year Club	League	G.	IP.	W.	L.	Pct.	H.	R.	ER.	SO.	BB.	ERA.
1989—Los Angeles	National	1	1	0	0	.000	0	1	1	0	3	9.00

WILLIAM AUGUSTUS HATCHER
(Billy)

Born October 4, 1960, at Williams, Ariz.
Height, 5.09. Weight, 185.
Throws and bats righthanded.
Attended Yavapai Community College, Prescott, Ariz.

Shares major league record for most doubles, game (4), August 21, 1990.
Major League stolen bases: 1984 (2), 1985 (2), 1986 (38), 1987 (53), 1988 (32), 1989 (24), 1990 (30). Total—181.
Tied for National League lead in double plays by outfielders with 6 in 1987.
Led American Association in being hit by pitch with 9 in 1984.
Led New York-Pennsylvania League in being hit by pitch with 8 in 1981.

Year Club	League	Pos.	G.	AB.	R.	H.	2B.	3B.	HR.	RBI.	B.A.	PO.	A.	E.	F.A.
1981—Geneva...................	NYP	OF	•75	289	57	81	15	3	4	40	.280	138	7	11	.930
1982—Salinas	Calif.	OF	138	549	92	171	18	8	8	59	.311	235	10	12	.953
1983—Midland................	Texas	OF	135	545	★132	163	33	11	10	80	.299	286	17	•13	.959
1984—Iowa	A. A.	OF	150	595	96	164	27	18	9	59	.276	303	15	7	.978
1984—Chicago	Nat.	OF	8	9	1	1	0	0	0	0	.111	2	1	0	1.000
1985—Iowa	A. A.	OF	67	279	39	78	14	5	5	19	.280	157	4	4	.976
1985—Chicago†‡	Nat.	OF	53	163	24	40	12	1	2	10	.245	77	2	1	.988
1986—Houston§	Nat.	OF	127	419	55	108	15	4	6	36	.258	226	7	4	.983
1987—Houston x	Nat.	OF	141	564	96	167	28	3	11	63	.296	276	16	4	.986
1988—Houston	Nat.	OF	145	530	79	142	25	4	7	52	.268	280	7	5	.983
1989—Hou.y-Pit.z	Nat.	OF	135	481	59	111	19	3	4	51	.231	250	1	2	.992
1990—Cincinnati	Nat.	OF	139	504	68	139	28	5	5	25	.276	308	10	1	★.997
Major League Totals—7 Years................			748	2670	382	708	127	20	35	237	.265	1419	44	17	.989

Selected by Chicago Cubs' organization in 6th round of free-agent draft, January 13, 1981.
†On disabled list, August 19 to September 3, 1985.
‡Traded with a player to be named later to Houston Astros for Outfielder Jerry Mumphrey, December 16, 1985; Houston organization acquired Pitcher Steve Engel to complete deal, July 24, 1986.
§On disabled list, June 28 to July 13, 1986.
xOn disabled list, July 7 to July 22, 1987.
yTraded to Pittsburgh Pirates for Outfielder Glenn Wilson, August 18, 1989.
zTraded to Cincinnati Reds for Pitcher Mike Roesler and Infielder Jeff Richardson, April 3, 1990.

CHAMPIONSHIP SERIES RECORD

Shares Championship Series record for most at-bats, game (7), October 15, 1986 (16 innings).

Year Club	League	Pos.	G.	AB.	R.	H.	2B.	3B.	HR.	RBI.	B.A.	PO.	A.	E.	F.A.
1986—Houston	Nat.	OF	6	25	4	7	0	0	1	2	.280	11	0	1	.917
1990—Cincinnati	Nat.	OF	4	15	2	5	1	0	1	2	.333	5	1	0	1.000
Championship Series Totals—2 Years.....			10	40	6	12	1	0	2	4	.300	16	1	1	.944

WORLD SERIES RECORD

Holds record for highest batting average, series (.750), 1990; most consecutive hits, series (7), October 16 (3), 17 (4), 1990.
Shares record for most at-bats, inning (2), October 19, 1990, third inning.

Year Club	League	Pos.	G.	AB.	R.	H.	2B.	3B.	HR.	RBI.	B.A.	PO.	A.	E.	F.A.
1990—Cincinnati	Nat.	OF	4	12	6	9	4	1	0	2	.750	11	0	0	1.000

MELTON ANDREW HAWKINS
(Andy)

Born January 21, 1960, at Waco, Tex.
Height, 6.03. Weight, 223.
Throws and bats righthanded.

Pitched no-hit game against Chicago White Sox in which he completed eight innings but lost, 4-0, July 1, 1990.
Led Pacific Coast League in shutouts with 6 in 1982.
Led Texas League in complete games with 14 and tied for lead in games started by pitchers with 27 in 1981.
Led Northwest League in balks with 4 in 1978.

Year Club	League	G.	IP.	W.	L.	Pct.	H.	R.	ER.	SO.	BB.	ERA.
1978—Walla Walla	Northwest	14	102	8	3	.727	95	52	24	73	45	2.12
1979—Reno	California	27	188	8	13	.381	★232	143	★117	130	97	5.60
1980—Reno	California	26	171	13	10	.565	183	108	81	124	79	4.26
1981—Amarillo..	Texas	27	200	11	10	.524	★209	100	★93	144	48	4.19
1982—Hawaii	P. Coast	18	132⅔	9	7	.563	108	49	32	91	47	2.17
1982—San Diego	National	15	63⅔	2	5	.286	66	33	29	25	27	4.10
1983—Las Vegas..	P. Coast	14	85⅓	6	4	.600	110	67	61	50	27	6.43
1983—San Diego	National	21	119⅔	5	7	.417	106	50	39	59	48	2.93

Year Club	League	G.	IP.	W.	L.	Pct.	H.	R.	ER.	SO.	BB.	ERA.
1984—San Diego	National	36	146	8	9	.471	143	90	76	77	72	4.68
1985—San Diego	National	33	228⅔	18	8	.692	229	88	80	69	65	3.15
1986—San Diego	National	37	209⅓	10	8	.556	218	111	100	117	75	4.30
1987—San Diego†	National	24	117⅔	3	10	.231	131	71	66	51	49	5.05
1988—San Diego‡	National	33	217⅔	14	11	.560	196	88	81	91	76	3.35
1989—New York	American	34	208⅓	15	15	.500	238	*127	●111	98	76	4.80
1990—New York	American	28	157⅔	5	12	.294	156	101	94	74	82	5.37
National League Totals—7 Years		199	1102⅔	60	58	.508	1089	531	471	489	412	3.84
American League Totals—2 Years		62	366	20	27	.426	394	228	205	172	158	5.04
Major League Totals—9 Years		261	1468⅔	80	85	.485	1483	759	676	661	570	4.14

Selected by San Diego Padres' organization in 1st round (fifth player selected) of free-agent draft, June 6, 1978.
†On disabled list, July 29 to September 1, 1987.
‡Granted free agency, November 4, 1988; signed by New York Yankees, December 8, 1988.

CHAMPIONSHIP SERIES RECORD

Year Club	League	G.	IP.	W.	L.	Pct.	H.	R.	ER.	SO.	BB.	ERA.
1984—San Diego	National	3	3⅔	0	0	.000	0	0	0	1	2	0.00

WORLD SERIES RECORD

Year Club	League	G.	IP.	W.	L.	Pct.	H.	R.	ER.	SO.	BB.	ERA.
1984—San Diego	National	3	12	1	1	.500	4	1	1	4	6	0.75

CHARLES DEWAYNE HAYES
(Charlie)

Born May 29, 1965, at Hattiesburg, Miss.
Height, 6.00. Weight, 205.
Throws and bats righthanded.

Major League stolen bases: 1989 (3), 1990 (4). Total—7.
Led National League third basemen in assists with 324 and tied for lead in total chances with 465 in 1990.
Led Pacific Coast League in grounding into double plays with 19 in 1988.
Led Texas League third basemen in total chances with 334 in 1987.
Led Texas League third basemen in double plays with 27 in 1986.

Year Club	League	Pos.	G.	AB.	R.	H.	2B.	3B.	HR.	RBI.	B.A.	PO.	A.	E.	F.A.
1983—Great Falls†	Pion.	3B-OF	34	111	9	29	4	2	0	9	.261	13	32	9	.833
1984—Clinton	Midw.	3B	116	392	41	96	17	2	2	51	.245	68	216	28	.910
1985—Fresno	Calif.	3B	131	467	73	132	17	2	4	68	.283	*100	233	18	*.949
1986—Shreveport	Texas	3B	121	434	52	107	23	2	5	45	.247	89	*259	25	.933
1987—Shreveport	Texas	3B	128	487	66	148	33	3	14	75	.304	*100	*212	22	*.934
1988—Phoenix	P. C.	OF-3B	131	492	71	151	26	4	7	71	.307	206	100	23	.930
1988—San Francisco	Nat.	OF-3B	7	11	0	1	0	0	0	0	.091	5	0	0	1.000
1989—Phoenix	P. C.	3-O-1-S-2	61	229	25	65	15	1	7	27	.284	76	76	8	.950
1989—S.F.‡-Phi.	Nat.	3B	87	304	26	78	15	1	8	43	.257	51	174	22	.911
1989—Scranton/W.-B.	Int.	3B	7	27	4	11	3	1	1	3	.407	8	8	0	1.000
1990—Philadelphia	Nat.	3B-1B-2B	152	561	56	145	20	0	10	57	.258	151	329	20	.960
Major League Totals—3 Years			246	876	82	224	35	1	18	100	.256	207	503	42	.944

Selected by San Francisco Giants' organization in 4th round of free-agent draft, June 6, 1983.
†On disabled list, July 20, 1983 through remainder of season.
‡Traded with Pitchers Dennis Cook and Terry Mulholland to Philadelphia Phillies for Pitcher Steve Bedrosian and a player to be named later, June 18, 1989; San Francisco Giants' organization acquired Infielder Rick Parker to complete deal, August 7, 1989.

VON FRANCIS HAYES

Born August 31, 1958, at Stockton, Calif.
Height, 6.05. Weight, 186.
Throws right and bats lefthanded.
Attended St. Mary's College, Moraga, Calif.

Shares major league record for most home runs (2) and most total bases (8), inning, June 11, 1985, first inning.
Major League stolen bases: 1981 (8), 1982 (32), 1983 (20), 1984 (48), 1985 (21), 1986 (24), 1987 (16), 1988 (20), 1989 (28), 1990 (16). Total—233.
Hit three home runs in a game, August 29, 1989.
Led Midwest League third basemen in fielding percentage with .930 in 1980.
Named Midwest League Most Valuable Player, 1980.

Year Club	League	Pos.	G.	AB.	R.	H.	2B.	3B.	HR.	RBI.	B.A.	PO.	A.	E.	F.A.
1980—Waterloo	Midw.	3B-SS	134	492	105	*162	*33	3	15	90	*.329	94	291	30	.928
1981—Cleveland	Amer.	OF-3B	43	109	21	28	8	2	1	17	.257	30	4	3	.919
1981—Charleston	Int.	3B-1B	105	382	58	120	19	6	10	73	.314	96	222	19	.944
1982—Cleveland†	Amer.	OF-3B-1B	150	527	65	132	25	3	14	82	.250	323	17	6	.983
1983—Philadelphia‡	Nat.	OF	124	351	45	93	9	5	6	32	.265	165	7	5	.972
1984—Philadelphia	Nat.	OF	152	561	85	164	27	6	16	67	.292	341	2	4	.988
1985—Philadelphia	Nat.	OF	152	570	76	150	30	4	13	70	.263	368	9	6	.984
1986—Philadelphia	Nat.	1B-OF	158	610	●107	186	*46	2	19	98	.305	1247	100	13	.990
1987—Philadelphia	Nat.	1B-OF	158	556	84	154	36	5	21	84	.277	1216	80	13	.990
1988—Philadelphia§	Nat.	1B-OF-3B	104	367	43	100	28	2	6	45	.272	756	58	9	.989
1989—Philadelphia	Nat.	OF-1B-3B	154	540	93	140	27	2	26	78	.259	426	47	9	.981
1990—Philadelphia ¤	Nat.	OF	120	467	70	122	11	3	17	73	.261	272	8	6	.979

Year Club League	Pos.	G.	AB.	R.	H.	2B.	3B.	HR.	RBI.	B.A.	PO.	A.	E.	F.A.
1990—Clearwater .... Fla. St.	OF	2	6	0	1	1	0	0	0	.167	3	0	0	1.000
American League Totals—2 Years		193	636	86	160	33	5	15	99	.252	353	21	9	.977
National League Totals—8 Years		1131	4022	603	1109	217	29	124	547	.276	4791	311	65	.987
Major League Totals—10 Years		1324	4658	689	1269	250	34	139	646	.272	5144	332	74	.987

Selected by Cleveland Indians' organization in 7th round of free-agent draft, June 5, 1979.

†Traded to Philadelphia Phillies for Second Baseman Manny Trillo, Outfielder George Vukovich, Infielder Julio Franco, Pitcher Jay Baller and Catcher Jerry Willard, December 9, 1982.

‡On disabled list, March 27 to April 12, 1983.

§On disabled list, July 15 to September 2, 1988.

xOn disabled list, June 28 to July 13, 1990; included rehabilitation disability assignment to Clearwater, July 9 to July 13, 1990.

CHAMPIONSHIP SERIES RECORD

Year Club League	Pos.	G.	AB.	R.	H.	2B.	3B.	HR.	RBI.	B.A.	PO.	A.	E.	F.A.
1983—Philadelphia .... Nat.	PH-OF	2	2	0	0	0	0	0	0	.000	0	0	0	.000

WORLD SERIES RECORD

Year Club League	Pos.	G.	AB.	R.	H.	2B.	3B.	HR.	RBI.	B.A.	PO.	A.	E.	F.A.
1983—Philadelphia .... Nat.	PH-OF	4	3	0	0	0	0	0	0	.000	1	0	0	1.000

ALL-STAR GAME RECORD

Year League	Pos.	AB.	R.	H.	2B.	3B.	HR.	RBI.	B.A.	PO.	A.	E.	F.A.
1989—National	OF	1	0	1	0	0	0	1	1.000	0	0	0	.000

MICHAEL THOMAS HEATH
(Mike)

Born February 5, 1955, at Tampa, Fla.

Height, 5.11. Weight, 180.

Throws and bats righthanded.

Major League stolen bases: 1979 (1), 1980 (3), 1981 (3), 1982 (8), 1983 (3), 1984 (7), 1985 (7), 1986 (6), 1987 (1), 1988 (1), 1989 (7), 1990 (7). Total—54.

Led American League catchers in assists with 66 and double plays with 10 in 1989.

Led New York-Pennsylvania League shortstops in double plays with 42 in 1974.

Tied for Appalachian League lead in sacrifice hits with 7 in 1973.

Year Club League	Pos.	G.	AB.	R.	H.	2B.	3B.	HR.	RBI.	B.A.	PO.	A.	E.	F.A.
1973—Johnson City .... Appal.	SS-2B-3B	48	166	17	29	5	2	0	10	.175	83	137	24	.902
1974—Oneonta .... NYP	SS	65	234	51	66	6	3	3	34	.282	114	170	*27	.913
1975—Fort Lauderdale† .Fla. St.	SS	98	376	43	87	7	3	1	23	.231	184	256	31	.934
1976—Fort Lauderdale‡ .Fla. St.	SS-3B-C-P	80	267	28	71	16	3	2	30	.266	143	121	16	.943
1977—West Haven .... East.	C-3B	98	352	58	94	13	5	8	42	.267	492	72	16	.972
1978—West Haven .... East.	C-SS	66	217	43	64	16	1	8	27	.295	335	53	10	.975
1978—New York§ .... Amer.	C	33	92	6	21	3	1	0	8	.228	151	11	5	.970
1979—Tucson x .... P. C.	C	54	196	21	53	8	2	1	28	.270	183	24	7	.967
1979—Oakland .... Amer.	OF-C-3B	74	258	19	66	8	0	3	27	.256	167	32	5	.975
1980—Oakland .... Amer.	C-OF	92	305	27	74	10	2	1	33	.243	292	20	4	.987
1981—Oakland .... Amer.	*C-OF	84	301	26	71	7	1	8	30	.236	399	45	*10	.978
1982—Oakland y .... Amer.	C-OF-3B	101	318	43	77	18	4	3	39	.242	368	54	12	.972
1983—Oakland z .... Amer.	C-OF-3B	96	345	45	97	17	0	6	33	.281	362	47	11	.974
1984—Oakland .... Amer.	C-O-3-S	140	475	49	118	21	5	13	64	.248	495	56	8	.986
1985—Oakland a .... Amer.	C-OF-3B	138	436	71	109	18	6	13	55	.250	539	67	12	.981
1986—St. Louis b .... Nat.	C-OF	65	190	19	39	8	1	4	25	.205	260	30	10	.967
1986—Detroit .... Amer.	C-3B	30	98	11	26	3	0	4	11	.265	145	9	3	.981
1987—Detroit c .... Amer.	C-O-I	93	270	34	76	16	0	8	33	.281	384	43	5	.988
1988—Detroit .... Amer.	C-OF	86	219	24	54	7	2	5	18	.247	361	24	6	.985
1989—Detroit .... Amer.	C-3B-OF	122	396	38	104	16	2	10	43	.263	584	68	10	.985
1990—Detroit de .... Amer.	C-OF-SS	122	370	46	100	18	2	7	38	.270	588	54	13	.980
American League Totals—13 Years		1211	3883	439	993	162	25	81	432	.256	4835	530	104	.981
National League Totals—1 Year		65	190	19	39	8	1	4	25	.205	260	30	10	.967
Major League Totals—13 Years		1276	4073	458	1032	170	26	85	457	.253	5095	560	114	.980

Selected by New York Yankees' organization in 2nd round of free-agent draft, June 5, 1973.

†On Syracuse disabled list, August 2 to September 16, 1975.

‡On disabled list, June 29 to July 13, 1976.

§Traded with Pitchers Sparky Lyle, Larry McCall and Dave Rajsich, Shortstop Domingo Ramos and cash to Texas Rangers for Outfielders Juan Beniquez and Greg Jemison and Pitchers Mike Griffin, Paul Mirabella and Dave Righetti, November 10, 1978.

xTraded with Third Baseman Dave Chalk and cash to Oakland A's for Pitcher John Henry Johnson, June 15, 1979.

yOn disabled list, March 28 to April 20, 1982.

zOn disabled list, April 25 to May 25, 1983.

aTraded with Pitcher Tim Conroy to St. Louis Cardinals for Pitcher Joaquin Andujar, December 10, 1985.

bTraded to Detroit Tigers for Pitcher Ken Hill and a player to be named later, August 10, 1986; St. Louis Cardinals acquired First Baseman Mike Laga to complete deal, September 2, 1986.

cGranted free agency, November 9, 1987; re-signed by Tigers, December 1, 1987.

dOn disabled list, August 2 and August 3, 1990.

eGranted free agency, December 7, 1990.

DIVISION SERIES RECORD

Year Club League	Pos.	G.	AB.	R.	H.	2B.	3B.	HR.	RBI.	B.A.	PO.	A.	E.	F.A.
1981—Oakland .... Amer.	C	2	8	0	0	0	0	0	0	.000	9	1	0	1.000

CHAMPIONSHIP SERIES RECORD

Year Club	League	Pos.	G.	AB.	R.	H.	2B.	3B.	HR.	RBI.	B.A.	PO.	A.	E.	F.A.
1981—Oakland	Amer.	C-OF	3	6	1	2	0	0	0	0	.333	3	1	0	1.000
1987—Detroit	Amer.	C	3	7	1	2	0	0	1	2	.286	14	0	0	1.000
Championship Series Totals—2 Years			6	13	2	4	0	0	1	2	.308	17	1	0	1.000

WORLD SERIES RECORD

Year Club	League	Pos.	G.	AB.	R.	H.	2B.	3B.	HR.	RBI.	B.A.	PO.	A.	E.	F.A.
1978—New York	Amer.	C	1	0	0	0	0	0	0	0	.000	0	0	0	.000

PITCHING RECORD

Year Club	League	G.	IP.	W.	L.	Pct.	H.	R.	ER.	SO.	BB.	ERA.
1976—Fort Lauderdale	Florida St.	1	1	0	0	.000	1	0	0	1	0	0.00

NEAL HEATON

Born March 3, 1960, at Jamaica, N. Y.
Height, 6.01. Weight, 195.
Throws and bats lefthanded.
Attended University of Miami, Coral Gables, Fla.

Major League saves: 1983 (7), 1986 (1), 1988 (2). Total—10.
Named lefthanded pitcher on THE SPORTING NEWS College Baseball All-America Team, 1981.

Year Club	League	G.	IP.	W.	L.	Pct.	H.	R.	ER.	SO.	BB.	ERA.
1981—Chattanooga	Southern	11	77	4	4	.500	61	42	34	50	27	3.97
1982—Charleston	Int'national	29	172⅔	10	5	.667	194	97	77	105	66	4.01
1982—Cleveland	American	8	31	0	2	.000	32	21	18	14	16	5.23
1983—Cleveland	American	39	149⅓	11	7	.611	157	79	69	75	44	4.16
1984—Cleveland	American	38	198⅔	12	15	.444	231	128	115	75	75	5.21
1985—Cleveland	American	36	207⅔	9	17	.346	244	119	113	82	80	4.90
1986—Cleveland†-Minnesota‡	American	33	198⅔	7	15	.318	201	102	90	90	81	4.08
1987—Montreal	National	32	193⅓	13	10	.565	207	103	97	105	37	4.52
1988—Montreal§x	National	32	97⅓	3	10	.231	98	54	54	43	43	4.99
1989—Pittsburgh y	National	42	147⅓	6	7	.462	127	55	50	67	55	3.05
1990—Pittsburgh	National	30	146	12	9	.571	143	66	56	68	38	3.45
American League Totals—5 Years		154	785⅓	39	56	.411	865	449	405	336	296	4.64
National League Totals—4 Years		136	584	34	36	.486	575	278	257	283	173	3.96
Major League Totals—9 Years		290	1369⅓	73	92	.442	1440	727	662	619	469	4.35

Selected by New York Mets' organization in 1st round (first player selected) of free-agent draft, January 9, 1979.
Selected by Cleveland Indians' organization in 2nd round of free-agent draft, June 8, 1981.
†Traded to Minnesota Twins for Pitcher John Butcher, June 20, 1986.
‡Traded with Pitchers Al Cardwood and Yorkis Perez and Catcher Jeff Reed to Montreal Expos for Pitcher Jeff Reardon and Catcher Tom Nieto, February 3, 1987.
§On disabled list, April 8 to April 29, 1988.
xTraded to Pittsburgh Pirates for a player to be named later, March 28, 1989; Montreal Expos acquired Pitcher Brett Gideon to complete deal, March 30, 1989.
yGranted free agency, November 13, 1989; re-signed by Pirates, December 6, 1989.

ALL-STAR GAME RECORD

Member of National League All-Star Team in 1990; did not play.

DANIEL WILLIAM HEEP
(Danny)

Born July 3, 1957, at San Antonio, Tex.
Height, 5.11. Weight, 177.
Throws and bats lefthanded.
Received degree in teaching and political science from St. Mary's University, San Antonio, Tex.

Major League stolen bases: 1983 (3), 1984 (3), 1985 (2), 1986 (1), 1987 (1), 1988 (2). Total—12.
Led Southern League in total bases with 274 in 1979.
Named Southern League co-Most Valuable Player, 1979.

Year Club	League	Pos.	G.	AB.	R.	H.	2B.	3B.	HR.	RBI.	B.A.	PO.	A.	E.	F.A.
1978—Daytona Beach	Fla. St.	OF	66	212	29	72	18	2	2	24	.340	89	9	2	.980
1979—Columbus	South.	OF	138	523	103	*171	30	5	21	84	.327	211	12	6	.974
1979—Houston	Nat.	OF	14	14	0	2	0	0	0	2	.143	7	0	0	1.000
1980—Tucson	P. C.	1B-OF	96	376	63	129	28	5	17	69	*.343	810	53	8	.991
1980—Houston	Nat.	1B	33	87	6	24	8	0	0	6	.276	188	8	2	.990
1981—Houston†	Nat.	1B-OF	33	96	6	24	3	0	0	11	.250	198	9	2	.990
1981—Tuscon	P. C.	1B-OF	78	285	55	96	23	5	11	60	.337	635	44	12	.983
1982—Houston‡	Nat.	OF-1B	85	198	16	47	14	1	4	22	.237	192	6	1	.995
1983—New York	Nat.	OF-1B	115	253	30	64	12	0	8	21	.253	159	11	0	1.000
1984—New York	Nat.	OF-1B	99	199	36	46	9	2	1	12	.231	137	7	4	.973
1985—New York	Nat.	OF-1B	95	271	26	76	17	0	7	42	.280	154	5	4	.975
1986—New York§	Nat.	OF	86	195	24	55	8	2	5	33	.282	83	2	1	.988
1987—San Antonio	Texas	OF	11	47	6	16	1	0	2	9	.340	9	1	0	1.000
1987—Los Angeles	Nat.	OF-1B	60	98	7	16	4	0	0	9	.163	52	6	1	.983
1988—Los Angeles x	Nat.	OF-1B-P	95	149	14	36	2	0	0	11	.242	129	10	3	.979

Year	Club	League	Pos.	G.	AB.	R.	H.	2B.	3B.	HR.	RBI.	B.A.	PO.	A.	E.	F.A.
1989—Boston		Amer.	OF-1B	113	320	36	96	17	0	5	49	.300	216	14	3	.987
1990—Boston yz		Amer.	OF-1B-P	41	69	3	12	1	1	0	8	.174	42	4	1	.979
National League Totals—10 Years				715	1560	165	390	77	5	25	169	.250	1299	64	18	.987
American League Totals—2 Years				154	389	39	108	18	1	5	57	.278	258	18	4	.986
Major League Totals—12 Years				869	1949	204	498	95	6	30	226	.256	1557	82	22	.987

Selected by Houston Astros' organization in 2nd round of free-agent draft, June 6, 1978.
†On disabled list, April 19 to May 4, 1981.
‡Traded to New York Mets for Pitcher Mike Scott, December 10, 1982.
§Granted free agency, November 12, 1986; signed by Los Angeles Dodgers' organization, June 12, 1987.
xReleased, December 21, 1988; signed by Boston Red Sox, February 6, 1989.
yOn disabled list, June 28 to September 2, 1990.
zGranted free agency, November 5, 1990.

CHAMPIONSHIP SERIES RECORD

Year	Club	League	Pos.	G.	AB.	R.	H.	2B.	3B.	HR.	RBI.	B.A.	PO.	A.	E.	F.A.
1980—Houston		Nat.	PH	1	1	0	0	0	0	0	0	.000	0	0	0	.000
1986—New York		Nat.	PH-OF	5	4	0	1	0	0	0	1	.250	0	0	0	.000
1988—Los Angeles		Nat.	PH	3	1	0	0	0	0	0	0	.000	0	0	0	.000
1990—Boston		Amer.	PH	2	2	0	0	0	0	0	0	.000	0	0	0	.000
Championship Series Totals—4 Years				11	8	0	1	0	0	0	1	.125	0	0	0	.000

WORLD SERIES TOTALS

Year	Club	League	Pos.	G.	AB.	R.	H.	2B.	3B.	HR.	RBI.	B.A.	PO.	A.	E.	F.A.
1986—New York		Nat.	PH-O-DH	5	11	0	1	0	0	0	2	.091	1	0	0	1.000
1988—Los Angeles		Nat.	PH-O-DH	3	8	0	2	1	0	0	0	.250	0	0	0	.000
World Series Totals—2 Years				8	19	0	3	1	0	0	2	.158	1	0	0	1.000

PITCHING RECORD

Year	Club	League	G.	IP.	W.	L.	Pct.	H.	R.	ER.	SO.	BB.	ERA.
1988—Los Angeles		National	1	2	0	0	.000	2	2	2	0	0	9.00
1990—Boston		American	1	1	0	0	.000	4	1	1	0	0	9.00
Major League Totals—2 Years			2	3	0	0	.000	6	3	3	0	0	9.00

SCOTT MATHEW HEMOND

Born November 18, 1965, at Taunton, Mass.
Height, 6.00. Weight, 205.
Throws and bats righthanded.
Attended University of South Florida, Tampa, Fla.
Led Southern League third basemen in assists with 299 and total chances with 427 in 1988.
Named catcher on THE SPORTING NEWS College Baseball All-America Team, 1986.

Year	Club	League	Pos.	G.	AB.	R.	H.	2B.	3B.	HR.	RBI.	B.A.	PO.	A.	E.	F.A.
1986—Madison		Midw.	C	22	85	9	26	2	0	2	13	.306	121	11	2	.985
1987—Madison		Midw.	C-OF	90	343	60	99	21	4	8	52	.289	408	53	16	.966
1987—Huntsville		South.	C-3B	33	110	10	20	3	1	1	8	.182	161	32	6	.970
1988—Huntsville		South.	3B-C	133	482	51	106	22	4	9	53	.220	93	302	38	.912
1989—Huntsville		South.	3B-C	132	490	89	130	26	6	5	62	.265	272	198	31	.938
1989—Oakland		Amer.	PR	4	0	2	0	0	0	0	0	.000	0	0	0	.000
1990—Tacoma†		P. C.	2-C-3-S	72	218	32	53	11	0	8	35	.243	138	177	12	.963
1990—Oakland		Amer.	3B-2B	7	13	0	2	0	0	0	1	.154	2	5	0	1.000
Major League Totals—2 Years				11	13	2	2	0	0	0	1	.154	2	5	0	1.000

Selected by Kansas City Royals' organization in 5th round of free-agent draft, June 6, 1983.
Selected by Oakland Athletics' organization in 1st round (12th player selected) of free-agent draft, June 2, 1986.
†On disabled list, May 18 to July 6, 1990.

DAVID LEE HENDERSON
(Dave)

Born July 21, 1958, at Dos Palos, Calif.
Height, 6.02. Weight, 210.
Throws and bats righthanded.
Nephew of Joe Henderson, pitcher with Chicago
White Sox and Cincinnati Reds, 1974, 1976 and 1977.
Major League stolen bases: 1981 (2), 1982 (2), 1983 (9), 1984 (5), 1985 (6), 1986 (2), 1987 (3), 1988 (2), 1989 (8), 1990 (3). Total—42.

Year	Club	League	Pos.	G.	AB.	R.	H.	2B.	3B.	HR.	RBI.	B.A.	PO.	A.	E.	F.A.
1977—Bellingham		N'west	OF	65	251	47	79	14	2	●16	63	.315	136	5	★11	.928
1978—Stockton		Calif.	OF	117	409	48	95	16	4	7	63	.232	204	12	14	.939
1979—San Jose		Calif.	OF	136	507	103	152	23	3	27	99	.300	264	18	4	.986
1980—Spokane†		P. C.	OF	109	341	48	95	26	1	7	50	.279	258	9	7	.974
1981—Seattle		Amer.	OF	59	126	17	21	3	0	6	13	.167	105	4	0	1.000
1981—Spokane		P. C.	OF	80	272	47	76	23	1	12	50	.279	146	7	3	.981
1982—Seattle‡		Amer.	OF	104	324	47	82	17	1	14	48	.253	249	11	4	.985
1983—Seattle		Amer.	OF	137	484	50	130	24	5	17	55	.269	304	17	6	.982
1984—Seattle§		Amer.	OF	112	350	42	98	23	0	14	43	.280	242	11	3	.988

Year	Club	League	Pos.	G.	AB.	R.	H.	2B.	3B.	HR.	RBI.	B.A.	PO.	A.	E.	F.A.
1985—Seattle....................	Amer.	OF	139	502	70	121	28	2	14	68	.241	335	8	5	.986
1986—Sea. x-Bos.	Amer.	OF	139	388	59	103	22	4	15	47	.265	231	11	5	.980
1987—Boston y.................	Amer.	OF	75	184	30	43	10	0	8	25	.234	114	0	5	.958
1987—San Francisco z ...	Nat.	OF	15	21	2	5	2	0	0	1	.238	10	1	0	1.000
1988—Oakland a	Amer.	OF	146	507	100	154	38	1	24	94	.304	382	5	7	.982
1989—Oakland...............	Amer.	OF	152	579	77	145	24	3	15	80	.250	385	5	9	.977
1990—Oakland bc...........	Amer.	OF	127	450	65	122	28	0	20	63	.271	319	5	4	.988
American League Totals—10 Years				1190	3894	557	1019	217	16	147	536	.262	2666	77	48	.983
National League Totals—1 Year				15	21	2	5	2	0	0	1	.238	10	1	0	1.000
Major League Totals—10 Years				1205	3915	559	1024	219	16	147	537	.262	2676	78	48	.983

Selected by Seattle Mariners' organization in 1st round (26th player selected) of free-agent draft, June 7, 1977.

†On disabled list, June 26 to July 22, 1980.

‡On disabled list, May 3 to May 18, 1982.

§On disabled list, August 10 to August 29, 1984.

xTraded with Infielder Spike Owen to Boston Red Sox for Infielder Rey Quinones, a player to be named later and cash, August 19, 1986; as part of deal, Seattle Mariners claimed Pitchers Mike Brown and Mike Trujillo on waivers from Boston, August 22, 1986. Seattle acquired Outfielder John Christensen to complete deal, September 25, 1986.

yTraded to San Francisco Giants for a player to be named later, September 1, 1987; Boston Red Sox acquired Outfielder Randy Kutcher to complete deal, December 9, 1987.

zGranted free agency, November 9, 1987; signed by Oakland A's, December 21, 1987.

aGranted free agency, November 4, 1988; re-signed by Athletics, December 1, 1988.

bOn disabled list, August 21 to September 21, 1990.

cGranted free agency, December 7, 1990; re-signed by Athletics, December 11, 1990.

CHAMPIONSHIP SERIES RECORD

Established Championship Series record for most strikeouts, four-game Series (7), 1988.

Year	Club	League	Pos.	G.	AB.	R.	H.	2B.	3B.	HR.	RBI.	B.A.	PO.	A.	E.	F.A.
1986—Boston....................	Amer.	OF	5	9	3	1	0	0	1	4	.111	11	0	0	1.000
1988—Oakland.................	Amer.	OF	4	16	2	6	1	0	1	4	.375	11	0	2	.846
1989—Oakland.................	Amer.	OF	5	19	4	5	3	0	1	1	.263	22	0	0	1.000
1990—Oakland.................	Amer.	OF	2	6	0	1	0	0	0	1	.167	7	0	0	1.000
Championship Series Totals—4 Years				16	50	9	13	4	0	3	10	.260	51	0	2	.962

WORLD SERIES RECORD

Shares World Series record for most home runs, two consecutive innings (2), October 27, 1989, fourth and fifth innings.

Year	Club	League	Pos.	G.	AB.	R.	H.	2B.	3B.	HR.	RBI.	B.A.	PO.	A.	E.	F.A.
1986—Boston....................	Amer.	OF	7	25	6	10	1	1	2	5	.400	22	0	0	1.000
1988—Oakland.................	Amer.	OF	5	20	1	6	2	0	1	1	.300	12	0	0	1.000
1989—Oakland.................	Amer.	OF	4	13	6	4	2	0	2	4	.308	13	0	0	1.000
1990—Oakland.................	Amer.	PH-OF	4	13	2	3	1	0	0	0	.231	7	0	0	1.000
World Series Totals—4 Years				20	71	15	23	6	1	4	10	.324	54	0	0	1.000

RICKEY HENLEY HENDERSON

Born December 25, 1958, at Chicago, Ill.
Height, 5.10. Weight, 195.
Throws left and bats righthanded.

Holds major league records for most home runs as leadoff batter, lifetime (45); most years leading league in stolen bases (10); most times caught stealing, season (42), 1982.

Holds modern major league record for most stolen bases, season (130), 1982.

Holds American League records for most home runs as leadoff batter, season (9), 1986; most stolen bases, lifetime (936); most years (10) and most consecutive years (7), 50 or more stolen bases; most times caught stealing, lifetime (211).

Shares American League records for most years leading league, stolen bases (9); most stolen bases, two consecutive games (7), July 3, 4, 1983.

Major League stolen bases: 1979 (33), 1980 (100), 1981 (56), 1982 (130), 1983 (108), 1984 (66), 1985 (80), 1986 (87), 1987 (41), 1988 (93), 1989 (77), 1990 (65). Total—936.

Led American League in bases on balls received with 116 in 1982, 103 in 1983 and 126 in 1989.

Led American League in stolen bases with 100 in 1980, 56 in 1981, 130 in 1982, 108 in 1983, 66 in 1984, 80 in 1985, 87 in 1986, 93 in 1988, 77 in 1989 and 65 in 1990.

Led American League in caught stealing with 26 in 1980, 22 in 1981, 42 in 1982, 19 in 1983 and tied for lead with 18 in 1986.

Led American League outfielders in total chances with 341 in 1981.

Tied for American League lead in double plays by outfielders with 5 in 1988.

Led Eastern League in stolen bases with 81 and caught stealing with 28 in 1978.

Led California League in stolen bases with 95 and caught stealing with 22 in 1977.

Led Eastern League outfielders in double plays with 4 in 1978.

Named American League Most Valuable Player by Baseball Writers' Association of America, 1990.

Won THE SPORTING NEWS Golden Shoe Award, 1983.

Won THE SPORTING NEWS Silver Shoe Award, 1982.

Named outfielder on THE SPORTING NEWS American League All-Star Team, 1981, 1985 and 1990.

Named outfielder on THE SPORTING NEWS American League All-Star fielding team, 1981.

Named outfielder on THE SPORTING NEWS American League Silver Slugger team, 1981, 1985 and 1990.

Year	Club	League	Pos.	G.	AB.	R.	H.	2B.	3B.	HR.	RBI.	B.A.	PO.	A.	E.	F.A.
1976—Boise	N'west.	OF	46	140	34	47	13	2	3	23	.336	99	3	*12	.895
1977—Modesto.................	Calif.	OF	134	481	120	166	18	4	11	69	.345	278	15	*20	.936
1978—Jersey City	East.	OF	133	455	81	141	14	4	0	34	.310	305	●15	7	.979

Year Club League	Pos.	G.	AB.	R.	H.	2B.	3B.	HR.	RBI.	B.A.	PO.	A.	E.	F.A.
1979—Ogden .... P. C.	OF	71	259	66	80	11	8	3	26	.309	149	6	6	.963
1979—Oakland.................. Amer.	OF	89	351	49	96	13	3	1	26	.274	215	5	6	.973
1980—Oakland.................. Amer.	OF	158	591	111	179	22	4	9	53	.303	407	15	7	.984
1981—Oakland.................. Amer.	OF	108	423	*89	*135	18	7	6	35	.319	*327	7	7	.979
1982—Oakland.................. Amer.	OF	149	536	119	143	24	4	10	51	.267	379	2	9	.977
1983—Oakland.................. Amer.	OF	145	513	105	150	25	7	9	48	.292	349	9	3	.992
1984—Oakland†............... Amer.	OF	142	502	113	147	27	4	16	58	.293	341	7	11	.969
1985—Fort Lauderdale‡ Fla. St.	OF	3	6	5	1	0	1	0	3	.167	6	0	0	1.000
1985—New York............ Amer.	OF	143	547	*146	172	28	5	24	72	.314	439	7	9	.980
1986—New York............ Amer.	OF	153	608	*130	160	31	5	28	74	.263	426	4	6	.986
1987—New York§........... Amer.	OF	95	358	78	104	17	3	17	37	.291	189	3	4	.980
1988—New York............ Amer.	OF	140	554	118	169	30	2	6	50	.305	320	7	12	.965
1989—N.Y.x-Oak.y.......... Amer.	OF	150	541	●113	148	26	3	12	57	.274	335	6	4	.988
1990—Oakland.................. Amer.	OF	136	489	*119	159	33	3	28	61	.325	289	5	5	.983
Major League Totals—12 Years.............		1608	6013	1290	1762	294	50	166	622	.293	4016	77	83	.980

Selected by Oakland A's organization in 4th round of free-agent draft, June 8, 1976.

†Traded with Pitcher Bert Bradley and cash to New York Yankees for Outfielder Stan Javier and Pitchers Jay Howell, Jose Rijo, Eric Plunk and Tim Birtsas, December 5, 1984.

‡On New York disabled list, March 30 to April 22, 1985; included rehabilitation disability assignment to Fort Lauderdale, April 19 to April 22, 1985.

§On disabled list, June 5 to June 29 and July 26 to September 1, 1987.

xTraded to Oakland Athletics for Pitchers Greg Cadaret and Eric Plunk and Outfielder Luis Polonia, June 21, 1989.

yGranted free agency, November 13, 1989; re-signed by Athletics, November 28, 1989.

DIVISION SERIES RECORD

Year Club League	Pos.	G.	AB.	R.	H.	2B.	3B.	HR.	RBI.	B.A.	PO.	A.	E.	F.A.
1981—Oakland.................. Amer.	OF	3	11	3	2	0	0	0	0	.182	8	0	0	1.000

CHAMPIONSHIP SERIES RECORD

Holds records for most stolen bases, lifetime (12), series (8), 1989 and game (4), October 4, 1989.

Shares records for most at-bats, hits and singles, inning (2), October 6, 1990, ninth inning; most runs, series (8), 1989; most stolen bases, inning (2), October 4, 1989, fourth and seventh innings.

Shares American League record for most bases on balls, series (7), 1989.

Year Club League	Pos.	G.	AB.	R.	H.	2B.	3B.	HR.	RBI.	B.A.	PO.	A.	E.	F.A.
1981—Oakland.................. Amer.	OF	3	11	0	4	2	1	0	1	.364	6	0	1	.857
1989—Oakland.................. Amer.	OF	5	15	8	6	1	1	2	5	.400	13	0	1	.929
1990—Oakland.................. Amer.	OF	4	17	1	5	0	0	0	3	.294	10	0	0	1.000
Championship Series Totals—3 Years.....		12	43	9	15	3	2	2	9	.349	29	0	2	.935

WORLD SERIES RECORD

Shares World Series record for most at-bats, nine-inning game (6), October 28, 1989.

Year Club League	Pos.	G.	AB.	R.	H.	2B.	3B.	HR.	RBI.	B.A.	PO.	A.	E.	F.A.
1989—Oakland.................. Amer.	OF	4	19	4	9	1	2	1	3	.474	9	0	0	1.000
1990—Oakland.................. Amer.	OF	4	15	2	5	2	0	1	1	.333	12	1	0	1.000
World Series Totals—2 Years		8	34	6	14	3	2	2	4	.412	21	1	0	1.000

ALL-STAR GAME RECORD

Shares All-Star Game record for most singles, game (3), July 13, 1982.

Year League	Pos.	AB.	R.	H.	2B.	3B.	HR.	RBI.	B.A.	PO.	A.	E.	F.A.
1980—American	OF	1	0	0	0	0	0	0	.000	0	0	0	.000
1982—American	OF	4	1	3	0	0	0	0	.750	3	0	1	.750
1983—American	OF	1	0	0	0	0	0	1	.000	0	0	0	.000
1984—American	OF	2	0	0	0	0	0	0	.000	0	0	0	.000
1985—American	OF	3	1	1	0	0	0	0	.333	1	0	0	1.000
1986—American	OF	3	0	0	0	0	0	0	.000	2	0	0	1.000
1987—American	OF	3	0	1	0	0	0	0	.333	0	0	0	.000
1988—American	OF	2	0	1	0	0	0	0	.500	1	0	0	1.000
1990—American	OF	3	0	0	0	0	0	0	.000	2	0	0	1.000
All-Star Game Totals—9 Years...................		22	2	6	0	0	0	1	.273	9	0	1	.900

THOMAS ANTHONY HENKE
Name pronounced HEN-key.

(Tom)

Born December 21, 1957, at Kansas City, Mo.
Height, 6.05. Weight, 225.
Throws and bats righthanded.
Attended East Central College, Union, Mo.

Major League saves: 1983 (1), 1984 (2), 1985 (13), 1986 (27), 1987 (34), 1988 (25), 1989 (20), 1990 (32). Total—154.
Led American League in games finished in relief with 62 and saves with 34 in 1987.
Tied for International League lead in saves with 18 in 1985.
Named International League Pitcher of the Year, 1985.

Year Club League	G.	IP.	W.	L.	Pct.	H.	R.	ER.	SO.	BB.	ERA.
1980—Sarasota Rangers......................... Gulf Coast	8	38	3	3	.500	33	11	4	34	12	0.95
1980—Asheville...................... S. Atlantic	5	23	0	2	.000	25	21	20	19	20	7.83
1981—Asheville...................... S. Atlantic	28	92	8	6	.571	77	36	30	67	35	2.93

Year Club	League	G.	IP.	W.	L.	Pct.	H.	R.	ER.	SO.	BB.	ERA.
1981—Tulsa	Texas	15	32	4	3	.571	31	16	14	37	14	3.94
1982—Tulsa	Texas	*52	87⅔	3	6	.333	69	35	26	100	40	2.67
1982—Texas	American	8	15⅔	1	0	1.000	14	2	2	9	8	1.15
1983—Oklahoma City	Am. Assoc.	47	77⅔	9	6	.600	71	33	26	90	33	3.01
1983—Texas	American	8	16	1	0	1.000	16	6	6	17	4	3.38
1984—Texas	American	25	28⅓	1	1	.500	36	21	20	25	20	6.35
1984—Oklahoma City†	Am. Assoc.	39	64⅔	6	2	.750	59	21	19	65	25	2.64
1985—Syracuse	Int'national	39	51⅓	2	1	.667	13	5	5	60	18	0.88
1985—Toronto	American	28	40	3	3	.500	29	12	9	42	8	2.03
1986—Toronto	American	63	91⅓	9	5	.643	63	39	34	118	32	3.35
1987—Toronto	American	72	94	0	6	.000	62	27	26	128	25	2.49
1988—Toronto	American	52	68	4	4	.500	60	23	22	66	24	2.91
1989—Toronto	American	64	89	8	3	.727	66	20	19	116	25	1.92
1990—Toronto	American	61	74⅔	2	4	.333	58	18	18	75	19	2.17
Major League Totals—9 Years		381	517	29	26	.527	404	168	156	596	165	2.72

Selected by Seattle Mariners' organization in 20th round of free-agent draft, June 5, 1979.
Selected by Chicago Cubs' organization in secondary phase of free-agent draft, January 8, 1980.
Selected by Texas Rangers' organization in secondary phase of free-agent draft, June 3, 1980.
†Selected by Toronto Blue Jays' organization in player compensation pool draft, January 24, 1985. (Toronto received compensation for Texas Rangers' signing of free agent Designated Hitter Cliff Johnson, a Type A player, December 5, 1984.

CHAMPIONSHIP SERIES RECORD

Shares American League Championship Series record for most games won, series (2), 1985.

Year Club	League	G.	IP.	W.	L.	Pct.	H.	R.	ER.	SO.	BB.	ERA.
1985—Toronto	American	3	6⅓	2	0	1.000	5	3	3	4	4	4.26
1989—Toronto	American	3	2⅔	0	0	.000	0	0	0	3	0	0.00
Championship Series Totals—2 Years		6	9	2	0	1.000	5	3	3	7	4	3.00

ALL-STAR GAME RECORD

Year League	IP.	W.	L.	Pct.	H.	R.	ER.	SO.	BB.	ERA.
1987—American	2⅔	0	0	.000	2	0	0	1	0	0.00

MICHAEL ALAN HENNEMAN
(Mike)

Born December 11, 1961, at St. Charles, Mo.
Height, 6.04. Weight, 195.
Throws and bats righthanded.
Attended Oklahoma State University, Stillwater, Okla.

Major League saves: 1987 (7), 1988 (22), 1989 (8), 1990 (22). Total—59.
Led American League in intentional bases on balls issued with 15 in 1989 and tied for lead with 10 in 1988.
Named American League Rookie Pitcher of the Year by THE SPORTING NEWS, 1987.

Year Club	League	G.	IP.	W.	L.	Pct.	H.	R.	ER.	SO.	BB.	ERA.
1984—Birmingham	Southern	29	59⅓	4	2	.667	48	22	16	39	33	2.43
1985—Birmingham	Southern	46	70⅓	3	5	.375	88	50	45	40	28	5.76
1986—Nashville	Am. Assoc.	31	58	2	5	.286	57	27	19	39	23	2.95
1987—Toledo	Int'national	11	18⅓	1	1	.500	5	3	3	19	3	1.47
1987—Detroit†	American	55	96⅔	11	3	.786	86	36	32	75	30	2.98
1988—Detroit‡	American	65	91⅓	9	6	.600	72	23	19	58	24	1.87
1989—Detroit§	American	60	90	11	4	.733	84	46	37	69	51	3.70
1990—Detroit	American	69	94⅓	8	6	.571	90	36	32	50	33	3.05
Major League Totals—4 Years		249	372⅓	39	19	.672	332	141	120	252	138	2.90

Selected by Toronto Blue Jays' organization in 27th round of free-agent draft, June 7, 1982.
Selected by Philadelphia Phillies' organization in secondary phase of free-agent draft, June 6, 1983.
Selected by Detroit Tigers' organization in 4th round of free-agent draft, June 4, 1984.
†Struck out in only at-bat.
‡On disabled list, May 22 to June 6, 1988.
§On disabled list, April 24 to May 15, 1989.

CHAMPIONSHIP SERIES RECORD

Year Club	League	G.	IP.	W.	L.	Pct.	H.	R.	ER.	SO.	BB.	ERA.
1987—Detroit	American	3	5	1	0	1.000	6	6	6	3	6	10.80

ALL-STAR GAME RECORD

Member of American League All-Star Team in 1989; did not play.

RANDALL PHILIP HENNIS

Born December 16, 1965, at Clearlake, Calif.
Height, 6.06. Weight, 220.
Throws and bats righthanded.
Attended UCLA, Los Angeles, Calif.

Tied for Pacific Coast League lead in games started by pitchers with 28 in 1990.

Year Club	League	G.	IP.	W.	L.	Pct.	H.	R.	ER.	SO.	BB.	ERA.
1987—Auburn	NYP	13	72⅔	3	•9	.250	67	41	37	40	33	4.58
1988—Osceola	Florida St.	14	82⅔	7	3	.700	64	34	22	48	28	2.40

Year Club	League	G.	IP.	W.	L.	Pct.	H.	R.	ER.	SO.	BB.	ERA.
1989—Columbus	Southern	28	171	9	9	.500	151	75	68	101	78	3.58
1990—Tucson	P. Coast	28	159⅓	10	8	.556	153	87	78	101	92	4.41
1990—Houston	National	3	9⅔	0	0	.000	1	0	0	4	3	0.00
Major League Totals—1 Year		3	9⅔	0	0	.000	1	0	0	4	3	0.00

Selected by New York Yankees' organization in 4th round of free-agent draft, June 4, 1984.
Selected by Houston Astros' organization in 2nd round of free-agent draft, June 2, 1987.

DWAYNE ALLEN HENRY

Born February 16, 1962, at Elkton, Md.
Height, 6.03. Weight, 205.
Throws and bats righthanded.

Major League saves: 1985 (3), 1988 (1), 1989 (1). Total—5.

Year Club	League	G.	IP.	W.	L.	Pct.	H.	R.	ER.	SO.	BB.	ERA.
1980—Sarasota Rangers	Gulf Coast	11	54	5	1	.833	36	23	16	47	28	2.67
1981—Asheville	S. Atlantic	25	134	8	7	.533	120	81	66	86	58	4.43
1982—Burlington†	Midwest	4	18⅔	2	0	1.000	6	0	0	25	6	0.00
1983—Tulsa‡	Texas	9	14	0	0	.000	16	14	9	14	19	5.79
1983—Sarasota Rangers	Gulf Coast	3	9	0	0	.000	10	6	4	11	1	4.00
1984—Tulsa	Texas	33	85	5	8	.385	65	42	32	79	60	3.39
1984—Texas	American	3	4⅓	0	1	.000	5	4	4	2	7	8.31
1985—Tulsa	Texas	34	81⅓	7	6	.538	51	32	24	97	44	2.66
1985—Texas	American	16	21	2	2	.500	16	7	6	20	7	2.57
1986—Texas§	American	19	19⅓	1	0	1.000	14	11	10	17	22	4.66
1986—Oklahoma City	Am. Assoc.	28	44⅓	2	1	.667	51	30	29	41	27	5.89
1987—Oklahoma City	Am. Assoc.	30	69	4	4	.500	66	39	38	55	50	4.96
1987—Texas	American	5	10	0	0	.000	12	10	10	7	9	9.00
1988—Oklahoma City	Am. Assoc.	46	75⅔	5	5	.500	57	51	47	98	54	5.59
1988—Texas x	American	11	10⅓	0	1	.000	15	10	10	10	9	8.71
1989—Richmond	Int'national	41	84⅔	11	5	.688	43	28	23	101	61	2.44
1989—Atlanta	National	12	12⅔	0	2	.000	12	6	6	16	5	4.26
1990—Atlanta	National	34	38⅓	2	2	.500	41	26	24	34	25	5.63
1990—Richmond y	Int'national	13	27	1	1	.500	12	7	7	36	16	2.33
American League Totals—5 Years		54	65	3	4	.429	62	42	40	56	54	5.54
National League Totals—2 Years		46	51	2	4	.333	53	32	30	50	30	5.29
Major League Totals—7 Years		100	116	5	8	.385	115	74	70	106	84	5.43

Selected by Texas Rangers' organization in 2nd round of free-agent draft, June 3, 1980.
†On disabled list, May 4, 1982 through remainder of season.
‡On disabled list, April 8 to July 9, 1983.
§On disabled list, May 31 to July 8, 1986; included rehabilitation disability assignment to Oklahoma City, June 18 to July 8, 1986.
xTraded to Atlanta Braves for Pitcher David Miller and cash, March 30, 1989.
yReleased, November 13, 1990.

FLOYD BLUFORD HENRY III
(Butch)

Born October 7, 1968, at El Paso, Tex.
Height, 6.01. Weight, 195.
Throws and bats lefthanded.

Year Club	League	G.	IP.	W.	L.	Pct.	H.	R.	ER.	SO.	BB.	ERA.
1987—Billings	Pioneer	9	35	4	0	1.000	37	21	18	38	12	4.63
1988—Cedar Rapids	Midwest	27	187	16	2	*.889	144	59	47	163	56	2.26
1989—Chattanooga†	Southern	7	26⅓	1	3	.250	22	12	10	19	12	3.42
1990—Chattanooga‡	Southern	24	143⅓	8	8	.500	151	74	67	95	58	4.21

Selected by Cincinnati Reds' organization in 15th round of free-agent draft, June 2, 1987.
†On disabled list, April 28, 1989 through remainder of season.
‡Traded with Catcher Terry McGriff and Pitcher Keith Kaiser, September 7, 1990, completing deal in which Houston Astros traded Second Baseman Bill Doran to Cincinnati Reds for three players to be named later, August 30, 1990.

PATRICK GEORGE HENTGEN
(Pat)

Born November 13, 1968, at Detroit, Mich.
Height, 6.02. Weight, 200.
Throws and bats righthanded.

Led Florida State League pitchers in games started with 30 in 1988.
Led South Atlantic League pitchers in games started with 31 in 1987.

Year Club	League	G.	IP.	W.	L.	Pct.	H.	R.	ER.	SO.	BB.	ERA.
1986—St. Catharines	NYP	13	40	0	4	.000	38	27	20	30	30	4.50
1987—Myrtle Beach	S. Atlantic	32	*188	11	5	.688	145	62	49	131	60	2.35
1988—Dunedin	Florida St.	31	151⅓	3	12	.200	139	80	58	125	65	3.45
1989—Dunedin	Florida St.	29	151⅓	9	8	.529	123	53	45	148	71	2.68
1990—Knoxville	Southern	28	153⅓	9	5	.643	121	57	52	142	68	3.05

Selected by Toronto Blue Jays' organization in 5th round of free-agent draft, June 2, 1986.

GILBERT HEREDIA
(Gil)

Born October 26, 1965, at Nogales, Ariz.
Height, 6.01. Weight, 190.
Throws and bats righthanded.
Attended Pima Community College, Tucson, Ariz., and
University of Arizona, Tucson, Ariz.

Year Club	League	G.	IP.	W.	L.	Pct.	H.	R.	ER.	SO.	BB.	ERA.
1987—Everett	Northwest	3	20	2	0	1.000	24	8	8	14	1	3.60
1987—Fresno	California	11	80⅔	5	3	.625	62	28	26	60	23	2.90
1988—San Jose	California	27	*206⅓	13	12	.520	●216	107	80	121	46	3.49
1989—Shreveport†	Texas	7	24⅔	1	0	1.000	28	10	7	8	4	2.55
1989—San Luis	Mexican	24	180⅔	14	9	.609	183	73	60	125	35	2.99
1990—Phoenix	P. Coast	29	147	9	7	.563	159	81	67	75	37	4.10

Selected by Pittsburgh Pirates' organization in 1st round (16th player selected) of free-agent draft, January 17, 1984.
Selected by Baltimore Orioles' organization in 6th round of free-agent draft, January 9, 1985.
Selected by San Francisco Giants' organization in 9th round of free-agent draft, June 2, 1987.
†Loaned to San Luis Potosi and returned.

CARLOS ALBERTO HERNANDEZ

Born May 24, 1967, at Bolivar, Venezuela.
Height, 5.11. Weight, 185.
Throws and bats righthanded.

Led Texas League catchers in total chances with 737 in 1989.
Tied for Gulf Coast League lead in double plays by catcher with 3 in 1986.

Year Club	League	Pos.	G.	AB.	R.	H.	2B.	3B.	HR.	RBI.	B.A.	PO.	A.	E.	F.A.
1985—Braden. Dodgers .	Gulf C.	3B-1B	22	49	3	12	1	0	0	0	.245	48	16	2	.970
1986—Sarasota Dodgers	Gulf C.	C-3B	57	205	19	64	7	0	1	31	.312	217	36	10	.962
1987—Bakersfield	Calif.	C	48	162	22	37	6	1	3	22	.228	181	26	8	.963
1988—Bakersfield	Calif.	C	92	333	37	103	15	2	5	52	.309	480	88	14	.976
1988—Albuquerque	P. C.	C	3	8	0	1	0	0	0	1	.125	11	0	1	.917
1989—San Antonio	Texas	C	99	370	37	111	16	3	8	41	.300	*629	*90	*18	.976
1989—Albuquerque	P. C.	C	4	14	1	3	0	0	0	1	.214	23	3	3	.897
1990—Albuquerque†	P. C.	C	52	143	11	45	8	1	0	16	.315	207	31	8	.967
1990—Los Angeles	Nat.	C	10	20	2	4	1	0	0	1	.200	37	2	0	1.000
Major League Totals—1 Year			10	20	2	4	1	0	0	1	.200	37	2	0	1.000

Signed as free agent by Los Angeles Dodgers' organization, October 10, 1984.
†On disabled list, May 27 to June 20, 1990.

FRANCIS XAVIER HERNANDEZ
(Known by middle name.)

Born August 16, 1965, at Port Arthur, Tex.
Height, 6.02. Weight, 185.
Throws right and bats lefthanded.
Attended University of Southwestern Louisiana, Lafayette, La.

Year Club	League	G.	IP.	W.	L.	Pct.	H.	R.	ER.	SO.	BB.	ERA.
1986—St. Catharines	NYP	13	70⅔	5	5	.500	55	27	21	69	16	2.67
1987—St. Catharines	NYP	13	55	3	3	.500	57	39	31	49	16	5.07
1988—Myrtle Beach	S. Atlantic	23	148	13	6	.684	116	52	42	111	28	2.55
1988—Knoxville	Southern	11	68⅓	2	4	.333	73	32	22	33	15	2.90
1989—Knoxville	Southern	4	24	1	1	.500	25	11	11	17	11	4.13
1989—Syracuse	Int'national	15	99⅓	5	6	.455	95	42	39	47	22	3.53
1989—Toronto†	American	7	22⅔	1	0	1.000	25	15	12	7	8	4.76
1990—Houston	National	34	62⅓	2	1	.667	60	34	32	24	24	4.62
American League Totals—1 Year		7	22⅔	1	0	1.000	25	15	12	7	8	4.76
National League Totals—1 Year		34	62⅓	2	1	.667	60	34	32	24	24	4.62
Major League Totals—2 Years		41	85	3	1	.750	85	49	44	31	32	4.66

Selected by Toronto Blue Jays' organization in 4th round of free-agent draft, June 2, 1986.
†Drafted by Houston Astros, December 4, 1989.

JEREMY STUART HERNANDEZ

Born July 6, 1966, at Burbank, Calif.
Height, 6.05. Weight, 195.
Throws and bats righthanded.
Attended California State University, Northridge, Calif.

Led Texas League in home runs allowed with 18 in 1990.

Year Club	League	G.	IP.	W.	L.	Pct.	H.	R.	ER.	SO.	BB.	ERA.
1987—Erie	NYP	16	99⅓	5	4	.556	87	36	31	62	41	2.81
1988—Springfield†	Midwest	24	147⅓	12	6	.667	133	73	58	97	34	3.54
1989—Charleston, S.C.	S. Atlantic	10	58⅔	3	5	.375	65	37	23	39	16	3.53
1989—Riverside	California	9	67	5	2	.714	55	17	13	65	11	1.75
1989—Wichita	Texas	4	19	2	1	.667	30	18	18	9	8	8.53
1990—Wichita	Texas	26	155	7	6	.538	163	92	78	101	50	4.53

Selected by St. Louis Cardinals' organization in 2nd round of free-agent draft, June 2, 1987.
†Traded to Charleston, S.C. (San Diego Padres' organization) for Outfielder Randell Byers, April 24, 1989.

KEITH HERNANDEZ

Born October 20, 1953, at San Francisco, Calif.
Height, 6.00. Weight, 205.
Throws and bats lefthanded.
Attended College of San Mateo, San Mateo, Calif.
Son of John Hernandez, minor league infielder, 1941 through 1950; and brother of Gary Hernandez, first baseman-outfielder in St. Louis Cardinals' organization, 1972 through 1975.

Holds major league records for most game-winning RBIs, season (24), 1985; most game-winning RBIs, lifetime (129); most years leading league in double plays by first baseman (6); most assists by first baseman, lifetime (1,682).

Shares National League records for most grand slams, month (2), September, 1977; fewest errors by first baseman for leader in errors, season (13), 1983.

Major League stolen bases: 1976 (4), 1977 (7), 1978 (13), 1979 (11), 1980 (14), 1981 (12), 1982 (19), 1983 (9), 1984 (2), 1985 (3), 1986 (2), 1988 (2). Total—98.

Hit for the cycle, July 4, 1985.

Led National League in bases on balls received with 94 in 1986.

Led National League in intentional bases on balls received with 19 in 1982.

Led National League first basemen in putouts with 1,054 in 1981 and 1,586 in 1982.

Led National League first basemen in double plays with 146 in 1977, 145 in 1979, 146 in 1980, 99 in 1981, 147 in 1983 and 127 in 1984.

Led National League first basemen in total chances with 1,643 in 1979, 1,732 in 1982, 1,578 in 1983 and 1,457 in 1987.

Led National League in game-winning RBIs with 24 in 1985 and tied for lead with 21 in 1982.

Led Texas League first basemen in double plays with 101 in 1973.

Named National League Player of the Year by THE SPORTING NEWS, 1979.

Named National League co-Most Valuable Player by Baseball Writers' Association of America, 1979.

Named first baseman on THE SPORTING NEWS National League All-Star Team, 1979, 1980 and 1984 through 1986.

Named first baseman on THE SPORTING NEWS National League All-Star fielding team, 1978 through 1988.

Named first baseman on THE SPORTING NEWS National League Silver Slugger team, 1980 and 1984.

Year—Club	League	Pos.	G.	AB.	R.	H.	2B.	3B.	HR.	RBI.	B.A.	PO.	A.	E.	F.A.
1972—St. Petersburg†	Fla. St.	1B	84	309	38	79	16	5	5	41	.256	682	52	7	.991
1972—Tulsa	A. A.	1B	11	29	5	7	1	0	0	1	.241	54	2	0	1.000
1973—Arkansas	Texas	1B	105	388	62	101	20	2	3	52	.260	960	61	9	*.991
1973—Tulsa	A. A.	1B	31	120	20	40	6	1	5	25	.333	289	15	1	.997
1974—Tulsa‡	A. A.	1B-OF	102	353	67	124	18	6	14	63	*.351	690	50	12	.984
1974—St. Louis	Nat.	1B	14	34	3	10	1	2	0	2	.294	70	1	2	.973
1975—Tulsa	A. A.	●1B-OF	85	324	70	107	29	3	10	48	.330	597	53	●13	.980
1975—St. Louis	Nat.	1B	64	188	20	47	8	2	3	20	.250	469	36	2	.996
1976—St. Louis	Nat.	1B	129	374	54	108	21	5	7	46	.289	862	●107	10	.990
1977—St. Louis	Nat.	1B	161	560	90	163	41	4	15	91	.291	1453	106	12	.992
1978—St. Louis	Nat.	1B	159	542	90	138	32	4	11	64	.255	1436	96	10	.994
1979—St. Louis	Nat.	1B	161	610	*116	210	*48	11	11	105	*.344	*1489	*146	8	.995
1980—St. Louis	Nat.	1B	159	595	*111	191	39	8	16	99	.321	1572	115	9	.995
1981—St. Louis	Nat.	1B-OF	103	376	65	115	27	4	8	48	.306	1056	86	3	.997
1982—St. Louis	Nat.	1B-OF	160	579	79	173	33	6	7	94	.299	1591	135	11	.994
1983—St.L.§-N.Y.	Nat.	1B	150	538	77	160	23	7	12	63	.297	*1418	147	●13	.992
1984—New York	Nat.	1B	154	550	83	171	31	0	15	94	.311	1214	*142	8	.994
1985—New York	Nat.	1B	158	593	87	183	34	4	10	91	.309	1310	*139	4	*.997
1986—New York	Nat.	1B	149	551	94	171	34	1	13	83	.310	1199	149	5	*.996
1987—New York	Nat.	1B	154	587	87	170	28	2	18	89	.290	1298	*149	10	.993
1988—New York x	Nat.	1B	95	348	43	96	16	0	11	55	.276	734	77	2	.998
1989—New York y	Nat.	1B	75	215	18	50	8	0	4	19	.233	405	31	4	.991
1989—Port St. Lucie z	Fla. St.	1B	4	16	1	6	1	0	0	1	.375	23	0	0	1.000
1990—Cleveland a	Amer.	1B	43	130	7	26	2	0	1	8	.200	340	20	2	.994
1990—Sarasota Indians	Gulf C.	1B	5	11	3	5	1	0	1	2	.455	10	1	0	1.000
National League Totals—16 Years			2045	7240	1117	2156	424	60	161	1063	.298	17576	1662	113	.994
American League Totals—1 Year			43	130	7	26	2	0	1	8	.200	340	20	2	.994
Major League Totals—17 Years			2088	7370	1124	2182	426	60	162	1071	.296	17916	1682	115	.994

Selected by St. Louis Cardinals' organization in 42nd round of free-agent draft, June 8, 1971.

†On disabled list, April 10 to May 30, 1972.

‡On disabled list, April 16 to May 20, 1974.

§Traded to New York Mets for Pitchers Neil Allen and Rick Ownbey, June 15, 1983.

xOn disabled list, June 7 to June 22 and June 24 to August 5, 1988.

yOn disabled list, May 18 to July 13, 1989; included rehabilitation disability assignment to Port St. Lucie, July 7 to July 13, 1989.

zGranted free agency, November 13, 1989; signed by Cleveland Indians, December 7, 1989.

aOn disabled list, May 27 to June 15, June 18 to July 12 and August 1, 1990 through remainder of season; included rehabilitation disability assignment to Sarasota Indians, July 1 to July 12, 1990.

CHAMPIONSHIP SERIES RECORD

Shares Championship Series records for most at-bats, game (7), October 15, 1986 (16 innings) and inning (2), October 7, 1982, sixth inning.

Year—Club	League	Pos.	G.	AB.	R.	H.	2B.	3B.	HR.	RBI.	B.A.	PO.	A.	E.	F.A.
1982—St. Louis	Nat.	1B	3	12	3	4	0	0	0	1	.333	35	1	0	1.000
1986—New York	Nat.	1B	6	26	3	7	1	1	0	3	.269	67	12	0	1.000
1988—New York	Nat.	1B	7	26	2	7	0	0	1	5	.269	57	4	1	.984
Championship Series Totals—3 Years			16	64	8	18	1	1	1	9	.281	159	17	1	.994

WORLD SERIES RECORD

Year—Club	League	Pos.	G.	AB.	R.	H.	2B.	3B.	HR.	RBI.	B.A.	PO.	A.	E.	F.A.
1982—St. Louis	Nat.	1B	7	27	4	7	2	0	1	8	.259	62	7	2	.972
1986—New York	Nat.	1B	7	26	1	6	0	0	0	4	.231	48	4	1	.981
World Series Totals—2 Years			14	53	5	13	2	0	1	12	.245	110	11	3	.976

ALL-STAR GAME RECORD

Year League	Pos.	AB.	R.	H.	2B.	3B.	HR.	RBI.	B.A.	PO.	A.	E.	F.A.
1979—National	PH	1	0	0	0	0	0	0	.000	0	0	0	.000
1980—National	PH-1B	2	0	2	0	0	0	0	1.000	5	0	0	1.000
1984—National	1B	1	0	0	0	0	0	0	.000	1	0	0	1.000
1986—National	1B	4	0	0	0	0	0	0	.000	5	0	0	1.000
1987—National	1B	2	0	1	0	0	0	0	.500	4	2	0	1.000
All-Star Game Totals—5 Years		10	0	3	0	0	0	0	.300	15	2	0	1.000

ROBERTO MANUEL HERNANDEZ

Born November 11, 1964, at Santurce, Puerto Rico.
Height, 6.04. Weight, 220.
Throws and bats righthanded.
Attended University of South Carolina, Aiken, S.C.

Year Club	League	G.	IP.	W.	L.	Pct.	H.	R.	ER.	SO.	BB.	ERA.
1986—Salem	Northwest	10	55	2	2	.500	57	37	28	38	42	4.58
1987—Quad City†	Midwest	7	21	2	3	.400	24	21	16	21	12	6.86
1988—Quad City	Midwest	24	164⅔	9	10	.474	157	70	58	114	48	3.17
1988—Midland	Texas	3	12⅓	0	2	.000	16	13	9	7	8	6.57
1989—Midland	Texas	12	64	2	7	.222	94	57	49	42	30	6.89
1989—Palm Springs‡	California	7	42⅔	1	4	.200	49	27	22	33	16	4.64
1989—South Bend	Midwest	4	24⅓	1	1	.500	19	9	9	17	7	3.33
1990—Birmingham	Southern	17	108	8	5	.615	103	57	44	62	43	3.67
1990—Vancouver	P. Coast	11	79⅓	3	5	.375	73	33	25	49	26	2.84

Selected by California Angels' organization in 1st round (16th player selected) of free-agent draft, June 2, 1986.
†On disabled list, May 6 to May 21 and June 4 to August 14, 1987.
‡Traded with Outfielder Mark Doran to Chicago White Sox' organization for Outfielder Mark Davis and a player to be named later, August 2, 1989.

THOMAS MITCHELL HERR
(Tom)

Born April 4, 1956, at Lancaster, Pa.
Height, 6.00. Weight, 196.
Throws right and bats left and righthanded.
Attended University of Delaware, Newark, Del.

Shares major league record for highest fielding average, second baseman, lifetime (.989).
Major league stolen bases: 1979 (1), 1980 (9), 1981 (23), 1982 (25), 1983 (6), 1984 (13), 1985 (31), 1986 (22), 1987 (19), 1988 (13), 1989 (10), 1990 (7). Total—179.
Led National League in sacrifice flies with 13 in 1985 and 12 in 1987.
Led National League second basemen in double plays with 74 in 1981, 106 in 1984, 121 in 1986 and tied for lead with 94 in 1990.
Led National League second basemen in total chances with 590 in 1981.
Led Florida State League in stolen bases with 50 in 1977.
Led Florida State League second basemen in double plays with 91 in 1977.
Named second baseman on THE SPORTING NEWS National League All-Star Team, 1985.

Year Club	League	Pos.	G.	AB.	R.	H.	2B.	3B.	HR.	RBI.	B.A.	PO.	A.	E.	F.A.
1975—Johnson City	Appal.	2B-SS	42	133	29	41	8	1	0	15	.308	74	125	5	.975
1976—St. Petersburg	Fla. St.	SS-2B	82	275	47	74	6	1	0	21	.269	133	211	18	.950
1977—St. Petersburg	Fla. St.	2B	136	★515	★80	★156	13	7	1	53	.303	★348	★430	21	★.974
1978—Arkansas	Texas	2B	89	335	70	98	23	4	3	45	.293	207	280	13	.974
1978—Springfield	A. A.	2B	33	86	16	24	6	1	0	8	.279	45	63	7	.939
1979—Springfield	A. A.	2B	109	423	74	124	20	6	6	48	.293	225	324	10	★.982
1979—St. Louis	Nat.	2B	14	10	4	2	0	0	0	1	.200	12	11	0	1.000
1980—Springfield	A. A.	2B-3B	37	141	29	44	6	2	1	16	.312	29	52	1	.988
1980—St. Louis	Nat.	2B-SS	76	222	29	55	12	5	0	15	.248	124	184	7	.978
1981—St. Louis	Nat.	2B	103	411	50	110	14	9	0	46	.268	211	★374	5	★.992
1982—St. Louis	Nat.	2B	135	493	83	131	19	4	0	36	.266	263	427	9	.987
1983—St. Louis†	Nat.	2B	89	313	43	101	14	4	2	31	.323	178	245	6	.986
1983—Arkansas	Texas	2B	3	9	0	4	3	0	0	1	.444	4	9	0	1.000
1984—St. Louis	Nat.	2B	145	558	67	154	23	2	4	49	.276	328	452	6	.992
1985—St. Louis	Nat.	2B	159	596	97	180	38	3	8	110	.302	337	448	12	.985
1986—St. Louis	Nat.	2B	152	559	48	141	30	4	2	61	.252	352	414	9	.988
1987—St. Louis‡	Nat.	2B	141	510	73	134	29	0	2	83	.263	306	350	7	.989
1988—St. Louis§	Nat.	2B	15	50	4	13	0	0	1	3	.260	28	35	1	.984
1988—Minnesota xyz	Amer.	2B-SS	86	304	42	80	16	0	1	21	.263	140	195	4	.988
1989—Philadelphia	Nat.	2B	151	561	65	161	25	6	2	37	.287	281	415	7	.990
1990—Phila.a-N.Y	Nat.	2B	146	547	48	143	26	3	5	60	.261	275	349	7	.989
National League Totals—12 Years			1326	4830	611	1325	230	40	26	532	.274	2695	3704	76	.988
American League Totals—1 Year			86	304	42	80	16	0	1	21	.263	140	195	4	.988
Major League Totals—12 Years			1412	5134	653	1405	246	40	27	553	.274	2835	3899	80	.988

Signed as free agent by St. Louis Cardinals' organization, August 22, 1974.
†On disabled list, March 25 to April 29 and August 9, 1983 through remainder of season; included rehabilitation disability assignment to Arkansas, April 18 to April 29, 1983.
‡On disabled list, April 24 to May 12, 1987.
§Traded to Minnesota Twins for Outfielder Tom Brunansky, April 22, 1988.
xOn disabled list, June 21 to July 22 and July 25 to August 18, 1988.
yTraded with Catcher Tom Nieto and Outfielder Eric Bullock to Philadelphia Phillies for Pitcher Shane Rawley and cash, October 24, 1988.

zGranted free agency, November 4, 1988; re-signed by Phillies, November 17, 1988.
aTraded to New York Mets for Pitcher Rocky Elli and First Baseman Nikco Riesgo, August 30, 1990.

CHAMPIONSHIP SERIES RECORD

Shares Championship Series record for most doubles, series (4), 1985.

Year	Club	League	Pos.	G.	AB.	R.	H.	2B.	3B.	HR.	RBI.	B.A.	PO.	A.	E.	F.A.
1982—St. Louis		Nat.	2B	3	13	1	3	1	0	0	0	.231	6	10	0	1.000
1985—St. Louis		Nat.	2B	6	21	2	7	4	0	1	6	.333	13	12	0	1.000
1987—St. Louis		Nat.	2B	7	27	0	6	0	0	0	3	.222	12	11	1	.958
Championship Series Totals—3 Years				16	61	3	16	5	0	1	9	.262	31	33	1	.985

WORLD SERIES RECORD

Established World Series record for most double plays started, second baseman, seven-game Series (5), 1985.
Established World Series record for most runs batted in on sacrifice fly (2), October 16, 1982 (second inning).

Year	Club	League	Pos.	G.	AB.	R.	H.	2B.	3B.	HR.	RBI.	B.A.	PO.	A.	E.	F.A.
1982—St. Louis		Nat.	2B	7	25	2	4	2	0	0	5	.160	11	19	1	.968
1985—St. Louis		Nat.	2B	7	26	2	4	2	0	0	0	.154	11	13	0	1.000
1987—St. Louis		Nat.	2B	7	28	2	7	0	0	1	1	.250	23	17	0	1.000
World Series Totals—3 Years				21	79	6	15	4	0	1	6	.190	45	49	1	.989

ALL-STAR GAME RECORD

Year	League	Pos.	AB.	R.	H.	2B.	3B.	HR.	RBI.	B.A.	PO.	A.	E.	F.A.
1985—National		2B	3	1	1	1	0	0	0	.333	0	1	0	1.000

OREL LEONARD HERSHISER IV

Name pronounced Hersh-HYZ-ur.

Born September 16, 1958, at Buffalo, N. Y.
Height, 6.03. Weight, 190.
Throws and bats righthanded.
Attended Bowling Green State University, Bowling Green, O.
Brother of Gordie Hershiser, pitcher in Los Angeles Dodgers' organization, 1987 and 1988.

Holds major league record for most consecutive scoreless innings, season (59), August 30, sixth inning, through September 28, tenth inning, 1988.
Shares National League records for fewest games lost for leader, season (15), 1989; most shutouts, month (5), September, 1988.
Major League saves: 1983 (1), 1984 (2), 1987 (1), 1988 (1). Total—5.
Led National League in shutouts with 8 in 1988 and tied for lead with 4 in 1984.
Tied for National League lead in complete games with 15 in 1988.
Tied for National League lead in sacrifice hits by batters with 19 in 1988.
Led Pacific Coast League in intentional bases on balls issued with 8 in 1983.
Named Major League Player of the Year by THE SPORTING NEWS, 1988.
Named National League Pitcher of the Year by THE SPORTING NEWS, 1988.
Won National League Cy Young Memorial Award, 1988.
Named righthanded pitcher on THE SPORTING NEWS National League All-Star Team, 1988.
Named pitcher on THE SPORTING NEWS National League All-Star fielding team, 1988.

Year	Club	League	G.	IP.	W.	L.	Pct.	H.	R.	ER.	SO.	BB.	ERA.
1979—Clinton		Midwest	15	43	4	0	1.000	33	15	10	33	17	2.09
1980—San Antonio		Texas	49	109	5	9	.357	120	59	43	75	59	3.55
1981—San Antonio		Texas	42	102	7	6	.538	94	54	53	95	50	4.68
1982—Albuquerque		P. Coast	47	123⅔	9	6	.600	121	73	51	93	63	3.71
1983—Albuquerque		P. Coast	49	134⅓	10	8	.556	132	73	61	95	57	4.09
1983—Los Angeles		National	8	8	0	0	.000	7	6	3	5	6	3.38
1984—Los Angeles		National	45	189⅔	11	8	.579	160	65	56	150	50	2.66
1985—Los Angeles		National	36	239⅔	19	3	*.864	179	72	54	157	68	2.03
1986—Los Angeles		National	35	231⅓	14	14	.500	213	112	99	153	86	3.85
1987—Los Angeles		National	37	*264⅔	16	16	.500	247	105	90	190	74	3.06
1988—Los Angeles		National	35	*267	●23	8	.742	208	73	67	178	73	2.26
1989—Los Angeles		National	35	*256⅔	15	●15	.500	226	75	66	178	77	2.31
1990—Los Angeles†		National	4	25⅓	1	1	.500	26	12	12	16	4	4.26
Major League Totals—8 Years			235	1482⅓	99	65	.604	1266	520	447	1027	438	2.71

Selected by Los Angeles Dodgers' organization in 17th round of free-agent draft, June 5, 1979.
†On disabled list, April 27, 1990 through remainder of season.

CHAMPIONSHIP SERIES RECORD

Holds Championship Series record for most innings pitched, series (24⅔), 1988.
Shares Championship Series record for most wild pitches, total series (3).
Holds National League Championship Series record for most hit batsmen, game (2), October 12, 1988.
Shares National League Championship Series records for most complete games total series (2); most hit bastmen total series (2) and series (2), 1988.

Year	Club	League	G.	IP.	W.	L.	Pct.	H.	R.	ER.	SO.	BB.	ERA.
1985—Los Angeles		National	2	15⅓	1	0	1.000	17	6	6	5	6	3.52
1988—Los Angeles		National	4	24⅔	1	0	1.000	18	5	3	15	7	1.09
Championship Series Totals—2 Years			6	40	2	0	1.000	35	11	9	20	13	2.03

WORLD SERIES RECORD

Year	Club	League	G.	IP.	W.	L.	Pct.	H.	R.	ER.	SO.	BB.	ERA.
1988—Los Angeles		National	2	18	2	0	1.000	7	2	2	17	6	1.00

Year League	IP.	W.	L.	Pct.	H.	R.	ER.	SO.	BB.	ERA.
1987—National	2	0	0	.000	1	0	0	0	1	0.00
1988—National	1	0	0	.000	0	0	0	0	0	0.00
All-Star Game Totals—2 Years	3	0	0	.000	1	0	0	0	1	0.00

Member of National League All-Star Team in 1989; did not play.

JOSEPH THOMAS HESKETH
(Joe)

Born February 15, 1959, at Lackawanna, N. Y.
Height, 6.02. Weight, 170.
Throws and bats lefthanded.
Attended State University of New York, Buffalo, N. Y.

Major League saves: 1984 (1), 1987 (1), 1988 (9), 1989 (3), 1990 (5). Total—19.
Tied for American Association lead in shutouts with 2 in 1983.
Named American Association Pitcher of the Year, 1984.

Year Club	League	G.	IP.	W.	L.	Pct.	H.	R.	ER.	SO.	BB.	ERA.
1980—West Palm Beach	Florida St.	11	75	8	2	.800	71	30	16	43	32	1.92
1980—Memphis	Southern	3	20	1	0	1.000	20	13	9	20	7	4.05
1981—Memphis†	Southern					(Did Not Play)						
1982—Memphis‡	Southern					(Did Not Play)						
1982—West Palm Beach	Florida St.	8	45⅔	3	2	.600	41	16	14	24	16	2.76
1983—Memphis	Southern	11	74	6	4	.600	82	38	25	22	25	3.04
1983—Wichita	Am. Assoc.	15	88⅓	5	5	.500	98	53	50	41	46	5.09
1984—Indianapolis	Am. Assoc.	22	147⅔	12	3	.800	120	60	50	135	54	3.05
1984—Montreal	National	11	45	2	2	.500	38	12	9	32	15	1.80
1985—Montreal§	National	25	155⅓	10	5	.667	125	52	43	113	45	2.49
1986—Montreal x	National	15	82⅔	6	5	.545	92	46	46	67	31	5.01
1987—Bradenton Expos	Gulf Coast	2	4⅓	0	0	.000	7	4	4	8	0	8.31
1987—Jacksonville	Southern	6	19⅔	1	0	1.000	18	6	5	22	4	2.29
1987—Montreal	National	18	28⅔	0	0	.000	23	12	10	31	15	3.14
1988—Indianapolis	Am. Assoc.	8	11	0	0	.000	10	5	4	16	5	3.27
1988—Montreal	National	60	72⅔	4	3	.571	63	30	23	64	35	2.85
1989—Montreal y	National	43	48⅓	6	4	.600	54	34	31	44	26	5.77
1989—Indianapolis	Am. Assoc.	5	9⅓	0	0	.000	11	4	4	9	5	3.86
1990—Montreal z-Atlanta a	National	33	34	1	2	.333	32	23	20	24	14	5.29
1990—Boston	American	12	25⅔	0	4	.000	37	12	10	26	11	3.51
National League Totals—7 Years		205	466⅔	29	21	.580	427	209	182	375	181	3.51
American League Totals—1 Year		12	25⅔	0	4	.000	37	12	10	26	11	3.51
Major League Totals—7 Years		217	492⅓	29	25	.537	464	221	192	401	192	3.51

Selected by Montreal Expos' organization in 2nd round of free-agent draft, June 3, 1980.
†On disabled list, April 9, 1981, through remainder of season.
‡On disabled list, April 8 to July 8, 1982.
§On disabled list, August 24, 1985 through remainder of season.
xOn disabled list, July 4, 1986 through remainder of season.
yOn disabled list, August 18 to September 8, 1989.
zClaimed on waivers by Atlanta Braves, April 30, 1990.
aReleased, July 24, 1990; signed by Boston Red Sox, July 31, 1990.

ERIC PAUL HETZEL

Born September 25, 1963, at Crowley, La.
Height, 6.03. Weight, 180.
Throws and bats righthanded.
Attended Eastern Oklahoma State College, Wilburton,
Okla., and Louisiana State University, Baton Rouge, La.

Year Club	League	G.	IP.	W.	L.	Pct.	H.	R.	ER.	SO.	BB.	ERA.
1985—Greensboro	S. Atlantic	15	76	7	5	.853	87	54	47	82	48	5.57
1986—Greensboro†	S. Atlantic					(Did not play)						
1987—Winter Haven	Florida St.	26	192⅔	10	12	.455	186	94	76	136	87	3.55
1988—Pawtucket	Int'national	22	127⅓	6	10	.375	129	67	56	122	51	3.96
1989—Pawtucket	Int'national	12	80	4	4	.500	65	27	22	79	32	2.48
1989—Boston‡	American	12	50⅓	2	3	.400	61	39	35	33	28	6.26
1990—Pawtucket	Int'national	19	108⅔	6	5	.545	85	51	44	90	74	3.64
1990—Boston	American	9	35	1	4	.200	39	28	23	20	21	5.91
Major League Totals—2 Years		21	85⅓	3	7	.300	100	67	58	53	49	6.12

Selected by Boston Red Sox' organization in 5th round of free-agent draft, January 11, 1983.
Selected by Kansas City Royals' organization in 2nd round of free-agent draft, January 17, 1984.
Selected by Pittsburgh Pirates' organization in secondary phase of free-agent draft, June 4, 1984.
Selected by Boston Red Sox' organization in secondary phase of free-agent draft, June 3, 1985.
†On disabled list, April 9, 1986 through entire season.
‡On disabled list, August 3 to August 24, 1989; included rehabilitation disability assignment to Pawtucket, August 18 to August 24, 1989.

JAMES GREGORY HIBBARD
(Greg)

Born September 13, 1964, at New Orleans, La.
Height, 6.00. Weight, 190.
Throws and bats lefthanded.
Attended Mississippi Gulf Coast Junior College, Perkinston, Miss.,
and University of Alabama, Tuscaloosa, Ala.

Year Club	League	G.	IP.	W.	L.	Pct.	H.	R.	ER.	SO.	BB.	ERA.
1986—Eugene	Northwest	26	39	5	2	.714	30	23	15	44	19	3.46
1987—Appleton	Midwest	9	64⅔	7	2	.778	53	17	8	61	18	1.11
1987—Fort Myers	Florida St.	3	24	2	1	.667	20	5	5	20	3	1.88
1987—Memphis†	Southern	16	106	7	6	.538	102	48	38	56	21	3.23
1988—Vancouver	P. Coast	25	144⅓	11	11	.500	155	74	66	65	44	4.12
1989—Vancouver	P. Coast	9	58	2	3	.400	47	24	17	45	11	2.64
1989—Chicago	American	23	137⅓	6	7	.462	142	58	49	55	41	3.21
1990—Chicago	American	33	211	14	9	.609	202	80	74	92	55	3.16
Major League Totals—2 Years		56	348⅓	20	16	.556	344	138	123	147	96	3.18

Selected by Houston Astros' organization in 8th round of free-agent draft, January 17, 1984.
Selected by Kansas City Royals' organization in 16th round of free-agent draft, June 2, 1986.
†Traded with Pitchers Melido Perez, John Davis and Chuck Mount to Chicago White Sox for Pitcher Floyd Bannister and Third Baseman Dave Cochrane, December 10, 1987.

KEVIN JOHN HICKEY

Born February 25, 1956, at Chicago, Ill.
Height, 6.01. Weight, 200.
Throws and bats lefthanded.

Major League saves: 1981 (3), 1982 (6), 1983 (5), 1989 (2), 1990 (1). Total—17.
Led Eastern League in home runs allowed with 20 and balks with 6 in 1980.
Led Midwest League in balks with 5 in 1979.

Year Club	League	G.	IP.	W.	L.	Pct.	H.	R.	ER.	SO.	BB.	ERA.
1978—Paintsville	Ap'lachian	9	36	2	4	.333	37	19	16	24	23	4.00
1979—Appleton	Midwest	29	121	5	10	.333	122	64	48	100	71	3.57
1980—Glens Falls	Eastern	26	169	9	7	.563	184	92	81	80	73	4.31
1981—Chicago	American	41	44	0	2	.000	38	22	18	17	18	3.68
1982—Chicago	American	60	78	4	4	.500	73	32	26	38	30	3.00
1983—Chicago†‡	American	23	20⅔	1	2	.333	23	14	12	8	11	5.23
1984—Appleton	Midwest	10	49⅔	4	3	.571	45	18	13	40	11	2.36
1984—Denver§	Am. Assoc.	16	47⅓	2	2	.500	61	39	33	20	23	6.27
1984—Columbus	Int'national	5	9⅓	1	1	.500	14	10	9	3	8	8.68
1985—Albany x-Reading	Eastern	44	60⅓	5	5	.500	53	22	18	44	22	2.69
1986—Portland y	P. Coast	33	65	1	3	.250	76	54	47	44	29	6.51
1987—Hawaii z-Phoenix a	P. Coast	46	82⅔	4	5	.444	88	52	46	48	36	5.01
1988—Charlotte	Southern	6	9⅔	1	1	.500	10	4	4	7	8	3.72
1988—Rochester	Int'national	27	37	2	0	1.000	31	7	6	24	9	1.46
1989—Baltimore	American	51	49⅓	2	3	.400	38	16	16	28	23	2.92
1990—Baltimore	American	37	26⅓	1	3	.250	26	16	15	17	13	5.13
1990—Rochester	Int'national	16	23⅓	2	1	.667	31	15	15	28	7	5.79
Major League Totals—5 Years		212	218⅓	8	14	.364	198	100	87	108	95	3.59

Signed as free agent by Chicago White Sox' organization, August 18, 1977.
†On disabled list, August 1 to September 5, 1983.
‡Released, March 26, 1984; re-signed by Chicago White Sox' organization, April 2, 1984.
§Traded with Pitcher Doug Drabek to New York Yankees' organization, August 13, 1984, completing deal in which New York traded Infielder Roy Smalley to Chicago White Sox for two players to be named later, July 18, 1984.
xReleased, May 25, 1985; signed by Reading (Philadelphia Phillies' organization), June 1, 1985.
yReleased, September 30, 1986; signed by Hawaii (Chicago White Sox' organization), March 11, 1987.
zReleased, August 21, 1987; signed by Phoenix (San Francisco Giants' organization), August 22, 1987.
aGranted free agency, October 15, 1987; signed by Charlotte (Baltimore Orioles' organization), December 18, 1987.

TEODORO HIGUERA (VALENZUELA)

Name pronounced Tea-O-door-RO HE-gare-uh Val-en-ZWAY-luh.

(Ted)

Born November 9, 1958, at Los Mochis, Mexico.
Height, 5.10. Weight, 180.
Throws left and bats left and righthanded.

Tied for Mexican League lead in games started by pitchers with 27 and complete games with 18 in 1983.
Named lefthanded pitcher on THE SPORTING NEWS American League All-Star Team, 1986.
Named American League Rookie Pitcher of the Year by THE SPORTING NEWS, 1985.

Year Club	League	G.	IP.	W.	L.	Pct.	H.	R.	ER.	SO.	BB.	ERA.
1979—Ciudad Juarez	Mexican	2	1	0	1	.000	4	5	5	1	4	45.00
1980—Ciudad Juarez†	Mexican	19	117	8	3	.727	111	30	24	76	59	1.85
1980—Ciudad Juarez‡	Mexican	8	49	2	5	.286	44	22	20	29	17	3.67
1981—Ciudad Juarez	Mexican	28	203	16	9	.640	207	81	70	157	69	3.10
1982—Ciudad Juarez	Mexican	24	142⅓	9	12	.429	163	77	64	74	53	4.05
1983—Ciudad Juarez§	Mexican	27	★222	●17	8	.680	177	61	50	★165	68	2.03
1984—El Paso	Texas	19	121	8	7	.533	116	57	35	99	43	★2.60
1984—Vancouver	P. Coast	8	40	1	4	.200	49	26	21	29	14	4.73

Year Club	League	G.	IP.	W.	L.	Pct.	H.	R.	ER.	SO.	BB.	ERA.
1985—Milwaukee....................................	American	32	212⅓	15	8	.652	186	105	92	127	63	3.90
1986—Milwaukee....................................	American	34	248⅓	20	11	.645	226	84	77	207	74	2.79
1987—Milwaukee....................................	American	35	261⅔	18	10	.643	236	120	112	240	87	3.85
1988—Milwaukee....................................	American	31	227⅓	16	9	.640	168	66	62	192	59	2.45
1989—El Paso x	Texas	1	5	0	1	.000	5	2	1	4	1	1.80
1989—Milwaukee....................................	American	22	135⅓	9	6	.600	125	56	52	91	48	3.46
1990—Milwaukee yz	American	27	170	11	10	.524	167	80	71	129	50	3.76
Major League Totals—6 Years...........................		181	1255	89	54	.622	1108	511	466	986	381	3.34

†20-team season.
‡6-team season.
§Sold to Vancouver (Milwaukee Brewers' organization), September 13, 1983.
xOn Milwaukee disabled list, March 25 to May 1, 1989; included rehabilitation disability assignment to El Paso, April 9 to April 28, 1989.
yOn disabled list, June 14 to June 29, 1990.
zGranted free agency, November 5, 1990; re-signed by Brewers, December 5, 1990.

ALL-STAR GAME RECORD

Year League	IP.	W.	L.	Pct.	H.	R.	ER.	SO.	BB.	ERA.
1986—American	3	0	0	.000	1	0	0	2	1	0.00

DONALD EARL HILL
(Donnie)

Born November 12, 1960, at Pomona, Calif.
Height, 5.10. Weight, 160.
Throws right and bats left and righthanded.
Attended Orange Coast College, Costa Mesa, Calif.; and Arizona State University, Tempe, Ariz.

Major League stolen bases: 1983 (1), 1984 (1), 1985 (9), 1986 (5), 1987 (1), 1988 (3), 1990 (1). Total—21.
Tied for Eastern League lead in sacrifice flies with 8 in 1982.

Year Club	League	Pos.	G.	AB.	R.	H.	2B.	3B.	HR.	RBI.	B.A.	PO.	A.	E.	F.A.
1981—Modesto.................	Calif.	SS-2B	46	149	21	29	3	0	6	22	.195	44	84	22	.853
1982—West Haven†	East.	SS-3B	132	405	66	103	21	3	10	59	.254	141	301	29	.938
1983—Tacoma‡...............	P. C.	SS	93	322	45	101	19	2	14	63	.314	148	256	18	.957
1983—Oakland.................	Amer.	SS	53	158	20	42	7	0	2	15	.266	87	136	9	.961
1984—Oakland§..............	Amer.	SS-2B-3B	73	174	21	40	6	0	2	16	.230	102	128	12	.950
1984—Tacoma	P. C.	SS-2B	42	141	28	46	12	3	2	24	.326	71	92	4	.976
1985—Oakland.................	Amer.	2B	123	393	45	112	13	2	3	48	.285	228	320	15	.973
1986—Oakland x	Amer.	2B-3B-SS	108	339	37	96	16	2	4	29	.283	104	213	9	.972
1987—Chicago y..............	Amer.	2B-3B	111	410	57	98	14	6	9	46	.239	167	278	14	.969
1987—Hawaii	P. C.	2B	7	23	10	9	2	0	2	6	.391	11	11	0	1.000
1988—Chicago	Amer.	2B-3B	83	221	17	48	6	1	2	20	.217	118	152	8	.971
1988—Vancouver z...........	P. C.	2B	7	26	5	9	4	0	0	7	.346	4	10	1	.933
1989—Tacoma a	P. C.	2-3-S-P	58	180	26	47	7	2	4	23	.261	69	102	7	.966
1990—California bc..........	Amer.	2-S-3-1-P	103	352	36	93	18	2	3	32	.264	194	255	11	.976
Major League Totals—7 Years.................			654	2047	233	529	80	13	25	206	.258	1000	1482	78	.970

Selected by Houston Astros' organization in 5th round of free-agent draft, January 8, 1980.
Selected by San Francisco Giants' organization in secondary phase of free-agent draft, June 3, 1980.
Selected by Oakland A's organization in secondary phase of free-agent draft, June 8, 1981.
†On temporary inactive list, April 13 to April 23, 1982.
‡On disabled list, April 30 to May 10, 1983.
§On disabled list, May 3 to May 18, 1984.
xTraded to Chicago White Sox for Pitcher Gene Nelson and a player to be named later, December 11, 1986; Oakland A's acquired Pitcher Bruce Tanner to complete deal, December 18, 1986.
yOn disabled list, May 30 to June 14 and July 29 to August 13, 1987; included rehabilitation disability assignment to Hawaii, June 6 to June 14, 1987.
zReleased, March 9, 1989; signed by Tacoma (Oakland Athletics' organization), March 22, 1989.
aReleased, August 9, 1989; signed by Edmonton (California Angels' organization), January 5, 1990.
bOn disabled list, August 25 to September 11, 1990.
cGranted free agency, November 5, 1990; re-signed by Angels, December 19, 1990.

PITCHING RECORD

Year Club	League	G.	IP.	W.	L.	Pct.	H.	R.	ER.	SO.	BB.	ERA.
1989—Tacoma.............................	P. Coast	1	1	0	0	.000	1	0	0	0	0	0.00
1990—California.............................	American	1	1	0	0	.000	0	0	0	1	1	0.00
Major League Totals—1 Year..............................		1	1	0	0	.000	0	0	0	1	1	0.00

GLENALLEN HILL

Born March 22, 1965, at Santa Cruz, Calif.
Height, 6.02. Weight, 210.
Throws and bats righthanded.

Major League stolen bases: 1989 (2), 1990 (8). Total—10.
Led International League in total bases with 279 and slugging percentage with .578 in 1989.
Led International League batters in strikeouts with 152 in 1987.
Led Southern League in total bases with 287, strikeouts with 153 and tied for lead in sacrifice flies with 13 in 1986.
Led Carolina League batters in strikeouts with 211 in 1985.
Led South Atlantic League batters in strikeouts with 150 in 1984.

Year Club	League	Pos.	G.	AB.	R.	H.	2B.	3B.	HR.	RBI.	B.A.	PO.	A.	E.	F.A.
1983—Medicine Hat........	Pion.	OF	46	133	34	63	3	4	6	27	.256	63	3	6	.917
1984—Florence..............	S. Atl.	OF	129	440	75	105	19	5	16	64	.239	281	9	16	.948
1985—Kinston................	Carol.	OF	131	466	57	98	13	0	20	56	.210	234	12	13	.950
1986—Knoxville.............	South.	OF	141	*570	87	159	23	6	*31	96	.279	230	9	*21	.919
1987—Syracuse	Int.	OF	*137	536	65	126	25	6	16	77	.235	176	10	10	.949
1988—Syracuse	Int.	OF	51	172	21	40	7	0	4	19	.233	101	2	1	.990
1988—Knoxville.............	South.	OF	79	269	37	71	13	2	12	38	.264	130	6	5	.965
1989—Syracuse	Int.	OF	125	483	*86	*155	31	*15	*21	72	.321	242	3	*7	.972
1989—Toronto	Amer.	OF	19	52	4	15	0	0	1	7	.288	27	0	1	.964
1990—Toronto†	Amer.	OF	84	260	47	60	11	3	12	32	.231	115	4	2	.983
Major League Totals—2 Years................			103	312	51	75	11	3	13	39	.240	142	4	3	.980

Selected by Toronto Blue Jays' organization in 9th round of free-agent draft, June 6, 1983.
†On disabled list, July 6 to July 21, 1990.

KENNETH WADE HILL
(Ken)

Born December 14, 1965, at Lynn, Mass.
Height, 6.02. Weight, 175.
Throws and bats righthanded.

Shares National League record for fewest games lost for leader, season (15), 1989.

Year Club	League	G.	IP.	W.	L.	Pct.	H.	R.	ER.	SO.	BB.	ERA.
1985—Gastonia................	S. Atlantic	15	69	3	6	.333	60	51	38	48	57	4.96
1986—Gastonia................	S. Atlantic	22	122⅔	9	5	.643	95	51	38	86	80	2.79
1986—Glens Falls†	Eastern	1	7	0	1	.000	4	4	4	4	6	5.14
1986—Arkansas....................	Texas	3	18	1	2	.333	18	10	9	9	7	4.50
1987—Arkansas....................	Texas	18	53⅔	3	5	.375	60	33	31	48	30	5.20
1988—St. Louis‡	National	4	14	0	1	.000	16	9	8	6	6	5.14
1988—Arkansas....................	Texas	22	115⅓	9	9	.500	129	76	63	107	50	4.92
1989—Louisville	Am. Assoc.	3	18	0	2	.000	13	8	7	18	10	3.50
1989—St. Louis....................	National	33	196⅔	7	●15	.318	186	92	83	112	*99	3.80
1990—St. Louis....................	National	17	78⅔	5	6	.455	79	49	48	58	33	5.49
1990—Louisville	Am. Assoc.	12	85⅓	6	1	.857	47	20	17	104	27	1.79
Major League Totals—3 Years............................		54	289⅓	12	22	.353	281	150	139	176	138	4.32

Signed as free agent by Detroit Tigers' organization, February 14, 1985.
†Traded with a player to be named later to St. Louis Cardinals for Catcher Mike Heath, August 10, 1986; St. Louis acquired First Baseman Mike Laga to complete deal, September 2, 1986.
‡On disabled list, March 26 to May 9, 1988.

MILTON GILES HILL
(Milt)

Born August 22, 1965, at Atlanta, Ga.
Height, 6.00. Weight, 180.
Throws and bats righthanded.
Attended DeKalb College, Clarkston, Ga., and Georgia College, Milledgeville, Ga.

Year Club	League	G.	IP.	W.	L.	Pct.	H.	R.	ER.	SO.	BB.	ERA.
1987—Billings....................	Pioneer	21	32⅔	3	1	.750	25	10	6	40	4	1.65
1988—Cedar Rapids....................	Midwest	44	78⅓	9	4	.692	52	21	18	69	17	2.07
1989—Chattanooga	Southern	51	70	6	5	.545	49	19	16	63	28	2.06
1990—Nashville....................	Am. Assoc.	48	71⅓	4	4	.500	51	20	18	58	18	2.27

Selected by Atlanta Braves' organization in 23rd round of free-agent draft, June 3, 1985.
Selected by Cincinnati Reds' organization in 28th round of free-agent draft, June 2, 1987.

SHAWN PATRICK HILLEGAS
Name pronounced HILL-uh-gus.

Born August 21, 1964, at Dos Palos, Calif.
Height, 6.02. Weight, 223.
Throws and bats righthanded.
Attended Middle Georgia College, Cochran, Ga.

Major League saves: 1989 (3).

Year Club	League	G.	IP.	W.	L.	Pct.	H.	R.	ER.	SO.	BB.	ERA.
1984—Vero Beach....................	Florida St.	13	93⅓	5	3	.625	71	25	19	64	33	1.83
1985—San Antonio....................	Texas	23	139½	4	10	.286	134	72	49	56	67	3.17
1986—San Antonio....................	Texas	17	132½	9	5	.643	107	60	45	97	58	3.06
1986—Albuquerque	P. Coast	9	46⅔	1	5	.167	48	35	32	43	31	6.17
1987—Albuquerque	P. Coast	24	165⅔	13	5	.722	172	79	62	105	64	3.37
1987—Los Angeles	National	12	58	4	3	.571	52	27	23	51	31	3.57
1988—Albuquerque	P. Coast	16	100⅔	6	4	.600	93	44	39	66	22	3.49
1988—Los Angeles†	National	11	56⅓	3	4	.429	54	26	26	30	17	4.13
1988—Chicago....................	American	6	40	3	2	.600	30	16	14	26	18	3.15
1989—Chicago....................	American	50	119⅔	7	11	.389	132	67	63	76	51	4.74
1990—Vancouver....................	P. Coast	36	67⅓	5	3	.625	49	22	13	52	15	1.74
1990—Chicago‡....................	American	7	11⅓	0	0	.000	4	1	1	5	5	0.79
National League Totals—2 Years........................		23	114⅔	7	7	.500	106	53	49	81	48	3.85
American League Totals—3 Years....................		63	171	10	13	.435	166	84	78	107	74	4.11
Major League Totals—4 Years............................		86	285⅔	17	20	.459	272	137	127	188	122	4.00

Selected by California Angels' organization in 26th round of free-agent draft, June 6, 1983.
Selected by Los Angeles Dodgers' organization in secondary phase of free-agent draft, January 17, 1984.
†Traded to Chicago White Sox, September 2, 1988, completing deal in which Chicago traded Pitcher Rick Horton to Los Angeles Dodgers for a player to be named later, August 30, 1988.
‡Traded with Pitcher Eric King to Cleveland Indians for Outfielder Cory Snyder and Infielder Lindsay Foster, December 4, 1990.

JOHN ERIC HILLMAN
(Known by middle name.)

Born April 27, 1966, at Gary, Ind.
Height, 6.10. Weight, 225.
Throws and bats lefthanded.
Attended Eastern Illinois University, Charleston, Ill.

Year Club	League	G.	IP.	W.	L.	Pct.	H.	R.	ER.	SO.	BB.	ERA.
1987—Little Falls	NYP	13	79	6	4	.600	84	44	37	80	30	4.22
1988—Columbia	S. Atlantic	17	73	1	6	.143	73	54	45	60	43	3.95
1989—Columbia	S. Atlantic	9	33⅔	2	1	.667	28	17	7	33	21	1.87
1989—St. Lucie	Florida St.	19	88⅓	6	6	.500	96	59	54	67	53	5.50
1990—St. Lucie	Florida St.	4	27	2	0	1.000	15	2	2	23	8	0.67
1990—Jackson	Texas	15	89⅓	6	5	.545	92	42	39	61	30	3.93

Selected by New York Mets' organization in 16th round of free-agent draft, June 2, 1987.

HOWARD JAMES HILTON

Born January 3, 1964, at Oxnard, Calif.
Height, 6.03. Weight, 230.
Throws and bats righthanded.
Attended Oxnard College, Oxnard, Calif., and
University of Arkansas, Fayetteville, Ark.

Led New York-Pennsylvania League in intentional bases on balls issued with 8 in 1985.

Year Club	League	G.	IP.	W.	L.	Pct.	H.	R.	ER.	SO.	BB.	ERA.
1985—Erie	NYP	24	65⅓	3	7	.300	73	46	31	66	26	4.27
1986—St. Petersburg	Florida St.	36	62⅔	4	5	.444	53	21	17	49	28	2.44
1987—Springfield	Midwest	★62	107⅓	8	6	.571	77	33	25	107	17	2.10
1988—Arkansas	Texas	66	102	8	7	.533	90	39	30	90	46	2.65
1989—Louisville	Am. Assoc.	★70	96⅓	12	5	.706	86	44	40	77	42	3.74
1990—St. Louis	National	2	3	0	0	.000	2	0	0	2	3	0.00
1990—Louisville	Am. Assoc.	56	80	4	3	.571	73	40	32	55	34	3.60
Major League Totals—1 Year		2	3	0	0	.000	2	0	0	2	3	0.00

Selected by St. Louis Cardinals' organization in 22nd round of free-agent draft, June 3, 1985.

CHRISTOPHER ALLEN HOILES
(Chris)

Born March 20, 1965, at Bowling Green, O.
Height, 6.00. Weight, 213.
Throws and bats righthanded.
Attended Eastern Michigan University, Ypsilanti, Mich.

Led Eastern League in slugging percentage with .500 in 1988.
Led Appalachian League in game-winning RBIs with 10 and total bases with 143 in 1986.
Led Appalachian League first basemen in putouts with 515, total chances with 551 and fielding percentage with .996 in 1986.
Tied for Eastern League lead in double plays by catchers with 5 in 1988.

Year Club	League	Pos.	G.	AB.	R.	H.	2B.	3B.	HR.	RBI.	B.A.	PO.	A.	E.	F.A.
1986—Bristol	Appal.	1B-C	●68	253	42	81	★19	2	13	★57	.320	563	38	4	.993
1987—Glens Falls	East.	C-1B-3B	108	380	47	105	12	0	13	53	.276	406	88	11	.978
1988—Glens Falls†	East.	C-1B	103	360	67	102	21	3	●17	73	.283	438	57	7	.986
1988—Toledo	Int.	C	22	69	4	11	1	0	2	6	.159	71	2	1	.986
1989—Rochester‡	Int.	C-1B	96	322	41	79	19	1	10	51	.245	431	33	7	.985
1989—Baltimore	Amer.	C	6	9	0	1	1	0	0	1	.111	11	0	0	1.000
1990—Rochester	Int.	C-1B	74	247	52	86	20	1	18	56	.348	268	13	5	.983
1990—Baltimore	Amer.	C-1B	23	63	7	12	3	0	1	6	.190	62	6	0	1.000
Major League Totals—2 Years			29	72	7	13	4	0	1	7	.181	73	6	0	1.000

Selected by Detroit Tigers' organization in 19th round of free-agent draft, June 2, 1986.
†Traded with Pitchers Cesar Mejia and Robinson Garces to Baltimore Orioles, September 9, 1988, to complete deal in which Baltimore traded Outfielder Fred Lynn to Detroit Tigers for three players to be named later, August 31, 1988.
‡On disabled list, June 18 to July 7, 1989.

DAVID MICHAELS HOLLINS
(Dave)

Born May 25, 1966, at Buffalo, N.Y.
Height, 6.01. Weight, 195.
Throws right and bats left and righthanded.
Attended University of South Carolina, Columbia, S.C.

Led Texas League in sacrifice flies with 10 in 1989.
Led Northwest League in intentional bases on balls received with 7 in 1987.
Led Northwest League third basemen in total chances with 241 in 1987.

— 217 —

Year Club	League	Pos.	G.	AB.	R.	H.	2B.	3B.	HR.	RBI.	B.A.	PO.	A.	E.	F.A.
1987—Spokane	N'west	3B	75	278	52	86	14	4	2	44	.309	*59	*167	15	*.938
1988—Riverside	Calif.	3B-1B	139	516	90	157	32	1	9	92	.304	102	248	29	.923
1989—Wichita†	Texas	3B	131	459	69	126	29	4	9	79	.275	77	209	25	.920
1990—Philadelphia	Nat.	3B-1B	72	114	14	21	0	0	5	15	.184	27	37	4	.941
Major League Totals—1 Year..................			72	114	14	21	0	0	5	15	.184	27	37	4	.941

Selected by San Diego Padres' organization in 6th round of free-agent draft, June 2, 1987.

†Drafted by Philadelphia Phillies, December 4, 1989.

BRIAN SCOTT HOLMAN

Born January 25, 1965, at Denver, Colo.
Height, 6.04. Weight, 185.
Throws and bats righthanded.

Led Southern League in complete games with 6 in 1987.
Named Southern League Pitcher of the Year, 1987.

Year Club	League	G.	IP.	W.	L.	Pct.	H.	R.	ER.	SO.	BB.	ERA.
1983—Jamestown†	NYP	2	5⅓	0	0	.000	7	7	7	5	4	11.81
1984—West Palm Beach	Florida St.	4	8	0	3	.000	14	19	16	14	21	18.00
1984—Gastonia..........................	S. Atlantic	20	90⅔	5	8	.385	76	58	48	94	98	4.76
1985—West Palm Beach	Florida St.	25	143⅓	9	9	.500	124	79	63	103	90	3.96
1986—Jacksonville....................	Southern	27	157⅔	11	9	.550	146	111	90	118	*122	5.14
1987—Jacksonville....................	Southern	22	151⅓	14	5	.737	114	52	42	115	56	*2.50
1987—Indianapolis	Am. Assoc.	6	34⅔	0	4	.000	41	28	24	27	33	6.23
1988—Indianapolis	Am. Assoc.	14	91⅓	8	1	.889	78	26	24	70	30	2.36
1988—Montreal........................	National	18	100⅓	4	8	.333	101	39	36	58	34	3.23
1989—Montreal‡......................	National	10	31⅔	1	2	.333	34	18	17	23	15	4.83
1989—Seattle...........................	American	23	159⅔	8	10	.444	160	68	61	82	62	3.44
1990—Seattle§.........................	American	28	189⅔	11	11	.500	188	92	85	121	66	4.03
National League Totals—2 Years......................		28	132	5	10	.333	135	57	53	81	49	3.61
American League Totals—2 Years		51	349⅓	19	21	.475	348	160	146	203	128	3.76
Major League Totals—3 Years........................		79	481⅓	24	31	.436	483	217	199	284	177	3.72

Selected by Montreal Expos' organization in 1st round (16th player selected) of free-agent draft, June 6, 1983.

†On disabled list, August 3, 1983 through remainder of season.

‡Traded with Pitchers Randy Johnson and Gene Harris to Seattle Mariners for Pitcher Mark Langston and a player to be named later, May 25, 1989; Indianapolis (Montreal Expos' organization) acquired Pitcher Mike Campbell to complete deal, July 31, 1989.

§Batted once in order (reached on error) after designated hitter moved to first base.

DARREN LEE HOLMES

Born April 25, 1966, at Asheville, N.C.
Height, 6.00. Weight, 200.
Throws and bats righthanded.

Year Club	League	G.	IP.	W.	L.	Pct.	H.	R.	ER.	SO.	BB.	ERA.
1984—Great Falls....................................	Pioneer	18	44⅔	2	5	.286	53	41	33	29	30	6.65
1985—Vero Beach..................................	Florida St.	33	63⅔	4	3	.571	57	31	22	46	35	3.11
1986—Vero Beach†................................	Florida St.	11	64⅔	3	6	.333	55	30	21	59	39	2.92
1987—Vero Beach..................................	Florida St.	19	99⅔	6	4	.600	111	60	50	46	53	4.52
1988—San Luis Potosi‡..........................	Mexican	23	139⅔	9	9	.500	151	88	72	110	92	4.64
1988—Albuquerque................................	P. Coast	2	5⅓	0	1	.000	6	3	3	1	1	5.06
1989—San Antonio................................	Texas	17	110⅓	5	8	.385	102	59	47	81	44	3.83
1989—Albuquerque................................	P. Coast	9	38⅔	1	4	.200	50	32	32	31	18	7.45
1990—Albuquerque................................	P. Coast	56	92⅔	12	2	*.857	78	34	32	99	39	3.11
1990—Los Angeles§...............................	National	14	17⅓	0	1	.000	15	10	10	19	11	5.19
Major League Totals—1 Year.............................		14	17⅓	0	1	.000	15	10	10	19	11	5.19

Selected by Los Angeles Dodgers' organization in 16th round of free-agent draft, June 4, 1984.

†On disabled list, June 5, 1986 through remainder of season.

‡Loaned to San Luis Potosi and returned.

§Traded to Milwaukee Brewers for Catcher Bert Heffernan, December 20, 1990.

BRIAN JOHN HOLTON

Born November 29, 1959, at McKeesport, Pa.
Height, 6.00. Weight, 207.
Throws and bats righthanded.
Attended Louisburg College, Louisburg, N. C.

Major League saves: 1987 (2), 1988 (1). Total—3.
Tied for Pacific Coast League lead in games started by pitchers with 27 in 1986.
Tied for Texas League lead in complete games with 16 in 1980.
Tied for California League lead in shutouts with 3 in 1979.

Year Club	League	G.	IP.	W.	L.	Pct.	H.	R.	ER.	SO.	BB.	ERA.
1978—Clinton†	Midwest	14	79	6	4	.600	94	51	38	54	23	4.33
1979—Lodi	California	10	72	7	0	1.000	47	26	21	72	32	2.63
1979—San Antonio......................................	Texas	13	51	3	5	.375	50	24	21	40	25	3.71
1980—San Antonio......................................	Texas	27	207	●15	10	.600	204	93	79	139	65	3.43
1981—Albuquerque	P. Coast	26	191	16	6	.727	215	94	73	73	51	3.44
1982—Albuquerque	P. Coast	32	161⅓	12	8	.600	191	102	92	76	60	5.13
1983—Albuquerque‡	P. Coast	20	97⅔	7	5	.583	113	76	69	70	50	6.36

— 218 —

Year Club	League	G.	IP.	W.	L.	Pct.	H.	R.	ER.	SO.	BB.	ERA.
1984—Albuquerque §x	P. Coast	12	32	0	0	.000	39	23	20	15	9	5.63
1985—Albuquerque	P. Coast	27	179⅔	9	10	.474	183	83	72	86	40	3.61
1985—Los Angeles	National	3	4	1	1	.500	9	7	4	1	1	9.00
1986—Albuquerque	P. Coast	27	*182⅔	10	10	.500	200	90	74	105	20	3.78
1986—Los Angeles	National	12	24⅓	2	3	.400	28	13	12	24	6	4.44
1987—Los Angeles	National	53	83⅓	3	2	.600	87	39	36	58	32	3.89
1988—Los Angeles y	National	45	84⅔	7	3	.700	69	19	16	49	26	1.70
1989—Baltimore	American	39	116⅓	5	7	.417	140	63	52	51	39	4.02
1990—Baltimore	American	33	58	2	3	.400	68	31	29	27	21	4.50
1990—Rochester z	Int'national	9	15⅔	1	4	.200	26	16	16	18	6	9.19
National League Totals—4 Years		113	196⅓	13	9	.591	193	78	68	132	65	3.12
American League Totals—2 Years		72	174⅓	7	10	.412	208	94	81	78	60	4.18
Major League Totals—6 Years		185	370⅔	20	19	.513	401	172	149	210	125	3.62

Selected by Los Angeles Dodgers' organization in 1st round (22nd player selected) of free-agent draft, January 10, 1978.

†On temporary inactive list, June 12 to July 7, 1978.

‡On disabled list, June 28 to July 15, 1983.

§On disabled list, April 7 to July 11, 1984.

xGranted free agency, October 15, 1984; re-signed by Dodgers' organization, October 22, 1984.

yTraded with Pitcher Ken Howell and Shortstop Juan Bell to Baltimore Orioles for First Baseman Eddie Murray, December 4, 1988.

zGranted free agency, October 15, 1990.

CHAMPIONSHIP SERIES RECORD

Year Club	League	G.	IP.	W.	L.	Pct.	H.	R.	ER.	SO.	BB.	ERA.
1988—Los Angeles	National	3	4	0	0	.000	2	1	1	2	1	2.25

WORLD SERIES RECORD

Year Club	League	G.	IP.	W.	L.	Pct.	H.	R.	ER.	SO.	BB.	ERA.
1988—Los Angeles	National	1	2	0	0	.000	0	0	0	0	1	0.00

FREDERICK WAYNE HONEYCUTT
(Rick)

Born June 29, 1954, at Chattanooga, Tenn.
Height, 6.01. Weight, 190.
Throws and bats lefthanded.
Received bachelor of science degree in health education from
University of Tennessee, Knoxville, Tenn.

Major League saves: 1985 (1), 1988 (7), 1989 (12), 1990 (7). Total—27.
Tied for New York-Pennsylvania League lead in complete games with 7 in 1976.

Year Club	League	G.	IP.	W.	L.	Pct.	H.	R.	ER.	SO.	BB.	ERA.
1976—Niagara Falls†	NYP	13	*97	5	3	.625	91	36	28	*98	20	2.60
1977—Shreveport‡§	Texas	21	135	10	6	.625	144	53	37	82	42	*2.47
1977—Seattle	American	10	29	0	1	.000	26	16	14	17	11	4.34
1978—Seattle x	American	26	134	5	11	.313	150	81	73	50	49	4.90
1979—Seattle	American	33	194	11	12	.478	201	103	87	83	67	4.04
1980—Seattle y	American	30	203	10	17	.370	221	99	89	79	60	3.95
1981—Texas	American	20	128	11	6	.647	120	49	47	40	17	3.30
1982—Texas	American	30	164	5	17	.227	201	103	96	64	54	5.27
1983—Texas z	American	25	174⅔	14	8	.636	168	59	47	56	37	*2.42
1983—Los Angeles	National	9	39	2	3	.400	46	26	25	18	13	5.77
1984—Los Angeles	National	29	183⅔	10	9	.526	180	72	58	75	51	2.84
1985—Los Angeles	National	31	142	8	12	.400	141	71	54	67	49	3.42
1986—Los Angeles	National	32	171	11	9	.550	164	71	63	100	45	3.32
1987—Los Angeles a	National	27	115⅔	2	12	.143	133	74	59	92	45	4.59
1987—Oakland b	American	7	23⅔	1	4	.200	25	17	14	10	9	5.32
1988—Oakland b	American	55	79⅔	3	2	.600	74	36	31	47	25	3.50
1989—Oakland	American	64	76⅔	2	2	.500	56	26	20	52	26	2.35
1990—Oakland c	American	63	63⅓	2	2	.500	46	23	19	38	22	2.70
American League Totals—11 Years		363	1270	64	82	.438	1288	612	537	536	377	3.81
National League Totals—5 Years		128	651⅓	33	45	.423	664	314	259	352	203	3.58
Major League Totals—14 Years		491	1921⅓	97	127	.433	1952	926	796	888	580	3.73

Selected by Baltimore Orioles' organization in 14th round of free-agent draft, June 6, 1972.

Selected by Pittsburgh Pirates' organization in 17th round of free-agent draft, June 8, 1976.

†Played two games as first baseman and one game as shortstop.

‡Traded to Seattle Mariners, August 22, 1977, completing deal in which Seattle traded Pitcher Dave Pagan to Pittsburgh Pirates for a player to be named later, July 27, 1977.

§Appeared as shortstop with no chances.

xOn disabled list, May 20 to June 26, 1978.

yTraded with Catcher Larry Cox, Outfielders Willie Horton and Leon Roberts and Shortstop Mario Mendoza to Texas Rangers with Ken Clay, Steve Finch and Jerry Don Gleaton, Shortstop Rick Auerbach and Outfielder Richie Zisk, December 12, 1980.

zTraded to Los Angeles Dodgers for Pitcher Dave Stewart and a player to be named later, August 19, 1983; Texas Rangers acquired Pitcher Ricky Wright to complete deal, September 16, 1983.

aTraded to Oakland Athletics for a player to be named later, August 29, 1987; Los Angeles Dodgers acquired Pitcher Tim Belcher to complete deal, September 3, 1987.

bGranted free agency, November 4, 1988; re-signed by Athletics, December 21, 1988.

cMade an out in both appearances as a pinch-hitter and appeared in one game as a pinch-runner.

CHAMPIONSHIP SERIES RECORD

Year Club	League	G.	IP.	W.	L.	Pct.	H.	R.	ER.	SO.	BB.	ERA.
1983—Los Angeles	National	2	1⅔	0	0	.000	4	4	4	2	0	21.60
1985—Los Angeles	National	2	1⅓	0	0	.000	4	2	2	1	2	13.50
1988—Oakland....................................	American	3	2	1	0	1.000	0	0	0	0	2	0.00
1989—Oakland....................................	American	3	1⅔	0	0	.000	6	6	6	1	5	32.40
1990—Oakland....................................	American	3	1⅔	0	0	.000	0	0	0	0	0	0.00
Championship Series Totals—5 Years................		13	8⅓	1	0	1.000	14	12	12	4	9	12.96

WORLD SERIES RECORD

Year Club	League	G.	IP.	W.	L.	Pct.	H.	R.	ER.	SO.	BB.	ERA.
1988—Oakland....................................	American	3	3⅓	1	0	1.000	0	0	0	5	0	0.00
1989—Oakland....................................	American	3	2⅔	0	0	.000	4	2	2	2	0	6.75
1990—Oakland....................................	American	1	1⅔	0	0	.000	2	0	0	0	1	0.00
World Series Totals—3 Years		7	7⅔	1	0	1.000	6	2	2	7	1	2.35

ALL-STAR GAME RECORD

Year League	IP.	W.	L.	Pct.	H.	R.	ER.	SO.	BB.	ERA.
1983—American	2	0	0	.000	5	2	2	0	0	9.00

Member of American League All-Star Team in 1980; did not play.

JOHN NICKLAUS HOOVER

Born November 22, 1962, at Fresno, Calif.
Height, 6.02. Weight, 190.
Throws and bats righthanded.
Received degree from Fresno State University, Fresno, Calif. in 1984.

Led Southern League pitchers in games started with 29 in 1985.
Member of 1984 U.S. Olympic baseball team.

Year Club	League	G.	IP.	W.	L.	Pct.	H.	R.	ER.	SO.	BB.	ERA.
1984—Rochester	Int'national	5	19	2	3	.400	19	14	11	13	11	5.21
1985—Charlotte......................................	Southern	29	183	8	*16	.333	186	108	96	●128	81	4.72
1986—Charlotte†....................................	Southern	8	39	2	4	.333	52	35	33	9	34	7.62
1986—Miami..	Florida St.	2	3⅔	0	1	.000	10	10	9	3	8	22.09
1986—Hagerstown	Carolina	3	18	2	0	1.000	10	2	1	13	13	0.50
1987—Charlotte‡....................................	Southern	22	140	9	8	.529	151	78	71	100	51	4.56
1988—Jacksonville§	Southern	29	159⅔	10	11	.476	161	90	73	121	58	4.11
1989—Tulsa...	Texas	21	125	9	6	.600	125	53	47	77	37	3.38
1990—Tulsa...	Texas	4	23⅔	2	1	.667	29	12	9	18	11	3.42
1990—Oklahoma City x-Indianapolis ....Am. Assoc.		28	97⅓	4	5	.444	120	73	64	47	39	5.92
1990—Texas y..	American	2	4⅔	0	0	.000	8	6	6	0	3	11.57
Major League Totals—1 Year................		2	4⅔	0	0	.000	8	6	6	0	3	11.57

Selected by New York Yankees' organization in 20th round of free-agent draft, June 6, 1983.
Selected by Baltimore Orioles' organization in 1st round (25th player selected) of free-agent draft, June 4, 1984.
†On disabled list, April 24 to June 8, 1986.
‡Traded with Pitchers Doug Cinnella and Rick Carriger to Montreal Expos for Pitchers Jay Tibbs and Al Cardwood, February 16, 1988.
§Released, April 2, 1989; signed by Tulsa (Texas Rangers' organization), May 3, 1989.
xReleased, July 21, 1990; signed by Indianapolis (Montreal Expos' organization), August 18, 1990.
yGranted free agency, October 15, 1990.

SAMUEL LEE HORN
(Sam)

Born November 2, 1963, at Dallas, Tex.
Height, 6.05. Weight, 250.
Throws and bats lefthanded.

Shares American League record for most home runs, first two major league games (2), July 25 and 26, 1987.
Led International League in slugging percentage with .649 in 1987.
Led Carolina League in slugging percentage with .538 in 1984.
Tied for International League lead in intentional bases on balls received with 10 in 1988.

Year Club	League	Pos.	G.	AB.	R.	H.	2B.	3B.	HR.	RBI.	B.A.	PO.	A.	E.	F.A.
1982—Elmira	NYP	1B	61	213	47	64	13	1	11	48	.300	368	29	11	.973
1983—Winston-Salem† ... Carol.		1B	68	217	33	52	9	0	9	29	.240	363	24	10	.975
1984—Winston-Salem ..... Carol.		1B	127	403	67	126	22	3	21	89	.313	978	*70	*29	.973
1985—New Britain .... East.		1B	134	457	64	129	*32	0	11	82	.282	751	63	*23	.973
1986—New Britain .... East.		1B	100	345	41	85	13	0	8	46	.246	356	28	9	.977
1986—Pawtucket .... Int.		1B	20	77	8	15	2	0	3	14	.195	61	4	0	1.000
1987—Pawtucket .... Int.		1B	94	333	57	107	19	0	30	84	.321	28	2	2	.938
1987—Boston.................... Amer.		DH	46	158	31	44	7	0	14	34	.278	0	0	0	.000
1988—Boston.................... Amer.		DH	24	61	4	9	0	0	2	8	.148	0	0	0	.000
1988—Pawtucket .... Int.		1B	83	279	33	65	10	0	10	31	.233	6	1	1	.875
1989—Boston‡................. Amer.		1B	33	54	1	8	2	0	4	4	.148	5	0	0	1.000
1989—Pawtucket§ .... Int.		DH	51	164	15	38	9	1	8	27	.232	0	0	0	.000
1990—Baltimore x........ Amer.		1B	79	246	30	61	13	0	14	45	.248	58	6	2	.970
1990—Rochester .... Int.		1B	17	58	16	24	3	0	9	26	.414	27	1	2	.933
1990—Hagerstown .... East.		DH	7	23	2	6	2	0	1	3	.261	0	0	0	.000
Major League Totals—4 Years................			182	519	66	122	22	0	30	91	.235	63	6	2	.972

Selected by Boston Red Sox' organization in 1st round (16th player selected) of free-agent draft, June 7, 1982.

†On disabled list, April 28 to June 23, 1983.

‡On disabled list, June 8 to July 28, 1989; included rehabilitation disability assignment to Pawtucket, July 13 to July 28, 1989.

§Released, December 20, 1989; signed by Rochester (Baltimore Orioles' organization), February 20, 1990.

xOn disabled list, May 8 to May 29, 1990; included rehabilitation disability assignment to Rochester, May 21 to May 29, 1990.

RICKY NEAL HORTON
(Rick)

Born July 30, 1959, at Poughkeepsie, N.Y.
Height, 6.02. Weight, 197.
Throws and bats lefthanded.
Received bachelor of science degree in engineering from
University of Virginia, Charlottesville, Va. in 1982.
Brother of David Horton, infielder in St. Louis Cardinals' organization, 1986 and 1987.

Major League saves: 1984 (1), 1985 (1), 1986 (3), 1987 (7), 1988 (2), 1990 (1). Total—15.
Led American Association in balks with 7 in 1983.

Year	Club	League	G.	IP.	W.	L.	Pct.	H.	R.	ER.	SO.	BB.	ERA.
1980—St. Petersburg	Florida St.	6	25	0	2	.000	29	18	17	13	17	6.12
1980—Gastonia	S. Atlantic	14	42	2	4	.333	30	21	17	30	25	3.64
1981—St. Petersburg	Florida St.	28	100	7	3	.700	101	52	49	66	49	4.41
1982—Arkansas	Texas	16	108⅔	9	6	.600	83	45	38	90	52	3.15
1982—Louisville	Am. Assoc.	8	36⅓	2	3	.400	47	31	27	37	11	6.69
1983—Louisville	Am. Assoc.	30	157	10	6	.625	177	99	84	92	58	4.82
1984—St. Louis	National	37	125⅔	9	4	.692	140	53	48	76	39	3.44
1985—St. Louis	National	49	89⅔	3	2	.600	84	30	29	59	34	2.91
1986—St. Louis†	National	42	100⅓	4	3	.571	77	25	25	49	26	2.24
1986—Springfield	Midwest	1	2	0	0	.000	2	0	0	2	0	0.00
1987—St. Louis‡§	National	67	125	8	3	.727	127	58	53	55	42	3.82
1988—Chicago x	American	52	109⅓	6	10	.375	120	64	59	28	36	4.86
1988—Los Angeles	National	12	9	1	1	.500	11	7	5	8	2	5.00
1989—Los Angeles y-St. Louis	National	34	72⅓	0	3	.000	85	39	39	26	21	4.85
1989—Louisville z	Am. Assoc.	2	9	1	0	1.000	8	1	1	1	2	1.00
1990—St. Louis a	National	32	42	1	1	.500	52	25	23	18	22	4.93
1990—Denver b	Am. Assoc.	5	24⅓	3	1	.750	37	17	13	10	7	4.81
National League Totals—7 Years		273	564	26	17	.605	576	237	222	291	186	3.54
American League Totals—1 Year		52	109⅓	6	10	.375	120	64	59	28	36	4.86
Major League Totals—7 Years		325	673⅓	32	27	.542	696	301	281	319	222	3.76

Selected by San Francisco Giants' organization in 20th round of free-agent draft, June 7, 1977.

Selected by St. Louis Cardinals' organization in 4th round of free-agent draft, June 3, 1980.

†On disabled list, May 25 to June 24, 1986; included rehabilitation disability assignment to Springfield, June 20 to June 24, 1986.

‡Appeared as an outfielder with no chances.

§Traded with Outfielder Lance Johnson and cash to Chicago White Sox for Pitcher Jose DeLeon, February 9, 1988.

xTraded to Los Angeles Dodgers for a player to be named later, August 30, 1988; Chicago White Sox acquired Pitcher Shawn Hillegas to complete deal, September 2, 1988.

yReleased, July 16, 1989; signed by Louisville (St. Louis Cardinals' organization), July 20, 1989.

zGranted free agency, November 13, 1989; re-signed by Cardinals, December 6, 1989.

aReleased, July 25, 1990; signed by Denver (Milwaukee Brewers' organization), August 10, 1990.

bReleased, September 5, 1990.

CHAMPIONSHIP SERIES RECORD

Year	Club	League	G.	IP.	W.	L.	Pct.	H.	R.	ER.	SO.	BB.	ERA.
1985—St. Louis	National	3	3	0	0	.000	4	4	4	1	2	12.00
1987—St. Louis	National	1	3	0	0	.000	2	0	0	2	0	0.00
1988—Los Angeles	National	4	4⅓	0	0	.000	4	0	0	3	2	0.00
Championship Series Totals—3 Years		8	10⅓	0	0	.000	10	4	4	6	4	3.48

WORLD SERIES RECORD

Year	Club	League	G.	IP.	W.	L.	Pct.	H.	R.	ER.	SO.	BB.	ERA.
1985—St. Louis	National	3	4	0	0	.000	4	3	3	5	5	6.75
1987—St. Louis	National	2	3	0	0	.000	5	2	2	1	0	6.00
World Series Totals—2 Years		5	7	0	0	.000	9	5	5	6	5	6.43

CHARLES OLIVER HOUGH
Name pronounced Huff.
(Charlie)

Born January 5, 1948, at Honolulu, Haw.
Height, 6.02. Weight, 190.
Throws and bats righthanded.
Son of Dick Hough, minor league third baseman, 1933.

Shares major league record for most strikeouts, inning (4), July 4, 1988, first inning.
Holds American League record for most balks, season (9), 1987.
Major League saves: 1970 (2), 1973 (5), 1974 (1), 1975 (4), 1976 (18), 1977 (22), 1978 (7), 1980 (1), 1981 (1). Total—61.
Led American League in hit batsmen with 19 in 1987 and 11 in 1990.
Led American League pitchers in games started with 40 in 1987 and tied for lead with 36 in 1984.

Led American League pitchers in complete games with 17 in 1984.
Led American League in balks with 9 in 1987.
Tied for American League lead in home runs allowed with 28 in 1989.
Led Pacific Coast League in intentional bases on balls issued with 13 in 1972.
Led Pacific Coast League in saves with 18 in 1970.
Led Texas League in home runs allowed with 17 in 1969.
Named Pacific Coast League Pitcher of the Year, 1972.

Year Club	League	G.	IP.	W.	L.	Pct.	H.	R.	ER.	SO.	BB.	ERA.
1966—Ogden	Pioneer	21	68	5	●7	.417	82	56	36	68	29	4.76
1967—Santa Barbara	California	20	165	14	4	★.778	129	50	41	138	43	2.24
1967—Albuquerque	Texas	7	36	2	1	.667	57	31	28	25	10	7.00
1968—Albuquerque†	Texas	27	121	6	10	.375	145	72	53	74	26	3.94
1969—Albuquerque	Texas	27	163	10	9	.526	190	87	74	113	42	4.09
1970—Spokane	P. Coast	49	134	12	8	.600	98	43	29	90	44	1.95
1970—Los Angeles	National	8	17	0	0	.000	18	11	10	8	11	5.29
1971—Spokane‡	P. Coast	47	117	10	8	.556	95	56	51	104	52	3.92
1971—Los Angeles	National	4	4	0	0	.000	3	3	2	4	3	4.50
1972—Albuquerque§	P. Coast	58	125	14	5	.737	109	47	33	95	60	2.38
1972—Los Angeles	National	2	3	0	0	.000	2	1	1	4	2	3.00
1973—Los Angeles	National	37	72	4	2	.667	52	24	22	70	45	2.75
1974—Los Angeles	National	49	96	9	4	.692	65	45	40	63	40	3.75
1975—Los Angeles	National	38	61	3	7	.300	43	25	20	34	34	2.95
1976—Los Angeles	National	77	143	12	8	.600	102	43	35	81	77	2.20
1977—Los Angeles	National	70	127	6	12	.333	98	53	47	105	70	3.33
1978—Los Angeles	National	55	93	5	5	.500	69	38	34	66	48	3.29
1979—Los Angeles	National	42	151	7	5	.583	152	88	80	76	66	4.77
1980—Los Angeles x	National	19	32	1	3	.250	37	21	20	25	21	5.63
1980—Texas	American	16	61	2	2	.500	54	30	27	47	37	3.98
1981—Texas	American	21	82	4	1	.800	61	30	27	69	31	2.96
1982—Texas	American	34	228	16	13	.552	217	111	100	128	72	3.95
1983—Texas	American	34	252	15	13	.536	219	96	89	152	95	3.18
1984—Texas	American	36	266	16	14	.533	★260	127	111	164	94	3.76
1985—Texas	American	34	250⅓	14	16	.467	198	102	92	141	83	3.31
1986—Oklahoma City y	Am. Assoc.	1	5	0	1	.000	7	5	5	3	1	9.00
1986—Texas	American	33	230⅓	17	10	.630	188	115	97	146	89	3.79
1987—Texas	American	40	★285⅓	18	13	.581	238	★159	120	223	124	3.79
1988—Texas	American	34	252	15	16	.484	202	111	93	174	★126	3.32
1989—Texas z	American	30	182	10	13	.435	168	97	88	94	95	4.35
1990—Texas a	American	32	218⅔	12	12	.500	190	108	99	114	119	4.07
National League Totals—11 Years		401	799	47	46	.505	641	352	311	536	417	3.50
American League Totals—11 Years		344	2307⅔	139	123	.531	1995	1086	943	1452	965	3.68
Major League Totals—21 Years		745	3106⅔	186	169	.524	2636	1438	1254	1988	1382	3.63

Selected by Los Angeles Dodgers' organization in 8th round of free-agent draft, June 9, 1966.
†On temporary inactive list, June 19 to July 1, 1968.
‡On temporary inactive list, July 10 to July 24, 1971.
§On temporary inactive list June 12 to June 15, July 22 to July 24 and August 7 to August 12, 1972.
xSold to Texas Rangers, July 11, 1980.
yOn Texas disabled list, March 25 to May 6, 1986; included rehabilitation disability assignment to Oklahoma City, May 2 to May 6, 1986.
zOn disabled list, July 20 to August 4, 1989.
aGranted free agency, November 5, 1990; signed by Chicago White Sox, December 20, 1990.

CHAMPIONSHIP SERIES RECORD

Year Club	League	G.	IP.	W.	L.	Pct.	H.	R.	ER.	SO.	BB.	ERA.
1974—Los Angeles	National	1	2⅓	0	0	.000	4	2	2	2	0	7.71
1977—Los Angeles	National	1	2	0	0	.000	2	1	1	3	0	4.50
1978—Los Angeles	National	1	2	0	0	.000	1	1	1	1	0	4.50
Championship Series Totals—3 Years		3	6⅓	0	0	.000	7	4	4	6	0	5.68

WORLD SERIES RECORD

Tied World Series record for most wild pitches, inning and game (2), October 15, 1978 (seventh inning).

Year Club	League	G.	IP.	W.	L.	Pct.	H.	R.	ER.	SO.	BB.	ERA.
1974—Los Angeles	National	1	2	0	0	.000	0	0	0	4	1	0.00
1977—Los Angeles	National	2	5	0	0	.000	3	1	1	5	0	1.80
1978—Los Angeles	National	2	5⅓	0	0	.000	10	5	5	5	2	8.44
World Series Totals—3 Years		5	12⅓	0	0	.000	13	6	6	14	3	4.38

ALL-STAR GAME RECORD

Year League	IP.	W.	L.	Pct.	H.	R.	ER.	SO.	BB.	ERA.
1986—American	1⅔	0	0	.000	2	2	1	3	0	5.40

BATTING RECORD

Year Club	League	Pos.	G.	AB.	R.	H.	2B.	3B.	HR.	RBI.	B.A.	PO.	A.	E.	F.A.
1967—Santa Barbara	Calif.	P-1B	28	72	8	14	2	0	0	4	.194	15	25	2	.953
1968—Albuquerque	Texas	P-1B-3B	56	83	10	21	4	0	0	6	.253	43	25	4	.944
1969—Albuquerque	Texas	P-3B	31	57	10	12	0	0	1	9	.211	10	19	2	.935
1970—Spokane	P. C.	P-OF-1B	49	33	1	6	0	0	1	3	.182	7	28	3	.921
1971—Spokane	P. C.	P-OF	48	36	2	10	0	0	0	3	.278	6	20	1	.963
1972—Albuquerque	P. C.	P-OF	58	34	4	9	1	0	0	5	.265	3	27	0	1.000

STEVEN BERNARD HOWARD
(Steve)

Born December 7, 1963, at Oakland, Calif.
Height, 6.02. Weight, 205.
Throws and bats righthanded.
Attended Laney College, Oakland, Calif.

Led Pacific Coast League batters in strikeouts with 135 in 1989.
Led Southern League in being hit by pitch with 12 in 1987.
Led Northwest League batters in strikeouts with 89 in 1984.
Tied for Pacific Coast League lead in double plays by outfielders with 4 in 1989.

Year Club	League	Pos.	G.	AB.	R.	H.	2B.	3B.	HR.	RBI.	B.A.	PO.	A.	E.	F.A.
1983—Idaho Falls	Pion.	OF	61	203	40	45	4	4	6	33	.222	77	2	6	.929
1984—Madison	Midw.	OF	44	123	13	21	4	0	2	14	.171	36	0	4	.900
1984—Medford	N'west	OF	53	185	26	39	4	1	4	24	.211	55	2	5	.919
1985—Modesto	Calif.	OF	110	349	59	77	15	3	14	64	.221	101	1	11	.903
1986—Modesto†	Calif.	OF	98	302	64	70	11	4	9	53	.232	156	2	12	.929
1987—Huntsville	South.	OF	133	439	79	112	17	4	13	66	.255	197	1	●15	.930
1988—Huntsville	South.	OF	128	461	70	114	19	6	17	78	.247	211	5	11	.952
1989—Tacoma	P. C.	OF	107	341	51	83	10	2	13	60	.243	170	7	6	.967
1990—Tacoma	P. C.	OF	97	330	55	89	18	4	10	45	.270	124	4	5	.962
1990—Oakland‡	Amer.	OF	21	52	5	12	4	0	0	1	.231	14	0	1	.933
Major League Totals—1 Year			21	52	5	12	4	0	0	1	.231	14	0	1	.933

Selected by Oakland Athletics' organization in 8th round of free-agent draft, January 11, 1983.
†On disabled list, June 30 to July 22, 1986.
‡Granted free agency, December 20, 1990.

THOMAS SYLVESTER HOWARD

Born December 11, 1964, at Middletown, O.
Height, 6.02. Weight, 200.
Throws right and bats left and righthanded.
Attended Ball State University, Muncie, Ind.

Named outfielder on THE SPORTING NEWS College Baseball All-America Team, 1986.

Year Club	League	Pos.	G.	AB.	R.	H.	2B.	3B.	HR.	RBI.	B.A.	PO.	A.	E.	F.A.
1986—Spokane	N'west	OF	13	55	16	23	3	3	2	17	.418	24	3	0	1.000
1986—Reno	Calif.	OF	61	223	35	57	7	3	10	39	.256	104	5	6	.948
1987—Wichita	Texas	OF	113	401	72	133	27	4	14	60	.332	226	6	6	.975
1988—Wichita	Texas	OF	29	103	15	31	9	2	0	16	.301	51	2	2	.964
1988—Las Vegas	P. C.	OF	44	167	29	42	9	1	0	15	.251	74	3	2	.975
1989—Las Vegas†	P. C.	OF	80	303	45	91	18	3	3	31	.300	178	7	2	.989
1990—Las Vegas	P. C.	OF	89	341	58	112	26	8	5	51	.328	159	6	2	.988
1990—San Diego	Nat.	OF	20	44	4	12	2	0	0	0	.273	19	0	1	.950
Major League Totals—1 Year			20	44	4	12	2	0	0	0	.273	19	0	1	.950

Selected by San Diego Padres' organization in 1st round (11th player selected) of free-agent draft, June 2, 1986.
†On disabled list, June 5 to July 17, 1989.

JACK ROBERT HOWELL

Born August 18, 1961, at Tucson, Ariz.
Height, 6.00. Weight, 190.
Throws right and bats lefthanded.
Attended Pima Community College, Tucson, Ariz., and University of Arizona, Tucson, Ariz.

Major League stolen bases: 1985 (1), 1986 (2), 1987 (4), 1988 (2), 1990 (3). Total—12.
Led American League third basemen in total chances with 428 in 1989.
Led California League third basemen in fielding percentage with .943, assists with 259, double plays with 23 and total chances with 368 in 1984.

Year Club	League	Pos.	G.	AB.	R.	H.	2B.	3B.	HR.	RBI.	B.A.	PO.	A.	E.	F.A.
1983—Salem	N'west	3B-2B	21	76	23	30	2	5	3	12	.395	19	32	11	.823
1984—Redwood	Calif.	3B-1B	135	451	62	111	21	5	5	64	.246	96	260	21	.944
1985—Edmonton†	P. C.	3B-SS	79	284	55	106	22	3	13	48	.373	130	12	.943
1985—California	Amer.	3B	43	137	19	27	4	0	5	18	.197	33	75	8	.931
1986—Edmonton	P. C.	3B	44	156	39	56	17	3	3	28	.359	28	84	8	.933
1986—California	Amer.	3B-OF	63	151	26	41	14	2	4	21	.272	38	57	2	.979
1987—California	Amer.	OF-3B-2B	138	449	64	110	18	5	23	64	.245	185	95	7	.976
1988—California	Amer.	3B-OF	154	500	59	127	32	2	16	63	.254	97	249	17	.953
1989—California	Amer.	★3B-OF	144	474	56	108	19	4	20	52	.228	97	★322	11	★.974
1990—California‡	Amer.	3B-SS-1B	105	316	35	72	19	1	8	33	.228	76	196	18	.938
1990—Edmonton	P. C.	3B-1B	20	75	14	25	7	1	2	15	.333	22	33	1	.982
Major League Totals—6 Years			647	2027	259	485	106	14	76	251	.239	526	994	63	.960

Signed as free agent by California Angels' organization, August 6, 1983.
†On disabled list, June 21 to July 7, 1985.
‡On disabled list, May 23 to June 9, 1990.

CHAMPIONSHIP SERIES RECORD

Year Club	League	Pos.	G.	AB.	R.	H.	2B.	3B.	HR.	RBI.	B.A.	PO.	A.	E.	F.A.
1986—California	Amer.	PH	2	1	0	0	0	0	0	0	.000	0	0	0	.000

JAY CANFIELD HOWELL

Born November 26, 1955, at Miami, Fla.
Height, 6.03. Weight, 220.
Throws and bats righthanded.
Attended University of Colorado, Boulder, Colo.

Major League saves: 1984 (7), 1985 (29), 1986 (16), 1987 (16), 1988 (21), 1989 (28), 1990 (16). Total—133.
Tied for American Association lead in shutouts with 2 in 1982.
Tied for American Association lead in balks with 6 in 1981.
Named American Association Pitcher of the Year, 1982.

Year Club	League	G.	IP.	W.	L.	Pct.	H.	R.	ER.	SO.	BB.	ERA.
1976—Eugene	Northwest	13	73	5	4	.556	65	30	24	79	34	2.96
1977—Tampa	Florida St.	23	158	7	13	.350	141	60	52	99	52	2.96
1978—Nashville	Southern	28	166	9	14	.391	134	70	57	★173	55	3.09
1979—Indianapolis	Am. Assoc.	24	128	10	10	.500	121	82	73	79	84	5.13
1980—Indianapolis	Am. Assoc.	25	98	5	11	.313	95	70	55	73	71	5.05
1980—Cincinnati†	National	5	3	0	0	.000	8	5	5	1	0	15.00
1981—Iowa	Am. Assoc.	23	144	5	10	.333	141	74	60	90	62	3.75
1981—Chicago	National	10	22	2	0	1.000	23	13	12	10	10	4.91
1982—Iowa‡	Am. Assoc.	20	141⅓	13	4	★.765	102	45	37	139	48	★2.36
1982—Columbus	Int'national	5	37⅓	2	1	.667	18	13	10	33	19	2.41
1982—New York	American	6	28	2	3	.400	42	25	24	21	13	7.71
1983—New York§	American	19	82	1	5	.167	89	53	49	61	35	5.38
1984—New York x	American	61	103⅔	9	4	.692	86	33	31	109	34	2.69
1985—Oakland	American	63	98	9	8	.529	98	32	31	68	31	2.85
1986—Oakland y	American	38	53⅓	3	6	.333	53	23	20	42	23	3.38
1986—Modesto	California	2	2	0	0	.000	5	3	3	1	1	13.50
1987—Oakland za	American	36	44⅓	3	4	.429	48	30	29	35	21	5.89
1988—Los Angeles b	National	50	65	5	3	.625	44	16	15	70	21	2.08
1989—Los Angeles	National	56	79⅔	5	3	.625	60	15	14	55	22	1.58
1990—Los Angeles c	National	45	66	5	5	.500	59	17	16	59	20	2.18
National League Totals—5 Years		166	235⅔	17	11	.607	194	66	62	195	73	2.37
American League Totals—6 Years		223	409⅓	27	30	.474	416	196	184	336	157	4.05
Major League Totals—11 Years		389	645	44	41	.518	610	262	246	531	230	3.43

Selected by Cincinnati Reds' organization in 12th round of free-agent draft, June 5, 1973.
Selected by Cincinnati Reds' organization in 31st round of free-agent draft, June 8, 1976.
†Traded to Chicago Cubs for Catcher Mike O'Berry, October 17, 1980.
‡Traded to New York Yankees' organization, August 2, 1982, completing deal in which Chicago Cubs acquired Second Baseman Pat Tabler from New York on waivers for two players to be named later, August 19, 1981; New York acquired Pitcher Bill Caudill as partial completion of deal, April 1, 1982.
§On disabled list, August 3, 1983 through remainder of season.
xTraded with Outfielder Stan Javier and Pitchers Jose Rijo, Eric Plunk and Tim Birtsas to Oakland A's for Outfielder Rickey Henderson, Pitcher Bert Bradley and cash, December 5, 1984.
yOn disabled list, April 30 to May 18 and May 27 to July 20, 1986; included rehabilitation disability assignment to Modesto, July 11 to July 16, 1986.
zOn disabled list, August 25, 1987 through remainder of season.
aAs part of an eight-player, three-team deal, New York Mets traded Pitcher Jesse Orosco to Oakland Athletics, December 11, 1987. Oakland then traded Orosco along with Shortstop Alfredo Griffin and Pitcher Jay Howell to Los Angeles Dodgers for Pitchers Bob Welch, Matt Young and Jack Savage. Oakland then traded Savage along with Pitchers Wally Whitehurst and Kevin Tapani to New York.
bOn disabled list, June 21 to July 7, 1988.
cOn disabled list, April 23 to May 17, 1990.

CHAMPIONSHIP SERIES RECORD

Year Club	League	G.	IP.	W.	L.	Pct.	H.	R.	ER.	SO.	BB.	ERA.
1988—Los Angeles	National	2	⅔	0	1	.000	1	2	2	1	2	27.00

WORLD SERIES RECORD

Year Club	League	G.	IP.	W.	L.	Pct.	H.	R.	ER.	SO.	BB.	ERA.
1988—Los Angeles	National	2	2⅔	0	1	.000	3	1	1	2	1	3.38

ALL-STAR GAME RECORD

Year League	IP.	W.	L.	Pct.	H.	R.	ER.	SO.	BB.	ERA.
1987—American	2	0	1	.000	3	2	2	3	0	9.00
1989—National	1	0	0	.000	1	0	0	1	0	0.00
All-Star Game Totals—2 Years	3	0	1	.000	4	2	2	4	0	6.00

Member of American League All-Star Team in 1985; did not play.

KENNETH HOWELL JR.

(Ken)

Born November 28, 1960, at Detroit, Mich.
Height, 6.03. Weight, 228.
Throws and bats righthanded.
Attended Tuskegee Institute, Tuskegee Institute, Ala.

Major League saves: 1984 (6), 1985 (12), 1986 (12), 1987 (1). Total—31.
Led National League in wild pitches with 21 in 1989.
Tied for Texas League lead in games started by pitchers with 27 in 1983.

Year Club	League	G.	IP.	W.	L.	Pct.	H.	R.	ER.	SO.	BB.	ERA.
1982—Vero Beach	Florida St.	11	59⅔	5	4	.556	58	40	28	37	36	4.22
1983—San Antonio	Texas	27	169⅓	8	11	.421	171	98	83	116	101	4.41
1983—Albuquerque	P. Coast	1	3	0	0	.000	4	3	3	1	1	9.00
1984—Albuquerque†	P. Coast	18	72⅓	8	2	.800	79	48	37	58	37	4.60
1984—Los Angeles	National	32	51⅓	5	5	.500	51	21	19	54	9	3.33
1985—Los Angeles	National	56	86	4	7	.364	66	41	36	85	35	3.77
1986—Los Angeles	National	62	97⅔	6	12	.333	86	48	42	104	63	3.87
1987—Los Angeles	National	40	55	3	4	.429	54	32	30	60	29	4.91
1987—Albuquerque	P. Coast	2	13	1	0	1.000	6	1	0	13	7	0.00
1988—Bakersfield‡	California	3	13⅔	0	1	.000	8	5	2	13	9	1.32
1988—Albuquerque	P. Coast	18	107⅓	10	1	★.909	92	43	39	95	42	3.27
1988—Los Angeles§x	National	4	12⅔	0	1	.000	16	10	9	12	4	6.39
1989—Philadelphia	National	33	204	12	12	.500	155	84	78	164	86	3.44
1990—Philadelphia y	National	18	106⅔	8	7	.533	106	60	55	70	49	4.64
Major League Totals—7 Years		245	613⅓	38	48	.442	534	296	269	549	275	3.95

Selected by Los Angeles Dodgers' organization in 3rd round of free-agent draft, June 7, 1982.

†On disabled list, April 7 to April 17, 1984.

‡On Los Angeles disabled list, March 20 to May 25 and June 17 to July 8, 1988; included rehabilitation disability assignment to Bakersfield, May 7 to May 11 and May 17 to May 25, 1988; and to Albuquerque, May 12 to May 16 and June 24 to July 8, 1988.

§Traded with Pitcher Brian Holton and Shortstop Juan Bell to Baltimore Orioles for First Baseman Eddie Murray, December 4, 1988.

xTraded with Pitcher Gordon Dillard by Baltimore Orioles to Philadelphia Phillies for Outfielder Phil Bradley, December 8, 1988.

yOn disabled list, July 6 to July 31 and August 1, 1990 through remainder of season.

CHAMPIONSHIP SERIES RECORD

Year Club	League	G.	IP.	W.	L.	Pct.	H.	R.	ER.	SO.	BB.	ERA.
1985—Los Angeles	National	1	2	0	0	.000	0	0	0	2	0	0.00

PATRICK O'NEAL HOWELL
(Pat)

Born August 31, 1968, at Mobile, Ala.
Height, 5.11. Weight, 155.
Throws right and bats left and righthanded.
Led South Atlantic League in stolen bases with 79 in 1990.
Led South Atlantic League outfielders in total chances with 334 in 1990.

Year Club	League	Pos.	G.	AB.	R.	H.	2B.	3B.	HR.	RBI.	B.A.	PO.	A.	E.	F.A.
1987—Kingsport†	Appal.	OF	34	92	14	20	2	0	1	5	.217	35	4	1	.975
1988—Kingsport†	Appal.	OF	66	251	43	67	6	3	0	16	.267	122	5	1	★.992
1989—Pittsfield†	NYP	OF	56	231	41	67	4	3	1	26	.290	113	5	3	.975
1990—Columbia‡	S. Atl.	OF	135	★573	98	151	15	5	1	37	.264	★303	16	15	.955

Selected by New York Mets' organization in 9th round of free-agent draft, June 2, 1987.

†Batted righthanded only.

‡Drafted by Minnesota Twins, December 3, 1990.

DANN PAUL JOHN HOWITT

Born February 13, 1964, at Battle Creek, Mich.
Height, 6.05. Weight, 205.
Throws right and bats lefthanded.
Attended Michigan State University, East Lansing, Mich.,
and California State University, Fullerton, Calif.
Brother of Shaun Howitt, outfielder in Kansas City Royals' organization, 1972.
Led Southern League in total bases with 253 in 1989.
Led Southern League first basemen in fielding percentage with .992 in 1989.
Led California League outfielders in double plays with 6 in 1987.
Tied for Northwest League lead in double plays by outfielders with 2 in 1986.

Year Club	League	Pos.	G.	AB.	R.	H.	2B.	3B.	HR.	RBI.	B.A.	PO.	A.	E.	F.A.
1986—Medford	N'west	OF	66	208	36	66	9	2	6	37	.317	83	5	4	.957
1987—Modesto	Calif.	OF-1B	109	336	44	70	11	2	8	42	.208	263	23	6	.979
1988—Modesto	Calif.	OF-1B	132	480	75	121	20	2	18	86	.252	475	42	12	.977
1988—Tacoma	P. C.	OF-1B	4	15	1	2	1	0	0	0	.133	14	0	0	1.000
1989—Huntsville	South.	1B-OF-P	138	509	78	143	28	2	26	111	.281	965	74	9	.991
1989—Oakland	Amer.	1B-OF	3	3	0	0	0	0	0	0	.000	2	0	0	1.000
1990—Tacoma	P. C.	1B-OF-3B	118	437	58	116	30	1	11	69	.265	608	74	11	.984
1990—Oakland	Amer.	OF-1B-3B	14	22	3	3	0	1	0	1	.136	34	1	0	1.000
Major League Totals—2 Years		17	25	3	3	0	1	0	1	.120	36	1	0	1.000

Selected by Oakland Athletics' organization in 18th round of free-agent draft, June 2, 1986.

PITCHING RECORD

Year Club	League	G.	IP.	W.	L.	Pct.	H.	R.	ER.	SO.	BB.	ERA.
1989—Huntsville	Southern	2	2	0	0	.000	2	1	0	2	0	0.00

KENT ALAN HRBEK

Name pronounced HER-beck.

Born May 21, 1960, at Minneapolis, Minn.
Height, 6.04. Weight, 250.
Throws right and bats lefthanded.

Major League stolen bases: 1982 (3), 1983 (4), 1984 (1), 1985 (1), 1986 (2), 1987 (5), 1989 (3), 1990 (5). Total—24.
Led California League in slugging percentage with .630 and tied for lead in sacrifice flies with 9 in 1981.
Named California League Most Valuable Player, 1981.

Year	Club	League	Pos.	G.	AB.	R.	H.	2B.	3B.	HR.	RBI.	B.A.	PO.	A.	E.	F.A.
1979—Elizabethton†‡	.....	Appal.	1B	17	59	5	12	2	0	1	11	.203	126	11	2	.986
1980—Wisc. Rapids§	....	Midw.	1B	115	419	74	112	16	0	19	76	.267	1005	81	*20	.982
1981—Visalia	....	Calif.	1B	121	462	119	175	25	5	27	111	*.379	1034	53	11	*.989
1981—Minnesota	....	Amer.	1B	24	67	5	16	5	0	1	7	.239	124	4	0	1.000
1982—Minnesota	....	Amer.	1B	140	532	82	160	21	4	23	92	.301	1174	88	9	.993
1983—Minnesota	....	Amer.	1B	141	515	75	153	41	5	16	84	.297	1151	89	13	.990
1984—Minnesota	....	Amer.	1B	149	559	80	174	31	3	27	107	.311	1320	99	14	.990
1985—Minnesota	....	Amer.	1B	158	593	78	165	31	2	21	93	.278	1339	114	8	.995
1986—Minnesota	....	Amer.	1B	149	550	85	147	27	1	29	91	.267	1218	104	10	.992
1987—Minnesota	....	Amer.	1B	143	477	85	136	20	1	34	90	.285	1179	68	5	.996
1988—Minnesota	....	Amer.	1B	143	510	75	159	31	0	25	76	.312	842	57	3	.997
1989—Minnesota xy	....	Amer.	1B	109	375	59	102	17	0	25	84	.272	723	60	4	.995
1990—Minnesota	....	Amer.	*1B-3B	143	492	61	141	26	0	22	79	.287	1057	83	3	*.997
Major League Totals—10 Years		....		1299	4670	685	1353	250	16	223	803	.290	10127	766	69	.994

Selected by Minnesota Twins' organization in 17th round of free-agent draft, June 6, 1978.
†On Wisconsin Rapids disabled list, April 13 to June 21, 1979.
‡On Elizabethton disabled list, July 22 to September 6, 1979.
§On disabled list, May 27 to June 6, 1980.
xOn disabled list, May 16 to June 26, 1989.
yGranted free agency, November 13, 1989; re-signed by Twins, December 6, 1989.

CHAMPIONSHIP SERIES RECORD

Year	Club	League	Pos.	G.	AB.	R.	H.	2B.	3B.	HR.	RBI.	B.A.	PO.	A.	E.	F.A.
1987—Minnesota	....	Amer.	1B	5	20	4	3	0	0	1	1	.150	40	3	0	1.000

WORLD SERIES RECORD

Shares World Series records for most grand slams, game (1), October 24, 1987; most runs batted in, inning (4), October 24, 1987, sixth inning.

Year	Club	League	Pos.	G.	AB.	R.	H.	2B.	3B.	HR.	RBI.	B.A.	PO.	A.	E.	F.A.
1987—Minnesota	....	Amer.	1B	7	24	4	5	0	0	1	6	.208	68	2	0	1.000

ALL-STAR GAME RECORD

Year	League	Pos.	AB.	R.	H.	2B.	3B.	HR.	RBI.	B.A.	PO.	A.	E.	F.A.
1982—American	....	PH	1	0	0	0	0	0	0	.000	0	0	0	.000

REX ALLEN HUDLER

Born September 2, 1960, at Tempe, Ariz.
Height, 6.00. Weight, 180.
Throws and bats righthanded.

Major League stolen bases: 1986 (1), 1988 (29), 1989 (15), 1990 (18). Total—63.
Led International League second basemen in double plays with 95 in 1984.

Year	Club	League	Pos.	G.	AB.	R.	H.	2B.	3B.	HR.	RBI.	B.A.	PO.	A.	E.	F.A.
1978—Oneonta	....	NYP	SS	58	221	33	62	5	5	0	24	.281	123	21	21	.906
1979—Fort Lauderdale†	Fla. St.	S-3-2-O	116	414	37	104	14	1	1	25	.251	164	314	45	.914
1980—Fort Lauderdale‡	Fla. St.	3-2-O-1	37	125	14	26	4	0	0	6	.208	55	71	5	.962
1980—Greensboro	....	S. Atl.	2B	20	75	7	17	3	1	2	9	.227	51	52	5	.954
1981—Fort Lauderdale§	Fla. St.	2-S-3-O	79	259	35	77	11	1	2	26	.297	104	238	19	.947
1982—Nashville	....	South.	2B-SS-OF	89	299	27	71	14	1	0	24	.237	136	219	20	.947
1982—Fort Lauderdale	..	Fla. St.	2B	9	32	2	8	1	0	1	6	.250	23	25	2	.960
1983—Fort Lauderdale	..	Fla. St.	2B-SS	91	345	55	93	15	2	2	50	.270	195	245	15	.967
1983—Columbus	....	Int.	2B-3B-SS	40	118	17	36	5	0	1	11	.305	55	95	4	.974
1984—Columbus	....	Int.	2B	114	394	49	115	26	1	1	35	.292	266	348	16	.975
1984—New York	....	Amer.	2B	9	7	2	1	1	0	0	0	.143	4	7	0	1.000
1985—Columbus	....	Int.	2-S-O-3-1	106	380	62	95	13	4	3	18	.250	192	234	17	.962
1985—New York x	....	Amer.	2B-1B-SS	20	51	4	8	0	1	0	1	.157	42	51	2	.979
1986—Rochester	....	Int.	2-3-O-S	77	219	29	57	12	3	2	13	.260	135	191	15	.956
1986—Baltimore	....	Amer.	2B-3B	14	1	1	0	0	0	0	0	.000	2	3	1	.833
1987—Rochester yz	....	Int.	OF-2B-SS	31	106	22	27	5	1	5	10	.255	51	15	2	.971
1988—Indianapolis	....	A. A.	O-2-S-3	67	234	36	71	11	3	7	25	.303	102	96	4	.980
1988—Montreal	....	Nat.	2B-SS-OF	77	216	38	59	14	2	4	14	.273	116	168	10	.966
1989—Montreal	....	Nat.	2B-OF-SS	92	155	21	38	7	0	6	13	.245	59	59	7	.944
1990—Mont.a-St.L.	......	Nat.	O-2-1-3-S	93	220	31	62	11	2	7	22	.282	158	42	5	.976
American League Totals—3 Years		....		43	59	7	9	1	1	0	1	.153	48	61	3	.973
National League Totals—3 Years		....		262	591	90	159	32	4	17	49	.269	333	269	22	.965
Major League Totals—6 Years		....		305	650	97	168	33	5	17	50	.258	381	330	25	.966

Selected by New York Yankees' organization in 1st round (18th player selected) of free-agent draft, June 6, 1978.
†On disabled list, May 18 to May 31, 1979.
‡On disabled list, May 10 to June 15, 1980.

§On disabled list, May 11 to June 11, 1981.
xTraded with Pitcher Rich Bordi to Baltimore Orioles for Oufielder Gary Roenicke and a player to be named later, December 12, 1985; New York Yankees acquired Outfielder Leo Hernandez to complete deal, December 16, 1985.
yOn Baltimore disabled list, March 23 to June 16, 1987; included rehabilitation disability assignment to Rochester, May 28 to June 16, 1987.
zGranted free agency, October 15, 1987; signed by Indianapolis (Montreal Expos' organization) December 18, 1987.
aTraded to St. Louis Cardinals for Pitcher John Costello, April 23, 1990.

MICHAEL KALE HUFF
(Mike)

Born August 11, 1963, at Honolulu, Haw.
Height, 6.01. Weight, 180.
Throws and bats righthanded.
Received bachelor of science degree in industrial
engineering from Northwestern University, Evanston, Ill., in 1985.

Tied for Texas League lead in double plays by outfielders with 4 in 1988.

Year Club	League	Pos.	G.	AB.	R.	H.	2B.	3B.	HR.	RBI.	B.A.	PO.	A.	E.	F.A.
1985—Great Falls	Pion.	OF	•70	247	70	78	6	6	0	35	.316	120	5	5	.962
1986—Vero Beach	Fla. St.	OF	113	362	73	106	6	8	2	32	.293	257	10	1	.996
1987—San Antonio†	Texas	OF	31	135	23	42	5	1	3	18	.311	52	2	2	.964
1988—San Antonio	Texas	OF	102	395	68	120	18	10	2	40	.304	222	12	2	.992
1988—Albuquerque	P. C.	OF	2	4	0	1	1	0	0	0	.250	2	0	0	1.000
1989—Albuquerque	P. C.	OF-2B	115	471	75	150	29	7	10	78	.318	209	13	2	.991
1989—Los Angeles	Nat.	OF	12	25	4	5	1	0	1	2	.200	18	0	0	1.000
1990—Albuquerque‡	P. C.	OF-2B	★138	474	99	154	28	11	7	84	.325	285	29	5	.984
Major League Totals—1 Year			12	25	4	5	1	0	1	2	.200	18	0	0	1.000

Selected by Los Angeles Dodgers' organization in 16th round of free-agent draft, June 3, 1985.
†On disabled list, May 11, 1987 through remainder of season.
‡Drafted by Cleveland Indians, December 3, 1990.

KEITH WILLS HUGHES

Born September 12, 1963, at Bryn Mawr, Pa.
Height, 6.03. Weight, 210.
Throws and bats lefthanded.

Major League stolen bases: 1988 (1).
Tied for South Atlantic League lead in intentional bases on balls received with 5 in 1983.

Year Club	League	Pos.	G.	AB.	R.	H.	2B.	3B.	HR.	RBI.	B.A.	PO.	A.	E.	F.A.
1982—Bend	N'west	OF	55	179	29	46	10	2	3	26	.257	90	6	5	.950
1983—Spartanburg	S. Atl.	OF-1B	131	484	80	159	31	4	15	90	.329	171	5	7	.962
1984—Reading†	East.	OF-1B	70	230	35	60	7	5	2	20	.261	117	7	9	.932
1984—Nashville	South.	OF	21	50	6	9	0	0	0	5	.180	19	0	0	1.000
1985—Albany	East.	OF-2B	104	361	53	97	22	5	10	54	.269	218	18	3	.988
1985—Columbus	Int.	OF	18	54	7	16	4	0	3	8	.296	25	0	2	.926
1986—Albany‡	East.	OF-1B	94	323	44	99	21	3	7	37	.307	247	17	7	.974
1986—Columbus	Int.	OF	2	8	0	1	0	0	0	0	.125	6	0	1	.857
1987—Columbus-Maine	Int.	OF-1B	90	316	48	93	15	4	17	57	.294	149	2	7	.956
1987—New York§	Amer.	PH	4	4	0	0	0	0	0	0	.000	0	0	0	.000
1987—Philadelphia x	Nat.	OF	37	76	8	20	2	0	0	10	.263	26	0	1	.963
1988—Rochester	Int.	OF	77	274	44	74	13	2	7	49	.270	159	2	3	.982
1988—Baltimore	Amer.	OF	41	108	10	21	4	2	2	14	.194	59	4	2	.969
1989—Rochester yz	Int.	OF-1B	83	285	44	78	20	4	2	43	.274	180	7	5	.974
1990—Tidewater	Int.	OF-1B	117	379	77	117	24	5	10	53	.309	262	18	6	.979
1990—New York a	Nat.	OF	8	9	0	0	0	0	0	0	.000	5	0	0	1.000
American League Totals—2 Years			45	112	10	21	4	2	2	14	.188	59	4	2	.969
National League Totals—2 Years			45	85	8	20	2	0	0	10	.235	31	0	1	.969
Major League Totals—3 Years			90	197	18	41	6	2	2	24	.208	90	4	3	.969

Signed as free agent by Philadelphia Phillies' organization, August 24, 1981.
†Traded with Pitcher Marty Bystrom to New York Yankees for Pitcher Shane Rawley, June 30, 1984.
‡On disabled list, July 22 to August 26, 1986.
§Traded with Infielder Shane Turner to Philadelphia Phillies' organization for Outfielder Mike Easler, June 10, 1987.
xTraded with Infielder Rick Schu and Outfielder Jeff Stone to Baltimore Orioles for Outfielder Mike Young and a player to be named later, March 21, 1988; Philadelphia Phillies acquired Outfielder Frank Bellino to complete deal, June 14, 1988.
yOn disabled list, July 5, 1989 through remainder of season.
zTraded with Pitcher Cesar Mejia to New York Mets for Pitcher John Mitchell and Outfielder Joaquin Contreras, December 5, 1989.
aReleased, November 13, 1990; signed by Columbus (New York Yankees' organization), January 7, 1991.

MARK LAWRENCE HUISMANN

Born May 11, 1958, at Lincoln, Neb.
Height, 6.03. Weight, 195.
Throws and bats righthanded.
Received bachelor of science degree in business and finance from
Colorado State University, Fort Collins, Colo., in 1980.

Major League saves: 1984 (3), 1986 (5), 1987 (2), 1989 (1). Total—11.

Led International League in games finished in relief with 45 in 1988.
Led American Association in saves with 33 and games finished in relief with 56 in 1985.
Named American Association Pitcher of the Year, 1985.

Year	Club	League	G.	IP.	W.	L.	Pct.	H.	R.	ER.	SO.	BB.	ERA.
1980—Sarasota Royals-Blue	Gulf Coast	28	59	1	2	.333	50	20	16	46	14	2.44
1981—Charleston	S. Atlantic	28	44	3	2	.600	36	16	8	42	17	1.64
1981—Fort Myers	Florida St.	14	21	3	1	.750	15	9	8	19	16	3.43
1982—Fort Myers	Florida St.	14	23	3	1	.750	16	1	1	21	4	0.39
1982—Jacksonville	Southern	36	54⅔	4	4	.500	52	18	13	60	15	2.14
1983—Jacksonville	Southern	37	61⅓	6	3	.667	60	25	22	46	25	3.23
1983—Omaha	Am. Assoc.	17	24⅓	0	2	.000	16	7	5	25	9	1.85
1983—Kansas City	American	13	30⅔	2	1	.667	29	20	19	20	17	5.58
1984—Kansas City	American	38	75	3	3	.500	84	38	35	54	21	4.20
1984—Omaha	Am. Assoc.	15	19	2	0	1.000	11	0	0	18	5	0.00
1985—Omaha	Am. Assoc.	*59	89⅓	5	5	.500	70	20	20	70	14	2.01
1985—Kansas City	American	9	18⅔	1	0	1.000	14	4	4	9	3	1.93
1986—Kansas City†-Seattle	American	46	97⅓	3	4	.429	98	47	41	72	25	3.79
1987—Seattle‡-Cleveland	American	26	50	2	3	.400	48	32	28	38	12	5.04
1987—Buffalo§	Am. Assoc.	13	33⅓	1	1	.500	43	32	28	31	8	7.56
1988—Toledo	Int'national	48	57⅔	4	6	.400	50	20	12	61	15	1.87
1988—Detroit x	American	5	5⅓	1	0	1.000	6	3	3	6	2	5.06
1989—Rochester	Int'national	16	21	2	1	.667	9	4	4	20	3	1.71
1989—Baltimore yz	American	8	11⅓	0	0	.000	13	8	8	13	0	6.35
1990—Buffalo	Am. Assoc.	49	76	6	2	.750	69	23	22	32	15	2.61
1990—Pittsburgh a	National	2	3	1	0	1.000	6	5	3	2	1	9.00
American League Totals—7 Years		145	288⅓	12	11	.522	292	152	138	214	80	4.31
National League Totals—1 Year		2	3	1	0	1.000	6	5	3	2	1	9.00
Major League Totals—8 Years		147	291⅓	13	11	.542	298	157	141	216	81	4.36

Selected by Chicago Cubs' organization in 23rd round of free-agent draft, June 5, 1979.
Signed as free agent by Kansas City Royals' organization, June 16, 1980.
†Traded to Seattle Mariners for Catcher Terry Bell, May 21, 1986.
‡Traded to Cleveland Indians for Outfielder Dave Gallagher, May 12, 1987.
§Released, March 17, 1988; signed by Toledo (Detroit Tigers' organization), March 23, 1988.
xReleased, February 22, 1989; signed by Rochester (Baltimore Orioles' organization), March 1, 1989.
yOn disabled list, June 11, 1989 through remainder of season.
zReleased, October 3, 1989; signed by Buffalo (Pittsburgh Pirates' organization), March 7, 1990.
aGranted free agency, October 15, 1990.

CHAMPIONSHIP SERIES RECORD

Year	Club	League	G.	IP.	W.	L.	Pct.	H.	R.	ER.	SO.	BB.	ERA.
1984—Kansas City	American	1	2⅔	0	0	.000	6	3	2	2	1	6.75

TIMOTHY CRAIG HULETT
Name pronounced HUGH-lit.

(Tim)

Born January 12, 1960, at Springfield, Ill.
Height, 6.00. Weight, 195.
Throws and bats righthanded.
Attended Miami-Dade Community College (North), Miami, Fla.,
and University of South Florida, Tampa, Fla.

Major League stolen bases: 1983 (1), 1984 (1), 1985 (6), 1986 (4), 1990 (1). Total—13.
Tied for American League lead in errors by third basemen with 23 in 1985.
Led American Association in sacrifice flies with 9 in both 1983 and 1988.
Led International League third basemen in double plays with 23 in 1989.
Led American Association second basemen in total chances with 730 in 1983.
Led Eastern League second basemen in putouts with 343, assists with 386, double plays with 95, fielding percentage with .975 and total chances with 748 in 1982.
Led Eastern League second basemen in putouts with 332, assists with 415, double plays with 112 and total chances with 763 in 1981.

Year	Club	League	Pos.	G.	AB.	R.	H.	2B.	3B.	HR.	RBI.	B.A.	PO.	A.	E.	F.A.
1980—Glens Falls	East.	SS	6	23	2	4	0	0	0	0	.174	14	13	2	.931
1980—Iowa	A. A.	3B	3	8	1	2	0	0	0	0	.250	0	6	3	.667
1980—Appleton	Midw.	2B-3B-SS	79	278	49	72	11	1	13	47	.259	162	258	17	.961
1981—Glens Falls	East.	2B-3B	134	437	59	99	27	1	10	55	.227	333	422	16	.979
1982—Glens Falls	East.	2B-SS	●140	*536	*113	145	28	5	22	87	.271	352	398	21	.973
1983—Denver	A. A.	2B	133	477	77	130	19	4	21	88	.273	*286	*424	*20	.973
1983—Chicago	Amer.	2B	6	5	0	1	0	0	0	0	.200	8	6	2	.875
1984—Chicago	Amer.	3B-2B	8	7	1	0	0	0	0	0	.000	4	15	0	1.000
1984—Denver	A. A.	2B-3B-SS	139	475	72	125	32	6	16	80	.263	269	371	28	.958
1985—Chicago	Amer.	3B-2B-OF	141	395	52	106	19	4	5	37	.268	117	256	24	.940
1986—Chicago	Amer.	3B-2B	150	520	53	120	16	5	17	44	.231	179	331	15	.971
1987—Chicago	Amer.	3B-2B	68	240	20	52	10	0	7	28	.217	55	142	9	.956
1987—Hawaii†	P. C.	3B-2B	42	157	13	37	5	2	1	24	.236	47	81	11	.921
1988—Indianapolis‡	A. A.	3B-2B	126	427	36	100	29	2	7	59	.234	118	211	25	.929
1989—Rochester	Int.	3-S-2-P	122	461	61	129	32	12	3	50	.280	149	289	20	.956
1989—Baltimore	Amer.	2B-3B	33	97	12	27	5	0	3	18	.278	70	71	4	.972
1990—Rochester§	Int.	2B-SS-3B	14	43	10	16	2	1	2	4	.372	22	35	1	.983
1990—Baltimore	Amer.	3B-2B	53	153	16	39	7	1	3	16	.255	44	101	4	.973
Major League Totals—7 Years			459	1417	154	345	57	10	35	143	.243	477	922	58	.960

Selected by Texas Rangers' organization in 39th round of free-agent draft, June 6, 1978.
Selected by Chicago White Sox' organization in secondary phase of free-agent draft, January 8, 1980.
†Traded to Montreal Expos for a player to be named later, April 13, 1988; Chicago White Sox acquired Second Baseman Edgar Caceres to complete deal, June 15, 1988.
‡Granted free agency, October 15, 1988; signed by Rochester (Baltimore Orioles' organization), November 21, 1988.
§On Baltimore disabled list, April 4 to June 12, 1990; included rehabilitation disability assignment to Rochester, May 29 to June 12, 1990.

PITCHING RECORD

Year Club	League	G.	IP.	W.	L.	Pct.	H.	R.	ER.	SO.	BB.	ERA.
1989—Rochester	Int'national	1	⅔	0	0	.000	0	0	0	0	0	0.00

MICHAEL BUTLER HUMPHREYS
(Mike)

Born April 10, 1967, at Dallas, Tex.
Height, 6.00. Weight, 185.
Throws and bats righthanded.
Attended Texas Tech University, Lubbock, Tex.

Tied for Northwest League lead in game-winning RBIs with 9 in 1988.
Tied for Northwest League lead in putouts by outfielders with 180 in 1988.

Year Club	League	Pos.	G.	AB.	R.	H.	2B.	3B.	HR.	RBI.	B.A.	PO.	A.	E.	F.A.
1988—Spokane	N'west	*OF-1B	76	303	*67	93	16	•5	6	59	.307	181	6	5	*.974
1989—Riverside	Calif.	OF-3B-1B	117	420	77	121	26	1	13	66	.288	251	10	7	.974
1990—Wichita	Texas	OF	116	421	*92	116	21	4	17	79	.276	277	8	5	.983
1990—Las Vegas	P. C.	OF	12	42	7	10	1	0	2	6	.238	19	5	0	1.000

Selected by San Diego Padres' organization in 15th round of free-agent draft, June 1, 1988.

TODD RANDOLPH HUNDLEY

Born May 27, 1969, at Martinsville, Va.
Height, 5.11. Weight, 170.
Throws right and bats left and righthanded.
Attended William Rainey Harper College, Palatine, Ill.
Son of Randy Hundley, catcher with San Francisco Giants, Chicago Cubs,
Minnesota Twins and San Diego Padres, 1964 through 1977; and minor league manager
in Chicago Cubs' organization, 1979 and 1980.

Led South Atlantic League in intentional bases on balls received with 10 and grounded into double plays with 20 in 1989.
Led South Atlantic League catchers in putouts with 826 and total chances with 930 in 1989.

Year Club	League	Pos.	G.	AB.	R.	H.	2B.	3B.	HR.	RBI.	B.A.	PO.	A.	E.	F.A.
1987—Little Falls	NYP	C	34	103	12	15	4	0	1	10	.146	181	25	7	.967
1988—Little Falls	NYP	C	52	176	23	33	8	0	2	18	.188	345	54	8	.980
1988—St. Lucie	Fla. St.	C	1	1	0	0	0	0	0	0	.000	4	0	1	.800
1989—Columbia	S. Atl.	C-OF	125	439	67	118	23	4	11	66	.269	829	91	13	.986
1990—Jackson	Texas	C-3B	81	279	27	74	12	2	1	35	.265	474	63	9	.984
1990—New York	Nat.	C	36	67	8	14	6	0	0	2	.209	162	8	2	.988
Major League Totals—1 Year			36	67	8	14	6	0	0	2	.209	162	8	2	.988

Selected by New York Mets' organization in 2nd round of free-agent draft, June 2, 1987.

BRIAN RONALD HUNTER

Born March 4, 1968, at El Toro, Calif.
Height, 6.00. Weight, 195.
Throws left and bats righthanded.
Attended Cerritos College, Norwalk, Calif.

Tied for Southern League lead in sacrifice flies with 9 in 1989.
Led Midwest League first basemen in errors with 21 in 1988.
Led Appalachian League first basemen in double plays with 43 in 1987.

Year Club	League	Pos.	G.	AB.	R.	H.	2B.	3B.	HR.	RBI.	B.A.	PO.	A.	E.	F.A.
1987—Pulaski	Appal.	1B-OF	65	251	38	58	10	2	8	30	.231	498	29	11	.975
1988—Burlington	Midw.	1B-OF	117	417	58	108	17	0	•22	71	.259	987	69	22	.980
1988—Durham	Carol.	OF-1B	13	49	13	17	3	0	3	9	.347	52	6	0	1.000
1989—Greenville	South.	OF-1B	124	451	57	114	19	2	19	82	.253	248	15	4	.985
1990—Richmond	Int.	OF-1B	43	137	13	27	4	0	5	16	.197	126	5	3	.978
1990—Greenville	South.	OF-1B	88	320	45	77	13	1	14	55	.241	189	19	8	.963

Selected by Atlanta Braves' organization in 8th round of free-agent draft, June 2, 1987.

BRUCE VEE HURST

Born March 24, 1958, at St. George, Utah.
Height, 6.03. Weight, 219.
Throws and bats lefthanded.
Attended Dixie College, St. George, Utah.

Shares major league record for fewest complete games for leader, season (10), 1989.
Led American League in balks with 4 in 1985.
Tied for National League lead in shutouts with 4 in 1990.
Tied for National League lead in complete games with 10 in 1989.

Year Club	League	G.	IP.	W.	L.	Pct.	H.	R.	ER.	SO.	BB.	ERA.
1976—Elmira	NYP	9	42	3	2	.600	25	18	14	40	38	3.00
1977—Winter Haven†	Florida St.	13	91	5	4	.556	77	28	21	69	25	2.08
1978—Bristol‡	Eastern	6	33	1	3	.250	32	15	10	35	17	2.73
1979—Winter Haven	Florida St.	12	84	8	2	.800	57	22	18	64	20	1.93
1979—Bristol	Eastern	16	113	9	4	.692	108	56	45	91	49	3.58
1980—Pawtucket	Int'national	17	105	8	6	.571	101	52	46	54	50	3.94
1980—Boston	American	12	31	2	2	.500	39	33	31	16	16	9.00
1981—Pawtucket	Int'national	32	157	12	7	.632	143	68	50	99	71	2.87
1981—Boston	American	5	23	2	0	1.000	23	11	11	11	12	4.30
1982—Boston	American	28	117	3	7	.300	161	87	75	53	40	5.77
1983—Boston	American	33	211⅓	12	12	.500	241	102	96	115	62	4.09
1984—Boston	American	33	218	12	12	.500	232	106	95	136	88	3.92
1985—Boston	American	35	229⅓	11	13	.458	243	123	115	189	70	4.51
1986—Boston§	American	25	174⅓	13	8	.619	169	63	58	167	50	2.99
1987—Boston	American	33	238⅔	15	13	.536	239	124	117	190	76	4.41
1988—Boston xy	American	33	216⅔	18	6	.750	222	98	88	166	65	3.66
1989—San Diego	National	33	244⅔	15	11	.577	214	84	73	179	66	2.69
1990—San Diego	National	33	223⅔	11	9	.550	188	85	78	162	63	3.14
American League Totals—9 Years		237	1459⅓	88	73	.547	1569	747	686	1043	479	4.23
National League Totals—2 Years		66	468⅓	26	20	.565	402	169	151	341	129	2.90
Major League Totals—11 Years		303	1927⅔	114	93	.551	1971	916	837	1384	608	3.91

Selected by Boston Red Sox' organization in 1st round (22nd player selected) of free-agent draft, June 8, 1976.
†On disabled list, August 8 to September 14, 1977.
‡On disabled list, May 23 to September 21, 1978.
§On disabled list, June 3 to July 18, 1986.
xOn disabled list, July 8 to July 24, 1988.
yGranted free agency, November 4, 1988; signed by San Diego Padres, December 8, 1988.

CHAMPIONSHIP SERIES RECORD

Shares Championship Series record for most games lost, series (2), 1988.

Year Club	League	G.	IP.	W.	L.	Pct.	H.	R.	ER.	SO.	BB.	ERA.
1986—Boston	American	2	15	1	0	1.000	18	5	4	8	1	2.40
1988—Boston	American	2	13	0	2	.000	10	4	4	12	5	2.77
Championship Series Totals—2 Years		4	28	1	2	.333	28	9	8	20	6	2.57

WORLD SERIES RECORD

Year Club	League	G.	IP.	W.	L.	Pct.	H.	R.	ER.	SO.	BB.	ERA.
1986—Boston	American	3	23	2	0	1.000	18	5	5	17	6	1.96

ALL-STAR GAME RECORD

Member of American League All-Star Team in 1987; did not play.

JEFFREY KENT HUSON
(Jeff)

Born August 15, 1964, at Scottsdale, Ariz.
Height, 6.03. Weight, 180.
Throws right and bats lefthanded.
Attended Glendale Community College, Glendale, Ariz., and University of Wyoming, Laramie, Wyo.

Major League stolen bases: 1988 (2), 1989 (3), 1990 (12). Total—17.
Led Southern League in stolen bases with 56 in 1988.

Year Club	League	Pos.	G.	AB.	R.	H.	2B.	3B.	HR.	RBI.	B.A.	PO.	A.	E.	F.A.
1986—Burlington	Midw.	SS-3B-2B	133	457	85	132	19	1	16	72	.289	183	324	37	.932
1986—Jacksonville	South.	3B	1	4	0	0	0	0	0	0	.000	0	1	0	1.000
1987—W. Palm Beach	Fla. St.	SS-OF-2B	131	455	54	130	15	4	1	53	.286	234	347	34	.945
1988—Jacksonville	South.	S-2-O-3	128	471	72	117	18	1	0	34	.248	217	285	26	.951
1988—Montreal	Nat.	S-2-3-O	20	42	7	13	2	0	0	3	.310	18	41	4	.937
1989—Indianapolis	A. A.	SS-OF-2B	102	378	70	115	17	4	3	35	.304	172	214	17	.958
1989—Montreal†	Nat.	SS-2B-3B	32	74	1	12	5	0	0	2	.162	40	65	8	.929
1990—Texas	Amer.	SS-3B-2B	145	396	57	95	12	2	0	28	.240	183	304	19	.962
National League Totals—2 Years			52	116	8	25	7	0	0	5	.216	58	106	12	.932
American League Totals—1 Year			145	396	57	95	12	2	0	28	.240	183	304	19	.962
Major League Totals—3 Years			197	512	65	120	19	2	0	33	.234	241	410	31	.955

Signed as free agent by Montreal Expos' organization, August 18, 1985.
†Traded to Oklahoma City (Texas Rangers' organization) for Pitcher Drew Hall, April 2, 1990.

RODNEY CRAIG IMES

Born November 19, 1966, at Cumberland, Md.
Height, 6.05. Weight, 210.
Throws and bats righthanded.
Attended Old Dominion University, Norfolk, Va.

Led Eastern League in complete games with 9 in 1989.
Tied for American Association lead in games started by pitchers with 29 in 1990.
Named Eastern League Pitcher of the Year, 1989.

Year Club	League	G.	IP.	W.	L.	Pct.	H.	R.	ER.	SO.	BB.	ERA.
1987—Oneonta	NYP	4	27⅔	4	0	1.000	16	1	1	10	5	0.33
1987—Prince William	Carolina	10	68⅓	2	3	.400	68	35	30	49	20	3.95
1988—Prince William	Carolina	11	77	4	5	.444	82	47	38	67	32	4.44
1988—Albany	Eastern	7	49⅓	4	1	.800	46	21	15	24	16	2.74
1988—Fort Lauderdale	Florida St.	8	57⅔	6	2	.750	48	18	11	47	17	1.72
1989—Albany†	Eastern	24	171⅔	*17	6	.739	143	56	52	128	41	2.73
1990—Nashville	Am. Assoc.	29	169⅔	10	8	.556	175	82	70	97	68	3.71

Selected by New York Yankees' organization in 16th round of free-agent draft, June 2, 1987.
†Traded with First Baseman Hal Morris to Cincinnati Reds for Pitcher Tim Leary and Outfielder Van Snider, December 12, 1989.

PETER JOSEPH INCAVIGLIA
(Pete)

Born April 2, 1964, at Pebble Beach, Calif.
Height, 6.01. Weight, 230.
Throws and bats righthanded.
Attended Oklahoma State University, Stillwater, Okla.
Son of Tom Incaviglia, minor league infielder, 1948 through 1950 and 1955; and brother of Tony Incaviglia, minor league third baseman, 1979 through 1983.

Shares major league record for most doubles, inning (2), May 11, 1986 (second game), fourth inning.
Major League stolen bases: 1986 (3), 1987 (9), 1988 (6), 1989 (5), 1990 (3). Total—26.
Led American League batters in strikeouts with 185 in 1986 and tied for lead with 153 in 1988.
Received reported $175,000 bonus to sign with Texas Rangers, 1985.
Named designated hitter on THE SPORTING NEWS College Baseball All-America Team, 1985.

Year Club	League	Pos.	G.	AB.	R.	H.	2B.	3B.	HR.	RBI.	B.A.	PO.	A.	E.	F.A.
1986—Texas†	Amer.	OF	153	540	82	135	21	2	30	88	.250	157	6	●14	.921
1987—Texas	Amer.	OF	139	509	85	138	26	4	27	80	.271	216	8	●13	.945
1988—Texas	Amer.	OF	116	418	59	104	19	3	22	54	.249	172	12	2	.989
1989—Texas‡	Amer.	OF	133	453	48	107	27	4	21	81	.236	213	7	6	.973
1990—Texas	Amer.	OF	153	529	59	123	27	0	24	85	.233	290	12	8	.974
Major League Totals—5 Years			694	2449	333	607	120	13	124	388	.248	1048	45	43	.962

Selected by San Francisco Giants' organization in 10th round of free-agent draft, June 7, 1982.
Selected by Montreal Expos' organization in 1st round (eighth player selected) of free-agent draft, June 3, 1985.
†Traded to Texas Rangers' organization for Pitcher Bob Sebra and Infielder Jim Anderson, November 2, 1985.
‡On disabled list, June 15 to June 30, 1989.

FERMIN ALEXIS INFANTE

Name pronounced En-fawn-tay.
(Known by middle name.)
Born December 4, 1961, at Barquisimeto, Venezuela.
Height, 5.10. Weight, 188.
Throws and bats righthanded.

Major League stolen bases: 1989 (1).
Led International League shortstops in errors with 23 in 1988.
Led International League shortstops in total chances with 699 and double plays with 84 in 1985.
Led South Atlantic League shortstops in total chances with 646 in 1983.

Year Club	League	Pos.	G.	AB.	R.	H.	2B.	3B.	HR.	RBI.	B.A.	PO.	A.	E.	F.A.
1982—Bradenton Jays	Gulf C.	SS	37	137	17	40	7	2	0	15	.292	47	117	5	.970
1983—Florence	S. Atl.	SS	128	480	88	134	25	3	4	56	.279	*197	393	*56	.913
1984—Knoxville	South.	SS	67	253	28	67	13	1	2	29	.265	92	204	18	.943
1984—Syracuse	Int.	SS	72	225	27	50	6	1	0	7	.222	88	229	21	.938
1985—Syracuse	Int.	SS	136	453	63	109	10	5	2	39	.241	*225	*432	*42	.940
1986—Syracuse†	Int.	SS	57	193	27	53	6	2	0	15	.275	73	172	14	.946
1987—Syracuse	Int.	S-3-O-2	107	319	40	72	7	4	2	30	.226	111	260	20	.949
1987—Toronto	Amer.	PR	1	0	0	0	0	0	0	0	.000	0	0	0	.000
1988—Syracuse	Int.	SS-3B-2B	97	340	48	102	15	4	2	28	.300	143	240	25	.939
1988—Toronto	Amer.	3B-SS	19	15	7	3	0	0	0	0	.200	4	6	1	.909
1989—Syracuse	Int.	2B-3B-SS	67	250	39	52	5	0	0	17	.208	108	166	12	.958
1989—Toronto‡	Amer.	SS-3B-2B	20	12	1	2	0	0	0	0	.167	6	13	0	1.000
1990—Atlanta	Nat.	2B-3B-SS	20	28	3	1	1	0	0	0	.036	22	24	2	.958
1990—Richmond	Int.	2B	31	96	8	23	3	0	1	12	.240	52	74	4	.969
American League Totals—3 Years			40	27	8	5	0	0	0	0	.185	10	19	1	.967
National League Totals—1 Year			20	28	3	1	1	0	0	0	.036	22	24	2	.958
Major League Totals—4 Years			60	55	11	6	1	0	0	0	.109	32	43	3	.962

Signed as free agent by Toronto Blue Jays' organization, December 8, 1981.
†On disabled list, June 18, 1986 through remainder of season.
‡Sold to Atlanta Braves, November 20, 1989.

JEFFREY DAVID INNIS
(Jeff)

Born July 5, 1962, at Decatur, Ill.
Height, 6.00. Weight, 170.
Throws and bats righthanded.
Attended University of Illinois, Champaign, Ill.

Major League saves: 1990 (1).
Led Texas League in saves with 25 in 1986.

Year Club	League	G.	IP.	W.	L.	Pct.	H.	R.	ER.	SO.	BB.	ERA.
1983—Little Falls	NYP	28	46	8	0	1.000	29	8	7	68	28	1.37
1984—Jackson	Texas	42	59⅓	6	5	.545	65	34	28	63	40	4.25
1985—Lynchburg	Carolina	53	77	6	3	.667	46	26	20	91	40	2.34
1986—Jackson	Texas	56	92	4	5	.444	69	30	25	75	24	2.45
1987—Tidewater	Int'national	29	44⅓	6	1	.857	26	10	10	28	16	2.03
1987—New York	National	17	25⅔	0	1	.000	29	9	9	28	4	3.16
1988—Tidewater	Int'national	34	48⅓	0	5	.000	43	22	19	43	25	3.54
1988—New York	National	12	19	1	1	.500	19	6	4	14	2	1.89
1989—Tidewater	Int'national	25	29⅔	3	1	.750	28	9	7	14	8	2.12
1989—New York	National	29	39⅔	0	1	.000	38	16	14	16	8	3.18
1990—New York	National	18	26⅓	1	3	.250	19	9	7	12	10	2.39
1990—Tidewater	Int'national	40	52⅔	5	2	.714	34	11	10	42	17	1.71
Major League Totals—4 Years		76	110⅔	2	6	.250	105	40	34	70	24	2.77

Selected by New York Mets' organization in 13th round of free-agent draft, June 6, 1983.

DARYL KEITH IRVINE

Born November 15, 1964, at Harrisonburg, Va.
Height, 6.03. Weight, 195.
Throws and bats righthanded.
Attended Ferrum Junior College, Ferrum, Va.

Led Eastern League in games finished in relief with 45 in 1989.
Led Eastern League in wild pitches with 16 in 1987.

Year Club	League	G.	IP.	W.	L.	Pct.	H.	R.	ER.	SO.	BB.	ERA.
1985—Greensboro†	S. Atlantic	8	37	4	2	.667	46	26	18	19	17	4.38
1986—Winter Haven	Florida St.	26	161	9	8	.529	162	73	57	73	67	3.19
1987—New Britain	Eastern	37	127	4	13	.235	156	101	75	70	59	5.31
1988—New Britain	Eastern	39	125⅓	5	11	.313	113	62	43	82	57	3.09
1989—New Britain	Eastern	★54	91⅓	4	6	.400	74	24	13	50	23	1.28
1990—Pawtucket	Int'national	42	50	2	5	.286	47	24	18	35	19	3.24
1990—Boston	American	11	17⅓	1	1	.500	15	10	9	9	10	4.67
Major League Totals—1 Year		11	17⅓	1	1	.500	15	10	9	9	10	4.67

Selected by Boston Red Sox' organization in 3rd round of free-agent draft, January 17, 1984.
Selected by Toronto Blue Jays' organization in secondary phase of free-agent draft, June 4, 1984.
Selected by Boston Red Sox' organization in secondary phase of free-agent draft, January 9, 1985.
†On disabled list, June 2 to July 15, 1985.

DANNY LYNN JACKSON

Born January 5, 1962, at San Antonio, Tex.
Height, 6.00. Weight, 205.
Throws left and bats righthanded.
Attended University of Oklahoma, Norman, Okla., and
Trinidad State Junior College, Trinidad, Colo.
Brother of Mike Jackson, fourth-round selection of Kansas City Kings in 1983 NBA draft.

Major League saves: 1986 (1).
Tied for National League lead in complete games with 15 in 1988.
Tied for American Association lead in complete games with 10 in 1984.
Tied for American Association lead in shutouts with 2 in 1983 and 3 in 1984.
Named lefthanded pitcher on THE SPORTING NEWS National League All-Star Team, 1988.

Year Club	League	G.	IP.	W.	L.	Pct.	H.	R.	ER.	SO.	BB.	ERA.
1982—Charleston	S. Atlantic	13	96⅓	10	1	.909	80	37	28	62	39	2.62
1982—Jacksonville†	Southern	14	98	7	2	.778	78	30	26	74	42	2.39
1983—Omaha	Am. Assoc.	23	136	7	8	.467	126	74	60	93	73	3.97
1983—Kansas City	American	4	19	1	1	.500	26	12	11	9	6	5.21
1984—Kansas City	American	15	76	2	6	.250	84	41	36	40	35	4.26
1984—Omaha	Am. Assoc.	16	110⅓	5	4	.385	91	50	45	82	45	3.67
1985—Kansas City	American	32	208	14	12	.538	209	94	79	114	76	3.42
1986—Kansas City‡	American	32	185⅔	11	12	.478	177	83	66	115	79	3.20
1987—Kansas City§	American	36	224	9	18	.333	219	115	100	152	109	4.02
1988—Cincinnati	National	35	260⅔	●23	8	.742	206	86	79	161	71	2.73
1989—Cincinnati x	National	20	115⅔	6	11	.353	122	78	72	70	57	5.60
1990—Cincinnati y	National	22	117⅓	6	6	.500	119	54	47	76	40	3.61
1990—Nashville	Am. Assoc.	2	11	1	0	1.000	9	0	0	3	4	0.00
1990—Charleston, W.V. z	S. Atlantic	1	3	0	0	.000	2	2	2	2	1	6.00
American League Totals—5 Years		119	712⅔	37	49	.430	715	345	292	430	305	3.69
National League Totals—3 Years		77	493⅔	35	25	.583	447	218	198	307	168	3.61
Major League Totals—8 Years		196	1206⅓	72	74	.493	1162	563	490	737	473	3.66

Selected by Oakland A's organization in 24th round of free-agent draft, June 3, 1980.
Selected by Kansas City Royals' organization in secondary phase of free-agent draft, January 17, 1982.
†On disabled list, September 8, 1982 through remainder of season.
‡On disabled list, April 4 to April 21, 1986.
§Traded with Shortstop Angel Salazar to Cincinnati Reds for Pitcher Ted Power and Shortstop Kurt Stillwell, November 6, 1987.
xOn disabled list, June 18 to July 6 and July 25 to September 1, 1989.

zGranted free agency, November 5, 1990; signed by Chicago Cubs, November 21, 1990.

CHAMPIONSHIP SERIES RECORD

Year Club	League	G.	IP.	W.	L.	Pct.	H.	R.	ER.	SO.	BB.	ERA.
1985—Kansas City	American	2	10	1	0	1.000	10	0	0	7	1	0.00
1990—Cincinnati	National	2	11⅓	1	0	1.000	8	3	3	8	7	2.38
Championship Series Totals—2 Years		4	21⅓	2	0	1.000	18	3	3	15	8	1.27

WORLD SERIES RECORD

Year Club	League	G.	IP.	W.	L.	Pct.	H.	R.	ER.	SO.	BB.	ERA.
1985—Kansas City	American	2	16	1	1	.500	9	3	3	12	5	1.69
1990—Cincinnati	National	1	2⅔	0	0	.000	6	4	3	0	2	10.13
World Series Totals—2 Years		3	18⅔	1	1	.500	15	7	6	12	7	2.89

ALL-STAR GAME RECORD

Member of National League All-Star Team in 1988; did not play.

DARRIN JAY JACKSON

Born August 22, 1963, at Los Angeles, Calif.
Height, 6.00. Weight, 185.
Throws and bats righthanded.

Major League stolen bases: 1988 (4), 1989 (1), 1990 (3). Total—8.
Led Gulf Coast League outfielders in total chances with 127 in 1981.
Tied for American Association lead in double plays by outfielders with 6 in 1987.
Tied for Texas League lead in double plays with 6 in 1984.

Year Club	League	Pos.	G.	AB.	R.	H.	2B.	3B.	HR.	RBI.	B.A.	PO.	A.	E.	F.A.
1981—Sarasota Cubs	Gulf C.	OF	62	210	29	39	5	0	1	15	.186	★121	5	1	.992
1982—Quad Cities	Midw.	OF	132	529	86	146	23	5	5	48	.276	266	9	8	.972
1983—Salinas	Calif.	OF	129	509	70	126	18	5	6	54	.248	237	15	13	.951
1984—Midland	Texas	OF	132	496	63	134	18	2	15	54	.270	286	★19	8	.974
1985—Iowa	A. A.	OF	10	40	0	7	2	1	0	1	.175	19	0	0	1.000
1985—Pittsfield	East.	OF	91	325	38	82	10	1	3	30	.252	221	5	0	1.000
1985—Chicago	Nat.	OF	5	11	0	1	0	0	0	0	.091	7	0	0	1.000
1986—Pittsfield	East.	OF	137	●520	82	139	28	2	15	64	.267	320	★16	7	.980
1987—Iowa	A. A.	OF	132	474	81	130	32	5	23	81	.274	290	15	6	.981
1987—Chicago	Nat.	OF	7	5	2	4	1	0	0	0	.800	1	0	0	1.000
1988—Chicago	Nat.	OF	100	188	29	50	11	3	6	20	.266	116	1	2	.983
1989—Chi.†-S.D.	Nat.	OF	70	170	17	37	7	0	4	20	.218	121	5	5	.962
1989—Iowa	A. A.	OF	30	120	18	31	4	1	7	17	.258	66	12	0	1.000
1990—San Diego	Nat.	OF	58	113	10	29	3	0	3	9	.257	63	1	1	.985
1990—Las Vegas	P. C.	OF	29	98	14	27	4	0	5	15	.276	61	4	0	1.000
Major League Totals—5 Years			240	487	58	121	22	3	13	49	.248	308	7	8	.975

Selected by Chicago Cubs' organization in 2nd round of free-agent draft, June 8, 1981.

†Traded with Pitcher Calvin Schiraldi and a player to be named later to San Diego Padres for Outfielder Marvell Wynne and Infielder Luis Salazar, August 30, 1989; San Diego acquired First Baseman Phil Stephenson to complete deal, September 5, 1989.

MICHAEL RAY JACKSON
(Mike)

Born December 22, 1964, at Houston, Tex.
Height, 6.00. Weight, 200.
Throws and bats righthanded.
Attended Hill Junior College, Hillsboro, Tex.

Major League saves: 1987 (1), 1988 (4), 1989 (7), 1990 (3). Total—15.
Tied for American League lead in intentional bases on balls issued with 10 in 1988.
Tied for National League lead in balks with 8 in 1987.
Led Carolina League in balks with 7 in 1985.

Year Club	League	G.	IP.	W.	L.	Pct.	H.	R.	ER.	SO.	BB.	ERA.
1984—Spartanburg	S. Atlantic	14	80⅔	7	2	.778	53	35	24	77	50	2.68
1985—Peninsula	Carolina	31	125⅓	7	9	.438	127	71	64	96	53	4.60
1986—Reading	Eastern	30	43⅓	2	3	.400	25	9	8	42	22	1.66
1986—Portland	P. Coast	17	22⅔	3	1	.750	18	8	8	23	13	3.18
1986—Philadelphia	National	9	13⅓	0	0	.000	12	5	5	3	4	3.38
1987—Philadelphia†	National	55	109⅓	3	10	.231	88	55	51	93	56	4.20
1987—Maine‡	Int'national	2	11	1	0	1.000	9	2	1	13	5	0.82
1988—Seattle	American	62	99⅓	6	5	.545	74	37	29	76	43	2.63
1989—Seattle	American	65	99⅓	4	6	.400	81	43	35	94	54	3.17
1990—Seattle	American	63	77⅓	5	7	.417	64	42	39	69	44	4.54
National League Totals—2 Years		64	122⅔	3	10	.231	100	60	56	96	60	4.11
American League Totals—3 Years		190	276	15	18	.455	219	122	103	239	141	3.36
Major League Totals—5 Years		254	398⅔	18	28	.391	319	182	159	335	201	3.59

Selected by Philadelphia Phillies' organization in 29th round of free-agent draft, June 6, 1983.
Selected by Philadelphia Phillies' organization in secondary phase of free-agent draft, January 17, 1984.

†On disabled list, August 6 to August 21, 1987.
‡Traded with Outfielders Glenn Wilson and Dave Brundage to Seattle Mariners for Outfielder Phil Bradley and Pitcher Tim Fortugno, December 9, 1987.

VINCENT EDWARD JACKSON
(Bo)

Born November 30, 1962, at Bessemer, Ala.
Height, 6.01. Weight, 225.
Throws and bats righthanded.
Attended Auburn University, Auburn, Ala.

Shares major league records for most consecutive home runs (4), July 17 (3), August 26 (1), 1990; most strikeouts, nine-inning game (5), April 18, 1987; most strikeouts, inning (2), April 8, 1987, fourth inning.
Major League stolen bases: 1986 (3), 1987 (10), 1988 (27), 1989 (26), 1990 (15). Total—81.
Hit three home runs in a game, July 17, 1990.
Led American League batters in strikeouts with 172 in 1989.

Year Club	League	Pos.	G.	AB.	R.	H.	2B.	3B.	HR.	RBI.	B.A.	PO.	A.	E.	F.A.
1986—Memphis†	South.	OF	53	184	30	51	9	3	7	25	.277	116	8	7	.947
1986—Kansas City	Amer.	OF	25	82	9	17	2	1	2	9	.207	29	2	4	.886
1987—Kansas City	Amer.	OF	116	396	46	93	17	2	22	53	.235	180	9	9	.955
1988—Kansas City‡	Amer.	OF	124	439	63	108	16	4	25	68	.246	246	11	7	.973
1989—Kansas City§	Amer.	OF	135	515	86	132	15	6	32	105	.256	224	11	8	.967
1990—Kansas City x	Amer.	OF	111	405	74	110	16	1	28	78	.272	230	8	12	.952
Major League Totals—5 Years			511	1837	278	460	66	14	109	313	.250	909	41	40	.960

Selected by New York Yankees' organization in 2nd round of free-agent draft, June 7, 1982.
Selected by California Angels' organization in 20th round of free-agent draft, June 3, 1985.
Selected by Kansas City Royals' organization in 4th round of free-agent draft, June 2, 1986.
†On temporary inactive list, June 20 to June 30, 1986.
‡On disabled list, June 1 to July 2, 1988.
§On disabled list, July 25 to August 9, 1989.
xOn disabled list, July 18 to August 26, 1990.

ALL-STAR GAME RECORD

Shares All-Star Game record for hitting home run in first at-bat, July 11, 1989.

Year League	Pos.	AB.	R.	H.	2B.	3B.	HR.	RBI.	B.A.	PO.	A.	E.	F.A.
1989—American	OF	4	1	2	0	0	1	2	.500	2	0	0	1.000

RECORD AS FOOTBALL PLAYER

Heisman Trophy winner, 1985.
Named college football Player of the Year by THE SPORTING NEWS, 1985.
Named as running back on THE SPORTING NEWS College All-America Team, 1985.
Selected by Tampa Bay in 1st round (1st player selected) of 1986 NFL draft.
Selected by Birmingham in 1986 USFL territorial draft.
On reserve/did not sign entire 1986 football season through April 27, 1987.
Selected by Los Angeles Raiders in 7th round (183rd player selected) of 1987 NFL draft.
Signed by Los Angeles Raiders, July 17, 1987.
On reserve/did not report, August 27 through October 23, 1987; activated, October 24, 1987.
On reserve/did not report, August 22 through October 11, 1988; reported, October 12, 1988.
Activated from reserve/did not report, October 15, 1988.
On reserve/did not report, July 21 through October 10, 1989; activated, October 11, 1989.
On reserve/did not report, July 17 through October 14, 1990.
Reinstated and granted roster exemption, October 15 through October 19, 1990; activated, October 20, 1990.

Year Club	G.	RUSHING Att.	Yds.	Avg.	TD.	PASS RECEIVING P.C.	Yds.	Avg.	TD.	—TOTAL— TD.	Pts.	F.
1987—Los Angeles Raiders NFL	7	81	554	6.8	4	16	136	8.5	2	6	36	2
1988—Los Angeles Raiders NFL	10	136	580	4.3	3	9	79	8.8	0	3	18	5
1989—Los Angeles Raiders NFL	11	173	950	5.5	4	9	69	7.7	0	4	24	1
1990—Los Angeles Raiders NFL	10	125	698	5.6	5	6	68	11.3	0	5	30	3
Pro Totals—4 Years	38	515	2782	5.4	16	40	352	8.8	2	18	108	11

Additional pro statistics: Recovered one fumble, 1987; recovered two fumbles, 1988.
Played in Pro Bowl (NFL All-Star Game) following 1990 season.

BROOK WALLACE JACOBY JR.

Born November 23, 1959, at Philadelphia, Pa.
Height, 5.11. Weight, 195.
Throws and bats righthanded.
Attended Ventura College, Ventura, Calif.
Son of Brook Jacoby Sr., minor league pitcher, 1956 through 1958.

Major League stolen bases: 1984 (3), 1985 (2), 1986 (2), 1987 (2), 1988 (2), 1989 (2), 1990 (1). Total—14.
Hit three home runs in a game, July 3, 1987.
Tied for American League lead in putouts by third basemen with 134 in 1987.
Led International League third basemen in total chances with 331 and double plays with 22 in 1982.

Year Club	League	Pos.	G.	AB.	R.	H.	2B.	3B.	HR.	RBI.	B.A.	PO.	A.	E.	F.A.
1979—Kingsport	Appal.	OF	8	28	3	7	2	0	0	1	.250	9	0	0	1.000
1979—Bradenton	Gulf C.	OF	42	160	24	43	11	1	3	35	.269	65	7	4	.947
1980—Anderson	S. Atl.	OF-3B	132	496	82	147	*40	4	19	*108	.296	219	30	10	.961
1980—Savannah	South.	3B	3	8	0	1	0	0	0	0	.125	0	2	0	1.000
1981—Savannah	South.	3B-OF	140	507	59	148	28	3	24	82	.292	103	232	31	.915

Year Club	League	Pos.	G.	AB.	R.	H.	2B.	3B.	HR.	RBI.	B.A.	PO.	A.	E.	F.A.
1981—Atlanta	Nat.	3B	11	10	0	2	0	0	0	1	.200	3	4	0	1.000
1982—Richmond.............	Int.	3B	134	501	74	150	21	3	18	58	.299	83	*229	*19	*.943
1983—Richmond.............	Int.	3B	133	489	88	154	32	2	25	100	.315	62	247	18	.945
1983—Atlanta†	Nat.	3B	4	8	0	0	0	0	0	0	.000	0	2	0	1.000
1984—Cleveland‡...........	Amer.	3B-SS	126	439	64	116	19	3	7	40	.264	86	188	14	.951
1985—Cleveland.............	Amer.	3B-2B	161	606	72	166	26	3	20	87	.274	114	319	19	.958
1986—Cleveland.............	Amer.	3B	158	583	83	168	30	4	17	80	.288	109	292	25	.941
1987—Cleveland.............	Amer.	●3B-1B	155	540	73	162	26	4	32	69	.300	192	261	●22	.954
1988—Cleveland.............	Amer.	3B	152	552	59	133	25	0	9	49	.241	99	298	10	.975
1989—Cleveland.............	Amer.	3B	147	519	49	141	26	5	13	64	.272	92	268	17	.955
1990—Cleveland.............	Amer.	3B-1B	155	553	77	162	24	4	14	75	.293	628	186	6	.993
National League Totals—2 Years...........			15	18	0	2	0	0	0	1	.111	3	6	0	1.000
American League Totals—7 Years			1054	3792	477	1048	176	23	112	464	.276	1320	1812	113	.965
Major League Totals—9 Years................			1069	3810	477	1050	176	23	112	465	.276	1323	1818	113	.965

Selected by Atlanta Braves' organization in 7th round of free-agent draft, January 9, 1979.

†Traded with Outfielder Brett Butler to Cleveland Indians, October 21, 1983, completing deal in which Atlanta Braves acquired Pitcher Len Barker for three players to be named later, August 28, 1983. Cleveland acquired Pitcher Rick Behenna as partial completion of deal, September 2, 1983.

‡On disabled list, August 20, 1984 through remainder of season.

ALL-STAR GAME RECORD

Year League	Pos.	AB.	R.	H.	2B.	3B.	HR.	RBI.	B.A.	PO.	A.	E.	F.A.
1986—American	PH-3B	1	0	0	0	0	0	0	.000	1	1	0	1.000
1990—American	PH	1	0	0	0	0	0	0	.000	0	0	0	.000
All-Star Game Totals—2 Years....................		2	0	0	0	0	0	0	.000	1	1	0	1.000

DION JAMES

Born November 9, 1962, at Philadelphia, Pa.
Height, 6.01. Weight, 170.
Throws and bats lefthanded.

Major League stolen bases: 1983 (1), 1984 (10), 1987 (10), 1988 (9), 1989 (2), 1990 (5). Total—37.
Led California League outfielders in fielding percentage with .988 in 1981.

Year Club	League	Pos.	G.	AB.	R.	H.	2B.	3B.	HR.	RBI.	B.A.	PO.	A.	E.	F.A.
1980—Butte	Pion.	OF-1B	59	224	57	71	14	1	0	27	.317	80	4	7	.923
1980—Burlington	Midw.	OF	3	10	0	1	0	0	0	1	.100	8	1	0	1.000
1981—Stockton	Calif.	OF-1B	124	451	70	137	17	3	2	49	.304	250	10	3	.989
1982—El Paso†	Texas	OF	106	422	103	136	25	3	9	72	.322	237	9	7	.972
1983—Vancouver..........	P. C.	OF	129	467	84	157	29	5	8	68	.336	289	6	2	.993
1983—Milwaukee..........	Amer.	OF	11	20	1	2	0	0	0	1	.100	12	1	0	1.000
1984—Milwaukee..........	Amer.	OF	128	387	52	114	19	5	1	30	.295	252	7	3	.989
1985—Vancouver‡.........	P. C.	OF	10	37	2	4	2	0	0	5	.108	17	0	0	1.000
1985—Milwaukee..........	Amer.	OF	18	49	5	11	1	0	0	3	.224	20	0	0	1.000
1986—Vancouver§.........	P. C.	OF-1B	130	485	85	137	25	6	6	55	.282	348	7	5	.986
1987—Atlanta	Nat.	OF	134	494	80	154	37	6	10	61	.312	262	4	1	*.996
1988—Atlanta	Nat.	OF	132	386	46	99	17	5	3	30	.256	222	5	3	.987
1989—Atlanta x..............	Nat.	OF-1B	63	170	15	44	7	0	1	11	.259	126	7	0	1.000
1989—Cleveland...........	Amer.	OF-1B	71	245	26	75	11	0	4	29	.306	85	1	3	.966
1990—Cleveland y	Amer.	1B-OF	87	248	28	68	15	2	1	22	.274	282	17	4	.987
American League Totals—5 Years			315	949	112	270	46	7	6	85	.285	651	26	10	.985
National League Totals—3 Years			329	1050	141	297	61	11	14	102	.283	610	16	4	.994
Major League Totals—7 Years................			644	1999	253	567	107	18	20	187	.284	1261	42	14	.989

Selected by Milwaukee Brewers' organization in 1st round (25th player selected) of free-agent draft, June 3, 1980.

†On disabled list, July 1 to August 1, 1982.

‡On Milwaukee disabled list, March 31 to April 28 and May 20 to September 1, 1985; included rehabilitation disability assignment to Vancouver, April 12 to April 28, 1985.

§Traded to Atlanta Braves for Outfielder Brad Komminsk, January 20, 1987.

xTraded to Cleveland Indians for Outfielder Oddibe McDowell, July 2, 1989.

yReleased, October 30, 1990.

DONALD CHRISTOPHER JAMES
(Chris)

Born October 4, 1962, at Rusk, Tex.
Height, 6.01. Weight, 190.
Throws and bats righthanded.
Attended Blinn College, Brenham, Tex.
Brother of Craig James, running back with Washington Federals
and New England Patriots, 1983 through 1988.

Major League stolen bases: 1987 (3), 1988 (7), 1989 (5), 1990 (4). Total—19.
Tied for Pacific Coast League lead in being hit by pitch with 7 in 1985.
Led South Atlantic League in total bases with 257 and tied for lead in being hit by pitch with 12 in 1983.
Led Pacific Coast League outfielders in total chances with 351 in 1985.

Year Club	League	Pos.	G.	AB.	R.	H.	2B.	3B.	HR.	RBI.	B.A.	PO.	A.	E.	F.A.
1982—Bend......................	N'west	3B-OF	63	227	47	72	*19	3	12	50	.317	93	54	10	.936
1983—Spartanburg..........	S. Atl.	OF-3B	129	499	94	148	23	4	26	*121	.297	150	88	16	.937
1984—Reading.................	East.	*3B-OF	128	457	66	117	19	*12	8	57	.256	104	209	*39	.889
1985—Portland................	P. C.	OF	135	507	78	160	35	8	11	73	.316	*328	16	7	.980

Year	Club	League	Pos.	G.	AB.	R.	H.	2B.	3B.	HR.	RBI.	B.A.	PO.	A.	E.	F.A.
1986—Portland	P. C.	OF-3B	69	266	30	64	6	2	12	41	.241	83	44	8	.941
1986—Philadelphia†	Nat.	OF	16	46	5	13	3	0	1	5	.283	19	0	0	1.000
1987—Philadelphia	Nat.	OF	115	358	48	105	20	6	17	54	.293	198	5	2	.990
1987—Maine	Int.	OF-3B	13	40	5	9	2	1	0	3	.225	22	4	0	1.000
1988—Philadelphia	Nat.	OF-3B	150	566	57	137	24	1	19	66	.242	282	51	9	.974
1989—Phi.‡-S.D.§	Nat.	OF-3B	132	482	55	117	17	2	13	65	.243	215	27	7	.972
1990—Cleveland	Amer.	OF	140	528	62	158	32	4	12	70	.299	25	1	0	1.000
National League Totals—4 Years			413	1452	165	372	64	9	50	190	.256	714	83	18	.978
American League Totals—1 Year			140	528	62	158	32	4	12	70	.299	25	1	0	1.000
Major League Totals—5 Years			553	1980	227	530	96	13	62	260	.268	739	84	18	.979

Signed as free agent by Philadelphia Phillies' organization, October 30, 1981.

†On disabled list, May 6 to July 21, 1986; included rehabilitation disability assignment to Portland, July 3 to July 21, 1986.

‡Traded to San Diego Padres for Infielder Randy Ready and Outfielder John Kruk, June 2, 1989.

§Traded with Catcher Sandy Alomar and Third Baseman Carlos Baerga to Cleveland Indians for Outfielder Joe Carter, December 6, 1989.

MICHAEL ELMO JAMES
(Mike)

Born August 15, 1967, at Fort Walton Beach, Fla.
Height, 6.03. Weight, 180.
Throws and bats righthanded.
Attended Lurleen B. Wallace State Junior College, Andalusia, Ala.

Year	Club	League	G.	IP.	W.	L.	Pct.	H.	R.	ER.	SO.	BB.	ERA.
1988—Great Falls	Pioneer	14	67	7	1	*.875	61	36	28	59	41	3.76
1989—Bakersfield	California	27	159⅔	11	8	.579	144	82	67	127	78	3.78
1990—San Antonio	Texas	26	157	11	4	.733	144	73	58	97	78	3.32

Selected by Los Angeles Dodgers' organization in 43rd round of free-agent draft, June 2, 1987.

STANLEY JULIAN JAVIER
Name pronounced HAAV-e-AIR.
(Stan)

Born September 1, 1965, at San Francisco Macoris, D. R.
Height, 6.00. Weight, 185.
Throws right and bats left and righthanded.
Son of Julian Javier, infielder with St. Louis Cardinals and Cincinnati Reds, 1960 through 1972.

Major League stolen bases: 1986 (8), 1987 (3), 1988 (20), 1989 (12), 1990 (15). Total—58.
Led Southern League in bases on balls received with 112 in 1985.

Year	Club	League	Pos.	G.	AB.	R.	H.	2B.	3B.	HR.	RBI.	B.A.	PO.	A.	E.	F.A.
1981—Johnson City	Appal.	OF	53	144	30	36	5	4	3	19	.250	53	2	3	.948
1982—Johnson City†	Appal.	OF	57	185	45	51	3	●4	8	36	.276	94	8	4	.962
1983—Greensboro	S. Atl.	OF	129	489	109	152	*34	6	12	77	.311	250	10	15	.945
1984—New York	Amer.	OF	7	7	1	1	0	0	0	0	.143	3	0	0	1.000
1984—Nashville‡	South.	OF	76	262	40	76	17	4	7	38	.290	202	4	7	.967
1984—Columbus	Int.	OF	32	99	12	22	3	1	0	7	.222	77	4	2	.976
1985—Huntsville	South.	OF	140	486	105	138	22	8	9	64	.284	363	8	7	.981
1986—Tacoma	P. C.	OF-1B	69	248	50	81	16	2	4	51	.327	172	9	6	.968
1986—Oakland	Amer.	OF	59	114	13	23	8	0	0	8	.202	118	1	0	1.000
1987—Oakland§	Amer.	OF-1B	81	151	22	28	3	1	2	9	.185	149	5	3	.981
1987—Tacoma	P. C.	OF-1B	15	51	6	11	2	0	0	2	.216	26	0	2	.929
1988—Oakland x	Amer.	OF-1B	125	397	49	102	13	3	2	35	.257	274	7	5	.983
1989—Oakland y	Amer.	OF-2B-1B	112	310	42	77	12	3	1	28	.248	221	8	2	.991
1990—Oakland z	Amer.	OF	19	33	4	8	0	2	0	3	.242	19	0	0	1.000
1990—Los Angeles	Nat.	OF	104	276	56	84	9	4	3	24	.304	204	2	0	1.000
American League Totals—6 Years			403	1012	131	239	36	9	5	83	.236	784	21	10	.988
National League Totals—1 Year			104	276	56	84	9	4	3	24	.304	204	2	0	1.000
Major League Totals—6 Years			507	1288	187	323	45	13	8	107	.251	988	23	10	.990

Signed as free agent by St. Louis Cardinals' organization, March 26, 1981.

†Traded with shortstop Bob Meacham to New York Yankees' organization for Outfielder Bob Helsom and Pitchers Marty Mason and Steve Fincher, December 14, 1982.

‡Traded with Pitchers Jay Howell, Jose Rijo, Eric Plunk and Tim Birtsas to Oakland A's for Outfielder Rickey Henderson, Pitcher Bert Bradley and cash, December 5, 1984.

§On disabled list, August 3 to September 1, 1987; included rehabilitation disability assignment to Tacoma, August 20 to September 1, 1987.

xOn disabled list, August 18 to September 2, 1988.

yOn disabled list, July 7 to July 24, 1989.

zTraded to Los Angeles Dodgers for Second Baseman Willie Randolph, May 13, 1990.

CHAMPIONSHIP SERIES RECORD

Year	Club	League	Pos.	G.	AB.	R.	H.	2B.	3B.	HR.	RBI.	B.A.	PO.	A.	E.	F.A.
1988—Oakland	Amer.	OF-PR	2	4	0	2	0	0	0	1	.500	5	0	0	1.000
1989—Oakland	Amer.	OF	1	2	0	0	0	0	0	0	.000	1	0	0	1.000
Championship Series Totals—2 Years			3	6	0	2	0	0	0	1	.333	6	0	0	1.000

Year Club League	Pos.	G.	AB.	R.	H.	2B.	3B.	HR.	RBI.	B.A.	PO.	A.	E.	F.A.
1988—Oakland................. Amer.	PR-OF	3	4	0	2	0	0	0	2	.500	1	0	0	1.000
1989—Oakland................. Amer.	OF	1	0	0	0	0	0	0	0	.000	0	0	0	.000
World Series Totals—2 Years		4	4	0	2	0	0	0	2	.500	1	0	0	1.000

JAMES MICHAEL JEFFCOAT
(Mike)

Born August 3, 1959, at Pine Bluff, Ark.
Height, 6.02. Weight, 189.
Throws and bats lefthanded.
Attended Louisiana Tech University, Ruston, La.

Major League saves: 1984 (1), 1990 (5). Total—6.

Year Club League	G.	IP.	W.	L.	Pct.	H.	R.	ER.	SO.	BB.	ERA.
1980—Waterloo..................... Midwest	4	6	0	0	.000	12	12	4	7	3	6.00
1980—Batavia......................... NYP	12	68	4	3	.571	65	40	30	71	45	3.97
1981—Waterloo..................... Midwest	25	147	10	8	.556	151	71	63	109	78	3.86
1982—Waterloo..................... Midwest	9	62	5	4	.556	58	29	28	68	15	4.06
1982—Chattanooga .... Southern	18	128⅓	8	8	.500	122	49	41	107	51	2.88
1983—Charleston .... Int'natonal	26	167	12	8	.600	187	95	84	96	46	4.53
1983—Cleveland................... American	11	32⅔	1	3	.250	32	13	12	9	13	3.31
1984—Cleveland................... American	63	75⅓	5	2	.714	82	28	25	41	24	2.99
1985—Cleveland†................. American	9	9⅔	0	0	.000	8	5	3	4	6	2.79
1985—Phoenix....................... P. Coast	10	59⅔	4	5	.444	64	26	24	28	9	3.62
1985—San Francisco .... National	19	22	0	2	.000	27	13	13	10	6	5.32
1986—Phoenix‡..................... P. Coast	54	75	7	2	.778	81	40	35	57	31	4.20
1987—Oklahoma City .... Am. Assoc.	26	159⅔	11	8	.579	193	99	85	101	41	4.79
1987—Texas............................ American	2	7	0	1	.000	11	10	10	1	4	12.86
1988—Texas............................ American	5	10	0	2	.000	19	13	13	5	5	11.70
1988—Oklahoma City .... Am. Assoc.	22	157⅓	9	5	.643	137	53	49	95	41	2.80
1989—Oklahoma City .... Am. Assoc.	11	72⅔	4	4	.500	81	31	26	50	21	3.22
1989—Texas............................ American	22	130⅔	9	6	.600	139	65	52	64	33	3.58
1990—Texas§......................... American	44	110⅔	5	6	.455	122	57	55	58	28	4.47
American League Totals—7 Years	156	376	20	20	.500	413	191	170	182	113	4.07
National League Totals—1 Year........................	19	22	0	2	.000	27	13	13	10	6	5.32
Major League Totals—7 Years............................	175	398	20	22	.476	440	204	183	192	119	4.14

Selected by St. Louis Cardinals' organization in 30th round of free-agent draft, June 7, 1977.
Selected by Cleveland Indians' organization in 13th round of free-agent draft, June 3, 1980.
†Traded with Infielder Luis Quinones to San Francisco Giants' organization for Shortstop Johnnie LeMaster, May 7, 1985.
‡Released, October 21, 1986; signed by Texas Rangers' organization, December 18, 1986.
§On disabled list, July 22 to August 18 and August 21 to September 5, 1990.

GREGORY SCOTT JEFFERIES
(Gregg)

Born August 1, 1967, at Burlingame, Calif.
Height, 5.10. Weight, 180.
Throws right and bats left and righthanded.

Major League stolen bases: 1988 (5), 1989 (21), 1990 (11). Total—37.
Tied for International League lead in intentional bases on balls received with 10 in 1988.
Led Texas League in intentional bases on balls received with 18 in 1987.
Led Carolina League in slugging percentage with .549 in 1986.
Led International League third basemen in assists with 240 in 1988.
Named Texas League Most Valuable Player, 1987.
Named Carolina League Most Valuable Player, 1986.
Named Appalachian League Player of the Year, 1985.

Year Club League	Pos.	G.	AB.	R.	H.	2B.	3B.	HR.	RBI.	B.A.	PO.	A.	E.	F.A.
1985—Kingsport............... Appal.	SS-2B	47	166	27	57	18	2	3	29	.343	78	130	21	.908
1985—Columbia .... S. Atl.	2B-SS	20	64	7	18	2	2	1	12	.281	28	26	2	.964
1986—Columbia .... S. Atl.	SS	25	112	29	38	6	1	5	24	.339	36	83	7	.944
1986—Lynchburg............ Carol.	SS	95	390	66	138	25	9	11	80	★.354	138	273	20	.954
1986—Jackson .... Texas	SS-3B	5	19	1	8	1	1	0	7	.421	7	9	1	.941
1987—Jackson .... Texas	SS-3B	134	510	81	187	★48	5	20	101	.367	167	388	35	.941
1987—New York.............. Nat.	PH	6	6	0	3	1	0	0	2	.500	0	0	0	.000
1988—Tidewater.............. Int.	3-S-2-O	132	504	62	142	28	4	7	61	.282	110	330	27	.942
1988—New York.............. Nat.	3B-2B	29	109	19	35	8	2	6	17	.321	33	46	2	.975
1989—New York.............. Nat.	2B-3B	141	508	72	131	28	2	12	56	.258	242	280	14	.974
1990—New York.............. Nat.	2B-3B	153	604	96	171	★40	3	15	68	.283	242	341	16	.973
Major League Totals—4 Years.................	329	1227	187	340	77	7	33	143	.277	517	667	32	.974

Selected by New York Mets' organization in 1st round (20th player selected) of free-agent draft, June 3, 1985.

CHAMPIONSHIP SERIES RECORD

Year Club League	Pos.	G.	AB.	R.	H.	2B.	3B.	HR.	RBI.	B.A.	PO.	A.	E.	F.A.
1988—New York............. Nat.	3B	7	27	2	9	2	0	0	1	.333	5	8	1	.929

REGINALD JIROD JEFFERSON
(Reggie)

Born September 25, 1968, at Tallahassee, Fla.
Height, 6.04. Weight, 210.
Throws left and bats right and lefthanded.
Led Gulf Coast League first basemen in total chances with 624 in 1986.

Year	Club	League	Pos.	G.	AB.	R.	H.	2B.	3B.	HR.	RBI.	B.A.	PO.	A.	E.	F.A.
1986—Sarasota Reds		Gulf C.	1B	59	208	28	54	4	●5	3	33	.260	★581	★36	7	.989
1987—Billings		Pion.	1B	8	22	10	8	1	0	1	9	.364	21	1	0	1.000
1987—Cedar Rapids†		Midw.	1B	15	54	9	12	5	0	3	11	.222	120	11	1	.992
1988—Cedar Rapids†		Midw.	1B	135	517	76	149	26	2	18	★90	.288	1084	91	13	.989
1989—Chattanooga		South.	1B	135	487	66	140	19	3	17	80	.287	1004	79	16	.985
1990—Nashville‡		A. A.	1B	37	126	24	34	11	2	5	23	.270	314	20	4	.988

Selected by Cincinnati Reds' organization in 3rd round of free-agent draft, June 2, 1986.
†Batted lefthanded only.
‡On disabled list, May 25, 1990 through remainder of season.

STANLEY JEFFERSON
(Stan)

Born December 4, 1962, at New York, N.Y.
Height, 5.11. Weight, 180.
Throws right and bats left and righthanded.
Attended Bethune-Cookman College, Daytona Beach, Fla.
Major League stolen bases: 1987 (34), 1988 (5), 1989 (10), 1990 (9). Total—58.
Led Texas League in stolen bases with 39 in 1985.
Led New York-Pennsylvania League in stolen bases with 35 in 1983.
Named outfielder on THE SPORTING NEWS College Baseball All-America Team, 1983.

Year	Club	League	Pos.	G.	AB.	R.	H.	2B.	3B.	HR.	RBI.	B.A.	PO.	A.	E.	F.A.
1983—Little Falls†		NYP	OF	71	281	57	90	5	1	9	36	.320	★153	7	4	.976
1984—Lynchburg†		Carol.	OF	128	493	★113	142	20	●9	5	47	.288	265	11	8	.972
1985—Jackson		Texas	OF	133	524	97	145	21	6	8	30	.277	276	9	7	.976
1986—Tidewater‡		Int.	OF	95	369	60	107	19	4	2	37	.290	219	5	2	.991
1986—New York§		Nat.	OF	14	24	6	5	1	0	1	3	.208	13	0	0	1.000
1987—San Diego x		Nat.	OF	116	422	59	97	8	7	8	29	.230	232	3	3	.987
1988—San Diego		Nat.	OF	49	111	16	16	1	2	1	4	.144	62	0	0	1.000
1988—Las Vegas y		P. C.	OF	74	278	60	88	14	6	4	33	.317	163	4	7	.960
1989—N.Y.z-Bal.		Amer.	OF	45	139	20	34	7	0	4	21	.245	82	3	1	.988
1989—Col.-Roch.		Int.	OF	84	321	43	83	14	9	3	36	.259	150	3	4	.975
1990—Balt.a-Cleve.		Amer.	OF	59	117	22	27	8	0	2	10	.231	70	4	1	.987
1990—Colorado Springs		P. C.	OF	33	119	27	41	9	3	3	17	.345	69	6	0	1.000
National League Totals—3 Years				179	557	81	118	10	9	10	36	.212	307	3	3	.990
American League Totals—2 Years				104	256	42	61	15	0	6	31	.238	152	7	2	.988
Major League Totals—5 Years				283	813	123	179	25	9	16	67	.220	459	10	5	.989

Selected by New York Mets' organization in 1st round (20th player selected) of free-agent draft, June 6, 1983.
†Batted righthanded only.
‡On disabled list, July 25 to August 14, 1986.
§Traded with Outfielders Shawn Abner and Kevin Mitchell and Pitchers Kevin Armstrong and Kevin Brown to San Diego Padres for Outfielder Kevin McReynolds, Pitcher Gene Walter and Infielder Adam Ging, December 11, 1986.
xOn disabled list, April 13 to May 7 and May 30 to June 14, 1987.
yTraded with Pitchers Jimmy Jones and Lance McCullers to New York Yankees for First Baseman-Outfielder Jack Clark and Pitcher Pat Clements, October 24, 1988.
zTraded to Rochester (Baltimore Orioles' organization) for Pitcher John Hayden, July 20, 1989.
aClaimed on waivers by Cleveland Indians, May 7, 1990.

CHRISTOPHER JOHN JELIC
(Chris)

Born December 16, 1963, at Pittsburgh, Pa.
Height, 5.11. Weight, 180.
Throws and bats righthanded.
Attended University of Pittsburgh, Pittsburgh, Pa.
Led Texas League in passed balls with 16 in 1988.

Year	Club	League	Pos.	G.	AB.	R.	H.	2B.	3B.	HR.	RBI.	B.A.	PO.	A.	E.	F.A.
1985—Eugene		N'west	C	42	144	24	45	7	3	2	22	.313	263	36	1	★.997
1986—Fort Myers†		Fla. St.	C	108	348	50	89	11	5	5	50	.256	482	82	●21	.964
1987—Lynchburg		Carol.	C	71	224	47	74	8	5	8	48	.330	346	45	9	.978
1987—Jackson		Texas	C-OF	50	183	22	45	10	2	5	24	.246	267	35	8	.974
1988—Jackson		Texas	C	88	273	29	57	13	1	4	25	.209	498	59	6	.989
1989—Jackson‡		Texas	3B-1B-C	86	249	32	64	11	1	7	37	.257	279	87	11	.971
1990—Tidewater‡		Int.	3B-1B-C	92	265	39	81	21	1	4	49	.306	145	94	13	.948
1990—New York x		Nat.	OF	4	11	2	1	0	0	1	1	.091	1	0	0	1.000
Major League Totals—1 Year				4	11	2	1	0	0	1	1	.091	1	0	0	1.000

Selected by Kansas City Royals' organization in 2nd round of free-agent draft, June 3, 1985.
†Traded with Pitcher David Cone to New York Mets for Catcher Ed Hearn and Pitchers Rick Anderson and Mauro Gozzo, March 27, 1987.
‡On disabled list, April 8 to April 23, 1989.

§On disabled list, May 26 to June 14, 1990.
xReleased, November 13, 1990.

LARRY STEVEN JELTZ
(Steve)

Born May 28, 1959, at Paris, France.
Height, 5.11. Weight, 190.
Throws right and bats left and righthanded.
Attended University of Kansas, Lawrence, Kan.

Major League stolen bases: 1984 (2), 1985 (1), 1986 (6), 1987 (1), 1988 (3), 1989 (4), 1990 (1). Total—18.
Switch-hit home runs in one game, June 8, 1989.
Led Carolina League second basemen in double plays with 84 in 1981.
Tied for Carolina League lead in caught stealing with 15 in 1981.

Year	Club	League	Pos.	G.	AB.	R.	H.	2B.	3B.	HR.	RBI.	B.A.	PO.	A.	E.	F.A.
1980—Spartanburg†	S. Atl.		2B	31	107	19	31	2	1	0	8	.290	51	61	4	.966
1981—Peninsula	Carol.		2B	133	482	81	112	18	0	2	32	.232	★293	★369	25	.964
1982—Reading	East.		2B-SS-3B	126	380	61	92	10	3	7	28	.242	251	297	22	.961
1983—Portland	P. C.		3-2-S-O	71	181	34	48	6	1	0	16	.265	106	113	11	.952
1983—Philadelphia	Nat.		2B-SS-3B	13	8	0	1	0	1	0	1	.125	4	5	0	1.000
1984—Portland	P. C.		S-2-O-3	134	436	68	96	10	9	2	46	.220	270	349	28	.957
1984—Philadelphia	Nat.		SS-3B	28	68	7	14	0	1	1	7	.206	37	93	1	.992
1985—Philadelphia	Nat.		SS	89	196	17	37	4	1	0	12	.189	106	215	14	.958
1985—Portland	P. C.		SS	21	71	6	21	4	1	1	9	.296	28	66	4	.959
1986—Philadelphia	Nat.		SS	145	439	44	96	11	4	0	36	.219	229	406	22	.967
1987—Philadelphia	Nat.		SS-OF	114	293	37	68	9	6	0	12	.232	192	271	14	.971
1987—Maine	Int.		SS	24	72	6	24	7	0	0	3	.333	45	79	6	.954
1988—Philadelphia	Nat.		SS	148	379	39	71	11	4	0	27	.187	195	368	14	.976
1989—Philadelphia‡	Nat.		S-3-2-O	116	263	28	64	7	3	4	25	.243	111	205	6	.981
1990—Kansas City§	Amer.		2-S-O-3	74	103	11	16	4	0	0	10	.155	58	98	4	.975
National League Totals—7 Years				653	1646	172	351	42	20	5	120	.213	874	1563	71	.972
American League Totals—1 Year				74	103	11	16	4	0	0	10	.155	58	98	4	.975
Major League Totals—8 Years				727	1749	183	367	46	20	5	130	.210	932	1661	75	.972

Selected by Philadelphia Phillies' organization in 9th round of free-agent draft, June 3, 1980.
†On disabled list, July 27, 1980 through remainder of season.
‡Traded to Kansas City Royals for Pitcher Jose DeJesus, March 31, 1990.
§Granted free agency, November 5, 1990.

JAMES DOUGLAS JENNINGS
(Doug)

Born September 30, 1964, at Atlanta, Ga.
Height, 5.10. Weight, 170.
Throws and bats lefthanded.
Attended Brevard Community College, Cocoa, Fla.

Led Pacific Coast League in bases on balls received with 93 and being hit by pitch with 16 in 1989.
Led Texas League in bases on balls received with 94 and being hit by pitch with 13 in 1987.
Led California League in bases on balls received with 117 in 1986.
Led Pacific Coast League first basemen in errors with 12 in 1989.

Year	Club	League	Pos.	G.	AB.	R.	H.	2B.	3B.	HR.	RBI.	B.A.	PO.	A.	E.	F.A.
1984—Salem	N'west		OF	52	173	29	45	7	1	1	17	.260	82	5	9	.906
1985—Quad Cities	Midw.		OF	95	319	50	81	17	7	5	54	.254	187	12	11	.948
1986—Palm Springs	Calif.		OF	129	429	95	136	31	9	17	89	.317	205	10	6	.973
1987—Midland†	Texas		OF	126	464	106	157	33	1	●30	104	.338	145	6	6	.962
1988—Oakland‡	Amer.		OF-1B	71	101	9	21	6	0	1	15	.208	85	5	1	.989
1988—Tacoma	P. C.		OF-1B	16	49	12	16	1	0	0	9	.327	26	1	1	.964
1989—Tacoma	P. C.		1B-OF-P	137	497	★99	136	35	5	11	64	.274	842	34	14	.984
1989—Oakland	Amer.		OF	4	4	0	0	0	0	0	0	.000	2	0	0	1.000
1990—Tacoma	P. C.		OF-1B	60	208	32	72	19	1	6	30	.346	123	7	5	.963
1990—Oakland	Amer.		OF-1B	64	156	19	30	7	2	2	14	.192	90	1	1	.989
Major League Totals—3 Years				139	261	28	51	13	2	3	29	.195	177	6	2	.989

Selected by California Angels' organization in 2nd round of free-agent draft, January 17, 1984.
†Drafted by Oakland Athletics, December 7, 1987.
‡On disabled list, June 27 to July 31, 1988; included rehabilitation disability assignment to Tacoma, July 15 to July 31, 1988.

CHAMPIONSHIP SERIES RECORD

Year	Club	League	Pos.	G.	AB.	R.	H.	2B.	3B.	HR.	RBI.	B.A.	PO.	A.	E.	F.A.
1990—Oakland	Amer.		OF	1	1	0	0	0	0	0	0	.000	0	0	0	.000

WORLD SERIES RECORD

Year	Club	League	Pos.	G.	AB.	R.	H.	2B.	3B.	HR.	RBI.	B.A.	PO.	A.	E.	F.A.
1990—Oakland	Amer.		PH	1	1	0	1	0	0	0	0	1.000	0	0	0	.000

PITCHING RECORD

Year	Club	League	G.	IP.	W.	L.	Pct.	H.	R.	ER.	SO.	BB.	ERA.
1989—Tacoma	P. Coast		2	3	0	0	.000	4	1	1	1	0	3.00

CHRISTOPHER AUBRY JOHNSON
(Chris)

Born December 7, 1968, at Chattanooga, Tenn.
Height, 6.07. Weight, 200.
Throws and bats righthanded.

Year Club	League	G.	IP.	W.	L.	Pct.	H.	R.	ER.	SO.	BB.	ERA.
1987—Helena	Pioneer	12	60⅓	5	0	1.000	55	32	27	54	21	4.03
1988—Beloit	Midwest	26	130	8	10	.444	137	66	57	99	42	3.95
1989—Beloit	Midwest	25	138⅔	9	9	.500	118	63	49	118	50	3.18
1990—Stockton	California	23	142	13	6	.684	121	56	47	112	54	2.98

Selected by Milwaukee Brewers' organization in 2nd round of free-agent draft, June 2, 1987.

DAVID WAYNE JOHNSON
(Dave)

Born October 24, 1959, at Baltimore, Md.
Height, 5.11. Weight, 179.
Throws and bats righthanded.
Attended Community College of Baltimore, Baltimore, Md.

Pitched 3-0 no-hit victory against Portland, July 23, 1987.
Led American League in home runs allowed with 30 in 1990.
Led American Association pitchers in complete games with 9 and tied for games started with 29 in 1988.
Tied for Pacific Coast League lead in complete games with 9 in 1987.

Year Club	League	G.	IP.	W.	L.	Pct.	H.	R.	ER.	SO.	BB.	ERA.
1982—Greenwood	S. Atlantic	16	58⅓	4	4	.500	50	32	25	41	41	3.86
1983—Alexandria	Carolina	46	113⅔	7	5	.583	100	52	38	95	42	3.01
1984—Prince William	Carolina	13	88⅓	7	5	.583	60	22	13	48	35	1.32
1984—Nashua	Eastern	12	83⅔	1	8	.111	95	52	45	47	31	4.84
1985—Nashua	Eastern	34	153	6	9	.400	129	66	53	84	45	3.12
1986—Hawaii	P. Coast	22	150⅓	8	7	.533	150	68	53	71	35	★3.17
1987—Vancouver	P. Coast	23	153⅔	8	10	.444	133	74	60	76	68	3.51
1987—Pittsburgh	National	5	6⅓	0	0	.000	13	7	7	4	2	9.95
1988—Buffalo†‡	Am. Assoc.	29	192⅓	★15	12	.556	★213	93	75	90	55	3.51
1989—Rochester	Int'national	18	105	7	6	.538	104	45	38	60	31	3.26
1989—Baltimore	American	14	89⅓	4	7	.364	90	44	42	26	28	4.23
1990—Baltimore§	American	30	180	13	9	.591	196	83	82	68	43	4.10
National League Totals—1 Year		5	6⅓	0	0	.000	13	7	7	4	2	9.95
American League Totals—2 Years		44	269⅓	17	16	.515	286	127	124	94	71	4.14
Major League Totals—3 Years		49	275⅔	17	16	.515	299	134	131	98	73	4.28

Selected by Kansas City Royals' organization in 5th round of free-agent draft, January 13, 1981.
Signed as free agent by Pittsburgh Pirates' organization, June 10, 1982.
†Granted free agency, October 15, 1988; signed by Houston Astros, December 22, 1988.
‡Traded with Outfielder Victor Hithe by Houston Astros to Baltimore Orioles for Catcher Carl Nichols, March 31, 1989.
§On disabled list, August 15 to September 4, 1990.

HOWARD MICHAEL JOHNSON

Born November 29, 1960, at Clearwater, Fla.
Height, 5.10. Weight, 195.
Throws right and bats right and lefthanded.
Attended St. Petersburg Junior College, St. Petersburg, Fla.

Holds National League record for most home runs, switch-hitter, season (36), 1987, 1989.
Major League stolen bases: 1982 (7), 1984 (10), 1985 (6), 1986 (8), 1987 (32), 1988 (23), 1989 (41), 1990 (34). Total—161.
Tied for National League lead in game-winning RBIs with 16 in 1987.
Led Florida State League in sacrifice hits with 16 in 1980.
Led American Association third basemen in double plays with 19 in 1982.
Led Florida State League third basemen in double plays with 21 in 1980.
Named third baseman on THE SPORTING NEWS National League All-Star Team, 1989.
Named third baseman on THE SPORTING NEWS National League Silver Slugger team, 1989.

Year Club	League	Pos.	G.	AB.	R.	H.	2B.	3B.	HR.	RBI.	B.A.	PO.	A.	E.	F.A.
1979—Lakeland	Fla. St.	3B-SS-OF	132	456	49	107	9	6	3	49	.235	130	240	36	.911
1980—Lakeland	Fla. St.	3B	130	474	83	135	★28	1	10	69	.285	★110	★264	13	★.966
1981—Birmingham	South.	3B	138	488	84	130	28	7	22	83	.266	103	218	26	.925
1982—Evansville	A. A.	3B-OF	98	366	70	116	16	4	23	67	.317	69	139	23	.900
1982—Detroit	Amer.	3B-OF	54	155	23	49	5	0	4	14	.316	36	40	7	.916
1983—Detroit	Amer.	3B	27	66	11	14	0	0	3	5	.212	10	30	7	.851
1983—Evansville†	A. A.	3B	3	9	1	2	1	0	0	0	.222	1	11	2	.857
1984—Detroit‡	Amer.	3-S-1-O	116	355	43	88	14	1	12	50	.248	63	150	14	.938
1985—New York	Nat.	3B-SS-OF	126	389	38	94	18	4	11	46	.242	78	190	18	.937
1986—New York§	Nat.	3B-SS-OF	88	220	30	54	14	0	10	39	.245	52	136	20	.904
1987—New York	Nat.	3B-SS-OF	157	554	93	147	22	1	36	99	.265	118	305	26	.942
1988—New York	Nat.	3B-SS	148	495	85	114	21	1	24	68	.230	110	274	18	.955
1989—New York	Nat.	3B-SS	153	571	●104	164	41	3	36	101	.287	97	217	24	.929
1990—New York	Nat.	3B-SS	154	590	89	144	37	3	23	90	.244	150	335	28	.945
American League Totals—3 Years			197	576	77	151	19	1	19	69	.262	109	220	28	.922
National League Totals—6 Years			826	2819	439	717	153	12	140	443	.254	605	1457	134	.939
Major League Totals—9 Years			1023	3395	516	868	172	13	159	512	.256	714	1677	162	.937

Selected by New York Yankees' organization in 23rd round of free-agent draft, June 6, 1978.
Selected by Detroit Tigers' organization in secondary phase of free-agent draft, January 9, 1979.
†On disabled list, June 2 to August 8, 1983.
‡Traded to New York Mets for Pitcher Walt Terrell, December 7, 1984.
§On disabled list, June 2 to June 23, 1986.

CHAMPIONSHIP SERIES RECORD

Year Club	League	Pos.	G.	AB.	R.	H.	2B.	3B.	HR.	RBI.	B.A.	PO.	A.	E.	F.A.
1986—New York	Nat.	PH	2	2	0	0	0	0	0	0	.000	0	0	0	.000
1988—New York	Nat.	SS-3-PH	6	18	3	1	0	0	0	0	.056	6	9	1	.938
Championship Series Totals—2 Years			8	20	3	1	0	0	0	0	.050	6	9	1	.938

WORLD SERIES RECORD

Year Club	League	Pos.	G.	AB.	R.	H.	2B.	3B.	HR.	RBI.	B.A.	PO.	A.	E.	F.A.
1984—Detroit	Amer.	PH	1	1	0	0	0	0	0	0	.000	0	0	0	.000
1986—New York	Nat.	3B-PH-SS	2	5	0	0	0	0	0	0	.000	1	0	0	1.000
World Series Totals—2 Years			3	6	0	0	0	0	0	0	.000	1	0	0	1.000

ALL-STAR GAME RECORD

Year League	Pos.	AB.	R.	H.	2B.	3B.	HR.	RBI.	B.A.	PO.	A.	E.	F.A.
1989—National	3B	3	0	1	0	0	0	1	.333	0	0	0	.000

WILLIAM JEFFREY JOHNSON
(Jeff)

Born August 4, 1966, at Durham, N.C.
Height, 6.03. Weight, 200.
Throws left and bats righthanded.
Attended University of North Carolina, Charlotte, N.C.

Year Club	League	G.	IP.	W.	L.	Pct.	H.	R.	ER.	SO.	BB.	ERA.
1988—Oneonta	NYP	14	87⅔	6	1	.857	67	35	29	91	39	2.98
1989—Prince William	Carolina	25	138⅔	4	10	.286	125	59	45	99	55	2.92
1990—Fort Lauderdale	Florida St.	17	103⅔	6	8	.429	101	55	42	84	25	3.65
1990—Albany	Eastern	9	60⅔	4	3	.571	44	14	11	41	15	1.63

Selected by New York Yankees' organization in 6th round of free-agent draft, June 1, 1988.

KENNETH LANCE JOHNSON

(Known by middle name.)

Born July 7, 1963, at Lincoln Heights, O.
Height, 5.11. Weight, 155.
Throws and bats lefthanded.
Attended Triton College, River Grove, Ill.,
and University of South Alabama, Mobile, Ala.

Major League stolen bases: 1987 (6), 1988 (6), 1989 (16), 1990 (36). Total—64.
Led American League in caught stealing with 22 in 1990.
Led Pacific Coast League in caught stealing with 18 in 1989.
Led Texas League in stolen bases with 49 and caught stealing with 15 in 1986.
Led Pacific Coast League outfielders in total chances with 273 in 1989.
Led Pacific Coast League outfielders in double plays with 5 in 1988.
Led American Association outfielders in total chances with 333 in 1987.
Led New York-Pennsylvania League outfielders in total chances with 201 in 1984.
Named American Association Most Valuable Player, 1987.

Year Club	League	Pos.	G.	AB.	R.	H.	2B.	3B.	HR.	RBI.	B.A.	PO.	A.	E.	F.A.
1984—Erie	NYP	OF	71	283	*63	*96	7	5	1	28	.339	*188	5	8	.960
1985—St. Petersburg	Fla. St.	OF	129	497	68	134	17	10	2	55	.270	338	16	5	.986
1986—Arkansas	Texas	OF	127	445	82	128	24	6	2	33	.288	262	11	7	.975
1987—Louisville	A. A.	OF	116	477	89	159	21	11	5	50	.333	*319	6	●8	.976
1987—St. Louis†	Nat.	OF	33	59	4	13	2	1	0	7	.220	27	0	2	.931
1988—Chicago	Amer.	OF	33	124	11	23	4	1	0	6	.185	63	1	2	.970
1988—Vancouver	P. C.	OF	100	411	71	126	12	6	2	36	.307	262	9	5	.982
1989—Vancouver	P. C.	OF	106	408	69	124	11	7	0	28	.304	*261	7	5	.982
1989—Chicago	Amer.	OF	50	180	28	54	8	2	0	16	.300	113	0	2	.983
1990—Chicago	Amer.	OF	151	541	76	154	18	9	1	51	.285	353	5	10	.973
National League Totals—1 Year			33	59	4	13	2	1	0	7	.220	27	0	2	.931
American League Totals—3 Years			234	845	115	231	30	12	1	73	.273	529	6	14	.974
Major League Totals—4 Years			267	904	119	244	32	13	1	80	.270	556	6	16	.972

Selected by Pittsburgh Pirates' organization in 30th round of free-agent draft, June 8, 1981.
Selected by Seattle Mariners' organization in 31st round of free-agent draft, June 7, 1982.
Selected by St. Louis Cardinals' organization in 6th round of free-agent draft, June 4, 1984.
†Traded with Pitcher Rick Horton and cash to Chicago White Sox for Pitcher Jose DeLeon, February 9, 1988.

CHAMPIONSHIP SERIES RECORD

Year Club	League	Pos.	G.	AB.	R.	H.	2B.	3B.	HR.	RBI.	B.A.	PO.	A.	E.	F.A.
1987—St. Louis	Nat.	PR	1	0	1	0	0	0	0	0	.000	0	0	0	.000

WORLD SERIES RECORD

Year Club	League	Pos.	G.	AB.	R.	H.	2B.	3B.	HR.	RBI.	B.A.	PO.	A.	E.	F.A.
1987—St. Louis	Nat.	PR	1	0	0	0	0	0	0	0	.000	0	0	0	.000

RANDALL DAVID JOHNSON
(Randy)

Born September 10, 1963, at Walnut Creek, Calif.
Height, 6.10. Weight, 225.
Throws left and bats righthanded.
Attended University of Southern California, Los Angeles, Calif.

Pitched 2-0 no-hit victory against Detroit Tigers, June 2, 1990.
Led American Association in balks with 20 in 1988.
Tied for Florida State League lead in games started by pitchers with 26 in 1986.

Year Club	League	G.	IP.	W.	L.	Pct.	H.	R.	ER.	SO.	BB.	ERA.
1985—Jamestown	NYP	8	27⅓	0	3	.000	29	22	18	21	24	5.93
1986—West Palm Beach	Florida St.	26	119⅔	8	7	.533	89	49	42	133	*94	3.16
1987—Jacksonville	Southern	25	140	11	8	.579	100	63	58	*163	128	3.73
1988—Indianapolis	Am. Assoc.	20	113⅓	8	7	.533	85	52	41	111	72	3.26
1988—Montreal	National	4	26	3	0	1.000	23	8	7	25	7	2.42
1989—Montreal	National	7	29⅔	0	4	.000	29	25	22	26	26	6.67
1989—Indianapolis†	Am. Assoc.	3	18	1	1	.500	13	5	4	17	9	2.00
1989—Seattle	American	22	131	7	9	.438	118	75	64	104	70	4.40
1990—Seattle	American	33	219⅔	14	11	.560	174	103	89	194	*120	3.65
National League Totals—2 Years		11	55⅔	3	4	.429	52	33	29	51	33	4.69
American League Totals—2 Years		55	350⅔	21	20	.512	292	178	153	298	190	3.93
Major League Totals—3 Years		66	406⅓	24	24	.500	344	211	182	349	223	4.03

Selected by Atlanta Braves' organization in 3rd round of free-agent draft, June 7, 1982.
Selected by Montreal Expos' organization in 2nd round of free-agent draft, June 3, 1985.

†Traded with Pitchers Brian Holman and Gene Harris to Seattle Mariners for Pitcher Mark Langston and a player to be named later, May 25, 1989; Indianapolis (Montreal Expos' organization) acquired Pitcher Mike Campbell to complete deal, July 31, 1989.

ALL-STAR GAME RECORD

Member of American League All-Star Team in 1990; did not play.

WALLACE DARNELL JOHNSON
(Wally)

Born December 25, 1956, at Gary, Ind.
Height, 5.11. Weight, 185.
Throws right and bats right and lefthanded.
Received degree in accounting from Indiana State University, Terre Haute, Ind., in 1979.

Major League stolen bases: 1981 (1), 1982 (4), 1983 (1), 1986 (6), 1987 (5), 1989 (1), 1990 (1). Total—19.
Led Florida State League in stolen bases with 58 and caught stealing with 22 in 1980.
Named Florida State League Southern Division Most Valuable Player, 1980.

Year Club	League	Pos.	G.	AB.	R.	H.	2B.	3B.	HR.	RBI.	B.A.	PO.	A.	E.	F.A.
1979—Jamestown	NYP	2B	70	*284	60	96	11	6	6	42	.338	157	155	17	.948
1980—W. Palm Beach	Fla. St.	2B-OF	126	488	86	*163	17	5	3	49	*.334	294	350	31	.954
1980—Memphis	South.	2B	4	13	1	1	1	0	0	0	.077	5	12	0	1.000
1981—Memphis†	South.	2B-OF	28	102	15	37	9	0	1	18	.363	44	52	10	.906
1981—Denver	A. A.	2B-OF	59	215	39	64	13	4	0	16	.298	72	116	7	.964
1981—Montreal	Nat.	PH	11	9	1	2	0	1	0	3	.222	1	2	0	1.000
1982—Montreal	Nat.	2B	36	57	5	11	0	2	0	2	.193	22	18	2	.952
1982—Wichita	A. A.	2B-OF	76	298	62	105	12	4	6	36	.352	128	79	12	.945
1983—Wichita	A. A.	OF	16	53	7	14	3	1	0	6	.264	26	0	2	.929
1983—Mont.‡-S. F.	Nat.	2B	10	10	1	2	0	0	0	1	.200	3	2	0	1.000
1983—Phoenix§	P. C.	2B	63	229	42	66	8	2	2	26	.288	105	150	15	.944
1984—Jacksonville	South.	DH	31	117	18	35	5	0	1	12	.299	0	0	0	.000
1984—Indianapolis	A. A.	OF-1B-2B	97	357	50	101	12	2	3	38	.283	350	39	5	.987
1984—Montreal	Nat.	1B	17	24	3	5	0	0	0	4	.208	27	3	1	.968
1985—Indianapolis x	A. A.	OF-1B-2B	127	431	68	133	13	3	3	36	.309	240	14	5	.981
1986—Indianapolis	A. A.	1B-OF	61	225	27	58	15	4	0	26	.258	188	14	3	.985
1986—Montreal	Nat.	1B	61	127	13	36	3	1	1	10	.283	204	17	2	.991
1987—Montreal	Nat.	1B	75	85	7	21	5	0	1	14	.247	68	2	2	.972
1988—Montreal	Nat.	1B-2B	86	94	7	29	5	1	0	3	.309	80	9	1	.989
1989—Montreal	Nat.	1B	85	114	9	31	3	1	2	17	.272	130	7	4	.972
1990—Montreal y	Nat.	1B	47	49	6	8	1	0	1	5	.163	39	0	0	1.000
1990—Indianapolis z	A. A.	1B	11	40	6	12	1	0	1	11	.300	65	7	1	.986
1990—Tacoma a	P. C.	1B-OF	6	18	5	6	1	1	0	2	.333	21	0	0	1.000
Major League Totals—9 Years			428	569	52	145	17	6	5	59	.255	574	60	12	.981

Selected by Montreal Expos' organization in 6th round of free-agent draft, June 5, 1979.
†On disabled list, April 29 to May 15, 1981.
‡Traded to San Francisco Giants for Outfielder Mike Vail, May 25, 1983.
§Released, March 27, 1984; signed by Jacksonville (Montreal Expos' organization), April 1, 1984.
xGranted free agency, October 15, 1985; re-signed by Expos, January 22, 1986.
yOn disabled list, July 10 to July 25, 1990; included rehabilitation disability assignment to Indianapolis, July 16 to July 25, 1990.
zReleased, August 11, 1990; signed by Tacoma (Oakland Athletics' organization), August 28, 1990.
aGranted free agency, October 15, 1990.

DIVISION SERIES RECORD

Year Club	League	Pos.	G.	AB.	R.	H.	2B.	3B.	HR.	RBI.	B.A.	PO.	A.	E.	F.A.
1981—Montreal	Nat.	PH	2	2	0	1	0	0	0	1	.500	0	0	0	.000

BARRY LOUIS JONES

Born February 15, 1963, at Centerville, Ind.
Height, 6.04. Weight, 225.
Throws and bats righthanded.
Attended Indiana University, Bloomington, Ind.

Major League saves: 1986 (3), 1987 (1), 1988 (3), 1989 (1), 1990 (1). Total—9.

Year Club	League	G.	IP.	W.	L.	Pct.	H.	R.	ER.	SO.	BB.	ERA.
1984—Watertown	NYP	14	86⅔	6	3	.667	75	41	33	61	49	3.43
1985—Prince William	Carolina	28	37⅓	3	2	.600	26	7	5	42	19	1.21
1985—Nashua	Eastern	23	29	3	2	.600	19	6	5	24	10	1.55
1985—Hawaii	P. Coast	1	3	0	0	.000	5	5	3	2	1	9.00
1986—Hawaii	P. Coast	35	48	3	6	.333	41	20	19	28	20	3.56
1986—Pittsburgh	National	26	37⅓	3	4	.429	29	16	12	29	21	2.89
1987—Pittsburgh	National	32	43⅓	2	4	.333	55	34	27	28	23	5.61
1987—Vancouver	P. Coast	20	25⅓	1	2	.333	21	9	9	27	14	3.20
1988—Pittsburgh†	National	42	56⅓	1	1	.500	57	21	19	31	21	3.04
1988—Chicago	American	17	26	2	2	.500	15	7	7	17	17	2.42
1989—Chicago‡	American	22	30⅓	3	2	.600	22	12	8	17	8	2.37
1989—Sarasota White Sox	Gulf Coast	7	18⅓	0	1	.000	12	7	3	14	5	1.47
1990—Chicago§	American	65	74	11	4	.733	62	20	19	45	33	2.31
National League Totals—3 Years		100	137	6	9	.400	141	71	58	88	65	3.81
American League Totals—3 Years		104	130⅓	16	8	.667	99	39	34	79	58	2.35
Major League Totals—5 Years		204	267⅓	22	17	.564	240	109	92	167	123	3.10

Selected by Texas Rangers' organization in 6th round of free-agent draft, June 8, 1981.
Selected by Pittsburgh Pirates' organization in 3rd round of free-agent draft, June 4, 1984.
†Traded to Chicago White Sox for Pitcher Dave LaPoint, August 13, 1988.
‡On disabled list, May 4 to August 24, 1989; included rehabilitation disability assignment to Sarasota, June 29 to July 18, 1989.
§Traded with Outfielder Ivan Calderon to Montreal Expos for Outfielder Tim Raines, Pitcher Jeff Carter and a player to be named later, December 23, 1990.

DOUGLAS REID JONES
(Doug)

Born June 24, 1957, at Covina, Calif.
Height, 6.02. Weight, 195.
Throws and bats righthanded.
Attended Central Arizona College, Coolidge, Ariz., and Butler University, Indianapolis, Ind.

Major League saves: 1986 (1), 1987 (8), 1988 (37), 1989 (32), 1990 (43). Total—121.
Led Midwest League in complete games with 16 and tied for lead in shutouts with 3 in 1979.
Tied for Eastern League lead in intentional bases on balls issued with 8 in 1985.

Year Club	League	G.	IP.	W.	L.	Pct.	H.	R.	ER.	SO.	BB.	ERA.
1978—Newark†	NYP	15	38	2	4	.333	49	30	22	27	15	5.21
1979—Burlington	Midwest	28	★190	10	10	.500	144	63	37	115	73	★1.75
1980—Stockton	California	11	76	6	2	.750	63	32	24	54	31	2.84
1980—Vancouver	P. Coast	8	53	3	2	.600	52	19	19	28	15	3.23
1980—Holyoke	Eastern	8	62	5	3	.625	57	23	20	39	26	2.90
1981—El Paso	Texas	15	90	5	7	.417	121	67	58	62	28	5.80
1981—Vancouver	P. Coast	11	80	5	3	.625	79	29	27	38	22	3.04
1982—Milwaukee	American	4	2⅔	0	0	.000	5	3	3	1	1	10.13
1982—Vancouver	P. Coast	23	106	5	8	.385	109	48	35	60	31	2.97
1983—Vancouver‡	P. Coast	3	7	0	1	.000	10	8	8	4	5	10.29
1984—Vancouver§	P. Coast	3	8	1	0	1.000	9	9	9	2	3	10.13
1984—El Paso x	Texas	16	109⅓	6	8	.429	120	61	52	62	35	4.28
1985—Waterbury	Eastern	39	116	9	4	.692	123	59	47	113	36	3.65
1986—Maine	Int'national	43	116⅓	6	5	.455	105	35	27	98	27	★2.09
1986—Cleveland	American	11	18	1	0	1.000	18	5	5	12	6	2.50
1987—Cleveland	American	49	91⅓	6	5	.545	101	45	32	87	24	3.15
1987—Buffalo	Am. Assoc.	23	61⅔	5	2	.714	49	18	14	61	12	2.04
1988—Cleveland	American	51	83⅓	3	4	.429	69	26	21	72	16	2.27
1989—Cleveland	American	59	80⅔	7	10	.412	76	25	21	65	13	2.34
1990—Cleveland	American	66	84⅓	5	5	.500	66	26	24	55	22	2.56
Major League Totals—6 Years		240	360⅓	22	24	.478	335	130	106	292	82	2.65

Selected by Milwaukee Brewers' organization in 3rd round of free-agent draft, January 10, 1978.
†On disabled list, June 20 to July 12, 1978.
‡On disabled list, April 11 to September 1, 1983.
§On disabled list, April 25 to May 30, 1984.
xGranted free agency, October 15, 1984; signed by Waterbury (Cleveland Indians' organization), April 3, 1985.

ALL-STAR GAME RECORD

Year League	IP.	W.	L.	Pct.	H.	R.	ER.	SO.	BB.	ERA.
1988—American	⅔	0	0	.000	0	0	0	1	0	0.00
1989—American	1⅓	0	0	.000	1	0	0	0	0	0.00
All-Star Game Totals—2 Years	2	0	0	.000	1	0	0	1	0	0.00

Member of American League All-Star Team in 1990; did not play.

JAMES CONDIA JONES
(Jimmy)

Born April 20, 1964, at Dallas, Tex.
Height, 6.02. Weight, 190.
Throws and bats righthanded.

Shares modern major league record for fewest hits allowed, first major league game, nine innings (1), September 21, 1986.
Tied for Pacific Coast League lead in games started by pitchers with 27 in 1986.

Year Club	League	G.	IP.	W.	L.	Pct.	H.	R.	ER.	SO.	BB.	ERA.
1982—Walla Walla	Northwest	14	78⅓	4	6	.400	64	49	28	78	71	3.22
1983—Reno	California	17	116⅔	7	5	.583	96	50	35	79	49	2.70
1984—Beaumont†	Texas	13	85⅔	7	2	.778	63	28	20	49	39	2.10
1985—Beaumont‡	Texas	16	85	7	5	.583	84	51	44	57	66	4.66
1986—Las Vegas	P. Coast	28	157⅔	9	10	.474	168	84	77	114	72	4.40
1986—San Diego	National	3	18	2	0	1.000	10	6	5	15	3	2.50
1987—Las Vegas	P. Coast	4	24⅓	2	0	1.000	24	16	16	11	8	5.92
1987—San Diego	National	30	145⅔	9	7	.563	154	85	67	51	54	4.14
1988—San Diego§	National	29	179	9	14	.391	192	98	82	82	44	4.12
1989—Columbus	Int'national	20	124	8	6	.571	110	54	52	94	31	3.77
1989—New York	American	11	48	2	1	.667	56	29	28	25	16	5.25
1990—Columbus	Int'national	11	73	5	2	.714	46	20	19	78	35	2.34
1990—New York x	American	17	50	1	2	.333	72	42	35	25	23	6.30
National League Totals—3 Years		62	342⅔	20	21	.488	356	189	154	148	101	4.04
American League Totals—2 Years		28	98	3	3	.500	128	71	63	50	39	5.79
Major League Totals—5 Years		90	440⅔	23	24	.489	484	260	217	198	140	4.43

Selected by San Diego Padres' organization in 1st round (third player selected) of free-agent draft, June 7, 1982.
†On disabled list, July 13, 1984 through remainder of season.
‡On disabled list, June 29 to July 11 and July 28, 1985 through remainder of season.
§Traded with Pitcher Lance McCullers and Outfielder Stan Jefferson to New York Yankees for First Baseman Outfielder Jack Clark and Pitcher Pat Clements, October 24, 1988.
xGranted free agency, October 4, 1990.

RONALD GLEN JONES
(Ron)

Born June 11, 1964, at Seguin, Tex.
Height, 5.10. Weight, 214.
Throws right and bats lefthanded.
Attended Wharton County Junior College, Wharton, Tex.
Nephew of Alvin Jones, outfielder in Atlanta Braves'
organization, 1973 through 1976.

Major League stolen bases: 1989 (1).
Led Florida State League in total bases with 216 and slugging percentage with .524 in 1986.
Led Northwest League in game-winning RBIs with 10 in 1985.
Tied for International League lead in game-winning RBIs with 11 and sacrifice flies with 8 in 1988.
Tied for International League lead in double plays by outfielders with 4 in 1988.
Named Florida State League Most Valuable Player, 1986.

Year Club	League	Pos.	G.	AB.	R.	H.	2B.	3B.	HR.	RBI.	B.A.	PO.	A.	E.	F.A.
1985—Bend	N'west	OF	73	286	54	90	13	1	10	60	.315	88	4	★11	.893
1986—Clearwater	Fla. St.	OF	108	412	76	●153	18	★12	7	73	★.371	196	9	2	.990
1986—Portland†	P. C.	OF	11	34	4	4	1	0	0	2	.118	11	2	0	1.000
1987—Maine	Int.	OF	90	316	33	78	13	4	7	32	.247	178	4	3	.984
1988—Maine	Int.	OF	125	445	64	119	15	3	16	★75	.267	191	14	7	.967
1988—Philadelphia	Nat.	OF	33	124	15	36	6	1	8	26	.290	70	1	0	1.000
1989—Philadelphia‡	Nat.	OF	12	31	7	9	0	0	2	4	.290	27	1	0	1.000
1990—Scranton/W.-B.	Int.	OF	44	148	13	39	4	1	3	26	.264	46	1	1	.979
1990—Philadelphia§	Nat.	OF	24	58	5	16	2	0	3	7	.276	25	1	0	1.000
Major League Totals—3 Years			69	213	27	61	8	1	13	37	.286	122	3	0	1.000

Selected by Toronto Blue Jays' organization in 14th round of free-agent draft, June 7, 1982.
Selected by Montreal Expos' organization in secondary phase of free-agent draft, January 11, 1983.
Signed as free agent by Philadelphia Phillies' organization, October 20, 1984.
†On disabled list, August 8, 1986 through remainder of season.
‡On disabled list, April 19, 1989 through remainder of season.
§On disabled list, July 1, 1990 through remainder of season.

TRACY DONALD JONES

Born March 31, 1961, at Inglewood, Calif.
Height, 6.03. Weight, 220.
Throws and bats righthanded.
Attended Loyola Marymount University, Los Angeles, Calif.
Brother of Terry Jones, infielder in California Angels' and Kansas City Royals'
organizations, 1984 through 1988.

Major League stolen bases: 1986 (7), 1987 (31), 1988 (18), 1989 (3), 1990 (1). Total—60.

Year	Club	League	Pos.	G.	AB.	R.	H.	2B.	3B.	HR.	RBI.	B.A.	PO.	A.	E.	F.A.
1983—Tampa	Fla. St.	O-3-1-S	53	118	27	32	5	3	1	15	.271	54	12	11	.857
1983—Eugene	N'west	2B-3B-OF	55	203	42	54	12	0	1	26	.266	81	68	12	.925
1984—Tampa†	Fla. St.	OF	86	307	50	95	14	3	4	41	.309	150	6	0	1.000
1985—Vermont	East.	OF	75	284	40	90	12	3	4	31	.317	117	4	1	.992
1985—Denver	A. A.	OF	51	205	43	69	12	0	10	31	.337	93	2	0	1.000
1986—Cincinnati‡	Nat.	OF-1B	46	86	16	30	3	0	2	10	.349	46	1	0	1.000
1987—Cincinnati	Nat.	OF	117	359	53	104	17	3	10	44	.290	189	2	2	.990
1988—Cinc.§x-Mon.	Nat.	OF	90	224	29	66	6	1	3	24	.295	96	2	2	.980
1988—Nashville y	A. A.	OF	2	6	2	3	1	0	0	1	.500	2	1	0	1.000
1989—San Francisco z	Nat.	OF	40	97	5	18	4	0	0	12	.186	35	0	0	1.000
1989—Detroit a	Amer.	OF	46	158	17	41	10	0	3	26	.259	72	0	1	.986
1990—Det. b-Sea. c	Amer.	OF	75	204	23	53	8	1	6	24	.260	68	3	2	.973
National League Totals—4 Years			293	766	103	218	30	4	15	90	.285	366	5	4	.989
American League Totals—2 Years			121	362	40	94	18	1	9	50	.260	140	3	3	.979
Major League Totals—5 Years			414	1128	143	312	48	5	24	140	.277	506	8	7	.987

Selected by New York Mets' organization in 4th round of free-agent draft, June 7, 1982.
Selected by Cincinnati Reds' organization in secondary phase of free-agent draft, January 11, 1983.
†On disabled list, July 18 to September 18, 1984.
‡On disabled list, May 23 to June 15 and July 10 to September 1, 1986.
§On disabled list, May 5 to May 22 and May 26 to June 20, 1988; included rehabilitation disability assignment to Nashville, June 18 and June 19, 1988.
xTraded with Pitcher Pat Pacillo to Montreal Expos for Catcher Jeff Reed, Outfielder Herm Winningham and Pitcher Randy St. Claire, July 13, 1988.
yTraded to San Francisco Giants for Outfielder Mike Aldrete, December 8, 1988.
zTraded to Detroit Tigers for Outfielder Pat Sheridan, June 18, 1989.
aOn disabled list, August 17, 1989 through remainder of season.
bTraded to Seattle Mariners for Outfielder Darnell Coles, June 18, 1990.
cOn disabled list, August 9, 1990 through remainder of season.

WILLIAM TIMOTHY JONES
(Tim)

Born December 1, 1962, at Sumter, S. C.
Height, 5.10. Weight, 172.
Throws right and bats lefthanded.
Received degree in health service from The Citadel,
Charleston, S.C., in 1985.

Major League stolen bases: 1988 (4), 1989 (1), 1990 (3). Total—8.
Tied for Appalachian League lead in sacrifice flies with 5 in 1985.
Led Appalachian League shortstops in putouts with 105 and double plays with 30 in 1985.

Year	Club	League	Pos.	G.	AB.	R.	H.	2B.	3B.	HR.	RBI.	B.A.	PO.	A.	E.	F.A.
1985—Johnson City	Appal.	SS-3B	68	★235	33	75	10	1	3	48	.319	109	148	23	.918
1986—St. Petersburg	Fla. St.	SS	39	142	19	43	3	2	0	27	.254	67	125	8	.960
1986—Arkansas	Texas	SS	96	284	36	76	15	1	2	27	.268	142	277	24	.946
1987—Arkansas	Texas	SS-2B	61	176	23	58	12	0	3	26	.330	80	151	9	.963
1987—Louisville	A. A.	SS	73	276	48	78	14	3	4	43	.283	112	221	13	.962
1988—Louisville	A. A.	SS	103	370	63	95	21	2	6	38	.257	145	302	15	★.968
1988—St. Louis	Nat.	SS-2B-3B	31	52	2	14	0	0	0	3	.269	26	40	1	.985
1989—St. Louis	Nat.	2-S-3-O-C	42	75	11	22	6	0	0	7	.293	33	48	2	.976
1990—St. Louis	Nat.	S-2-3-P	67	128	9	28	7	1	1	12	.219	43	105	7	.955
Major League Totals—3 Years			140	255	22	64	13	1	1	22	.251	102	193	10	.967

Selected by St. Louis Cardinals' organization in 2nd round of free-agent draft, June 3, 1985.

PITCHING RECORD

Year	Club	League	G.	IP.	W.	L.	Pct.	H.	R.	ER.	SO.	BB.	ERA.
1990—St. Louis	National	1	1⅓	0	0	.000	1	2	1	0	2	6.75

PAUL SCOTT JORDAN
(Ricky)

Born May 26, 1965, at Richmond, Calif.
Height, 6.03. Weight, 210.
Throws and bats righthanded.

Shares major league record by hitting home run in first at-bat, July 17, 1988.
Major League stolen bases: 1988 (1), 1990 (2). Total—7.
Tied for Eastern League lead in sacrifice flies with 9 in 1987.
Led Eastern League first basemen in total chances with 1,255 and double plays with 110 in 1987.
Led Eastern League first basemen in double plays with 100 in 1986.

Year	Club	League	Pos.	G.	AB.	R.	H.	2B.	3B.	HR.	RBI.	B.A.	PO.	A.	E.	F.A.
1983—Helena	Pion.	1B	60	247	32	73	7	1	5	33	.296	486	35	7	.986
1984—Spartanburg	S. Atl.	1B	128	490	72	143	23	4	10	76	.292	1129	69	14	.988
1985—Clearwater	Fla. St.	1B	★139	528	60	146	22	8	7	62	.277	1252	86	★20	.985
1986—Reading	East.	★1B-OF	133	478	44	131	19	3	2	60	.274	1052	87	★17	.985
1987—Reading	East.	1B	132	475	78	151	28	3	16	95	.318	★1193	54	8	.994
1988—Maine	Int.	1B	87	338	42	104	23	1	7	36	.308	809	41	4	.995
1988—Philadelphia	Nat.	1B	69	273	41	84	15	1	11	43	.308	579	35	5	.992
1989—Philadelphia	Nat.	1B	144	523	63	149	22	3	12	75	.285	1271	61	9	.993
1990—Philadelphia†	Nat.	1B	92	324	32	78	21	0	5	44	.241	743	37	4	.995

Year	Club	League	Pos.	G.	AB.	R.	H.	2B.	3B.	HR.	RBI.	B.A.	PO.	A.	E.	F.A.
1990—Scranton/W.-B......	Int.	1B	27	104	8	29	1	0	2	11	.279	225	8	1	.996
Major League Totals—3 Years			305	1120	136	311	58	4	28	162	.278	2593	133	18	.993

Selected by Philadelphia Phillies' organization in 1st round (22nd player selected) of free-agent draft, June 6, 1983.

†On disabled list, June 13 to July 4, 1990; included rehabilitation disability assignment to Scranton/Wilkes-Barre, June 29 to July 4, 1990.

TERRY ALLEN JORGENSEN

Born September 2, 1966, at Kewaunee, Wis.
Height, 6.04. Weight, 210.
Throws and bats righthanded.
Attended University of Wisconsin, Oshkosh, Wis.

Tied for Southern League lead in sacrifice flies with 9 in 1989.
Led Pacific Coast League third basemen in putouts with 102 and errors with 34 in 1990.
Led Southern League third basemen in total chances with 406 and tied for lead in double plays with 21 in 1989.

Year	Club	League	Pos.	G.	AB.	R.	H.	2B.	3B.	HR.	RBI.	B.A.	PO.	A.	E.	F.A.
1987—Kenosha	Midw.	OF	67	254	37	80	17	0	7	33	.315	54	4	5	.921
1988—Orlando	South.	3B	135	472	53	116	27	4	3	43	.246	101	216	*39	.890
1989—Orlando	South.	3B	135	514	84	135	27	5	13	101	.263	*99	*274	33	.919
1989—Minnesota	Amer.	3B	10	23	1	4	1	0	0	2	.174	4	19	1	.958
1990—Portland	P. C.	3B-SS-2B	123	440	43	114	28	3	10	50	.259	104	206	35	.899
Major League Totals—1 Year			10	23	1	4	1	0	0	2	.174	4	19	1	.958

Selected by Minnesota Twins' organization in 2nd round of free-agent draft, June 2, 1987.

DOMINGO FELIX JOSE

(Known by middle name.)
Born May 8, 1965, at Santo Domingo, D. R.
Height, 6.01. Weight, 190.
Throws right and bats left and righthanded.

Major League stolen bases: 1988 (1), 1990 (12). Total—13.

Year	Club	League	Pos.	G.	AB.	R.	H.	2B.	3B.	HR.	RBI.	B.A.	PO.	A.	E.	F.A.
1984—Idaho Falls	Pion.	OF	45	152	16	33	6	0	1	18	.217	48	6	1	.982
1985—Madison	Midw.	OF	117	409	46	89	13	3	3	33	.218	187	9	12	.942
1986—Modesto	Calif.	OF	127	516	77	147	22	8	14	77	.285	215	12	14	.942
1987—Huntsville	South.	OF	91	296	29	67	11	1	5	42	.226	131	7	8	.945
1988—Tacoma	P. C.	OF	134	508	72	161	29	5	12	83	.317	253	11	8	.971
1988—Oakland	Amer.	OF	8	6	2	2	1	0	0	1	.333	8	0	0	1.000
1989—Tacoma	P. C.	OF	104	387	59	111	26	0	14	63	.287	186	7	*10	.951
1989—Oakland	Amer.	OF	20	57	3	11	2	0	0	5	.193	35	2	1	.974
1990—Oakland†	Amer.	OF	101	341	42	90	12	0	8	39	.264	212	5	5	.977
1990—St. Louis	Nat.	OF	25	85	12	23	4	1	3	13	.271	42	0	0	1.000
American League Totals—3 Years			129	404	47	103	15	0	8	45	.255	255	7	6	.978
National League Totals—1 Year			25	85	12	23	4	1	3	13	.271	42	0	0	1.000
Major League Totals—3 Years			154	489	59	126	19	1	11	58	.258	297	7	6	.981

Signed as free agent by Oakland A's organization, January 3, 1984.

†Traded with Third Baseman Stan Royer and Pitcher Daryl Green to St. Louis Cardinals for Outfielder Willie McGee, August 29, 1990.

WALLACE KEITH JOYNER
(Wally)

Born June 16, 1962, at Atlanta, Ga.
Height, 6.02. Weight, 203.
Throws and bats lefthanded.
Attended Brigham Young University, Provo, Utah.

Shares major league record for most home runs, month of October (4), 1987.
Major League stolen bases: 1986 (5), 1987 (8), 1988 (8), 1989 (3), 1990 (2). Total—26.
Hit three home runs in a game, October 3, 1987.
Led American League in sacrifice flies with 12 in 1986.
Led American League first basemen in total chances with 1,520 and double plays with 148 in 1988.
Tied for Eastern League lead in intentional bases on balls received with 8 in 1984.
Led Pacific Coast League first basemen in total chances with 1,229 and double plays with 121 in 1985.

Year	Club	League	Pos.	G.	AB.	R.	H.	2B.	3B.	HR.	RBI.	B.A.	PO.	A.	E.	F.A.
1983—Peoria	Midw.	1B	54	192	25	63	16	2	3	33	.328	480	45	6	.989
1984—Waterbury	East.	1B-OF	134	467	81	148	24	7	12	72	.317	906	86	9	.991
1985—Edmonton	P. C.	1B	126	477	68	135	29	5	12	73	.283	*1107	*107	●15	.988
1986—California	Amer.	1B	154	593	82	172	27	3	22	100	.290	1222	139	15	.989
1987—California	Amer.	1B	149	564	100	161	33	1	34	117	.285	1276	92	10	.993
1988—California	Amer.	1B	158	597	81	176	31	2	13	85	.295	*1369	*143	8	.995
1989—California	Amer.	1B	159	593	78	167	30	2	16	79	.282	*1487	99	4	*.997
1990—California†	Amer.	1B	83	310	35	83	15	0	8	41	.268	727	62	4	.995
Major League Totals—5 Years			703	2657	376	759	136	8	93	422	.286	6061	535	41	.994

Selected by California Angels' organization in 3rd round of free-agent draft, June 6, 1983.

†On disabled list, July 12, 1990 through remainder of season.

DAVID CHRISTOPHER JUSTICE
(Dave)

Born April 14, 1966, at Cincinnati, O.
Height, 6.03. Weight, 200.
Throws and bats lefthanded.
Attended Thomas More College, Crestview Hills, Ky.

Major League stolen bases: 1989 (2), 1990 (11). Total—13.
Tied for Appalachian League lead in sacrifice flies with 5 in 1985.
Named National League Rookie Player of the Year by THE SPORTING NEWS, 1990.
Named National League Rookie of the Year by Baseball Writers' Association of America, 1990.

Year Club	League	Pos.	G.	AB.	R.	H.	2B.	3B.	HR.	RBI.	B.A.	PO.	A.	E.	F.A.
1985—Pulaski	Appal.	OF	66	204	39	50	8	0	●10	46	.245	86	2	4	.957
1986—Sumter	S. Atl.	OF	61	220	48	66	16	0	10	61	.300	124	7	4	.970
1986—Durham	Carol.	OF-1B	67	229	47	64	9	1	12	44	.279	163	5	1	.994
1987—Greenville	South.	OF	93	348	38	79	12	4	6	40	.227	199	4	8	.962
1988—Richmond	Int.	OF	70	227	27	46	9	1	8	28	.203	136	5	4	.972
1988—Greenville	South.	OF	58	198	34	55	13	1	9	37	.278	100	3	5	.954
1989—Richmond	Int.	OF-1B	115	391	47	102	24	3	12	58	.261	220	15	6	.975
1989—Atlanta	Nat.	OF	16	51	7	12	3	0	1	3	.235	24	0	0	1.000
1990—Richmond	Int.	OF-1B	12	45	7	16	5	1	2	7	.356	23	4	2	.931
1990—Atlanta	Nat.	1B-OF	127	439	76	124	23	2	28	78	.282	604	42	14	.979
Major League Totals—2 Years			143	490	83	136	26	2	29	81	.278	628	42	14	.980

Selected by Atlanta Braves' organization in 4th round of free-agent draft, June 3, 1985.

JEFFREY PATRICK KAISER
(Jeff)

Born July 24, 1960, at Wyandotte, Mich.
Height, 6.03. Weight, 195.
Throws left and bats righthanded.
Received bachelor of arts degree in business administration from
Western Michigan University, Kalamazoo, Mich.

Year Club	League	G.	IP.	W.	L.	Pct.	H.	R.	ER.	SO.	BB.	ERA.
1982—Medford	Northwest	15	78	8	1	*.889	91	56	46	69	57	5.31
1983—Modesto	California	25	164⅔	12	9	.571	160	84	70	102	80	3.83
1984—Albany	Eastern	7	47⅔	5	1	.833	36	11	10	20	15	1.89
1984—Tacoma†	P. Coast	14	74⅔	4	7	.364	81	52	38	38	28	4.58
1985—Oakland	American	15	16⅔	0	0	.000	25	32	27	10	20	14.58
1985—Tacoma‡	P. Coast	27	46⅓	4	2	.667	33	10	9	36	18	1.75
1986—Tacoma§x	P. Coast	34	110⅔	4	4	.500	123	70	53	63	52	4.31
1987—Buffalo	Am. Assoc.	22	71⅓	5	3	.625	87	52	41	53	32	5.17
1987—Cleveland y	American	2	3⅓	0	0	.000	4	6	6	2	3	16.20
1988—Colorado Springs	P. Coast	36	53	3	2	.600	56	23	22	47	19	3.74
1988—Cleveland	American	3	2⅔	0	0	.000	2	0	0	0	1	0.00
1989—Colorado Springs	P. Coast	31	45⅓	3	6	.333	64	29	22	46	18	4.37
1989—Cleveland z	American	6	3⅔	0	1	.000	5	5	3	4	5	7.36
1990—Colorado Springs	P. Coast	25	43	2	2	.500	36	16	14	46	22	2.93
1990—Cleveland a	American	5	12⅔	0	0	.000	16	5	5	9	7	3.55
Major League Totals—5 Years		31	39	0	1	.000	52	48	41	25	36	9.46

Selected by Toronto Blue Jays' organization in 7th round of free-agent draft, June 8, 1981.
Selected by Oakland A's organization in 10th round of free-agent draft, June 7, 1982.
†On disabled list, July 20 to August 3, 1984.
‡On disabled list, June 21 to July 7, 1985.
§On disabled list, May 4 to May 14, 1986.
xTraded to Cleveland Indians for Pitcher Curt Wardle, February 23, 1987.
yOn disabled list, August 9 to August 31, 1987.
zGranted free agency, April 5, 1990; re-signed by Indians' organization, April 11, 1990.
aOn disabled list, July 8 to September 4, 1990; included rehabilitation disability assignment to Colorado Springs, August 8 to September 4, 1990.

KEITH WADE KAISER

Born May 24, 1967, at San Antonio, Tex.
Height, 6.04. Weight, 205.
Throws right and bats left and righthanded.
Attended New Mexico State University, Las Cruces, N.M.

Led Southern League in hit batsmen with 12 and tied for lead in home runs allowed with 21 in 1990.
Led South Atlantic League in wild pitches with 17 in 1988.

Year Club	League	G.	IP.	W.	L.	Pct.	H.	R.	ER.	SO.	BB.	ERA.
1986—Sarasota Reds	Gulf Coast	11	28⅓	0	4	.000	28	22	10	14	25	3.18
1987—Billings	Pioneer	13	76	6	5	.545	67	37	26	71	39	3.08
1988—Greensboro	S. Atlantic	28	186	11	9	.550	135	67	52	159	*101	2.52
1989—Chattanooga	Southern	28	158	5	13	.278	169	*110	*97	105	86	5.53
1990—Chattanooga†	Southern	33	171	9	11	.450	166	*122	*109	123	*109	5.74

Selected by Cincinnati Reds' organization in 21st round of free-agent draft, June 3, 1985.
Signed as free agent by Cincinnati Reds' organization, July 7, 1986.
†Traded with Catcher Terry McGriff and Pitcher Butch Henry, September 7, 1990, completing deal in which Houston Astros traded Second Baseman Bill Doran to Cincinnati Reds for three players to be named later, August 30, 1990.

RONALD JOSEPH KARKOVICE
Name pronounced CAR-koh-vice.
(Ron)
Born August 8, 1963, at Union, N. J.
Height, 6.01. Weight, 215.
Throws and bats righthanded.

Major League stolen bases: 1986 (1), 1987 (3), 1988 (4), 1990 (2). Total—10.
Led Gulf Coast League batters in strikeouts with 73 in 1982.
Led Eastern League catchers in double plays with 13 in 1985.
Led Midwest League catchers in fielding percentage with .996 in 1983.
Led Gulf Coast League catchers in total chances with 394 and tied for lead in double plays with 5 in 1982.

Year	Club	League	Pos.	G.	AB.	R.	H.	2B.	3B.	HR.	RBI.	B.A.	PO.	A.	E.	F.A.
1982—Sarasota W.S.	Gulf C.	C		60	214	34	56	6	0	7	32	.262	★331	★51	12	.970
1983—Appleton	Midw.	C-OF		97	326	54	78	17	3	13	48	.239	682	91	4	.995
1984—Glens Falls	East.	C		88	260	37	56	9	1	13	39	.215	442	★68	11	.979
1984—Denver	A. A.	C		31	86	7	19	1	0	2	10	.221	149	28	3	.983
1985—Glens Falls	East.	C		99	324	37	70	9	3	11	37	.216	573	★103	★14	.980
1986—Birmingham	South.	C		97	319	63	90	13	1	20	53	.282	463	72	10	.982
1986—Chicago	Amer.	C		37	97	13	24	7	0	4	13	.247	227	19	1	.996
1987—Chicago	Amer.	C		39	85	7	6	0	0	2	7	.071	147	20	3	.982
1987—Hawaii	P. C.	C-OF		34	104	15	19	3	0	4	11	.183	108	13	3	.976
1988—Vancouver	P. C.	C		39	116	12	29	10	0	2	13	.250	202	16	3	.986
1988—Chicago	Amer.	C		46	115	10	20	4	0	3	9	.174	190	24	1	.995
1989—Chicago	Amer.	C		71	182	21	48	9	2	3	24	.264	299	47	5	.986
1990—Chicago	Amer.	C		68	183	30	45	10	0	6	20	.246	296	31	2	.994
Major League Totals—5 Years				261	662	81	143	30	2	18	73	.216	1159	141	12	.991

Selected by Chicago White Sox' organization in 1st round (14th player selected) of free-agent draft, June 7, 1982.

ERIC PETER KARROS
Born November 4, 1967, at Hackensack, N. J.
Height, 6.04. Weight, 205.
Throws and bats righthanded.
Attended UCLA, Los Angeles, Calif.

Led Texas League in total bases with 282 in 1990.
Led Texas League first basemen in total chances with 1,337 and double plays with 129 in 1990.
Led California League first basemen in putouts with 1,232 and assists with 110 in 1989.
Led Pioneer League first basemen in errors with 14 in 1988.

Year	Club	League	Pos.	G.	AB.	R.	H.	2B.	3B.	HR.	RBI.	B.A.	PO.	A.	E.	F.A.
1988—Great Falls	Pion.	1B-3B	66	268	68	98	12	1	12	55	.366	516	31	19	.966
1989—Bakersfield	Calif.	1B-3B	★142	545	86	★165	★40	1	15	86	.303	1238	113	19	.986
1990—San Antonio	Texas	1B	●131	509	91	★179	★45	2	18	78	★.352	★1223	★106	8	★.994

Selected by Los Angeles Dodgers' organization in 6th round of free-agent draft, June 1, 1988.

ROBERTO CONRADO KELLY
Born October 1, 1964, at Panama City, Panama.
Height, 6.02. Weight, 195.
Throws and bats righthanded.
Attended Jose Dolores Moscote College, Panama.

Shares major league record for fewest double plays by outfielder, season, 150 or more games (0), 1990.
Major League stolen bases: 1987 (9), 1988 (5), 1989 (35), 1990 (42). Total—91.
Led American League outfielders in total chances with 430 in 1990.
Led International League in stolen bases with 51 in 1987.
Led International League outfielders in total chances with 345 in 1987.

Year	Club	League	Pos.	G.	AB.	R.	H.	2B.	3B.	HR.	RBI.	B.A.	PO.	A.	E.	F.A.
1982—Bradenton Yanks	Gulf C.	SS-OF	31	86	13	17	1	1	1	18	.198	47	79	19	.869
1983—Oneonta	NYP	OF-3B	48	167	17	36	1	2	2	17	.216	70	3	5	.936
1983—Greensboro	S. Atl.	OF	20	49	6	13	0	0	0	3	.265	30	2	0	1.000
1984—Greensboro	S. Atl.	Of-1B	111	361	68	86	13	2	1	26	.238	228	5	4	.983
1985—Fort Lauderdale†	Fla. St.	OF	114	417	86	103	4	★13	3	38	.247	187	1	1	.995
1986—Albany‡	East.	OF	86	299	42	87	11	4	2	43	.291	206	8	7	.968
1987—Columbus	Int.	OF	118	471	77	131	19	8	13	62	.278	★331	4	10	.971
1987—New York	Amer.	OF	23	52	12	14	3	0	1	7	.269	42	0	2	.955
1988—New York§	Amer.	OF	38	77	9	19	4	1	1	7	.247	70	1	1	.986
1988—Columbus	Int.	OF	30	120	25	40	8	1	3	16	.333	51	1	0	1.000
1989—New York x	Amer.	OF	137	441	65	133	18	3	9	48	.302	353	9	6	.984
1990—New York	Amer.	OF	★162	641	85	183	32	4	15	61	.285	420	5	5	.988
Major League Totals—4 Years			360	1211	171	349	57	8	26	123	.288	885	15	14	.985

Signed as free agent by New York Yankees' organization, February 21, 1982.
†Switch-hitter.
‡On disabled list, July 10 to August 23, 1986.
§On disabled list, June 29 to September 1, 1988.
xOn disabled list, May 26 to June 12, 1989.

TERRENCE EDWARD KENNEDY
(Terry)

Born June 4, 1956, at Euclid, O.
Height, 6.04. Weight, 220.
Throws right and bats lefthanded.
Attended Florida State University, Tallahassee, Fla.

Son of Bob Kennedy, third baseman-outfielder with Chicago AL, Cleveland, Baltimore, Detroit and Brooklyn, 1939 through 1957; scout, Cleveland, 1958 through 1961; minor league manager, Chicago Cubs' organization, 1962; coach, Chicago Cubs, 1963 and 1964; Chicago Cubs executive, 1965; minor league manager, Los Angeles Dodgers' organization, 1966; coach, Atlanta Braves, 1967; manager, Oakland A's, 1968; Director of Player Development, St. Louis Cardinals, 1969 through 1976; Executive Vice President, Chicago Cubs, 1977 through 1981; Houston Astros Vice-President-Baseball Operations, 1982 through 1985; and San Francisco Giants Vice-President-Baseball Operations since 1986; brother of Bob Kennedy Jr., pitcher in St. Louis Cardinals' organization, 1971 through 1975; scout, Seattle Mariners, 1976; scout, Chicago Cubs, 1977 through 1981; scout with Houston Astros, 1982 through 1985.

Shares National League record for most doubles by catcher, season (40), 1982.
Major League stolen bases: 1982 (1), 1983 (1), 1984 (1), 1987 (1), 1989 (1), 1990 (1). Total—6.
Led National League catchers in double plays with 12 in 1981 and tied for lead with 11 in 1982 and 12 in 1985.
Named catcher on THE SPORTING NEWS National League Silver Slugger team, 1983.
Named College Player of the Year by THE SPORTING NEWS, 1977.
Received reported $100,000 bonus to sign with St. Louis Cardinals, 1977.
Named catcher on THE SPORTING NEWS College Baseball All-America Team, 1976 and 1977.

Year—Club	League	Pos.	G.	AB.	R.	H.	2B.	3B.	HR.	RBI.	B.A.	PO.	A.	E.	F.A.
1977—Johnson City	Appal.	C-1B	12	39	14	23	7	2	3	15	.590	66	3	1	.986
1977—St. Petersburg	Fla. St.	C	45	166	22	41	8	0	4	22	.247	168	22	6	.969
1978—Arkansas	Texas	C-OF	69	239	55	69	14	0	10	54	.289	365	30	7	.983
1978—Springfield	A. A.	C-1B	64	230	35	76	13	0	10	46	.330	331	26	7	.981
1978—St. Louis	Nat.	C	10	29	0	5	0	0	0	2	.172	46	4	1	.980
1979—Springfield	A. A.	C	84	294	35	86	18	1	13	64	.293	434	38	13	.973
1979—St. Louis	Nat.	C	33	109	11	31	7	0	2	17	.284	135	7	1	.993
1980—St. Louis†	Nat.	C-OF	84	248	28	63	12	3	4	34	.254	231	22	7	.973
1981—San Diego	Nat.	C	101	382	32	115	24	1	2	41	.301	465	63	★20	.964
1982—San Diego	Nat.	C-1B	153	562	75	166	42	1	21	97	.295	777	66	9	.989
1983—San Diego	Nat.	C-1B	149	549	47	156	27	2	17	98	.284	807	82	12	.987
1984—San Diego	Nat.	C	148	530	54	127	16	1	14	57	.240	708	54	14	.982
1985—San Diego	Nat.	C-1B	143	532	54	139	27	1	10	74	.261	662	68	10	.986
1986—San Diego‡	Nat.	C	141	432	46	114	22	1	12	57	.264	692	70	8	.990
1987—Baltimore	Amer.	C	143	512	51	128	13	1	18	62	.250	750	★58	6	.993
1988—Baltimore§	Amer.	C	85	265	20	60	10	0	3	16	.226	332	23	2	.994
1989—San Francisco x	Nat.	C-1B	125	355	19	85	15	0	5	34	.239	519	47	8	.986
1990—San Francisco	Nat.	C	107	303	25	84	22	0	2	26	.277	390	38	4	.991
National League Totals—11 Years			1194	4031	391	1085	214	10	89	537	.269	5432	521	94	.984
American League Totals—2 Years			228	777	71	188	23	1	21	78	.242	1082	81	8	.993
Major League Totals—13 Years			1422	4808	462	1273	237	11	110	615	.265	6514	602	102	.986

Selected by St. Louis Cardinals' organization in 1st round (sixth player selected) of free-agent draft, June 7, 1977.
†Traded with Catcher Steve Swisher, Pitchers John Littlefield, Al Olmsted, Kim Seaman and John Urrea and Infielder Mike Phillips to San Diego Padres for Pitchers Rollie Fingers and Bob Shirley, Catcher-First Baseman Gene Tenace and a player to be named later, December 8, 1980; St. Louis Cardinals' organization acquired catcher Bob Geren to complete deal, December 10, 1980.
‡Traded with Pitcher Mark Williamson to Baltimore Orioles for Pitcher Storm Davis, October 30, 1986.
§Traded to San Francisco Giants for Catcher Bob Melvin, January 24, 1989.
xGranted free agency, November 13, 1989; re-signed by Giants, December 8, 1989.

CHAMPIONSHIP SERIES RECORD

Year—Club	League	Pos.	G.	AB.	R.	H.	2B.	3B.	HR.	RBI.	B.A.	PO.	A.	E.	F.A.
1984—San Diego	Nat.	C	5	18	2	4	0	0	0	1	.222	28	4	0	1.000
1989—San Francisco	Nat.	C	5	16	0	3	1	0	0	0	.188	26	1	0	1.000
Championship Series Totals—2 Years			10	34	2	7	1	0	0	1	.206	54	5	0	1.000

WORLD SERIES RECORD

Year—Club	League	Pos.	G.	AB.	R.	H.	2B.	3B.	HR.	RBI.	B.A.	PO.	A.	E.	F.A.
1984—San Diego	Nat.	C	5	19	2	4	1	0	1	3	.211	30	2	0	1.000
1989—San Francisco	Nat.	C	4	12	1	2	0	0	0	2	.167	23	1	1	.960
World Series Totals—2 Years			9	31	3	6	1	0	1	5	.194	53	3	1	.982

ALL-STAR GAME RECORD

Year—League	Pos.	AB.	R.	H.	2B.	3B.	HR.	RBI.	B.A.	PO.	A.	E.	F.A.
1981—National	PH	1	0	0	0	0	0	0	.000	0	0	0	.000
1985—National	C	2	0	1	0	0	0	1	.500	0	0	1	.000
1987—American	C	2	0	0	0	0	0	0	.000	3	1	0	1.000
All-Star Game Totals—3 Years		5	0	1	0	0	0	1	.200	3	1	1	.800

Member of National League All-Star Team in 1983; did not play.

—DID YOU KNOW—

That the Cardinals fielded their first last-place team since 1918?

CHARLES PATRICK KERFELD
(Charley)

Born September 28, 1963, at Knob Noster, Mo.
Height, 6.07. Weight, 250.
Throws and bats righthanded.
Attended Yavapai College, Prescott, Ariz.

Major League saves: 1986 (7), 1990 (2). Total—9.
Led South Atlantic League pitchers in complete games with 12 and tied for lead in games started with 28 in 1983.
Named South Atlantic League Pitcher of the Year, 1983.

Year	Club	League	G.	IP.	W.	L.	Pct.	H.	R.	ER.	SO.	BB.	ERA.
1983—Asheville	S. Atlantic	28	*192	*16	10	.615	171	84	62	189	85	2.91
1984—Columbus†	Southern	24	162⅔	14	9	.609	140	80	54	118	79	2.99
1984—Tucson	P. Coast	1	3⅔	0	1	.000	6	4	4	3	1	9.82
1985—Tucson	P. Coast	26	163⅓	10	11	.476	176	95	80	123	74	4.41
1985—Houston	National	11	44⅓	4	2	.667	44	22	20	30	25	4.06
1986—Houston‡	National	61	93⅔	11	2	.846	71	32	27	77	42	2.59
1987—Houston§	National	21	29⅔	0	2	.000	34	22	22	17	21	6.67
1987—Tucson	P. Coast	32	62⅔	4	4	.500	61	36	33	59	27	4.74
1988—Columbus x	Southern	13	64	2	7	.222	63	36	32	63	21	4.50
1989—Tucson	P. Coast	53	73⅓	3	11	.214	89	56	45	77	55	5.52
1989—Osceola	Florida St.	5	7⅔	0	0	.000	4	2	1	8	3	1.17
1990—Houston y-Atlanta za	National	30	34	3	3	.500	40	28	25	31	29	6.62
1990—Richmond b	Int'national	15	21⅓	2	0	1.000	22	10	8	24	16	3.38
Major League Totals—4 Years		123	201⅔	18	9	.667	189	104	94	155	117	4.20

Selected by Philadelphia Phillies' organization in 24th round of free-agent draft, June 8, 1981.
Selected by Seattle Mariners' organization in secondary phase of free-agent draft, January 12, 1982.
Selected by Houston Astros' organization in secondary phase of free-agent draft, June 7, 1982.
†On disabled list, June 4 to June 28, 1984.
‡On disabled list, June 14 to July 2, 1986.
§On disabled list, July 31 to September 21, 1987.
xOn Houston disabled list, March 27 to April 21, 1988.
yTraded to Atlanta Braves for Outfielder Kevin Dean and a player to be named later, April 28, 1990; Houston Astros acquired Pitcher Lee Ellis Johnson to complete deal, October 29, 1990.
zOn disabled list, June 9 to June 24, 1990.
aReleased, July 23, 1990; re-signed by Braves' organization, July 27, 1990.
bGranted free agency, October 15, 1990.

CHAMPIONSHIP SERIES RECORD

Year	Club	League	G.	IP.	W.	L.	Pct.	H.	R.	ER.	SO.	BB.	ERA.
1986—Houston	National	3	4	0	1	.000	2	1	1	4	1	2.25

JAMES EDWARD KEY
(Jimmy)

Born April 22, 1961, at Huntsville, Ala.
Height, 6.01. Weight, 185.
Throws left and bats righthanded.
Attended Clemson University, Clemson, S. C.

Major League saves: 1984 (10).
Named American League Pitcher of the Year by THE SPORTING NEWS, 1987.
Named lefthanded pitcher on THE SPORTING NEWS American League All-Star Team, 1987.

Year	Club	League	G.	IP.	W.	L.	Pct.	H.	R.	ER.	SO.	BB.	ERA.
1982—Medicine Hat	Pioneer	5	31⅓	2	1	.667	27	12	8	25	10	2.30
1982—Florence	S. Atlantic	9	58	5	2	.714	59	33	24	49	18	3.72
1983—Knoxville	Southern	14	101	6	5	.545	86	35	32	57	40	2.85
1983—Syracuse	Int'national	16	89⅓	4	8	.333	87	58	41	71	33	4.13
1984—Toronto	American	63	62	4	5	.444	70	37	32	44	32	4.65
1985—Toronto†	American	35	212⅔	14	6	.700	188	77	71	85	50	3.00
1986—Toronto	American	36	232	14	11	.560	222	98	92	141	74	3.57
1987—Toronto	American	36	261	17	8	.680	210	93	80	161	66	*2.76
1988—Toronto‡	American	21	131⅓	12	5	.706	127	55	48	65	30	3.29
1988—Dunedin	Florida St.	4	21⅓	2	0	1.000	15	2	0	11	1	0.00
1989—Toronto§	American	33	216	13	14	.481	226	99	93	118	27	3.88
1990—Toronto x	American	27	154⅔	13	7	.650	169	79	73	88	22	4.25
1990—Dunedin	Florida St.	3	18	2	0	1.000	21	7	5	14	3	2.50
Major League Totals—7 Years		251	1269⅔	87	56	.608	1212	538	489	702	301	3.47

Selected by Chicago White Sox' organization in 10th round of free-agent draft, June 5, 1979.
Selected by Toronto Blue Jays' organization in 3rd round of free-agent draft, June 7, 1982.
†Appeared in one game as a pinch-runner.
‡On disabled list, April 15 to June 29, 1988; included rehabilitation disability assignment to Dunedin, June 10 to June 27, 1988.
§On disabled list, August 4 to August 19, 1989.
xOn disabled list, May 23 to June 22, 1990; included rehabilitation disability assignment to Dunedin, June 7 to June 18, 1990.

CHAMPIONSHIP SERIES RECORD

Year	Club	League	G.	IP.	W.	L.	Pct.	H.	R.	ER.	SO.	BB.	ERA.
1985—Toronto	American	2	8⅔	0	1	.000	15	5	5	5	2	5.19
1989—Toronto	American	1	6	1	0	1.000	7	3	3	2	2	4.50
Championship Series Totals—2 Years		3	14⅔	1	1	.500	22	8	8	7	4	4.91

Year League	IP.	W.	L.	Pct.	H.	R.	ER.	SO.	BB.	ERA.
1985—American	⅓	0	0	.000	0	0	0	0	0	0.00

DANA ERVIN KIECKER

Name pronounced Kicker.
Born February 25, 1961, at Sleepy Eye, Minn.
Height, 6.03. Weight, 180.
Throws and bats righthanded.
Attended St. Cloud State University, St. Cloud, Minn.

Led Florida State League in games started by pitchers with 29 in 1985.
Tied for Eastern League lead in balks with 5 in 1986.

Year Club	League	G.	IP.	W.	L.	Pct.	H.	R.	ER.	SO.	BB.	ERA.
1983—Elmira	NYP	16	*111⅔	11	5	.688	92	50	34	78	44	2.74
1984—Winston-Salem	Carolina	29	137⅔	6	11	.353	142	86	67	82	55	4.38
1985—Winter Haven	Florida St.	29	*193⅔	12	●12	.500	176	72	56	60	59	2.60
1986—New Britain	Eastern	24	156⅓	7	12	.368	*171	88	72	71	48	4.14
1987—New Britain	Eastern	39	153	7	10	.412	164	76	65	66	66	3.82
1988—Pawtucket	Int'national	23	132⅓	7	7	.500	120	65	54	74	46	3.67
1988—New Britain	Eastern	1	6	1	0	1.000	3	0	0	1	0	0.00
1989—Pawtucket	Int'national	28	147⅓	8	9	.471	163	83	60	87	36	3.67
1990—Boston	American	32	152	8	9	.471	145	74	67	93	54	3.97
Major League Totals—1 Year		32	152	8	9	.471	145	74	67	93	54	3.97

Selected by Boston Red Sox' organization in 8th round of free-agent draft, June 6, 1983.

Year Club	League	G.	IP.	W.	L.	Pct.	H.	R.	ER.	SO.	BB.	ERA.
1990—Boston	American	1	5⅔	0	0	.000	6	1	1	2	1	1.59

DARRYL ANDREW KILE

Born December 2, 1968, at Garden Grove, Calif.
Height, 6.05. Weight, 185.
Throws and bats righthanded.
Attended Chaffey College, Alta Loma, Calif.

Tied for Southern League lead in shutouts with 2 in 1989.

Year Club	League	G.	IP.	W.	L.	Pct.	H.	R.	ER.	SO.	BB.	ERA.
1988—Sarasota Astros	Gulf Coast	12	59⅔	5	3	.625	48	34	21	54	33	3.17
1989—Columbus	Southern	20	125⅔	11	6	.647	74	47	36	108	68	2.58
1989—Tucson	P. Coast	6	25⅔	2	1	.667	33	20	17	18	13	5.96
1990—Tucson	P. Coast	26	123⅓	5	10	.333	147	97	91	77	68	6.64

Selected by Houston Astros' organization in 30th round of free-agent draft, June 2, 1987.

PAUL NELSON KILGUS

Born February 2, 1962, at Bowling Green, Ky.
Height, 6.01. Weight, 185.
Throws and bats lefthanded.
Received bachelor of science degree in biology from University of Kentucky, Lexington, Ky., in 1984.

Major League saves: 1989 (2).

Year Club	League	G.	IP.	W.	L.	Pct.	H.	R.	ER.	SO.	BB.	ERA.
1984—Tri-Cities	Northwest	14	78⅓	7	5	.583	87	38	25	60	31	2.87
1985—Salem	Carolina	38	84⅓	3	1	.750	69	28	19	67	26	2.03
1986—Tulsa	Texas	41	103⅔	3	7	.300	102	56	43	59	36	3.73
1987—Oklahoma City	Am. Assoc.	21	24⅔	2	0	1.000	23	12	11	14	10	4.01
1987—Texas	American	25	89⅓	2	7	.222	95	45	41	42	31	4.13
1988—Texas†	American	32	203⅓	12	15	.444	190	105	94	88	71	4.16
1989—Chicago	National	35	145⅔	6	10	.375	164	90	71	61	49	4.39
1989—Iowa‡	Am. Assoc.	1	9	1	0	1.000	9	3	3	5	2	3.00
1990—Toronto	American	11	16⅓	0	0	.000	19	11	11	7	7	6.06
1990—Syracuse§	Int'national	20	125⅔	6	8	.429	116	47	41	75	39	2.94
American League Totals—3 Years		68	309	14	22	.389	304	161	146	137	109	4.25
National League Totals—1 Year		35	145⅔	6	10	.375	164	90	71	61	49	4.39
Major League Totals—4 Years		103	454⅔	20	32	.385	468	251	217	198	158	4.30

Selected by Texas Rangers' organization in 43rd round of free-agent draft, June 4, 1984.
†Traded with Pitchers Mitch Williams and Steve Wilson, Infielders Curtis Wilkerson and Luis Benitez and Outfielder Pablo Delgado to Chicago Cubs for Outfielder Rafael Palmeiro and Pitchers Jamie Moyer and Drew Hall, December 5, 1988.
‡Traded to Toronto Blue Jays for Pitcher Jose Nunez, December 7, 1989.
§Traded to Baltimore Orioles for Pitcher Mickey Weston, December 14, 1990.

Year Club	League	G.	IP.	W.	L.	Pct.	H.	R.	ER.	SO.	BB.	ERA.
1989—Chicago	National	1	3	0	0	.000	4	0	0	1	1	0.00

ERIC STEVEN KING

Born April 10, 1964, at Oxnard, Calif.
Height, 6.02. Weight, 218.
Throws and bats righthanded.

Shares major league record for most putouts by pitcher, nine-inning game (6), July 8, 1986.
Major League saves: 1986 (3), 1987 (9), 1988 (3). Total—15.

Year Club	League	G.	IP.	W.	L.	Pct.	H.	R.	ER.	SO.	BB.	ERA.
1983—Great Falls	Pioneer	20	56½	3	4	.429	58	31	27	61	14	4.31
1984—Clinton	Midwest	35	147½	5	10	.333	142	74	55	124	76	3.36
1985—Shreveport†‡	Texas	15	104⅔	5	3	.625	74	34	27	80	30	2.32
1986—Nashville	Am. Assoc.	6	38½	3	2	.600	29	16	15	38	16	3.52
1986—Detroit	American	33	138⅓	11	4	.733	108	54	54	79	63	3.51
1987—Detroit	American	55	116	6	9	.400	111	67	63	89	60	4.89
1988—Toledo	Int'national	10	69	3	4	.429	54	26	25	51	23	3.26
1988—Detroit	American	23	68⅔	4	1	.800	60	28	26	45	34	3.41
1989—Chicago§	American	25	159⅓	9	10	.474	144	69	60	72	64	3.39
1990—Chicago x	American	25	151	12	4	.750	135	59	55	70	40	3.28
1990—Sarasota y	Florida St.	2	8	1	0	1.000	8	4	2	5	2	2.25
Major League Totals—5 Years		161	633⅓	42	28	.600	558	277	258	355	261	3.67

Signed as free agent by San Francisco Giants' organization, June 11, 1983.
†On suspended list, July 3 to July 13, 1985, then transferred to disabled list, July 13 to July 27, 1985.
‡Traded with Pitcher Dave LaPoint and Catcher Matt Nokes to Detroit Tigers for Pitcher Juan Berenguer, Catcher Bob Melvin and a player to be named later, October 7, 1985; San Francisco Giants acquired Pitcher Scott Medvin to complete deal, December 11, 1985.
§Traded to Chicago White Sox for Outfielder Kenny Williams, March 23, 1989.
xOn disabled list, August 1 to September 1, 1990; included rehabilitation disability assignment to Sarasota, August 23 to August 31, 1990.
yTraded with Pitcher Shawn Hillegas to Cleveland Indians for Outfielder Cory Snyder and Infielder Lindsay Foster, December 4, 1990.

CHAMPIONSHIP SERIES RECORD

Year Club	League	G.	IP.	W.	L.	Pct.	H.	R.	ER.	SO.	BB.	ERA.
1987—Detroit	American	2	5⅓	0	0	.000	3	1	1	4	2	1.69

JEFFREY WAYNE KING
(Jeff)

Born December 26, 1964, at Marion, Ind.
Height, 6.01. Weight, 180.
Throws and bats righthanded.
Attended University of Arkansas, Fayetteville, Ark.
Son of Jack King, minor league catcher, 1954 and 1955; and brother of James King, shortstop drafted by Philadelphia Phillies' organization in 1982 and Seattle Mariners' organization in 1984.

Major League stolen bases: 1989 (4), 1990 (3). Total—7.
Led Carolina League in slugging percentage with .565 in 1987.
Received reported $180,000 bonus to sign with Pittsburgh Pirates, 1986.
Named College Player of the Year by THE SPORTING NEWS, 1986.
Named third baseman on THE SPORTING NEWS College Baseball All-America Team, 1986.

Year Club	League	Pos.	G.	AB.	R.	H.	2B.	3B.	HR.	RBI.	B.A.	PO.	A.	E.	F.A.
1986—Prince William	Carol.	3B	37	132	18	31	4	1	6	20	.235	25	50	8	.904
1987—Salem	Carol.	1B-3B	90	310	68	86	9	1	26	71	.277	572	106	13	.981
1987—Harrisburg	East.	1B	26	100	12	24	7	0	2	25	.240	107	10	1	.992
1988—Harrisburg	East.	3B	117	411	49	105	21	1	14	66	.255	97	208	24	.927
1989—Buffalo	A. A.	1B-3B	51	169	26	43	5	2	6	29	.254	213	61	8	.972
1989—Pittsburgh	Nat.	1-3-2-S	75	215	31	42	13	3	5	19	.195	403	59	4	.991
1990—Pittsburgh	Nat.	3B-1B	127	371	46	91	17	1	14	53	.245	61	215	18	.939
Major League Totals—2 Years			202	586	77	133	30	4	19	72	.227	464	274	22	.971

Selected by Chicago Cubs' organization in 23rd round of free-agent draft, June 6, 1983.
Selected by Pittsburgh Pirates' organization in 1st round (first player selected) of free-agent draft, June 2, 1986.

CHAMPIONSHIP SERIES RECORD

Year Club	League	Pos.	G.	AB.	R.	H.	2B.	3B.	HR.	RBI.	B.A.	PO.	A.	E.	F.A.
1990—Pittsburgh	Nat.	PH-3B	5	10	0	1	0	0	0	0	.100	1	4	0	1.000

MICHAEL SCOTT KINGERY
(Mike)

Born March 29, 1961, at St. James, Minn.
Height, 6.00. Weight, 185.
Throws and bats lefthanded.
Attended Willmar Community College, Willmar, Minn.;
and St. Cloud State University, St. Cloud, Minn.

Major League stolen bases: 1986 (7), 1987 (7), 1988 (3), 1989 (1), 1990 (6). Total—24.
Led Florida State League in intentional bases on balls received with 11 in 1983.
Tied for South Atlantic League lead in double plays by outfielders with 5 in 1982.

Year Club	League	Pos.	G.	AB.	R.	H.	2B.	3B.	HR.	RBI.	B.A.	PO.	A.	E.	F.A.
1980—K.C. Royals-Gold . Gulf C.		OF	44	143	12	32	3	3	0	13	.224	78	5	2	.976
1981—Charleston†	S. Atl.	OF	69	213	33	57	3	4	3	25	.268	80	7	4	.956

Year Club	League	Pos.	G.	AB.	R.	H.	2B.	3B.	HR.	RBI.	B.A.	PO.	A.	E.	F.A.
1982—Charleston	S. Atl.	OF	140	513	65	163	19	4	8	75	.318	250	21	7	.975
1983—Fort Myers	Fla. St.	OF	123	436	68	116	9	7	2	51	.266	200	16	5	.977
1984—Memphis	South.	OF	139	455	65	135	19	3	4	58	.297	291	18	6	.981
1985—Omaha	A. A.	OF	132	444	51	113	25	6	2	49	.255	247	17	5	.981
1986—Omaha	A. A.	OF	79	298	47	99	14	8	3	47	.332	171	10	1	.995
1986—Kansas City‡	Amer.	OF	62	209	25	54	8	5	3	14	.258	102	6	3	.973
1987—Seattle	Amer.	OF	120	354	38	99	25	4	9	52	.280	226	15	2	.992
1988—Seattle	Amer.	OF-1B	57	123	21	25	6	0	1	9	.203	102	6	2	.982
1988—Calgary	P. C.	OF-1B	47	170	29	54	12	2	1	14	.318	144	4	3	.980
1989—Calgary	P. C.	OF-1B	107	396	72	115	22	9	4	47	.290	289	10	1	.997
1989—Seattle§	Amer.	OF	31	76	14	17	3	0	2	6	.224	70	0	0	1.000
1990—Phoenix	P. C.	OF	35	100	12	24	9	2	1	16	.240	61	4	1	.985
1990—San Francisco	Nat.	OF	105	207	24	61	7	1	0	24	.295	126	7	3	.978
American League Totals—4 Years			270	762	98	195	42	9	15	81	.256	500	27	7	.987
National League Totals—1 Year			105	207	24	61	7	1	0	24	.295	126	7	3	.978
Major League Totals—5 Years			375	969	122	256	49	10	15	105	.264	626	34	10	.985

Signed as free agent by Kansas City Royals' organization, August 27, 1979.

†On disabled list, July 29 to August 15, 1981.

‡Traded with Pitchers Scott Bankhead and Steve Shields to Seattle Mariners for Outfielder Danny Tartabull and Pitcher Rick Luecken, December 10, 1986.

§Granted free agency, April 6, 1990; signed by Phoenix (San Francisco Giants' organization), April 14, 1990.

MATTHEW ROY KINZER
(Matt)

Born June 17, 1963, at Indianapolis, Ind.
Height, 6.02. Weight, 210.
Throws and bats righthanded.
Attended Purdue University, West Lafayette, Ind.

Year Club	League	G.	IP.	W.	L.	Pct.	H.	R.	ER.	SO.	BB.	ERA.
1984—Arkansas	Texas	14	82⅔	5	6	.455	97	48	41	41	27	4.46
1985—Springfield†	Midwest	11	58⅓	5	4	.556	56	26	24	36	21	3.70
1986—St. Petersburg	Florida St.	22	134	10	7	.588	129	49	43	80	42	2.89
1987—Arkansas	Texas	17	91⅓	5	6	.455	82	57	48	74	34	4.73
1988—Arkansas	Texas	16	29	3	0	1.000	26	11	10	34	3	3.10
1988—Louisville	Am. Assoc.	46	80	6	2	.750	73	34	33	53	24	3.71
1989—Louisville	Am. Assoc.	51	72	1	4	.200	69	28	26	62	14	3.25
1989—St. Louis‡	National	8	13⅓	0	2	.000	25	20	19	8	4	12.82
1990—Toledo	Int'national	15	18	0	3	.000	15	7	5	25	8	2.50
1990—Detroit§x	American	1	1⅔	0	0	.000	3	3	3	1	3	16.20
1990—Hagerstown y	Eastern	3	3⅔	0	1	.000	0	1	0	3	2	0.00
National League Totals—1 Year		8	13⅓	0	2	.000	25	20	19	8	4	12.82
American League Totals—1 Year		1	1⅔	0	0	.000	3	3	3	1	3	16.20
Major League Totals—2 Years		9	15	0	2	.000	28	23	22	9	7	13.20

Selected by Cleveland Indians' organization in 6th round of free-agent draft, June 8, 1981.

Selected by St. Louis Cardinals' organization in 2nd round of free-agent draft, June 4, 1984.

†On disabled list, August 2, 1985 through remainder of season.

‡Traded with First Baseman Jim Lindeman to Detroit Tigers for Second Baseman Pat Austin, Catcher Bill Henderson and Pitcher Marcos Betances, December 6, 1989.

§On disabled list, June 5 to July 5, 1990.

xReleased, July 12, 1990; signed by Hagerstown (Baltimore Orioles' organization), August 3, 1990.

yReleased, August 14, 1990.

RECORD AS FOOTBALL PLAYER

Signed as replacement player by Detroit Lions, September 24, 1987.
Released by Detroit Lions, October 16, 1987.

		——PUNTING——		
Year Club	G.	No.	Avg.	Blk.
1987—Detroit NFL	1	7	34.0	0

ROBERT WAYNE KIPPER
(Bob)

Born July 8, 1964, at Aurora, Ill.
Height, 6.02. Weight, 180.
Throws left and bats righthanded.

Pitched seven-inning, 9-0 no-hit victory against San Jose, June 10, 1984 (second game).
Major League saves: 1989 (4), 1990 (3). Total—7.
Tied for National League lead in balks with 5 in 1990.
Named California League Pitcher of the Year, 1984.

Year Club	League	G.	IP.	W.	L.	Pct.	H.	R.	ER.	SO.	BB.	ERA.
1982—Salem	Northwest	13	76⅔	6	5	.545	62	46	38	65	52	4.46
1983—Peoria†	Midwest	22	127⅔	5	8	.385	112	77	66	105	52	4.65
1984—Redwood	California	26	185	★18	8	.692	147	61	42	98	65	★2.04
1985—California	American	2	3⅓	0	1	.000	7	8	8	0	3	21.60
1985—Midland‡	Texas	9	49⅔	3	3	.500	52	22	17	31	10	3.08
1985—Edmonton§x-Hawaii	P. Coast	7	49⅔	3	0	1.000	36	15	11	42	12	1.99
1985—Pittsburgh	National	5	24⅔	1	2	.333	21	16	14	13	7	5.11

Year Club	League	G.	IP.	W.	L.	Pct.	H.	R.	ER.	SO.	BB.	ERA.
1986—Pittsburgh y	National	20	114	6	8	.429	123	60	51	81	34	4.03
1986—Nashua	Eastern	4	18⅓	0	1	.000	14	7	7	19	3	3.44
1987—Pittsburgh	National	24	110⅔	5	9	.357	117	74	73	83	52	5.94
1987—Vancouver	P. Coast	6	25⅓	0	2	.000	23	7	5	22	4	1.78
1988—Pittsburgh	National	50	65	2	6	.250	54	33	27	39	26	3.74
1989—Pittsburgh z	National	52	83	3	4	.429	55	29	27	58	33	2.93
1990—Buffalo a	Am. Assoc.	5	4⅔	0	0	.000	6	4	4	6	1	7.71
1990—Pittsburgh	National	41	62⅔	5	2	.714	44	24	21	35	26	3.02
American League Totals—1 Year		2	3⅓	0	1	.000	7	8	8	0	3	21.60
National League Totals—6 Years		192	460	22	31	.415	414	236	213	309	178	4.17
Major League Totals—6 Years		194	463⅓	22	32	.407	421	244	221	309	181	4.29

Selected by California Angels' organization in 1st round (eighth player selected) of free-agent draft, June 7, 1982.

†On disabled list, July 20 to August 8, 1983.

‡On disabled list, May 31 to June 10, 1985.

§Loaned to Hawaii (Pittsburgh Pirates' organization), August 2, 1985; returned, August 16, 1985.

xTraded to Pittsburgh Pirates' organization, August 16, 1985, completing deal in which Pittsburgh traded Pitchers John Candelaria and Al Holland and Outfielder George Hendrick to California Angels for Pitcher Pat Clements, Outfielder Mike Brown and a player to be named later, August 2, 1985.

yOn disabled list, June 29 to September 1, 1986; included rehabilitation disability assignment to Nashua, August 14 to September 1, 1986.

zOn disabled list, July 31 to September 1, 1989.

aOn Pittsburgh disability list, March 30 to May 7, 1990; included rehabilitation disability assignment to Buffalo, April 26 to May 7, 1990.

RONALD DALE KITTLE
(Ron)

Born January 5, 1958, at Gary, Ind.
Height, 6.04. Weight, 230.
Throws and bats righthanded.

Shares major league record for most home runs, month of October (4), 1985.
Major League stolen bases: 1983 (8), 1984 (3), 1985 (1), 1986 (4). Total—16.
Led American League batters in strikeouts with 150 in 1983.
Led Pacific Coast League in total bases with 355, slugging percentage with .752 and tied for lead in being hit by pitch with 10 in 1982.
Led Eastern League in total bases with 270 and slugging percentage with .694 in 1981.
Named American League Rookie Player of the Year by THE SPORTING NEWS, 1983.
Named American League Rookie of the Year by Baseball Writers' Association of America, 1983.
Named Minor League Player of the Year by THE SPORTING NEWS, 1982.
Named Pacific Coast League Most Valuable Player, 1982.
Named Eastern League Most Valuable Player, 1981.

Year Club	League	Pos.	G.	AB.	R.	H.	2B.	3B.	HR.	RBI.	B.A.	PO.	A.	E.	F.A.
1977—Clinton†	Midw.	OF	22	53	9	10	4	0	0	3	.189	16	0	0	1.000
1977—Lethbridge	Pion.	OF	34	100	22	25	3	0	7	21	.250	29	2	6	.838
1978—Clinton‡	Midw.	OF	13	35	2	5	2	1	0	4	.143	4	1	1	.833
1979—Knoxville	South.	OF-C	53	157	28	43	9	1	6	26	.274	44	1	6	.980
1979—Appleton	Midw.	OF-C	35	120	18	31	3	1	2	12	.258	33	1	2	.972
1980—Appleton	Midw.	C-OF	61	209	31	66	15	3	12	56	.316	56	9	1	.985
1980—Glens Falls§	East.	OF	17	65	11	20	3	1	4	9	.308	24	4	3	.903
1981—Glens Falls x	East.	OF	109	389	97	127	17	3	★40	★103	.326	28	0	3	.903
1982—Edmonton	P. C.	OF-C	127	472	★121	163	22	10	★50	★144	.345	149	15	8	.953
1982—Chicago	Amer.	OF	20	29	3	7	2	0	1	7	.241	3	0	0	1.000
1983—Chicago	Amer.	OF	145	520	75	132	19	3	35	100	.254	234	7	9	.964
1984—Chicago	Amer.	OF	139	466	67	100	15	0	32	74	.215	226	14	7	.972
1985—Chicago y	Amer.	OF	116	379	51	87	12	0	26	58	.230	88	2	1	.989
1985—Buffalo	A. A.	OF	6	21	3	7	2	0	2	5	.333	2	0	0	1.000
1986—Chi. z-N.Y.	Amer.	OF	116	376	42	82	13	0	21	60	.218	39	3	0	1.000
1987—New York a	Amer.	OF	59	159	21	44	5	0	12	28	.277	4	1	0	1.000
1987—Columbus b	Int.	DH	4	18	3	4	0	0	0	1	.222	0	0	0	.000
1988—Cleveland c	Amer.	DH	75	225	31	58	8	0	18	43	.258	0	0	0	.000
1989—Chicago d	Amer.	1B-OF	51	169	26	51	10	0	11	37	.302	216	12	4	.983
1990—Chi.e-Balt.f	Amer.	1B	105	338	33	78	16	0	18	46	.231	176	6	2	.989
Major League Totals—9 Years			826	2661	349	639	100	3	174	453	.240	986	45	23	.978

Signed as free agent by Los Angeles Dodgers' organization, July 5, 1977.

†On disabled list, April 30 to May 14, 1977.

‡Released, July 7, 1978; signed by Knoxville (Chicago White Sox' organization), September 4, 1978.

§On disabled list, July 27 to August 31, 1980.

xOn disabled list, April 21 to May 10, 1981.

yOn disabled list, July 4 to July 25, 1985; included rehabilitation disability assignment to Buffalo, July 19 to July 25, 1985.

zTraded with Infielder Wayne Tolleson and Catcher Joel Skinner to New York Yankees for Catcher Ron Hassey, Shortstop Carlos Martinez and a player to be named later, July 30, 1986; New York traded Catcher Bill Lindsey to Chicago White Sox' organization to complete deal, December 24, 1986.

aOn disabled list, July 7 to August 16, 1987; included rehabilitation disability assignment to Columbus, August 14 to August 16, 1987.

bReleased, December 21, 1987; signed by Cleveland Indians, February 9, 1988.

cGranted free agency, November 4, 1988; signed by Chicago White Sox, November 26, 1988.

dOn disabled list, June 11, 1989 through remainder of season.
eTraded to Baltimore Orioles for Outfielder Phil Bradley, July 30, 1990.
fGranted free agency, December 15, 1990.

CHAMPIONSHIP SERIES RECORD

Year Club	League	Pos.	G.	AB.	R.	H.	2B.	3B.	HR.	RBI.	B.A.	PO.	A.	E.	F.A.
1983—Chicago	Amer.	OF	3	7	1	2	1	0	0	0	.286	3	0	0	1.000

ALL-STAR GAME RECORD

Year League	Pos.	AB.	R.	H.	2B.	3B.	HR.	RBI.	B.A.	PO.	A.	E.	F.A.
1983—American	OF	2	1	1	0	0	0	0	.500	1	0	0	1.000

JOSEPH CHARLES KLINK
(Joe)

Born February 3, 1962, at Johnstown, Pa.
Height, 5.11. Weight, 175.
Throws and bats lefthanded.
Attended Biscayne College, Miami, Fla.

Major League saves: 1990 (1).
Led Southern League in saves with 26 in 1989.

Year Club	League	G.	IP.	W.	L.	Pct.	H.	R.	ER.	SO.	BB.	ERA.
1983—Columbia	S. Atlantic	12	25⅓	2	2	.500	24	16	13	14	14	4.62
1984—Columbia	S. Atlantic	31	38⅔	5	4	.556	30	19	15	49	28	3.49
1985—Lynchburg†	Carolina	44	51⅔	3	3	.500	41	16	13	59	26	2.26
1986—Orlando	Southern	45	68	4	5	.444	59	24	19	63	37	2.51
1987—Minnesota‡	American	12	23	0	1	.000	37	18	17	17	11	6.65
1987—Portland‡	P. Coast	12	23	0	0	.000	25	14	11	14	13	4.30
1988—Huntsville	Southern	21	34⅔	1	2	.333	25	6	3	30	14	0.78
1988—Tacoma	P. Coast	27	38⅔	2	1	.667	47	29	22	32	17	5.12
1989—Huntsville	Southern	57	60⅔	4	4	.500	46	19	19	59	23	2.82
1989—Tacoma	P. Coast	6	6⅔	0	0	.000	2	0	0	5	2	0.00
1990—Oakland	American	40	39⅔	0	0	.000	34	9	9	19	18	2.04
Major League Totals—2 Years		52	62⅔	0	1	.000	71	27	26	36	29	3.73

Selected by New York Mets' organization in 36th round of free-agent draft, June 6, 1983.
†Traded with Pitcher Bill Latham and Outfielder Billy Beane to Minnesota Twins for Second Baseman Tim Teufel and Outfielder Pat Crosby, January 16, 1986.
‡Traded to Oakland Athletics for a player to be named later, March 31, 1988; Minnesota Twins' organization acquired Pitcher Russ Kibler to complete deal, June 25, 1988.

WORLD SERIES RECORD

Year Club	League	G.	IP.	W.	L.	Pct.	H.	R.	ER.	SO.	BB.	ERA.
1990—Oakland	American	1	0	0	0	.000	0	0	0	0	1	0.00

BRENT BRADLEY KNACKERT

Born August 1, 1969, at Los Angeles, Calif.
Height, 6.03. Weight, 190.
Throws and bats righthanded.

Year Club	League	G.	IP.	W.	L.	Pct.	H.	R.	ER.	SO.	BB.	ERA.
1987—Sarasota White Sox	Gulf Coast	12	72⅔	6	2	.750	55	28	23	60	15	2.85
1988—Tampa	Florida St.	23	142	10	8	.556	132	58	50	78	46	3.17
1989—Sarasota†‡	Florida St.	35	98	8	5	.615	85	41	32	80	35	2.94
1990—Seattle	American	24	37⅓	1	1	.500	50	28	27	28	21	6.51
Major League Totals—1 Year		24	37⅓	1	1	.500	50	28	27	28	21	6.51

Selected by Chicago White Sox' organization in 2nd round of free-agent draft, June 2, 1987.
†Drafted by New York Mets, December 4, 1989.
‡Claimed on waivers by Seattle Mariners, April 5, 1990.

ROBERT WESLEY KNEPPER

Name pronounced NEPP-ur.

(Bob)

Born May 25, 1954, at Akron, O.
Height, 6.02. Weight, 210.
Throws and bats lefthanded.

Shares National League record for fewest assists by pitcher, season, for leader in assists (47), 1986.
Major League saves: 1982 (1).
Led National League in shutouts with 6 in 1978 and tied for lead with 5 in 1986.
Tied for National League lead in hit batsmen with 8 in 1980.
Led California League pitchers in games started with 30 and tied for lead in complete games with 16 in 1974.
Tied for Pacific Coast League lead in shutouts with 3 in 1976.
Named National League Comeback Player of the Year by THE SPORTING NEWS, 1981.

Year Club	League	G.	IP.	W.	L.	Pct.	H.	R.	ER.	SO.	BB.	ERA.
1972—Great Falls	Pioneer	12	68	7	1	.875	53	20	11	75	19	1.46
1973—Decatur	Midwest	11	79	7	2	.778	65	28	17	68	23	1.94
1973—Fresno	California	13	71	2	8	.200	78	54	32	66	35	4.06

Year Club	League	G.	IP.	W.	L.	Pct.	H.	R.	ER.	SO.	BB.	ERA.
1974—Fresno	California	30	*238	*20	5	●.800	*239	103	84	*247	80	3.18
1975—Phoenix	P. Coast	26	155	11	11	.500	169	101	79	94	78	4.59
1976—Phoenix	P. Coast	29	205	14	10	.583	209	105	98	130	64	4.30
1976—San Francisco	National	4	25	1	2	.333	26	9	9	11	7	3.24
1977—Phoenix	P. Coast	10	51	3	6	.333	68	51	42	24	25	7.41
1977—San Francisco	National	27	166	11	9	.550	151	73	62	100	72	3.36
1978—San Francisco	National	36	260	17	11	.607	218	85	76	147	85	2.63
1979—San Francisco	National	34	207	9	12	.429	241	117	107	123	77	4.65
1980—San Francisco†	National	35	215	9	16	.360	242	114	98	103	61	4.10
1981—Houston	National	22	157	9	5	.643	128	41	38	75	38	2.18
1982—Houston	National	33	180	5	15	.250	193	100	89	108	60	4.45
1983—Houston	National	35	203	6	13	.316	202	93	72	125	71	3.19
1984—Houston	National	35	233⅔	15	10	.600	223	93	83	140	55	3.20
1985—Houston	National	37	241	15	13	.536	253	●119	95	131	54	3.55
1986—Houston	National	40	258	17	12	.586	232	100	90	143	62	3.14
1987—Houston	National	33	177⅔	8	*17	.320	226	118	104	76	54	5.27
1988—Houston	National	27	175	14	5	.737	156	70	61	103	67	3.14
1989—Houston‡-San Francisco§	National	35	165	7	12	.368	190	98	94	64	75	5.13
1990—Phoenix	P. Coast	4	24⅔	1	2	.333	21	14	10	13	9	3.65
1990—San Francisco x	National	12	44⅓	3	3	.500	56	28	28	24	19	5.68
Major League Totals—15 Years		445	2707⅔	146	155	.485	2737	1258	1106	1473	857	3.68

Selected by San Francisco Giants' organization in 2nd round of free-agent draft, June 6, 1972.
†Traded with Outfielder Chris Bourjos to Houston Astros for Third Baseman Enos Cabell, December 8, 1980.
‡Released, July 28, 1989; signed by San Francisco Giants, August 4, 1989.
§Granted free agency, November 13, 1989; re-signed by Giants' organization, April 5, 1990.
xReleased, June 26, 1990.

DIVISION SERIES RECORD

Year Club	League	G.	IP.	W.	L.	Pct.	H.	R.	ER.	SO.	BB.	ERA.
1981—Houston	National	1	5	0	1	.000	6	3	3	4	2	5.40

CHAMPIONSHIP SERIES RECORD

Year Club	League	G.	IP.	W.	L.	Pct.	H.	R.	ER.	SO.	BB.	ERA.
1986—Houston	National	2	15⅓	0	0	.000	13	7	6	9	1	3.52

ALL-STAR GAME RECORD

Year League	IP.	W.	L.	Pct.	H.	R.	ER.	SO.	BB.	ERA.
1981—National	2	0	0	.000	1	0	0	3	2	0.00
1988—National	1	0	0	.000	2	1	1	0	1	9.00
All-Star Game Totals—2 Years	3	0	0	.000	3	1	1	3	3	3.00

RANDY DUANE KNORR

Born November 12, 1968, at San Gabriel, Calif.
Height, 6.02. Weight, 205.
Throws and bats righthanded.

Led South Atlantic League catchers in passed balls with 25 and total chances with 960 in 1988.

Year Club	League	Pos.	G.	AB.	R.	H.	2B.	3B.	HR.	RBI.	B.A.	PO.	A.	E.	F.A.
1986—Medicine Hat†	Pion.	1B	55	215	21	58	13	0	4	52	.270	451	29	10	.980
1987—Myrtle Beach	S. Atl.	C-1B-2B	46	129	17	34	4	0	6	21	.264	95	7	1	.990
1987—Medicine Hat	Pion.	C	26	106	21	31	7	0	10	24	.292	70	5	4	.949
1988—Myrtle Beach	S. Atl.	C	117	364	43	85	13	0	9	42	.234	*870	75	15	.984
1989—Dunedin‡	Fla. St.	C	33	122	13	32	6	0	6	22	.262	186	20	2	.990
1990—Knoxville	South.	C	116	392	51	108	12	1	13	64	.276	599	72	15	.978

Selected by Toronto Blue Jays' organization in 10th round of free-agent draft, June 2, 1986.
†On disabled list, June 24 to July 4, 1986.
‡On disabled list, May 10, 1989 through remainder of season.

MARK RICHARD KNUDSON

Name pronounced NOOD-sun.

Born October 28, 1960, at Denver, Colo.
Height, 6.05. Weight, 200.
Throws and bats righthanded.
Attended Colorado State University, Fort Collins, Colo.

Year Club	League	G.	IP.	W.	L.	Pct.	H.	R.	ER.	SO.	BB.	ERA.
1982—Daytona Beach	Florida St.	12	60⅓	2	6	.250	75	35	32	15	23	4.77
1983—Daytona Beach	Florida St.	12	78⅔	5	3	.625	80	29	21	47	22	2.40
1983—Columbus	Southern	13	69⅔	4	5	.444	82	40	33	28	21	4.26
1984—Columbus	Southern	14	101	4	5	.444	100	32	25	54	27	2.23
1984—Tucson	P. Coast	13	84	4	6	.400	93	41	34	42	20	3.64
1985—Tucson	P. Coast	24	146	8	5	.615	171	69	65	68	37	4.01
1985—Houston†	National	2	11	0	2	.000	21	11	11	4	3	9.00
1986—Tucson‡-Vancouver	P. Coast	17	106⅔	6	6	.500	124	54	49	63	26	4.13
1986—Houston	National	9	42⅔	1	5	.167	48	23	20	20	15	4.22
1986—Milwaukee	American	4	17⅔	0	1	.000	22	15	15	9	5	7.64
1987—Denver	Am. Assoc.	14	78⅓	7	2	.778	89	53	51	37	30	5.86
1987—Milwaukee	American	15	62	4	4	.500	88	46	37	26	14	5.37

Year Club	League	G.	IP.	W.	L.	Pct.	H.	R.	ER.	SO.	BB.	ERA.
1988—Denver	Am. Assoc.	24	164⅓	11	8	.579	180	67	62	66	33	3.40
1988—Milwaukee	American	5	16	0	0	.000	17	3	2	7	2	1.13
1989—Milwaukee	American	40	123⅔	8	5	.615	110	50	46	47	29	3.35
1990—Milwaukee	American	30	168⅓	10	9	.526	187	84	77	56	40	4.12
National League Totals—2 Years		11	53⅔	1	7	.167	69	34	31	24	18	5.20
American League Totals—5 Years		94	387⅔	22	19	.537	424	198	177	145	90	4.11
Major League Totals—6 Years		105	441⅓	23	26	.469	493	232	208	169	108	4.24

Selected by Houston Astros' organization in 3rd round of free-agent draft, June 7, 1982.

†On disabled list, July 15 to August 5, 1985.

‡Traded to Milwaukee Brewers' organization, August 21, 1986, completing deal in which Milwaukee traded Pitcher Danny Darwin to Houston Astros for Pitcher Don August and a player to be named later, August 15, 1986.

BRAD LYNN KOMMINSK

Name pronounced KOMM-insk.

Born April 4, 1961, at Lima, O.
Height, 6.02. Weight, 205.
Throws and bats righthanded.

Major League stolen bases: 1984 (18), 1985 (10), 1987 (1), 1989 (8), 1990 (1). Total—38.
Led American Association batters in strikeouts with 127 in 1987.
Led International League batters in strikeouts with 124 in 1986.
Led International League in slugging percentage with .596 and tied for lead in game-winning RBIs with 14 in 1983.
Led Carolina League in total bases with 278 and grounding into double plays with 24 in 1981.
Led Appalachian League batters in strikeouts with 74 and stolen bases with 20 in 1979.
Led International League third basemen in errors with 28 in 1986.
Named Carolina League Most Valuable Player, 1981.
Received reported $72,000 bonus to sign with Atlanta Braves, 1979.

Year Club	League	Pos.	G.	AB.	R.	H.	2B.	3B.	HR.	RBI.	B.A.	PO.	A.	E.	F.A.
1979—Kingsport	Appal.	OF	59	185	37	41	9	1	7	34	.222	112	1	2	.983
1980—Anderson	S. Atl.	OF	121	425	86	111	17	5	20	67	.261	217	5	12	.949
1981—Durham	Carol.	OF	132	459	108	●148	27	2	33	★104	★.322	154	7	10	.942
1982—Savannah	South.	OF	133	454	88	124	18	7	26	78	.273	158	6	10	.943
1982—Richmond	Int.	OF	5	17	4	6	1	0	2	5	.353	10	0	0	1.000
1983—Richmond	Int.	OF	117	413	94	138	24	6	24	103	.334	179	4	3	.984
1983—Atlanta	Nat.	OF	19	36	2	8	2	0	0	4	.222	16	1	1	.944
1984—Richmond	Int.	OF	42	144	23	37	11	3	5	28	.257	66	4	3	.959
1984—Atlanta	Nat.	OF	90	301	37	61	10	0	8	36	.203	135	2	1	.993
1985—Atlanta	Nat.	OF	106	300	52	68	12	3	4	21	.227	161	2	7	.959
1986—Richmond	Int.	3B-OF-1B	133	465	67	109	22	4	13	65	.234	127	200	30	.916
1986—Atlanta†	Nat.	3B-OF	5	5	1	2	0	0	0	1	.400	1	2	0	1.000
1987—Denver	A. A.	OF	135	494	110	147	31	4	★32	95	.298	269	16	5	.983
1987—Milwaukee	Amer.	OF	7	15	0	1	0	0	0	0	.067	10	0	0	1.000
1988—Denver‡	A. A.	OF	105	348	55	83	18	3	16	57	.239	210	6	4	.982
1989—Colorado Springs§	P. C.	OF	54	190	30	55	17	0	9	34	.289	119	0	1	.992
1989—Cleveland x	Amer.	OF	71	198	27	47	8	2	8	33	.237	181	3	1	.995
1990—San Francisco y	Nat.	OF	8	5	2	1	0	0	0	0	.200	3	0	0	1.000
1990—Baltimore	Amer.	OF	46	101	18	24	4	0	3	8	.238	67	2	0	1.000
1990—Rochester	Int.	OF	28	79	7	23	2	0	1	8	.291	38	2	2	.952
American League Totals—3 Years			124	314	45	72	12	2	11	41	.229	258	5	1	.996
National League Totals—5 Years			228	647	94	140	24	3	12	92	.216	316	7	9	.973
Major League Totals—7 Years			352	961	139	212	36	5	23	133	.221	574	12	10	.983

Selected by Atlanta Braves' organization in 1st round (fourth player selected) of free-agent draft, June 5, 1979.

†Traded to Milwaukee Brewers for Outfielder Dion James, January 20, 1987.

‡Granted free agency, October 15, 1988; signed by Colorado Springs (Cleveland Indians' organization), December 21, 1988.

§On Cleveland disabled list, April 9 to May 4, 1989.

xClaimed on waivers by San Francisco Giants, April 5, 1990.

yClaimed on waivers by Baltimore Orioles, May 2, 1990.

JOSEPH WAYNE KRAEMER
(Joe)

Born September 10, 1964, at Olympia, Wash.
Height, 6.02. Weight, 185.
Throws and bats lefthanded.
Attended Lower Columbia College, Longview, Wash.,
and Portland State University, Portland, Ore.

Year Club	League	G.	IP.	W.	L.	Pct.	H.	R.	ER.	SO.	BB.	ERA.
1985—Wytheville	Ap'lachian	22	45⅔	4	2	.667	33	21	17	52	36	3.35
1986—Peoria	Midwest	45	66⅓	6	3	.667	50	17	8	78	12	1.09
1987—Winston-Salem	Carolina	41	52⅔	3	2	.600	49	20	16	43	41	2.73
1987—Iowa	Am. Assoc.	5	2⅔	1	0	1.000	8	8	8	2	5	27.00
1988—Iowa	Am. Assoc.	20	26	3	3	.500	19	14	13	26	17	4.50
1988—Pittsfield	Eastern	15	95	5	5	.500	84	37	29	47	43	2.75
1989—Iowa	Am. Assoc.	27	181⅔	8	10	.444	180	81	70	113	50	3.47
1989—Chicago	National	1	3⅔	0	1	.000	7	6	2	5	2	4.91
1990—Chicago	National	18	25	0	0	.000	31	25	20	16	14	7.20
1990—Iowa	Am. Assoc.	20	122	7	6	.538	113	56	51	84	40	3.76
Major League Totals—2 Years		19	28⅔	0	1	.000	38	31	22	21	16	6.91

Selected by New York Mets' organization in 2nd round of free-agent draft, January 11, 1983.
Selected by Seattle Mariners' organization in 6th round of free-agent draft, January 17, 1984.
Selected by Chicago Cubs' organization in 16th round of free-agent draft, June 3, 1985.

RANDALL JOHN KRAMER
(Randy)

Born September 20, 1960, at Palo Alto, Calif.
Height, 6.02. Weight, 180.
Throws and bats righthanded.
Attended San Jose City College, San Jose, Calif.

Major League saves: 1989 (2).
Tied for Northwest League lead in games started by pitchers with 15 and wild pitches with 13 in 1984.

Year Club	League	G.	IP.	W.	L.	Pct.	H.	R.	ER.	SO.	BB.	ERA.
1982—Sarasota Rangers	Gulf Coast	2	2⅔	0	0	.000	2	0	0	0	0	0.00
1983—Burlington	Midwest	26	132⅔	6	8	.429	131	97	76	113	92	5.16
1984—Salem	Carolina	12	53	2	8	.200	63	66	58	35	34	9.85
1984—Tri-Cities	Northwest	15	84	5	6	.455	83	62	47	74	∗58	5.04
1985—Salem	Carolina	25	115⅓	7	11	.389	143	∗99	∗86	86	77	6.71
1986—Kinston†-Salem	Carolina	25	43⅓	3	3	.500	43	26	23	38	28	4.78
1986—Tulsa‡	Texas	26	39	0	3	.000	40	22	19	32	19	4.38
1987—Harrisburg	Eastern	26	49⅔	4	5	.444	62	43	35	43	29	6.34
1987—Vancouver	P. Coast	11	17⅔	0	0	.000	16	14	12	16	19	6.11
1988—Buffalo	Am. Assoc.	28	∗198⅓	10	8	.556	161	85	69	120	50	3.13
1988—Pittsburgh	National	5	10	1	2	.333	12	6	6	7	1	5.40
1989—Buffalo	Am. Assoc.	5	14⅓	1	0	1.000	15	5	2	8	7	1.26
1989—Pittsburgh	National	35	111⅓	5	9	.357	90	53	49	52	61	3.96
1990—Pittsburgh§-Chicago	National	22	46	0	3	.000	47	25	23	27	21	4.50
1990—Buffalo x	Am. Assoc.	18	73⅔	6	1	.857	55	29	21	58	33	2.57
Major League Totals—3 Years		62	167⅓	6	14	.300	149	84	78	86	83	4.20

Selected by San Diego Padres' organization in 26th round of free-agent draft, June 6, 1978.
Selected by Houston Astros' organization in 2nd round of free-agent draft, January 12, 1982.
Selected by Texas Rangers' organization in secondary phase of free-agent draft, June 7, 1982.
†Loaned to Kinston (Independent), April 2, 1986; returned, May 20, 1986.
‡Traded to Pittsburgh Pirates for Pitcher Jeff Zaske, September 30, 1986.
§Traded to Chicago Cubs for Pitcher Greg Kallevig, September 3, 1990.
xReleased, December 17, 1990.

THOMAS JOSEPH KRAMER
(Tom)

Born January 9, 1968, at Cincinnati, O.
Height, 6.00. Weight, 185.
Throws right and bats left and righthanded.
Attended John A. Logan College, Carterville, Ill.

Led Midwest League in complete games with 10 in 1988.

Year Club	League	G.	IP.	W.	L.	Pct.	H.	R.	ER.	SO.	BB.	ERA.
1987—Burlington	Ap'lachian	12	71⅔	7	3	.700	57	31	24	71	26	3.01
1988—Waterloo	Midwest	27	∗198⅔	14	7	.667	173	70	56	152	60	2.54
1989—Kinston	Carolina	18	131⅔	9	5	.643	97	44	38	89	44	2.60
1989—Canton-Akron	Eastern	10	43⅓	1	6	.143	58	34	30	26	20	6.23
1990—Kinston	Carolina	16	98	7	4	.636	82	34	31	96	29	2.85
1990—Canton-Akron	Eastern	12	72	6	3	.667	67	25	24	46	14	3.00

Selected by Cleveland Indians' organization in 5th round of free-agent draft, June 2, 1987.

JAMES EDWARD KREMERS
(Jimmy)

Born October 8, 1965, at Little Rock, Ark.
Height, 6.03. Weight, 205.
Throws right and bats lefthanded.
Attended University of Arkansas, Fayetteville, Ark.

Led Southern League catchers in total chances with 743 and passed balls with 19 in 1989.

Year Club	League	Pos.	G.	AB.	R.	H.	2B.	3B.	HR.	RBI.	B.A.	PO.	A.	E.	F.A.
1988—Sumter	S. Atl.	C	72	256	30	68	12	3	5	42	.266	51	13	0	1.000
1989—Greenville	South.	C	121	388	41	91	19	1	16	58	.235	∗649	∗86	8	.989
1990—Richmond	Int.	C-1B	63	190	25	44	8	0	6	24	.232	309	40	4	.989
1990—Atlanta	Nat.	C	29	73	7	8	1	1	1	2	.110	107	10	1	.992
Major League Totals—1 Year			29	73	7	8	1	1	1	2	.110	107	10	1	.992

Selected by Cincinnati Reds' organization in 8th round of free-agent draft, June 2, 1987.
Selected by Atlanta Braves' organization in 2nd round of free-agent draft, June 1, 1988.

—DID YOU KNOW—

That Los Angeles pitchers hurled the most complete games (29) in the majors in 1990 while Toronto pitched the fewest (six)?

CHAD MICHAEL KREUTER

Name pronounced CREWT-ur.

Born August 26, 1964, in Marin County, Calif.
Height, 6.02. Weight, 190.
Throws and bats righthanded.
Attended Pepperdine University, Malibu, Calif.

Shares major league record for most hits, inning, first major league game (2), September 14, 1988, fifth inning.
Led American League in passed balls with 21 in 1989.
Tied for Texas League lead in double plays by catchers with 9 in 1988.
Led Carolina League catchers in double plays with 17 and tied for lead in assists with 113 in 1986.

Year Club	League	Pos.	G.	AB.	R.	H.	2B.	3B.	HR.	RBI.	B.A.	PO.	A.	E.	F.A.
1985—Burlington	Midw.	C	69	199	25	53	9	0	4	26	.266	349	34	8	.980
1986—Salem	Carol.	C-OF-3B	125	387	55	85	21	2	6	49	.220	613	115	★21	.972
1987—Charlotte	Fla. St.	C-OF-3B	85	281	36	61	18	1	9	40	.217	380	54	8	.982
1988—Tulsa†	Texas	C	108	358	46	95	24	6	3	51	.265	603	71	●13	.981
1988—Texas†	Amer.	C	16	51	3	14	2	1	1	5	.275	93	8	1	.990
1989—Texas†	Amer.	C	87	158	16	24	3	0	5	9	.152	453	26	4	.992
1989—Oklahoma City†	A. A.	C	26	87	10	22	3	0	0	6	.253	146	14	2	.988
1990—Texas	Amer.	C	22	22	2	1	1	0	0	2	.045	39	4	1	.977
1990—Oklahoma City	A. A.	C	92	291	41	65	17	1	7	35	.223	559	64	10	.984
Major League Totals—3 Years			125	231	21	39	6	1	6	16	.169	585	38	6	.990

Selected by Texas Rangers' organization in 5th round of free-agent draft, June 3, 1985.
†Switch-hitter.

WILLIAM CULP KRUEGER

Name pronounced CREW-ger.

(Bill)

Born April 24, 1958, at Waukegan, Ill.
Height, 6.05. Weight, 205.
Throws and bats lefthanded.
Received bachelor of arts degree in business administration from
University of Portland, Portland, Ore. in 1979.

Pitched seven-inning 2-0 no-hit victory against Phoenix, August 14, 1987 (second game).
Major League saves: 1986 (1), 1989 (3). Total—4.
Led Pacific Coast League in shutouts with 4 in 1988.
Tied for Eastern League lead in games started by pitchers with 27 and shutouts with 3 in 1982.

Year Club	League	G.	IP.	W.	L.	Pct.	H.	R.	ER.	SO.	BB.	ERA.
1980—Medford	Northwest	9	44	0	4	.000	54	38	25	48	29	5.11
1981—Modesto	California	16	98	3	5	.375	87	49	40	76	52	3.67
1981—West Haven	Eastern	11	68	3	6	.333	74	36	27	36	31	3.57
1982—West Haven	Eastern	28	181	15	9	.625	160	69	57	163	81	2.83
1983—Oakland†	American	17	109⅔	7	6	.538	104	54	44	58	53	3.61
1984—Tacoma	P. Coast	5	31⅔	2	2	.500	29	17	13	20	21	3.69
1984—Oakland	American	26	142	10	10	.500	156	95	75	61	85	4.75
1985—Oakland	American	32	151⅓	9	10	.474	165	95	76	56	69	4.52
1985—Tacoma	P. Coast	2	9⅔	0	1	.000	12	10	10	10	6	9.31
1986—Oakland‡	American	11	34⅓	1	2	.333	40	25	23	10	13	6.03
1986—Madison	Midwest	1	2	0	0	.000	1	0	0	1	1	0.00
1986—Tacoma	P. Coast	8	52⅓	3	3	.500	53	32	27	41	27	4.64
1987—Oakland	American	9	5⅔	0	3	.000	9	7	6	2	8	9.53
1987—Tacoma§-Albuquerque	P. Coast	24	146⅓	9	7	.563	158	74	66	97	66	4.06
1987—Los Angeles x	National	2	2⅓	0	0	.000	3	2	0	2	1	0.00
1988—Albuquerque	P. Coast	27	173⅓	★15	5	.750	167	74	58	114	69	★3.01
1988—Los Angeles yz	National	1	2⅓	0	0	.000	4	3	3	1	2	11.57
1989—Denver	Am. Assoc.	2	13⅓	1	1	.500	10	4	3	9	6	2.03
1989—Milwaukee	American	34	93⅔	3	2	.600	96	43	40	72	33	3.84
1990—Milwaukee a	American	30	129	6	8	.429	137	70	57	64	54	3.98
1990—Beloit b	Midwest	1	6	1	0	1.000	4	1	1	4	0	1.50
American League Totals—7 Years			159	665⅔	36	41	.468	707	389	321	323	315	4.34
National League Totals—2 Years			3	4⅔	0	0	.000	7	5	3	3	3	5.79
Major League Totals—8 Years			162	670⅓	36	41	.468	714	394	324	326	318	4.35

Signed as free agent by Oakland A's organization, July 12, 1980.
†On disabled list, August 5, 1983 through remainder of season.
‡On disabled list, May 6 to August 8, 1986; included rehabilitation disability assignment to Madison, July 4 to July 8, and Tacoma, July 10 to July 18 and July 21 to July 27, 1986.
§Traded to Los Angeles Dodgers' organization for Pitcher Tim Meeks, June 23, 1987.
xReleased, November 12, 1987; re-signed by Dodgers' organization, January 1, 1988.
yTraded to Pittsburgh Pirates for Pitcher Jim Neidlinger, October 3, 1988.
zReleased, March 28, 1989; signed by Denver (Milwaukee Brewers' organization), April 7, 1989.
aOn disabled list, August 10 to August 31, 1990; included rehabilitation disability assignment to Beloit, August 29 to August 31, 1990.
bGranted free agency, November 5, 1990; signed by Seattle Mariners, December 19, 1990.

—DID YOU KNOW—
That the Yankees' 67-95 record last season was their worst since 1913?

JOHN MARTIN KRUK

Born February 9, 1961, at Charleston, W. Va.
Height, 5.10. Weight, 204.
Throws and bats lefthanded.
Attended Allegany Community College, Cumberland, Md.

Major League stolen bases: 1986 (2), 1987 (18), 1988 (5), 1989 (3), 1990 (10). Total—38.
Led Texas League in sacrifice flies with 13 in 1983.
Led Pacific Coast League outfielders in double plays with 4 in 1984.

Year	Club	League	Pos.	G.	AB.	R.	H.	2B.	3B.	HR.	RBI.	B.A.	PO.	A.	E.	F.A.
1981—Walla Walla	N'west	OF-1B	63	157	31	38	10	0	1	13	.242	108	5	2	.983
1982—Reno	Calif.	OF-1B	125	441	82	137	30	8	11	92	.311	253	11	7	.974
1983—Beaumont	Texas	OF-1B-P	133	498	94	170	41	9	10	88	.341	304	22	8	.976
1984—Las Vegas	P. C.	OF	115	340	56	111	25	6	11	57	.326	183	7	2	.990
1985—Las Vegas	P. C.	OF-1B	123	422	61	148	29	4	7	59	★.351	356	18	7	.982
1986—San Diego	Nat.	OF-1B	122	278	33	86	16	2	4	38	.309	139	6	3	.980
1986—Las Vegas	P. C.	OF-1B	6	28	6	13	3	1	0	9	.464	22	1	0	1.000
1987—San Diego	Nat.	1B-OF	138	447	72	140	14	2	20	91	.313	911	78	5	.995
1988—San Diego	Nat.	1B-OF	120	378	54	91	17	1	9	44	.241	634	37	3	.996
1989—S.D.†‡-Phi.§	Nat.	OF-1B	112	357	53	107	13	6	8	44	.300	212	9	4	.982
1990—Philadelphia	Nat.	OF-1B	142	443	52	129	25	8	7	67	.291	543	45	4	.993
Major League Totals—5 Years			634	1903	264	553	85	19	48	284	.291	2439	175	19	.993

Selected by Pittsburgh Pirates' organization in 3rd round of free-agent draft, January 13, 1981.
Selected by San Diego Padres' organization in secondary phase of free-agent draft, June 8, 1981.
†On disabled list, May 5 to May 21, 1989.
‡Traded with Infielder Randy Ready to Philadelphia Phillies for Outfielder Chris James, June 2, 1989.
§On disabled list, July 3 to July 28, 1989.

PITCHING RECORD

Year	Club	League	G.	IP.	W.	L.	Pct.	H.	R.	ER.	SO.	BB.	ERA.
1983—Beaumont	Texas	3	5	0	0	.000	5	0	0	3	2	0.00

JEFFREY WILLIAM KUNKEL
(Jeff)

Born March 25, 1962, at West Palm Beach, Fla.
Height, 6.02. Weight, 180.
Throws and bats righthanded.
Attended Rider College, Lawrenceville, N.J.

Son of Bill Kunkel, pitcher with Kansas City A's and New York Yankees, 1961 through 1963; umpire, Florida
State League, 1966; Southern League, 1967 and 1968; and American League umpire, 1968 through 1984.
Major League stolen bases: 1984 (4), 1989 (3), 1990 (2). Total—9.
Named shortstop on THE SPORTING NEWS College Baseball All-America Team, 1983.

Year	Club	League	Pos.	G.	AB.	R.	H.	2B.	3B.	HR.	RBI.	B.A.	PO.	A.	E.	F.A.
1983—Burlington	Midw.	SS	31	122	22	35	7	1	6	18	.287	38	88	13	.906
1983—Tulsa	Texas	SS-2B	37	130	21	37	14	0	5	25	.285	68	106	9	.951
1984—Tulsa†	Texas	SS	47	177	30	56	16	1	4	22	.316	64	103	16	.913
1984—Texas	Amer.	SS	50	142	13	29	2	3	3	7	.204	81	120	17	.922
1985—Oklahoma City	A. A.	SS-OF	99	370	40	72	8	6	5	43	.195	152	308	26	.947
1985—Texas	Amer.	SS	2	4	1	1	0	0	0	0	.250	2	5	0	1.000
1986—Oklahoma City	A. A.	SS	55	111	409	50	100	16	4	11	51	.244	135	272	19	.955
1986—Texas	Amer.	SS	8	13	3	3	0	0	1	2	.231	4	6	3	.769
1987—Oklahoma City‡	A. A.	S-O-2-3	58	193	31	49	9	3	9	34	.254	65	100	5	.971
1987—Texas	Amer.	2-3-O-1-S	15	32	1	7	0	0	1	2	.219	19	27	3	.939
1988—Oklahoma City	A. A.	SS-OF	56	203	28	44	11	4	5	21	.217	68	151	7	.969
1988—Texas	Amer.	2-S-3-O-P	55	154	14	35	8	3	2	15	.227	78	119	8	.961
1989—Texas	Amer.	S-O-2-3-P	108	293	39	79	21	2	8	29	.270	143	168	22	.934
1990—Texas§	Amer.	S-3-2-O	99	200	17	34	11	1	3	17	.170	101	172	11	.961
1990—Oklahoma City	A. A.	SS-3B	4	19	0	8	1	0	0	3	.421	7	11	0	1.000
Major League Totals—7 Years			337	838	88	188	42	9	18	72	.224	428	617	64	.942

Selected by Texas Rangers' organization in 1st round (third player selected) of free-agent draft, June 6, 1983.
†On disabled list, April 10 to May 12 and May 17 to June 4, 1984.
‡On Texas disabled list, March 25 to May 6, 1987; included rehabilitation disability assignment to Oklahoma City,
April 17 to May 6, 1987.
§On disabled list, June 24 to July 26, 1990; included rehabilitation disability assignment to Oklahoma City, July 12 to
July 20, 1990.

PITCHING RECORD

Year	Club	League	G.	IP.	W.	L.	Pct.	H.	R.	ER.	SO.	BB.	ERA.
1988—Texas	American	1	1	0	0	.000	0	0	0	1	0	0.00
1989—Texas	American	1	1⅔	0	0	.000	4	4	4	0	3	21.60
Major League Totals—2 Years		2	2⅔	0	0	.000	4	4	4	1	3	13.50

RANDY SCOTT KUTCHER

Born April 20, 1960, at Anchorage, Alaska.
Height, 5.11. Weight, 175.
Throws and bats righthanded.

Major League stolen bases: 1986 (6), 1987 (1), 1989 (3), 1990 (3). Total—13.
Led International League third basemen in errors with 21 in 1988.

Year—Club	League	Pos.	G.	AB.	R.	H.	2B.	3B.	HR.	RBI.	B.A.	PO.	A.	E.	F.A.
1979—Great Falls	Pion.	SS	65	245	55	62	8	2	2	25	.253	79	109	29	.866
1980—Clinton	Midw.	SS-3B	138	525	72	133	17	•8	3	46	.253	204	365	39	.936
1981—Fresno	Calif.	S-O-2-3	41	161	28	44	10	2	3	26	.273	66	80	18	.890
1981—Shreveport	Texas	SS	77	249	36	71	13	4	4	20	.285	112	212	18	.947
1982—Shreveport	Texas	SS-OF	116	397	56	98	18	2	3	31	.247	183	142	18	.948
1983—Phoenix	P. C.	S-O-2-3-C	104	275	45	75	11	4	3	45	.273	152	138	15	.951
1984—Phoenix	P. C.	O-S-3-2-C	103	336	37	93	17	3	2	31	.277	177	80	11	.959
1985—Phoenix†	P. C.	OF-2B	97	228	36	54	15	2	1	20	.237	143	9	4	.974
1986—Phoenix	P. C.	S-O-2-3-C	55	208	47	72	14	4	11	39	.346	93	89	16	.919
1986—San Francisco	Nat.	O-S-3-2	71	186	28	44	9	1	7	16	.237	111	11	1	.992
1987—Phoenix	P. C.	O-3-2-S-1	92	349	68	89	15	5	6	53	.255	153	116	15	.947
1987—San Francisco‡	Nat.	O-2-3-S	14	16	7	3	1	1	0	1	.188	14	5	0	1.000
1988—Pawtucket	Int.	3B-OF-2B	86	331	40	77	12	2	4	27	.233	73	138	22	.906
1988—Boston	Amer.	OF-3B	19	12	2	2	1	0	0	0	.167	6	5	1	.917
1989—Boston§	Amer.	OF-3B-C	77	160	28	36	10	3	2	18	.225	112	8	3	.976
1990—Boston	Amer.	OF-3B-2B	63	74	18	17	4	1	1	5	.230	55	26	0	1.000
1990—Pawtucket	Int.	SS-3B	35	136	18	43	8	1	1	14	.316	57	97	7	.957
National League Totals—2 Years			85	202	35	47	10	2	7	17	.233	125	16	1	.993
American League Totals—3 Years			159	246	48	55	15	4	3	23	.224	173	39	4	.981
Major League Totals—5 Years			244	448	83	102	25	6	10	40	.228	298	55	5	.986

Selected by San Francisco Giants' organization in 4th round of free-agent draft, June 5, 1979.

†Granted free agency, October 15, 1985; re-signed by Giants, February 3, 1986.

‡Traded to Boston Red Sox, December 9, 1987, completing deal in which Boston traded Outfielder Dave Henderson to San Francisco Giants for a player to be named later, September 1, 1987.

§On disabled list, August 28 to September 12, 1989.

CHAMPIONSHIP SERIES RECORD

Year—Club	League	Pos.	G.	AB.	R.	H.	2B.	3B.	HR.	RBI.	B.A.	PO.	A.	E.	F.A.
1990—Boston	Amer.	PR	2	0	0	0	0	0	0	0	.000	0	0	0	.000

JERRY SCOTT KUTZLER

Born March 25, 1965, at Waukegan, Ill.
Height, 6.01. Weight, 175.
Throws right and bats lefthanded.
Attended William Penn College, Oskaloosa, Ia.

Led Florida State League pitchers in complete games with 12 in 1988.
Named Florida State League Pitcher of the Year, 1988.

Year—Club	League	G.	IP.	W.	L.	Pct.	H.	R.	ER.	SO.	BB.	ERA.
1987—Sarasota White Sox	Gulf Coast	4	20	1	1	.500	14	13	11	16	7	4.95
1987—Peninsula	Carolina	10	63⅔	5	2	.714	53	34	29	30	24	4.10
1988—Tampa	Florida St.	26	184	∗16	7	.696	154	73	57	100	39	2.79
1989—Birmingham	Southern	14	99⅓	9	4	.692	95	50	40	85	27	3.62
1989—Vancouver	P. Coast	12	80	5	5	.500	76	37	34	36	20	3.83
1990—Vancouver	P. Coast	19	113⅔	5	7	.417	124	64	53	73	34	4.20
1990—Chicago	American	7	31⅓	2	1	.667	38	23	21	21	14	6.03
Major League Totals—1 Year		7	31⅓	2	1	.667	38	23	21	21	14	6.03

Selected by Chicago White Sox' organization in 6th round of free-agent draft, June 2, 1987.

MICHAEL JAMES LaCOSS
(Mike)

Born May 30, 1956, at Glendale, Calif.
Height, 6.04. Weight, 200.
Throws and bats righthanded.

Major League saves: 1981 (1), 1983 (1), 1984 (3), 1985 (1), 1989 (6). Total—12.
Tied for American Association lead in shutouts with 3 in 1978.

Year—Club	League	G.	IP.	W.	L.	Pct.	H.	R.	ER.	SO.	BB.	ERA.
1974—Billings	Pioneer	13	87	6	5	.545	81	40	27	58	38	2.79
1975—Tampa	Florida St.	23	151	4	7	.412	131	61	48	72	41	2.86
1976—Three Rivers	Eastern	25	162	12	10	.545	148	66	53	80	53	2.94
1977—Indianapolis	Am. Assoc.	27	186	11	∗13	.458	181	93	80	104	65	3.87
1978—Indianapolis	Am. Assoc.	19	130	11	5	.688	129	62	50	67	49	3.46
1978—Cincinnati	National	16	96	4	8	.333	104	56	48	31	46	4.50
1979—Cincinnati	National	35	206	14	8	.636	202	92	80	73	79	3.50
1980—Cincinnati	National	34	169	10	12	.455	207	101	87	59	68	4.63
1981—Cincinnati†	National	20	78	4	7	.364	102	55	53	22	30	6.12
1982—Houston	National	41	115	6	6	.500	107	41	37	51	54	2.90
1983—Houston‡	National	38	138	5	7	.417	142	81	68	53	56	4.43
1984—Houston§	National	39	132	7	5	.583	132	64	59	86	55	4.02
1985—Kansas City	American	21	40⅔	1	1	.500	49	25	23	26	29	5.09
1985—Omaha x	Am. Assoc.	4	22⅓	1	2	.333	23	12	8	11	15	3.22
1986—San Francisco y	National	37	204⅓	10	13	.435	179	99	81	86	70	3.57
1987—San Francisco z	National	39	171	13	10	.565	184	78	70	79	63	3.68
1988—San Francisco a	National	19	114⅓	7	7	.500	99	55	46	70	47	3.62
1989—San Francisco	National	45	150⅓	10	10	.500	143	62	53	78	65	3.17
1990—San Francisco b	National	13	77⅔	6	4	.600	75	37	34	39	39	3.94

Year Club	League	G.	IP.	W.	L.	Pct.	H.	R.	ER.	SO.	BB.	ERA.
1990—San Jose c...............................	California	1	6	1	0	1.000	5	1	1	6	0	1.50
National League Totals—12 Years......................		376	1651⅔	96	97	.497	1676	821	716	727	672	3.90
American League Totals—1 Year		21	40⅔	1	1	.500	49	25	23	26	29	5.09
Major League Totals—13 Years.........................		397	1692⅓	97	98	.497	1725	846	739	753	701	3.93

Selected by Cincinnati Reds' organization in 3rd round of free-agent draft, June 5, 1974.

†Sold on waivers to Houston Astros, April 4, 1982.

‡On disabled list, June 17 to July 8, 1983.

§Granted free agency, November 8, 1984; signed by Kansas City Royals' organization, February 19, 1985.

xReleased, November 6, 1985; signed by San Francisco Giants' organization, February 3, 1986.

yGranted free agency, November 12, 1986; re-signed by Giants, December 12, 1986.

zGranted free agency, November 9, 1987; re-signed by Giants, November 24, 1987.

aOn disabled list, July 17 to September 8, 1988.

bOn disabled list, May 3 to August 9, 1990; included rehabilitation disability assignment to San Jose, August 5 to August 9, 1990.

cGranted free agency, December 7, 1990.

CHAMPIONSHIP SERIES RECORD

Year Club	League	G.	IP.	W.	L.	Pct.	H.	R.	ER.	SO.	BB.	ERA.
1979—Cincinnati	National	1	1⅔	0	1	.000	1	2	2	0	4	10.80
1987—San Francisco	National	2	3⅓	0	0	.000	1	0	0	2	3	0.00
1989—San Francisco	National	1	3	0	0	.000	7	3	3	2	0	9.00
Championship Series Totals—3 Years................		4	8	0	1	.000	9	5	5	4	7	5.63

WORLD SERIES RECORD

Year Club	League	G.	IP.	W.	L.	Pct.	H.	R.	ER.	SO.	BB.	ERA.
1989—San Francisco	National	2	4⅓	0	0	.000	4	3	3	2	3	6.23

ALL-STAR GAME RECORD

Year League	IP.	W.	L.	Pct.	H.	R.	ER.	SO.	BB.	ERA.
1979—National	1⅓	0	0	.000	1	0	0	0	0	0.00

MICHAEL RUSSELL LAGA
(Mike)

Born June 14, 1960, at Ridgewood, N. J.
Height, 6.02. Weight, 210.
Throws and bats lefthanded.
Attended Bergen Community College, Paramus, N. J.,
and Fairleigh Dickinson University, Teaneck, N. J.

Major League stolen bases: 1982 (1).

Led American Association in intentional bases on balls received with 12 in 1987.

Led American Association in sacrifice flies with 7 in 1985.

Led American Association in being hit by pitch with 13 in 1982.

Led American Association first basemen in double plays with 101 in 1985.

Led American Association first basemen in total chances with 1,221 in 1982 and 1,146 in 1985.

Year Club	League	Pos.	G.	AB.	R.	H.	2B.	3B.	HR.	RBI.	B.A.	PO.	A.	E.	F.A.
1980—Lakeland................	Fla. St.	1B	122	407	60	111	14	6	12	74	.273	1025	84	★18	.984
1981—Birmingham	South.	1B	142	547	89	158	28	7	31	86	.289	1193	★105	★23	.983
1982—Evansville	A. A.	1B	126	444	77	111	15	3	34	90	.250	★1135	68	18	.985
1982—Detroit....................	Amer.	1B	27	88	6	23	9	0	3	11	.261	163	4	1	.994
1983—Evansville	A. A.	1B	105	355	46	82	24	1	16	58	.231	835	62	★11	.988
1983—Detroit....................	Amer.	1B	12	21	2	4	0	0	0	2	.190	9	1	0	1.000
1984—Evansville	A. A.	1B	●153	569	86	151	30	9	30	94	.265	1008	92	14	.987
1984—Detroit....................	Amer.	1B	9	11	1	6	0	0	0	1	.545	12	1	0	1.000
1985—Nashville................	A. A.	1B	117	430	58	113	30	2	20	79	.263	★1024	★111	11	.990
1985—Detroit....................	Amer.	1B	9	36	3	6	1	0	2	6	.167	33	5	1	.974
1986—Detroit†..................	Amer.	1B	15	45	6	9	1	0	3	8	.200	98	7	0	1.000
1986—Nashville................	A. A.	1B	12	41	4	9	3	0	2	7	.220	109	16	2	.984
1986—St. Louis‡..............	Nat.	1B	18	46	7	10	4	0	3	8	.217	109	14	0	1.000
1987—St. Louis................	Nat.	1B	17	29	4	4	1	0	1	4	.138	66	7	2	.973
1987—Louisville	A. A.	1B	116	418	80	127	35	2	29	91	.304	922	67	11	.989
1988—Louisville§	A. A.	1B	13	49	4	10	2	0	1	5	.204	74	3	1	.987
1988—St. Louis x..............	Nat.	1B	41	100	5	13	0	0	1	4	.130	293	17	0	1.000
1989—Phoenix	P. C.	1B	126	449	55	108	20	9	23	68	.241	1064	93	6	.995
1989—San Francisco	Nat.	1B	17	20	1	4	1	0	1	7	.200	16	1	0	1.000
1990—San Francisco	Nat.	1B	23	27	4	5	1	0	2	4	.185	33	5	0	1.000
1990—Phoenix y	P. C.	1B	89	309	63	92	18	3	22	71	.298	760	64	3	.996
American League Totals—5 Years			72	201	18	48	11	0	8	28	.239	315	18	2	.994
National League Totals—5 Years............			116	222	21	36	7	0	8	27	.162	517	44	2	.996
Major League Totals—9 Years................			188	423	39	84	18	0	16	55	.199	832	62	4	.996

Selected by Detroit Tigers' organization in 1st round (17th player selected) of free-agent draft, January 8, 1980.

†On disabled list, May 15 to September 1, 1986; included rehabilitation disability assignment to Nashville, August 8 to August 27, 1986.

‡Traded to St. Louis Cardinals, September 2, 1986, completing deal in which St. Louis traded Catcher Mike Heath to Detroit Tigers for Pitcher Ken Hill and a player to be named later, August 10, 1986.

§On St. Louis disabled list, March 26 to July 14, 1988; included rehabilitation disability assignment to Louisville, June 28 to July 14, 1988.

xReleased, November 8, 1988; signed by Phoenix (San Francisco Giants' organization), January 25, 1989.

yReleased, October 25, 1990.

STEVEN MICHAEL LAKE
(Steve)

Born March 14, 1957, at Inglewood, Calif.
Height, 6.01. Weight, 199.
Throws and bats righthanded.
Cousin of Mike Lake, minor league pitcher, 1941 through 1946.

Major League stolen bases: 1985 (1).
Led Appalachian League in passed balls with 15 in 1975.

Year Club	League	Pos.	G.	AB.	R.	H.	2B.	3B.	HR.	RBI.	B.A.	PO.	A.	E.	F.A.
1975—Bluefield	Appal.	C	49	162	17	45	12	0	3	24	.278	254	★39	9	.970
1976—Miami	Fla. St.	PH	1	1	0	1	0	0	0	1	1.000	0	0	0	.000
1977—Miami	Fla. St.	C	79	232	25	55	10	1	2	24	.237	357	47	6	.985
1978—Miami†‡	Fla. St.	C	69	223	19	57	10	0	2	26	.256	300	49	6	.983
1979—Stockton§	Calif.	C	94	329	36	93	12	3	6	40	.283	504	73	8	.986
1980—Holyoke	East.	C-OF	102	325	26	84	9	2	2	44	.258	445	107	10	.982
1981—Vancouver x	P. C.	C	109	348	27	80	14	1	2	38	.230	502	102	7	.989
1982—Tucson y	P. C.	C	112	378	42	100	15	4	3	45	.265	504	91	12	.980
1983—Chicago	Nat.	C	38	85	9	22	4	1	1	7	.259	115	22	0	1.000
1984—Chicago z	Nat.	C	25	54	4	12	4	0	2	7	.222	72	13	4	.955
1984—Midland	Texas	C	9	25	2	4	0	0	0	1	.160	46	7	0	1.000
1985—Chicago	Nat.	C	58	119	5	18	2	0	1	11	.151	182	25	1	.995
1986—Chi. a-St.L.	Nat.	C	36	68	8	20	2	0	2	14	.294	105	9	2	.983
1986—Iowa-Louisville	A. A.	C	33	98	5	24	6	0	0	13	.245	140	21	2	.988
1987—St. Louis	Nat.	C	74	179	19	45	7	2	2	19	.251	253	21	1	.996
1988—St. Louis b	Nat.	C	36	54	5	15	3	0	1	4	.278	51	8	1	.983
1989—Philadelphia cd	Nat.	C	58	155	9	39	5	1	2	14	.252	262	33	3	.990
1990—Philadelphia e	Nat.	C	29	80	4	20	2	0	0	6	.250	115	19	1	.993
Major League Totals—8 Years			354	794	63	191	29	4	11	82	.241	1155	150	13	.990

Selected by Baltimore Orioles' organization in 3rd round of free-agent draft, June 4, 1975.
†On disabled list, April 17 to May 16, 1978.
‡Sold to Milwaukee Brewers' organization, December 21, 1978.
§On disabled list, June 20 to July 6, 1979.
xLoaned to Tucson (Houston Astros' organization), April 5, 1982; returned, September 7, 1982.
yTraded to Chicago Cubs for a player to be named later, April 1, 1983; Milwaukee Brewers' organization acquired Pitcher Rich Buonantony to complete deal, October 24, 1983.
zOn disabled list, May 14 to August 3, 1984; included rehabilitation disability assignment to Midland, July 23 to August 3, 1984.
aReleased, July 15, 1986; signed by Louisville (St. Louis Cardinals' organization), July 24, 1986.
bTraded with Outfielder Curt Ford to Philadelphia Phillies for Outfielder Milt Thompson, December 16, 1988.
cOn disabled list, August 28, 1989 through remainder of season.
dGranted free agency, November 13, 1989; re-signed by Phillies, December 6, 1989.
eOn disabled list, July 21 to September 1, 1990.

CHAMPIONSHIP SERIES RECORD

Year Club	League	Pos.	G.	AB.	R.	H.	2B.	3B.	HR.	RBI.	B.A.	PO.	A.	E.	F.A.
1984—Chicago	Nat.	C	1	1	0	1	1	0	0	0	1.000	0	0	0	.000

WORLD SERIES RECORD

Year Club	League	Pos.	G.	AB.	R.	H.	2B.	3B.	HR.	RBI.	B.A.	PO.	A.	E.	F.A.
1987—St. Louis	Nat.	C	3	3	0	1	0	0	0	1	.333	8	1	0	1.000

DENNIS PATRICK LAMP

Born September 23, 1952, at Los Angeles, Calif.
Height, 6.03. Weight, 215.
Throws and bats righthanded.

Major League saves: 1982 (5), 1983 (15), 1984 (9), 1985 (2), 1986 (2), 1989 (2). Total—35.

Year Club	League	G.	IP.	W.	L.	Pct.	H.	R.	ER.	SO.	BB.	ERA.
1971—Caldwell	Pioneer	14	46	1	2	.333	51	39	33	43	32	6.46
1972—Bradenton Cubs	Gulf Coast	14	70	7	2	.778	56	20	15	56	21	1.93
1973—Quincy	Midwest	13	89	6	4	.600	67	32	26	71	29	2.63
1973—Midland	Texas	9	48	2	4	.333	54	29	25	23	11	4.69
1974—Key West	Florida St.	8	49	1	5	.167	39	15	8	20	14	1.47
1974—Midland	Texas	24	60	1	1	.500	70	38	31	42	22	4.65
1975—Midland	Texas	37	127	7	5	.583	112	52	47	71	54	3.33
1976—Wichita	Am. Assoc.	30	153	8	★14	.364	182	94	69	98	52	4.06
1977—Wichita	Am. Assoc.	20	129	11	★.733	54	42	52	23	2.93
1977—Chicago	National	11	30	0	2	.000	43	21	21	12	8	6.30
1978—Chicago	National	37	224	7	15	.318	221	96	82	73	56	3.29
1979—Chicago	National	38	200	11	10	.524	200	96	78	86	46	3.51
1980—Chicago†	National	41	203	10	14	.417	259	★123	★117	83	82	5.19
1981—Chicago	American	27	127	7	6	.538	103	41	34	71	43	2.41
1982—Chicago§	American	44	189⅔	11	8	.579	206	96	84	78	59	3.99
1983—Chicago‡	American	49	116⅓	7	7	.500	123	52	48	44	29	3.71
1984—Toronto	American	56	85	8	8	.500	97	53	43	45	38	4.55
1985—Toronto	American	53	105⅔	11	0	1.000	96	42	39	68	27	3.32
1986—Toronto§x	American	40	73	2	6	.250	93	50	41	30	23	5.05
1987—Tacoma	P. Coast	6	12⅓	1	0	1.000	9	4	4	10	8	2.92
1987—Oakland y	American	36	56⅔	1	3	.250	76	38	32	36	22	5.08

Year Club	League	G.	IP.	W.	L.	Pct.	H.	R.	ER.	SO.	BB.	ERA.
1988—Boston za	American	46	82⅔	7	6	.538	92	39	32	49	19	3.48
1989—Boston b	American	42	112⅓	4	2	.667	96	37	29	61	27	2.32
1990—Boston	American	47	105⅔	3	5	.375	114	61	55	49	30	4.68
National League Totals—4 Years		127	657	28	41	.406	746	336	298	254	192	4.08
American League Totals—10 Years		440	1054	61	51	.545	1096	509	437	531	317	3.73
Major League Totals—14 Years		567	1711	89	92	.492	1842	845	735	785	509	3.87

Selected by Chicago Cubs' organization in 3rd round of free-agent draft, June 8, 1971.
†Traded to Chicago White Sox for Pitcher Ken Kravec, March 28, 1981.
‡Granted free agency, November 7, 1983; signed by Toronto Blue Jays as Type A player, January 10, 1984. (Pitcher Tom Seaver selected from player compensation pool by Chicago White Sox, January 20, 1984.)
§Released, October 20, 1986; signed by Cleveland Indians, February 5, 1987.
xReleased, March 23, 1987; signed by Oakland Athletics' organization, April 27, 1987.
yGranted free agency, October 19, 1987; signed by Pawtucket (Boston Red Sox' organization), January 5, 1988.
zOn disabled list, August 9 to August 27, 1988.
aGranted free agency, November 4, 1988; re-signed by Red Sox, November 20, 1988.
bGranted free agency, November 13, 1989; re-signed by Red Sox, December 6, 1989.

CHAMPIONSHIP SERIES RECORD

Year Club	League	G.	IP.	W.	L.	Pct.	H.	R.	ER.	SO.	BB.	ERA.
1983—Chicago	American	3	2	0	0	.000	0	1	0	1	2	0.00
1985—Toronto	American	3	9⅓	0	0	.000	2	0	0	10	1	0.00
1990—Boston	American	1	⅓	0	0	.000	2	4	4	0	2	108.00
Championship Series Totals—3 Years		7	11⅔	0	0	.000	4	5	4	11	5	3.09

THOMAS MICHAEL LAMPKIN
(Tom)

Born March 4, 1964, at Cincinnati, O.
Height, 5.11. Weight, 185.
Throws right and bats lefthanded.
Attended University of Portland, Portland, Ore.

Year Club	League	Pos.	G.	AB.	R.	H.	2B.	3B.	HR.	RBI.	B.A.	PO.	A.	E.	F.A.
1986—Batavia	NYP	C	63	190	24	49	5	1	1	20	.258	323	36	8	.978
1987—Waterloo	Midw.	C	118	398	49	106	19	2	7	55	.266	689	★100	15	.981
1988—Williamsport	East.	C	80	263	38	71	10	0	3	23	.270	431	60	9	.982
1988—Colorado Springs	P. C.	C	34	107	14	30	5	0	0	7	.280	171	28	5	.975
1988—Cleveland	Amer.	C	4	4	0	0	0	0	0	0	.000	3	0	0	1.000
1989—Colorado Springs†	P. C.	C	63	209	26	67	10	3	4	32	.231	305	21	8	.976
1990—Col. Sp.‡-L.Vegas	P. C.	C-2B	70	201	32	45	7	5	1	18	.224	315	36	12	.967
1990—San Diego	Nat.	C	26	63	4	14	0	1	1	4	.222	91	10	3	.971
American League Totals—1 Year			4	4	0	0	0	0	0	0	.000	3	0	0	1.000
National League Totals—1 Year			26	63	4	14	0	1	1	4	.222	91	10	3	.971
Major League Totals—2 Years			30	67	4	14	0	1	1	4	.209	94	10	3	.972

Selected by Cleveland Indians' organization in 11th round of free-agent draft, June 2, 1986.
†On disabled list, July 6, 1989 through remainder of season.
‡Traded to San Diego Padres for Outfielder Alex Cole, July 11, 1990.

LESTER WAYNE LANCASTER
(Les)

Born April 21, 1962, at Dallas, Tex.
Height, 6.02. Weight, 200.
Throws and bats righthanded.
Attended Dallas Baptist College, Dallas, Tex., and University of Arkansas, Fayetteville, Ark.

Major League saves: 1988 (5), 1989 (8), 1990 (6). Total—19.
Tied for National League lead in balks with 8 in 1987.
Led Appalachian League in complete games with 7 and intentional bases on balls issued with 5 in 1985.

Year Club	League	G.	IP.	W.	L.	Pct.	H.	R.	ER.	SO.	BB.	ERA.
1985—Wytheville	Ap'lachian	20	★102	7	4	.636	★98	49	41	★81	24	3.62
1986—Winston-Salem	Carolina	13	97	8	3	.727	88	37	30	52	30	2.78
1986—Pittsfield	Eastern	14	88	5	6	.455	105	46	41	49	34	4.19
1987—Chicago	National	27	132⅓	8	3	.727	138	76	72	78	51	4.90
1987—Iowa	Am. Assoc.	15	67	5	3	.625	59	24	24	62	17	3.22
1988—Chicago†	National	44	85⅔	4	6	.400	89	42	36	36	34	3.78
1989—Iowa	Am. Assoc.	17	91⅓	5	7	.417	76	38	27	56	43	2.66
1989—Chicago	National	42	72⅔	4	2	.667	60	12	11	56	15	1.36
1990—Chicago‡	National	55	109	9	5	.643	121	57	56	65	40	4.62
1990—Iowa	Am. Assoc.	6	17⅔	0	1	.000	20	10	8	15	5	4.08
Major League Totals—4 Years		168	399⅔	25	16	.610	408	187	175	235	140	3.94

Selected by New York Yankees' organization in 24th round of free-agent draft, June 8, 1981.
Selected by Texas Rangers' organization in 39th round of free-agent draft, June 6, 1983.
Signed as free agent by Chicago Cubs' organization, June 13, 1985.
†On disabled list, July 24 to August 14 and August 20 to September 4, 1988.
‡Appeared in one game as an outfielder with no chances.

CHAMPIONSHIP SERIES RECORD

Year Club	League	G.	IP.	W.	L.	Pct.	H.	R.	ER.	SO.	BB.	ERA.
1989—Chicago	National	3	6	1	1	.500	6	4	4	3	1	6.00

RICHARD ANTHONY LANCELLOTTI
(Rick)

Born July 5, 1957, at Providence, R.I.
Height, 6.02. Weight, 210.
Throws and bats lefthanded.
Attended Glassboro State College, Glassboro, N.J.

Led Pacific Coast League in game-winning RBIs with 19 and being hit by pitch with 11 in 1984.
Led Eastern League in total bases with 296 in 1979.
Tied for International League lead in intentional bases on balls received with 10 in 1989.
Named Eastern League Most Valuable Player, 1979.

Year Club	League	Pos.	G.	AB.	R.	H.	2B.	3B.	HR.	RBI.	B.A.	PO.	A.	E.	F.A.
1977—Charleston	W. Car.	OF	73	239	37	63	14	4	9	31	.264	103	5	7	.939
1978—Salem	Carol.	OF	133	439	67	106	15	3	15	60	.241	198	15	*13	.942
1979—Buffalo	East.	OF	138	506	95	145	14	7	*41	●107	.287	190	13	16	.927
1980—Portland	P. C.	OF	61	199	25	44	8	0	7	29	.221	62	3	1	.985
1980—Buffalo†	East.	OF	30	107	19	28	1	0	10	21	.262	61	3	3	.955
1980—Amarillo	Texas	OF	22	79	15	30	8	1	4	15	.380	24	0	0	1.000
1981—Hawaii	P. C.	OF-1B	132	482	67	122	23	5	19	84	.253	404	17	5	.988
1982—Hawaii	P. C.	1B-OF	136	500	76	136	31	4	20	95	.272	304	16	4	.988
1982—San Diego‡	Nat.	1B-OF	17	39	2	7	2	0	0	4	.179	63	2	1	.985
1983—Wich.§-Ok. C.x	A. A.	1B-OF	64	218	27	45	11	0	8	35	.206	334	25	5	.986
1983—Las Vegas	P. C.	1B-OF	30	116	21	35	8	0	9	32	.302	47	3	2	.962
1984—Las Vegas y	P. C.	OF-1B	133	522	88	150	29	6	29	*131	.287	340	23	12	.968
1985—Tidewater z	Int.	1B	91	316	32	57	9	0	10	28	.180	701	38	10	.987
1985—Phoenix a	P. C.	OF-1B	33	119	17	25	4	2	6	29	.210	136	3	1	.993
1986—Phoenix	P. C.	OF-1B	122	440	81	121	20	3	*31	106	.275	501	33	12	.978
1986—San Francisco b	Nat.	OF-1B	15	18	2	4	0	0	2	6	.222	7	0	0	1.000
1987—Hiroshima	Japan	....	121	403	....	88	....	....	39	83	.218	Figures Unavailable			
1988—Hiroshima c	Japan	....	79	264	33	50	....	....	19	50	.189	Figures Unavailable			
1989—Pawtucket	Int.	1B-OF	109	350	50	89	16	0	17	56	.254	714	52	8	.990
1990—Pawtucket	Int.	1B-OF-P	127	430	63	96	15	1	20	61	.223	461	36	4	.992
1990—Boston d	Amer.	1B	4	8	0	0	0	0	0	1	.000	20	2	0	1.000
National League Totals—2 Years			32	57	4	11	2		2	10	.193	70	2	1	.986
American League Totals—1 Year			4	8	0	0	0	0	0	1	.000	20	2	0	1.000
Major League Totals—3 Years			36	65	4	11	2	0	2	11	.169	90	4	1	.989

Selected by Pittsburgh Pirates' organization in 11th round of free-agent draft, June 7, 1977.

†Traded with Outfielder Luis Salazar to San Diego Padres' organization for Infielder Kurt Bevacqua and a player to be named later, August 5, 1980; Pittsburgh Pirates' organization acquired Pitcher Mark Lee to complete deal, August 12, 1980.

‡Sold to Wichita (Montreal Expos' organization), October 7, 1982.

§Released, May 30, 1983; signed by Oklahoma City (Texas Rangers' organization), June 10, 1983.

xReleased, July 26, 1983; signed by Las Vegas (San Diego Padres' organization), August 2, 1983.

yGranted free agency, October 15, 1984; signed by Tidewater (New York Mets' organization), March 31, 1985.

zSold to Phoenix (San Francisco Giants' organization), July 31, 1985.

aGranted free agency, October 15, 1985; re-signed by Giants' organization, February 7, 1986.

bReleased, November 10, 1986; signed by Hiroshima Carp of Japanese Baseball League, Spring 1987.

cSigned by Boston Red Sox' organization, May 17, 1989.

dGranted free agency, October 15, 1990.

PITCHING RECORD

Year Club	League	G.	IP.	W.	L.	Pct.	H.	R.	ER.	SO.	BB.	ERA.
1990—Pawtucket	Int'national	1	1	0	0	.000	3	3	3	0	0	27.00

THOMAS WILLIAM LANDRUM
(Bill)

Born August 17, 1958, at Columbia, S.C.
Height, 6.02. Weight, 205.
Throws and bats righthanded.
Attended Spartanburg Methodist College, Spartanburg, S.C., and received bachelor of science degree from University of South Carolina, Columbia, S.C. in 1980.
Son of Joe Landrum, pitcher with Brooklyn Dodgers, 1950 and 1952.

Major League saves: 1987 (2), 1989 (26), 1990 (13). Total—41.

Year Club	League	G.	IP.	W.	L.	Pct.	H.	R.	ER.	SO.	BB.	ERA.
1980—Sarasota Cubs†	Gulf Coast	11	37	2	0	1.000	37	21	17	27	11	4.14
1981—Tampa	Florida St.	17	83	6	8	.429	87	44	35	52	22	3.80
1982—Waterbury	Eastern	*58	112⅓	10	6	.625	109	63	51	104	65	4.09
1983—Waterbury	Eastern	17	29⅔	1	1	.500	17	5	5	33	14	1.52
1983—Indianapolis‡	Am. Assoc.	15	17⅔	1	3	.250	20	6	6	21	6	3.06
1984—Wichita§	Am. Assoc.	47	130⅓	7	4	.636	12	58	50	120	52	3.45
1985—Denver	Am. Assoc.	29	138	6	6	.500	148	72	61	88	49	3.98
1986—Denver x	Am. Assoc.	24	36⅓	1	3	.250	36	20	14	36	25	3.47
1986—Cincinnati	National	10	13⅓	0	0	.000	23	11	10	14	4	6.75
1987—Cincinnati	National	44	65	3	2	.600	68	35	34	42	34	4.71
1987—Nashville y	Am. Assoc.	19	38⅔	4	0	1.000	30	9	9	47	19	2.09
1988—Iowa	Am. Assoc.	9	21⅓	1	0	1.000	13	7	7	22	6	2.95
1988—Chicago z	National	7	12⅓	1	0	1.000	19	8	8	6	3	5.84
1990—Pittsburgh	National	56	81	2	3	.400	60	18	15	51	28	1.67

Year Club	League	G.	IP.	W.	L.	Pct.	H.	R.	ER.	SO.	BB.	ERA.
1989—Buffalo	Am. Assoc.	5	25⅓	3	0	1.000	16	2	2	20	6	0.71
1990—Pittsburgh	National	54	71⅔	7	3	.700	69	22	17	39	21	2.13
Major League Totals—5 Years		171	243⅓	13	8	.619	239	94	84	152	90	3.11

Signed as free agent by Chicago Cubs' organization, June 22, 1980.
†Released, October 20, 1980; signed by Billings (Cincinnati Reds' organization), February 7, 1981.
‡On disabled list, July 19 to August 4, 1983.
§Drafted by Chicago White Sox, December 3, 1984; returned, March 30, 1985.
xOn disabled list, April 29 to June 21, 1986.
yTraded to Chicago Cubs for Infielder Luis Quinones, April 1, 1988.
zGranted free agency, October 15, 1988; signed by Pittsburgh Pirates, January 12, 1989.

CHAMPIONSHIP SERIES RECORD

Year Club	League	G.	IP.	W.	L.	Pct.	H.	R.	ER.	SO.	BB.	ERA.
1990—Pittsburgh	National	2	2	0	0	.000	0	0	0	1	0	0.00

MARK EDWARD LANGSTON

Born August 20, 1960, at San Diego, Calif.
Height, 6.02. Weight, 183.
Throws left and bats righthanded.
Attended San Jose State University, San Jose, Calif.

Holds major league record for fewest assists by pitcher for leader, season (42), 1990.
Pitched seven innings, combining with Mike Witt in 1-0 nine-inning no-hit victory against Seattle Mariners, April 11, 1990.
Named pitcher on THE SPORTING NEWS American League All-Star fielding team, 1987 and 1988.
Named American League Rookie Pitcher of the Year by THE SPORTING NEWS, 1984.

Year Club	League	G.	IP.	W.	L.	Pct.	H.	R.	ER.	SO.	BB.	ERA.
1981—Bellingham	Northwest	13	85	7	3	.700	81	37	32	97	46	3.39
1982—Bakersfield	California	26	177⅓	12	7	.632	143	71	50	161	102	2.54
1983—Chattanooga	Southern	28	198	14	9	.609	187	104	79	142	102	3.59
1984—Seattle	American	35	225	17	10	.630	188	99	85	★204	★118	3.40
1985—Seattle†	American	24	126⅔	7	14	.333	122	85	77	72	91	5.47
1986—Seattle	American	37	239⅓	12	14	.462	234	★142	★129	★245	123	4.85
1987—Seattle	American	35	272	19	13	.594	242	132	116	★262	114	3.84
1988—Seattle	American	35	261⅓	15	11	.577	222	108	97	235	110	3.34
1989—Seattle‡	American	10	73⅓	4	5	.444	60	30	29	60	19	3.56
1989—Montreal§	National	24	176⅔	12	9	.571	138	57	47	175	93	2.39
1990—California	American	33	223	10	17	.370	215	120	109	195	104	4.40
American League Totals—7 Years		209	1420⅔	84	84	.500	1283	716	642	1273	679	4.07
National League Totals—1 Year		24	176⅔	12	9	.571	138	57	47	175	93	2.39
Major League Totals—7 Years		233	1597⅓	96	93	.508	1421	773	689	1448	772	3.88

Selected by Chicago Cubs' organization in 15th round of free-agent draft, June 6, 1978.
Selected by Seattle Mariners' organization in 3rd round of free-agent draft, June 8, 1981.
†On disabled list, June 7 to July 22, 1985.
‡Traded with a player to be named later to Montreal Expos for Pitchers Randy Johnson, Brian Holman and Gene Harris, May 25, 1989; Indianapolis (Montreal Expos' organization) acquired Pitcher Mike Campbell to complete deal, July 31, 1989.
§Granted free agency, November 13, 1989; signed by California Angels, December 1, 1989.

ALL-STAR GAME RECORD

Year League		IP.	W.	L.	Pct.	H.	R.	ER.	SO.	BB.	ERA.
1987—American		2	0	0	.000	0	0	0	3	0	0.00

RAYMOND L. LANKFORD
(Ray)

Born June 5, 1967, at Modesto, Calif.
Height, 5.11. Weight, 180.
Throws and bats lefthanded.
Attended Modesto Junior College, Modesto, Calif.

Major League stolen bases: 1990 (8).
Led Midwest League in total bases with 242 in 1988.
Led Appalachian League in caught stealing with 11 in 1987.
Tied for American Association lead in intentional bases on balls received with 9 in 1990.
Led American Association outfielders in total chances with 352 in 1990.
Led Texas League outfielders in total chances with 387 in 1989.
Led Appalachian League outfielders in total chances with 155 in 1987.
Named Texas League Most Valuable Player, 1989.

Year Club	League	Pos.	G.	AB.	R.	H.	2B.	3B.	HR.	RBI.	B.A.	PO.	A.	E.	F.A.
1987—Johnson City	Appal.	OF	66	253	45	78	17	4	3	32	.308	★143	7	5	.968
1988—Springfield	Midw.	OF	135	532	90	151	26	★16	11	66	.284	284	5	7	.976
1989—Arkansas	Texas	OF	★134	498	98	★158	28	★12	11	98	.317	★367	9	11	.972
1990—Louisville	A. A.	OF	132	473	61	123	25	8	10	72	.260	★333	8	●11	.969
1990—St. Louis	Nat.	OF	39	126	12	36	10	1	3	12	.286	92	1	1	.989
Major League Totals—1 Year			39	126	12	36	10	1	3	12	.286	92	1	1	.989

Selected by Chicago Cubs' organization in 3rd round of free-agent draft, January 14, 1986.
Selected by St. Louis Cardinals' organization in 3rd round of free-agent draft, June 2, 1987.

CARNEY RAY LANSFORD

Born February 7, 1957, at San Jose, Calif.
Height, 6.02. Weight, 195.
Throws and bats righthanded.
Brother of Phil Lansford, infielder in Cleveland Indians' and Toronto Blue Jays' organizations,
1978 through 1981; and Joe Lansford, first baseman with San Diego Padres, 1982 and 1983.

Major League stolen bases: 1978 (20), 1979 (20), 1980 (14), 1981 (15), 1982 (9), 1983 (3), 1984 (9), 1985 (2), 1986 (16), 1987 (28), 1988 (29), 1989 (37), 1990 (16). Total—217.
Hit three home runs in a game, September 1, 1979.
Led American League in sacrifice flies with 11 in 1980.
Led American League third basemen in fielding percentage with .980 in 1987, .979 in 1988 and .970 in 1990.
Led Texas League third basemen in double plays with 16 in 1977.
Named third baseman on THE SPORTING NEWS American League All-Star Team, 1989.
Named third baseman on THE SPORTING NEWS American League Silver Slugger team, 1981.

Year Club League	Pos.	G.	AB.	R.	H.	2B.	3B.	HR.	RBI.	B.A.	PO.	A.	E.	F.A.
1975—Idaho Falls† .... Pion.	3B-SS	8	27	5	6	2	0	1	1	.222	8	14	9	.710
1976—Quad Cities........... Midw.	3B-OF-SS	121	418	87	120	19	5	14	86	.287	130	215	36	.906
1977—El Paso..................... Texas	3B	120	443	98	147	17	3	18	94	.332	★110	★210	15	★.955
1978—California‡............. Amer.	3B-SS	121	453	63	133	23	2	8	52	.294	94	186	18	.940
1979—California.............. Amer.	3B	157	654	114	188	30	5	19	79	.287	★135	263	7	★.983
1980—California§............. Amer.	3B	151	602	87	157	27	3	15	80	.261	★151	250	19	.955
1981—Boston.................... Amer.	3B	102	399	61	134	23	3	4	52	★.336	70	180	13	.951
1982—Boston xy.............. Amer.	3B	128	482	65	145	28	4	11	63	.301	83	216	10	.968
1983—Oakland z.............. Amer.	3B-SS	80	299	43	92	16	2	10	45	.308	60	163	10	.957
1984—Oakland................. Amer.	3B	151	597	70	179	31	5	14	74	.300	137	268	18	.957
1985—Oakland a.............. Amer.	3B	98	401	51	111	18	2	13	46	.277	85	119	5	.976
1986—Oakland................. Amer.	3B-1B-2B	151	591	80	168	16	4	19	72	.284	480	170	6	.991
1987—Oakland................. Amer.	3B-1B	151	554	89	160	27	4	19	76	.289	156	258	7	.983
1988—Oakland................. Amer.	3B-1B-2B	150	556	80	155	20	2	7	57	.279	125	221	7	.980
1989—Oakland................. Amer.	3B-1B	148	551	81	185	28	2	2	52	.336	195	188	13	.967
1990—Oakland b............. Amer.	3B-1B	134	507	58	136	15	1	3	50	.268	128	195	9	.973
Major League Totals—13 Years.............		1722	6646	942	1943	302	39	144	798	.292	1899	2677	142	.970

Selected by California Angels' organization in 3rd round of free-agent draft, June 4, 1975.
†On disabled list, July 21 to September 30, 1975.
‡On disabled list, June 11 to July 7, 1978.
§Traded with Pitcher Mark Clear and Outfielder Rick Miller to Boston Red Sox for Shortstop Rick Burleson and Third Baseman Butch Hobson, December 10, 1980.
xOn disabled list, June 24 to July 21, 1982.
yTraded with Outfielder Garry Hancock and a player to be named later to Oakland A's for Outfielder Tony Armas and Catcher Jeff Newman, December 6, 1982; Oakland acquired Pitcher Jerry King to complete deal, December 20, 1982.
zOn disabled list, May 19 to June 7, 1983.
aOn disabled list, July 26 to August 28, 1985.
bOn disabled list, July 12 to July 27, 1990.

CHAMPIONSHIP SERIES RECORD

Year Club League	Pos.	G.	AB.	R.	H.	2B.	3B.	HR.	RBI.	B.A.	PO.	A.	E.	F.A.
1979—California............... Amer.	3B	4	17	2	5	0	0	0	3	.294	4	8	0	1.000
1988—Oakland................. Amer.	3B	4	17	4	5	1	0	1	2	.294	7	8	0	1.000
1989—Oakland................. Amer.	3B	3	11	2	5	0	0	0	4	.455	1	2	0	1.000
1990—Oakland................. Amer.	3B	4	16	2	7	1	0	0	2	.438	3	11	0	1.000
Championship Series Totals—4 Years.....		15	61	10	22	2	0	1	11	.361	15	29	0	1.000

WORLD SERIES RECORD

Shares World Series record for most runs, game (4), October 27, 1989.

Year Club League	Pos.	G.	AB.	R.	H.	2B.	3B.	HR.	RBI.	B.A.	PO.	A.	E.	F.A.
1988—Oakland................. Amer.	3B	5	18	2	3	0	0	0	1	.167	8	7	0	1.000
1989—Oakland................. Amer.	3B	4	16	5	7	1	0	1	4	.438	5	5	0	1.000
1990—Oakland................. Amer.	3B	4	15	0	4	0	0	0	1	.267	1	14	0	1.000
World Series Totals—3 Years		13	49	7	14	1	0	1	6	.286	14	26	0	1.000

ALL-STAR GAME RECORD

Year League	Pos.	AB.	R.	H.	2B.	3B.	HR.	RBI.	B.A.	PO.	A.	E.	F.A.
1988—American	3B	1	0	0	0	0	0	0	.000	0	1	0	1.000

DAVID JEFFREY LaPOINT
(Dave)

Born July 29, 1959, at Glens Falls, N. Y.
Height, 6.03. Weight, 231.
Throws and bats lefthanded.

Pitched 4-0 no-hit victory against Reno, July 25, 1979.
Major League saves: 1980 (1).
Led National League in wild pitches with 15 in 1984.
Tied for American Association lead in complete games with 9 in 1981.
Tied for California League lead in shutouts with 3 and complete games with 11 in 1979.
Tied for Midwest League lead in home runs allowed with 20 in 1978.

Year Club	League	G.	IP.	W.	L.	Pct.	H.	R.	ER.	SO.	BB.	ERA.
1977—Newark	NYP	13	69	5	2	.714	73	40	36	60	22	4.70
1978—Burlington	Midwest	25	161	12	12	.500	177	98	72	134	41	4.02
1979—Stockton	California	27	180	12	10	.545	144	74	63	*208	85	3.15
1980—Vancouver†	P. Coast	17	93	7	4	.636	71	48	29	64	45	2.81
1980—Milwaukee‡	American	5	15	1	0	1.000	17	14	10	5	13	6.00
1981—Springfield	Am. Assoc.	25	172	13	9	.591	160	83	61	*129	66	3.19
1981—St. Louis	National	3	11	1	0	1.000	12	5	5	4	2	4.09
1982—St. Louis	National	42	152⅔	9	3	.750	170	63	58	81	52	3.42
1983—St. Louis	National	37	191⅓	12	9	.571	191	92	84	113	84	3.95
1984—St. Louis§x	National	33	193	12	10	.545	205	94	85	130	77	3.96
1985—San Francisco y	National	31	206⅔	7	17	.292	215	99	82	122	74	3.57
1986—Detroit z	American	16	67⅔	3	6	.333	85	49	43	36	32	5.72
1986—San Diego a	National	24	61⅓	1	4	.200	67	37	29	41	24	4.26
1987—St. Louis	National	6	16	1	1	.500	26	12	12	8	5	6.75
1987—Louisville b	Am. Assoc.	14	91⅔	5	5	.500	93	45	41	70	27	4.03
1987—Chicago c	American	14	82⅔	6	3	.667	69	29	27	43	31	2.94
1988—Chicago d	American	25	161⅓	10	11	.476	151	69	61	79	47	3.40
1988—Pittsburgh e	National	8	52	4	2	.667	54	18	16	19	10	2.77
1989—New York f	American	20	113⅔	6	9	.400	146	73	71	51	45	5.62
1990—New York g	American	28	157⅔	7	10	.412	180	84	72	67	57	4.11
American League Totals—6 Years		108	598	33	39	.458	648	318	284	281	225	4.27
National League Totals—8 Years		184	884	47	46	.505	940	420	371	518	328	3.78
Major League Totals—11 Years		292	1482	80	85	.485	1588	738	655	799	553	3.98

Selected by Milwaukee Brewers' organization in 10th round of free-agent draft, June 7, 1977.

†On disabled list, May 6 to May 17 and June 6 to July 15, 1980.

‡Traded with Pitcher Lary Sorensen and Outfielders Sixto Lezcano and David Green to St. Louis Cardinals for Pitchers Pete Vuckovich and Rollie Fingers and Catcher Ted Simmons, December 12, 1980.

§On disabled list, June 15 to June 30, 1984.

xTraded with First Basemen David Green and Gary Rajsich and Shortstop Jose Gonzalez (Jose Uribe) to San Francisco Giants for Outfielder-First Baseman Jack Clark, February 1, 1985.

yTraded with Catcher Matt Nokes and Pitcher Eric King to Detroit Tigers for Pitcher Juan Berenguer, Catcher Bob Melvin and a player to be named later, October 7, 1985; San Francisco Giants acquired Pitcher Scott Medvin to complete deal, December 11, 1985.

zTraded to San Diego Padres for Pitcher Mark Thurmond, July 9, 1986.

aReleased, December 20, 1986; signed by St. Louis Cardinals, January 19, 1987.

bTraded to Chicago White Sox for Pitcher Bryce Hulstrom, July 30, 1987.

cGranted free agency, November 9, 1987; re-signed by White Sox, February 9, 1988.

dTraded to Pittsburgh Pirates for Pitcher Barry Jones, August 13, 1988.

eGranted free agency, November 4, 1988; signed by New York Yankees, December 3, 1988.

fOn disabled list, June 30 to July 17 and August 3, 1989 through remainder of season.

gGranted free agency, December 7, 1990.

WORLD SERIES RECORD

Year Club	League	G.	IP.	W.	L.	Pct.	H.	R.	ER.	SO.	BB.	ERA.
1982—St. Louis	National	2	8⅓	0	0	.000	10	6	3	3	2	3.24

BARRY LOUIS LARKIN

Born April 28, 1964, at Cincinnati, O.
Height, 6.00. Weight, 185.
Throws and bats righthanded.
Attended University of Michigan, Ann Arbor, Mich.

Major League stolen bases: 1986 (8), 1987 (21), 1988 (40), 1989 (10), 1990 (30). Total—109.
Tied for National League lead in double plays by shortstops with 86 in 1990.
Led American Association in slugging percentage with .525 in 1986.
Named shortstop on THE SPORTING NEWS National League All-Star Team, 1988 and 1990.
Named shortstop on THE SPORTING NEWS National League Silver Slugger team, 1988 through 1990.
Named American Association Most Valuable Player, 1986.
Named shortstop on THE SPORTING NEWS College Baseball All-America Team, 1985.
Member of 1984 U.S. Olympic baseball team.

Year Club	League	Pos.	G.	AB.	R.	H.	2B.	3B.	HR.	RBI.	B.A.	PO.	A.	E.	F.A.
1985—Vermont	East.	SS	72	255	42	68	13	2	1	31	.267	110	166	17	.942
1986—Denver	A. A.	SS-2B	103	413	67	136	31	10	10	51	.329	172	287	18	.962
1986—Cincinnati	Nat.	SS-2B	41	159	27	45	4	3	3	19	.283	51	125	4	.978
1987—Cincinnati†	Nat.	SS	125	439	64	107	16	2	12	43	.244	168	358	19	.965
1988—Cincinnati	Nat.	SS	151	588	91	174	32	5	12	56	.296	231	470	●29	.960
1989—Cincinnati‡	Nat.	SS	97	325	47	111	14	4	4	36	.342	142	267	10	.976
1989—Nashville	A. A.	SS	2	5	2	5	1	0	0	0	1.000	1	3	0	1.000
1990—Cincinnati	Nat.	SS	158	614	85	185	25	6	7	67	.301	254	*469	17	.977
Major League Totals—5 Years			572	2125	314	622	91	20	38	221	.293	846	1689	79	.970

Selected by Cincinnati Reds' organization in 2nd round of free-agent draft, June 7, 1982.

Selected by Cincinnati Reds' organization in 1st round (fourth player selected) of free-agent draft, June 3, 1985.

†On disabled list, April 13 to May 2, 1987.

‡On disabled list, July 11 to September 1, 1989; included rehabilitation disability assignment to Nashville, August 27 to September 1, 1989.

CHAMPIONSHIP SERIES RECORD

Year Club	League	Pos.	G.	AB.	R.	H.	2B.	3B.	HR.	RBI.	B.A.	PO.	A.	E.	F.A.
1990—Cincinnati	Nat.	SS	6	23	5	6	2	0	0	1	.261	21	15	1	.973

WORLD SERIES RECORD

Shares record for most at-bats, inning (2), October 19, 1990, third inning.

Year	Club	League	Pos.	G.	AB.	R.	H.	2B.	3B.	HR.	RBI.	B.A.	PO.	A.	E.	F.A.
1990—Cincinnati		Nat.	SS	4	17	3	6	1	1	0	1	.353	1	14	0	1.000

ALL-STAR GAME RECORD

Year	League	Pos.	AB.	R.	H.	2B.	3B.	HR.	RBI.	B.A.	PO.	A.	E.	F.A.
1988—National		SS	2	0	0	0	0	0	0	.000	0	1	0	1.000
1990—National		PR-SS	0	0	0	0	0	0	0	.000	1	2	0	1.000
All-Star Game Totals—2 Years			2	0	0	0	0	0	0	.000	1	3	0	1.000

Member of National League All-Star Team in 1989; did not play.

EUGENE THOMAS LARKIN
(Gene)

Born October 24, 1962, at Flushing, N. Y.
Height, 6.03. Weight, 205.
Throws right and bats left and righthanded.
Received degree from Columbia University, New York, N. Y.

Major League stolen bases: 1987 (1), 1988 (3), 1989 (5), 1990 (5). Total—14.
Led American League in being hit by pitch with 15 in 1988.
Led California League in sacrifice flies with 14 in 1985.
Tied for Southern League lead in sacrifice flies with 13 in 1986.
Led California League first basemen in double plays with 140 in 1985.
Led Appalachian League first basemen in double plays with 54 in 1984.

Year	Club	League	Pos.	G.	AB.	R.	H.	2B.	3B.	HR.	RBI.	B.A.	PO.	A.	E.	F.A.
1984—Elizabethton	Appal.	1B	57	193	29	63	13	1	6	37	.326	478	19	6	★.988
1985—Visalia	Calif.	1B	●142	528	90	161	25	3	13	●106	.305	★1227	62	12	.991
1986—Orlando	South.	1B-3B	142	529	85	●170	29	6	15	104	.321	923	53	13	.987
1987—Portland	P. C.	1B-OF	35	129	17	39	9	0	1	14	.302	191	22	4	.982
1987—Minnesota	Amer.	1B	85	233	23	62	11	2	4	28	.266	165	10	2	.989
1988—Minnesota	Amer.	1B	149	505	56	135	30	2	8	70	.267	466	28	3	.994
1989—Minnesota	Amer.	1B-OF	136	446	61	119	25	1	6	46	.267	524	28	4	.993
1990—Minnesota†	Amer.	OF-1B	119	401	46	108	26	4	5	42	.269	299	18	2	.994
Major League Totals—4 Years			489	1585	186	424	92	9	23	186	.268	1454	84	11	.993

Selected by Minnesota Twins' organization in 20th round of free-agent draft, June 4, 1984.
†On disabled list, July 14 to July 30, 1990.

CHAMPIONSHIP SERIES RECORD

Year	Club	League	Pos.	G.	AB.	R.	H.	2B.	3B.	HR.	RBI.	B.A.	PO.	A.	E.	F.A.
1987—Minnesota	Amer.	PH	1	1	0	1	1	0	0	1	1.000	0	0	0	.000

WORLD SERIES RECORD

Year	Club	League	Pos.	G.	AB.	R.	H.	2B.	3B.	HR.	RBI.	B.A.	PO.	A.	E.	F.A.
1987—Minnesota	Amer.	1B-PH	5	3	1	0	0	0	0	0	.000	1	0	0	1.000

MICHAEL EUGENE LaVALLIERE

Name pronounced Luh-VAL-yur.

(Mike)

Born August 18, 1960, at Charlotte, N. C.
Height, 5.10. Weight, 205.
Throws right and bats lefthanded.
Attended University of Lowell, Lowell, Mass.
Son of Guy LaValliere, minor league catcher, 1952 and 1955 through 1961.

Major League stolen bases: 1988 (3).
Named catcher on THE SPORTING NEWS National League All-Star Team, 1988.
Named catcher on THE SPORTING NEWS National League All-Star fielding team, 1987.

Year	Club	League	Pos.	G.	AB.	R.	H.	2B.	3B.	HR.	RBI.	B.A.	PO.	A.	E.	F.A.
1981—Spartanburg	S. Atl.	3B-OF	39	123	15	33	9	0	2	23	.268	16	32	5	.906
1982—Peninsula	Carol.	C-3B	66	178	20	49	4	2	2	23	.275	306	35	6	.983
1983—Reading	East.	C-3B-P	81	218	24	64	16	2	4	43	.294	243	59	4	.987
1984—Reading	East.	C-3-2-P	55	147	19	37	6	0	6	22	.252	113	45	2	.988
1984—Portland	P. C.	C	37	122	20	38	6	3	5	21	.311	186	16	1	.995
1984—Philadelphia†‡	Nat.	C	6	7	0	0	0	0	0	0	.000	20	2	0	1.000
1985—St. Louis	Nat.	C	12	34	2	5	1	0	0	6	.147	48	5	0	1.000
1985—Louisville§	A. A.	C	83	231	19	47	12	1	4	26	.203	420	53	5	.990
1986—St. Louis x	Nat.	C	110	303	18	71	10	2	3	30	.234	468	47	6	.988
1987—Pittsburgh	Nat.	C	121	340	33	102	19	0	1	36	.300	584	70	5	.992
1988—Pittsburgh	Nat.	C	120	352	24	92	18	0	2	47	.261	565	55	8	.987
1989—Pittsburgh y	Nat.	C	68	190	15	60	10	0	2	23	.316	306	24	3	.991
1989—Buffalo	A. A.	C	7	18	0	2	0	0	0	1	.111	15	1	0	1.000
1990—Pittsburgh	Nat.	C	96	279	27	72	15	0	3	31	.258	478	36	5	.990
Major League Totals—7 Years			533	1505	119	402	73	2	11	173	.267	2469	239	27	.990

Signed as free agent by Philadelphia Phillies' organization, July 12, 1981.
†Traded to St. Louis Cardinals for a player to be named later, December 3, 1984; returned due to injured status, December 13, 1984.

‡Granted free agency, December 23, 1984; signed by Louisville (St. Louis Cardinals' organization), January 23, 1985.
§On disabled list, July 18 to July 29, 1985.
xTraded with Outfielder Andy Van Slyke and Pitcher Mike Dunne to Pittsburgh Pirates for Catcher Tony Pena, April 1, 1987.
yOn disabled list, April 17 to July 4, 1989; included rehabilitation disability assignment to Buffalo, June 26 to July 4, 1989.

CHAMPIONSHIP SERIES RECORD

Year Club	League	Pos.	G.	AB.	R.	H.	2B.	3B.	HR.	RBI.	B.A.	PO.	A.	E.	F.A.
1990—Pittsburgh.............	Nat.	C	3	6	1	0	0	0	0	0	.000	17	2	0	1.000

PITCHING RECORD

Year Club	League	G.	IP.	W.	L.	Pct.	H.	R.	ER.	SO.	BB.	ERA.
1983—Reading................	Eastern	4	3⅓	0	0	.000	3	3	2	2	2	5.40
1984—Reading................	Eastern	1	1	0	0	.000	3	2	2	1	1	18.00

VANCE AARON LAW

Born October 1, 1956, at Boise, Ida.
Height, 6.01. Weight, 190.
Throws and bats righthanded.
Attended Brigham Young University, Provo, Utah.
Son of Vern Law, pitcher with Pittsburgh Pirates, 1950, 1951 and 1954 through 1967.

Holds American League record for longest errorless game by third baseman (25 innings), May 8, finished May 9, 1984.

Shares American League record for most innings played by third baseman, game (25), May 8, finished May 9, 1984.

Major League stolen bases: 1980 (2), 1981 (1), 1982 (4), 1983 (3), 1984 (4), 1985 (6), 1986 (3), 1987 (8), 1988 (1), 1989 (2). Total—34.

Led Pacific Coast League in sacrifice hits with 14 in 1979.

Year Club	League	Pos.	G.	AB.	R.	H.	2B.	3B.	HR.	RBI.	B.A.	PO.	A.	E.	F.A.
1978—Bradenton Pir.	Gulf C.	SS	1	3	0	1	0	0	0	0	.333	2	5	0	1.000
1978—Salem....................	Carol.	SS	60	213	48	68	13	7	2	30	.319	96	180	22	.926
1979—Portland................	P. C.	SS-3B-2B	131	448	62	139	16	8	2	52	.310	201	308	22	.959
1980—Portland................	P. C.	SS	96	339	59	100	23	5	5	54	.295	169	295	14	.971
1980—Pittsburgh.............	Nat.	2B-SS-3B	25	74	11	17	2	2	0	3	.230	31	54	3	.966
1981—Pittsburgh.............	Nat.	2B-SS-3B	30	67	1	9	0	1	0	3	.134	50	58	0	1.000
1981—Portland†‡............	P. C.	2B-SS-3B	88	310	55	86	14	9	5	43	.277	168	218	9	.977
1982—Chicago	Amer.	S-3-2-O	114	359	40	101	20	1	5	54	.281	156	313	26	.947
1983—Chicago	Amer.	3-2-S-O	145	408	55	99	21	5	4	42	.243	94	311	14	.967
1984—Chicago§	Amer.	3-2-O-S	151	481	60	121	18	2	17	59	.252	119	246	16	.958
1985—Montreal	Nat.	2-1-3-O	147	519	75	138	30	6	10	52	.266	420	402	12	.986
1986—Montreal	Nat.	2-1-3-P-O	112	360	37	81	17	2	5	44	.225	273	299	4	.993
1987—Montreal x	Nat.	2-1-3-P	133	436	52	119	27	1	12	56	.273	258	308	11	.981
1988—Chicago	Nat.	3B-OF	151	556	73	163	29	2	11	78	.293	112	272	19	.953
1989—Chicago y..............	Nat.	3B-OF	130	408	38	96	22	3	7	42	.235	76	168	13	.949
1990—Chunichi z.............	Central	......	122	457	....	143	....	....	29	78	.313	Figures Unavailable			
National League Totals—7 Years...........			728	2420	287	623	127	17	45	278	.257	1220	1561	62	.978
American League Totals—3 Years			410	1248	155	321	59	8	26	155	.257	369	870	56	.957
Major League Totals—10 Years...............			1138	3668	442	944	186	25	71	433	.257	1589	2431	118	.971

Selected by Pittsburgh Pirates' organization in 38th round of free-agent draft, June 6, 1978.
†On disabled list, July 5 to July 15, 1981.
‡Traded with Pitcher Ernie Camacho to Chicago White Sox for Pitchers Ross Baumgarten and Butch Edge, March 21, 1982.
§Traded to Montreal Expos for Pitcher Bob James, December 7, 1984.
xGranted free agency, November 9, 1987; signed by Chicago Cubs, December 14, 1987.
yReleased, January 2, 1990; sold to Chunichi Dragons of Japanese Baseball League, January 4, 1990.
zSigned by Oakland Athletics, January 7, 1991.

CHAMPIONSHIP SERIES RECORD

Year Club	League	Pos.	G.	AB.	R.	H.	2B.	3B.	HR.	RBI.	B.A.	PO.	A.	E.	F.A.
1983—Chicago	Amer.	3B	4	11	0	2	0	0	0	1	.182	1	9	1	.909
1989—Chicago	Nat.	PH-3B	2	3	0	0	0	0	0	0	.000	0	0	0	.000
Championship Series Totals—2 Years.....			6	14	0	2	0	0	0	1	.143	1	9	1	.909

ALL-STAR GAME RECORD

Year League	Pos.	AB.	R.	H.	2B.	3B.	HR.	RBI.	B.A.	PO.	A.	E.	F.A.
1988—National	2B	0	0	0	0	0	0	0	.000	0	0	0	.000

PITCHING RECORD

Year Club	League	G.	IP.	W.	L.	Pct.	H.	R.	ER.	SO.	BB.	ERA.
1986—Montreal	National	3	4	0	0	.000	3	2	1	0	2	2.25
1987—Montreal	National	3	3⅓	0	0	.000	5	2	2	2	0	5.40
Major League Totals—2 Years...........................		6	7⅓	0	0	.000	8	4	3	2	2	3.68

—DID YOU KNOW—

That after a 20-7 loss to Milwaukee last July 8, the Angels' team earned-run average climbed from 3.55 to 3.75?

THOMAS JAMES LAWLESS
(Tom)

Born December 19, 1956, at Erie, Pa.
Height, 5.11. Weight, 165.
Throws and bats righthanded.
Received bachelor of arts degree in political science from
Pennsylvania State University-Behrend, Erie, Pa.

Major League stolen bases: 1982 (16), 1984 (7), 1985 (2), 1986 (8), 1987 (2), 1988 (6), 1989 (12). Total—53.
Led American Association in stolen bases with 46 in 1983.
Led Florida State League in sacrifice hits with 13 and stolen bases with 60 in 1979.
Led Pioneer League shortstops in putouts with 116 in 1978.

Year Club	League	Pos.	G.	AB.	R.	H.	2B.	3B.	HR.	RBI.	B.A.	PO.	A.	E.	F.A.
1978—Billings	Pioneer	SS-2B	63	254	64	70	5	•7	5	35	.276	117	186	24	.927
1979—Tampa	Fla. St.	2B	131	469	66	126	9	5	1	39	.269	*296	376	17	*.975
1980—Waterbury	East.	2B	130	498	83	137	20	7	2	29	.275	*316	333	14	.979
1981—Waterbury	East.	2B	136	522	77	152	20	10	8	50	.291	323	379	15	.979
1982—Indianapolis	A. A.	2B-SS	86	351	76	108	18	6	2	28	.308	185	251	13	.971
1982—Cincinnati	Nat.	2B	49	165	19	35	6	0	0	4	.212	87	136	5	.978
1983—Indianapolis	A. A.	2B	115	423	93	118	23	3	13	35	.279	255	303	17	.970
1984—Cinc.†-Mont.	Nat.	2B-3B	54	97	11	23	3	0	1	2	.237	50	52	1	.990
1984—Wich.-Ind.‡	A. A.	3B-2B-SS	50	173	36	47	5	5	4	23	.272	53	103	4	.975
1985—Louisville	A. A.	3B-OF	31	124	16	36	9	1	1	12	.290	20	58	3	.963
1985—St. Louis	Nat.	3B-2B	47	58	8	12	3	1	0	8	.207	19	44	1	.984
1986—St. Louis	Nat.	3B-2B-OF	46	39	5	11	1	0	0	3	.282	11	15	2	.929
1987—St. Louis§	Nat.	2B-3B-OF	19	25	5	2	1	0	0	0	.080	5	15	0	1.000
1988—St. Louis x	Nat.	3-O-2-1	54	65	9	10	2	1	1	3	.154	23	29	0	1.000
1989—Toronto y	Amer.	O-3-2-C	59	70	20	16	1	0	0	3	.229	39	26	3	.956
1990—Toronto z	Amer.	3B-OF-2B	15	12	1	1	0	0	0	1	.083	11	4	1	.938
National League Totals—6 Years			269	449	57	93	16	2	2	20	.207	195	291	9	.982
American League Totals—2 Years			74	82	21	17	1	0	0	4	.207	50	30	4	.952
Major League Totals—8 Years			343	531	78	110	17	2	2	24	.207	245	321	13	.978

Selected by Cincinnati Reds' organization in 17th round of free-agent draft, June 6, 1978.
†Traded to Montreal Expos' organization for First Baseman-Outfielder Pete Rose, August 16, 1984.
‡Sold to Louisville (St. Louis Cardinals' organization), March 25, 1985, completing deal in which St. Louis traded Pitcher Mickey Mahler to Montreal Expos for a player to be named later, February 6, 1985.
§On disabled list, August 21 to September 5, 1987.
xReleased, December 21, 1988; signed by Toronto Blue Jays, January 23, 1989.
yGranted free agency, November 13, 1989; re-signed by Blue Jays, December 7, 1989.
zReleased, July 22, 1990.

CHAMPIONSHIP SERIES RECORD

Year Club	League	Pos.	G.	AB.	R.	H.	2B.	3B.	HR.	RBI.	B.A.	PO.	A.	E.	F.A.
1987—St. Louis	Nat.	3B-PH-O	3	6	0	2	0	0	0	0	.333	1	4	0	1.000

WORLD SERIES RECORD

Year Club	League	Pos.	G.	AB.	R.	H.	2B.	3B.	HR.	RBI.	B.A.	PO.	A.	E.	F.A.
1985—St. Louis	Nat.	PR	1	0	0	0	0	0	0	0	.000	0	0	0	.000
1987—St. Louis	Nat.	3B	3	10	1	1	0	0	1	3	.100	3	6	1	.900
World Series Totals—2 Years			4	10	1	1	0	0	1	3	.100	3	6	1	.900

TIMOTHY JOSEPH LAYANA
(Tim)

Born March 2, 1964, at Inglewood, Calif.
Height, 6.02. Weight, 195.
Throws and bats righthanded.
Attended Loyola Marymount University, Los Angeles, Calif.

Major League saves: 1990 (2).
Led Eastern League in saves with 17 in 1989.

Year Club	League	G.	IP.	W.	L.	Pct.	H.	R.	ER.	SO.	BB.	ERA.
1986—Oneonta	NYP	3	19	2	0	1.000	10	5	5	24	5	2.37
1986—Fort Lauderdale	Florida St.	11	68⅓	5	4	.556	59	19	17	52	19	2.24
1987—Columbus	Int'national	13	70	4	5	.444	77	37	37	36	37	4.76
1987—Albany	Eastern	8	46⅓	2	4	.333	51	28	26	19	18	5.05
1987—Prince William	Carolina	7	22⅔	2	1	.667	29	22	16	17	11	6.35
1988—Columbus	Int'national	11	47⅔	1	7	.125	54	34	32	25	25	6.04
1988—Albany	Eastern	14	87	5	7	.417	90	52	42	42	30	4.34
1989—Albany†	Eastern	40	67⅔	7	4	.636	53	17	13	48	15	1.73
1990—Cincinnati	National	55	80	5	3	.625	71	33	31	53	44	3.49
Major League Totals—1 Year		55	80	5	3	.625	71	33	31	53	44	3.49

Selected by Chicago White Sox' organization in 28th round of free-agent draft, June 7, 1982.
Selected by New York Mets' organization in 5th round of free-agent draft, June 3, 1985.
Selected by New York Yankees' organization in 3rd round of free-agent draft, June 2, 1986.
†Drafted by Cincinnati Reds, December 4, 1989.

RICHARD MAX LEACH JR.
(Rick)

Born May 4, 1957, at Ann Arbor, Mich.
Height, 6.00. Weight, 195.
Throws and bats lefthanded.
Attended University of Michigan, Ann Arbor, Mich.

Major League stolen bases: 1982 (4), 1983 (2), 1989 (2). Total—8.
Led International League in sacrifice flies with 12 in 1985.
Tied for International League lead in assists by outfielders with 13 in 1985.
Selected by Denver Broncos in 5th round of 1979 NFL draft.
Received reported $200,000 bonus to sign with Detroit Tigers, 1979.
Named outfielder on THE SPORTING NEWS College Baseball All-America Team, 1979.

Year	Club	League	Pos.	G.	AB.	R.	H.	2B.	3B.	HR.	RBI.	B.A.	PO.	A.	E.	F.A.
1979—Lakeland†	Fla. St.	OF	48	168	21	51	10	1	2	23	.304	104	8	3	.974
1980—Evansville	A. A.	1B-OF	126	430	69	117	14	1	5	58	.272	767	62	9	.989
1981—Evansville	A. A.	1B	13	44	8	18	5	0	2	16	.409	129	16	2	.986
1981—Detroit	Amer.	1B-OF	54	83	9	16	3	1	1	11	.193	149	14	0	1.000
1982—Detroit‡	Amer.	1B-OF	82	218	23	52	7	2	3	12	.239	430	29	2	.996
1982—Evansville	A. A.	DH	11	38	6	11	2	0	0	2	.289	0	0	0	.000
1983—Detroit§	Amer.	1B-OF	99	242	22	60	17	0	3	26	.248	465	45	4	.992
1984—Syracuse	Int.	OF-1B	23	79	16	24	6	2	3	8	.304	70	4	2	.974
1984—Toronto	Amer.	OF-1B-P	65	88	11	23	6	2	0	7	.261	92	14	0	1.000
1985—Syracuse	Int.	OF-1B	136	533	77	151	24	2	15	79	.283	675	66	10	.987
1985—Toronto	Amer.	1B-OF	16	35	2	7	0	1	0	1	.200	78	6	1	.988
1986—Toronto	Amer.	OF-1B	110	246	35	76	14	1	5	39	.309	107	5	3	.974
1987—Toronto	Amer.	OF-1B	98	195	26	55	13	1	3	25	.282	57	1	1	.993
1988—Toronto x	Amer.	OF-1B	87	199	21	55	13	1	0	23	.276	93	5	0	1.000
1989—Texas y	Amer.	OF-1B	110	239	32	65	14	1	1	23	.272	74	2	3	.962
1990—San Francisco z	Nat.	OF-1B	78	174	24	51	13	0	2	16	.293	123	5	1	.992
American League Totals—9 Years			721	1545	181	409	87	10	16	167	.265	1545	121	14	.992
National League Totals—1 Year			78	174	24	51	13	0	2	16	.293	123	5	1	.992
Major League Totals—10 Years			799	1719	205	460	100	10	18	183	.268	1668	126	15	.992

Selected by Philadelphia Phillies' organization in 11th round of free-agent draft, June 4, 1975.
Selected by Philadelphia Phillies' organization in 24th round of free-agent draft, June 6, 1978.
Selected by Detroit Tigers' organization in 1st round (13th player selected) of free-agent draft, June 5, 1979.
†On disabled list, June 18 to June 29, 1979.
‡On disabled list, April 12 to May 17, 1982; included rehabilitation disability assignment to Evansville, May 6 to May 17, 1982.
§Released, March 24, 1984; signed by Toronto Blue Jays' organization, April 3, 1984.
xGranted free agency, November 4, 1988; signed by Texas Rangers, January 23, 1989.
yGranted free agency, November 13, 1989; signed by San Francisco Giants, April 8, 1990.
zOn disqualified list, August 7, 1990 through remainder of season.

PITCHING RECORD

Year	Club	League	G.	IP.	W.	L.	Pct.	H.	R.	ER.	SO.	BB.	ERA.
1984—Toronto	American	1	1	0	0	.000	2	3	3	0	2	27.00

TERRY HESTER LEACH

Born March 13, 1954, at Selma, Ala.
Height, 6.00. Weight, 191.
Throws and bats righthanded.
Received business administration degree in personnel management-industrial relations
from Auburn University, Auburn University, Ala.

Major League saves: 1982 (3), 1985 (1), 1988 (3), 1990 (2). Total—9.
Led Gulf States League in home runs allowed with 12 in 1976.

Year	Club	League	G.	IP.	W.	L.	Pct.	H.	R.	ER.	SO.	BB.	ERA.
1976—Baton Rouge†‡	Gulf States	5	19	2	0	1.000	43	21	13	15	14	6.16
1977—Greenwood	W. Carol.	20	67	3	2	.600	47	25	19	67	24	2.55
1978—Savannah§	Southern	9	25	1	0	1.000	24	17	14	21	13	5.04
1978—Kinston	Carolina	34	66	5	4	.556	57	29	24	46	25	3.27
1979—Savannah	Southern	40	92	2	9	.182	77	33	20	68	26	1.96
1979—Richmond	Int'national	7	14	3	1	.750	14	3	3	12	4	1.93
1980—Savannah xy	Southern	22	87	5	1	.833	83	36	31	58	17	3.21
1980—Jackson	Texas	8	54	5	1	.833	50	16	9	30	15	1.50
1981—Tidewater	Int'national	15	76	5	2	.714	63	27	23	42	19	2.72
1981—Jackson	Texas	8	58	5	1	.833	47	14	11	43	12	1.71
1981—New York	National	21	35	1	1	.500	26	11	10	16	12	2.57
1982—Tidewater	Int'national	30	48⅔	4	1	.800	48	20	16	34	10	2.96
1982—New York	National	21	45⅓	2	1	.667	46	22	21	30	18	4.17
1983—Tidewater	Int'national	37	113	5	7	.417	120	66	56	66	42	4.46
1984—Richmond b-Tidewater	Int'national	43	95	11	4	.733	98	42	32	59	30	3.03
1985—Tidewater	Int'national	24	45⅓	1	0	1.000	33	12	8	25	8	1.59
1985—New York	National	22	55⅔	3	4	.429	48	19	18	30	14	2.91
1986—Tidewater	Int'national	34	79⅔	4	4	.500	69	30	22	55	21	2.49
1986—New York	National	6	6⅔	0	0	.000	6	3	2	4	3	2.70
1987—New York c	National	44	131⅓	11	1	.917	132	54	47	61	29	3.22
1988—New York	National	52	92	7	2	.778	95	32	26	51	24	2.54
1989—New York d	National	10	21⅓	0	0	.000	19	11	10	2	4	4.22

Year Club	League	G.	IP.	W.	L.	Pct.	H.	R.	ER.	SO.	BB.	E..
1989—Kansas City e	American	30	73⅓	5	6	.455	78	46	34	34	36	4.1b
1990—Minnesota	American	55	81⅔	2	5	.286	84	31	29	46	21	3.20
National League Totals—7 Years		176	387⅓	24	9	.727	372	152	134	194	104	3.11
American League Totals—2 Years		85	155⅓	7	11	.389	162	77	63	80	57	3.65
Major League Totals—8 Years		261	542⅔	31	20	.608	534	229	197	274	161	3.27

Selected by Boston Red Sox' organization in 7th round of free-agent draft, January 7, 1976.

†Signed as free agent by Baton Rouge (Independent), June 29, 1976; released when Baton Rouge withdrew from league, August 13, 1976.

‡Signed by Greenwood (Atlanta Braves' organization) as free agent, May 28, 1977.

§Loaned to Kinston (Independent), June 3, 1978; returned, October 25, 1978.

xOn disabled list, June 12 to July 23, 1980.

yReleased, July 23, 1980; signed by Jackson (New York Mets' organization), July 27, 1980.

zTraded to Chicago Cubs' organization for Pitchers Jim Adamczak and Mitch Cook, September 26, 1983.

aTraded by Chicago Cubs' organization to Atlanta Braves' organization for Pitcher Ron Meridith, April 4, 1984.

bReleased, May 25, 1984; signed by New York Mets' organization, May 26, 1984.

cOn disabled list, July 12 to July 27, 1987.

dTraded to Kansas City Royals for a player to be named later, June 9, 1989; New York Mets acquired Pitcher Aguedo Vasquez to complete deal, October 1, 1989.

eReleased, April 2, 1990; signed by Minnesota Twins, April 7, 1990.

CHAMPIONSHIP SERIES RECORD

Year Club	League	G.	IP.	W.	L.	Pct.	H.	R.	ER.	SO.	BB.	ERA.
1988—New York	National	3	5	0	0	.000	4	0	0	4	1	0.00

TIMOTHY JAMES LEARY
(Tim)

Born December 23, 1958, at Santa Monica, Calif.
Height, 6.03. Weight, 212.
Throws and bats righthanded.
Attended UCLA, Los Angeles, Calif.

Major League saves: 1987 (1).
Led American League in wild pitches with 23 in 1990.
Tied for National League lead in intentional bases on balls issued with 15 in 1989.
Led Texas League in shutouts with 6 in 1980.
Named National League Comeback Player of the Year by THE SPORTING NEWS, 1988.
Named pitcher on National League Silver Slugger team, 1988.
Named Texas League Most Valuable Player, 1980.
Named righthanded pitcher on THE SPORTING NEWS College Baseball All-America Team, 1979.

Year Club	League	G.	IP.	W.	L.	Pct.	H.	R.	ER.	SO.	BB.	ERA.
1979—Jackson†	Texas					(Did not play)						
1980—Jackson	Texas	26	173	●15	8	.652	150	67	53	138	62	2.76
1981—New York‡	National	1	2	0	0	.000	0	0	0	3	1	0.00
1981—Tidewater	Int'national	6	34	1	3	.250	27	16	14	15	27	3.71
1982—Tidewater§	Int'national					(Did not play)						
1983—Tidewater	Int'national	27	160⅓	8	★16	.333	170	100	78	106	73	4.38
1983—New York	National	2	10⅔	1	1	.500	15	10	4	9	4	3.38
1984—New York	National	20	53⅔	3	3	.500	61	28	24	29	18	4.02
1984—Tidewater x	Int'national	10	53⅓	4	4	.500	47	26	24	27	42	4.05
1985—Vancouver	P. Coast	27	177⅔	10	7	.588	174	85	79	136	57	4.00
1985—Milwaukee	American	5	33⅓	1	4	.200	40	18	15	29	8	4.05
1986—Milwaukee y	American	33	188⅓	12	12	.500	216	97	88	110	53	4.21
1987—Los Angeles	National	39	107⅔	3	11	.214	121	62	57	61	36	4.76
1988—Los Angeles	National	35	228⅔	17	11	.607	201	87	74	180	56	2.91
1989—Los Angeles z-Cincinnati a	National	33	207	8	14	.364	205	84	81	123	68	3.52
1990—New York b	American	31	208	9	★19	.321	202	105	95	138	78	4.11
National League Totals—6 Years		130	609⅔	32	40	.444	603	271	240	405	183	3.54
American League Totals—3 Years		69	429⅔	22	35	.386	458	220	198	277	139	4.15
Major League Totals—9 Years		199	1039⅓	54	75	.419	1061	491	438	682	322	3.79

Selected by New York Mets' organization in 1st round (second player selected) of free-agent draft, June 5, 1979.

†On disabled list, July 19 to October 1, 1979.

‡On disabled list, April 16 to August 1, 1981.

§On disabled list, April 13, 1982 through remainder of season.

xTraded to Milwaukee Brewers' organization as part of a six-player, four-team deal in which Kansas City Royals acquired Catcher Jim Sundberg from Milwaukee, Texas Rangers acquired Catcher Don Slaught from Kansas City, New York Mets' organization acquired Pitcher Frank Wills from Kansas City and Milwaukee acquired Pitcher Danny Darwin and a player to be named later from Texas, January 18, 1985; Milwaukee organization acquired Catcher Bill Hance from Texas to complete deal, January 30, 1985.

yTraded with Pitcher Tim Crews to Los Angeles Dodgers for First Baseman Greg Brock, December 10, 1986.

zTraded with Shortstop Mariano Duncan to Cincinnati Reds for Outfielder Kal Daniels and Infielder Lenny Harris, July 18, 1989.

aTraded with Outfielder Van Snider to New York Yankees for First Baseman Hal Morris and Pitcher Rodney Imes, December 12, 1989.

bGranted free agency, November 5, 1990; re-signed by Yankees, November 19, 1990.

CHAMPIONSHIP SERIES RECORD

Year Club	League	G.	IP.	W.	L.	Pct.	H.	R.	ER.	SO.	BB.	ERA.
1988—Los Angeles	National	2	4⅓	0	1	.000	8	4	3	3	3	6.23

Year Club	League	G.	IP.	W.	L.	Pct.	H.	R.	ER.	SO.	BB.	ERA.
1988—Los Angeles	National	2	6⅔	0	0	.000	6	1	1	4	2	1.35

MANUEL LORA LEE
(Manny)

Born June 17, 1965, at San Pedro de Macoris, D. R.
Height, 5.09. Weight, 166.
Throws right and bats left and righthanded.
Major League stolen bases: 1985 (1), 1987 (2), 1988 (3), 1989 (4), 1990 (3). Total—13.

Year Club	League	Pos.	G.	AB.	R.	H.	2B.	3B.	HR.	RBI.	B.A.	PO.	A.	E.	F.A.
1982—Kingsport	Appal.	2B-SS	16	54	2	12	1	0	0	3	.222	34	34	6	.919
1983—Sarasota Mets	Gulf C.	2B-SS	32	97	8	24	2	1	0	12	.247	44	79	8	.939
1983—Little Falls	NYP	2B	17	45	10	13	0	0	0	5	.289	34	40	3	.961
1984—Columbia†‡§	S. Atl.	SS-2B	102	346	84	114	12	5	2	33	★.329	126	277	34	.922
1985—Toronto	Amer.	2B-SS-3B	64	40	9	8	0	0	0	0	.200	34	56	3	.968
1986—Syracuse	Int.	SS-2B	76	236	34	58	6	1	1	19	.246	132	237	18	.953
1986—Knoxville	South.	SS-2B	41	158	21	43	1	2	0	11	.272	70	117	8	.959
1986—Toronto	Amer.	2B-SS-3B	35	78	8	16	0	1	1	7	.205	36	76	2	.982
1987—Toronto	Amer.	2B-SS	56	121	14	31	2	3	1	11	.256	77	110	5	.974
1987—Syracuse	Int.	SS	74	251	25	71	9	5	3	26	.283	120	177	23	.928
1988—Toronto x	Amer.	2B-SS-3B	116	381	38	111	16	3	2	38	.291	250	308	12	.979
1989—Toronto y	Amer.	2-S-3-O	99	300	27	78	9	2	3	34	.260	152	201	11	.970
1990—Toronto	Amer.	★2B-SS	117	391	45	95	12	4	6	41	.243	265	301	4	★.993
Major League Totals—6 Years			487	1311	141	339	39	13	13	131	.259	814	1052	37	.981

Signed as free agent by New York Mets' organization, May 10, 1982.
†On disabled list, April 9 to April 22, 1984.
‡Traded with Outfielder Gerald Young to Houston Astros, August 31, 1984, as partial completion of deal in which New York Mets acquired Infielder Ray Knight for three players to be named later, August 28, 1984; Houston acquired Pitcher Mitch Cook to complete deal, September 10, 1984.
§Drafted by Toronto Blue Jays, December 3, 1984.
xOn disabled list, March 28 to April 12 and May 12 to June 1, 1988.
yOn disabled list, April 30 to June 6, 1989.

CHAMPIONSHIP SERIES RECORD

Year Club	League	Pos.	G.	AB.	R.	H.	2B.	3B.	HR.	RBI.	B.A.	PO.	A.	E.	F.A.
1985—Toronto	Amer.	PR-2B	1	0	0	0	0	0	0	0	.000	0	0	0	.000
1989—Toronto	Amer.	2B	2	8	2	2	0	0	0	0	.250	4	1	0	1.000
Championship Series Totals—2 Years			3	8	2	2	0	0	0	0	.250	4	1	0	1.000

MARK OWEN LEE

Born July 20, 1964, at Williston, N. D.
Height, 6.03. Weight, 198.
Throws and bats lefthanded.
Attended Trinidad State Junior College, Trinidad, Colo.,
and Florida International University, Miami, Fla.

Year Club	League	G.	IP.	W.	L.	Pct.	H.	R.	ER.	SO.	BB.	ERA.
1985—Bristol	Ap'lachian	15	33	3	0	1.000	18	5	4	40	12	1.09
1986—Lakeland	Florida St.	41	62⅔	2	5	.286	73	44	36	39	21	5.17
1987—Glens Falls	Eastern	7	8⅓	0	0	.000	13	9	8	3	1	8.64
1987—Lakeland	Florida St.	30	53	3	2	.600	48	17	15	42	18	2.55
1988—Lakeland	Florida St.	10	19	1	0	1.000	16	7	3	15	4	1.42
1988—Glens Falls	Eastern	14	26	3	0	1.000	27	10	7	25	4	2.42
1988—Toledo†	Int'national	22	19⅓	0	1	.000	18	7	6	13	7	2.79
1988—Kansas City	American	4	5	0	0	.000	6	2	2	0	1	3.60
1989—Memphis‡	Southern	25	122⅔	5	11	.313	149	84	71	79	44	5.21
1990—Stockton	California	5	7⅔	1	0	1.000	5	2	2	7	3	2.35
1990—Denver	Am. Assoc.	20	28	3	1	.750	25	7	7	35	6	2.25
1990—Milwaukee	American	11	21⅓	1	0	1.000	20	5	5	14	4	2.11
Major League Totals—2 Years		15	26⅓	1	0	1.000	26	7	7	14	5	2.39

Selected by Detroit Tigers' organization in 15th round of free-agent draft, June 3, 1985.
†Traded with Catcher Rey Palacios to Kansas City Royals for Pitcher Ted Power, August 31, 1988.
‡Released, March 31, 1990, signed by Stockton (Milwaukee Brewers' organization), May 23, 1990.

TERRY JAMES LEE

Born March 13, 1962, at San Francisco, Calif.
Height, 6.05. Weight, 220.
Throws and bats righthanded.
Attended Chemeketa Community College, Salem, Ore.;
and Boise State University, Boise, Ida.

Led Eastern League first basemen in double plays with 93 in 1984.

Year Club	League	Pos.	G.	AB.	R.	H.	2B.	3B.	HR.	RBI.	B.A.	PO.	A.	E.	F.A.
1982—Eugene	N'west	OF-1B	32	117	23	30	5	3	4	21	.256	123	7	1	.992
1983—Cedar Rapids	Midw.	★1-O-3	123	405	60	106	★31	1	19	67	.262	946	64	8	★.992
1984—Vermont	East.	1B	134	422	56	102	10	2	11	47	.242	★1105	85	★16	.987

Year	Club	League	Pos.	G.	AB.	R.	H.	2B.	3B.	HR.	RBI.	B.A.	PO.	A.	E.	F.A.
1985—Vermont	East.	1B-OF-3B	121	409	56	118	20	2	12	62	.289	599	59	10	.985
1986—Denver†	A. A.	1B	34	104	10	25	2	1	2	10	.240	240	25	1	.996
1987—Denver‡	A. A.	(Did Not Play)													
1988—Greensboro	S. Atl.	1B	25	56	8	18	5	0	2	9	.321	39	2	0	1.000
1989—Chattanooga	South.	OF-1B	51	177	23	46	13	0	5	27	.260	66	3	1	.986
1989—Nashville	A. A.	1B	13	47	5	11	4	0	0	3	.234	118	13	2	.985
1990—Chattanooga	South.	1B	43	156	25	51	8	1	8	20	.327	331	27	6	.984
1990—Nashville	A. A.	1B	72	260	38	79	18	1	15	67	.304	592	47	5	.992
1990—Cincinnati	Nat.	1B	12	19	1	4	1	0	0	3	.211	28	3	0	1.000
Major League Totals—1 Year				12	19	1	4	1	0	0	3	.211	28	3	0	1.000

Signed as free agent by Cincinnati Reds' organization, July 30, 1982.
†On disabled list, June 9, 1986 through remainder of season.
‡On disabled list, April 1, 1987 through entire season.

CRAIG LINDSAY LEFFERTS

Born September 29, 1957, in Munich, West Germany.
Height, 6.01. Weight, 210.
Throws and bats lefthanded.
Attended University of Arizona, Tucson, Ariz.

Major League saves: 1983 (1), 1984 (10), 1985 (2), 1986 (4), 1987 (6), 1988 (11), 1989 (20), 1990 (23). Total—77.

Year	Club	League	G.	IP.	W.	L.	Pct.	H.	R.	ER.	SO.	BB.	ERA.
1980—Geneva	NYP	12	94	9	1	∗.900	74	35	29	∗99	24	2.78
1981—Midland	Texas	26	185	12	●12	.500	203	95	85	135	36	4.14
1982—Iowa†	Am.Assoc.	18	97⅓	8	5	.615	97	50	33	71	25	3.05
1983—Chicago‡	National	56	89	3	4	.429	80	35	31	60	29	3.13
1984—San Diego	National	62	105⅔	3	4	.429	88	29	25	56	24	2.13
1985—San Diego	National	60	83⅓	7	6	.538	75	34	31	48	30	3.35
1986—San Diego	National	∗83	107⅔	9	8	.529	98	41	37	72	44	3.09
1987—San Diego§-San Francisco	National	77	98⅔	5	5	.500	92	47	42	57	33	3.83
1988—San Francisco	National	64	92⅓	3	8	.273	74	33	30	58	23	2.92
1989—San Francisco x	National	70	107	2	4	.333	93	38	32	71	22	2.69
1990—San Diego	National	56	78⅔	7	5	.583	68	26	22	60	22	2.52
Major League Totals—8 Years		528	762⅓	39	44	.470	668	283	250	482	227	2.95

Selected by Kansas City Royals' organization in 6th round of free-agent draft, June 5, 1979.
Selected by Chicago Cubs' organization in 9th round of free-agent draft, June 3, 1980.
†On disabled list, April 24 to June 4, 1982.
‡Traded with First Baseman Carmelo Martinez and Third Baseman Fritz Connally to San Diego Padres for Pitcher Scott Sanderson, December 7, 1983.
§Traded with Pitcher Dave Dravecky and Infielder Kevin Mitchell to San Francisco Giants for Third Baseman Chris Brown and Pitchers Keith Comstock, Mark Davis and Mark Grant, July 4, 1987.
xGranted free agency, November 13, 1989; signed by San Diego Padres, December 6, 1989.

CHAMPIONSHIP SERIES RECORD

Year	Club	League	G.	IP.	W.	L.	Pct.	H.	R.	ER.	SO.	BB.	ERA.
1984—San Diego	National	3	4	2	0	1.000	1	0	0	1	1	0.00
1987—San Francisco	National	3	2	0	0	.000	3	0	0	0	1	0.00
1989—San Francisco	National	2	1	0	0	.000	1	1	1	1	2	9.00
Championship Series Totals—3 Years		8	7	2	0	1.000	5	1	1	2	4	1.29

WORLD SERIES RECORD

Year	Club	League	G.	IP.	W.	L.	Pct.	H.	R.	ER.	SO.	BB.	ERA.
1984—San Diego	National	3	6	0	0	.000	2	0	0	7	1	0.00
1989—San Francisco	National	3	2⅔	0	0	.000	2	1	1	1	2	3.38
World Series Totals—2 Years		6	8⅔	0	0	.000	4	1	1	8	3	1.04

CHARLES LOUIS LEIBRANDT JR.
(Charlie)

Born October 4, 1956, at Chicago, Ill.
Height, 6.03. Weight, 200.
Throws left and bats righthanded.
Received bachelor of science degree in business management from
Miami University, Oxford, O.

Holds major league record for fewest assists by pitcher, for leader in assists (43), 1986.
Major League saves: 1982 (2).
Tied for American Association lead in shutouts with 3 in 1984.
Tied for American Association lead in games started by pitchers with 26 in 1979.

Year	Club	League	G.	IP.	W.	L.	Pct.	H.	R.	ER.	SO.	BB.	ERA.
1978—Eugene	Northwest	3	20	2	0	1.000	24	13	9	18	5	4.05
1978—Tampa	Florida St.	6	47	4	1	.800	26	4	4	40	17	0.77
1978—Indianapolis	Am. Assoc	4	29	2	1	.667	20	9	9	12	12	2.79
1979—Indianapolis	Am. Assoc.	27	162	8	●14	.364	146	67	53	100	65	2.94
1979—Cincinnati	National	3	4	0	0	.000	2	2	0	1	2	0.00
1980—Cincinnati	National	36	174	10	9	.526	200	84	82	62	54	4.24
1981—Indianapolis	Am. Assoc.	25	169	9	7	.563	149	76	55	101	75	2.93
1981—Cincinnati	National	7	30	1	1	.500	28	12	12	9	15	3.60
1982—Cincinnati	National	36	107⅔	5	7	.417	130	68	61	34	48	5.10

Year Club	League	G.	IP.	W.	L.	Pct.	H.	R.	ER.	SO.	BB.	ERA.
1983—Indianapolis†-Omaha	Am. Assoc.	27	185⅓	9	10	.474	181	113	88	128	77	4.27
1984—Omaha..	Am. Assoc.	9	72⅔	7	1	.875	51	14	10	38	16	1.24
1984—Kansas City..................................	American	23	143¾	11	7	.611	158	65	58	53	38	3.63
1985—Kansas City..................................	American	33	237⅔	17	9	.654	223	86	71	108	68	2.69
1986—Kansas City..................................	American	35	231⅓	14	11	.560	238	112	105	108	63	4.09
1987—Kansas City‡................................	American	35	240⅓	16	11	.593	235	104	91	151	74	3.41
1988—Kansas City..................................	American	35	243	13	12	.520	244	98	86	125	62	3.19
1989—Kansas City§................................	American	33	161	5	11	.313	196	98	92	73	54	5.14
1990—Greenville x.................................	Southern	2	13	1	0	1.000	5	4	0	12	5	0.00
1990—Atlanta y.....................................	National	24	162⅓	9	11	.450	164	72	57	76	35	3.16
National League Totals—5 Years.......................		106	478	25	28	.472	524	238	212	182	154	3.99
American League Totals—6 Years.....................		194	1257	76	61	.555	1294	563	503	618	359	3.60
Major League Totals—11 Years..........................		300	1735	101	89	.532	1818	801	715	800	513	3.71

Selected by Cincinnati Reds' organization in 9th round of free-agent draft, June 6, 1978.

†Traded to Kansas City Royals for Pitcher Bob Tufts, June 7, 1983.

‡Granted free agency, November 9, 1987; re-signed by Royals, January 7, 1988.

§Traded with Pitcher Rick Luecken to Atlanta Braves for First Baseman Gerald Perry and Pitcher Jim Lemasters, December 15, 1989.

xOn Atlanta disabled list, March 26 to June 3, 1990; included rehabilitation disability assignment to Greenville, May 21 to June 3, 1990.

yGranted free agency, December 7, 1990; re-signed by Braves, December 20, 1990.

CHAMPIONSHIP SERIES RECORD

Shares Championship Series record for most games lost, series (2), 1985.

Year Club	League	G.	IP.	W.	L.	Pct.	H.	R.	ER.	SO.	BB.	ERA.
1979—Cincinnati.......................................	National	1	⅓	0	0	.000	0	0	0	0	0	0.00
1984—Kansas City..................................	American	1	8	0	1	.000	3	1	1	6	4	1.13
1985—Kansas City..................................	American	3	15⅓	1	2	.333	17	9	9	6	4	5.28
Championship Series Totals—3 Years................		5	23⅔	1	3	.250	20	10	10	12	8	3.80

WORLD SERIES RECORD

Year Club	League	G.	IP.	W.	L.	Pct.	H.	R.	ER.	SO.	BB.	ERA.
1985—Kansas City..................................	American	2	16⅓	0	1	.000	10	5	5	10	4	2.76

JOHN WILLIAM LEISTER

Name pronounced LIE-ster.

Born January 3, 1961, at San Antonio, Tex.
Height, 6.02. Weight, 215.
Throws and bats righthanded.
Attended Michigan State University, East Lansing, Mich.

Led International League in wild pitches with 12 in 1989.

Year Club	League	G.	IP.	W.	L.	Pct.	H.	R.	ER.	SO.	BB.	ERA.
1984—Winter Haven...............................	Florida St.	31	175⅓	12	12	.500	173	90	66	103	93	3.39
1985—New Britain	Eastern	27	105	8	6	.571	91	48	37	68	49	3.17
1986—Pawtucket†..................................	Int'national	23	134⅔	8	7	.533	125	68	61	78	81	4.08
1987—Pawtucket....................................	Int'national	21	145⅔	11	5	.688	136	69	61	92	52	3.77
1987—Boston...	American	8	30⅓	0	2	.000	49	31	31	16	12	9.20
1988—Pawtucket....................................	Int'national	28	167	6	16	.273	161	90	80	112	75	4.31
1989—Pawtucket....................................	Int'national	38	128⅓	7	7	.500	101	58	56	104	70	3.93
1990—Pawtucket‡..................................	Int'national	19	95	2	10	.167	114	65	61	47	39	5.78
1990—Boston...	American	2	5⅔	0	0	.000	7	5	3	3	4	4.76
Major League Totals—2 Years............................		10	36	0	2	.000	56	36	34	19	16	8.50

Selected by New York Mets' organization in 20th round of free-agent draft, June 5, 1979.

Selected by Oakland A's organization in 6th round of free-agent draft, June 6, 1983.

Selected by Boston Red Sox' organization in secondary phase of free-agent draft, January 17, 1984.

†On disabled list, June 26 to July 11, 1986.

‡On disabled list, July 31 to August 13, 1990.

RECORD AS FOOTBALL PLAYER

Selected by Michigan in 1983 USFL territorial draft.

Signed as free agent by Pittsburgh Steelers, June 20, 1983.

Released by Pittsburgh Steelers, August 29, 1983; signed by Michigan Panthers, October 24, 1983.

Placed on reserve/left team, January 30, 1984.

Not protected in merger of Michigan Panthers and Oakland Invaders, December 6, 1984.

ALOIS TERRY LEITER

Name pronounced LIE-ter.

(Al)

Born October 23, 1965, at Toms River, N. J.
Height, 6.03. Weight, 215.
Throws and bats lefthanded.
Brother of Kurt Leiter, pitcher in Baltimore Orioles' organization,
1982 through 1984; and Miami (Independent), 1986; and brother of Mark Leiter,
pitcher in New York Yankees' organization.

Year Club	League	G.	IP.	W.	L.	Pct.	H.	R.	ER.	SO.	BB.	ERA.
1984—Oneonta	NYP	10	57	3	2	.600	52	32	23	48	26	3.63
1985—Oneonta	NYP	6	38	3	2	.600	27	14	10	34	25	2.37
1985—Fort Lauderdale	Florida St.	17	82	1	6	.143	87	70	59	44	57	6.48
1986—Fort Lauderdale	Florida St.	22	117⅔	4	8	.333	96	64	53	101	90	4.05
1987—Columbus	Int'national	5	23⅓	1	4	.200	21	18	16	23	15	6.17
1987—Albany	Eastern	15	78	3	3	.500	64	34	29	71	37	3.35
1987—New York	American	4	22⅔	2	2	.500	24	16	16	28	15	6.35
1988—New York†	American	14	57⅓	4	4	.500	49	27	25	60	33	3.92
1988—Columbus	Int'national	4	13	0	2	.000	5	7	5	12	14	3.46
1989—New York‡-Toronto§	American	5	33⅓	1	2	.333	32	23	21	26	23	5.67
1989—Dunedin	Florida St.	3	8	0	2	.000	11	5	5	4	5	5.63
1990—Dunedin	Florida St.	6	24	0	0	.000	18	8	7	14	12	2.63
1990—Syracuse x	Int'national	15	78	3	8	.273	59	43	40	69	68	4.62
1990—Toronto	American	4	6⅓	0	0	.000	1	0	0	5	2	0.00
Major League Totals—4 Years		27	119⅔	7	8	.467	106	66	62	119	73	4.66

Selected by New York Yankees' organization in 2nd round of free-agent draft, June 4, 1984.

†On disabled list, June 22 to July 26, 1988; included rehabilitation disability assignment to Columbus, July 17 to July 25, 1988.

‡Traded to Toronto Blue Jays for Outfielder Jesse Barfield, April 30, 1989.

§On disabled list, May 11, 1989 through remainder of season; included rehabilitation disability assignment to Dunedin, August 12 to August 29, 1989.

xOn disabled list, May 20 to June 13, 1990.

MARK EDWARD LEITER

Name pronounced LIE-ter.

Born April 13, 1963, at Joliet, Ill.
Height, 6.03. Weight, 210.
Throws and bats righthanded.
Attended Connors State College, Warner, Okla., and Ramapo College, Mahwah, N.J.
Brother of Al Leiter, pitcher with Toronto Blue Jays; and Kurt Leiter,
pitcher in Baltimore Orioles' organization, 1982 through
1984; and Miami (Independent), 1986.

Year Club	League	G.	IP.	W.	L.	Pct.	H.	R.	ER.	SO.	BB.	ERA.
1983—Bluefield	Ap'lachian	6	36⅔	2	1	.667	33	17	11	35	13	2.70
1983—Hagerstown	Carolina	8	36	1	5	.167	42	31	29	18	28	7.25
1984—Hagerstown	Carolina	27	139⅓	8	●13	.381	132	96	87	105	★108	5.62
1985—Hagerstown	Carolina	34	83⅓	2	8	.200	77	44	32	82	29	3.46
1985—Charlotte	Southern	5	6⅓	0	1	.000	3	1	1	8	2	1.42
1986—Charlotte†	Southern						(Did Not Play)					
1987—Charlotte‡	Southern						(Did Not Play)					
1988—Charlotte§x	Southern						(Did Not Play)					
1989—Fort Lauderdale	Florida St.	6	35⅓	2	2	.500	27	9	6	22	5	1.53
1989—Columbus	Int'national	22	90	9	6	.600	102	50	50	70	34	5.00
1990—Columbus	Int'national	30	122⅔	9	4	.692	114	56	49	115	27	3.60
1990—New York	American	8	26⅓	1	1	.500	33	20	20	21	9	6.84
Major League Totals—1 Year		8	26⅓	1	1	.500	33	20	20	21	9	6.84

Selected by Baltimore Orioles' organization in 4th round of free-agent draft, January 11, 1983.

†On disabled list, April 10, 1986 through entire season.

‡On disabled list, April 10, 1987 through entire season.

§On disabled list, April 10, 1988 through entire season.

xReleased, June 13, 1988; signed by Fort Lauderdale (New York Yankees' organization), September 29, 1988.

SCOTT THOMAS LEIUS

Name pronounced LAY-us.

Born September 24, 1965, at Yonkers, N.Y.
Height, 6.03. Weight, 180.
Throws and bats righthanded.
Attended Concordia College, Bronxville, N.Y.

Led Midwest League shortstops in double plays with 74 in 1987.
Led Appalachian League shortstops in assists with 174 and double plays with 33 in 1986.

Year Club	League	Pos.	G.	AB.	R.	H.	2B.	3B.	HR.	RBI.	B.A.	PO.	A.	E.	F.A.
1986—Elizabethton	Appal.	SS-3B	61	237	37	66	14	1	4	23	.278	67	176	18	.931
1987—Kenosha	Midw.	SS	126	414	65	99	16	4	8	51	.239	183	331	31	.943
1988—Visalia	Calif.	SS	93	308	44	73	14	4	3	46	.237	154	234	15	.963
1989—Orlando†	South.	SS	99	346	49	105	22	2	4	45	★.303	148	257	22	.948
1990—Portland	P. C.	SS-2B	103	352	34	81	13	5	2	23	.229	155	323	18	.964
1990—Minnesota	Amer.	SS-3B	14	25	4	6	1	0	1	4	.240	20	25	0	1.000
Major League Totals—1 Year			14	25	4	6	1	0	1	4	.240	20	25	0	1.000

Selected by Minnesota Twins' organization in 13th round of free-agent draft, June 2, 1986.

†On disabled list, August 3, 1989 through remainder of season.

MARK ALAN LEMKE

Name pronounced LEM-kee.

Born August 13, 1965, at Utica, N.Y.
Height, 5.09. Weight, 165.
Throws right and bats left and righthanded.

— 277 —

Led Southern League in total bases with 239 in 1988.
Led International League second basemen in total chances with 731 and double plays with 105 in 1989.
Led Southern League second basemen in total chances with 739 and double plays with 105 in 1988.
Led Carolina League second basemen in double plays with 83 in 1987.
Led Gulf Coast League second basemen in assists with 207, total chances with 391 and double plays with 39 in 1984.

Year	Club	League	Pos.	G.	AB.	R.	H.	2B.	3B.	HR.	RBI.	B.A.	PO.	A.	E.	F.A.
1983—Bradenton Braves	Gulf C.		2B	53	209	37	55	6	0	0	19	.263	81	101	11	.943
1984—Anderson	S. Atl.		2B-3B	42	121	18	18	2	0	0	5	.149	67	83	4	.974
1984—Bradenton Braves	Gulf C.		*2B-SS	•63	*243	41	67	11	0	3	32	.276	*175	209	9	*.977
1985—Sumter	S. Atl.		2B	90	231	25	50	6	0	0	20	.216	119	174	11	.964
1986—Sumter	S. Atl.		3B-2B	126	448	99	122	24	2	18	66	.272	134	274	16	.962
1987—Durham	Carol.		*2B-3B	127	489	75	143	28	3	20	68	.292	248	*355	11	*.982
1987—Greenville	South.		3B	6	26	0	6	0	0	0	4	.231	4	12	1	.941
1988—Greenville	South.		2B	•143	*567	81	*153	30	4	16	80	.270	*281	*440	18	.976
1988—Atlanta	Nat.		2B	16	58	8	13	4	0	0	2	.224	47	51	3	.970
1989—Richmond	Int.		2B	*146	*518	69	143	22	7	5	61	.276	*299	*417	*15	.979
1989—Atlanta	Nat.		2B	14	55	4	10	2	1	2	10	.182	25	40	0	1.000
1990—Atlanta†	Nat.		3B-2B-SS	102	239	22	54	13	0	0	21	.226	90	193	4	.986
1990—Bradenton Brav...	Gulf C.		2B-3B	4	11	2	4	0	0	1	5	.364	5	11	1	.941
Major League Totals—3 Years				132	352	34	77	19	1	2	33	.219	162	284	7	.985

Selected by Atlanta Braves' organization in 27th round of free-agent draft, June 6, 1983.
†On disabled list, May 29 to July 17, 1990; included rehabilitation disability assignment to Bradenton, July 9 to July 17, 1990.

CHESTER EARL LEMON
(Chet)

Born February 12, 1955, at Jackson, Miss.
Height, 6.00. Weight, 190.
Throws and bats righthanded.
Attended Pepperdine University, Malibu, Calif., and Cerritos College, Norwalk, Calif.
Cousin of Eric Yarber, wide receiver-kick returner with Washington Redskins, 1986 and 1987.

Holds American League records for most chances accepted by outfielder, season (524), 1977; most putouts by outfielder, season (512), 1977; most years by outfielder, 400 or more putouts (5).
Shares American League record for most years by outfielder, 500 or more putouts (1), 1977.
Major League stolen bases: 1975 (1), 1976 (13), 1977 (8), 1978 (5), 1979 (7), 1980 (6), 1981 (5), 1982 (1), 1984 (5), 1986 (2), 1988 (1), 1989 (1), 1990 (3). Total—58.
Led American League in being hit by pitch with 13 in 1979, 13 in 1981, 15 in 1982 and 20 in 1983.
Led American League outfielders in total chances with 536 in 1977.

Year	Club	League	Pos.	G.	AB.	R.	H.	2B.	3B.	HR.	RBI.	B.A.	PO.	A.	E.	F.A.
1972—Coos Bay-N. B.	N'west		SS-3B	38	140	33	40	8	1	2	16	.286	56	94	16	.904
1972—Burlington	Midw.		3B-SS	33	129	18	33	5	0	1	8	.256	24	62	13	.869
1973—Burlington	Midw.		3B-SS	113	392	73	121	21	1	19	*88	.309	102	215	36	.898
1974—Birmingham†	South.		3B-SS	79	272	52	79	22	2	10	61	.290	84	135	23	.905
1975—Tucson‡	P. C.		3B-OF	65	243	43	68	7	2	5	33	.280	60	70	19	.872
1975—Denver	A. A.		3B-OF	70	254	40	78	15	6	8	49	.307	39	76	19	.858
1975—Chicago	Amer.		3B-OF	9	35	2	9	2	0	0	1	.257	5	7	1	.923
1976—Chicago	Amer.		OF	132	451	46	111	15	5	4	38	.246	353	12	3	.992
1977—Chicago	Amer.		OF	150	553	99	151	38	4	19	67	.273	*512	12	12	.978
1978—Chicago§	Amer.		OF	105	357	51	107	24	6	13	55	.300	284	8	5	.983
1979—Chicago	Amer.		OF	148	556	79	177	•44	2	17	86	.318	411	10	10	.977
1980—Chicago	Amer.		OF-2B	147	514	76	150	32	6	11	51	.292	347	11	7	.981
1981—Chicago x	Amer.		OF	94	328	50	99	23	6	9	50	.302	240	2	4	.948
1982—Detroit	Amer.		OF	125	436	75	116	20	1	19	52	.266	242	11	4	.984
1983—Detroit	Amer.		OF	145	491	78	125	21	5	24	69	.255	406	6	5	.988
1984—Detroit	Amer.		OF	141	509	77	146	34	6	20	76	.287	427	6	2	.995
1985—Detroit	Amer.		OF	145	517	69	137	28	4	18	68	.265	411	6	4	.990
1986—Detroit	Amer.		OF	126	403	45	101	21	3	12	53	.251	316	6	5	.985
1987—Detroit	Amer.		OF	146	470	75	130	30	3	20	75	.277	350	4	3	.992
1988—Detroit	Amer.		OF	144	512	67	135	29	4	17	64	.264	296	8	8	.974
1989—Detroit	Amer.		OF	127	414	45	98	19	2	7	47	.237	189	6	3	.985
1990—Detroit y	Amer.		OF	104	322	39	83	16	4	5	32	.258	209	7	6	.973
Major League Totals—16 Years				1988	6868	973	1875	396	61	215	884	.273	4998	122	82	.984

Selected by Oakland A's organization in 1st round (20th player selected) of free-agent draft, June 6, 1972.
†On disabled list, July 16 to September 16, 1974.
‡Traded with Pitcher Dave Hamilton to Chicago White Sox for Pitchers Stan Bahnsen and Lee (Skip) Pitlock, June 15, 1975.
§On disabled list, August 12 to August 27, 1978.
xTraded to Detroit Tigers for Outfielder Steve Kemp, November 27, 1981.
yOn disabled list, June 20 to July 5, 1990.

CHAMPIONSHIP SERIES RECORD

Year	Club	League	Pos.	G.	AB.	R.	H.	2B.	3B.	HR.	RBI.	B.A.	PO.	A.	E.	F.A.
1984—Detroit	Amer.		OF	3	13	1	0	0	0	0	0	.000	9	0	0	1.000
1987—Detroit	Amer.		OF	5	18	4	5	0	0	2	4	.278	13	0	0	1.000
Championship Series Totals—2 Years				8	31	5	5	0	0	2	4	.161	22	0	0	1.000

WORLD SERIES RECORD

Year	Club	League	Pos.	G.	AB.	R.	H.	2B.	3B.	HR.	RBI.	B.A.	PO.	A.	E.	F.A.
1984—Detroit	Amer.		OF	5	17	1	5	0	0	0	1	.294	15	0	0	1.000

Year League	Pos.	AB.	R.	H.	2B.	3B.	HR.	RBI.	B.A.	PO.	A.	E.	F.A.
1978—American	OF	0	0	0	0	0	0	0	.000	0	0	1	.000
1979—American	OF	2	1	0	0	0	0	0	.000	2	0	0	1.000
1984—American	OF	2	0	1	0	0	0	0	.500	0	0	0	.000
All-Star Game Totals—3 Years		4	1	1	0	0	0	0	.250	2	0	1	.667

PATRICK ORLANDO LENNON

Born April 27, 1968, at Whiteville, N.C.
Height, 6.02. Weight, 200.
Throws and bats righthanded.

Led Midwest League third basemen in errors with 39 in 1987.

Year Club	League	Pos.	G.	AB.	R.	H.	2B.	3B.	HR.	RBI.	B.A.	PO.	A.	E.	F.A.
1986—Bellingham	N'west	SS-3B	51	169	35	41	5	2	3	27	.243	57	90	27	.845
1987—Wausau	Midw.	3B-SS	98	319	54	80	21	3	7	34	.251	73	190	40	.868
1988—Vermont	East.	3B	95	321	44	83	9	3	9	40	.259	81	143	*28	.889
1989—Williamsport	East.	OF-3B	66	248	32	65	14	2	3	31	.262	67	20	14	.861
1990—San Bernardino	Calif.	3B-OF	44	163	29	47	6	2	8	30	.288	29	40	7	.908
1990—Williamsport	East.	OF-3B	49	167	24	49	6	4	5	22	.293	62	40	10	.911

Selected by Seattle Mariners' organization in 1st round (eighth player selected) of free-agent draft, June 2, 1986.

JEFFREY N. LEONARD

Born September 22, 1955, at Philadelphia, Pa.
Height, 6.04. Weight, 205.
Throws and bats righthanded.

Major League stolen bases: 1979 (23), 1980 (4), 1981 (5), 1982 (18), 1983 (26), 1984 (17), 1985 (11), 1986 (16), 1987 (16), 1988 (17), 1989 (6), 1990 (4). Total—163.
Hit for the cycle, June 27, 1985.
Named National League Rookie Player of the Year by THE SPORTING NEWS, 1979.

Year Club	League	Pos.	G.	AB.	R.	H.	2B.	3B.	HR.	RBI.	B.A.	PO.	A.	E.	F.A.
1973—Bellingham	N'west	OF	55	187	30	52	4	3	2	20	.278	46	2	5	.906
1974—Orangeburg	W. Car.	OF	8	15	0	1	0	0	0	1	.067	5	1	1	.857
1974—Bellingham	N'west	OF	78	278	47	90	12	4	3	43	.324	115	7	6	.953
1975—Bakersfield	Calif.	OF	106	320	44	89	11	3	4	37	.278	137	5	7	.953
1976—Lodi	Calif.	OF	133	509	93	168	29	9	8	85	.330	214	13	*15	.938
1976—Albuquerque	P. C.	OF	7	27	2	8	2	1	1	6	.296	14	0	0	1.000
1977—San Antonio	Texas	OF	122	468	75	147	17	10	12	70	.314	241	12	8	.969
1977—Los Angeles	Nat.	OF	11	10	1	3	0	1	0	2	.300	7	0	0	1.000
1978—Albuquerque†	P. C.	OF	133	502	111	*183	23	14	11	93	*.365	216	8	6	.974
1978—Houston	Nat.	OF	8	26	2	10	2	0	0	4	.385	16	1	0	1.000
1979—Houston	Nat.	OF	134	411	47	119	15	5	0	47	.290	227	6	10	.959
1980—Houston	Nat.	OF	88	216	29	46	7	5	3	20	.213	161	9	3	.983
1981—Hou.‡-S.F.	Nat.	OF-1B	44	145	21	42	12	4	4	29	.290	152	5	1	.994
1981—Phoenix	P. C.	OF	47	187	38	75	17	3	7	45	.401	90	2	2	.979
1982—San Francisco§	Nat.	OF-1B	80	278	32	72	16	1	9	49	.259	137	2	9	.939
1982—Phoenix	P. C.	OF	17	59	14	21	5	0	4	12	.356	5	0	0	1.000
1983—San Francisco	Nat.	OF	139	516	74	144	17	7	21	87	.279	253	17	7	.975
1984—San Francisco	Nat.	OF	136	514	76	155	27	2	21	86	.302	247	14	8	.970
1985—San Francisco	Nat.	OF	133	507	49	122	20	3	17	62	.241	203	10	5	.977
1986—San Francisco x	Nat.	OF	89	341	48	95	11	3	6	42	.279	158	4	5	.970
1987—San Francisco	Nat.	OF	131	503	70	141	29	4	19	63	.280	193	7	7	.966
1988—San Francisco yz	Nat.	OF	44	160	12	41	8	1	2	20	.256	74	0	1	.987
1988—Milwaukee a	Amer.	OF	94	374	45	88	19	0	8	44	.235	191	4	3	.985
1989—Seattle	Amer.	OF	150	566	69	144	20	1	24	93	.254	54	0	1	.982
1990—Seattle b	Amer.	OF	134	478	39	120	20	0	10	75	.251	118	0	2	.983
National League Totals—12 Years			1037	3627	461	990	164	36	102	511	.273	1828	75	56	.971
American League Totals—3 Years			378	1418	153	352	59	1	42	212	.248	363	6	6	.984
Major League Totals—14 Years			1415	5045	614	1342	223	37	144	723	.266	2191	81	62	.973

Signed as free agent by Los Angeles Dodgers' organization, June 7, 1973.
†Traded to Houston Astros, September 11, 1978, completing deal in which Los Angeles Dodgers acquired Catcher Joe Ferguson for two players to be named later, July 1, 1978; Houston acquired Shortstop Rafael Landestoy as partial completion of deal, July 7, 1978.
‡Traded with First Baseman-Outfielder Dave Bergman to San Francisco Giants for First Baseman Mike Ivie, April 20, 1981.
§On disabled list, May 23 to July 19, 1982; included rehabilitation disability assignment to Phoenix, July 1 to July 19, 1982.
xOn disabled list, July 31, 1986 through remainder of season.
yOn disabled list, March 29 to April 13, 1988.
zTraded to Milwaukee Brewers for Shortstop Ernest Riles, June 8, 1988.
aGranted free agency, November 4, 1988; signed by Seattle Mariners, December 7, 1988.
bReleased, October 12, 1990.

CHAMPIONSHIP SERIES RECORD

Shares Championship Series record for most home runs, series (4), 1987.
Shares National League Championship Series record for most total bases, series (22), 1987.

Year Club	League	Pos.	G.	AB.	R.	H.	2B.	3B.	HR.	RBI.	B.A.	PO.	A.	E.	F.A.
1980—Houston	Nat.	PH-OF	3	3	0	0	0	0	0	0	.000	2	1	0	1.000
1987—San Francisco	Nat.	OF	7	24	5	10	0	0	4	5	.417	14	1	0	1.000
Championship Series Totals—2 Years			10	27	5	10	0	0	4	5	.370	16	2	0	1.000

Year League	Pos.	AB.	R.	H.	2B.	3B.	HR.	RBI.	B.A.	PO.	A.	E.	F.A.
1987—National	OF	2	0	0	0	0	0	0	.000	0	0	0	.000
1989—American	PH	1	0	0	0	0	0	0	.000	0	0	0	.000
All-Star Game Totals—2 Years		3	0	0	0	0	0	0	.000	0	0	0	.000

MARK DAVID LEONARD

Born August 14, 1964, at Mountain View, Calif.
Height, 6.01. Weight, 195.
Throws right and bats lefthanded.
Attended University of California, Santa Barbara, Calif.

Led California League in total bases with 283, game-winning RBIs with 17, sacrifice flies with 11 and intentional bases on balls received with 13 in 1988.

Year Club	League	Pos.	G.	AB.	R.	H.	2B.	3B.	HR.	RBI.	B.A.	PO.	A.	E.	F.A.
1986—Ever.†-Tri-Cities	N'west	OF-1B-C	38	128	21	33	6	0	4	17	.258	63	2	4	.942
1987—Clinton	Midw.	1B	128	413	57	132	31	2	15	80	.320	610	47	9	.986
1988—San Jose	Calif.	OF-1B	★142	510	102	176	★50	6	15	★118	.345	178	120	9	.971
1989—Shreveport	Texas	OF	63	219	29	68	15	3	10	52	.311	90	5	0	1.000
1989—Phoenix‡	P. C.	OF	27	78	7	21	4	0	0	6	.269	29	1	3	.909
1990—Phoenix	P. C.	OF	109	390	76	130	22	2	19	82	.333	120	3	1	.992
1990—San Francisco§	Nat.	OF	11	17	3	3	1	0	1	2	.176	10	0	0	1.000
Major League Totals—1 Year			11	17	3	3	1	0	1	2	.176	10	0	0	1.000

Selected by San Francisco Giants' organization in 29th round of free-agent draft, June 2, 1986.
†Loaned to Tri-Cities (Co-op), June 23, 1986; returned, September 1, 1986.
‡On disabled list, August 6, 1989 through remainder of season.
§On disabled list, August 8 to September 5, 1990; included rehabilitation disability assignment to Phoenix, August 27 to September 5, 1990.

DARREN JOEL LEWIS

Born August 28, 1967, at Berkeley, Calif.
Height, 6.00. Weight, 175.
Throws and bats righthanded.
Attended Chabot College, Hayward, Calif., and University
of California, Berkeley, Calif.

Major League stolen bases: 1990 (2).
Led California League outfielders in total chances with 324 in 1989.

Year Club	League	Pos.	G.	AB.	R.	H.	2B.	3B.	HR.	RBI.	B.A.	PO.	A.	E.	F.A.
1988—Scottsdale A's	Ariz.	OF	5	15	8	5	3	0	0	4	.333	15	1	0	1.000
1988—Madison	Midw.	OF-2B	60	199	38	49	4	1	0	11	.246	195	3	4	.980
1989—Modesto	Calif.	OF	129	503	74	150	23	5	4	39	.298	★311	8	5	.985
1989—Huntsville	South.	OF	9	31	7	10	1	1	1	7	.323	16	0	0	1.000
1990—Huntsville	South.	OF	71	284	52	84	11	3	3	23	.296	186	6	0	1.000
1990—Tacoma	P. C.	OF	60	247	32	72	5	2	2	26	.291	132	9	2	.986
1990—Oakland†	Amer.	OF	25	35	4	8	0	0	0	1	.229	33	0	0	1.000
Major League Totals—1 Year			25	35	4	8	0	0	0	1	.229	33	0	0	1.000

Selected by Los Angeles Dodgers' organization in 6th round of free-agent draft, January 14, 1986.
Selected by Toronto Blue Jays' organization in 45th round of free-agent draft, June 2, 1987.
Selected by Oakland Athletics' organization in 18th round of free-agent draft, June 1, 1988.
†Traded with a player to be named later to San Francisco Giants for Infielder Ernest Riles, December 4, 1990; San Francisco acquired Pitcher Pedro Pena to complete deal, December 17, 1990.

SCOTT ALLEN LEWIS

Born December 5, 1965, at Grants Pass, Ore.
Height, 6.03. Weight, 178.
Throws and bats righthanded.
Attended University of Nevada, Las Vegas, Nev.

Led California League in balks with 9 in 1989.
Tied for Pacific Coast League lead in complete games with 6 in 1990.

Year Club	League	G.	IP.	W.	L.	Pct.	H.	R.	ER.	SO.	BB.	ERA.
1988—Bend	Northwest	9	61⅔	5	3	.625	63	33	24	53	12	3.50
1988—Quad City	Midwest	3	21⅓	1	2	.333	19	12	11	20	5	4.64
1988—Palm Springs	California	2	8	0	1	.000	12	5	5	7	2	5.63
1989—Midland	Texas	25	162⅓	11	12	.478	195	★121	89	104	55	4.93
1990—Edmonton	P. Coast	27	177⅔	13	11	.542	198	90	77	124	35	3.90
1990—California	American	2	16⅓	1	1	.500	10	4	4	9	2	2.20
Major League Totals—1 Year		2	16⅓	1	1	.500	10	4	4	9	2	2.20

Selected by California Angels' organization in 11th round of free-agent draft, June 1, 1988.

JAMES JOSEPH LEYRITZ
(Jim)

Born December 27, 1963, at Lakewood, O.
Height, 6.00. Weight, 190.
Throws and bats righthanded.
Attended Middle Georgia College, Cochran, Ga., and
University of Kentucky, Lexington, Ky.

Major League stolen bases: 1990 (2).
Led Florida State League in passed balls with 25 in 1987.
Tied for Eastern League lead in being hit by pitch with 9 in 1989.

Year Club	League	Pos.	G.	AB.	R.	H.	2B.	3B.	HR.	RBI.	B.A.	PO.	A.	E.	F.A.
1986—Fort Lauderdale ..	Fla. St.	C	12	34	3	10	1	1	0	1	.294	32	8	1	.976
1986—Oneonta...............	NYP	C	23	91	12	33	3	1	4	15	.363	170	21	2	.990
1987—Fort Lauderdale ..	Fla. St.	C	102	374	48	115	22	0	6	51	.307	458	*76	13	.976
1988—Albany.................	East.	C-3B-1B	112	382	40	92	18	3	5	50	.241	418	73	6	.988
1989—Albany.................	East.	C-OF-3B	114	375	53	118	18	2	10	66	*.315	421	41	3	.994
1990—Columbus.............	Int.	3-2-1-O-C	59	204	36	59	11	1	8	32	.289	75	96	13	.929
1990—New York............	Amer.	3B-OF-C	92	303	28	78	13	1	5	25	.257	117	107	13	.945
Major League Totals—1 Year..................			92	303	28	78	13	1	5	25	.257	117	107	13	.945

Signed as free agent by New York Yankees' organization, August 24, 1985.

DAVID ALEXANDER LIDDELL

(Dave)

Born June 15, 1966, at Los Angeles, Calif.
Height, 5.11. Weight, 190.
Throws and bats righthanded.

Year Club	League	Pos.	G.	AB.	R.	H.	2B.	3B.	HR.	RBI.	B.A.	PO.	A.	E.	F.A.
1984—Pikeville................	Appal.	C-1B	22	46	3	3	1	0	0	1	.065	81	4	4	.955
1985—Wytheville............	Appal.	C	36	104	21	24	5	0	4	11	.231	204	18	5	*.978
1986—Peoria†.................	Midw.	C	37	125	12	33	4	1	3	15	.264	206	22	5	.979
1986—Columbia	S. Atl.	C	18	54	8	12	2	0	2	10	.222	134	15	1	.993
1986—Lynchburg.............	Carol.	C	9	29	5	3	0	0	1	3	.103	63	7	2	.972
1987—Columbia	S. Atl.	C	23	53	6	11	3	0	0	3	.208	90	16	8	.930
1987—Jackson	Texas	C	10	25	2	3	0	0	0	0	.120	51	3	4	.931
1987—Lynchburg.............	Carol.	C	31	102	18	26	6	0	4	17	.255	174	15	7	.964
1988—Reno	Calif.	C-1B	26	70	11	23	8	0	0	12	.329	134	19	1	.994
1988—St. Lucie...............	Fla. St.	C	57	165	23	41	5	2	1	13	.248	299	35	9	.974
1989—Tidewater.............	Int.	C	24	73	8	11	2	0	2	7	.151	127	10	1	.993
1989—Jackson	Texas	C	62	191	15	34	8	0	1	8	.178	347	53	5	.988
1990—Tidewater.............	Int.	C	73	189	16	40	5	0	2	15	.212	384	34	9	.979
1990—New York‡...........	Nat.	C	1	1	1	1	0	0	0	0	1.000	1	0	0	1.000
Major League Totals—1 Year..................			1	1	1	1	0	0	0	0	1.000	1	0	0	1.000

Selected by Chicago Cubs' organization in 4th round of free-agent draft, June 4, 1984.
†Traded with Pitcher Dave Lenderman to Columbia (New York Mets' organization) for Pitcher Ed Lynch, June 30, 1986.
‡Granted free agency, October 15, 1990; signed by Nashville (Cincinnati Reds' organization), November 6, 1990.

DEREK JANSEN LILLIQUIST

Born February 20, 1966, at Winter Park, Fla.
Height, 6.00. Weight, 214.
Throws and bats lefthanded.
Attended University of Georgia, Athens, Ga.

Named lefthanded pitcher on THE SPORTING NEWS College Baseball All-American Team, 1987.

Year Club	League	G.	IP.	W.	L.	Pct.	H.	R.	ER.	SO.	BB.	ERA.
1987—Bradenton Braves........................	Gulf Coast	2	13	0	0	.000	3	0	0	16	2	0.00
1987—Durham..............................	Carolina	3	25	2	1	.667	13	9	8	29	6	2.88
1988—Richmond...........................	Int'national	28	170⅔	10	12	.455	179	70	64	80	36	3.38
1989—Atlanta	National	32	165⅔	8	10	.444	202	87	73	79	34	3.97
1990—Atlanta†-San Diego	National	28	122	5	11	.313	136	74	72	63	42	5.31
1990—Richmond...........................	Int'national	5	35	4	0	1.000	31	11	10	24	11	2.57
Major League Totals—2 Years....................		60	287⅔	13	21	.382	338	161	145	142	76	4.54

Selected by Boston Red Sox' organization in 15th round of free-agent draft, June 4, 1984.
Selected by Atlanta Braves in 1st round (sixth player selected) of free-agent draft, June 2, 1987.
†Traded to San Diego Padres for Pitcher Mark Grant, July 12, 1990.

JOSE LIND (SALGADO)

Name pronounced Leend.
Born May 1, 1964, at Toabaja, P. R.
Height, 5.11. Weight, 170.
Throws and bats righthanded.
Brother of Orlando Lind, pitcher in Minnesota Twins' organization; and cousin of Onix Concepcion, infielder with Kansas City Royals and Pittsburgh Pirates, 1980 through 1985 and 1987.

Major League stolen bases: 1987 (2), 1988 (15), 1989 (15), 1990 (8). Total—40.
Led National League second basemen in total chances with 786 in 1990.
Led Pacific Coast League second basemen in double plays with 84 and total chances with 764 in 1987.
Led Eastern League second basemen in total chances with 705 and double plays with 84 in 1986.

Year Club	League	Pos.	G.	AB.	R.	H.	2B.	3B.	HR.	RBI.	B.A.	PO.	A.	E.	F.A.
1983—Bradenton Pir.	Gulf C.	2B-SS	45	163	26	49	3	4	0	18	.301	102	125	9	.962
1984—Macon..................	S. Atl.	2B-SS	121	396	39	82	5	2	0	30	.207	271	306	32	.947
1985—Prince William	Carol.	2-S-3-O	105	377	42	104	9	4	0	28	.276	164	221	14	.965
1986—Nashua	East.	2B	134	•520	58	137	18	5	1	33	.263	*314	*378	13	*.982
1987—Vancouver............	P. C.	2B	128	*533	75	143	16	3	3	30	.268	*311	*432	21	.973

Year Club League	Pos.	G.	AB.	R.	H.	2B.	3B.	HR.	RBI.	B.A.	PO.	A.	E.	F.A.
1987—Pittsburgh............. Nat.	2B	35	143	21	46	8	4	0	11	.322	53	139	1	.995
1988—Pittsburgh............. Nat.	2B	154	611	82	160	24	4	2	49	.262	333	473	11	.987
1989—Pittsburgh............. Nat.	2B	153	578	52	134	21	3	2	48	.232	309	438	18	.976
1990—Pittsburgh............. Nat.	2B	152	514	46	134	28	5	1	48	.261	★330	449	7	.991
Major League Totals—4 Years................		494	1846	201	474	81	16	5	156	.257	1025	1499	37	.986

Signed as free agent by Pittsburgh Pirates' organization, December 3, 1982.

CHAMPIONSHIP SERIES RECORD

Year Club League	Pos.	G.	AB.	R.	H.	2B.	3B.	HR.	RBI.	B.A.	PO.	A.	E.	F.A.
1990—Pittsburgh............. Nat.	2B	6	21	1	5	1	1	1	2	.238	19	19	0	1.000

JAMES WILLIAM LINDEMAN
(Jim)

Born January 10, 1962, at Evanston, Ill.
Height, 6.01. Weight, 200.
Throws and bats righthanded.
Attended Bradley University, Peoria, Ill.

Major League stolen bases: 1986 (1), 1987 (3). Total—4.

Year Club League	Pos.	G.	AB.	R.	H.	2B.	3B.	HR.	RBI.	B.A.	PO.	A.	E.	F.A.
1983—St. Petersburg....... Fla. St.	3B	70	232	45	64	13	1	8	37	.276	36	98	26	.838
1984—Springfield........... Midw.	3B-SS	94	354	69	169	15	2	18	66	.271	78	175	30	.894
1984—Arkansas................ Texas	3B	40	137	14	26	4	3	0	13	.190	26	67	6	.939
1985—Arkansas................ Texas	3B	128	450	54	127	30	6	10	63	.282	74	238	24	.929
1986—Louisville .... A. A.	1B-3B-OF	139	509	82	128	38	5	20	★96	.251	718	110	19	.978
1986—St. Louis................ Nat.	1B-3B-OF	19	55	7	14	1	0	1	6	.255	118	10	1	.992
1987—St. Louis†............... Nat.	OF-1B	75	207	20	43	13	0	8	28	.208	196	14	3	.986
1987—Louisville .... A. A.	OF	20	78	11	24	3	1	4	10	.308	14	1	1	.938
1988—St. Louis‡.............. Nat.	OF-1B	17	43	3	9	1	0	2	7	.209	36	2	1	.974
1988—Louisville .... A. A.	OF-1B	73	261	32	66	18	4	2	30	.253	308	23	4	.988
1989—St. Louis§.............. Nat.	1B-OF	73	45	8	5	1	0	0	2	.111	93	6	1	.990
1989—Louisville x........... A. A.	OF-1B	29	109	18	33	8	1	5	20	.303	52	5	2	.966
1990—Toledo .... Int.	1B-OF-3B	109	374	48	85	17	2	12	50	.227	709	53	8	.990
1990—Detroit................... Amer.	1B-OF	12	32	5	7	1	0	2	8	.219	5	0	0	1.000
National League Totals—4 Years............		184	350	38	71	16	0	11	43	.203	443	32	6	.988
American League Totals—1 Year..........		12	32	5	7	1	0	2	8	.219	5	0	0	1.000
Major League Totals—5 Years................		196	382	43	78	17	0	13	51	.204	448	32	6	.988

Selected by St. Louis Cardinals' organization in 1st round (24th player selected) of free-agent draft, June 6, 1983.
†On disabled list, May 12 to May 29 and June 4 to July 4, 1987; included rehabilitation disability assignment to Louisville, May 26 to May 29 and June 17 to July 4, 1987.
‡On disabled list, April 22 to July 5, 1988; included rehabilitation disability assignment to Louisville, June 16 to July 5, 1988.
§On disabled list, July 10 to August 10, 1989; included rehabilitation disability assignment to Louisville, July 26 to August 10, 1989.
xTraded with Pitcher Matt Kinzer to Detroit Tigers for Second Baseman Pat Austin, Catcher Bill Henderson and Pitcher Marcus Betances, December 6, 1989.

CHAMPIONSHIP SERIES RECORD

Year Club League	Pos.	G.	AB.	R.	H.	2B.	3B.	HR.	RBI.	B.A.	PO.	A.	E.	F.A.
1987—St. Louis................. Nat.	1B-PH	5	13	1	4	0	0	1	3	.308	33	2	0	1.000

WORLD SERIES RECORD

Year Club League	Pos.	G.	AB.	R.	H.	2B.	3B.	HR.	RBI.	B.A.	PO.	A.	E.	F.A.
1987—St. Louis................. Nat.	1B-PH-O	6	15	3	5	1	0	0	2	.333	28	2	3	.909

MICHAEL SHAWN LINSKEY
(Mike)

Born June 18, 1966, at Baltimore, Md.
Height, 6.05. Weight, 220.
Throws and bats lefthanded.
Received degree in sports management from James Madison
University, Harrisonburg, Va.

Year Club	League	G.	IP.	W.	L.	Pct.	H.	R.	ER.	SO.	BB.	ERA.
1988—Erie	NYP	10	55	3	3	.500	46	24	19	50	18	3.11
1989—Frederick	Carolina	9	61⅓	2	2	.500	47	7	6	46	16	0.88
1989—Hagerstown	Eastern	18	128	10	6	.625	108	45	40	90	35	2.81
1990—Hagerstown	Eastern	8	55	7	1	.875	40	16	9	40	14	1.47
1990—Rochester	Int'national	19	110⅔	7	9	.438	116	60	44	54	28	3.58

Selected by Pittsburgh Pirates' organization in 20th round of free-agent draft, June 4, 1984.
Selected by Baltimore Orioles' organization in 9th round of free-agent draft, June 1, 1988.

—DID YOU KNOW—

That the Milwaukee Brewers were shut out only five times in 1990, the fewest in the majors?

NELSON ARTURO LIRIANO

Name pronounced Leer-E-anno.
Born June 3, 1964, at Puerto Plata, D. R.
Height, 5.10. Weight, 172.
Throws right and bats left and righthanded.
Major League stolen bases: 1987 (13), 1988 (12), 1989 (16), 1990 (8). Total—49.
Led International League second basemen in double plays with 96 and total chances with 611 in 1987.
Led Carolina League second basemen in double plays with 79 in 1985.

Year	Club	League	Pos.	G.	AB.	R.	H.	2B.	3B.	HR.	RBI.	B.A.	PO.	A.	E.	F.A.
1983—Florence		S. Atl.	2B	129	478	87	124	24	5	6	57	.259	214	323	34	.940
1984—Kinston		Carol.	2B	132	*512	68	126	22	4	5	50	.246	260	*357	*21	.967
1985—Kinston		Carol.	2B	134	451	68	130	23	1	6	36	.288	*261	328	•25	.959
1986—Knoxville		South.	2B-3B-SS	135	557	88	159	25	*15	7	59	.285	239	324	22	.962
1987—Syracuse		Int.	2B	130	531	72	133	19	•10	10	55	.250	*246	*346	*19	.969
1987—Toronto		Amer.	2B	37	158	29	38	6	2	2	10	.241	83	107	1	.995
1988—Toronto		Amer.	2B-3B	99	276	36	73	6	2	3	23	.264	121	177	12	.961
1988—Syracuse		Int.	2B	8	31	2	6	1	1	0	1	.194	14	23	0	1.000
1989—Toronto		Amer.	2B	132	418	51	110	26	3	5	53	.263	267	330	12	.980
1990—Tor.†-Minn.		Amer.	2B-SS	103	355	46	83	12	9	1	28	.234	176	260	11	.975
Major League Totals—4 Years				371	1207	162	304	50	16	11	114	.252	647	874	36	.977

Signed as free agent by Toronto Blue Jays' organization, November 1, 1982.
†Traded with Outfielder Pedro Munoz to Minnesota Twins for Pitcher John Candelaria, July 27, 1990.

CHAMPIONSHIP SERIES RECORD

Year	Club	League	Pos.	G.	AB.	R.	H.	2B.	3B.	HR.	RBI.	B.A.	PO.	A.	E.	F.A.
1989—Toronto		Amer.	2B	3	7	1	3	0	0	0	1	.429	4	3	1	.875

JON GREGORY LITTON
(Greg)

Born July 13, 1964, at New Orleans, La.
Height, 6.00. Weight, 190.
Throws and bats righthanded.
Attended Pensacola Junior College, Pensacola, Fla.
Major League stolen bases: 1990 (1).
Led Texas League second basemen in putouts with 262, assists with 369 and total chances with 655 in 1986.
Led California League second basemen in total chances with 749 in 1985.

Year	Club	League	Pos.	G.	AB.	R.	H.	2B.	3B.	HR.	RBI.	B.A.	PO.	A.	E.	F.A.
1984—Everett		N'west	2B-3B	62	243	29	57	12	2	4	26	.235	135	160	17	.977
1985—Fresno		Calif.	*2B-OF	141	*564	88	150	*33	7	12	103	.266	269	*453	28	.963
1986—Shreveport		Texas	*2-S-O	131	455	46	112	30	3	10	55	.246	265	373	*24	.964
1987—Shreveport		Texas	2B-SS	72	254	34	66	6	3	8	33	.260	117	199	3	.991
1987—Phoenix		P. C.	2B-SS	60	203	24	44	8	2	1	22	.217	146	173	8	.976
1988—Shreveport		Texas	3B-2B-SS	116	432	58	120	35	5	11	64	.278	116	247	13	.965
1989—Phoenix		P. C.	2-S-3-1-C	30	89	6	16	4	2	2	6	.180	48	50	4	.961
1989—San Francisco		Nat.	3-2-S-O-C	71	143	12	36	5	3	4	17	.252	44	66	3	.973
1990—Phoenix†		P. C.	OF-2B-3B	6	22	3	6	1	0	0	4	.273	6	7	2	.867
1990—San Francisco		Nat.	O-2-S-3	93	204	17	50	9	1	1	24	.245	90	43	1	.993
Major League Totals—2 Years				164	347	29	86	14	4	5	41	.248	134	109	4	.984

Selected by San Francisco Giants' organization in 1st round (10th player selected) of free-agent draft, January 17, 1984.
†On San Francisco disabled list, March 28 to April 21, 1990; included rehabilitation disability assignment to Phoenix, April 15 to April 21, 1990.

CHAMPIONSHIP SERIES RECORD

Year	Club	League	Pos.	G.	AB.	R.	H.	2B.	3B.	HR.	RBI.	B.A.	PO.	A.	E.	F.A.
1989—San Francisco		Nat.	PH-3B	1	1	0	1	0	0	0	0	1.000	0	0	0	.000

WORLD SERIES RECORD

Year	Club	League	Pos.	G.	AB.	R.	H.	2B.	3B.	HR.	RBI.	B.A.	PO.	A.	E.	F.A.
1989—San Francisco		Nat.	PH-2B-3B	2	6	1	3	1	0	1	3	.500	2	3	0	1.000

DEREK ROBERT LIVERNOIS

Born April 17, 1967, at Inglewood, Calif.
Height, 6.00. Weight, 170.
Throws right and bats lefthanded.

Year	Club	League	G.	IP.	W.	L.	Pct.	H.	R.	ER.	SO.	BB.	ERA.
1985—Elmira	NYP	17	47	2	3	.400	44	26	20	55	18	3.83
1986—Greensboro	S. Atlantic	25	159⅔	12	7	.632	142	72	47	164	73	2.65
1987—Winter Haven†	Florida St.	20	113⅓	7	7	.500	133	80	62	64	48	4.92
1988—Winter Haven‡	Florida St.	7	40	3	3	.500	39	18	14	25	12	3.15
1989—Lynchburg	Carolina	26	159⅓	10	8	.556	147	75	62	*151	48	3.50
1990—New Britain§	Eastern	15	95⅔	9	2	.818	80	24	21	67	31	1.98

Selected by Boston Red Sox' organization in 15th round of free-agent draft, June 3, 1985.
†On disabled list, July 7 to July 19, 1987.
‡On disabled list, June 16 to July 26, 1988.
§On disabled list, May 8 to July 12, 1990.

SCOTT LOUIS LIVINGSTONE

Born July 15, 1965, at Dallas, Tex.
Height, 6.00. Weight, 185.
Throws right and bats lefthanded.
Attended Texas A&M University, College Station, Tex.

Tied for Eastern League lead in total chances by third baseman with 360 in 1989.
Named designated hitter on THE SPORTING NEWS College Baseball All-America Team, 1987 and 1988.

Year Club	League	Pos.	G.	AB.	R.	H.	2B.	3B.	HR.	RBI.	B.A.	PO.	A.	E.	F.A.
1988—Lakeland................	Fla. St.	3B	53	180	28	51	8	1	2	25	.283	30	115	8	.948
1989—London	East.	3B-SS	124	452	46	98	18	1	14	71	.217	100	265	25	.936
1990—Toledo†	Int.	3B	103	345	44	94	19	0	6	36	.272	66	181	13	.950

Selected by Toronto Blue Jays' organization in 6th round of free-agent draft, June 4, 1984.
Selected by New York Yankees' organization in 26th round of free-agent draft, June 2, 1986.
Selected by Oakland Athletics' organization in 3rd round of free-agent draft, June 2, 1987.
Selected by Detroit Tigers' organization in 2nd round of free-agent draft, June 1, 1988.
†On disabled list, July 14 to July 23 and July 28 to August 7, 1990.

KENNETH LOFTON
(Kenny)

Born May 31, 1967, at East Chicago, Ind.
Height, 6.00. Weight, 180.
Throws and bats lefthanded.
Attended University of Arizona, Tucson, Ariz.

Year Club	League	Pos.	G.	AB.	R.	H.	2B.	3B.	HR.	RBI.	B.A.	PO.	A.	E.	F.A.
1988—Auburn	NYP	OF	48	187	23	40	6	1	1	14	.214	94	5	4	.961
1989—Auburn	NYP	OF	34	110	21	29	3	1	0	8	.264	37	4	8	.837
1989—Asheville...............	S. Atl.	OF	22	82	14	27	2	0	1	9	.329	38	1	2	.951
1990—Osceola..................	Fla. St.	OF	124	481	98	∗159	15	5	2	35	.331	246	13	7	.974

Selected by Houston Astros' organization in 17th round of free-agent draft, June 1, 1988.

STEPHEN PAUL LOMBARDOZZI
(Steve)

Born April 26, 1960, at Malden, Mass.
Height, 6.00. Weight, 183.
Throws and bats righthanded.
Attended Gulf Coast Community College, Panama City, Fla.,
and University of Florida, Gainesville, Fla.

Brother of Chris Lombardozzi, shortstop in New York Yankees' organization, 1985 through 1988.

Major League stolen bases: 1985 (3), 1986 (3), 1987 (5), 1988 (2). Total—13.
Led California League shortstops in fielding percentage with .947 in 1982.

Year Club	League	Pos.	G.	AB.	R.	H.	2B.	3B.	HR.	RBI.	B.A.	PO.	A.	E.	F.A.
1981—Elizabethton	Appal.	SS	65	246	48	79	13	2	6	38	.321	89	192	14	∗.953
1982—Visalia	Calif.	SS-OF-P	122	441	81	131	24	1	6	67	.297	185	393	33	.946
1983—Orlando	South.	SS-2B	137	492	76	143	23	6	3	52	.291	203	364	33	.945
1984—Toledo	Int.	2B-SS	119	385	57	96	15	1	9	31	.249	237	310	14	.975
1985—Toledo	Int.	2B-3B-SS	118	451	55	119	21	3	14	48	.264	272	324	17	.972
1985—Minnesota.............	Amer.	2B	28	54	10	20	4	1	0	6	.370	31	80	2	.982
1986—Minnesota.............	Amer.	2B	156	453	53	103	20	5	8	33	.227	289	407	6	∗.991
1987—Minnesota.............	Amer.	2B	136	432	51	103	19	3	8	38	.238	245	356	14	.977
1988—Minnesota†...........	Amer.	2B-SS-3B	103	287	34	60	15	2	3	27	.209	152	237	5	.987
1989—Houston	Nat.	2B-3B	21	37	5	8	3	1	1	3	.216	20	28	4	.923
1989—Tucson..................	P. C.	2B-SS	114	401	66	103	21	2	5	46	.257	170	285	15	.968
1990—Houston‡..............	Nat.	PH	2	1	0	0	0	0	0	0	.000	0	0	0	.000
1990—Columbus§............	South.	2B-SS	6	20	1	4	0	0	1	2	.200	4	10	2	.875
1990—Toledo x...............	Int.	SS-2B-3B	62	210	31	52	11	3	6	23	.248	81	143	8	.966
American League Totals—4 Years			423	1226	148	286	58	11	19	104	.233	717	1080	27	.985
National League Totals—2 Years............			23	38	5	8	3	1	1	3	.211	20	28	4	.923
Major League Totals—6 Years................			446	1264	153	294	61	12	20	107	.233	737	1108	31	.983

Selected by Minnesota Twins' organization in 9th round of free-agent draft, June 8, 1981.
†Traded to Houston Astros for three players to be named later, March 21, 1989; Minnesota Twins acquired Outfielder Ramon Cedeno and Pitcher Gordon Farmer, September 16, 1989; and Second Baseman Mica Lewis, June 2, 1990, to complete deal.
‡On disabled list, April 15 to May 28, 1990; included rehabilitation disability assignment to Columbus, May 17 to May 24, 1990.
§Released, May 28, 1990; signed by Toledo (Detroit Tigers' organization), June 9, 1990.
xGranted free agency, October 15, 1990.

CHAMPIONSHIP SERIES RECORD

Year Club	League	Pos.	G.	AB.	R.	H.	2B.	3B.	HR.	RBI.	B.A.	PO.	A.	E.	F.A.
1987—Minnesota.............	Amer.	2B-PR	5	15	2	4	7	0	0	1	.267	8	9	1	.944

Year	Club	League	Pos.	G.	AB.	R.	H.	2B.	3B.	HR.	RBI.	B.A.	PO.	A.	E.	F.A.
1987—Minnesota		Amer.	2B	6	17	3	7	1	0	1	4	.412	9	24	0	1.000

PITCHING RECORD

Year	Club	League	G.	IP.	W.	L.	Pct.	H.	R.	ER.	SO.	BB.	ERA.
1982—Visalia		California	1	1	0	1	.000	5	4	4	2	0	36.00

WILLIAM DOUGLAS LONG
(Bill)

Born February 29, 1960, at Cincinnati, O.
Height, 6.00. Weight, 190.
Throws and bats righthanded.
Attended Miami University, Oxford, O.

Major League saves: 1987 (1), 1988 (2), 1989 (1), 1990 (5). Total—9.

Year	Club	League	G.	IP.	W.	L.	Pct.	H.	R.	ER.	SO.	BB.	ERA.
1981—Salem		Carolina	14	87	9	2	.818	*81	31	27	80	28	2.79
1982—Amarillo		Texas	27	*198⅓	12	10	.545	*222	116	97	117	53	4.40
1983—Las Vegas		P. Coast	18	62⅓	5	5	.500	99	66	53	41	28	7.65
1983—Beaumont		Texas	10	65⅓	2	5	.286	80	47	41	33	28	5.65
1984—Beaumont†		Texas	25	159⅔	●14	5	.737	149	56	52	114	67	2.93
1985—Buffalo		Am. Assoc.	25	151⅓	*13	6	.684	146	69	59	71	43	3.51
1985—Chicago		American	4	14	0	1	.000	25	17	16	13	5	10.29
1986—Buffalo‡		Am. Assoc.	22	146	9	9	.500	159	73	63	86	44	3.88
1987—Hawaii		P. Coast	2	13	2	0	1.000	15	7	6	6	4	4.15
1987—Chicago		American	29	169	8	8	.500	179	85	82	72	28	4.37
1988—Chicago		American	47	174	8	11	.421	187	89	78	77	43	4.03
1989—Chicago		American	30	98⅔	5	5	.500	101	49	43	51	37	3.92
1989—Vancouver		P. Coast	3	26	1	2	.333	17	8	8	14	2	2.77
1990—Chicago§		American	4	5⅔	0	1	.000	6	5	4	2	2	6.35
1990—Chicago xy		National	42	55⅔	6	1	.857	66	29	27	32	21	4.37
American League Totals—5 Years			114	461⅓	21	26	.447	498	245	223	215	115	4.35
National League Totals—1 Year			42	55⅔	6	1	.857	66	29	27	32	21	4.37
Major League Totals—5 Years			156	517	27	27	.500	564	274	250	247	136	4.35

Selected by San Diego Padres' organization in 2nd round of free-agent draft, June 8, 1981.
†Traded with Pitcher Tim Lollar, Third Baseman Luis Salazar and Shortstop Ozzie Guillen to Chicago White Sox for Pitchers LaMarr Hoyt, Kevin Kristan and Todd Simmons, December 6, 1984.
‡On disabled list, May 12 to June 16, 1986.
§Traded to Chicago Cubs for Pitcher Frank Campos, April 30, 1990.
xOn disabled list, June 7 to June 28, 1990.
yReleased, December 18, 1990.

ANTHONY EUGENE LONGMIRE
(Tony)

Born August 12, 1968, at Vallejo, Calif.
Height, 6.01. Weight, 195.
Throws right and bats left and righthanded.

Year	Club	League	Pos.	G.	AB.	R.	H.	2B.	3B.	HR.	RBI.	B.A.	PO.	A.	E.	F.A.
1986—Bradenton Pir.		Gulf C.	OF	15	40	6	11	2	1	0	6	.275	19	0	2	.905
1987—Macon		S. Atl.	OF	127	445	63	117	15	4	5	62	.263	167	5	8	.956
1988—Salem†‡		Carol.	OF	64	218	46	60	12	2	11	40	.275	91	3	3	.969
1988—Harrisburg		East.	OF	32	94	7	14	2	2	0	4	.149	46	2	2	.960
1989—Salem†		Carol.	OF	14	62	8	20	3	1	1	6	.323	14	3	0	1.000
1989—Harrisburg†		East.	OF	37	127	15	37	7	0	3	22	.291	62	1	2	.969
1990—Harrisburg§x		East.	OF	24	91	9	27	6	0	1	13	.297	46	4	2	.962

Selected by Pittsburgh Pirates' organization in 8th round of free-agent draft, June 2, 1986.
†Batted lefthanded only.
‡On disabled list, August 27, 1988 through remainder of season.
§On disabled list, April 10 to May 24 and June 25, 1990 through remainder of season.
xTraded to Philadelphia Phillies, September 28, 1990, completing deal in which Philadelphia traded Outfielder/First Baseman Carmelo Martinez to Pittsburgh Pirates for Outfielders Wes Chamberlain and Julio Peguero and a player to be named later, August 30, 1990.

LUIS ANTONIO LOPEZ

Born September 1, 1964, at Brooklyn, N.Y.
Height, 6.01. Weight, 190.
Throws and bats righthanded.

Led Texas League in being hit by pitch with 13 in 1988.
Led California League in total bases with 276 and in game-winning RBIs with 16 in 1987.
Led California League catchers in fielding percentage with .989 in 1987.
Led Pioneer League first basemen in errors with 16 in 1984.
Named California League Most Valuable Player, 1987.

Year	Club	League	Pos.	G.	AB.	R.	H.	2B.	3B.	HR.	RBI.	B.A.	PO.	A.	E.	F.A.
1984—Great Falls	Pion.	1B-C	68	275	60	90	15	5	6	61	.327	527	42	17	.971
1985—Vero Beach	Fla. St.	1B-C	120	382	47	106	18	2	1	43	.277	655	46	14	.980
1986—Vero Beach	Fla. St.	C-1B	122	434	52	124	21	3	1	60	.286	688	72	15	.981
1987—Bakersfield	Calif.	C-1B	*142	*550	89	*181	*43	2	16	96	.329	928	85	14	.986
1988—San Antonio	Texas	1B-C	124	470	56	116	16	3	7	65	.247	1036	87	18	.984
1989—San Antonio	Texas	O-1-3-C	99	327	46	87	17	0	10	51	.266	214	40	5	.981
1989—Albuquerque	P. C.	3B-OF	19	75	17	37	7	0	2	16	.493	22	12	1	.971
1990—Albuquerque	P. C.	1-C-3-S	128	448	65	158	23	2	11	81	*.353	494	33	7	.987
1990—Los Angeles†	Nat.	1B	6	6	0	0	0	0	0	0	.000	4	0	0	1.000
Major League Totals—1 Year			6	6	0	0	0	0	0	0	.000	4	0	0	1.000

Selected by Los Angeles Dodgers' organization in 2nd round of free-agent draft, June 6, 1983.
†Released, December 13, 1990.

VANCE ODELL LOVELACE

Born August 9, 1963, at Tampa, Fla.
Height, 6.05. Weight, 235.
Throws and bats lefthanded.

Led Florida State League in hit batsmen with 25, wild pitches with 25 and tied for lead in balks with 6 in 1983.

Year	Club	League	G.	IP.	W.	L.	Pct.	H.	R.	ER.	SO.	BB.	ERA.
1981—Sarasota Cubs	Gulf Coast	7	30	0	5	.000	27	22	11	31	26	3.30
1982—Quad Cities†‡	Midwest	21	94	4	6	.400	62	67	52	107	94	4.98
1983—Vero Beach	Florida St.	24	115	8	10	.444	104	80	61	95	93	4.77
1984—San Antonio§	Texas	16	65	3	7	.300	48	39	28	52	73	3.88
1985—San Antonio	Texas	7	23⅔	0	4	.000	22	27	20	12	30	7.61
1985—Vero Beach x	Florida St.	11	29⅓	1	2	.333	31	22	20	26	23	6.14
1986—Midland	Texas	23	42⅓	2	4	.333	45	46	42	27	58	8.93
1986—Palm Springs	California	6	17⅔	0	1	.000	21	23	18	16	30	9.17
1987—Midland	Texas	53	83⅔	3	3	.500	73	40	30	91	60	3.23
1988—Edmonton	P. Coast	46	69⅓	1	3	.250	79	48	47	56	57	6.10
1988—California	American	3	1⅓	0	0	.000	2	2	2	0	3	13.50
1989—California	American	1	1	0	0	.000	0	0	0	1	1	0.00
1989—Edmonton y	P. Coast	37	48⅔	0	7	.000	42	42	32	40	55	5.92
1990—Calgary	P. Coast	56	70	5	5	.500	64	33	27	40	44	3.47
1990—Seattle z	American	5	2⅓	0	0	.000	3	1	1	1	6	3.86
Major League Totals—3 Years		9	4⅔	0	0	.000	5	3	3	2	10	5.79

Selected by Chicago Cubs' organization in 1st round (16th player selected) of free-agent draft, June 8, 1981.
†On disabled list, April 20 to May 6, 1982.
‡Traded with Outfielder Dan Cataline to Los Angeles Dodgers' organization for Third Baseman Ron Cey, January 19, 1983.
§On disabled list, April 28 to May 24, 1984.
xDrafted by California Angels' organization, December 11, 1985.
yGranted free agency, October 15, 1989; signed by Calgary (Seattle Mariners' organization), December 18, 1989.
zGranted free agency, October 15, 1990.

RICHARD FRED LUECKEN

Name pronounced LOO-ken.

(Rick)

Born November 15, 1960, at McAllen, Tex.
Height, 6.06. Weight, 210.
Throws and bats righthanded.
Attended Texas A&M University, College Station, Tex.

Major League saves: 1989 (1), 1990 (1). Total—2.

Year	Club	League	G.	IP.	W.	L.	Pct.	H.	R.	ER.	SO.	BB.	ERA.
1983—Bellingham	Northwest	14	78⅓	5	4	.556	70	39	31	83	37	3.56
1984—Chattanooga	Southern	26	163⅔	11	*13	.458	166	85	69	90	88	3.79
1985—Calgary†	P. Coast	18	111	4	8	.333	111	70	66	44	39	6.93
1986—Chattanooga‡§	Southern	17	88⅔	6	7	.462	106	57	52	55	42	5.28
1987—Memphis	Southern	28	146	9	9	.500	163	86	77	88	53	4.75
1988—Memphis	Southern	21	24⅔	4	1	.800	17	8	6	30	7	2.19
1988—Omaha	Am. Assoc.	26	40	5	0	1.000	45	10	9	27	15	2.03
1989—Omaha	Am. Assoc.	36	46⅔	4	1	.800	33	14	12	39	22	2.31
1989—Kansas City x	American	19	23⅔	2	1	.667	23	9	9	16	13	3.42
1990—Atlanta	National	36	53	1	4	.200	73	36	34	35	30	5.77
1990—Richmond y	Int'national	8	13⅓	1	1	.500	11	3	2	15	8	1.35
1990—Toronto z	American	1	1	0	0	.000	2	1	1	0	1	9.00
American League Totals—2 Years		20	24⅔	2	1	.667	25	10	10	16	14	3.65
National League Totals—1 Year		36	53	1	4	.200	73	36	34	35	30	5.77
Major League Totals—2 Years		56	77⅔	3	5	.375	98	46	44	51	44	5.10

Selected by San Francisco Giants' organization in 1st round (18th player selected) of free-agent draft, June 5, 1979.
Selected by Cincinnati Reds' organization in 12th round of free-agent draft, June 7, 1982.
Selected by Seattle Mariners' organization in 27th round of free-agent draft, June 6, 1983.
†On disabled list, April 11 to April 25, June 9 to July 2 and August 20, 1985 through remainder of season.
‡On disabled list, June 18 to August 14, 1986.
§Traded with Outfielder Danny Tartabull to Kansas City Royals for Pitchers Scott Bankhead and Steve Shields and Outfielder Mike Kingery, December 10, 1986.

xTraded with Pitcher Charlie Leibrandt to Atlanta Braves for First Baseman Gerald Perry and Pitcher Jim Lemasters, December 15, 1989.
yClaimed on waivers by Toronto Blue Jays, September 24, 1990.
zReleased, October 26, 1990.

URBANO RAFAEL LUGO

Born August 12, 1962, at Falcon, Venezuela.
Height, 5.11. Weight, 197.
Throws and bats righthanded.
Son of Urbano Lugo, pitcher in Mexican League, 1967 through 1970 and 1973.

Year Club	League	G.	IP.	W.	L.	Pct.	H.	R.	ER.	SO.	BB.	ERA.
1982—Danville	Midwest	10	24	0	2	.000	35	30	27	13	16	10.13
1982—Salem	Northwest	14	90⅔	7	3	.700	74	45	29	62	61	2.88
1983—Peoria	Midwest	15	107	8	5	.615	82	39	30	96	28	2.52
1983—Redwood	California	11	64⅔	5	5	.500	59	36	28	58	31	3.90
1984—Waterbury	Eastern	24	164⅓	13	8	.619	135	63	51	117	68	2.79
1985—Edmonton	P. Coast	4	25⅔	2	0	1.000	20	14	13	19	14	4.56
1985—California†	American	20	83	3	4	.429	86	36	34	42	29	3.69
1986—Midland‡	Texas	2	11	1	1	.500	9	2	2	4	4	1.64
1986—Edmonton	P. Coast	16	100⅓	8	6	.571	110	58	52	53	41	4.66
1986—California	American	6	21⅓	1	1	.500	21	9	9	9	6	3.80
1987—California	American	7	28	0	2	.000	42	34	29	24	18	9.32
1987—Edmonton	P. Coast	15	90⅔	4	3	.571	89	46	37	47	46	3.67
1988—Edmonton	P. Coast	38	116⅓	9	6	.600	148	74	68	69	47	5.26
1988—California§	American	1	2	0	0	.000	2	2	2	1	1	9.00
1989—Indianapolis	Am. Assoc.	22	122⅓	12	4	*.750	100	53	40	79	41	2.94
1989—Montreal x	National	3	4	0	0	.000	4	3	3	3	0	6.75
1990—Detroit	American	13	24⅓	2	0	1.000	30	19	19	12	13	7.03
1990—Toledo y	Int'national	29	66⅓	2	2	.500	56	30	29	43	27	3.93
American League Totals—5 Years		47	158⅔	6	7	.462	181	100	93	88	67	5.28
National League Totals—1 Year		3	4	0	0	.000	4	3	3	3	0	6.75
Major League Totals—6 Years		50	162⅔	6	7	.462	185	103	96	91	67	5.31

Signed as free agent by California Angels' organization, January 31, 1982.
†On disabled list, August 22 to September 6, 1985.
‡On California disabled list, March 31 to June 5, 1986; included rehabilitation disability assignment to Midland, May 15 to June 4, 1986.
§Released, March 31, 1989; signed by Indianapolis (Montreal Expos' organization), April 4, 1989.
xGranted free agency, October 15, 1989; signed by Detroit Tigers, April 8, 1990.
yGranted free agency, October 15, 1990.

SCOTT EDWARD LUSADER

Named pronounced Loo-SAY-der.

Born September 30, 1964, at Chicago, Ill.
Height, 5.10. Weight, 165.
Throws and bats lefthanded.
Received bachelor of science degree in marketing
from University of Florida, Gainesville, Fla.

Shares major league record for most errors, outfielder, inning (3), September 9, 1989, first inning.
Major League stolen bases: 1987 (1), 1989 (3). Total—4.

Year Club	League	Pos.	G.	AB.	R.	H.	2B.	3B.	HR.	RBI.	B.A.	PO.	A.	E.	F.A.
1985—Lakeland	Fla. St.	OF	27	97	16	28	5	1	2	22	.289	47	3	3	.943
1985—Birmingham	South.	OF	21	77	13	26	3	4	2	14	.338	49	1	0	1.000
1986—Glens Falls	East.	OF	136	479	74	134	23	3	11	59	.280	275	13	●11	.963
1987—Toledo	Int.	OF	136	505	78	136	29	8	17	80	.269	274	11	6	.979
1987—Detroit	Amer.	OF	23	47	8	15	3	1	1	8	.319	29	0	1	.967
1988—Toledo	Int.	OF-1B	89	329	38	86	11	5	4	46	.261	193	0	3	.985
1988—Detroit	Amer.	OF	16	16	3	1	0	0	1	3	.063	7	0	0	1.000
1989—Toledo†	Int.	OF	44	153	17	37	9	1	2	15	.242	111	5	4	.967
1989—Detroit‡	Amer.	OF	40	103	15	26	4	0	1	8	.252	56	0	4	.933
1989—Tucson	P. C.	OF	33	121	15	30	3	1	2	13	.248	80	2	4	.953
1990—Toledo	Int.	OF	76	268	35	67	12	1	4	25	.250	140	5	4	.973
1990—Detroit	Amer.	OF	45	87	13	21	2	0	2	16	.241	53	1	1	.982
Major League Totals—4 Years			124	253	39	63	9	1	5	35	.249	145	1	6	.961

Selected by Detroit Tigers' organization in 6th round of free-agent draft, June 3, 1985.
†On Detroit disabled list, March 27 to May 5, 1989; included rehabilitation disability assignment to Toledo, April 21 to May 5, 1989.
‡Loaned to Tucson (Houston Astros' organization), July 13, 1989; returned, September 2, 1989.

FREDRIC MICHAEL LYNN
(Fred)

Born February 3, 1952, at Chicago, Ill.
Height, 6.01. Weight, 190.
Throws and bats lefthanded.
Attended University of Southern California, Los Angeles, Calif.

Holds American League record for most doubles, rookie season (47), 1975.
Shares American League record for most total bases, game (16), June 18, 1975.

Major League stolen bases: 1975 (10), 1976 (14), 1977 (2), 1978 (3), 1979 (2), 1980 (12), 1981 (1), 1982 (7), 1983 (2), 1984 (2), 1985 (7), 1986 (2), 1987 (3), 1988 (2), 1989 (1), 1990 (2). Total—72.
Hit three home runs in a game, June 18, 1975.
Hit for the cycle, May 13, 1980.
Led American League in slugging percentage with .566 in 1975 and .637 in 1979.
Named American League Player of the Year by THE SPORTING NEWS, 1975.
Named American League Most Valuable Player by Baseball Writers' Association of America, 1975.
Named American League Rookie of the Year by Baseball Writers' Association of America, 1975.
Named American League Rookie Player of the Year by THE SPORTING NEWS, 1975.
Named outfielder on THE SPORTING NEWS American League All-Star Team, 1975, 1978 and 1979.
Named outfielder on THE SPORTING NEWS American League All-Star fielding team, 1975 and 1978 through 1980.
Received reported $40,000 bonus to sign with Boston Red Sox, 1973.
Named outfielder on THE SPORTING NEWS College Baseball All-America Team, 1972 and 1973.

Year Club	League	Pos.	G.	AB.	R.	H.	2B.	3B.	HR.	RBI.	B.A.	PO.	A.	E.	F.A.
1973—Bristol	East.	OF	53	162	26	42	9	4	6	36	.259	79	3	5	.943
1974—Pawtucket	Int.	OF	124	415	65	117	19	2	21	68	.282	247	12	7	.974
1974—Boston	Amer.	OF	15	43	5	18	2	2	2	10	.419	18	2	0	1.000
1975—Boston	Amer.	OF	145	528	*103	175	*47	7	21	105	.331	404	11	7	.983
1976—Boston	Amer.	OF	132	507	76	159	32	8	10	65	.314	367	13	6	.984
1977—Boston†	Amer.	OF	129	497	81	129	29	5	18	76	.260	333	7	2	.994
1978—Boston	Amer.	OF	150	541	75	161	33	3	22	82	.298	408	11	7	.984
1979—Boston	Amer.	OF	147	531	116	177	42	1	39	122	*.333	381	10	5	.987
1980—Boston‡	Amer.	OF	110	415	67	125	32	3	12	61	.301	302	11	2	.994
1981—California	Amer.	OF	76	256	28	56	8	1	5	31	.219	176	4	4	.978
1982—California	Amer.	OF	138	472	89	141	38	1	21	86	.299	317	6	3	.991
1983—California	Amer.	OF	117	437	56	119	20	3	22	74	.272	274	8	2	.993
1984—California§	Amer.	OF	142	517	84	140	28	4	23	79	.271	321	12	6	.982
1985—Baltimore x	Amer.	OF	124	448	59	118	12	1	23	68	.263	314	6	2	.994
1986—Baltimore	Amer.	OF	112	397	67	114	13	1	23	67	.287	244	2	4	.984
1987—Baltimore y	Amer.	OF	111	396	49	100	24	0	23	60	.253	229	2	2	.991
1988—Balt. za-Det	Amer.	OF	114	391	46	96	14	1	25	56	.246	257	3	2	.992
1989—Detroit bc	Amer.	OF	117	353	44	85	11	1	11	46	.241	119	5	1	.992
1990—San Diego d	Nat.	OF	90	196	18	47	3	1	6	23	.240	92	1	0	1.000
American League Totals—16 Years			1879	6729	1045	1913	385	42	300	1088	.284	4464	113	55	.988
National League Totals—1 Year			90	196	18	47	3	1	6	23	.240	92	1	0	1.000
Major League Totals—17 Years			1969	6925	1063	1960	388	43	306	1111	.283	4556	114	55	.988

Selected by New York Yankees' organization in 3rd round of free-agent draft, June 4, 1970.
Selected by Boston Red Sox' organization in 2nd round of free-agent draft, June 5, 1973.
†On disabled list, March 24 to May 6, 1977.
‡Traded with Pitcher Steve Renko to California Angels for Pitchers Frank Tanana and Jim Dorsey and Outfielder Joe Rudi, January 23, 1981.
§Granted free agency, November 8, 1984; signed by Baltimore Orioles, December 11, 1984. (Pitcher Donnie Moore selected from player compensation pool by California Angels, January 24, 1985.)
xOn disabled list, June 11 to June 27, 1986.
yOn disabled list, July 21 to August 5, 1987.
zOn disabled list, July 15 to August 12, 1988.
aTraded to Detroit Tigers for three players to be named later, August 31, 1988; Baltimore Orioles acquired Catcher Chris Hoiles and Pitchers Cesar Mejia and Robinson Garces to complete deal, September 9, 1988.
bOn disabled list, June 8 to June 23, 1989.
cGranted free agency, November 13, 1989; signed by San Diego Padres, December 6, 1989.
dGranted free agency, November 5, 1990.

CHAMPIONSHIP SERIES RECORD

Holds American League Championship Series record for highest batting average, series (.611), 1982.
Shares Championship Series record for most hits, series (11), 1982.

Year Club	League	Pos.	G.	AB.	R.	H.	2B.	3B.	HR.	RBI.	B.A.	PO.	A.	E.	F.A.
1975—Boston	Amer.	OF	3	11	1	4	1	0	0	3	.364	12	1	1	.929
1982—California	Amer.	OF	5	18	5	11	2	0	1	5	.611	16	0	1	.941
Championship Series Totals—2 Years			8	29	6	15	3	0	1	8	.517	28	1	2	.935

WORLD SERIES RECORD

Year Club	League	Pos.	G.	AB.	R.	H.	2B.	3B.	HR.	RBI.	B.A.	PO.	A.	E.	F.A.
1975—Boston	Amer.	OF	7	25	3	7	1	0	1	5	.280	23	1	0	1.000

ALL-STAR GAME RECORD

Holds All-Star Game records for most grand slams, game (1), July 6, 1983; most runs batted in, inning (4), July 6, 1983, third inning.

Year League	Pos.	AB.	R.	H.	2B.	3B.	HR.	RBI.	B.A.	PO.	A.	E.	F.A.
1975—American	PH-OF	2	0	0	0	0	0	0	.000	1	0	0	1.000
1976—American	OF	3	1	1	0	0	1	1	.333	1	0	0	1.000
1977—American	OF	1	1	0	0	0	0	0	.000	2	0	0	1.000
1978—American	OF	4	0	1	0	0	0	0	.250	3	0	0	1.000
1979—American	OF	1	1	1	0	0	1	2	1.000	0	0	0	.000
1980—American	OF	3	1	1	0	0	1	2	.333	2	0	0	1.000
1981—American	PH	1	0	1	0	0	0	1	1.000	0	0	0	.000
1982—American	OF	2	0	0	0	0	0	0	.000	0	0	0	.000
1983—American	OF	3	1	1	0	0	1	4	.333	1	0	0	1.000
All-Star Game Totals—9 Years		20	5	6	0	0	4	10	.300	9	0	0	1.000

BARRY STEPHEN LYONS

Born June 3, 1960, at Biloxi, Miss.
Height, 6.01. Weight, 200.
Throws and bats righthanded.
Attended Delta State University, Cleveland, Miss.

Led Texas League in grounding into double plays with 19 and tied for lead in game-winning RBIs with 16 in 1985.
Led Texas League catchers in errors with 19 in 1985.
Led Carolina League catchers in assists with 72 and fielding percentage with .989 in 1984.
Named Carolina League Player of the Year, 1984.

Year Club	League	Pos.	G.	AB.	R.	H.	2B.	3B.	HR.	RBI.	B.A.	PO.	A.	E.	F.A.
1982—Shelby	S. Atl.	C-1B	45	164	23	46	12	0	4	46	.280	226	21	8	.969
1983—Lynchburg	Carol.	C	2	7	0	1	0	0	0	2	.143	21	4	0	1.000
1983—Columbia	S. Atl.	C-1B-OF	92	316	55	94	9	2	5	45	.297	387	33	17	.961
1984—Lynchburg	Carol.	C-1B-OF	115	412	59	130	17	3	12	87	.316	894	86	13	.987
1985—Jackson	Texas	C-1B	126	486	69	149	34	6	11	108	.307	834	65	23	.975
1986—New York	Nat.	C	6	9	1	0	0	0	0	2	.000	16	0	1	.941
1986—Tidewater†	Int.	1B-C	61	234	28	69	16	0	4	46	.295	423	25	6	.987
1987—New York	Nat.	C	53	130	15	33	4	1	4	24	.254	223	17	4	.984
1988—New York	Nat.	C-1B	50	91	5	21	7	1	0	11	.231	130	9	3	.979
1989—New York‡	Nat.	C	79	235	15	58	13	0	3	27	.247	463	29	10	.980
1989—Tidewater	Int.	C-1B	5	20	1	2	0	1	0	2	.100	43	5	1	.980
1990—N. Y.§x-L. A.	Nat.	C	27	85	9	20	0	0	3	9	.235	183	12	4	.980
1990—Tidewater	Int.	C-1B	57	164	8	28	5	0	0	17	.171	291	23	5	.984
Major League Totals—5 Years			215	550	45	132	24	2	10	73	.240	1015	67	22	.980

Selected by Detroit Tigers' organization in 25th round of free-agent draft, June 8, 1981.
Selected by New York Mets' organization in 15th round of free-agent draft, June 7, 1982.
†On disabled list, August 4, 1986 through remainder of season.
‡On disabled list, June 27 to July 25, 1989; included rehabilitation disability assignment to Tidewater, July 19 to July 25, 1989.
§On disabled list, May 16 to July 9, 1990; included rehabilitation disability assignment to Tidewater, June 19 to July 9, 1990.
xReleased, September 4, 1990; signed by Los Angeles Dodgers, September 21, 1990.

STEPHEN JOHN LYONS
(Steve)

Born June 3, 1960, at Tacoma, Wash.
Height, 6.03. Weight, 195.
Throws right and bats lefthanded.
Attended Oregon State University, Corvallis, Ore.

Major League stolen bases: 1985 (12), 1986 (4), 1987 (3), 1988 (1), 1989 (9), 1990 (1). Total—30.
Led American League third basemen in double plays with 36 in 1988.
Led International League third basemen in putouts with 98, errors with 25 and total chances with 332 in 1984.

Year Club	League	Pos.	G.	AB.	R.	H.	2B.	3B.	HR.	RBI.	B.A.	PO.	A.	E.	F.A.
1981—Winston-Salem	Carol.	OF-SS	64	252	43	61	9	3	6	40	.242	137	23	8	.952
1982—Bristol	East.	OF-SS	135	460	86	112	23	3	13	58	.243	275	11	9	.969
1983—New Britain	East.	3-O-S-P	132	456	83	112	24	7	7	62	.246	145	207	17	.954
1984—Pawtucket	Int.	3B-OF-SS	131	444	80	119	21	2	17	62	.268	141	211	26	.931
1985—Boston	Amer.	OF-3B-SS	133	371	52	98	14	3	5	30	.264	253	6	7	.974
1986—Boston†-Chicago	Amer.	OF-3B-1B	101	247	30	56	9	3	1	20	.227	175	11	4	.979
1986—Buffalo	A. A.	3-S-O-1	20	74	18	22	5	1	3	8	.297	36	41	4	.951
1987—Chicago	Amer.	3B-OF-2B	76	193	26	54	11	1	1	19	.280	69	101	4	.977
1987—Hawaii	P. C.	O-2-3-S	47	167	26	48	11	0	2	16	.285	73	71	3	.980
1988—Chicago	Amer.	3-O-2-C-1	146	472	59	127	28	3	5	45	.269	128	243	29	.928
1989—Chicago	Amer.	1-O-C	140	443	51	117	21	3	2	50	.264	414	245	15	.978
1990—Chicago	Amer.	I-O-P	94	146	22	28	6	1	1	11	.192	244	54	5	.983
Major League Totals—6 Years			690	1872	240	480	89	14	15	175	.256	1283	660	64	.968

Selected by Boston Red Sox' organization in 1st round (19th player selected) of free-agent draft, June 8, 1981.
†Traded to Chicago White Sox for Pitcher Tom Seaver, June 29, 1986.

PITCHING RECORD

Year Club	League	G.	IP.	W.	L.	Pct.	H.	R.	ER.	SO.	BB.	ERA.
1983—New Britain	Eastern	3	3⅓	1	0	1.000	3	1	1	2	1	2.45
1990—Chicago	American	1	2	0	0	.000	2	1	1	1	4	4.50
Major League Totals—1 Year		1	2	0	0	.000	2	1	1	1	4	4.50

KEVIN CHRISTIAN MAAS

Born January 20, 1965, at Castro Valley, Calif.
Height, 6.03. Weight, 206.
Throws and bats lefthanded.
Attended University of California, Berkeley, Calif.
Brother of Jason Maas, outfielder in New York Yankees' organization.

Major League stolen bases: 1990 (1).

Year Club	League	Pos.	G.	AB.	R.	H.	2B.	3B.	HR.	RBI.	B.A.	PO.	A.	E.	F.A.
1986—Oneonta	NYP	1B	28	101	14	36	10	0	0	18	.356	222	19	1	.996
1987—Fort Lauderdale	Fla. St.	1B	116	439	77	122	28	4	11	73	.278	667	51	10	.986
1988—Prince William	Carol.	1B	29	108	24	32	7	0	12	35	.296	288	25	5	.984

Year	Club	League	Pos.	G.	AB.	R.	H.	2B.	3B.	HR.	RBI.	B.A.	PO.	A.	E.	F.A.
1988—Albany	East.		1B	109	372	66	98	14	3	16	55	.263	902	73	12	.988
1989—Columbus†	Int.		OF	83	291	42	93	23	2	6	45	.320	78	3	3	.964
1990—Columbus	Int.		1B	57	194	37	55	15	2	13	38	.284	219	19	4	.983
1990—New York	Amer.		1B	79	254	42	64	9	0	21	41	.252	486	35	9	.983
Major League Totals—1 Year				79	254	42	64	9	0	21	41	.252	486	35	9	.983

Selected by New York Yankees' organization in 22nd round of free-agent draft, June 2, 1986.
†On disabled list, April 19 to April 30 and July 27, 1989 through remainder of season.

ROBERT JOSEPH MacDONALD
(Rob)

Born April 27, 1965, at East Orange, N.J.
Height, 6.03. Weight, 208.
Throws and bats lefthanded.
Attended Rutgers University, New Brunswick, N.J.

Led South Atlantic League in games finished in relief with 48 in 1988.

Year	Club	League	G.	IP.	W.	L.	Pct.	H.	R.	ER.	SO.	BB.	ERA.
1987—St. Catharines	NYP	1	4	0	0	.000	8	4	2	4	0	4.50
1987—Myrtle Beach	S. Atlantic	10	20⅔	2	1	.667	24	18	13	12	7	5.66
1988—Myrtle Beach	S. Atlantic	52	53⅓	3	4	.429	42	13	10	43	18	1.69
1989—Knoxville	Southern	43	63	3	5	.375	52	27	23	58	23	3.29
1989—Syracuse	Int'national	12	16	1	0	1.000	16	10	10	12	6	5.63
1990—Syracuse	Int'national	9	8⅓	0	2	.000	4	5	5	6	9	5.40
1990—Knoxville	Southern	36	57	1	2	.333	37	17	12	54	29	1.89
1990—Toronto	American	4	2⅓	0	0	.000	0	0	0	0	2	0.00
Major League Totals—1 Year		4	2⅓	0	0	.000	0	0	0	0	2	0.00

Selected by Toronto Blue Jays' organization in 19th round of free-agent draft, June 2, 1987.

MICHAEL ANDREW MACFARLANE
(Mike)

Born April 12, 1964, at Stockton, Calif.
Height, 6.01. Weight, 200.
Throws and bats righthanded.
Attended University of Santa Clara, Santa Clara, Calif.

Major League stolen bases: 1990 (1).

Year	Club	League	Pos.	G.	AB.	R.	H.	2B.	3B.	HR.	RBI.	B.A.	PO.	A.	E.	F.A.
1985—Memphis	South.	C	65	223	29	60	15	4	8	39	.269	295	24	9	.973
1986—Memphis†	South.	DH	40	141	26	34	7	2	12	29	.241	0	0	0	.000
1987—Omaha	A. A.	C	87	302	53	79	25	1	13	50	.262	408	37	6	.987
1987—Kansas City	Amer.	C	8	19	0	4	1	0	0	3	.211	29	2	0	1.000
1988—Kansas City	Amer.	C	70	211	25	56	15	0	4	26	.265	309	18	2	.994
1988—Omaha	A. A.	C	21	76	8	18	7	2	2	8	.237	85	5	1	.989
1989—Kansas City	Amer.	C	69	157	13	35	6	0	2	19	.223	249	17	1	.996
1990—Kansas City	Amer.	C	124	400	37	102	24	4	6	58	.255	660	23	6	.991
Major League Totals—4 Years			271	787	75	197	46	4	12	106	.250	1247	60	9	.993

Selected by Kansas City Royals' organization in 4th round of free-agent draft, June 3, 1985.
†On disabled list, April 9 to July 9, 1986.

JULIO S. MACHADO

Born December 1, 1965, at Zulia, Venezuela.
Height, 5.09. Weight, 165.
Throws and bats righthanded.

Major League saves: 1990 (3).

Year	Club	League	G.	IP.	W.	L.	Pct.	H.	R.	ER.	SO.	BB.	ERA.
1985—Spartanburg	S. Atlantic	32	81⅓	4	5	.444	75	50	39	71	38	4.32
1986—Spartanburg	S. Atlantic	43	79⅔	2	5	.286	68	39	33	81	52	3.73
1987—Clearwater	Florida St.	7	34⅔	2	0	1.000	31	11	10	32	19	2.60
1987—Reading	Eastern	21	108⅓	4	5	.444	112	70	57	89	40	4.74
1988—Reading	Eastern	26	63	6	1	.857	69	41	38	52	34	5.43
1988—Clearwater†	Florida St.	13	36⅔	1	4	.200	34	13	12	45	14	2.95
1989—St. Lucie	Florida St.	4	10⅔	1	0	1.000	5	0	0	14	3	0.00
1989—Jackson	Texas	32	57	3	5	.375	42	23	18	67	27	2.84
1989—Tidewater	Int'national	14	29	1	2	.333	16	2	2	37	17	0.62
1989—New York	National	10	11	0	1	.000	9	4	4	14	3	3.27
1990—New York	National	27	34⅓	4	1	.800	32	13	12	27	17	3.15
1990—Tidewater‡	Int'national	16	21⅓	0	1	.000	16	7	4	24	8	1.69
1990—Milwaukee	American	10	13	0	0	.000	9	1	1	12	8	0.69
National League Totals—2 Years		37	45⅓	4	2	.667	41	17	16	41	20	3.18
American League Totals—1 Year		10	13	0	0	.000	9	1	1	12	8	0.69
Major League Totals—2 Years		47	58⅓	4	2	.667	50	18	17	53	28	2.62

Signed as free agent by Philadelphia Phillies' organization, April 10, 1985.
†Released, March, 1989; signed by St. Lucie (New York Mets' organization), April, 1989.
‡Traded with Pitcher Kevin Brown to Milwaukee Brewers, September 7, 1990, as partial completion of deal in which Milwaukee traded Catcher Charlie O'Brien and a player to be named later to New York Mets for two players to be named later, August 30, 1990; New York acquired Pitcher Kevin Carmody to complete deal, September 11, 1990.

SHANE LEE MACK

Born December 7, 1963, at Los Angeles, Calif.
Height, 6.00. Weight, 190.
Throws and bats righthanded.
Attended UCLA, Los Angeles, Calif.
Brother of Quinn Mack, outfielder in Montreal Expos' organization.

Major League stolen bases: 1987 (4), 1988 (5), 1990 (13). Total—22.
Tied for Texas League lead in being hit by pitch with 7 in 1986.
Led Texas League outfielders in double plays with 4 in 1986.
Member of 1984 U.S. Olympic baseball team.
Named outfielder on THE SPORTING NEWS College Baseball All-America Team, 1984.

Year—Club	League	Pos.	G.	AB.	R.	H.	2B.	3B.	HR.	RBI.	B.A.	PO.	A.	E.	F.A.
1985—Beaumont	Texas	OF-3B	125	430	59	112	23	3	6	55	.260	252	12	7	.974
1986—Beaumont	Texas	OF	115	452	61	127	26	3	15	68	.281	255	●14	8	.971
1986—Las Vegas	P. C.	OF	19	69	13	25	1	6	0	6	.362	43	0	2	.956
1987—Las Vegas	P. C.	OF	39	152	38	51	11	1	5	26	.336	97	3	1	.990
1987—San Diego	Nat.	OF	105	238	28	57	11	3	4	25	.239	159	1	3	.982
1988—Las Vegas	P. C.	OF	55	196	43	68	7	1	10	40	.347	116	7	3	.976
1988—San Diego	Nat.	OF	56	119	13	29	3	0	0	12	.244	110	4	2	.983
1989—Las Vegas†‡	P. C.	OF	24	80	10	18	3	1	1	8	.225	59	3	1	.984
1990—Minnesota	Amer.	OF	125	313	50	102	10	4	8	44	.326	230	8	3	.988
National League Totals—2 Years			161	357	41	86	14	3	4	37	.241	269	5	5	.982
American League Totals—1 Year			125	313	50	102	10	4	8	44	.326	230	8	3	.988
Major League Totals—3 Years			286	670	91	188	24	7	12	81	.281	499	13	8	.985

Selected by Kansas City Royals' organization in 4th round of free-agent draft, June 8, 1981.
Selected by San Diego Padres' organization in 1st round (11th player selected) of free-agent draft, June 4, 1984.
†On San Diego disabled list, March 25 to May 4, 1989.
‡Drafted by Minnesota Twins, December 4, 1989.

LONNIE LEE MACLIN JR.

Born February 17, 1967, at Clayton, Mo.
Height, 5.11. Weight, 160.
Throws and bats lefthanded.
Attended St. Louis Community College at Meramec, Kirkwood, Mo.

Year—Club	League	Pos.	G.	AB.	R.	H.	2B.	3B.	HR.	RBI.	B.A.	PO.	A.	E.	F.A.
1987—Johnson City	Appal.	OF	62	229	45	69	6	1	3	22	.301	70	1	6	.922
1988—St. Petersburg	Fla. St.	OF	51	175	22	33	3	1	3	12	.189	79	1	0	1.000
1988—Savannah	S. Atl.	OF	46	119	10	28	3	0	0	9	.235	104	7	1	.991
1989—Springfield	Midw.	OF	103	315	33	78	10	3	3	34	.248	135	7	5	.966
1990—St. Petersburg	Fla. St.	OF	31	119	18	46	6	3	2	17	.387	65	3	4	.944
1990—Arkansas	Texas	OF	74	264	32	82	14	5	2	25	.311	111	5	5	.959
1990—Louisville	A. A.	OF	17	58	9	18	3	2	0	6	.310	39	0	1	.975

Selected by Cincinnati Reds' organization in 10th round of free-agent draft, January 14, 1986.
Selected by St. Louis Cardinals' organization in secondary phase of free-agent draft, June 2, 1986.

GREGORY ALAN MADDUX
(Greg)

Born April 14, 1966, at San Angelo, Tex.
Height, 6.00. Weight, 170.
Throws and bats righthanded.
Brother of Mike Maddux, pitcher with Philadelphia Phillies and Los Angeles Dodgers, 1986 through 1990.

Shares major league record for most putouts by pitcher, game (7), April 29, 1990.
Tied for National League lead in games started by pitchers with 35 in 1990.
Led National League in intentional bases on balls issued with 16 in 1988.
Led American Association in hit batsmen with 12 in 1986.
Led Appalachian League in hit batsmen with 8 and tied for lead in shutouts with 2 in 1984.
Tied for American Association lead in shutouts with 2 in both 1986 and 1987.
Named pitcher on THE SPORTING NEWS National League All-Star fielding team, 1990.

Year—Club	League	G.	IP.	W.	L.	Pct.	H.	R.	ER.	SO.	BB.	ERA.
1984—Pikeville	Ap'lachian	14	85⅔	6	2	.750	63	35	25	62	41	2.63
1985—Peoria	Midwest	27	186	13	9	.591	176	86	66	125	52	3.19
1986—Pittsfield	Eastern	8	62⅔	4	3	.571	49	22	19	35	15	2.69
1986—Iowa	Am. Assoc.	18	128⅓	10	1	*.909	127	49	43	65	30	3.02
1986—Chicago	National	6	31	2	4	.333	44	20	19	20	11	5.52
1987—Chicago	National	30	155⅔	6	14	.300	181	111	97	101	74	5.61
1987—Iowa	Am. Assoc.	4	27⅔	3	0	1.000	17	3	3	22	12	0.98
1988—Chicago	National	34	249	18	8	.692	230	97	88	140	81	3.18
1989—Chicago	National	35	238⅓	19	12	.613	222	90	78	135	82	2.95
1990—Chicago	National	35	237	15	15	.500	*242	*116	91	144	71	3.46
Major League Totals—5 Years		140	911	60	53	.531	919	434	373	540	319	3.68

Selected by Chicago Cubs' organization in 2nd round of free-agent draft, June 4, 1984.

Shares Championship Series record for most earned runs allowed, series (11), 1989.
Holds National League Championship Series record for most runs allowed, series (12), 1989.

Year Club	League	G.	IP.	W.	L.	Pct.	H.	R.	ER.	SO.	BB.	ERA.
1989—Chicago	National	2	7⅓	0	1	.000	13	12	11	5	4	13.50

Appeared as pinch-runner for Chicago Cubs in 1989 Championship Series.

ALL-STAR GAME RECORD
Member of National League All-Star team in 1988; did not play.

MICHAEL AUSLEY MADDUX
(Mike)

Born August 27, 1961, at Dayton, O.
Height, 6.02. Weight, 180.
Throws and bats righthanded.
Attended University of Texas, El Paso, Tex.
Brother of Greg Maddux, pitcher with Chicago Cubs.

Major League saves: 1989 (1).

Year Club	League	G.	IP.	W.	L.	Pct.	H.	R.	ER.	SO.	BB.	ERA.
1982—Bend	Northwest	11	65⅓	3	6	.333	68	35	29	59	26	3.99
1983—Spartanburg	S. Atlantic	13	84⅓	4	6	.400	98	62	51	85	47	5.44
1983—Peninsula	Carolina	14	99⅓	8	4	.667	92	46	40	78	35	3.62
1983—Reading	Eastern	1	3	0	0	.000	4	2	2	2	1	6.00
1984—Reading	Eastern	20	116	3	●12	.200	143	82	65	77	49	5.04
1984—Portland	P. Coast	8	44⅔	2	4	.333	58	32	29	22	17	5.84
1985—Portland	P. Coast	27	166	9	12	.429	195	106	98	96	51	5.31
1986—Portland	P. Coast	12	84	5	2	.714	70	26	22	65	22	2.36
1986—Philadelphia	National	16	78	3	7	.300	88	56	47	44	34	5.42
1987—Maine	Int'national	18	103⅓	6	6	.500	116	58	50	71	26	4.35
1987—Philadelphia	National	7	17	2	0	1.000	17	5	5	15	5	2.65
1988—Philadelphia†	National	25	88⅔	4	3	.571	91	41	37	59	34	3.76
1988—Maine	Int'national	5	23⅔	0	2	.000	25	18	11	18	10	4.18
1989—Philadelphia	National	16	43⅔	1	3	.250	52	29	25	26	14	5.15
1989—Scranton/Wilkes-Barre‡	Int'national	19	123	7	7	.500	119	55	50	100	26	3.66
1990—Albuquerque	P. Coast	20	108	8	5	.615	122	59	51	85	32	4.25
1990—Los Angeles§	National	11	20⅔	0	1	.000	24	15	15	11	4	6.53
Major League Totals—5 Years		75	248	10	14	.417	272	146	129	155	91	4.68

Selected by Cincinnati Reds' organization in 36th round of free-agent draft, June 5, 1979.
Selected by Philadelphia Phillies' organization in 5th round of free-agent draft, June 7, 1982.
†On disabled list, April 21 to June 1, 1988; included rehabilitation disability assignment to Maine, May 13 to May 22, 1988.
‡Released, November 20, 1989; signed by Los Angeles Dodgers, December 21, 1989.
§Granted free agency, October 15, 1990.

DAVID JOSEPH MAGADAN
(Dave)

Born September 30, 1962, at Tampa, Fla.
Height, 6.03. Weight, 200.
Throws right and bats lefthanded.
Attended University of Alabama, University, Ala.
Cousin of Lou Piniella, manager with Cincinnati Reds.

Major League stolen bases: 1989 (1), 1990 (2). Total—3.
Led National League first basemen in fielding percentage with .998 in 1990.
Led Texas League in bases on balls received with 106 in 1985.
Led Carolina League in intentional bases on balls received with 10 in 1984.
Led International League third basemen in fielding percentage with .934, assists with 283 and double plays with 31 in 1986.
Led Texas League third basemen in putouts with 87, assists with 275 and total chances with 393 in 1985.
Named designated hitter on THE SPORTING NEWS College Baseball All-America Team, 1983.

Year Club	League	Pos.	G.	AB.	R.	H.	2B.	3B.	HR.	RBI.	B.A.	PO.	A.	E.	F.A.
1983—Columbia	S. Atl.	1B	64	220	41	74	13	1	3	32	.336	520	37	7	.988
1984—Lynchburg†	Carol.	1B	112	371	78	130	22	4	0	62	★.350	896	64	16	.984
1985—Jackson	Texas	★3B-1B	134	466	84	144	22	0	0	76	.309	106	276	★31	.925
1986—Tidewater	Int.	3B-1B	133	473	68	147	33	6	1	64	.311	78	284	25	.935
1986—New York	Nat.	1B	10	18	3	8	0	0	0	3	.444	48	5	0	1.000
1987—New York‡	Nat.	3B-1B	85	192	21	61	13	1	3	24	.318	88	92	4	.978
1988—New York§	Nat.	1B-3B	112	314	39	87	15	0	1	35	.277	459	99	10	.982
1989—New York	Nat.	1B-3B	127	374	47	107	22	3	4	41	.286	587	89	7	.990
1990—New York	Nat.	1B-3B	144	451	74	148	28	6	6	72	.328	837	99	3	.997
Major League Totals—5 Years			478	1349	184	411	78	10	14	175	.305	2019	384	24	.990

Selected by Boston Red Sox' organization in 12th round of free-agent draft, June 3, 1980.
Selected by New York Mets' organization in 2nd round of free-agent draft, June 6, 1983.
†On disabled list, August 7 to September 10, 1984.
‡On disabled list, March 29 to April 17, 1987.
§On disabled list, May 5 to May 20, 1988.

Year	Club	League	Pos.	G.	AB.	R.	H.	2B.	3B.	HR.	RBI.	B.A.	PO.	A.	E.	F.A.
1988—New York		Nat.	PH	3	3	0	0	0	0	0	0	.000	0	0	0	.000

EVERARDO MAGALLANES

Name pronounced Mag-a-YEA-nes.

(Ever)

Born November 6, 1965, at Chihuahua, Mexico.
Height, 5.10. Weight, 165.
Throws right and bats lefthanded.
Attended Texas A&M University, College Station, Tex.

Year	Club	League	Pos.	G.	AB.	R.	H.	2B.	3B.	HR.	RBI.	B.A.	PO.	A.	E.	F.A.
1987—Kinston		Carol.	SS	58	205	20	50	4	3	2	23	.244	79	169	17	.936
1988—Kinston		Carol.	SS-2B	119	396	67	104	13	3	1	45	.263	216	351	34	.943
1989—Canton-Akron		East.	2B-SS	74	241	26	67	5	0	0	18	.278	155	199	11	.970
1989—Colorado Springs		P. C.	SS-2B	12	44	2	11	1	0	1	3	.250	16	37	2	.964
1990—Colorado Springs		P. C.	SS-2B-3B	125	377	60	116	17	3	1	63	.308	207	359	33	.945

Selected by New York Mets' organization in 31st round of free-agent draft, June 2, 1986.
Selected by Cleveland Indians' organization in 10th round of free-agent draft, June 2, 1987.

JOSEPH DAVID MAGRANE

(Joe)

Born July 2, 1964, at Des Moines, Ia.
Height, 6.06. Weight, 230.
Throws left and bats righthanded.
Attended University of Arizona, Tucson, Ariz.

Tied for National League lead in hit batsmen with 10 in 1987.
Tied for American Association lead in shutouts with 2 and complete games with 8 in 1986.

Year	Club	League	G.	IP.	W.	L.	Pct.	H.	R.	ER.	SO.	BB.	ERA.
1985—Johnson City		Ap'lachian	6	30	2	1	.667	15	4	2	31	11	0.60
1985—St. Petersburg		Florida St.	5	34⅔	3	1	.750	21	8	4	17	14	1.04
1986—Arkansas		Texas	13	89⅓	8	4	.667	66	29	24	66	31	2.42
1986—Louisville		Am. Assoc.	15	113⅓	9	6	.600	93	34	26	72	33	2.06
1987—Louisville		Am. Assoc.	3	23⅓	1	0	1.000	16	7	5	17	3	1.93
1987—St. Louis†		National	27	170⅓	9	7	.563	157	75	67	101	60	3.54
1988—St. Louis‡		National	24	165⅓	5	9	.357	133	57	40	100	51	★2.18
1988—Louisville		Am. Assoc.	4	20	2	1	.667	19	7	7	18	7	3.15
1989—St. Louis§		National	34	234⅔	18	9	.667	219	81	76	127	72	2.91
1990—St. Louis		National	31	203⅓	10	17	.370	204	86	81	100	59	3.59
Major League Totals—4 Years			116	773⅔	42	42	.500	713	299	264	428	242	3.07

Selected by Pittsburgh Pirates' organization in 3rd round of free-agent draft, June 7, 1982.
Selected by St. Louis Cardinals' organization in 1st round (18th player selected) of free-agent draft, June 3, 1985.
†On disabled list, May 30 to June 18, 1987.
‡On disabled list, April 17 to June 11, 1988; included rehabilitation disability assignment to Louisville, May 23 to June 11, 1988.
§On disabled list, April 15 to April 30, 1989.

CHAMPIONSHIP SERIES RECORD

Year	Club	League	G.	IP.	W.	L.	Pct.	H.	R.	ER.	SO.	BB.	ERA.
1987—St. Louis		National	1	4	0	0	.000	4	4	4	3	2	9.00

WORLD SERIES RECORD

Year	Club	League	G.	IP.	W.	L.	Pct.	H.	R.	ER.	SO.	BB.	ERA.
1987—St. Louis		National	2	7⅓	0	1	.000	9	7	7	5	5	8.59

RICHARD KEITH MAHLER

Name pronounced MAY-ler.

(Rick)

Born August 5, 1953, at Austin, Tex.
Height, 6.01. Weight, 202.
Throws and bats righthanded.
Attended Trinity University, San Antonio, Tex.
Brother of Mickey Mahler, pitcher with Atlanta Braves,
Pittsburgh Pirates, California Angels, Montreal Expos, Detroit Tigers,
Texas Rangers and Toronto Blue Jays, 1977 through 1982, 1985 and 1986.

Holds major league record for most game-winning runs batted in by pitcher, season (3), 1985.
Shares major league record for most years leading league in runs allowed (3).
Shares National League record for most shutouts in season openers, lifetime (3).
Major League saves: 1981 (2), 1990 (4). Total—6.
Led National League in hit batsmen with 10 in 1989.
Led National League pitchers in games started with 39 in 1985 and tied for lead with 39 in 1986.

Year Club	League	G.	IP.	W.	L.	Pct.	H.	R.	ER.	SO.	BB.	ERA.
1975—Kingsport	Ap'lachian	26	64	2	2	.500	52	23	21	58	26	2.95
1976—Greenwood	W. Carol.	31	105	6	6	.500	96	49	34	68	49	2.91
1977—Savannah	Southern	17	86	6	2	.750	71	31	22	53	38	2.30
1977—Richmond	Int'national	14	40	0	2	.000	45	29	27	25	23	6.08
1978—Richmond	Int'national	32	126	9	5	.643	130	65	55	66	53	3.93
1979—Richmond	Int'national	24	54	4	6	.400	46	26	20	40	18	3.33
1979—Atlanta	National	15	22	0	0	.000	28	16	15	12	11	6.14
1980—Richmond	Int'national	29	188	12	6	.667	172	68	54	101	80	2.59
1980—Atlanta	National	2	4	0	0	.000	2	1	1	1	0	2.25
1981—Atlanta	National	34	112	8	6	.571	109	41	35	54	43	2.81
1982—Atlanta	National	39	205⅓	9	10	.474	213	105	96	105	62	4.21
1983—Atlanta	National	10	14⅓	0	0	.000	16	8	8	7	9	5.02
1983—Richmond	In'national	24	162⅔	12	7	.632	165	102	89	103	85	4.92
1984—Atlanta	National	38	222	13	10	.565	209	86	77	106	62	3.12
1985—Atlanta	National	39	266⅔	17	15	.531	*272	116	103	107	79	3.48
1986—Atlanta	National	39	237⅔	14	*18	.438	*283	*139	*129	137	95	4.88
1987—Atlanta	National	39	197	8	13	.381	212	118	109	95	85	4.98
1988—Atlanta†	National	39	249	9	16	.360	*279	*125	*102	131	42	3.69
1989—Cincinnati	National	40	220⅔	9	13	.409	*242	*113	94	102	51	3.83
1990—Cincinnati‡	National	35	134⅔	7	6	.538	134	67	64	68	39	4.28
1990—Nashville§	Am. Assoc.	1	7⅓	0	1	.000	6	2	2	5	3	2.45
Major League Totals—12 Years		369	1885⅓	94	107	.468	1999	935	833	925	578	3.98

Signed as free agent by Atlanta Braves' organization, June 16, 1975.

†Granted free agency, November 4, 1988; signed by Cincinnati Reds, December 2, 1988.

‡On disabled list, May 17 to June 1, 1990; included rehabilitation disability assignment to Nashville, May 29 and May 30, 1990.

§Granted free agency, November 5, 1990.

CHAMPIONSHIP SERIES RECORD

Year Club	League	G.	IP.	W.	L.	Pct.	H.	R.	ER.	SO.	BB.	ERA.
1982—Atlanta	National	1	1⅔	0	0	.000	3	0	0	0	2	0.00
1990—Cincinnati	National	1	1⅔	0	0	.000	2	0	0	0	0	0.00
Championship Series Totals—2 Years		2	3⅓	0	0	.000	5	0	0	0	2	0.00

CANDIDO MALDONADO (GUADARRAMA)
(Candy)

Born September 5, 1960, at Humacao, Puerto Rico.
Height, 6.00. Weight, 195.
Throws and bats righthanded.

Shares major league record for most sacrifice flies, game (3), August 29, 1987.
Major League stolen bases: 1985 (1), 1986 (4), 1987 (8), 1988 (6), 1989 (4), 1990 (3). Total—26.
Hit for the cycle, May 4, 1987.
Led California League in total bases with 247 in 1980.
Tied for Pioneer League lead in sacrifice flies with 6 in 1978.
Named California League co-Most Valuable Player, 1980.

Year Club	League	Pos.	G.	AB.	R.	H.	2B.	3B.	HR.	RBI.	B.A.	PO.	A.	E.	F.A.
1978—Lethbridge	Pion.	OF	57	210	45	61	15	5	12	48	.290	112	6	8	.937
1979—Clinton	Midw.	OF	50	158	25	37	13	1	2	26	.234	81	5	2	.977
1979—Lethbridge	Pion.	OF	59	234	42	70	*20	3	5	33	.299	81	5	4	.956
1980—Lodi†	Calif.	OF	121	456	75	139	27	3	25	*102	.305	211	13	11	.953
1981—Albuquerque	P. C.	OF	126	460	96	154	40	9	21	104	.335	221	21	8	.968
1981—Los Angeles	Nat.	OF	11	12	0	1	0	0	0	0	.083	8	0	0	1.000
1982—Albuquerque	P. C.	OF	138	541	91	163	28	6	24	96	.301	303	15	10	.970
1982—Los Angeles	Nat.	OF	6	4	0	0	0	0	0	0	.000	5	0	0	1.000
1983—Los Angeles	Nat.	OF	42	62	5	12	1	1	1	6	.194	26	0	0	1.000
1983—Albuquerque	P. C.	OF-3B	38	144	23	46	6	1	4	20	.319	66	11	4	.951
1984—Los Angeles	Nat.	OF-3B	116	254	25	68	14	0	5	28	.268	124	5	8	.942
1985—Los Angeles‡	Nat.	OF	121	213	20	48	7	1	5	19	.225	121	6	2	.984
1986—San Francisco	Nat.	OF-3B	133	405	49	102	31	3	18	85	.252	161	11	3	.983
1987—San Francisco§	Nat.	OF	118	442	69	129	28	4	20	85	.292	176	7	5	.973
1988—San Francisco	Nat.	OF	142	499	53	127	23	1	12	68	.255	251	5	10	.962
1989—San Francisco x	Nat.	OF	129	345	39	75	23	0	9	41	.217	181	6	5	.974
1990—Cleveland y	Amer.	OF	155	590	76	161	32	2	22	95	.273	293	9	2	.993
National League Totals—9 Years			818	2236	260	562	127	10	70	332	.251	1053	40	33	.971
American League Totals—1 Year			155	590	76	161	32	2	22	95	.273	293	9	2	.993
Major League Totals—10 Years			973	2826	336	723	159	12	92	427	.256	1346	49	35	.976

Signed as free agent by Los Angeles Dodgers' organization, June 6, 1978.

†On disabled list, August 16 to September 16, 1980.

‡Traded to San Francisco Giants for Catcher Alex Trevino, December 11, 1985.

§On disabled list, June 28 to August 7, 1987.

xGranted free agency, November 13, 1989; signed by Cleveland Indians, November 28, 1989.

yGranted free agency, November 5, 1990.

CHAMPIONSHIP SERIES RECORD

Year Club	League	Pos.	G.	AB.	R.	H.	2B.	3B.	HR.	RBI.	B.A.	PO.	A.	E.	F.A.
1983—Los Angeles	Nat.	PH	2	2	0	0	0	0	0	0	.000	0	0	0	.000
1985—Los Angeles	Nat.	OF-PH	4	7	0	1	0	0	0	1	.143	4	0	1	.800

Year Club League	Pos.	G.	AB.	R.	H.	2B.	3B.	HR.	RBI.	B.A.	PO.	A.	E.	F.A.
1987—San Francisco ...... Nat.	OF	5	19	2	4	1	0	0	2	.211	7	0	0	1.000
1989—San Francisco ...... Nat.	PH-OF	3	3	1	0	0	0	0	1	.000	2	0	0	1.000
Championship Series Totals—4 Years.....		14	31	3	5	1	0	0	4	.161	13	0	1	.929

WORLD SERIES RECORD

Year Club League	Pos.	G.	AB.	R.	H.	2B.	3B.	HR.	RBI.	B.A.	PO.	A.	E.	F.A.
1989—San Francisco ...... Nat.	OF-PH	4	11	1	1	0	1	0	0	.091	5	0	0	1.000

CARLOS CESAR MALDONADO

Born October 18, 1966, at Chepo, Panama.
Height, 6.01. Weight, 210.
Throws and bats righthanded.

Led Southern League in games finished in relief with 48 in 1990.

Year Club	League	G.	IP.	W.	L.	Pct.	H.	R.	ER.	SO.	BB.	ERA.
1986—Sarasota Royals............................	Gulf Coast	10	34⅓	0	2	.000	29	10	7	16	10	1.83
1987—Sarasota Royals............................	Gulf Coast	20	58	5	1	.833	32	18	16	56	19	2.48
1987—Appleton	Midwest	2	2⅓	0	0	.000	4	3	3	4	3	11.57
1988—Baseball City	Florida St.	16	52⅔	1	5	.167	46	35	31	44	39	5.30
1989—Baseball City†	Florida St.	28	76⅔	11	3	.786	47	14	10	66	24	1.17
1990—Memphis....................................	Southern	55	77⅓	4	5	.444	61	29	25	77	37	2.91
1990—Kansas City................................	American	4	6	0	0	.000	9	6	6	9	4	9.00
Major League Totals—1 Year................		4	6	0	0	.000	9	6	6	9	4	9.00

Signed as free agent by Kansas City Royals' organization, April 28, 1986.
†On Appleton disabled list, April 7 to May 12, 1989.

ROBERT WILLIAM MALLOY
(Bob)

Born November 24, 1964, at Garland, Tex.
Height, 6.05. Weight, 200.
Throws and bats righthanded.
Attended University of Virginia, Charlottesville, Va.

Year Club	League	G.	IP.	W.	L.	Pct.	H.	R.	ER.	SO.	BB.	ERA.
1986—Sarasota Rangers†	Gulf Coast					(Did not play)						
1987—Gastonia.......................................	S. Atlantic	9	57	5	0	1.000	51	21	16	66	13	2.53
1987—Texas..	American	2	11	0	0	.000	13	11	8	8	3	6.55
1987—Tulsa..	Texas	16	92	2	10	.167	97	55	50	73	39	4.89
1988—Tulsa..	Texas	12	71⅓	1	7	.125	93	53	41	29	24	5.17
1988—Port Charlotte	Florida St.	13	82	4	6	.400	65	30	27	44	26	2.96
1989—Tulsa‡..	Texas	34	125⅓	10	9	.526	142	75	65	54	35	4.67
1990—Jacksonville................................	Southern	8	43⅓	4	1	.800	34	17	16	25	16	3.32
1990—Indianapolis................................	Am. Assoc.	23	33⅓	2	2	.500	31	15	14	31	8	3.78
1990—Montreal	National	1	2	0	0	.000	1	0	0	1	1	0.00
American League Totals—1 Year		2	11	0	0	.000	13	11	8	8	3	6.55
National League Totals—1 Year		1	2	0	0	.000	1	0	0	1	1	0.00
Major League Totals—2 Years................		3	13	0	0	.000	14	11	8	9	4	5.54

Selected by Oakland Athletics' organization in 30th round of free-agent draft, June 3, 1985.
Selected by Texas Rangers' organization in 19th round of free-agent draft, June 2, 1986.
†On disabled list, July 5, 1986 through entire season.
‡Drafted by Indianapolis (Montreal Expos' organization), December 5, 1989.

CHARLES RAY MALONE JR.
(Chuck)

Born July 8, 1965, at Harrisburg, Ark.
Height, 6.07. Weight, 250.
Throws and bats righthanded.
Attended Arkansas State University, State University, Ark.,
and Three Rivers Community College, Poplar Bluff, Mo.

Year Club	League	G.	IP.	W.	L.	Pct.	H.	R.	ER.	SO.	BB.	ERA.
1986—Bend..	Northwest	21	54⅔	2	6	.250	47	38	31	60	50	5.10
1987—Clearwater	Florida St.	34	120	6	8	.429	105	55	52	100	63	3.90
1988—Reading.......................................	Eastern	22	126⅔	12	7	.632	107	63	53	117	*88	3.77
1988—Maine..	Int'national	6	27⅔	1	4	.200	28	27	21	38	24	6.83
1989—Reading.......................................	Eastern	33	106	5	7	.417	64	61	49	107	106	4.16
1990—Scranton/Wilkes-Barre................	Int'national	26	76	4	3	.571	47	57	54	79	78	6.39
1990—Philadelphia	National	7	7⅓	1	0	1.000	3	4	3	7	11	3.68
Major League Totals—1 Year................		7	7⅓	1	0	1.000	3	4	3	7	11	3.68

Selected by Philadelphia Phillies' organization in 5th round of free-agent draft, January 14, 1986.

KELLY JOHN MANN

Born August 17, 1967, at Santa Monica, Calif.
Height, 6.03. Weight, 215.
Throws and bats righthanded.

Tied for New York-Pennsylvania League lead in double plays by catchers with 7 in 1986.

Year Club League	Pos.	G.	AB.	R.	H.	2B.	3B.	HR.	RBI.	B.A.	PO.	A.	E.	F.A.
1985—Wytheville............ Appal.	C	26	75	6	15	3	0	1	10	.200	118	11	5	.963
1986—Geneva................... NYP	C	60	191	17	37	1	0	2	15	.194	419	49	8	.983
1986—Peoria................... Midw.	C	3	13	4	6	2	0	0	4	.462	26	1	1	.964
1987—Peoria................... Midw.	C	95	287	24	73	16	1	4	45	.254	582	63	9	.986
1988—Winston-Salem ..... Carol.	C	94	307	32	84	11	0	8	40	.274	668	52	13	.982
1988—Pittsfield .... East.	C	22	51	7	10	3	0	0	3	.196	95	20	4	.966
1989—Charlotte†.............. South.	C-1B	117	345	37	85	14	1	8	56	.246	612	84	9	.987
1989—Atlanta.................. Nat.	C	7	24	1	5	2	0	0	1	.208	48	5	0	1.000
1990—Greenville .... South.	C	50	155	25	49	13	0	7	27	.316	249	38	5	.983
1990—Richmond.............. Int.	C	63	203	18	41	13	0	3	20	.202	353	49	7	.983
1990—Atlanta.................. Nat.	C	11	28	2	4	1	0	1	2	.143	40	3	0	1.000
Major League Totals—2 Years		18	52	3	9	3	0	1	3	.173	88	8	0	1.000

Selected by Chicago Cubs' organization in 20th round of free-agent draft, June 3, 1985.

†Traded with Pitcher Pat Gomez to Atlanta Braves, September 1, 1989, completing deal in which Atlanta traded Pitcher Paul Assenmacher to Chicago Cubs for two players to be named later, August 24, 1989.

RAMON MANON

Name pronounced MIN-yawn.

Born January 20, 1968, at Santo Domingo, Dominican Republic.
Height, 6.00. Weight, 150.
Throws and bats righthanded.

Year Club	League	G.	IP.	W.	L.	Pct.	H.	R.	ER.	SO.	BB.	ERA.
1986—Sarasota Yankees .... Gulf Coast	11	28	0	4	.000	31	22	16	13	22	5.14
1987—Prince William .... Carolina	23	39⅓	2	3	.400	45	36	32	28	41	7.32
1988—Fort Lauderdale† .... Florida St.	4	22⅓	2	0	1.000	13	5	5	13	12	2.01
1989—Fort Lauderdale‡ .... Florida St.	22	122⅓	7	9	.438	91	62	48	100	53	3.53
1990—Texas§... American	1	2	0	0	.000	3	3	3	0	3	13.50
1990—Fort Lauderdale .... Florida St.	11	35½	2	3	.400	39	26	23	40	23	5.86
1990—Albany x....................................... Eastern	9	25⅔	1	2	.333	24	19	17	21	29	5.96
Major League Totals—1 Year..............................	1	2	0	0	.000	3	3	3	0	3	13.50

Signed as free agent by New York Yankees' organization, October 18, 1985.
†On disabled list, June 22, 1988 through remainder of season.
‡Drafted by Texas Rangers, December 4, 1989.
§Returned to New York Yankees' organization, April 30, 1990.
xOn disabled list, May 29 to June 5, 1990.

REYES FRED ELOY MANRIQUE

Name pronounced Man-REE-kee.

(Fred)

Born November 5, 1961, at Bolivar, Venezuela.
Height, 6.01. Weight, 175.
Throws and bats righthanded.

Major League stolen bases: 1986 (1), 1987 (5), 1988 (6), 1989 (4), 1990 (2). Total—18.
Led American Association in grounding into double plays with 19 in 1986.
Led American Association shortstops in errors with 25 and double plays with 86 in 1986.
Led International League second basemen in errors with 22 in 1983 and 24 in 1984.

Year Club League	Pos.	G.	AB.	R.	H.	2B.	3B.	HR.	RBI.	B.A.	PO.	A.	E.	F.A.
1979—Dunedin .... Fla. St.	SS	5	15	0	2	0	0	0	0	.133	4	7	3	.786
1979—Medicine Hat........ Pion.	SS	66	270	47	81	8	●10	0	30	.300	103	208	★37	.894
1980—Kinston................... Carol.	SS-OF	111	390	49	108	9	5	7	50	.277	120	192	37	.894
1981—Knoxville† .... South.	SS	115	469	62	131	15	6	5	42	.279	161	330	45	.916
1981—Toronto .... Amer.	SS-3B	14	28	1	4	0	0	0	1	.143	10	27	3	.925
1982—Syracuse‡ .... Int.	2B-3B-SS	103	362	41	91	9	2	4	37	.251	186	255	24	.948
1983—Syracuse .... Int.	2-S-3-O	128	485	55	130	22	8	10	50	.268	211	351	36	.940
1984—Syracuse .... Int.	2B-SS-3B	129	517	63	146	15	5	6	45	.282	233	389	28	.957
1984—Toronto§ .... Amer.	2B	10	9	0	3	0	0	0	1	.333	5	10	1	.938
1985—Indianapolis .... A. A.	3B-SS-2B	123	409	46	98	21	5	8	37	.240	126	249	19	.952
1985—Montreal x .... Nat.	2B-SS-3B	9	13	5	4	1	1	1	1	.308	5	10	0	1.000
1986—Louisville .... A. A.	SS-2B	133	520	79	148	19	6	9	51	.285	208	421	26	.960
1986—St. Louis y .... Nat.	3B-2B	13	17	2	3	0	0	1	1	.176	1	3	0	1.000
1987—Chicago .... Amer.	2B-SS	115	298	30	77	13	3	4	29	.258	176	286	7	.985
1988—Chicago .... Amer.	2B-SS	140	345	43	81	10	6	5	37	.235	241	343	13	.978
1989—Chicago z-Texas a Amer.	2B-SS-3B	119	378	46	111	25	1	4	52	.294	177	250	21	.953
1990—Minnesota .... Amer.	2B	69	228	22	54	10	0	5	29	.237	104	155	7	.974
1990—Portland b .... P. C.	PH	1	1	0	1	0	0	0	1	1.000	0	0	0	.000
American League Totals—6 Years		467	1286	142	330	58	10	18	149	.257	713	1071	52	.972
National League Totals—2 Years		22	30	7	7	1	1	2	2	.233	6	13	0	1.000
Major League Totals—8 Years.................		489	1316	149	337	59	11	20	151	.256	719	1084	52	.972

Signed as free agent by Toronto Blue Jays' organization, November 24, 1978.
†On disabled list, April 9 to April 19, 1981.
‡On disabled list, June 27 to July 12, 1982.
§Sold to Montreal Expos, April 7, 1985.
xTraded to St. Louis Cardinals for Catcher Tom Nieto, March 31, 1986.
yTraded to Chicago White Sox for Pitcher Bill Dawley, December 22, 1986.

zTraded to Outfielder Harold Baines to Texas Rangers for Shortstop Scott Fletcher, Outfielder Sammy Sosa and Pitcher Wilson Alvarez, July 29, 1989.
aTraded to Minnesota Twins for Pitcher Jeff Satzinger and cash, April 13, 1990.
bReleased, August 8, 1990; signed by California Angels, December 7, 1990.

JEFFREY PAUL MANTO
(Jeff)

Born August 23, 1964, at Bristol, Pa.
Height, 6.03. Weight, 210.
Throws and bats righthanded.
Attended Temple University, Philadelphia, Pa.

Led Texas League in grounding into double plays with 17 in 1988.
Led Pacific Coast League third basemen in assists with 265, fielding percentage with .943 and double plays with 22 in 1989.
Led California League third basemen in assists with 245 and total chances with 365 in 1987.
Named Texas League Most Valuable Player, 1988.

Year	Club	League	Pos.	G.	AB.	R.	H.	2B.	3B.	HR.	RBI.	B.A.	PO.	A.	E.	F.A.
1985—Quad Cities		Midw.	OF-3B	74	233	34	46	5	2	11	34	.197	87	8	3	.969
1986—Quad Cities†		Midw.	3B	73	239	31	59	13	0	8	49	.247	48	114	28	.853
1987—Palm Springs		Calif.	3B-1B	112	375	61	96	21	4	7	63	.256	93	246	37	.902
1988—Midland		Texas	●3B-2B-1B	120	408	88	123	23	3	24	101	.301	82	208	●32	.901
1989—Edmonton‡		P. C.	3B-1B	127	408	89	113	25	3	23	67	.277	140	266	21	.951
1990—Colorado Springs		P. C.	3B-1B	96	316	73	94	27	1	18	82	.297	340	131	10	.979
1990—Cleveland		Amer.	1B-3B	30	76	12	17	5	1	2	14	.224	185	24	2	.991
Major League Totals—1 Year				30	76	12	17	5	1	2	14	.224	185	24	2	.991

Selected by New York Yankees' organization in 35th round of free-agent draft, June 7, 1982.
Selected by California Angels' organization in 14th round of free-agent draft, June 3, 1985.
†On disabled list, July 16, 1986 through remainder of season.
‡Traded with Pitcher Colin Charland to Cleveland Indians for Pitcher Scott Bailes, January 9, 1990.

KIRT DEAN MANWARING

Born July 15, 1965, at Elmira, N. Y.
Height, 5.11. Weight, 190.
Throws and bats righthanded.
Attended Coastal Carolina College, Conway, S. C.

Major League stolen bases: 1989 (2).
Led Texas League catchers in double plays with 8 and total chances with 688 in 1987.

Year	Club	League	Pos.	G.	AB.	R.	H.	2B.	3B.	HR.	RBI.	B.A.	PO.	A.	E.	F.A.
1986—Clinton		Midw.	C	49	147	18	36	7	1	2	16	.245	243	31	5	.982
1987—Shreveport		Texas	C	98	307	27	82	13	2	2	22	.267	603	★81	4	.994
1987—San Francisco		Nat.	C	6	7	0	1	0	0	0	0	.143	9	1	1	.909
1988—Phoenix		P. C.	C	81	273	29	77	12	2	2	35	.282	411	51	6	.987
1988—San Francisco		Nat.	C	40	116	12	29	7	0	1	15	.250	162	24	4	.979
1989—San Francisco†		Nat.	C	85	200	14	42	4	2	0	18	.210	289	32	6	.982
1990—Phoenix		P. C.	C	74	247	20	58	10	2	3	14	.235	352	45	4	★.990
1990—San Francisco		Nat.	C	8	13	0	2	0	1	0	1	.154	22	3	0	1.000
Major League Totals—4 Years				139	336	26	74	11	3	1	34	.220	482	60	11	.980

Selected by Boston Red Sox' organization in 12th round of free-agent draft, June 6, 1983.
Selected by San Francisco Giants' organization in 2nd round of free-agent draft, June 2, 1986.
†On disabled list, August 31 to September 15, 1989.

CHAMPIONSHIP SERIES RECORD

Year	Club	League	Pos.	G.	AB.	R.	H.	2B.	3B.	HR.	RBI.	B.A.	PO.	A.	E.	F.A.
1989—San Francisco		Nat.	PH-C	3	2	0	0	0	0	0	0	.000	5	0	0	1.000

WORLD SERIES RECORD

Year	Club	League	Pos.	G.	AB.	R.	H.	2B.	3B.	HR.	RBI.	B.A.	PO.	A.	E.	F.A.
1989—San Francisco		Nat.	C	1	1	1	1	1	0	0	0	1.000	0	0	0	.000

PAUL PATRICK MARAK

Born August 2, 1965, at Lakenheath, England.
Height, 6.02. Weight, 175.
Throws and bats righthanded.
Attended Trinidad State Junior College, Trinidad, Colo.

Tied for Pioneer League lead in wild pitches with 12 in 1986.

Year	Club	League	G.	IP.	W.	L.	Pct.	H.	R.	ER.	SO.	BB.	ERA.
1985—Bradenton Braves		Gulf Coast	12	63	2	6	.250	80	58	39	33	36	5.57
1986—Idaho Falls		Pioneer	12	61	2	5	.286	82	57	34	52	25	5.02
1987—Sumter		S. Atlantic	50	118	12	5	.706	101	50	41	98	44	3.13
1988—Durham		Carolina	32	100⅔	7	4	.636	90	40	30	84	33	2.68
1988—Greenville		Southern	12	16⅓	0	0	.000	25	19	19	9	11	10.47
1989—Greenville		Southern	43	121⅔	8	7	.533	102	53	41	81	47	3.03
1989—Richmond		Int'national	2	4	0	1	.000	8	4	4	2	4	9.00
1990—Richmond		Int'national	32	148	9	8	.529	130	49	41	75	50	★2.49
1990—Atlanta		National	7	39	1	2	.333	39	16	16	15	19	3.69
Major League Totals—1 Year			7	39	1	2	.333	39	16	16	15	19	3.69

Selected by Atlanta Braves' organization in 11th round of free-agent draft, January 9, 1985.

MICHAEL ALLEN MARSHALL
(Mike)

Born January 12, 1960, at Libertyville, Ill.
Height, 6.05. Weight, 215.
Throws and bats righthanded.

Major League stolen bases: 1982 (2), 1983 (7), 1984 (4), 1985 (3), 1986 (4), 1988 (4), 1989 (2). Total—26.
Led California League in total bases with 301 in 1979.
Led Pacific Coast League first basemen in double plays with 136 in 1981.
Led Texas League first basemen in double plays with 120 in 1980.
Named Minor League Player of the Year by THE SPORTING NEWS, 1981.
Named Pacific Coast League Most Valuable Player, 1981.
Named California League co-Most Valuable Player, 1979.

Year—Club	League	Pos.	G.	AB.	R.	H.	2B.	3B.	HR.	RBI.	B.A.	PO.	A.	E.	F.A.
1978—Lethbridge	Pion.	1B-OF	65	256	48	83	15	2	12	70	.324	308	16	7	.979
1979—Lodi	Calif.	1B	137	525	101	*186	*37	3	24	116	*.354	1173	71	20	.984
1980—San Antonio	Texas	1B	134	470	95	151	21	6	16	82	.321	*1157	64	●16	.987
1981—Albuquerque	P. C.	1B	128	467	*114	174	25	7	*34	*137	*.373	1127	54	9	.992
1981—Los Angeles	Nat.	1B-3B-OF	14	25	2	5	3	0	0	1	.200	14	2	0	1.000
1982—Albuquerque	P. C.	OF-1B-3B	66	255	74	99	20	1	14	58	.388	113	3	4	.966
1982—Los Angeles	Nat.	OF-1B	49	95	10	23	3	0	5	9	.242	122	5	2	.984
1983—Los Angeles	Nat.	OF-1B	140	465	47	132	17	1	17	65	.284	395	21	6	.986
1984—Los Angeles†	Nat.	OF-1B	134	495	68	127	27	0	21	65	.257	331	17	5	.986
1985—Los Angeles‡	Nat.	OF-1B	135	518	72	152	27	2	28	95	.293	265	12	4	.986
1986—Los Angeles§	Nat.	OF	103	330	47	77	11	0	19	53	.233	149	8	6	.963
1987—Los Angeles x	Nat.	OF	104	402	45	118	19	0	16	72	.294	147	4	2	.987
1988—Los Angeles y	Nat.	OF-1B	144	542	63	150	27	2	20	82	.277	605	49	7	.989
1989—Los Angeles za	Nat.	OF	105	377	41	98	21	1	11	42	.260	179	2	4	.978
1990—New York bc	Nat.	1B-OF	53	163	24	39	8	1	6	27	.239	277	24	2	.993
1990—Boston	Amer.	1B-OF	30	112	10	32	6	1	4	12	.286	55	7	1	.984
1990—Pawtucket	Int.	OF	6	23	5	7	0	0	2	4	.304	1	0	0	1.000
National League Totals—10 Years			981	3412	419	921	163	7	143	511	.270	2484	144	38	.986
American League Totals—1 Year			30	112	10	32	6	1	4	12	.286	55	7	1	.984
Major League Totals—10 Years			1011	3524	429	953	169	8	147	523	.270	2539	151	39	.986

Selected by Los Angeles Dodgers' organization in 6th round of free-agent draft, June 6, 1978.
†On disabled list, May 13 to June 3, 1984.
‡On disabled list, June 20 to July 18, 1985.
§On disabled list, July 20 to August 4, 1986.
xOn disabled list, May 6 to May 29 and August 21 to September 5, 1987.
yGranted free agency, November 4, 1988; re-signed by Dodgers, November 13, 1988.
zOn disabled list, May 31 to July 1, 1989.
aTraded with Pitcher Alejandro Pena to New York Mets for Outfielder Juan Samuel, December 20, 1989.
bOn disabled list, July 13 to July 28, 1990.
cTraded to Boston Red Sox for Pitcher Greg Hansell, Outfielder Ed Perozo and a player to be named later, July 27, 1990; New York Mets acquired Catcher Paul Williams to complete deal, November 19, 1990.

DIVISION SERIES RECORD

Year—Club	League	Pos.	G.	AB.	R.	H.	2B.	3B.	HR.	RBI.	B.A.	PO.	A.	E.	F.A.
1981—Los Angeles	Nat.	PH	1	1	0	0	0	0	0	0	.000	0	0	0	.000

CHAMPIONSHIP SERIES RECORD

Shares National League Championship Series record for most at-bats, series (30), 1988.

Year—Club	League	Pos.	G.	AB.	R.	H.	2B.	3B.	HR.	RBI.	B.A.	PO.	A.	E.	F.A.
1983—Los Angeles	Nat.	1B-OF	4	15	1	2	1	0	1	2	.133	22	2	0	1.000
1985—Los Angeles	Nat.	OF	6	23	1	5	2	0	1	3	.217	8	0	0	1.000
1988—Los Angeles	Nat.	OF	7	30	3	7	1	1	0	5	.233	14	0	0	1.000
1990—Boston	Amer.	PH	3	3	0	1	0	0	0	0	.333	0	0	0	.000
Championship Series Totals—4 Years			20	71	5	15	4	1	2	10	.211	44	2	0	1.000

WORLD SERIES RECORD

Year—Club	League	Pos.	G.	AB.	R.	H.	2B.	3B.	HR.	RBI.	B.A.	PO.	A.	E.	F.A.
1988—Los Angeles	Nat.	OF	5	13	2	3	0	1	1	3	.231	6	0	0	1.000

ALL-STAR GAME RECORD

Member of National League All-Star Team in 1984; did not play.

NORBERTO EDONAL MARTIN

Name pronounced Mar-TEEN.

Born December 10, 1966, at Santo Domingo, Dominican Republic.
Height, 5.10. Weight, 165.
Throws right and bats left and righthanded.

Year—Club	League	Pos.	G.	AB.	R.	H.	2B.	3B.	HR.	RBI.	B.A.	PO.	A.	E.	F.A.
1984—Sarasota W.S.	Gulf C.	*SS-OF	56	205	36	56	8	2	1	30	.273	66	149	*37	.853
1985—Appleton	Midw.	SS	30	196	15	19	2	0	0	5	.198	39	86	12	.912
1985—Niagara Falls	NYP	SS	60	217	22	55	9	0	1	13	.253	85	173	35	.881
1986—Peninsula†	Carol.						(Did Not Play)								
1986—Appleton‡	Midw.	SS	9	33	4	10	2	0	0	2	.303	13	16	6	.829

Year Club League	Pos.	G.	AB.	R.	H.	2B.	3B.	HR.	RBI.	B.A.	PO.	A.	E.	F.A.
1986—Sarasota W.S........ Gulf C.	PR	1	0	0	0	0	0	0	0	.000	0	0	0	.000
1987—Charleston, W.Va.S. Atl.	SS-OF-2B	68	250	44	78	14	1	5	35	.312	84	152	25	.904
1987—Peninsula.............. Carol.	2B	41	162	21	42	6	1	1	18	.259	94	108	15	.931
1988—Tampa................... Fla. St.	2B	101	360	44	93	10	4	2	33	.258	196	268	20	.959
1989—Tampa§.................Fla. St.						(Did Not Play)								
1990—Vancouver............ P. C.	2B	130	508	77	135	20	4	3	45	.266	283	324	17	.973

Signed as free agent by Chicago White Sox' organization, March 27, 1984.
†On disabled list, April 10 to May 5, 1986.
‡On disabled list, May 14, 1986 through remainder of season.
§On disabled list, April 7, 1989 through entire season.

CARLOS ALBERTO MARTINEZ

Born August 11, 1965, at La Guaira, Venezuela.
Height, 6.05. Weight, 175.
Throws and bats righthanded.

Major League stolen bases: 1988 (1), 1989 (4). Total—5.

Year Club League	Pos.	G.	AB.	R.	H.	2B.	3B.	HR.	RBI.	B.A.	PO.	A.	E.	F.A.
1984—Sara. Yankees...... Gulf C.	SS	31	91	9	14	1	1	0	4	.154	53	103	14	.918
1985—Fort Lauderdale .. Fla. St.	SS	93	311	39	77	15	7	6	44	.248	123	254	25	.938
1986—Fort Lauderdale† Fla. St.	SS	5	16	1	1	0	0	0	0	.063	7	18	0	1.000
1986—Albany‡................. East.	SS-3B	69	253	34	70	18	2	8	39	.277	120	161	32	.898
1986—Buffalo................... A. A.	SS-3B	17	54	6	16	1	0	2	6	.296	24	20	5	.898
1987—Birmingham .... South.	3B	9	30	2	7	1	0	0	0	.233	5	17	2	.917
1987—Hawaii.................... P. C.	OF-3B-SS	83	304	32	75	15	1	3	36	.247	109	91	18	.917
1988—Birmingham .... South.	OF-3B-SS	133	498	67	138	22	3	14	73	.277	196	139	20	.944
1988—Chicago................ Amer.	3B	17	55	5	9	1	0	0	0	.164	7	33	4	.909
1989—Vancouver............ P. C.	1B	18	64	12	25	3	1	2	9	.391	178	10	1	.995
1989—Chicago§ .... Amer.	3B-1B-OF	109	350	44	105	22	0	5	32	.300	283	134	20	.954
1989—South Bend .... Midw.	3B	3	11	2	6	3	0	0	3	.545	0	9	3	.750
1990—Chicago .... Amer.	1B-OF	92	272	18	61	6	5	4	24	.224	632	38	8	.988
Major League Totals—3 Years............		218	677	67	175	29	5	9	56	.258	922	205	32	.972

Signed as free agent by New York Yankees' organization, November 17, 1983.
†On disabled list, April 11 to May 1, 1986.
‡Traded with Catcher Ron Hassey and a player to be named later to Chicago White Sox for Catcher Joel Skinner, Infielder Wayne Tolleson and Outfielder-Designated Hitter Ron Kittle, July 30, 1986; New York Yankees traded Catcher Bill Lindsey to Chicago organization to complete deal, December 24, 1986.
§On disabled list, June 22 to July 13, 1989; included rehabilitation disability assignment to South Bend, July 8 to July 12, 1989.

CARMELO MARTINEZ (SALGADO)

Born July 28, 1960, at Dorado, Puerto Rico.
Height, 6.02. Weight, 211.
Throws and bats righthanded.
Attended Central College of Bayamon, Bayamon, Puerto Rico.
Cousin of Edgar Martinez, third baseman with Seattle Mariners.

Shares major league record by hitting home run in first major league at-bat, August 22, 1983.
Major League stolen bases: 1984 (1), 1986 (1), 1987 (5), 1988 (1), 1990 (2). Total—10.
Tied for National League lead in sacrifice flies with 10 in 1984.
Led American Association first basemen in total chances with 1,283 and tied for lead in double plays with 99 in 1983.
Led Texas League first basemen in putouts with 1,087, total chances with 1,180 and double plays with 102 in 1982.

Year Club League	Pos.	G.	AB.	R.	H.	2B.	3B.	HR.	RBI.	B.A.	PO.	A.	E.	F.A.
1979—Sarasota Cubs ...... Gulf C.	OF-1B	40	143	18	29	4	0	1	23	.203	139	9	6	.961
1980—Quad Cities........... Midw.	O-1-3-2-S	128	460	65	118	23	0	12	64	.257	433	99	13	.976
1981—Midland................. Texas	3-O-2-1	116	392	65	116	22	1	21	84	.296	61	80	24	.855
1982—Midland................. Texas	1B-OF	131	467	100	156	35	4	27	93	.334	1098	78	17	.986
1983—Iowa .... A. A.	*1B-2B	123	458	76	115	25	1	*31	94	.251	*1191	*83	9	.993
1983—Chicago† .... Nat.	1B-3B-OF	29	89	8	23	3	0	6	16	.258	233	17	2	.992
1984—San Diego .... Nat.	OF-1B	149	488	64	122	28	2	13	66	.250	317	15	8	.976
1985—San Diego‡ .... Nat.	OF-1B	150	514	64	130	28	1	21	72	.253	302	14	7	.978
1986—San Diego .... Nat.	OF-1B-3B	113	244	28	58	10	0	9	25	.238	142	14	2	.987
1987—San Diego .... Nat.	OF-1B	139	447	59	122	21	2	15	70	.273	591	42	9	.986
1988—San Diego .... Nat.	OF-1B	121	365	48	86	12	0	18	65	.236	430	32	4	.991
1989—San Diego§ .... Nat.	OF-1B	111	267	23	59	12	2	6	39	.221	225	18	2	.992
1990—Phila.xy-Pitt.......... Nat.	1B-OF	83	217	26	52	9	0	10	35	.240	374	29	2	.995
Major League Totals—8 Years............		895	2631	320	652	123	7	98	388	.248	2614	181	36	.987

Signed as free agent by Chicago Cubs' organization, December 9, 1978.
†Traded with Pitcher Craig Lefferts and Third Baseman Fritz Connally to San Diego Padres for Pitcher Scott Sanderson, December 7, 1983.
‡On disabled list, March 31 to April 15, 1985.
§Granted free agency, November 13, 1989; signed by Philadelphia Phillies, December 1, 1989.
xOn disabled list, May 29 to June 13, 1990.
yTraded to Pittsburgh Pirates for Outfielders Wes Chamberlain and Julio Peguero and a player to be named later, August 30, 1990; Philadelphia Phillies acquired Outfielder Tony Longmire to complete deal, September 28, 1990.

Year Club	League	Pos.	G.	AB.	R.	H.	2B.	3B.	HR.	RBI.	B.A.	PO.	A.	E.	F.A.
1984—San Diego	Nat.	OF	5	17	1	3	0	0	0	0	.176	6	0	0	1.000
1990—Pittsburgh	Nat.	1B	2	8	0	2	2	0	0	2	.250	15	1	0	1.000
Championship Series Totals—2 Years			7	25	1	5	2	0	0	2	.200	21	1	0	1.000

WORLD SERIES RECORD

Year Club	League	Pos.	G.	AB.	R.	H.	2B.	3B.	HR.	RBI.	B.A.	PO.	A.	E.	F.A.
1984—San Diego	Nat.	OF	5	17	0	3	0	0	0	0	.176	7	0	1	.875

CONSTANTINO MARTINEZ
(Tino)

Born December 7, 1967, at Tampa, Fla.
Height, 6.02. Weight, 205.
Throws right and bats lefthanded.
Attended University of Tampa, Tampa, Fla.

Led Eastern League in intentional bases on balls received with 13 in 1989.
Tied for Pacific Coast League lead in intentional bases on balls received with 11 in 1990.
Led Pacific Coast League first basemen in total chances with 1,159 and double plays with 117 in 1990.
Led Eastern League first basemen in double plays with 106 and total chances with 1,348 in 1989.
Received reported $115,000 bonus to sign with Seattle Mariners, 1988.
Member of 1988 U.S. Olympic baseball team.
Named first baseman on THE SPORTING NEWS College Baseball All-America Team, 1988.

Year Club	League	Pos.	G.	AB.	R.	H.	2B.	3B.	HR.	RBI.	B.A.	PO.	A.	E.	F.A.
1989—Williamsport	East.	1B	*137	*509	51	131	29	2	13	64	.257	*1260	*81	7	*.995
1990—Calgary	P. C.	*1B-3B	128	453	83	145	28	1	17	93	.320	*1051	*98	10	*.991
1990—Seattle	Amer.	1B	24	68	4	15	4	0	0	5	.221	155	12	0	1.000
Major League Totals—1 Year			24	68	4	15	4	0	0	5	.221	155	12	0	1.000

Selected by Boston Red Sox' organization in 3rd round of free-agent draft, June 3, 1985.
Selected by Seattle Mariners' organization in 1st round (14th player selected) of free-agent draft, June 1, 1988.

DAVID MARTINEZ
(Dave)

Born September 26, 1964, at New York, N.Y.
Height, 5.10, Weight, 170.
Throws and bats lefthanded.
Attended Valencia Community College, Orlando, Fla.

Major League stolen bases: 1986 (4), 1987 (16), 1988 (23), 1989 (23), 1990 (13). Total—79.

Year Club	League	Pos.	G.	AB.	R.	H.	2B.	3B.	HR.	RBI.	B.A.	PO.	A.	E.	F.A.
1983—Quad Cities	Midw.	OF	44	119	17	29	6	2	0	10	.244	47	8	1	.982
1983—Geneva	NYP	OF	64	241	35	63	15	2	5	33	.261	132	6	8	.945
1984—Quad Cities†	Midw.	OF	12	41	6	9	2	2	0	5	.220	13	2	1	.938
1985—Winston-Salem	Carol.	OF	115	386	52	132	14	4	5	54	*.342	206	11	7	.969
1986—Iowa	A. A.	OF	83	318	52	92	11	5	5	32	.289	214	7	2	.991
1986—Chicago	Nat.	OF	53	108	13	15	1	1	1	7	.139	77	2	1	.988
1987—Chicago	Nat.	OF	142	459	70	134	18	8	8	36	.292	283	10	6	.980
1988—Chi.‡-Mon.	Nat.	OF	138	447	51	114	13	6	6	46	.255	281	4	6	.979
1989—Montreal	Nat.	OF	126	361	41	99	16	7	3	27	.274	199	7	7	.967
1990—Montreal	Nat.	OF-P	118	391	60	109	13	5	11	39	.279	257	6	3	.989
Major League Totals—5 Years			577	1766	235	471	61	27	29	155	.267	1097	29	23	.980

Selected by Texas Rangers' organization in 40th round of free-agent draft, June 7, 1982.
Selected by Chicago Cubs' organization in secondary phase of free-agent draft, January 11, 1983.
†On disabled list, April 27, 1984 through remainder of season.
‡Traded to Montreal Expos for Outfielder Mitch Webster, July 14, 1988.

PITCHING RECORD

Year Club	League	G.	IP.	W.	L.	Pct.	H.	R.	ER.	SO.	BB.	ERA.
1990—Montreal	National	1	⅓	0	0	.000	2	2	2	0	2	54.00

DAVID De LEON MARTINEZ

Born September 18, 1963, at Austin, Tex.
Height, 6.00. Weight, 190.
Throws and bats righthanded.
Attended Blinn College, Brenham, Tex.

Tied for Northwest League lead in games started by pitchers with 15 in 1984.

Year Club	League	G.	IP.	W.	L.	Pct.	H.	R.	ER.	SO.	BB.	ERA.
1984—Salem	Northwest	15	90	3	8	.273	88	53	43	62	43	4.30
1985—Quad Cities†	Midwest	18	100⅓	5	7	.417	101	67	56	75	61	5.02
1986—Palm Springs‡	California	18	94½	6	4	.600	106	63	55	41	58	5.25
1987—Midland	Texas	12	72⅓	3	6	.333	71	49	45	46	44	5.60
1988—Midland§	Texas					(Did Not Play)						
1989—Midland	Texas	22	109⅓	9	5	.643	117	76	63	53	59	5.19
1990—Palm Springs	California	12	55½	0	6	.000	59	32	29	37	16	4.72
1990—Midland x	Texas	34	71⅓	6	6	.500	95	47	41	74	30	5.17

Selected by California Angels' organization in 1st round (fifth player selected) of free-agent draft, January 17, 1984.
†On disabled list, May 13 to June 14, 1985.
‡On disabled list, June 13 to July 26, 1986.
§On disabled list, April 1, 1988 through entire season.
xTraded with Pitcher Mike Hook to Baltimore Orioles for Outfielder Dave Gallagher, December 4, 1990.

EDGAR MARTINEZ

Born January 2, 1963, at New York, N. Y.
Height, 5.11. Weight, 175.
Throws and bats righthanded.
Attended American College, Puerto Rico.
Cousin of Carmelo Martinez, outfielder-first baseman with Pittsburgh Pirates.
Shares American League record for most errors, game (4), May 6, 1990.
Major League stolen bases: 1989 (2), 1990 (1). Total—3.
Led Southern League in sacrifice flies with 12 in 1985.
Led Pacific Coast League third basemen in double plays with 31 and total chances with 389 in 1987.
Led Southern League third basemen in double plays with 34 and total chances with 360 in 1985.

Year Club	League	Pos.	G.	AB.	R.	H.	2B.	3B.	HR.	RBI.	B.A.	PO.	A.	E.	F.A.
1983—Bellingham	N'west	3B	32	104	14	18	1	1	0	5	.173	22	58	6	.930
1984—Wausau	Midw.	3B	126	433	72	131	32	2	15	66	.303	85	246	25	.930
1985—Chattanooga	South.	3B	111	357	43	92	15	5	3	47	.258	★94	★247	19	★.947
1985—Calgary	P. C.	3B-2B	20	68	8	24	7	1	0	14	.353	15	44	4	.937
1986—Chattanooga	South.	★3B-2B	132	451	71	119	29	5	6	74	.264	94	263	15	★.960
1987—Calgary	P. C.	3B	129	438	75	144	31	1	10	66	.329	★91	★278	20	.949
1987—Seattle	Amer.	3B	13	43	6	16	5	2	0	5	.372	13	19	0	1.000
1988—Calgary	P. C.	3B-2B	95	331	63	120	19	4	8	64	★.363	48	185	20	.921
1988—Seattle	Amer.	3B	14	32	0	9	4	0	0	5	.281	5	8	1	.929
1989—Seattle	Amer.	3B	65	171	20	41	5	0	2	20	.240	40	72	6	.949
1989—Calgary	P. C.	3B-2B	32	113	30	39	11	0	3	23	.345	22	56	12	.867
1990—Seattle	Amer.	3B	144	487	71	147	27	2	11	49	.302	89	259	★27	.928
Major League Totals—4 Years			236	733	97	213	41	4	13	79	.291	147	358	34	.937

Signed as free agent by Seattle Mariners' organization, December 19, 1982.

JOSE DENNIS MARTINEZ

(Known by middle name.)

Born May 14, 1955, at Granada, Nicaragua.
Height, 6.01. Weight, 183.
Throws and bats righthanded.

Major League saves: 1977 (4), 1980 (1). Total—5.
Led American League pitchers in games started with 39 and complete games with 18 in 1979.
Tied for National League lead in balks with 10 in 1988.
Led International League in complete games with 16 in 1976.
Named International League Pitcher of the Year, 1976.

Year Club	League	G.	IP.	W.	L.	Pct.	H.	R.	ER.	SO.	BB.	ERA.
1974—Miami	Florida St.	25	179	15	6	.714	124	48	41	164	53	2.06
1975—Miami	Florida St.	20	145	12	4	.750	125	54	42	114	35	2.61
1975—Asheville	Southern	6	45	4	1	.800	45	16	13	18	12	2.60
1975—Rochester	Int'national	2	5	0	0	.000	7	4	3	4	2	5.40
1976—Rochester	Int'national	25	180	★14	8	.636	148	64	50	★140	50	★2.50
1976—Baltimore	American	4	28	1	2	.333	23	8	8	18	8	2.57
1977—Baltimore	American	42	167	14	7	.667	157	86	76	107	64	4.10
1978—Baltimore	American	40	276	16	11	.593	257	121	108	142	93	3.25
1979—Baltimore	American	40	★292	15	16	.484	279	129	119	132	78	3.67
1980—Baltimore†	American	25	100	6	4	.600	103	44	44	42	44	3.96
1980—Miami	Florida St.	2	12	0	0	.000	3	1	0	7	5	0.00
1981—Baltimore	American	25	179	●14	5	.737	173	84	66	88	62	3.32
1982—Baltimore	American	40	252	16	12	.571	262	123	118	111	87	4.21
1983—Baltimore	American	32	153	7	16	.304	209	108	94	71	45	5.53
1984—Baltimore	American	34	141⅔	6	9	.400	145	81	79	77	37	5.02
1985—Baltimore	American	33	180	13	11	.542	203	110	103	68	63	5.15
1986—Baltimore‡	American	4	6⅔	0	0	.000	11	5	5	2	2	6.75
1986—Rochester§	Int'national	4	19⅓	2	1	.667	18	14	13	14	9	6.05
1986—Montreal x	National	19	98	3	6	.333	103	52	50	63	28	4.59
1987—Miami y	Florida St.	3	19	1	1	.500	21	14	13	11	3	6.16
1987—Indianapolis	Am. Assoc.	7	38⅓	3	2	.600	32	20	19	30	13	4.46
1987—Montreal z	National	22	144⅔	11	4	★.733	133	59	53	84	40	3.30
1988—Montreal	National	34	235⅓	15	13	.536	215	94	71	120	55	2.72
1989—Montreal	National	34	232	16	7	.696	227	88	82	142	49	3.18
1990—Montreal	National	32	226	10	11	.476	191	80	74	156	49	2.95
American League Totals—11 Years		319	1775⅓	108	93	.537	1822	899	820	858	583	4.16
National League Totals—5 Years		141	936	55	41	.573	869	373	330	565	221	3.17
Major League Totals—15 Years		460	2711⅓	163	134	.549	2691	1272	1150	1423	804	3.82

Signed as free agent by Baltimore Orioles' organization, December 10, 1973.
†On disabled list, March 28 to April 20 and June 3 to July 10, 1980; included rehabilitation disability assignment to Miami, July 1 to July 10, 1980.
‡On disabled list, April 28 to June 16, 1986; included rehabilitation disability assignment to Rochester, May 21 to June 10, 1986.

§Traded to Montreal Expos for a player to be named later, June 16, 1986; Baltimore Orioles acquired Infielder Rene Gonzales to complete deal, December 16, 1986.
xGranted free agency, November 12, 1986; signed by Miami (Independent), April 14, 1987.
yReleased, May 6, 1987; signed by Montreal Expos' organization, May 6, 1987.
zGranted free agency, November 9, 1987; re-signed by Expos, December 18, 1987.

CHAMPIONSHIP SERIES RECORD

Year Club	League	G.	IP.	W.	L.	Pct.	H.	R.	ER.	SO.	BB.	ERA.
1979—Baltimore	American	1	8⅓	0	0	.000	8	3	3	4	0	3.24

WORLD SERIES RECORD

Year Club	League	G.	IP.	W.	L.	Pct.	H.	R.	ER.	SO.	BB.	ERA.
1979—Baltimore	American	2	2	0	0	.000	6	4	4	0	0	18.00

Eligible for 1983 World Series with Baltimore Orioles; did not play.

ALL-STAR GAME RECORD

Year League	IP.	W.	L.	Pct.	H.	R.	ER.	SO.	BB.	ERA.
1990—National	1	0	0	.000	0	0	0	1	0	0.00

RAMON JAIME MARTINEZ

Born March 22, 1968, at Santo Domingo, D. R.
Height, 6.04. Weight, 172.
Throws and bats righthanded.

Led National League in complete games with 12 in 1990.
Member of 1984 Dominican Republic Olympic baseball team.

Year Club	League	G.	IP.	W.	L.	Pct.	H.	R.	ER.	SO.	BB.	ERA.
1985—Bradenton Dodgers	Gulf Coast	23	59	4	1	.800	57	30	17	42	23	2.59
1986—Bakersfield	California	20	106	4	8	.333	119	73	56	78	63	4.75
1987—Vero Beach	Florida St.	25	170⅓	16	5	.762	128	45	41	148	78	2.17
1988—San Antonio	Texas	14	95	8	4	.667	79	29	26	89	34	2.46
1988—Albuquerque	P. Coast	10	58⅔	5	2	.714	43	24	18	49	32	2.76
1988—Los Angeles	National	9	35⅔	1	3	.250	27	17	15	23	22	3.79
1989—Albuquerque	P. Coast	18	113	10	2	.833	92	40	35	127	50	2.79
1989—Los Angeles	National	15	98⅔	6	4	.600	79	39	35	89	41	3.19
1990—Los Angeles	National	33	234⅓	20	6	.769	191	89	76	223	67	2.92
Major League Totals—3 Years		57	368⅔	27	13	.675	297	145	126	335	130	3.08

Signed as free agent by Los Angeles Dodgers' organization, September 1, 1984.

ALL-STAR GAME RECORD

Year League	IP.	W.	L.	Pct.	H.	R.	ER.	SO.	BB.	ERA.
1990—National	1	0	0	.000	0	0	0	1	2	0.00

JOHN ROBERT MARZANO

Born February 14, 1963, at Philadelphia, Pa.
Height, 5.11. Weight, 197.
Throws and bats righthanded.
Attended Temple University, Philadelphia, Pa.

Led Eastern League in being hit by pitch with 12 in 1986.
Member of 1984 U.S. Olympic baseball team.
Named catcher on THE SPORTING NEWS College Baseball All-America Team, 1984.

Year Club	League	Pos.	G.	AB.	R.	H.	2B.	3B.	HR.	RBI.	B.A.	PO.	A.	E.	F.A.
1985—New Britain	East.	C	103	350	36	86	14	6	4	51	.246	530	70	12	.980
1986—New Britain†	East.	C-3B	118	445	55	126	28	2	10	62	.283	509	76	14	.977
1987—Pawtucket	Int.	C	70	255	46	72	22	0	10	35	.282	326	36	8	.978
1987—Boston	Amer.	C	52	168	20	41	11	0	5	24	.244	337	24	5	.986
1988—Boston	Amer.	C	10	29	3	4	1	0	0	1	.138	77	4	0	1.000
1988—Pawtucket	Int.	C	33	111	7	22	2	1	0	5	.198	151	24	8	.956
1988—New Britain	East.	C	35	112	11	23	6	1	0	5	.205	117	11	3	.977
1989—Pawtucket	Int.	C	106	322	27	68	11	0	8	36	.211	574	62	10	.985
1989—Boston	Amer.	C	7	18	5	8	3	0	1	3	.444	29	4	0	1.000
1990—Boston	Amer.	C	32	83	8	20	4	0	0	6	.241	153	14	0	1.000
1990—Pawtucket	Int.	C-3B	26	75	16	24	4	1	2	8	.320	100	12	0	1.000
Major League Totals—4 Years			101	298	36	73	19	0	6	34	.245	596	46	5	.992

Selected by Minnesota Twins' organization in 3rd round of free-agent draft, June 8, 1981.
Selected by Boston Red Sox' organization in 1st round (14th player selected) of free-agent draft, June 4, 1984.
†On disabled list, June 13 to June 28, 1986.

GREGORY INMAN MATHEWS
(Greg)

Born May 17, 1962, at Harbor City, Calif.
Height, 6.02. Weight, 180.
Throws left and bats righthanded.
Attended Santa Ana College, Santa Ana, Calif.; and
California State University, Fullerton, Calif.

Tied for American Association lead in shutouts with 2 in 1986 and 1987.

Year	Club	League	G.	IP.	W.	L.	Pct.	H.	R.	ER.	SO.	BB.	ERA.
1984—Erie	NYP	3	15	0	1	.000	16	15	15	9	8	9.00
1984—Johnson City	Ap'lachian	5	31⅓	2	3	.400	27	12	9	21	13	2.59
1984—Savannah	S. Atlantic	6	27⅓	1	0	1.000	24	10	9	21	15	2.96
1985—St. Petersburg	Florida St.	16	122	13	1	*.929	76	17	15	96	47	*1.11
1985—Louisville	Am. Assoc.	12	74	6	4	.600	61	33	24	47	26	2.92
1986—Louisville†	Am. Assoc.	7	45⅓	3	3	.500	44	19	13	20	14	2.58
1986—St. Louis	National	23	145⅓	11	8	.579	139	61	59	67	44	3.65
1987—St. Louis	National	32	197⅔	11	11	.500	184	87	82	108	71	3.73
1987—Louisville	Am. Assoc.	3	22	3	0	1.000	18	5	5	20	3	2.05
1988—St. Louis‡	National	13	68	4	6	.400	61	34	32	31	33	4.24
1988—Louisville	Am. Assoc.	5	16	0	1	.000	15	14	13	8	9	7.31
1989—St. Louis§	National	(Did not play)										
1989—Louisville	Am. Assoc.	1	0	0	0	.000	0	1	1	0	1	......
1990—St. Louis	National	11	50⅔	0	5	.000	53	34	30	18	30	5.33
1990—Louisville	Am. Assoc.	4	13⅔	0	2	.000	18	15	14	6	12	9.22
1990—Arkansas x	Texas	1	7	0	1	.000	4	2	2	4	1	2.57
Major League Totals—4 Years		79	461⅔	26	30	.464	437	216	203	224	178	3.96

Selected by Minnesota Twins' organization in 9th round of free-agent draft, January 12, 1982.
Selected by St. Louis Cardinals' organization in 10th round of free-agent draft, June 4, 1984.
†On disabled list, April 25 to May 12, 1986.
‡On disabled list, May 14 to August 16, 1988; included rehabilitation disability assignment to Arkansas, June 7 to June 13, 1988; and Louisville, July 26 to August 12, 1988.
§On disabled list, March 25, 1989 through entire season; included rehabilitation disability assignment to Louisville, April 25 to May 2, 1989.
xGranted free agency, October 16, 1990.

CHAMPIONSHIP SERIES RECORD

Year	Club	League	G.	IP.	W.	L.	Pct.	H.	R.	ER.	SO.	BB.	ERA.
1987—St. Louis	National	2	10⅓	1	0	1.000	6	5	4	10	3	3.48

WORLD SERIES RECORD

Year	Club	League	G.	IP.	W.	L.	Pct.	H.	R.	ER.	SO.	BB.	ERA.
1987—St. Louis	National	1	3⅔	0	0	.000	2	1	1	3	2	2.45

DONALD ARTHUR MATTINGLY
(Don)

Born April 20, 1961, at Evansville, Ind.
Height, 6.00. Weight, 193.
Throws and bats lefthanded.
Brother of Randy Mattingly, selected by Cleveland Browns in 4th round of 1973 NFL draft; and quarterback with Saskatchewan Roughriders and Hamilton Tiger-Cats of CFL, 1974 through 1976.

Holds major league records for most home runs, seven consecutive games (9), July 8 through 17, 1987, and eight consecutive games (10), July 8 through 18, 1987; most grand slams, season (6), 1987; most at-bats without a stolen base, season (677), 1986.

Shares major league records for most doubles, inning (2), April 11, 1987, seventh inning; most consecutive games, one or more home runs (8), July 8 through 18, 1987; most sacrifice flies, game (3), May 3, 1986; most putouts and chances accepted by first baseman, nine-inning game (22), July 20, 1987.

Holds American League record for most at-bats by lefthander, season (677), 1986; most consecutive games, one or more long hits, season (10), July 7 through 19, 1987.

Major League stolen bases: 1984 (1), 1985 (2), 1987 (1), 1988 (1), 1989 (3), 1990 (1). Total—9.
Led American League in total bases with 370 in 1985 and 388 in 1986.
Led American League in slugging percentage with .573 in 1986.
Led American League in game-winning RBIs with 21 in 1985 and tied for lead with 15 in 1986.
Led American League in sacrifice flies with 15 in 1985.
Led American League first basemen in fielding percentage with .996 in 1984 and 1986.
Led American League first basemen in putouts with 1,377 and total chances with 1,483 in 1986.
Tied for American League lead in double plays by first basemen with 154 in 1985.
Led South Atlantic League in sacrifice flies with 12 in 1980.
Named Major League Player of the Year by THE SPORTING NEWS, 1985.
Named American League Player of the Year by THE SPORTING NEWS, 1984 through 1986.
Named American League Most Valuable Player by Baseball Writers' Association of America, 1985.
Named first baseman on THE SPORTING NEWS American League All-Star Team, 1984 through 1987.
Named first baseman on THE SPORTING NEWS American League All-Star fielding team, 1985 through 1989.
Named first baseman on THE SPORTING NEWS American League Silver Slugger team, 1985 through 1987.
Named South Atlantic League Most Valuable Player, 1980.
Received reported $22,000 bonus to sign with New York Yankees, 1979.

Year	Club	League	Pos.	G.	AB.	R.	H.	2B.	3B.	HR.	RBI.	B.A.	PO.	A.	E.	F.A.
1979—Oneonta	NYP	OF-1B	53	166	20	58	10	2	3	31	.349	29	2	2	.939
1980—Greensboro	S. Atl.	OF-1B	133	494	92	*177	32	5	9	105	*.358	205	16	8	.976
1981—Nashville	South.	OF-1B	141	547	74	173	*35	4	7	98	.316	846	69	12	.987
1982—Columbus	Int.	OF-1B	130	476	67	150	24	2	10	75	.315	271	17	5	.983
1982—New York	Amer.	OF-1B	7	12	0	2	0	0	0	1	.167	15	1	0	1.000
1983—New York	Amer.	OF-1B-2B	91	279	34	79	15	4	4	32	.283	350	15	3	.992
1983—Columbus	Int.	1B-OF	43	159	35	54	11	3	8	37	.340	325	29	1	.997
1984—New York	Amer.	1B-OF	153	603	91	*207	*44	2	23	110	*.343	1143	126	6	.995
1985—New York	Amer.	1B	159	652	107	211	*48	3	35	*145	.324	1318	87	7	*.995
1986—New York	Amer.	1B-3B	162	677	117	*238	*53	2	31	113	.352	1378	111	7	.996
1987—New York†	Amer.	1B	141	569	93	186	38	2	30	115	.327	1239	91	5	*.996
1988—New York‡	Amer.	1B-OF	144	599	94	186	37	0	18	88	.311	1250	99	9	.993

Year Club	League	Pos.	G.	AB.	R.	H.	2B.	3B.	HR.	RBI.	B.A.	PO.	A.	E.	F.A.
1989—New York.............	Amer.	1B-OF	158	631	79	191	37	2	23	113	.303	1276	87	7	.995
1990—New York§...........	Amer.	1B-OF	102	394	40	101	16	0	5	42	.256	800	78	3	.997
Major League Totals—9 Years................			1117	4416	655	1401	288	15	169	759	.317	8769	695	47	.995

Selected by New York Yankees' organization in 19th round of free-agent draft, June 5, 1979.
†On disabled list, June 9 to June 24, 1987.
‡On disabled list, May 27 to June 14, 1988.
§On disabled list, July 26 to September 11, 1990.

ALL-STAR GAME RECORD

Year League	Pos.	AB.	R.	H.	2B.	3B.	HR.	RBI.	B.A.	PO.	A.	E.	F.A.
1984—American	PH	1	0	0	0	0	0	0	.000	0	0	0	.000
1985—American	1B	1	0	0	0	0	0	0	.000	4	0	0	1.000
1986—American	PH-1B	3	0	0	0	0	0	0	.000	7	0	0	1.000
1987—American	1B	1	0	0	0	0	0	0	.000	10	0	0	1.000
1988—American	1B	2	0	0	0	0	0	0	.000	2	1	1	.750
1989—American	1B	1	0	1	1	0	0	0	1.000	4	0	0	1.000
All-Star Game Totals—6 Years..................		9	0	1	1	0	0	0	.111	27	1	1	.966

ROBERT JOHN MAURER
(Rob)

Born January 7, 1967, at Evansville, Ind.
Height, 6.03. Weight, 200.
Throws and bats lefthanded.
Attended University of Evansville, Evansville, Ind.
Tied for Pioneer League lead in intentional bases on balls received with 3 in 1988.
Led Florida State League first basemen in double plays with 105 in 1989.
Led Pioneer League first basemen in double plays with 65 in 1988.

Year Club	League	Pos.	G.	AB.	R.	H.	2B.	3B.	HR.	RBI.	B.A.	PO.	A.	E.	F.A.
1988—Butte	Pion.	1B	63	233	65	91	18	3	8	60	*.391	519	*41	6	.989
1989—Port Charlotte......	Fla. St.	1B	132	456	69	126	18	9	6	51	.276	1094	*105	14	.988
1990—Tulsa	Texas	1B	104	367	55	110	31	4	21	78	.300	939	72	11	.989

Selected by Texas Rangers' organization in 6th round of free-agent draft, June 1, 1988.

TIMOTHY EDWARD MAUSER
(Tim)

Born October 4, 1966, at Fort Worth, Tex.
Height, 6.00. Weight, 185.
Throws and bats righthanded.
Attended Texas Christian University, Fort Worth, Tex.
Pitched 9-0 no-hit victory against New Britain, August 30, 1989 (second game).

Year Club	League	G.	IP.	W.	L.	Pct.	H.	R.	ER.	SO.	BB.	ERA.
1988—Spartanburg...................................	S. Atlantic	4	23	2	1	.667	15	6	5	18	5	1.96
1988—Reading..	Eastern	5	28⅓	2	3	.400	27	14	11	17	6	3.49
1989—Clearwater.....................................	Florida St.	16	107	6	7	.462	105	40	32	73	40	2.69
1989—Reading..	Eastern	11	72	7	4	.636	62	36	29	54	33	3.63
1990—Reading..	Eastern	8	46⅓	3	4	.429	35	20	17	40	15	3.30
1990—Scranton/Wilkes-Barre.................	Int'national	16	98⅓	5	7	.417	75	48	40	54	34	3.66

Selected by Philadelphia Phillies' organization in 3rd round of free-agent draft, June 1, 1988.

DERRICK BRANT MAY

Born July 14, 1968, at Rochester, N.Y.
Height, 6.04. Weight, 205.
Throws right and bats lefthanded.
Son of Dave May, outfielder with Baltimore Orioles, Milwaukee Brewers,
Atlanta Braves, Texas Rangers and Pittsburgh Pirates, 1967 through 1978.
Major League stolen bases: 1990 (1).
Tied for Carolina League lead in double plays by outfielders with 4 in 1988.

Year Club	League	Pos.	G.	AB.	R.	H.	2B.	3B.	HR.	RBI.	B.A.	PO.	A.	E.	F.A.
1986—Wytheville.............	Appal.	OF	54	178	25	57	6	1	0	23	.320	47	3	5	.909
1987—Peoria.....................	Midw.	OF	128	439	60	131	19	8	9	52	.298	181	13	8	.960
1988—Winston-Salem	Carol.	OF	130	485	76	●148	29	*9	8	65	.305	209	13	10	.957
1989—Charlotte...............	South.	OF	136	491	72	145	26	5	9	70	.295	239	8	●13	.950
1990—Iowa	A. A.	OF-1B	119	459	55	136	27	1	8	69	.296	159	10	8	.955
1990—Chicago	Nat.	OF	17	61	8	15	3	0	1	11	.246	34	1	1	.972
Major League Totals—1 Year..................			17	61	8	15	3	0	1	11	.246	34	1	1	.972

Selected by Chicago Cubs' organization in 1st round (ninth player selected) of free-agent draft, June 2, 1986.

BRENT DANEM MAYNE

Born April 19, 1968, at Loma Linda, Calif.
Height, 6.01. Weight, 195.
Throws right and bats lefthanded.
Attended Orange Coast College, Costa Mesa, Calif., and
California State University, Fullerton, Calif.

Received reported $138,000 bonus to sign with Kansas City Royals, 1989.

Year Club	League	Pos.	G.	AB.	R.	H.	2B.	3B.	HR.	RBI.	B.A.	PO.	A.	E.	F.A.
1989—Baseball City†	Fla. St.	C	7	24	5	13	3	1	0	8	.542	31	2	0	1.000
1990—Memphis	South.	C	115	412	48	110	16	3	2	61	.267	591	61	11	.983
1990—Kansas City	Amer.	C	5	13	2	3	0	0	0	1	.231	29	3	1	.970
Major League Totals—1 Year			5	13	2	3	0	0	0	1	.231	29	3	1	.970

Selected by Kansas City Royals' organization in 1st round (13th player selected) of free-agent draft, June 5, 1989.
†On disabled list, July 24, 1989 through remainder of season.

LARRY RANDALL McCAMENT
(Randy)

Born July 29, 1962, at Albuquerque, N.M.
Height, 6.03. Weight, 180.
Throws and bats righthanded.
Attended Grand Canyon College, Phoenix, Ariz.

Led Northwest League in shutouts with 2 in 1985.

Year Club	League	G.	IP.	W.	L.	Pct.	H.	R.	ER.	SO.	BB.	ERA.
1985—Everett	Northwest	14	*105⅔	7	3	.700	98	46	34	66	20	2.90
1986—Fresno	California	54	86⅔	4	4	.500	87	36	24	61	24	2.49
1986—Shreveport	Texas	8	19½	2	1	.667	16	7	6	16	4	2.79
1987—Shreveport	Texas	52	79½	4	3	.571	78	28	21	39	18	2.38
1988—Phoenix	P. Coast	19	25	0	1	.000	40	26	21	7	16	7.56
1988—Shreveport	Texas	24	42	3	4	.429	56	29	25	15	14	5.36
1989—Phoenix	P. Coast	22	37⅓	3	0	1.000	40	15	15	13	12	3.62
1989—San Francisco	National	25	36⅔	1	1	.500	32	22	16	12	23	3.93
1990—Phoenix	P. Coast	46	78½	3	3	.500	99	40	33	32	32	3.79
1990—San Francisco	National	3	6	0	0	.000	8	2	2	5	5	3.00
Major League Totals—2 Years		28	42⅔	1	1	.500	40	24	18	17	28	3.80

Selected by Cleveland Indians' organization in 16th round of free-agent draft, June 4, 1984.
Selected by San Francisco Giants' organization in 15th round of free-agent draft, June 3, 1985.

GREGORY O'NEIL McCARTHY
(Greg)

Born October 30, 1968, at Norwalk, Conn.
Height, 6.04. Weight, 195.
Throws and bats lefthanded.

Year Club	League	G.	IP.	W.	L.	Pct.	H.	R.	ER.	SO.	BB.	ERA.
1987—Utica	NYP	20	29⅔	4	1	.800	14	9	3	40	23	0.91
1988—Spartanburg	S. Atlantic	34	64⅔	4	2	.667	52	36	29	65	52	4.04
1989—Spartanburg	S. Atlantic	24	112	5	8	.385	90	58	52	115	80	4.18
1990—Clearwater†	Florida St.	42	59⅔	1	3	.250	47	33	23	67	38	3.47

Selected by Philadelphia Phillies' organization in 36th round of free-agent draft, June 2, 1987.
†Drafted by Montreal Expos, December 3, 1990.

KIRK EDWARD McCASKILL

Born April 9, 1961, at Kapuskasing, Ont., Canada.
Height, 6.01. Weight, 205.
Throws and bats righthanded.
Attended University of Vermont, Burlington, Vt.
Son of Ted McCaskill, center with Minnesota North Stars (NHL)
and Los Angeles Sharks (WHA), 1967-68, 1972-73 and 1973-74.

Year Club	League	G.	IP.	W.	L.	Pct.	H.	R.	ER.	SO.	BB.	ERA.
1982—Salem	Northwest	11	71⅓	5	5	.500	63	43	34	87	51	4.29
1983—Redwood	California	16	108⅓	6	5	.545	78	39	28	100	60	2.33
1983—Nashua†	Eastern	13	87	4	8	.333	90	47	43	63	43	4.45
1984—Edmonton	P. Coast	24	143	7	11	.389	162	104	91	75	74	5.73
1985—Edmonton	P. Coast	3	17⅔	1	1	.500	17	7	4	18	6	2.04
1985—California	American	30	189⅔	12	12	.500	189	105	99	102	64	4.70
1986—California	American	34	246⅓	17	10	.630	207	98	92	202	92	3.36
1987—California‡	American	14	74⅔	4	6	.400	84	52	47	56	34	5.67
1987—Palm Springs	California	2	10	2	0	1.000	4	1	0	7	3	0.00
1987—Edmonton	P. Coast	1	6	1	0	1.000	3	2	2	4	4	3.00
1988—California§	American	23	146⅓	8	6	.571	155	78	70	98	61	4.31
1989—California	American	32	212	15	10	.600	202	73	69	107	59	2.93
1990—California	American	29	174⅓	12	11	.522	161	77	63	78	72	3.25
Major League Totals—6 Years		162	1043⅓	68	55	.553	998	483	440	643	382	3.80

Selected by California Angels' organization in 4th round of free-agent draft, June 7, 1982.
†On suspended list, August 30, 1983; then transferred to disqualified list, September 26, 1983 through April 25, 1984.
‡On disabled list, April 24 to July 11, 1987; included rehabilitation disability assignment to Palm Springs, June 24 to July 2, and Edmonton, July 3 to July 8, 1987.
§On disabled list, August 9, 1988 through remainder of season.

Holds Championship Series record for most runs allowed, series (13), 1986.
Shares Championship Series records for most games lost, series (2), 1986; most hits allowed, inning (6), October 14, 1986, third inning.

Year Club	League	G.	IP.	W.	L.	Pct.	H.	R.	ER.	SO.	BB.	ERA.
1986—California	American	2	9⅓	0	2	.000	16	13	8	7	5	7.71

RECORD AS HOCKEY PLAYER

Year Team	League	Games	G.	A.	Pts.	Pen.
1983-84—Sherbrooke Jets (a)	AHL	78	10	12	22	21

(a)—June, 1981—Drafted by Winnipeg Jets in 1981 NHL entry draft. Fourth Jets pick, 64th overall, fourth round.

PAUL WILLIAM McCLELLAN

Born February 8, 1966, at San Mateo, Calif.
Height, 6.02. Weight, 180.
Throws and bats righthanded.
Attended College of San Mateo, San Mateo, Calif.

Led Texas League in balks with 22 in 1988.

Year Club	League	G.	IP.	W.	L.	Pct.	H.	R.	ER.	SO.	BB.	ERA.
1986—Everett	Northwest	13	86⅓	5	4	.556	71	39	32	74	46	3.34
1987—Clinton	Midwest	28	177⅓	12	10	.545	141	86	64	★209	100	3.25
1988—Shreveport	Texas	27	167	10	12	.455	146	89	75	128	62	4.04
1989—Shreveport	Texas	12	84⅓	8	3	.727	56	26	21	56	35	2.24
1989—Phoenix	P. Coast	9	56⅔	3	4	.429	56	34	31	25	29	4.92
1990—Phoenix	P. Coast	28	171⅓	7	★16	.304	192	112	99	102	78	5.17
1990—San Francisco	National	4	7⅔	0	1	.000	14	10	10	2	6	11.74
Major League Totals—1 Year		4	7⅔	0	1	.000	14	10	10	2	6	11.74

Selected by Atlanta Braves' organization in 25th round of free-agent draft, June 3, 1985.
Selected by San Francisco Giants' organization in secondary phase of free-agent draft, January 14, 1986.

LLOYD GLENN McCLENDON

Born January 11, 1959, at Gary, Ind.
Height, 5.11. Weight, 195.
Throws and bats righthanded.
Attended Valparaiso University, Valparaiso, Ind.

Major League stolen bases: 1987 (1), 1988 (4), 1989 (6), 1990 (1). Total—12.

Year Club	League	Pos.	G.	AB.	R.	H.	2B.	3B.	HR.	RBI.	B.A.	PO.	A.	E.	F.A.
1980—Kingsport	Appal.	C	14	46	7	15	2	0	1	9	.326	19	5	3	.889
1980—Little Falls	NYP	C	40	117	25	32	9	1	3	20	.274	203	20	7	.970
1981—Lynchburg	Carol.	C-3B	103	363	55	91	12	6	7	57	.251	437	74	17	.968
1982—Lynchburg†‡	Carol.	C-3B	108	384	61	105	25	1	18	78	.273	492	87	15	.975
1983—Waterbury	East.	C-3B-1B	123	434	58	114	19	2	15	57	.263	466	99	8	.986
1984—Vermont	East.	C-1-3-O	60	202	36	56	16	0	7	27	.277	174	24	3	.985
1984—Wichita	A.A.	3B-1B-C	48	152	28	45	13	1	6	28	.296	143	45	4	.979
1985—Denver	A.A.	1-3-C-O	114	379	57	105	18	5	16	79	.277	470	104	17	.971
1986—Denver	A.A.	1-O-C-3	132	433	75	112	30	1	★24	88	.259	656	45	11	.985
1987—Cincinnati	Nat.	C-1-3-O	45	72	8	15	5	0	2	13	.208	80	5	2	.977
1987—Nashville	A. A.	1B-C	26	84	11	24	6	0	3	14	.286	72	3	1	.987
1988—Cincinnati	Nat.	C-O-1-3	72	137	9	30	4	0	3	14	.219	197	13	4	.981
1988—Nashville§	A. A.	OF-C	2	7	0	1	0	0	0	0	.143	2	2	0	1.000
1989—Iowa	A. A.	1B-OF-C	34	109	18	35	10	0	4	13	.321	115	6	6	.953
1989—Chicago	Nat.	O-1-3-C	92	259	47	74	12	1	12	40	.286	310	18	6	.982
1990—Chi.x-Pit.	Nat.	OF-1B-C	53	110	6	18	3	0	2	12	.164	120	9	1	.992
1990—Iowa	A. A.	1-3-O-C	25	91	14	26	2	0	2	10	.286	125	12	2	.986
Major League Totals—4 Years			262	578	70	137	24	1	19	79	.237	707	45	13	.983

Selected by New York Mets' organization in 8th round of free-agent draft, June 3, 1980.
†On disabled list, April 4 to April 27, 1982.
‡Traded with Pitcher Charlie Puleo and Outfielder Jason Felice to Cincinnati Reds for Pitcher Tom Seaver, December 16, 1982.
§Traded to Chicago Cubs for Outfielder Rolando Roomes, December 9, 1988.
xTraded to Pittsburgh Pirates for a player to be named later, September 7, 1990. Chicago Cubs acquired Pitcher Mike Pomeranz to complete deal, September 28, 1990.

CHAMPIONSHIP SERIES RECORD

Year Club	League	Pos.	G.	AB.	R.	H.	2B.	3B.	HR.	RBI.	B.A.	PO.	A.	E.	F.A.
1989—Chicago	Nat.	PH-C-OF	3	3	0	2	0	0	0	0	.667	3	0	0	1.000

ROBERT CRAIG McCLURE
(Bob)

Born April 29, 1953, at Oakland, Calif.
Height, 5.11. Weight, 188.
Throws left and bats righthanded.
Attended College of San Mateo, San Mateo, Calif.

Major League saves: 1975 (1), 1977 (0), 1978 (9), 1979 (5), 1980 (10), 1984 (1), 1985 (3), 1986 (6), 1987 (5), 1988 (3), 1989 (3). Total—52.

Led American League in balks with 6 in 1983.
Tied for Pioneer League lead in shutouts with 3 in 1973.

Year Club	League	G.	IP.	W.	L.	Pct.	H.	R.	ER.	SO.	BB.	ERA.
1973—Billings	Pioneer	14	94	*10	2	.833	64	41	22	110	67	2.11
1974—Omaha	Am. Assoc.	21	136	5	8	.385	140	71	58	88	65	3.84
1975—Jacksonville†	Southern	9	42	3	2	.600	31	18	11	39	23	2.36
1975—Kansas City	American	12	15	1	0	1.000	4	0	0	15	14	0.00
1976—Omaha	Am. Assoc.	21	133	9	8	.529	133	61	44	91	41	2.98
1976—Kansas City‡	American	8	4	0	0	.000	3	4	4	3	8	9.00
1977—Milwaukee	American	68	71	2	1	.667	64	25	20	57	34	2.54
1978—Milwaukee	American	44	65	2	6	.250	53	30	27	47	30	3.74
1979—Milwaukee	American	36	51	5	2	.714	53	29	22	37	24	3.88
1980—Milwaukee	American	52	91	5	8	.385	83	34	31	47	37	3.07
1981—Burlington	Midwest	4	14	0	2	.000	19	15	15	11	11	9.64
1981—Milwaukee§	American	4	8	0	0	.000	7	3	3	6	4	3.38
1982—Milwaukee x	American	34	172⅔	12	7	.632	160	90	81	99	74	4.22
1983—Milwaukee y	American	24	142	9	9	.500	152	75	71	68	68	4.50
1984—Milwaukee	American	39	139¾	4	8	.333	154	76	68	68	52	4.38
1985—Milwaukee	American	38	85⅔	4	1	.800	91	43	41	57	30	4.31
1986—Milwaukee z	American	13	16⅓	2	1	.667	18	7	7	11	10	3.86
1986—Montreal	National	52	62⅔	2	5	.286	53	22	21	42	23	3.02
1987—Montreal a	National	52	52⅓	6	1	.857	47	30	20	33	20	3.44
1988—Montreal b-New York c	National	33	30	2	3	.400	35	18	18	19	8	5.40
1989—California	American	48	52⅓	6	1	.857	39	14	9	36	15	1.55
1990—Palm Springs d	California	2	3	0	0	.000	0	0	0	6	1	0.00
1990—California	American	11	7	2	0	1.000	7	6	5	6	3	6.43
American League Totals—14 Years		431	920⅔	54	44	.551	888	436	389	557	403	3.80
National League Totals—3 Years		137	145	10	9	.526	135	70	59	94	51	3.66
Major League Totals—16 Years		568	1065⅔	64	53	.547	1023	506	448	651	454	3.78

Selected by Los Angeles Dodgers' organization in 3rd round of free-agent draft, January 10, 1973.
Selected by Kansas City Royals' organization in secondary phase of free-agent draft, June 5, 1973.
†On disabled list, April 15 to May 13 and June 5 to July 25, 1975.
‡Traded to Milwaukee Brewers, March 15, 1977; completing deal in which Kansas City Royals traded Infielder Jamie Quirk, Outfielder Jim Wohlford and a player to be named later to Milwaukee for Pitcher Jim Colborn and Catcher Darrell Porter, December 6, 1976.
§On disabled list, March 28 to September 1, 1981; included rehabilitation disability assignment to Burlington, August 7 to August 24, 1981.
xGranted free agency, November 10, 1982; re-signed by Brewers, December 6, 1982.
yOn disabled list, August 22 to September 12, 1983.
zSold to Montreal Expos, June 8, 1986.
aGranted free agency, November 9, 1987; re-signed by Expos, December 7, 1987.
bReleased, July 2, 1988; signed by New York Mets, July 13, 1988.
cReleased, October 27, 1988; signed by California Angels, January 12, 1989.
dOn California disabled list, April 6 to August 14, 1990; included rehabilitation disability assignment to Palm Springs, August 3 to August 14, 1990.

DIVISION SERIES RECORD

Year Club	League	G.	IP.	W.	L.	Pct.	H.	R.	ER.	SO.	BB.	ERA.
1981—Milwaukee	American	3	3⅓	0	0	.000	4	0	0	2	0	0.00

CHAMPIONSHIP SERIES RECORD

Year Club	League	G.	IP.	W.	L.	Pct.	H.	R.	ER.	SO.	BB.	ERA.
1982—Milwaukee	American	1	1⅔	1	0	1.000	2	0	0	0	0	0.00

WORLD SERIES RECORD

Year Club	League	G.	IP.	W.	L.	Pct.	H.	R.	ER.	SO.	BB.	ERA.
1982—Milwaukee	American	5	4⅓	0	2	.000	5	2	2	5	3	4.15

RODNEY DUNCAN McCRAY

Born September 13, 1963, at Detroit, Mich.
Height, 5.10. Weight, 175.
Throws and bats righthanded.
Attended Santa Monica College, Santa Monica, Calif.,
and West Los Angeles College, Culver City, Calif.

Major League stolen bases: 1990 (6).
Led Florida State League in bases on balls received with 96 in 1989.
Led California League in stolen bases with 65 in 1987.
Led South Atlantic League in caught stealing with 32 in 1986.
Led California League outfielders in total chances with 271 in 1987.
Tied for Northwest League lead in assists by outfielders with 3 in 1984.

Year Club	League	Pos.	G.	AB.	R.	H.	2B.	3B.	HR.	RBI.	B.A.	PO.	A.	E.	F.A.
1984—Spokane	N'west	OF	71	244	40	50	6	1	1	20	.205	124	*13	4	.972
1985—Charleston	S. Atl.	OF	117	373	81	77	8	1	1	27	.206	177	13	13	.936
1986—Charleston	S. Atl.	OF	123	417	88	107	13	3	4	33	.257	271	*17	6	.980
1987—Reno†	Calif.	OF	117	413	69	87	11	5	0	26	.211	*251	13	7	.974
1988—South Bend	Midw.	OF	107	306	48	65	10	2	1	24	.212	218	15	10	.959
1989—Sarasota	Fla. St.	OF	124	422	81	112	19	4	1	34	.265	296	9	4	*.987
1990—Birmingham	South.	OF	60	188	36	37	2	2	1	16	.197	156	8	4	.976
1990—Chicago	Amer.	OF	32	6	8	0	0	0	0	0	.000	8	0	0	1.000
1990—Vancouver	P. C.	OF	19	53	7	12	4	2	0	6	.226	50	4	2	.964
Major League Totals—1 Year			32	6	8	0	0	0	0	0	.000	8	0	0	1.000

Selected by Chicago White Sox' organization in 1st round (13th player selected) of free-agent draft, January 12 1982.

Selected by Oakland A's organization in secondary phase of free-agent draft, June 7, 1982.

Selected by Los Angeles Dodgers' organization in secondary phase of free-agent draft, January 11, 1983.

Selected by San Diego Padres' organization in 9th round of free-agent draft, January 17, 1984.

†Drafted by Chicago White Sox' organization, December 8, 1987.

LANCE GRAYE McCULLERS

Born March 8, 1964, at Tampa, Fla.
Height, 6.01. Weight, 213.
Throws and bats righthanded.

Major League saves: 1985 (5), 1986 (5), 1987 (16), 1988 (10), 1989 (3). Total—39.
Tied for Pacific Coast League lead in hit batsmen with 6 in 1985.

Year Club	League	G.	IP.	W.	L.	Pct.	H.	R.	ER.	SO.	BB.	ERA.
1982—Helena	Pioneer	13	87	6	4	.600	89	44	36	62	33	3.72
1983—Spartanburg†	S. Atlantic	22	136⅓	9	6	.600	139	79	61	87	57	4.03
1984—Miami	Florida St.	22	106⅓	6	4	.600	92	37	30	94	45	2.54
1984—Beaumont‡	Texas	8	55⅓	4	1	.800	38	13	13	48	35	2.11
1985—Las Vegas	P. Coast	24	149⅓	11	8	.579	135	75	66	148	83	3.98
1985—San Diego	National	21	35	0	2	.000	23	15	9	27	16	2.31
1986—San Diego	National	70	136	10	10	.500	103	46	42	92	58	2.78
1987—San Diego	National	78	123⅓	8	10	.444	115	60	51	126	59	3.72
1988—San Diego§	National	60	97⅔	3	6	.333	70	29	27	81	55	2.49
1989—New York	American	52	84⅔	4	3	.571	83	46	43	82	37	4.57
1990—Columbus	Int'national	3	3	0	0	.000	0	0	0	2	2	0.00
1990—New York xy-Detroit za	American	20	44⅔	2	0	1.000	32	19	15	31	19	3.02
National League Totals—4 Years		229	392	21	28	.429	311	150	129	326	188	2.96
American League Totals—2 Years		72	129⅓	6	3	.667	115	65	58	113	56	4.04
Major League Totals—6 Years		301	521⅓	27	31	.466	426	215	187	439	244	3.23

Selected by Philadelphia Phillies' organization in 2nd round of free-agent draft, June 7, 1982.

†Traded with Pitchers Marty Decker, Darren Burroughs and Ed Wojna to San Diego Padres, September 20, 1983, as partial completion of deal in which San Diego traded Outfielder Sixto Lezcano and a player to be named later to Philadelphia Phillies for four players to be named later, August 31, 1983; Philadelphia organization acquired Pitcher Steve Fireovid to complete deal, October 11, 1983.

‡On disabled list, September 7, 1984 through remainder of season.

§Traded with Pitcher Jimmy Jones and Outfielder Stan Jefferson to New York Yankees for First Baseman-Outfielder Jack Clark and Pitcher Pat Clements, October 24, 1988.

xOn New York disabled list, April 7 to April 24, 1990; included rehabilitation disability assignment to Columbus, April 17 to April 23, 1990.

yTraded with Pitcher Clay Parker to Detroit Tigers for Catcher Matt Nokes, June 4, 1990.

zOn disabled list, July 19, 1990 through remainder of season.

aGranted free agency, December 20, 1990.

TERRENCE KEITH McDANIEL
(Terry)

Born December 6, 1966, at Kansas City, Mo.
Height, 5.09. Weight, 195.
Throws and bats righthanded.

Led South Atlantic League batters in strikeouts with 173 in 1988.
Led Florida State League outfielders in double plays with 5 in 1989.
Tied for New York-Pennsylvania League lead in double plays by outfielders with 3 in 1987.

Year Club	League	Pos.	G.	AB.	R.	H.	2B.	3B.	HR.	RBI.	B.A.	PO.	A.	E.	F.A.
1986—Kingsport	Appal.	OF	41	114	24	48	5	1	6	21	.246	68	★11	3	.963
1987—Little Falls†	NYP	OF	70	237	51	57	4	2	5	31	.241	101	★15	★9	.928
1988—Columbia	S. Atl.	OF	127	449	76	111	16	6	5	43	.247	211	7	11	.952
1988—St. Lucie	Fla. St.	OF	4	12	1	3	0	0	0	0	.250	5	0	1	.833
1989—St. Lucie‡	Fla. St.	OF	105	351	70	81	17	11	7	43	.231	214	★16	4	.983
1990—Jackson§	Texas	OF	67	234	34	67	14	2	5	37	.286	129	3	4	.971

Selected by New York Mets' organization in 6th round of free-agent draft, January 14, 1986.

†Switch-hitter.

‡On disabled list, June 7 to June 17, 1989.

§On disabled list, May 17 to June 5, July 15 to August 8 and August 12, 1990 through remainder of season.

LARRY BENARD McDONALD
(Ben)

Born November 24, 1967, at Baton Rouge, La.
Height, 6.07. Weight, 210.
Throws and bats righthanded.
Attended Louisiana State University, Baton Rouge, La.

Member of 1988 U.S. Olympic baseball team.
Named College Player of the Year by THE SPORTING NEWS, 1989.
Named righthanded pitcher on THE SPORTING NEWS College Baseball All-America Team, 1989.
Received reported $350,000 bonus to sign with Baltimore Orioles, 1989.

Year Club	League	G.	IP.	W.	L.	Pct.	H.	R.	ER.	SO.	BB.	ERA.
1989—Frederick	Carolina	2	9	0	0	.000	10	2	2	9	0	2.00
1989—Baltimore	American	6	7⅓	1	0	1.000	8	7	7	3	4	8.59

Year Club	League	G.	IP.	W.	L.	Pct.	H.	R.	ER.	SO.	BB.	ERA.
1990—Hagerstown†	Eastern	3	11	0	1	.000	11	8	8	15	3	6.55
1990—Rochester	Int'national	7	44	3	3	.500	33	18	14	37	21	2.86
1990—Baltimore	American	21	118⅔	8	5	.615	88	36	32	65	35	2.43
Major League Totals—2 Years		27	126	9	5	.643	96	43	39	68	39	2.79

Selected by Atlanta Braves' organization in 27th round of free-agent draft, June 2, 1986.
Selected by Baltimore Orioles' organization in 1st round (first player selected) of free-agent draft, June 5, 1989.
†On Baltimore disabled list, April 6 to May 22, 1990; included rehabilitation disability assignment to Hagerstown, April 24 to April 29 and May 14, 1990; and Rochester, April 30 to May 13 and May 15 to May 21, 1990.

JACK BURNS McDOWELL

Born January 16, 1966, at Van Nuys, Calif.
Height, 6.05. Weight, 179.
Throws and bats righthanded.
Attended Stanford University, Stanford, Calif.

Received reported $175,000 bonus to sign with Chicago White Sox, 1987.

Year Club	League	G.	IP.	W.	L.	Pct.	H.	R.	ER.	SO.	BB.	ERA.
1987—Sarasota White Sox	Gulf Coast	2	7	0	1	.000	4	3	2	12	1	2.57
1987—Birmingham	Southern	4	20⅔	1	2	.333	19	20	18	17	8	7.84
1987—Chicago	American	4	28	3	0	1.000	16	6	6	15	6	1.93
1988—Chicago	American	26	158⅔	5	10	.333	147	85	70	84	68	3.97
1989—Vancouver	P. Coast	16	86⅔	5	6	.455	97	60	59	65	50	6.13
1990—Sarasota White Sox	Gulf Coast	4	24	2	0	1.000	19	2	2	25	4	0.75
1990—Chicago	American	33	205	14	9	.609	189	93	87	165	77	3.82
Major League Totals—3 Years		63	391⅔	22	19	.537	352	184	163	264	151	3.75

Selected by Boston Red Sox' organization in 20th round of free-agent draft, June 4, 1984.
Selected by Chicago White Sox' organization in 1st round (fifth player selected) of free-agent draft, June 2, 1987.

ODDIBE McDOWELL JR.

First name pronounced OH-da-bee.

Born August 25, 1962, at Hollywood, Fla.
Height, 5.09. Weight, 160.
Throws and bats lefthanded.
Attended Miami-Dade Community College (North), Miami, Fla., and
Arizona State University, Tempe, Ariz.

Shares major league record for most putouts by outfielder, game (12), July 20, 1985 (15 innings).
Shares American League record for most chances accepted by outfielder, game (12), July 20, 1985 (15 innings).
Major League stolen bases: 1985 (25), 1986 (33), 1987 (24), 1988 (33), 1989 (27), 1990 (13). Total—155.
Hit for the cycle, July 23, 1985.
Member of 1984 U.S. Olympic baseball team.
Named outfielder on THE SPORTING NEWS College Baseball All-America Team, 1983 and 1984.

Year Club	League	Pos.	G.	AB.	R.	H.	2B.	3B.	HR.	RBI.	B.A.	PO.	A.	E.	F.A.
1985—Oklahoma City	A. A.	OF	31	125	32	50	7	8	2	18	.400	72	4	1	.987
1985—Texas	Amer.	OF	111	406	63	97	14	5	18	42	.239	282	9	2	.993
1986—Texas	Amer.	OF	154	572	105	152	24	7	18	49	.266	325	13	3	.991
1987—Texas	Amer.	OF	128	407	65	98	26	4	14	52	.241	263	5	3	.989
1988—Texas	Amer.	OF	120	437	55	108	19	5	6	37	.247	267	2	3	.989
1988—Oklahoma City†	A. A.	OF	18	70	9	20	3	1	1	6	.286	50	1	0	1.000
1989—Cleveland‡	Amer.	OF	69	239	33	53	5	2	3	22	.222	124	5	1	.992
1989—Atlanta	Nat.	OF	76	280	56	85	18	4	7	24	.304	179	2	4	.978
1990—Atlanta	Nat.	OF	113	305	47	74	14	0	7	25	.243	134	2	4	.971
American League Totals—5 Years			582	2061	321	508	88	23	59	202	.246	1261	34	12	.991
National League Totals—2 Years			189	585	103	159	32	4	14	49	.272	313	4	8	.975
Major League Totals—6 Years			771	2646	424	667	120	27	73	251	.252	1574	38	20	.988

Selected by St. Louis Cardinals' organization in 4th round of free-agent draft, January 13, 1981.
Selected by Texas Rangers' organization in secondary phase of free-agent draft, June 8, 1981.
Selected by New York Yankees' organization in secondary phase of free-agent draft, January 12, 1982.
Selected by Toronto Blue Jays' organization in secondary phase of free-agent draft, June 7, 1982.
Selected by Minnesota Twins' organization in secondary phase of free-agent draft, June 6, 1983.
Selected by Texas Rangers' organization in 1st round (12th player selected) of free-agent draft, June 4, 1984.
†Traded with First Baseman Pete O'Brien and Second Baseman Jerry Browne to Cleveland Indians for Second Baseman Julio Franco, December 6, 1988.
‡Traded to Atlanta Braves for Outfielder Dion James, July 2, 1989.

ROGER ALAN McDOWELL

Born December 21, 1960, at Cincinnati, O.
Height, 6.01. Weight, 185.
Throws and bats righthanded.
Attended Bowling Green State University, Bowling Green, O.

Major League saves: 1985 (17), 1986 (22), 1987 (25), 1988 (16), 1989 (23), 1990 (22). Total—125.
Led National League in games finished in relief with 60 in 1990.

Year Club	League	G.	IP.	W.	L.	Pct.	H.	R.	ER.	SO.	BB.	ERA.
1982—Shelby	S. Atlantic	12	71⅓	6	4	.600	61	34	26	40	30	3.28
1982—Lynchburg	Carolina	4	29⅓	2	0	1.000	26	12	7	23	11	2.15
1983—Jackson	Texas	27	172⅓	11	12	.478	203	111	93	115	71	4.86

Year Club	League	G.	IP.	W.	L.	Pct.	H.	R.	ER.	SO.	BB.	ERA.
1984—Jackson†	Texas	3	7⅓	0	0	.000	9	3	3	8	1	3.68
1985—New York	National	62	127⅓	6	5	.545	108	43	40	70	37	2.83
1986—New York‡	National	75	128	14	9	.609	107	48	43	65	42	3.02
1987—New York§	National	56	88⅔	7	5	.583	95	41	41	32	28	4.16
1988—New York	National	62	89	5	5	.500	80	31	26	46	31	2.63
1989—New York x-Philadelphia	National	69	92	4	8	.333	79	36	20	47	38	1.96
1990—Philadelphia	National	72	86⅓	6	8	.429	92	41	37	39	35	3.86
Major League Totals—6 Years		396	611⅓	42	40	.512	561	240	207	299	211	3.05

Selected by New York Mets' organization in 3rd round of free-agent draft, June 7, 1982.
†On disabled list, April 10 to August 14, 1984.
‡Appeared in one game as an outfielder with no chances.
§On disabled list, March 29 to May 14, 1987.
xTraded with Outfielder Lenny Dykstra and a player to be named later to Philadelphia Phillies for Outfielder Juan Samuel, June 18, 1989; Philadelphia organization acquired Pitcher Tom Edens to complete deal, July 27, 1989.

CHAMPIONSHIP SERIES RECORD

Year Club	League	G.	IP.	W.	L.	Pct.	H.	R.	ER.	SO.	BB.	ERA.
1986—New York	National	2	7	0	0	.000	1	0	0	3	0	0.00
1988—New York	National	4	6	0	1	.000	6	3	3	5	2	4.50
Championship Series Totals—2 Years		6	13	0	1	.000	7	3	3	8	2	2.08

WORLD SERIES RECORD

Year Club	League	G.	IP.	W.	L.	Pct.	H.	R.	ER.	SO.	BB.	ERA.
1986—New York	National	5	7⅓	1	0	1.000	10	5	4	2	6	4.91

CHARLES DWAYNE McELROY
(Chuck)

Born October 1, 1967, at Galveston, Tex.
Height, 6.00. Weight, 160.
Throws and bats lefthanded.

Year Club	League	G.	IP.	W.	L.	Pct.	H.	R.	ER.	SO.	BB.	ERA.
1986—Utica	NYP	14	94⅔	4	6	.400	85	40	31	91	28	2.95
1987—Spartanburg	S. Atlantic	24	130⅓	14	4	.778	117	51	45	115	48	3.11
1987—Clearwater	Florida St.	2	7⅓	1	0	1.000	1	1	0	7	4	0.00
1988—Reading	Eastern	28	160	9	12	.429	●173	89	∗80	92	70	4.50
1989—Reading	Eastern	32	47	3	1	.750	39	14	14	39	14	2.68
1989—Scranton/Wilkes-Barre	Int'national	14	15⅓	1	2	.333	13	6	5	12	11	2.93
1989—Philadelphia	National	11	10⅓	0	0	.000	12	2	2	8	4	1.74
1990—Philadelphia	National	16	14	0	1	.000	24	13	12	16	10	7.71
1990—Scranton/Wilkes-Barre	Int'national	57	76	6	8	.429	62	24	23	78	34	2.72
Major League Totals—2 Years		27	24⅓	0	1	.000	36	15	14	24	14	5.18

Selected by Philadelphia Phillies' organization in 8th round of free-agent draft, June 2, 1986.

ANDREW JOSEPH McGAFFIGAN
(Andy)

Born October 25, 1956, at West Palm Beach, Fla.
Height, 6.03. Weight, 190.
Throws and bats righthanded.
Attended Palm Beach Junior College, Lake Worth, Fla., and
received degree from Florida Southern College, Lakeland, Fla., in 1978.
Major League saves: 1983 (2), 1984 (1), 1986 (2), 1987 (12), 1988 (4), 1989 (2), 1990 (1). Total—24.
Named Southern League Pitcher of the Year, 1980.

Year Club	League	G.	IP.	W.	L.	Pct.	H.	R.	ER.	SO.	BB.	ERA.
1978—Oneonta	NYP	2	12	0	1	.000	14	8	6	13	9	4.50
1978—Fort Lauderdale	Florida St.	11	66	4	5	.444	45	28	21	36	20	2.86
1979—West Haven	Eastern	23	144	10	6	.625	136	75	61	113	54	3.81
1980—Nashville†	Southern	31	170	15	5	.750	139	62	45	125	62	∗2.38
1981—Columbus‡	Int'national	17	103	8	6	.571	85	45	37	57	37	3.23
1981—New York§	American	2	7	0	0	.000	5	3	2	2	3	2.57
1982—Phoenix x	P. Coast	18	96	1	6	.143	115	72	64	64	51	6.00
1982—San Francisco	National	4	8	1	0	1.000	5	1	0	4	1	0.00
1983—San Francisco y	National	43	134⅓	3	9	.250	131	67	64	93	39	4.29
1984—Montreal z-Cincinnati	National	30	69	3	6	.333	60	28	27	57	23	3.52
1985—Denver	Am. Assoc.	26	106⅔	11	5	.688	105	43	35	91	37	2.95
1985—Cincinnati a	National	15	94⅓	3	3	.500	88	40	39	83	30	3.72
1986—Montreal	National	48	142⅔	10	5	.667	114	49	42	104	55	2.65
1987—Montreal	National	69	120⅓	5	2	.714	105	38	32	100	42	2.39
1988—Montreal b	National	63	91⅓	6	0	1.000	81	31	28	71	37	2.76
1989—Montreal cd	National	57	75	3	5	.375	85	40	39	40	30	4.68
1990—San Francisco e	National	4	4⅔	0	0	.000	10	9	9	4	4	17.36
1990—Omaha	Am. Assoc.	10	17	2	1	.667	22	7	7	17	5	3.71
1990—Kansas City f	American	24	78⅔	4	3	.571	75	40	27	49	28	3.09
American League Totals—2 Years		26	85⅔	4	3	.571	80	43	29	51	31	3.05
National League Totals—9 Years		333	739⅔	34	30	.531	679	303	280	556	261	3.41
Major League Totals—10 Years		359	825⅓	38	33	.535	759	346	309	607	292	3.37

Selected by Cincinnati Reds' organization in 36th round of free-agent draft, June 5, 1974.
Selected by Chicago White Sox' organization in 5th round of free-agent draft, January 7, 1976.
Selected by New York Yankees' organization in 6th round of free-agent draft, June 6, 1978.
†On disabled list, September 1 to September 22, 1980.
‡On disabled list, April 10 to June 14, 1981.
§Traded with Outfielder Ted Wilborn to San Francisco Giants' organization for Pitcher Doyle Alexander, March 30, 1982.
· xOn disabled list, June 20 to August 13, 1982.
yTraded to Montreal Expos, March 31, 1984, as compensation for the injury that Pitcher Fred Breining arrived with in trade of February 27, 1984, which sent Breining and Outfielder Max Venable to Montreal for First Baseman Al Oliver. (Breining remained with Montreal.)
zTraded with Pitcher Jim Jefferson to Cincinnati Reds for First Baseman Dan Driessen, July 26, 1984.
aTraded with Pitchers Jay Tibbs and John Stuper and Catcher Dann Bilardello to Montreal Expos for Pitcher Bill Gullickson and Catcher Sal Butera, December 19, 1985.
bOn disabled list, June 15 to July 2, 1988.
cOn disabled list, August 18 to September 2, 1989.
dTraded to San Francisco Giants for a player to be named later, April 7, 1990; Montreal Expos' organization acquired Infielder Steve Hecht to complete deal, June 26, 1990.
eReleased, April 25, 1990; signed by Omaha (Kansas City Royals' organization), May 9, 1990.
fGranted free agency, November 5, 1990; re-signed by Royals, December 8, 1990.

WILLIE DEAN McGEE

Born November 2, 1958, at San Francisco, Calif.
Height, 6.01. Weight, 195.
Throws right and bats right and lefthanded.
Attended Diablo Valley College, Pleasant Hill, Calif.
Cousin of Dennis Hood, outfielder in Seattle Mariners' organization.

Holds modern National League record for highest batting average, switch-hitter, season, 100 or more games (.353), 1985.
Major League stolen bases: 1982 (24), 1983 (39), 1984 (43), 1985 (56), 1986 (19), 1987 (16), 1988 (41), 1989 (8), 1990 (31). Total—277.
Hit for the cycle, June 23, 1984.
Led National League in grounding into double plays with 24 in 1987.
Named National League Player of the Year by THE SPORTING NEWS, 1985.
Named National League Most Valuable Player by Baseball Writers' Association of America, 1985.
Named outfielder on THE SPORTING NEWS National League All-Star Team, 1985.
Named outfielder on THE SPORTING NEWS National League All-Star fielding team, 1983, 1985 and 1986.
Named outfielder on THE SPORTING NEWS National League Silver Slugger team, 1985.

Year Club	League	Pos.	G.	AB.	R.	H.	2B.	3B.	HR.	RBI.	B.A.	PO.	A.	E.	F.A.
1977—Oneonta	NYP	OF	65	225	31	53	4	3	2	22	.236	103	5	10	.915
1978—Fort Lauderdale	Fla. St.	OF	124	423	62	106	6	6	0	37	.251	243	12	9	.966
1979—West Haven	East.	OF	49	115	21	28	3	1	1	8	.243	88	3	3	.968
1979—Fort Lauderdale	Fla. St.	OF	46	176	25	56	8	3	1	18	.318	103	3	2	.981
1980—Nashville†	South.	OF	78	223	35	63	4	5	1	22	.283	127	6	6	.957
1981—Nashville‡§	South.	OF	100	388	77	125	20	5	7	63	.322	203	10	6	.973
1982—Louisville x	A. A.	OF	13	55	11	16	2	2	1	3	.291	40	0	1	.976
1982—St. Louis	Nat.	OF	123	422	43	125	12	8	4	56	.296	245	3	11	.958
1983—St. Louis y	Nat.	OF	147	601	75	172	22	8	5	75	.286	385	7	5	.987
1983—Arkansas	Texas	OF	7	29	5	8	1	1	0	2	.276	7	0	0	1.000
1984—St. Louis z	Nat.	OF	145	571	82	166	19	11	6	50	.291	374	10	6	.985
1985—St. Louis	Nat.	OF	152	612	114	*216	26	*18	10	82	*.353	382	11	9	.978
1986—St. Louis a	Nat.	OF	124	497	65	127	22	7	7	48	.256	325	9	3	*.991
1987—St. Louis	Nat.	OF-SS	153	620	76	177	37	11	11	105	.285	354	10	7	.981
1988—St. Louis	Nat.	OF	137	562	73	164	24	6	3	50	.292	348	9	9	.975
1989—St. Louis b	Nat.	OF	58	199	23	47	10	2	3	17	.236	118	2	3	.976
1989—Louisville	A. A.	OF	8	27	5	11	4	0	0	4	.407	20	1	1	.955
1990—St. Louis c	Nat.	OF	125	501	76	168	32	5	3	62	*.335	341	13	*16	.957
1990—Oakland d	Amer.	OF	29	113	23	31	3	2	0	15	.274	72	1	1	.986
National League Totals—9 Years			1164	4585	627	1362	204	76	52	545	.297	2872	74	69	.977
American League Totals—1 Year			29	113	23	31	3	2	0	15	.274	72	1	1	.986
Major League Totals—9 Years			1193	4698	650	1393	207	78	52	560	.297	2744	75	70	.977

Selected by Chicago White Sox' organization in 7th round of free-agent draft, June 8, 1976.
Selected by New York Yankees' organization in secondary phase of free-agent draft, January 11, 1977.
†On disabled list, May 22 to June 7 and July 14 to August 7, 1980.
‡On disabled list, April 24 to June 4, 1981.
§Traded to St. Louis Cardinals' organization for Pitcher Bob Sykes, October 21, 1981.
xOn disabled list, April 13 to April 23, 1982.
yOn disabled list, March 30 to April 29, 1983; included rehabilitation disability assignment to Arkansas, April 18 to April 29, 1983.
zOn disabled list, July 12 to July 27, 1984.
aOn disabled list, August 3 to August 27, 1986.
bOn disabled list, June 7 to July 18 and July 26 to August 14, 1989; included rehabilitation disability assignment to Louisville, July 8 to July 18, 1989.
cTraded to Oakland Athletics for Outfielder Felix Jose, Third Baseman Stan Royer and Pitcher Daryl Green, August 29, 1990.
dGranted free agency, November 5, 1990; signed by San Francisco Giants, December 3, 1990.

CHAMPIONSHIP SERIES RECORD

Shares Championship Series records for most triples, series (2), 1982; most times caught stealing, series (3), 1985.

Holds National League Championship Series record for most triples, total series, (3).
Shares National League Championship Series record for most times caught stealing, total series (4).

Year	Club	League	Pos.	G.	AB.	R.	H.	2B.	3B.	HR.	RBI.	B.A.	PO.	A.	E.	F.A.
1982—St. Louis	Nat.	OF	3	13	4	4	0	2	1	5	.308	12	0	1	.923
1985—St. Louis	Nat.	OF	6	26	6	7	1	0	0	3	.269	18	0	0	1.000
1987—St. Louis	Nat.	OF	7	26	2	8	1	1	0	2	.308	16	0	0	1.000
1990—Oakland	Amer.	O-PR-DH	3	9	3	2	1	0	0	0	.222	2	0	0	1.000
Championship Series Totals—4 Years			19	74	15	21	3	3	1	10	.284	48	0	1	.980

WORLD SERIES RECORD

Year	Club	League	Pos.	G.	AB.	R.	H.	2B.	3B.	HR.	RBI.	B.A.	PO.	A.	E.	F.A.
1982—St. Louis	Nat.	OF	6	25	6	6	0	0	2	5	.240	24	0	0	1.000
1985—St. Louis	Nat.	OF	7	27	2	7	2	0	1	2	.259	15	0	0	1.000
1987—St. Louis	Nat.	OF	7	27	2	10	2	0	0	4	.370	21	1	1	.957
1990—Oakland	Amer.	OF-PH	4	10	1	2	1	0	0	0	.200	5	0	0	1.000
World Series Totals—4 Years			24	89	11	25	5	0	3	11	.281	65	1	1	.985

ALL-STAR GAME RECORD

Year	League	Pos.	AB.	R.	H.	2B.	3B.	HR.	RBI.	B.A.	PO.	A.	E.	F.A.
1983—National	OF	2	0	1	0	0	0	0	0	.500	2	0	0	1.000
1985—National	OF	2	0	1	1	0	0	2	.500	1	0	0	1.000
1987—National	OF	4	0	0	0	0	0	0	.000	2	0	0	1.000
1988—National	PR-OF	2	0	0	0	0	0	0	.000	1	0	0	1.000
All-Star Game Totals—4 Years		10	0	2	1	0	0	2	.200	6	0	0	1.000

FREDERICK STANLEY McGRIFF
(Fred)

Born October 31, 1963, at Tampa, Fla.
Height, 6.03. Weight, 208.
Throws and bats lefthanded.

Major League stolen bases: 1987 (3), 1988 (6), 1989 (7), 1990 (5). Total—21.
Led American League first basemen in total chances with 1,592 and double plays with 148 in 1989.
Tied for International League lead in intentional bases on balls received with 8 and grounding into double plays with 16 in 1986.
Led Gulf Coast League in bases on balls received with 48 and tied for lead in game-winning RBIs with 6 in 1982.
Led International League first basemen in total chances with 1,314 and double plays with 108 in 1986.
Named first baseman on THE SPORTING NEWS American League All-Star Team, 1989.
Named first baseman on THE SPORTING NEWS American League Silver Slugger team, 1989.

Year	Club	League	Pos.	G.	AB.	R.	H.	2B.	3B.	HR.	RBI.	B.A.	PO.	A.	E.	F.A.
1981—Bradenton Yanks	Gulf C.	1B	29	81	6	12	2	0	0	9	.148	176	8	7	.963
1982—Braden. Yanks†	Gulf C.	1B	62	217	38	59	11	1	*9	●41	.272	514	*56	8	.986
1983—Florence	S. Atl.	1B	33	119	26	37	3	1	7	26	.311	250	14	6	.978
1983—Kinston	Carol.	1B	94	350	53	85	14	1	21	57	.243	784	57	10	.988
1984—Knoxville	South.	1B	56	189	29	47	13	2	9	25	.249	481	45	10	.981
1984—Syracuse	Int.	1B	70	238	28	56	10	1	13	28	.235	644	45	3	.996
1985—Syracuse‡	Int.	1B	51	176	19	40	8	2	5	20	.227	433	37	5	.989
1986—Syracuse	Int.	*1B-OF	133	468	69	121	23	4	19	74	.259	*1219	*85	10	*.992
1986—Toronto	Amer.	1B	3	5	1	1	0	0	0	0	.200	3	0	0	1.000
1987—Toronto	Amer.	1B	107	295	58	73	16	0	20	43	.247	108	7	2	.983
1988—Toronto	Amer.	1B	154	536	100	151	35	4	34	82	.282	1344	93	5	*.997
1989—Toronto	Amer.	1B	161	551	98	148	27	3	*36	92	.269	1460	115	*17	.989
1990—Toronto§	Amer.	1B	153	557	91	167	21	1	35	88	.300	1246	126	6	.996
Major League Totals—5 Years			578	1944	348	540	99	8	125	305	.278	4161	341	30	.993

Selected by New York Yankees' organization in 9th round of free-agent draft, June 8, 1981.
†Traded with Outfielder Dave Collins, Pitcher Mike Morgan and a reported $400,000 to Toronto Blue Jays for Outfielder-Catcher Tom Dodd and Pitcher Dale Murray, December 9, 1982.
‡On disabled list, June 5 to August 14, 1985.
§Traded with Shortstop Tony Fernandez to San Diego Padres for Outfielder Joe Carter and Second Baseman Roberto Alomar, December 5, 1990.

CHAMPIONSHIP SERIES RECORD

Year	Club	League	Pos.	G.	AB.	R.	H.	2B.	3B.	HR.	RBI.	B.A.	PO.	A.	E.	F.A.
1989—Toronto	Amer.	1B	5	21	1	3	0	0	0	3	.143	35	2	1	.974

TERENCE ROY McGRIFF
(Terry)

Born September 23, 1963, at Fort Pierce, Fla.
Height, 6.02. Weight, 195.
Throws and bats righthanded.

Major League stolen bases: 1988 (1).
Led American Association catchers in double plays with 8 1986 and tied for lead with 10 in 1989.
Led American Association in passed balls with 10 in 1986.
Led Eastern League catchers in total chances with 731 in 1985.

Year	Club	League	Pos.	G.	AB.	R.	H.	2B.	3B.	HR.	RBI.	B.A.	PO.	A.	E.	F.A.
1981—Billings	Pion.	C-1B	42	96	15	26	3	0	1	15	.271	166	14	7	.963
1982—Eugene	N'west	C	53	190	23	46	10	2	4	31	.242	320	*43	8	.978

Year	Club	League	Pos.	G.	AB.	R.	H.	2B.	3B.	HR.	RBI.	B.A.	PO.	A.	E.	F.A.
1983—Tampa	Fla. St.	C	87	260	21	66	11	3	5	45	.254	403	67	7	.985
1984—Tampa	Fla. St.	C	110	345	48	96	19	0	7	41	.278	576	88	16	.976
1985—Vermont	East.	C	110	363	52	92	10	4	13	60	.253	*636	89	6	*.992
1986—Denver	A. A.	C	108	340	54	99	22	1	9	54	.291	411	*59	11	.977
1987—Nashville	A. A.	C	67	228	36	62	11	3	10	33	.272	343	36	3	.992
1987—Cincinnati	Nat.	C	34	89	6	20	3	0	2	11	.225	160	14	3	.983
1988—Cincinnati	Nat.	C	35	96	9	19	3	0	1	4	.198	177	14	2	.990
1988—Nashville	A. A.	C	35	97	8	21	3	1	1	12	.216	175	10	4	.979
1989—Cincinnati	Nat.	C	6	11	1	3	0	0	0	2	.273	23	3	2	.929
1989—Nashville	A. A.	C	102	335	42	94	24	1	5	28	.281	534	74	9	.985
1990—Cinc.†-Hou.	Nat.	C	6	9	0	0	0	0	0	0	.000	13	2	1	.938
1990—Nashville	A. A.	C	94	325	44	91	17	0	9	54	.280	564	59	9	.986
Major League Totals—4 Years			81	205	16	42	6	0	3	17	.205	373	33	8	.981

Selected by Cincinnati Reds' organization in 8th round of free-agent draft, June 8, 1981.

†Traded with Pitchers Keith Kaiser and Butch Henry, September 7, 1990, completing deal in which Houston Astros traded Second Baseman Bill Doran to Cincinnati Reds for three players to be named later, August 30, 1990.

WILLIAM PATRICK McGUIRE JR.
(Bill)

Born February 14, 1964, at Omaha, Neb.
Height, 6.03. Weight, 215.
Throws and bats righthanded.
Attended University of Nebraska, Lincoln, Neb.

Led California League catchers in double plays with 16 in 1986.
Tied for Pacific Coast League lead in sacrifice hits with 11 in 1990.
Tied for Pacific Coast League lead in double plays with 9 in 1990.

Year	Club	League	Pos.	G.	AB.	R.	H.	2B.	3B.	HR.	RBI.	B.A.	PO.	A.	E.	F.A.
1985—Wausau	Midw.	C	56	191	24	47	9	0	3	15	.246	304	26	9	.973
1986—Salinas	Calif.	C	116	368	49	110	22	1	6	62	.299	713	83	*20	.975
1987—Chattanooga	South.	C	79	259	21	59	10	0	3	29	.228	477	43	6	.989
1988—Vermont	East.	C	49	136	16	28	3	0	5	24	.206	280	43	7	.979
1988—Calgary	P. C.	C	37	117	17	27	7	0	2	15	.231	215	19	1	.996
1988—Seattle	Amer.	C	9	16	1	3	0	0	0	2	.188	29	3	0	1.000
1989—Calgary	P. C.	C	83	268	39	74	17	0	7	38	.276	467	55	7	.987
1989—Seattle	Amer.	C	14	28	2	5	0	0	1	4	.179	62	6	0	1.000
1990—Calgary	P. C.	C	118	358	47	82	12	2	7	46	.229	650	*81	*17	.977
Major League Totals—2 Years			23	44	3	8	0	0	1	6	.182	91	9	0	1.000

Selected by Cleveland Indians' organization in 25th round of free-agent draft, June 7, 1982.
Selected by Seattle Mariners' organization in 1st round (27th player selected) of free-agent draft, June 3, 1985.

MARK DAVID McGWIRE

Born October 1, 1963, at Pomona, Calif.
Height, 6.05. Weight, 225.
Throws and bats righthanded.
Attended University of Southern California, Los Angeles, Calif.
Brother of Dan McGwire, quarterback at San Diego State University.

Holds major league records for most home runs (49) and extra bases on long hits (183) by rookie, season, 1987.
Shares major league record for most home runs, two consecutive games (5), June 27 and 28, 1987.
Shares modern major league record for most runs, two consecutive games (9), June 27 and 28, 1987.
Holds American League record for highest slugging average by rookie, season (.618), 1987.
Hit three home runs in a game, June 27, 1987.
Major League stolen bases: 1987 (1), 1989 (1), 1990 (2). Total—4.
Led American League in slugging percentage with .618 in 1987.
Led American League in bases on balls received with 110 in 1990.
Led American League first basemen in total chances with 1,429 in 1990.
Led California League third basemen in assists with 239 and total chances with 354 in 1985.
Named first baseman on THE SPORTING NEWS American League All-Star fielding team, 1990.
Named American League Rookie Player of the Year by THE SPORTING NEWS, 1987.
Named American League Rookie of the Year by Baseball Writers' Association of America, 1987.
Member of 1984 U.S. Olympic baseball team.
Named College Player of the Year by THE SPORTING NEWS, 1984.
Named first baseman on THE SPORTING NEWS College Baseball All-America Team, 1984.

Year	Club	League	Pos.	G.	AB.	R.	H.	2B.	3B.	HR.	RBI.	B.A.	PO.	A.	E.	F.A.
1984—Modesto	Calif.	1B	16	55	7	11	3	0	1	1	.200	107	6	1	.991
1985—Modesto	Calif.	3B-1B	138	489	95	134	23	3	●24	●106	.274	105	240	33	.913
1986—Huntsville	South	3B	55	195	40	59	15	0	10	53	.303	34	124	16	.908
1986—Tacoma	P. C.	3B	78	280	42	89	21	5	13	59	.318	53	126	25	.877
1986—Oakland	Amer.	3B	18	53	10	10	1	0	3	9	.189	10	20	6	.833
1987—Oakland	Amer.	1B-3B-OF	151	557	97	161	28	4	*49	118	.289	1176	101	13	.990
1988—Oakland	Amer.	1B-OF	155	550	87	143	22	1	32	99	.260	1228	88	9	.993
1989—Oakland†	Amer.	1B	143	490	74	113	17	0	33	95	.231	1170	114	6	.995
1990—Oakland	Amer.	1B	156	523	87	123	16	0	39	108	.235	*1329	95	5	.997
Major League Totals—5 Years			623	2173	355	550	84	5	156	429	.253	4913	418	39	.993

Selected by Montreal Expos' organization in 8th round of free-agent draft, June 8, 1981.
Selected by Oakland A's organization in 1st round (10th player selected) of free-agent draft, June 4, 1984.
†On disabled list, April 11 to April 26, 1989.

CHAMPIONSHIP SERIES RECORD

Year	Club	League	Pos.	G.	AB.	R.	H.	2B.	3B.	HR.	RBI.	B.A.	PO.	A.	E.	F.A.
1988—Oakland		Amer.	1B	4	15	4	5	0	0	1	3	.333	24	2	0	1.000
1989—Oakland		Amer.	1B	5	18	3	7	1	0	1	3	.389	46	1	1	.979
1990—Oakland		Amer.	1B	4	13	2	2	0	0	0	2	.154	40	0	0	1.000
Championship Series Totals—3 Years				13	46	9	14	1	0	2	8	.304	110	3	1	.991

WORLD SERIES RECORD

Year	Club	League	Pos.	G.	AB.	R.	H.	2B.	3B.	HR.	RBI.	B.A.	PO.	A.	E.	F.A.
1988—Oakland		Amer.	1B	5	17	1	1	0	0	1	1	.059	40	3	0	1.000
1989—Oakland		Amer.	1B	4	17	0	5	1	0	0	1	.294	28	2	0	1.000
1990—Oakland		Amer.	1B	4	14	1	3	0	0	0	0	.214	42	1	2	.956
World Series Totals—3 Years				13	48	2	9	1	0	1	2	.188	110	6	2	.983

ALL-STAR GAME RECORD

Year	League	Pos.	AB.	R.	H.	2B.	3B.	HR.	RBI.	B.A.	PO.	A.	E.	F.A.
1987—American		1B	3	0	0	0	0	0	0	.000	7	0	1	.875
1988—American		1B	2	0	1	0	0	0	0	.500	8	0	0	1.000
1989—American		1B	3	0	1	0	0	0	0	.333	5	0	0	1.000
1990—American		1B	2	0	0	0	0	0	0	.000	7	0	0	1.000
All-Star Game Totals—4 Years			10	0	2	0	0	0	0	.200	27	0	1	.964

TIMOTHY ALLEN McINTOSH
(Tim)

Born March 21, 1965, at Crystal, Minn.
Height, 5.11. Weight, 195.
Throws and bats righthanded.
Attended University of Minnesota, Minneapolis, Minn.

Led Midwest League in game-winning RBIs with 14 in 1987.
Led American Association catchers in errors with 19 and passed balls with 13 in 1990.
Led California League catchers in assists with 99 and double plays with 14 in 1988.

Year	Club	League	Pos.	G.	AB.	R.	H.	2B.	3B.	HR.	RBI.	B.A.	PO.	A.	E.	F.A.
1986—Beloit		Midw.	OF	49	173	26	45	3	2	4	21	.260	98	4	4	.962
1987—Beloit		Midw.	C	130	461	83	139	30	3	20	85	.302	624	71	6	*.991
1988—Stockton		Calif.	C-OF	138	519	81	147	32	6	15	92	.283	779	101	17	.981
1989—El Paso		Texas	C-OF	120	463	72	139	30	3	17	93	.300	474	59	17	.969
1990—Denver		A. A.	C-OF	116	416	72	120	21	3	18	74	.288	577	72	20	.970
1990—Milwaukee		Amer.	C	5	5	1	1	0	0	1	1	.200	6	1	1	.875
Major League Totals—1 Year				5	5	1	1	0	0	1	1	.200	6	1	1	.875

Selected by Milwaukee Brewers' organization in 3rd round of free-agent draft, June 2, 1986.

JEFFERSON ALAN McKNIGHT
(Jeff)

Born February 18, 1963, at Conway, Ark.
Height, 6.00. Weight, 188.
Throws right and bats left and righthanded.
Attended Westark Community College, Fort Smith, Ark.
Son of Jim McKnight, infielder with Chicago Cubs, 1960 and 1962.

Led International League in bases on balls received with 79 in 1989.

Year	Club	League	Pos.	G.	AB.	R.	H.	2B.	3B.	HR.	RBI.	B.A.	PO.	A.	E.	F.A.
1983—Little Falls†		NYP	SS	39	115	10	25	3	1	0	9	.217	43	72	16	.878
1984—Columbia†		S. Atl.	S-2-3-1-O	95	251	31	64	10	1	1	27	.255	115	144	21	.925
1985—Columbia†		S. Atl.	O-1-P	67	159	26	42	6	1	1	24	.264	92	16	4	.964
1985—Lynchburg†		Carol.	S-3-2-O	49	150	19	33	6	1	0	21	.220	47	106	12	.927
1986—Jackson†		Texas	O-I-P	132	469	71	118	24	3	4	55	.252	400	154	19	.967
1987—Jackson†		Texas	O-3-1-2-S	16	59	5	12	3	0	2	8	.203	22	27	1	.980
1987—Tidewater		Int.	I-O-P	87	184	21	47	7	3	2	25	.255	141	119	9	.967
1988—Tidewater†		Int.	O-2-S-1-3	113	345	36	88	14	0	2	25	.255	180	155	15	.957
1989—Tidewater		Int.	I-O-C	116	425	84	106	19	2	9	48	.249	665	172	15	.982
1989—New York‡		Nat.	2-1-S-3	6	12	2	3	0	0	0	0	.250	4	5	1	.900
1990—Rochester		Int.	O-S-1-2	100	339	56	95	21	3	7	45	.280	211	144	14	.962
1990—Baltimore		Amer.	1-O-2-S	29	75	11	15	2	0	1	4	.200	106	20	0	1.000
National League Totals—1 Year				6	12	2	3	0	0	0	0	.250	4	5	1	.900
American League Totals—1 Year				29	75	11	15	2	0	1	4	.200	106	20	0	1.000
Major League Totals—2 Years				35	87	13	18	2	0	1	4	.207	110	25	1	.993

Selected by Baltimore Orioles' organization in 28th round of free-agent draft, June 7, 1982.
Selected by New York Mets' organization in secondary phase of free-agent draft, January 11, 1983.
†Batted lefthanded only.
‡Released, September 29, 1989; signed by Rochester (Baltimore Orioles' organization), December 5, 1989.

RECORD AS PITCHER

Year	Club	League	G.	IP.	W.	L.	Pct.	H.	R.	ER.	SO.	BB.	ERA.
1985—Columbia		S. Atlantic	3	4	0	0	.000	4	5	4	8	3	9.00
1986—Jackson		Texas	5	6	0	0	.000	4	1	1	1	1	1.50
1987—Tidewater		Int'national	1	2	0	0	.000	0	0	0	0	0	0.00

MARK TREMELL McLEMORE

Born October 4, 1964, at San Diego, Calif.
Height, 5.11. Weight, 195.
Throws right and bats left and righthanded.

Major League stolen bases: 1987 (25), 1988 (13), 1989 (6), 1990 (1). Total—45.
Led Pacific Coast League second basemen in total chances with 597 and double plays with 95 in 1989.
Led California League second basemen in assists with 400 and double plays with 84 in 1984.

Year Club	League	Pos.	G.	AB.	R.	H.	2B.	3B.	HR.	RBI.	B.A.	PO.	A.	E.	F.A.
1982—Salem	N'west	2B-SS	55	165	42	49	6	2	0	25	.297	81	125	11	.947
1983—Peoria	Midw.	2B-SS	95	329	42	79	7	3	0	18	.240	170	250	24	.946
1984—Redwood	Calif.	2B-SS	134	482	102	142	8	3	0	45	.295	274	429	25	.966
1985—Midland†	Texas	2B-SS	117	458	80	124	17	6	2	46	.271	301	339	19	.971
1986—Midland	Texas	2B	63	237	54	75	9	1	1	29	.316	155	194	13	.964
1986—Edmonton	P. C.	2B	73	286	41	79	13	1	0	23	.276	173	215	7	.982
1986—California	Amer.	2B	5	4	0	0	0	0	0	0	.000	3	10	0	1.000
1987—California	Amer.	2B-SS	138	433	61	102	13	3	3	41	.236	293	363	17	.975
1988—California‡	Amer.	2B-3B	77	233	38	56	11	2	2	16	.240	108	178	6	.979
1988—Palm Springs	Calif.	2B	11	44	9	15	3	1	0	6	.341	18	24	1	.977
1988—Edmonton	P. C.	2B	12	45	7	12	3	0	0	6	.267	35	33	1	.986
1989—Edmonton	P. C.	2B	114	430	60	105	13	2	2	34	.244	★264	323	10	★.983
1989—California	Amer.	2B	32	103	12	25	3	1	0	14	.243	55	88	5	.966
1990—Cal.§x-Cleve.	Amer.	2B-SS-3B	28	60	6	9	2	0	0	2	.150	37	39	4	.950
1990—Edm.-Col.Spr.	P. C.	2B-SS-3B	23	93	15	25	4	0	1	10	.269	47	72	6	.952
1990—Palm Springs y	Calif.	2B	6	22	3	6	0	0	0	2	.273	20	22	0	1.000
Major League Totals—5 Years			280	833	117	192	29	6	5	73	.230	496	678	32	.973

Selected by California Angels' organization in 9th round of free-agent draft, June 7, 1982.
†On disabled list, May 15 to May 27, 1985.
‡On disabled list, May 24 to August 2, 1988; included rehabilitation disability assignment to Palm Springs, July 7 to July 21, 1988; and Edmonton, July 22 to July 27, 1988.
§On disabled list, May 17 to August 17, 1990; included rehabilitation disability assignment to Edmonton, May 24 to June 6, 1990; and Palm Springs, August 9 to August 13, 1990.
xTraded to Colorado Springs (Cleveland Indians' organization), August 17, 1990, completing deal in which Cleveland traded Catcher Ron Tingley to California Angels for a player to be named later, September 6, 1989.
yReleased, December 13, 1990.

JOE CRAIG McMURTRY

(Known by middle name.)
Born November 5, 1959, at Temple, Tex.
Height, 6.05. Weight, 195.
Throws and bats righthanded.
Attended McLennan Community College, Waco, Tex.

Major League saves: 1985 (1), 1988 (3). Total—4.
Tied for International League lead in games started by pitchers with 32 in 1982.
Named National League Rookie Pitcher of the Year by THE SPORTING NEWS, 1983.
Named International League Pitcher of the Year, 1982.

Year Club	League	G.	IP.	W.	L.	Pct.	H.	R.	ER.	SO.	BB.	ERA.
1980—Savannah	Southern	14	86	7	4	.636	82	40	34	37	35	3.56
1981—Savannah	Southern	28	202	★15	11	.577	168	87	62	111	95	2.76
1982—Richmond	Int'national	32	★210	★17	9	.654	198	98	89	96	107	3.81
1983—Atlanta	National	36	224⅔	15	9	.625	204	86	77	105	88	3.08
1984—Atlanta	National	37	183⅓	9	17	.346	184	100	88	99	102	4.32
1985—Atlanta	National	17	45	0	3	.000	56	36	33	28	27	6.60
1985—Richmond	Int'national	16	107⅓	7	5	.583	88	43	39	74	51	3.27
1986—Atlanta†	National	37	79⅔	1	6	.143	82	46	42	50	43	4.74
1986—Greenville‡	Southern	3	15	1	1	.500	13	10	10	12	9	6.00
1987—Knoxville§	Southern	12	78	4	2	.667	64	28	24	56	20	2.77
1987—Syracuse x	Int'national	9	53⅔	5	3	.625	46	23	21	31	15	3.52
1988—Oklahoma City	Am. Assoc.	9	49⅔	2	5	.286	55	27	24	35	21	4.35
1988—Texas	American	32	60	3	3	.500	37	16	15	35	24	2.25
1989—Texas y	American	19	23	0	0	.000	29	21	19	14	13	7.43
1989—Sarasota Rangers	Gulf Coast	4	8	0	1	.000	3	2	1	10	2	1.13
1989—Oklahoma City z	Am. Assoc.	1	3	0	0	.000	2	1	1	1	1	3.00
1990—Texas a	American	23	41⅔	0	3	.000	43	25	20	14	30	4.32
1990—Oklahoma City b	Am. Assoc.	6	26⅔	1	1	.500	31	15	8	19	21	2.70
National League Totals—4 Years		127	532⅔	25	35	.417	526	268	240	282	260	4.06
American League Totals—3 Years		74	124⅔	3	6	.333	109	62	54	63	67	3.90
Major League Totals—7 Years		201	657⅓	28	41	.406	635	330	294	345	327	4.03

Selected by Atlanta Braves' organization in 1st round (fourth player selected) of free-agent draft, January 8, 1980.
†On disabled list, July 27 to September 1, 1986; included rehabilitation disability assignment to Greenville, August 14 to September 1, 1986.
‡Traded to Toronto Blue Jays for Second Baseman Damaso Garcia and Pitcher Luis Leal, February 2, 1987.
§On Toronto disabled list, March 30 to June 18, 1987; included rehabilitation disability assignment to Knoxville, May 29 to June 17, 1987.
xGranted free agency, November 22, 1987; signed by Texas Rangers, December 8, 1987.
yOn disabled list, April 18 to May 5 and May 25 to August 20, 1989; included rehabilitation disability assignment to Sarasota Rangers, August 5 to August 14, 1989; then transferred to Oklahoma City, August 15 to August 20, 1989.
zGranted free agency, November 13, 1989; re-signed by Rangers' organization, January 5, 1990.
aReleased, April 25, 1990; re-signed by Rangers' organization, May 10, 1990.
bGranted free agency, November 5, 1990.

BRIAN WESLEY McRAE

Born August 27, 1967, at Bradenton, Fla.
Height, 6.00. Weight, 180.
Throws right and bats left and righthanded.
Son of Hal McRae, outfielder with Cincinnati Reds and Kansas City Royals, 1968 and
1970 through 1987; coach with Kansas City Royals, 1987; minor league instructor in
Pittsburgh Pirates' organization, 1988 and 1989; and currently coach with Montreal Expos.
Major League stolen bases: 1990 (4).
Led Northwest League second basemen in total chances with 373 in 1986.
Tied for Southern League lead in double plays by outfielders with 5 in 1989.

Year	Club	League	Pos.	G.	AB.	R.	H.	2B.	3B.	HR.	RBI.	B.A.	PO.	A.	E.	F.A.
1985—Sarasota Royals...	Gulf C.	2B-SS	60	217	40	58	6	5	0	23	.267	116	142	18	.935
1986—Eugene	N'west	2B	72	306	*66	82	10	3	1	29	.268	146	*214	13	*.965
1987—Fort Myers	Fla. St.	2B	131	481	62	121	14	1	1	31	.252	*284	346	18	.972
1988—Baseball City	Fla. St.	2B	30	107	18	33	2	0	1	11	.308	70	103	4	.977
1988—Memphis	South.	2B	91	288	33	58	13	1	4	15	.201	147	231	18	.955
1989—Memphis	South.	OF	138	*533	72	121	18	8	5	42	.227	249	11	5	.981
1990—Memphis	South.	OF	116	470	78	126	24	6	10	64	.268	265	8	7	.975
1990—Kansas City	Amer.	OF	46	168	21	48	8	3	2	23	.286	120	1	0	1.000
Major League Totals—1 Year				46	168	21	48	8	3	2	23	.286	120	1	0	1.000

Selected by Kansas City Royals' organization in 1st round (17th player selected) of free-agent draft, June 3, 1985.

WALTER KEVIN McREYNOLDS

(Known by middle name.)
Born October 16, 1959, at Little Rock, Ark.
Height, 6.01. Weight, 215.
Throws and bats righthanded.
Attended University of Arkansas, Fayetteville, Ark.

Holds major league record for most stolen bases with no caught stealing, season (21), 1988.
Shares major league records for fewest assists by outfielder for leader, season (14), 1990; fewest double plays by
outfielder, season, 150 or more games (0), 1987.
Major League stolen bases: 1983 (2), 1984 (3), 1985 (4), 1986 (8), 1987 (14), 1988 (21), 1989 (15), 1990 (9). Total—76.
Hit for the cycle, August 1, 1989.
Led National League outfielders in double plays with 5 in 1988.
Led National League outfielders in total chances with 436 in 1984 and 445 in 1985.
Led Pacific Coast League in total bases with 328 in 1983.
Named outfielder on THE SPORTING NEWS National League All-Star Team, 1988.
Named Minor League Player of the Year by THE SPORTING NEWS, 1983.
Named Pacific Coast League Player of the Year, 1983.
Named California League Most Valuable Player, 1982.
Received reported $125,000 bonus to sign with San Diego Padres, 1982.
Named outfielder on THE SPORTING NEWS College Baseball All-America Team, 1981.

Year	Club	League	Pos.	G.	AB.	R.	H.	2B.	3B.	HR.	RBI.	B.A.	PO.	A.	E.	F.A.
1982—Reno	Calif.	OF	90	338	83	127	17	5	*28	98	*.376	52	7	3	.952
1982—Amarillo	Texas	OF	40	162	30	57	8	3	5	39	.352	76	3	2	.975
1983—Las Vegas	P. C.	OF	113	446	98	168	*46	9	●32	116	.377	257	3	9	.967
1983—San Diego	Nat.	OF	39	140	15	31	3	1	4	14	.221	87	4	1	.989
1984—San Diego	Nat.	OF	147	525	68	146	26	6	20	75	.278	*422	10	4	.991
1985—San Diego	Nat.	OF	152	564	61	132	24	4	15	75	.234	*430	12	3	.993
1986—San Diego†	Nat.	OF	158	560	89	161	31	6	26	96	.288	332	9	8	.977
1987—New York	Nat.	OF	151	590	86	163	32	5	29	95	.276	286	8	4	.987
1988—New York	Nat.	OF	147	552	82	159	30	2	27	99	.288	252	*18	4	.985
1989—New York	Nat.	OF	148	545	74	148	25	3	22	85	.272	307	10	●10	.969
1990—New York	Nat.	OF	147	521	75	140	23	1	24	82	.269	237	●14	3	.988
Major League Totals—8 Years			1089	3997	550	1080	194	28	167	621	.270	2353	85	37	.985

Selected by Milwaukee Brewers' organization in 18th round of free-agent draft, June 6, 1978.
Selected by San Diego Padres' organization in 1st round (sixth player selected) of free-agent draft, June 8, 1981.
†Traded with Pitcher Gene Walter and Infielder Adam Ging to New York Mets for Outfielders Shawn Abner,
Stanley Jefferson and Kevin Mitchell and Pitchers Kevin Armstrong and Kevin Brown, December 11, 1986.

CHAMPIONSHIP SERIES RECORD

Shares National League Championship Series record for most hits, game (4), October 11, 1988.

Year	Club	League	Pos.	G.	AB.	R.	H.	2B.	3B.	HR.	RBI.	B.A.	PO.	A.	E.	F.A.
1984—San Diego	Nat.	OF	4	10	2	3	0	0	1	4	.300	10	0	0	1.000
1988—New York	Nat.	OF	7	28	4	7	2	0	2	4	.250	19	0	0	1.000
Championship Series Totals—2 Years			11	38	6	10	2	0	3	8	.263	29	0	0	1.000

LARRY DEAN McWILLIAMS

Born February 10, 1954, at Wichita, Kan.
Height, 6.05. Weight, 181.
Throws and bats lefthanded.
Attended Paris Junior College, Paris, Tex.

Shares major league record for most strikeouts by batter, inning (2), April 22, 1979, fourth inning.
Major League saves: 1982 (1), 1984 (1), 1988 (1). Total—3.
Named lefthanded pitcher on THE SPORTING NEWS National League All-Star Team, 1983.

Year Club	League	G.	IP.	W.	L.	Pct.	H.	R.	ER.	SO.	BB.	ERA.
1974—Greenwood†	W. Carol.	11	64	4	3	.571	64	26	20	61	23	2.81
1975—Greenwood‡	W. Carol.	17	93	8	4	.667	83	36	29	71	18	2.81
1976—Greenwood	W. Carol.	8	48	2	2	.500	40	19	14	44	13	2.63
1976—Savannah	Southern	16	74	3	8	.273	82	41	38	37	33	4.62
1977—Savannah	Southern	26	158	8	9	.471	153	70	59	139	64	3.36
1978—Richmond	Int'national	15	108	6	5	.545	87	36	34	78	41	2.83
1978—Atlanta	National	15	99	9	3	.750	84	38	31	42	35	2.82
1979—Atlanta§	National	13	66	3	2	.600	69	41	41	32	22	5.59
1980—Atlanta	National	30	164	9	14	.391	188	97	90	77	39	4.94
1981—Richmond	Int'national	29	178	●13	10	.565	174	98	●86	157	79	4.35
1981—Atlanta	National	6	38	2	1	.667	31	13	13	23	8	3.08
1982—Atlanta x-Pittsburgh	National	46	159⅓	8	8	.500	158	79	68	118	44	3.84
1983—Pittsburgh	National	35	238	15	8	.652	205	99	86	199	87	3.25
1984—Pittsburgh	National	34	227⅓	12	11	.522	226	86	74	149	78	2.93
1985—Pittsburgh y	National	30	126⅓	7	9	.438	139	70	66	52	62	4.70
1986—Pittsburgh z	National	49	122⅓	3	11	.214	129	75	70	80	49	5.15
1987—Greenville	Southern	7	33	1	2	.333	33	24	20	27	26	5.45
1987—Atlanta a	National	9	20⅓	0	1	.000	25	15	13	13	7	5.75
1987—Oklahoma City b	Am. Assoc.	7	22⅓	1	4	.200	44	29	28	13	20	11.28
1988—St. Louis c	National	42	136	6	9	.400	130	64	59	70	45	3.90
1989—Philadelphia d	National	40	120⅔	2	11	.154	123	67	55	54	49	4.10
1989—Kansas City	American	8	32⅔	2	2	.500	31	15	15	24	8	4.13
1990—Kansas City e	American	13	8⅓	0	0	.000	10	9	9	7	9	9.72
National League Totals—12 Years		349	1517⅓	76	88	.463	1507	744	666	909	525	3.95
American League Totals—2 Years		21	41	2	2	.500	41	24	24	31	17	5.27
Major League Totals—13 Years		370	1558⅓	78	90	.464	1548	768	690	940	542	3.99

Selected by Atlanta Braves' organization in 1st round (sixth player selected) of free-agent draft, January 9, 1974.
†On disabled list, July 22 to September 25, 1974.
‡On disabled list, April 11 to June 3, 1975.
§On disabled list, May 18 to June 15 and July 7 to September 1, 1979.
xTraded to Pittsburgh Pirates for Pitcher Pascual Perez and a player to be named later, June 30, 1982; Atlanta Braves' organization acquired Shortstop Carlos Rios to complete deal, September 8, 1982.
yOn disabled list, May 17 to June 8 and August 18 to September 3, 1985.
zReleased, April 6, 1987; signed by Greenville (Atlanta Braves' organization), May 18, 1987.
aReleased, July 25, 1987; signed by Oklahoma City (Texas Rangers' organization), August 6, 1987.
bReleased, February 2, 1988; signed by St. Louis Cardinals, February 12, 1988.
cGranted free agency, November 4, 1988; signed by Philadelphia Phillies, January 30, 1989.
dTraded by Kansas City Royals for a player to be named later, September 2, 1989; Reading (Philadelphia Phillies' organization) acquired Catcher Jeff Hulse to complete deal, October 21, 1989.
eReleased, May 14, 1990.

RUSSELL LOREN MEACHAM
(Rusty)

Born January 27, 1968, at Stuart, Fla.
Height, 6.03. Weight, 155.
Throws and bats righthanded.
Attended Indian River Community College, Ft. Pierce, Fla.

Tied for Eastern League lead in shutouts with 3 and complete games with 9 in 1990.
Tied for Appalachian League lead in shutouts with 2 in 1988.

Year Club	League	G.	IP.	W.	L.	Pct.	H.	R.	ER.	SO.	BB.	ERA.
1988—Fayetteville	S. Atlantic	6	24⅔	0	3	.000	37	19	17	16	6	6.20
1988—Bristol	Ap'lachian	13	75⅓	●9	1	●.900	55	14	12	85	22	★1.43
1989—Fayetteville	S. Atlantic	16	102	10	3	.769	103	33	26	74	23	2.29
1989—Lakeland	Florida St.	11	64⅔	5	4	.556	59	15	14	39	12	1.95
1990—London	Eastern	26	178	★15	9	.625	161	70	62	123	36	3.13

Selected by Detroit Tigers' organization in 33rd round of free-agent draft, June 2, 1987.

MICHAEL RAY MEADOWS
(Louie)

Born April 29, 1961, in Onslow County, N. C.
Height, 5.11. Weight, 190.
Throws and bats lefthanded.
Attended North Carolina State University, Raleigh, N. C.

Major League stolen bases: 1986 (1), 1988 (4), 1989 (1). Total—6.

Year Club	League	Pos.	G.	AB.	R.	H.	2B.	3B.	HR.	RBI.	B.A.	PO.	A.	E.	F.A.
1982—Asheville	S. Atl.	OF	66	228	43	72	9	1	10	41	.316	87	4	13	.875
1983—Daytona Beach	Fla. St.	OF	112	382	68	112	25	14	9	71	.293	169	5	4	.978
1984—Daytona Beach	Fla. St.	OF-1B	70	252	49	76	14	10	6	44	.302	323	17	5	.986
1984—Columbus	South.	OF-1B	65	225	33	63	17	4	8	36	.280	150	6	3	.981
1985—Columbus	South.	OF-1B	140	476	76	111	16	8	14	67	.233	514	32	12	.978
1986—Tucson†	P. C.	OF-1B	82	290	42	87	14	8	10	52	.300	203	15	9	.960
1986—Houston	Nat.	OF	6	6	1	2	0	0	0	0	.333	0	0	0	.000
1987—Tucson	P. C.	OF-1B	129	426	70	110	21	★14	10	76	.258	252	8	7	.974
1988—Tucson	P. C.	OF-1B	85	280	42	71	16	9	5	43	.254	415	28	5	.989
1988—Houston	Nat.	OF	35	42	5	8	0	1	2	3	.190	18	1	0	1.000
1989—Tucson	P. C.	OF-1B	53	179	32	44	9	2	6	27	.246	109	5	3	.974

Year Club League	Pos.	G.	AB.	R.	H.	2B.	3B.	HR.	RBI.	B.A.	PO.	A.	E.	F.A.
1989—Houston................. Nat.	OF-1B	31	51	5	9	0	0	3	10	.176	13	0	0	1.000
1990—Tucson................... P. C.	OF	25	84	16	25	3	3	3	18	.298	23	0	1	.958
1990—Hou.‡-Phila............ Nat.	OF	30	28	4	3	0	0	0	0	.107	8	0	0	1.000
1990—Scranton/W.-B.§... Int.	OF	48	172	29	47	6	2	4	18	.273	99	3	1	.990
Major League Totals—4 Years...............		102	127	15	22	0	1	5	13	.173	39	1	0	1.000

Selected by Houston Astros' organization in 2nd round of free-agent draft, June 7, 1982.

†On disabled list, July 21, 1986 through remainder of season.

‡Granted free agency, June 13, 1990; signed by Scranton/Wilkes-Barre (Philadelphia Phillies' organization), July 4, 1990.

§Granted free agency, October 15, 1990.

SCOTT HOWARD MEDVIN

Born September 16, 1961, at North Olmsted, O.
Height, 6.00. Weight, 190.
Throws and bats righthanded.
Received bachelor of arts degree in management from Baldwin-Wallace College, Berea, O.

Year Club	League	G.	IP.	W.	L.	Pct.	H.	R.	ER.	SO.	BB.	ERA.
1984—Wausau†..	Midwest	40	65⅔	4	2	.667	62	36	26	53	35	3.56
1985—Lakeland‡....................................	Florida St.	31	51⅔	5	4	.556	48	20	16	47	20	2.79
1985—Birmingham	Southern	13	23	3	3	.500	14	10	8	17	12	3.13
1986—Shreveport	Texas	49	93⅔	8	6	.571	71	32	25	68	42	2.40
1987—Shreveport	Texas	37	78⅔	7	1	.875	59	19	15	71	41	1.72
1987—Phoenix§-Vancouver x................	P. Coast	13	22⅓	0	1	.000	22	17	13	16	18	5.24
1988—Buffalo...	Am. Assoc.	39	56	5	4	.556	38	18	15	49	25	2.41
1988—Pittsburgh..................................	National	17	27⅔	3	0	1.000	23	16	15	16	9	4.88
1989—Buffalo...	Am. Assoc.	54	86	7	6	.538	65	29	22	84	46	2.30
1989—Pittsburgh..................................	National	6	6⅓	0	1	.000	6	5	4	4	5	5.68
1990—Buffalo y	Am. Assoc.	13	24⅔	2	2	.500	13	7	4	10	11	1.46
1990—Calgary	P. Coast	43	50⅔	1	3	.250	47	30	28	31	24	4.97
1990—Seattle...	American	5	4⅓	0	1	.000	7	4	3	1	2	6.23
National League Totals—2 Years........................		23	34	3	1	.750	29	21	19	20	14	5.03
American League Totals—1 Year........................		5	4⅓	0	1	.000	7	4	3	1	2	6.23
Major League Totals—3 Years........................		28	38⅓	3	2	.600	36	25	22	21	16	5.17

Signed as free agent by Detroit Tigers' organization, September 27, 1983.

†Loaned to Wausau (Seattle Mariners' organization), April 4, 1984; returned, September 5, 1984.

‡Traded to San Francisco Giants, December 11, 1985, completing deal in which San Francisco traded Pitchers Dave LaPoint and Eric King and Catcher Matt Nokes to Detroit Tigers for Pitcher Juan Berenguer, Catcher Bob Melvin and a player to be named later, October 7, 1985.

§Traded with Pitcher Jeff Robinson to Pittsburgh Pirates for Pitcher Rick Reuschel, August 21, 1987.

xDrafted by Houston Astros, December 7, 1987; returned, April 4, 1988.

yTraded to Calgary (Seattle Mariners' organization) for Pitcher Lee Hancock, May 18, 1990.

JOSE LUIS MELENDEZ

Born September 2, 1965, at Naguabo, Puerto Rico.
Height, 6.02. Weight, 175.
Throws and bats righthanded.

Year Club	League	G.	IP.	W.	L.	Pct.	H.	R.	ER.	SO.	BB.	ERA.
1984—Watertown	NYP	15	91	5	7	.417	61	37	28	68	40	2.77
1985—Prince William†	Carolina	9	44⅓	3	2	.600	25	17	12	41	26	2.44
1986—Prince William	Carolina	28	186⅓	13	10	.565	141	75	54	146	81	2.61
1987—Harrisburg	Eastern	6	18⅓	1	3	.250	28	24	22	13	11	10.80
1987—Salem..	Carolina	20	116⅓	9	6	.600	96	62	59	86	56	4.56
1988—Salem..	Carolina	8	53⅔	4	2	.667	55	26	24	50	19	4.02
1988—Harrisburg‡...............................	Eastern	22	71⅓	5	3	.625	46	20	18	38	19	2.27
1989—Williamsport...............................	Eastern	11	73⅓	3	4	.429	54	23	20	56	22	2.45
1989—Calgary	P. Coast	17	40⅔	1	2	.333	42	27	26	24	19	5.75
1990—Calgary	P. Coast	45	124⅔	11	4	.733	119	61	54	95	44	3.90
1990—Seattle...	American	3	5⅓	0	0	.000	8	8	7	7	3	11.81
Major League Totals—1 Year............................		3	5⅓	0	0	.000	8	8	7	7	3	11.81

Signed as free agent by Pittsburgh Pirates' organization, August 29, 1983.

†On disabled list, May 3 to May 25 and June 9 to August 12, 1985.

‡Drafted by Calgary (Seattle Mariners' organization), December 5, 1988.

ROBERT PAUL MELVIN
(Bob)

Born October 28, 1961, at Palo Alto, Calif.
Height, 6.04. Weight, 205.
Throws and bats righthanded.
Attended University of California, Berkeley, Calif.,
and Canada College, Redwood City, Calif.

Major League stolen bases: 1986 (3), 1989 (1). Total—4.

Year—Club	League	Pos.	G.	AB.	R.	H.	2B.	3B.	HR.	RBI.	B.A.	PO.	A.	E.	F.A.
1981—Macon	S. Atl.	C	114	412	56	112	19	1	14	64	.272	456	67	2	*.996
1982—Birmingham†	South.	*C-1B-3B	98	364	33	86	12	1	13	52	.236	638	54	9	*.987
1983—Birmingham	South.	C-1B-2B	78	285	43	82	14	2	10	56	.288	404	30	2	.995
1983—Evansville	A. A.	C-1B	45	142	10	27	6	0	2	11	.190	213	16	1	.996
1984—Evansville	A. A.	C-1B	44	141	12	35	13	0	0	11	.248	214	21	1	.996
1984—Birmingham	South.	C-1B-3B	69	271	34	73	14	1	2	33	.269	341	38	4	.990
1985—Nashville	A. A.	C-1B-OF	53	177	27	48	7	1	9	24	.271	276	28	2	.993
1985—Detroit‡	Amer.	C	41	82	10	18	4	1	0	4	.220	175	13	2	.989
1986—San Francisco	Nat.	C-3B	89	268	24	60	14	2	5	25	.224	443	60	6	.988
1987—San Francisco§	Nat.	C-1B	84	246	31	49	8	0	11	31	.199	414	44	1	.998
1988—San Francisco	Nat.	C-1B	92	273	23	64	13	1	8	27	.234	406	31	7	.984
1988—Phoenix x	P. C.	C	21	75	11	23	5	0	2	9	.307	123	6	1	.992
1989—Baltimore y	Amer.	C	85	278	22	67	10	1	1	32	.241	303	20	3	.991
1990—Baltimore	Amer.	C-1B	93	301	30	73	14	1	5	37	.243	365	26	1	.997
American League Totals—3 Years			219	661	62	158	28	3	6	73	.239	843	59	6	.993
National League Totals—3 Years			265	787	78	173	35	3	24	83	.220	1263	135	14	.990
Major League Totals—6 Years			484	1448	140	331	63	6	30	156	.229	2106	194	20	.991

Selected by Baltimore Orioles' organization in 3rd round of free-agent draft, June 5, 1979.
Selected by Detroit Tigers' organization in secondary phase of free-agent draft, January 13, 1981.
†On disabled list, May 1 to May 25, 1982.
‡Traded with Pitcher Juan Berenguer and a player to be named later to San Francisco Giants for Pitchers Dave LaPoint and Eric King and Catcher Matt Nokes, October 7, 1985; San Francisco acquired Pitcher Scott Medvin to complete deal, December 11, 1985.
§On disabled list, July 11 to July 26, 1987.
xTraded to Baltimore Orioles for Catcher Terry Kennedy, January 24, 1989.
yOn disabled list, April 22 to May 7, 1989.

CHAMPIONSHIP SERIES RECORD

Year—Club	League	Pos.	G.	AB.	R.	H.	2B.	3B.	HR.	RBI.	B.A.	PO.	A.	E.	F.A.
1987—San Francisco	Nat.	PH-C	3	7	0	3	0	0	0	0	.429	14	1	0	1.000

ORLANDO MERCADO (RODRIGUEZ)

Born November 7, 1961, at Arecibo, Puerto Rico.
Height, 6.00. Weight, 195.
Throws and bats righthanded.

Major League stolen bases: 1983 (2), 1984 (1), 1989 (1). Total—4.
Led Eastern League in passed balls with 23 in 1980.
Led California League in passed balls with 24 in 1979.

Year—Club	League	Pos.	G.	AB.	R.	H.	2B.	3B.	HR.	RBI.	B.A.	PO.	A.	E.	F.A.
1978—Bellingham	N'west	C	38	49	7	6	2	0	0	5	.122	184	20	4	.981
1979—San Jose	Calif.	C-1B	110	335	53	86	18	2	10	54	.257	629	71	17	.976
1980—Lynn	East.	C-1B	117	396	55	101	25	6	11	71	.255	607	78	11	.984
1981—Spokane	P. C.	C-OF	95	312	32	67	21	2	4	31	.215	446	60	13	.975
1982—Salt Lake City	P. C.	C-O-1-3	90	321	43	90	19	2	16	66	.280	497	43	13	.976
1982—Seattle	Amer.	C	9	17	1	2	0	0	1	6	.118	31	1	0	1.000
1983—Seattle	Amer.	C	66	178	10	35	11	2	1	16	.197	342	27	2	.995
1983—Salt Lake City	P. C.	C-3B	26	88	12	20	2	1	2	12	.227	131	13	2	.986
1984—Seattle	Amer.	C	30	78	5	17	3	1	0	5	.218	118	10	1	.992
1984—Salt Lake City†	P. C.	C-1B-OF	29	109	18	39	9	2	6	22	.358	169	18	2	.989
1985—Oklahoma City‡	A. A.	C	59	206	20	52	7	1	8	29	.252	268	26	4	.987
1986—Oklahoma City	A. A.	C	48	172	20	47	11	1	3	25	.273	234	29	8	.970
1986—Texas§	Amer.	C	46	102	7	24	1	1	1	7	.235	240	25	1	.996
1987—Detroit x	Amer.	C	10	22	2	3	0	0	0	1	.136	40	8	1	.980
1987—Albuquerque	P. C.	C	69	205	22	57	18	0	2	27	.278	327	47	6	.984
1987—Los Angeles y	Nat.	C	7	5	1	3	1	0	0	1	.600	13	0	0	1.000
1988—Oakland	Amer.	C	16	24	3	3	0	0	1	1	.125	45	2	2	.959
1988—Tacoma z	P. C.	C-1B-OF	53	148	16	33	6	0	2	19	.223	228	22	2	.9992
1989—Portland	P. C.	C	57	196	17	58	20	1	4	29	.296	295	19	6	.981
1989—Minnesota a	Amer.	C	19	38	1	4	0	0	0	1	.105	73	9	0	1.000
1990—N.Y.b-Mont.	Nat.	C	50	98	10	21	1	0	3	7	.214	239	9	2	.992
1990—Tidewater	Int.	C	24	72	5	19	4	0	1	10	.264	133	12	0	1.000
American League Totals—7 Years			196	459	29	88	15	4	4	37	.192	889	82	7	.993
National League Totals—2 Years			57	103	11	24	2	0	3	8	.233	252	9	2	.992
Major League Totals—8 Years			253	562	40	112	17	4	7	45	.199	1141	91	9	.993

Signed as free agent by Seattle Mariners' organization, January 6, 1978.
†Traded to Texas Rangers' organization for Catcher Donnie Scott, April 4, 1985.
‡On disabled list, July 10 to September 19, 1985.
§Traded to Detroit Tigers for a player to be named later, March 24, 1987; Texas Rangers' organization acquired Outfielder Ruben Guzman to complete deal, May 8, 1987.
xTraded to Los Angeles Dodgers' organization for Pitcher Balvino Galvez, May 5, 1987.
yReleased, November 12, 1987; signed by Tacoma (Oakland Athletics' organization), January 14, 1988.
zGranted free agency, October 15, 1988; signed by Portland (Minnesota Twins' organization), December 30, 1988.
aGranted free agency, October 15, 1989; signed by Tidewater (New York Mets' organization), December 12, 1989.
bClaimed on waivers by Montreal Expos, August 30, 1990.

ORLANDO LUIS MERCED

Born November 2, 1966, at San Juan, Puerto Rico.
Height, 5.11. Weight, 170.
Throws right and bats righthanded.

Year	Club	League	Pos.	G.	AB.	R.	H.	2B.	3B.	HR.	RBI.	B.A.	PO.	A.	E.	F.A.
1985—Bradenton Pir.	..... Gulf C.		SS-3B-1B	40	136	16	31	6	0	1	13	.228	46	78	28	.816
1986—Macon	...... S. Atl.		OF-3B	65	173	20	34	4	1	2	24	.197	53	15	13	.840
1986—Watertown	.... NYP		3B-1B-OF	27	89	12	16	0	1	3	9	.180	49	28	10	.885
1987—Macon†	.... S. Atl.		OF	4	4	1	0	0	0	0	0	.000	1	1	0	1.000
1987—Watertown‡	.... NYP		2B	4	12	4	5	0	1	0	3	.417	11	7	2	.900
1988—Augusta	.... S. Atl.		2B-3B-SS	37	136	19	36	6	3	1	17	.265	35	39	7	.914
1988—Salem	.... Carol.		3-2-O-1-S	80	298	47	87	12	7	7	42	.292	77	183	31	.893
1989—Harrisburg	.... East.		1B-OF-3B	95	341	43	82	16	4	6	48	.240	435	32	10	.979
1989—Buffalo	.... A. A.		1B-OF-3B	35	129	18	44	5	3	1	16	.341	173	15	3	.984
1990—Buffalo	.... A. A.		1B-3B-OF	101	378	52	99	12	6	9	55	.262	689	83	20	.975
1990—Pittsburgh	.... Nat.		OF-C	25	24	3	5	1	0	0	0	.208	0	0	0	.000
Major League Totals—1 Year	....			25	24	3	5	1	0	0	0	.208	0	0	0	.000

Signed as free agent by Pittsburgh Pirates' organization, February 22, 1985.
†On disabled list, April 18 to April 28, 1987.
‡On disabled list, June 23, 1987 through remainder of season.

LUIS ROBERTO MERCEDES

Born February 20, 1968, at San Pedro de Macoris, Dominican Republic.
Height, 6.00. Weight, 180.
Throws and bats righthanded.

Year	Club	League	Pos.	G.	AB.	R.	H.	2B.	3B.	HR.	RBI.	B.A.	PO.	A.	E.	F.A.
1988—Bluefield	.... Appal.		2B	59	215	36	59	8	4	0	20	.274	127	152	★26	.915
1989—Frederick	.... Carol.		2B	108	401	62	124	12	5	3	36	★.309	204	305	25	.953
1990—Hagerstown	...... East.		OF	108	416	71	139	12	4	3	37	.334	157	5	●9	.947

Signed as free agent by Baltimore Orioles' organization, February 16, 1987.

KENT FRANKLIN MERCKER

Born February 1, 1968, at Dublin, O.
Height, 6.02. Weight, 195.
Throws and bats lefthanded.

Major League saves: 1990 (7).
Tied for International League lead in games started by pitchers with 27 in 1989.
Named Carolina League co-Pitcher of the Year, 1988.

Year	Club	League	G.	IP.	W.	L.	Pct.	H.	R.	ER.	SO.	BB.	ERA.
1986—Bradenton Braves	.... Gulf Coast		9	47⅓	4	3	.571	37	21	13	42	16	2.47
1987—Durham	.... Carolina		3	11⅔	0	1	.000	11	8	7	14	6	5.40
1988—Durham	.... Carolina		19	127⅔	11	4	.733	102	44	39	159	47	★2.75
1988—Greenville	.... Southern		9	48⅓	3	1	.750	36	20	18	60	26	3.35
1989—Richmond	.... Int'national		27	168⅔	9	12	.429	107	66	60	★144	★95	3.20
1989—Atlanta	.... National		2	4½	0	0	.000	8	6	6	4	6	12.46
1990—Richmond†	.... Int'national		12	58⅓	5	4	.556	60	30	23	69	27	3.55
1990—Atlanta	.... National		36	48⅓	4	7	.364	43	22	17	39	24	3.17
Major League Totals—2 Years	....		38	52⅔	4	7	.364	51	28	23	43	30	3.93

Selected by Atlanta Braves' organization in 1st round (fifth player selected) of free-agent draft, June 2, 1986.
†On Atlanta disabled list, March 30 to May 6, 1990.

MATTHEW BATES MERULLO
(Matt)

Born August 4, 1965, at Winchester, Mass.
Height, 6.02. Weight, 200.
Throws right and bats lefthanded.
Attended University of North Carolina, Chapel Hill, N.C.
Grandson of Lennie Merullo, Sr., infielder with Chicago Cubs, 1941 through 1947;
and son of Len Merullo, Jr., minor league infielder, 1961 through 1964.

Led Southern League catchers in errors with 18 in 1990.
Led Southern League in passed balls with 21 in 1988.

Year	Club	League	Pos.	G.	AB.	R.	H.	2B.	3B.	HR.	RBI.	B.A.	PO.	A.	E.	F.A.
1986—Peninsula	.... Carol.		C	64	208	21	63	12	2	3	35	.303	225	26	6	.979
1987—Daytona Beach	.... Fla. St.		C-1B-OF	70	250	26	65	11	6	4	47	.260	227	28	6	.977
1987—Birmingham	.... South.		C	48	167	13	46	7	0	2	17	.275	278	24	8	.974
1988—Birmingham	.... South.		C-1B	125	449	58	117	26	0	6	60	.261	640	60	14	.980
1989—Vancouver	.... P. C.		C	3	9	0	2	1	0	0	2	.222	19	1	1	.952
1989—Chicago	.... Amer.		C	31	81	5	18	1	0	1	8	.222	100	10	3	.973
1989—Birmingham	.... South.		C	33	119	19	35	6	0	3	23	.294	149	10	1	.994
1990—Birmingham	.... South.		C-1B	102	378	57	110	26	1	8	50	.291	561	51	24	.962
Major League Totals—1 Year	....			31	81	5	18	1	0	1	8	.222	100	10	3	.973

Selected by Chicago White Sox' organization in 7th round of free-agent draft, June 2, 1986.

JOSE RAMON MESA

Born May 22, 1966, at Azua, Dominican Republic.
Height, 6.03. Weight, 219
Throws and bats righthanded.

Led Southern League pitchers in games started with 35 in 1987.
Led Gulf Coast League in shutouts with 3 in 1982.
Tied for Carolina League lead in hit batsmen with 9 in 1985.

Year	Club	League	G.	IP.	W.	L.	Pct.	H.	R.	ER.	SO.	BB.	ERA.
1982—Bradenton Blue Jays	Gulf Coast	13	83⅓	6	4	.600	58	34	25	40	20	2.70
1983—Florence	S. Atlantic	28	141½	6	12	.333	153	★116	86	91	93	5.48
1984—Florence	S. Atlantic	7	38⅓	4	3	.571	38	24	16	35	25	3.76
1984—Kinston†	Carolina	10	50⅔	5	2	.714	51	23	22	24	28	3.91
1985—Kinston	Carolina	30	106⅔	5	10	.333	110	89	73	71	79	6.16
1986—Ventura County	California	24	142⅓	10	6	.625	141	71	61	113	58	3.86
1986—Knoxville	Southern	9	41⅓	2	2	.500	40	32	20	30	23	4.35
1987—Knoxville‡	Southern	35	★193⅓	10	●13	.435	★206	★131	★112	115	104	5.21
1987—Baltimore	American	6	31⅓	1	3	.250	38	23	21	17	15	6.03
1988—Rochester§	Int'national	11	15⅔	0	3	.000	21	20	15	15	14	8.62
1989—Rochester x	Int'national	7	10	0	2	.000	10	6	6	3	6	5.40
1989—Hagerstown	Eastern	3	13	0	0	.000	9	2	2	12	4	1.38
1990—Hagerstown	Eastern	15	79	5	5	.500	77	35	30	72	30	3.42
1990—Rochester	Int'national	4	26	1	2	.333	21	11	7	23	12	2.42
1990—Baltimore	American	7	46⅔	3	2	.600	37	20	20	24	27	3.86
Major League Totals—2 Years		13	78	4	5	.444	75	43	41	41	42	4.73

Signed as free agent by Toronto Blue Jays' organization, October 31, 1981.
†On disabled list, August 27, 1984 through remainder of season.
‡Traded to Baltimore Orioles, September 4, 1987, completing deal in which Baltimore traded Pitcher Mike Flanagan to Toronto Blue Jays for Pitcher Oswald Peraza and a player to be named later, August 31, 1987.
§On disabled list, April 18 to May 16 and June 30, 1988 through remainder of season.
xOn disabled list, May 27, 1989 through remainder of season.

HENSLEY FILEMON MEULENS

Born June 23, 1967, at Curacao, Netherlands Antilles.
Height, 6.03. Weight, 212.
Throws and bats righthanded.

Major League stolen bases: 1990 (1).
Led International League in total bases with 245 in 1990.
Led Gulf Coast League batters in strikeouts with 66 in 1986.
Tied for Eastern League lead in being hit by pitch with 9 in 1989.
Led Gulf Coast League third basemen in total chances with 178 in 1986.
Tied for Eastern League lead in double plays by third basemen with 18 in 1988.
Named International League Player of the Year, 1990.

Year	Club	League	Pos.	G.	AB.	R.	H.	2B.	3B.	HR.	RBI.	B.A.	PO.	A.	E.	F.A.
1986—Sarasota Yankees	Gulf C.	3B	59	219	36	51	10	4	4	31	.233	★40	★118	20	.888
1987—Prince William	Carol.	3B	116	430	76	129	23	2	28	103	.300	96	224	★37	.896
1987—Fort Lauderdale	Fla. St.	3B	17	58	2	10	3	0	0	2	.172	18	37	7	.887
1988—Albany	East.	3B	79	278	50	68	9	1	13	40	.245	57	162	23	.905
1988—Columbus	Int.	3B	55	209	27	48	9	1	6	22	.230	39	111	14	.915
1989—Albany	East.	3B	104	335	55	86	8	2	11	45	.257	67	172	★29	.892
1989—Columbus	Int.	3B	14	45	8	13	4	0	1	3	.289	11	27	3	.927
1989—New York	Amer.	3B	8	28	2	5	0	0	0	1	.179	5	23	4	.875
1990—Columbus	Int.	OF-1B-3B	136	480	81	137	20	5	26	96	.285	359	51	13	.969
1990—New York	Amer.	OF	23	83	12	20	7	0	3	10	.241	49	3	2	.963
Major League Totals—2 Years			31	111	14	25	7	0	3	11	.225	54	26	6	.930

Signed as free agent by New York Yankees' organization, October 31, 1985.

BRIAN S. MEYER

Born January 29, 1963, at Camden, N. J.
Height, 6.01. Weight, 190.
Throws and bats righthanded.
Attended Rollins College, Winter Park, Fla.
Nephew of Jack Meyer, pitcher with Philadelphia Phillies, 1955 through 1961.

Major League saves: 1989 (1), 1990 (1). Total—2.
Led Pacific Coast League in games finished in relief with 45 and tied for lead in intentional bases on balls issued with 8 in 1990.
Led Southern League in games finished in relief with 59 in 1988.
Led Florida State League in saves with 25 in 1987.
Led New York-Pennsylvania League in games finished in relief with 28 in 1986.

Year	Club	League	G.	IP.	W.	L.	Pct.	H.	R.	ER.	SO.	BB.	ERA.
1986—Auburn	NYP	★32	56⅔	5	2	.714	44	14	9	66	10	1.43
1987—Osceola	Florida St.	52	77	8	9	.471	58	26	17	58	23	1.99
1988—Columbus	Southern	62	83⅓	4	3	.571	61	23	21	68	36	2.27
1988—Houston	National	8	12⅓	0	0	.000	9	2	2	10	4	1.46
1989—Tucson	P. Coast	58	80⅓	5	4	.556	81	36	25	56	33	2.80
1989—Houston	National	12	18	0	1	.000	16	13	9	13	13	4.50

Year	Club	League	G.	IP.	W.	L.	Pct.	H.	R.	ER.	SO.	BB.	ERA.
1990—Tucson		P. Coast	64	100	5	7	.417	91	43	33	54	38	2.97
1990—Houston		National	14	20⅓	0	4	.000	16	7	5	6	6	2.21
Major League Totals—3 Years			34	50⅔	0	5	.000	41	22	16	29	23	2.84

Selected by Houston Astros' organization in 16th round of free-agent draft, June 2, 1986.

GARY ROGER MIELKE

Name pronounced MILL-kee.

Born January 28, 1963, at St. James, Minn.
Height, 6.03. Weight, 199.
Throws and bats righthanded.
Attended Mankato State University, Mankato, Minn.

Major League saves: 1989 (1).

Year	Club	League	G.	IP.	W.	L.	Pct.	H.	R.	ER.	SO.	BB.	ERA.
1985—Sarasota Rangers		Gulf Coast	19	37⅔	2	2	.500	25	8	4	49	14	0.96
1986—Tulsa		Texas	24	47	2	0	1.000	41	22	18	48	32	3.45
1986—Salem		Carolina	37	52⅔	4	4	.500	48	25	23	49	20	3.93
1987—Tulsa		Texas	28	45⅓	3	3	.500	34	18	15	46	10	2.98
1987—Oklahoma City		Am. Assoc.	28	37⅓	2	4	.333	36	20	17	34	16	4.10
1987—Texas		American	3	3	0	0	.000	3	2	2	3	1	6.00
1988—Oklahoma City		Am. Assoc.	38	59⅔	6	5	.545	50	21	19	42	22	2.87
1989—Oklahoma City		Am. Assoc.	18	40⅔	3	3	.500	28	7	5	40	10	1.11
1989—Texas		American	43	49⅔	1	0	1.000	52	18	18	26	25	3.26
1990—Texas†		American	33	41	0	3	.000	42	17	17	13	15	3.73
1990—Oklahoma City‡		Am. Assoc.	5	5⅔	0	0	.000	5	2	1	7	4	1.59
Major League Totals—3 Years			79	93⅔	1	3	.250	97	37	37	42	41	3.56

Selected by Texas Rangers' organization in 26th round of free-agent draft, June 3, 1985.

†On disabled list, May 28 to July 24, 1990; included rehabilitation disability assignment to Oklahoma City, July 12 to July 24, 1990.

‡Granted free agency, November 15, 1990.

ROBERT MILACKI

(Bob)

Born July 28, 1964, at Trenton, N. J.
Height, 6.04. Weight, 235.
Throws and bats righthanded.
Attended Yavapai College, Prescott, Ariz.

Lost no-hitter in 12th inning against Chattanooga, May 28, 1987.
Tied for American League lead in games started by pitchers with 36 in 1989.
Led International League in complete games with 11 and tied for lead in shutouts with 3 in 1988.

Year	Club	League	G.	IP.	W.	L.	Pct.	H.	R.	ER.	SO.	BB.	ERA.
1984—Hagerstown†		Carolina	15	77⅔	4	5	.444	69	35	29	62	48	3.36
1985—Daytona Beach‡		Florida St.	8	38⅓	1	4	.200	32	23	17	24	26	3.99
1985—Hagerstown§		Carolina	7	40⅔	3	2	.600	32	16	12	37	22	2.66
1986—Hagerstown		Carolina	13	60⅔	4	5	.444	69	59	32	46	37	4.75
1986—Miami		Florida St.	12	67⅓	4	4	.500	70	36	28	41	27	3.74
1986—Charlotte		Southern	1	5⅓	0	1	.000	7	4	4	6	4	6.75
1987—Charlotte		Southern	29	148	11	9	.550	168	86	75	101	66	4.56
1988—Charlotte		Southern	5	37⅔	3	1	.750	26	11	10	29	12	2.39
1988—Rochester		Int'national	24	176⅔	12	8	.600	174	62	53	103	65	2.70
1988—Baltimore		American	3	25	2	0	1.000	9	2	2	18	9	0.72
1989—Baltimore		American	37	243	14	12	.538	233	105	101	113	88	3.74
1990—Baltimore x		American	27	135⅓	5	8	.385	143	73	67	60	61	4.46
Major League Totals—3 Years			67	403⅓	21	20	.512	385	180	170	191	158	3.79

Selected by San Diego Padres' organization in 1st round (ninth player selected) of free-agent draft, January 11, 1983.

Selected by Baltimore Orioles' organization in secondary phase of free-agent draft, June 6, 1983.

†On disabled list, July 2 to August 28, 1984.
‡On disabled list, April 12 to May 11, 1985.
§On disabled list, July 5 to August 24, 1985.
xOn disabled list, July 31 to September 1, 1990.

KEITH ALAN MILLER

Born June 12, 1963, at Midland, Mich.
Height, 5.11. Weight, 180.
Throws and bats righthanded.
Attended Oral Roberts University, Tulsa, Okla.

Major League stolen bases: 1987 (8), 1989 (6), 1990 (16). Total—30.
Tied for Texas League lead in being hit by pitch with 7 in 1986.

Year	Club	League	Pos.	G.	AB.	R.	H.	2B.	3B.	HR.	RBI.	B.A.	PO.	A.	E.	F.A.
1985—Lynchburg	Carol.	3B-2B-OF	89	325	51	98	16	5	7	54	.302	103	203	25	.924
1985—Jackson	Texas	2B-SS	46	165	17	37	8	1	3	22	.224	108	132	8	.968
1986—Jackson†	Texas	2B	94	353	80	116	23	4	5	36	.329	198	272	19	.961
1987—Tidewater	Int.	2B-OF	53	202	29	50	9	1	6	22	.248	112	129	5	.980
1987—New York‡	Nat.	2B	25	51	14	19	2	2	0	1	.373	21	38	2	.967

Year Club	League	Pos.	G.	AB.	R.	H.	2B.	3B.	HR.	RBI.	B.A.	PO.	A.	E.	F.A.
1988—Tidewater............. Int.		2-S-3-O	42	171	23	48	11	1	1	15	.281	81	111	12	.941
1988—New York............. Nat.		2-S-3-O	40	70	9	15	1	1	1	5	.214	34	24	5	.921
1989—Tidewater............. Int.		2-O-S-3	48	184	33	49	8	2	1	15	.266	89	109	8	.961
1989—New York............. Nat.		2-O-S-3	57	143	15	33	7	0	1	7	.231	90	52	5	.966
1990—New York§........... Nat.		OF-2B-SS	88	233	42	60	8	0	1	12	.258	168	21	4	.979
Major League Totals—4 Years...............			210	497	80	127	18	3	3	25	.256	313	135	16	.966

Selected by Cleveland Indians' organization in 24th round of free-agent draft, June 5, 1981.

Selected by New York Yankees' organization in 2nd round of free-agent draft, June 4, 1984 (contract was later voided after it was discovered he had a pre-existing knee injury).

Signed as free agent by New York Mets' organization, September 6, 1984.

†On disabled list, April 8 to May 20, 1986.

‡On disabled list, June 29 to September 1, 1987; included rehabilitation disability assignment to Tidewater, August 21 to September 1, 1987.

§On disabled list, April 25 to May 17 and August 15 to September 1, 1990.

MICHAEL DARREN MILLER
(Mike)

Born April 14, 1967, at Kirkwood, Mo.
Height, 6.04. Weight, 200.
Throws and bats righthanded.
Attended St. Louis Community College at Meramec, Kirkwood, Mo.

Year Club	League	G.	IP.	W.	L.	Pct.	H.	R.	ER.	SO.	BB.	ERA.
1987—Little Falls.................................. NYP		13	76⅓	2	5	.286	87	40	34	44	12	4.01
1988—Columbia .... S. Atlantic		31	163⅓	14	8	.636	146	64	50	98	28	2.76
1988—St. Lucie .... Florida St.		1	7	0	1	.000	2	1	0	5	2	0.00
1989—St. Lucie .... Florida St.		26	★200⅓	13	6	.684	177	64	53	130	28	2.38
1990—Jackson† .... Texas		22	139	7	7	.500	113	54	45	95	32	2.91

Selected by New York Mets' organization in 4th round of free-agent draft, June 2, 1987.

†Claimed on waivers by Boston Red Sox, November 20, 1990.

RANDALL ANDRE MILLIGAN
(Randy)

Born November 27, 1961, at San Diego, Calif.
Height, 6.01. Weight, 235.
Throws and bats righthanded.
Attended San Diego Mesa College, San Diego, Calif.

Major League stolen bases: 1988 (1), 1989 (9), 1990 (6). Total—16.

Hit three home runs in a game, June 9, 1990.

Led International League batters in total bases with 272, bases on balls received with 91 and tied for lead in intentional bases on balls received with 10 in 1987.

Named Minor League Player of the Year by THE SPORTING NEWS, 1987.

Named International League Player of the Year, 1987.

Year Club	League	Pos.	G.	AB.	R.	H.	2B.	3B.	HR.	RBI.	B.A.	PO.	A.	E.	F.A.
1981—Shelby.................... S. Atl.		OF-SS	130	406	90	115	16	6	7	58	.283	174	5	14	.927
1982—Lynchburg............ Carol.		OF-1B	118	420	63	113	10	6	5	55	.269	341	12	11	.970
1983—Lynchburg............ Carol.		1B-OF	106	349	60	102	13	5	5	56	.292	558	41	13	.979
1984—Jackson† .... Texas		1B	62	193	32	53	5	0	9	34	.275	475	67	8	.985
1985—Jackson .... Texas		1B	119	391	60	121	22	2	13	77	.309	726	49	11	.986
1986—Tidewater............. Int.		1B	21	60	3	5	0	0	0	3	.083	60	4	1	.985
1986—Jackson .... Texas		1B	78	269	53	85	11	3	7	53	.316	684	62	6	.992
1987—Tidewater............. Int.		1B-OF	136	457	★99	149	28	4	29	★103	★.326	858	88	10	.990
1987—New York‡........... Nat.		PH-PR	3	1	0	0	0	0	0	0	.000	0	0	0	.000
1988—Pittsburgh.............. Nat.		1B-OF	40	82	10	18	5	0	3	8	.220	213	15	3	.987
1988—Buffalo§ .... A. A.		1B-OF	63	221	37	61	15	3	2	30	.276	551	48	5	.992
1989—Baltimore .... Amer.		1B	124	365	56	98	23	5	12	45	.268	914	83	5	.995
1990—Baltimore x.......... Amer.		1B	109	362	64	96	20	1	20	60	.265	846	87	9	.990
National League Totals—2 Years...........			43	83	10	18	5	0	3	8	.217	213	15	3	.987
American League Totals—2 Years			233	727	120	194	43	6	32	105	.267	1760	170	14	.993
Major League Totals—4 Years................			276	810	130	212	48	6	35	113	.262	1973	185	17	.992

Selected by New York Mets' organization in 1st round (third player selected) of free-agent draft, January 13, 1981.

†On disabled list, July 11, 1984 through remainder of season.

‡Traded with Pitcher Scott Henion to Pittsburgh Pirates for Catcher Mackey Sasser and Pitcher Tim Drummond, March 26, 1988.

§Traded to Baltimore Orioles for a player to be named later, November 9, 1988; Pittsburgh acquired Pitcher Pete Blohm to complete deal, December 7, 1988.

xOn disabled list, August 10 to September 28, 1990.

ALAN BERNARD MILLS

Born October 18, 1966, at Lakeland, Fla.
Height, 6.01. Weight, 190.
Throws right and bats left and righthanded.
Attended Polk Community College, Winter Haven, Fla.

Year Club	League	G.	IP.	W.	L.	Pct.	H.	R.	ER.	SO.	BB.	ERA.
1986—Salem†	Northwest	14	83⅔	6	6	.500	77	58	43	50	60	4.63
1987—Prince William	Carolina	35	85⅔	2	11	.154	102	75	58	53	64	6.09
1988—Prince William	Carolina	42	93⅔	3	8	.273	93	56	43	59	43	4.13
1989—Prince William	Carolina	26	39⅔	6	1	.857	22	5	4	44	13	0.91
1989—Fort Lauderdale	Florida St.	22	31	1	4	.200	40	15	13	25	9	3.77
1990—New York	American	36	41⅔	1	5	.167	48	21	19	24	33	4.10
1990—Columbus	Int'national	17	29⅓	3	3	.500	22	11	11	30	14	3.38
Major League Totals—1 Year		36	41⅔	1	5	.167	48	21	19	24	33	4.10

Selected by Boston Red Sox' organization in 1st round (13th player selected) of free-agent draft, January 14, 1986.
Selected by California Angels' organization in secondary phase of free-agent draft, June 2, 1986.
†Traded to New York Yankees' organization, June 22, 1987, completing deal in which California Angels traded Pitcher Ron Romanick and a player to be named later to New York for Catcher Butch Wynegar, December 19, 1986.

BLAS MINOR JR.

Born March 20, 1966, at Merced, Calif.
Height, 6.03. Weight, 200.
Throws and bats righthanded.
Attended Merced College, Merced, Calif., and
Arizona State University, Tempe, Ariz.

Year Club	League	G.	IP.	W.	L.	Pct.	H.	R.	ER.	SO.	BB.	ERA.
1988—Princeton	Ap'lachian	15	16⅓	0	1	.000	18	10	8	23	5	4.41
1989—Salem	Carolina	39	86⅔	3	5	.375	91	43	35	62	31	3.63
1990—Harrisburg	Eastern	38	94	6	4	.600	81	41	32	98	29	3.06
1990—Buffalo	Am. Assoc.	1	2⅔	0	1	.000	2	1	1	2	2	3.38

Selected by Kansas City Royals' organization in 11th round of free-agent draft, January 9, 1985.
Selected by Philadelphia Phillies' organization in secondary phase of free-agent draft, June 3, 1985.
Selected by Philadelphia Phillies' organization in secondary phase of free-agent draft, January 14, 1986.
Selected by Pittsburgh Pirates' organization in 6th round of free-agent draft, June 1, 1988.

GREGORY BRIAN MINTON
(Greg)

Born July 29, 1951, at Lubbock, Tex.
Height, 6.02. Weight, 207.
Throws right and bats left and righthanded.
Attended San Diego Mesa College, San Diego, Calif.

Major League saves: 1979 (4), 1980 (19), 1981 (21), 1982 (30), 1983 (22), 1984 (19), 1985 (4), 1986 (5), 1987 (11), 1988 (7), 1989 (8). Total—150.
Led National League in intentional bases on balls issued with 20 in 1984 and 18 in 1985.
Led National League in games finished in relief with 44 in 1981 and 66 in 1982.
Tied for American League lead in intentional bases on balls issued with 10 in 1988.
Led Pacific Coast League in wild pitches with 18 in 1977.
Led Pacific Coast League in balks with 6 in 1975.

Year Club	League	G.	IP.	W.	L.	Pct.	H.	R.	ER.	SO.	BB.	ERA.
1970—Billings†	Pioneer	16	40	1	4	.200	37	23	14	36	16	3.15
1971—Waterloo	Midwest	27	124	11	6	.647	118	52	42	117	55	3.05
1972—San José‡	California	28	178	12	12	.500	182	117	78	153	77	3.94
1973—Phoenix	P. Coast	5	13	0	0	.000	11	6	6	4	8	4.15
1973—Amarillo	Texas	38	122	5	11	.313	138	87	61	77	48	4.50
1974—Fresno	California	13	96	10	1	.909	85	32	24	81	18	2.25
1974—Amarillo	Texas	6	29	1	4	.200	42	26	19	21	10	5.90
1975—Phoenix	P. Coast	42	177	10	6	.625	178	73	51	76	76	2.59
1975—San Francisco	National	4	17	1	1	.500	19	14	13	6	11	6.88
1976—San Francisco	National	10	26	0	3	.000	32	18	14	7	12	4.85
1976—Phoenix§	P. Coast	13	74	4	5	.444	91	57	46	31	32	5.59
1977—Phoenix	P. Coast	29	161	14	6	*.700	188	93	87	77	70	4.86
1977—San Francisco	National	2	14	1	1	.500	14	8	7	5	4	4.50
1978—Phoenix	P. Coast	14	92	7	4	.636	97	54	46	32	38	4.50
1978—San Francisco	National	11	16	0	1	.000	22	14	14	6	8	7.88
1979—San Francisco x	National	46	80	4	3	.571	59	25	16	33	27	1.80
1980—San Francisco	National	68	91	4	6	.400	81	28	25	42	34	2.47
1981—San Francisco	National	55	84	4	5	.444	84	28	27	29	36	2.89
1982—San Francisco	National	78	123	10	4	.714	108	29	25	58	42	1.83
1983—San Francisco	National	73	106⅔	7	11	.389	117	51	42	38	47	3.54
1984—San Francisco	National	74	124⅓	4	9	.308	130	60	52	48	57	3.76
1985—San Francisco	National	68	96⅔	5	4	.556	98	42	38	37	54	3.54
1986—San Francisco y	National	48	68⅔	4	4	.500	63	35	30	34	34	3.93
1987—San Francisco z	National	15	23⅓	1	0	1.000	30	9	9	9	10	3.47
1987—California a	American	41	76	5	4	.556	71	28	26	35	29	3.08
1988—Palm Springs b	California	2	4	0	0	.000	3	0	0	4	1	0.00
1988—California	American	44	79	4	5	.444	67	37	25	46	34	2.85
1989—California cd	American	62	90	4	3	.571	76	22	22	42	37	2.20
1990—California e	American	11	15⅓	1	1	.500	11	4	4	4	7	2.35
1990—Midland f	Texas	4	5⅔	0	0	.000	3	0	0	1	1	0.00
National League Totals—13 Years		552	870⅔	45	52	.464	857	361	312	352	376	3.23
American League Totals—4 Years		158	260⅓	14	13	.519	225	91	77	127	107	2.66
Major League Totals—16 Years		710	1131	59	65	.476	1082	452	389	479	483	3.10

Selected by Kansas City Royals' organization in 3rd round of free-agent draft, January 17, 1970.
†Appeared in two games as an outfielder with one putout.
‡Traded to San Francisco Giants for Catcher Fran Healy, April 2, 1973.
§On disabled list, July 24 to August 5, 1976.
xOn disabled list, March 26 to May 31, 1979.
yOn disabled list, July 22 to August 14, 1986.
zReleased, May 28, 1987; signed by California Angels, June 1, 1987.
aGranted free agency, November 9, 1987; re-signed by Angels, December 3, 1987.
bOn California disabled list, March 26 to May 11, 1988; included rehabilitation disability assignment to Palm Springs, May 7 to May 11, 1988.
cOn disabled list, June 23 to July 8, 1989.
dReleased, February 3, 1990; re-signed by Angels, February 21, 1990.
eOn disabled list, April 18 to July 6 and July 9 to September 1, 1990; included rehabilitation disability assignment to Midland, August 21 to August 31, 1990.
fGranted free agency, November 5, 1990.

ALL-STAR GAME RECORD

Year	League	IP.	W.	L.	Pct.	H.	R.	ER.	SO.	BB.	ERA.
1982—National		⅔	0	0	.000	0	0	0	0	1	0.00

GINO MICHAEL MINUTELLI

Born May 23, 1964, at Wilmington, Del.
Height, 6.00. Weight, 185.
Throws and bats lefthanded.
Attended Southwestern College, Chula Vista, Calif.

Led Southern League in balks with 13 in 1990.

Year	Club	League	G.	IP.	W.	L.	Pct.	H.	R.	ER.	SO.	BB.	ERA.
1985—Tri-Cities		Northwest	20	57	4	•8	.333	61	57	51	79	57	8.05
1986—Cedar Rapids		Midwest	27	152⅔	15	5	.750	133	73	62	149	76	3.66
1987—Tampa		Florida St.	17	104⅓	7	6	.538	98	51	44	70	48	3.80
1987—Vermont		Eastern	6	39⅔	4	1	.800	34	15	14	39	16	3.18
1988—Chattanooga†		Southern	2	5⅔	0	1	.000	6	2	1	3	4	1.59
1989—Plant City‡		Gulf Coast	1	1	0	0	.000	0	0	0	0	1	0.00
1989—Chattanooga		Southern	6	29	1	1	.500	28	19	17	20	23	5.28
1990—Chattanooga		Southern	17	108⅓	9	5	.643	106	52	48	75	46	3.99
1990—Nashville		Am. Assoc.	11	78⅓	5	2	.714	65	34	28	61	31	3.22
1990—Cincinnati		National	2	1	0	0	.000	0	1	1	0	2	9.00
Major League Totals—1 Year			2	1	0	0	.000	0	1	1	0	2	9.00

Signed as free agent by Cincinnati Reds' organization, May 19, 1985.
†On disabled list, April 12 to April 23 and April 27, 1988 through remainder of season.
‡On disabled list, April 1 to August 1, 1989.

PAUL THOMAS MIRABELLA

Born March 20, 1954, at Belleville, N. J.
Height, 6.02. Weight, 185.
Throws and bats lefthanded.
Attended Montclair State University, Upper Montclair, N. J.

Major League saves: 1978 (1), 1982 (3), 1984 (3), 1987 (2), 1988 (4). Total—13.
Tied for Pacific Coast League lead in balks with 4 in 1978.
Tied for Texas League lead in shutouts with 4 and games started by pitchers with 26 in 1977.
Tied for Western Carolinas League lead in balks with 5 in 1976.

Year	Club	League	G.	IP.	W.	L.	Pct.	H.	R.	ER.	SO.	BB.	ERA.
1976—Asheville		W. Carol.	22	149	10	7	.588	149	77	66	*136	69	3.99
1977—Tulsa		Texas	26	176	12	7	.632	167	90	75	112	70	3.83
1978—Tucson		P. Coast	22	143	9	6	.600	158	77	63	85	68	3.97
1978—Texas†		American	10	28	3	2	.600	30	18	18	23	17	5.79
1979—Columbus		Int'national	22	144	11	7	.611	129	75	62	98	50	3.88
1979—New York‡		American	10	14	0	4	.000	16	15	14	4	10	9.00
1980—Syracuse		Int'national	4	31	1	2	.333	28	13	9	23	8	2.61
1980—Toronto		American	33	131	5	12	.294	151	73	63	53	66	4.33
1981—Syracuse		Int'national	22	153	11	7	.611	150	63	52	79	53	3.06
1981—Toronto§x		American	8	15	0	0	.000	20	16	12	9	7	7.20
1982—Texas y		American	40	50⅔	1	1	.500	46	28	27	29	22	4.80
1983—Rochester		Int'national	19	76⅓	3	5	.375	87	44	31	32	29	3.66
1983—Baltimore z		American	3	9⅔	0	0	.000	9	6	6	4	7	5.59
1983—Portland a		P. Coast	5	14⅓	0	1	.000	19	13	12	11	10	7.53
1984—Seattle		American	52	68	2	5	.286	74	39	33	41	32	4.37
1985—Calgary		P. Coast	53	68⅓	4	4	.556	84	34	31	42	29	4.08
1985—Seattle		American	10	13⅔	0	0	.000	9	4	2	8	4	1.32
1986—Seattle		American	8	6⅓	0	0	.000	13	7	6	6	3	8.53
1986—Calgary b		P. Coast	47	68⅓	3	4	.429	92	48	45	42	24	5.93
1987—Denver		Am. Assoc.	25	39	5	1	.833	39	11	10	28	10	2.31
1987—Milwaukee		American	29	29⅓	2	1	.667	30	20	16	14	16	4.91
1988—Denver		Am. Assoc.	8	9⅔	0	0	.000	9	3	1	7	4	0.93
1988—Milwaukee c		American	38	60	2	2	.500	44	12	11	33	21	1.65
1989—Milwaukee d		American	13	15⅓	0	0	.000	18	14	13	6	8	7.63
1989—Beloit e		Midwest	2	5	0	0	.000	3	0	0	6	0	0.00
1990—Milwaukee f		American	44	59	4	2	.667	66	32	26	28	27	3.97
Major League Totals—13 Years			298	500	19	29	.396	526	284	247	258	239	4.45

Selected by Minnesota Twins' organization in 16th round of free-agent draft, June 4, 1975.

Selected by Texas Rangers' organization in secondary phase of free-agent draft, January 7, 1976.

†Traded with Pitchers Mike Griffin and Dave Righetti and Outfielders Juan Beniquez and Greg Jemison to New York Yankees for Pitchers Sparky Lyle, Larry McCall and Dave Rajsich, Catcher Mike Heath, Shortstop Domingo Ramos and cash, November 10, 1978.

‡Traded with First Baseman Chris Chambliss and Infielder Damaso Garcia to Toronto Blue Jays for Catcher Rick Cerone, Pitcher Tom Underwood and Outfielder Ted Wilborn, November 1, 1979.

§Traded to Chicago Cubs' organization for a player to be named later, December 28, 1981; Toronto Blue Jays' organization acquired Pitcher Dave Geisel to complete deal, March 25, 1982.

xTraded with a player to be named later and cash to Texas Rangers for Second Baseman Bump Wills, March 26, 1982; Texas organization acquired Pitcher Paul Semall to complete deal, April 21, 1982.

yReleased, March 26, 1983; signed by Rochester (Baltimore Orioles' organization), April 16, 1983.

zSold to Portland (Philadelphia Phillies' organization), August 12, 1983.

aGranted free agency, October 20, 1983; signed by Seattle Mariners, January 23, 1984.

bGranted free agency, October 15, 1986; signed by Denver (Milwaukee Brewers' organization), February 14, 1987.

cOn disabled list, August 15 to August 30, 1988.

dOn disabled list, April 25 to May 10 and May 22 to September 1, 1989; included rehabilitation disability assignment to Beloit, August 23 to September 1, 1989.

eReleased, November 9, 1989; re-signed by Brewers, April 8, 1990.

fGranted free agency, November 5, 1990.

ANGEL MIRANDA

Born November 9, 1969, at Arecibo, Puerto Rico.
Height, 6.01. Weight, 160.
Throws and bats lefthanded.

Year	Club	League	G.	IP.	W.	L.	Pct.	H.	R.	ER.	SO.	BB.	ERA.
1987—Butte†-Helena	Pioneer	25	43⅓	1	2	.333	27	22	15	60	26	3.12
1988—Stockton	California	16	26⅓	0	1	.000	20	30	21	36	37	7.18
1988—Helena	Pioneer	14	60⅔	5	2	.714	54	32	26	75	58	3.86
1989—Beloit	Midwest	43	63	6	5	.545	39	13	6	88	32	0.86
1990—Stockton	California	52	108⅓	9	4	.692	75	37	32	138	49	2.66

Signed as free agent by Milwaukee Brewers' organization, March 4, 1987.

†Loaned to Butte (Co-op), March 4, 1987; returned, Summer, 1987.

JOHN KYLE MITCHELL

Born August 11, 1965, at Dickson, Tenn.
Height, 6.02. Weight, 189.
Throws and bats righthanded.
Brother of Charlie Mitchell, pitcher in Boston Red Sox' and
Minnesota Twins' organization, 1982 through 1986.

Pitched 4-0 no-hit victory against Indianapolis, June 27, 1988 (first game).
Led Florida State League in wild pitches with 21 in 1984.
Named International League Pitcher of the Year, 1986.

Year	Club	League	G.	IP.	W.	L.	Pct.	H.	R.	ER.	SO.	BB.	ERA.
1983—Elmira	NYP	16	75⅓	5	6	.455	78	57	41	72	41	4.90
1984—Winter Haven	Florida St.	27	★183⅔	16	9	.640	160	84	64	109	66	3.14
1985—New Britain†	Eastern	26	190⅓	12	8	.600	143	71	57	108	61	2.70
1986—Tidewater	Int'national	27	172⅓	12	9	.571	162	78	65	83	59	3.39
1986—New York	National	4	10	0	1	.000	10	4	4	2	4	3.60
1987—Tidewater	Int'national	8	48⅔	3	2	.600	44	24	18	16	20	3.33
1987—New York	National	20	111⅔	3	6	.333	124	64	51	57	36	4.11
1988—Tidewater	Int'national	27	★190	10	9	.526	164	76	60	65	45	2.84
1988—New York	National	1	1	0	0	.000	2	0	0	1	1	0.00
1989—Tidewater	Int'national	26	178⅓	11	11	.500	169	78	60	86	57	3.03
1989—New York‡	National	2	3	0	1	.000	3	7	2	4	4	6.00
1990—Baltimore	American	24	114⅓	6	6	.500	133	63	59	43	48	4.64
1990—Rochester	Int'national	8	46	5	0	1.000	39	9	8	15	9	1.57
National League Totals—4 Years		27	125⅔	3	8	.273	139	75	57	64	45	4.08
American League Totals—1 Year		24	114⅓	6	6	.500	133	63	59	43	48	4.64
Major League Totals—5 Years		51	240	9	14	.391	272	138	116	107	93	4.35

Selected by Boston Red Sox' organization in 7th round of free-agent draft, June 6, 1983.

†Traded with Pitchers Bob Ojeda, Tom McCarthy and Chris Bayer to New York Mets for Pitchers Calvin Schiraldi and Wes Gardner and Outfielders John Christensen and LaSchelle Tarver, November 13, 1985.

‡Traded with Outfielder Joaquin Contreras to Baltimore Orioles for Outfielder Keith Hughes and Pitcher Cesar Mejia, December 5, 1989.

KEVIN DARRELL MITCHELL

Born January 13, 1962, at San Diego, Calif.
Height, 5.11. Weight, 210.
Throws and bats righthanded.
Cousin of Keith Mitchell, outfielder in Atlanta Braves' organization.

Holds major league record for most intentional bases on balls, righthanded batter, season (32), 1989.
Major League stolen bases: 1986 (3), 1987 (9), 1988 (5), 1989 (3), 1990 (4). Total—24.
Hit three home runs in a game, May 25, 1990.
Led National League in total bases with 345, intentional bases on balls received with 32 and slugging percentage with .635 in 1989.
Led International League third basemen in assists with 215 in 1984.

Named Major League Player of the Year by THE SPORTING NEWS, 1989.
Named National League Player of the Year by THE SPORTING NEWS, 1989.
Named National League Most Valuable Player by Baseball Writers' Association of America, 1989.
Named outfielder on THE SPORTING NEWS National League All-Star Team, 1989.
Named outfielder on THE SPORTING NEWS National League Silver Slugger team, 1989.

Year Club	League	Pos.	G.	AB.	R.	H.	2B.	3B.	HR.	RBI.	B.A.	PO.	A.	E.	F.A.
1981—Kingsport	Appal.	3B-OF	62	221	39	74	9	2	7	45	.335	44	102	18	.890
1982—Lynchburg†	Carol.	3B	29	85	19	27	5	1	1	16	.318	11	33	10	.815
1983—Jackson	Texas	*3B-OF	120	441	75	132	25	2	15	85	.299	81	*224	21	.936
1984—Tidewater	Int.	3B-1B-OF	120	432	51	105	21	3	10	54	.243	114	220	22	.938
1984—New York	Nat.	3B	7	14	0	3	0	0	0	1	.214	1	4	1	.833
1985—Tidewater‡	Int.	*3B-1B	95	348	44	101	24	2	9	43	.290	56	209	*22	.923
1986—New York§	Nat.	O-S-3-1	108	328	51	91	22	2	12	43	.277	158	69	10	.958
1987—S.D. x-S.F.	Nat.	3B-OF-SS	131	464	68	130	20	2	22	70	.280	76	240	15	.955
1988—San Francisco	Nat.	3B-OF	148	505	60	127	25	7	19	80	.251	118	205	22	.936
1989—San Francisco	Nat.	OF-3B	154	543	100	158	34	6	*47	*125	.291	305	10	7	.978
1990—San Francisco	Nat.	OF	140	524	90	152	24	2	35	93	.290	295	9	9	.971
Major League Totals—6 Years			688	2378	369	661	125	19	135	412	.278	953	537	64	.959

Signed as free agent by New York Mets' organization, November 16, 1980.
†On disabled list, July 21, 1982 through remainder of season.
‡On disabled list, July 12 to July 30, 1985.
§Traded with Outfielders Shawn Abner and Stanley Jefferson and Pitchers Kevin Armstrong and Kevin Brown to San Diego Padres for Outfielder Kevin McReynolds, Pitcher Gene Walter and Infielder Adam Ging, December 11, 1986.
xTraded with Pitchers Dave Dravecky and Craig Lefferts to San Francisco Giants for Third Baseman Chris Brown and Pitchers Keith Comstock, Mark Davis and Mark Grant, July 4, 1987.

CHAMPIONSHIP SERIES RECORD

Shares National League Championship Series record for most at-bats, series (30), 1987.

Year Club	League	Pos.	G.	AB.	R.	H.	2B.	3B.	HR.	RBI.	B.A.	PO.	A.	E.	F.A.
1986—New York	Nat.	OF	2	8	1	2	0	0	0	0	.250	3	0	0	1.000
1987—San Francisco	Nat.	3B	7	30	2	8	1	0	1	2	.267	4	11	1	.938
1989—San Francisco	Nat.	OF	5	17	5	6	0	0	2	7	.353	15	1	1	.941
Championship Series Totals—3 Years			14	55	8	16	1	0	3	9	.291	22	12	2	.944

WORLD SERIES RECORD

Year Club	League	Pos.	G.	AB.	R.	H.	2B.	3B.	HR.	RBI.	B.A.	PO.	A.	E.	F.A.
1986—New York	Nat.	PH-O-DH	5	8	1	2	0	0	0	0	.250	0	2	0	1.000
1989—San Francisco	Nat.	OF	4	17	2	5	0	0	1	2	.294	10	0	1	.909
World Series Totals—2 Years			9	25	3	7	0	0	1	2	.280	10	2	1	.923

ALL-STAR GAME RECORD

Year League	Pos.	AB.	R.	H.	2B.	3B.	HR.	RBI.	B.A.	PO.	A.	E.	F.A.
1989—National	OF	4	1	2	0	0	0	1	.500	0	0	0	.000
1990—National	OF	2	0	0	0	0	0	0	.000	1	0	0	1.000
All-Star Game Totals—2 Years		6	1	2	0	0	0	1	.333	1	0	0	1.000

KEVIN PAUL MMAHAT

Name pronounced Ma-ma-hat.
Born November 9, 1964, at Memphis, Tenn.
Height, 6.05. Weight, 220.
Throws and bats lefthanded.
Attended Tulane University, New Orleans, La.

Year Club	League	G.	IP.	W.	L.	Pct.	H.	R.	ER.	SO.	BB.	ERA.
1987—Sarasota Rangers†	Gulf Coast	12	53⅓	3	3	.500	37	22	19	60	30	3.21
1988—Albany	Eastern	6	38½	2	3	.400	30	19	17	32	24	3.99
1988—Fort Lauderdale	Florida St.	17	102⅓	7	7	.500	95	60	47	78	57	4.13
1989—Albany	Eastern	8	51⅓	5	1	.833	35	11	9	48	19	1.58
1989—Columbus	Int'national	15	82	3	4	.429	70	44	35	50	49	3.84
1989—New York	American	4	7⅔	0	2	.000	13	12	11	3	8	12.91
1990—Columbus	Int'national	20	115	11	5	.688	99	52	48	81	61	3.76
Major League Totals—1 Year		4	7⅔	0	2	.000	13	12	11	3	8	12.91

Selected by Texas Rangers' organization in 31st round of free-agent draft, June 2, 1987.
†Sold to Albany (New York Yankees' organization), June 20, 1988.

DALE ROBERT MOHORCIC

Name pronounced Muh-HORR-sick.
Born January 25, 1956, at Cleveland, O.
Height, 6.03. Weight, 220.
Throws and bats righthanded.
Attended Cuyahoga Community College (Metro), Cleveland, O.,
and Cleveland State University, Cleveland, O.

Shares major league record for most consecutive games pitched as relief pitcher (13), August 6 through 20, 1986.
Major League saves: 1986 (7), 1987 (16), 1988 (6), 1989 (2), 1990 (2). Total—33.
Tied for Northwest League lead in shutouts with 2 in 1978.

Year Club	League	G.	IP.	W.	L.	Pct.	H.	R.	ER.	SO.	BB.	ERA.
1978—Victoria†	Northwest	14	98	6	5	.545	84	39	22	73	36	2.02
1979—Dunedin‡	Florida St.	23	106	4	7	.364	134	59	52	52	27	4.42
1980—Salem	Carolina	47	111	7	5	.583	91	38	27	85	32	2.18
1981—Portland	P. Coast	40	93	5	3	.625	103	54	45	39	41	4.35
1982—Buffalo§	Eastern	44	57⅔	2	8	.200	71	41	32	40	23	4.99
1983—Lynn	Eastern	18	34⅔	3	1	.750	35	20	14	13	17	3.63
1983—Hawaii	P. Coast	15	69	6	6	.500	90	42	38	30	21	4.96
1984—Hawaii x	P. Coast	9	57⅓	1	3	.250	67	29	25	21	17	3.92
1985—Oklahoma City y	Amer. Assoc.	40	84⅔	3	7	.300	72	32	27	47	21	2.87
1986—Oklahoma City	Amer. Assoc.	16	37⅔	4	4	.500	34	16	10	24	11	2.39
1986—Texas	American	58	79	2	4	.333	86	25	22	29	15	2.51
1987—Texas z	American	74	99⅓	7	6	.538	88	34	33	48	19	2.99
1988—Texas ab-New York	American	56	74⅔	4	8	.333	83	42	35	44	29	4.22
1989—New York	American	32	57⅔	2	1	.667	65	41	32	24	18	4.99
1989—Columbus c	Int'national	16	26⅔	1	2	.333	18	12	3	12	10	1.01
1990—Indianapolis	Am. Assoc.	13	16	2	0	1.000	11	3	2	9	3	1.13
1990—Montreal d	National	34	53	1	2	.333	56	21	19	29	18	3.23
American League Totals—4 Years		220	310⅔	15	19	.441	322	142	122	145	81	3.53
National League Totals—1 Year		34	53	1	2	.333	56	21	19	29	18	3.23
Major League Totals—5 Years		254	363⅔	16	21	.432	378	163	141	174	99	3.49

Signed as free agent by Victoria, June 11, 1978.
†Sold to Toronto Blue Jays' organization, September 25, 1978.
‡Released, January 8, 1980; signed by Pittsburgh Pirates' organization, April 5, 1980.
§On disabled list, May 27 through July 2, 1982.
xGranted free agency, October 15, 1984; signed by Oklahoma City (Texas Rangers' organization), May 19, 1985.
yGranted free agency, October 15, 1985; re-signed by Oklahoma City (Texas Rangers' organization), February 18, 1986.
zOn disabled list, August 12 to August 27, 1987.
aOn disabled list, March 26 to April 27, 1988.
bTraded to New York Yankees for Pitcher Cecilio Guante, August 30, 1988.
cReleased, November 8, 1989; signed by Indianapolis (Montreal Expos' organization), December 7, 1989.
dReleased, December 3, 1990.

PAUL LEO MOLITOR

Born August 22, 1956, at St. Paul, Minn.
Height, 6.00. Weight, 185.
Throws and bats righthanded.
Attended University of Minnesota, Minneapolis, Minn.

Shares major league record for most stolen bases, inning (3), July 26, 1987, first inning.
Hit three home runs in a game, May 12, 1982.
Major League stolen bases: 1978 (30), 1979 (33), 1980 (34), 1981 (10), 1982 (41), 1983 (41), 1984 (1), 1985 (21), 1986 (20) 1987 (45), 1988 (41), 1989 (27), 1990 (18). Total—362.
Led American League third basemen in errors with 29 and double plays with 48 in 1982.
Named American League Rookie Player of the Year by THE SPORTING NEWS, 1978.
Named Midwest League Most Valuable Player, 1977.
Received reported $100,000 bonus to sign with Milwaukee Brewers, 1977.
Named shortstop on THE SPORTING NEWS College Baseball All-America Team, 1977.
Named designated hitter on THE SPORTING NEWS American League All-Star Team, 1987.
Named designated hitter on THE SPORTING NEWS American League Silver Slugger team, 1987 and 1988.

Year Club	League	Pos.	G.	AB.	R.	H.	2B.	3B.	HR.	RBI.	B.A.	PO.	A.	E.	F.A.
1977—Burlington	Midw.	SS	64	228	52	79	12	0	8	50	.346	83	207	28	.912
1978—Milwaukee	Amer.	2B-SS-3B	125	521	73	142	26	4	6	45	.273	253	401	22	.967
1979—Milwaukee	Amer.	2B-SS	140	584	88	188	27	16	9	62	.322	309	440	16	.979
1980—Milwaukee†	Amer.	2B-SS-3B	111	450	81	137	29	2	9	37	.304	260	336	20	.968
1981—Milwaukee‡	Amer.	OF	64	251	45	67	11	0	2	19	.267	119	4	3	.976
1982—Milwaukee	Amer.	3B-SS	160	*666	*136	201	26	8	19	71	.302	134	350	32	.938
1983—Milwaukee	Amer.	3B	152	608	95	164	28	6	15	47	.270	105	343	16	.966
1984—Milwaukee§	Amer.	3B	13	46	3	10	1	0	0	6	.217	7	21	2	.933
1985—Milwaukee x	Amer.	3B	140	576	93	171	28	3	10	48	.297	126	263	19	.953
1986—Milwaukee y	Amer.	3B-OF	105	437	62	123	24	6	9	55	.281	86	171	15	.945
1987—Milwaukee za	Amer.	3B-2B	118	465	*114	164	*41	5	16	75	.353	60	113	5	.972
1988—Milwaukee	Amer.	3B-2B	154	609	115	190	34	6	13	60	.312	87	188	17	.942
1989—Milwaukee b	Amer.	3B-2B	155	615	84	194	35	4	11	56	.315	106	287	18	.956
1990—Milwaukee c	Amer.	2B-1B-3B	103	418	64	119	27	6	12	45	.285	463	222	10	.986
1990—Beloit	Milw.	DH	1	4	1	2	0	0	1	1	.500	0	0	0	.000
Major League Totals—13 Years			1540	6246	1053	1870	337	66	131	626	.299	2115	3139	195	.964

Selected by St. Louis Cardinals' organization in 28th round of free-agent draft, June 5, 1974.
Selected by Milwaukee Brewers' organization in 1st round (third player selected) of free-agent draft, June 7, 1977.
†On disabled list, June 24 to July 18, 1980.
‡On disabled list, May 3 to August 12, 1981.
§On disabled list, May 2, 1984 through remainder of season.
xOn disabled list, August 13 to August 28, 1985.
yOn disabled list, May 10 to May 30, June 2 to June 17 and June 19 to July 8, 1986.
zOn disabled list, April 30 to May 26 and June 27 to July 16, 1987.
aGranted free agency, November 9, 1987, re-signed by Brewers, January 5, 1988.
bOn disabled list, March 30 to April 14, 1989.
cOn disabled list, April 2 to April 27 and June 17 to July 30, 1990; included rehabilitation disability assignment to Beloit, July 28, 1990.

DIVISION SERIES RECORD

Year	Club	League	Pos.	G.	AB.	R.	H.	2B.	3B.	HR.	RBI.	B.A.	PO.	A.	E.	F.A.
1981—Milwaukee		Amer.	OF	5	20	2	5	0	0	1	1	.250	12	0	0	1.000

CHAMPIONSHIP SERIES RECORD

Year	Club	League	Pos.	G.	AB.	R.	H.	2B.	3B.	HR.	RBI.	B.A.	PO.	A.	E.	F.A.
1982—Milwaukee		Amer.	3B	5	19	4	6	1	0	2	5	.316	4	11	2	.882

WORLD SERIES RECORD

Holds World Series records for most hits (5) and singles (5), game, October 12, 1982.
Shares World Series record for most at-bats, nine-inning game (6), October 12, 1982.

Year	Club	League	Pos.	G.	AB.	R.	H.	2B.	3B.	HR.	RBI.	B.A.	PO.	A.	E.	F.A.
1982—Milwaukee		Amer.	3B	7	31	5	11	0	0	0	3	.355	4	9	0	1.000

ALL-STAR GAME RECORD

Year	League	Pos.	AB.	R.	H.	2B.	3B.	HR.	RBI.	B.A.	PO.	A.	E.	F.A.
1985—American		3B-OF	1	0	0	0	0	0	0	.000	0	0	0	.000
1988—American		2B	3	0	0	0	0	0	0	.000	1	2	0	1.000
All-Star Game Totals—2 Years			4	0	0	0	0	0	0	.000	1	2	0	1.000

Named to American League All-Star Team in 1980; replaced due to injury.

RICHARD MONTELEONE

Name pronounced Mon-ta-lee-YONE.

(Rich)

Born March 22, 1963, at Tampa, Fla.
Height, 6.02. Weight, 234.
Throws and bats righthanded.

Led Appalachian League pitchers in home runs allowed with 8 in 1982.

Year	Club	League	G.	IP.	W.	L.	Pct.	H.	R.	ER.	SO.	BB.	ERA.
1982—Bristol		Ap'lachian	12	71⅔	4	6	.400	66	41	31	52	23	3.89
1983—Lakeland		Florida St.	24	142⅓	9	8	.529	146	80	65	124	80	4.11
1983—Birmingham		Southern	3	15	1	1	.500	25	12	12	9	6	7.20
1984—Birmingham		Southern	19	123⅔	7	8	.467	116	69	64	74	67	4.66
1984—Evansville		Am. Assoc.	11	64	5	3	.625	64	33	32	42	36	4.50
1985—Nashville†		Am. Assoc.	27	145⅓	6	12	.333	149	89	82	97	87	5.08
1986—Calgary		P. Coast	39	158⅔	8	12	.400	177	108	93	101	*89	5.28
1987—Seattle		American	3	7	0	0	.000	10	5	5	2	4	6.43
1987—Calgary		P. Coast	51	65⅓	6	*13	.316	59	45	40	38	63	5.51
1988—Calgary‡-Edmonton		P. Coast	30	122⅓	4	7	.364	141	84	69	97	27	5.08
1988—California		American	3	4⅓	0	0	.000	4	0	0	3	1	0.00
1989—Edmonton		P. Coast	13	57	3	6	.333	50	23	22	47	16	3.47
1989—California		American	24	39⅔	2	2	.500	39	15	14	27	13	3.18
1990—Edmonton§		P. Coast	5	14	1	0	1.000	7	3	3	9	4	1.93
1990—Columbus		Int'national	38	64⅓	4	4	.500	51	17	16	60	23	2.24
1990—New York		American	5	7⅓	0	1	.000	8	5	5	8	2	6.14
Major League Totals—4 Years			35	58⅓	2	3	.400	61	25	24	40	20	3.70

Selected by Detroit Tigers' organization in 1st round (20th player selected) of free-agent draft, June 7, 1982.
†Traded to Seattle Mariners for Third Baseman Darnell Coles, December 12, 1985.
‡Released, May 9, 1988; signed by Edmonton (California Angels' organization), May 13, 1988.
§Traded with Outfielder Claudell Washington to New York Yankees for Outfielder Luis Polonia, April 28, 1990.

JEFFREY THOMAS MONTGOMERY

(Jeff)

Born January 7, 1962, at Wellston, O.
Height, 5.11. Weight, 180.
Throws and bats righthanded.
Received bachelor of science degree in computer science from
Marshall University, Huntington, W. Va., in 1984.

Major League saves: 1988 (1), 1989 (18), 1990 (24). Total—43.
Tied for Florida State League lead in saves with 14 in 1984.

Year	Club	League	G.	IP.	W.	L.	Pct.	H.	R.	ER.	SO.	BB.	ERA.
1983—Billings		Pioneer	20	44⅔	6	2	.750	31	13	12	90	13	2.42
1984—Tampa		Florida St.	31	44⅓	5	3	.625	29	15	12	56	30	2.44
1984—Vermont		Eastern	22	25⅓	2	0	1.000	14	7	6	20	24	2.13
1985—Vermont		Eastern	*53	101	5	3	.625	63	25	23	89	48	2.05
1986—Denver		Am. Assoc.	30	151⅔	11	7	.611	162	88	74	78	57	4.39
1987—Nashville†		Am. Assoc.	24	139	8	5	.615	132	76	64	121	51	4.14
1987—Cincinnati†		National	14	19⅓	2	2	.500	25	15	14	13	9	6.52
1988—Omaha		Am. Assoc.	20	28⅓	1	2	.333	15	6	6	36	11	1.91
1988—Kansas City		American	45	62⅔	7	2	.778	54	25	24	47	30	3.45
1989—Kansas City		American	63	92	7	3	.700	66	16	14	94	25	1.37
1990—Kansas City		American	73	94⅓	6	5	.545	81	36	25	94	34	2.39
National League Totals—1 Year			14	19⅓	2	2	.500	25	15	14	13	9	6.52
American League Totals—3 Years			181	249	20	10	.667	201	77	63	235	89	2.28
Major League Totals—4 Years			195	268⅓	22	12	.647	226	92	77	248	98	2.58

Selected by Cincinnati Reds' organization in 9th round of free-agent draft, June 6, 1983.
†Traded to Kansas City Royals for Outfielder Van Snider, February 15, 1988.

BRADLEY ALAN MOORE
(Brad)

Born June 21, 1964, at Loveland, Colo.
Height, 6.01. Weight, 185.
Throws and bats righthanded.
Attended Garden City Community College, Garden City, Kan.,
and Grand Canyon College, Phoenix, Ariz.
Led International League in intentional bases on balls issued with 10 in 1989.

Year Club	League	G.	IP.	W.	L.	Pct.	H.	R.	ER.	SO.	BB.	ERA.
1986—Bend	Northwest	16	33⅔	2	5	.286	32	29	22	35	22	5.88
1987—Clearwater	Florida St.	53	67⅓	4	7	.364	63	23	15	42	21	2.00
1987—Reading	Eastern	9	18⅓	0	1	.000	12	2	2	13	4	0.98
1988—Reading	Eastern	57	70⅔	4	6	.400	57	30	24	39	33	3.06
1988—Philadelphia	National	5	5⅔	0	0	.000	4	0	0	2	4	0.00
1989—Scranton/Wilkes-Barre	Int'national	∗61	97	6	10	.375	86	41	36	67	49	3.34
1990—Philadelphia	National	3	2⅔	0	0	.000	4	1	1	1	2	3.38
1990—Scranton/Wilkes-Barre	Int'national	35	101⅔	3	7	.300	97	48	42	45	28	3.72
1990—Reading†	Eastern	1	6	1	0	1.000	2	0	0	4	1	0.00
Major League Totals—2 Years		8	8⅓	0	0	.000	8	1	1	3	6	1.08

Signed as free agent by Philadelphia Phillies' organization, June 25, 1986.
†Granted free agency, October 11, 1990.

MICHAEL WAYNE MOORE
(Mike)

Born November 26, 1959, at Eakly, Okla.
Height, 6.04. Weight, 205.
Throws and bats righthanded.
Attended Oral Roberts University, Tulsa, Okla.
Major League saves: 1986 (1), 1988 (1). Total—2.
Tied for American League lead in games started by pitchers with 37 in 1986.
Received reported $100,000 bonus to sign with Seattle Mariners, 1981.
Named righthanded pitcher on THE SPORTING NEWS College Baseball All-America Team, 1981.

Year Club	League	G.	IP.	W.	L.	Pct.	H.	R.	ER.	SO.	BB.	ERA.
1981—Lynn	Eastern	13	94	6	5	.545	83	42	38	81	34	3.64
1982—Seattle	American	28	144⅓	7	14	.333	159	91	86	73	79	5.36
1982—Salt Lake City	P. Coast	1	8	0	0	.000	9	4	4	6	5	4.50
1983—Seattle	American	22	128	6	8	.429	130	75	67	108	60	4.71
1983—Salt Lake City	P. Coast	11	82⅓	4	4	.500	78	48	33	80	54	3.61
1984—Seattle	American	34	212	7	17	.292	236	127	117	158	85	4.97
1985—Seattle	American	35	247	17	10	.630	230	100	95	155	70	3.46
1986—Seattle	American	38	266	11	13	.458	∗279	141	127	146	94	4.30
1987—Seattle†	American	33	231	9	∗19	.321	∗268	145	∗121	115	84	4.71
1988—Seattle‡	American	37	228⅔	9	15	.375	196	104	96	182	63	3.78
1989—Oakland	American	35	241⅔	19	11	.633	193	82	70	172	83	2.61
1990—Oakland	American	33	199⅓	13	15	.464	204	113	103	73	84	4.65
Major League Totals—9 Years		295	1898	98	122	.445	1895	978	882	1182	702	4.18

Selected by St. Louis Cardinals' organization in 3rd round of free-agent draft, June 6, 1978.
Selected by Seattle Mariners' organization in 1st round (first player selected) of free-agent draft, June 8, 1981.
†Made an out in only appearance as a pinch-hitter.
‡Granted free agency, November 4, 1988; signed by Oakland Athletics, November 28, 1988.

CHAMPIONSHIP SERIES RECORD

Year Club	League	G.	IP.	W.	L.	Pct.	H.	R.	ER.	SO.	BB.	ERA.
1989—Oakland	American	1	7	1	0	1.000	3	1	0	3	2	0.00
1990—Oakland	American	1	6	1	0	1.000	4	1	1	5	1	1.50
Championship Series Totals—2 Years		2	13	2	0	1.000	7	2	1	8	3	0.69

WORLD SERIES RECORD

Shares World Series record for most wild pitches, game (2), October 15, 1989.

Year Club	League	G.	IP.	W.	L.	Pct.	H.	R.	ER.	SO.	BB.	ERA.
1989—Oakland	American	2	13	2	0	1.000	9	3	3	10	3	2.08
1990—Oakland	American	1	2⅔	0	1	.000	8	6	2	1	0	6.75
World Series Totals—2 Years		3	15⅔	2	1	.667	17	9	5	11	3	2.87

ALL-STAR GAME RECORD

Year League	IP.	W.	L.	Pct.	H.	R.	ER.	SO.	BB.	ERA.
1989—American	1	0	0	.000	0	0	0	1	0	0.00

—DID YOU KNOW—

That Dodgers rookie Jose Offerman, homerless in 454 minor league at-bats in 1990, stroked a four master in his first big-league at-bat on August 19?

MICHAEL ROBERT MORANDINI
(Mickey)

Born April 22, 1966, at Kittanning, Pa.
Height, 5.11. Weight, 170.
Throws right and bats lefthanded.
Attended Indiana University, Bloomington, Ind.

Major League stolen bases: 1990 (3).
Led International League second basemen in total chances with 701 in 1990.
Member of 1988 U.S. Olympic baseball team.

Year Club	League	Pos.	G.	AB.	R.	H.	2B.	3B.	HR.	RBI.	B.A.	PO.	A.	E.	F.A.
1989—Spartanburg	S. Atl.	SS	63	231	43	78	19	1	1	30	.338	87	198	10	.966
1989—Clearwater	Fla. St.	SS	17	63	14	19	4	1	0	4	.302	20	59	2	.975
1989—Reading	East.	SS	48	188	39	66	12	1	5	29	.351	73	137	10	.955
1990—Scranton/W.-B.	Int.	*2B-SS	139	503	76	131	24	*10	1	31	.260	*271	*419	11	.984
1990—Philadelphia	Nat.	2B	25	79	9	19	4	0	1	3	.241	37	61	1	.990
Major League Totals—1 Year			25	79	9	19	4	0	1	3	.241	37	61	1	.990

Selected by Pittsburgh Pirates' organization in 7th round of free-agent draft, June 2, 1987.
Selected by Philadelphia Phillies' organization in 5th round of free-agent draft, June 1, 1988.

MICHAEL THOMAS MORGAN
(Mike)

Born October 8, 1959, at Tulare, Calif.
Height, 6.02. Weight, 222.
Throws and bats righthanded.

Major League saves: 1986 (1), 1988 (1). Total—2.
Tied for National League lead in shutouts with 4 in 1990.
Tied for International League lead in shutouts with 4 in 1984.
Received reported $50,000 bonus to sign with Oakland A's, 1978.

Year Club	League	G.	IP.	W.	L.	Pct.	H.	R.	ER.	SO.	BB.	ERA.
1978—Oakland	American	3	12	0	3	.000	19	12	10	0	8	7.50
1978—Vancouver	P. Coast	14	92	5	6	.455	109	67	57	31	54	5.58
1979—Ogden	P. Coast	13	101	5	5	.500	93	48	39	42	49	3.48
1979—Oakland	American	13	77	2	10	.167	102	57	51	17	50	5.96
1980—Ogden†‡	P. Coast	20	115	6	9	.400	135	79	69	46	77	5.40
1981—Nashville§	Southern	26	169	8	7	.533	164	97	83	100	83	4.42
1982—New York x	American	30	150⅓	7	11	.389	167	77	73	71	67	4.37
1983—Toronto y	American	16	45⅓	0	3	.000	48	26	26	22	21	5.16
1983—Syracuse	Int'national	5	19⅓	0	3	.000	20	12	12	17	13	5.59
1984—Syracuse z	Int'national	34	*185⅔	13	11	.542	167	●101	84	105	●100	4.07
1985—Seattle a	American	2	6	1	1	.500	11	8	8	2	5	12.00
1985—Calgary	P. Coast	1	2	0	0	.000	3	1	1	0	0	4.50
1986—Seattle	American	37	216⅓	11	●17	.393	243	122	109	116	86	4.53
1987—Seattle b	American	34	207	12	17	.414	245	117	107	85	53	4.65
1988—Baltimore c	American	22	71⅓	1	6	.143	70	45	43	29	23	5.43
1988—Rochester d	Int'national	3	17	0	2	.000	19	10	9	7	6	4.76
1989—Los Angeles	National	40	152⅔	8	11	.421	130	51	43	72	33	2.53
1990—Los Angeles	National	33	211	11	15	.423	216	100	88	106	60	3.75
American League Totals—8 Years		157	785⅓	34	68	.333	905	464	427	342	313	4.89
National League Totals—2 Years		73	363⅔	19	26	.422	346	151	131	178	93	3.24
Major League Totals—10 Years		230	1149	53	94	.361	1251	615	558	520	406	4.37

Selected by Oakland A's organizaton in 1st round (fourth player selected) of free-agent draft, June 6, 1978.
†On disabled list, May 14 to June 27, 1980.
‡Traded to New York Yankees for Shortstop Fred Stanley and a player to be named later, November 3, 1980; Oakland A's acquired Second Baseman Brian Doyle to complete deal, November 17, 1980.
§On disabled list, April 9 to April 22, 1981.
xTraded with Outfielder-First Baseman Dave Collins, First Baseman Fred McGriff and a reported $400,000 to Toronto Blue Jays for Pitcher Dale Murray and Outfielder-Catcher Tom Dodd, December 9, 1982.
yOn disabled list, July 2 to August 23, 1983; included rehabilitation disability assignment to Syracuse, August 1 to August 18, 1983.
zDrafted by Seattle Mariners, December 3, 1984.
aOn disabled list, April 17, 1985 through remainder of season; included rehabilitation disability assignment to Calgary, July 19 to July 22, 1985.
bTraded to Baltimore Orioles for Pitcher Ken Dixon, December 9, 1987.
cOn disabled list, June 9 to July 19 and August 12, 1988 through remainder of season; included rehabilitation disability assignment to Rochester, June 30 to July 17, 1988.
dTraded to Los Angeles Dodgers for Outfielder Mike Devereaux, March 12, 1989.

RUSSELL LEE MORMAN
(Russ)

Born April 28, 1962, at Independence, Mo.
Height, 6.04. Weight, 215.
Throws and bats righthanded.
Attended Iowa Western Community College, Clarinda, Ia.,
and Wichita State University, Wichita, Kan.

Shares major league record for most hits, inning, first major league game (2), August 3, 1986, fourth inning.

Major League stolen bases: 1986 (1), 1989 (1). Total—2.
Led Eastern League in slugging percentage with .512 in 1985.
Led Midwest League in game-winning RBIs with 15 in 1984.
Led American Association third basemen in double plays with 23 in 1986.
Led Eastern League first basemen in assists with 79 in 1985.
Named first baseman on THE SPORTING NEWS College Baseball All-America Team, 1983.

Year	Club	League	Pos.	G.	AB.	R.	H.	2B.	3B.	HR.	RBI.	B.A.	PO.	A.	E.	F.A.
1983—Glens Falls	East.		1B	71	233	29	57	9	1	3	32	.245	591	43	7	.989
1984—Appleton	Midw.		1B-OF	122	424	68	111	17	7	7	80	.262	823	43	10	.989
1985—Glens Falls	East.		*1-3-O	119	422	64	131	24	5	17	81	.310	905	81	12	*.988
1985—Buffalo	A. A.		1B	21	64	16	19	3	1	7	14	.297	144	7	2	.987
1986—Buffalo	A. A.		3B-OF	106	365	52	97	17	2	13	57	.266	87	201	24	.923
1986—Chicago	Amer.		1B	49	159	18	40	5	0	4	17	.252	342	26	4	.989
1987—Hawaii	P. C.		1B-OF	89	294	52	79	19	2	9	53	.269	410	28	3	.993
1988—Vancouver	P. C.		1B-OF	69	257	40	77	8	1	5	45	.300	370	21	3	.992
1988—Chicago	Amer.		1B-OF	40	75	8	18	2	0	0	3	.240	114	5	2	.983
1989—Vancouver	P. C.		1B-OF	61	216	18	60	14	1	1	23	.278	163	12	3	.983
1989—Chicago†	Amer.		1B	37	58	5	13	2	0	0	8	.224	157	13	2	.988
1990—Omaha	A. A.		1-O-3-2	121	436	67	130	14	9	13	81	.298	665	59	5	.993
1990—Kansas City	Amer.		OF-1B	12	37	5	10	4	2	1	3	.270	27	4	0	1.000
Major League Totals—4 Years				138	329	36	81	13	2	5	31	.246	640	48	8	.989

Selected by Kansas City Royals' organization in 7th round of free-agent draft, January 13, 1981.
Selected by Chicago White Sox' organization in 1st round (28th player selected) of free-agent draft, June 6, 1983.
†Released, November 20, 1989; signed by Omaha (Kansas City Royals' organization), December 21, 1989.

JOHN DANIEL MORRIS

Born February 23, 1961, at Freeport, N.Y.
Height, 6.01. Weight, 185.
Throws and bats lefthanded.
Attended Seton Hall University, South Orange, N.J.

Major League stolen bases: 1986 (6), 1987 (5), 1989 (1). Total—12.
Led Southern League outfielders in total chances with 343 in 1985.
Named Southern League Most Valuable Player, 1983.
Named outfielder on THE SPORTING NEWS College Baseball All-America Team, 1982.

Year	Club	League	Pos.	G.	AB.	R.	H.	2B.	3B.	HR.	RBI.	B.A.	PO.	A.	E.	F.A.
1982—Fort Myers	Fla. St.		OF	45	137	21	39	7	2	2	17	.285	64	2	2	.971
1983—Jacksonville	South.		OF	140	490	96	141	27	8	23	92	.288	260	8	3	*.989
1984—Omaha	A. A.		OF	148	492	77	133	24	4	15	60	.270	*359	7	4	*.989
1985—Omaha†-Louis.	A. A.		OF	130	466	64	117	25	6	5	50	.251	*330	11	2	*.994
1986—Louisville‡	A. A.		OF	60	213	30	50	13	7	1	24	.235	132	6	2	.986
1986—St. Louis	Nat.		OF	39	100	8	24	0	1	1	14	.240	68	0	1	.986
1987—Louisville	A. A.		OF	14	47	13	16	5	2	3	12	.340	20	2	0	1.000
1987—St. Louis	Nat.		OF	101	157	22	41	6	4	3	23	.261	86	0	1	.989
1988—Louisville§	A. A.		OF	13	40	3	4	0	0	0	0	.100	8	0	0	1.000
1988—St. Louis	Nat.		OF	20	38	3	11	2	1	0	3	.289	12	0	2	.857
1989—St. Louis	Nat.		OF	96	117	8	28	4	1	2	14	.239	45	0	0	1.000
1990—St. Louis xy	Nat.		OF	18	18	0	2	0	0	0	0	.111	4	0	0	1.000
Major League Totals—5 Years				274	430	41	106	12	7	6	54	.247	215	0	4	.982

Selected by Kansas City Royals' organization in 1st round (10th player selected) of free-agent draft, June 7, 1982.
†Traded to St. Louis Cardinals' organization for Outfielder Lonnie Smith, May 17, 1985.
‡On disabled list, May 7 to June 11 and June 28 to July 8, 1986.
§On St. Louis disabled list, March 20 to September 2, 1988; included rehabilitation disability assignment to Louisville, August 17 to September 2, 1988.
xOn disabled list, June 5, 1990 through remainder of season.
yGranted free agency, October 9, 1990; signed by Scranton/Wilkes-Barre (Philadelphia Phillies' organization), January 10, 1991.

CHAMPIONSHIP SERIES RECORD

Year	Club	League	Pos.	G.	AB.	R.	H.	2B.	3B.	HR.	RBI.	B.A.	PO.	A.	E.	F.A.
1987—St. Louis	Nat.		OF	2	3	0	0	0	0	0	0	.000	1	0	0	1.000

WORLD SERIES RECORD

Year	Club	League	Pos.	G.	AB.	R.	H.	2B.	3B.	HR.	RBI.	B.A.	PO.	A.	E.	F.A.
1987—St. Louis	Nat.		OF	1	2	0	0	0	0	0	0	.000	2	0	0	1.000

JOHN SCOTT MORRIS
(Jack)

Born May 16, 1955, at St. Paul, Minn.
Height, 6.03. Weight, 200.
Throws and bats righthanded.
Attended Brigham Young University, Provo, Utah.

Holds American League record for most consecutive starting assignments, lifetime (396).
Holds American League records for most wild pitches, season (24), 1987; most seasons leading league, wild pitches (4).
Shares American League records for fewest complete games for leader, season (11), 1990; most wild pitches, game (5), August 3, 1987 (10 innings).
Pitched 4-0 no-hit victory against Chicago White Sox, April 7, 1984.

Led American League in intentional bases on balls issued with 13 and tied for lead in complete games with 11 and games started by pitchers with 36 in 1990.
Led American League in shutouts with 6 in 1986.
Led American League in wild pitches with 18 in 1983, 14 in 1984, 15 in 1985 and 24 in 1987.
Named American League Pitcher of the Year by THE SPORTING NEWS, 1981.
Named righthanded pitcher on THE SPORTING NEWS American League All-Star Team, 1981.

Year Club	League	G.	IP.	W.	L.	Pct.	H.	R.	ER.	SO.	BB.	ERA.
1976—Montgomery	Southern	12	36	2	3	.400	37	31	25	18	36	6.25
1977—Evansville	Am. Assoc.	20	135	6	7	.462	141	68	54	95	42	3.60
1977—Detroit	American	7	46	1	1	.500	38	20	19	28	23	3.72
1978—Detroit	American	28	106	3	5	.375	107	57	51	48	49	4.33
1979—Evansville	Am. Assoc.	5	34	2	2	.500	22	13	9	28	18	2.38
1979—Detroit	American	27	198	17	7	.708	179	76	72	113	59	3.27
1980—Detroit	American	36	250	16	15	.516	252	125	116	112	87	4.18
1981—Detroit	American	25	198	●14	7	.667	153	69	67	97	★78	3.05
1982—Detroit	American	37	266⅓	17	16	.515	247	131	120	135	96	4.06
1983—Detroit†	American	37	★293⅔	20	13	.606	257	117	109	★232	83	3.34
1984—Detroit	American	35	240⅓	19	11	.633	221	108	96	148	87	3.60
1985—Detroit‡	American	35	257	16	11	.593	212	102	95	191	110	3.33
1986—Detroit§	American	35	267	21	8	.724	229	105	97	223	82	3.27
1987—Detroit xy	American	34	266	18	11	.621	227	111	100	208	93	3.38
1988—Detroit	American	34	235	15	13	.536	225	115	103	168	83	3.94
1989—Detroit z	American	24	170⅓	6	14	.300	189	102	92	115	59	4.86
1989—Lakeland	Florida St.	3	8	0	0	.000	7	2	2	2	0	2.25
1990—Detroit a	American	36	249⅔	15	18	.455	231	★144	★125	162	97	4.51
Major League Totals—14 Years		430	3043⅓	198	150	.569	2767	1382	1262	1980	1086	3.73

Selected by Detroit Tigers' organization in 5th round of free-agent draft, June 8, 1976.
†Appeared in seven games as a pinch-runner.
‡Appeared in one game as a pinch-runner.
§Granted free agency, November 12, 1986; re-signed by Tigers, December 19, 1986.
xMade an out in only appearance as a pinch-hitter.
yGranted free agency, November 9, 1987; re-signed by Tigers, December 29, 1987.
zOn disabled list, May 25 to July 24, 1989; included rehabilitation disability assignment to Lakeland, July 10 to July 24, 1989.
aGranted free agency, December 7, 1990.

CHAMPIONSHIP SERIES RECORD

Year Club	League	G.	IP.	W.	L.	Pct.	H.	R.	ER.	SO.	BB.	ERA.
1984—Detroit	American	1	7	1	0	1.000	5	1	1	4	1	1.29
1987—Detroit	American	1	8	0	1	.000	6	6	6	7	3	6.75
Championship Series Totals—2 Years		2	15	1	1	.500	11	7	7	11	4	4.20

Appeared as pinch-runner for Detroit Tigers in one game of 1987 Championship Series.

WORLD SERIES RECORD

Shares World Series record for most wild pitches, game (2), October 13, 1984.

Year Club	League	G.	IP.	W.	L.	Pct.	H.	R.	ER.	SO.	BB.	ERA.
1984—Detroit	American	2	18	2	0	1.000	13	4	4	13	3	2.00

ALL-STAR GAME RECORD

Year League	IP.	W.	L.	Pct.	H.	R.	ER.	SO.	BB.	ERA.
1981—American	2	0	0	.000	2	0	0	2	1	0.00
1984—American	2	0	0	.000	2	0	0	2	1	0.00
1985—American	2⅔	0	1	.000	5	2	2	1	1	6.75
1987—American	2	0	0	.000	1	0	0	2	1	0.00
All-Star Game Totals—4 Years	8⅔	0	1	.000	10	2	2	7	4	2.08

WILLIAM HAROLD MORRIS
(Hal)

Born April 9, 1965, at Fort Rucker, Ala.
Height, 6.04. Weight, 215.
Throws and bats lefthanded.
Attended University of Michigan, Ann Arbor, Mich.

Major League stolen bases: 1990 (9).

Year Club	League	Pos.	G.	AB.	R.	H.	2B.	3B.	HR.	RBI.	B.A.	PO.	A.	E.	F.A.
1986—Oneonta	NYP	1B	36	127	26	48	9	2	3	30	.378	317	26	3	.991
1986—Albany†	East.	1B	25	79	7	17	5	0	0	4	.215	203	19	2	.991
1987—Albany	East.	1B-OF	135	★530	65	★173	31	4	5	73	.326	1086	79	17	.986
1988—Columbus	Int.	OF-1B	121	452	41	134	19	4	3	38	.296	543	26	8	.986
1988—New York	Amer.	OF	15	20	1	2	0	0	0	0	.100	7	0	0	1.000
1989—Columbus	Int.	1B-OF	111	417	70	136	24	1	17	66	★.326	636	67	9	.987
1989—New York‡	Amer.	OF-1B	15	18	2	5	0	0	0	4	.278	12	0	0	1.000
1990—Cincinnati	Nat.	1B-OF	107	309	50	105	22	3	7	36	.340	595	53	4	.994
1990—Nashville	A. A.	OF	16	64	8	22	5	0	1	10	.344	23	1	1	.960
American League Totals—2 Years			30	38	3	7	0	0	0	4	.184	19	0	0	1.000
National League Totals—1 Year			107	309	50	105	22	3	7	36	.340	595	53	4	.994
Major League Totals—3 Years			137	347	53	112	22	3	7	40	.323	614	53	4	.994

Selected by New York Yankees' organization in 8th round of free-agent draft, June 2, 1986.

†On disabled list, August 14, 1986 through remainder of season.
‡Traded with Pitcher Rodney Imes to Cincinnati Reds for Pitcher Tim Leary and Outfielder Van Snider, December 12, 1989.

CHAMPIONSHIP SERIES RECORD

Year Club	League	Pos.	G.	AB.	R.	H.	2B.	3B.	HR.	RBI.	B.A.	PO.	A.	E.	F.A.
1990—Cincinnati	Nat.	1B-PH	5	12	3	5	1	0	0	1	.417	20	2	0	1.000

WORLD SERIES RECORD

Year Club	League	Pos.	G.	AB.	R.	H.	2B.	3B.	HR.	RBI.	B.A.	PO.	A.	E.	F.A.
1990—Cincinnati	Nat.	1B-DH	4	14	0	1	0	0	0	2	.071	18	1	0	1.000

LLOYD ANTHONY MOSEBY

Born November 5, 1959, at Portland, Ark.
Height, 6.03. Weight, 200.
Throws right and bats lefthanded.

Major League stolen bases: 1980 (4), 1981 (11), 1982 (11), 1983 (27), 1984 (39), 1985 (37), 1986 (32), 1987 (39), 1988 (31), 1989 (24), 1990 (17). Total—272.
Led Florida State League in total bases with 237 and tied for lead in being hit by pitch with 10 in 1979.
Led Pioneer League in being hit by pitch with 11 and tied for lead in caught stealing with 7 in 1978.
Named outfielder on THE SPORTING NEWS American League All-Star Team, 1983.
Named outfielder on THE SPORTING NEWS American League Silver Slugger team, 1983.

Year Club	League	Pos.	G.	AB.	R.	H.	2B.	3B.	HR.	RBI.	B.A.	PO.	A.	E.	F.A.
1978—Medicine Hat	Pion.	OF	67	253	65	77	12	4	10	38	.304	76	3	6	.929
1979—Dunedin	Fla. St.	OF	129	446	*89	*148	23	6	18	84	.332	190	11	9	.957
1980—Syracuse	Int.	OF	37	146	28	47	8	6	3	19	.322	83	1	3	.966
1980—Toronto	Amer.	OF	114	389	44	89	24	1	9	46	.229	208	12	4	.982
1981—Toronto	Amer.	OF	100	378	36	88	16	2	9	43	.233	259	4	3	.989
1982—Toronto	Amer.	OF	147	487	51	115	20	9	9	52	.236	361	4	3	.992
1983—Toronto	Amer.	OF	151	539	104	170	31	7	18	81	.315	399	10	7	.983
1984—Toronto	Amer.	OF	158	592	97	166	28	•15	18	92	.280	473	8	5	.990
1985—Toronto	Amer.	OF	152	584	92	151	30	7	18	70	.259	394	7	8	.980
1986—Toronto	Amer.	OF	152	589	89	149	24	5	21	86	.253	371	6	6	.984
1987—Toronto	Amer.	OF	155	592	106	167	27	4	26	96	.282	294	7	6	.980
1988—Toronto†	Amer.	OF	128	472	77	113	17	7	10	42	.239	304	2	5	.984
1989—Toronto‡	Amer.	OF	135	502	72	111	25	3	11	43	.221	288	3	4	.986
1990—Detroit§	Amer.	OF	122	431	64	107	16	5	14	51	.248	288	9	5	.983
Major League Totals—11 Years			1514	5555	832	1426	258	65	163	702	.257	3639	72	56	.985

Selected by Toronto Blue Jays' organization in 1st round (second player selected) of free-agent draft, June 6, 1978.
†On disabled list, July 31 to August 16, 1988.
‡Granted free agency, November 13, 1989.; signed by Detroit Tigers, December 7, 1989.
§On disabled list, June 26 to July 13, 1990.

CHAMPIONSHIP SERIES RECORD

Year Club	League	Pos.	G.	AB.	R.	H.	2B.	3B.	HR.	RBI.	B.A.	PO.	A.	E.	F.A.
1985—Toronto	Amer.	OF	7	31	5	7	1	0	0	4	.226	16	0	0	1.000
1989—Toronto	Amer.	OF	5	16	4	5	0	0	1	2	.313	15	0	0	1.000
Championship Series Totals—2 Years			12	47	9	12	1	0	1	6	.255	31	0	0	1.000

ALL-STAR GAME RECORD

Year League	Pos.	AB.	R.	H.	2B.	3B.	HR.	RBI.	B.A.	PO.	A.	E.	F.A.
1986—American	OF	0	0	0	0	0	0	0	.000	0	0	0	.000

JOHN WILLIAM MOSES

Born August 9, 1957, at Los Angeles, Calif.
Height, 5.10. Weight, 170.
Throws left and bats left and righthanded.
Attended Golden West College, Huntington Beach, Calif., and
University of Arizona, Tucson, Ariz.

Major League stolen bases: 1982 (5), 1983 (11), 1984 (1), 1985 (5), 1986 (25), 1987 (23), 1988 (11), 1989 (14), 1990 (2). Total—97.
Tied for American League lead in caught stealing with 18 in 1986.
Led Midwest League in caught stealing with 21 and bases on balls received with 103 in 1981.
Tied for Midwest League lead in sacrifice hits with 13 in 1981.
Led Eastern League outfielders in double plays with 6 in 1982.

Year Club	League	Pos.	G.	AB.	R.	H.	2B.	3B.	HR.	RBI.	B.A.	PO.	A.	E.	F.A.
1980—Bellingham	N'west	OF	60	227	55	60	5	2	2	32	.264	92	6	3	.970
1981—Wausau	Midw.	OF	123	429	*102	120	24	3	3	48	.280	204	10	5	.977
1982—Lynn	East.	OF	128	466	87	133	25	6	6	52	.285	259	*20	0	*1.000
1982—Seattle	Amer.	OF	22	44	7	14	5	1	1	3	.318	16	2	1	.947
1983—Seattle	Amer.	OF	93	130	19	27	4	1	0	6	.208	87	8	2	.979
1983—Salt Lake City	P. C.	OF	16	65	14	17	4	0	0	10	.262	26	0	0	1.000
1984—Chattanooga	South.	OF	53	182	27	46	6	3	0	12	.253	107	4	2	.982
1984—Salt Lake City	P. C.	OF	70	276	45	76	11	5	0	27	.275	161	8	1	.994
1984—Seattle	Amer.	OF	19	35	3	12	1	1	0	2	.343	26	1	0	1.000
1985—Calgary	P. C.	OF-1B	113	473	75	152	*37	1	5	47	.321	316	12	4	.988
1985—Seattle	Amer.	OF	33	62	4	12	0	0	0	3	.194	35	1	0	1.000

— 334 —

Year Club	League	Pos.	G.	AB.	R.	H.	2B.	3B.	HR.	RBI.	B.A.	PO.	A.	E.	F.A.
1986—Calgary	P. C.	OF	39	148	31	48	3	1	3	18	.324	93	3	1	.990
1986—Seattle....................	Amer.	OF-1B	103	399	56	102	16	3	3	34	.256	249	11	5	.981
1987—Seattle†‡...............	Amer.	OF-1B	116	390	58	96	16	4	3	38	.246	271	7	4	.986
1988—Portland.................	P. C.	OF	17	66	13	23	3	1	0	6	.348	40	0	0	1.000
1988—Minnesota............	Amer.	OF	105	206	33	65	10	3	2	12	.316	123	1	0	1.000
1989—Minnesota............	Amer.	OF-1B-P	129	242	33	68	12	3	1	31	.281	168	3	2	.988
1990—Minnesota§...........	Amer.	OF-1B-P	115	172	26	38	3	1	1	14	.221	108	2	0	1.000
Major League Totals—9 Years.................			735	1680	239	434	67	17	11	143	.258	1083	36	14	.988

Selected by Seattle Mariners' organization in 16th round of free-agent draft, June 3, 1980.
†Released, December 21, 1987; signed by Cleveland Indians, January 19, 1988.
‡Released, March 29, 1988; signed by Portland (Minnesota Twins' organization), April 5, 1988.
§Granted free agency, November 5, 1990.

PITCHING RECORD

Year Club	League	G.	IP.	W.	L.	Pct.	H.	R.	ER.	SO.	BB.	ERA.
1989—Minnesota..............	American	1	1	0	0	.000	0	0	0	0	1	0.00
1990—Minnesota..............	American	2	2	0	0	.000	5	3	3	0	2	13.50
Major League Totals—2 Years............................		3	3	0	0	.000	5	3	3	0	3	9.00

JAMIE MOYER

Born November 18, 1962, at Sellersville, Pa.
Height, 6.00. Weight, 170.
Throws and bats lefthanded.
Attended St. Joseph's University, Philadelphia, Pa.
Son-in-law of Digger Phelps, basketball coach at University of Notre Dame.

Year Club	League	G.	IP.	W.	L.	Pct.	H.	R.	ER.	SO.	BB.	ERA.
1984—Geneva...............	NYP	14	*104⅔	●9	3	.750	59	27	22	*120	31	1.89
1985—Winston-Salem	Carolina	12	94	8	2	.800	82	36	24	94	22	2.30
1985—Pittsfield	Eastern	15	96⅔	7	6	.538	99	49	40	51	32	3.72
1986—Pittsfield	Eastern	6	41	3	1	.750	27	10	4	42	16	0.88
1986—Iowa............................	Am. Assoc.	6	42⅓	3	2	.600	25	14	12	25	11	2.55
1986—Chicago......................	National	16	87⅓	7	4	.636	107	52	49	45	42	5.05
1987—Chicago......................	National	35	201	12	15	.444	210	127	*114	147	97	5.10
1988—Chicago†....................	National	34	202	9	15	.375	212	84	78	121	55	3.48
1989—Texas‡......................	American	15	76	4	9	.308	84	51	41	44	33	4.86
1989—Sarasota Rangers........................	Gulf Coast	3	11	1	0	1.000	8	4	2	18	1	1.64
1989—Tulsa............................	Texas	2	12⅓	1	1	.500	16	8	7	9	3	5.11
1990—Texas§......................	American	33	102⅓	2	6	.250	115	59	53	58	39	4.66
National League Totals—3 Years........................		85	490⅓	28	34	.452	529	263	241	313	194	4.42
American League Totals—2 Years		48	178⅓	6	15	.286	199	110	94	102	72	4.74
Major League Totals—5 Years............................		133	668⅔	34	49	.410	728	373	335	415	266	4.51

Selected by Chicago Cubs' organization in 6th round of free-agent draft, June 4, 1984.
†Traded with Outfielder Rafael Palmeiro and Pitcher Drew Hall to Texas Rangers for Pitchers Mitch Williams, Paul Kilgus and Steve Wilson, Infielders Curtis Wilkerson and Luis Benitez and Outfielder Pablo Delgado, December 5, 1988.
‡On disabled list, May 31 to September 1, 1989; included rehabilitation disability assignment to Sarasota Rangers, August 5 to August 14, 1989; and Tulsa, August 15 to August 24, 1989.
§Released, November 13, 1990; signed by Louisville (St. Louis Cardinals' organization), January 9, 1991.

TERENCE JOHN MULHOLLAND
(Terry)

Born March 9, 1963, at Uniontown, Pa.
Height, 6.03. Weight, 207.
Throws left and bats righthanded.
Attended Marietta College, Marietta, O.

Pitched 6-0 no-hit victory against San Francisco, August 15, 1990.
Led Pacific Coast League pitchers in games started with 29 in 1987.
Led Texas League in shutouts with 3 in 1985.

Year Club	League	G.	IP.	W.	L.	Pct.	H.	R.	ER.	SO.	BB.	ERA.
1984—Everett......................	Northwest	3	19	1	0	1.000	10	2	0	15	4	0.00
1984—Fresno......................	California	9	42⅔	5	2	.714	32	17	14	39	36	2.95
1985—Shreveport	Texas	26	176⅔	9	8	.529	166	79	57	122	87	2.90
1986—Phoenix......................	P. Coast	17	111	8	5	.615	112	60	55	77	56	4.46
1986—San Francisco	National	15	54⅔	1	7	.125	51	33	30	27	35	4.94
1987—Phoenix......................	P. Coast	37	172⅓	7	12	.368	200	*124	●97	94	90	5.07
1988—Phoenix......................	P. Coast	19	100⅔	7	3	.700	116	45	40	57	44	3.58
1988—San Francisco†	National	9	46	2	1	.667	50	20	19	18	7	3.72
1989—Phoenix......................	P. Coast	13	78⅓	4	5	.444	67	30	26	61	26	2.99
1989—San Francisco‡-Philadelphia...............National		25	115⅓	4	7	.364	137	66	63	66	36	4.92
1990—Philadelphia§	National	33	180⅔	9	10	.474	172	78	67	75	42	3.34
1990—Scranton/Wilkes-Barre................Int'national		1	6	0	1	.000	9	4	2	2	2	3.00
Major League Totals—4 Years............................		82	396⅔	16	25	.390	410	197	179	186	120	4.06

Selected by San Francisco Giants' organization in 1st round (24th player selected) of free-agent draft, June 4, 1984.
†On disabled list, August 1, 1988 through remainder of season.

‡Traded with Pitchers Dennis Cook and Third Baseman Charlie Hayes to Philadelphia Phillies for Pitcher Steve Bedrosian and a player to be named later, June 18, 1989; San Francisco Giants' organization acquired Infielder Rick Parker to complete deal, August 7, 1989.

§On disabled list, June 12 to June 28, 1990; included rehabilitation disability assignment to Scranton/Wilkes-Barre, June 23 and June 24, 1990.

STEVEN RANCE MULLINIKS

Name pronounced MUL-in-iks.

(Known by middle name.)

Born January 15, 1956, at Tulare, Calif.
Height, 6.00. Weight, 175.
Throws right and bats lefthanded.
Son of Harvey Mulliniks, pitcher in New York Yankees' organization, 1956 and 1957.

Major League stolen bases: 1977 (1), 1978 (2), 1982 (3), 1984 (2), 1985 (2), 1986 (1), 1987 (1), 1988 (1), 1990 (2). Total—15.

Led American League third basemen in fielding percentage with .968 in 1984.

Led Pacific Coast League shortstops in fielding percentage with .968 in 1979.

Year Club	League	Pos.	G.	AB.	R.	H.	2B.	3B.	HR.	RBI.	B.A.	PO.	A.	E.	F.A.
1974—Idaho Falls	Pion.	SS	66	202	28	44	8	3	0	24	.218	*110	*170	*33	.895
1975—Quad Cities	Midw.	SS	52	186	34	50	6	2	1	21	.269	82	136	17	.928
1975—Salinas	Calif.	SS-2B	59	209	38	54	8	0	0	10	.258	88	146	14	.944
1976—El Paso†	Texas	SS-2B	90	333	81	105	22	4	7	51	.315	140	247	20	.951
1977—Salt Lake City	P. C.	SS	58	220	48	68	17	3	11	51	.309	116	207	15	.956
1977—California	Amer.	SS	78	271	36	73	13	2	3	21	.269	112	229	13	.963
1978—Salt Lake City	P. C.	SS	34	127	34	39	6	2	3	21	.307	65	109	12	.935
1978—California	Amer.	SS	50	119	6	22	3	1	1	6	.185	68	93	8	.953
1979—Salt Lake City	P. C.	SS-2B	116	402	94	138	21	7	3	59	.343	204	331	17	.969
1979—California‡	Amer.	SS	22	68	7	10	0	0	1	8	.147	46	43	4	.957
1980—Kansas City	Amer.	SS-2B	36	54	8	14	3	0	0	6	.259	30	53	1	.988
1981—Kansas City§	Amer.	2B-SS-3B	24	44	6	10	3	0	0	5	.227	25	39	5	.928
1982—Toronto	Amer.	3B-SS	112	311	32	76	25	0	4	35	.244	69	154	14	.941
1983—Toronto	Amer.	3B-SS-2B	129	364	54	100	34	3	10	49	.275	77	185	7	.974
1984—Toronto	Amer.	3B-SS-2B	125	343	41	111	21	5	3	42	.324	67	152	8	.965
1985—Toronto	Amer.	3B	129	366	55	108	26	1	10	57	.295	75	162	7	*.971
1986—Toronto x	Amer.	*3B-2B	117	348	50	90	22	0	11	45	.259	60	176	6	*.975
1987—Toronto	Amer.	3B-SS	124	332	37	103	28	1	11	44	.310	29	137	13	.927
1988—Toronto y	Amer.	3B	119	337	49	101	21	1	12	48	.300	3	5	0	1.000
1989—Toronto	Amer.	3B	103	273	25	65	11	2	3	29	.238	15	50	1	.985
1990—Toronto z	Amer.	3B-1B	57	97	11	28	4	0	2	16	.289	23	25	2	.960
Major League Totals—14 Years			1225	3327	417	911	214	16	71	411	.274	699	1503	89	.961

Selected by California Angels' organization in 3rd round of free-agent draft, June 5, 1974.

†On disabled list, May 4 to June 9 and September 2 to September 24, 1976.

‡Traded with First Baseman Willie Aikens to Kansas City Royals for Outfielder Al Cowens, Shortstop Todd Cruz and a player to be named later, December 6, 1979; California Angels acquired Pitcher Craig Eaton to complete deal, April 1, 1980.

§Traded to Toronto Blue Jays for Pitcher Phil Huffman, March 25, 1982.

xOn disabled list, August 6 to September 1, 1986.

yOn disabled list, April 12 to May 2, 1988.

zGranted free agency, November 5, 1990; re-signed by Blue Jays, December 4, 1990.

CHAMPIONSHIP SERIES RECORD

Year Club	League	Pos.	G.	AB.	R.	H.	2B.	3B.	HR.	RBI.	B.A.	PO.	A.	E.	F.A.
1985—Toronto	Amer.	PH-3B	5	11	1	4	1	0	1	3	.364	1	4	0	1.000
1989—Toronto	Amer.	PH	1	1	0	0	0	0	0	0	.000	0	0	0	.000
Championship Series Totals—2 Years			6	12	1	4	1	0	1	3	.333	1	4	0	1.000

MICHAEL ANTHONY MUNOZ

(Mike)

Born July 12, 1965, at Baldwin Park, Calif.
Height, 6.02. Weight, 195.
Throws and bats lefthanded.
Attended California State Poly University, Pomona, Calif.

Tied for Pacific Coast League lead in intentional bases on balls issued with 8 in 1989.

Year Club	League	G.	IP.	W.	L.	Pct.	H.	R.	ER.	SO.	BB.	ERA.
1986—Great Falls	Pioneer	14	81⅓	4	4	.500	85	44	29	49	38	3.21
1987—Bakersfield	California	52	118	8	7	.533	125	68	49	80	43	3.74
1988—San Antonio	Texas	56	71⅔	7	2	.778	63	18	8	71	24	1.00
1989—Albuquerque	P. Coast	60	79	6	4	.600	72	32	27	81	40	3.08
1989—Los Angeles	National	3	2⅔	0	0	.000	5	5	5	3	2	16.88
1990—Los Angeles	National	8	5⅔	0	1	.000	6	2	2	2	3	3.18
1990—Albuquerque†	P. Coast	49	59⅓	4	1	.800	65	33	28	40	19	4.25
Major League Totals—2 Years		11	8⅓	0	1	.000	11	7	7	5	5	7.56

Selected by Los Angeles Dodgers' organization in 3rd round of free-agent draft, June 2, 1986.

†Traded to Detroit Tigers for Pitcher Mike Wilkins, September 30, 1990.

PEDRO JAVIER MUNOZ

Born September 19, 1968, at Ponce, Puerto Rico.
Height, 5.11. Weight, 170.
Throws and bats righthanded.

Major League stolen bases: 1990 (3).
Tied for South Atlantic League lead in intentional bases on balls received with 4 in 1987.

Year	Club	League	Pos.	G.	AB.	R.	H.	2B.	3B.	HR.	RBI.	B.A.	PO.	A.	E.	F.A.
1985—Bradenton Jays....	Gulf C.		OF	40	145	14	38	3	0	2	17	.262	46	2	1	.980
1986—Florence	S. Atl.		OF	122	445	69	131	16	5	14	82	.294	197	14	9	.959
1987—Dunedin†	Fla. St.		OF	92	341	55	80	11	5	8	44	.235	4	1	0	1.000
1988—Dunedin	Fla. St.		OF	133	481	59	141	21	7	8	73	.293	164	8	*15	.920
1989—Knoxville	South.		OF	122	442	54	118	15	4	19	65	.267	55	3	1	.983
1990—Syracuse‡	Int.		OF	86	317	41	101	22	3	7	56	.319	110	4	6	.950
1990—Portland	P. C.		OF	30	110	19	35	4	0	5	21	.318	51	1	3	.945
1990—Minnesota	Amer.		OF	22	85	13	23	4	1	0	5	.271	34	1	1	.972
Major League Totals—1 Year				22	85	13	23	4	1	0	5	.271	34	1	1	.972

Signed as free agent by Toronto Blue Jays' organization, May 31, 1985.
†On disabled list, July 30 to August 28, 1987.
‡Traded with Second Baseman Nelson Liriano to Minnesota Twins for Pitcher John Candelaria, July 27, 1990.

DALE BRYAN MURPHY

Born March 12, 1956, at Portland, Ore.
Height, 6.04. Weight, 215.
Throws and bats righthanded.
Attended Portland Community College, Portland, Ore. and Brigham Young University, Provo, Utah.

Shares major league records for most home runs (2) and runs batted in (6), inning, July 27, 1989, sixth inning; most years leading league in games, outfielder (6); fewest double plays by outfielder, season, 150 or more games (0), 1983; fewest double plays by outfielder, season, for leader in double plays (4), 1981 and 1985.
Shares National League record for most intentional bases on balls by righthander, season, (29), 1987.
Major League stolen bases: 1978 (11), 1979 (6), 1980 (9), 1981 (14), 1982 (23), 1983 (30), 1984 (19), 1985 (10), 1986 (7), 1987 (16), 1988 (3), 1989 (3), 1990 (9). Total—160.
Hit three home runs in a game, May 18, 1979.
Led National League in grounding into double plays with 24 in 1988 and 22 in 1990.
Led National League in intentional bases on balls received with 29 in 1987.
Led National League in bases on balls received with 90 in 1985.
Led National League in total bases with 332 in 1984.
Led National League in slugging percentage with .540 in 1983 and .547 in 1984.
Led National League batters in strikeouts with 145 in 1978, 133 in 1980 and tied for lead with 141 in 1985.
Led National League first basemen in errors with 20 in 1978.
Tied for National League lead in double plays by outfielders with 4 in 1981 and 1985.
Tied for International League lead in total bases with 249 in 1977.
Led International League catchers in putouts with 510, passed balls with 14 and tied for lead in double plays with 7 in 1977.
Named National League Player of the Year by THE SPORTING NEWS, 1982 and 1983.
Named National League Most Valuable Player by Baseball Writers' Association of America, 1982 and 1983.
Named outfielder on THE SPORTING NEWS National League All-Star Team, 1982 through 1985.
Named outfielder on THE SPORTING NEWS National League All-Star fielding team, 1982 through 1986.
Named outfielder on THE SPORTING NEWS National League Silver Slugger team, 1982 through 1985.

Year	Club	League	Pos.	G.	AB.	R.	H.	2B.	3B.	HR.	RBI.	B.A.	PO.	A.	E.	F.A.
1974—Kingsport	Appal.		C	54	181	28	46	7	0	5	31	.254	389	28	7	.983
1975—Greenwood	W. Car.		C-1B	131	443	48	101	20	1	5	48	.228	723	81	18	.978
1976—Savannah	South.		C	104	352	37	94	13	5	12	55	.267	444	40	10	.980
1976—Richmond	Int.		C-OF	18	50	10	13	1	1	4	8	.260	60	9	4	.945
1976—Atlanta	Nat.		C	19	65	3	17	6	0	0	9	.262	100	13	3	.974
1977—Richmond	Int.		C-1B	127	466	71	142	●33	4	22	*90	.305	600	50	15	.977
1977—Atlanta	Nat.		C	18	76	5	24	8	1	2	14	.316	114	11	6	.954
1978—Atlanta	Nat.		1B-C	151	530	66	120	14	3	23	79	.226	1220	105	23	.983
1979—Atlanta†	Nat.		1B-C	104	384	53	106	7	2	21	57	.276	812	57	20	.978
1980—Atlanta	Nat.		OF-1B	156	569	98	160	27	2	33	89	.281	384	15	6	.985
1981—Atlanta	Nat.		OF-1B	104	369	43	91	12	1	13	50	.247	264	11	5	.982
1982—Atlanta	Nat.		OF	●162	598	113	168	23	2	36	●109	.281	407	6	9	.979
1983—Atlanta	Nat.		OF	*162	589	131	178	24	4	36	*121	.302	373	10	6	.985
1984—Atlanta	Nat.		OF	*162	607	94	176	32	8	●36	100	.290	369	10	5	.987
1985—Atlanta	Nat.		OF	●162	616	*118	185	32	2	*37	111	.300	334	8	7	.980
1986—Atlanta	Nat.		OF	160	614	89	163	29	7	29	83	.265	303	6	6	.981
1987—Atlanta	Nat.		OF	159	566	115	167	27	1	44	105	.295	325	14	8	.977
1988—Atlanta	Nat.		OF	156	592	77	134	35	4	24	77	.226	340	15	3	.992
1989—Atlanta	Nat.		OF	154	574	60	131	16	0	20	84	.228	331	5	5	.985
1990—Atl.‡-Phila.	Nat.		OF	154	563	60	138	23	1	24	83	.245	321	7	5	.985
Major League Totals—15 Years				1983	7312	1125	1958	315	38	378	1171	.268	5997	293	117	.982

Selected by Atlanta Braves' organization in 1st round (fifth player selected) of free-agent draft, June 5, 1974.
†On disabled list, May 25 to July 19, 1979.
‡Traded with a player to be named later to Philadelphia Phillies for Pitcher Jeff Parrett and two players to be named later, August 3, 1990; Scranton/Wilkes-Barre (Philadelphia Phillies' organization) acquired Pitcher Tommy Greene on August 9, 1990 and Atlanta Braves acquired Outfielder Jim Vatcher on August 9, 1990 and Shortstop Victor Rosario on September 4, 1990 to complete deal.

Year	Club	League	Pos.	G.	AB.	R.	H.	2B.	3B.	HR.	RBI.	B.A.	PO.	A.	E.	F.A.
1982—Atlanta		Nat.	OF	3	11	1	3	0	0	0	0	.273	8	0	0	1.000

ALL-STAR GAME RECORD

Year	League	Pos.	AB.	R.	H.	2B.	3B.	HR.	RBI.	B.A.	PO.	A.	E.	F.A.
1980—National		OF	1	0	0	0	0	0	0	.000	0	0	0	.000
1982—National		OF	2	1	0	0	0	0	0	.000	2	0	0	1.000
1983—National		OF	3	0	1	0	0	0	1	.333	0	0	0	.000
1984—National		OF	3	1	2	0	0	1	1	.667	0	0	0	.000
1985—National		OF	3	0	1	1	0	0	0	.333	1	0	0	1.000
1986—National		OF	2	0	0	0	0	0	0	.000	2	0	0	1.000
1987—National		OF	1	0	0	0	0	0	0	.000	1	0	0	1.000
All-Star Game Totals—7 Years			15	2	4	1	0	1	2	.267	6	0	0	1.000

ROBERT ALBERT MURPHY JR.
(Rob)

Born May 26, 1960, at Miami, Fla.
Height, 6.02. Weight, 215.
Throws and bats lefthanded.
Attended University of Florida, Gainesville, Fla.

Major League saves: 1986 (1), 1987 (3), 1988 (3), 1989 (9), 1990 (7). Total—23.
Tied for Eastern League lead in saves with 15 in 1984.

Year	Club	League	G.	IP.	W.	L.	Pct.	H.	R.	ER.	SO.	BB.	ERA.
1981—Tampa		Florida St.	25	105	6	8	.429	109	73	53	58	67	4.54
1982—Cedar Rapids		Midwest	31	89	3	7	.300	92	62	40	96	61	4.04
1983—Cedar Rapids		Midwest	36	140⅔	6	10	.375	120	66	52	137	69	3.33
1984—Vermont		Eastern	45	69⅔	2	3	.400	57	23	21	69	35	2.71
1985—Denver		Am. Assoc.	41	84	5	5	.500	94	55	43	66	57	4.61
1985—Cincinnati		National	2	3	0	0	.000	2	2	2	1	2	6.00
1986—Denver		Am. Assoc.	27	42⅔	3	4	.429	33	12	9	36	24	1.90
1986—Cincinnati		National	34	50⅓	6	0	1.000	26	4	4	36	21	0.72
1987—Cincinnati		National	87	100⅔	8	5	.615	91	37	34	99	32	3.04
1988—Cincinnati†		National	★76	84⅔	0	6	.000	69	31	29	74	38	3.08
1989—Boston		American	74	105	5	7	.417	97	38	32	107	41	2.74
1990—Boston		American	68	57	0	6	.000	85	46	40	54	32	6.32
National League Totals—4 Years			199	238⅔	14	11	.560	188	74	69	210	93	2.60
American League Totals—2 Years			142	162	5	13	.278	182	84	72	161	73	4.00
Major League Totals—6 Years			341	400⅔	19	24	.442	370	158	141	371	166	3.17

Selected by Milwaukee Brewers' organization in 29th round of free-agent draft, June 6, 1978.
Selected by Cincinnati Reds' organization in secondary phase of free-agent draft, January 13, 1981.
†Traded with First Baseman Nick Esasky to Boston Red Sox for First Baseman Todd Benzinger, Pitcher Jeff Sellers and a player to be named later, December 13, 1988; Cincinnati Reds acquired Pitcher Luis Vasquez to complete deal, January 12, 1989.

CHAMPIONSHIP SERIES RECORD

Year	Club	League	G.	IP.	W.	L.	Pct.	H.	R.	ER.	SO.	BB.	ERA.
1990—Boston		American	1	⅔	0	0	.000	2	1	1	0	1	13.50

EDDIE CLARENCE MURRAY

Born February 24, 1956, at Los Angeles, Calif.
Height, 6.02. Weight, 224.
Throws right and bats left and righthanded.
Attended California State University, Los Angeles, Calif.
Brother of Rich Murray, first baseman with San Francisco Giants, 1980 and 1983;
Leon Murray, first baseman in San Franciso Giants' organization, 1970;
Charles Murray, minor league outfielder, 1962 through 1966
and 1969; and Venice Murray, first baseman in
San Francisco Giants' organization, 1978.

Shares major league records for most games, switch-hit home runs, lifetime (10), and season (2), 1982, 1987 and 1990.
Holds American League records for most consecutive games, one or more hits by switch-hitter, season (22), 1984; most game-winning runs batted in, lifetime (117); most intentional bases on balls by switch-hitter, season (25), 1984.
Holds National League record for fewest double plays by first baseman, season, 150 or more games (88), 1990.
Major League stolen bases: 1978 (6), 1979 (10), 1980 (7), 1981 (2), 1982 (7), 1983 (5), 1984 (10), 1985 (5), 1986 (3), 1987 (1), 1988 (5), 1989 (7), 1990 (8). Total—76.
Hit three home runs in a game, August 29, 1979 (second game), September 14, 1980 (13 innings) and August 26, 1985.
Switch-hit home runs in one game 10 times: August 3, 1977, August 29, 1979 (two righthanded and one lefthanded); August 16, 1981, April 24, 1982, August 26, 1982, August 26, 1985 (two lefthanded and one righthanded), May 8, 1987, May 9, 1987, April 18, 1990 and June 9, 1990.
Led American League in bases on balls received with 107 and game-winning RBIs with 19 in 1984.
Led American League in intentional bases on balls received with 25 in 1984 and tied for lead with 18 in 1982.
Tied for National League lead in intentional bases on balls received with 21 in 1990.
Led National League first basemen in double plays with 122 in 1989.
Led American League first basemen in double plays with 152 in 1984, 146 in 1987 and tied for lead with 154 in 1985.
Led American League first basemen in total chances with 1,615 in 1978, 1,694 in 1984 and 1,526 in 1987.
Led American League first basemen in putouts with 1,504 in 1978.

Led Florida State League in total bases with 212 in 1974.
Led Florida State League first basemen in double plays with 113 in 1974.
Named American League Rookie of the Year by Baseball Writers' Association of America, 1977.
Named first baseman on THE SPORTING NEWS National League All-Star Team, 1990.
Named first baseman on THE SPORTING NEWS American League All-Star Team, 1983.
Named first baseman on THE SPORTING NEWS American League All-Star fielding team, 1982 through 1984.
Named first baseman on THE SPORTING NEWS National League Silver Slugger team, 1990.
Named first baseman on THE SPORTING NEWS American League Silver Slugger team, 1983 and 1984.
Named Appalachian League Player of the Year, 1973.

Year Club	League	Pos.	G.	AB.	R.	H.	2B.	3B.	HR.	RBI.	B.A.	PO.	A.	E.	F.A.
1973—Bluefield	Appal.	1B	50	188	34	54	6	0	11	32	.287	421	14	13	.971
1974—Miami	Fla. St.	1B	131	460	64	133	★29	7	12	63	.289	★1114	★51	★25	.979
1974—Asheville	South.	1B	2	7	1	2	2	0	0	2	.286	17	0	0	1.000
1975—Asheville	South.	1B-3B	124	436	66	115	13	5	17	68	.264	637	58	15	.979
1976—Charlotte	South.	1B	88	299	46	89	15	2	12	46	.298	746	45	9	.989
1976—Rochester	Int.	1B-OF-3B	54	168	35	46	6	2	11	40	.274	291	13	5	.984
1977—Baltimore	Amer.	OF-1B	160	611	81	173	29	2	27	88	.283	482	20	4	.992
1978—Baltimore	Amer.	1B-3B	161	610	85	174	32	3	27	95	.285	1507	112	6	.996
1979—Baltimore	Amer.	1B	159	606	90	179	30	2	25	99	.295	★1456	107	10	.994
1980—Baltimore	Amer.	1B	158	621	100	186	36	2	32	116	.300	1369	77	9	.994
1981—Baltimore	Amer.	1B	99	378	57	111	21	2	●22	★78	.294	899	★91	1	★.999
1982—Baltimore	Amer.	1B	151	550	87	174	30	1	32	110	.316	1269	97	4	★.997
1983—Baltimore	Amer.	1B	156	582	115	178	30	3	33	111	.306	1393	114	10	.993
1984—Baltimore	Amer.	1B	●162	588	97	180	26	3	29	110	.306	★1538	★143	13	.992
1985—Baltimore	Amer.	1B	156	583	111	173	37	1	31	124	.297	1338	152	★19	.987
1986—Baltimore†	Amer.	1B	137	495	61	151	25	1	17	84	.305	1045	88	13	.989
1987—Baltimore	Amer.	1B	160	618	89	171	28	3	30	91	.277	1371	145	10	.993
1988—Baltimore‡	Amer.	1B	161	603	75	171	27	2	28	84	.284	867	106	11	.989
1989—Los Angeles	Nat.	★1B-3B	160	594	66	147	29	1	20	88	.247	1316	★137	6	★.996
1990—Los Angeles	Nat.	1B	155	558	96	184	22	3	26	95	.330	1180	113	10	.992
American League Totals—12 Years			1820	6845	1048	2021	351	25	333	1190	.295	14534	1252	110	.993
National League Totals—2 Years			315	1152	162	331	51	4	46	183	.287	2496	250	16	.994
Major League Totals—14 Years			2135	7997	1210	2352	402	29	379	1373	.294	17030	1502	126	.993

Selected by Baltimore Orioles' organization in 3rd round of free-agent draft, June 5, 1973.

†On disabled list, July 10 to August 7, 1986.

‡Traded to Los Angeles Dodgers for Pitchers Brian Holton and Ken Howell and Shortstop Juan Bell, December 4, 1988.

CHAMPIONSHIP SERIES RECORD

Shares Championship Series record for most runs, game (4), October 7, 1983.

Year Club	League	Pos.	G.	AB.	R.	H.	2B.	3B.	HR.	RBI.	B.A.	PO.	A.	E.	F.A.
1979—Baltimore	Amer.	1B	4	12	3	5	0	0	1	5	.417	44	3	2	.959
1983—Baltimore	Amer.	1B	4	15	5	4	0	0	1	3	.267	34	3	1	.974
Championship Series Totals—2 Years			8	27	8	9	0	0	2	8	.333	78	6	3	.966

WORLD SERIES RECORD

Year Club	League	Pos.	G.	AB.	R.	H.	2B.	3B.	HR.	RBI.	B.A.	PO.	A.	E.	F.A.
1979—Baltimore	Amer.	1B	7	26	3	4	1	0	1	2	.154	60	7	0	1.000
1983—Baltimore	Amer.	1B	5	20	2	5	0	0	2	3	.250	46	1	1	.979
World Series Totals—2 Years			12	46	5	9	1	0	3	5	.196	106	8	1	.991

ALL-STAR GAME RECORD

Year League	Pos.	AB.	R.	H.	2B.	3B.	HR.	RBI.	B.A.	PO.	A.	E.	F.A.
1981—American	PH-1B	2	0	0	0	0	0	0	.000	2	1	0	1.000
1982—American	PH-1B	1	0	0	0	0	0	0	.000	4	0	0	1.000
1983—American	1B	2	0	0	0	0	0	0	.000	4	0	0	1.000
1984—American	1B	2	0	1	1	0	0	0	.500	3	0	0	1.000
1985—American	1B	3	0	0	0	0	0	0	.000	5	2	0	1.000
All-Star Game Totals—5 Years		10	0	1	1	0	0	0	.100	18	3	0	1.000

Member of American League All-Star Team in 1978 and 1986; did not play.

JEFFREY JOSEPH MUSSELMAN
(Jeff)

Born June 21, 1963, at Doylestown, Pa.
Height, 6.00. Weight, 185.
Throws and bats lefthanded.
Received bachelor of arts degree in economics from Harvard University, Cambridge, Mass., in 1985.

Major League saves: 1987 (1).
Tied for Pioneer League lead in games started by pitchers with 15 in 1985.

Year Club	League	G.	IP.	W.	L.	Pct.	H.	R.	ER.	SO.	BB.	ERA.
1985—Medicine Hat	Pioneer	16	88	6	4	.600	75	41	39	96	44	3.99
1986—Ventura County	California	26	154⅔	7	7	.500	122	67	52	165	59	3.03
1986—Knoxville	Southern	7	41⅓	5	1	.833	33	17	13	38	25	2.83
1986—Toronto	American	6	5⅓	0	0	.000	8	7	6	4	5	10.13
1987—Toronto	American	68	89	12	5	.706	75	43	41	54	54	4.15
1988—Dunedin†	Florida St.	2	5⅔	0	0	.000	6	3	2	4	1	3.18
1988—Syracuse	Int'national	10	49	4	1	.800	42	20	16	31	17	2.94

Year Club	League	G.	IP.	W.	L.	Pct.	H.	R.	ER.	SO.	BB.	ERA.
1988—Toronto	American	15	85	8	5	.615	80	34	30	39	30	3.18
1989—Toronto‡	American	5	11	0	1	.000	19	15	13	3	9	10.64
1989—Syracuse§	Int'national	10	57⅓	5	2	.714	62	24	24	30	24	3.77
1989—New York	National	20	26⅓	3	2	.600	27	11	9	11	14	3.08
1990—New York	National	28	32	0	2	.000	40	22	20	14	11	5.63
1990—Tidewater x	Int'national	10	56⅓	4	3	.571	60	24	22	31	16	3.51
American League Totals—4 Years		94	190⅓	20	11	.645	182	99	90	100	98	4.26
National League Totals—2 Years		48	58⅓	3	4	.429	67	33	29	25	25	4.47
Major League Totals—5 Years		142	248⅔	23	15	.605	249	132	119	125	123	4.31

Selected by Toronto Blue Jays' organization in 6th round of free-agent draft, June 3, 1985.

†On Toronto disabled list, March 22 to June 15, 1988; included rehabilitation disability assignment to Dunedin, May 23 to May 27, 1988.

‡On disabled list, April 19 to June 27, 1989; included rehabilitation disability assignment to Syracuse, June 7 to June 26, 1989.

§Traded with Pitcher Mike Brady to New York Mets for a player to be named later, July 31, 1989; Toronto Blue Jays acquired Outfielder Mookie Wilson to complete deal, August 1, 1989.

xGranted free agency, December 20, 1990.

JEFFREY THOMAS MUTIS
(Jeff)

Born December 20, 1966, at Allentown, Pa.
Height, 6.02. Weight, 185.
Throws and bats lefthanded.
Attended Lafayette College, Easton, Pa.

Tied for Eastern League lead in shutouts with 3 in 1990.

Year Club	League	G.	IP.	W.	L.	Pct.	H.	R.	ER.	SO.	BB.	ERA.
1988—Burlington	Ap'lachian	3	22	3	0	1.000	8	1	1	20	6	0.41
1988—Kinston†	Carolina	1	5⅔	1	0	1.000	6	1	1	2	3	1.59
1989—Kinston‡	Carolina	16	99⅔	7	3	.700	87	42	29	68	20	2.62
1990—Canton-Akron	Eastern	26	165	11	10	.524	*178	73	58	94	44	3.16

Selected by Cleveland Indians' organization in 34th round of free-agent draft, June 3, 1985.
Selected by Cleveland Indians' organization in 1st round (27th player selected) of free-agent draft, June 1, 1988.
†On disabled list, July 20, 1988 through remainder of season.
‡On disabled list, July 6 to July 31 and August 1, 1989 through remainder of season.

GREGORY RICHARD MYERS
(Greg)

Born April 14, 1966, at Riverside, Calif.
Height, 6.02. Weight, 205.
Throws right and bats lefthanded.

Led International League catchers in total chances with 698 in 1987.
Led California League catchers in total chances with 967 in 1986.

Year Club	League	Pos.	G.	AB.	R.	H.	2B.	3B.	HR.	RBI.	B.A.	PO.	A.	E.	F.A.
1984—Medicine Hat	Pion.	C	38	133	20	42	9	0	2	20	.316	216	24	4	.984
1985—Florence	S. Atl.	C	134	489	52	109	19	2	5	62	.223	551	61	7	*.989
1986—Ventura	Calif.	C	124	451	65	133	23	4	20	79	.295	*849	99	19	.980
1987—Syracuse	Int.	C	107	342	35	84	19	1	10	47	.246	*637	50	11	.984
1987—Toronto	Amer.	C	7	9	1	1	0	0	0	0	.111	24	1	0	1.000
1988—Syracuse†	Int.	C	34	120	18	34	7	1	7	21	.283	63	9	1	.986
1989—Knoxville‡	South.	C	29	90	11	30	10	0	5	19	.333	130	12	1	.993
1989—Toronto	Amer.	C	17	44	0	5	2	0	0	1	.114	46	6	0	1.000
1989—Syracuse	Int.	C	24	89	8	24	6	0	1	11	.270	60	7	1	.985
1990—Toronto§	Amer.	C	87	250	33	59	7	1	5	22	.236	411	30	3	.993
1990—Syracuse	Int.	C	3	11	0	2	1	0	0	2	.182	14	0	0	1.000
Major League Totals—3 Years			111	303	34	65	9	1	5	23	.215	481	37	3	.994

Selected by Toronto Blue Jays' organization in 3rd round of free-agent draft, June 4, 1984.
†On disabled list, June 17, 1988 through remainder of season.
‡On Toronto disabled list, March 26 to June 5, 1989; included rehabilitation disability assignment to Knoxville, May 17 to June 5, 1989.
§On disabled list, May 5 to May 25, 1990; included rehabilitation disability assignment to Syracuse, May 21 to May 24, 1990.

RANDALL KIRK MYERS
(Randy)

Born September 19, 1962, at Vancouver, Wash.
Height, 6.01. Weight, 208.
Throws and bats lefthanded.
Attended Clark College, Vancouver, Wash.

Shares National League record for most consecutive strikeouts by relief pitcher, game (6), September 8, 1990.
Major League saves: 1987 (6), 1988 (26), 1989 (24), 1990 (31). Total—87.
Tied for Carolina League lead in complete games with 7 in 1984.
Tied for South Atlantic League lead in games started by pitchers with 28 in 1983.
Tied for Appalachian League lead in games started by pitchers with 13 and balks with 3 in 1982.
Named Carolina League Pitcher of the Year, 1984.

Year Club	League	G.	IP.	W.	L.	Pct.	H.	R.	ER.	SO.	BB.	ERA.
1982—Kingsport	Ap'lachian	13	74⅓	6	3	.667	68	49	34	●86	69	4.12
1983—Columbia	S. Atlantic	28	173⅓	14	10	.583	146	94	70	164	108	3.63
1984—Lynchburg	Carolina	23	157	13	5	.722	123	46	36	171	61	★2.06
1984—Jackson	Texas	5	35	2	1	.667	29	14	8	35	16	2.06
1985—Jackson	Texas	19	120⅓	4	8	.333	99	61	53	116	69	3.96
1985—Tidewater	Int'national	8	44	1	1	.500	40	13	9	25	20	1.84
1985—New York	National	1	2	0	0	.000	0	0	0	2	1	0.00
1986—Tidewater	Int'national	45	65	6	7	.462	44	19	17	79	44	2.35
1986—New York	National	10	10⅔	0	0	.000	11	5	5	13	9	4.22
1987—New York	National	54	75	3	6	.333	61	36	33	92	30	3.96
1987—Tidewater	Int'national	5	7⅓	0	0	.000	6	4	4	13	4	4.91
1988—New York	National	55	68	7	3	.700	45	15	13	69	17	1.72
1989—New York†	National	65	84⅓	7	4	.636	62	23	22	88	40	2.35
1990—Cincinnati	National	66	86⅔	4	6	.400	59	24	20	98	38	2.08
Major League Totals—6 Years		251	326⅔	21	19	.525	238	103	93	362	135	2.56

Selected by Cincinnati Reds' organization in 3rd round of free-agent draft, January 12, 1982.
Selected by New York Mets' organization in secondary phase of free-agent draft, June 7, 1982.
†Traded with Pitcher Kip Gross to Cincinnati Reds for Pitcher John Franco and Outfielder Don Brown, December 6, 1989.

CHAMPIONSHIP SERIES RECORD
Shares National League record for most saves, series (3), 1990.

Year Club	League	G.	IP.	W.	L.	Pct.	H.	R.	ER.	SO.	BB.	ERA.
1988—New York	National	3	4⅔	2	0	1.000	1	0	0	0	2	0.00
1990—Cincinnati	National	4	5⅔	0	0	.000	2	0	0	7	3	0.00
Championship Series Totals—2 Years		7	10⅓	2	0	1.000	3	0	0	7	5	0.00

WORLD SERIES RECORD

Year Club	League	G.	IP.	W.	L.	Pct.	H.	R.	ER.	SO.	BB.	ERA.
1990—Cincinnati	National	3	3	0	0	.000	2	0	0	3	0	0.00

ALL-STAR GAME RECORD

Year League	IP.	W.	L.	Pct.	H.	R.	ER.	SO.	BB.	ERA.
1990—National	1	0	0	.000	1	0	0	0	2	0.00

CHRISTOPHER WILLIAM NABHOLZ
(Chris)

Born January 5, 1967, at Harrisburg, Pa.
Height, 6.05. Weight, 210.
Throws and bats lefthanded.
Attended Towson State University, Towson, Md.

Year Club	League	G.	IP.	W.	L.	Pct.	H.	R.	ER.	SO.	BB.	ERA.
1989—Rockford	Midwest	24	161⅓	13	5	.722	132	54	39	149	41	2.18
1990—Jacksonville	Southern	11	74⅓	7	2	.778	62	28	25	77	27	3.03
1990—Montreal	National	11	70	6	2	.750	43	23	22	53	32	2.83
1990—Indianapolis	Am. Assoc.	10	63⅓	0	6	.000	66	38	34	44	28	4.83
Major League Totals—1 Year		11	70	6	2	.750	43	23	22	53	32	2.83

Selected by Cleveland Indians' organization in 30th round of free-agent draft, June 3, 1985.
Selected by Montreal Expos' organization in 2nd round of free-agent draft, June 1, 1988.

TIMOTHY JAMES NAEHRING
(Tim)

Born February 1, 1967, at Cincinnati, O.
Height, 6.02. Weight, 190.
Throws and bats righthanded.
Attended Miami University, Oxford, O.

Year Club	League	Pos.	G.	AB.	R.	H.	2B.	3B.	HR.	RBI.	B.A.	PO.	A.	E.	F.A.
1988—Elmira	NYP	SS	19	59	6	18	3	0	1	13	.305	25	51	6	.927
1988—Winter Haven	Fla. St.	SS	42	141	17	32	7	0	0	10	.227	77	136	20	.914
1989—Lynchburg	Carol.	SS	56	209	24	63	7	1	4	37	.301	72	131	12	.944
1989—Pawtucket	Int.	SS-3B	79	273	32	75	16	1	3	31	.275	118	192	21	.937
1990—Pawtucket	Int.	SS-3B-2B	82	290	45	78	16	1	15	47	.269	126	240	16	.958
1990—Boston†	Amer.	SS-3B-2B	24	85	10	23	6	0	2	12	.271	36	66	9	.919
Major League Totals—1 Year			24	85	10	23	6	0	2	12	.271	36	66	9	.919

Selected by Boston Red Sox' organization in 8th round of free-agent draft, June 1, 1988.
†On disabled list, August 16, 1990 through remainder of season.

CHARLES HARRISON NAGY

Born May 5, 1967, at Bridgeport, Conn.
Height, 6.03. Weight, 200.
Throws right and bats lefthanded.
Attended University of Connecticut, Storrs, Conn.
Led Eastern League in shutouts with 4 in 1989.
Tied for Eastern League lead in complete games with 9 in 1990.

Named Carolina League Pitcher of the Year, 1989.
Received reported $125,000 bonus to sign with Cleveland Indians' organization, 1988.
Member of 1988 U.S. Olympic baseball team.

Year Club	League	G.	IP.	W.	L.	Pct.	H.	R.	ER.	SO.	BB.	ERA.
1989—Kinston	Carolina	13	95⅓	8	4	.667	69	22	16	99	24	1.51
1989—Canton-Akron	Eastern	15	94	4	5	.444	102	44	35	65	32	3.35
1990—Canton-Akron	Eastern	23	175	13	8	.619	132	62	49	99	39	2.52
1990—Cleveland	American	9	45⅔	2	4	.333	58	31	30	26	21	5.91
Major League Totals—1 Year		9	45⅔	2	4	.333	58	31	30	26	21	5.91

Selected by Cleveland Indians' organization in 1st round (17th player selected) of free-agent draft, June 1, 1988.

JAIME NAVARRO

Born March 27, 1967, at Bayamon, Puerto Rico.
Height, 6.04. Weight, 210.
Throws and bats righthanded.
Attended Miami-Dade Community College-New World Center, Miami, Fla.
Son of Julio Navarro, pitcher with Los Angeles Dodgers, Detroit Tigers and Atlanta Braves,
1962 through 1966 and 1970; scout in Chicago Cubs' organization, 1980 through 1985;
and minor league coach with Atlanta Braves' organization, 1988.

Major League saves: 1990 (1).
Led American League in balks with 5 in 1990.

Year Club	League	G.	IP.	W.	L.	Pct.	H.	R.	ER.	SO.	BB.	ERA.
1987—Helena	Pioneer	13	85⅓	4	3	.571	87	37	34	95	18	3.57
1988—Stockton	California	26	174⅔	15	5	.750	148	70	60	151	74	3.09
1989—El Paso	Texas	11	76⅔	5	2	.714	61	29	21	78	35	2.47
1989—Denver	Am. Assoc.	3	20	1	1	.500	24	8	8	17	7	3.60
1989—Milwaukee	American	19	109⅔	7	8	.467	119	47	38	56	32	3.12
1990—Milwaukee	American	32	149⅓	8	7	.533	176	83	74	75	41	4.46
1990—Denver	Am. Assoc.	6	40⅔	2	3	.400	41	27	19	28	14	4.20
Major League Totals—2 Years		51	259	15	15	.500	295	130	112	131	73	3.89

Selected by Baltimore Orioles' organization in 2nd round of free-agent draft, January 14, 1986.
Selected by Baltimore Orioles' organization in secondary phase of free-agent draft, June 2, 1986.
Selected by Milwaukee Brewers' organization in 3rd round of free-agent draft, June 2, 1987.

JEFFREY DAVID NEELY
(Jeff)

Born August 9, 1965, at Tacoma, Wash.
Height, 6.04. Weight, 195.
Throws and bats righthanded.
Attended University of Portland, Portland, Ore.
Led Eastern League in intentional bases on balls issued with 10 in 1990.

Year Club	League	G.	IP.	W.	L.	Pct.	H.	R.	ER.	SO.	BB.	ERA.
1988—Bradenton Pirates	Gulf Coast	14	35⅓	4	3	.571	29	15	10	29	4	2.55
1989—Augusta	S. Atlantic	54	95⅔	10	8	.556	62	17	13	93	26	1.22
1990—Salem	Carolina	6	7⅓	0	1	.000	5	2	2	11	3	2.45
1990—Harrisburg	Eastern	40	65⅔	4	4	.500	49	22	13	62	18	1.78
1990—Buffalo	Am. Assoc.	6	8⅔	1	0	1.000	5	4	4	5	4	4.15

Signed as free agent by Pittsburgh Pirates' organization, June 14, 1988.

JAMES LLEWELYN NEIDLINGER
(Jim)

Born September 24, 1964, at Vallejo, Calif.
Height, 6.04. Weight, 180.
Throws right and bats left and righthanded.
Attended Marin Community College, Kentfield, Calif.

Pitched 2-0 no-hit victory against Glens Falls, July 1, 1986.
Tied for Carolina League lead in games started by pitchers with 26 in 1985.
Named Eastern League Pitcher of the Year, 1986.

Year Club	League	G.	IP.	W.	L.	Pct.	H.	R.	ER.	SO.	BB.	ERA.
1984—Mason	S. Atlantic	25	166	9	8	.529	138	65	51	113	85	2.77
1985—Prince William	Carolina	26	165⅓	8	●13	.381	141	86	79	143	83	4.30
1986—Nashua	Eastern	22	163⅔	12	7	.632	135	57	44	98	44	★2.42
1986—Hawaii	P. Coast	4	27⅔	2	1	.667	33	14	12	14	9	3.90
1987—Harrisburg	Eastern	26	170⅔	11	8	.579	183	92	75	96	61	3.96
1988—Harrisburg	Eastern	40	124⅔	5	8	.385	135	54	39	88	25	2.82
1988—Buffalo†	Am. Assoc.	3	4⅓	0	0	.000	7	3	3	4	1	6.23
1989—Albuquerque	P. Coast	34	139⅔	8	6	.571	164	77	63	97	37	4.06
1990—Albuquerque	P. Coast	20	119⅔	8	5	.615	129	70	57	81	34	4.29
1990—Los Angeles	National	12	74	5	3	.625	67	30	27	46	15	3.28
Major League Totals—1 Year		12	74	5	3	.625	67	30	27	46	15	3.28

Signed as free agent by Pittsburgh Pirates' organization, March 4, 1984.
†Traded to Los Angeles Dodgers' organization for Pitcher Bill Krueger, October 3, 1988.

ROBERT AUGUSTUS NELSON II
(Rob)

Born May 17, 1964, at Pasadena, Calif.
Height, 6.04. Weight, 215.
Throws and bats lefthanded.
Attended Mount San Antonio College, Walnut, Calif.

Major League stolen bases: 1989 (1).
Led Pacific Coast League batters in strikeouts with 133 in 1987 and 130 in 1988.
Led Pacific Coast League in sacrifice flies with 13 in 1986.
Led Midwest League batters in strikeouts with 140 in 1984.
Led Pacific Coast League first basemen in total chances with 1,359 in 1986.
Led Midwest League first basemen in double plays with 111 and total chances with 1,279 in 1984.

Year Club	League	Pos.	G.	AB.	R.	H.	2B.	3B.	HR.	RBI.	B.A.	PO.	A.	E.	F.A.
1983—Idaho Falls	Pion.	1B	54	196	42	57	12	2	12	38	.291	418	32	6	.986
1984—Madison	Midw.	1B	136	487	71	120	25	2	19	85	.246	*1173	*89	17	.987
1985—Huntsville	South.	1B	140	499	68	116	25	0	32	98	.232	1101	86	*23	.981
1986—Tacoma	P. C.	1B	139	508	77	140	26	4	20	108	.276	*1228	*121	10	.992
1986—Oakland	Amer.	1B	5	9	1	2	1	0	0	0	.222	3	1	1	.800
1987—Oakland	Amer.	1B	7	24	1	4	1	0	0	0	.167	49	11	2	.968
1987—Tacoma†	P. C.	1B-OF	120	413	68	89	19	3	20	74	.215	971	70	7	.993
1987—San Diego	Nat.	1B	10	11	0	1	0	0	0	1	.091	14	0	0	1.000
1988—Las Vegas	P. C.	1B-OF	116	388	68	101	23	1	23	77	.260	632	50	6	.991
1988—San Diego	Nat.	1B	7	21	4	4	0	0	1	3	.190	48	5	1	.981
1989—Las Vegas	P. C.	1B	56	185	35	49	11	1	7	26	.265	451	31	7	.986
1989—San Diego	Nat.	1B	42	82	6	16	0	1	3	7	.195	201	23	2	.991
1990—San Diego	Nat.	PH	5	5	0	0	0	0	0	0	.000	0	0	0	.000
1990—Las Vegas‡	P. C.	1B	112	390	56	103	18	1	20	90	.264	764	59	10	.988
American League Totals—2 Years			12	33	2	6	2	0	0	0	.182	52	12	3	.955
National League Totals—4 Years			64	119	10	21	0	1	4	11	.178	263	28	3	.990
Major League Totals—5 Years			76	152	12	27	2	1	4	11	.178	315	40	6	.983

Selected by Houston Astros' organization in 27th round of free-agent draft, June 7, 1982.
Selected by Atlanta Braves' organization in secondary phase of free-agent draft, January 11, 1983.
Selected by Oakland A's organization in secondary phase of free-agent draft, June 6, 1983.
†Traded to San Diego Padres, September 8, 1987, completing deal in which San Diego traded Pitcher Storm Davis to Oakland Athletics for two players to be named later, August 30, 1987. San Diego acquired Pitcher Dave Leiper as partial completion of deal, August 31, 1987.
‡Granted free agency, October 15, 1990; signed by Chicago White Sox, January 8, 1991.

WAYLAND EUGENE NELSON II
(Gene)

Born December 3, 1960, at Tampa, Fla.
Height, 6.00. Weight, 172.
Throws and bats righthanded.

Major League saves: 1984 (1), 1985 (2), 1986 (6), 1987 (3), 1988 (3), 1989 (3), 1990 (5). Total—23.
Major League stolen bases: 1988 (1).
Led Florida State League in shutouts with 5 and complete games with 16 in 1980.

Year Club	League	G.	IP.	W.	L.	Pct.	H.	R.	ER.	SO.	BB.	ERA.
1978—Sarasota Rangers	Gulf Coast	14	52	5	0	•1.000	41	18	13	28	20	2.25
1979—Asheville†	W. Carol.	33	155	13	5	*.722	149	77	62	96	44	3.60
1980—Fort Lauderdale	Florida St.	27	196	*20	3	*.870	146	51	43	130	70	1.97
1981—New York‡	American	8	39	3	1	.750	40	24	21	16	23	4.85
1981—Fort Lauderdale	Florida St.	2	10	0	0	.000	9	6	6	8	5	5.40
1981—Columbus§	Int'national	5	32	4	0	1.000	9	9	9	37	14	2.53
1982—Seattle	American	22	122⅔	6	9	.400	133	70	63	71	60	4.62
1982—Salt Lake City	P. Coast	5	37⅓	1	3	.250	36	18	14	22	28	3.35
1983—Salt Lake City x	P. Coast	16	99	9	4	.692	115	65	57	74	28	5.18
1983—Seattle	American	10	32	0	3	.000	38	29	28	11	21	7.88
1984—Salt Lake City y	P. Coast	17	112	6	8	.429	138	75	70	89	54	5.63
1984—Chicago	American	20	74⅔	3	5	.375	72	38	37	36	17	4.46
1985—Chicago z	American	46	145⅔	10	10	.500	144	74	69	101	67	4.26
1986—Chicago a	American	54	114⅔	6	6	.500	118	52	49	70	41	3.85
1987—Oakland	American	54	123⅔	6	5	.545	120	58	54	94	35	3.93
1988—Oakland b	American	54	111⅔	9	6	.600	93	42	38	67	38	3.06
1989—Oakland cd	American	50	80	3	5	.375	60	33	29	70	30	3.26
1990—Oakland	American	51	74⅔	3	3	.500	55	14	13	38	17	1.57
Major League Totals—10 Years		369	918⅔	49	53	.480	873	434	401	574	349	3.93

Selected by Texas Rangers' organization in 29th round of free-agent draft, June 6, 1978.
†Traded with Pitcher Ray Fontenot to New York Yankees' organization for Pitchers Bob Polinsky, Neal Mersch and Mark Softy, October 8, 1979; completing deal in which New York traded Outfielder Mickey Rivers and three players to be named later to Texas Rangers for Third Baseman Amos Lewis and two players to be named later, August 1, 1979.
‡On disabled list, April 10 to May 4, 1981; included rehabilitation disability assignment to Ft. Lauderdale, April 17 to May 4, 1981.
§Traded with Pitcher Bill Caudill, a player to be named later and cash to Seattle Mariners for Pitcher Shane Rawley, April 1, 1982; Seattle organization acquired Outfielder Bobby Brown to complete deal, April 6, 1982.
xOn disabled list, June 25 to July 31, 1983.
yTraded with Pitcher Jerry Don Gleaton to Chicago White Sox for Pitcher Salome Barojas, June 27, 1984.

zHad one at-bat with no hits.
aTraded with a player to be named later to Oakland A's for Infielder Donnie Hill, December 11, 1986; Oakland acquired Pitcher Bruce Tanner to complete deal, December 18, 1986.
bAppeared in three games as a pinch-runner.
cOn disabled list, April 8 to April 23, 1989.
dAppeared in one game as a pinch-runner.

CHAMPIONSHIP SERIES RECORD

Shares American League Championship Series record for most games won, series (2), 1988.

Year Club	League	G.	IP.	W.	L.	Pct.	H.	R.	ER.	SO.	BB.	ERA.
1988—Oakland	American	2	4⅔	2	0	1.000	5	0	0	0	1	0.00
1989—Oakland	American	1	1⅓	0	0	.000	1	0	0	2	0	0.00
1990—Oakland	American	1	1⅔	0	0	.000	3	0	0	0	0	0.00
Championship Series Totals—3 Years		4	7⅔	2	0	1.000	9	0	0	2	1	0.00

WORLD SERIES RECORD

Year Club	League	G.	IP.	W.	L.	Pct.	H.	R.	ER.	SO.	BB.	ERA.
1988—Oakland	American	3	6⅓	0	0	.000	4	1	1	3	3	1.42
1989—Oakland	American	2	1	0	0	.000	4	6	6	1	2	54.00
1990—Oakland	American	2	5	0	0	.000	3	0	0	0	2	0.00
World Series Totals—3 Years		7	12⅓	0	0	.000	11	7	7	4	7	5.11

ALBERT DWAYNE NEWMAN
(Al)

Born June 30, 1960, at Kansas City, Mo.
Height, 5.09. Weight, 188.
Throws right and bats left and righthanded.
Attended Chaffey College, Alta Loma, Calif., and
San Diego State University, San Diego, Calif.

Major League stolen bases: 1985 (2), 1986 (11), 1987 (15), 1988 (12), 1989 (25), 1990 (13). Total—78.
Led Southern League in sacrifice hits with 18 in 1982.
Led Texas League shortstops in double plays with 58 in 1984.
Led Southern League second basemen in total chances with 776 in 1982.

Year Club	League	Pos.	G.	AB.	R.	H.	2B.	3B.	HR.	RBI.	B.A.	PO.	A.	E.	F.A.
1982—Memphis	South.	2B	142	494	85	136	16	8	1	41	.275	★356	●388	★32	.959
1983—Wichita	A. A.	2B	38	124	20	30	6	1	0	16	.242	73	96	5	.971
1983—Memphis†‡	South.	2B	52	194	18	49	5	2	0	13	.253	111	123	14	.944
1984—Beaumont§	Texas	SS	88	318	69	80	8	0	0	23	.252	138	250	27	.935
1984—Indianapolis	A. A.	2-3-O-S	37	123	13	37	3	0	0	11	.301	49	79	2	.985
1985—Indianapolis	A. A.	2B-SS	87	301	42	85	16	2	0	23	.282	144	250	10	.975
1985—Montreal	Nat.	2B-SS	25	29	7	5	1	0	0	1	.172	19	36	0	1.000
1986—Montreal x	Nat.	2B-SS	95	185	23	37	3	0	1	8	.200	98	161	11	.959
1987—Minnesota	Amer.	S-2-3-O	110	307	44	68	15	5	0	29	.221	120	225	5	.986
1988—Minnesota	Amer.	3B-SS-2B	105	260	35	58	7	0	0	19	.223	97	155	6	.977
1989—Minnesota	Amer.	2-3-S-O	141	446	62	113	18	2	0	38	.253	191	282	16	.967
1990—Minnesota	Amer.	2-S-3-O	144	388	43	94	14	0	1	30	.242	190	304	13	.974
National League Totals—2 Years			120	214	30	42	4	0	1	9	.196	117	197	11	.966
American League Totals—4 Years			500	1401	184	333	54	7	0	116	.238	598	966	40	.975
Major League Totals—6 Years			620	1615	214	375	58	7	1	125	.232	715	1163	51	.974

Selected by California Angels' organization in 3rd round of free-agent draft, January 9, 1979.
Selected by Texas Rangers' organization in 3rd round of free-agent draft, January 8, 1980.
Selected by New York Mets' organization in secondary phase of free-agent draft, June 3, 1980.
Selected by Montreal Expos' organization in secondary phase of free-agent draft, June 8, 1981.
†On disabled list, July 23 to August 16, 1983.
‡Traded with Pitcher Scott Sanderson to San Diego Padres for Pitcher Gary Lucas, December 7, 1983.
§Traded to Montreal Expos' organization for Pitcher Greg Harris, July 20, 1984.
xTraded to Minnesota Twins for Pitcher Mike Shade, February 20, 1987.

CHAMPIONSHIP SERIES RECORD

Year Club	League	Pos.	G.	AB.	R.	H.	2B.	3B.	HR.	RBI.	B.A.	PO.	A.	E.	F.A.
1987—Minnesota	Amer.	2B	1	2	0	0	0	0	0	0	.000	0	1	0	1.000

WORLD SERIES RECORD

Year Club	League	Pos.	G.	AB.	R.	H.	2B.	3B.	HR.	RBI.	B.A.	PO.	A.	E.	F.A.
1987—Minnesota	Amer.	PR-2-PH	4	5	0	1	0	0	0	0	.200	1	2	0	1.000

CARL EDWARD NICHOLS

Born October 14, 1962, at Los Angeles, Calif.
Height, 6.00. Weight, 192.
Throws and bats righthanded.

Led Pacific Coast League catchers in assists with 76 in 1989.
Led International League catchers in fielding percentage with .988, double plays with 9 and passed balls with 9 in 1987.
Led Southern League catchers in putouts with 693 and total chances with 818 in 1986.
Led California League catchers in total chances with 897 in 1984.
Led New York-Pennsylvania League catchers in assists with 47 and tied for lead in double plays with 6 in 1983.

Year Club	League	Pos.	G.	AB.	R.	H.	2B.	3B.	HR.	RBI.	B.A.	PO.	A.	E.	F.A.
1980—Bluefield................	Appal.	C-1B-OF	37	85	24	18	2	2	0	10	.212	129	13	2	.986
1981—Miami....................	Fla. St.	C-1-S-3-O	16	31	1	6	0	0	0	3	.194	34	9	6	.878
1981—Hagerstown†........	Carol.	C-O-S-2	38	81	8	22	4	0	1	6	.272	131	21	3	.981
1982—Macon..................	S. Atl.	C-OF-1B	84	257	33	55	10	2	0	30	.214	391	49	21	.954
1983—San Jose..............	Calif.	C-OF-3B	54	152	16	31	4	0	1	12	.204	204	39	17	.935
1983—Newark.................	NYP	C-O-3-S	66	217	40	63	14	0	5	26	.290	348	56	10	.976
1984—S.J.‡-Red.§...........	Calif.	*C-OF	121	389	53	88	14	2	4	54	.226	*769	*112	17	.981
1985—Charlotte..............	South.	C-OF-1B	115	331	45	78	11	2	2	37	.236	496	71	15	.984
1986—Charlotte..............	Sŏuth.	*C-OF	118	439	63	118	26	1	14	72	.269	700	*110	16	.981
1986—Baltimore.............	Amer.	C	5	5	0	0	0	0	0	0	.000	11	0	0	1.000
1987—Rochester.............	Int.	C-OF	108	364	45	93	15	3	11	52	.255	617	65	9	.987
1987—Baltimore.............	Amer.	C	13	21	4	8	1	0	0	3	.381	39	3	0	1.000
1988—Baltimore.............	Amer.	C-OF	18	47	2	9	1	0	0	1	.191	71	13	1	.988
1988—Rochester x..........	Int.	C-OF-3B	75	193	20	44	7	1	3	16	.228	335	44	8	.979
1989—Tucson..................	P. C.	C-OF	104	340	45	87	27	1	4	27	.256	553	77	11	.983
1989—Houston................	Nat.	C	8	13	0	1	0	0	0	2	.077	16	1	0	1.000
1990—Tucson..................	P. C.	C-OF-1B	58	170	24	43	11	0	4	33	.253	242	36	6	.979
1990—Houston y..............	Nat.	C-1B-OF	32	49	7	10	3	0	0	11	.204	86	10	3	.970
American League Totals—3 Years........			36	73	6	17	2	0	0	4	.233	121	16	1	.993
National League Totals—2 Years............			40	62	7	11	3	0	0	13	.177	102	11	3	.974
Major League Totals—5 Years.................			76	135	13	28	5	0	0	17	.207	223	27	4	.984

Selected by Baltimore Orioles' organization in 4th round of free-agent draft, June 3, 1980.

†Loaned to Macon (Detroit Tigers' organization), April 8, 1982; returned, September 15, 1982.

‡Loaned to San Jose (Independent), April 10, 1984; returned, June 9, 1984.

§Loaned to Redwood (California Angels' organization), June 9, 1984; returned, September 10, 1984.

xTraded to Houston Astros for Pitcher Dave Johnson and Outfielder Victor Hithe, March 31, 1989.

yOn disabled list, August 24 to September 15, 1990.

RODNEY LEA NICHOLS

(Rod)

Born December 29, 1964, at Burlington, Ia.
Height, 6.02. Weight, 190.
Throws and bats righthanded.
Attended University of New Mexico, Albuquerque, N.M.

Tied for Pacific Coast League lead in shutouts with 2 in 1990.

Year Club	League	G.	IP.	W.	L.	Pct.	H.	R.	ER.	SO.	BB.	ERA.
1985—Batavia............................	NYP	13	84	5	5	.500	74	40	28	93	33	3.00
1986—Waterloo†.....................	Midwest	20	115⅓	8	5	.615	128	56	52	83	21	4.06
1987—Kinston.........................	Carolina	9	56	4	2	.667	53	27	25	61	14	4.02
1987—Williamsport...................	Eastern	16	100	4	3	.571	107	53	41	60	33	3.69
1988—Kinston‡.......................	Carolina	4	24	3	1	.750	26	13	12	19	15	4.50
1988—Colorado Springs...........	P. Coast	10	58⅔	2	6	.250	69	41	37	43	17	5.74
1988—Cleveland......................	American	11	69⅓	1	7	.125	73	41	39	31	23	5.06
1989—Colorado Springs§.........	P. Coast	10	65⅓	8	1	.889	52	28	26	41	30	3.58
1989—Cleveland......................	American	15	71⅔	4	6	.400	81	42	35	42	24	4.40
1990—Cleveland......................	American	4	16	0	3	.000	24	14	14	3	6	7.88
1990—Colorado Springs...........	P. Coast	22	133⅓	12	9	.571	160	84	76	74	48	5.13
Major League Totals—3 Years...................		30	157	5	16	.238	178	97	88	76	53	5.04

Selected by Cleveland Indians' organization in 5th round of free-agent draft, June 3, 1985.

†On disabled list, July 12 to August 18, 1986.

‡On Cleveland disabled list, March 26 to May 12, 1988.

§On Cleveland disabled list, March 19 to June 12, 1989; including rehabilitation disability assignment to Colorado Springs, May 24 to June 12, 1989.

THOMAS EDWARD NIEDENFUER

Name pronounced NEED-un-fyoor.

(Tom)

Born August 13, 1959, at St. Louis Park, Minn.
Height, 6.05. Weight, 230.
Throws and bats righthanded.
Attended Washington State University, Pullman, Wash.
Husband of Judy Landers, television actress.

Major League saves: 1981 (2), 1982 (9), 1983 (11), 1984 (11), 1985 (19), 1986 (11), 1987 (14), 1988 (18), 1990 (2). Total—97.

Year Club	League	G.	IP.	W.	L.	Pct.	H.	R.	ER.	SO.	BB.	ERA.
1981—San Antonio....................	Texas	36	90	13	3	*.813	61	19	18	95	34	1.80
1981—Los Angeles....................	National	17	26	3	1	.750	25	11	11	12	6	3.81
1982—Albuquerque....................	P. Coast	4	10⅔	2	0	1.000	6	0	0	15	2	0.00
1982—Los Angeles....................	National	55	69⅔	3	4	.429	71	22	21	60	25	2.71
1983—Los Angeles....................	National	66	94⅔	8	3	.727	55	22	20	66	29	1.90
1984—Los Angeles†..................	National	33	47⅓	2	5	.286	39	14	13	45	23	2.47
1985—Los Angeles....................	National	64	106⅓	7	9	.438	86	32	32	102	24	2.71
1986—Los Angeles‡..................	National	60	80	6	6	.500	86	35	33	55	29	3.71
1987—Los Angeles§..................	National	15	16⅓	1	0	1.000	13	5	5	10	9	2.76
1987—Baltimore.......................	American	45	52⅓	3	5	.375	55	32	29	37	22	4.99

Year Club	League	G.	IP.	W.	L.	Pct.	H.	R.	ER.	SO.	BB.	ERA.
1988—Baltimore x	American	52	59	3	4	.429	59	23	23	40	19	3.51
1989—Seattle y	American	25	36⅓	0	3	.000	46	29	27	15	15	6.69
1989—Calgary z	P. Coast	13	18⅔	1	2	.333	23	13	11	11	7	5.30
1990—Louisville	Am. Assoc.	5	7⅓	0	0	.000	5	2	2	7	4	2.45
1990—St. Louis a	National	52	65	0	6	.000	66	26	25	32	25	3.46
National League Totals—8 Years		362	505⅓	30	34	.469	441	167	160	382	170	2.85
American League Totals—3 Years		122	147⅔	6	12	.333	160	84	79	92	56	4.81
Major League Totals—10 Years		484	653	36	46	.439	601	251	239	474	226	3.29

Selected by Los Angeles Dodgers' organization in 36th round of free-agent draft, June 7, 1977.
Signed as free agent by Los Angeles Dodgers' organization, August 14, 1980.
†On disabled list, July 16 to July 31 and August 5 to September 11, 1984.
‡On disabled list, August 19 to September 3, 1986.
§Traded to Baltimore Orioles for Outfielder John Shelby and Pitcher Brad Havens, May 22, 1987.
xGranted free agency, November 4, 1988; signed by Seattle Mariners, December 7, 1988.
yOn disabled list, April 12 to May 30, 1989; included rehabilitation disability assignment to Calgary, May 21 to May 30, 1989.
zReleased, April 6, 1990; signed by Louisville (St. Louis Cardinals' organization), April 10, 1990.
aGranted free agency, November 5, 1990.

DIVISION SERIES RECORD

Year Club	League	G.	IP.	W.	L.	Pct.	H.	R.	ER.	SO.	BB.	ERA.
1981—Los Angeles	National	1	⅓	0	0	.000	1	0	0	1	1	0.00

CHAMPIONSHIP SERIES RECORD

Shares Championship Series record for most games lost, series (2), 1985.

Year Club	League	G.	IP.	W.	L.	Pct.	H.	R.	ER.	SO.	BB.	ERA.
1981—Los Angeles	National	1	⅓	0	0	.000	2	0	0	0	0	0.00
1983—Los Angeles	National	2	2	0	0	.000	0	0	0	3	1	0.00
1985—Los Angeles	National	3	5⅔	0	2	.000	5	4	4	5	2	6.35
Championship Series Totals—3 Years		6	8	0	2	.000	7	4	4	8	3	4.50

WORLD SERIES RECORD

Year Club	League	G.	IP.	W.	L.	Pct.	H.	R.	ER.	SO.	BB.	ERA.
1981—Los Angeles	National	2	5	0	0	.000	3	2	0	0	1	0.00

THOMAS ANDREW NIETO

Name pronounced Nee-AY-toh.

(Tom)

Born October 27, 1960, at Downey, Calif.
Height, 6.01. Weight, 210.
Throws and bats righthanded.
Attended Cerritos College, Norwalk, Calif., and
Oral Roberts University, Tulsa, Okla.

Tied for American Association lead in being hit by pitch with 8 in 1983.

Year Club	League	Pos.	G.	AB.	R.	H.	2B.	3B.	HR.	RBI.	B.A.	PO.	A.	E.	F.A.
1981—Arkansas	Texas	C	62	184	12	33	2	0	2	19	.179	270	37	8	.975
1982—Arkansas†	Texas	C	96	298	33	72	11	3	5	31	.242	466	58	3	*.994
1983—Louisville	A. A.	C	115	383	44	104	17	1	5	52	.272	605	71	*15	.978
1984—Louisville	A. A.	C	77	253	23	70	12	1	7	34	.277	446	43	8	.984
1984—St. Louis	Nat.	C	33	86	7	24	4	0	3	12	.279	135	18	1	.994
1985—St. Louis‡	Nat.	C	95	253	15	57	10	2	0	34	.225	384	28	4	.990
1986—Montreal§	Nat.	C	30	65	5	13	3	1	1	7	.200	123	11	3	.978
1986—Indianapolis x	A. A.	C	53	167	21	50	16	0	3	19	.299	295	25	9	.973
1987—Minnesota y	Amer.	C	41	105	7	21	7	1	1	12	.200	210	17	1	.996
1987—Portland	P. C.	C	38	110	10	25	5	0	0	3	.227	193	15	5	.977
1988—Minnesota	Amer.	C	24	60	1	4	0	0	0	0	.067	108	6	1	.991
1988—Portland z	P. C.	C	53	158	11	44	7	2	3	21	.278	276	25	6	.980
1989—Scr./Wil.-Barre a . Int.		C	46	136	8	26	3	0	1	7	.191	236	25	7	.974
1989—Philadelphia	Nat.	C	11	20	1	3	0	0	0	0	.150	63	2	0	1.000
1990—Scranton/W.-B.b .. Int.		C	37	112	9	25	2	0	2	15	.223	189	15	0	1.000
1990—Philadelphia c	Nat.	C	17	30	1	5	0	0	0	4	.167	57	5	1	.984
National League Totals—5 Years			186	454	29	102	17	3	4	57	.225	762	64	9	.989
American League Totals—2 Years			65	165	8	25	7	1	1	12	.152	318	23	2	.994
Major League Totals—7 Years			251	619	37	127	24	4	5	69	.205	1080	87	11	.991

Selected by Minnesota Twins' organization in 31st round of free-agent draft, June 5, 1979.
Selected by Pittsburgh Pirates' organization in secondary phase of free-agent draft, January 8, 1980.
Selected by St. Louis Cardinals' organization in 3rd round of free-agent draft, June 8, 1981.
†On disabled list, June 19 to June 30, 1982.
‡Traded to Montreal Expos for Infielder Fred Manrique, March 31, 1986.
§On disabled list, August 21 to September 11, 1986; included rehabilitation disability assignment to Indianapolis, September 3 to September 10, 1986.
xTraded with Pitcher Jeff Reardon to Minnesota Twins for Pitchers Neal Heaton, Al Cardwood and Yorkis Perez and Catcher Jeff Reed, February 3, 1987.
yOn disabled list, May 18 to July 22, 1987; included rehabilitation disability assignment to Portland, July 12 to July 22, 1987.

zTraded with Second Baseman Tom Herr and Outfielder Eric Bullock to Philadelphia Phillies for Pitcher Shane Rawley and cash, October 24, 1988.

aOn Philadelphia disabled list, March 29 to June 2, 1989; included rehabilitation disability assignment to Scranton/Wilkes-Barre, May 1 to May 20, 1989.

bOn Philadelphia disabled list, March 29 to April 20, 1990.

cGranted free agency, October 15, 1990.

CHAMPIONSHIP SERIES RECORD

Year Club	League	Pos.	G.	AB.	R.	H.	2B.	3B.	HR.	RBI.	B.A.	PO.	A.	E.	F.A.
1985—St. Louis	Nat.	C	1	3	1	0	0	0	0	0	.000	7	0	0	1.000

WORLD SERIES RECORD

Year Club	League	Pos.	G.	AB.	R.	H.	2B.	3B.	HR.	RBI.	B.A.	PO.	A.	E.	F.A.
1985—St. Louis	Nat.	C	2	5	0	0	0	0	0	1	.000	23	1	0	1.000

ALBERT SAMUEL NIPPER
(Al)

Born April 2, 1959, at San Diego, Calif.
Height, 6.00. Weight, 194.
Throws and bats righthanded.
Attended Northeast Missouri State University, Kirksville, Mo.

Major League saves: 1988 (1).
Led Florida State League in complete games with 15 in 1981.

Year Club	League	G.	IP.	W.	L.	Pct.	H.	R.	ER.	SO.	BB.	ERA.
1980—Winter Haven	Florida St.	16	85	6	4	.600	82	29	24	48	49	2.54
1981—Winter Haven	Florida St.	29	*212	14	8	.636	191	59	40	139	60	*1.70
1982—Bristol†	Eastern	19	115	6	7	.462	108	50	47	66	45	3.68
1983—New Britain	Eastern	10	67	4	3	.571	46	26	21	42	25	2.82
1983—Pawtucket	Int'national	18	109⅓	9	4	.692	108	62	54	58	54	4.45
1983—Boston	American	3	16	1	1	.500	17	4	4	5	7	2.25
1984—Boston	American	29	182⅔	11	6	.647	183	86	79	84	52	3.89
1985—Boston‡	American	25	162	9	12	.429	157	83	73	85	82	4.06
1986—Boston§	American	26	159	10	12	.455	186	108	95	79	47	5.38
1987—Boston xy	American	30	174	11	12	.478	196	115	105	89	62	5.43
1988—Chicago za	National	22	80	2	4	.333	72	37	37	27	34	3.04
1989—						(Out of Organized Baseball)						
1990—Cleveland b	American	9	24	2	3	.400	35	19	18	12	19	6.75
1990—Colorado Springs b	P. Coast	17	89⅓	5	5	.500	80	53	47	47	56	4.74
American League Totals—6 Years		122	717⅔	44	46	.489	774	415	374	354	269	4.69
National League Totals—1 Year		22	80	2	4	.333	72	37	27	27	34	3.04
Major League Totals—7 Years		144	797⅔	46	50	.479	846	452	401	381	303	4.52

Selected by Boston Red Sox' organization in 8th round of free-agent draft, June 3, 1980.

†On disabled list, June 26 to July 25, 1982.

‡On disabled list, March 25 to April 15, 1985; included rehabilitation disability assignment to Pawtucket, March 31 to April 15, 1985.

§On disabled list, May 19 to June 25, 1986.

xOn disabled list, July 20 to August 13, 1987.

yTraded with Pitcher Calvin Schiraldi to Chicago Cubs for Pitcher Lee Smith, December 8, 1987.

zOn disabled list, May 28 to June 23 and August 12 to September 2, 1988.

aReleased, March 28, 1989; signed by Colorado Springs (Cleveland Indians' organization), February 20, 1990.

bReleased, October 4, 1990.

WORLD SERIES RECORD

Year Club	League	G.	IP.	W.	L.	Pct.	H.	R.	ER.	SO.	BB.	ERA.
1986—Boston	American	2	6⅓	0	1	.000	10	5	5	2	2	7.11

OTIS JUNIOR NIXON

Born January 9, 1959, at Evergreen, N.C.
Height, 6.02. Weight, 180.
Throws right and bats right and lefthanded.
Attended Louisburg College, Louisburg, N.C.
Brother of Donell Nixon, outfielder with Seattle Mariners, San Francisco Giants
and Baltimore Orioles, 1987 through 1990.

Major League stolen bases: 1984 (12), 1985 (20), 1986 (23), 1987 (2), 1988 (46), 1989 (37), 1990 (50). Total—190.
Led International League in stolen bases with 94 and caught stealing with 29 in 1983.
Led Southern League in bases on balls received with 110 in 1981.
Led South Atlantic League in bases on balls received with 113 and stolen bases with 67 in 1980.
Led Appalachian League in bases on balls received with 57 in 1979.
Led International League outfielders in fielding percentage with .992, putouts with 363 and total chances with 371 in 1983.
Led Appalachian League third basemen in fielding percentage with .945, putouts with 52, assists with 120, and double plays with 12 in 1979.

Year Club	League	Pos.	G.	AB.	R.	H.	2B.	3B.	HR.	RBI.	B.A.	PO.	A.	E.	F.A.
1979—Paintsville	Appal.	3B-SS	63	203	58	58	10	3	1	25	.286	54	122	11	.941
1980—Greensboro	S. Atl.	3B-SS	136	493	*124	137	12	5	3	48	.278	164	308	36	.929
1981—Nashville	South.	SS	127	407	89	102	9	2	0	20	.251	198	348	*56	.907
1982—Nashville	South.	SS-2B	72	283	47	80	3	2	0	20	.283	126	211	23	.936

Year Club	League	Pos.	G.	AB.	R.	H.	2B.	3B.	HR.	RBI.	B.A.	PO.	A.	E.	F.A.
1982—Columbus..............	Int.	2B-SS	59	207	43	58	4	0	0	14	.280	104	169	14	.951
1983—Columbus..............	Int.	OF-2B	138	*557	*129	*162	11	6	0	41	.291	385	24	4	.990
1983—New York†..........	Amer.	OF	13	14	2	2	0	0	0	0	.143	14	1	1	.938
1984—Cleveland..............	Amer.	OF	49	91	16	14	0	0	0	1	.154	81	3	0	1.000
1984—Maine...................	Int.	OF	72	253	42	70	5	1	0	22	.277	206	7	1	.995
1985—Cleveland..............	Amer.	OF	104	162	34	38	4	0	3	9	.235	129	5	4	.971
1986—Cleveland..............	Amer.	OF	105	95	33	25	4	1	0	8	.263	90	3	3	.969
1987—Cleveland..............	Amer.	OF	19	17	2	1	0	0	0	1	.059	21	0	0	1.000
1987—Buffalo‡.................	A. A.	OF	59	249	51	71	13	4	2	23	.285	170	3	3	.983
1988—Indianapolis..........	A. A.	OF	67	235	52	67	6	3	0	19	.285	130	1	1	.992
1988—Montreal..............	Nat.	OF	90	271	47	66	8	2	0	15	.244	176	2	1	.994
1989—Montreal..............	Nat.	OF	126	258	41	56	7	2	0	21	.217	160	2	2	.988
1990—Montreal..............	Nat.	OF-SS	119	231	46	58	6	2	1	20	.251	149	6	1	.994
American League Totals—5 Years........			290	379	87	80	8	1	3	19	.211	335	12	8	.977
National League Totals—3 Years...........			335	760	134	180	21	6	1	56	.237	485	10	4	.992
Major League Totals—8 Years.................			625	1139	221	260	29	7	4	75	.228	820	22	12	.986

Selected by Cincinnati Reds' organization in 21st round of free-agent draft, June 6, 1978.
Selected by California Angels' organization in secondary phase of free-agent draft, January 9, 1979.
Selected by New York Yankees' organization in secondary phase of free-agent draft, June 5, 1979.
†Traded with Pitcher George Frazier and a player to be named later to Cleveland Indians for Third Baseman Toby Harrah and a player to be named later, February 5, 1984; New York organization acquired Pitcher Rick Browne and Cleveland organization acquired Pitcher Guy Elston to complete deal, February 8, 1984.
‡Granted free agency, October 15, 1987; signed by Indianapolis (Montreal Expos' organization), March 5, 1988.

ROBERT DONELL NIXON

(Known by middle name.)
Born December 31, 1961, at Evergreen, N. C.
Height, 6.01. Weight, 185.
Throws and bats righthanded.
Attended Louisburg College, Louisburg, N. C.
Brother of Otis Nixon, outfielder with Montreal Expos.

Shares major league record for most times caught stealing, inning (2), July 6, 1988, sixth inning.
Major League stolen bases: 1987 (21), 1988 (11), 1989 (10), 1990 (5). Total—47.
Led Pacific Coast League in stolen bases with 46 in 1987.
Led Southern League in stolen bases with 102 in 1984.
Led California League in stolen bases with 144 and caught stealing with 24 in 1983.
Led Midwest League in stolen bases with 85 in 1982.

Year Club	League	Pos.	G.	AB.	R.	H.	2B.	3B.	HR.	RBI.	B.A.	PO.	A.	E.	F.A.
1981—Wausau†.................	Midw.	1B-2B-OF	59	204	35	58	7	2	5	26	.284	252	9	3	.989
1982—Wausau....................	Midw.	*3B-1B	116	461	102	156	18	7	11	56	.338	*87	187	*49	.848
1982—Lynn......................	Midw.	3B	6	24	5	7	2	1	0	1	.292	0	2	0	1.000
1983—Bakersfield...........	Calif.	*3B-OF	135	542	*116	174	27	4	4	51	.321	98	249	*51	.872
1984—Chattanooga	South.	OF-3B	140	536	99	144	25	5	4	57	.269	262	6	8	.971
1985—Seattle‡..................	Amer.						(Did not play)								
1986—Chattanooga§.........	South.	OF	4	18	2	6	1	0	0	0	.333	7	0	1	.875
1986—Calgary	P. C.	OF	8	35	3	12	1	1	0	1	.343	15	2	0	1.000
1987—Seattle...................	Amer.	OF	46	132	17	33	4	0	3	12	.250	76	1	0	1.000
1987—Calgary	P. C.	OF-1B	82	328	72	106	18	1	5	52	.323	168	1	6	.966
1988—Calgary x	P. C.	OF	40	160	28	45	7	0	3	10	.281	0	0	0	.000
1988—San Francisco y ..	Nat.	OF	59	78	15	27	3	0	0	6	.346	59	0	1	.983
1989—San Francisco y ..	Nat.	OF	95	166	23	44	2	0	1	15	.265	87	0	3	.967
1990—Rochester..............	Int.	OF	85	291	54	72	3	4	2	26	.247	145	2	4	.974
1990—Baltimore z	Amer.	OF	8	20	1	5	2	0	0	2	.250	5	0	0	1.000
American League Totals—2 Years........			54	152	18	38	6	0	3	14	.250	81	1	0	1.000
National League Totals—2 Years...........			154	244	38	71	5	0	1	21	.291	146	0	4	.973
Major League Totals—4 Years.................			208	396	56	109	11	0	4	35	.275	227	1	4	.983

Selected by Seattle Mariners' organization in 10th round of free-agent draft, June 3, 1980.
†On disabled list, July 7, 1981 through remainder of season.
‡On disabled list, April 8, 1985 through entire season.
§On Calgary disabled list, April 11 to August 1, 1986.
xTraded to San Francisco Giants, June 23, 1988, completing deal in which San Francisco traded Pitcher Rod Scurry to Seattle Mariners for a player to be named later, March 19, 1988.
yReleased, April 8, 1990; signed by Rochester (Baltimore Orioles' organization), April 16, 1990.
zGranted free agency, September 20, 1990.

CHAMPIONSHIP SERIES RECORD

Year Club	League	Pos.	G.	AB.	R.	H.	2B.	3B.	HR.	RBI.	B.A.	PO.	A.	E.	F.A.
1989—San Francisco	Nat.	OF-PR	3	3	0	0	0	0	0	0	.000	2	0	1	.667

WORLD SERIES RECORD

Year Club	League	Pos.	G.	AB.	R.	H.	2B.	3B.	HR.	RBI.	B.A.	PO.	A.	E.	F.A.
1989—San Francisco	Nat.	PH-OF	2	5	1	1	0	0	0	0	.200	2	0	0	1.000

—DID YOU KNOW—

That Franklin Stubbs set a Houston club record for lefthanded hitters by belting 23 home runs in 1990?

MILCIADES ARTURO NOBOA JR.
Name pronounced Nah-BO-ah.
(Junior)
Born November 10, 1964, at Azua, D. R.
Height, 5.10. Weight, 165.
Throws and bats righthanded.

Major League stolen bases: 1984 (1), 1987 (1), 1990 (4). Total—6.
Led Eastern League in sacrifice hits with 17 in 1984.
Led Midwest League in sacrifice hits with 18 in 1983.
Tied for American Association lead in sacrifice flies with 8 in 1989.
Led American Association second basemen in fielding percentage with .986 in 1989.
Led Midwest League second basemen in putouts with 257 and double plays with 81 in 1983.

Year	Club	League	Pos.	G.	AB.	R.	H.	2B.	3B.	HR.	RBI.	B.A.	PO.	A.	E.	F.A.
1981—Batavia	NYP	2B	50	162	15	49	8	0	0	6	.302	82	100	*18	.910
1982—Waterloo	Midw.	SS	121	385	69	96	12	5	0	23	.249	*207	306	46	.918
1983—Waterloo	Midw.	2B-SS	132	449	64	115	22	3	1	29	.256	260	355	24	.962
1984—Buffalo	East.	2B	117	383	55	97	18	4	1	45	.253	228	305	*18	.967
1984—Cleveland	Amer.	2B	23	11	3	4	0	0	0	0	.364	7	13	0	1.000
1985—Maine	Int.	2B	122	403	62	116	11	2	5	32	.288	270	379	14	.979
1986—Maine	Int.	2B-SS-3B	108	399	44	114	21	1	4	32	.286	160	252	13	.969
1987—Buffalo	A. A.	2B-SS-3B	43	149	26	47	6	2	0	14	.315	70	108	11	.942
1987—Cleveland†	Amer.	2B-SS-3B	39	80	7	18	2	1	0	7	.225	28	66	3	.969
1988—Edmonton	P. C.	2-S-O-3	50	159	24	47	6	1	0	17	.296	86	145	7	.971
1988—California‡	Amer.	2B-SS-3B	21	16	4	1	0	0	0	0	.063	8	24	1	.970
1989—Indianapolis	A. A.	2B-SS	117	467	61	*159	21	8	2	62	*.340	170	305	10	.979
1989—Montreal	Nat.	2B-SS-3B	21	44	3	10	0	0	0	1	.227	17	45	0	1.000
1990—Montreal	Nat.	2-O-3-S-P	81	158	15	42	7	2	0	14	.266	47	52	2	.980
American League Totals—3 Years			83	107	14	23	2	1	0	7	.215	43	103	4	.973
National League Totals—2 Years			102	202	18	52	7	2	0	15	.257	64	97	2	.988
Major League Totals—5 Years			185	309	32	75	9	3	0	22	.243	107	200	6	.981

Signed as free agent by Cleveland Indians' organization, May 26, 1981.
†Traded to California Angels for Outfielder Ted Milner, March 30, 1988.
‡Granted free agency, October 15, 1988; signed by Indianapolis (Montreal Expos' organization), January 4, 1989.

PITCHING RECORD

Year	Club	League	G.	IP.	W.	L.	Pct.	H.	R.	ER.	SO.	BB.	ERA.
1990—Montreal	National	1	⅔	0	0	.000	0	0	0	0	1	0.00

PAUL DAVID NOCE
Born December 16, 1959, at San Francisco, Calif.
Height, 5.10. Weight, 175.
Throws and bats righthanded.
Attended Washington State University, Pullman, Wash.

Tied major league record for most times caught stealing, inning (2), June 26, 1987 (third inning).
Major League stolen bases: 1987 (5).

Year	Club	League	Pos.	G.	AB.	R.	H.	2B.	3B.	HR.	RBI.	B.A.	PO.	A.	E.	F.A.
1981—Reno	Calif.	SS	37	134	29	36	1	2	3	22	.269	28	94	16	.884
1982—Reno	Calif.	3B-SS	56	185	23	48	7	5	2	20	.259	56	128	13	.934
1982—Salem	Carol.	3-S-2-O-1	59	204	16	40	2	3	4	19	.196	39	76	12	.906
1983—Miami	Fla. St.	S-3-O-2-C	65	220	26	59	11	4	0	23	.268	94	147	16	.938
1983—Reno	Calif.	2-S-3-O-C	61	237	48	73	16	2	6	30	.308	101	177	14	.952
1984—Reno†	Calif.	3B	9	35	8	15	2	1	0	4	.429	9	12	2	.913
1984—Midland	Texas	SS-3B-2B	109	364	49	105	16	5	4	29	.288	135	264	28	.934
1985—Iowa	A. A.	O-3-2-S	89	258	31	58	8	4	5	25	.225	64	73	9	.938
1986—Iowa	A. A.	2B	7	5	1	1	0	0	1	1	.200	3	2	0	1.000
1986—Pittsfield	East.	SS	114	410	*87	126	26	*14	7	56	.307	180	340	28	.949
1987—Iowa	A. A.	2-S-3-O	47	167	30	45	5	3	7	25	.269	88	139	7	.970
1987—Chicago	Nat.	2B-SS-3B	70	180	17	41	9	2	3	14	.228	117	157	5	.982
1988—Iowa‡-Ind.§	A. A.	S-2-3-1-O	106	340	42	80	11	4	4	24	.235	144	225	16	.959
1989—Calgary x	P. C.	SS-2B-3B	134	510	95	142	28	●10	3	42	.278	206	403	13	.979
1990—Nashville	A. A.	I-O-C	100	293	46	64	10	2	4	18	.218	139	199	19	.947
1990—Cincinnati y	Nat.	PH	1	1	0	1	0	0	0	0	1.000	0	0	0	.000
Major League Totals—2 Years			71	181	17	42	9	2	3	14	.232	117	157	5	.982

Selected by San Diego Padres' organization in 25th round of free-agent draft, June 6, 1978.
Selected by San Diego Padres' organization in 14th round of free-agent draft, June 8, 1981.
†Traded to Chicago Cubs' organization for Outfielder Terry Austin, April 23, 1984.
‡Traded to Indianapolis (Montreal Expos' organization) for Pitcher Bryan Oelkers, July 28, 1988.
§Granted free agency, October 15, 1988; signed by Calgary (Seattle Mariners' organization), April 2, 1989.
xGranted free agency, October 15, 1989; signed by Nashville (Cincinnati Reds' organization), January 5, 1990.
yGranted free agency, October 3, 1990.

MATTHEW DODGE NOKES
(Matt)
Born October 31, 1963, at San Diego, Calif.
Height, 6.01. Weight, 191.
Throws right and bats lefthanded.

Major League stolen bases: 1987 (2), 1989 (1), 1990 (2). Total—5.
Led Texas League catchers in double plays with 6 in 1985.
Led California League catchers in double plays with 9 in 1983.
Led Pioneer League in passed balls with 19 in 1981.
Tied for American Association lead in errors by catchers with 13 in 1986.
Named catcher on THE SPORTING NEWS American League All-Star Team, 1987.
Named catcher on THE SPORTING NEWS American League Silver Slugger team, 1987.

Year Club	League	Pos.	G.	AB.	R.	H.	2B.	3B.	HR.	RBI.	B.A.	PO.	A.	E.	F.A.
1981—Great Falls	Pion.	C	44	146	14	33	6	2	0	13	.226	288	35	★13	.961
1982—Clinton	Midw.	C	82	247	19	53	12	0	3	23	.215	363	41	13	.969
1983—Fresno	Calif.	C	125	429	62	138	26	6	14	82	.322	595	62	16	.976
1984—Shreveport	Texas	C	97	308	32	89	19	2	11	61	.289	400	31	8	.982
1985—Shreveport	Texas	C	105	344	52	101	24	1	14	56	.294	520	40	12	.979
1985—San Francisco†	Nat.	C	19	53	3	11	2	0	2	5	.208	84	2	2	.977
1986—Nashville	A. A.	C-1B-OF	125	428	55	122	25	4	10	71	.285	502	50	18	.968
1986—Detroit	Amer.	C	7	24	2	8	1	0	1	2	.333	43	2	0	1.000
1987—Detroit	Amer.	C-OF-3B	135	461	69	133	14	2	32	87	.289	600	32	5	.992
1988—Detroit	Amer.	C	122	382	53	96	18	0	16	53	.251	574	45	7	.989
1989—Detroit‡	Amer.	C	87	268	15	67	10	0	9	39	.250	235	26	6	.978
1990—Det.§-N.Y.	Amer.	C-OF	136	351	33	87	9	1	11	40	.248	237	34	2	.993
National League Totals—1 Year			19	53	3	11	2	0	2	5	.208	84	2	2	.977
American League Totals—5 Years			487	1486	172	391	52	3	69	221	.263	1689	139	20	.989
Major League Totals—6 Years			506	1539	175	402	54	3	71	226	.261	1773	141	22	.989

Selected by San Francisco Giants' organization in 20th round of free-agent draft, June 8, 1981.

†Traded with Pitchers Dave LaPoint and Eric King to Detroit Tigers for Pitcher Juan Berenguer, Catcher Bob Melvin and a player to be named later, October 7, 1985; San Francisco Giants acquired Pitcher Scott Medvin to complete deal, December 11, 1985.

‡On disabled list, June 19 to August 3, 1989.

§Traded to New York Yankees for Pitchers Lance McCullers and Clay Parker, June 4, 1990.

CHAMPIONSHIP SERIES RECORD

Year Club	League	Pos.	G.	AB.	R.	H.	2B.	3B.	HR.	RBI.	B.A.	PO.	A.	E.	F.A.
1987—Detroit	Amer.	PH-DH-C	5	14	2	2	0	0	1	2	.143	11	2	0	1.000

ALL-STAR GAME RECORD

Year League	Pos.	AB.	R.	H.	2B.	3B.	HR.	RBI.	B.A.	PO.	A.	E.	F.A.
1987—American	C	2	0	0	0	0	0	0	.000	8	0	0	1.000

DICKIE RAY NOLES

Born November 19, 1956, at Charlotte, N. C.
Height, 6.02. Weight, 190.
Throws and bats righthanded.

Major League saves: 1980 (6), 1985 (1), 1987 (4). Total—11.
Led Eastern League in hit batsmen with 15 in 1978.
Led Carolina League in games started by pitchers with 27 in 1977.
Led Western Carolinas League in hit batsmen with 13 in 1976.
Tied for International League lead in saves with 19 in 1989.
Tied for Carolina League lead in hit batsmen with 11 in 1977.
Tied for Western Carolinas League lead in home runs allowed with 13 in 1976.

Year Club	League	G.	IP.	W.	L.	Pct.	H.	R.	ER.	SO.	BB.	ERA.
1975—Auburn	NYP	9	50	2	2	.500	49	30	20	31	27	3.60
1976—Spartanburg	W. Carol.	24	137	4	★16	.200	166	★110	★90	95	65	5.91
1977—Peninsula	Carolina	27	★199	10	11	.476	188	103	81	114	78	3.66
1978—Reading	Eastern	27	159	12	8	.600	177	100	75	78	72	4.25
1979—Oklahoma City†	Am. Assoc.	12	76	6	4	.600	69	38	33	48	28	3.91
1979—Philadelphia	National	14	90	3	4	.429	80	40	38	42	38	3.80
1979—Reading	Eastern	1	9	0	1	.000	7	5	4	2	4	4.00
1980—Philadelphia	National	48	81	1	4	.200	80	42	35	57	42	3.89
1981—Oklahoma City‡	Am. Assoc.	22	104	6	6	.500	85	45	38	82	46	3.29
1981—Philadelphia§	National	13	58	2	2	.500	57	30	27	34	23	4.19
1982—Chicago x	National	31	171	10	13	.435	180	99	84	85	61	4.42
1983—Chicago y	National	24	116⅓	5	10	.333	133	69	61	59	37	4.72
1983—Quad Cities	Midwest	3	12	0	1	.000	19	11	7	12	5	5.25
1984—Chicago z	National	21	50⅔	2	2	.500	60	29	29	14	16	5.15
1984—Texas	American	18	57⅔	2	3	.400	60	38	33	39	30	5.15
1985—Texas ab	American	28	110⅓	4	8	.333	129	67	62	59	33	5.06
1986—Cleveland c	American	32	54⅔	3	2	.600	56	33	31	32	30	5.10
1986—Maine d	Int'national	3	10	0	1	.000	11	6	5	4	4	4.50
1987—Chicago e	National	41	64⅓	4	2	.667	59	31	25	33	27	3.50
1987—Pittsfield f	Eastern	1	3	0	1	.000	4	2	2	5	1	6.00
1987—Iowa	Am. Assoc.	3	5	0	1	.000	8	6	6	3	3	10.80
1987—Detroit g	American	4	2	0	0	.000	2	1	1	0	1	4.50
1988—Rochester	Int'national	31	130	10	5	.667	124	57	45	59	31	3.12
1988—Baltimore h	American	2	3⅓	0	2	.000	11	10	9	1	0	24.30
1989—Columbus i	Int'national	42	87⅔	5	2	.714	77	43	36	66	34	3.70
1990—Scranton/Wilkes-Barre	Int'national	26	37⅔	3	2	.600	31	15	14	18	14	3.35
1990—Philadelphia jk	National	1	⅓	0	1	.000	2	1	1	0	0	27.00
National League Totals—8 Years		193	631⅓	27	38	.415	651	341	300	324	244	4.27
American League Totals—5 Years		84	228	9	15	.375	258	149	136	131	94	5.37
Major League Totals—11 Years		277	859⅔	36	53	.404	909	490	436	455	338	4.56

Selected by Philadelphia Phillies' organization in 4th round of free-agent draft, June 4, 1975.
†On disabled list, April 13 to April 24, 1979.
‡Appeared as outfielder with no chances.
§Traded with Catcher Keith Moreland and Pitcher Dan Larson to Chicago Cubs for Pitcher Mike Krukow and cash, December 8, 1981.
xOn disabled list, June 13 to July 4, 1982.
yOn disabled list, April 12 to June 4, 1983; included rehabilitation disability assignment to Quad Cities, May 21 to June 4, 1983.
zTraded to Texas Rangers for two players to be named later, July 2, 1984; Chicago Cubs' organization acquired Pitcher Tim Henry and Infielder Jorge Gomez to complete deal, December 11, 1984.
aOn disabled list, June 24 to July 14, 1985.
bReleased, December 20, 1985; signed by Maine (Cleveland Indians' organization), February 8, 1986.
cOn disabled list, April 18 to June 18, 1986; included rehabilitation disability assignment to Maine, June 7 to June 18, 1986.
dGranted free agency, November 12, 1986; signed by Chicago Cubs, April 6, 1987.
eOn disabled list, July 2 to August 21, 1987; included rehabilitation disability assignment to Pittsfield, August 10, and Iowa, August 14 to August 21, 1987.
fTraded to Detroit Tigers for a player to be named later, September 22, 1987; returned, October 23, 1987.
gGranted free agency, November 9, 1987; signed by Rochester (Baltimore Orioles' organization), April 2, 1988.
hReleased, November 17, 1988; signed by New York Yankees, December 22, 1988.
iReleased, October, 1989; signed by Scranton/Wilkes-Barre (Philadelphia Phillies' organization), April 6, 1990.
jOn disabled list, May 9 to July 30, 1990; included rehabilitation disability assignment to Scranton/Wilkes-Barre, June 14 to July 13, 1990.
kGranted free agency, October 15, 1990.

DIVISION SERIES RECORD

Year Club	League	G.	IP.	W.	L.	Pct.	H.	R.	ER.	SO.	BB.	ERA.
1981—Philadelphia	National	1	4	0	0	.000	4	2	2	5	2	4.50

CHAMPIONSHIP SERIES RECORD

Year Club	League	G.	IP.	W.	L.	Pct.	H.	R.	ER.	SO.	BB.	ERA.
1980—Philadelphia	National	2	2⅔	0	0	.000	1	0	0	0	3	0.00

WORLD SERIES RECORD

Year Club	League	G.	IP.	W.	L.	Pct.	H.	R.	ER.	SO.	BB.	ERA.
1980—Philadelphia	National	1	4⅔	0	0	.000	5	1	1	6	2	1.93

MICHAEL KELVIN NORRIS
(Mike)

Born March 19, 1955, at San Francisco, Calif.
Height, 6.02. Weight, 190.
Throws and bats righthanded.
Attended City College of San Francisco, San Francisco, Calif.

Pitched shutout in first major league game, April 10, 1975.
Led American League in wild pitches with 14 in 1981.
Tied for American League lead in balks with 4 in 1980 and 5 in 1981.
Named pitcher on THE SPORTING NEWS American League All-Star fielding team, 1980 and 1981.
Received reported $25,000 bonus to sign with Oakland Athletics, 1973.

Year Club	League	G.	IP.	W.	L.	Pct.	H.	R.	ER.	SO.	BB.	ERA.
1973—Burlington	Midwest	20	110	8	4	.667	81	38	27	130	40	2.21
1974—Birmingham†	Southern	21	109	7	8	.467	107	64	49	103	65	4.05
1975—Oakland‡	American	4	17	1	0	1.000	6	2	0	5	8	0.00
1976—Tucson	P. Coast	5	33	2	1	.667	28	15	14	19	23	3.82
1976—Oakland	American	24	96	4	5	.444	91	53	51	44	56	4.78
1977—San José§	P. Coast	6	46	3	2	.600	42	18	18	35	18	3.52
1977—Oakland x	American	16	77	2	7	.222	77	45	41	35	31	4.79
1978—Vancouver	P. Coast	7	42	3	3	.500	42	28	27	32	27	5.79
1978—Jersey City y	Eastern	9	66	2	6	.250	58	35	25	51	36	3.41
1978—Oakland	American	14	49	0	5	.000	46	34	30	36	35	5.51
1979—Oakland z	American	29	146	5	8	.385	146	87	78	96	94	4.81
1980—Oakland	American	33	284	22	9	.710	215	88	80	180	83	2.54
1981—Oakland	American	23	173	12	9	.571	145	77	72	78	63	3.75
1982—Oakland a	American	28	166⅓	7	11	.389	154	103	88	83	84	4.76
1983—Oakland b	American	16	88⅔	4	5	.444	68	42	37	63	36	3.76
1983—Tacoma	P. Coast	1	4	0	0	.000	6	6	4	3	1	9.00
1984—Oakland c	American					(Did not play)						
1985—Modesto de	California	2	13	1	0	1.000	4	1	0	6	1	0.00
1986—San Jose f	California	11	56⅓	4	3	.571	48	18	9	62	8	1.44
1987-88						(Out of Organized Baseball)						
1989—Huntsville	Southern	1	5⅓	1	0	1.000	6	0	0	3	0	0.00
1989—Tacoma	P.Coast	23	82	6	6	.500	78	39	29	72	27	3.18
1990—Oakland g	American	14	27	1	0	1.000	24	10	9	16	9	3.00
Major League Totals—10 Years		201	1124	58	59	.496	972	541	486	636	499	3.89

Selected by Oakland Athletics' organization in 1st round (24th player selected) of free-agent draft, January 10, 1973.
†On disabled list, June 14 to June 24, 1974.
‡On disabled list, April 28 to September 19, 1975.
§On disabled list, August 27 to September 6, 1977.
xStruck out in only appearance as a pinch-hitter.

yOn suspended list, May 19 to May 28, 1978.
zOn disabled list, July 12 to August 7, 1979.
aOn disabled list, June 17 to July 8, 1982.
bOn disabled list, June 18 to July 26 and August 11, 1983 through remainder of season; included rehabilitation disability assignment to Tacoma, July 6 to July 26, 1983.
cOn disabled list, March 31, 1984 through entire season.
dOn Oakland disabled list, March 29, 1985 through entire season; included rehabilitation disability assignment to Modesto, June 13 to June 25, 1985.
eGranted free agency, November 12, 1985; signed by San Jose (Independent), March 7, 1986.
fSigned by Tacoma (Oakland Athletics' organization), April 6, 1989.
gReleased, July 15, 1990.

DIVISION SERIES RECORD

Year Club	League	G.	IP.	W.	L.	Pct.	H.	R.	ER.	SO.	BB.	ERA.
1981—Oakland	American	1	9	1	0	1.000	4	0	0	2	3	0.00

CHAMPIONSHIP SERIES RECORD

Year Club	League	G.	IP.	W.	L.	Pct.	H.	R.	ER.	SO.	BB.	ERA.
1981—Oakland	American	1	7⅓	0	1	.000	6	3	3	4	2	3.68

ALL-STAR GAME RECORD

Year League	IP.	W.	L.	Pct.	H.	R.	ER.	SO.	BB.	ERA.
1981—American	1	0	0	.000	2	1	1	1	0	9.00

RANDALL WILLIAM NOSEK
(Randy)

Born January 8, 1967, at Omaha, Neb.
Height, 6.04. Weight, 215.
Throws and bats righthanded.

Year Club	League	G.	IP.	W.	L.	Pct.	H.	R.	ER.	SO.	BB.	ERA.
1986—Gastonia	S. Atlantic	12	52⅓	4	5	.444	56	41	35	37	49	6.02
1986—Bristol	Ap'lachian	11	63½	6	4	.600	58	38	32	48	45	4.55
1987—Fayetteville	S. Atlantic	16	77⅔	4	11	.267	69	63	40	57	63	4.64
1988—Lakeland	Florida St.	8	30⅔	0	4	.000	29	17	13	11	16	3.82
1989—London	Eastern	22	123⅔	8	10	.444	113	75	68	62	100	4.95
1989—Detroit	American	2	5⅓	0	2	.000	7	8	8	4	10	13.50
1989—Toledo	Int'national	1	1	0	0	.000	2	4	4	0	4	36.00
1990—Toledo	Int'national	22	109⅓	5	8	.385	112	70	63	55	66	5.19
1990—Detroit	American	3	7	1	1	.500	7	7	6	3	9	7.71
Major League Totals—2 Years		5	12⅓	1	3	.250	14	15	14	7	19	10.22

Selected by Detroit Tigers' organization in 1st round (26th player selected) of free-agent draft, June 3, 1985.

RAFAEL ANGEL NOVOA

Born October 26, 1967, at New York, N.Y.
Height, 6.00. Weight, 185.
Throws and bats lefthanded.
Received degree from Villanova University, Villanova, Pa.

Major League saves: 1990 (1).

Year Club	League	G.	IP.	W.	L.	Pct.	H.	R.	ER.	SO.	BB.	ERA.
1989—Everett	Northwest	3	15	0	1	.000	20	11	8	20	8	4.80
1989—Clinton	Midwest	13	63⅔	5	4	.556	58	20	18	61	18	2.54
1990—Clinton	Midwest	15	97⅔	9	2	.818	73	32	26	113	30	2.40
1990—Shreveport	Texas	11	71⅔	5	4	.556	60	21	21	65	25	2.64
1990—San Francisco	National	7	18⅔	0	1	.000	21	14	14	14	13	6.75
Major League Totals—1 Year		7	18⅔	0	1	.000	21	14	14	14	13	6.75

Selected by San Francisco Giants' organization in 9th round of free-agent draft, June 5, 1989.

EDWIN NUNEZ (MARTINEZ)

Name pronounced NOON-yez.

Born May 27, 1963, at Humacao, Puerto Rico.
Height, 6.05. Weight, 240.
Throws and bats righthanded.

Major League saves: 1984 (7), 1985 (16), 1987 (12), 1989 (1), 1990 (6). Total—42.
Led Midwest League in complete games with 13 in 1981.

Year Club	League	G.	IP.	W.	L.	Pct.	H.	R.	ER.	SO.	BB.	ERA.
1979—Bellingham	Northwest	6	39	4	1	.800	39	14	9	30	5	2.08
1980—Wausau	Midwest	22	138	9	7	.563	145	71	57	91	58	3.72
1981—Wausau	Midwest	25	★186	★16	3	.842	143	61	51	★205	58	2.47
1982—Seattle†	American	8	35⅓	1	2	.333	36	18	18	27	16	4.58
1982—Salt Lake City‡	P. Coast	11	55⅓	4	3	.571	40	26	21	42	23	3.42
1983—Seattle	American	14	37	0	4	.000	40	21	18	35	22	4.38
1983—Salt Lake City§	P. Coast	14	77½	4	4	.500	99	70	61	52	36	7.10
1984—Salt Lake City x	P. Coast	18	27⅔	3	2	.600	24	12	11	26	12	3.58
1984—Seattle	American	37	67⅔	2	2	.500	55	26	24	57	21	3.19
1985—Seattle	American	70	90⅓	7	3	.700	79	36	31	58	34	3.09
1986—Seattle y	American	14	21⅔	1	2	.333	25	15	14	17	5	5.82

— 352 —

Year—Club	League	G.	IP.	W.	L.	Pct.	H.	R.	ER.	SO.	BB.	ERA.
1986—Calgary	P. Coast	6	14	1	2	.333	19	13	11	17	4	7.07
1987—Seattle z	American	48	47⅓	3	4	.429	45	20	20	34	18	3.80
1988—Seattle	American	14	29⅓	1	4	.200	45	33	26	19	14	7.98
1988—Calgary a	P. Coast	3	15⅓	2	0	1.000	15	9	8	12	4	4.70
1988—New York b	National	10	14	1	0	1.000	21	7	7	8	3	4.50
1989—Toledo	Int'national	13	59⅓	1	5	.167	47	20	17	53	18	2.58
1989—Detroit	American	27	54	3	4	.429	49	33	25	41	36	4.17
1990—Detroit cd	American	42	80⅓	3	1	.750	65	26	20	66	37	2.24
American League Totals—9 Years		274	463	21	26	.447	439	228	196	354	203	3.81
National League Totals—1 Year		10	14	1	0	1.000	21	7	7	8	3	4.50
Major League Totals—9 Years		284	477	22	26	.458	460	235	203	362	206	3.83

Signed as free agent by Seattle Mariners' organization, March 17, 1979.
†On disabled list, April 23 to May 15, 1982.
‡On disabled list, June 4 to June 29, 1982.
§On disabled list, June 30 to July 14, 1983.
xOn disabled list, May 12 to June 3, 1984.
yOn disabled list, April 5 to April 29 and May 1 to May 16, 1986.
zOn disabled list, May 20 to June 4, 1987.
aTraded to New York Mets for Pitcher Gene Walter, July 11, 1988.
bReleased, March 28, 1989; signed by Toledo (Detroit Tigers' organization), April 1, 1989.
cOn disabled list, July 8 to August 14, 1990.
dGranted free agency, November 5, 1990; signed by Milwaukee Brewers, December 4, 1990.

JOSE NUNEZ

Name pronounced NOON-yez.

Born January 13, 1964, at Jarabocoa, D. R.
Height, 6.03. Weight, 190.
Throws and bats righthanded.

Year—Club	League	G.	IP.	W.	L.	Pct.	H.	R.	ER.	SO.	BB.	ERA.
1984—Charleston	S. Atlantic	25	170	14	8	.636	★167	91	62	106	54	3.28
1985—Fort Myers†	Florida St.	11	44⅓	3	2	.600	32	14	12	23	12	2.44
1986—Memphis	Southern	13	48⅔	2	6	.250	52	43	29	36	51	5.36
1986—Fort Myers‡	Florida St.	14	87⅓	8	2	.800	73	31	24	59	32	2.47
1987—Toronto	American	37	97	5	2	.714	91	57	54	99	58	5.01
1988—Syracuse	Int'national	12	71⅓	5	4	.556	62	26	23	67	16	2.90
1988—Toronto§	American	13	29⅓	0	1	.000	28	11	10	18	17	3.07
1989—Syracuse	Int'national	40	134⅓	11	11	.500	116	51	33	122	55	★2.21
1989—Toronto x	American	6	10⅔	0	0	.000	8	3	3	14	2	2.53
1990—Chicago	National	21	60⅔	4	7	.364	61	47	44	40	34	6.53
1990—Iowa	Am. Assoc.	16	107⅓	7	6	.538	105	51	47	109	32	3.94
American League Totals—3 Years		56	137	5	3	.625	127	71	67	131	77	4.40
National League Totals—1 Year		21	60⅔	4	7	.364	61	47	44	40	34	6.53
Major League Totals—4 Years		77	197⅔	9	10	.474	188	118	111	171	111	5.05

Signed as free agent by Kansas City Royals' organization, November 11, 1983.
†On disabled list, May 30 to June 19 and July 1 to August 24, 1985.
‡Drafted by Toronto Blue Jays, December 8, 1986.
§On disabled list, June 3 to June 18, 1988.
xTraded to Chicago Cubs for Pitcher Paul Kilgus, December 7, 1989.

KENNETH RAY OBERKFELL

Name pronounced OH-burk-fell.

(Ken)

Born May 4, 1956, at Maryville, Ill.
Height, 6.01. Weight, 210.
Throws right and bats lefthanded.
Attended Belleville Area Junior College, Belleville, Ill.

Major League stolen bases: 1979 (4), 1980 (4), 1981 (13), 1982 (11), 1983 (12), 1984 (2), 1985 (1), 1986 (7), 1987 (3), 1988 (4), 1990 (1). Total—62.
Led National League third basemen in double plays with 23 and tied for lead in total chances with 338 in 1981.
Led National League second basemen in fielding percentage with .985 in 1979.

Year—Club	League	Pos.	G.	AB.	R.	H.	2B.	3B.	HR.	RBI.	B.A.	PO.	A.	E.	F.A.
1975—Johnson City	Appal.	SS	17	54	15	19	3	0	1	8	.352	21	58	4	.952
1975—St. Petersburg	Fla. St.	SS	41	134	14	47	6	1	0	22	.351	71	107	6	.967
1976—Arkansas	Texas	2B-SS	128	456	64	131	19	2	3	47	.287	259	321	18	.970
1977—New Orleans	A. A.	2B-SS	120	418	67	105	18	5	4	32	.251	205	325	17	.969
1977—St. Louis	Nat.	2B	9	9	0	1	0	0	0	1	.111	3	4	0	1.000
1978—Springfield	A. A.	3B-2B-SS	64	242	41	69	13	4	6	38	.285	77	113	6	.969
1978—St. Louis	Nat.	2B-3B	24	50	7	6	1	0	0	0	.120	30	48	1	.987
1979—St. Louis†	Nat.	2B-3B-SS	135	369	53	111	19	5	1	35	.301	223	343	9	.984
1980—St. Louis†	Nat.	2B-3B	116	422	58	128	27	6	3	46	.303	227	340	7	.988
1981—St. Louis	Nat.	3B-SS	102	376	43	110	12	6	2	45	.293	77	247	15	.956
1982—St. Louis‡	Nat.	★3B-2B	137	470	55	136	22	5	2	34	.289	80	305	11	★.972
1983—St. Louis	Nat.	★3B-2B-SS	151	488	62	143	26	5	3	38	.293	132	303	18	★.960
1984—St. L.§-Atl.x	Nat.	3B-2B-SS	100	324	38	87	19	2	1	21	.269	64	173	8	.967
1985—Atlanta	Nat.	3B-2B	134	412	30	112	19	4	3	35	.272	88	257	12	.966

Year Club	League	Pos.	G.	AB.	R.	H.	2B.	3B.	HR.	RBI.	B.A.	PO.	A.	E.	F.A.
1986—Atlanta	Nat.	3B-2B	151	503	62	136	24	3	5	48	.270	116	335	11	.976
1987—Atlanta y	Nat.	3B-2B	135	508	59	142	29	2	3	48	.280	89	265	7	.981
1988—Atl.z-Pit.	Nat.	3-2-S-1	140	476	49	129	22	4	3	42	.271	107	237	15	.958
1989—Pit.a-S.F.b	Nat.	3B-1B-2B	97	156	19	42	6	1	2	17	.269	131	47	4	.978
1990—Houston c	Nat.	3B-1B-2B	77	150	10	31	6	1	1	12	.207	93	52	4	.973
Major League Totals—14 Years.............			1508	4713	545	1314	232	44	29	422	.279	1460	2956	122	.973

Signed as free agent by St. Louis Cardinals' organization, May 4, 1975.
†On disabled list, May 11 to June 20, 1980.
‡On disabled list, March 31 to April 23, 1982.
§Traded to Atlanta Braves for Pitcher Ken Dayley and First Baseman Mike Jorgensen, June 15, 1984.
xOn disabled list, August 27, 1984 through remainder of season.
yOn disabled list, June 26 to July 11, 1987.
zTraded with cash to Pittsburgh Pirates for a player to be named later, August 28, 1988; Atlanta Braves acquired Outfielder Tommy Gregg to complete deal, September 1, 1988.
aTraded to San Francisco Giants for Pitcher Roger Samuels, May 10, 1989.
bGranted free agency, November 13, 1989; signed by Houston Astros, December 6, 1989.
cOn disabled list, June 19 to July 4, 1990.

CHAMPIONSHIP SERIES RECORD

Tied Championship Series record for most at-bats, three-game Series (15).

Year Club	League	Pos.	G.	AB.	R.	H.	2B.	3B.	HR.	RBI.	B.A.	PO.	A.	E.	F.A.
1982—St. Louis.................	Nat.	3B	3	15	1	3	0	0	0	2	.200	2	4	1	.857
1989—San Francisco	Nat.	PH-3B	3	4	0	0	0	0	0	0	.000	0	1	0	1.000
Championship Series Totals—2 Years.....			6	19	1	3	0	0	0	2	.158	2	5	1	.875

WORLD SERIES RECORD

Year Club	League	Pos.	G.	AB.	R.	H.	2B.	3B.	HR.	RBI.	B.A.	PO.	A.	E.	F.A.
1982—St. Louis...............	Nat.	3B	7	24	4	7	1	0	0	1	.292	3	21	1	.960
1989—San Francisco	Nat.	PH-3B	4	6	1	2	0	0	0	0	.333	0	5	1	.833
World Series Totals—2 Years			11	30	5	9	1	0	0	1	.300	3	26	2	.935

CHARLES HUGH O'BRIEN
(Charlie)

Born May 1, 1961, at Tulsa, Okla.
Height, 6.02. Weight, 190.
Throws and bats righthanded.
Attended McClennan Community College, Waco, Tex., and Wichita State University, Wichita, Kan.

Year Club	League	Pos.	G.	AB.	R.	H.	2B.	3B.	HR.	RBI.	B.A.	PO.	A.	E.	F.A.
1982—Medford	N'west	C	17	60	11	17	3	0	3	14	.283	116	18	4	.971
1982—Modesto.................	Calif.	C	41	140	23	42	6	0	3	32	.300	239	44	5	.983
1983—Albany†	East.	C-1B	92	285	50	83	12	1	14	56	.291	478	82	11	.981
1984—Modesto‡...............	Calif.	C	9	32	8	9	2	0	1	5	.281	41	8	0	1.000
1984—Tacoma.................	P. C.	C-OF	69	195	33	44	11	0	9	22	.226	260	39	0	1.000
1985—Huntsville	South.	C	33	115	20	24	5	0	7	16	.209	182	29	5	.977
1985—Oakland.................	Amer.	C	16	11	3	3	1	0	0	1	.273	23	0	1	.958
1985—Modesto.................	Calif.	C	9	27	5	8	4	1	1	2	.296	33	8	1	.976
1985—Tacoma§...............	P. C.	C	18	57	5	9	4	0	0	7	.158	110	9	3	.975
1986—Vancouver.............	P. C.	C	6	17	1	2	0	0	0	1	.118	22	3	2	.926
1986—El Paso..................	Texas	C-OF-1B	92	336	72	109	20	3	15	75	.324	437	43	4	.992
1987—Denver	A. A.	C	80	266	37	75	12	1	8	35	.282	415	53	6	.987
1987—Milwaukee.............	Amer.	C	10	35	2	7	3	1	0	0	.200	78	11	0	1.000
1988—Denver	A. A.	C	48	153	16	43	5	0	4	25	.281	243	44	3	.990
1988—Milwaukee.............	Amer.	C	40	118	12	26	6	0	2	9	.220	210	20	2	.991
1989—Milwaukee.............	Amer.	C	62	188	22	44	10	0	6	35	.234	314	36	5	.986
1990—Milwaukee x	Amer.	C	46	145	11	27	7	2	0	11	.186	217	24	2	.992
1990—New York..............	Nat.	C	28	68	6	11	3	0	0	9	.162	191	21	3	.986
American League Totals—5 Years			174	497	50	107	27	3	8	56	.215	842	91	10	.989
National League Totals—1 Year.............			28	68	6	11	3	0	0	9	.162	191	21	3	.986
Major League Totals—5 Years................			202	565	56	118	30	3	8	65	.209	1033	112	13	.989

Selected by Texas Rangers' organization in 14th round of free-agent draft, June 6, 1978.
Selected by Seattle Mariners' organization in 21st round of free-agent draft, June 8, 1981.
Selected by Oakland A's organization in 5th round of free-agent draft, June 7, 1982.
†On disabled list, July 31, 1983 through remainder of season.
‡On Albany disabled list, April 13 to May 15, 1984.
§Traded with Infielder Steve Kiefer and Pitchers Mike Fulmer and Pete Kendrick to Milwaukee Brewers for Pitcher Moose Haas, March 30, 1986.
xTraded with a player to be named later to New York Mets for two players to be named later, August 30, 1990; Milwaukee Brewers acquired Pitchers Julio Machado and Kevin Brown on September 7, 1990 and New York acquired Pitcher Kevin Carmody on September 11, 1990 to complete deal.

—DID YOU KNOW—

That Luis Rivera hit Boston's first grand slam of 1990 in the team's 131st game? In the 132nd game, Mike Greenwell stroked an inside-the-park slam.

PETER MICHAEL O'BRIEN
(Pete)

Born February 9, 1958, at Santa Monica, Calif.
Height, 6.02. Weight, 195.
Throws and bats lefthanded.
Attended Monterrey Peninsula College, Monterrey, Calif.; and
University of Nebraska, Lincoln, Neb.

Shares major league record for most double plays started by first baseman, nine-inning game (3), May 22, 1984.
Major League stolen bases: 1982 (1), 1983 (5), 1984 (3), 1985 (5), 1986 (4), 1988 (1), 1989 (3). Total—22.
Led American League first basemen in assists with 120 in 1983.

Year	Club	League	Pos.	G.	AB.	R.	H.	2B.	3B.	HR.	RBI.	B.A.	PO.	A.	E.	F.A.
1979—Sarasota Rangers	Gulf C.		1B	50	189	39	46	10	2	0	31	.243	*465	*44	7	.986
1980—Asheville	S. Atl.		1B	134	505	98	149	34	2	17	94	.295	*1227	*96	14	.990
1981—Tulsa	Texas		1B	110	382	57	109	19	3	17	78	.285	973	95	11	.990
1982—Denver	A. A.		OF-1B	128	477	92	148	21	1	25	102	.310	418	37	8	.983
1982—Texas	Amer.		OF-1B	20	67	13	16	4	1	4	13	.239	39	3	0	1.000
1983—Texas	Amer.		1B-OF	154	524	53	124	24	5	8	53	.237	1191	121	11	.992
1984—Texas	Amer.		1B-OF	142	520	57	149	26	2	18	80	.287	1271	105	11	.992
1985—Texas	Amer.		1B	159	573	69	153	34	3	22	92	.267	1457	98	8	.995
1986—Texas	Amer.		1B	156	551	86	160	23	3	23	90	.290	1224	115	11	.992
1987—Texas	Amer.		*1B-OF	159	569	84	163	26	1	23	88	.286	1233	*146	11	.992
1988—Texas†	Amer.		1B	156	547	57	149	24	1	16	71	.272	1346	140	8	.995
1989—Cleveland‡	Amer.		1B	155	554	75	144	24	1	12	55	.260	1359	114	9	.994
1990—Seattle§	Amer.		1B-OF	108	366	32	82	18	0	5	27	.224	852	76	5	.995
Major League Totals—9 Years				1209	4271	526	1140	203	17	131	569	.267	9972	918	74	.993

Selected by Texas Rangers' organization in 15th round of free-agent draft, June 5, 1979.

†Traded with Outfielder Oddibe McDowell and Second Baseman Jerry Browne to Cleveland Indians for Second Baseman Julio Franco, December 6, 1988.

‡Granted free agency, November 13, 1989; signed by Seattle Mariners, December 7, 1989.

§On disabled list, May 5 to June 19, 1990.

RONALD JOHN OESTER
Name pronounced O-ster.
(Ron)

Born May 5, 1956, at Cincinnati, O.
Height, 6.02. Weight, 195.
Throws right and bats left and righthanded.

Major League stolen bases: 1980 (6), 1981 (2), 1982 (5), 1983 (2), 1984 (7), 1985 (5), 1986 (9), 1987 (2), 1989 (1), 1990 (1)
Total—40.
Led National League second basemen in total chances with 861 in 1986.
Led American Association shortstops in double plays with 102 in 1978.
Led Eastern League shortstops in double plays with 84 in 1976.
Led Pioneer League shortstops in double plays with 27 in 1974.

Year	Club	League	Pos.	G.	AB.	R.	H.	2B.	3B.	HR.	RBI.	B.A.	PO.	A.	E.	F.A.
1974—Billings	Pion.		SS	53	167	23	52	11	1	0	21	.311	87	141	27	.894
1975—Tampa	Fla. St.		SS	117	375	40	82	3	4	0	25	.219	174	358	34	.940
1976—Three Rivers	East.		SS	138	447	57	110	14	4	0	44	.246	*233	*408	38	.944
1977—Indianapolis	A. A.		SS	134	455	60	116	16	5	3	33	.255	203	*386	39	.938
1978—Indianapolis	A. A.		SS	●135	514	78	133	21	4	7	49	.259	*300	*428	32	.958
1978—Cincinnati	Nat.		SS	6	8	1	3	0	0	0	1	.375	3	9	0	1.000
1979—Indianapolis	A. A.		SS	●136	509	62	143	19	6	2	33	.281	*244	397	31	.954
1979—Cincinnati	Nat.		SS	6	3	0	0	0	0	0	0	.000	1	2	0	1.000
1980—Cincinnati	Nat.		2B-SS-3B	100	303	40	84	16	2	2	20	.277	161	224	10	.975
1981—Cincinnati	Nat.		2B-SS	105	354	45	96	16	7	5	42	.271	213	341	11	.981
1982—Cincinnati	Nat.		2B-SS-3B	151	549	63	143	19	4	9	47	.260	304	403	22	.970
1983—Cincinnati	Nat.		2B	157	549	63	145	23	5	11	58	.264	315	413	17	.977
1984—Cincinnati	Nat.		2B-SS	150	553	54	134	26	3	3	38	.242	357	388	15	.980
1985—Cincinnati	Nat.		2B	152	526	59	155	26	3	1	34	.295	366	457	9	.989
1986—Cincinnati	Nat.		2B	153	523	52	135	23	2	8	44	.258	●367	475	19	.978
1987—Cincinnati†‡	Nat.		2B	69	237	28	60	9	6	2	23	.253	183	186	10	.974
1988—Nashville	A. A.		2B	12	37	4	7	1	0	0	3	.189	15	28	4	.915
1988—Chattanooga	South.		2B	14	46	5	14	2	0	1	6	.304	19	25	1	.978
1988—Cincinnati§	Nat.		2B-SS	54	150	20	42	7	0	0	10	.280	110	113	1	.996
1989—Cincinnati x	Nat.		2B-SS	109	305	23	75	15	0	1	14	.246	215	249	7	.985
1990—Cincinnati y	Nat.		2B-3B	64	154	10	46	10	1	0	13	.299	80	90	4	.977
Major League Totals—13 Years				1276	4214	458	1118	190	33	42	344	.265	2675	3350	125	.980

Selected by Cincinnati Reds' organization in 9th round of free-agent draft, June 5, 1974.

†On disabled list, July 6, 1987 through remainder of season.

‡Released, October 21, 1987; re-signed by Reds' organization, January 29, 1988.

§Granted free agency, November 4, 1988; re-signed by Reds, December 2, 1988.

xOn disabled list, June 7 to July 17, 1989.

yGranted free agency, November 5, 1990.

CHAMPIONSHIP SERIES RECORD

Year	Club	League	Pos.	G.	AB.	R.	H.	2B.	3B.	HR.	RBI.	B.A.	PO.	A.	E.	F.A.
1990—Cincinnati	Nat.		PH-2B	4	3	1	1	0	0	0	0	.333	0	1	0	1.000

Year	Club	League	Pos.	G.	AB.	R.	H.	2B.	3B.	HR.	RBI.	B.A.	PO.	A.	E.	F.A.
1990—Cincinnati		Nat.	PH	1	1	0	1	0	0	0	1	1.000	0	0	0	.000

JOSE ANTONIO OFFERMAN (DONO)

Born November 8, 1968, at San Pedro de Macoris, Dominican Republic.
Height, 6.00. Weight, 160.
Throws right and bats left and righthanded.

Shares major league record by hitting home run in first at-bat, August 19, 1990.
Major League stolen bases: 1990 (1).
Led Pacific Coast League in stolen bases with 60 and tied for lead in caught stealing with 18 in 1990.
Led Pioneer League in stolen bases with 57 and tied for lead in caught stealing with 10 in 1988.
Named Minor League Player of the Year by THE SPORTING NEWS, 1990.
Named Pacific Coast League Player of the Year, 1990.

Year	Club	League	Pos.	G.	AB.	R.	H.	2B.	3B.	HR.	RBI.	B.A.	PO.	A.	E.	F.A.
1988—Great Falls		Pion.	SS	60	251	75	83	11	5	2	28	.331	82	143	18	*.926
1989—Bakersfield		Calif.	SS	62	245	53	75	9	4	2	22	.306	94	179	30	.901
1989—San Antonio		Texas	SS	68	278	47	80	6	3	2	22	.288	106	168	20	.932
1990—Albuquerque		P. C.	*SS-2B	117	454	104	148	16	11	0	56	.326	174	361	*36	.937
1990—Los Angeles		Nat.	SS	29	58	7	9	0	0	1	7	.155	30	40	4	.946
Major League Totals—1 Year				29	58	7	9	0	0	1	7	.155	30	40	4	.946

Signed as free agent by Los Angeles Dodgers' organization, July 24, 1986.

ROBERT MICHAEL OJEDA

Name pronounced Oh-HEED-a.

(Bob)

Born December 17, 1957, at Los Angeles, Calif.
Height, 6.01. Weight, 195.
Throws and bats lefthanded.
Attended College of the Sequoias, Visalia, Calif.

Major League saves: 1985 (1).
Tied for American League lead in shutouts with 5 in 1984.
Tied for International League lead in balks with 3 in 1980.
Tied for Florida State League lead in games started by pitchers with 29 in 1979.
Named International League Pitcher of the Year, 1981.

Year	Club	League	G.	IP.	W.	L.	Pct.	H.	R.	ER.	SO.	BB.	ERA.
1978—Elmira		NYP	18	43	1	6	.143	45	32	23	35	43	4.81
1979—Winter Haven		Florida St.	29	200	15	7	.682	163	66	54	150	84	2.43
1980—Pawtucket		Int'national	19	123	6	7	.462	107	54	44	78	56	3.22
1980—Boston		American	7	26	1	1	.500	39	20	20	12	14	6.92
1981—Pawtucket		Int'national	25	173	12	9	.571	136	52	41	113	73	*2.13
1981—Boston		American	10	66	6	2	.750	50	25	23	28	25	3.14
1982—Boston†		American	22	78⅓	4	6	.400	95	53	49	52	29	5.63
1983—Boston		American	29	173⅔	12	7	.632	173	85	78	94	73	4.04
1984—Boston‡		American	33	216⅔	12	12	.500	211	106	96	137	96	3.99
1985—Boston§		American	39	157⅔	9	11	.450	166	74	70	102	48	4.00
1986—New York		National	32	217⅓	18	5	*.783	185	72	62	148	52	2.57
1987—New York x		National	10	46⅓	3	5	.375	45	23	20	21	10	3.88
1988—New York		National	29	190⅓	10	13	.435	158	74	61	133	33	2.88
1989—New York		National	31	192	13	11	.542	179	83	74	95	78	3.47
1990—New York y		National	38	118	7	6	.538	123	53	48	62	40	3.66
American League Totals—6 Years			140	718⅓	44	39	.530	734	363	336	425	285	4.21
National League Totals—5 Years			140	764	51	40	.560	690	305	265	459	213	3.12
Major League Totals—11 Years			280	1482⅓	95	79	.546	1424	668	601	884	498	3.65

Signed as free agent by Boston Red Sox' organization, May 20, 1978.
†On disabled list, August 20 to September 10, 1982.
‡On disabled list, August 16 to September 1, 1984.
§Traded with Pitchers Tom McCarthy, John Mitchell and Chris Bayer to New York Mets for Pitchers Calvin Schiraldi and Wes Gardner and Outfielders John Christensen and LaSchelle Tarver, November 13, 1985.
xOn disabled list, May 11 to September 1, 1987.
yTraded with Pitcher Greg Hansell to Los Angeles Dodgers for Outfielder Hubie Brooks, December 15, 1990.

Shares National League Championship Series record for most hits allowed, game (10), October 9, 1986.

Year	Club	League	G.	IP.	W.	L.	Pct.	H.	R.	ER.	SO.	BB.	ERA.
1986—New York		National	2	14	1	0	1.000	15	4	4	6	4	2.57

Year	Club	League	G.	IP.	W.	L.	Pct.	H.	R.	ER.	SO.	BB.	ERA.
1986—New York		National	2	13	1	0	1.000	13	3	3	9	5	2.08

—DID YOU KNOW—

That Kansas City's George Brett is the only major leaguer to win batting titles in three different decades (1976, 1980, 1990)?

JOHN GARRETT OLERUD

Name pronounced OL-uh-rude.

Born August 5, 1968, at Bellevue, Wash.
Height, 6.05. Weight, 218.
Throws and bats lefthanded.
Attended Washington State University, Pullman, Wash.
Son of John E. Olerud, minor league catcher, 1965 through 1970.

Year Club	League	Pos.	G.	AB.	R.	H.	2B.	3B.	HR.	RBI.	B.A.	PO.	A.	E.	F.A.
1989—Toronto	Amer.	1B	6	8	2	3	0	0	0	0	.375	19	2	0	1.000
1990—Toronto	Amer.	1B	111	358	43	95	15	1	14	48	.265	133	10	2	.986
Major League Totals—2 Years			117	366	45	98	15	1	14	48	.268	152	12	2	.988

Selected by New York Mets' organization in 27th round of free-agent draft, June 2, 1986.
Selected by Toronto Blue Jays' organization in 3rd round of free-agent draft, June 5, 1989.

STEVEN ROBERT OLIN
(Steve)

Born October 10, 1965, at Portland, Ore.
Height, 6.02. Weight, 190.
Throws and bats righthanded.
Attended Portland State University, Portland, Ore.

Major League saves: 1989 (1), 1990 (1). Total—2.
Led Pacific Coast League in saves with 24 in 1989.
Led Appalachian League in games finished in relief with 25 in 1987.

Year Club	League	G.	IP.	W.	L.	Pct.	H.	R.	ER.	SO.	BB.	ERA.
1987—Burlington	Ap'lachian	●26	57⅓	4	4	.500	42	21	15	75	17	2.35
1988—Waterloo	Midwest	29	39⅓	3	0	1.000	26	7	6	48	14	1.37
1988—Kinston	Carolina	33	56⅔	5	2	.714	49	23	19	45	15	3.02
1989—Colorado Springs	P. Coast	42	50⅓	4	1	.800	34	18	18	46	15	3.22
1989—Cleveland	American	25	36	1	4	.200	35	16	15	24	14	3.75
1990—Cleveland	American	50	92⅓	4	4	.500	96	41	35	64	26	3.41
1990—Colorado Springs	P. Coast	14	27⅓	3	1	.750	18	9	2	30	15	0.66
Major League Totals—2 Years		75	128⅓	5	8	.385	131	57	50	88	40	3.51

Selected by Cleveland Indians' organization in 16th round of free-agent draft, June 2, 1987.

OMAR OLIVARES (PALQ)

Born July 6, 1967, at Mayaguez, Puerto Rico.
Height, 6.01. Weight, 185.
Throws and bats righthanded.

Tied for Texas League lead in hit batsmen with 10 in 1989.

Year Club	League	G.	IP.	W.	L.	Pct.	H.	R.	ER.	SO.	BB.	ERA.
1987—Charleston, S.C.	S. Atlantic	31	170⅓	4	14	.222	182	107	87	86	57	4.60
1988—Charleston, S.C.	S. Atlantic	24	185⅓	13	6	.684	166	63	46	94	43	2.23
1988—Riverside	California	4	23⅓	3	0	1.000	18	9	3	16	9	1.16
1989—Wichita†	Texas	26	*185⅔	12	11	.522	175	87	70	79	61	3.39
1990—Louisville	Am. Assoc.	23	159⅓	10	11	.476	127	58	50	88	59	2.82
1990—St. Louis	National	9	49⅓	1	1	.500	45	17	16	20	17	2.92
Major League Totals—1 Year		9	49⅓	1	1	.500	45	17	16	20	17	2.92

Signed as free agent by San Diego Padres' organization, September 15, 1986.
†Traded to St. Louis Cardinals for Outfielder Alex Cole and Pitcher Steve Peters, February 27, 1990.

JOSEPH MELTON OLIVER
(Joe)

Born July 24, 1965, at Memphis, Tenn.
Height, 6.03. Weight, 210.
Throws and bats righthanded.

Major League stolen bases: 1990 (1).
Tied for National League lead in passed balls with 16 in 1990.
Led Florida State League catchers in assists with 84 and passed balls with 33 in 1985.
Led Midwest League catchers in passed balls with 30 and total chances with 855 in 1984.
Led Pioneer League catchers in putouts with 425, assists with 38 and total chances with 468 in 1983.

Year Club	League	Pos.	G.	AB.	R.	H.	2B.	3B.	HR.	RBI.	B.A.	PO.	A.	E.	F.A.
1983—Billings	Pion.	★C-1B	56	186	21	40	4	0	4	28	.215	426	39	5	★.989
1984—Cedar Rapids	Midw.	C	102	335	34	73	11	0	3	29	.218	★757	85	13	.985
1985—Tampa	Fla. St.	C-1B	112	386	38	104	23	2	7	62	.269	615	94	16	.978
1986—Vermont†	East.	C	84	282	32	78	18	1	6	41	.277	383	62	14	.969
1987—Vermont	East.	C-1B	66	236	31	72	13	2	10	60	.305	247	35	10	.966
1988—Nashville	A. A.	C	73	220	19	45	7	2	4	24	.205	413	37	7	.985
1988—Chattanooga	South.	C	28	105	9	26	6	0	3	12	.248	176	15	0	1.000
1989—Nashville	A. A.	★C-1B	71	233	22	68	13	0	6	31	.292	388	37	★13	.970
1989—Cincinnati	Nat.	C	49	151	13	41	8	0	3	23	.272	260	21	4	.986
1990—Cincinnati	Nat.	C	121	364	34	84	23	0	8	52	.231	686	59	6	★.992
Major League Totals—2 Years			170	515	47	125	31	0	11	75	.243	946	80	10	.990

Selected by Cincinnati Reds' organization in 2nd round of free-agent draft, June 6, 1983.
†On disabled list, April 23 to May 6, 1986.

Year Club	League	Pos.	G.	AB.	R.	H.	2B.	3B.	HR.	RBI.	B.A.	PO.	A.	E.	F.A.
1990—Cincinnati	Nat.	C	5	14	1	2	0	0	0	0	.143	27	1	0	1.000

WORLD SERIES RECORD

Year Club	League	Pos.	G.	AB.	R.	H.	2B.	3B.	HR.	RBI.	B.A.	PO.	A.	E.	F.A.
1990—Cincinnati	Nat.	C	4	18	2	6	3	0	0	2	.333	27	1	3	.903

FRANCISCO JAVIER OLIVERAS (NOA)

Born January 31, 1963, at Santurce, Puerto Rico.
Height, 5.10. Weight, 180.
Throws and bats righthanded.

Major League stolen bases: 1990 (2).
Tied for Southern League lead in home runs allowed with 27 in 1986.

Year Club	League	G.	IP.	W.	L.	Pct.	H.	R.	ER.	SO.	BB.	ERA.
1981—Miami	Florida St.	19	108	6	5	.545	103	55	46	80	48	3.83
1981—Charlotte	Southern	4	16	0	2	.000	23	10	10	10	7	5.63
1982—Charlotte†	Southern	24	162⅓	10	9	.526	132	71	64	97	64	3.55
1983—Charlotte‡	Southern	25	151⅓	8	*14	.364	173	94	78	89	73	4.64
1984—Charlotte	Southern	19	75	3	7	.300	68	45	35	52	39	4.20
1984—Rochester§	Int'national	12	40⅔	1	3	.250	58	37	36	39	19	7.97
1985—Charlotte x	Southern	12	57	2	1	.667	57	40	30	20	25	6.64
1985—Daytona Beach y	Florida St.	3	23⅔	3	0	1.000	13	6	5	25	9	1.90
1985—Beaumont	Texas	7	27	3	1	.750	23	17	15	24	9	5.00
1986—Charlotte	Southern	33	194	12	9	.571	185	112	90	127	71	4.18
1987—Charlotte	Southern	23	100	6	3	.667	99	43	40	67	21	3.60
1987—Rochester z	Int'national	6	27	3	0	1.000	31	14	13	18	7	4.33
1988—Orlando	Southern	7	43	3	1	.750	44	24	23	42	18	4.81
1988—Portland	P. Coast	21	133⅔	11	10	.524	134	69	64	95	43	4.31
1989—Portland	P. Coast	17	97⅔	6	4	.600	108	54	54	54	24	4.98
1989—Minnesota	American	12	55⅔	3	4	.429	64	28	28	24	15	4.53
1990—Portland a	P. Coast	11	62	3	4	.429	44	23	20	56	22	2.90
1990—San Francisco b	National	33	55⅓	2	2	.500	47	22	17	41	21	2.77
1990—San Jose	California	1	3⅔	0	0	.000	4	2	1	3	1	2.45
American League Totals—1 Year		12	55⅔	3	4	.429	64	28	28	24	15	4.53
National League Totals—1 Year		33	55⅓	2	2	.500	47	22	17	41	21	2.77
Major League Totals—2 Years		45	111	5	6	.455	111	50	45	65	36	3.65

Signed as free agent by Baltimore Orioles' organization, September 10, 1980.
†On disabled list, July 9 to July 23, 1982.
‡On disabled list, April 22 to May 9, 1983.
§On disabled list, July 30 to August 18, 1984.
xLoaned to Daytona Beach (Co-op), June 1, 1985; returned, July 4, 1985.
yLoaned to Beaumont (San Diego Padres' organization), July 31, 1985; returned, September 1, 1985.
zGranted free agency, October 15, 1987; signed by Portland (Minnesota Twins' organization), December, 1987.
aTraded to San Francisco Giants for a player to be named later, May 30, 1990; Visalia (Minnesota Twins' organization) acquired Pitcher Ed Gustafson to complete deal, September 26, 1990.
bOn disabled list, July 11 to August 4, 1990; included rehabilitation disability assignment to San Jose, July 30 to August 3, 1990.

GREGG WILLIAM OLSON

Born October 11, 1966, at Omaha, Neb.
Height, 6.04. Weight, 209.
Throws and bats righthanded.
Attended Auburn University, Auburn, Ala.

Holds American League record for most saves by rookie (27), 1989.
Major League saves: 1989 (27), 1990 (37). Total—64.
Named American League Rookie of the Year by Baseball Writers' Association of America, 1989.
Received reported $200,000 bonus to sign with Baltimore Orioles, 1988.
Named righthanded pitcher on THE SPORTING NEWS College Baseball All-America Team, 1988.

Year Club	League	G.	IP.	W.	L.	Pct.	H.	R.	ER.	SO.	BB.	ERA.
1988—Hagerstown	Carolina	8	9	1	0	1.000	5	2	2	9	2	2.00
1988—Charlotte	Southern	8	15⅓	0	1	.000	24	13	10	22	6	5.87
1988—Baltimore	American	10	11	1	1	.500	10	4	4	9	10	3.27
1989—Baltimore	American	64	85	5	2	.714	57	17	16	90	46	1.69
1990—Baltimore	American	64	74⅓	6	5	.545	57	20	20	74	31	2.42
Major League Totals—3 Years		138	170⅓	12	8	.600	124	41	40	173	87	2.11

Selected by Baltimore Orioles' organization in 1st round (fourth player selected) of free-agent draft, June 1, 1988.

ALL-STAR GAME RECORD

Member of American League All-Star Team in 1990; did not play.

GREGORY WILLIAM OLSON
(Greg)

Born September 6, 1960, at Marshall, Minn.
Height, 6.00. Weight, 200.
Throws and bats righthanded.
Attended University of Minnesota, Minneapolis, Minn.

Major League stolen bases: 1990 (1).
Led Carolina League catchers in total chances with 973 in 1983.
Tied for International League lead in passed balls with 15 in 1988.

Year Club League	Pos.	G.	AB.	R.	H.	2B.	3B.	HR.	RBI.	B.A.	PO.	A.	E.	F.A.
1982—Lynchburg............ Carol.	C-3B	32	91	10	24	1	0	0	5	.264	149	26	6	.967
1983—Lynchburg............ Carol.	C	107	318	56	73	7	0	0	22	.230	*881	*82	10	*.990
1984—Jackson .... Texas	C	74	234	27	55	9	0	0	22	.235	511	51	9	.984
1985—Jackson .... Texas	C	69	211	21	57	7	0	1	32	.270	353	56	6	.986
1986—Jackson .... Texas	C	64	196	28	39	5	1	2	16	.199	347	49	4	.990
1986—Tidewater............ Int.	C	19	55	11	18	1	0	0	7	.327	104	13	3	.975
1987—Tidewater............ Int.	C	47	120	15	34	8	1	2	15	.283	219	12	3	.987
1988—Tidewater†.......... Int.	C-OF	115	344	39	92	19	1	6	48	.267	600	64	7	.990
1989—Portland............... P. C.	C-3B	79	247	38	58	8	2	6	38	.235	440	32	5	.990
1989—Minnesota‡........... Amer.	C	3	2	0	1	0	0	0	0	.500	4	0	0	1.000
1990—Richmond........... Int.	C	3	7	0	0	0	0	0	0	.000	17	2	0	1.000
1990—Atlanta .... Amer.	C-3B	100	298	36	78	12	1	7	36	.262	501	43	7	.987
American League Totals—1 Year		3	2	0	1	0	0	0	0	.500	4	0	0	1.000
National League Totals—1 Year		100	298	36	78	12	1	7	36	.262	501	43	7	.987
Major League Totals—2 Years		103	300	36	79	12	1	7	36	.263	505	43	7	.987

Selected by New York Mets' organization in 7th round of free-agent draft, June 7, 1982.
†Granted free agency, October 15, 1988; signed by Portland (Minnesota Twins' organization), November 30, 1988.
‡Granted free agency, October 15, 1989; signed by Richmond (Atlanta Braves' organization), November 6, 1989.

ALL-STAR GAME RECORD

Year League	Pos.	AB.	R.	H.	2B.	3B.	HR.	RBI.	B.A.	PO.	A.	E.	F.A.
1990—National...............................	PH-C	1	0	0	0	0	0	0	.000	0	0	0	.000

THOMAS PATRICK O'MALLEY
(Tom)

Born December 25, 1960, at Orange, N. J.
Height, 6.00. Weight, 190.
Throws right and bats lefthanded.

Major League stolen bases: 1983 (2).
Tied for International League lead in intentional bases on balls received with 10 in 1989.
Led American Association third basemen in fielding percentage with .955 in 1988.
Led International League third basemen in fielding percentage with .964 in 1985 and .966 in 1989.
Led International League third basemen in assists with 231 and total chances with 322 in 1989.
Led International League third basemen with putouts with 90 in 1985.
Named International League Player of the Year, 1989.

Year Club League	Pos.	G.	AB.	R.	H.	2B.	3B.	HR.	RBI.	B.A.	PO.	A.	E.	F.A.
1979—Great Falls............ Pion.	2-S-O-3	42	119	13	29	6	1	1	20	.244	41	34	9	.893
1980—Fresno .... Calif.	3B	122	435	67	125	20	9	3	74	.287	69	253	22	*.936
1981—Shreveport .... Texas	3B	123	467	50	135	23	6	6	53	.289	94	237	15	.957
1982—Phoenix................. P. C.	3B	26	96	23	43	11	1	3	15	.448	12	44	6	.903
1982—San Francisco† ...... Nat.	3B-SS-2B	92	291	26	80	12	4	2	27	.275	60	161	8	.965
1983—San Francisco .... Nat.	3B	135	410	40	106	16	1	5	45	.259	70	213	18	.940
1984—Phoenix.................. P. C.	3B-1B	105	387	44	134	20	2	5	72	.346	227	134	15	.960
1984—San Francisco‡ ...... Nat.	3B	13	25	2	3	0	0	0	0	.120	5	8	0	1.000
1984—Chicago§ .... Amer.	3B	12	16	0	2	0	0	0	3	.125	2	1	0	1.000
1985—Nashville x........... A. A	3B	33	128	13	39	8	0	1	12	.305	16	62	9	.897
1985—Rochester .... Int.	3B-1B	102	358	62	108	13	1	10	44	.302	92	207	11	.965
1985—Baltimore .... Amer.	3B	8	14	1	1	0	0	1	2	.071	2	3	1	.833
1986—Rochester .... Int.	3B-2B	59	212	36	65	10	0	9	30	.307	46	111	8	.952
1986—Baltimore y........... Amer.	3B	56	181	19	46	9	0	1	18	.254	37	98	9	.938
1987—Oklahoma City ..... A. A.	3B	109	431	83	134	27	2	12	70	.311	*112	198	9	*.972
1987—Texas..................... Amer.	3B-2B	45	117	10	32	8	0	1	12	.274	21	56	3	.962
1988—Oklahoma City z .. A. A.	3B-1B-2B	*138	522	68	152	26	4	9	72	.291	118	246	16	.958
1988—Montreal a .... Nat.	3B	14	27	3	7	0	0	0	2	.259	4	15	2	.905
1989—Tidewater............. Int.	3B-1B	132	492	64	145	29	0	15	*84	.295	127	235	11	.971
1989—New York .... Nat.	3B	9	11	2	6	2	0	0	8	.545	2	1	0	1.000
1990—New York b .... Nat.	3B-1B	82	121	14	27	7	0	3	14	.223	41	33	2	.974
National League Totals—6 Years...........		345	885	87	229	37	5	10	96	.259	182	431	30	.953
American League Totals—4 Years		121	328	30	81	17	0	3	35	.247	62	158	13	.944
Major League Totals—9 Years................		466	1213	117	310	54	5	13	131	.256	244	589	43	.951

Selected by San Francisco Giants' organization in 16th round of free-agent draft, June 5, 1979.
†On disabled list, August 16 to September 6, 1982.
‡Traded to Chicago White Sox for two players to be named later, September 1, 1984; San Francisco Giants acquired Pitcher Mike Trujillo and First Baseman Pat Adams to complete deal, September 7, 1984.
§Released, April 1, 1985; signed by Nashville (Detroit Tigers' organization), April 8, 1985.
xTraded to Rochester (Baltimore Orioles' organization) for Catcher Luis Rosado, May 21, 1985.
yGranted free agency, October 15, 1986; signed by Texas Rangers' organization, December 3, 1986.
zTraded to Montreal Expos for a player to be named later, September 1, 1988; Texas Rangers' organization acquired First Baseman Jack Daugherty to complete deal, September 13, 1988.
aTraded with Catcher Mark Bailey to New York Mets for Pitcher Steve Frey, March 28, 1989.
bSold to Hanshin Tigers of Japanese Baseball League, October 25, 1990.

RANDALL JEFFREY O'NEAL
(Randy)

Born August 30, 1960, at Ashland, Ky.
Height, 6.02. Weight, 195.
Throws and bats righthanded.
Attended Palm Beach Junior College, Lake Worth, Fla.,
and University of Florida, Gainesville, Fla.

Pitched seven-inning, 4-0 no-hit victory against Winter Haven, August 23, 1981 (first game).
Major League saves: 1985 (1), 1986 (2). Total—3.
Tied for American Association lead in balks with 6 in 1984.

Year Club	League	G.	IP.	W.	L.	Pct.	H.	R.	ER.	SO.	BB.	ERA.
1981—Lakeland	Florida St.	13	69	4	5	.444	59	27	22	31	18	2.87
1982—Birmingham	Southern	27	185	11	7	.611	169	83	70	105	71	3.41
1983—Evansville	Am. Assoc.	23	140⅓	8	10	.444	159	80	66	70	45	4.23
1984—Evansville	Am. Assoc.	25	166⅓	9	10	.474	152	82	66	110	59	3.57
1984—Detroit	American	4	18⅔	2	1	.667	16	7	7	12	6	3.38
1985—Nashville	Am. Assoc.	10	67⅔	5	4	.556	57	29	27	44	19	3.59
1985—Detroit	American	28	94⅓	5	5	.500	82	42	34	52	36	3.24
1986—Detroit	American	37	122⅔	3	7	.300	121	69	59	68	44	4.33
1986—Nashville†	Am. Assoc.	4	28⅓	1	2	.333	28	16	15	15	9	4.76
1987—Atlanta-St. Louis	National	17	66	4	2	.667	81	42	39	37	26	5.32
1987—Richmond‡	Int'national	1	5	0	1	.000	4	3	2	5	1	3.60
1987—Louisville	Am. Assoc.	7	47⅓	3	1	.750	54	27	24	19	10	4.56
1988—Louisville	Am. Assoc.	10	60⅔	3	5	.375	59	30	25	33	21	3.71
1988—St. Louis§x	National	10	53	2	3	.400	57	29	27	20	10	4.58
1989—Scranton/Wilkes-Barre	Int'national	18	96	4	4	.500	82	33	27	71	23	2.53
1989—Philadelphia y	National	20	39	0	1	.000	46	28	27	29	9	6.23
1990—San Francisco z	National	26	47	1	0	1.000	58	23	20	30	18	3.83
1990—Phoenix	P. Coast	7	39⅓	5	0	1.000	34	14	13	25	8	2.97
1990—San Jose a	California	1	3	0	0	.000	4	1	1	2	0	3.00
American League Totals—3 Years		69	235⅔	10	13	.435	219	118	100	132	86	3.82
National League Totals—4 Years		73	205	7	6	.538	242	122	113	116	63	4.96
Major League Totals—7 Years		142	440⅔	17	19	.472	461	240	213	248	149	4.35

Selected by Montreal Expos' organization in 4th round of free-agent draft, January 9, 1979.
Selected by Minnesota Twins' organization in secondary phase of free-agent draft, June 5, 1979.
Selected by Milwaukee Brewers' organization in secondary phase of free-agent draft, January 8, 1980.
Selected by Cincinnati Reds' organization in secondary phase of free-agent draft, June 3, 1980.
Selected by Detroit Tigers' organization in secondary phase of free-agent draft, June 8, 1981.
†Traded with Pitcher Chuck Cary to Atlanta Braves for Outfielders Terry Harper and Freddy Tiburcio, January 27, 1987.
‡Traded to St. Louis Cardinals' organization for Pitcher Joe Boever, July 25, 1987.
§On disabled list, June 10 to August 11, 1988; included rehabilitation disability assignment to Louisville, July 26 to August 11, 1988.
xGranted free agency, October 15, 1988; signed by Scranton/Wilkes-Barre (Philadelphia Phillies' organization), December 2, 1988.
yReleased, October 4, 1989; signed by Phoenix (San Francisco Giants' organization), January 20, 1990.
zOn disabled list, August 4 to August 27, 1990; included rehabilitation disability assignment to San Jose, August 22 to August 26, 1990.
aReleased, October 3, 1990.

PAUL ANDREW O'NEILL

Born February 25, 1963, at Columbus, O.
Height, 6.04. Weight, 215.
Throws and bats lefthanded.
Attended Otterbein College, Westerville, O.
Son of Charles W. O'Neill, minor league pitcher, 1945 through 1948.

Major League stolen bases: 1987 (2), 1988 (8), 1989 (20), 1990 (13). Total—43.
Tied for American Association lead in game-winning RBIs with 13 in 1985.
Led American Association outfielders in assists with 19 and double plays with 8 in 1985.

Year Club	League	Pos.	G.	AB.	R.	H.	2B.	3B.	HR.	RBI.	B.A.	PO.	A.	E.	F.A.
1981—Billings	Pion.	OF	66	241	37	76	7	2	3	29	.315	87	4	5	.948
1982—Cedar Rapids	Midw.	OF	116	386	50	105	19	2	8	71	.272	137	7	8	.947
1983—Tampa	Fla. St.	OF-1B	121	413	62	115	23	7	8	51	.278	218	14	10	.959
1983—Waterbury	East.	OF	14	43	6	12	0	0	0	6	.279	26	0	0	1.000
1984—Vermont	East.	OF	134	475	70	126	31	5	16	76	.265	246	5	7	.973
1985—Denver	A. A.	OB-1B	*137	*509	63	*155	*32	3	7	74	.305	248	20	7	.975
1985—Cincinnati	Nat.	OF	5	12	1	4	1	0	0	1	.333	3	1	0	1.000
1986—Cincinnati	Nat.	PH	3	2	0	0	0	0	0	0	.000	0	0	0	.000
1986—Denver†	A. A.	OF	55	193	20	49	9	2	5	27	.254	98	7	4	.963
1987—Cincinnati	Nat.	OF-1B-P	84	160	24	41	14	1	7	28	.256	90	2	4	.958
1987—Nashville	A. A.	OF	11	37	12	11	0	0	3	6	.297	19	1	0	1.000
1988—Cincinnati	Nat.	OF-1B	145	485	58	122	25	3	16	73	.252	410	13	6	.986
1989—Cincinnati‡	Nat.	OF	117	428	49	118	24	2	15	74	.276	223	7	4	.983
1989—Nashville	A. A.	OF	4	12	1	4	0	0	0	0	.333	7	1	0	1.000
1990—Cincinnati	Nat.	OF	145	503	59	136	28	0	16	78	.270	271	12	2	.993
Major League Totals—6 Years			499	1590	191	421	92	6	54	254	.265	997	35	16	.985

Selected by Cincinnati Reds' organization in 4th round of free-agent draft, June 8, 1981.
†On disabled list, May 10 to July 16, 1986.

‡On disabled list, July 21 to September 1, 1989; included rehabilitation disability assignment to Nashville, August 27 to September 1, 1989.

CHAMPIONSHIP SERIES RECORD

Year Club	League	Pos.	G.	AB.	R.	H.	2B.	3B.	HR.	RBI.	B.A.	PO.	A.	E.	F.A.
1990—Cincinnati	Nat.	OF	5	17	1	8	3	0	1	4	.471	9	2	0	1.000

WORLD SERIES RECORD

Year Club	League	Pos.	G.	AB.	R.	H.	2B.	3B.	HR.	RBI.	B.A.	PO.	A.	E.	F.A.
1990—Cincinnati	Nat.	OF	4	12	2	1	0	0	0	1	.083	11	0	0	1.000

PITCHING RECORD

Year Club	League	G.	IP.	W.	L.	Pct.	H.	R.	ER.	SO.	BB.	ERA.
1987—Cincinnati	National	1	2	0	0	.000	2	3	3	2	4	13.50

STEVEN ONTIVEROS

Name pronounced Ahn-tih-VAIR-oss.

(Steve)

Born March 5, 1961, at Tularosa, N.M.
Height, 6.00. Weight, 190.
Throws and bats righthanded.
Received bachelor of science degree in physical education
from University of Michigan, Ann Arbor, Mich.

Major League saves: 1985 (8), 1986 (10), 1987 (1). Total—19.

Year Club	League	G.	IP.	W.	L.	Pct.	H.	R.	ER.	SO.	BB.	ERA.
1982—Medford	Northwest	4	8	1	0	1.000	3	0	0	9	4	0.00
1982—West Haven†	Eastern	16	27	2	2	.500	34	26	19	28	12	6.33
1983—Albany	Eastern	32	129⅔	8	4	.667	131	62	54	91	36	3.75
1984—Tacoma‡	P. Coast	2	11⅓	1	1	.500	18	11	10	6	5	7.94
1985—Madison	Midwest	5	30⅔	3	1	.750	23	10	7	26	6	2.05
1985—Tacoma§	P. Coast	15	33⅔	3	0	1.000	26	13	11	30	21	2.94
1985—Oakland	American	39	74⅔	1	3	.250	45	17	16	36	19	1.93
1986—Oakland xy	American	46	72⅔	2	2	.500	72	40	38	54	25	4.71
1987—Tacoma z	P. Coast	1	3	0	0	.000	1	1	1	1	2	3.00
1987—Oakland	American	35	150⅔	10	8	.556	141	78	67	97	50	4.00
1988—Oakland abc	American	10	54⅔	3	4	.429	57	32	28	30	21	4.61
1989—Philadelphia d	National	6	30⅔	2	1	.667	34	15	13	12	15	3.82
1989—Scranton/Wilkes-Barre..............	Int'national	1	3⅓	0	0	.000	3	0	0	0	3	0.00
1990—Clearwater e	Florida St.	3	7⅔	0	0	.000	4	2	2	2	3	2.35
1990—Reading	Eastern	2	6	0	2	.000	7	6	6	8	2	9.00
1990—Philadelphia	National	5	10	0	0	.000	9	3	3	6	3	2.70
American League Totals—4 Years		130	352⅔	16	17	.485	315	167	149	217	115	3.80
National League Totals—2 Years		11	40⅔	2	1	.667	43	18	16	18	18	3.54
Major League Totals—6 Years		141	393⅓	18	18	.500	358	185	165	235	133	3.78

Selected by Oakland A's organization in 2nd round of free-agent draft, June 7, 1982.
†On temporarily inactive list, July 27 to August 6, 1982.
‡On disabled list, April 16 to August 8, 1984.
§On disabled list, April 16 to April 28, 1985.
xAppeared in one game as a pinch-runner.
yOn disabled list, July 24 to September 14, 1986.
zOn Oakland disabled list, March 30 to April 24, 1987; included rehabilitation disability assignment to Tacoma, April 21 to April 24, 1987.
aAppeared in two games as a pinch-runner.
bOn disabled list, June 12 to August 2 and August 3, 1988 through remainder of season.
cReleased, December 21, 1988; signed by Philadelphia Phillies' organization, February 16, 1989.
dOn disabled list, April 20 to June 6 and June 21, 1989 through remainder of season; included rehabilitation disability assignment to Scranton/Wilkes-Barre, May 14 to May 22 and June 28, 1989.
eOn Philadelphia disabled list, March 30 to September 8, 1990; included rehabilitation disability assignment to Clearwater, August 2 to August 16, 1990; and Reading, August 17 to August 19 and August 27 to September 2, 1990.

DANIEL CHARLES OPPERMAN

(Dan)

Born November 13, 1968, at Las Vegas, Nev.
Height, 6.02. Weight, 175.
Throws and bats righthanded.

Led Texas League pitchers in games started with 27 in 1990.

Year Club	League	G.	IP.	W.	L.	Pct.	H.	R.	ER.	SO.	BB.	ERA.
1987—Great Falls†	Pioneer				(Did not play)							
1988—Great Falls‡	Pioneer				(Did not play)							
1989—Vero Beach§	Florida St.	19	61	0	7	.000	51	26	24	35	24	3.54
1990—San Antonio.....................................	Texas	27	155⅔	12	8	.600	153	75	59	96	62	3.41

Selected by Los Angeles Dodgers' organization in 1st round (eighth player selected) of free-agent draft, June 2, 1987.
†On disabled list, July 17, 1987 through entire season.
‡On disabled list, June 16, 1988 through entire season.
§On disabled list, July 12 to August 3, 1989.

JOSE MANUEL OQUENDO

Name pronounced Oh-KEN-doh.

Born July 4, 1963, at Rio Piedras, Puerto Rico.
Height, 5.10. Weight, 160.
Throws right and bats left and righthanded.

Holds major league records for highest fielding percentage (.996) and fewest errors (3), second baseman, season, 150 or more games, 1990.

Shares major league record for fewest double plays by second baseman, season, 150 or more games (65), 1990.

Shares National League record for highest fielding average, second basemen, season, 150 or more games (.994), 1989.

Major League stolen bases: 1983 (8), 1984 (10), 1986 (2), 1987 (4), 1988 (4), 1989 (3), 1990 (1). Total—32.

Led National League second basemen in putouts with 346, assists with 500, total chances with 851 and double plays with 106 in 1989.

Led National League second basemen in fielding percentage with .994 in 1989 and .996 in 1990.

Led American Association in sacrifice hits with 15 in 1985.

Led International League in sacrifice hits with 14 in 1982.

Led Carolina League in sacrifice hits with 13 in 1980.

Led American Association shortstops in total chances with 591 in 1985.

Led Northwest League shortstops in errors with 40 in 1979.

Year	Club	League	Pos.	G.	AB.	R.	H.	2B.	3B.	HR.	RBI.	B.A.	PO.	A.	E.	F.A.
1979—Grays Harbor	N'west	*SS-2B	64	220	24	50	8	0	1	14	.227	90	177	*40	.870
1980—Lynchburg	Carol.	SS	109	301	38	51	10	3	0	26	.169	126	358	31	*.940
1981—Lynchburg	Carol.	SS	124	393	59	98	8	6	0	38	.249	169	390	23	*.961
1982—Tidewater	Int.	SS	114	337	40	72	8	3	0	22	.214	186	337	25	.954
1983—Tidewater	Int.	SS	13	34	3	4	0	0	0	3	.118	20	23	4	.915
1983—New York	Nat.	SS	120	328	29	70	7	0	1	17	.213	182	326	21	.960
1984—New York	Nat.	SS	81	189	23	42	5	0	0	10	.222	95	152	7	.972
1984—Tidewater†	Int.	SS	38	113	8	18	1	0	1	8	.159	54	111	2	.988
1985—Louisville	A. A.	SS	133	384	38	81	8	1	1	30	.211	*227	341	23	.961
1986—St. Louis	Nat.	S-2-3-O	76	138	20	41	4	1	0	13	.297	52	94	8	.948
1987—St. Louis	Nat.	I-O-P	116	248	43	71	9	0	1	24	.286	149	133	4	.986
1988—St. Louis	Nat.	I-O-C-P	148	451	36	125	10	1	7	46	.277	268	315	11	.981
1989—St. Louis	Nat.	2B-SS-1B	●163	556	59	162	28	7	1	48	.291	356	523	6	.993
1990—St. Louis	Nat.	2B-SS	156	469	38	118	17	5	1	37	.252	294	403	4	.994
Major League Totals—7 Years				860	2379	248	629	80	14	11	195	.264	1396	1946	61	.982

Signed as free agent by New York Mets' organization, April 15, 1979.

†Traded with Pitcher Mark Jason Davis to St. Louis Cardinals' organization for Shortstop Argenis Salazar and Pitcher John Young, April 2, 1985.

CHAMPIONSHIP SERIES RECORD

Year	Club	League	Pos.	G.	AB.	R.	H.	2B.	3B.	HR.	RBI.	B.A.	PO.	A.	E.	F.A.
1987—St. Louis	Nat.	O-3B-PH	5	12	3	2	0	0	1	4	.167	7	0	0	1.000

WORLD SERIES RECORD

Year	Club	League	Pos.	G.	AB.	R.	H.	2B.	3B.	HR.	RBI.	B.A.	PO.	A.	E.	F.A.
1987—St. Louis	Nat.	OF-3B	7	24	2	6	0	0	0	2	.250	8	10	0	1.000

PITCHING RECORD

Year	Club	League	G.	IP.	W.	L.	Pct.	H.	R.	ER.	SO.	BB.	ERA.
1987—St. Louis	National	1	1	0	0	.000	4	3	3	0	1	27.00
1988—St. Louis	National	1	4	0	1	.000	4	2	2	1	6	4.50
Major League Totals—2 Years			2	5	0	1	.000	8	5	5	1	7	9.00

JESSE OROSCO

Name pronounced Oh-ROSS-koh.

Born April 21, 1957, at Santa Barbara, Calif.
Height, 6.02. Weight, 185.
Throws left and bats righthanded.
Attended Santa Barbara City College, Santa Barbara, Calif.

Major League saves: 1981 (1), 1982 (4), 1983 (17), 1984 (31), 1985 (17), 1986 (21), 1987 (16), 1988 (9), 1989 (3), 1990 (2). Total—121.

Led Appalachian League in intentional bases on balls issued with 5 in 1978.

Year	Club	League	G.	IP.	W.	L.	Pct.	H.	R.	ER.	SO.	BB.	ERA.
1978—Elizabethton†	Ap'lachian	20	40	4	4	.500	29	7	5	48	20	1.13
1979—Tidewater	Int'national	16	81	4	4	.500	82	45	35	55	43	3.89
1979—New York	National	18	35	1	2	.333	33	20	19	22	22	4.89
1980—Jackson	Texas	37	71	4	4	.500	52	36	29	85	62	3.68
1981—Tidewater	Int'national	46	87	9	5	.643	80	39	32	81	32	3.31
1981—New York	National	8	17	0	1	.000	13	4	3	18	6	1.59
1982—New York	National	54	109⅓	4	10	.286	92	37	33	89	40	2.72
1983—New York	National	62	110	13	7	.650	76	27	18	84	38	1.47
1984—New York	National	60	87	10	6	.625	58	29	25	85	34	2.59
1985—New York	National	54	79	8	6	.571	66	26	24	68	34	2.73
1986—New York‡	National	58	81	8	6	.571	64	23	21	62	35	2.33
1987—New York§	National	58	77	3	9	.250	78	41	38	78	31	4.44
1988—Los Angeles x	National	55	53	3	2	.600	41	18	16	43	30	2.72

Year Club	League	G.	IP.	W.	L.	Pct.	H.	R.	ER.	SO.	BB.	ERA.
1989—Cleveland	American	69	78	3	4	.429	54	20	18	79	26	2.08
1990—Cleveland	American	55	64⅔	5	4	.556	58	35	28	55	38	3.90
National League Totals—9 Years		427	648½	50	49	.505	521	225	197	549	270	2.73
American League Totals—2 Years		124	142⅔	8	8	.500	112	55	46	134	64	2.90
Major League Totals—11 Years		551	791	58	57	.504	633	280	243	683	334	2.76

Selected by St. Louis Cardinals' organization in 7th round of free-agent draft, January 11, 1977.
Selected by Minnesota Twins' organization in 2nd round of free-agent draft, January 10, 1978.
†Traded to New York Mets, February 7, 1979, completing deal in which Minnesota Twins traded Pitcher Greg Field and a player to be named later to New York for Pitcher Jerry Koosman, December 8, 1978.
‡Appeared in one game as an outfielder with one putout.
§As part of an eight-player, three-team deal, New York Mets traded Pitcher Jesse Orosco to Oakland Athletics, December 11, 1987. Oakland then traded Orosco along with shortstop Alfredo Griffin and Pitcher Jay Howell to Los Angeles Dodgers for Pitchers Bob Welch, Matt Young and Jack Savage. Oakland then traded Savage along with Pitchers Wally Whitehurst and Kevin Tapani to New York.
xGranted free agency, November 4, 1988; signed by Cleveland Indians, December 3, 1988.

CHAMPIONSHIP SERIES RECORD

Holds Championship Series record for most games won, series (3), 1986.

Year Club	League	G.	IP.	W.	L.	Pct.	H.	R.	ER.	SO.	BB.	ERA.
1986—New York	National	4	8	3	0	1.000	5	3	3	10	2	3.38
1988—Los Angeles	National	4	2⅓	0	0	.000	4	2	2	0	3	7.71
Championship Series Totals—2 Years		8	10⅓	3	0	1.000	9	5	5	10	5	4.35

WORLD SERIES RECORD

Year Club	League	G.	IP.	W.	L.	Pct.	H.	R.	ER.	SO.	BB.	ERA.
1986—New York	National	4	5⅔	0	0	.000	2	0	0	6	0	0.00

ALL-STAR GAME RECORD

Year League		IP.	W.	L.	Pct.	H.	R.	ER.	SO.	BB.	ERA.
1983—National		⅓	0	0	.000	0	0	0	1	0	0.00

Member of National League All-Star Team in 1984; did not play.

JOSEPH MICHAEL ORSULAK
(Joe)

Born May 31, 1962, at Glen Ridge, N.J.
Height, 6.01. Weight, 200.
Throws and bats lefthanded.

Major League stolen bases: 1984 (3), 1985 (24), 1986 (24), 1988 (9), 1989 (5), 1990 (6). Total—71.
Led Pacific Coast League outfielders in total chances with 367 and double plays with 8 in 1983.
Tied for South Atlantic League lead in double plays by outfielders with 4 in 1981.

Year Club	League	Pos.	G.	AB.	R.	H.	2B.	3B.	HR.	RBI.	B.A.	PO.	A.	E.	F.A.
1981—Greenwood†	S. Atl.	OF	118	460	80	145	18	8	6	70	.315	249	16	4	*.985
1982—Alexandria	Carol.	OF-1B	129	463	92	134	18	4	14	65	.289	286	7	10	.967
1983—Hawaii	P. C.	OF	139	538	87	154	12	●13	10	58	.286	★341	●18	8	.978
1983—Pittsburgh	Nat.	OF	7	11	0	2	0	0	0	1	.182	2	2	0	1.000
1984—Hawaii	P. C.	OF	98	388	51	110	19	12	3	53	.284	258	6	2	.992
1984—Pittsburgh	Nat.	OF	32	67	12	17	1	2	0	3	.254	41	1	0	1.000
1985—Pittsburgh‡	Nat.	OF	121	397	54	119	14	6	0	21	.300	229	10	6	.976
1986—Pittsburgh	Nat.	OF	138	401	60	100	19	6	2	19	.249	193	11	4	.981
1987—Vancouver§x	P. C.	OF	39	143	20	33	6	1	1	12	.231	58	2	2	.968
1988—Baltimore	Amer.	OF	125	379	48	109	21	3	8	27	.288	228	6	5	.979
1989—Baltimore	Amer.	OF	123	390	59	111	22	5	7	55	.285	250	10	4	.985
1990—Baltimore	Amer.	OF	124	413	49	111	14	3	11	57	.269	267	5	3	.989
National League Totals—4 Years			298	876	126	238	34	14	2	44	.272	465	24	10	.980
American League Totals—3 Years			372	1182	156	331	57	11	26	139	.280	745	21	12	.985
Major League Totals—7 Years			670	2058	282	569	91	25	28	183	.276	1210	45	22	.983

Selected by Pittsburgh Pirates' organization in 6th round of free-agent draft, June 3, 1980.
†On temporarily inactive list, July 10 to July 27, 1981.
‡On disabled list, May 25 to June 9, 1985.
§On Pittsburgh disabled list, March 31 to May 22, 1987; included rehabilitation disability assignment to Vancouver, May 4 to May 22, 1987.
xTraded to Baltimore Orioles for Shortstop Terry Crowley Jr. and Third Baseman Rico Rossy, November 6, 1987.

ADALBERTO ORTIZ JR. (COLON)

Name pronounced Orr-TEEZ.

(Junior)

Born October 24, 1959, at Humacao, Puerto Rico.
Height, 5.11. Weight, 181.
Throws and bats righthanded.
Brother of Alexander Ortiz, minor league outfielder, 1978 and 1979.

Major League stolen bases: 1983 (1), 1984 (1), 1985 (1), 1988 (1), 1989 (2). Total—6.
Led Pacific Coast League catchers in putouts with 744 and double plays with 17 in 1982.
Led Carolina League catchers in double plays with 12 in 1979.
Tied for Western Carolinas League lead in passed balls with 22 in 1978

Year Club	League	Pos.	G.	AB.	R.	H.	2B.	3B.	HR.	RBI.	B.A.	PO.	A.	E.	F.A.
1977—Charleston†	W. Car.	C	21	53	2	14	3	0	0	10	.264	93	13	4	.964
1977—Bradenton Pir.	Gulf C.	C	34	118	11	24	5	1	1	12	.203	76	14	4	.957
1978—Charleston‡	W. Car.	C	41	122	12	26	4	0	1	16	.213	198	44	7	.972
1979—Salem	Carol.	*C-1B	108	396	35	112	21	2	5	66	.283	632	*84	*17	.977
1980—Buffalo	East.	C	126	515	79	*178	25	1	12	78	*.346	497	91	16	.974
1980—Portland	P. C.	C	8	27	1	3	0	1	0	3	.111	42	10	0	1.000
1981—Portland	P. C.	C	105	346	49	93	14	7	2	46	.269	606	76	15	.978
1982—Portland	P. C.	*C-O-1	124	449	46	131	22	0	6	57	.292	751	*110	*19	.978
1982—Pittsburgh	Nat.	C	7	15	1	3	1	0	0	0	.200	27	3	0	1.000
1983—Pitt.§-N.Y.	Nat.	C	73	193	11	48	5	0	0	12	.249	293	31	11	.967
1984—New York x	Nat.	C	40	91	6	18	3	0	0	11	.198	136	13	3	.980
1985—Pittsburgh	Nat.	C	23	72	4	21	2	0	1	5	.292	115	14	2	.985
1986—Pittsburgh	Nat.	C	49	110	11	37	6	0	0	14	.336	165	13	3	.983
1987—Pittsburgh	Nat.	C	75	192	16	52	8	1	1	22	.271	313	39	9	.975
1988—Pittsburgh y	Nat.	C	49	118	8	33	6	0	2	18	.280	152	23	3	.983
1989—Pittsburgh z	Nat.	C	91	230	16	50	6	1	1	22	.217	334	32	2	.995
1990—Minnesota	Amer.	C	71	170	18	57	7	1	0	18	.335	247	25	0	1.000
National League Totals—8 Years			407	1021	73	262	37	2	5	104	.257	1535	168	33	.981
American League Totals—1 Year			71	170	18	57	7	1	0	18	.335	247	25	0	1.000
Major League Totals—9 Years			478	1191	91	319	44	3	5	122	.268	1782	193	33	.984

Signed as free agent by Pittsburgh Pirates' organization, January 18, 1977.
†On temporary inactive list, June 18 to June 22, 1977.
‡On disabled list, June 16 to September 5, 1978.
§Traded with Pitcher Art Ray to New York Mets for Outfielder Marvell Wynne and Pitcher Steve Senteney, June 14, 1983.
xDrafted by Pittsburgh Pirates, December 3, 1984.
yOn disabled list, July 28 to September 5, 1988.
zTraded with Pitcher Orlando Lind to Minnesota Twins for Pitcher Mike Pomeranz, April 4, 1990.

JAVIER VICTOR ORTIZ

Name pronounced Orr-TEEZ.

Born January 22, 1963, at Boston, Mass.
Height, 6.04. Weight, 220.
Throws and bats righthanded.
Attended University of Florida, Gainesville, Fla., and Miami-Dade Community College (South), Miami, Fla.

Major League stolen bases: 1990 (1).
Led Midwest League in slugging percentage with .561 in 1983.
Tied for Texas League lead in being hit by pitch with 7 in 1986.
Led American Association in sacrifice flies with 10 in 1987.

Year Club	League	Pos.	G.	AB.	R.	H.	2B.	3B.	HR.	RBI.	B.A.	PO.	A.	E.	F.A.
1983—Burlington	Midwest	OF	101	378	72	133	23	4	16	79	*.352	126	7	10	.930
1984—Tulsa	Texas	OF	94	325	42	97	21	3	8	53	.298	115	13	8	.941
1985—Tulsa†	Texas	OF-1B	86	304	47	75	12	3	5	31	.247	264	15	9	.969
1986—Tulsa	Texas	OF	110	378	52	114	29	3	14	65	.302	178	7	*11	.944
1987—Oklahoma City‡...	A. A.	OF	119	381	58	105	23	7	15	69	.276	209	16	6	.974
1988—San Antonio§.........	Texas	OF-1B	51	182	35	53	13	2	8	33	.291	116	2	2	.983
1989—Albu.x-Tucson.......	P. Coast	OF	81	260	47	66	10	0	11	36	.254	130	7	8	.945
1990—Tucson..................	P. Coast	OF	49	179	36	63	16	2	5	39	.352	98	4	2	.981
1990—Houston y	National	OF	30	77	7	21	5	1	1	10	.273	44	1	1	.978
Major League Totals—1 Year..................			30	77	7	21	5	1	1	10	.273	44	1	1	.978

Selected by Texas Rangers' organization in 1st round (fourth player selected) of free-agent draft, January 11, 1983.
†On disabled list, April 9 to May 21, 1985.
‡Traded to Oklahoma City (Los Angeles Dodgers' organization) for Pitcher Scott May, December 12, 1987.
§On disabled list, June 6 to August 24, 1988.
xTraded to Tucson (Houston Astros' organization) for Pitcher Ed Vosberg, July 22, 1989.
yOn disabled list, July 27, 1990 through remainder of season.

JOHN ANDREW ORTON

Born December 8, 1965, at Santa Cruz, Calif.
Height, 6.01. Weight, 195.
Throws and bats righthanded.
Attended California State Poly University, San Luis Obispo, Calif.

Led Texas League catchers in fielding percentage with .994 and double plays with 12 in 1989.

Year Club	League	Pos.	G.	AB.	R.	H.	2B.	3B.	HR.	RBI.	B.A.	PO.	A.	E.	F.A.
1987—Salem.....................	N'west	OF-C	51	176	31	46	8	1	8	36	.261	271	15	6	.979
1987—Midland	Texas	C	5	13	1	2	1	0	0	0	.154	26	5	1	.969
1988—Palm Springs†	Calif.	C	68	230	42	46	6	1	1	28	.200	235	27	8	.970
1989—Midland	Texas	C-1B	99	344	51	80	20	6	10	53	.233	466	56	4	.992
1989—California..............	Amer.	C	16	39	4	7	1	0	0	4	.179	76	7	1	.988
1990—California..............	Amer.	C	31	84	8	16	5	0	1	6	.190	139	15	2	.987
1990—Edmonton..............	P. C.	C	50	174	29	42	8	0	6	26	.241	277	36	7	.978
Major League Totals—2 Years................			47	123	12	23	6	0	1	10	.187	215	22	3	.988

Selected by New York Mets' organization in 17th round of free-agent draft, June 4, 1984.
Selected by California Angels' organization in 1st round (25th player selected) of free-agent draft, June 2, 1987.
†On disabled list, June 14 to August 5, 1988.

ALFONSO OSUNA JR.
(Al)

Born August 10, 1965, at Inglewood, Calif.
Height, 6.03. Weight, 200.
Throws left and bats righthanded.
Attended Cerritos College, Norwalk, Calif., and
Stanford University, Stanford, Calif.

Year Club	League	G.	IP.	W.	L.	Pct.	H.	R.	ER.	SO.	BB.	ERA.
1987—Auburn	NYP	8	15⅔	1	0	1.000	16	16	10	20	14	5.74
1987—Asheville	S. Atlantic	14	19⅔	2	0	1.000	20	6	6	20	6	2.75
1988—Asheville	S. Atlantic	31	50	6	1	.857	41	19	11	41	25	1.98
1988—Osceola	Florida St.	8	11⅔	0	1	.000	12	9	9	5	9	6.94
1989—Osceola	Florida St.	46	67⅔	3	4	.429	50	27	20	62	27	2.66
1990—Columbus	Southern	●60	69⅓	7	5	.583	57	30	26	82	33	3.38
1990—Houston	National	12	11⅓	2	0	1.000	10	6	6	6	6	4.76
Major League Totals—1 Year		12	11⅓	2	0	1.000	10	6	6	6	6	4.76

Selected by Baltimore Orioles' organization in 5th round of free-agent draft, January 9, 1985.
Selected by San Diego Padres' organization in secondary phase of free-agent draft, June 3, 1985.
Selected by Houston Astros' organization in 16th round of free-agent draft, June 2, 1987.

DAVID ALAN OTTO
(Dave)

Born November 12, 1964, at Chicago, Ill.
Height, 6.07. Weight, 210.
Throws and bats lefthanded.
Attended University of Missouri, Columbia, Mo.

Led Pacific Coast League pitchers in wild pitches with 18 and tied for games started with 28 in 1989.

Year Club	League	G.	IP.	W.	L.	Pct.	H.	R.	ER.	SO.	BB.	ERA.
1985—Medford	Northwest	11	42⅓	2	2	.500	42	27	19	27	22	4.04
1986—Madison	Midwest	26	169	13	7	.650	154	72	50	125	71	2.66
1987—Madison	Midwest	1	3	0	0	.000	2	0	0	2	0	0.00
1987—Huntsville	Southern	9	50	4	1	.800	36	14	13	25	11	2.34
1987—Oakland	American	3	6	0	0	.000	7	6	6	3	1	9.00
1988—Tacoma	P. Coast	21	127⅔	4	9	.308	124	71	50	80	63	3.52
1988—Oakland	American	3	10	0	0	.000	9	2	2	7	6	1.80
1989—Tacoma	P. Coast	29	169	10	13	.435	164	84	69	122	61	3.67
1989—Oakland	American	1	6⅔	0	0	.000	6	2	2	4	2	2.70
1990—Oakland†	American	2	2⅓	0	0	.000	3	3	2	2	3	7.71
1990—Tacoma‡	P. Coast	2	2	0	0	.000	3	1	1	2	1	4.50
Major League Totals—4 Years		9	25	0	0	.000	25	13	12	16	12	4.32

Selected by Baltimore Orioles' organization in 2nd round of free-agent draft, June 7, 1982.
Selected by Oakland A's organization in 2nd round of free-agent draft, June 3, 1985.
†On disabled list, April 29, 1990 through remainder of season; included rehabilitation disability assignment to Tacoma, May 14 and May 15, 1990.
‡Granted free agency, December 20, 1990.

SPIKE DEE OWEN

Born April 19, 1961, at Cleburne, Tex.
Height, 5.10. Weight, 170.
Throws right and bats left and righthanded.
Attended University of Texas, Austin, Tex.

Brother of Dave Owen, shortstop with Chicago Cubs and Kansas City Royals, 1983 through 1985 and 1988.
Shares modern major league record for most runs, game (6), August 21, 1986.
Holds National League record for most consecutive errorless games by shortstop, season (63), April 9 through June 22, 1990.
Major League stolen bases: 1983 (10), 1984 (16), 1985 (11), 1986 (4), 1987 (11), 1989 (3), 1990 (8). Total—63.
Led American League shortstops in total chances with 767 and double plays with 133 in 1986.
Named shortstop on THE SPORTING NEWS College Baseball All-America Team, 1982.

Year Club	League	Pos.	G.	AB.	R.	H.	2B.	3B.	HR.	RBI.	B.A.	PO.	A.	E.	F.A.
1982—Lynn	East.	SS	78	241	32	64	9	2	1	27	.266	106	207	9	.972
1983—Salt Lake City	P. C.	SS	72	256	58	68	8	9	1	32	.266	111	212	14	.958
1983—Seattle	Amer.	SS	80	306	36	60	11	3	2	21	.196	122	233	11	.970
1984—Seattle	Amer.	SS	152	530	67	130	18	8	3	43	.245	245	463	17	.977
1985—Seattle†	Amer.	SS	118	352	41	91	10	6	6	37	.259	196	361	14	.975
1986—Seattle‡-Boston	Amer.	SS	154	528	67	122	24	7	1	45	.231	279	467	21	.973
1987—Boston	Amer.	SS	132	437	50	113	17	7	2	48	.259	164	336	13	.975
1988—Boston§	Amer.	SS	89	257	40	64	14	1	5	18	.249	102	192	10	.967
1989—Montreal x	Nat.	SS	142	437	52	102	17	4	6	41	.233	232	388	13	★.979
1990—Montreal	Nat.	SS	149	453	55	106	24	5	5	35	.234	216	340	6	★.989
American League Totals—6 Years			725	2410	301	580	94	32	19	212	.241	1120	2052	86	.974
National League Totals—2 Years			291	890	107	208	41	9	11	76	.234	448	728	19	.984
Major League Totals—8 Years			1016	3300	408	788	135	41	30	288	.239	1568	2780	105	.976

Selected by Seattle Mariners' organization in 1st round (sixth player selected) of free-agent draft, June 7, 1982.
†On disabled list, July 15 to August 1, 1985.

‡Traded with Outfielder Dave Henderson to Boston Red Sox for Infielder Rey Quinones, a player to be named later and cash, August 19, 1986; as part of deal, Seattle Mariners claimed Pitchers Mike Brown and Mike Trujillo on waivers from Boston, August 22, 1986. Seattle acquired Outfielder John Christensen to complete deal, September 25, 1986.

§Traded with Pitcher Dan Gakeler to Montreal Expos for Pitcher John Dopson and Shortstop Luis Rivera, December 8, 1988.

xOn disabled list, July 17 to August 1, 1989.

CHAMPIONSHIP SERIES RECORD

Year Club	League	Pos.	G.	AB.	R.	H.	2B.	3B.	HR.	RBI.	B.A.	PO.	A.	E.	F.A.
1986—Boston....................	Amer.	SS	7	21	5	9	0	1	0	3	.429	12	21	5	.868
1988—Boston....................	Amer.	PH	1	0	0	0	0	0	0	0	.000	0	0	0	.000
Championship Series Totals—2 Years.....			8	21	5	9	0	1	0	3	.429	12	21	5	.868

WORLD SERIES RECORD

Year Club	League	Pos.	G.	AB.	R.	H.	2B.	3B.	HR.	RBI.	B.A.	PO.	A.	E.	F.A.
1986—Boston....................	Amer.	SS	7	20	2	6	0	0	0	2	.300	10	13	0	1.000

MICHAEL TIMOTHY PAGLIARULO
Name pronounced Pal-ya-ROO-lo.
(Mike)

Born March 15, 1960, at Medford, Mass.
Height, 6.02. Weight, 195.
Throws right and bats lefthanded.
Attended University of Miami, Coral Gables, Fla.
Son of Charles Pagliarulo, infielder in Chicago Cubs' organization, 1958.

Major League stolen bases: 1986 (4), 1987 (1), 1988 (1), 1989 (3), 1990 (1). Total—10.
Led New York-Pennsylvania League in intentional bases on balls received with 8 in 1981.
Led Southern League third basemen in total chances with 433 in 1983.
Led New York-Pennsylvania League third basemen in total chances with 214 in 1981.

Year Club	League	Pos.	G.	AB.	R.	H.	2B.	3B.	HR.	RBI.	B.A.	PO.	A.	E.	F.A.
1981—Oneonta.................	NYP	3B	72	245	32	53	9	4	2	28	.216	40	*159	15	.930
1982—Greensboro...........	S. Atl.	3B	123	403	79	113	22	0	22	79	.280	73	*278	27	.929
1983—Nashville...............	South.	3B	135	450	82	117	19	4	19	80	.260	*98	*315	20	*.954
1984—Columbus...............	Int.	3B-SS	58	146	24	31	5	1	7	25	.212	27	95	13	.904
1984—New York..............	Amer.	3B	67	201	24	48	15	3	7	34	.239	44	106	7	.955
1985—New York..............	Amer.	3B	138	380	55	91	16	2	19	62	.239	67	187	13	.951
1986—New York..............	Amer.	3B-SS	149	504	71	120	24	3	28	71	.238	104	283	19	.953
1987—New York..............	Amer.	3B-1B	150	522	76	122	26	3	32	87	.234	97	297	17	.959
1988—New York‡..........	Amer.	3B	125	444	46	96	20	1	15	67	.216	82	232	19	.943
1989—New York‡..........	Amer.	3B	74	223	19	44	10	0	4	16	.197	25	122	10	.936
1989—San Diego.............	Nat.	3B	50	148	12	29	7	0	3	14	.196	19	83	7	.936
1990—San Diego§	Nat.	3B	128	398	29	101	23	2	7	38	.254	79	200	13	.955
American League Totals—6 Years			703	2274	291	521	111	12	105	337	.229	419	1227	85	.951
National League Totals—2 Years.............			178	546	41	130	30	2	10	52	.238	98	283	20	.950
Major League Totals—7 Years			881	2820	332	651	141	14	115	389	.231	517	1510	105	.951

Selected by New York Yankees' organization in 6th round of free-agent draft, June 8, 1981.
†On disabled list, July 25 to August 11, 1988.
‡Traded with Pitcher Don Schulze to San Diego Padres for Pitcher Walt Terrell and a player to be named later, July 22, 1989; New York Yankees acquired Pitcher Fred Toliver to complete deal, September 27, 1989.
§Granted free agency, November 5, 1990.

THOMAS ALAN PAGNOZZI
Name pronounced Pag-NOHZ-ee.
(Tom)

Born July 30, 1962, at Tucson, Ariz.
Height, 6.01. Weight, 190.
Throws and bats righthanded.
Attended Central Arizona College, Coolidge, Ariz.,
and University of Arkansas, Fayetteville, Ark.
Brother of Tim Pagnozzi, shortstop in Philadelphia Phillies' organization, 1976;
and Mike Pagnozzi, pitcher in Baltimore Orioles' organization, 1975 through 1978.

Major League stolen bases: 1987 (1), 1990 (1). Total—2.

Year Club	League	Pos.	G.	AB.	R.	H.	2B.	3B.	HR.	RBI.	B.A.	PO.	A.	E.	F.A.
1983—Erie	NYP	C	45	168	28	52	9	1	6	22	.310	183	20	3	.985
1983—Macon.................	S. Atl.	C	18	57	7	14	2	1	0	6	.246	125	18	8	.947
1984—Springfield...........	Midw.	C	114	396	57	112	20	4	10	68	.283	667	*90	12	.984
1985—Arkansas...............	Texas	C-1B	41	139	15	43	7	1	5	29	.309	243	27	1	.996
1985—Louisville	A. A.	C	76	268	29	72	13	2	5	40	.269	266	25	4	.986
1986—Louisville	A. A.	C	30	106	12	31	4	0	1	18	.292	160	19	3	.984
1987—Louisville	A. A.	C-3B	84	320	53	100	20	2	14	71	.313	427	43	6	.987
1987—St. Louis.................	Nat.	C-1B	27	48	8	9	1	0	2	9	.188	61	5	0	1.000
1988—St. Louis.................	Nat.	1B-C-3B	81	195	17	55	9	0	0	15	.282	340	30	4	.989
1989—St. Louis.................	Nat.	C-1B-3B	52	80	3	12	2	0	0	3	.150	100	9	2	.982
1990—St. Louis.................	Nat.	C-1B	69	220	20	61	15	0	2	23	.277	345	39	4	.990
Major League Totals—4 Years			229	543	48	137	27	0	4	50	.252	846	83	10	.989

Selected by Milwaukee Brewers' organization in 24th round of free-agent draft, January 12, 1982.
Selected by St. Louis Cardinals' organization in 8th round of free agent draft, June 6, 1983.

CHAMPIONSHIP SERIES RECORD

Year	Club	League	Pos.	G.	AB.	R.	H.	2B.	3B.	HR.	RBI.	B.A.	PO.	A.	E.	F.A.
1987—St. Louis	Nat.	PH	1	1	0	0	0	0	0	0	0	.000	0	0	0	.000

WORLD SERIES RECORD

Year	Club	League	Pos.	G.	AB.	R.	H.	2B.	3B.	HR.	RBI.	B.A.	PO.	A.	E.	F.A.
1987—St. Louis	Nat.	DH-PH	2	4	0	1	0	0	0	0	0	.250	0	0	0	.000

ROBERT REY PALACIOS

Name pronounced Pah-LAH-see-os.

(Known by middle name.)
Born November 8, 1962, at Brooklyn, N. Y.
Height, 5.10. Weight, 190.
Throws and bats righthanded.
Attended Kingsborough Community College, Brooklyn, N. Y.

Major League stolen bases: 1990 (2).
Led International League in sacrifice flies with 9 in 1987.
Led International League catchers in putouts with 789, total chances with 890 and tied for lead in double plays with 7 and passed balls with 15 in 1988.
Led International League catchers in assists with 66 in 1987 and 82 in 1988.
Led International League catchers in errors with 19 in 1988 and tied for lead with 13 in 1987.
Led Eastern League catchers in putouts with 603, assists with 86, errors with 20, total chances with 709 and double plays with 8 in 1986.
Tied for Appalachian League lead in double plays by catchers with 2 in 1984.

Year	Club	League	Pos.	G.	AB.	R.	H.	2B.	3B.	HR.	RBI.	B.A.	PO.	A.	E.	F.A.
1983—Bristol	Appal.	C	47	139	28	42	7	1	7	28	.302	187	22	7	.968
1984—Lakeland†	Fla. St.	3B-1B-C	107	373	44	92	21	4	2	53	.247	285	105	19	.954
1985—Lakeland	Fla. St.	C-1B	85	280	35	65	11	1	2	27	.232	410	45	13	.972
1985—Birmingham	South.	C-3B-1B	35	110	14	29	4	0	2	16	.264	153	43	8	.961
1986—Glens Falls	East.	C-3B-1B	135	461	66	116	20	4	16	66	.252	703	140	26	.970
1987—Toledo	Int.	C-3-1-O	133	449	50	116	22	2	13	60	.258	569	122	22	.969
1988—Toledo‡	Int.	C-1-O-2-3	132	409	38	94	26	1	5	27	.230	811	84	20	.978
1988—Kansas City	Amer.	C-3B	5	11	2	1	0	0	0	0	.091	17	1	0	1.000
1989—Kansas City	Amer.	3-1-C-O	55	47	12	8	2	0	1	8	.170	96	15	2	.982
1989—Omaha	A. A.	C-3B-OF	34	90	13	16	6	0	1	6	.178	164	20	5	.974
1990—Kansas City§	Amer.	C-1-3-O	41	56	8	13	3	0	2	9	.232	122	7	1	.992
1990—Omaha x	A. A.	3B-C	4	15	2	2	0	1	0	0	.133	5	5	1	.909
Major League Totals—3 Years			101	114	22	22	5	0	3	17	.193	235	23	3	.989

Signed as free agent by Detroit Tigers' organization, August 16, 1982.
†On disabled list, April 17 to May 21, 1984.
‡Traded with Pitcher Mark Lee to Kansas City Royals for Pitcher Ted Power, August 31, 1988.
§On disabled list, July 31 to August 31 and September 17, 1990 through remainder of season; included rehabilitation disability assignment to Omaha, August 24 to August 30, 1990.
xReleased, October 4, 1990.

VICENTE PALACIOS (HERNANDEZ)

Name pronounced Pah-LAH-see-os.

(Vince)

Born July 19, 1963, at Mataloma, Mex.
Height, 6.03. Weight, 180.
Throws and bats righthanded.

Led Pacific Coast League in shutouts with 5 in 1987.
Led Mexican League in balks with 3 in 1983.
Tied for Eastern League lead in balks with 4 in 1985.

Year	Club	League	G.	IP.	W.	L.	Pct.	H.	R.	ER.	SO.	BB.	ERA.
1982—Aguila	Mexican						(Did not play)						
1983—Aguila	Mexican	22	165⅓	12	6	.667	121	53	48	125	60	2.61
1984—Aguila†	Mexican	24	128	7	8	.468	117	64	50	120	79	3.52
1984—Glens Falls	Eastern	5	25⅓	1	2	.333	23	12	7	10	11	2.49
1985—Glens Falls‡	Eastern	8	39⅔	1	1	.500	44	25	21	20	29	4.76
1985—Mexico City Reds	Mexican	13	74⅓	7	2	.778	86	44	32	49	44	3.87
1986—Aguila§xy	Mexican	23	138⅔	5	14	.263	157	75	68	121	78	4.41
1987—Vancouver	P. Coast	27	*185	13	5	.722	140	63	53	*148	85	*2.58
1987—Pittsburgh	National	6	29⅓	2	1	.667	27	14	14	13	9	4.30
1988—Pittsburgh	National	7	24⅓	1	2	.333	28	18	18	15	15	6.66
1988—Buffalo	Am. Assoc.	5	31⅔	3	0	1.000	26	7	7	23	5	1.99
1989—Buffalo z	Am. Assoc.	2	10	0	2	.000	9	8	8	8	8	7.20
1990—Buffalo	Am. Assoc.	28	183⅔	13	7	.650	173	77	70	137	53	3.43
1990—Pittsburgh	National	7	15	0	0	.000	4	0	0	8	2	0.00
Major League Totals—3 Years		20	68⅔	3	3	.500	59	32	32	36	26	4.19

Signed as free agent by Aguila of Mexican League, April 23, 1982.
†Sold to Chicago White Sox' organization, July 20, 1984.
‡Loaned to Mexico City Reds of Mexican League, May 28, 1985; returned, September 3, 1985.

§Loaned to Aguila of Mexican League, April 5, 1986; returned, September 1, 1986.
xReleased, November 10, 1986; signed by Pittsburgh Pirates' organization, December 4, 1986.
yDrafted by Milwaukee Brewers, December 8, 1986; returned, April 3, 1987.
zOn disabled list, April 1 to June 12 and July 4, 1989 through remainder of season.

DONN STEVEN PALL

Born January 11, 1962, at Chicago, Ill.
Height, 6.01. Weight, 180.
Throws and bats righthanded.
Received degree from University of Illinois, Champaign, Ill., in 1985.

Major League saves: 1989 (6), 1990 (2). Total—8.
Tied for Gulf Coast League lead in complete games with 4 and shutouts with 2 in 1985.

Year	Club	League	G.	IP.	W.	L.	Pct.	H.	R.	ER.	SO.	BB.	ERA.
1985—Sarasota White Sox	Gulf Coast	13	*86	●7	5	.583	68	34	16	63	10	1.67
1986—Appleton	Midwest	11	78	5	5	.500	71	29	20	51	14	2.31
1986—Birmingham	Southern	21	73	3	4	.429	77	38	36	41	27	4.44
1987—Birmingham	Southern	30	158	8	11	.421	173	100	75	139	63	4.27
1988—Vancouver	P. Coast	44	72⅔	5	2	.714	61	21	18	41	20	2.23
1988—Chicago	American	17	28⅔	0	2	.000	39	11	11	16	8	3.45
1989—Chicago	American	53	87	4	5	.444	90	35	32	58	19	3.31
1989—South Bend	Midwest	2	3⅓	0	0	.000	1	0	0	4	0	0.00
1990—Chicago	American	56	76	3	5	.375	63	33	28	39	24	3.32
Major League Totals—3 Years		126	191⅔	7	12	.368	192	79	71	113	51	3.33

Selected by Chicago White Sox' organization in 23rd round of free-agent draft, June 3, 1985.
†On disabled list, May 19 to June 2, 1989; included rehabilitation disability assignment to South Bend, May 30 to June 2, 1989.

RAFAEL CORRALES PALMEIRO

Name pronounced Pal-MAIR-oh.

Born September 24, 1964, at Havana, Cuba.
Height, 6.00. Weight, 188.
Throws and bats lefthanded.
Received degree in commercial art from Mississippi State University, Starkville, Miss.

Major League stolen bases: 1986 (1), 1987 (2), 1988 (12), 1989 (4), 1990 (3). Total—22.
Led Eastern League in total bases with 225, sacrifice flies with 13 and intentional bases on balls received with 13 in 1986.
Named outfielder on THE SPORTING NEWS College Baseball All-America Team, 1985.
Named Eastern League Most Valuable Player, 1986.

Year	Club	League	Pos.	G.	AB.	R.	H.	2B.	3B.	HR.	RBI.	B.A.	PO.	A.	E.	F.A.
1985—Peoria	Midw.	OF	73	279	34	83	22	4	5	51	.297	113	7	1	.992
1986—Pittsfield	East.	OF	●140	509	66	*156	29	2	12	*95	.306	248	9	3	*.988
1986—Chicago	Nat.	OF	22	73	9	18	4	0	3	12	.247	34	2	4	.900
1987—Iowa	A. A.	OF-1B	57	214	36	64	14	3	11	41	.299	150	13	2	.988
1987—Chicago	Nat.	OF-1B	84	221	32	61	15	1	14	30	.276	176	9	1	.995
1988—Chicago†	Nat.	OF-1B	152	580	75	178	41	5	8	53	.307	322	11	5	.985
1989—Texas	Amer.	1B	156	559	76	154	23	4	8	64	.275	1167	*119	12	.991
1990—Texas	Amer.	1B	154	598	72	*191	35	6	14	89	.319	1215	91	7	.995
National League Totals—3 Years		258	874	116	257	60	6	25	95	.294	532	22	10	.982
American League Totals—2 Years		310	1157	148	345	58	10	22	153	.298	2382	210	19	.993
Major League Totals—5 Years		568	2031	264	602	118	16	47	248	.296	2914	232	29	.991

Selected by New York Mets' organization in 8th round of free-agent draft, June 7, 1982.
Selected by Chicago Cubs' organization in 1st round (22nd player selected) of free-agent draft, June 3, 1985.
†Traded with Pitchers Jamie Moyer and Drew Hall to Texas Rangers for Pitchers Mitch Williams, Paul Kilgus and Steve Wilson, Infielders Curtis Wilkerson and Luis Benitez and Outfielder Pablo Delgado, December 5, 1988.

ALL-STAR GAME RECORD

Year	League	Pos.	AB.	R.	H.	2B.	3B.	HR.	RBI.	B.A.	PO.	A.	E.	F.A.
1988—National		PH-OF	0	0	0	0	0	0	0	.000	1	0	0	1.000

JAMES FRANKLIN PANKOVITS
(Jim)

Born August 6, 1955, at Pennington Gap, Va.
Height, 5.10. Weight, 175.
Throws and bats righthanded.
Attended University of South Carolina, Columbia, S.C.

Major League stolen bases: 1984 (2), 1985 (1), 1986 (1), 1987 (2), 1988 (2). Total—8.
Led International League in sacrifice hits with 11 in 1990.
Led Appalachian League second basemen in assists with 212 and double plays with 47 in 1976.
Named third baseman on THE SPORTING NEWS College Baseball All-America Team, 1976.

Year	Club	League	Pos.	G.	AB.	R.	H.	2B.	3B.	HR.	RBI.	B.A.	PO.	A.	E.	F.A.
1976—Covington	Appal.	2B	●70	275	50	68	9	2	5	31	.247	165	212	18	.954
1977—Cocoa†	Fla. St.	SS-3B	91	326	27	74	9	3	2	20	.227	2	3	0	1.000
1978—Columbus	South.	SS	137	509	67	122	19	7	10	43	.240	4	8	2	.857
1978—Charleston	Int.	2B	3	7	0	1	0	0	0	0	.143	5	3	0	1.000

Year	Club	League	Pos.	G.	AB.	R.	H.	2B.	3B.	HR.	RBI.	B.A.	PO.	A.	E.	F.A.
1979—Columbus	South.		SS	92	346	53	91	10	3	10	45	.263	0	13	0	1.000
1979—Charleston	Int.		2B	22	59	7	10	3	1	0	3	.169	43	53	4	.960
1980—Tucson	P. C.		2B-3B-SS	64	213	36	53	8	4	2	26	.249	110	128	9	.964
1981—Tucson	P. C.		O-3-2-S	122	450	83	127	34	9	7	64	.282	93	75	22	.884
1982—Hawaii‡§	P. C.		3B-2B-OF	139	494	84	132	25	7	15	77	.267	192	162	22	.941
1983—Tucson	P. C.		2B	126	450	77	129	25	6	11	62	.287	215	322	25	.956
1984—Tucson	P. C.		2B	49	187	41	62	12	3	7	39	.332	103	176	8	.972
1984—Houston	Nat.		2B-SS-OF	53	81	6	23	7	0	1	14	.284	22	22	3	.936
1985—Houston x	Nat.		O-2-S-3	75	172	24	42	3	0	4	14	.244	81	38	2	.983
1986—Houston	Nat.		2B-OF-C	70	113	12	32	6	1	1	7	.283	42	58	4	.962
1987—Tucson	P. C.		2-3-1-O-S	34	101	17	33	7	2	4	25	.327	67	49	3	.975
1987—Houston	Nat.		2B-OF-3B	50	61	7	14	2	0	1	8	.230	19	15	0	1.000
1988—Houston y	Nat.		2B-3B-1B	68	140	13	31	7	1	2	12	.221	48	80	11	.921
1989—Buffalo z	A. A.		2B	30	83	5	15	2	1	2	8	.181	48	59	4	.964
1989—Albuquerque a	P. C.		2B-OF-3B	82	295	39	74	10	3	4	37	.251	132	166	17	.946
1990—Pawtucket	Int.		2B-OF	122	468	64	108	26	3	9	52	.231	267	148	13	.970
1990—Boston	Amer.		2B	2	0	0	0	0	0	0	0	.000	0	0	0	.000
National League Totals—5 Years				316	567	62	142	25	2	9	55	.250	212	213	20	.955
American League Totals—1 Year				2	0	0	0	0	0	0	0	.000	0	0	0	.000
Major League Totals—6 Years				318	567	62	142	25	2	9	55	.250	212	213	20	.955

Selected by Houston Astros' organization in 4th round of free-agent draft, June 8, 1976.
†On disabled list, May 22 to June 24, 1977.
‡Traded to Hawaii (San Diego Padres' organization) for Outfielder Doug Lulay, March 28, 1982.
§Granted free agency, October 22, 1982; re-signed by Astros' organization, January 23, 1983.
xOn disabled list, July 3 to July 18 and July 26 to August 22, 1985.
yReleased, November 17, 1988; signed by Buffalo (Pittsburgh Pirates' organization), February 22, 1989.
zSold to Albuquerque (Los Angeles Dodgers' organization), May 23, 1989.
aGranted free agency, October 15, 1989; signed by Pawtucket (Boston Red Sox' organization), February 5, 1990.

CHAMPIONSHIP SERIES RECORD

Year	Club	League	Pos.	G.	AB.	R.	H.	2B.	3B.	HR.	RBI.	B.A.	PO.	A.	E.	F.A.
1986—Houston	Nat.		PH	2	2	0	0	0	0	0	0	.000	0	0	0	.000

JOHNNY ALFONSO PAREDES (ISAMBERT)

Born September 2, 1962, at Maracaibo, Venezuela.
Height, 5.11. Weight, 165.
Throws and bats righthanded.

Major League stolen bases: 1988 (5).

Year	Club	League	Pos.	G.	AB.	R.	H.	2B.	3B.	HR.	RBI.	B.A.	PO.	A.	E.	F.A.
1982—Helena	Pioneer		3B-2B-SS	34	105	17	32	4	1	1	7	.305	28	63	7	.929
1983—Spartanburg†	S. Atl.		3B-1B-2B	46	130	14	31	0	3	0	11	.238	98	59	11	.925
1984—W. Palm Beach	Fla. St.		2B	112	438	64	111	11	1	0	32	.253	275	295	15	★.974
1985—W. Palm Beach	Fla. St.		2B	101	322	65	84	7	4	2	34	.261	184	281	9	★.981
1985—Jacksonville	South.		2B	21	73	11	23	2	0	0	5	.315	47	51	2	.980
1986—Jacksonville	South.		O-S-2-3-1	122	472	86	135	15	5	6	34	.286	230	189	19	.957
1987—Indianapolis	A. A.		2B	130	493	80	154	19	6	8	47	.312	234	387	14	.978
1988—Indianapolis	A. A.		2B-3B	101	400	69	118	17	3	4	46	.295	220	275	10	.980
1988—Montreal	Nat.		2B-OF	35	91	6	17	2	0	1	10	.187	46	77	3	.976
1989—Montreal‡§	Nat.		(Did not play)													
1990—Detroit x	Amer.		2B	6	8	2	1	0	0	0	0	.125	4	7	1	.917
1990—Indianapolis	A. A.		2B	94	322	46	84	7	1	3	17	.261	179	248	12	.973
1990—Montreal y	Nat.		2B	3	6	0	2	1	0	0	1	.333	1	7	1	.889
National League Totals—2 Years				38	97	6	19	3	0	1	11	.196	47	84	4	.970
American League Totals—1 Year				6	8	2	1	0	0	0	0	.125	4	7	1	.917
Major League Totals—2 Years				44	105	8	20	3	0	1	11	.190	51	91	5	.966

Signed as free agent by Philadelphia Phillies' organization, June 22, 1982.
†Released, September 19, 1983; signed by Gastonia (Montreal Expos' organization), January 12, 1984.
‡On disabled list, March 31 to September 28, 1989.
§Drafted by Detroit Tigers, December 4, 1989.
xReturned to Montreal Expos' organization, May 1, 1990.
yReleased, October 3, 1990.

MARK ALAN PARENT

Born September 16, 1961, at Ashland, Ore.
Height, 6.05. Weight, 240.
Throws and bats righthanded.

Major League stolen bases: 1989 (1), 1990 (1). Total—2.
Led Pacific Coast League catchers in fielding percentage with .988 in 1987.
Led Carolina League catchers in double plays with 16 in 1981.
Led Northwest League catchers in fielding percentage with .979 in 1980.

Year	Club	League	Pos.	G.	AB.	R.	H.	2B.	3B.	HR.	RBI.	B.A.	PO.	A.	E.	F.A.
1979—Walla Walla	N'west		C-OF	40	126	8	24	4	0	1	11	.190	229	34	6	.978
1980—Reno	Calif.		C	30	99	8	20	3	0	0	12	.202	128	23	2	.987
1980—Grays Harbor	N'west		C-1B	66	230	29	55	11	2	7	32	.230	381	38	9	.979
1981—Salem	Carol.		C	123	438	44	103	16	3	6	47	.235	★694	87	★28	.965
1982—Amarillo	Texas		C	26	89	12	17	3	1	1	13	.191	100	6	2	.981

Year	Club	League	Pos.	G.	AB.	R.	H.	2B.	3B.	HR.	RBI.	B.A.	PO.	A.	E.	F.A.
1982—Salem	Carol.	C-1B	99	360	39	81	15	2	6	41	.225	475	64	12	.978
1983—Beaumont†	Texas	C	81	282	38	71	22	1	7	33	.252	464	71	10	*.982
1984—Beaumont‡	Texas	C-1B	111	380	52	109	24	3	7	60	.287	674	68	7	.991
1985—Las Vegas	P. C.	C-1B	105	361	36	87	23	3	7	45	.241	586	54	6	.991
1986—Las Vegas	P. C.	C-1B	86	267	29	77	10	4	5	40	.288	344	40	5	.987
1986—San Diego	Nat.	C	8	14	1	2	0	0	0	0	.143	16	0	2	.889
1987—Las Vegas‡	P. C.	C-1-3-O	105	387	50	113	23	2	4	43	.292	556	58	8	.987
1987—San Diego	Nat.	C	12	25	0	2	0	0	0	2	.080	36	3	0	1.000
1988—San Diego	Nat.	C	41	118	9	23	3	0	6	15	.195	203	15	3	.986
1989—San Diego	Nat.	C-1B	52	141	12	27	4	0	7	21	.191	246	17	0	1.000
1990—San Diego§	Nat.	C	65	189	13	42	11	0	3	16	.222	324	31	3	.992
Major League Totals—5 Years			178	487	35	96	18	0	16	54	.197	825	66	8	.991

Selected by San Diego Padres' organization in 4th round of free-agent draft, June 5, 1979.
†On suspended list, August 27, 1983 through remainder of season.
‡On disabled list, September 4, 1984 through remainder of season.
§Traded to Texas Rangers for Third Baseman Scott Coolbaugh, December 12, 1990.

DAVID GENE PARKER
(Dave)

Born June 9, 1951, at Jackson, Miss.
Height, 6.05. Weight, 230.
Throws right and bats lefthanded.

Shares major league record for most home runs, month of October (4), 1985; fewest errors by outfielder, season, for leader in errors (9), 1986.
Major League stolen bases: 1973 (1), 1974 (3), 1975 (8), 1976 (19), 1977 (17), 1978 (20), 1979 (20), 1980 (10), 1981 (6), 1982 (7), 1983 (12), 1984 (11), 1985 (5), 1986 (1), 1987 (7), 1990 (4). Total—151.
Led American League in sacrifice flies with 14 in 1990.
Led National League in grounding into double plays with 26 in 1985.
Led National League in total bases with 340 in 1978, 350 in 1985 and 304 in 1986.
Led National League in slugging percentage with .541 in 1975 and .585 in 1978.
Led National League in intentional bases on balls received with 23 in 1978 and tied for lead with 24 in 1985.
Tied for National League lead in game-winning RBIs with 16 in 1987.
Tied for National League lead in sacrifice flies with 9 in 1979.
Led National League outfielders in total chances with 430 and double plays with 9 in 1977.
Led Carolina League in total bases with 270 and stolen bases with 38 in 1972.
Tied for Gulf Coast League lead in total bases with 107 in 1970.
Named National League Player of the Year by THE SPORTING NEWS, 1978.
Named National League Most Valuable Player by Baseball Writers' Association of America, 1978.
Named designated hitter on THE SPORTING NEWS American League All-Star Team, 1990.
Named outfielder on THE SPORTING NEWS National League All-Star Team, 1975, 1977, 1978, 1985 and 1986.
Named outfielder on THE SPORTING NEWS National League All-Star fielding team, 1977 through 1979.
Named designated hitter on THE SPORTING NEWS American League Silver Slugger team, 1990.
Named outfielder on THE SPORTING NEWS National League Silver Slugger team, 1985 and 1986.
Named Carolina League Most Valuable Player, 1972.

Year	Club	League	Pos.	G.	AB.	R.	H.	2B.	3B.	HR.	RBI.	B.A.	PO.	A.	E.	F.A.
1970—Bradenton Pir.	Gulf C.	●OF-P	61	239	34	75	8	3	●6	41	.314	92	11	●8	.928
1971—Waterbury	East.	OF	30	114	10	26	4	1	0	7	.228	43	5	6	.889
1971—Monroe	W. Car.	OF	71	268	49	96	16	4	11	48	.358	104	8	10	.918
1972—Salem	Carol.	OF	135	*523	*91	*162	*30	6	22	*101	*.310	*250	*20	*20	.931
1973—Charleston	Int.	OF	84	309	44	98	20	7	9	57	.317	144	11	7	.957
1973—Pittsburgh	Nat.	OF	54	139	17	40	9	1	4	14	.288	77	3	3	.964
1974—Pittsburgh†	Nat.	OF-1B	73	220	27	62	10	3	4	29	.282	154	8	4	.976
1975—Pittsburgh	Nat.	OF	148	558	75	172	35	10	25	101	.308	311	7	9	.972
1976—Pittsburgh	Nat.	OF	138	537	82	168	28	10	13	90	.313	294	13	*14	.956
1977—Pittsburgh	Nat.	*OF-2B	159	637	107	*215	*44	8	21	88	*.338	*389	*26	*15	.965
1978—Pittsburgh‡	Nat.	OF	148	581	102	194	32	12	30	117	*.334	302	12	*13	.960
1979—Pittsburgh	Nat.	OF	158	622	109	193	45	7	25	94	.310	341	15	*15	.960
1980—Pittsburgh	Nat.	OF	139	518	71	153	31	1	17	79	.295	235	14	9	.965
1981—Pittsburgh§	Nat.	OF	67	240	29	62	14	3	9	48	.258	110	1	7	.941
1982—Pittsburgh x	Nat.	OF	73	244	41	66	19	3	6	29	.270	108	2	5	.957
1983—Pittsburgh y	Nat.	OF	144	552	68	154	29	4	12	69	.279	282	3	8	.973
1984—Cincinnati	Nat.	OF	156	607	73	173	28	0	16	94	.285	296	6	8	.974
1985—Cincinnati	Nat.	OF	160	635	88	198	*42	4	34	*125	.312	329	12	10	.972
1986—Cincinnati	Nat.	OF	*162	637	89	174	31	3	31	116	.273	278	9	●9	.970
1987—Cincinnati z	Nat.	OF-1B	153	589	77	149	28	0	26	97	.253	354	17	11	.971
1988—Oakland a	Amer.	OF-1B	101	377	43	97	18	1	12	55	.257	63	5	3	.958
1989—Oakland b	Amer.	OF	144	553	56	146	27	0	22	97	.264	2	0	0	1.000
1990—Milwaukee	Amer.	1B	157	610	71	176	30	3	21	92	.289	24	0	1	.960
National League Totals—15 Years			1932	7316	1055	2173	425	69	273	1190	.297	3860	147	140	.966
American League Totals—3 Years			402	1540	170	419	75	4	55	244	.272	89	5	4	.959
Major League Totals—18 Years			2334	8856	1225	2592	500	73	328	1434	.293	3949	152	144	.966

Selected by Pittsburgh Pirates' organization in 14th round of free-agent draft, June 4, 1970.
†On disabled list, June 7 to June 28 and July 5 to July 31, 1974.
‡On disabled list, July 1 to July 16, 1978.
§On disabled list, May 14 to May 29, 1981.
xOn disabled list, May 12 to June 7 and July 29 to September 7, 1982.
yGranted free agency, November 7, 1983; signed by Cincinnati Reds, December 7, 1983.
zTraded to Oakland A's for Pitchers Jose Rijo and Tim Birtsas, December 8, 1987.

aOn disabled list, July 5 to August 21, 1988.
bGranted free agency, November 13, 1989; signed by Milwaukee Brewers, December 3, 1989.

CHAMPIONSHIP SERIES RECORD

Year	Club	League	Pos.	G.	AB.	R.	H.	2B.	3B.	HR.	RBI.	B.A.	PO.	A.	E.	F.A.
1974—Pittsburgh		Nat.	OF-PH	3	8	0	1	0	0	0	0	.125	4	1	0	1.000
1975—Pittsburgh		Nat.	OF	3	10	2	0	0	0	0	0	.000	13	1	0	1.000
1979—Pittsburgh		Nat.	OF	3	12	2	4	0	0	0	2	.333	9	0	0	1.000
1988—Oakland		Amer.	DH-OF	3	12	1	3	1	0	0	0	.250	1	0	1	.500
1989—Oakland		Amer.	DH	4	16	2	3	0	0	2	3	.188	0	0	0	.000
Championship Series Totals—5 Years				16	58	7	11	1	0	2	5	.190	27	2	1	.967

WORLD SERIES RECORD

Year	Club	League	Pos.	G.	AB.	R.	H.	2B.	3B.	HR.	RBI.	B.A.	PO.	A.	E.	F.A.
1979—Pittsburgh		Nat.	OF	7	29	2	10	3	0	0	4	.345	13	1	1	.933
1988—Oakland		Amer.	OF-DH	4	15	0	3	0	0	0	0	.200	4	0	0	1.000
1989—Oakland		Amer.	DH-PH	3	9	2	2	1	0	1	2	.222	0	0	0	.000
World Series Totals—3 Years				14	53	4	15	4	0	1	6	.283	17	1	1	.947

ALL-STAR GAME RECORD

Year	League	Pos.	AB.	R.	H.	2B.	3B.	HR.	RBI.	B.A.	PO.	A.	E.	F.A.
1977—National		OF	3	1	1	0	0	0	0	.333	2	0	0	1.000
1979—National		OF	3	0	1	0	0	0	1	.333	0	2	0	1.000
1980—National		OF	2	0	0	0	0	0	0	.000	0	0	0	.000
1981—National		OF	3	1	1	0	0	1	1	.333	1	0	0	1.000
1985—National		OF	2	0	0	0	0	0	0	.000	1	0	0	1.000
1986—National		OF	2	0	1	0	0	0	0	.500	0	0	0	.000
All-Star Game Totals—6 Years			15	2	4	0	0	1	2	.267	4	2	0	1.000

Member of American League All-Star Team in 1990; did not play.

PITCHING RECORD

Year	Club	League	G.	IP.	W.	L.	Pct.	H.	R.	ER.	SO.	BB.	ERA.
1970—Bradenton Pirates		Gulf Coast	1	4	0	0	.000	7	2	2	2	1	4.50

JAMES CLAYTON PARKER
(Clay)

Born December 19, 1962, at Columbia, La.
Height, 6.02. Weight, 185.
Throws and bats righthanded.
Attended Louisiana State University, Baton Rouge, La.

Year	Club	League	G.	IP.	W.	L.	Pct.	H.	R.	ER.	SO.	BB.	ERA.
1985—Bellingham		Northwest	10	63⅔	6	1	*.857	40	16	11	69	16	*1.55
1986—Wausau		Midwest	26	178	8	7	.533	171	77	57	154	39	2.88
1987—Chattanooga		Southern	16	112	7	5	.583	103	47	34	60	14	2.73
1987—Calgary		P. Coast	12	86	8	1	.889	78	35	28	44	28	2.93
1987—Seattle†		American	3	7⅔	0	0	.000	15	10	9	8	4	10.57
1988—Columbus‡		Int'national	10	49⅔	2	2	.500	49	21	18	51	9	3.26
1989—Columbus		Int'national	5	38	3	0	1.000	25	9	7	25	10	1.66
1989—New York§		American	22	120	4	5	.444	123	53	49	53	31	3.68
1990—New York x-Detroit		American	29	73	3	3	.500	64	29	29	40	32	3.58
1990—Columbus-Toledo		Int'national	9	54	2	5	.286	58	23	20	34	13	3.33
Major League Totals—3 Years			54	200⅔	7	8	.467	202	92	87	101	67	3.90

Selected by Minnesota Twins' organization in 21st round of free-agent draft, June 4, 1984.
Selected by Seattle Mariners' organization in 15th round of free-agent draft, June 3, 1985.
†Traded with Pitchers Lee Guetterman and Wade Taylor to New York Yankees for Pitcher Steve Trout and Outfielder Henry Cotto, December 22, 1987.
‡On disabled list, April 13 to April 22, June 1 to June 23 and June 28 to August 21, 1988.
§On disabled list, June 10 to July 1, 1989.
xTraded with Pitcher Lance McCullers to Detroit Tigers for Catcher Matt Nokes, June 4, 1990.

RICHARD ALLEN PARKER
(Rick)

Born March 20, 1963, at Kansas City, Mo.
Height, 6.00. Weight, 185.
Throws and bats righthanded.
Attended Southwest Missouri State University, Springfield, Mo.,
and University of Texas, Austin, Tex.

Major League stolen bases: 1990 (6).

Year	Club	League	Pos.	G.	AB.	R.	H.	2B.	3B.	HR.	RBI.	B.A.	PO.	A.	E.	F.A.
1985—Bend		N'west	SS	55	205	45	51	9	1	2	20	.249	79	143	25	.899
1986—Spartanburg		S. Atl.	SS	62	233	39	69	7	3	5	28	.296	87	169	18	.934
1986—Clearwater		Fla. St.	SS	63	218	24	51	10	2	0	15	.234	94	197	21	.933
1987—Clearwater		Fla. St.	2B-SS-3B	101	330	56	83	13	3	3	34	.252	130	234	27	.931
1988—Reading		East.	3-O-1-2-S	116	362	50	93	13	3	3	47	.257	174	114	18	.941
1989—Reading†		East.	3B-OF-SS	103	388	59	92	7	*9	3	32	.237	123	91	22	.907
1989—Phoenix		P. C.	3B-OF-SS	18	68	5	18	2	2	0	11	.265	25	32	1	.983

Year Club	League	Pos.	G.	AB.	R.	H.	2B.	3B.	HR.	RBI.	B.A.	PO.	A.	E.	F.A.
1990—Phoenix	P. C.	3B-OF-2B	44	173	38	58	7	4	1	18	.335	57	51	2	.982
1990—San Francisco	Nat.	O-2-S-3	54	107	19	26	5	0	2	14	.243	45	3	2	.960
Major League Totals—1 Year			54	107	19	26	5	0	2	14	.243	45	3	2	.960

Selected by Philadelphia Phillies' organization in 16th round of free-agent draft, June 3, 1985.

†Traded to Phoenix (San Francisco Giants' organization), August 7, 1989, completing deal in which Philadelphia Phillies traded Pitcher Steve Bedrosian and a player to be named later to San Francisco Giants for Pitchers Dennis Cook and Terry Mulholland and Third Baseman Charlie Hayes, June 18, 1989.

JEFFREY DALE PARRETT
(Jeff)

Born August 26, 1961, at Indianapolis, Ind.
Height, 6.03. Weight, 193.
Throws and bats righthanded.
Attended University of Kentucky, Lexington, Ky.

Major League saves: 1987 (6), 1988 (6), 1989 (6), 1990 (2). Total—20.

Year Club	League	G.	IP.	W.	L.	Pct.	H.	R.	ER.	SO.	BB.	ERA.
1983—Paintsville	Ap'lachian	3	17	2	0	1.000	12	6	4	21	8	2.12
1983—Beloit	Midwest	10	47	2	2	.500	40	26	21	34	29	4.02
1984—Beloit	Midwest	29	91⅓	4	3	.571	76	50	46	95	71	4.52
1985—Stockton†	California	45	127⅔	7	4	.636	97	50	39	120	75	*2.75
1986—Montreal	National	12	20⅓	0	1	.000	19	11	11	21	13	4.87
1986—Indianapolis	Am. Assoc.	25	69	2	5	.286	54	44	38	76	35	4.96
1987—Montreal	National	45	62	7	6	.538	53	33	29	56	30	4.21
1987—Indianapolis	Am. Assoc.	20	22⅓	2	1	.667	15	5	5	17	13	2.01
1988—Montreal‡§	National	61	91⅔	12	4	.750	66	29	27	62	45	2.65
1989—Philadelphia x	National	72	105⅔	12	6	.667	90	43	35	98	44	2.98
1990—Philadelphia y-Atlanta	National	67	108⅔	5	10	.333	119	62	56	86	55	4.64
Major League Totals—5 Years		257	388⅓	36	27	.571	347	178	158	323	187	3.66

Selected by Milwaukee Brewers' organization in 9th round of free-agent draft, June 6, 1983.

†Drafted by Montreal Expos, December 10, 1985.

‡On disabled list, July 16 to August 14, 1988.

§Traded with Pitcher Floyd Youmans to Philadelphia Phillies for Pitcher Kevin Gross, December 6, 1988.

xOn disabled list, April 29 to May 22, 1989.

yTraded with two players to be named later to Atlanta Braves for Outfielder Dale Murphy and a player to be named later, August 3, 1990; Scranton/Wilkes-Barre (Philadelphia Phillies' organization) acquired Pitcher Tommy Greene on August 9, 1990 and Atlanta acquired Outfielder Jim Vatcher on August 9, 1990 and Shortstop Victor Rosario on September 4, 1990 to complete deal.

LANCE MICHAEL PARRISH

Born June 15, 1956, at McKeesport, Pa.
Height, 6.03. Weight, 224.
Throws and bats righthanded.

Major League stolen bases: 1979 (6), 1980 (6), 1981 (2), 1982 (3), 1983 (1), 1984 (2), 1985 (2), 1989 (1), 1990 (2). Total—25.

Led American League in sacrifice flies with 13 in 1983.
Led American League catchers in assists with 88 in 1990.
Led American League catchers in double plays with 11 in 1984 and 15 in 1990.
Led American League catchers in total chances with 772 in 1983.
Led American League in passed balls with 21 in 1979 and tied for lead with 17 in 1980.
Led National League catchers in passed balls with 12 in 1988 and tied for lead in double plays with 11 in 1988.
Led Appalachian League batters in strikeouts with 92 in 1974.
Led American Association in double plays with 10 and passed balls with 21 in 1977.
Led Southern League in passed balls with 22 in 1976.
Led Florida State League catchers in double plays with 8 and passed balls with 31 in 1975.
Named catcher on THE SPORTING NEWS American League All-Star Team, 1982 and 1984.
Named catcher on THE SPORTING NEWS American League All-Star fielding team, 1983 through 1985.
Named catcher on THE SPORTING NEWS American League Silver Slugger team, 1980, 1982 through 1984, 1986 and 1990.

Year Club	League	Pos.	G.	AB.	R.	H.	2B.	3B.	HR.	RBI.	B.A.	PO.	A.	E.	F.A.
1974—Bristol	Appal.	3B-OF	68	253	45	54	11	1	11	46	.213	36	83	22	.844
1975—Lakeland	Fla. St.	C	100	341	30	75	15	2	5	37	.220	460	50	7	.986
1976—Montgomery	South.	C	107	340	46	75	9	2	14	55	.221	*600	*79	11	*.984
1977—Evansville	A. A.	C	115	416	74	116	21	2	25	90	.279	*722	*82	11	*.987
1977—Detroit	Amer.	C	12	46	10	9	2	0	3	7	.196	76	6	0	1.000
1978—Detroit	Amer.	C	85	288	37	63	11	3	14	41	.219	353	39	5	.987
1979—Detroit	Amer.	C	143	493	65	136	26	3	19	65	.276	707	*79	9	.989
1980—Detroit	Amer.	C-1B-OF	144	553	79	158	34	6	24	82	.286	607	67	7	.990
1981—Detroit	Amer.	C	96	348	39	85	18	2	10	46	.244	407	40	3	.993
1982—Detroit	Amer.	C-OF	133	486	75	138	19	2	32	87	.284	627	76	8	.989
1983—Detroit	Amer.	C	155	605	80	163	42	3	27	114	.269	695	73	4	.995
1984—Detroit	Amer.	C	147	578	75	137	16	2	33	98	.237	720	67	7	.991
1985—Detroit	Amer.	C	140	549	64	150	27	1	28	98	.273	695	53	5	.993
1986—Detroit†‡	Amer.	C	91	327	53	84	6	1	22	62	.257	483	48	6	.989
1987—Philadelphia	Nat.	C	130	466	42	114	21	0	17	67	.245	724	66	9	.989
1988—Philadelphia§x	Nat.	C-1B	123	424	44	91	17	2	15	60	.215	640	73	9	.988

Year Club	League	Pos.	G.	AB.	R.	H.	2B.	3B.	HR.	RBI.	B.A.	PO.	A.	E.	F.A.
1989—California	Amer.	C	124	433	48	103	12	1	17	50	.238	638	63	5	.993
1990—California	Amer.	C-1B	133	470	54	126	14	0	24	70	.268	794	90	6	.993
American League Totals—12 Years			1403	5176	679	1352	227	24	253	820	.261	6802	701	65	.991
National League Totals—2 Years			253	890	86	205	38	2	32	127	.230	1364	139	18	.988
Major League Totals—14 Years			1656	6066	765	1557	265	26	285	947	.257	8166	840	83	.991

Selected by Detroit Tigers' organization in 1st round (16th player selected) of free-agent draft, June 5, 1974.
†On disabled list, July 31 to September 29, 1986.
‡Granted free agency, November 12, 1986; signed by Philadelphia Phillies, March 13, 1987.
§On disabled list, July 13 to July 28, 1987.
xTraded to California Angels for Pitcher David Holdridge, October 3, 1988.

CHAMPIONSHIP SERIES RECORD

Year Club	League	Pos.	G.	AB.	R.	H.	2B.	3B.	HR.	RBI.	B.A.	PO.	A.	E.	F.A.
1984—Detroit	Amer.	C	3	12	1	3	1	0	1	3	.250	21	2	0	1.000

WORLD SERIES RECORD

Year Club	League	Pos.	G.	AB.	R.	H.	2B.	3B.	HR.	RBI.	B.A.	PO.	A.	E.	F.A.
1984—Detroit	Amer.	C	5	18	3	5	1	0	1	2	.278	30	3	1	.971

ALL-STAR GAME RECORD

Year League	Pos.	AB.	R.	H.	2B.	3B.	HR.	RBI.	B.A.	PO.	A.	E.	F.A.
1980—American	C	1	0	0	0	0	0	0	.000	0	0	0	.000
1982—American	C	2	0	1	1	0	0	0	.500	2	3	0	1.000
1983—American	C	2	0	0	0	0	0	0	.000	1	0	0	1.000
1984—American	C	2	0	0	0	0	0	0	.000	3	1	1	.800
1986—American	C	3	0	0	0	0	0	0	.000	4	0	0	1.000
1988—National	C	1	0	0	0	0	0	0	.000	0	0	0	.000
1990—American	PH-C	1	1	1	0	0	0	0	1.000	3	0	0	1.000
All-Star Game Totals—7 Years		12	1	2	1	0	0	0	.167	13	4	1	.944

Named to American League All-Star Team for 1985 game; replaced due to injury by Rich Gedman.

DANIEL ANTHONY PASQUA

Name Pronounced PASS-quah.

(Dan)

Born October 17, 1961, at Yonkers, N. Y.
Height, 6.00. Weight, 205.
Throws and bats lefthanded.
Attended William Paterson College, Wayne, N.J.

Major League stolen bases: 1986 (2), 1988 (1), 1989 (1), 1990 (1). Total—5.
Led American League outfielders in fielding percentage with .996 in 1988.
Led International League in slugging percentage with .599 in 1985.
Led Southern League batters in strikeouts with 148 in 1984.
Named International League Player of the Year, 1985.
Named Appalachian League Player of the Year, 1982.

Year Club	League	Pos.	G.	AB.	R.	H.	2B.	3B.	HR.	RBI.	B.A.	PO.	A.	E.	F.A.
1982—Paintsville	Appal.	OF	60	239	43	72	10	2	★16	●63	.301	114	4	4	.967
1982—Oneonta	NYP	OF	4	17	3	5	1	0	2	4	.294	2	1	1	.750
1983—Fort Lauderdale	Fla. St.	OF	131	451	83	123	25	10	19	84	.273	213	8	5	.978
1983—Columbus	Int.	OF	1	3	0	0	0	0	0	0	.000	5	0	0	1.000
1984—Nashville	South.	OF	136	460	78	112	14	3	★33	91	.243	244	11	★12	.955
1985—Columbus	Int.	OF	78	287	52	92	16	5	18	69	.321	141	9	4	.974
1985—New York	Amer.	OF	60	148	17	31	3	1	9	25	.209	72	2	0	1.000
1986—Columbus	Int.	OF	32	110	25	32	3	3	6	20	.291	62	0	3	.954
1986—New York	Amer.	OF-1B	102	280	44	82	17	0	16	45	.293	172	4	2	.989
1987—New York	Amer.	OF-1B	113	318	42	74	7	1	17	42	.233	214	10	2	.991
1987—Columbus†	Int.	OF	23	85	16	29	6	0	6	15	.341	55	0	1	.982
1988—Chicago	Amer.	OF-1B	129	422	48	96	16	2	20	50	.227	316	14	2	.994
1989—Chicago‡	Amer.	OF	73	246	26	61	9	1	11	47	.248	149	3	1	.993
1990—Chicago	Amer.	OF	112	325	43	89	27	3	13	58	.274	71	5	3	.962
Major League Totals—6 Years			589	1739	220	433	79	8	86	267	.249	994	38	10	.990

Selected by New York Yankees' organization in 3rd round of free-agent draft, June 7, 1982.
†Traded with Catcher Mark Salas and Pitcher Steve Rosenberg to Chicago White Sox for Pitchers Richard Dotson and Scott Nielsen, November 12, 1987.
‡On disabled list, April 6 to May 14 and August 21, 1989 through remainder of season.

KENNETH BRIAN PATTERSON

(Ken)

Born July 8, 1964, at Costa Mesa, Calif.
Height, 6.04. Weight, 210.
Throws and bats lefthanded.
Attended McLennan Community College, Waco, Tex., and Baylor University, Waco, Tex.

Major League saves: 1988 (1), 1990 (2). Total—3.
Led New York-Pennsylvania League in shutouts with 4 in 1986.

Year Club	League	G.	IP.	W.	L.	Pct.	H.	R.	ER.	SO.	BB.	ERA.
1985—Oneonta	NYP	6	22⅓	2	2	.500	23	14	12	21	14	4.84
1986—Fort Lauderdale	Florida St.	5	18⅔	0	2	.000	30	20	16	13	16	7.71
1986—Oneonta†	NYP	15	100⅓	9	3	.750	67	25	15	102	45	*1.35
1987—Daytona Beach	Florida St.	9	42⅔	1	3	.250	46	34	30	36	31	6.33
1987—Hawaii	P. Coast	3	3⅓	0	0	.000	1	0	0	5	3	0.00
1988—Vancouver	P. Coast	55	86⅓	6	5	.545	64	37	31	89	36	3.23
1988—Chicago	American	9	20⅔	0	2	.000	25	11	11	8	7	4.79
1989—Chicago	American	50	65⅔	6	1	.857	64	37	33	43	28	4.52
1989—Vancouver	P. Coast	2	9	0	1	.000	6	2	1	17	1	1.00
1990—Chicago	American	43	66⅓	2	1	.667	58	27	25	40	34	3.39
Major League Totals—3 Years		102	152⅔	8	4	.667	147	75	69	91	69	4.07

Selected by Philadelphia Phillies' organization in 29th round of free-agent draft, June 7, 1982.
Selected by Baltimore Orioles' organization in secondary phase of free-agent draft, January 11, 1983.
Selected by Philadelphia Phillies' organization in secondary phase of free-agent draft, June 6, 1983.
Selected by New York Yankees' organization in 3rd round of free-agent draft, June 3, 1985.
†Traded with a player to be named later to Chicago White Sox for Infielder-Outfielder Jerry Royster and Infielder Mike Soper, August 26, 1987; White Sox acquired Pitcher Jeff Pries to complete deal, September 19, 1987.

ROBERT CHANDLER PATTERSON
(Bob)

Born May 16, 1959, at Jacksonville, Fla.
Height, 6.02. Weight, 192.
Throws left and bats righthanded.
Received degree in industrial technology from East Carolina University, Greenville, N.C.

Major League saves: 1989 (1), 1990 (5). Total—6.

Year Club	League	G.	IP.	W.	L.	Pct.	H.	R.	ER.	SO.	BB.	ERA.
1982—Sarasota Padres	Gulf Coast	8	52	4	3	.571	60	18	17	65	7	2.94
1982—Reno	California	4	25⅓	1	0	1.000	28	11	10	10	5	3.55
1983—Beaumont	Texas	43	116⅔	8	4	.667	107	61	52	97	36	4.01
1984—Las Vegas	P. Coast	*60	143⅓	8	9	.471	129	63	52	97	37	3.27
1985—Las Vegas	P. Coast	42	186⅓	10	11	.476	187	80	65	146	52	3.14
1985—San Diego†	National	3	4	0	0	.000	13	11	11	1	3	24.75
1986—Hawaii	P. Coast	25	156	9	6	.600	146	68	59	*137	44	3.40
1986—Pittsburgh	National	11	36⅓	2	3	.400	49	20	20	20	5	4.95
1987—Pittsburgh	National	15	43	1	4	.200	49	34	32	27	22	6.70
1987—Vancouver	P. Coast	14	89	5	2	.714	62	21	21	92	30	2.12
1988—Buffalo‡	Am. Assoc.	4	31	2	0	1.000	26	12	8	20	4	2.32
1989—Buffalo	Am. Assoc.	31	177⅓	12	6	.667	177	69	66	103	35	3.35
1989—Pittsburgh	National	12	26⅔	4	3	.571	23	13	12	20	8	4.05
1990—Pittsburgh	National	55	94⅔	8	5	.615	88	33	31	70	21	2.95
Major League Totals—5 Years		96	204⅔	15	15	.500	222	111	106	138	59	4.66

Selected by San Diego Padres' organization in 21st round of free-agent draft, June 7, 1982.
†Traded to Pittsburgh Pirates for Outfielder Marvell Wynne, April 3, 1986.
‡On disabled list, April 28, 1988 through remainder of season.

CHAMPIONSHIP SERIES RECORD

Year Club	League	G.	IP.	W.	L.	Pct.	H.	R.	ER.	SO.	BB.	ERA.
1990—Pittsburgh	National	2	1	0	0	.000	1	0	0	0	2	0.00

DAVID LEE PAVLAS
(Dave)

Born August 12, 1962, at Frankfurt, West Germany.
Height, 6.07. Weight, 195.
Throws and bats righthanded.
Attended Rice University, Houston, Tex.

Led American Association in hit batsmen with 10 in 1990.
Named Carolina League Pitcher of the Year, 1986.

Year Club	League	G.	IP.	W.	L.	Pct.	H.	R.	ER.	SO.	BB.	ERA.
1985—Peoria	Midwest	17	110	8	3	.727	90	40	32	86	32	2.62
1986—Winston-Salem	Carolina	28	173⅓	14	6	.700	172	91	74	143	57	3.84
1987—Pittsfield†	Eastern	7	45	6	1	.857	49	25	19	27	17	3.80
1987—Tulsa	Texas	13	59⅔	1	6	.143	79	51	51	46	27	7.69
1988—Tulsa	Texas	26	77⅓	5	2	.714	52	26	17	69	18	1.98
1988—Oklahoma City	Am. Assoc.	13	52⅓	3	1	.750	59	29	26	40	28	4.47
1989—Oklahoma City‡	Am. Assoc.	29	143⅔	2	*14	.125	175	89	75	94	67	4.70
1990—Iowa	Am. Assoc.	53	99⅓	8	3	.727	84	38	36	96	48	3.26
1990—Chicago	National	13	21⅓	2	0	1.000	23	7	5	12	6	2.11
Major League Totals—1 Year		13	21⅓	2	0	1.000	23	7	5	12	6	2.11

Signed as free agent by Chicago Cubs' organization, December 15, 1984.
†Traded to Texas Rangers' organization, June 6, 1987, completing deal in which Texas traded Pitcher Mike Mason to Chicago Cubs for a player to be named later, May 15, 1987.
‡Sold to Chicago Cubs' organization, January 3, 1990.

WILLIAM JOSEPH PECOTA
(Bill)

Born February 16, 1960, at Redwood City, Calif.
Height, 6.02. Weight, 190.
Throws and bats righthanded.
Attended De Anza College, Cupertino, Calif.

Major League stolen bases: 1987 (5), 1988 (7), 1989 (5), 1990 (8). Total—25.
Led American Association third basemen in assists with 217 and total chances with 337 in 1986.
Led American Association third basemen in total chances with 372 and double plays with 22 in 1985.
Led Southern League third basemen in total chances with 434 in 1984.

Year	Club	League	Pos.	G.	AB.	R.	H.	2B.	3B.	HR.	RBI.	B.A.	PO.	A.	E.	F.A.
1981—Sara.Roy.-Blue		Gulf C.	C-3B-2B	61	208	*61	66	11	4	3	22	.317	112	45	6	.963
1982—Fort Myers		Fla. St.	3B	135	482	71	115	16	6	4	49	.239	109	243	15	.959
1983—Fort Myers		Fla. St.	3B	65	234	48	63	7	2	5	33	.269	46	114	7	.958
1983—Jacksonville		South.	3B-SS	72	260	38	63	9	1	5	25	.242	54	135	19	.909
1984—Memphis		South.	3B	145	543	84	131	19	2	9	50	.241	*142	267	25	*.942
1985—Omaha		A. A.	*3-S-O	130	409	47	98	17	3	1	34	.240	*111	*247	14	*.962
1986—Omaha		A. A.	3B-SS-OF	139	474	48	125	26	2	4	54	.264	125	238	11	.971
1986—Kansas City		Amer.	3B-SS	12	29	3	6	2	0	0	2	.207	7	31	1	.974
1987—Omaha		A. A.	3B-SS-2B	35	126	31	39	8	1	2	16	.310	38	78	8	.935
1987—Kansas City		Amer.	SS-3B-2B	66	156	22	43	5	1	3	14	.276	67	135	6	.971
1988—Kansas City		Amer.	I-O-C	90	178	25	37	3	3	1	15	.208	98	145	6	.976
1989—Kansas City		Amer.	S-O-2-3-1	65	83	21	17	4	2	3	5	.205	50	79	2	.985
1989—Omaha		A. A.	S-3-2-O	64	248	34	63	12	1	3	40	.254	96	206	8	.974
1990—Kansas City		Amer.	2-S-3-O-1	87	240	43	58	15	2	5	20	.242	160	195	5	.986
1990—Omaha		A. A.	3B-2B-SS	29	116	30	35	6	0	4	13	.302	32	80	1	.991
Major League Totals—5 Years				320	686	114	161	29	8	12	56	.235	382	585	20	.980

Selected by Kansas City Royals' organization in 10th round of free-agent draft, January 13, 1981.

ALEJANDRO PENA (VASQUEZ)

Born June 25, 1959, at Cambiaso, Dominican Republic.
Height, 6.01. Weight, 203.
Throws and bats righthanded.

Major League saves: 1981 (2), 1983 (1), 1986 (1), 1987 (11), 1988 (12), 1989 (5), 1990 (5). Total—37.
Tied for National League lead in shutouts with 4 in 1984.
Led Pacific Coast League in saves with 22 in 1981.

Year	Club	League	G.	IP.	W.	L.	Pct.	H.	R.	ER.	SO.	BB.	ERA.
1979—Clinton		Midwest	21	71	3	3	.500	53	39	33	57	44	4.18
1980—Vero Beach		Florida St.	35	73	10	3	.769	57	32	26	46	41	3.21
1981—Albuquerque		P. Coast	38	56	2	5	.286	36	12	10	40	21	1.61
1981—Los Angeles		National	14	25	1	1	.500	18	8	8	14	11	2.88
1982—Los Angeles		National	29	35⅔	0	2	.000	37	24	19	20	21	4.79
1982—Albuquerque		P. Coast	16	28⅔	1	1	.500	37	18	17	27	10	5.34
1983—Los Angeles		National	34	177	12	9	.571	152	67	54	120	51	2.75
1984—Los Angeles		National	28	199⅓	12	6	.667	186	67	55	135	46	*2.48
1985—Los Angeles†		National	2	4⅓	0	1	.000	7	5	4	2	3	8.31
1986—Vero Beach‡		Florida St.	4	15⅔	0	2	.000	22	15	13	11	4	7.47
1986—Los Angeles		National	24	70	1	2	.333	74	40	38	46	30	4.89
1987—Los Angeles§		National	37	87⅓	2	7	.222	82	41	34	76	37	3.50
1988—Los Angeles x		National	60	94⅓	6	7	.462	75	29	20	83	27	1.91
1989—Los Angeles yz		National	53	76	4	3	.571	62	20	18	75	18	2.13
1990—New York		National	52	76	3	3	.500	71	31	27	76	22	3.20
Major League Totals—10 Years			333	845	41	41	.500	764	332	277	647	266	2.95

Signed as free agent by Los Angeles Dodgers' organization, September 10, 1978.
†On disabled list, April 8 to September 5, 1985.
‡On Los Angeles disabled list, March 23 to May 26, 1986; included rehabilitation disability assignment to Vero Beach, May 2 to May 19, 1986.
§On disabled list, July 27 to August 17, 1987.
xGranted free agency, November 4, 1988; re-signed by Dodgers, November 7, 1988.
yOn disabled list, July 8 to July 23, 1989.
zTraded with Outfielder Mike Marshall to New York Mets for Outfielder Juan Samuel, December 20, 1989.

CHAMPIONSHIP SERIES RECORD

Year	Club	League	G.	IP.	W.	L.	Pct.	H.	R.	ER.	SO.	BB.	ERA.
1981—Los Angeles		National	2	2⅓	0	0	.000	1	0	0	0	0	0.00
1983—Los Angeles		National	1	2⅔	0	0	.000	4	2	2	3	1	6.75
1988—Los Angeles		National	3	4⅓	1	1	.500	1	2	2	1	5	4.15
Championship Series Totals—3 Years			6	9⅓	1	1	.500	6	4	4	4	6	3.86

WORLD SERIES RECORD

Year	Club	League	G.	IP.	W.	L.	Pct.	H.	R.	ER.	SO.	BB.	ERA.
1988—Los Angeles		National	2	5	1	0	1.000	2	0	0	7	1	0.00

Eligible for 1981 World Series with Los Angeles Dodgers; did not play.

ANTONIO FRANCISCO PENA (PADILLA)
(Tony)

Born June 4, 1957, at Monte Cristi, Dominican Republic.
Height, 6.00. Weight, 184.
Throws and bats righthanded.
Brother of Ramon Pena, pitcher with Detroit Tigers, 1989; and related
to Jose Pena, catcher in San Francisco Giants' organization, 1983 through 1989.

Major League stolen bases: 1981 (1), 1982 (2), 1983 (6), 1984 (12), 1985 (12), 1986 (9), 1987 (6), 1988 (6), 1989 (5), 1990 (8). Total—67.

Tied for National League lead in grounding into double plays with 21 in 1986.
Led American League catchers in putouts with 864 and total chances with 943 in 1990.
Led National League catchers in fielding percentage with .994 in 1988.
Led National League catchers in assists with 100 in 1985.
Led National League catchers in double plays with 15 in 1984 and 13 in 1989.
Led National League catchers in total chances with 1,075 in 1983, 999 in 1984 and 1,034 in 1985.
Led Eastern League catchers in double plays with 14 in 1979.
Led Carolina League catchers in double plays with 9 in 1977.
Tied for Carolina League lead in passed balls with 16 in 1977.
Named catcher on THE SPORTING NEWS National League All-Star Team, 1983.
Named catcher on THE SPORTING NEWS National League All-Star fielding team, 1983 through 1985.

Year—Club	League	Pos.	G.	AB.	R.	H.	2B.	3B.	HR.	RBI.	B.A.	PO.	A.	E.	F.A.
1976—Bradenton Pir.	Gulf C.	O-1-C-3	33	110	10	23	2	2	1	11	.209	108	14	4	.968
1976—Charleston	W. Car.	C	14	49	4	11	2	0	1	8	.224	64	7	2	.973
1977—Charleston	W. Car.	C	29	101	10	24	4	0	3	16	.238	172	19	6	.970
1977—Salem	Carol.	C	84	319	36	88	15	3	7	46	.276	★470	★66	★17	.969
1978—Shreveport	Texas	C	104	348	34	80	14	0	8	42	.230	637	54	★25	.965
1979—Buffalo	East.	C	134	515	89	161	16	4	34	97	.313	★768	★120	★26	.972
1980—Portland	P. C.	C	124	452	57	148	24	13	9	77	.327	★639	85	●23	.969
1980—Pittsburgh	Nat.	C	8	21	1	9	1	1	0	1	.429	38	2	2	.952
1981—Pittsburgh	Nat.	C	66	210	16	63	9	1	2	17	.300	286	41	5	.985
1982—Pittsburgh	Nat.	C	138	497	53	147	28	4	11	63	.296	763	89	16	.982
1983—Pittsburgh	Nat.	C	151	542	51	163	22	3	15	70	.301	★976	90	9	.992
1984—Pittsburgh	Nat.	C	147	546	77	156	27	2	15	78	.286	★895	★95	9	.991
1985—Pittsburgh	Nat.	C-1B	147	546	53	136	27	2	10	59	.249	925	102	12	.988
1986—Pittsburgh†	Nat.	★C-1B	144	510	56	147	26	2	10	52	.288	824	99	★18	.981
1987—St. Louis‡	Nat.	C-1B-OF	116	384	40	82	13	4	5	44	.214	624	51	8	.988
1987—Louisville	A. A.	C	2	8	0	3	0	0	0	0	.375	7	1	0	1.000
1988—St. Louis	Nat.	C-1B	149	505	55	133	23	1	10	51	.263	796	72	6	.993
1989—St. Louis§	Nat.	C-OF	141	424	36	110	17	2	4	37	.259	675	70	2	★.997
1990—Boston	Amer.	C-1B	143	491	62	129	19	1	7	56	.263	866	74	5	.995
American League Totals—1 Year			143	491	62	129	19	1	7	56	.263	866	74	5	.995
National League Totals—10 Years			1207	4185	438	1146	193	22	82	472	.274	6802	711	87	.989
Major League Totals—11 Years			1350	4676	500	1275	212	23	89	528	.273	7668	785	92	.989

Signed as free agent by Pittsburgh Pirates' organization, July 22, 1975.

†Traded to St. Louis Cardinals for Outfielder Andy Van Slyke, Catcher Mike LaValliere and Pitcher Mike Dunne, April 1, 1987.

‡On disabled list, April 11 to May 22, 1987; included rehabilitation disability assignment to Louisville, May 19 to May 22, 1987.

§Granted free agency, November 13, 1989; signed by Boston Red Sox, November 27, 1989.

CHAMPIONSHIP SERIES RECORD

Year—Club	League	Pos.	G.	AB.	R.	H.	2B.	3B.	HR.	RBI.	B.A.	PO.	A.	E.	F.A.
1987—St. Louis	Nat.	C	7	21	5	8	0	1	0	0	.381	55	5	0	1.000
1990—Boston	Amer.	C	4	14	0	3	0	0	0	0	.214	22	4	1	.963
Championship Series Totals—2 Years			11	35	5	11	0	1	0	0	.314	77	9	1	.989

WORLD SERIES RECORD

Year—Club	League	Pos.	G.	AB.	R.	H.	2B.	3B.	HR.	RBI.	B.A.	PO.	A.	E.	F.A.
1987—St. Louis	Nat.	C-DH	7	22	2	9	1	0	0	4	.409	32	1	1	.971

ALL-STAR GAME RECORD

Year—League	Pos.	AB.	R.	H.	2B.	3B.	HR.	RBI.	B.A.	PO.	A.	E.	F.A.
1982—National	PR-C	1	0	0	0	0	0	0	.000	3	0	0	1.000
1984—National	C	0	0	0	0	0	0	0	.000	2	0	0	1.000
1985—National	C	1	0	0	0	0	0	0	.000	4	1	0	1.000
1986—National	PR	0	0	0	0	0	0	0	.000	0	0	0	.000
1989—National	PH-C	2	0	0	0	0	0	0	.000	2	0	0	1.000
All-Star Game Totals—5 Years		4	0	0	0	0	0	0	.000	11	1	0	1.000

GERONIMO PENA

Born March 29, 1967, at Distrito Nacional, D. R.
Height, 6.01. Weight, 170.
Throws right and bats left and righthanded.

Major League stolen bases: 1990 (1).
Led American Association in being hit by pitch with 18 in 1990.
Led South Atlantic League in stolen bases with 80 in 1987.
Led Appalachian League in intentional bases on balls received with 4 in 1986.

Led American Association third basemen in errors with 20 in 1990.
Led Florida State League second basemen in total chances with 723 and double plays with 103 in 1988.
Led South Atlantic League shortstops in putouts with 324, assists with 342, total chances with 695 and double plays with 80 in 1987.

Year Club	League	Pos.	G.	AB.	R.	H.	2B.	3B.	HR.	RBI.	B.A.	PO.	A.	E.	F.A.
1986—Johnson City†	Appal.	2B	56	202	★55	60	7	4	3	20	.297	108	144	7	.973
1987—Savannah†	S. Atl.	★2B-SS	134	505	95	136	28	3	9	51	.269	325	343	★29	.958
1988—St. Petersburg	Fla. St.	2B	130	484	82	125	25	10	4	35	.258	★301	★402	20	★.972
1989—St. Petersburg‡	Fla. St.	2B	6	21	2	4	1	0	0	2	.190	9	19	1	.966
1989—Arkansas	Texas	2B	77	267	61	79	16	8	9	44	.296	177	208	14	.965
1990—Louisville	A. A.	2B-3B	118	390	65	97	24	6	6	35	.249	153	261	27	.939
1990—St. Louis	Nat.	2B	18	45	5	11	2	0	0	2	.244	24	30	1	.982
Major League Totals—1 Year			18	45	5	11	2	0	0	2	.244	24	30	1	.982

Signed as free agent by St. Louis Cardinals' organization, August 9, 1984.
†Batted righthanded only.
‡On St. Louis disabled list, March 25 to June 5, 1989; included rehabilitation disability assignment to St. Petersburg, May 29 to June 5, 1989.

TERRY LEE PENDLETON

Born July 16, 1960, at Los Angeles, Calif.
Height, 5.09. Weight, 178.
Throws right and bats left and righthanded.
Attended Oxnard College, Oxnard, Calif. and Fresno State University, Fresno, Calif.

Major League stolen bases: 1984 (20), 1985 (17), 1986 (24), 1987 (19), 1988 (3), 1989 (9), 1990 (7). Total—99.
Led National League third basemen in total chances with 524 in 1986, 512 in 1987 and 520 in 1989.
Led National League third basemen in double plays with 36 in 1986.
Led American Association third basemen in putouts with 88 and fielding percentage with .964 in 1984.
Named third baseman on THE SPORTING NEWS National League All-Star fielding team, 1987 and 1989.

Year Club	League	Pos.	G.	AB.	R.	H.	2B.	3B.	HR.	RBI.	B.A.	PO.	A.	E.	F.A.
1982—Johnson City	Appal.	2B	43	181	38	58	14	●4	4	27	.320	79	105	17	.915
1982—St. Petersburg	Fla. St.	2B	20	69	4	18	2	1	1	7	.261	41	51	2	.979
1983—Arkansas†	Texas	2B	48	185	29	51	10	3	4	20	.276	94	135	7	.970
1984—Louisville	A. A.	3B-2B	91	330	52	98	23	5	4	44	.297	91	157	10	.961
1984—St. Louis	Nat.	3B	67	262	37	85	16	3	1	33	.324	59	155	13	.943
1985—St. Louis‡	Nat.	3B	149	559	56	134	16	3	5	69	.240	129	361	18	.965
1986—St. Louis	Nat.	★3B-OF	159	578	56	138	26	5	1	59	.239	★133	★371	20	.962
1987—St. Louis	Nat.	3B	159	583	82	167	29	4	12	96	.286	117	★369	26	.949
1988—St. Louis§	Nat.	3B	110	391	44	99	20	2	6	53	.253	75	239	12	.963
1989—St. Louis	Nat.	3B	162	613	83	162	28	5	13	74	.264	113	★392	15	★.971
1990—St. Louis xy	Nat.	3B	121	447	46	103	20	2	6	58	.230	91	248	19	.947
Major League Totals—7 Years			927	3433	404	888	155	24	44	442	.259	717	2135	123	.959

Selected by St. Louis Cardinals' organization in 7th round of free-agent draft, June 7, 1982.
†On disabled list, April 8 to May 23 and July 16 to September 5, 1983.
‡On disabled list June 15 to June 30, 1985.
§On disabled list, May 28 to June 24, 1988.
xOn disabled list, April 24 to May 9, 1990.
yGranted free agency, November 5, 1990; signed by Atlanta Braves, December 3, 1990.

CHAMPIONSHIP SERIES RECORD

Shares Championship Series record for most at-bats, inning (2), October 13, 1985, second inning.

Year Club	League	Pos.	G.	AB.	R.	H.	2B.	3B.	HR.	RBI.	B.A.	PO.	A.	E.	F.A.
1985—St. Louis	Nat.	3B	6	24	2	5	1	0	0	4	.208	6	18	1	.960
1987—St. Louis	Nat.	3B	6	19	3	4	0	1	0	1	.211	3	11	0	1.000
Championship Series Totals—2 Years			12	43	5	9	1	1	0	5	.209	9	29	1	.974

WORLD SERIES RECORD

Year Club	League	Pos.	G.	AB.	R.	H.	2B.	3B.	HR.	RBI.	B.A.	PO.	A.	E.	F.A.
1985—St. Louis	Nat.	3B	7	23	3	6	1	1	0	3	.261	6	14	1	.952
1987—St. Louis	Nat.	DH-PH	3	7	2	3	0	0	0	1	.429	0	0	0	.000
World Series Totals—2 Years			10	30	5	9	1	1	0	4	.300	6	14	1	.952

MELIDO T. PEREZ

Born February 15, 1966, at San Cristobal, D. R.
Height, 6.04. Weight, 180.
Throws and bats righthanded.
Brother of Pascual Perez, pitcher with New York Yankees; Vladimir Perez,
pitcher in New York Mets' organization; Dario Perez, pitcher in Kansas City Royals'
organization; Carlos Perez, pitcher in Montreal Expos' organization;
and Valerio Perez, pitcher in Kansas City Royals' organization, 1983 and 1984.

Pitched six-inning, 8-0 no-hit victory against New York Yankees, July 12, 1990.
Led Midwest League in complete games with 13 in 1986.
Tied for Northwest League lead in games started by pitchers with 15, balks with 2 and home runs allowed with 13 in 1985.

Year Club	League	G.	IP.	W.	L.	Pct.	H.	R.	ER.	SO.	BB.	ERA.
1984—Charleston	S. Atlantic	16	89	5	7	.417	99	52	43	55	19	4.35
1985—Eugene	Northwest	17	101	6	7	.462	116	65	★61	88	35	5.44

Year	Club	League	G.	IP.	W.	L.	Pct.	H.	R.	ER.	SO.	BB.	ERA.
1986—Burlington	Midwest	28	170⅓	10	12	.455	148	83	70	153	49	3.70
1987—Fort Myers	Florida St.	8	64⅓	4	3	.571	51	20	17	51	7	2.38
1987—Memphis	Southern	20	133⅔	8	5	.615	125	60	51	126	20	3.43
1987—Kansas City†	American	3	10⅓	1	1	.500	18	12	9	5	5	7.84
1988—Chicago	American	32	197	12	10	.545	186	105	83	138	72	3.79
1989—Chicago	American	31	183⅓	11	14	.440	187	106	102	141	90	5.01
1990—Chicago	American	35	197	13	14	.481	177	111	101	161	86	4.61
Major League Totals—4 Years		101	587⅔	37	39	.487	568	334	295	445	253	4.52

Signed as free agent by Kansas City Royals' organization, July 22, 1983.
†Traded with Pitchers John Davis, Chuck Mount and Greg Hibbard to Chicago White Sox for Pitcher Floyd Bannister and Infielder Dave Cochrane, December 10, 1987.

MICHAEL IRVIN PEREZ
(Mike)

Born October 19, 1964, at Yauco, Puerto Rico.
Height, 6.00. Weight, 185.
Throws and bats righthanded.
Attended San Jose City College, San Jose, Calif.,
and Troy State University, Troy, Ala.

Major League saves: 1990 (1).
Led American Association in saves with 31 and games finished in relief with 50 in 1990.
Led Texas League in saves with 33 and games finished in relief with 51 in 1989.
Led Midwest League in saves with 41 and games finished in relief with 51 in 1987.

Year	Club	League	G.	IP.	W.	L.	Pct.	H.	R.	ER.	SO.	BB.	ERA.
1986—Johnson City	Ap'lachian	18	72⅔	3	5	.375	69	35	24	72	22	2.97
1987—Springfield	Midwest	58	84⅓	6	2	.750	47	12	8	119	21	0.85
1988—Arkansas	Texas	11	14⅓	1	3	.250	18	18	18	17	13	11.30
1988—St. Petersburg	Florida St.	35	43⅓	2	2	.500	24	12	10	45	16	2.08
1989—Arkansas	Texas	57	76⅔	4	6	.400	68	34	31	74	32	3.64
1990—Louisville	Am. Assoc.	•57	67⅓	7	7	.500	64	34	32	69	33	4.28
1990—St. Louis	National	13	13⅔	1	0	1.000	12	6	6	5	3	3.95
Major League Totals—1 Year		13	13⅔	1	0	1.000	12	6	6	5	3	3.95

Selected by St. Louis Cardinals' organization in 12th round of free-agent draft, June 2, 1986.

PASCUAL GROSS PEREZ

Born May 17, 1957, at San Cristobal, Dominican Republic.
Height, 6.03. Weight, 183.
Throws and bats righthanded.
Brother of Melido Perez, pitcher with Chicago White Sox; Vladimir Perez, pitcher in
New York Mets' organization; Dario Perez, pitcher in Kansas City Royals' organization;
Carlos Perez, pitcher in Montreal Expos' organization; and Valerio Perez,
pitcher in Kansas City Royals' organization, 1983 and 1984.

Pitched five-inning, 1-0 no-hit victory against Philadelphia Phillies, September 24, 1988.
Tied for National League lead in balks with 10 in 1988.
Led Western Carolinas League in balks with 6 in 1977.
Tied for American Association lead in shutouts with 2 in 1987.
Tied for Carolina League lead in shutouts with 5 in 1978.
Named American Association Pitcher of the Year, 1987.

Year	Club	League	G.	IP.	W.	L.	Pct.	H.	R.	ER.	SO.	BB.	ERA.
1976—Bradenton Pirates†	Gulf Coast	10	56	2	5	.286	51	41	29	34	35	4.66
1977—Charleston	W. Carol.	25	156	10	5	.667	153	80	69	96	60	3.98
1978—Salem	Carolina	24	152	11	7	.611	133	70	44	126	51	2.61
1978—Columbus	Int'national	1	5	0	0	.000	4	0	0	4	1	0.00
1979—Portland‡	P. Coast	20	103	9	7	.563	121	70	63	51	47	5.50
1980—Portland	P. Coast	24	160	12	10	.545	172	76	72	105	48	4.05
1980—Pittsburgh	National	2	12	0	1	.000	15	6	5	7	2	3.75
1981—Portland	P. Coast	5	31	1	2	.333	40	19	17	11	14	4.94
1981—Pittsburgh	National	17	86	2	7	.222	92	50	38	46	34	3.98
1982—Portland§	P. Coast	19	106⅓	4	9	.308	111	59	57	59	37	4.82
1982—Richmond	Int'national	5	43	5	0	1.000	32	7	6	27	8	1.26
1982—Atlanta	National	16	79⅓	4	4	.500	85	35	27	29	17	3.06
1983—Atlanta	National	33	215⅓	15	8	.652	213	88	82	144	51	3.43
1984—Atlanta x	National	30	211⅔	14	8	.636	208	96	88	145	51	3.74
1985—Atlanta yza	National	22	95⅓	1	13	.071	115	72	65	57	57	6.14
1986—					(Out of Organized Baseball)							
1987—Indianapolis	Am. Assoc.	19	133	9	7	.563	128	65	56	125	34	★3.79
1987—Montreal	National	10	70⅓	7	0	1.000	52	21	18	58	16	2.30
1988—Montreal b	National	27	188	12	8	.600	133	59	51	131	44	2.44
1988—Indianapolis	Am. Assoc.	2	7⅔	0	0	.000	4	1	1	7	4	1.17
1989—Montreal c	National	33	198⅓	9	13	.409	178	85	73	152	45	3.31
1990—New York d	American	3	14	1	2	.333	8	3	2	12	3	1.29
1990—Fort Lauderdale	Florida St.	1	3	0	0	.000	3	2	2	1	1	6.00
American League Totals—1 Year		3	14	1	2	.333	8	3	2	12	3	1.29
National League Totals—9 Years		190	1156⅓	64	62	.508	1091	512	447	769	317	3.48
Major League Totals—10 Years		193	1170⅓	65	64	.504	1099	515	449	781	320	3.45

Signed as free agent by Pittsburgh Pirates' organization, January 27, 1976.

†On suspended list, August 26 to August 28, 1976.
‡On disabled list, July 16 to August 14, 1979.
§Traded with a player to be named later to Atlanta Braves' organization for Pitcher Larry McWilliams, June 30, 1982; Atlanta organization acquired Shortstop Carlos Rios to complete deal, September 8, 1982.
xOn suspended list, April 3 to May 1, 1984.
yOn disabled list, May 5 to May 25, June 1 to June 22 and August 13 to September 3, 1985.
zOn suspended list, July 22, 1985; then transferred to restricted list, July 25 to August 4, 1985.
aReleased, April 1, 1986; signed by Indianapolis (Montreal Expos' organization), February 16, 1987.
bOn disabled list, May 8 to June 21, 1988; included rehabilitation disability assignment to Indianapolis, June 13 to June 21, 1988.
cGranted free agency, November 13, 1989; signed by New York Yankees, November 21, 1989.
dOn disabled list, April 26, 1990 through remainder of season; included rehabilitation disability assignment to Tampa, May 21 to May 31, 1990 (did not pitch there); and Fort Lauderdale, June 5 to June 10, 1990.

CHAMPIONSHIP SERIES RECORD

Year	Club	League	G.	IP.	W.	L.	Pct.	H.	R.	ER.	SO.	BB.	ERA.
1982—Atlanta		National	2	8⅔	0	1	.000	10	5	5	4	2	5.19

ALL-STAR GAME RECORD

Year	League	IP.	W.	L.	Pct.	H.	R.	ER.	SO.	BB.	ERA.
1983—National		⅔	0	0	.000	3	2	2	1	1	27.00

ANTONIO LLAMAS PEREZCHICA
(Tony)

Born April 20, 1966, at Mexicali, Mex.
Height, 5.11. Weight, 175.
Throws and bats righthanded.

Led Midwest League shortstops in total chances with 599 in 1985.

Year	Club	League	Pos.	G.	AB.	R.	H.	2B.	3B.	HR.	RBI.	B.A.	PO.	A.	E.	F.A.
1984—Everett		N'west	SS	33	119	10	23	6	1	0	10	.193	45	73	18	.868
1985—Clinton		Midw.	SS	127	452	54	109	21	●8	4	40	.241	★224	332	43	.928
1986—Fresno		Calif.	SS-3B	126	452	65	126	30	8	9	54	.279	224	303	42	.926
1987—Shreveport		Texas	SS-2B	89	332	44	106	24	1	11	47	.319	144	258	16	.962
1988—Phoenix		P. C.	2B-SS-OF	134	517	79	158	18	●10	9	64	.306	255	381	29	.956
1988—San Francisco		Nat.	2B	7	8	1	1	0	0	0	1	.125	5	5	0	1.000
1989—Phoenix†		P. C.	2B-SS	94	307	40	71	11	3	8	33	.231	155	224	8	.979
1990—San Francisco		Nat.	2B-SS	4	3	1	1	0	0	0	0	.333	2	0	0	1.000
1990—Phoenix		P. C.	2B-SS-3B	105	392	55	105	22	6	9	49	.268	199	325	22	.960
Major League Totals—2 Years				11	11	2	2	0	0	0	1	.182	7	5	0	1.000

Selected by San Francisco Giants' organization in 3rd round of free-agent draft, June 4, 1984.
†On disabled list, April 21 to May 5 and August 19 to August 31, 1989.

GERALD JUNE PERRY

Born October 30, 1960, at Savannah, Ga.
Height, 6.00. Weight, 190.
Throws right and bats lefthanded.
Nephew of Dan Driessen, first baseman with Cincinnati Reds, Montreal Expos, San Francisco Giants, Houston Astros and St. Louis Cardinals, 1973 through 1987.

Major League stolen bases: 1984 (15), 1985 (9), 1987 (42), 1988 (29), 1989 (10), 1990 (17). Total—122.
Led International League in game-winning RBIs with 17 and tied for lead in intentional bases on balls received with 8 in 1986.
Led Carolina League first basemen in double plays with 109 in 1980.
Led Gulf Coast League first basemen in double plays with 46 in 1978.

Year	Club	League	Pos.	G.	AB.	R.	H.	2B.	3B.	HR.	RBI.	B.A.	PO.	A.	E.	F.A.
1978—Bradenton Brav...		Gulf C.	1B	★55	191	32	51	★12	3	1	26	.267	★479	★37	6	★.989
1979—Greenwood		W. Car.	1B	109	400	69	133	17	4	9	71	★.333	881	59	19	.980
1980—Durham		Carol.	1B	138	497	102	124	19	5	15	92	.249	★1296	93	16	.989
1981—Savannah		South.	1B	137	476	71	132	18	3	19	84	.277	1221	86	18	.986
1982—Richmond		Int.	1B	133	492	94	146	22	4	15	92	.297	1110	94	●17	.986
1983—Richmond		Int.	1B	113	423	81	133	21	8	13	71	.314	943	88	11	.989
1983—Atlanta		Nat.	1B-OF	27	39	5	14	2	0	1	6	.359	55	0	1	.982
1984—Atlanta		Nat.	1B-OF	122	347	52	92	12	2	7	47	.265	550	28	12	.980
1985—Atlanta		Nat.	1B-OF	110	238	22	51	5	0	3	13	.214	541	37	9	.985
1986—Richmond		Int.	OF-1B	107	384	69	125	30	5	10	75	.326	394	25	7	.984
1986—Atlanta		Nat.	OF-1B	29	70	6	19	2	0	2	11	.271	24	1	2	.926
1987—Atlanta		Nat.	1B-OF	142	533	77	144	35	2	12	74	.270	1297	72	14	.990
1988—Atlanta†		Nat.	1B	141	547	61	164	29	1	8	74	.300	1282	106	●17	.988
1989—Atlanta‡§		Nat.	1B	72	266	24	67	11	0	4	21	.252	618	51	9	.987
1990—Kansas City x		Amer.	1B	133	465	57	118	22	2	8	57	.254	394	40	6	.986
American League Totals—1 Year				133	465	57	118	22	2	8	57	.254	394	40	6	.986
National League Totals—7 Years				643	2040	247	551	96	5	37	246	.270	4367	295	64	.986
Major League Totals—8 Years				776	2505	304	669	118	7	45	303	.267	4761	335	70	.986

Selected by Atlanta Braves' organization in 11th round of free-agent draft, June 6, 1978.
†On disabled list, June 19 to July 4, 1988.
‡On disabled list, June 6 to June 21 and July 10, 1989 through remainder of season.
§Traded with Pitcher Jim Lemasters to Kansas City Royals for Pitchers Charlie Leibrandt and Rick Luecken, December 15, 1989.
xGranted free agency, November 5, 1990; signed by St. Louis Cardinals, December 13, 1990.

Year	League	Pos.	AB.	R.	H.	2B.	3B.	HR.	RBI.	B.A.	PO.	A.	E.	F.A.
1988—National		PH	1	0	0	0	0	0	0	.000	0	0	0	.000

WILLIAM PATRICK PERRY
(Pat)

Born February 4, 1959, at Taylorville, Ill.
Height, 6.01. Weight, 190.
Throws and bats lefthanded.
Attended Lincoln Land Community College, Springfield, Ill.

Major League saves: 1986 (2), 1987 (2), 1988 (1), 1989 (1). Total—6.
Tied for Gulf Coast League lead in shutouts with 2 in 1978.

Year	Club	League	G.	IP.	W.	L.	Pct.	H.	R.	ER.	SO.	BB.	ERA.
1978—Sarasota Astros	Gulf Coast	12	35	2	4	.333	29	15	9	35	14	2.31
1979—Daytona Beach	Florida St.	12	51	2	3	.400	64	31	30	30	16	5.29
1979—Sarasota Astros	Gulf Coast	9	49	3	1	.750	55	21	20	24	16	3.67
1980—Daytona Beach	Florida St.	22	115	9	5	.643	121	51	38	54	46	2.97
1981—Columbus	Southern	27	51	3	1	.750	54	40	36	35	38	6.35
1981—Daytona Beach	Florida St.	9	20	2	0	1.000	11	6	6	22	7	2.70
1982—Columbus†	Southern	22	37⅔	4	0	1.000	32	19	17	28	18	4.06
1983—Columbus‡§	Southern	11	49	5	2	.714	60	30	22	27	21	4.04
1983—Buffalo x	Eastern	4	5⅓	0	0	.000	8	5	4	4	4	6.75
1983—Springfield	Midwest	6	24½	1	1	.500	17	6	6	31	5	2.22
1984—Arkansas	Texas	25	48⅔	4	2	.667	34	8	6	51	17	1.11
1984—Louisville	Am. Assoc.	21	44⅔	4	3	.571	35	12	11	43	21	2.22
1985—Louisville	Am. Assoc.	45	91	4	3	.571	56	33	24	63	39	2.37
1985—St. Louis	National	6	12⅓	1	0	1.000	3	0	0	6	3	0.00
1986—St. Louis	National	46	68⅔	2	3	.400	59	31	29	34	34	3.80
1986—Louisville	Am. Assoc.	5	11	1	0	1.000	8	6	4	7	6	3.27
1987—St. Louis y-Cincinnati	National	57	81	5	2	.714	60	34	32	39	25	3.56
1988—Cincinnati z-Chicago a	National	47	58⅔	4	4	.500	61	32	27	35	16	4.14
1988—Iowa	Am. Assoc.	2	3	0	0	.000	0	0	0	4	0	0.00
1989—Chicago b	National	19	35⅔	0	1	.000	23	8	7	20	16	1.77
1989—Iowa c	Am. Assoc.	5	4⅓	1	0	1.000	3	3	3	4	6	6.23
1990—Bakersfield d	California	3	5	0	0	.000	3	3	2	7	1	3.60
1990—Los Angeles e	National	7	6⅔	0	0	.000	9	7	6	2	5	8.10
Major League Totals—6 Years		182	263	12	10	.545	215	112	101	131	99	3.46

Selected by Houston Astros' organization in 2nd round of free-agent draft, January 10, 1978.
†On disabled list, May 6 to May 24 and August 1, 1982 through remainder of season.
‡On disabled list, May 24 to June 15, 1983.
§Released, June 24, 1983; signed by Buffalo (Cleveland Indians' organization), July 1, 1983.
xReleased, July 12, 1983; signed by Springfield (St. Louis Cardinals' organization), August 3, 1983.
yTraded to Cincinnati Reds for a player to be named later, August 31, 1987; St. Louis Cardinals acquired Pitcher Scott Terry to complete deal, September 3, 1987.
zTraded to Chicago Cubs for First Baseman Leon Durham and cash, May 19, 1988.
aOn disabled list, August 20 to September 10, 1988.
bOn disabled list, June 17 to September 29, 1989; included rehabilitation disability assignment to Iowa, July 14 to July 27, 1989.
cReleased, December 13, 1989; signed by Los Angeles Dodgers, January 26, 1990.
dOn Los Angeles disabled list, March 31 to May 22 and June 11 to September 1, 1990; included rehabilitation disability assignment to Bakersfield, May 13 to May 21, 1990.
eGranted free agency, November 16, 1990.

ADAM CHARLES PETERSON

Born December 11, 1965, at Long Beach, Calif.
Height, 6.03. Weight, 190.
Throws and bats righthanded.

Tied for Pacific Coast League lead in shutouts with 2 in 1990.
Tied for Pacific Coast League lead in complete games with 6 in 1989.

Year	Club	League	G.	IP.	W.	L.	Pct.	H.	R.	ER.	SO.	BB.	ERA.
1984—Sarasota White Sox	Gulf Coast	12	43	1	4	.200	49	39	26	31	19	5.44
1985—Niagara Falls	NYP	14	92⅓	7	6	.538	74	39	31	79	34	3.02
1986—Peninsula	Carolina	24	147	9	8	.529	150	92	75	84	58	4.59
1986—Birmingham	Southern	6	32⅓	1	3	.250	34	16	15	21	16	4.18
1987—Birmingham	Southern	26	170⅔	12	9	.571	165	79	74	124	73	3.90
1987—Chicago	American	1	4	0	0	.000	8	6	6	1	3	13.50
1988—Vancouver	P. Coast	28	171	14	7	.667	161	69	63	103	81	3.32
1988—Chicago	American	2	6	0	1	.000	6	9	9	5	6	13.50
1989—Vancouver	P. Coast	25	172	14	5	.737	141	60	52	116	71	2.72
1989—Chicago	American	3	5⅓	0	1	.000	13	9	9	3	2	15.19
1990—Vancouver	P. Coast	6	43	4	1	.800	26	11	10	30	15	2.09
1990—Chicago	American	20	85	2	5	.286	90	46	43	29	26	4.55
Major League Totals—4 Years		26	100⅓	2	7	.222	117	70	67	38	37	6.01

Selected by Chicago White Sox' organization in 5th round of free-agent draft, June 4, 1984.

EUGENE JAMES PETRALLI JR.

Name pronounced Puh-TRA-lee.

(Geno)

Born September 25, 1959, at Sacramento, Calif.
Height, 6.01. Weight, 190.
Throws right and bats lefthanded.
Attended Sacramento City College, Sacramento, Calif.
Son of Gene Petralli, minor league first baseman, 1948 through 1951 and 1953.

Holds modern major league record for most passed balls, season (35), 1987.

Shares modern major league record for most passed balls, game (6), August 30, 1987; most passed balls, inning (4), August 22, 1987, seventh inning.

Major League stolen bases: 1983 (1), 1985 (1), 1986 (3). Total—5.

Led American League in passed balls with 35 in 1987 and 20 in both 1988 and 1990.

Led International League catchers in putouts with 633, assists with 86, errors with 19, double plays with 10 and total chances with 738 in 1982.

Tied for Pioneer League lead in passed balls with 27 in 1978.

Year	Club	League	Pos.	G.	AB.	R.	H.	2B.	3B.	HR.	RBI.	B.A.	PO.	A.	E.	F.A.
1978—Medicine Hat†	Pion.		C-3B	65	242	42	68	14	5	2	40	.281	238	68	19	.942
1979—Dunedin†‡	Fla. St.		C-3B-OF	52	184	18	53	13	0	1	24	.288	206	42	5	.980
1979—Syracuse†	Int.		C	18	56	6	13	0	1	0	7	.232	67	12	1	.988
1980—Knoxville†	South.		C-1B-OF	116	382	42	109	20	2	3	38	.285	569	82	18	.973
1981—Syracuse†§	Int.		C	45	151	17	40	11	0	0	16	.265	188	30	6	.973
1982—Syracuse†	Int.		C-1B-3B	126	395	57	114	19	3	9	58	.289	674	89	20	.974
1982—Toronto†	Amer.		C-3B	16	44	3	16	2	0	0	1	.364	51	4	1	.982
1983—Syracuse†	Int.		C-1B	104	327	39	80	9	2	3	40	.245	541	68	7	.989
1983—Toronto†	Amer.		C	6	4	0	0	0	0	0	0	.000	7	0	0	1.000
1984—Toronto† x	Amer.		C	3	3	0	0	0	0	0	0	.000	1	1	0	1.000
1984—Maine† y	Int.		C-O-1	23	83	9	18	3	0	0	5	.217	122	11	6	.957
1985—Maine z	Int.		C	2	7	0	1	0	0	0	1	.143	12	1	1	.929
1985—Oklahoma City	A. A.		C	27	80	11	21	8	0	1	5	.263	108	14	3	.976
1985—Texas†	Amer.		C	42	100	7	27	2	0	0	11	.270	179	16	2	.990
1986—Texas†	Amer.		C-3B	69	137	17	35	9	3	2	18	.255	163	14	4	.978
1987—Texas†	Amer.		C-3-1-2-O	101	202	28	61	11	2	7	31	.302	370	34	5	.988
1988—Texas	Amer.		C-3-1-2	129	351	35	99	14	2	7	36	.282	421	54	10	.979
1989—Texas a	Amer.		C	70	184	18	56	7	0	4	23	.304	258	15	3	.989
1989—Tulsa	Texas		C	5	13	2	3	0	0	1	1	.231	6	1	0	1.000
1990—Texas	Amer.		C-3B-2B	133	325	28	83	13	1	0	21	.255	602	46	6	.991
Major League Totals—9 Years				569	1350	136	377	58	8	20	141	.279	2052	184	31	.986

Selected by Toronto Blue Jays' organization in 3rd round of free-agent draft, January 10, 1978.

†Switch-hitter.

‡On suspended list, April 13 to April 27, 1979.

§On disabled list, May 6 to June 1 and June 28 to August 18, 1981.

xSold to Maine (Cleveland Indians' organization), May 8, 1984.

yOn disabled list, July 11, 1984 through remainder of season.

zReleased, April 23, 1985; signed by Oklahoma City (Texas Rangers' organization), May 17, 1985.

aOn disabled list, May 27 to June 11 and June 27 to August 19, 1989; included rehabilitation disability assignment to Tulsa, August 14 to August 19, 1989.

DANIEL JOSEPH PETRY

Name pronounced PEE-tree.

(Dan)

Born November 13, 1958, at Palo Alto, Calif.
Height, 6.04. Weight, 215.
Throws and bats righthanded.

Led American League pitchers in games started with 38 and home runs allowed with 37 in 1983.

Year	Club	League	G.	IP.	W.	L.	Pct.	H.	R.	ER.	SO.	BB.	ERA.
1976—Bristol	Ap'lachian	14	79	2	3	.400	54	42	33	51	⋆56	3.76
1977—Lakeland	Florida St.	25	145	10	11	.476	139	68	55	68	68	3.41
1978—Montgomery	Southern	14	92	6	7	.462	70	38	25	69	41	2.45
1978—Evansville	Am. Assoc.	13	71	4	3	.571	59	38	36	50	33	4.56
1979—Evansville	Am. Assoc.	15	91	4	3	.571	92	60	49	55	37	4.85
1979—Detroit	American	15	98	6	5	.545	90	46	43	43	33	3.95
1980—Evansville	Am. Assoc.	4	30	2	0	1.000	21	11	9	16	12	2.70
1980—Detroit	American	27	165	10	9	.526	156	82	72	88	83	3.93
1981—Detroit	American	23	141	10	9	.526	115	53	47	79	57	3.00
1982—Detroit	American	35	246	15	9	.625	220	98	88	132	100	3.22
1983—Detroit	American	38	266⅓	19	11	.633	256	126	116	122	99	3.92
1984—Detroit	American	35	233⅓	18	8	.692	231	94	84	144	66	3.24
1985—Detroit	American	34	238⅔	15	13	.536	190	98	89	109	81	3.36
1986—Detroit†	American	20	116	5	10	.333	122	78	60	56	53	4.66
1986—Lakeland	Florida St.	3	10⅓	1	1	.500	13	8	8	6	1	6.97
1987—Detroit‡	American	30	134⅔	9	7	.563	148	101	84	93	76	5.61
1988—California§	American	22	139⅔	3	9	.250	139	70	68	64	59	4.38
1988—Palm Springs	California	3	15	1	2	.333	19	14	11	11	11	6.60
1989—California x	American	19	51	3	2	.600	53	32	31	21	23	5.47
1990—Detroit y	American	32	149⅔	10	9	.526	148	78	74	73	77	4.45
Major League Totals—12 Years		330	1979⅓	123	101	.549	1868	956	856	1024	807	3.89

Selected by Detroit Tigers' organization in 4th round of free-agent draft, June 8, 1976.
†On disabled list, June 6 to August 19, 1986; included rehabilitation disability assignment to Lakeland, July 30 to August 19, 1986.
‡Traded to California Angels for Outfielder Gary Pettis, December 5, 1987.
§On disabled list, June 26 to August 30, 1988; included rehabilitation disability assignment to Palm Springs, August 13 to August 30, 1988.
xGranted free agency, November 13, 1989; signed by Toledo (Detroit Tigers' organization), January 22, 1990.
yGranted free agency, November 5, 1990; re-signed by Tigers, December 19, 1990.

CHAMPIONSHIP SERIES RECORD

Year Club	League	G.	IP.	W.	L.	Pct.	H.	R.	ER.	SO.	BB.	ERA.
1984—Detroit	American	1	7	0	0	.000	4	2	2	4	1	2.57
1987—Detroit	American	1	3⅓	0	0	.000	1	1	0	1	0	0.00
Championship Series Totals—2 Years		2	10⅓	0	0	.000	5	3	2	5	1	1.74

WORLD SERIES RECORD

Year Club	League	G.	IP.	W.	L.	Pct.	H.	R.	ER.	SO.	BB.	ERA.
1984—Detroit	American	2	8	0	1	.000	14	8	8	4	5	9.00

ALL-STAR GAME RECORD

Year League	IP.	W.	L.	Pct.	H.	R.	ER.	SO.	BB.	ERA.
1985—American	⅓	0	0	.000	0	2	2	1	3	54.00

GARY GEORGE PETTIS

Born April 3, 1958, at Oakland, Calif.
Height, 6.01. Weight, 160.
Throws right and bats left and righthanded.
Attended Laney College, Oakland, Calif.
Brother of Stacey Pettis, outfielder in Pittsburgh Pirates' and California Angels' organizations,
1981 through 1987.

Shares major league record for most putouts by outfielder, game (12), June 4, 1985 (15 innings).
Shares American League record for most chances accepted by outfielder, game (12), June 4, 1985 (15 innings).
Major League stolen bases: 1983 (8), 1984 (48), 1985 (56), 1986 (50), 1987 (24), 1988 (44), 1989 (43), 1990 (38). Total—311.
Led American League outfielders in total chances with 478 in 1986.
Led Pacific Coast League in stolen bases with 53 in 1982.
Named outfielder on THE SPORTING NEWS American League All-Star fielding team, 1985, 1986 and 1988 through 1990.

Year Club	League	Pos.	G.	AB.	R.	H.	2B.	3B.	HR.	RBI.	B.A.	PO.	A.	E.	F.A.
1979—Idaho Falls	Pion.	3B-SS-2B	50	198	39	63	10	●10	3	26	.318	59	94	24	.864
1980—Salinas	Calif.	OF-SS-3B	118	393	71	94	15	3	2	31	.239	206	36	13	.949
1981—Holyoke	East.	OF	120	421	77	112	8	9	3	36	.266	237	5	4	.984
1982—Spokane	P. C.	OF	133	528	108	152	22	★14	1	59	.288	★345	9	6	★.983
1982—California	Amer.	OF	10	5	5	1	0	0	1	1	.200	5	1	0	1.000
1983—Edmonton	P. C.	OF	132	529	★138	151	27	8	11	52	.285	325	10	5	.985
1983—California	Amer.	OF	22	85	19	25	2	3	3	6	.294	49	5	1	.982
1984—California	Amer.	OF	140	397	63	90	11	6	2	29	.227	337	11	6	.983
1985—California†	Amer.	OF	125	443	67	114	10	8	1	32	.257	368	13	4	.990
1986—California	Amer.	OF	154	539	93	139	23	4	5	58	.258	★462	9	7	.985
1987—California	Amer.	OF	133	394	49	82	13	2	1	17	.208	344	2	7	.980
1987—Edmonton‡	P. C.	OF	8	16	6	2	1	0	0	1	.125	7	1	1	.889
1988—Detroit§	Amer.	OF	129	458	65	96	14	4	3	36	.210	361	5	5	.987
1989—Toledo x	Int.	OF	6	21	6	7	1	0	1	3	.333	9	1	0	1.000
1989—Detroit y	Amer.	OF	119	444	77	114	8	6	1	18	.257	325	1	4	.988
1990—Texas	Amer.	OF	136	423	66	101	16	8	3	31	.239	285	10	2	.993
Major League Totals—9 Years			968	3188	504	762	97	41	20	228	.239	2536	57	36	.986

Selected by California Angels' organization in 6th round of free-agent draft, January 9, 1979.
†On disabled list, July 5 to July 31, 1985.
‡Traded to Detroit Tigers for Pitcher Dan Petry, December 5, 1987.
§On disabled list, July 30 to August 15, 1988.
xOn disabled list, March 26 to May 15, 1989; included rehabilitation disability assignment to Toledo, May 6 to May 15, 1989.
yGranted free agency, November 13, 1989; signed by Texas Rangers, November 24, 1989.

CHAMPIONSHIP SERIES RECORD

Shares Championship Series record for most sacrifice hits, series (2), 1986.

Year Club	League	Pos.	G.	AB.	R.	H.	2B.	3B.	HR.	RBI.	B.A.	PO.	A.	E.	F.A.
1986—California	Amer.	OF	7	26	4	9	1	0	1	4	.346	28	0	1	.966

KENNETH ALLEN PHELPS
(Ken)

Born August 6, 1954, at Seattle, Wash.
Height, 6.01. Weight, 204.
Throws and bats lefthanded.
Attended Washington State University, Pullman, Wash.; Mesa Community College,
Mesa, Ariz., and received bachelor of science degree in physical education from
Arizona State University, Tempe, Ariz.

Major League stolen bases: 1984 (3), 1985 (2), 1986 (2), 1987 (1), 1988 (1), 1990 (1). Total—10.
Led American Association in total bases with 320 in 1982.
Led American Association in bases on balls received with 128 in 1980 and 108 in 1982.
Led Southern League in bases on balls received with 99 in 1978.
Tied for American Association lead in intentional bases on balls received with 12 in 1982.
Led American Association first basemen in double plays with 111 in 1979, 103 in 1980 and 108 in 1982.
Named American Association Most Valuable Player, 1982.

Year Club League	Pos.	G.	AB.	R.	H.	2B.	3B.	HR.	RBI.	B.A.	PO.	A.	E.	F.A.
1976—Sarasota Royals... Gulf C.	1B	28	98	20	29	6	3	3	28	.296	166	16	2	.989
1976—Waterloo................ Midw.	1B	25	72	12	19	8	0	1	10	.264	205	12	3	.986
1977—Daytona Beach .... Fla. St.	1B	40	145	22	50	7	0	5	32	.345	341	31	8	.979
1977—Jacksonville......... South.	1B	81	262	30	51	6	3	5	40	.195	691	38	10	.986
1978—Jacksonville.......... South.	1B	124	381	65	94	20	0	16	61	.247	1028	66	16	.986
1979—Omaha.................... A. A.	1B	130	430	71	114	26	3	20	77	.265	★1129	80	★13	.989
1980—Omaha.................... A. A.	1B	133	442	80	130	30	3	23	72	.294	★1154	51	12	.990
1980—Kansas City........... Amer.	1B	3	4	0	0	0	0	0	0	.000	14	0	0	1.000
1981—Kansas City........... Amer.	1B	21	22	1	3	0	1	0	1	.136	4	1	0	1.000
1981—Omaha†................. A. A.	1B	19	66	9	22	8	1	5	21	.333	169	15	2	.989
1982—Wichita................. A. A.	1B	132	453	112	151	23	4	★46	★141	.333	1047	74	14	.988
1982—Montreal‡............. Nat.	PH	10	8	0	2	0	0	0	0	.250	0	0	0	.000
1983—Seattle.................... Amer.	1B	50	127	10	30	4	1	7	16	.236	164	16	0	1.000
1983—Salt Lake City....... P. C.	1B	74	270	81	92	29	6	24	82	.341	535	37	7	.988
1984—Seattle§................. Amer.	1B	101	290	52	70	9	0	24	51	.241	72	4	1	.987
1984—Salt Lake City....... P. C.	1B	12	45	7	14	3	0	3	13	.311	25	5	0	1.000
1985—Seattle.................... Amer.	1B	61	116	18	24	3	0	9	24	.207	31	2	0	1.000
1986—Seattle.................... Amer.	1B	125	344	69	85	16	4	24	64	.247	487	34	9	.983
1987—Seattle.................... Amer.	1B	120	332	68	86	13	1	27	68	.259	8	0	0	1.000
1988—Sea. x-N.Y............. Amer.	1B	117	297	54	78	13	0	24	54	.263	18	2	1	.952
1989—N.Y.y-Oak.z.......... Amer.	1B	97	194	26	47	4	0	7	29	.242	56	2	1	.983
1990—Oak.a-Cleve.b........ Amer.	1B	56	120	10	18	2	0	1	6	.150	111	10	1	.992
American League Totals—10 Years		751	1846	308	441	64	7	123	313	.239	965	71	13	.988
National League Totals—1 Year.............		10	8	0	2	0	0	0	0	.250	0	0	0	.000
Major League Totals—11 Years..............		761	1854	308	443	64	7	123	313	.239	965	71	13	.988

Selected by Atlanta Braves' organization in 8th round of free-agent draft, June 6, 1972.
Selected by New York Yankees' organization in 1st round (11th player selected) of free-agent draft, January 9, 1974.
Selected by Philadelphia Phillies' organization in secondary phase of free-agent draft, June 5, 1974.
Selected by Kansas City Royals' organization in 15th round of free-agent draft, June 8, 1976.
†Traded to Montreal Expos' organization for Pitcher Grant Jackson, January 19, 1982.
‡Sold to Seattle Mariners, March 31, 1983.
§On disabled list, April 7 to May 18, 1984; included rehabilitation disability assignment to Salt Lake City, May 4 to May 18, 1984.
xTraded to New York Yankees for Outfielder Jay Buhner, Pitcher Rich Balabon and a player to be named later, July 21, 1988; Seattle Mariners acquired Pitcher Troy Evers to complete deal, October 12, 1988.
yTraded to Oakland Athletics for Pitcher Scott Holcomb, August 30, 1989.
zGranted free agency, November 13, 1989; re-signed by Athletics, December 8, 1989.
aSold to Cleveland Indians, June 17, 1990.
bGranted free agency, November 5, 1990.

CHAMPIONSHIP SERIES RECORD

Year Club League	Pos.	G.	AB.	R.	H.	2B.	3B.	HR.	RBI.	B.A.	PO.	A.	E.	F.A.
1989—Oakland................. Amer.	PH	1	1	0	1	1	0	0	0	1.000	0	0	0	.000

WORLD SERIES RECORD

Year Club League	Pos.	G.	AB.	R.	H.	2B.	3B.	HR.	RBI.	B.A.	PO.	A.	E.	F.A.
1989—Oakland................. Amer.	PH	1	1	0	0	0	0	0	0	.000	0	0	0	.000

KEITH ANTHONY PHILLIPS
(Tony)

Born April 25, 1959, at Atlanta, Ga.
Height, 5.10. Weight, 175.
Throws right and bats right and lefthanded.
Attended New Mexico Military Institute, Roswell, N.M.

Shares major league record for most assists by second baseman, nine-inning game (12), July 6, 1986.
Major League stolen bases: 1982 (2), 1983 (16), 1984 (10), 1985 (3), 1986 (15), 1987 (7), 1989 (3), 1990 (19). Total—75.
Hit for the cycle, May 16, 1986.
Led Eastern League in being hit by pitch with 10 in 1981.
Led Southern League in bases on balls received with 98 in 1980.

Year Club League	Pos.	G.	AB.	R.	H.	2B.	3B.	HR.	RBI.	B.A.	PO.	A.	E.	F.A.
1978—W. Palm Beach†.. Fla. St.	3B-SS-2B	32	54	8	9	0	0	0	3	.167	13	33	5	.902
1978—Jamestown............ NYP	SS-2B-3B	52	152	24	29	5	2	1	17	.191	73	146	16	.932
1979—W. Palm Beach.... Fla. St.	2B-SS	60	203	30	47	5	1	0	18	.232	120	156	21	.929
1979—Memphis................ South.	SS-2B	52	156	31	44	4	2	3	11	.282	68	134	18	.914
1980—Memphis‡§........... South.	★SS-2B	136	502	100	125	18	4	5	41	.249	226	408	★42	.938
1981—West Haven .... East.	SS	131	461	79	114	25	3	9	64	.247	200	391	★33	.947
1981—Tacoma................. P. C.	2B-SS	4	11	1	4	1	0	0	2	.364	8	10	0	1.000
1982—Tacoma................. P. C.	SS	86	300	76	89	18	5	4	47	.297	138	236	30	.926
1982—Oakland................. Amer.	SS	40	81	11	17	2	2	0	8	.210	46	95	7	.953
1983—Oakland................. Amer.	SS-2B-3B	148	412	54	102	12	3	4	35	.248	218	383	30	.952

Year Club	League	Pos.	G.	AB.	R.	H.	2B.	3B.	HR.	RBI.	B.A.	PO.	A.	E.	F.A.
1984—Oakland	Amer.	SS-2B-OF	154	451	62	120	24	3	4	37	.266	255	391	28	.958
1985—Tacoma x	P. C.	3B-2B	20	69	9	9	1	0	0	5	.130	15	36	4	.927
1985—Oakland	Amer.	3B-2B	42	161	23	45	12	2	4	17	.280	54	103	3	.981
1986—Oakland y	Amer.	2-3-O-S	118	441	76	113	14	5	5	52	.256	191	326	13	.975
1987—Oakland z	Amer.	2-3-S-O	111	379	48	91	20	0	10	46	.240	179	299	14	.972
1987—Tacoma a	P. C.	2B-3B	7	26	5	9	2	1	1	6	.346	8	10	0	1.000
1988—Tacoma	P. C.	S-O-2-3	16	59	10	16	0	0	2	8	.271	25	27	2	.963
1988—Oakland b	Amer.	3-O-2-S-1	79	212	32	43	8	4	2	17	.203	84	80	10	.943
1989—Oakland c	Amer.	2-3-S-O-1	143	451	48	118	15	6	4	47	.262	184	321	15	.971
1990—Detroit	Amer.	3-2-S-O	152	573	97	144	23	5	8	55	.251	180	368	23	.960
Major League Totals—9 Years			987	3161	451	793	130	30	41	314	.251	1391	2366	143	.963

Selected by Seattle Mariners' organization in 16th round of free-agent draft, June 7, 1977.

Selected by Montreal Expos' organization in secondary phase of free-agent draft, January 10, 1978.

†On temporary inactive list, April 11 to May 4, 1978.

‡Traded with cash to San Diego Padres for First Baseman Willie Montanez, August 31, 1980.

§Traded with Pitcher Eric Mustad and Infielder Kevin Bell to Oakland A's organization for Pitcher Bob Lacey and Pitcher Roy Moretti, March 27, 1981.

xOn Oakland disabled list, March 26 to August 22, 1985; included rehabilitation disability assignment to Tacoma, July 30 to August 5 and August 7 to August 20, 1985.

yOn disabled list, August 14 to October 3, 1986.

zOn disabled list, July 12 to August 28, 1987; included rehabilitation disability assignment to Tacoma, August 20 to August 28, 1987.

aReleased, December 21, 1987; re-signed by Athletics, March 9, 1988.

bOn disabled list, May 18 to July 8, 1988; included rehabilitation disability assignment to Tacoma, June 16 to July 4, 1988.

cGranted free agency, November 13, 1989; signed by Detroit Tigers, December 5, 1989.

CHAMPIONSHIP SERIES RECORD

Year Club	League	Pos.	G.	AB.	R.	H.	2B.	3B.	HR.	RBI.	B.A.	PO.	A.	E.	F.A.
1988—Oakland	Amer.	OF-2B	2	7	0	2	1	0	0	0	.286	10	0	0	1.000
1989—Oakland	Amer.	2B-3B	5	18	1	3	1	0	0	1	.167	4	14	0	1.000
Championship Series Totals—2 Years			7	25	1	5	2	0	0	1	.200	14	14	0	1.000

WORLD SERIES RECORD

Year Club	League	Pos.	G.	AB.	R.	H.	2B.	3B.	HR.	RBI.	B.A.	PO.	A.	E.	F.A.
1988—Oakland	Amer.	OF-2B	2	4	1	1	0	0	0	0	.250	3	5	0	1.000
1989—Oakland	Amer.	2B-3B-OF	4	17	2	4	1	0	1	3	.235	8	15	0	1.000
World Series Totals—2 Years			6	21	3	5	1	0	1	3	.238	11	20	0	1.000

JEFFREY MARK PICO
(Jeff)

Born February 12, 1966, at Antioch, Calif.
Height, 6.02. Weight, 170.
Throws and bats righthanded.

Shares major league record for pitching shutout, first major league game, May 31, 1988.

Major League saves: 1988 (1), 1989 (2), 1990 (2). Total—5.

Tied for Appalachian League lead in games started by pitchers with 13 in 1984.

Year Club	League	G.	IP.	W.	L.	Pct.	H.	R.	ER.	SO.	BB.	ERA.
1984—Pikeville	Ap'lachian	13	73⅓	2	3	.400	65	35	27	46	29	3.31
1985—Peoria	Midwest	27	179⅓	11	10	.524	186	76	61	109	56	3.06
1986—Winston-Salem	Carolina	27	166	12	8	.600	165	75	59	116	54	3.20
1987—Pittsfield	Eastern	12	79	4	4	.500	74	38	34	52	23	3.87
1987—Iowa	Am. Assoc.	16	93⅔	6	5	.545	118	57	50	45	27	4.80
1988—Iowa	Am. Assoc.	10	68⅓	5	2	.714	67	28	17	40	18	2.24
1988—Chicago	National	29	112⅔	6	7	.462	108	57	52	57	37	4.15
1989—Chicago	National	53	90⅔	3	1	.750	99	43	38	38	31	3.77
1989—Iowa	Am. Assoc.	2	6⅓	1	0	1.000	5	0	0	2	0	0.00
1990—Chicago	National	31	92	4	4	.500	120	53	49	37	37	4.79
1990—Iowa	Am. Assoc.	1	4⅔	0	0	.000	7	3	3	1	0	5.79
Major League Totals—3 Years		113	295⅓	13	12	.520	327	153	139	132	105	4.24

Selected by Chicago Cubs' organization in 13th round of free-agent draft, June 4, 1984.

PHILLIP ALAN PLANTIER
(Phil)

Born January 27, 1969, at Manchester, N.H.
Height, 6.00. Weight, 175.
Throws right and bats lefthanded.

Led International League batters in slugging percentage with .549 and strikeouts with 148 in 1990.

Led Carolina League in total bases with 242, slugging percentage with .546 and tied for lead in intentional bases on balls received with 7 in 1989.

Named Carolina League Most Valuable Player, 1989.

Year Club	League	Pos.	G.	AB.	R.	H.	2B.	3B.	HR.	RBI.	B.A.	PO.	A.	E.	F.A.
1987—Elmira	NYP	3B	28	80	7	14	2	0	2	9	.175	12	34	12	.793
1988—Winter Haven	Fla. St.	OF-3B-2B	111	337	29	81	13	1	4	32	.240	106	72	18	.908

Year	Club	League	Pos.	G.	AB.	R.	H.	2B.	3B.	HR.	RBI.	B.A.	PO.	A.	E.	F.A.
1989—Lynchburg............	Carol.		OF	131	443	73	133	26	1	*27	*105	.300	140	10	8	.949
1990—Pawtucket............	Int.		OF	123	430	83	109	22	3	*33	79	.253	245	8	*14	.948
1990—Boston..................	Amer.		OF	14	15	1	2	1	0	0	3	.133	0	0	0	.000
Major League Totals—1 Year..................				14	15	1	2	1	0	0	3	.133	0	0	0	.000

Selected by Boston Red Sox' organization in 11th round of free-agent draft, June 2, 1987.

DANIEL THOMAS PLESAC
(Dan)

Born February 4, 1962, at Gary, Ind.
Height, 6.05. Weight, 215.
Throws and bats lefthanded.
Attended North Carolina State University, Raleigh, N.C.

Major League saves: 1986 (14), 1987 (23), 1988 (30), 1989 (24). Total—124.
Led Appalachian League pitchers in balks with 3 and tied for lead in games started with 14 in 1983.

Year	Club	League	G.	IP.	W.	L.	Pct.	H.	R.	ER.	SO.	BB.	ERA.
1983—Paintsville	Ap'lachian	14	82⅓	*9	1	*.900	76	44	32	*85	57	3.50
1984—Stockton	California	16	108⅓	6	6	.500	106	51	40	101	50	3.32
1984—El Paso	Texas	7	39	2	2	.500	43	19	15	24	16	3.46
1985—El Paso.........................	Texas	25	150⅓	12	5	.706	171	91	83	128	68	4.97
1986—Milwaukee....................	American	51	91	10	7	.588	81	34	30	75	29	2.97
1987—Milwaukee....................	American	57	79⅓	5	6	.455	63	30	23	89	23	2.61
1988—Milwaukee....................	American	50	52⅓	1	2	.333	46	14	14	52	12	2.41
1989—Milwaukee....................	American	52	61⅓	3	4	.429	47	16	16	52	17	2.35
1990—Milwaukee....................	American	66	69	3	7	.300	67	36	34	65	31	4.43
Major League Totals—5 Years............................		276	353	22	26	.458	304	130	117	333	112	2.98

Selected by St. Louis Cardinals' organization in 2nd round of free-agent draft, June 3, 1980.
Selected by Milwaukee Brewers' organization in 1st round (26th player selected) of free-agent draft, June 6, 1983.

ALL-STAR GAME RECORD

Year	League	IP.	W.	L.	Pct.	H.	R.	ER.	SO.	BB.	ERA.
1987—American	1	0	0	.000	0	0	0	1	0	0.00
1988—American	⅓	0	0	.000	0	0	0	1	0	0.00
1989—American	0	0	0	.000	1	0	0	0	0	....
All-Star Game Totals—3 Years.................................	1⅓	0	0	.000	1	0	0	2	0	0.00

ERIC VAUGHN PLUNK

Born September 3, 1963, at Wilmington, Calif.
Height, 6.05. Weight, 217.
Throws and bats righthanded.
Attended California State University at Dominguez Hills, Carson, Calif.

Major League saves: 1987 (2), 1988 (5), 1989 (1). Total—8.
Led American League in balks with 6 in 1986.
Tied for Florida State League lead in shutouts with 4 in 1983 and balks with 7 in 1984.

Year	Club	League	G.	IP.	W.	L.	Pct.	H.	R.	ER.	SO.	BB.	ERA.
1981—Bradenton Yankees.....................	Gulf Coast	11	54	3	4	.429	56	29	23	47	20	3.83
1982—Paintsville	Ap'lachian	12	64	6	3	.667	63	35	33	59	30	4.64
1983—Fort Lauderdale†	Florida St.	20	125	8	10	.444	115	55	38	109	63	2.74
1984—Fort Lauderdale‡	Florida St.	28	176⅓	12	12	.500	153	85	56	*152	*123	2.86
1985—Huntsville	Southern	13	79⅓	8	2	.800	61	36	30	68	56	3.40
1985—Tacoma	P. Coast	11	53	0	5	.000	51	41	34	43	50	5.77
1986—Tacoma	P. Coast	6	32⅔	2	3	.400	25	18	17	31	33	4.68
1986—Oakland.....................	American	26	120⅓	4	7	.364	91	75	71	98	102	5.21
1987—Oakland.....................	American	32	95	4	6	.400	91	53	50	90	62	4.74
1987—Tacoma	P. Coast	24	34⅔	1	1	.500	21	8	6	56	17	1.56
1988—Oakland§.....................	American	49	78	7	2	.778	62	27	26	79	39	3.00
1989—Oakland x-New York	American	50	104⅓	8	6	.571	82	43	38	85	64	3.28
1990—New York	American	47	72⅔	6	3	.667	58	27	22	67	43	2.72
Major League Totals—5 Years............................		204	470⅓	29	24	.547	384	225	207	419	310	3.96

Selected by New York Yankees' organization in 4th round of free-agent draft, June 8, 1981.
†On disabled list, August 11 to August 26, 1983.
‡Traded with Outfielder Stan Javier and Pitchers Jay Howell, Jose Rijo and Tim Birtsas to Oakland A's for Outfielder Rickey Henderson, Pitcher Bert Bradley and cash, December 5, 1984.
§On disabled list, July 2 to July 17, 1988.
xTraded with Pitcher Greg Cadaret and Outfielder Luis Polonia to New York Yankees for Outfielder Rickey Henderson, June 21, 1989.

CHAMPIONSHIP SERIES RECORD

Year	Club	League	G.	IP.	W.	L.	Pct.	H.	R.	ER.	SO.	BB.	ERA.
1988—Oakland..	American	1	⅓	0	0	.000	1	0	0	1	0	0.00

WORLD SERIES RECORD

Year	Club	League	G.	IP.	W.	L.	Pct.	H.	R.	ER.	SO.	BB.	ERA.
1988—Oakland..	American	2	1⅔	0	0	.000	0	0	0	3	0	0.00

GUSTAVO ADOLFO POLIDOR
(Gus)

Born October 26, 1961, at Caracas, Venezuela.
Height, 6.00. Weight, 180.
Throws and bats righthanded.

Major League stolen bases: 1989 (3).
Led Pacific Coast League shortstops in fielding percentage with .986 in 1986.
Led Pacific Coast League shortstops in double plays with 93 in 1985 and tied for lead with 92 in 1986.
Led Pacific Coast League shortstops in total chances with 669 in 1985.
Tied for Eastern League lead in double plays by shortstops with 69 in 1983.

Year Club	League	Pos.	G.	AB.	R.	H.	2B.	3B.	HR.	RBI.	B.A.	PO.	A.	E.	F.A.
1981—Holyoke	East.	SS	130	479	46	119	17	3	2	47	.248	192	375	32	.947
1982—Holyoke†	East.	SS	56	208	17	47	7	0	2	23	.226	74	149	21	.914
1983—Nashua	East.	*SS-3B	105	329	32	69	7	2	0	21	.210	208	283	*37	.930
1984—Waterbury	East.	*SS-P	119	394	42	88	11	1	1	32	.223	*200	322	27	*.951
1985—Edmonton	P. C.	SS	132	460	56	131	18	7	2	51	.285	*250	*396	23	.966
1985—California	Amer.	SS-OF	2	1	1	1	0	0	0	0	1.000	0	2	0	1.000
1986—Edmonton	P. C.	S-2-1-3	119	476	72	143	27	5	5	61	.300	213	316	7	.987
1986—California	Amer.	2B-SS-3B	6	19	1	5	1	0	0	1	.263	10	13	0	1.000
1987—California	Amer.	SS-3B-2B	63	137	12	36	3	0	2	15	.263	46	92	2	.986
1988—California‡	Amer.	SS-3B-2B	54	81	4	12	3	0	0	4	.148	31	54	1	.988
1988—Edmonton§	P. C.	SS-1B	11	33	6	12	4	0	0	7	.364	20	23	2	.956
1989—Milwaukee	Amer.	3B-2B-SS	79	175	15	34	7	0	0	14	.194	78	123	12	.944
1990—Milwaukee	Amer.	3B-2B-SS	18	15	0	1	0	0	0	1	.067	2	13	0	1.000
1990—Denver x	A. A.	SS-2B-3B	46	165	17	50	8	0	1	16	.303	83	112	6	.970
Major League Totals—6 Years			222	428	33	89	14	0	2	35	.208	167	297	15	.969

Signed as free agent by California Angels' organization, January 5, 1981.
†On disabled list, June 22 to July 14 and July 26, 1982 through remainder of season.
‡On disabled list, June 14 to July 1, 1988.
§Traded to Milwaukee Brewers for Catcher Bill Schroeder, December 7, 1988.
xReleased, December 6, 1990.

PITCHING RECORD

Year Club	League	G.	IP.	W.	L.	Pct.	H.	R.	ER.	SO.	BB.	ERA.
1984—Waterbury	Eastern	1	1	0	0	.000	0	0	0	0	1	0.00

LUIS ANDREW POLONIA (ALMONTE)

Born October 12, 1964, at Santiago City, D. R.
Height, 5.08. Weight, 150.
Throws and bats lefthanded.

Major League stolen bases: 1987 (29), 1988 (24), 1989 (22), 1990 (21). Total—96.
Led Pacific Coast League in caught stealing with 21 in 1986.
Led Midwest League in caught stealing with 24 in 1984.

Year Club	League	Pos.	G.	AB.	R.	H.	2B.	3B.	HR.	RBI.	B.A.	PO.	A.	E.	F.A.
1984—Madison†	Midw.	OF	135	*528	103	*162	21	10	8	64	.307	202	9	10	.955
1985—Huntsville†	South.	OF	130	515	82	149	15	*18	2	36	.289	236	13	12	.954
1986—Tacoma†	P. C.	OF	134	*549	98	*165	20	4	3	63	.301	*318	8	10	.970
1987—Tacoma†	P. C.	OF	14	56	18	18	1	2	0	8	.321	28	1	1	.967
1987—Oakland	Amer.	OF	125	435	78	125	16	10	4	49	.287	235	2	5	.979
1988—Tacoma†	P. C.	OF	65	254	58	85	13	5	2	27	.335	129	7	7	.951
1988—Oakland	Amer.	OF	84	288	51	84	11	4	2	27	.292	155	3	2	.988
1989—Oak.‡-N.Y.	Amer.	OF	125	433	70	130	17	6	3	46	.300	231	9	4	.984
1990—N.Y.§-Calif.	Amer.	OF	120	403	52	135	7	9	2	35	.335	142	3	3	.980
Major League Totals—4 Years			454	1559	251	474	51	29	11	157	.304	763	17	14	.982

Signed as free agent by Oakland A's organization, January 3, 1984.
†Switch-hitter.
‡Traded with Pitchers Greg Cadaret and Eric Plunk to New York Yankees for Outfielder Rickey Henderson, June 21, 1989.
§Traded to California Angels for Outfielder Claudell Washington and Pitcher Rich Monteleone, April 28, 1990.

CHAMPIONSHIP SERIES RECORD

Year Club	League	Pos.	G.	AB.	R.	H.	2B.	3B.	HR.	RBI.	B.A.	PO.	A.	E.	F.A.
1988—Oakland	Amer.	PR-O-PH	3	5	0	2	0	0	0	0	.400	2	0	0	1.000

WORLD SERIES RECORD

Year Club	League	Pos.	G.	AB.	R.	H.	2B.	3B.	HR.	RBI.	B.A.	PO.	A.	E.	F.A.
1988—Oakland	Amer.	PH-OF	3	9	1	1	0	0	0	0	.111	2	0	0	1.000

JAMES RICHARD POOLE
(Jim)

Born April 28, 1966, at Rochester, N.Y.
Height, 6.02. Weight, 190.
Throws and bats lefthanded.
Attended Georgia Tech, Atlanta, Ga.

Led Florida State League in games finished in relief with 50 in 1989.

Year Club	League	G.	IP.	W.	L.	Pct.	H.	R.	ER.	SO.	BB.	ERA.
1988—Vero Beach	Florida St.	10	14⅓	1	1	.500	13	7	6	12	9	3.77
1989—Vero Beach	Florida St.	*60	78⅓	11	4	.733	57	16	14	93	24	1.61
1989—Bakersfield	California	1	1⅔	0	0	.000	2	1	0	1	0	0.00
1990—San Antonio	Texas	54	63⅔	6	7	.462	55	31	17	77	27	2.40
1990—Los Angeles†	National	16	10⅔	0	0	.000	7	5	5	6	8	4.22
Major League Totals—1 Year		16	10⅔	0	0	.000	7	5	5	6	8	4.22

Selected by Los Angeles Dodgers' organization in 34th round of free-agent draft, June 2, 1987.
Selected by Los Angeles Dodgers' organization in 9th round of free-agent draft, June 1, 1988.
†Traded with cash to Texas Rangers for Pitchers Steve Allen and David Lynch, December 30, 1990.

MARK STEVEN PORTUGAL

Born October 30, 1962, at Los Angeles, Calif.
Height, 6.00. Weight, 190.
Throws and bats righthanded.

Major League saves: 1986 (1), 1988 (3). Total—4.
Led Appalachian League in wild pitches with 12, home runs allowed with 11 and tied for lead in hit batsmen with 5 in 1981.

Year Club	League	G.	IP.	W.	L.	Pct.	H.	R.	ER.	SO.	BB.	ERA.
1981—Elizabethton	Ap'lachian	14	85	7	1	.875	65	41	35	65	39	3.71
1982—Wisconsin Rapids	Midwest	36	119	9	8	.529	110	62	53	95	62	4.01
1983—Visalia	California	24	131⅓	10	5	.667	142	77	61	132	84	4.18
1984—Orlando	Southern	27	196	14	7	.667	171	80	65	110	113	2.98
1985—Toledo†	Int'national	19	128⅔	8	5	.615	129	60	54	89	60	3.78
1985—Minnesota	American	6	24⅓	1	3	.250	24	16	15	12	14	5.55
1986—Toledo	Int'national	6	45	5	1	.833	34	15	13	30	23	2.60
1986—Minnesota	American	27	112⅔	6	10	.375	112	56	54	67	50	4.31
1987—Minnesota	American	13	44	1	3	.250	58	40	38	28	24	7.77
1987—Portland	P. Coast	17	102	1	10	.091	108	75	68	69	50	6.00
1988—Portland	P. Coast	3	19⅔	2	0	1.000	15	3	3	9	8	1.37
1988—Minnesota‡§	American	26	57⅔	3	3	.500	60	30	29	31	17	4.53
1989—Tucson	P. Coast	17	116⅔	7	5	.583	107	55	49	90	32	3.78
1989—Houston	National	20	108	7	1	.875	91	34	33	86	37	2.75
1990—Houston	National	32	196⅔	11	10	.524	187	90	79	136	67	3.62
American League Totals—4 Years		72	238⅔	11	19	.367	254	142	136	138	105	5.13
National League Totals—2 Years		52	304⅔	18	11	.621	278	124	112	222	104	3.31
Major League Totals—6 Years		124	543⅓	29	30	.492	532	266	248	360	209	4.11

Signed as free agent by Minnesota Twins' organization, October 23, 1980.
†On disabled list, July 22 to August 2, 1985.
‡On disabled list, August 7 to August 28, 1988.
§Traded to Houston Astros for a player to be named later, December 4, 1988; Minnesota Twins' organization acquired Pitcher Todd McClure to complete deal, December 7, 1988.

DENNIS CLAY POWELL

Born August 13, 1963, at Moultrie, Ga.
Height, 6.03. Weight, 200.
Throws left and bats righthanded.

Major League saves: 1985 (1), 1989 (2). Total—3.
Led Gulf Coast League in shutouts with 2 in 1983.

Year Club	League	G.	IP.	W.	L.	Pct.	H.	R.	ER.	SO.	BB.	ERA.
1983—Bradenton Dodgers	Gulf Coast	11	74	8	2	.800	52	22	12	*103	23	1.46
1984—Vero Beach	Florida St.	4	26	1	1	.500	19	7	4	14	12	1.38
1984—San Antonio	Texas	24	168	9	8	.529	153	81	63	82	87	3.38
1985—Albuquerque	P. Coast	18	111⅓	9	0	1.000	106	40	34	55	48	2.74
1985—Los Angeles	National	16	29⅓	1	1	.500	30	19	17	19	13	5.22
1986—Los Angeles†	National	27	65⅓	2	7	.222	65	32	31	31	25	4.27
1986—Albuquerque‡	P. Coast	7	41⅔	3	3	.500	45	23	19	27	15	4.10
1987—Calgary	P. Coast	20	117⅓	4	8	.333	145	80	64	65	48	4.52
1987—Seattle	American	16	34⅓	1	3	.250	32	13	12	17	15	3.15
1988—Calgary	P. Coast	21	108	6	4	.600	116	57	50	81	49	4.17
1988—Seattle	American	12	18⅔	1	3	.250	29	20	18	15	11	8.68
1989—Seattle	American	43	45	2	2	.500	49	25	25	27	21	5.00
1989—Calgary	P. Coast	18	25⅓	3	2	.600	21	10	6	15	12	2.13
1990—Seattle§-Milwaukee	American	11	42⅓	0	4	.000	64	40	33	23	21	7.02
1990—Denver x	Am. Assoc.	11	62⅓	4	4	.500	63	34	25	46	21	3.61
National League Totals—2 Years		43	94⅔	3	8	.273	95	51	48	50	38	4.56
American League Totals—4 Years		82	140⅓	4	12	.250	174	98	88	82	68	5.64
Major League Totals—6 Years		125	235	7	20	.259	269	149	136	132	106	5.21

Signed as free agent by Los Angeles Dodgers' organization, May 17, 1983.
†On disabled list, April 30 to June 6, 1986.
‡Traded with Infielder Mike Watters to Seattle Mariners for Pitcher Matt Young, December 10, 1986.
§Granted free agency, May 1, 1990; signed by Denver (Milwaukee Brewers' organization), May 7, 1990.
xGranted free agency, October 15, 1990.

TED HENRY POWER

Born January 31, 1955, at Guthrie, Okla.
Height, 6.04. Weight, 220.
Throws and bats righthanded.
Attended Kansas State University, Manhattan, Kan.

Major League saves: 1983 (2), 1984 (11), 1985 (27), 1986 (1), 1990 (7). Total—48.

Year Club	League	G.	IP.	W.	L.	Pct.	H.	R.	ER.	SO.	BB.	ERA.
1976—Lodi	California	13	51	1	3	.250	46	34	26	58	44	4.59
1977—San Antonio†	Texas	12	72	5	3	.625	51	35	31	60	55	3.88
1978—San Antonio‡	Texas	25	101	6	5	.545	92	57	45	97	75	4.01
1979—San Antonio	Texas	10	64	5	1	.833	69	44	37	52	43	5.20
1979—Albuquerque	P. Coast	18	101	5	5	.500	95	59	52	69	82	4.63
1980—Albuquerque	P. Coast	26	155	13	7	.650	160	93	78	113	95	4.53
1981—Albuquerque	P. Coast	27	187	★18	3	★.857	165	84	74	111	★103	3.56
1981—Los Angeles	National	5	14	1	3	.250	16	6	5	7	7	3.21
1982—Los Angeles	National	12	33⅔	1	1	.500	38	27	25	15	23	6.68
1982—Albuquerque§	P. Coast	14	73	5	4	.556	77	51	42	54	49	5.18
1983—Cincinnati	National	49	111	5	6	.455	120	62	56	57	49	4.54
1984—Cincinnati	National	★78	108⅔	9	7	.563	93	37	34	81	46	2.82
1985—Cincinnati	National	64	80	8	6	.571	65	27	24	42	45	2.70
1986—Cincinnati	National	56	129	10	6	.625	115	59	53	95	52	3.70
1987—Cincinnati x	National	34	204	10	13	.435	213	115	102	133	71	4.50
1988—Kansas City yz-Detroit ab	American	26	99	6	7	.462	121	67	65	57	38	5.91
1989—Louisville	American	8	37	4	3	.571	29	13	13	36	15	3.16
1989—St. Louis bc	National	23	97	7	7	.500	96	47	40	43	21	3.71
1990—Pittsburgh ef	National	40	51⅔	1	3	.250	50	23	21	42	17	3.66
National League Totals—9 Years		361	829	52	52	.500	806	403	360	515	331	3.91
American League Totals—1 Year		26	99	6	7	.462	121	67	65	57	38	5.91
Major League Totals—10 Years		387	928	58	59	.496	927	470	425	572	369	4.12

Selected by Los Angeles Dodgers' organization in 5th round of free-agent draft, June 8, 1976.
†On disabled list, July 18 to July 29 and August 20 to September 4, 1977.
‡On disabled list, July 5 to July 21, 1978.
§Traded to Cincinnati Reds for cash and Infielder Michael James Ramsey, October 15, 1982.
xTraded with Shortstop Kurt Stillwell to Kansas City Royals for Pitcher Danny Jackson and Shortstop Angel Salazar, November 6, 1987.
yOn disabled list, June 18 to July 4, 1988.
zTraded to Detroit Tigers for Catcher Rey Palacios and Pitcher Mark Lee, August 31, 1988.
aGranted free agency, November 4, 1988; re-signed by Tigers, December 7, 1988.
bReleased, March 25, 1989; signed by Louisville (St. Louis Cardinals' organization), March 28, 1989.
cOn disabled list, May 17 to June 19, 1989; included rehabilitation disability assignment to Louisville, June 9 to June 19, 1989.
dGranted free agency, November 13, 1989; signed by Pittsburgh Pirates, November 20, 1989.
eOn disabled list, June 5 to July 14 and August 5 to August 20, 1990.
fGranted free agency, November 5, 1990; signed by Cincinnati Reds, December 14, 1990.

CHAMPIONSHIP SERIES RECORD

Year Club	League	G.	IP.	W.	L.	Pct.	H.	R.	ER.	SO.	BB.	ERA.
1990—Pittsburgh	National	3	5	0	0	.000	6	2	2	3	2	3.60

JAMES ARTHUR PRESLEY
(Jim)

Born October 23, 1961, at Pensacola, Fla.
Height, 6.01. Weight, 190.
Throws and bats righthanded.
Attended Pensacola Junior College, Pensacola, Fla.

Holds major league record for fewest putouts by third baseman, season, 150 or more games (82), 1985.
Shares major league record for most home runs, opening day of season (2), April 8, 1986.
Major League stolen bases: 1984 (1), 1985 (2), 1987 (2), 1988 (3), 1990 (1). Total—9.
Hit three home runs in a game, September 1, 1986.
Led National League third basemen in errors with 25 in 1990.
Led American League third baseman in assists with 311 and total chances with 445 in 1987.
Led Eastern League in game-winning RBIs with 16 in 1982.
Led Midwest League in being hit by pitch with 12 in 1980.
Led Eastern League third basemen in assists with 247 and total chances with 365 in 1982.
Led Southern League third basemen in double plays with 29 in 1983.

Year Club	League	Pos.	G.	AB.	R.	H.	2B.	3B.	HR.	RBI.	B.A.	PO.	A.	E.	F.A.
1979—Bellingham	N'west	SS	48	138	20	27	4	1	1	12	.196	42	127	27	.862
1980—Wausau	Midw.	3-S-2-1	126	429	45	105	21	1	12	52	.245	161	235	22	.947
1981—Wausau	Midw.	3B	57	208	48	58	10	0	12	53	.279	32	105	9	.938
1981—Lynn	East.	3B-2B	64	210	32	54	7	1	8	36	.257	49	110	11	.935
1982—Lynn	East.	★3B-OF	133	462	65	123	24	0	22	79	.266	84	250	★35	.905
1983—Chattanooga	South.	3B-SS	131	461	70	122	31	5	14	90	.265	122	329	27	.944
1984—Salt Lake City	P. C.	3B	69	265	43	84	13	4	13	56	.317	53	140	12	.941
1984—Seattle	Amer.	3B	70	251	27	57	12	1	10	36	.227	48	113	7	.958
1985—Seattle	Amer.	3B	155	570	71	157	33	1	28	84	.275	82	335	17	.961
1986—Seattle	Amer.	3B	155	616	83	163	33	4	27	107	.265	110	308	15	.965
1987—Seattle	Amer.	3B-SS	152	575	78	142	23	6	24	88	.247	113	315	21	.953
1988—Seattle	Amer.	3B	150	544	50	125	26	0	14	62	.230	112	234	22	.940

Year Club	League	Pos.	G.	AB.	R.	H.	2B.	3B.	HR.	RBI.	B.A.	PO.	A.	E.	F.A.
1989—Seattle†	Amer.	3B-1B	117	390	42	92	20	1	12	41	.236	222	169	18	.956
1990—Atlanta‡	Nat.	3B-1B	140	541	59	131	34	1	19	72	.242	178	242	26	.942
American League Totals—6 Years			799	2946	351	736	147	13	115	418	.250	687	1474	100	.956
National League Totals—1 Year			140	541	59	131	34	1	19	72	.242	178	242	26	.942
Major League Totals—7 Years			939	3487	410	867	181	14	134	490	.249	865	1716	126	.953

Selected by Seattle Mariners' organization in 4th round of free-agent draft, June 5, 1979.
†Traded to Atlanta Braves for Pitcher Gary Eave and Third Baseman Ken Pennington, January 24, 1990.
‡Granted free agency, November 5, 1990.

ALL-STAR GAME RECORD

Member of American League All-Star Team in 1986; did not play.

JOSEPH WALTER PRICE
(Joe)

Born November 29, 1956, at Inglewood, Calif.
Height, 6.04. Weight, 215.
Throws left and bats righthanded.
Attended Oklahoma State University, Stillwater, Okla., and
University of Oklahoma, Norman, Okla.

Major League saves: 1981 (4), 1982 (3), 1985 (1), 1987 (1), 1988 (4). Total—13.

Year Club	League	G.	IP.	W.	L.	Pct.	H.	R.	ER.	SO.	BB.	ERA.
1977—Billings	Pioneer	15	94	6	5	.545	83	50	39	97	42	3.73
1978—Tampa	Florida St.	23	165	10	4	.714	123	40	27	128	51	1.47
1978—Nashville	Southern	2	10	0	0	.000	7	3	3	10	3	2.70
1979—Nashville	Southern	22	109	6	6	.500	101	58	48	69	41	3.96
1980—Indianapolis	Am. Assoc.	11	79	4	4	.500	64	36	34	83	30	3.87
1980—Cincinnati	National	24	111	7	3	.700	95	45	44	44	37	3.57
1981—Cincinnati	National	41	54	6	1	.857	42	19	15	41	18	2.50
1982—Cincinnati	National	59	72⅔	3	4	.429	73	26	23	71	32	2.85
1983—Cincinnati†	National	21	144	10	6	.625	118	46	46	83	46	2.88
1984—Cincinnati	National	30	171⅔	7	13	.350	176	91	80	129	61	4.19
1985—Cincinnati‡	National	26	64⅔	2	2	.500	59	35	28	52	23	3.90
1986—Cincinnati§x	National	25	41⅔	1	2	.333	49	30	25	30	22	5.40
1987—Phoenix	P. Coast	17	61⅓	6	0	1.000	45	21	17	49	40	2.49
1987—San Francisco y	National	20	35	2	2	.500	19	10	10	42	13	2.57
1988—San Francisco z	National	38	61⅔	1	6	.143	59	33	27	49	27	3.94
1989—San Francisco a	National	7	14	1	1	.500	16	9	9	10	4	5.79
1989—Boston bc	American	31	70½	2	5	.286	71	35	34	52	30	4.35
1990—Baltimore de	American	50	65⅓	3	4	.429	62	29	26	54	24	3.58
National League Totals—10 Years		291	770⅓	40	40	.500	706	344	307	551	283	3.59
American League Totals—2 Years		81	135⅔	5	9	.357	133	64	60	106	54	3.98
Major League Totals—11 Years		372	906	45	49	.479	839	408	367	657	337	3.65

Selected by Cincinnati Reds' organization in 4th round of free-agent draft, June 7, 1977.
†On disabled list, August 7 to September 1, 1983.
‡On disabled list, July 23 to August 8 and August 29 to September 13, 1985.
§On disabled list, July 17 to September 1, 1986.
xGranted free agency, November 12, 1986; signed by San Francisco Giants, February 5, 1987.
yGranted free agency, November 9, 1987; re-signed by San Francisco Giants, December 14, 1987.
zOn disabled list, May 9 to June 3 and August 17 to September 2, 1988.
aReleased, May 1, 1989; signed by Boston Red Sox, May 5, 1989.
bOn suspended list, September 10 to September 14, 1989.
cGranted free agency, November 13, 1989; signed by Baltimore Orioles, January 12, 1990.
dOn disabled list, June 27 to July 15, 1990.
eGranted free agency, November 5, 1990.

CHAMPIONSHIP SERIES RECORD

Year Club	League	G.	IP.	W.	L.	Pct.	H.	R.	ER.	SO.	BB.	ERA.
1987—San Francisco	National	2	5⅔	1	0	1.000	3	0	0	7	1	0.00

THOMAS ALBERT PRINCE
(Tom)

Born August 13, 1964, at Kankakee, Ill.
Height, 5.11. Weight, 185.
Throws and bats righthanded.
Attended Kankakee Community College, Kankakee, Ill.

Major League stolen bases: 1989 (1).
Led Eastern League catchers in double plays with 9 and total chances with 721 in 1987.
Led Carolina League catchers in total chances with 954 and passed balls with 15 in 1986.
Led South Atlantic League catchers in total chances with 930, double plays with 10 and passed balls with 27 in 1985.

Year Club	League	Pos.	G.	AB.	R.	H.	2B.	3B.	HR.	RBI.	B.A.	PO.	A.	E.	F.A.
1984—Watertown	NYP	C-3B	23	69	6	14	3	0	2	13	.203	155	26	2	.989
1984—Bradenton Pir.	Gulf C.	C-1B	18	48	4	11	0	0	1	6	.229	75	16	4	.958
1985—Macon	S. Atl.	C	124	360	60	75	20	1	10	42	.208	*810	*101	*19	.980
1986—Prince William	Carol.	C	121	395	59	100	34	1	10	47	.253	*821	●113	20	.979

Year Club League	Pos.	G.	AB.	R.	H.	2B.	3B.	HR.	RBI.	B.A.	PO.	A.	E.	F.A.
1987—Harrisburg .... East.	C	113	365	41	112	23	2	6	54	.307	*622	*88	●11	.985
1987—Pittsburgh .... Nat.	C	4	9	1	2	1	0	1	2	.222	14	3	0	1.000
1988—Buffalo .... A. A.	C	86	304	35	79	16	0	14	42	.260	456	51	*12	.977
1988—Pittsburgh .... Nat.	C	29	74	3	13	2	0	0	6	.176	108	8	2	.983
1989—Buffalo .... A. A.	C	65	183	21	37	8	1	6	33	.202	312	22	5	.985
1989—Pittsburgh .... Nat.	C	21	52	1	7	4	0	0	5	.135	85	11	4	.960
1990—Pittsburgh .... Nat.	C	4	10	1	1	0	0	0	0	.100	16	1	0	1.000
1990—Buffalo .... A. A.	C-1B	94	284	38	64	13	0	7	37	.225	461	62	8	.985
Major League Totals—4 Years		58	145	6	23	7	0	1	13	.159	223	23	6	.976

Selected by Atlanta Braves' organization in 8th round of free-agent draft, January 11, 1983.
Selected by Atlanta Braves' organization in secondary phase of free-agent draft, June 6, 1983.
Selected by Pittsburgh Pirates' organization in secondary phase of free-agent draft, January 17, 1984.

KIRBY PUCKETT

Born March 14, 1961, at Chicago, Ill.
Height, 5.08. Weight, 210.
Throws and bats righthanded.
Attended Bradley University, Peoria, Ill., and Triton College, River Grove, Ill.

Shares major league records for most doubles, game (4), May 13, 1989; most doubles, two consecutive games (6), May 13 (4), 14 (2), 1989; most at-bats, season, no sacrifice flies (680), 1986.
Shares modern major league record for most hits, first game in majors, nine innings (4), May 8, 1984.
Holds American League record for most hits, two consecutive nine-inning games (10), August 29 and 30, 1987.
Shares American League record for most seasons, 400 or more putouts, outfielder (5).
Major League stolen bases: 1984 (14), 1985 (21), 1986 (20), 1987 (12), 1988 (6), 1989 (11), 1990 (5). Total—89.
Collected six hits in one game, August 30, 1987.
Hit for the cycle, August 1, 1986.
Led American League in total bases with 358 in 1988.
Led American League outfielders in total chances with 492 in 1985, 465 in 1988 and 455 in 1989.
Led Appalachian League in total bases with 135 and tied for lead in stolen bases with 43 in 1982.
Led California League outfielders in double plays with 5 in 1983.
Named outfielder on THE SPORTING NEWS American League All-Star Team, 1986 through 1989.
Named outfielder on THE SPORTING NEWS American League All-Star fielding team, 1986 through 1989.
Named outfielder on THE SPORTING NEWS American League Silver Slugger team, 1986 through 1989.
Named California League Player of the Year, 1983.

Year Club League	Pos.	G.	AB.	R.	H.	2B.	3B.	HR.	RBI.	B.A.	PO.	A.	E.	F.A.
1982—Elizabethton .... Appal.	OF	65	*275	*65	*105	15	3	3	35	*.382	133	*11	5	.966
1983—Visalia .... Calif.	OF	138	*548	105	172	29	7	9	97	.314	253	*22	5	.982
1984—Toledo .... Int.	OF	21	80	9	21	2	0	1	5	.263	35	1	3	.923
1984—Minnesota .... Amer.	OF	128	557	63	165	12	5	0	31	.296	438	*16	3	.993
1985—Minnesota .... Amer.	OF	161	*691	80	199	29	13	4	74	.288	*465	19	8	.984
1986—Minnesota .... Amer.	OF	161	680	119	223	37	6	31	96	.328	429	8	6	.986
1987—Minnesota .... Amer.	OF	157	624	96	●207	32	5	28	99	.332	341	8	5	.986
1988—Minnesota .... Amer.	OF	158	*657	109	*234	42	5	24	121	.356	*450	12	3	.994
1989—Minnesota .... Amer.	OF	159	635	75	*215	45	4	9	85	*.339	*438	13	4	.991
1990—Minnesota .... Amer.	O-2-3-S	146	551	82	164	40	3	12	80	.298	354	9	4	.989
Major League Totals—7 Years		1070	4395	624	1407	237	41	108	586	.320	2915	85	33	.989

Selected by Minnesota Twins' organization in 1st round (third player selected) of free-agent draft, January 12, 1982.

CHAMPIONSHIP SERIES RECORD

Shares American League Championship Series record for most at-bats, game (6), October 12, 1987.

Year Club League	Pos.	G.	AB.	R.	H.	2B.	3B.	HR.	RBI.	B.A.	PO.	A.	E.	F.A.
1987—Minnesota .... Amer.	OF	5	24	3	5	1	0	1	3	.208	7	0	0	1.000

WORLD SERIES RECORD

Shares World Series records for most at-bats, inning (2), October 18, 1987, fourth inning; most runs, game (4), October 24, 1987.

Year Club League	Pos.	G.	AB.	R.	H.	2B.	3B.	HR.	RBI.	B.A.	PO.	A.	E.	F.A.
1987—Minnesota .... Amer.	OF	7	28	5	10	1	1	0	3	.357	15	1	1	.941

ALL-STAR GAME RECORD

Year League	Pos.	AB.	R.	H.	2B.	3B.	HR.	RBI.	B.A.	PO.	A.	E.	F.A.
1986—American	OF	3	0	1	0	0	0	0	.333	5	0	0	1.000
1987—American	PH-OF	4	0	0	0	0	0	0	.000	1	0	0	1.000
1988—American	OF	1	0	0	0	0	0	0	.000	1	0	0	1.000
1989—American	OF	3	1	1	0	0	0	0	.333	0	0	0	.000
1990—American	PH-OF	1	0	1	0	0	0	0	1.000	1	0	0	1.000
All-Star Game Totals—5 Years		12	1	3	0	0	0	0	.250	8	0	0	1.000

TERRANCE STEPHEN PUHL

Name pronounced Pool.

(Terry)

Born July 8, 1956, at Melville, Saskatchewan, Canada.
Height, 6.02. Weight, 197.
Throws right and bats lefthanded.

Holds major league record for highest fielding percentage by outfielder, lifetime, 1,000 or more games (.993).

Shares major league records for highest fielding percentage by outfielder, season, 150 or more games (1.000), 1979; fewest errors by outfielder, season, 150 or more games (0), 1979.

Major League stolen bases: 1977 (10), 1978 (32), 1979 (30), 1980 (27), 1981 (22), 1982 (17), 1983 (24), 1984 (13), 1985 (6) 1986 (3), 1987 (1), 1988 (22), 1989 (9), 1990 (1). Total—217.

Year Club	League	Pos.	G.	AB.	R.	H.	2B.	3B.	HR.	RBI.	B.A.	PO.	A.	E.	F.A.
1974—Covington	Appal.	OF	59	211	42	60	11	0	0	21	.284	89	2	2	.978
1975—Dubuque	Midw.	OF-1B	104	346	57	115	10	2	0	28	.332	230	11	7	.971
1976—Columbus	South.	OF	28	98	13	28	5	0	1	14	.286	76	1	2	.975
1976—Memphis	Int.	OF	105	372	50	99	17	3	1	39	.266	191	5	3	.985
1977—Charleston	Int.	OF	78	285	53	87	12	6	4	33	.305	189	4	3	.985
1977—Houston	Nat.	OF	60	229	40	69	13	5	0	10	.301	119	3	1	.992
1978—Houston	Nat.	OF	149	585	87	169	25	6	3	35	.289	386	6	3	.992
1979—Houston	Nat.	OF	157	600	87	172	22	4	8	49	.287	352	7	0	*1.000
1980—Houston	Nat.	OF	141	535	75	151	24	5	13	55	.282	311	14	3	.991
1981—Houston	Nat.	OF	96	350	43	88	19	4	3	28	.251	185	5	0	●1.000
1982—Houston	Nat.	OF	145	507	64	133	17	9	8	50	.262	257	4	3	.989
1983—Houston	Nat.	OF	137	465	66	136	25	7	8	44	.292	220	4	2	.991
1984—Houston†	Nat.	OF	132	449	66	135	19	7	9	55	.301	213	6	3	.986
1985—Houston‡	Nat.	OF	57	194	34	55	14	3	2	23	.284	92	3	0	1.000
1986—Houston§	Nat.	OF	81	172	17	42	10	0	3	14	.244	65	0	0	1.000
1987—Houston	Nat.	OF	90	122	9	28	5	0	2	15	.230	48	0	1	.980
1988—Houston	Nat.	OF	113	234	42	71	7	2	3	19	.303	116	2	2	.983
1989—Houston	Nat.	OF-1B	121	354	41	96	25	4	0	27	.271	212	3	0	1.000
1990—Houston xy	Nat.	OF-1B	37	41	5	12	1	0	0	8	.293	9	0	0	1.000
Major League Totals—14 Years			1516	4837	676	1357	226	56	62	432	.281	2585	57	18	.993

Signed as free agent by Houston Astros' organization, September 19, 1973.

†On disabled list, April 13 to April 30, 1984.

‡On disabled list, April 22 to May 7, June 13 to June 28, July 19 to August 15 and August 26, 1985 through remainder of season.

§On disabled list, March 30 to April 15 and July 2 to July 23, 1986.

xOn disabled list, May 10 to June 28 and August 7, 1990 through remainder of season.

yGranted free agency, November 5, 1990; signed by New York Mets, December 13, 1990.

DIVISION SERIES RECORD

Year Club	League	Pos.	G.	AB.	R.	H.	2B.	3B.	HR.	RBI.	B.A.	PO.	A.	E.	F.A.
1981—Houston	Nat.	OF	5	21	2	4	1	0	0	0	.190	7	1	0	1.000

CHAMPIONSHIP SERIES RECORD

Shares Championship Series record for most singles, game (4), October 12, 1980 (10 innings).

Shares National League Championship Series record for most singles, series (8), 1980.

Year Club	League	Pos.	G.	AB.	R.	H.	2B.	3B.	HR.	RBI.	B.A.	PO.	A.	E.	F.A.
1980—Houston	Nat.	PH-OF	5	19	4	10	2	0	0	3	.526	13	0	0	1.000
1986—Houston	Nat.	PH	3	3	0	2	0	0	0	0	.667	0	0	0	.000
Championship Series Totals—2 Years			8	22	4	12	2	0	0	3	.545	13	0	0	1.000

ALL-STAR GAME RECORD

Member of National League All-Star Team for 1978 game; did not play.

THOMAS RAYMOND QUINLAN
(Tom)

Born March 27, 1968, at St. Paul, Minn.
Height, 6.03. Weight, 210.
Throws and bats righthanded.

Led Southern League batters in strikeouts with 157 in 1990.

Led Southern League third basemen in putouts with 103 in 1990.

Led South Atlantic League third basemen in putouts with 96 and double plays with 29 and tied for lead in total chances with 368 in 1987.

Tied for Southern League lead in double plays by third basemen with 21 in 1989.

Year Club	League	Pos.	G.	AB.	R.	H.	2B.	3B.	HR.	RBI.	B.A.	PO.	A.	E.	F.A.
1987—Myrtle Beach	S. Atl.	3B-1B	132	435	42	97	20	3	5	51	.223	107	232	40	.894
1988—Knoxville†	South.	3B-1B	98	326	33	71	19	1	8	47	.218	87	188	25	.917
1989—Knoxville	South.	3B	139	452	62	95	21	3	16	57	.210	81	259	34	.909
1990—Knoxville	South.	3B-SS	141	481	70	124	24	6	15	51	.258	106	259	31	.922
1990—Toronto	Amer.	3B	1	2	0	1	0	0	0	0	.500	0	1	0	1.000
Major League Totals—1 Year			1	2	0	1	0	0	0	0	.500	0	1	0	1.000

Selected by Toronto Blue Jays' organization in 27th round of free-agent draft, June 2, 1986.

†On disabled list, June 10 to July 14, 1989.

LUIS RAUL QUINONES

Name pronounced Key-NO-nez.

Born April 28, 1962, at Ponce, Puerto Rico.
Height, 5.11. Weight, 180.
Throws right and bats left and righthanded.

Shares major league record for most plate appearances, inning (3), August 3, 1989, first inning.

Major League stolen bases: 1983 (1), 1986 (3), 1988 (1), 1989 (2), 1990 (1). Total—8.

Led Carolina League shortstops in double plays with 77 in 1981.
Tied for Northwest League lead in double plays by shortstops with 33 in 1980.

Year	Club	League	Pos.	G.	AB.	R.	H.	2B.	3B.	HR.	RBI.	B.A.	PO.	A.	E.	F.A.
1980—Grays Harbor	N'west	SS	56	156	33	35	2	2	0	11	.224	70	157	24	.904
1981—Salem	Carol.	●SS-2B	123	455	64	102	10	4	7	37	.224	208	341	●53	.912
1982—Salem	Carol.	SS	41	173	32	48	1	4	5	28	.277	41	99	15	.903
1982—Amarillo†	Texas	SS	95	411	69	120	19	7	11	60	.292	164	288	31	.936
1983—Albany	East.	2B-OF-SS	56	213	35	51	5	0	6	23	.239	101	138	13	.948
1983—Oakland	Amer.	2-O-3-S	19	42	5	8	2	1	0	4	.190	22	24	1	.979
1983—Tacoma‡	P. C.	SS-OF-2B	45	133	14	35	3	1	2	14	.263	62	97	9	.946
1984—Maine	Int.	*SS-OF-2B	131	473	71	127	27	3	8	60	.268	217	330	*43	.927
1985—Maine§	Int.	SS-OF	14	45	4	8	2	1	1	2	.178	19	12	0	1.000
1985—Phoenix	P. C.	SS-2B-3B	85	304	46	78	13	7	8	47	.257	106	236	13	.963
1986—Phoenix	P. C.	SS	14	55	7	14	4	1	0	7	.255	23	37	3	.952
1986—San Francisco xy.	Nat.	SS-3B-2B	71	106	13	19	1	3	0	11	.179	28	66	8	.922
1987—Iowa	A. A.	SS-2B	77	287	44	91	14	*12	11	62	.317	93	122	14	.939
1987—Chicago z	Nat.	SS-2B-3B	49	101	12	22	6	0	0	8	.218	35	58	3	.969
1988—Nashville	A. A.	SS-3B-1B	114	417	42	115	28	6	9	53	.276	164	285	25	.947
1988—Cincinnati	Nat.	SS-3B-2B	23	52	4	12	3	0	1	11	.231	15	37	2	.963
1989—Nashville	A. A.	3B-2B-SS	45	176	19	40	9	2	4	24	.227	38	75	13	.897
1989—Cincinnati	Nat.	2B-3B-SS	97	340	43	83	13	4	12	34	.244	112	213	10	.970
1990—Cincinnati	Nat.	3-2-S-1	83	145	10	35	7	0	2	17	.241	44	85	6	.956
American League Totals—1 Year			19	42	5	8	2	1	0	4	.190	22	24	1	.979
National League Totals—5 Years			323	744	82	171	30	7	15	81	.230	234	459	29	.960
Major League Totals—6 Years			342	786	87	179	32	8	15	85	.228	256	483	30	.961

Signed as free agent by San Diego Padres' organization, April 28, 1980.
†Drafted by Oakland A's, December 6, 1982.
‡Traded to Cleveland Indians, December 8, 1983, completing deal in which Cleveland traded Catcher Jim Essian to Oakland A's for a player to be named later, December 5, 1983.
§Traded with Pitcher Mike Jeffcoat to San Francisco Giants' organization for Shortstop Johnnie LeMaster, May 7, 1985.
xReleased, November 10, 1986; signed by Tacoma (Oakland A's organization), January 22, 1987.
yTraded to Chicago Cubs for Third Baseman Ron Cey, January 30, 1987.
zTraded to Cincinnati Reds for Pitcher Bill Landrum, April 1, 1988.

CHAMPIONSHIP SERIES RECORD

Year	Club	League	Pos.	G.	AB.	R.	H.	2B.	3B.	HR.	RBI.	B.A.	PO.	A.	E.	F.A.
1990—Cincinnati	Nat.	PH	3	2	1	1	0	0	0	2	.500	0	0	0	.000

CARLOS NARCIS QUINTANA

Born August 26, 1965, at Estado Miranda, Venezuela.
Height, 6.02. Weight, 195.
Throws and bats righthanded.

Major League stolen bases: 1990 (1).
Led International League outfielders in assists with 15 in 1988.

Year	Club	League	Pos.	G.	AB.	R.	H.	2B.	3B.	HR.	RBI.	B.A.	PO.	A.	E.	F.A.
1985—Elmira	NYP	OF	65	220	27	61	8	0	4	35	.277	55	5	3	.952
1986—Greensboro	S. Atl.	OF-1B	126	443	97	144	19	4	11	81	.325	224	12	9	.963
1987—New Britain	East.	OF	56	206	31	64	11	3	2	31	.311	100	4	2	.981
1988—Pawtucket	Int.	OF-1B	131	471	67	134	25	3	16	66	.285	525	44	11	.981
1988—Boston	Amer.	OF	5	6	1	2	0	0	0	2	.333	4	0	0	1.000
1989—Pawtucket	Int.	1B-OF	82	272	45	78	11	2	11	52	.287	398	27	2	.995
1989—Boston†	Amer.	OF-1B	34	77	6	16	5	0	0	6	.208	31	0	2	.939
1990—Boston	Amer.	*1B-OF	149	512	56	147	28	0	7	67	.287	1190	*137	*17	.987
Major League Totals—3 Years			188	595	63	165	33	0	7	75	.277	1225	137	19	.986

Signed as free agent by Boston Red Sox' organization, November 26, 1984.
†On disabled list, June 22 to July 7, 1989.

CHAMPIONSHIP SERIES RECORD

Year	Club	League	Pos.	G.	AB.	R.	H.	2B.	3B.	HR.	RBI.	B.A.	PO.	A.	E.	F.A.
1990—Boston	Amer.	1B	4	13	0	0	0	0	0	1	.000	29	2	0	1.000

JAMES PATRICK QUIRK
(Jamie)

Born October 22, 1954, at Whittier, Calif.
Height, 6.04. Weight, 200.
Throws right and bats lefthanded.
Attended Whittier College, Whittier, Calif.

Major League stolen bases: 1980 (3), 1987 (1), 1988 (1). Total—5.
Led American Association in passed balls with 23 in 1985.
Led American Association third basemen in double plays with 31 in 1975.
Led Pioneer League shortstops in double plays with 16 in 1972.

Year	Club	League	Pos.	G.	AB.	R.	H.	2B.	3B.	HR.	RBI.	B.A.	PO.	A.	E.	F.A.
1972—Billings	Pion.	SS	55	208	29	53	9	4	5	37	.255	*63	*162	*28	*.889
1973—San Jose	Calif.	SS	132	429	58	99	12	7	8	45	.231	160	330	39	.926
1974—Jacksonville	South.	SS	46	163	16	37	7	2	3	21	.227	75	133	20	.912

Year	Club	League	Pos.	G.	AB.	R.	H.	2B.	3B.	HR.	RBI.	B.A.	PO.	A.	E.	F.A.
1974—Omaha	A. A.		SS-3B-2B	53	203	27	57	10	2	10	31	.281	64	141	14	.936
1975—Omaha	A. A.		3B	127	445	62	122	23	4	13	64	.274	109	*254	16	*.958
1975—Kansas City	Amer.		OF-3B	14	39	2	10	0	0	1	5	.256	19	3	2	.917
1976—Kansas City†	Amer.		SS-3B-1B	64	114	11	28	6	0	1	15	.246	9	14	2	.920
1977—Milwaukee	Amer.		OF-3B	93	221	16	48	14	1	3	13	.217	19	4	2	.920
1978—Spokane‡	P. C.		3B-1B	97	343	58	100	20	2	12	63	.292	235	142	20	.950
1978—Kansas City§	Amer.		3B-SS	17	29	3	6	2	0	0	2	.207	11	16	2	.931
1979—Kansas City	Amer.		C-SS-3B	51	79	8	24	6	1	1	11	.304	16	9	1	.960
1980—Kansas City	Amer.		C-3-O-1	62	163	13	45	5	0	5	21	.276	78	66	8	.947
1981—Kansas City	Amer.		C-3-2-O	46	100	8	25	7	0	0	10	.250	63	23	4	.956
1982—Kansas City xy	Amer.		C-1-3-O	36	78	8	18	3	0	1	5	.231	110	12	0	1.000
1983—St. Louis za	Nat.		C-3B-SS	48	86	3	18	2	1	2	11	.209	68	13	6	.931
1984—Denver	A. A.		C-3-O-1-P	70	201	23	42	6	3	2	24	.209	212	67	11	.962
1984—Chi. b-Cle. c	Amer.		3B-C	4	3	1	1	0	0	1	2	.333	1	0	0	1.000
1985—Omaha	A. A.		C-1B-3B	104	324	33	79	5	1	8	48	.244	525	67	14	.977
1985—Kansas City d	Amer.		C-1B	19	57	3	16	3	1	0	4	.281	66	8	1	.987
1986—Kansas City	Amer.		C-3-1-O	80	219	24	47	10	0	8	26	.215	303	64	4	.989
1987—Kansas City fg	Amer.		C-SS	109	296	24	70	17	0	5	33	.236	532	40	8	.986
1988—Kansas City h	Amer.		C-1B-3B	84	196	22	47	7	1	8	25	.240	412	34	8	.982
1989—N.Y. i-Oak j-Bal	Amer.		C-3-1-O-S	47	85	6	15	2	0	1	10	.176	129	15	1	.993
1989—Tacoma k	P. C.		C-1B	14	47	5	8	2	0	1	5	.170	89	7	2	.980
1990—Oakland l	Amer.		C-1-3-O	56	121	12	34	5	1	3	26	.281	168	18	5	.974
American League Totals—15 Years				782	1800	161	434	87	5	38	208	.241	1936	326	48	.979
National League Totals—1 Year				48	86	3	18	2	1	2	11	.209	68	13	6	.931
Major League Totals—16 Years				830	1886	164	452	89	6	40	219	.240	2004	339	54	.977

Selected by Kansas City Royals' organization in 1st round (18th player selected) of free-agent draft, June 6, 1972.

†Traded with Outfielder Jim Wohlford and a player to be named later to Milwaukee Brewers for Pitcher Jim Colborn and Catcher Darrell Porter, December 6, 1976; Milwaukee acquired Pitcher Bob McClure to complete deal, March 15, 1977.

‡Traded to Kansas City Royals for Pitcher Gerry Ako and cash, August 3, 1978.

§On disabled list, August 14 to September 5, 1978.

xOn disabled list, August 10 to September 1, 1982.

yGranted free agency, November 10, 1982; signed by St. Louis Cardinals, February 16, 1983.

zReleased, March 26, 1984; named St. Louis Cardinals coach, April 13, 1984.

aSigned by Chicago White Sox' organization, May 23, 1984.

bSold to Cleveland Indians, September 24, 1984.

cReleased, October 15, 1984; signed by Kansas City Royals' organization, February 25, 1985.

dGranted free agency, November 12, 1985; re-signed by Royals, November 27, 1985.

eGranted free agency, November 12, 1986; re-signed by Royals, December 17, 1986.

fOn disabled list, July 21 to August 5, 1987.

gGranted free agency, November 9, 1987; re-signed by Royals, January 25, 1988.

hGranted free agency, November 4, 1988; signed by New York Yankees, December 20, 1988.

iReleased, May 16, 1989; signed by Tacoma (Oakland Athletics' organization), May 27, 1989.

jReleased, July 24, 1989; signed by Baltimore Orioles, August 5, 1989.

kReleased, November 2, 1989; signed by Oakland Athletics, December 13, 1989.

lGranted free agency, November 5, 1990; signed by Oakland Athletics, November 28, 1990.

CHAMPIONSHIP SERIES RECORD

Year	Club	League	Pos.	G.	AB.	R.	H.	2B.	3B.	HR.	RBI.	B.A.	PO.	A.	E.	F.A.
1976—Kansas City	Amer.		PH-DH	4	7	1	1	0	1	0	2	.143	0	0	0	.000
1985—Kansas City	Amer.		PH	1	1	0	0	0	0	0	0	.000	0	0	0	.000
1990—Oakland	Amer.		PH	1	1	0	1	0	0	0	0	1.000	0	0	0	.000
Championship Series Totals—3 Years				6	9	1	2	0	1	0	2	.222	0	0	0	.000

WORLD SERIES RECORD

Year	Club	League	Pos.	G.	AB.	R.	H.	2B.	3B.	HR.	RBI.	B.A.	PO.	A.	E.	F.A.
1990—Oakland	Amer.		C	1	3	0	0	0	0	0	0	.000	2	2	0	1.000

Eligible for 1980 and 1985 World Series with Kansas City Royals; did not play.

PITCHING RECORD

Year	Club	League	G.	IP.	W.	L.	Pct.	H.	R.	ER.	SO.	BB.	ERA.
1984—Denver	Am. Assoc.		2	2	0	0	.000	6	3	3	0	0	13.50

DANIEL RAYMOND QUISENBERRY

Name pronounced QUIZ-en-berry.

(Dan)

Born February 7, 1953, at Santa Monica, Calif.
Height, 6.02. Weight, 185.
Throws and bats righthanded.
Attended Orange Coast College, Costa Mesa, Calif., LaVerne College, LaVerne, Calif.,
and Fresno Pacific College, Fresno, Calif.

Holds American League record for most saves, lifetime (238).

Major League saves: 1979 (5), 1980 (33), 1981 (18), 1982 (35), 1983 (45), 1984 (44), 1985 (37), 1986 (12), 1987 (8), 1988 (1), 1989 (6). Total—244.

Led American League in games finished in relief with 68 in both 1980 and 1982, 62 in 1983 and 76 in 1985.

Led American League in saves with 35 in 1982, 45 in 1983, 44 in 1984, 37 in 1985 and tied for lead with 33 in 1980.

Tied for Southern League lead in saves with 15 in 1978.

Named American League Fireman of the Year by THE SPORTING NEWS, 1980 and 1982 through 1985.

Year Club	League	G.	IP.	W.	L.	Pct.	H.	R.	ER.	SO.	BB.	ERA.
1975—Waterloo	Midwest	20	44	3	2	.600	40	16	12	31	6	2.45
1975—Jacksonville	Southern	6	8	0	1	.000	5	3	2	2	4	2.25
1976—Jacksonville	Southern	9	12	0	1	.000	8	6	3	6	2	2.25
1976—Waterloo	Midwest	34	42	2	1	.667	28	4	3	19	9	0.64
1977—Jacksonville	Southern	33	74	3	1	.750	61	18	11	33	11	1.34
1978—Jacksonville	Southern	48	64	4	2	.667	62	22	17	29	12	2.39
1979—Omaha	Am. Assoc.	26	35	2	1	.667	29	15	14	16	10	3.60
1979—Kansas City	American	32	40	3	2	.600	42	16	14	13	7	3.15
1980—Kansas City	American	*75	128	12	7	.632	129	47	44	37	27	3.09
1981—Kansas City	American	40	62	1	4	.200	59	16	12	20	15	1.74
1982—Kansas City	American	72	136⅔	9	7	.563	126	43	39	46	12	2.57
1983—Kansas City	American	*69	139	5	3	.625	118	35	30	48	11	1.94
1984—Kansas City	American	72	129⅓	6	3	.667	121	39	38	41	12	2.64
1985—Kansas City	American	*84	129	8	9	.471	142	41	34	54	16	2.37
1986—Kansas City	American	62	81⅓	3	7	.300	92	30	25	36	24	2.77
1987—Kansas City	American	47	49	4	1	.800	58	15	15	17	10	2.76
1988—Kansas City†	American	20	25⅓	0	1	.000	32	11	10	9	5	3.55
1988—St. Louis	National	33	38	2	0	1.000	54	26	26	19	6	6.16
1989—St. Louis‡	National	63	78⅓	3	1	.750	78	25	23	37	14	2.64
1990—San Francisco§	National	5	6⅔	0	1	.000	13	12	10	2	3	13.50
American League Totals—10 Years		573	919⅔	51	44	.537	919	293	261	321	139	2.55
National League Totals—3 Years		101	123	5	2	.714	145	63	59	58	23	4.32
Major League Totals—12 Years		674	1042⅔	56	46	.549	1064	356	320	379	162	2.76

Signed as free agent by Kansas City Royals' organization, June 7, 1975.
†Released, July 4, 1988; signed by St. Louis Cardinals, July 14, 1988.
‡Released by St. Louis Cardinals, October 11, 1989; signed by San Francisco Giants, January 28, 1990.
§On voluntarily retired list, April 30, 1990.

DIVISION SERIES RECORD

Year Club	League	G.	IP.	W.	L.	Pct.	H.	R.	ER.	SO.	BB.	ERA.
1981—Kansas City	American	1	1	0	0	.000	1	0	0	0	0	0.00

CHAMPIONSHIP SERIES RECORD

Shares American League Championship Series record for most games pitched, series (4), 1985.

Year Club	League	G.	IP.	W.	L.	Pct.	H.	R.	ER.	SO.	BB.	ERA.
1980—Kansas City	American	2	4⅔	1	0	1.000	4	1	0	1	2	0.00
1984—Kansas City	American	1	3	0	1	.000	2	2	1	1	1	3.00
1985—Kansas City	American	4	4⅔	0	1	.000	7	4	2	3	0	3.86
Championship Series Totals—3 Years		7	12⅓	1	2	.333	13	7	3	5	3	2.19

WORLD SERIES RECORD

Year Club	League	G.	IP.	W.	L.	Pct.	H.	R.	ER.	SO.	BB.	ERA.
1980—Kansas City	American	6	10⅓	1	2	.333	10	6	6	0	3	5.23
1985—Kansas City	American	4	4⅓	1	0	1.000	5	1	1	3	3	2.08
World Series Totals—2 Years		10	14⅔	2	2	.500	15	7	7	3	6	4.30

ALL-STAR GAME RECORD

Year League		IP.	W.	L.	Pct.	H.	R.	ER.	SO.	BB.	ERA.
1982—American		2	0	0	.000	3	1	1	1	0	4.50
1983—American		1	0	0	.000	1	0	0	1	0	0.00
All-Star Game Totals—2 Years		3	0	0	.000	4	1	1	2	0	3.00

Member of American League All-Star Team in 1984; did not play.

SCOTT DAVID RADINSKY

Born March 3, 1968, at Glendale, Calif.
Height, 6.03. Weight, 190.
Throws and bats lefthanded.

Major League saves: 1990 (4).

Year Club	League	G.	IP.	W.	L.	Pct.	H.	R.	ER.	SO.	BB.	ERA.
1986—Sarasota White Sox	Gulf Coast	7	26⅔	1	0	1.000	24	20	10	18	17	3.38
1987—Peninsula	Carolina	12	39	1	7	.125	43	30	25	37	32	5.77
1987—Sarasota White Sox	Gulf Coast	11	58⅓	3	3	.500	43	23	15	41	39	2.31
1988—Sarasota White Sox	Gulf Coast	5	3⅓	0	0	.000	2	2	2	7	4	5.40
1989—South Bend	Midwest	53	61⅔	7	5	.583	39	21	12	83	19	1.75
1990—Chicago	American	62	52⅓	6	1	.857	47	29	28	46	36	4.82
Major League Totals—1 Year		62	52⅓	6	1	.857	47	29	28	46	36	4.82

Selected by Chicago White Sox' organization in 3rd round of free-agent draft, June 2, 1986.

TIMOTHY RAINES
(Tim)

Born September 16, 1959, at Sanford, Fla.
Height, 5.08. Weight, 185.
Throws right and bats left and righthanded.
Brother of Ned Raines, minor league outfielder, 1978 through 1980.

Holds major league records for highest stolen base percentage, lifetime, 300 or attempts (.857); most intentional bases on balls by switch-hitter, season (26), 1987.

Shares major league record for fewest double plays by outfielder, season, for leader in double plays (4), 1985.

Major League stolen bases: 1979 (2), 1980 (5), 1981 (71), 1982 (78), 1983 (90), 1984 (75), 1985 (70), 1986 (70), 1987 (50), 1988 (33), 1989 (41), 1990 (49). Total—634.

Switch-hit home runs in one game, July 16, 1988.

Hit for the cycle, August 16, 1987.

Led National League in stolen bases with 71 in 1981, 78 in 1982, 90 in 1983 and 75 in 1984.

Led National League outfielders in assists with 21 in 1983.

Led American Association in stolen bases with 77 in 1980.

Won THE SPORTING NEWS Gold Shoe Award, 1984.

Named outfielder on THE SPORTING NEWS National League All-Star Team, 1983 and 1986.

Named outfielder on THE SPORTING NEWS National League Silver Slugger team, 1986.

Named National League Rookie Player of the Year by THE SPORTING NEWS, 1981.

Named Minor League Player of the Year by THE SPORTING NEWS, 1980.

Year — Club	League	Pos.	G.	AB.	R.	H.	2B.	3B.	HR.	RBI.	B.A.	PO.	A.	E.	F.A.
1977—Sarasota Expos	Gulf C.	2B-3B-OF	49	161	28	45	6	2	0	21	.280	79	72	13	.921
1978—W. Palm Beach†	Fla. St.	2B-SS	100	359	67	103	10	0	0	23	.287	219	273	24	.953
1979—Memphis	South.	2B	●145	552	★104	160	25	10	5	50	.290	★341	★413	★23	.970
1979—Montreal	Nat.	PR	6	0	3	0	0	0	0	0	.000	0	0	0	.000
1980—Denver	A. A.	2B	108	429	105	152	23	●11	6	64	★.354	226	338	16	.972
1980—Montreal	Nat.	2B-OF	15	20	5	1	0	0	0	0	.050	15	16	0	1.000
1981—Montreal	Nat.	OF-2B	88	313	61	95	13	7	5	37	.304	162	8	4	.977
1982—Montreal	Nat.	OF-2B	156	647	90	179	32	8	4	43	.277	293	126	8	.981
1983—Montreal	Nat.	OF-2B	156	615	★133	183	32	8	11	71	.298	314	23	4	.988
1984—Montreal	Nat.	OF-2B	160	622	106	192	●38	9	8	60	.309	420	8	6	.986
1985—Montreal	Nat.	OF	150	575	115	184	30	13	11	41	.320	284	8	2	.993
1986—Montreal‡	Nat.	OF	151	580	91	194	35	10	9	62	★.334	270	13	6	.979
1987—Montreal	Nat.	OF	139	530	★123	175	34	8	18	68	.330	297	9	4	.987
1988—Montreal§	Nat.	OF	109	429	66	116	19	7	12	48	.270	235	5	3	.988
1989—Montreal	Nat.	OF	145	517	76	148	29	6	9	60	.286	253	7	1	.996
1990—Montreal xy	Nat.	OF	130	457	65	131	11	5	9	62	.287	239	3	6	.976
Major League Totals—12 Years			1405	5305	934	1598	273	81	96	552	.301	2782	226	44	.986

Selected by Montreal Expos' organization in 5th round of free-agent draft, June 7, 1977.

†On disabled list, May 23 to June 5, 1978.

‡Granted free agency, November 12, 1986; re-signed by Expos, May 2, 1987.

§On disabled list, June 24 to July 9, 1988.

xOn disabled list, June 25 to July 10, 1990.

yTraded with Pitcher Jeff Carter and a player to be named later to Chicago White Sox for Outfielder Ivan Calderon and Pitcher Barry Jones, December 23, 1990.

CHAMPIONSHIP SERIES RECORD

Year — Club	League	Pos.	G.	AB.	R.	H.	2B.	3B.	HR.	RBI.	B.A.	PO.	A.	E.	F.A.
1981—Montreal	Nat.	OF	5	21	1	5	2	0	0	1	.238	9	0	0	1.000

ALL-STAR GAME RECORD

Year — League	Pos.	AB.	R.	H.	2B.	3B.	HR.	RBI.	B.A.	PO.	A.	E.	F.A.
1981—National	PR-OF	0	0	0	0	0	0	0	.000	1	0	0	1.000
1982—National	OF	1	0	0	0	0	0	0	.000	0	0	0	.000
1983—National	OF	3	0	0	0	0	0	0	.000	2	0	0	1.000
1984—National	OF	1	0	0	0	0	0	0	.000	4	0	0	1.000
1985—National	PH-OF	0	1	0	0	0	0	0	.000	0	0	0	.000
1986—National	PH-OF	2	0	0	0	0	0	0	.000	1	0	0	1.000
1987—National	OF	3	0	3	0	1	0	2	1.000	1	0	0	1.000
All-Star Game Totals—7 Years		10	1	3	0	1	0	2	.300	9	0	0	1.000

RAFAEL EMILIO RAMIREZ (PEGUERO)

Born February 18, 1959, at San Pedro de Macoris, Dominican Republic.

Height, 5.11. Weight, 190.

Throws and bats righthanded.

Shares major league records for most doubles, game (4), May 21, 1986, 13 innings; most double plays by shortstop, extra-inning game (6), June 27, 1982 (14 innings); most years leading league, errors, shortstop (6).

Holds National League record for fewest putouts by shortstop, season, for leader in most putouts (251), 1984.

Major League stolen bases: 1980 (2), 1981 (7), 1982 (27), 1983 (16), 1984 (14), 1985 (2), 1986 (19), 1987 (6), 1988 (3), 1989 (3), 1990 (10). Total—109.

Led National League shortstops in double plays with 130 in 1982, 116 in 1983, 115 in 1985 and tied for lead with 94 in 1984.

Led National League shortstops in total chances with 866 in 1982 and 724 in 1984.

Year — Club	League	Pos.	G.	AB.	R.	H.	2B.	3B.	HR.	RBI.	B.A.	PO.	A.	E.	F.A.
1977—Brad. Braves	Gulf C.	SS-OF	49	175	20	31	2	1	4	19	.177	52	94	32	.820
1978—Greenwood	W. Car.	SS	81	282	54	77	15	3	6	46	.273	119	229	★43	.890
1978—Savannah	South.	SS	38	131	14	27	4	0	2	13	.206	61	123	15	.925
1979—Savannah†	South.	SS	113	386	47	80	17	3	10	39	.207	134	282	★38	.916
1980—Richmond‡	Int.	SS	80	281	33	79	15	3	5	38	.281	117	294	23	.947
1980—Atlanta	Nat.	SS	50	165	17	44	6	1	2	11	.267	63	140	11	.949
1981—Atlanta	Nat.	SS	95	307	30	67	16	2	2	20	.218	181	306	★30	.942
1982—Atlanta	Nat.	SS	157	609	74	169	24	4	10	52	.278	★300	528	★38	.956
1983—Atlanta	Nat.	SS	152	622	82	185	13	5	7	58	.297	232	490	★39	.949
1984—Atlanta	Nat.	SS	145	591	51	157	22	4	2	48	.266	★251	443	●30	.959

Year Club	League	Pos.	G.	AB.	R.	H.	2B.	3B.	HR.	RBI.	B.A.	PO.	A.	E.	F.A.
1985—Atlanta .... Nat.		SS	138	568	54	141	25	4	5	58	.248	214	451	*32	.954
1986—Atlanta .... Nat.		SS-3B-OF	134	496	57	119	21	1	8	33	.240	156	371	29	.948
1987—Atlanta§x .... Nat.		SS-3B	56	179	22	47	12	0	1	21	.263	66	110	10	.946
1988—Houston .... Nat.		SS	155	566	51	156	30	5	6	59	.276	232	408	23	.965
1989—Houston .... Nat.		SS	151	537	46	132	20	2	6	54	.246	189	326	*30	.945
1990—Houston y .... Nat.		SS	132	445	44	116	19	3	2	37	.261	190	321	25	.953
Major League Totals—11 Years			1365	5085	528	1333	208	31	51	451	.262	2074	3894	297	.953

Signed as free agent by Atlanta Braves' organization, September 28, 1976.

†On disabled list, April 16 to April 27, 1979.

‡On disabled list, June 23 to July 17, 1980.

§On disabled list, July 2 to September 25, 1987.

xTraded with cash to Houston Astros for Third Baseman Ed Whited and Pitcher Mike Stoker, December 8, 1987.

yOn disabled list, July 12 to July 27, 1990.

CHAMPIONSHIP SERIES RECORD

Year Club	League	Pos.	G.	AB.	R.	H.	2B.	3B.	HR.	RBI.	B.A.	PO.	A.	E.	F.A.
1982—Atlanta .... Nat.		SS	3	11	1	2	0	0	0	1	.182	5	11	1	.941

ALL-STAR GAME RECORD

Member of National League All-Star Team in 1984; did not play.

DOMINGO ANTONIO RAMOS

Born March 29, 1958, at Santiago, Dominican Republic.
Height, 5.10. Weight, 170.
Throws and bats righthanded.

Major League stolen bases: 1983 (3), 1984 (2), 1989 (1). Total—6.
Tied for International League lead in sacrifice flies with 6 in 1981.

Year Club	League	Pos.	G.	AB.	R.	H.	2B.	3B.	HR.	RBI.	B.A.	PO.	A.	E.	F.A.
1975—Oneonta .... NYP		SS-3B	49	166	29	39	4	1	0	21	.235	60	143	14	.935
1976—Fort Lauderdale ...Fla. St.		SS	103	328	34	79	11	3	0	29	.241	150	343	35	.934
1976—Syracuse .... Int.		SS	11	39	7	10	2	1	0	8	.256	13	20	2	.943
1977—West Haven .... East.		SS	129	431	55	106	18	6	2	50	.246	222	433	23	*.966
1978—Tacoma .... P. C.		SS	91	314	43	74	13	3	0	30	.236	155	290	28	.941
1978—West Haven .... East.		SS	40	134	16	34	2	2	1	13	.254	40	128	6	.966
1978—New York†‡ .... Amer.		SS	1	0	0	0	0	0	0	0	.000	0	0	0	.000
1979—Syr.§-Colum. x .... Int.		SS	115	376	38	92	11	4	1	28	.245	211	323	26	.954
1980—Syracuse .... Int.		SS	84	319	45	80	8	4	4	27	.251	160	240	28	.935
1980—Toronto .... Amer.		SS-2B	5	16	0	2	0	0	0	0	.125	5	10	0	1.000
1981—Syracuse y .... Int.		SS-3B-2B	96	320	42	82	4	5	0	31	.256	158	248	19	.955
1982—Salt Lake City .... P. C.		SS	112	427	75	134	19	8	6	56	.314	174	288	19	.960
1982—Seattle.................... Amer.		SS	8	26	3	4	2	0	0	1	.154	9	14	2	.920
1983—Seattle.................... Amer.		2B-SS-3B	53	127	14	36	4	0	2	10	.283	51	109	8	.952
1984—Seattle.................... Amer.		3-S-1-2	59	81	6	15	2	0	0	2	.185	51	49	5	.952
1985—Seattle.................... Amer.		S-2-1-3	75	168	19	33	6	0	1	15	.196	87	119	10	.954
1986—Seattle.................... Amer.		SS-2B-3B	49	99	8	18	2	0	0	5	.182	55	93	6	.961
1987—Seattle z................ Amer.		SS-3B-2B	42	103	9	32	6	0	2	11	.311	47	88	5	.964
1988—Colo. Spr. a-Edm.. P. C.		3B-SS-2B	50	165	30	46	10	2	2	25	.279	45	107	9	.944
1988—Clev.-Calif.b.......... Amer.		2-3-1-S-O	32	61	10	14	1	0	0	5	.230	37	43	1	.988
1989—Chicago .... Nat.		SS-3B	85	179	18	47	6	2	1	19	.263	49	142	11	.946
1990—Chicago .... Nat.		3B-SS-2B	98	226	22	60	5	0	2	17	.265	62	100	10	.942
American League Totals—9 Years			324	681	69	154	23	0	5	49	.226	342	525	37	.959
National League Totals—2 Years			183	405	40	107	11	2	3	36	.264	111	242	21	.944
Major League Totals—11 Years			507	1086	109	261	34	2	8	85	.240	453	767	58	.955

Signed as free agent by New York Yankees' organization, May 27, 1975.

†Traded with Pitchers Sparky Lyle, Larry McCall and Dave Rajsich, Catcher Mike Heath and cash to Texas Rangers for Outfielders Juan Beniquez and Greg Jemison and Pitchers Mike Griffin, Paul Mirabella and Dave Righetti, November 10, 1978.

‡Loaned to Toronto Blue Jays' organization, April 5, 1979.

§Loaned to New York Yankees' organization, July 30, 1979; returned to Texas Rangers, September 28, 1979.

xSold to Toronto Blue Jays, November 5, 1979.

yDrafted by Seattle Mariners, December 7, 1981.

zReleased, December 21, 1987; signed by Colorado Springs (Cleveland Indians' organization), February 1, 1988.

aReleased, August 5, 1988; signed by Edmonton (California Angels' organization), August 17, 1988.

bGranted free agency, November 4, 1988; signed by Iowa (Chicago Cubs' organization), December 14, 1988.

CHAMPIONSHIP SERIES RECORD

Year Club	League	Pos.	G.	AB.	R.	H.	2B.	3B.	HR.	RBI.	B.A.	PO.	A.	E.	F.A.
1989—Chicago .... Nat.		PH	1	1	0	0	0	0	0	0	.000	0	0	0	.000

WILLIAM LARRY RANDOLPH JR.
(Willie)

Born July 6, 1954, at Holly Hill, S. C.
Height, 5.11. Weight, 171.
Throws and bats righthanded.
Brother of Terry Randolph, defensive back with Green Bay Packers, 1977.

Shares major league record for most assists by second baseman in extra-inning game since 1900 (13), August 25, 1976 (19 innings).

Holds American League record for most chances accepted by second baseman in extra-inning game (20), August 25, 1976 (19 innings).

Major League stolen bases: 1975 (1), 1976 (37), 1977 (13), 1978 (36), 1979 (33), 1980 (30), 1981 (14), 1982 (16), 1983 (12), 1984 (10), 1985 (16), 1986 (15), 1987 (11), 1988 (8), 1989 (7), 1990 (7). Total—266.

Led American League in bases on balls received with 119 in 1980.
Led American League second basemen in double plays with 128 in 1979 and 112 in 1984.
Led American League second basemen in total chances with 846 in 1979.
Led Eastern League in bases on balls received with 110 in 1974.
Led Western Carolinas League in bases on balls received with 90 and tied for lead in sacrifice flies with 8 in 1973.
Named second baseman on THE SPORTING NEWS American League All-Star Team, 1977, 1980 and 1987.
Named second baseman on THE SPORTING NEWS American League Silver Slugger team, 1980.

Year	Club	League	Pos.	G.	AB.	R.	H.	2B.	3B.	HR.	RBI.	B.A.	PO.	A.	E.	F.A.
1972—Bradenton Pir.	..... Gulf C.		SS-OF	44	167	21	53	6	5	0	10	.317	85	116	24	.893
1973—Charleston	.... W. Car.		2B	121	428	93	120	25	6	8	51	.280	*285	308	*24	.961
1974—Thetford Mines	.... East.		2B	135	461	*103	117	28	6	12	53	.254	269	319	21	.966
1975—Charleston	.... Int.		2B	91	313	41	106	13	5	7	42	.339	189	250	16	.965
1975—Pittsburgh†	.... Nat.		2B-3B	30	61	9	10	1	0	0	3	.164	34	45	6	.929
1976—New York	.... Amer.		2B	125	430	59	115	15	4	1	40	.267	307	415	19	.974
1977—New York	.... Amer.		2B	147	551	91	151	28	11	4	40	.274	350	454	16	.980
1978—New York‡	.... Amer.		2B	134	499	87	139	18	6	3	42	.279	296	400	16	.978
1979—New York	.... Amer.		2B	153	574	98	155	15	13	5	61	.270	*355	*478	13	.985
1980—New York	.... Amer.		2B	138	513	99	151	23	7	7	46	.294	361	401	19	.976
1981—New York	.... Amer.		2B	93	357	59	83	14	3	2	24	.232	205	268	*11	.977
1982—New York	.... Amer.		2B	144	553	85	155	21	4	3	36	.280	352	380	14	.981
1983—New York§	.... Amer.		2B	104	420	73	117	21	1	2	38	.279	265	298	12	.979
1984—New York	.... Amer.		2B	142	564	86	162	24	2	2	31	.287	334	419	13	.983
1985—New York	.... Amer.		2B	143	497	75	137	21	2	5	40	.276	303	425	11	.985
1986—New York x	.... Amer.		2B	141	492	76	136	15	2	5	50	.276	313	381	*20	.972
1987—New York y	.... Amer.		2B	120	449	96	137	24	2	7	67	.305	286	338	12	.981
1988—New York za	.... Amer.		2B	110	404	43	93	20	1	2	34	.230	254	339	7	.988
1989—Los Angeles	.... Nat.		2B	145	549	62	155	18	0	2	36	.282	260	412	9	.987
1990—Los Angeles b	...... Nat.		2B	26	96	15	26	4	0	1	9	.271	50	73	4	.969
1990—Oakland cd	...... Amer.		2B	93	292	37	75	9	3	1	21	.257	148	240	7	.982
National League Totals—3 Years		....		201	706	86	191	23	0	3	48	.271	344	530	19	.979
American League Totals—14 Years		....		1787	6595	1064	1806	268	61	49	570	.274	4129	5236	190	.980
Major League Totals—16 Years		....		1988	7301	1150	1997	291	61	52	618	.274	4473	5766	209	.980

Selected by Pittsburgh Pirates' organization in 7th round of free-agent draft, June 6, 1972.
†Traded with Pitchers Ken Brett and Dock Ellis to New York Yankees for Pitcher Doc Medich, December 11, 1975.
‡On disabled list, June 23 to July 14, 1978.
§On disabled list, June 27 to July 12 and July 13 to August 5, 1983.
xGranted free agency, November 12, 1986; re-signed by Yankees, January 8, 1987.
yOn disabled list, July 15 to August 14, 1987.
zOn disabled list, June 10 to June 25 and August 3 to August 28, 1988.
aGranted free agency, October 24, 1988; signed by Los Angeles Dodgers, December 10, 1988.
bTraded to Oakland Athletics for Outfielder Stan Javier, May 13, 1990.
cOn disabled list, July 15 to August 1, 1990.
dGranted free agency, November 5, 1990.

DIVISION SERIES RECORD

Year	Club	League	Pos.	G.	AB.	R.	H.	2B.	3B.	HR.	RBI.	B.A.	PO.	A.	E.	F.A.
1981—New York	.... Amer.		2B	5	20	0	4	0	0	0	1	.200	7	10	0	1.000

CHAMPIONSHIP SERIES RECORD

Shares American League Championship Series record for most times grounding into double play, total series (4).

Year	Club	League	Pos.	G.	AB.	R.	H.	2B.	3B.	HR.	RBI.	B.A.	PO.	A.	E.	F.A.
1975—Pittsburgh	.... Nat.		PH-PR-2	2	2	1	0	0	0	0	0	.000	0	1	0	1.000
1976—New York	.... Amer.		2B	5	17	0	2	0	0	0	1	.118	8	14	0	1.000
1977—New York	.... Amer.		2B	5	18	4	5	1	0	0	2	.278	13	9	0	1.000
1980—New York	.... Amer.		2B	3	13	0	5	2	0	0	1	.385	2	9	0	1.000
1981—New York	.... Amer.		2B	3	12	2	4	0	0	1	2	.333	12	12	0	1.000
1990—Oakland	.... Amer.		PR-2B	4	8	1	3	0	0	0	3	.375	5	9	0	1.000
Championship Series Totals—6 Years		.....		22	70	8	19	3	0	1	9	.271	40	54	0	1.000

WORLD SERIES RECORD

Year	Club	League	Pos.	G.	AB.	R.	H.	2B.	3B.	HR.	RBI.	B.A.	PO.	A.	E.	F.A.
1976—New York	.... Amer.		2B	4	14	1	1	0	0	0	0	.071	13	8	0	1.000
1977—New York	.... Amer.		2B	6	25	5	4	2	0	1	1	.160	13	14	0	1.000
1981—New York	.... Amer.		2B	6	18	5	4	1	1	2	3	.222	13	11	0	1.000
1990—Oakland	.... Amer.		2B	4	15	0	4	0	0	0	0	.267	14	12	0	1.000
World Series Totals—4 Years		....		20	72	11	13	3	1	3	4	.181	53	45	0	1.000

ALL-STAR GAME RECORD

Shares All-Star Game record for most at-bats, nine-inning game (5), July 19, 1977.

Year	League	Pos.	AB.	R.	H.	2B.	3B.	HR.	RBI.	B.A.	PO.	A.	E.	F.A.
1977—American	....	2B	5	0	1	0	0	0	1	.200	2	6	0	1.000
1980—American	....	2B	4	0	2	0	0	0	0	.500	0	3	2	.600
1981—American	....	2B	3	0	1	0	0	0	0	.333	0	5	0	1.000

Year League	Pos.	AB.	R.	H.	2B.	3B.	HR.	RBI.	B.A.	PO.	A.	E.	F.A.
1987—American	2B	1	0	0	0	0	0	0	.000	0	1	0	1.000
1989—National	2B	1	0	0	0	0	0	0	.000	0	0	0	.000
All-Star Game Totals—5 Years		14	0	4	0	0	0	1	.286	2	15	2	.895

Named to American League All-Star Team for 1976 game; replaced due to injury.

DENNIS LEE RASMUSSEN

Born April 18, 1959, at Los Angeles, Calif.
Height, 6.07. Weight, 233.
Throws and bats lefthanded.
Attended Creighton University, Omaha, Neb.
Grandson of Wilbur Lee (Bill) Brubaker, infielder with Pittsburgh
Pirates and Boston Braves, 1932 through 1940 and 1943.

Led National League in home runs allowed with 28 in 1990.
Led Eastern League in wild pitches with 18 in 1981.
Tied for International League lead in games started by pitchers with 28 in 1983.

Year Club	League	G.	IP.	W.	L.	Pct.	H.	R.	ER.	SO.	BB.	ERA.
1980—Salinas	California	11	76	4	6	.400	69	51	46	63	52	5.45
1981—Holyoke	Eastern	24	156	8	12	.400	134	95	69	125	99	3.98
1982—Spokane†	P. Coast	27	171⅔	11	8	.579	166	110	96	162	★113	5.03
1983—Columbus‡	Int'national	28	181	●13	10	.565	161	106	92	★187	108	4.57
1983—San Diego§	National	4	13⅔	0	0	.000	10	5	3	13	8	1.98
1984—Columbus	Int'national	6	43⅔	4	1	.800	24	15	15	30	27	3.09
1984—New York	American	24	147⅔	9	6	.600	127	79	75	110	60	4.57
1985—New York	American	22	101⅔	3	5	.375	97	56	45	63	42	3.98
1985—Columbus	Int'national	7	45	0	3	.000	41	24	19	43	25	3.80
1986—New York	American	31	202	18	6	.750	160	91	87	131	74	3.88
1987—New York	American	26	146	9	7	.563	145	78	77	89	55	4.75
1987—Columbus x	Int'national	1	7	1	0	1.000	5	1	1	4	0	1.29
1987—Cincinnati	National	7	45⅓	4	1	.800	39	22	20	39	12	3.97
1988—Cincinnati y-San Diego	National	31	204⅔	16	10	.615	199	84	78	112	58	3.43
1989—San Diego	National	33	183⅔	10	10	.500	190	100	87	87	72	4.26
1990—San Diego z	National	32	187⅔	11	15	.423	217	110	94	86	62	4.51
National League Totals—5 Years		107	635	41	36	.532	655	321	282	337	212	4.00
American League Totals—4 Years		103	597⅓	39	24	.619	529	304	284	393	231	4.28
Major League Totals—8 Years		210	1232⅓	80	60	.571	1184	625	566	730	443	4.13

Selected by Pittsburgh Pirates' organization in 18th round of free-agent draft, June 7, 1977.
Selected by California Angels' organization in 1st round (17th player selected) of free-agent draft, June 3, 1980.
†Traded to New York Yankees, November 24, 1982, completing deal in which New York traded Pitcher Tommy John to California Angels for a player to be named later, August 31, 1982.
‡Traded with Second Baseman Edwin Rodriguez to San Diego Padres, September 12, 1983, completing deal in which San Diego traded Pitcher John Montefusco to New York Yankees for two players to be named later, August 26, 1983.
§Traded with a player to be named later to New York Yankees' organization for Third Baseman Graig Nettles, March 30, 1984; New York organization acquired Pitcher Darin Cloninger to complete deal, April 26, 1984.
xTraded to Cincinnati Reds for Pitcher Bill Gullickson, August 26, 1987.
yTraded to San Diego Padres for Pitcher Candy Sierra, June 8, 1988.
zGranted free agency, November 5, 1990; re-signed by Padres, January 9, 1991.

JOHNNY CORNELIUS RAY

Born March 1, 1957, at Chouteau, Okla.
Height, 5.11. Weight, 189.
Throws right and bats right and lefthanded.
Attended Northeastern Oklahoma A & M, Miami, Okla.; and
University of Arkansas, Fayetteville, Ark.

Major League stolen bases: 1982 (16), 1983 (18), 1984 (11), 1985 (13), 1986 (6), 1987 (4), 1988 (4), 1989 (6), 1990 (2). Total—80.
Tied for National League lead in grounding into double plays with 21 in 1986.
Led National League second basemen in total chances with 914 in 1982.
Named National League Rookie Player of the Year by THE SPORTING NEWS, 1982.
Named second baseman on THE SPORTING NEWS American League All-Star Team, 1988.
Named second baseman on THE SPORTING NEWS National League Silver Slugger team, 1983.

Year Club	League	Pos.	G.	AB.	R.	H.	2B.	3B.	HR.	RBI.	B.A.	PO.	A.	E.	F.A.
1979—Sarasota Astros	Gulf C.	3B-2B	37	132	25	41	8	1	3	25	.311	25	51	11	.874
1979—Daytona Beach	Fla. St.	3B-SS-2B	24	68	6	15	1	2	1	10	.221	21	38	8	.881
1980—Columbus	South.	2B-3B-OF	138	497	86	161	32	6	10	72	.324	203	331	24	.957
1981—Tucson†	P. C.	2B	131	525	111	183	★50	10	5	83	.349	309	369	19	.973
1981—Pittsburgh	Nat.	2B	31	102	10	25	11	0	0	6	.245	52	96	2	.987
1982—Pittsburgh	Nat.	2B	●162	647	79	182	30	7	7	63	.281	★381	★512	★21	.977
1983—Pittsburgh	Nat.	2B	151	576	68	163	●38	7	5	53	.283	319	452	13	.983
1984—Pittsburgh	Nat.	2B	155	555	75	173	●38	6	6	67	.312	331	400	12	.984
1985—Pittsburgh	Nat.	2B	154	594	67	163	33	3	7	70	.274	305	423	18	.976
1986—Pittsburgh	Nat.	2B	155	579	67	174	33	0	7	78	.301	280	479	5	.993
1987—Pittsburgh‡	Nat.	2B	123	472	48	129	19	3	5	54	.273	248	358	12	.981
1987—California	Amer.	2B	30	127	16	44	11	0	0	15	.346	52	90	2	.986
1988—California	Amer.	2B-OF	153	602	75	184	42	7	6	83	.306	269	328	20	.968
1989—California§	Amer.	2B	134	530	52	153	16	3	5	62	.289	279	403	11	.984

Year Club League	Pos.	G.	AB.	R.	H.	2B.	3B.	HR.	RBI.	B.A.	PO.	A.	E.	F.A.
1990—California xy......... Amer.	2B	105	404	47	112	23	0	5	43	.277	241	295	7	.987
National League Totals—7 Years............		931	3525	414	1009	202	26	37	391	.286	1916	2720	83	.982
American League Totals—4 Years		422	1663	190	493	92	10	16	203	.296	841	1116	40	.980
Major League Totals—10 Years...............		1353	5188	604	1502	294	36	53	594	.290	2757	3836	123	.982

Selected by Houston Astros' organization in 12th round of free-agent draft, June 5, 1979.

†Traded with two players to be named later to Pittsburgh Pirates for Second Baseman Phil Garner, August 31, 1981; Pittsburgh organization acquired Pitcher Randy Niemann and Outfielder Kevin Houston to complete deal, September 9, 1981.

‡Traded to California Angels for Third Baseman Billie Merrifield and a player to be named later, August 29, 1987; Pittsburgh Pirates acquired Pitcher Miguel Garcia to complete deal, September 3, 1987.

§On disabled list, April 6 to April 21, 1989.

xOn disabled list, June 9 to June 30, 1990.

yReleased, December 20, 1990; signed by Yakult Swallows of Japanese Baseball League, December 20, 1990.

ALL-STAR GAME RECORD

Year League	Pos.	AB.	R.	H.	2B.	3B.	HR.	RBI.	B.A.	PO.	A.	E.	F.A.
1988—American	PH	1	0	0	0	0	0	0	.000	0	0	0	.000

RANDY MAX READY

Born January 8, 1960, at San Mateo, Calif.
Height, 5.11. Weight, 184.
Throws and bats righthanded.
Attended California State University, Hayward,
Calif., and Mesa College, Grand Junction, Colo.

Shares American League record for most innings played by third baseman, game (25), May 8, finished May 9, 1984 (fielded 24⅓ innings).

Major League stolen bases: 1986 (2), 1987 (7), 1988 (6), 1989 (4), 1990 (3). Total—22.

Led Pacific Coast League in bases on balls received with 99 in 1983.

Led Texas League in total bases with 281 in 1982.

Led Texas League third basemen in double plays with 27 and total chances with 456 in 1982.

Led Midwest League third basemen in double plays with 22 in 1981.

Year Club League	Pos.	G.	AB.	R.	H.	2B.	3B.	HR.	RBI.	B.A.	PO.	A.	E.	F.A.
1980—Butte .... Pion.	SS-2B-3B	61	226	*65	85	*23	4	8	50	*.376	86	174	22	.922
1981—Burlington .... Midw.	3B	110	367	74	113	17	0	17	56	.308	72	216	21	*.932
1982—El Paso.................. Texas	3B	132	475	*122	*178	33	5	20	99	*.375	*115	*312	●29	.936
1983—Vancouver............. P. C.	3B	116	407	82	134	28	1	13	59	.329	136	231	24	.939
1983—Milwaukee............. Amer.	3B	12	37	8	15	3	2	1	6	.405	5	8	0	1.000
1984—Milwaukee............. Amer.	3B	37	123	13	23	6	1	3	13	.187	29	76	6	.946
1984—Vancouver†........... P. C.	2B-3B	43	151	48	49	7	4	3	18	.325	74	125	6	.971
1985—Milwaukee‡........... Amer.	OF-3B-2B	48	181	29	48	9	5	1	21	.265	93	14	1	.991
1985—Vancouver............. P. C.	OF-3B-2B	52	190	33	62	12	3	4	29	.326	60	35	7	.931
1986—Milwaukee§........... Amer.	OF-2B-3B	23	79	8	15	4	0	1	4	.190	35	21	3	.949
1986—San Diego x .... Nat.	3B	1	3	0	0	0	0	0	0	.000	0	2	1	.667
1986—Las Vegas y .... P. C.	3B-OF	10	38	5	14	4	0	1	8	.368	12	10	0	1.000
1987—San Diego .... Nat.	3B-2B-OF	124	350	69	108	26	6	12	54	.309	124	220	15	.958
1988—San Diego .... Nat.	3B-2B-OF	114	331	43	88	16	2	7	39	.266	112	153	11	.960
1989—S.D.z-Phi................ Nat.	OF-3B-2B	100	254	37	67	13	2	8	26	.264	80	72	9	.944
1990—Philadelphia .... Nat.	OF-2B	101	217	26	53	9	1	1	26	.244	78	86	2	.988
American League Totals—4 Years		120	420	58	101	22	8	6	44	.240	162	119	10	.966
National League Totals—5 Years............		440	1155	175	316	64	11	28	145	.274	394	533	38	.961
Major League Totals—10 Years...............		560	1575	233	417	86	19	34	189	.265	556	652	48	.962

Selected by Milwaukee Brewers' organization in 5th round of free-agent draft, June 3, 1980.

†On disabled list, August 21, 1984 through remainder of season.

‡On disabled list, April 30 to June 19, 1985; included rehabilitation disability assignment to Vancouver, June 1 to June 19, 1985.

§Traded to San Diego Padres for a player to be named later, June 12, 1986; San Diego traded Infielder Tim Pyznarski to Milwaukee Brewers' organization to complete deal, October 29, 1986.

xOn disabled list, June 19 to July 7, 1986.

yOn disabled list, July 22, 1986 through remainder of season.

zTraded with Outfielder John Kruk to Philadelphia Phillies for Outfielder Chris James, June 2, 1989.

JEFFREY JAMES REARDON
(Jeff)

Born October 1, 1955, at Pittsfield, Mass.
Height, 6.00. Weight, 200.
Throws and bats righthanded.
Attended University of Massachusetts, Amherst, Mass.

Major League saves: 1979 (2), 1980 (6), 1981 (8), 1982 (26), 1983 (21), 1984 (23), 1985 (41), 1986 (35), 1987 (31), 1988 (42), 1989 (31), 1990 (21). Total—287.

Led National League in saves with 41 in 1985.

Led Carolina League in shutouts with 3 in 1977.

Named American League Co-Fireman of the Year by THE SPORTING NEWS, 1987.

Named National League Fireman of the Year by THE SPORTING NEWS, 1985.

Year Club League	G.	IP.	W.	L.	Pct.	H.	R.	ER.	SO.	BB.	ERA.
1977—Lynchburg...................... Carolina	16	101	8	3	.727	89	42	37	60	30	3.30
1978—Jackson .... Texas	28	163	*17	4	*.810	128	56	46	115	65	2.53

Year	Club	League	G.	IP.	W.	L.	Pct.	H.	R.	ER.	SO.	BB.	ERA.
1979—Tidewater†	Int'national	30	69	5	2	.714	46	18	16	64	21	2.09
1979—New York	National	18	21	1	2	.333	12	7	4	10	9	1.71
1980—New York	National	61	110	8	7	.533	96	36	32	101	47	2.62
1981—New York‡-Montreal	National	43	70	3	0	1.000	48	17	17	49	21	2.19
1982—Montreal	National	75	109	7	4	.636	87	28	25	86	36	2.06
1983—Montreal	National	66	92	7	9	.438	87	34	31	78	44	3.03
1984—Montreal	National	68	87	7	7	.500	70	31	28	79	37	2.90
1985—Montreal	National	63	87⅔	2	8	.200	68	31	31	67	26	3.18
1986—Montreal§	National	62	89	7	9	.438	83	42	39	67	26	3.94
1987—Minnesota	American	63	80⅓	8	8	.500	70	41	40	83	28	4.48
1988—Minnesota	American	63	73	2	4	.333	68	21	20	56	15	2.47
1989—Minnesota x	American	65	73	5	4	.556	68	33	33	46	12	4.07
1990—Boston y	American	47	51⅓	5	3	.625	39	19	18	33	19	3.16
National League Totals—8 Years		456	665⅔	42	46	.477	551	226	207	537	246	2.80
American League Totals—4 Years		238	277⅔	20	19	.513	245	114	111	218	74	3.60
Major League Totals—12 Years		694	943⅓	62	65	.488	796	340	318	755	320	3.03

Selected by Montreal Expos' organization in 23rd round of free-agent draft, June 5, 1973.
Signed as free agent by New York Mets' organization, June 14, 1977.
†On disabled list, June 13 to June 24 and June 29 to July 26, 1979.
‡Traded with Outfielder Dan Norman to Montreal Expos for Outfielder Ellis Valentine, May 29, 1981.
§Traded with Catcher Tom Nieto to Minnesota Twins for Pitchers Neal Heaton, Al Cardwood and Yorkis Perez and Catcher Jeff Reed, February 3, 1987.
xGranted free agency, November 13, 1989; signed by Boston Red Sox, December 6, 1989.
yOn disabled list, July 30 to September 12, 1990.

DIVISION SERIES RECORD

Year	Club	League	G.	IP.	W.	L.	Pct.	H.	R.	ER.	SO.	BB.	ERA.
1981—Montreal	National	3	4⅓	0	1	.000	1	1	1	2	1	2.08

CHAMPIONSHIP SERIES RECORD

Shares American League Championship Series record for most games pitched, series (4), 1987.

Year	Club	League	G.	IP.	W.	L.	Pct.	H.	R.	ER.	SO.	BB.	ERA.
1981—Montreal	National	1	1	0	0	.000	3	3	3	0	0	27.00
1987—Minnesota	American	4	5⅓	1	1	.500	7	3	3	5	3	5.06
1990—Boston	American	1	2	0	0	.000	3	2	2	0	1	9.00
Championship Series Totals—3 Years		6	8⅓	1	1	.500	13	8	8	5	4	8.64

WORLD SERIES RECORD

Year	Club	League	G.	IP.	W.	L.	Pct.	H.	R.	ER.	SO.	BB.	ERA.
1987—Minnesota	American	4	4⅔	0	0	.000	5	0	0	3	0	0.00

ALL-STAR GAME RECORD

Year	League	IP.	W.	L.	Pct.	H.	R.	ER.	SO.	BB.	ERA.
1985—National		1	0	0	.000	1	0	0	1	0	0.00

Member of National League All-Star Team in 1986; did not play.
Member of American League All-Star Team in 1988; did not play.

GARY EUGENE REDUS

Name pronounced REE-dus.

Born November 1, 1956, at Athens, Ala.
Height, 6.01. Weight, 185.
Throws and bats righthanded.

Major League stolen bases: 1982 (11), 1983 (39), 1984 (48), 1985 (48), 1986 (25), 1987 (52), 1988 (31), 1989 (25), 1990 (11). Total—290.
Hit for the cycle, August 25, 1989.
Led American Association in stolen bases with 54 and tied for lead in sacrifice flies with 9 in 1982.
Led Florida State League in total bases with 220 in 1980.
Led Pioneer League in total bases with 199, stolen bases with 42 and tied for lead in sacrifice flies with 6 in 1978.
Tied for Western Carolinas League lead in errors by second basemen with 20 in 1979.
Named Pioneer League Player of the Year, 1978.

Year	Club	League	Pos.	G.	AB.	R.	H.	2B.	3B.	HR.	RBI.	B.A.	PO.	A.	E.	F.A.
1978—Billings	Pion.	2B	68	253	*100	*117	19	6	17	62	*.462	124	*185	*28	.917
1979—Nashville	South.	OF	36	109	7	19	2	1	0	7	.174	74	3	3	.963
1979—Greensboro	W. Car.	2B-OF	83	309	79	86	17	1	16	52	.278	172	193	21	.946
1980—Tampa	Fla. St.	OF-3B-1B	128	452	78	136	18	9	16	68	.301	213	84	27	.917
1981—Waterbury	East.	OF-1B	138	477	71	119	26	4	20	75	.249	667	34	14	.980
1982—Indianapolis	A. A.	OF	122	439	112	146	29	9	24	93	.333	223	10	7	.971
1982—Cincinnati	Nat.	OF	20	83	12	18	3	2	1	7	.217	29	3	1	.970
1983—Cincinnati	Nat.	OF	125	453	90	112	20	9	17	51	.247	235	11	7	.972
1984—Cincinnati	Nat.	OF	123	394	69	100	21	3	7	22	.254	200	6	7	.967
1985—Cincinnati†	Nat.	OF	101	246	51	62	14	4	6	28	.252	140	3	2	.986
1986—Philadelphia‡	Nat.	OF	90	340	62	84	22	4	11	33	.247	185	8	4	.980
1986—Reading§	East.	OF	6	24	4	6	1	0	0	0	.250	11	1	1	.923
1987—Chicago	Amer.	OF	130	475	78	112	26	6	12	48	.236	262	13	6	.979
1988—Chicago x	Amer.	OF	77	262	42	69	10	4	6	34	.263	140	7	2	.987
1988—Pittsburgh y	Nat.	OF	30	71	12	14	2	0	2	4	.197	42	2	2	.957

Year—Club	League	Pos.	G.	AB.	R.	H.	2B.	3B.	HR.	RBI.	B.A.	PO.	A.	E.	F.A.
1989—Pittsburgh z	Nat.	1B-OF	98	279	42	79	18	7	6	33	.283	583	55	9	.986
1990—Pittsburgh a	Nat.	1B-OF	96	227	32	56	15	3	6	23	.247	461	36	8	.984
National League Totals—8 Years			683	2093	370	525	115	32	56	201	.251	1875	124	40	.980
American League Totals—2 Years			207	737	120	181	36	10	18	82	.246	402	20	8	.981
Major League Totals—9 Years			890	2830	490	706	151	42	74	283	.249	2277	144	48	.981

Selected by Boston Red Sox' organization in 17th round of free-agent draft, June 7, 1977.
Selected by Cincinnati Reds' organization in 15th round of free-agent draft, June 6, 1978.
†Traded with Pitcher Tom Hume to Philadelphia Phillies for Pitchers John Denny and Jeff Gray, December 11, 1985.
‡On disabled list, April 28 to July 1, 1986; included rehabilitation disability assignment to Reading, June 23 to June 30, 1986.
§Traded to Chicago White Sox for Pitcher Joe Cowley and cash, March 26, 1987.
xTraded to Pittsburgh Pirates for Outfielder Mike Diaz, August 19, 1988.
yGranted free agency, November 4, 1988; re-signed by Pirates, November 15, 1988.
zOn disabled list, March 27 to April 11 and July 25 to August 9, 1989.
aGranted free agency, November 5, 1990; re-signed by Pirates, December 10, 1990.

CHAMPIONSHIP SERIES RECORD

Year—Club	League	Pos.	G.	AB.	R.	H.	2B.	3B.	HR.	RBI.	B.A.	PO.	A.	E.	F.A.
1990—Pittsburgh	Nat.	PH-1B	5	8	1	2	0	0	0	0	.250	16	0	0	1.000

DARREN DOUGLAS REED

Born October 16, 1965, at Ventura, Calif.
Height, 6.01. Weight, 190.
Throws and bats righthanded.
Attended Ventura College, Ventura, Calif.

Major League stolen bases: 1990 (1).
Led International League in grounding into double plays with 15 in 1989.

Year—Club	League	Pos.	G.	AB.	R.	H.	2B.	3B.	HR.	RBI.	B.A.	PO.	A.	E.	F.A.
1984—Oneonta	NYP	OF-C	40	113	17	26	7	0	2	9	.230	41	2	2	.956
1985—Fort Lauderdale	Fla. St.	OF	100	369	63	117	21	4	10	61	.317	191	8	7	.966
1986—Albany†	East.	OF	51	196	22	45	11	1	4	27	.230	78	2	5	.941
1987—Albany	East.	OF	107	404	68	129	23	4	20	79	.319	174	6	4	.978
1987—Columbus‡	Int.	OF	21	79	15	26	3	3	8	16	.329	33	2	1	.972
1988—Tidewater	Int.	OF-C	101	345	31	83	26	0	9	47	.241	170	5	4	.978
1989—Tidewater	Int.	OF	133	444	57	119	30	6	4	50	.268	232	★19	5	.980
1990—Tidewater	Int.	OF	104	359	58	95	21	6	17	74	.265	222	11	4	.983
1990—New York	Nat.	OF	26	39	5	8	4	1	1	2	.205	20	1	1	.955
Major League Totals—1 Year			26	39	5	8	4	1	1	2	.205	20	1	1	.955

Selected by Oakland A's organization in 10th round of free-agent draft, January 17, 1984.
Selected by New York Yankees' organization in secondary phase of free-agent draft, June 4, 1984.
†On disabled list, June 17, 1986 through remainder of season.
‡Traded with Catcher Phil Lombardi and Pitcher Steve Frey to New York Mets for Shortstop Rafael Santana and Pitcher Victor Garcia, December 11, 1987.

JEFFREY SCOTT REED
(Jeff)

Born November 12, 1962, at Joliet, Ill.
Height, 6.02. Weight, 190.
Throws right and bats lefthanded.
Brother of Curtis Reed, outfielder in San Diego Padres' and
Chicago White Sox' organizations 1977 through 1984.

Holds modern National League record for most errors by catcher, inning (3), July 28, 1987, seventh inning.
Major League stolen bases: 1986 (1), 1988 (1). Total—2.
Led International League catchers in total chances with 720 in 1985.
Led Southern League catchers in total chances with 714 and double plays with 12 in 1983.
Led California League catchers in total chances with 758 and tied for lead in double plays with 9 in 1982.

Year—Club	League	Pos.	G.	AB.	R.	H.	2B.	3B.	HR.	RBI.	B.A.	PO.	A.	E.	F.A.
1980—Elizabethton	Appal.	C	65	225	39	64	15	1	1	20	.284	269	★41	9	.972
1981—Wisconsin Rapids	Midw.	C	106	312	63	73	12	1	4	34	.234	547	★93	7	.989
1981—Orlando	South.	C	3	4	0	1	0	0	0	0	.250	4	1	0	1.000
1982—Visalia	Calif.	C	125	395	69	130	19	2	5	54	.329	★642	●106	10	.987
1983—Orlando	South.	C	118	379	52	100	16	5	6	45	.264	★618	★88	8	★.989
1983—Toledo	Int.	C	14	41	5	7	1	1	0	3	.171	77	6	1	.988
1984—Minnesota	Amer.	C	18	21	3	3	3	0	0	1	.143	41	2	1	.977
1984—Toledo	Int.	C	94	301	30	80	16	3	3	35	.266	546	43	5	★.992
1985—Toledo	Int.	C	122	404	53	100	15	3	5	36	.248	★627	★81	12	.983
1985—Minnesota	Amer.	C	7	10	2	2	0	0	0	0	.200	9	3	0	1.000
1986—Minnesota	Amer.	C	68	165	13	39	6	1	2	9	.236	332	19	2	.994
1986—Toledo†	Int.	C	25	71	10	22	5	3	1	14	.310	108	22	2	.985
1987—Montreal‡	Nat.	C	75	207	15	44	11	0	1	21	.213	357	36	12	.970
1987—Indianapolis	A. A.	C	5	17	0	3	0	0	0	0	.176	27	2	0	1.000
1988—Mont.§-Cinc.	Nat.	C	92	265	20	60	9	2	1	16	.226	468	38	3	.994
1988—Indianapolis	A. A.	C	8	22	1	7	3	0	0	1	.318	30	11	0	1.000
1989—Cincinnati	Nat.	C	102	287	16	64	11	0	3	23	.223	504	50	7	.988

Year Club	League	Pos.	G.	AB.	R.	H.	2B.	3B.	HR.	RBI.	B.A.	PO.	A.	E.	F.A.
1990—Cincinnati............. Nat.		C	72	175	12	44	8	1	3	16	.251	358	26	5	.987
American League Totals—3 Years........			93	196	18	44	9	1	2	10	.224	382	24	3	.993
National League Totals—4 Years...........			341	934	63	212	39	3	8	76	.227	1687	150	27	.986
Major League Totals—7 Years.................			434	1130	81	256	48	4	10	86	.227	2069	174	30	.987

Selected by Minnesota Twins' organization in 1st round (12th player selected) of free-agent draft, June 3, 1980.

†Traded with Pitchers Neal Heaton, Al Cardwood and Yorkis Perez to Montreal Expos for Pitcher Jeff Reardon and Catcher Tom Nieto, February 3, 1987.

‡On disabled list, April 20 to May 25, 1987; included rehabilitation disability assignment to Indianapolis, May 19 to May 25, 1987.

§Traded with Outfielder Herm Winningham and Pitcher Randy St. Claire to Cincinnati Reds for Outfielder Tracy Jones and Pitcher Pat Pacillo, July 13, 1988.

CHAMPIONSHIP SERIES RECORD

Year Club	League	Pos.	G.	AB.	R.	H.	2B.	3B.	HR.	RBI.	B.A.	PO.	A.	E.	F.A.
1990—Cincinnati............. Nat.		C	4	7	0	0	0	0	0	0	.000	24	1	0	1.000

JERRY MAXWELL REED

Born October 8, 1955, at Bryson City, N.C.
Weight, 6.01. Weight, 190.
Throws and bats righthanded.
Received bachelor of science degree in education from
Western Carolina University, Cullowhee, N.C. in 1977.

Major League saves: 1985 (8), 1987 (7), 1988 (1), 1990 (2). Total—18.
Tied for Eastern League lead in intentional bases on balls issued with 9 in 1979.

Year Club	League	G.	IP.	W.	L.	Pct.	H.	R.	ER.	SO.	BB.	ERA.
1977—Auburn	NYP	*32	56	3	5	.375	63	35	30	36	24	4.82
1978—Spartanburg...................................	W. Carol.	39	66	7	2	.778	36	22	10	31	34	1.36
1978—Peninsula......................................	Carolina	15	24	1	0	1.000	9	3	2	11	5	0.75
1979—Reading...	Eastern	45	80	11	4	.733	67	25	17	37	28	1.91
1980—Oklahoma City	Am. Assoc.	33	97	6	5	.545	128	62	53	36	42	4.92
1980—Reading...	Eastern	8	17	1	1	.500	17	6	6	10	10	3.18
1981—Reading...	Eastern	56	80	5	4	.556	80	34	29	62	29	3.26
1981—Philadelphia	National	4	5	0	1	.000	7	4	4	5	6	7.20
1982—Oklahoma City	Am. Assoc.	25	131⅔	6	7	.462	135	78	64	73	59	4.37
1982—Philadelphia†	National	7	8⅔	1	0	1.000	11	6	5	1	3	5.19
1982—Cleveland.....................................	American	6	15⅔	1	1	.500	15	6	6	10	3	3.45
1983—Charleston....................................	Int'national	21	145⅓	10	6	.625	141	70	58	57	67	3.59
1983—Cleveland.....................................	American	7	21⅓	0	0	.000	26	19	17	11	9	7.17
1984—Maine...	Int'national	27	179⅓	12	6	.667	*193	86	72	77	57	3.61
1985—Maine...	Int'national	14	95⅓	8	5	.615	88	41	36	47	37	3.40
1985—Cleveland‡....................................	American	33	72⅓	3	5	.375	67	41	33	37	19	4.11
1986—Calgary	P. Coast	19	41	2	1	.667	45	24	21	20	17	4.61
1986—Seattle§...	American	11	34⅔	4	0	1.000	38	13	12	16	13	3.12
1987—Seattle x..	American	39	81⅔	1	2	.333	79	32	31	51	24	3.42
1987—Calgary	P. Coast	1	3	0	0	.000	1	0	0	3	0	0.00
1988—Seattle...	American	46	86⅓	1	1	.500	82	42	38	48	33	3.96
1989—Seattle...	American	52	101⅔	7	7	.500	89	44	36	50	43	3.19
1990—Seattle y-Boston z.......................	American	33	52⅓	2	2	.500	63	31	28	19	19	4.82
National League Totals—2 Years......................		11	13⅔	1	1	.500	18	10	9	6	9	5.93
American League Totals—8 Years....................		227	466	19	18	.514	459	228	201	242	163	3.88
Major League Totals—9 Years............................		238	479⅔	20	19	.513	477	238	210	248	172	3.94

Selected by Minnesota Twins' organization in 11th round of free-agent draft, June 5, 1973.

Selected by Philadelphia Phillies' organization in 22nd round of free-agent draft, June 7, 1977.

†Traded with Pitcher Roy Smith and Outfielder Wil Culmer to Cleveland Indians for Pitcher John Denny, September 12, 1982.

‡Released, April 1, 1986; signed by Calgary (Seattle Mariners' organization), April 11, 1986.

§On disabled list, August 4, 1986 through remainder of season.

xOn disabled list, July 25 to August 20, 1987; included rehabilitation disability assignment to Calgary, August 16 to August 20, 1987.

yReleased, April 25, 1990; signed by Boston Red Sox, May 3, 1990.

zReleased, August 12, 1990.

JODY ERIC REED

Born July 26, 1962, at Tampa, Fla.
Height, 5.09. Weight, 165.
Throws and bats righthanded.
Attended Manatee Junior College, Bradenton, Fla., and received degree in criminology
from Florida State University, Tallahassee, Fla., in 1985.

Major League stolen bases: 1987 (1), 1988 (1), 1989 (4), 1990 (4). Total—10.
Led Florida State League in bases on balls received with 94 in 1985.
Led International League shortstops in total chances with 683 and double plays with 86 in 1987.
Led Florida State League shortstops in double plays with 101 in 1985.

Year Club	League	Pos.	G.	AB.	R.	H.	2B.	3B.	HR.	RBI.	B.A.	PO.	A.	E.	F.A.
1984—Winter Haven....... Fla. St.		SS	77	273	46	74	14	1	0	20	.271	128	271	26	.939
1985—Winter Haven....... Fla. St.		SS	134	489	*95	157	25	1	0	45	*.321	*256	*478	37	*.952
1986—New Britain .... East.		SS	60	218	33	50	12	1	0	11	.229	114	190	14	.956

Year—Club	League	Pos.	G.	AB.	R.	H.	2B.	3B.	HR.	RBI.	B.A.	PO.	A.	E.	F.A.
1986—Pawtucket	Int.	SS	69	227	27	64	11	0	1	30	.282	115	222	12	.966
1987—Pawtucket	Int.	SS	136	510	77	151	22	2	7	51	.296	★236	★427	20	.971
1987—Boston	Amer.	SS-2B-3B	9	30	4	9	1	1	0	8	.300	11	26	0	1.000
1988—Boston†	Amer.	SS-2B-3B	109	338	60	99	23	1	1	28	.293	147	282	11	.975
1989—Boston	Amer.	S-2-3-O	146	524	76	151	42	2	3	40	.288	255	423	19	.973
1990—Boston	Amer.	2B-SS	155	598	70	173	●45	0	5	51	.289	278	478	16	.979
Major League Totals—4 Years			419	1490	210	432	111	4	9	127	.290	691	1209	46	.976

Selected by Texas Rangers' organization in 3rd round of free-agent draft, January 12, 1982.
Selected by San Francisco Giants' organization in secondary phase of free-agent draft, June 7, 1982.
Selected by Texas Rangers' organization in secondary phase of free-agent draft, June 6, 1983.
Selected by Boston Red Sox' organization in 8th round of free-agent draft, June 4, 1984.
†Appeared in one game as a pinch-runner.

CHAMPIONSHIP SERIES RECORD

Year—Club	League	Pos.	G.	AB.	R.	H.	2B.	3B.	HR.	RBI.	B.A.	PO.	A.	E.	F.A.
1988—Boston	Amer.	SS	4	11	0	3	1	0	0	0	.273	3	10	0	1.000
1990—Boston	Amer.	2B-SS	4	15	0	2	0	0	0	1	.133	11	11	0	1.000
Championship Series Totals—2 Years			8	26	0	5	1	0	0	1	.192	14	21	0	1.000

RICHARD ALLEN REED
(Rick)

Born August 16, 1964, at Huntington, W. Va.
Height, 6.00. Weight, 195.
Throws and bats righthanded.
Attended Marshall University, Huntington, W. Va.

Major League saves: 1990 (1).

Year—Club	League	G.	IP.	W.	L.	Pct.	H.	R.	ER.	SO.	BB.	ERA.
1986—Bradenton Pirates	Gulf Coast	8	24	0	2	.000	20	12	10	15	6	3.75
1986—Macon	S. Atlantic	1	6⅓	0	0	.000	5	3	2	1	2	2.84
1987—Macon	S. Atlantic	46	93⅔	8	4	.667	80	38	26	92	29	2.50
1988—Salem	Carolina	15	72⅓	6	2	.750	56	28	22	73	17	2.74
1988—Harrisburg	Eastern	2	16	1	0	1.000	11	2	2	17	2	1.13
1988—Buffalo	Am. Assoc.	10	77	5	2	.714	62	15	14	50	12	1.64
1988—Pittsburgh	National	2	12	1	0	1.000	10	4	4	6	2	3.00
1989—Buffalo	Am. Assoc.	20	125⅔	9	8	.529	130	58	52	75	28	3.72
1989—Pittsburgh	National	15	54⅔	1	4	.200	62	35	34	34	11	5.60
1990—Buffalo	Am. Assoc.	15	91	7	4	.636	82	37	35	63	21	3.46
1990—Pittsburgh	National	13	53⅔	2	3	.400	62	32	26	27	12	4.36
Major League Totals—3 Years		30	120⅓	4	7	.364	134	71	64	67	25	4.79

Selected by Pittsburgh Pirates' organization in 26th round of free-agent draft, June 2, 1986.

KEVIN MICHAEL REIMER

Born June 28, 1964, at Macon, Ga.
Height, 6.02. Weight, 220.
Throws right and bats lefthanded.
Attended Orange Coast College, Costa Mesa, Calif.,
and California State University, Fullerton, Calif.
Son of Gerry Reimer, minor league first baseman-outfielder, 1958 through 1968.

Led Texas League in game-winning RBIs with 12 and tied for intentional bases on balls received with 9 in 1988.

Year—Club	League	Pos.	G.	AB.	R.	H.	2B.	3B.	HR.	RBI.	B.A.	PO.	A.	E.	F.A.
1985—Burlington	Midw.	1B-OF	80	292	25	67	12	0	8	33	.229	685	29	15	.979
1986—Salem	Carol.	OF-1B	133	453	57	111	21	2	16	76	.245	412	27	32	.932
1987—Charlotte	Fla. St.	OF	74	271	36	66	13	7	6	34	.244	31	0	2	.939
1988—Tulsa	Texas	OF	133	486	74	147	30	★11	21	76	.302	63	1	7	.901
1988—Texas	Amer.	OF	12	25	2	3	0	0	1	2	.120	0	0	0	.000
1989—Oklahoma City	A. A.	OF	133	514	59	137	37	7	10	73	.267	73	2	6	.926
1989—Texas	Amer.	DH-PH	3	5	0	0	0	0	0	0	.000	0	0	0	.000
1990—Oklahoma City	A. A.	1B-OF	51	198	24	56	18	2	4	33	.283	170	11	2	.989
1990—Texas	Amer.	OF	64	100	5	26	9	1	2	15	.260	12	0	2	.857
Major League Totals—3 Years			79	130	7	29	9	1	3	17	.223	12	0	2	.857

Selected by Texas Rangers' organization in 11th round of free-agent draft, June 3, 1985.

RICKY EUGENE REUSCHEL

Name pronounced RUSH-ul.

(Rick)

Born May 16, 1949, at Quincy, Ill.
Height, 6.03. Weight, 250.
Throws and bats righthanded.
Attended Western Illinois University, Macomb, Ill.

Brother of Paul Reuschel, pitcher with Chicago Cubs and Cleveland Indians, 1975 through 1978.

Shares major league record for most putouts, pitcher, inning (3), April 25, 1975, third inning.
Major League saves: 1975 (1), 1976 (1), 1977 (1), 1985 (1), 1990 (1). Total—5.
Tied for National League lead in complete games with 12 and shutouts with 4 in 1987.
Tied for National League lead in hit batsmen with 8 in 1986.
Tied for National League lead in games started by pitchers with 38 in 1980 and 36 in 1988.

Tied for National League lead in sacrifice hits by batters with 19 in 1988.
Led Northern League pitchers in complete games with 7 and tied for lead in games started with 14 in 1970.
Named righthanded pitcher on THE SPORTING NEWS National League All-Star Team, 1977.
Named National League Comeback Player of the Year by THE SPORTING NEWS, 1985.
Named pitcher on THE SPORTING NEWS National League All-Star fielding team, 1985 and 1987.

Year Club	League	G.	IP.	W.	L.	Pct.	H.	R.	ER.	SO.	BB.	ERA.
1970—Huron	Northern	14	102	9	2	.818	96	52	40	88	22	3.52
1971—San Antonio†	Texas	16	121	8	4	.667	105	40	31	81	15	2.31
1972—Wichita	Am. Assoc.	12	102	9	2	.818	78	30	15	72	30	1.32
1972—Chicago	National	21	129	10	8	.556	127	46	42	87	29	2.93
1973—Chicago	National	36	237	14	15	.483	244	95	79	168	62	3.00
1974—Chicago	National	41	241	13	12	.520	262	130	115	160	83	4.29
1975—Chicago	National	38	234	11	*17	.393	244	116	97	155	67	3.73
1976—Chicago	National	38	260	14	12	.538	260	*117	100	146	64	3.46
1977—Chicago	National	39	252	20	10	.667	233	84	78	166	74	2.79
1978—Chicago	National	35	243	14	15	.483	235	98	92	115	54	3.41
1979—Chicago	National	36	239	18	12	.600	251	104	96	125	75	3.62
1980—Chicago	National	38	257	11	13	.458	*281	111	97	140	76	3.40
1981—Chicago‡	National	13	86	4	7	.364	87	40	33	53	23	3.45
1981—New York	American	12	71	4	4	.500	75	24	21	22	10	2.66
1982—New York§	American					(Did not play)						
1983—Columbus xy	Int'national	4	16	0	1	.000	21	9	9	7	6	5.06
1983—Quad Cities	Midwest	13	70⅔	3	4	.429	73	29	19	56	9	2.42
1983—Chicago	National	4	20⅔	1	1	.500	18	9	9	9	10	3.92
1984—Chicago za	National	19	92⅓	5	5	.500	123	57	53	43	23	5.17
1985—Hawaii	P. Coast	8	54	6	2	.750	52	18	15	46	12	2.50
1985—Pittsburgh	National	31	194	14	8	.636	153	58	49	138	52	2.27
1986—Pittsburgh	National	35	215⅔	9	16	.360	232	106	95	125	57	3.96
1987—Pittsburgh b-San Francisco	National	34	227	13	9	.591	207	91	78	107	42	3.09
1988—San Francisco	National	36	245	19	11	.633	242	88	85	92	42	3.12
1989—San Francisco c	National	32	208⅓	17	8	.680	195	75	68	111	54	2.94
1990—San Francisco d	National	15	87	3	6	.333	102	40	38	49	31	3.93
National League Totals—18 Years		541	3468	210	185	.532	3496	1465	1304	1989	918	3.38
American League Totals—1 Year		12	71	4	4	.500	75	24	21	22	10	2.66
Major League Totals—18 Years		553	3539	214	189	.531	3571	1489	1325	2011	928	3.37

Selected by Chicago Cubs' organization in 3rd round of free-agent draft, June 4, 1970.

†On temporary inactive list, July 2, 1971; transferred to military list, July 8, 1971 through April 10, 1972.

‡Traded to New York Yankees for Pitcher Doug Bird, $400,000 and a player to be named later, June 12, 1981; Chicago Cubs acquired Pitcher Mike Griffin to complete deal, August 5, 1981.

§On disabled list, March 23, 1982 through remainder of season.

xOn New York disabled list, April 4 to June 9, 1983; included rehabilitation disability assignment to Columbus, May 23 to June 9, 1983.

yReleased, June 9, 1983; signed by Quad Cities (Chicago Cubs' organization), June 28, 1983.

zOn disabled list, March 27 to April 21 and August 23 to September 1, 1984.

aGranted free agency, November 8, 1984; signed by Pittsburgh Pirates' organization, February 28, 1985.

bTraded to San Francisco Giants for Pitchers Jeff Robinson and Scott Medvin, August 21, 1987.

cOn disabled list, July 30 to August 16, 1989.

dOn disabled list, May 30 to September 17, 1990.

DIVISION SERIES RECORD

Year Club	League	G.	IP.	W.	L.	Pct.	H.	R.	ER.	SO.	BB.	ERA.
1981—New York	American	1	6	0	1	.000	4	2	2	3	1	3.00

CHAMPIONSHIP SERIES RECORD

Tied National League Championship Series record for most earned runs allowed, seven-game Series (7), 1987.

Year Club	League	G.	IP.	W.	L.	Pct.	H.	R.	ER.	SO.	BB.	ERA.
1987—San Francisco	National	2	10	0	1	.000	15	8	7	2	2	6.30
1989—San Francisco	National	2	8⅔	1	1	.500	12	6	5	5	2	5.19
Championship Series Totals—2 Years		4	18⅔	1	2	.333	27	14	12	7	4	5.79

WORLD SERIES RECORD

Year Club	League	G.	IP.	W.	L.	Pct.	H.	R.	ER.	SO.	BB.	ERA.
1981—New York	American	2	3⅔	0	0	.000	7	3	2	2	3	4.91
1989—San Francisco	National	1	4	0	1	.000	5	5	5	2	4	11.25
World Series Totals—2 Years		3	7⅔	0	1	.000	12	8	7	4	7	8.22

ALL-STAR GAME RECORD

Shares All-Star Game record for most home runs allowed, inning (2), July 11, 1989, first inning.

Year League	IP.	W.	L.	Pct.	H.	R.	ER.	SO.	BB.	ERA.
1977—National	1	0	0	.000	1	0	0	0	0	0.00
1987—National	1⅓	0	0	.000	1	0	0	1	0	0.00
1989—National	1	0	0	.000	3	2	2	0	0	18.00
All-Star Game Totals—3 Years	3⅓	0	0	.000	5	2	2	1	0	0.00

—DID YOU KNOW—

That Los Angeles' Ramon Martinez was 13-0 against N.L. West division rivals en route to a 20-6 season in 1990?

JERRY REUSS
Name pronounced Royce.

Born June 19, 1949, at St. Louis, Mo.
Height, 6.05. Weight, 227.
Throws and bats lefthanded.
Attended Southern Illinois University, Carbondale, Ill., Central Missouri State College,
Warrensburg, Mo., and University of California, Santa Barbara, Calif.

Shares major league record for most grand slams allowed, lifetime (9).
Pitched 8-0 no-hit victory against San Francisco Giants, June 27, 1980.
Major League saves: 1972 (1), 1976 (2), 1979 (3), 1980 (3), 1984 (1), 1986 (1). Total—11.
Led National League in shutouts with 6 in 1980.
Led National League in hit batsmen with 10 in 1972.
Tied for National League lead in games started by pitchers with 40 in 1973.
Led American Association pitchers in games started with 29 in 1969.
Led Texas League in wild pitches with 16 in 1968.
Named National League Comeback Player of the Year by THE SPORTING NEWS, 1980.
Received reported $30,000 bonus to sign with St. Louis Cardinals, 1967.

Year—Club	League	G.	IP.	W.	L.	Pct.	H.	R.	ER.	SO.	BB.	ERA.
1967—Sarasota Cards	Gulf Coast	2	7	0	0	.000	7	6	4	6	3	5.14
1967—Cedar Rapids	Midwest	9	58	2	5	.286	44	20	12	63	19	1.86
1967—Tulsa	P. Coast	1	1	0	0	.000	2	6	6	1	4	54.00
1968—Arkansas	Texas	17	112	7	8	.467	75	43	27	86	45	2.17
1969—Tulsa	Am. Assoc.	30	★186	●13	11	.542	188	●112	84	★151	116	4.06
1969—St. Louis	National	1	7	1	0	1.000	2	0	0	3	3	0.00
1970—Tulsa	Am. Assoc.	11	85	7	2	.778	69	26	20	69	28	2.12
1970—St. Louis	National	20	127	7	8	.467	132	62	58	74	49	4.11
1971—St. Louis†	National	36	211	14	14	.500	228	125	112	131	109	4.78
1972—Houston	National	33	192	9	13	.409	177	101	89	174	83	4.17
1973—Houston‡	National	41	279	16	13	.552	271	123	116	177	★117	3.74
1974—Pittsburgh	National	35	260	16	11	.593	259	115	101	105	101	3.50
1975—Pittsburgh	National	32	237	18	11	.621	224	73	67	131	78	2.54
1976—Pittsburgh	National	31	209	14	9	.609	209	98	82	108	51	3.53
1977—Pittsburgh	National	33	208	10	13	.435	225	109	95	116	71	4.11
1978—Pittsburgh§	National	23	83	3	2	.600	97	48	45	42	23	4.88
1979—Los Angeles	National	39	160	7	14	.333	178	88	63	83	60	3.54
1980—Los Angeles	National	37	229	18	6	.750	193	74	64	111	40	2.52
1981—Los Angeles	National	22	153	10	4	.714	138	44	39	51	27	2.29
1982—Los Angeles	National	39	254⅔	18	11	.621	232	98	88	138	50	3.11
1983—Los Angeles	National	32	223⅓	12	11	.522	233	94	73	143	50	2.94
1984—Los Angeles x	National	30	99	5	7	.417	102	51	42	44	31	3.82
1985—Los Angeles	National	34	212⅔	14	10	.583	210	78	69	84	58	2.92
1986—Los Angeles y	National	19	74	2	6	.250	96	57	48	29	17	5.84
1987—Los Angeles z-Cincinnati	National	8	36⅔	0	5	.000	54	32	31	12	12	7.61
1987—Nashville a	Am. Assoc.	2	12	0	2	.000	16	8	8	4	6	6.00
1987—California bc	American	17	82⅓	4	5	.444	112	60	48	37	17	5.25
1988—Chicago	American	32	183	13	9	.591	183	79	70	73	43	3.44
1989—Chicago d-Milwaukee efg	American	30	140⅓	9	9	.500	171	88	80	40	34	5.13
1990—Columbus	Southern	10	21⅔	1	0	1.000	23	4	4	11	4	1.66
1990—Tucson h	P. Coast	5	5⅓	0	0	.000	18	14	9	3	2	15.19
1990—Buffalo	Am. Assoc.	14	61⅓	4	4	.500	73	25	24	29	12	3.52
1990—Pittsburgh i	National	4	7⅔	0	0	.000	8	3	3	1	3	3.52
National League Totals—20 Years		549	3263	194	168	.536	3268	1473	1285	1757	1033	3.54
American League Totals—3 Years		79	405⅔	26	23	.531	466	227	198	150	94	4.39
Major League Totals—22 Years		628	3668⅔	220	191	.535	3734	1700	1483	1907	1127	3.64

Selected by St. Louis Cardinals' organization in 2nd round of free-agent draft, June 6, 1967.
†Traded to Houston Astros for Pitchers Scipio Spinks and Lance Clemons, April 15, 1972.
‡Traded to Pittsburgh Pirates for Catcher Milt May, October 31, 1973.
§Traded to Los Angeles Dodgers for Pitcher Rick Rhoden, April 9, 1979.
xOn disabled list, June 8 to July 12, 1984.
yOn disabled list, July 17 to September 3, 1986.
zReleased, April 10, 1987; signed by Nashville (Cincinnati Reds' organization), April 18, 1987.
aReleased, June 14, 1987; signed by California Angels, June 19, 1987.
bOn disabled list, August 1 to August 16, 1987.
cGranted free agency, November 9, 1987; signed by Chicago White Sox, March 29, 1988.
dTraded to Milwaukee Brewers for Pitcher Brian Drahman, July 31, 1989.
eOn disabled list, August 25 to September 9, 1989.
fReleased, November 8, 1989; signed by Chicago White Sox, March, 1990.
gReleased, April 3, 1990; signed by Columbus (Houston Astros' organization), April 14, 1990.
hReleased, May 14, 1990; signed by Buffalo (Pittsburgh Pirates' organization), July 7, 1990.
iGranted free agency, November 5, 1990.

DIVISION SERIES RECORD

Year—Club	League	G.	IP.	W.	L.	Pct.	H.	R.	ER.	SO.	BB.	ERA.
1981—Los Angeles	National	2	18	1	0	1.000	10	0	0	7	5	0.00

CHAMPIONSHIP SERIES RECORD

Holds Championship Series records for most games lost and most consecutive games lost, total series (7); most runs allowed, inning (7), October 13, 1985, second inning.
Shares Championship Series records for most games lost, series (2), 1974, 1983; most runs allowed, total series (25).

Year Club	League	G.	IP.	W.	L.	Pct.	H.	R.	ER.	SO.	BB.	ERA.
1974—Pittsburgh	National	2	9⅔	0	2	.000	7	4	4	3	8	3.72
1975—Pittsburgh	National	1	2⅔	0	1	.000	4	4	4	1	4	13.50
1981—Los Angeles	National	1	7	0	1	.000	7	4	4	2	1	5.14
1983—Los Angeles	National	2	12	0	2	.000	14	6	6	4	3	4.50
1985—Los Angeles	National	1	1⅔	0	1	.000	5	7	2	0	1	10.80
Championship Series Totals—5 Years		7	33	0	7	.000	37	25	20	10	17	5.45

WORLD SERIES RECORD

Year Club	League	G.	IP.	W.	L.	Pct.	H.	R.	ER.	SO.	BB.	ERA.
1981—Los Angeles	National	2	11⅔	1	1	.500	10	5	5	8	3	3.86

ALL-STAR GAME RECORD

Year League	IP.	W.	L.	Pct.	H.	R.	ER.	SO.	BB.	ERA.
1975—National	3	0	0	.000	3	0	0	2	0	0.00
1980—National	1	1	0	1.000	0	0	0	3	0	0.00
All-Star Game Totals—2 Years	4	1	0	1.000	3	0	0	5	0	0.00

HAROLD CRAIG REYNOLDS

Born November 26, 1960, at Eugene, Ore.
Height, 5.11. Weight, 165.
Throws right and bats left and righthanded.
Attended San Diego State University, San Diego, Calif.; Canada College,
Redwood City, Calif., and California State University, Long Beach, Calif.
Brother of Larry Reynolds, shortstop-outfielder in Texas Rangers' and St. Louis Cardinals' organizations,
1979 through 1984; and Don Reynolds, outfielder with San Diego Padres, 1978 and 1979;
and minor league instructor in Seattle Mariners' organization, 1988.

Shares major league record for most assists by second baseman, nine-inning game (12), August 27, 1986.
Shares American League record for most years leading league in errors, second baseman (4).
Major League stolen bases: 1984 (1), 1985 (3), 1986 (30), 1987 (60), 1988 (35), 1989 (25), 1990 (31). Total—185.
Led American League in stolen bases with 60 in 1987.
Led American League in caught stealing with 20 in 1987 and 29 in 1988.
Led American League second basemen in double plays with 111 in 1986, 1987 and 1988.
Led American League second basemen in total chances with 874 in 1987, 792 in 1988, 834 in 1989 and 848 in 1990.
Led Pacific Coast League in sacrifice hits with 14 in 1983.
Led Eastern League in caught stealing with 20 in 1982.
Led Midwest League in stolen bases with 69 in 1981.
Tied for Pacific Coast League lead in caught stealing with 17 in 1984.
Led Pacific Coast League second basemen in double plays with 104 and total chances with 747 in 1984.
Led Pacific Coast League second basemen in putouts with 286 and total chances with 723 in 1983.
Led Midwest League second basemen in double plays with 82 in 1981.
Named second baseman on THE SPORTING NEWS American League All-Star fielding team, 1988 through 1990.

Year Club	League	Pos.	G.	AB.	R.	H.	2B.	3B.	HR.	RBI.	B.A.	PO.	A.	E.	F.A.
1981—Wausau	Midw.	2B-OF-3B	127	493	98	146	23	3	11	59	.296	259	386	27	.960
1982—Lynn	East.	2B	102	375	58	102	14	4	2	48	.272	202	232	19	.958
1983—Salt Lake City	P. C.	*2B-SS	136	534	84	165	20	9	1	72	.309	287	*410	*27	.963
1983—Seattle	Amer.	2B	20	59	8	12	4	1	0	1	.203	30	48	2	.975
1984—Salt Lake City	P. C.	2B	135	*558	94	165	22	6	3	54	.296	*326	*396	*25	*.967
1984—Seattle	Amer.	2B	10	10	3	3	0	0	0	0	.300	8	12	0	1.000
1985—Seattle	Amer.	2B	67	104	15	15	3	1	0	6	.144	69	123	8	.960
1985—Calgary	P. C.	2B	52	212	36	77	11	3	5	30	.363	119	171	13	.957
1986—Calgary	P. C.	2B	29	118	20	37	7	0	1	7	.314	64	83	4	.974
1986—Seattle	Amer.	2B	126	445	46	99	19	4	1	24	.222	278	415	16	.977
1987—Seattle	Amer.	2B	160	530	73	146	31	8	1	35	.275	*347	*507	*20	.977
1988—Seattle	Amer.	2B	158	598	61	169	26	●11	4	41	.283	303	*471	*18	.977
1989—Seattle	Amer.	2B	153	613	87	184	24	9	0	43	.300	311	*506	*17	.980
1990—Seattle	Amer.	2B	160	*642	100	162	36	5	5	55	.252	*330	*499	●19	.978
Major League Totals—8 Years			854	3001	393	790	143	39	11	205	.263	1676	2581	100	.977

Selected by San Diego Padres' organization in 5th round of free-agent draft, June 5, 1979.
Selected by Seattle Mariners' organization in secondary phase of free-agent draft, June 3, 1980.

ALL-STAR GAME RECORD

Year League	Pos.	AB.	R.	H.	2B.	3B.	HR.	RBI.	B.A.	PO.	A.	E.	F.A.
1987—American	2B	3	0	0	0	0	0	0	.000	4	4	0	1.000
1988—American	2B	1	0	0	0	0	0	0	.000	1	1	0	1.000
All-Star Game Totals—2 Years		4	0	0	0	0	0	0	.000	5	5	0	1.000

ROBERT JAMES REYNOLDS
(R. J.)

Born April 19, 1960, at Sacramento, Calif.
Height, 6.00. Weight, 180.
Throws right and bats left and righthanded.
Attended Cosumnes River College, Sacramento, Calif.;
and Sacramento City College, Sacramento, Calif.

Shares major league record for fewest errors by outfielder, season, for leader in errors (9), 1986.
Major League stolen bases: 1983 (5), 1984 (7), 1985 (18), 1986 (16), 1987 (14), 1988 (15), 1989 (22), 1990 (12). Total—109.

Led Texas League outfielders in double plays with 8 in 1983.
Led Florida State League outfielders in double plays with 6 and total chances with 395 in 1981.
Led California League outfielders in double plays with 6 in 1980.

Year	Club	League	Pos.	G.	AB.	R.	H.	2B.	3B.	HR.	RBI.	B.A.	PO.	A.	E.	F.A.
1980—Lodi	Calif.	OF	86	299	33	84	6	3	4	31	.281	188	10	12	.943
1981—Vero Beach	Fla. St.	OF	132	502	62	139	9	11	2	49	.277	★368	20	7	.982
1982—Lodi	Calif.	OF	108	403	67	126	19	3	6	35	.313	212	12	6	.974
1982—San Antonio	Texas	OF	3	12	3	2	0	0	1	2	.167	10	1	0	1.000
1983—San Antonio	Texas	OF	133	504	103	170	25	3	18	89	.337	255	●18	12	.958
1983—Los Angeles	Nat.	OF	24	55	5	13	0	0	2	11	.236	25	2	2	.931
1984—Albuquerque	P. C.	OF	47	199	38	69	10	4	3	30	.347	104	4	6	.947
1984—Los Angeles†	Nat.	OF	73	240	24	62	12	2	2	24	.258	104	4	3	.973
1985—L.A.‡§-Pitt.	Nat.	OF	104	337	44	95	15	7	3	42	.282	159	6	6	.965
1986—Pittsburgh	Nat.	OF	118	402	63	108	30	2	9	48	.269	190	2	●9	.955
1987—Pittsburgh	Nat.	OF	117	335	47	87	24	1	7	51	.260	134	7	1	.993
1988—Pittsburgh	Nat.	OF	130	323	35	80	14	2	6	51	.248	142	7	4	.974
1989—Pittsburgh	Nat.	OF	125	363	45	98	16	2	6	48	.270	200	6	2	.990
1990—Pittsburgh xy	Nat.	OF	95	215	25	62	10	1	0	19	.288	102	3	3	.972
Major League Totals—8 Years				786	2270	288	605	121	17	35	294	.267	1056	37	30	.973

Selected by Los Angeles Dodgers' organization in 2nd round of free-agent draft, January 8, 1980.
†On disabled list, July 2 to July 17, 1984.
‡On disabled list, April 8 to April 23 and July 10 to August 2, 1985.
§Traded to Pittsburgh Pirates, September 3, 1985, as partial completion of deal in which Los Angeles Dodgers acquired Third Baseman Bill Madlock for three players to be named later, August 31, 1985; Pittsburgh acquired Outfielder Cecil Espy and First Baseman Sid Bream to complete deal, September 9, 1985.
xOn disabled list, August 8 to August 23, 1990.
yGranted free agency, November 5, 1990; signed by Yokohama Taiyo Whales of Japanese Baseball League, November 14, 1990.

CHAMPIONSHIP SERIES RECORD

Year	Club	League	Pos.	G.	AB.	R.	H.	2B.	3B.	HR.	RBI.	B.A.	PO.	A.	E.	F.A.
1990—Pittsburgh	Nat.	PH-OF	6	10	0	2	0	0	0	0	.200	2	0	1	.667

RONN DWAYNE REYNOLDS

Born September 28, 1958, at Wichita, Kan.
Height, 6.00. Weight, 205.
Throws and bats righthanded.
Attended Garden City Community College, Garden City, Kan.,
and University of Arkansas, Fayetteville, Ark.

Tied for Texas League lead in being hit by pitch with 10 in 1982.
Led Texas League catchers in putouts with 583 and total chances with 651 in 1982.

Year	Club	League	Pos.	G.	AB.	R.	H.	2B.	3B.	HR.	RBI.	B.A.	PO.	A.	E.	F.A.
1980—Little Falls	NYP	C	15	44	6	8	1	1	1	8	.182	85	3	2	.978
1980—Lynchburg	Carol.	C	36	105	14	21	3	0	2	17	.200	206	23	3	.987
1981—Jackson	Texas	C	88	272	16	64	12	1	2	30	.235	493	67	12	.979
1982—Jackson	Texas	C-3B-OF	123	431	50	110	13	1	10	43	.255	585	57	14	.979
1982—New York	Nat.	C	2	4	0	0	0	0	0	0	.000	3	0	0	1.000
1983—Tidewater	Int.	C	40	128	8	27	8	0	0	9	.211	209	27	1	.996
1983—New York	Nat.	C	24	66	4	13	1	0	0	2	.197	99	14	7	.942
1984—Tidewater	Int.	C-1B	90	280	35	73	11	0	11	46	.261	457	25	7	.986
1985—New York	Nat.	C	28	43	4	9	2	0	0	1	.209	86	9	1	.990
1985—Tidewater†	Int.	C	3	10	0	3	1	0	0	2	.300	5	2	0	1.000
1986—Portland	P. C.	C-1B	51	165	13	38	9	4	2	22	.230	228	23	2	.992
1986—Philadelphia‡	Nat.	C	43	126	8	27	4	0	3	10	.214	198	16	2	.991
1987—Tucson	P. C.	C-1B	81	210	22	42	10	0	3	16	.200	297	40	9	.974
1987—Houston§	Nat.	C	38	102	5	17	4	0	1	7	.167	216	16	6	.975
1988—Denver	A. A.	C-1B	83	271	36	65	13	1	9	33	.240	448	46	8	.984
1989—Denver xy	A. A.	C-1B	10	30	1	8	3	0	0	0	.267	31	3	0	1.000
1990—Las Vegas	P. C.	C-1B	81	247	35	63	17	0	9	41	.255	338	26	6	.984
1990—San Diego	Nat.	C	8	15	1	1	1	0	0	1	.067	26	2	0	1.000
Major League Totals—6 Years				143	356	22	67	12	0	4	21	.188	628	57	16	.977

Selected by Oakland A's organization in 5th round of free-agent draft, June 5, 1979.
Selected by New York Mets' organization in 5th round of free-agent draft, June 3, 1980.
†Traded with Pitcher Jeff Bittiger to Philadelphia Phillies for Pitcher Rodger Cole and First Baseman Ronnie Gideon, January 16, 1986.
‡Traded to Houston Astros' organization for Pitcher Jeff Calhoun, April 2, 1987.
§Released, October 13, 1987; signed by Milwaukee Brewers, January 19, 1988.
xOn disabled list, April 5 to August 8, 1989.
yGranted free agency, October 15, 1989; signed by Las Vegas (San Diego Padres' organization), January 11, 1990.

KARL DERRICK RHODES

Born August 21, 1968, at Cincinnati, O.
Height, 5.11. Weight, 170.
Throws and bats lefthanded.

Major League stolen bases: 1990 (4).
Tied for Southern League lead in double plays by outfielders with 5 in 1989.

Year Club	League	Pos.	G.	AB.	R.	H.	2B.	3B.	HR.	RBI.	B.A.	PO.	A.	E.	F.A.
1986—Sarasota Astros....	Gulf C.	OF	*62	222	36	65	10	3	0	22	.293	113	6	0	*1.000
1987—Asheville...............	S. Atl.	OF	129	413	62	104	16	4	3	50	.252	163	14	9	.952
1988—Osceola..................	Fla. St.	OF-2B	132	452	69	128	4	2	1	34	.283	232	14	2	.992
1989—Columbus..............	South.	OF	●143	520	81	134	25	5	4	63	.258	262	15	11	.962
1990—Tucson..................	P. C.	OF	107	385	68	106	24	11	3	59	.275	214	*20	8	.967
1990—Houston.................	Nat.	OF	39	86	12	21	6	1	1	3	.244	61	2	3	.955
Major League Totals—1 Year..................			39	86	12	21	6	1	1	3	.244	61	2	3	.955

Selected by Houston Astros' organization in 3rd round of free-agent draft, June 2, 1986.

RUSSELL EARL RICHARDS
(Rusty)

Born January 27, 1965, at Houston, Tex.
Height, 6.04. Weight, 210.
Throws right and bats lefthanded.
Attended Austin Community College, Austin, Tex.,
and University of Texas, Austin, Tex.

Tied for International League lead in games started by pitchers with 27 in 1989.

Year Club	League	G.	IP.	W.	L.	Pct.	H.	R.	ER.	SO.	BB.	ERA.
1986—Bradenton Braves........................	Gulf Coast	12	19⅓	0	0	.000	17	8	5	15	7	2.33
1987—Sumter................................	S. Atlantic	10	48	3	3	.500	45	28	17	39	17	3.19
1987—Durham................................	Carolina	22	125	6	10	.375	138	73	63	62	50	4.54
1988—Durham................................	Carolina	1	3⅓	1	0	1.000	0	0	0	3	0	0.00
1988—Greenville	Southern	28	147	10	7	.588	125	46	43	96	42	2.63
1989—Richmond..........................	Int'national	27	167⅔	11	11	.500	*178	76	71	85	54	3.81
1989—Atlanta..............................	National	2	9⅓	0	0	.000	10	5	5	4	6	4.82
1990—Richmond..........................	Int'national	30	140⅓	6	9	.400	159	83	71	56	73	4.55
1990—Atlanta..............................	National	1	1	0	0	.000	2	3	3	0	1	27.00
Major League Totals—2 Years.....................		3	10⅓	0	0	.000	12	8	8	4	7	6.97

Selected by Philadelphia Phillies' organization in 7th round of free-agent draft, January 14, 1986.
Signed as free agent by Atlanta Braves' organization, June 19, 1986.

JEFFREY SCOTT RICHARDSON
(Jeff)

Born August 29, 1963, at Wichita, Kan.
Height, 6.03. Weight, 203.
Throws and bats righthanded.
Attended Connors State College, Warner, Okla.

Led Carolina League pitchers in games started with 28 in 1987.

Year Club	League	G.	IP.	W.	L.	Pct.	H.	R.	ER.	SO.	BB.	ERA.
1984—Medicine Hat†..............................	Pioneer	18	70	4	6	.400	96	67	56	39	32	7.20
1985—Little Falls..	NYP	11	62⅓	4	3	.571	58	32	25	56	32	3.61
1985—Columbia	S. Atlantic	5	35⅔	3	2	.600	25	11	7	33	11	1.77
1986—Lynchburg.........................	Carolina	32	171	13	5	.722	183	96	80	93	82	4.21
1986—Jackson.............................	Texas	1	3	0	1	.000	6	8	6	2	4	18.00
1987—Lynchburg‡.......................	Carolina	29	154	6	12	.333	180	103	84	79	68	4.91
1988—Palm Springs...............................	California	44	69	0	4	.000	66	24	19	56	27	2.48
1989—Palm Springs...............................	California	24	26⅔	4	2	.667	19	15	12	25	9	4.05
1989—Midland..	Texas	19	22⅔	0	1	.000	9	4	4	12	5	1.59
1990—Edmonton..	P. Coast	38	48⅓	5	0	1.000	46	17	10	31	27	1.86
1990—California..	American	1	⅓	0	0	.000	1	0	0	0	0	0.00
Major League Totals—1 Year.........................		1	⅓	0	0	.000	1	0	0	0	0	0.00

Selected by New York Mets' organization in 19th round of free-agent draft, June 7, 1982.
Selected by Chicago White Sox' organization in secondary phase of free-agent draft, January 17, 1984.
Selected by Toronto Blue Jays' organization in secondary phase of free-agent draft, June 4, 1984.
†Released, April 1, 1985; signed by Little Falls (New York Mets' organization), May 9, 1985.
‡Traded with Pitcher Shane Young to California Angels for Pitcher John Candelaria, September 15, 1987.

DAVID ALLEN RIGHETTI
Name pronounced Ri-GET-tee.
(Dave)

Born November 28, 1958, at San Jose, Calif.
Height, 6.04. Weight, 210.
Throws and bats lefthanded.
Attended San Jose City College, San Jose, Calif.
Son of Leo Righetti, minor league infielder, 1944 through 1949 and 1951 through 1957;
Brother of Steven Righetti, third baseman in Texas Rangers' organization, 1977 through 1979.

Pitched 4-0 no-hit victory against Boston Red Sox, July 4, 1983.
Major League saves: 1982 (1), 1984 (31), 1985 (29), 1986 (46), 1987 (31), 1988 (25), 1989 (25), 1990 (36). Total—224.
Led American League in saves with 46 and games finished in relief with 68 in 1986.
Named American League Co-Fireman of the Year by THE SPORTING NEWS, 1987.
Named American League Fireman of the Year by THE SPORTING NEWS, 1986.
Named American League Rookie Pitcher of the Year by THE SPORTING NEWS, 1981.
Named American League Rookie of the Year by Baseball Writers' Association of America, 1981.

Year Club	League	G.	IP.	W.	L.	Pct.	H.	R.	ER.	SO.	BB.	ERA.
1977—Asheville	W. Carol.	17	109	11	3	*.786	98	47	38	101	53	3.14
1978—Tulsa†‡	Texas	13	91	5	5	.500	66	40	32	127	49	3.16
1979—West Haven§	Eastern	11	69	4	3	.571	45	23	15	78	45	1.96
1979—Columbus x	Int'national	8	40	3	2	.600	22	13	13	44	19	2.93
1979—New York	American	3	17	0	1	.000	10	7	7	13	10	3.71
1980—Columbus	Int'national	24	142	6	10	.375	124	79	73	139	*101	4.63
1981—Columbus	Int'national	7	45	5	0	1.000	30	8	5	50	26	1.00
1981—New York†	American	15	105	8	4	.667	75	25	24	89	38	2.06
1982—New York	American	33	183	11	10	.524	155	88	77	163	*108	3.79
1982—Columbus	Int'national	4	25⅔	1	0	1.000	22	11	8	33	12	2.81
1983—New York	American	31	217	14	8	.636	194	96	83	169	67	3.44
1984—New York y	American	64	96⅓	5	6	.455	79	29	25	90	37	2.34
1985—New York‡	American	74	107	12	7	.632	96	36	33	92	45	2.78
1986—New York	American	74	106⅔	8	8	.500	88	31	29	83	35	2.45
1987—New York z	American	60	95	8	6	.571	95	45	37	77	44	3.51
1988—New York	American	60	87	5	4	.556	86	35	34	70	37	3.52
1989—New York	American	55	69	2	6	.250	73	32	23	51	26	3.00
1990—New York a	American	53	53	1	1	.500	48	24	21	43	26	3.57
Major League Totals—11 Years		522	1136	74	61	.548	999	448	393	940	473	3.11

Selected by Texas Rangers' organization in 1st round (ninth player selected) of free-agent draft, January 11, 1977.

†On disabled list, July 31 to September 2, 1978.

‡Traded with Pitchers Mike Griffin and Paul Mirabella and Outfielders Juan Beniquez and Greg Jemison to New York Yankees for Pitchers Sparky Lyle, Larry McCall and Dave Rajsich, Catcher Mike Heath, Shortstop Domingo Ramos and cash, November 10, 1978.

§On disabled list, May 21 to June 28, 1979.

xOn disabled list, June 28 to July 20 and August 2 to August 23, 1979.

yOn disabled list, June 17 to July 2, 1984.

zGranted free agency, November 9, 1987; re-signed by Yankees, December 23, 1987.

aGranted free agency, November 5, 1990; signed by San Francisco Giants, December 4, 1990.

DIVISION SERIES RECORD

Year Club	League	G.	IP.	W.	L.	Pct.	H.	R.	ER.	SO.	BB.	ERA.
1981—New York	American	2	9	2	0	1.000	8	1	1	10	3	1.00

CHAMPIONSHIP SERIES RECORD

Year Club	League	G.	IP.	W.	L.	Pct.	H.	R.	ER.	SO.	BB.	ERA.
1981—New York	American	1	6	1	0	1.000	4	0	0	4	2	0.00

WORLD SERIES RECORD

Year Club	League	G.	IP.	W.	L.	Pct.	H.	R.	ER.	SO.	BB.	ERA.
1981—New York	American	1	2	0	0	.000	5	3	3	1	2	13.50

ALL-STAR GAME RECORD

Year League	IP.	W.	L.	Pct.	H.	R.	ER.	SO.	BB.	ERA.
1986—American	⅔	0	0	.000	2	0	0	0	0	0.00
1987—American	⅓	0	0	.000	1	0	0	0	0	0.00
All-Star Game Totals—2 Years	1	0	0	.000	3	0	0	0	0	0.00

JOSE ANTONIO RIJO (ABREAU)

Name pronounced REE-ho.

Born May 13, 1965, at San Cristobal, Dominican Republic.

Height, 6.02. Weight, 210.

Throws and bats righthanded.

Son-in-law of Juan Marichal, Hall of Fame pitcher with San Francisco Giants, Boston Red Sox and Los Angeles Dodgers, 1960 through 1975; and scout for Oakland A's, 1983 through 1985.

Major League saves: 1984 (2), 1986 (1). Total—3.

Tied for National League lead in balks with 5 in 1990.

Led Pacific Coast League in balks with 11 in 1985.

Led Florida State League in complete games with 15 and tied for lead in shutouts with 4 in 1983.

Named Florida State League Most Valuable Player, 1983.

Year Club	League	G.	IP.	W.	L.	Pct.	H.	R.	ER.	SO.	BB.	ERA.
1981—Bradenton Yankees	Gulf Coast	11	22	3	3	.500	37	16	11	22	7	4.50
1982—Paintsville	Ap'lachian	13	79⅓	8	4	.667	76	33	22	66	22	2.50
1983—Fort Lauderdale	Florida St.	21	160⅓	*15	5	.750	129	38	30	152	43	*1.68
1983—Nashville	Southern	5	40⅓	3	2	.600	31	12	12	32	22	2.68
1984—New York	American	24	62⅓	2	8	.200	74	40	33	47	33	4.76
1984—Columbus†	Int'national	11	65⅓	3	3	.500	67	35	32	47	40	4.41
1985—Tacoma	P. Coast	24	149	7	10	.412	116	64	48	*179	*108	2.90
1985—Oakland	American	12	63⅔	6	4	.600	57	26	25	65	28	3.53
1986—Oakland	American	39	193⅔	9	11	.450	172	116	100	176	108	4.65
1987—Oakland	American	21	82⅓	2	7	.222	106	67	54	67	41	5.90
1987—Tacoma‡	P. Coast	9	54⅔	2	4	.333	44	27	24	67	28	3.95
1988—Cincinnati§	National	49	162	13	8	.619	120	47	43	160	63	2.39
1989—Cincinnati x	National	19	111	7	6	.538	101	39	35	86	48	2.84
1990—Cincinnati y	National	29	197	14	8	.636	151	65	59	152	78	2.70
1990—Nashville	Am. Assoc.	1	4⅓	0	0	.000	5	4	4	2	2	8.31
American League Totals—4 Years		96	402	19	30	.388	409	249	212	355	210	4.75
National League Totals—3 Years		97	470	34	22	.607	372	151	137	398	189	2.62
Major League Totals—7 Years		193	872	53	52	.505	781	400	349	753	399	3.60

Signed as free agent by New York Yankees' organization, August 1, 1980.
†Traded with Outfielder Stan Javier and Pitchers Jay Howell, Eric Plunk and Tim Birtsas to Oakland A's for Outfielder Rickey Henderson, Pitcher Bert Bradley and cash, December 5, 1984.
‡Traded with Pitcher Tim Birtsas to Cincinnati Reds for Outfielder Dave Parker, December 8, 1987.
§On disabled list, August 18 to September 8, 1988.
xOn disabled list, July 17 to September 1, 1989.
yOn disabled list, June 29 to July 21, 1990; included rehabilitation disability assignment to Nashville, July 16 to July 20, 1990.

CHAMPIONSHIP SERIES RECORD

Year Club	League	G.	IP.	W.	L.	Pct.	H.	R.	ER.	SO.	BB.	ERA.
1990—Cincinnati	National	2	12⅓	1	0	1.000	10	6	6	15	7	4.38

WORLD SERIES RECORD

Year Club	League	G.	IP.	W.	L.	Pct.	H.	R.	ER.	SO.	BB.	ERA.
1990—Cincinnati	National	2	15⅓	2	0	1.000	9	1	1	14	5	0.59

ERNEST RILES

Born October 2, 1960, at Bainbridge, Ga.
Height, 6.01. Weight, 175.
Throws right and bats lefthanded.
Attended Middle Georgia College, Cochran, Ga.

Major League stolen bases: 1985 (2), 1986 (7), 1987 (3), 1988 (3). Total—15.
Led California League in bases on balls received with 84 in 1982.
Led Texas League shortstops in total chances with 670 and double plays with 77 in 1983.
Led California League shortstops in double plays with 95 and tied for lead in total chances with 692 in 1982.

Year Club	League	Pos.	G.	AB.	R.	H.	2B.	3B.	HR.	RBI.	B.A.	PO.	A.	E.	F.A.
1981—Butte	Pion.	SS-3B-2B	67	256	63	89	11	2	4	43	.348	97	217	27	.921
1982—Stockton	Calif.	SS	138	447	60	128	23	6	2	56	.286	204	★451	37	.947
1983—El Paso	Texas	SS	130	476	109	166	31	3	13	91	.349	★193	★445	32	★.952
1984—Vancouver	P. C.	SS	123	424	59	113	19	7	3	54	.267	★190	316	17	.967
1985—Vancouver	P. C.	SS	30	118	19	41	7	1	2	20	.347	47	120	6	.965
1985—Milwaukee	Amer.	SS	116	448	54	128	12	7	5	45	.286	183	310	22	.957
1986—Milwaukee	Amer.	SS	145	524	69	132	24	2	9	47	.252	212	327	20	.964
1987—El Paso†	Texas	SS	41	153	45	52	10	0	6	24	.340	70	127	10	.952
1987—Milwaukee	Amer.	3B-SS	83	276	38	72	11	1	4	38	.261	76	152	13	.946
1988—Milwaukee‡	Amer.	3B-SS	41	127	7	32	6	1	1	9	.252	36	64	4	.962
1988—San Francisco	Nat.	3B-2B-SS	79	187	26	55	7	2	3	28	.294	46	133	3	.984
1989—San Francisco	Nat.	3-2-S-O	122	302	43	84	13	2	7	40	.278	69	144	9	.959
1990—San Francisco§	Nat.	SS-2B-3B	92	155	22	31	2	1	8	21	.200	53	105	3	.981
American League Totals—4 Years			385	1375	168	364	53	11	19	139	.265	507	853	59	.958
National League Totals—3 Years			293	644	91	170	22	5	18	89	.264	168	382	15	.973
Major League Totals—6 Years			678	2019	259	534	75	16	37	228	.264	675	1235	74	.963

Selected by Seattle Mariners' organization in 21st round of free-agent draft, June 3, 1980.
Selected by Milwaukee Brewers' organization in secondary phase of free-agent draft, January 13, 1981.
†On Milwaukee disabled list, March 26 to June 3, 1987; included rehabilitation disability assignment to El Paso, May 13 to June 2, 1987.
‡Traded to San Francisco Giants for Outfielder Jeffrey Leonard, June 8, 1988.
§Traded to Oakland Athletics for Outfielder Darren Lewis and a player to be named later, December 4, 1990; San Francisco Giants acquired Pitcher Pedro Pena to complete deal, December 17, 1990.

CHAMPIONSHIP SERIES RECORD

Year Club	League	Pos.	G.	AB.	R.	H.	2B.	3B.	HR.	RBI.	B.A.	PO.	A.	E.	F.A.
1989—San Francisco	Nat.	PH	1	1	0	0	0	0	0	0	.000	0	0	0	.000

WORLD SERIES RECORD

Year Club	League	Pos.	G.	AB.	R.	H.	2B.	3B.	HR.	RBI.	B.A.	PO.	A.	E.	F.A.
1989—San Francisco	Nat.	DH-PH	4	8	0	0	0	0	0	0	.000	0	0	0	.000

CALVIN EDWIN RIPKEN JR.
(Cal)

Born August 24, 1960, at Havre de Grace, Md.
Height, 6.04. Weight, 225.
Throws and bats righthanded.

Son of Cal Ripken, Sr., minor league catcher, 1957 through 1962 and 1964; minor league manager, 1961 through 1974; scout, Baltimore Orioles, 1975; manager, Baltimore Orioles, 1987 through April 11, 1988; and coach with Baltimore Orioles, 1976 through 1986 and since 1989; brother of Billy Ripken, second baseman with Baltimore Orioles; and nephew of Bill Ripken, minor league outfielder, 1947 through 1949.

Holds major league records for most at-bats without a triple, season (646), 1989; most consecutive games by shortstop, lifetime (1,384), July 1, 1982 through October 3, 1990; highest fielding percentage by shortstop, season (.996), 1990; fewest errors by shortstop, season, 150 or more games (3), 1990; most consecutive errorless games by shortstop, season (95), April 14 through July 27, 1990; most consecutive chances accepted by shortstop, season and lifetime (431), April 14 to July 28, first game, 1990.

Shares major league record for most years leading league in games by shortstop (6).

Holds American League record for most home runs, shortstop, lifetime (217); most assists by shortstop, season (583), 1984.

Shares American League records for most years leading league in putouts (4), shortstop.

Major League stolen bases: 1982 (3), 1984 (2), 1985 (2), 1986 (4), 1987 (3), 1988 (2), 1989 (3), 1990 (3). Total—22.

Hit for the cycle, May 6, 1984.

Tied for American League lead in sacrifice flies with 10 in 1988.

Tied for American League lead in game-winning RBIs with 15 in 1986.

Led American League shortstops in total chances with 831 in 1983, 906 in 1984 and 815 in 1989.

Led American League shortstops in double plays with 113 in 1983, 122 in 1984, 123 in 1985 and 119 in 1989.

Tied for Southern League lead in sacrifice flies with 9 in 1980.

Led Southern League third basemen in fielding percentage with .933, putouts with 119, assists with 268, and double plays with 34 in 1980.

Tied for Appalachian League lead in double plays by shortstops with 31 in 1978.

Named Major League Player of the Year by THE SPORTING NEWS, 1983.

Named American League Player of the Year by THE SPORTING NEWS, 1983.

Named American League Most Valuable Player by Baseball Writers' Association of America, 1983.

Named American League Rookie Player of the Year by THE SPORTING NEWS, 1982.

Named American League Rookie of the Year by Baseball Writers' Association of America, 1982.

Named shortstop on THE SPORTING NEWS American League All-Star Team, 1983 through 1985 and 1989.

Named shortstop on THE SPORTING NEWS Silver Slugger team, 1983 through 1986 and 1989.

Year—Club	League	Pos.	G.	AB.	R.	H.	2B.	3B.	HR.	RBI.	B.A.	PO.	A.	E.	F.A.
1978—Bluefield	Appal.	SS	63	239	27	63	7	1	0	24	.264	*92	204	*33	.900
1979—Miami	Fla. St.	3B-SS-2B	105	393	51	119	*28	1	5	54	.303	149	260	30	.932
1979—Charlotte	South.	3B	17	61	6	11	0	1	3	8	.180	13	26	3	.929
1980—Charlotte	South.	3B-SS	●144	522	91	144	28	5	25	78	.276	151	341	35	.934
1981—Rochester	Int.	3B-SS	114	437	74	126	31	4	23	75	.288	128	320	21	.955
1981—Baltimore	Amer.	SS-3B	23	39	1	5	0	0	0	0	.128	13	30	3	.935
1982—Baltimore	Amer.	SS-3B	160	598	90	158	32	5	28	93	.264	221	440	19	.972
1983—Baltimore	Amer.	SS	●162	*663	*121	*211	*47	2	27	102	.318	272	*534	25	.970
1984—Baltimore	Amer.	SS	●162	641	103	195	37	7	27	86	.304	*297	*583	26	.971
1985—Baltimore	Amer.	SS	161	642	116	181	32	5	26	110	.282	*286	474	26	.967
1986—Baltimore	Amer.	SS	162	627	98	177	35	1	25	81	.282	240	*482	13	.982
1987—Baltimore	Amer.	SS	*162	624	97	157	28	3	27	98	.252	240	*480	20	.973
1988—Baltimore	Amer.	SS	161	575	87	152	25	1	23	81	.264	*284	480	21	.973
1989—Baltimore	Amer.	SS	●162	646	80	166	30	0	21	93	.257	*276	*531	8	.990
1990—Baltimore	Amer.	SS	161	600	78	150	28	4	21	84	.250	242	435	3	*.996
Major League Totals—10 Years			1476	5655	871	1552	294	28	225	828	.274	2371	4469	164	.977

Selected by Baltimore Orioles' organization in 2nd round of free-agent draft, June 6, 1978.

CHAMPIONSHIP SERIES RECORD

Year—Club	League	Pos.	G.	AB.	R.	H.	2B.	3B.	HR.	RBI.	B.A.	PO.	A.	E.	F.A.
1983—Baltimore	Amer.	SS	4	15	5	6	2	0	0	1	.400	7	11	0	1.000

WORLD SERIES RECORD

Year—Club	League	Pos.	G.	AB.	R.	H.	2B.	3B.	HR.	RBI.	B.A.	PO.	A.	E.	F.A.
1983—Baltimore	Amer.	SS	5	18	2	3	0	0	0	1	.167	6	14	0	1.000

ALL-STAR GAME RECORD

Year—League	Pos.	AB.	R.	H.	2B.	3B.	HR.	RBI.	B.A.	PO.	A.	E.	F.A.
1983—American	SS	0	0	0	0	0	0	0	.000	1	0	0	1.000
1984—American	SS	3	0	0	0	0	0	0	.000	0	0	0	.000
1985—American	SS	3	0	1	0	0	0	0	.333	2	1	0	1.000
1986—American	SS	4	0	0	0	0	0	0	.000	0	1	0	1.000
1987—American	SS	2	0	1	0	0	0	0	.500	0	5	0	1.000
1988—American	SS	3	0	0	0	0	0	0	.000	1	4	0	1.000
1989—American	SS	3	0	1	1	0	0	0	.333	0	0	0	.000
1990—American	SS	2	0	0	0	0	0	0	.000	1	1	0	1.000
All-Star Game Totals—8 Years		20	0	3	1	0	0	0	.150	5	12	0	1.000

WILLIAM OLIVER RIPKEN
(Billy)

Born December 16, 1964, at Havre de Grace, Md.

Height, 6.01. Weight, 183.

Throws and bats righthanded.

Son of Cal Ripken, Sr., minor league catcher, 1957 through 1962 and 1964; minor league manager, 1961 through 1974; scout, Baltimore Orioles, 1975; manager, Baltimore Orioles, 1987 through April 11, 1988; and coach with Baltimore Orioles, 1976 through 1986 and since 1989; brother of Cal Ripken, Jr., shortstop with Baltimore Orioles; and nephew of Bill Ripken, minor league outfielder, 1947 through 1949.

Major League stolen bases: 1987 (4), 1988 (8), 1989 (1), 1990 (5). Total—18.

Tied for American League lead in sacrifice hits with 17 in 1990.

Tied for Southern League lead in grounding into double plays with 21 in 1986.

Led Southern League second basemen in total chances with 723 and double plays with 79 in 1986.

Year—Club	League	Pos.	G.	AB.	R.	H.	2B.	3B.	HR.	RBI.	B.A.	PO.	A.	E.	F.A.
1982—Bluefield	Appal.	SS-3B-2B	27	45	8	11	1	0	0	4	.244	15	17	3	.914
1983—Bluefield	Appal.	SS-3B	48	152	24	33	6	0	0	13	.217	82	145	23	.908
1984—Hagerstown†	Carol.	SS-2B	115	409	48	94	15	3	2	40	.230	187	358	28	.951
1985—Charlotte	South.	SS	18	51	2	7	1	0	0	3	.137	18	52	4	.946
1985—Daytona Beach‡	Fla. St.	SS-3B-2B	67	222	23	51	11	0	0	18	.230	90	198	8	.973
1985—Hagerstown	Carol.	3B-2B	14	47	9	12	0	1	0	0	.255	14	37	2	.962
1986—Charlotte	South.	2B	141	530	58	142	20	3	5	62	.268	*305	*395	*23	.968
1987—Rochester	Int.	2B-SS	74	238	32	68	15	0	0	11	.286	154	200	9	.975
1987—Baltimore	Amer.	2B	58	234	27	72	9	0	2	20	.308	133	162	3	.990

Year Club League	Pos.	G.	AB.	R.	H.	2B.	3B.	HR.	RBI.	B.A.	PO.	A.	E.	F.A.
1988—Baltimore .... Amer.	2B-3B	150	512	52	106	18	1	2	34	.207	310	440	12	.984
1989—Baltimore§ .... Amer.	2B	115	318	31	76	11	2	2	26	.239	255	335	9	.985
1990—Baltimore x........... Amer.	2B	129	406	48	118	28	1	3	38	.291	250	366	8	.987
Major League Totals—4 Years.................		452	1470	158	372	66	4	9	118	.253	948	1303	32	.986

Selected by Baltimore Orioles' organization in 11th round of free-agent draft, June 7, 1982.
†On disabled list, April 20 to May 3, 1984.
‡On disabled list, June 23 to July 6, 1985.
§On disabled list, March 27 to April 14 and August 23 to September 7, 1989.
xOn disabled list, August 5 to August 20, 1990.

KEVIN D. RITZ

Born June 8, 1965, at Eatonstown, N. J.
Height, 6.04. Weight, 195.
Throws and bats righthanded.
Attended William Penn College, Oskaloosa, Ia., and Indian Hills Community College, Centerville, Ia.

Year Club	League	G.	IP.	W.	L.	Pct.	H.	R.	ER.	SO.	BB.	ERA.
1986—Gastonia..........................	S. Atlantic	7	36⅓	1	2	.333	29	19	17	34	21	4.21
1986—Lakeland.........................	Florida St.	18	85⅔	3	9	.250	114	60	53	39	45	5.57
1987—Glens Falls	Eastern	25	152⅔	8	8	.500	171	95	83	78	71	4.89
1988—Glens Falls	Eastern	26	136⅔	8	10	.444	115	68	58	75	70	3.82
1989—Toledo.............................	Int'national	16	102⅔	7	8	.467	95	48	36	74	60	3.16
1989—Detroit.............................	American	12	74	4	6	.400	75	41	36	56	44	4.38
1990—Toledo.............................	Int'national	20	89⅔	3	6	.333	93	68	52	57	59	5.22
1990—Detroit.............................	American	4	7⅓	0	4	.000	14	12	9	3	14	11.05
Major League Totals—2 Years............................		16	81⅓	4	10	.286	89	53	45	59	58	4.98

Selected by San Francisco Giants' organization in 4th round of free-agent draft, January 9, 1985.
Selected by Detroit Tigers' organization in secondary phase of free-agent draft, June 3, 1985.

LUIS ANTONIO RIVERA

Born January 3, 1964, at Cidra, Puerto Rico.
Height, 5.09. Weight, 170.
Throws and bats righthanded.
Major League stolen bases: 1986 (1), 1988 (3), 1989 (2), 1990 (4). Total—10.
Led American Association in double plays with 84 in 1987.
Led Southern League shortstops in total chances with 643 and double plays with 107 in 1985.
Led Florida State League shortstops in assists with 436, errors with 51, total chances with 704 and double plays with 95 in 1983.
Tied for Florida State League lead in total chances by shortstops with 626 in 1984.

Year Club League	Pos.	G.	AB.	R.	H.	2B.	3B.	HR.	RBI.	B.A.	PO.	A.	E.	F.A.
1982—San Jose .... Calif.	SS	130	476	53	123	20	3	3	49	.258	226	389	55	.918
1983—W. Palm Beach.... Fla. St.	SS	129	419	63	95	18	5	5	53	.227	217	436	51	.928
1984—W. Palm Beach.... Fla. St.	SS	124	439	54	100	23	0	6	43	.228	★198	★389	39	.938
1985—Jacksonville .... South.	SS	138	★538	74	129	20	2	16	72	.240	★198	★412	33	.949
1986—Indianapolis .... A. A.	SS	108	407	60	100	17	5	7	43	.246	178	330	24	.955
1986—Montreal .... Nat.	SS	55	166	20	34	11	1	0	13	.205	64	119	9	.953
1987—Indianapolis .... A. A.	SS	108	433	73	135	26	3	8	53	.312	190	291	18	.964
1987—Montreal .... Nat.	SS	18	32	0	5	2	0	0	1	.156	9	27	3	.923
1988—Montreal† .... Nat.	SS	123	371	35	83	17	3	4	30	.224	160	301	18	.962
1989—Pawtucket .... Int.	SS-3B	43	175	22	44	9	0	1	13	.251	53	106	9	.946
1989—Boston................... Amer.	SS-2B	93	323	35	83	17	1	5	29	.257	127	240	16	.958
1990—Boston................... Amer.	SS-2B-3B	118	346	38	78	20	0	7	45	.225	187	310	18	.965
National League Totals—3 Years...........		196	569	55	122	30	4	4	44	.214	233	447	30	.958
American League Totals—2 Years		211	669	73	161	37	1	12	74	.241	314	550	34	.962
Major League Totals—5 Years................		407	1238	128	283	67	5	16	118	.229	547	997	64	.960

Signed as free agent by Montreal Expos' organization, September 22, 1981.
†Traded with Pitcher John Dopson to Boston Red Sox for Shortstop Spike Owen and Pitcher Dan Gakeler, December 8, 1988.

CHAMPIONSHIP SERIES RECORD

Year Club League	Pos.	G.	AB.	R.	H.	2B.	3B.	HR.	RBI.	B.A.	PO.	A.	E.	F.A.
1990—Boston................... Amer.	SS	4	9	1	2	1	0	0	0	.222	6	16	1	.957

LEON JOSEPH ROBERTS III
(Bip)

Born October 27, 1963, at Berkeley, Calif.
Height, 5.07. Weight, 160.
Throws right and bats left and righthanded.
Attended Chabot College, Hayward, Calif.; and University of Nevada, Las Vegas, Nev.
Major League stolen bases: 1986 (14), 1989 (21), 1990 (46). Total—81.
Tied for Eastern League lead in stolen bases with 40 in 1985.
Led Carolina League second basemen in total chances with 654 and double plays with 91 in 1984.
Led South Atlantic League second basemen in fielding percentage with .962 and tied for lead in double plays with 76 in 1983.

Year Club League	Pos.	G.	AB.	R.	H.	2B.	3B.	HR.	RBI.	B.A.	PO.	A.	E.	F.A.
1982—Bradenton Pir. ..... Gulf C.	2B	6	23	4	7	1	0	0	1	.304	14	15	0	1.000
1982—Greenwood........... S. Atl.	2B	33	107	15	23	3	1	0	6	.215	52	82	7	.950
1983—Greenwood........... S. Atl.	2B-SS	122	438	78	140	20	5	6	63	.320	273	311	24	.961
1984—Prince William .... Carol.	2B	134	498	81	*150	25	5	8	77	.301	*282	352	20	*.969
1985—Nashua†‡ .... East.	2B	105	401	64	109	19	5	1	23	.272	217	249	•29	.941
1986—San Diego§ .... Nat.	2B	101	241	34	61	5	2	1	12	.253	166	172	10	.971
1987—Las Vegas.............. P. C.	2B-OF-3B	98	359	66	110	18	10	1	38	.306	147	150	8	.974
1988—Las Vegas.............. P. C.	3B-OF-2B	100	343	73	121	21	8	7	51	.353	103	130	17	.932
1988—San Diego .... Nat.	2B-3B	5	9	1	3	0	0	0	0	.333	2	3	1	.833
1989—San Diego .... Nat.	O-3-S-2	117	329	81	99	15	8	3	25	.301	134	113	9	.965
1990—San Diego .... Nat.	O-3-S-2	149	556	104	172	36	3	9	44	.309	227	160	13	.968
Major League Totals—4 Years................		372	1135	220	335	56	13	13	81	.295	529	448	33	.967

Selected by Pittsburgh Pirates' organization in 5th round of free-agent draft, June 8, 1981.
Selected by Pittsburgh Pirates' organization in secondary phase of free-agent draft, June 7, 1982.
†On suspended list, June 30 to July 3, 1985.
‡Drafted by San Diego Padres, December 10, 1985.
§On disabled list, May 21 to June 5, 1986.

WILLIAM JOSEPH ROBIDOUX
Name pronounced ROW-ba-doe.
(Billy Jo)
Born January 13, 1964, at Ware, Mass.
Height, 6.01. Weight, 200.
Throws right and bats lefthanded.

Major League stolen bases: 1988 (1).
Led Pacific Coast League in intentional bases on balls received with 9 in 1989.
Led Texas League in total bases with 297 and slugging percentage with .577 in 1985.
Led Texas League first basemen in putouts with 1,025, assists with 68, fielding percentage with .988, total chances with 1,106 and double plays with 102 in 1985.
Named Texas League Most Valuable Player, 1985.

Year Club League	Pos.	G.	AB.	R.	H.	2B.	3B.	HR.	RBI.	B.A.	PO.	A.	E.	F.A.
1982—Pikeville† .... Appal.	3B-1B	54	167	28	48	10	1	0	13	.287	57	54	15	.881
1983—Beloit .... Midw.	3B-1B-2B	126	435	70	138	30	1	10	61	.317	104	163	25	.914
1984—Stockton .... Calif.	3B-1B	97	333	50	93	18	1	5	67	.279	323	98	15	.966
1985—El Paso .... Texas	1B-OF-3B	133	515	*111	*176	*46	3	23	*132	*.342	1030	69	15	.987
1985—Milwaukee.............. Amer.	OF-1B	18	51	5	9	2	0	3	8	.176	64	6	0	1.000
1986—Milwaukee‡.......... Amer.	1B	56	181	15	41	8	0	1	21	.227	326	29	5	.986
1986—Beloit .... Midw.	1B	7	16	3	4	2	0	0	2	.250	12	2	0	1.000
1986—El Paso .... Texas	1B	30	114	30	37	9	0	10	34	.325	269	11	1	.996
1987—Milwaukee.............. Amer.	1B	23	62	9	12	0	0	0	4	.194	53	4	1	.983
1987—Denver§ .... A. A.	1B-3B	30	116	27	33	9	3	3	15	.284	184	14	5	.975
1988—Denver .... A. A.	1B	70	240	43	70	24	0	8	42	.292	570	48	8	.987
1988—Milwaukee x .... Amer.	1B	33	91	9	23	5	0	0	5	.253	212	25	4	.983
1989—Chicago .... Amer.	1B-OF	16	39	2	5	2	0	0	1	.128	93	7	1	.990
1989—Vancouver y .... P. C.	1B	73	246	36	78	19	2	11	42	.317	440	41	5	.990
1990—Boston z .... Amer.	1B	27	44	3	8	4	0	1	4	.182	49	4	1	.981
1990—Pawtucket a.......... Int.	DH-PH	22	54	5	11	1	0	3	7	.204	0	0	0	.000
Major League Totals—6 Years................		173	468	43	98	21	0	5	43	.209	797	75	12	.986

Selected by Milwaukee Brewers' organization in 6th round of free-agent draft, June 7, 1982.
†On disabled list, June 21 to July 1, 1982.
‡On disabled list, May 13 to June 11 and July 8 to August 20, 1986; included rehabilitation disability assignment to Beloit, June 4 to June 11, and to El Paso, August 1 to August 20, 1986.
§On disabled list, July 16, 1987 through remainder of season.
xGranted free agency, October 15, 1988; signed by Chicago White Sox, October 30, 1988.
yGranted free agency, October 15, 1989; signed by Pawtucket (Boston Red Sox' organization), December 13, 1989.
zOn disabled list, April 27 to June 28, 1990.
aReleased, December 4, 1990.

DON ALLEN ROBINSON
Born June 8, 1957, at Ashland, Ky.
Height, 6.04. Weight, 240.
Throws and bats righthanded.

Major League saves: 1978 (1), 1980 (1), 1981 (2), 1984 (10), 1985 (3), 1986 (14), 1987 (19), 1988 (6). Total—56.
Tied for National League lead in home runs allowed with 26 in 1982.
Led Western Carolinas League in complete games with 11 in 1976.
Tied for Gulf Coast League lead in hit batsmen with 6 in 1975.
Named National League Rookie Pitcher of the Year by THE SPORTING NEWS, 1978.
Named pitcher on THE SPORTING NEWS National League Silver Slugger team, 1982, 1989 and 1990.

Year Club League	G.	IP.	W.	L.	Pct.	H.	R.	ER.	SO.	BB.	ERA.
1975—Bradenton Pirates......... Gulf Coast	10	66	2	3	.400	51	23	18	*70	31	2.45
1976—Charleston .... W. Carol.	25	*172	12	9	.571	146	79	62	132	64	3.24
1977—Shreveport .... Texas	18	112	7	6	.538	113	58	51	103	41	4.06
1977—Columbus† .... Int'national	1	5	1	0	1.000	7	0	0	3	1	0.00
1978—Pittsburgh................ National	35	228	14	6	.700	203	98	88	135	57	3.47
1979—Pittsburgh................ National	29	161	8	8	.500	171	74	69	96	52	3.86
1980—Pittsburgh‡................ National	29	160	7	10	.412	157	74	71	103	45	3.99

Year Club	League	G.	IP.	W.	L.	Pct.	H.	R.	ER.	SO.	BB.	ERA.
1981—Pittsburgh§	National	16	38	0	3	.000	47	27	25	17	23	5.92
1982—Pittsburgh	National	38	227	15	13	.536	213	★123	108	165	103	4.28
1983—Pittsburgh x	National	9	36⅓	2	2	.500	43	21	18	28	21	4.46
1983—Lynn	Eastern	2	6⅔	0	1	.000	9	6	6	5	2	8.10
1984—Pittsburgh y	National	51	122	5	6	.455	99	45	41	110	49	3.02
1985—Pittsburgh	National	44	95⅓	5	11	.313	95	49	41	65	42	3.87
1986—Pittsburgh z	National	50	69⅓	3	4	.429	61	27	26	53	27	3.38
1986—Prince William	Carolina	3	12⅔	1	1	.500	13	7	1	13	1	0.71
1987—Pittsburgh a-San Francisco	National	67	108	11	7	.611	105	42	41	79	40	3.42
1988—San Francisco	National	51	176⅔	10	5	.667	152	63	48	122	49	2.45
1989—San Francisco	National	34	197	12	11	.522	184	80	75	96	37	3.43
1990—San Jose b	California	2	7	1	0	1.000	6	3	3	8	1	3.86
1990—San Francisco	National	26	157⅔	10	7	.588	173	84	80	78	41	4.57
Major League Totals—13 Years		479	1776⅓	102	93	.523	1703	807	731	1147	586	3.70

Selected by Pittsburgh Pirates' organization in 3rd round of free-agent draft, June 4, 1975.

†On disabled list, July 28 to September 6, 1977.

‡On disabled list, March 31 to May 1, 1980.

§On disabled list, May 2 to June 6 and August 2 to August 26, 1981.

xOn disabled list, March 29 to June 10 and July 29 to September 2, 1983; included rehabilitation disability assignment to Lynn, April 29 to May 18, 1983.

yAppeared in one game as an outfielder with two putouts.

zOn disabled list, April 21 to June 7, 1986; included rehabilitation disability assignment to Prince William, May 24 to June 7, 1986.

aTraded to San Francisco Giants for Catcher Mackey Sasser and $50,000, July 31, 1987.

bOn San Francisco disabled list, March 28 to May 23, 1990; included rehabilitation disability assignment to San Jose, May 9 to May 22, 1990.

CHAMPIONSHIP SERIES RECORD

Year Club	League	G.	IP.	W.	L.	Pct.	H.	R.	ER.	SO.	BB.	ERA.
1979—Pittsburgh	National	2	2	1	0	1.000	0	0	0	3	1	0.00
1987—San Francisco	National	3	3	0	1	.000	3	3	3	3	0	9.00
1989—San Francisco	National	1	1⅔	1	0	1.000	3	1	0	0	0	0.00
Championship Series Totals—3 Years		6	6⅔	2	1	.667	6	4	3	6	1	4.05

WORLD SERIES RECORD

Year Club	League	G.	IP.	W.	L.	Pct.	H.	R.	ER.	SO.	BB.	ERA.
1979—Pittsburgh	National	4	5	1	0	1.000	4	3	3	3	6	5.40
1989—San Francisco	National	1	1⅔	0	1	.000	4	4	4	0	1	21.60
World Series Totals—2 Years		5	6⅔	1	1	.500	8	7	7	3	7	9.45

JEFFREY DANIEL ROBINSON
(Jeff)

Born December 13, 1960, at Santa Ana, Calif.
Height, 6.04. Weight, 200.
Throws and bats righthanded.
Attended California State University, Fullerton, Calif.

Shares major league record by striking out side on 9 pitches, September 7, 1987, eighth inning.
Major League saves: 1986 (8), 1987 (14), 1988 (9), 1989 (4). Total—35.
Tied for National League lead in hit batsmen with 7 in 1984.
Tied for Pacific Coast League lead in games started by pitchers with 29 in 1985.

Year Club	League	G.	IP.	W.	L.	Pct.	H.	R.	ER.	SO.	BB.	ERA.
1983—Fresno	California	14	94⅔	7	6	.538	88	35	24	78	21	2.28
1984—San Francisco	National	34	171⅔	7	15	.318	195	99	87	102	52	4.56
1985—Phoenix	P. Coast	29	161	9	9	.500	192	107	92	80	60	5.14
1985—San Francisco	National	8	12⅓	0	0	.000	16	11	7	8	10	5.11
1986—San Francisco†	National	64	104⅓	6	3	.667	92	46	39	90	32	3.36
1987—San Francisco‡-Pittsburgh	National	81	123⅓	8	9	.471	89	43	39	101	54	2.85
1988—Pittsburgh	National	75	124⅔	11	5	.688	113	44	42	87	39	3.03
1989—Pittsburgh§	National	50	141⅓	7	13	.350	161	92	72	95	59	4.58
1990—New York x	American	54	88⅔	3	6	.333	82	35	34	43	34	3.45
National League Totals—6 Years		312	677⅔	39	45	.464	666	335	286	483	246	3.80
American League Totals—1 Year		54	88⅔	3	6	.333	82	35	34	43	34	3.45
Major League Totals—7 Years		366	766⅓	42	51	.452	748	370	320	526	280	3.76

Selected by Toronto Blue Jays' organization in 17th round of free-agent draft, June 5, 1979.

Selected by Detroit Tigers' organization in 14th round of free-agent draft, June 7, 1982.

Selected by San Francisco Giants' organization in 2nd round of free-agent draft, June 6, 1983.

†Appeared in one game as an outfielder with no chances.

‡Traded with Pitcher Scott Medvin to Pittsburgh Pirates for Pitcher Rick Reuschel, August 21, 1987.

§Traded with Pitcher Willie Smith to New York Yankees for Catcher Don Slaught, December 4, 1989.

xGranted free agency, November 5, 1990.

—DID YOU KNOW—

That Montreal rookie pitcher Chris Nabholz fashioned a 6-0 start with the Expos following an 0-6 stint at Class AAA Indianapolis in 1990?

JEFFREY MARK ROBINSON
(Jeff)

Born December 14, 1961, at Ventura, Calif.
Height, 6.06. Weight, 240.
Throws and bats righthanded.
Attended Azusa Pacific University, Azusa, Calif.

Year Club	League	G.	IP.	W.	L.	Pct.	H.	R.	ER.	SO.	BB.	ERA.
1983—Lakeland	Florida St.	11	50	2	5	.286	61	38	33	23	19	5.94
1984—Lakeland	Florida St.	10	61⅔	2	3	.400	62	30	23	33	26	3.36
1984—Birmingham	Southern	20	113	6	6	.500	111	64	59	47	56	4.70
1985—Birmingham†	Southern	22	115	4	8	.333	142	79	65	67	59	5.09
1986—Nashville	Am. Assoc.	25	150	10	7	.588	162	85	73	72	72	4.38
1987—Detroit	American	29	127⅓	9	6	.600	132	86	76	98	54	5.37
1988—Detroit‡	American	24	172	13	6	.684	121	61	57	114	72	2.98
1989—Detroit§	American	16	78	4	5	.444	76	47	41	40	46	4.73
1989—Lakeland	Florida St.	4	11	0	0	.000	12	8	8	5	4	6.55
1990—Detroit	American	27	145	10	9	.526	141	101	96	76	88	5.96
Major League Totals—4 Years		96	522⅓	36	26	.581	470	295	270	328	260	4.65

Selected by San Diego Padres' organization in 40th round of free-agent draft, June 3, 1980.
Selected by Detroit Tigers' organization in 3rd round of free-agent draft, June 6, 1983.
†On disabled list, June 28 to July 10, 1985.
‡On disabled list, August 24, 1988 through remainder of season.
§On disabled list, May 15 to May 31 and June 11 to July 26, 1989; included rehabilitation disability assignment to Lakeland, July 10 to July 26, 1989.
xTraded to Baltimore Orioles for Catcher Mickey Tettleton, January 11, 1991.

CHAMPIONSHIP SERIES RECORD

Year Club	League	G.	IP.	W.	L.	Pct.	H.	R.	ER.	SO.	BB.	ERA.
1987—Detroit	American	1	⅓	0	0	.000	1	0	0	0	0	0.00

RONALD DEAN ROBINSON
(Ron)

Born March 24, 1962, at Exeter, Calif.
Height, 6.04. Weight, 235.
Throws and bats righthanded.

Major League saves: 1985 (1), 1986 (14), 1987 (4). Total—19.

Year Club	League	G.	IP.	W.	L.	Pct.	H.	R.	ER.	SO.	BB.	ERA.
1980—Tampa	Florida St.	13	76	4	6	.400	76	32	28	44	16	3.32
1981—Cedar Rapids	Midwest	24	169	10	8	.556	136	58	42	165	55	2.24
1982—Waterbury	Eastern	32	178⅓	13	7	.650	166	78	65	149	65	3.28
1983—Waterbury	Eastern	20	142⅔	7	9	.438	132	66	57	82	60	3.60
1983—Indianapolis	Am. Assoc.	4	30⅔	4	0	1.000	22	13	11	20	7	3.23
1984—Wichita	Am. Assoc.	25	150⅓	9	6	.600	168	86	77	98	60	4.61
1984—Cincinnati	National	12	39⅔	1	2	.333	35	18	12	24	13	2.72
1985—Denver	Am. Assoc.	6	39⅔	2	1	.667	39	17	12	24	12	2.72
1985—Cincinnati	National	33	108⅓	7	7	.500	107	53	48	76	32	3.99
1986—Cincinnati	National	70	116⅔	10	3	.769	110	44	42	117	43	3.24
1987—Cincinnati	National	48	154	7	5	.583	148	71	63	99	43	3.68
1988—Cincinnati†	National	17	78⅔	3	7	.300	88	47	36	38	26	4.12
1988—Nashville	Am. Assoc.	2	3⅔	0	0	.000	4	3	3	4	3	7.36
1989—Nashville‡	Am. Assoc.	3	19	2	0	1.000	12	5	4	11	6	1.89
1989—Chattanooga	Southern	1	5	0	0	.000	3	1	1	5	1	1.80
1989—Cincinnati	National	15	83⅓	5	3	.625	80	36	31	36	28	3.35
1990—Cincinnati§	National	6	31⅓	2	2	.500	36	18	17	14	14	4.88
1990—Milwaukee	American	22	148⅓	12	5	.706	158	60	48	57	37	2.91
National League Totals—7 Years		201	612	35	29	.547	604	287	249	404	199	3.66
American League Totals—1 Year		22	148⅓	12	5	.706	158	60	48	57	37	2.91
Major League Totals—7 Years		223	760⅓	47	34	.580	762	347	297	461	236	3.52

Selected by Cincinnati Reds' organization in 1st round (19th player selected) of free-agent draft, June 3, 1980.
†On disabled list, June 25 to July 18 and July 20 to September 2, 1988; included rehabilitation disability assignment to Nashville, August 15 to September 2, 1988.
‡On Cincinnati disabled list, March 19 to July 17, 1989; included rehabilitation disability assignment to Nashville, June 26 to July 2, 1989; then transferred to Chattanooga, July 3, 1989.
§Traded with Pitcher Bob Sebra to Milwaukee Brewers for Outfielder Glenn Braggs and Infielder Billy Bates, June 9, 1990.

MICHAEL JOSEPH ROCHFORD
(Mike)

Born March 14, 1963, at Methuen, Mass.
Height, 6.04. Weight, 205.
Throws and bats lefthanded.
Attended Santa Fe Community College, Gainsville, Fla.

Led International League in balks with 5 in 1984.
Tied for International League lead in complete games with 9 in 1989.
Tied for Carolina League lead in games started by pitchers with 29 in 1983.

Year Club	League	G.	IP.	W.	L.	Pct.	H.	R.	ER.	SO.	BB.	ERA.
1982—Elmira	NYP	16	85⅔	6	4	.600	99	53	40	66	26	4.20
1983—Winston-Salem	Carolina	29	210⅓	16	11	.593	182	85	70	165	57	3.00
1984—Pawtucket	Int'national	31	141⅓	8	10	.444	156	88	77	73	59	4.90
1985—New Britain	Eastern	14	93⅓	8	5	.615	84	39	31	42	41	2.99
1985—Pawtucket	Int'national	12	72	5	2	.714	74	34	33	47	32	4.13
1986—Pawtucket	Int'national	28	170⅔	11	10	.524	178	76	67	70	50	3.53
1987—Pawtucket	Int'national	22	123⅔	8	8	.500	144	65	63	42	38	4.58
1988—Pawtucket	Int'national	52	81⅔	1	5	.167	68	30	28	47	29	3.09
1988—Boston	American	2	2⅓	0	0	.000	4	0	0	1	1	0.00
1989—Pawtucket	Int'national	37	163⅓	9	6	.600	139	52	43	76	43	2.37
1989—Boston	American	4	4	0	0	.000	4	7	3	1	4	6.75
1990—Boston	American	2	4	0	1	.000	10	10	8	0	4	18.00
1990—Pawtucket	Int'national	9	43⅓	3	3	.500	36	19	13	31	13	2.70
Major League Totals—3 Years		8	10⅓	0	1	.000	18	17	11	2	9	9.58

Selected by Boston Red Sox' organization in 1st round (17th player selected) of free-agent draft, January 12, 1982.

HENRY ANDERSON RODRIGUEZ (LORENZO)

Born November 8, 1967, at Santo Domingo, Dominican Republic.
Height, 6.01. Weight, 180.
Throws and bats lefthanded.

Led Texas League in sacrifice flies with 14 in 1990.
Tied for Gulf Coast League lead in intentional bases on balls received with 7 in 1987.
Named Texas League Most Valuable Player, 1990.

Year Club	League	Pos.	G.	AB.	R.	H.	2B.	3B.	HR.	RBI.	B.A.	PO.	A.	E.	F.A.
1987—Sarasota Dodg.	Gulf C.	1B-SS	49	148	23	49	7	3	0	15	*.331	309	23	6	.982
1988—Salem	N'west	1B	72	291	47	84	14	4	2	39	.289	585	*38	7	.989
1989—Vero Beach	Fla. St.	1B-OF	126	433	53	123	*33	1	10	73	.284	1072	66	12	.990
1989—Bakersfield	Calif.	1B	3	9	2	2	0	0	1	2	.222	8	0	0	1.000
1990—San Antonio	Texas	OF	129	495	82	144	22	9	*28	*109	.291	223	5	10	.958

Signed as free agent by Los Angeles Dodgers' organization, July 14, 1985.

RICARDO RODRIGUEZ
(Rick)

Born September 21, 1960, at Oakland, Calif.
Height, 6.02. Weight, 200.
Throws and bats righthanded.
Attended Chabot College, Hayward, Calif., and University of California, Riverside, Calif.

Year Club	League	G.	IP.	W.	L.	Pct.	H.	R.	ER.	SO.	BB.	ERA.
1981—Modesto	California	11	63	2	5	.286	68	51	37	28	28	5.29
1982—Modesto†	California	15	105⅔	8	2	.800	100	38	32	70	41	2.73
1983—Tacoma‡	P. Coast	10	58	1	4	.200	61	32	25	25	28	3.88
1984—Modesto§	California	2	13⅓	0	0	.000	11	3	3	6	5	2.03
1984—Tacoma	P. Coast	6	16⅓	0	1	.000	21	17	16	9	7	8.82
1984—Albany	Eastern	10	42⅔	5	1	.833	54	33	25	29	19	5.27
1985—Modesto	California	16	103⅔	8	1	.889	103	42	38	50	41	3.30
1985—Huntsville	Southern	8	50	2	1	.667	40	18	13	25	13	2.34
1985—Tacoma	P. Coast	7	13⅓	0	1	.000	18	9	6	5	7	4.05
1986—Huntsville	Southern	9	16	0	0	.000	17	11	9	14	7	5.06
1986—Tacoma	P. Coast	26	139	7	8	.467	144	82	61	76	59	3.95
1986—Oakland	American	3	16⅓	1	2	.333	17	12	12	2	7	6.61
1987—Oakland	American	15	24⅓	1	0	1.000	32	8	8	9	15	2.96
1987—Tacoma x	P. Coast	21	92⅓	5	4	.556	90	39	34	52	36	3.31
1988—Colorado Springs	P. Coast	19	126⅔	8	6	.571	112	49	43	55	43	3.06
1988—Cleveland y	American	10	33	1	2	.333	43	28	26	9	17	7.09
1989—Vancouver z	P. Coast	13	61⅓	2	5	.286	90	47	43	26	22	6.31
1990—Phoenix	P. Coast	14	41⅔	4	2	.667	36	24	22	21	22	4.75
1990—San Francisco	National	3	3⅓	0	0	.000	5	3	3	2	2	8.10
American League Totals—3 Years		28	73⅔	3	4	.429	92	48	46	20	39	5.62
National League Totals—1 Year		3	3⅓	0	0	.000	5	3	3	2	2	8.10
Major League Totals—4 Years		31	77	3	4	.429	97	51	49	22	41	5.73

Selected by Oakland A's organization in 2nd round of free-agent draft, June 8, 1981.
†On disabled list, May 15 to July 23, 1982.
‡On disabled list, April 10 to May 14 and July 1, 1983 through remainder of season.
§On Tacoma disabled list, April 7 to May 23 and June 12 to June 22, 1984.
xReleased, December 21, 1987; signed by Cleveland Indians, January 15, 1988.
yGranted free agency, October 15, 1988; signed by Chicago White Sox' organization, November 8, 1988.
zGranted free agency, October 15, 1989; signed by Phoenix (San Francisco Giants' organization), June 24, 1990.

RICHARD ANTHONY RODRIGUEZ
(Rich)

Born March 1, 1963, at Los Angeles, Calif.
Height, 5.11. Weight, 200.
Throws and bats lefthanded.
Attended University of Tennessee, Knoxville, Tenn.

Major League saves: 1990 (1).

Led Texas League in intentional bases on balls issued with 11 in 1989.
Tied for New York-Pennsylvania League lead in intentional bases on balls issued with 7 in 1984.

Year Club	League	G.	IP.	W.	L.	Pct.	H.	R.	ER.	SO.	BB.	ERA.
1984—Little Falls	NYP	25	35⅓	2	1	.667	28	21	11	27	36	2.80
1985—Columbia	S. Atlantic	49	80⅓	6	3	.667	89	41	36	71	36	4.03
1986—Lynchburg	Carolina	36	45⅓	2	1	.667	37	20	18	38	19	3.57
1986—Jackson	Texas	13	33	3	4	.429	51	35	33	15	15	9.00
1987—Lynchburg	Carolina	★69	68	3	1	.750	69	23	21	59	26	2.78
1988—Jackson†	Texas	47	78½	2	7	.222	66	35	25	68	42	2.87
1989—Wichita	Texas	54	74⅓	8	3	.727	74	30	30	40	37	3.63
1990—Las Vegas	P. Coast	27	59	3	4	.429	50	24	23	46	22	3.51
1990—San Diego	National	32	47⅔	1	1	.500	52	17	15	22	16	2.83
Major League Totals—1 Year		32	47⅔	1	1	.500	52	17	15	22	16	2.83

Selected by Kansas City Royals' organization in 17th round of free-agent draft, June 8, 1981.
Selected by New York Mets' organization in 9th round of free-agent draft, June 4, 1984.
†Traded to Wichita (San Diego Padres' organization) for First Basemen Brad Pounders and Bill Stevenson, January 13, 1989.

ROSARIO RODRIGUEZ

Born July 8, 1969 at Los Moches, Mexico.
Height, 6.00. Weight, 195.
Throws left and bats righthanded.

Year Club	League	G.	IP.	W.	L.	Pct.	H.	R.	ER.	SO.	BB.	ERA.
1987—Sarasota Reds	Gulf Coast	17	64⅓	1	5	.167	64	32	22	33	21	3.08
1988—Greensboro	S. Atlantic	23	65⅓	6	4	.600	49	15	11	53	24	1.52
1988—Cedar Rapids	Midwest	13	70	3	4	.429	73	41	31	47	25	3.99
1989—Chattanooga	Southern	28	44⅓	3	0	1.000	48	24	22	36	18	4.47
1989—Cincinnati	National	7	4⅓	1	1	.500	3	2	2	0	3	4.15
1990—Nashville	Am. Assoc.	5	4⅓	0	1	.000	4	5	5	1	3	10.38
1990—Chattanooga	Southern	36	53⅔	2	2	.500	52	29	26	39	48	4.36
1990—Cincinnati†	National	9	10⅓	0	0	.000	15	7	7	8	2	6.10
Major League Totals—2 Years		16	14⅔	1	1	.500	18	9	9	8	5	5.52

Signed as free agent by Cincinnati Reds' organization, March 16, 1987.
†Claimed on waivers by Pittsburgh Pirates, December 20, 1990.

MICHAEL JOSEPH ROESLER

Name pronounced RESS-ler.

(Mike)

Born September 12, 1963, at Fort Wayne, Ind.
Height, 6.05. Weight, 205.
Throws and bats righthanded.
Attended Ball State University, Muncie, Ind.

Year Club	League	G.	IP.	W.	L.	Pct.	H.	R.	ER.	SO.	BB.	ERA.
1985—Billings	Pioneer	13	88⅔	8	2	.800	72	32	23	73	28	2.33
1986—Cedar Rapids	Midwest	32	163	9	13	.409	165	95	83	135	80	4.58
1987—Tampa	Florida St.	28	36⅓	7	2	.778	30	14	9	29	15	2.23
1987—Vermont	Eastern	22	27⅓	4	2	.667	28	10	10	19	10	3.29
1988—Chattanooga	Southern	16	20⅓	1	1	.500	16	5	5	13	8	2.21
1988—Nashville	Am. Assoc.	32	41⅓	3	2	.600	44	25	23	31	27	5.01
1989—Nashville	Am. Assoc.	40	69⅓	6	4	.600	63	30	25	53	39	3.25
1989—Cincinnati†	National	17	25	0	1	.000	22	11	11	14	9	3.96
1990—Pittsburgh	National	5	6	1	0	1.000	5	2	2	4	2	3.00
1990—Buffalo	Am. Assoc.	24	42	0	3	.000	50	25	20	19	17	4.29
1990—Harrisburg	Eastern	10	23⅔	2	1	.667	29	14	12	11	6	4.56
Major League Totals—2 Years		22	31	1	1	.500	27	13	13	18	11	3.77

Selected by Cincinnati Reds' organization in 17th round of free-agent draft, June 3, 1985.
†Traded with Infielder Jeff Richardson to Pittsburgh Pirates for Outfielder Billy Hatcher, April 3, 1990.

KENNETH SCOTT ROGERS

(Kenny)

Born November 10, 1964, at Savannah, Ga.
Height, 6.01. Weight, 205.
Throws and bats lefthanded.

Major League saves: 1989 (2), 1990 (15). Total—17.

Year Club	League	G.	IP.	W.	L.	Pct.	H.	R.	ER.	SO.	BB.	ERA.
1982—Sarasota Rangers	Gulf Coast	2	3	0	0	.000	0	0	0	4	0	0.00
1983—Sarasota Rangers	Gulf Coast	15	53⅓	4	1	.800	40	21	14	36	20	2.36
1984—Burlington	Midwest	39	92⅔	4	7	.364	87	52	41	93	33	3.98
1985—Daytona Beach	Florida St.	6	10	0	1	.000	12	9	8	9	11	7.20
1985—Burlington	Midwest	33	95	2	5	.286	67	34	30	96	62	2.84
1986—Tulsa†	Texas	10	26⅓	0	3	.000	39	30	29	23	18	9.91
1986—Salem	Carolina	12	66	2	7	.222	75	54	46	46	26	6.27
1987—Charlotte	Florida St.	5	17	0	3	.000	17	13	9	14	8	4.76
1987—Tulsa	Texas	28	69	1	5	.167	80	51	41	59	35	5.35
1988—Tulsa	Texas	13	83⅓	4	6	.400	73	43	37	76	34	4.00

Year Club	League	G.	IP.	W.	L.	Pct.	H.	R.	ER.	SO.	BB.	ERA.
1988—Port Charlotte	Florida St.	8	35⅓	2	0	1.000	22	8	5	26	11	1.27
1989—Texas	American	73	73⅔	3	4	.429	60	28	24	63	42	2.93
1990—Texas	American	69	97⅔	10	6	.625	93	40	34	74	42	3.13
Major League Totals—2 Years		142	171⅓	13	10	.565	153	68	58	137	84	3.05

Selected by Texas Rangers' organization in 39th round of free-agent draft, June 7, 1982.
†On disabled list, April 12 to April 30, 1986.

DAVID GRANT ROHDE

Name pronounced ROH-dee.

(Dave)

Born May 8, 1964, at Los Altos, Calif.
Height, 6.02. Weight, 180.
Throws right and bats left and righthanded.
Attended Saddleback Community College, Mission Viejo, Calif.,
and University of Arizona, Tucson, Ariz.

Led Southern League second basemen in fielding percentage with .987 in 1988.

Year Club	League	Pos.	G.	AB.	R.	H.	2B.	3B.	HR.	RBI.	B.A.	PO.	A.	E.	F.A.
1986—Auburn†	NYP	SS	61	207	41	54	6	4	2	22	.261	90	158	16	.939
1987—Osceola†	Fla. St.	2B-SS	103	377	57	108	15	1	5	42	.286	165	305	20	.959
1988—Columbus†	South.	2B-SS	142	486	76	130	20	2	4	53	.267	251	356	25	.960
1989—Columbus	South.	3B-2B-SS	67	254	40	71	5	2	2	27	.280	70	127	17	.921
1989—Tucson	P. C.	SS-3B	75	234	35	68	7	3	1	30	.291	108	232	13	.963
1990—Houston	Nat.	2B-3B-SS	58	98	8	18	4	0	0	5	.184	28	70	0	1.000
1990—Tucson	P. C.	2B-SS	47	170	42	60	10	2	0	20	.353	76	137	7	.968
Major League Totals—1 Year			58	98	8	18	4	0	0	5	.184	28	70	0	1.000

Selected by Houston Astros' organization in 5th round of free-agent draft, June 2, 1986.
†Batted righthanded only.

MELQUIADES ROJAS

Name pronounced ROH-hass.

(Mel or Hiti)

Born December 10, 1966, at Haina, Dominican Republic.
Throws and bats righthanded.
Height, 5.11. Weight, 175.
Nephew of Felipe Alou, outfielder with San Francisco, Milwaukee-Atlanta Braves, Oakland, New York Yankees, Montreal and Milwaukee Brewers, 1958 through 1974; coach with Montreal Expos, 1979, 1980 and 1984; and minor league manager in Montreal Expos' organization, 1977, 1978, 1981 through 1983 and since 1985; nephew of Jesus Alou, outfielder with San Francisco, Houston, Oakland and New York Yankees, 1963 through 1975, 1978 and 1979, and scout with Montreal Expos since 1983; nephew of Matty Alou, outfielder with San Francisco, Pittsburgh, St. Louis, Oakland, New York Yankees and San Diego, 1960 through 1974; nephew of Jose Alou, outfielder in Montreal Expos' organization, 1987 through 1989; and brother of Francisco Rojas, outfielder in San Francisco Giants' organization, 1978 and 1979.

Major League saves: 1990 (1).

Year Club	League	G.	IP.	W.	L.	Pct.	H.	R.	ER.	SO.	BB.	ERA.
1986—Bradenton Expos	Gulf Coast	13	55⅓	4	5	.444	63	39	30	34	37	4.88
1987—Burlington	Midwest	25	158⅔	8	9	.471	146	84	67	100	67	3.80
1988—Rockford†	Midwest	12	73⅓	6	4	.600	52	30	20	72	29	2.45
1988—West Palm Beach‡	Florida St.	2	5	1	0	1.000	4	2	2	4	1	3.60
1989—Jacksonville	Southern	34	112	10	7	.588	62	39	31	104	57	2.49
1990—Indianapolis	Am. Assoc.	17	97⅔	2	4	.333	84	42	34	64	47	3.13
1990—Montreal	National	23	40	3	1	.750	34	17	16	26	24	3.60
Major League Totals—1 Year		23	40	3	1	.750	34	17	16	26	24	3.60

Signed as free agent by Montreal Expos' organization, November 7, 1985.
†On disabled list, May 7 to June 14, 1988.
‡On disabled list, August 8, 1988 through remainder of season.

EDGARDO ROMERO

(Ed)

Born December 9, 1957, at Santurce, Puerto Rico.
Height, 5.11. Weight, 180.
Throws and bats righthanded.
Attended Engineer College, Mayaquez, Puerto Rico.

Major League stolen bases: 1980 (2), 1983 (1), 1984 (3), 1985 (1), 1986 (2). Total—9.
Led Pacific Coast League shortstops in double plays with 97 in 1979.
Led Midwest League shortstops in total chances with 647 and double plays with 64 in 1976.

Year Club	League	Pos.	G.	AB.	R.	H.	2B.	3B.	HR.	RBI.	B.A.	PO.	A.	E.	F.A.
1976—Burlington	Midwest	SS	●129	462	58	101	23	1	1	32	.219	187	★419	41	.937
1977—Holyoke	East.	SS	121	457	63	118	19	6	1	38	.258	203	372	41	.933
1977—Milwaukee	Amer.	SS	10	25	4	7	1	0	0	2	.280	9	24	1	.971
1978—Spokane	P. C.	SS-3B	129	440	73	123	27	2	4	52	.280	221	349	32	.947
1979—Vancouver	P. C.	SS	139	515	65	134	26	6	0	39	.260	215	★414	26	.960
1980—Vancouver	P. C.	SS-2B	50	172	19	47	7	1	0	16	.273	72	153	6	.974
1980—Milwaukee	Amer.	SS-2B-3B	42	104	20	27	7	0	1	10	.260	60	102	12	.931
1981—Milwaukee	Amer.	SS-3B-2B	44	91	6	18	3	0	1	10	.198	61	102	6	.964

Year Club	League	Pos.	G.	AB.	R.	H.	2B.	3B.	HR.	RBI.	B.A.	PO.	A.	E.	F.A.
1982—Milwaukee............ Amer.		2-S-3-O	52	144	18	36	8	0	1	7	.250	103	113	7	.969
1983—Milwaukee............ Amer.		S-O-3-2	59	145	17	46	7	0	1	18	.317	59	58	5	.959
1984—Milwaukee............ Amer.		3-S-2-1-O	116	357	36	90	12	0	1	31	.252	141	256	18	.957
1985—Milwaukee†......... Amer.		S-2-O-3	88	251	24	63	11	1	0	21	.251	157	219	8	.979
1986—Boston.............. Amer.		S-3-2-O	100	233	41	49	11	0	2	23	.210	111	159	12	.957
1987—Boston.................. Amer.		2-S-3-1	88	235	23	64	5	0	0	14	.272	122	151	6	.978
1988—Boston‡............. Amer.		3-S-2-1	31	75	3	18	3	0	0	5	.240	21	42	0	1.000
1989—Bos.§-Milw.... Amer.		2B-3B-SS	61	163	17	34	7	0	0	9	.209	82	127	4	.981
1989—Atlanta xy............. Nat.		2B-SS-3B	7	19	1	5	1	0	1	1	.263	7	25	1	.970
1990—Detroit z................ Amer.		3B	32	70	8	16	3	0	0	4	.229	15	41	1	.982
American League Totals—12 Years......			723	1893	217	468	78	1	7	154	.247	941	1394	80	.967
National League Totals—1 Year.............			7	19	1	5	1	0	1	1	.263	7	25	1	.970
Major League Totals—12 Years...............			730	1912	218	473	79	1	8	155	.247	948	1419	81	.967

Signed as free agent by Milwaukee Brewers' organization, November 14, 1975.
†Traded to Boston Red Sox for Pitcher Mark Clear, December 11, 1985.
‡On disabled list, June 6 to July 21, 1988.
§Released, August 5, 1989; signed by Atlanta Braves, August 12, 1989.
xTraded to Milwaukee Brewers for a player to be named later, August 23, 1989; Atlanta Braves acquired Pitcher Jay Aldrich to complete deal, September 1, 1989.
yGranted free agency, November 13, 1989; signed by Detroit Tigers, January 15, 1990.
zReleased, July 15, 1990.

DIVISION SERIES RECORD

Year Club	League	Pos.	G.	AB.	R.	H.	2B.	3B.	HR.	RBI.	B.A.	PO.	A.	E.	F.A.
1981—Milwaukee............ Amer.		2B	1	2	1	1	0	0	0	0	.500	2	2	0	1.000

CHAMPIONSHIP SERIES RECORD

Year Club	League	Pos.	G.	AB.	R.	H.	2B.	3B.	HR.	RBI.	B.A.	PO.	A.	E.	F.A.
1986—Boston.................. Amer.		PR-SS	1	2	0	0	0	0	0	0	.000	0	0	0	.000
1988—Boston.................. Amer.		PR	1	0	0	0	0	0	0	0	.000	0	0	0	.000
Championship Series Totals—2 Years.....			2	2	0	0	0	0	0	0	.000	0	0	0	.000

WORLD SERIES RECORD

Year Club	League	Pos.	G.	AB.	R.	H.	2B.	3B.	HR.	RBI.	B.A.	PO.	A.	E.	F.A.
1986—Boston.................. Amer.		PR-SS	3	1	0	0	0	0	0	0	.000	0	1	0	1.000

Eligible for 1982 World Series with Milwaukee Brewers; did not play.

KEVIN ANDREW ROMINE
Name pronounced Ro-MINE.

Born May 23, 1961, at Exeter, N.H.
Height, 5.11. Weight, 204.
Throws and bats righthanded.
Attended Orange Coast College, Costa Mesa, Calif., and
Arizona State University, Tempe, Ariz.

Major League stolen bases: 1985 (1), 1986 (2), 1988 (2), 1989 (1), 1990 (4). Total—10.
Tied for Eastern League lead in double plays by outfielders with 4 in 1983.
Named outfielder on THE SPORTING NEWS College Baseball All-America Team, 1982.

Year Club	League	Pos.	G.	AB.	R.	H.	2B.	3B.	HR.	RBI.	B.A.	PO.	A.	E.	F.A.
1982—Winter Haven....... Fla. St.		OF	55	201	24	51	4	4	3	22	.254	97	6	3	.972
1983—New Britain .... East.		OF	132	467	74	122	26	5	11	80	.261	211	12	4	.982
1984—Pawtucket†.......... Int.		OF	113	336	62	85	10	1	12	72	.253	202	12	5	.977
1985—Pawtucket‡....... Int.		OF	106	403	43	98	20	1	5	33	.243	246	9	8	.970
1985—Boston.................. Amer.		OF	24	28	3	6	2	0	0	1	.214	20	1	0	1.000
1986—Pawtucket............ Int.		OF	71	257	30	75	8	3	4	32	.292	162	2	2	.988
1986—Boston.................. Amer.		OF	35	35	6	9	2	0	0	2	.257	45	1	0	1.000
1987—Pawtucket............ Int.		OF	129	491	72	131	24	1	11	52	.267	311	6	3	.991
1987—Boston.................. Amer.		OF	9	24	5	7	2	0	0	2	.292	10	1	0	1.000
1988—Boston.................. Amer.		OF	57	78	17	15	2	1	1	6	.192	44	0	2	.957
1988—Pawtucket............ Int.		OF	41	148	18	53	6	1	4	26	.358	71	5	0	1.000
1989—Pawtucket............ Int.		OF-1B	27	90	9	27	3	0	2	7	.300	49	4	1	.981
1989—Boston.................. Amer.		OF	92	274	30	75	13	0	1	23	.274	157	9	3	.982
1990—Boston.................. Amer.		OF	70	136	21	37	7	0	2	14	.272	81	0	2	.976
Major League Totals—6 Years...............			287	575	82	149	28	1	4	48	.259	357	12	7	.981

Selected by California Angels' organization in 3rd round of free-agent draft, January 8, 1980.
Selected by Philadelphia Phillies' organization in secondary phase of free-agent draft, June 3, 1980.
Selected by Boston Red Sox' organization in second round of free-agent draft, June 7, 1982.
†On disabled list, July 18 to July 31, 1984.
‡On disabled list, July 6 to July 17, 1985.

CHAMPIONSHIP SERIES RECORD

Year Club	League	Pos.	G.	AB.	R.	H.	2B.	3B.	HR.	RBI.	B.A.	PO.	A.	E.	F.A.
1988—Boston.................. Amer.		PR	2	0	1	0	0	0	0	0	.000	0	0	0	.000

—DID YOU KNOW—

That the Cubs' Ryne Sandberg belted an N.L.-high 40 homers in 1990, becoming the first second sacker to top the league since Rogers Hornsby in 1925?

ROLANDO AUDLEY ROOMES

Born February 15, 1962, in Jamaica, West Indies.
Height, 6.03. Weight, 180.
Throws and bats righthanded.

Holds major league record for most putouts, rightfielder, game (12), July 28, 1989 (17 innings).
Major League stolen bases: 1989 (12).
Led American Association batters in strikeouts with 134 in 1988.
Led Eastern League batters in strikeouts with 135 in 1987.
Led Midwest League batters in strikeouts with 167 in 1983.
Led New York-Pennsylvania League outfielders in double plays with 4 in 1982.

Year Club	League	Pos.	G.	AB.	R.	H.	2B.	3B.	HR.	RBI.	B.A.	PO.	A.	E.	F.A.
1980—Sarasota Cubs	Gulf C.	OF	19	48	11	7	1	0	2	3	.146	19	1	4	.833
1981—Sarasota Cubs	Gulf C.	OF	63	207	31	48	4	9	2	25	.232	80	7	5	.946
1982—Quad Cities	Midw.	OF	31	80	11	12	1	0	3	8	.150	50	1	3	.944
1982—Geneva	NYP	OF	65	251	57	80	11	3	22	59	.319	129	8	8	.945
1983—Quad Cities	Midw.	OF	122	416	47	89	6	4	9	40	.214	216	*22	14	.944
1984—Lodi	Calif.	OF	116	377	52	100	12	2	13	52	.265	194	11	8	.962
1985—Winston-Salem	Carol.	OF	131	433	57	105	19	6	13	51	.242	254	14	6	.978
1986—Winston-Salem	Carol.	OF	19	68	10	15	3	0	6	14	.238	22	0	0	1.000
1986—Pittsfield	East.	OF	79	191	24	52	5	3	7	42	.272	91	4	7	.931
1987—Pittsfield	East.	OF	129	503	100	155	19	*12	21	95	.308	268	13	6	.979
1988—Chicago	Nat.	OF	17	16	3	3	0	0	0	0	.188	5	0	1	.833
1988—Iowa†	A. A.	OF	112	419	65	126	19	5	16	66	.301	247	12	9	.966
1989—Nashville	A. A.	OF	25	92	13	25	3	1	4	10	.272	57	2	1	.983
1989—Cincinnati	Nat.	OF	107	315	36	83	18	5	7	34	.263	201	4	4	.981
1990—Cinc.‡-Mont.	Nat.	OF	46	75	6	17	0	1	2	8	.227	39	1	0	1.000
1990—Indianapolis§	A. A.	OF	53	198	22	46	5	1	7	31	.232	129	3	5	.964
Major League Totals—3 Years			170	406	45	103	18	6	9	42	.254	245	5	5	.980

Signed as free agent by Chicago Cubs' organization, July 14, 1980.
†Traded to Cincinnati Reds for Catcher Lloyd McClendon, December 9, 1988.
‡Claimed on waivers by Montreal Expos, June 18, 1990.
§Released, December 3, 1990.

VICTOR MANUEL ROSARIO

Born August 26, 1966, at Hato Mayor del Rey, Dominican Republic.
Height, 5.11. Weight, 145.
Throws and bats righthanded.

Led International League shortstops in total chances with 638 and double plays with 76 in 1990.

Year Club	League	Pos.	G.	AB.	R.	H.	2B.	3B.	HR.	RBI.	B.A.	PO.	A.	E.	F.A.
1984—Elmira	NYP	SS	23	27	2	3	0	0	0	0	.111	8	22	4	.882
1985—Elmira	NYP	SS	59	177	11	36	8	1	1	14	.203	70	130	24	.893
1986—Greensboro†	S. Atl.	SS	26	93	12	28	5	1	4	19	.301	37	65	9	.919
1986—Day.B.‡-Win.Hav.	Fla. St.	SS-2B	20	55	6	12	2	0	0	5	.218	25	30	6	.902
1987—Greensboro	S. Atl.	SS	109	370	43	81	9	0	10	48	.219	155	303	44	.912
1988—New Britain§x	East.	SS	101	347	28	90	14	1	1	26	.259	159	274	25	.945
1989—Reading	East.	SS	64	213	16	50	8	0	3	16	.235	91	171	13	.953
1989—Scranton/W.-B.	Int.	SS	56	151	16	39	7	0	0	16	.258	58	127	11	.944
1990—Scranton/W.-B.y	Int.	SS	●143	477	45	120	23	6	5	42	.252	*206	*396	*36	.944
1990—Atlanta	Nat.	SS-2B	9	7	3	1	0	0	0	0	.143	3	4	0	1.000
Major League Totals—1 Year			9	7	3	1	0	0	0	0	.143	3	4	0	1.000

Signed as free agent by Boston Red Sox' organization, December 5, 1983.
†Switch-hitter
‡Loaned to Daytona Beach (Texas Rangers' organization), July, 1986; returned, July, 1986.
§Traded to Jacksonville (Montreal Expos' organization) for Pitcher John Trautwein, August 31, 1988.
xTraded by Montreal Expos' organization to Philadelphia Phillies' organization for Pitcher Tim Sossamon, March 28, 1989.
yTraded to Atlanta Braves, September 4, 1990, as partial completion of deal in which Atlanta traded Outfielder Dale Murphy and a player to be named later to Philadelphia Phillies for Pitcher Jeff Parrett and two players to be named later, August 3, 1990. Scranton/Wilkes-Barre (Philadelphia Phillies' organization) acquired Pitcher Tommy Greene on August 9, 1990 and Atlanta acquired Outfielder Jim Vatcher on August 9, 1990 to complete deal.

ROBERT RICHARD ROSE
(Bobby)

Born March 15, 1967, at Covina, Calif.
Height, 5.11. Weight, 187.
Throws and bats righthanded.

Led Texas League in slugging percentage with .541 in 1989.
Led Pacific Coast League second basemen in errors with 21 in 1990.

Year Club	League	Pos.	G.	AB.	R.	H.	2B.	3B.	HR.	RBI.	B.A.	PO.	A.	E.	F.A.
1985—Salem	N'west	SS-1B	50	167	15	37	6	2	0	16	.222	58	112	22	.885
1986—Quad Cities	Midw.	SS-2B	129	467	67	118	21	5	7	56	.253	176	297	40	.922
1987—						(Out of Organized Baseball)									
1988—Quad City	Midw.	3B-1B	135	483	75	137	23	3	13	78	.284	127	179	30	.911
1988—Palm Springs	Calif.	DH	1	3	0	1	0	0	0	1	.333	0	0	0	.000
1989—Midland	Texas	3B-2B	99	351	64	126	21	5	11	73	*.359	102	203	17	.947
1989—California	Amer.	3B-2B	14	38	4	8	1	2	1	3	.211	10	21	2	.939

Year Club League	Pos.	G.	AB.	R.	H.	2B.	3B.	HR.	RBI.	B.A.	PO.	A.	E.	F.A.
1990—Edmonton............. P. C.	2B-3B-SS	134	502	84	142	27	10	9	68	.283	225	376	25	.960
1990—California......... Amer.	2B-3B	7	13	5	5	0	0	1	2	.385	3	7	0	1.000
Major League Totals—2 Years...............		21	51	9	13	1	2	2	5	.255	13	28	2	.953

Selected by California Angels' organization in 5th round of free-agent draft, June 3, 1985.

STEVEN ALAN ROSENBERG
(Steve)

Born October 31, 1964, at Brooklyn, N.Y.
Height, 6.00. Weight, 185.
Throws and bats lefthanded.
Attended University of Florida, Gainesville, Fla.

Major League saves: 1988 (1).

Year Club League	G.	IP.	W.	L.	Pct.	H.	R.	ER.	SO.	BB.	ERA.
1986—Oneonta.................... NYP	4	9	0	0	.000	4	1	1	10	2	1.00
1986—Fort Lauderdale .... Florida St.	25	29⅔	6	1	.857	24	7	7	26	18	2.12
1987—Albany............................... Eastern	32	40	4	4	.500	33	11	10	24	12	2.25
1987—Columbus†.................................. Int'national	21	35⅓	4	1	.800	43	17	16	27	18	4.08
1988—Vancouver................................. P. Coast	20	24⅓	2	0	1.000	15	9	9	17	11	3.33
1988—Chicago............................... American	33	46	0	1	.000	53	22	22	28	19	4.30
1989—Chicago............................... American	38	142	4	13	.235	148	92	78	77	58	4.94
1990—Vancouver............................. P. Coast	40	88⅓	6	5	.545	66	43	35	74	44	3.57
1990—Chicago............................... American	6	10	1	0	1.000	10	6	6	4	5	5.40
Major League Totals—3 Years...............	77	198	5	14	.263	211	120	106	109	82	4.82

Selected by New York Yankees' organization in 4th round of free-agent draft, June 2, 1986.
†Traded with Outfielder Dan Pasqua and Catcher Mark Salas to Chicago White Sox for Pitchers Richard Dotson and Scott Nielsen, November 12, 1987.

MARK JOSEPH ROSS

Born August 8, 1957, at Galveston, Tex.
Height, 6.00. Weight, 200.
Throws and bats righthanded.
Received bachelor of business degree in finance from Texas A&M University, College Station, Tex., in 1979.

Major League saves: 1985 (1).
Led Pacific Coast League in games finished in relief with 45 and saves with 20 in 1984.
Led Southern League in games finished in relief with 59, intentional bases on balls issued with 12 and tied for lead in saves with 22 in 1981.

Year Club League	G.	IP.	W.	L.	Pct.	H.	R.	ER.	SO.	BB.	ERA.
1979—Sarasota Astros........................... Gulf Coast	2	7	1	0	1.000	5	3	3	2	1	3.86
1980—Daytona Beach .... Florida St.	30	58	5	3	.625	50	14	11	39	11	1.71
1980—Columbus.................................. Southern	14	27	2	2	.500	30	11	11	13	4	3.67
1981—Columbus.................................. Southern	*64	116	8	10	.444	103	35	29	70	32	*2.25
1982—Tucson..................................... P. Coast	43	83	4	3	.571	106	55	45	35	32	4.88
1982—Houston................................... National	4	6	0	0	.000	3	1	1	4	0	1.50
1983—Columbus†.................................. Southern	13	27⅓	1	1	.500	27	8	8	12	16	2.63
1983—Tucson..................................... P. Coast	6	6⅓	0	2	.000	14	10	7	2	4	9.95
1984—Tucson..................................... P. Coast	57	92	5	6	.455	88	35	30	32	24	2.93
1984—Houston................................... National	2	2⅓	1	0	1.000	1	0	0	1	0	0.00
1985—Tucson..................................... P. Coast	46	77	8	5	.615	109	38	31	31	21	3.62
1985—Houston‡................................... National	8	13	0	2	.000	12	7	7	3	2	4.85
1986—Tucson§................................... P. Coast	48	73⅓	5	5	.500	99	37	34	26	20	4.17
1987—Vancouver............................... P. Coast	32	89⅓	5	6	.455	87	40	30	48	21	3.02
1987—Pittsburgh x............................... National	1	1	0	0	.000	1	1	1	0	0	9.00
1988—Syracuse .... Int'national	17	99⅔	3	8	.273	101	50	40	57	19	3.61
1988—Toronto................................. American	3	7⅓	0	0	.000	5	6	4	4	4	4.91
1989—Syracuse y................................. Int'national	26	95	8	5	.615	102	43	31	58	11	2.94
1990—Buffalo................................. Am. Assoc.	47	71⅓	6	8	.429	73	23	16	36	12	2.02
1990—Pittsburgh................................... National	9	12⅔	1	0	1.000	11	5	5	5	4	3.55
National League Totals—5 Years......................	24	35	2	2	.500	28	14	14	13	6	3.60
American League Totals—1 Year	3	7⅓	0	0	.000	5	6	4	4	4	4.91
Major League Totals—6 Years............................	27	42⅓	2	2	.500	33	20	18	17	10	3.83

Selected by Houston Astros' organization in 7th round of free-agent draft, June 5, 1979.
†On Tucson disabled list, April 11 to June 27, 1983.
‡Traded to St. Louis Cardinals for a player to be named later, December 9, 1985.
§Granted free agency, October 15, 1986; signed by Vancouver (Pittsburgh Pirates' organization), December 4, 1986.
xGranted free agency, October 15, 1987; signed by Syracuse (Toronto Blue Jays' organization), February 22, 1988.
yGranted free agency, October 15, 1989; signed by Buffalo (Pittsburgh Pirates' organization), January 14, 1990.

RICHARD GARNET ROWLAND
(Rich)

Born February 25, 1967, at Cloverdale, Calif.
Height, 6.01. Weight, 210.
Throws and bats righthanded.
Attended Mendocino Community College, Ukiah, Calif.

Year Club League	Pos.	G.	AB.	R.	H.	2B.	3B.	HR.	RBI.	B.A.	PO.	A.	E.	F.A.
1988—Bristol.................... Appal.	C	56	186	29	51	10	1	4	41	.274	253	31	7	.976
1989—Fayetteville.......... S. Atl.	C	108	375	43	102	17	1	9	59	.272	527	66	11	.982
1990—London .... East.	C	47	161	22	46	10	0	8	30	.286	231	24	3	.988
1990—Toledo .... Int.	C	62	192	28	50	12	0	7	22	.260	305	39	*13	.964
1990—Detroit................... Amer.	C	7	19	3	3	1	0	0	0	.158	29	0	1	.967
Major League Totals—1 Year.................		7	19	3	3	1	0	0	0	.158	29	0	1	.967

Selected by Detroit Tigers' organization in 17th round of free-agent draft, June 1, 1988.

STANLEY DEAN ROYER
(Stan)

Born August 31, 1967, at Olney, Ill.
Height, 6.03. Weight, 195.
Throws and bats righthanded.
Attended Eastern Illinois University, Charleston, Ill.

Led Southern League third basemen in assists with 269, total chances with 387 and double plays with 28 in 1990.
Led California League third basemen in total chances with 342 in 1989.
Led Northwest League third basemen in total chances with 231 in 1988.
Named Northwest League Most Valuable Player, 1988.
Received reported $105,000 to sign with Oakland Athletics, 1988.

Year Club League	Pos.	G.	AB.	R.	H.	2B.	3B.	HR.	RBI.	B.A.	PO.	A.	E.	F.A.
1988—Southern Oregon . N'west	3B	73	286	47	91	19	3	6	48	.318	*50	*158	23	*.900
1989—Modesto................. Calif.	3B	127	476	54	120	28	1	11	69	.252	*99	220	23	*.933
1989—Tacoma................. P. C.	3B	6	19	2	5	1	0	0	2	.263	4	9	4	.765
1990—Huntsville†........... South.	*3-O-S	137	527	69	136	29	3	14	89	.258	88	271	*38	.904
1990—Louisville .... A. A.	3B	4	15	1	4	1	1	0	4	.267	0	7	0	1.000

Selected by Atlanta Braves' organization in 10th round of free-agent draft, June 3, 1985.
Selected by Oakland Athletics' organization in 1st round (16th player selected) of free-agent draft, June 1, 1988.
†Traded with Outfielder Felix Jose and Pitcher Daryl Green to St. Louis Cardinals for Outfielder Willie McGee, August 29, 1990.

BRUCE WAYNE RUFFIN

Born October 4, 1963, at Lubbock, Tex.
Height, 6.02. Weight, 213.
Throws left and bats right and lefthanded.
Attended University of Texas, Austin, Tex.

Major League stolen bases: 1988 (3).

Year Club	League	G.	IP.	W.	L.	Pct.	H.	R.	ER.	SO.	BB.	ERA.
1985—Clearwater .... Florida St.		14	97	5	5	.500	87	33	31	74	34	2.88
1986—Reading.. Eastern		16	90⅓	8	4	.667	89	41	33	68	26	3.29
1986—Philadelphia .... National		21	146⅓	9	4	.692	138	53	40	70	44	2.46
1987—Philadelphia .... National		35	204⅔	11	14	.440	236	118	99	93	73	4.35
1988—Philadelphia .... National		55	144⅓	6	10	.375	151	86	71	82	80	4.43
1989—Philadelphia .... National		24	125⅔	6	10	.375	152	69	62	70	62	4.44
1989—Scranton/Wilkes-Barre................Int'national		9	50	5	1	.833	44	28	26	44	39	4.68
1990—Philadelphia .... National		32	149	6	13	.316	178	99	89	79	62	5.38
Major League Totals—5 Years............................		167	770	38	51	.427	855	425	361	394	321	4.22

Selected by Philadelphia Phillies' organization in 31st round of free-agent draft, June 7, 1982.
Selected by Philadelphia Phillies' organization in 2nd round of free-agent draft, June 3, 1985.

SCOTT DREW RUSKIN

Born June 8, 1963, at Jacksonville, Fla.
Height, 6.02. Weight, 185.
Throws left and bats righthanded.
Attended University of Florida, Gainesville, Fla.

Major League saves: 1990 (2).

Year Club	League	G.	IP.	W.	L.	Pct.	H.	R.	ER.	SO.	BB.	ERA.
1989—Salem................ Carolina		14	84⅔	4	5	.444	71	35	21	92	33	2.23
1989—Harrisburg .... Eastern		12	63	2	3	.400	64	38	34	56	32	4.86
1990—Pittsburgh‡-Montreal ....National		67	75⅓	3	2	.600	75	28	23	57	38	2.75
Major League Totals—1 Year............................		67	75⅓	3	2	.600	75	28	23	57	38	2.75

RECORD AS OUTFIELDER

Year Club League	Pos.	G.	AB.	R.	H.	2B.	3B.	HR.	RBI.	B.A.	PO.	A.	E.	F.A.
1986—Bradenton Pir. ..... Gulf C.	DH	11	31	3	11	1	0	0	4	.355	0	0	0	.000
1987—Macon†................... S. Atl.	OF-1B	81	239	37	71	9	2	9	42	.297	183	11	6	.970
1987—Salem..................... Carol.	1B-OF	23	83	16	25	3	1	3	11	.301	154	16	1	.994
1988—Salem..................... Carol.	OF-1B	26	96	16	28	8	2	4	16	.292	83	6	4	.957
1988—Harrisburg .... East.	OF-1B	90	309	27	69	14	3	3	32	.223	233	12	8	.968

Selected by Cincinnati Reds' organization in 14th round of free-agent draft, June 8, 1981.
Selected by Texas Rangers' organization in 4th round of free-agent draft, June 4, 1984.
Selected by Cleveland Indians' organization in 3rd round of free-agent draft, June 3, 1985.
Selected by Montreal Expos' organization in secondary phase of free-agent draft, January 14, 1986.
Selected by Pittsburgh Pirates' organization in secondary phase of free-agent draft, June 2, 1986.
†On disabled list, April 7 to April 28, 1987.

‡Traded with Shortstop Willie Greene and a player to be named later to Montreal Expos for Pitcher Zane Smith, August 8, 1990; Montreal acquired Outfielder Moises Alou to complete deal, August 16, 1990.

JEFFREY LEE RUSSELL
(Jeff)

Born September 2, 1961, at Cincinnati, O.
Height, 6.03. Weight, 205.
Throws and bats righthanded.
Attended Gulf Coast Community College, Panama City, Fla.

Major League saves: 1986 (2), 1987 (3), 1989 (38), 1990 (10). Total—53.
Led American League in saves with 38 and games finished in relief with 66 in 1989.
Named American League Fireman of the Year by THE SPORTING NEWS, 1989.

Year	Club	League	G.	IP.	W.	L.	Pct.	H.	R.	ER.	SO.	BB.	ERA.
1980—Eugene		Northwest	13	90	6	5	.545	80	47	30	75	50	3.00
1981—Tampa		Florida St.	22	143	10	4	.714	109	51	32	92	48	2.01
1982—Waterbury†		Eastern	14	79⅔	6	4	.600	67	27	21	88	23	2.37
1983—Indianapolis		Am. Assoc.	18	119	5	5	.500	106	51	47	98	44	3.55
1983—Cincinnati		National	10	68⅓	4	5	.444	58	30	23	40	22	3.03
1984—Cincinnati		National	33	181⅔	6	★18	.250	186	97	86	101	65	4.26
1985—Denver‡§-Oklahoma City		Am. Assoc.	18	115⅓	7	4	.636	105	55	52	94	51	4.06
1985—Texas		American	13	62	3	6	.333	85	55	52	44	27	7.55
1986—Oklahoma City		Am. Assoc.	11	70⅔	4	1	.800	63	32	31	34	38	3.95
1986—Texas		American	37	82	5	2	.714	74	40	31	54	31	3.40
1987—Port Charlotte x		Florida St.	2	11	0	0	.000	8	3	3	3	5	2.45
1987—Oklahoma City		Am. Assoc.	4	6⅓	0	0	.000	5	1	1	5	1	1.42
1987—Texas		American	52	97⅓	5	4	.556	109	56	48	56	52	4.44
1988—Texas y		American	34	188⅔	10	9	.526	183	86	80	88	66	3.82
1989—Texas		American	71	72⅔	6	4	.600	45	21	16	77	24	1.98
1990—Texas z		American	27	25⅓	1	5	.167	23	15	12	16	16	4.26
1990—Charlotte		Florida St.	1	1	0	1	.000	1	1	1	0	0	......
National League Totals—2 Years			43	250	10	23	.303	244	127	109	141	87	3.92
American League Totals—6 Years			234	528	30	30	.500	519	273	239	335	216	4.07
Major League Totals—8 Years			277	778	40	53	.430	763	400	348	476	303	4.03

Selected by Cincinnati Reds' organization in 5th round of free-agent draft, June 5, 1979.
†On disabled list, May 5 to June 10 and July 28, 1982 through remainder of season.
‡On disabled list, May 22 to June 10, 1985.
§Traded to Texas Rangers' organization, July 23, 1985, completing deal in which Texas traded Third Baseman Buddy Bell to Cincinnati Reds for Outfielder Duane Walker and a player to be named later, July 19, 1985.
xOn Texas disabled list, March 25 to May 15, 1987; included rehabilitation disability assignment to Port Charlotte, April 26 to May 4, and to Oklahoma City, May 5 to May 15, 1987.
yMade an out in only appearance as a pinch-hitter.
zOn disabled list, May 29 to September 10, 1990; included rehabilitation disability assignment to Charlotte, July 30 to August 3, 1990.

ALL-STAR GAME RECORD

Year	League	IP.	W.	L.	Pct.	H.	R.	ER.	SO.	BB.	ERA.
1988—American		1	0	0	.000	1	0	0	0	1	0.00
1989—American		1	0	0	.000	1	1	1	0	1	9.00
All-Star Game Totals—2 Years		2	0	0	.000	2	1	1	0	2	4.50

JOHN WILLIAM RUSSELL

Born January 5, 1961, at Oklahoma City, Okla.
Height, 6.00. Weight, 195.
Throws and bats righthanded.
Attended University of Oklahoma, Norman, Okla.

Major League stolen bases: 1985 (2), 1990 (1). Total—3.
Led National League in passed balls with 17 in 1986.
Tied for Pacific Coast League lead in passed balls with 13 in 1983.

Year	Club	League	Pos.	G.	AB.	R.	H.	2B.	3B.	HR.	RBI.	B.A.	PO.	A.	E.	F.A.
1982—Reading	East.		C-OF-1B	77	263	26	53	10	5	6	30	.202	354	44	12	.971
1983—Portland	P. C.		C-O-3	128	445	71	113	23	3	27	76	.254	551	58	12	.981
1984—Portland	P. C.		OF-1B-C	93	350	75	101	22	5	19	77	.289	182	18	5	.976
1984—Philadelphia	Nat.		OF-C	39	99	11	28	8	1	2	11	.283	51	1	0	1.000
1985—Philadelphia	Nat.		OF-1B	81	216	22	47	12	0	9	23	.218	170	9	4	.978
1985—Portland	P. C.		OF-C-1B	16	49	8	15	2	2	4	11	.306	24	1	1	.962
1986—Philadelphia	Nat.		C	93	315	35	76	21	2	13	60	.241	498	39	13	.976
1987—Philadelphia	Nat.		OF-C	24	62	5	9	1	0	3	8	.145	48	1	1	.980
1987—Maine	Int.		OF-C-3B	44	143	15	29	6	1	7	24	.203	107	14	2	.984
1988—Maine	Int.		C-O-3-1	110	394	50	90	18	0	13	52	.228	363	54	10	.977
1988—Philadelphia†	Nat.		C	22	49	5	12	1	0	2	4	.245	77	9	5	.945
1989—Atlanta‡	Nat.		C-O-1-3-P	74	159	14	29	2	0	2	9	.182	194	28	4	.982
1990—Oklahoma City	A. A.		C	6	22	7	9	4	0	2	6	.409	30	1	1	.969
1990—Texas	Amer.		C-O-1-3	68	128	16	35	4	0	2	8	.273	148	11	3	.981
National League Totals—6 Years				333	900	92	201	45	3	31	115	.223	1040	87	27	.977
American League Totals—1 Year				68	128	16	35	4	0	2	8	.273	148	11	3	.981
Major League Totals—7 Years				401	1028	108	236	49	3	33	123	.230	1188	98	30	.977

Selected by Montreal Expos' organization in 4th round of free-agent draft, June 5, 1979.

Selected by Philadelphia Phillies' organization in 1st round (13th player selected) of free-agent draft, June 7, 1982.
†Sold to Atlanta Braves, March 25, 1989.
‡Released, April 6, 1990; signed by Oklahoma City (Texas Rangers' organization), May 8, 1990.
§Granted free agency, October 22, 1990.

PITCHING RECORD

Year	Club	League	G.	IP.	W.	L.	Pct.	H.	R.	ER.	SO.	BB.	ERA.
1989—Atlanta		National	1	⅓	0	0	.000	0	0	0	0	0	0.00

MARK DWAYNE RYAL

Name pronounced Rile.
Born April 28, 1960, at Henryetta, Okla.
Height, 6.01. Weight, 197.
Throws and bats lefthanded.

Major League stolen bases: 1986 (1).
Led Pacific Coast League in intentional bases on balls received with 10 in 1986.
Led American Association in grounding into double plays with 21 in 1983.
Tied for American Association lead in intentional bases on balls received with 12 in 1982 and 9 in 1990.

Year	Club	League	Pos.	G.	AB.	R.	H.	2B.	3B.	HR.	RBI.	B.A.	PO.	A.	E.	F.A.
1978—Sarasota Royals	Gulf C.		OF	27	83	11	20	0	1	0	10	.241	37	4	0	1.000
1979—Fort Myers	Fla. St.		OF	107	360	27	79	12	1	4	34	.219	199	15	3	.986
1980—Fort Myers	Fla. St.		OF	123	440	60	117	21	3	5	51	.266	174	8	2	.989
1981—Jacksonville	South.		OF	123	457	50	122	15	2	14	69	.267	237	8	11	.957
1981—Omaha	A. A.		OF	6	19	2	4	0	0	0	1	.211	9	1	0	1.000
1982—Omaha	A. A.		★OF-1B	129	473	69	135	27	2	20	77	.285	242	★18	6	.977
1982—Kansas City	Amer.		OF	6	13	0	1	0	0	0	0	.077	9	0	1	.900
1983—Omaha	A. A.		OF-1B	132	454	61	118	28	5	9	57	.260	203	11	8	.964
1984—Omaha†	A. A.		1B-OF	131	435	56	103	18	1	13	64	.237	680	58	16	.979
1985—Buffalo	A. A.		OF	106	392	50	104	21	1	13	66	.265	175	10	2	.989
1985—Chicago‡	Amer.		OF	12	33	4	5	3	0	0	3	.152	21	0	0	1.000
1986—Edmonton	P. C.		1B-OF	127	479	72	163	33	4	14	84	.340	734	50	7	.991
1986—California	Amer.		OF-1B	13	32	6	12	0	0	2	5	.375	32	2	1	.971
1987—California	Amer.		OF-1B	58	100	7	20	6	0	5	18	.200	50	1	3	.944
1987—Edmonton§	P. C.		OF-1B	16	49	10	21	3	2	0	12	.429	44	0	0	1.000
1988—Louisville x	A. A.		OF-1B	94	336	35	86	25	1	11	62	.256	153	16	1	.994
1989—Philadelphia	Nat.		1B-OF	29	33	2	8	2	0	0	5	.242	17	0	0	1.000
1989—Scranton/W.-B.y	Int.		OF-1B	59	210	16	59	14	0	2	21	.281	117	4	0	1.000
1990—Buffalo	A. A.		1B-OF	109	371	49	124	★34	2	9	49	★.334	385	38	4	.991
1990—Pittsburgh	Nat.		OF	9	12	0	1	0	0	0	0	.083	4	0	0	1.000
American League Totals—4 Years				89	178	17	38	9	0	7	26	.213	112	3	5	.958
National League Totals—2 Years				38	45	2	9	2	0	0	5	.200	21	0	0	1.000
Major League Totals—6 Years				127	223	19	47	11	0	7	31	.211	133	3	5	.965

Selected by Kansas City Royals' organization in 3rd round of free-agent draft, June 6, 1978.
†Released, September 4, 1984; signed by Chicago White Sox' organization, December 28, 1984.
‡Granted free agency, October 15, 1985; signed by California Angels, January 21, 1986.
§Released, March 29, 1988. signed by Louisville (St. Louis Cardinals' organization), April 30, 1988.
xGranted free agency, October 15, 1988; signed by Scranton/Wilkes-Barre (Philadelphia Phillies' organization), November 11, 1988.
yGranted free agency, October 15, 1989; signed by Buffalo (Pittsburgh Pirates' organization), January 15, 1990.

LYNN NOLAN RYAN JR.

(Known by middle name.)

Born January 31, 1947, at Refugio, Tex.
Height, 6.02. Weight, 210.
Throws and bats righthanded.
Attended Alvin Junior College, Alvin, Tex.

Holds major league records for most strikeouts, lifetime (5,308); most years, 100 or more strikeouts, (22); most games, 15 or more strikeouts, lifetime (25); most games, 10 or more strikeouts, lifetime (207); most years, 300 or more strikeouts (6); most years, 200 or more strikeouts (14); most games, 10 or more strikeouts, season (23), 1973; most strikeouts, three consecutive games (including extra innings—27⅓) (47), August 12, 16 and 20, 1974; most strikeouts by losing pitcher, extra-inning game (19), August 20, 1974 (11 innings); most seasons leading league, bases on balls allowed (8); most bases on balls, lifetime (2,614); most no-hit games, lifetime (6); most low-hit (one or zero) games, lifetime (18); most wild pitches, lifetime (257).

Holds modern major league records for most consecutive seasons, 300 or more strikeouts (3); most strikeouts, season (383), 1973.

Shares major league records for striking out side on nine pitches, April 19, 1968, third inning and July 9, 1972, second inning; most consecutive seasons, 100 or more strikeouts (21), 1970 through 1990; most no-hit games, season (2), 1973; most clubs shut out, season (8), 1972; most consecutive seasons leading major leagues, bases on balls allowed (3); most strikeouts, three consecutive nine-inning games (41), August 7, 12 and 16, 1974.

Holds American League record for most years, 200 or more strikeouts (9); most games, 10 or more strikeouts, lifetime (140); most games, 15 or more strikeouts, lifetime (22); most no-hit games, lifetime (5).

Shares American League records for most consecutive strikeouts, game (8), July 9, 1972 and July 15, 1973; most strikeouts, two consecutive games (32), August 7 (13), 12 (19), 1974; most low-hit (one or zero) games, lifetime (14) and season (3), 1973; most seasons leading league, errors by pitcher (4).

Pitched 5-0 no-hit victory against Oakland Athletics, June 11, 1990.
Pitched 5-0 no-hit victory against Los Angeles Dodgers, September 26, 1981.
Pitched 1-0 no-hit victory against Baltimore Orioles, June 1, 1975.

Pitched 4-0 no-hit victory against Minnesota Twins, September 28, 1974.
Pitched 6-0 no-hit victory against Detroit Tigers, July 15, 1973.
Pitched 3-0 no-hit victory against Kansas City Royals, May 15, 1973.
Major League saves: 1969 (1), 1970 (1), 1973 (1). Total—3.
Led National League in hit batsmen with 8 in 1982.
Led National League in wild pitches with 16 in 1981 and 15 in 1986.
Led American League in shutouts with 9 in 1972, 7 in 1976, and tied for lead with 5 in 1979.
Led American League in wild pitches with 18 in 1972, 21 in 1977, 13 in 1978 and 19 in 1989.
Tied for American League lead in complete games with 22 in 1977.
Tied for National League lead in sacrifice hits by hitters with 14 in 1985.
Led Western Carolinas League pitchers in games started with 28 in 1966.
Tied for Appalachian League lead in hit batsmen with 8 in 1965.
Named Man of the Year by THE SPORTING NEWS, 1990.
Named American League Pitcher of the Year by THE SPORTING NEWS, 1977.
Named righthanded pitcher on THE SPORTING NEWS American League All-Star Team, 1977.
Named Western Carolinas Pitcher of the Year, 1966.

Year	Club	League	G.	IP.	W.	L.	Pct.	H.	R.	ER.	SO.	BB.	ERA.
1965—Marion	Ap'lachian	13	78	3	6	.333	61	47	38	115	56	4.38
1966—Greenville	W. Carol.	29	183	*17	2	.895	109	59	51	*272	*127	2.51
1966—Williamsport	Eastern	3	19	0	2	.000	9	6	2	35	12	0.95
1966—New York	National	2	3	0	1	.000	5	5	5	6	3	15.00
1967—Winter Haven†	Florida St.	1	4	0	0	.000	1	1	1	5	2	2.25
1967—Jacksonville‡	Int'national	3	7	1	0	1.000	3	1	0	18	3	0.00
1968—New York§	National	21	134	6	9	.400	93	50	46	133	75	3.09
1969—New York	National	25	89	6	3	.667	60	38	35	92	53	3.54
1970—New York	National	27	132	7	11	.389	86	59	50	125	97	3.41
1971—New York x	National	30	152	10	14	.417	125	78	67	137	116	3.97
1972—California	American	39	284	19	16	.543	166	80	72	*329	*157	2.28
1973—California	American	41	326	21	16	.568	238	113	104	*383	*162	2.87
1974—California	American	42	*333	22	16	.579	221	127	107	*367	*202	2.89
1975—California	American	28	198	14	12	.538	152	90	76	186	132	3.45
1976—California	American	39	284	17	*18	.486	193	117	106	*327	*183	3.36
1977—California	American	37	299	19	16	.543	198	110	92	*341	*204	2.77
1978—California y	American	31	235	10	13	.435	183	106	97	*260	*148	3.71
1979—California z	American	34	223	16	14	.533	169	104	89	*223	114	3.59
1980—Houston	National	35	234	11	10	.524	205	100	87	200	*98	3.35
1981—Houston	National	21	149	11	5	.688	99	34	28	140	68	*1.69
1982—Houston	National	35	250⅓	16	12	.571	196	100	88	245	*109	3.16
1983—Houston a	National	29	196⅓	14	9	.609	134	74	65	183	101	2.98
1984—Houston b	National	30	183⅔	12	11	.522	143	78	62	197	69	3.04
1985—Houston	National	35	232	10	12	.455	205	108	98	209	95	3.80
1986—Houston c	National	30	178	12	8	.600	119	72	66	194	82	3.34
1987—Houston	National	34	211⅔	8	16	.333	154	75	65	*270	87	*2.76
1988—Houston d	National	33	220	12	11	.522	186	98	86	*228	87	3.52
1989—Texas	American	32	239⅓	16	10	.615	162	96	85	*301	98	3.20
1990—Texas e	American	30	204	13	9	.591	137	86	78	*232	74	3.44
National League Totals—14 Years		387	2365	135	132	.506	1810	969	848	2359	1140	3.23
American League Totals—10 Years		353	2625⅓	167	140	.544	1819	1029	906	2949	1474	3.11
Major League Totals—24 Years		740	4990⅓	302	272	.526	3629	1998	1754	5308	2614	3.16

Selected by New York Mets' organization in 8th round of free-agent draft, June, 1965.
†On military list, January 3 to May 13, 1967.
‡On disabled list, July 16 to August 30, 1967.
§On disabled list, July 30 to August 30, 1968.
xTraded with Pitcher Don Rose, Outfielder Leroy Stanton and Catcher Francisco Estrada to California Angels for Infielder Jim Fregosi, December 10, 1971.
yOn disabled list, June 14 to July 5, 1978.
zGranted free agency, November 1, 1979; signed by Houston Astros, November 19, 1979.
aOn disabled list, March 25 to April 17 and May 3 to June 6, 1983.
bOn disabled list, June 2 to June 17 and June 18 to July 3, 1984.
cOn disabled list, June 1 to June 24 and July 28 to August 12, 1986.
dGranted free agency, November 4, 1988; signed by Texas Rangers, December 7, 1988.
eOn disabled list, May 18 to June 6, 1990.

DIVISION SERIES RECORD

Year	Club	League	G.	IP.	W.	L.	Pct.	H.	R.	ER.	SO.	BB.	ERA.
1981—Houston	National	2	15	1	1	.500	6	4	3	14	3	1.80

CHAMPIONSHIP SERIES RECORD

Shares Championship Series records for most strikeouts, total series (46); most consecutive strikeouts, game (4), October 3, 1979.

Year	Club	League	G.	IP.	W.	L.	Pct.	H.	R.	ER.	SO.	BB.	ERA.
1969—New York	National	1	7	1	0	1.000	3	2	2	7	2	2.57
1979—California	American	1	7	0	0	.000	4	3	1	8	3	1.29
1980—Houston	National	2	13⅓	0	0	.000	16	8	8	14	3	5.40
1986—Houston	National	2	14	0	1	.000	9	6	6	17	1	3.86
Championship Series Totals—4 Years		6	41⅓	1	1	.500	32	19	17	46	9	3.70

WORLD SERIES RECORD

Year	Club	League	G.	IP.	W.	L.	Pct.	H.	R.	ER.	SO.	BB.	ERA.
1969—New York	National	1	2⅓	0	0	.000	1	0	0	3	2	0.00

Year League	IP.	W.	L.	Pct.	H.	R.	ER.	SO.	BB.	ERA.
1973—American	2	0	0	.000	2	2	2	2	2	9.00
1979—American	2	0	0	.000	5	3	3	2	1	13.50
1981—National	1	0	0	.000	0	0	0	1	0	0.00
1985—National	3	0	0	.000	2	0	0	2	2	0.00
1989—American	2	1	0	1.000	1	0	0	3	0	0.00
All-Star Game Totals—5 Years	10	1	0	1.000	10	5	5	10	5	4.50

Member of American League All-Star Team for the 1972 and 1975 games; did not play.
Named to American League All-Star Team to replace Frank Tanana for 1977 game; declined.

BRET WILLIAM SABERHAGEN

Born April 11, 1964, at Chicago Heights, Ill.
Height, 6.01. Weight, 195.
Throws and bats righthanded.

Major League saves: 1984 (1).
Led American League in complete games with 12 in 1989.
Named American League Pitcher of the Year by THE SPORTING NEWS, 1985 and 1989.
Won American League Cy Young Memorial Award, 1985 and 1989.
Named righthanded pitcher on THE SPORTING NEWS American League All-Star Team, 1985 and 1989.
Named pitcher on THE SPORTING NEWS American League All-Star fielding team, 1989.
Named American League Comeback Player of the Year by THE SPORTING NEWS, 1987.

Year Club	League	G.	IP.	W.	L.	Pct.	H.	R.	ER.	SO.	BB.	ERA.
1983—Fort Myers	Florida St.	16	109⅔	10	5	.667	98	34	28	82	19	2.30
1983—Jacksonville	Southern	11	77⅓	6	2	.750	66	31	25	48	29	2.91
1984—Kansas City†	American	38	157⅔	10	11	.476	138	71	61	73	36	3.48
1985—Kansas City	American	32	235⅓	20	6	.769	211	79	75	158	38	2.87
1986—Kansas City‡	American	30	156	7	12	.368	165	77	72	112	29	4.15
1987—Kansas City	American	33	257	18	10	.643	246	99	96	163	53	3.36
1988—Kansas City	American	35	260⅔	14	16	.467	*271	122	110	171	59	3.80
1989—Kansas City§	American	36	*262⅓	*23	6	*.793	209	74	63	193	43	*2.16
1990—Kansas City x	American	20	135	5	9	.357	146	52	49	87	28	3.27
Major League Totals—7 Years		224	1464	97	70	.581	1386	574	526	957	286	3.23

Selected by Kansas City Royals' organization in 19th round of free-agent draft, June 7, 1982.
†Appeared in one game as a pinch-runner.
‡On disabled list, August 10 to September 1, 1986.
§Appeared in three games as a pinch-runner.
xOn disabled list, July 16 to September 10, 1990.

Year Club	League	G.	IP.	W.	L.	Pct.	H.	R.	ER.	SO.	BB.	ERA.
1984—Kansas City	American	1	8	0	0	.000	6	3	2	5	1	2.25
1985—Kansas City	American	2	7⅓	0	0	.000	12	5	5	6	2	6.14
Championship Series Totals—2 Years		3	15⅓	0	0	.000	18	8	7	11	3	4.11

Year Club	League	G.	IP.	W.	L.	Pct.	H.	R.	ER.	SO.	BB.	ERA.
1985—Kansas City	American	2	18	2	0	1.000	11	1	1	10	1	0.50

Year League	IP.	W.	L.	Pct.	H.	R.	ER.	SO.	BB.	ERA.
1987—American	3	0	0	.000	1	0	0	0	0	0.00
1990—American	2	1	0	1.000	0	0	0	1	0	0.00
All-Star Game Totals—2 Years	5	1	0	1.000	1	0	0	1	0	0.00

CHRISTOPHER ANDREW SABO
(Chris)

Born January 19, 1962, at Detroit, Mich.
Height, 6.00. Weight, 185.
Throws and bats righthanded.
Attended University of Michigan, Ann Arbor, Mich.

Shares major league record for most assists, third baseman, nine-inning game (11), April 7, 1988.
Major League stolen bases: 1988 (46), 1989 (14), 1990 (25). Total—85.
Led National League third basemen in double plays with 31 in 1988.
Led Eastern League third basemen in assists with 236 in 1985.
Led Eastern League third basemen in fielding percentage with .943 in 1984.
Named National League Rookie of the Year by Baseball Writers' Association of America, 1988.
Named third baseman on THE SPORTING NEWS College Baseball All-America Team, 1983.

Year Club	League	Pos.	G.	AB.	R.	H.	2B.	3B.	HR.	RBI.	B.A.	PO.	A.	E.	F.A.
1983—Cedar Rapids	Midw.	3B	77	274	43	75	11	6	12	37	.274	43	130	9	.951
1984—Vermont	East.	3B-2B	125	441	44	94	19	1	5	38	.213	80	210	21	.932
1985—Vermont	East.	3B-SS	124	428	66	119	19	0	11	46	.278	97	236	18	.949
1986—Denver	A. A.	3B	129	432	83	118	26	2	10	60	.273	83	202	9	*.969
1987—Nashville	A. A.	3B	91	315	56	92	19	3	7	51	.292	43	137	12	.938
1988—Cincinnati	Nat.	*3B-SS	137	538	74	146	40	2	11	44	.271	75	318	14	*.966
1989—Cincinnati†	Nat.	3B	82	304	40	79	21	1	6	29	.260	36	145	11	.943

Year Club League	Pos.	G.	AB.	R.	H.	2B.	3B.	HR.	RBI.	B.A.	PO.	A.	E.	F.A.
1989—Nashville................ A. A.	3B	7	30	0	5	2	0	0	3	.167	7	5	1	.923
1990—Cincinnati .... Nat.	3B	148	567	95	153	38	2	25	71	.270	70	273	12	*.966
Major League Totals—3 Years.................		367	1409	209	378	99	5	42	144	.268	181	736	37	.961

Selected by Montreal Expos' organization in 30th round of free-agent draft, June 3, 1980.
Selected by Cincinnati Reds' organization in 2nd round of free-agent draft, June 6, 1983.
†On disabled list, June 27 to September 1, 1989; included rehabilitation disability assignment to Nashville, August 7 to August 11, 1989.

CHAMPIONSHIP SERIES RECORD

Year Club League	Pos.	G.	AB.	R.	H.	2B.	3B.	HR.	RBI.	B.A.	PO.	A.	E.	F.A.
1990—Cincinnati .... Nat.	3B	6	22	1	5	0	0	1	3	.227	7	7	0	1.000

WORLD SERIES RECORD

Shares record for most home runs, two consecutive innings (2), October 19, 1990, second and third innings.

Year Club League	Pos.	G.	AB.	R.	H.	2B.	3B.	HR.	RBI.	B.A.	PO.	A.	E.	F.A.
1990—Cincinnati .... Nat.	3B	4	16	2	9	1	0	2	5	.563	3	14	0	1.000

ALL-STAR GAME RECORD

Year League	Pos.	AB.	R.	H.	2B.	3B.	HR.	RBI.	B.A.	PO.	A.	E.	F.A.
1988—National	PR	0	0	0	0	0	0	0	.000	0	0	0	.000
1990—National	3B	2	0	0	0	0	0	0	.000	0	2	0	1.000
All-Star Game Totals—2 Years....................		2	0	0	0	0	0	0	.000	0	2	0	1.000

MARK BRUCE SALAS

Name pronounced SAL-us.
Born March 8, 1961, at Montebello, Calif.
Height, 6.00. Weight, 205.
Throws right and bats lefthanded.

Major League stolen bases: 1986 (3).
Tied for Florida State League lead in sacrifice flies with 10 in 1981.
Tied for Appalachian League lead in passed balls with 10 in 1979.

Year Club League	Pos.	G.	AB.	R.	H.	2B.	3B.	HR.	RBI.	B.A.	PO.	A.	E.	F.A.
1979—Johnson City .... Appal.	C	53	144	23	35	4	2	5	23	.243	194	19	6	.973
1980—Gastonia................ S. Atl.	C	98	267	42	67	8	3	9	46	.251	452	41	5	*.990
1981—St. Petersburg...... Fla St.	•C-1B	100	321	26	78	9	2	2	52	.243	387	66	•13	.972
1982—Arkansas................ Texas	C	27	76	4	17	4	0	0	5	.224	88	15	1	.990
1982—Louisville† .... A. A.	C	7	22	1	4	0	0	0	1	.182	16	3	1	.950
1982—Nashville................ South.	C	43	137	19	35	7	0	6	20	.255	267	24	7	.977
1983—Arkansas................ Texas	C-OF	131	473	76	144	25	4	20	82	.304	334	41	4	.989
1984—Louisville .... A. A.	C-OF	95	316	28	77	20	2	12	48	.244	260	28	7	.976
1984—St. Louis‡.............. Nat.	C-OF	14	20	1	2	1	0	0	1	.100	13	2	0	1.000
1985—Minnesota.............. Amer.	C	120	360	51	108	20	5	9	41	.300	529	39	5	.991
1986—Minnesota§........... Amer.	C	91	258	28	60	7	4	8	33	.233	358	32	8	.980
1987—Minn. x-N. Y. ..... Amer.	C-OF	72	160	21	40	6	0	6	21	.250	258	16	1	.996
1987—Columbus y............ Int.	C	12	43	5	10	1	0	2	4	.233	46	5	0	1.000
1988—Chicago z............. Amer.	C	75	196	17	49	7	0	3	9	.250	251	35	6	.979
1989—Colorado Springs. P. C.	C-1B-OF	46	146	27	46	10	2	6	20	.315	86	5	1	.989
1989—Cleveland a .... Amer.	C	30	77	4	17	4	1	2	7	.221	3	1	0	1.000
1990—Detroit................... Amer.	C-3B	74	164	18	38	3	0	9	24	.232	227	23	3	.988
National League Totals—1 Year.............		14	20	1	2	1	0	0	1	.100	13	2	0	1.000
American League Totals—6 Years		462	1215	139	312	47	10	37	135	.257	1626	146	23	.987
Major League Totals—7 Years.................		476	1235	140	314	48	10	37	136	.254	1639	148	23	.987

Selected by St. Louis Cardinals' organization in 18th round of free-agent draft, June 5, 1979.
†Loaned to Nashville (New York Yankees' organization), June 30, 1982; returned, September 13, 1982.
‡Drafted by Minnesota Twins, December 3, 1984.
§On disabled list, May 24 to June 17, 1986.
xTraded to New York Yankees for Pitcher Joe Niekro and cash, June 7, 1987.
yTraded with Outfielder Dan Pasqua and Pitcher Steve Rosenberg to Chicago White Sox for Pitchers Richard Dotson and Scott Nielsen, November 12, 1987.
zReleased, March 28, 1989; signed by Cleveland Indians, April 1, 1989.
aReleased, December 1, 1989; signed by Detroit Tigers, April 8, 1990.

LUIS ERNESTO GARCIA SALAZAR

Born May 19, 1956, at Barcelona, Venezuela.
Height, 5.09. Weight, 180.
Throws and bats righthanded.

Major League stolen bases: 1980 (11), 1981 (11), 1982 (32), 1983 (24), 1984 (11), 1985 (14), 1987 (3), 1988 (6), 1989 (1), 1990 (3). Total—116.
Led National League third basemen in errors with 26 and tied for lead in double plays with 28 in 1982.
Led Eastern League outfielders in putouts with 312 and tied for lead in double plays with 3 in 1979.

Year Club League	Pos.	G.	AB.	R.	H.	2B.	3B.	HR.	RBI.	B.A.	PO.	A.	E.	F.A.
1974—Sarasota Royals†. Gulf C.	SS	2	4	0	1	0	0	0	1	.250	0	2	0	1.000
1976—Niagara Falls .... NYP	SS-OF	42	151	18	36	3	4	1	17	.238	71	49	17	.876
1977—Salem.................... Carol.	SS-3B-2B	116	433	72	117	17	5	11	48	.270	157	294	45	.909
1978—Salem.................... Carol.	OF-3B-SS	126	472	55	138	20	4	3	49	.292	160	77	19	.926

Year	Club	League	Pos.	G.	AB.	R.	H.	2B.	3B.	HR.	RBI.	B.A.	PO.	A.	E.	F.A.
1979—Buffalo	East.		OF-3B	*139	*561	*108	*181	17	5	27	86	.323	321	42	13	.965
1980—Port.‡-Hawaii	P. C.		OF	127	497	91	157	23	15	9	64	.316	304	11	8	.975
1980—San Diego	Nat.		3B-OF	44	169	28	57	4	7	1	25	.337	39	88	7	.948
1981—San Diego	Nat.		3B-OF	109	400	37	121	19	6	3	38	.303	108	191	14	.955
1982—San Diego	Nat.		3B-SS-OF	145	524	55	127	15	5	8	62	.242	133	326	29	.941
1983—San Diego	Nat.		3B-SS	134	481	52	124	16	2	14	45	.258	122	274	21	.950
1984—San Diego§x	Nat.		3B-OF-SS	93	228	20	55	7	2	3	17	.241	87	97	6	.968
1985—Chicago	Amer.		OF-3B-1B	122	327	39	80	18	2	10	45	.245	180	57	10	.960
1986—Appleton y	Midw.		3B	21	79	9	16	1	0	2	4	.203	9	39	5	.906
1986—Chicago z	Amer.		DH-PH	4	7	1	1	0	0	0	0	.143	0	0	0	.000
1987—Las Vegas	P. C.		OF	4	17	2	5	2	0	1	3	.294	5	0	0	1.000
1987—San Diego a	Nat.		3-S-O-P-1	84	189	13	48	5	0	3	17	.254	56	95	9	.944
1988—Detroit b	Amer.		O-S-3-2-1	130	452	61	122	14	1	12	62	.270	199	151	10	.972
1989—S.D.c-Chi.	Nat.		3-O-S-1	121	326	34	92	12	2	9	34	.282	79	154	10	.959
1990—Chicago	Nat.		3B-OF	115	410	44	104	13	3	12	47	.254	96	137	12	.951
National League Totals—8 Years				845	2727	283	728	91	27	53	285	.267	720	1362	108	.951
American League Totals—3 Years				256	786	101	203	32	3	22	107	.258	379	208	20	.967
Major League Totals—11 Years				1101	3513	384	931	123	30	75	392	.265	1099	1570	128	.954

Signed as free agent by Kansas City Royals' organization, November 29, 1973.

†Released, July 8, 1974; signed by Pittsburgh Pirates' organization, November 23, 1975.

‡Traded with Outfielder Rick Lancellotti to San Diego Padres' organization for Infielder Kurt Bevacqua and a player to be named later, August 4, 1980; Pittsburgh Pirates' organization acquired Pitcher Mark Lee to complete deal, August 12, 1980.

§On disabled list, May 15 to June 11, 1984.

xTraded with Pitchers Tim Lollar and Bill Long and Shortstop Ozzie Guillen to Chicago White Sox for Pitchers LaMarr Hoyt, Kevin Kristan and Todd Simmons, December 6, 1984.

yOn Chicago disabled list, April 4 to August 8, August 16 to September 1 and September 8, 1986 through remainder of season; included rehabilitation disability assignment to Appleton, July 17 to August 6, 1986.

zReleased, December 19, 1986; signed by San Diego Padres' organization, April 2, 1987.

aGranted free agency, October 20, 1987; signed by Toledo (Detroit Tigers' organization), February 20, 1988.

bTraded to San Diego Padres for Shortstop Mike Brumley, March 23, 1989.

cTraded with Outfielder Marvell Wynne to Chicago Cubs for Pitcher Calvin Schiraldi, Outfielder Darrin Jackson and a player to be named later, August 30, 1989; San Diego Padres acquired First Baseman Phil Stephenson to complete deal, September 5, 1989.

CHAMPIONSHIP SERIES RECORD

Year	Club	League	Pos.	G.	AB.	R.	H.	2B.	3B.	HR.	RBI.	B.A.	PO.	A.	E.	F.A.
1984—San Diego	Nat.		3B-PH-OF	3	5	0	1	0	1	0	0	.200	1	3	0	1.000
1989—Chicago	Nat.		3B	5	19	2	7	0	1	1	2	.368	4	5	1	.900
Championship Series Totals—2 Years				8	24	2	8	0	2	1	2	.333	5	8	1	.929

WORLD SERIES RECORD

Year	Club	League	Pos.	G.	AB.	R.	H.	2B.	3B.	HR.	RBI.	B.A.	PO.	A.	E.	F.A.
1984—San Diego†	Nat.		3B-OF	4	3	0	1	0	0	0	0	.333	1	0	0	1.000

†Also appeared as a pinch-runner and pinch-hitter.

PITCHING RECORD

Year	Club	League	G.	IP.	W.	L.	Pct.	H.	R.	ER.	SO.	BB.	ERA.
1987—San Diego	National		2	2	0	0	.000	2	1	1	0	1	4.50

WILLIAM ALBERT SAMPEN
(Bill)

Born January 18, 1963, at Lincoln, Ill.
Height, 6.01. Weight, 185.
Throws and bats righthanded.
Attended McMurray College, Jacksonville, Ill.

Major League saves: 1990 (2).

Tied for Eastern League lead in games started by pitchers with 26 in 1989.

Year	Club	League	G.	IP.	W.	L.	Pct.	H.	R.	ER.	SO.	BB.	ERA.
1985—Watertown	NYP		5	10	0	0	.000	9	3	2	11	7	1.80
1986—Watertown	NYP		9	29⅔	0	3	.000	27	18	14	29	13	4.25
1987—Salem	Carolina		26	152⅓	9	8	.529	126	77	65	137	72	3.84
1988—Harrisburg†	Eastern		13	82⅔	6	3	.667	72	38	34	65	27	3.70
1988—Salem	Carolina		8	51⅓	3	3	.500	47	22	19	59	14	3.33
1989—Harrisburg‡	Eastern		26	165⅔	11	9	.550	148	75	59	134	40	3.21
1990—Montreal	National		59	90⅓	12	7	.632	94	34	30	69	33	2.99
Major League Totals—1 Year			59	90⅓	12	7	.632	94	34	30	69	33	2.99

Selected by Pittsburgh Pirates' organization in 12th round of free-agent draft, June 3, 1985.

†On disabled list, April 6 to May 5, 1988.

‡Drafted by Montreal Expos, December 4, 1989.

—DID YOU KNOW—

That 1990 N.L. Rookie of the Year Dave Justice belted 23 of his 28 home runs after the All-Star break, tying Detroit's Cecil Fielder for the second-half high?

JUAN MILTON SAMUEL

Name pronounced SAHM-well.

Born December 9, 1960, at San Pedro de Macoris, D.R.
Height, 5.11. Weight, 170.
Throws and bats righthanded.

Holds major league records for most at-bats by righthander, season (701), 1984; fewest sacrifice hits, most at-bats, season (0 and 701), 1984.

Shares major league records for most consecutive seasons leading league in strikeouts (4), 1984 through 1987; most assists by second baseman, nine-inning game (12), April 20, 1985.

Holds National League record for most at-bats, season (701), 1984.

Major League stolen bases: 1983 (3), 1984 (72), 1985 (53), 1986 (42), 1987 (35), 1988 (33), 1989 (42), 1990 (38). Total—318.

Led National League batters in strikeouts with 168 in 1984, 142 in 1986, 162 in 1987 and tied for lead with 141 in 1985.

Led National League second basemen in putouts with 343 and double plays with 92 in 1988.

Led National League second basemen in total chances with 826 in 1987.

Led Carolina League in total bases with 283 and tied for lead in being hit by pitch with 15 in 1982.

Led Northwest League batters in strikeouts with 87 and caught stealing with 10 in 1980.

Led Carolina League second basemen in double plays with 82 and total chances with 721 in 1982.

Led South Atlantic League second basemen in double plays with 82 and total chances with 737 in 1981.

Named second baseman on THE SPORTING NEWS National League All-Star Team, 1987.

Named second baseman on THE SPORTING NEWS National League Silver Slugger team, 1987.

Named National League Rookie Player of the Year by THE SPORTING NEWS, 1984.

Named Carolina League Most Valuable Player, 1982.

Year	Club	League	Pos.	G.	AB.	R.	H.	2B.	3B.	HR.	RBI.	B.A.	PO.	A.	E.	F.A.
1980—Central Oregon	N'west		2B	69	*298	66	84	11	2	17	44	.282	162	188	*30	.921
1981—Spartanburg.........	S. Atl.		2B	135	512	88	127	22	8	11	74	.248	*280	*409	*50	.932
1982—Peninsula..............	Carol.		2B	135	494	*111	158	29	6	28	94	.320	*244	*442	*35	.951
1983—Reading................	East.		2B	47	184	36	43	10	0	11	39	.234	121	127	14	.947
1983—Portland...............	P. C.		2B	65	261	59	86	14	8	15	52	.330	110	168	15	.949
1983—Philadelphia	Nat.		2B	18	65	14	18	1	2	2	5	.277	44	54	9	.916
1984—Philadelphia	Nat.		2B	160	*701	105	191	36	●19	15	69	.272	388	438	*33	.962
1985—Philadelphia	Nat.		2B	161	*663	101	175	31	13	19	74	.264	*389	463	15	.983
1986—Philadelphia†	Nat.		2B	145	591	90	157	36	12	16	78	.266	290	440	*25	.967
1987—Philadelphia	Nat.		2B	160	*655	113	178	37	*15	28	100	.272	*374	434	*18	.978
1988—Philadelphia	Nat.		2B-OF-3B	157	629	68	153	32	9	12	67	.243	351	387	16	.979
1989—Phi.‡§-N.Y.x	Nat.		OF	137	532	69	125	16	2	11	48	.235	339	6	4	.989
1990—Los Angeles y	Nat.		2B-OF	143	492	62	119	24	3	13	52	.242	273	262	16	.971
Major League Totals—8 Years................				1081	4328	622	1116	213	75	116	493	.258	2448	2484	136	.973

Signed as free agent by Philadelphia Phillies' organization, April 29, 1980.

†On disabled list, April 13 to May 2, 1986.

‡On disabled list, April 1 to April 19, 1989.

§Traded to New York Mets for Outfielder Lenny Dykstra, Pitcher Roger McDowell and a player to be named later, June 18, 1989; Philadelphia Phillies' organization acquired Pitcher Tom Edens to complete deal, July 27, 1989.

xTraded to Los Angeles Dodgers for Pitcher Alejandro Pena and Outfielder Mike Marshall, December 20, 1989.

yGranted free agency, November 5, 1990; re-signed by Dodgers, December 16, 1990.

CHAMPIONSHIP SERIES RECORD

Year	Club	League	Pos.	G.	AB.	R.	H.	2B.	3B.	HR.	RBI.	B.A.	PO.	A.	E.	F.A.
1983—Philadelphia	Nat.		PR	1	0	0	0	0	0	0	0	.000	0	0	0	.000

WORLD SERIES RECORD

Year	Club	League	Pos.	G.	AB.	R.	H.	2B.	3B.	HR.	RBI.	B.A.	PO.	A.	E.	F.A.
1983—Philadelphia	Nat.		PR-PH	3	1	0	0	0	0	0	0	.000	0	0	0	.000

ALL-STAR GAME RECORD

Established All-Star Game record for most putouts by second baseman, game (7), July 14, 1987.

Tied All-Star Game record for most chances accepted by second baseman, game (9), July 14, 1987.

Year	League	Pos.	AB.	R.	H.	2B.	3B.	HR.	RBI.	B.A.	PO.	A.	E.	F.A.
1987—National...		2B	4	0	0	0	0	0	0	.000	7	2	0	1.000

Member of National League All-Star Team in 1984; did not play.

ISRAEL SANCHEZ JR.

Born August 20, 1963, at Falcon, Cuba.
Height, 5.09. Weight, 170.
Throws and bats lefthanded.

Major League saves: 1988 (1).

Year	Club	League	G.	IP.	W.	L.	Pct.	H.	R.	ER.	SO.	BB.	ERA.
1982—Sarasota Royals...........................	Gulf Coast	12	61	3	5	.375	63	41	31	49	36	4.57
1983—Charleston...................................	S. Atlantic	30	163	10	6	.625	172	92	65	130	70	3.59
1984—Fort Myers†...............................	Florida St.	14	66⅔	3	3	.500	62	30	27	63	29	3.65
1985—Fort Myers‡..............................	Florida St.	28	98⅓	8	6	.571	72	32	23	86	27	2.11
1986—Memphis....................................	Southern	28	184⅓	13	7	.650	190	97	71	141	55	3.47
1986—Omaha..	Am. Assoc.	1	3	0	1	.000	4	3	3	2	2	9.00
1987—Omaha..	Am. Assoc.	23	124⅔	5	12	.294	162	74	64	74	46	4.62
1988—Omaha..	Am. Assoc.	15	102	7	4	.636	102	36	33	85	36	2.91
1988—Kansas City................................	American	19	35⅔	3	2	.600	36	20	18	14	18	4.54
1989—Baseball City§x	Florida St.	3	8	1	0	1.000	7	3	0	4	2	0.00

Year Club	League	G.	IP.	W.	L.	Pct.	H.	R.	ER.	SO.	BB.	ERA.
1990—Baseball City	Florida St.	7	16⅔	1	1	.500	18	8	2	17	1	1.08
1990—Memphis	Southern	15	29	1	2	.333	21	11	10	32	8	3.10
1990—Kansas City y	American	11	9⅔	0	0	.000	16	9	9	5	3	8.38
Major League Totals—2 Years		30	45⅓	3	2	.600	52	29	27	19	21	5.36

Selected by Kansas City Royals' organization in 9th round of free-agent draft, June 7, 1982.

†On disabled list, May 26 to June 18 and June 29 to August 22, 1984.

‡On disabled list, April 12 to May 1, 1985.

§On Kansas City disabled list, March 21, 1989 through entire season; included rehabilitation disability assignment to Baseball City, July 22 to August 4, 1989.

xReleased, December 7, 1989; re-signed by Royals' organization, February 16, 1990.

yGranted free agency, October 3, 1990.

RYNE DEE SANDBERG

Born September 18, 1959, at Spokane, Wash.
Height, 6.02. Weight, 180.
Throws and bats righthanded.

Holds major league record for most consecutive errorless games, second baseman, lifetime (123), June 21 through May 17, 1990, and season (90), June 21 through October 1, 1989.

Shares major league records for highest fielding average, second baseman, lifetime (.989); most assists by second baseman, nine-inning game (12), June 12, 1983.

Holds National League record for highest fielding average by second baseman, season (.994), 1986.

Major League stolen bases: 1982 (32), 1983 (37), 1984 (32), 1985 (54), 1986 (34), 1987 (21), 1988 (25), 1989 (15), 1990 (25). Total—275.

Led National League in total bases with 344 in 1990.

Led National League second basemen in total chances with 914 in 1983, 870 in 1984 and 824 in 1988.

Led National League second basemen in assists with 571 and double plays with 126 in 1983.

Led Eastern League shortstops in fielding percentage with .964, assists with 386 and double plays with 81 in 1980.

Led Western Carolinas League shortstops in double plays with 80 in 1979.

Led Pioneer League shortstops in double plays with 39 in 1978.

Named Major League Player of the Year by THE SPORTING NEWS, 1984.

Named National League Player of the Year by THE SPORTING NEWS, 1984.

Named National League Most Valuable Player by Baseball Writers' Association of America, 1984.

Named second baseman on THE SPORTING NEWS National League All-Star Team, 1984 and 1988 through 1990.

Named second baseman on THE SPORTING NEWS National League All-Star fielding team, 1983 through 1990.

Named second baseman on THE SPORTING NEWS National League Silver Slugger team, 1984, 1985 and 1988 through 1990.

Received reported $30,000 bonus to sign with Philadelphia Phillies, 1978.

Year Club	League	Pos.	G.	AB.	R.	H.	2B.	3B.	HR.	RBI.	B.A.	PO.	A.	E.	F.A.
1978—Helena	Pion.	SS	56	190	34	59	6	6	1	23	.311	92	★200	24	.924
1979—Spartanburg	W. Car.	SS	★138	★539	83	133	21	7	4	47	.247	134	★467	35	★.945
1980—Reading	East.	SS-3B	129	490	95	152	21	12	11	79	.310	156	388	20	.965
1981—Oklahoma City	A. A.	SS-2B	133	519	78	152	17	5	9	62	.293	229	396	21	.967
1981—Philadelphia†	Nat.	SS-2B	13	6	2	1	0	0	0	0	.167	7	7	0	1.000
1982—Chicago	Nat.	3B-2B	156	635	103	172	33	5	7	54	.271	136	373	12	.977
1983—Chicago	Nat.	★2B-SS	158	633	94	165	25	4	8	48	.261	330	572	13	★.986
1984—Chicago	Nat.	2B	156	636	★114	200	36	●19	19	84	.314	314	★550	6	★.993
1985—Chicago	Nat.	2B-SS	153	609	113	186	31	6	26	83	.305	353	501	12	.986
1986—Chicago	Nat.	2B	154	627	68	178	28	5	14	76	.284	309	★492	5	★.994
1987—Chicago‡	Nat.	2B	132	523	81	154	25	2	16	59	.294	294	375	10	.985
1988—Chicago	Nat.	2B	155	618	77	163	23	8	19	69	.264	291	★522	11	.987
1989—Chicago	Nat.	2B	157	606	●104	176	25	5	30	76	.290	294	466	6	.992
1990—Chicago	Nat.	2B	155	615	★116	188	30	3	★40	100	.306	278	★469	8	.989
Major League Totals—10 Years			1389	5508	872	1583	256	57	179	649	.287	2606	4327	83	.988

Selected by Philadelphia Phillies' organization in 20th round of free-agent draft, June 6, 1978.

†Traded with Shortstop Larry Bowa to Chicago Cubs for Shortstop Ivan DeJesus, January 27, 1982.

‡On disabled list, June 14 to July 11, 1987.

CHAMPIONSHIP SERIES RECORD

Year Club	League	Pos.	G.	AB.	R.	H.	2B.	3B.	HR.	RBI.	B.A.	PO.	A.	E.	F.A.
1984—Chicago	Nat.	2B	5	19	3	7	2	0	0	2	.368	13	18	1	.969
1989—Chicago	Nat.	2B	5	20	6	8	3	1	1	4	.400	7	11	0	1.000
Championship Game Totals—2 Years			10	39	9	15	5	1	1	6	.385	20	29	1	.980

ALL-STAR GAME RECORD

Year League	Pos.	AB.	R.	H.	2B.	3B.	HR.	RBI.	B.A.	PO.	A.	E.	F.A.
1984—National	2B	4	0	1	0	0	0	0	.250	0	0	0	.000
1985—National	2B	1	1	0	0	0	0	0	.000	0	3	0	1.000
1986—National	2B	3	0	0	0	0	0	0	.000	0	2	1	.667
1987—National	2B	2	0	0	0	0	0	0	.000	0	2	0	1.000
1988—National	2B	4	0	1	0	0	0	0	.250	2	2	0	1.000
1989—National	2B	3	0	0	0	0	0	0	.000	2	4	0	1.000
1990—National	2B	3	0	0	0	0	0	0	.000	1	2	0	1.000
All-Star Game Totals—7 Years		20	1	2	0	0	0	0	.100	5	15	1	.952

—DID YOU KNOW—

That Terry Mulholland's 1990 no-hitter was the first pitched in Philadelphia by a Phillies' hurler since 1898?

DEION LUWYNN SANDERS

Born August 9, 1967, at Fort Myers, Fla.
Height, 6.01. Weight, 195.
Throws and bats lefthanded.
Attended Florida State University, Tallahassee, Fla.

Major League stolen bases: 1989 (1), 1990 (8). Total—9.

Year Club	League	Pos.	G.	AB.	R.	H.	2B.	3B.	HR.	RBI.	B.A.	PO.	A.	E.	F.A.
1988—Sarasota Yanks....	Gulf C.	OF	17	75	7	21	4	2	0	6	.280	33	1	2	.944
1988—Fort Lauderdale..	Fla. St.	OF	6	21	5	9	2	0	0	2	.429	22	2	0	1.000
1988—Columbus..............	Int.	OF	5	20	3	3	1	0	0	0	.150	13	0	0	1.000
1989—Albany	East.	OF	33	119	28	34	2	2	1	6	.286	79	3	0	1.000
1989—New York.............	Amer.	OF	14	47	7	11	2	0	2	7	.234	30	1	1	.969
1989—Columbus..............	Int.	OF	70	259	38	72	12	7	5	30	.278	165	0	4	.976
1990—New York†...........	Amer.	OF	57	133	24	21	2	2	3	9	.158	69	2	2	.973
1990—Columbus‡............	Int.	OF	22	84	21	27	7	1	2	10	.321	49	1	0	1.000
Major League Totals—2 Years.................			71	180	31	32	4	2	5	16	.178	99	3	3	.971

Selected by Kansas City Royals' organization in 6th round of free-agent draft, June 3, 1985.
Selected by New York Yankees' organization in 30th round of free-agent draft, June 1, 1988.
†On disqualified list, August 1 to September 24, 1990.
‡Released, September 24, 1990.

RECORD AS FOOTBALL PLAYER

Named as defensive back on The Sporting News College Football All-America Team, 1986 through 1988.
Selected by Atlanta in 1st round (5th player selected) of 1989 NFL draft.
Signed by Atlanta Falcons, September 7, 1989.

		INTERCEPTIONS			–PUNT RETURNS–			—KICKOFF RET.—			—TOTAL—		
Year Club	G.	No.	Yds.	Avg. TD.	No.	Yds.	Avg. TD.	No.	Yds.	Avg. TD.	TD.	Pts.	F.
1989—Atlanta NFL	15	5	52	10.4 0	28	307	11.0 *1	35	725	20.7 0	1	6	2
1990—Atlanta NFL	16	3	153	51.0 2	29	250	8.6 1	39	851	21.8 0	3	18	4
Pro Totals—2 Years.......	31	8	205	25.6 2	57	557	9.8 2	74	1576	21.3 0	4	24	6

Additional pro statistics: Recovered one fumble and caught one pass for minus eight yards, 1989.

SCOTT DOUGLAS SANDERSON

Born July 22, 1956, at Dearborn, Mich.
Height, 6.05. Weight, 198.
Throws and bats righthanded.
Attended Vanderbilt University, Nashville, Tenn.

Shares National League record for most consecutive home runs allowed, inning (3), July 11, 1982, second inning.
Major League saves: 1979 (1), 1983 (1), 1986 (1), 1987 (2). Total—5.

Year Club	League	G.	IP.	W.	L.	Pct.	H.	R.	ER.	SO.	BB.	ERA.
1977—West Palm Beach	Florida St.	10	57	5	2	.714	58	22	17	37	23	2.68
1978—Memphis.........................	Southern	9	58	5	3	.625	55	32	26	44	19	4.03
1978—Denver...........................	Am. Assoc.	9	49	4	2	.667	47	35	33	36	30	6.06
1978—Montreal........................	National	10	61	4	2	.667	52	20	17	50	21	2.51
1979—Montreal........................	National	34	168	9	8	.529	148	69	64	138	54	3.43
1980—Montreal........................	National	33	211	16	11	.593	206	76	73	125	56	3.11
1981—Montreal........................	National	22	137	9	7	.563	122	50	45	77	31	2.96
1982—Montreal........................	National	32	224	12	12	.500	212	98	86	158	58	3.46
1983—Montreal†‡.....................	National	18	81⅓	6	7	.462	98	50	42	55	20	4.65
1984—Chicago§.......................	National	24	140⅔	8	5	.615	140	54	49	76	24	3.14
1984—Lodi................................	California	1	5	0	1	.000	7	2	2	2	0	3.60
1985—Chicago x........................	National	19	121	5	6	.455	100	49	42	80	27	3.12
1986—Chicago y........................	National	37	169⅔	9	11	.450	165	85	79	124	37	4.19
1987—Chicago y........................	National	32	144⅔	8	9	.471	156	72	69	106	50	4.29
1988—Peoria z..........................	Midwest	1	5	0	0	.000	4	1	0	3	0	0.00
1988—Iowa	Am. Assoc.	3	13⅓	1	0	1.000	13	7	7	4	2	4.73
1988—Chicago a.......................	National	11	15⅓	1	2	.333	13	9	9	6	3	5.28
1989—Chicago b.......................	National	37	146⅓	11	9	.550	155	69	64	86	31	3.94
1990—Oakland cd.....................	American	34	206⅓	17	11	.607	205	99	89	128	66	3.88
National League Totals—12 Years......................		309	1620	98	89	.524	1567	701	639	1081	412	3.55
American League Totals—1 Year.........................		34	206⅓	17	11	.607	205	99	89	128	66	3.88
Major League Totals—13 Years........................		343	1826⅓	115	100	.535	1772	800	728	1209	478	3.59

Selected by Kansas City Royals' organization in 11th round of free-agent draft, June 5, 1974.
Selected by Montreal Expos' organization in 3rd round of free-agent draft, June 7, 1977.
†On disabled list, July 5 to September 1, 1983.
‡Traded with Infielder Al Newman to San Diego Padres for Pitcher Gary Lucas, December 7, 1983; Traded by San Diego to Chicago Cubs for First Baseman Carmelo Martinez, Pitcher Craig Lefferts and Third Baseman Fritz Connally, December 7, 1983.
§On disabled list, June 1 to July 5, 1984; included rehabilitation disability assignment to Lodi, June 29 to July 5, 1984.
xOn disabled list, August 14, 1985 through remainder of season.
yOn disabled list, March 29 to April 24 and June 22 to July 7, 1987.
zOn Chicago disabled list, April 5 to August 23, 1988; included rehabilitation disability assignment to Peoria, June 25 to June 29, 1988; and Iowa, June 30 to July 11, 1988.
aGranted free agency, November 4, 1988; re-signed by Cubs, December 7, 1988.
bGranted free agency, November 13, 1989; signed by Oakland Athletics, December 13, 1989.
cGranted free agency, November 5, 1990; re-signed by Athletics, December 19, 1990.
dSold to New York Yankees, December 31, 1990.

DIVISION SERIES RECORD

Year Club	League	G.	IP.	W.	L.	Pct.	H.	R.	ER.	SO.	BB.	ERA.
1981—Montreal	National	1	2⅔	0	0	.000	4	4	2	2	2	6.75

CHAMPIONSHIP SERIES RECORD

Year Club	League	G.	IP.	W.	L.	Pct.	H.	R.	ER.	SO.	BB.	ERA.
1984—Chicago	National	1	4⅔	0	0	.000	6	3	3	2	1	5.79
1989—Chicago	National	1	2	0	0	.000	2	0	0	1	0	0.00
Championship Series Totals—2 Years		2	6⅔	0	0	.000	8	3	3	3	1	4.05

WORLD SERIES RECORD

Year Club	League	G.	IP.	W.	L.	Pct.	H.	R.	ER.	SO.	BB.	ERA.
1990—Oakland	American	2	1⅔	0	0	.000	4	2	2	0	1	10.80

ANDRES CONFESOR SANTANA

Born March 19, 1968, at San Pedro de Macoris, D.R.
Height, 5.11. Weight, 150.
Throws right and bats left and righthanded.

Led Pioneer League in stolen bases with 45 and caught stealing with 10 in 1987.
Led Midwest League in caught stealing with 23 in 1988.
Led Pioneer League shortstops in total chances with 337 in 1987.

Year Club	League	Pos.	G.	AB.	R.	H.	2B.	3B.	HR.	RBI.	B.A.	PO.	A.	E.	F.A.
1987—Pocatello	Pion.	SS	67	256	51	67	2	3	0	9	.262	94	*202	*41	.878
1988—Clinton	Midw.	SS	118	450	77	126	4	1	0	24	.280	154	301	50	.901
1988—Shreveport	Texas	SS	11	36	3	6	0	0	0	3	.167	20	29	1	.980
1989—San Jose	Calif.	SS	18	69	14	18	3	0	0	3	.261	22	46	8	.895
1990—Shreveport	Texas	SS	92	336	50	98	5	4	0	24	.292	131	207	33	.911
1990—San Francisco	Nat.	SS	6	2	0	0	0	0	0	1	.000	2	1	0	1.000
Major League Totals—1 Year			6	2	0	0	0	0	0	1	.000	2	1	0	1.000

Signed as free agent by San Francisco Giants' organization, November 22, 1985.

RAFAEL FRANCISCO SANTANA (DeLaCRUZ)

Born January 31, 1958, at La Romana, Dominican Republic.
Height, 6.01. Weight, 156.
Throws and bats righthanded.

Holds National League record for fewest assists by shortstop, season, 150 or more games (396), 1985.
Major League stolen bases: 1985 (1), 1987 (1), 1988 (1). Total—3.
Led New York-Pennsylvania League in sacrifice hits with 8 in 1977.
Led Texas League shortstops in fielding percentage with .955 and tied for lead in double plays with 79 in 1981.

Year Club	League	Pos.	G.	AB.	R.	H.	2B.	3B.	HR.	RBI.	B.A.	PO.	A.	E.	F.A.
1977—Oneonta	NYP	SS	60	157	26	41	5	0	0	23	.261	62	162	*37	.892
1978—Fort Lauderdale	Fla. St.	SS	131	431	37	111	8	5	0	35	.258	166	372	*48	.918
1979—Fort Lauderdale	Fla. St.	SS-3B-2B	133	472	62	124	9	6	0	41	.263	160	351	16	.970
1980—Nashville	South.	SS	86	275	33	64	4	3	0	20	.233	125	247	25	.937
1980—Fort Lauderdale†	Fla. St.	SS	51	168	20	38	2	0	1	17	.226	81	158	9	.964
1981—Arkansas	Texas	SS-3B-2B	110	326	34	76	14	3	0	19	.233	154	350	23	.956
1981—Springfield	A. A.	SS-3B	2	8	3	4	1	0	1	2	.500	1	8	3	.750
1982—Louisville	A. A.	3B-2B-SS	121	430	65	123	15	3	3	53	.286	163	275	11	.976
1983—St. Louis	Nat.	2B-SS-3B	30	14	1	3	0	0	0	2	.214	3	8	4	.733
1983—Louisville‡	A. A.	3-2-S-1	45	167	19	47	9	1	0	20	.281	60	117	10	.947
1984—Tidewater	Int.	S-3-2-1	77	255	34	71	6	0	1	23	.278	107	232	14	.960
1984—New York§	Nat.	SS	51	152	14	42	11	1	1	12	.276	92	104	6	.970
1985—New York	Nat.	SS	154	529	41	136	19	1	1	29	.257	*301	396	25	.965
1986—New York	Nat.	SS-2B	139	394	38	86	11	0	1	28	.218	203	369	16	.973
1987—New York x	Nat.	SS	139	439	41	112	21	2	5	44	.255	213	396	17	.973
1988—New York	Amer.	SS	148	480	50	115	12	1	4	38	.240	202	421	22	.966
1989—New York yz	Amer.						(Did Not Play)								
1990—Cleveland a	Amer.	SS	7	13	3	3	0	0	1	3	.231	2	9	0	1.000
National League Totals—5 Years			513	1528	135	379	62	4	8	115	.248	812	1273	68	.968
American League Totals—2 Years			155	493	53	118	12	1	5	41	.239	204	430	22	.966
Major League Totals—7 Years			668	2021	188	497	74	5	13	156	.246	1016	1703	90	.968

Signed as free agent by New York Yankees' organization, August 31. 1976.

†Traded to St. Louis Cardinals for a player to be named later, February 16, 1981; New York Yankees' organization acquired Pitcher George Frazier to complete deal, June 7, 1981.

‡Released, January 17, 1984; signed by Tidewater (New York Mets' organization), January 17, 1984.

§On disabled list, August 25 to September 9, 1984.

xTraded with Pitcher Victor Garcia to New York Yankees for Outfielder Darren Reed, Catcher Phil Lombardi and Pitcher Steve Frey, December 11, 1987.

yOn disabled list, March 19, 1989 through entire season.

zReleased, November 20, 1989; signed by Cleveland Indians, January 10, 1990.

aReleased, April 25, 1990.

CHAMPIONSHIP SERIES RECORD

Year Club	League	Pos.	G.	AB.	R.	H.	2B.	3B.	HR.	RBI.	B.A.	PO.	A.	E.	F.A.
1986—New York	Nat.	SS	6	17	0	3	0	0	0	0	.176	13	18	0	1.000

Year	Club	League	Pos.	G.	AB.	R.	H.	2B.	3B.	HR.	RBI.	B.A.	PO.	A.	E.	F.A.
1986—New York		Nat.	SS	7	20	3	5	0	0	0	2	.250	11	17	1	.966

BENITO SANTIAGO (RIVERA)

Name pronounced Sahn-tee-AH-goh.

Born March 9, 1965, at Ponce, P.R.
Height, 6.01. Weight, 185.
Throws and bats righthanded.

Holds major league record for most consecutive games batted safely by rookie, season (34), August 25 through October 2, 1987.
Major League stolen bases: 1987 (21), 1988 (15), 1989 (11), 1990 (5). Total—52.
Led National League in passed balls with 14 in 1989.
Tied for National League lead in double plays by catchers with 11 in 1988.
Led Pacific Coast League catchers in total chances with 655 in 1986.
Led Texas League in passed balls with 16 in 1985.
Led Florida State League catchers in double plays with 12 and passed balls with 26 in 1983.
Led National League in passed balls with 22 in 1987.
Named catcher on THE SPORTING NEWS National League All-Star Team, 1987 and 1989.
Named catcher on THE SPORTING NEWS National League All-Star fielding team, 1988 through 1990.
Named catcher on THE SPORTING NEWS National League Silver Slugger team, 1987, 1988 and 1990.
Named National League Rookie Player of the Year by THE SPORTING NEWS, 1987.
Named National League Rookie of the Year by Baseball Writers' Association of America, 1987.

Year	Club	League	Pos.	G.	AB.	R.	H.	2B.	3B.	HR.	RBI.	B.A.	PO.	A.	E.	F.A.
1983—Miami		Fla. St.	C	122	429	34	106	25	3	5	56	.247	471	*69	*21	.963
1984—Reno		Calif.	C	114	416	64	116	20	6	16	83	.279	692	96	25	.969
1985—Beaumont†		Texas	*C-1B-3B	101	372	55	111	16	6	5	52	.298	525	*78	15	.976
1986—Las Vegas		P. C.	C	117	437	55	125	26	3	17	71	.286	*563	71	*21	.968
1986—San Diego		Nat.	C	17	62	10	18	2	0	3	6	.290	80	7	5	.946
1987—San Diego		Nat.	C	146	546	64	164	33	2	18	79	.300	817	80	*22	.976
1988—San Diego		Nat.	C	139	492	49	122	22	2	10	46	.248	725	*75	*12	.985
1989—San Diego		Nat.	C	129	462	50	109	16	3	16	62	.236	685	81	*20	.975
1990—San Diego‡		Nat.	C	100	344	42	93	8	5	11	53	.270	538	51	12	.980
1990—Las Vegas		P. C.	C	6	20	5	6	2	0	1	8	.300	25	5	0	1.000
Major League Totals—5 Years				531	1906	215	506	81	12	58	246	.265	2845	294	71	.978

Signed as free agent by San Diego Padres' organization, September 1, 1982.

†On disabled list, June 21 to July 2, 1985.

‡On disabled list, June 15 to August 10, 1990; included rehabilitation disability assignment to Las Vegas, August 2 to August 9, 1990.

Year	League	Pos.	AB.	R.	H.	2B.	3B.	HR.	RBI.	B.A.	PO.	A.	E.	F.A.
1989—National		C	1	0	0	0	0	0	0	.000	0	0	1	.000

Named to National League All-Star Team for 1990 game; did not play due to injury.

NELSON GIL SANTOVENIA

Name pronounced San-toe-VAYN-yuh.

Born July 27, 1961, at Pino del Rio, Cuba.
Height, 6.03. Weight, 205.
Throws and bats righthanded.
Attended Miami-Dade Community College (South), Miami, Fla.,
and University of Miami, Coral Gables, Fla.

Major League stolen bases: 1988 (2), 1989 (2). Total—4.
Led Southern League catchers in putouts with 785 and total chances with 867 in 1987.
Led Southern League in passed balls with 21 in 1983.
Tied for Southern League lead in double plays by catchers with 9 in 1984.

Year	Club	League	Pos.	G.	AB.	R.	H.	2B.	3B.	HR.	RBI.	B.A.	PO.	A.	E.	F.A.
1982—W. Palm Beach		Fla. St.	C	40	118	8	29	4	0	1	12	.246	127	21	5	.967
1983—Memphis		South.	C	94	318	27	77	13	0	3	44	.242	490	69	*15	.974
1984—Jacksonville†		South.	C	90	255	27	55	9	0	5	29	.216	464	•64	4	.992
1985—Jacksonville		South.	C	57	184	15	40	6	0	2	15	.217	281	20	9	.971
1985—Indianapolis		A. A.	C	28	75	5	16	2	0	0	4	.213	135	20	1	.994
1986—Jacksonville		South.	C-OF	31	72	15	22	7	0	4	11	.306	97	14	1	.991
1986—Indianapolis		A. A.	C	18	57	6	12	1	0	1	2	.211	80	14	1	.989
1987—Jacksonville		South.	C-1B	117	394	56	110	17	0	19	63	.279	790	71	11	.987
1987—Montreal		Nat.	C	2	1	0	0	0	0	0	0	.000	1	0	0	1.000
1988—Indianapolis		A. A.	C	27	91	9	28	5	0	2	13	.308	198	23	3	.987
1988—Montreal‡		Nat.	C-1B	92	309	26	73	20	2	8	41	.236	465	63	9	.983
1989—Montreal§		Nat.	C-1B	97	304	30	76	14	1	5	31	.250	564	66	12	.981
1990—Montreal x		Nat.	C	59	163	13	31	3	1	6	28	.190	264	24	6	.980
1990—Indianapolis		A. A.	C	11	44	3	14	2	0	1	10	.318	40	7	1	.979
Major League Totals—4 Years				250	777	69	180	37	4	19	100	.232	1294	153	27	.982

Selected by Philadelphia Phillies' organization in 29th round of free-agent draft, June 5, 1979.

Selected by Montreal Expos' organization in 3rd round of free-agent draft, June 8, 1981.

Selected by Montreal Expos' organization in secondary phase of free-agent draft, June 7, 1982.

†On suspended list, May 24 to May 31, 1984.

‡On disabled list, June 4 to June 20, 1988.

MACK DANIEL SASSER JR.
(Mackey)

Born August 3, 1962, at Fort Gaines, Ga.
Height, 6.01. Weight, 210.
Throws right and bats lefthanded.
Attended George C. Wallace Community College, Dothan, Ala.,
and Troy State University, Troy, Ala.

Led Texas League in intentional bases on balls received with 13 in 1986.
Led California League in total bases with 245 and tied for lead in game-winning RBIs with 16 in 1985.
Led Pacific Coast League catchers in putouts with 584, errors with 16 and total chances with 663 in 1987.
Led California League in passed balls with 19 in 1985.

Year	Club	League	Pos.	G.	AB.	R.	H.	2B.	3B.	HR.	RBI.	B.A.	PO.	A.	E.	F.A.
1984—Clinton	Midw.	1-3-O-C	118	428	57	125	20	5	6	65	.292	526	95	17	.973
1984—Fresno	Calif.	OF-3B-1B	16	62	8	17	1	1	0	6	.274	24	15	4	.907
1985—Fresno	Calif.	O-C-1-3	133	497	79	168	27	4	14	102	.338	402	42	14	.969
1986—Shreveport	Texas	C-1B-OF	120	441	52	129	29	5	5	72	.293	577	66	10	.985
1987—Phoe.†-Vanc.	P. C.	C-3B-1B	115	400	53	127	24	1	3	56	.318	588	72	18	.973
1987—S.F.-Pitt.‡	Nat.	C	14	27	2	5	0	0	0	2	.185	29	0	0	1.000
1988—New York	Nat.	C-3B-OF	60	123	9	35	10	1	1	17	.285	235	17	6	.977
1989—New York	Nat.	C-3B	72	182	17	53	14	2	1	22	.291	335	19	3	.992
1990—New York	Nat.	*C-1B	100	270	31	83	14	0	6	41	.307	501	43	*14	.975
Major League Totals—4 Years			246	602	59	176	38	3	8	82	.292	1100	79	23	.981

Selected by San Francisco Giants' organization in 5th round of free-agent draft, January 17, 1984.
†Traded with $50,000 to Pittsburgh Pirates' organization for Pitcher Don Robinson, July 31, 1987.
‡Traded with Pitcher Tim Drummond to New York Mets for First Baseman Randy Milligan and Pitcher Scott Henion, March 26, 1988.

CHAMPIONSHIP SERIES RECORD

Year	Club	League	Pos.	G.	AB.	R.	H.	2B.	3B.	HR.	RBI.	B.A.	PO.	A.	E.	F.A.
1988—New York	Nat.	PH-C	4	5	0	1	0	0	0	0	.200	2	0	0	1.000

JOHN JOSEPH SAVAGE
(Jack)

Born April 22, 1964, at Louisville, Ky.
Height, 6.00. Weight, 185.
Throws and bats righthanded.
Attended University of Kentucky, Lexington, Ky.

Major League saves: 1990 (1).
Led Texas League in intentional bases on balls issued with 12 in 1987.
Led California League in intentional bases on balls with 11 in 1986.
Tied for Pioneer League lead in saves with 8 in 1985.

Year	Club	League	G.	IP.	W.	L.	Pct.	H.	R.	ER.	SO.	BB.	ERA.
1985—Great Falls	Pioneer	24	44⅔	5	1	.833	26	5	5	51	18	1.01
1986—Bakersfield	California	44	77⅔	5	8	.385	82	45	39	77	45	4.52
1987—San Antonio	Texas	49	69⅓	5	6	.455	64	22	20	67	31	2.60
1987—Albuquerque	P. Coast	13	15	0	4	.000	20	15	7	13	11	4.20
1987—Los Angeles†	National	3	3⅓	0	0	.000	4	1	1	0	0	2.70
1988—Tidewater	Int'national	43	88⅓	5	8	.385	67	37	31	46	37	3.16
1989—Tidewater‡	Int'national	33	42⅔	3	2	.600	41	21	17	28	21	3.59
1990—Portland	P. Coast	16	20⅔	1	2	.333	17	8	3	25	11	1.31
1990—Minnesota	American	17	26	0	2	.000	37	26	24	12	11	8.31
National League Totals—1 Year		3	3⅓	0	0	.000	4	1	1	0	0	2.70
American League Totals—1 Year		17	26	0	2	.000	37	26	24	12	11	8.31
Major League Totals—2 Years		20	29⅓	0	2	.000	41	27	25	12	11	7.67

Selected by Los Angeles Dodgers' organization in 8th round of free-agent draft, June 3, 1985.
†As part of an eight-player three-team deal, New York Mets traded Pitcher Jesse Orosco to Oakland Athletics, December 11, 1987. Oakland then traded Orosco along with Shortstop Alfredo Griffin and Pitcher Jay Howell to Los Angeles Dodgers for Pitchers Bob Welch, Matt Young and Jack Savage. Oakland then traded Savage along with Pitchers Wally Whitehurst and Kevin Tapani to New York.
‡Traded to Minnesota Twins, October 16, 1989, completing deal in which Minnesota traded Pitcher Frank Viola to New York Mets for Pitchers Rick Aguilera and David West and three players to be named later, July 31, 1989. Portland (Minnesota Twins' organization) acquired Pitchers Kevin Tapani and Tim Drummond as partial completion of deal, August 1, 1989.

STEPHEN LOUIS SAX
(Steve)

Born January 29, 1960, at Sacramento, Calif.
Height, 6.00. Weight, 183.
Throws and bats righthanded.
Brother of David Sax, catcher in New York Yankees' organization.

Major League stolen bases: 1981 (5), 1982 (49), 1983 (56), 1984 (34), 1985 (27), 1986 (40), 1987 (37), 1988 (42), 1989 (43), 1990 (43). Total—376.

Led National League in caught stealing with 30 in 1983.
Led American League second basemen in double plays with 117 in 1989.
Led Florida State League second basemen in double plays with 91 in 1980.
Named second baseman on THE SPORTING NEWS National League All-Star Team, 1986.
Named second baseman on THE SPORTING NEWS National League Silver Slugger team, 1986.
Named National League Rookie of the Year by Baseball Writers' Association of America, 1982.
Named Texas League Most Valuable Player, 1981.

Year	Club	League	Pos.	G.	AB.	R.	H.	2B.	3B.	HR.	RBI.	B.A.	PO.	A.	E.	F.A.
1978—Lethbridge	Pion.		SS	39	131	24	43	6	3	0	21	.328	21	40	9	.871
1979—Clinton	Midw.		OF-2B-3B	115	386	64	112	15	2	2	52	.290	111	75	18	.912
1980—Vero Beach	Fla. St.		★2B-OF	●139	●530	78	150	18	8	3	61	.283	★360	★438	20	★.976
1981—San Antonio	Texas		2B	115	485	94	168	23	3	8	52	★.346	255	298	17	.970
1981—Los Angeles	Nat.		2B	31	119	15	33	2	0	2	9	.277	64	93	4	.975
1982—Los Angeles	Nat.		2B	150	638	88	180	23	7	4	47	.282	347	452	19	.977
1983—Los Angeles	Nat.		2B	155	623	94	175	18	5	5	41	.281	331	399	★30	.961
1984—Los Angeles	Nat.		2B	145	569	70	138	24	4	1	35	.243	318	450	21	.973
1985—Los Angeles†	Nat.		★2B-3B	136	488	62	136	8	4	1	42	.279	330	358	★22	.969
1986—Los Angeles	Nat.		2B	157	633	91	210	43	4	6	56	.332	●367	432	16	.980
1987—Los Angeles	Nat.		2B-OF-3B	157	610	84	171	22	7	6	46	.280	343	420	14	.982
1988—Los Angeles‡	Nat.		2B	160	★632	70	175	19	4	5	57	.277	276	429	14	.981
1989—New York	Amer.		2B	158	●651	88	205	26	3	5	63	.315	312	460	10	★.987
1990—New York	Amer.		2B	155	615	70	160	24	2	4	42	.260	292	457	10	.987
National League Totals—8 Years				1091	4312	574	1218	159	35	30	333	.282	2376	3033	140	.975
American League Totals—2 Years				313	1266	158	365	50	5	9	105	.288	604	917	20	.987
Major League Totals—10 Years				1404	5578	732	1583	209	40	39	438	.284	2980	3950	160	.977

Selected by Los Angeles Dodgers' organization in 9th round of free-agent draft, June 6, 1978.
†On disabled list, April 19 to May 4, 1985.
‡Granted free agency, November 4, 1988; signed by New York Yankees, November 23, 1988.

DIVISION SERIES RECORD

Year	Club	League	Pos.	G.	AB.	R.	H.	2B.	3B.	HR.	RBI.	B.A.	PO.	A.	E.	F.A.
1981—Los Angeles	Nat.		2B	1	0	0	0	0	0	0	0	.000	0	0	0	.000

CHAMPIONSHIP SERIES RECORD

Shares Championship Series record for most stolen bases, inning (2), October 9, 1988, third inning.
Holds National League Championship Series records for most runs, series (7), 1988.
Shares National League Championship Series records for most at-bats (30), singles (8) and stolen bases (5), series, 1988; most stolen bases, game (3), October 9, 1988 (12 innings).

Year	Club	League	Pos.	G.	AB.	R.	H.	2B.	3B.	HR.	RBI.	B.A.	PO.	A.	E.	F.A.
1981—Los Angeles	Nat.		2B	1	0	0	0	0	0	0	0	.000	0	1	0	1.000
1983—Los Angeles	Nat.		2B	4	16	0	4	0	0	0	0	.250	11	12	0	1.000
1985—Los Angeles	Nat.		2B	6	20	1	6	3	0	0	1	.300	11	21	0	1.000
1988—Los Angeles	Nat.		2B	7	30	7	8	0	0	0	3	.267	12	22	0	1.000
Championship Series Totals—4 Years				18	66	8	18	3	0	0	4	.273	34	56	0	1.000

WORLD SERIES RECORD

Year	Club	League	Pos.	G.	AB.	R.	H.	2B.	3B.	HR.	RBI.	B.A.	PO.	A.	E.	F.A.
1981—Los Angeles	Nat.		PH-PR-2	2	1	0	0	0	0	0	0	.000	0	0	0	.000
1988—Los Angeles	Nat.		2B	5	20	3	6	0	0	0	0	.300	11	11	0	1.000
World Series Totals—2 Years				7	21	3	6	0	0	0	0	.286	11	11	0	1.000

ALL-STAR GAME RECORD

Year	League	Pos.	AB.	R.	H.	2B.	3B.	HR.	RBI.	B.A.	PO.	A.	E.	F.A.
1982—National		PR-2B	1	0	1	0	0	0	0	1.000	2	0	1	.667
1983—National		2B	3	1	1	0	0	0	1	.333	2	0	1	.667
1986—National		2B	1	0	1	0	0	0	1	1.000	0	1	0	1.000
1989—American		2B	1	0	0	0	0	0	0	.000	1	3	0	1.000
1990—American		2B	1	0	0	0	0	0	0	.000	0	1	0	1.000
All-Star Game Totals—5 Years			7	1	3	0	0	0	2	.429	5	5	2	.833

JEFFREY SCOTT SCHAEFER
(Jeff)

Born May 31, 1960, at Patchogue, N. Y.
Height, 5.10. Weight, 170.
Throws and bats righthanded.
Attended University of Maryland, College Park, Md.

Major League stolen bases: 1989 (1), 1990 (4). Totals—5.
Led Pacific Coast League shortstops in total chances with 679 in 1988.
Led Texas League shortstops in total chances with 521 and double plays with 73 in 1987.
Led Southern League second basemen in fielding percentage with .982 in 1984.
Led Appalachian League second basemen in total chances with 365 and double plays with 56 in 1981.

Year	Club	League	Pos.	G.	AB.	R.	H.	2B.	3B.	HR.	RBI.	B.A.	PO.	A.	E.	F.A.
1981—Bluefield	Appal.		2B	62	250	45	67	7	2	1	31	.268	★170	★189	6	.984
1982—Hagerstown	Carol.		2B	18	60	4	6	0	0	0	7	.100	39	41	3	.964
1982—Charlotte	South.		2-3-O-S	106	331	35	83	15	0	3	32	.251	231	232	22	.955
1983—Hagerstown	Carol.		2B-SS	68	229	32	61	15	4	1	16	.266	145	197	7	.980
1983—Charlotte	South.		2B-SS	51	182	20	43	7	2	2	28	.236	102	166	11	.961

Year Club	League	Pos.	G.	AB.	R.	H.	2B.	3B.	HR.	RBI.	B.A.	PO.	A.	E.	F.A.
1984—Rochester	Int.	SS-3B-2B	31	91	10	24	5	1	0	3	.264	44	84	2	.985
1984—Charlotte	South.	2B-SS	99	383	47	90	8	0	4	31	.235	249	264	9	.983
1985—Charlotte	South.	S-2-3-O	49	181	19	47	7	1	2	19	.260	84	112	7	.966
1985—Rochester†	Int.	2B-SS	68	187	17	37	4	0	2	12	.198	134	195	5	.985
1986—Midland‡§	Texas	SS-2B	114	406	50	109	17	1	6	41	.268	192	342	31	.945
1987—San Antonio x	Texas	SS	101	368	39	112	18	2	0	37	.304	165	★330	26	.950
1988—Vancouver	P. C.	SS	131	450	53	111	30	2	1	59	.247	★227	★417	★35	.948
1989—Vancouver	P. C.	2B-SS-OF	88	294	32	67	13	2	3	22	.228	177	232	10	.976
1989—Chicago y	Amer.	SS-2B-3B	15	10	2	1	0	0	0	0	.100	5	7	2	.857
1990—Calgary	P. C.	SS-3B-OF	49	170	24	41	9	2	0	19	.241	86	139	8	.966
1990—Seattle	Amer.	3B-SS-2B	55	107	11	22	3	0	0	6	.206	52	87	5	.965
Major League Totals—2 Years			70	117	13	23	3	0	0	6	.197	57	94	7	.956

Selected by Baltimore Orioles' organization in 12th round of free-agent draft, June 8, 1981.
†Sold to Edmonton (California Angels' organization), January 21, 1986.
‡On disabled list, May 21 to May 31, 1986.
§Drafted by San Antonio (Los Angeles Dodgers' organization), December 9, 1986.
xGranted free agency, October 15, 1987; signed by Vancouver (Chicago White Sox' organization), November 16, 1987.
yGranted free agency, October 15, 1989; signed by Calgary (Seattle Mariners' organization), November 13, 1989.

DANIEL ERNEST SCHATZEDER
Name pronounced SHOT-zay-dur.
(Dan)
Born December 1, 1954, at Elmhurst, Ill.
Height, 6.00. Weight, 195.
Throws and bats lefthanded.
Received degree in business administration from University of Denver, Denver, Colo., in 1976.

Major League saves: 1979 (1), 1983 (2), 1984 (1), 1986 (2), 1988 (3), 1989 (1). Total—10.

Year Club	League	G.	IP.	W.	L.	Pct.	H.	R.	ER.	SO.	BB.	ERA.
1976—West Palm Beach	Florida St.	10	64	5	3	.625	49	22	19	49	20	2.67
1976—Quebec City	Eastern	5	28	2	3	.400	38	16	14	19	10	4.50
1977—Quebec City	Eastern	8	62	5	3	.625	39	20	19	59	15	2.76
1977—Denver†	Am. Assoc.	9	36	2	2	.500	45	25	24	28	14	6.00
1977—Montreal	National	6	22	2	1	.667	16	6	6	14	13	2.45
1978—Denver	Am. Assoc.	4	28	3	0	1.000	24	11	9	19	11	2.89
1978—Montreal	National	29	144	7	7	.500	108	54	49	69	68	3.06
1979—Montreal‡	National	32	162	10	5	.667	136	57	51	106	59	2.83
1980—Detroit§	American	32	193	11	13	.458	178	88	86	94	58	4.01
1981—Detroit x	American	17	71	6	8	.429	74	49	48	20	29	6.08
1982—San Francisco y-Montreal	National	39	69⅓	1	6	.143	84	46	41	33	24	5.23
1982—Phoenix	P. Coast	1	3⅔	0	0	.000	10	6	5	1	3	12.27
1983—Montreal z	National	58	87	5	2	.714	88	34	31	48	25	3.21
1984—Montreal	National	36	136	7	7	.500	112	44	41	89	36	2.71
1985—Montreal a	National	24	104⅓	3	5	.375	101	52	44	64	31	3.80
1985—Indianapolis	Am. Assoc.	1	3	0	0	.000	2	0	0	3	1	0.00
1986—Montreal b-Philadelphia	National	55	88⅓	6	5	.545	81	43	32	47	35	3.26
1987—Philadelphia c	National	26	37⅔	3	1	.750	40	21	17	28	14	4.06
1987—Minnesota d	American	30	43⅔	3	1	.750	64	37	31	30	18	6.39
1988—Cleveland e-Minnesota	American	25	26⅓	0	3	.000	34	21	19	17	7	6.49
1988—Portland f	P. Coast	13	86⅔	6	4	.600	82	26	25	55	24	2.60
1989—Tucson	P. Coast	11	16	0	2	.000	15	8	7	15	10	3.94
1989—Houston gh	National	36	56⅔	4	1	.800	64	33	28	46	28	4.45
1990—Houston i-New York j	National	51	69⅔	1	3	.250	66	23	17	39	23	2.20
National League Totals—11 Years		392	977	49	43	.533	896	413	357	583	356	3.29
American League Totals—4 Years		104	334	20	25	.444	350	195	184	161	112	4.96
Major League Totals—14 Years		496	1311	69	68	.504	1246	608	541	744	468	3.71

Selected by Montreal Expos' organization in 3rd round of free-agent draft, June 8, 1976.
†On disabled list, July 5 to August 30, 1977.
‡Traded to Detroit Tigers for Outfielder Ron LeFlore, December 7, 1979.
§On disabled list, May 27 to June 17, 1980.
xTraded with Pitcher Mike Chris to San Francisco Giants for Outfielder Larry Herndon, December 9, 1981.
ySold to Montreal Expos, June 15, 1982.
zGranted free agency, November 7, 1983; re-signed by Expos, December 19, 1983.
aOn disabled list, June 21 to July 23 and August 7 to September 1, 1985; included rehabilitation disability assignment to Indianapolis, July 19 to July 23, 1985.
bTraded with Infielder Skeeter Barnes to Philadelphia Phillies for Infielder Tom Foley and Pitcher Lary Sorensen, July 24, 1986.
cTraded with cash to Minnesota Twins for Pitcher Danny Clay and Third Baseman Tom Schwarz, June 24, 1987.
dReleased, December 21, 1987; signed by Cleveland Indians, February 9, 1988.
eReleased, June 22, 1988; signed by Portland (Minnesota Twins' organization), June 27, 1988.
fGranted free agency, November 4, 1988; signed by Houston Astros, January 30, 1989.
gOn disabled list, July 19 to September 6, 1989; included rehabilitation disability assignment to Tucson, August 18 to August 31, 1989.
hGranted free agency, November 13, 1989; re-signed by Astros, December 19, 1989.
iTraded to New York Mets for Pitcher Steve LaRose and Infielder Nick Davis, September 10, 1990.
jGranted free agency, November 5, 1990; signed by Kansas City Royals, December 4, 1990.

Year Club	League	G.	IP.	W.	L.	Pct.	H.	R.	ER.	SO.	BB.	ERA.
1987—Minnesota	American	2	4⅓	0	0	.000	2	0	0	5	0	0.00

WORLD SERIES RECORD

Year Club	League	G.	IP.	W.	L.	Pct.	H.	R.	ER.	SO.	BB.	ERA.
1987—Minnesota	American	3	4⅓	1	0	1.000	4	3	3	3	3	6.23

CURTIS MONTAGUE SCHILLING
(Curt)

Born November 14, 1966, at Phoenix, Ariz.
Height, 6.04. Weight, 215.
Throws and bats righthanded.
Attended Yavapai College, Prescott, Ariz.

Major League saves: 1990 (3).
Tied for International League lead in games started by pitchers with 27, shutouts with 3, complete games with 9 and balks with 6 in 1989.

Year Club	League	G.	IP.	W.	L.	Pct.	H.	R.	ER.	SO.	BB.	ERA.
1986—Elmira	NYP	16	93⅔	7	3	.700	92	34	27	75	30	2.59
1987—Greensboro	S. Atlantic	29	184	8	★15	.348	179	96	78	★189	65	3.82
1988—New Britain†	Eastern	21	106	8	5	.615	91	44	35	62	40	2.97
1988—Charlotte	Southern	7	45⅓	5	2	.714	36	19	16	32	23	3.18
1988—Baltimore	American	4	14⅔	0	3	.000	22	19	16	4	10	9.82
1989—Rochester	Int'national	27	★185⅓	●13	11	.542	176	76	66	109	59	3.21
1989—Baltimore	American	5	8⅔	0	1	.000	10	6	6	6	3	6.23
1990—Rochester	Int'national	15	87⅓	4	4	.500	95	46	38	83	25	3.92
1990—Baltimore‡	American	35	46	1	2	.333	38	13	13	32	19	2.54
Major League Totals—3 Years		44	69⅓	1	6	.143	70	38	35	42	32	4.54

Selected by Boston Red Sox' organization in 2nd round of free-agent draft, January 14, 1986.
†Traded with Outfielder Brady Anderson to Baltimore Orioles for Pitcher Mike Boddicker, July 29, 1988.
‡Traded with Pitcher Pete Harnisch and Outfielder Steve Finley to Houston Astros for First Baseman Glenn Davis, January 10, 1991.

CALVIN DREW SCHIRALDI

Born June 16, 1962, at Houston, Tex.
Height, 6.05. Weight, 215.
Throws and bats righthanded.
Attended University of Texas, Austin, Tex.

Major League saves: 1986 (9), 1987 (6), 1988 (1), 1989 (4), 1990 (1). Total—21.
Named Texas League Pitcher of the Year, 1984.

Year Club	League	G.	IP.	W.	L.	Pct.	H.	R.	ER.	SO.	BB.	ERA.
1983—Jackson	Texas	7	38⅔	3	3	.500	41	28	25	26	29	5.82
1983—Lynchburg	Carolina	6	30⅓	4	1	.800	28	16	15	41	17	4.45
1984—Jackson	Texas	23	156⅓	●14	3	★.824	118	58	50	131	69	2.88
1984—Tidewater	Int'national	4	31⅓	3	1	.750	18	6	4	24	10	1.15
1984—New York	National	5	17⅓	0	2	.000	20	13	11	16	10	5.71
1985—Tidewater	Int'national	17	100⅓	4	5	.444	91	50	39	76	56	3.50
1985—New York†‡	National	10	26⅓	2	1	.667	43	27	26	21	11	8.89
1986—Pawtucket	Int'national	31	44	4	3	.571	32	19	14	59	20	2.86
1986—Boston	American	25	51	4	2	.667	36	8	8	55	15	1.41
1987—Boston§	American	62	83⅔	8	5	.615	75	45	41	93	40	4.41
1988—Chicago x	National	29	166⅓	9	13	.409	166	87	81	140	63	4.38
1989—Chicago y-San Diego	National	59	100	6	7	.462	72	40	39	71	63	3.51
1990—San Diego	National	42	104	3	8	.273	105	59	51	74	60	4.41
National League Totals—5 Years		145	414	20	31	.392	406	226	208	322	207	4.52
American League Totals—2 Years		87	134⅔	12	7	.632	111	53	49	148	55	3.27
Major League Totals—7 Years		232	548⅔	32	38	.457	517	279	257	470	262	4.22

Selected by Chicago White Sox' organization in 17th round of free-agent draft, June 3, 1980.
Selected by New York Mets' organization in 1st round (27th player selected) of free-agent draft, June 6, 1983.
†On disabled list, May 15 to May 30, 1985.
‡Traded with Pitcher Wes Gardner and Outfielders John Christensen and LaSchelle Tarver to Boston Red Sox for Pitchers Bob Ojeda, Tom McCarthy, John Mitchell and Chris Bayer, November 13, 1985.
§Traded with Pitcher Al Nipper to Chicago Cubs for Pitcher Lee Smith, December 8, 1987.
xOn disabled list, May 13 to May 28 and August 5 to August 20, 1988.
yTraded with Outfielder Darrin Jackson and a player to be named later to San Diego Padres for Outfielder Marvell Wynne and Infielder Luis Salazar, August 30, 1989; San Diego acquired First Baseman Phil Stephenson to complete deal, September 5, 1989.

CHAMPIONSHIP SERIES RECORD

Shares American League Championship Series record for most games pitched, series (4), 1986.

Year Club	League	G.	IP.	W.	L.	Pct.	H.	R.	ER.	SO.	BB.	ERA.
1986—Boston	American	4	6	0	1	.000	5	2	1	9	3	1.50

WORLD SERIES RECORD

Year Club	League	G.	IP.	W.	L.	Pct.	H.	R.	ER.	SO.	BB.	ERA.
1986—Boston	American	3	4	0	2	.000	7	7	6	2	3	13.50

DAVID JOSEPH SCHMIDT
(Dave)

Born April 22, 1957, at Niles, Mich.
Height, 6.01. Weight, 194.
Throws and bats righthanded.
Attended Los Angeles Valley College, Van Nuys, Calif., and UCLA, Los Angeles, Calif.

Major League saves: 1981 (1), 1982 (6), 1983 (2), 1984 (12), 1985 (5), 1986 (8), 1987 (1), 1988 (2), 1990 (13). Total—50.

Year Club	League	G.	IP.	W.	L.	Pct.	H.	R.	ER.	SO.	BB.	ERA.
1979—Sarasota Rangers	Gulf Coast	7	30	2	2	.500	30	19	14	27	8	4.20
1980—Asheville	S. Atlantic	12	91	8	1	.889	76	32	20	67	13	1.98
1980—Tulsa	Texas	12	73	4	6	.400	90	42	36	46	28	4.44
1981—Tulsa	Texas	3	24	1	1	.500	17	5	5	17	6	1.88
1981—Texas	American	14	32	0	1	.000	31	11	11	13	11	3.09
1981—Wichita	Am. Assoc.	12	87	2	5	.286	90	47	47	49	26	4.86
1982—Texas	American	33	109⅔	4	6	.400	118	45	39	69	25	3.20
1983—Texas†	American	31	46⅓	3	3	.500	42	20	20	29	14	3.88
1984—Texas	American	43	70⅓	6	6	.500	69	30	20	46	20	2.56
1985—Texas‡	American	51	85⅔	7	6	.538	81	36	30	46	22	3.15
1986—Chicago§	American	49	92⅓	3	6	.333	94	37	34	67	27	3.31
1987—Baltimore	American	35	124	10	5	.667	128	57	52	70	26	3.77
1988—Baltimore	American	41	129⅔	8	5	.615	129	58	49	67	38	3.40
1989—Baltimore x	American	38	156⅔	10	13	.435	196	102	99	46	36	5.69
1990—Jacksonville y	Southern	3	6	0	1	.000	4	3	3	4	0	4.50
1990—Montreal z	National	34	48	3	3	.500	58	26	23	22	13	4.31
American League Totals—9 Years		335	846⅔	51	51	.500	888	396	354	453	219	3.76
National League Totals—1 Year		34	48	3	3	.500	58	26	23	22	13	4.31
Major League Totals—10 Years		369	894½	54	54	.500	946	422	377	475	232	3.79

Selected by Texas Rangers' organization in 26th round of free-agent draft, June 5, 1979.

†On disabled list, March 25 to May 1, 1983.

‡Traded with Infielder Wayne Tolleson to Chicago White Sox for Pitcher Ed Correa, Infielder Scott Fletcher and a player to be named later, November 25, 1985; Texas Rangers acquired Infielder Jose Mota to complete deal, December 12, 1985.

§Released, December 19, 1986; signed by Baltimore Orioles, January 22, 1987.

xGranted free agency, November 13, 1989; signed by Montreal Expos, December 13, 1989.

yOn Montreal disabled list, March 29 to May 2 and July 26, 1990 through remainder of season; included rehabilitation disability assignment to Jacksonville, April 24 to April 29, 1990.

zGranted free agency, November 5, 1990.

RICHARD CRAIG SCHOFIELD
(Dick)

Born November 21, 1962, at Springfield, Ill.
Height, 5.10. Weight, 179.
Throws and bats righthanded.
Son of John Richard (Dick) Schofield, infielder with St. Louis Cardinals, Pittsburgh, San Francisco, New York Yankees, Los Angeles Dodgers, Boston and Milwaukee Brewers, 1953 through 1971.

Major League stolen bases: 1984 (5), 1985 (11), 1986 (23), 1987 (19), 1988 (20), 1989 (9), 1990 (3). Total—90.
Led American League shortstops in double plays with 125 in 1988.
Led Pioneer League in bases on balls received with 68 in 1981.
Received reported $100,000 bonus to sign with California Angels, 1981.

Year Club	League	Pos.	G.	AB.	R.	H.	2B.	3B.	HR.	RBI.	B.A.	PO.	A.	E.	F.A.
1981—Idaho Falls	Pion.	*SS-2B	66	226	59	63	10	1	6	31	.279	*102	201	22	.932
1982—Danville	Midw.	SS	92	308	80	111	21	*10	12	53	*.360	129	249	23	.943
1982—Redwood	Calif.	SS	33	102	15	25	3	3	1	8	.245	35	103	3	.979
1982—Spokane	P. C.	SS-3B	7	30	4	9	4	1	1	12	.300	7	20	0	1.000
1983—Edmonton	P. C.	SS-3B	139	521	91	148	30	7	16	94	.284	220	402	30	.954
1983—California	Amer.	SS	21	54	4	11	2	0	3	4	.204	24	67	7	.929
1984—California†	Amer.	SS	140	400	39	77	10	3	4	21	.193	218	420	12	*.982
1985—California	Amer.	SS	147	438	50	96	19	3	8	41	.219	261	397	25	.963
1986—California	Amer.	SS	139	458	67	114	17	6	13	57	.249	246	389	18	.972
1987—California‡	Amer.	*SS-2B	134	479	52	120	17	3	9	46	.251	205	351	9	*.984
1988—California	Amer.	SS	155	527	61	126	11	6	6	34	.239	278	492	13	*.983
1989—California§	Amer.	SS	91	302	42	69	11	2	4	26	.228	118	276	7	.983
1990—Edmonton x	P. C.	SS	5	18	4	7	1	0	1	4	.389	6	14	1	.952
1990—California	Amer.	SS	99	310	41	79	8	1	1	18	.255	170	318	17	.966
Major League Totals—8 Years			926	2968	356	692	95	24	48	247	.233	1520	2710	108	.975

Selected by California Angels' organization in 1st round (third player selected) of free-agent draft, June 8, 1981.

†On disabled list, July 1 to July 24, 1984.

‡On disabled list, July 13 to August 11, 1987.

§On disabled list, April 12 to May 6 and August 11 to September 21, 1989.

xOn California disabled list, March 31 to June 6, 1990; included rehabilitation disability assignment to Edmonton, May 31 to June 5, 1990.

CHAMPIONSHIP SERIES RECORD

Year Club	League	Pos.	G.	AB.	R.	H.	2B.	3B.	HR.	RBI.	B.A.	PO.	A.	E.	F.A.
1986—California	Amer.	SS	7	30	4	9	1	0	1	2	.300	13	23	2	.947

MICHAEL RALPH SCHOOLER
(Mike)

Born August 10, 1962, at Anaheim, Calif.
Height, 6.03. Weight, 220.
Throws and bats righthanded.
Attended Golden West College, Huntington, Beach, Calif.,
and California State University, Fullerton, Calif.

Major League saves: 1988 (15), 1989 (33), 1990 (30). Total—78.

Year Club	League	G.	IP.	W.	L.	Pct.	H.	R.	ER.	SO.	BB.	ERA.
1985—Bellingham	Northwest	10	55⅓	4	3	.571	42	24	18	48	15	2.93
1986—Wausau	Midwest	26	166⅓	12	10	.545	166	83	62	171	44	3.35
1987—Chattanooga	Southern	28	175	13	8	.619	183	87	77	144	48	3.96
1988—Calgary	P. Coast	26	33⅔	4	4	.500	33	19	12	47	6	3.21
1988—Seattle	American	40	48⅓	5	8	.385	45	21	19	54	24	3.54
1989—Seattle	American	67	77	1	7	.125	81	27	24	69	19	2.81
1990—Seattle†	American	49	56	1	4	.200	47	18	14	45	16	2.25
Major League Totals—3 Years		156	181⅓	7	19	.269	173	66	57	168	59	2.83

Selected by Seattle Mariners' organization in 2nd round of free-agent draft, June 3, 1985.
†On disabled list, August 25, 1990 through remainder of season.

ALFRED WILLIAM SCHROEDER III
Name pronounced SHRO-der.
(Bill)

Born September 7, 1958, at Baltimore, Md.
Height, 6.02. Weight, 200.
Throws and bats righthanded.
Attended Clemson University, Clemson, S. C.

Major League stolen bases: 1986 (1), 1987 (5). Total—6.
Led Pacific Coast League batters in strikeouts with 136 and game-winning RBIs with 15 in 1982.
Led California League batters in strikeouts with 141 in 1980.
Led Pioneer League in total bases with 170 in 1979.
Led California League catchers in total chances with 759 in 1980.
Tied for Pacific Coast League lead in passed balls with 13 in 1983.

Year Club	League	Pos.	G.	AB.	R.	H.	2B.	3B.	HR.	RBI.	B.A.	PO.	A.	E.	F.A.
1979—Butte	Pion.	C-1B	65	242	73	86	16	7	18	77	.355	474	50	9	.983
1980—Stockton	Calif.	*C-1B	123	437	68	117	20	3	18	97	.268	669	96	7	*.991
1981—El Paso	Texas	C-OF	95	335	41	87	20	2	15	61	.260	511	49	10	.982
1982—Vancouver	P. C.	C	116	425	66	113	16	3	22	77	.266	569	77	7	*.989
1983—Vancouver	P. C.	C	82	304	51	87	13	3	20	70	.286	399	68	6	*.987
1983—Milwaukee	Amer.	C	23	73	7	13	2	1	3	7	.178	92	5	2	.980
1984—Milwaukee	Amer.	C-1B	61	210	29	54	6	0	14	25	.257	277	24	4	.987
1985—Milwaukee†	Amer.	C-1B	53	194	18	47	8	0	8	25	.242	216	23	3	.988
1986—El Paso‡	Texas	C	8	26	5	6	3	0	1	2	.231	26	2	0	1.000
1986—Milwaukee	Amer.	C-1B	64	217	32	46	14	0	7	19	.212	307	25	1	.997
1987—Milwaukee	Amer.	C-1B	75	250	35	83	12	0	14	42	.332	373	27	2	.995
1988—Milwaukee§	Amer.	C-1B	41	122	9	19	2	0	5	10	.156	197	21	0	1.000
1988—Denver x	A. A.	C	6	17	4	4	2	1	0	3	.235	16	3	0	1.000
1989—California y	Amer.	C-1B	41	138	16	28	2	0	6	15	.203	252	32	3	.990
1990—Palm Springs z	Calif.	C	6	12	2	4	1	0	0	1	.333	18	4	0	1.000
1990—California a	Amer.	C-1B	18	58	7	13	3	0	4	9	.224	100	10	0	1.000
Major League Totals—8 Years			376	1262	153	303	49	1	61	152	.240	1814	167	15	.992

Selected by Milwaukee Brewers' organization in 8th round of free-agent draft, June 5, 1979.
†On disabled list, May 15 to June 14 and June 22 to July 19, 1985.
‡On Milwaukee disabled list, March 29 to May 4, 1986; included rehabilitation disability assignment to El Paso, April 24 to May 4, 1986.
§On disabled list, July 27 to August 15, 1988; included rehabilitation disability assignment to Denver, August 5 to August 12, 1988.
xTraded to California Angels for Infielder Gus Polidor, December 7, 1988.
yOn disabled list, August 11 to August 29, 1989.
zOn California disabled list, April 4 to July 2, 1990; included rehabilitation disability assignment to Edmonton, May 31 to June 2, 1990 (did not play); and Palm Springs, June 21 to June 27, 1990.
aReleased, October 11, 1990.

RICHARD SPENCER SCHU
Name pronounced Shoo.
(Rick)

Born January 26, 1962, at Philadelphia, Pa.
Height, 6.00. Weight, 185.
Throws and bats righthanded.
Attended Sacramento City College, Sacramento, Calif.
Son of Ken Schu, minor league pitcher, 1955 and 1956.

Shares major league record for most doubles, inning (2), October 3, 1985, third inning.
Major League stolen bases: 1985 (8), 1986 (2), 1988 (6), 1989 (1). Total—17.
Led Pacific Coast League third basemen in total chances with 390 in 1984.

Year	Club	League	Pos.	G.	AB.	R.	H.	2B.	3B.	HR.	RBI.	B.A.	PO.	A.	E.	F.A.
1981—Bend	N'west	3B-2B-SS	68	258	41	69	10	0	2	42	.267	55	137	24	.889
1982—Spartanburg	S. Atl.	3B-2B-SS	125	429	78	117	28	1	12	60	.273	157	257	45	.902
1983—Peninsula	Carol.	3B-SS-2B	122	444	69	119	22	3	14	63	.268	82	252	30	.918
1983—Portland	P. C.	3B-SS	9	29	7	11	2	1	1	3	.379	6	12	2	.900
1984—Portland	P. C.	3B	140	552	70	166	35	●14	12	82	.301	★109	★254	★27	.931
1984—Philadelphia	Nat.	3B	17	29	12	8	2	1	2	5	.276	7	13	1	.952
1985—Portland	P. C.	SS-3B	42	150	19	42	8	3	4	22	.280	36	91	11	.920
1985—Philadelphia	Nat.	3B	112	416	54	105	21	4	7	24	.252	86	191	20	.933
1986—Philadelphia	Nat.	3B	92	208	32	57	10	1	8	25	.274	42	94	13	.913
1987—Philadelphia†‡	Nat.	3B-1B	92	196	24	46	6	3	7	23	.235	193	71	10	.964
1988—Baltimore§	Amer.	3B-1B	89	270	22	69	9	4	4	20	.256	94	110	11	.949
1989—Balt.x-Det.	Amer.	3-2-1-S	99	266	25	57	11	0	7	21	.214	59	126	12	.939
1989—Rochester y	Int.	3B-1B	28	94	11	21	6	1	1	10	.223	50	39	5	.947
1990—California	Amer.	3-1-O-2	61	157	19	42	8	0	6	14	.268	104	81	11	.944
1990—Edmonton	P. C.	1B-3B-OF	18	60	8	18	7	0	1	8	.300	83	20	2	.981
National League Totals—4 Years			313	849	122	216	39	9	24	77	.254	328	369	44	.941
American League Totals—3 Years			249	693	66	168	28	4	17	55	.242	257	317	34	.944
Major League Totals—7 Years			562	1542	188	384	67	13	41	132	.249	585	686	78	.942

Signed as free agent by Philadelphia Phillies' organization, November 25, 1980.

†On disabled list, August 19 to September 3, 1987.

‡Traded with Outfielders Jeff Stone and Keith Hughes to Baltimore Orioles for Outfielder Mike Young and a player to be named later, March 21, 1988; Philadelphia Phillies acquired Outfielder Frank Bellino to complete deal, June 14, 1988.

§On disabled list, April 22 to May 7, June 6 to June 21 and August 12 to August 29, 1988.

xSold to Detroit Tigers, May 19, 1989.

yReleased, December 8, 1989; signed by Edmonton (California Angels' organization), February 5, 1990.

JEFFREY ALAN SCHULZ
(Jeff)

Born June 2, 1961, at Evansville, Ind.
Height, 6.01. Weight, 190.
Throws right and bats lefthanded.
Attended Western Kentucky University, Bowling Green, Ky.,
and Indiana State University, Evansville, Ind.

Year	Club	League	Pos.	G.	AB.	R.	H.	2B.	3B.	HR.	RBI.	B.A.	PO.	A.	E.	F.A.
1983—Butte	Pion.	OF	61	211	44	69	12	2	7	55	.327	59	6	4	.942
1984—Charleston	S. Atl.	OF	69	265	52	89	14	3	5	54	.336	115	12	4	.969
1984—Fort Myers	Fla. St.	OF	59	204	23	64	10	0	0	26	.314	110	10	0	1.000
1985—Memphis	South.	OF	136	488	73	149	15	5	4	53	.305	263	12	11	.962
1986—Omaha	A. A.	OF	123	400	40	121	19	4	2	61	.303	119	5	5	.961
1987—Omaha	A. A.	OF-1B	99	316	25	81	12	7	4	36	.256	163	8	2	.988
1988—Omaha	A. A.	OF	101	359	37	103	20	3	5	41	.287	105	7	7	.941
1989—Omaha	A. A.	OF	95	331	31	92	19	5	2	37	.278	132	6	3	.979
1989—Kansas City	Amer.	OF	7	9	0	2	0	0	0	1	.222	6	0	0	1.000
1990—Omaha	A. A.	OF-1B	69	231	35	69	16	1	4	27	.299	86	2	0	1.000
1990—Kansas City†‡	Amer.	OF	30	66	5	17	5	1	0	6	.258	33	0	2	.943
Major League Totals—2 Years			37	75	5	19	5	1	0	7	.253	39	0	2	.951

Selected by Kansas City Royals' organization in 23rd round of free-agent draft, June 6, 1983.

†On disabled list, August 7 to September 5, 1990.

‡Released, December 3, 1990.

MICHAEL SCOTT SCHWABE
Name pronounced SHWOBB-bee.
(Mike)

Born July 12, 1964, at Fort Dodge, Ia.
Height, 6.04. Weight, 200.
Throws and bats righthanded.
Attended Rancho Santiago College, Santa Ana, Calif.,
and Arizona State University, Tempe, Ariz.

Year	Club	League	G.	IP.	W.	L.	Pct.	H.	R.	ER.	SO.	BB.	ERA.
1987—Bristol	Ap'lachian	4	12⅔	2	1	.667	8	8	6	7	3	4.26
1987—Fayetteville	S. Atlantic	11	22	1	1	.500	18	10	6	23	2	2.45
1987—Lakeland	Florida St.	5	18	2	1	.667	12	6	6	9	8	3.00
1988—Lakeland	Florida St.	40	111⅔	9	0	1.000	88	24	20	80	14	1.61
1988—Glens Falls	Eastern	8	18	0	2	.000	16	9	7	11	5	3.50
1989—London	Eastern	8	25⅓	3	0	1.000	25	7	3	22	5	1.07
1989—Detroit	American	13	44⅔	2	4	.333	58	33	30	13	16	6.04
1989—Toledo	Int'national	13	62⅓	5	3	.625	60	20	18	32	10	2.60
1990—Toledo	Int'national	51	108	6	5	.545	112	58	46	69	22	3.83
1990—Detroit†	American	1	3⅔	0	0	.000	5	1	1	1	0	2.45
Major League Totals—2 Years		14	48⅓	2	4	.333	63	34	31	14	16	5.77

Selected by Minnesota Twins' organization in 8th round of free-agent draft, January 14, 1986.

Selected by Minnesota Twins' organization in secondary phase of free-agent draft, June 2, 1986.

Selected by Detroit Tigers' organization in 21st round of free-agent draft, June 2, 1987.

†Released, December 5, 1990.

MICHAEL LORRI SCIOSCIA
Name pronounced SO-sha.
(Mike)
Born November 27, 1958, at Upper Darby, Pa.
Height, 6.02. Weight, 229.
Throws right and bats lefthanded.
Attended Pennsylvania State University, University Park, Pa.

Major League stolen bases: 1980 (1), 1982 (2), 1984 (2), 1985 (3), 1986 (3), 1987 (7), 1990 (4). Total—22.
Led National League catchers in total chances with 1,016 in 1987, 915 in 1989 and 910 in 1990.
Led National League in passed balls with 11 in 1981.
Tied for Pacific Coast League lead in being hit by pitch with 7 in 1979.
Led Pacific Coast League catchers in double plays with 19 and passed balls with 22 in 1979.
Led Midwest League catchers in errors with 20 and double plays with 12 in 1978.
Named catcher on THE SPORTING NEWS National League All-Star Team, 1990.

Year	Club	League	Pos.	G.	AB.	R.	H.	2B.	3B.	HR.	RBI.	B.A.	PO.	A.	E.	F.A.
1976—Bellingham	N'west.		C	46	151	25	42	6	0	7	26	.278	202	35	14	.944
1977—Clinton	Midw.		C-1B	121	364	58	92	20	1	7	44	.253	764	95	22	.975
1978—San Antonio†	Texas		C	58	204	29	61	16	0	2	34	.299	214	17	4	.983
1979—Albuquerque	P. C.		C	143	461	80	155	34	0	3	68	.336	★690	★86	★15	.981
1980—Albuquerque	P. C.		C	52	160	33	53	11	1	3	33	.331	207	19	5	.978
1980—Los Angeles‡	Nat.		C	54	134	8	34	5	1	1	8	.254	226	26	2	.992
1981—Los Angeles	Nat.		C	93	290	27	80	10	0	2	29	.276	493	48	7	.987
1982—Los Angeles	Nat.		C	129	365	31	80	11	1	5	38	.219	631	57	10	.986
1983—Los Angeles§	Nat.		C	12	35	3	11	3	0	1	7	.314	55	4	0	1.000
1984—Los Angeles x	Nat.		C	114	341	29	93	18	0	5	38	.273	701	64	12	.985
1985—Los Angeles	Nat.		C	141	429	47	127	26	3	7	53	.296	818	66	●13	.986
1986—Los Angeles y	Nat.		C	122	374	36	94	18	1	5	26	.251	756	64	15	.982
1987—Los Angeles z	Nat.		C	142	461	44	122	26	1	6	38	.265	★925	80	11	.989
1988—Los Angeles	Nat.		C	130	408	29	105	18	0	3	35	.257	748	63	7	.991
1989—Los Angeles	Nat.		C	133	408	40	102	16	0	10	44	.250	★822	★82	11	.988
1990—Los Angeles	Nat.		C	135	435	46	115	25	0	12	66	.264	★842	58	10	.989
Major League Totals—11 Years				1205	3680	340	963	176	7	57	382	.262	7017	612	98	.987

Selected by Los Angeles Dodgers' organization in 1st round (19th player selected) of free-agent draft, June 8, 1976.
†On disabled list, May 19 to August 4, 1978.
‡On disabled list, April 10 to April 20, 1980.
§On disabled list, May 15, 1983 through remainder of season.
xOn disabled list, May 6 to May 21, 1984.
yOn disabled list, June 10 to July 15, 1986.
zOn disabled list, June 1 to June 16, 1987.

DIVISION SERIES RECORD

Year	Club	League	Pos.	G.	AB.	R.	H.	2B.	3B.	HR.	RBI.	B.A.	PO.	A.	E.	F.A.
1981—Los Angeles	Nat.		C	4	13	0	2	0	0	0	1	.154	21	3	0	1.000

CHAMPIONSHIP SERIES RECORD

Year	Club	League	Pos.	G.	AB.	R.	H.	2B.	3B.	HR.	RBI.	B.A.	PO.	A.	E.	F.A.
1981—Los Angeles	Nat.		C	5	15	1	2	0	0	1	1	.133	27	1	0	1.000
1985—Los Angeles	Nat.		C	6	16	2	4	0	0	0	1	.250	31	4	1	.972
1988—Los Angeles	Nat.		C	7	22	3	8	1	0	1	2	.364	37	4	0	1.000
Championship Series Totals—3 Years				18	53	6	14	1	0	2	4	.264	95	9	1	.990

WORLD SERIES RECORD

Year	Club	League	Pos.	G.	AB.	R.	H.	2B.	3B.	HR.	RBI.	B.A.	PO.	A.	E.	F.A.
1981—Los Angeles	Nat.		C-PH	3	4	1	1	0	0	0	0	.250	7	1	0	1.000
1988—Los Angeles	Nat.		C	4	14	0	3	0	0	0	1	.214	28	0	1	.966
World Series Totals—2 Years				7	18	1	4	0	0	0	1	.222	35	1	1	.973

ALL-STAR GAME RECORD

Year	League	Pos.	AB.	R.	H.	2B.	3B.	HR.	RBI.	B.A.	PO.	A.	E.	F.A.
1989—National		C	1	0	0	0	0	0	0	.000	3	0	0	1.000
1990—National		C	2	0	0	0	0	0	0	.000	6	0	0	1.000
All-Star Game Totals—2 Years			3	0	0	0	0	0	0	.000	9	0	0	1.000

MICHAEL WARREN SCOTT
(Mike)

Born April 26, 1955, at Santa Monica, Calif.
Height, 6.03. Weight, 215.
Throws and bats righthanded.
Attended Pepperdine University, Malibu, Calif.

Shares major league record for most strikeouts, inning (4), September 3, 1986, fifth inning.
Pitched 2-0 no-hit victory against San Francisco Giants, September 25, 1986.
Major League saves: 1982 (3).
Tied for National League lead in games started by pitchers with 36 in 1987.
Tied for National League lead in shutouts with 5 in 1986.
Led Texas League in complete games with 14 and tied for lead in balks with 3 in 1977.

Tied for International League lead in games started by pitchers with 29 in 1978 and balks with 3 in 1980.
Named National League Pitcher of the Year by THE SPORTING NEWS, 1986.
Won National League Cy Young Memorial Award, 1986.
Named righthanded pitcher on THE SPORTING NEWS National League All-Star Team, 1986 and 1989.

Year	Club	League	G.	IP.	W.	L.	Pct.	H.	R.	ER.	SO.	BB.	ERA.
1976—Jackson	Texas	7	44	3	3	.500	34	20	14	19	14	2.86
1977—Jackson	Texas	25	*187	*14	10	.583	132	77	61	97	55	2.94
1977—Tidewater	Int'national	2	2	0	1	.000	4	5	4	0	3	18.00
1978—Tidewater	Int'national	29	192	10	10	.500	196	105	84	93	83	3.94
1979—Tidewater	Int'national	18	99	8	4	.667	103	37	35	40	27	3.18
1979—New York	National	18	52	1	3	.250	59	35	31	21	20	5.37
1980—Tidewater	Int'national	27	170	13	7	.650	165	69	56	88	64	2.96
1980—New York	National	6	29	1	1	.500	40	14	14	13	8	4.34
1981—New York	National	23	136	5	10	.333	130	65	59	54	34	3.90
1982—New York†	National	37	147	7	13	.350	185	100	84	63	60	5.14
1983—Houston‡	National	24	145	10	6	.625	143	67	60	73	46	3.72
1984—Houston	National	31	154	5	11	.313	179	96	80	83	43	4.68
1985—Houston	National	36	221⅔	18	8	.692	194	91	81	137	80	3.29
1986—Houston	National	37	*275⅓	18	10	.643	182	73	68	*306	72	*2.22
1987—Houston	National	36	247⅔	16	13	.552	199	94	89	233	79	3.23
1988—Houston§	National	32	218⅔	14	8	.636	162	74	71	190	53	2.92
1989—Houston	National	33	229	*20	10	.667	180	87	79	172	62	3.10
1990—Houston	National	32	205⅔	9	13	.409	194	102	87	121	66	3.81
Major League Totals—12 Years		345	2061	124	106	.539	1847	898	803	1466	623	3.51

Selected by New York Mets' organization in 2nd round of free-agent draft, June 8, 1976.
†Traded to Houston Astros for Outfielder-First Baseman Danny Heep, December 10, 1982.
‡On disabled list, April 5 to May 4, 1983.
§On disabled list, June 22 to July 13, 1988.

CHAMPIONSHIP SERIES RECORD

Holds Championship Series record for most consecutive scoreless innings, series (16), 1986.
Shares Championship Series records for most complete games, series (2), 1986; most strikeouts (4), and consecutive strikeouts (4), game, October 8, 1986.
Shares National League Championship Series records for most complete games, total series (2); most consecutive scoreless innings, total series (16).

Year	Club	League	G.	IP.	W.	L.	Pct.	H.	R.	ER.	SO.	BB.	ERA.
1986—Houston	National	2	18	2	0	1.000	8	1	1	19	1	0.50

ALL-STAR GAME RECORD

Year	League	IP.	W.	L.	Pct.	H.	R.	ER.	SO.	BB.	ERA.
1986—National		1	0	0	.000	1	1	1	2	0	9.00
1987—National		2	0	0	.000	1	0	0	1	0	0.00
All-Star Game Totals—2 Years		3	0	0	.000	2	1	1	3	0	3.00

Named to National League All-Star Team for 1989 game; replaced due to injury by Rick Sutcliffe.

WILLIAM SCOTT SCUDDER
(Known by middle name.)

Born February 14, 1968, at Paris, Tex.
Height, 6.02. Weight, 185.
Throws and bats righthanded.

Pitched 4-0 no-hit victory against Wausau, May 20, 1988.

Year	Club	League	G.	IP.	W.	L.	Pct.	H.	R.	ER.	SO.	BB.	ERA.
1986—Billings	Pioneer	12	52⅔	1	3	.250	43	34	28	38	36	4.78
1987—Cedar Rapids	Midwest	26	153⅔	7	12	.368	129	86	70	128	76	4.10
1988—Cedar Rapids	Midwest	16	102⅓	7	3	.700	61	30	23	126	41	2.02
1988—Chattanooga	Southern	11	70	7	0	1.000	53	24	23	52	30	2.96
1989—Nashville	Am. Assoc.	12	80⅔	6	2	.750	54	27	24	64	48	2.68
1989—Cincinnati	National	23	100⅓	4	9	.308	91	54	50	66	61	4.49
1990—Nashville	Am. Assoc.	11	80⅔	7	1	.875	53	27	21	60	32	2.34
1990—Cincinnati	National	21	71⅔	5	5	.500	74	41	39	42	30	4.90
Major League Totals—2 Years		44	172	9	14	.391	165	95	89	108	91	4.66

Selected by Cincinnati Reds' organization in 1st round (17th player selected) of free-agent draft, June 2, 1986.

CHAMPIONSHIP SERIES RECORD

Year	Club	League	G.	IP.	W.	L.	Pct.	H.	R.	ER.	SO.	BB.	ERA.
1990—Cincinnati	National	1	1	0	0	.000	1	0	0	1	0	0.00

WORLD SERIES RECORD

Year	Club	League	G.	IP.	W.	L.	Pct.	H.	R.	ER.	SO.	BB.	ERA.
1990—Cincinnati	National	1	1⅓	0	0	.000	0	0	0	2	2	0.00

RUDY CABALLERO SEANEZ
Born October 20, 1968, at Brawley, Calif.
Height, 5.10. Weight, 185.
Throws and bats righthanded.

Pitched 4-0 no-hit victory against Pulaski, August 2, 1986.

Year Club	League	G.	IP.	W.	L.	Pct.	H.	R.	ER.	SO.	BB.	ERA.
1986—Burlington	Ap'lachian	13	76	5	2	.714	59	37	27	56	32	3.20
1987—Waterloo†	Midwest	10	34⅔	0	4	.000	35	29	26	23	23	6.75
1988—Waterloo	Midwest	22	113⅓	6	6	.500	98	69	59	93	68	4.69
1989—Kinston	Carolina	25	113	8	10	.444	94	66	52	149	*111	4.14
1989—Colorado Springs	P. Coast	1	1	0	0	.000	1	0	0	0	0	0.00
1989—Cleveland	American	5	5	0	0	.000	1	2	2	7	4	3.60
1990—Canton-Akron	Eastern	15	16⅔	1	0	1.000	9	4	4	27	12	2.16
1990—Cleveland	American	24	27⅓	2	1	.667	22	17	17	24	25	5.60
1990—Colorado Springs	P. Coast	12	12	1	4	.200	15	10	9	7	10	6.75
Major League Totals—2 Years		29	32⅓	2	1	.667	23	19	19	31	29	5.29

Selected by Cleveland Indians' organization in 4th round of free-agent draft, June 10, 1986.

†On disabled list, May 4 to July 11 and August 9 to August 29, 1987.

RAYMOND MARK SEARAGE
(Ray)

Born May 1, 1955, at Freeport, N.Y.
Height, 6.01. Weight, 201.
Throws and bats lefthanded.
Attended West Liberty State College, West Liberty, W. Va.

Major League saves: 1981 (1), 1984 (6), 1985 (1), 1986 (1), 1987 (2). Total—11.
Led International League in wild pitches with 14 in 1982.

Year Club	League	G.	IP.	W.	L.	Pct.	H.	R.	ER.	SO.	BB.	ERA.
1976—Sara. W. Sox-Sara. Cards	Gulf Coast	11	32	1	3	.250	24	17	15	31	22	4.22
1977—St. Petersburg	Florida St.	13	19	0	0	.000	11	7	6	12	12	2.84
1977—Johnson City	Ap'lachian	8	41	3	2	.600	38	23	22	27	21	4.83
1978—Gastonia	W. Carol.	39	110	8	3	.727	86	40	34	86	68	2.78
1979—Arkansas†	Texas	42	89	10	4	.714	73	27	22	63	46	2.22
1980—Tidewater	Int'national	19	30	1	0	1.000	35	24	23	20	20	6.90
1980—Jackson	Texas	14	70	4	5	.444	54	32	26	71	26	3.34
1981—Tidewater	Int'national	18	27	2	0	1.000	29	10	7	23	13	2.33
1981—New York‡	National	26	37	1	0	1.000	34	16	15	16	17	3.65
1982—Charleston§	Int'national	38	114	2	7	.222	112	73	62	87	87	4.89
1983—Charleston x	Int'national	31	134	7	7	.500	146	94	84	77	76	5.64
1984—Vancouver	P. Coast	33	76⅓	6	3	.667	62	29	26	59	44	3.07
1984—Milwaukee	American	21	38⅓	2	1	.667	20	3	3	29	16	0.70
1985—Milwaukee	American	33	38	1	4	.200	54	27	25	36	24	5.92
1985—Vancouver	P. Coast	23	26	2	0	1.000	22	10	7	31	12	2.42
1986—Milwaukee yz-Chicago	American	46	51	1	1	.500	44	20	19	36	28	3.35
1986—Vancouver	P. Coast	20	25	2	0	1.000	12	5	4	20	8	1.44
1987—Chicago	American	58	55⅔	2	3	.400	56	28	26	33	24	4.20
1987—Hawaii a	P. Coast	3	7⅓	0	1	.000	6	5	3	5	3	3.68
1988—Albuquerque	P. Coast	51	60	2	3	.400	62	39	34	58	25	5.10
1989—Los Angeles b	National	41	35⅔	3	4	.429	29	15	14	24	18	3.53
1989—Albuquerque	P. Coast	2	8	0	1	.000	8	3	2	7	2	2.25
1990—Los Angeles c	National	29	33⅓	1	0	1.000	30	11	10	19	10	2.78
1990—Bakersfield d	California	10	14	1	2	.333	8	5	5	17	8	3.21
National League Totals—3 Years		96	105	5	4	.556	93	42	39	59	45	3.34
American League Totals—4 Years		158	183	6	9	.400	174	78	73	134	92	3.59
Major League Totals—7 Years		254	288	11	13	.458	267	120	112	193	137	3.50

Selected by St. Louis Cardinals' organization in 22nd round of free-agent draft, June 8, 1976.

†Traded to New York Mets' organization for Catcher Jody Davis, December 10, 1979.

‡Traded to Cleveland Indians for Shortstop Tom Veryzer, January 8, 1982.

§Traded on a conditional basis to San Diego Padres for a player to be named later, December 15, 1982; returned, March 28, 1983.

xGranted free agency, October 20, 1983; signed by Vancouver (Milwaukee Brewers' organization), November 4, 1983.

yLoaned to Buffalo (Chicago White Sox' organization), July 17, 1986; returned, July 23, 1986.

zTraded to Chicago White Sox for Pitcher Al Jones and Outfielder Tom Hartley, July 23, 1986.

aReleased, March 25, 1988; signed by Albuquerque (Los Angeles Dodgers' organization), April 5, 1988.

bOn disabled list, May 31 to July 8, 1989; included rehabilitation disability assignment to Albuquerque, June 29 to July 8, 1989.

cOn disabled list, May 11 to July 2 and August 15 to September 11, 1990; included rehabilitation disability assignment to Bakersfield, June 8 to June 10, 1990.

dReleased, December 15, 1990.

WILLIAM STEPHEN SEARCY
(Steve)

Born June 4, 1964, at Knoxville, Tenn.
Height, 6.01. Weight, 195.
Throws and bats lefthanded.
Attended University of Tennessee, Knoxville, Tenn.

Led International League in hit batsmen with 12 in 1988.
Tied for Eastern League lead in games started by pitchers with 27 in 1986.
Named International League Pitcher of the Year, 1988.

Year Club	League	G.	IP.	W.	L.	Pct.	H.	R.	ER.	SO.	BB.	ERA.
1985—Bristol	Ap'lachian	4	22	1	1	.500	15	6	5	24	2	2.05
1985—Birmingham	Southern	7	36⅔	2	2	.500	39	17	13	19	23	3.19
1986—Glens Falls	Eastern	27	172	11	6	.647	166	79	63	*139	74	3.30
1987—Toledo	Int'national	10	53⅓	3	4	.429	49	26	25	54	32	4.22
1988—Toledo	Int'national	27	170	●13	7	.650	131	61	49	*176	79	2.59
1988—Detroit	American	2	8	0	2	.000	8	6	5	5	4	5.63
1989—Toledo†	Int'national	9	37	2	3	.400	41	36	31	26	37	7.54
1989—Lakeland	Florida St.	9	52⅔	2	3	.400	40	21	15	44	33	2.56
1989—Detroit	American	8	22⅓	1	1	.500	27	16	15	11	12	6.04
1990—Toledo	Int'national	17	104⅔	10	5	.667	71	40	34	105	52	2.92
1990—Detroit	American	16	75⅓	2	7	.222	76	44	39	66	51	4.66
Major League Totals—3 Years		26	105⅔	3	10	.231	111	66	59	82	67	5.03

Selected by Detroit Tigers' organization in 3rd round of free-agent draft, June 3, 1985.
†On Detroit disabled list, March 27 to May 5, 1989.

ROBERT BUSH SEBRA

Name pronounced SEBB-ruh.

(Bob)

Born December 11, 1961, at Ridgewood, N.J.
Height, 6.02. Weight, 195.
Throws and bats righthanded.
Attended University of Nebraska, Lincoln, Neb.

Major League saves: 1989 (1).
Tied for American Association lead in home runs allowed with 17 in 1985.
Named American Association Pitcher of the Year, 1988.

Year Club	League	G.	IP.	W.	L.	Pct.	H.	R.	ER.	SO.	BB.	ERA.
1983—Tri-Cities	Northwest	12	58⅓	4	3	.571	48	36	26	70	29	4.01
1984—Tulsa	Texas	17	100⅓	10	5	.667	86	45	38	90	41	3.41
1984—Oklahoma City	Am. Assoc.	9	53⅓	4	4	.500	37	23	20	38	25	3.38
1985—Oklahoma City	Am. Assoc.	22	138⅔	10	6	.625	121	62	59	84	57	3.83
1985—Texas†	American	7	20⅓	0	2	.000	26	17	17	13	14	7.52
1986—Indianapolis	Am. Assoc.	20	126	9	2	.818	108	59	48	91	70	3.43
1986—Montreal	National	17	91⅓	5	5	.500	82	39	36	66	25	3.55
1987—Montreal	National	36	177⅓	6	15	.286	184	99	87	156	67	4.42
1988—Indianapolis‡	Am. Assoc.	29	174⅓	12	6	.667	154	71	57	126	59	2.94
1988—Philadelphia	National	3	11⅓	1	2	.333	15	11	10	7	10	7.94
1989—Scranton/Wilkes-Barre	Int'national	11	64⅔	3	4	.429	61	36	34	56	21	4.73
1989—Philadelphia§-Cincinnati	National	21	55⅓	2	3	.400	65	36	32	35	28	5.20
1989—Nashville	Am. Assoc.	11	18	0	0	.000	15	6	5	15	10	2.50
1990—Nashville x-Denver	Am. Assoc.	44	63⅓	4	3	.571	61	26	23	69	24	3.27
1990—Milwaukee yz	American	10	11	1	2	.333	20	10	10	4	5	8.18
American League Totals—2 Years		17	31⅓	1	4	.200	46	27	27	17	19	7.76
National League Totals—4 Years		77	335⅓	14	25	.359	346	185	165	264	130	4.43
Major League Totals—6 Years		94	366⅔	15	29	.341	392	212	192	281	149	4.71

Selected by Detroit Tigers' organization in 4th round of free-agent draft, June 3, 1980.
Selected by Texas Rangers' organization in 5th round of free-agent draft, June 6, 1983.
†Traded with Infielder Jim Anderson to Montreal Expos for Outfielder Pete Incaviglia, November 2, 1985.
‡Traded to Philadelphia Phillies for Pitcher Travis Chambers, September 1, 1988.
§Traded to Cincinnati Reds for a player to be named later, July 13, 1989; Philadelphia Phillies' organization acquired Pitcher Jeff Gray to complete deal, September 6, 1989.
xTraded with Pitcher Ron Robinson to Milwaukee Brewers for Outfielder Glenn Braggs and Infielder Billy Bates, June 9, 1990.
yOn suspended list, September 25 to September 29, 1990.
zReleased, October 1, 1990.

DAVID VINCENT SEGUI

Born July 19, 1966, at Kansas City, Kan.
Height, 6.01. Weight, 195.
Throws left and bats left and righthanded.
Attended Kansas City Community College, Kansas City, Kan.,
and Louisiana Tech University, Ruston, La.
Son of Diego Segui, pitcher with Kansas City/Oakland Athletics, Washington Senators,
Seattle Pilots, St. Louis Cardinals, Boston Red Sox and Seattle Mariners,
1962 through 1975 and 1977; pitcher in Mexican League, 1978 through 1985;
and minor league coach in San Francisco Giants' organization since 1986;
and brother of Dan Segui, infielder in New York Mets' organization.

Year Club	League	Pos.	G.	AB.	R.	H.	2B.	3B.	HR.	RBI.	B.A.	PO.	A.	E.	F.A.
1988—Hagerstown	Carol.	1B-OF	60	190	35	51	12	4	3	31	.268	342	25	9	.976
1989—Frederick	Carol.	1B	83	284	43	90	19	0	10	50	.317	707	47	4	.995
1989—Hagerstown	East.	1B	44	173	22	56	14	1	1	27	.324	381	30	1	.998
1990—Rochester	Int.	1B-OF	86	307	55	103	28	0	2	51	.336	704	62	3	.996
1990—Baltimore	Amer.	1B	40	123	14	30	7	0	2	15	.244	283	26	3	.990
Major League Totals—1 Year			40	123	14	30	7	0	2	15	.244	283	26	3	.990

Selected by Baltimore Orioles' organization in 18th round of free-agent draft, June 2, 1987.

KEVIN LEE SEITZER

Born March 26, 1962, at Springfield, Ill.
Height, 5.11. Weight, 180.
Throws and bats righthanded.
Received bachelor of science degree in industrial electronics from
Eastern Illinois University, Charleston, Ill.

Major League stolen bases: 1987 (12), 1988 (10), 1989 (17), 1990 (7). Total—46.
Collected six hits in one game, August 2, 1987.
Led American League third basemen in errors with 22 in 1987.
Led South Atlantic League in bases on balls received with 118 in 1984.
Tied for American Association lead in being hit by pitch with 9 in 1986.
Led South Atlantic League third basemen in total chances with 409 in 1984.
Led Pioneer League third basemen in assists with 122 and total chances with 172 in 1983.
Named South Atlantic League Most Valuable Player, 1984.

Year	Club	League	Pos.	G.	AB.	R.	H.	2B.	3B.	HR.	RBI.	B.A.	PO.	A.	E.	F.A.
1983—Butte	Pion.		3B-SS	68	238	60	82	14	1	2	45	.345	52	124	21	.893
1984—Charleston	S. Atl.		3B	●141	489	★96	★145	26	5	8	79	.297	80	★279	★50	.878
1985—Fort Myers	Fla. St.		1B-3B	90	290	61	91	10	5	3	46	.314	569	88	9	.986
1985—Memphis	South.		3B-1B-OF	52	187	26	65	6	2	1	20	.348	79	51	10	.929
1986—Memphis	South.		1B	4	11	4	3	0	0	0	1	.273	28	3	1	.969
1986—Omaha	A. A.		OF-1B-3B	129	432	86	138	20	11	13	74	.319	338	39	9	.977
1986—Kansas City	Amer.		1B-OF-3B	28	96	16	31	4	1	2	11	.323	224	19	3	.988
1987—Kansas City	Amer.		3B-1B-OF	161	641	105	●207	33	8	15	83	.323	290	315	24	.962
1988—Kansas City	Amer.		★3B-OF	149	559	90	170	32	5	5	60	.304	93	297	★26	.938
1989—Kansas City	Amer.		3-S-O-1	160	597	78	168	17	2	4	48	.281	118	277	20	.952
1990—Kansas City	Amer.		3B-2B	158	622	91	171	31	5	6	38	.275	118	281	19	.955
Major League Totals—5 Years				656	2515	380	747	117	21	32	240	.297	843	1189	92	.957

Selected by Kansas City Royals' organization in 11th round of free-agent draft, June 6, 1983.

ALL-STAR GAME RECORD

Year	League	Pos.	AB.	R.	H.	2B.	3B.	HR.	RBI.	B.A.	PO.	A.	E.	F.A.
1987—American		3B	2	0	0	0	0	0	0	.000	0	0	0	.000

MICHAEL TYRONE SHARPERSON
(Mike)

Born October 4, 1961, at Orangeburg, S.C.
Height, 6.03. Weight, 191.
Throws and bats righthanded.
Attended DeKalb Community College South, Decatur, Ga.

Major League stolen bases: 1987 (2), 1990 (15). Total—17.
Led International League second basemen in putouts with 286 and total chances with 666 in 1985.
Led Southern League second basemen in total chances with 775 and double plays with 103 in 1984.
Tied for International League lead in double plays by third basemen with 16 in 1987.

Year	Club	League	Pos.	G.	AB.	R.	H.	2B.	3B.	HR.	RBI.	B.A.	PO.	A.	E.	F.A.
1982—Florence	S. Atl.		SS-3B	111	326	51	83	16	1	3	33	.255	136	261	33	.923
1983—Kinston†	Carol.		S-3-2-C	90	361	55	96	8	1	5	41	.266	148	286	19	.958
1984—Knoxville	South.		2B	140	542	86	165	25	7	4	48	.304	★331	★423	21	.973
1985—Syracuse	Int.		2B-SS	134	★536	★86	★155	19	★7	1	59	.289	291	372	17	.975
1986—Syracuse	Int.		2B-3B	133	519	★86	★150	18	★9	4	45	.289	258	376	18	.972
1987—Toronto	Amer.		2B	32	96	4	20	4	1	0	9	.208	64	69	4	.971
1987—Syracuse‡	Int.		3B-2B	88	338	67	101	21	5	5	26	.299	81	152	8	.967
1987—Albuquerque	Nat.		3B-2B	10	33	7	9	2	0	0	1	.273	4	28	1	.970
1988—Albuquerque	P. C.		2B-3B-SS	56	210	55	67	10	2	0	30	.319	88	173	12	.956
1988—Los Angeles	Nat.		2B-3B-SS	46	59	8	16	1	0	0	4	.271	19	31	2	.962
1989—Albuquerque	P. C.		2B-3B-SS	98	359	81	111	15	7	3	48	.309	114	250	14	.963
1989—Los Angeles	Nat.		2-1-3-S	27	28	2	7	3	0	0	5	.250	11	8	0	1.000
1990—Los Angeles	Nat.		3-S-2-1	129	357	42	106	14	2	3	36	.297	152	193	15	.958
American League Totals—1 Year				32	96	4	20	4	1	0	9	.208	64	69	4	.971
National League Totals—4 Years				212	477	59	138	20	2	3	46	.289	186	260	18	.961
Major League Totals—4 Years				244	573	63	158	24	3	3	55	.276	250	329	22	.963

Selected by Pittsburgh Pirates' organization in 41st round of free-agent draft, June 5, 1979.
Selected by Montreal Expos' organization in secondary phase of free-agent draft, January 8, 1980.
Selected by Detroit Tigers' organization in 4th round of free-agent draft, January 13, 1981.
Selected by Toronto Blue Jays' organization in secondary phase of free-agent draft, June 8, 1981.
†On disabled list, August 14, 1983 through remainder of season.
‡Traded to Los Angeles Dodgers for Pitcher Juan Guzman, September 22, 1987.

CHAMPIONSHIP SERIES RECORD

Year	Club	League	Pos.	G.	AB.	R.	H.	2B.	3B.	HR.	RBI.	B.A.	PO.	A.	E.	F.A.
1988—Los Angeles	Nat.		PH-S-3	2	1	0	0	0	0	0	1	.000	1	0	0	1.000

—DID YOU KNOW—

That Pittsburgh starters Doug Drabek, Bob Walk and John Smiley were a combined 22-3 against the National League West in 1990?

JEFFREY LEE SHAW
(Jeff)

Born July 7, 1966, at Washington Court House, O.
Height, 6.02. Weight, 185.
Throws and bats righthanded.
Attended Cuyahoga Community College-Western Campus, Parma, O.

Led Eastern League in hit batsmen with 14 in 1989.
Led Midwest League pitchers in games started with 28 and shutouts with 4 in 1987.
Tied for Eastern League lead in games started by pitchers with 27 in 1988.

Year Club	League	G.	IP.	W.	L.	Pct.	H.	R.	ER.	SO.	BB.	ERA.
1986—Batavia	NYP	14	88⅔	8	4	.667	79	32	24	71	35	2.44
1987—Waterloo	Midwest	28	184⅓	11	11	.500	192	89	72	117	56	3.52
1988—Williamsport	Eastern	27	163⅔	5	*19	.208	●173	*94	66	61	75	3.63
1989—Canton-Akron	Eastern	30	154⅓	7	10	.412	134	84	62	95	67	3.62
1990—Colorado Springs	P. Coast	17	98⅔	10	3	.769	98	54	47	55	52	4.29
1990—Cleveland	American	12	48⅔	3	4	.429	73	38	36	25	20	6.66
Major League Totals—1 Year		12	48⅔	3	4	.429	73	38	36	25	20	6.66

Selected by Cleveland Indians' organization in 1st round (first player selected) of free-agent draft, January 14, 1986.

LARRY KENT SHEETS

Born December 6, 1959, at Staunton, Va.
Height, 6.03. Weight, 236.
Throws right and bats lefthanded.
Received degree in health and physical education from
Eastern Mennonite College, Harrisonburg, Va. in 1986.

Major League stolen bases: 1986 (2), 1987 (1), 1988 (1), 1989 (1), 1990 (1). Total—6.
Led International League outfielders in double plays with 5 in 1984.

Year Club	League	Pos.	G.	AB.	R.	H.	2B.	3B.	HR.	RBI.	B.A.	PO.	A.	E.	F.A.
1978—Bluefield	Appal.	OF-1B	67	225	32	60	9	2	11	*48	.267	121	8	4	.970
1979—Miami†	Fla. St.						(Did not play)								
1979—Bluefield	Appal.	OF	3	12	2	4	2	0	0	2	.333	1	0	0	1.000
1980—Bluefield‡	Appal.	OF	37	124	29	47	9	1	*14	47	.379	40	3	2	.956
1980—Charlotte	South.	OF	13	48	1	9	4	0	0	5	.188	4	1	0	1.000
1981—Rochester§	Int.						(Did not play)								
1982—Rochester x	Int.						(Did not play)								
1982—Hagerstown y	Carol.	OF	88	324	46	96	21	0	18	59	.296	123	5	6	.955
1983—Charlotte	South.	OF-1B	138	503	72	145	*37	3	●25	87	.288	256	15	7	.975
1983—Rochester	Int.	OF	3	13	1	2	1	0	0	2	.154	5	0	1	.833
1984—Rochester	Int.	OF	134	431	76	130	26	4	13	67	.302	201	*19	2	.991
1984—Baltimore	Amer.	OF	8	16	3	7	1	0	1	2	.438	12	1	0	1.000
1985—Baltimore	Amer.	OF-1B	113	328	43	86	8	0	17	50	.262	12	1	1	.929
1986—Baltimore z	Amer.	O-1-3-C	112	338	42	92	17	1	18	60	.272	90	8	3	.970
1987—Baltimore	Amer.	OF-1B	135	469	74	148	23	0	31	94	.316	243	7	7	.973
1988—Baltimore	Amer.	OF-1B	136	452	38	104	19	1	10	47	.230	159	12	4	.977
1989—Baltimore a	Amer.	DH	102	304	33	74	12	1	7	33	.243	0	0	0	.000
1990—Detroit b	Amer.	OF	131	360	40	94	17	2	10	52	.261	98	7	2	.981
Major League Totals—7 Years			737	2267	273	605	97	5	94	338	.267	614	36	17	.975

Selected by Baltimore Orioles' organization in 2nd round of free-agent draft, June 6, 1978.
†On suspended list, May 1 to August 29, 1979.
‡On restricted list, June 18 to June 23, 1980.
§On restricted list, April 14 to May 28 and June 18, 1981 through remainder of season.
xOn suspended list, April 13, 1982; then transferred to restricted list, April 23 to May 13, 1982.
yOn disabled list, August 23, 1982 through remainder of season.
zOn disabled list, June 30 to July 17, 1986.
aTraded to Detroit Tigers for Infielder Mike Brumley, January 10, 1990.
bGranted free agency, November 5, 1990.

GARY ANTONIAN SHEFFIELD

Born November 18, 1968, at Tampa, Fla.
Height, 5.11. Weight, 190.
Throws and bats righthanded.
Nephew of Dwight Gooden, pitcher with New York Mets.

Major League stolen bases: 1988 (3), 1989 (10), 1990 (25). Total—38.
Led California League shortstops in double plays with 77 in 1987.
Led Pioneer League shortstops in double plays with 34 in 1986.
Named Minor League co-Player of the Year by THE SPORTING NEWS, 1988.

Year Club	League	Pos.	G.	AB.	R.	H.	2B.	3B.	HR.	RBI.	B.A.	PO.	A.	E.	F.A.
1986—Helena	Pion.	SS	57	222	53	81	12	2	15	*71	.365	97	149	24	.911
1987—Stockton	Calif.	SS	129	469	84	130	23	3	17	*103	.277	235	345	39	.937
1988—El Paso	Texas	SS-3B-OF	77	296	70	93	19	3	19	65	.314	130	206	23	.936
1988—Denver	A. A.	3B-SS	57	212	42	73	9	5	9	54	.344	54	97	8	.950
1988—Milwaukee	Amer.	SS	24	80	12	19	1	0	4	12	.238	39	48	3	.967
1989—Milwaukee†	Amer.	SS-3B	95	368	34	91	18	0	5	32	.247	100	238	16	.955
1989—Denver	A. A.	SS	7	29	3	4	1	1	0	0	.138	2	6	0	1.000
1990—Milwaukee‡	Amer.	3B	125	487	67	143	30	1	10	67	.294	98	254	25	.934
Major League Totals—3 Years			244	935	113	253	49	1	19	111	.271	237	540	44	.946

Selected by Milwaukee Brewers' organization in 1st round (sixth player selected) of free-agent draft, June 2, 1986.
†On disabled list, July 14 to September 9, 1989.
‡On suspended list, August 31 to September 3, 1990.

JOHN T. SHELBY

Born February 23, 1958, at Lexington, Ky.
Height, 6.01. Weight, 175.
Throws right and bats right and lefthanded.
Attended Columbia State Community College, Columbia, Tenn.

Holds National League record for most strikeouts by switch-hitter, season (128), 1988.
Major League stolen bases: 1981 (2), 1983 (15), 1984 (12), 1985 (5), 1986 (18), 1987 (16), 1988 (16), 1989 (10), 1990 (4). Total—98.
Led Florida State League outfielders in double plays with 7 in 1979.
Led Appalachian League outfielders in double plays with 3 in 1978.

Year Club	League	Pos.	G.	AB.	R.	H.	2B.	3B.	HR.	RBI.	B.A.	PO.	A.	E.	F.A.
1977—Bluefield	Appal.	OF	60	211	28	54	9	1	0	1	.256	90	•12	7	.936
1978—Miami	Fla. St.	OF	13	26	4	6	1	0	0	3	.231	14	2	2	.889
1978—Bluefield	Appal.	OF	64	248	49	70	9	1	6	25	.282	128	*11	6	.959
1979—Miami	Fla. St.	OF	132	478	50	96	11	6	3	38	.201	*252	•22	8	.972
1980—Charlotte	South.	OF	134	*560	66	135	27	11	6	51	.241	*361	*21	*16	.960
1981—Charlotte	South.	OF	62	251	40	59	11	4	2	21	.235	120	3	10	.925
1981—Rochester	Int.	OF	76	326	42	86	21	8	3	32	.264	189	8	6	.970
1981—Baltimore	Amer.	OF	7	2	2	0	0	0	0	0	.000	1	0	0	1.000
1982—Rochester	Int.	OF	133	*548	92	153	26	6	16	52	.279	331	13	8	.977
1982—Baltimore	Amer.	OF	26	35	8	11	3	0	1	2	.314	20	1	0	1.000
1983—Baltimore	Amer.	OF	126	325	52	84	15	2	5	27	.258	200	9	4	.981
1984—Baltimore	Amer.	OF	128	383	44	80	12	5	6	30	.209	261	9	2	.993
1985—Rochester	Int.	OF	52	206	31	59	16	4	8	21	.286	124	4	1	.992
1985—Baltimore	Amer.	OF-2B	69	205	28	58	6	2	7	27	.283	148	4	3	.981
1986—Baltimore	Amer	OF	135	404	54	92	14	4	11	49	.228	222	5	5	.978
1987—Baltimore	Amer.	OF	21	32	4	6	0	0	1	3	.188	25	0	0	1.000
1987—Rochester†	Int.	OF	6	24	5	6	2	0	1	2	.250	14	0	0	1.000
1987—Los Angeles	Nat.	OF	120	476	61	132	26	0	21	69	.277	269	9	8	.972
1988—Los Angeles‡	Nat.	OF	140	494	65	130	23	6	10	64	.263	329	7	6	.982
1989—Los Angeles	Nat.	OF	108	345	28	63	11	1	1	12	.183	220	3	2	.991
1989—Albuquerque§	P. C.	OF	32	126	20	36	7	3	4	21	.286	75	2	1	.987
1990—Los Angeles x	Nat.	OF	25	24	2	6	1	0	0	2	.250	8	0	0	1.000
1990—Toledo	Int.	OF	5	19	2	6	1	0	0	1	.316	17	0	0	1.000
1990—Detroit y	Amer.	OF	78	222	22	55	9	3	4	20	.248	138	5	4	.973
American League Totals—8 Years			590	1608	214	386	59	16	35	158	.240	1015	33	18	.983
National League Totals—4 Years			393	1339	156	331	61	7	32	147	.247	826	19	16	.981
Major League Totals—10 Years			983	2947	370	717	120	23	67	305	.243	1841	52	34	.982

Selected by Baltimore Orioles' organization in 1st round (19th player selected) of free-agent draft, January 11, 1977.
†Traded with Pitcher Brad Havens to Los Angeles Dodgers for Pitcher Tom Niedenfuer, May 22, 1987.
‡On disabled list, April 22 to May 12, 1988.
§Granted free agency, November 13, 1989; re-signed by Dodgers, December 19, 1989.
xReleased, June 2, 1990; signed by Toledo (Detroit Tigers' organization), June 13, 1990.
yGranted free agency, November 5, 1990; re-signed by Tigers, November 26, 1990.

CHAMPIONSHIP SERIES RECORD

Shares Championship Series record for most strikeouts, series (12), 1988.

Year Club	League	Pos.	G.	AB.	R.	H.	2B.	3B.	HR.	RBI.	B.A.	PO.	A.	E.	F.A.
1983—Baltimore	Amer.	OF-PH	3	9	1	2	0	0	0	0	.222	3	0	0	1.000
1988—Los Angeles	Nat.	OF	7	24	3	4	0	0	0	3	.167	19	0	0	1.000
Championship Series Totals—2 Years			10	33	4	6	0	0	0	3	.182	22	0	0	1.000

WORLD SERIES RECORD

Year Club	League	Pos.	G.	AB.	R.	H.	2B.	3B.	HR.	RBI.	B.A.	PO.	A.	E.	F.A.
1983—Baltimore	Amer.	PH-OF	5	9	1	4	0	0	0	1	.444	10	0	0	1.000
1988—Los Angeles	Nat.	OF	5	18	0	4	1	0	0	1	.222	14	0	0	1.000
World Series Totals—2 Years			10	27	1	8	1	0	0	2	.296	24	0	0	1.000

TIMOTHY SHAWN SHERRILL
(Tim)

Born September 10, 1965, at Harrison, Ark.
Height, 5.11. Weight, 170.
Throws and bats lefthanded.
Attended North Arkansas Community College, Harrison,
Ark., and University of Arkansas, Fayetteville, Ark.

Tied for Appalachian League lead in saves with 8 in 1987.

Year Club	League	G.	IP.	W.	L.	Pct.	H.	R.	ER.	SO.	BB.	ERA.
1987—Johnson City	Ap'lachian	25	42	3	4	.429	25	18	14	62	18	3.00
1988—Savannah	S. Atlantic	31	45⅓	3	2	.600	26	12	9	62	13	1.79
1988—St. Petersburg	Florida St.	16	23⅓	2	0	1.000	14	4	4	25	8	1.54
1989—St. Petersburg	Florida St.	52	68	4	0	1.000	52	19	16	48	23	2.12
1989—Savannah	S. Atlantic	3	3⅔	0	0	.000	3	0	0	6	2	0.00

Year Club	League	G.	IP.	W.	L.	Pct.	H.	R.	ER.	SO.	BB.	ERA.
1990—Louisville	Am. Assoc.	52	61⅓	4	3	.571	49	17	17	57	21	2.49
1990—St. Louis..	National	8	4⅓	0	0	.000	10	5	3	3	3	6.23
Major League Totals—1 Year...............................		8	4⅓	0	0	.000	10	5	3	3	3	6.23

Selected by St. Louis Cardinals' organization in 18th round of free-agent draft, June 2, 1987.

ERIC VAUGHN SHOW
Name rhymes with Chow.

Born May 19, 1956, at Riverside, Calif.
Height, 6.01. Weight, 182.
Throws and bats righthanded.
Attended University of California, Riverside, Calif.

Major League saves: 1981 (3), 1982 (3), 1990 (1). Total—7.
Led Texas League in hit batsmen with 10 in 1980.

Year Club	League	G.	IP.	W.	L.	Pct.	H.	R.	ER.	SO.	BB.	ERA.
1978—Walla Walla	Northwest	11	60	5	2	.714	47	28	19	43	20	2.85
1979—Reno	California	28	169	13	9	.591	144	79	67	186	92	3.57
1980—Amarillo.............................	Texas	26	166	12	6	.667	141	81	69	144	81	3.74
1981—Hawaii	P. Coast	34	85	7	3	.700	67	30	24	70	35	2.54
1981—San Diego	National	15	23	1	3	.250	17	9	8	22	9	3.13
1982—San Diego	National	47	150	10	6	.625	117	49	44	88	48	2.64
1983—San Diego	National	35	200⅔	15	12	.556	201	97	93	120	74	4.17
1984—San Diego	National	32	206⅔	15	9	.625	175	88	78	104	88	3.40
1985—San Diego	National	35	233	12	11	.522	212	95	80	141	87	3.09
1986—San Diego†	National	24	136⅓	9	5	.643	109	47	45	94	69	2.97
1987—San Diego	National	34	206⅓	8	16	.333	188	99	88	117	85	3.84
1988—San Diego	National	32	234⅔	16	11	.593	201	86	85	144	53	3.26
1989—San Diego‡	National	16	106⅓	8	6	.571	113	59	50	66	39	4.23
1990—San Diego§	National	39	106⅓	6	8	.429	131	74	68	55	41	5.76
Major League Totals—10 Years..........		309	1603⅓	100	87	.535	1464	703	639	951	593	3.59

Selected by Minnesota Twins' organization in 36th round of free-agent draft, June 5, 1974.
Selected by San Diego Padres' organization in 18th round of free-agent draft, June 6, 1978.
†On disabled list, July 8 to July 31 and August 28, 1986 through remainder of season.
‡On disabled list, July 6, 1989 through remainder of season.
§Granted free agency, November 5, 1990; signed by Oakland Athletics, December 10, 1990.

CHAMPIONSHIP SERIES RECORD

Year Club	League	G.	IP.	W.	L.	Pct.	H.	R.	ER.	SO.	BB.	ERA.
1984—San Diego	National	2	5⅓	0	1	.000	8	8	8	2	4	13.50

WORLD SERIES RECORD

Year Club	League	G.	IP.	W.	L.	Pct.	H.	R.	ER.	SO.	BB.	ERA.
1984—San Diego	National	1	2⅔	0	1	.000	4	4	3	2	1	10.13

TERRANCE DARNELL SHUMPERT
(Terry)

Born August 16, 1966, at Paducah, Ky.
Height, 5.11. Weight, 190.
Throws and bats righthanded.
Attended University of Kentucky, Lexington, Ky.

Major League stolen bases: 1990 (3).

Year Club	League	Pos.	G.	AB.	R.	H.	2B.	3B.	HR.	RBI.	B.A.	PO.	A.	E.	F.A.
1987—Eugene...................	N'west	2B	48	186	38	54	16	1	4	22	.290	81	107	11	.945
1988—Appleton...............	Midw.	2B-OF	114	422	64	102	★37	2	7	38	.242	235	266	20	.962
1989—Omaha...................	A. A.	2B	113	355	54	88	29	2	4	22	.248	218	295	★22	.959
1990—Omaha...................	A. A.	2B	39	153	24	39	6	4	2	12	.255	72	95	7	.960
1990—Kansas City†.........	Amer.	2B	32	91	7	25	6	1	0	8	.275	56	74	3	.977
Major League Totals—1 Year.................			32	91	7	25	6	1	0	8	.275	56	74	3	.977

Selected by Kansas City Royals' organization in 2nd round of free-agent draft, June 2, 1987.
†On disabled list, June 3 to September 10, 1990; included rehabilitation disability assignment to Omaha, August 7 to August 25, 1990.

RUBEN ANGEL SIERRA (GARCIA)

Born October 6, 1965, at Rio Piedras, Puerto Rico.
Height, 6.01. Weight, 200.
Throws right and bats left and righthanded.

Major League stolen bases: 1986 (7), 1987 (16), 1988 (18), 1989 (8), 1990 (9). Total—58.
Switch-hit home runs in one game, September 13, 1986, August 27, 1988 and June 8, 1989.
Led American League in total bases with 344 and slugging percentage with .543 in 1989.
Led American League in sacrifice flies with 12 in 1987.
Led American League outfielders in double plays with 6 in 1987.
Named American League Player of the Year by THE SPORTING NEWS, 1989.
Named outfielder on THE SPORTING NEWS American League All-Star Team, 1989.
Named outfielder on THE SPORTING NEWS American League Silver Slugger team, 1989.

Year Club League	Pos.	G.	AB.	R.	H.	2B.	3B.	HR.	RBI.	B.A.	PO.	A.	E.	F.A.
1983—Sarasota Rang.†... Gulf C.	OF	48	182	26	44	7	3	1	26	.242	67	6	4	.948
1984—Burlington .... Midw.	OF	●138	482	55	127	33	5	6	75	.263	239	18	★20	.928
1985—Tulsa .... Texas	OF	★137	★545	63	138	34	★8	13	74	.253	234	12	★15	.943
1986—Oklahoma City ..... A. A.	OF	46	189	31	56	11	2	9	41	.296	114	4	2	.983
1986—Texas .... Amer.	OF	113	382	50	101	13	10	16	55	.264	200	7	6	.972
1987—Texas .... Amer.	OF	158	★643	97	169	35	4	30	109	.263	272	●17	11	.963
1988—Texas .... Amer.	OF	156	615	77	156	32	2	23	91	.254	310	11	7	.979
1989—Texas .... Amer.	OF	●162	634	101	194	35	★14	29	★119	.306	313	13	9	.973
1990—Texas .... Amer.	OF	159	608	70	170	37	2	16	96	.280	283	7	10	.967
Major League Totals—5 Years................		748	2882	395	790	152	32	114	470	.274	1378	55	43	.971

Signed as free agent by Texas Rangers' organization, November 21, 1982.
†Batted righthanded only.

ALL-STAR GAME RECORD

Year League	Pos.	AB.	R.	H.	2B.	3B.	HR.	RBI.	B.A.	PO.	A.	E.	F.A.
1989—American	OF	3	1	2	0	0	0	1	.667	1	0	0	1.000

MICHAEL HOWARD SIMMS
(Mike)

Born January 12, 1967, at Orange, Calif.
Height, 6.04. Weight, 185.
Throws and bats righthanded.
Led Pacific Coast League batters in strikeouts with 135 in 1990.
Led South Atlantic League batters in total bases with 264 and strikeouts with 167 in 1987.
Led South Atlantic League first basemen in total chances with 1,158 in 1987.

Year Club League	Pos.	G.	AB.	R.	H.	2B.	3B.	HR.	RBI.	B.A.	PO.	A.	E.	F.A.
1985—Sarasota Astros.... Gulf C.	1B	21	70	10	19	2	1	3	18	.271	186	7	5	.975
1986—Sarasota Astros.... Gulf C.	1B	54	181	33	47	14	1	4	37	.260	433	28	7	.985
1987—Asheville................ S. Atl.	★1B-3B	133	469	93	128	19	0	★39	100	.273	★1089	52	★19	.984
1988—Osceola................. Fla. St.	1B	123	428	63	104	19	1	16	73	.243	1143	41	22	.982
1989—Columbus.............. South.	1B	109	378	64	97	21	3	20	81	.257	938	44	10	.990
1990—Tucson.................. P. C.	★1-3-O	124	421	75	115	34	5	13	72	.273	1013	75	★19	.983
1990—Houston .... Nat.	1B	12	13	3	4	1	0	1	2	.308	20	1	0	1.000
Major League Totals—1 Year..................		12	13	3	4	1	0	1	2	.308	20	1	0	1.000

Selected by Houston Astros' organization in 6th round of free-agent draft, June 3, 1985.

DOUGLAS EUGENE SIMONS
(Doug)

Born September 15, 1966, at Bakersfield, Calif.
Height, 6.00. Weight, 160.
Throws and bats lefthanded.
Attended Oxnard College, Calif.; and
Pepperdine University, Malibu, Calif.

Year Club	League	G.	IP.	W.	L.	Pct.	H.	R.	ER.	SO.	BB.	ERA.
1988—Visalia .... California	17	107⅓	6	5	.545	100	59	47	123	46	3.94
1989—Visalia .... California	14	90⅔	6	2	.750	77	33	15	79	33	1.49
1989—Orlando .... Southern	14	87⅓	7	3	.700	83	39	37	58	37	3.81
1990—Orlando† .... Southern	29	188	★15	12	.556	160	76	53	109	43	2.54

Selected by Los Angeles Dodgers' organization in 45th round of free-agent draft, June 2, 1987.
Selected by Minnesota Twins' organization in 9th round of free-agent draft, June 1, 1988.
†Drafted by New York Mets, December 3, 1990.

MATTHEW STEPHEN SINATRO
(Matt)

Born March 22, 1960, at West Hartford, Conn.
Height, 5.09. Weight, 174.
Throws and bats righthanded.
Major League stolen bases: 1981 (1), 1990 (1). Total—2.
Tied for Western Carolinas League lead in caught stealing with 15 in 1979.
Led Southern League catchers in total chances with 537 in 1984.
Led International League catchers in total chances with 710 in 1983.
Led Southern League catchers in double plays with 10 in 1980.

Year Club League	Pos.	G.	AB.	R.	H.	2B.	3B.	HR.	RBI.	B.A.	PO.	A.	E.	F.A.
1978—Kingsport.............. Appal.	C	35	112	15	23	7	0	0	6	.205	198	26	2	.991
1979—Greenwood........... W. Car.	C	120	385	54	97	16	4	7	57	.252	639	69	11	.985
1980—Savannah.............. South.	C	122	449	76	125	16	1	11	50	.278	514	70	15	.975
1981—Richmond............. Int.	C	121	430	43	101	13	2	6	53	.235	738	78	12	.986
1981—Atlanta .... Nat.	C	12	32	4	9	1	1	0	4	.281	56	10	0	1.000
1982—Atlanta .... Nat.	C	37	81	10	11	2	0	1	4	.136	112	25	0	1.000
1982—Richmond............. Int.	C	72	246	39	62	7	1	8	29	.252	423	53	5	.990
1983—Richmond............. Int.	C	110	365	36	77	11	1	4	41	.211	★642	60	8	.989
1983—Atlanta .... Nat.	C	7	12	0	2	0	0	0	2	.167	24	5	1	.967
1984—Atlanta .... Nat.	C	2	4	0	0	0	0	0	0	.000	4	0	0	1.000

Year Club League	Pos.	G.	AB.	R.	H.	2B.	3B.	HR.	RBI.	B.A.	PO.	A.	E.	F.A.
1984—Greenville† .... South.	C	101	352	36	80	16	1	5	49	.227	*466	●64	7	.987
1985—Greenville .... South.	C	49	172	25	48	4	1	6	28	.279	265	49	7	.978
1985—Richmond‡.............. Int.	C	24	67	7	19	3	0	1	8	.284	89	8	3	.970
1986—Richmond§x .... Int.	C-3B	28	66	8	13	2	0	2	7	.197	124	18	2	.986
1986—Buffalo y .... A. A.	C	11	32	4	8	3	0	0	3	.250	60	7	4	.944
1987—Tacoma................. P. C.	C-3B-OF	79	215	30	54	13	0	5	32	.251	370	50	12	.972
1987—Oakland z.............. Amer.	C	6	3	0	0	0	0	0	0	.000	4	0	0	1.000
1988—Tacoma................. P. C.	C-OF	77	234	28	54	8	1	2	23	.231	361	48	7	.983
1988—Oakland ab........... Amer.	C	10	9	1	3	2	0	0	5	.333	21	2	0	1.000
1989—Tuc.cd-Cal. .... P. C.	C	46	128	13	33	6	0	0	12	.258	224	28	6	.977
1989—Detroit.................. Amer.	C	13	25	2	3	0	0	0	1	.120	42	2	0	1.000
1990—Seattle.................. Amer.	C	30	50	2	15	1	0	0	4	.300	112	16	1	.992
1990—Calgary e .... P. C.	C	9	20	1	6	0	0	1	2	.300	33	1	0	1.000
National League Totals—4 Years............		58	129	14	22	3	1	1	10	.171	196	40	1	.996
American League Totals—4 Years		59	87	5	21	3	0	0	10	.241	179	20	1	.995
Major League Totals—8 Years................		117	216	19	43	6	1	1	20	.199	375	60	2	.995

Selected by Atlanta Braves' organization in 2nd round of free-agent draft, June 6, 1978.

†Granted free agency, October 15, 1984; re-signed by Atlanta Braves' organization, December 11, 1984.

‡On disabled list, July 2 to August 1, 1985.

§On suspended list, July 6 to August 15, 1986.

xReleased, August 15, 1986; signed by Buffalo (Chicago White Sox' organization), August 20, 1986.

yGranted free agency, October 15, 1986; signed by Tacoma (Oakland Athletics' organization), April 1, 1987.

zReleased, October 15, 1987; re-signed by Athletics' organization, January 5, 1988.

aOn disabled list, August 19 to September 3, 1988.

bTraded to Tucson (Houston Astros' organization) for Catcher-Outfielder Troy Afenir, April 6, 1989.

cSold to Detroit Tigers, June 19, 1989.

dSold to Calgary (Seattle Mariners' organization), August 5, 1989.

eGranted free agency, October 5, 1990.

DOUGLAS RANDALL SISK
(Doug)

Born September 26, 1957, at Renton, Wash.
Height, 6.02. Weight, 210.
Throws and bats righthanded.
Attended Green River Community College, Auburn, Wash., and received bachelor of science degree
in criminal justice from Washington State University, Pullman, Wash.

Major League saves: 1982 (1), 1983 (11), 1984 (15), 1985 (2), 1986 (1), 1987 (3). Total—33.
Led Appalachian League pitchers in games started with 15 in 1980.

Year Club	League	G.	IP.	W.	L.	Pct.	H.	R.	ER.	SO.	BB.	ERA.
1980—Kingsport........................	Ap'lachian	15	*98	●8	5	.615	*91	46	29	41	45	2.66
1981—Lynchburg	Carolina	36	83	3	2	.600	78	35	30	61	32	3.25
1981—Jackson	Texas	14	25	3	0	1.000	23	11	10	15	12	3.60
1982—Jackson	Texas	44	138	11	8	.611	136	59	41	53	58	*2.67
1982—New York	National	8	8⅔	0	1	.000	5	1	1	4	4	1.04
1983—New York	National	67	104⅓	5	4	.556	88	38	26	33	59	2.24
1984—New York†	National	50	77⅔	1	3	.250	57	24	18	32	54	2.09
1985—New York	National	42	73	4	5	.444	86	48	43	26	40	5.30
1985—Tidewater	Int'national	4	15	0	2	.000	15	12	12	4	13	7.20
1986—Tidewater	Int'national	9	30	2	3	.400	34	16	14	19	9	4.20
1986—New York	National	41	70⅔	4	2	.667	77	31	24	31	31	3.06
1987—New York‡	National	55	78	3	1	.750	83	38	30	37	22	3.46
1988—Baltimore§	American	52	94⅓	3	3	.500	109	43	39	26	45	3.72
1988—Rochester x	Int'national	6	10⅔	0	2	.000	15	7	7	5	3	5.91
1989—					(Out of Organized Baseball)							
1990—Colorado Springs y	P. Coast	8	7⅔	1	0	1.000	8	8	6	7	5	7.04
1990—Tidewater z...................	Int'national	8	41⅔	5	1	.833	39	16	13	20	10	2.81
1990—Atlanta ab.....................	National	3	2⅓	0	0	.000	1	1	1	1	4	3.86
National League Totals—7 Years......................		266	414⅔	17	16	.515	397	181	143	164	214	3.10
American League Totals—1 Year		52	94⅓	3	3	.500	109	43	39	26	45	3.72
Major League Totals—8 Years............................		318	509	20	19	.513	506	224	182	190	259	3.22

Signed as free agent by New York Mets' organization, June 10, 1980.

†On disabled list, August 9 to August 29, 1984.

‡Traded to Baltimore Orioles for Pitcher Blaine Beatty and a player to be named later, December 8, 1987; New York Mets acquired Pitcher Greg Talamantez to complete deal, December 11, 1987.

§On disabled list, June 27 to July 22, 1988; included rehabilitation disability assignment to Rochester, July 3 to July 21, 1988.

xReleased, October 3, 1988; signed by Colorado Springs (Cleveland Indians' organization), December 15, 1989.

yReleased, June 9, 1990; signed by Tidewater (New York Mets' organization), June 12, 1990.

zTraded to Atlanta Braves for Pitcher Tony Valle, July 22, 1990.

aOn disabled list, July 28 to August 28, 1990.

bReleased, August 28, 1990.

CHAMPIONSHIP SERIES RECORD

Year Club	League	G.	IP.	W.	L.	Pct.	H.	R.	ER.	SO.	BB.	ERA.
1986—New York........................	National	1	1	0	0	.000	1	0	0	0	1	0.00

WORLD SERIES RECORD

Year Club	League	G.	IP.	W.	L.	Pct.	H.	R.	ER.	SO.	BB.	ERA.
1986—New York........................	National	1	⅔	0	0	.000	0	0	0	1	1	0.00

JOEL PATRICK SKINNER

Born February 21, 1961, at La Jolla, Calif.
Height, 6.04. Weight, 205.
Throws and bats righthanded.
Attended San Diego Mesa College, San Diego, Calif.
Son of Bob Skinner, outfielder-first baseman with Pittsburgh Pirates, Cincinnati Reds and St. Louis
Cardinals, 1954 through 1966; manager, Philadelphia Phillies, 1968 and 1969, manager,
San Diego Padres, 1977; coach, San Diego Padres, 1977; coach, California Angels, 1978;
coach with Pittsburgh Pirates, 1979 through 1985; and coach with Atlanta Braves, 1986 through May 22, 1988.

Major League stolen bases: 1984 (1), 1986 (1), 1989 (1). Total—3.
Led American Association batters in strikeouts with 115 and tied for lead in grounding into double plays with 16 in 1985.
Led American Association catchers in total chances with 698 and double plays with 13 in 1985.
Tied for South Atlantic League lead in double plays by catchers with 7 in 1980.

Year Club	League	Pos.	G.	AB.	R.	H.	2B.	3B.	HR.	RBI.	B.A.	PO.	A.	E.	F.A.
1980—Shelby	S. Atl.	C	100	324	36	73	15	2	7	27	.225	536	63	18	.971
1981—Greenwood†‡	S. Atl.	C	117	428	48	114	25	2	11	63	.266	766	42	★22	.974
1982—Glens Falls	East.	C	120	422	49	107	11	6	7	65	.254	726	80	12	.985
1983—Denver	A. A.	C	108	361	55	94	15	5	12	50	.260	550	54	5	.992
1983—Chicago	Amer.	C	6	11	2	3	0	0	0	1	.273	20	4	1	.960
1984—Denver§	A. A.	C	42	141	27	40	6	0	10	27	.284	255	24	5	.982
1984—Chicago	Amer.	C	43	80	4	17	2	0	0	3	.213	171	11	2	.989
1985—Buffalo	A. A.	C	115	390	47	94	13	0	12	59	.241	★623	★65	10	.986
1985—Chicago	Amer.	C	22	44	9	15	4	1	1	5	.341	94	8	3	.971
1986—Chi. x-N.Y.	Amer.	C	114	315	23	73	9	1	5	37	.232	507	37	9	.984
1987—New York	Amer.	C	64	139	9	19	4	0	3	14	.137	232	18	4	.984
1987—Columbus	Int.	C	49	178	19	43	10	2	6	27	.242	226	25	4	.984
1988—New York	Amer.	C-OF-1B	88	251	23	57	15	0	4	23	.227	396	16	4	.990
1989—Cleveland y	Amer.	C	79	178	10	41	10	0	1	13	.230	280	22	3	.990
1990—Cleveland	Amer.	C	49	139	16	35	4	1	2	16	.252	222	16	1	.996
Major League Totals—8 Years			465	1157	96	260	48	3	16	112	.225	1922	132	27	.987

Selected by Pittsburgh Pirates' organization in 36th round of free-agent draft, June 5, 1979.
†On disabled list, June 1 to June 13, 1981.
‡Selected by Chicago White Sox' organization in player compensation pool draft, February 2, 1982. (Chicago received compensation for Philadelphia Phillies' signing of free agent Pitcher Ed Farmer, a Type A player, January 28, 1982.)
§On disabled list, July 23, 1984 through remainder of season.
xTraded with Outfielder-Designated Hitter Ron Kittle and Infielder Wayne Tolleson to New York Yankees for Catcher Ron Hassey, Shortstop Carlos Martinez and a player to be named later, July 30, 1986; New York traded Catcher Bill Lindsey to Chicago White Sox' organization to complete deal, December 24, 1986.
yTraded with Outfielder Turner Ward to Cleveland Indians for Outfielder Mel Hall, March 19, 1989.

DONALD MARTIN SLAUGHT
(Don)

Born September 11, 1958, at Long Beach, Calif.
Height, 6.01. Weight, 190.
Throws and bats righthanded.
Attended El Camino College, Torrance, Calif., and received bachelor of
science degree in economics from UCLA, Los Angeles, Calif. in 1983.

Major League stolen bases: 1983 (3), 1985 (5), 1986 (3), 1988 (1), 1989 (1). Total—13.

Year Club	League	Pos.	G.	AB.	R.	H.	2B.	3B.	HR.	RBI.	B.A.	PO.	A.	E.	F.A.
1980—Fort Myers	Fla. St.	C	50	176	13	46	9	0	2	16	.261	175	34	4	.981
1981—Jacksonville	South.	C-1B	96	379	45	127	21	2	6	44	.335	482	61	9	.984
1981—Omaha†	A. A.	C	22	71	10	21	4	0	2	8	.296	91	7	3	.970
1982—Omaha‡	A. A.	C	53	206	29	55	10	1	4	16	.267	216	25	5	.980
1982—Kansas City	Amer.	C	43	115	14	32	6	0	3	8	.278	156	7	1	.994
1983—Kansas City§	Amer.	C	83	276	21	86	13	4	0	28	.312	299	18	12	.964
1984—Kansas City x	Amer.	C	124	409	48	108	27	4	4	42	.264	547	44	11	.982
1985—Texas y	Amer.	C	102	343	34	96	17	4	8	35	.280	550	33	6	.990
1986—Texas z	Amer.	C	95	314	39	83	17	1	13	46	.264	533	40	4	.993
1986—Oklahoma City	A. A.	C	3	12	2	4	1	0	0	1	.333	6	1	0	1.000
1987—Texas a	Amer.	C	95	237	25	53	15	2	8	16	.224	429	39	7	.985
1988—New York b	Amer.	C	97	322	33	91	25	1	9	43	.283	496	24	●11	.979
1989—New York c	Amer.	C	117	350	34	88	21	3	5	38	.251	493	44	5	.991
1990—Pittsburgh de	Nat.	C	84	230	27	69	18	3	4	29	.300	345	36	8	.979
American League Totals—8 Years			756	2366	248	637	141	19	50	256	.269	3503	249	57	.985
National League Totals—1 Year			84	230	27	69	18	3	4	29	.300	345	36	8	.979
Major League Totals—9 Years			840	2596	275	706	159	22	54	285	.272	3848	285	65	.985

Selected by Milwaukee Brewers' organization in 19th round of free-agent draft, June 5, 1979.
Selected by Kansas City Royals' organization in 7th round of free-agent draft, June 3, 1980.
†On disabled list, August 16 to September 29, 1981.
‡On disabled list, April 21 to May 15, 1982.
§On disabled list, May 16 to June 1, 1983.
xTraded to Texas Rangers as part of a six-player, four-team deal in which Kansas City Royals acquired Catcher Jim Sundberg from Milwaukee Brewers, New York Mets' organization acquired Pitcher Frank Wills from Kansas City, Milwaukee acquired Pitcher Danny Darwin and a player to be named later from Texas and Pitcher Tim Leary from New York, January 18, 1985; Milwaukee organization acquired Catcher Bill Hance from Texas to complete deal, January 30, 1985.

yOn disabled list, August 9 to August 26, 1985.
zOn disabled list, May 18 to July 4, 1986; included rehabilitation disability assignment to Oklahoma City, July 1 to July 4, 1986.
aTraded to New York Yankees for a player to be named later, November 2, 1987; Texas Rangers acquired Pitcher Brad Arnsberg to complete deal, November 10, 1987.
bOn disabled list, May 15 to June 20, 1988.
cTraded to Pittsburgh Pirates for Pitchers Jeff Robinson and Willie Smith, December 20, 1989.
dOn disabled list, June 30 to July 16, 1990.
eGranted free agency, November 5, 1990; re-signed by Pirates, December 19, 1990.

CHAMPIONSHIP SERIES RECORD

Year Club	League	Pos.	G.	AB.	R.	H.	2B.	3B.	HR.	RBI.	B.A.	PO.	A.	E.	F.A.
1984—Kansas City	Amer.	C	3	11	0	4	0	0	0	0	.364	17	0	3	.850
1990—Pittsburgh	Nat.	C	4	11	0	1	1	0	0	1	.091	22	1	1	.958
Championship Series Totals—2 Years		7	22	0	5	1	0	0	1	.227	39	1	4	.909

JOHN PATRICK SMILEY

Born March 17, 1965 at Phoenixville, Pa.
Height, 6.04. Weight, 200.
Throws and bats lefthanded.

Major League saves: 1987 (4).
Tied for Gulf Coast League lead in home runs allowed with 5 in 1983.

Year Club	League	G.	IP.	W.	L.	Pct.	H.	R.	ER.	SO.	BB.	ERA.
1983—Bradenton Pirates	Gulf Coast	12	65⅓	3	4	.429	69	45	43	42	27	5.92
1984—Macon†	S. Atlantic	21	130	5	11	.313	119	73	57	73	41	3.95
1985—Prince William	Carolina	10	56	2	2	.500	64	36	32	45	27	5.14
1985—Macon	S. Atlantic	16	88⅔	3	8	.273	84	55	46	70	37	4.67
1986—Prince William	Carolina	48	90	2	4	.333	64	35	31	93	40	3.10
1986—Pittsburgh	National	12	11⅔	1	0	1.000	4	6	5	9	4	3.86
1987—Pittsburgh	National	63	75	5	5	.500	69	49	48	58	50	5.76
1988—Pittsburgh	National	34	205	13	11	.542	185	81	74	129	46	3.25
1989—Pittsburgh	National	28	205⅓	12	8	.600	174	78	64	123	49	2.81
1990—Pittsburgh‡	National	26	149⅓	9	10	.474	161	83	77	86	36	4.64
Major League Totals—5 Years		163	646⅓	40	34	.541	593	297	268	405	185	3.73

Selected by Pittsburgh Pirates' organization in 12th round of free-agent draft, June 6, 1983.
†On disabled list, April 27 to May 27, 1984.
‡On disabled list, May 19 to July 1, 1990.

CHAMPIONSHIP SERIES RECORD

Year Club	League	G.	IP.	W.	L.	Pct.	H.	R.	ER.	SO.	BB.	ERA.
1990—Pittsburgh	National	1	2	0	0	.000	2	0	0	0	0	0.00

BRYN NELSON SMITH

First name pronounced Brin.

Born August 11, 1955, at Marietta, Ga.
Height, 6.02. Weight, 205.
Throws and bats righthanded.
Attended Allan Hancock College, Santa Maria, Calif.

Major League saves: 1982 (3), 1983 (3). Total—6.
Tied for American Association lead in complete games with 9 in 1981.
Tied for Southern League lead in complete games with 16 in 1977 and 12 in 1980.
Named American Association Pitcher of the Year, 1981.

Year Club	League	G.	IP.	W.	L.	Pct.	H.	R.	ER.	SO.	BB.	ERA.
1975—Miami	Florida St.	26	139	11	7	.611	117	48	33	93	59	2.14
1976—Miami	Florida St.	23	164	10	10	.500	140	72	51	119	62	2.80
1977—Charlotte†	Southern	27	★206	★15	11	.577	★195	78	63	103	57	2.75
1978—Denver	Am. Assoc.	11	54	0	6	.000	79	48	41	25	14	6.83
1978—Memphis‡	Southern	11	69	4	6	.400	53	28	19	48	31	2.48
1979—Memphis	Southern	27	184	11	10	.524	175	80	69	115	74	3.38
1980—Memphis	Southern	27	181	10	9	.526	179	75	56	110	54	2.78
1981—Denver	Am. Assoc.	29	★183	★15	5	★.750	166	80	62	127	42	3.05
1981—Montreal	National	7	13	1	0	1.000	14	4	4	9	3	2.77
1982—Wichita	Am. Assoc.	3	23⅔	2	0	1.000	21	5	5	15	2	1.90
1982—Montreal	National	47	79⅓	2	4	.333	81	43	37	50	23	4.20
1983—Montreal	National	49	155⅓	6	11	.353	142	51	43	101	43	2.49
1984—Montreal	National	28	179	12	13	.480	178	72	66	101	51	3.32
1985—Montreal	National	32	222⅓	18	5	.783	193	85	72	127	41	2.91
1986—Montreal§	National	30	187⅓	10	8	.556	182	101	82	105	63	3.94
1987—West Palm Beach x	Florida St.	4	17⅔	0	2	.000	19	10	8	16	1	4.08
1987—Montreal y	National	26	150⅓	10	9	.526	164	81	73	94	31	4.37
1988—Montreal	National	32	198	12	10	.545	179	79	66	122	32	3.00
1989—Montreal z	National	33	215⅔	10	11	.476	177	76	68	129	54	2.84
1990—St. Louis a	National	26	141⅓	9	8	.529	160	81	67	78	30	4.27
Major League Totals—10 Years		310	1541⅓	90	79	.533	1470	673	578	916	371	3.37

Selected by St. Louis Cardinals' organization in the 49th round of free-agent draft, June 5, 1973.
Signed as free agent by Baltimore Orioles' organization, December 18, 1974.

†Traded with Pitchers Rudy May and Randy Miller by Baltimore Orioles' organization to Montreal Expos' organization for Pitchers Don Stanhouse and Joe Kerrigan and Outfielder Gary Roenicke, December 7, 1977.
‡On disabled list, August 5 to August 17, 1978.
§Released, December 20, 1986; re-signed by Expos, February 27, 1987.
xOn Montreal disabled list, March 23 to May 1, 1987; included rehabilitation disability assignment to West Palm Beach, April 10, 1987.
yGranted free agency, November 9, 1987; re-signed by Expos, December 16, 1987.
zGranted free agency, November 13, 1989; signed by St. Louis Cardinals, November 28, 1989.
aOn disabled list, July 28 to September 6, 1990.

DARYL CLINTON SMITH

Born July 29, 1960, at Baltimore, Md.
Height, 6.04. Weight, 185.
Throws and bats righthanded.
Attended Essex Community College, Baltimore, Md.

Year Club	League	G.	IP.	W.	L.	Pct.	H.	R.	ER.	SO.	BB.	ERA.
1980—Asheville	S. Atlantic	22	66	5	3	.625	72	40	35	30	41	4.77
1980—Sarasota Rangers	Gulf Coast	4	12	1	1	.500	13	9	6	4	4	4.50
1981—Asheville	S. Atlantic	29	160	•16	5	.762	136	65	49	64	57	2.76
1982—Tulsa	Texas	9	37⅔	2	5	.286	51	35	30	18	24	7.17
1982—Burlington	Midwest	19	80⅔	3	5	.375	78	40	30	32	40	3.35
1983—Salem	Carolina	13	55⅔	1	2	.333	53	30	26	35	32	4.20
1983—Tulsa†	Texas	6	14⅓	0	0	.000	14	3	3	5	6	1.88
1984—Tulsa	Texas	7	10⅔	0	1	.000	18	17	17	6	9	14.34
1984—Salem‡	Carolina	16	67	6	3	.667	67	40	32	38	44	4.30
1985—Waterloo	Midwest	1	4⅔	0	0	.000	4	1	1	5	2	1.93
1985—Waterbury	Eastern	16	53⅔	2	2	.500	42	25	21	38	37	3.52
1986—Waterbury§	Eastern	21	89	4	3	.571	71	37	35	55	48	3.54
1987—Willamsport x-Reading	Eastern	21	87⅓	7	3	.700	86	46	38	58	46	3.92
1987—Maine y	Int'national	4	22⅓	1	3	.250	21	18	17	16	13	6.75
1988—Birmingham z	Southern	40	53	1	4	.200	42	25	19	44	27	3.23
1989—					(Out of Organized Baseball)							
1990—Memphis	Southern	21	48⅓	2	1	.667	46	27	17	48	23	3.17
1990—Omaha	Am. Assoc.	11	64	6	2	.750	59	25	22	56	32	3.09
1990—Kansas City a	American	2	6⅔	0	1	.000	5	3	3	6	4	4.05
Major League Totals—1 Year		2	6⅔	0	1	.000	5	3	3	6	4	4.05

Selected by Texas Rangers' organization in 6th round of free-agent draft, January 8, 1980.
†On disabled list, June 24 through July 9 and July 10, 1983 through remainder of season.
‡Released, April 6, 1985; signed by Waterloo (Cleveland Indians' organization), May 21, 1985.
§On disabled list, May 2 to June 3, 1986.
xReleased, April 30, 1987; signed by Reading (Philadelphia Phillies' organization), May 4, 1987.
yGranted free agency, October 15, 1987; signed by Vancouver (Chicago White Sox' organization), December 7, 1987.
zReleased, February, 1989; signed by Memphis (Kansas City Royals' organization), March 22, 1990.
aGranted free agency, October 15, 1990.

DAVID STANLEY SMITH JR.
(Dave)

Born January 21, 1955, at San Francisco, Calif.
Height, 6.01. Weight, 195.
Throws and bats righthanded.
Attended San Diego State University, San Diego, Calif.

Major League saves: 1980 (10), 1981 (8), 1982 (11), 1983 (6), 1984 (5), 1985 (27), 1986 (33), 1987 (24), 1988 (27), 1989 (25), 1990 (23). Total—199.
Tied for National League lead in balks with 5 in 1990.

Year Club	League	G.	IP.	W.	L.	Pct.	H.	R.	ER.	SO.	BB.	ERA.
1976—Covington	Ap'lachian	15	97	5	5	.500	80	40	29	71	28	2.69
1977—Cocoa	Florida St.	14	93	7	5	.583	97	40	32	81	31	3.10
1977—Columbus	Southern	9	54	3	5	.375	52	2	21	29	24	3.50
1978—Columbus	Southern	26	181	10	13	.435	170	89	70	114	88	3.48
1979—Charleston	Int'national	34	160	7	8	.467	159	80	65	90	44	3.66
1980—Houston	National	57	103	7	5	.583	90	24	22	85	32	1.92
1981—Houston	National	42	75	5	3	.625	54	26	23	52	23	2.76
1982—Houston†	National	49	63⅓	5	4	.556	69	30	27	28	31	3.84
1983—Houston	National	42	72⅔	3	1	.750	72	32	25	41	36	3.10
1984—Houston	National	53	77⅓	5	4	.556	60	22	19	45	20	2.21
1985—Houston	National	64	79⅓	9	5	.643	69	26	20	40	17	2.27
1986—Houston	National	54	56	4	7	.364	39	17	17	46	22	2.73
1987—Houston‡	National	50	60	2	3	.400	39	13	11	73	21	1.65
1988—Houston	National	51	57⅓	4	5	.444	60	26	17	38	19	2.67
1989—Houston	National	52	58	3	4	.429	49	20	17	31	19	2.64
1990—Houston§	National	49	60⅓	6	6	.500	45	18	16	50	20	2.39
Major League Totals—11 Years		563	762⅓	53	47	.530	646	254	214	529	260	2.53

Selected by Houston Astros' organization in 8th round of free-agent draft, June 8, 1976.
†On disabled list, June 27 to July 18, 1982.
‡Granted free agency, November 9, 1987; re-signed by Astros, January 8, 1988.
§Granted free agency, December 7, 1990; signed by Chicago Cubs, December 17, 1990.

Year	Club	League	G.	IP.	W.	L.	Pct.	H.	R.	ER.	SO.	BB.	ERA.
1981—Houston		National	2	2⅓	0	0	.000	2	1	1	4	0	3.86

CHAMPIONSHIP SERIES RECORD

Year	Club	League	G.	IP.	W.	L.	Pct.	H.	R.	ER.	SO.	BB.	ERA.
1980—Houston		National	3	2⅓	1	0	1.000	4	1	1	4	2	3.86
1986—Houston		National	2	2	0	1	.000	2	2	2	2	3	9.00
Championship Series Totals—2 Years			5	4⅓	1	1	.500	6	3	3	6	5	6.23

ALL-STAR GAME RECORD

Year	League	IP.	W.	L.	Pct.	H.	R.	ER.	SO.	BB.	ERA.
1990—National		⅔	0	0	.000	1	0	0	1	2	0.00

Member of National League All-Star Team in 1986; did not play.

GREGORY ALLEN SMITH
(Greg)

Born April 5, 1967, at Baltimore, Md.
Height, 5.11. Weight, 170.
Throws right and bats left and righthanded.

Major League stolen bases: 1990 (1).
Led Southern League second basemen in total chances with 621 and double plays with 59 in 1989.
Led Midwest League shortstops in errors with 48 and tied for lead in putouts with 189 in 1987.

Year	Club	League	Pos.	G.	AB.	R.	H.	2B.	3B.	HR.	RBI.	B.A.	PO.	A.	E.	F.A.
1985—Wytheville	Appal.		SS	51	179	28	42	6	2	0	15	.235	56	160	24	.900
1986—Peoria	Midw.		SS-2B	53	170	24	43	6	3	2	26	.253	65	101	15	.917
1987—Peoria	Midw.		SS-2B	124	444	69	120	23	5	6	56	.270	193	347	49	.917
1988—Winston-Salem	Carol.		2B-1B	95	361	62	101	12	2	4	29	.280	162	236	16	.961
1989—Charlotte	South.		2B	126	467	59	138	23	6	5	64	.296	★253	★348	20	.968
1989—Chicago	Nat.		2B	4	5	1	2	0	0	0	2	.400	4	3	2	.778
1990—Chicago	Nat.		SS-2B	18	44	4	9	2	1	0	5	.205	20	38	3	.951
1990—Iowa†	A. A.		SS-3B	105	398	54	116	19	1	5	44	.291	155	303	18	.962
Major League Totals—2 Years				22	49	5	11	2	1	0	7	.224	24	41	5	.929

Selected by Chicago Cubs' organization in 2nd round of free-agent draft, June 3, 1985.
†Traded to Los Angeles Dodgers for Infielder Jose Vizcaino, December 14, 1990.

JOHN DWIGHT SMITH

(Known by middle name.)
Born November 8, 1963, at Tallahassee, Fla.
Height, 5.11. Weight, 175.
Throws right and bats lefthanded.
Attended Spartanburg Methodist College, Spartanburg, S.C.

Major League stolen bases: 1989 (9), 1990 (11). Total—20.
Led Eastern League in total bases with 270, stolen bases with 60 and tied for lead in caught stealing with 18 in 1987.
Led Appalachian League in stolen bases with 47 in 1984.
Led Midwest League outfielders in total chances with 296 in 1986.
Tied for Appalachian League lead in double plays by outfielders with 3 in 1984.

Year	Club	League	Pos.	G.	AB.	R.	H.	2B.	3B.	HR.	RBI.	B.A.	PO.	A.	E.	F.A.
1984—Pikeville	Appal.		OF	61	195	42	46	6	2	1	17	.236	77	8	●9	.904
1985—Geneva	NYP		OF	73	232	44	67	11	2	4	32	.289	81	4	7	.924
1986—Peoria	Midw.		OF	124	471	92	146	22	★11	11	57	.310	★272	11	13	.956
1987—Pittsfield	East.		OF	130	498	★111	168	28	10	18	72	.337	214	8	●14	.941
1988—Iowa	A. A.		OF	129	505	76	148	26	3	9	48	.293	216	11	★15	.938
1989—Iowa	A. A.		OF	21	83	11	27	7	3	2	7	.325	39	2	4	.911
1989—Chicago	Nat.		OF	109	343	52	111	19	6	9	52	.324	188	7	5	.975
1990—Chicago	Nat.		OF	117	290	34	76	15	0	6	27	.262	139	4	2	.986
Major League Totals—2 Years				226	633	86	187	34	6	15	79	.295	327	11	7	.980

Selected by Toronto Blue Jays' organization in 3rd round of free-agent draft, January 17, 1984.
Selected by Chicago Cubs' organization in secondary phase of free-agent draft, June 4, 1984.

CHAMPIONSHIP SERIES RECORD

Shares record for most at-bats, inning (2), October 5, 1989, first inning.

Year	Club	League	Pos.	G.	AB.	R.	H.	2B.	3B.	HR.	RBI.	B.A.	PO.	A.	E.	F.A.
1989—Chicago	Nat.		OF	4	15	2	3	1	0	0	0	.200	10	0	0	1.000

LEE ARTHUR SMITH

Born December 4, 1957, at Jamestown, La.
Height, 6.06. Weight, 250.
Throws and bats righthanded.
Attended Northwestern State University, Natchitoches, La.

Major League saves: 1981 (1), 1982 (17), 1983 (29), 1984 (33), 1985 (33), 1986 (31), 1987 (36), 1988 (29), 1989 (25), 1990. (31). Total—265.
Led National League in games finished in relief with 57 in 1985 and tied for lead with 56 in 1983.
Led National League in saves with 29 in 1983.

Tied for American Association lead in wild pitches with 16 in 1980.
Named National League co-Fireman of the Year by THE SPORTING NEWS, 1983.

Year Club	League	G.	IP.	W.	L.	Pct.	H.	R.	ER.	SO.	BB.	ERA.
1975—Bradenton Cubs	Gulf Coast	10	62	3	5	.375	35	23	16	35	*49	2.32
1976—Pompano Beach	Florida St.	26	101	4	8	.333	120	76	60	52	74	5.35
1977—Pompano Beach	Florida St.	26	130	10	4	.714	131	67	62	82	85	4.29
1978—Midland	Texas	30	155	8	10	.444	161	122	103	71	*128	5.98
1979—Midland	Texas	35	104	9	5	.643	122	65	57	46	85	4.93
1980—Wichita	Am. Assoc.	50	90	4	7	.364	70	49	37	63	56	3.70
1980—Chicago	National	18	22	2	0	1.000	21	9	7	17	14	2.86
1981—Chicago	National	40	67	3	6	.333	57	31	26	50	31	3.49
1982—Chicago	National	72	117	2	5	.286	105	38	35	99	37	2.69
1983—Chicago	National	66	103⅓	4	10	.286	70	23	19	91	41	1.65
1984—Chicago	National	69	101	9	7	.563	98	42	41	86	35	3.65
1985—Chicago	National	65	97⅔	7	4	.636	87	35	33	112	32	3.04
1986—Chicago†	National	66	90⅓	9	9	.500	69	32	31	93	42	3.09
1987—Chicago‡	National	62	83⅔	4	10	.286	84	30	29	96	32	3.12
1988—Boston	American	64	83⅔	4	5	.444	72	34	26	96	37	2.80
1989—Boston	American	64	70⅔	6	1	.857	53	30	28	96	33	3.57
1990—Boston§	American	11	14⅓	2	1	.667	13	4	3	17	9	1.88
1990—St. Louis	National	53	68⅔	3	4	.429	58	20	16	70	20	2.10
National League Totals—9 Years		511	750⅔	43	55	.439	649	260	237	714	284	2.84
American League Totals—3 Years		139	168⅔	12	7	.632	138	68	57	209	79	3.04
Major League Totals—11 Years		650	919⅓	55	62	.470	787	328	294	923	363	2.88

Selected by Chicago Cubs' organization in 2nd round of free-agent draft, June 4, 1975.
†On disabled list, April 21 to May 6, 1986.
‡Traded to Boston Red Sox for Pitchers Al Nipper and Calvin Schiraldi, December 8, 1987.
§Traded to St. Louis Cardinals for Outfielder Tom Brunansky, May 4, 1990.

CHAMPIONSHIP SERIES RECORD

Year Club	League	G.	IP.	W.	L.	Pct.	H.	R.	ER.	SO.	BB.	ERA.
1984—Chicago	National	2	2	0	1	.000	3	2	2	3	0	9.00
1988—Boston	American	2	3⅓	0	1	.000	6	3	3	4	1	8.10
Championship Series Totals—2 Years		4	5⅓	0	2	.000	9	5	5	7	1	8.44

ALL-STAR GAME RECORD

Year League	IP.	W.	L.	Pct.	H.	R.	ER.	SO.	BB.	ERA.
1983—National	1	0	0	.000	2	2	1	1	0	9.00
1987—National	3	1	0	1.000	2	0	0	4	0	0.00
All-Star Game Totals—2 Years	4	1	0	1.000	4	2	1	5	0	2.25

LeROY PURDY SMITH III
(Roy)

Born September 6, 1961, at Mt. Vernon, N.Y.
Height, 6.03. Weight, 212.
Throws and bats righthanded.
Attended Fordham University, Bronx, N.Y.

Major League saves: 1989 (1).
Tied for Carolina League lead in shutouts with 3 in 1980.
Named Carolina League Pitcher of the Year, 1980.

Year Club	League	G.	IP.	W.	L.	Pct.	H.	R.	ER.	SO.	BB.	ERA
1979—Helena	Pioneer	5	36	5	0	1.000	21	16	10	42	16	2.50
1980—Peninsula	Carolina	27	163	*17	6	.739	101	54	47	134	63	2.60
1981—Reading	Eastern	27	161	11	8	.579	123	92	79	117	97	4.42
1982—Reading†	Eastern	26	166	10	8	.556	141	81	71	122	82	3.85
1983—Charleston	Int'national	27	155⅓	6	8	.429	166	101	89	95	75	5.16
1984—Maine	Int'national	12	80⅔	5	4	.556	77	47	39	48	29	4.35
1984—Cleveland	American	22	86⅓	5	5	.500	91	49	44	55	40	4.59
1985—Maine	Int'national	15	109⅓	10	4	.714	84	33	29	65	29	2.39
1985—Cleveland‡§	American	12	62⅓	1	4	.200	84	40	37	28	17	5.34
1986—Minnesota	American	5	10⅓	0	2	.000	13	8	8	8	5	6.97
1986—Toledo xy	Int'national	9	53⅔	2	1	.667	42	12	9	39	16	1.51
1987—Portland	P. Coast	24	166⅓	9	12	.429	176	84	70	106	41	3.79
1987—Minnesota	American	7	16⅓	1	0	1.000	20	10	9	8	6	4.96
1988—Portland	P. Coast	22	150	12	9	.571	152	82	72	110	31	4.32
1988—Minnesota	American	9	37	3	0	1.000	29	12	11	17	12	2.68
1989—Minnesota	American	32	172⅓	10	6	.625	180	82	75	92	51	3.92
1990—Minnesota z	American	32	153⅓	5	10	.333	191	91	82	87	47	4.81
Major League Totals—7 Years		119	538	25	27	.481	608	292	266	295	178	4.45

Selected by Philadelphia Phillies' organization in 3rd round of free-agent draft, June 5, 1979.
†Traded with Pitcher Jerry Reed and Outfielder Wil Culmer to Cleveland Indians for Pitcher John Denny, September 12, 1982.
‡On disabled list, July 3 to August 1, 1985; included rehabilitation disability assignment to Maine, July 27 to July 30, 1985.
§Traded with Pitcher Ramon Romero to Minnesota Twins for Pitchers Ken Schrom and Bryan Oelkers, January 7, 1986.
xOn disabled list, June 7 to July 3, 1986.
yReleased, December 20, 1986; re-signed by Minnesota Twins' organization, February 24, 1987.
zReleased, December 2, 1990.

LONNIE SMITH

Born December 22, 1955, at Chicago, Ill.
Height, 5.09. Weight, 170.
Throws and bats righthanded.

Shares major league record for fewest double plays by outfielder, season, for leader in double plays (4), 1983.
Shares modern National League record for most stolen bases, game, (5), September 4, 1982.
Major League stolen bases: 1978 (4), 1979 (2), 1980 (33), 1981 (21), 1982 (68), 1983 (43), 1984 (50), 1985 (52), 1986 (26), 1987 (9), 1988 (4), 1989 (25), 1990 (10). Total—347.
Led National League in being hit by pitch with 9 in 1982 and 1984 and tied for lead with 9 in 1983.
Tied for National League lead in caught stealing with 26 in 1982.
Tied for National League lead in double plays by outfielders with 4 in 1983.
Led International League in bases on balls received with 66 in 1988.
Led American Association in stolen bases with 66 and caught stealing with 19 in 1978.
Led Western Carolinas League in stolen bases with 56 and tied for lead in caught stealing with 14 in 1975.
Led American Association outfielders in double plays with 5 in 1978.
Named National League Comeback Player of the Year by THE SPORTING NEWS, 1989.
Named National League Rookie Player of the Year by THE SPORTING NEWS, 1980.
Named outfielder on THE SPORTING NEWS National League All-Star Team, 1982.

Year—Club	League	Pos.	G.	AB.	R.	H.	2B.	3B.	HR.	RBI.	B.A.	PO.	A.	E.	F.A.
1974—Auburn	NYP	OF	61	210	48	60	10	4	5	27	.286	143	6	●9	.943
1975—Spartanburg	W. Car.	OF	131	465	★114	★150	23	4	7	40	.323	★317	9	11	.967
1976—Oklahoma City	A. A.	OF	134	483	★93	149	24	9	8	54	.308	200	4	★14	.936
1977—Oklahoma City	A. A.	OF	125	477	91	132	14	10	4	41	.277	231	8	★13	.948
1978—Oklahoma City†	A. A.	OF	125	480	103	151	20	5	7	43	.315	274	★21	★12	.961
1978—Philadelphia	Nat.	OF	17	4	6	0	0	0	0	0	.000	5	1	0	1.000
1979—Oklahoma City	A. A.	OF	110	451	★106	149	26	9	7	44	.330	268	13	★12	.959
1979—Philadelphia	Nat.	OF	17	30	4	5	2	0	0	3	.167	19	1	0	1.000
1980—Philadelphia	Nat.	OF	100	298	69	101	14	4	3	20	.339	121	2	4	.969
1981—Philadelphia‡	Nat.	OF	62	176	40	57	14	3	2	11	.324	91	10	3	.971
1982—St. Louis	Nat.	OF	156	592	★120	182	35	8	8	69	.307	303	●16	10	.970
1983—St. Louis§	Nat.	OF	130	492	83	158	31	5	8	45	.321	225	14	★15	.941
1984—St. Louis	Nat.	OF	145	504	77	126	20	4	6	49	.250	184	★18	●11	.948
1985—St. Louis x	Nat.	OF	28	96	15	25	2	2	0	7	.260	43	1	0	1.000
1985—Kansas City	Amer.	OF	120	448	77	115	23	4	6	41	.257	195	10	9	.958
1986—Kansas City yz	Amer.	OF	134	508	80	146	25	7	8	44	.287	245	5	9	.965
1987—Omaha	A. A.	OF	40	149	36	49	9	1	7	33	.329	51	1	3	.945
1987—Kansas City a	Amer.	OF	48	167	26	42	7	1	3	8	.251	52	2	5	.915
1988—Richmond	Int.	OF	93	290	58	87	13	5	9	51	.300	120	6	2	.984
1988—Atlanta	Nat.	OF	43	114	14	27	3	0	3	9	.237	59	2	2	.968
1989—Atlanta b	Nat.	OF	134	482	89	152	34	4	21	79	.315	289	3	2	.993
1990—Atlanta	Nat.	OF	135	466	72	142	27	9	9	42	.305	254	6	12	.956
National League Totals—11 Years			967	3254	589	975	182	39	60	334	.300	1593	74	59	.966
American League Totals—3 Years			302	1123	183	303	55	12	17	93	.270	492	17	23	.957
Major League Totals—13 Years			1269	4377	772	1278	237	51	77	427	.292	2085	91	82	.964

Selected by Philadelphia Phillies' organization in 1st round (third player selected) of free-agent draft, June 5, 1974.
†On disabled list, April 14 to April 25, 1978.
‡Traded with a player to be named later to Cleveland Indians for Catcher Bo Diaz, November 20, 1981; Traded by Cleveland to St. Louis Cardinals for Pitchers Lary Sorensen and Silvio Martinez, November 20, 1981. Cleveland organization acquired Pitcher Scott Munninghoff to complete first deal, December 9, 1981.
§On disabled list, June 11 to July 8, 1983.
xTraded to Kansas City Royals for Outfielder John Morris, May 17, 1985.
yOn disabled list, April 13 to May 4, 1986.
zGranted free agency, November 12, 1986; re-signed by Royals' organization, May 18, 1987.
aReleased, December 15, 1987; signed by Richmond (Atlanta Braves' organization), March 12, 1988.
bOn disabled list, May 20 to June 13, 1989.

DIVISION SERIES RECORD

Year—Club	League	Pos.	G.	AB.	R.	H.	2B.	3B.	HR.	RBI.	B.A.	PO.	A.	E.	F.A.
1981—Philadelphia	Nat.	OF	5	19	1	5	1	0	0	0	.263	6	1	0	1.000

CHAMPIONSHIP SERIES RECORD

Year—Club	League	Pos.	G.	AB.	R.	H.	2B.	3B.	HR.	RBI.	B.A.	PO.	A.	E.	F.A.
1980—Philadelphia	Nat.	PR-OF	3	5	2	3	0	0	0	0	.600	2	1	0	1.000
1982—St. Louis	Nat.	OF	3	11	1	3	0	0	0	1	.273	2	0	0	1.000
1985—Kansas City	Amer.	OF	7	28	2	7	2	0	0	1	.250	8	3	1	.917
Championship Series Totals—3 Years			13	44	5	13	2	0	0	2	.295	12	4	1	.941

WORLD SERIES RECORD

Year—Club	League	Pos.	G.	AB.	R.	H.	2B.	3B.	HR.	RBI.	B.A.	PO.	A.	E.	F.A.
1980—Philadelphia	Nat.	PR-O-DH	6	19	2	5	1	0	0	1	.263	4	1	0	1.000
1982—St. Louis	Nat.	OF-DH	7	28	6	9	4	1	0	1	.321	11	0	0	1.000
1985—Kansas City	Amer.	OF	7	27	4	9	3	0	0	4	.333	7	2	0	1.000
World Series Totals—3 Years			20	74	12	23	8	1	0	6	.311	22	3	0	1.000

ALL-STAR GAME RECORD

Year	League	Pos.	AB.	R.	H.	2B.	3B.	HR.	RBI.	B.A.	PO.	A.	E.	F.A.
1982—National		OF	0	0	0	0	0	0	0	.000	1	0	0	1.000

MICHAEL ANTHONY SMITH
(Mike)

Born October 31, 1963, at San Antonio, Tex.
Height, 6.03. Weight, 190.
Throws and bats righthanded.
Attended Ranger Junior College, Ranger, Tex.

Led Southern League in hit batsmen with 10 in 1988.
Tied for Eastern League lead in games started by pitchers with 27 in 1987.
Tied for Midwest League lead in wild pitches with 19 in 1986.

Year Club	League	G.	IP.	W.	L.	Pct.	H.	R.	ER.	SO.	BB.	ERA.
1984—Sarasota Reds	Gulf Coast	11	67	2	4	.333	65	33	27	65	24	3.63
1985—Billings	Pioneer	7	33⅔	2	2	.500	24	15	11	24	24	2.94
1985—Cedar Rapids	Midwest	8	44⅓	5	1	.833	38	20	16	28	22	3.25
1986—Cedar Rapids	Midwest	28	★191	10	10	.500	155	88	71	172	106	3.35
1987—Vermont	Eastern	27	171⅓	8	12	.400	152	78	64	104	★117	3.36
1988—Chattanooga†	Southern	28	194⅓	9	10	.474	160	90	69	141	★98	3.20
1989—Rochester	Int'national	36	56	2	4	.333	45	23	20	48	22	3.21
1989—Baltimore	American	13	20	2	0	1.000	25	19	17	12	14	7.65
1990—Rochester	Int'national	29	123⅓	9	6	.600	118	76	68	112	73	4.96
1990—Baltimore‡	American	2	3	0	0	.000	4	4	4	2	1	12.00
Major League Totals—2 Years		15	23	2	0	1.000	29	23	21	14	15	8.22

Selected by San Diego Padres' organization in 4th round of free-agent draft, January 11, 1983.
Selected by Cincinnati Reds' organization in 5th round of free-agent draft, January 17, 1984.
†Drafted by Baltimore Orioles, December 5, 1988; Cincinnati Reds turned down right to reclaim.
‡Released, December 3, 1990.

OSBORNE EARL SMITH
(Ozzie)

Born December 26, 1954, at Mobile, Ala.
Height, 5.10. Weight, 160.
Throws right and bats left and righthanded.
Received degree from California Polytechnic State University, San Luis Obispo, Calif.

Holds major league records for most assists by shortstop, season (621), 1980; most years with 500 or more assists by shortstop (8); fewest chances accepted for leader, shortstop, season (692), 1989; most years leading league in assists and chances accepted, shortstop (8).

Shares major league record for most double plays by shortstop, extra-inning game (6), August 25, 1979 (19 innings).

Shares National League records for most consecutive years leading league in assists by shortstop (4), 1979 through 1982; most years leading league in fielding average by shortstop, 100 or more games (6); highest fielding average by shortstop, season, 150 or more games (.987), 1987.

Shares modern National League record for most consecutive years leading league in fielding average by shortstop, 100 or more games (4), 1984 through 1987.

Major League stolen bases: 1978 (40), 1979 (28), 1980 (57), 1981 (22), 1982 (25), 1983 (34), 1984 (35), 1985 (31), 1986 (31), 1987 (43), 1988 (57), 1989 (29), 1990 (32). Total—464.

Led National League in sacrifice hits with 28 in 1978 and 23 in 1980.

Led National League shortstops in total chances with 933 in 1980, 658 in 1981, 844 in 1983, 827 in 1985, 771 in 1987, 775 in 1988 and 709 in 1989.

Led National League shortstops in double plays with 113 in 1980, 111 in 1987 and tied for lead with 94 in 1984 and 96 in 1986.

Led Northwest League in stolen bases with 30 in 1977.
Led Northwest League shortstops in double plays with 40 in 1977.

Named shortstop on THE SPORTING NEWS National League All-Star Team, 1982 and 1984 through 1987.
Named shortstop on THE SPORTING NEWS National League All-Star fielding team, 1980 through 1990.
Named shortstop on THE SPORTING NEWS National League Silver Slugger team, 1987.

Year Club	League	Pos.	G.	AB.	R.	H.	2B.	3B.	HR.	RBI.	B.A.	PO.	A.	E.	F.A.
1977—Walla Walla	N'west	SS	●68	★287	★69	87	10	2	1	35	.303	130	★254	23	★.943
1978—San Diego	Nat.	SS	159	590	69	152	17	6	1	46	.258	264	548	25	.970
1979—San Diego	Nat.	SS	156	587	77	124	18	6	0	27	.211	256	★555	20	.976
1980—San Diego	Nat.	SS	158	609	67	140	18	5	0	35	.230	★288	★621	24	.974
1981—San Diego†	Nat.	SS	●110	★450	53	100	11	2	0	21	.222	220	★422	16	★.976
1982—St. Louis	Nat.	SS	140	488	58	121	24	1	2	43	.248	279	★535	13	★.984
1983—St. Louis	Nat.	SS	159	552	69	134	30	6	3	50	.243	★304	519	21	.975
1984—St. Louis‡	Nat.	SS	124	412	53	106	20	5	1	44	.257	233	437	12	★.982
1985—St. Louis	Nat.	SS	158	537	70	148	22	3	6	54	.276	264	★549	14	★.983
1986—St. Louis	Nat.	SS	153	514	67	144	19	4	0	54	.280	229	453	15	★.978
1987—St. Louis	Nat.	SS	158	600	104	182	40	4	0	75	.303	245	★516	10	★.987
1988—St. Louis	Nat.	SS	153	575	80	155	27	1	3	51	.270	234	★519	22	.972
1989—St. Louis§	Nat.	SS	155	593	82	162	30	8	2	50	.273	209	★483	17	.976
1990—St. Louis	Nat.	SS	143	512	61	130	21	1	1	50	.254	212	378	12	.980
Major League Totals—13 Years			1926	7019	910	1798	297	52	19	600	.256	3237	6535	221	.978

Selected by Detroit Tigers' organization in 7th round of free-agent draft, June 8, 1976.
Selected by San Diego Padres' organization in 4th round of free-agent draft, June 7, 1977.
†Traded to St. Louis Cardinals for Shortstop Garry Templeton, February 11, 1982.
‡On disabled list, July 14 to August 19, 1984.
§On disabled list, March 31 to April 15, 1989.

Year	Club	League	Pos.	G.	AB.	R.	H.	2B.	3B.	HR.	RBI.	B.A.	PO.	A.	E.	F.A.
1982—St. Louis		Nat.	SS	3	9	0	5	0	0	0	3	.556	4	11	0	1.000
1985—St. Louis		Nat.	SS	6	23	4	10	1	1	1	3	.435	6	16	0	1.000
1987—St. Louis		Nat.	SS	7	25	2	5	0	1	0	1	.200	10	19	1	.967
Championship Series Totals—3 Years				16	57	6	20	1	2	1	7	.351	20	46	1	.985

WORLD SERIES RECORD

Year	Club	League	Pos.	G.	AB.	R.	H.	2B.	3B.	HR.	RBI.	B.A.	PO.	A.	E.	F.A.
1982—St. Louis		Nat.	SS	7	24	3	5	0	0	0	1	.208	22	17	0	1.000
1985—St. Louis		Nat.	SS	7	23	1	2	0	0	0	0	.087	10	16	1	.963
1987—St. Louis		Nat.	SS	7	28	3	6	0	0	0	2	.214	7	19	0	1.000
World Series Totals—3 Years				21	75	7	13	0	0	0	3	.173	39	52	1	.989

ALL-STAR GAME RECORD

Year	League	Pos.	AB.	R.	H.	2B.	3B.	HR.	RBI.	B.A.	PO.	A.	E.	F.A.
1981—National		SS	0	0	0	0	0	0	0	.000	1	0	0	1.000
1982—National		PR-SS	0	0	0	0	0	0	0	.000	0	1	0	1.000
1983—National		SS	2	1	1	0	0	0	0	.500	0	0	0	.000
1984—National		SS	3	0	0	0	0	0	0	.000	3	0	0	1.000
1985—National		SS	4	0	0	0	0	0	0	.000	1	3	0	1.000
1986—National		SS	1	0	0	0	0	0	0	.000	3	2	0	1.000
1987—National		SS	2	0	0	0	0	0	0	.000	3	2	1	.833
1988—National		SS	2	0	0	0	0	0	0	.000	1	4	0	1.000
1989—National		SS	4	0	1	0	0	0	0	.250	1	3	0	1.000
1990—National		SS	1	0	0	0	0	0	0	.000	1	1	0	1.000
All-Star Game Totals—10 Years			19	1	2	0	0	0	0	.105	14	16	1	.968

PETER JOHN SMITH
(Pete)

Born February 27, 1966, at Abington, Mass.
Height, 6.02. Weight, 200.
Throws and bats righthanded.

Led National League in balks with 7 in 1989.

Year	Club	League	G.	IP.	W.	L.	Pct.	H.	R.	ER.	SO.	BB.	ERA.
1984—Sarasota Phillies		Gulf Coast	8	37	1	2	.333	28	11	6	35	16	1.46
1985—Clearwater†		Florida St.	26	153	12	10	.545	135	68	56	80	80	3.29
1986—Greenville		Southern	24	104⅔	1	8	.111	117	88	68	64	78	5.85
1987—Greenville		Southern	29	177⅓	9	9	.500	162	76	66	119	67	3.35
1987—Atlanta		National	6	31⅔	1	2	.333	39	21	17	11	14	4.83
1988—Atlanta		National	32	195⅓	7	15	.318	183	89	80	124	88	3.69
1989—Atlanta		National	28	142	5	14	.263	144	83	75	115	57	4.75
1990—Atlanta‡		National	13	77	5	6	.455	77	45	41	56	24	4.79
1990—Greenville		Southern	2	3⅓	0	0	.000	1	0	0	2	0	0.00
Major League Totals—4 Years			79	446	18	37	.327	443	238	213	306	183	4.30

Selected by Philadelphia Phillies' organization in 1st round (21st player selected) of free-agent draft, June 4, 1984.
†Traded with Catcher Ozzie Virgil to Atlanta Braves for Pitcher Steve Bedrosian and Outfielder Milt Thompson, December 10, 1985.
‡On disabled list, June 25 to September 3, 1990; included rehabilitation disability assignment to Greenville, August 26 to September 2, 1990.

ZANE WILLIAM SMITH

Born December 28, 1960, at Madison, Wis.
Height, 6.02. Weight, 195.
Throws and bats lefthanded.
Attended Indiana State University, Terre Haute, Ind.

Major League saves: 1986 (1), 1989 (2). Total—3.
Led National League hitters in sacrifice hits with 14 in 1987.
Tied for National League lead in games started by pitchers with 36 in 1987.
Named lefthanded pitcher on THE SPORTING NEWS National League All-Star Team, 1987.

Year	Club	League	G.	IP.	W.	L.	Pct.	H.	R.	ER.	SO.	BB.	ERA.
1982—Anderson		S. Atlantic	12	63	5	3	.625	65	53	48	32	34	6.86
1983—Durham		Carolina	27	170⅔	9	●15	.375	183	109	93	126	83	4.90
1984—Greenville		Southern	9	60	7	0	1.000	47	13	11	35	23	1.65
1984—Richmond		Int'national	19	123⅔	7	4	.636	113	62	57	68	65	4.15
1984—Atlanta		National	3	20	1	0	1.000	16	7	5	16	13	2.25
1985—Atlanta†		National	42	147	9	10	.474	135	70	62	85	80	3.80
1986—Atlanta		National	38	204⅔	8	16	.333	209	109	92	139	105	4.05
1987—Atlanta		National	36	242	15	10	.600	245	★130	110	130	91	4.09
1988—Atlanta‡		National	23	140⅓	5	10	.333	159	72	67	59	44	4.30
1989—Atlanta§-Montreal		National	48	147	1	13	.071	141	76	57	93	52	3.49
1990—Montreal x-Pittsburgh y		National	33	215⅓	12	9	.571	196	77	61	130	50	2.55
Major League Totals—7 Years			223	1116⅓	51	68	.429	1101	541	454	652	435	3.66

Selected by Atlanta Braves' organization in 3rd round of free-agent draft, June 7, 1982.
†On disabled list, August 5 to September 1, 1985.
‡On disabled list, August 25, 1988 through remainder of season.

§Traded to Montreal Expos for Pitchers Sergio Valdez and Nate Minshey and Outfielder Kevin Dean, July 2, 1989.
xTraded to Pittsburgh Pirates for Pitcher Scott Ruskin, Shortstop Willie Greene and a player to be named later, August 8, 1990; Montreal Expos acquired Outfielder Moises Alou to complete deal, August 16, 1990.
yGranted free agency, November 5, 1990; re-signed by Pirates, December 6, 1990.

CHAMPIONSHIP SERIES RECORD

Shares record for most games lost, series (2), 1990.

Year Club	League	G.	IP.	W.	L.	Pct.	H.	R.	ER.	SO.	BB.	ERA.
1990—Pittsburgh	National	2	9	0	2	.000	14	6	6	8	1	6.00

JOHN ANDREW SMOLTZ

Born May 15, 1967, at Detroit, Mich.
Height, 6.03. Weight, 185.
Throws and bats righthanded.

Led National League in wild pitches with 14 in 1990.
Tied for Florida State League lead in balks with 6 in 1986.

Year Club	League	G.	IP.	W.	L.	Pct.	H.	R.	ER.	SO.	BB.	ERA.
1986—Lakeland†	Florida St.	17	96	7	8	.467	86	44	38	47	31	3.56
1987—Glens Falls	Eastern	21	130	4	10	.286	131	89	82	86	81	5.68
1987—Richmond	Int'national	3	16	0	1	.000	17	11	11	5	11	6.19
1988—Richmond	Int'national	20	135⅓	10	5	.667	118	49	42	115	37	2.79
1988—Atlanta	National	12	64	2	7	.222	74	40	39	37	33	5.48
1989—Atlanta	National	29	208	12	11	.522	160	79	68	168	72	2.94
1990—Atlanta	National	34	231⅓	14	11	.560	206	109	99	170	*90	3.85
Major League Totals—3 Years		75	503⅓	28	29	.491	440	228	206	375	195	3.68

Selected by Detroit Tigers' organization in 22nd round of free-agent draft, June 3, 1985.
†Traded to Atlanta Braves for pitcher Doyle Alexander, August 12, 1987.

ALL-STAR GAME RECORD

Year League	IP.	W.	L.	Pct.	H.	R.	ER.	SO.	BB.	ERA.
1989—National	1	0	1	.000	2	1	1	0	0	9.00

JAMES CORY SNYDER

(Known by middle name.)

Born November 11, 1962, at Englewood, Calif.
Height, 6.03. Weight, 185.
Throws and bats righthanded.
Attended Brigham Young University, Provo, Utah.
Son of Jim Snyder, infielder in Milwaukee Braves' organization, 1961 and 1962.

Major League stolen bases: 1986 (2), 1987 (5), 1988 (5), 1989 (6), 1990 (1). Total—19.
Hit three home runs in a game, May 21, 1987.
Led Eastern League in total bases with 255, game-winning RBIs with 14 and sacrifice flies with 12 in 1985.
Led Eastern League third basemen in putouts with 132, total chances with 391 and double plays with 26 in 1985.
Named Eastern League Most Valuable Player, 1985.
Member of 1984 U.S. Olympic baseball team.
Named shortstop on THE SPORTING NEWS College Baseball All-America Team, 1984.

Year Club	League	Pos.	G.	AB.	R.	H.	2B.	3B.	HR.	RBI.	B.A.	PO.	A.	E.	F.A.
1985—Waterbury	East.	3B-SS	*139	512	77	144	25	1	*28	*94	.281	134	231	33	.917
1986—Maine	Int.	3B-SS	49	192	25	58	19	0	9	32	.302	46	87	8	.943
1986—Cleveland	Amer.	OF-SS-3B	103	416	58	113	21	1	24	69	.272	213	84	10	.967
1987—Cleveland	Amer.	OF-SS	157	577	74	136	24	2	33	82	.236	313	53	15	.961
1988—Cleveland	Amer.	OF	142	511	71	139	24	3	26	75	.272	314	*16	5	.985
1989—Cleveland†	Amer.	*OF-SS	132	489	49	105	17	0	18	59	.215	297	32	1	*.997
1989—Canton-Akron	East.	OF	4	11	3	5	0	0	0	2	.455	5	2	0	1.000
1990—Cleveland‡	Amer.	OF-SS	123	438	46	102	27	3	14	55	.233	229	18	7	.972
Major League Totals—5 Years			657	2431	298	595	113	9	115	340	.245	1366	203	38	.976

Selected by Cleveland Indians' organization in 1st round (fourth player selected) of free-agent draft, June 4, 1984.
†On disabled list, July 14 to July 30, 1989; included rehabilitation disability assignment to Canton-Akron, July 24 to July 30, 1989.
‡Traded with Infielder Lindsay Foster to Chicago White Sox for Pitchers Eric King and Shawn Hillegas, December 4, 1990.

LUIS SOJO

Name pronounced SOW-ho.

Born January 3, 1966, at Barquisimeto, Venezuela.
Height, 5.11. Weight, 165.
Throws and bats righthanded.

Major League stolen bases: 1990 (1).
Led International League in sacrifice flies with 9 in 1990.

Year Club	League	Pos.	G.	AB.	R.	H.	2B.	3B.	HR.	RBI.	B.A.	PO.	A.	E.	F.A.
1986—				(Played in Dominican Republic League)											
1987—Myrtle Beach	S. Atl.	S-2-3-O	72	223	23	47	5	4	2	15	.211	104	123	14	.942
1988—Myrtle Beach	S. Atl.	SS	135	*536	83	*155	22	5	5	56	.289	191	407	28	.955
1989—Syracuse	Int.	*SS-2B	121	482	54	133	20	5	3	54	.276	170	348	23	*.957
1990—Syracuse	Int.	2B-SS	75	297	39	88	12	3	6	25	.296	138	212	10	.972
1990—Toronto†	Amer.	2-S-O-3	33	80	14	18	3	0	1	9	.225	34	31	5	.929
Major League Totals—1 Year			33	80	14	18	3	0	1	9	.225	34	31	5	.929

Signed as free agent by Toronto Blue Jays' organization, January 3, 1986.

†Traded with Outfielder Junior Felix and a player to be named later to California Angels for Outfielder Devon White, Pitcher Willie Fraser and a player to be named later, December 2, 1990; Toronto Blue Jays acquired Pitcher Marcus Moore and California acquired Catcher Ken Rivers to complete deal, December 4, 1990.

PAUL ANTHONY SORRENTO

Born November 17, 1965, at Somerville, Mass.
Height, 6.02. Weight, 210.
Throws right and bats lefthanded.
Attended Florida State University, Tallahassee, Fla.

Major League stolen bases: 1990 (1).
Led Southern League first basemen in double plays with 103 in 1989.

Year Club League	Pos.	G.	AB.	R.	H.	2B.	3B.	HR.	RBI.	B.A.	PO.	A.	E.	F.A.
1986—Quad Cities............ Midw.	OF	53	177	33	63	11	2	6	34	.356	83	7	1	.989
1986—Palm Springs........ Calif.	OF	16	62	5	15	3	0	1	7	.242	16	1	1	.944
1987—Palm Springs....... Calif.	OF	114	370	66	83	14	2	8	45	.224	123	10	4	.971
1988—Palm Springs†...... Calif.	1B-OF	133	465	91	133	30	6	14	99	.286	719	55	18	.977
1989—Orlando .... South.	1B	140	509	81	130	*35	2	27	*112	.255	1070	41	*24	.979
1989—Minnesota............ Amer.	1B	14	21	2	5	0	0	0	1	.238	13	0	0	1.000
1990—Portland................. P. C.	1B-OF	102	354	59	107	27	1	19	72	.302	695	52	13	.983
1990—Minnesota............ Amer.	1B	41	121	11	25	4	1	5	13	.207	118	7	1	.992
Major League Totals—2 Years...............		55	142	13	30	4	1	5	14	.211	131	7	1	.993

Selected by California Angels' organization in 4th round of free-agent draft, June 2, 1986.

†Traded with Pitchers Mike Cook and Rob Wassenaar to Minnesota Twins for Pitchers Bert Blyleven and Kevin Trudeau, November 3, 1988.

SAMUEL SOSA
(Sammy)

Born November 10, 1968, at San Pedro de Macoris, D.R.
Height, 6.00. Weight, 175.
Throws and bats righthanded.

Major League stolen bases: 1989 (7), 1990 (32). Total—39.
Led Gulf Coast League in total bases with 96 in 1986.
Tied for South Atlantic League lead in double plays by outfielders with 4 in 1987.

Year Club League	Pos.	G.	AB.	R.	H.	2B.	3B.	HR.	RBI.	B.A.	PO.	A.	E.	F.A.
1986—Sarasota Rangers Gulf C.	OF	61	229	38	63	*19	1	4	28	.275	92	9	•6	.944
1987—Gastonia................. S. Atl.	OF	129	519	73	145	27	4	11	59	.279	183	12	17	.920
1988—Port Charlotte...... Fla. St.	OF	131	507	70	116	13	*12	9	51	.229	227	11	7	.971
1989—Tulsa .... Texas	OF	66	273	45	81	15	4	7	31	.297	110	7	4	.967
1989—Texas†-Chicago.... Amer.	OF	58	183	27	47	8	0	4	13	.257	94	2	4	.960
1989—Oklahoma City ..... A. A.	OF	10	39	2	4	2	0	0	3	.103	22	0	2	.917
1989—Vancouver............. P. C.	OF	13	49	7	18	3	0	1	5	.367	43	1	0	1.000
1990—Chicago .... Amer.	OF	153	532	72	124	26	10	15	70	.233	315	14	*13	.962
Major League Totals—2 Years................		211	715	99	171	34	10	19	83	.239	409	16	17	.962

Signed as free agent by Texas Rangers' organization, July 30, 1985.

†Traded with Shortstop Scott Fletcher and Pitcher Wilson Alvarez to Chicago White Sox for Outfielder Harold Baines and Infielder Fred Manrique, July 29, 1989.

WILLIAM JAMES SPIERS III

Name pronounced SPY-ers.

(Bill)

Born June 5, 1966, at Orangeburg, S.C.
Height, 6.02. Weight, 190.
Throws right and bats lefthanded.
Attended Clemson University, Clemson, S.C.

Major League stolen bases: 1989 (10), 1990 (11). Totals—21.
Named shortstop on THE SPORTING NEWS College Baseball All-America Team, 1987.

Year Club League	Pos.	G.	AB.	R.	H.	2B.	3B.	HR.	RBI.	B.A.	PO.	A.	E.	F.A.
1987—Helena................... Pion.	SS	6	22	4	9	1	0	0	3	.409	8	6	6	.700
1987—Beloit .... Midw.	SS	64	258	43	77	10	1	3	26	.298	111	160	20	.931
1988—Stockton .... Calif.	SS	84	353	68	95	17	3	5	52	.269	140	240	19	.952
1988—El Paso.................. Texas	SS	47	168	22	47	5	2	3	21	.280	73	141	13	.943
1989—Milwaukee............ Amer.	S-3-2-1	114	345	44	88	9	3	4	33	.255	164	295	21	.956
1989—Denver .... A. A.	SS	14	47	9	17	2	1	2	8	.362	32	33	2	.970
1990—Denver† .... A. A.	SS	11	38	6	12	0	0	1	7	.316	22	23	2	.957
1990—Milwaukee............ Amer.	SS	112	363	44	88	15	3	2	36	.242	159	326	12	.976
Major League Totals—2 Years................		226	708	88	176	24	6	6	69	.249	323	621	33	966

Selected by Milwaukee Brewers' organization in 1st round (13th player selected) of free-agent draft, June 2, 1987.

†On Milwaukee disabled list, April 6 to May 15, 1990; included rehabilitation disability assignment to Denver, April 27 to May 14, 1990.

STEVEN MICHAEL SPRINGER
(Steve)

Born February 11, 1961, at Long Beach, Calif.
Height, 6.01. Weight, 190.
Throws and bats righthanded.
Attended Golden West College, Huntington Beach, Calif., and
received degree from University of Utah, Salt Lake City, Utah.

Led South Atlantic League in game-winning RBIs with 18 in 1984.
Led International League second basemen in errors with 21 and double plays with 86 in 1986.

Year Club	League	Pos.	G.	AB.	R.	H.	2B.	3B.	HR.	RBI.	B.A.	PO.	A.	E.	F.A.
1982—Little Falls	NYP	OF-3B	67	244	49	60	11	0	11	38	.246	90	14	8	.929
1983—Columbia	S. Atl.	2B-OF-3B	130	488	99	*165	24	9	12	88	.338	250	217	23	.953
1984—Jackson	Texas	2-S-3-O	103	362	41	99	21	3	5	40	.273	144	245	24	.942
1985—Tidewater	Int.	2B-3B	126	479	59	125	20	4	7	56	.261	234	379	15	.976
1986—Tidewater	Int.	2-3-O-S	117	440	52	120	19	6	4	46	.273	235	338	23	.961
1987—Tidewater	Int.	3-2-S-O	132	467	65	131	23	4	7	54	.281	158	337	26	.950
1988—Tidewater†	Int.	2B-3B-OF	97	337	42	88	15	0	2	25	.261	134	216	11	.958
1988—Vancouver	P. C.	3B-2B-SS	27	105	15	28	4	1	2	9	.267	15	57	3	.959
1989—Vancouver‡	P. C.	2B-3B	137	520	61	144	21	3	8	56	.277	214	367	19	.968
1990—Colo. Sp.§-L. Veg.	P. C.	2-3-S-O	95	324	46	88	26	5	8	52	.272	134	223	16	.957
1990—Cleveland x	Amer.	3B	4	12	1	2	0	0	0	1	.167	2	3	0	1.000
Major League Totals—1 Year			4	12	1	2	0	0	0	1	.167	2	3	0	1.000

Selected by New York Mets' organization in 20th round of free-agent draft, June 7, 1982.

†Traded with Pitcher Tom McCarthy to Chicago White Sox' organization for Outfielder Vince Harris and Catcher/First Baseman Mike Maksudian, August 3, 1988.

‡Granted free agency, October 15, 1989; signed by Colorado Springs (Cleveland Indians' organization), December 15, 1989.

§Released, July 31, 1990; signed by Las Vegas (San Diego Padres' organization), August 1, 1990.

xGranted free agency, October 15, 1990; signed by Seattle Mariners' organization, January 16, 1991.

ROBERT MICHAEL STANLEY
(Mike)

Born June 25, 1963, at Fort Lauderdale, Fla.
Height, 6.01. Weight, 185.
Throws and bats righthanded.
Attended University of Florida, Gainesville, Fla.

Major League stolen bases: 1986 (1), 1987 (3), 1989 (1), 1990 (1). Total—6.

Year Club	League	Pos.	G.	AB.	R.	H.	2B.	3B.	HR.	RBI.	B.A.	PO.	A.	E.	F.A.
1985—Salem	Carol.	1B-C	4	9	2	5	0	0	0	3	.556	19	1	1	.952
1985—Burlington	Midw.	C-1B-OF	13	42	8	13	2	0	1	6	.310	45	2	0	1.000
1985—Tulsa	Texas	C-1-O-2	46	165	24	51	10	0	3	17	.309	289	18	6	.981
1986—Tulsa	Texas	C-1B-3B	67	235	41	69	16	2	6	35	.294	379	45	2	.995
1986—Texas	Amer.	3B-C-OF	15	30	4	10	3	0	1	1	.333	14	8	1	.957
1986—Oklahoma City	A. A.	C-3B-1B	56	202	37	74	13	3	5	49	.366	206	55	9	.967
1987—Oklahoma City	A. A.	C-1B	46	182	43	61	8	3	13	54	.335	277	32	2	.994
1987—Texas	Amer.	C-1B-OF	78	216	34	59	8	1	6	37	.273	389	26	7	.983
1988—Texas†	Amer.	C-1B-3B	94	249	21	57	8	0	3	27	.229	342	17	4	.989
1989—Texas‡	Amer.	C-1B-3B	67	122	9	30	3	1	1	11	.246	117	8	3	.977
1990—Texas§	Amer.	C-3B-1B	103	189	21	47	8	1	2	19	.249	261	25	4	.986
Major League Totals—5 Years			357	806	89	203	30	3	13	95	.252	1123	84	19	.985

Selected by Texas Rangers' organization in 16th round of free-agent draft, June 3, 1985.

†On disabled list, July 24 to August 14, 1988.

‡On disabled list, August 18 to September 2, 1989.

§Granted free agency, November 15, 1990.

WILLIAM MICHAEL STANTON
(Mike)

Born June 2, 1967, at Houston, Tex.
Height, 6.01. Weight, 190.
Throws and bats lefthanded.
Attended Alvin Community College, Alvin, Tex.

Major League saves: 1989 (7), 1990 (2). Total—9.

Year Club	League	G.	IP.	W.	L.	Pct.	H.	R.	ER.	SO.	BB.	ERA.
1987—Pulaski	Ap'lachian	15	83⅓	4	8	.333	64	37	30	82	42	3.24
1988—Burlington	Midwest	30	154	11	5	.688	154	86	62	160	69	3.62
1988—Durham	Carolina	2	12⅓	1	0	1.000	14	3	2	14	5	1.46
1989—Greenville	Southern	47	51⅓	4	1	.800	32	10	9	58	31	1.58
1989—Richmond	Int'national	13	20	2	0	1.000	6	0	0	20	13	0.00
1989—Atlanta	National	20	24	0	1	.000	17	4	4	27	8	1.50
1990—Atlanta†	National	7	7	0	3	.000	16	16	14	7	4	18.00
1990—Greenville	Southern	4	5⅔	0	1	.000	7	1	1	4	3	1.59
Major League Totals—2 Years		27	31	0	4	.000	33	20	18	34	12	5.23

Selected by Atlanta Braves' organization in 13th round of free-agent draft, June 2, 1987.

†On disabled list, April 27, 1990 through remainder of season; included rehabilitation disability assignment to Greenville, May 31 to June 5 and August 21 to August 29, 1990.

MATTHEW SCOTT STARK
(Matt)

Born January 21, 1965, at Whittier, Calif.
Height, 6.04. Weight, 245.
Throws and bats righthanded.

Tied for Southern League lead in sacrifice flies with 12 in 1990.
Led Southern League catchers in double plays with 12 in 1986.

Year	Club	League	Pos.	G.	AB.	R.	H.	2B.	3B.	HR.	RBI.	B.A.	PO.	A.	E.	F.A.
1983—Medicine Hat	Pion.		C	60	206	29	58	6	0	8	49	.282	215	19	10	.959
1984—Florence†	S. Atl.		C	69	205	24	46	7	1	3	27	.224	383	36	12	.972
1985—Florence	S. Atl.		C	110	381	66	113	15	0	13	70	.297	392	36	17	.962
1985—Knoxville	South.		C	18	53	3	13	1	0	1	3	.245	85	8	4	.959
1986—Knoxville	South.		C	120	424	63	125	21	0	17	72	.295	665	73	16	.979
1987—Toronto‡	Amer.		C	5	12	0	1	0	0	0	0	.083	25	1	0	1.000
1987—Knoxville	South.		C	25	87	10	26	3	2	2	18	.299	18	3	0	1.000
1988—Knoxville§xy	South.		C	97	334	37	89	17	1	11	54	.266	78	9	1	.989
1989—						(Out of Organized Baseball)										
1990—Birmingham	South.		C-1B	129	453	69	140	26	0	14	*109	.309	6	0	0	1.000
1990—Chicago	Amer.		DH-PH	8	16	0	4	1	0	0	3	.250	0	0	0	.000
Major League Totals—3 Years				13	28	0	5	1	0	0	3	.179	25	1	0	1.000

Selected by Toronto Blue Jays' organization in 1st round (ninth player selected) of free-agent draft, June 6, 1983.
†On disabled list, July 7, 1984 through remainder of season.
‡On disabled list, April 16 to May 6, 1987.
§On Toronto disabled list, March 22 to June 17, 1988; included rehabilitation disability assignment to Knoxville, May 28 to June 16, 1988.
xDrafted by Atlanta Braves, December 5, 1988.
yReleased, March 27, 1989; signed by Birmingham (Chicago White Sox' organization), January 23, 1990.

TERRY LEE STEINBACH

Born March 2, 1962, at New Ulm, Minn.
Height, 6.01. Weight, 195.
Throws and bats righthanded.
Attended University of Minnesota, Minneapolis, Minn.
Brother of Tom Steinbach, outfielder in Seattle Mariners' organization, 1983.

Shares major league record by hitting home run in first major league at-bat, September 12, 1986.
Major League stolen bases: 1987 (1), 1988 (3), 1989 (1). Total—5.
Led Southern League in passed balls with 22 in 1986.
Led Midwest League third basemen in double plays with 31 in 1984.
Led Northwest League third basemen in assists with 122 and tied for lead in errors with 17 in 1983.
Named Southern League Most Valuable Player, 1986.

Year	Club	League	Pos.	G.	AB.	R.	H.	2B.	3B.	HR.	RBI.	B.A.	PO.	A.	E.	F.A.
1983—Medford	N'west		3B-OF-1B	62	219	42	69	16	0	6	38	.315	105	124	21	.916
1984—Madison	Midw.		3B-1B-P	135	474	57	140	24	6	11	79	.295	107	257	27	.931
1985—Huntsville	South.		C-3-1-O-P	128	456	64	124	31	3	9	72	.272	187	43	6	.975
1986—Huntsville	South.		C-1B-3B	138	505	113	164	33	2	24	*132	.325	620	73	14	.980
1986—Oakland	Amer.		C	6	15	3	5	0	0	2	4	.333	21	4	1	.962
1987—Oakland	Amer.		C-3B-1B	122	391	66	111	16	3	16	56	.284	642	44	10	.986
1988—Oakland†	Amer.		C-3-1-O	104	351	42	93	19	1	9	51	.265	536	58	9	.985
1989—Oakland	Amer.		C-O-1-3	130	454	37	124	13	1	7	42	.273	612	47	11	.984
1990—Oakland‡	Amer.		C-1B	114	379	32	95	15	2	9	57	.251	401	31	5	.989
Major League Totals—5 Years				476	1590	180	428	63	7	43	210	.269	2212	184	36	.985

Selected by Cleveland Indians' organization in 16th round of free-agent draft, June 3, 1980.
Selected by Oakland A's organization in 9th round of free-agent draft, June 6, 1983.
†On disabled list, May 6 to June 1, 1988.
‡On disabled list, July 3 to July 28, 1990.

CHAMPIONSHIP SERIES RECORD

Year	Club	League	Pos.	G.	AB.	R.	H.	2B.	3B.	HR.	RBI.	B.A.	PO.	A.	E.	F.A.
1988—Oakland	Amer.		C	2	4	0	1	0	0	0	0	.250	12	0	0	1.000
1989—Oakland	Amer.		C-DH	4	15	0	3	0	0	0	1	.200	17	0	0	1.000
1990—Oakland	Amer.		C	3	11	2	5	0	0	0	1	.455	11	0	0	1.000
Championship Series Totals—3 Years				9	30	2	9	0	0	0	2	.300	13	0	0	1.000

WORLD SERIES RECORD

Year	Club	League	Pos.	G.	AB.	R.	H.	2B.	3B.	HR.	RBI.	B.A.	PO.	A.	E.	F.A.
1988—Oakland	Amer.		C-DH	3	11	0	4	1	0	0	0	.364	11	3	0	1.000
1989—Oakland	Amer.		C	4	16	3	4	0	1	1	7	.250	27	2	0	1.000
1990—Oakland	Amer.		C	3	8	0	1	0	0	0	0	.125	8	1	0	1.000
World Series Totals—3 Years				10	35	3	9	1	1	1	7	.257	46	6	0	1.000

ALL-STAR GAME RECORD

Shares All-Star Game record for hitting home run in first at-bat, July 12, 1988.

Year	League	Pos.	AB.	R.	H.	2B.	3B.	HR.	RBI.	B.A.	PO.	A.	E.	F.A.
1988—American		C	1	1	1	0	0	1	2	1.000	3	1	1	.800
1989—American		C	3	0	1	0	0	0	0	.333	6	1	0	1.000
All-Star Game Totals—2 Years			4	1	2	0	0	1	2	.500	9	2	1	.917

Year Club	League	G.	IP.	W.	L.	Pct.	H.	R.	ER.	SO.	BB.	ERA.
1984—Madison	Midwest	2	3	0	0	.000	2	4	3	0	4	9.00
1985—Huntsville	Southern	1	1	0	0	.000	0	0	0	0	0	0.00

CARL RAY STEPHENS JR.

(Known by middle name.)

Born September 22, 1962, at Houston, Tex.
Height, 6.00. Weight, 190.
Throws and bats righthanded.
Attended Middle Georgia College, Cochran, Ga.,
and Troy State University, Troy, Ala.

Led American Association catchers in total chances with 661 and passed balls with 13 in 1988.

Year Club	League	Pos.	G.	AB.	R.	H.	2B.	3B.	HR.	RBI.	B.A.	PO.	A.	E.	F.A.
1985—Erie	NYP	C	9	31	3	9	1	1	1	5	.290	68	17	1	.988
1985—Savannah	S. Atl.	C	39	127	11	26	6	0	0	6	.205	229	30	4	.985
1986—Savannah	S. Atl.	C	95	325	52	71	10	0	13	56	.218	570	★70	12	.982
1986—Louisville	A. A.	C	12	31	2	6	1	0	1	2	.194	38	6	1	.978
1987—Arkansas..............	Texas	C	100	307	35	77	20	0	8	42	.251	553	75	5	.992
1987—Louisville	A. A.	C	9	30	1	4	0	0	0	2	.133	53	4	1	.983
1988—Louisville	A. A.	C	115	355	26	67	13	2	3	25	.189	★590	★64	7	★.989
1989—Arkansas..............	Texas	C	112	363	49	95	14	0	7	44	.262	545	63	9	.985
1990—Louisville	A. A.	C	98	294	20	65	8	1	3	27	.221	552	55	8	.987
1990—St. Louis.................	Nat.	C	5	15	2	2	1	0	1	1	.133	31	2	0	1.000
Major League Totals—1 Year.................			5	15	2	2	1	0	1	1	.133	31	2	0	1.000

Selected by St. Louis Cardinals' organization in 6th round of free-agent draft, June 3, 1985.

PHILLIP RAYMOND STEPHENSON

(Phil)

Born September 19, 1960, at Guthrie, Okla.
Height, 6.01. Weight, 201.
Throws and bats lefthanded.
Received bachelor of arts degree in business management from Wichita State University, Wichita, Kan.
Brother of Gene Stephenson, baseball coach at Wichita State University.

Major League stolen bases: 1989 (1), 1990 (2). Total—3.
Led American Association in intentional bases on balls received with 9 in 1989 and tied for lead with 9 in 1988.
Led American Association in slugging percentage with .566 in 1988.
Led Eastern League in bases on balls received with 114 in 1983 and 129 in 1986.
Tied for Eastern League lead in sacrifice flies with 10 in 1983.
Led American Association first basemen in double plays with 103 in 1988.
Led Eastern League first basemen in putouts with 1,164 and total chances with 1,332 in 1986.
Named first baseman on The Sporting News College Baseball All-America Team, 1981.

Year Club	League	Pos.	G.	AB.	R.	H.	2B.	3B.	HR.	RBI.	B.A.	PO.	A.	E.	F.A.
1982—Modesto.................	Calif.	1B	64	212	39	60	14	2	5	26	.283	436	39	4	.992
1983—Albany	East.	●1B-OF	133	436	90	122	●30	3	19	77	.280	771	85	●14	.984
1984—Tacoma.................	P. C.	OF-1B	124	398	70	120	25	1	10	69	.302	418	40	9	.981
1985—Tacoma†...............	P. C.	OF-1B	56	171	30	36	11	0	5	24	.211	117	6	5	.961
1985—Midland‡..............	Texas	1B-OF	50	176	39	52	14	0	7	41	.295	340	27	3	.992
1986—Pittsfield	East.	★1B-OF-P	●140	423	72	115	29	2	12	68	.272	1165	★163	5	★.996
1987—Iowa	A. A.	1B-OF	105	298	53	91	24	2	10	56	.305	735	71	10	.988
1988—Iowa	A. A.	1B	118	426	69	125	28	11	22	81	.293	925	★88	10	.990
1989—Chi.§x-S.D.............	Nat.	1B-OF	27	38	4	9	0	0	2	2	.237	42	4	1	.979
1989—Iowa	A. A.	1B-OF	84	290	52	87	17	3	13	62	.300	648	51	7	.990
1990—San Diego	Nat.	1B	103	182	26	38	9	1	4	19	.209	345	36	1	.997
Major League Totals—2 Years.................			130	220	30	47	9	1	6	21	.214	387	40	2	.995

Selected by Montreal Expos' organization in 5th round of free-agent draft, June 8, 1981.
Selected by Oakland A's organization in 3rd round of free-agent draft, June 7, 1982.
†Loaned to Midland (California Angels' organization), July 7, 1985; returned, September 10, 1985.
‡Traded with Third Baseman Bob Bathe to Chicago Cubs for Second Baseman Gary Jones and Pitcher John Cox, January 17, 1986.
§On disabled list, May 27 to June 11, 1989.
xTraded to San Diego Padres, September 5, 1989, completing deal in which Chicago Cubs traded Pitcher Calvin Schiraldi, Outfielder Darrin Jackson and a player to be named later to San Diego for Outfielder Marvell Wynne and Infielder Luis Salazar, August 30, 1989.

PITCHING RECORD

Year Club	League	G.	IP.	W.	L.	Pct.	H.	R.	ER.	SO.	BB.	ERA.
1986—Pittsfield	Eastern	3	4	0	0	.000	1	0	0	1	2	0.00

DeWAIN LEE STEVENS

(Known by middle name.)

Born July 10, 1967, at Kansas City, Mo.
Height, 6.04. Weight, 219.
Throws and bats lefthanded.

Major League stolen bases: 1990 (1).

Tied for Pacific Coast League lead in intentional bases on balls received with 11 in 1990.
Tied for Northwest League lead in game-winning RBIs with 8 in 1986.
Led Texas League outfielders in errors with 12 in 1988.
Led California League first basemen in putouts with 1,028, assists with 66 and fielding percentage with .986 in 1987.

Year Club	League	Pos.	G.	AB.	R.	H.	2B.	3B.	HR.	RBI.	B.A.	PO.	A.	E.	F.A.
1986—Salem	N'west	OF-1B	72	267	45	75	18	2	6	47	.281	231	18	5	.980
1987—Palm Springs	Calif.	1B-OF	140	532	82	130	29	2	19	97	.244	1031	68	18	.984
1988—Midland	Texas	OF-1B	116	414	79	123	26	4	23	76	.297	217	16	14	.943
1989—Edmonton	P. C.	1B-OF	127	446	72	110	29	9	14	74	.247	635	40	7	.990
1990—Edmonton	P. C.	OF-1B	90	338	57	99	31	2	16	66	.293	284	10	6	.980
1990—California	Amer.	1B	67	248	28	53	10	0	7	32	.214	597	36	4	.994
Major League Totals—1 Year			67	248	28	53	10	0	7	32	.214	597	36	4	.994

Selected by California Angels' organization in 1st round (22nd player selected) of free-agent draft, June 2, 1986.

DAVID KEITH STEWART
(Dave)

Born February 19, 1957, at Oakland, Calif.
Height, 6.02. Weight, 200.
Throws and bats righthanded.
Attended Merritt College, Oakland, Calif., and California State University, Hayward, Calif.

Shares American League record for fewest complete games for leader, season (11), 1990.
Pitched 5-0 no-hit victory against Toronto Blue Jays, June 29, 1990.
Major League saves: 1981 (6), 1982 (1), 1983 (8), 1985 (4). Total—19.
Led American League in balks with 16 in 1988.
Led American League pitchers in games started with 37 in 1988 and tied for lead with 36 in both 1989 and 1990.
Tied for American League lead in complete games with 14 in 1988 and 11 in 1990.
Tied for American League lead in shutouts with 4 in 1990.
Led Pacific Coast League pitchers in games started with 29 in 1980.
Tied for Texas League lead in games started by pitchers with 28 in 1978.
Tied for Midwest League lead in complete games with 15, shutouts with 3 and balks with 3 in 1977.
Named righthanded pitcher on THE SPORTING NEWS American League All-Star Team, 1988.

Year Club	League	G.	IP.	W.	L.	Pct.	H.	R.	ER.	SO.	BB.	ERA.
1975—Bellingham	Northwest	22	49	0	5	.000	59	46	30	37	49	5.51
1976—Danville	Midwest	4	10	0	2	.000	17	20	18	10	16	16.20
1976—Bellingham	Northwest	24	50	1	1	.500	47	35	28	53	58	5.04
1977—Clinton	Midwest	24	176	★17	4	★.810	152	52	42	144	72	2.15
1977—Albuquerque	P. Coast	1	6	1	0	1.000	4	3	3	3	6	4.50
1978—San Antonio	Texas	28	★193	14	12	.538	181	99	79	130	97	3.68
1978—Los Angeles	National	1	2	0	0	.000	1	0	0	1	0	0.00
1979—Albuquerque	P. Coast	28	170	11	12	.478	198	112	99	105	81	5.24
1980—Albuquerque	P. Coast	31	★202	●15	10	.600	189	94	83	125	89	3.70
1981—Los Angeles	National	32	43	4	3	.571	40	13	12	29	14	2.51
1982—Los Angeles	National	45	146⅓	9	8	.529	137	72	62	80	49	3.81
1983—Los Angeles†	National	46	76	5	2	.714	67	28	25	54	33	2.96
1983—Texas	American	8	59	5	2	.714	50	15	14	24	17	2.14
1984—Texas	American	32	192⅓	7	14	.333	193	106	101	119	87	4.73
1985—Texas‡	American	42	81⅓	0	6	.000	86	53	49	64	37	5.42
1985—Philadelphia	National	4	4⅓	0	0	.000	5	4	3	2	4	6.23
1986—Philadelphia§	National	8	12⅓	0	0	.000	15	9	9	9	4	6.57
1986—Tacoma	P. Coast	1	3	0	0	.000	4	1	0	3	1	0.00
1986—Oakland	American	29	149⅓	9	5	.643	137	67	62	102	65	3.74
1987—Oakland	American	37	261⅓	●20	13	.606	224	121	107	205	105	3.68
1988—Oakland	American	37	★275⅔	21	12	.636	240	111	99	192	110	3.23
1989—Oakland	American	36	257⅔	21	9	.700	★260	105	95	155	69	3.32
1990—Oakland	American	36	★267	22	11	.667	226	84	76	166	83	2.56
National League Totals—6 Years		136	284	18	13	.581	265	126	111	175	104	3.52
American League Totals—8 Years		257	1543⅓	105	72	.593	1416	662	603	1027	573	3.52
Major League Totals—11 Years		393	1827⅔	123	85	.591	1681	788	714	1202	677	3.52

Selected by Los Angeles Dodgers' organization in 16th round of free-agent draft, June 4, 1975.
†Traded with a player to be named later to Texas Rangers for Pitcher Rick Honeycutt, August 19, 1983; Texas acquired Pitcher Ricky Wright to complete deal, September 16, 1983.
‡Traded to Philadelphia Phillies for Pitcher Rick Surhoff, September 13, 1985.
§Released, May 9, 1986; signed by Tacoma (Oakland A's organization), May 23, 1986.

DIVISION SERIES RECORD

Year Club	League	G.	IP.	W.	L.	Pct.	H.	R.	ER.	SO.	BB.	ERA.
1981—Los Angeles	National	2	⅔	0	2	.000	4	3	3	1	0	40.50

CHAMPIONSHIP SERIES RECORD

Holds record for most games won, lifetime (5).
Shares American League record for most games won, series (2), 1989.

Year Club	League	G.	IP.	W.	L.	Pct.	H.	R.	ER.	SO.	BB.	ERA.
1988—Oakland	American	2	13⅓	1	0	1.000	9	2	2	11	6	1.35
1989—Oakland	American	2	16	2	0	1.000	13	5	5	9	3	2.81
1990—Oakland	American	2	16	2	0	1.000	8	2	2	4	2	1.13
Championship Series Totals—3 Years		6	45⅓	5	0	1.000	30	9	9	24	11	1.79

WORLD SERIES RECORD

Year Club	League	G.	IP.	W.	L.	Pct.	H.	R.	ER.	SO.	BB.	ERA.
1981—Los Angeles	National	2	1⅔	0	0	.000	1	0	0	1	2	0.00
1988—Oakland	American	2	14⅓	0	1	.000	12	7	5	5	5	3.14
1989—Oakland	American	2	16	2	0	1.000	10	3	3	14	2	1.69
1990—Oakland	American	2	13	0	2	.000	10	6	4	5	6	2.77
World Series Totals—4 Years		8	45	2	3	.400	33	16	12	25	15	2.40

ALL-STAR GAME RECORD

Year League	IP.	W.	L.	Pct.	H.	R.	ER.	SO.	BB.	ERA.
1989—American	1	0	0	.000	3	2	2	0	2	18.00

DAVID ANDREW STIEB

Name pronounced Steeb.

(Dave)

Born July 22, 1957, at Santa Ana, Calif.
Height, 6.01. Weight, 195.
Throws and bats righthanded.
Attended Santa Ana College, Santa Ana, Calif., and
Southern Illinois University, Carbondale, Ill.
Brother of Steve Stieb, catcher in Atlanta Braves' organization, 1979 through 1981.

Shares major league record for most consecutive one-hit games (2), September 24 and 30, 1988.
Shares American League record for most low-hit (no-hit and one-hit) games, season (3), 1988.
Pitched 3-0 no-hit victory against Cleveland Indians, September 2, 1990.
Major League saves: 1986 (1).
Led American League in hit batsmen with 14 in 1983, 11 in 1984, 15 in 1986, 13 in 1989 and tied for lead with 11 in 1981.
Led American League in complete games with 19 and shutouts with 5 in 1982.
Named American League Pitcher of the Year by THE SPORTING NEWS, 1982.
Named righthanded pitcher on THE SPORTING NEWS American League All-Star Team, 1982.
Named outfielder on THE SPORTING NEWS College Baseball All-America Team, 1978.

Year Club	League	G.	IP.	W.	L.	Pct.	H.	R.	ER.	SO.	BB.	ERA.
1978—Dunedin	Florida St.	4	26	2	0	1.000	23	10	6	8	1	2.08
1979—Dunedin	Florida St.	8	51	5	0	1.000	54	30	24	38	28	4.24
1979—Syracuse	Int'national	7	51	5	2	.714	39	15	12	20	14	2.12
1979—Toronto	American	18	129	8	8	.500	139	70	62	52	48	4.33
1980—Toronto†	American	34	243	12	15	.444	232	108	100	108	83	3.70
1981—Toronto	American	25	184	11	10	.524	148	70	65	89	61	3.18
1982—Toronto	American	38	★288⅓	17	14	.548	★271	116	104	141	75	3.25
1983—Toronto	American	36	278	17	12	.586	223	105	94	187	93	3.04
1984—Toronto	American	35	★267	16	8	.667	215	87	84	198	88	2.83
1985—Toronto	American	36	265	14	13	.519	206	89	73	167	96	★2.48
1986—Toronto‡	American	37	205	7	12	.368	239	128	108	127	87	4.74
1987—Toronto	American	33	185	13	9	.591	164	92	84	115	87	4.09
1988—Toronto‡	American	32	207⅓	16	8	.667	157	76	70	147	79	3.04
1989—Toronto	American	33	206⅔	17	8	.680	164	83	77	101	76	3.35
1990—Toronto	American	33	208⅔	18	6	.750	179	73	68	125	64	2.93
Major League Totals—12 Years		390	2667	166	123	.574	2337	1097	989	1557	937	3.34

Selected by Toronto Blue Jays' organization in 5th round of free-agent draft, June 6, 1978.
†Appeared in one game as outfielder with no chances and had one at-bat.
‡Appeared in one game as a pinch-runner.

CHAMPIONSHIP SERIES RECORD

Holds American League Championship Series record for most strikeouts, series (18), 1985.
Shares Championship Series record for most games lost, series (2), 1989.

Year Club	League	G.	IP.	W.	L.	Pct.	H.	R.	ER.	SO.	BB.	ERA.
1985—Toronto	American	3	20⅓	1	1	.500	11	7	7	18	10	3.10
1989—Toronto	American	2	11⅓	0	2	.000	12	8	8	10	6	6.35
Championship Series Totals—2 Years		5	31⅔	1	3	.250	23	15	15	28	16	4.26

ALL-STAR GAME RECORD

Shares All-Star Game records for most wild pitches, game and inning (2), July 8, 1980, seventh inning.

Year League	IP.	W.	L.	Pct.	H.	R.	ER.	SO.	BB.	ERA.
1980—American	1	0	0	.000	1	1	0	0	2	0.00
1981—American	1⅔	0	0	.000	1	0	0	1	1	0.00
1983—American	3	1	0	1.000	0	1	0	4	1	0.00
1984—American	2	0	1	.000	3	2	1	2	0	4.50
1985—American	1	0	0	.000	0	0	0	2	1	0.00
1988—American	1	0	0	.000	1	0	0	0	0	0.00
1990—American	2	0	0	.000	0	0	0	1	1	0.00
All-Star Game Totals—7 Years	11⅔	1	1	.500	6	4	1	10	6	0.77

RECORD AS OUTFIELDER

Year Club	League	Pos.	G.	AB.	R.	H.	2B.	3B.	HR.	RBI.	B.A.	PO.	A.	E.	F.A.
1978 Dunedin	Fla. St.	OF P	35	00	10	19	3	0	1	9	.192	85	7	3	.968

KURT ANDREW STILLWELL

Born June 4, 1965, at Glendale, Calif.
Height, 5.11. Weight, 175.
Throws right and bats left and righthanded.
Son of Ron Stillwell, infielder with Washington Senators, 1961 and 1962; and brother of Rod Stillwell,
shortstop in Kansas City Royals' organization.

Shares American League record for fewest errors for leader by shortstop, season (24), 1990.
Major League stolen bases: 1986 (6), 1987 (4), 1988 (6), 1989 (9). Total—25.

Year Club	League	Pos.	G.	AB.	R.	H.	2B.	3B.	HR.	RBI.	B.A.	PO.	A.	E.	F.A.
1983—Billings	Pion.	SS	65	250	47	81	10	1	2	44	.324	73	137	*30	.875
1984—Cedar Rapids	Midw.	SS	112	382	63	96	15	1	4	33	.251	156	245	25	.941
1985—Denver†	A. A.	SS-3B	59	182	28	48	7	4	1	22	.264	103	135	25	.905
1986—Cincinnati	Nat.	SS	104	279	31	64	6	1	0	26	.229	107	205	16	.951
1986—Denver	A. A.	SS	10	30	2	7	0	0	0	2	.233	14	21	5	.875
1987—Cincinnati‡	Nat.	SS-2B-3B	131	395	54	102	20	7	4	33	.258	144	247	23	.944
1988—Kansas City	Amer.	SS	128	459	63	115	28	5	10	53	.251	170	349	13	.976
1989—Kansas City§	Amer.	SS	130	463	52	121	20	7	7	54	.261	179	334	16	.970
1990—Kansas City	Amer.	SS	144	506	60	126	35	4	3	51	.249	181	350	*24	.957
National League Totals—2 Years			235	674	85	166	26	8	4	59	.246	251	452	39	.947
American League Totals—3 Years			402	1428	175	362	83	16	20	158	.254	530	1033	53	.967
Major League Totals—5 Years			637	2102	260	528	109	24	24	217	.251	781	1485	92	.961

Selected by Cincinnati Reds' organization in 1st round (second player selected) of free-agent draft, June 6, 1983.
†On disabled list, August 9, 1985 through remainder of season.
‡Traded with Pitcher Ted Power to Kansas City Royals for Pitcher Danny Jackson and Shortstop Angel Salazar,
November 6, 1987.
§On disabled list, July 6 to August 3, 1989.

ALL-STAR GAME RECORD

Year League	Pos.	AB.	R.	H.	2B.	3B.	HR.	RBI.	B.A.	PO.	A.	E.	F.A.
1988—American	SS	0	0	0	0	0	0	0	.000	1	0	0	1.000

JEFFERY GLEN STONE
(Jeff)

Born December 26, 1960, at Kennett, Mo.
Height, 6.00. Weight, 180.
Throws right and bats lefthanded.
Twin brother of Jerome Stone, outfielder in Philadelphia Phillies organization, 1984 through 1985.

Major League stolen bases: 1983 (4), 1984 (27), 1985 (15), 1986 (19), 1987 (3), 1988 (4), 1989 (3). Total—75.
Led Carolina League in stolen bases with 94 in 1982.
Led South Atlantic League in being hit by pitch with 15 and stolen bases with 123 in 1981.
Led South Atlantic League outfielders in total chances with 290 in 1981.
Named Eastern League Most Valuable Player, 1983.

Year Club	League	Pos.	G.	AB.	R.	H.	2B.	3B.	HR.	RBI.	B.A.	PO.	A.	E.	F.A.
1980—Central Oregon	N'west	OF	55	241	52	63	12	4	0	19	.261	116	4	4	.968
1981—Spartanburg	S. Atl.	OF	134	516	*108	143	13	9	3	53	.277	*264	11	15	.948
1982—Peninsula	Carol.	OF	*137	*559	110	166	18	*13	2	50	.297	●276	9	8	.973
1983—Reading†	East.	OF	125	492	*109	156	25	10	9	67	.317	226	6	9	.963
1983—Philadelphia	Nat.	OF	9	4	2	3	0	2	0	3	.750	0	0	0	.000
1984—Portland	P. C.	OF	82	355	59	109	15	●14	7	34	.307	194	7	12	.944
1984—Philadelphia‡	Nat.	OF	51	185	27	67	4	6	1	15	.362	75	1	7	.916
1985—Philadelphia	Nat.	OF	88	264	36	70	4	3	3	11	.265	82	4	3	.966
1985—Portland	P. C.	OF	67	252	58	83	16	8	2	28	.329	103	6	6	.948
1986—Portland	P. C.	OF	31	118	25	40	4	1	2	9	.339	60	0	1	.984
1986—Philadelphia	Nat.	OF	82	249	32	69	6	4	6	19	.277	103	8	2	.982
1987—Maine	Int.	OF	40	151	22	35	6	2	1	10	.232	89	1	2	.978
1987—Philadelphia§x	Nat.	OF	66	125	19	32	7	1	1	16	.256	32	3	0	1.000
1988—Baltimore y	Amer.	OF	26	61	4	10	1	0	0	1	.164	23	3	1	.963
1988—Rochester z	Int.	OF	71	267	39	74	12	5	3	27	.277	102	9	3	.974
1989—Oklahoma City	A.A.	OF	13	39	4	7	2	0	0	1	.179	6	0	1	.857
1989—Texas a-Boston	Amer.	OF	40	51	8	9	1	2	0	6	.176	8	0	0	1.000
1989—Pawtucket b	Int.	OF	57	196	30	55	10	2	4	22	.281	70	1	2	.973
1990—Pawtucket	Int.	OF	112	393	51	110	28	1	8	41	.280	182	7	4	.979
1990—Boston c	Amer.	PH-DH	10	2	1	1	0	0	0	1	.500	0	0	0	.000
National League Totals—5 Years			296	827	116	241	21	16	11	64	.291	292	16	12	.963
American League Totals—3 Years			76	114	13	20	2	2	0	8	.175	31	3	1	.971
Major League Totals—8 Years			372	941	129	261	23	18	11	72	.277	323	19	13	.963

Signed as free agent by Philadelphia Phillies' organization, August 26, 1979.
†On disabled list, May 11 to May 21, 1983.
‡On disabled list, July 7 to August 6, 1984; included rehabilitation disability assignment to Portland, August 2 to
August 6, 1984.
§On disabled list, June 16 to July 20, 1987; included rehabilitation disability assignment to Maine, July 1 to July 20,
1987.
xTraded with Infielder Rick Schu and Outfielder Keith Hughes to Baltimore Orioles for Outfielder Mike Young and
a player to be named later, March 21, 1988; Philadelphia Phillies acquired Outfielder Frank Bellino to complete deal,
June 14, 1988.
yOn disabled list, April 29 to June 12, 1988; included rehabilitation disability assignment to Rochester, May 24 to
June 12, 1988.

zReleased, December 5, 1988; signed by Oklahoma City (Texas Rangers' organization), February 25, 1989.
aSold to Boston Red Sox, June 26, 1989.
bReleased, October 12, 1989; signed by Pawtucket (Boston Red Sox' organization), December 13, 1989.
cReleased, November 20, 1990.

MELVIN LEON STOTTLEMYRE JR.
(Mel)

Born December 28, 1963, at Prosser, Wash.
Height, 6.00. Weight 190.
Throws and bats righthanded.
Attended University of Nevada, Las Vegas, Nev.
Son of Mel Stottlemyre Sr., pitcher with the New York Yankees, 1964 through 1974; minor league
pitching instructor, Seattle Mariners' organization, 1977 through 1981; and coach with
the New York Mets since 1984; nephew of Jeff Stottlemyre, pitcher in Seattle Mariners'
organization, 1980 through 1983; and brother of Todd Stottlemyre, pitcher with Toronto Blue Jays.

Year	Club	League	G.	IP.	W.	L.	Pct.	H.	R.	ER.	SO.	BB.	ERA.
1985—Asheville†	S. Atlantic	14	78⅔	5	4	.556	65	33	24	70	38	2.75
1986—Osceola	Florida St.	9	35⅔	0	7	.000	48	38	31	25	26	7.82
1986—Asheville	S. Atlantic	7	34⅓	3	1	.750	32	13	8	28	12	2.10
1987—Columbus‡-Memphis	Southern	20	127⅓	7	6	.538	125	68	61	85	41	4.31
1988—Memphis§	Southern	7	45	3	2	.600	41	18	12	29	14	2.40
1989—Omaha	Am. Assoc.	7	7⅔	1	1	.500	6	4	2	9	3	2.35
1989—Baseball City	Florida St.	13	23⅔	1	2	.333	30	14	13	25	9	4.94
1989—Memphis	Southern	16	22⅔	3	0	1.000	15	4	4	18	9	1.59
1990—Omaha	Am. Assoc.	29	41⅔	2	1	.667	26	9	7	33	11	1.51
1990—Kansas City	American	13	31⅓	0	1	.000	35	18	17	14	12	4.88
Major League Totals—1 Year		13	31⅓	0	1	.000	35	18	17	14	12	4.88

Selected by Seattle Mariners' organization in 28th round of free-agent draft, June 7, 1982.
Selected by Houston Astros' organization in secondary phase of free-agent draft, January 9, 1985.
†On disabled list, July 23, 1985 through remainder of season.
‡Traded to Kansas City Royals' organization for Shortstop Buddy Biancalana, July 29, 1987.
§On disabled list, May 20, 1988 through remainder of season.

TODD VERNON STOTTLEMYRE

Born May 20, 1965, at Yakima, Wash.
Height, 6.03. Weight, 195.
Throws right and bats lefthanded.
Attended Yakima Valley College, Yakima, Wash.
Son of Mel Stottlemyre Sr., pitcher with New York Yankees, 1964 through 1974; minor league
pitching instructor, Seattle Mariners' organization, 1977 through 1981; and coach with
New York Mets since 1984; nephew of Jeff Stottlemyre, pitcher in Seattle
Mariners' organization, 1980 through 1983;
and brother of Mel Stottlemyre Jr., pitcher with Kansas City Royals.
Led International League pitchers in games started with 34 in 1987.

Year	Club	League	G.	IP.	W.	L.	Pct.	H.	R.	ER.	SO.	BB.	ERA.
1986—Ventura County	California	17	103⅔	9	4	.692	76	39	28	104	36	2.43
1986—Knoxville	Southern	18	99	8	7	.533	93	56	46	81	49	4.18
1987—Syracuse	Int'national	34	186⅔	11	●13	.458	189	●103	∗92	143	∗87	4.44
1988—Toronto	American	28	98	4	8	.333	109	70	62	67	46	5.69
1988—Syracuse	Int'national	7	48⅓	5	0	1.000	36	12	11	51	8	2.05
1989—Toronto	American	27	127⅔	7	7	.500	137	56	55	63	44	3.88
1989—Syracuse	Int'national	10	55⅔	3	2	.600	46	23	20	45	15	3.23
1990—Toronto	American	33	203	13	17	.433	214	101	98	115	69	4.34
Major League Totals—3 Years		88	428⅔	24	32	.429	460	227	215	245	159	4.51

Selected by New York Yankees' organization in 5th round of free-agent draft, June 6, 1983.
Selected by St. Louis Cardinals' organization in secondary phase of free-agent draft, January 9, 1985.
Selected by Toronto Blue Jays' organization in secondary phase of free-agent draft, June 3, 1985.

CHAMPIONSHIP SERIES RECORD

Year	Club	League	G.	IP.	W.	L.	Pct.	H.	R.	ER.	SO.	BB.	ERA.
1989—Toronto	American	1	5	0	1	.000	7	4	4	3	2	7.20

DARRYL EUGENE STRAWBERRY

Born March 12, 1962, at Los Angeles, Calif.
Height, 6.06. Weight, 200.
Throws and bats lefthanded.
Brother of Michael Strawberry, outfielder in Los Angeles Dodgers' organization, 1980 and 1981.
Hit three home runs in a game, August 5, 1985.
Major League stolen bases: 1983 (19), 1984 (27), 1985 (26), 1986 (28), 1987 (36), 1988 (29), 1989 (11), 1990 (15)
Total—191.
Led National League in slugging percentage with .545 in 1988.
Led Texas League in slugging percentage with .602, bases on balls received with 100 and caught stealing with 22 in
1982.
Named outfielder on THE SPORTING NEWS National League All-Star Team, 1988 and 1990.
Named outfielder on THE SPORTING NEWS National League Silver Slugger team, 1988 and 1990.
Named National League Rookie Player of the Year by THE SPORTING NEWS, 1983.
Named National League Rookie of the Year by Baseball Writers' Association of America, 1983.

Named Texas League Most Valuable Player, 1982.
Received reported $210,000 bonus to sign with New York Mets, 1980.

Year	Club	League	Pos.	G.	AB.	R.	H.	2B.	3B.	HR.	RBI.	B.A.	PO.	A.	E.	F.A.
1980—Kingsport	Appal.	OF	44	157	27	42	5	2	5	20	.268	55	4	3	.952
1981—Lynchburg	Carol.	OF	123	420	84	107	22	6	13	78	.255	173	8	13	.933
1982—Jackson	Texas	OF	129	435	93	123	19	9	★34	97	.283	211	8	9	.961
1983—Tidewater	Int.	OF	16	57	12	19	4	1	3	13	.333	22	0	4	.846
1983—New York	Nat.	OF	122	420	63	108	15	7	26	74	.257	232	8	4	.984
1984—New York	Nat.	OF	147	522	75	131	27	4	26	97	.251	276	11	6	.980
1985—New York†	Nat.	OF	111	393	78	109	15	4	29	79	.277	211	5	2	.991
1986—New York	Nat.	OF	136	475	76	123	27	5	27	93	.259	226	10	6	.975
1987—New York	Nat.	OF	154	532	108	151	32	5	39	104	.284	272	6	8	.972
1988—New York	Nat.	OF	153	543	101	146	27	3	★39	101	.269	297	4	9	.971
1989—New York	Nat.	OF	134	476	69	107	26	1	29	77	.225	272	4	8	.972
1990—New York‡	Nat.	OF	152	542	92	150	18	1	37	108	.277	268	10	3	.989
Major League Totals—8 Years			1109	3903	662	1025	187	30	252	733	.263	2054	58	46	.979

Selected by New York Mets' organization in 1st round (first player selected) of free-agent draft, June 3, 1980.
†On disabled list, May 12 to June 28, 1985.
‡Granted free agency, November 5, 1990; signed by Los Angeles Dodgers, November 8, 1990.

CHAMPIONSHIP SERIES RECORD

Shares Championship Series record for most strikeouts, series (12), 1986.
Shares National League Championship Series record for most at-bats, series (30), 1988.

Year	Club	League	Pos.	G.	AB.	R.	H.	2B.	3B.	HR.	RBI.	B.A.	PO.	A.	E.	F.A.
1986—New York	Nat.	OF	6	22	4	5	1	0	2	5	.227	9	0	0	1.000
1988—New York	Nat.	OF	7	30	5	9	2	0	1	6	.300	11	0	0	1.000
Championship Series Totals—2 Years			13	52	9	14	3	0	3	11	.269	20	0	0	1.000

WORLD SERIES RECORD

Year	Club	League	Pos.	G.	AB.	R.	H.	2B.	3B.	HR.	RBI.	B.A.	PO.	A.	E.	F.A.
1986—New York	Nat.	OF	7	24	4	5	1	0	1	1	.208	19	0	0	1.000

ALL-STAR GAME RECORD

Year	League	Pos.	AB.	R.	H.	2B.	3B.	HR.	RBI.	B.A.	PO.	A.	E.	F.A.
1984—National		OF	2	0	1	0	0	0	0	.500	0	0	0	.000
1985—National		OF	1	2	1	0	0	0	0	1.000	3	0	0	1.000
1986—National		OF	2	0	1	0	0	0	0	.500	1	0	0	1.000
1987—National		OF	2	0	0	0	0	0	0	.000	0	0	0	.000
1988—National		OF	4	0	1	0	0	0	0	.250	4	0	0	1.000
1990—National		OF	1	0	0	0	0	0	0	.000	3	1	1	.800
All-Star Game Totals—6 Years			12	2	4	0	0	0	0	.333	11	1	1	.923

Named to National League All-Star Team for 1989 game; did not play due to injury.

FRANKLIN LEE STUBBS

Born October 21, 1960, at Laurinburg, N.C.
Height, 6.02. Weight, 209.
Throws and bats lefthanded.
Attended Virginia Tech., Blacksburg, Va.

Shares major league record for fewest putouts by first baseman, game (0), July 25, 1990.
Major League stolen bases: 1984 (2), 1986 (7), 1987 (8), 1988 (11), 1989 (3), 1990 (19). Total—50.
Led National League first basemen in fielding percentage with .994 in 1987.
Named first baseman on THE SPORTING NEWS College Baseball All-America Team, 1982.

Year	Club	League	Pos.	G.	AB.	R.	H.	2B.	3B.	HR.	RBI.	B.A.	PO.	A.	E.	F.A.
1982—Vero Beach†	Fla. St.	1B	16	54	6	11	1	1	3	5	.204	134	3	3	.979
1983—San Antonio	Texas	1B-OF	47	173	35	54	8	3	12	52	.312	425	23	5	.989
1983—Albuquerque	P. C.	OF-1B	76	267	49	74	16	3	16	58	.277	106	3	6	.948
1984—Albuquerque	P. C.	OF-1B	29	108	26	35	5	5	6	24	.324	36	4	2	.952
1984—Los Angeles	Nat.	1B-OF	87	217	22	42	2	3	8	17	.194	417	37	4	.991
1985—Albuquerque	P. C.	1B-OF	132	421	86	118	23	5	32	93	.280	945	87	14	.987
1985—Los Angeles	Nat.	1B	10	9	0	2	0	0	0	2	.222	11	0	0	1.000
1986—Los Angeles	Nat.	OF-1B	132	420	55	95	11	1	23	58	.226	244	14	7	.974
1987—Los Angeles‡	Nat.	1B-OF	129	386	48	90	16	3	16	52	.233	830	79	5	.995
1988—Los Angeles	Nat.	1B-OF	115	242	30	54	13	0	8	34	.223	530	57	13	.978
1989—Los Angeles§x	Nat.	OF-1B	69	103	11	30	6	0	4	15	.291	70	5	3	.962
1990—Houston y	Nat.	1B-OF	146	448	59	117	23	2	23	71	.261	609	43	6	.991
Major League Totals—7 Years			688	1825	225	430	71	9	82	249	.236	2711	235	38	.987

Selected by Los Angeles Dodgers' organization in 1st round (19th player selected) of free-agent draft, June 7, 1982.
†On disabled list, July 5, 1982 through remainder of season.
‡On disabled list, August 3 to August 24, 1987.
§On disabled list, August 20, 1989 through remainder of season.
xTraded to Houston Astros for Pitcher Terry Wells, April 1, 1990.
yGranted free agency, November 5, 1990; signed by Milwaukee Brewers, December 5, 1990.

CHAMPIONSHIP SERIES RECORD

Year	Club	League	Pos.	G.	AB.	R.	H.	2B.	3B.	HR.	RBI.	B.A.	PO.	A.	E.	F.A.
1988—Los Angeles	Nat.	1B-PH	4	8	0	2	0	0	0	0	.250	16	2	0	1.000

Year	Club	League	Pos.	G.	AB.	R.	H.	2B.	3B.	HR.	RBI.	B.A.	PO.	A.	E.	F.A.
1988—Los Angeles		Nat.	1B	5	17	3	5	2	0	0	2	.294	34	0	0	1.000

WILLIAM JAMES SURHOFF
(B. J.)

Born August 4, 1964, at Bronx, N.Y.
Height, 6.01. Weight, 200.
Throws right and bats lefthanded.
Attended University of North Carolina, Chapel Hill, N.C.
Son of Dick Surhoff, forward with New York Knicks and Milwaukee Hawks of the
National Basketball Association, 1952-53 and 1953-54; and brother of
Rich Surhoff, pitcher with Philadelphia Phillies and Texas Rangers, 1985.

Major League stolen bases: 1987 (11), 1988 (21), 1989 (14), 1990 (18). Total—64.
Tied for Pacific Coast League lead in double plays by catchers with 10 in 1986.
Named College Player of the Year by THE SPORTING NEWS, 1985.
Member of 1984 U. S. Olympic baseball team.
Named catcher on THE SPORTING NEWS College Baseball All-America Team, 1985.

Year	Club	League	Pos.	G.	AB.	R.	H.	2B.	3B.	HR.	RBI.	B.A.	PO.	A.	E.	F.A.
1985—Beloit	Midw.		C	76	289	39	96	13	4	7	58	.332	475	44	3	.994
1986—Vancouver	P. C.		C	116	458	71	141	19	3	5	59	.308	539	70	7	*.989
1987—Milwaukee	Amer.		C-3B-1B	115	395	50	118	22	3	7	68	.299	648	56	11	.985 •
1988—Milwaukee	Amer.		C-3-1-S-O	139	493	47	121	21	0	5	38	.245	550	94	8	.988
1989—Milwaukee	Amer.		C-3B	126	436	42	108	17	4	5	55	.248	530	58	10	.983
1990—Milwaukee†	Amer.		C-3B	135	474	55	131	21	4	6	59	.276	619	62	12	.983
Major League Totals—4 Years				515	1798	194	478	81	11	23	220	.266	2347	270	41	.985

Selected by New York Yankees' organization in 5th round of free-agent draft, June 7, 1982.
Selected by Milwaukee Brewers' organization in 1st round (first player selected) of free-agent draft, June 3, 1985.
†On suspended list, August 23 to August 25, 1990.

RICHARD LEE SUTCLIFFE
(Rick)

Born June 21, 1956, at Independence, Mo.
Height, 6.07. Weight, 215.
Throws right and bats lefthanded.
Brother of Terry Sutcliffe, pitcher in Los Angeles Dodgers' organization, 1979 through 1981.

Shares major league record for fewest games won, season, for leader (18), 1987.
Major League saves: 1980 (5), 1982 (1). Total—6.
Led National League in intentional bases on balls issued with 14 in 1987.
Led California League pitchers in games started with 28 in 1975.
Tied for Northwest League lead in shutouts with 2 in 1974.
Named National League Pitcher of the Year by THE SPORTING NEWS, 1984.
Won National League Cy Young Memorial Award, 1984.
Named righthanded pitcher on THE SPORTING NEWS National League All-Star Team, 1984.
Named National League Comeback Player of the Year by THE SPORTING NEWS, 1987.
Named National League Rookie Pitcher of the Year by THE SPORTING NEWS, 1979.
Named National League Rookie of the Year by Baseball Writers' Association of America, 1979.
Received reported $80,000 bonus to sign with Los Angeles Dodgers, 1974.

Year	Club	League	G.	IP.	W.	L.	Pct.	H.	R.	ER.	SO.	BB.	ERA.
1974—Bellingham	Northwest		17	95	10	3	.769	79	42	35	69	48	3.32
1975—Bakersfield	California		28	193	8	*16	.333	*214	*115	*89	91	68	4.15
1976—Waterbury	Eastern		30	187	10	11	.476	*187	90	66	121	45	3.18
1976—Los Angeles	National		1	5	0	0	.000	2	0	0	3	1	0.00
1977—Albuquerque†	P. Coast		17	77	3	10	.231	96	67	55	48	63	6.43
1978—Albuquerque	P. Coast		30	184	13	6	.684	179	101	91	99	92	4.45
1978—Los Angeles	National		2	2	0	0	.000	2	0	0	1	0	0.00
1979—Los Angeles	National		39	242	17	10	.630	217	104	93	117	97	3.46
1980—Los Angeles	National		42	110	3	9	.250	122	73	68	59	55	5.56
1981—Los Angeles‡§	National		14	47	2	2	.500	41	24	21	16	20	4.02
1982—Cleveland	American		34	216	14	8	.636	174	81	71	142	98	*2.96
1983—Cleveland	American		36	243⅓	17	11	.607	251	131	116	160	102	4.29
1984—Cleveland x	American		15	94⅓	4	5	.444	111	60	54	58	46	5.15
1984—Chicago y	National		20	150⅓	16	1	*.941	123	53	45	155	39	2.69
1985—Chicago z	National		20	130	8	8	.500	119	51	46	102	44	3.18
1986—Chicago a	National		28	176⅔	5	14	.263	166	92	91	122	96	4.64
1987—Chicago	National		34	237⅓	*18	10	.643	223	106	97	174	106	3.68
1988—Chicago b	National		32	226	13	14	.481	232	97	97	144	70	3.86
1989—Chicago	National		35	229	16	11	.593	202	98	93	153	69	3.66
1990—Iowa c	Am. Assoc.		2	12⅔	0	2	.000	18	13	11	12	7	7.82
1990—Chicago	National		5	21⅔	0	2	.000	25	14	14	7	12	5.91
National League Totals—12 Years			272	1577	98	81	.547	1474	712	665	1052	610	3.80
American League Totals—3 Years			85	553⅔	35	24	.593	536	272	241	360	246	3.92
Major League Totals—14 Years			357	2130⅔	133	105	.559	2010	984	906	1412	856	3.83

Selected by Los Angeles Dodgers' organization in 1st round (21st player selected) of free-agent draft, June 5, 1974.
†On disabled list, May 3 to May 24, 1977.
‡On disabled list, August 14 to September 5, 1981.

§Traded with Second Baseman Jack Perconte to Cleveland Indians for Outfielder Jorge Orta, Catcher Jack Fimple and Pitcher Larry White, December 9, 1981.

xTraded with Catcher Ron Hassey and Pitcher George Frazier to Chicago Cubs for Outfielders Mel Hall and Joe Carter and Pitchers Don Schulze and Darryl Banks, June 13, 1984.

yGranted free agency, November 8, 1984; re-signed by Cubs, December 14, 1984.

zOn disabled list, May 20 to June 7, July 8 to July 23 and July 29 to September 27, 1985.

aOn disabled list, June 30 to August 3, 1986.

bOn disabled list, May 21 to June 11, 1988.

cOn Chicago disabled list, March 31 to August 29, 1990; included rehabilitation disability assignment to Iowa, April 26 to May 1, 1990.

CHAMPIONSHIP SERIES RECORD

Shares Championship Series record for hitting home run in first series at-bat, October 2, 1984.

Year Club	League	G.	IP.	W.	L.	Pct.	H.	R.	ER.	SO.	BB.	ERA.
1984—Chicago	National	2	13⅓	1	1	.500	9	6	5	10	8	3.38
1989—Chicago	National	1	6	0	0	.000	5	3	3	2	4	4.50
Championship Series Totals—2 Years		3	19⅓	1	1	.500	14	9	8	12	12	3.72

ALL-STAR GAME RECORD

Year League	IP.	W.	L.	Pct.	H.	R.	ER.	SO.	BB.	ERA.
1987—National	2	0	0	.000	1	0	0	0	1	0.00
1989—National	1	0	0	.000	4	2	2	0	0	18.00
All-Star Game Totals—2 Years	3	0	0	.000	5	2	2	0	1	6.00

Member of American League All-Star Team in 1983; did not play.

GLENN EDWARD SUTKO

Born May 9, 1968, at Atlanta, Ga.
Height, 6.03. Weight, 225.
Throws and bats righthanded.
Attended Spartanburg Methodist College, Spartanburg,
S.C., and Dekalb College, Dunwoody, Ga.

Year Club	League	Pos.	G.	AB.	R.	H.	2B.	3B.	HR.	RBI.	B.A.	PO.	A.	E.	F.A.
1988—Billings	Pion.	C	30	84	3	13	2	1	1	8	.155	141	15	5	.969
1989—Greensboro	S. Atl.	C	109	333	44	78	21	0	7	41	.234	676	77	11	.986
1990—Cedar Rapids†	Midw.	C	4	10	0	3	0	0	0	0	.300	21	2	0	1.000
1990—Chattanooga	South.	C-1B	53	174	12	29	7	1	2	11	.167	351	33	4	.990
1990—Cincinnati	Nat.	C	1	1	0	0	0	0	0	0	.000	3	0	0	1.000
Major League Totals—1 Year			1	1	0	0	0	0	0	0	.000	3	0	0	1.000

Selected by Cincinnati Reds' organization in 45th round of free-agent draft, June 2, 1987.

†On disabled list, May 29 to July 12, 1990.

DALE CURTIS SVEUM

Name pronounced Swaim.

Born November 23, 1963, at Richmond, Calif.
Height, 6.03. Weight, 185.
Throws right and bats left and righthanded.

Major League stolen bases: 1986 (4), 1987 (2), 1988 (1). Total—7.
Hit three home runs in a game, July 17, 1987.
Switch-hit home runs in one game, July 17, 1987 and June 12, 1988.
Led American League third basemen in errors with 26 in 1986.
Led Texas League in total bases with 256 in 1984.
Led Texas League third basemen in putouts with 111 in 1984.
Led California League third basemen in assists with 261 in 1983.

Year Club	League	Pos.	G.	AB.	R.	H.	2B.	3B.	HR.	RBI.	B.A.	PO.	A.	E.	F.A.
1982—Pikeville	Appal.	SS-3B	58	223	29	52	13	1	2	21	.233	84	158	36	.871
1983—Stockton	Calif.	3B-SS	135	533	70	139	26	5	5	70	.261	105	281	40	.906
1984—El Paso	Texas	*3B-SS	131	523	92	*172	*41	8	9	84	.329	113	259	*30	.925
1985—Vancouver	P. C.	3B-SS	122	415	42	98	17	3	6	48	.236	81	200	26	.915
1986—Vancouver	P. C.	3B	28	105	16	31	3	2	1	23	.295	22	54	4	.950
1986—Milwaukee†	Amer.	3B-SS-2B	91	317	35	78	13	2	7	35	.246	92	179	30	.900
1987—Milwaukee	Amer.	SS-2B	153	535	86	135	27	3	25	95	.252	242	396	23	.965
1988—Milwaukee	Amer.	SS-2B	129	467	41	113	14	4	9	51	.242	209	375	*27	.956
1989—Beloit‡	Midw.	DH	6	15	0	2	1	0	0	2	.133	0	0	0	.000
1989—Stockton	Calif.	DH	11	43	5	8	0	0	1	5	.186	0	0	0	.000
1990—Milwaukee	Amer.	3-2-1-S	48	117	15	23	7	0	1	12	.197	59	63	6	.953
1990—Denver	A. A.	3-S-1-2	57	218	25	63	17	2	2	26	.289	134	102	12	.952
Major League Totals—4 Years			421	1436	177	349	61	9	42	193	.243	602	1013	86	.949

Selected by Milwaukee Brewers' organization in 1st round (25th player selected) of free-agent draft, June 7, 1982.

†On disabled list, July 23 to August 9, 1986.

‡On Milwaukee disabled list, March 19, 1989 through entire season; included rehabilitation disability assignment to Beloit, June 30 to July 5, 1989; then transferred to Stockton, July 6 to July 18, 1989.

—DID YOU KNOW—

That the Oakland Athletics in 1990 became the first team since the 1973-75 Los Angeles Dodgers to lead their league in ERA for three straight seasons?

RUSSELL HOWARD SWAN
(Russ)

Born January 3, 1964, at Fremont, Calif.
Height, 6.04. Weight, 215.
Throws and bats lefthanded.
Attended Spokane Falls Community College, Spokane, Wash.,
and Texas A&M University, College Station, Tex.

Year Club	League	G.	IP.	W.	L.	Pct.	H.	R.	ER.	SO.	BB.	ERA.
1986—Everett	Northwest	7	46	5	0	1.000	30	17	11	45	22	2.15
1986—Clinton	Midwest	7	43⅔	3	3	.500	36	18	15	37	8	3.09
1987—Fresno	California	12	64	6	3	.667	54	40	27	59	29	3.80
1988—San Jose	California	11	76⅔	7	0	1.000	53	28	19	62	26	2.23
1989—Shreveport	Texas	11	75⅓	2	3	.400	62	25	22	56	22	2.63
1989—San Francisco	National	2	6⅔	0	2	.000	11	10	8	2	4	10.80
1989—Phoenix	P. Coast	14	83	4	3	.571	75	37	31	49	29	3.36
1990—San Francisco	National	2	2⅓	0	1	.000	6	4	1	1	4	3.86
1990—Phoenix†-Calgary	P. Coast	11	56⅔	3	6	.333	69	35	28	35	27	4.45
1990—Seattle‡	American	11	47	2	3	.400	42	22	19	15	18	3.64
National League Totals—2 Years		4	9	0	3	.000	17	14	9	3	8	9.00
American League Totals—1 Year		11	47	2	3	.400	42	22	19	15	18	3.64
Major League Totals—2 Years		15	56	2	6	.250	59	36	28	18	26	4.50

Selected by Houston Astros' organization in 2nd round of free-agent draft, January 17, 1984.
Selected by Seattle Mariners' organization in secondary phase of free-agent draft, June 4, 1984.
Selected by San Francisco Giants' organization in 9th round of free-agent draft, June 2, 1986.
†Traded to Seattle Mariners for Pitcher Gary Eave, May 24, 1990.
‡On disabled list, July 8 to September 1, 1990; included rehabilitation disability assignment to Calgary, August 16 to August 31, 1990.

WILLIAM CHARLES SWIFT
(Bill)

Born October 27, 1961, at Portland, Maine.
Height, 6.00. Weight, 180.
Throws and bats righthanded.
Attended University of Maine, Orono, Maine.

Major League saves: 1989 (1), 1990 (6). Total—7.
Member of 1984 U.S. Olympic baseball team.

Year Club	League	G.	IP.	W.	L.	Pct.	H.	R.	ER.	SO.	BB.	ERA.
1985—Chattanooga†	Southern	7	39	2	1	.667	34	16	16	21	21	3.69
1985—Seattle	American	23	120⅔	6	10	.375	131	71	64	55	48	4.77
1986—Seattle	American	29	115⅓	2	9	.182	148	85	70	55	55	5.46
1986—Calgary	P. Coast	10	57	4	4	.500	57	33	25	29	22	3.95
1987—Calgary‡	P. Coast	5	18⅓	0	0	.000	32	22	18	5	13	8.84
1988—Seattle	American	38	174⅔	8	12	.400	199	99	89	47	65	4.59
1989—San Bernardino§	California	2	10	1	0	1.000	8	0	0	4	2	0.00
1989—Seattle	American	37	130	7	3	.700	140	72	64	45	38	4.43
1990—Seattle	American	55	128	6	4	.600	135	46	34	42	21	2.39
Major League Totals—5 Years		182	668⅔	29	38	.433	753	373	321	244	227	4.32

Selected by Minnesota Twins' organization in 2nd round of free-agent draft, June 6, 1983.
Selected by Seattle Mariners' organization in 1st round (second player selected) of free-agent draft, June 4, 1984.
†On disabled list, May 6 to May 21, 1985.
‡On disabled list, April 22, 1987 through remainder of season.
§On Seattle disabled list, March 28 to April 27, 1989; included rehabilitation disability assignment to San Bernardino, April 18 to April 27, 1989.

FOREST GREGORY SWINDELL
(Greg)

Born January 2, 1965, at Fort Worth, Tex.
Height, 6.03. Weight, 225.
Throws left and bats left and righthanded.
Attended University of Texas, Austin, Tex.

Named lefthanded pitcher on THE SPORTING NEWS College Baseball All-America Team, 1985 and 1986.

Year Club	League	G.	IP.	W.	L.	Pct.	H.	R.	ER.	SO.	BB.	ERA.
1986—Waterloo	Midwest	3	18	2	1	.667	12	2	2	25	3	1.00
1986—Cleveland	American	9	61⅔	5	2	.714	57	35	29	46	15	4.23
1987—Cleveland†	American	16	102⅓	3	8	.273	112	62	58	97	37	5.10
1988—Cleveland	American	33	242	18	14	.563	234	97	86	180	45	3.20
1989—Cleveland‡	American	28	184⅓	13	6	.684	170	71	69	129	51	3.37
1990—Cleveland	American	34	214⅔	12	9	.571	245	110	105	135	47	4.40
Major League Totals—5 Years		120	805	51	39	.567	818	375	347	587	195	3.88

Selected by Cleveland Indians' organization in 1st round (second player selected) of free-agent draft, June 2, 1986.
†On disabled list, June 30, 1987 through remainder of season.
†On disabled list, July 26 to August 30, 1989.

Year	League	IP.	W.	L.	Pct.	H.	R.	ER.	SO.	BB.	ERA.
1989—American		1⅔	0	0	.000	2	0	0	3	0	0.00

PATRICK SEAN TABLER
(Pat)

Born February 2, 1958, at Hamilton, O.
Height, 6.02. Weight, 200.
Throws and bats righthanded.

Major League stolen bases: 1983 (2), 1984 (3), 1986 (3), 1987 (5), 1988 (3). Total—16.
Led Southern League in game-winning RBIs with 13 in 1980.
Led American Association third basemen in total chances with 361 in 1982.
Tied for American Association lead in sacrifice flies with 9 in 1982.

Year	Club	League	Pos.	G.	AB.	R.	H.	2B.	3B.	HR.	RBI.	B.A.	PO.	A.	E.	F.A.
1976—Oneonta	NYP	3B-OF	65	238	27	55	3	0	1	20	.231	79	71	12	.926
1977—Fort Lauderdale	Fla. St.	3B	110	391	35	93	7	1	1	36	.238	87	209	★35	.894
1978—Fort Lauderdale	Fla. St.	1B-3B-OF	138	455	56	124	9	5	5	70	.273	855	88	15	.984
1979—Fort Lauderdale	Fla. St.	O-3-2-1	75	247	39	78	12	4	2	33	.316	102	41	11	.929
1979—West Haven	East.	2B-OF	56	190	33	57	15	3	6	36	.300	124	169	13	.958
1980—Nashville	South.	2B	136	479	82	142	38	8	16	83	.296	262	361	★27	.958
1981—Columbus†‡	Int.	2B-3B	52	179	41	53	14	3	11	33	.296	66	116	14	.929
1981—Iowa	A. A.	2B	63	222	41	68	13	3	6	37	.306	110	141	4	.984
1981—Chicago	Nat.	2B	35	101	11	19	3	1	1	5	.188	70	93	3	.982
1982—Iowa	A. A.	★3B-1B	129	441	89	151	32	★11	17	105	.342	★112	★215	★34	.906
1982—Chicago§x	Nat.	3B	25	85	9	20	4	2	1	7	.235	23	33	3	.949
1983—Charleston	Int.	3B	4	14	2	3	0	1	0	2	.214	2	4	3	.667
1983—Cleveland	Amer.	OF-3B-2B	124	430	56	125	23	5	6	65	.291	197	55	11	.958
1984—Cleveland	Amer.	1-O-3-2	144	473	66	137	21	3	10	68	.290	532	89	7	.989
1985—Cleveland	Amer.	1B-3B-2B	117	404	47	111	18	3	5	59	.275	744	77	14	.983
1986—Cleveland y	Amer.	1B	130	473	61	154	29	2	6	48	.326	846	84	9	.990
1986—Maine	Int.	DH	3	12	5	3	1	0	0	1	.250	0	0	0	.000
1987—Cleveland	Amer.	1B	151	553	66	170	34	3	11	86	.307	650	75	●12	.984
1988—Clev. z-K.C.	Amer.	OF-1B-3B	130	444	53	125	22	3	2	66	.282	182	10	5	.975
1989—Kansas City	Amer.	O-1-2-3	123	390	36	101	11	1	2	42	.259	217	25	4	.984
1990—Kansas City a	Amer.	OF-3B-1B	75	195	12	53	14	0	1	19	.272	101	10	2	.982
1990—New York b	Nat.	OF	17	43	6	12	1	1	1	10	.279	20	1	0	1.000
National League Totals—3 Years			77	229	26	51	8	4	3	22	.223	113	127	6	.976
American League Totals—8 Years			994	3362	397	976	172	20	43	453	.290	3469	425	64	.984
Major League Totals—10 Years			1071	3591	423	1027	180	24	46	475	.286	3582	552	70	.983

Selected by New York Yankees' organization in 1st round (16th player selected) of free-agent draft, June 8, 1976.

†Loaned to Iowa (Chicago Cubs' organization), June 12, 1981; returned, August 19, 1981.

‡Acquired on waivers by Chicago Cubs for two players to be named later, August 19, 1981; New York Yankees acquired Pitcher Bill Caudill, April 1, 1982, and New York organization acquired Pitcher Jay Howell, August 2, 1982, to complete deal.

§Traded with Pitchers Dick Tidrow and Randy Martz and Infielder Scott Fletcher to Chicago White Sox for Pitchers Steve Trout and Warren Brusstar, January 25, 1983.

xTraded to Cleveland Indians for Shortstop Jerry Dybzinski, April 1, 1983.

yOn disabled list, June 11 to June 30, 1986; included rehabilitation disability assignment to Maine, June 26 to June 30, 1986.

zTraded to Kansas City Royals for Pitcher Bud Black, June 3, 1988.

aTraded to New York Mets for Pitcher Archie Corbin, August 30, 1990.

bGranted free agency, November 5, 1990; signed by Toronto Blue Jays, December 5, 1990.

ALL-STAR GAME RECORD

Year	League	Pos.	AB.	R.	H.	2B.	3B.	HR.	RBI.	B.A.	PO.	A.	E.	F.A.
1987—American		PH	1	0	0	0	0	0	0	.000	0	0	0	.000

FRANK DARYL TANANA
Name rhymes with Banana.

Born July 3, 1953, at Detroit, Mich.
Height, 6.03. Weight, 195.
Throws and bats lefthanded.
Attended California State University, Fullerton, Calif.
Son of Frank Richard Tanana, minor league outfielder, 1952 through 1956.

Shares American League record for most consecutive hits allowed, start of game (5), May 18, 1980.
Major League saves: 1990 (1).
Led American League in balks with 8 in 1978 and tied for lead with 4 in 1984.
Led American League in shutouts with 7 in 1977.
Led Texas League in complete games with 15 in 1973.
Named American League Rookie Pitcher of the Year by THE SPORTING NEWS, 1974.
Named lefthanded pitcher on THE SPORTING NEWS American League All-Star Team, 1976 and 1977.
Named Texas League Pitcher of the Year, 1973.

Year	Club	League	G.	IP.	W.	L.	Pct.	H.	R.	ER.	SO.	BB.	ERA.
1971—Idaho Falls†	Pioneer		...	...	...	...	...	...	...	...	...	...	...
1972—Quad Cities	Midwest	19	129	7	2	.778	111	48	40	134	57	2.79
1973—El Paso	Texas	26	★206	16	6	.727	170	72	62	★197	63	2.71
1973—Salt Lake City	P. Coast	2	14	1	0	1.000	11	5	4	15	2	2.57

Year Club	League	G.	IP.	W.	L.	Pct.	H.	R.	ER.	SO.	BB.	ERA.
1973—California	American	4	26	2	2	.500	20	11	9	22	8	3.12
1974—California	American	39	269	14	19	.424	262	104	93	180	77	3.11
1975—California	American	34	257	16	9	.640	211	80	75	*269	73	2.63
1976—California	American	34	288	19	10	.655	212	88	78	261	73	2.44
1977—California	American	31	241	15	9	.625	201	72	68	205	61	*2.54
1978—California	American	33	239	18	12	.600	239	108	97	137	60	3.65
1979—California‡	American	18	90	7	5	.583	93	44	39	46	25	3.90
1980—California§	American	32	204	11	12	.478	223	107	94	113	45	4.15
1981—Boston x	American	24	141	4	10	.286	142	70	63	78	43	4.02
1982—Texas	American	30	194⅓	7	•18	.280	199	102	91	87	55	4.21
1983—Texas	American	29	159⅓	7	9	.438	144	70	56	108	49	3.16
1984—Texas	American	35	246⅓	15	15	.500	234	117	89	141	81	3.25
1985—Texas y-Detroit	American	33	215	12	14	.462	220	112	102	159	57	4.27
1986—Detroit	American	32	188⅓	12	9	.571	196	95	87	119	65	4.16
1987—Detroit z	American	34	218⅔	15	10	.600	216	106	95	146	56	3.91
1988—Detroit	American	32	203	14	11	.560	213	105	95	127	64	4.21
1989—Detroit a	American	33	223⅔	10	14	.417	227	105	89	147	74	3.58
1990—Detroit	American	34	176⅓	9	8	.529	190	104	104	114	66	5.31
Major League Totals—18 Years		541	3580	207	196	.514	3442	1600	1424	2459	1032	3.58

Selected by California Angels' organization in 1st round (13th player selected) of free-agent draft, June 8, 1971.

†Appeared in one game as pinch-runner (did not pitch due to a sore arm).

‡On disabled list, July 9 to September 4, 1979.

§Traded with Pitcher Jim Dorsey and Outfielder Joe Rudi to Boston Red Sox for Outfielder Fred Lynn and Pitcher Steve Renko, January 23, 1981.

xGranted free agency, November 13, 1981; signed by Texas Rangers, January 6, 1982.

yTraded to Detroit Tigers for Pitcher Duane James, June 20, 1985.

zGranted free agency, November 9, 1987.

aGranted free agency, November 13, 1989; re-signed by Tigers, November 20, 1989.

CHAMPIONSHIP SERIES RECORD

Holds records for most hit batsmen, total series (4) and series (3), 1987; most hit batsmen, game (3), October 11, 1987.

Year Club	League	G.	IP.	W.	L.	Pct.	H.	R.	ER.	SO.	BB.	ERA.
1979—California	American	1	5	0	0	.000	6	2	2	3	2	3.60
1987—Detroit	American	1	5⅓	0	1	.000	6	4	3	1	4	5.06
Championship Series Totals—2 Years		2	10⅓	0	1	.000	12	6	5	4	6	4.35

ALL-STAR GAME RECORD

Year League		IP.	W.	L.	Pct.	H.	R.	ER.	SO.	BB.	ERA.
1976—American		2	0	0	.000	3	3	3	0	1	6.00

Named to American League All-Star Team for the 1977 game; replaced due to injury.

Named to American League All-Star Team for 1978 game; did not play.

KEVIN RAY TAPANI
Name pronounced TAP-uh-nee.

Born February 18, 1964, at Des Moines, Ia.
Height, 6.00. Weight, 180.
Throws and bats righthanded.
Received degree in finance from Central Michigan University, Mt. Pleasant, Mich., in 1987.

Year Club	League	G.	IP.	W.	L.	Pct.	H.	R.	ER.	SO.	BB.	ERA.
1986—Medford	Northwest	2	8⅓	1	0	1.000	6	3	0	9	3	0.00
1986—Modesto	California	11	69	6	1	.857	74	26	19	44	22	2.48
1986—Huntsville	Southern	1	6	1	0	1.000	8	4	4	2	1	6.00
1986—Tacoma	P. Coast	1	2⅓	0	1	.000	5	6	4	1	1	15.43
1987—Modesto†	California	24	148⅓	10	7	.588	122	74	62	121	60	3.76
1988—St. Lucie	Florida St.	3	19	1	0	1.000	17	5	3	11	4	1.42
1988—Jackson	Texas	24	62⅓	5	1	.833	46	23	19	35	19	2.74
1989—Tidewater	Int'national	17	109	7	5	.583	113	49	42	63	25	3.47
1989—New York‡	National	3	7⅓	0	0	.000	5	3	3	2	4	3.68
1989—Portland	P. Coast	6	41	4	2	.667	38	15	10	30	12	2.20
1989—Minnesota	American	5	32⅔	2	2	.500	34	15	14	21	8	3.86
1990—Minnesota§	American	28	159⅓	12	8	.600	164	75	72	101	29	4.07
National League Totals—1 Year		3	7⅓	0	0	.000	5	3	3	2	4	3.68
American League Totals—2 Years		33	192	14	10	.583	198	90	86	122	37	4.03
Major League Totals—2 Years		36	199⅓	14	10	.583	203	93	89	124	41	4.02

Selected by Chicago Cubs' organization in 9th round of free-agent draft, June 3, 1985.

Selected by Oakland Athletics' organization in 2nd round of free-agent draft, June 2, 1986.

†As part of an eight-player, three-team deal, New York Mets traded Pitcher Jesse Orosco to Oakland Athletics, December 11, 1987. Oakland then traded Orosco along with Shortstop Alfredo Griffin and Pitcher Jay Howell to Los Angeles Dodgers for Pitchers Bob Welch, Matt Young and Jack Savage. Oakland then traded Savage along with Pitchers Wally Whitehurst and Kevin Tapani to New York.

‡Traded with Pitcher Tim Drummond to Portland (Minnesota Twins' organization), August 1, 1989, as partial completion of deal in which Minnesota Twins traded Pitcher Frank Viola to New York Mets for Pitchers Rick Aguilera and David West and three players to be named later, July 31, 1989. Minnesota acquired Pitcher Jack Savage to complete deal, October 16, 1989.

§On disabled list, August 17 to September 10, 1990.

DANILO TARTABULL (MORA)
(Danny)

Born October 30, 1962, at Miami, Fla.
Height, 6.01. Weight, 205.
Throws and bats righthanded.
Son of Jose Tartabull, outfielder with Kansas City A's, Boston Red Sox and Oakland A's, 1962
through 1970; and minor league manager in Houston Astros' organization, 1982 through 1984;
and brother of Jose Tartabull, Jr., outfielder in Seattle Mariners' organization, 1986 through 1988.

Major League stolen bases: 1985 (1), 1986 (4), 1987 (9), 1988 (8), 1989 (4), 1990 (1). Total—27.
Led American League in game-winning RBIs with 21 in 1987.
Led Pacific Coast League in slugging percentage with .615 and total bases with 291 in 1985.
Led Pacific Coast League shortstops in errors with 35 in 1985.
Led Pacific Coast League shortstops in double plays with 68 in 1984.
Led Florida State League third basemen in errors with 29 in 1981.
Named Pacific Coast League Player of the Year, 1985.
Named Florida State League Most Valuable Player, 1981.

Year	Club	League	Pos.	G.	AB.	R.	H.	2B.	3B.	HR.	RBI.	B.A.	PO.	A.	E.	F.A.
1980—Billings	Pion.	3B-OF-2B	59	157	33	47	10	0	2	27	.299	34	54	14	.863
1981—Tampa	Fla. St.	3B-2B	127	422	86	131	*28	10	14	81	*.310	150	248	39	.911
1982—Waterbury†	East.	2B	126	409	64	93	17	3	17	63	.227	237	306	*32	.944
1983—Chattanooga	South.	2B	128	481	95	145	32	7	13	66	.301	252	405	23	.966
1984—Salt Lake City	P. C.	SS	116	418	69	127	22	9	13	73	.304	181	333	24	.955
1984—Seattle	Amer.	SS-2B	10	20	3	6	1	0	2	7	.300	8	21	2	.935
1985—Calgary	P. C.	SS-3B	125	473	102	142	14	3	*43	*109	.300	181	399	36	.942
1985—Seattle	Amer.	SS-3B	19	61	8	20	7	1	1	7	.328	28	43	4	.947
1986—Seattle‡§	Amer.	OF-2B-3B	137	511	76	138	25	6	25	96	.270	233	111	18	.950
1987—Kansas City	Amer.	OF	158	582	95	180	27	3	34	101	.309	228	11	6	.976
1988—Kansas City	Amer.	OF	146	507	80	139	38	3	26	102	.274	227	8	9	.963
1989—Kansas City x	Amer.	OF	133	441	54	118	22	0	18	62	.268	108	3	2	.982
1990—Kansas City y	Amer.	OF	88	313	41	84	19	0	15	60	.268	81	1	3	.965
Major League Totals—7 Years				691	2435	357	685	139	13	121	435	.281	913	198	44	.962

Selected by Cincinnati Reds' organization in 3rd round of free-agent draft, June 3, 1980.
†Selected by Seattle Mariners' organization in player compensation pool draft, January 20, 1983. (Seattle received compensation for Chicago White Sox' signing of free-agent Pitcher Floyd Bannister, December 13, 1982.)
‡On disabled list, May 15 to May 30, 1986.
§Traded with Pitcher Rick Luecken to Kansas City Royals for Pitchers Scott Bankhead and Steve Shields and Outfielder Mike Kingery, December 10, 1986.
xOn disabled list, June 15 to June 30, 1989.
yOn disabled list, April 11 to May 18 and July 14 to July 31, 1990.

DONALD CLYDE TAYLOR
(Dorn)

Born August 11, 1958, at Abington, Pa.
Height, 6.02. Weight, 180.
Throws and bats righthanded.
Led American Association in home runs allowed with 15 in 1989.
Tied for American Association lead in games started by pitchers with 29 in 1990.

Year	Club	League	G.	IP.	W.	L.	Pct.	H.	R.	ER.	SO.	BB.	ERA.
1982—Greenwood	S. Atlantic	27	164⅔	9	8	.529	128	57	42	133	92	*2.30
1983—Alexandria	Carolina	28	35⅓	2	7	.222	38	33	31	22	30	7.90
1983—Greenwood	S. Atlantic	12	81⅔	6	3	.667	73	35	32	79	40	3.53
1984—Prince William	Carolina	25	161⅔	11	5	.688	133	68	61	148	67	3.40
1985—Nashua†	Eastern	26	112⅔	6	9	.400	101	63	54	64	57	4.31
1986—Nashua‡	Eastern	33	62⅔	2	2	.500	42	13	11	57	26	1.58
1986—Hawaii	P. Coast	5	31⅓	3	1	.750	22	10	7	29	12	2.01
1987—Vancouver	P. Coast	9	57⅔	0	3	.000	46	20	17	47	29	2.65
1987—Pittsburgh§	National	14	53⅓	2	3	.400	48	35	34	37	28	5.74
1987—Harrisburg	Eastern	3	8	1	0	1.000	6	0	0	10	1	0.00
1988—Buffalo	Am. Assoc.	22	139	10	8	.556	125	45	33	65	44	*2.14
1989—Pittsburgh	National	9	10⅔	1	1	.500	14	6	6	3	5	5.06
1989—Buffalo	Am. Assoc.	25	170⅔	10	8	.556	145	61	49	103	51	2.58
1990—Buffalo x	Am. Assoc.	30	*195	14	6	.700	170	74	63	112	51	2.91
1990—Baltimore y	American	4	3⅔	0	1	.000	4	3	1	4	2	2.45
National League Totals—2 Years		23	64	3	4	.429	62	41	40	40	33	5.63
American League Totals—1 Year		4	3⅔	0	1	.000	4	3	1	4	2	2.45
Major League Totals—3 Years		27	67⅔	3	5	.375	66	44	41	44	35	5.45

Signed as free agent by Pittsburgh Pirates' organization, December 11, 1981.
†On disabled list, July 5 to July 21, 1985.
‡On disabled list, April 11 to April 21, 1986.
§On disabled list, July 3 to July 30, 1987; included rehabilitation disability assignment to Harrisburg, July 16 to July 30, 1987.
xTraded to Baltimore Orioles, September 5, 1990, completing deal in which Baltimore traded Pitcher Jay Tibbs to Pittsburgh Pirates for a player to be named later, June 25, 1990.
yReleased, October 10, 1990.

RODNEY SCOTT TAYLOR

(Known by middle name.)

Born August 2, 1967, at Defiance, O.
Height, 6.01. Weight, 185.
Throws and bats lefthanded.
Attended Bowling Green State University, Bowling Green, O.

Year Club	League	G.	IP.	W.	L.	Pct.	H.	R.	ER.	SO.	BB.	ERA.
1988—Elmira	NYP	2	3⅔	1	0	1.000	2	0	0	8	3	0.00
1989—Lynchburg†	Carolina	19	81	5	3	.625	61	33	26	99	25	2.89
1990—Lynchburg	Carolina	13	89	5	6	.455	76	36	27	120	30	2.73
1990—New Britain‡	Eastern	5	27⅓	0	2	.000	23	8	5	27	13	1.65

Selected by Boston Red Sox' organization in 28th round of free-agent draft, June 1, 1988.
†On disabled list, June 15 to July 4, 1989.
‡On disabled list, July 13, 1990 through remainder of season.

WADE ERIC TAYLOR

Born October 19, 1965, at Mobile, Ala.
Height, 6.01. Weight, 185.
Throws and bats righthanded.
Attended Jefferson Davis Junior College, Brewton, Ala.,
and University of Miami, Coral Gables, Fla.

Tied for International League lead in shutouts with 3 in 1990.

Year Club	League	G.	IP.	W.	L.	Pct.	H.	R.	ER.	SO.	BB.	ERA.
1987—Bellingham†	Northwest	12	58⅓	3	5	.375	58	31	29	53	22	4.47
1988—Fort Lauderdale	Florida St.	24	122⅔	4	11	.267	109	53	47	90	57	3.45
1989—Prince William	Carolina	25	142⅔	9	8	.529	131	63	53	104	56	3.34
1990—Albany	Eastern	12	84⅓	6	4	.600	71	30	27	44	18	2.88
1990—Columbus	Int'national	14	98⅔	6	4	.600	91	25	24	57	30	2.19

Selected by Toronto Blue Jays' organization in 9th round of free-agent draft, January 14, 1986.
Selected by Los Angeles Dodgers' organization in secondary phase of free-agent draft, June 2, 1986.
Signed as free agent by Seattle Mariners' organization, June 30, 1987.
†Traded with Pitchers Lee Guetterman and Clay Parker to New York Yankees for Pitcher Steve Trout and Henry Cotto, December 22, 1987.

ANTHONY CHARLES TELFORD

Born March 6, 1966, at San Jose, Calif.
Height, 6.00. Weight, 184.
Throws and bats righthanded.
Attended San Jose State University, San Jose, Calif.

Year Club	League	G.	IP.	W.	L.	Pct.	H.	R.	ER.	SO.	BB.	ERA.
1987—Newark	NYP	6	17⅔	1	0	1.000	16	2	2	27	3	1.02
1987—Hagerstown	Carolina	2	11⅓	1	0	1.000	9	2	2	10	5	1.59
1987—Rochester	Int'national	1	2	0	0	.000	0	0	0	3	3	0.00
1988—Hagerstown†	Carolina	1	7	1	0	1.000	3	0	0	10	0	0.00
1989—Frederick‡§	Carolina	9	25⅔	2	1	.667	25	15	12	19	12	4.21
1990—Frederick	Carolina	8	53⅔	4	2	.667	35	15	10	49	11	1.68
1990—Hagerstown	Eastern	14	96	10	2	*.833	80	26	21	73	25	1.97
1990—Baltimore	American	8	36⅓	3	3	.500	43	22	20	20	19	4.95
Major League Totals—1 Year		8	36⅓	3	3	.500	43	22	20	20	19	4.95

Selected by Baltimore Orioles' organization in 3rd round of free-agent draft, June 2, 1987.
†On disabled list, April 20, 1988 through remainder of season.
‡On Frederick disabled list, April 7 to April 18, 1989.
§On Erie disabled list, June 16 to June 30, 1989.

GARRY LEWIS TEMPLETON

Born March 24, 1956, at Lockney, Tex.
Height, 6.00. Weight, 209.
Throws right and bats left and righthanded.
Brother of Ken Templeton, outfielder in Oakland A's organization, 1972 through 1974; son of
Spiavia Templeton, former infielder in the Negro Leagues.

Shares major league records by collecting 100 or more hits righthanded and lefthanded, season, 1979; most consecutive seasons leading league, three-base hits (3), 1977 through 1979; most intentional bases on balls, game (4), July 5, 1985 (12 innings).

Shares modern major league record for most three-base hits by switch hitter, season, (19), 1979; most intentional bases on balls, game (4), July 5, 1985 (12 innings).

Major League stolen bases: 1976 (11), 1977 (28), 1978 (34), 1979 (26), 1980 (31), 1981 (8), 1982 (27), 1983 (16), 1984 (8), 1985 (16), 1986 (10), 1987 (14), 1988 (9), 1989 (1), 1990 (1). Total—239.

Led National League in intentional bases on balls received with 23 in 1984 and tied for lead with 24 in 1985.

Led National League shortstops in total chances with 848 in 1978 and 851 in 1979.

Led National League shortstops in double plays with 108 in 1978.

Tied for National League lead in caught stealing with 24 in 1977.

Tied for National League lead in double plays by shortstops with 102 in 1979.

Named shortstop on THE SPORTING NEWS National League All-Star Team, 1977, 1979 and 1980.

Named shortstop on THE SPORTING NEWS National League Silver Slugger team, 1980 and 1984.

Received reported $40,000 bonus to sign with St. Louis Cardinals, 1974.

Year Club	League	Pos.	G.	AB.	R.	H.	2B.	3B.	HR.	RBI.	B.A.	PO.	A.	E.	F.A.
1974—Sarasota Cards.....	Gulf C.	SS	18	71	11	19	1	0	3	10	.268	15	41	3	.949
1974—St. Petersburg	Fla. St.	SS	23	95	3	20	1	0	0	2	.211	42	64	7	.938
1975—St. Petersburg	Fla. St.	SS	82	349	50	92	7	8	1	32	.264	130	253	29	.930
1975—Arkansas................	Texas	SS	42	177	36	71	9	4	2	20	.401	60	131	18	.914
1976—Tulsa......................	A. A.	*S-3-O	106	443	65	142	24	*15	6	38	.321	*178	319	34	.936
1976—St. Louis................	Nat.	SS	53	213	32	62	8	2	1	17	.291	111	172	24	.922
1977—St. Louis................	Nat.	SS	153	621	94	200	19	*18	8	79	.322	285	453	32	.958
1978—St. Louis................	Nat.	SS	155	647	82	181	31	*13	2	47	.280	*285	523	*40	.953
1979—St. Louis................	Nat.	SS	154	672	105	*211	32	*19	9	62	.314	*292	525	*34	.960
1980—St. Louis†..............	Nat.	SS	118	504	83	161	19	9	4	43	.319	223	451	*29	.959
1981—St. Louis‡§..............	Nat.	SS	80	333	47	96	16	8	1	33	.288	160	272	18	.960
1982—San Diego	Nat.	SS	141	563	76	139	25	8	6	64	.247	220	422	26	.961
1983—San Diego x	Nat.	SS	126	460	39	121	20	2	3	40	.263	219	355	24	.960
1984—San Diego	Nat.	SS	148	493	40	127	19	3	2	35	.258	225	407	26	.960
1985—San Diego	Nat.	SS	148	546	63	154	30	2	6	55	.282	245	460	23	.968
1986—San Diego	Nat.	SS	147	510	42	126	21	2	2	44	.247	207	358	20	.966
1987—San Diego	Nat.	SS	148	510	42	113	13	5	5	48	.222	*253	447	20	.972
1988—San Diego y	Nat.	SS-3B	110	362	35	90	15	7	3	36	.249	170	316	16	.968
1989—San Diego	Nat.	SS	142	506	43	129	26	3	6	40	.255	232	409	20	.970
1990—San Diego	Nat.	SS	144	505	45	125	25	3	9	59	.248	214	367	●26	.957
Major League Totals—15 Years..............			1967	7445	868	2035	319	104	67	702	.273	3341	5937	378	.961

Selected by St. Louis Cardinals' organization in 1st round (13th player selected) of free-agent draft, June 5, 1974.
†On disabled list, July 24 to August 14 and August 24 to September 8, 1980.
‡On suspended list, August 26, 1981; then transferred to disabled list, August 28 to September 14, 1981.
§Traded to San Diego Padres for Shortstop Ozzie Smith, February 11, 1982.
xOn disabled list, April 28 to May 17, 1983.
yGranted free agency, November 4, 1988; re-signed by Padres, December 6, 1988.

CHAMPIONSHIP SERIES RECORD

Year Club	League	Pos.	G.	AB.	R.	H.	2B.	3B.	HR.	RBI.	B.A.	PO.	A.	E.	F.A.
1984—San Diego	Nat.	SS	5	15	2	5	1	0	0	2	.333	19	11	1	.968

WORLD SERIES RECORD

Year Club	League	Pos.	G.	AB.	R.	H.	2B.	3B.	HR.	RBI.	B.A.	PO.	A.	E.	F.A.
1984—San Diego	Nat.	SS	5	19	1	6	1	0	0	0	.316	8	11	0	1.000

ALL-STAR GAME RECORD

Year League	Pos.	AB.	R.	H.	2B.	3B.	HR.	RBI.	B.A.	PO.	A.	E.	F.A.
1977—National	SS	1	1	1	1	0	0	0	1.000	1	2	1	.750
1985—National	PH	1	0	1	0	0	0	0	1.000	0	0	0	.000
All-Star Game Totals—2 Years....................		2	1	2	1	0	0	0	1.000	1	2	1	.750

Named to National League All-Star Team for 1979 game; declined.

CHARLES WALTER TERRELL

Name pronounced TEAR-el.

(Walt)

Born May 11, 1958, at Jeffersonville, Ind.
Height, 6.01. Weight, 215.
Throws right and bats lefthanded.
Received degree from Morehead State University, Morehead, Ky. in 1980.

Tied for International League lead in intentional bases on balls issued with 9 in 1982.
Named International League Pitcher of the Year, 1983.

Year Club	League	G.	IP.	W.	L.	Pct.	H.	R.	ER.	SO.	BB.	ERA.
1980—Sarasota Rangers........................	Gulf Coast	7	38	3	2	.600	20	11	6	23	12	1.42
1980—Asheville........................	S. Atlantic	3	8	1	1	.500	11	9	6	5	8	6.75
1981—Tulsa†...............................	Texas	27	174	●15	7	.682	158	74	60	123	63	3.10
1982—Tidewater‡......................	Int'national	21	138⅔	7	8	.467	130	69	61	74	72	3.96
1982—New York	National	3	21	0	3	.000	22	12	8	8	14	3.43
1983—Tidewater......................	Int'national	12	86⅔	10	1	*.909	76	34	30	58	44	3.12
1983—New York	National	21	133⅔	8	8	.500	123	57	53	59	55	3.57
1984—New York§	National	33	215	11	12	.478	232	99	84	114	80	3.52
1985—Detroit............................	American	34	229	15	10	.600	221	107	98	130	95	3.85
1986—Detroit............................	American	34	217⅓	15	12	.556	199	116	110	93	98	4.56
1987—Detroit............................	American	35	244⅔	17	10	.630	254	123	110	143	94	4.05
1988—Lakeland x	Florida St.	2	9⅔	1	1	.500	13	7	7	6	1	6.52
1988—Detroit y	American	29	206⅓	7	16	.304	199	101	91	84	78	3.97
1989—San Diego z	National	19	123⅓	5	13	.278	134	65	55	63	26	4.01
1989—New York a	American	13	83	6	5	.545	102	52	48	30	24	5.20
1990—Pittsburgh b...................	National	16	82⅔	2	7	.222	98	59	54	34	33	5.88
1990—Detroit............................	American	13	75⅓	6	4	.600	86	39	38	30	24	4.54
National League Totals—5 Years........................		92	575⅔	26	43	.377	609	292	254	278	208	3.97
American League Totals—6 Years		158	1055⅔	66	57	.537	1061	538	495	510	413	4.22
Major League Totals—9 Years....................		250	1631⅓	92	100	.479	1670	830	749	788	621	4.13

Selected by New York Mets' organization in 15th round of free-agent draft, June 5, 1979.
Selected by Texas Rangers' organization in 33rd round of free-agent draft, June 3, 1980.

†Traded with Pitcher Ron Darling to New York Mets' organization for Outfielder Lee Mazzilli, April 1, 1982.
‡On disabled list, July 19 to August 2, 1982.
§Traded to Detroit Tigers for Third Baseman Howard Johnson, December 7, 1984.
xOn Detroit disabled list, April 1 to April 30, 1988; included rehabilitation disability assignment to Lakeland, April 16 to April 26, 1988.
yTraded to San Diego Padres for Infielders Chris Brown and Keith Moreland, October 28, 1988.
zTraded with a player to be named later to New York Yankees for Third Baseman Mike Pagliarulo and Pitcher Don Schulze, July 22, 1989; New York acquired Pitcher Fred Toliver to complete deal, September 27, 1989.
aGranted free agency, November 13, 1989; signed by Pittsburgh Pirates, November 29, 1989.
bReleased, July 24, 1990; signed by Detroit Tigers, July 28, 1990.

CHAMPIONSHIP SERIES RECORD

Year	Club	League	G.	IP.	W.	L.	Pct.	H.	R.	ER.	SO.	BB.	ERA.
1987—Detroit	American	1	6	0	0	.000	7	6	6	4	4	9.00

SCOTT RAY TERRY

Born November 21, 1959, at Hobbs, N.M.
Height, 5.11. Weight, 195.
Throws and bats righthanded.
Received degree from Southwestern University, Georgetown, Tex., in 1982.

Major League saves: 1988 (3), 1989 (2), 1990 (2). Total—7.
Led American Association in complete games with 10 in 1987.
Led Eastern League in shutouts with 6 in 1984.
Tied for American Association lead in games started by pitchers with 28 and wild pitches with 14 in 1985.

Year	Club	League	G.	IP.	W.	L.	Pct.	H.	R.	ER.	SO.	BB.	ERA.
1983—Tampa	Florida St.	30	59⅓	3	3	.500	60	34	28	52	30	4.25
1984—Vermont	Eastern	20	144	14	3	*.824	110	31	24	100	43	*1.50
1984—Wichita†	Am. Assoc.	2	9⅓	0	0	.000	13	6	6	6	7	5.79
1985—Denver	Am. Assoc.	28	178⅔	11	12	.478	*203	*105	*88	101	76	4.43
1986—Denver	Am. Assoc.	10	19⅓	1	2	.333	22	13	5	13	8	2.33
1986—Cincinnati	National	28	55⅔	1	2	.333	66	40	38	32	32	6.14
1987—Nashville‡	Am. Assoc.	27	*181⅔	11	10	.524	199	94	80	91	48	3.96
1987—St. Louis	National	11	13⅓	0	0	.000	13	5	5	9	8	3.38
1988—St. Louis§	National	51	129⅓	9	6	.600	119	48	42	65	34	2.92
1988—Louisville	Am. Assoc.	3	5	0	0	.000	2	0	0	1	1	0.00
1989—St. Louis x	National	31	148⅔	8	10	.444	142	65	59	69	43	3.57
1990—St. Louis	National	50	72	2	6	.250	75	45	38	35	27	4.75
Major League Totals—5 Years		171	419	20	24	.455	415	203	182	210	144	3.91

Selected by Cincinnati Reds' organization in 12th round of free-agent draft, June 3, 1980.
†On disabled list, August 8 to September 18, 1984.
‡Traded to St. Louis Cardinals, September 3, 1987, completing deal in which St. Louis traded Pitcher Pat Perry to Cincinnati Reds for a player to be named later, August 31, 1987.
§On disabled list, June 27 to July 24, 1988; included rehabilitation disability assignment to Louisville, July 18 to July 24, 1988.
xOn disabled list, August 14 to September 5, 1989.

RECORD AS OUTFIELDER

Year	Club	League	Pos.	G.	AB.	R.	H.	2B.	3B.	HR.	RBI.	B.A.	PO.	A.	E.	F.A.
1980—Billings	Pion.	OF	67	251	39	65	9	3	4	45	.259	104	●10	5	.958
1981—Cedar Rapids	Midw.	OF	113	351	32	68	9	0	5	31	.194	147	5	5	.968
1982—Cedar Rapids	Midw.	OF	108	335	50	85	16	3	12	54	.254	156	10	8	.954
1983—Tampa	Fla. St.	OF-P	66	105	14	25	6	2	0	12	.238	60	16	3	.962

MICKEY LEE TETTLETON

Born September 16, 1960, at Oklahoma City, Okla.
Height, 6.02. Weight, 208.
Throws right and bats left and righthanded.
Attended Oklahoma State University, Stillwater, Okla.

Holds major league record for most strikeouts by switch-hitter, season (160), 1990.
Major League stolen bases: 1985 (2), 1986 (7), 1987 (1), 1989 (3), 1990 (2). Total—15.
Switch-hit home runs in one game, June 13, 1988.
Tied for Eastern League lead in intentional bases on balls received with 8 in 1984.
Named catcher on THE SPORTING NEWS American League All-Star Team, 1989.
Named catcher on THE SPORTING NEWS American League Silver Slugger team, 1989.

Year	Club	League	Pos.	G.	AB.	R.	H.	2B.	3B.	HR.	RBI.	B.A.	PO.	A.	E.	F.A.
1981—Modesto	Calif.	C-OF-1B	48	138	28	34	3	0	5	19	.246	235	31	14	.950
1982—Modesto†	Calif.	C-OF	88	253	44	63	18	0	8	37	.249	424	36	8	.983
1983—Modesto	Calif.	C-OF	124	378	55	92	18	2	7	62	.243	582	46	11	.983
1984—Albany	East.	*C-O-1-3-S	86	281	32	65	18	0	5	47	.231	368	42	3	*.993
1984—Oakland	Amer.	C	33	76	10	20	2	1	1	5	.263	112	10	1	.992
1985—Oakland‡	Amer.	C	78	211	23	53	12	0	3	15	.251	344	24	4	.989
1985—Modesto	Calif.	C	4	14	1	3	3	0	0	2	.214	20	1	0	1.000
1986—Oakland§	Amer.	C	90	211	26	43	9	0	10	35	.204	463	32	8	.984
1986—Modesto	Calif.	C	15	42	14	10	1	0	2	8	.238	40	3	2	.956
1987—Oakland x	Amer.	C-1B	82	211	19	41	3	0	8	26	.194	435	29	6	.987
1987—Modesto y	Calif.	C	3	11	4	4	1	0	2	2	.364	5	0	0	1.000
1988—Rochester	Int.	C-OF	19	41	9	10	3	1	1	4	.244	71	7	3	.963
1988—Baltimore	Amer.	C	86	283	31	74	11	1	11	37	.261	361	31	3	.992

Year Club League	Pos.	G.	AB.	R.	H.	2B.	3B.	HR.	RBI.	B.A.	PO.	A.	E.	F.A.
1989—Baltimore z .... Amer.	C	117	411	72	106	21	2	26	65	.258	297	42	2	.994
1990—Baltimore ab........ Amer.	C-1B-OF	135	444	68	99	21	2	15	51	.223	458	39	5	.990
Major League Totals—7 Years.................		621	1847	249	436	79	6	74	234	.236	2470	207	29	.989

Selected by Oakland A's organization in 5th round of free-agent draft, June 8, 1981.

†On disabled list, July 16 to August 13, 1982.

‡On disabled list, August 4 to August 25, 1985; included rehabilitation disability assignment to Modesto, August 21 to August 25, 1985.

§On disabled list, May 9 to June 16, 1986; included rehabilitation disability assignment to Modesto, May 23 to June 13, 1986.

xOn disabled list, July 22 to August 6, 1987; included rehabilitation disability assignment to Modesto, August 2 to August 6, 1987.

yReleased, March 28, 1988; signed by Rochester (Baltimore Orioles' organization), April 5, 1988.

zOn disabled list, August 5 to September 2, 1989.

aGranted free agency, November 5, 1990; re-signed by Orioles, December 19, 1990.

bTraded to Detroit Tigers for Pitcher Jeff Robinson, January 11, 1991.

ALL-STAR GAME RECORD

Year League	Pos.	AB.	R.	H.	2B.	3B.	HR.	RBI.	B.A.	PO.	A.	E.	F.A.
1989—American	C	1	0	0	0	0	0	0	.000	2	0	0	1.000

TIMOTHY SHAWN TEUFEL

Name pronounced TUFF-el.

(Tim)

Born July 7, 1958, at Greenwich, Conn.
Height, 6.00. Weight, 175.
Throws and bats righthanded.
Attended St. Petersburg Junior College, St. Petersburg, Fla.,
and Clemson University, Clemson, S. C.

Holds American League record for fewest double plays by second baseman, season, 150 or more games (81), 1984.

Major League stolen bases: 1984 (1), 1985 (4), 1986 (1), 1987 (3), 1989 (1). Total—10.

Led International League second basemen in putouts with 304, assists with 394, total chances with 711 and double plays with 109 in 1983.

Named International League Player of the Year, 1983.

Named second baseman on THE SPORTING NEWS College Baseball All-America Team, 1980.

Year Club League	Pos.	G.	AB.	R.	H.	2B.	3B.	HR.	RBI.	B.A.	PO.	A.	E.	F.A.
1980—Orlando .... South.	2B	86	287	38	76	15	3	11	47	.265	196	246	17	.963
1981—Orlando .... South.	2B	128	416	69	103	21	5	17	60	.248	312	376	20	.972
1982—Orlando .... South.	2B	100	340	52	96	12	4	9	56	.282	231	185	15	.965
1982—Toledo .... Int.	2B	45	149	25	42	10	4	6	20	.282	99	139	3	.988
1983—Toledo .... Int.	2B-SS	136	471	103	152	27	6	27	100	.323	306	401	14	.981
1983—Minnesota............. Amer.	2B-SS	21	78	11	24	7	1	3	6	.308	47	58	1	.991
1984—Minnesota............. Amer.	2B	157	568	76	149	30	3	14	61	.262	315	★485	13	.984
1985—Minnesota†........... Amer.	2B	138	434	58	113	24	3	10	50	.260	237	352	12	.980
1986—New York .... Nat.	2B-1B-3B	93	279	35	69	20	1	4	31	.247	143	174	9	.972
1987—New York‡........... Nat.	2B-1B	97	299	55	92	29	0	14	61	.308	139	214	11	.970
1988—New York§........... Nat.	2B-1B	90	273	35	64	20	0	4	31	.234	175	213	7	.982
1989—New York x .... Nat.	2B-1B	83	219	27	56	7	2	2	15	.256	261	112	10	.974
1990—New York .... Nat.	1B-2B-3B	80	175	28	43	11	0	10	24	.246	141	58	4	.980
American League Totals—3 Years		316	1080	145	286	61	7	27	117	.265	599	895	26	.983
National League Totals—5 Years............		443	1245	180	324	87	3	34	162	.260	859	771	41	.975
Major League Totals—8 Years.................		759	2325	325	610	148	10	61	279	.262	1458	1666	67	.979

Selected by Milwaukee Brewers' organization in 16th round of free-agent draft, June 6, 1978.

Selected by Chicago White Sox' organization in secondary phase of free-agent draft, June 5, 1979.

Selected by Minnesota Twins' organization in 2nd round of free-agent draft, June 3, 1980.

†Traded with Outfielder Pat Crosby to New York Mets for Outfielder Billy Beane and Pitchers Bill Latham and Joe Klink, January 16, 1986.

‡On disabled list, June 16 to July 1, 1987.

§On disabled list, May 17 to June 11, 1988.

xOn disabled list, June 5 to June 23, 1989.

CHAMPIONSHIP SERIES RECORD

Year Club League	Pos.	G.	AB.	R.	H.	2B.	3B.	HR.	RBI.	B.A.	PO.	A.	E.	F.A.
1986—New York............. Nat.	2B	2	6	0	1	0	0	0	0	.167	2	8	0	1.000
1988—New York............. Nat.	2B	1	3	0	0	0	0	0	0	.000	1	3	0	1.000
Championship Series Totals—2 Years.....		3	9	0	1	0	0	0	0	.111	3	11	0	1.000

WORLD SERIES RECORD

Year Club League	Pos.	G.	AB.	R.	H.	2B.	3B.	HR.	RBI.	B.A.	PO.	A.	E.	F.A.
1986—New York............. Nat.	2B	3	9	1	4	1	0	1	1	.444	3	3	1	.857

ROBERT ALAN TEWKSBURY

(Bob)

Born November 30, 1960, at Concord, N. H.
Height, 6.04. Weight, 200.
Throws and bats righthanded.
Attended Rutgers University, New Brunswick, N.J., and St. Leo College, St. Leo, Fla.

Major League saves: 1990 (1).
Led Florida State League in shutouts with 5 and tied for lead in complete games with 13 in 1982.

Year Club	League	G.	IP.	W.	L.	Pct.	H.	R.	ER.	SO.	BB.	ERA.
1981—Oneonta	NYP	14	85	7	3	.700	85	43	34	62	37	3.40
1982—Fort Lauderdale	Florida St.	24	181⅓	*15	4	.789	146	46	38	92	47	*1.88
1983—Fort Lauderdale†	Florida St.	2	16	2	0	1.000	6	1	0	5	1	0.00
1983—Nashville	Southern	7	51	5	1	.833	49	20	16	15	10	2.82
1984—Nashville‡	Southern	26	172	11	9	.550	185	69	54	78	42	2.83
1985—Albany§	Eastern	17	106⅔	6	5	.545	101	48	42	63	19	3.54
1985—Columbus	Int'national	6	44	3	0	1.000	27	5	5	21	5	1.02
1986—New York	American	23	130⅓	9	5	.643	144	58	48	49	31	3.31
1986—Columbus	Int'national	2	10	1	0	1.000	6	3	3	4	2	2.70
1987—New York x	American	8	33⅓	1	4	.200	47	26	25	12	7	6.75
1987—Columbus	Int'national	11	74⅔	6	1	.857	68	23	21	32	11	2.53
1987—Chicago y	National	7	18	0	4	.000	32	15	13	10	13	6.50
1988—Iowa	Am. Assoc.	10	67	4	2	.667	73	28	28	43	10	3.76
1988—Chicago za	National	1	3⅓	0	0	.000	6	5	3	1	2	8.10
1989—Louisville	Am. Assoc.	28	*189	●13	5	.722	170	63	51	72	34	2.43
1989—St. Louis	National	7	30	1	0	1.000	25	12	11	17	10	3.30
1990—St. Louis	National	28	145⅓	10	9	.526	151	67	56	50	15	3.47
1990—Louisville	Am. Assoc.	6	40⅔	3	2	.600	41	15	11	22	3	2.43
American League Totals—2 Years		31	163⅔	10	9	.526	191	84	73	61	38	4.01
National League Totals—4 Years		43	196⅔	11	13	.458	214	99	83	78	40	3.80
Major League Totals—5 Years		74	360⅓	21	22	.488	405	183	156	139	78	3.90

Selected by New York Yankees' organization in 19th round of free-agent draft, June 8, 1981.
†On disabled list, April 8 to June 7, 1983.
‡On disabled list, April 9 to April 27, 1984.
§On disabled list, June 10 to June 25, 1985.
xTraded with Pitchers Rich Scheid and Dean Wilkins to Chicago Cubs for Pitcher Steve Trout, July 13, 1987.
yOn disabled list, August 13, 1987 through remainder of season.
zOn disabled list, May 22 to June 12, 1988.
aGranted free agency, October 15, 1988.

ROBERT THOMAS THIGPEN
(Bobby)

Born July 17, 1963, at Tallahassee, Fla.
Height, 6.03. Weight, 195.
Throws and bats righthanded.
Attended Seminole Community College, Sanford, Fla., and
Mississippi State University, Starkville, Miss.

Holds major league record for most saves, season, (57), 1990.
Major League saves: 1986 (7), 1987 (16), 1988 (34), 1989 (34), 1990 (57). Total—148.
Led American League in games finished in relief with 59 in 1988 and 73 in 1990.
Led American League in saves with 57 in 1990.
Led Southern League in hit batsmen with 11 in 1986.
Named American League Fireman of the Year by THE SPORTING NEWS, 1990.

Year Club	League	G.	IP.	W.	L.	Pct.	H.	R.	ER.	SO.	BB.	ERA.
1985—Niagara Falls	NYP	28	52⅓	2	3	.400	30	12	10	74	19	1.72
1985—Appleton	Midwest	1	2⅔	1	0	1.000	1	0	0	4	1	0.00
1986—Birmingham	Southern	25	159⅔	8	11	.421	182	97	83	90	54	4.68
1986—Chicago	American	20	35⅔	2	0	1.000	26	7	7	20	12	1.77
1987—Chicago	American	51	89	7	5	.583	86	30	27	52	24	2.73
1987—Hawaii	P. Coast	9	52⅔	2	3	.400	72	38	36	17	14	6.15
1988—Chicago	American	68	90	5	8	.385	96	38	33	62	33	3.30
1989—Chicago	American	61	79	2	6	.250	62	34	33	47	40	3.76
1990—Chicago	American	*77	88⅔	4	6	.400	60	20	18	70	32	1.83
Major League Totals—5 Years		277	382⅓	20	25	.444	330	129	118	251	141	2.78

Selected by Milwaukee Brewers' organization in 7th round of free-agent draft, January 11, 1983.
Selected by Chicago White Sox' organization in 4th round of free-agent draft, June 3, 1985.

ALL-STAR GAME RECORD

Year League	IP.	W.	L.	Pct.	H.	R.	ER.	SO.	BB.	ERA.
1990—American	1	0	0	.000	0	0	0	1	0	0.00

ANDRES PERES THOMAS

Born November 10, 1963, at Santo Domingo, Dominican Republic.
Height, 6.01. Weight, 185.
Throws and bats righthanded.

Major League stolen bases: 1986 (4), 1987 (6), 1988 (7), 1989 (3), 1990 (2). Total—22.
Led National League shortstops in double plays with 90 in 1988.

Year Club	League	Pos.	G.	AB.	R.	H.	2B.	3B.	HR.	RBI.	B.A.	PO.	A.	E.	F.A.
1982—Bradenton Brav...	Gulf C.	SS	44	143	18	37	2	1	1	14	.259	61	136	20	.908
1983—Anderson	S. Atl.	SS	61	251	33	79	8	4	1	20	.315	61	197	24	.915
1983—Durham	Carol.	SS	70	290	17	72	14	0	2	41	.248	107	222	32	.911
1984—Durham†	Carol.	SS	114	460	64	121	18	4	7	44	.263	156	361	34	.938
1985—Greenville	South.	SS-OF	114	458	53	114	18	4	9	59	.249	155	339	31	.941
1985—Richmond	Int.	SS	11	28	3	5	0	0	1	6	.179	15	30	3	.938

Year Club	League	Pos.	G.	AB.	R.	H.	2B.	3B.	HR.	RBI.	B.A.	PO.	A.	E.	F.A.
1985—Atlanta	Nat.	SS	15	18	6	5	0	0	0	2	.278	6	17	2	.920
1986—Atlanta	Nat.	SS	102	323	26	81	17	2	6	32	.251	143	290	19	.958
1987—Atlanta‡	Nat.	SS	82	324	29	75	11	0	5	39	.231	128	276	20	.953
1988—Atlanta	Nat.	SS	153	606	54	153	22	2	13	68	.252	230	456	●29	.959
1989—Atlanta ,.................	Nat.	SS	141	554	41	118	18	0	13	57	.213	231	400	29	.956
1990—Atlanta§	Nat.	SS-3B	84	278	26	61	8	0	5	30	.219	104	200	10	.968
Major League Totals—6 Years................			577	2103	182	493	76	4	42	228	.234	842	1639	109	.958

Signed as free agent by Atlanta Braves' organization, December 16, 1981.
†On suspended list, August 28, 1984 through remainder of season.
‡On disabled list, April 20 to May 13 and August 10, 1987 through remainder of season.
§On disabled list, July 30 to August 16, 1990.

FRANK EDWARD THOMAS

Born May 27, 1968, at Columbus, Ga.
Height, 6.05. Weight, 240.
Throws and bats righthanded.
Attended Auburn University, Auburn, Ala.

Led Southern League in bases on balls received with 112 and slugging percentage with .581 in 1990.
Received reported $175,000 bonus to sign with Chicago White Sox, 1989.
Named first baseman on THE SPORTING NEWS College Baseball All-America Team, 1989.

Year Club	League	Pos.	G.	AB.	R.	H.	2B.	3B.	HR.	RBI.	B.A.	PO.	A.	E.	F.A.
1989—Sarasota W.S........	Gulf C.	1B	17	52	8	19	5	0	1	11	.365	130	8	2	.986
1989—Sarasota	Fla. St.	1B	55	188	27	52	9	1	4	30	.277	420	31	7	.985
1990—Birmingham	South.	1B	109	353	85	114	27	5	18	71	.323	954	77	14	.987
1990—Chicago	Amer.	1B	60	191	39	63	11	3	7	31	.330	428	26	5	.989
Major League Totals—1 Year...................			60	191	39	63	11	3	7	31	.330	428	26	5	.989

Selected by Chicago White Sox' organization in 1st round (seventh player selected) of free-agent draft, June 5, 1989.

MILTON BERNARD THOMPSON
(Milt)

Born January 5, 1959, at Washington, D.C.
Height, 5.11. Weight, 170.
Throws right and bats lefthanded.
Attended Howard University, Washington, D.C.

Major League stolen bases: 1984 (14), 1985 (9), 1986 (19), 1987 (46), 1988 (17), 1989 (27), 1990 (25). Total—157.
Led International League in total chances with 341 in 1984.
Led Southern League in stolen bases with 68 and caught stealing with 19 in 1982.
Led Southern League outfielders in total chances with 336 in 1982.

Year Club	League	Pos.	G.	AB.	R.	H.	2B.	3B.	HR.	RBI.	B.A.	PO.	A.	E.	F.A.
1979—Greenwood...........	W. Car.	OF	53	145	31	27	4	1	2	16	.186	85	8	3	.969
1979—Kingsport..............	Appal.	OF	26	94	22	31	8	4	1	11	.330	58	4	1	.984
1980—Durham.................	Carol.	OF	68	255	49	74	12	3	2	36	.290	159	8	5	.971
1980—Savannah	South.	OF	71	278	35	83	7	3	1	15	.299	133	11	6	.960
1981—Savannah	South.	OF	140	493	92	135	18	2	4	31	.274	226	17	8	.968
1982—Savannah	South.	OF	●144	526	83	132	20	7	6	45	.251	★312	10	14	.958
1982—Richmond..............	Int.	OF	3	6	2	1	0	0	0	0	.167	4	0	0	1.000
1983—Richmond..............	Int.	OF	12	32	12	8	1	0	0	3	.250	30	0	1	.968
1983—Savannah	South.	OF-1B	115	386	84	117	21	4	5	36	.303	295	15	7	.978
1984—Richmond..............	Int.	OF	134	503	●91	145	11	3	4	40	.288	★317	13	11	.968
1984—Atlanta	Nat.	OF	25	99	16	30	1	0	2	4	.303	37	6	2	.956
1985—Richmond..............	Int.	OF	82	312	52	98	10	1	2	22	.314	209	3	4	.981
1985—Atlanta†	Nat.	OF	73	182	17	55	7	2	0	6	.302	78	2	3	.964
1986—Philadelphia	Nat.	OF	96	299	38	75	7	1	6	23	.251	212	1	2	.991
1986—Portland.................	P. C.	OF	41	161	26	56	10	2	1	16	.348	101	1	1	.990
1987—Philadelphia	Nat.	OF	150	527	86	159	26	9	7	43	.302	354	4	4	.989
1988—Philadelphia‡	Nat.	OF	122	378	53	109	16	2	2	33	.288	278	5	5	.983
1989—St. Louis.................	Nat.	OF	155	545	60	158	28	8	4	68	.290	348	5	8	.978
1990—St. Louis.................	Nat.	OF	135	418	42	91	14	7	6	30	.218	232	4	7	.971
Major League Totals—7 Years.................			756	2448	312	677	99	29	28	207	.277	1539	27	31	.981

Selected by Atlanta Braves' organization in 2nd round of free-agent draft, January 9, 1979.
†Traded with Pitcher Steve Bedrosian to Philadelphia Phillies for Catcher Ozzie Virgil and Pitcher Pete Smith, December 10, 1985.
‡Traded to St. Louis Cardinals for Catcher Steve Lake and Outfielder Curt Ford, December 16, 1988.

RICHARD NEIL THOMPSON
(Rich)

Born November 1, 1958, at New York, N.Y.
Height, 6.03. Weight, 215.
Throws right and bats left and righthanded.
Received bachelor of arts degree in economics from Amherst College, Amherst, Mass.
in 1980, and attended Baylor University School of Law, Waco, Tex.

Major League saves: 1985 (5).

Year Club	League	G.	IP.	W.	L.	Pct.	H.	R.	ER.	SO.	BB.	ERA.
1980—Batavia	NYP	7	12	2	0	1.000	12	3	1	16	6	0.75
1981—Waterloo	Midwest	28	122	5	6	.455	112	67	56	109	55	4.13
1982—Chattanooga	Southern	50	78	7	6	.538	69	39	35	55	36	4.04
1983—Buffalo	Eastern	43	78⅔	3	7	.300	67	33	25	61	46	2.86
1984—Buffalo†	Eastern	51	104⅔	9	7	.563	96	48	39	81	47	3.35
1985—Maine	Int'national	4	9	0	0	.000	6	1	1	2	2	1.00
1985—Cleveland‡	American	57	80	3	8	.273	95	63	56	30	48	6.30
1986—Vancouver§x	P. Coast	23	40⅔	1	1	.500	47	35	33	24	18	7.30
1987—Albany	Eastern	5	10⅓	0	0	.000	14	12	11	2	7	9.58
1987—Columbus y	Int'national	2	4	0	0	.000	6	2	2	3	2	4.50
1987—Jacksonville z-Memphis	Southern	15	31	1	0	1.000	35	20	18	27	11	5.23
1988—Memphis	Southern	20	80⅓	3	5	.375	87	44	37	53	17	4.15
1988—Omaha a	Am. Assoc.	17	96⅓	6	7	.462	94	36	31	46	15	2.90
1989—Indianapolis	Am. Assoc.	23	161⅓	9	6	.600	146	46	37	73	37	*2.06
1989—Montreal	National	19	33	0	2	.000	27	11	8	15	11	2.18
1990—Indianapolis b	Am. Assoc.	15	24⅔	3	2	.600	31	16	15	14	10	5.47
1990—Montreal c	National	1	1	0	0	.000	1	0	0	0	0	0.00
American League Totals—1 Year		57	80	3	8	.273	95	63	56	30	48	6.30
National League Totals—2 Years		20	34	0	2	.000	28	11	8	15	11	2.12
Major League Totals—3 Years		77	114	3	10	.231	123	74	64	45	59	5.05

Selected by Cleveland Indians' organization in 7th round of free-agent draft, June 3, 1980.
†On disabled list, August 9 to August 19, 1984.
‡Traded to Milwaukee Brewers for Pitcher Scott Roberts, December 16, 1985.
§On disabled list, July 14 to August 2, 1986.
xGranted free agency, October 15, 1986; signed by Albany (New York Yankees' organization), March 17, 1987.
yReleased, May 18, 1987; signed by Jacksonville (Montreal Expos' organization), June, 1987.
zReleased, July, 1987; signed by Memphis (Kansas City Royals' organization), August 10, 1987.
aReleased, March, 1989; signed by Indianapolis (Montreal Expos' organization), March 15, 1989.
bOn disabled list, July 13, 1990 through remainder of season.
cReleased, September 4, 1990.

ROBERT RANDALL THOMPSON
(Robby)

Born May 10, 1962, at West Palm Beach, Fla.
Height, 5.11. Weight, 170.
Throws and bats righthanded.
Attended Palm Beach Junior College, Lake Worth, Fla.,
and University of Florida, Gainesville, Fla.

Major League stolen bases: 1986 (12), 1987 (16), 1988 (14), 1989 (12), 1990 (14). Total—68.
Established major league record for most times caught stealing, game (4), June 27, 1986, 12 innings.
Led National League in sacrifice hits with 18 in 1986.
Tied for National League lead in being hit by pitch with 13 in 1989.
Tied for National League lead in double plays by second basemen with 94 in 1990.
Named National League Rookie Player of the Year by THE SPORTING NEWS, 1986.
Led Texas League second basemen in putouts with 291, total chances with 664 and double plays with 91 in 1985.

Year Club	League	Pos.	G.	AB.	R.	H.	2B.	3B.	HR.	RBI.	B.A.	PO.	A.	E.	F.A.
1983—Fresno	Calif.	2B	64	220	33	57	8	1	4	23	.259	118	185	11	.965
1984—Fresno	Calif.	2B-SS-3B	102	325	53	81	11	0	8	43	.249	182	280	24	.951
1985—Shreveport	Texas	*2B-SS	121	449	85	117	20	7	9	40	.261	292	366	12	*.982
1986—San Francisco†	Nat.	2B-SS	149	549	73	149	27	3	7	47	.271	255	451	17	.976
1987—San Francisco†	Nat.	2B	132	420	62	110	26	5	10	44	.262	246	341	17	.972
1988—San Francisco	Nat.	2B	138	477	66	126	24	6	7	48	.264	255	365	14	.978
1989—San Francisco	Nat.	2B	148	547	91	132	26	*11	13	50	.241	307	425	8	.989
1990—San Francisco	Nat.	2B	144	498	67	122	22	3	15	56	.245	287	441	8	.989
Major League Totals—5 Years			711	2491	359	639	125	28	52	245	.257	1350	2023	64	.981

Selected by Oakland A's organization in 2nd round of free-agent draft, January 12, 1982.
Selected by Seattle Mariners' organization in secondary phase of free-agent draft, June 7, 1982.
Selected by San Francisco Giants' organization in secondary phase of free-agent draft, June 6, 1983.
†On disabled list, April 28 to May 13, 1987.

CHAMPIONSHIP SERIES RECORD

Year Club	League	Pos.	G.	AB.	R.	H.	2B.	3B.	HR.	RBI.	B.A.	PO.	A.	E.	F.A.
1987—San Francisco	Nat.	2B-PH	7	20	4	2	0	1	1	2	.100	11	19	1	.968
1989—San Francisco	Nat.	2B	5	18	5	5	0	0	2	3	.278	10	13	0	1.000
Championship Series Totals—2 Years			12	38	9	7	0	1	3	5	.184	21	32	1	.981

WORLD SERIES RECORD

Year Club	League	Pos.	G.	AB.	R.	H.	2B.	3B.	HR.	RBI.	B.A.	PO.	A.	E.	F.A.
1989—San Francisco	Nat.	2B-PH	4	11	0	1	0	0	0	2	.091	4	10	0	1.000

ALL-STAR GAME RECORD

Named to National League All-Star Team for 1988 game; replaced due to injury by Bob Walk.

—DID YOU KNOW—

That the Yankees tied a major league record by collecting eight consecutive hits before Baltimore retired a batter last September 25?

RICHARD WILLIAM THON
(Dickie)

Born June 20, 1958, at South Bend, Ind.
Height, 5.11. Weight, 175.
Throws and bats righthanded.
Grandson of Fred Thon, minor league pitcher, 1940.

Shares National League record for fewest triples, season, for league leader in triples (10), 1982.
Major League stolen bases: 1980 (7), 1981 (6), 1982 (37), 1983 (34), 1985 (8), 1986 (6), 1987 (3), 1988 (19), 1989 (6), 1990 (12). Total—138.
Led National League in game-winning RBIs with 18 in 1983.
Tied for National League lead in double plays by shortstops with 86 in 1990.
Named shortstop on THE SPORTING NEWS National League All-Star Team, 1983.
Named shortstop on THE SPORTING NEWS National League Silver Slugger team, 1983.

Year Club	League	Pos.	G.	AB.	R.	H.	2B.	3B.	HR.	RBI.	B.A.	PO.	A.	E.	F.A.
1976—Quad Cities	Midw.	SS	69	246	46	68	11	4	1	32	.276	96	193	32	.900
1977—Salinas	Calif.	SS	56	225	48	71	13	2	4	44	.316	95	162	13	.952
1977—Salt Lake City	P. C.	SS	77	274	47	79	9	3	8	43	.288	129	242	26	.935
1978—Salt Lake City	P. C.	2B-SS	130	439	67	113	17	3	1	47	.257	273	380	26	.962
1979—Salt Lake City	P. C.	SS-2B	38	162	25	47	3	1	2	21	.290	70	120	11	.945
1979—California	Amer.	2B-SS-3B	35	56	6	19	3	0	0	8	.339	38	46	8	.913
1980—Salt Lake City	P. C.	2B-SS	40	155	28	61	14	2	2	28	.394	81	107	12	.940
1980—California†	Amer.	S-2-3-1	80	267	32	68	12	2	0	15	.255	70	124	10	.951
1981—Houston	Nat.	2B-SS-3B	49	95	13	26	6	0	0	3	.274	53	63	6	.951
1982—Houston	Nat.	SS-3B-2B	136	496	73	137	31	*10	3	36	.276	183	*412	17	.972
1983—Houston	Nat.	SS	154	619	81	177	28	9	20	79	.286	258	*533	28	.966
1984—Houston‡	Nat.	SS	5	17	3	6	0	1	0	1	.353	8	13	0	1.000
1985—Houston§x	Nat.	SS	84	251	26	63	6	1	6	29	.251	106	218	11	.967
1986—Houston y	Nat.	SS	106	278	24	69	13	1	3	21	.248	142	210	10	.945
1987—Tucson z	P. C.	SS	14	48	10	13	4	0	0	6	.271	22	40	7	.899
1987—Houston ab	Nat.	SS	32	66	6	14	1	0	1	3	.212	21	53	6	.925
1988—San Diego c	Nat.	SS-2B-3B	95	258	36	68	12	2	1	18	.264	84	171	12	.955
1989—Philadelphia	Nat.	SS	136	435	45	118	18	4	15	60	.271	174	380	16	.972
1990—Philadelphia d	Nat.	SS	149	552	54	141	20	4	8	48	.255	222	439	25	.964
American League Totals—2 Years			115	323	38	87	15	2	0	23	.269	108	170	18	.939
National League Totals—10 Years			946	3067	361	819	135	32	57	298	.267	1251	2492	131	.966
Major League Totals—12 Years			1061	3390	399	906	150	34	57	321	.267	1359	2662	149	.964

Signed as free agent by California Angels' organization, November 23, 1975.
†Traded to Houston Astros for Pitcher Ken Forsch, April 1, 1981.
‡On disabled list, April 9, 1984 through remainder of season.
§On disabled list, May 19 to June 8, 1985.
xGranted free agency, November 12, 1985; re-signed by Astros, January 7, 1986.
yOn disabled list, June 6 to June 23, 1986.
zOn Houston restricted list, April 3 to April 18, 1987; then transferred to disabled list, April 19 to May 10, 1987; included rehabilitation disability assignment to Tucson, April 19 to May 8, 1987.
aOn disqualified list, July 4, 1987 through remainder of season.
bGranted free agency, November 9, 1987; signed by San Diego Padres, February 18, 1988.
cSold to Philadelphia Phillies, January 27, 1989.
dOn suspended list, June 29 to July 1, 1990.

DIVISION SERIES RECORD

Year Club	League	Pos.	G.	AB.	R.	H.	2B.	3B.	HR.	RBI.	B.A.	PO.	A.	E.	F.A.
1981—Houston	Nat.	SS-PH	4	11	0	2	0	0	0	0	.182	5	10	1	.938

CHAMPIONSHIP SERIES RECORD

Year Club	League	Pos.	G.	AB.	R.	H.	2B.	3B.	HR.	RBI.	B.A.	PO.	A.	E.	F.A.
1979—California	Amer.	PR-SS	1	0	1	0	0	0	0	0	.000	0	0	0	.000
1986—Houston	Nat.	SS-PH	6	12	1	3	0	0	1	1	.250	6	9	0	1.000
Championship Series Totals—2 Years			7	12	2	3	0	0	1	1	.250	6	9	0	1.000

ALL-STAR GAME RECORD

Year League	Pos.	AB.	R.	H.	2B.	3B.	HR.	RBI.	B.A.	PO.	A.	E.	F.A.
1983—National	PH-SS	3	0	1	0	0	0	0	.333	0	2	0	1.000

LOUIS THORNTON JR.
(Lou)

Born April 26, 1963, at Montgomery, Ala.
Height, 6.00. Weight, 175.
Throws right and bats lefthanded.

Major League stolen bases: 1985 (1), 1989 (2). Total—3.
Led Appalachian League outfielders in errors with 9 in 1982.

Year Club	League	Pos.	G.	AB.	R.	H.	2B.	3B.	HR.	RBI.	B.A.	PO.	A.	E.	F.A.
1981—Kingsport	Appal.	1B	48	153	23	32	7	0	2	17	.209	338	43	16	.960
1982—Kingsport	Appal.	OF-1B-3B	57	210	29	44	9	2	5	29	.210	182	7	13	.940
1983—Columbia	S. Atl.	OF	119	448	80	120	24	6	11	73	.268	193	18	11	.950
1984—Lynchburg†	Carolina	OF-1B	131	505	78	139	25	7	6	67	.275	250	13	11	.960
1985—Toronto	Amer.	OF	56	72	18	17	1	1	1	8	.236	44	0	2	.957
1986—Syracuse‡	Int.	OF	64	231	34	60	4	2	2	28	.260	114	5	4	.967

Year Club	League	Pos.	G.	AB.	R.	H.	2B.	3B.	HR.	RBI.	B.A.	PO.	A.	E.	F.A.
1987—Syracuse	Int.	OF	122	464	64	123	10	5	9	47	.265	199	6	10	.953
1987—Toronto	Amer.	OF	12	2	5	1	0	0	0	0	.500	0	0	0	.000
1988—Syracuse	Int.	OF-3B	69	246	23	51	12	3	4	22	.207	106	31	12	.919
1988—Toronto§x	Amer.	OF	11	2	1	0	0	0	0	0	.000	1	0	0	1.000
1989—Buffalo y	A. A.	OF	28	96	8	20	3	1	1	7	.208	48	3	1	.981
1989—Tidewater	Int.	OF-1B-3B	71	229	34	62	10	2	2	20	.271	148	11	3	.981
1989—New York	Nat.	OF	13	13	5	4	1	0	0	1	.308	9	0	0	1.000
1990—New York	Nat.	OF	3	0	0	0	0	0	0	0	.000	1	0	0	1.000
1990—Tidewater z............	Int.	OF-1B	109	379	42	86	9	4	4	38	.227	204	11	7	.968
American League Totals—3 Years			79	76	24	18	1	1	1	8	.237	45	0	2	.957
National League Totals—2 Years...........			16	13	5	4	1	0	0	1	.308	10	0	0	1.000
Major League Totals—5 Years...............			95	89	29	22	2	1	1	9	.247	55	0	2	.965

Selected by New York Mets' organization in 19th round of free-agent draft, June 8, 1981.

†Drafted by Toronto Blue Jays, December 3, 1984.

‡On disabled list, May 29 to September 1, 1986.

§Granted free agency, October 15, 1988; signed by Denver (Milwaukee Brewers' organization), February, 1989.

xTraded to Pittsburgh Pirates, March 26, 1989, completing deal in which Pittsburgh traded Catcher Ruben Rodriguez to Milwaukee Brewers for a player to be named later, March 17, 1989.

yReleased, May 3, 1989; signed by Tidewater (New York Mets' organization), June 9, 1989.

zGranted free agency, October 15, 1990.

CHAMPIONSHIP SERIES RECORD

Year Club	League	Pos.	G.	AB.	R.	H.	2B.	3B.	HR.	RBI.	B.A.	PO.	A.	E.	F.A.
1985—Toronto	Amer.	PR	2	0	1	0	0	0	0	0	.000	0	0	0	.000

GARY MONTEZ THURMAN JR.

Born November 12, 1964, at Indianapolis, Ind.
Height, 5.10. Weight, 175.
Throws and bats righthanded.

Shares American League record for most stolen bases with no caught stealing, season (16), 1989.
Major League stolen bases: 1987 (7), 1988 (5), 1989 (16), 1990 (1). Total—29.
Led American Association in stolen bases with 58 in 1987.
Led Florida State League in stolen bases with 70 in 1985.
Led Gulf Coast League batters in strikeouts with 58 in 1983.
Tied for South Atlantic League lead in caught stealing with 17 in 1984.
Led Gulf Coast League outfielders in total chances with 143 in 1983, South Atlantic League outfielders with 329 in 1984 and Florida State League outfielders with 396 in 1985.
Tied for American Association lead in double plays by outfielders with 6 in 1987.

Year Club	League	Pos.	G.	AB.	R.	H.	2B.	3B.	HR.	RBI.	B.A.	PO.	A.	E.	F.A.
1983—Sarasota Royals...	Gulf C.	OF	59	203	32	52	8	2	0	19	.256	★127	★13	3	.979
1984—Charleston............	S. Atl.	OF	129	478	71	109	6	8	6	51	.228	★311	5	13	.960
1985—Fort Myers............	Fla. St.	OF	134	453	68	137	9	9	0	45	.302	★368	18	10	.975
1986—Memphis...............	South.	OF	131	525	88	164	24	12	7	62	.312	277	5	11	.962
1986—Omaha..................	A. A.	OF	3	2	1	1	0	0	0	0	.500	2	0	0	1.000
1987—Omaha..................	A. A.	OF	115	450	88	132	14	9	8	39	.293	283	11	●8	.974
1987—Kansas City..........	Amer.	OF	27	81	12	24	2	0	0	5	.296	61	5	2	.971
1988—Omaha..................	A. A.	OF	106	422	77	106	12	6	3	40	.251	195	16	6	.972
1988—Kansas City..........	Amer.	OF	35	66	6	11	1	0	0	2	.167	36	1	2	.949
1989—Kansas City†........	Amer.	OF	72	87	24	17	2	1	0	5	.195	54	2	3	.949
1989—Omaha..................	A. A.	OF	17	64	5	14	3	2	0	3	.219	34	1	2	.946
1990—Kansas City..........	Amer.	OF	23	60	5	14	3	0	0	3	.233	32	0	0	1.000
1990—Omaha..................	A. A.	OF	98	381	65	126	14	8	0	26	.331	163	6	6	.966
Major League Totals—4 Years...............			157	294	47	66	8	1	0	15	.224	183	8	7	.965

Selected by Kansas City Royals' organization in 1st round (21st player selected) of free-agent draft, June 6, 1983.

†On disabled list, March 26 to April 13 and May 10 to July 26, 1989; included rehabilitation disability assignment to Omaha, June 15 to July 26, 1989.

MARK ANTHONY THURMOND

Born September 12, 1956, at Houston, Tex.
Height, 6.00. Weight, 190.
Throws and bats lefthanded.
Received bachelor of science degree in finance from
Texas A&M University, College Station, Tex. in 1979.

Major League saves: 1985 (2), 1986 (3), 1987 (5), 1988 (3), 1989 (4), 1990 (4). Total—21.
Named lefthanded pitcher on THE SPORTING NEWS National League All-Star Team, 1984.
Tied for Texas League lead in games started by pitchers with 27 in 1981.

Year Club	League	G.	IP.	W.	L.	Pct.	H.	R.	ER.	SO.	BB.	ERA.
1979—Amarillo............................	Texas	17	62	3	5	.375	89	52	39	46	31	5.66
1980—Amarillo†...........................	Texas	26	156	10	9	.526	164	80	67	125	61	3.87
1981—Amarillo............................	Texas	27	193	12	5	.706	202	86	70	128	56	3.26
1982—Hawaii...............................	P. Coast	28	194⅓	12	10	.545	202	88	77	106	58	3.57
1983—Las Vegas..........................	P. Coast	19	63	6	1	.857	63	28	23	38	24	3.29
1983—San Diego	National	21	115⅓	7	3	.700	104	40	34	49	33	2.65
1984—San Diego	National	32	178⅔	14	8	.636	174	70	59	57	55	2.97
1985—San Diego	National	36	138⅓	7	11	.389	154	70	61	57	44	3.97
1986—San Diego‡	National	17	70⅔	3	7	.300	96	58	51	32	27	6.50
1986—Detroit...............................	American	25	51⅔	4	1	.800	44	13	11	17	17	1.92

Year Club	League	G.	IP.	W.	L.	Pct.	H.	R.	ER.	SO.	BB.	ERA.
1987—Detroit§	American	48	61⅔	0	1	.000	83	32	29	21	24	4.23
1988—Baltimore	American	43	74⅔	1	8	.111	80	43	38	29	27	4.58
1988—Rochester	Int'national	8	54⅓	5	3	.625	40	22	16	25	18	2.65
1989—Baltimore x	American	49	90	2	4	.333	102	43	39	34	17	3.90
1990—Tucson y	P. Coast	9	11	0	0	.000	11	4	4	6	1	3.27
1990—San Francisco z	National	43	56⅔	2	3	.400	53	26	21	24	18	3.34
National League Totals—5 Years		149	559⅔	33	32	.508	581	264	226	219	177	3.63
American League Totals—4 Years		165	278	7	14	.333	309	131	117	101	85	3.79
Major League Totals—8 Years		314	837⅔	40	46	.465	890	395	343	320	262	3.69

Selected by San Diego Padres' organization in 24th round of free-agent draft, June 6, 1978.
Selected by San Diego Padres' organization in 5th round of free-agent draft, June 5, 1979.
†On disabled list, July 5 to July 16, 1980.
‡Traded to Detroit Tigers for Pitcher Dave LaPoint, July 9, 1986.
§Traded to Baltimore Orioles for Third Baseman Ray Knight, February 27, 1988.
xGranted free agency, November 13, 1989; signed by Tucson (Houston Astros' organization), February 1, 1990.
yTraded to San Francisco Giants for a player to be named later, May 1, 1990; deal settled with cash.
zGranted free agency, November 5, 1990.

CHAMPIONSHIP SERIES RECORD

Year Club	League	G.	IP.	W.	L.	Pct.	H.	R.	ER.	SO.	BB.	ERA.
1984—San Diego	National	1	3⅔	0	1	.000	7	4	4	1	2	9.82
1987—Detroit	American	1	⅓	0	0	.000	0	0	0	0	0	0.00
Championship Series Totals—2 Years		2	4	0	1	.000	7	4	4	1	2	9.00

WORLD SERIES RECORD

Year Club	League	G.	IP.	W.	L.	Pct.	H.	R.	ER.	SO.	BB.	ERA.
1984—San Diego	National	2	5⅓	0	1	.000	12	6	6	2	3	10.13

JAY LINDSEY TIBBS

Born January 4, 1962, at Birmingham, Ala.
Height, 6.01. Weight, 183.
Throws and bats righthanded.

Year Club	League	G.	IP.	W.	L.	Pct.	H.	R.	ER.	SO.	BB.	ERA.
1980—Kingsport	Ap'lachian	12	76	3	7	.300	88	54	37	45	32	4.38
1981—Lynchburg	Carolina	15	72	2	7	.222	89	65	55	41	34	6.88
1981—Shelby	W. Carol.	13	89	4	8	.333	87	56	38	57	33	3.84
1982—Lynchburg†	Carolina	7	38⅓	2	4	.333	42	28	24	31	23	5.63
1982—Jackson	Texas	1	3⅓	0	0	.000	2	1	0	3	1	0.00
1983—Lynchburg‡	Carolina	28	203⅔	14	8	.636	172	94	66	170	96	2.92
1984—Jackson	Texas	6	37⅓	1	2	.333	28	15	13	31	19	3.13
1984—Tidewater§	Int'national	8	41⅓	3	5	.375	44	27	24	27	23	5.23
1984—Wichita	Am. Assoc.	4	27⅔	3	0	1.000	22	13	11	14	8	3.58
1984—Cincinnati	National	14	100⅔	6	2	.750	87	34	32	40	33	2.86
1985—Cincinnati	National	35	218	10	16	.385	216	111	95	98	83	3.92
1985—Denver x	Am. Assoc.	4	31⅔	1	2	.333	20	10	8	15	12	2.27
1986—Montreal	National	35	190⅓	7	9	.438	181	96	84	117	70	3.97
1987—Montreal	National	19	83	4	5	.444	95	55	46	54	34	4.99
1987—Indianapolis y	Am. Assoc.	12	81⅓	5	5	.500	64	31	27	55	22	2.99
1988—Rochester	Int'national	4	25⅓	3	1	.750	22	12	8	18	9	2.84
1988—Baltimore	American	30	158⅔	4	15	.211	184	103	95	82	63	5.39
1989—Rochester	Int'national	4	29	3	0	1.000	22	3	3	14	10	0.93
1989—Baltimore z	American	10	54⅓	5	0	1.000	62	17	17	30	20	2.82
1990—Baltimore a	American	10	50⅔	2	7	.222	55	34	32	23	14	5.68
1990—Pittsburgh	National	5	7	1	0	1.000	7	2	2	4	2	2.57
1990—Buffalo b	Am. Assoc.	2	3	0	0	.000	3	1	1	1	2	3.00
National League Totals—5 Years		108	599	28	32	.467	586	298	259	313	222	3.89
American League Totals—3 Years		50	263⅔	11	22	.333	301	154	144	135	97	4.92
Major League Totals—7 Years		158	862⅔	39	54	.419	887	452	403	448	319	4.20

Selected by New York Mets' organization in 2nd round of free-agent draft, June 3, 1980.
†On disabled list, July 21 to August 29, 1982.
‡Drafted by Philadelphia Phillies, December 5, 1983; returned, March 29, 1984.
§Traded with Third Baseman Eddie Williams and Pitcher Matt Bullinger to Cincinnati Reds' organization for Pitcher Bruce Berenyi, June 15, 1984.
xTraded with Pitchers Andy McGaffigan and John Stuper and Catcher Dann Bilardello to Montreal Expos for Pitcher Bill Gullickson and Catcher Sal Butera, December 19, 1985.
yTraded with Pitcher Al Cardwood to Baltimore Orioles for Pitchers John Hoover, Doug Cinnella and Rick Carriger, February 16, 1988.
zOn disabled list, July 3, 1989 through remainder of season.
aTraded to Pittsburgh Pirates for a player to be named later, June 25, 1990; Baltimore Orioles acquired Pitcher Dorn Taylor to complete deal, September 5, 1990.
bGranted free agency, October 15, 1990.

MICHAEL AUGUST TIMLIN
(Mike)

Born March 10, 1966, at Midland, Tex.
Height, 6.04. Weight, 205.
Throws and bats righthanded.
Attended Southwestern University, Georgetown, Tex.

Led South Atlantic League in hit batsmen with 19 in 1988.

Year Club	League	G.	IP.	W.	L.	Pct.	H.	R.	ER.	SO.	BB.	ERA.
1987—Medicine Hat	Pioneer	13	75⅓	4	8	.333	79	50	43	66	26	5.14
1988—Myrtle Beach	S. Atlantic	35	151	10	6	.625	119	68	48	106	77	2.86
1989—Dunedin	Florida St.	33	88⅔	5	8	.385	90	44	32	64	36	3.25
1990—Dunedin	Florida St.	42	50⅓	7	2	.778	36	11	8	46	16	1.43
1990—Knoxville	Southern	17	26	1	2	.333	20	6	5	21	7	1.73

Selected by Toronto Blue Jays' organization in 5th round of free-agent draft, June 2, 1987.

RONALD IRVIN TINGLEY
(Ron)

Born May 27, 1959, at Presque Isle, Maine.
Height, 6.02. Weight, 180.
Throws and bats righthanded.

Year Club	League	Pos.	G.	AB.	R.	H.	2B.	3B.	HR.	RBI.	B.A.	PO.	A.	E.	F.A.
1977—Walla Walla	N'west	OF	21	33	8	5	0	0	1	3	.152	5	2	0	1.000
1978—Walla Walla	N'west	OF-C	43	140	22	29	2	0	2	21	.207	149	16	8	.954
1979—Santa Clara	Calif.	C-OF-P	52	143	11	29	4	1	0	17	.203	258	42	8	.974
1979—Amarillo	Texas	C-OF	30	90	16	23	4	1	1	6	.256	133	17	4	.974
1980—Reno†	Calif.	C-OF	65	204	37	61	3	3	3	35	.299	333	46	10	.974
1981—Amarillo	Texas	C-1B-OF	116	379	72	109	9	★10	13	60	.288	607	47	11	.983
1982—Hawaii	P. C.	C	115	362	45	95	13	8	6	42	.262	540	77	12	.981
1982—San Diego	Nat.	C	8	20	0	2	0	0	0	0	.100	40	4	2	.957
1983—Las Vegas	P. C.	C	92	294	44	83	15	6	10	48	.282	449	55	12	.977
1984—Salt Lake City‡§	P. C.	C	3	2	1	1	0	0	1	1	.500	3	0	0	1.000
1985—Calgary x	P. C.	C-OF	83	277	36	70	11	3	11	47	.253	399	51	10	.978
1986—Rich.y-Maine	Int.	C	58	174	13	35	2	1	3	13	.201	280	23	6	.981
1987—Buffalo	A. A.	C-1B-3B	57	167	27	45	8	5	5	30	.269	306	37	6	.983
1988—Colorado Springs	P. C.	C	44	130	11	37	5	1	3	20	.285	234	22	0	1.000
1988—Cleveland	Amer.	C	9	24	1	4	0	0	1	2	.167	48	6	0	1.000
1989—Colo. Springs z	P. C.	C-1B	66	207	28	54	8	2	6	39	.261	349	45	12	.970
1989—California	Amer.	C	4	3	0	1	0	0	0	0	.333	7	1	1	.889
1990—Edmonton	P. C.	C	54	172	27	46	9	2	5	23	.267	284	35	8	.976
1990—California ab	Amer.	C	5	3	0	0	0	0	0	0	.000	12	0	0	1.000
National League Totals—1 Year			8	20	0	2	0	0	0	0	.100	40	4	2	.957
American League Totals—3 Years			18	30	1	5	0	0	1	2	.167	67	7	1	.987
Major League Totals—4 Years			26	50	1	7	0	0	1	2	.140	107	11	3	.975

Selected by San Diego Padres' organization in 10th round of free-agent draft, June 7, 1977.
†On disabled list, April 10 to April 29, 1980.
‡On disabled list, April 7 to August 10, 1984.
§Granted free agency, October 15, 1984; signed by Calgary (Seattle Mariners' organization), January 15, 1985.
xGranted free agency, October 15, 1985; signed by Richmond (Atlanta Braves' organization), November 19, 1985.
yReleased, June 19, 1986; signed by Maine (Cleveland Indians' organization), June 23, 1986.
zTraded to California Angels for a player to be named later, September 6, 1989; Colorado Springs (Cleveland Indians' organization) acquired Infielder Mark McLemore to complete deal, August 17, 1990.
aOn disabled list, August 4 to September 1, 1990.
bGranted free agency, October 15, 1990.

PITCHING RECORD

Year Club	League	G.	IP.	W.	L.	Pct.	H.	R.	ER.	SO.	BB.	ERA.
1979—Santa Clara	California	1	1	0	0	.000	4	5	1	2	2	9.00

LEE OWEN TINSLEY

Born March 4, 1969, at Shelbyville, Ky.
Height, 5.10. Weight, 180.
Throws right and bats left and righthanded.

Led Midwest League batters in strikeouts with 177 in 1989 and 175 in 1990.
Led Northwest League batters in strikeouts with 106, bases on balls received with 66, stolen bases with 42 and tied for lead in caught stealing with 10 in 1988.
Led Midwest League outfielders in total chances with 320 in 1990.

Year Club	League	Pos.	G.	AB.	R.	H.	2B.	3B.	HR.	RBI.	B.A.	PO.	A.	E.	F.A.
1987—Medford	N'west	OF	45	132	22	23	3	2	0	13	.174	77	2	4	.952
1988—Southern Oregon	N'west	OF	72	256	56	64	8	2	3	28	.250	127	6	6	.957
1989—Madison	Midw.	OF	123	397	51	72	10	2	6	31	.181	274	7	8	.972
1990—Madison	Midw.	OF	132	482	88	121	14	12	12	59	.251	★302	7	11	.966

Selected by Oakland Athletics' organization in 1st round (11th player selected) of free-agent draft, June 2, 1987.

JIMMY WAYNE TOLLESON
(Known by middle name.)

Born September 22, 1955, at Spartanburg, S. C.
Height, 5.09. Weight, 160.
Throws right and bats left and righthanded.
Received degree from Western Carolina University, Cullowhee, N. C., in 1978.
Brother of Mike Tolleson, outfielder in Cleveland Indians' organization, 1984.

Major League stolen bases: 1981 (2), 1982 (1), 1983 (33), 1984 (22), 1985 (21), 1986 (17), 1987 (5), 1988 (1), 1989 (5), 1990 (1). Total—108.

Year	Club	League	Pos.	G.	AB.	R.	H.	2B.	3B.	HR.	RBI.	B.A.	PO.	A.	E.	F.A.
1978—Asheville	W. Car.		3B-SS	70	212	35	57	4	1	0	21	.269	85	175	20	.929
1979—Tulsa	Texas		SS	130	418	43	98	9	7	1	36	.234	179	413	★41	.935
1980—Tulsa	Texas		SS	131	452	69	124	19	7	1	30	.274	161	395	31	.947
1981—Wichita	A. A.		3-S-2-O	107	375	58	98	9	4	3	38	.261	96	259	15	.959
1981—Texas	Amer.		3B-SS	14	24	6	4	0	0	0	1	.167	5	8	0	1.000
1982—Texas	Amer.		SS-3B-2B	38	70	6	8	1	0	0	2	.114	47	70	5	.959
1982—Denver	A. A.		SS	71	266	48	64	9	3	4	27	.241	97	195	6	.980
1983—Texas	Amer.		2B-SS	134	470	64	122	13	2	3	20	.260	268	372	17	.974
1984—Texas	Amer.		2-S-3-O	118	338	35	72	9	2	0	9	.213	195	287	10	.980
1985—Texas†	Amer.		SS-2B-3B	123	323	45	101	9	5	1	18	.313	149	255	14	.967
1986—Chi.‡-N.Y.	Amer.		S-3-2-O	141	475	61	126	16	5	3	43	.265	147	327	14	.971
1987—New York§	Amer.		SS-3B	121	349	48	77	4	0	1	22	.221	162	326	15	.970
1988—Fort Lauderdale x	Fla. St.		SS	4	18	2	5	0	0	0	5	.278	6	13	2	.905
1988—Columbus	Int.		SS-3B	8	27	4	5	0	0	0	1	.185	7	20	1	.964
1988—New York	Amer.		2B-3B-SS	21	59	8	15	2	0	0	5	.254	28	54	3	.965
1989—New York z	Amer.		SS-3B-2B	80	140	16	23	5	2	1	9	.164	45	107	7	.956
1990—New York a	Amer.		SS-2B-3B	73	74	12	11	1	1	0	4	.149	57	86	2	.986
Major League Totals—10 Years				863	2322	301	559	60	17	9	133	.241	1103	1892	87	.972

Selected by Pittsburgh Pirates' organization in 12th round of free-agent draft, June 7, 1977.
Selected by Texas Rangers' organization in 8th round of free-agent draft, June 6, 1978.
†Traded with Pitcher Dave Schmidt to Chicago White Sox for Pitcher Ed Correa, Infielder Scott Fletcher and a player to be named later, November 25, 1985; Texas Rangers acquired Infielder Jose Mota to complete deal, December 12, 1985.
‡Traded with Outfielder-Designated Hitter Ron Kittle and Catcher Joel Skinner to New York Yankees for Catcher Ron Hassey, Shortstop Carlos Martinez and a player to be named later, July 30, 1986; New York traded Catcher Bill Lindsey to Chicago White Sox' organization to complete deal, December 24, 1986.
§On disabled list, August 19 to September 3, 1987.
xOn New York disabled list, April 4 to June 10, June 20 to July 14, July 17 to August 11 and August 14 to September 11, 1988; included rehabilitation disability assignment to Fort Lauderdale, April 16 to April 24, and to Columbus, May 19 to May 28, 1988.
yGranted free agency, November 4, 1988; re-signed by Yankees, December 18, 1988.
zOn disabled list, March 25 to April 16, 1989.
aReleased, October 5, 1990.

ANDY LEE TOMBERLIN

Born November 7, 1966, at Monroe, N.C.
Height, 5.11. Weight, 160.
Throws and bats lefthanded.

Year	Club	League	Pos.	G.	AB.	R.	H.	2B.	3B.	HR.	RBI.	B.A.	PO.	A.	E.	F.A.
1988—Burlington	Midw.		OF	43	134	24	46	7	3	3	18	.343	62	6	3	.958
1988—Durham	Carol.		OF	83	256	43	77	16	3	6	35	.301	152	2	3	.981
1989—Durham	Carol.		OF-1B-P	119	363	63	102	13	2	16	61	.281	442	16	1	.998
1990—Greenville	South.		OF-P	60	196	31	61	9	1	4	25	.311	95	4	3	.971
1990—Richmond	Int.		OF-1B	80	283	36	86	19	3	4	31	.304	180	9	4	.979

Signed as free agent by Atlanta Braves' organization, August 16, 1985.

RECORD AS PITCHER

Year	Club	League	G.	IP.	W.	L.	Pct.	H.	R.	ER.	SO.	BB.	ERA.
1986—Sumter	S. Atlantic	13	25⅓	1	0	1.000	18	17	13	22	27	4.62
1986—Pulaski	Ap'lachian	3	17	2	0	1.000	13	4	4	15	9	2.12
1987—Pulaski	Ap'lachian	12	44⅔	4	2	.667	35	23	22	51	29	4.43
1989—Durham	Carolina	1	1	0	0	.000	2	2	2	2	2	18.00
1990—Greenville	Southern	1	1	0	0	.000	1	0	0	1	1	0.00

RANDY LEON TOMLIN

Born June 14, 1966, at Bainbridge, Md.
Height, 5.11. Weight, 180.
Throws and bats lefthanded.
Attended Liberty University, Lynchburg, Va.

Pitched 1-0 no-hit victory against Kinston, May 28, 1989.
Tied for Eastern League lead in shutouts with 3 in 1990.

Year	Club	League	G.	IP.	W.	L.	Pct.	H.	R.	ER.	SO.	BB.	ERA.
1988—Watertown	NYP	15	103⅓	7	5	.583	75	31	25	87	25	2.18
1989—Salem	Carolina	21	138⅔	12	6	.667	131	60	50	99	43	3.25
1989—Harrisburg	Eastern	5	32	2	2	.500	18	6	3	31	6	0.84
1990—Harrisburg	Eastern	19	126⅓	9	6	.600	101	43	32	92	34	2.28
1990—Buffalo	Am. Assoc.	3	8	0	0	.000	12	3	3	3	1	3.38
1990—Pittsburgh	National	12	77⅔	4	4	.500	62	24	22	42	12	2.55
Major League Totals—1 Year			12	77⅔	4	4	.500	62	24	22	42	12	2.55

Selected by Pittsburgh Pirates' organization in 18th round of free-agent draft, June 1, 1988.

—DID YOU KNOW—

That the no-hitters pitched by Fernando Valenzuela and Dave Stewart last June 29 were the majors' first same-day no-hitters since April 22, 1898?

KELVIN CURTIS TORVE

Born January 10, 1960, at Rapid City, S.D.
Height, 6.03. Weight, 185.
Throws right and bats lefthanded.
Received bachelor of science degree in marketing from Oral Roberts University, Tulsa, Okla.

Led Texas League in intentional bases on balls received with 11 and tied for lead in sacrifice flies with 9 in 1982.
Led Pacific Coast League first basemen in total chances with 1,310 and double plays with 111 in 1989.

Year—Club	League	Pos.	G.	AB.	R.	H.	2B.	3B.	HR.	RBI.	B.A.	PO.	A.	E.	F.A.
1981—Clinton	Midw.	1B	57	211	27	55	10	0	1	27	.261	538	41	4	.993
1982—Shreveport	Texas	1B	127	449	66	137	29	7	15	84	.305	1040	★96	17	.985
1983—Phoenix	P. C.	1B	115	392	58	102	21	5	4	54	.260	730	53	10	.987
1984—Shreveport†	Texas	1B-SS	114	316	59	94	21	5	16	62	.297	668	58	4	.995
1985—Charlotte	South.	1B-OF	134	482	85	140	●34	1	15	77	.290	1077	68	9	.992
1986—Rochester	Int.	1B	109	356	39	86	16	1	4	41	.242	555	51	5	.992
1987—Rochester‡	Int.	1B	86	252	27	66	10	0	9	32	.262	632	48	3	.996
1988—Portland	P. C.	1B	103	385	58	116	28	2	9	47	.301	864	62	2	★.998
1988—Minnesota	Amer.	1B	12	16	1	3	0	0	1	2	.188	14	1	0	1.000
1989—Portland§	P. C.	1B	137	499	62	145	★41	2	8	62	.291	★1206	★102	2	★.998
1990—Tidewater	Int.	1B-OF	115	402	62	122	25	1	11	76	.303	839	77	15	.984
1990—New York x	Nat.	1B-OF	20	38	0	11	4	0	0	2	.289	65	0	0	1.000
American League Totals—1 Year			12	16	1	3	0	0	1	2	.188	14	1	0	1.000
National League Totals—1 Year			20	38	0	11	4	0	0	2	.289	65	0	0	1.000
Major League Totals—2 Years			32	54	1	14	4	0	1	4	.259	79	1	0	1.000

Selected by San Francisco Giants' organization in 2nd round of free-agent draft, June 8, 1981.
†Traded to Baltimore Orioles' organization for Pitcher Tommy Alexander, April 9, 1985.
‡Granted free agency, October 15, 1987; signed by Portland (Minnesota Twins' organization), January 18, 1988.
§Granted free agency, October 15, 1989; signed by Tidewater (New York Mets' organization), December 13, 1989.
xGranted free agency, October 15, 1990.

ALAN STUART TRAMMELL

Name pronounced TRAM-mull.

Born February 21, 1958, at Garden Grove, Calif.
Height, 6.00. Weight, 175.
Throws and bats righthanded.

Major League stolen bases: 1978 (3), 1979 (17), 1980 (12), 1981 (10), 1982 (19), 1983 (30), 1984 (19), 1985 (14), 1986 (25), 1987 (21), 1988 (7), 1989 (10), 1990 (12). Total—199.
Led American League in sacrifice hits with 16 in 1981 and 15 in 1983.
Led American League shortstops in double plays with 102 in 1984.
Named American League Comeback Player of the Year by THE SPORTING NEWS, 1983.
Named shortstop on THE SPORTING NEWS American League All-Star Team, 1987, 1988 and 1990.
Named shortstop on THE SPORTING NEWS American League All-Star fielding team, 1980, 1981, 1983 and 1984.
Named shortstop on THE SPORTING NEWS American League Silver Slugger team, 1987, 1988 and 1990.
Named Southern League Most Valuable Player, 1977.

Year—Club	League	Pos.	G.	AB.	R.	H.	2B.	3B.	HR.	RBI.	B.A.	PO.	A.	E.	F.A.
1976—Bristol	Appal.	SS	41	140	27	38	2	2	0	7	.271	59	131	12	.941
1976—Montgomery	South.	SS	21	56	4	10	0	0	0	2	.179	40	64	2	.981
1977—Montgomery	South.	SS	134	454	78	132	9	★19	3	50	.291	188	397	27	.956
1977—Detroit	Amer.	SS	19	43	6	8	0	0	0	0	.186	15	34	2	.961
1978—Detroit	Amer.	SS	139	448	49	120	14	6	2	34	.268	239	421	14	.979
1979—Detroit	Amer.	SS	142	460	68	127	11	4	6	50	.276	245	388	26	.961
1980—Detroit	Amer.	SS	146	560	107	168	21	5	9	65	.300	225	412	13	.980
1981—Detroit	Amer.	SS	105	392	52	101	15	3	2	31	.258	181	347	9	.983
1982—Detroit	Amer.	SS	157	489	66	126	34	3	9	57	.258	259	459	16	.978
1983—Detroit	Amer.	SS	142	505	83	161	31	2	14	66	.319	236	367	13	.979
1984—Detroit†	Amer.	SS	139	555	85	174	34	5	14	69	.314	180	314	10	.980
1985—Detroit	Amer.	SS	149	605	79	156	21	7	13	57	.258	225	400	15	.977
1986—Detroit	Amer.	SS	151	574	107	159	33	7	21	75	.277	238	445	22	.969
1987—Detroit	Amer.	SS	151	597	109	205	34	3	28	105	.343	222	421	19	.971
1988—Detroit‡	Amer.	SS	128	466	73	145	24	1	15	69	.311	195	355	11	.980
1989—Detroit§	Amer.	SS	121	449	54	109	20	3	5	43	.243	188	396	9	.985
1990—Detroit	Amer.	SS	146	559	71	170	37	1	14	89	.304	232	409	14	.979
Major League Totals—14 Years			1835	6702	1009	1929	329	50	152	810	.288	2880	5168	193	.977

Selected by Detroit Tigers' organization in 2nd round of free-agent draft, June 8, 1976.
†On disabled list, July 9 to July 31, 1984.
‡On disabled list, June 29 to July 17, 1988.
§On disabled list, June 4 to June 23, 1989.

CHAMPIONSHIP SERIES RECORD

Year—Club	League	Pos.	G.	AB.	R.	H.	2B.	3B.	HR.	RBI.	B.A.	PO.	A.	E.	F.A.
1984—Detroit	Amer.	SS	3	11	2	4	0	1	1	3	.364	1	8	0	1.000
1987—Detroit	Amer.	SS	5	20	3	4	1	0	0	2	.200	6	9	1	.938
Championship Series Totals—2 Years			8	31	5	8	1	1	1	5	.258	7	17	1	.960

WORLD SERIES RECORD

Tied World Series records for batting in all club's runs, game, most (4), October 13, 1984; most hits, five-game Series (9), 1984.

Year—Club	League	Pos.	G.	AB.	R.	H.	2B.	3B.	HR.	RBI.	B.A.	PO.	A.	E.	F.A.
1984—Detroit	Amer.	SS	5	20	5	9	1	0	2	6	.450	8	9	1	.944

Year League	Pos.	AB.	R.	H.	2B.	3B.	HR.	RBI.	B.A.	PO.	A.	E.	F.A.
1980—American	SS	0	0	0	0	0	0	0	.000	0	0	0	.000
1985—American	SS	1	0	0	0	0	0	0	.000	0	0	0	.000
1987—American	PH	1	0	0	0	0	0	0	.000	0	0	0	.000
1990—American	PH	1	0	0	0	0	0	0	.000	0	0	0	.000
All-Star Game Totals—4 Years		3	0	0	0	0	0	0	.000	0	0	0	.000

Named to American League All-Star Team for 1984 game; replaced due to injury by Alfredo Griffin.
Named to American League All-Star Team for 1988 game; replaced due to injury by Cal Ripken Jr.

BRIAN LEE TRAXLER

Born September 26, 1967, at Waukegan, Ill.
Height, 5.10. Weight, 200.
Throws and bats lefthanded.
Attended University of New Orleans, New Orleans, La.

Year Club League	Pos.	G.	AB.	R.	H.	2B.	3B.	HR.	RBI.	B.A.	PO.	A.	E.	F.A.
1988—Vero Beach........ Fla. St.	1B	72	260	30	76	14	0	2	34	.292	538	56	8	.987
1989—San Antonio........... Texas	1B	63	228	37	79	7	0	9	44	.346	529	52	4	.993
1989—Albuquerque........ P. C.	1B	64	239	33	72	10	3	3	30	.301	552	61	4	.994
1990—Albuquerque........ P. C.	1B-P	98	318	43	88	23	0	7	53	.277	730	47	9	.989
1990—Los Angeles .... Nat.	1B	9	11	0	1	1	0	0	0	.091	6	2	0	1.000
Major League Totals—1 Year		9	11	0	1	1	0	0	0	.091	6	2	0	1.000

Selected by Los Angeles Dodgers' organization in 16th round of free-agent draft, June 1, 1988.

PITCHING RECORD

Year Club	League	G.	IP.	W.	L.	Pct.	H.	R.	ER.	SO.	BB.	ERA.
1990—Albuquerque.................. P. Coast	1	1	0	0	.000	0	0	0	1	1	0.00

HUGH JEFFERY TREADWAY
(Jeff)

Born January 22, 1963, at Columbus, Ga.
Weight, 5.11. Weight, 170.
Throws right and bats lefthanded.
Attended Middle Georgia College, Cochran, Ga.,
and University of Georgia, Athens, Ga.

Major League stolen bases: 1987 (1), 1988 (2), 1989 (3), 1990 (3). Total—9.
Hit three home runs in a game, May 26, 1990.

Year Club League	Pos.	G.	AB.	R.	H.	2B.	3B.	HR.	RBI.	B.A.	PO.	A.	E.	F.A.
1984—Tampa.................... Fla. St.	3B-2B	119	372	44	115	16	0	0	44	.309	128	184	25	.926
1985—Vermont .... East.	2B	129	431	63	130	17	1	2	49	.302	271	332	15	.976
1986—Vermont .... East.	2B	33	122	18	41	8	1	1	16	.336	68	102	5	.971
1986—Denver .... A. A.	2B-3B	72	204	20	67	11	4	3	23	.328	75	153	6	.974
1987—Nashville............... A. A.	2B	123	409	66	129	28	5	7	59	.315	236	362	12	★.980
1987—Cincinnati............. Nat.	2B	23	84	9	28	4	0	2	4	.333	44	48	4	.958
1988—Cincinnati†‡......... Nat.	2B-3B	103	301	30	76	19	4	2	23	.252	189	253	8	.982
1989—Atlanta .... Nat.	2B-3B	134	473	58	131	18	3	8	40	.277	273	341	12	.981
1990—Atlanta .... Nat.	2B	128	474	56	134	20	2	11	59	.283	241	360	15	.976
Major League Totals—4 Years		388	1332	153	369	61	9	23	126	.277	747	1002	39	.978

Selected by Montreal Expos' organization in 18th round of free-agent draft, January 13, 1981.
Signed as free agent by Cincinnati Reds' organization, January 29, 1984.
†On disabled list, August 28 to September 24, 1988.
†Sold to Atlanta Braves, March 25, 1989.

ALEJANDRO TREVINO (CASTRO)
(Alex)

Born August 26, 1957, at Monterrey, Nuevo Leon, Mex.
Height, 5.11. Weight, 179.
Throws and bats righthanded.
Attended University of Nuevo Leon, Monterrey, Mex.
Brother of Bobby Trevino, outfielder with California Angels, 1968; manager, Tabasco, 1977,
Tampico, 1979, and Toluca, 1980.

Major League stolen bases: 1979 (2), 1981 (3), 1982 (3), 1984 (5), 1987 (1), 1988 (5). Total—19.
Led Midwest League catchers in putouts with 847 and assists with 102 in 1977.
Led Carolina League in passed balls with 18 in 1976.

Year Club League	Pos.	G.	AB.	R.	H.	2B.	3B.	HR.	RBI.	B.A.	PO.	A.	E.	F.A.
1973—Victoria†............... Mx. Cen.	C-OF	12	26	3	6	1	0	0	2	.231	26	5	1	.969
1974—Marion.................. Appal.	C-SS	12	16	0	1	0	0	0	1	.063	15	0	0	1.000
1975—Marion.................. Appal.	C-2B-OF	22	60	10	12	1	0	0	3	.200	96	8	6	.963
1976—Lynchburg............ Carol.	C-3-2-S	94	284	17	57	11	2	0	31	.201	400	130	18	.967
1977—Wausau................. Midw.	C-2-1-3	128	422	57	100	10	0	2	36	.237	865	110	15	.985
1978—Tidewater............. Int.	C-3B	87	262	44	77	13	2	5	37	.294	303	68	11	.971
1978—New York............. Nat.	C-3B	6	12	3	3	0	0	0	0	.250	12	4	0	1.000
1979—New York............. Nat.	C-3B-2B	79	207	24	56	11	1	0	20	.271	229	71	9	.971

Year	Club	League	Pos.	G.	AB.	R.	H.	2B.	3B.	HR.	RBI.	B.A.	PO.	A.	E.	F.A.
1980—New York	Nat.	C-3B-2B	106	355	26	91	11	2	0	37	.256	450	76	16	.970
1981—New York‡	Nat.	C-2-0-3	56	149	17	39	2	0	0	10	.262	215	25	9	.964
1982—Cincinnati	Nat.	*C-3B	120	355	24	89	10	3	1	33	.251	725	61	*17	.979
1983—Cincinnati	Nat.	C-3B-2B	74	167	14	36	8	1	1	13	.216	359	32	5	.987
1984—Cinc.§-Atl.	Nat.	C	85	272	36	66	16	0	3	28	.243	403	61	5	.989
1985—Atl. x-S.F. y	Nat.	C-3B	57	157	17	34	10	1	6	19	.217	299	19	7	.978
1986—Los Angeles	Nat.	C-1B	89	202	31	53	13	0	4	26	.262	304	46	11	.970
1987—Los Angeles z	Nat.	C-OF-3B	72	144	16	32	7	1	3	16	.222	206	22	3	.987
1988—Tucson	P. C.	C-OF-3B	15	45	5	10	3	1	0	3	.222	39	10	2	.961
1988—Houston a	Nat.	C-OF	78	193	19	48	17	0	2	13	.249	360	24	9	.977
1989—Houston	Nat.	C-1B-3B	59	131	15	38	7	1	2	16	.290	173	13	2	.989
1990—Hou.b-N.Y.c-Cin.d	Nat.	C-1B	58	86	3	19	5	0	1	13	.221	172	9	4	.978
Major League Totals—13 Years			939	2430	245	604	117	10	23	244	.249	3907	463	97	.978

Signed as free agent by Victoria, May 16, 1973.

†Sold to New York Mets' organization, May 22, 1974.

‡Traded with Pitchers Jim Kern and Greg Harris to Cincinnati Reds for Outfielder George Foster, February 10, 1982.

§Traded to Atlanta Braves for player to be named later, April 24, 1984; deal settled with reported $50,000 in July, 1984.

xTraded to San Francisco Giants for Catcher-Outfielder John Rabb, April 17, 1985.

yTraded to Los Angeles Dodgers for Outfielder Candy Maldonado, December 11, 1985.

zReleased, April 4, 1988; signed by Tucson (Houston Astros' organization), April 12, 1988.

aGranted free agency, November 4, 1988; re-signed by Astros, December 21, 1988.

bReleased, July 27, 1990; signed by New York Mets, August 3, 1990.

cClaimed on waivers by Cincinnati Reds, September 7, 1990.

dGranted free agency, December 2, 1990; signed by St. Louis Cardinals, January 2, 1991.

RICHARD ALAN TRLICEK

Name pronounced TRILL-a-check.

(Rick)

Born April 26, 1969, at Houston, Tex.
Height, 6.03. Weight, 200.
Throws and bats righthanded.

Year	Club	League	G.	IP.	W.	L.	Pct.	H.	R.	ER.	SO.	BB.	ERA.
1987—Utica	NYP	10	37⅓	2	5	.286	43	28	17	22	31	4.10
1988—Batavia†	NYP	8	31⅔	2	3	.400	27	32	26	26	31	7.39
1989—Sumter	S. Atlantic	15	93⅔	6	5	.545	73	40	27	72	40	2.59
1989—Durham‡	Carolina	1	8	0	0	.000	3	2	1	4	1	1.13
1990—Dunedin	Florida St.	26	154⅓	5	8	.385	128	74	64	125	72	3.73

Selected by Philadelphia Phillies' organization in 4th round of free-agent draft, June 2, 1987.

†Released, March 23, 1989; signed by Atlanta Braves' organization, April 2, 1989.

‡Traded to Toronto Blue Jays for Catcher Ernie Whitt and Outfielder Kevin Batiste, December 17, 1989.

EDDIE JACK TUCKER

(Scooter)

Born November 18, 1966, at Greenville, Miss.
Height, 6.02. Weight, 205.
Throws and bats righthanded.
Attended Delta State University, Cleveland, Miss.

Year	Club	League	Pos.	G.	AB.	R.	H.	2B.	3B.	HR.	RBI.	B.A.	PO.	A.	E.	F.A.
1988—Everett	N'west	C	45	153	24	40	5	0	3	23	.261	237	23	1	.996
1989—Clinton	Midw.	C-OF	126	426	44	105	20	2	3	43	.246	649	60	10	.986
1990—San Jose	Calif.	C-OF	123	439	59	123	28	2	5	71	.280	599	88	11	.984

Selected by San Francisco Giants' organization in 5th round of free-agent draft, June 1, 1988.

JOHN THOMAS TUDOR

Born February 2, 1954, at Schenectady, N.Y.
Height, 6.00. Weight, 185.
Throws and bats lefthanded.
Attended North Shore Community College, Beverly, Mass. and received bachelor of science degree in criminal justice from Georgia Southern College, Statesboro, Ga.

Pitched seven-inning, 2-0 no-hit victory against Reading, June 28, 1977.
Major League saves: 1981 (1).
Led National League in shutouts with 10 in 1985.
Named lefthanded pitcher on THE SPORTING NEWS National League All-Star Team, 1985.
Named National League Comeback Player of the Year by THE SPORTING NEWS, 1990.

Year	Club	League	G.	IP.	W.	L.	Pct.	H.	R.	ER.	SO.	BB.	ERA.
1976—Winston-Salem	Carolina	25	82	5	2	.714	77	26	25	76	28	2.74
1977—Bristol	Eastern	27	115	6	5	.545	113	57	45	78	35	3.52
1977—Pawtucket	Int'national	4	4	1	1	.500	5	1	1	1	3	2.25
1978—Pawtucket	Int'national	26	105	7	4	.636	100	46	36	83	56	3.09
1979—Pawtucket	Int'national	25	163	10	11	.476	145	73	53	103	52	2.93
1979—Boston	American	6	28	1	2	.333	39	23	20	11	9	6.43
1980—Pawtucket	Int'national	12	74	4	5	.444	67	36	30	51	33	3.65
1980—Boston	American	16	92	8	5	.615	81	35	31	45	31	3.03

Year Club	League	G.	IP.	W.	L.	Pct.	H.	R.	ER.	SO.	BB.	ERA.
1981—Boston	American	18	79	4	3	.571	74	44	40	44	28	4.56
1982—Boston	American	32	195⅔	13	10	.565	215	90	79	146	59	3.63
1983—Boston†	American	34	242	13	12	.520	236	122	110	136	81	4.09
1984—Pittsburgh‡	National	32	212	12	11	.522	200	81	77	117	56	3.27
1985—St. Louis	National	36	275	21	8	.724	209	68	59	169	49	1.93
1986—St. Louis§	National	30	219	13	7	.650	197	81	71	107	53	2.92
1987—St. Louis x	National	16	96	10	2	.833	100	43	41	54	32	3.84
1987—Louisville	Am. Assoc.	2	8	1	0	1.000	11	8	7	3	1	7.88
1988—St. Louis yz-Los Angeles	National	30	197⅔	10	8	.556	189	60	51	87	41	2.32
1989—Vero Beach a	Florida St.	1	5	1	0	1.000	1	1	1	5	0	1.80
1989—Bakersfield	California	1	6⅔	0	0	.000	4	2	1	6	2	1.35
1989—Los Angeles b	National	6	14⅓	0	0	.000	17	5	5	9	6	3.14
1990—St. Louis cd	National	25	146⅓	12	4	.750	120	48	39	63	30	2.40
American League Totals—5 Years		106	636⅔	39	32	.549	645	314	280	382	208	3.96
National League Totals—7 Years		175	1160⅓	78	40	.661	1032	386	373	606	267	2.66
Major League Totals—12 Years		281	1797	117	72	.619	1677	700	623	988	475	3.12

Selected by New York Mets' organization in 21st round of free-agent draft, June 4, 1975.
Selected by Boston Red Sox' organization in secondary phase of free-agent draft, January 7, 1976.
†Traded to Pittsburgh Pirates for Outfielder Mike Easler, December 6, 1983.
‡Traded with Outfielder Brian Harper to St. Louis Cardinals for Outfielder-First Baseman George Hendrick and Catcher Steve Barnard, December 12, 1984.
§On disabled list, September 16, 1986 through remainder of season.
xOn disabled list, April 20 to July 30, 1987; included rehabilitation disability assignment to Louisville, July 22 to July 30, 1987.
yOn disabled list, March 26 to April 25, 1988.
zTraded to Los Angeles Dodgers for Infielder Pedro Guerrero, August 16, 1988.
aOn Los Angeles disabled list, March 31 to June 27 and July 8 to September 2, 1989; included rehabilitation disability assignment to Vero Beach, June 7 to June 17, 1989; then transferred to Bakersfield, June 18 to June 27, 1989.
bGranted free agency, November 13, 1989; signed by St. Louis Cardinals, December 14, 1989.
cOn disabled list, August 11 to September 2, 1990.
dGranted free agency, November 5, 1990.

CHAMPIONSHIP SERIES RECORD

Shares National League Championship Series record for most hits allowed, game (10), October 7, 1987.

Year Club	League	G.	IP.	W.	L.	Pct.	H.	R.	ER.	SO.	BB.	ERA.
1985—St. Louis	National	2	12⅔	1	1	.500	10	5	4	8	3	2.84
1987—St. Louis	National	2	15⅓	1	1	.500	16	5	3	12	5	1.76
1988—Los Angeles	National	1	5	0	0	.000	8	4	4	1	1	7.20
Championship Series Totals—3 Years		5	33	2	2	.500	34	14	11	21	9	3.00

WORLD SERIES RECORD

Year Club	League	G.	IP.	W.	L.	Pct.	H.	R.	ER.	SO.	BB.	ERA.
1985—St. Louis	National	3	18	2	1	.667	15	6	6	14	7	3.00
1987—St. Louis	National	2	11	1	1	.500	15	7	7	8	3	5.73
1988—Los Angeles	National	1	1⅓	0	0	.000	0	0	0	1	0	0.00
World Series Totals—3 Years		6	30⅓	3	2	.600	30	13	13	23	10	3.86

JOSEPH FRANCIS TUREK
(Joe)

Born November 1, 1966, at Ambler, Pa.
Height, 6.02. Weight, 180.
Throws and bats righthanded.
Attended West Chester University, West Chester, Pa.

Year Club	League	G.	IP.	W.	L.	Pct.	H.	R.	ER.	SO.	BB.	ERA.
1987—Billings	Pioneer	9	15⅓	0	2	.000	18	11	10	10	10	5.87
1987—Sarasota Reds	Gulf Coast	3	22	3	0	1.000	15	6	5	19	10	2.05
1988—Greensboro	S. Atlantic	19	111⅓	10	3	.769	91	44	34	91	32	2.75
1989—Cedar Rapids	Midwest	25	149	9	11	.450	120	77	62	138	77	3.74
1990—Cedar Rapids†	Midwest	25	169⅓	13	6	.684	131	54	44	154	61	2.34

Selected by Cincinnati Reds' organization in 10th round of free-agent draft, June 2, 1987.
†Drafted by Oakland Athletics, December 3, 1990.

WILLIAM MATTHEW TURNER
(Matt)

Born February 18, 1967, at Lexington, Ky.
Height, 6.05. Weight, 215.
Throws and bats righthanded.
Attended Middle Georgia College, Cochran, Ga.

Tied for South Atlantic League lead in balks with 6 in 1987.

Year Club	League	G.	IP.	W.	L.	Pct.	H.	R.	ER.	SO.	BB.	ERA.
1986—Pulaski	Ap'lachian	18	48⅔	1	3	.250	55	36	25	48	28	4.62
1987—Sumter	S. Atlantic	39	93⅔	2	3	.400	91	61	49	102	48	4.71
1988—Burlington	Midwest	7	34⅓	1	3	.250	43	27	25	26	16	6.55
1988—Sumter	S. Atlantic	7	15⅔	1	0	1.000	17	8	8	7	3	4.60
1989—Durham	Carolina	53	118	9	9	.500	95	38	32	114	47	2.44

Year Club	League	G.	IP.	W.	L.	Pct.	H.	R.	ER.	SO.	BB.	ERA.
1990—Greenville	Southern	40	67⅔	6	4	.600	59	24	20	60	29	2.66
1990—Richmond.......................................	Int'national	22	42	2	3	.400	44	20	18	36	16	3.86

Signed as free agent by Atlanta Braves' organization, May 21, 1986.

JOSE ALTA URIBE

(Name pronounced Yoo-REE-bay.)
(Formerly known as Jose Alta Gonzalez.)

Born January 21, 1960, at San Cristobal, D. R.
Height, 5.10. Weight, 170.
Throws right and bats left and righthanded.

Major League stolen bases: 1984 (1), 1985 (8), 1986 (22), 1987 (12), 1988 (14), 1989 (6), 1990 (5). Total—68.
Led National League shortstops in double plays with 85 in 1989.
Led American Association in sacrifice hits with 14 in 1983.
Led American Association shortstops in total chances with 720 and double plays with 96 in 1984.
Led American Association shortstops in total chances with 664 and double plays with 90 in 1983.
Led Texas League shortstops in double plays with 88 in 1982.

Year Club	League	Pos.	G.	AB.	R.	H.	2B.	3B.	HR.	RBI.	B.A.	PO.	A.	E.	F.A.
1981—St. Petersburg†	Fla. St.	SS	128	463	54	124	15	2	0	40	.268	171	★387	32	.946
1982—Arkansas...............	Texas	SS	123	465	73	115	17	7	0	41	.247	185	385	36	.941
1982—Louisville	A. A.	SS	8	28	5	10	2	0	0	4	.357	15	18	1	.971
1983—Louisville	A. A.	SS	122	423	64	120	19	6	3	44	.284	206	425	★33	.950
1984—Louisville	A. A.	SS	145	484	68	135	20	2	3	46	.279	★233	★455	★32	★.956
1984—St. Louis‡...............	Nat.	SS-2B	8	19	4	4	0	0	0	3	.211	7	15	1	.957
1985—San Francisco	Nat.	SS-2B	147	476	46	113	20	4	3	26	.237	209	438	26	.961
1986—San Francisco	Nat.	SS	157	453	46	101	15	1	3	43	.223	249	444	16	.977
1987—San Francisco§ ...	Nat.	SS	95	309	44	90	16	5	5	30	.291	145	286	13	.971
1988—San Francisco x...	Nat.	SS	141	493	47	124	10	7	3	35	.252	212	404	19	.970
1989—San Francisco	Nat.	SS	151	453	34	100	12	6	1	30	.221	225	436	18	.973
1990—San Francisco	Nat.	SS	138	415	35	103	8	6	1	24	.248	182	373	20	.965
Major League Totals—7 Years................			837	2618	256	635	81	29	16	191	.243	1229	2396	113	.970

Signed as free agent by New York Yankees' organization, February 18, 1977.
†Released, July 5, 1977; signed by St. Louis Cardinals' organization, August 18, 1980.
‡Traded with First Basemen David Green and Gary Rajsich and Pitcher Dave LaPoint to San Francisco Giants for Outfielder-First Baseman Jack Clark, February 1, 1985.
§On disabled list, April 11 to April 30, May 5 to May 20 and May 28 to July 4, 1987.
xOn disabled list, May 31 to June 16, 1988.

CHAMPIONSHIP SERIES RECORD

Year Club	League	Pos.	G.	AB.	R.	H.	2B.	3B.	HR.	RBI.	B.A.	PO.	A.	E.	F.A.
1987—San Francisco	Nat.	SS	7	26	1	7	1	0	0	2	.269	11	20	1	.969
1989—San Francisco	Nat.	SS	5	17	2	4	1	0	0	1	.235	6	9	2	.882
Championship Series Totals—2 Years.....			12	43	3	11	2	0	0	3	.256	17	29	3	.939

WORLD SERIES RECORD

Year Club	League	Pos.	G.	AB.	R.	H.	2B.	3B.	HR.	RBI.	B.A.	PO.	A.	E.	F.A.
1989—San Francisco	Nat.	SS	3	5	1	1	0	0	0	0	.200	1	3	0	1.000

EFRAIN ANTONIO VALDEZ

Born June 11, 1966, at Nizao de Bani, Dominican Republic.
Height, 5.11. Weight, 170.
Throws and bats lefthanded.

Tied for Pacific Coast League lead in intentional bases on balls issued with 8 in 1990.

Year Club	League	G.	IP.	W.	L.	Pct.	H.	R.	ER.	SO.	BB.	ERA.
1983—Spokane	Northwest	13	29⅔	0	0	.000	40	32	23	27	17	6.98
1984—Spokane†	Northwest	13	16⅔	1	2	.333	26	18	14	15	8	7.56
1985—	(Out of Organized Baseball)											
1986—San Luis Potosi‡....................	Mexican	26	164⅓	11	8	.579	176	105	84	82	76	4.60
1986—Tulsa	Texas	4	12⅓	0	1	.000	12	8	8	4	6	5.84
1987—Tulsa	Texas	11	49⅓	1	4	.200	62	44	39	38	24	7.11
1988—Tulsa§	Texas	43	63⅓	6	5	.545	63	37	32	52	24	4.55
1989—Canton-Akron	Eastern	44	75⅓	2	4	.333	60	26	18	55	13	2.15
1990—Colorado Springs	P. Coast	46	75⅔	4	2	.667	72	38	32	52	30	3.81
1990—Cleveland.......................	American	13	23⅔	1	1	.500	20	10	8	13	14	3.04
Major League Totals—1 Year.............................		13	23⅔	1	1	.500	20	10	8	13	14	3.04

Signed as free agent by San Diego Padres' organization, May 4, 1983.
†Sold to Texas Rangers' organization, December 10, 1984.
‡Loaned to San Luis Potosi.
§Drafted by Cleveland Indians' organization, December 6, 1988.

RAFAEL EMILIO VALDEZ (DIAZ)

Born December 17, 1968, at Nizao Boni, Dominican Republic.
Height, 5.11. Weight, 185.
Throws and bats righthanded.

Pitched 2-0 perfect game against Reno, July 20, 1989.
Led South Atlantic League shortstops in errors with 46 in 1986.

Year Club	League	G.	IP.	W.	L.	Pct.	H.	R.	ER.	SO.	BB.	ERA.
1988—Charleston, S.C.	S. Atlantic	28	152⅓	11	4	.733	117	42	38	100	46	2.25
1989—Riverside	California	21	143⅓	10	5	.667	89	40	36	137	58	2.26
1989—Wichita	Texas	6	41⅔	5	0	1.000	28	10	9	26	24	1.94
1990—San Diego	National	3	5⅔	0	1	.000	11	7	7	3	2	11.12
1990—Las Vegas	P. Coast	17	86	4	7	.364	82	58	47	79	65	4.92
Major League Totals—1 Year		3	5⅔	0	1	.000	11	7	7	3	2	11.12

Signed as free agent by San Diego Padres' organization, March 6, 1985.

RECORD AS INFIELDER

Year Club	League	Pos.	G.	AB.	R.	H.	2B.	3B.	HR.	RBI.	B.A.	PO.	A.	E.	F.A.
1986—Charleston	S. Atl.	SS-2B	90	260	25	55	15	3	3	27	.212	112	204	47	.877
1987—Charleston, S.C.	S. Atl.	SS	127	435	42	115	16	2	5	44	.264	145	343	53	.902

SERGIO SANCHEZ VALDEZ

Born September 7, 1965, at Elias Pina, D.R.
Height, 6.01. Weight, 190.
Throws and bats righthanded.

Tied for American Association lead in shutouts with 2 in 1987.
Tied for Florida State League lead in shutouts with 4 in 1986.
Tied for New York-Pennsylvania League lead in games started by pitchers with 15 in 1985.

Year Club	League	G.	IP.	W.	L.	Pct.	H.	R.	ER.	SO.	BB.	ERA.
1983—Calgary	Pioneer	13	72⅔	6	3	.667	88	55	45	41	31	5.57
1984—West Palm Beach†	Florida St.	5	11⅓	0	0	.000	15	11	11	6	8	8.74
1984—Jamestown	NYP	13	76	2	7	.222	78	47	34	46	33	4.03
1985—Utica	NYP	15	105⅔	6	5	.545	98	53	36	86	36	3.07
1986—West Palm Beach	Florida St.	24	145⅔	★16	6	.727	119	48	40	108	46	2.47
1986—Montreal	National	5	25	0	4	.000	39	20	19	20	11	6.84
1987—Indianapolis	Am. Assoc.	27	158⅓	10	7	.588	191	108	90	★128	64	5.12
1988—Indianapolis	Am. Assoc.	14	84	5	4	.556	80	38	32	61	28	3.43
1989—Indianapolis‡	Am. Assoc.	19	90⅔	6	3	.667	78	38	33	81	26	3.28
1989—Atlanta	National	19	32⅔	1	2	.333	31	24	22	26	17	6.06
1990—Atlanta§	National	6	5⅓	0	0	.000	6	4	4	3	3	6.75
1990—Cleveland	American	24	102⅓	6	6	.500	109	62	54	63	35	4.75
1990—Colorado Springs	P. Coast	7	43⅓	4	3	.571	55	29	25	33	13	5.19
National League Totals—3 Years		30	63	1	6	.143	76	48	45	49	31	6.43
American League Totals—1 Year		24	102⅓	6	6	.500	109	62	54	63	35	4.75
Major League Totals—3 Years		54	165⅓	7	12	.368	185	110	99	112	66	5.39

Signed as free agent by Montreal Expos' organizaton, June 18, 1983.
†On disabled list, May 17 to June 3, 1984.
‡Traded with Pitchers Nate Minchey and Outfielder Kevin Dean to Atlanta Braves for Pitcher Zane Smith, July 2, 1989.
§Claimed on waivers by Cleveland Indians, April 30, 1990.

FERNANDO VALENZUELA (ANGUAMEA)

Name pronounced Val-en-ZWAY-luh.

Born November 1, 1960, at Navajoa, Sonora, Mexico.
Height, 5.11. Weight, 202.
Throws and bats lefthanded.

Shares modern major league record for most shutout games won or tied, rookie year (8), 1981.
Shares National League record for fewest assists by pitcher, season, for leader in assists (47), 1986.
Pitched 6-0 no-hit victory against St. Louis Cardinals, June 29, 1990.
Major League saves: 1980 (1), 1988 (1). Total—2.
Led National League in wild pitches with 14 in 1987.
Led National League in complete games with 11 in 1981, 20 in 1986 and tied for lead with 12 in 1987.
Led National League in shutouts with 8 in 1981.
Tied for National League lead in games started by pitchers with 25 in 1981.
Led Mexican Center League in wild pitches with 13 in 1978.
Named Major League Player of the Year by THE SPORTING NEWS, 1981.
Named National League Pitcher of the Year by THE SPORTING NEWS, 1981.
Won National League Cy Young Memorial Award, 1981.
Named National League Rookie Pitcher of the Year by THE SPORTING NEWS, 1981.
Named National League Rookie of the Year by Baseball Writers' Association of America, 1981.
Named lefthanded pitcher on THE SPORTING NEWS National League All-Star Team, 1981 and 1986.
Named pitcher on THE SPORTING NEWS National League All-Star fielding team, 1986.
Named pitcher on THE SPORTING NEWS National League Silver Slugger team, 1981 and 1983.

Year Club	League	G.	IP.	W.	L.	Pct.	H.	R.	ER.	SO.	BB.	ERA.
1978—Guanajuato	Mex. Cent.	16	93	5	6	.455	88	46	23	★91	46	2.23
1979—Yucatan†	Mexican	26	181	10	12	.455	157	68	50	141	70	2.49
1979—Lodi	California	3	24	1	2	.333	21	10	3	18	3	1.13
1980—San Antonio	Texas	27	174	13	9	.591	156	70	60	★162	70	3.10
1980—Los Angeles	National	10	18	2	0	1.000	8	2	0	16	5	0.00
1981—Los Angeles	National	25	★192	13	7	.650	140	55	53	★180	61	2.48
1982—Los Angeles‡	National	37	285	19	13	.594	247	105	91	199	83	2.87
1983—Los Angeles	National	35	257	15	10	.600	245	★122	107	189	99	3.75

Year	Club	League	G.	IP.	W.	L.	Pct.	H.	R.	ER.	SO.	BB.	ERA.
1984—Los Angeles	National	34	261	12	17	.414	218	109	88	240	*106	3.03
1985—Los Angeles	National	35	272⅓	17	10	.630	211	92	74	208	101	2.45
1986—Los Angeles	National	34	269⅓	*21	11	.656	226	104	94	242	85	3.14
1987—Los Angeles	National	34	251	14	14	.500	*254	120	111	190	*124	3.98
1988—Los Angeles§	National	23	142⅓	5	8	.385	142	71	67	64	76	4.24
1989—Los Angeles xy	National	31	196⅔	10	13	.435	185	89	75	116	98	3.43
1990—Los Angeles z	National	33	204	13	13	.500	223	112	*104	115	77	4.59
Major League Totals—11 Years		331	2348⅔	141	116	.549	2099	981	864	1759	915	3.31

†Sold to Los Angeles Dodgers' organization, July 6, 1979.
‡Appeared in one game as an outfielder with no chances.
§On disabled list, July 31 to September 26, 1988.
xAppeared in one game as a first baseman with two putouts.
yGranted free agency, November 13, 1989; re-signed by Dodgers, December 15, 1989.
zGranted free agency, November 5, 1990; re-signed by Dodgers, December 19, 1990.

DIVISION SERIES RECORD

Year	Club	League	G.	IP.	W.	L.	Pct.	H.	R.	ER.	SO.	BB.	ERA.
1981—Los Angeles	National	2	17	1	0	1.000	10	2	2	10	3	1.06

CHAMPIONSHIP SERIES RECORD

Holds National League Championship Series records for most bases on balls allowed, series (10), 1985; most bases on balls, game (8), October 14, 1985.
Shares National League Championship Series record for most wild pitches, total series (3).

Year	Club	League	G.	IP.	W.	L.	Pct.	H.	R.	ER.	SO.	BB.	ERA.
1981—Los Angeles	National	2	14⅔	1	1	.500	10	4	4	10	5	2.45
1983—Los Angeles	National	1	8	1	0	1.000	7	1	1	5	4	1.13
1985—Los Angeles	National	2	14⅓	1	0	1.000	11	3	3	13	10	1.88
Championship Series Totals—3 Years		5	37	3	1	.750	28	8	8	28	19	1.95

WORLD SERIES RECORD

Year	Club	League	G.	IP.	W.	L.	Pct.	H.	R.	ER.	SO.	BB.	ERA.
1981—Los Angeles	National	1	9	1	0	1.000	9	4	4	6	7	4.00

ALL-STAR GAME RECORD

Shares All-Star Game record for most consecutive strikeouts, game (5), July 15, 1986.

Year	League	IP.	W.	L.	Pct.	H.	R.	ER.	SO.	BB.	ERA.
1981—National		1	0	0	.000	2	0	0	0	0	0.00
1982—National		⅔	0	0	.000	0	0	0	0	2	0.00
1984—National		2	0	0	.000	2	0	0	3	0	0.00
1985—National		1	0	0	.000	0	0	0	1	1	0.00
1986—National		3	0	0	.000	1	0	0	5	0	0.00
All-Star Game Totals—5 Years		7⅔	0	0	.000	5	0	0	9	3	0.00

Member of National League All-Star Team in 1983; did not play.

JULIO E. VALERA

Born October 13, 1968, at San Sebastian, Puerto Rico.
Height, 6.02. Weight, 185.
Throws and bats righthanded.

Year	Club	League	G.	IP.	W.	L.	Pct.	H.	R.	ER.	SO.	BB.	ERA.
1986—Kingsport	Ap'lachian	13	76⅓	3	●10	.231	91	58	44	64	29	5.19
1987—Columbia	S. Atlantic	22	125⅓	8	7	.533	114	53	39	97	31	2.80
1988—Columbia	S. Atlantic	30	191	15	11	.577	171	77	68	144	51	3.20
1989—St. Lucie	Florida St.	6	45	4	2	.667	34	5	5	45	6	1.00
1989—Jackson	Texas	19	137⅓	10	6	.625	123	47	38	107	36	*2.49
1989—Tidewater	Int'national	2	13	1	1	.500	8	3	3	10	5	2.08
1990—Tidewater	Int'national	24	158	10	10	.500	146	66	53	133	39	3.02
1990—New York	National	3	13	1	1	.500	20	11	10	4	7	6.92
Major League Totals—1 Year		3	13	1	1	.500	20	11	10	4	7	6.92

Signed as free agent by New York Mets' organization, February 6, 1986.

DAVID VALLE

Name pronounced Valley.

(Dave)

Born October 30, 1960, at Bayside, N. Y.
Height, 6.02. Weight, 200.
Throws and bats righthanded.
Brother of John Valle, minor league outfielder, 1972 through 1984.

Major League stolen bases: 1987 (2), 1990 (1). Total—3.
Led Northwest League catchers in double plays with 6 and tied for lead in passed balls with 23 in 1978.

Year	Club	League	Pos.	G.	AB.	R.	H.	2B.	3B.	HR.	RBI.	B.A.	PO.	A.	E.	F.A.
1978—Bellingham	N'west	C	57	167	12	34	2	0	2	21	.204	*338	65	10	.976
1979—Alexandria†	Carol.	C	58	169	17	36	5	0	6	25	.213	290	44	11	.968
1980—San Jose	Calif.	*C-P	119	430	81	126	14	0	12	70	.293	570	*102	17	.975
1981—Lynn‡	East.	C	93	318	38	82	16	0	11	54	.258	445	56	6	.988

Year Club	League	Pos.	G.	AB.	R.	H.	2B.	3B.	HR.	RBI.	B.A.	PO.	A.	E.	F.A.
1982—Salt Lake City.......	P. C.	C-1B	75	234	28	49	11	1	4	28	.209	347	49	11	.973
1983—Chattanooga§	South.	C-1B	53	176	20	42	11	0	3	22	.239	239	24	4	.985
1984—Salt Lake City x ...	P. C.	C	86	284	54	79	13	1	12	54	.278	433	34	6	.987
1984—Seattle..................	Amer.	C	13	27	4	8	1	0	1	4	.296	56	5	0	1.000
1985—Seattle y	Amer.	C	31	70	2	11	1	0	0	4	.157	117	7	3	.976
1985—Calgary	P. C.	C	42	131	17	45	8	0	6	26	.344	202	11	1	.995
1986—Calgary	P. C.	C	105	353	71	110	21	2	21	72	.312	404	61	6	.987
1986—Seattle..................	Amer.	C-1B	22	53	10	18	3	0	5	15	.340	90	3	2	.979
1987—Seattle z................	Amer.	C-1B-OF	95	324	40	83	16	3	12	53	.256	422	34	5	.989
1988—Seattle a	Amer.	C-1B	93	290	29	67	15	2	10	50	.231	490	47	6	.989
1989—Seattle b	Amer.	C	94	316	32	75	10	3	7	34	.237	496	52	4	.993
1989—Calgary	P. C.	C	2	6	0	0	0	0	0	0	.000	6	0	0	1.000
1990—Seattle c...............	Amer.	★C-1B	107	308	37	66	15	0	7	33	.214	633	44	2	★.997
Major League Totals—7 Years................			455	1388	154	328	61	8	42	193	.236	2304	192	22	.991

Selected by Seattle Mariners' organization in 2nd round of free-agent draft, June 6, 1978.

†On disabled list, July 26 to August 25, 1979.

‡On disabled list, June 24 to July 3, 1981.

§On disabled list, April 13 to June 20 and June 27 to July 7, 1983.

xOn disabled list, May 4 to May 17 and June 9 to June 25, 1984.

yOn disabled list, April 26 to July 19, 1985; included rehabilitation disability assignment to Calgary, June 26 to July 12, 1985.

zOn disabled list, April 17 to May 7, 1987.

aOn disabled list, July 23 to September 2, 1988.

bOn disabled list, May 30 to July 6, 1989; included rehabilitation disability assignment to Calgary, July 4 to July 6, 1989.

cOn disabled list, May 18 to June 17, 1990.

PITCHING RECORD

Year Club	League	G.	IP.	W.	L.	Pct.	H.	R.	ER.	SO.	BB.	ERA.
1980—San Jose.............................	California	1	1	0	0	.000	1	0	0	2	2	0.00

BRANDY G. VANN

Born December 9, 1966, at Oklahoma City, Okla.
Height, 6.00. Weight, 205.
Throws and bats righthanded.
Attended Butler County Community College, El Dorado, Kan.

Tied for Midwest League lead in shutouts with 3 in 1988.

Year Club	League	G.	IP.	W.	L.	Pct.	H.	R.	ER.	SO.	BB.	ERA.
1986—Salem..............................	Northwest	20	51	3	0	1.000	56	53	40	46	51	7.06
1987—Quad City.........................	Midwest	27	167⅓	7	15	.318	140	90	74	110	96	3.98
1988—Quad City.........................	Midwest	27	173⅔	10	11	.476	142	73	59	146	81	3.06
1989—Palm Springs...................	California	29	169	11	14	.400	185	★97	●79	95	58	4.21
1990—Palm Springs...................	California	28	26⅓	1	0	1.000	17	8	6	29	12	2.05
1990—Midland†..........................	Texas	32	52⅓	2	5	.286	59	26	24	43	27	4.13

Selected by California Angels' organization in 1st round (21st player selected) of free-agent draft, January 14, 1986.
†Drafted by Milwaukee Brewers, December 3, 1990.

TODD MATTHEW VAN POPPEL

Born December 9, 1971, at Hinsdale, Ill.
Height, 6.05. Weight, 210.
Throws and bats righthanded.
Received reported $500,000 bonus to sign with Oakland Athletics, 1990.

Year Club	League	G.	IP.	W.	L.	Pct.	H.	R.	ER.	SO.	BB.	ERA.
1990—Southern Oregon ....Northwest		5	24	1	1	.500	10	5	3	32	9	1.13
1990—Madison	Midwest	3	13⅔	2	1	.667	8	11	6	17	10	3.95

Selected by Oakland Athletics' organization in 1st round (14th player selected) of free-agent draft, June 4, 1990.

ANDREW JAMES VAN SLYKE
(Andy)

Born December 21, 1960, at Utica, N.Y.
Height, 6.02. Weight, 195.
Throws right and bats lefthanded.

Shares Major League record for fewest double plays by outfielder, season, for leader in double plays (4), 1985.
Major League stolen bases: 1983 (21), 1984 (28), 1985 (34), 1986 (21), 1987 (34), 1988 (30), 1989 (16), 1990 (14). Total—198.
Led National League in sacrifice flies with 13 in 1988.
Led National League outfielders in total chances with 422 in 1988.
Tied for National League lead in double plays by outfielders with 4 in 1985, 6 in 1987 and 5 in 1989.
Named National League Player of the Year by THE SPORTING NEWS, 1988.
Named outfielder on THE SPORTING NEWS National League All-Star Team, 1988.
Named outfielder on THE SPORTING NEWS National League All-Star fielding team, 1988 through 1990.
Named outfielder on THE SPORTING NEWS National League Silver Slugger team, 1988.
Received reported $50,000 bonus to sign with St. Louis Cardinals, 1979.

Year	Club	League	Pos.	G.	AB.	R.	H.	2B.	3B.	HR.	RBI.	B.A.	PO.	A.	E.	F.A.
1979—Johnson City†	Appal.							(Did not play)								
1980—Gastonia	S. Atl.		OF	126	426	62	115	15	4	8	59	.270	177	16	●16	.923
1981—St. Petersburg‡	Fla. St.		OF	94	282	42	62	11	3	1	25	.220	168	10	5	.973
1982—Arkansas	Texas		OF	123	416	83	116	13	*11	16	70	.279	266	17	7	.976
1983—Louisville	A. A.		3B-1B-OF	54	220	52	81	21	4	6	41	.368	201	78	16	.946
1983—St. Louis	Nat.		OF-3B-1B	101	309	51	81	15	5	8	38	.262	203	59	6	.978
1984—St. Louis	Nat.		OF-3B-1B	137	361	45	88	16	4	7	50	.244	357	82	8	.982
1985—St. Louis	Nat.		OF-1B	146	424	61	110	25	6	13	55	.259	237	13	1	.996
1986—St. Louis§	Nat.		OF-1B	137	418	48	113	23	7	13	61	.270	415	34	8	.982
1987—Pittsburgh	Nat.		OF-1B	157	564	93	165	36	11	21	82	.293	338	10	4	.989
1988—Pittsburgh	Nat.		OF	154	587	101	169	23	*15	25	100	.288	*406	12	4	.991
1989—Pittsburgh x	Nat.		OF-1B	130	476	64	113	18	9	9	53	.237	344	9	4	.989
1990—Pittsburgh	Nat.		OF	136	493	67	140	26	6	17	77	.284	326	6	8	.976
Major League Totals—8 Years				1098	3632	530	979	182	63	113	516	.270	2626	225	43	.985

Selected by St. Louis Cardinals' organization in 1st round (sixth player selected) of free-agent draft, June 5, 1979.
†On disabled list, June 8, 1979 through entire season.
‡On disabled list, April 10 to May 14, 1981.
§Traded with Catcher Mike LaValliere and Pitcher Mike Dunne to Pittsburgh Pirates for Catcher Tony Pena, April 1, 1987.
xOn disabled list, April 17 to May 12, 1989.

CHAMPIONSHIP SERIES RECORD

Year	Club	League	Pos.	G.	AB.	R.	H.	2B.	3B.	HR.	RBI.	B.A.	PO.	A.	E.	F.A.
1985—St. Louis	Nat.		OF-PR	5	11	1	1	0	0	0	1	.091	6	0	0	1.000
1990—Pittsburgh	Nat.		OF	6	24	3	5	1	1	0	3	.208	13	1	0	1.000
Championship Series Totals—2 Years				11	35	4	6	1	1	0	4	.171	19	1	0	1.000

WORLD SERIES RECORD

Year	Club	League	Pos.	G.	AB.	R.	H.	2B.	3B.	HR.	RBI.	B.A.	PO.	A.	E.	F.A.
1985—St. Louis	Nat.		O-PH-PR	6	11	0	1	0	0	0	0	.091	8	0	0	1.000

ALL-STAR GAME RECORD

Year	League	Pos.	AB.	R.	H.	2B.	3B.	HR.	RBI.	B.A.	PO.	A.	E.	F.A.
1988—National		OF	2	0	0	0	0	0	0	.000	2	0	0	1.000

GARY ANDREW VARSHO

Born June 20, 1961, at Marshfield, Wis.
Height, 5.11. Weight, 190.
Throws right and bats lefthanded.
Attended University of Wisconsin, Oshkosh, Wis.

Major League stolen bases: 1988: (5), 1989 (3), 1990 (2). Total—10.
Led American Association in caught stealing with 17 in 1987.
Led Eastern League in stolen bases with 45 in 1986 and tied for lead with 40 in 1985.
Led Texas League second basemen in total chances with 650 in 1984.
Led California League second basemen in double plays with 71 in 1983.

Year	Club	League	Pos.	G.	AB.	R.	H.	2B.	3B.	HR.	RBI.	B.A.	PO.	A.	E.	F.A.
1982—Quad Cities	Midw.		2B	76	271	52	68	9	4	3	40	.251	190	180	14	.964
1983—Salinas	Calif.		2B	131	490	69	129	16	*13	3	57	.263	284	339	●33	.950
1984—Midland	Texas		2B	128	429	65	112	15	6	8	50	.261	*286	335	*29	.955
1985—Pittsfield	East.		1B-OF	115	418	62	101	14	6	3	37	.242	670	51	6	.992
1986—Pittsfield†	East.		OF-1B-2B	107	399	75	106	18	5	13	44	.266	213	14	6	.974
1987—Iowa	A. A.		OF	132	504	87	152	23	9	9	48	.302	227	18	6	.976
1988—Iowa	A. A.		OF	66	234	46	65	16	5	4	26	.278	120	6	2	.984
1988—Chicago	Nat.		OF	46	73	6	20	3	0	0	5	.274	29	0	3	.906
1989—Chicago	Nat.		OF	61	87	10	16	4	2	0	6	.184	25	1	2	.929
1989—Iowa	A. A.		OF	31	112	13	26	3	1	2	13	.232	67	4	3	.959
1990—Iowa	A. A.		OF-1B-3B	63	229	35	69	9	0	7	33	.301	202	15	7	.969
1990—Chicago	Nat.		OF	46	48	10	12	4	0	0	1	.250	2	0	0	1.000
Major League Totals—3 Years				153	208	26	48	11	2	0	12	.231	56	1	5	.919

Selected by Chicago Cubs' organization in 5th round of free-agent draft, June 7, 1982.
†On disabled list, August 13, 1986 through remainder of season.

LUIS EDUARDO VASQUEZ

Born March 23, 1967, at Estrada Bolivar, Venezuela.
Height, 6.01. Weight, 180.
Throws and bats righthanded.

Led American Association in games started by pitchers with 29 in 1989.

Year	Club	League	G.	IP.	W.	L.	Pct.	H.	R.	ER.	SO.	BB.	ERA.
1985—Elmira	NYP	18	57⅓	2	4	.333	50	28	22	42	24	3.45
1986—Winter Haven	Florida St.	31	159⅓	15	3	●.833	145	65	60	92	58	3.39
1987—New Britain†	Eastern	10	61	3	2	.600	63	23	19	26	19	2.80
1988—New Britain	Eastern	15	112⅓	3	9	.250	87	46	31	97	28	2.48
1988—Pawtucket‡	Int'national	12	75⅓	5	4	.556	74	37	30	73	15	3.58
1989—Nashville	Am. Assoc.	29	162⅓	11	13	.458	170	91	83	115	84	4.60
1990—Nashville	Am. Assoc.	18	99	4	6	.400	85	46	40	54	59	3.64

Signed as free agent by Boston Red Sox' organization, January 24, 1985.

†On disabled list, July 1 to July 14 and July 17, 1987 through remainder of season.

‡Traded to Cincinnati Reds, January 12, 1989, completing deal in which Cincinnati traded First Baseman Nick Esasky and Pitcher Rob Murphy to Boston Red Sox for First Baseman Todd Benzinger, Pitcher Jeff Sellers and a player to be named later, December 13, 1988.

JAMES ERNEST VATCHER
(Jim)

Born May 27, 1966, at Santa Monica, Calif.
Height, 5.09, Weight, 165.
Throws and bats righthanded.
Attended West Los Angeles College, Culver City, Calif.,
and California State University, Northridge, Calif.

Led South Atlantic League in bases on balls received with 89 in 1988.
Tied for New York-Pennsylvania League lead in double plays by outfielders with 3 in 1987.

Year	Club	League	Pos.	G.	AB.	R.	H.	2B.	3B.	HR.	RBI.	B.A.	PO.	A.	E.	F.A.
1987—Utica	NYP	OF-SS	67	249	44	67	15	2	3	21	.269	116	12	3	.977
1988—Spartanburg	S. Atl.	OF	●137	496	★90	150	32	2	12	72	.302	224	13	4	.983
1989—Clearwater	Fla. St.	OF-2B-3B	92	349	51	105	30	5	4	46	.301	163	35	8	.961
1989—Reading	East.	OF	48	171	27	56	11	3	4	32	.327	76	5	1	.988
1990—Scranton/W.-B.	Int.	OF-3B	55	181	30	46	12	4	5	22	.254	88	24	2	.982
1990—Phila.†-Atlanta	Nat.	OF	57	73	7	19	2	1	1	7	.260	27	0	0	1.000
Major League Totals—1 Year			57	73	7	19	2	1	1	7	.260	27	0	0	1.000

Selected by Philadelphia Phillies' organization in 20th round of free-agent draft, June 2, 1987.

†Traded to Atlanta Braves, August 9, 1990, as partial completion of deal in which Atlanta traded Outfielder Dale Murphy and a player to be named later to Philadelphia Phillies for Pitcher Jeff Parrett and two players to be named later, August 3, 1990. Scranton/Wilkes-Barre (Philadelphia Phillies' organization) acquired Pitcher Tommy Greene on August 9, 1990 and Atlanta acquired Shortstop Victor Rosario on September 4, 1990 to complete deal.

GREGORY LAMONT VAUGHN
(Greg)

Born July 3, 1965, at Sacramento, Calif.
Height, 6.00. Weight, 195.
Throws and bats righthanded.
Attended Sacramento City College, Sacramento, Calif.,
and University of Miami, Coral Gables, Fla.

Major League stolen bases: 1989 (4), 1990 (7). Total—11.
Led American Association in slugging percentage with .548 in 1989.
Led Texas League in total bases with 279 in 1988.
Led Midwest League in total bases with 292 in 1987.
Named American Association Most Valuable Player, 1989.
Named Midwest League co-Most Valuable Player, 1987.

Year	Club	League	Pos.	G.	AB.	R.	H.	2B.	3B.	HR.	RBI.	B.A.	PO.	A.	E.	F.A.
1986—Helena	Pion.	OF	66	258	64	75	13	2	16	54	.291	99	5	3	.972
1987—Beloit	Midw.	OF	139	492	★120	150	31	6	★33	105	.305	247	11	10	.963
1988—El Paso	Texas	OF	131	505	★104	152	★39	2	★28	★105	.301	216	12	7	.970
1989—Denver	A. A.	OF	110	387	74	107	17	5	★26	★92	.276	140	4	3	.980
1989—Milwaukee	Amer.	OF	38	113	18	30	3	0	5	23	.265	32	1	2	.943
1990—Milwaukee†	Amer.	OF	120	382	51	84	26	2	17	61	.220	195	8	7	.967
Major League Totals—2 Years			158	495	69	114	29	2	22	84	.230	227	9	9	963

Selected by St. Louis Cardinals' organization in 5th round of free-agent draft, January 17, 1984.
Selected by Milwaukee Brewers' organization in secondary phase of free-agent draft, June 4, 1984.
Selected by Pittsburgh Pirates' organization in secondary phase of free-agent draft, January 9, 1985.
Selected by California Angels' organization in secondary phase of free-agent draft, June 3, 1985.
Selected by Milwaukee Brewers' organization in secondary phase of free-agent draft, June 2, 1986.

†On disabled list, May 26 to June 10, 1990.

MAURICE SAMUEL VAUGHN
(Mo)

Born December 15, 1967, at Norwalk, Conn.
Height, 6.01. Weight, 225.
Throws right and bats lefthanded.
Attended Seton Hall University, South Orange, N.J.

Year	Club	League	Pos.	G.	AB.	R.	H.	2B.	3B.	HR.	RBI.	B.A.	PO.	A.	E.	F.A.
1989—New Britain	East.	1B	73	245	28	68	15	0	8	38	.278	541	45	●10	.983
1990—Pawtucket	Int.	1B	108	386	62	114	26	1	22	72	.295	828	60	11	.988

Selected by Boston Red Sox' organization in 1st round (23rd player selected) of free-agent draft, June 9, 1989.

—DID YOU KNOW—

That after grounding into two triple plays, a major league record, against the Twins last July 17, the Red Sox tied an A.L. mark the next day by hitting into six double plays, also against Minnesota?

RANDY LEE VELARDE
Name pronounced Vel-ARE-dee.

Born November 24, 1962, at Midland, Tex.
Height, 6.00. Weight, 190.
Throws and bats righthanded.
Attended Lubbock Christian College, Lubbock, Tex.

Major League stolen bases: 1988 (1).
Led Midwest League shortstops in errors with 52 in 1986.

Year Club	League	Pos.	G.	AB.	R.	H.	2B.	3B.	HR.	RBI.	B.A.	PO.	A.	E.	F.A.
1985—Niagara Falls	NYP	O-S-2-3	67	218	28	48	7	3	1	16	.220	124	117	15	.941
1986—Appleton	Midw.	SS-3B-OF	124	417	55	105	31	4	11	50	.252	205	300	54	.903
1986—Buffalo†	A. A.	SS	9	20	2	4	1	0	0	2	.200	9	28	3	.925
1987—Albany	East.	SS-OF	71	263	40	83	20	2	7	32	.316	128	254	17	.957
1987—Columbus..............	Int.	SS	49	185	21	59	10	6	5	33	.319	100	164	16	.943
1987—New York.............	Amer.	SS	8	22	1	4	0	0	0	1	.182	8	20	2	.933
1988—Columbus..............	Int.	SS-2B-3B	78	293	39	79	23	4	5	37	.270	123	271	25	.940
1988—New York.............	Amer.	2B-SS-3B	48	115	18	20	6	0	5	12	.174	72	98	8	.955
1989—Columbus..............	Int.	SS-3B	103	387	59	103	26	3	11	53	.266	150	295	22	.953
1989—New York‡...........	Amer.	3B-SS	33	100	12	34	4	2	2	11	.340	26	61	4	.956
1990—New York.............	Amer.	3-S-O-2	95	229	21	48	6	2	5	19	.210	70	159	12	.950
Major League Totals—4 Years................			184	466	52	106	16	4	12	43	.227	176	338	26	.952

Selected by Chicago White Sox' organization in 19th round of free-agent draft, June 3, 1985.

†Traded with Pitcher Pete Filson to New York Yankees for Pitcher Scott Nielsen and Infielder Mike Soper, January 5, 1987.

‡On disabled list, August 9 to August 29, 1989.

WILLIAM McKINLEY VENABLE JR.
(Max)

Born June 6, 1957, at Phoenix, Ariz.
Height, 5.10. Weight, 185.
Throws right and bats lefthanded.

Major League stolen bases: 1979 (3), 1980 (8), 1981 (3), 1982 (9), 1983 (15), 1984 (1), 1985 (11), 1986 (7), 1990 (5). Total—62.
Led American Association in sacrifice hits with 11 in 1987.

Year Club	League	Pos.	G.	AB.	R.	H.	2B.	3B.	HR.	RBI.	B.A.	PO.	A.	E.	F.A.
1976—Bellingham†	N'west	OF	51	162	25	35	2	0	1	16	.216	58	4	8	.886
1977—Clinton..................	Midw.	OF-2B	125	425	72	115	19	4	9	63	.271	149	13	13	.926
1978—Lodi‡...................	Calif.	OF	•140	566	134	180	30	9	17	101	.318	220	8	8	.966
1979—San Francisco	Nat.	OF	55	85	12	14	1	1	0	3	.165	30	2	3	.914
1979—Shreveport	Texas	OF	18	69	11	16	1	2	0	3	.232	28	2	1	.968
1979—Phoenix................	P. C.	OF	38	150	27	46	5	4	0	11	.307	96	4	3	.971
1980—Phoenix................	P. C.	OF	78	312	52	89	10	10	5	40	.285	179	7	4	.979
1980—San Francisco	Nat.	OF	64	138	13	37	5	0	0	10	.268	61	0	0	1.000
1981—Phoenix§..............	P. C.	OF	104	428	81	122	24	10	8	48	.285	263	6	3	.989
1981—San Francisco	Nat.	OF	18	32	2	6	0	2	0	1	.188	12	0	0	1.000
1982—San Francisco x...	Nat.	OF	71	125	17	28	2	1	1	7	.224	66	6	1	.986
1982—Phoenix................	P. C.	OF	8	32	5	8	1	2	0	3	.250	16	0	0	1.000
1983—San Francisco y...	Nat.	OF	94	228	28	50	7	4	6	27	.219	141	5	1	.993
1984—Indianapolis..........	A. A.	OF	99	330	57	82	13	3	9	47	.248	183	4	4	.979
1984—Montreal...............	Nat.	OF	38	71	7	17	2	0	2	7	.239	33	0	0	1.000
1985—Indy. z-Den.	A. A.	OF	46	172	27	42	7	5	4	19	.244	93	2	1	.990
1985—Cincinnati	Nat.	OF	77	135	21	39	12	3	0	10	.289	60	3	0	1.000
1986—Cincinnati a	Nat.	OF	108	147	17	31	7	1	2	15	.211	63	0	2	.969
1987—Nashville...............	A. A.	OF	116	400	57	108	16	4	2	28	.270	212	5	5	.977
1987—Cincinnati bcd.......	Nat.	OF	7	7	2	1	0	0	0	2	.143	3	0	0	1.000
1988—Yucatan e.............	Mex.	OF	13	47	14	15	0	1	1	8	.319	31	1	0	1.000
1989—Edmonton.............	P. C.	OF	95	329	52	89	14	4	1	45	.271	189	9	2	.990
1989—California..............	Amer.	OF	20	53	7	19	4	0	0	4	.358	21	0	0	1.000
1990—California f...........	Amer.	OF	93	189	26	49	9	3	4	21	.259	112	3	3	.975
National League Totals—9 Years...........			532	968	119	223	36	12	11	82	.230	469	16	7	.986
American League Totals—2 Years.........			113	242	33	68	13	3	4	25	.281	133	3	3	.978
Major League Totals—11 Years.........			645	1210	152	291	49	15	15	107	.240	602	19	10	.984

Selected by Los Angeles Dodgers' organization in 3rd round of free-agent draft, June 8, 1976.

†On disabled list, June 26 to July 10, 1976.

‡Drafted by San Francisco Giants, December 4, 1978.

§On disabled list, April 23 to May 16, 1981.

xOn disabled list, April 21 to June 1, 1982; included rehabilitation disability assignment to Phoenix, May 22 to June 1, 1982.

yTraded to Montreal Expos' organization, March 31, 1984, completing deal in which Montreal traded First Baseman Al Oliver to San Francisco Giants for Pitcher Fred Breining and a player to be named later, February 27, 1984. (San Francisco traded Pitcher Andy McGaffigan to Montreal, March 31, 1984, as compensation for the injury that Breining arrived with. Breining remained with Montreal.)

zTraded to Cincinnati Reds' organization for Infielder Skeeter Barnes, April 26, 1985.

aReleased, March 29, 1987; re-signed by Reds' organization, April 9, 1987.

bGranted free agency, October 15, 1987; signed by Baltimore Orioles, February, 1988.

cReleased, March 1988; signed by Nashville (Cincinnati Reds' organization), July 11, 1988.

dLoaned to Yucatan of Mexican League, July, 1988; returned, September, 1988.

ROBIN MARK VENTURA

Born July 14, 1967, at Santa Maria, Calif.
Height, 6.01. Weight, 192.
Throws right and bats lefthanded.
Attended Oklahoma State University, Stillwater, Okla.

Major League stolen bases: 1990 (1).
Led Southern League in intentional bases on balls received with 12 in 1989.
Tied for Southern League lead in double plays by third basemen with 21 in 1989.
Member of 1988 U.S. Olympic baseball team.
Named College Player of the Year by THE SPORTING NEWS, 1987 and 1988.
Named third baseman on THE SPORTING NEWS College Baseball All-America Team, 1987 and 1988.

Year	Club	League	Pos.	G.	AB.	R.	H.	2B.	3B.	HR.	RBI.	B.A.	PO.	A.	E.	F.A.
1989—Birmingham		South.	★3-1-2	129	454	75	126	25	2	3	67	.278	108	249	27	★.930
1989—Chicago		Amer.	3B	16	45	5	8	3	0	0	7	.178	17	33	2	.962
1990—Chicago		Amer.	3B-1B	150	493	48	123	17	1	5	54	.249	116	268	25	.939
Major League Totals—2 Years				166	538	53	131	20	1	5	61	.243	133	301	27	.941

Selected by Chicago White Sox' organization in 1st round (10th player selected) of free-agent draft, June 1, 1988.

RANDOLPH RUHLAND VERES

Name pronounced VER-es.

(Randy)

Born November 25, 1965, at San Francisco, Calif.
Height, 6.03. Weight, 190.
Throws and bats righthanded.
Attended Sacramento City College, Sacramento, Calif.

Major League saves: 1990 (1).

Year	Club	League	G.	IP.	W.	L.	Pct.	H.	R.	ER.	SO.	BB.	ERA.
1985—Helena		Pioneer	13	77⅓	7	4	.636	66	43	33	67	36	3.84
1986—Beloit†		Midwest	23	113⅓	4	12	.250	132	78	49	87	52	3.89
1987—Beloit		Midwest	21	127	10	6	.625	132	63	44	98	52	3.12
1988—Stockton		California	20	110	8	4	.667	94	54	41	96	77	3.35
1988—El Paso		Texas	6	39⅓	3	2	.600	35	18	16	31	12	3.66
1989—El Paso		Texas	8	43⅓	2	3	.400	43	29	23	41	25	4.78
1989—Denver		Am. Assoc.	17	107	6	7	.462	108	57	47	80	38	3.95
1989—Milwaukee		American	3	8⅓	0	1	.000	9	5	4	8	4	4.32
1990—Denver		Am. Assoc.	16	50⅓	1	6	.143	60	36	29	36	27	5.19
1990—Milwaukee		American	26	41⅔	0	3	.000	38	17	17	16	16	3.67
Major League Totals—2 Years			29	50	0	4	.000	47	22	21	24	20	3.78

Selected by New York Mets' organization in 32nd round of free-agent draft, June 4, 1984.
Selected by Milwaukee Brewers' organization in secondary phase of free-agent draft, January 9, 1985.
†On disabled list, August 17, 1986 through remainder of season.

HECTOR VILLANUEVA (BALASQUIDE)

Born October 2, 1964, at San Juan, Puerto Rico.
Height, 6.01. Weight, 220.
Throws and bats righthanded.
Attended University of Alabama, Birmingham, Ala.

Major League stolen bases: 1990 (1).
Led Eastern League in bases on balls received with 71 in 1988.
Led Carolina League in sacrifice flies with 12 in 1986.

Year	Club	League	Pos.	G.	AB.	R.	H.	2B.	3B.	HR.	RBI.	B.A.	PO.	A.	E.	F.A.
1985—Geneva		NYP	C	1	0	0	0	0	0	0	0	.000	0	0	0	.000
1985—Peoria		Midw.	C	65	193	22	45	7	0	1	19	.233	322	43	12	.968
1986—Winston-Salem		Carol.	C-1B	125	412	58	131	20	2	13	100	.318	653	72	6	.992
1987—Pittsfield†		East.	C-1B	109	391	59	107	31	0	14	70	.274	489	58	4	.993
1988—Pittsfield		East.	1B-C-3B	127	436	50	137	24	3	10	75	.314	840	98	11	.988
1989—Iowa		A. A.	C-1B	120	444	46	112	25	1	12	57	.252	618	67	6	.991
1990—Iowa		A. A.	C-1B	52	177	20	47	7	1	8	34	.266	263	27	0	1.000
1990—Chicago		Nat.	C-1B	52	114	14	31	4	1	7	18	.272	170	10	2	.989
Major League Totals—1 Year				52	114	14	31	4	1	7	18	.272	170	10	2	.989

Signed as free agent by Chicago Cubs' organization, March 26, 1985.
†On disabled list, June 7 to June 22, 1987.

FRANK JOHN VIOLA JR.

Name pronounced Vy-OH-luh.

Born April 19, 1960, at Hempstead, N.Y.
Height, 6.04. Weight, 209.
Throws and bats lefthanded.
Attended St. John's University, Jamaica, N.Y.

Tied for National League lead in games started by pitchers with 35 in 1990.
Tied for American League lead in games started by pitchers with 37 in 1986.

Named American League Pitcher of the Year by THE SPORTING NEWS, 1988.
Won American League Cy Young Memorial Award, 1988.
Named lefthanded pitcher on THE SPORTING NEWS National League All-Star Team, 1990.
Named lefthanded pitcher on THE SPORTING NEWS American League All-Star Team, 1988.

Year Club	League	G.	IP.	W.	L.	Pct.	H.	R.	ER.	SO.	BB.	ERA.
1981—Orlando	Southern	17	97	5	4	.556	112	47	37	50	33	3.43
1982—Toledo	Int'national	8	58	2	3	.400	61	27	25	34	18	3.88
1982—Minnesota	American	22	126	4	10	.286	152	77	73	84	38	5.21
1983—Minnesota	American	35	210	7	15	.318	242	*141	*128	127	92	5.49
1984—Minnesota	American	35	257⅔	18	12	.600	225	101	92	149	73	3.21
1985—Minnesota	American	36	250⅔	18	14	.563	262	*136	114	135	68	4.09
1986—Minnesota	American	37	245⅔	16	13	.552	257	136	123	191	83	4.51
1987—Minnesota	American	36	251⅓	17	10	.630	230	91	81	197	66	2.90
1988—Minnesota	American	35	255⅓	*24	7	*.774	236	80	75	193	54	2.64
1989—Minnesota†	American	24	175⅔	8	12	.400	171	80	74	138	47	3.79
1989—New York	National	12	85⅓	5	5	.500	75	35	32	73	27	3.38
1990—New York	American	35	*249⅔	20	12	.625	227	83	74	182	60	2.67
American League Totals—8 Years		260	1772⅔	112	93	.546	1775	842	760	1214	521	3.86
National League Totals—2 Years		47	335	25	17	.595	302	118	106	255	87	2.85
Major League Totals—9 Years		307	2107⅔	137	110	.555	2077	960	866	1469	608	3.70

Selected by Kansas City Royals' organization in 16th round of free-agent draft, June 6, 1978.
Selected by Minnesota Twins' organization in 2nd round of free-agent draft, June 8, 1981.
†Traded to New York Mets for Pitchers Rick Aguilera and David West and three players to be named later, July 31, 1989; Portland (Minnesota Twins' organization) acquired Pitchers Kevin Tapani and Tim Drummond on August 1, 1989, and Minnesota acquired Pitcher Jack Savage to complete deal, October 16, 1989.

CHAMPIONSHIP SERIES RECORD

Year Club	League	G.	IP.	W.	L.	Pct.	H.	R.	ER.	SO.	BB.	ERA.
1987—Minnesota	American	2	12	1	0	1.000	14	8	7	9	5	5.25

WORLD SERIES RECORD

Year Club	League	G.	IP.	W.	L.	Pct.	H.	R.	ER.	SO.	BB.	ERA.
1987—Minnesota	American	3	19⅓	2	1	.667	17	8	8	16	3	3.72

ALL-STAR GAME RECORD

Year League	IP.	W.	L.	Pct.	H.	R.	ER.	SO.	BB.	ERA.
1988—American	2	1	0	1.000	0	0	0	1	0	0.00
1990—National	1	0	0	.000	1	0	0	0	0	0.00
All-Star Game Totals—2 Years	3	1	0	1.000	1	0	0	1	0	0.00

OSVALDO JOSE VIRGIL JR.
(Ozzie)

Born December 7, 1956, at Mayaguez, Puerto Rico.
Height, 6.01. Weight, 195.
Throws and bats righthanded.
Son of Ozzie Virgil, infielder-catcher with New York N.L., Detroit, Kansas City, Baltimore, Pittsburgh and San Francisco, 1956 through 1958, 1960 through 1962, 1965, 1966 and 1969; coach, San Francisco Giants, 1970 through 1972, 1974 and 1975; scout, San Francisco Giants, 1973; coach, Montreal Expos, 1976 through 1981; coach, San Diego Padres, 1982 through 1985; and coach with Seattle Mariners, 1986 through June 6, 1988.

Major League stolen bases: 1984 (1), 1986 (1), 1988 (2). Total—4.
Led Carolina League in total bases with 234 in 1978.
Named Carolina League Most Valuable Player, 1978.

Year Club	League	Pos.	G.	AB.	R.	H.	2B.	3B.	HR.	RBI.	B.A.	PO.	A.	E.	F.A.
1976—Auburn	NYP	C	39	113	10	16	1	2	1	10	.142	153	14	5	.971
1977—Spartanburg	W. Car.	C	107	365	53	103	21	1	14	54	.282	502	*68	18	.969
1978—Peninsula	Carol.	C	126	409	79	124	21	1	*29	*98	.303	581	45	8	.987
1979—Reading	East.	C	128	429	57	99	17	1	8	66	.231	532	64	12	.980
1980—Reading	East.	C-1B	135	456	92	123	15	2	28	*104	.270	592	62	16	.976
1980—Philadelphia	Nat.	C	1	5	1	1	1	0	0	0	.200	4	0	0	1.000
1981—Oklahoma City†	A. A.	C	83	275	41	63	11	2	11	44	.229	201	28	4	.983
1981—Philadelphia	Nat.	C	6	6	0	0	0	0	0	0	.000	2	0	0	1.000
1982—Philadelphia	Nat.	C	49	101	11	24	6	0	3	8	.238	173	14	7	.964
1983—Philadelphia	Nat.	C	55	140	11	30	7	0	6	23	.214	228	24	9	.966
1984—Philadelphia	Nat.	C	141	456	61	119	21	2	18	68	.261	722	58	6	.992
1985—Philadelphia‡	Nat.	C	131	426	47	105	16	3	19	55	.246	667	52	4	*.994
1986—Atlanta	Nat.	C	114	359	45	80	9	0	15	48	.223	682	93	13	.984
1987—Atlanta	Nat.	C	123	429	57	106	13	1	27	72	.247	654	74	8	.989
1988—Atlanta§	Nat.	C	107	320	23	82	10	0	9	31	.256	448	45	5	.990
1989—Syracuse	Int.	C	43	146	15	38	4	0	4	18	.260	155	10	0	1.000
1989—Toronto x	Amer.	C	9	11	2	2	1	0	1	2	.182	1	0	1	1.000
1990—Toronto	Amer.	C	3	5	0	0	0	0	0	0	.000	1	0	0	1.000
1990—Syracuse	Int.	C-1B	28	84	5	12	2	0	0	7	.143	147	14	2	.988
National League Totals—9 Years			727	2242	256	547	83	6	97	305	.244	3580	360	52	.987
American League Totals—2 Years			12	16	2	2	1	0	1	2	.125	2	0	0	1.000
Major League Totals—11 Years			739	2258	258	549	84	6	98	307	.243	3582	360	52	.987

Selected by Philadelphia Phillies' organization in 6th round of free-agent draft, June 8, 1976.

†On disabled list, April 14 to April 27 and June 2 to June 29, 1981.
‡Traded with Pitcher Pete Smith to Atlanta Braves for Pitcher Steve Bedrosian and Outfielder Milt Thompson, December 10, 1985.
§Granted free agency, November 4, 1988; signed by Syracuse (Toronto Blue Jays' organization), June 24, 1989.
xReleased, October 20, 1989; re-signed by Blue Jays' organization, February 2, 1990.

CHAMPIONSHIP SERIES RECORD

Year Club	League	Pos.	G.	AB.	R.	H.	2B.	3B.	HR.	RBI.	B.A.	PO.	A.	E.	F.A.
1983—Philadelphia	Nat.	PH	1	1	0	0	0	0	0	0	.000	0	0	0	.000

WORLD SERIES RECORD

Year Club	League	Pos.	G.	AB.	R.	H.	2B.	3B.	HR.	RBI.	B.A.	PO.	A.	E.	F.A.
1983—Philadelphia	Nat.	PH-C	3	2	0	1	0	0	0	1	.500	1	0	0	1.000

ALL-STAR GAME RECORD

Year League	Pos.	AB.	R.	H.	2B.	3B.	HR.	RBI.	B.A.	PO.	A.	E.	F.A.
1985—National	C	1	0	1	0	0	0	2	1.000	3	0	0	1.000
1987—National	C	2	1	1	0	0	0	0	.500	7	0	0	1.000
All-Star Game Totals—2 Years		3	1	2	0	0	0	2	.667	10	0	0	1.000

JOSE LUIS VIZCAINO (PIMENTAL)

Born March 26, 1968, at Palenque, Dominican Republic.
Height, 6.01. Weight, 150.
Throws right and bats left and righthanded.

Major League stolen bases: 1990 (1).
Led Pacific Coast League shortstops in total chances with 611 and double plays with 82 in 1989.
Led Gulf Coast League shortstops in double plays with 23 in 1987.

Year Club	League	Pos.	G.	AB.	R.	H.	2B.	3B.	HR.	RBI.	B.A.	PO.	A.	E.	F.A.
1987—Sarasota Dodgers	Gulf C.	SS-1B	49	150	26	38	5	1	0	12	.253	73	107	13	.933
1988—Bakersfield	Calif.	SS	122	433	77	126	11	4	0	38	.291	185	340	30	.946
1989—Albuquerque	P. C.	SS	129	434	60	123	10	4	1	44	.283	★191	★390	★30	.951
1989—Los Angeles	Nat.	SS	7	10	2	2	0	0	0	0	.200	6	9	2	.882
1990—Albuquerque	P. C.	2B-SS	81	276	46	77	10	2	2	38	.279	141	229	14	.964
1990—Los Angeles†	Nat.	SS-2B	37	51	3	14	1	1	0	2	.275	23	27	2	.962
Major League Totals—2 Years			44	61	5	16	1	1	0	2	.262	29	36	4	.942

Signed as free agent by Los Angeles Dodgers' organization, February 18, 1986.
†Traded to Chicago Cubs for Infielder Greg Smith, December 14, 1990.

OMAR ENRIQUE VIZQUEL

Name pronounced Vis-KEL.

Born April 24, 1967, at Caracas, Venezuela.
Height, 5.09. Weight, 165.
Throws right and bats left and righthanded.

Major League stolen bases: 1989 (1), 1990 (4). Total—5.
Led Midwest League shortstops in fielding with .969 in 1986.

Year Club	League	Pos.	G.	AB.	R.	H.	2B.	3B.	HR.	RBI.	B.A.	PO.	A.	E.	F.A.
1984—Butte†	Pion.	SS-2B	15	45	7	14	2	0	0	4	.311	13	29	5	.894
1985—Bellingham†	N'west	SS-2B	50	187	24	42	9	0	5	17	.225	85	175	19	.932
1986—Wausau†	Midw.	SS-2B	105	352	60	75	13	2	4	28	.213	153	328	16	.968
1987—Salinas†	Calif.	SS-2B	114	407	61	107	12	8	0	38	.263	81	295	25	.938
1988—Vermont†	East.	SS	103	374	54	95	18	2	2	35	.254	173	268	19	★.959
1988—Calgary	P. C.	SS	33	107	10	24	2	3	1	12	.224	43	92	6	.957
1989—Calgary	P. C.	SS	7	28	3	6	2	0	0	3	.214	15	14	0	1.000
1989—Seattle	Amer.	SS	143	387	45	85	7	3	1	20	.220	208	388	18	.971
1990—Calgary‡	P. C.	SS	48	150	18	35	6	2	0	8	.233	70	142	6	.972
1990—San Bernardino	Calif.	SS	6	28	5	7	0	0	0	3	.250	11	21	3	.914
1990—Seattle	Amer.	SS	81	255	19	63	3	2	2	18	.247	103	239	7	.980
Major League Totals—2 Years			224	642	64	148	10	5	3	38	.231	311	627	25	.974

Signed as free agent by Seattle Mariners' organization, April 1, 1984.
†Batted righthanded only.
‡On Seattle disabled list, April 7 to May 13, 1990; included rehabilitation disability assignment to Calgary, May 3 to May 7, 1990; and San Bernardino, May 8 to May 12, 1990.

EDWARD JOHN VOSBERG

(Ed)

Born September 28, 1961, at Tucson, Ariz.
Height, 6.01. Weight, 190.
Throws and bats lefthanded.
Attended University of Arizona, Tucson, Ariz.

Led Pacific Coast League in balks with 11 in 1987.
Tied for Texas League lead in games started by pitchers with 27 in both 1984 and 1985.

Year Club	League	G.	IP.	W.	L.	Pct.	H.	R.	ER.	SO.	BB.	ERA.
1983—Reno	California	15	97⅔	6	6	.500	111	61	42	70	39	3.87
1983—Beaumont	Texas	1	7	1	0	1.000	2	0	0	1	2	0.00

Year Club	League	G.	IP.	W.	L.	Pct.	H.	R.	ER.	SO.	BB.	ERA.
1984—Beaumont	Texas	27	183⅔	13	●11	.542	196	87	70	100	74	3.43
1985—Beaumont	Texas	27	175	9	11	.450	178	92	76	124	69	3.91
1986—Las Vegas	P. Coast	25	129⅔	7	8	.467	136	80	68	93	64	4.72
1986—San Diego	National	5	13⅔	0	1	.000	17	11	10	8	9	6.59
1987—Las Vegas	P. Coast	34	167⅔	9	8	.529	154	88	73	98	97	3.92
1988—Las Vegas†	P. Coast	45	128	11	7	.611	137	67	59	75	56	4.15
1989—Tucson‡-Albuquerque§	P. Coast	35	107⅔	6	8	.429	139	78	72	86	54	6.02
1990—Phoenix	P. Coast	24	34	1	3	.250	36	14	10	28	16	2.65
1990—San Francisco x	National	18	24⅓	1	1	.500	21	16	15	12	12	5.55
Major League Totals—2 Years		23	38	1	2	.333	38	27	25	20	21	5.92

Selected by St. Louis Cardinals' organization in 3rd round of free-agent draft, June 5, 1979.
Selected by Toronto Blue Jays' organization in 11th round of free-agent draft, June 7, 1982.
Selected by San Diego Padres' organization in 3rd round of free-agent draft, June 6, 1983.
†Traded to Houston Astros' organization for Catcher Dan Walters, December 13, 1988.
‡Traded to Los Angeles Dodgers' organization, August 1, 1989, completing deal in which Los Angeles' organization traded Outfielder Javier Ortiz to Houston Astros' organization for a player to be named later, July 22, 1989.
§Granted free agency, October 15, 1989; signed by Phoenix (San Francisco Giants' organization), March 13, 1990.
xGranted free agency, October 15, 1990; signed by California Angels, December 4, 1990.

HECTOR RAUL WAGNER

Born November 26, 1968 at Los Mamelles, Santo Domingo, D.R.
Height, 6.03. Weight, 185.
Throws and bats righthanded.

Year Club	League	G.	IP.	W.	L.	Pct.	H.	R.	ER.	SO.	BB.	ERA.
1987—Sarasota Royals	Gulf Coast	13	53	1	3	.250	63	26	18	28	12	3.06
1988—Eugene	Northwest	15	85⅔	4	●9	.308	76	46	35	67	28	3.68
1989—Appleton	Midwest	24	130⅓	6	11	.353	149	79	66	71	29	4.56
1990—Memphis	Southern	40	133⅓	12	4	.750	114	37	30	63	41	2.03
1990—Kansas City	American	5	23⅓	0	2	.000	32	24	21	14	11	8.10
Major League Totals—1 Year		5	23⅓	0	2	.000	32	24	21	14	11	8.10

Signed as free agent by Kansas City Royals' organization, May 13, 1986.

JAMES WALEWANDER

Name pronounced WHALE-wonn-der.

(Jim)

Born May 2, 1961, at Chicago, Ill.
Height, 5.10. Weight, 155.
Throws right and bats left and righthanded.
Attended Iowa State University, Ames, Iowa.

Major League stolen bases: 1987 (2), 1988 (11), 1990 (1). Total—14.
Led International League in bases on balls received with 90 and being hit by pitch with 11 in 1990.
Led Appalachian League in stolen bases with 35 in 1983.
Led Florida State League second basemen in total chances with 698 in 1985.
Led Florida State League second basemen in putouts with 329 in 1984.
Led Appalachian League second basemen in assists with 188, total chances with 325 and double plays with 33 in 1983.

Year Club	League	Pos.	G.	AB.	R.	H.	2B.	3B.	HR.	RBI.	B.A.	PO.	A.	E.	F.A.
1983—Bristol	Appal.	2B-SS	●73	★285	56	91	14	2	4	28	.319	140	222	16	.958
1984—Lakeland	Fla. St.	2B-SS-3B	137	502	70	136	16	2	0	36	.271	342	341	23	.967
1985—Lakeland	Fla. St.	2B	129	499	80	141	13	7	0	36	.283	267	★417	14	.980
1985—Birmingham	South.	2B	14	45	3	13	0	1	0	2	.289	22	33	1	.982
1986—Glens Falls	East.	2B-3B-SS	124	440	59	107	10	6	1	31	.243	207	291	18	.965
1987—Toledo	Int.	2B	59	210	27	57	9	1	0	12	.271	129	139	12	.957
1987—Detroit	Amer.	2B-3B-SS	53	54	24	13	3	1	1	4	.241	26	58	1	.988
1988—Detroit	Amer.	2B-SS-3B	88	175	23	37	5	0	0	6	.211	125	154	6	.979
1988—Toledo	Int.	2B	4	11	4	5	2	0	0	2	.455	12	10	1	.957
1989—Toledo†	Int.	2B-SS-3B	133	484	53	109	15	3	7	38	.225	182	282	24	.951
1990—Columbus	Int.	2-3-S-1	131	368	80	92	14	5	1	31	.250	216	282	22	.958
1990—New York‡	Amer.	2B-3B-SS	9	5	1	1	1	0	0	1	.200	4	5	0	1.000
Major League Totals—3 Years			150	234	48	51	9	1	1	11	.218	155	217	7	.982

Selected by Detroit Tigers' organization in 9th round of free-agent draft, June 6, 1983.
†Granted free agency, October 15, 1989; signed by Columbus (New York Yankees' organization), December 27, 1989.
‡Granted free agency, October 15, 1990.

ROBERT VERNON WALK

(Bob)

Born November 26, 1956, at Van Nuys, Calif.
Height, 6.04. Weight, 217.
Throws and bats righthanded.
Attended College of the Canyons, Valencia, Calif.

Major League saves: 1986 (2), 1990 (1). Total—3.
Led National League in wild pitches with 13 in 1988.
Led Pacific Coast League in complete games with 12 in 1985.

Led International League in complete games with 11 and tied for lead in games started by pitchers with 28 and home runs allowed with 22 in 1983.

Led Carolina League in hit batsmen with 13 in 1978.

Year Club	League	G.	IP.	W.	L.	Pct.	H.	R.	ER.	SO.	BB.	ERA.
1977—Spartanburg	W. Carol.	15	99	6	9	.400	90	55	40	66	46	3.64
1977—Peninsula	Carolina	8	36	0	2	.000	44	31	17	23	20	4.25
1978—Peninsula	Carolina	26	187	13	8	.619	147	58	44	150	64	2.12
1979—Reading	Eastern	24	185	12	7	.632	156	62	46	*135	77	*2.24
1980—Oklahoma City	Am. Assoc.	8	49	5	1	.833	39	21	16	36	17	2.94
1980—Philadelphia†	National	27	152	11	7	.611	163	82	77	94	71	4.56
1981—Atlanta‡	National	12	43	1	4	.200	41	25	22	16	23	4.60
1981—Richmond	Int'national	4	22	2	1	.667	18	7	6	13	11	2.45
1982—Atlanta	National	32	164⅓	11	9	.550	179	101	89	84	59	4.87
1983—Richmond	Int'national	28	*185	11	12	.478	179	*119	*107	123	102	5.21
1983—Atlanta§	National	1	3⅔	0	0	.000	7	3	3	4	2	7.36
1984—Hawaii	P. Coast	18	127⅓	9	5	.643	100	39	32	85	42	*2.26
1984—Pittsburgh x	National	2	10⅓	1	1	.500	8	5	3	10	4	2.61
1985—Hawaii	P. Coast	24	173	*16	5	.762	143	57	51	124	61	*2.65
1985—Pittsburgh	National	9	58⅔	2	3	.400	60	27	24	40	18	3.68
1986—Pittsburgh	National	44	141⅔	7	8	.467	129	66	59	78	64	3.75
1987—Pittsburgh	National	39	117	8	2	.800	107	52	43	78	51	3.31
1988—Pittsburgh y	National	32	212⅔	12	10	.545	183	75	64	81	65	2.71
1989—Pittsburgh z	National	33	196	13	10	.565	208	106	96	83	65	4.41
1990—Pittsburgh a	National	26	129⅔	7	5	.583	136	59	54	73	36	3.75
Major League Totals—10 Years		257	1229	73	59	.553	1221	601	534	641	458	3.91

Selected by California Angels' organization in 5th round of free-agent draft, January 9, 1975.
Selected by Philadelphia Phillies' organization in 5th round of free-agent draft, January 7, 1976.
Selected by Philadelphia Phillies' organization in secondary phase of free-agent draft, June 8, 1976.
†Traded to Atlanta Braves for Outfielder Gary Matthews, March 25, 1981.
‡On disabled list, May 26 to August 9, 1981.
§Released, March 26, 1984; signed by Pittsburgh Pirates' organization, April 3, 1984.
xOn disabled list, July 23, 1984 through remainder of season.
yGranted free agency, November 4, 1988; re-signed by Pirates, November 27, 1988.
zOn disabled list, June 9 to June 24, 1989.
aOn disabled list, June 20 to July 14 and August 6 to August 25, 1990.

CHAMPIONSHIP SERIES RECORD

Year Club	League	G.	IP.	W.	L.	Pct.	H.	R.	ER.	SO.	BB.	ERA.
1982—Atlanta	National	1	1	0	0	.000	2	1	1	1	1	9.00
1990—Pittsburgh	National	2	13	1	1	.500	11	7	7	8	2	4.85
Championship Series Totals—2 Years		3	14	1	1	.500	13	8	8	9	3	5.14

WORLD SERIES RECORD

Year Club	League	G.	IP.	W.	L.	Pct.	H.	R.	ER.	SO.	BB.	ERA.
1980—Philadelphia	National	1	7	1	0	1.000	8	6	6	3	3	7.71

ALL-STAR GAME RECORD

Year League	IP.	W.	L.	Pct.	H.	R.	ER.	SO.	BB.	ERA.
1988—National	⅓	0	0	.000	0	0	0	0	0	0.00

GREGORY LEE WALKER
(Greg)

Born October 6, 1959, at Douglas, Ga.
Height, 6.03. Weight, 210.
Throws right and bats lefthanded.

Major League stolen bases: 1983 (2), 1984 (8), 1985 (5), 1986 (1), 1987 (2), 1990 (1). Total—19.

Led Midwest League first basemen in double plays with 108 in 1980.

Year Club	League	Pos.	G.	AB.	R.	H.	2B.	3B.	HR.	RBI.	B.A.	PO.	A.	E.	F.A.
1977—Auburn†	NYP	1B	33	98	12	25	1	2	2	8	.255	5	0	0	1.000
1978—Spartanburg	W. Car.	1B-3B-C	100	341	51	71	16	2	11	47	.208	538	50	13	.978
1979—Peninsula‡	Carol.	1B	122	446	59	125	*27	4	10	61	.280	973	53	19	.982
1980—Appleton	Midw.	1B	135	464	88	130	20	3	21	*98	.280	*1298	*88	10	*.993
1981—Glens Falls	East.	1B	135	508	*117	*163	*33	2	22	86	.321	*1215	77	11	.992
1982—Edmonton§	P. C.	1B	35	117	18	41	8	0	3	12	.350	94	11	0	1.000
1982—Chicago	Amer.	DH	11	17	3	7	2	1	2	7	.412	0	0	0	.000
1983—Chicago	Amer.	1B	118	307	32	83	16	3	10	55	.270	426	19	7	.985
1984—Chicago	Amer.	1B	136	442	62	130	29	2	24	75	.294	791	51	4	.995
1985—Chicago	Amer.	1B	*163	601	77	155	38	4	24	92	.258	1217	97	8	.994
1986—Chicago x	Amer.	1B	78	282	37	78	10	6	13	51	.277	670	57	5	.993
1987—Chicago	Amer.	1B	157	566	85	145	33	2	27	94	.256	*1402	80	9	.994
1988—Chicago y	Amer.	1B	99	377	45	93	22	1	8	42	.247	935	41	7	.993
1989—Chicago z	Amer.	1B	77	233	25	49	14	0	5	26	.210	373	17	5	.987
1990—Chi.a-Balt.	Amer.	1B	16	39	2	6	0	0	0	2	.154	14	1	0	1.000
1990—Rochester b	Int.	1B	22	66	14	20	6	0	2	11	.303	4	1	1	.833
Major League Totals—9 Years			765	2864	368	746	164	19	113	444	.260	5828	363	45	.993

Selected by Philadelphia Phillies' organization in 20th round of free-agent draft, June 7, 1977.
†On disabled list, June 21, 1977 through remainder of season.
‡Drafted by Iowa (Chicago White Sox' organization), December 4, 1979.

§On disabled list, April 23 to July 27, 1982.
xOn disabled list, April 15 to May 14 and August 3, 1986 through remainder of season.
yOn disabled list, July 30, 1988 through remainder of season.
zOn disabled list, April 27 to May 13, 1989.
aReleased, April 30, 1990; signed by Rochester (Baltimore Orioles' organization), May 4, 1990.
bReleased, July 3, 1990.

CHAMPIONSHIP SERIES RECORD

Year Club	League	Pos.	G.	AB.	R.	H.	2B.	3B.	HR.	RBI.	B.A.	PO.	A.	E.	F.A.
1983—Chicago	Amer.	PH-1B	2	3	0	1	0	0	0	0	.333	7	1	0	1.000

LARRY KENNETH ROBERT WALKER

Born December 1, 1966, at Maple Ridge, British Columbia, Canada.
Height, 6.02. Weight, 205.
Throws right and bats lefthanded.

Major League stolen bases: 1989 (1), 1990 (21). Total—22.
Tied for Southern League lead in game-winning RBIs with 19 in 1987.

Year Club	League	Pos.	G.	AB.	R.	H.	2B.	3B.	HR.	RBI.	B.A.	PO.	A.	E.	F.A.
1985—Utica	NYP	1B-3B	62	215	24	48	8	2	2	26	.223	354	62	8	.981
1986—Burlington	Midw.	OF-3B	95	332	67	96	12	6	29	74	.289	106	51	10	.940
1986—W. Palm Beach	Fla. St.	OF	38	113	20	32	7	5	4	16	.283	44	5	0	1.000
1987—Jacksonville	South.	OF	128	474	91	136	25	7	26	83	.287	263	9	9	.968
1988—Montreal†	South.					(Did not play)									
1989—Indianapolis	A.A.	OF	114	385	68	104	18	2	12	59	.270	241	∗18	∗11	.959
1989—Montreal	Nat.	OF	20	47	4	8	0	0	0	4	.170	19	2	0	1.000
1990—Montreal	Nat.	OF	133	419	59	101	18	3	19	51	.241	249	12	4	.985
Major League Totals—2 Years			153	466	63	109	18	3	19	55	.234	268	14	4	.986

Signed as free agent by Montreal Expos' organization, November 14, 1984.
†On disabled list, April 4, 1988 through entire season.

MICHAEL AARON WALKER
(Mike)

Born June 23, 1965, at Houston, Tex.
Height, 6.03. Weight, 205.
Throws and bats righthanded.
Attended University of Houston, Houston, Tex.

Year Club	League	G.	IP.	W.	L.	Pct.	H.	R.	ER.	SO.	BB.	ERA.
1986—Watertown	NYP	16	103⅓	4	●10	.286	∗116	∗71	∗52	81	46	4.53
1987—Harrisburg	Eastern	4	15	0	2	.000	20	17	15	9	9	9.00
1987—Salem	Carolina	21	135⅔	12	5	.706	140	67	56	91	57	3.71
1988—Salem	Carolina	5	37	2	2	.500	42	17	13	29	9	3.16
1988—Harrisburg	Eastern	13	74⅓	2	7	.222	76	40	29	47	15	3.51
1988—Buffalo	Am. Assoc.	8	55	2	3	.400	52	18	17	26	8	2.78
1989—Buffalo†	Am. Assoc.	3	17	0	1	.000	12	13	10	5	13	5.29
1989—Calgary	P. Coast	18	88	6	7	.462	119	74	63	46	37	6.44
1990—Calgary	P. Coast	25	144⅔	5	11	.313	176	92	86	64	45	5.35

Selected by Pittsburgh Pirates' organization in 2nd round of free-agent draft, June 2, 1986.
†Traded with Pitcher Mike Dunne and Outfielder Mark Merchant to Seattle Mariners for Shortstop Rey Quinones and Pitcher Bill Wilkinson, April 21, 1989.

MICHAEL CHARLES WALKER
(Mike)

Born October 4, 1966, at Brooksville, Fla.
Height, 6.01. Weight, 195.
Throws and bats righthanded.
Attended Seminole Community College, Sanford, Fla.

Led Pacific Coast League pitchers in home runs allowed with 21, hit batsmen with 14 and tied for lead in games started with 28 in 1989.
Led Eastern League pitchers in wild pitches with 17 and tied for lead in games started with 27 in 1988.
Led Midwest League in complete games with 8 in 1987.

Year Club	League	G.	IP.	W.	L.	Pct.	H.	R.	ER.	SO.	BB.	ERA.
1986—Burlington	Ap'lachian	14	70⅓	4	6	.400	75	∗65	●46	42	45	5.89
1987—Waterloo	Midwest	23	145⅓	11	7	.611	133	74	58	144	68	3.59
1987—Kingston	Carolina	3	20⅔	3	0	1.000	17	7	6	19	14	2.61
1988—Williamsport	Eastern	28	∗164⅓	∗15	7	.682	162	82	68	∗144	74	3.72
1988—Cleveland	American	3	8⅔	0	1	.000	8	7	7	10	7	7.27
1989—Colorado Springs	P. Coast	28	168	6	∗15	.286	193	∗124	∗108	97	∗93	5.79
1990—Colorado Springs	P. Coast	18	79	2	7	.222	96	62	49	50	36	5.58
1990—Canton-Akron	Eastern	1	7	1	0	1.000	4	0	0	3	4	0.00
1990—Cleveland	American	18	75⅔	2	6	.250	82	49	41	34	42	4.88
Major League Totals—2 Years		21	84⅓	2	7	.222	90	56	48	41	52	5.12

Selected by Montreal Expos' organization in 14th round of free-agent draft, June 4, 1984.
Selected by Montreal Expos' organization in secondary phase of free-agent draft, January 9, 1985.
Selected by Cleveland Indians' organization in 2nd round of free-agent draft, January 14, 1986.

TIMOTHY CHARLES WALLACH
(Tim)

Born September 14, 1957, at Huntington Park, Calif.
Height, 6.03. Weight, 200.
Throws and bats righthanded.
Attended Saddleback Junior College, Mission Viejo, Calif., and
California State University, Fullerton, Calif.

Shares major league record by hitting home run in first major league at-bat, September 6, 1980.
Major League stolen bases: 1982 (6), 1984 (3), 1985 (9), 1986 (8), 1987 (9), 1988 (2), 1989 (3), 1990 (6). Total—46.
Hit three home runs in a game, May 4, 1987.
Led National League in grounding into double plays with 21 in 1989.
Led National League in being hit by pitch with 10 in 1986.
Tied for National League lead in game-winning RBIs with 16 in 1987.
Led National League third basemen in putouts with 123 in 1988.
Led National League third basemen in total chances with 515 in 1984 and 549 in 1985.
Led National League third basemen in double plays with 29 in 1984, 34 in 1985 and tied for lead with 31 in 1988.
Led American Association in total bases with 295, game-winning RBIs with 16 and tied for lead in sacrifice flies with 9 in 1980.
Named third baseman on THE SPORTING NEWS National League All-Star Team, 1985 and 1987.
Named third baseman on THE SPORTING NEWS National League All-Star fielding team, 1985, 1988 and 1990.
Named third baseman on THE SPORTING NEWS National League Silver Slugger team, 1985 and 1987.
Named College Player of the Year by THE SPORTING NEWS College Baseball All-America Team, 1979.

Year	Club	League	Pos.	G.	AB.	R.	H.	2B.	3B.	HR.	RBI.	B.A.	PO.	A.	E.	F.A.
1979—Memphis	South.	1B-3B	75	257	50	84	16	4	18	51	.327	290	35	4	.988
1980—Denver	A. A.	3B-OF-1B	134	512	103	144	29	7	36	124	.281	222	147	21	.946
1980—Montreal	Nat.	OF-1B	5	11	1	2	0	0	1	2	.182	12	0	0	1.000
1981—Montreal	Nat.	OF-1B-3B	71	212	19	50	9	1	4	13	.236	207	31	1	.996
1982—Montreal	Nat.	★3-O-1	158	596	89	160	31	3	28	97	.268	★132	287	23	.948
1983—Montreal	Nat.	3B	156	581	54	156	33	3	19	70	.269	★151	262	19	.956
1984—Montreal	Nat.	★3B-SS	160	582	55	143	25	4	18	72	.246	★162	★332	21	.959
1985—Montreal	Nat.	3B	155	569	70	148	36	3	22	81	.260	★148	★383	18	.967
1986—Montreal	Nat.	3B	134	480	50	112	22	1	18	71	.233	94	270	16	.958
1987—Montreal	Nat.	★3B-P	153	593	89	177	★42	4	26	123	.298	★128	292	21	.952
1988—Montreal	Nat.	3B-2B	159	592	52	152	32	5	12	69	.257	124	329	18	.962
1989—Montreal	Nat.	3B-P	154	573	76	159	●42	0	13	77	.277	113	302	18	.958
1990—Montreal	Nat.	3B	161	626	69	185	37	5	21	98	.296	128	309	21	954
Major League Totals—11 Years			1466	5415	624	1444	309	29	182	773	.267	1399	2800	176	.960

Selected by California Angels' organization in 8th round of free-agent draft, June 6, 1978.
Selected by Montreal Expos' organization in 1st round (10th player selected) of free-agent draft, June 5, 1979.

DIVISION SERIES RECORD

Year	Club	League	Pos.	G.	AB.	R.	H.	2B.	3B.	HR.	RBI.	B.A.	PO.	A.	E.	F.A.
1981—Montreal	Nat.	OF	4	4	1	1	1	0	0	0	.250	4	0	0	1.000

CHAMPIONSHIP SERIES RECORD

Year	Club	League	Pos.	G.	AB.	R.	H.	2B.	3B.	HR.	RBI.	B.A.	PO.	A.	E.	F.A.
1981—Montreal	Nat.	PH	1	1	0	0	0	0	0	0	.000	0	0	0	.000

ALL-STAR GAME RECORD

Year	League	Pos.	AB.	R.	H.	2B.	3B.	HR.	RBI.	B.A.	PO.	A.	E.	F.A.
1984—National		3B	1	0	0	0	0	0	0	.000	0	0	0	.000
1985—National		3B	2	1	1	1	0	0	0	.500	1	1	0	1.000
1987—National		3B	3	0	0	0	0	0	0	.000	0	2	0	1.000
1989—National		3B	1	0	0	0	0	0	0	.000	0	0	0	.000
1990—National		3B	2	0	0	0	0	0	0	.000	0	0	0	.000
All-Star Game Totals—5 Years			9	1	1	1	0	0	0	.111	1	3	0	1.000

PITCHING RECORD

Year	Club	League	G.	IP.	W.	L.	Pct.	H.	R.	ER.	SO.	BB.	ERA.
1987—Montreal	National	1	1	0	0	.000	1	0	0	0	0	0.00
1989—Montreal	National	1	1	0	0	.000	2	1	1	0	0	9.00
Major League Totals—2 Years		2	2	0	0	.000	3	1	1	0	0	4.50

DENNIS MARTIN WALLING
(Denny)

Born April 17, 1954, at Neptune, N.J.
Height, 6.01. Weight, 185.
Throws right and bats lefthanded.
Attended Brookdale Community College, Lincroft, N.J., and
Clemson University, Clemson, S.C.
Brother of Gregory Walling, minor league outfielder, 1967.

Major League stolen bases: 1978 (9), 1979 (3), 1980 (4), 1981 (2), 1982 (4), 1983 (2), 1984 (7), 1985 (5), 1986 (1), 1987 (5), 1988 (2). Total—44.
Named outfielder on THE SPORTING NEWS College Baseball All-America Team, 1975.

Year	Club	League	Pos.	G.	AB.	R.	H.	2B.	3B.	HR.	RBI.	B.A.	PO.	A.	E.	F.A.
1975—Oakland	Amer.	OF	6	8	0	1	1	0	0	2	.125	3	0	0	1.000
1976—Chattanooga	South.	OF	115	369	48	95	15	5	9	42	.257	241	8	2	★.992

Year—Club	League	Pos.	G.	AB.	R.	H.	2B.	3B.	HR.	RBI.	B.A.	PO.	A.	E.	F.A.
1976—Oakland	Amer.	OF	3	11	1	3	0	0	0	0	.273	8	0	1	.889
1977—San Jose†‡	P. C.	OF	3	10	1	3	0	0	0	4	.300	8	0	0	1.000
1977—Charleston	Int.	OF	29	89	17	31	4	1	4	14	.348	66	0	0	1.000
1977—Houston	Nat.	OF	6	21	1	6	0	1	0	6	.286	14	0	0	1.000
1978—Houston	Nat.	OF	120	247	30	62	11	3	3	36	.251	140	4	3	.980
1979—Houston	Nat.	OF	82	147	21	48	8	4	3	31	.327	65	2	1	.985
1980—Houston	Nat.	1B-OF	100	284	30	85	6	5	3	29	.299	525	31	6	.989
1981—Houston	Nat.	1B-OF	65	158	23	37	6	0	5	23	.234	226	9	2	.992
1982—Houston	Nat.	OF-1B	85	146	22	30	4	1	1	14	.205	167	11	1	.994
1983—Houston§	Nat.	1B-3B-OF	100	135	24	40	5	3	3	19	.296	134	29	6	.964
1984—Houston x	Nat.	3B-1B-OF	87	249	37	70	11	5	3	31	.281	116	102	7	.969
1985—Houston	Nat.	3B-1B-OF	119	345	44	93	20	1	7	45	.270	326	124	12	.974
1986—Houston	Nat.	3B-OF-1B	130	382	54	119	23	1	13	58	.312	108	161	9	.968
1987—Houston y	Nat.	3B-1B-OF	110	325	45	92	21	4	5	33	.283	175	119	10	.967
1988—Hou. za-St.L.	Nat.	3B-OF-1B	84	234	22	56	13	2	1	21	.239	73	112	9	.954
1988—Tucson	P. C.	3B	5	16	2	3	1	0	0	4	.188	4	10	1	.933
1989—St. Louis b	Nat.	1B-3B-OF	69	79	9	24	7	0	1	11	.304	67	9	4	.950
1990—St. Louis c	Nat.	1B-3B-OF	78	127	7	28	5	0	1	19	.220	103	26	0	1.000
American League Totals—2 Years			9	19	1	4	1	0	0	2	.210	11	0	1	.917
National League Totals—14 Years			1235	2879	369	790	140	30	49	376	.274	2239	739	70	.977
Major League Totals—16 Years			1244	2898	370	794	141	30	49	378	.274	2250	739	71	.977

Selected by San Francisco Giants' organization in 8th round of free-agent draft, June 5, 1974.
Selected by Oakland A's organization in secondary phase of free-agent draft, June 4, 1975.
†On disabled list, April 18 to June 15, 1977.
‡Traded with cash to Houston Astros' organization for Outfielder Willie Crawford, June 15, 1977.
§Granted free agency, November 7, 1983; re-signed by Astros, December 20, 1983.
xOn disabled list, May 2 to May 24, 1984.
yOn disabled list, March 28 to April 17, 1987.
zOn disabled list, June 20 to August 6, 1988; included rehabilitation disability assignment to Tucson, July 29 to August 3, 1988.
aTraded to St. Louis Cardinals for Pitcher Bob Forsch, August 31, 1988.
bOn disabled list, May 24, to June 8, 1989.
cGranted free agency, November 5, 1990.

DIVISION SERIES RECORD

Year—Club	League	Pos.	G.	AB.	R.	H.	2B.	3B.	HR.	RBI.	B.A.	PO.	A.	E.	F.A.
1981—Houston	Nat.	PH-1B	3	6	0	2	0	0	0	1	.333	6	1	1	.875

CHAMPIONSHIP SERIES RECORD

Year—Club	League	Pos.	G.	AB.	R.	H.	2B.	3B.	HR.	RBI.	B.A.	PO.	A.	E.	F.A.
1980—Houston	Nat.	1-O-PH	3	9	2	1	0	0	0	2	.111	6	0	0	1.000
1986—Houston	Nat.	3B-PH	5	19	1	3	1	0	0	2	.158	3	6	0	1.000
Championship Series Totals—2 Years			8	28	3	4	1	0	0	4	.143	9	6	0	1.000

DAVID PETER WALSH
(Dave)

Born September 25, 1960, at Arlington, Mass.
Height, 6.01. Weight, 185.
Throws and bats lefthanded.
Received bachelor of arts degree in English from
University of California, Santa Barbara, Calif.

Major League saves: 1990 (1).

Year—Club	League	G.	IP.	W.	L.	Pct.	H.	R.	ER.	SO.	BB.	ERA.
1982—Medicine Hat	Pioneer	13	26	1	2	.333	35	30	16	22	18	5.54
1983—Florence	S. Atlantic	41	99⅔	10	2	*.833	95	53	37	90	34	3.34
1984—Kinston	Carolina	3	7⅔	1	1	.500	8	2	2	9	2	2.35
1984—Knoxville	Southern	23	119⅓	5	8	.385	111	54	43	60	64	3.24
1984—Syracuse	Int'national	9	28⅔	1	1	.500	40	23	21	15	15	6.59
1985—Knoxville†	Southern	38	154	11	8	.579	147	89	77	103	89	4.50
1986—Ventura County‡	California	15	59⅓	6	3	.667	65	41	34	43	26	5.16
1986—Knoxville	Southern	11	28⅔	2	0	1.000	30	21	18	15	32	5.65
1987—Knoxville	Southern	24	67⅔	2	4	.333	72	52	41	42	46	5.45
1988—Nuevo Laredo§x	Mexican	18	125	14	1	*.933	82	28	24	141	77	*1.73
1989—Albuquerque	P. Coast	6	27	1	2	.333	27	15	15	18	17	5.00
1989—San Antonio	Texas	38	55⅔	2	4	.250	72	47	26	63	30	3.72
1990—Albuquerque	P. Coast	47	62	6	0	1.000	50	21	18	66	31	2.61
1990—Los Angeles	National	20	16⅓	1	0	1.000	15	12	7	15	6	3.86
Major League Totals—1 Year		20	16⅓	1	0	1.000	15	12	7	15	6	3.86

Selected by Toronto Blue Jays' organization in 9th round of free-agent draft, June 7, 1982.
†On disabled list, July 24 to August 4, 1985.
‡On disabled list, July 2 to August 22, 1986.
§Loaned to Nuevo Laredo of Mexican League.
xGranted free agency, October 15, 1988; signed by Albuquerque (Los Angeles Dodgers' organization), January 27, 1989.

JEROME O'TERRELL WALTON

Born July 8, 1965, at Newnan, Ga.
Height, 6.01. Weight, 175.
Throws and bats righthanded.
Attended Enterprise State Junior College, Enterprise, Ala.

Major League stolen bases: 1989 (24), 1990 (14). Total—38.
Led Midwest League in caught stealing with 25 in 1987.
Led Appalachian League outfielders in putouts with 128, total chances with 131 and tied for lead in double plays with 2 in 1986.
Named National League Rookie Player of the Year by THE SPORTING NEWS, 1989.
Named National League Rookie of the Year by Baseball Writers' Association of America, 1989.

Year Club	League	Pos.	G.	AB.	R.	H.	2B.	3B.	HR.	RBI.	B.A.	PO.	A.	E.	F.A.
1986—Wytheville	Appal.	OF-3B	62	229	48	66	7	4	5	34	.288	130	7	3	.979
1987—Peoria	Midw.	OF	128	472	102	158	24	11	6	38	.335	255	9	7	.974
1988—Pittsfield	East.	OF	120	414	64	137	26	2	3	49	.331	270	11	2	*.993
1989—Chicago†	Nat.	OF	116	475	64	139	23	3	5	46	.293	289	2	3	.990
1989—Iowa	A. A.	OF	4	18	4	6	1	0	1	3	.333	8	0	0	1.000
1990—Chicago‡	Nat.	OF	101	392	63	103	16	2	2	21	.263	247	3	6	.977
1990—Iowa	A. A.	OF	4	16	3	3	0	0	1	1	.188	6	1	0	1.000
Major League Totals—2 Years			217	867	127	242	39	5	7	67	.279	536	5	9	.984

Selected by Chicago Cubs' organization in 2nd round of free-agent draft, January 14, 1986.
†On disabled list, May 11 to June 11, 1989; included rehabilitation disability assignment to Iowa, June 6 to June 11, 1989.
‡On disabled list, June 18 to August 2, 1990; included rehabilitation disability assignment to Iowa, July 29 to August 1, 1990.

CHAMPIONSHIP SERIES RECORD

Shares Championship Series records for most at-bats (2), hits (2) and singles (2), inning, October 5, 1989, first inning.

Year Club	League	Pos.	G.	AB.	R.	H.	2B.	3B.	HR.	RBI.	B.A.	PO.	A.	E.	F.A.
1989—Chicago	Nat.	OF	5	22	4	8	0	0	0	2	.364	11	0	0	1.000

STEVEN LEE WAPNICK
(Steve)

Born September 25, 1965, at Panorama City, Calif.
Height, 6.02. Weight, 200.
Throws and bats righthanded.
Attended Moorpark College, Moorpark, Calif.,
and Fresno State University, Fresno, Calif.

Year Club	League	G.	IP.	W.	L.	Pct.	H.	R.	ER.	SO.	BB.	ERA.
1987—St. Catharines	NYP	20	65⅔	3	4	.429	53	28	22	63	21	3.02
1988—Myrtle Beach	S. Atlantic	*54	60⅓	4	3	.571	44	18	15	69	31	2.24
1989—Dunedin	Florida St.	24	66	4	0	1.000	48	19	15	59	22	2.05
1989—Knoxville	Southern	12	18⅓	1	0	1.000	12	1	1	20	7	0.49
1989—Syracuse†	Int'national	6	13	1	0	1.000	9	1	1	10	5	0.69
1990—Detroit‡	American	4	7	0	0	.000	8	5	5	6	10	6.43
1990—Syracuse	Int'national	11	16	0	1	.000	16	9	9	19	6	5.06
Major League Totals—1 Year		4	7	0	0	.000	8	5	5	6	10	6.43

Selected by San Diego Padres' organization in 2nd round of free-agent draft, January 9, 1985.
Selected by Oakland Athletics' organization in secondary phase of free-agent draft, June 3, 1985.
Selected by Toronto Blue Jays' organization in 30th round of free-agent draft, June 2, 1987.
†Drafted by Detroit Tigers, December 4, 1989.
‡Returned to Syracuse (Toronto Blue Jays' organization), May 1, 1990.

GARY LAMELL WARD

Born December 6, 1953, at Los Angeles, Calif.
Height, 6.02. Weight, 202.
Throws and bats righthanded.
Father of Agee Ward, forward at Fullerton State.

Major League stolen bases: 1981 (5), 1982 (13), 1983 (8), 1984 (7), 1985 (26), 1986 (12), 1987 (9), 1989 (1), 1990 (2). Total—83.
Hit for the cycle, September 18, 1980 (first game).
Led American League outfielders in double plays with 4 in 1981.
Led New York-Pennsylvania League first basemen in errors with 12 in 1973.
Tied for Midwest League lead in assists by outfielders with 18 in 1974.

Year Club	League	Pos.	G.	AB.	R.	H.	2B.	3B.	HR.	RBI.	B.A.	PO.	A.	E.	F.A.
1973—Geneva	NYP	1B-OF-3B	61	211	36	57	13	1	10	38	.270	336	20	14	.962
1974—Wisconsin Rapids	Midw.	OF-1B	126	*467	*104	122	12	5	26	78	.261	184	19	11	.949
1975—Orlando	South.	OF-C	124	438	45	117	18	5	8	71	.267	204	10	4	.982
1976—Orlando	South.	OF	132	475	50	119	17	2	9	65	.251	235	●16	●10	.962
1977—Tacoma	P. C.	OF-3B	125	413	62	97	15	8	8	43	.235	212	34	10	.961
1978—Toledo	Int.	*O-1-3	139	511	82	150	20	12	14	79	.294	260	6	*13	.953
1979—Toledo	Int.	OF	134	506	75	133	16	9	13	67	.263	323	12	●11	.968
1979—Minnesota	Amer.	DH-PH	10	14	2	4	0	0	0	1	.286	0	0	0	.000
1980—Toledo†	Int.	OF-1B	128	496	82	140	22	8	13	66	.282	269	14	8	.973
1980—Minnesota	Amer.	OF	13	41	11	19	6	2	1	10	.463	14	0	0	1.000

Year	Club	League	Pos.	G.	AB.	R.	H.	2B.	3B.	HR.	RBI.	B.A.	PO.	A.	E.	F.A.
1981—Minnesota	Amer.		OF	85	295	42	78	7	6	3	29	.264	185	8	5	.975
1982—Minnesota	Amer.		OF	152	570	85	165	33	7	28	91	.289	343	13	4	.989
1983—Minnesota‡	Amer.		OF	157	623	76	173	34	5	19	88	.278	374	★24	9	.978
1984—Texas	Amer.		OF	155	602	97	171	21	7	21	79	.284	376	11	5	.987
1985—Texas	Amer.		OF	154	593	77	170	28	7	15	70	.287	304	11	10	.969
1986—Texas§	Amer.		OF	105	380	54	120	15	2	5	51	.316	237	8	1	.996
1987—New York	Amer.		OF-1B	146	529	65	131	22	1	16	78	.248	318	10	3	.991
1988—New York	Amer.		OF-1B-3B	91	231	26	52	8	0	4	24	.225	220	5	2	.991
1989—N.Y.x-Det.	Amer.		OF-1B	113	292	27	74	11	2	9	30	.253	234	16	3	.988
1990—Detroit yz	Amer.		OF-1B	106	309	32	79	11	2	9	46	.256	164	2	2	.988
Major League Totals—12 Years				1287	4479	594	1236	196	41	130	597	.276	2769	108	44	.985

Signed as free agent by Minnesota Twins' organization, August 29, 1972.

†On disabled list, April 16 to April 26, 1980.

‡Traded to Texas Rangers for Pitchers Mike Smithson and John Butcher and Catcher Sam Sorce, December 7, 1983.

§Granted free agency, November 12, 1986; signed by New York Yankees, December 24, 1986.

xReleased, April 16, 1989; signed by Detroit Tigers, April 23, 1989.

yOn disabled list, June 9 to June 24, 1990.

zGranted free agency, November 5, 1990.

ALL-STAR GAME RECORD

Year	League	Pos.	AB.	R.	H.	2B.	3B.	HR.	RBI.	B.A.	PO.	A.	E.	F.A.
1983—American		PH	1	0	0	0	0	0	0	.000	0	0	0	.000
1985—American		PH	1	0	0	0	0	0	0	.000	0	0	0	.000
All-Star Game Totals—2 Years			2	0	0	0	0	0	0	.000	0	0	0	.000

ROBERT COLBY WARD

(Known by middle name.)

Born January 2, 1964, at Lansing, Mich.
Height, 6.02. Weight, 185.
Throws and bats righthanded.
Attended Brigham Young University, Provo, Utah.

Major League saves: 1990 (1).

Year	Club	League	G.	IP.	W.	L.	Pct.	H.	R.	ER.	SO.	BB.	ERA.
1986—Salem	Northwest	27	53⅓	4	6	.400	43	24	19	74	22	3.21
1987—Palm Springs	California	54	88⅔	7	7	.500	74	37	26	85	42	2.64
1988—Midland	Texas	26	40⅓	9	2	.818	42	17	12	32	19	2.68
1988—Edmonton	P. Coast	23	31	0	2	.000	23	13	11	17	16	3.19
1989—Edmonton†-Colorado Springs.	P. Coast	41	78	4	2	.667	99	56	45	57	40	5.19
1990—Colorado Springs	P. Coast	43	63	4	3	.571	45	23	14	56	30	2.00
1990—Cleveland	American	22	36	1	3	.250	31	17	17	23	21	4.25
Major League Totals—1 Year		22	36	1	3	.250	31	17	17	23	21	4.25

Selected by Milwaukee Brewers' organization in 15th round of free-agent draft, June 3, 1985.

Selected by California Angels' organization in 11th round of free-agent draft, June 2, 1986.

†Traded to Colorado Springs (Cleveland Indians' organization), July 15, 1989, completing deal in which Cleveland traded Catcher Brian Dorsett to California Angels for a player to be named later, June 7, 1988.

ROY DUANE WARD

(Known by middle name.)

Born May 28, 1964, at Parkview, N.M.
Height, 6.04. Weight, 215.
Throws and bats righthanded.

Major League saves: 1988 (15), 1989 (15), 1990 (11). Total—41.

Year	Club	League	G.	IP.	W.	L.	Pct.	H.	R.	ER.	SO.	BB.	ERA.
1982—Bradenton Braves	Gulf Coast	8	45⅔	2	3	.400	45	25	23	31	24	4.53
1982—Anderson	S. Atlantic	5	23⅔	1	2	.333	24	16	14	18	15	5.32
1983—Durham	Carolina	28	178⅓	11	13	.458	165	103	85	115	75	4.29
1984—Greenville†	Southern	21	104⅔	4	9	.308	108	71	58	54	57	4.99
1985—Greenville	Southern	28	150	11	10	.524	141	83	70	100	★105	4.20
1985—Richmond	Int'national	5	5⅓	0	1	.000	8	9	7	3	8	11.81
1986—Atlanta	National	10	16	0	1	.000	22	13	13	8	8	7.31
1986—Richmond‡-Syracuse	Int'national	20	117⅔	7	5	.583	125	56	52	67	52	3.98
1986—Toronto	American	2	2	0	1	.000	3	4	3	1	4	13.50
1987—Toronto	American	12	11⅔	1	0	1.000	14	9	9	10	12	6.94
1987—Syracuse	Int'national	46	76⅓	2	2	.500	59	35	33	67	42	3.89
1988—Toronto	American	64	111⅔	9	3	.750	101	46	41	91	60	3.30
1989—Toronto	American	66	114⅔	4	10	.286	94	55	48	122	58	3.77
1990—Toronto	American	73	127⅔	2	8	.200	101	51	49	112	42	3.45
National League Totals—1 Year		10	16	0	1	.000	22	13	13	8	8	7.31
American League Totals—5 Years		217	367⅔	16	22	.421	313	165	150	336	176	3.67
Major League Totals—5 Years		227	383⅔	16	23	.410	335	178	163	344	184	3.82

Selected by Atlanta Braves' organization in 1st round (ninth player selected) of free-agent draft, June 7, 1982.

†On disabled list, May 7 to May 29 and July 14 to August 7, 1984.

‡Traded to Toronto Blue Jays for Pitcher Doyle Alexander, July 6, 1986.

Year Club	League	G.	IP.	W.	L.	Pct.	H.	R.	ER.	SO.	BB.	ERA.
1989—Toronto	American	2	3⅔	0	0	.000	6	3	3	5	3	7.36

TURNER MAX WARD

Born April 11, 1965, at Orlando, Fla.
Height, 6.02. Weight, 200.
Throws right and bats left and righthanded.
Attended University of South Alabama, Mobile, Ala.
Major League stolen bases: 1990 (3).
Led Pacific Coast League outfielders in total chances with 306 in 1990.

Year Club	League	Pos.	G.	AB.	R.	H.	2B.	3B.	HR.	RBI.	B.A.	PO.	A.	E.	F.A.
1986—Oneonta.................	NYP	OF-1B-3B	63	221	42	62	4	1	1	19	.281	97	6	5	.954
1987—Fort Lauderdale..	Fla. St.	OF-3B	130	493	83	145	15	2	7	55	.294	332	11	8	.977
1988—Columbus†	Int.	OF	134	490	55	123	24	1	7	50	.251	233	5	1	★.996
1989—Sarasota Indians‡	Gulf C.	DH	4	15	2	3	0	0	0	1	.200	0	0	0	.000
1989—Canton-Akron	East.	OF	30	93	19	28	5	1	0	3	.301	2	0	0	1.000
1990—Colorado Springs.	P. C.	★OF-2B	133	495	89	148	24	9	6	65	.299	★292	7	9	.971
1990—Cleveland..............	Amer.	OF	14	46	10	16	2	1	1	10	.348	20	2	1	.957
Major League Totals—1 Year..................			14	46	10	16	2	1	1	10	.348	20	2	1	.957

Selected by New York Yankees' organization in 18th round of free-agent draft, June 2, 1986.
†Traded with Catcher Joel Skinner to Cleveland Indians' organization for Outfielder Mel Hall, March 19, 1989.
‡On disabled list, April 7 to July 24, 1989.

CLAUDELL WASHINGTON

Born August 31, 1954, at Los Angeles, Calif.
Height, 6.02. Weight, 195.
Throws and bats lefthanded.
Brother of Don Washington, outfielder in Los Angeles Dodgers' and
Oakland A's organizations, 1975 through 1977.
Hit three home runs in a game, July 14, 1979 and June 22, 1980.
Major League stolen bases: 1974 (6), 1975 (40), 1976 (37), 1977 (21), 1978 (5), 1979 (19), 1980 (21), 1981 (12), 1982 (33), 1983 (31), 1984 (21), 1985 (14), 1986 (10), 1987 (10), 1988 (15), 1989 (13), 1990 (4). Total—312.
Led Midwest League in total bases with 218 in 1973.

Year Club	League	Pos.	G.	AB.	R.	H.	2B.	3B.	HR.	RBI.	B.A.	PO.	A.	E.	F.A.
1972—C's Bay-N. Bend....	N'west.	OF	33	111	13	31	3	2	2	15	.279	37	1	6	.864
1973—Burlington	Midw.	OF	108	447	★92	144	25	5	13	81	.322	149	10	★15	.914
1974—Birmingham	South.	OF	74	294	64	106	23	3	11	55	.361	116	5	13	.903
1974—Oakland.................	Amer.	OF	73	221	16	63	10	5	0	19	.285	63	2	1	.985
1975—Oakland.................	Amer.	OF	148	590	86	182	24	7	10	77	.308	305	8	7	.978
1976—Oakland†‡.............	Amer.	●OF	134	490	65	126	20	6	5	53	.257	276	10	●11	.963
1977—Texas§	Amer.	OF	129	521	63	148	31	2	12	68	.284	255	11	6	.978
1978—Tex. x-Chi. y	Amer.	OF	98	356	34	90	16	5	6	33	.253	170	6	8	.957
1979—Chicago	Amer.	OF	131	471	79	132	33	5	13	66	.280	256	7	7	.974
1980—Chicago z	Amer.	OF	32	90	15	26	4	2	1	12	.289	41	1	3	.933
1980—New York a	Nat.	OF	79	284	38	78	16	4	10	42	.275	123	12	3	.978
1981—Atlanta b	Nat.	OF	85	320	37	93	22	3	5	37	.291	145	5	1	.993
1982—Atlanta	Nat.	OF	150	563	94	150	24	6	16	80	.266	221	9	12	.950
1983—Atlanta	Nat.	OF	134	496	75	138	24	8	9	44	.278	218	8	6	.974
1984—Atlanta c	Nat.	OF	120	416	62	119	21	2	17	61	.286	170	4	6	.967
1985—Atlanta	Nat.	OF	122	398	62	110	14	6	15	43	.276	122	3	5	.962
1986—Atlanta de.............	Nat.	OF	40	137	17	37	11	0	5	14	.270	44	1	2	.957
1986—New York f	Amer.	OF	54	135	19	32	5	0	6	16	.237	66	0	1	.985
1987—New York g	Amer.	OF	102	312	42	87	17	0	9	44	.279	166	3	2	.988
1988—New York h	Amer.	OF	126	455	62	140	22	3	11	64	.308	309	5	5	.984
1989—California i	Amer.	OF	110	418	53	114	18	4	13	42	.273	187	6	5	.975
1990—Calif. j-N.Y. kl.......	Amer.	OF	45	114	7	19	2	1	1	9	.167	61	3	0	1.000
American League Totals—12 Years			1182	4173	541	1159	202	40	87	503	.278	2155	62	56	.975
National League Totals—7 Years...........			730	2614	385	725	132	29	77	321	.277	1043	42	35	.969
Major League Totals—17 Years..............			1912	6787	926	1884	334	69	164	824	.278	3198	104	91	.973

Signed as free agent by Oakland A's organization, July 7, 1972.
†On disabled list, August 16 to September 1, 1976.
‡Traded to Texas Rangers for Pitcher Jim Umbarger, Infielder Rodney Scott and cash estimated at $100,000, March 26, 1977.
§On disabled list, May 27 to June 11, 1977.
xTraded with Outfielder Rusty Torres and cash to Chicago White Sox for Outfielder Bobby Bonds, May 16, 1978.
yOn disabled list, May 22 to June 16, 1978.
zTraded to New York Mets for Pitcher Jesse Anderson, June 7, 1980.
aGranted free agency, October 31, 1980; signed by Atlanta Braves, November 15, 1980.
bOn disabled list, June 5 to August 9, 1981.
cOn disabled list, May 30 to June 14, 1984.
dOn disabled list, May 18 to June 16, 1986.
eTraded with Shortstop Paul Zuvella to New York Yankees for Outfielder Ken Griffey, June 30, 1986.
fGranted free agency, November 12, 1986; re-signed by Yankees, December 7, 1986.
gOn disabled list, May 18 to June 2, 1987.
hGranted free agency, October 24, 1988; signed by California Angels, January 17, 1989.
iOn disabled list, July 1 to July 18, 1989.

kOn disabled list, June 19, 1990 through remainder of season.
lReleased, October 4, 1990.

CHAMPIONSHIP SERIES RECORD

Year Club	League	Pos.	G.	AB.	R.	H.	2B.	3B.	HR.	RBI.	B.A.	PO.	A.	E.	F.A.
1974—Oakland	Amer.	OF-PH	4	11	1	3	1	0	0	0	.273	11	0	0	1.000
1975—Oakland	Amer.	OF-DH	3	12	1	3	1	0	0	1	.250	1	0	2	.333
1982—Atlanta	Nat.	OF	3	9	0	3	0	0	0	0	.333	5	1	0	1.000
Championship Series Totals—3 Years			10	32	2	9	2	0	0	1	.281	17	1	2	.900

WORLD SERIES RECORD

Tied World Series record for most positions played, Series (3), 1974 (all three outfield positions).

Year Club	League	Pos.	G.	AB.	R.	H.	2B.	3B.	HR.	RBI.	B.A.	PO.	A.	E.	F.A.
1974—Oakland	Amer.	OF-PH	5	7	1	4	0	0	0	0	.571	3	0	0	1.000

ALL-STAR GAME RECORD

Year League	Pos.	AB.	R.	H.	2B.	3B.	HR.	RBI.	B.A.	PO.	A.	E.	F.A.
1975—American	PR-OF	1	0	1	0	0	0	0	1.000	1	0	0	1.000
1984—National	OF	2	0	1	1	0	0	0	.500	1	0	0	1.000
All-Star Game Totals—2 Years		3	0	2	1	0	0	0	.667	2	0	0	1.000

GARY ANTHONY WAYNE

Born November 30, 1962, at Dearborn, Mich.
Height, 6.03. Weight, 192.
Throws and bats lefthanded.
Attended University of Michigan, Ann Arbor, Mich.

Major League saves: 1989 (1).
Led Florida State League in saves with 25 in 1986.

Year Club	League	G.	IP.	W.	L.	Pct.	H.	R.	ER.	SO.	BB.	ERA.
1984—West Palm Beach	Florida St.	13	74⅓	3	5	.375	70	38	32	46	49	3.87
1985—Jacksonville	Southern	21	102	3	12	.200	108	67	60	62	70	5.29
1985—West Palm Beach	Florida St.	8	30⅔	2	2	.500	37	23	19	18	22	5.58
1986—West Palm Beach	Florida St.	47	61⅓	2	5	.286	48	16	11	55	25	1.61
1987—Jacksonville	Southern	56	80⅓	5	1	.833	56	23	21	78	35	2.35
1988—Indianapolis†‡	Am. Assoc.	8	7⅓	0	0	.000	9	5	5	6	3	6.14
1989—Minnesota	American	60	71	3	4	.429	55	28	26	41	36	3.30
1990—Minnesota	American	38	38⅔	1	1	.500	38	19	18	28	13	4.19
1990—Portland	P. Coast	22	31⅔	2	4	.333	29	14	12	30	13	3.41
Major League Totals—2 Years		98	109⅔	4	5	.444	93	47	44	69	49	3.61

Selected by Oakland A's organization in 23rd round of free-agent draft, June 6, 1983.
Selected by Montreal Expos' organization in 4th round of free-agent draft, June 4, 1984.
†On disabled list, April 7 to August 24, 1988.
‡Drafted by Minnesota Twins, December 5, 1988.

LEONARD IRELL WEBSTER
(Lenny)

Born February 10, 1965, at New Orleans, La.
Height, 5.09. Weight, 185.
Throws and bats righthanded.
Attended Grambling State University, Grambling, La.

Led Midwest League in game-winning RBIs with 14 in 1988.
Named Midwest League Most Valuable Player, 1988.

Year Club	League	Pos.	G.	AB.	R.	H.	2B.	3B.	HR.	RBI.	B.A.	PO.	A.	E.	F.A.
1986—Kenosha	Midw.	C	22	65	2	10	2	0	0	8	.154	87	9	0	1.000
1986—Elizabethton	Appal.	C	48	152	29	35	4	0	3	14	.230	88	11	3	.971
1987—Kenosha	Midw.	C	52	140	17	35	7	0	3	17	.250	228	29	5	.981
1988—Kenosha	Midw.	C	129	465	82	134	23	2	11	87	.288	606	96	14	.980
1989—Visalia	Calif.	C	63	231	36	62	7	0	5	39	.268	352	57	4	.990
1989—Orlando	South.	C	59	191	29	45	7	0	2	17	.236	293	46	4	.988
1989—Minnesota	Amer.	C	14	20	3	6	2	0	0	1	.300	32	0	0	1.000
1990—Orlando	South.	C	126	455	69	119	31	0	8	71	.262	629	70	9	.987
1990—Minnesota	Amer.	C	2	6	1	2	1	0	0	0	.333	9	0	0	1.000
Major League Totals—2 Years			16	26	4	8	3	0	0	1	.308	41	0	0	1.000

Selected by Minnesota Twins' organization in 16th round of free-agent draft, June 7, 1982.
Selected by Minnesota Twins' organization in 21st round of free-agent draft, June 3, 1985.

MITCHELL DEAN WEBSTER
(Mitch)

Born May 16, 1959, at Larned, Kan.
Height, 6.01. Weight, 185.
Throws left and bats left and righthanded.

Shares major league record for fewest double plays by outfielder, season, 150 or more games (0), 1987.
Major League stolen bases: 1985 (15), 1986 (36), 1987 (33), 1988 (22), 1989 (14), 1990 (22). Total—142.
Led International League outfielders in double plays with 5 and total chances with 385 in 1982.

Year Club	League	Pos.	G.	AB.	R.	H.	2B.	3B.	HR.	RBI.	B.A.	PO.	A.	E.	F.A.
1977—Lethbridge	Pion	OF	55	168	45	59	4	0	0	31	.351	81	3	8	.913
1978—Clinton	Midw.	OF	45	157	18	38	3	1	0	9	.242	92	6	7	.933
1978—Lethbridge	Pion.	OF	55	182	58	58	5	1	0	18	.319	77	3	0	*1.000
1979—Clinton†	Midw.	OF	123	473	95	*154	17	7	2	40	*.326	*272	10	10	.966
1980—Syracuse	Int.	OF	49	161	23	35	4	2	1	12	.217	112	3	5	.958
1980—Kinston	Carol.	OF	65	258	43	76	7	3	0	28	.295	129	8	5	.965
1981—Knoxville	South.	OF	140	554	89	163	26	6	1	42	.294	317	7	10	.970
1982—Syracuse	Int.	OF	137	513	95	144	21	7	13	68	.281	*367	16	2	*.995
1983—Syracuse	Int.	OF-1B	135	462	77	120	26	8	9	45	.260	266	16	10	.966
1983—Toronto	Amer.	OF	11	11	2	2	0	0	0	0	.182	5	0	0	1.000
1984—Toronto	Amer.	OF-1B	26	22	9	5	2	1	0	4	.227	16	0	2	.889
1984—Syracuse	Int.	OF	95	360	60	108	22	5	3	25	.300	239	7	7	.972
1985—Toronto	Amer.	OF	4	1	0	0	0	0	0	0	.000	0	0	0	.000
1985—Syracuse‡	Int.	OF	47	189	32	52	5	3	3	23	.275	83	10	1	.989
1985—Montreal	Nat.	OF	74	212	32	58	8	2	11	30	.274	133	3	1	.993
1986—Montreal	Nat.	OF	151	576	89	167	31	*13	8	49	.290	325	12	8	.977
1987—Montreal	Nat.	OF	156	588	101	165	30	8	15	63	.281	266	8	5	.982
1988—Mont.§-Chi.	Nat.	OF	151	523	69	136	16	8	6	39	.260	322	3	6	.982
1989—Chicago xy	Nat.	OF	98	272	40	70	12	4	3	19	.257	161	3	6	.965
1990—Cleveland	Amer.	OF-1B	128	437	58	110	20	6	12	55	.252	345	3	5	.986
American League Totals—4 Years			169	471	69	117	22	7	12	59	.248	366	3	7	.981
National League Totals—5 Years			630	2171	331	596	97	35	43	200	.275	1207	29	26	.979
Major League Totals—8 Years			799	2642	400	713	119	42	55	259	.270	1573	32	33	.980

Selected by Los Angeles Dodgers' organization in 23rd round of free-agent draft, June 7, 1977.

†Drafted by Syracuse (Toronto Blue Jays' organization), December 4, 1979.

‡Traded to Montreal Expos for a player to be named later, June 22, 1985; Toronto Blue Jays' organization acquired Pitcher Cliff Young to complete deal, September 10, 1985.

§Traded to Chicago Cubs for Outfielder Dave Martinez, July 14, 1988.

xOn disabled list, May 14 to May 29, 1989.

yTraded to Cleveland Indians for Outfielder Dave Clark, November 20, 1989.

CHAMPIONSHIP SERIES RECORD

Year Club	League	Pos.	G.	AB.	R.	H.	2B.	3B.	HR.	RBI.	B.A.	PO.	A.	E.	F.A.
1989—Chicago	Nat.	PH-OF	3	3	0	1	0	0	0	0	.333	0	0	0	.000

WILLIAM EDWARD WEGMAN
(Bill)

Born December 19, 1962, at Cincinnati, O.
Height, 6.05. Weight, 220.
Throws and bats righthanded.

Led Pacific Coast League in home runs allowed with 21 in 1985.
Led California League in balks with 5 and tied for lead in complete games with 15 and shutouts with 4 in 1983.

Year Club	League	G.	IP.	W.	L.	Pct.	H.	R.	ER.	SO.	BB.	ERA.
1981—Butte	Pioneer	14	82	6	5	.545	94	51	38	47	44	4.17
1982—Beloit	Midwest	25	179⅔	12	6	.667	176	77	56	129	38	2.81
1983—Stockton	California	24	186⅔	*16	5	.762	149	33	27	135	45	*1.30
1984—El Paso	Texas	10	64	4	5	.444	62	25	19	42	15	2.67
1984—Vancouver†	P. Coast	6	27⅔	0	3	.000	30	11	6	16	8	1.95
1985—Vancouver	P. Coast	28	188	10	11	.476	187	93	84	113	52	4.02
1985—Milwaukee	American	3	17⅔	2	0	1.000	17	8	7	6	3	3.57
1986—Milwaukee‡	American	35	198⅓	5	12	.294	217	120	113	82	43	5.13
1987—Milwaukee§	American	34	225	12	11	.522	229	113	106	102	53	4.24
1988—Milwaukee xy	American	32	199	13	13	.500	207	104	91	84	50	4.12
1989—Milwaukee z	American	11	51	2	6	.250	69	44	38	27	21	6.71
1990—Denver	Am. Assoc.	3	13⅔	1	0	1.000	10	5	5	14	7	3.29
1990—Milwaukee a	American	8	29⅔	2	2	.500	37	21	16	20	6	4.85
1990—Beloit	Midwest	1	2	0	0	.000	1	0	0	2	1	0.00
Major League Totals—6 Years		123	720⅔	36	44	.450	776	410	371	321	176	4.63

Selected by Milwaukee Brewers' organization in 5th round of free-agent draft, June 8, 1981.

†On disabled list, June 18 to August 11, 1984.

‡Appeared in two games as a pinch-runner.

§On disabled list, August 7 to August 22, 1987.

xAppeared in one game as a pinch-runner.

yOn disabled list, May 21 to June 7, 1988.

zOn disabled list, June 1, 1989 through remainder of season.

aOn disabled list, June 3, 1990 through remainder of season; included rehabilitation disability assignment to Beloit, June 27, 1990.

JOHN PAUL WEHNER

Born June 29, 1967, at Pittsburgh, Pa.
Height, 6.03. Weight, 205.
Throws and bats righthanded.
Attended Indiana University, Bloomington, Ind.

Led Eastern League third basemen in total chances with 476 and double plays with 40 in 1990.
Led Carolina League third basemen in total chances with 403 and tied for lead in double plays with 24 in 1989.
Led New York-Pennsylvania League third basemen in double plays with 14 and total chances with 219 in 1988.

Year Club League	Pos.	G.	AB.	R.	H.	2B.	3B.	HR.	RBI.	B.A.	PO.	A.	E.	F.A.
1988—Watertown .... NYP	3B	70	265	41	73	6	0	3	31	.275	★65	137	17	.922
1989—Salem .... Carol.	3B	★137	★515	69	★155	32	6	14	73	.301	★89	★278	36	.911
1990—Harrisburg .... East.	3B	●138	★511	71	147	27	1	4	62	.288	★109	★317	★50	.895

Selected by Pittsburgh Pirates' organization in 7th round of free-agent draft, June 1, 1988.

WALTER WILLIAM WEISS JR.
(Walt)

Born November 28, 1963, at Tuxedo, N. Y.
Height, 6.00. Weight, 175.
Throws right and bats left and righthanded.
Attended University of North Carolina, Chapel Hill, N. C.
Major League stolen bases: 1987 (1), 1988 (4), 1989 (6), 1990 (9). Total—20.
Named American League Rookie Player of the Year by THE SPORTING NEWS, 1988.
Named American League Rookie of the Year by Baseball Writers' Association of America, 1988.

Year Club League	Pos.	G.	AB.	R.	H.	2B.	3B.	HR.	RBI.	B.A.	PO.	A.	E.	F.A.
1985—Pocatello.............. Pion.	SS	40	158	19	49	9	3	0	21	.310	51	126	11	.941
1985—Modesto................ Calif.	SS	30	122	17	24	4	1	0	7	.197	36	97	7	.950
1986—Madison .... Midw.	SS	84	322	50	97	15	5	2	54	.301	143	251	20	.952
1986—Huntsville .... South.	SS	46	160	19	40	2	1	0	13	.250	72	142	11	.951
1987—Huntsville .... South.	SS	91	337	43	96	16	2	1	32	.285	152	259	17	.960
1987—Oakland................. Amer.	SS	16	26	3	12	4	0	0	1	.462	8	30	1	.974
1987—Tacoma................. P. C.	SS	46	179	35	47	4	3	0	17	.263	76	140	11	.952
1988—Oakland................. Amer.	SS	147	452	44	113	17	3	3	39	.250	254	431	15	.979
1989—Oakland†.............. Amer.	SS	84	236	30	55	11	0	3	21	.233	106	195	15	.953
1989—Tacoma................. P. C.	SS	2	9	1	1	1	0	0	1	.111	0	3	1	.750
1989—Modesto................ Calif.	SS	5	8	1	3	0	0	0	1	.375	6	9	0	1.000
1990—Oakland‡.............. Amer.	SS	138	445	50	118	17	1	2	35	.265	194	373	12	.979
Major League Totals—4 Years................		385	1159	127	298	49	4	8	96	.257	562	1029	43	.974

Selected by Baltimore Orioles' organization in 10th round of free-agent draft, June 7, 1982.
Selected by Oakland A's organization in 1st round (11th player selected) of free-agent draft, June 3, 1985.
†On disabled list, May 18 to July 31, 1989; included rehabilitation disability assignment to Tacoma, July 18 to July 25, 1989; and Modesto, July 26 to July 31, 1989.
‡On disabled list, August 23 to September 7, 1990.

CHAMPIONSHIP SERIES RECORD

Year Club League	Pos.	G.	AB.	R.	H.	2B.	3B.	HR.	RBI.	B.A.	PO.	A.	E.	F.A.
1988—Oakland................. Amer.	SS	4	15	2	5	2	0	0	2	.333	7	10	0	1.000
1989—Oakland................. Amer.	SS-PR	4	9	2	1	1	0	0	0	.111	5	9	0	1.000
1990—Oakland................. Amer.	SS	2	7	2	0	0	0	0	0	.000	2	7	1	.900
Championship Series Totals—3 Years.....		10	31	6	6	3	0	0	2	.194	14	26	1	.976

WORLD SERIES RECORD

Year Club League	Pos.	G.	AB.	R.	H.	2B.	3B.	HR.	RBI.	B.A.	PO.	A.	E.	F.A.
1988—Oakland................. Amer.	SS	5	16	1	1	0	0	0	0	.063	5	11	1	.941
1989—Oakland................. Amer.	SS	4	15	3	2	0	0	1	1	.133	7	8	0	1.000
World Series Totals—2 Years		9	31	4	3	0	0	1	1	.097	12	19	1	.969

ROBERT LYNN WELCH
(Bob)

Born November 3, 1956, at Detroit, Mich.
Height, 6.03. Weight, 195.
Throws and bats righthanded.
Attended Eastern Michigan University, Ypsilanti, Mich.
Major League saves: 1978 (3), 1979 (5). Total—8.
Tied for National League lead in shutouts with 4 in 1987.
Named American League Pitcher of the Year by THE SPORTING NEWS, 1990.
Won American League Cy Young Memorial Award, 1990.
Named righthanded pitcher on THE SPORTING NEWS American League All-Star Team, 1990.

Year Club League	G.	IP.	W.	L.	Pct.	H.	R.	ER.	SO.	BB.	ERA.
1977—San Antonio.................... Texas	14	71	4	5	.444	94	44	35	56	17	4.44
1978—Albuquerque .... P. Coast	11	69	5	1	.833	72	33	29	53	19	3.78
1978—Los Angeles .... National	23	111	7	4	.636	92	28	25	66	26	2.03
1979—Los Angeles .... National	25	81	5	6	.455	82	42	36	64	32	4.00
1980—Los Angeles .... National	32	214	14	9	.609	190	85	78	141	79	3.28
1981—Los Angeles .... National	23	141	9	5	.643	141	56	54	88	41	3.45
1982—Los Angeles† .... National	36	235⅔	16	11	.593	199	94	88	176	81	3.36
1983—Los Angeles .... National	31	204	15	12	.556	164	73	60	156	72	2.65
1984—Los Angeles .... National	31	178⅔	13	13	.500	191	86	75	126	58	3.78
1985—Los Angeles‡ .... National	23	167⅓	14	4	.778	141	49	43	96	35	2.31
1985—Vero Beach.................... Florida St.	3	17	0	0	.000	15	4	4	9	1	2.12
1986—Los Angeles .... National	33	235⅔	7	13	.350	227	95	86	183	55	3.28
1987—Los Angeles§ .... National	35	251⅔	15	9	.625	204	94	90	196	86	3.22
1988—Oakland .... American	36	244⅔	17	9	.654	237	107	99	158	81	3.64

Year Club	League	G.	IP.	W.	L.	Pct.	H.	R.	ER.	SO.	BB.	ERA.
1989—Oakland x	American	33	209⅔	17	8	.680	191	82	70	137	78	3.00
1990—Oakland y	American	35	238	*27	6	*.818	214	90	78	127	77	2.95
National League Totals—10 Years		292	1820	115	86	.572	1631	702	635	1292	565	3.14
American League Totals—3 Years		104	692⅓	61	23	.726	642	279	247	422	236	3.21
Major League Totals—13 Years		396	2512⅓	176	109	.618	2273	981	882	1714	801	3.16

Selected by Chicago Cubs' organization in 14th round of free-agent draft, June 5, 1974.
Selected by Los Angeles Dodgers' organization in 1st round (20th player selected) of free-agent draft, June 7, 1977.
†Appeared in one game as outfielder with no chances.
‡On disabled list, April 29 to June 5, 1985; included rehabilitation disability assignment to Vero Beach, May 21 to June 5, 1985.
§As part of an eight-player, three-team deal, New York Mets traded Pitcher Jesse Orosco to Oakland Athletics, December 11, 1987. Oakland then traded Orosco along with Shortstop Alfredo Griffin and Pitcher Jay Howell to Los Angeles Dodgers for Pitchers Bob Welch, Matt Young and Jack Savage. Oakland then traded Savage along with Pitchers Wally Whitehurst and Kevin Tapani to New York.
xOn disabled list, June 13 to June 30, 1989.
yGranted free agency, November 5, 1990; re-signed by Athletics, December 15, 1990.

DIVISION SERIES RECORD

Year Club	League	G.	IP.	W.	L.	Pct.	H.	R.	ER.	SO.	BB.	ERA.
1981—Los Angeles	National	1	1	0	0	.000	0	0	0	1	1	0.00

CHAMPIONSHIP SERIES RECORD

Holds record for most series pitched (7).
Shares record for most bases on balls allowed, inning (4), October 12, 1985, first inning.

Year Club	League	G.	IP.	W.	L.	Pct.	H.	R.	ER.	SO.	BB.	ERA.
1978—Los Angeles	National	1	4⅓	1	0	1.000	2	1	1	5	0	2.08
1981—Los Angeles	National	3	1⅔	0	0	.000	2	1	1	2	0	5.40
1983—Los Angeles	National	1	1⅓	0	1	.000	0	2	1	0	2	6.75
1985—Los Angeles	National	1	2⅔	0	1	.000	5	4	2	2	6	6.75
1988—Oakland	American	1	1⅔	0	0	.000	6	5	5	0	2	27.00
1989—Oakland	American	1	5⅔	1	0	1.000	8	2	2	4	1	3.18
1990—Oakland	American	1	7⅓	1	0	1.000	6	1	1	4	3	1.23
Championship Series Totals—7 Years		9	24⅔	3	2	.600	29	16	13	17	14	4.74

WORLD SERIES RECORD

Year Club	League	G.	IP.	W.	L.	Pct.	H.	R.	ER.	SO.	BB.	ERA.
1978—Los Angeles	National	3	4⅓	0	1	.000	4	3	3	6	2	6.23
1981—Los Angeles	National	1	0	0	0	.000	3	2	2	0	1	....
1988—Oakland	American	1	5	0	0	.000	6	1	1	8	3	1.80
1990—Oakland	American	1	7⅓	0	0	.000	9	4	4	2	2	4.91
World Series Totals—4 Years		6	16⅔	0	1	.000	22	10	10	16	8	5.40

Eligible for 1989 World Series with Oakland Athletics; did not play.

ALL-STAR GAME RECORD

Year League	IP.	W.	L.	Pct.	H.	R.	ER.	SO.	BB.	ERA.
1980—National	3	0	0	.000	5	2	2	4	1	6.00
1990—American	2	0	0	.000	1	0	0	1	0	0.00
All-Star Game Totals—2 Years	5	0	0	.000	6	2	2	5	1	3.60

DAVID LEE WELLS

Born May 20, 1963, at Torrance, Calif.
Height, 6.04. Weight, 225.
Throws and bats lefthanded.

Major League saves: 1987 (1), 1988 (4), 1989 (2), 1990 (3). Total—10.

Year Club	League	G.	IP.	W.	L.	Pct.	H.	R.	ER.	SO.	BB.	ERA.
1982—Medicine Hat	Pioneer	12	64⅓	4	3	.571	71	42	37	53	32	5.18
1983—Kinston	Carolina	25	157	6	5	.545	141	81	65	115	71	3.73
1984—Kinston	Carolina	7	42	1	6	.143	51	29	22	44	19	4.71
1984—Knoxville†	Southern	8	59	3	2	.600	58	22	17	34	17	2.59
1985—Syracuse‡	Int'national					(Did not play)						
1986—Florence	S. Atlantic	4	12⅔	0	0	.000	7	6	5	14	9	3.55
1986—Ventura	California	5	19	2	1	.667	13	5	4	26	4	1.89
1986—Knoxville§	Southern	10	40	1	3	.250	42	24	18	32	18	4.05
1986—Syracuse	Int'national	3	3⅔	0	1	.000	6	4	4	2	1	9.82
1987—Syracuse	Int'national	43	109⅓	4	6	.400	102	49	47	106	32	3.87
1987—Toronto	American	18	29⅓	4	3	.571	37	14	13	32	12	3.99
1988—Toronto	American	41	64⅓	3	5	.375	65	36	33	56	31	4.62
1988—Syracuse	Int'national	6	5⅔	0	0	.000	7	1	0	8	2	0.00
1989—Toronto	American	54	86⅓	7	4	.636	66	25	23	78	28	2.40
1990—Toronto	American	43	189	11	6	.647	165	72	66	115	45	3.14
Major League Totals—4 Years		156	369	25	18	.581	333	147	135	281	116	3.29

Selected by Toronto Blue Jays' organization in 2nd round of free-agent draft, June 7, 1982.
†On disabled list, June 28, 1984, through remainder of season.
‡On disabled list, April 10, 1985, through entire season.
§On disabled list, July 7 to August 20, 1986.

Year Club	League	G.	IP.	W.	L.	Pct.	H.	R.	ER.	SO.	BB.	ERA.
1989—Toronto	American	1	1	0	0	.000	0	1	0	1	2	0.00

TERRY WELLS

Born September 10, 1963, at Kankakee, Ill.
Height, 6.03. Weight, 205.
Throws and bats lefthanded.
Attended University of Illinois, Champaign, Ill.

Led Pacific Coast League in wild pitches with 17 in 1990.
Led South Atlantic League in home runs allowed with 20 in 1986.

Year Club	League	G.	IP.	W.	L.	Pct.	H.	R.	ER.	SO.	BB.	ERA.
1985—Auburn	NYP	13	62⅓	4	4	.500	35	19	19	46	51	2.74
1986—Asheville	S. Atlantic	26	136⅔	12	6	.667	125	87	69	125	83	4.54
1987—Osceola	Florida St.	26	130⅓	7	9	.438	118	74	69	93	82	4.76
1988—Columbus	Southern	37	108⅓	5	5	.500	92	58	55	109	85	4.57
1989—Columbus	Southern	23	46⅔	2	3	.400	44	25	24	38	31	4.63
1989—Tucson†	P. Coast	26	48⅓	0	5	.000	57	32	31	47	36	5.77
1990—Albuquerque	P. Coast	24	115	8	6	.571	83	64	59	86	87	4.62
1990—Los Angeles‡	National	5	20⅔	1	2	.333	25	23	18	18	14	7.84
Major League Totals—1 Year		5	20⅔	1	2	.333	25	23	18	18	14	7.84

Selected by Cleveland Indians' organization in 11th round of free-agent draft, June 8, 1981.
Selected by Chicago White Sox' organization in 8th round of free-agent draft, June 4, 1984.
Selected by Houston Astros' organization in 8th round of free-agent draft, June 3, 1985.
†Traded to Los Angeles Dodgers for First Baseman/Outfielder Franklin Stubbs, April 1, 1990.
†Granted free agency, December 20, 1990.

STEVEN JOHN WENDELL
(Turk)

Born May 19, 1967, at Pittsfield, Mass.
Height, 6.03. Weight, 175.
Throws right and bats lefthanded.
Attended Quinnipiac College, Hamden, Conn.

Led Midwest League in shutouts with 5 and tied for lead in complete games with 9 in 1989.
Led Appalachian League in complete games with 6 in 1988.

Year Club	League	G.	IP.	W.	L.	Pct.	H.	R.	ER.	SO.	BB.	ERA.
1988—Pulaski	Ap'lachian	14	★101	3	●8	.273	85	50	43	87	30	3.83
1989—Burlington	Midwest	22	159	9	11	.550	127	63	39	153	41	2.21
1989—Greenville	Southern	1	3⅔	0	0	.000	7	5	4	3	1	9.82
1989—Durham	Carolina	3	24	2	0	1.000	13	4	3	27	6	1.13
1990—Durham	Carolina	6	38⅔	1	3	.250	24	10	8	26	15	1.86
1990—Greenville	Southern	36	91	4	9	.308	105	70	58	85	48	5.74

Selected by Atlanta Braves' organization in 5th round of free-agent draft, June 1, 1988.

DAVID LEE WEST

Born September 1, 1964, at Memphis, Tenn.
Height, 6.06. Weight, 220.
Throws and bats lefthanded.

Won 3-0 no-hit victory against Spartanburg, August 14, 1985.
Led New York-Pennsylvania League in wild pitches with 16 in 1984.
Tied for Texas League lead in shutouts with 2 in 1987.

Year Club	League	G.	IP.	W.	L.	Pct.	H.	R.	ER.	SO.	BB.	ERA.
1983—Sarasota Mets	Gulf Coast	12	53⅔	2	4	.333	41	28	17	56	52	2.85
1984—Columbia	S. Atlantic	12	60⅔	3	5	.375	41	47	42	60	68	6.23
1984—Little Falls	NYP	13	62	6	4	.600	43	35	23	79	62	3.34
1985—Columbia	S. Atlantic	26	150	10	9	.526	105	97	76	194	★111	4.56
1986—Lynchburg	Carolina	13	75	1	6	.143	76	50	43	70	53	5.16
1986—Columbia	S. Atlantic	13	92⅔	10	3	.769	74	41	30	101	56	2.91
1987—Jackson	Texas	25	166⅔	10	7	.588	152	67	52	★186	★81	2.81
1988—Tidewater	Int'national	23	160⅓	12	4	★.750	106	42	32	143	★97	★1.80
1988—New York	National	2	6	1	0	1.000	6	2	2	3	3	3.00
1989—Tidewater	Int'national	12	87⅓	7	4	.636	60	31	23	69	29	2.37
1989—New York†	National	11	24⅓	0	2	.000	25	20	20	19	14	7.40
1989—Minnesota	American	10	39⅓	3	2	.600	48	29	28	31	19	6.41
1990—Minnesota‡	American	29	146⅓	7	9	.438	142	88	83	92	78	5.10
National League Totals—2 Years		13	30⅓	1	2	.333	31	22	22	22	17	6.53
American League Totals—2 Years		39	185⅔	10	11	.476	190	117	111	123	97	5.38
Major League Totals—3 Years		52	216	11	13	.458	221	139	133	145	114	5.54

Selected by New York Mets' organization in 4th round of free-agent draft, June 6, 1983.
†Traded with Pitcher Rick Aguilera and three players to be named later to Minnesota Twins for Pitcher Frank Viola, July 31, 1989; Portland (Minnesota Twins' organization) acquired Pitchers Kevin Tapani and Tim Drummond on August 1, 1989, and Minnesota acquired Pitcher Jack Savage to complete deal, October 16, 1989.
‡On disabled list, September 7, 1990 through remainder of season.

MICHAEL LEE WESTON
(Mickey)

Born March 26, 1961, at Flint, Mich.
Height. 6.01. Weight, 187.
Throws and bats righthanded.
Attended Eastern Michigan University, Ypsilanti, Mich.

Major League saves: 1989 (1).

Year	Club	League	G.	IP.	W.	L.	Pct.	H.	R.	ER.	SO.	BB.	ERA.
1982—Little Falls	NYP	17	92⅓	7	6	.538	105	63	52	67	22	5.07
1983—Columbia	S. Atlantic	37	74⅔	2	2	.500	87	48	36	46	22	4.34
1984—Columbia	S. Atlantic	32	63⅔	6	5	.545	58	27	13	40	27	1.84
1985—Lynchburg	Carolina	49	100⅓	6	5	.545	81	29	24	62	22	2.15
1986—Jackson†	Texas	34	70⅔	4	4	.500	73	40	34	36	27	4.33
1987—Jackson	Texas	58	82	8	4	.667	96	39	31	50	18	3.40
1988—Jackson	Texas	30	125⅓	8	5	.615	127	50	31	61	20	★2.23
1988—Tidewater‡	Int'national	4	29⅔	2	1	.667	21	6	5	16	5	1.52
1989—Rochester	Int'national	23	112	8	3	.727	103	30	26	51	19	2.09
1989—Baltimore§	American	7	13	1	0	1.000	18	8	8	7	2	5.54
1990—Rochester	Int'national	29	109⅓	11	1	★.917	93	36	24	58	22	1.98
1990—Baltimore x	American	9	21	0	1	.000	28	20	18	9	6	7.71
Major League Totals—2 Years		16	34	1	1	.500	46	28	26	16	8	6.88

Selected by New York Mets' organization in 12th round of free-agent draft, June 7, 1982.

†On disabled list, April 8 to April 18 and May 23 to June 25, 1986.

‡Granted free agency, October 15, 1988; signed by Rochester (Baltimore Orioles' organization.), November 28, 1988.

§On disabled list, June 23 to August 22, 1989; included rehabilitation disability assignment to Rochester, August 2 to August 21, 1989.

xTraded to Toronto Blue Jays for Pitcher Paul Kilgus, December 14, 1990.

JOHN KARL WETTELAND

Born August 21, 1966, at San Mateo, Calif.
Height, 6.02. Weight, 195.
Throws and bats righthanded.
Attended College of San Mateo, San Mateo, Calif.

Major League saves: 1989 (1).
Led Texas League in wild pitches with 22 in 1988.
Tied for Florida State League lead in home runs allowed with 11 and wild pitches with 17 in 1987.

Year	Club	League	G.	IP.	W.	L.	Pct.	H.	R.	ER.	SO.	BB.	ERA.
1985—Great Falls	Pioneer	11	20⅔	1	1	.500	17	10	9	23	15	3.92
1986—Bakersfield	California	15	67	0	7	.000	71	50	43	38	46	5.78
1986—Great Falls	Pioneer	12	69⅓	4	3	.571	70	51	42	59	40	5.45
1987—Vero Beach†	Florida St.	27	175⅔	12	7	.632	150	81	61	144	92	3.13
1988—San Antonio	Texas	25	162⅓	10	8	.556	141	74	70	140	●77	3.88
1989—Albuquerque	P. Coast	10	69	5	3	.625	61	28	28	73	20	3.65
1989—Los Angeles	National	31	102⅔	5	8	.385	81	46	43	96	34	3.77
1990—Los Angeles	National	22	43	2	4	.333	44	28	23	36	17	4.81
1990—Albuquerque	P. Coast	8	29	2	2	.500	27	19	18	26	13	5.59
Major League Totals—2 Years		53	145⅔	7	12	.368	125	74	66	132	51	4.08

Selected by New York Mets' organization in 12th round of free-agent draft, June 4, 1984.

Selected by Los Angeles Dodgers' organization in secondary phase of free-agent draft, January 9, 1985.

†Drafted by Detroit Tigers, December 7, 1987; returned, March 29, 1988.

LOUIS RODMAN WHITAKER
(Lou)

Born May 12, 1957, at Brooklyn, N.Y.
Height, 5.11. Weight, 180.
Throws right and bats lefthanded.

Major League stolen bases: 1977 (2), 1978 (7), 1979 (20), 1980 (8), 1981 (5), 1982 (11), 1983 (17), 1984 (6), 1985 (6), 1986 (13), 1987 (13), 1988 (2), 1989 (6), 1990 (8). Total—124.

Led American League second basemen in total chances with 811 and double plays with 120 in 1982.

Led Florida State League second basemen in double plays with 30 in 1976.

Named second baseman on THE SPORTING NEWS American League All-Star Team, 1983 and 1984.

Named second baseman on THE SPORTING NEWS American League All-Star fielding team, 1983 through 1985.

Named second baseman on THE SPORTING NEWS American League Silver Slugger team, 1983 through 1985 and 1987.

Named American League Rookie of the Year by Baseball Writers' Association of America, 1978.

Named Florida State League Most Valuable Player, 1976.

Year	Club	League	Pos.	G.	AB.	R.	H.	2B.	3B.	HR.	RBI.	B.A.	PO.	A.	E.	F.A.
1975—Bristol	Appal.	3B-SS	42	114	17	27	6	1	1	17	.237	38	82	16	.882
1976—Lakeland	Fla. St.	3B	124	343	★70	129	12	5	1	62	.297	★99	★267	★30	★.924
1977—Montgomery†	South.	2B	107	396	★81	111	13	4	3	48	.280	208	285	15	.970
1977—Detroit	Amer.	2B	11	32	5	8	1	0	0	2	.250	17	18	0	1.000
1978—Detroit	Amer.	2B	139	484	71	138	12	7	3	58	.285	301	458	17	.978
1979—Detroit‡	Amer.	2B	127	423	75	121	14	8	3	42	.286	280	369	9	.986
1980—Detroit	Amer.	2B	145	477	68	111	19	1	1	45	.233	340	428	12	.985
1981—Detroit	Amer.	2B	●109	335	48	88	14	4	5	36	.263	227	★354	9	.985
1982—Detroit	Amer.	2B	152	560	76	160	22	8	15	65	.286	331	★470	10	★.988

— 514 —

Year	Club	League	Pos.	G.	AB.	R.	H.	2B.	3B.	HR.	RBI.	B.A.	PO.	A.	E.	F.A.
1983—Detroit	Amer.	2B	161	643	94	206	40	6	12	72	.320	299	447	13	.983
1984—Detroit	Amer.	2B	143	558	90	161	25	1	13	56	.289	290	405	15	.979
1985—Detroit	Amer.	2B	152	609	102	170	29	8	21	73	.279	314	414	11	.985
1986—Detroit	Amer.	2B	144	584	95	157	26	6	20	73	.269	276	421	11	.984
1987—Detroit	Amer.	2B	149	604	110	160	38	6	16	59	.265	275	416	17	.976
1988—Detroit	Amer.	2B	115	403	54	111	18	2	12	55	.275	218	284	8	.984
1989—Detroit	Amer.	2B	148	509	77	128	21	1	28	85	.251	★327	393	11	.985
1990—Detroit	Amer.	2B	132	472	75	112	22	2	18	60	.237	286	372	6	.991
Major League Totals—14 Years			1827	6693	1040	1831	301	60	167	781	.274	3581	5249	149	.983

Selected by Detroit Tigers' organization in 5th round of free-agent draft, June 4, 1975.
†On disabled list, May 3 to May 14, 1977.
‡On disabled list, June 13 to June 28, 1979.

CHAMPIONSHIP SERIES RECORD

Shares Championship Series record for most bases on balls, series (7), 1987.

Year	Club	League	Pos.	G.	AB.	R.	H.	2B.	3B.	HR.	RBI.	B.A.	PO.	A.	E.	F.A.
1984—Detroit	Amer.	2B	3	14	3	2	0	0	0	0	.143	5	6	0	1.000
1987—Detroit	Amer.	2B	5	17	4	3	0	0	1	1	.176	11	14	0	1.000
Championship Series Totals—2 Years			8	31	7	5	0	0	1	1	.161	16	20	0	1.000

WORLD SERIES RECORD

Year	Club	League	Pos.	G.	AB.	R.	H.	2B.	3B.	HR.	RBI.	B.A.	PO.	A.	E.	F.A.
1984—Detroit	Amer.	2B	5	18	6	5	2	0	0	0	.278	15	18	0	1.000

ALL-STAR GAME RECORD

Year	League	Pos.	AB.	R.	H.	2B.	3B.	HR.	RBI.	B.A.	PO.	A.	E.	F.A.
1983—American	PH-2B	1	1	1	0	1	0	2	1.000	1	0	0	1.000
1984—American	2B	3	0	2	1	0	0	0	.667	0	5	0	1.000
1985—American	2B	2	0	0	0	0	0	0	.000	1	1	0	1.000
1986—American	2B	2	1	1	0	0	1	2	.500	0	3	0	1.000
All-Star Game Totals—4 Years		8	2	4	1	1	1	4	.500	2	9	0	1.000

Named to American League All-Star Team for 1987 game; replaced due to injury by Harold Reynolds.

DEVON MARKES WHITE

First name pronounced De-VON.

Born December 29, 1962, at Kingston, Jamaica.
Height, 6.02. Weight, 182.
Throws right and bats left and righthanded.

Shares major league record for most stolen bases, inning (3), September 9, 1989, sixth inning.
Major League stolen bases: 1985 (3), 1986 (6), 1987 (32), 1988 (17), 1989 (44), 1990 (21). Total—123.
Switch-hit home runs in game, June 23, 1987 and June 29, 1990.
Led American League outfielders in total chances with 449 in 1987.
Led Pacific Coast League in stolen bases with 42 in 1986.
Led Pacific Coast League outfielders in total chances with 339 in 1986.
Led California League outfielders in total chances with 351 in 1984.
Led Midwest League outfielders in total chances with 286 in 1983.
Named outfielder on THE SPORTING NEWS American League All-Star fielding team, 1988 and 1989.

Year	Club	League	Pos.	G.	AB.	R.	H.	2B.	3B.	HR.	RBI.	B.A.	PO.	A.	E.	F.A.
1981—Idaho Falls	Pion.	OF-3B-1B	30	106	10	19	2	0	0	10	.179	33	10	3	.935
1982—Danville†	Midw.	OF	57	186	21	40	6	1	1	11	.215	89	3	8	.920
1983—Peoria	Midw.	OF	117	430	69	109	17	6	13	66	.253	267	8	11	.962
1983—Nashua	East.	OF	17	70	11	18	7	2	0	2	.257	37	0	3	.925
1984—Redwood	Calif.	OF	138	520	101	147	25	5	7	55	.283	★322	16	13	.963
1985—Midland	Texas	OF	70	260	52	77	10	4	4	35	.296	176	10	4	.979
1985—Edmonton	P. C.	OF	66	277	53	70	16	5	4	39	.253	205	6	2	.991
1985—California	Amer.	OF	21	7	7	1	0	0	0	0	.143	10	1	0	1.000
1986—Edmonton‡	P. C.	OF	112	461	84	134	25	10	14	60	.291	317	●16	6	.982
1986—California	Amer.	OF	29	51	8	12	1	1	1	3	.235	49	0	2	.961
1987—California	Amer.	OF	159	639	103	168	33	5	24	87	.263	★424	16	9	.980
1988—California§	Amer.	OF	122	455	76	118	22	2	11	51	.259	364	7	9	.976
1989—California	Amer.	OF	156	636	86	156	18	13	12	56	.245	430	10	5	.989
1990—California x	Amer.	OF	125	443	57	96	17	3	11	44	.217	302	11	9	.972
1990—Edmonton x	P. C.	OF	14	55	9	20	4	4	0	6	.364	31	1	3	.914
Major League Totals—6 Years			612	2231	337	551	91	24	59	241	.247	1579	45	34	.979

Selected by California Angels' organization in 6th round of free-agent draft, June 8, 1981.
†On suspended list, June 11 to June 12 and July 19, 1982 through remainder of season.
‡On disabled list, May 12 to May 22, 1986.
§On disabled list, May 7 to June 10, 1988.
xTraded with Pitcher Willie Fraser and a player to be named later to Toronto Blue Jays for Outfielder Junior Felix, Infielder Luis Sojo and a player to be named later, December 2, 1990; Toronto acquired Pitcher Marcus Moore and California Angels acquired Catcher Ken Rivers to complete deal, December 4, 1990.

CHAMPIONSHIP SERIES RECORD

Year	Club	League	Pos.	G.	AB.	R.	H.	2B.	3B.	HR.	RBI.	B.A.	PO.	A.	E.	F.A.
1986—California	Amer.	OF-PR	4	2	2	1	0	0	0	0	.500	3	0	0	1.000

Year	League	Pos.	AB.	R.	H.	2B.	3B.	HR.	RBI.	B.A.	PO.	A.	E.	F.A.
1989—American		OF	1	0	0	0	0	0	0	.000	0	0	0	.000

FRANK WHITE JR.

Born September 4, 1950, at Greenville, Miss.
Height, 5.11. Weight, 190.
Throws and bats righthanded.
Attended Manatee Junior College, Bradenton, Fla., and
Longview Community College, Lee's Summit, Mo.

Hit for the cycle, September 26, 1979 and August 3, 1982.
Major League stolen bases: 1973 (3), 1974 (3), 1975 (11), 1976 (20), 1977 (23), 1978 (13), 1979 (28), 1980 (19), 1981 (4), 1982 (10), 1983 (13), 1984 (5), 1985 (10), 1986 (4), 1987 (1), 1988 (7), 1989 (3), 1990 (1). Total—178.
Led American League second basemen in total chances with 849 in 1985.
Led Gulf Coast League in stolen bases with 18 in 1971.
Led Gulf Coast League shortstops in double plays with 27 in 1971.
Named second baseman on THE SPORTING NEWS American League All-Star Team, 1978.
Named second baseman on THE SPORTING NEWS American League All-Star fielding team, 1977 through 1982, 1986 and 1987.
Named second baseman on THE SPORTING NEWS American League Silver Slugger team, 1986.

Year	Club	League	Pos.	G.	AB.	R.	H.	2B.	3B.	HR.	RBI.	B.A.	PO.	A.	E.	F.A.
1971—Sarasota Royals...	Gulf C.		SS	50	158	31	39	6	3	1	21	.247	70	★149	17	★.928
1972—San Jose	Calif.		SS	49	187	44	55	7	2	10	26	.294	77	138	14	.939
1972—Jacksonville	South.		SS	91	333	34	84	12	2	2	23	.252	124	306	31	.933
1973—Omaha	A. A.		2B-SS	86	348	49	92	19	2	4	32	.264	163	221	21	.948
1973—Kansas City	Amer.		SS-2B	51	139	20	31	6	1	0	5	.223	71	121	12	.941
1974—Kansas City	Amer.		2B-SS-3B	99	204	19	45	6	3	1	18	.221	119	189	12	.963
1975—Kansas City	Amer.		2-S-3-C	111	304	43	76	10	2	7	36	.250	182	275	12	.974
1976—Kansas City	Amer.		2B-SS	152	446	39	102	17	6	2	46	.229	296	479	23	.971
1977—Kansas City	Amer.		★2B-SS	152	474	59	116	21	5	5	20	.245	310	437	8	★.989
1978—Kansas City	Amer.		2B	143	461	66	127	24	6	7	50	.275	325	385	16	.978
1979—Kansas City†	Amer.		2B	127	467	73	124	26	4	10	48	.266	317	332	12	.982
1980—Kansas City	Amer.		2B	154	560	70	148	23	4	7	60	.264	395	448	10	.988
1981—Kansas City	Amer.		2B	94	364	35	91	17	1	9	38	.250	226	263	6	.988
1982—Kansas City	Amer.		2B	145	524	71	156	45	6	11	56	.298	★361	389	★17	.978
1983—Kansas City	Amer.		2B	146	549	52	143	35	6	11	77	.260	★390	442	8	★.990
1984—Kansas City‡	Amer.		2B	129	479	58	130	22	5	17	56	.271	299	425	11	.985
1985—Kansas City	Amer.		2B	149	563	62	140	25	1	22	69	.249	342	★490	★17	.980
1986—Kansas City	Amer.		2B-SS-3B	151	566	76	154	37	3	22	84	.272	317	441	10	.987
1987—Kansas City	Amer.		2B	154	563	67	138	32	2	17	78	.245	320	458	10	.987
1988—Kansas City	Amer.		2B	150	537	48	126	25	1	8	58	.235	293	426	4	★.994
1989—Kansas City§	Amer.		2B-OF	135	418	34	107	22	1	2	36	.256	238	407	10	.985
1990—Kansas City xy	Amer.		2B-OF	82	241	20	52	14	1	2	21	.216	142	218	8	.978
Major League Totals—18 Years				2324	7859	912	2006	407	58	160	886	.255	4943	6625	206	.983

Signed as free agent by Kansas City Royals' organization, July 2, 1970.
†On disabled list, May 9 to June 11, 1979.
‡On disabled list, July 6 to July 21, 1984.
§Granted free agency, November 13, 1989; re-signed by Royals, December 7, 1989.
xOn disabled list, April 27 to May 14, 1990.
yGranted free agency, November 5, 1990.

DIVISION SERIES RECORD

Year	Club	League	Pos.	G.	AB.	R.	H.	2B.	3B.	HR.	RBI.	B.A.	PO.	A.	E.	F.A.
1981—Kansas City	Amer.		2B	3	11	1	2	0	0	0	0	.182	5	6	1	.917

CHAMPIONSHIP SERIES RECORD

Year	Club	League	Pos.	G.	AB.	R.	H.	2B.	3B.	HR.	RBI.	B.A.	PO.	A.	E.	F.A.
1976—Kansas City	Amer.		2B-PR	4	8	2	1	0	0	0	0	.125	6	11	0	1.000
1977—Kansas City	Amer.		2B	5	18	1	5	1	0	0	2	.278	13	16	0	1.000
1978—Kansas City	Amer.		2B	4	13	1	3	0	0	0	2	.231	9	12	0	1.000
1980—Kansas City	Amer.		2B	3	11	3	6	1	0	1	3	.545	9	10	1	.950
1984—Kansas City	Amer.		2B	3	11	1	1	0	0	0	0	.091	7	3	0	1.000
1985—Kansas City	Amer.		2B	7	25	1	5	0	0	0	3	.200	9	28	0	1.000
Championship Series Totals—6 Years				26	86	9	21	2	0	1	10	.244	53	80	1	.993

WORLD SERIES RECORD

Year	Club	League	Pos.	G.	AB.	R.	H.	2B.	3B.	HR.	RBI.	B.A.	PO.	A.	E.	F.A.
1980—Kansas City	Amer.		2B	6	25	0	2	0	0	0	0	.080	13	21	2	.944
1985—Kansas City	Amer.		2B	7	28	4	7	3	0	1	6	.250	10	20	0	1.000
World Series Totals—2 Years				13	53	4	9	3	0	1	6	.170	23	41	2	.970

ALL-STAR GAME RECORD

Year	League	Pos.	AB.	R.	H.	2B.	3B.	HR.	RBI.	B.A.	PO.	A.	E.	F.A.
1978—American		2B	1	0	0	0	0	0	0	.000	1	2	0	1.000
1979—American		2B	2	0	0	0	0	0	0	.000	2	2	0	1.000
1981—American		PR-2B	1	0	0	0	0	0	0	.000	1	0	0	1.000
1982—American		2B	1	0	0	0	0	0	0	.000	2	1	0	1.000
1986—American		PH-2B	2	1	1	0	0	1	1	.500	1	1	0	1.000
All-Star Game Totals—5 Years			7	1	1	0	0	1	1	.143	7	6	0	1.000

WALTER RICHARD WHITEHURST
(Wally)

Born April 11, 1964, at Shreveport, La.
Height, 6.03. Weight, 185.
Throws and bats righthanded.
Attended University of New Orleans, New Orleans, La.

Major League saves: 1990 (2).
Tied for Southern League lead in shutouts with 3 in 1987.
Tied for Midwest League lead in shutouts with 4 in 1986.
Tied for Northwest League lead in hit batsmen with 7 and balks with 2 in 1985.

Year Club	League	G.	IP.	W.	L.	Pct.	H.	R.	ER.	SO.	BB.	ERA.
1985—Medford	Northwest	14	88	7	5	.583	92	51	35	●91	29	3.58
1985—Modesto	California	2	10	1	0	1.000	10	3	2	5	5	1.80
1986—Madison	Midwest	8	61	6	1	.857	42	8	4	57	16	0.59
1986—Huntsville	Southern	19	104⅔	9	5	.643	114	66	54	54	46	4.64
1987—Huntsville†	Southern	28	183⅓	11	10	.524	192	104	81	106	42	3.98
1988—Tidewater	Int'national	26	165	10	11	.476	145	65	56	113	32	3.05
1989—Tidewater	Int'national	21	133	8	7	.533	123	54	48	95	32	3.25
1989—New York	National	9	14	0	1	.000	17	7	7	9	5	4.50
1990—New York	National	38	65⅔	1	0	1.000	63	27	24	46	9	3.29
1990—Tidewater	Int'national	2	9	1	0	1.000	7	2	2	10	1	2.00
Major League Totals—2 Years		47	79⅔	1	1	.500	80	34	31	55	14	3.50

Selected by Oakland A's organization in 3rd round of free-agent draft, June 3, 1985.

†As part of an eight-player, three-team deal, New York Mets traded Pitcher Jesse Orosco to Oakland Athletics, December 11, 1987. Oakland then traded Orosco along with Shortstop Alfredo Griffin and Pitcher Jay Howell to Los Angeles Dodgers for Pitchers Bob Welch, Matt Young and Jack Savage. Oakland then traded Savage along with Pitchers Wally Whitehurst and Kevin Tapani to New York.

MARK ANTHONY WHITEN

Name pronounced WHITT-en.

Born November 25, 1966, at Pensacola, Fla.
Height, 6.03. Weight, 215.
Throws right and bats left and righthanded.
Attended Pensacola Junior College, Pensacola, Fla.

Major League stolen bases: 1990 (2).
Led Southern League in being hit by pitch with 11 in 1989.
Led South Atlantic League in being hit by pitch with 16 and tied for lead in intentional bases on balls received with 10 in 1987.
Tied for Pioneer League lead in being hit by pitch with 6 in 1986.
Led South Atlantic League outfielders in total chances with 322 and tied for lead in double plays by outfielders with 4 in 1987.

Year Club	League	Pos.	G.	AB.	R.	H.	2B.	3B.	HR.	RBI.	B.A.	PO.	A.	E.	F.A.
1986—Medicine Hat	Pion.	OF	●70	270	53	81	16	3	10	44	.300	111	9	★10	.923
1987—Myrtle Beach†	S. Atl.	OF	★139	494	90	125	22	5	15	64	.253	★292	★18	12	.963
1988—Dunedin†	Fla. St.	OF	99	385	61	97	8	5	7	37	.252	200	★21	9	.961
1988—Knoxville†	South.	OF	28	108	20	28	3	1	2	9	.259	62	3	4	.942
1989—Knoxville†	South.	OF	129	423	75	109	13	6	12	47	.258	223	17	8	.968
1990—Syracuse	Int.	OF	104	390	65	113	19	4	14	48	.290	158	14	6	.966
1990—Toronto	Amer.	OF	33	88	12	24	1	1	2	7	.273	60	3	0	1.000
Major League Totals—1 Year			33	88	12	24	1	1	2	7	.273	60	3	0	1.000

Selected by Toronto Blue Jays' organization in 5th round of free-agent draft, January 14, 1986.
†Batted righthanded only.

EDDIE LEE WHITSON
(Ed)

Born May 19, 1955, at Johnson City, Tenn.
Height, 6.03. Weight, 202.
Throws and bats righthanded.

Major League saves: 1978 (4), 1979 (1), 1982 (2), 1983 (1). Total—8.
Led National League in home runs allowed with 36 in 1987.
Led Carolina League in complete games with 16 in 1976.
Led Western Carolinas League in hit batsmen with 15 in 1975.

Year Club	League	G.	IP.	W.	L.	Pct.	H.	R.	ER.	SO.	BB.	ERA.
1974—Bradenton Pirates	Gulf Coast	8	44	1	4	.200	45	28	21	25	15	4.30
1975—Charleston	W. Carol.	24	142	8	★15	.348	140	★96	★80	120	99	5.07
1976—Salem	Carolina	26	★203	●15	9	.625	168	75	57	★186	65	2.53
1977—Columbus	Int'national	26	175	8	13	.381	175	74	65	120	68	3.34
1977—Pittsburgh	National	5	16	1	0	1.000	11	6	6	10	9	3.38
1978—Columbus	Int'national	7	51	2	2	.500	56	25	21	55	10	3.71
1978—Pittsburgh	National	43	74	5	6	.455	66	31	27	64	37	3.28
1979—Pittsburgh†-San Francisco	National	37	158	7	11	.389	151	83	72	93	75	4.10
1980—San Francisco	National	34	212	11	13	.458	222	88	73	90	56	3.10
1981—San Francisco‡	National	22	123	6	9	.400	130	61	55	65	47	4.02
1982—Cleveland§	American	40	107⅔	4	2	.667	91	43	39	61	58	3.26
1983—San Diego x	National	31	144⅓	5	7	.417	143	73	69	81	50	4.30
1983—Las Vegas	P. Coast	3	12	1	0	1.000	15	9	9	11	5	6.75

Year Club	League	G.	IP.	W.	L.	Pct.	H.	R.	ER.	SO.	BB.	ERA.
1984—San Diego y	National	31	189	14	8	.636	181	72	68	103	42	3.24
1985—New York	American	30	158⅔	10	8	.556	201	100	86	89	43	4.88
1986—New York za	American	14	37	5	2	.714	54	37	31	27	23	7.54
1986—San Diego	National	17	75⅓	1	7	.125	85	48	47	46	37	5.59
1987—San Diego	National	36	205⅔	10	13	.435	197	113	108	135	64	4.73
1988—San Diego	National	34	205⅓	13	11	.542	202	93	86	118	45	3.77
1989—San Diego	National	33	227	16	11	.593	198	77	67	117	48	2.66
1990—San Diego	National	32	228⅔	14	9	.609	215	73	66	127	47	2.60
National League Totals—12 Years		355	1858⅔	103	105	.495	1801	818	744	1049	557	3.60
American League Totals—3 Years		84	303⅓	19	12	.613	346	180	156	177	124	4.63
Major League Totals—14 Years		439	2162	122	117	'.510	2147	998	900	1226	681	3.75

Selected by Pittsburgh Pirates' organization in 6th round of free-agent draft, June 5, 1974.

†Traded with Pitchers Fred Breining and Al Holland to San Francisco Giants for Infielders Bill Madlock and Lenny Randle and Pitcher Dave Roberts, June 28, 1979.

‡Traded to Cleveland Indians for Second Baseman Duane Kuiper, November 16, 1981.

§Traded to San Diego Padres for Pitcher Juan Eichelberger and First Baseman-Outfielder Broderick Perkins, November 18, 1982.

xOn disabled list, April 18 to May 28, 1983; included rehabilitation disability assignment to Las Vegas, May 10 to May 28, 1983.

yGranted free agency, November 8, 1984; signed by New York Yankees, December 27, 1984.

zOn disabled list, April 30 to May 21, 1986.

aTraded to San Diego Padres for Pitcher Tim Stoddard, July 9, 1986.

CHAMPIONSHIP SERIES RECORD

Year Club	League	G.	IP.	W.	L.	Pct.	H.	R.	ER.	SO.	BB.	ERA.
1984—San Diego	National	1	8	1	0	1.000	5	1	1	6	2	1.13

WORLD SERIES RECORD

Year Club	League	G.	IP.	W.	L.	Pct.	H.	R.	ER.	SO.	BB.	ERA.
1984—San Diego	National	1	⅔	0	0	.000	5	3	3	0	0	40.50

ALL-STAR GAME RECORD

Member of National League All-Star Team in 1980; did not play.

LEO ERNEST WHITT
(Ernie)

Born June 13, 1952, Detroit, Mich.
Height, 6.02. Weight, 205.
Throws right and bats lefthanded.
Attended Macomb County Community College, Warren, Mich.

Major League stolen bases: 1980 (1), 1981 (5), 1982 (3), 1983 (1), 1985 (3), 1988 (4), 1989 (5). Total—22.
Hit three home runs in a game, September 14, 1987.
Led American League catchers in total chances with 863 in 1987.
Led International League in passed balls with 16 in 1978.
Led Eastern League catchers in fielding percentage with .992 in 1974.
Tied for Carolina League lead in double plays by catchers with 7 in 1973.
Named catcher on THE SPORTING NEWS American League All-Star Team, 1988.

Year Club	League	Pos.	G.	AB.	R.	H.	2B.	3B.	HR.	RBI.	B.A.	PO.	A.	E.	F.A.
1972—Williamsport	NYP	1B	1	4	1	2	1	0	0	0	.500	8	1	0	1.000
1972—Winter Haven	Fla. St.	C-1B-OF	31	82	3	15	1	1	0	7	.183	151	14	5	.971
1973—Winston-Salem	Carol.	C-OF-1B	130	424	63	123	23	3	1	50	.290	686	70	15	.980
1974—Bristol	East.	C-OF-1B	111	385	55	96	10	1	9	56	.249	557	50	6	.990
1975—Bristol†	East.	C-OF	82	252	29	64	9	1	2	19	.254	357	36	7	.982
1976—Bristol	East.	C	26	87	12	19	2	3	1	10	.218	127	25	1	.993
1976—Rhode Island	Int.	C-1-O-3	90	304	33	81	16	2	7	42	.266	487	59	9	.984
1976—Boston‡	Amer.	C	8	18	4	4	2	0	1	3	.222	24	0	0	1.000
1977—Charleston	Int.	C-3B	29	94	12	24	6	0	0	7	.255	129	28	7	.957
1977—Toronto§	Amer.	C	23	41	4	7	3	0	0	6	.171	62	4	0	1.000
1978—Syracuse	Int.	C-1B-OF	121	399	50	98	16	3	12	53	.246	673	79	7	.991
1978—Toronto	Amer.	C	2	4	0	0	0	0	0	0	.000	7	1	0	1.000
1979—Syracuse	Int.	*C-OF-3B	114	382	32	95	18	4	7	43	.249	494	69	3	*.995
1980—Toronto	Amer.	C	106	295	23	70	12	2	6	34	.237	436	56	7	.986
1981—Toronto	Amer.	C	74	195	16	46	9	0	1	16	.236	297	46	3	.991
1982—Toronto	Amer.	C	105	284	28	74	14	2	11	42	.261	406	30	8	.982
1983—Toronto	Amer.	C	123	344	53	88	15	2	17	56	.256	554	50	5	.992
1984—Toronto x	Amer.	C	124	315	35	75	12	1	15	46	.238	583	40	4	.994
1985—Toronto	Amer.	C	139	412	55	101	21	2	19	64	.245	649	38	8	.988
1986—Toronto yz	Amer.	C	131	395	48	106	19	2	16	56	.268	709	41	7	.991
1987—Toronto	Amer.	C	135	446	57	120	24	1	19	75	.269	*803	55	5	.994
1988—Toronto	Amer.	C	127	398	63	100	11	2	16	70	.251	643	43	4	.994
1989—Toronto a	Amer.	C	129	385	42	101	24	1	11	53	.262	550	43	5	.992
1990—Atlanta b	Nat.	C	67	180	14	31	8	0	2	10	.172	296	42	3	.991
1990—Greenville c	South.	C	4	12	1	4	1	0	0	0	.333	14	1	0	1.000
American League Totals—13 Years			1226	3532	428	892	166	15	132	521	.253	5723	447	56	.991
National League Totals—1 Year			67	180	14	31	8	0	2	10	.172	296	42	3	.991
Major League Totals—14 Years			1293	3712	442	923	174	15	134	531	.249	6019	489	59	.991

Selected by Boston Red Sox' organization in 15th round of free-agent draft, June 6, 1972.

†On disabled list, April 11 to June 13, 1975.
‡Selected by Toronto Blue Jays in American League expansion draft, November 5, 1976.
§On disabled list, August 17 to September 27, 1977.
xOn disabled list, June 16 to July 1, 1984.
yOn disabled list, April 15 to April 30, 1986; included rehabilitation disability assignment to Syracuse, April 28 to April 30, 1986.
zGranted free agency, November 12, 1986; re-signed by Blue Jays, January 8, 1987.
aTraded with Outfielder Kevin Batiste to Atlanta Braves for Pitcher Rick Trlicek, December 17, 1989.
bOn disabled list, June 3 to July 30, 1990; included rehabilitation disability assignment to Greenville, July 24 to July 29, 1990.
cReleased, October 15, 1990.

CHAMPIONSHIP SERIES RECORD

Year	Club	League	Pos.	G.	AB.	R.	H.	2B.	3B.	HR.	RBI.	B.A.	PO.	A.	E.	F.A.
1985—Toronto		Amer.	C	7	21	1	4	1	0	0	2	.190	50	3	0	1.000
1989—Toronto		Amer.	C	5	16	1	2	0	0	1	3	.125	32	2	0	1.000
Championship Series Totals—2 Years				12	37	2	6	1	0	1	5	.162	82	5	0	1.000

ALL-STAR GAME RECORD

Year	League	Pos.	AB.	R.	H.	2B.	3B.	HR.	RBI.	B.A.	PO.	A.	E.	F.A.
1985—American		C	0	0	0	0	0	0	0	.000	2	0	0	1.000

KEVIN DEAN WICKANDER

Born January 4, 1965, at Fort Dodge, Ia.
Height, 6.02. Weight, 200.
Throws and bats lefthanded.
Attended Grand Canyon College, Phoenix, Ariz.

Year	Club	League	G.	IP.	W.	L.	Pct.	H.	R.	ER.	SO.	BB.	ERA.
1986—Batavia		NYP	11	46⅓	3	4	.429	30	19	14	63	27	2.72
1987—Kinston		Carolina	25	147⅓	9	6	.600	128	69	56	118	75	3.42
1988—Williamsport		Eastern	24	28⅔	1	0	1.000	14	3	2	33	9	0.63
1988—Colorado Springs		P. Coast	19	32⅔	0	2	.000	44	30	26	22	27	7.16
1989—Colorado Springs		P. Coast	45	42⅔	1	3	.250	40	14	14	41	27	2.95
1989—Cleveland		American	2	2⅔	0	0	.000	6	1	1	0	2	3.38
1990—Cleveland†		American	10	12⅓	0	1	.000	14	6	5	10	4	3.65
Major League Totals—2 Years			12	15	0	1	.000	20	7	6	10	6	3.60

Selected by Cleveland Indians' organization in 2nd round of free-agent draft, June 2, 1986.
†On disabled list, May 31, 1990 through remainder of season.

CURTIS VERNON WILKERSON
(Curt)

Born April 26, 1961, at Petersburg, Va.
Height, 5.09. Weight, 173.
Throws right and bats left and righthanded.

Major League stolen bases: 1983 (3), 1984 (12), 1985 (14), 1986 (9), 1987 (6), 1988 (9), 1989 (4), 1990 (2). Total—59.
Tied for Texas League lead in sacrifice hits with 11 in 1982.

Year	Club	League	Pos.	G.	AB.	R.	H.	2B.	3B.	HR.	RBI.	B.A.	PO.	A.	E.	F.A.
1980—Sarasota Rangers	Gulf C.		SS-2B	37	105	15	20	2	0	0	8	.190	38	86	17	.879
1981—Asheville		S. Atl.	SS-2B	106	333	45	68	7	3	0	19	.204	188	372	28	.952
1982—Burlington		Midw.	SS-2B	56	198	18	50	6	0	0	13	.253	78	159	16	.937
1982—Tulsa		Texas	SS	72	266	32	71	6	3	2	14	.267	102	225	18	.948
1983—Oklahoma City†	A. A.		SS	89	343	51	107	19	4	3	31	.312	135	272	19	.955
1983—Texas		Amer.	SS-2B-3B	16	35	7	6	0	1	0	1	.171	18	31	1	.980
1984—Texas		Amer.	SS-2B	153	484	47	120	12	0	1	26	.248	227	391	30	.954
1985—Texas		Amer.	SS-2B	129	360	35	88	11	6	0	22	.244	165	328	21	.959
1986—Texas		Amer.	2B-SS	110	236	27	56	10	3	0	15	.237	125	199	13	.961
1987—Texas		Amer.	SS-2B-3B	85	138	28	37	5	3	2	14	.268	79	98	6	.967
1988—Texas‡		Amer.	2B-SS-3B	117	338	41	99	12	5	0	28	.293	186	299	15	.970
1989—Chicago		Nat.	3-2-S-O	77	160	18	39	4	2	1	10	.244	42	91	8	.943
1990—Chicago§		Nat.	3-2-S-O	77	186	21	41	5	1	0	16	.220	49	93	14	.910
American League Totals—6 Years				610	1591	185	406	50	18	3	106	.255	800	1346	86	.961
National League Totals—2 Years				154	346	39	80	9	3	1	26	.231	91	184	22	.926
Major League Totals—8 Years				764	1937	224	486	59	21	4	132	.251	891	1530	108	.957

Selected by Texas Rangers' organization in 4th round of free-agent draft, June 3, 1980.
†On disabled list, May 19 to June 21, 1983.
‡Traded with Pitchers Mitch Williams, Paul Kilgus and Steve Wilson, Infielder Luis Benitez and Outfielder Pablo Delgado to Chicago Cubs for Outfielder Rafael Palmeiro and Pitchers Jamie Moyer and Drew Hall, December 5, 1988.
§Granted free agency, November 5, 1990; signed by Pittsburgh Pirates, January 9, 1991.

CHAMPIONSHIP SERIES RECORD

Year	Club	League	Pos.	G.	AB.	R.	H.	2B.	3B.	HR.	RBI.	B.A.	PO.	A.	E.	F.A.
1989—Chicago		Nat.	PR-3B-PH	3	2	1	1	0	0	0	0	.500	0	0	0	.000

DEAN ALLAN WILKINS

Born August 24, 1966, at Chicago, Ill.
Height, 6.01. Weight, 170.
Throws and bats righthanded.
Attended San Diego Mesa College, San Diego, Calif.

Major League saves: 1990 (1).
Led Eastern League in saves with 26 and games finished in relief with 49 in 1988.

Year Club	League	G.	IP.	W.	L.	Pct.	H.	R.	ER.	SO.	BB.	ERA.
1986—Oneonta	NYP	15	83⅓	9	0	*1.000	64	32	29	80	24	3.13
1987—Fort Lauderdale	Florida St.	15	105⅔	8	5	.615	95	41	32	76	39	2.73
1987—Albany†	Eastern	2	12	0	0	.000	18	11	9	8	1	6.75
1987—Winston-Salem	Carolina	13	50⅓	4	4	.500	49	31	23	29	24	4.11
1988—Pittsfield	Eastern	●59	71⅔	5	7	.417	53	25	13	59	30	1.63
1989—Iowa	Am. Assoc.	38	138	8	11	.421	149	74	65	82	58	4.24
1989—Chicago	National	11	15⅔	1	0	1.000	13	9	9	14	9	5.17
1990—Chicago	National	7	7⅓	0	0	.000	11	8	8	3	7	9.82
1990—Iowa‡	Am. Assoc.	52	73	6	2	.750	75	37	30	61	38	3.70
Major League Totals—2 Years		18	23	1	0	1.000	24	17	17	17	16	6.65

Selected by New York Yankees' organization in 2nd round of free-agent draft, January 14, 1986.
†Traded with Pitchers Rick Scheid and Bob Tewksbury to Chicago Cubs for Pitcher Steve Trout, July 13, 1987.
‡Drafted by Houston Astros, December 3, 1990.

RICHARD DAVID WILKINS
(Rick)

Born July 4, 1967, at Jacksonville, Fla.
Height, 6.02. Weight, 210.
Throws right and bats lefthanded.
Attended Florida Community College, Jacksonville, Fla.,
and Furman University, Greenville, S.C.

Led Appalachian League in intentional bases on balls received with 8 in 1987.
Led Southern League catchers in total chances with 857, double plays with 11 and passed balls with 15 in 1990.
Led Carolina League catchers in total chances with 860 and tied for lead in double plays with 8 in 1989.
Led Midwest League catchers in total chances with 984 in 1988.
Led Appalachian League catchers in putouts with 483, total chances with 540 and fielding percentage with .989 and tied for lead in double plays with 6 in 1987.

Year Club	League	Pos.	G.	AB.	R.	H.	2B.	3B.	HR.	RBI.	B.A.	PO.	A.	E.	F.A.
1987—Geneva	NYP	C-1B	75	243	35	61	8	2	8	43	.251	503	51	7	.988
1988—Peoria	Midw.	C	137	490	54	119	30	1	8	63	.243	*864	*101	*19	.981
1989—Winston-Salem	Carol.	C	132	445	61	111	24	1	12	54	.249	*764	*78	*18	.979
1990—Charlotte	South.	C	127	449	48	102	18	1	17	71	.227	*740	*103	14	.984

Selected by Chicago Cubs' organization in 23rd round of free-agent draft, June 2, 1986.

GERALD DUANE WILLARD JR.
(Jerry)

Born March 14, 1960, at Oxnard, Calif.
Height, 6.02. Weight, 195.
Throws right and bats lefthanded.
Attended Oxnard College, Oxnard, Calif.

Major League stolen bases: 1984 (1).
Led Pacific Coast League in passed balls with 18 in 1990.
Led Pacific Coast League catchers in double plays with 12 in 1989.
Led International League catchers in assists with 78 in 1983.

Year Club	League	Pos.	G.	AB.	R.	H.	2B.	3B.	HR.	RBI.	B.A.	PO.	A.	E.	F.A.
1980—Central Oregon	N'west	C	65	231	53	85	21	1	5	59	.368	283	37	*18	.947
1981—Peninsula	Carol.	C	107	334	43	87	17	1	12	60	.260	319	28	3	.991
1982—Reading	East.	C	81	281	43	82	10	1	12	51	.292	534	64	13	.979
1982—Oklahoma City†	A. A.	C	36	95	13	22	5	0	2	14	.232	169	35	8	.962
1983—Charleston	Int.	C-3B-OF	127	396	61	119	22	2	19	77	.301	613	79	12	.983
1984—Cleveland	Amer.	C	87	246	21	55	8	1	10	37	.224	335	35	7	.981
1985—Cleveland	Amer.	C	104	300	39	81	13	0	7	36	.270	427	52	5	.990
1985—Maine‡	Int.	C	11	40	5	9	3	0	1	4	.225	56	11	2	.971
1986—Tacoma	P. C.	C	22	62	7	16	5	0	1	12	.258	100	7	1	.991
1986—Oakland	Amer.	C	75	161	17	43	7	0	4	26	.267	300	12	2	.994
1987—Tacoma	P. C.	O-C-1-3	67	215	42	64	15	0	6	38	.298	117	14	4	.970
1987—Oakland§x	Amer.	1B-3B	7	6	1	1	0	0	0	0	.167	1	0	0	1.000
1988—						(Out of Organized Baseball)									
1989—Birmingham	South.	C	5	10	5	3	1	0	0	1	.300	38	4	2	.955
1989—Vancouver y	P. C.	C-1B	90	283	32	78	18	1	7	38	.276	435	56	1	.998
1990—Vancouver	P. C.	C-1B	121	380	66	106	21	0	20	76	.279	550	74	12	.981
1990—Chicago z	Amer.	C	3	3	0	0	0	0	0	0	.000	0	0	0	.000
Major League Totals—5 Years			276	716	78	180	28	1	21	99	.251	1063	99	14	.988

Signed as free agent by Philadelphia Phillies' organization, December 20, 1979.
†Traded with Second Baseman Manny Trillo, Infielder Julio Franco, Outfielder George Vukovich and Pitcher Jay Baller to Cleveland Indians for Outfielder Von Hayes, December 9, 1982.
‡Released, April 1, 1986; signed by Tacoma (Oakland A's organization), April 4, 1986.
§On disabled list, May 11 to June 29, 1987.

xReleased, October 12, 1987; signed by Vancouver (Chicago White Sox' organization), February 10, 1989.
yOn disabled list, May 10 to May 24, 1989.
zReleased, November 30, 1990.

BERNABE WILLIAMS (FIGUEROA)
(Bernie)

Born September 13, 1968, at San Juan, Puerto Rico.
Height, 6.02. Weight, 180.
Throws right and bats left and righthanded.

Led Eastern League in bases on balls received with 98, stolen bases with 39 and caught stealing with 18 in 1990.
Tied for Gulf Coast League lead in caught stealing with 12 in 1986.
Led Eastern League outfielders in total chances with 307 and tied for lead in double plays with 4 in 1990.
Led Gulf Coast League outfielders in total chances with 123 in 1986.

Year	Club	League	Pos.	G.	AB.	R.	H.	2B.	3B.	HR.	RBI.	B.A.	PO.	A.	E.	F.A.
1986—Sarasota Yanks†	Gulf C.		OF	61	230	*45	62	5	3	2	25	.270	*117	3	3	.976
1987—Fort Lauderdale†	Fla. St.		OF	25	71	11	11	3	0	0	4	.155	49	1	0	1.000
1987—Oneonta†	NYP		OF	25	93	13	32	4	0	0	15	.344	40	0	2	1.000
1988—Prince William†‡	Carol.		OF	92	337	72	113	16	7	7	45	*.335	186	8	5	.975
1989—Columbus	Int.		OF	50	162	21	35	8	1	2	16	.216	112	2	1	.991
1989—Albany	East.		OF	91	314	63	79	11	8	11	42	.252	180	5	5	.974
1990—Albany	East.		OF	134	466	*91	131	28	5	8	54	.281	*288	15	4	.987

Signed as free agent by New York Yankees' organization, September 13, 1985.
†Batted righthanded only.
‡On disabled list, July 15, 1988 through remainder of season.

EDWARD LAQUAN WILLIAMS
(Eddie)

Born November 1, 1964, at Shreveport, La.
Height, 6.00. Weight, 192.
Throws and bats righthanded.

Major League stolen bases: 1989 (1).
Led Pacific Coast League in being hit by pitch with 12 in 1988.
Led American Association in being hit by pitch with 15 in 1987.
Led Midwest League in being hit by pitch with 15 in 1985.
Led American Association third basemen in total chances with 352 and double plays with 24 in 1987.
Named Midwest League Most Valuable Player, 1985.

Year	Club	League	Pos.	G.	AB.	R.	H.	2B.	3B.	HR.	RBI.	B.A.	PO.	A.	E.	F.A.
1983—Little Falls	NYP		3B	50	190	30	50	6	2	6	28	.263	50	53	13	.888
1984—Columbia†	S. Atl.		3B	43	152	17	28	4	2	3	24	.184	24	76	16	.862
1984—Tampa	Fla. St.		3B	50	138	20	35	8	0	2	16	.254	25	43	11	.861
1985—Cedar Rapids‡	Midw.		3B	119	406	71	106	13	3	20	83	.261	83	204	33	.897
1986—Cleveland	Amer.		OF	5	7	2	1	0	0	0	1	.143	0	0	0	.000
1986—Waterbury	East.		3B	62	214	24	51	10	0	7	30	.238	39	100	15	.903
1987—Buffalo	A. A.		*3B-SS	131	488	90	142	29	2	22	85	.291	88	*237	*27	.923
1987—Cleveland	Amer.		3B	22	64	9	11	4	0	1	4	.172	17	37	1	.982
1988—Colorado Springs	P. C.		3B-SS-1B	101	365	53	110	24	3	12	58	.301	93	177	29	.903
1988—Cleveland§	Amer.		3B	10	21	3	4	0	0	0	1	.190	3	18	0	1.000
1989—Chicago	Amer.		3B	66	201	25	55	8	0	3	10	.274	37	123	16	.909
1989—Vancouver x	P. C.		3B-1B	35	114	12	28	8	0	1	13	.246	8	10	4	.818
1990—Las Vegas	P. C.		3B-1B	93	348	59	110	29	2	17	75	.316	106	121	17	.930
1990—San Diego y	Nat.		3B	14	42	5	12	3	0	3	4	.286	5	21	3	.897
American League Totals—4 Years				103	293	39	71	12	0	4	16	.242	57	178	17	.933
National League Totals—1 Year				14	42	5	12	3	0	3	4	.286	5	21	3	.897
Major League Totals—5 Years				117	335	44	83	15	0	7	20	.248	62	199	20	.929

Selected by New York Mets' organization in 1st round (fourth player selected) of free-agent draft, June 6, 1983.
†Traded with Pitchers Matt Bullinger and Jay Tibbs to Cincinnati Reds for Pitcher Bruce Berenyi, June 15, 1984.
‡Drafted by Cleveland Indians, December 10, 1985.
§Traded to Chicago White Sox for Pitchers Joel Davis and Ed Wojna, January 23, 1989.
xGranted free agency, October 15, 1989; signed by Las Vegas (San Diego Padres' organization), December 21, 1989.
ySold to Daiei Hawks of Japanese Baseball League, December 2, 1990.

GERALD FLOYD WILLIAMS

Born August 10, 1966, at New Orleans, La.
Height, 6.02. Weight, 190.
Throws and bats righthanded.
Attended Grambling State University, Grambling, La.

Led Carolina League outfielders in total chances with 307 in 1989.

Year	Club	League	Pos.	G.	AB.	R.	H.	2B.	3B.	HR.	RBI.	B.A.	PO.	A.	E.	F.A.
1987—Oneonta	NYP		OF	29	115	26	42	6	2	2	29	.365	68	3	3	.959
1988—Prince William	Carol.		OF	54	159	20	29	3	0	2	18	.182	71	2	3	.961
1988—Fort Lauderdale	Fla. St.		OF	63	212	21	40	7	2	2	17	.189	163	2	6	.965
1989—Prince William	Carol.		OF	134	454	63	104	19	6	13	69	.229	*.292	7	8	.974
1990—Fort Lauderdale	Fla. St.		OF	50	204	25	59	4	5	7	43	.289	115	1	3	.975
1990—Albany	East.		OF	96	324	54	81	17	2	13	58	.250	210	6	7	.969

Selected by New York Yankees' organization in 14th round of free-agent draft, June 2, 1987.

JIMMY WILLIAMS

Born May 18, 1965, at Butler, Ala.
Height, 6.07. Weight, 232.
Throws and bats lefthanded.

Year Club	League	G.	IP.	W.	L.	Pct.	H.	R.	ER.	SO.	BB.	ERA.
1984—Great Falls	Pioneer	8	11	0	1	.000	10	14	11	9	16	9.00
1984—Bradenton Dodgers	Gulf Coast	2	3	0	0	.000	4	4	0	1	4	0.00
1985—Bradenton Dodgers	Gulf Coast	13	66⅔	4	4	.500	54	35	28	59	*55	3.78
1986—Vero Beach†	Florida St.	30	60	1	1	.500	47	35	29	40	66	4.35
1987—Visalia	California	13	85	7	4	.636	66	38	21	81	62	2.22
1988—Visalia	California	37	51	3	4	.429	41	23	21	55	33	3.71
1989—Orlando	Southern	43	53⅓	6	4	.600	50	23	18	62	35	3.04
1989—Portland	P. Coast	16	23⅔	3	2	.600	24	15	11	22	18	4.18
1990—Portland‡	P. Coast	51	84	4	6	.400	73	64	47	62	74	5.04

Selected by Los Angeles Dodgers' organization in 10th round of free-agent draft, June 4, 1984.
†Traded with Pitcher Carl Thomas to Minnesota Twins' organization for Outfielder Tom Thomas, June 19, 1987.
‡Traded to San Francisco Giants, December 18, 1990, completing deal in which San Francisco traded Pitcher Steve Bedrosian to Minnesota Twins for Pitcher Johnny Ard and a player to be named later, December 5, 1990.

KENNETH ROYAL WILLIAMS
(Kenny)

Born April 6, 1964, at Berkeley, Calif.
Height, 6.01. Weight, 195.
Throws and bats righthanded.
Attended Stanford University, Stanford, Calif.

Major League stolen bases: 1986 (1), 1987 (21), 1988 (6), 1989 (9), 1990 (9). Total—46.
Received reported $165,000 bonus to sign with Chicago White Sox, 1982.

Year Club	League	Pos.	G.	AB.	R.	H.	2B.	3B.	HR.	RBI.	B.A.	PO.	A.	E.	F.A.
1982—Sarasota W. Sox	Gulf C.	OF	31	104	19	31	2	1	1	11	.298	61	2	0	1.000
1983—Appleton	Midw.	OF	124	415	60	96	18	2	12	53	.231	218	10	10	.958
1984—Appleton	Midw.	OF	38	147	23	42	11	2	5	26	.286	58	5	2	.969
1984—Glens Falls	East.	OF	97	309	35	76	7	5	8	47	.246	173	10	5	.973
1985—Glens Falls	East.	OF	133	*520	*87	130	16	6	16	66	.250	296	*20	*14	.958
1986—Buffalo	A. A.	OF	50	189	21	40	4	2	4	15	.212	100	8	1	.991
1986—Birmingham	South.	OF	68	272	41	90	16	5	6	40	.331	192	3	8	.961
1986—Chicago	Amer.	OF	15	31	2	4	0	0	1	1	.129	18	1	0	1.000
1987—Hawaii	P. C.	OF	35	134	19	36	4	4	3	14	.269	75	1	2	.974
1987—Chicago	Amer.	OF	116	391	48	110	18	2	11	50	.281	303	5	6	.981
1988—Chicago†	Amer.	OF-3B	73	220	18	35	4	2	8	28	.159	87	69	17	.902
1988—Vancouver‡	P. C.	OF	16	60	8	15	2	1	1	7	.250	23	0	0	1.000
1989—Detroit§	Amer.	OF-1B	94	258	29	53	5	1	6	23	.205	180	11	4	.979
1989—Toledo	Int.	OF	14	51	8	13	2	0	3	8	.255	27	1	0	1.000
1990—Det. x-Tor.	Amer.	OF	106	155	23	25	8	1	0	13	.161	103	5	0	1.000
Major League Totals—5 Years			404	1055	120	227	35	6	26	115	.215	691	91	27	.967

Selected by Chicago White Sox' organization in 3rd round of free-agent draft, June 7, 1982.
†On disabled list, May 25 to June 30, 1988.
‡Traded to Detroit Tigers for Pitcher Eric King, March 23, 1989.
§On disabled list, June 23 to July 29, 1989; included rehabilitation disability assignment to Toledo, July 14 to July 29, 1989.
xClaimed on waivers by Toronto Blue Jays, June 18, 1990.

MATTHEW DERRICK WILLIAMS
(Matt)

Born November 28, 1965, at Bishop, Calif.
Height, 6.02. Weight, 210.
Throws and bats righthanded.
Attended University of Nevada, Las Vegas, Nev.

Major League stolen bases: 1987 (4), 1989 (1), 1990 (7). Total—12.
Led National League third basemen in double plays with 33 and tied for lead in total chances with 465 in 1990.
Named third baseman on THE SPORTING NEWS National League All-Star Team, 1990.
Named third baseman on THE SPORTING NEWS National League Silver Slugger team, 1990.
Named shortstop on THE SPORTING NEWS College Baseball All-America Team, 1986.

Year Club	League	Pos.	G.	AB.	R.	H.	2B.	3B.	HR.	RBI.	B.A.	PO.	A.	E.	F.A.
1986—Everett	N'west	SS	4	17	3	4	0	1	1	10	.235	5	10	2	.882
1986—Clinton	Midw.	SS	68	250	32	60	14	3	7	29	.240	89	150	10	.960
1987—Phoenix	P. C.	3B-2B-SS	56	211	36	61	15	2	6	37	.289	53	136	14	.931
1987—San Francisco	Nat.	SS-3B	84	245	28	46	9	2	8	21	.188	110	234	9	.975
1988—Phoenix	P. C.	3-S-2-O	82	306	45	83	19	1	12	51	.271	56	173	13	.946
1988—San Francisco	Nat.	3B-SS	52	156	17	32	6	1	8	19	.205	48	108	7	.957
1989—San Francisco	Nat.	3B-SS	84	292	31	59	18	1	18	50	.202	90	168	10	.963
1989—Phoenix	P. C.	3B-SS-OF	76	284	61	91	20	2	26	61	.320	57	197	11	.958
1990—San Francisco	Nat.	3B	159	617	87	171	27	2	33	*122	.277	*140	306	19	.959
Major League Totals—4 Years			379	1310	163	308	60	6	67	212	.235	388	816	45	.964

Selected by New York Mets organization in 27th round of free-agent draft, June 6, 1983.
Selected by San Francisco Giants organization in 1st round (third player selected) of free-agent draft, June 2, 1986.

CHAMPIONSHIP SERIES RECORD

Holds National League Championship Series record for most runs batted in, series (9), 1989.

Year	Club	League	Pos.	G.	AB.	R.	H.	2B.	3B.	HR.	RBI.	B.A.	PO.	A.	E.	F.A.
1989—San Francisco		Nat.	3B-SS	5	20	2	6	1	0	2	9	.300	5	12	0	1.000

WORLD SERIES RECORD

Year	Club	League	Pos.	G.	AB.	R.	H.	2B.	3B.	HR.	RBI.	B.A.	PO.	A.	E.	F.A.
1989—San Francisco		Nat.	3B-SS	4	16	1	2	0	0	1	1	.125	4	12	0	1.000

ALL-STAR GAME RECORD

Year	League	Pos.	AB.	R.	H.	2B.	3B.	HR.	RBI.	B.A.	PO.	A.	E.	F.A.
1990—National		PH	1	0	0	0	0	0	0	.000	0	0	0	.000

MITCHELL STEVEN WILLIAMS
(Mitch)

Born November 17, 1964, at Santa Ana, Calif.
Height, 6.04. Weight, 205.
Throws and bats lefthanded.
Brother of Bruce Williams, pitcher in Milwaukee Brewers' organization, 1981 through 1985.

Major League saves: 1986 (8), 1987 (6), 1988 (18), 1989 (36), 1990 (16). Total—84.
Established major league record for most games pitched by rookie (80), 1986.
Led Northwest League pitchers in wild pitches with 14 and tied for lead in games started with 14 and balks with 2 in 1983.

Year	Club	League	G.	IP.	W.	L.	Pct.	H.	R.	ER.	SO.	BB.	ERA.
1982—Walla Walla		Northwest	12	58⅓	3	4	.429	37	37	31	66	★72	4.78
1983—Reno		California	11	58	1	7	.125	58	56	46	44	60	7.14
1983—Spokane		Northwest	14	92⅓	7	6	.538	84	51	●46	87	55	4.48
1984—Reno†‡		California	26	164	9	8	.529	163	113	91	165	127	4.99
1985—Salem		Carolina	22	99	6	9	.400	57	64	60	138	★117	5.45
1985—Tulsa		Texas	6	33	2	2	.500	17	24	17	37	48	4.64
1986—Texas		American	★80	98	8	6	.571	69	39	39	90	79	3.58
1987—Texas		American	85	108⅔	8	6	.571	63	47	39	129	94	3.23
1988—Texas§x		American	67	68	2	7	.222	48	38	35	61	47	4.63
1989—Chicago		National	★76	81⅔	4	4	.500	71	27	24	67	52	2.64
1990—Chicago y		National	59	66⅓	1	8	.111	60	38	29	55	50	3.93
American League Totals—3 Years			232	274⅔	18	19	.486	180	124	113	280	220	3.70
National League Totals—2 Years			135	148	5	12	.294	131	65	53	122	102	3.22
Major League Totals—5 Years			367	422⅔	23	31	.426	311	189	166	402	322	3.53

Selected by San Diego Padres' organization in 8th round of free-agent draft, June 7, 1982.
†Drafted by Texas Rangers, December 3, 1984; returned, April 6, 1985.
‡Traded to Texas Rangers for Third Baseman Randy Asadoor, April 6, 1985.
§On suspended list, May 2 to May 4, 1988.
xTraded with Pitchers Paul Kilgus and Steve Wilson, Infielders Curtis Wilkerson and Luis Benitez and Outfielder Pablo Delgado to Chicago Cubs for Outfielder Rafael Palmeiro and Pitchers Jamie Moyer and Drew Hall, December 5, 1988.
yOn disabled list, June 12 to July 12, 1990.

CHAMPIONSHIP SERIES RECORD

Year	Club	League	G.	IP.	W.	L.	Pct.	H.	R.	ER.	SO.	BB.	ERA.
1989—Chicago		National	2	1	0	0	.000	1	0	0	2	0	0.00

ALL-STAR GAME RECORD

Year	League	IP.	W.	L.	Pct.	H.	R.	ER.	SO.	BB.	ERA.
1989—National		1	0	0	.000	0	0	0	1	1	0.00

MARK ALAN WILLIAMSON

Born July 21, 1959, at Corpus Christi, Tex.
Height, 6.00. Weight, 171.
Throws and bats righthanded.
Attended Grossmont College, El Cajon, Calif., and received degree in mechanical engineering from San Diego State University, San Diego, Calif.

Major League saves: 1987 (3), 1988 (2), 1989 (9), 1990 (1). Total—15.
Led American League in intentional bases on balls issued with 15 in 1987.
Tied for Pacific Coast League lead in saves with 16 in 1986.
Tied for California League lead in intentional bases on balls issued with 10 in 1984.

Year	Club	League	G.	IP.	W.	L.	Pct.	H.	R.	ER.	SO.	BB.	ERA.
1982—Reno		California	26	41	7	5	.583	34	24	20	30	18	4.39
1983—Beaumont		Texas	47	82⅔	6	3	.667	90	45	37	39	30	4.03
1984—Reno		California	56	93	10	12	.455	105	41	30	69	23	2.90
1985—Beaumont		Texas	42	78⅔	10	9	.526	72	27	25	64	23	2.86
1986—Las Vegas†		P. Coast	★65	104⅓	10	3	★.769	103	47	39	81	36	3.36
1987—Baltimore		American	61	125	8	9	.471	122	59	56	73	41	4.03
1987—Rochester		Int'national	1	4	0	1	.000	6	3	3	1	1	6.75
1988—Baltimore		American	37	117⅔	5	8	.385	125	70	64	69	40	4.90
1988—Rochester		Int'national	12	29⅔	2	3	.400	38	11	11	25	5	3.34

Year Club	League	G.	IP.	W.	L.	Pct.	H.	R.	ER.	SO.	BB.	ERA.
1989—Baltimore	American	65	107⅓	10	5	.667	105	35	35	55	30	2.93
1990—Baltimore‡	American	49	85⅓	8	2	.800	65	25	21	60	28	2.21
Major League Totals—4 Years		212	435⅓	31	24	.564	417	189	176	257	139	3.64

Selected by Kansas City Royals' organization in 12th round of free-agent draft, June 8, 1981.
Selected by San Diego Padres' organization in 4th round of free-agent draft, June 7, 1982.
†Traded with Catcher Terry Kennedy to Baltimore Orioles for Pitcher Storm Davis, October 30, 1986.
‡On disabled list, March 31 to April 22 and August 19, 1990 through remainder of season.

FRANK LEE WILLS JR.

Born October 26, 1958, at New Orleans, La.
Height, 6.02. Weight, 210.
Throws and bats righthanded.
Attended Tulane University, New Orleans, La.

Pitched seven-inning, 1-0 no-hit victory against Tacoma, May 31, 1985 (first game).
Major League saves: 1985 (1), 1986 (4), 1987 (1). Total—6.
Tied for Southern League lead in wild pitches with 15 in 1981.
Named righthanded pitcher on THE SPORTING NEWS College Baseball All-America Team, 1980.

Year Club	League	G.	IP.	W.	L.	Pct.	H.	R.	ER.	SO.	BB.	ERA.
1980—Sarasota Royals-Blue	Gulf Coast	4	23	2	0	1.000	18	7	5	20	8	1.96
1980—Charleston	S. Atlantic	9	57	2	5	.286	59	33	23	48	32	3.63
1981—Jacksonville	Southern	27	192	9	14	.391	199	104	85	174	91	3.98
1982—Omaha	Am. Assoc.	41	107⅓	7	10	.412	110	71	62	77	*81	5.20
1983—Jacksonville	Southern	8	54⅓	5	2	.714	44	19	15	40	23	2.48
1983—Omaha	Am. Assoc.	16	95	4	11	.267	96	56	50	65	45	4.74
1983—Kansas City	American	6	34⅔	2	1	.667	35	17	16	23	15	4.15
1984—Omaha	Am. Assoc.	15	89⅔	7	4	.636	75	32	28	69	49	2.81
1984—Kansas City†‡§	American	10	37	2	3	.400	39	21	21	21	13	5.11
1985—Calgary	P. Coast	9	46⅓	4	3	.571	44	27	25	31	25	4.86
1985—Seattle x	American	24	123	5	11	.313	122	85	82	67	68	6.00
1986—Maine y	Int'national	22	31⅓	4	3	.571	37	10	10	21	10	2.87
1986—Cleveland	American	26	40⅓	4	4	.500	43	23	22	32	16	4.91
1987—Buffalo	Am. Assoc.	36	56⅔	3	2	.600	53	28	21	45	22	3.34
1987—Cleveland z	American	6	5⅓	0	1	.000	3	3	3	4	7	5.06
1988—Syracuse	Int'national	25	80⅔	6	4	.600	70	40	29	53	25	3.24
1988—Toronto a	American	10	20⅔	0	0	.000	22	12	12	19	6	5.23
1989—Syracuse	Int'national	14	17	1	0	1.000	8	7	3	13	8	1.59
1989—Toronto	American	24	71⅓	3	1	.750	65	31	29	41	30	3.66
1990—Toronto	American	44	99	6	4	.600	101	54	52	72	38	4.73
Major League Totals—8 Years		150	431⅓	22	25	.468	430	246	237	279	193	4.95

Selected by Kansas City Royals' organization in 1st round (16th player selected) of free-agent draft, June 3, 1980.
†On disabled list, August 1 to August 16, 1984.
‡Traded to New York Mets' organization as part of a six-player, four-team deal in which Kansas City Royals acquired Catcher Jim Sundberg from Milwaukee Brewers, Texas Rangers acquired Catcher Don Slaught from Kansas City, Milwaukee acquired Pitcher Danny Darwin and a player to be named later from Texas and Pitcher Tim Leary from New York, January 18, 1985; Milwaukee organization acquired Catcher Bill Hance from Texas to complete deal, January 30, 1985.
§Traded to Seattle Mariners' organization for Pitcher Wray Bergendahl, March 29, 1985.
xReleased, March 20, 1986; signed by Maine (Cleveland Indians' organization), March 27, 1986.
yOn disabled list, May 4 to May 31, 1986.
zReleased, March 29, 1988; signed by Knoxville (Toronto Blue Jays' organization), April 7, 1988.
aReleased, October 28, 1988; re-signed by Blue Jays' organization, January 12, 1989.

CRAIG WILSON

Born November 28, 1964, at Anne Arundel County, Md.
Height, 5.11. Weight, 175.
Throws and bats righthanded.
Attended Anne Arundel Community College, Arnold, Md.

Led American Association third basemen in assists with 264, errors with 26, total chances with 386 and double plays with 28 in 1988.
Led Midwest League second basemen in total chances with 653 and double plays with 86 in 1986.
Led Midwest League third basemen in fielding with .932 in 1985.

Year Club	League	Pos.	G.	AB.	R.	H.	2B.	3B.	HR.	RBI.	B.A.	PO.	A.	E.	F.A.
1984—Erie	NYP	2B-3B-SS	72	282	53	83	18	4	7	46	.294	169	206	14	.964
1985—Springfield	Midw.	3B-2B	133	504	64	132	16	4	8	52	.262	156	293	27	.943
1986—Springfield	Midw.	2B	127	496	106	136	17	6	1	49	.274	*292	*343	18	*.972
1987—St. Petersburg	Fla. St.	3B-2B	38	162	35	58	6	4	0	28	.358	35	91	6	.955
1987—Louisville	A. A.	2B-3B	21	70	10	15	2	0	1	8	.214	22	51	2	.973
1987—Arkansas	Texas	2-3-S-O	66	238	37	69	13	1	1	26	.290	117	164	8	.972
1988—Louisville	A. A.	*3B-2B	133	497	59	127	27	2	1	46	.256	98	271	*26	.934
1989—Arkansas	Texas	2B-3B	55	224	41	71	12	1	1	40	.317	127	150	12	.958
1989—Louisville	A.A.	2B-3B	75	278	37	81	18	3	1	30	.291	130	151	18	.940
1989—St. Louis	Nat.	3B	6	4	1	1	0	0	0	1	.250	1	0	1	.500
1990—Louisville	A. A.	2B-3B	57	204	30	57	9	2	2	23	.279	78	139	12	.948
1990—St. Louis	Nat.	3-O-2-1	55	121	13	30	2	0	0	7	.248	45	30	1	.987
Major League Totals—2 Years			61	125	14	31	2	0	0	8	.248	46	30	2	.974

Selected by St. Louis Cardinals' organization in 20th round of free-agent draft, June 4, 1984.

GLENN DWIGHT WILSON

Born December 22, 1958, at Baytown, Tex.
Height, 6.01. Weight, 190.
Throws and bats righthanded.
Attended Sam Houston State University, Huntsville, Tex.

Shares major league record for fewest double plays by outfielder, season, for leader in double plays (4), 1985.
Major League stolen bases: 1982 (2), 1983 (1), 1984 (7), 1985 (7), 1986 (5), 1987 (3), 1988 (1), 1989 (1). Total—27.
Led National League outfielders in assists with 18 in 1987.
Led National League outfielders in double plays with 5 in 1986, 6 in 1990 and tied for lead with 4 in 1985.
Received reported $60,000 bonus to sign with Detroit Tigers, 1980.
Named third baseman on THE SPORTING NEWS College Baseball All-America Team, 1980.

Year	Club	League	Pos.	G.	AB.	R.	H.	2B.	3B.	HR.	RBI.	B.A.	PO.	A.	E.	F.A.
1980—Montgomery	South.	3B	77	284	36	75	16	2	7	31	.264	56	189	★33	.881
1981—Birmingham	South.	OF	124	496	77	152	24	6	18	82	.306	292	18	5	.984
1981—Evansville	A. A.	OF-1B	10	37	5	9	2	0	2	7	.243	16	2	0	1.000
1982—Detroit	Amer.	OF	84	322	39	94	15	1	12	34	.292	215	8	3	.987
1982—Evansville†	A. A.	OF	42	165	24	46	7	2	10	33	.279	96	6	3	.971
1983—Detroit‡	Amer.	OF	144	503	55	135	25	6	11	65	.268	225	12	3	.988
1984—Philadelphia	Nat.	OF-3B	132	341	28	82	21	3	6	31	.240	153	7	7	.958
1985—Philadelphia	Nat.	OF	161	608	73	167	39	5	14	102	.275	343	★18	★12	.968
1986—Philadelphia	Nat.	OF	155	584	70	158	30	4	15	84	.271	331	★20	4	.989
1987—Philadelphia§	Nat.	★OF-P	154	569	55	150	21	2	14	54	.264	315	19	★11	.968
1988—Seattle x	Amer.	OF	78	284	28	71	10	1	3	17	.250	140	4	3	.980
1988—Pittsburgh y	Nat.	OF	37	126	11	34	8	0	2	15	.270	66	1	1	.985
1989—Pitt. z-Hou.	Nat.	OF-1B	128	432	50	115	26	4	11	64	.266	249	13	6	.978
1990—Houston a	Nat.	OF-1B	118	368	42	90	14	0	10	55	.245	227	12	6	.976
American League Totals—3 Years			306	1109	122	300	50	8	26	116	.271	580	24	9	.985
National League Totals—7 Years			885	3028	329	796	159	18	72	405	.263	1684	90	47	.974
Major League Totals—9 Years			1191	4137	451	1096	209	26	98	521	.265	2264	114	56	.977

Selected by Detroit Tigers' organization in 1st round (18th player selected) of free-agent draft, June 3, 1980.
†On disabled list, May 27 to June 9 and June 17 to June 27, 1982.
‡Traded with Catcher-First Baseman John Wockenfuss to Philadelphia Phillies for First Baseman Dave Bergman and Pitcher Willie Hernandez, March 24, 1984.
§Traded with Outfielder Dave Brundage and Pitcher Mike Jackson to Seattle Mariners for Outfielder Phil Bradley and Pitcher Tim Fortugno, December 9, 1987.
xTraded to Pittsburgh Pirates for Outfielder Darnell Coles, July 22, 1988.
yOn disabled list, August 5 to August 20, 1988.
zTraded to Houston Astros for Outfielder Billy Hatcher, August 18, 1989.
aGranted free agency, November 5, 1990.

ALL-STAR GAME RECORD

Year	League	Pos.	AB.	R.	H.	2B.	3B.	HR.	RBI.	B.A.	PO.	A.	E.	F.A.
1985—National		PH	1	0	0	0	0	0	0	.000	0	0	0	.000

PITCHING RECORD

Year	Club	League	G.	IP.	W.	L.	Pct.	H.	R.	ER.	SO.	BB.	ERA.
1987—Philadelphia	National	1	1	0	0	.000	0	0	0	1	0	0.00

STEPHEN DOUGLAS WILSON

(Steve)

Born December 13, 1964, at Victoria, British Columbia, Can.
Height, 6.04. Weight, 195.
Throws and bats lefthanded.
Attended University of Portland, Portland, Ore.

Major League saves: 1989 (2), 1990 (1). Total—3.
Played semi-pro baseball with Alaska Goldpanners.

Year	Club	League	G.	IP.	W.	L.	Pct.	H.	R.	ER.	SO.	BB.	ERA.
1985—Burlington	Midwest	21	72⅔	3	5	.375	71	44	37	76	27	4.58
1986—Tulsa	Texas	24	136⅔	7	13	.350	117	83	74	95	★103	4.87
1987—Charlotte	Florida St.	20	107	9	5	.643	81	41	29	80	44	2.44
1988—Tulsa	Texas	25	165⅓	15	7	.682	147	72	58	132	53	3.16
1988—Texas†	American	3	7⅔	0	0	.000	7	5	5	1	4	5.87
1989—Chicago	National	53	85⅔	6	4	.600	83	43	40	65	31	4.20
1990—Chicago	National	45	139	4	9	.308	140	77	74	95	43	4.79
American League Totals—1 Year		3	7⅔	0	0	.000	7	5	5	1	4	5.87
National League Totals—2 Years		98	224⅔	10	13	.435	223	120	114	160	74	4.57
Major League Totals—3 Years		101	232⅓	10	13	.435	230	125	119	161	78	4.61

Selected by Texas Rangers' organization in 4th round of free-agent draft, June 3, 1985.
†Traded with Pitchers Mitch Williams and Paul Kilgus, Infielders Curtis Wilkerson and Luis Benitez and Outfielder Pablo Delgado to Chicago Cubs for Outfielder Rafael Palmeiro and Pitchers Jamie Moyer and Drew Hall, December 5, 1988.

CHAMPIONSHIP SERIES RECORD

Year	Club	League	G.	IP.	W.	L.	Pct.	H.	R.	ER.	SO.	BB.	ERA.
1989—Chicago	National	2	3⅔	0	1	.000	3	5	2	4	1	4.91

TREVOR KIRK WILSON

Born June 7, 1966, at Torrance, Calif.
Height, 6.00. Weight, 195.
Throws and bats lefthanded.
Attended Oregon State University, Corvallis, Ore.

Tied for Northwest League lead in balks with 2 in 1985.

Year	Club	League	G.	IP.	W.	L.	Pct.	H.	R.	ER.	SO.	BB.	ERA.
1985—Everett		Northwest	17	55⅓	2	4	.333	67	36	26	50	26	4.23
1986—Clinton		Midwest	34	130⅔	6	11	.353	126	70	62	84	64	4.27
1987—Clinton		Midwest	26	161⅓	10	6	.625	130	60	36	146	77	2.01
1988—Shreveport		Texas	12	72⅔	5	4	.556	55	19	15	53	23	1.86
1988—Phoenix		P. Coast	11	51⅔	2	3	.400	49	35	29	49	33	5.05
1988—San Francisco		National	4	22	0	2	.000	25	14	10	15	8	4.09
1989—Phoenix		P. Coast	23	115⅓	7	7	.500	109	49	40	77	76	3.12
1989—San Francisco		National	14	39⅓	2	3	.400	28	20	19	22	24	4.35
1990—Phoenix		P. Coast	11	66	5	5	.500	63	31	28	45	44	3.82
1990—San Francisco†		National	27	110⅓	8	7	.533	87	52	49	66	49	4.00
Major League Totals—3 Years			45	171⅔	10	12	.455	140	86	78	103	81	4.09

Selected by San Francisco Giants' organization in 8th round of free-agent draft, June 3, 1985.
†On disabled list, August 22 to September 6, 1990.

WILLIAM HAYWARD WILSON
(Mookie)

Born February 9, 1956, at Bamberg, S. C.
Height, 5.10. Weight, 175.
Throws right and bats right and lefthanded.
Attended Spartanburg Methodist College, Spartanburg, S. C.,
and University of South Carolina, Columbia, S. C.
Brother of John Wilson, outfielder in New York Mets' organization, 1982 through 1987; and
Phil Wilson, outfielder in Minnesota Twins' organization, 1984 through 1989.

Major League stolen bases: 1980 (7), 1981 (24), 1982 (58), 1983 (54), 1984 (46), 1985 (24), 1986 (25), 1987 (21), 1988 (15), 1989 (19), 1990 (23). Total—316.
Led National League outfielders in double plays with 6 in 1984.

Year	Club	League	Pos.	G.	AB.	R.	H.	2B.	3B.	HR.	RBI.	B.A.	PO.	A.	E.	F.A.
1977—Wausau	Midw.		OF	68	245	50	71	10	2	6	32	.290	150	8	9	.946
1978—Jackson	Texas		OF	132	497	72	145	13	*15	7	72	.292	282	10	7	.977
1979—Tidewater	Int.		OF	*141	529	84	141	22	10	5	36	.267	317	11	7	.979
1980—Tidewater	Int.		OF	132	515	*92	*152	11	*14	4	44	.295	*350	11	7	.981
1980—New York	Nat.		OF	27	105	16	26	5	3	0	4	.248	72	1	2	.973
1981—New York	Nat.		OF	92	328	49	89	8	8	3	14	.271	226	3	4	.983
1982—New York	Nat.		OF	159	639	90	178	25	9	5	55	.279	415	12	5	.988
1983—New York	Nat.		OF	152	*638	91	176	25	6	7	51	.276	422	5	7	.984
1984—New York	Nat.		OF	154	587	88	162	28	10	10	54	.276	396	8	4	.990
1985—New York†	Nat.		OF	93	337	56	93	16	8	6	26	.276	216	0	8	.964
1986—Tidewater	Int.		OF	9	31	4	8	1	0	0	4	.258	19	1	0	1.000
1986—New York‡	Nat.		OF	123	381	61	110	17	5	9	45	.289	228	7	5	.979
1987—New York	Nat.		OF	124	385	58	115	19	7	9	34	.299	205	3	8	.963
1988—New York	Nat.		OF	112	378	61	112	17	5	8	41	.296	200	4	5	.976
1989—New York§	Nat.		OF	80	249	22	51	10	1	3	18	.205	152	2	4	.975
1989—Toronto x	Amer.		OF	54	238	32	71	9	1	2	17	.298	111	2	1	.991
1990—Toronto	Amer.		OF	147	588	81	156	36	4	3	51	.265	370	5	3	.992
National League Totals—10 Years				1116	4027	592	1112	170	62	60	342	.276	2532	45	52	.980
American League Totals—2 Years				201	826	113	227	45	5	5	68	.275	481	7	4	.992
Major League Totals—11 Years				1317	4853	705	1339	215	67	65	410	.276	3013	52	56	.982

Selected by Los Angeles Dodgers' organization in 4th round of free-agent draft, January 7, 1976.
Selected by New York Mets' organization in 2nd round of free-agent draft, June 7, 1977.
†On disabled list, July 2 to September 1, 1985.
‡On New York disabled list, March 30 to May 9, 1986; included rehabilitation disability assignment to Tidewater, April 26 to May 9, 1986.
§Traded to Toronto Blue Jays, August 1, 1989, completing deal in which Toronto traded Pitcher Jeff Musselman and Pitcher Mike Brady to New York Mets for a player to be named later, July 31, 1989.
xGranted free agency, November 13, 1989; re-signed by Blue Jays, November 27, 1989.

CHAMPIONSHIP SERIES RECORD

Shares record for most at-bats, game (7), October 15, 1986 (16 innings).

Year	Club	League	Pos.	G.	AB.	R.	H.	2B.	3B.	HR.	RBI.	B.A.	PO.	A.	E.	F.A.
1986—New York	Nat.		OF	6	26	2	3	0	0	0	1	.115	16	1	0	1.000
1988—New York	Nat.		OF-PH	4	13	2	2	0	0	0	1	.154	6	0	0	1.000
1989—Toronto	Amer.		OF	5	19	2	5	0	0	0	2	.263	10	0	0	1.000
Championship Series Totals—3 Years				15	58	6	10	0	0	0	4	.172	32	1	0	1.000

WORLD SERIES RECORD

Year	Club	League	Pos.	G.	AB.	R.	H.	2B.	3B.	HR.	RBI.	B.A.	PO.	A.	E.	F.A.
1986—New York	Nat.		OF	7	26	3	7	1	0	0	0	.269	15	2	0	1.000

WILLIE JAMES WILSON

Born July 9, 1955, at Montgomery, Ala.
Height, 6.03. Weight, 195.
Throws right and bats left and righthanded.

Holds major league records for most at-bats season (705), 1980; most at-bats by switch-hitter, season (705), 1980.

Shares major league records by collecting 100 or more hits righthanded and lefthanded, season, 1980; for most hits by switch-hitter, season (230), 1980.

Holds American League records for most triples by switch-hitter, season (21), 1985; highest stolen base percentage, lifetime, 300 or more attempts (.837).

Shares American League records for most years leading league in triples (5); most consecutive stolen bases without caught stealing (32), July 23 through September 23, 1980; fewest times caught stealing, season, 50 or more stolen bases (8), 1983.

Major League stolen bases: 1976 (2), 1977 (6), 1978 (46), 1979 (83), 1980 (79), 1981 (34), 1982 (37), 1983 (59), 1984 (47), 1985 (43), 1986 (34), 1987 (59), 1988 (35), 1989 (24), 1990 (24). Total—612.

Switch-hit home runs in one game, June 15, 1979.

Led American League in stolen bases with 83 in 1979.

Led Gulf Coast League in stolen bases with 24 in 1974, Midwest League with 76 in 1975 and American Association with 74 in 1977.

Led Midwest League in being hit by pitch with 13 in 1975.

Named outfielder on THE SPORTING NEWS American League All-Star fielding team, 1980.

Named outfielder on THE SPORTING NEWS American League Silver Slugger team, 1980 and 1982.

Named Midwest League Most Valuable Player, 1975.

Received reported $90,000 bonus to sign with Kansas City Royals, 1974.

Year	Club	League	Pos.	G.	AB.	R.	H.	2B.	3B.	HR.	RBI.	B.A.	PO.	A.	E.	F.A.
1974—Sarasota Royals	Gulf C.	OF	47	155	30	39	3	5	1	14	.252	92	8	4	.962
1975—Waterloo	Midw.	OF	127	486	92	★132	18	4	8	73	.272	249	●17	★17	.940
1976—Jacksonville	South.	OF	107	388	54	98	13	6	1	35	.253	273	5	8	.972
1976—Kansas City	Amer.	OF	12	6	0	1	0	0	0	0	.167	6	1	1	.875
1977—Omaha	A. A.	OF	132	495	67	139	10	6	4	47	.281	★278	7	11	.963
1977—Kansas City	Amer.	OF	13	34	10	11	2	0	0	1	.324	24	0	1	.960
1978—Kansas City	Amer.	OF	127	198	43	43	8	2	0	16	.217	171	6	4	.978
1979—Kansas City	Amer.	OF	154	588	113	185	18	13	6	49	.315	384	12	6	.985
1980—Kansas City	Amer.	OF	161	★705	★133	★230	28	●15	3	49	.326	482	9	6	.988
1981—Kansas City	Amer.	OF	102	439	54	133	10	7	1	32	.303	299	★14	4	.987
1982—Kansas City	Amer.	OF	136	585	87	194	19	★15	3	46	★.332	215	8	3	.987
1983—Kansas City†‡	Amer.	OF	137	576	90	159	22	8	2	33	.276	354	3	9	.975
1984—Kansas City	Amer.	OF	128	541	81	163	24	9	2	44	.301	383	6	4	.990
1985—Kansas City	Amer.	OF	141	605	87	168	25	★21	4	43	.278	378	4	2	.995
1986—Kansas City	Amer.	OF	156	631	77	170	20	7	9	44	.269	408	4	3	.993
1987—Kansas City	Amer.	OF	146	610	97	170	18	★15	4	30	.279	342	3	1	★.997
1988—Kansas City	Amer.	OF	147	591	81	155	17	●11	1	37	.262	365	1	4	.989
1989—Kansas City§x	Amer.	OF	112	383	58	97	17	7	3	43	.253	252	2	6	.977
1990—Kansas City y	Amer.	OF	115	307	49	89	13	3	2	42	.290	187	2	0	1.000
Major League Totals—15 Years				1787	6799	1060	1968	241	133	40	509	.289	4250	75	54	.988

Selected by Kansas City Royals' organization in 1st round (18th player selected) of free-agent draft, June 5, 1974.

†On disabled list, August 21 to September 6, 1983.

‡On suspended list, December 15, 1983 through May 15, 1984.

§On disabled list, May 27 to June 17, 1989.

xGranted free agency, November 13, 1989; re-signed by Royals, December 7, 1989.

yGranted free agency, November 5, 1990; signed by Oakland Athletics, December 3, 1990.

DIVISION SERIES RECORD

Year	Club	League	Pos.	G.	AB.	R.	H.	2B.	3B.	HR.	RBI.	B.A.	PO.	A.	E.	F.A.
1981—Kansas City	Amer.	OF	3	13	0	4	0	0	0	1	.308	6	0	0	1.000

CHAMPIONSHIP SERIES RECORD

Year	Club	League	Pos.	G.	AB.	R.	H.	2B.	3B.	HR.	RBI.	B.A.	PO.	A.	E.	F.A.
1978—Kansas City	Amer.	PR-OF	3	4	0	1	0	0	0	0	.250	2	0	0	1.000
1980—Kansas City	Amer.	OF	3	13	2	4	2	1	0	4	.308	6	1	0	1.000
1984—Kansas City	Amer.	OF	3	13	0	2	0	0	0	0	.154	10	0	0	1.000
1985—Kansas City	Amer.	OF	7	29	5	9	0	0	1	2	.310	12	0	0	1.000
Championship Series Totals—4 Years			16	59	7	16	2	1	1	6	.271	30	1	0	1.000

WORLD SERIES RECORD

Holds record for most strikeouts, series (12), 1980.

Shares record for most at-bats, inning (2), October 18, 1980, first inning.

Year	Club	League	Pos.	G.	AB.	R.	H.	2B.	3B.	HR.	RBI.	B.A.	PO.	A.	E.	F.A.
1980—Kansas City	Amer.	OF	6	26	3	4	1	0	0	0	.154	15	1	0	1.000
1985—Kansas City	Amer.	OF	7	30	2	11	0	1	0	3	.367	19	1	0	1.000
World Series Totals—2 Years			13	56	5	15	1	1	0	3	.268	34	2	0	1.000

ALL-STAR GAME RECORD

Year	League	Pos.	AB.	R.	H.	2B.	3B.	HR.	RBI.	B.A.	PO.	A.	E.	F.A.
1982—American		OF	2	0	0	0	0	0	0	.000	1	0	0	1.000
1983—American		OF	1	0	1	1	0	0	1	1.000	2	0	0	1.000
All-Star Game Totals—2 Years			3	0	1	1	0	0	1	.333	3	0	0	1.000

DAVID MARK WINFIELD
(Dave)

Born October 3, 1951, at St. Paul, Minn.
Height, 6.06. Weight, 220.
Throws and bats righthanded.
Received degree from University of Minnesota, Minneapolis, Minn.

Major League stolen bases: 1974 (9), 1975 (23), 1976 (26), 1977 (16), 1978 (21), 1979 (15), 1980 (23), 1981 (11), 1982 (5), 1983 (15), 1984 (6), 1985 (19), 1986 (6), 1987 (5), 1988 (9). Total—209.
Led National League in total bases with 333 and intentional bases on balls received with 24 in 1979.
Named outfielder on THE SPORTING NEWS American League All-Star Team, 1982 through 1984.
Named outfielder on THE SPORTING NEWS National League All-Star Team, 1979.
Named outfielder on THE SPORTING NEWS American League All-Star fielding team, 1982 through 1985 and 1987.
Named outfielder on THE SPORTING NEWS National League All-Star fielding team, 1979 and 1980.
Named outfielder on THE SPORTING NEWS American League Silver Slugger team, 1981 through 1985.
Named American League Comeback Player of the Year by THE SPORTING NEWS, 1990.
Received reported $100,000 bonus to sign with San Diego Padres, 1973.
Selected by Atlanta Hawks in 5th round (79th player selected) of 1973 NBA draft.
Selected by Utah Stars in 6th round (58th player selected) of 1973 ABA draft.
Selected by Minnesota Vikings in 17th round (429th player selected) of 1973 NFL draft.
Named outfielder on THE SPORTING NEWS College Baseball All-America Team, 1973.

Year Club	League	Pos.	G.	AB.	R.	H.	2B.	3B.	HR.	RBI.	B.A.	PO.	A.	E.	F.A.
1973—San Diego	Nat.	OF-1B	56	141	9	39	4	1	3	12	.277	65	1	3	.957
1974—San Diego	Nat.	OF	145	498	57	132	18	4	20	75	.265	276	11	●12	.960
1975—San Diego	Nat.	OF	143	509	74	136	20	2	15	76	.267	302	9	9	.972
1976—San Diego	Nat.	OF	137	492	81	139	26	4	13	69	.283	304	*15	6	.982
1977—San Diego	Nat.	OF	157	615	104	169	29	7	25	92	.275	368	15	11	.972
1978—San Diego	Nat.	OF-1B	158	587	88	181	30	5	24	97	.308	328	8	7	.980
1979—San Diego	Nat.	OF	159	597	97	184	27	10	34	*118	.308	344	14	5	.986
1980—San Diego†	Nat.	OF	162	558	89	154	25	6	20	87	.276	273	20	4	.987
1981—New York	Amer.	OF	105	388	52	114	25	1	13	68	.294	196	1	3	.985
1982—New York‡	Amer.	OF	140	539	84	151	24	8	37	106	.280	279	*17	8	.974
1983—New York	Amer.	OF	152	598	99	169	26	8	32	116	.283	313	5	7	.978
1984—New York§	Amer.	OF	141	567	106	193	34	4	19	100	.340	306	3	2	.994
1985—New York	Amer.	OF	155	633	105	174	34	6	26	114	.275	316	13	3	.991
1986—New York	Amer.	OF-3B	154	565	90	148	31	5	24	104	.262	292	9	5	.984
1987—New York	Amer.	OF	156	575	83	158	22	1	27	97	.275	253	6	3	.989
1988—New York x	Amer.	OF	149	559	96	180	37	2	25	107	.322	276	3	3	.989
1989—New York x	Amer.						(Did not play)								
1990—N.Y.y-Calif.	Amer.	OF	132	475	70	127	21	2	21	78	.267	177	7	2	.989
National League Totals—8 Years			1117	3997	599	1134	179	39	154	626	.284	2260	93	57	.976
American League Totals—9 Years			1284	4899	785	1414	254	37	224	890	.289	2408	64	36	.986
Major League Totals—17 Years			2401	8896	1384	2548	433	76	378	1516	.286	4668	157	93	.981

Selected by Baltimore Orioles' organization in 40th round of free-agent draft, June 5, 1969.
Selected by San Diego Padres' organization in 1st round (fourth player selected) of free-agent draft, June 5, 1973.
†Granted free agency, October 22, 1980; signed by New York Yankees, December 15, 1980.
‡On disabled list, May 20 to June 4, 1982.
§On disabled list, April 16 to May 1, 1984.
xOn disabled list, March 19, 1989 through entire season.
yTraded to California Angels for Pitcher Mike Witt, May 11, 1990.

DIVISION SERIES RECORD

Year Club	League	Pos.	G.	AB.	R.	H.	2B.	3B.	HR.	RBI.	B.A.	PO.	A.	E.	F.A.
1981—New York	Amer.	OF	5	20	2	7	3	0	0	0	.350	10	1	0	1.000

CHAMPIONSHIP SERIES RECORD

Year Club	League	Pos.	G.	AB.	R.	H.	2B.	3B.	HR.	RBI.	B.A.	PO.	A.	E.	F.A.
1981—New York	Amer.	OF	3	13	2	2	1	0	0	2	.154	6	0	0	1.000

WORLD SERIES RECORD

Year Club	League	Pos.	G.	AB.	R.	H.	2B.	3B.	HR.	RBI.	B.A.	PO.	A.	E.	F.A.
1981—New York	Amer.	OF	6	22	0	1	0	0	0	1	.045	13	1	0	1.000

ALL-STAR GAME RECORD

Holds All-Star Game record for most doubles, lifetime (7).
Shares All-Star Game records for most at-bats, nine-inning game (5), July 17, 1979; most consecutive games, one or more hits (7).

Year League	Pos.	AB.	R.	H.	2B.	3B.	HR.	RBI.	B.A.	PO.	A.	E.	F.A.
1977—National	OF	2	0	2	1	0	0	2	1.000	1	0	0	1.000
1978—National	OF	2	1	1	0	0	0	0	.500	1	0	0	1.000
1979—National	OF	5	1	1	1	0	0	1	.200	3	0	0	1.000
1980—National	OF	2	0	0	0	0	0	0	.000	2	0	0	1.000
1981—American	OF	4	0	0	0	0	0	0	.000	0	1	0	1.000
1982—American	OF	2	0	1	0	0	0	0	.500	0	0	0	.000
1983—American	OF	3	2	3	1	0	0	1	1.000	3	0	0	1.000
1984—American	OF	4	0	1	1	0	0	0	.250	2	1	0	1.000
1985—American	OF	3	0	1	0	0	0	0	.333	0	0	0	.000
1986—American	OF	1	0	1	1	0	0	0	1.000	0	0	0	.000
1987—American	OF	5	0	1	1	0	0	0	.200	2	0	0	1.000
1988—American	OF	3	1	1	1	0	0	0	.333	1	0	0	1.000
All-Star Game Totals—12 Years		36	6	13	7	0	0	5	.361	15	2	0	1.000

HERMAN S. WINNINGHAM JR.
(Herm)

Born December 1, 1961, at Orangeburg, S.C.
Height, 5.11. Weight, 185.
Throws right and bats lefthanded.
Attended DeKalb Community College South, Decatur, Ga.

Shares modern major league record for most triples, game (3), August 15, 1990, 12 innings.
Major League stolen bases: 1984 (2), 1985 (20), 1986 (12), 1987 (29), 1988 (12), 1989 (14), 1990 (6). Total—95.

Year Club	League	Pos.	G.	AB.	R.	H.	2B.	3B.	HR.	RBI.	B.A.	PO.	A.	E.	F.A.
1981—Kingsport	Appal.	OF	58	204	44	52	7	4	2	14	.255	128	3	2	★.985
1982—Lynchburg	Carol.	OF	120	430	65	127	20	5	6	61	.295	235	6	5	.980
1983—Jackson	Texas	OF	78	288	54	102	13	6	4	41	.354	157	5	6	.964
1983—Tidewater†	Int.	OF	29	113	18	30	5	2	1	11	.265	70	1	3	.959
1984—Tidewater	Int.	OF	115	406	50	114	20	3	3	47	.281	228	8	4	.983
1984—New York‡	Nat.	OF	14	27	5	11	1	1	0	5	.407	7	0	0	1.000
1985—Montreal§	Nat.	OF	125	312	30	74	6	5	3	21	.237	229	6	4	.983
1985—Indianapolis	A. A.	OF	11	35	3	6	0	0	0	2	.171	22	0	1	.957
1986—Montreal	Nat.	OF-SS	90	185	23	40	6	3	4	11	.216	97	2	2	.980
1986—Indianapolis	A. A.	OF	51	201	35	54	5	7	4	24	.269	106	3	1	.991
1987—Montreal	Nat.	OF	137	347	34	83	20	3	4	41	.239	225	5	6	.975
1988—Mont. x-Cinc.	Nat.	OF	100	203	16	47	3	4	0	21	.232	128	1	1	.992
1988—Indianapolis	A. A.	OF	3	10	2	2	0	1	0	1	.200	6	0	0	1.000
1989—Cincinnati y	Nat.	OF	115	251	40	63	11	3	3	13	.251	146	3	3	.980
1990—Cincinnati	Nat.	OF	84	160	20	41	8	5	3	17	.256	89	3	0	1.000
Major League Totals—7 Years			665	1485	168	359	55	24	17	129	.242	921	20	16	.983

Selected by Pittsburgh Pirates' organization in 38th round of free-agent draft, June 5, 1979.
Selected by Milwaukee Brewers' organization in secondary phase of free-agent draft, January 8, 1980.
Selected by Montreal Expos' organization in secondary phase of free-agent draft, June 3, 1980.
Selected by New York Mets' organization in secondary phase of free-agent draft, January 13, 1981.
†On disabled list, August 9 to September 20, 1983.
‡Traded with Infielder Hubie Brooks, Catcher Mike Fitzgerald and Pitcher Floyd Youmans to Montreal Expos for Catcher Gary Carter, December 10, 1984.
§On disabled list, June 24 to July 13, 1985; included rehabilitation disability assignment to Indianapolis, July 4 to July 13, 1985.
xTraded with Catcher Jeff Reed and Pitcher Randy St. Claire to Cincinnati Reds for Outfielder Tracy Jones and Pitcher Pat Pacillo, July 13, 1988.
yOn disabled list, June 6 to June 21, 1989.

CHAMPIONSHIP SERIES RECORD

Year Club	League	Pos.	G.	AB.	R.	H.	2B.	3B.	HR.	RBI.	B.A.	PO.	A.	E.	F.A.
1990—Cincinnati	Nat.	PH-OF	3	7	1	2	1	0	0	1	.286	7	0	0	1.000

WORLD SERIES RECORD

Year Club	League	Pos.	G.	AB.	R.	H.	2B.	3B.	HR.	RBI.	B.A.	PO.	A.	E.	F.A.
1990—Cincinnati	Nat.	PH-OF	2	4	1	2	0	0	0	0	.500	3	0	0	1.000

MICHAEL ATWATER WITT
(Mike)

Born July 20, 1960, at Fullerton, Calif.
Height, 6.07. Weight, 203.
Throws and bats righthanded.
Attending Cypress Junior College, Cypress, Calif.

Pitched 1-0 perfect game against Texas Rangers, September 30, 1984.
Pitched two innings in combination with Mark Langston in 1-0 no-hit victory against Seattle Mariners, April 11, 1990.
Major League saves: 1983 (5), 1990 (1). Total—6.
Tied for American League lead in hit batsmen with 11 in 1981.

Year Club	League	G.	IP.	W.	L.	Pct.	H.	R.	ER.	SO.	BB.	ERA.
1978—Idaho Falls	Pioneer	13	86	7	1	.875	88	45	34	79	26	3.56
1979—Salinas	California	30	141	8	10	.444	156	96	80	94	70	5.11
1980—Salinas	California	13	90	7	3	.700	85	30	21	76	35	2.10
1980—El Paso	Texas	12	70	5	5	.500	72	53	45	64	39	5.79
1981—California	American	22	129	8	9	.471	123	60	47	75	47	3.28
1982—California	American	33	179⅔	8	6	.571	177	77	70	85	47	3.51
1983—California	American	43	154	7	14	.333	173	90	84	77	75	4.91
1984—California	American	34	246⅔	15	11	.577	227	103	95	196	84	3.47
1985—California	American	35	250	15	9	.625	228	115	99	180	98	3.56
1986—California	American	34	269	18	10	.643	218	95	85	208	73	2.84
1987—California†	American	36	247	16	14	.533	252	128	110	192	84	4.01
1988—California	American	34	249⅔	13	16	.448	263	★130	115	133	87	4.15
1989—California	American	33	220	9	15	.375	252	119	●111	123	48	4.54
1990—California‡-New York§x	American	26	117	5	9	.357	106	62	52	74	47	4.00
Major League Totals—10 Years		330	2062	114	113	.502	2019	979	868	1343	690	3.79

Selected by California Angels' organization in 4th round of free-agent draft, June 6, 1978.
†Granted free agency, November 9, 1987; re-signed by Angels, December 22, 1987.
‡Traded to New York Yankees for Outfielder Dave Winfield, May 11, 1990.
§On disabled list, June 9 to August 7, 1990.
xGranted free agency, December 7, 1990; re-signed by Yankees, January 2, 1991.

Year	Club	League	G.	IP.	W.	L.	Pct.	H.	R.	ER.	SO.	BB.	ERA.
1982—California	American	1	3	0	0	.000	2	2	2	3	2	6.00
1986—California	American	2	17⅔	1	0	1.000	13	5	5	8	2	2.55
Championship Series Totals—2 Years			3	20⅔	1	0	1.000	15	7	7	11	4	3.05

ALL-STAR GAME RECORD

Member of American League All-Star Team in 1986 and 1987; did not play.

ROBERT ANDREW WITT
(Bobby)

Born May 11, 1964, at Canton, Mass.
Height, 6.02. Weight, 205.
Throws and bats righthanded.
Attended University of Oklahoma, Norman, Okla.

Shares major league record for most strikeouts, inning (4), August 2, 1987, second inning.
Led American League in wild pitches with 22 in 1986 and tied for lead with 16 in 1988.
Named as righthanded pitcher on THE SPORTING NEWS College Baseball All-America Team, 1985.
Member of 1984 U.S. Olympic baseball team.

Year	Club	League	G.	IP.	W.	L.	Pct.	H.	R.	ER.	SO.	BB.	ERA.
1985—Tulsa	Texas	11	35	0	6	.000	26	26	25	39	44	6.43
1986—Texas	American	31	157⅔	11	9	.550	130	104	96	174	★143	5.48
1987—Texas†‡	American	26	143	8	10	.444	114	82	78	160	★140	4.91
1987—Oklahoma City	Am. Assoc.	1	5	1	0	1.000	5	5	5	2	3	9.00
1987—Tulsa	Texas	1	5	0	1	.000	5	9	3	2	6	5.40
1988—Texas	American	22	174⅓	8	10	.444	134	83	76	148	101	3.92
1988—Oklahoma City	Am. Assoc.	11	76⅔	4	6	.400	69	42	37	70	47	4.34
1989—Texas	American	31	194⅓	12	13	.480	182	123	●111	166	★114	5.14
1990—Texas§	American	33	222	17	10	.630	197	98	83	221	110	3.36
Major League Totals—5 Years			143	891⅓	56	52	.519	757	490	444	869	608	4.48

Selected by Cincinnati Reds' organization in 7th round of free-agent draft, June 7, 1982.
Selected by Texas Rangers' organization in 1st round (third player selected) of free-agent draft, June 3, 1985.
†On disabled list, May 21 to June 20, 1987; included rehabilitation disability assignment to Oklahoma City, June 7 to June 12, and Tulsa, June 13, 1987.
‡Struck out in only at-bat.
§Appeared in two games as a pinch-runner.

TODD ROLAND WORRELL

Name pronounced Wor-RELL.

Born September 28, 1959, at Arcadia, Calif.
Height, 6.05. Weight, 210.
Throws and bats righthanded.
Received bachelor of science degree in Christian education from
Biola College, La Mirada, Calif.
Brother of Tim Worrell, pitcher in San Diego Padres' organization.

Holds major league record for most saves by rookie (36), 1986.
Major League saves: 1985 (5), 1986 (36), 1987 (33), 1988 (32), 1989 (20). Total—126.
Led National League in games finished in relief with 60, saves with 36 and intentional bases on balls issued with 16 in 1986.
Named National League Rookie Pitcher of the Year by THE SPORTING NEWS, 1986.
Named National League Rookie of the Year by Baseball Writers' Association of America, 1986.
Named National League Fireman of the Year by THE SPORTING NEWS, 1986.
Named righthanded pitcher on THE SPORTING NEWS College Baseball All-America Team, 1982.

Year	Club	League	G.	IP.	W.	L.	Pct.	H.	R.	ER.	SO.	BB.	ERA.
1982—Erie	NYP	9	51⅔	4	1	.800	52	23	19	57	15	3.31
1983—Louisville	Am. Assoc.	15	79⅔	4	2	.667	76	49	42	46	42	4.74
1983—Arkansas	Texas	10	70⅓	5	2	.714	57	33	24	74	37	3.07
1984—Arkansas	Texas	18	100⅓	3	10	.231	109	72	50	88	67	4.49
1984—St. Petersburg	Florida St.	8	47⅓	3	2	.600	41	22	11	33	24	2.09
1985—Louisville	Am. Assoc.	34	127⅔	8	6	.571	114	59	51	★126	47	3.60
1985—St. Louis	National	17	21⅔	3	0	1.000	17	7	7	17	7	2.91
1986—St. Louis†	National	74	103⅔	9	10	.474	86	29	24	73	41	2.08
1987—St. Louis‡	National	75	94⅔	8	6	.571	86	29	28	92	34	2.66
1988—St. Louis	National	68	90	5	9	.357	69	32	30	78	34	3.00
1989—St. Louis‡§	National	47	51⅔	3	5	.375	42	21	17	41	26	2.96
1989—Louisville	Am. Assoc.	1	1	0	0	.000	0	0	0	1	0	0.00
1990—St. Louis x	National					(Did not play)						
Major League Totals—5 Years			281	361⅔	28	30	.483	300	118	106	301	142	2.64

Selected by St. Louis Cardinals' organization in 1st round (21st player selected) of free-agent draft, June 7, 1982.
†Appeared in two games as an outfielder with no chances.
‡Appeared in one game as an outfielder with no chances.
§On disabled list, May 14 to June 7, 1989; included rehabilitation disability assignment to Louisville, June 6 and June 7, 1989.
xOn disabled list, March 31, 1990 through entire season.

Year Club	League	G.	IP.	W.	L.	Pct.	H.	R.	ER.	SO.	BB.	ERA.
1985—St. Louis	National	4	6⅓	1	0	1.000	4	1	1	3	2	1.42
1987—St. Louis	National	3	4⅓	0	0	.000	4	1	1	6	1	2.08
Championship Series Totals—2 Years		7	10⅔	1	0	1.000	8	2	2	9	3	1.69

Appeared as an outfielder in one game of 1987 Championship Series.

WORLD SERIES RECORD

Shares World Series record for most consecutive strikeouts, game (6), October 24, 1985.

Year Club	League	G.	IP.	W.	L.	Pct.	H.	R.	ER.	SO.	BB.	ERA.
1985—St. Louis	National	3	4⅔	0	1	.000	4	2	2	6	2	3.86
1987—St. Louis	National	4	7	0	0	.000	6	1	1	3	4	1.29
World Series Totals—2 Years		7	11⅔	0	1	.000	10	3	3	9	6	2.31

ALL-STAR GAME RECORD

Year League	IP.	W.	L.	Pct.	H.	R.	ER.	SO.	BB.	ERA.
1988—National	1	0	0	.000	0	0	0	0	0	0.00

CRAIG RICHARD WORTHINGTON

Born April 17, 1965, at Los Angeles, Calif.
Height, 6.00. Weight, 202.
Throws and bats righthanded.
Attended Cerritos College, Norwalk, Calif.

Major League stolen bases: 1988 (1), 1989 (1), 1990 (1). Total—3.
Led Carolina League in game-winning RBIs with 16 in 1986.
Led International League third basemen in total chances with 310 in 1987 and 319 in 1988.
Tied for International League lead in double plays by third basemen with 16 in 1987.
Named American League Rookie Player of the Year by THE SPORTING NEWS, 1989.
Named International League Player of the Year, 1988.

Year Club	League	Pos.	G.	AB.	R.	H.	2B.	3B.	HR.	RBI.	B.A.	PO.	A.	E.	F.A.
1985—Bluefield	Appal.	3B	39	129	33	44	9	1	7	20	.341	32	68	12	.893
1986—Hagerstown	Carol.	3B	132	480	85	144	35	1	15	★105	.300	92	249	32	.914
1987—Rochester	Int.	3B	109	383	46	99	14	1	7	50	.258	★79	★211	★20	★.935
1988—Rochester	Int.	★3B-SS	121	430	53	105	25	1	16	73	.244	★91	209	19	.940
1988—Baltimore	Amer.	3B	26	81	5	15	2	0	2	4	.185	20	53	3	.961
1989—Baltimore	Amer.	3B	145	497	57	123	23	0	15	70	.247	113	277	20	.951
1990—Baltimore	Amer.	3B	133	425	46	96	17	0	8	44	.226	90	218	18	.945
Major League Totals—3 Years			304	1003	108	234	42	0	25	118	.233	223	548	41	.950

Selected by New York Mets' organization in 6th round of free-agent draft, January 17, 1984.
Selected by Houston Astros' organization in secondary phase of free-agent draft, June 4, 1984.
Selected by Chicago Cubs' organization in secondary phase of free-agent draft, January 9, 1985.
Selected by Baltimore Orioles' organization in secondary phase of free-agent draft, June 3, 1985.

RICHARD JAMES WRONA

Name pronounced RHO-nah.

(Rick)

Born December 10, 1963, at Tulsa, Okla.
Height, 6.01. Weight, 185.
Throws and bats righthanded.
Attended Wichita State University, Wichita, Kan.
Brother of Bill Wrona, infielder in Chicago Cubs' organization.

Major League stolen bases: 1990 (1).

Year Club	League	Pos.	G.	AB.	R.	H.	2B.	3B.	HR.	RBI.	B.A.	PO.	A.	E.	F.A.
1985—Peoria†	Midw.	C	6	16	2	4	1	0	0	2	.250	31	1	2	.941
1985—Winston-Salem†	Carol.	C	20	49	4	11	4	0	0	2	.224	90	10	3	.971
1986—Winston-Salem	Carol.	C-O-3-1	91	267	43	68	15	0	4	32	.255	464	74	11	.980
1987—Pittsfield	East.	C-1B	70	218	22	48	10	3	1	25	.220	299	49	9	.975
1988—Pittsfield	East.	C	5	6	0	0	0	0	0	1	.000	11	1	0	1.000
1988—Iowa	A. A.	C	83	193	28	51	9	0	2	23	.264	347	36	7	.982
1988—Chicago	Nat.	C	4	6	0	0	0	0	0	0	.000	11	0	1	1.000
1989—Chicago	Nat.	C	38	92	11	26	2	1	2	14	.283	158	15	3	.983
1989—Iowa	A. A.	C-1B-OF	60	189	15	41	8	3	2	13	.217	340	41	6	.984
1990—Chicago	Nat.	C	16	29	3	5	0	0	0	0	.172	55	9	2	.970
1990—Iowa	A. A.	C-1B	58	146	16	33	4	0	2	15	.226	311	37	6	.983
Major League Totals—3 Years			58	127	14	31	2	1	2	14	.244	224	25	5	.980

Selected by Chicago Cubs' organization in 5th round of free-agent draft, June 3, 1985.
†Switch-hitter.

CHAMPIONSHIP SERIES RECORD

Year Club	League	Pos.	G.	AB.	R.	H.	2B.	3B.	HR.	RBI.	B.A.	PO.	A.	E.	F.A.
1989—Chicago	Nat.	C	2	5	0	0	0	0	0	0	.000	9	1	0	1.000

MARVELL WYNNE

Name pronounced Win.
Born December 17, 1959, at Chicago, Ill.
Height, 5.11. Weight, 180.
Throws and bats lefthanded.

Major League stolen bases: 1983 (12), 1984 (24), 1985 (10), 1986 (11), 1987 (11), 1988 (3), 1989 (6), 1990 (3). Total—80.
Led South Atlantic League in total bases with 256 in 1980.
Led South Atlantic League outfielders in assists with 17 in 1980.
Tied for International League lead in game-winning RBIs with 14 in 1982.
Tied for Gulf Coast League lead in being hit by pitch with 5 in 1979.

Year Club	League	Pos.	G.	AB.	R.	H.	2B.	3B.	HR.	RBI.	B.A.	PO.	A.	E.	F.A.
1979—Sarasota Royals...	Gulf C.	OF	50	190	21	54	6	4	4	28	.284	108	9	4	.967
1980—Charleston†	S. Atl.	OF-2B-3B	137	*547	106	152	20	*15	18	98	.278	281	19	13	.958
1981—Jackson	Texas	OF	127	497	69	142	29	2	4	50	.286	267	21	6	.980
1982—Tidewater	Int.	OF	130	512	76	118	15	7	10	65	.230	283	13	12	.961
1983—Tidewater‡	Int.	OF	51	175	32	50	13	1	3	29	.286	114	5	2	.983
1983—Pittsburgh	Nat.	OF	103	366	66	89	16	2	7	26	.243	223	3	4	.983
1984—Pittsburgh	Nat.	OF	154	653	77	174	24	11	0	39	.266	373	8	4	.990
1985—Pittsburgh§x	Nat.	OF	103	337	21	69	6	3	2	18	.205	229	7	3	.987
1986—San Diego	Nat.	OF	137	288	34	76	19	2	7	37	.264	203	3	3	.986
1987—San Diego y	Nat.	OF	98	188	17	47	8	2	2	24	.250	100	2	2	.981
1988—San Diego	Nat.	OF	128	333	37	88	13	4	11	42	.264	216	5	3	.987
1989—S.D. z-Chi.	Nat.	OF	125	342	27	83	13	2	7	39	.243	177	7	6	.968
1990—Chicago a	Nat.	OF	92	186	21	38	8	2	4	19	.204	108	3	1	.991
Major League Totals—8 Years			940	2693	300	664	107	28	40	244	.247	1629	38	26	.985

Signed as free agent by Kansas City Royals' organization, September 3, 1978.
†Traded with Pitcher John Skinner to New York Mets' organization for Pitcher Juan Berenguer, March 31, 1981.
‡Traded with Pitcher Steve Senteney to Pittsburgh Pirates for Catcher Junior Ortiz and Pitcher Arthur Ray, June 14, 1983.
§On disabled list, April 20 to May 5 and June 3 to June 18, 1985.
xTraded to San Diego Padres for Pitcher Bob Patterson, April 3, 1986.
yOn disabled list, June 10 to June 25, 1987.
zTraded with Infielder Luis Salazar to Chicago Cubs for Pitcher Calvin Schiraldi, Outfielder Darrin Jackson and a player to be named later, August 30, 1989; San Diego Padres acquired First Baseman Phil Stephenson to complete deal, September 5, 1989.
aSold to Hanshin Tigers of Japanese Baseball League, November 1, 1990.

CHAMPIONSHIP SERIES RECORD

Year Club	League	Pos.	G.	AB.	R.	H.	2B.	3B.	HR.	RBI.	B.A.	PO.	A.	E.	F.A.
1989—Chicago	Nat.	PH-OF	4	6	0	1	0	0	0	0	.167	3	0	0	1.000

ERIC GIRARD YELDING

Born February 22, 1965, at Montrose, Ala.
Height, 5.11. Weight, 165.
Thows and bats righthanded.
Attended Chipola Junior College, Marianna, Fla.

Major League stolen bases: 1989 (11), 1990 (64). Total—75.
Led National League in caught stealing with 25 in 1990.
Led International League in stolen bases with 59 and caught stealing with 23 in 1988.
Led Carolina League in stolen bases with 62 and caught stealing with 26 in 1985.
Led Pioneer League in caught stealing with 11 in 1984.
Led International League second basemen in errors with 21 in 1988.
Led California League shortstops in total chances with 573 in 1986.

Year Club	League	Pos.	G.	AB.	R.	H.	2B.	3B.	HR.	RBI.	B.A.	PO.	A.	E.	F.A.
1984—Medicine Hat	Pion.	OF	67	*304	61	94	14	6	4	29	.309	99	9	13	.893
1985—Kinston	Carol.	OF	135	526	59	137	14	4	2	31	.260	310	10	9	.973
1986—Ventura County ...	Calif.	SS	131	*560	83	157	14	7	4	40	.280	*231	284	*58	.899
1987—Myrtle Beach	S. Atl.	SS	88	357	53	109	12	2	1	31	.305	126	226	45	.887
1987—Knoxville	South.	SS	39	150	23	30	6	1	0	7	.200	64	92	14	.918
1988—Syracuse†	Int.	2B-SS	●138	*556	●69	139	15	2	1	38	.250	222	310	35	.938
1989—Houston‡	Nat.	SS-2B-OF	70	90	19	21	2	0	0	9	.233	37	57	3	.969
1990—Houston	Nat.	O-S-2-3	142	511	69	130	9	5	1	28	.254	315	124	17	.963
Major League Totals—2 Years			212	601	88	151	11	5	1	37	.251	352	181	20	.964

Selected by Toronto Blue Jays' organization in 1st round (19th player selected) of free-agent draft, January 17, 1984.
†Drafted by Chicago Cubs, December 5, 1988.
‡Claimed on waivers by Houston Astros, April 3, 1989.

RICHARD MARTIN YETT
(Rich)

Born October 6, 1962, at Pomona, Calif.
Height, 6.02. Weight, 187.
Throws and bats righthanded.

Major League saves: 1986 (1), 1987 (1). Total—2.
Led International League in wild pitches with 16 in 1985.

Year Club	League	G.	IP.	W.	L.	Pct.	H.	R.	ER.	SO.	BB.	ERA.
1980—Elizabethton	Ap'lachian	10	52	3	4	.429	46	30	25	35	19	4.33
1981—Wisconsin Rapids	Midwest	25	164	12	6	.667	147	87	67	121	77	3.68
1982—Visalia	California	27	196⅔	16	9	.640	183	98	80	121	97	3.66
1983—Orlando†	Southern	24	162	8	10	.444	153	82	68	93	78	3.78
1984—Toledo	Int'national	26	174⅔	12	9	.571	159	71	63	129	66	3.25
1985—Minnesota	American	1	⅓	0	0	.000	1	1	1	0	2	27.00
1985—Toledo‡-Maine	Int'national	25	165	9	11	.450	162	82	76	99	★101	4.15
1986—Maine	Int'national	1	6	0	0	.000	7	3	3	2	2	4.50
1986—Cleveland	American	39	78⅔	5	3	.625	84	48	45	50	37	5.15
1987—Cleveland	American	37	97⅔	3	9	.250	96	63	57	59	49	5.25
1987—Buffalo	Am. Assoc.	7	44⅓	3	3	.500	38	17	15	33	18	3.05
1988—Cleveland§	American	23	134⅓	9	6	.600	146	72	69	71	55	4.62
1988—Williamsport	Eastern	1	3⅓	0	1	.000	6	6	3	4	3	8.10
1988—Colorado Springs	P. Coast	2	8	0	1	.000	10	8	8	5	3	9.00
1989—Cleveland x	American	32	99	5	6	.455	111	56	55	47	47	5.00
1990—Minnesota	American	4	4⅓	0	0	.000	6	2	1	2	1	2.08
1990—Portland	P. Coast	22	100⅔	4	6	.400	117	72	69	58	60	6.17
Major League Totals—6 Years		136	414⅓	22	24	.478	444	242	228	229	191	4.95

Selected by Minnesota Twins' organization in 26th round of free-agent draft, June 3, 1980.

†On disabled list, April 8 to April 25, 1983.

‡Traded to Cleveland Indians' organization, September 17, 1985, completing deal in which Cleveland traded Pitcher Bert Blyleven to Minnesota Twins for Pitcher Curt Wardle, Outfielder Jim Weaver, Infielder Jay Bell and a player to be named later, August 1, 1986.

§On disabled list, June 14 to July 18, 1988; included rehabilitation disability assignment to Williamsport, June 29 to July 18, 1988.

xReleased, December 21, 1989; signed by Minnesota Twins, December 29, 1989.

MICHAEL DAVID YORK
(Mike)

Born September 6, 1964, at Oak Park, Ill.
Height, 6.01. Weight, 192.
Throws and bats righthanded.

Year Club	League	G.	IP.	W.	L.	Pct.	H.	R.	ER.	SO.	BB.	ERA.
1983—Oneonta†	NYP	9	11	0	0	.000	19	13	10	3	8	8.18
1984—Sarasota White Sox‡	Gulf Coast	5	14⅔	1	0	1.000	18	9	6	19	9	3.68
1985—Bristol	Ap'lachian	21	38	●9	2	●.818	24	12	10	31	34	2.37
1986—Lakeland	Florida St.	16	40⅔	1	3	.250	49	42	29	29	43	6.42
1986—Gastonia§	S. Atlantic	22	34	2	2	.500	26	15	13	27	27	3.44
1987—Macon	S. Atlantic	28	165⅔	★17	6	.739	129	71	56	169	★88	3.04
1988—Salem	Carolina	13	84	9	2	●.818	65	31	25	77	52	2.68
1988—Harrisburg	Eastern	13	82⅓	0	5	.000	92	43	34	61	45	3.72
1989—Harrisburg	Eastern	18	121	11	5	.688	105	37	31	106	40	2.31
1989—Buffalo	Am. Assoc.	8	41	1	3	.250	48	29	27	28	25	5.93
1990—Buffalo	Am. Assoc.	27	158⅔	8	7	.533	165	87	74	130	●78	4.20
1990—Pittsburgh	National	4	12⅔	1	1	.500	13	5	4	4	5	2.84
Major League Totals—1 Year		4	12⅔	1	1	.500	13	5	4	4	5	2.84

Selected by New York Yankees' organization in 40th round of free-agent draft, June 7, 1982.

†Released, July 22, 1983; signed by Sarasota White Sox (Chicago White Sox' organization), July 18, 1984.

‡Released, April 8, 1985; signed by Lakeland (Detroit Tigers' organization), June 9, 1985.

§Released, August 29, 1986; signed by Pittsburgh Pirates' organization, October 11, 1986.

ANTHONY WAYNE YOUNG

Born January 19, 1966, at Houston, Tex.
Height, 6.02. Weight, 200.
Throws and bats righthanded.
Attended University of Houston, Houston, Tex.

Named Texas League Pitcher of the Year, 1990.

Year Club	League	G.	IP.	W.	L.	Pct.	H.	R.	ER.	SO.	BB.	ERA.
1987—Little Falls	NYP	14	53⅔	3	4	.429	58	37	27	48	25	4.53
1988—Little Falls	NYP	15	73⅔	3	5	.375	51	33	18	75	34	2.20
1989—Columbia†	S. Atlantic	21	129	9	6	.600	115	60	50	127	55	3.49
1990—Jackson‡	Texas	23	158	★15	3	★.833	116	38	29	95	52	★1.65

Selected by Montreal Expos' organization in 10th round of free-agent draft, June 4, 1984.

Selected by New York Mets' organization in 38th round of free-agent draft, June 2, 1987.

†On disabled list, July 19, 1989 through remainder of season.

‡On disabled list, June 11 to June 18, 1990.

CLIFFORD RAPHAEL YOUNG
(Cliff)

Born August 2, 1964, at Willis, Tex.
Height, 6.04. Weight, 210.
Throws and bats lefthanded.

Led Southern League in games started by pitchers with 31 in 1986.
Led Florida State League in home runs allowed with 13 in 1986.

Year Club	League	G.	IP.	W.	L.	Pct.	H.	R.	ER.	SO.	BB.	ERA.
1983—Calgary	Pioneer	13	79⅓	7	1	.875	98	55	45	72	32	5.11
1984—Gastonia†	S. Atlantic	24	144⅓	8	10	.444	117	77	67	121	68	4.18
1985—West Palm Beach‡	Florida St.	25	153⅔	15	5	.750	149	77	68	112	57	3.98
1986—Knoxville§x...........................	Southern	31	★203⅔	12	★14	.462	★232	111	88	121	71	3.89
1987—Knoxville	Southern	42	119⅓	8	9	.471	148	76	59	81	43	4.45
1988—Syracuse y	Int'national	33	147⅓	9	6	.600	133	68	56	75	32	3.42
1989—Edmonton	P. Coast	31	139	8	9	.471	158	80	74	89	32	4.79
1990—Edmonton	P. Coast	30	52	7	4	.636	45	15	14	30	10	2.42
1990—California	American	17	30⅔	1	1	.500	40	14	12	19	7	3.52
Major League Totals—1 Year		17	30⅔	1	1	.500	40	14	12	19	7	3.52

Selected by Montreal Expos' organization in 5th round of free-agent draft, June 6, 1983.

†On suspended list, May 23 to May 30, 1984.

‡Traded to Toronto Blue Jays' organization, September 10, 1985, completing deal in which Toronto traded Outfielder Mitch Webster to Montreal Expos for a player to be named later, June 22, 1985.

§On disabled list, August 20 to August 30, 1986.

xDrafted by Oakland Athletics, December 8, 1986; returned, April 6, 1987.

yTraded to California Angels for Pitcher DeWayne Buice, March 9, 1989.

CURTIS ALLEN YOUNG
(Curt)

Born April 16, 1960, at Saginaw, Mich.
Height, 6.01. Weight, 175.
Throws left and bats righthanded.
Attended Central Michigan University, Mt. Pleasant, Mich.

Led California League pitchers in games started with 28 in 1982.

Year Club	League	G.	IP.	W.	L.	Pct.	H.	R.	ER.	SO.	BB.	ERA.
1981—Medford	Northwest	8	53	2	2	.500	45	27	25	49	32	4.25
1981—Modesto	California	5	31	2	1	.667	28	15	12	22	16	3.48
1982—Modesto	California	28	205	15	8	.652	189	90	79	162	81	3.47
1983—Tacoma	P. Coast	27	158⅔	12	9	.571	94	89	109	52	5.05
1983—Oakland	American.	8	9	0	1	.000	17	17	16	5	5	16.00
1984—Tacoma	P. Coast	14	95⅓	6	4	.600	88	45	40	61	28	3.78
1984—Oakland	American	20	108⅔	9	4	.692	118	53	49	41	31	4.06
1985—Oakland†	American	19	46	0	4	.000	57	38	37	19	22	7.24
1985—Modesto	California	2	5⅔	0	0	.000	7	4	3	3	6	4.76
1985—Tacoma	P. Coast	3	15	2	0	1.000	10	7	6	8	7	3.60
1986—Tacoma	P. Coast	4	27	4	0	1.000	16	7	6	28	6	2.00
1986—Oakland	American	29	198	13	9	.591	176	88	76	116	57	3.45
1987—Oakland‡§	American	31	203	13	7	.650	194	102	92	124	44	4.08
1988—Oakland	American	26	156⅓	11	8	.579	162	77	72	69	50	4.14
1989—Oakland	American	25	111	5	9	.357	117	56	46	55	47	3.73
1990—Oakland x	American	26	124⅓	9	6	.600	124	70	67	56	53	4.85
Major League Totals—8 Years		184	956⅓	60	48	.556	965	501	455	485	309	4.28

Selected by Oakland A's organization in 4th round of free-agent draft, June 8, 1981.

†On disabled list, May 3 to July 5, 1985; included rehabilitation disability assignment to Modesto, June 29 to July 5, 1985.

‡On disabled list, June 30 to July 20, 1987.

§Had one at-bat with no hits.

xAppeared in one game as a pinch-runner.

CHAMPIONSHIP SERIES RECORD

Year Club	League	G.	IP.	W.	L.	Pct.	H.	R.	ER.	SO.	BB.	ERA.
1988—Oakland	American	1	1⅓	0	0	.000	1	1	0	2	0	0.00

WORLD SERIES RECORD

Year Club	League	G.	IP.	W.	L.	Pct.	H.	R.	ER.	SO.	BB.	ERA.
1988—Oakland	American	1	1	0	0	.000	1	0	0	0	0	0.00
1990—Oakland	American	1	1	0	0	.000	1	0	0	0	0	0.00
World Series Totals—2 Years		2	2	0	0	.000	2	0	0	0	0	0.00

Eligible for 1989 World Series with Oakland Athletics; did not play.

GERALD ANTHONY YOUNG

Born October 22, 1964, in Tele, Honduras.
Height, 6.02. Weight, 185.
Throws right and bats left and righthanded.

Major League stolen bases: 1987 (26), 1988 (65), 1989 (34), 1990 (6). Total—131.

Led National League in caught stealing with 25 in 1989 and tied for lead with 27 in 1988.

Led National League outfielders in total chances with 428 and tied for lead in double plays with 5 in 1989.

Led Southern League in stolen bases with 54 and caught stealing with 27 in 1986.

Tied for Appalachian League lead in being hit by pitch with 6 in 1982.

Led Appalachian League shortstops in errors with 38 in 1982.

Tied for Florida State League lead in double plays by outfielders with 5 in 1985.

Year—Club	League	Pos.	G.	AB.	R.	H.	2B.	3B.	HR.	RBI.	B.A.	PO.	A.	E.	F.A.
1982—Kingsport	Appal.	SS-2B-3B	59	197	27	35	6	1	0	15	.178	79	170	39	.865
1983—Sarasota Mets	Gulf C.	OF-SS	56	177	34	42	7	2	1	14	.237	88	9	7	.933
1984—Columbia†	S. Atl.	OF	124	396	69	84	14	3	1	52	.212	254	7	4	.985
1985—Osceola	Fla. St.	OF	133	474	88	121	20	9	3	48	.255	251	11	5	.981
1986—Columbus	South.	OF	136	539	101	151	30	4	9	62	.280	317	22	13	.963
1987—Tucson	P. C.	OF	86	340	59	99	15	5	2	31	.291	232	7	7	.972
1987—Houston	Nat.	OF	71	274	44	88	9	2	1	15	.321	143	5	3	.980
1988—Houston	Nat.	OF	149	576	79	148	21	9	0	37	.257	357	10	3	.992
1989—Houston	Nat.	OF	146	533	71	124	17	3	0	38	.233	★412	★15	1	★.998
1990—Houston	Nat.	OF	57	154	15	27	4	1	1	4	.175	99	4	1	.990
1990—Tucson	P. C.	OF	49	183	37	61	7	4	0	24	.333	112	8	6	.952
Major League Totals—4 Years			423	1537	209	387	51	15	2	94	.252	1011	34	8	.992

Selected by New York Mets' organization in 5th round of free-agent draft, June 7, 1982.

†Traded with Infielder Manny Lee to Houston Astros, August 31, 1984, as partial completion of deal in which New York Mets acquired Infielder Ray Knight for three players to be named later, August 28, 1984; Houston acquired Pitcher Mitch Cook to complete deal, September 10, 1984.

MATTHEW JOHN YOUNG
(Matt)

Born August 9, 1958, at Pasadena, Calif.
Height, 6.03. Weight, 205.
Throws and bats lefthanded.
Attended Pasadena City College, Pasadena, Calif., and
UCLA, Los Angeles, Calif.

Shares major league record for most strikeouts, innings (4), September 9, 1990, first inning.
Major League saves: 1985 (1), 1986 (13), 1987 (11). Total—25.

Year—Club	League	G.	IP.	W.	L.	Pct.	H.	R.	ER.	SO.	BB.	ERA.
1980—Bellingham	Northwest	12	73	4	5	.444	73	46	40	53	62	4.93
1981—Lynn	Eastern	14	81	3	9	.250	80	47	36	57	38	4.00
1982—Salt Lake City	P. Coast	29	176	12	10	.545	192	113	91	118	75	4.65
1983—Seattle	American	33	203⅔	11	15	.423	178	86	74	130	79	3.27
1984—Seattle†	American	22	113½	6	8	.429	141	81	72	73	57	5.72
1984—Salt Lake City	P. Coast	6	41⅔	6	0	1.000	32	9	7	37	20	1.51
1985—Seattle	American	37	218⅓	12	★19	.387	242	135	119	136	76	4.91
1986—Seattle‡	American	65	103⅔	8	6	.571	108	50	44	82	46	3.82
1987—Los Angeles§	National	47	54⅓	5	8	.385	62	30	27	42	17	4.47
1988—Oakland xy	American					(Did not play)						
1989—Modesto z	California	3	12	0	0	.000	9	1	1	13	6	0.75
1989—Tacoma	P. Coast	2	11	1	1	.500	8	4	3	6	5	2.45
1989—Oakland a	American	26	37⅓	1	4	.200	42	31	28	27	31	6.75
1990—Seattle b	American	34	225⅓	8	18	.308	198	106	88	176	107	3.51
American League Totals—6 Years		217	901⅔	46	70	.397	909	489	425	624	396	4.24
National League Totals—1 Year		47	54⅓	5	8	.385	62	30	27	42	17	4.47
Major League Totals—7 Years		264	956	51	78	.395	971	519	452	666	413	4.26

Selected by Boston Red Sox' organization in 2nd round of free-agent draft, January 10, 1978.
Selected by Seattle Mariners' organization in 2nd round of free-agent draft, June 3, 1980.
†On disabled list, July 4 to July 29, 1984.
‡Traded to Los Angeles Dodgers for Pitcher Dennis Powell and Infielder Mike Watters, December 10, 1986.
§As part of an eight-player, three-team deal, New York Mets traded Pitcher Jesse Orosco to Oakland Athletics, December 11, 1987. Oakland then traded Orosco along with Shortstop Alfredo Griffin and Pitcher Jay Howell to Los Angeles Dodgers for Pitchers Bob Welch, Matt Young and Jack Savage. Oakland then traded Savage along with Pitchers Wally Whitehurst and Kevin Tapani to New York.
xOn disabled list, April 3, 1988 through entire season.
yReleased, December 21, 1988; re-signed by Athletics, January 19, 1989.
zOn Oakland disabled list, March 19 to June 13, 1989; included rehabilitation disability assignment to Modesto, May 16 and May 25 to June 2, 1989; and Tacoma, June 3 to June 9, 1989.
aGranted free agency, November 13, 1989; signed by Seattle Mariners, December 15, 1989.
bGranted free agency, November 5, 1990; signed by Boston Red Sox, December 4, 1990.

CHAMPIONSHIP SERIES RECORD

Year—Club	League	G.	IP.	W.	L.	Pct.	H.	R.	ER.	SO.	BB.	ERA.
1989—Oakland	American	1	⅓	0	0	.000	0	0	0	0	2	0.00

WORLD SERIES RECORD

Eligible for 1989 World Series with Oakland Athletics; did not play.

ALL-STAR GAME RECORD

Year—League			IP.	W.	L.	Pct.	H.	R.	ER.	SO.	BB.	ERA.
1983—American			1	0	0	.000	0	0	0	1	0	0.00

ROBIN R. YOUNT

Born September 16, 1955, at Danville, Ill.
Height, 6.00. Weight, 180.
Throws and bats righthanded.
Brother of Larry Yount, pitcher with Houston Astros, 1971.

Major League stolen bases: 1974 (7), 1975 (12), 1976 (16), 1977 (16), 1978 (16), 1979 (11), 1980 (20), 1981 (4), 1982 (14), 1983 (12), 1984 (14), 1985 (10), 1986 (14), 1987 (19), 1988 (22), 1989 (19), 1990 (15). Total—241.

Hit for the cycle, June 12, 1988.
Led American League in total bases with 367 and slugging percentage with .578 in 1982.
Led American League outfielders in fielding percentage with .997 in 1986.
Led American League shortstops in double plays with 104 and total chances with 831 in 1976.
Named Major League Player of the Year by THE SPORTING NEWS, 1982.
Named American League Player of the Year by THE SPORTING NEWS, 1982.
Named American League Most Valuable Player by Baseball Writers' Association of America, 1982 and 1989.
Named outfielder on THE SPORTING NEWS American League All-Star Team, 1989.
Named shortstop on THE SPORTING NEWS American League All-Star Team, 1978, 1980 and 1982.
Named shortstop on THE SPORTING NEWS American League All-Star fielding team, 1982.
Named outfielder on THE SPORTING NEWS American League Silver Slugger team, 1989.
Named shortstop on THE SPORTING NEWS American League Silver Slugger team, 1980 and 1982.

Year	Club	League	Pos.	G.	AB.	R.	H.	2B.	3B.	HR.	RBI.	B.A.	PO.	A.	E.	F.A.
1973—Newark	NYP		SS	64	242	29	69	15	3	3	25	.285	43	85	18	.877
1974—Milwaukee	Amer.		SS	107	344	48	86	14	5	3	26	.250	148	327	19	.962
1975—Milwaukee	Amer.		SS	147	558	67	149	28	2	8	52	.267	273	402	★44	.939
1976—Milwaukee	Amer.		●SS-OF	●161	638	59	161	19	3	2	54	.252	●290	510	31	.963
1972—Milwaukee	Amer.		SS	154	605	66	174	34	4	4	49	.288	256	449	29	.964
1978—Milwaukee†	Amer.		SS	127	502	66	147	23	9	9	71	.293	246	453	30	.959
1979—Milwaukee	Amer.		SS	149	577	72	154	26	5	8	51	.267	267	517	25	.969
1980—Milwaukee	Amer.		SS	143	611	121	179	★49	10	23	87	.293	239	455	28	.961
1981—Milwaukee	Amer.		SS	96	377	50	103	15	5	10	49	.273	161	370	8	★.985
1982—Milwaukee	Amer.		SS	156	635	129	★210	●46	12	29	114	.331	253	★489	24	.969
1983—Milwaukee	Amer.		SS	149	578	102	178	42	★10	17	80	.308	256	420	19	.973
1984—Milwaukee	Amer.		SS	160	624	105	186	27	7	16	80	.298	199	402	18	.971
1985—Milwaukee	Amer.		OF-1B	122	466	76	129	26	3	15	68	.277	267	5	8	.971
1986—Milwaukee	Amer.		OF-1B	140	522	82	163	31	7	9	46	.312	365	9	2	.995
1987—Milwaukee	Amer.		OF	158	635	99	198	25	9	21	103	.312	380	5	5	.987
1988—Milwaukee	Amer.		OF	★162	621	92	190	38	●11	13	91	.306	444	12	2	.996
1989—Milwaukee‡	Amer.		OF	160	614	101	195	38	9	21	103	.318	361	8	7	.981
1990—Milwaukee	Amer.		OF	158	587	98	145	17	5	17	77	.247	★422	3	4	.991
Major League Totals—17 Years				2449	9494	1433	2747	498	116	225	1201	.289	4827	4836	300	.970

Selected by Milwaukee Brewers' organization in 1st round (third player selected) of free-agent draft, June 5, 1973.
†On disabled list, March 28 to May 3, 1978.
‡Granted free agency, November 13, 1989; re-signed by Brewers, December 19, 1989.

DIVISION SERIES RECORD

Year	Club	League	Pos.	G.	AB.	R.	H.	2B.	3B.	HR.	RBI.	B.A.	PO.	A.	E.	F.A.
1981—Milwaukee	Amer.		SS	5	19	4	6	0	1	0	1	.316	6	16	1	.957

CHAMPIONSHIP SERIES RECORD

Year	Club	League	Pos.	G.	AB.	R.	H.	2B.	3B.	HR.	RBI.	B.A.	PO.	A.	E.	F.A.
1982—Milwaukee	Amer.		SS	5	16	1	4	0	0	0	0	.250	11	12	1	.958

WORLD SERIES RECORD

Shares World Series record for most at-bats, nine-inning game (6), October 12, 1982.

Year	Club	League	Pos.	G.	AB.	R.	H.	2B.	3B.	HR.	RBI.	B.A.	PO.	A.	E.	F.A.
1982—Milwaukee	Amer.		SS	7	29	6	12	3	0	1	6	.414	20	19	3	.929

ALL-STAR GAME RECORD

Year	League	Pos.	AB.	R.	H.	2B.	3B.	HR.	RBI.	B.A.	PO.	A.	E.	F.A.
1980—American		SS	2	0	0	0	0	0	0	.000	3	2	0	1.000
1982—American		SS	3	0	0	0	0	0	0	.000	0	2	0	1.000
1983—American		SS	2	1	0	0	0	0	1	.000	0	1	0	1.000
All-Star Game Totals—3 Years			7	1	0	0	0	0	1	.000	3	5	0	1.000

CLINTON WAYNE ZAVARAS
(Clint)

Born January 4, 1967, at Denver, Colo.
Height, 6.01. Weight, 175.
Throws and bats righthanded.

Year	Club	League	G.	IP.	W.	L.	Pct.	H.	R.	ER.	SO.	BB.	ERA.
1985—Bellingham	Northwest		12	56⅓	4	7	.364	49	37	35	62	47	5.59
1986—Wausau	Midwest		17	91⅓	6	6	.500	68	45	34	98	67	3.35
1987—Salinas	California		26	139⅔	7	12	.368	102	87	69	180	101	4.45
1988—Vermont	Eastern		24	128⅔	10	7	.588	115	67	56	120	54	3.92
1989—Calgary	P. Coast		21	110⅓	6	9	.400	105	77	74	89	56	6.04
1989—Seattle	American		10	52	1	6	.143	49	33	30	31	30	5.19
1990—Seattle†	American						(Did Not Play)						
Major League Totals—1 Year			10	52	1	6	.143	49	33	30	31	30	5.19

Selected by Seattle Mariners' organization in 3rd round of free-agent draft, June 3, 1985.
†On disabled list, April 2, 1990 through entire season.

TODD EDWARD ZEILE

Born September 9, 1965, at Van Nuys, Calif.
Height, 6.01. Weight, 190.
Throws and bats righthanded.
Attended UCLA, Los Angeles, Calif.
Husband of Julianne McNamara, former Olympic gymnast.

Major League stolen bases: 1990 (2).
Led New York-Pennsylvania League in sacrifice flies with 6 in 1986.
Led American Association catchers in fielding percentage with .992 and passed balls with 17 in 1989.
Led Texas League catchers in putouts with 687 and total chances with 761 in 1988.
Tied for New York-Pennsylvania League lead in double plays by catchers with 7 in 1986.
Named Midwest League Co-Most Valuable Player, 1987.

Year	Club	League	Pos.	G.	AB.	R.	H.	2B.	3B.	HR.	RBI.	B.A.	PO.	A.	E.	F.A.
1986—Erie	NYP		C	70	248	40	64	14	1	14	*63	.258	407	*66	8	.983
1987—Springfield	Midw.		C-3B	130	487	94	142	24	4	25	*106	.292	867	79	14	.985
1988—Arkansas	Texas		C-OF-1B	129	430	95	117	33	2	19	75	.272	697	66	10	.987
1989—Louisville	A. A.		C-3B-1B	118	453	71	131	26	3	19	85	.289	583	71	6	.991
1989—St. Louis	Nat.		C	28	82	7	21	3	1	1	8	.256	125	10	4	.971
1990—St. Louis	Nat.		C-3-1-O	144	495	62	121	25	3	15	57	.244	648	106	15	.980
Major League Totals—2 Years				172	577	69	142	28	4	16	65	.246	773	116	19	.979

Selected by Kansas City Royals' organization in 30th round of free-agent draft, June 6, 1983.
Selected by St. Louis Cardinals' organization in 2nd round of free-agent draft, June 2, 1986.

EDWARD JAMES ZOSKY
(Eddie)

Born February 10, 1968, at Whittier, Calif.
Height, 6.00. Weight, 175.
Throws and bats righthanded.
Attended Fresno State University, Fresno, Calif.

Led Southern League shortstops in double plays with 80 in 1990.
Received reported $182,500 bonus to sign with Toronto Blue Jays, 1989.
Named shortstop on THE SPORTING NEWS College Baseball All-America Team, 1989.

Year	Club	League	Pos.	G.	AB.	R.	H.	2B.	3B.	HR.	RBI.	B.A.	PO.	A.	E.	F.A.
1989—Knoxville	South.		SS	56	208	21	46	5	3	2	14	.221	94	135	8	.966
1990—Knoxville	South.		SS	115	450	53	122	20	7	3	45	.271	*196	295	31	*.941

Selected by New York Mets' organization in 5th round of free-agent draft, June 2, 1986.
Selected by Toronto Blue Jays' organization in 1st round (19th player selected) of free-agent draft, June 5, 1989.

PLAYER MOVES

The following player deals involve players in the Register with the transactions occurring after January 6, 1991, and through January 28, 1991:

BACKMAN, WALLY: Signed by Philadelphia Phillies, January 10, 1991.

BARRETT, MARTY: Signed by San Diego Padres, January 8, 1991.

BATHE, BILL: Signed by Nippon Ham Fighters of Japanese Baseball League, January 7, 1991.

BILARDELLO, DANN: Signed by San Diego Padres, January 15, 1991.

CANSECO, OZZIE: Sold to Kinetsu Buffaloes of Japanese Baseball League, January 7, 1991.

CARTER, GARY: Invited to spring training with Los Angeles Dodgers.

CERONE, RICK: Released by New York Yankees, January 14, 1991; signed by New York Mets, January 21, 1991.

CERUTTI, JOHN: Signed by Detroit Tigers, January 15, 1991.

DAVIS, GLENN: Traded to Baltimore Orioles for Pitchers Pete Harnisch and Curt Schilling and Outfielder Steve Finley, January 10, 1991.

DEMPSEY, RICK: Invited to spring training with Milwaukee Brewers.

DORSETT, BRIAN: Signed by San Diego Padres, January 15, 1991.

EDENS, TOM: Signed by Portland (Minnesota Twins' organization), January 14, 1991.

FINLEY, STEVE: Traded with Pitchers Pete Harnisch and Curt Schilling to Houston Astros for First Baseman Glenn Davis, January 10, 1991.

FOSSAS, TONY: Signed by Boston Red Sox' organization, January 23, 1991.

GAETTI, GARY: Signed by California Angels, January 24, 1991.

GONZALES, RENE: Traded to Toronto Blue Jays for Pitcher Rob Blumberg, January 15, 1991.

GOSSAGE, RICH: Invited to spring training with Texas Rangers.

HARNISCH, PETE: Traded with Pitcher Curt Schilling and Outfielder Steve Finley to Houston Astros for First Baseman Glenn Davis, January 10, 1991.

HEATH, MIKE: Signed by Atlanta Braves, January 22, 1991.

KITTLE, RON: Signed by Cleveland Indians' organization, January 20, 1991.

MATHEWS, GREG: Signed by Kansas City Royals, January 21, 1991.

McMURTRY, CRAIG: Re-signed by Texas Rangers' organization, January 8, 1991.

OTTO, DAVE: Signed by Colorado Springs (Cleveland Indians' organization), January 16, 1991.

PAGLIARULO, MIKE: Signed by Minnesota Twins, January 25, 1991.

ROBINSON, JEFF D.: Signed by California Angels, January 17, 1991.

Major League Managers

GEORGE LEE ANDERSON
(Sparky)
Detroit Tigers

Born February 22, 1934, at Bridgewater, S. D.
Height, 5.09. Weight, 168.
Threw and batted righthanded.

Major League stolen bases: 1959 (6).
Led International League in sacrifice hits with 15 in 1960.
Led Western League in sacrifice hits with 20 in 1954.
Tied for Texas League lead in sacrifice hits with 22 in 1955.
Led Texas League second basemen in double plays with 117 in 1955, Pacific Coast League with 135 in 1957 and International League with 104 in 1958 and 89 in 1960.
Led California League shortstops in double plays with 83 in 1953.

Year	Club	League	Pos.	G.	AB.	R.	H.	2B.	3B.	HR.	RBI.	B.A.	PO.	A.	E.	F.A.
1953—Santa Barbara	Calif.	SS	●141	★598	98	157	21	4	5	55	.263	★277	395	32	.955
1954—Pueblo	West.	2B	147	497	72	147	13	5	0	62	.296	★397	432	20	●.976
1955—Fort Worth	Texas	2B	158	594	86	158	24	1	0	42	.266	★456	★469	18	★.981
1956—Montreal	Int.	2B	140	453	65	135	17	5	0	47	.298	372	391	15	.981
1957—Los Angeles	P. C.	★●2B-SS	●168	619	74	161	15	0	2	35	.260	★524	★488	●15	★.985
1958—Montreal†	Int.	2B	●155	580	78	156	35	5	2	56	.269	★387	★464	10	★.983
1959—Philadelphia	Nat.	2B	152	477	42	104	9	3	0	34	.218	343	403	12	.984
1960—Toronto	Int.	2B	148	543	67	123	11	5	5	21	.227	319	★416	12	.984
1961—Toronto	Int.	2B	97	275	30	66	17	0	0	22	.240	189	203	6	.985
1962—Toronto	Int.	2B	124	432	56	111	18	2	2	38	.257	282	327	8	★.987
1963—Toronto	Int.	2B	116	358	56	89	12	5	3	25	.249	226	256	6	★.988
Major League Totals—1 Year				152	477	42	104	9	3	0	34	.218	343	403	12	.984

†Recalled by Los Angeles Dodgers; traded to Philadelphia Phillies for Pitchers Jim Golden and Gene Snyder and Outfielder Eldon (Rip) Repulski, December 23, 1958.

RECORD AS MANAGER

Named American League Manager of the Year by THE SPORTING NEWS, 1987.

Year	Club	League	Position	W.	L.	Year	Club	League	Position	W.	L.
1964—Toronto	Int.		Fifth	80	72	1979—Detroit z	Amer.		Fifth(E)	56	50
1965—Rock Hill	W. Carol.		Eighth	24	40	1980—Detroit	Amer.		Fifth(E)	84	78
(Second Half)			†First	35	23	1981—Detroit a	Amer.			60	49
1966—St. Petersburg	Fla. St.		Second	42	24	1982—Detroit	Amer.		Fourth(E)	83	79
(Second Half)			‡First	49	21	1983—Detroit	Amer.		Second(E)	92	70
1967—Modesto	Calif.		§Second	38	32	1984—Detroit	Amer.		First(E)	104	58
(Second Half)			xFirst	41	29	1985—Detroit	Amer.		Third(E)	84	77
1968—Asheville	South.		First	86	54	1986—Detroit	Amer.		Third(E)	87	75
1970—Cincinnati	Nat.		First(W)	102	60	1987—Detroit	Amer.		First(E)	98	64
1971—Cincinnati	Nat.		yFourth(W)	79	83	1988—Detroit	Amer.		Second(E)	88	74
1972—Cincinnati	Nat.		First(W)	95	59	1989—Detroit b	Amer.		Seventh(E)	59	103
1973—Cincinnati	Nat.		First(W)	99	63	1990—Detroit	Amer.		Third(E)	79	83
1974—Cincinnati	Nat.		Second(W)	98	64	American League Totals—12 Years				974	860
1975—Cincinnati	Nat.		First(W)	108	54	National League Totals—9 Years				863	586
1976—Cincinnati	Nat.		First(W)	102	60	Major League Totals—21 Years				1837	1446
1977—Cincinnati	Nat.		Second(W)	88	74						
1978—Cincinnati	Nat.		Second(W)	92	69						

†Won playoff against Salisbury (First Half winner), two games to none.
‡Lost playoff against Leesburg (First Half winner), three games to two.
§Tied for position with Santa Barbara.
xLost playoff against San Jose (First Half winner), two games to none.
yTied for position with Houston Astros.
zReplaced Les Moss (and interim manager Dick Tracewski) with club in fifth place (record of 29-26), June 14, 1979.
aFirst Half.... Fourth (E) (record of 31-26); Second Half.... Third (E) (record of 29-23).
bTook time out and replaced by interim manager Dick Tracewski, May 19 through June 4, 1989 (record of 9-8).
Coach, San Diego Padres, 1969.
Manager, American League All-Star Team, 1985.
Manager, National League All-Star Team, 1971, 1973, 1976 and 1977.
Coach, National League All-Star Team, 1974.
Coach, American League All-Star Team, 1982 and 1984.

CHAMPIONSHIP SERIES RECORD

Year	Club	League	W.	L.
1970—Cincinnati	National	3	0
1972—Cincinnati	National	3	2
1973—Cincinnati	National	2	3
1975—Cincinnati	National	3	0
1976—Cincinnati	National	3	0
1984—Detroit	American	3	0
1987—Detroit	American	1	4
Championship Series Totals—7 Years		18	9

WORLD SERIES RECORD

Year	Club	League	W.	L.
1970—Cincinnati	National	1	4
1972—Cincinnati	National	3	4
1975—Cincinnati	National	4	3
1976—Cincinnati	National	4	0
1984—Detroit	American	4	1
World Series Totals—5 Years		16	12

ROBERT JOE COX
(Bobby)
Atlanta Braves

Born May 21, 1941, at Tulsa, Okla.
Height, 6.00. Weight, 185.
Threw and batted righthanded.
Attended Reedley Junior College, Reedley, Calif.

Major League stolen bases: 1968 (3).
Led Alabama-Florida League shortstops in double plays with 71 in 1961.
Received reported $40,000 bonus to sign with Los Angeles Dodgers, 1959.

Year	Club	League	Pos.	G.	AB.	R.	H.	2B.	3B.	HR.	RBI.	B.A.	PO.	A.	E.	F.A.
1960—Reno		Calif.	2B	125	440	99	112	20	5	13	75	.255	282	★385	★39	.945
1961—Salem		N'west	2B	14	44	3	9	2	0	0	2	.205	25	25	2	.962
1961—Panama City		Ala.-Fl.	2B	92	335	66	102	27	4	17	73	.304	220	247	8	★.983
1962—Salem		N'west	3B-2B	★141	514	83	143	26	7	16	82	.278	174	296	28	.944
1963—Albuquerque		Texas	3B	17	53	5	15	2	0	2	5	.283	8	27	1	.972
1963—Great Falls		Pion.	3B	109	407	103	137	★31	4	19	85	.337	82	211	21	★.933
1964—Albuquerque		Texas	2B	138	523	98	152	29	13	16	91	.291	★322	★415	★28	.963
1965—Salt Lake City		P. C.	★3B-2B	136	473	58	125	32	1	12	55	.264	133	337	22	★.955
1966—Tacoma		P. C.	3B-2B	10	34	2	4	1	0	0	4	.118	23	15	0	1.000
1966—Austin		Texas	2B-3B	92	339	35	77	11	1	7	30	.227	140	216	12	.967
1967—Richmond†		Int.	3B-1B	99	350	52	104	17	4	14	51	.297	84	136	8	.965
1968—New York		Amer.	3B	135	437	33	100	15	1	7	41	.229	98	279	17	.957
1969—New York		Amer.	3B-2B	85	191	17	41	7	1	2	17	.215	50	147	11	.947
1970—Syracuse‡		Int.	3B-SS-2B	90	251	34	55	15	0	9	30	.219	86	163	13	.950
1971—Fort Lauderdale§		Fla. St.	2B	4	9	1	1	0	0	0	0	.111	4	5	0	1.000
Major League Totals—2 Years				220	628	50	141	22	2	9	58	.224	148	426	28	.953

†Recalled by Atlanta Braves; traded to New York Yankees for Catcher Bob Tillman and Pitcher Dale Roberts (latter transferred to Richmond), December 7, 1967.
‡On disabled list, May 28 through June 18, 1970.
§Player-manager.

PITCHING RECORD

Year	Club	League	G.	IP.	W.	L.	Pct.	H.	R.	ER.	SO.	BB.	ERA.
1971—Fort Lauderdale	Florida St.		3	10	1	0	1.000	15	9	6	4	5	5.40

RECORD AS MANAGER

Named Major League Manager of the Year by THE SPORTING NEWS, 1985.

Year	Club	League	Position	W.	L.	Year	Club	League	Position	W.	L.
1971—Fort Lauderdale	Fla. St.	Fourth(E)	71	70		1982—Toronto	Amer.	xSixth(E)	78	84	
1972—West Haven	East.	†First(A.)	84	56		1983—Toronto	Amer.	Fourth(E)	89	73	
1973—Syracuse	Int.	Third(Am.)	76	70		1984—Toronto	Amer.	Second(E)	89	73	
1974—Syracuse	Int.	Second(N)	74	70		1985—Toronto	Amer.	First(E)	99	62	
1975—Syracuse	Int.	Third	72	64		1990—Atlanta y	Nat.	Sixth(W)	40	57	
1976—Syracuse	Int.	‡Second	82	57		American League Totals—4 Years				355	292
1978—Atlanta	Nat.	Sixth(W)	69	93		National League Totals—5 Years				306	380
1979—Atlanta	Nat.	Sixth(W)	66	94		Major League Totals—8 Years				661	672
1980—Atlanta	Nat.	Fourth(W)	81	80							
1981—Atlanta§	Nat.		50	56							

†Defeated Three Rivers in playoff, three games to none.
‡Won playoffs by defeating Memphis, three games to none; and Richmond (finals), three games to one.
§First Half. . . . Fourth (W) (record of 25-29); Second Half. . . . Fifth (W) (record of 25-27).
xTied for position with Cleveland Indians.
yReplaced Russ Nixon with club in sixth place (record of 25-40), June 22, 1990.
Coach, New York Yankees, 1977.
Coach, American League All-Star Team, 1985.

CHAMPIONSHIP SERIES RECORD

Year	Club	League	W.	L.
1985—Toronto	American		3	4

ROGER LEE CRAIG
San Francisco Giants

Born February 17, 1931, at Durham, N. C.
Height, 6.04. Weight, 196.
Threw and batted righthanded.
Attended North Carolina State College, Raleigh, N. C.

Shares major league record for most 1-0 games lost, season (5), 1963.
Shares National League record for most consecutive losses, season (18), May 4 through August 4, 1963.
Tied for National League lead in shutouts with 4 in 1959.

Year	Club	League	G.	IP.	W.	L.	Pct.	H.	R.	ER.	SO.	BB.	ERA.
1950—Newport News	Piedmont	6	19	0	1	.000	22	17	15	7	23	7.11
1950—Valdosta	Ga.-Fla.	23	167	14	7	.667	136	86	58	152	150	3.13
1951—Newport News	Piedmont	38	21	14	11	.560	175	109	90	119	★175	3.67
1952-53—Elmira	Eastern					(In Military Service)						

Year Club	League	G.	IP.	W.	L.	Pct.	H.	R.	ER.	SO.	BB.	ERA.
1954—Elmira	Eastern	3	2	0	0	.000	4	6	2	1	2	9.00
1954—Pueblo	Western	6	14	1	1	.500	14	17	15	8	19	9.64
1954—Newport News	Piedmont	20	125	8	3	.727	107	44	35	108	56	2.50
1955—Montreal	Int'national	22	117	10	2	.833	105	48	46	68	64	3.54
1955—Brooklyn	National	21	91	5	3	.625	81	37	28	48	43	2.77
1956—Brooklyn	National	35	199	12	11	.522	169	90	82	109	87	3.71
1957—Brooklyn	National	32	111	6	9	.400	102	58	57	69	47	4.62
1958—Los Angeles	National	9	32	2	1	.667	30	20	16	16	12	4.50
1958—St. Paul	Am. Assoc.	28	182	5	●17	.227	180	100	79	119	77	3.91
1959—Spokane	P. Coast	14	96	6	7	.462	86	39	34	46	26	3.19
1959—Los Angeles	National	29	153	11	5	.688	122	49	35	76	45	2.06
1960—Los Angeles	National	21	116	8	3	.727	99	48	42	69	43	3.26
1961—Los Angeles†	National	40	113	5	6	.455	130	87	77	63	52	6.13
1962—New York	National	42	233	10	★24	.294	261	133	117	118	70	4.52
1963—New York‡	National	46	236	5	★22	.185	249	117	99	108	58	3.78
1964—St. Louis§	National	39	166	7	9	.438	180	76	60	84	35	3.25
1965—Cincinnati x	National	40	64	1	4	.200	74	33	26	30	25	3.66
1966—Philadelphia	National	14	23	2	1	.667	31	15	14	13	5	5.48
1966—Seattle	P. Coast	6	22	0	1	.000	15	11	6	11	9	4.50
1968—Albuquerque	Texas	1	4	0	0	.000	3	0	0	2	2	0.00
Major League Totals—12 Years		368	1537	74	98	.430	1528	763	653	803	522	3.82

†Selected by New York Mets in National League expansion draft, October 10, 1961.
‡Traded to St. Louis Cardinals for Pitcher Bill Wakefield and Outfielder George Altman, November 4, 1963.
§Traded to Cincinnati Reds with Outfielder Charlie James for Pitcher Bob Purkey and a player to be named later, December 14, 1964.
xReleased by Cincinnati Reds and signed by Philadelphia Phillies, April 11, 1966.

WORLD SERIES RECORD

Year Club	League	G.	IP.	W.	L.	Pct.	H.	R.	ER.	SO.	BB.	ERA.
1955—Brooklyn	National	1	6	1	0	1.000	4	2	2	4	5	3.00
1956—Brooklyn	National	2	6	0	1	.000	10	8	8	4	3	12.00
1959—Los Angeles	National	2	9⅓	0	1	.000	15	9	9	8	5	8.68
1964—St. Louis	National	2	5	1	0	1.000	2	0	0	9	3	0.00
World Series Totals—3 Years		7	26⅓	2	2	.500	31	19	19	25	16	6.49

RECORD AS MANAGER

Year Club	League	Position	W.	L.	Year Club	League	Position	W.	L.
1968—Albuquerque	Texas	Second(W)	70	69	1987—San Francisco	Nat.	First(W)	90	72
1978—San Diego	Nat.	Fourth(W)	84	78	1988—San Francisco	Nat.	Fourth(W)	83	79
1979—San Diego	Nat.	Fifth(W)	68	93	1989—San Francisco	Nat.	First(W)	92	70
1985—San Francisco†	Nat.	Sixth(W)	6	12	1990—San Francisco	Nat.	Third(W)	85	77
1986—San Francisco	Nat.	Third(W)	83	79	Major League Totals—8 Years			591	560

†Replaced Jim Davenport with club in sixth place (record of 56-88), September 18, 1985.
Scout, Los Angeles Dodgers, 1967; coach, San Diego Padres, 1969 through 1972; minor league pitching instructor, Los Angeles Dodgers, 1973; coach, Houston Astros, 1974 and 1975; coach, San Diego Padres, 1976 and 1977; named manager of Padres (replacing Alvin Dark), March 21, 1978; coach, Detroit Tigers, 1980 through 1984; scout, Detroit Tigers, March 2, 1985 through September 18, 1985.
Manager, National League All-Star Team, 1990.
Coach, National League All-Star Team, 1987 and 1988.

CHAMPIONSHIP SERIES RECORD

Year Club	League	W.	L.
1987—San Francisco	National	3	4
1989—San Francisco	National	4	1
Championship Series Totals—2 Years		7	5

WORLD SERIES RECORD

Year Club	League	W.	L.
1989—San Francisco	National	0	4

CLARENCE EDWIN GASTON
(Cito)
Toronto Blue Jays

Born March 17, 1944, at San Antonio, Tex.
Height, 6.04. Weight, 210.
Threw and batted righthanded.
Led New York-Pennsylvania League in total bases with 255 in 1966.

Year Club	League	Pos.	G.	AB.	R.	H.	2B.	3B.	HR.	RBI.	B.A.	PO.	A.	E.	F.A.
1964—Binghamton	NYP	OF	11	21	1	5	2	0	1	4	.238	8	0	1	.889
1964—Greenville	W. Car.	OF	49	165	15	38	6	3	0	16	.230	62	5	5	.931
1965—W. Palm Beach	Fla. St.	OF	70	202	14	38	5	3	0	9	.188	111	4	5	.958
1966—Batavia	NYP	OF	114	433	84	143	18	5	★28	★104	.330	214	12	13	.946
1966—Austin	Texas	OF	4	10	2	3	1	1	0	4	.300	10	0	0	1.000
1967—Austin	Texas	OF	136	505	72	154	24	6	10	70	.305	274	8	12	.959
1967—Atlanta	Nat.	OF	9	25	1	3	0	1	0	1	.120	7	1	2	.800
1968—Richmond	Int.	OF	21	71	9	17	4	0	2	8	.239	43	0	0	1.000
1968—Shreveport†	Texas	OF	96	340	49	95	15	4	6	57	.279	203	3	9	.958
1969—San Diego	Nat.	OF	129	391	20	90	11	7	2	28	.230	243	12	11	.959

Year Club	League	Pos.	G.	AB.	R.	H.	2B.	3B.	HR.	RBI.	B.A.	PO.	A.	E.	F.A.
1970—San Diego	Nat.	OF	146	584	92	186	26	9	29	93	.318	310	7	8	.975
1971—San Diego	Nat.	OF	141	518	57	118	13	9	17	61	.228	271	8	5	.982
1972—San Diego‡	Nat.	OF	111	379	30	102	14	0	7	44	.269	158	10	4	.977
1973—San Diego	Nat.	OF	133	476	51	119	18	4	16	57	.250	198	16	●12	.947
1974—San Diego§	Nat.	OF	106	267	19	57	11	0	6	33	.213	119	7	1	.992
1975—Atlanta	Nat.	OF-1B	64	141	17	34	4	0	6	15	.241	80	2	3	.965
1976—Atlanta	Nat.	OF-1B	69	134	15	39	4	0	4	25	.291	58	2	1	.984
1977—Atlanta	Nat.	OF-1B	56	85	6	23	4	0	3	21	.271	44	4	1	.980
1978—Atl. x-Pitts. yza	Nat.	OF-1B	62	120	6	28	1	0	1	9	.233	66	2	3	.958
1979—Leon	Mex.	OF	24	83	5	28	2	0	1	8	.337	24	0	0	1.000
1980—Leon	Mex.	1B	48	185	16	44	5	0	4	27	.238	126	3	3	.977
Major League Totals—11 Years			1026	3120	314	799	106	30	91	387	.256	1554	71	51	.970

†Selected by San Diego Padres from Atlanta in expansion draft, October 14, 1968.
‡On disabled list, May 17 to June 2, 1972.
§Traded to Atlanta Braves for Pitcher Danny Frisella, November 7, 1974.
xSold to Pittsburgh Pirates, September 22, 1978.
yGranted free agency, November 2, 1978; signed by Santo Domingo of Mexican League, April 10, 1979.
zOn suspended list, June 21 to July 21, 1979.
aReleased, July 22, 1979; signed by Leon of Mexican League, July 22, 1979.

ALL-STAR GAME RECORD

Year League	Pos.	AB.	R.	H.	2B.	3B.	HR.	RBI.	B.A.	PO.	A.	E.	F.A.
1970—National	OF	2	0	0	0	0	0	0	.000	2	0	0	1.000

RECORD AS MANAGER

Year Club	League	Position	W.	L.
1989—Toronto†	Amer.	First(E)	77	49
1990—Toronto	Amer.	Second(E)	86	76
Major League Totals—2 Years			155	119

†Replaced Jimy Williams with club in seventh place (record of 12-24), May 15, 1989.
Minor League instructor, Atlanta Braves' organization, 1981, coach, Toronto Blue Jays, 1982 through May 15, 1989.

CHAMPIONSHIP SERIES RECORD

Year Club	League	W.	L.
1989—Toronto	American	1	4

DERREL McKINLEY HARRELSON
(Bud)

(Named by brother, who couldn't say Derrel so he called him "Bubba"
and it ended up "Bud".)

New York Mets

Born June 6, 1944, at Niles, Calif.
Height, 5.10. Weight, 155.
Threw right and batted left and righthanded.
Attended San Francisco State College, San Francisco, Calif.

Shares major league record for most assists, shortstop, extra-inning game, (14), May 24, 1973 (19 innings).
Named shortstop on THE SPORTING NEWS National League All-Star Team, 1971.
Named shortstop on THE SPORTING NEWS National League All-Star fielding team, 1971.

Year Club	League	Pos.	G.	AB.	R.	H.	2B.	3B.	HR.	RBI.	B.A.	PO.	A.	E.	F.A.
1963—Salinas†	Calif.	SS	36	136	21	30	2	2	1	9	.221	41	99	18	.886
1964—Salinas	Calif.	SS	135	441	65	102	12	5	3	48	.231	215	347	34	*.943
1965—Buffalo	Int.	SS	131	446	37	112	15	1	2	36	.251	243	350	*31	.950
1965—New York	Nat.	SS	19	37	3	4	1	1	0	0	.108	28	36	3	.955
1966—Jacksonville	Int.	SS	117	389	56	86	8	5	1	26	.221	194	379	28	.953
1966—New York	Nat.	SS	33	99	20	22	2	4	0	4	.222	52	91	1	.993
1967—New York	Nat.	SS	151	540	59	137	16	4	1	28	.254	254	467	32	.958
1968—New York‡	Nat.	SS	111	402	38	88	7	3	0	14	.219	199	317	15	.972
1969—New York§	Nat.	SS	123	395	42	98	11	6	0	24	.248	243	347	19	.969
1970—New York	Nat.	SS	157	564	72	137	18	8	1	42	.243	*305	401	21	.971
1971—New York	Nat.	SS	142	547	55	138	16	6	0	32	.252	257	441	16	.978
1972—New York x	Nat.	SS	115	418	54	90	10	4	1	24	.215	191	334	16	.970
1973—New York y	Nat.	SS	106	356	35	92	12	3	0	20	.258	153	315	10	.979
1974—New York	Nat.	SS	106	331	48	75	10	0	1	13	.227	196	325	17	.968
1975—New York z	Nat.	SS	34	73	5	16	2	0	0	3	.219	44	67	7	.941
1976—New York	Nat.	SS	118	359	34	84	12	4	1	26	.234	183	330	20	.962
1977—New York a	Nat.	SS	107	269	25	48	6	2	1	12	.178	141	239	6	.984
1978—Philadelphia b	Nat.	2B-SS	71	103	16	22	1	0	0	9	.214	72	109	4	.978
1979—Philadelphia c	Nat.	2-S-3-O	53	71	7	20	6	0	0	7	.282	63	71	4	.971
1980—Texas de	Amer.	SS-2B	87	180	26	49	6	0	1	9	.272	121	222	18	.950
National League Totals—15 Years			1446	4564	513	1071	130	45	6	258	.235	2381	3890	191	.970
American League Totals—1 Year			87	180	26	49	6	0	1	9	.272	121	222	18	.950
Major League Totals—16 Years			1533	4744	539	1120	136	45	7	267	.236	2502	4112	209	.969

Signed as free agent by New York Mets' organization, June 7, 1963.
†On disabled list, July 17 to September 8, 1963.
‡On military list, May 23 to June 12, 1968.

§On military list, June 25 to July 11, 1969.
xOn disabled list, August 3 to August 25, 1972.
yOn disabled list, June 5 to July 8 and August 3 to August 18, 1973.
zOn disabled list, May 27 to September 1, 1975.
aTraded to Philadelphia Phillies for Second Baseman Fred Andrews and cash, March 23, 1978.
bGranted free agency, November 2, 1978; signed by Philadelphia Phillies, May 25, 1979.
cReleased, April 4, 1980; signed by Texas Rangers, May 7, 1980.
dOn disabled list, July 17 to September 1, 1980.
eGranted free agency, October 25, 1980.

CHAMPIONSHIP SERIES RECORD

Year Club	League	Pos.	G.	AB.	R.	H.	2B.	3B.	HR.	RBI.	B.A.	PO.	A.	E.	F.A.
1969—New York	Nat.	SS	3	11	2	2	1	1	0	3	.182	6	6	1	.923
1973—New York	Nat.	SS	5	18	1	3	0	0	0	2	.167	12	14	0	1.000
Championship Series Totals—2 Years			8	29	3	5	1	1	0	5	.172	18	20	1	.974

WORLD SERIES RECORD

Year Club	League	Pos.	G.	AB.	R.	H.	2B.	3B.	HR.	RBI.	B.A.	PO.	A.	E.	F.A.
1969—New York	Nat.	SS	5	17	1	3	0	0	0	0	.176	12	17	0	1.000
1973—New York	Nat.	SS	7	24	2	6	1	0	0	1	.250	11	24	0	1.000
World Series Totals—2 Years			12	41	3	9	1	0	0	1	.220	23	41	0	1.000

ALL-STAR GAME RECORD

Year League	Pos.	AB.	R.	H.	2B.	3B.	HR.	RBI.	B.A.	PO.	A.	E.	F.A.
1970—National	SS	3	2	2	0	0	0	0	.667	0	4	0	1.000
1971—National	SS	2	0	0	0	0	0	0	.000	1	2	0	1.000
All-Star Game Totals—2 Years		5	2	2	0	0	0	0	.400	1	6	0	1.000

RECORD AS MANAGER

Named New York-Pennsylvania League Manager of the Year, 1984.

Year Club	League	Position	W.	L.
1984—Little Falls	NYP	†First(E)	44	31
1985—Columbia‡	S. Atl.		22	13
1990—New York§	Nat.	Second(E)	71	49
Major League Totals—1 Year			71	49

†Defeated Newark, two games to one, for championship.
‡Named New York Mets coach, May 17, 1985.
§Replaced Dave Johnson with club in fourth place (record of 20-22), May 29, 1990.
Coach, New York Mets, May 17, 1985 through May 28, 1990.

ARTHUR HENRY HOWE JR.
(Art)
Houston Astros

Born December 15, 1946, at Pittsburgh, Pa.
Height, 6.01. Weight, 185.
Threw and batted righthanded.
Received bachelor of science degree in business administration
from University of Wyoming, Laramie, Wyo. in 1969.

Major League stolen bases: 1975 (1), 1978 (2), 1979 (3), 1980 (1), 1981 (1), 1982 (2). Total—10.
Led International League third basemen in errors with 22 and double plays with 24 in 1972.
Tied for Carolina League lead in putouts by third basemen with 95 in 1971.

Year Club	League	Pos.	G.	AB.	R.	H.	2B.	3B.	HR.	RBI.	B.A.	PO.	A.	E.	F.A.
1971—Salem	Carol.	3B-SS	114	382	77	133	27	7	12	79	*.348	110	221	21	.940
1972—Charleston†	Int.	3B-2B-SS	109	365	68	99	21	3	14	53	.271	105	248	24	.936
1973—Charleston‡	Int.	3B-2B-SS	119	372	50	85	20	1	8	44	.228	141	229	21	.946
1974—Charleston	Int.	3B	60	207	26	70	17	4	8	36	.338	35	90	9	.933
1974—Pittsburgh	Nat.	3B-SS	29	74	10	18	4	1	1	5	.243	11	49	4	.938
1975—Charleston	Int.	3B-2B	11	42	4	15	1	3	0	3	.357	15	23	1	.974
1975—Pittsburgh§	Nat.	3B-SS	63	146	13	25	9	0	1	10	.171	19	89	7	.939
1976—Memphis	Int.	3B-1B	74	259	50	92	21	3	12	59	.355	93	120	14	.934
1976—Houston	Nat.	3B-2B	21	29	0	4	1	0	0	0	.138	17	16	1	.970
1977—Houston	Nat.	2B-3B-SS	125	413	44	109	23	7	8	58	.264	213	333	8	.986
1978—Houston	Nat.	2B-3B-1B	119	420	46	123	33	3	7	55	.293	240	302	13	.977
1979—Houston	Nat.	2B-3B-1B	118	355	32	88	15	2	6	33	.248	188	261	7	.985
1980—Houston	Nat.	1-3-2-S	110	321	34	91	12	5	10	46	.283	598	86	10	.986
1981—Houston	Nat.	3B-1B	103	361	43	107	22	4	3	36	.296	67	206	9	.968
1982—Houston x	Nat.	3B-1B	110	365	29	87	15	1	5	38	.238	344	174	7	.987
1983—Houston yz	Nat.					(Did not play)									
1984—St. Louis	Nat.	3-1-2-S	89	139	17	30	5	0	2	12	.216	71	80	3	.981
1985—St. Louis a	Nat.	1B-3B	4	3	0	0	0	0	0	0	.000	5	1	0	1.000
Major League Totals—12 Years			891	2626	268	682	139	23	43	293	.260	1773	1597	69	.980

Signed as free agent by Pittsburgh Pirates' organization, June, 1971.
†On disabled list, August 17 to September 2, 1972.
‡On disabled list, April 13 to May 6, 1973.
§Traded to Houston Astros, January 6, 1976, completing deal in which Houston traded Second Baseman Tommy Helms to Pittsburgh Pirates for a player to be named later, December 12, 1975.

xOn disabled list, May 12 to June 19, 1982.
yOn disabled list, March 27, 1983 through remainder of season.
zGranted free agency, November 7, 1983; signed by St. Louis Cardinals, March 21, 1984.
aReleased, April 22, 1985.

DIVISION SERIES RECORD

Year Club	League	Pos.	G.	AB.	R.	H.	2B.	3B.	HR.	RBI.	B.A.	PO.	A.	E.	F.A.
1981—Houston	Nat.	3B	5	17	1	4	0	0	1	1	.235	6	9	0	1.000

CHAMPIONSHIP SERIES RECORD

Year Club	League	Pos.	G.	AB.	R.	H.	2B.	3B.	HR.	RBI.	B.A.	PO.	A.	E.	F.A.
1974—Pittsburgh	Nat.	PH	1	1	0	0	0	0	0	0	.000	0	0	0	.000
1980—Houston	Nat.	1B-PH	5	15	0	3	1	1	0	2	.200	29	3	0	1.000
Championship Series Totals—2 Years			6	16	0	3	1	1	0	2	.188	29	3	0	1.000

RECORD AS MANAGER

Year Club	League	Position	W.	L.
1989—Houston	Nat.	Third(W)	86	76
1990—Houston	Nat.	†Fourth(W)	75	87
Major League Totals—2 Years			161	163

Coach, Texas Rangers, May 21, 1985 through 1988.
†Tied for position with San Diego Padres.

JAY THOMAS KELLY
(Tom)
Minnesota Twins

Born August 15, 1950, at Graceville, Minn.
Height, 5.11. Weight, 185.
Threw and batted lefthanded.
Attended Mesa Community College, Mesa, Ariz., and Monmouth College, West Long Branch, N. J.
Son of Joe Kelly, former pitcher in St. Louis Cardinals'
and New York Giants' organizations.

Led International League in bases on balls received with 91 in 1978.
Led New York-Pennsylvania League in stolen bases with 16 in 1968.
Led Pacific Coast League outfielders in double plays with 6 in 1972.

Year Club	League	Pos.	G.	AB.	R.	H.	2B.	3B.	HR.	RBI.	B.A.	PO.	A.	E.	F.A.
1968—Newark	NYP	OF	65	218	50	69	11	4	2	10	.317	*144	*9	3	.981
1969—Clinton	Midw.	OF	100	269	47	60	10	2	6	35	.223	158	15	4	.977
1970—Jacksonville†‡	South.	OF-1B	93	266	33	64	10	1	8	38	.241	204	19	4	.982
1971—Charlotte	South.	1B-OF	100	303	50	89	17	0	6	41	.294	508	38	9	.984
1972—Tacoma	P. C.	OF-1B	132	407	76	114	19	2	10	52	.280	282	19	10	.968
1973—Tacoma	P. C.	OF-1B	114	337	67	87	10	2	17	49	.258	200	20	6	.973
1974—Tacoma	P. C.	OF-1B	115	357	68	110	16	0	18	69	.308	514	41	3	.985
1975—Tacoma	P. C.	OF-1B	62	202	38	51	5	0	9	29	.252	185	12	6	.970
1975—Minnesota§	Amer.	1B-OF	49	127	11	23	5	0	1	11	.181	360	28	6	.985
1976—Rochester	Int.	OF-1B	127	405	71	117	19	3	18	70	.289	323	28	4	.989
1977—Tacoma xyz	P. C.	1B-OF-P	113	363	80	99	12	1	12	64	.273	251	15	6	.978
1978—Toledo ab	Int.	1B-OF	119	325	47	74	13	0	10	49	.228	556	46	5	.992
Major League Totals—1 Year			49	127	11	23	5	0	1	11	.181	360	28	6	.985

†On temporary inactive list, April 16 to April 20, April 25 to April 30 and August 21, 1970 through remainder of season.
‡Released, April 6, 1971; signed by Charlotte (Minnesota Twins' organization), April 28, 1971.
§Loaned to Rochester (Baltimore Orioles' organization), April 5, 1976; returned, September 22, 1976.
xOn temporary inactive list, April 15 to April 19, 1977.
yPlayer-manager.
zOn disabled list, July 25 to August 4, 1977.
aPlayer-coach.
bReleased, December 18, 1978.

PITCHING RECORD

Year Club	League	G.	IP.	W.	L.	Pct.	H.	R.	ER.	SO.	BB.	ERA.
1977—Tacoma	P. Coast	1	3	0	0	.000	2	2	2	0	3	6.00

RECORD AS MANAGER

Named Southern League Manager of the Year, 1981.
Named California League Co-Manager of the Year, 1980.
Named California League Manager of the Year, 1979.

Year Club	League	Position	W.	L.	Year Club	League	Position	W.	L.
1977—Tacoma†	P. Coast	Third(W)	28	26	(Second Half)		Second(E)	43	32
1979—Visalia	Calif.	‡First(S)	44	26	1986—Minnesota y	Amer.	Sixth(W)	12	11
(Second Half)		Second(S)	42	28	1987—Minnesota	Amer.	First(W)	85	77
1980—Visalia	Calif.	Fourth(S)	27	43	1988—Minnesota	Amer.	Second(W)	91	71
(Second Half)		§First(S)	44	26	1989—Minnesota	Amer.	Fifth(W)	80	82
1981—Orlando	South.	xFirst(E)	42	27	1990—Minnesota	Amer.	Seventh(W)	74	88
(Second Half)		Third(E)	37	36	Major League Totals—5 Years			342	329
1982—Orlando	South.	Fifth(E)	31	38					

‡Lost to San Jose, two games to one in semifinals.
§Defeated Fresno, two games to none in semifinals, and lost to Stockton, three games to none for championship.
xDefeated Savannah, three games to one in semifinals, and defeated Nashville, three games to one for championship.
yReplaced Ray Miller with club in seventh place (record of 59-80), September 12, 1986.
Manager, American League All-Star Team, 1988.
Coach, Minnesota Twins, 1983 through September 11, 1986.

CHAMPIONSHIP SERIES RECORD						WORLD SERIES RECORD				
Year	Club	League	W.	L.		Year	Club	League	W.	L.
1987—Minnesota		American	4	1		1987—Minnesota		American	4	3

ANTHONY La RUSSA JR.
(Tony)
Oakland Athletics

Born October 4, 1944, at Tampa, Fla.
Height, 6.00. Weight, 185.
Threw and batted righthanded.
Attended University of Tampa, Tampa, Fla., and received degree in industrial management from University of Southern Florida, Tampa, Fla.; and received law degree from Florida State University, Tallahassee, Fla. in 1980.

Led International League in being hit by pitch with 11 in 1972.
Received reported $50,000 bonus to sign with Kansas City A's, 1962.

Year	Club	League	Pos.	G.	AB.	R.	H.	2B.	3B.	HR.	RBI.	B.A.	PO.	A.	E.	F.A.
1962—Daytona Beach	Fla. St.	SS	64	225	37	58	7	0	1	32	.258	135	173	38	.890
1962—Binghamton	East.	SS-2B	12	43	3	8	0	0	0	4	.186	20	27	8	.855
1963—Kansas City	Amer.	SS-2B	34	44	4	11	1	1	0	1	.250	29	25	2	.964
1964—Lewiston†	N'west	2B-SS	90	329	50	77	22	1	1	25	.234	188	218	18	.958
1965—Birmingham‡	South.	2B	75	259	24	50	11	2	1	18	.193	202	161	21	.945
1966—Modesto	Calif.	2B	81	316	67	92	20	1	7	54	.291	201	212	20	.954
1966—Mobile	South.	2B	51	170	20	50	9	4	4	26	.294	117	133	10	.962
1967—Birmingham§	South.	2B	41	139	12	32	6	1	5	22	.230	88	120	5	.977
1968—Oakland	Amer.	PH	5	3	0	1	0	0	0	0	.333	0	0	0	.000
1968—Vancouver	P. C.	2B	122	455	55	109	16	8	5	29	.240	249	321	14	*.976
1969—Iowa	A. A.	2B	67	235	37	72	11	1	4	27	.306	177	222	15	.964
1969—Oakland	Amer.	PH	8	8	0	0	0	0	0	0	.000	0	0	0	.000
1970—Iowa	A. A.	2B	22	88	13	22	5	0	2	5	.250	52	59	3	.974
1970—Oakland	Amer.	2B	52	106	6	21	4	1	0	6	.198	67	89	5	.969
1971—Iowa	A. A.	2-3-S-O	28	107	21	31	5	1	2	11	.290	70	85	2	.987
1971—Oakland x	Amer.	2B-SS-3B	23	8	3	0	0	0	0	0	.000	8	7	2	.882
1971—Atlanta	Nat.	2B	9	7	1	2	0	0	0	0	.286	8	6	1	.933
1972—Richmond y	Int.	2B	122	389	68	120	13	2	10	42	.308	305	289	20	.967
1973—Wichita	A. A.	2B-1B-3B	106	392	82	123	16	0	5	75	.314	423	213	26	.961
1973—Chicago z	Nat.	PR	1	0	1	0	0	0	0	0	.000	0	0	0	.000
1974—Charleston a	Int.	2B	139	457	50	119	17	1	8	35	.260	262	*378	17	.974
1975—Denver	A. A.	3-O-S-2	118	354	87	99	23	2	7	46	.280	95	91	10	.949
1976—Iowa bc	A. A.	INF-O-P	107	332	53	86	11	0	4	34	.259	132	160	22	.930
1977—New Orleans de	A. A.	2B-3B	50	128	17	24	2	2	3	6	.188	66	87	7	.956
American League Totals—5 Years			122	169	13	33	5	2	0	7	.195	104	121	9	.962
National League Totals—2 Years			10	7	2	2	0	0	0	0	.286	8	6	1	.933
Major League Totals—6 Years			132	176	15	35	5	2	0	7	.199	112	127	10	.960

†On disabled list, May 9 to September 8, 1964.
‡On disabled list, June 3 to July 15, 1965.
§On disabled list, April 12 to May 6 and July 3 to September 5, 1967.
xSold to Atlanta Braves, August 14, 1971.
yTraded to Chicago Cubs for Pitcher Tom Phoebus, October 20, 1972.
zSold to Pittsburgh Pirates' organization.
aReleased, April 4, 1975; signed by Chicago White Sox' organization, April 7, 1975.
bOn disabled list, August 8 to August 18, 1976.
cSold to St. Louis Cardinals' organization, December 13, 1976.
dNamed coach, June 20, 1977.
eReleased, September 29, 1977.

PITCHING RECORD

Year	Club	League	G.	IP.	W.	L.	Pct.	H.	R.	ER.	SO.	BB.	ERA.
1976—Iowa		Am. Assoc.	3	3	0	0	.000	3	1	1	0	0	3.00

—DID YOU KNOW—

That San Francisco became the first team since the 1925-27 Yankees to have three different players win consecutive RBI titles: Matt Williams in 1990, Kevin Mitchell in 1989 and Will Clark in 1988?

Shares major league record for most clubs managed, season (2), 1986.
Named Major League Manager of the Year by THE SPORTING NEWS, 1983.
Named American League Manager of the Year, 1988.

Year	Club	League	Position	W.	L.	Year	Club	League	Position	W.	L.
1978—Knoxville	South.	First(W)	49	21	1985—Chicago		Amer.	Third(W)	85	77	
(Second Half)†		Third(W)	4	4	1986—Chicago z		Amer.	Sixth(W)	26	38	
1979—Iowa‡	A. A.	Second(E)	54	52	1986—Oakland a		Amer.	bThird(W)	45	34	
1979—Chicago§	Amer.	Fifth(W)	27	27	1987—Oakland		Amer.	Third(W)	81	81	
1980—Chicago	Amer.	Fifth(W)	70	90	1988—Oakland		Amer.	First(W)	104	58	
1981—Chicago x	Amer.		54	52	1989—Oakland		Amer.	First(W)	99	63	
1982—Chicago	Amer.	Third(W)	87	75	1990—Oakland		Amer.	First(W)	103	59	
1983—Chicago	Amer.	First(W)	99	63							
1984—Chicago	Amer.	yFifth(W)	74	88	Major League Totals—12 Years				954	805	

†Replaced by Joe Jones, July 3, 1978.
‡Replaced by Joe Sparks, August 3, 1979.
§Replaced Don Kessinger with club in fifth place (record of 46-60), August 3, 1979.
xFirst Half. . . . Third (W) (record of 31-22); Second Half. . . . Sixth (W) (record of 23-30).
yTied for position with Seattle Mariners.
zReplaced by interim manager Doug Rader, June 20, 1986.
aReplaced manager Jackie Moore (record of 29-44) and interim manager Jeff Newman (record of 2-8) with club in seventh place (combined record of 31-52), July 7, 1986.
bTied for position with Kansas City Royals.
Manager, American League All-Star Team, 1989 and 1990.
Coach, Chicago White Sox, July 3 through remainder of 1978 season.
Coach, American League All-Star Team, 1984 and 1987.

CHAMPIONSHIP SERIES RECORD

Year	Club	League	W.	L.
1983—Chicago	American	1	3	
1988—Oakland	American	4	0	
1989—Oakland	American	4	1	
1990—Oakland	American	4	0	
Championship Series Totals—4 Years		13	4	

WORLD SERIES RECORD

Year	Club	League	W.	L.
1988—Oakland	American	1	4	
1989—Oakland	American	4	0	
1990—Oakland	American	0	4	
World Series Totals—3 Years		5	8	

THOMAS CHARLES LASORDA
Name pronounced Luh-SORR-duh.
(Tom)
Los Angeles Dodgers

Born September 22, 1927, at Norristown, Pa.
Height, 5.09. Weight, 195.
Threw and batted lefthanded.

Shares National League record for most wild pitches, inning (3), May 5, 1955, first inning.
Led International League in complete games with 16 and tied for lead in shutouts with 5 in 1958.
Led Canadian-American League in wild pitches with 20 in 1948 and led International League with 14 in 1953.
Named International League Pitcher of the Year, 1958.

Year	Club	League	G.	IP.	W.	L.	Pct.	H.	R.	ER.	SO.	BB.	ERA.
1945—Concord	N. C. State	27	121	3	12	.200	115	84	55	91	100	4.09
1946-47—†	E. Shore					(In Military Service)						
1948—Schenectady‡§	Can.-Am.	32	192	9	12	.429	180	122	99	195	153	4.64
1949—Greenville	Sally	45	178	7	7	.500	141	81	58	151	138	2.93
1950—Montreal	Int'national	31	146	9	4	.692	136	73	60	85	82	3.70
1951—Montreal	Int'national	31	165	12	8	.600	145	75	64	80	87	3.49
1952—Montreal	Int'national	33	182	14	5	.737	156	90	74	77	93	3.66
1953—Montreal	Int'national	36	208	17	8	.680	171	77	65	122	94	2.81
1954—Montreal	Int'national	23	154	14	5	.737	142	66	60	77	79	3.51
1954—Brooklyn	National	4	9	0	0	.000	8	5	5	5	5	5.00
1955—Brooklyn	National	4	4	0	0	.000	5	6	6	4	6	13.50
1955—Montreal x	Int'national	22	143	9	8	.529	125	58	52	92	62	3.27
1956—Kansas City y	American	18	45	0	4	.000	40	38	31	28	45	6.20
1956—Denver	Am. Assoc.	16	83	3	4	.429	94	54	46	54	34	4.99
1957—Denver z	Am. Assoc.	6	17	0	2	.000	29	25	23	8	6	12.18
1957—Los Angeles	P. Coast	29	132	7	10	.412	134	73	57	72	59	3.90
1958—Montreal	Int'national	34	★230	★18	6	.750	191	77	64	126	76	2.50
1959—Montreal	Int'national	29	188	12	8	.600	192	93	80	64	77	3.83
1960—Montreal a	Int'national	12	45	2	5	.286	79	48	41	17	24	8.20
American League Totals—1 Year		18	45	0	4	.000	40	38	31	28	45	6.20
National League Totals—2 Years		8	13	0	0	.000	13	11	11	9	11	7.62
Major League Totals—3 Years		26	58	0	4	.000	53	49	42	37	56	6.52

†On National Defense list, May 14, 1946 through February 2, 1948.
‡On disabled list, July 9 to July 19, 1948.
§Drafted by Nashua (Brooklyn Dodgers' organization) from Philadelphia Phillies' organization, November 24, 1948.
xSold by Brooklyn Dodgers' organization to Kansas City Athletics for an estimated $35,000, March 2, 1956.
yTraded to New York Yankees for Pitcher Wally Burnette and cash, July 11, 1956.
zSold by New York Yankees' organization to Brooklyn Dodgers' organization, May 26, 1957.
aReleased, July 9, 1960.

RECORD AS MANAGER

Named National League co-Manager of the Year by THE SPORTING NEWS, 1988.
Named Minor League Manager of the Year by THE SPORTING NEWS, 1970.
Named Pacific Coast League co-Manager of the Year, 1970.
Named Pioneer League Manager of the Year, 1967.

Year Club	League	Position	W.	L.	Year Club	League	Position	W.	L.
1965—Pocatello	Pion.	†Second	33	33	1981—Los Angeles y	Nat.		63	47
1966—Ogden	Pion.	First	39	27	1982—Los Angeles	Nat.	Second(W)	88	74
1967—Ogden	Pion.	First	41	25	1983—Los Angeles	Nat.	First(W)	91	71
1968—Ogden	Pion.	First	39	25	1984—Los Angeles	Nat.	Fourth(W)	79	83
1969—Spokane	P. C.	Second(N)	71	73	1985—Los Angeles	Nat.	First(W)	95	67
1970—Spokane	P. C.	‡First(N)	94	52	1986—Los Angeles	Nat.	Fifth(W)	73	89
1971—Spokane	P. C.	Third(N)	69	76	1987—Los Angeles	Nat.	Fourth(W)	73	89
1972—Albuquerque	P. C.	§First(E)	92	56	1988—Los Angeles	Nat.	First(W)	94	67
1976—Los Angeles x	Nat.	Second(W)	2	2	1989—Los Angeles	Nat.	Fourth(W)	77	83
1977—Los Angeles	Nat.	First(W)	98	64	1990—Los Angeles	Nat.	Second(W)	86	76
1978—Los Angeles	Nat.	First(W)	95	67	Major League Totals—15 Years			1185	1033
1979—Los Angeles	Nat.	Third(W)	79	83					
1980—Los Angeles	Nat.	Second(W)	92	71					

†Tied for position with Magic Valley.
‡Won championship playoff against Hawaii, four games to none.
§Won championship playoff against Eugene, three games to one.
xReplaced retiring Walter Alston with club in second place (record of 90-68), September 29, 1976.
yFirst Half. . . . First(W) (record of 36-21); Second Half. . . . Fourth(W) (record of 27-26).
Scout, Los Angeles Dodgers, 1961 through 1965; manager Los Angeles farm team in Arizona Instructional League, 1969; coach, Los Angeles Dodgers, 1973 through 1976.
Manager, National League All-Star Team, 1978, 1979, 1982 and 1989.
Coach, National League All-Star Team, 1977, 1983, 1984 and 1986.

DIVISION SERIES RECORD

Year Club	League	W.	L.
1981—Los Angeles	National	3	2

CHAMPIONSHIP SERIES RECORD

Year Club	League	W.	L.
1977—Los Angeles	National	3	1
1978—Los Angeles	National	3	1
1981—Los Angeles	National	3	2
1983—Los Angeles	National	1	3
1985—Los Angeles	National	2	4
1988—Los Angeles	National	4	3
Championship Series Totals—6 Years		16	14

WORLD SERIES RECORD

Year Club	League	W.	L.
1977—Los Angeles	National	2	4
1978—Los Angeles	National	2	4
1981—Los Angeles	National	4	2
1988—Los Angeles	National	4	1
World Series Totals—4 Years		12	11

JAMES KENNETH LEFEBVRE

Name pronounced Luh-FEE-ver.

(Jim)
Seattle Mariners

Born January 7, 1943, at Inglewood, Calif.
Height, 6.00. Weight, 185.
Threw right and batted right and lefthanded.

Led California League second basemen in double plays with 79 in 1962.
Led Northwest League second basemen in double plays with 109 in 1963.
Named National League Rookie of the Year by Baseball Writers' Association of America, 1965.

Year—Club	League	Pos.	G.	AB.	R.	H.	2B.	3B.	HR.	RBI.	B.A.	PO.	A.	E.	F.A.
1962—Reno	Calif.	2B	138	541	139	177	33	4	39	130	.327	345	313	27	.961
1963—Salem	N'west	2B	139	474	82	134	29	9	17	92	.283	∗316	327	∗35	.948
1964—Spokane†	P. C.	2B	55	200	26	53	10	1	6	31	.265	123	126	8	.969
1965—Los Angeles	Nat.	2B	157	544	57	136	21	4	12	69	.250	349	429	24	.970
1966—Los Angeles	Nat.	2B-3B	152	544	69	149	23	3	24	74	.274	268	389	16	.976
1967—Los Angeles	Nat.	3B-2B-1B	136	494	51	129	18	5	8	50	.261	173	321	18	.965
1968—Los Angeles	Nat.	2-3-O-1	84	286	23	69	12	1	5	31	.241	179	161	8	.977
1969—Los Angeles	Nat.	3B-2B-1B	95	275	29	65	15	2	4	44	.236	154	185	6	.983
1970—Los Angeles	Nat.	2B-3B-1B	109	314	33	79	15	1	4	44	.252	168	212	6	.984
1971—Los Angeles	Nat.	2B-3B	119	388	40	95	14	2	12	68	.245	247	274	9	.983
1972—Los Angeles‡	Nat.	2B-3B	70	169	11	34	8	0	5	24	.201	70	99	4	.977
1973—Lotte	Pac.	1-2-3-O	111	400	50	106	12	2	29	63	.265	763	77	7	.992
1974—Lotte	Pac.	1B-3B	82	279	37	79	12	2	14	52	.283	580	32	4	.994
1975—Lotte	Pac.	1B	47	151	13	39	5	0	9	24	.258	252	13	0	1.000
1976—Lotte	Pac.	1B	90	268	22	65	8	0	8	37	.243	506	32	3	.994
Major League Totals—8 Years			922	3014	313	756	126	18	74	404	.251	1608	2070	91	.976

—DID YOU KNOW—

That the Astros and Yankees were the only teams that failed to connect for a grand slam in 1990?

---

†On military list, March 15 to July 18, 1964.
‡Released, November 27, 1972; signed with Lotte Orions of Japanese Baseball League.

WORLD SERIES RECORD

Year Club	League	Pos.	G.	AB.	R.	H.	2B.	3B.	HR.	RBI.	B.A.	PO.	A.	E.	F.A.
1965—Los Angeles	Nat.	2B	3	10	2	4	0	0	0	0	.400	3	7	1	.909
1966—Los Angeles	Nat.	2B	4	12	1	2	0	0	1	1	.167	10	10	0	1.000
World Series Totals—2 Years			7	22	3	6	0	0	1	1	.273	13	17	1	.968

ALL-STAR GAME RECORD

Year League	Pos.	AB.	R.	H.	2B.	3B.	HR.	RBI.	B.A.	PO.	A.	E.	F.A.
1966—National	2B	2	0	0	0	0	0	0	.000	2	0	0	1.000

RECORD AS MANAGER

Named Pacific Coast League Manager of the Year, 1985 and 1986.

Year Club	League	Position	W.	L.	Year Club	League	Position	W.	L.
1978—Lethbridge	Pion.	Fifth	33	35	1989—Seattle	Amer.	Sixth(W)	73	89
1985—Phoenix	P. C.	Second(S)	37	33	1990—Seattle	Amer.	Fifth(W)	77	85
(Second Half)		†First(S)	43	29	Major League Totals—2 Years			150	174
1986—Phoenix	P. C.	‡First(S)	43	28					
(Second Half)		Second(S)	38	33					

†Defeated Hawaii, three games to none in semifinals; lost to Vancouver, three games to none, for championship.
‡Lost to Las Vegas, three games to two in semifinals.
Coach, Lotte Orions, 1977; coach, Los Angeles Dodgers, September 24, 1978 through 1979; coach, San Francisco Giants, 1980 and 1982; Director of Player Development, San Francisco Giants, 1983 and 1984; coach, Oakland Athletics, 1987 and 1988.
Coach, American League All-Star Team, 1990.

JAMES RICHARD LEYLAND

Named pronounced LEE-lund.

(Jim)

Pittsburgh Pirates

Born December 15, 1944, at Toledo, O.
Height, 5.11. Weight, 170.
Threw and batted righthanded.

Year Club	League	Pos.	G.	AB.	R.	H.	2B.	3B.	HR.	RBI.	B.A.	PO.	A.	E.	F.A.
1964—Lakeland†	Fla. St.	C	52	129	8	25	0	1	0	8	.194	268	17	6	.979
1964—Cocoa Tigers	Rookie	C	24	52	2	12	1	1	0	4	.231	122	15	3	.979
1965—Jamestown	NYP	C-3B-P	82	211	18	50	7	2	1	21	.237	318	36	6	.983
1966—Rocky Mount	Carol.	C	67	173	24	42	6	0	0	16	.243	369	23	1	.997
1967—Montgomery	South.	C	62	171	11	40	3	0	1	16	.234	350	25	6	.984
1968—Montgomery	South.	C-3B-SS	81	264	19	51	3	0	1	20	.193	511	43	7	.988
1969—Montgomery	South.	C	16	39	1	8	0	0	0	1	.205	64	6	3	.959
1969—Lakeland	Fla. St.	C-P	60	179	20	43	8	0	1	16	.240	321	28	4	.989
1970—Montgomery‡	South.	C	2	3	0	0	0	0	0	0	.000	6	0	1	.857

Signed as free agent by Detroit Tigers' organization, September 21, 1963.
†On disabled list, June 15 to June 27, 1964.
‡Player-coach.

PITCHING RECORD

Year Club	League	G.	IP.	W.	L.	Pct.	H.	R.	ER.	SO.	BB.	ERA.
1965—Jamestown	NYP	1	2	0	0	.000	2	0	0	1	0	0.00
1969—Lakeland	Florida St.	1	2	0	0	.000	4	2	2	1	0	9.00

RECORD AS MANAGER

Named National League Manager of the Year by THE SPORTING NEWS, 1990.
Named National League co-Manager of the Year by THE SPORTING NEWS, 1988.
Named American Association Manager of the Year, 1979.
Named Florida State League Manager of the Year, 1977 and 1978.

Year Club	League	Position	W.	L.	Year Club	League	Position	W.	L.
1971—Bristol	Appal.	Third(S)	31	35	1979—Evansville	A. A.	yFirst(E)	78	58
1972—Clinton	Midw.	Fifth(N)	22	41	1980—Evansville	A. A.	Second(E)	61	74
(Second Half)		Fourth(N)	27	36	1981—Evansville	A. A.	zFirst(E)	73	63
1973—Clinton	Midw.	Second(N)	36	26	1985—Chicago	Amer.	aFourth(W)	1	1
(Second Half)		†First(N)	37	25	1986—Pittsburgh	Nat.	Sixth(E)	64	98
1974—Montgomery	South.	Third(W)	61	76	1987—Pittsburgh	Nat.	bFourth(E)	80	82
1975—Clinton	Midw.	Fourth(S)	29	31	1988—Pittsburgh	Nat.	Second(E)	85	75
(Second Half)		Second(S)	38	30	1989—Pittsburgh	Nat.	Fifth(E)	74	88
1976—Lakeland	Fla. St.	‡Second(N)	74	64	1990—Pittsburgh	Nat.	First(E)	95	67
1977—Lakeland	Fla. St.	§First(N)	85	53	Major League Totals—6 Years			399	411
1978—Lakeland	Fla. St.	Fourth(N)	31	38					
(Second Half)		xFirst(N)	47	22					

†Lost playoff to Wisconsin Rapids, two games to none.
‡Defeated Miami, two games to none in semifinals, and defeated Tampa, two games to none for championship.
§Defeated Miami, two games to none in semifinals, and defeated St. Petersburg, three games to one for championship.

xDefeated St. Petersburg, one game to none for Northern Division championship, and lost to Miami, two games to one for championship.
yDefeated Oklahoma City, four games to two for championship.
zLost to Denver, three games to one in semifinals.
aNamed interim manager, replacing Tony La Russa who was suspended, with club in fourth place, August 10 and 11, 1985.
bTied for position with Philadelphia Phillies.
Coach, Detroit Tigers' organization, 1970 through June 5, 1971; Coach, Chicago White Sox, 1982 through 1985.
Coach, National League All-Star Team, 1990.

CHAMPIONSHIP SERIES RECORD

Year	Club	League	W.	L.
1990—Pittsburgh		National	2	4

NICOLAS TOMAS LEYVA
(Nick)
Philadelphia Phillies

Born August 16, 1953, at Ontario, Calif.
Height, 5.11. Weight, 165.
Threw and batted righthanded.
Attended University of La Verne, La Verne, Calif.

Year Club	League	Pos.	G.	AB.	R.	H.	2B.	3B.	HR.	RBI.	B.A.	PO.	A.	E.	F.A.
1975—Sarasota Cards	Gulf C.	3B-SS	4	18	3	5	2	0	0	4	.278	8	11	4	.826
1975—St. Petersburg	Fla. St.	3B-SS	47	157	16	42	8	2	0	21	.268	48	105	7	.956
1976—St. Petersburg	Fla. St.	3B-SS	70	237	32	66	11	0	2	28	.278	69	128	7	.966
1976—Arkansas	Texas	2B-3B-SS	48	153	16	38	4	1	3	26	.248	60	87	6	.961
1977—Arkansas†	Texas	I-O-P	84	213	24	57	4	2	3	30	.268	102	119	11	.953

Selected by St. Louis Cardinals' organization in 24th round of free-agent draft, June 4, 1975.
†Released, December 12, 1977.

PITCHING RECORD

Year Club	League	G.	IP.	W.	L.	Pct.	H.	R.	ER.	SO.	BB.	ERA.
1977—Arkansas	Texas	2	4	0	0	.000	6	5	0	0	0	0.00

RECORD AS MANAGER

Named Texas League Manager of the Year, 1983.

Year Club	League	Position	W.	L.
1978—Johnson City	Appal.	Second	37	33
1979—Johnson City	Appal.	Fifth	25	43
1980—Gastonia†	S. Atl.	Third(N)	37	33
(Second Half)		Second(N)	37	33
1981—St. Petersburg	Fla. St.	Third(N)	33	36
(Second Half)		Second(N)	36	27
1982—St. Petersburg‡	Fla. St.	Fourth(N)	26	30
1982—Arkansas§	Texas	Third(E)	12	7
(Second Half)		Second(E)	38	31
1983—Arkansas	Texas	Fourth(E)	30	38
(Second Half)x		First(E)	39	29
1989—Philadelphia	Nat.	Sixth(E)	67	95
1990—Philadelphia	Nat.	yFourth(E)	77	85
Major League Totals—2 Years			144	180

†Lost playoffs to Greensboro, two games to one.
‡Manager through May 31, 1982.
§Shared first half managing duties with Gaylen Pitts.
xLost playoffs to Jackson, two games to none.
yTied for position with Chicago Cubs.
Coach, St. Louis Cardinals, 1984 through 1988.

JOHN FRANCIS McNAMARA
Cleveland Indians

Born June 4, 1932, at Sacramento, Calif.
Height, 5.10. Weight, 175.
Threw and batted righthanded.
Attended Sacramento State College, Sacramento, Calif.

Led Northwest League in sacrifice hits with 18 in 1959.
Led Northwest League catchers in double plays with 15 in 1958, 10 in 1959 and 14 in 1962.

Year Club	League	Pos.	G.	AB.	R.	H.	2B.	3B.	HR.	RBI.	B.A.	PO.	A.	E.	F.A.
1951—Fresno	Calif.	C	60	182	20	38	2	0	0	12	.209	284	46	11	.968
1952—Houston	Texas	....	6	13	0	1	0	0	0	0	.077	....	....	....	....
1952—Lynchburg	Pied.	C	102	303	25	54	8	0	0	19	.178	489	57	8	★.986
1953—Winston-Salem	Carol.					(In Military Service)									
1954—Omaha†	West.					(In Military Service)									
1955—Lewiston	N'west	C	129	427	49	102	24	4	1	54	.239	544	★93	●15	.977
1956—Sacramento	P. C.	C	76	181	22	31	5	1	1	18	.171	256	25	0	1.000
1956—Albuquerque	West.	C	29	83	11	23	2	2	1	9	.277	191	23	1	.995
1957—Tulsa	Texas	C	19	47	5	7	2	0	0	5	.149	92	9	2	.981
1957—Amarillo	West.	C	43	93	17	26	8	0	0	21	.280	177	13	3	.984
1958—Lewiston	N'west	C	133	439	62	117	20	2	2	63	.276	★892	★76	9	.991
1959—Lewiston	N'west	C	141	491	74	122	25	4	1	44	.248	714	★84	8	.990
1960—Lewiston	N'west	C	120	387	62	98	19	2	0	42	.253	★726	48	7	★.991
1961—Lewiston	N'west	C	77	204	28	54	6	0	0	27	.265	368	37	4	.990
1962—Lewiston	N'west	C	93	281	41	77	11	2	1	33	.274	670	74	8	★.989

Year	Club	League	Pos.	G.	AB.	R.	H.	2B.	3B.	HR.	RBI.	B.A.	PO.	A.	E.	F.A.
1963—Binghamton	East.		C	69	199	19	45	10	1	0	24	.226	483	34	2	.996
1964—Dallas	P. C.		C-3B	13	13	1	6	0	0	0	1	.194	58	7	0	1.000
1965—Birmingham	South.						(Did Not Play)									
1966—Mobile	South.		C	8	17	3	4	0	0	0	0	.235	44	1	0	1.000
1967—Birmingham	South.		C	2	6	1	0	0	0	0	1	.000	10	1	0	1.000

†Released by St. Louis Cardinals' organization, April 16, 1955.

PITCHING RECORD

Year	Club	League	G.	IP.	W.	L.	Pct.	H.	R.	ER.	SO.	BB.	ERA.
1960—Lewiston		Northwest	5	....	0	0	.000	....	....	....	....	....	....
1961—Lewiston		Northwest	4	....	0	0	.000	....	....	....	....	....	....
1962—Lewiston		Northwest	4	9	0	0	.000	13	6	6	3	2	6.00
1963—Binghamton		Eastern	1	1	0	0	.000	0	0	0	0	0	0.00

RECORD AS MANAGER

Named Major League Co-Manager of the Year by THE SPORTING NEWS, 1986.

Year	Club	League	Position	W.	L.
1959—Lewiston	N'west		Second	36	34
(Second Half)			Third	39	32
1960—Lewiston	N'west		Third	38	29
(Second Half)			Third	40	34
1961—Lewiston	N'west		†First	41	25
(Second Half)			Second	43	31
1962—Lewiston	N'west		Fifth	31	38
(Second Half)			Fourth	35	37
1963—Binghamton	East.		Fourth	65	75
1964—Dallas	P. C.		Sixth(E)	53	104
1965—Birmingham	South.		Eighth	54	85
1966—Mobile	South.		First	88	52
1967—Birmingham	South.		First	84	55
1969—Oakland‡	Amer.		Second(W)	8	5
1970—Oakland	Amer.		Second(W)	89	73
1974—San Diego	Nat.		Sixth(W)	60	102
1975—San Diego	Nat.		Fourth(W)	71	91
1976—San Diego	Nat.		Fifth(W)	73	89
1977—San Diego§	Nat.		Fifth(W)	20	28
1979—Cincinnati	Nat.		First(W)	90	71
1980—Cincinnati	Nat.		Third(W)	89	73
1981—Cincinnati x	Nat.			66	42
1982—Cincinnati y	Nat.		Sixth(W)	34	58
1983—California	Amer.		zFifth	70	92
1984—California	Amer.		zSecond(W)	81	81
1985—Boston	Amer.		Fifth(E)	81	81
1986—Boston	Amer.		First(E)	95	66
1987—Boston	Amer.		Fifth(E)	78	84
1988—Boston a	Amer.		Fourth(E)	43	42
1990—Cleveland	Amer.		Fourth(E)	77	85

American League Totals—9 Years ... 622 609
National League Totals—8 Years ... 503 554
Major League Totals—17 Years ... 1125 1163

†Won playoff by defeating Yakima (Second Half winner), four games to one.
‡Replaced Hank Bauer with club in second place (record of 80-69), September 19, 1969.
§Replaced by Alvin Dark, May 30, 1977 (Bob Skinner served as interim manager, May 29).
xFirst Half....Second (W) (record of 35-21); Second Half....Second (W) (record of 31-21).
yReplaced by Russ Nixon, July 21, 1982.
zTied for position with Minnesota Twins.
aReplaced by Joe Morgan, July 14, 1988.
Coach, Oakland Athletics, 1968 and 1969; San Francisco Giants, 1971 through 1973; California Angels, 1978.
Manager, American League All-Star Team, 1987.
Coach, American League All-Star Team, 1986.
Coach, National League All-Star Team, 1976, 1980 and 1982.

CHAMPIONSHIP SERIES RECORD

Year	Club	League	W.	L.
1979—Cincinnati	National		0	3
1986—Boston	American		4	3
Championship Series Totals—2 Years			4	6

WORLD SERIES RECORD

Year	Club	League	W.	L.
1986—Boston	American		3	4

CARL HARRISON MERRILL
(Stump)
New York Yankees

Born February 15, 1944, at Brunswick, Me.
Height, 5.08. Weight, 190.
Threw right and batted lefthanded.
Received bachelor of science degree and master of science degree in education
from University of Maine, Orono, Me.

Year	Club	League	Pos.	G.	AB.	R.	H.	2B.	3B.	HR.	RBI.	B.A.	PO.	A.	E.	F.A.
1966—Tidewater	Carol.		C	6	11	1	2	0	0	0	0	.182	Figures	unavailable		
1966—Batavia	NYP		C	46	142	13	33	5	0	0	11	.211	385	30	7	.983
1967—Bakersfield	Calif.		C	29	59	12	15	1	0	0	6	.254	189	20	5	.977
1967—Eugene	N'west		C	46	122	19	26	4	2	0	12	.213	332	38	5	.987
1968—Reading	East.		C	42	95	8	18	4	0	0	5	.189	187	23	2	.991
1968—San Diego	P. C.		C	4	11	1	1	0	0	0	1	.091	16	0	1	.941
1969—Reading	East.		C	80	226	57	73	9	2	1	29	.252	435	44	20	.960
1970—Eugene†	P. C.		C	55	111	12	29	4	0	0	12	.261	176	21	1	.995
1971—Eugene	P. C.		C	77	157	21	38	9	1	1	15	.242	281	25	5	.984

—DID YOU KNOW—

That in 1990, Lonnie Smith became only the second Atlanta Brave, next to Ralph Garr, to post back-to-back .300 seasons?

Selected by Minnesota Twins' organization in 23rd round of free-agent draft, June 8, 1965.
Selected by Baltimore Orioles' organization in secondary phase of free-agent draft, January 29, 1966.
Signed as free agent by Philadelphia Phillies' organization, June 9, 1966.
†On Reading temporarily inactive list, April 24 to May 16, 1970.

RECORD AS MANAGER

Named Eastern League Manager of the Year, 1979.

Year	Club	League	Position	W.	L.	Year	Club	League	Position	W.	L.
1978—West Haven	East.		Second	39	31		(Second Half)		Third(S)	36	28
	(Second Half)		Second	43	26	1984—Columbus	Int.		xFirst	82	57
1979—West Haven	East.		First	42	28	1985—Columbus y	Int.		azThird	65	52
	(Second Half)		First	41	28	1988—Wichita b	East.		cFourth	47	42
1980—Nashville	South.		Second(W)	46	25	1989—Prince William d	Carol.		Fourth(S)	12	16
	(Second Half)		†First(W)	51	21		(Second Half)		eFirst(S)	42	27
1981—Nashville	South.		Second(W)	38	32	1990—Columbus f	Int.		First(W)	33	25
	(Second Half)		‡First(W)	43	30	1990—New York g	Amer.		Seventh(E)	49	64
1982—Fort Lauderdale	Fla. St.		First(S)	47	21						
	(Second Half)		§Second(S)	35	29	Major League Totals—1 Year				49	64
1983—Fort Lauderdale	Fla. St.		Second(S)	41	26						

†Lost to Memphis, three games to one, in semifinals.
‡Defeated Memphis, three games to one, in semifinals, and lost to Orlando, three games to one, for championship.
§Defeated Vero Beach, two games to one, in semifinals, and defeated Tampa, three games to two, for championship.
xLost to Pawtucket, three games to one, in semifinals.
yReplaced Doug Holmquist (record of 10-12), May 7, 1985.
zTied for position with Tidewater Mets.
aDefeated Syracuse, three games to one, in semifinals, and lost to Tidewater, three games to one, for championship.
bReplaced Tommy Jones (record of 25-24), June 6, 1988.
cDefeated Glens Falls, three games to one, in semifinals, and defeated Vermont, three games to one, for championship.
dReplaced Mark Weidenmaier (record of 18-23), May 21, 1989.
eDefeated Lynchburg, two games to one, in semifinals, and defeated Durham, three games to one, for championship.
fPromoted to New York Yankees and replaced by Rick Down, June 5, 1990.
gReplaced Bucky Dent with club in seventh place (record of 18-31), June 6, 1990.
Pitching coach, West Haven (Eastern), 1977; coach, New York Yankees, April 28 to May 6, 1985; Minor League Coordinator, New York Yankees, beginning of 1988 through June 5, 1988.

JOSEPH MICHAEL MORGAN
(Joe)
Boston Red Sox

Born November 19, 1930, at Walpole, Mass.
Height, 5.10. Weight, 180.
Threw and batted lefthanded.
Received bachelor of science degree in history and government
from Boston College, Chestnut Hill, Mass., in 1953.

Named International League Player of the Year, 1964.

Year	Club	League	Pos.	G.	AB.	R.	H.	2B.	3B.	HR.	RBI.	B.A.	PO.	A.	E.	F.A.
1952—Hartford	East.		SS-3B	72	258	23	59	6	0	3	18	.228	141	237	22	.945
1953—Evansville†	I.I.I.		SS	78	301	53	74	10	5	4	29	.246	157	228	24	.941
1954-55—‡						(In U. S. Army)										
1956—Jacksonville	S. Atl.		SS	132	476	85	143	24	8	9	45	.300	209	421	37	.945
1957—Atlanta	S. A.		SS	149	551	111	174	31	8	12	77	.316	278	446	29	.961
1958—Wichita	A. A.		3B-SS	133	442	60	111	22	4	11	49	.251	120	271	23	.944
1959—Milwaukee	Nat.		2B	13	23	2	5	1	0	0	1	.217	9	12	2	.913
1959—Louisville§	A. A.		OF-3B	82	305	54	96	26	6	8	47	.315	134	22	5	.969
1959—Kansas City	Amer.		3B	20	21	2	4	0	1	0	3	.190	1	2	0	1.000
1960—Louisville x	A. A.		3B	55	174	35	49	5	2	4	29	.282	39	96	4	.971
1960—Philadelphia y	Nat.		3B	26	83	5	11	2	2	0	2	.133	24	42	2	.971
1960—Cleveland	Amer.		3B-OF	22	47	6	14	2	0	2	4	.298	11	22	4	.892
1961—Cleveland z	Amer.		OF	4	10	0	2	0	0	0	0	.200	6	0	0	1.000
1961—Charleston	Int.		3B	118	405	59	117	21	2	8	46	.289	79	184	15	.946
1962—Atlanta	Int.		3B-OF	142	474	70	132	15	4	16	70	.278	183	105	15	.950
1963—Atlanta	Int.		1B-OF-3B	131	406	61	114	12	3	12	70	.281	507	101	12	.981
1964—Jacksonville	Int.		3B-1B	143	476	77	138	24	4	16	66	.290	283	220	19	.964
1964—St. Louis	Nat.		PH	3	3	0	0	0	0	0	0	.000	0	0	0	.000
1965—J'cks'nv'lle abcde	Int.		3B-OF	93	270	31	56	8	2	5	24	.207	81	71	7	.956
1966—Raleigh	Carol.		3B	112	331	48	90	10	3	9	62	.272	66	169	10	.959
National League Totals—3 Years				42	109	7	16	3	2	0	3	.147	33	54	4	.956
American League Totals—3 Years				46	78	8	20	2	1	2	7	.256	18	24	4	.913
Major League Totals—4 Years				88	187	15	36	5	3	2	10	.193	51	78	8	.942

Signed as free agent by Boston Braves' organization, June 20, 1952.
†On restricted list, February 5 to June 12, 1953.
‡On National Defense Service list, November 17, 1953 through December 2, 1955.
§Sold to Kansas City A's, August 20, 1959; returned to Milwaukee Braves, April 15, 1960.
xTraded to Philadelphia Phillies for Shortstop Alvin Dark, June 23, 1960.

ySold to Cleveland Indians, August 9, 1960.

zTraded with cash and a player to be named later to St. Louis Cardinals for Outfielder Bob Nieman, May 10, 1961; St. Louis acquired Pitcher Mike Lee to complete deal, September 25, 1961.

aOn disabled list, April 17 to July 27, 1965.

bNon-player-coach, July 9 to July 16, 1965.

cPlayer-coach, July 17, 1965 through remainder of season.

dOn temporary inactive list, August 20, 1965 through remainder of season.

eReleased, January 11, 1966; signed by Raleigh (Pittsburgh Pirates' organization) as a player-manager, January 12, 1966.

RECORD OF MANAGER

Named Minor League Manager of the Year by THE SPORTING NEWS, 1973.
Named International League Manager of the Year, 1973 and 1977.
Named Eastern League Manager of the Year, 1969.
Named Carolina League Manager of the Year, 1966.

Year — Club	League	Position	W.	L.	Year — Club	League	Position	W.	L.
1966—Raleigh	Carol.	Third (W)	71	66	1978—Pawtucket	Int.	aSecond	81	59
1967—Raleigh	Carol.	†First(E)	77	65	1979—Pawtucket	Int.	Fifth	66	74
1968—York	East.	Fifth	58	82	1980—Pawtucket	Int.	Seventh	62	77
1969—York	East.	‡First	89	50	1981—Pawtucket	Int.	Sixth	67	73
1970—Columbus	Int.	§Second	81	59	1982—Pawtucket	Int.	Fifth	67	71
1971—Charleston	Int.	xThird	78	62	1988—Boston b	Amer.	First(E)	46	31
1973—Charleston	Int.	yFirst(N)	85	60	1989—Boston	Amer.	Third(E)	83	79
1974—Pawtucket	Int.	Fourth(N)	57	87	1990—Boston	Amer.	First(E)	88	74
1975—Pawtucket	Int.	Eighth	53	87	Major League Totals—3 Years			217	184
1976—Pawtucket	Int.	Fifth	68	70					
1977—Pawtucket	Int.	zFirst	80	60					

†Defeated Rocky Mount, one game to none in quarterfinals, and lost to Tidewater, two games to none in semifinals.

‡Losing to Pittsfield, one game to none in semifinals when playoffs were cancelled.

§Defeated Rochester, three games to two in semifinals, and lost to Syracuse, three games to one for championship.

xLost to Tidewater, three games to none in semifinals.

yDefeated Rochester, three games to none for championship, and lost to Pawtucket, three games to two for Governor's Cup.

zDefeated Richmond, three games to one in semifinals, and lost to Charleston, four games to none in Governor's Cup.

aDefeated Toledo, three games to two in semifinals, and lost to Richmond, four games to three for Governor's Cup.

bReplaced John McNamara with club in fourth place (record of 43-42), July 14, 1988.

Coach, American League All-Star Team, 1989.

Scout, Boston Red Sox, 1983 and 1984; coach, Pittsburgh Pirates, 1972; coach, Boston Red Sox, 1985 through July 13, 1988.

CHAMPIONSHIP SERIES RECORD

Year — Club	League	W.	L.
1988—Boston	American	0	4
1990—Boston	American	0	4
Championship Series Totals—2 Years		0	8

LOUIS VICTOR PINIELLA
Name pronounced Pin-ELLA.

(Lou)
Cincinnati Reds

Born August 28, 1943, at Tampa, Fla.
Height, 6.02. Weight, 199.
Threw and batted righthanded.
Attended University of Tampa, Tampa, Fla.
Cousin of Dave Magadan, infielder with New York Mets.

Tied major league record for most assists by outfielder, inning (2), May 27, 1974 (third inning).

Major League stolen bases: 1969 (2), 1970 (3), 1971 (5), 1972 (7), 1973 (5), 1974 (1), 1977 (2), 1978 (3), 1979 (3), 1983 (1). Total—32.

Led American League in grounding into double plays with 25 in 1972.

Named American League Rookie of the Year by Baseball Writers' Association of America, 1969.

Year — Club	League	Pos.	G.	AB.	R.	H.	2B.	3B.	HR.	RBI.	B.A.	PO.	A.	E.	F.A.
1962—Selma†	Ala.-Fl.	OF	70	278	40	75	10	5	8	44	.270	94	6	9	.917
1963—Peninsula	Carol.	OF	143	548	71	170	29	4	16	77	.310	271	*23	8	.974
1964—Aberdeen‡§	North.	OF	20	74	8	20	8	3	0	12	.270	37	1	1	.974
1964—Baltimore	Amer.	PH	4	1	0	0	0	0	0	0	.000	0	0	0	.000
1965—Elmira x	East.	OF	126	490	64	122	29	6	11	64	.249	176	5	7	.963
1966—Portland	P. C.	OF	133	457	47	132	22	3	7	52	.289	177	11	11	.945
1967—Portland	P. C.	OF	113	396	46	122	20	1	8	56	.308	199	7	6	.972
1968—Portland	P. C.	OF	88	331	49	105	15	3	13	62	.317	167	6	7	.961
1968—Cleveland yz	Amer.	OF	6	5	1	0	0	0	0	1	.000	1	0	0	1.000
1969—Kansas City	Amer.	OF	135	493	43	139	21	6	11	68	.282	278	13	7	.977
1970—Kansas City	Amer.	OF-1B	144	542	54	163	24	5	11	88	.301	250	6	4	.985
1971—Kansas City a	Amer.	OF	126	448	43	125	21	5	3	51	.279	201	6	3	.986
1972—Kansas City	Amer.	OF	151	574	65	179	*33	4	11	72	.312	275	8	7	.976

— 552 —

Year	Club	League	Pos.	G.	AB.	R.	H.	2B.	3B.	HR.	RBI.	B.A.	PO.	A.	E.	F.A.
1973—Kansas City b		Amer.	OF	144	513	53	128	28	1	9	69	.250	196	9	3	.986
1974—New York		Amer.	OF-1B	140	518	71	158	26	0	9	70	.305	270	16	3	.990
1975—New York c		Amer.	OF	74	199	7	39	4	1	0	22	.196	65	5	1	.986
1976—New York		Amer.	OF	100	327	36	92	16	6	3	38	.281	199	10	4	.981
1977—New York		Amer.	OF-1B	103	339	47	112	19	3	12	45	.330	86	3	2	.978
1978—New York		Amer.	OF	130	472	67	148	34	5	6	69	.314	213	4	7	.969
1979—New York		Amer.	OF	130	461	49	137	22	2	11	69	.297	204	13	4	.982
1980—New York		Amer.	OF	116	321	39	92	18	0	2	27	.287	157	8	5	.971
1981—New York d		Amer.	OF	60	159	16	44	9	0	5	18	.277	69	2	1	.986
1982—New York		Amer.	OF	102	261	33	80	17	1	6	37	.307	68	2	0	1.000
1983—New York e		Amer.	OF	53	148	19	43	9	1	2	16	.291	67	4	3	.959
1984—New York f		Amer.	OF	29	86	8	26	4	1	1	6	.302	40	3	0	1.000
Major League Totals—18 Years				1747	5867	651	1705	305	41	102	766	.291	2639	112	54	.981

Signed as free agent by Cleveland Indians' organization, June 9, 1962.

†Drafted by Washington Senators, November 26, 1962.

‡On military list, March 9 to July 20, 1964.

§Traded to Baltimore Orioles' organization, August 4, 1964, completing deal in which Baltimore traded Pitcher Lester (Buster) Narum to Washington Senators for cash and a player to be named later, March 31, 1964.

xTraded to Cleveland Indians' organization for Catcher Cam Carreon, March 10, 1966.

ySelected by Seattle Pilots in expansion draft, October 15, 1968.

zTraded by Seattle Pilots to Kansas City Royals for Outfielder Steve Whitaker and Pitcher John Gelnar, April 1, 1969.

aOn disabled list, May 5 to June 8, 1971.

bTraded with Pitcher Ken Wright to New York Yankees for Pitcher Lindy McDaniel, December 7, 1973.

cOn disabled list, June 17 to July 6, 1975.

dOn disabled list, August 23 to September 7, 1981.

eOn disabled list, March 30 to April 22, 1983.

fOn voluntarily retired list, June 17, 1984.

DIVISION SERIES RECORD

Year	Club	League	Pos.	G.	AB.	R.	H.	2B.	3B.	HR.	RBI.	B.A.	PO.	A.	E.	F.A.
1981—New York		Amer.	DH-PH	4	10	1	2	1	0	1	3	.200	0	0	0	.000

CHAMPIONSHIP SERIES RECORD

Year	Club	League	Pos.	G.	AB.	R.	H.	2B.	3B.	HR.	RBI.	B.A.	PO.	A.	E.	F.A.
1976—New York		Amer.	DH-PH	4	11	1	3	1	0	0	0	.273	0	0	0	.000
1977—New York		Amer.	OF-DH	5	21	1	7	3	0	0	2	.333	9	1	0	1.000
1978—New York		Amer.	OF	4	17	2	4	0	0	0	0	.235	13	0	0	1.000
1980—New York		Amer.	OF	2	5	1	1	0	0	1	1	.200	5	0	0	1.000
1981—New York		Amer.	PH-D-O	3	5	2	3	0	0	1	3	.600	0	0	0	.000
Championship Series Totals—5 Years				18	59	7	18	4	0	2	6	.305	27	1	0	1.000

WORLD SERIES RECORD

Tied World Series record for one or more hits, each game, six-game Series, 1978.

Year	Club	League	Pos.	G.	AB.	R.	H.	2B.	3B.	HR.	RBI.	B.A.	PO.	A.	E.	F.A.
1976—New York		Amer.	D-O-PH	4	9	1	3	1	0	0	0	.333	1	0	0	1.000
1977—New York		Amer.	OF	6	22	1	6	0	0	0	3	.273	16	1	1	.944
1978—New York		Amer.	OF	6	25	3	7	0	0	0	4	.280	14	1	0	1.000
1981—New York		Amer.	OF-PH	6	16	2	7	1	0	0	3	.438	7	0	0	1.000
World Series Totals—4 Years				22	72	7	23	2	0	0	10	.319	38	2	1	.976

ALL-STAR GAME RECORD

Year	League		Pos.	AB.	R.	H.	2B.	3B.	HR.	RBI.	B.A.	PO.	A.	E.	F.A.
1972—American			PH	1	0	0	0	0	0	0	.000	0	0	0	.000

RECORD AS MANAGER

Year	Club	League	Position	W.	L.
1986—New York		Amer.	Second(E)	90	72
1987—New York		Amer.	Fourth(E)	89	73
1988—New York†		Amer.	Fifth(E)	45	48
1990—Cincinnati		Nat.	First(W)	91	71
American League Totals—3 Years				224	193
National League Totals—1 Year				91	71
Major League Totals—4 Years				315	264

†Replaced Billy Martin with club in second place (record of 40-28), June 23, 1988.

Coach, New York Yankees, June 25, 1984 through 1985; Vice-President and General Manager, New York Yankees, beginning of 1988 season through June 22, 1988; and special advisor, New York Yankees, 1989.

CHAMPIONSHIP SERIES RECORD						WORLD SERIES RECORD				
Year	Club	League	W.	L.		Year	Club	League	W.	L.
1990—Cincinnati		National	4	2		1990—Cincinnati		National	4	0

—DID YOU KNOW—

That Texas' Bobby Witt led the majors with a 12-game winning streak in 1990?

DOUGLAS LEE RADER
(Doug)
California Angels

Born July 30, 1944, at Chicago, Ill.
Height, 6.03. Weight, 230.
Threw and batted righthanded.
Attended Illinois Wesleyan University, Bloomington, Ill.

Led National League third basemen in total chances with 479 in 1972.
Led National League third basemen in putouts with 147 in 1970.
Led National League third basemen in double plays with 39 in 1970 and tied for lead with 31 in 1972.
Named third baseman on THE SPORTING NEWS National League All-Star fielding team, 1970 through 1973.
Received reported $25,000 bonus to sign with Houston Astros, 1964.

Year	Club	League	Pos.	G.	AB.	R.	H.	2B.	3B.	HR.	RBI.	B.A.	PO.	A.	E.	F.A.
1965—Durham	Carol.	3B-OF	112	330	44	69	14	1	14	38	.209	111	185	21	.934
1966—Amarillo	Texas	3B	138	527	85	*153	21	12	16	74	.290	102	240	27	.927
1967—Oklahoma City	P. C.	3B	75	273	40	80	23	5	9	44	.293	47	110	12	.929
1967—Houston	Nat.	1B-3B	47	162	24	54	10	4	2	26	.333	270	33	8	.974
1968—Houston	Nat.	3B-1B	98	333	42	89	16	4	6	43	.267	130	171	22	.932
1969—Houston	Nat.	3B-1B	155	569	62	140	25	3	11	83	.246	140	307	26	.945
1970—Houston	Nat.	*3B-1B	156	576	90	145	25	3	25	87	.252	149	*357	18	*.966
1971—Houston	Nat.	3B	135	484	51	118	21	4	12	56	.244	93	275	●21	.946
1972—Houston	Nat.	3B	152	533	70	131	24	7	22	90	.237	119	*340	20	.958
1973—Houston	Nat.	3B	154	574	79	146	26	0	21	89	.254	*134	296	*25	.945
1974—Houston	Nat.	3B	152	533	61	137	27	3	17	78	.257	128	347	17	.965
1975—Houston†	Nat.	*3B-SS	129	448	41	100	23	2	12	48	.223	114	259	11	*.971
1976—San Diego	Nat.	3B	139	471	45	121	22	4	9	55	.257	109	318	20	.955
1977—San Diego‡	Nat.	3B	52	170	19	46	8	3	5	27	.271	43	104	6	.961
1977—Toronto§	Amer.	3B-1B-OF	96	313	47	75	18	2	13	40	.240	97	106	7	.967
National League Totals—11 Years			1369	4873	584	1227	227	37	142	682	.252	1429	2807	194	.956
American League Totals—1 Year			96	313	47	75	18	2	13	40	.240	97	106	7	.967
Major League Totals—11 Years			1465	5186	631	1302	245	39	155	722	.251	1526	2913	201	.957

Signed as free agent by Houston Colt .45s' organization, September 13, 1964.
†Traded to San Diego Padres for Pitchers Joe McIntosh and Larry Hardy, December 11, 1975.
‡Sold to Toronto Blue Jays, June 8, 1977.
§Released, March 18, 1978.

RECORD AS MANAGER

Year	Club	League	Position	W.	L.	Year	Club	League	Position	W.	L.
1980—Hawaii	P. C.	First(N)	40	25		1984—Texas	Amer.	Seventh(W)	69	92
(Second Half)		Third(N)	36	40		1985—Texas†	Amer.	Seventh(W)	9	23
1981—Hawaii	P. C.	First(N)	35	31		1986—Chicago‡	Amer.	Fifth(W)	1	1
(Second Half)		Third(N)	37	34		1989—California	Amer.	Third(W)	91	71
1982—Hawaii	P. C.	Second(S)	36	35		1990—California	Amer.	Fourth(W)	80	82
(Second Half)		Third(S)	37	36		Major League Totals—6 Years			327	354
1983—Texas	Amer.	Third(W)	77	85						

†Replaced by Bobby Valentine, May 16, 1985.
‡Served as interim manager, June 20 and June 21, 1986 before Jim Fregosi replaced Tony La Russa, June 22, 1986.
Coach, American League All-Star Team, 1989.
Coach, San Diego Padres, 1979; Coach, Chicago White Sox, 1986 and 1987; scout, California Angels, 1988.

GREGORY LEE RIDDOCH
(Greg)
San Diego Padres

Born July 17, 1946, at Greeley, Colo.
Height, 5.11. Weight, 175.
Threw and batted righthanded.
Received bachelor of arts degree in business administration and master's degree in
education from Colorado State College, Greeley, Colo.

Led Northern League third basemen in fielding percentage with .937 in 1969.

Year	Club	League	Pos.	G.	AB.	R.	H.	2B.	3B.	HR.	RBI.	B.A.	PO.	A.	E.	F.A.
1967—Tampa	Fla. St.	SS	63	213	19	38	6	3	1	19	.178	101	149	14	.947
1968—Tampa	Fla. St.	SS-3B	89	199	16	35	5	0	2	20	.176	95	115	14	.938
1969—Sioux Falls†	North.	3B-1B	64	253	42	81	8	4	8	30	.320	92	100	12	.941
1970—Asheville	South.	3B	132	448	25	92	16	1	1	22	.205	262	21	21	.947
1971—Three Rivers‡	East.	SS-3B-1B	78	201	14	34	8	1	1	8	.169	54	106	12	.930

Selected by Baltimore Orioles' organization in 49th round of free-agent draft, June 8, 1965.
Selected by Baltimore Orioles' organization in secondary phase of free-agent draft, June 7, 1966.
Selected by Baltimore Orioles' organization in secondary phase of free-agent draft, January 28, 1967.
Selected by Cincinnati Reds' organization in secondary phase of free-agent draft, June 7, 1967.

—DID YOU KNOW—

That the Texas Rangers led the majors with 37 victories and a .627 winning percentage in games decided by one run in 1990?

†On Tampa restricted list, April 16 to June 21, 1969.
‡Released, January 6, 1972.

RECORD AS MANAGER

Named Northwest League Manager of the Year, 1975.

Year	Club	League	Position	W.	L.	Year	Club	League	Position	W.	L.
1974—Seattle	N'west	Third(W)	45	39		1980—Eugene	N'west	§First(S)	37	33	
1975—Eugene	N'west	†First(S)	54	25		1981—Eugene	N'west	Third(S)	33	37	
1976—Eugene	N'west	Second(S)	37	34		1990—San Diego x	Nat.	yFifth(W)	38	44	
1977—Billings	Pion.	Sixth	23	46		Major League Totals—1 Year				38	44
1978—Eugene	N'west	‡First(S)	36	34							
1979—Eugene	N'west	Fourth(S)	30	41							

†Won championship playoff against Portland, two games to none.
‡Lost playoffs to Grays Harbor, one game to none (balance of playoff cancelled due to rain and wet grounds).
§Playoff series against Bellingham was tied at one game each when it was cancelled due to rain and wet grounds.
Eugene and Bellingham were declared co-champions.
xReplaced Jack McKeon with club in fourth place (record of 37-43), July 11, 1990.
yTied for position with Houston Astros.
Scouting Supervisor, Cincinnati Reds, 1982 and 1983; Assistant Director of Player Development, Cincinnati Reds, 1984; Director of Minor League Clubs, Cincinnati Reds, 1985; Associate Director of Minor Leagues and Scouting, San Diego Padres, January 1, 1986 through February 25, 1986; Director of Minor Leagues and Scouting, San Diego Padres, February 26, 1986 through October 27, 1986; Coach, San Diego Padres, October 28, 1986 through July 10, 1990.

FRANK ROBINSON
Baltimore Orioles

Born August 31, 1935, at Beaumont, Tex.
Height, 6.01. Weight, 194.
Threw and batted righthanded.
Attended Xavier University, Cincinnati, O.

Holds major league record for most consecutive seasons leading league, intentional bases on balls (4), 1961 through 1964 (tied in 1962).
Holds modern major league record for most times hit by pitch, rookie season (20), 1956.
Shares major league records for most home runs, bases filled, game (2), June 26, 1970; most home runs, bases filled, two successive at bats (2), June 26, 1970; most runs batted in, two successive innings (8), June 26, 1970, fifth and sixth innings; fewest putouts, first baseman, game (0), July 1, 1971; most home runs, rookie season (38), 1956; most years leading league, intentional bases on balls, since 1955 (4).
Hit three home runs in a game, August 22, 1959.
Hit for the cycle, May 2, 1959.
Won American League Triple Crown, 1966.
Led National League in slugging percentage with .595 in 1960, .611 in 1961 and .624 in 1962.
Led American League in total bases with 367 and in slugging percentage with .637 in 1966.
Led American League in being hit by pitch with 13 in 1969.
Led National League in being hit by pitch with 20 in 1956, 8 in 1959, 9 in 1960, 11 in 1962, 14 in 1963 and 18 in 1965.
Led National League in intentional bases on balls received with 23 in 1961, 20 in 1963, 20 in 1964 and tied for lead with 16 in 1962.
Led National League in sacrifice flies with 10 in 1961.
Led National League first basemen in double plays with 111 in 1959.
Tied for American League lead in sacrifice flies with 7 in 1966.
Named Major League Player of the Year by THE SPORTING NEWS, 1966.
Named American League Player of the Year by THE SPORTING NEWS, 1966.
Named American League Most Valuable Player by Baseball Writers' Association of America, 1966.
Named National League Player of the Year by THE SPORTING NEWS, 1961.
Named National League Most Valuable Player by Baseball Writers' Association of America, 1961.
Named National League Rookie of the Year by THE SPORTING NEWS, 1956.
Named National League Rookie of the Year by Baseball Writers' Association of America, 1956.
Named outfielder on THE SPORTING NEWS American League All-Star Team, 1966 and 1967.
Named outfielder on THE SPORTING NEWS National League All-Star Team, 1961 and 1962.
Named outfielder on THE SPORTING NEWS National League All-Star fielding team, 1958.
Elected to Hall of Fame, 1982.

Year	Club	League	Pos.	G.	AB.	R.	H.	2B.	3B.	HR.	RBI.	B.A.	PO.	A.	E.	F.A.
1953—Ogden	Pion.	OF-3B-1B	72	270	70	94	20	6	17	83	.348	105	28	18	.881
1954—Tulsa	Texas	2B-3B	8	30	4	8	0	0	0	1	.267	17	15	1	.970
1954—Columbia	Sally	OF-3B-2B	132	491	*112	165	32	9	25	110	.336	258	63	18	.947
1955—Columbia	Sally	OF-1B	80	243	50	64	15	7	12	52	.263	203	3	4	.981
1956—Cincinnati	Nat.	OF	152	572	*122	166	27	6	38	83	.290	323	5	8	.976
1957—Cincinnati	Nat.	OF-1B	150	611	97	197	29	5	29	75	.322	487	36	6	.989
1958—Cincinnati	Nat.	OF-3B	148	554	90	149	25	6	31	83	.269	314	24	6	.983
1959—Cincinnati	Nat.	1B-OF	146	540	106	168	31	4	36	125	.311	1049	78	18	.984
1960—Cincinnati	Nat.	1B-OF-3B	139	464	86	138	33	6	31	83	.297	775	62	10	.988
1961—Cincinnati	Nat.	OF-3B	153	545	117	176	32	7	37	124	.323	284	15	3	.990
1962—Cincinnati	Nat.	OF	162	609	*134	208	*51	2	39	136	.342	315	10	2	.994
1963—Cincinnati	Nat.	OF-1B	140	482	79	125	19	3	21	91	.259	238	13	4	.984
1964—Cincinnati	Nat.	OF	156	568	103	174	38	6	29	96	.306	279	7	4	.986
1965—Cincinnati†	Nat.	OF	156	582	109	172	33	5	33	113	.296	282	5	3	.990
1966—Baltimore	Amer.	OF-1B	155	576	*122	182	34	2	*49	*122	*.316	282	6	5	.983
1967—Baltimore	Amer.	OF-1B	129	479	83	149	23	7	30	94	.311	207	8	2	.991
1968—Baltimore	Amer.	OF-1B	130	421	69	113	27	1	15	52	.268	193	5	7	.966
1969—Baltimore	Amer.	OF-1B	148	539	111	166	19	5	32	100	.308	367	19	5	.987
1970—Baltimore	Amer.	OF-1B	132	471	88	144	24	1	25	78	.306	262	11	4	.986

Year	Club	League	Pos.	G.	AB.	R.	H.	2B.	3B.	HR.	RBI.	B.A.	PO.	A.	E.	F.A.
1971—Baltimore‡	Amer.	OF-1B	133	455	82	128	16	2	28	99	.281	449	20	11	.977
1972—Los Angeles§	Nat.	OF	103	342	41	86	6	1	19	59	.251	168	6	6	.967
1973—California	Amer.	OF	147	534	85	142	29	0	30	97	.266	38	3	1	.976
1974—Calif. x-Cleve.	Amer.	1B-OF	144	477	81	117	27	3	22	68	.245	23	0	1	.958
1975—Cleveland yz	Amer.	DH-PH	49	118	19	28	5	0	9	24	.237	0	0	0	.000
1976—Cleveland yab	Amer.	1B-OF	36	67	5	15	0	0	3	10	.224	11	0	0	1.000
National League Totals—11 Years			1605	5869	1084	1759	324	51	343	1068	.300	4514	261	70	.986
American League Totals—10 Years			1203	4137	745	1184	204	21	243	744	.286	1832	72	36	.981
Major League Totals—21 Years			2808	10006	1829	2943	528	72	586	1812	.294	6346	333	106	.984

†Traded to Baltimore Orioles for Outfielder Dick Simpson and Pitchers Milt Pappas and Jack Baldschun, December 9, 1965.

‡Traded with Pitcher Pete Richert to Los Angeles Dodgers for Pitchers Doyle Alexander and Bob O'Brien, Catcher Sergio Robles and First Baseman-Outfielder Royle Stillman, December 2, 1971.

§Traded with Infielders Billy Grabarkewitz and Bob Valentine and Pitchers Bill Singer and Mike Strahler to California Angels for Third Baseman Ken McMullen and Pitcher Andy Messersmith, November 28, 1972.

xReleased on waivers to Cleveland Indians, September 12, 1974; Indians assigned Outfielder Rusty Torres and Catcher Ken Suarez to Angels, December 4, 1974, to complete deal.

yPlayer-manager.

zOn disabled list, July 4 to July 23, 1975.

aOn disabled list, April 4 to April 26, 1976.

bReleased October 5, 1976.

CHAMPIONSHIP SERIES RECORD

Shares Championship Series records for hitting home runs in first at-bat, October 4, 1969; most at-bats, inning (2), October 3, 1970, fourth inning.

Year	Club	League	Pos.	G.	AB.	R.	H.	2B.	3B.	HR.	RBI.	B.A.	PO.	A.	E.	F.A.
1969—Baltimore	Amer.	OF	3	12	1	4	2	0	1	2	.333	2	0	1	.667
1970—Baltimore	Amer.	OF	3	10	3	2	0	0	1	2	.200	2	0	0	1.000
1971—Baltimore	Amer.	OF	3	12	2	1	1	0	0	1	.083	7	0	0	1.000
Championship Series Totals—3 Years			9	34	6	7	3	0	2	5	.206	11	0	1	.917

WORLD SERIES RECORD

Shares World Series record for most times hit by pitcher, total series (3), and game (2), October 8, 1961.

Year	Club	League	Pos.	G.	AB.	R.	H.	2B.	3B.	HR.	RBI.	B.A.	PO.	A.	E.	F.A.
1961—Cincinnati	Nat.	OF	5	15	3	3	2	0	1	4	.200	5	0	0	1.000
1966—Baltimore	Amer.	OF	4	14	4	4	0	1	2	3	.286	6	0	0	1.000
1969—Baltimore	Amer.	OF	5	16	2	3	0	0	1	1	.188	13	0	0	1.000
1970—Baltimore	Amer.	OF	5	22	5	6	0	0	2	4	.273	7	0	0	1.000
1971—Baltimore	Amer.	OF	7	25	5	7	0	0	2	2	.280	12	0	0	1.000
World Series Totals—5 Years			26	92	19	23	2	1	8	14	.250	43	0	0	1.000

ALL-STAR GAME RECORD

Year	League	Pos.	AB.	R.	H.	2B.	3B.	HR.	RBI.	B.A.	PO.	A.	E.	F.A.
1956—National		OF	2	0	0	0	0	0	0	.000	1	0	0	1.000
1957—National		OF	2	0	1	0	0	0	0	.500	5	0	0	1.000
1959—National (second game)		1B	3	1	3	0	0	1	1	1.000	3	0	1	.750
1961—National (first game)		OF	1	0	1	0	0	0	0	1.000	2	0	0	1.000
1962—National (second game)		OF	3	0	0	0	0	0	0	.000	1	0	0	1.000
1965—National		PH	1	0	0	0	0	0	0	.000	0	0	0	.000
1966—American		OF	4	0	0	0	0	0	0	.000	2	0	0	1.000
1969—American		OF	2	0	0	0	0	0	0	.000	0	0	0	.000
1970—American		OF	3	0	0	0	0	0	0	.000	1	0	0	1.000
1971—American		OF	2	1	1	0	0	1	2	.500	2	0	0	1.000
1974—American		PH	1	0	0	0	0	0	0	.000	0	0	0	.000
All-Star Game Totals—11 Years			24	2	6	0	0	2	3	.250	17	0	1	.944

Member of National League All-Star Team in 1959 (first game) and 1961 (second game); did not play.
Named to American League Team for 1967 game; replaced due to injury.

RECORD AS MANAGER

Named American League Manager of the Year by The Sporting News, 1989.

Year	Club	League	Position	W.	L.	Year	Club	League	Position	W.	L.
1975—Cleveland	Amer.	Fourth(E)	79	80	1988—Baltimore y	Amer.	Seventh(E)	54	101
1976—Cleveland	Amer.	Fourth(E)	81	78	1989—Baltimore	Amer.	Second(E)	87	75
1977—Cleveland†	Amer.	Sixth(E)	26	31	1990—Baltimore	Amer.	Fifth(E)	76	85
1978—Rochester‡	Int.	Sixth	58	64	National League Totals—4 Years			264	277
1981—San Francisco§	Nat.		56	55	American League Totals—6 Years			403	450
1982—San Francisco	Nat.	Third(W)	87	75	Major League Totals—10 Years			667	727
1983—San Francisco	Nat.	Fifth(W)	79	83					
1984—San Francisco x	Nat.	Sixth(W)	42	64					

†Replaced by Jeff Torborg, June 19, 1977.

‡Replaced interim manager Al Widmar (replacing Ken Boyer), May 8, 1978.

§First Half . . . Fifth (W) (record of 27-32); Second Half . . . Third (W) (record of 29-23).

xReplaced by interim manager Danny Ozark, August 5, 1984.

yReplaced Cal Ripken with club in seventh place (record of 0-6), April 12, 1988.

Coach, California Angels, July 11 through remainder of 1977 season; Coach, Baltimore Orioles, beginning of 1978 season through May 8, 1979, 1980 and 1985 through 1987; and Special Assistant to the President, Baltimore Orioles, beginning of 1988 through April 11, 1988.

Coach, American League All-Star Team, 1980 and 1990.

ROBERT LEROY RODGERS
(Bob or Buck)
Montreal Expos

Born August 16, 1938, at Delaware, O.
Height, 6.01. Weight, 190.
Threw right and batted left and righthanded.
Attended Ohio Wesleyan University, Delaware, O., and Ohio Northern
University, Ada, O.

Holds American League record for most games, by catcher, rookie season (150), 1962.
Shares American League record for fewest assists by catcher, season, 150 or more games (73), 1962.
Major League stolen bases: 1962 (1), 1963 (2), 1964 (4), 1965 (4), 1966 (3), 1967 (1), 1968 (2). Total—17.
Led American League catchers in double plays with 14 in 1962 and 14 in 1964.

Year—Club	League	Pos.	G.	AB.	R.	H.	2B.	3B.	HR.	RBI.	B.A.	PO.	A.	E.	F.A.
1956—Jamestown	Pony	OF	48	153	28	36	8	1	6	26	.235	43	6	3	.942
1957—Erie	NYP	*C-OF	114	430	79	127	26	4	12	80	.295	568	*77	*25	.963
1958—Lancaster	East.	C	19	63	8	16	3	0	3	8	.254	111	11	2	.984
1958—Idaho Falls	Pion.	*C-OF	99	378	73	115	15	6	12	74	.304	524	45	*20	.966
1959—Birmingham	South.	C	3	13	1	1	0	1	0	2	.077	28	0	1	.966
1959—Knoxville	Sally	*C-OF	105	355	53	102	18	6	7	55	.287	565	60	*13	.980
1960—Denver	A. A.	C	23	84	12	20	7	1	3	12	.238	127	15	4	.973
1960—Birmingham	South.	C	93	313	36	77	14	1	5	38	.246	456	*68	7	.987
1961—Dallas-Ft. W.†	A. A.	C	124	427	55	122	22	3	3	62	.286	*595	*70	11	.984
1961—Los Angeles	Amer.	C	16	56	8	18	2	0	2	13	.321	71	11	3	.965
1962—Los Angeles	Amer.	C	155	565	65	146	34	6	6	61	.258	826	73	●10	.989
1963—Los Angeles	Amer.	C	100	300	24	70	6	0	4	23	.233	416	48	*10	.979
1964—Los Angeles	Amer.	C	148	514	38	125	18	3	4	54	.243	884	*87	*13	.987
1965—California	Amer.	C	132	411	33	86	14	3	1	32	.209	682	52	7	.991
1966—California	Amer.	C	133	454	45	107	20	3	7	48	.236	662	*69	6	.992
1967—California	Amer.	*C-OF	139	429	29	94	13	3	6	41	.219	728	*73	7	.991
1968—California	Amer.	C	91	258	13	49	6	0	1	14	.190	407	50	7	.985
1969—Hawaii	P. C.	C-3B	44	145	15	37	5	0	0	12	.255	215	26	4	.984
1969—California	Amer.	C	18	49	4	9	1	0	0	2	.196	74	9	0	1.000
1975—California‡	Calif.	PH	4	3	1	1	0	0	0	0	.333	0	0	0	.000
1977—El Paso§	Texas	PH	1	0	0	0	0	0	0	0	.000	0	0	0	.000
Major League Totals—9 Years			932	3033	259	704	114	18	31	288	.232	4750	472	63	.988

†Selected by Los Angeles Angels from Detroit Tigers in American League expansion draft, December 14, 1960.
‡Player-manager, August 24 through September 15, 1975.
§Player-manager, July 15 through August 14, 1977.

RECORD AS MANAGER

Named National League Manager of the Year by THE SPORTING NEWS, 1987.
Named Minor League Manager of the Year by THE SPORTING NEWS, 1984.
Named American Association Manager of the Year, 1984.
Named Texas League Manager of the Year, 1977.

Year—Club	League	Position	W.	L.
1975—Salinas	Calif.	Fifth	35	35
(Second Half)		Sixth	32	38
1977—El Paso	Texas	First(W)	38	24
(Second Half)		†First(W)	40	28
1980—Milwaukee‡	Amer.	Third(E)	39	31
1981—Milwaukee§	Amer.		62	47
1982—Milwaukee x	Amer.	yFifth(E)	23	24
1984—Indianapolis	A. A.	zFirst	91	63
1985—Montreal	Nat.	Third(E)	84	77
1986—Montreal	Nat.	Fourth(E)	78	83
1987—Montreal	Nat.	Third(E)	91	71
1988—Montreal	Nat.	Third(E)	81	81
1989—Montreal	Nat.	Fourth(E)	81	81
1990—Montreal	Nat.	Third(E)	85	77
American League Totals—3 Years			124	102
National League Totals—6 Years			500	470
Major League Totals—9 Years			624	572

†Lost league championship to Arkansas, two games to none.
‡Began season as interim manager for ill George Bamberger who returned June 6, 1980, with club in second place (record of 26-21); named manager when Bamberger retired with club tied for fourth place (record of 73-66), September 7, 1980.
§First Half . . . Third (E) (record of 31-25); Second Half . . . First (E) (record of 31-22).
xReplaced by Harvey Kuenn, June 2, 1982.
yTied for position with Baltimore Orioles.
zLost semifinal playoff series to Louisville, four games to two.
Coach, National League All-Star Team, 1988 and 1989.
Coach, Minnesota Twins, 1970 through 1974; San Francisco Giants, 1976; Milwaukee Brewers, 1978 through 1980.

DIVISION SERIES RECORD

Year—Club	League	W.	L.
1981—Milwaukee	American	2	3

JEFFREY ALLEN TORBORG
(Jeff)
Chicago White Sox

Born November 26, 1941, at Westfield, N. J.
Height, 6.00. Weight, 195.
Threw and batted righthanded.
Received bachelor of science degree in education from Rutgers University, New Brunswick,

N. J.; and received master's degree in athletic administration from Montclair State College, Montclair, N. J. Father of Doug Torborg, pitcher in Pittsburgh Pirates' organization, 1987 and 1988.

Received reported $100,000 bonus to sign with Los Angeles Dodgers, 1963.

Year	Club	League	Pos.	G.	AB.	R.	H.	2B.	3B.	HR.	RBI.	B.A.	PO.	A.	E.	F.A.
1963—Albuquerque	Texas		C	64	184	19	41	10	3	1	18	.223	349	27	6	.984
1964—Los Angeles	Nat.		C	28	43	4	10	1	1	0	4	.233	80	4	2	.977
1965—Los Angeles	Nat.		C	56	150	8	36	5	1	3	13	.240	300	19	3	.991
1966—Los Angeles	Nat.		C	46	120	4	27	3	0	1	13	.225	269	17	4	.986
1967—Los Angeles	Nat.		C	76	196	11	42	4	1	2	12	.214	413	30	5	.989
1968—Los Angeles	Nat.		C	37	93	2	15	2	0	0	4	.161	206	20	2	.991
1969—Los Angeles	Nat.		C	51	124	7	23	4	0	0	7	.185	251	26	1	.996
1970—Los Angeles†	Nat.		C	64	134	11	31	8	0	1	17	.231	275	16	5	.983
1971—California‡	Amer.		C	55	123	6	25	5	0	0	5	.203	208	17	3	.987
1972—California§	Amer.		C	59	153	5	32	3	0	0	8	.209	383	28	1	.998
1973—California xyz	Amer.		C	102	255	20	56	7	0	1	18	.220	611	37	6	.991
National League Totals—7 Years				358	860	47	184	27	3	7	70	.214	1794	132	22	.989
American League Totals—3 Years				216	531	31	113	15	0	1	31	.213	1202	82	10	.990
Major League Totals—10 Years				574	1391	78	297	42	3	8	101	.214	2996	214	32	.990

†Sold to California Angels, March 13, 1971.
‡On disabled list, June 25 to July 27, 1971.
§On disabled list, May 21 to June 13, 1972.
xOn disabled list, July 13 to August 10, 1973.
yTraded to St. Louis Cardinals for Pitcher John Andrews, December 6, 1973.
zReleased, March 25, 1974.

RECORD AS MANAGER

Named American League Manager of the Year by THE SPORTING NEWS, 1990.

Year	Club	League	Position	W.	L.	Year	Club	League	Position	W.	L.
1977—Cleveland†	Amer.		Fifth(E)	45	59	1989—Chicago	Amer.		Seventh(W)	69	92
1978—Cleveland	Amer.		Sixth(E)	69	90	1990—Chicago	Amer.		Second(W)	94	68
1979—Cleveland‡	Amer.		Sixth(E)	43	52	Major League Totals—5 Years				320	361

†Replaced Frank Robinson with club in sixth place (record of 26-31), June 19, 1977.
‡Replaced by Dave Garcia, July 23, 1979.
Coach, Cleveland Indians, 1975 to June 18, 1977; coach, New York Yankees, July 26, 1979 through 1988.

JOSEPH PAUL TORRE
(Joe)
St. Louis Cardinals

Born July 18, 1940, at Brooklyn, N. Y.
Height, 6.01. Weight, 210.
Threw and batted righthanded.
Brother of Frank Torre, first baseman with Milwaukee Braves and Philadelphia Phillies, 1956 through 1960, 1962 and 1963.

Shares major league record for most times grounded into double play, nine-inning game (4), July 21, 1975.
Hit for the cycle, June 27, 1973.
Led National League in total bases with 352 in 1971.
Led National League in grounding into double plays with 26 in 1964, 22 in 1965, 22 in 1967 and 21 in 1968.
Led National League first basemen in assists with 102 and double plays with 144 in 1974.
Led National League catchers in double plays with 12 in 1967.
Led National League catchers in fielding percentage with .995 in 1964 and .996 in 1968.
Named Major League Player of the Year by THE SPORTING NEWS, 1971.
Named National League Player of the Year by THE SPORTING NEWS, 1971.
Named National League Most Valuable Player by Baseball Writers' Association of America, 1971.
Named third baseman on THE SPORTING NEWS National League All-Star Team, 1971.
Named catcher on THE SPORTING NEWS National League All-Star Team, 1964 through 1966.
Named catcher on THE SPORTING NEWS National League All-Star fielding team, 1965.

Year	Club	League	Pos.	G.	AB.	R.	H.	2B.	3B.	HR.	RBI.	B.A.	PO.	A.	E.	F.A.
1960—Eau Claire	North.		C	117	369	63	127	23	3	16	74	★.344	636	64	9	.987
1960—Milwaukee	Nat.		PH	2	2	0	1	0	0	0	0	.500	0	0	0	.000
1961—Louisville	A. A.		C	27	111	18	38	8	2	3	24	.342	185	14	2	.990
1961—Milwaukee	Nat.		C	113	406	40	113	21	4	10	42	.278	494	50	10	.982
1962—Milwaukee	Nat.		C	80	220	23	62	8	1	5	26	.282	325	39	5	.986
1963—Milwaukee	Nat.		C-1B-OF	142	501	57	147	19	4	14	71	.293	919	76	6	.994
1964—Milwaukee	Nat.		C-1B	154	601	87	193	36	5	20	109	.321	1081	94	7	.994
1965—Milwaukee	Nat.		C-1B	148	523	68	152	21	1	27	80	.291	1022	73	8	.993
1966—Atlanta	Nat.		C-1B	148	546	83	172	20	3	36	101	.315	874	87	12	.988
1967—Atlanta	Nat.		C-1B	135	477	67	132	18	1	20	68	.277	785	81	8	.991
1968—Atlanta†	Nat.		C-1B	115	424	45	115	11	2	10	55	.271	733	48	2	.997
1969—St. Louis	Nat.		1B-C	159	602	72	174	29	6	18	101	.289	1360	91	7	.995
1970—St. Louis	Nat.		C-3B-1B	●161	624	89	203	27	9	21	100	.325	651	162	13	.984
1971—St. Louis	Nat.		3B	161	634	97	★230	34	8	24	★137	★.363	★136	271	●21	.951
1972—St. Louis	Nat.		3B-1B	149	544	71	157	26	6	11	81	.289	336	198	15	.973
1973—St. Louis	Nat.		1B-3B	141	519	67	149	17	2	13	69	.287	881	128	12	.988
1974—St. Louis‡	Nat.		1B-3B	147	529	59	149	28	1	11	70	.282	1173	121	14	.989
1975—New York	Nat.		3B-1B	114	361	33	89	16	3	6	35	.247	172	157	15	.956

Year Club League	Pos.	G.	AB.	R.	H.	2B.	3B.	HR.	RBI.	B.A.	PO.	A.	E.	F.A.
1976—New York............. Nat.	1B-3B	114	310	36	95	10	3	5	31	.306	593	52	7	.989
1977—New York§............. Nat.	1B-3B	26	51	2	9	3	0	1	9	.176	83	3	1	.989
Major League Totals—18 Years...............		2209	7874	996	2342	344	59	252	1185	.297	11618	1731	163	.988

†Traded to St. Louis Cardinals for First Baseman Orlando Cepeda, March 17, 1969.
‡Traded to New York Mets for Pitchers Tommy Moore and Ray Sadecki, October 13, 1974.
§Player-manager, beginning May 31, until released as player, June 18, 1977.

ALL-STAR GAME RECORD

Year League	Pos.	AB.	R.	H.	2B.	3B.	HR.	RBI.	B.A.	PO.	A.	E.	F.A.
1964—National................	C	2	0	0	0	0	0	0	.000	5	0	0	1.000
1965—National................	C	4	1	1	0	0	1	2	.250	5	1	0	1.000
1966—National................	C	3	0	0	0	0	0	0	.000	5	0	0	1.000
1967—National................	C	2	0	0	0	0	0	0	.000	4	1	0	1.000
1970—National................	PH	1	0	0	0	0	0	0	.000	0	0	0	.000
1971—National................	3B	3	0	0	0	0	0	0	.000	1	0	0	1.000
1972—National................	3B	3	0	1	0	0	0	0	.333	1	2	0	1.000
1973—National................	1B-3B	3	0	0	0	0	0	0	.000	5	0	0	1.000
All-Star Game Totals—8 Years....................		21	1	2	0	0	1	2	.095	26	4	0	1.000

Member of National League All-Star Team for the 1963 game; did not play.

RECORD AS MANAGER

Year Club League	Position	W.	L.	Year Club League	Position	W.	L.
1977—New York†............. Nat.	Sixth(E)	49	68	1982—Atlanta .... Nat.	First(W)	89	73
1978—New York............... Nat.	Sixth(E)	66	96	1983—Atlanta .... Nat.	Second(W)	88	74
1979—New York............... Nat.	Sixth(E)	63	99	1984—Atlanta .... Nat.	§Second(W)	80	82
1980—New York............... Nat.	Fifth(E)	67	95	1990—St. Louis x............... Nat.	Sixth(E)	24	34
1981—New York‡............. Nat.		41	62	Major League Totals—9 Years.................		567	683

†Replaced Joe Frazier with club in sixth place (record of 15-30), May 31, 1977.
‡First Half . . . . Fifth (E) (record of 17-34); Second Half . . . . Fourth (E) (record of 24-28).
§Tied for position with Houston Astros.
xReplaced Whitey Herzog (record of 33-47) and interim manager Red Schoendienst (record 13-11) with club in sixth place (combined record of 46-58), August 1, 1990.
Coach, National League All-Star Team, 1983.

CHAMPIONSHIP SERIES RECORD

Year Club	League	W.	L.
1982—Atlanta .... National		0	3

THOMAS LYNN TREBELHORN
(Tom)
Milwaukee Brewers

Born January 27, 1948, at Portland, Ore.
Height, 5.11. Weight, 178.
Threw right and batted lefthanded.
Received bachelor of science degree in history and teaching
from Portland State University, Portland, Ore. in 1970.

Led Northwest League catchers in fielding percentage with .997 in 1971.
Led National League catchers in double plays with 5 in 1970.
Tied for Northwest League lead in double plays by catchers with 3 in 1972.

Year Club League	Pos.	G.	AB.	R.	H.	2B.	3B.	HR.	RBI.	B.A.	PO.	A.	E.	F.A.
1970—Bend.................. N'west	C-3-2-O	68	198	33	48	4	1	4	32	.242	296	48	12	.966
1971—Bend.................. N'west	C-OF	51	149	28	47	13	3	3	38	.315	282	33	2	.994
1972—Walla Walla† .... N'west	C	42	124	17	25	5	1	2	20	.202	272	19	4	.986
1973—Birmingham .... South.	3B-C-1B	33	89	9	18	5	0	2	13	.202	87	31	8	.937
1973—Burlington .... Midw.	C-1B	43	146	23	33	6	0	2	20	.226	298	25	5	.985
1974—Birmingham .... South.	C-3B	8	9	1	2	1	0	0	0	.222	13	1	1	.933
1974—Lewiston‡§ .... N'west	P	7	2	0	0	0	0	0	0	.000	1	2	0	1.000

Signed as free agent by Hawaii (Pacific Coast League), June 4, 1970.
†Sold to Oakland A's organization, September 2, 1972.
‡Player-coach.
§Released, June 17, 1975.

PITCHING RECORD

Year Club League	G.	IP.	W.	L.	Pct.	H.	R.	ER.	SO.	BB.	ERA.
1974—Lewiston .... Northwest	5	12	1	0	1.000	7	1	1	2	2	0.75

—DID YOU KNOW—

That Cincinnati won more night games (70-47) than any other N.L. team in 1990 but ranked 10th with a 21-24 mark in day games?

RECORD AS MANAGER

Year Club	League	Position	W.	L.	Year Club	League	Position	W.	L.
1975—Boise	N'west	Third(S)	39	39	1985—Vancouver‡	P. C.	Second(N)	38	34
1976—Boise	N'west	Third(S)	33	38	(Second Half)		First(N)	41	30
1977—Modesto	Calif.	Fourth	31	39	1986—Milwaukee§	Amer.	Sixth(E)	6	3
(Second Half)		Sixth	22	48	1987—Milwaukee	Amer.	Third(E)	91	71
1979—Batavia	NYP	Third(W)	37	34	1988—Milwaukee	Amer.	xThird(E)	87	75
1982—Portland	P. C.	Fifth(N)	32	39	1989—Milwaukee	Amer.	Fourth(E)	81	81
(Second Half)		Fifth(N)	33	40	1990—Milwaukee	Amer.	Sixth(E)	74	88
1983—Hawaii	P. C.	†Fourth(S)	32	40	Major League Totals—5 Years			339	318
(Second Half)		Second(S)	40	31					

†Tied for position with Phoenix.
‡Won division championship from Calgary, three games to none; won league championship from Phoenix, three games to none.
§Replaced retiring manager George Bamberger with club in sixth place (record of 71-81), September 26, 1986.
xTied for position with Toronto Blue Jays.
Coach, American League All-Star Team, 1988.
Coach, Cleveland Indians' organization, 1978; coach, Pittsburgh Pirates' organization, 1980 and 1981; coach, Milwaukee Brewers, 1984 and beginning of 1986 season through September 25, 1986.

ROBERT JOHN VALENTINE
(Bobby)
Texas Rangers

Born May 13, 1950, at Stamford, Conn.
Height, 5.10. Weight, 185.
Threw and batted righthanded.
Attended Arizona State University, Tempe, Ariz., and University of Southern California, Los Angeles, Calif.
Son-in-law of Ralph Branca, pitcher with Brooklyn Dodgers, Detroit Tigers
and New York Yankees, 1944 through 1954 and 1956.

Major League stolen bases: 1971 (5), 1972 (5), 1973 (6), 1974 (8), 1975 (1), 1978 (1), 1979 (1). Total—27.
Led Pioneer League in stolen bases with 20 in 1968.
Led Pacific Coast League in total bases with 324, sacrifice flies with 10 and double plays by shortstops with 106 in 1970.
Led Pioneer League outfielders in putouts with 107 and tied for lead in assists with 8 in 1987.
Named Pacific Coast League Player of the Year, 1970.

Year Club	League	Pos.	G.	AB.	R.	H.	2B.	3B.	HR.	RBI.	B.A.	PO.	A.	E.	F.A.
1968—Odgen	Pion.	OF-SS	62	224	★62	63	14	4	6	26	.281	111	10	6	.953
1969—Spokane	P. C.	★SS-OF	111	402	61	104	19	5	3	35	.259	166	254	★38	.917
1969—Los Angeles	Nat.	PR	5	0	3	0	0	0	0	0	.000	0	0	0	.000
1970—Spokane	P. C.	★SS-2B	●146	★621	★122	★211	★39	★16	14	80	★.340	★217	474	★54	.928
1971—Spokane	P. C.	SS	7	30	7	10	2	0	1	2	.333	13	18	3	.912
1971—Los Angeles	Nat.	S-3-2-O	101	281	32	70	10	2	1	25	.249	123	176	16	.949
1972—Los Angeles†	Nat.	2-3-O-S	119	391	42	107	11	2	3	32	.274	178	245	23	.948
1973—California‡	Amer.	SS-OF	32	126	12	38	5	2	1	13	.302	63	75	6	.958
1974—California§x	Amer.	OF-SS-3B	117	371	39	97	10	3	3	39	.261	160	116	17	.942
1975—Charleston	Int.	3B	56	175	27	41	4	0	1	17	.234	44	74	6	.952
1975—Salt Lake City	P. C.	1-O-3-2	46	147	29	45	6	1	0	17	.306	92	14	3	.972
1975—California y	Amer.	1B-3B-OF	26	57	5	16	2	0	0	5	.281	27	1	2	.933
1975—San Diego	Nat.	OF	7	15	1	2	0	0	1	1	.133	4	0	0	1.000
1976—Hawaii	P. C.	1-O-3-S	120	395	67	120	23	2	13	89	.304	578	47	4	.994
1976—San Diego	Nat.	OF-1B	15	49	3	18	4	0	0	4	.367	55	6	0	1.000
1977—S.D.z-N.Y.	Nat.	SS-1B-3B	86	150	13	23	4	0	2	13	.153	119	64	3	.984
1978—New York a	Nat.	2B-3B	69	160	17	43	7	0	1	18	.269	78	109	6	.969
1979—Seattle b	Amer.	S-O-2-3-C	62	98	9	27	6	0	0	7	.276	32	38	2	.972
National League Totals—7 Years			402	1046	111	263	36	4	8	93	.251	557	600	48	.960
American League Totals—4 Years			237	652	65	178	23	5	4	64	.273	282	230	27	.950
Major League Totals—10 Years			639	1698	176	441	59	9	12	157	.260	839	830	75	.957

Selected by Los Angeles Dodgers' organization in 1st round (fifth player selected) of free-agent draft, June 7, 1968.
†Traded with Infielder Billy Grabarkewitz, Outfielder Frank Robinson and Pitchers Bill Singer and Mike Strahler to California Angels for Pitcher Andy Messersmith and Third Baseman Ken McMullen, November 28, 1972.
‡On disabled list, May 17, 1973 through remainder of season.
§On disabled list, May 29 to June 13, 1974.
xLoaned to Charleston (Pittsburgh Pirates' organization), April 4, 1975; returned, June 20, 1975.
yTraded with a player to be named later to San Diego Padres for Pitcher Gary Ross, September 17, 1975; San Diego acquired Infielder Rudy Meoli to complete deal, November 4, 1975.
zTraded with Pitcher Paul Siebert to New York Mets for Infielder-Outfielder Dave Kingman, June 15, 1977.
aReleased, March 26, 1979; signed by Seattle Mariners, April 10, 1979.
bGranted free agency, November 1, 1979.

RECORD AS MANAGER

Year Club	League	Position	W.	L.	Year Club	League	Position	W.	L.
1985—Texas†	Amer.	Seventh(W)	53	76	1989—Texas	Amer.	Fourth(W)	83	79
1986—Texas	Amer.	Second(W)	87	75	1990—Texas	Amer.	Third(W)	83	79
1987—Texas	Amer.	‡Sixth(W)	75	87	Major League Totals—6 Years			451	487
1988—Texas	Amer.	Sixth(W)	70	91					

†Replaced Doug Rader with club in seventh place (record of 9-23), May 16, 1985.
‡Tied for position with California Angels.

Coach, American League All-Star Team, 1988.
    Scout and minor league instructor, San Diego Padres, 1981; minor league instructor, New York Mets, 1982; coach, New York Mets, 1983 through May 15, 1985.

JOHN DAVID WATHAN
Kansas City Royals

Born October 4, 1949, at Cedar Rapids, Ia.
Height, 6.02. Weight, 205.
Threw and batted righthanded.
Attended University of San Diego, San Diego, Calif., and
Mount Mercy College, Cedar Rapids, Ia.

Major League stolen bases: 1977 (2), 1978 (2), 1979 (2), 1980 (17), 1981 (11), 1982 (36), 1983 (28), 1984 (6), 1985 (1). Total—105.

Year Club	League	Pos.	G.	AB.	R.	H.	2B.	3B.	HR.	RBI.	B.A.	PO.	A.	E.	F.A.
1971—San Jose	Calif.	C-OF	64	215	37	56	11	2	1	29	.260	438	31	14	.971
1971—Waterloo	Midw.	C-OF-1B	43	147	31	41	4	4	3	21	.279	282	18	1	.997
1972—San Jose†	Calif.	C-1B-3B	48	148	25	40	8	0	4	15	.270	324	31	3	.992
1972—Omaha	A. A.	C	18	51	8	15	1	1	0	2	.294	94	5	1	.990
1972—Jacksonville	South.	C	16	54	6	17	3	1	0	3	.315	111	7	4	.967
1973—Jacksonville‡	South.	C-1B-3B	65	233	20	58	8	3	5	34	.249	294	28	4	.988
1974—Jacksonville	South.	1B-OF-C	120	428	63	105	14	2	7	47	.245	760	50	7	.991
1975—Omaha	A. A.	C-OF	104	360	42	109	14	4	8	46	.303	532	45	10	.983
1976—Omaha§	A. A.	C-OF	24	84	4	13	5	0	0	6	.155	128	14	4	.973
1976—Kansas City	Amer.	C-1B	27	42	5	12	1	0	0	5	.286	63	4	1	.985
1977—Kansas City	Amer.	C-1B	55	119	18	39	5	3	2	21	.328	156	9	2	.988
1978—Kansas City x	Amer.	1B-C	67	190	19	57	10	1	2	28	.300	385	28	2	.995
1979—Kansas City	Amer.	1B-C-OF	90	199	26	41	7	3	2	28	.206	336	24	3	.992
1980—Kansas City	Amer.	C-OF-1B	126	453	57	138	14	7	6	58	.305	472	33	8	.984
1981—Kansas City	Amer.	C-OF-1B	89	301	24	76	9	3	1	19	.252	316	28	7	.980
1982—Kansas City y	Amer.	C-1B	121	448	79	121	11	3	3	51	.270	482	40	10	.981
1983—Kansas City	Amer.	C-1B-OF	128	437	49	107	18	3	2	32	.245	615	58	9	.987
1984—Kansas City	Amer.	C-1B-OF	97	171	17	31	7	1	2	10	.181	304	31	6	.982
1985—Kansas City z	Amer.	C-1B	60	145	11	34	8	1	1	9	.234	259	29	4	.986
Major League Totals—10 Years			860	2505	305	656	90	25	21	261	.262	3388	284	52	.986

Selected by Kansas City Royals' organization in 4th round of free-agent draft, January 13, 1971.
†On disabled list, May 5 to May 30, 1972.
‡On disabled list, May 25 to June 28, 1973.
§On disabled list, July 29 to September 1, 1976.
xOn disabled list, June 16 to July 7, 1978.
yOn disabled list, July 6 to August 10, 1982.
zReleased and signed as coach, April 7, 1986.

DIVISION SERIES RECORD

Year Club	League	Pos.	G.	AB.	R.	H.	2B.	3B.	HR.	RBI.	B.A.	PO.	A.	E.	F.A.
1981—Kansas City	Amer.	C	3	10	1	3	0	0	0	0	.300	11	4	1	.938

CHAMPIONSHIP SERIES RECORD

Year Club	League	Pos.	G.	AB.	R.	H.	2B.	3B.	HR.	RBI.	B.A.	PO.	A.	E.	F.A.
1976—Kansas City	Amer.	C	1	0	0	0	0	0	0	0	.000	0	0	0	.000
1977—Kansas City	Amer.	C-1-D-PH	4	6	0	0	0	0	0	0	.000	19	0	0	1.000
1978—Kansas City	Amer.	1B	1	3	0	0	0	0	0	0	.000	7	0	0	1.000
1980—Kansas City	Amer.	OF-PH	3	6	1	0	0	0	0	0	.000	7	0	0	1.000
1984—Kansas City	Amer.	PR-DH	1	1	0	0	0	0	0	0	.000	0	0	0	.000
Championship Series Totals—5 Years			10	16	1	0	0	0	0	0	.000	33	0	0	1.000

WORLD SERIES RECORD

Year Club	League	Pos.	G.	AB.	R.	H.	2B.	3B.	HR.	RBI.	B.A.	PO.	A.	E.	F.A.
1980—Kansas City	Amer.	PH-OF-C	3	7	1	2	0	0	0	1	.286	7	1	0	1.000
1985—Kansas City	Amer.	PH-PR	2	1	0	0	0	0	0	0	.000	0	0	0	.000
World Series Totals—2 Years			5	8	1	2	0	0	0	1	.250	7	1	0	1.000

RECORD AS MANAGER

Year Club	League	Position	W.	L.	Year Club	League	Position	W.	L.
1987—Omaha	A. A.	Seventh†	64	76	1989—Kansas City	Amer.	Second(W)	92	70
1987—Kansas City‡	Amer.	Second(W)	21	15	1990—Kansas City	Amer.	Sixth(W)	75	86
1988—Kansas City	Amer.	Third(W)	84	77	Major League Totals—4 Years			272	248

†Tied for position with Nashville.
‡Replaced manager Billy Gardner with club in fourth place (record of 62-64), August 27, 1987.
Coach, Kansas City Royals, 1986.

—DID YOU KNOW—

That the A.L. witnessed three inside-the-park grand slams over a 19-day stretch in 1990: on August 14, by California's Luis Polonia; on August 30, by Chicago's Ron Karkovice, and on September 1, by Boston's Mike Greenwell?

DONALD WILLIAM ZIMMER
(Don)
Chicago Cubs

Born January 17, 1931, at Cincinnati, O.
Height, 5.10. Weight, 188.
Threw and batted righthanded.
Father of Tom Zimmer, minor league catcher in St. Louis Cardinals' organization, 1971 through 1975;
coach, St. Louis Cardinals' organization, 1975; coach, St. Louis Cardinals, 1976;
player-manager with Victoria in Lone Star League (Independent), 1977; manager with Butte in
Pioneer League (Co-op), 1978; manager in Pittsburgh Pirates' organization, 1979;
manager in California Angels' organization, 1980; and scout for San Francisco Giants since 1981.

Named American Association Rookie of the Year, 1953.

Year—Club	League	Pos.	G.	AB.	R.	H.	2B.	3B.	HR.	RBI.	B.A.	PO.	A.	E.	F.A.
1949—Cambridge	E. Shore	SS	71	304	56	69	14	3	4	30	.227	162	171	27	.925
1950—Hornell	Pony	*SS-3B	123	518	*146	163	34	5	*23	122	.315	*269	*367	45	*.934
1951—Elmira	East.	SS	137	546	94	149	28	2	9	70	.273	*326	414	38	*.951
1952—Mobile	South.	SS	153	613	107	190	32	7	17	91	.310	*355	*517	*52	.944
1953—St. Paul†	A. A.	SS	81	320	57	96	14	4	23	63	.300	165	264	21	.953
1954—St. Paul	A. A.	SS	73	268	54	78	9	6	17	53	.291	152	200	16	.957
1954—Brooklyn	Nat.	SS	24	33	3	6	0	1	0	0	.182	14	32	3	.939
1955—Brooklyn	Nat.	2B-SS-3B	88	280	38	67	10	1	15	50	.239	184	207	12	.970
1956—Brooklyn‡	Nat.	SS-3B-2B	17	20	4	6	1	0	0	2	.300	10	11	1	.955
1957—Brooklyn	Nat.	3B-SS-2B	84	269	23	59	9	1	6	19	.219	114	186	15	.952
1958—Los Angeles	Nat.	S-3-2-O	127	455	52	119	15	2	17	60	.262	281	395	26	.963
1959—Los Angeles§	Nat.	SS-3B-2B	97	249	21	41	7	1	4	28	.165	120	240	10	.973
1960—Chicago	Nat.	2-3-S-O	132	368	37	95	16	7	6	35	.258	211	274	16	.968
1961—Chicago x	Nat.	2B-3B-OF	128	477	57	120	25	4	13	40	.252	284	332	20	.969
1962—N.Y. y-Cinn. z	Nat.	3B-2B-SS	77	244	19	52	12	2	2	17	.213	77	129	11	.949
1963—Los Angeles a	Nat.	3B-2B-SS	22	23	4	5	1	0	1	2	.217	3	14	2	.895
1963—Washington	Amer.	3B-2B	83	298	37	74	12	1	13	44	.248	90	177	18	.937
1964—Washington	Amer.	3-O-C-2	121	341	38	84	16	2	12	38	.246	72	144	10	.956
1965—Washington b	Amer.	C-3B-2B	95	226	20	45	6	0	2	17	.199	181	81	12	.956
1966—Toei	Pacific	3B-SS	87	203	14	37	2	0	9	20	.182	101	143	11	.957
1967—Knoxville	South	P-3-1-C	25	49	2	10	3	0	0	5	.204	2	11	2	.846
1967—Buffalo	Int.	3B-OF	16	33	2	6	2	0	1	2	.182	4	9	3	.813
American League Totals—3 Years			299	865	95	203	34	3	27	99	.235	343	402	40	.949
National League Totals—10 Years			796	2418	258	570	96	19	64	253	.236	1298	1820	116	.964
Major League Totals—12 Years			1095	3283	353	773	130	22	91	352	.235	1641	2222	156	.961

†On disabled list, July 7, 1953 through remainder of season.
‡On disabled list, June 23, 1956 through remainder of season.
§Traded to Chicago Cubs for Pitcher Ron Perranoski, Infielder John Goryl, Outfielder Lee Handley and reported $25,000, April 8, 1960.
xSelected by New York Mets in Expansion Draft, October 10, 1961.
yTraded to Cincinnati Reds for Pitcher Robert G. Miller and Third Baseman Cliff Cook, May 6, 1962.
zTraded to Los Angeles Dodgers for Pitcher Scott Breeden, January 24, 1963.
aSold to Washington Senators, June 24, 1963.
bReleased, November 19, 1965; signed by Toei Flyers of Japanese Baseball League.

WORLD SERIES RECORD

Year—Club	League	Pos.	G.	AB.	R.	H.	2B.	3B.	HR.	RBI.	B.A.	PO.	A.	E.	F.A.
1955—Brooklyn	Nat.	2B	4	9	0	2	0	0	0	2	.222	4	8	2	.857
1959—Los Angeles	Nat.	SS	1	1	0	0	0	0	0	0	.000	0	1	0	1.000
World Series Totals—2 Years			5	10	0	2	0	0	0	2	.200	4	9	2	.867

ALL-STAR GAME RECORD

Year—League	Pos.	AB.	R.	H.	2B.	3B.	HR.	RBI.	B.A.	PO.	A.	E.	F.A.
1961—National (first game)	2B	1	0	0	0	0	0	0	.000	0	0	1	.000

PITCHING RECORD

Year—Club	League	G.	IP.	W.	L.	Pct.	H.	R.	ER.	SO.	BB.	ERA.
1967—Knoxville	Southern	12	27	0	0	.000	33	15	14	8	7	4.67

RECORD AS MANAGER

Named National League Manager of the Year by THE SPORTING NEWS, 1989.

Year—Club	League	Position	W.	L.	Year—Club	League	Position	W.	L.
1967—Knoxville	South.	†Sixth	26	46	1980—Boston z	Amer.	aThird(E)	82	73
1967—Buffalo	Int.	Seventh	33	40	1981—Texas b	Amer.		57	48
1968—Indianapolis	P. C.	Fifth(E)	66	78	1982—Texas c	Amer.	Sixth(W)	38	58
1969—Key West	Fla. St.	‡Third(S)	67	63	1988—Chicago	Nat.	Fourth(E)	77	85
1972—San Diego§	Nat.	Sixth(W)	54	88	1989—Chicago	Nat.	First(E)	93	69
1973—San Diego	Nat.	Sixth(W)	60	102	1990—Chicago	Nat.	dFourth(E)	77	85
1976—Boston x	Amer.	Third(E)	42	34	American League Totals—7 Years			506	410
1977—Boston	Amer.	ySecond(E)	97	64	National League Totals—5 Years			361	429
1978—Boston	Amer.	Second(E)	99	64	Major League Totals—12 Years			867	839
1979—Boston	Amer.	Third (E)	91	69					

†Transferred by Cincinnati Reds' organization from Knoxville to Buffalo, July 5, 1967.
‡Tied for position with Pompano Beach.

§Replaced Preston Gomez with club in fourth place (record of 4-7), April 27, 1972.
xReplaced Darrell Johnson with club in fifth place (record of 41-45), July 19, 1976.
yTied for position with Baltimore Orioles.
zReplaced by interim manager Johnny Pesky, October 1, 1980.
aTied for position with Milwaukee Brewers.
bFirst Half. . . . Second (W) (record of 33-22); Second Half. . . . Third (W) (record of 24-26).
cReplaced by Darrell Johnson, July 29, 1982.
dTied for position with Philadelphia Phillies.
Coach, Montreal Expos, 1971; San Diego Padres, 1972; Boston Red Sox, 1974 to July, 1976; coach, New York Yankees, 1983 and June 16, 1986 through remainder of season; coach, Chicago Cubs, 1984 through June 12, 1986; coach, San Francisco Giants, 1987.
Coach, National League All-Star Team, 1990.
Coach, American League All-Star Team, 1978 and 1981.

CHAMPIONSHIP SERIES RECORD

Year	Club	League	W.	L.
1989—Chicago		National	1	4

1991 Hall of Fame Enshrinees

RODNEY CLINE (ROD) CAREW

Born October 1, 1945, at Gatun, Panama.
Height, 6.00. Weight, 182.
Threw right and batted lefthanded.

Shares major league records for most times stealing home, season (7), 1969; most stolen bases, inning (3), May 18, 1969, third inning.

Shares American League records for most double plays by first baseman, game (6), August 29, 1977, first game (10 innings); most putouts by first baseman, game (32), April 13, 1982 (20 innings); most chances accepted by first baseman, game (34), April 13, 1982 (20 innings).

Led American League in intentional bases on balls received with 18 in 1975, 15 in 1977 and 19 in 1978.
Led American League first basemen in double plays with 149 in 1976 and 161 in 1977.
Led American League first basemen in assists with 121 in 1977.
Led American League first basemen in total chances with 1,590 in 1977.
Named Major League Player of the Year by THE SPORTING NEWS, 1977.
Named American League Player of the Year by THE SPORTING NEWS, 1977.
Named American League Most Valuable Player by Baseball Writers' Association of America, 1977.
Named American League Rookie Player of the Year by THE SPORTING NEWS, 1967.
Named American League Rookie of the Year by Baseball Writers' Association of America, 1967.
Named first baseman on THE SPORTING NEWS American League All-Star Team, 1977 and 1978.
Named second baseman on THE SPORTING NEWS American League All-Star Team, 1967 through 1969 and 1972 through 1975.
Named to Hall of Fame, 1991.

Year	Club	League	Pos.	G.	AB.	R.	H.	2B.	3B.	HR.	RBI.	B.A.	PO.	A.	E.	F.A.
1964—Melbourne Twins	Coc. Rk.		2B	37	123	17	40	5	●3	0	21	.325	86	48	7	.950
1965—Orlando	Fla. St.		2B	125	439	57	133	20	8	1	52	.303	290	328	●28	.957
1966—Wilson	Carol.		2B	112	383	64	112	19	3	1	30	.292	248	275	21	.961
1967—Minnesota	Amer.		2B	137	514	66	150	22	7	8	51	.292	289	314	15	.976
1968—Minnesota	Amer.		●2B-SS	127	461	46	126	27	2	1	42	.273	266	285	●18	.968
1969—Minnesota	Amer.		2B	123	458	79	152	30	4	8	56	*.332	244	302	17	.970
1970—Minnesota	Amer.		2B-1B	51	191	27	70	12	3	4	28	.366	79	122	8	.962
1971—Minnesota	Amer.		2B-3B	147	577	88	177	16	10	2	48	.307	324	331	16	.976
1972—Minnesota	Amer.		2B	142	535	61	170	21	6	0	51	*.318	331	378	16	.978
1973—Minnesota	Amer.		2B	149	580	98	*203	30	●11	6	62	*.350	383	413	13	.984
1974—Minnesota	Amer.		2B	153	599	86	*218	30	5	3	55	*.364	375	416	*33	.960
1975—Minnesota	Amer.		2B-1B	143	535	89	192	24	4	14	80	*.359	408	377	21	.974
1976—Minnesota	Amer.		1B-2B	156	605	97	200	29	12	9	90	.331	1398	110	16	.990
1977—Minnesota	Amer.		1B-2B	155	616	*128	*239	38	*16	14	100	*.388	1463	124	10	.994
1978—Minnesota†	Amer.		1B-2B-OF	152	564	85	188	26	10	5	70	*.333	1363	105	16	.989
1979—California	Amer.		1B	110	409	78	130	15	3	3	44	.318	804	55	10	.988
1980—California	Amer.		1B	144	540	74	179	34	7	3	59	.331	897	57	6	.994
1981—California	Amer.		1B	93	364	57	111	17	1	2	21	.305	877	60	5	.995
1982—California	Amer.		1B	138	523	88	167	25	5	3	44	.319	1339	94	12	.992
1983—California‡	Amer.		1B-2B	129	472	66	160	24	2	2	44	.339	891	42	6	.994
1984—California	Amer.		1B	93	329	42	97	8	1	3	31	.295	724	59	●15	.981
1985—California§	Amer.		1B	127	443	69	124	17	3	2	39	.280	1055	65	7	.994
Major League Totals—19 Years				2469	9315	1424	3053	445	112	92	1015	.328	13510	3709	260	.985

Signed as free agent by Minnesota Twins' organization, June 25, 1964.
†Traded to California Angels for Outfielder Ken Landreaux, Pitchers Paul Hartzell and Brad Havens and Third Baseman Dave Engle, February 3, 1979.
‡Granted free agency, November 7, 1983; re-signed by Angels, November 22, 1983.
§Granted free agency, November 12, 1985.

CHAMPIONSHIP SERIES RECORD

Tied Championship Series record for most two-base hits, four-game Series (3), 1979.
Tied American League Championship Series record for most hits, four-game Series (7), 1979.

Year	Club	League	Pos.	G.	AB.	R.	H.	2B.	3B.	HR.	RBI.	B.A.	PO.	A.	E.	F.A.
1969—Minnesota	Amer.		2B	3	14	0	1	0	0	0	0	.071	6	3	1	.900
1970—Minnesota	Amer.		PH	2	2	0	0	0	0	0	0	.000	0	0	0	.000
1979—California	Amer.		1B	4	17	4	7	3	0	0	1	.412	34	1	0	1.000
1982—California	Amer.		1B	5	17	2	3	1	0	0	0	.176	43	4	0	1.000
Championship Series Totals—4 Years				14	50	6	11	4	0	0	1	.220	83	8	1	.989

ALL-STAR GAME RECORD

Established All-Star Game record for most three-base hits, game (2), July 11, 1978.
Tied All-Star Game record for most at-bats, nine-inning game (5), July 15, 1975.

Year	League	Pos.	AB.	R.	H.	2B.	3B.	HR.	RBI.	B.A.	PO.	A.	E.	F.A.
1967—American		2B	3	0	0	0	0	0	0	.000	2	3	0	1.000
1968—American		2B	3	0	0	0	0	0	0	.000	2	2	0	1.000
1969—American		2B	3	0	0	0	0	0	0	.000	0	2	0	1.000
1971—American		2B	1	1	0	0	0	0	0	.000	1	2	0	1.000
1972—American		2B	2	0	1	0	0	0	1	.500	2	3	0	1.000
1973—American		2B	3	0	0	0	0	0	0	.000	5	1	0	1.000
1974—American		2B	1	1	0	0	0	0	0	.000	0	1	0	1.000
1975—American		2B	5	0	1	0	0	0	0	.200	3	1	0	1.000
1976—American		1B	3	0	0	0	0	0	0	.000	9	2	0	1.000

Year League	Pos.	AB.	R.	H.	2B.	3B.	HR.	RBI.	B.A.	PO.	A.	E.	F.A.
1977—American	1B	3	1	1	0	0	0	0	.333	7	0	0	1.000
1978—American	1B	4	2	2	0	2	0	0	.500	6	1	0	1.000
1980—American	1B	2	1	2	1	0	0	0	1.000	4	0	0	1.000
1981—American	1B	3	0	1	0	0	0	0	.333	12	0	0	1.000
1983—American	1B	3	2	2	0	0	0	1	.667	3	0	1	.750
1984—American	1B	2	0	0	0	0	0	0	.000	5	0	0	1.000
All-Star Game Totals—15 Years		41	8	10	1	2	0	2	.244	61	18	1	.988

Named to American League All-Star Team for 1970, 1979 and 1982 games; replaced due to injury.

FERGUSON ARTHUR JENKINS
(Fergie)

Born December 13, 1943, at Chatham, Ontario, Canada.
Height, 6.05. Weight, 210.
Threw and batted righthanded.

Shares major league records for most 1-0 games lost, season (5), 1968; most years leading league in home runs allowed (5).
Led American League in home runs allowed with 37 in 1975 and 40 in 1979.
Led National League in home runs allowed with 30 in 1967, 29 in 1971, 32 in 1972, 35 in 1973 and tied for lead with 26 in 1968.
Led American League in complete games with 29 in 1974.
Led National League in complete games with 20 in 1967, 24 in 1970 and 30 in 1971.
Led National League pitchers in games started with 40 in 1968, 42 in 1969 and tied for lead with 39 in 1971.
Led National League in balks with 4 in 1971.
Won National League Cy Young Memorial Award, 1971.
Named National League Pitcher of the Year by THE SPORTING NEWS, 1971.
Named American League Comeback Player of the Year by THE SPORTING NEWS, 1974.
Named righthanded pitcher on THE SPORTING NEWS National League All-Star Team, 1971, 1972.
Named pitcher on THE SPORTING NEWS National League All-Star Team, 1967.
Named to Hall of Fame, 1991.

Year Club	League	G.	IP.	W.	L.	Pct.	H.	R.	ER.	SO.	BB.	ERA.
1962—Miami	Florida St.	11	65	7	2	.778	34	10	7	69	19	0.97
1962—Buffalo	Int'national	3	13	1	1	.500	18	9	8	6	5	5.54
1963—Arkansas	Int'national	4	10	0	1	.000	13	7	7	13	3	6.30
1963—Miami	Florida St.	20	140	12	5	.706	110	66	53	135	59	3.41
1964—Chattanooga	Southern	21	139	10	6	.625	124	61	48	149	42	3.11
1964—Arkansas	P. Coast	11	57	5	5	.500	40	27	20	49	34	3.16
1965—Arkansas	P. Coast	32	122	8	6	.571	104	48	40	112	42	2.95
1965—Philadelphia	National	7	12	2	1	.667	7	3	3	10	2	2.25
1966—Philadelphia†-Chicago	National	61	184	6	8	.429	150	77	68	150	52	3.33
1967—Chicago	National	38	289	20	13	.606	230	101	90	236	83	2.80
1968—Chicago	National	40	308	20	15	.571	255	96	90	260	65	2.63
1969—Chicago	National	43	311	21	15	.583	284	122	111	★273	71	3.21
1970—Chicago	National	40	313	22	16	.579	265	128	●118	274	60	3.39
1971—Chicago	National	39	★325	★24	13	.649	★304	114	100	263	37	2.77
1972—Chicago	National	36	289	20	12	.625	253	111	★103	184	62	3.21
1973—Chicago‡	National	38	271	14	16	.467	267	133	117	170	57	3.89
1974—Texas	American	41	328	●25	12	.676	286	117	103	225	45	2.83
1975—Texas§	American	37	270	17	18	.486	261	130	118	157	56	3.93
1976—Boston	American	30	209	12	11	.522	201	85	76	142	43	3.27
1977—Boston x	American	28	193	10	10	.500	190	91	79	105	36	3.68
1978—Texas	American	34	249	18	8	.692	228	92	84	157	41	3.04
1979—Texas	American	37	259	16	14	.533	252	127	117	164	81	4.07
1980—Texas	American	29	198	12	12	.500	190	90	83	129	52	3.77
1981—Texas y	American	19	106	5	8	.385	122	55	53	63	40	4.50
1982—Chicago	National	34	217⅓	14	15	.483	221	92	76	134	68	3.15
1983—Chicago z	National	33	167⅓	6	9	.400	176	89	80	96	46	4.30
American League Totals—8 Years		255	1812	115	93	.553	1730	787	713	1142	394	3.54
National League Totals—11 Years		409	2686⅔	169	133	.560	2412	1066	956	2050	603	3.20
Major League Totals—19 Years		664	4498⅔	284	226	.557	4142	1853	1669	3192	997	3.34

Signed as free agent by Philadelphia Phillies' organization, June 15, 1962.
†Traded with Outfielder Adolfo Phillips and Outfielder/First Baseman John Herrnstein to Chicago Cubs for Pitchers Bob Buhl and Larry Jackson, April 21, 1966.
‡Traded to Texas Rangers for Infielders Bill Madlock and Vic Harris, October 25, 1973.
§Traded to Boston Red Sox for Outfielder Juan Beniquez, Pitcher Steve Barr, a player to be named later and an estimated $200,000, November 17, 1975; Texas Rangers acquired Pitcher Craig Skok to complete deal, December 12, 1975.
xTraded to Texas Rangers for Pitcher John Poloni and an estimated $20,000, December 14, 1977.
yGranted free agency, November 13, 1981; signed by Chicago Cubs, December 8, 1981.
zReleased, March 19, 1984.

ALL-STAR GAME RECORD

Shares record for most strikeouts, game (6), July 11, 1967.

Year League	IP.	W.	L.	Pct.	H.	R.	ER.	SO.	BB.	ERA.
1967—National	3	0	0	.000	3	1	1	6	0	3.00
1971—National	1	0	0	.000	3	2	2	0	0	18.00
All-Star Game Totals—2 Years	4	0	0	.000	6	3	3	6	0	6.75

Named to National League All-Star Team for 1972 game, did not play.

GAYLORD JACKSON PERRY

Born September 15, 1938, at Williamston, N.C.
Height, 6.04. Weight, 215.
Threw and batted righthanded.
Attended Campbell College, Buies Creek, N.C.
Brother of Jim Perry, pitcher with Cleveland Indians, Minnesota Twins,
Detroit Tigers and Oakland Athletics, 1959 through 1975.

Holds major league record by winning Cy Young Memorial Award in both leagues.
Pitched 1-0 no-hit victory against St. Louis Cardinals, September 17, 1968.
Major League saves: 1972 (1).
Led American League in wild pitches with 17 in 1973 and 13 in 1982.
Led American League in complete games with 29 in 1972 and 29 in 1973.
Led American League in intentional bases on balls issued with 16 in 1972.
Led National League in shutouts with 5 in 1970.
Led National League pitchers in games started with 41 in 1970.
Won National League Cy Young Memorial Award, 1978.
Won American League Cy Young Memorial Award, 1972.
Named righthanded pitcher on THE SPORTING NEWS National League All-Star Team, 1978.
Named righthanded pitcher on THE SPORTING NEWS American League All-Star Team, 1972.
Named Pacific Coast League Pitcher of the Year, 1961.
Received reported $90,000 bonus to sign with San Francisco Giants, 1958.
Named to Hall of Fame, 1991.

Year Club	League	G.	IP.	W.	L.	Pct.	H.	R.	ER.	SO.	BB.	ERA.
1958—St. Cloud	Northern	17	128	9	5	.643	97	40	34	111	48	2.39
1959—Corpus Christi	Texas	41	191	10	11	.476	*218	*120	86	119	69	4.05
1960—Tacoma	P. Coast	1	1	0	0	.000	1	1	1	0	0	9.00
1960—Rio Grande Valley	Texas	31	188	9	13	.409	164	68	59	120	77	*2.82
1961—Tacoma	P. Coast	33	*219	●16	10	.615	208	79	62	95	61	2.55
1962—San Francisco	National	13	43	3	1	.750	54	29	25	20	14	5.23
1962—Tacoma	P. Coast	22	156	10	7	.588	128	56	43	136	56	*2.48
1963—San Francisco	National	31	76	1	6	.143	84	41	34	52	29	4.03
1963—Tacoma	P. Coast	1	9	1	0	1.000	3	1	1	7	1	1.00
1964—San Francisco	National	44	206	12	11	.522	179	65	63	155	43	2.75
1965—San Francisco	National	47	196	8	12	.400	194	105	91	170	70	4.18
1966—San Francisco	National	36	256	21	8	.724	242	92	85	201	40	2.99
1967—San Francisco	National	39	293	15	17	.469	231	98	85	230	84	2.61
1968—San Francisco	National	39	291	16	15	.516	240	93	79	173	59	2.44
1969—San Francisco	National	40	*325	19	14	.576	290	115	90	233	91	2.49
1970—San Francisco	National	41	*329	●23	13	.639	*292	*138	117	214	84	3.20
1971—San Francisco†	National	37	280	16	12	.571	255	116	86	158	67	2.76
1972—Cleveland	American	41	343	●24	16	.600	253	79	73	234	82	1.92
1973—Cleveland	American	41	344	19	19	.500	315	143	129	238	115	3.38
1974—Cleveland	American	37	322	21	13	.618	230	98	90	216	99	2.52
1975—Cleveland‡-Texas	American	37	306	18	17	.514	277	127	110	233	70	3.24
1976—Texas	American	32	250	15	14	.517	232	93	90	143	52	3.24
1977—Texas§	American	34	238	15	12	.556	239	108	89	177	56	3.37
1978—San Diego	National	37	261	*21	6	*.778	241	96	79	154	66	2.72
1979—San Diego xy	National	32	233	12	11	.522	225	90	79	140	67	3.05
1980—Texas z-New York a	American	34	206	10	13	.435	224	107	84	135	64	3.67
1981—Atlanta b	National	23	151	8	9	.471	*182	70	66	60	24	3.93
1982—Seattle c	American	32	216⅔	10	12	.455	245	117	106	116	54	4.40
1983—Seattle d-Kansas City e	American	30	186⅓	7	14	.333	214	108	96	82	49	4.64
National League Totals—13 Years		459	2940	175	135	.565	2709	1148	979	1960	738	3.00
American League Totals—9 Years		318	2412	139	130	.517	2229	980	867	1574	641	3.24
Major League Totals—22 Years		777	5352	314	265	.542	4938	2128	1846	3534	1379	3.10

Signed as free agent for reported $90,000 by San Francisco Giants' organization, June 3, 1958.
†Traded with Shortstop Frank Duffy to Cleveland Indians for Pitcher Sam McDowell, November 29, 1971.
‡Traded to Texas Rangers for Pitchers Jim Bibby, Jackie Brown and Rick Waits and an estimated $100,000, June 12, 1975.
§Traded to San Diego Padres for Pitcher Dave Tomlin and $125,000, February 15, 1978.
xOn suspended list, September 5 to October 3, 1979.
yTraded with Third Baseman Tucker Ashford and Pitcher Joe Carroll to Texas Rangers for First Baseman Willie Montanez and a player to be named later, February 15, 1980; Hawaii (San Diego Padres' organization) purchased Infielder Tony Phillips to complete deal, September 11, 1980.
zTraded to New York Yankees for Pitcher Ken Clay and a player to be named later, August 14, 1980; Texas Rangers' organization acquired Outfielder Marvin Thompson to complete deal, October 1, 1980.
aGranted free agency, October 23, 1980; signed by Atlanta Braves, January 12, 1981.
bReleased, October 5, 1981; signed by Seattle Mariners, March 5, 1982.
cOn suspended list, September 17 to September 26, 1982.
dReleased, June 27, 1983; signed by Kansas City Royals, July 6, 1983.
eOn voluntarily retired list, September 24, 1983.

—DID YOU KNOW—

That by winning all 12 games against the New York Yankees in 1990, Oakland completed the first-ever season sweep against the Bronx Bombers?

CHAMPIONSHIP SERIES RECORD

Holds National League record for most hits allowed, Series (19), 1971.
Shares National League record for most hits allowed, game (10), October 6, 1971.

Year Club	League	G.	IP.	W.	L.	Pct.	H.	R.	ER.	SO.	BB.	ERA.
1971—San Francisco	National	2	14⅔	1	1	.500	19	11	10	11	3	6.14

ALL-STAR GAME RECORD

Year League	IP.	W.	L.	Pct.	H.	R.	ER.	SO.	BB.	ERA.
1966—National	2	1	0	1.000	1	0	0	1	1	0.00
1970—National	2	0	0	.000	4	2	2	0	1	9.00
1972—American	2	0	0	.000	3	2	2	1	0	9.00
1974—American	3	0	0	.000	3	1	1	4	0	3.00
1979—National	0	0	0	.000	3	1	1	0	0	......
All-Star Game Totals—5 Years	9	1	0	1.000	14	6	6	6	2	6.00

NOTES